Abnormal Psychology

Seventeenth Edition

Jill M. Hooley
Harvard University

James N. Butcher
University of Minnesota

Matthew K. Nock
Harvard University

Susan Mineka
Northwestern University

PEARSON

Boston   Columbus   Indianapolis   New York City   San Francisco
Amsterdam   Cape Town   Dubai   London   Madrid   Milan   Munich   Paris   Montréal   Toronto
Delhi   Mexico City   São Paulo   Sydney   Hong Kong   Seoul   Singapore   Taipei   Tokyo

VP, Product Development: Dickson Musslewhite
Senior Acquisitions Editor: Amber Chow
Director of Development: Brita Nordin
Sponsoring Editor: Carrie Brandon
Development Editor: Stephanie Ventura
Editorial Assistant: Stephany Harrington
Director of Product Marketing: Maggie Moylan
Director of Field Marketing: Jonathan Cottrell
Director, Program and Project Management: Lisa Iarkowski
Project Management Team Lead: Denise Forlow
Senior Project Manager: Sherry Lewis
Program Management Team Lead: Amber Mackey
Program Manager: Cecilia Turner
Field Marketing Manager: Kate Mitchell
Product Marketing Manager: Lindsey Prudhomme Gill
Marketing Assistant: Frank Alarcon
Operations Manager: Mary Fischer
Senior Operations Specialist: Carol Melville

Associate Director of Design: Blair Brown
Interior Design and Director: Kathryn Foot
Cover Art Director and Designer: Janet Slowik
Cover Art: (tl) Fritz Cohen/Corbis; (tc) Masterfile/Corbis; (tr) Patrik Giardino/Corbis; (l) Tony Anderson/Corbis; (cl) Kate Kunz/Corbis; (cr) Eugenio Marongiu/Corbis; (r) JAG Images/Corbis; (bl) Marnie Burkhart/Corbis; (bcl) Becky Yee/Corbis; (bcr) John Smith/Corbis; (br) Blue Images/Corbis
Digital Studio Team Lead: Peggy Bliss
Digital Studio Project Manager: Christopher Fegan
Media Project Managers: Pamela Weldin and Elissa Senra-Sargent
Full-Service Project Management and Composition: iEnergizer Aptara®, Ltd.
Printer/Binder: LSC/Kendallville
Cover Printer: Phoenix Color/Hagerstown

Acknowledgements of third-party content appear on page 730, which constitutes an extension of this copyright page.

Library of Congress Cataloging-in-Publication Data

Names: Hooley, Jill M., author. | Butcher, James Neal, author. | Nock, Matthew, author. | Mineka, Susan, author.
Title: Abnormal psychology.
Description: Seventeenth edition / Jill M. Hooley, James N. Butcher, Matthew K. Nock, Susan Mineka. | Boston : Pearson, [2017] | Revision of: Abnormal psychology / James N. Butcher, University of Minnesota, Susan Mineka, Northwestern University, Jill M. Hooley, Harvard University. Sixteenth edition. | Includes bibliographical references and index.
Identifiers: LCCN 2015041946 | ISBN 9780133852059 | ISBN 0133852059
Subjects: LCSH: Psychology, Pathological—Textbooks. | Psychiatry—Textbooks

2   16

PEARSON

Student Edition:
ISBN-10:   0-13-385205-9
ISBN-13: 978-0-13-385205-9

Books a la Carte:
ISBN-10:   0-13-422578-3
ISBN-13: 978-0-13-422578-4

Brief Contents

Contents

Features

What's New in DSM-5?
A Quick Guide

Many changes occurred from *DSM-IV-TR* to *DSM-5*. Here is a summary of some of the most important revisions. Many of these changes are highlighted in the "Thinking Critically about *DSM-5*" boxes throughout this edition.

- The chapters of the *DSM* have been reorganized to reflect a consideration of developmental and lifespan issues. Disorders that are thought to reflect developmental perturbations or that manifest early in life (e.g., neurodevelopmental disorders and disorders such as schizophrenia) are listed before disorders that occur later in life.

- The multiaxial system has been abandoned. No distinction is now made between Axis I and Axis II disorders.

- *DSM-5* allows for more gender-related differences to be taken into consideration for mental health problems.

- It is extremely important for the clinician to understand the client's cultural background in appraising mental health problems. *DSM-5* contains a structured interview that focuses on the patient's cultural background and characteristic approach to problems.

- The term *intellectual disability* is now used instead of the term *mental retardation*.

- A new diagnosis of autism spectrum disorder now encompasses autism, Asperger's disorder, and other forms of pervasive developmental disorder. The diagnosis of Asperger's disorder has been eliminated from the *DSM*.

- Changes to the diagnostic criteria for attention deficit disorder now mean that symptoms that occur before age 12 (rather than age 7) have diagnostic significance.

- A new diagnosis, called disruptive mood dysregulation disorder, has been added. This will be used to diagnose children up to age 18 who show persistent irritability and frequent episodes of extreme and uncontrolled behavior.

- The subtypes of schizophrenia have been eliminated.

- The special significance afforded to bizarre delusions with regard to the diagnosis of schizophrenia has been removed.

- Bipolar and related disorders are now described in a separate chapter of the *DSM* and are no longer listed with depressive disorders.

- Premenstrual dysphoric disorder has been promoted from the appendix of *DSM-IV-TR* and is now listed as a new diagnosis.

- A new diagnosis of persistent depressive disorder now subsumes dysthymia and chronic major depressive disorder.

- The bereavement exclusion has been removed in the diagnosis of major depressive episode.

- The diagnosis of phobia no longer requires that the person recognize that his or her anxiety is unreasonable.

- Panic disorder and agoraphobia have been unlinked and are now separate diagnoses in *DSM-5*.

- Obsessive-compulsive disorder is no longer classified as an anxiety disorder. *DSM-5* contains a new chapter that covers obsessive-compulsive and related disorders.

- New disorders in the obsessive-compulsive and related disorders category include hoarding disorder and excoriation (skin-picking) disorder.

- Posttraumatic stress disorder is no longer considered to be an anxiety disorder. Instead, it is listed in a new chapter that covers trauma- and stressor-related disorders.

- The diagnostic criteria for posttraumatic stress disorder have been significantly revised. The definition of what counts as a traumatic event has been clarified and made more explicit. *DSM-5* now also recognizes four-symptom clusters rather than the three noted in *DSM-IV-TR*.

- Dissociative fugue is no longer listed as a separate diagnosis. Instead, it is listed as a form of dissociative amnesia.

- The *DSM-IV-TR* diagnoses of hypochondriasis, somatoform disorder, and pain disorder have been removed and are now subsumed into the new diagnosis of somatic symptom disorder.

- Binge-eating disorder has been moved from the appendix of *DSM-IV-TR* and is now listed as an official diagnosis.

- The frequency of binge-eating and purging episodes has been reduced for the diagnosis of bulimia nervosa.

- Amenorrhea is no longer required for the diagnosis of anorexia nervosa.

- The *DSM-IV-TR* diagnoses of dementia and amnestic disorder have been eliminated and are now subsumed into a new category called major neurocognitive disorder.

- Mild neurocognitive disorder has been added as a new diagnosis.

- No changes have been made to the diagnostic criteria for personality disorders, although an alternative model is now offered as a guide for future research.

- Substance-related disorders are divided into two separate groups: substance use disorders and substance-induced disorders.

- A new disorder, gambling disorder, has been included in substance-related and addictive disorders.

- Included for the first time in Section III of *DSM-5* are several new disorders regarded as being in need of further study. These include attenuated psychosis syndrome, nonsuicidal self-injury disorder, Internet gaming disorder, and caffeine use disorder.

Preface

We are so excited about this course and hope that you are too! We (the authors) all took this course when we were undergraduate students because we were curious about abnormal aspects of human behavior. Why do some people become so depressed they can't get out of bed? Why do others have trouble controlling their use of alcohol and drugs? Why do some people become violent toward others, and in other cases toward themselves? We continue to be intensely curious about, and fascinated by, the answers to these and many other questions about abnormal human behavior. The purpose of this book is to provide a comprehensive (and hopefully engaging) introduction to the primary psychological disorders studied within abnormal psychology.

As you will learn, there are many different types of psychological disorders, and each is caused by the interaction of many different factors and can be considered from many different perspectives. We thought a lot about how best to present this information in a way that will be clear and engaging and will allow you to gain a solid, fundamental understanding of psychological disorders. As such, we use a biopsychosocial approach to provide a sophisticated appreciation of the total context in which abnormalities of behavior occur. This means that we present and describe the wide range of biological, psychological, and social factors that work together to lead to the development of psychological disorders. In addition, we discuss treatment approaches that target each of these different factors.

For ease of understanding we also present material on each disorder in a logical and consistent way. More specifically, we focus on three significant aspects: (1) the clinical picture, where we describe the symptoms of the disorder and its associated features; (2) factors involved in the development of the disorder; and (3) treatment approaches. In each case, we examine the evidence for biological, psychosocial (i.e., psychological and interpersonal), and sociocultural (the broader social environment of culture and subculture) influences. Because we wish never to lose sight of the person, we try to integrate as much case material as we can into each chapter. An additional feature of this book is a heavy focus on treatment. Although treatment is discussed in every chapter in the context of specific disorders, we also include a separate chapter that addresses issues in treatment more broadly. This provides students with increased understanding of a wide range of treatment approaches and permits more in-depth coverage than is possible in specific disorder–based chapters.

Abnormal Psychology has a long and distinguished tradition as an undergraduate text. Ever since James Coleman wrote the first edition many years ago, this textbook has been considered the most comprehensive in the field. Along the way there have been many changes. This is very much the case with this new edition. Perhaps the most exciting change, however, is the addition of Harvard Professor Matthew Nock to the author team. Matt, a recent MacArthur Award (aka, "Genius Grant") recipient, brings his brilliance, scholarship, and wry sense of humor to the book, providing fresh approaches and new perspectives. We are delighted that he has joined the author team and welcome him with great enthusiasm!

The Hooley-Butcher-Nock-Mineka author team is in a unique position to provide students with an integrated and comprehensive understanding of abnormal psychology. Each author is a noted researcher, an experienced teacher, and a licensed clinician. Each brings different areas of expertise and diverse research interests to the text. We are committed to excellence. We are also committed to making our text accessible to a broad audience. Our approach emphasizes the importance of research as well as the need to translate research findings into informed and effective clinical care for all who suffer from mental disorders. In this new edition, we seek to open up the fascinating world of abnormal psychology, providing students with comprehensive and up-to-date knowledge in a clear and engaging way. We hope that this newest edition conveys some of the passion and enthusiasm for the topic that we still experience every day.

Why Do You Need This New Edition?

The book you are reading is the seventeenth edition of *Abnormal Psychology*. Why so many revisions? And why not just use an old copy of the fifteenth or sixteenth edition? The reason is that our field is constantly making advances in our understanding of abnormal psychology. New research is being published all the time. As authors, it is important to us that these changes and new ways of thinking about the etiology, assessment, and treatment of psychological disorders are accurately presented in this text. Although many of the ideas and diagnostic concepts in the field of abnormal psychology have persisted for hundreds of years, changes in thinking often occur. And, at some point, events occur that force a rethinking of familiar topics. A major example here is the revision of the manual that is used to classify mental disorders (called the *DSM-5*). This new edition of *Abnormal Psychology* includes the most up-to-date information about *DSM-5* diagnostic categories, classifications, and criteria.

Every time we work on a revision of *Abnormal Psychology* we are reminded of how dynamic and vibrant our field is. Developments in areas such as genetics, brain imaging, behavioral observation, and classification, as well changes in social and government policy and in legal decisions, add to our knowledge base and stimulate new treatments for those whose lives are touched by mental disorders.

If you're wondering what exactly is so new in this edition of *Abnormal Psychology*, here are seven big revisions that we have made.

1. We have a new author! Matt Nock brings a fresh and new perspective to this authoritative and established text.

2. The seventeenth edition of *Abnormal Psychology* includes the most up-to-date and in-depth information about biological influences on the entire spectrum of behavioral abnormalities, while still maintaining a comprehensive and balanced biopsychosocial approach to understanding abnormal behavior.

3. As a result of the publication of *DSM-5*, the diagnostic criteria for many disorders have changed. This edition includes detailed boxes listing the current *DSM-5* diagnostic criteria for all the disorders covered in the book. Specific highlight boxes and discussions in the text also alert you to some of the most important changes in *DSM-5*.

4. Other feature boxes provide opportunities for critical thinking by illustrating some of the controversies associated with the changes that were (or were not) made. Throughout the text we also provide readers with different perspectives on the likely implications that these changes will have (or are having) for clinical diagnosis and research in psychopathology.

5. Reflecting the ever-changing field of abnormal psychology, hundreds of new references have been added, highlighting the newest and most important research findings.

6. Changes have been made in many chapters to improve the flow of the writing and enhance learning. The presentation of material in many chapters has also been reorganized to provide a more logical and coherent narrative.

7. Finally, at the beginning of each chapter, clearly defined learning objectives provide the reader with an overview of topics and issues that will be included in the chapter. These learning objectives also appear again in the specific sections to which they apply. This makes it easier for readers to identify what they should be learning in each section. At the end of each chapter a summary of the learning objectives is also provided. In Review questions at the end of major sections within chapters also provide additional opportunities for self-assessment and increased learning.

What's New

This new edition of *Abnormal Psychology* has been redesigned to reflect the newest and most relevant research findings, presented in a way that is engaging to the newest generation of students. We've done a lot of updating! Our focus has been on streamlining material throughout the book to decrease the length of each chapter while retaining all of the important information that students should be learning.

We have also done our best to include the most exciting changes and advances occurring in our field. For example, throughout the text, we have significantly increased the focus on the manifestation and treatment of psychological disorders around the globe, using data from a recently completed cross-national series of studies in more than 20 different countries. In Chapter 3, we have added a new and more accessible description of why correlation does not equal causation—and what does! In Chapter 5, we now adopt a more broad and integrative approach to the health consequences of stress, including a focus on the *mechanisms* through which stress is thought to cause physical health problems. Chapter 7 has been updated substantially and now includes more information about some of the problems most relevant to college students, such as suicide and self-injury.

New case studies have also been added throughout the book. Chapter 8, for example, has four new case studies, as well as two new highlight boxes. These illustrate recent neuroimaging research on patients with conversion disorder, as well as a very creative new approach to the treatment of this fascinating disorder. Chapter 11 has significant new material on how alcohol and drugs affect the brain, what causes hangovers, and information on new synthetic drugs that have recently hit the streets. In Chapter 13, the most current genetic findings concerning schizophrenia are described, and new developments in our understanding of the nature of dopamine abnormality in schizophrenia are discussed. A new Developments in Thinking highlight box also presents new ideas about the possibility that schizophrenia might be an immune function disorder. Chapter 15 has been reorganized and updated throughout; for instance, it now includes cutting-edge findings on the potential causes and most effective treatments for autism spectrum disorders. And throughout the book we have included information about some of the newest ways in which researchers and clinicians are treating psychological disorders, such as via the use of new smartphone apps, brain stimulation treatments, and assistive therapeutic robots! These are just a handful of the many changes we have made to give readers the most current perspectives possible. We want students to stay ahead of the curve and to provide them with the most up-to-date information we can. We also want to give students a sense of how and in what ways various fields are likely moving.

This edition also retains features that were very well received in the last edition. To assist both instructors and students, we continue to feature specialized boxes, highlighting many of the key changes that were made in *DSM-5*. In this edition, however, we also provide a detailed but accessible description of the RDoC approach.

As before, chapters begin with learning objectives. These orient the reader to the material that will be presented in each specific chapter. Learning objectives are also repeated by the section they apply to and summarized at the end of each chapter. Most chapters also begin with a case study (many of which are new) that illustrates the mental health problems to be addressed in the chapter. This serves to capture students' interest and attention right from the outset. Numerous new references, photographs, and illustrations have also been added. In short, outdated material has been replaced, current findings have been included, and new developments have been identified. Importantly, all of this has been accomplished without adding length to the book! We hope you enjoy this new edition.

Features and Pedagogy

The extensive research base and accessible organization of this book are supported by high-interest features and helpful pedagogy to further engage students and support learning. We also hope to encourage students to think in depth about the topics they are learning about through specific highlight features that emphasize critical thinking.

Features

FEATURE BOXES Special sections, called Developments in Research, Developments in Thinking, Developments in Practice, and The World Around Us, highlight topics of particular interest, focusing on applications of research to everyday life, current events, and the latest research methodologies, technologies, and findings.

CRITICAL THINKING Many of the revisions to *DSM-5* were highly contentious and controversial. A feature box called "Thinking Critically about *DSM-5*" introduces students to the revised *DSM* and encourages them to think critically about the implications of these changes.

UNRESOLVED ISSUES All chapters include end-of-chapter sections that demonstrate how far we have come

and how far we have yet to go in our understanding of psychological disorders. The topics covered here provide insight into the future of the field and expose students to some controversial topics.

Pedagogy

LEARNING OBJECTIVES Each chapter begins with learning objectives. These orient the reader to the material that will be presented in each specific chapter. Learning objectives are also repeated by the section they apply to and summarized at the end of each chapter. This provides students with an excellent tool for study and review. In this edition, sections of many chapters have also been reorganized and material has been streamlined whenever possible. All the changes that have been made are designed to improve the flow of the writing and enhance pedagogy.

CASE STUDIES Extensive case studies of individuals with various disorders are integrated in the text throughout the book. Some are brief excerpts; others are detailed analyses. These cases bring important aspects of the disorders to life. They also remind readers that the problems of abnormal psychology affect the lives of people—people from all kinds of diverse backgrounds who have much in common with all of us.

IN REVIEW QUESTIONS Review questions appear at the end of each major section within the chapter, providing regular opportunities for self-assessment as students read and further reinforce their learning.

***DSM-5* BOXES** Throughout the book these boxes contain the most up-to-date (*DSM-5*) diagnostic criteria for all of the disorders discussed. In a convenient and visually accessible form, they provide a helpful study tool that reflects current diagnostic practice. They also help students understand disorders in a real-world context.

RESEARCH CLOSE-UP TERMS Appearing throughout each chapter, these terms illuminate research methodologies. They are designed to give students a clearer understanding of some of the most important research concepts in the field of abnormal psychology.

CHAPTER SUMMARIES Each chapter ends with a summary of the essential points of the chapter organized around the learning objectives presented at the start of the chapter. These summaries use bulleted lists rather than formal paragraphs. This makes the information more accessible for students and easier to scan.

KEY TERMS Key terms are identified in each chapter. Key terms are also listed at the end of every chapter with page numbers referencing where they can be found in the body of the text. Key terms are also defined in the Glossary at the end of the text.

Supplements Package

REVEL™

EXPERIENCE DESIGNED FOR THE WAY TODAY'S STUDENTS READ, THINK, AND LEARN When students are engaged deeply, they learn more effectively and perform better in their courses. This simple fact inspired the creation of REVEL: an immersive learning experience designed for the way today's students read, think, and learn. Built in collaboration with educators and students nationwide, REVEL is the newest, fully digital way to deliver respected Pearson content.

REVEL enlivens course content with media interactives and assessments—integrated directly within the authors' narrative—that provide opportunities for students to read about and practice course material in tandem. This immersive experience boosts student engagement, which leads to better understanding of concepts and improved performance throughout the course.

Learn more about REVEL

www.pearsonhighered.com/revel

The seventeenth edition includes integrated videos and media content throughout, allowing students to explore topics more deeply at the point of relevancy.

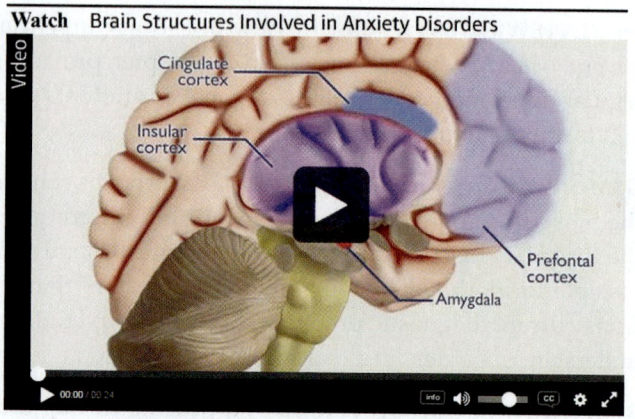

Revel also offers the ability for students to assess their content mastery by taking multiple-choice quizzes that offer instant feedback and by participating in a variety of writing assignments such as peer-reviewed questions and auto-graded assignments.

Speaking Out: Interviews with People Who Struggle with Psychological Disorders

This set of video segments allows students to see firsthand accounts of patients with various disorders. The interviews were conducted by licensed clinicians and range in length from 8 to 25 minutes. Disorders include major depressive disorder, obsessive-compulsive disorder, anorexia nervosa, PTSD, alcoholism, schizophrenia, autism, ADHD, bipolar disorder, social phobia, hypochondriasis, borderline personality disorder, and adjustment to physical illness. These video segments are available on DVD.

Volume 1: ISBN 0131933329

Volume 2: ISBN 0136003036

Volume 3: ISBN 0132308916

MyPsychLab (0205952372)

Available at www.MyPsychLab.com, MyPsychLab is an online homework, tutorial, and assessment program that truly engages students in learning. It helps students better prepare for class, quizzes, and exams—resulting in better performance in the course. It provides educators a dynamic set of tools for gauging individual and class performance:

Customizable—MyPsychLab is customizable. Instructors choose what students' course looks like. Homework, applications, and more can easily be turned on and off.

Blackboard Single Sign-on—MyPsychLab can be used by itself or linked to any course management system. Blackboard single sign-on provides deep linking to all New MyPsychLab resources.

Pearson eText and Chapter Audio—Like the printed text, students can highlight relevant passages and add notes. The Pearson eText can be accessed through laptops, iPads, and tablets. Download the free Pearson eText app to use on tablets. Students can also listen to their text with the Audio eText.

Assignment Calendar & Gradebook—A drag and drop assignment calendar makes assigning and completing work easy. The automatically graded assessment provides instant feedback and flows into the gradebook, which can be used in the MyPsychLab or exported.

Personalized Study Plan—Students' personalized plans promote better critical thinking skills. The study plan organizes students' study needs into sections, such as Remembering, Understanding, Applying, and Analyzing.

Instructor's Manual (0134319451)

A comprehensive tool for class preparation and management, each chapter includes teaching objectives; a chapter overview; a detailed lecture outline; a list of key terms; teaching resources, including lecture launchers, class activities, demonstrations, assignments, teaching tips, and handouts; a list of video, media, and Web resources; and a sample syllabus. Available for download on the Instructor's Resource Center at www.pearsonhighered.com.

Test Bank (0134474767)

The Test Bank is composed of approximately 2,000 fully referenced multiple-choice, completion, short-answer, and concise essay questions. Each question is accompanied by a page reference, difficulty level, skill type (factual, conceptual, or applied), topic, and a correct answer. Available for download on the Instructor's Resource Center at www.pearsonhighered.com.

MyTest (0134319478)

A powerful assessment-generation program that helps instructors easily create and print quizzes and exams. Questions and tests can be authored online, allowing instructors ultimate flexibility and the ability to efficiently manage assessments anytime, anywhere. Instructors can easily access existing questions and edit, create, and store questions using a simple drag-and-drop technique and Word-like controls. Data on each question provides information on difficulty level and the page number of the corresponding text discussion. For more information, go to www.PearsonMyTest.com.

Lecture PowerPoint Slides (0134319443)

The PowerPoint slides provide an active format for presenting concepts from each chapter and feature relevant figures and tables from the text. Available for download on the Instructor's Resource Center at www.pearsonhighered.com.

Enhanced Lecture PowerPoint Slides with Embedded Videos (0134474791) have been embedded with select Speaking Out video pertaining to each disorder chapter, enabling instructors to show videos within the context of their lecture.

PowerPoint Slides for Photos, Figures, and Tables (013447483X) contain only the photos, figures, and line art from the text. Available for download on the Instructor's Resource Center at www.pearsonhighered.com.

Acknowledgments

It takes each member of the author team more than a year of focused work to produce a new edition of this textbook. During this time, family and friends receive much less attention than they deserve. We are aware that a few lines of acknowledgment in a preface do little to compensate those close to us for all the inconveniences and absences they have endured. Nonetheless, Jill Hooley is ever grateful to Kip Schur for his patience, love, support, and ability to retain a sense of humor throughout the revision process. She also wishes to thank Tina Chou for her help with producing an image for Chapter 10. James Butcher would like to thank his wife, Carolyn L. Williams, and his children, Holly Butcher, Sherry Butcher, and Jay Butcher, for their

patience and support during this time. Matthew Nock would like to thank his wife, Keesha, and their children Matt Jr., Maya, and Georgina, for their patience (and tolerance). He is also grateful to Franchesca Ramirez and Nicole Murman for their assistance in the preparation of this edition. Finally, Susan Mineka thanks her graduate students, friends, and family for their patience and support.

The authors would like to express our most extreme gratitude, respect, and appreciation to our amazing development editor, Stephanie Ventura. Her insightful recommendations, editorial excellence, and all-around awesomeness made her a delight to work with. (*Note:* If they had let her edit this section, she would have caught that we just ended a sentence with a preposition. She's that good.) A big thank you also goes to Amber Chow, our acquisitions editor, for her leadership, guidance, advice, and support of this book. Without Amber's ability to manage every challenge that arose, this book might still be in the production stages. In addition, we are grateful to Carrie Brandon for all of her hard work, support, and especially for her instrumental role in creating new video for this edition. Another special thank you goes to Cecilia Turner, our program manager, for her expert coordination of all aspects of this project as well as to Donna Simons and Sherry Lewis for their skillful management of the production of this book. We also thank Laura Chadwick for her efforts to secure all the permissions necessary for the figures and photographs.

Many experts, researchers, and users of this book provided us with comments on individual chapters. We are extremely grateful for their input and feedback. Their knowledge and expertise help us keep this text current and accurate.

We are also especially grateful to the many reviewers who have given us invaluable feedback on this and previous editions of *Abnormal Psychology*: Joe Davis, CSU/SWC; Dan Fox, University of Houston; Marvin Lee, Tennessee State University; Stevie McKenna, Rutgers University; Loreto Prieto, Iowa State University; Hugh Riley, Baylor University; Edward Selby, Rutgers University; Tasia Smith, University of Florida; Stephanie Stein, Central Washington University; David Topor, Harvard University; Anthony Zoccolillo, Texas A&M; Angela Bragg, Mount Hood Community College; Greg Carey, University of Colorado; Louis Castonguay, Pennsylvania State University; Richard Cavasina, California University of Pennsylvania; Dianne Chambless, University of Pennsylvania; Lee Anna Clark, The University of Iowa; Barbara Cornblatt; William Paul Deal, University of Mississippi; Raymond L. Eastman, Stephen F. Austin State University; John F. Edens, Sam Houston State University; Colleen Ehrnstrom, University of Colorado at Boulder; William Fals-Stewart, The State University of New York at Buffalo; John P. Forsyth, The

State University of New York at Albany; Louis R. Franzini, San Diego State University; David H. Gleaves, Texas A&M University; Michael Green, University of California at Los Angeles; Steven Haynes, University of Hawaii at Manoa; Kathi Heffner, Ohio University; Daniel Holland, University of Arkansas at Little Rock; Steven Hollon, Vanderbilt University; Joanne Hoven Stohs, California State University Fullerton; Robert Howland, University of Pittsburgh, School of Medicine; Jean W. Hunt, Cumberland College; Alexandrea Hye-Young Park, Virginia Tech; William G. Iacono, University of Minnesota; Jessica Jablonski, University of Delaware; Erick Janssen, Indiana University; Sheri Johnson, University of Miami; Ann Kane, Barnstable High; Alan Kazdin, Yale University; Lynne Kemen, Hunter College; Carolin Keutzer, University of Oregon; John F. Kihlstrom, University of California at Berkeley; Gerald Koocher, Simmons College; David Kosson, Chicago Medical School; Marvin Lee, Tennessee State University; Brett Litz, Boston University; Brendan Maher, Harvard University; Richard McNally, Harvard University; Edwin Megargee, Florida State University; William Miller, University of New Mexico; Robin Morgan, Indiana University Southeast; Michael Neboschick, College of Charleston; Matthew Nock, Harvard University; Chris Patrick, Florida State University; Marcus Patterson, University of Massachusetts; John Daniel Paxton, Lorain County Community College; Walter Penk, Memorial Veterans Hospital, Bedford, MA; Diego Pizzagalli, Harvard University; Lauren Polvere, Concordia University; Andy Pomerantz, Southern Illinois University, Edwardsville; Harvey Richman, Columbus State University; Barry J. Ries, Minnesota State University; Lizabeth Roemer, University of Massachusetts at Boston; Rick Seime, Mayo Clinic; Frances Sessa, Pennsylvania State University, Abington; Brad Schmidt, Ohio State University; Kandy Stahl, Stephen F. Austin State University; Stephanie Stein, Central Washington University; Xuan Stevens, Florida International University; Eric Stice, University of Texas at Austin; Marcus Tye, Dowling College; Beverly Vchulek, Columbia College; Michael E. Walker, Stephen F. Austin State University; Clifton Watkins, University of North Texas; Nathan Weed, Central Michigan University; and Kenneth J. Zucker, Centre for Addiction and Mental Health, Ontario, Canada.

About the Authors

Jill M. Hooley
Harvard University

Jill M. Hooley is a professor of psychology at Harvard University. She is also the head of the experimental psychopathology and clinical psychology program at Harvard. Dr. Hooley was born in England and received a BSc in psychology from the University of Liverpool. This was followed by research work at Cambridge University. She then attended Magdalen College, Oxford, where she completed her DPhil. After a move to the United States and additional training in clinical psychology at SUNY Stony Brook, Dr. Hooley took a position at Harvard, where she has been a faculty member since 1985.

Dr. Hooley has a long-standing interest in psychosocial predictors of psychiatric relapse in patients with severe psychopathology such as schizophrenia and depression. Her research has been supported by grants from the National Institute of Mental Health and by the Borderline Personality Disorder Research Foundation. She uses fMRI to study emotion regulation in people who are vulnerable to depression and in people who are suffering from borderline personality disorder. Another area of research interest is nonsuicidal self-harming behaviors such as skin cutting or burning.

In 2000, Dr. Hooley received the Aaron T. Beck Award for Excellence in Psychopathology Research. She is also a past president of the Society for Research in Psychopathology. The author of many scholarly publications, Dr. Hooley was appointed Associate Editor for *Clinical Psychological Science* in 2012. She is also an associate editor for *Applied and Preventive Psychology* and serves on the editorial boards of several journals including the *Journal of Consulting and Clinical Psychology*, the *Journal of Family Psychology*, *Family Process*, and *Personality Disorders: Theory, Research and Treatment*. In 2015 Dr. Hooley received the Zubin Award for Lifetime Achievement in Psychopathology Research from the Society for Research in Psychopathology.

At Harvard, Dr. Hooley has taught graduate and undergraduate classes in introductory psychology, abnormal psychology, schizophrenia, mood disorders, clinical psychology, psychiatric diagnosis, and psychological treatment. Reflecting her commitment to the scientist-practitioner model, she also does clinical work specializing in the treatment of people with depression, anxiety disorders, and personality disorders.

James N. Butcher
Professor Emeritus, University of Minnesota

James N. Butcher was born in West Virginia. He enlisted in the army when he was 17 years old and served in the airborne infantry for 3 years, including a 1-year tour in Korea during the Korean War. After military service, he attended Guilford College, graduating in 1960 with a BA in psychology. He received an MA in experimental psychology in 1962 and a PhD in clinical psychology from the University of North Carolina at Chapel Hill. He was awarded Doctor Honoris Causa from the Free University of Brussels, Belgium, in 1990 and an honorary doctorate from the University of Florence, Florence, Italy, in 2005. He is currently professor emeritus in the Department of Psychology at the University of Minnesota. He was associate director and director of the clinical psychology program at the university for 19 years. He was a member of the University of Minnesota Press's MMPI Consultative Committee, which undertook the revision of the MMPI in 1989. He was formerly the editor of *Psychological Assessment*, a journal of the American Psychological Association, and serves as consulting editor or reviewer for numerous other journals in psychology and psychiatry. Dr. Butcher was actively involved in developing and organizing disaster response programs for dealing with human problems following airline disasters during his career. He organized a model crisis intervention disaster response for the Minneapolis-St. Paul Airport and organized and supervised the psychological services offered following two major airline disasters: Northwest Flight 255 in Detroit, Michigan, and Aloha Airlines on Maui. He is a fellow of the Society for Personality Assessment. He has published 60 books and more than 250 articles in the fields of abnormal psychology, cross-cultural psychology, and personality assessment.

Matthew K. Nock
Harvard University

Matthew Nock was born and raised in New Jersey. Matt received his BA from Boston University (1995), followed by two masters (2000, 2001) and a PhD from Yale University (2003). He also completed a clinical internship at Bellevue Hospital and the New York University Child Study Center (2003). Matt joined the faculty of Harvard University in 2003 and has been there ever since, currently serving as a Professor in the Department of Psychology. While an undergraduate, Matt became very interested in the question of why people do things to intentionally harm themselves and he has been conducting research aimed at answering this question ever since. His research is multidisciplinary in nature and uses a range of methodological approaches (e.g., epidemiologic surveys, laboratory-based experiments, and clinic-based studies) to better understand how these behaviors develop, how to predict them, and how to prevent their occurrence. His work is funded by research grants from the National Institutes of Health, Department of Defense, and several private foundations. Matt's research has been published in over 100 scientific papers and book chapters and has been recognized through the receipt of awards from the American Psychological Association, the Association for Behavioral and Cognitive Therapies, and the American Association of Suicidology. In 2011 he received a MacArthur Fellowship (aka, "Genius Grant") in recognition of his research on suicide and self-harm. At Harvard, Matt teaches courses on various topics including psychopathology, statistics, research methods, and cultural diversity. He has received numerous teaching and mentoring awards including the Roslyn Abramson Teaching Award and the Petra Shattuck Prize.

Susan Mineka
Northwestern University

Susan Mineka, born and raised in Ithaca, New York, received her undergraduate degree magna cum laude in psychology at Cornell University. She received a PhD in experimental psychology from the University of Pennsylvania and later completed a formal clinical retraining program from 1981 to 1984. She taught at the University of Wisconsin–Madison and at the University of Texas at Austin before moving to Northwestern University in 1987. Since 1987 she has been a professor of psychology at Northwestern, and from 1998 to 2006 she served as director of clinical training there. She has taught a wide range of undergraduate and graduate courses, including introductory psychology, learning, motivation, abnormal psychology, and cognitive-behavior therapy. Her current research interests include cognitive and behavioral approaches to understanding the etiology, maintenance, and treatment of anxiety and mood disorders. She is currently a Fellow of the American Psychological Association, the American Psychological Society, and the Academy of Cognitive Therapy. She has served as editor of the *Journal of Abnormal Psychology* (1990–1994). She also served as associate editor for *Emotion* from 2002 to 2006 and is on the editorial boards of several of the leading journals in the field. She was also president of the Society for the Science of Clinical Psychology (1994–1995) and was president of the Midwestern Psychological Association (1997). She also served on the American Psychological Association's Board of Scientific Affairs (1992–1994, chair 1994), on the Executive Board of the Society for Research in Psychopathology (1992–1994, 2000–2003), and on the Board of Directors of the American Psychological Society (2001–2004). During 1997 and 1998 she was a fellow at the Center for Advanced Study in the Behavioral Sciences at Stanford.

Chapter 1
Abnormal Psychology: Overview and Research Approaches

⋁ Learning Objectives

1.1 Explain how we define abnormality and classify mental disorders.

1.2 Describe the advantages and disadvantages of classification.

1.3 Explain how culture affects what is considered abnormal and describe two different culture-specific disorders.

1.4 Distinguish between incidence and prevalence and identify the most common and prevalent mental disorders.

1.5 Discuss why abnormal psychology research can be conducted in almost any setting.

1.6 Describe three different approaches used to gather information about mental disorders.

1.7 Explain why a control (or comparison group) is necessary to adequately test a hypothesis.

1.8 Discuss why correlational research designs are valuable, even though they cannot be used to make causal inferences.

1.9 Explain the key features of an experimental design.

Abnormal psychology is concerned with understanding the nature, causes, and treatment of mental disorders. The topics and problems within the field of abnormal psychology surround us every day. You have only to read a newspaper, flip through a magazine, surf the web, or sit through a movie to be exposed to some of the issues that clinicians and researchers deal with on a day-to-day basis. All too often, some celebrity is in the news because of a drug or alcohol problem, a suicide attempt, an eating disorder, or some other psychological difficulty. Countless books provide personal accounts of struggles with schizophrenia, depression, phobias, and panic attacks. Films and TV shows portray aspects of abnormal behavior with varying degrees of accuracy. And then there are the tragic news stories of mothers who kill their children, in which problems with depression, schizophrenia, or postpartum difficulties seem to be implicated.

Abnormal psychology can also be found much closer to home. Walk around any college campus, and you will see flyers about peer support groups for people with eating disorders, depression, and a variety of other disturbances. You may even know someone who has experienced a clinical problem. It may be a cousin with a cocaine habit, a roommate with bulimia, or a grandparent who is developing Alzheimer's disease. It may be a coworker of your mother's who is hospitalized for depression, a neighbor who is afraid to leave the house, or someone at your gym who works out intensely despite being worrisomely thin. It may even be the disheveled street person in the aluminum foil hat who shouts, "Leave me alone!" to voices only he can hear.

The issues of abnormal psychology capture our interest, demand our attention, and trigger our concern. They also compel us to ask questions. To illustrate further, let's consider two clinical cases.

Monique

Monique is a 24-year-old law student. She is attractive, neatly dressed, and clearly very bright. If you were to meet her, you would think that she had few problems in her life; but Monique has been drinking alcohol since she was 14, and she smokes marijuana every day. Although she describes herself as "just a social drinker," she drinks four or five glasses of wine when she goes out with friends and also drinks several glasses of wine a night when she is alone in her apartment in the evening. She frequently misses early morning classes because she feels too hung over to get out of bed. On several occasions her drinking has caused her to black out. Although she denies having any problems with alcohol, Monique admits that her friends and family have become very concerned about her and have suggested that she seek help. Monique, however, says, "I don't think I am an alcoholic because I never drink in the mornings." The previous week she decided to stop smoking marijuana entirely because she was concerned that she might have a drug problem. However, she found it impossible to stop and is now smoking regularly again.

Scott

Scott was born into an affluent family. There were no problems when he was born and he seemed to develop normally when he was a child. He went to a prestigious college and completed his degree in mathematics. Shortly afterwards, however, he began to isolate himself from his family and he abandoned his plans for graduate studies. He traveled to San Francisco, took an apartment in a run-down part of the city, became increasingly suspicious of people around him, and developed strange ideas about brain transfer technology. Shortly before Christmas, he received a package from a friend. As he opened the package, he reported that his "head exploded" and he began to hear voices, even though no one was around. The voices began to tell him what to do and what not to do. His concerned parents came out to visit him, but he refused to seek any help or return home to live with them. Shortly after, he left the city and, living as a homeless person, moved around the country, eventually making his way back to the East Coast. Throughout that time he was hearing voices every day—sometimes as many as five or six different ones. Eventually Scott's worried family located him and persuaded him to seek treatment. Although he has been hospitalized several times and been on many different medications in the intervening years, Scott still has symptoms of psychosis. His voices have never entirely gone away and they still dictate his behavior to a considerable extent. Now age 49, he lives in a halfway house, and works part-time shelving books in a university library.

Perhaps you found yourself asking questions as you read about Monique and Scott. For example, because Monique doesn't drink in the mornings, you might have

Fergie has spoken about her past struggles with substance abuse, specifically crystal meth.

wondered whether she could really have a serious alcohol problem. She does. This is a question that concerns the criteria that must be met before someone receives a particular diagnosis. Or perhaps you wondered whether other people in Monique's family likewise have drinking problems. They do. This is a question about what we call **family aggregation**—that is, whether a disorder runs in families.

You may also have been curious about what is wrong with Scott and why he is hearing voices. Questions about the age of onset of his symptoms as well as predisposing factors may have occurred to you. Scott has schizophrenia, a disorder that often strikes in late adolescence or early adulthood. Also, as Scott's case illustrates, it is not especially unusual for someone who develops schizophrenia to develop in a seemingly normal manner before suddenly becoming ill.

These cases, which describe real people, give some indication of just how profoundly lives can be derailed because of mental disorders. It is hard to read about difficulties such as these without feeling compassion for the people who are struggling. Still, in addition to compassion, clinicians and researchers who want to help people like Monique and Scott must have other attributes and skills. If we are to understand mental disorders, we must learn to ask the kinds of questions that will enable us to help the patients and families who have mental disorders. These questions are at the very heart of a research-based approach that looks to use scientific inquiry and careful observation to understand abnormal psychology.

Asking questions is an important aspect of being a psychologist. Psychology is a fascinating field, and abnormal psychology is one of the most interesting areas of psychology (although we are undoubtedly biased). Psychologists are trained to ask questions and to conduct research. Though not all people who are trained in abnormal psychology (this field is sometimes called psychopathology) conduct research, they still rely heavily on their scientific skills and ability both to ask questions and to put information together in coherent and logical ways. For example, when a clinician first sees a new client or patient, he or she asks many questions to try and understand the issues or problems related to that person. The clinician will also rely on current research to choose the most effective treatment. The best treatments of 20, 10, or even 5 years ago are not invariably the best treatments of today. Knowledge accumulates and advances are made—and research is the engine that drives all of these developments.

In this chapter, we outline the field of abnormal psychology and the varied training and activities of the people who work within its demands. First we describe the ways in which abnormal behavior is defined and classified so that researchers and mental health professionals can communicate with each other about the people they see. Some of the issues here are probably more complex and

controversial than you might expect. We also outline basic information about the extent of behavioral abnormalities in the population at large.

The second part of this chapter is devoted to research. We make every effort to convey to you how abnormal behavior is studied. Research is at the heart of progress and knowledge in abnormal psychology. The more you know and understand about how research is conducted, the more educated and aware you will be about what research findings do and do not mean.

What Do We Mean by Abnormality?

1.1 **Explain how we define abnormality and classify mental disorders.**

It may come as a surprise to you that there is still no universal agreement about what is meant by *abnormality* or *disorder*. This is not to say we do not have definitions; we do. However, a truly satisfactory definition will probably always remain elusive (Lilienfeld et al., 2013; Stein et al., 2010).

Indicators of Abnormality

Why does the definition of a mental disorder present so many challenges? A major problem is that there is no one behavior that makes someone abnormal. However, there are some clear elements or indicators of abnormality (Lilienfeld et al., 2013; Stein et al., 2010). No single indicator is sufficient in and of itself to define or determine abnormality. Nonetheless, the more that someone has difficulties in the following areas, the more likely he or she is to have some form of mental disorder:

1. **Subjective distress:** If people suffer or experience psychological pain we are inclined to consider this as indicative of abnormality. People with depression clearly report being distressed, as do people with anxiety disorders. But what of the patient who is manic and whose mood is one of elation? He or she may not be experiencing any distress. In fact, many such patients dislike taking medications because they do not want to lose their manic "highs." You may have a test tomorrow and be exceedingly worried. But we would hardly label your subjective distress abnormal. Although subjective distress is an element of abnormality in many cases, it is neither a sufficient condition (all that is needed) nor even a necessary condition (a feature that all cases of abnormality must show) for us to consider something as abnormal.

2. **Maladaptiveness:** Maladaptive behavior is often an indicator of abnormality. The person with anorexia may restrict her intake of food to the point where she

becomes so emaciated that she needs to be hospitalized. The person with depression may withdraw from friends and family and may be unable to work for weeks or months. Maladaptive behavior interferes with our well-being and with our ability to enjoy our work and our relationships. But not all disorders involve maladaptive behavior. Consider the con artist and the contract killer, both of whom have antisocial personality disorder. The first may be able glibly to talk people out of their life savings, the second to take someone's life in return for payment. Is this behavior maladaptive? Not for them, because it is the way in which they make their respective livings. We consider them abnormal, however, because their behavior is maladaptive for and toward society.

3. **Statistical deviancy:** The word *abnormal* literally means "away from the normal." But simply considering statistically rare behavior to be abnormal does not provide us with a solution to our problem of defining abnormality. Genius is statistically rare, as is perfect pitch. However, we do not consider people with such uncommon talents to be abnormal in any way. Also, just because something is statistically common doesn't make it normal. The common cold is certainly very common, but it is regarded as an illness nonetheless.

On the other hand, intellectual disability (which is statistically rare and represents a deviation from normal) is considered to reflect abnormality. This tells us that in defining abnormality we make value judgments. If something is statistically rare and undesirable (as is severely diminished intellectual functioning), we are more likely to consider it abnormal than something that is statistically rare and highly desirable (such as genius) or something that is undesirable but statistically common (such as rudeness).

As with most accomplished athletes, Venus and Serena Williams' physical ability is abnormal in a literal and statistical sense. Their behavior, however, would not be labeled as being abnormal by psychologists. Why not?

4. **Violation of the standards of society:** All cultures have rules. Some of these are formalized as laws. Others form the norms and moral standards that we are taught to follow. Although many social rules are arbitrary to some extent, when people fail to follow the conventional social and moral rules of their cultural group, we may consider their behavior abnormal. For example, driving a car or watching television would be considered highly abnormal for the Amish of Pennsylvania. However, both of these activities reflect normal everyday behavior for most other Pennsylvania residents.

Of course, much depends on the magnitude of the violation and on how commonly the rule is violated by others. As illustrated in the preceding example, a behavior is most likely to be viewed as abnormal when it violates the standards of society and is statistically deviant or rare. In contrast, most of us have parked illegally at some point. This failure to follow the rules is so statistically common that we tend not to think of it as abnormal. Yet when a mother drowns her children there is instant recognition that this is abnormal behavior.

5. **Social discomfort:** Not all rules are explicit. And not all rules bother us when they are violated. Nonetheless, when someone violates an implicit or unwritten social rule, those around him or her may experience a sense of discomfort or unease. Imagine that you are sitting in an almost empty bus. There are rows of unoccupied seats. Then someone comes in and sits down right next to you. How do you feel? Is the person's behavior abnormal? Why? The person is not breaking any formal rule. He or she has paid for a ticket and is permitted to sit anywhere he or she likes. But your sense of social discomfort ("Why did this person sit right next to me when there are so many empty seats available?") will probably incline you to think that this is an example of abnormal behavior. In other words, social discomfort is another potential way that we can recognize abnormality. But again, much depends on circumstances. If the person who gets on the bus is someone you know well, it might be more unusual if he or she did not join you.

6. **Irrationality and unpredictability:** As we have already noted, we expect people to behave in certain ways. Although a little unconventionality may add some spice to life, there is a point at which we are likely to consider a given unorthodox behavior abnormal. If a person sitting next to you suddenly began to scream and yell obscenities at nothing, you would probably regard that behavior as abnormal. It would be unpredictable, and it would make no sense to you. The disordered speech and the disorganized behavior of patients with schizophrenia are often irrational. Such behaviors are also a hallmark of the manic phases of bipolar disorder. Perhaps the most important factor, however, is our

evaluation of whether the person can control his or her behavior. Few of us would consider a roommate who began to recite speeches from *King Lear* to be abnormal if we knew that he was playing Lear in the next campus Shakespeare production—or even if he was a dramatic person given to extravagant outbursts. On the other hand, if we discovered our roommate lying on the floor, flailing wildly, and reciting Shakespeare, we might consider calling for assistance if this was entirely out of character and we knew of no reason why he should be behaving in such a manner.

7. **Dangerousness:** It seems quite reasonable to think that someone who is a danger to him- or herself or to another person must be psychologically abnormal. Indeed, therapists are required to hospitalize suicidal clients or contact the police (as well as the person who is the target of the threat) if they have a client who makes an explicit threat to harm another person. But, as with all of the other elements of abnormality, if we rely only on dangerousness as our sole feature of abnormality, we will run into problems. Is a soldier in combat mentally ill? What about someone who is an extremely bad driver? Both of these people may be a danger to others. Yet we would not consider them to be mentally ill. Why not? And why is someone who engages in extreme sports or who has a dangerous hobby (such as free diving, race car driving, or keeping poisonous snakes as pets) not immediately regarded as mentally ill? Just because we may be a danger to ourselves or to others does not mean we are mentally ill. Conversely, we cannot assume that someone diagnosed with a mental disorder must be dangerous. Although people with mental illness do commit serious crimes, serious crimes are also committed every day by people who have no signs of mental disorder. Indeed, research suggests that in people with mental illness, dangerousness is more the exception than the rule (Corrigan & Watson, 2005).

One final point bears repeating. Decisions about abnormal behavior always involve social judgments and are based on the values and expectations of society at large. This means that culture plays a role in determining what is and is not abnormal. In addition, because society is constantly shifting and becoming more or less tolerant of certain behaviors, what is considered abnormal or deviant in one decade may not be considered abnormal or deviant a decade or two later. At one time, homosexuality was classified as a mental disorder. But this is no longer the case (it was removed from the formal classification system in 1974). A generation ago, pierced noses and navels were regarded as highly deviant and prompted questions about a person's mental health. Now, however, such adornments are commonplace and attract little attention. What other behaviors can you think of that are now considered normal but were regarded as deviant in the past?

How important is dangerousness to the definition of mental illness? If we are a risk to ourselves or to others, does this mean we are mentally ill?

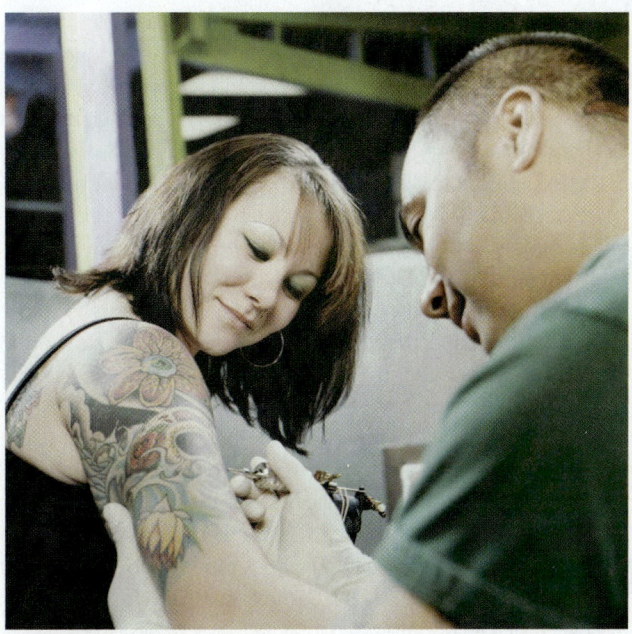

Tattoos, which were once regarded as highly deviant, are now quite commonplace and considered fashionable by many.

As you think about these issues, consider the person described in the World Around Us box. He is certainly an unusual human being. But is his behavior abnormal? Do you think everyone will agree about this?

The World Around Us

Extreme Generosity or Pathological Behavior?

Zell Kravinsky was a brilliant student who grew up in a working-class neighborhood in Philadelphia. He won prizes at school, and at the age of 12, he began investing in the stock market. Despite his abilities, his Russian immigrant parents were, in the words of a family friend, "steadfast in denying him any praise." Kravinsky eventually completed two Ph.D. degrees and indulged his growing interest in real estate. By the time he was 45 years old, he was married with children. His assets amounted to almost $45 million.

Although Kravinsky had a talent for making money, he found it difficult to spend it. He drove an old car, did not give his children pocket money, and lived with his family in a modest home. As his fortune grew, however, he began to talk to his friends about his plans to give all of his assets to charity. His philanthropy began in earnest when he and his wife gave two gifts, totaling $6.2 million, to the Centers for Disease Control Foundation. They also donated an apartment building to a school for the disabled in Philadelphia. The following year the Kravinskys gave real estate gifts worth approximately $30 million to Ohio State University.

Kravinsky's motivation for his donations was to help others. According to one of his friends, "He gave away the money because he had it and there were people who needed it. But it changed his way of looking at himself. He decided the purpose of his life was to give away things." After he had put some money aside in trust for his wife and his children, Kravinsky's personal assets were reduced to a house (on which he had a substantial mortgage), two minivans, and around $80,000 in stocks and cash. He had essentially given away his entire fortune.

Kravinsky's donations did not end when his financial assets became depleted. He began to be preoccupied with the idea of nondirected organ donations, in which an altruistic person gives an organ to a total stranger. When he learned that he could live quite normally with only one kidney, Kravinsky decided that the personal costs of giving away one of his kidneys were minimal compared to the benefits received by the kidney recipient. His wife, however, did not share his view. Although she had consented to bequeathing substantial sums of money to worthwhile charities, when it came to her husband offering his kidney, she could not support him.

For Kravinsky, however, the burden of refusing to help alleviate the suffering of someone in need was almost unbearable, even if it meant sacrificing his very own organs. He called the Albert Einstein Medical Center and spoke to a transplant coordinator. He met with a surgeon and then with a psychiatrist. Kravinsky told the psychiatrist that his wife did not support his desire to donate one of his kidneys. When the psychiatrist told him that he was doing something he did not have to do, Kravinsky's response was that he did need to make this sacrifice: "You're missing the whole point. It's as much a necessity as food, water, and air."

Is Zell Kravinsky's behavior abnormal, or is he a man with profound moral conviction and courage?

Three months later, Kravinsky left his home in the early hours of the morning, drove to the hospital, and donated his right kidney. He informed his wife after the surgery was over. In spite of the turmoil that his kidney donation created within his family, Kravinsky's mind turned back to philanthropy almost immediately. "I lay there in the hospital, and I thought about all my other good organs. When I do something good, I feel that I can do more. I burn to do more. It's a heady feeling." By the time he was discharged, he was wondering about giving away his one remaining kidney.

After the operation, Kravinsky experienced a loss of direction. He had come to view his life as a continuing donation. However, now that his financial assets and his kidney were gone, what could he provide to the less fortunate? Sometimes he imagines offering his entire body for donation. "My organs could save several people if I gave my whole body away." He acknowledges that he feels unable to hurt his family through the sacrifice of his life.

Several years after the kidney donation, Kravinsky still remains committed to giving away as much as possible. However, his actions have caused a tremendous strain in his marriage. In an effort to maintain a harmonious relationship with his wife, he is now involved in real estate and has bought his family a larger home. (Taken from I. Parker, 2004.)

Is Zell Kravinsky a courageous man of profound moral commitment? Or is his behavior abnormal and indicative of a mental disorder? Explain how you reached the conclusion you did.

DSM-5   Thinking Critically about *DSM-5*

What Is the *DSM* and Why Was It Revised?

The *Diagnostic and Statistical Manual of Mental Disorders* (*DSM*) provides all the information necessary (descriptions, lists of symptoms) to diagnose mental disorders. As such, it provides clinicians with specific diagnostic criteria for each disorder. This creates a common language so that a specific diagnosis means the same thing to one clinician as it does to another. In addition, providing descriptive information about the type and number of symptoms needed for each diagnosis helps ensure diagnostic accuracy and consistency (reliability). The *DSM* is also important for research. If patients could not be diagnosed reliably, it would be impossible to compare different treatments for patients with similar conditions. Although the *DSM* does not include information about treatment, clinicians need to have an accurate diagnosis in order to select the most appropriate treatment for their patients.

Since *DSM-I* was first published in 1952, the *DSM* has been revised from time to time. Revisions are important because they allow new scientific developments to be incorporated into how we think about mental disorders. The revision process for *DSM-5* had the goals of maintaining continuity with the previous edition (*DSM-IV*) as well as being guided by new research findings. But another guiding principle was that no constraints should be placed on the level of change that could be made. If this strikes you as a little contradictory, you are correct. Striking the right balance between change and continuity presented considerable challenges. It also created a great deal of controversy. As part of the revision process, experts in specific disorders were invited to join special *DSM-5* work groups and make specific recommendations for change. In some cases, the debates were so heated that people resigned from their work groups! Now that *DSM-5* is here, not everyone is happy with some of the changes that have been made. On the other hand, many of the revisions that have been made make a lot of sense. In the chapters that follow we highlight key changes in *DSM-5*. We also try to help you think critically about the reasons behind the specific modifications that were proposed and understand why they were accepted.

The *DSM-5* and the Definition of Mental Disorder

In the United States, the accepted standard for defining various types of mental disorders is the American Psychiatric Association's *Diagnostic and Statistical Manual of Mental Disorders*. This manual, commonly referred to as the *DSM*, is revised and updated from time to time. The current version, called *DSM-5*, was published in 2013. It is 947 pages long and contains a total of 541 diagnostic categories (Blashfield et al., 2014). This recent revision of the *DSM* has been the topic of much debate and controversy. In the Thinking Critically about *DSM-5* box we explain more about the *DSM* and discuss why a revision was necessary.

Although the *DSM* is widely used, it is not the only psychiatric classification system. The *International Classification of Diseases* (called *ICD-10* because it is now in its 10th revision) is produced by the World Health Organization (WHO). Chapter V of this document covers mental and behavioral disorders (WHO, 2015b). Although the *ICD-10* has much in common with *DSM-5*, it also many differences, with similar disorders having different names, for example. The *ICD-10* is used in many countries outside the United States and *ICD-11* is currently in development.

Within *DSM-5*, a mental disorder is defined as a syndrome that is present in an individual and that involves clinically significant disturbance in behavior, emotion regulation, or cognitive functioning. These disturbances are thought to reflect a dysfunction in biological, psychological, or developmental processes that are necessary for mental functioning. *DSM-5* also recognizes that mental disorders are usually associated with significant distress or disability in key areas of functioning such as social, occupational, or other activities. Predictable or culturally approved responses to common stressors or losses (such as death of a loved one) are excluded. It is also important that this dysfunctional pattern of behavior not stem from social deviance or conflicts that the person has with society as a whole.

This new *DSM-5* definition of mental illness was based on input from various *DSM-5* work groups as well as other sources (Broome & Bortolotti, 2010; First & Wakefield, 2010; Stein et al., 2010). Although this definition will still not satisfy everyone, it brings us even closer to a good working

Watch   What Does it Mean to Have a Mental Disorder?

idiosyncrasies: An unusual feature of a person.

description. Keep in mind that any definition of abnormality or mental disorder must be somewhat arbitrary. Rather than thinking of the *DSM* as a finished product, it should always be regarded as a work in progress, with regular updates and modifications to be expected. Although earlier versions of the *DSM* used Roman numerals to refer to each specific edition (e.g., *DSM-IV*), Arabic numerals are now being used instead of Roman numerals (5 versus V) to facilitate updating (e.g., *DSM-5.1*, *DSM-5.2*) in the future.

in review

- Why is abnormality so difficult to define?
- What characteristics help us recognize abnormality?

Classification and Diagnosis

1.2 **Describe the advantages and disadvantages of classification.**

If defining abnormality is so contentious and so difficult, why do we try to do it? One simple reason is that most sciences rely on classification (e.g., the periodic table in chemistry and the classification of living organisms into kingdoms, phyla, classes, and so on in biology). At the most fundamental level, classification systems provide us with a **nomenclature** (a naming system). This gives clinicians and researchers both a *common language* and *shorthand terms* for complex clinical conditions. Without having a common set of terms to describe specific clinical conditions, clinicians would have to talk at length about each patient individually to provide an overview of the patient's problems. But if there is a shared understanding of what the term "schizophrenia" means, for example, communication across professional boundaries is simplified and facilitated.

Another advantage of classification systems is that they enable us to *structure information* in a more helpful manner. Classification systems shape the way information is organized. For example, most classification systems typically place diagnoses that are thought to be related in some way close together. In *DSM-5*, the section on anxiety disorders includes disorders (such as panic disorder, specific phobia, and agoraphobia) that share the common features of fear and anxiety.

Organizing information within a classification system also allows us to study the different disorders that we classify and therefore to learn new things. In other words, *classification facilitates research*, which gives us more information and facilitates greater understanding, not only about what causes various disorders but also how they might best be treated. For example, thinking back to the cases you read about, Monique has alcohol and drug use disorders, and Scott has schizophrenia. Knowing what disorder each of them has is clearly very helpful, because Scott's treatment would be very different from Monique's.

A final effect of classification system usage is somewhat more mundane. As others have pointed out, the classification of mental disorders has social and political implications (see Keeley et al., 2015; Kirk & Kutchins, 1992). Simply put, *defining the domain* of what is considered to be pathological establishes the range of problems that the mental health profession can address. As a consequence, on a purely pragmatic level, it furthermore delineates which types of psychological difficulties warrant insurance reimbursement and the extent of such reimbursement.

What Are the Disadvantages of Classification?

Of course, a number of potential disadvantages are associated with the use of a discrete classification system. Classification, by its very nature, provides information in a shorthand form. However, using any form of shorthand inevitably leads to a *loss of information*. If we know the specific history, personality traits, idiosyncrasies, and familial relations of a person with a particular type of disorder (e.g., from reading a case summary), we naturally have much more information than if we were simply told the individual's diagnosis (e.g., schizophrenia). In other words, as we simplify through classification, we inevitably lose an array of personal details about the actual person who has the disorder.

Moreover, although things are improving, there can still be some **stigma** (disgrace) associated with having a psychiatric diagnosis. Stigma, of course, is hardly the fault of the diagnostic system itself. But even today, people are generally far more comfortable disclosing that they have a physical illness such as diabetes than they are admitting to any mental disorder. This is in part due to the fear (real or imagined) that speaking candidly about having a psychological disorder will result in unwanted social or occupational consequences or frank discrimination. Be honest. Have you ever described someone as "nuts," "crazy," or "a psycho"? Now think of the hurt that people with mental disorders experience when they hear such words. In one study, 96 percent of patients with schizophrenia reported that stigma was a routine part of their lives (Jenkins & Carpenter-Song, 2008). In spite of the large amount of information that is now available about mental health issues, the level of knowledge about mental illness (sometimes referred to as mental health literacy) is often very poor (Thornicroft et al., 2007). Stigma is a deterrent to seeking treatment for mental health problems. This is especially true for younger people, for men, and for ethnic minorities (Clement et al., 2015). Stigma is also a disproportionately greater deterrent to treatment seeking for two other groups: military personnel and (ironically) mental health professionals. Would you have predicted this? Why do you think this is the case?

Related to stigma is the problem of **stereotyping**. Stereotypes are automatic beliefs concerning other people that we unavoidably learn as a result of growing up in a particular culture (e.g., people who wear glasses are more intelligent; New Yorkers are rude). Because we may have heard about certain behaviors that can accompany mental disorders, we may automatically and incorrectly infer that these behaviors will also be present in any person we meet who has a psychiatric diagnosis. Negative stereotypes about psychiatric patients are also perpetuated in movies. If you have ever seen a horror movie you know that a common dominant theme involves the homicidal maniac. And an analysis of 55 horror films made between 2000 and 2012 has shown that it is people with psychosis who are most often portrayed as murderers (Goodwin, 2014). Stereotyping is also reflected in the comment "People like you don't go back to work" in the case example of James McNulty.

James McNulty

I have lived with bipolar disorder for more than 35 years—all of my adult life. The first 15 years were relatively conventional, at least on the surface. I graduated from an Ivy League university, started my own business, and began a career in local politics. I was married, the father of two sons. I experienced mood swings during these years, and as I got older the swings worsened. Eventually, I became so ill that I was unable to work, my marriage ended, I lost my business, and I became homeless.

At this point I had my most powerful experience with stigma. I was 38 years old. I had recently been discharged after a psychiatric hospitalization for a suicide attempt, I had no place to live, my savings were exhausted, and my only possession was a 4-year-old car. I contacted the mental health authorities in the state where I then lived and asked for assistance in dealing with my mental illness. I was told that to qualify for assistance I would need to sell my car and spend down the proceeds. I asked how I was supposed to get to work when I recovered enough to find a job. I was told, "Don't worry about going back to work. People like you don't go back to work." (McNulty, 2004)

Finally, stigma can be perpetuated by the problem of **labeling**. A person's self-concept may be directly affected by being given a diagnosis of schizophrenia, depression, or some other form of mental illness. How might you react if you were told something like this? Furthermore, once a group of symptoms is given a name and identified by means of a diagnosis, this diagnostic label can be hard to shake even if the person later makes a full recovery.

It is important to keep in mind, however, that diagnostic classification systems do not classify people. Rather, *they classify the disorders that people have*. And stigma may be less a consequence of the diagnostic label than a result of the disturbed behavior that got the person the diagnosis in the first place. In some situations, a diagnosis may even reduce stigma because it provides at least a partial explanation for a person's otherwise inexplicable behavior (Ruscio, 2004). Nonetheless, when we note that someone has an illness, we should take care not to define him or her by that illness.

Respectful and appropriate language should instead be used. At one time, it was quite common for mental health professionals to describe a given patient as "a schizophrenic" or "a manic-depressive." Now, however, it is widely acknowledged that it is more accurate (not to mention more considerate) to use what is called person-first language and say, "a person with schizophrenia," or "a person with bipolar disorder." Simply put, the person is not the diagnosis.

How Can We Reduce Prejudicial Attitudes Toward People Who Are Mentally Ill?

Negative reactions to people with mental illness are common and may be a fairly widespread phenomenon throughout the world. Using focus groups, Arthur and colleagues (2010) asked community residents in Jamaica about the concept of stigma. Some participants came from rural communities, others from more urban areas. Regardless of their gender, level of education, or where they lived, most participants described highly prejudicial attitudes toward those with mental illnesses. One middle-class male participant said, "We treat them as in a sense second class citizens, we stay far away from them, ostracize them, we just treat them bad" (see Arthur et al., 2010, p. 263). Fear of people who are mentally ill was also commonly expressed. A rural-dwelling middle-class man described a specific situation in the following way, "There is a mad lady on the

Are attitudes toward people who are mentally ill in Jamaica more benign than they are in more industrialized countries?

road named […]. Even the police are afraid of her because she throws stones at them. She is very, very terrible" (p. 261). Moreover, even when more kindly attitudes were expressed, fear was still a common response. One person put it simply, "You are fearful even though you may be sympathetic" (p. 262). In short, the results of this study suggest that stereotyping, labeling, and stigma toward people with mental illness are not restricted to industrialized countries. Although we might wish that it were otherwise, prejudicial attitudes are common. This highlights the need for anti-stigma campaigns.

For a long time, it was thought that educating people that mental illnesses were "real" brain disorders might be the solution. Sadly, however, this does not seem to be the case. Although there have been impressive increases in the proportion of people who now understand that mental disorders have neurobiological causes, this increased awareness has not resulted in decreases in stigma. In one study, Pescosolido and colleagues (2010) asked people in the community to read a vignette (brief description) about a person who showed symptoms of mental illness. Some people read a vignette about a person who had schizophrenia. Others read a vignette about someone with clinical depression or alcohol dependence. Importantly, no diagnostic labels were used to describe these people. The vignettes simply provided descriptive information. Nonetheless, the majority of the people who were surveyed in this study expressed an unwillingness to work with the person described in the vignette. They also did not want to have to socialize with them and did not want them to marry into their family. Moreover, the level of rejection that was shown was just as high as it was in a similar survey that was done 10 years earlier. Over that same 10-year period, however, many more people embraced a neurobiological understanding about the causes of mental illness. So what this study tells us is that just because people understand that mental illness is caused by problems in the brain doesn't mean that they are any less prejudiced toward those with mental illness. This is a disappointing conclusion for everyone who hoped that more scientific research into the biology of mental illness would lead to the elimination of stigma.

Stigma does seem to be reduced by having more contact with people in the stigmatized group (Corrigan et al., 2014; Couture & Penn, 2003). However, there may be barriers to this. Simply imagining interacting with a person who has a mental disorder can lead to distress and also to unpleasant physical reactions. In an interesting study, Graves and colleagues (2005) asked college students enrolled in a psychology course to imagine interacting with a person whose image was shown to them on a slide. As the slide was being presented, subjects were given some scripted biographical information that described the person. In some scripts, the target person was described as having been diagnosed with schizophrenia, although it was also mentioned that he or she

was "doing much better now." In other trials, the biographical description made no mention of any mental illness when the person on the slide was being described. Students who took part in the study reported more distress and had more muscle tension in their brows when they imagined interacting with a person with schizophrenia than when they imagined interacting with a person who did not have schizophrenia. Heart rate changes also suggested they were experiencing the imagined interactions with the patients as being more unpleasant than the interactions with the nonpatients. Finally, research participants who had more psychophysiological reactivity to the slides of the patients reported higher levels of stigma toward these patients. These findings suggest that people may tend to avoid those with mental illness because the psychophysiological arousal these encounters create is experienced as unpleasant.

in review

- What is stigma? How common is it?
- What challenges are involved in reducing stigma toward people with mental illness?

Culture and Abnormality

1.3   **Explain how culture affects what is considered abnormal and describe two different culture-specific disorders.**

Just as we must consider changing societal values and expectations in defining abnormality, so too must we consider differences across cultures. In fact, this is explicitly acknowledged in the *DSM-5* definition of *disorder*. Within a given culture, many shared beliefs and behaviors exist that are widely accepted and that may constitute one or more customary practices. For instance, many people in Christian countries believe that the number 13 is unlucky. The origins of this may be linked to the Last Supper, at which 13 people were present. Many of us try to be especially cautious on Friday the 13th. Some hotels and apartment buildings avoid having a 13th floor altogether. Similarly, there is frequently no bed numbered 13 in hospital wards.

The Japanese, in contrast, are not worried about the number 13. Rather, they attempt to avoid the number 4. This is because in Japanese the sound of the word for "four" is similar to the sound of the word for "death" (see Tseng, 2001, pp. 105–106).

There is also considerable variation in the way different cultures describe psychological distress. For example, there is no word for "depressed" in the languages of certain Native Americans, Alaska Natives, and Southeast Asian cultures (Manson, 1995). Of course, this does not mean that members from such cultural groups do not experience clinically significant depression. As the accompanying case illustrates,

There is no word for "depressed" in the languages of certain Native American tribes. Members of these communities tend to describe their symptoms of depression in physical rather than emotional terms.

however, the way some disorders present themselves may depend on culturally sanctioned ways of articulating distress.

Depression in a Native American Elder

JGH is a 71-year-old member of a Southwestern tribe who has been brought to a local Indian Health Service hospital by one of his granddaughters and is seen in the general medical outpatient clinic for multiple complaints. Most of Mr. GH's complaints involve nonlocalized pain. When asked to point to where he hurts, Mr. GH indicates his chest, then his abdomen, his knees, and finally moves his hands "all over." Barely whispering, he mentions a phrase in his native language that translates as "whole body sickness." His granddaughter notes that he "has not been himself" recently. Specifically, Mr. GH, during the past 3 or 4 months, has stopped attending or participating in many events previously important to him and central to his role in a large extended family and clan. He is reluctant to discuss this change in behavior as well as his feelings. When questioned more directly, Mr. GH acknowledges that he has had difficulty falling asleep, sleeps intermittently through the night, and almost always awakens at dawn's first light. He admits that he has not felt like eating in recent months but denies weight loss, although his clothes hang loosely in many folds. Trouble concentrating and remembering are eventually disclosed as well. Asked why he has not participated in family and clan events in the last several months, Mr. GH describes himself as "too tired and full of pain" and "afraid of disappointing people." Further pressing by the clinician is met with silence. Suddenly the patient states, "You know, my sheep haven't been doing well lately. Their

coats are ragged; they're thinner. They just wander aimlessly; even the ewes don't seem to care about the little ones." Physical examination and laboratory tests are normal. Mr. GH continues to take two tablets of acetaminophen daily for mild arthritic pain. Although he describes himself as a "recovering alcoholic," Mr. GH reports not having consumed alcohol during the last 23 years. He denies any prior episodes of depression or other psychiatric problems. (Manson, 1995, p. 488)

As is apparent in the case of JGH, culture can shape the clinical presentation of disorders like depression, which are present across cultures around the world (see Draguns & Tanaka-Matsumi, 2003). In China, for instance, individuals with depression frequently focus on physical concerns (fatigue, dizziness, headaches) rather than verbalizing their feelings of melancholy or hopelessness (Kleinman, 1986; Parker et al., 2001). This focus on physical pain rather than emotional pain is also noteworthy in Mr. GH's case.

Despite progressively increasing cultural awareness, we still know relatively little concerning cultural interpretation and expression of abnormal psychology (Arrindell, 2003). The vast majority of the psychiatric literature originates from Euro-American countries—that is, Western Europe, North America, and Australia/New Zealand (Patel & Kim, 2007; Patel & Sumathipala, 2001). To exacerbate this underrepresentation, research published in languages other than English tends to be disregarded (Draguns, 2001).

Prejudice toward people with mental illness seems to be found worldwide. However, some types of psychopathology appear to be highly culture specific: They are found only in certain areas of the world and seem to be highly linked to culturally bound concerns. A case in point is *taijin kyofusho*. This syndrome, which is an anxiety disorder, is quite prevalent in Japan. It involves a marked fear that one's body, body parts, or body functions may offend, embarrass, or otherwise make others feel uncomfortable. Often, people with this disorder are afraid of blushing or upsetting others by their gaze, facial expression, or body odor (Levine & Gaw, 1995).

Some disorders are highly culture specific. For example, taijin kyofusho is a disorder that is prevalent in Japan. It is characterized by the fear that one may upset others by one's gaze, facial expression, or body odor.

Another culturally rooted expression of distress, found in people of Latino descent, especially those from the Caribbean, is *ataque de nervios* or an "attack of nerves" (Lizardi et al., 2009; Lopez & Guarnaccia, 2005). This is a clinical syndrome that does not seem to correspond to any specific diagnosis within the *DSM*. The symptoms of an *ataque de nervios*, which is often triggered by a stressful event such as divorce or bereavement, include crying, trembling, and uncontrollable screaming. There is also a sense of being out of control. Sometimes the person may become physically or verbally aggressive. Alternately, the person may faint or experience a seizure-like fit. Once the *ataque* is over, the person may promptly resume his or her normal manner, with little or no memory of the incident.

As noted earlier, abnormal behavior is behavior that deviates from the norms of the society in which the person lives. Experiences such as hearing the voice of a dead relative might be regarded as normative in one culture (e.g., in many Native American tribes) yet abnormal in another cultural milieu. Nonetheless, certain unconventional actions and behaviors are almost universally considered to be the product of mental disorder.

Many years ago, the anthropologist Jane Murphy (1976) studied abnormal behavior in the Yoruba of Africa and the Yupik-speaking Eskimos living on an island in the Bering Sea. Both societies had words that were used to denote abnormality or "craziness." In addition, the clusters of behaviors that were considered to reflect abnormality in these cultures were behaviors that most of us would also regard as abnormal. These included hearing voices, laughing at nothing, defecating in public, drinking urine, and believing things that no one else believes. Why do you think these behaviors are universally considered to be abnormal?

in review

- In what ways can culture shape the clinical presentation of mental disorders?
- Are the same disorders always found worldwide, regardless of culture?

How Common Are Mental Disorders?

1.4 **Distinguish between incidence and prevalence and identify the most common and prevalent mental disorders.**

How many and what sort of people have diagnosable psychological disorders today? This is a significant question for a number of reasons. First, such information is essential when planning and establishing mental health services. Mental health planners require a precise understanding of the nature and extent of the psychological difficulties within a given area, state, or country because they are responsible for determining how resources such as funding of research projects or services provided by community mental health centers may be most effectively allocated. It would obviously be imprudent to have a treatment center filled with clinicians skilled in the treatment of anorexia nervosa (a very severe but relatively rare clinical problem) if there were few clinicians skilled in treating anxiety or depression, which are much more prevalent disorders.

Second, estimates of the frequency of mental disorders in different groups of people may provide valuable clues as to the causes of these disorders. For example, data from the United Kingdom have shown that schizophrenia is about three times more likely to develop in ethnic minorities than in the white population (Kirkbridge et al., 2006). Rates of schizophrenia in southeast London are also high relative to other parts of the country. This is prompting researchers to explore why this might be. Possible factors may be social class and neighborhood deprivation, as well as diet or exposure to infections or environmental contaminants.

Prevalence and Incidence

Before we can further discuss the impact of mental disorders upon society, we must clarify the way in which psychological problems are counted. **Epidemiology** is the study of the distribution of diseases, disorders, or health-related behaviors in a given population. Mental health epidemiology is the study of the distribution of mental disorders. A key component of an epidemiological survey is determining the frequencies of mental disorders. There are several ways of doing this. The term **prevalence** refers to the number of active cases in a population during any given period of time. Prevalence figures are typically expressed as percentages (i.e., the percentage of the population that has the disorder). Furthermore, there are several different types of prevalence estimates that can be made.

Point prevalence refers to the estimated proportion of actual, active cases of a disorder in a given population at a given point in time. For example, if we were to conduct a study and count the number of people who have major depressive disorder (i.e., clinical depression) on January 1 of next year, this would provide us with a point prevalence estimate of active cases of depression. A person who experienced depression during the months of November and December but who managed to recover by January 1 would not be included in our point prevalence calculation. The same is true of someone whose depression did not begin until January 2.

If, on the other hand, we wanted to calculate a **1-year prevalence** figure, we would count everyone who experienced depression at any point in time throughout the entire year. As you might imagine, this prevalence figure would be higher than the point prevalence figure because it would cover a much longer time. It would moreover include those people who had recovered before the point prevalence assessment as well as those whose disorders did not begin until after the point prevalence estimate was made.

Finally, we may also wish to obtain an estimate of the number of people who have had a particular disorder at any time in their lives (even if they are now recovered). This would provide us with a **lifetime prevalence** estimate. Because they extend over an entire lifetime and include both currently ill and recovered individuals, lifetime prevalence estimates tend to be higher than other kinds of prevalence estimates.

An additional term with which you should be familiar is **incidence**. This refers to the number of new cases that occur over a given period of time (typically 1 year). Incidence figures tend to be lower than prevalence figures because they exclude preexisting cases. In other words, if we were assessing the 1-year incidence of schizophrenia, we would not count people whose schizophrenia began before our given starting date (even if they were still ill) because they are not "new" cases of schizophrenia. On the other hand, someone who was quite well previously but then developed schizophrenia during our 1-year window would be included in our incidence estimate.

Prevalence Estimates for Mental Disorders

Now that you have an understanding of some basic terms, let's turn to the 1-year prevalence rates for several important disorders. The most comprehensive source of prevalence estimates for adults in the United States diagnosed with mental disorders is the National Comorbidity Survey Replication (NCS-R). It sampled the entire adult American population using a number of sophisticated methodological strategies (Kessler et al., 2004; Kessler, Berglund, Borges, et al., 2005; Kessler & Merikangas, 2004). Table 1.1 shows 1-year and lifetime prevalence estimates of the *DSM-IV* mental disorders assessed from the NCS-R study.

Table 1.1 Prevalence of Mental Disorders in Adults in the United States

	1-Year (%)	Lifetime (%)
Any anxiety disorder	18.1	28.8
Any mood disorder	9.5	20.8
Any substance-abuse disorder	3.8	14.6
Any disorder	26.2	46.4

SOURCES: Based on Kessler, R. C., Berglund, P., Borges, G., Nock, M., & Wang, P. S. (2005a). Trends in suicide ideation, plans, gestures, and attempts in the United States. *JAMA, 293*(20), 2487–95.; Kessler, R. C., Chiu, W. T., Demler, O., & Walters, E. E. (2005c). Prevalence, severity, and comorbidity of 12-month DSM-IV disorders in the National Comorbidity Survey Replication. *Arch. Gen. Psychiatry, 62*, 617–27.

Because *DSM-5* is so new, no comprehensive lifetime prevalence data using this revised version of the *DSM* are yet available. However, the lifetime prevalence of having any *DSM-IV* disorder is 46.4 percent. This means that almost half of the Americans who were questioned had been affected by mental illness at some point in their lives (Kessler, Berglund, Demler, et al., 2005). Although this figure may seem high, it may actually be an underestimate, as the NCS-R study did not assess for eating disorders, schizophrenia, or autism, for example. Neither did it include measures of most personality disorders. As you can see from Table 1.1, the most prevalent category of psychological disorders is anxiety disorders. The most common individual disorders are major depressive disorder, alcohol abuse, and specific phobias (e.g., fear of small animals, insects, flying, heights). Social phobias (e.g., fear of public speaking) are similarly very common (see Table 1.2).

Table 1.2 Most Common Individual Mental Disorders in the United States

Disorder	1-Year Prevalence (%)	Lifetime Prevalence (%)
Major depressive disorder	6.7	16.6
Alcohol abuse	3.1	13.2
Specific phobia	8.7	12.5
Social phobia	6.8	12.1
Conduct disorder	1.0	9.5

SOURCES: Based on Kessler, R. C., Berglund, P., Borges, G., Nock, M., & Wang, P. S. (2005a). Trends in suicide ideation, plans, gestures, and attempts in the United States. *JAMA, 293*(20), 2487–95.; Kessler, R. C., Chiu, W. T., Demler, O., & Walters, E. E. (2005c). Prevalence, severity, and comorbidity of 12-month DSM-IV disorders in the National Comorbidity Survey Replication. *Arch. Gen. Psychiatry, 62*, 617–27.

Although lifetime (and 12-month) rates of mental disorders appear to be quite high, it is important to remember that, in some cases, the duration of the disorder may be relatively brief (e.g., depression that lasts for a few weeks after the breakup of a romantic relationship). Furthermore, many people who meet criteria for a given disorder will not be seriously affected by it. For instance, in the NCS-R study, almost half (48 percent) of the people diagnosed with a specific phobia had disorders that were rated as mild in severity, and only 22 percent of phobias were regarded as severe (Kessler, Chiu, et al., 2005). Meeting diagnostic criteria for a particular disorder and being seriously impaired by that disorder are not necessarily synonymous. In the NCS-R data, 12-month rates of *serious* mental illness are estimated to be 5.8 percent for adults and 8.0 percent among adolescents (Kessler et al., 2012).

One problem with the NCS-R data is that they are now well over a decade old. Fortunately, another survey, called the National Survey on Drug Use and Health (NSDUH), is conducted every year. Although this survey does not include information about specific disorders, it can be used to provide the most recent information. As you can see from Figure 1.1, the most up-to-date estimates show that

Figure 1.1 Prevalence of Serious Mental Illness Among U.S. Adults (2012)

Rates of severe mental illness are higher in women, people ages 26 to 49, and some minority groups.

(Data courtesy of SAMHSA)

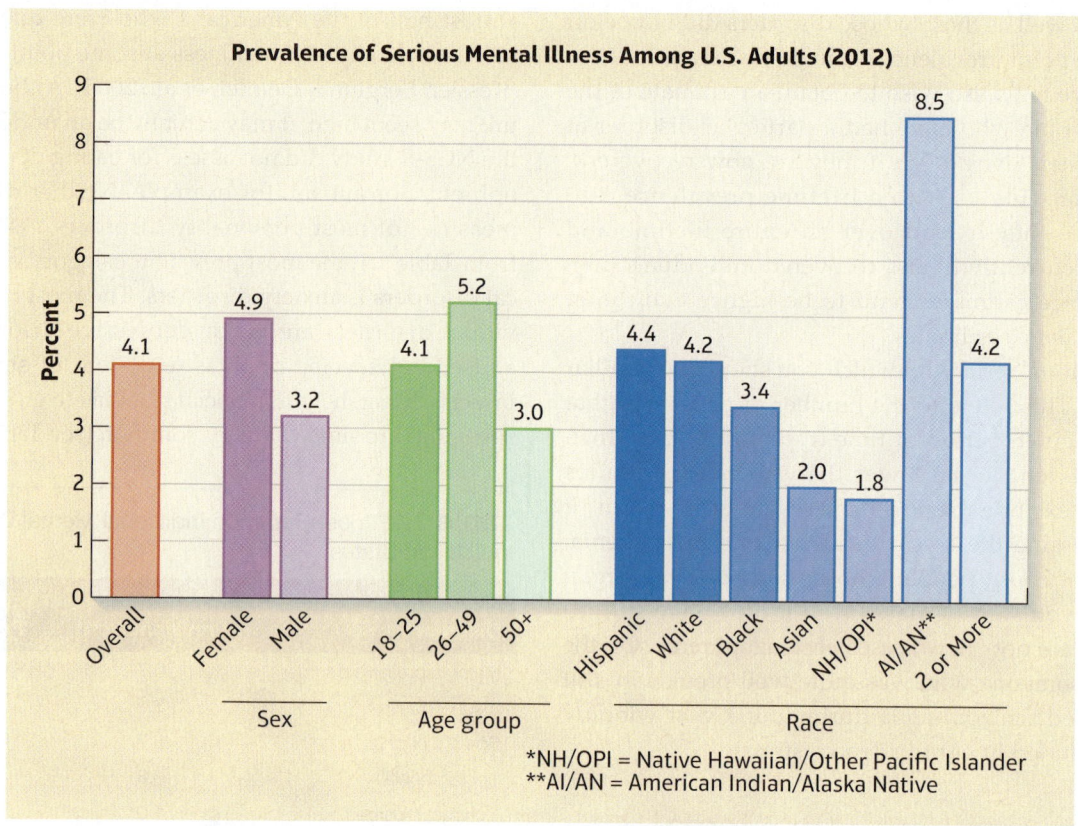

Prevalence of Serious Mental Illness Among U.S. Adults (2012)

*NH/OPI = Native Hawaiian/Other Pacific Islander
**AI/AN = American Indian/Alaska Native

the 1-year prevalence of serious mental illness (excluding substance use disorders) in adults in the United States is 4.1 percent overall. This is not too far from the 5.8 percent rate reported in the NCS-R (which did include substance use disorders). You can also see from the figure that rates of serious mental illness are higher in some groups than in others.

A final finding from the NCS-R study concerns the widespread occurrence of comorbidity among diagnosed disorders (Kessler, Chiu, et al., 2005). **Comorbidity** is the term used to describe the presence of two or more disorders in the same person. Comorbidity is especially high in people who have severe forms of mental disorders. In the NCS-R study, half of the individuals with a disorder rated as serious on a scale of severity (mild, moderate, and serious) had two or more additional disorders. An illustration of this would be a person who drinks excessively and who is simultaneously depressed and suffering from an anxiety disorder. In contrast, only 7 percent of the people who had a mild form of a disorder also had two or more other diagnosable conditions. What this indicates is that comorbidity is much more likely to occur in people who have the most serious forms of mental disorders. When the condition is mild, comorbidity is the exception rather than the rule.

Disorders do not always occur in isolation. A person who abuses alcohol may also be depressed or pathologically anxious. This is an example of comorbidity.

The Global Burden of Disease

Mental and substance use disorders are often disabling conditions. Worldwide, they account for over 7 percent of the global burden of disease. This is more than the burden of disease caused by HIV/AIDS, tuberculosis, diabetes, or transportation injuries. Because they are so common, anxiety disorders, depressive disorders, and substance use disorders together account for 184 million disability adjusted years of life (DALYs), where one DALY can be thought of as the loss of 1 year of otherwise "healthy" life. The disorder that results in the biggest global burden is depression, which accounts for more than 40 percent of the DALYs (see Figure 1.2). In terms of lost economic output caused by people with mental disorders being temporarily or permanently unable to work, estimates are that, worldwide, mental disorders will cost 16 trillion U.S. dollars (about 25 percent of global GDP in 2010) during the next 20 years. This is a staggering figure. It also does not include the costs of treatment or the personal (emotional) costs that living with a mental disorder can cause for the person and his or her family (Whiteford et al., 2013). All of this points to the need to find better ways to provide mental health services, especially in developing countries. In war-torn or resource-constrained environments, however, this presents numerous challenges.

Treatment

Although they may not be available to everyone, many treatments for psychological disorders exist. These include medications as well as different forms of psychotherapy. Each chapter of this book that covers specific disorders also includes a section describing how those disorders are treated. In addition, in Chapter 16 we discuss different approaches to treatment more broadly and describe different types of therapy in detail. However, it is important to emphasize that not all people with psychological disorders receive treatment. In some cases, people deny or minimize their suffering. Others try to cope on their own and may manage to recover without ever seeking aid from a mental health professional. As we noted earlier, stigma is a factor that makes some people especially reluctant to seek help (Clement et al., 2015). Even when they recognize that they have a problem, it is typical for individuals to wait a long time before deciding to seek help. Half of individuals with depression delay seeking treatment for more than 6 to 8 years. For anxiety disorders, the delay ranges from 9 to 23 years (Wang, Berglund, et al., 2005)!

When people with mental disorders do seek help, they are often treated by their family physician rather than by a mental health specialist (Wang, Berglund, et al., 2005). It is also the case that the vast majority of mental health treatment

Figure 1.2 The Burden of Mental Illness for Different Disorders Across the Lifespan

Disability adjusted life years (DALYs) for various mental and substance use disorders are shown according to age. DALYs represent the total (worldwide) number of otherwise healthy years of life that are lost or profoundly impacted because of the disorder. Depression causes the greatest total disability. This is because depression is a relatively common disorder.

(Adapted from Whiteford et al., 2013. *Global burden of disease attributable to mental and substance use disorders: findings from the Global Burden of Disease Study 2010.* Lancet, 382, 1580.)

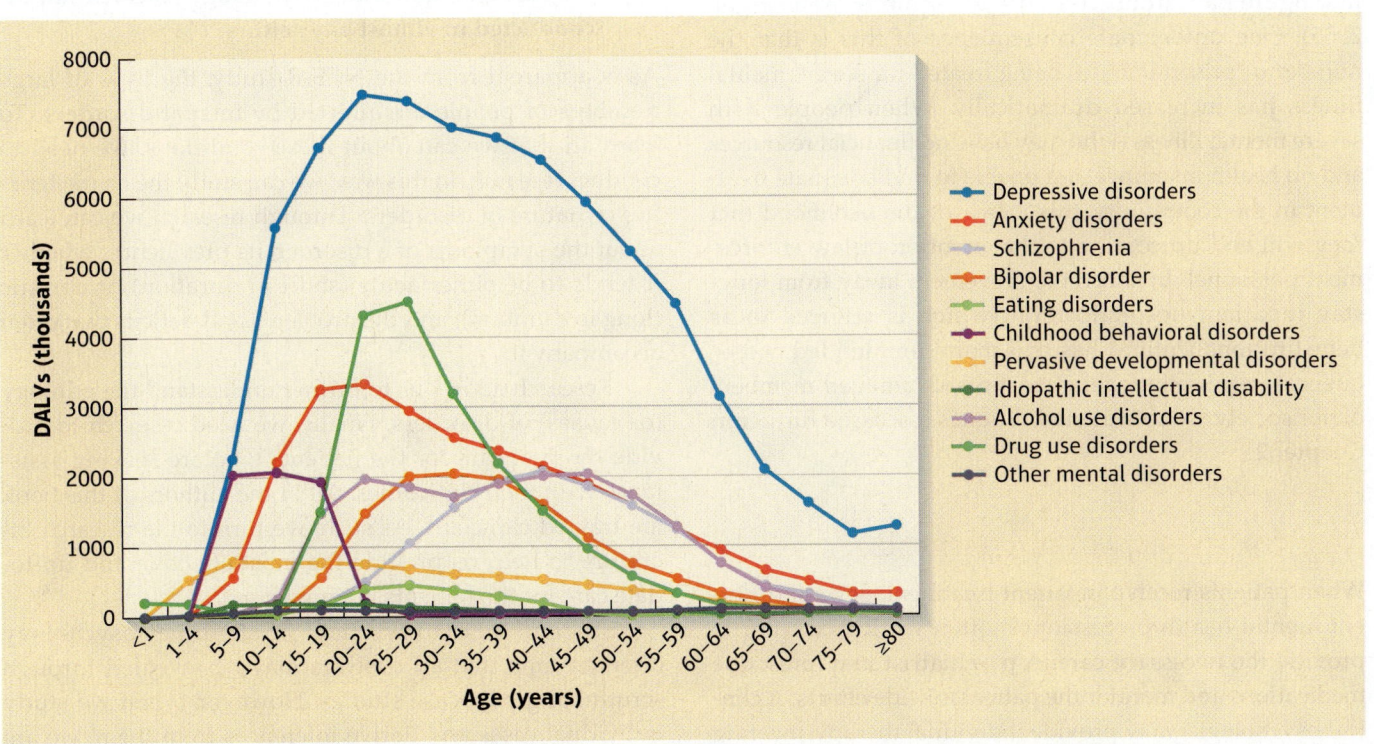

is now administered on an outpatient (as opposed to an inpatient) basis (O'Donnell et al., 2000). Outpatient treatment requires that a patient visit a mental health facility practitioner; however, the patient does not have to be admitted to the hospital or stay there overnight. A patient may attend a community mental health center, see a private therapist, or receive treatment through the outpatient department of a hospital.

Hospitalization and inpatient care are the preferred options for people who need more intensive treatment than can be provided on an outpatient basis. Various surveys indicate that admission to mental hospitals has decreased substantially during the past 45 years. The development of medications that control the symptoms of the most severe disorders is one reason for this change. Budget cuts have also forced many large state or county facilities to close. The limitations that insurance companies place on hospital admissions also contribute. If a hospital stay is not authorized by the insurance company, patients must seek treatment elsewhere.

Patients needing inpatient care are usually admitted to the psychiatric units of general hospitals, or to private psychiatric hospitals specializing in particular mental disorders. Stays in inpatient facilities tend to be much shorter than they were in the past (see Case et al., 2007; Lay et al., 2007). Patients receive additional treatment on an outpatient basis.

This trend away from the use of traditional hospitalization began several decades ago. Over time, there has been an enormous decrease in inpatient beds. For example, in 1955 there were 339 beds available in state mental hospitals per 100,000 people in the population. By the year 2000, that figure had dropped to just 22 (Lamb & Weinberger, 2005). One unfortunate consequence of this is that the number of prison inmates being treated for severe mental illness has increased dramatically. When people with severe mental illness (who may have no financial resources and no health insurance) are unable to find adequate treatment in the community, this increases the likelihood that they will end up coming to the attention of law enforcement personnel. In short, the movement away from long-stay inpatient hospitalization (which is referred to as deinstitutionalization) has had many unintended consequences, especially for the most disadvantaged members of our society. Deinstitutionalization is discussed further in Chapter 2.

Mental Health Professionals

When patients receive inpatient treatment, several different mental health professionals often work as a team to provide the necessary care. A psychiatrist may prescribe medications and monitor the patient for side effects. A clinical psychologist may provide individual therapy, meeting with the patient several times a week. A clinical social worker may help the patient resolve family problems, and a psychiatric nurse may check in with the patient on a daily basis to provide support and help the patient cope better in the hospital environment. The intensity of treatment that is typical in a hospital setting is designed to help the patient get better as rapidly as possible.

Patients treated in outpatient settings may also work with a team of professionals. However, the number of mental health specialists involved is typically much smaller. In some cases a patient will receive all treatment from a psychiatrist, who will prescribe medication and also provide psychotherapy. Other patients will receive medications from a psychiatrist and see a psychologist or a clinical social worker for regular therapy sessions. In other cases, depending on the type and severity of the problem, a patient (*client* is the preferred term in some settings) may see a counseling psychologist, a psychoanalyst, or a counselor who specializes in the treatment of drug and alcohol problems.

in review

- What is epidemiology?
- What is the difference between prevalence and incidence?
- What are the most common mental disorders?
- How is illness severity associated with comorbidity?

Research Approaches in Abnormal Psychology

1.5 Discuss why abnormal psychology research can be conducted in almost any setting.

As is apparent from the NCS-R study, the lives of large numbers of people are affected by mental disorders. To learn all that we can about these conditions, we need to conduct research. In this way, we can study the characteristics or nature of disorders. Through research we can learn about the symptoms of a disorder, its prevalence, whether it tends to be either **acute** (short in duration) or **chronic** (long in duration), and the problems and deficits that often accompany it.

Research allows us to further understand the **etiology** (or causes) of disorders. Finally, we need research to provide the best care for the patients who are seeking assistance with their difficulties. All of the authors of this book are trained clinicians. As such, we turn to the research literature to help us provide the most effective and up-to-date care for the patients whom we see.

Students new to the field of abnormal psychology often assume that all answers may be revealed through scrutinizing past case studies. However, when we study individual cases and derive inferences from them, we are as likely to develop errors in our thinking as we are to obtain knowledge. One such error is that we often attend only to data that confirm our view of how things are. For example, Dr. Smart might believe that drinking milk causes schizophrenia. When we ask Dr. Smart why he holds this view, he might say it is because every patient he has ever treated who has schizophrenia has drunk milk at some time in his or her life. Given that Dr. Smart has treated a lot of patients with schizophrenia and clearly has a great deal of experience with the disorder, we might be persuaded that he is right. Then along comes Dr. Notsofast. Dr. Notsofast decides to conduct a research study. He studies two groups of people: One group has schizophrenia; the other group does not have schizophrenia. Dr. Notsofast asks all of them about their milk-drinking habits. He finds that everyone has drunk milk at some point in his or her life and that there are no differences between the two groups with respect to their milk-drinking histories. As this simple example illustrates, research prevents us from being misled by natural errors in thinking. In short, research protects investigators from their own biases in perception and inference (Raulin & Lilienfeld, 2015).

Abnormal psychology research can be conducted in a variety of settings outside the research laboratory, including clinics, hospitals, schools, or prisons.

Abnormal psychology research can take place in clinics, hospitals, schools, prisons, and even highly unstructured contexts such as naturalistic observations of the homeless on the street. It is not the setting that determines whether a given research project may be undertaken. As Kazdin aptly points out (1998), "methodology is not merely a compilation of practices and procedures. Rather it is an approach toward problem solving, thinking, and acquiring knowledge." As such, research methodology (that is, the scientific processes and procedures we use to conduct research) is constantly evolving.

As new techniques become available (brain-imaging techniques and new statistical procedures, to name a few),

methodology in turn evolves. In the sections that follow, we introduce some fundamental research concepts so that you may begin to think critically like a clinical scientist. For further help, in some chapters we use a Research Close-Up to draw your attention to some key terms that are central to the comprehension of psychological research.

Sources of Information

1.6 **Describe three different approaches used to gather information about mental disorders.**

As humans, we often direct our attention to the people around us. If you were asked to describe your best friend, your father, or even the professor teaching your abnormal psychology class, you would undoubtedly have plenty to say. As is the case in virtually all other sciences, the foundation of psychological knowledge stems from observation. Indeed, a large amount of early knowledge was distilled from case studies in which specific individuals were described in great detail.

Case Studies

Astute clinicians such as the German psychiatrist Emil Kraepelin (1856–1926) and the Swiss psychiatrist Eugen Bleuler (1857–1939) provided us with detailed accounts of patients whom a modern-day reader would easily recognize as having disorders such as schizophrenia and manic depression. Alois Alzheimer (1864–1915) depicted a patient with an unusual clinical picture that subsequently became known as Alzheimer's disease. Sigmund Freud (1856–1939), the founder of psychoanalysis, published multiple clinical cases describing what we now recognize as phobia (the case of "Little Hans") and obsessive-compulsive disorder ("the Rat Man"). Such portrayals make for fascinating reading, even today.

Much can be learned when skilled clinicians use the **case study** method. Still, the information presented in them is subject to **bias** because the writer of the case study selects what information to include and what information to omit. Another concern is that the material in a case study is often relevant only to the individual being described. This means that the conclusions of a case study have low **generalizability**—that is, they cannot be used to draw conclusions about other cases even when those cases involve people with a seemingly similar abnormality. When there is only one observer and one subject, and when the observations are made in a relatively uncontrolled context and are anecdotal and impressionistic in nature, the conclusions we can draw are very narrow and may be mistaken. Nonetheless, case studies are an excellent way to illustrate clinical material. They can also provide some limited support for a particular theory or provide some negative evidence that can challenge a prevailing idea or assumption. Importantly, case studies can be a valuable source of new ideas and serve as a stimulus for research, and they may provide insight into unusual clinical conditions that are too rare to be studied in a more systematic way.

Self-Report Data

If we wish to study behavior in a more rigorous manner, how do we go about doing so? One approach is to collect **self-report data** from the people we wish to learn more about. This might involve having our research participants complete questionnaires of various types. Another way of collecting self-report data is from interviews. The researcher asks a series of questions and then records what the person says.

Asking people to report on their subjective experiences might appear to be an excellent way to collect information. However, as a research approach it has some limitations. Self-report data can sometimes be misleading. One problem is that people may not be very good reporters of their own subjective states or experiences. For example, when asked in an interview, one child may report that he has 20 "best friends." Yet, when we observe him, he may always be playing alone. Because people will occasionally lie, misinterpret the question, or desire to present themselves in a particularly favorable (or unfavorable) light, self-report data cannot always be regarded as highly accurate and truthful. This is something that anyone who has ever tried online dating knows only too well! And if you still need convincing, ask three people to tell you their weight. Then ask them to step on a scale. How likely is it that the weight they self-report will be the weight that appears when they step on the scale? What reasons do you think might explain the discrepancy?

Observational Approaches

When we collect information in a way that does not involve asking people directly (self-report), we are using some form of observational approach. Exactly how we go about this depends on what it is we seek to understand. For example, if we are studying aggressive children, we may wish to have trained observers record the number of times children who are classified as being aggressive hit, bite, push, punch, or kick their playmates. This would involve **direct observation** of the children's behavior.

We may also collect information about biological variables (such as heart rate) in our sample of aggressive children. Alternatively, we could collect information about stress hormones, such as cortisol, by asking the observed children to spit into a plastic container (because cortisol is found in saliva). We would then send the saliva samples to the lab for analysis. This, too, is a form of observational data; it tells us something that we want to know using a variable that is relevant to our interests.

Technology has advanced, and we are now developing methods to study behaviors, moods, and cognitions that have long been considered inaccessible. For example, brain-imaging techniques such as functional magnetic resonance imaging (fMRI) are now routinely used to study the working brain. We can study blood flow to various parts of the brain during memory tasks. We can even look at which brain areas influence imagination.

With other techniques such as transcranial magnetic stimulation (TMS; see Figure 1.3), which generates a magnetic field on the surface of the head, we can stimulate underlying brain tissue (see Eldaief et al., 2013). This can be done painlessly and noninvasively while the person receiving the TMS sits in an armchair. Using TMS, we can even take a particular area of the brain "off-line" for a few seconds and measure the behavioral consequences. In short, we can now collect observational data that would have been impossible to obtain in the past.

Figure 1.3

Researchers use technology, such as transcranial magnetic stimulation (TMS), to study how the brain works. TMS generates a magnetic field on the surface of the head through which underlying brain tissue is stimulated. Researchers can evaluate and measure behavioral consequences of this noninvasive and painless brain stimulation.

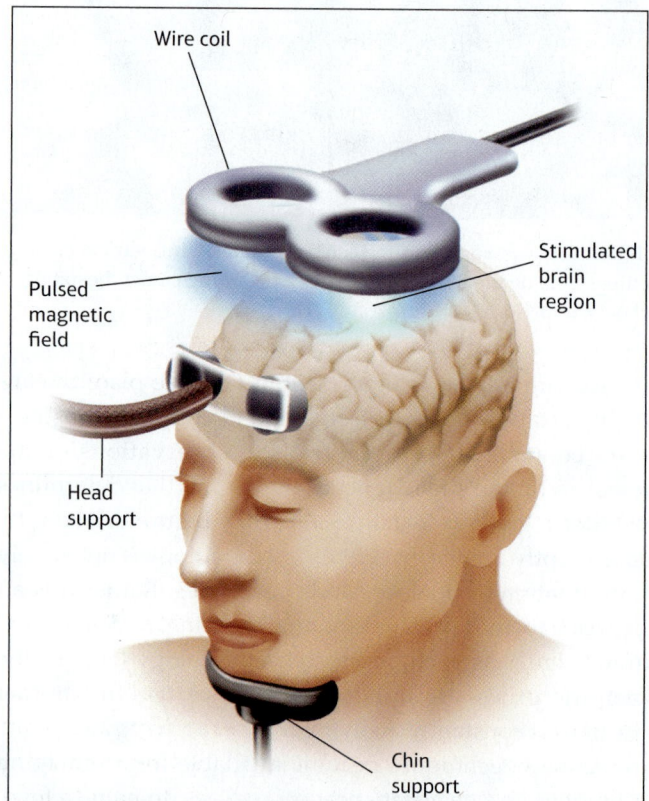

Wire coil

Pulsed magnetic field

Stimulated brain region

Head support

Chin support

In practice, much clinical research involves a mix of self-report and observational methods. Also, keep in mind that when we refer to observing behavior we mean much more than simply watching people. Observing behavior, in this context, refers to careful scrutiny of the conduct and manner of specific individuals (e.g., healthy people, people with depression, people with anxiety, people with schizophrenia). We may study social behavior in a sample of patients with depression by enlisting trained observers to record the frequency with which the patients smile or make eye contact. We may also ask the patients themselves to fill out self-report questionnaires that assess social skills. If we think that sociability in patients with depression may be related to (or correlated with) their severity of depression, we may further ask patients to complete self-report measures designed to assess that severity. We may even measure levels of certain substances in patients' blood, urine, or cerebrospinal fluid (the clear fluid that bathes the brain and that can be obtained by performing a lumbar puncture). Finally, we could possibly study the brains of patients with depression directly via brain-imaging approaches. These diverse sources of information would provide us with potentially valuable data, the basis of scientific inquiry.

in review

- What are the strengths and limitations of case studies?
- Why is it desirable not to rely solely on self-report data as a source of information?
- What is the difference between self-report and observational data?
- What range of measures could be considered to reflect observational data?

Forming and Testing Hypotheses

1.7   Explain why a control (or comparison group) is necessary to adequately test a hypothesis.

Research is all about asking questions. To make sense of behavior, researchers generate hypotheses. A **hypothesis** is an effort to explain, predict, or explore something. What distinguishes scientific hypotheses from the vague speculation that we all routinely engage in is that scientists attempt to test their hypotheses. In other words, they try to design research studies that will help them approach a fuller understanding of how and why things happen.

Anecdotal accounts such as case studies can be very valuable in helping us develop hypotheses, although case studies are not well suited for testing the hypotheses that they may have inspired. Other sources of hypotheses are unusual or unexpected research findings. One example is the higher-than-expected rate of suicide in women who

have had cosmetic breast augmentation (Sarwer et al., 2007). Consider for a moment why this association might exist. Possible explanations might include higher rates of psychopathology in women who seek breast augmentation, unrealistic expectations about the positive effects that the surgery would have on their lives, postoperative complications that could lead to depressed mood, and other factors such as preoperative body image dissatisfaction.

Although men generally have lower rates of depression than women, the rate of depression for Jewish men and women is equal. Why would this be? A correlation between higher rates of depression and lower rates of alcohol abuse in Jewish men provides interesting ground for further study.

Another observation in search of an explanation is the finding that, although men generally have lower rates of depression than women, this is not true of Jewish men. Why should Jewish men be more at risk for depression than non-Jewish men? One hypothesis is that there may be an interesting (and inverse) relationship between depression and alcohol use (Levav et al., 1997). Jewish men have lower rates of alcohol abuse and alcohol dependence than do non-Jewish men. Consistent with this idea, a study of members of Orthodox synagogues in London found no alcoholism and similar rates of depression in females and males (i.e., a 1:1 gender ratio instead of the typical 2:1 ratio; Loewenthal et al., 1995). Although much more remains to be uncovered, the hypothesis that higher rates of depression in Jewish men may be related to their lower rates of alcohol abuse appears to merit further study (see Loewenthal et al., 2003).

Hypotheses are vital because they frequently determine the therapeutic approaches used to treat a particular clinical problem. The ideas we have about what might be causing a client's difficulties will naturally shape the form of intervention we use when we provide treatment. For instance, suppose we are confronted with someone who washes his or her hands 60 to 100 times a day, causing serious injury to the skin and underlying tissues (this is an example of obsessive-compulsive disorder). If we believe that this behavior is a result of subtle problems in certain neural circuits, we may try to identify which circuits are dysfunctional in the hope of ultimately finding a means of correcting them (perhaps with medication).

On the other hand, if we view the excessive hand washing as reflecting a symbolic cleansing of sinful and unacceptable thoughts, we may try to unearth and address the sources of the person's excessive guilt and concern with morality. Finally, if we regard the hand washing as merely the product of unfortunate conditioning or learning, we may devise a means to extinguish the problematic behavior. In other words, our working hypotheses regarding the causes of different disorders very much shape the approaches we use when we study and treat the disorders.

Sampling and Generalization

We can occasionally glean instructive leads from careful scrutiny of a single case. However, this strategy rarely yields enough information to allow us to reach firm conclusions. Research in abnormal psychology is concerned with gaining enhanced understanding and, where possible, control of abnormal behavior (i.e., the ability to alter it in predictable ways). Edward, for instance, may accost women in supermarkets and try to lick their feet because his mother always gave him attention when, as a child, he tried on her shoes. In contrast, George may engage in the same behavior for an entirely different reason. We need to study a larger group of individuals with the same problem in order to discover which of our observations or hypotheses possess scientific credibility. The more people we study, the more confident we can be about our findings.

Whom should we include in our research study? In general, we want to study groups of individuals who have similar abnormalities of behavior. If we wanted to study people with panic disorder, a first step would be to determine criteria such as those provided in the current *DSM* for identifying people affected with this clinical disorder. We would then need to find people who fit our criteria. Ideally, we would study everyone in the world who met our criteria because these people constitute our population of interest. This, of course, is impossible to do, so instead we would try to get a representative sample of people who

are drawn from this underlying population. To do this, we would use a technique called **sampling**. What this means is that we would try to select people who are representative of the much larger group of individuals with panic disorder (in the same way that jury selection involves having a representative sample of eligible voters).

Ideally, we would like our smaller sample (our study group) to mirror the larger group (the underlying population) in all important ways (e.g., in severity and duration of disorder and in demographics such as age, gender, and marital status). If we could do everything perfectly, our research sample would be randomly selected from the larger population of people with panic disorder, which is tantamount to ensuring that every person in that population would have an equal chance of being included in our study. Such a procedure would automatically adjust for potential biases in sample selection. In practice, however, this does not happen, and researchers must simply do the best they can given real-world constraints (including the fact that some people don't wish to participate in a research study!).

Because finding research participants is not always easy, researchers sometimes use "samples of convenience" in their studies. This means that they study groups of people who are easily accessible to them and who are readily available. Have you noticed how much research is conducted using college students? Is this because college students are intrinsically fascinating people to study? Or are other factors in play here?

Why is so much research conducted using college students? What are the advantages and disadvantages of this?

An even more convenient strategy is to recruit participants online using approaches such as Amazon's Mechanical Turk. MTurk is an online labor market that connects "requesters" with "workers" who then complete surveys or other research-related tasks in return for a small payment (Shapiro et al., 2013). Although this makes life easier for researchers, there is (as usual) no free lunch. As you might expect, MTurk workers are not a representative sample of the population as a whole. Is your grandmother an

MTurk worker? Almost certainly not. Workers tend to be younger, overeducated, underemployed, less religious, and more liberal than people in the general population. In the United States, blacks and Hispanics are underrepresented and Asians are overrepresented in the MTurk worker pool relative to their presence in the population as a whole (Paolacci & Chandler, 2014).

Internal and External Validity

From a research perspective, the more representative our sample is, the better able we are to generalize (or extend the findings from our study) to the larger group. The extent to which we can generalize our findings beyond the study itself is called **external validity**. A research study that involves both males and females from all age groups, income levels, and educational levels is more representative of the underlying population (and will have greater external validity) than research using only female college students, for example. And when we study a group of people who all share a defining characteristic (e.g., a specific disorder), we may then be able to infer that additional commonalities that they share (such as a family history of depression or low levels of certain neurotransmitters) may be related to the disorder itself. Of course, this is based on the assumption that the characteristic in question is not widely shared by people who do not have the disorder.

Unlike external validity, which concerns the degree to which research findings from a specific study can be generalized to other samples, contexts, or times, **internal validity** reflects how confident we can be in the results of a particular given study. In other words, internal validity is the extent to which a study is methodologically sound, free of confounds, or other sources of error, and able to be used to draw valid conclusions. For example, suppose that a researcher is interested in how heart rate changes when participants are told that they are about to be given an electric shock. Imagine also how much faith you might have in the results of the research if participants who have just completed the study are allowed to chat in the waiting area with people who are just about to participate. What if the latter learn that, in reality, no shocks are given at all? How might this information change how subjects respond? Failure to control the exchange of information in this way clearly jeopardizes the integrity of the study and is a threat to its internal validity. Some subjects (those who have not been given prior information) will expect to receive real shocks; others will not because, unbeknownst to the experimenter, information has been leaked to them beforehand.

Criterion and Comparison Groups

To test their hypotheses, researchers use a **comparison group** (sometimes called a **control group**). This may be defined as a group of people who do not exhibit the disorder being studied but who are comparable in all other major respects to the **criterion group** (i.e., people with the disorder being studied). By "comparable" we might mean that the two groups are similar in age, number of males and females, educational level, and similar demographic variables. Typically, the comparison group is psychologically healthy, or "normal," according to certain specified criteria. We can then compare the two groups on the variables of interest.

To further illustrate the idea of criterion and control groups, let us return to our example about schizophrenia and milk. Dr. Smart's hypothesis was that drinking milk causes schizophrenia. However, when a group of patients with schizophrenia (the criterion group or the group of interest) was compared with a group of patients who did not have schizophrenia (the control group), it was clear that there were no differences in milk drinking between the two groups.

Using the controlled research approaches we have just described, researchers have learned much about many different psychological disorders. We can also use extensions of this approach not only to compare one cohort of patients with healthy controls but also to compare groups of patients with different disorders.

For example, Cutting and Murphy (1990) studied how well (1) patients with schizophrenia, (2) patients with depression or mania, and (3) healthy controls performed on a questionnaire testing social knowledge. This involved a series of multiple-choice questions that presented a social problem (e.g., "How would you tell a friend politely that he had stayed too long?"). Possible answer choices included responses such as "There's no more coffee left" and "You'd better go. I'm fed up with you staying too long." (In case you are wondering, both of these are incorrect choices; the preferred answer for this example was, "Excuse me. I've got an appointment with a friend.")

Consistent with the literature showing that social deficits are associated with schizophrenia, the patients with schizophrenia did worse on this test relative to both the healthy controls and the patients with depression or mania. The finding that the patients with schizophrenia did more poorly than the patients with depression or mania allowed the researchers to rule out the possibility that simply being a psychiatric patient is linked to poor social knowledge.

in review

- Explain what the term *representative sample* means.
- What is a sample of convenience?
- What is the difference between internal and external validity? How can external validity be maximized?
- Why are comparison or control groups so important?

Correlational Research Designs

A major goal of researchers in abnormal psychology is to learn about the causes of different disorders. For ethical and practical reasons, however, we often cannot do this directly. Perhaps we want to learn about factors that result in depression. We may hypothesize that the stress of losing a parent early in life may be important in this regard. Needless to say, we cannot create such situations and then see what unfolds!

Instead, the researcher uses what is known as a **correlational research** design. A correlational research design involves studying the world as it is. Unlike a true experimental research design (described later), correlational research does not involve any manipulation of variables. Rather, the researcher selects certain groups of interest (e.g., people who have recently been exposed to a great deal of stress, or people who lost a parent when they were growing up). She would then compare the groups on a variety of different measures (including, in this example, levels of depression).

Any time we study differences between individuals who have a particular disorder and those who do not, we are utilizing this type of correlational research design (see Figure 1.4). Essentially, we are capitalizing on the fact that the world works in ways that create natural groupings of people (people with specific disorders, people who have had traumatic experiences, people who win lotteries, etc.) whom we can then study. Using these types of research designs, we are able to identify factors that appear to be associated with depression, alcoholism, binge eating, or alternate psychological states of distress (for a more comprehensive description of this kind of research approach, see Kazdin, 1998).

Measuring Correlation

Correlational research takes things as they are and determines associations among observed phenomena. Do measures vary together in a direct, corresponding manner (known as a **positive correlation**—see Figure 1.5) such as in the example we mentioned earlier showing that breast augmentation surgery was correlated with increased risk of suicide? Or conversely, is there an inverse correlation, or **negative correlation**, between the variables of interest (such as high socioeconomic status and decreased risk of psychopathology)? Or finally, are the variables in question entirely independent of one another, or uncorrelated, such that a given state or level of one variable fails to predict reliably the degree of the other variable, as was the case with our example about milk and schizophrenia?

The strength of a **correlation** is measured by a **correlation coefficient**, which is denoted by the symbol r. A correlation runs from 0 to 1, with a number closer to 1 representing a stronger association between the two variables. The + sign or − sign indicates the direction of the association between the variables. For example, a positive correlation means that higher scores on one variable are associated with

---

Figure 1.4 Correlational Research Designs

In correlational research, data are collected from two different samples or groups and are then compared.

(Adapted from Petrie & Sabin, 2000. *Medical Statistics at a Glance*. Oxford, UK: Blackwell Science Ltd.)

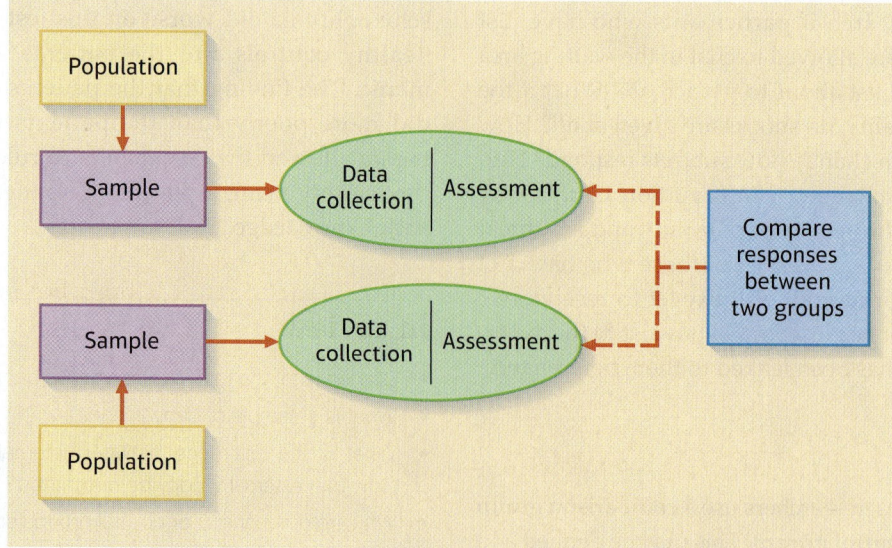

Figure 1.5

Scatterplots of data illustrating positive, negative, and no correlation between two variables. Dots indicate a given person's score on the two variables of interest. A strong positive correlation ($r = +1.0$) means that high scores on one variable are associated with high scores on the second variable, creating a forward-sloping straight line. For example, we would expect there to be a positive correlation between weight and the number of calories eaten per day. When there is a strong negative correlation ($r = -1.0$), high scores on the first variable are associated with low scores on the second variable, creating a backward-sloping straight line. A relevant example here would be the association between weight and time spent exercising per day. When there is no correlation ($r = 0$), scores on the independent variable tell us nothing about scores on the dependent variable. An example here might involve weight and astrological sign.

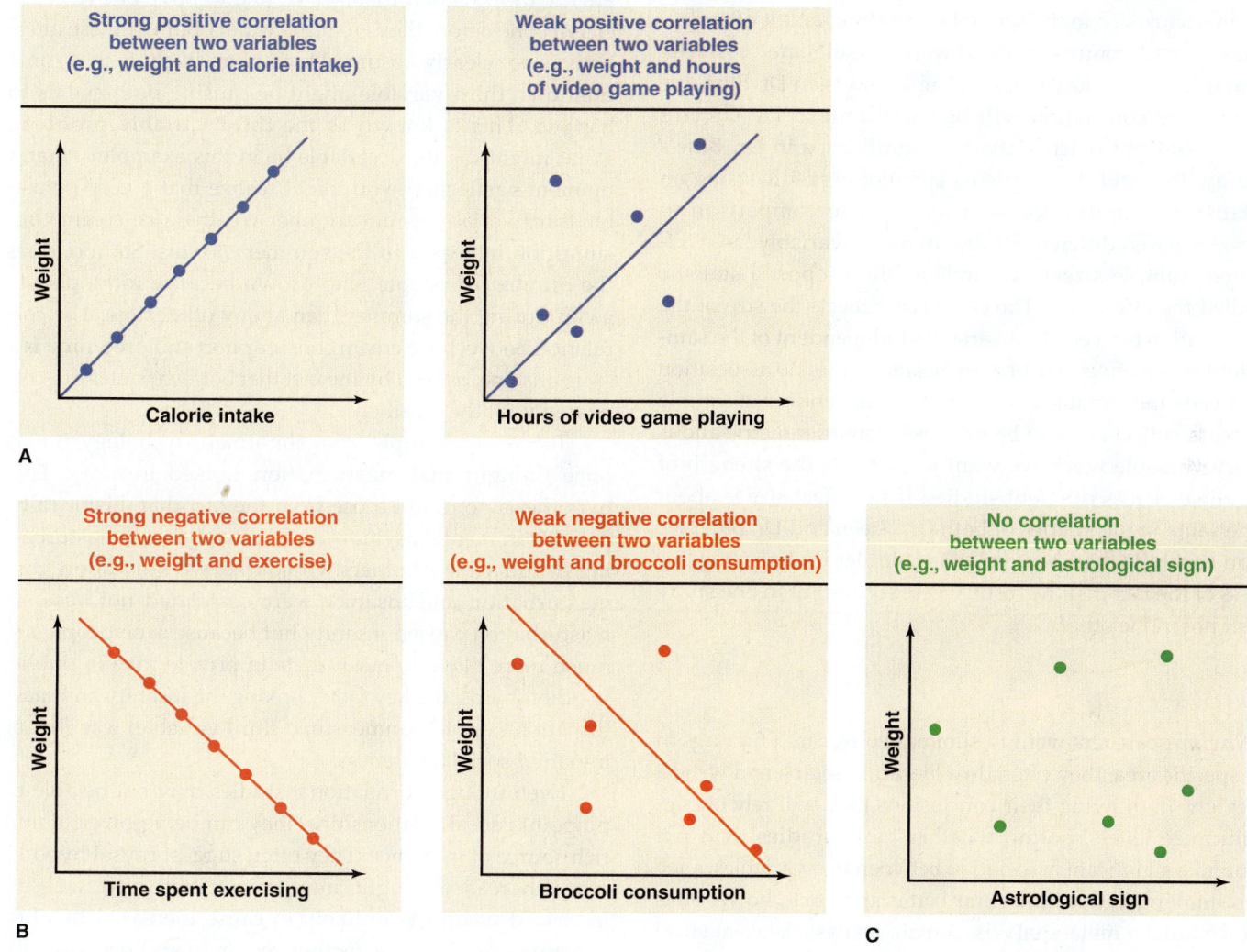

higher scores on the other variable, as might be the case for hours spent studying and grade point average. A negative correlation means that, as scores on one variable go up, scores on the other variable tend to go down. An example here might be the association between hours spent partying and grade point average.

Statistical Significance

If you read a research article, you are likely to see correlations reported in the text. Next to the correlation you will almost certainly see a notation that reads $p < .05$. This is the level of **statistical significance**. But what does this mean? Simply put, it means that the probability that the correlation would occur purely by chance is less than 5 out of 100. Researchers adopt this conventional level of significance and consider correlations that have a $p < .05$ to be statistically significant and worthy of attention. Of course, this does not mean that the result in question could not have occurred by chance; it simply means that it is not very likely.

Statistical significance is influenced not only by the magnitude or size of the correlation between the two variables but also by the sample size. A correlation of .30 will not be significant if the sample size is 20 people but will be significant if the sample size is 50 people. Correlations based on very large samples (e.g., 1,000 people) can be very small and yet still reach statistical significance. Conversely, correlations drawn from small samples need to be very large to reach statistical significance.

Effect Size

The fact that statistical significance is influenced by sample size creates a problem when we want to compare findings across studies. Suppose that Dr. Green reports a significant association between two variables in her study. But, in a second study, Dr. Blue reports no significant correlation between these same two variables. This is not an uncommon occurrence in the scientific literature, and it often creates a lot of confusion about whose results are "correct." But if Dr. Green has a larger sample size than Dr. Blue, the same-size correlation will be significant in Dr. Green's study but not reach statistical significance in Dr. Blue's study. To avoid the problems inherent in just focusing on statistical significance, and to facilitate comparison of results across different studies (which invariably have different sample sizes), researchers often report a statistic called the **effect size**. The effect size reflects the size of the association between two variables independent of the sample size. An effect size of zero means there is no association between the variables. Because it is independent of sample size, the effect size can be used as a common metric and is very valuable when we want to compare the strength of findings across different studies. If the effect size is about the same in the studies of both Dr. Green and Dr. Blue, we can conclude that they really had similar findings, regardless of the fact that the results were significant in one study but not in the other.

Meta-Analysis

When researchers want to summarize research findings in a specific area, they often do a literature search and write a review. In drawing their conclusions they will rely on significance levels, noting whether more studies than not found a significant association between two variables, such as smoking and health. A far better approach, however, is to conduct a **meta-analysis**. A meta-analysis is a statistical approach that calculates and then combines the effect sizes from all of the studies. Within a meta-analysis, each separate study can be thought of as being equivalent to an individual participant in a conventional research design. Because it uses effect sizes, a meta-analysis provides a better way to summarize research findings than is possible with a literature review.

Correlations and Causality

When it comes to correlations, one thing is very important to remember: Correlation does not mean causation. Just because two variables are correlated does not tell us anything about why they are correlated. This is true regardless of the size of the correlation. Many research investigations in abnormal psychology reveal that two (or more) things regularly occur together, such as poverty and diminished intellectual development, or depression and reported prior stressors. This in no way affirms that one factor is the cause of the other.

Consider, for example, the positive correlation that exists between ice cream consumption and drowning. Does this mean that eating ice cream compromises swimming ability and so leads to drowning? Or that people who are about to drown themselves like to have one final ice cream cone before they enter the water? Both of these alternatives are clearly absurd. Much more likely is that some unknown third variable might be causing both events to happen. This is known as the **third variable problem**. What might the third variable be in this example? After a moment's reflection, you might realize that a very plausible third variable is hot summer weather. Ice cream consumption increases in the summer months. So, too, does the number of people who drown because more people swim during the summer than at any other time. The correlation between ice cream consumption and drowning is a spurious one, caused by the fact that both variables are correlated with the weather.

To use an example from abnormal psychology, it was once thought that masturbation caused insanity. This hypothesis no doubt arose from the fact that, historically, patients in mental asylums could often be seen masturbating in full view of others. Of course, we now know that masturbation and insanity were correlated not because masturbation caused insanity but because sane people are much more likely to masturbate in private than in public. In other words, the key factor linking the insanity and masturbation (and the unmeasured third variable) was that of impaired social awareness.

Even though correlational studies may not be able to pinpoint causal relationships, they can be a powerful and rich source of inference. They often suggest causal hypotheses (increased height may cause increased weight; increased weight is unlikely to cause increased height), generate questions for further research, and occasionally provide crucial data that may confirm or refute specific hypotheses. Much of what we know about mental disorders is derived from correlational studies. The fact that we cannot manipulate many of the variables we study does not mean that we cannot learn a great deal from such approaches.

Retrospective versus Prospective Strategies

Correlational research designs can be used to study different groups of patients as they are at the time of the study (i.e., concurrently). For example, if we used brain imaging to look at the size of certain brain structures in patients with schizophrenia and in healthy controls, we would be using this type of approach. But if we wanted to learn what our patients were like before they developed a specific disorder, we might adopt a **retrospective research** strategy. This involves looking back in time. In other words, we would try to collect information about how the patients behaved early in their lives with the goal of identifying factors that might have been associated with what went wrong later. In some cases, our source material might be limited to a patient's recollections, the recollections of family members, material from diaries, or other records. A challenge with this technique is the potential for memories to be both faulty and selective.

Certain difficulties are involved with attempting to reconstruct the pasts of people already experiencing a disorder. Apart from the fact that a person who currently has a mental disorder may not be the most accurate or objective source of information, such a strategy invites investigators to discover what they already presume they will discover concerning background factors theoretically linked to a disorder. It invites biased procedure, unconscious or otherwise.

For instance, reports of a link between early sexual abuse and various forms of psychopathology began to emerge in the 1980s. After these reports came out, many therapists proceeded to suggest to their patients with such conditions that perhaps they too had been abused. For certain overzealous therapists, the fact that many patients had no memories of any abuse was taken as evidence that the painful memories had simply been "repressed." In other cases, a patient's simply having such common problems as difficulty sleeping or being easily startled was taken as evidence of past abuse. Over time, many patients became as convinced as their therapists that they must have been abused and that this accounted for their current difficulties. But for many patients, it simply was not the case that they had been abused. This underscores the pitfalls inherent in trying to reinterpret a person's past (or past behavior) in light of his or her current problems. Adherence to fundamental scientific principles is as crucial in the clinical domain as it is in the research laboratory.

Another approach is to use a **prospective research** strategy, which involves looking ahead in time. Here the idea is to identify individuals who have a higher-than-average likelihood of becoming psychologically disordered and to focus research attention on them before any disorder manifests. We can have much more confidence in our hypotheses about the causes of a disorder if we have been tracking influences and measuring them prior to the development of the illness in question. When our hypotheses correctly predict the behavioral problems that a group of individuals will later develop, we are much closer to establishing a causal relationship. A study that follows people over time and that tries to identify factors that predate the onset of a disorder employs a **longitudinal design**.

A prototypical illustration might be a study that follows, from infancy to adulthood, the children of mothers with schizophrenia. By collecting data on the children at regular intervals, researchers can compare those who later develop schizophrenia with those who do not, with the goal of identifying important differentiating factors. In another example of a longitudinal design, researchers have shown that adolescents who report suicidal thoughts at age 15 are much more likely to have psychological problems and to have attempted suicide by age 30 than people who do not have suicidal ideas in their teens (Reinherz et al., 2006).

in review

- What is the difference between a positive and a negative correlation?
- If two variables are correlated, does this mean that one variable causes the other? If so, why? If not, why not?

The Experimental Method in Abnormal Psychology

1.9 Explain the key features of an experimental design.

As you have already learned, even when we find strong positive or negative associations between variables, correlational research does not allow us to draw any conclusions about directionality (i.e., does variable A cause B, or does B cause A?). This is known as the *direction of effect problem*. To draw conclusions about causality and resolve questions of directionality, an **experimental research** approach must be used. In such cases, scientists control all factors except one—the factor that could have an effect on a variable or outcome of interest. They then actively manipulate (or influence) that one factor. The factor that is manipulated is referred to as the **independent variable**. If the outcome of interest, called the **dependent variable**, is observed to change as the manipulated factor is changed, then that independent variable can be regarded as a cause of the outcome (see Figure 1.6).

In Romania, children who are abandoned by their parents are traditionally raised in orphanages rather than in foster care. To study the cognitive effects of institutional versus other forms of care, researchers randomly assigned 136 children who had been institutionalized as babies to either remain in these institutions or be raised by foster families (see Nelson et al., 2007). These foster parents had been recruited for the study by the researchers. Another sample of children who lived with their birth families was also studied for comparison purposes. All the children received cognitive testing when they were 30, 42, and 54 months old. In this study, the independent variable is the living situation of the child (orphanage or foster care). The dependent variable is intellectual functioning.

Figure 1.6 Experimental Research Designs

In experimental research, participants are assessed at baseline and then randomly assigned to different groups (e.g., a treatment and a control condition). After the experiment or treatment is completed, data collected from the two different groups are then compared.

(Adapted from Petrie & Sabin, 2000. *Medical Statistics at a Glance*. Oxford, UK: Blackwell Science Ltd.)

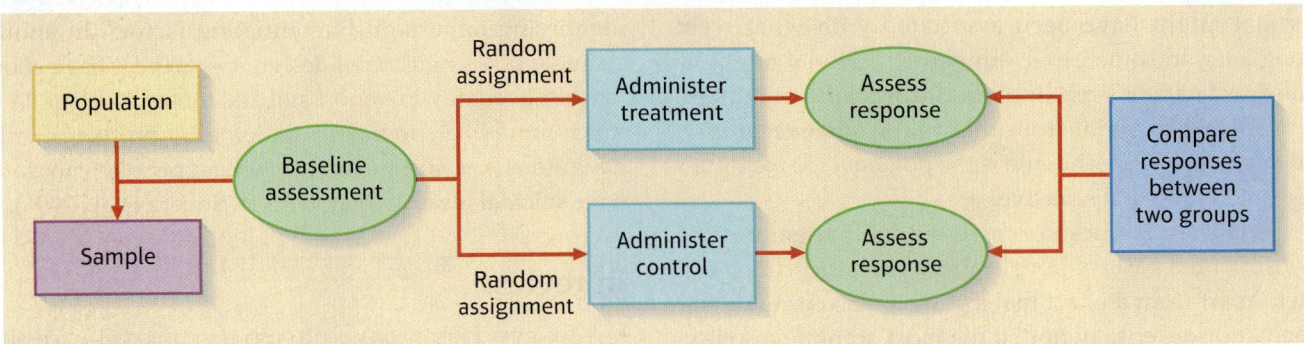

Did the children assigned to foster care fare better than the children who remained in institutions? The answer is yes. At both the 42-month and the 54-month assessments, the children in foster families had significantly higher scores on the measure of cognitive functioning than the children who remained institutionalized. We can therefore conclude that there was something about being raised in a foster family that was responsible for the increased intellectual development of these children. Sadly, however, the cognitive development of both groups of children was much lower than the intellectual functioning of children who were raised in typical families. The results of this unique study therefore tell us that, although foster care helps abandoned children, these children remain at a disadvantage relative to children who are raised by their biological families. However, based at least partially on the findings from this remarkable study, Romania no longer allows children without severe disabilities to be placed in institutional care.

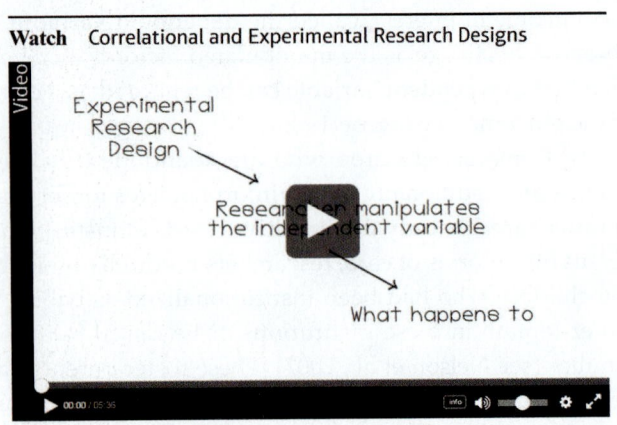

Watch Correlational and Experimental Research Designs

Studying the Efficacy of Therapy

Researchers in abnormal psychology are often interested in learning which treatments work for specific disorders. Used in the context of treatment research, the experimental method has proved to be indispensable. It is a relatively straightforward process to establish: A proposed treatment is given to a designated group of patients and withheld from a similar group of patients. Should the treated group show significantly more improvement than the untreated group, we can have confidence in the treatment's efficacy. We may not, however, know why the treatment works, although investigators are becoming increasingly sophisticated in fine-tuning their experiments to tease out the means by which therapeutic change is induced (e.g., Kazdin & Nock, 2003; Kleim et al., 2013; Ramseyer et al., 2014). The Developments in Research feature provides a nice example of a treatment research study. The findings of this study also show just how powerful placebo effects can be.

In treatment research it is important that the two groups (treated and untreated) be as equivalent as possible except for the presence or absence of the proposed active treatment. To facilitate this, patients are typically randomly assigned to the treatment condition or the no-treatment condition. **Random assignment** means that every research participant has an equal chance of being placed in the treatment or the no-treatment condition. Once a treatment has been established as effective, it can then be provided for members of the original control (untreated) group, leading to improved functioning for all those involved.

Sometimes, however, this "waiting list" control group strategy is deemed inadvisable for ethical or other reasons. Withholding a treatment that has been established as beneficial just to evaluate a new form of treatment may deprive control subjects of valuable clinical help for longer than would be considered appropriate. For this reason, stringent safeguards need to be in place regarding the potential costs versus benefits of conducting the particular research project.

In certain cases, an alternative research design may be called for in which two (or more) treatments are compared in differing yet comparable groups. This method is termed a *standard treatment comparison study*. Typically, the efficacy of the control condition has been previously established; thus, patients who are assigned to this condition are not disadvantaged. Instead, the question is whether patients who receive the new treatment improve to a greater extent than those receiving the control (established) treatment. Such comparative-outcome research has much to recommend it and is being increasingly employed (Kendall et al., 2004).

Single-Case Experimental Designs

Does experimental research always involve testing hypotheses by manipulating variables across groups? The simple answer is no. We have already noted the importance of case studies as a source of ideas and hypotheses. In addition, case studies can be used to develop and test therapy techniques within a scientific framework. Such approaches are called **single-case research designs** (Hayes, 1998; Kazdin, 1998). A central feature of such designs is that the same individual is studied over time. Behavior or performance at one point in time can then be compared to behavior or performance at a later time, after a specific intervention or treatment has been introduced. For example, using a single-case design, Wallenstein and Nock (2007) were able to show that exercise helped a 26-year-old female patient to significantly decrease the frequency of her nonsuicidal self-injuring behaviors, which included self-hitting and head-banging.

Developments in Research

Do Magnets Help with Repetitive-Stress Injury?

Magnets are often marketed to people who have chronic hand or wrist pain. This type of problem is known as repetitive-stress injury (RSI) and can be caused by extensive computer use. But do magnets really relieve the chronic pain that is associated with RSI? Testimonials notwithstanding, the only way to answer this question is by controlled research.

Pope and McNally (2002) randomly assigned college students with RSI to one of three groups. One group was asked to wear wristbands containing magnets for a 30-minute period (magnet group). A second group was also given seemingly identical bracelets to wear. In this case, however, and unknown both to the participants and to the assistant running the study, the magnets had been removed from the wristbands (sham group). A third group of subjects did not receive any magnets (no-treatment group).

You should note here that this study is an example of what we call a **double-blind study**. In other words, neither the subjects nor the experimenter who was working with the subjects knew who got the genuine magnets. The use of the wristbands with the magnets removed is called a **placebo treatment** condition (the word *placebo* comes from the Latin meaning "I shall please"). Placebo treatment conditions enable experimenters to control for the possibility that simply believing one is getting an effective type of treatment produces a therapeutic benefit. Finally, the no-treatment control group enables the experimenters to see what happens when they do not provide any treatment (or expectation of treatment) at all.

At the start of the study, all of the student participants completed a 4-minute typing test. This provided a measure of how many words they could type in this time period. Then, 30 minutes after wearing the magnets or fake wristbands (or, for the no-treatment subjects, after waiting 30 minutes), all participants completed another 4-minute typing test. In addition, those who had been assigned to either the genuine or the placebo magnet group were asked to rate their degree of pain relief (from no improvement to complete relief) using an 8-point scale.

What were the results? As might be expected, those people who had been assigned to the no-treatment group did not report that their level of pain changed in any appreciable way. This is hardly surprising because nothing had been done to them at all. They typed an average of about four more words on the second test (the posttest) than on the first (the pretest).

Did the people who wore the magnets do better than this? The answer is yes. Those who wore the genuine magnets reported that their pain was diminished. They also typed an average of 19 more words on the second typing test than they had on the first! In other words, with respect to both their self-report data (their pain improvement ratings) and their behavioral data (how rapidly they could type), they clearly did better than the no-treatment group.

Before you rush out to buy magnetic bracelets, however, let us look at the performance of the people who received the fake bracelets. Like the subjects who wore the genuine magnets, these participants also reported that their pain had improved. And, in fact, on the behavioral typing test, subjects in the placebo treatment group typed even more words on the second test (an average of 26 more words) than subjects who wore the real magnets did. With respect to their self-reports and their behavioral data, therefore, the group who wore the fake bracelets improved just as much as the group who wore the real magnets! On the basis of this study, then, we must conclude that magnet therapy works via the placebo effect, not because there is any genuine clinical benefit that comes from the magnets themselves. If you believe that the magnet will help your RSI, you do not actually need a magnet to bring about any clinical improvement. And this, in a nutshell, is why we need controlled research trials.

One of the most basic experimental designs in single-case research is called the **ABAB design**. The different letters refer to different phases of the intervention. The first A phase serves as a baseline condition. Here we simply collect data on or from the participant. Then, in the first B phase, we introduce our treatment. Perhaps the person's behavior changes in some way. Even if there is a change, however, we are not justified in concluding that it was due to the introduction of our treatment. Other factors might have coincided with its introduction, so any association between the treatment and the behavior change might be spurious. To establish whether it really was the treatment that was important, we therefore withdraw the treatment and see what happens. This is the reasoning behind the second A phase (i.e., at the ABA point). Finally, to demonstrate that the behavior observed during the B phase is attainable once again, we reinstate our treatment and see if the behavioral changes we saw in the first B phase become apparent again. To further clarify the logic behind the ABAB design, let's consider the case of Kris (see Rapp et al., 2000).

Kris

Kris was a 19-year-old female with severe intellectual impairments. Since the age of 3 she had pulled her hair out. This disorder is called *trichotillomania* (pronounced tri-ko-til-lo-mania). Kris's hair pulling was so severe that she had a bald area on her scalp that was approximately 2.5 inches in diameter.

The researchers used an ABAB experimental design (see Figure 1.7) to test a treatment for reducing Kris's hair pulling. In each phase, they used a video camera to observe Kris while she was alone in her room watching television. During the baseline phase (Phase A), observers measured the percentage of time that Kris spent either touching or manipulating her hair (42.5 percent of the time) as well as pulling hair (7.6 percent of the time).

In the treatment phase (Phase B), a 2.5-lb weight was put around Kris's wrist when she settled down to watch television. When she was wearing the wrist weight, Kris's hair manipulation and hair pulling were reduced to zero. This, of course, suggested that Kris's behavior had changed because she was wearing a weight on her wrist. To verify this, the wrist weight was withdrawn in the second A phase (i.e., ABA). Kris immediately started to touch and manipulate her hair again (55.9 percent). She also showed an increase in hair pulling (4 percent of the time).

When the wrist weight was reintroduced in the second B phase (ABAB), Kris's hair manipulation and pulling once again decreased, at least for a while. Although additional treatments were necessary (see Rapp et al., 2000), Kris's hair pulling was eventually eliminated entirely. Most important for our discussion, the ABAB design allowed the researchers to systematically explore, using experimental techniques and methods, the treatment approaches that might be beneficial for patients with trichotillomania.

Figure 1.7 An ABAB Experimental Design: Kris's Treatment

In the A phase, baseline data are collected. In the B phase, a treatment is introduced. This treatment is then withdrawn (second A phase) and then reinstated (second B phase). In this example, hair manipulation declines with use of wrist weights, returns to pretreatment (baseline) levels when they are withdrawn, and declines again when they are reintroduced.

(Data adapted from Rapp et al., 2000. Treatment of hair pulling and hair manipulation maintained by digital-tactile stimulation. *Behavior Therapy*, 31, pp. 381–93.)

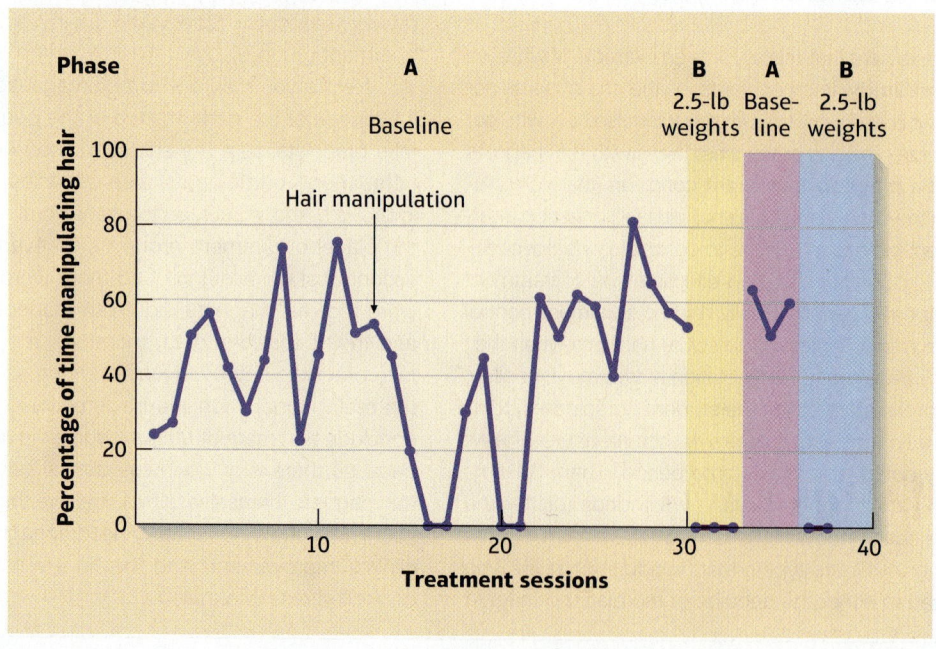

Animal Research

An additional way in which we can use the experimental method is by conducting research with animals. Although ethical considerations are still critical in animal research, we are able to perform studies using animal subjects that would not be possible to implement with humans (such as subjecting them to controlled environmental conditions or having them be raised by a different mother).

Of course, one major assumption is that the findings from animal studies can be generalized to humans. Experiments of this kind are generally known as **analogue studies**, in which we study not the true item of interest but an approximation to it. Analogue studies may also involve humans (e.g., when we try to study depression by studying healthy research participants whom we have made mildly and transiently sad).

One current model of depression, called "hopelessness depression," has its origins in early research conducted with animals (Seligman, 1975). Laboratory experiments with dogs had demonstrated that, when subjected to repeated experiences of painful, unpredictable, and inescapable electric shock, the dogs lost their ability to learn a simple escape response to avoid further shock in a different situation later on. They just sat and endured the pain.

Animal research allows behavioral scientists to manipulate and study behavior under controlled conditions that would not be possible to replicate using humans as subjects. However, results of this research may not hold up when extended to humans outside the laboratory in a real-world setting.

This observation led Seligman and his colleagues to argue that human depression (which he believed was analogous to the reaction of the helpless dogs) is a reaction to uncontrollable stressful events in which one's behavior has no effect on one's environment, leading to helplessness,

Unresolved Issues

Are We All Becoming Mentally Ill? The Expanding Horizons of Mental Disorder

The concept of mental disorder, as we have seen, suffers from the lack of a truly objective means of determining what is disordered and what is not. Moreover, inclusion of a disorder in the *DSM* is a prerequisite for health insurers' reimbursement of services rendered. It is therefore in the financial interests of mental health professionals to be more and more inclusive concerning the kinds of problems that might be regarded as "mentally disordered." Not surprisingly, there is often pressure to include in the *DSM* more and more kinds of socially undesirable behavior.

The *DSM* has been growing in size for many years as new disorders are added. But it is in the interests of the public at large to keep a close eye on proposed expansions of what is considered "mentally disordered." Failure to do so could eventually lead to a situation in which much of human behavior—save for the most bland, conformist, and conventional of conduct—would be declared a manifestation of a mental disorder. For example, when *DSM-5* was being developed, some groups lobbied for "apathy syndrome" and "parental alienation syndrome" to be considered as new disorders. But is being unmotivated or having a troubled relationship with your parents really a disorder? In the end, these proposals were rejected.

Accepted into *DSM-5*, however, were several newly proposed disorders that might still cause some to raise an eyebrow. These include "caffeine use disorder" and "Internet gaming disorder."

Internet gaming disorder is now listed in *DSM-5* as a new disorder in need of further study.

These have been added to *DSM-5* in a special section that is reserved for disorders still in need of further study. Although this does not mean that they are being formally accepted as official disorders, it is certainly a first step. What do you think of this? How close do you think we are getting to the point where all of us, by virtue of drinking too much coffee or spending too much time gaming are at risk of being considered mentally ill?

passivity, and depression. In other words, the findings from these animal studies provided the impetus for what first became known as the "learned helplessness theory of depression" (Abramson et al., 1978; Seligman, 1975) and is now termed "the hopelessness theory of depression" (Abramson et al., 1989). These theories of depression are not without their difficulties. Nevertheless, it is useful to remain aware of the broader message: Even though problems may arise when we generalize too readily from animal to human models of psychopathology, the learned helplessness analogy has generated much research and has allowed us to refine and develop our understanding of depression.

in review

- How is experimental research different from correlational research?
- In experimental research, which variable (independent or dependent) is manipulated?
- What is a placebo?
- Explain the process of performing an ABAB design. Why are such designs helpful to clinicians and researchers?

Summary

1.1   Explain how we define abnormality and classify mental disorders.

- A precise definition of *abnormality* remains elusive. Elements that can be helpful in considering whether something is abnormal include subjective distress, maladaptiveness, statistical deviancy, violation of societal norms, social discomfort, irrationality and unpredictability, and dangerousness.

- The *DSM* employs a category type of classification similar to that used in medicine. Disorders are regarded as discrete clinical entities, though not all clinical disorders may be best considered in this way.

- Even though it is not without problems, the *DSM* provides us with working criteria that help clinicians and researchers identify and study specific difficulties that affect the lives of many people. It is far from a "finished product." However, familiarity with the *DSM* is essential to significant study of the field.

1.2   Describe the advantages and disadvantages of classification.

- Classifying disorders provides a common language as well as a communication shorthand. It also allows us to structure information in an efficient manner and provides us with an organizational framework. This facilitates research and treatment. In addition, classification defines the domain of what is considered to be pathological. From a practical perspective, it delineates the types of psychological difficulties that warrant insurance reimbursement and identifies the disorders that mental health professionals treat.

- When we classify, we lose detailed personal information about the person with the disorder. Classification can also facilitate stigma, stereotyping, and labeling, although we should keep in mind that these problems are not caused by the classification system itself. Fear of being viewed negatively or being discriminated against may lead some people to avoid seeking treatment.

1.3   Explain how culture affects what is considered abnormal and describe two different culture-specific disorders.

- Culture shapes the presentation of clinical disorders in some cases. Culture also provides the backdrop against which we must evaluate whether a particular behavior is abnormal or not.

- Certain disorders appear to be highly culture specific. *Taijin kyofusho* is an anxiety disorder that is quite prevalent in Japan. It involves fear that one's body, body parts, or body functions may offend, embarrass, or make others feel uncomfortable. *Ataque de nervios* is another culturally rooted expression of distress. It is found in people of Latino descent, especially those from the Caribbean. This condition does not have a clear counterpart in the *DSM*. Symptoms can include crying, trembling, fainting, uncontrollable screaming, and a general feeling of loss of control.

1.4   Distinguish between incidence and prevalence and identify the most common and prevalent mental disorders.

- Epidemiology involves the study of the distribution and frequency of disorders. Incidence is the number of *new* cases that occur in a given period of time. Prevalence refers to the total number cases in a population during any specified period of time.

- Just under 50 percent of people will experience some form of mental disorder during the course of their lifetimes. Mood disorders and anxiety disorders are particularly common.

1.5 **Discuss why abnormal psychology research can be conducted in almost any setting.**

- Studying and drawing inferences from past case studies alone often leads to erroneous thinking as we often focus on data that confirm our ideas of how things are.

- Research prevents us from being misled by natural errors in thinking and can be conducted in clinics, hospitals, schools, prisons, and on the street. It is not the setting that determines whether a given research project may be undertaken. The importance lies in the researcher's methodology.

1.6 **Describe three different approaches used to gather information about mental disorders.**

- Information about mental disorders can be collected through case studies, self-report data, and observational approaches.

- Case studies can be a valuable source of new ideas and serve as a stimulus for research. They also may provide insight into unusual clinical conditions that are too rare to be studied in a more systematic way.

- Self-report data allows us to study behavior in a more rigorous manner. This type of research often involves having research participants complete questionnaires of various types or conducting interviews.

- When we collect information in a way that does not involve asking people directly, we are using some form of observational approach. Exactly how we go about this depends on what it is we seek to understand.

1.7 **Explain why a control (or comparison group) is necessary to adequately test a hypothesis.**

- Unless there is a control or comparison group, researchers cannot test their hypothesis adequately. The control group must be comparable in all major respects (age, educational level, proportion of males and females, etc.) to the criterion group (e.g., people with the disorder we want to learn about), except for the fact that they do not exhibit the disorder of interest. The control group could be psychologically healthy people, or could comprise people with a different disorder.

- Only when they are using a suitable control or comparison group can researchers compare the two groups on the variables of interest to see if there are significant differences.

1.8 **Discuss why correlational research designs are valuable, even though they cannot be used to make causal inferences.**

- Correlational research examines factors as they currently are, allowing us to identify factors that appear to be associated with certain disorders.

- Just because two variables are correlated does not mean that there is a causal relationship between them. Correlation does not equal causation.

1.9 **Explain the key features of an experimental design.**

- Experimental research involves manipulating one variable (the independent variable) and observing the effect this manipulation produces with regard to another variable (the dependent variable).

- Because the experimenter is changing the experimental conditions, experimental research designs permit causal inferences to be made.

- Although most experiments involve the study of groups, single-case experimental designs (e.g., ABAB designs) may also be used to make causal inferences in individual instances.

Key Terms

ABAB design, p. 28
abnormal psychology, p. 2
acute, p. 16
analogue studies, p. 29
bias, p. 17
case study, p. 17
chronic, p. 16
comorbidity, p. 14
comparison or control group, p. 21
correlation, p. 22
correlation coefficient, p. 22
correlational research, p. 22
criterion group, p. 21
dependent variable, p. 25
direct observation, p. 18
double-blind study, p. 27

effect size, p. 24
epidemiology, p. 12
etiology, p. 16
experimental research, p. 25
external validity, p. 21
family aggregation, p. 3
generalizability, p. 17
hypothesis, p. 19
incidence, p. 13
independent variable, p. 25
internal validity, p. 21
labeling, p. 9
lifetime prevalence, p. 13
longitudinal design, p. 25
meta-analysis, p. 24
negative correlation, p. 22

nomenclature, p. 8
1-year prevalence, p. 12
placebo treatment, p. 27
point prevalence, p. 12
positive correlation, p. 22
prevalence, p. 12
prospective research, p. 25
random assignment, p. 26
retrospective research, p. 25
sampling, p. 20
self-report data, p. 18
single-case research design, p. 27
statistical significance, p. 23
stereotyping, p. 8
stigma, p. 8
third variable problem, p. 24

Chapter 2
Historical and Contemporary Views of Abnormal Behavior

⌄ Learning Objectives

2.1 Explain how abnormal behavior has been viewed throughout history.

2.2 Describe the effect that humanism had on abnormal psychology.

2.3 Identify developments that led to the contemporary view of abnormal psychology.

An Artist in Bedlam

The most famous patient committed to the historic Bethlem Hospital in England (better known as Bedlam) during its long existence was a well-known and talented young artist, Richard Dadd (1817–1886). Dadd was born in Chatham, England, in 1817. His father was a successful chemist. Dadd attended the Kings School in Rochester and also studied art at the Royal Academy School in London. He showed a strong aptitude for drawing and painting and was admitted to the prestigious Royal Academy of Arts at the early age of 20. When he was 25, he was invited to accompany Sir Thomas Phillips, the former mayor of Newport, on a grand tour through Europe, Greece, Turkey, Syria, and Egypt to serve as the draftsman and painter for the expedition. During the trip, Dadd produced a number of exceptional paintings of people and places he encountered on the journey. The voyage was reportedly difficult and stressful, and at one point, during a trip up the Nile River, Dadd underwent a remarkable personality change, becoming delusional and increasingly aggressive and violent toward people he met. He was reported to have expressed an urge to kill the Pope. He experienced delusional beliefs—for example, that he had come under the influence of the Egyptian god Osiris.

When he returned from the trip in 1843, he was diagnosed as being mentally unsound because of his hallucinations and his strange, delusional beliefs. In an effort to restore him to health, his family took him to recuperate in a countryside village in Kent, England. The records indicate that one day he came to the conclusion that his father was the Devil in disguise, and on a walk in the countryside Dadd killed his father with a knife. He attempted to escape by fleeing to France; however, his aggressive behavior continued, and he attempted to kill a tourist with a razor. He was arrested by the police and was eventually returned to England. He was committed to Bethlem Royal Hospital, where he was held in the criminal ward for dangerous inmates. He remained in Bethlem Hospital for almost 20 years and was eventually transferred to Broadmoor Hospital, where he died in 1886. During his stay in both the Bethlem and Broadmoor hospitals he was allowed and encouraged to paint by the staff as part of his treatment. During this time he produced a number of paintings, many of which can be seen today in art museums.

Although he appears to have experienced symptoms of a mood disorder including acute mania (see Chapter 7), it is likely that Dadd suffered from paranoid schizophrenia (see Chapter 14 for further discussion). Interestingly, two of his siblings appeared to suffer from the same symptom pattern; thus, he may have been genetically predisposed to this condition (see Greysmith, 1979, and MacGregor, 1989, for a discussion of his life and artwork).

Historical Views of Abnormal Behavior

2.1 Explain how abnormal behavior has been viewed throughout history.

Our historical efforts to understand abnormal psychology include both humor and tragedy. In this chapter, we highlight some views of psychopathology and some of the treatments administered, from ancient times to the twenty-first century. In a broad sense, we will see a progression of beliefs from what we now consider superstition to those based on scientific awareness—from a focus on supernatural explanations to knowledge of natural causes. The course of this evolution has at times been marked by periods of advancement or unique, individual contributions, followed by long years of inactivity or unproductive, backward steps.

Although human life appeared on earth some 3 million or more years ago, written records extend back only a few thousand years. Thus, our knowledge of our early ancestors is limited. Two Egyptian papyri dating from the sixteenth century B.C. provide some clues to the earliest treatments of diseases and behavior disorders (Okasha & Okasha, 2000). The Edwin Smith papyrus (named after its nineteenth-century discoverer) contains detailed descriptions of the treatment of wounds and other surgical operations. In it, the brain is described—possibly for the first time in history—and the writing clearly shows that the brain was recognized as the site of mental functions. The Ebers papyrus offers another perspective on treatment. It covers internal medicine and the circulatory system but relies more on incantations and magic for explaining and curing diseases with unknown causes. Although surgical techniques may have been used, they were probably coupled with prayers, which reflected the prevailing view of the origin of mental illness.

Antisocial personality disorders, though not well addressed in psychiatry until the nineteenth century, have posed major problems to all societies. There is evidence from legal and religious literature that some people with personality problems posed serious challenges to earlier societies going back the beginning of civilization. In ancient Mesopotamia (before the eighth century B.C.) there was a clear recognition of the types of mental health problems that are currently described as personality disorders in contemporary diagnostic manuals, the ICD-10 and *DSM-5*. Antisocial personality problems were described on cuneiform tablets detailing an ancient Mesopotamian incantation that were found at the palace of Ashurbanipal in what is now Iraq (the tablets are currently in the British Museum). Those tablets include descriptions of antisocial behaviors such as irritability and aggressiveness; lack of remorse; hurting, mistreating or stealing from others; failing to conform to social norms with respect to lawful behaviors; impulsivity or failure to plan ahead; and showing irresponsible behaviors that mental health practitioners today encounter and recognize as personality disorders. The behavioral problems were dealt with not through medicine but through religious rites or incantations that were made by people who sought exorcism from antisocial traits and behaviors by repeating explicit phrases. A recent article by Abdul-Hamid and Stein (2013) provides interesting evidence of the comparability of these ancient views of behavior problems to contemporary diagnostic manuals and their management of them through religious rites.

The Ashurbanipal cuneiform tablet from Mesopotamia around 800 B.C. includes descriptions of antisocial behaviors such as irritability and aggressiveness; mistreating or stealing from others; and irresponsible behaviors that mental health practitioners today encounter and recognize as personality disorders.

Demonology, Gods, and Magic

References to abnormal behavior in early writings show that the Chinese, Egyptians, Hebrews, and Greeks often attributed such behavior to a demon or god who had taken possession of a person. Whether the "possession" was assumed to involve good spirits or evil spirits usually depended on the affected individual's symptoms. If a person's speech or behavior appeared to have a religious or mystical significance, it was usually thought that he or she was possessed by a good spirit or god. Such people were often treated with considerable awe and respect, for individuals believed they had supernatural powers.

Most possessions, however, were considered to be the work of an angry god or an evil spirit, particularly when a person became excited or overactive and engaged in behavior contrary to religious teachings. Among the ancient Hebrews, for example, such possessions were thought to represent the wrath and punishment of God. Moses is quoted in the Bible as saying, "The Lord shall smite thee with madness." Apparently this punishment was thought to involve the withdrawal of God's protection and the abandonment of the person to the forces of evil. In such cases, every effort was made to rid the person of the evil spirit. The primary type of treatment for demonic possession was exorcism, which included various techniques for casting an evil spirit out. These techniques varied but typically included magic, prayer, incantation, noisemaking, and the use of horrible-tasting concoctions made from sheep's dung and wine.

Hippocrates' Early Medical Concepts

The Greek temples of healing ushered in the Golden Age of Greece under the Athenian leader Pericles (461–429 B.C.). This period saw considerable progress in the understanding and treatment of mental disorders, in spite of the fact that Greeks of the time considered the human body sacred so little could be learned of human anatomy or physiology. During this period the Greek physician Hippocrates (460–377 B.C.), often referred to as the father of modern medicine, received his training and made substantial contributions to the field.

Hippocrates denied that deities and demons intervened in the development of illnesses and instead insisted that mental disorders, like other diseases, had natural causes and appropriate treatments. He believed that the brain was the central organ of intellectual activity and that mental disorders were due to brain pathology. He also emphasized the importance of heredity and predisposition and pointed out that injuries to the head could cause sensory and motor disorders.

Hippocrates classified all mental disorders into three general categories—mania, melancholia, and phrenitis (brain fever)—and gave detailed clinical descriptions of the specific disorders included in each category. He relied heavily on clinical observation, and his descriptions, which were based on daily clinical records of his patients, were surprisingly thorough.

Maher and Maher (1994) pointed out that the best known of the earlier paradigms for explaining personality or temperament is the doctrine of the four humors, associated with the name of Hippocrates and later with the Roman physician Galen. The four elements of the material world were thought to be earth, air, fire, and water, which had attributes of heat, cold, moisture, and dryness. These elements combined to form the four essential fluids of the body—blood (sanguis), phlegm, bile (choler), and black bile (melancholic). The fluids combined in different proportions within different individuals, and a person's temperament was determined by which of the humors was dominant. From this view came one of the earliest and longest lasting typologies of human behavior: the sanguine, the phlegmatic, the choleric, and the melancholic. Each of these "types" brought with it a set of personality attributes. For example, the person of sanguine temperament was optimistic, cheerful, and unafraid.

Hippocrates considered dreams to be important in understanding a patient's personality. On this point, he was a harbinger of a basic concept of modern psychodynamic psychotherapy. The treatments advocated by Hippocrates were far in advance of the exorcistic practices then prevalent. For the treatment of melancholia (see the Developments in Thinking box), for example, he prescribed a regular and tranquil life, sobriety and abstinence from all excesses, a vegetable diet, celibacy, exercise short of fatigue, and bleeding if indicated. He also recognized the importance of the environment and often removed his patients from their families.

Hippocrates' emphasis on the natural causes of diseases, on clinical observation, and on brain pathology as the root of mental disorders was truly revolutionary. Like his contemporaries, however, Hippocrates had little knowledge of physiology. He believed that hysteria (the appearance of physical illness in the absence of organic pathology) was restricted to women and was caused by the uterus wandering to various parts of the body, pining for children. For this "disease," Hippocrates recommended marriage as the best remedy.

Developments in Thinking

Melancholia Through the Ages

Although the modern mental health sciences have made great strides in defining, describing, classifying, determining the causes of, and treating psychological disorders, we should not ignore or minimize the contributions to understanding these conditions that were made by many individuals in antiquity. Actually, some mental health problems that are receiving a great deal of research and clinical attention today have been recognized and well described for millennia. One recent study of surviving letters from patients who were hospitalized in Edinborough Asylum between 1873 and 1906 concluded that mental health problems in the nineteenth century were very similar to those in our day (Beveridge, 1997). One such disorder is depression.

Perhaps no other mental disorder received so much attention from early scholars as depression, or (as it has been referred to in the past) melancholia. Efforts to understand melancholia have been undertaken by physicians, philosophers, writers, painters, and religious leaders in Western civilization for over 2,000 years. Moreover, conditions similar to depression are described in surviving writings from ancient Egypt (Okasha & Okasha, 2000). These disorders might have been viewed variously as medical conditions or religious states or human frailties; however, the symptom structure and behavior described were unmistakable.

Radden (2000) published an interesting compendium of important writings on melancholia that span 24 centuries, some highlights of which are provided here.

- Investigations into the nature of depression, beginning with Aristotle and Galen during the Greek and Roman eras, provide lucid descriptions of the disorder melancholia.
- Even in the Middle Ages, when scholarship and inquiry were hindered by a period of religious persecution that included the Spanish Inquisition, scholars were interested in mental states such as melancholia. Hildegard (1098–1179), a nun known as

the "first published woman physician," carried the Greek views of melancholia further by noting, among other things, that melancholia took different forms in men and women. Johann Weyer (1515–1588) provided astute descriptions of melancholia and examined characteristics of persons who might be so affected, even though these observations were often couched in terms of demonic possession—perhaps as a concession to leaders of the Inquisition in order to avoid persecution.

- The pre-modern view of melancholia as a disorder (without the taint of demonic possession or ancient Greek humors) was introduced by Philippe Pinel (1745–1826). A French physician widely recognized for his contributions to the humane treatment of people with mental disorders, Pinel also advanced our scholarly understanding of mental disorders such as melancholia by improving a classification schema and examining the causes of the disorder.
- Two early modern contributors to our understanding of depression were Wilhelm Griesinger (1817–1868) and Emil Kraepelin (1856–1926). Griesinger's views on the underlying biological basis for disorders such as melancholia focused the field of psychiatry on the need to seek biological determinants for disorders. Kraepelin is credited with preparing the way for the modern view of psychiatry. His classification schema is still cited today in contemporary writings as seminal in the evolution of diagnostic classification systems. He also identified manic depression as a major category of depression.

Even though much of our understanding of depression and our development of effective treatment methods has emerged during the past three decades, our debt to the ancients who struggled with describing and understanding this disorder needs to be recognized.

Hippocrates' (460–377 B.C.) belief that mental disease was the result of natural causes and brain pathology was revolutionary for its time.

The earliest use of the concept "delirium" to describe symptoms of mental disorders that result from fever or physical injury or brain trauma occurred in the first century A.D. by Celsus (Adamis et al., 2007).

Early Philosophical Conceptions of Consciousness

The Greek philosopher Plato (429–347 B.C.) studied individuals with mental disturbances who had committed criminal acts and how to deal with them. He wrote that such persons were, in some "obvious" sense, not responsible for their acts and should not receive punishment in the same way as normal persons. He also made provision for mental cases to be cared for in the community.

Plato viewed psychological phenomena as responses of the whole organism, reflecting its internal state and natural appetites. In *The Republic*, Plato emphasized the importance of individual differences in intellectual and other abilities and took into account sociocultural influences in shaping thinking and behavior. His ideas regarding treatment included a provision for "hospital" care for individuals who developed beliefs that ran counter to those of the broader social order. There they would be engaged periodically in conversations comparable to psychotherapy to promote the health of their souls (Milns, 1986). Despite these modern ideas, however,

Plato shared the belief that mental disorders were in part divinely caused.

The celebrated Greek philosopher Aristotle (384–322 B.C.), who was a pupil of Plato, wrote extensively on mental disorders. Among his most lasting contributions to psychology are his descriptions of consciousness. He held the view that "thinking" as directed would eliminate pain and help to attain pleasure. On the question of whether mental disorders could be caused by psychological factors such as frustration and conflict, Aristotle discussed the possibility and rejected it; his lead on this issue was widely followed. Aristotle generally subscribed to the Hippocratic theory of disturbances in the bile. For example, he thought that very hot bile generated amorous desires, verbal fluency, and suicidal impulses.

Later Greek and Roman Thought

Hippocrates' work was continued by some of the later Greek and Roman physicians. Particularly in Alexandria, Egypt (which became a center of Greek culture after its founding in 332 B.C. by Alexander the Great), medical practices developed to a higher level, and the temples dedicated to Saturn were first-rate sanatoria. Pleasant surroundings were considered of great therapeutic value for patients with mental illness, who were provided with constant activities including parties, dances, walks in the temple gardens, rowing along the Nile, and musical concerts. Physicians of this time also used a wide range of therapeutic measures including dieting, massage, hydrotherapy, gymnastics, and education, as well as some less desirable practices such as bleeding, purging, and mechanical restraints.

Asclepiades (c. 124–40 B.C.) was a Greek physician born at Prusa in Bithynia in Asia Minor and practiced medicine in Rome toward the end of the second century B.C. He developed a theory of disease that was based on the flow of atoms through the pores in the body and came up with treatments, such as massage, special diets, bathing, exercise, listening to music, and rest and quiet, to restore to the body (Stone, 1937).

One of the most influential Greek physicians was Galen (A.D. 130–200), who practiced in Rome. Although he elaborated on the Hippocratic tradition, he did not contribute much that was new to the treatment or clinical descriptions of mental disorders. Rather, he made a number of original contributions concerning the anatomy of the nervous system. (These findings were based on dissections of animals; human autopsies were still not allowed.) Galen also took a scientific approach to the field, dividing the causes of psychological disorders into physical and mental categories. Among the causes he named were injuries to the head, excessive use of alcohol, shock, fear, adolescence, menstrual changes, economic reversals, and disappointment in love.

Roman medicine reflected the characteristic pragmatism of the Roman people. Roman physicians wanted to make their patients comfortable and thus used pleasant physical therapies such as warm baths and massage. They also followed the principle of *contrariis contrarius* (or "opposite by opposite") by, for example, having their patients drink chilled wine while they were in a warm tub.

Galen (A.D. 130–200) believed that psychological disorders could have either physical causes, such as injuries to the head, or mental causes, such as disappointment in love.

Early Views of Mental Disorders in China

China was one of the earliest developed civilizations in which medicine and attention to mental disorders were introduced (Soong, 2006). The following passage is taken from an ancient Chinese medical text supposedly written by Huang Ti (c. 2674 B.C.), the third legendary emperor:

> The person suffering from excited insanity initially feels sad, eating and sleeping less; he then becomes grandiose, feeling that he is very smart and noble, talking and scolding day and night, singing, behaving strangely, seeing strange things, hearing strange voices, believing that he can see the devil or gods. (Tseng, 1973, p. 570)

Even at this early date, Chinese medicine was based on a belief in natural rather than supernatural causes for illnesses. For example, in the concept of yin and yang, the human body, like the cosmos, is divided into positive and

negative forces that both complement and contradict each other. If the two forces are balanced, the result is physical and mental health; if they are not, illness results. Thus, treatments focused on restoring balance (Tseng, 1973, p. 570).

Chinese medicine reached a relatively sophisticated level during the second century, and Chung Ching, who has been called the Hippocrates of China, wrote two well-known medical works around A.D. 200. Like Hippocrates, he based his views of physical and mental disorders on clinical observations, and he implicated organ pathologies as primary causes. However, he also believed that stressful psychological conditions could cause organ pathologies, and his treatments, like those of Hippocrates, utilized both drugs and the regaining of emotional balance through appropriate activities.

As in the West, Chinese views of mental disorders regressed to a belief in supernatural forces as causal agents. From the later part of the second century through the early part of the ninth century, ghosts and devils were implicated in "ghost-evil" insanity, which presumably resulted from possession by evil spirits. The "Dark Ages" in China, however, were neither so severe (in terms of the treatment of patients with mental illness) nor as long lasting as in the West. A return to biological, somatic (bodily) views and an emphasis on psychosocial factors occurred in the centuries that followed. During the past 50 years, China has been experiencing a broadening of ideas in mental health services and has been incorporating many ideas from Western psychiatry (Zhang & Lu, 2006).

Views of Abnormality During the Middle Ages

During the Middle Ages (about A.D. 500 to A.D. 1500), the more scientific aspects of Greek medicine survived in the Islamic countries of the Middle East. The first mental hospital was established in Baghdad in A.D. 792; it was soon followed by others in Damascus and Aleppo (Polvan, 1969). In these hospitals, individuals with mental disturbances received humane treatment. One outstanding figure in ancient medicine was Avicenna from Persia (c. 980–1037). Referred to as the "prince of physicians" (Campbell, 1926), he was the author of *The Canon of Medicine*, perhaps the most widely studied medical work ever written. In his writings, Avicenna frequently referred to hysteria, epilepsy, manic reactions, and melancholia. The following case study illustrates Avicenna's unique approach to the treatment of a young prince suffering from mental disorder.

An Early Treatment Case

A certain prince was afflicted with melancholia and suffered from the delusion that he was a cow. . . . He would low like a cow, causing annoyance to everyone, . . . crying, "Kill me so that a good stew may be made of my flesh." Finally . . . he would eat nothing. . . . Avicenna was persuaded to take the case. . . . First of all he sent a message to the patient bidding him be of good cheer because the butcher was coming to slaughter him, whereat . . . the sick man rejoiced. Some time afterward Avicenna, holding a knife in his hand, entered the sickroom saying, "Where is this cow that I may kill it?" The patient lowed like a cow to indicate where he was. By Avicenna's orders he was laid on the ground bound hand and foot. Avicenna then felt him all over and said, "He is too lean, and not ready to be killed; he must be fattened." Then they offered him suitable food of which he now partook eagerly, and gradually he gained strength, got rid of his delusion, and was completely cured. (Browne, 1921, pp. 88–89)

Ancient Persian physician Avicenna (c. 980–1037) approached the treatment of mental disorders with humane practices unknown to Western medical practitioners of the time.

During the Middle Ages in Europe, scientific inquiry into abnormal behavior was limited, and the treatment of individuals who were psychologically disturbed was characterized more often by ritual or superstition than by attempts to understand an individual's condition. In contrast to Avicenna's era in the Islamic countries of the Middle East or to the period of enlightenment during the seventeenth and eighteenth centuries, the Middle Ages in Europe were largely devoid of scientific thinking and humane treatment for those with mental illness.

Mental disorders were quite prevalent throughout the Middle Ages in Europe, especially toward the end of the period, when medieval institutions, social structures, and beliefs began to change drastically. During this time, supernatural explanations of the causes of mental illness grew in popularity. Within this environment, it obviously was difficult to make great strides in the understanding and treatment of abnormal behavior. Although the influence of theology was growing rapidly, "sin" was not always cited as a causal factor in mental illness. For example, Kroll and Bachrach (1984) examined 57 episodes of mental illness

ranging from madness and possession to alcohol abuse and epilepsy. They found sin implicated in only nine cases (16 percent). To understand better this elusive period of history, let us look at two events of the times, mass madness and exorcism, to see how they are related to views of abnormal behavior.

MASS MADNESS   During the last half of the Middle Ages in Europe, a peculiar trend emerged in efforts to understand abnormal behavior. It involved **mass madness**—the widespread occurrence of group behavior disorders that were apparently cases of hysteria. Whole groups of people were affected simultaneously. Dancing manias (epidemics of raving, jumping, dancing, and convulsions) were reported as early as the tenth century. One such episode that occurred in Italy early in the thirteenth century was known as **tarantism**—a disorder that included an uncontrollable impulse to dance that was often attributed to the bite of the southern European tarantula or wolf spider. This dancing mania later spread to Germany and the rest of Europe, where it was known as **Saint Vitus's dance**.

Isolated rural areas were also afflicted with outbreaks of **lycanthropy**—a condition in which people believed themselves to be possessed by wolves and imitated their behavior. In 1541 a case was reported in which a person suffering from lycanthropy told his captors, in confidence, that he was really a wolf but that his skin was smooth on the surface because all the hairs were on the inside (Stone, 1937). To cure him of his delusions, his extremities were amputated, following which he died, still uncured.

Mass madness occurred periodically all the way into the seventeenth century but had reached its peak during the fourteenth and fifteenth centuries—a period noted for social oppression, famine, and epidemic diseases. During this time, Europe was ravaged by a plague known as the Black Death, which killed millions (according to some estimates, 50 percent of the population of Europe died) and severely disrupted social organization. Undoubtedly, many of the peculiar cases of mass madness were related to the depression, fear, and wild mysticism engendered by the terrible events of this period. People simply could not believe that frightening catastrophes such as the Black Death could have natural causes and thus could be within their power to control, prevent, or even create.

Today, so-called mass hysteria occurs occasionally; the affliction usually mimics some type of physical disorder such as fainting spells or convulsive movements. A case of apparent mass hysteria occurred among hundreds of West Bank Palestinian girls in April 1983. This episode threatened to have serious political repercussions because some Arab leaders initially thought that the girls had been poisoned by Israelis. Health officials later concluded that psychological factors had played a key role in most of the cases (Hefez, 1985).

Ilechukwu (1992) describes an epidemic of mass hysteria that occurred in Nigeria in 1990 in which many men feared that their genitals had simply vanished. This fear of genital retraction accompanied by a fear of death is referred to as *koro* and has been widely documented in Southeast Asia. The afflicted persons believe this genital disappearance was caused by a supernatural occurrence in which they were robbed of their genitalia in order to benefit other people magically. Ilechukwu attributes some of this panic to male resentment of women's success during a period of social strain and the symbolic equation between masculine sexuality and economic, social, and creative prowess.

EXORCISM AND WITCHCRAFT   In the Middle Ages in Europe, management of people who were mentally disturbed was left largely to the clergy. Monasteries served as refuges and places of confinement. During the early medieval period, people with mental disturbances were typically treated with kindness. "Treatment" consisted of prayer, holy water, sanctified ointments, the breath or spittle of the priests, the touching of relics, visits to holy places, and mild forms of exorcism. In some monasteries and shrines, **exorcisms** were performed by the gentle "laying on of hands." Such methods were often joined with vaguely understood medical treatments derived mainly from Galen, which gave rise to prescriptions such as the following: "For a fiend-sick man: When a devil possesses a man, or controls him from within with disease, a spewdrink of lupin, bishopswort, henbane, garlic. Pound these together, add ale and holy water" (Cockayne, 1864–1866).

Interestingly, there has been a recent resurgence of superstition. For example, one can find those who believe that supernatural forces cause psychological problems and that "cures" should involve exorcism to rid people of unwanted characteristics or "spells." Fries (2001) reported on the tragedy of a woman who drowned her 4-year-old daughter in an exorcism ritual. The mother was attempting to rid her daughter of the demons that the mother believed possessed her. In another example, CBS News (2003) reported an incident in which a boy with autism was killed in an exorcism at a church in Milwaukee.

It had long been thought that during the Middle Ages many people with mental disturbances were accused of being witches and thus were punished and often killed (e.g., Zilboorg & Henry, 1941). But several more recent interpretations have questioned the extent to which this was so (Maher & Maher, 1985; Phillips, 2002). For example, in a review of the literature, Schoeneman (1984) notes that "the typical accused witch was not a mentally ill person but an impoverished woman with a sharp tongue and a bad temper" (p. 301). He concluded that "witchcraft was, in fact, never considered a variety of possession either by witch hunters, the general populace, or modern historians" (p. 306). To say "never" may be overstating the case; clearly,

some people with mental illness were punished as witches. Otherwise, as we will see in the next section, why did some physicians and thinkers go to great lengths to expose the fallacies of the connection? In the case of witchcraft and mental illness, the confusion may be due, in part, to confusion about demonic possession. Even Robert Burton (1576–1640), an enlightened scholar, in his classic work *The Anatomy of Melancholia* (1621), considered demonic possession a potential cause of mental disorder. There were two types of demonically possessed people: Those physically possessed were considered mad, whereas those spiritually possessed were likely to be considered witches. Over time, the distinctions between these two categories may have blurred in the eyes of historians, resulting in the perception that witchcraft and mental illness were connected more frequently in the medieval mind than was the case.

The changing view of the relationship between witchcraft and mental illness points to an even broader issue—the difficulties of interpreting historical events accurately. We will discuss this concept in more depth in the Unresolved Issues section at the end of this chapter.

---

in review

- What aspects of Hippocrates' alternative approach to mental disorders were truly revolutionary?
- What were the historical views of the disorder of melancholia (known as depression today)?
- What was the role of supernatural beliefs in efforts to understand mental disorders during the Middle Ages?
- What is mass madness? Give some examples of this phenomenon.

Toward Humanitarian Approaches

2.2   Describe the effect that humanism had on abnormal psychology.

During the latter part of the Middle Ages and the early Renaissance, scientific questioning reemerged and a movement emphasizing the importance of specifically human interests and concerns began—a movement (still with us today) that can be loosely referred to as humanism. Consequently, the superstitious beliefs that had hindered the understanding and therapeutic treatment of mental disorders began to be challenged.

The Resurgence of Scientific Questioning in Europe

Paracelsus (1490–1541), a Swiss physician, was an early critic of superstitious beliefs about possession. He insisted that the dancing mania was not a possession but a form of disease, and that it should be treated as such. He also postulated a conflict between the instinctual and spiritual natures of human beings, formulated the idea of psychic causes for mental illness, and advocated treatment by "bodily magnetism," later called hypnosis (Mora, 1967). Although Paracelsus rejected demonology, his view of abnormal behavior was colored by his belief in astral influences (*lunatic* is derived from the Latin word *luna*, or "moon"). He was convinced that the moon exerted a supernatural influence over the brain—an idea, incidentally, that persists even today.

Johann Weyer (1515–1588), a German physician and writer who wrote under the Latin name of Joannus Wierus, was so deeply disturbed by the imprisonment, torture, and burning of people accused of witchcraft that he made a careful study of the entire problem. About 1583 he published a book, *On the Deceits of the Demons*, that contains a step-by-step rebuttal of the *Malleus Maleficarum*, a witch-hunting handbook published in 1486 for use in recognizing and dealing with those suspected of being witches. In his book, Weyer argued that a considerable number, if not all, of those imprisoned, tortured, and burned for witchcraft were really sick in mind or body and that, consequently, great wrongs were being committed against innocent people. Weyer's work enjoyed the approval of a few outstanding physicians and theologians of his time. Mostly, however, it met with vehement protest and condemnation.

Weyer was one of the first physicians to specialize in mental disorders, and his wide experience and progressive views justify his reputation as the founder of modern psychopathology. Unfortunately, however, he was too far ahead of his time. He was scorned by his peers, many of whom called him "Weirus Hereticus" and "Weirus Insanus." His works were banned by the Church and remained so until the twentieth century.

The clergy, however, were also beginning to question the practices of the time. For example, St. Vincent de Paul (1576–1660), at the risk of his life, declared, "Mental disease is no different than bodily disease and Christianity demands of the humane and powerful to protect, and the skillful to relieve the one as well as the other" (Castiglioni, 1924).

In the face of such persistent advocates of science, who continued their testimonies throughout the next two centuries, demonology and superstition gave ground. These advocates gradually paved the way for the return of observation and reason, which culminated in the development of modern experimental and clinical approaches.

The Establishment of Early Asylums

From the sixteenth century on, special institutions called **asylums**—sanctuaries or places of refuge meant solely for the care of people with mental illness—grew in number. The early asylums were begun as a way of removing from society troublesome individuals who could not care for themselves. Although scientific inquiry into abnormal behavior was on the increase, most early asylums, often referred to as "madhouses," were not pleasant places or "hospitals" but primarily residences or storage places for people who were insane. The unfortunate residents lived and died amid conditions of incredible filth and cruelty.

The first asylum established in Europe was probably in Spain in 1409 (Villasante, 2003), although this point has been the subject of considerable discussion (Polo, 1997; Trope, 1997). Little is known about the treatment of patients in this asylum. In 1547 the monastery of St. Mary of Bethlem in London (initially founded as a monastery in 1247; see O'Donoghue, 1914) was officially made into an asylum by Henry VIII. Its name soon was contracted to "Bedlam," and it became widely known for its deplorable conditions and practices. The more violent patients were exhibited to the public for one penny a look, and the more harmless inmates were forced to seek charity on the streets of London. Tuke (1882) describes Ned Ward's account, in *History of the Insane in the British Isles*, of a visit to Bedlam:

> Accordingly we were admitted in thro' an iron gate, within which sat a brawny Cerberus, of an Idico-colour, leaning upon a money-box; we turned in through another Iron-Barricado, where we heard such a rattling of chains, drumming of doors, ranting, hollowing, singing, and running, that I could think of nothing but Don Quevedo's Vision where the lost souls broke loose and put Hell in an uproar. The first whimsey-headed wretch of this lunatic family that we observed, was a merry fellow in a straw cap, who was talking to himself, "that he had an army of Eagles at his command," then clapping his hand upon his

Johann Weyer (1515–1588), a sixteenth-century German physician, became so concerned over the torture and imprisonment of people accused of being witches that he wrote a book rebutting the church's witch-hunting handbook, the *Malleus Maleficarum*.

head, swore by his crown of moonshine, he would battle all the Stars in the Skies, but he would have some claret. . . . We then moved on till we found another remarkable figure worth our observing, who was peeping through his wicket, eating of bread and cheese, talking all the while like a carrier at his supper, chewing his words with his victuals, all that he spoke being in praise of bread and cheese: "bread was good with cheese, and cheese was good with bread, and bread and cheese was good together"; and abundance of such stuff; to which my friend and I, with others stood listening; at last he counterfeits a sneeze, and shot such a mouthful of bread and cheese amongst us, that every spectator had some share of his kindness, which made us retreat. (pp. 76–77)

Such asylums for those with mental illness were gradually established in other countries, including Mexico (1566) and France (1641). An asylum was established in Moscow in 1764, and the notorious Lunatics' Tower in Vienna was constructed in 1784. This structure was a showplace in Old Vienna, an ornately decorated round tower within which were square rooms. The doctors and "keepers" lived in the square rooms, while the patients were confined in the spaces between the walls of the rooms and the outside of the tower, where they were put on exhibit to the public for a small fee. These early asylums were primarily modifications of penal institutions, and the inmates were treated more like beasts than human beings.

In the United States, the Pennsylvania Hospital in Philadelphia, completed under the guidance of Benjamin Franklin in 1756, provided some cells or wards for patients with mental illness. The Public Hospital in Williamsburg, Virginia, constructed in 1768, was the first hospital in the United States devoted exclusively to patients with mental illness. The treatment of patients with mental illness in the United States was no better than that offered by European institutions, however. Zwelling's 1985 review of the Public Hospital's treatment methods shows that, initially, the philosophy of treatment involved the belief that the patients

Constructed in 1768, the Public Hospital in Williamsburg, Virginia was the first hospital in the United States devoted exclusively to patients with mental illness.

needed to choose rationality over **insanity**. Thus, the treatment techniques were aggressive, aimed at restoring a "physical balance in the body and brain." These techniques, though based on the scientific views of the day, were designed to intimidate patients. They included powerful drugs, water treatments, bleeding and blistering, electric shocks, and physical restraints. For example, a violent patient might be plunged into ice water or a listless patient into hot water; frenzied patients might be administered drugs to exhaust them; or patients might be bled in order to drain their system of "harmful" fluids.

Humanitarian Reform

Clearly, by the late eighteenth century, most mental hospitals in Europe and America were in significant need of reform. The humanitarian treatment of patients received great impetus from the work of Philippe Pinel (1745–1826) in France.

PINEL'S EXPERIMENT   In 1792, shortly after the first phase of the French Revolution, Pinel was placed in charge of La Bicêtre, a hospital in Paris. In this capacity, he received the grudging permission of the Revolutionary Commune to remove the chains from some of the inmates as an experiment to test his views that patients with mental illness should be treated with kindness and consideration—as sick people, not as vicious beasts or criminals. Had his experiment proved a failure, Pinel might have lost his head, but fortunately it was a great success. Chains were removed; sunny rooms were provided; patients were permitted to exercise on the hospital grounds; and kindness was extended to these poor beings, some of whom had been chained in dungeons for 30 or more years. The effect was almost miraculous. The previous noise, filth, and abuse were replaced by order and peace. Interestingly, a historical document, subsequently found in the French Archives, raises some question about the date at which humanitarian reforms were begun in France. The document, provided by Jean-Baptiste Pussin (Pinel's predecessor at La Bicêtre), indicated that he had been the head of the hospital beginning in 1784 and had removed some of the chains from patients and employed slightly more humane straitjackets instead. He also pointed out in the document that he had issued orders forbidding the staff from beating patients (Weiner, 1979).

TUKE'S WORK IN ENGLAND   At about the same time that Pinel was reforming La Bicêtre, an English Quaker named William Tuke (1732–1822) established the York Retreat, a pleasant country house where patients with mental illness lived, worked, and rested in a kindly, religious atmosphere (Narby, 1982). This retreat represented the culmination of a noble battle against the brutality, ignorance, and indifference of Tuke's time.

The Quakers believed in treating all people, even the insane, with kindness and acceptance. Their view that kind acceptance would help people with mental illness recover sparked the growth of more humane psychiatric treatment during a period when such patients were ignored and mistreated (Glover, 1984).

The Quaker retreat at York has continued to provide humane mental health treatment for over 200 years (Borthwick et al., 2001), even though the mental hospital movement spawned by its example evolved into large mental hospitals that became crowded and often offered less-than-humane treatment in the late nineteenth and early twentieth centuries. (See the photograph of the York Retreat today.)

As word of Pinel's amazing results spread to England, Tuke's small force of Quakers gradually gained the support of English medical practitioners such as Thomas Wakley and Samuel Hitch. In 1841 Hitch introduced trained nurses into the wards at the Gloucester Asylum and put trained supervisors at the head of the nursing staffs. These innovations, quite revolutionary at the time, not only improved the care of patients but also changed public attitudes toward people with mental disturbances. In 1842, following Wakley's lobbying for change, the Lunacy Inquiry Act was passed, which included a requirement that asylums and houses be effectively inspected every 4 months (Roberts, 1981) to ensure proper diet and the elimination of the use of restraints.

In 1845, the Country Asylums Act was passed in England, which required every county to provide asylum to "paupers and lunatics" (Scull, 1996). Britain's policy of providing more humane treatment of people with mental illness was substantially expanded to the colonies (Australia, Canada, India, West Indies, South Africa, etc.) after a widely publicized incident of maltreatment of patients that

This painting depicts Philippe Pinel supervising the unchaining of inmates at La Bicêtre hospital. Pinel's experiment represented both a great reform and a major step in devising humanitarian methods of treating mental disorders.

This picture shows a male ward of Bethlem Hospital under the new, more humane treatment approach. Walford (1878) pointed out that by 1815, there was no more "show for a penny" at Bethlem Hospital, and patients were afforded more humane living facilities and activities.

The historic mental health facility, the York Retreat, continues to provide services in York, England, over 200 years since it was founded by William Tuke in 1796. This mental health facility is sponsored by the Quakers and provides a broad range of services in both inpatient and outpatient care.

occurred in Kingston, Jamaica, prompted an audit of colonial facilities and practices. In Kingston, an article written by a former patient disclosed that the staff used "tanking" to control and punish patients with mental illness. During tanking, "lunatics" were routinely held under water in a bathing tank by nurses and sometimes other patients until they were near death (Swartz, 2010).

RUSH AND MORAL MANAGEMENT IN AMERICA The success of Pinel's and Tuke's humanitarian experiments revolutionized the treatment of patients with mental illness throughout the Western world. In the United States, this revolution was reflected in the work of Benjamin Rush (1745–1813), the founder of American psychiatry and also one of the signers of the Declaration of Independence. While he was associated with the Pennsylvania Hospital in 1783, Rush encouraged more humane treatment of patients with mental illness; wrote the first systematic treatise on psychiatry in America, *Medical Inquiries and Observations upon Diseases of the Mind* (1812); and was the first American to organize a course in psychiatry (see Gentile & Miller, 2009). But even he did not escape entirely from the established beliefs of his time. His medical theory was tainted with astrology, and his principal remedies were bloodletting and purgatives. In addition, he invented and used a device called the "tranquilizing chair," which was probably more torturous than tranquil for patients. The chair was thought to lessen the force of the blood on the head while the muscles were relaxed. Despite these limitations, we can consider Rush an important transitional figure between the old era and the new.

During the early part of this period of humanitarian reform, the use of moral management—a wide-ranging method of treatment that focused on a patient's social, individual, and occupational needs—became relatively widespread. This approach, which stemmed largely from the work of Pinel and Tuke, began in Europe during the late eighteenth century and in America during the early nineteenth century.

Moral management in asylums emphasized the patients' moral and spiritual development and the rehabilitation of their "character" rather than their physical or mental disorders, in part because very little effective treatment was available for these conditions at the time. The treatment or rehabilitation of the physical or mental disorders was usually attempted through manual labor and spiritual discussion, along with humane treatment.

Moral management achieved a high degree of effectiveness—which is all the more amazing because it was done without the benefit of the antipsychotic drugs used today and because many of the patients were probably suffering from syphilis, a then-incurable disease of the central nervous system. In the 20-year period between 1833 and 1853, Worcester State Hospital's discharge rate for patients who had been ill less than a year before admission was 71 percent. Even for patients with a longer preadmission disorder, the discharge rate was 59 percent (Bockhoven, 1972). In London, Walford (1878) reported that during a 100-year period ending in 1876, the "cure" rate was 45.7 percent for the famed Bedlam Hospital.

Despite its reported effectiveness in many cases, moral management was nearly abandoned by the latter part of the nineteenth century. The reasons were many and varied. Among the more obvious ones were ethnic prejudice against the rising immigrant population in hospitals, leading to tension between staff and patients; the failure of the movement's leaders to train their own replacements; and the overextension of hospital facilities, which reflected the misguided belief that bigger hospitals would differ from smaller ones only in size.

Two other reasons for the demise of moral management are, in retrospect, truly ironic. One was the rise of the mental hygiene movement, which advocated a method of treatment that focused almost exclusively on the physical well-being of hospitalized patients with mental illness. Although the patients' comfort levels improved under the mental hygienists, the patients received no help for their mental problems and thus were subtly condemned to helplessness and dependency.

Advances in biomedical science also contributed to the demise of moral management and the rise of the mental hygiene movement. These advances fostered the notion that all mental disorders would eventually yield to biological explanations and biologically based treatments (Luchins, 1989). Thus, the psychological and social environment of a patient was considered largely irrelevant; the best one could do was keep the patient comfortable until a biological cure was discovered. Needless to say, the anticipated biological cure-all did not arrive, and by the late 1940s and early 1950s, discharge rates were down to about 30 percent. Its negative effects on the use of moral management notwithstanding, the mental hygiene movement has accounted for many humanitarian accomplishments.

BENJAMIN FRANKLIN'S EARLY DISCOVERY OF THE POTENTIAL CURATIVE EFFECTS OF ELECTRIC SHOCK In school, most people learn about Benjamin Franklin's early experimentation with electricity in the early eighteenth century. His kite-flying during electric storms and its influence on the physical sciences is common knowledge. However, most people (even mental health professionals) are not aware that his work with electricity was among the earliest efforts to explore electric shock to treat mental illness, an insight he gained accidentally. His proposals for using electricity to treat melancholia (depression) grew out of his observations that a severe shock he had experienced altered his memories (see the informative discussion by Finger & Zaromb, 2006). Franklin published articles describing his experience and suggested that physicians further study this method for treating melancholia. Shortly afterward, one of his friends, a physician named Ingenhousz, reported a similar incident in which he observed alterations in his thinking following a shock he had received. He too called for clinical trials to study this phenomenon as a possible treatment for psychiatric patients. Although these early efforts suggested that electroshock was a potentially valuable treatment approach, medical research on the procedure was slow to develop. Rudolf Gottfried Arndt (1835–1900) from Germany treated a larger number of psychotic patients with electrotherapy (Arndt, 1878; see also discussion by Steinberg, 2013), but it was not until the twentieth century that Cerletti and Bini (1938), at the University of Rome, brought professional attention to electric shock as a treatment for depression.

DIX AND THE MENTAL HYGIENE MOVEMENT   Dorothea Dix (1802–1887) was an energetic New Englander who became a champion of poor and "forgotten" people who had been consigned to prisons and mental institutions for decades during the nineteenth century. Dix, herself a child of very difficult and impoverished circumstances (Viney, 1996), later became an important driving force in humane treatment for psychiatric patients. She worked as a schoolteacher as a young adult but was later forced into early retirement because of recurring attacks of tuberculosis. In 1841, she began to teach in a women's prison. Through this contact she became acquainted with the deplorable conditions in jails, almshouses, and asylums. In a "Memorial" submitted to the U.S. Congress in 1848, she stated that she had seen

> more than 9000 idiots, epileptics and insane in the United States, destitute of appropriate care and protection . . . bound with galling chains, bowed beneath fetters and heavy iron bails attached to drag-chains, lacerated with ropes, scourged with rods and terrified beneath storms of execration and cruel blows; now subject to jibes and scorn and torturing tricks; now abandoned to the most outrageous violations. (Zilboorg & Henry, 1941, pp. 583–584)

As a result of what she had seen, Dix carried on a zealous campaign between 1841 and 1881 that aroused people and legislatures to do something about the inhuman treatment accorded to people with mental illness. Through her efforts, the mental hygiene movement grew in America: Millions of dollars were raised to build suitable hospitals, and 20 states responded directly to her appeals. Not only was she instrumental in improving conditions in American hospitals but she also directed the opening of two large institutions in Canada and completely reformed the asylum system in Scotland and several other countries. She is credited with establishing 32 mental hospitals, an astonishing record given the ignorance and superstition that still prevailed in the field of mental health at that time. Dix rounded out her career by organizing the nursing forces of the Union Army during the Civil War. A resolution presented by the U.S. Congress in 1901 characterized her as "among the noblest examples of humanity in all history" (Karnesh, with Zucker, 1945, p. 18).

Later critics have claimed that establishing hospitals for people with mental illness and increasing the number of patients in them spawned overcrowded facilities and custodial care (Bockhoven, 1972; Dain, 1964). These critics have further claimed that housing patients in institutions away from society interfered with the treatment of the day (moral therapy) and deferred the search for more appropriate and effective treatments for mental disorders (Bockhoven, 1972). These criticisms, however, do not consider the context in which Dix's contributions were made

(see the Unresolved Issues section at the end of this chapter). Her advocacy of the humane treatment of people with mental illness stood in stark contrast to the cruel treatment common at the time.

Dorothea Dix (1802–1887) was a tireless reformer who made great strides in changing public attitudes toward people with mental illness.

THE MILITARY AND PEOPLE WITH MENTAL ILLNESS   Mental health treatment was also advanced by military medicine. The first mental health facility for treating war casualties with mental disabilities was opened by the Confederate Army during the American Civil War (Deutsch, 1944; Gabriel, 1987). An even more extensive and influential program of military psychiatry evolved in Germany during the late 1800s. Lengweiler (2003) reviewed the evolution of military psychiatry in Germany between the Franco-Prussian War in 1870 and World War I in 1914. During this period, psychiatrists, a number of whom made great contributions to the field of abnormal psychology (e.g., Emil Kraepelin and Richard von Krafft-Ebing), worked with the military administration, conducting research and training doctors to detect mental health problems that could interfere with performance of duty. One early research program illustrates the interplay between medicine and the military administration. Kraepelin, who viewed alcohol as a key cause of psychological problems among soldiers, conducted a research project evaluating the extent to which alcohol consumption adversely affected the soldiers' ability to fire their rifles effectively.

Nineteenth-Century Views of the Causes and Treatment of Mental Disorders

In the early part of the nineteenth century, mental hospitals were controlled essentially by laypersons because of the prominence of moral management in the treatment of "lunatics." Medical professionals—or "alienists," as psychiatrists were called at this time in reference to their treating the "alienated," or insane—had a relatively inconsequential role in the care of the insane and the management of the asylums of the day. Moreover, effective treatments for mental disorders were unavailable, the only measures being such procedures as drugging, bleeding, and purging, which produced few objective results. However, during the latter part of the century, alienists gained control of the insane asylums and incorporated the traditional moral management therapy into their other rudimentary physical medical procedures.

Over time, the alienists acquired more status and influence in society and became influential as purveyors of morality, touting the benefits of Victorian morality as important to good mental health. Mental disorders were only vaguely understood, and conditions such as melancholia (depression) were considered to be the result of nervous exhaustion. That is, psychiatrists of the time thought that emotional problems were caused by the expenditure of energy or by the depletion of bodily energies as a result of excesses in living. The mental deterioration or "shattered nerves" that supposedly resulted from a person's using up precious nerve force came to be referred to as "neurasthenia," a condition that involved pervasive feelings of low mood, lack of energy, and physical symptoms that were thought to be related to "lifestyle" problems brought on by the demands of civilization. These vague symptoms, viewed by the alienists/psychiatrists as a definable medical condition, were then considered treatable by medical men of the times.

Changing Attitudes Toward Mental Health in the Early Twentieth Century

It is difficult to partition modern views of abnormal behavior into discrete, uniform attitudes or to trace their historical precedents without appearing arbitrary and overly simplistic. However, a brief, selective overview here will bring us into the contemporary era and set the scene for our discussion of the major viewpoints and causal considerations discussed in Chapter 3. By the end of the nineteenth century, the mental hospital or asylum—"the big house on the hill"—with its fortress-like appearance, had become a familiar landmark in America. In it, patients with mental illness lived under relatively harsh conditions despite the inroads made by moral management. To the general public, however, the asylum was an eerie place and its occupants a strange and frightening lot. Little was done by the psychiatrists to educate the public or reduce the general fear of insanity. A principal reason for this silence, of course, was that early psychiatrists had few treatment strategies or effective procedures to help patients.

In the first half of the twentieth century, hospital care for people with mental illness afforded very little in the way of effective treatment. In many cases, the care was considered to be harsh, punitive, and inhumane.

Gradually, however, important strides were made toward changing the general public's attitude toward patients with mental illness. In America, the pioneering work of Dix was followed by that of Clifford Beers (1876–1943), whose book *A Mind That Found Itself* was first published in 1908. Beers, a Yale graduate, described his own mental collapse and told of the bad treatment he received in three typical institutions of the day. Although chains and other torture devices had long since been given up, the straitjacket was still widely used as a means of "quieting" excited patients. Beers experienced this treatment and supplied a vivid description of what such painful immobilization of the arms means to an overwrought mental patient in a widely read description of his experiences.

After Beers recovered in the home of a kind attendant, he launched a campaign to make people realize that such treatment was no way to handle the sick. He soon won the interest and support of many public-spirited individuals, including the eminent psychologist William James and the "dean of American psychiatry," Adolf Meyer.

The World Around Us

Chaining Mental Health Patients

Because of limited mental health treatment resources in some countries, it is not uncommon for people with mental illness to be chained. Westermeyer and Kroll (1978) conducted an epidemiologic study on the use of restraints for people with mental illness in 27 villages in Laos. They reported that people with mental illness who were aggressive toward others or who were considered to be a danger to themselves were sometimes restrained by being chained to posts. The woman from Laos in the photograph shown here suffered from a psychotic disorder and reportedly felt compelled to sweep her platform for 6 or 7 hours a day. She

Chained patient from Laos

was restrained at a Buddhist temple in order to keep her from wandering into the jungle (Westermeyer, 2001).

Treatment of patients at the Mohammad Ali Shah Shrine in eastern Afghanistan involves being fed only a small piece of bread, a raw chili, and water each day for 21 days. Their family is charged 20 pounds a month. Many patients are chained as a means of controlling their behavior.

Many temples in some countries provide homes for individuals who are psychologically disturbed, although the care is typically inadequate. For example, Erwady, India, near Madras, has 15 privately run homes, many of which are without electricity, tap water, toilet facilities, and beds. In 2000, six people died from waterborne disease at one of the Erwady asylums, prompting the government to direct an inquiry into the conditions of the mental health asylums. Later, fire swept through a palm-thatched shed that housed people with mental illness at one Erwady asylum, killing 25 patients and injuring 5 others, many of whom were chained to heavy stones or pillars (Associated Press, 2001). At the time of the fire, the asylum housed 46 residents; only 16 of the patients escaped uninjured.

What social factors today might prompt people in some societies to engage in the extreme action of chaining individuals with mental health problems? How would Philippe Pinel during the eighteenth century or Clifford Beers in the early twentieth century view these contemporary chaining events?

Mental Hospital Care in the Twentieth Century

The twentieth century began with a continued period of growth in asylums for people with mental illness; however, the fate of patients with mental illness during that century was neither uniform nor entirely positive (see the World Around Us box). At the beginning of the twentieth century, with the influence of enlightened people such as Clifford Beers, mental hospitals grew substantially in number—predominantly to house persons with severe mental disorders such as schizophrenia, depression, organic mental disorders, tertiary syphilis and paresis (syphilis of the brain), and severe alcoholism. By 1940 the public mental hospitals housed over 400,000 patients, roughly 90 percent of whom resided in large state-funded hospitals; the remainder resided in private hospitals (Grob, 1994). During this period, hospital stays were typically quite lengthy, and many individuals with mental illness were destined to be hospitalized for many years. For the first half of the twentieth century, hospital care was accompanied by little in the way of effective treatment, and the care was often harsh, punitive, and inhumane. The year 1946, however,

marked the beginning of an important period of change. In that year, Mary Jane Ward published a very influential book, *The Snake Pit*, which was popularized in a movie of the same name. This work called attention to the plight of patients with mental illness and helped to create concern over the need to provide more humane mental health care in the community in place of the overcrowded mental hospitals. Also in 1946, the National Institutes of Mental Health was organized and provided active support for research and training through psychiatric residencies and (later) clinical psychology training programs. Moreover, the Hill-Burton Act, a program that funded community mental health hospitals, was passed during this period. This legislation, along with the Community Mental Health Act of 1963, helped to create a far-reaching set of programs to develop outpatient psychiatric clinics, inpatient facilities in general hospitals, and community consultation and rehabilitation programs. Baker and colleagues (2012) discussed the broad extension of clinical psychology after World War II with the increased development of mental health services for veterans returning from the war.

The need for reform in psychiatric hospitals was a prominent concern of many professionals and laypersons alike during the 1950s and 1960s. A great deal of professional attention was given to the need to improve conditions in mental hospitals following the publication of another influential book, *Asylums*, by the sociologist Erving Goffman (1961). This book further exposed the inhumane treatment of patients with mental illness and provided a detailed account of neglect and maltreatment in mental hospitals. The movement to change the mental hospital environment was also enhanced significantly by scientific advances in the last half of the twentieth century, particularly the development of effective medications for many disorders—for example, the use of lithium in the treatment of manic depressive disorders (Cade, 1949) and the introduction of phenothiazines for the treatment of schizophrenia. (See Developments in Research and Chapter 17 for further discussion.)

During the latter decades of the twentieth century, our society had seemingly reversed its position with respect to the means of providing humane care for people with mental illness in the hospital environment. Vigorous efforts were made to close down mental hospitals and return people who were psychiatrically disturbed to the community, ostensibly as a means of providing more integrated and humane treatment than was available in the "isolated" environment of the psychiatric hospital and because of the success of medications (chlorpromazine) that emerged in the 1950s to alleviate psychotic symptoms (Alanen et al., 2009). Large numbers of psychiatric hospitals were closed, and there was a significant reduction in state and county mental hospital populations, from over half a million in 1950 (Lerman, 1981) to about 100,000 by the early 1990s (Narrow et al., 1993). These reductions are all the more impressive given that the U.S. population increased substantially during those years. This movement, referred to as **deinstitutionalization**, although motivated by benevolent goals, has also created great difficulties for many people with psychological challenges and for many communities as well (see Chapter 17).

As a phenomenon, deinstitutionalization is an international movement. For example, there has been a shift in the locus of care of patients with chronic psychiatric illnesses from psychiatric hospitals to community-based residential services in Hong Kong (Chan, 2001), in the Netherlands (Pijl et al., 2001), and in Finland (Korkeila et al., 1998). Some countries have experienced extensive deinstitutionalization during the past 20 years. For example, in England and Wales during the last decades of the twentieth century, only 14 of 130 psychiatric institutions remained open; and Australia showed a 90 percent reduction in hospital beds during the same period (Goldney, 2003). In a follow-up study of patients from 22 hospitals in Italy, D'Avanzo and colleagues (2003) report that all were closed and 39 percent of the patients in these hospitals had been discharged to nursing homes, 29 percent to residential facilities, and 29 percent to other psychiatric hospitals; only 2 percent were returned to their families.

The original impetus behind the deinstitutionalization policy was that it was considered more humane (and cost effective) to treat disturbed people outside of large mental hospitals because doing so would prevent people from acquiring negative adaptations to hospital confinement. Many professionals were concerned that the mental hospitals were becoming permanent refuges for disturbed people who were "escaping" from the demands of everyday living and were settling into a chronic sick role with a permanent excuse for letting other people take care of them. There was great hope that new medications would promote a healthy readjustment and enable former patients to live more productive lives outside the hospital. In a recent review on the influence of deinstitutionalization on discharged patients, Kunitoh (2013) found that, although many symptoms and social behavioral problems remained unchanged, both living skills and quality of life were improved after discharge. However, many former patients have not fared well in community living and authorities now frequently speak of the "abandonment" of chronic patients to a cruel and harsh existence. Evidence of this failure to treat psychiatric patients successfully in the community can be readily seen in our cities: Many of the people living on the streets in large cities today are homeless and have mental illnesses. The problems caused by deinstitutionalization appear to be due, in no small part, to the failure of society to develop ways to fill the gaps in mental health services in the community (Grob, 1994).

Freed from the confines of institutionalized care, or abandoned by society? Many homeless people suffer from one or more mental disorders. Deinstitutionalization, though motivated by benevolent goals, has created great difficulties for many individuals with psychological disturbances who have been released to a cruel and harsh existence.

The mental institution, once thought to be the most humane way to manage the problems of people with severe mental illnesses, came to be seen as obsolete or as an evil alternative, more of a problem than a solution to mental health problems. By the end of the twentieth century, inpatient mental hospitals had been substantially replaced by community-based care, day treatment hospitals, and outreach.

The twentieth century closed on a note of uncertainty with respect to the best ways to manage the needs of severely disturbed psychiatric patients. It is clear that closing mental hospitals and providing treatment for severely disturbed people in the community has not proved to be the panacea it was touted to be only a few years ago (Whitaker, 2009). As we will discuss further in Chapter 17, deinstitutionalization has created problems for both patients and society as a whole. The role of the psychiatric hospital in helping those with severe psychiatric problems is likely to undergo further evolution as society again finds itself unable to deal effectively with the problems that severe mental illness can create if ignored or left unattended (see Grob, 1994).

in review

- Describe the changing views toward mental illness that evolved as scientific thinking came to have greater influence in Europe in the sixteenth and seventeenth centuries.
- Discuss the development of the psychiatric hospital.
- Describe the historical development of humanitarian reform, and give some of the reasons why it occurred.
- Describe the changes in social attitudes that brought about major changes in the way persons with mental disorders have been treated.

The Emergence of Contemporary Views of Abnormal Behavior

2.3   Identify developments that led to the contemporary view of abnormal psychology.

While the mental hygiene movement was gaining ground in the United States during the latter years of the nineteenth century, great technological discoveries occurred both at home and abroad. These advances helped usher in what we know today as the scientific, or experimentally oriented, view of abnormal behavior and the application of scientific knowledge to the treatment of individuals with mental disturbances. In this section we describe four major themes in abnormal psychology that spanned the nineteenth and twentieth centuries and generated powerful influences on our contemporary perspectives in abnormal behavior: (1) biological discoveries, (2) the development of a classification system for mental disorders, (3) the emergence of psychological causation views, and (4) experimental psychological research developments.

Biological Discoveries: Establishing the Link Between the Brain and Mental Disorder

Advances in the study of biological and anatomical factors as underlying both physical and mental disorders developed during this period. A major biomedical breakthrough, for example, came with the discovery of the organic factors underlying general paresis—syphilis of the brain. One of the most serious mental illnesses of the day, general paresis produced paralysis and insanity and typically caused death within 2 to 5 years as a result of brain deterioration. This scientific discovery, however, did not occur overnight; it required the combined efforts of many scientists and researchers for nearly a century.

GENERAL PARESIS AND SYPHILIS   The discovery of a cure for general paresis began in 1825, when the French physician A. L. J. Bayle (1799–1858) differentiated general paresis as a specific type of mental disorder. Bayle gave a complete and accurate description of the symptom pattern of paresis and convincingly presented his reasons for believing paresis to be a distinct disorder. Many years later, in 1897, the Viennese psychiatrist Richard von Krafft-Ebing conducted experiments involving the inoculation of patients with paresis with matter from syphilitic sores. None of the patients developed secondary symptoms of syphilis, which led to the conclusion that they must previously have been infected. This crucial experiment established the relationship between general paresis and syphilis. It was almost a decade later, in 1906, when August von Wassermann devised a blood test for syphilis. This development made it possible to check for the presence of the deadly bacteria in the bloodstream of an individual before the more serious consequences of infection appeared.

Finally, in 1917, Julius von Wagner-Jauregg, chief of the psychiatric clinic of the University of Vienna, introduced the malarial fever treatment of syphilis and paresis because he knew that the high fever associated with malaria killed off the bacteria. He infected nine patients with paresis with the blood of a malaria-infected soldier and found marked improvement in paretic symptoms in three patients and apparent recovery in three others. By 1925 several hospitals in the United States were incorporating the new malarial treatment for paresis into their hospital treatments. One of the earliest controlled studies of malarial treatment for paresis was conducted by Bahr and Brutsch in Indiana in 1928. They found that out of the 100 patients studied, 37 percent of patients with paresis showed significant recovery, 25 percent had been discharged, and 21 percent of those had returned to their previous or similar occupations. Today, of course, we have penicillin as an effective, simpler treatment of syphilis, but the early malarial treatment represented the first clear-cut conquest of a mental disorder by medical science. The field of abnormal psychology had come a long way—from superstitious beliefs to scientific proof of how brain pathology can cause a specific disorder. This breakthrough raised great hopes in the medical community that organic bases would be found for many other mental disorders—perhaps for all of them.

BRAIN PATHOLOGY AS A CAUSAL FACTOR   With the emergence of modern experimental science in the early part of the eighteenth century, knowledge of anatomy, physiology, neurology, chemistry, and general medicine increased rapidly. Scientists began to focus on diseased body organs as the cause of physical ailments. It was the next logical step for these researchers to assume that mental disorder was an illness based on the pathology of an organ—in this case, the brain. In 1757 Albrecht von Haller (1708–1777), in his *Elementa physiologae corporis humani*, emphasized the importance of the brain in psychic functions and advocated postmortem dissection to study the brains of the insane. The first systematic presentation of this viewpoint, however, was made by the German psychiatrist Wilhelm Griesinger (1817–1868). In his textbook *The Pathology and Therapy of Psychic Disorders*, published in 1845, Griesinger insisted that all mental disorders could be explained in terms of brain pathology. Following the discovery that brain deterioration resulted in general paresis, other successes followed. Alois Alzheimer and other investigators established the brain pathology in cerebral arteriosclerosis and in the senile mental disorders. Eventually, in the twentieth century, the organic pathologies underlying the toxic mental disorders (disorders caused by toxic substances such as lead), certain types of mental retardation, and other mental illnesses were discovered.

Along with the advancements in mental health treatment in the twentieth century came some unfortunate missteps. During the early years of the twentieth century, Henry Cotton, a psychiatrist at a New Jersey hospital, developed a theory that mental health problems such as schizophrenia could be cured by removing the infections that he believed caused the condition. He used surgical procedures to remove all of a person's teeth or body parts such as tonsils, parts of the colon, testicles, or ovaries in order to reduce the infection (Scull, 2005). In the 1920s through the 1940s, an American psychiatrist, Walter Freeman, followed the strategies developed by Italian psychiatrist Egas Moniz to treat severe mental disorders using surgical procedures called *lobotomies*. Freeman modified the surgery used by Moniz, using an ice pick to sever the neural connections in the brain after entering through the patient's eye sockets (see discussion on lobotomy by El-Hai, 2005). These surgical efforts to treat mental disorder were considered to be ineffective and inappropriate by many in the profession at the time and

were eventually discredited, although lobotomy is still used in some rare cases.

It is important to note here that although the discovery of the organic bases of mental disorders addressed the "how" behind causation, it did not, in most cases, address the "why." This is sometimes true even today. For example, although we know what causes certain "presenile" mental disorders—brain pathology—we do not yet know why some individuals are afflicted and others are not. Nonetheless, we can predict quite accurately the courses of these disorders. This ability is due not only to a greater understanding of the organic factors involved but also, in large part, to the work of a follower of Griesinger, Emil Kraepelin.

The Development of a Classification System

Emil Kraepelin (1856–1926), another German psychiatrist, played a dominant role in the early development of the biological viewpoint. His textbook *Compendium der Psychiatrie*, published in 1883, not only emphasized the importance of brain pathology in mental disorders but also made several related contributions that helped establish this viewpoint. The most important of these contributions was

Emil Kraepelin (1856–1926) was a German psychiatrist who developed an early synthesis and classification system of the hundreds of mental disorders by grouping diseases together based on common patterns of symptoms. Kraepelin also demonstrated that mental disorders showed specific patterns in the genetics, course, and outcome of disorders.

his system of classification of mental disorders, which became the forerunner of today's *DSM* classification (see Chapters 1 and 4). Kraepelin noted that certain symptom patterns occurred together regularly enough to be regarded as specific types of mental disease. He then proceeded to describe and clarify these types of mental disorders, working out a scheme of classification that is the basis of our present system. Integrating all of the clinical material underlying this classification was a Herculean task and represented a major contribution to the field of psychopathology.

Kraepelin saw each type of mental disorder as distinct from the others and thought that the course of each was as predetermined and predictable as the course of measles. Thus, the outcome of a given type of disorder could presumably be predicted even if it could not yet be controlled. Such claims led to widespread interest in the accurate description and classification of mental disorders.

Development of the Psychological Basis of Mental Disorder

Despite the emphasis on biological research, understanding of the psychological factors in mental disorders was progressing as well. The first major steps were taken by Sigmund Freud (1856–1939), the most frequently cited psychological

Developments in Research

The Search for Medications to Cure Mental Disorders

For centuries physicians have sought a medicinal cure for mental disorders. One of the earliest known treatises on the use of drugs to treat mental disorders is the work of the Roman physician Galen (A.D. 130–200). His writing details both the concoction of various medications and the clinical use of drug therapy with patients experiencing mental disorders. Most of his medications were laxatives and emetics (purgatives) that were used to cleanse the body of nonhuman materials believed to be causing the person's ills. During the Middle Ages, another notable but highly controversial physician-chemist named Paracelsus (1490–1541) experimented with various chemicals as medications to treat human disorders. He even used a substance referred to as "mummy powder" (ground up particles of mummies) and various other, seemingly more potent substances such as mercury.

A more recent phase in the development of psychotropic medicine began in the 1950s. The root *Rauwolfia serpentina* had been used for centuries as an herbal folk medicine in India, where it had been prescribed for a wide array of afflictions, including insanity. In the early 1950s the active ingredient in *Rauwolfia*, reserpine, was isolated by a Swiss drug company, and in 1953 psychiatrist R. A. Hakim wrote a prize-winning paper on using *Rauwolfia* to treat psychosis (as cited in Gupta et al., 1943). Today reserpine has been surpassed as a treatment for psychoses because of the development of other drugs and because of its side effects, and it is mostly used in the treatment of hypertension.

The second psychoactive drug to emerge in the 1950s as a treatment for severe mental disorder was chlorpromazine. A German chemist named Bernthsen, searching for compounds that would operate as dyes, first developed the drug in the latter part of the nineteenth century. He synthesized a compound that is referred to as phenothiazine. Paul Erlich, a medical researcher and father of the field of chemotherapy, thought that this compound might be effective in treating human diseases by killing nonhuman cells while preserving human tissue. The drug was first tried as a means of treating malaria, and by the 1930s it was being employed as an anesthetic. In 1951, the French surgeon Henri Laborit employed the drug as an "artificial hibernator" to prevent shock among surgical patients. It was not until 1952 that two French psychiatrists, Jean Delay and Pierre Deniker, finding that the drug reduced psychotic symptoms, began to use chlorpromazine to treat psychiatric patients.

The almost magical impact of antipsychotic medication was immediately felt in the psychiatric community in the United States. By 1956, the first year of widespread use of reserpine and chlorpromazine, the impact on psychiatric hospitalization had begun to show a remarkable effect. The previously increasing admission rate to psychiatric hospitals leveled off at 560,000 psychiatric inpatients in the United States. This number had dropped to 490,000 by 1964 and to 300,000 by 1971. Currier (2000) reported that the number of inpatient psychiatric beds decreased sharply during the past generation, both in absolute numbers and as a percentage of total hospital beds in seven countries including the United States. The drop in available hospital beds between and 1960 and 1994 was from 4 per thousand to less than 1.3 per thousand of the population. In the United States, the available bed reductions were fostered by the movement for deinstitutionalization and the development of managed care. In Europe and other regions, the number of beds decreased largely as a result of intense government pressure to curtail health care budgets. Interestingly, the need for psychiatric inpatient care has remained despite the closing of public mental health hospitals. Hutchins and colleagues (2011) point out that the number of private mental hospitals doubled between 1976 and 1992 and that two-thirds of all psychiatric hospitals and half of all inpatient beds were in private facilities.

The effectiveness of drugs in reducing psychotic symptoms has also led researchers to develop more specific causal hypotheses for mental disorders such as schizophrenia. Researchers have noted that antipsychotic drugs such as the phenothiazines modify the levels of dopamine, a neurotransmitter associated with schizophrenia. These observations have led theoreticians to the "dopamine hypothesis"—that the metabolism of dopamine is associated with the cause of schizophrenia.

Sources: Frankenburg (1994); Green (1951); Moriarty et al. (1984); Pachter (1951).

theorist of the twentieth century (Street, 1994). During five decades of observation, treatment, and writing, Freud developed a comprehensive theory of psychopathology that emphasized the inner dynamics of unconscious motives (often referred to as *psychodynamics*) that are at the heart of the **psychoanalytic perspective**. The methods he used to study and treat patients came to be called **psychoanalysis**. We can trace the ancestral roots of psychoanalysis to a somewhat unexpected place—the study of hypnosis, especially in its relation to hysteria. (For a contemporary discussion of hysteria, see Brown, 2006.) Hypnosis, an induced state of relaxation in which a person is highly open to suggestion, first came into widespread use in late-eighteenth- and early-nineteenth-century France.

MESMERISM Our efforts to understand psychological causation of mental disorder start with Franz Anton Mesmer (1734–1815), an Austrian physician who further developed the ideas of Paracelsus (the influential sixteenth-century physician and scholar; see Developments in Research) about the influence of the planets on the human body. Mesmer believed that the planets affected a universal magnetic fluid in the body, the distribution of which determined health or disease. In attempting to find cures for mental disorders, Mesmer concluded that all people possessed magnetic forces that could be used to influence the distribution of the magnetic fluid in other people, thus effecting cures.

Mesmer attempted to put his views into practice in Vienna and various other cities, but it was in Paris in 1778 that he gained a broad following. There, he opened a clinic in which he treated all kinds of diseases by using "animal magnetism." In a dark room, patients were seated around a tub containing various chemicals, and iron rods protruding from the tub were applied to the affected areas of the patients' bodies. Accompanied by music, Mesmer appeared in a lilac robe, passing from one patient to another and touching each one with his hands or his wand. By this means, Mesmer was reportedly able to remove hysterical anesthesias and paralyses. He also demonstrated most of the phenomena later connected with the use of hypnosis.

Mesmer was eventually branded a charlatan by his medical colleagues and an appointed body of noted scholars that included the American scientist Benjamin Franklin (Van Doren, 1938). The committee conducted what have been referred to as the first psychological experiments (Dingfelder, 2010), or tests such as tricking a woman into believing that she had been influenced by magnetism. The committee concluded that the real source of Mesmer's power was in the patients and not in "magnetism." Mesmer was forced to leave Paris and quickly faded into obscurity. His methods and results, however, were at the center of scientific controversy for many

years—in fact, **mesmerism**, as his technique came to be known, was as much a source of heated discussion in the early nineteenth century as psychoanalysis became in the early twentieth century. This discussion led to renewed interest in hypnosis itself as an explanation of the "cures" that took place.

Franz Anton Mesmer (1734–1815) believed that the distribution of magnetic fluid in the body was responsible for determining health or disease. He further thought that all people possessed magnetic forces that could be used to influence the distribution of fluid in others, thus effecting cures. In this painting of his therapy, Mesmer stands on the far right, holding a wand. He was eventually branded a fraud by his colleagues. His theories did, however, demonstrate most of the phenomena later connected with the use of hypnosis.

Even after mesmerism was discredited in France, this method of inducing a trance and its perceived potential for treating illness had a long life in the United States. The magical powers of mesmerism were introduced in 1836 and intrigued a number of Americans, ranging from the poet Emerson to the physician Benjamin Rush, with speculations about its higher mental powers and its potential application as an anesthetic for surgical procedures (Schmit, 2005). A number of lecturers traveled the United States illustrating its medical use and giving demonstrations, including to the U.S. Congress. The early mesmerists, though considered to be "quacks" by many physicians, had an influence on medical practice until the introduction of ether as a surgical anesthetic (Schmit, 2005). In spite of its limitations, mesmerism clearly had an influence on psychology and hypnosis for many years and came to be influential in spiritual movements such as Christian Science in the nineteenth century.

THE NANCY SCHOOL Ambrose August Liébeault (1823–1904), a French physician who practiced in the town of Nancy, used hypnosis successfully in his practice. Also in Nancy at the time was a professor of medicine, Hippolyte Bernheim (1840–1919), who became interested in the relationship between hysteria and hypnosis. His interest was piqued by Liébeault's success in using hypnosis to cure a patient whom Bernheim had been treating unsuccessfully by more conventional methods for 4 years (Selling, 1943).

Bernheim and Liébeault worked together to develop the hypothesis that hypnotism and hysteria were related and that both were due to suggestion (Brown & Menninger, 1940). Their hypothesis was based on two lines of evidence: (1) The phenomena observed in hysteria—such as paralysis of an arm, inability to hear, and anesthetic areas in which an individual could be stuck with a pin without feeling pain (all of which occurred when there was apparently nothing organically wrong)—could be produced in normal subjects by means of hypnosis and (2) the same symptoms also could be removed by means of hypnosis. Thus, it seemed likely that hysteria was a sort of self-hypnosis. The physicians who accepted this view ultimately came to be known as adherents of the **Nancy School**.

Meanwhile, Jean Charcot (1825–1893), who was head of the Salpêtrière Hospital in Paris and the leading neurologist of his time, had been experimenting with some of the phenomena described by the mesmerists. As a result of his research, Charcot disagreed with the findings of the Nancy School and insisted that degenerative brain changes led to hysteria. In this, Charcot was eventually proved wrong, but work on the problem by so outstanding a scientist did a great deal to awaken medical and scientific interest in hysteria.

The dispute between Charcot and the Nancy School was one of the major debates of medical history, and many harsh words were spoken on both sides. The adherents to the Nancy School finally triumphed. This first recognition of a psychologically caused mental disorder spurred more research on the behavior underlying hysteria and other disorders. Soon it was suggested that psychological factors were also involved in anxiety states, phobias, and other psychopathologies. Eventually, Charcot himself was won over to the new point of view and did much to promote the study of psychological factors in various mental disorders.

The debate over whether mental disorders are caused by biological or psychological factors continues to this day. The Nancy School–Charcot debate represented a major step forward for psychology, however. Toward the end of the nineteenth century, it became clear that mental disorders could have psychological bases, biological bases, or both. But a major question remained to be answered: How do the psychologically based mental disorders actually develop?

THE BEGINNINGS OF PSYCHOANALYSIS   The first systematic attempt to answer this question was made by Sigmund Freud (1856–1939). Freud was a brilliant, young Viennese neurologist who received an appointment as lecturer on nervous diseases at the University of Vienna. In 1885 he went to study under Charcot and later became acquainted with the work of Liébeault and Bernheim at Nancy. He was impressed by their use of hypnosis with patients experiencing hysteria and came away convinced that powerful mental processes could remain hidden from consciousness.

On his return to Vienna, Freud worked in collaboration with another Viennese physician, Josef Breuer (1842–1925), who had incorporated an interesting innovation into the use of hypnosis with his patients. Unlike hypnotists before them, Freud and Breuer directed patients to talk freely about their problems while under hypnosis. The patients usually displayed considerable emotion and, on awakening from their hypnotic states, felt a significant emotional release, which was called a **catharsis**. This simple innovation in the use of hypnosis proved to be of great significance: It not only helped patients discharge their emotional tensions by discussing their problems but also revealed to the therapist the nature of the difficulties that had brought about certain symptoms. The patients, on awakening, saw no relationship between their problems and their hysterical symptoms.

It was this approach that led to the discovery of the **unconscious**—the portion of the mind that contains experiences of which a person is unaware—and with it the belief that processes outside of a person's awareness can play an important role in determining behavior. In 1893, Freud and Breuer published a joint paper titled *On the Psychical Mechanisms of Hysterical Phenomena*, which was one of the great milestones in the study of the dynamics of the conscious and unconscious. Freud soon discovered, moreover, that he could dispense with hypnosis entirely. By encouraging patients to say whatever came into their minds without regard to logic or propriety, Freud found that patients would eventually overcome inner obstacles to remembering and would discuss their problems freely.

Psychoanalysis was introduced to North America at a famous meeting at Clark University in Worcester, Massachusetts, in 1909. Among those present were (back row) A. A. Brill, Ernest Jones, and Sandor Ferenczi; (front row) Sigmund Freud, G. Stanley Hall, and Carl Jung.

Two related methods enabled him to understand patients' conscious and unconscious thought processes. One method, **free association**, involved having patients talk freely about themselves, thereby providing information about their feelings, motives, and so forth. A second method, **dream analysis**, involved having patients record and describe their dreams. These techniques helped analysts and patients gain insights and achieve a better understanding of the patients' emotional problems. Freud devoted the rest of his long and energetic life to the development and elaboration of psychoanalytic principles. His views were formally introduced to American scientists in 1909, when he was invited to deliver a series of lectures at Clark University by the eminent psychologist G. Stanley Hall (1844–1924), who was then president of the university. These lectures created a great deal of controversy and helped popularize psychoanalytic concepts with scientists as well as with the general public.

Watch Thinking Like a Psychologist: Assessing Treatment Effectiveness

1895 Freud's talking therapy

We will discuss the psychoanalytic viewpoint further in Chapter 3. Freud's lively and seminal views attracted a substantial following over his long career, and interest in his ideas persists today, more than 100 years after he began writing. Numerous other clinician-theorists—such as Carl Jung, Alfred Adler, and Harry Stack Sullivan—launched "spin-off" theories that have elaborated on the psychoanalytic viewpoint. More will also be said of these views in Chapter 3. Here we will examine the early development of psychological research and explore the evolution of the behavioral perspective on abnormal behavior.

The Evolution of the Psychological Research Tradition: Experimental Psychology

The origins of much of the scientific thinking in contemporary psychology lie in early rigorous efforts to study psychological processes objectively, as demonstrated by Wilhelm Wundt (1832–1920) and William James (1842–1910). Although the early work of these experimental psychologists did not bear directly on clinical practice or on our understanding of abnormal behavior, this tradition was clearly influential a few decades later in molding the thinking of the psychologists who brought these rigorous attitudes into the clinic. (For a discussion of the history of clinical psychology, see Benjamin, 2014, and Shriver, 2015.)

THE EARLY PSYCHOLOGY LABORATORIES In 1879 Wilhelm Wundt established the first experimental psychology laboratory at the University of Leipzig. While studying the psychological factors involved in memory and sensation, Wundt and his colleagues devised many basic experimental methods and strategies. Wundt directly influenced early contributors to the empirical study of abnormal behavior such as William James, G. Stanley Hall, and a student of Wundt's, J. McKeen Cattell (1860–1944) (Benjamin, 2014); they followed his experimental methodology and also applied some of his research strategies to study clinical problems. For example, Cattell brought Wundt's experimental methods to the United States and used them to assess individual differences in mental processing. He and other students of Wundt's work established research laboratories throughout the United States.

It was not until 1896, however, that another of Wundt's students, Lightner Witmer (1867–1956), combined research with application and established the first American psychological clinic at the University of Pennsylvania. At Witmer's clinic both research and therapy were conducted, with a focus on the problems of children with mental deficiencies. Witmer, considered to be the founder of clinical psychology (McReynolds, 1996, 1997), was influential in encouraging others to become involved in this new profession. Other clinics were soon established. One clinic of great importance was the Chicago Juvenile Psychopathic Institute (later called the Institute of Juvenile Research), established in 1909 by William Healy (1869–1963). Healy was the first to view juvenile delinquency as a symptom of urbanization, not as a result of inner psychological problems. In so doing, he was among the first to recognize a new area of causation—environmental, or sociocultural, factors.

By the first decade of the twentieth century, psychological laboratories and clinics were burgeoning, and a great deal of research was being generated (Goodwin, 2011). The rapid and objective communication of scientific findings was perhaps as important in the development of modern psychology as the collection and interpretation of research findings. This period saw the origin of many scientific journals for the propagation of research and theoretical discoveries, and as the years have passed, the number of journals has grown. The American Psychological

Association publishes numerous scientific journals, many of which focus on research into abnormal behavior and personality functioning.

THE BEHAVIORAL PERSPECTIVE Although psychoanalysis dominated thought about abnormal behavior at the end of the nineteenth century and in the early twentieth century, another school—behaviorism—emerged out of experimental psychology to challenge its supremacy. Behavioral psychologists believed that the study of subjective experience—through the techniques of free association and dream analysis—did not provide acceptable scientific data because such observations were not open to verification by other investigators. In their view, only the study of directly observable behavior—and the stimuli and reinforcing conditions that "control" it—could serve as a basis for formulating scientific principles of human behavior.

The **behavioral perspective** is organized around a central theme: the role of learning in human behavior. Although this perspective was initially developed through research in the laboratory rather than through clinical practice, its implications for explaining and treating maladaptive behavior soon became evident.

Classical Conditioning The origins of the behavioral view of abnormal behavior and its treatment are tied to experimental work on the type of learning known as **classical conditioning**—a form of learning in which a neutral stimulus is paired repeatedly with an unconditioned stimulus that naturally elicits an unconditioned behavior. After repeated pairings, the neutral stimulus becomes a conditioned stimulus that elicits a conditioned response. This work began with the discovery of the conditioned reflex by Russian physiologist Ivan Pavlov (1849–1936). Around the turn of the twentieth century, Pavlov demonstrated that dogs would gradually begin to salivate in response to a nonfood stimulus such as a bell after the stimulus had been regularly accompanied by food.

Pavlov's discoveries in classical conditioning excited a young American psychologist, John B. Watson (1878–1958), who was searching for objective ways to study human behavior. Watson reasoned that if psychology was to become a true science, it would have to abandon the subjectivity of inner sensations and other "mental" events and limit itself to what could be objectively observed. What better way to do this than to observe systematic changes in behavior brought about simply by rearranging stimulus conditions? Watson thus changed the focus of psychology to the study of overt behavior rather than the study of theoretical mentalistic constructs, an approach he called **behaviorism**.

Ivan Pavlov (1849–1936), a pioneer in demonstrating the part conditioning plays in behavior, is shown here with the staff and some of the apparatus used to condition reflexes in dogs.

Watson, a man of impressive energy and demeanor, saw great possibilities in behaviorism, and he was quick to point them out to his fellow scientists and a curious public. He boasted that through conditioning he could train any healthy child to become whatever sort of adult one wished. He also challenged the psychoanalysts and the more biologically oriented psychologists of his day by suggesting that abnormal behavior was the product of unfortunate, inadvertent earlier conditioning and could be modified through reconditioning.

By the 1930s Watson had had an enormous impact on American psychology. Watson's approach placed heavy emphasis on the role of the social environment in conditioning personality development and behavior, both normal and abnormal. Today's behaviorally oriented psychologists still accept many of the basic tenets of Watson's doctrine, although they are more cautious in their claims.

Operant Conditioning While Pavlov and Watson were studying stimulus–response conditioning, E. L. Thorndike (1874–1949) and subsequently B. F. Skinner (1904–1990) were exploring a different kind of conditioning, one in which the consequences of behavior influence behavior. Behavior that operates on the environment may be instrumental in producing certain outcomes, and those outcomes, in turn, determine the likelihood that the behavior will be repeated on similar occasions. For example, Thorndike studied how cats could learn a particular response, such as pulling a chain, if that response was followed by food reinforcement. This type of learning came to be called instrumental conditioning and was later renamed **operant conditioning** by Skinner. Both terms are still used today. In Skinner's view, behavior is "shaped" when something reinforces a particular activity of an organism—which makes it possible "to shape an animal's behavior almost as a sculptor shapes a lump of clay" (Skinner, 1951, pp. 26–27).

B. F. Skinner (1904–1990) formulated the concept of operant conditioning, in which reinforcers can be used to make a response more or less probable and frequent.

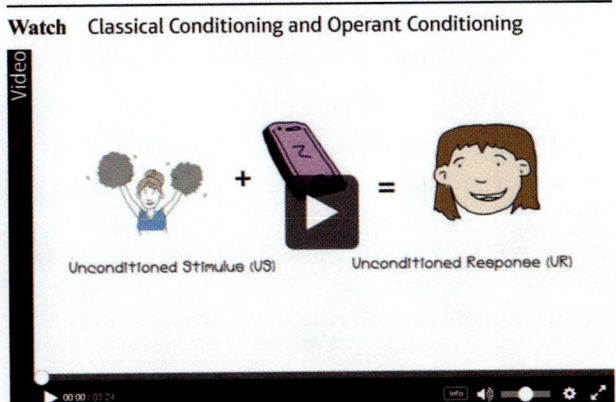

Watch Classical Conditioning and Operant Conditioning

Unconditioned Stimulus (US) + = Unconditioned Response (UR)

In this chapter we have touched on several important trends in the evolution of the field of abnormal psychology and have recounted the contributions of numerous individuals from history who have shaped our current views. The vast amount of information available can cause confusion and controversy when efforts are made to obtain an integrated view of behavior and causation. We may have left supernatural beliefs behind, but we have moved into something far more complex in trying to determine the role of natural factors—be they biological, psychological, or sociocultural—in abnormal behavior. For a recap of some of the key contributors to the field of abnormal psychology, see Table 2.1.

in review

- Compare the views of the Nancy School with those of Charcot. How did this debate influence modern psychology?
- Evaluate the impact of the work of Freud and that of Watson on psychology today.
- How did early experimental science help to establish brain pathology as a causal factor in mental disorders?
- Describe the historical development of the behavioral view in psychology.

Table 2.1 Major Figures in the Early History of Abnormal Psychology

The Ancient World

Hippocrates

Hippocrates (460–377 B.C.) A Greek physician who believed that mental disease was the result of natural causes and brain pathology rather than demonology.

Plato (429–347 B.C.) A Greek philosopher who believed that patients with mental illness should be treated humanely and should not be held responsible for their actions.

Aristotle (384–322 B.C.) A Greek philosopher and a pupil of Plato who believed in the Hippocratic theory that various agents, or humors, within the body, when imbalanced, were responsible for mental disorders. Aristotle rejected the notion of psychological factors as causes of mental disorders.

Galen (A.D. 130–200) A Greek physician who contributed much to our understanding of the nervous system. Galen divided the causes of mental disorders into physical and mental categories.

Galen

The Middle Ages

Avicenna

Avicenna (c. 980–1037) An ancient Persian physician who promoted principles of humane treatment for people with mental disturbances at a time when Western approaches to mental illness were inhumane.

Hildegard (1098–1179) A remarkable woman, known as the "Sybil of the Rhine," who used curative powers of natural objects for healing and wrote treatises about natural history and medicinal uses of plants.

The Sixteenth Through the Eighteenth Centuries

Paracelsus (1490–1541) A Swiss physician who rejected demonology as a cause of abnormal behavior. Paracelsus believed in psychic causes of mental illness.

Teresa of Avila (1515–1582) A Spanish nun, since canonized, who argued that mental disorder was an illness of the mind.

Johann Weyer (1515–1588) A German physician who argued against demonology and was ostracized by his peers and the Church for his progressive views.

Robert Burton (1576–1640) An Oxford scholar who wrote a classic, influential treatise on depression, *The Anatomy of Melancholia*, in 1621.

William Tuke (1732–1822) An English Quaker who established the York Retreat, where patients with mental illness lived in humane surroundings.

Philippe Pinel (1745–1826) A French physician who pioneered the use of moral management in La Bicêtre and La Salpêtrière hospitals in France, where patients with mental illness were treated in a humane way.

Benjamin Rush (1745–1813) An American physician and the founder of American psychiatry, who used moral management, based on Pinel's humanitarian methods, to treat people with mental disturbances.

Benjamin Rush

The Nineteenth and Early Twentieth Centuries

Dorothea Dix (1802–1887) An American teacher who founded the mental hygiene movement in the United States, which focused on the physical well-being of patients with mental illness in hospitals.

Clifford Beers (1876–1943) An American who campaigned to change public attitudes toward patients with mental illness after his own experiences in mental institutions.

Franz Anton Mesmer (1734–1815) An Austrian physician who conducted early investigations into hypnosis as a medical treatment.

Emil Kraepelin (1856–1926) A German psychiatrist who developed the first diagnostic system.

Sigmund Freud (1856–1939) The founder of the school of psychological therapy known as psychoanalysis.

Dorothea Dix

Wilhelm Wundt (1832–1920) A German scientist who established the first experimental psychology laboratory in 1879 and subsequently influenced the empirical study of abnormal behavior.

Sigmund Freud

J. McKeen Cattell (1860–1944) An American psychologist who adopted Wundt's methods and studied individual differences in mental processing.

Lightner Witmer (1867–1956) An American psychologist who established the first psychological clinic in the United States, focusing on problems of children with mental deficiencies. He also founded the journal *The Psychological Clinic* in 1907.

William Healy (1869–1963) An American psychologist who established the Chicago Juvenile Psychopathic Institute and advanced the idea that mental illness was due to environmental, or sociocultural, factors.

Ivan Pavlov (1849–1936) A Russian physiologist who published classical studies in the psychology of learning.

John B. Watson (1878–1958) An American psychologist who conducted early research into learning principles and came to be known as the father of behaviorism.

B. F. Skinner (1904–1990) An American learning theorist who developed the school of learning known as operant conditioning and was influential in incorporating behavioral principles into influencing behavioral change.

John B. Watson

B.F. Skinner

Unresolved Issues

Interpreting Historical Events

Understanding current events and phenomena depends to a substantial degree on having an accurate understanding of the historical development of knowledge. Many psychologists hold the view that psychological theorizing can be advanced by greater use of historical data (McGuire, 1994). This chapter has attempted to provide a historical perspective on some of the concepts you will encounter in the chapters that follow. You might think that looking back in history to get a picture of events that occurred long ago would not be a difficult task—that it would be a simple matter of reviewing some history books and some publications from the time in question. However, different and conflicting views as to the importance and relevance of historical events in contemporary psychology have emerged. The traditional view maintains that historical events are stepping stones for understanding contemporary events, while a "New History" approach minimizes this cumulative and often celebratory approach and questions the cumulative knowledge aspect. Instead, this approach favors considering history as "national habits or characteristics of a culture that does not necessarily serve as cumulative force in the advancement of knowledge" (for an interesting discussion of historical approaches see Lovett, 2006). The distinction here is whether past developments in acquiring knowledge and understanding build on each other to create a more accurate picture or whether such developments should be viewed independently in their own context.

Regardless of one's view of the historical approach, those who try to understand the historical context of particular phenomena or ideas are sometimes confronted with what Burton (2001) referred to as the tenacity of historical misinformation. He pointed out that there is one discouraging theme in the history of science—the widespread acceptance of false accounts. He noted that it is not uncommon for psychological findings and theories to be exaggerated or distorted and that the exaggerations frequently spread much further through public sources than do the authentic facts. For example, he noted the widespread acceptance, and inclusion in many textbooks, of inaccurate restatements of the widely cited study of Little Albert's fear of furry objects:

Little Albert

Little Albert was the famous toddler who, originally unafraid of rats, exhibited such a fear when J. B. Watson and Rayner (1920) paired the presence of a rat with a loud noise. Harris (1979), Samelson (1980), and Gilovich (1991) are among the critics who have noted how frequently and consistently this case is misrepresented and exaggerated. J. B. Watson and Rayner described pairing the loud noise with the rat and later testing Albert's reaction to a rat and a rabbit, as well as to blocks, a seal coat, cotton wool, the hair of Watson and some assistants, and a Santa Claus mask. Albert never reacted to the blocks or the assistants' hair, always reacted to the rat, and reacted to the other objects with various degrees of agitation that were sometimes vividly described but sometimes merely (and vaguely) termed "negative reaction." According to Harris (1979, p. 153), secondary sources have erroneously reported the testing of "a fur pelt, . . . a man's beard, . . . a cat, a pup, a fur muff, . . . a white furry glove, . . . Albert's aunt, who supposedly wore fur, . . . either the fur coat or the fur neckpiece of Albert's mother, . . . and even a teddy bear." (pp. 228–229)

Another factor that can affect the quality of historical information is that our views of history and our understanding of events are sometimes open to reinterpretation. As Schudson (1995) points out, "Collective memory, more than individual memory, at least in liberal pluralistic societies, is provisional. It is always open to contestation" (p. 16). Any number of obstacles can stand in the way of our gaining an accurate picture of the attitudes and behaviors of people who lived hundreds of years ago. This has certainly been the case with our views of the Middle Ages (Kroll & Bachrach, 1984).

The foremost problem in retrospective psychological analysis is that we cannot rely on direct observation, a hallmark of psychological research. Instead, we must turn to written documents or historical surveys of the times. Although these sources are often full of fascinating information, they may not reveal directly the information we seek; we must therefore extrapolate "facts" from the information we have, which is not always an easy task. We are restricted in our conclusions by the documents or sources available to us. Attempting to learn about people's attitudes and subtle social perceptions hundreds of years ago by examining surviving church documents or biographical accounts is less than ideal. First, we inevitably view these documents out of the context in which they were written. Second, we do not know whether the authors had ulterior motives or what the real purposes of the documents were. For example, some historians have concluded erroneously that people of the Middle Ages considered sin to be a major causal factor in mental illness. This misconception may have been due in part to zealous authors invoking "God's punishment" against the victims of mental illnesses who happened to be their enemies. Apparently, if the victims happened to be friends, sin was typically not mentioned as a causal factor (Kroll & Bachrach, 1984). Such writings, of course, are biased, but we may have no way of knowing this. The fewer the sources surveyed, the more likely that any existing bias will go undetected.

In other cases, concepts important to historical interpretation may have quite a different meaning to us today than they had in the past, or the meaning may simply be unclear. Kroll and Bachrach (1984) point out that the concept of "possession," so critical to our views of the Middle Ages, is a very vague and complex concept for which we have no helpful natural models. Our language fails us, except for colorful analogies and metaphors. Just as the term *nervous breakdown* means different things to different people, so too *possession* means and meant many different things and undoubtedly had a different range of meanings to medieval persons from what it has to us. This kind of uncertainty can make definitive assessments of things that happened during the Middle Ages difficult, if not impossible (Phillips, 2002).

Bias can come into play during interpretation also. Our interpretations of historical events or previously held beliefs can be colored by our own views of what is normal and what is abnormal. In fact, it is difficult to conduct a retrospective analysis without taking current perspectives and values as a starting point. For example, our modern beliefs about the Middle Ages have led, says Schoeneman (1984), to our contemporary misinterpretation that during the fifteenth and sixteenth centuries people with mental illness were typically accused of being witches. For most of us, this mistaken interpretation makes sense simply because we do not understand the medieval perspective on witchcraft.

Although reevaluations of the Middle Ages have discredited the view that demonology, sin, and witchcraft played key roles in the medieval understanding of mental illness, it is also clear that in some cases these concepts were associated with mental illness. Where does the truth lie? It appears that the last word has not been written on the Middle Ages, nor on any period of our history for that matter. At best, historical views—and, therefore, retrospective psychological studies—must be regarded as working hypotheses that are open to change as new perspectives are applied to history and as "new" historical documents are discovered.

Summary

2.1 Explain how abnormal behavior has been viewed throughout history.

- Understanding of abnormal behavior has not evolved smoothly or uniformly over the centuries; the steps have been uneven, with great gaps in between, and unusual—even bizarre—views or beliefs have often sidetracked researchers and theorists.

- The dominant social, economic, and religious views of the times have had a profound influence over how people have viewed abnormal behavior.

- In the ancient world, superstitious explanations for mental disorders were followed by the emergence of medical concepts in many places such as Egypt and Greece; many of these concepts were developed and refined by Roman physicians.

- After the fall of Rome near the end of the fifth century A.D., superstitious views dominated popular thinking about mental disorders for over 1,000 years. In the fifteenth and sixteenth centuries, it was still widely believed, even by scholars, that some of the people experiencing mental disturbances were possessed by a devil.

2.2 Describe the effect that humanism had on abnormal psychology.

- Great strides have been made in our understanding of abnormal behavior. For example, during the latter part of the Middle Ages and the early Renaissance, a spirit of scientific questioning reappeared in Europe, and several noted physicians spoke out against inhumane treatments. There was a general movement away from superstitions and "magic" toward reasoned, scientific studies.

- With recognition of a need for the special treatment of people with mental illness came the founding of various "asylums" toward the end of the sixteenth century. However, institutionalization led to the isolation and maltreatment of patients. Slowly this situation was recognized, and in the eighteenth century further efforts were made to help afflicted individuals by providing them with better living conditions and humane treatment, although these improvements were the exception rather than the rule.

- The nineteenth and early twentieth centuries witnessed a number of scientific and humanitarian advances. The work of Philippe Pinel in France, of William Tuke in England, and of Benjamin Rush and Dorothea Dix in the United States prepared the way for several important developments in contemporary abnormal psychology, such as moral management. Among these were the gradual acceptance of patients with mental illness as afflicted individuals who need and deserve professional attention; the successful application of biomedical methods to disorders; and the growth of scientific research into the biological, psychological, and sociocultural roots of abnormal behavior.

- The reform of mental hospitals continued into the twentieth century, but during the last four decades of the century, there was a strong movement to close mental hospitals and release people into the community. This movement remains controversial in the early part of the twenty-first century.

2.3 Identify developments that led to the contemporary view of abnormal psychology.

- In the nineteenth century, great technological discoveries and scientific advancements that were made in the biological sciences enhanced the understanding and treatment of individuals with mental illness. One major biomedical breakthrough came with the discovery of the organic factors underlying general paresis—syphilis of the brain—one of the most serious mental illnesses of the day.

- Beginning in the early part of the eighteenth century, knowledge of anatomy, physiology, neurology, chemistry, and general medicine increased rapidly. These advances led to the identification of the biological, or organic, pathology underlying many physical ailments.

- The development of a psychiatric classification system by Kraepelin played a dominant role in the early development of the biological viewpoint. Kraepelin's work (a forerunner to the *DSM* system) helped to establish the importance of brain pathology in mental disorders and made several related contributions that helped establish this viewpoint.

- The first major steps toward understanding psychological factors in mental disorders occurred with mesmerism and the Nancy School, followed by the work of Sigmund Freud. During five decades of observation, treatment, and writing, he developed a theory of psychopathology, known as *psychoanalysis*, that emphasized the inner dynamics of unconscious motives. During the past half-century, other clinicians have modified and revised Freud's theory, which has thus evolved into new psychodynamic perspectives.

- Scientific investigation into psychological factors and human behavior began to make progress in the latter part of the nineteenth century. The end of the nineteenth century and the early twentieth century saw experimental psychology evolve into clinical psychology with the development of clinics to study, as well as intervene in, abnormal behavior.

- Paralleling this development was the work of Pavlov in understanding learning and conditioning. Behaviorism emerged as an explanatory model in abnormal psychology. The behavioral perspective is organized around a central theme—that learning plays an important role in human behavior. Although this perspective was initially developed through research in the laboratory (unlike psychoanalysis, which emerged out of clinical practice with disturbed individuals), it has been shown to have important implications for explaining and treating maladaptive behavior.

- Understanding the history of psychopathology—its forward steps and missteps alike—helps us understand the emergence of modern concepts of abnormal behavior.

Key Terms

asylums, p. 40
behavioral perspective, p. 54
behaviorism, p. 54
catharsis, p. 52
classical conditioning, p. 54
deinstitutionalization, p. 47
dream analysis, p. 53
exorcisms, p. 39

free association, p. 53
insanity, p. 41
lycanthropy, p. 38
mass madness, p. 38
mental hygiene
    movement, p. 43
mesmerism, p. 51
moral management, p. 43

Nancy School, p. 52
operant conditioning, p. 54
psychoanalysis, p. 51
psychoanalytic perspective, p. 51
Saint Vitus's dance, p. 38
tarantism, p. 38
unconscious, p. 52

Chapter 3
Causal Factors and Viewpoints

⌄ Learning Objectives

3.1 Distinguish between risk factors and causes of abnormal behavior.

3.2 List the perspectives that psychologists take to understand the causes of abnormal behavior.

3.3 Explain what the biological perspective tells us about abnormal behavior and also explain the biological causal factors of abnormal behavior.

3.4 Describe the most prominent psychological perspectives on abnormal psychology.

3.5 Describe three social factors known to contribute to abnormal behavior.

3.6 Explain how cultural differences can influence perceptions of abnormal behavior.

We saw in the last chapter that speculation about the causes of abnormal behavior goes back very far in human history. From early times, those who observed disordered behavior grappled with the question of its cause, and many people believed that abnormal behavior was the work of gods or demons. Hippocrates proposed a disease model suggesting that an imbalance in the four bodily humors produced abnormal behavior, with each humor connected with certain kinds of behavior. More recently, disorders such as schizophrenia and autism were thought to be caused by poor parenting practices or the administration of vaccines.

Each attempt at identifying a cause brought with it a theory, or model, of abnormal behavior. Today we are still puzzling over the causes of abnormal behavior, and speculation about causes continues to give rise to new models of abnormality. Since about 1900, several important schools of thought have developed elaborate models to explain the origins of abnormal behavior and to suggest how it might be treated. We discuss the most influential of these theoretical perspectives in this chapter, paying special attention to the different types of causal factors that each perspective has identified. First, however, we need to address the very nature of the concept of causation as it is applied to abnormal behavior.

Risk Factors and Causes of Abnormal Behavior

3.1 **Distinguish between risk factors and causes of abnormal behavior.**

Central to the field of abnormal psychology are questions about what causes people to experience mental distress and to behave maladaptively. If we knew the causes for given disorders, we might be able to prevent conditions that lead to them and perhaps reverse those that maintain them. We could also classify and diagnose disorders better if we clearly understood their causes rather than relying on clusters of symptoms, as we usually must do now.

Although understanding the causes of abnormal behavior is a desirable goal, it is enormously difficult to achieve because human behavior is so complex. Even the simplest human behavior, such as speaking or writing a single word, relies on various biological processes (e.g., the development of different brain regions), as well as thousands of prior social experiences. Attempting to understand a person's life in causal terms is a task of enormous magnitude, whether it be a fairly normal or adaptive life or a life characterized by severe mental disorders.

One of the primary goals of clinical psychology, like science more generally, is to understand the nature of relationships among variables of interest. As you learned in Chapter 1, we can learn about relationships among variables by observing them and measuring the extent to which two variables or events co-occur (i.e., co-vary or correlate). In trying to understand what causes different kinds of psychopathology, an important first step is to observe what variables are associated with such outcomes. A variable (X) that is associated with an outcome of interest (Y) is considered to be a **correlate** of that outcome. For instance, the experience of physical abuse during childhood (X) is associated with greater risk of depression later in life (Y), so abuse is said to be *correlated* with depression. But just knowing that two things are correlated doesn't tell you if one *caused* the other (see Kraemer et al., 1997, and Figure 3.1). If, and only if, X is shown to precede Y in time can we infer that X is a **risk factor** for Y. That is, it is a factor or characteristic that is associated with an increased risk of developing condition Y. The next question we want to ask is if X can be changed. If it can, then it is considered to be a **variable risk factor** for outcome Y. If not, then it is considered a **fixed marker** of outcome Y, as is the case with a history of abuse during childhood. The key question for causality is whether changing X leads to a change in Y. If not, then X would be considered a **variable marker** of Y. If so, then and only then, would we consider X to be a **causal risk factor** for condition Y. Many correlates and risk factors may seem like they could be causes of our outcome of interest, but in order to know for sure, we must conduct studies to test the nature of these associations.

Necessary, Sufficient, and Contributory Causes

With these distinctions in mind, it is important to note that there are different types of causal relations in the **etiology**, or causal pattern, of abnormal behavior. A **necessary cause** (X) is a characteristic that *must* exist for a disorder (Y) to occur. For example, general paresis (Y)—a degenerative brain disorder—cannot develop unless a person has previously contracted syphilis (X). Or more generally, if Y occurs, then X must have preceded it. Another example is Huntington's chorea—a rare degenerative brain disorder of the central nervous system—which can develop only if the person has the necessary gene (*IT15*, or the Huntington's gene—see Chapter 14). To date, most mental disorders have not been found to have necessary causes, although there continues to be a search for such causes.

A **sufficient cause** of a disorder is a condition that guarantees the occurrence of a disorder. For example, one current theory hypothesizes that hopelessness (X) is a sufficient cause of depression (Y) (Abramson et al., 1995, 1989). Or, more generally, if X occurs, then Y will also occur. According to this theory, if you are hopeless enough about your future, then you will become depressed. However, a sufficient cause may not be a necessary cause. Continuing

Figure 3.1 From Correlation to Causation

Virtually all areas of science share an interest in understanding how variables are related to each other. Are they correlated? Does one actually cause the other? This helpful diagram created by Kraemer and colleagues (1997) is designed to help determine the status of potential causal factors. To use it, ask yourself: "Can it be shown that. . . ." Then start at the top-left box and work your way down.

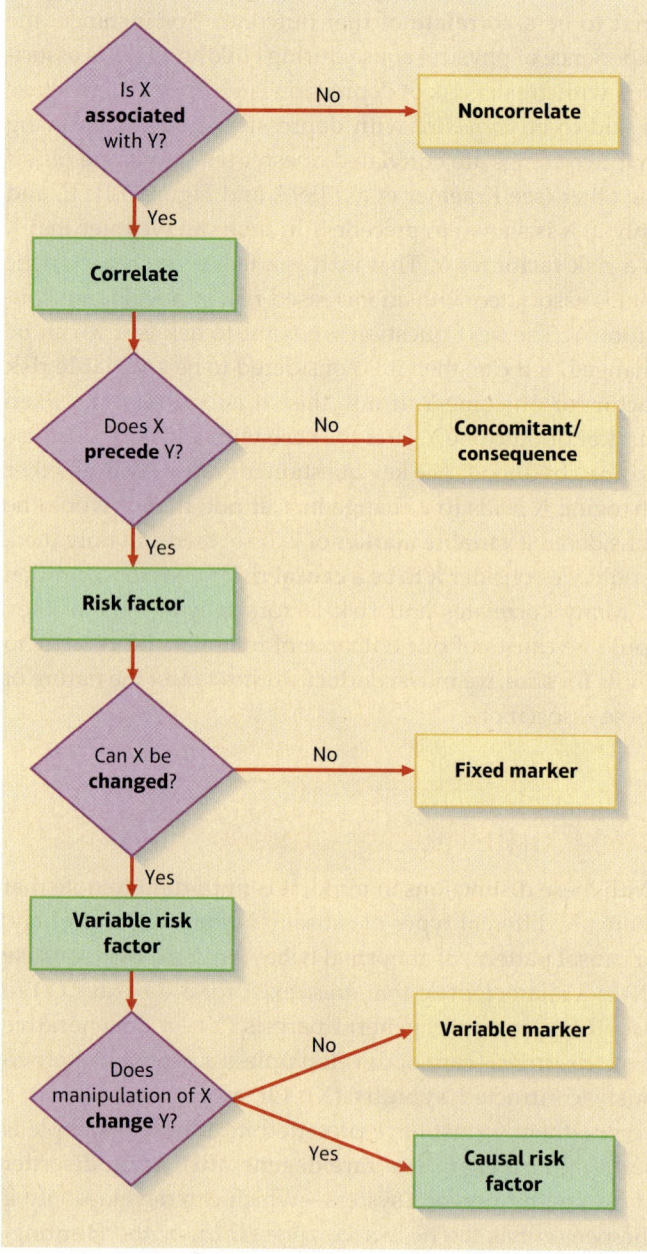

could increase the probability that a child will later have difficulty in handling close personal relationships or could increase the probability that being rejected in a relationship in adulthood will precipitate depression. We say here that parental rejection could be a contributory cause for the person's later difficulties, but it is neither necessary nor sufficient (Abramson et al., 1989, 1995).

Negative life events can contribute to the development of mental disorders, but may not be necessary or sufficient in themselves. The destruction caused by Hurricane Katrina is one example. Many, but not all, of those affected by the hurricane had elevated symptoms of mental disorders in the years following the storm.

In addition to distinguishing among necessary, sufficient, and contributory causes of abnormal behavior, we must also consider the time frame under which the different causes operate. Some causal factors occurring relatively early in life may not show their effects for many years; these would be considered *distal risk factors* (or distal *causal* factors if the conditions described in Figure 3.1 are satisfied) that may contribute to a predisposition to develop a disorder. For example, loss of a parent early in life, or having abusive or neglectful parents as a child or adolescent, may serve as a distal contributory cause predisposing a person to depression or antisocial behaviors later in life. By contrast, other factors operate shortly before the occurrence of the symptoms of a disorder; these would be considered *proximal risk factors*. Sometimes a proximal factor may be a condition that proves too much for a child or adult and triggers the onset of a disorder. A crushing disappointment at school or work or severe difficulties with a school friend or a marital partner are examples of more proximal factors that could lead to depression. In other cases, proximal factors might involve biological changes such as damage to certain parts of the left hemisphere of the brain, which can lead to depression.

A *reinforcing contributory cause* is a condition that tends to maintain maladaptive behavior that is already occurring.

with the depression example, Abramson and colleagues (1989) acknowledge that hopelessness is not a necessary cause of depression; there are other causes of depression as well. Finally, what we study most often in psychopathology research are **contributory causes**. A contributory cause is one that increases the probability of a disorder developing but is neither necessary nor sufficient for the disorder to occur. More generally, if X occurs, then the probability of Y occurring increases. For example, parental rejection

An example is the extra attention, sympathy, and relief from unwanted responsibility that may come when a person is ill; these pleasant experiences may unintentionally discourage recovery. Another example occurs when a depressed person's behavior alienates friends and family, leading to a greater sense of rejection that reinforces the existing depression (Joiner & Timmons, 2009).

For many forms of psychopathology, we do not yet have a clear understanding of whether there are necessary or sufficient causes, although answering this question remains the goal of much current research. We do, however, have a good understanding of many of the risk factors for most forms of psychopathology. Some of the distal risk factors, to be discussed later in this chapter, set up vulnerability during childhood to some disorder later in life. Other more proximal risk factors appear to bring on a disorder directly, and still others may contribute to maintenance of a disorder. This complex picture is further complicated by the fact that what may be a proximal risk factor for a problem at one stage in life may also serve as a distal risk factor that sets up a predisposition for another disorder later in life. For example, the death of a parent can be a proximal risk factor of a child's subsequent grief reaction, which might last a few months or a year; however, the parent's death may also serve as a distal risk factor that increases the probability that when the child grows up he or she will become depressed in response to certain stressors.

Feedback and Bidirectionality in Abnormal Behavior

Traditionally in the sciences, the task of determining cause-and-effect relationships has focused on isolating the condition X (cause) that can be demonstrated to lead to condition Y (effect). For example, when the alcohol content of the blood reaches a certain level, alcoholic intoxication occurs. When more than one causal factor is involved, as is often the case, the term *causal pattern* is used. Here, conditions A, B, C, and so on, lead to condition Y. In either case, this concept of cause follows a simple linear model in which a given variable or set of variables leads to a result either immediately or later. However, in the behavioral sciences, we deal with a multitude of interacting causes, and often have difficulty distinguishing between what is a cause and what is an effect. This occurs because effects can serve as feedback that can in turn influence the causes. In other words, the effects of feedback and the existence of mutual, two-way (bidirectional) influences must be taken into account.

Consider the following example, which illustrates that our concepts of causal relationships must take into account the complex factors of bidirectionality of feedback.

Perceived Hostility

A boy with a history of disturbed interactions with his parents routinely misinterprets the intentions of his peers as being hostile. He develops defensive strategies to counteract the supposed hostility of those around him such as rejecting the efforts of others to be friendly, which he misinterprets as patronizing. Confronted by the boy's prickly behavior, those around him become defensive, hostile, and rejecting, thus confirming and strengthening the boy's distorted expectations. What is the cause of this boy's problems with his peers? His interactions with his parents? His tendency to misinterpret the intentions of others? His defensiveness? The response of his peers? Each seems to contribute; however, teasing these all apart and understanding if and how they contribute to his problems is an extremely challenging task. Welcome to the world of psychopathology research!

Diathesis–Stress Models

Scientists try to understand how variables work together to cause outcomes of interest using conceptual models that distinguish between different types of causal factors. Many mental disorders are believed to develop when someone who has a preexisting *vulnerability* for that disorder experiences a major *stressor*. Models describing this kind of situation are commonly known as **diathesis–stress models** of abnormal behavior (e.g., Ingram & Luxton, 2005; Meehl, 1962; Monroe & Simons, 1991). A vulnerability, or **diathesis**, is a predisposition toward developing a disorder that can derive from biological, psychological, or sociocultural causal factors. **Stress**, the response or experience of an individual to demands that he or she perceives as taxing or exceeding his or her personal resources, will be the focus of Chapter 5. Stress often occurs when an individual experiences chronic or episodic events that are undesirable and lead to behavioral, physiological, and cognitive accommodations (Schneiderman et al., 2005).

To translate these terms into the types of causal factors described earlier, the diathesis results from one or more relatively distal necessary or contributory causes, but is generally not sufficient to cause the disorder. Instead, there must be a more proximal factor (the stressor), which may also be contributory or necessary but is generally not sufficient by itself to cause the disorder except in someone with the diathesis. It is important to note that factors contributing to the development of a diathesis are themselves sometimes highly potent stressors, as when a child experiences the death of a parent and may thereby acquire a predisposition or diathesis for becoming depressed later in life.

Researchers have proposed several different ways in which a diathesis and stress may combine to produce a disorder (Ingram & Luxton, 2005). In what is called the *additive model*, the diathesis and the stress sum together, and when one is high the other can be low, and vice versa. Thus, a person with no diathesis or a very low level of diathesis could still develop a disorder when faced with truly severe stress. In other words, individuals who have a high level of a diathesis may need only a small amount of stress before a disorder develops, but those who have a very low level of a diathesis may need to experience a large amount of stress for a disorder to develop. In what is called an *interactive model*, some amount of diathesis must be present before stress will have any effect. Thus, someone with no diathesis will never develop the disorder, no matter how much stress he or she experiences, whereas someone with the diathesis will demonstrate an increasing likelihood of developing the disorder with increasing levels of stress. More complex models are also possible because diatheses often exist on a continuum, ranging from zero to high levels. Each of these possibilities is illustrated in Figure 3.2.

Figure 3.2 Diathesis–Stress Model

(a) Interactive model of diathesis-stress interaction. (b) Additive model of diathesis–stress interaction.

(Adapted from S. M. Monroe & A. D. Simons (1991). Diathesis–stress theories in the context of life stress research: Implications for the depressive disorders. *Psychological Bulletin*, 110, 406–425.)

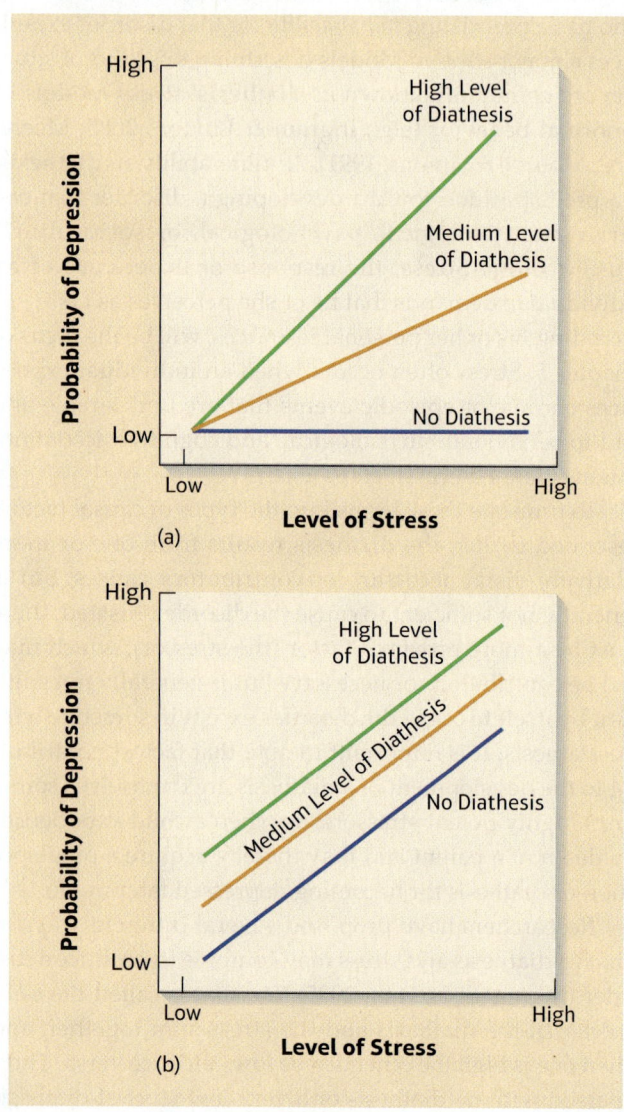

In contrast to risk factors that increase the likelihood of negative outcomes, **protective factors** decrease the likelihood of negative outcomes among those at risk (Kraemer et al., 1997). Note that a protective factor is not simply the absence of a risk factor, but instead is something that actively buffers against the likelihood of a negative outcome among those with some risk factor(s). One important protective factor in childhood is having a family environment in which at least one parent is warm and supportive, allowing the development of a good attachment relationship between the child and parent that can protect against the harmful effects of an abusive parent (Masten & Coatsworth, 1998).

Protective factors are not necessarily positive experiences. Indeed, sometimes exposure to stressful experiences that are dealt with successfully can promote a sense of self-confidence or self-esteem and thereby serve as a protective factor. Thus, some stressors paradoxically promote coping. This "steeling" or "inoculation" effect is more likely to occur with moderate stressors than with mild or extreme stressors (Barlow, 2002; Hetherington, 1991; Rutter, 1987). Some protective factors have nothing to do with experiences at all but are simply some quality or attribute of a person. For example, adolescents who score high on emotional intelligence are less likely to show negative outcomes following childhood abuse (Cha & Nock, 2009).

Protective factors most often, but not always, lead to **resilience**—the ability to adapt successfully to even very difficult circumstances. An example is the child who perseveres and does well in school despite his or her parent's drug addiction or physical abuse. More generally, the term *resilience* has been used to describe the phenomenon that "some individuals have a relatively good outcome despite suffering risk experiences that would be expected to bring about serious sequelae" (Rutter, 2007, p. 205). A more everyday way of thinking of resilience is in terms of "overcoming the odds" against you. There is increasing evidence that if a child's fundamental systems of adaptation (such as intelligence and cognitive development, ability to self-regulate, motivation to achieve mastery, effective parenting, and well-functioning neurobiological systems for handling stress) are operating normally, then most threatening circumstances will have minimal impact on him or her (Masten, 2001; Sapienza & Masten, 2011). Problems tend to arise when one or more of these systems of adaptation is weak to begin with (e.g., low intelligence or poorly functioning neurobiological systems for handling stress; Lester et al., 2006) or when a serious stressor damages one or more of these systems (e.g., when a parent dies). Problems can also arise when the level of challenge far exceeds human capacity to adapt (e.g., exposure to chronic trauma in war or chronic maltreatment in abusive families; Ungar, 2015). We should also note, however, that resilience should not be thought of as an all-or-none capacity, and some research suggests that resilient children (that is, those who show high social competence despite high stress) may also experience considerable self-reported emotional distress. Moreover, children who show resilience in one domain may show significant difficulties in other domains.

A child growing up under conditions of adversity may be protected from problems later in life if he or she has a warm and supportive relationship with some adult, such as a grandparent. Encouraging children to learn, explore, ask questions, and try new experiences—while providing a safe and supportive environment—is an important aspect of a protective relationship.

In sum, we can distinguish between causes of abnormal behavior that lie within and are part of the biological makeup or prior experience of a person—diatheses, vulnerabilities, or predispositions—and causes that pertain to current challenges in a person's life—stressors. Typically, neither the diathesis nor the stress is by itself sufficient to cause the disorder, but in combination they can sometimes lead the individual to behave abnormally. In addition, we can examine protective factors, which may derive either from particular types of experiences or from certain qualities of the person, that can promote resilience in the face of vulnerability and stress. The following scenario illustrates some of these concepts.

Nature and Nurture

Melinda and Tracy were identical twins whose parents were killed in a car accident when they were a year old. Their mother and grandmother both had histories of recurrent clinical depression. The twins were separately adopted into two loving middle-class families without a history of depression. Melinda's adoptive family provided a loving and supportive environment and supported her through school and college. Tracy's adoptive parents, by contrast, soon divorced, and she was raised by her adoptive mother, who developed a serious dependence on alcohol and who could not hold a job. Her mother's living circumstances deteriorated and Tracy was forced to change schools four times. Because of her adoptive mother's alcohol and other mental problems, she was unable to provide Tracy with a consistently loving and supportive environment, and when she was drunk she frequently punished Tracy for no good reason. Tracy somehow managed to graduate from high school and supported herself through a state college. Both Tracy and Melinda married after they graduated from college but, by age 27, both marriages resulted in divorce. Although Melinda developed some depressive symptoms for the first 6 weeks following the divorce, the depression was not severe and she quickly recovered. Tracy, by contrast, developed a major depressive episode that lasted for over a year.

In this example, both Tracy and Melinda have identical genetic makeup and therefore the same genetic diathesis for depression. Both had experienced the same distal stressor (death of parents at an early age), and the same proximal stressor (divorce) at age 27. However, Melinda had many protective factors growing up (loving and supportive family and adequate resources) that Tracy did not have (lack of a loving and supportive mother and inadequate resources). Thus, Melinda showed resilience in the face of her divorce but Tracy did not.

This discussion should make it very clear that diathesis–stress models need to be considered in a broad framework of *multicausal developmental models*. Specifically, in the course of development a child may acquire a variety of cumulative risk factors that may interact to determine his or her risk for psychopathology. These risk factors also interact with a variety of protective processes, and sometimes with stressors, to determine whether the child develops in a normal and adaptive way—as opposed to showing signs of maladaptive behavior and psychopathology—in childhood, adolescence, or adulthood. Note also that to understand what is abnormal, one must always have a good understanding of normal human development at biological, psychological, and sociocultural levels of analysis. This has been the focus of the rapidly growing field of **developmental psychopathology**, which concentrates on determining what is abnormal at any point in development by comparing and contrasting it with the normal and expected changes that occur in the course of development. For example, an intense fear of the dark in a 3- to 5-year-old child may not be considered abnormal, given that most children have at least one specific fear that they bring into early adolescence. However, an intense fear of the dark that causes considerable distress and avoidance behavior in a high school or college-age student would be considered a phobia.

in review

- What is a necessary cause? A sufficient cause? A contributory cause?
- What is a diathesis–stress model of abnormal behavior?
- Define the terms *protective factors* and *resilience*. Give examples of each.
- Explain why diathesis–stress models need to be considered as multicausal developmental models.

Perspectives to Understanding the Causes of Abnormal Behavior

3.2   List the perspectives that psychologists take to understand the causes of abnormal behavior.

Students are often perplexed by the fact that in the behavioral sciences several competing explanations are often offered for the same thing. For instance, what causes depression? There are many different perspectives from which we can study this question. One way is to take a biological perspective in which we try to understand how factors such as genetics, neurobiology, and hormonal responses can influence psychopathology, a strategy that has become increasingly common in recent years. Another is to take a psychological perspective and try to understand how dysfunctional thoughts, feelings, and behaviors can lead to psychopathology. Yet another is to take a sociocultural perspective in which we try to understand how social and cultural factors can influence the way that we think about abnormal behavior. Of course, these different perspectives overlap, so an integrated approach is needed to provide a full understanding of the origins of various forms of psychopathology. Thus, in recent years, many theorists recognize the need for a more integrative, **biopsychosocial viewpoint** that acknowledges that biological, psychological, and social factors all interact and play a role in psychopathology and treatment. Moreover, the cultural context in which each of these factors plays out influences how we think about behavior, both normal and abnormal.

With this in mind, we now turn to the major different perspectives themselves. We present the key ideas of each perspective, along with information about attempts to evaluate its validity. We also describe the kinds of causal factors that each model tends to emphasize.

in review

- What are the three traditional perspectives that have dominated the study of abnormal behavior in recent years?
- What is the central idea of the more current biopsychosocial perspective?

The Biological Perspective

3.3   Explain what the biological perspective tells us about abnormal behavior and also explain the biological causal factors of abnormal behavior.

As we saw in Chapter 2 in the discussion of general paresis and its link to syphilis, the traditional biological viewpoint focuses on mental disorders as diseases, many of the primary symptoms of which are cognitive, emotional, or behavioral. Mental disorders are thus viewed as disorders of the central nervous system, the autonomic nervous system, and/or the endocrine system that are either inherited or caused by some pathological process. At one time, people who adopted this viewpoint hoped to find simple biological explanations. Today, however, most people recognize that such explanations are rarely simple, and many also acknowledge that psychological and sociocultural causal factors play important roles as well.

The disorders first recognized as having biological or organic components were those associated with gross destruction of brain tissue. These disorders are neurological diseases—that is, they result from the disruption of brain functioning by physical or biochemical means and often involve psychological or behavioral aberrations. For example, damage to certain areas in the brain can cause memory loss, and damage to the left hemisphere that occurs during a stroke can cause depression.

However, most mental disorders are not caused by neurological damage per se. For example, abnormalities in neurotransmitter systems in the brain can lead to mental disorders without causing damage to the brain. Moreover, the bizarre content of delusions and other abnormal mental states like hallucinations can never be caused simply and directly by brain damage. Consider the example of a person with schizophrenia or general paresis who claims to be Napoleon. The content of such delusions must be the by-product of some sort of functional integration of different neural structures, some of which have been "programmed" by personality and learning based on past experience (e.g., having learned who Napoleon was).

We focus here on four categories of biological factors that seem particularly relevant to the development of maladaptive behavior: (1) genetic vulnerabilities, (2) brain dysfunction and neural plasticity, (3) neurotransmitter and hormonal abnormalities in the brain or other parts of the central nervous system, and (4) temperament. Each of these categories encompasses a number of conditions that influence the quality and functioning of our bodies and our behavior. They are often not independent of each other but rather interact with one another. Moreover, different factors may play more or less important roles in different people.

Genetic Vulnerabilities

Genes are very long molecules of DNA (deoxyribonucleic acid) that are present at various locations on chromosomes. **Chromosomes** are the chain-like structures within a cell nucleus that contain the genes. Genes are the carriers of the information that we inherit from our parents (individuals have two copies of each gene—one from each of our parents), and each gene exists in two or more alternate forms called *alleles*. Genes don't fully determine whether a person develops a mental disorder; however, there is substantial evidence that most mental disorders show at least some genetic influence (Plomin et al., 2013; Rutter, 2006a). Some of these genetic influences, such as broad temperamental features, are first apparent in newborns and children. For example, some children are just naturally more shy or anxious, whereas others are more outgoing (Fox et al., 2010; Kagan & Fox, 2006). However, some genetic sources of vulnerability do not manifest themselves until adolescence or adulthood, when most mental disorders appear for the first time.

Each human cell has 23 pairs of chromosomes (46 total) containing genetic materials that encode the hereditary plan for each individual. One copy of each chromosome comes from the mother and one from the father. Twenty-two of these chromosome pairs determine, by their biochemical action, an individual's general anatomical and other physiological characteristics. The remaining pair, the *sex chromosomes*, determines the individual's sex. If both of these are X chromosomes, the offspring is a female (XX). If the sex chromosome inherited from the father is a Y chromosome, the offspring is a male (XY). (See Figure 3.3.)

Research in developmental genetics has shown that abnormalities in the structure or number of chromosomes can be associated with major defects or disorders. For example, Down syndrome is a type of intellectual disability in which there is a trisomy (a set of three chromosomes instead of two) in chromosome 21 (see Chapter 15). Here the extra chromosome is the primary cause of the disorder. Anomalies may also occur in the sex chromosomes, producing a variety of complications, such as ambiguous sexual characteristics, that may predispose a person to develop abnormal behavior.

More typically, however, personality traits and mental disorders are not affected by chromosomal abnormalities per se. Instead they are more often influenced either by abnormalities in some of the genes on the chromosomes or by naturally occurring variations of genes known as *polymorphisms*. Although you will often hear about

---

Figure 3.3 Human Chromosome Pairs

A normal human male has 23 pairs of chromosomes, including an X chromosome and a Y chromosome.

(Adapted from "Human Chromosome Pairs," from Thomas D. Gelehrter et al. (1998). *Principles of Medical Genetics*. Reprinted with permission of Lippincott/Williams & Wilkins and Dr. Thomas D. Gelehrter.)

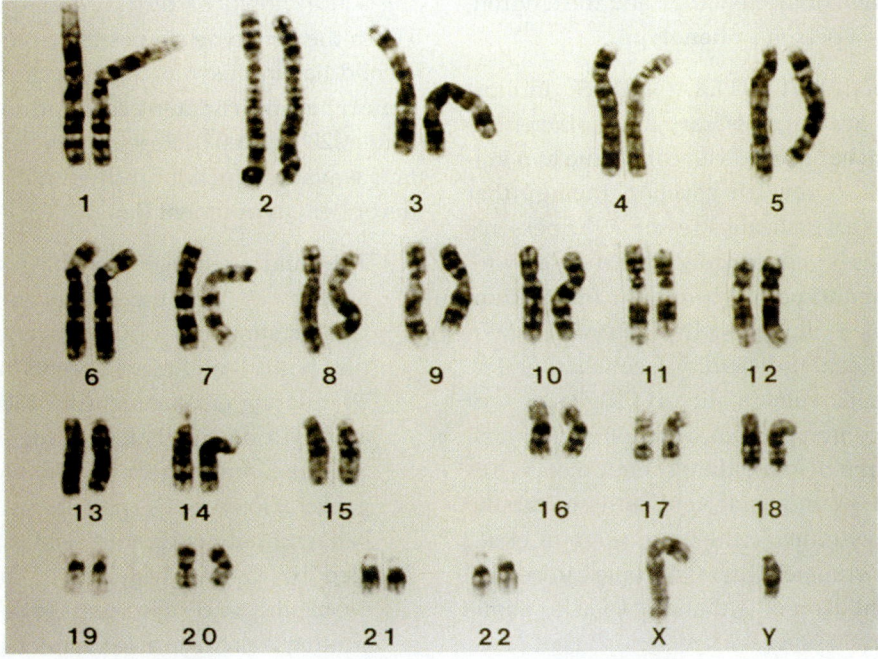

discoveries that "the gene" for a particular disorder has been discovered, vulnerabilities to mental disorders are almost always **polygenic**, which means they are influenced by multiple genes or by multiple polymorphisms of genes, with any one gene having only very small effects (Kendler, 2005; Plomin et al., 2013). In other words, a genetically vulnerable person has usually inherited a large number of genes, or polymorphisms of genes, that operate together in an additive or interactive fashion to increase vulnerability. Collectively these genes may lead to structural abnormalities in the central nervous system, to abnormalities in the regulation of brain chemistry and hormonal balance, or to excesses or deficiencies in the reactivity of the autonomic nervous system, which is involved in mediating many of our emotional responses.

In the field of abnormal psychology, genetic influences rarely express themselves in a simple and straightforward manner. This is because behavior, unlike some physical characteristics such as eye color, is not determined exclusively by genetic endowment; it is a product of the organism's interaction with the environment. In other words, genes can affect behavior only indirectly. Gene "expression" is normally not a simple outcome of the information encoded in DNA but is, rather, the end product of an intricate process that may be influenced by the internal (e.g., intrauterine) and external environment. Indeed, certain genes can actually be "turned on," or activated, and "turned off," or deactivated, in response to environmental influences such as stress.

THE RELATIONSHIP OF GENOTYPES TO PHENOTYPES
A person's total genetic endowment is referred to as her or his **genotype** and, except for identical twins, no two humans ever begin life with the same genetic makeup. The observed structural and functional characteristics that result from an interaction of the genotype and the environment are referred to as a person's **phenotype**.

GENOTYPE–ENVIRONMENT INTERACTIONS In most cases, genetic factors are not necessary and sufficient to cause mental disorders but instead can contribute to a vulnerability or diathesis to develop psychopathology that only happens if there is a significant stressor in the person's life (as in the diathesis–stress models described above). This is known as a **genotype–environment interaction**. One important example is illustrated by a disorder known as PKU-induced intellectual disability (see Chapter 15). Children with the genetic vulnerability to PKU react very differently to many common foods with phenylalanine than do normal children because they cannot metabolize the phenylalanine (an amino acid), and as its metabolic products build up, they damage the brain (Plomin et al., 2013; Rutter, 2006b). Fortunately, this syndrome can be prevented if the young child's diet is changed so as to eliminate foods with phenylalanine.

Another example occurs in people at genetic risk for depression, who have been shown to be more likely to respond to stressful life events by becoming depressed than are people without the genetic risk factors who experience the same stressful life events (Moffitt et al., 2005, 2006). In one landmark study of nearly 850 young adults who were followed since age 3, investigators found evidence for a genotype–environment interaction involving several variants on a specific gene involved in the transport of the neurotransmitter serotonin. The variants of this gene that a person had affected the likelihood that she or he would develop major depression in her or his 20s, but only when considered in interaction with life stress (Caspi et al., 2003). Specifically, individuals with one variant of the gene (two short alleles) who also experienced four or more major life stressors had twice the probability of developing major depression than individuals with another variant of the gene (two long alleles) who also experienced four or more major life stressors (see Chapter 7 for more details). Since then, this basic pattern of results has been replicated in many studies (although not in all), with recent evidence suggesting that the effects are robust if sophisticated interview-based measures of life stress are used (Uher & McGuffin, 2010; see also Karg et al., 2011).

GENOTYPE–ENVIRONMENT CORRELATIONS In many cases, genes can actually shape the environmental experiences a child has, thus affecting the phenotype in important ways. For example, a child who is genetically predisposed to aggressive behavior may be rejected by his or her peers in early grades because of the aggressive behavior. Such rejection may lead the child to go on to associate with similarly aggressive and delinquent peers in later grades, leading to an increased likelihood of developing a full-blown pattern of delinquency in adolescence. When the genotype shapes the environmental experiences a child has in this way, we refer to this phenomenon as a **genotype–environment correlation** (Plomin et al., 2013; Rutter, 2006a, 2007). Researchers have found three important ways in which an individual's genotype may shape his or her environment (Jang, 2005; Plomin et al., 2013).

1. The child's genotype may have what has been termed a *passive effect* on the environment, resulting from the genetic similarity of parents and children. For example, highly intelligent parents may provide a highly stimulating environment for their child, thus creating an environment that will interact in a positive way with the child's genetic endowment for high intelligence. Conversely, parents who exhibit antisocial behavior tend to create a risky environment characterized by family dysfunction, thereby increasing the probability of certain mental disorders in their children (Rutter, 2006b; see also Chapter 10).

2. The child's genotype may evoke particular kinds of reactions from the social and physical environment—a so-called *evocative effect*. For example, active, happy babies evoke more positive responses from others than do passive, unresponsive infants (Lytton, 1980). Similarly, musically talented children may be picked out at school and given special opportunities (Plomin et al., 2013).

3. The child's genotype may play a more active role in shaping the environment—a so-called *active effect*. In this case the child seeks out or builds an environment that is congenial—a phenomenon known as "niche building." For example, extraverted children may seek the company of others, thereby enhancing their own tendencies to be sociable (Baumrind, 1991; Plomin et al., 2013).

METHODS FOR STUDYING GENETIC INFLUENCES
Although advances are beginning to be made in studying genetic factors that are associated with psychopathology, for the most part we are not yet able to isolate, on the genes themselves, specific defects for mental disorders. Instead, most of the information we have on the role of genetic factors in mental disorders is based not on studies of genes but on studies of people who are related to each other. Three primary methods have traditionally been used in **behavior genetics**, the field that focuses on studying the heritability of mental disorders (as well as other aspects of psychological functioning): (1) the family history method, (2) the twin method, and (3) the adoption method. More recently, two additional methods, linkage studies and association studies, have also been developed.

The **family history** (or pedigree) **method** requires that an investigator observe samples of relatives of each *proband* or *index case* (the subject, or carrier, of the trait or disorder in question) to see whether the incidence increases in proportion to the degree of hereditary relationship. In addition, the incidence of the disorder in a normal population is compared (as a control) with its incidence among the relatives of the index cases. The main limitation of this method is that people who are more closely related genetically also tend to share more similar environments, which makes it difficult to disentangle genetic and environmental effects.

The **twin method** is the second approach used to study genetic influences on abnormal behavior. *Identical (monozygotic) twins* share the same genetic endowment because they develop from a single zygote, or fertilized egg. Thus, if a given disorder or trait were completely heritable, one would expect the **concordance rate**—the percentage of twins sharing the disorder or trait—to be 100 percent. That is, if one identical twin had a particular disorder, the other twin would as well. However, there are no forms of psychopathology where the concordance rates for identical

twins are this high, so we can safely conclude that no mental disorders are completely heritable. Nevertheless, as we will see, there are relatively high concordance rates for identical twins in some of the more severe forms of psychopathology. These concordance rates are particularly meaningful when they differ from those found for nonidentical (i.e., dizygotic) twins. *Dizygotic twins* develop from two different fertilized eggs and so do not share any more genes than do siblings from the same parents. One would therefore expect concordance rates for a disorder to be much lower for dizygotic (DZ) than for monozygotic (MZ) twins if the disorder had a strong genetic component. Evidence for genetic transmission of a trait or a disorder can be obtained by comparing the concordance rates between identical and nonidentical twins. For most of the disorders we will discuss, concordance rates are indeed much lower for nonidentical twins than for identical twins.

Some researchers have argued that finding higher concordance rates for a disorder in monozygotic twins than in dizygotic twins is not conclusive evidence of a genetic contribution because it is always possible that identical twins are treated more similarly by their parents and others than are nonidentical twins (Bouchard & Propping, 1993; Torgersen, 1993). However, research has provided evidence that the genetic similarity is more important than

These identical twins from Bouchard's University of Minnesota Study of Twins Reared Apart pose here with Dr. Nancy Segal, co-director of the project. Mark Newman (left) and Gerry Levey (right) were separated at birth and raised by different parents. Both were dedicated firefighters in different New Jersey towns and met after someone mistook one of them at a firemen's convention for his twin. Both had highly similar patterns of baldness and were 6'4" tall. They both loved Budweiser beer (which they both held by placing their pinky finger under the beer can) as well as Chinese and Italian food. Both had been smokers until recently, when one had quit. They both also liked hunting and fishing and always carried knives. These eerie similarities between identical twins reared apart have been observed in many other such twins as well (Segal, 2005).

the similarity of the parents' behavior (Plomin et al., 2013). Nevertheless, the ideal study of genetic factors in psychopathology involves identical twins who have been reared apart in significantly different environments. Unfortunately, finding such twins is extremely difficult (there are probably only a few hundred pairs in the United States), and so only a few such small studies have been done.

The **adoption method**, the third method used to study genetic influences, capitalizes on the fact that adoption creates a situation in which individuals who do not share a common family environment are nonetheless genetically related. In one variation on this method, the biological parents of individuals who have a given disorder (and who were adopted away shortly after birth) are compared with the biological parents of individuals without the disorder (who also were adopted away shortly after birth) to determine their rates of disorder. If there is a genetic influence, one expects to find higher rates of the disorder in the biological relatives of those with the disorder than in those without the disorder. In another variation, researchers compare the rates of disorder in the adopted-away offspring of biological parents who have a disorder with those seen in the adopted-away offspring of normal biological parents. If there is a genetic influence, then there should be higher rates of disorder in the adopted-away offspring of the biological parents who have the disorder.

Watch   Genetic Mechanisms and Behavioral Genetics

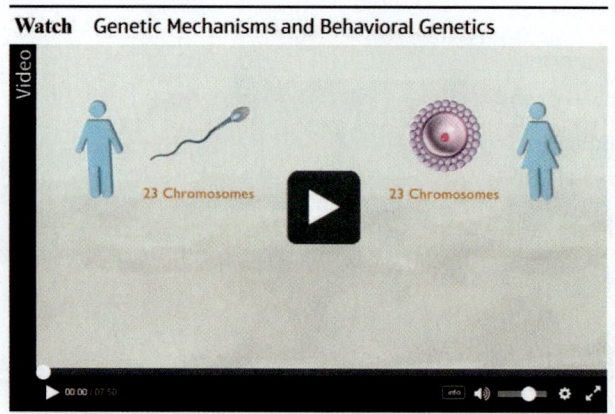

Although pitfalls can arise in interpreting each of these methods, if the results from studies using all three strategies converge, one can draw reasonably strong conclusions about the genetic influence on a disorder. The Developments in Thinking box considers various misconceptions about studies of genetics and psychopathology.

SEPARATING GENETIC AND ENVIRONMENTAL INFLUENCES   Because all of the three types of heritability studies separate heredity from environment to some extent, they also allow for testing the influence of environmental factors and even for differentiating "shared" and "nonshared" environmental influences. *Shared environmental influences* are those that would make children in a family

more similar, whether the influence occurs within the family (e.g., family discord and poverty) or in the environment (e.g., two high-quality schools, with one twin going to each). *Nonshared environmental influences* are those in which the children in a family differ. These would include unique experiences at school and also some unique features of upbringing in the home, such as a parent treating one child in a qualitatively different way from another. An example of nonshared influences occurs when parents who are quarreling and showing hostility to one another draw some children into the conflict while others are able to remain outside it. For many important psychological characteristics and forms of psychopathology, nonshared influences have appeared to be more important—that is, experiences that are specific to a child may do more to influence his or her behavior and adjustment than experiences shared by all children in the family (Plomin et al., 2013; Rutter, 1991, 2006a).

LINKAGE ANALYSIS AND ASSOCIATION STUDIES
More recent molecular genetic methods used to study genetic influences on mental disorders include *linkage analysis* and *association studies*. Whereas the methods previously described attempt to obtain quantitative estimates of the degree of genetic influence for different disorders, linkage analysis and association studies attempt to determine the actual location of genes responsible for mental disorders. Considerable excitement surrounds such work because identifying the location of genes for certain disorders could provide promising leads for new forms of treatment and even prevention of those disorders.

Linkage analysis studies of mental disorders capitalize on several currently known locations on chromosomes of genes for other inherited physical characteristics or biological processes (such as eye color or blood group). For example, researchers might conduct a large family pedigree study on schizophrenia, looking at all known relatives of a person with schizophrenia going back several generations. At the same time, however, they might also keep track of something like the eye color of each individual (as well as which *DSM* diagnoses they have). Eye color might be chosen because it has a known genetic marker located on a particular chromosome. If the researchers found that the familial patterns for schizophrenia in one family pedigree (a sample of all relatives) were closely linked to the familial patterns for eye color in the same pedigree, they could infer that a gene affecting schizophrenia might be located very nearby on the chromosome that contains the known genetic marker for eye color. In other words, in this case one would expect all members of a particular family pedigree with schizophrenia to have the same eye color (e.g., blue), even though all members of a different family pedigree with schizophrenia might have brown eyes.

Developments in Thinking

Nature, Nurture, and Psychopathology: A New Look at an Old Topic

People have abundant misconceptions and stereotypes about studies of genetic influences on behavior, traits, and psychopathology, many stemming from outdated ideas that nature and nurture are separate rather than in constant interplay. Indeed, as we have seen in the examples of genotype–environment correlations and interactions, "In the great majority of cases, both psychological traits and mental disorders are multifactorial in origin—meaning that they involve some kind of combination, and interplay, among several genetic factors providing contributions to susceptibility or liability and several environmental factors that similarly play a part in the causal pathway" (Rutter, 2006a, p. 29). Several of the more important misconceptions are presented here (Plomin et al., 2013; Rutter, 1991, 2006a).

1. **Misconception:** Strong genetic effects mean that environmental influences must be unimportant. *Fact:* Even if we are discussing a trait or disorder that has a strong genetic influence, environmental factors can have a major impact on the level of that trait (Rutter, 2006a). Height, for example, is strongly genetically determined, and yet nutritional factors have a very large effect on the actual height a person attains. Between 1900 and 1960 the average height of boys reared in London increased about 4 inches, thanks only to improvements in diet (Tizard, 1975).

2. **Misconception:** Genes provide a limit to potential. *Fact:* One's potential can change if one's environment changes, as the height example above illustrates. Another example comes from children born to socially disadvantaged parents but who are adopted and reared with socially advantaged parents. These children have a mean IQ about 12 points higher than those reared in the socially disadvantaged environment (Capron & Duyme, 1989; see also Duyme et al., 2004).

3. **Misconception:** Genetic strategies are of no value for studying environmental influences. *Fact:* The opposite is true because genetic research strategies provide critical tests of environmental influences on personality and psychopathology (Rutter, 2006a). For example, because monozygotic twins have identical genes, concordance rates of less than 100 percent clearly illustrate the importance of environmental influences (Bouchard & Loehlin, 2001; Rutter, 2006a).

4. **Misconception:** Genetic effects diminish with age. *Fact:* Although many people assume that genetic effects should be maximal at birth, with environmental influences getting stronger with increasing age, it is now evident that this is not always true (Plomin, 1986; Rutter, 2006a). For height, weight, and IQ, dizygotic twins are almost as alike as monozygotic twins in early infancy, but over time dizygotic twins show greater differences than monozygotic twins. For whatever reasons, many genetic effects on psychological characteristics increase with age up to at least middle childhood or even young adulthood. Moreover, other genetic effects do not appear until much later in life, as in cases like Huntington's disease, to be discussed in Chapter 14.

5. **Misconception:** Disorders that run in families must be genetic, and those that do not run in families must not be genetic. *Fact:* Many examples contradict these misconceptions. For example, teenage-onset juvenile delinquency tends to run in families, and yet this seems to be due primarily to environmental rather than genetic influences (Plomin et al., 2013; Rutter, 2006a). Conversely, autism is such a rare disorder that it doesn't appear to run in families (only about 3 percent of siblings have the disorder), and yet there seems to be a very powerful genetic effect (Plomin et al., 2013; Rutter, 2006a).

A number of published studies during the past 20 years using linkage analysis have provided evidence supporting, for example, the location of a gene for bipolar disorder on chromosome 11 and the location of genes for schizophrenia on particular parts of chromosomes 22, 6, 8, and 1. However, numerous other studies have failed to replicate these results. Therefore, most results are considered inconclusive at the present time (Carey, 2003; Rutter, 2006a). Part of the problem in coming up with replicable results in such studies is that most of these disorders are influenced by many different genes spread over multiple chromosomes. To date, these linkage analysis techniques have been most successful in locating the genes for single-gene brain disorders such as Huntington's disease (Plomin et al., 2013; Rutter, 2006a).

Association studies start with two large groups of individuals, one group with and one group without a given disorder. Researchers then compare the frequencies in these two groups of certain genetic markers that are known to be located on particular chromosomes (such as eye color or blood group). If one or more of the known genetic markers occur with much higher frequency in the individuals with the disorder than in the people without the disorder, the researchers infer that one or more genes associated with the disorder are located on the same chromosome. Ideally, the search for gene candidates for a given disorder starts with known genes for some biological process that is disrupted in the disorder (see Moffitt et al., 2005). For example, one study found that the genetic markers for certain aspects of dopamine functioning were present significantly more frequently in the children with hyperactivity than in the children without hyperactivity. This led researchers to infer that some of the genes involved with hyperactivity are located near the known genetic markers for dopamine functioning (Thapar et al., 2006; see also Plomin et al., 2013). For most mental disorders that are known to be influenced polygenically, association studies are more promising than linkage studies for identifying small effects of any particular gene.

In summary, studies using linkage and association methodologies hold tremendous promise for identifying new prevention or treatment approaches. However, at present that promise has not been fulfilled because of difficulties in producing replicable results.

Brain Dysfunction and Neural Plasticity

Specific brain lesions with observable defects in brain tissue are rarely a primary cause of psychiatric disorders. However, advances in understanding how more subtle deficiencies of brain structure or function are implicated in many mental disorders have been increasing at a rapid pace in the past few decades. Some of these advances come from the increased availability of sophisticated new neuroimaging techniques to study the function and structure of the brain (see Chapter 4 for more details). Research has revealed that genetic factors guide brain development—so these different pieces of the biological puzzle are all related (Hibar et al., 2015). However, we also know that genetic programs for brain development are not so rigid and deterministic as was once believed (Gottesman & Hanson, 2005; Thompson & Nelson, 2001). Instead, there is considerable *neural plasticity*—flexibility of the brain in making changes in organization and function in response to pre- and postnatal experiences, stress, diet, disease, drugs, maturation, and so forth. Existing neural circuits can be modified, or new neural circuits can be generated (Fox et al., 2010; Kolb et al., 2003). The effects can be either beneficial or detrimental to the individual, depending on the circumstances.

that were less negatively affected by brain injury that occurred early in development than those without the same positive prenatal experiences (Kolb et al., 2003). One example of negative effects of prenatal experiences comes from an experiment in which pregnant monkeys exposed to unpredictable loud sounds had infants that were jittery and showed neurochemical abnormalities (specifically, elevated levels of circulating catecholamines; Schneider, 1992). Many *postnatal environmental events* also affect the brain development of the infant and child (Nelson & Bloom, 1997; Thompson & Nelson, 2001). For example, the formation of new neural connections (or synapses) after birth is dramatically affected by the experiences a young organism has (Rosenzweig et al., 2002). Rats reared in enriched environments (as opposed to in isolation) show heavier and thicker cell development in certain portions of the cortex (as well as more synapses per neuron). Similar but less extensive changes can occur in older animals exposed to enriched environments. Physical exercise, such as running, also has been shown to lead to neurogenesis (the creation of new brain cells; Stranahan et al., 2007). Indeed, neural plasticity continues to some extent throughout the life span (so get up and go for a jog after you finish this chapter!).

Research on neural and behavioral plasticity, in combination with the work described earlier on genotype–environment correlations, makes it clear why developmental psychopathologists have been devoting increasing attention to a **developmental systems approach** (Masten, 2006; Spencer et al., 2009), which acknowledges that genetics influences neural activity, which in turn influences behavior, which in turn influences the environment, but also that these influences are bidirectional. Thus, Figure 3.4 illustrates this first direction of influence but also shows how various aspects of our environment (physical, social, and cultural) also influence our behavior, which in turn

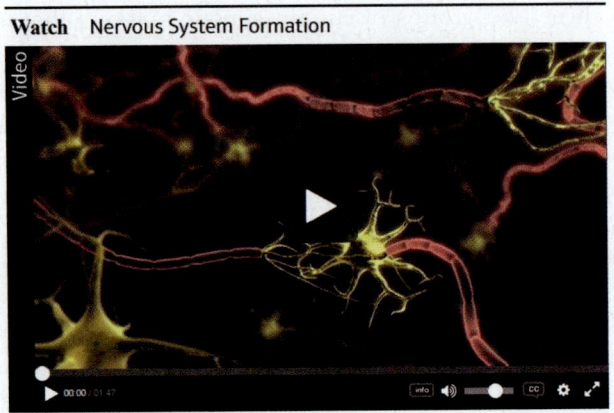

Watch Nervous System Formation

Video

One example of the positive effects of *prenatal experiences* comes from an experiment in which pregnant rats housed in complex, enriched environments had offspring

Figure 3.4 Bidirectional Influences

A systems view of psychobiological development.

(Adapted from Gilbert Gottlieb. 1992. *Individual Development and Evolution: The Genesis of Novel Behavior*. New York: Oxford University Press. Reprinted by permission of Lawrence Erlbaum Associates.)

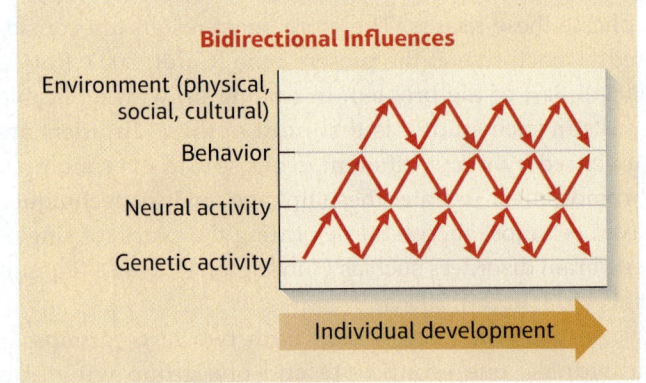

affects our neural activity, and this in turn can even influence genetic activity (Gottesman & Hanson, 2005; Gottlieb & Halpern, 2002; Masten, 2006).

Imbalances of Neurotransmitters and Hormones

In order for the brain to function adequately, neurons, or nerve cells, must communicate effectively with one another. This communication is done through the transmission of electrical nerve impulses. Nerve impulses travel from the cell body or dendrites of one neuron (nerve cell) down the axon. Although there is only one axon for each neuron, axons have branches at their ends called axon endings. These are the sites where neurotransmitter substances are released into the **synapse**—a tiny fluid-filled space between the axon endings of one neuron (the presynaptic neuron) and the dendrites or cell body of another neuron (the postsynaptic neuron). These interneuronal transmissions are accomplished by **neurotransmitters**—chemical substances that are released into the synapse by the presynaptic neuron when a nerve impulse occurs. The neurotransmitter substances released into the synapse then act on the postsynaptic membrane of the dendrite (or cell body) of the receiving neuron, which has specialized receptor sites where the neurotransmitter substances pass on their message. The neurotransmitters can stimulate that postsynaptic neuron to either initiate an impulse or inhibit impulse transmission. Both kinds of messages are important.

Watch The Basics: How the Brain Works

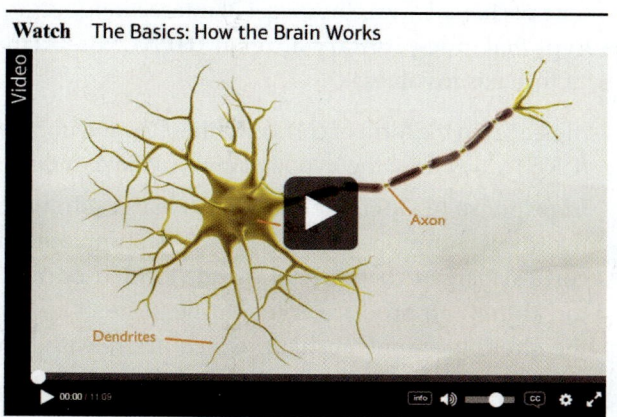

Once the neurotransmitter substance is released into the synapse, it does not stay around indefinitely (otherwise, the receiving neuron would continue firing in the absence of a real impulse). Sometimes the neurotransmitters are quickly destroyed by an enzyme such as monoamine oxidase, and sometimes they are returned to storage vesicles in the axon endings by a reuptake mechanism—a process of reabsorption by which the neurotransmitters are reabsorbed or effectively sucked back up into the axon ending. The enzyme monoamine oxidase is also present in

the presynaptic terminal and can destroy excess neurotransmitters there too.

There are many different kinds of neurotransmitters; some increase the likelihood that the postsynaptic neuron will "fire" (produce an impulse), and others inhibit the impulse. Whether the neural message is successfully transmitted to the postsynaptic neuron depends, among other things, on the concentration of certain neurotransmitters within the synapse.

IMBALANCES OF NEUROTRANSMITTER SYSTEMS The belief that imbalances in neurotransmitters in the brain can result in abnormal behavior is one of the basic tenets of the biological perspective today, although currently most researchers agree that this is only part of the causal pattern involved in the etiology of most disorders. Sometimes psychological stress can bring on *neurotransmitter imbalances*. These imbalances can be created in a variety of ways:

- There may be excessive production and release of the neurotransmitter substance into the synapses, causing a functional excess in levels of that neurotransmitter.

- There may be dysfunctions in the normal processes by which neurotransmitters, once released into the synapse, are deactivated. Ordinarily this deactivation occurs either through a process of reuptake of the released neurotransmitter from the synapse into the axon endings or through a process of degradation by certain enzymes that may be present in the synapse and in the presynaptic axon endings.

- Finally, there may be problems with the receptors in the postsynaptic neuron, which may be either abnormally sensitive or abnormally insensitive.

Neurons that are sensitive to a particular neurotransmitter tend to cluster together, forming neural paths between different parts of the brain known as *chemical circuits*. As we will see, different disorders are thought to stem from different patterns of neurotransmitter imbalances in various brain areas (Lambert & Kinsley, 2005; Thompson, 2000). Medications used to treat various disorders are often believed to operate by correcting these imbalances. For example, the widely prescribed antidepressants Prozac and Zoloft are designed to slow the reuptake of the neurotransmitter serotonin, thereby prolonging how long serotonin remains in the synapse (see Chapters 7 and 16).

Although over a hundred neurotransmitters have been discovered to date, five different kinds of neurotransmitters have been most extensively studied in relationship to psychopathology: (1) norepinephrine, (2) dopamine, (3) serotonin, (4) glutamate, and (5) gamma aminobutyric acid (known as GABA; Carlson, 2007; Lambert & Kinsley, 2005; Thompson, 2000). The first three belong to a class of neurotransmitters called *monoamines* because each is synthesized from a single amino acid (*monoamine* means "one amine"). Norepinephrine has been implicated as playing an important role in the emergency reactions our bodies show when we are exposed to an acutely stressful or dangerous situation, as well as in attention, orientation, and basic motives (see Chapters 5 and 6). Some of the functions of dopamine include pleasure and cognitive processing, and it has been implicated in schizophrenia (see Chapter 13) as well as in addictive disorders (see Chapter 11). Serotonin has been found to have important effects on the way we think and process information from our environment as well as on behaviors and moods. Not surprisingly, then, it seems to play an important role in emotional disorders such as anxiety and depression, as well as in suicide, as we will see in Chapters 6 and 7. In Chapter 13 we discuss the excitatory neurotransmitter glutamate, which has been implicated in schizophrenia. Finally, in Chapter 6, we discuss the neurotransmitter GABA, which is strongly implicated in reducing anxiety as well as other emotional states characterized by high levels of arousal. Each will be discussed at greater length when the relevant disorders are discussed.

Given that many forms of psychopathology have been associated with various abnormalities in neurotransmitter functioning and with altered sensitivities of receptor sites, it is not surprising that many of the medications used to treat various disorders have the synapse as their site of action. For example, certain medications act to increase or decrease the concentrations of pertinent neurotransmitters in the synaptic gap. They may do so by blocking the reuptake process, by altering the sensitivity of the receptor sites, or by affecting the actions of the enzymes that ordinarily break down the neurotransmitter substances. Medications that facilitate the effects of a neurotransmitter on the postsynaptic neuron are called *agonists*, and those that oppose or inhibit the effects of a neurotransmitter on a postsynaptic neuron are called *antagonists*.

HORMONAL IMBALANCES Some forms of psychopathology have also been linked to *hormonal imbalances*. **Hormones** are chemical messengers secreted by a set of endocrine glands in our bodies. Each of the endocrine glands produces and releases its own set of hormones directly into our bloodstream. The hormones then travel and directly affect target cells in various parts of our brain and body, influencing diverse events such as fight-or-flight reactions, sexual responses, physical growth, and many other physical expressions of mental states. Our central nervous system is linked to the endocrine system (in what is known as the *neuroendocrine system*) by the effects of the hypothalamus on the **pituitary gland**, which is the master gland of the body, producing a variety of hormones that regulate or control the other endocrine glands (see Figure 3.5).

Figure 3.5 Major Glands of the Endocrine System

This figure illustrates some of the major glands of the endocrine system, which produce and release hormones into the bloodstream. The hypothalamic-pituitary-adrenal axis is also shown (red arrows). The hypothalamus and pituitary are closely connected, and the hypothalamus periodically sends hormone signals to the pituitary (the master gland), which in turn sends another hormone to the cortical part of the adrenal glands (above the kidneys) to release epinephrine and the stress hormone cortisol.

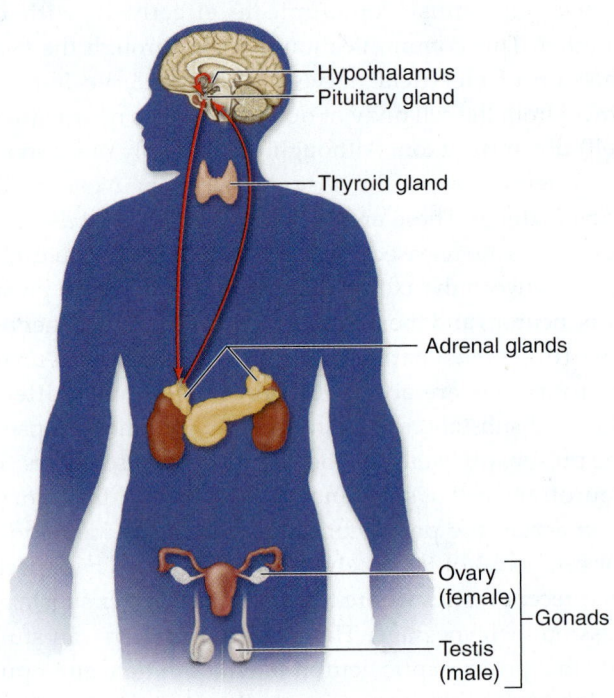

One particularly important set of interactions occurs in the **hypothalamic-pituitary-adrenal (HPA) axis**. Activation of this axis involves:

1. Messages in the form of corticotropin-releasing hormone (CRH) travel from the hypothalamus to the pituitary.

2. In response to CRH, the pituitary releases adrenocorticotropic hormone (ACTH), which stimulates the cortical part of the adrenal gland (located on top of the kidney) to produce epinephrine (adrenaline) and the stress hormone **cortisol**, which are released into the general circulation. Cortisol mobilizes the body to deal with stress.

3. Cortisol in turn provides negative feedback to the hypothalamus and pituitary to decrease their release of CRH and ACTH, which in turn reduces the release of adrenaline and cortisol. This negative feedback system operates much as a thermostat does to regulate temperature.

As we will see, malfunctioning of this negative feedback system has been implicated in various forms of psychopathology such as depression and posttraumatic stress disorder.

Sex hormones are produced by the gonadal glands, and imbalance in these (such as the male hormones, the *androgens*) can also contribute to maladaptive behavior. Moreover, gonadal hormonal influences on the developing nervous system also seem to contribute to some of the differences between behavior in men and in women (Hayward, 2003; Hines, 2004).

Temperament

Temperament refers to a child's reactivity and characteristic ways of self-regulation, which is believed to be biologically programmed. When we say that babies differ in temperament, we mean that they show differences in their characteristic emotional and arousal responses to various stimuli and in their tendency to approach, withdraw, or attend to various situations (Rothbart, Derryberry, & Hershey, 2000). Some babies naturally are startled by slight sounds or cry when sunlight hits their faces; others are seemingly insensitive to such stimulation. These behaviors are strongly influenced by genetic factors, but prenatal and postnatal environmental factors also play a role in their development (Goldsmith, 2003; Rothbart, Derryberry, & Hershey, 2000).

Our early temperament is thought to be the basis from which our personality develops. Starting at about 2 to 3 months of age, approximately five dimensions of temperament can be identified: fearfulness, irritability/frustration, positive affect, activity level, and attentional persistence/ effortful control, although some of these emerge later than others. These seem to be related to the three important dimensions of adult personality: (1) neuroticism or negative emotionality, (2) extraversion or positive emotionality, and (3) constraint (conscientiousness and agreeableness; Rothbart & Bates, 2006; Watson et al., 1994). The infant dimensions of fearfulness and irritability, which show few gender differences (Else-Quest et al., 2006), correspond to the adult dimension of neuroticism—the disposition to experience negative affect. The infant dimensions of positive affect and possibly activity level seem related to the adult dimension of extraversion, and the infant dimension of attentional persistence and effortful control seems related to the adult dimension of constraint or control. One quantitative review concluded that, on average, boys show slightly higher levels of activity and intense pleasure than do girls, whereas girls, on average, seem to have greater control of their impulses and greater ability to regulate their attention (Else-Quest et al., 2006). At least some aspects of temperament show a moderate degree of stability from late in the first year of life through at least middle childhood, although temperament can also change (Kagan, 2003).

Just as we saw in the discussion of genotype–environment correlations, the temperament of an infant or young child has profound effects on a variety of important developmental processes. For example, a child with a fearful temperament has many opportunities for the classical conditioning of fear to situations in which fear is provoked; later the child may learn to avoid entering those feared situations, and evidence suggests that he or she may be especially likely to learn to fear social situations (Fox et al., 2010; Kagan, 2003). In addition, children with high levels of positive affect and activity are more likely to show high levels of mastery motivation, whereas children with high levels of fear and sadness are less likely to show mastery motivation (Posner & Rothbart, 2007).

Finally, children with high levels of negative emotionality are more difficult for parents to be supportive of, and different parents have different styles of parenting such children. This seems to be true especially in families with lower socioeconomic status, which are, on average, less supportive of difficult children than families of mid to high socioeconomic status. The latter families seem to be more resourceful in adapting their parenting styles when faced with such high negative emotionality in a child (Paulussen-Hoogeboom et al., 2007).

Not surprisingly, temperament may also set the stage for the development of various forms of psychopathology later in life. For example, children who are fearful and hypervigilant in many novel or unfamiliar situations have been labeled *behaviorally inhibited* by Kagan, Fox, and their colleagues. This trait has a significant heritable component (Kagan, 2003) and, when it is stable, is a risk factor for the development of anxiety disorders later in childhood and probably in adulthood (Fox et al., 2010; Kagan, 2003). Conversely, 2-year-old children who are highly *uninhibited*, showing little fear of anything, may have difficulty learning

Temperament is consistent over time, causing us to have similar reactions in similar contexts.

moral standards for their behavior from parents or society (Frick, Cornell, Bodin, et al., 2003; Rothbart, Ahadi, & Evans, 2000), and they have been shown at age 13 to exhibit more aggressive and delinquent behavior (Schwartz et al., 1996). If these personality ingredients are combined with high levels of hostility, the stage also might be set for the development of conduct disorder and antisocial personality disorder (Harpur et al., 1993).

The Impact of the Biological Viewpoint

Biological discoveries have profoundly affected the way we think about human behavior. We now recognize the important role of biochemical factors and innate characteristics, many of which are genetically determined, in both normal and abnormal behavior. However, as Gorenstein (1992) and others argued two decades ago, there are several common errors in the way many people interpret the meaning of recent biological advances. It is incorrect to think—as some prominent biological researchers have—that establishing biological differences between, for example, individuals with schizophrenia and those without schizophrenia in and of itself substantiates that schizophrenia is an illness (e.g., Andreasen, 1984; Kety, 1974). All behavioral traits (introversion and extraversion, for example, or high and low sensation seeking) have biological characteristics, yet we do not label these traits as illnesses. Thus, the decision about what constitutes a mental illness or disorder ultimately still rests on clinical judgment regarding the functional effects of the disordered behavior—specifically whether it leads to clinically significant distress or impairment in functioning. Establishing the biological substrate does not bear on this issue because all behavior—normal and abnormal—has a biological substrate.

As Gorenstein (1992) also pointed out, the effects of psychological events are always *mediated* through the activities of the central nervous system because *all* our thoughts, feelings, and behaviors occur as biological events in the brain. However, we must remember that biology alone does not shape our thoughts, feelings, and behaviors; they instead occur via interaction with social events in our environment. As noted earlier, we must draw from multiple perspectives in order to fully understand abnormal (and normal) behavior.

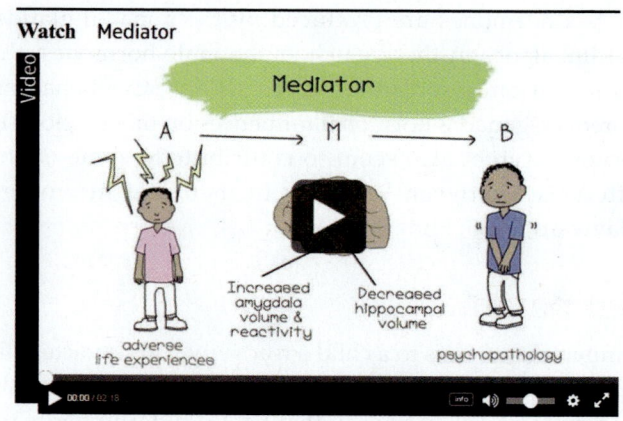

At a more general level, we must remind ourselves again that few, if any, mental disorders are independent of people's personalities or of the problems they face in trying to live their lives. We will examine perspectives that emphasize these psychological and sociocultural considerations in the sections that follow, keeping in mind that the ultimate challenge will be to integrate these varying perspectives into a theoretically consistent biopsychosocial perspective on psychopathology.

in review

- What is the relationship between an individual's genotype and phenotype, and how can genotypes shape and interact with the environment?
- Describe at least two methods for studying genetic influences on abnormal behavior.
- What do we mean by "neural plasticity"?
- Describe the sequence of events involved in the transmission of nerve impulses.
- Explain how neurotransmitter and hormonal abnormalities might produce abnormal behavior.
- What is temperament, and why is it important for the origins of abnormal behavior?

The Psychological Perspective

3.4 Describe the most prominent psychological perspectives on abnormal psychology.

There are many more psychological than biological interpretations of abnormal behavior, reflecting a wider range of opinions on how best to understand humans as people with motives, desires, perceptions, thoughts, and so on, rather than just as biological organisms. In this section we examine in some depth three perspectives on human nature and behavior that have been particularly influential: psychodynamic, behavioral, and cognitive-behavioral.

Research Close-Up

Mediator

A mediator (or mediating variable) lies between two other variables and helps explain the relationship between them. You can think of it as being like an intermediate variable, hence the name.

These three viewpoints represent distinct and sometimes conflicting orientations, but they are in many ways complementary. They all emphasize the importance of early experience and an awareness of psychological processes within an individual, as well as how these are influenced by social factors. The Developments in Thinking box later in this chapter presents a few of the major themes of two additional psychological perspectives: the humanistic and existential perspectives.

The Psychodynamic Perspective

As we noted in Chapter 2, Sigmund Freud founded the *psychoanalytic school*, which emphasized the role of unconscious motives and thoughts and their dynamic interrelationships in the determination of both normal and abnormal behavior. A key concept here is the *unconscious.* According to Freud, the conscious part of the mind represents a relatively small area, whereas the unconscious part, like the submerged part of an iceberg, is the much larger portion. In the depths of the unconscious are the hurtful memories, forbidden desires, and other experiences that have been repressed—that is, pushed out of consciousness. However, Freud believed that unconscious material continues to seek expression and emerges in fantasies, dreams, slips of the tongue, and so forth. Until such unconscious material is brought to awareness and integrated into the conscious part of the mind—for example, through psychoanalysis (a form of psychotherapy Freud developed; see Chapter 16)—it may lead to irrational and maladaptive behavior. For our purposes, a general overview of the principles of classical psychoanalytic theory will suffice (see Luborsky & Barrett, 2006, or any of Freud's original works for more information). We then discuss several of the newer *psychodynamic perspectives*, which were the second generation of theories that stemmed in some important ways out of Freud's original psychoanalytic theory and yet also departed from it in significant ways.

FUNDAMENTALS OF FREUD'S PSYCHOANALYTIC THEORY

The Structure of Personality: Id, Ego, and Superego   In an effort to explain human behavior, Freud theorized that a person's behavior results from the interaction of three key components of the personality or psyche: the id, ego, and superego. The **id** is the source of instinctual drives and is the first structure to appear in infancy. These drives are inherited and are considered to be of two opposing types: (1) *life instincts*, which are constructive drives primarily of a sexual nature and which constitute the **libido**, the basic emotional and psychic energy of life; and (2) *death instincts*, which are destructive drives that tend toward aggression, destruction, and eventual death. Freud used the term *sexual* in a broad sense to refer to almost anything pleasurable,

from eating to painting. The id operates on the **pleasure principle**, engaging in completely selfish and pleasure-oriented behavior, concerned only with the immediate gratification of instinctual needs without reference to reality or moral considerations. Although the id can generate mental images and wish-fulfilling fantasies, referred to as **primary process thinking**, it cannot undertake the realistic actions needed to meet instinctual demands.

According to Freud's theory, a second part of the personality that he called the **ego** develops after the first few months of life. The ego mediates between the demands of the id and the realities of the external world. For example, during toilet training the child learns to control a bodily function to meet parental and societal expectations, and it is the developing ego that assumes the role of mediating between the physical needs of the body/id and the need to find an appropriate place and time. One of the basic functions of the ego is to meet id demands, but in such a way as to ensure the well-being and survival of the individual. This role requires the use of reason and other intellectual resources in dealing with the external world, as well as the exercise of control over id demands. The ego's adaptive measures are referred to as **secondary process thinking**, and the ego operates on the **reality principle**.

Freud viewed id demands, especially sexual and aggressive strivings, as inherently in conflict with the rules and prohibitions imposed by society. He postulated that as a child grows and gradually learns the rules of parents and society regarding right and wrong, a third part of the personality gradually emerges from the ego—the **superego**. The superego is the outgrowth of internalizing the taboos and moral values of society concerning what is right and wrong. It is essentially what we refer to as the *conscience*. As the superego develops, it becomes an inner control system that deals with the uninhibited desires of the id. Because the ego mediates among the desires of the id, the demands of reality, and the moral constraints of the superego, it is often called the *executive branch of the personality*.

Freud believed that the interplay of id, ego, and superego is of crucial significance in determining behavior. Often inner mental conflicts arise because the three subsystems are striving for different goals. If unresolved, these **intrapsychic conflicts** lead to mental disorder.

Anxiety, Defense Mechanisms, and the Unconscious   The concept of *anxiety*—generalized feelings of fear and apprehension—is prominent in the psychoanalytic viewpoint because Freud believed that it plays a key causal role in most of the forms of psychopathology discussed in this text. He believed that the anxiety is sometimes overtly experienced, and at other times it is repressed and then transformed into and manifested in other overt symptoms such as conversion blindness or paralysis (see Chapter 8).

Anxiety is almost universally experienced at some point. This woman shows her anxiety while awaiting news about the outcome of surgery on her sick child.

Anxiety is the body's natural warning system that signals impending danger and the need to take corrective action. Indeed, it is the anxiety that humans experience when they see a fast-approaching tiger (or bus) that keeps us alive and allows us to procreate and pass this trait on. However, when it is extreme, persistent, and occurs outside the context of real danger, anxiety can be considered problematic or even pathological. Freud believed that in many instances, the ego can cope with elevated anxiety through rational measures (i.e., we talk ourselves down). However, Freud suggested that when our anxiety exists only in our unconscious and we are not aware of it, it cannot be dealt with through rational measures. In these cases the ego resorts to irrational protective measures that are referred to as **ego-defense mechanisms**, some of which are described in Table 3.1. These defense mechanisms, Freud proposed, reduce anxiety by helping a person push painful ideas out of consciousness (such as when we "forget" a dental appointment) rather than by dealing directly with the problem. These mechanisms result in a distorted view of reality, although some are clearly more adaptive than others.

Psychosexual Stages of Development   In addition to his concept of the structure of personality, Freud also proposed that there are five **psychosexual stages of development** that we all pass through from infancy through puberty.

Table 3.1 Ego-Defense Mechanisms

Mechanism	Example
Displacement. Discharging pent-up feelings, often of hostility, on objects less dangerous than those arousing the feelings.	A woman harassed by her boss at work initiates an argument with her husband.
Fixation. Attaching oneself in an unreasonable or exaggerated way to some person, or arresting emotional development on a childhood or adolescent level.	An unmarried, middle-aged man still depends on his mother to provide his basic needs.
Projection. Attributing one's unacceptable motives or characteristics to others.	An expansionist-minded dictator of a totalitarian state is convinced that neighboring countries are planning to invade.
Rationalization. Using contrived explanations to conceal or disguise unworthy motives for one's behavior.	A fanatical racist uses ambiguous passages from the scriptures to justify his hostile actions toward minorities.
Reaction formation. Preventing the awareness or expression of unacceptable desires by an exaggerated adoption of seemingly opposite behavior.	A man troubled by homosexual urges initiates a zealous community campaign to stamp out gay bars.
Regression. Retreating to an earlier developmental level involving less mature behavior and responsibility.	A man with shattered self-esteem reverts to childlike "showing off" and exhibits his genitals to young girls.
Repression. Preventing painful or dangerous thoughts from entering consciousness.	A mother's occasional murderous impulses toward her hyperactive 2-year-old are denied access to awareness.
Sublimation. Channeling frustrated sexual energy into substitutive activities.	A sexually frustrated artist paints wildly erotic pictures.

SOURCE: Based on A. Freud (1946) and *DSM-IV-TR* (American Psychiatric Association, 2000).

Each stage is characterized by a dominant mode of achieving libidinal (sexual) pleasure:

1. **Oral stage:** During the first 2 years of life, the mouth is the principal erogenous zone: An infant's greatest source of gratification is sucking, a process that is necessary for feeding.

2. **Anal stage:** From ages 2 to 3, the anus provides the major source of pleasurable stimulation during the time when toilet training is often going on and there are urges both for retention and for elimination.

3. **Phallic stage:** From ages 3 to 5 or 6, self-manipulation of the genitals provides the major source of pleasurable sensation.

4. **Latency period:** From ages 6 to 12, sexual motivations recede in importance as a child becomes preoccupied with developing skills and other activities.

5. **Genital stage:** After puberty, the deepest feelings of pleasure come from sexual relations.

Freud believed that appropriate gratification during each stage is important if a person is to avoid being stuck, or *fixated*, at that level. For example, he maintained that an infant who does not receive adequate oral gratification may, in adult life, be prone to excessive eating or other forms of oral stimulation, such as biting fingernails, smoking, or drinking.

The demands of the id are evident in early childhood. According to Freud, babies pass through an oral stage, in which sucking is a dominant pleasure.

The Oedipus Complex and the Electra Complex   In general, each psychosexual stage of development places demands on a child and arouses conflicts that Freud believed must be resolved in order to avoid later fixations. One of the most important conflicts occurs during the phallic stage, when the pleasures of self-stimulation and accompanying fantasies pave the way for the **Oedipus complex**. According to Greek mythology, Oedipus unknowingly killed his father and married his mother. Each young boy, Freud thought, symbolically relives the Oedipus drama. He longs for his mother sexually and views his father as a hated rival; however, each young boy also fears that his father will punish his son's lust by cutting off his penis. This **castration anxiety** forces the boy to repress his sexual desire for his mother and his hostility toward his father. Eventually, if all goes well, the boy identifies with his father and comes to have only harmless affection for his mother, channeling his sexual impulses toward another woman.

The **Electra complex** is the female counterpart of the Oedipus complex and is also drawn from a Greek tragedy. It is based on the view that each girl desires to possess her father and to replace her mother. Freud also believed that each girl at this stage experiences *penis envy*, wishing she could be more like her father and brothers. She emerges from the complex when she comes to identify with her mother and settles for a promissory note: One day she will have a man of her own who can give her a baby—which unconsciously serves as a type of penis substitute.

Resolution of this conflict is considered essential if a young adult of either sex is to develop satisfactory heterosexual relationships. The psychoanalytic perspective holds that the best we can hope for is to reach a compromise among our warring inclinations—and to realize as much instinctual gratification as possible with minimal punishment and guilt. This perspective thus presents a deterministic view of human behavior that minimizes rationality and freedom of self-determination. On a group level, it interprets violence, war, and related phenomena as the inevitable products of the aggressive and destructive instincts present in human nature.

NEWER PSYCHODYNAMIC PERSPECTIVES   In seeking to understand his patients and develop his theories, Freud was chiefly concerned with the workings of the id, its nature as a source of energy, and the manner in which this id energy could be channeled or transformed. He also focused on the superego and the role of conscience but paid relatively little attention to the importance of the ego. Later theorists developed some of Freud's basic ideas in three somewhat different directions.

Ego Psychology   One new direction was that taken by his daughter Anna Freud (1895–1982), who was much more concerned with how the *ego* performs its central functions as the "executive" of personality. She and some of the other influential second-generation psychodynamic theorists refined and elaborated on the ego-defense mechanisms and put the ego in the foreground, giving it an important organizing role in personality development (e.g., Freud, 1946). According to this view, psychopathology develops when the ego does not function adequately to control or

Anna Freud (1895–1982) studied the important role of the ego in normal and abnormal development and elaborated the theory of ego-defense reactions.

delay impulse gratification or does not make adequate use of defense mechanisms when faced with internal conflicts. This school became known as **ego psychology**.

Object-Relations Theory   A second new psychodynamic perspective was object-relations theory, developed by a number of prominent theorists including Melanie Klein, Margaret Mahler, W. R. D. Fairburn, and D. W. Winnicott, starting in the 1930s and 1940s. Although there are many variations on **object-relations theory**, they share a focus on individuals' interactions with real and imagined other people (external and internal objects) and on the relationships that people experience between their external and internal objects. *Object* in this context refers to the symbolic representation of another person in the infant's or child's environment, most often a parent. Through a process of *introjection*, a child symbolically incorporates into his or her personality (through images and memories) important people in his or her life. For example, a child might internalize images of a punishing father; that image then becomes a harsh self-critic, influencing how the child behaves. The general notion is that internalized objects could have various conflicting properties—such as exciting or attractive versus hostile, frustrating, or rejecting—and also that these objects could split off from the central ego and maintain independent existences, thus giving rise to inner conflicts. An individual experiencing such splitting among internalized objects is, so to speak, "the servant of many masters" and cannot therefore lead an integrated, orderly life.

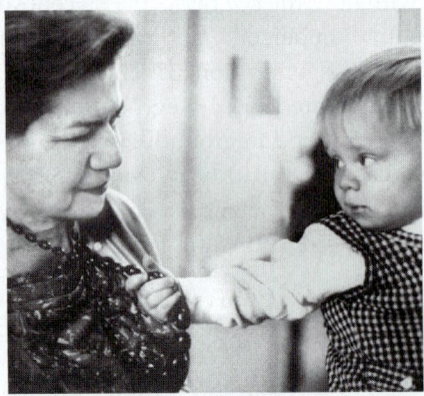

Margaret Mahler (1897–1985) elaborated the object-relations approach, which many see as the main focus of contemporary psychoanalysis.

For example, Otto Kernberg, an influential American psychoanalyst, has a theory that people with *borderline personality disorder*, whose chief characteristic is instability (especially in personal relationships), are unable to achieve a full and stable personal identity (self) because of an inability to integrate and reconcile pathological internalized objects (Kernberg 1985, 1996; Kernberg & Michels, 2009). Because of their inability to structure their internal world in such a way that the people they know (including themselves) can have a mixture of both good and bad

traits, they also perceive the external world in abrupt extremes. For example, a person may be "all good" one moment and "all bad" the next (Koenigsberg et al., 2000).

The Interpersonal Perspective   A third set of second-generation psychodynamic theorists focused on social determinants of behavior. We are social beings, and much of what we are is a product of our relationships with others. It is logical to expect that much of psychopathology reflects this fact—that psychopathology is rooted in the unfortunate tendencies we have developed while dealing with our interpersonal environments. This is the focus of the **interpersonal perspective**, which began with the defection in 1911 of Alfred Adler (1870–1937) from the psychoanalytic viewpoint of his teacher, Sigmund Freud, and emphasizes social and cultural forces rather than inner instincts as determinants of behavior. In Adler's view, people are inherently social beings motivated primarily by the desire to belong to and participate in a group.

Over time, a number of other psychodynamic theorists also took issue with psychoanalytic theory for its neglect of crucial social factors. Among the best known of these theorists are Erich Fromm (1900–1980) and Karen Horney (1885–1952). Fromm focused on the orientations, or dispositions (exploitive, for example), that people adopted in their interactions with others. He believed that when these orientations to the social environment were maladaptive, they served as the bases of much psychopathology. Horney independently developed a similar view and, in particular, vigorously rejected Freud's demeaning psychoanalytic view of women (for instance, the idea that women experience penis envy).

Erich Fromm (1900–1980) focused on the orientations that people adopt in their interactions with others. He believed that these basic orientations to the social environment were the bases of much psychopathology.

Erik Erikson (1902–1994) also extended the interpersonal aspects of psychoanalytic theory. He elaborated and broadened Freud's psychosexual stages into more socially oriented concepts, describing crises or conflicts that occurred at eight stages, each of which could be resolved in a healthy or unhealthy way. For example, Erikson believed that during what Freud called the "oral stage," when a child is preoccupied with oral gratification, a child's real development centers on learning either "basic trust" or "basic mistrust" of her or his social world. Achieving a certain level of trust, for instance, is necessary for later competence in many areas of life.

Erik Erikson (1902–1994) elaborated and broadened Freud's psychosexual stages into more socially oriented concepts. Erikson described conflicts that occurred at eight stages, each of which could be resolved in a healthy or unhealthy way.

Attachment Theory   Finally, John Bowlby's **attachment theory**, which can in many ways be seen as having its roots in the interpersonal and object-relations perspectives, has become an enormously influential theory in child psychology and child psychiatry as well as in adult psychopathology. Drawing on Freud and others from these perspectives, Bowlby's theory (1969, 1973, 1980) emphasizes the importance of early experience, especially early experience with attachment relationships, as laying the foundation for later functioning throughout childhood, adolescence, and adulthood. He stresses the importance of the quality of parental care to the development of secure attachments, but he also sees the infant as playing a more active role in shaping the course of his or her own development than had most of the earlier theorists (Carlson & Sroufe, 1995; Rutter et al., 2009; Sroufe et al., 2000).

IMPACT OF THE PSYCHOANALYTIC PERSPECTIVE
Freud's psychoanalytic theory can be seen as the first systematic approach to showing how human psychological processes can result in mental disorders. Much as the biological perspective had replaced superstition with organic pathology as the suspected cause of mental disorders for many psychiatrists and psychologists, the psychoanalytic perspective replaced brain pathology with intrapsychic conflict and exaggerated ego defenses as the suspected cause of at least some mental disorders.

Freud greatly advanced our understanding of both normal and abnormal behavior. Many of his original concepts have become fundamental to our thinking about human nature and behavior and have even had an important influence on the intellectual history of Western civilization. Two of Freud's contributions stand out as particularly noteworthy:

1. He developed therapeutic techniques such as free association and dream analysis for becoming acquainted with both the conscious and the unconscious aspects of mental life (see Chapter 16). Freud emphasized several points that have been incorporated (in modified forms) into current thinking: (a) there are psychological factors outside our conscious awareness that influence our behavior; (b) early childhood experiences can have an important and lasting impact on the development of both normal and abnormal personality; and (c) sexual factors can play a large role in human behavior and mental disorders. Although, as we have said, Freud used the term *sexual* in a much broader sense than usual, the idea struck a common chord, and the role of sexual factors in human behavior was finally brought out into the open as an appropriate topic for scientific investigation (see Chapter 12).

2. He demonstrated that certain abnormal mental phenomena occur in an attempt to cope with difficult problems and are simply exaggerations of normal ego-defense mechanisms. This realization that the same psychological principles apply to both normal and abnormal behavior dissipated much of the mystery and fear surrounding mental disorders.

After years of prominence, the psychoanalytic perspective came under attack from many directions. Two important criticisms of traditional psychoanalytic theory center on its failure as a scientific theory to explain abnormal behavior. First, many believe that it fails to realize the scientific limits of personal reports of experience as the primary mode of obtaining information. Second, there is a lack of scientific evidence to support many of its explanatory assumptions or the effectiveness of traditional psychoanalysis. In addition, Freudian theory in particular has been criticized for an overemphasis on the sex drive, for its demeaning view of women, for pessimism about basic human nature, for exaggerating the role of unconscious processes, and for failing to consider motives toward personal growth and fulfillment.

IMPACT OF NEWER PSYCHODYNAMIC PERSPECTIVES
The second generation of psychodynamic theorists has done much to improve scientific efforts to measure concepts such as a person's core (but unconscious) conflictual relationships (e.g., Horowitz et al., 1991; Luborsky & Barrett, 2006). Some progress has also been made in understanding

how psychodynamic therapy works and in documenting its effectiveness for certain problems (e.g., Crits-Christoph et al., 2004; Shedler, 2010). In addition, Bowlby's attachment theory has generated an enormous amount of research supporting many of its basic tenets about normal and abnormal child development and adult psychopathology (e.g., Grossman et al., 2005; Rutter et al., 2009).

The focus of interpersonal therapy is on alleviating problem-causing relationships and on helping people achieve more satisfactory relationships. In recent years, major progress has been made in documenting that interpersonal psychotherapy for certain disorders such as depression, bulimia, and some personality disorders can be as effective, or nearly as effective, as cognitive-behavioral treatment—considered by many to be the treatment of choice for these disorders (Benjamin, 2004; Hollon et al., 2006; Wilson & Fairburn, 2007).

The Developments in Thinking box presents two further psychological perspectives that developed in the middle of the twentieth century in part because their founders did not believe that psychodynamic theories acknowledged a person's freedom of choice or the concept of free will.

Developments in Thinking

The Humanistic and Existential Perspectives

The Humanistic Perspective

The *humanistic perspective* views human nature as basically "good." Paying less attention to unconscious processes and past causes, it emphasizes present conscious processes and places strong emphasis on people's inherent capacity for responsible self-direction. Humanistic psychologists think that much of the empirical research designed to investigate causal factors is too simplistic to uncover the complexities of human behavior. Instead, this perspective is concerned with processes such as love, hope, creativity, values, meaning, personal growth, and self-fulfillment. Although these abstract processes are not readily subject to empirical investigation, certain underlying themes and principles of humanistic psychology can be identified, including the self as a unifying theme and a focus on values and personal growth.

In using the concept of *self* as a unifying theme, humanistic psychologists emphasize the importance of individuality. Among humanistic psychologists, Carl Rogers (1902–1987) developed the most systematic formulation of the *self-concept*, based largely on his pioneering research into the nature of the psychotherapeutic process. Rogers (1951, 1959) stated his views in a series of propositions that may be summarized as follows:

- Each individual exists in a private world of experience of which the *I*, *me*, or *myself* is the center.
- The most basic striving of an individual is toward the maintenance, enhancement, and actualization of the self, and his or her inner tendencies are toward health and wholeness under normal conditions.
- Perceived threat to the self is followed by a defense, including a tightening of perception and behavior and the introduction of self-defense mechanisms.

Humanistic psychologists emphasize that values and the process of choice are key in guiding our behavior and achieving meaningful and fulfilling lives. Each of us must develop values and a sense of our own identity based on our own experiences rather than blindly accepting the values of others; otherwise, we deny our own experiences and lose touch with our own feelings. Only in this way can we become *self-actualizing*, meaning that we are achieving our full potential. According to this view, psychopathology is essentially the blocking or distortion of personal growth and the natural tendency toward physical and mental health. Chapter 16 presents the humanistic approach to psychotherapy.

The Existential Perspective

The *existential perspective* resembles the humanistic view in its emphasis on the uniqueness of each individual, the quest for values and meaning, and the existence of freedom for self-direction and self-fulfillment. However, it takes a less optimistic view of human beings and places more emphasis on their irrational tendencies and the difficulties inherent in self-fulfillment—particularly in a modern, bureaucratic, and dehumanizing mass society. In short, living is much more of a "confrontation" for the existentialists than for the humanists. Existential thinkers are especially concerned with the inner experiences of an individual in his or her attempts to understand and deal with the deepest human problems. Existentialism has several basic themes:

- *Existence and essence.* Our existence is a given, but what we make of it—our essence—is up to us. Our essence is created by our choices because our choices reflect the values on which we base and order our lives.
- *Meaning and value.* The will-to-meaning is a basic human tendency to find satisfying values and guide one's life by them.
- *Existential anxiety and the encounter with nothingness.* Nonbeing, or nothingness, which in its final form is death, is the inescapable fate of all human beings. The awareness of our inevitable death and its implications for our living can lead to existential anxiety, a deep concern over whether we are living meaningful and fulfilling lives.

Thus, existential psychologists focus on the importance of establishing values and acquiring a level of spiritual maturity worthy of the freedom and dignity bestowed by one's humanness. Avoiding such central issues creates corrupted, meaningless, and wasted lives. Much abnormal behavior, therefore, is seen as the product of a failure to deal constructively with existential despair and frustration.

The Behavioral Perspective

The behavioral perspective arose in the early twentieth century in part as a reaction against the unscientific methods of psychoanalysis. Behavioral psychologists believed that the study of subjective experience (e.g., free association and dream analysis) did not provide acceptable scientific data because such observations were not open to verification by other investigators. In their view, only the study of directly observable behavior and of the stimuli and reinforcing conditions that control it could serve as a basis for understanding human behavior, normal and abnormal.

Importantly, this perspective was developed through laboratory research rather than clinical practice with patients; however, its implications for explaining and treating maladaptive behavior soon became evident. As we noted in Chapter 2, the roots of the behavioral perspective are in Pavlov's study of classical conditioning and in Thorndike's study of instrumental conditioning (later renamed operant conditioning by Skinner; today both terms are used). The behavioral approach really came together with the 1924 publication of Watson's book *Behaviorism*.

Learning—the modification of behavior as a consequence of experience—is the central theme of the behavioral approach. Because most human behavior is learned, the behaviorists addressed the question of how learning occurs. Behaviorists focus on the effects of environmental conditions (stimuli) on the acquisition, modification, and possible elimination of various types of response patterns, both adaptive and maladaptive.

CLASSICAL CONDITIONING A specific stimulus may come to elicit a specific response through the process of **classical conditioning**. For example, although food naturally elicits salivation, a stimulus that reliably precedes and signals the presentation of food will also come to elicit salivation (Pavlov, 1927). In this case, food is the *unconditioned stimulus* (UCS) and salivation the *unconditioned response* (UCR). A stimulus that signals food delivery and eventually elicits salivation is called a *conditioned stimulus* (CS). Conditioning has occurred when presentation of the conditioned stimulus alone elicits salivation—the *conditioned response* (CR). The same general process occurs when a neutral CS is paired with a painful or frightening stimulus such as a mild electric shock or loud noise, as illustrated in Figure 3.6, although in this case fear rather than salivation is conditioned.

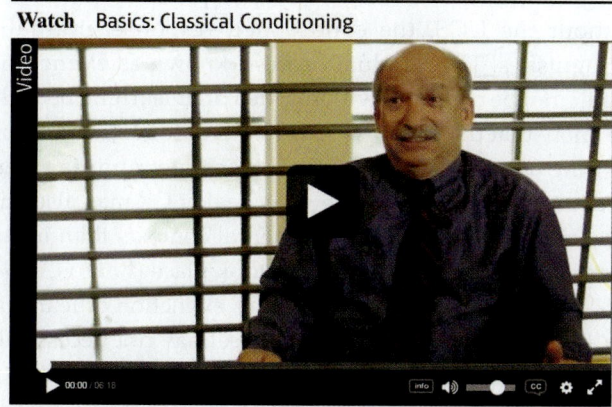

Watch   Basics: Classical Conditioning

The hallmark of classical conditioning is that a formerly neutral stimulus—the CS—acquires the capacity to elicit biologically adaptive responses through repeated pairings with the UCS (e.g., Bouton, 2007; Domjan, 2009). However, we also now know that this process of classical conditioning is not as blind or automatic as was once thought. Rather, it seems that animals (and people) actively

---

Figure 3.6 Classical Conditioning

Before conditioning, the CS is neutral and has no capacity to elicit fear. However, after being repeatedly followed by a painful or frightening UCS that elicits pain, fear, or distress, the CS gradually acquires the capacity to elicit a fear CR. If there are also interspersed trials in which the UCS occurs without being preceded by the CS, conditioning does not occur because in this case the CS is not a reliable predictor of the occurrence of the UCS.

Classical Conditioning

Prior to conditioning:
Conditioned stimulus (neutral) (CS) ....Orientation response to light
    (light)
Unconditioned stimulus (UCS) ....Unconditioned response (UCR)
    (painful stimulus)   (pain and fear)

During conditioning:
Conditioned stimulus (light) (CS)
                 + ...Conditioned response (fear) (CR)
Unconditioned stimulus (UCS)
    (painful stimulus)

Following conditioning:
Conditioned stimulus (alone) (CS) ....Conditioned response (fear) (CR)

acquire information about what CSs allow them to predict, expect, or prepare for an upcoming biologically significant event (the UCS). That is, they learn what is often called a *stimulus-stimulus expectancy*. Indeed, only CSs that provide reliable and nonredundant information about the occurrence of a UCS acquire the capacity to elicit CRs (Hall, 1994; Rescorla, 1988). For example, if UCSs occur as often without being preceded by a CS as they do with the CS, conditioning will not occur because the CS in this case does not provide reliable information about the occurrence of the UCS.

Classically conditioned responses are well maintained over time; that is, they are not simply forgotten (even over many years). However, if a CS is repeatedly presented without the UCS, the conditioned response gradually extinguishes. This gradual process, known as **extinction**, should not be confused with the idea of unlearning because we know that the response may return at some future point in time (a phenomenon Pavlov called **spontaneous recovery**). Moreover, a somewhat weaker CR may also still be elicited in different environmental contexts than in the one where the extinction process took place (Bouton, 1994, 2002; Bouton et al., 2006). Thus, any extinction of fear that has taken place in a therapist's office may not necessarily generalize completely and automatically to other contexts outside the therapist's office (see Craske & Mystkowski, 2006; Mystkowski & Mineka, 2007). As we shall see later, these principles of extinction and spontaneous recovery have important implications for many forms of behavioral treatment.

Classical conditioning is important in abnormal psychology because many physiological and emotional responses can be conditioned, including those related to fear, anxiety, or sexual arousal and those stimulated by drugs of abuse. Thus, for example, one can learn a fear of the dark if fear-producing stimuli (such as frightening dreams or fantasies) occur regularly in the dark, or one can acquire a fear of snakes if bitten by a snake (Mineka & Sutton, 2006; Mineka & Zinbarg, 2006). In addition, a young man who has his first few powerful sexual experiences (UCR) with a very attractive woman (UCS) wearing some form of distinctive clothing (CS—such as black fishnet stockings) may find in the future that he becomes very sexually aroused (CR) simply upon seeing fishnet stockings.

OPERANT CONDITIONING   In **operant (or instrumental) conditioning**, an individual learns how to achieve a desired goal. The goal in question may be to obtain something that is rewarding or to escape from something that is unpleasant. Essential here is the concept of **reinforcement**, which refers either to the delivery of a reward or pleasant stimulus, or to the removal of or escape from an aversive stimulus. New responses are learned and tend to recur if they are reinforced. Although it was originally thought

that instrumental conditioning consisted of simple strengthening of a stimulus–response connection every time that reinforcement occurred, it is now believed that the animal or person learns a *response–outcome expectancy* (e.g., Domjan, 2005)—that is, learns that a response will lead to a reward outcome. If sufficiently motivated for that outcome (e.g., being hungry), the person will make the response that he or she has learned produces the outcome (e.g., opening the refrigerator).

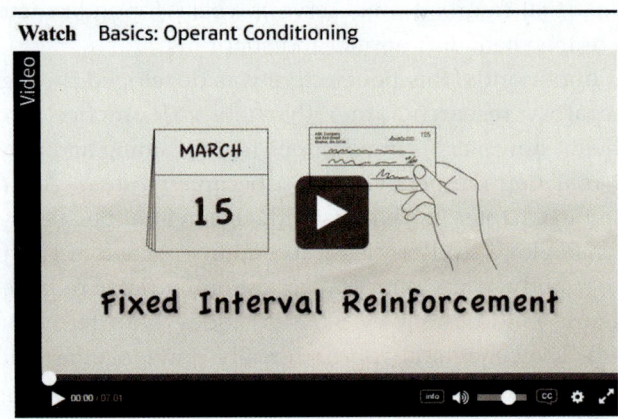

Watch   Basics: Operant Conditioning

Initially a high rate of reinforcement may be necessary to establish an instrumental response, but lesser rates are usually sufficient to maintain it. In fact, an instrumental response appears to be especially persistent when reinforcement is intermittent—when the reinforcing stimulus does not invariably follow the response—as demonstrated in gambling, when occasional wins seem to maintain high rates of responding. However, when reinforcement is consistently withheld over time, the conditioned response—whether classical or instrumental—gradually extinguishes. In short, the subject eventually stops making the response.

A special problem arises in situations in which a subject has been conditioned to anticipate an aversive event and so consistently avoids those situations. For example, a boy who has nearly drowned in a swimming pool may develop a fear of water and a *conditioned avoidance response* in which he consistently avoids all large bodies of water. According to one influential theory, when he sees a pond, lake, or swimming pool, he feels anxious; running away and avoiding contact lessens his anxiety and thus is reinforcing. As a result, his avoidance response is highly resistant to extinction. It also prevents him from having experiences with water that could bring about extinction of his fear. In later discussions, we will see that conditioned avoidance responses play a role in many patterns of abnormal behavior.

As we grow up, instrumental learning becomes an important mechanism for discriminating between what will prove rewarding and what will prove unrewarding—and thus for acquiring the behaviors essential for coping with our world. Unfortunately, what we learn is not always useful in the long run. We may learn to value things (such as cigarettes or alcohol) that seem attractive in the short run but that can actually hurt us in the long run, or we may learn coping patterns (such as helplessness, bullying, or other irresponsible behaviors) that are maladaptive rather than adaptive in the long run.

GENERALIZATION AND DISCRIMINATION In both classical and instrumental conditioning, when a response is conditioned to one stimulus or set of stimuli, it can be evoked by other, similar stimuli; this process is called **generalization**. A person who fears bees, for example, may generalize that fear to all flying insects. A process complementary to generalization is **discrimination**, which occurs when a person learns to distinguish between similar stimuli and to respond differently to them based on which ones are followed by reinforcement. For example, because red strawberries taste good and green ones do not, a conditioned discrimination will occur if a person has experience with both.

The concepts of generalization and discrimination have many implications for the development of maladaptive behavior. Although generalization enables us to use past experiences in sizing up new situations, the possibility of making inappropriate generalizations always exists, as when a troubled adolescent fails to discriminate between friendly and hostile teasing from peers. In some instances, an important discrimination seems to be beyond an individual's capability (as when a bigoted person deals with others on the basis of stereotypes rather than as individuals) and may lead to inappropriate and maladaptive behavior.

OBSERVATIONAL LEARNING Human and nonhuman primates are also capable of **observational learning**—that is, learning through observation alone, without directly experiencing an unconditioned stimulus (for classical conditioning) or a reinforcement (for instrumental conditioning). For instance, children can acquire new fears by simply observing a parent or peer behaving fearfully with some object or situation that the child did not initially fear. In this case, they experience the fear of the parent or peer vicariously, and that fear becomes attached to the formerly neutral object (Mineka & Oehlberg, 2008; Mineka & Sutton, 2006). For observational instrumental learning, Bandura did a classic series of experiments in the 1960s on how children observationally learned various novel, aggressive responses toward a large Bobo doll after they had observed models being reinforced for these responses (see Bandura, 1969). Although the children themselves were never directly reinforced for showing these novel aggressive responses, they nonetheless showed them when given the opportunity to interact with the Bobo doll themselves. The possibilities for observational conditioning of both classical and instrumental responses greatly

expand our opportunities for learning both adaptive and maladaptive behavior.

IMPACT OF THE BEHAVIORAL PERSPECTIVE Because there was so much resistance from well-entrenched supporters of psychoanalysis, behavior therapy did not become well established as a powerful way of viewing and treating abnormal behavior until the 1960s and 1970s. By then, the behavioral assault on the prevailing psychodynamic doctrine of the time (Salter, 1949; Wolpe, 1958) was well under way and important evidence had been gathered on the power of behavior therapy techniques.

By means of a relatively few basic concepts, the behavioral perspective attempts to explain the acquisition, modification, and extinction of nearly all types of behavior. Maladaptive behavior is viewed as essentially the result of (1) a failure to learn necessary adaptive behaviors or competencies, such as how to establish satisfying personal relationships, and/or (2) the learning of ineffective or maladaptive responses. Maladaptive behavior is thus the result of learning that has gone awry and is defined in terms of specific, observable, undesirable responses.

For the behavior therapist, the focus of therapy is on changing specific behaviors and emotional responses—eliminating undesirable reactions and learning desirable ones. For example, fears and phobias can be successfully treated by prolonged exposure to the feared objects or situations—an extinction procedure derived from principles of extinction of classical conditioning. Or an inappropriate sexual attraction to a deviant stimulus (such as prepubertal children) can be altered by pairing pictures of the deviant stimuli with a foul odor or another unpleasant stimulus. Classic work using the principles of instrumental conditioning also showed that institutionalized people with chronic mental illness can be retaught basic living skills such as clothing and feeding themselves through the use of tokens that are earned for appropriate behavior and that can be turned in for desirable rewards (candy, time watching television, passes to go outside, etc.).

The behavioral approach is well known for its precision and objectivity, for its wealth of research, and for its demonstrated effectiveness in changing specific behaviors. A behavior therapist specifies what behavior is to be changed and how it is to be changed. Later, the effectiveness of the therapy can be evaluated objectively by the degree to which the stated goals have been achieved. Nevertheless, the behavioral perspective has been criticized for several reasons. One early criticism was that behavior therapy was concerned only with symptoms, not underlying causes. However, this criticism has been considered unfair by many contemporary behavior therapists, given that successful symptom-focused treatment often has very positive effects on other aspects of a person's life (e.g., Borkovec et al., 1995; Lenz & Demal, 2000). Still others have argued that the behavioral approach oversimplifies human behavior and is unable to explain all of its complexities. This latter criticism stems at least in part from misunderstandings about current developments in behavioral approaches (e.g., Bouton, 2007; Bouton et al., 2001; Mineka & Oehlberg, 2008; Mineka & Zinbarg, 2006). Whatever its limitations, the behavioral perspective has had a tremendous impact on contemporary views of human nature, behavior, and psychopathology.

The Cognitive-Behavioral Perspective

Since the 1950s many psychologists, including some learning theorists, focused on cognitive processes and their impact on behavior. Cognitive psychology involves the study of basic information-processing mechanisms such as attention and memory, as well as higher mental processes such as thinking, planning, and decision making. The current emphasis within psychology as a whole on understanding all of these facets of normal human cognition originally began as a reaction against the relatively mechanistic nature of the traditional, radical behavioral viewpoint (espoused by Watson and Skinner), including its failure to attend to the importance of mental processes—both in their own right and for their influence on emotions and behavior.

Albert Bandura (b. 1925), a learning theorist who developed an early cognitive-behavioral perspective, placed considerable emphasis on the cognitive aspects of learning. Bandura stressed that human beings regulate behavior by internal symbolic processes—thoughts. That is, we learn by *internal reinforcement*. According to Bandura, we prepare ourselves for difficult tasks, for example, by visualizing what the consequences would be if we did not perform them. Thus we take our automobiles to the garage in the fall and have the antifreeze checked because we can "see" ourselves stranded on a road in winter. We do not always require external reinforcement to alter our behavior patterns; our cognitive abilities allow us to solve many problems internally. Bandura (1974) went so far as to say that human beings have "a capacity for self-direction" (p. 861). Bandura later developed a theory of *self-efficacy*, the belief that one can achieve desired goals (1986, 1997). He posited that cognitive-behavioral treatments work in large part by improving self-efficacy.

Other cognitive-behavioral theorists abandoned the learning theory framework more vigorously than did Bandura and focused almost exclusively on cognitive processes and their impact on behavior. Today the cognitive or **cognitive-behavioral perspective** on abnormal behavior generally focuses on how thoughts and information processing can become distorted and lead to maladaptive emotions and behavior. One central construct

Albert Bandura (b. 1925) stressed that people learn more by internal than external reinforcement. They can visualize the consequences of their actions rather than rely exclusively on environmental reinforcements.

for this perspective is the concept of a schema, which was adapted from cognitive psychology by Aaron Beck (b. 1921), another pioneering cognitive theorist (e.g., Beck, 1967; Neisser, 1967, 1982). A **schema** is an underlying representation of knowledge that guides the current processing of information and often leads to distortions in attention, memory, and comprehension. People develop different schemas based on their temperament, abilities, and experiences.

SCHEMAS AND COGNITIVE DISTORTIONS Our schemas about the world around us and about ourselves (self-schemas) are our guides, one might say, through the complexities of living in the world as we understand it. We all have schemas about other people (for example, expectations that they are lazy or very career oriented). We also have schemas about social roles (for example, expectations about what the appropriate behaviors for a widow are) and about events (for example, what sequences of events are appropriate for a particular situation such as someone coping with a loss; Bodenhausen & Morales, 2013;

Clark, Beck, & Alford, 1999). Our **self-schemas** include our views on who we are, what we might become, and what is important to us. Other aspects of our self-schemas concern our notions of the various roles we occupy or might occupy in our social environment such as "woman," "man," "student," "parent," "physician," "American," and so on. Most people have clear ideas about at least some of their own personal attributes and less clear ideas about other attributes (Fiske & Taylor, 1991; Kunda, 1999).

Our self-schemas—our frames of reference for who we are, what we might become, and what is important to us—influence our choice of goals and our confidence in attaining them. Until his mid-30s, Ang Lee was an unemployed stay-at-home dad. He eventually pursued his dream of making movies, and soon thereafter went on to write and/or direct award-winning films such as *Sense and Sensibility, Crouching Tiger, Hidden Dragon*, and *Life of Pi*. It was likely a self-schema that he is a filmmaker that led him to continue to pursue his dream for so long.

Schemas about the world and self-schemas are vital to our ability to engage in effective and organized behavior because they enable us to focus on the most relevant and important bits of information among the amazingly complex array of information that is available to our senses. However, schemas are also sources of psychological vulnerabilities because some of our schemas or certain aspects of our self-schemas may be distorted and inaccurate. In addition, we often hold some schemas—even distorted ones—with conviction, making them resistant to change.

This is in part because we are usually not completely conscious of our schemas. In other words, although our daily decisions and behavior are largely shaped by these frames of reference, we may be unaware of the assumptions on which they are based—or even of making assumptions at all. We think that we are simply seeing things the way they are and often do not consider the fact that other views of the "real" world might be possible or that other rules for what is "right" might exist.

We tend to work new experiences into our existing cognitive frameworks, even if the new information has to be reinterpreted or distorted to make it fit—a process known as *assimilation*. In other words, we are likely to cling to existing assumptions and to reject or distort new information that contradicts them. *Accommodation*—changing our existing frameworks to make it possible to incorporate new information that doesn't fit—is more difficult and threatening, especially when important assumptions are challenged. Accommodation is, of course, a basic goal of psychological therapies—explicitly in the case of the cognitive and cognitive-behavioral therapies, but deeply embedded in virtually all other approaches as well.

According to Beck (1967; Beck et al., 2005), different forms of psychopathology are characterized by different maladaptive schemas that have developed as a function of adverse early learning experiences. These maladaptive schemas lead to the distortions in thinking that are characteristic of certain disorders such as anxiety, depression, and personality disorders. In addition to studying the nature of dysfunctional schemas associated with different forms of psychopathology, researchers have also studied several different patterns of distorted information processing exhibited by people with various forms of psychopathology. This

Aaron Beck (b. 1921) pioneered the development of cognitive theories of depression, anxiety, and personality disorders. He also developed highly effective cognitive-behavioral treatments for these disorders.

research has illuminated the cognitive mechanisms that may be involved in causing or maintaining certain disorders. For example, individuals who are depressed show memory biases favoring negative information over positive or neutral information. Such biases are likely to help reinforce or maintain one's current depressed state (e.g., Joormann, 2009; Mathews & MacLeod, 2005).

Another important feature of information processing is that a great deal of information is processed *nonconsciously*, or outside of our awareness. Note that the term *nonconscious* does not refer to Freud's concept of the *unconscious*, in which primitive emotional conflicts are thought to simmer. Instead, the term *nonconscious mental activity* as studied by cognitive psychologists is simply a descriptive term for mental processes that are occurring without our being aware of them. One example relevant to psychopathology is that anxious people seem to have their attention drawn to threatening information even when that information is presented subliminally (that is, without the person's awareness; e.g., Mathews & MacLeod, 2005). Another relevant example occurs in the well-known phenomenon of *implicit memory*, which is demonstrated when a person's behavior reveals that she or he remembers a previously learned word or activity even though she or he cannot consciously remember it. For example, if someone asks you for your old home phone number from about 10 years ago, you may not be able to recall it (no explicit memory for it), but if you picked up a phone you might dial it correctly (intact implicit memory for it).

ATTRIBUTIONS, ATTRIBUTIONAL STYLE, AND PSYCHOPATHOLOGY   *Attribution theory* has also contributed significantly to the cognitive-behavioral approach (Fiske & Taylor, 1991; Gotlib & Abramson, 1999). **Attribution** is simply the process of assigning causes to things that happen. We may attribute behavior to external events such as rewards or punishments ("He did it for the money"), or we may assume that the causes are internal and derive from traits within ourselves or others ("He did it because he is so generous"). Causal attributions help us explain our own or other people's behaviors and make it possible to predict what we or others are likely to do in the future. A student who fails a test may attribute the failure to a lack of intelligence (a personal trait) or to ambiguous test questions or unclear directions (environmental causes).

Attribution theorists have been interested in whether different forms of psychopathology are associated with distinctive and dysfunctional attributional styles. *Attributional style* is a characteristic way in which an individual tends to assign causes to bad events or good events. For example, people with depression tend to attribute bad events to internal, stable, and global causes ("I failed the test because I'm stupid" as opposed to "I failed the test because the teacher was in a bad mood and graded it unfairly"). However inaccurate our attributions may be, they become important parts of our view of the world and can have significant effects on our emotional well-being (Abramson et al., 1978; Mineka et al., 2002). Interestingly, nondepressed people tend to have what is called a *self-serving bias* in which they are more likely to make internal, stable, and global attributions for positive rather than negative events (e.g., Mezulis et al., 2004).

The cognitive perspective suggests that it is not events, but our attributions about events, that influence our feelings and behaviors. For instance, if you are home alone at night and hear a strange noise, you may believe it was caused by the wind and do nothing. But, if you believe it was caused by an intruder, you may grab a large knife (and a large phone), like Drew Barrymore in the classic movie *Scream*.

COGNITIVE THERAPY   Beck, who is generally considered the founder of cognitive therapy, has been enormously influential in the development of cognitive-behavioral treatment approaches to various forms of psychopathology. Following Beck's lead, cognitive-behavioral theorists and clinicians have simply shifted their focus from overt behavior itself to the underlying cognitions assumed to be producing the maladaptive emotions and behavior. Fundamental to Beck's perspective is the idea that the way we interpret events and experiences determines our emotional reactions to them. Suppose, for example, that you are sitting in your living room and hear a crash in the adjacent dining room. You remember that you left the window open in the dining room and conclude that a gust of wind must have knocked over your favorite vase, which was sitting on the table. What would your emotional reaction be? Probably you would be annoyed or angry with yourself either for having left the window open or for having left the vase out (or both!). By contrast, suppose you conclude that a burglar must have climbed in the open window. What would your emotional reaction be then? In all likelihood, you would feel frightened. Thus, your interpretation of the crash you heard in the next room fundamentally determines your emotional reaction to it. Moreover, certain individuals with prominent danger schemas may be especially prone to making the burglar assumption in this example, leaving them at risk for anxiety and worry.

One central issue for cognitive therapy, then, is how best to alter distorted and maladaptive cognitions, including the underlying maladaptive schemas that lead to different disorders and their associated emotions. For example, cognitive-behavioral clinicians are concerned with their clients' self-statements—that is, with what their clients say to themselves by way of interpreting their experiences. People who interpret what happens in their lives as a negative reflection of their self-worth are likely to feel depressed; people who interpret the sensation that their heart is racing as meaning that they may have a heart attack and die are likely to have a panic attack. Cognitive-behavioral clinicians use a variety of techniques designed to alter whatever negative cognitive biases the client harbors (e.g., see Barlow, 2008; Beck et al., 2004; Hollon & Beck, 1994; Hollon et al., 2006). This is in contrast to, for example, psychodynamic practice, which assumes that diverse problems are due to a limited array of intrapsychic conflicts (such as an unresolved Oedipus complex) and tends not to focus treatment directly on a person's particular problems or complaints. Many widely used cognitive-behavioral therapies will be described in later chapters.

THE IMPACT OF THE COGNITIVE-BEHAVIORAL PERSPECTIVE The cognitive-behavioral viewpoint has had a powerful impact on contemporary clinical psychology. Many researchers and clinicians have found support for the principle of altering human behavior through changing the way people think about themselves and others. Many traditional behaviorists, however, have remained skeptical of the cognitive-behavioral viewpoint. B. F. Skinner (1990), in his last major address, remained true to behaviorism. He questioned the move away from principles of operant conditioning. He reminded his audience that cognitions are not observable phenomena and, as such, cannot be relied on as solid empirical data. Although

Skinner is gone, this debate will surely continue in some form. Indeed, Wolpe (1988, 1993), another founder of behavior therapy, also remained highly critical of the cognitive perspective until his death in 1997. However, these criticisms have seemed to be decreasing in recent years as more and more evidence accumulates for the efficacy of cognitive-behavioral treatments for various disorders ranging from schizophrenia to anxiety, depression, and personality disorders (e.g., Barlow, 2008; Butler et al., 2006; Tolin, 2010). This approach has also been greatly advanced by the accumulation of sophisticated information-processing studies of the effects of emotion on cognition and behavior (e.g., Joormann & Quinn, 2014; Ochsner et al., 2012). This is because such studies do not rely on the self-report techniques that were originally central to this approach, and which are especially open to the kinds of criticisms raised by Skinner and Wolpe.

What the Adoption of a Perspective Does and Does Not Do

Each of the psychological perspectives on human behavior—psychodynamic, behavioral, and cognitive-behavioral—contributes to our understanding of psychopathology, but none alone can account for the complex variety of human maladaptive behaviors. Because different causal perspectives influence which components of maladaptive behavior the observer focuses on, each perspective depends on generalizations from limited observations and research. For example, in attempting to explain a complex disorder such as alcohol dependence, the more traditional psychodynamic viewpoint focuses on intrapsychic conflict and anxiety that the person attempts to reduce through the intake of alcohol. The more recent interpersonal variant on the psychodynamic perspective focuses on difficulties in a person's past and present relationships that contribute to drinking. The behavioral viewpoint focuses on faulty learning of habits to reduce stress (drinking alcohol) and environmental conditions that may be exacerbating or maintaining the condition; and the cognitive-behavioral viewpoint focuses on maladaptive thinking including deficits in problem solving and information processing, such as irrational beliefs about the need for alcohol to reduce stress.

Thus, which perspective we adopt has important consequences: It influences our *perception of maladaptive behavior*, the *types of evidence we look for*, and *the way in which we are likely to interpret data*. A wide range of psychological causal factors have been implicated in the origins of maladaptive behavior, and some of these different viewpoints provide contrasting (or sometimes complementary) explanations for how the causal factors exert their effects. (See Figure 3.7.)

Figure 3.7 Three Major Psychological Perspectives on Alcohol Dependence

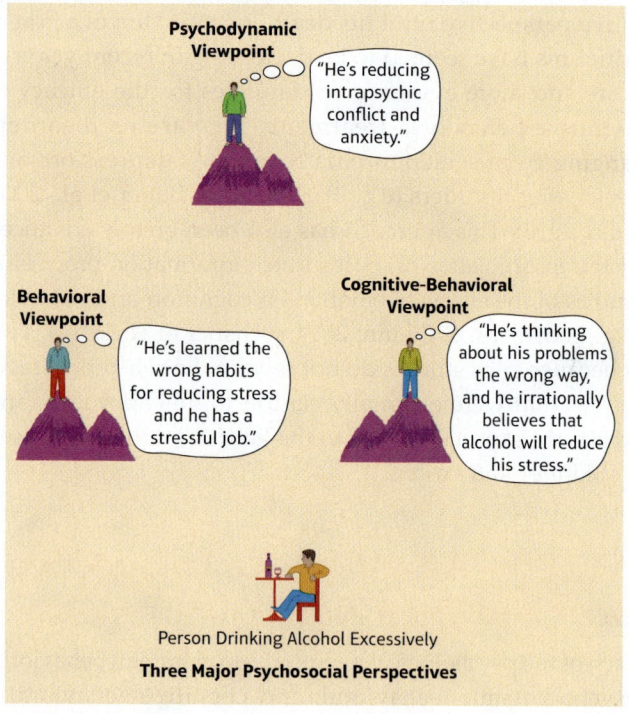

in review

- Contrast the newer psychodynamic perspectives—ego psychology, object-relations theory, and the interpersonal and attachment theory perspectives—with the earlier, Freudian perspective.
- What is the central theme of the behavioral perspective, and what has been its impact?
- How do classical and operant conditioning, generalization, discrimination, and observational learning contribute to the origins of abnormal behavior?
- What is the focus of the cognitive-behavioral perspective, and what has been its impact?
- Why are schemas and self-schemas so important for understanding abnormal behavior and its treatment?
- What role do cognitive distortions and attributions have in psychopathology, according to the cognitive-behavioral perspective?

The Social Perspective

3.5 Describe three social factors known to contribute to abnormal behavior.

We begin life with a great capacity to learn from experience. What we learn from our experiences may help us face challenges resourcefully and may lead to resilience in the face of future stressors. Unfortunately, some of our experiences may be much less helpful in our later lives, and we may be deeply influenced by factors in early childhood over which we have no control. One good example of ways

in which the events in one child's life may be vastly different from those in another child's life is whether they are *predictable* or *controllable*. Exposure to multiple uncontrollable and unpredictable frightening events is likely to leave a person vulnerable to anxiety and negative affect, a central problem in a number of mental disorders such as anxiety and depression (Barlow, 2002; Mineka & Zinbarg, 2006). It is important to note that a person exposed to the same frequency and intensity of negative outcomes that are predictable and/or controllable will experience less stress and be less likely to develop anxiety or depression.

In this section we examine the types of social factors that make people vulnerable to disorder or that may precipitate disorder. Social factors are environmental influences—often unpredictable and uncontrollable negative events—that can negatively affect a person psychologically, making him or her less resourceful in coping with events. We will focus on several different types of social factors that can each have important detrimental effects on a child's socioemotional development: (1) early deprivation or trauma, (2) problems in parenting style, (3) marital discord and divorce, (4) low socioeconomic status and unemployment, (5) maladaptive peer relationships, and (6) prejudice and discrimination.

Early Deprivation or Trauma

Children who do not have the resources that are typically supplied by parents or parental surrogates may be left with deep and sometimes irreversible psychological scars. The needed resources range from food and shelter to love and attention. Deprivation of such resources can occur in several forms. The most severe manifestations of deprivation are usually seen among abandoned or orphaned children, who may be either institutionalized or placed in a succession of unwholesome and inadequate foster homes. However, it can also occur in intact families where, for one reason or another, parents are unable (for instance, because of mental disorder) or unwilling to provide close and frequent human attention and nurturing.

INSTITUTIONALIZATION In some cases children are raised in an institution where, compared with an ordinary home, there is likely to be significantly less warmth and physical contact; less intellectual, emotional, and social stimulation; and a lack of encouragement and help in positive learning. Current estimates are that worldwide up to 8 million children live in orphanages (Bos et al., 2011). Research done when institutionalization was more common in the United States and the United Kingdom makes it clear that the long-range prognosis for most children who suffer early and prolonged environmental and social deprivation through institutionalization is unfavorable, especially if the institutionalization lasts longer than 6 months (Beckett et al., 2006; Kreppner et al., 2007; Wiik et al., 2011).

Many children institutionalized in infancy and early childhood show severe emotional, behavioral, and learning problems and are at risk for disturbed attachment relationships and psychopathology (e.g., Bos et al., 2011; Ellis et al., 2004; Smyke et al., 2007).

These problems seem to be mediated, at least in part, by reduced brain development (McLaughlin et al., 2010). Indeed, children raised in institutions from an early age show significant reductions in both gray and white matter volume. In one recent study, researchers compared children raised in Romanian orphanages to never-institutionalized Romanian children. Importantly, the children raised in orphanages were then randomly assigned to either remain in the orphanage or to participate in a foster care intervention. Interestingly, assignment to the foster care intervention was not associated with any significant changes in total gray matter—having been institutionalized was associated with lower total gray matter volume (Sheridan et al., 2012; Figure 3.8). However, the children in the foster care condition showed smaller decreases in white matter volume to the point where they were not significantly different from the never-institutionalized children. This suggests that some effects of institutionalization are persistent, but that with intervention some of the effects of early deprivation can be at least partially reversed.

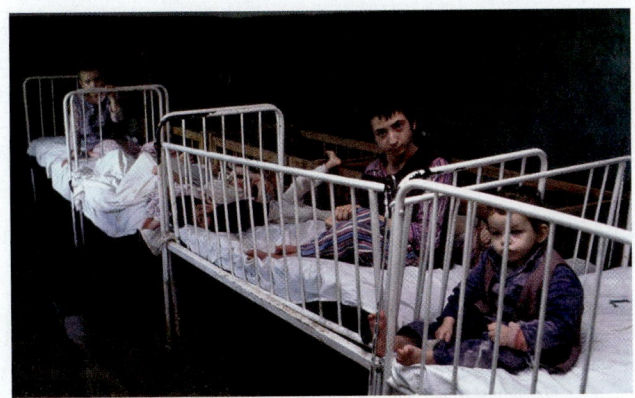

These Romanian orphans spend most of their days in their cribs. The lack of physical contact and social stimulation and support causes many children who are often institutionalized starting in infancy and early childhood to show severe emotional, behavioral, and learning problems. They are also at elevated risk for psychopathology.

Fortunately, the results of this line of research have had a major impact on public policy in this and some other societies, which have recognized the need to place such children in foster or adoptive families rather than in institutions (Johnson, 2000). Accordingly, conducting research on the effects of institutionalization in Western societies is less urgent today—and less feasible—than it once was. Unfortunately, however, enlightened policies have not been implemented in some Eastern European

Figure 3.8 Reduced Brain Development in Institutionalized Children

(a) A study by Sheridan and colleagues (2012) showed that children raised in deprived environments (a Romanian orphanage in this case) have less total cortical gray matter than those in a never-institutionalized group, regardless of whether they were later placed in a more enriched foster care intervention (the "foster care group" or FCG) or not (the "care as usual group" or CAU). (b) The same study by Sheridan and colleagues showed that although the FCG intervention did not counteract the earlier effects of deprivation, it did seem to lessen the decrease in total cortical white matter associated with earlier deprivation, as shown in this figure.

(From Sheridan et al., 2012.)

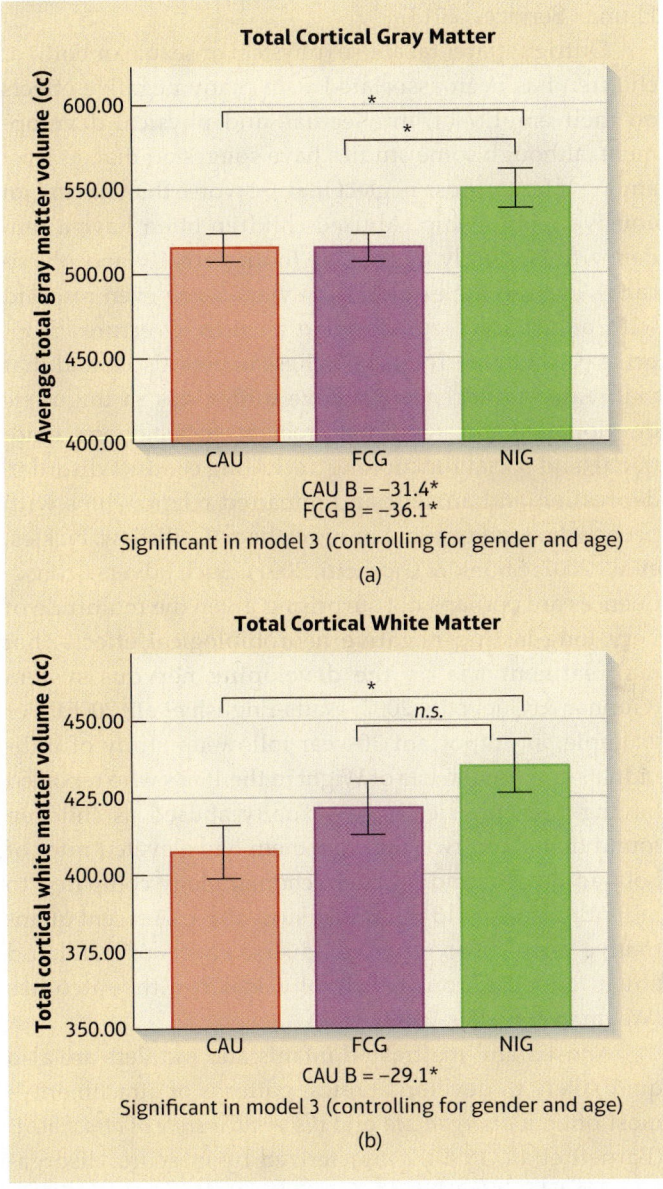

countries and in some other parts of the world, where the plight of children in orphanages has often been deplorable (Johnson, 2000). In general, early institutionalization is associated with long-lasting negative effects, and the earlier children are adopted out of orphanages the better they do (see Johnson, 2000, for a review).

NEGLECT AND ABUSE IN THE HOME Most infants subjected to parental deprivation are not separated from their parents and placed in institutions; rather, they suffer from maltreatment in their own home. In the United States, there are nearly 4 million reports of child maltreatment each year and approximately 20 percent are verified as actual, documented maltreatment. This means that 9 out of every 1,000 children are known to be victims of abuse or neglect, with countless numbers of other unreported cases. The majority (78 percent) of these cases are cases of neglect, with physical abuse (18 percent) and sexual abuse (9 percent) being less common (U.S. Department of Health and Human Services, 2013).

Outright parental abuse (physical or sexual or both) of children has been associated with many negative effects on their emotional, intellectual, and physical development, although some studies have suggested that, at least among infants, gross neglect may be worse than having an abusive relationship. Abused children often have a tendency to be overly aggressive (both verbally and physically), even to the extent of bullying. Some even respond with anger and aggression to friendly overtures from peers (Cicchetti & Toth, 2005). Researchers also found that maltreated children often have difficulties in linguistic development and significant problems in behavioral, emotional, and social functioning, including conduct disorder, depression and anxiety, and impaired relationships with peers, who tend to avoid or reject them (Collishaw, Pickles, et al., 2007; Shonk & Cicchetti, 2001). Such adverse consequences are perhaps not surprising given the multitude of very long-lasting negative neurobiological effects that maltreatment has on the developing nervous system (Gunnar & Quevedo, 2007; Watts-English et al., 2006). For example, an important 30-year follow-up study of individuals born on the Isle of Wight in the 1960s who reported having been physically or sexually abused as children found that about two-thirds of them had elevated rates of both adolescent and adult psychopathology compared to individuals who did not report such abuse. A recent quantitative review also reported adverse effects of childhood abuse on numerous adult physical health outcomes (Wegman & Stetler, 2009).

Abused and maltreated infants and toddlers are also quite likely to develop atypical patterns of attachment—most often a *disorganized* and *disoriented style of attachment* (Barnett et al., 1999), characterized by insecure, disorganized, and inconsistent behavior with the primary caregiver. Such a child might at one point act dazed and show frozen behavior when reunited with his or her caregiver. However, at another point he or she might actually approach the caregiver but then immediately reject and avoid her. A significant portion of these children continue to show these confused patterns of relating to their caregiver up to at least age 13, after which they often expect others to treat them in a similar negative manner and to not expect that they will fare well in such relationships. Consequently, they may selectively avoid new relationships and experiences that could correct their expectations (Shields et al., 2001).

These effects of early abuse may endure into adolescence and adulthood. For example, previously abused or neglected children have, on average, lower levels of education, employment, and earnings (Currie & Widom, 2010). Childhood physical abuse predicts both familial and nonfamilial violence in adolescence and adulthood, especially in abused men (Cicchetti & Toth, 1995b; Serbin & Karp, 2004). Thus, a significant proportion of parents who reject or abuse their children have themselves been the victims of parental rejection. Their early history of rejection or abuse would clearly have had damaging effects on their schemas and self-schemas, and they were probably unable to internalize good models of parenting (e.g., Serbin & Karp, 2004; Shields et al., 2001). Estimates suggest that there is about a 30 percent chance of this pattern of intergenerational transmission of abuse (Kaufman & Zigler, 1989).

It is important to remember that maltreated children—whether the maltreatment comes from abuse or from deprivation—can improve to at least some extent when the caregiving environment improves (Cicchetti & Toth, 1995a; Emery & Laumann-Billings, 1998). Moreover, there are always a range of effects, and those children who are least likely to show these negative outcomes tend to have one or more protective factors such as a good relationship with some adult during childhood, a higher IQ, positive school experiences, or physical attractiveness.

SEPARATION Bowlby (1960, 1973) first summarized the traumatic effects, for children from 2 to 5 years old, of being separated from their parents during prolonged periods of hospitalization. First, there are the short-term or acute effects of the separation, which can include significant despair during the separation as well as detachment from the parents upon reunion; Bowlby considered this to be a normal response to prolonged separation, even in infants with a *secure attachment*. However, he also found evidence that children who undergo a number of such separations may develop an *insecure attachment*. In addition, there can be longer-term effects of early separation from one or both parents. For example, such separations can cause an increased vulnerability to stressors in adulthood, making it more likely that the person will become depressed (Bowlby, 1980) or show other psychiatric symptoms (Canetti et al., 2000; Carlson et al., 2003). As with other early traumatic experiences, the long-term effects of separation depend heavily on whether support and reassurance are given a child by parents or other significant people, which is most likely if the child has a secure relationship with at least one parent (Canetti et al., 2000). Interestingly, many children who experience even a parent's death do not exhibit discernible long-term effects (Canetti et al., 2000).

Watch Separation Anxiety Across Cultures

Problems in Parenting Style

Even in the absence of severe deprivation, neglect, or trauma, many kinds of deviations in parenting can have profound effects on a child's subsequent ability to cope with life's challenges and thus can create a child's vulnerability to various forms of psychopathology. Therefore, although their explanations vary considerably, the psychological viewpoints on causes of psychopathology all focus on the behavioral tendencies a child acquires in the course of early social interaction with others—chiefly parents or parental surrogates (Parke, 2004; Sroufe et al., 2000).

It is important to note that a parent–child relationship is always bidirectional: As in any continuing relationship, the behavior of each person affects the behavior of the other. For instance, children who are anxious, irritable, and impulsive may be more difficult to care for, and can elicit anxiety, irritability, and impulsiveness in their parents. The parents' behavior may in turn lead to worsening in the child's behavior (Crouter & Booth, 2003; Rutter, 2006a).

Problems with parenting style can have profound effects on a child's subsequent ability to cope with life's challenges and thus create vulnerability to various forms of psychopathology.

PARENTAL PSYCHOPATHOLOGY Parents who have various forms of psychopathology (including schizophrenia, depression, antisocial personality disorder, and alcohol use problems) tend to have one or more children who are at heightened risk for a wide range of developmental difficulties (unless protective factors are also present; Brennan et al., 2003; Masten, 2007). The focus of most research in this area has been on mothers, but there is good evidence that fathers with mental disorders or others who are minimally involved in caretaking in infancy can also make significant contributions to child and adolescent psychopathology, especially to problems such as depression, conduct disorder, delinquency, and attention-deficit disorder (Boyce et al., 2006; Phares et al., 2002). Although some of these effects undoubtedly have a genetic component, many researchers believe that genetic influences cannot account for all of the adverse effects that parental psychopathology can have on children (Hammen, 2009; Sher et al., 2005).

Consider some examples. Although many children of people with serious alcohol abuse problems do not have difficulties, others have elevated rates of truancy, substance abuse, and a greater likelihood of dropping out of school, as well as higher levels of anxiety and depression and lower levels of self-esteem (Leonard & Eiden, 2007; Marmorstein et al., 2009). In addition, the children of parents who are seriously depressed are at enhanced risk for depression and other disorders themselves (Burt et al., 2005; Hammen, 2009), at least partly because depression makes for unskillful parenting—notably including either intrusive or withdrawn behavior (Field et al., 2006), excessive criticism, and ineffectiveness in managing and disciplining the children (Rogosch et al., 2004). Not surprisingly, children of mothers with depression also are more likely than children of nondepressed mothers to live in environments with high levels of stress (Hammen, 2009).

PARENTING STYLES: WARMTH AND CONTROL Researchers have been interested in how parenting styles—including their disciplinary styles—affect children's behavior over the course of development. A parenting style reflects an attitude and values that are expressed toward a child across a wide range of settings (Williams et al., 2009). Four types of parenting styles have been identified that seem to be related to different developmental outcomes for children: (1) authoritative, (2) authoritarian, (3) permissive/indulgent, and (4) neglectful/uninvolved. These styles vary in the degree of *parental warmth* (amount of support, encouragement, and affection versus shame, rejection, and hostility) and in the degree of *parental control* (extent of discipline and monitoring versus leaving the children largely unsupervised; Manzeske & Stright, 2009; Morris, 2001). (See Figure 3.9.) Parental control includes both behavioral control (rewards and punishments) and psychological control (e.g., expression of approval versus disapproval, or guilt induction).

Healthy parenting styles are those that reflect warmth and clear limits and restrictions regarding certain kinds of behaviors while allowing considerable freedom within certain boundaries. The children raised in these environments tend to be energetic and friendly and show general competencies for dealing with others.

Authoritative Parenting   The *authoritative style* is one in which the parents are both very warm and very careful to set clear standards and limits on certain kinds of behaviors while allowing considerable freedom within these limits.

They tend to be attentive and sensitive to their children's needs while still enforcing their limits. This style of parenting is associated with the most positive early social development; the children tend to be energetic and friendly and to show development of general competencies for dealing with others and with their environments (Baumrind, 1993; Simons et al., 2005). They also usually have secure attachment relationships and show high levels of overall well-being, as well as good school performance when followed into late adolescence (Berk, 2003; Slicker & Thornberry, 2002). Not surprisingly they also are less likely to exhibit either emotional disorders (e.g., anxiety and depression) or behavioral problems (e.g., conduct problems and delinquency) (Williams et al., 2009). Authoritative parenting also seems to promote resilience in children living in highly stressful contexts (Salem-Pickartz & Donnelly, 2007).

Authoritarian Parenting   Parents with an *authoritarian style* are high on control but low on warmth. They often appear quite cold and demanding, favoring punitive methods if their children disobey. Their children tend to be conflicted, irritable, and moody (Baumrind, 1993; Siegler et al., 2003). When followed into adolescence, these children tend to be lower in social and academic competence than children of authoritative parents, with boys doing particularly poorly in social and cognitive skills. Boys with authoritarian fathers—especially those high on hostility—are also at heightened risk of engaging in substance abuse and other delinquent activity (Bronte-Tinkew et al., 2006; Hoeve et al.,

Figure 3.9 Parenting Styles

Authoritative	Authoritarian	Permissive/ Indulgent	Neglectful/ Uninvolved
Parents are high on warmth and moderate on control, very careful to set clear limits and restrictions regarding certain kinds of behaviors. **Research Shows:** Children tend to be friendly and to show development of general competencies for dealing with others and with their environments.	Parents are low on warmth and high on control and often cold and demanding. **Research Shows:** Children tend to be conflicted, irritable, and moody. When followed into adolescence, these children have more negative outcomes, the boys doing particularly poorly in social and cognitive skills.	Parents are high on warmth and low on control and discipline. **Research Shows:** Children tend to be impulsive and aggressive. Overly indulged children are characteristically spoiled, selfish, impatient, inconsiderate, and demanding.	Parents are low on warmth and low on control. **Research Shows:** Children tend to be moody and to have low self-esteem and conduct problems later in childhood. They also have problems with peer relations and with academic performance.

2009). If such authoritarian parents also use overly severe discipline in the form of physical punishment—as opposed to the withdrawal of approval and privileges—the result tends to be increased aggressive behavior on the part of the child (Berk, 2003).

Permissive/Indulgent Parenting   Parents with a *permissive/indulgent style* are high on warmth but low on discipline and control. This lenient style of parenting is associated with impulsive and aggressive behavior in childhood and adolescence (Baumrind, 1967; Hetherington & Parke, 1993). Overly indulged children are characteristically spoiled, selfish, impatient, inconsiderate, and demanding (Baumrind, 1971, 1975). In adolescence, they tend to do less well academically and to show more antisocial behaviors (Steinberg et al., 2006). Confusion and difficulties in adjustment may occur when "reality" forces them to reassess their assumptions about themselves and the world.

Neglectful/Uninvolved Parenting   Finally, parents who are low both on warmth and on control exhibit the *neglectful/uninvolved style*. They tend to be disengaged and not supportive of their children. This style of parental uninvolvement is associated with disruptions in attachment during early childhood (Egeland & Sroufe, 1981; Karavasilis et al., 2003) and with moodiness, low self-esteem, and conduct problems later in childhood. These children of uninvolved parents also have problems with peer relations and with academic performance (Hetherington & Parke, 1993; see also Berk, 2003).

Marital Discord and Divorce

Disturbed parent–child patterns such as parental rejection are rarely found in severe form unless the total familial context is also abnormal. Thus, disturbed family structure is an overarching risk factor that increases an individual's vulnerability to particular stressors. We will distinguish between intact families where there is significant marital discord and families that have been disrupted by divorce or separation.

MARITAL DISCORD   All couples argue, but when taken to an extreme, marital discord can have damaging psychological effects on both adults and their children (e.g., Amato, 2006; Amato & Booth, 2001; Parke, 2004). More severe cases of marital discord may expose children to one or more of the stressors we have already discussed: child abuse or neglect, the effects of living with a parent with a serious mental disorder, authoritarian or neglectful/uninvolved parenting, and spouse abuse. But even less severe cases of marital discord also have negative effects on many children. For example, children of parents with high levels of overt conflict show a greater disposition to behave aggressively toward both their peers and their

parents than children from less conflictual marriages (Cummings et al., 2004; Du Rocher Schudlich, et al., 2004). College students who report high levels of marital conflict in their parents also show elevated conflict in their own romantic relationships, which in turn is linked to poorer quality of their own romantic relationships (Cui & Fincham, 2010). Interestingly, children can be buffered against many of the damaging effects of marital conflict if one or both parents have the following characteristics: warmth, proneness to giving praise and approval, and ability to inhibit rejecting behavior toward their children (Katz & Gottman, 1997). Longitudinal studies have documented that the damaging effects of serious marital discord on children continue into adulthood: The offspring's own marriages are more likely to be marked by discord (whether or not the parents divorced). Some of this intergenerational transmission of marital discord may be the result of the offspring having learned negative interaction styles by observing their own parents' marital interactions (Amato, 2006; Amato & Booth, 2001).

DIVORCED FAMILIES   Nearly 20 percent of marriages end in divorce around the world, and the United States' rate is among the highest at 40 percent (Breslau et al., 2011). Estimates suggest that approximately 20 percent of children under the age of 18 are living in a single-parent household—some with unwed parents and some with divorced parents.

Effects of Divorce on Parents   Unhappy marriages are difficult, but ending a marital relationship can also be enormously stressful for the adults, both mentally and physically. The negative effects are often temporary, with most people being able to adapt constructively within 2 to 3 years, but some adults never fully recover (Amato, 2000; Hetherington, 2003a). Divorced and separated persons are overrepresented among psychiatric patients, although the *direction of the causal relationship* is not always clear. It should also be recognized, however, that divorce actually benefits some individuals (Amato, 2000, 2010)—with some evidence that women are more likely to benefit than men (Hetherington, 2003a). There is also some evidence that individuals who were in high-distress marriages before divorce are more likely to show an increase in happiness than are individuals who were in low-distress marriages before divorce (Amato & Hohmann-Marriott, 2007). In addition, favorable adjustment after divorce is positively associated with higher income, dating someone steadily, remarriage, having had relatively favorable attitudes toward divorce before it happened, and being the partner who initiated the divorce (Amato, 2000).

Effects of Divorce on Children   Divorce can have traumatic effects on children, too. Feelings of insecurity and rejection may be aggravated by conflicting loyalties. Delinquency and a wide range of other psychological problems such as anxiety and depression are much more frequent among children and adolescents from divorced families than among those from intact families, although it is likely that a contributing factor here is prior or continuing parental strife (Strohschein, 2005). However, findings also show that, on average, such children had shown these problems to some degree even before their parents divorced (Amato, 2010; Strohschein, 2005). In addition, the adverse effects of divorce on adaptive functioning may persist into adulthood. On average, compared to young adults from families without divorce, young adults from divorced families have somewhat lower educational attainment, lower incomes, lower life satisfaction, and an increased probability of being on welfare and having children out of wedlock (Chase-Lansdale et al., 1995; Hetherington et al., 1998). Children from divorced families are also more likely to have their own marriages end in divorce (Amato & DeBoer, 2001; Hetherington, 2003b). There is evidence that these effects even occurred in a subsequent third generation. Specifically, in a study of nearly 700 grandparents and their grandchildren, Amato and Cheadle (2005) found that divorce in the grandparents was associated with lower education, more marital discord, and weaker parental ties in the grandchildren.

Research Close-Up
Direction of the Causal Relationship

Recall that, in a correlational or observational study, an association between two variables does not allow us to make inferences about causal direction. For example, divorce could precipitate psychological problems. Alternatively, people with psychological disorders might be more likely to have problematic marriages and end up divorced.

Nevertheless, many children adjust quite well to the divorce of their parents. Indeed, a quantitative review of 92 studies on parental divorce and the well-being of children, conducted on 13,000 children from 1950 to 1990, concluded that the average negative effects of divorce on children are actually quite modest, as are the negative effects persisting into adulthood (Amato & Keith, 1991b). Amato and Keith (1991a, 1991b) also found that the negative effects of divorce seemed to decrease from the 1950s through the 1980s (particularly since 1970), perhaps because the stigma of divorce was decreasing. However, a follow-up review of 67 such studies published in the 1990s showed no further decreases in these negative effects since 1990 (Amato, 2001).

The effects of divorce on children are often more favorable than the effects of remaining in a home torn by marital conflict and dissension (Amato, 2010; Amato & Keith, 1991b). At one time it was thought that the detrimental effects of divorce might be minimized if a successful remarriage provided an adequate environment for childrearing. Unfortunately, however, the Amato and Keith (1991b) review revealed that children living with a stepparent were often no better off than children living with a single parent, although this was truer for girls than for boys. Other studies have shown that children—especially very young children—living with a stepparent are at increased risk for physical abuse (injury and even death) by the stepparent relative to children living with two biological parents (Daly & Wilson, 1988, 1996).

Low Socioeconomic Status and Unemployment

In our society the lower the socioeconomic class, the higher the incidence of mental and physical disorders (Caracci & Mezzich, 2001; Conger & Donnellan, 2007). The strength of this inverse correlation varies with different types of mental disorder, however. For example, antisocial personality disorder is strongly related to socioeconomic status (SES), occurring about 3 times as often in the lowest income category as in the highest income category, whereas depressive disorders occur only about 1.5 times as often in the lowest income category as in the highest income category (Kessler & Zhao, 1999; Monroe et al., 2009).

There are many reasons for this general inverse association. One factor is that some people with mental disorders slide down to the lower rungs of the economic ladder and remain there, sometimes because they do not have the economic or personal resources to climb back up (Gottesman, 1991) and sometimes because of prejudice and stigma against those with mental illness (Caracci & Mezzich, 2001). Another factor is that, on average, people who live in poverty encounter more—and more severe—stressors in their lives, than do more affluent people, and they usually have fewer resources for dealing with them (Twenge & Campbell, 2002).

Children and adolescents from lower SES families also tend to have more psychological problems. One recent, large-scale study of U.S. adolescents examined different measures of low SES and found that adolescents' *perceptions* of their social status are most strongly linked to higher rates of mental disorders, more so than factors like family income (McLaughlin, Costello, et al., 2012). It is important to keep in mind that many children from lower SES homes do very well, especially those with higher IQs and those with adequate relationships at home, in school, and with peers (Felsman & Valliant, 1987; Long & Valliant, 1984; Masten & Coatsworth, 1995).

Studies have repeatedly found unemployment—with its financial hardships, self-devaluation, and emotional distress—to be associated with enhanced vulnerability to psychopathology (e.g., Dooley et al., 2000; Grzywacz & Dooley, 2003; Thomas et al., 2007). In particular, rates of depression, marital problems, and somatic (bodily) complaints increase during periods of unemployment but usually normalize when employment rates recover (Jones, 1992; Murphy & Athanasou, 1999). These effects occur even when mental health status before unemployment is taken into account. Not surprisingly, the wives of unemployed men are also adversely affected, exhibiting higher levels of anxiety, depression, and hostility, which seem to be at least partially caused by the distress of the unemployed husband (Dew et al., 1987). Children too can be seriously affected. In the worst cases, unemployed fathers are much more likely to engage in child abuse (Cicchetti & Lynch, 1995; Dew et al., 1991).

Finally, economic crises since 1990 have centered not only on unemployment but also on the effects that corporate restructuring and downsizing have had on upper-middle-class people, many of whom find themselves having to look for jobs requiring lower skills and paying much lower incomes than they earned in the past. In other cases people are forced to work only part time and often do not make enough to live on. Several large studies of people who were underemployed (or who had inadequate employment) found that rates of depression were comparable or nearly comparable to those seen in unemployed individuals (Dooley & Prause, 2004; Dooley et al., 2000; Grzywacz & Dooley, 2003).

Maladaptive Peer Relationships

Learning how to navigate the world as a child can be a difficult and confusing task. Learning how to successfully navigate relationships with your peers can be even harder. Many children and adolescents are able to develop healthy and adaptive peer relationships with no major disruptions. However, some will experience different types of problems, such as becoming a bully or the victim of some form of intentional exclusion or aggression. Unfortunately, such problems in peer relationships are associated with an increased risk of psychological disorders.

Several studies have found bullies to show high levels of both proactive aggression (where they initiate the aggressive behavior) and reactive aggression (where they overreact when confronted; Salmivalli, 2010; Salmivalli & Nieminen, 2002). Although some bullies probably behave this way because of deficits in social skills, others have a more sophisticated understanding of social behavior, which enables them to manipulate and organize their peers (often driven by status goals) so that they can avoid being caught while making others suffer (Salmivalli, 2010). Most children report having negative attitudes toward bullying; however, studies suggest that when bullying actually occurs most students do nothing to intervene or support

the victim (and as many as 20 to 30 percent actually encourage the bully; Salmivalli, 2010; Salmivalli & Voeten, 2004). A small percentage (approximately 20 percent), however, do take the side of the victim and may even help defend him or her. Victims who have one or more classmates defend them show less distress and higher self-esteem.

In recent years a new form of particularly insidious bullying has emerged as an enormous problem in many North American schools. *Cyberbullying*, as it is called, includes sending offensive, harassing, or intimidating messages over the Internet, spreading ugly rumors on certain Internet sites, and spreading someone's very personal information (Willard, 2007). Some estimate that as many as one-third of teenagers who use the Internet engage in cyberbullying (Li, 2007; Scharnberg, 2007). The psychological consequences of cyberbullying on the victims can be very serious—including anxiety, school phobia, lower self-esteem, suicidal ideation, and occasional cases of suicide (Thomas, 2006).

Cyberbulling has emerged as a new and especially troublesome form of bullying. Amanda Todd, a 15-year-old high school student, was repeatedly bullied online, leading to problems with anxiety, depression, drug use, and ultimately to her suicide.

Fortunately, there is another side to this coin. Peer relations can be difficult, but they can also be sources of key learning experiences that stand an individual in good stead for many years. For a resourceful child, the winning and losing and the successes and failures of the school years provide excellent training in coming to grips with the real world and with her or his developing self—its capabilities and limitations, its attractive and unattractive qualities. The experience of intimacy with a friend has its beginning in this period of intense social involvement. If all goes well, a child emerges into adolescence with a considerable repertoire of social knowledge and skills that add up to social competence. Such resources can be strong protective factors against parental rejection, frustration, demoralization, despair, and mental disorder (Masten, 2007; Sentse et al., 2010).

SOURCES OF POPULARITY VERSUS REJECTION What determines which children will be popular and which will be rejected? There seem to be two types of popular children—the prosocial and the antisocial types. *Prosocial* popular children communicate with their peers in friendly and assertive yet cooperative ways. They tend to be good students relative to their less popular peers (Zettergreen, 2003). *Antisocial* popular children—usually boys—tend to be "tough boys" who may be athletically skilled but who do poorly academically. They tend to be highly aggressive and defiant of authority (Berk, 2003).

Juvenile socializing is a risky business in which a child's hard-won prestige in a group is probably perceived as being constantly in jeopardy. Actually, reputation and status in a group tend to be stable, and a child who has been rejected by peers is likely to continue to have problems in peer relationships.

Much attention has been devoted to determining why some children are persistently rejected by their peers and the consequences of such rejection. There also appear to be two types of rejected children—those who are too aggressive and those who are very withdrawn (Ladd, 2006). The rejected children who are aggressive take an excessively demanding or aggressive approach when interacting with their peers. They often take offense too readily and attribute hostile intent to the teasing of their peers, thus escalating confrontations to unintended levels (Dodge, 2006; Reijntjes et al., 2011). Indeed, the tendency to attribute hostile intent to others in grade 8 has been shown to predict levels of antisocial behavior in grade 11 (Lansford et al., 2006). Such children also tend to take a more punitive and less forgiving attitude toward such situations (Coie et al., 1991; Crick & Dodge, 1994). This may be especially likely in children who have been maltreated by their parents and have therefore developed maladaptive mental representations of caregivers and expect maltreatment. Expecting maltreatment, they may approach social situations with hyperarousal, anxiety, and angry reactivity, which may be

consistent with what they have experienced at home but is out of synch with the context they share with peers (Cicchetti & Toth, 2005; Shields et al., 2001). In addition, having a poor ability to understand a peer's emotions (such as fear and sadness) in kindergarten also predicts aggressive behavior toward peers in the third grade (Dodge et al., 2002).

The second subset of children who may become chronic victims of rejection are not aggressive but, rather, are highly unassertive and quite submissive toward their peers, often because of social anxiety and fear of being scorned or attacked (Schwartz et al., 1993). Such isolation is likely to have serious consequences because it often leads to peer rejection, which in turn deprives a child of further opportunities to learn the rules of social behavior and interchange, rules that become more sophisticated and subtle with increasing age (Coie, 1990; Ladd, 2006). Repeated social failure or becoming the victim of bullies is the usual result, which has further damaging effects on self-confidence and self-esteem and sometimes leads to loneliness, depression, and anxiety, especially during the elementary school years (Burks et al., 1995; Ladd, 2006).

In summary, children who fail to establish satisfactory relationships with peers during the developmental years are deprived of a crucial set of background experiences and are at higher-than-average risk for a variety of negative outcomes in adolescence and adulthood including depression, school dropout, suicidal ideation, and delinquency (Heilbron & Prinstein, 2010). However, one should also remember that peer social problems may also be early markers of disorders that have a heritable component but do not become full blown until later in adolescence or adulthood. Peer social problems may reflect some heritable diathesis, but they also serve as stressors that make it more likely that the underlying vulnerability will lead to full-blown disorder later.

Prejudice and Discrimination in Race, Gender, and Ethnicity

Many members of our society are repeatedly subjected to prejudice (prejudgment based on personal characteristics) and discrimination (unjust treatment of others based on perceived group membership) based on their gender, race (i.e., the category to which others assign a person based on their physical characteristics, such as skin color), and ethnicity (i.e., a social group with a common culture, history, and homeland). Prejudice and discrimination can occur anywhere—on the street, on college campuses, in schools, or in the workplace. For example, two common types of discrimination that occur in the workplace are (1) *access discrimination*, wherein members of a certain group (e.g., women, people of a certain race or ethnicity) are not hired because of their personal characteristics, and (2) *treatment discrimination*, wherein certain types of people are given a job but are paid less and receive fewer opportunities for promotion (Eagly & Carli, 2007; Eagly & Karau, 2002). Beyond the obvious financial effects of such treatment, prejudice and discrimination can lead to higher levels of stress and can have negative downstream effects on a person's physical and mental health.

Indeed, prejudice against minority groups may help to explain why these groups sometimes show increased prevalence of certain mental disorders such as depression (Cohler et al., 1995; Kessler et al., 1994). One possible reason for this is that perceived discrimination may serve as a stressor that threatens self-esteem, which in turn increases psychological distress (e.g., Cassidy et al., 2004). A recent study of Arab and Muslim Americans 2 years after the bombing of the World Trade Center in New York found increased psychological distress, lower levels of happiness, and increased health problems in those who had experienced personal or familial prejudice, discrimination, or violence (Padela & Heisler, 2010).

Experimental laboratory studies have tested how prejudice and discrimination may "get under the skin" to increase the likelihood of negative health outcomes. Such studies have shown that the experience or perception of racial discrimination leads to increases in anger and cardiovascular reactivity (Mendes et al., 2008). In addition, discrimination increases risk-taking behavior, an effect that is partially mediated (or explained) by increased cardiovascular reactivity (Jamieson et al., 2013). Perceived discrimination also predicts lower levels of well-being for women (Ryff et al., 2003).

The Impact of the Social Perspective

With our increased understanding of social influences on mental health, what was previously an almost exclusive concern with individuals' minds has broadened to include a concern with how factors in peoples' environment can influence the occurrence of mental disorders. Research in this area has led to programs designed to improve the social conditions that foster maladaptive behavior and mental disorder, and to community facilities for the early detection, treatment, and long-range prevention of mental disorder. In Chapter 17 we will examine some clinical facilities and other programs—both governmental and private—that have been established as a result of community efforts.

in review

- What are the most important effects of a child's being exposed to early deprivation or abuse?
- What kinds of influences do different parenting styles tend to have on children's development?
- What is the typical range of effects that divorce and marital discord can have on children? What about effects on adults?

- What effects do low SES and unemployment have on adults and children?
- How can prejudice and discrimination have adverse effects on the development of abnormal behavior?

The Cultural Perspective

3.6 Explain how cultural differences can influence perceptions of abnormal behavior.

Understanding the causes of abnormal behavior also requires taking into account the cultural context in which the behavior occurs. Indeed, what is considered to be normal and abnormal differs in different places around the world. Sociology and anthropology have shown that individual personality development reflects the larger society—its institutions, norms, values, and ideas—as well as the immediate family and other groups. Studies in these disciplines have illuminated the relationship between various sociocultural conditions and mental disorders (for example, the relationship between the particular stressors in a given society and the types of mental disorders that typically occur in it). Further studies showed that the patterns of both physical and mental disorders within a given society could change over time as sociocultural conditions change. These discoveries have added important new dimensions to modern perspectives on abnormal behavior (Fabrega, 2001; Tsai et al., 2001; Westermeyer & Janca, 1997).

The cultural perspective is concerned with the impact of culture on the definition and manifestation of mental disorders. The relationships are complex. However, cross-cultural research can enhance our knowledge about the range of variation that is possible in human behavioral and emotional development and can generate ideas about what causes normal and abnormal behavior—ideas that can later be tested more rigorously in the laboratory (Canino & Alegria, 2008).

Universal and Culture-Specific Symptoms of Disorders

Research supports the view that many psychological disturbances—in both adults and children—are universal, appearing in most cultures studied (Butcher, 2005; Kessler & Ustun, 2008). Examining such issues is, of course, never easy because of the need to adapt psychological tests across barriers of language and culture and to validate their use in other cultures. One example of such research has shown that when some tests are translated into the language of different cultures, they need to be adapted so that they are appropriate for the new cultural context. In addition, care must be taken not to miss what may be culture-specific elements of various disorders such as anxiety and depression (Sue & Chang, 2003; Weisz, Weiss, et al., 2006).

Cultural factors influence the form and course of certain disorders. For example, in Western societies people suffering from stress frequently will become depressed. In China, stress is not manifested as depression but in physical problems such as fatigue and weakness.

The Minnesota Multiphasic Personality Inventory (MMPI-2; see Chapter 4) is the best validated and most widely used test that has been adapted for use in many cultures (e.g., Butcher, 2011). For example, the basic pattern of disturbed thoughts and behaviors that we call schizophrenia can be found among nearly all peoples, although the prevalence and symptoms vary to some degree (Woo & Oei, 2007). Moreover, certain psychological symptoms, as measured, are consistently found among similarly diagnosed clinical groups in many other countries. For example, Butcher (1996a) found that psychiatric patients from Italy, Switzerland, Chile, India, Greece, and the United States who were diagnosed with paranoid schizophrenia produced similar general personality and symptom patterns on the MMPI. The same MMPI-2 pattern was also found to occur among patients with schizophrenia in Japan (Hayama, 1999).

Nevertheless, although some universal symptoms and patterns of symptoms appear, sociocultural factors often influence which disorders develop, the forms they take, how prevalent they are, and their courses. For example, the prevalence of major depressive disorder varies widely across the cultures of the world. In one study conducted in 10 countries around the world, the prevalence ranged from 3 percent in Japan to nearly 17 percent in the United States (Andrade et al., 2004). Differences can also emerge in the prognosis or outcomes of several severe mental disorders in different countries. Several international studies have found a more favorable course of schizophrenia in developing countries than in developed countries (Kulhara & Chakrabarti, 2001).

In another example, Kleinman (1986, 1988) compared the ways in which Chinese people (in Taiwan and the People's Republic of China) and Westerners deal with stress. He found that in Western societies, depression was a frequent reaction to individual stress. In China, on the other hand, he noted a relatively low rate of reported depression (Kleinman, 2004). Instead, the effects of stress were more typically manifested in physical problems such as fatigue, weakness, and other complaints. Moreover, Kleinman and Good (1985) surveyed the experience of depression across cultures. Their data show that important elements of depression in Western societies—for example, the acute sense of guilt typically experienced—do not appear in many other cultures. They also point out that the symptoms of depression, such as sadness, hopelessness, unhappiness, and a lack of pleasure in the things of the world and in social relationships, have dramatically different meanings in different societies. For Buddhists, seeking pleasure from things of the world and social relationships is the basis of all suffering; a willful disengagement is thus the first step toward achieving enlightenment. For Shi'ite Muslims in Iran, grief is a religious experience associated with recognition of the tragic consequences of living justly in an unjust world; the ability to experience grief fully is thus a marker of depth of personality and understanding.

In addition to the influence of culture on the symptoms experienced in different cultures, there are also entire patterns of symptoms in certain cultures that are unlike the patterns experienced in most other parts of the world. Although a variety of these culture-specific manifestations of mental disorders will be discussed in various parts of this text, the few discussed here serve to illustrate the general idea. In recent years, for example, a phenomenon known as *hikikomori* has emerged as quite common in Japan, affecting as many as 700,000 individuals. This is a disorder of acute social withdrawal in which young people just remain in their room in their parents' house and refuse social interactions for at least 6 months, but often for many years. Hikikomori seems to be caused, at least in part, by a combination of shy temperament, parental rejection, poor parental attachment, and social exclusion by peers (Krieg & Dickie, 2013). These potential causal factors are universal, but the outcome or manifestation of the resulting abnormal behavior can look different in different cultures. Other examples of culture-specific manifestations of mental disorders will be covered in subsequent chapters (such as *koro* and *taijin kyofusho* discussed in Chapter 6).

Culture and Over- and Undercontrolled Behavior

Studies of the prevalence of different kinds of childhood psychopathology in different cultures raise some fascinating issues. In cultures such as that of Thailand, adults are highly intolerant of *undercontrolled behavior* such as aggression, disobedience, and disrespectful acts in their children (Weisz et al., 2003). Children are explicitly taught to be polite and deferential and to inhibit any expression of anger. This raises interesting questions about whether childhood problems stemming from undercontrolled behavior are lower in Thailand than in the United States, where such behavior seems to be tolerated to a greater extent. It also raises the question of whether problems related to *overcontrolled behavior* such as shyness, anxiety, and depression would be overrepresented in Thailand relative to the United States.

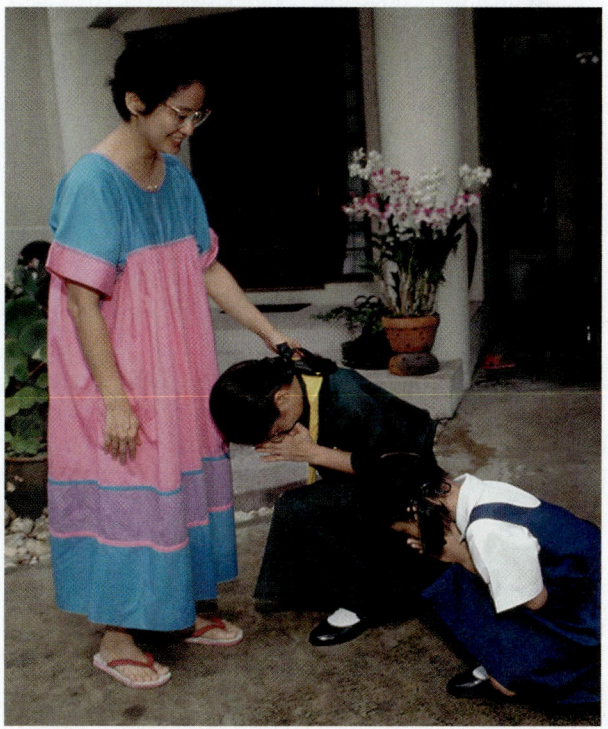

In Thailand, children tend to exhibit *overcontrolled behavior* and are explicitly taught by their parents to be polite and deferential and to inhibit any expression of anger. This is in contrast to American children, whose parents tend to tolerate undercontrolled behavior to a greater extent.

Two cross-national studies (Weisz et al., 1987), confirmed that Thai children and adolescents do indeed have a greater prevalence of overcontrolled problems than do American children. Although there were no differences in the rate of undercontrolled behavior problems between the two countries, there were differences in the kinds of undercontrolled behavior problems reported. For example, Thai adolescents had higher scores than American adolescents on indirect and subtle forms of undercontrol not involving interpersonal aggression such as having difficulty concentrating or being cruel to animals. American adolescents, on the other hand, had higher scores than Thai adolescents on behaviors like fighting, bullying, and disobeying at school (Weisz et al., 1993). In addition, these investigators found that Thai and American parents differ a good deal in which problems they will bring for treatment. In general, Thai parents seem less likely than American parents to refer their children for psychological treatment (Weisz & Weiss, 1991; Weisz et al., 1997). This may be in part because of their Buddhist belief in the transience of problems and their optimism that their child's behavior will improve. Alternatively, Thai parents may not refer their children with undercontrolled problems for treatment simply because these problems are so unacceptable that the parents are embarrassed to go public with them (Weisz et al., 1997).

Cultural differences in psychopathology may also result from differences in what cultures consider to be the ideal kinds of parent–child attachment relationships. The World Around Us box discusses research on cultural differences in what Japanese and Western cultures believe to be the nature of ideal versus disordered attachment relationships.

in review

- Give an example of universal and culture-specific symptoms of disorders.
- What cultural factors help account for differences in problems involving overcontrolled and undercontrolled behavior in Thai versus American children?

The World Around Us

Culture and Attachment Relationships

Recently, research has shown that there are significant cross-cultural differences in views of ideal parent–child attachment relationships. Accordingly, there are different views of what constitutes disordered attachment relationships that can increase risk for psychopathology. Views on the function of good attachment relationships (and the nature of disordered attachment) in Western cultures have been found to differ rather dramatically from those seen in Japan (Rothbaum, Weisz, et al., 2000, 2001). In Western societies, secure attachment relationships are thought to occur when a mother responds in a sensitive fashion to a child's signals (e.g., signs of hunger or discomfort) yet gradually allows the child to explore the environment and develop some autonomy. In the United States one study found that teachers similarly prefer to respond to explicit expression of needs and to foster children's independence and self-expression, which would also foster secure attachments (Rothbaum et al., 2006). Importantly, securely attached children (relative to insecurely attached children) are thought to be less anxious and depressed, better able to cope with negative emotional states, and better able to form close relationships with peers.

However, in Japan, parents' goals are to anticipate all the child's needs and thereby avoid any exposure to stress such as hunger or discomfort and to foster dependency (Rothbaum, Weisz, et al., 2000, 2001). Japanese teachers also prefer to anticipate their students' needs and to foster dependency on other tasks (Rothbaum et al., 2006). Accordingly, children who are considered securely attached in Japan are very dependent on their mothers (and teachers), and independent children are thought to have disturbed attachments. Moreover, because the Japanese value social harmony, children who are dependent and emotionally restrained and who express their feelings only indirectly are the ones viewed as competent; they also tend to be self-critical and self-effacing. This is very different from Western cultures, where children who show exploration and autonomy and are willing to express strong feelings and even disagreement openly are considered to be socially competent. Such children in Western cultures also tend to have positive self-views (Rothbaum, Weisz, et al., 2000).

Given such differences, it is not surprising that different clinical interventions are viewed as appropriate for children with behavior problems in these two cultures. For example, American therapists often help their clients to develop their own separate identities and assume that expression of negative feelings toward others (including parents) may be necessary. By contrast, Japanese therapists are more likely to encourage clients to be grateful to others (especially their parents) and encourage devotion (see Rothbaum, Weisz, et al., 2000, 2001).

Mismatches between cultural expectations and children's behavior can lead to that behavior being considered abnormal. Based on what you have learned so far, when would that behavior be considered a mental disorder?

Unresolved Issues

Theoretical Perspectives and the Causes of Abnormal Behavior

The perspectives described in this chapter are theoretical constructions devised to orient psychologists in the study of abnormal behavior. As a set of hypothetical guidelines, each perspective emphasizes the importance and integrity of its own position to the exclusion of other explanations. Most psychodynamically oriented clinicians, for example, value those traditional writings and beliefs consistent with Freudian or later psychodynamic theories, and they minimize or ignore the teachings of opposing viewpoints. They usually adhere to prescribed practices of psychodynamic therapy and do not use other methods such as exposure therapy.

Advantages of Having a Theoretical Perspective

Theoretical integrity and adherence to a systematic viewpoint have a key advantage: They ensure a consistent approach to one's practice or research efforts. Once mastered, the methodology can guide a practitioner or researcher through the complex web of human problems. But such adherence to a theory has its disadvantages. By excluding other possible explanations, it can blind researchers to other factors that may be equally important. The fact is that none of the theories devised to date addresses the whole spectrum of abnormality—each is limited in some way in its focus.

Two general trends have occurred as a result. First, the original model or theory may be revised by expanding or modifying some elements of the system. The many examples of such modified interpretations include Adler's and Erikson's modifications of Freudian theory and the more recent cognitive-behavioral approach's modification of behavior therapy. But many of the early Freudian theorists did not accept the neo-Freudian additions, and some classical behavior therapists today still do not accept the revisions proposed by cognitive behaviorists. Therefore, the second trend has been for theoretical viewpoints to multiply and coexist—each with its own proponents—rather than being assimilated into previous views.

The Eclectic Approach

Alternatively, aspects of two or more diverse approaches may be combined in a more general, eclectic approach. In practice, many psychologists have responded to the existence of many perspectives by adopting an eclectic stance; that is, they accept working ideas from several viewpoints and incorporate whichever they find useful. For example, a psychologist using an eclectic approach might accept causal explanations from psychodynamic theory while applying techniques of anxiety reduction from behavior therapy. Another psychologist might combine techniques from the cognitive-behavioral approach with those from the interpersonal approach. Purists in the field—those who advocate a single viewpoint—are skeptical about eclecticism, claiming that an eclectic approach tends to lack integrity and produces a "crazy quilt" of inconsistent practice with little rationale. This criticism may be true, but the approach certainly seems to work for many psychotherapists.

Typically, those who use an eclectic approach to treatment make no attempt to synthesize the theoretical perspectives. Although this approach can work in practical settings, it is not successful at a theoretical level because the underlying principles of many of the theoretical perspectives are incompatible as they now stand. Thus, the eclectic approach still falls short of the final goal, which is to tackle the theoretical clutter and develop a single, comprehensive, internally consistent viewpoint that accurately reflects what we know empirically about abnormal behavior.

The Biopsychosocial Unified Approach

At present, the only attempt at such a unified perspective that has been developing is called the *biopsychosocial perspective.* This viewpoint reflects the conviction that most disorders are the result of many causal factors—biological, psychological, and sociocultural—interacting with one another. Moreover, for any given person, the particular combination of causal factors may be unique, or at least not widely shared by large numbers of people with the same disorder. For example, some children may become delinquents primarily because of having a heavy genetic loading for antisocial behavior, whereas others may become delinquent primarily because of environmental influences such as living in an area with a large number of gangs. Therefore, we can still hope to achieve a scientific understanding of many of the causes of abnormal behavior even if we cannot predict such behavior with exact certainty in each individual case and are often left with some "unexplained" influences.

Summary

3.1 Distinguish between risk factors and causes of abnormal behavior.

- In considering the causes of abnormal behavior, it is important to distinguish among necessary, sufficient, and contributory causal factors, as well as between relatively distal causal factors and those that are more proximal.

- Usually the occurrence of abnormal or maladaptive behavior is considered to be the joint product of a person's predisposition or vulnerability (diathesis) to disorder and of certain stressors that challenge his or her coping resources.

- The concept of protective factors is important for understanding why some people with both a diathesis and a stressor may remain resilient and not develop a disorder.

3.2 List the perspectives that psychologists take to understand the causes of abnormal behavior.

This chapter discusses biological, psychological, social, and cultural perspectives, each of which tends to emphasize the importance of causal factors of a characteristic type. Ultimately we strive for an integrative biopsychosocial viewpoint.

3.3 Explain what the biological perspective tells us about abnormal behavior and also explain the biological causal factors of abnormal behavior.

- In examining biologically based vulnerabilities, we must consider abnormalities in genetics, brain dysfunction and neural plasticity, neurotransmitter and hormonal abnormalities in the brain or other parts of the central nervous system, and temperament.

- Genetic vulnerabilities can affect the development of mental disorders through multiple mechanisms, including ways in which the genotype may affect the phenotype (genotype–environment correlations) and ways in which they affect an individual's susceptibility to environmental influences (genotype–environment interactions).

- Methods for studying the extent of genetic versus environmental influences include the family history method, the twin method, and the adoption method. More recently, linkage analysis and association studies are beginning to contribute knowledge about the exact location of genes contributing to mental disorders.

- Studies of neural plasticity have shown that genetic programs for brain development are not as fixed as once believed and that existing neural circuits can often be modified based on experience.

- Many different neurotransmitter and hormonal abnormalities contribute to the development of mental disorders because of the effects they exert on different relevant brain and body areas for different disorders.

- Temperament is strongly influenced by genetic factors and refers to a baby's characteristic ways of reacting to the environment and his or her ways of self-regulation. It forms the basis of our adult personality, which in turn influences our vulnerability to different disorders.

3.4 Describe the most prominent psychological perspectives on abnormal psychology.

- In examining psychologically based vulnerabilities, three primary perspectives have developed since the end of the nineteenth century: psychodynamic, behavioral, and cognitive-behavioral.

- The oldest psychological viewpoint on abnormal behavior is Freudian psychoanalytic theory. For many years this view was preoccupied with questions about libidinal (id) energies and their containment.

- More recently, four second-generation psychodynamic theories departed in significant ways from Freud's original ideas.

- Anna Freud's ego psychology focused on the important role of the ego in normal and abnormal behavior, with special attention focused on ego-defense reactions.

- Object-relations theorists focused on the role of the quality of very early (pre-Oedipal) mother–infant relationships for normal development.

- The originators of the interpersonal perspective took exception to the Freudian emphasis on the internal determinants of motivation and behavior and instead emphasized the social and cultural forces that shape behavior.

- Attachment theory, which has roots in both the interpersonal and object-relations perspectives, emphasizes the importance of early experiences with attachment relationships for laying the foundation for later child, adolescent, and adult development.

- Psychoanalysis and closely related therapeutic approaches are termed *psychodynamic* in recognition of their attention to inner, often unconscious forces.

- The behavioral perspective focuses on the role of learning in human behavior and attributes maladaptive behavior either to a failure to learn appropriate behaviors or to the learning of maladaptive behaviors.

- The primary forms of learning studied are classical conditioning and operant (instrumental) conditioning. The effects of each are modified by principles of generalization and discrimination. Observational learning is also important.

- Adherents of the behavioral viewpoint attempt to alter maladaptive behavior by extinguishing it or providing training in new, more adaptive behaviors.

- The cognitive-behavioral viewpoint attempts to incorporate the complexities of human cognition, and how it can become distorted, into an understanding of the causes of psychopathology.

- People's schemas and self-schemas play a central role in the way they process information, in how they attribute outcomes to causes, and in their values. The efficiency, accuracy, and coherence of a person's schemas and self-schemas and attributions appear to provide an important protection against breakdown.

- Treatments developed from the cognitive-behavioral perspective attempt to alter maladaptive thinking and improve a person's abilities to solve problems and to achieve goals.

3.5 **Describe three social factors known to contribute to abnormal behavior.**

- Sources of psychologically determined vulnerability include early deprivation or trauma, problems in parenting style, marital discord and divorce, low socioeconomic status and unemployment, maladaptive peer relationships, and prejudice and discrimination.

3.6 **Explain how cultural differences can influence perceptions of abnormal behavior.**

- The cultural perspective is concerned with the contribution of cultural variables to mental disorder.

- Although many serious mental disorders are fairly universal, the form that some disorders take and their prevalence vary widely among different cultures.

- The biopsychosocial approach is promising, but in many ways it is merely a descriptive acknowledgment of the complex interactions among biological, psychological, and sociocultural risk factors rather than a clearly articulated theory of how they interact.

Key Terms

adoption method, p. 70
association studies, p. 71
attachment theory, p. 81
attribution, p. 88
behavior genetics, p. 69
biopsychosocial viewpoint, p. 66
castration anxiety, p. 79
causal risk factor, p. 61
chromosomes, p. 67
classical conditioning, p. 83
cognitive-behavioral
   perspective, p. 86
concordance rate, p. 69
contributory cause, p. 62
correlate, p. 61

cortisol, p. 74
developmental psychopathology, p. 65
developmental systems
   approach, p. 72
diathesis, p. 63
diathesis–stress models, p. 63
discrimination, p. 85
ego, p. 77
ego-defense mechanisms, p. 78
ego psychology, p. 80
Electra complex, p. 79
etiology, p. 61
extinction, p. 84
family history method, p. 69
fixed marker, p. 61

generalization, p. 85
genes, p. 67
genotype, p. 68
genotype–environment
   correlation, p. 68
genotype–environment
   interaction, p. 68
hikikomori, p. 100
hormones, p. 74
hypothalamic-pituitary-adrenal
   (HPA) axis, p. 74
id, p. 77
interpersonal perspective, p. 80
intrapsychic conflicts, p. 77
learning, p. 83

Chapter 4
Clinical Assessment and Diagnosis

 Learning Objectives

4.1 Identify the basic elements in assessment.

4.2 Describe the factors involved in the assessment of the physical organism.

4.3 Explain the interview process, clinical observation, and testing in psychosocial assessment.

4.4 Evaluate the case study of a woman who experienced violence in the workplace.

4.5 Discuss how practitioners integrate assessment data in treatment planning.

4.6 Explain the process for classifying abnormal behavior.

The assessment of the personality and motivation of others has been of interest to people since antiquity. Hathaway (1965) pointed out that one of the earliest descriptions of using behavioral observation in assessing personality can be found in the Old Testament. Gideon relied on observations of his men who trembled with fear to consider whether they were fit for duty; Gideon also observed how soldiers chose to drink water from a stream as a means of selecting effective men for battle. In ancient Rome, Tacitus provided examples in which the appraisal of a person's personality entered into their leader's judgments about them. Tacitus (translated by Grant, 1956, p. 36) points out that Emperor Tiberius evaluated his subordinates in his meetings by often pretending to be hesitant in order to detect what the leading men were thinking.

Psychological assessment is one of the oldest and most widely developed branches of contemporary psychology, dating back to the work of Galton (1879) in the nineteenth century (Butcher, 2010; Weiner & Greene, 2008). In this chapter we focus on the initial clinical assessment and on arriving at a clinical diagnosis according to *DSM-5*. **Psychological assessment** refers to a procedure by which clinicians, using psychological tests, observation, and interviews, develop a summary of the client's symptoms and problems. **Clinical diagnosis** is the process through which a clinician arrives at a general "summary classification" of the patient's symptoms by following a clearly defined system such as *DSM-5* or *ICD-10* (*International Classification of Diseases*), the latter published by the World Health Organization (WHO).

Assessment is an ongoing process and may be important at various points during treatment, not just at the beginning—for example, to examine the client's progress in treatment or to evaluate the outcome. In the initial clinical assessment, an attempt is usually made to identify the main dimensions of a client's problem and to predict the probable course of events under various conditions. It is at this initial stage that crucial decisions have to be made—such as what (if any) treatment approach is to be offered, whether the problem will require hospitalization, to what extent family members will need to be included as co-clients, and so on. Sometimes these decisions must be made quickly, as in emergency conditions, and without critical information. As will be seen, various psychological measurement instruments are employed to maximize assessment efficiency in this type of pretreatment examination process (Harwood & Beutler, 2009).

A less obvious, but equally important, function of pretreatment assessment is establishing baselines for various psychological functions so that the effects of treatment can be measured. For example, Kamphaus, Reynolds, and Dever (2014) showed the importance of childhood assessment screening for determining the behavioral and emotional risk children experience in schools as a means of ensuring adequate adjustment and performance later. Criteria based on these measurements may be established as part of the treatment plan such that the therapy is considered successful and is terminated only when the client's behavior meets these predetermined criteria. Also, as we will see in later chapters, comparison of posttreatment with pretreatment assessment results is an essential feature of many research projects designed to evaluate the effectiveness of various therapies.

In this chapter, we review some of the more commonly used assessment procedures and show how the data obtained can be integrated into a coherent clinical picture for making decisions about referral and treatment. Our survey includes a discussion of physical, neurological, and neuropsychological assessment; the clinical interview; behavioral observation; and personality assessment through the use of projective and objective psychological tests. Later in the chapter we examine the process of arriving at a clinical diagnosis using *DSM-5*.

Let us look first at what exactly a clinician is trying to learn during the psychological assessment of a client.

The Basic Elements in Assessment

4.1   Identify the basic elements in assessment.

What does a clinician need to know? First, of course, the **presenting problem**, or major symptoms and behavior the client is experiencing, must be identified. Is it a situational problem precipitated by some environmental stressor such as divorce or unemployment, a manifestation of a more pervasive and long-term disorder, or some combination of the two? Is there any evidence of recent deterioration in cognitive functioning? What is the duration of the current complaint, and how is the person dealing with the problem? What, if any, prior help has been sought? Are there indications of self-defeating behavior and personality deterioration, or is the individual using available personal and environmental resources in a good effort to cope? How pervasively has the problem affected the person's performance of important social roles? Does the individual's symptomatic behavior fit any of the diagnostic patterns in the *DSM-5*?

The Relationship Between Assessment and Diagnosis

It is important to have an adequate classification of the presenting problem for a number of reasons. Clinically, knowledge of a person's type of disorder can help in planning and managing the appropriate treatment. Administratively, it is essential to know the range of diagnostic problems that are represented in the client population and for which treatment facilities need to be available. If most clients at a facility have been diagnosed as having personality disorders, for example, then the staffing, physical environment, and treatment facilities should be arranged accordingly, with appropriate security and clearly established rules. In many cases, a formal diagnosis is necessary before insurance claims can be filed to cover a client's treatment costs. Thus, the nature of the difficulty needs to be understood as clearly as possible, including a diagnostic categorization if appropriate (see the "Classifying Abnormal Behavior" section at the end of this chapter).

Taking a Social or Behavioral History

For most clinical purposes, assigning a formal diagnostic classification per se is much less important than having a clear understanding of the individual's behavioral history, intellectual functioning, personality characteristics, and environmental pressures and resources. That is, an adequate assessment includes much more than the diagnostic label. For example, it should include an objective description of the person's behavior. How does the person characteristically respond to other people? Are there excesses in behavior present, such as eating or drinking too much? Are there notable deficits, for example, in social skills? How appropriate is the person's behavior? Is the person manifesting behavior that is plainly unresponsive or uncooperative? Excesses, deficits, and appropriateness are key dimensions to be noted if the clinician is to understand the particular disorder that has brought the individual to the clinic or hospital.

PERSONALITY FACTORS Assessment should include a description of any relevant long-term personality characteristics. Has the person typically responded in deviant ways to particular kinds of situations—for example, those requiring submission to legitimate authority? Are there personality traits or behavior patterns that predispose the individual to behave in maladaptive ways? Does the person tend to become enmeshed with others to the point of losing his or her identity, or is he or she so self-absorbed that intimate relationships are not possible? Is the person able to accept help from others? Is the person capable of genuine affection and of accepting appropriate responsibility for the welfare of others? Such questions are at the heart of many assessment efforts.

THE SOCIAL CONTEXT It is also important to assess the social context in which the individual functions. What kinds of environmental demands are typically placed on the person, and what supports or special stressors exist in her or his life situation? For example, being the primary

caretaker for a spouse suffering from Alzheimer's disease is so challenging that it can result in significant psychological impairment, especially where outside supports are lacking.

The diverse and often conflicting bits of information about the individual's personality traits, behavior patterns, environmental demands, and so on, must then be integrated into a consistent and meaningful picture. Some clinicians refer to this picture as a "dynamic formulation" because it not only describes the current situation but also includes hypotheses about what is driving the person to behave in maladaptive ways. At this point in the assessment, the clinician should have a plausible explanation for why a normally passive and mild-mannered man suddenly flew into a rage and started breaking up furniture, for example. The formulation should allow the clinician to develop hypotheses about the client's future behavior as well. What is the likelihood of improvement or deterioration if the person's problems are left untreated? Which behaviors should be the initial focus of change, and what treatment methods are likely to be most efficient in producing this change? How much change might be expected from a particular type of treatment?

Where feasible, decisions about treatment are made collaboratively with the consent and approval of the individual. In cases of severe disorder, however, they may have to be made without the client's participation or, in rare instances, even without consulting responsible family members. As has already been indicated, knowledge of the person's strengths and resources is important; in short, what qualities does the client bring to treatment that can enhance the chances of improvement? Because a wide range of factors can play important roles in causing and maintaining maladaptive behavior, assessment may involve the coordinated use of physical, psychological, and environmental assessment procedures. Moreover, as we have indicated, the nature and comprehensiveness of clinical assessments vary with the problem and the treatment

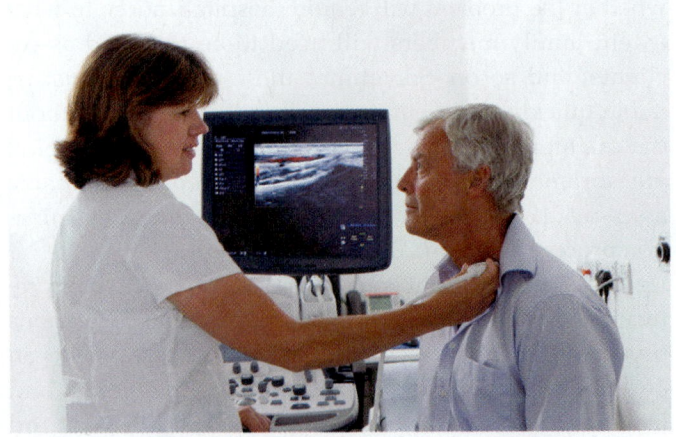

Some patients with cognitive deterioration are difficult to evaluate and to provide health care for, often requiring special facilities.

agency's facilities. Assessment by phone in a suicide prevention center (Stolberg & Bongar, 2009), for example, is quite different from assessment aimed at developing a treatment plan for a person who has come to a clinic for help (Perry, 2009).

Ensuring Culturally Sensitive Assessment Procedures

Increasingly, practitioners are being asked to conduct psychological evaluations for clients from diverse ethnic and language backgrounds. In both clinical and court settings, for example, a psychologist might be referred a client who has limited English language skills and low exposure to American mores, values, and laws. It is critical for the psychologist to be informed of the issues involved in multicultural assessment (often referred to as **cultural competence**) and to use testing procedures that have been adapted and validated for culturally diverse clients (Butcher et al., 2015).

Psychological assessment of clients from diverse ethnic backgrounds has increased greatly in recent years. The growing number of minorities requiring a clinical or forensic evaluation comes about, in part, from the influx of immigrants or refugees, many of whom encounter adjustment difficulties. The U.S. Census Bureau (2014) reports that the Hispanic population now makes up 17 percent of the U.S. population. People of Hispanic origin are now the largest ethnic minority group in the United States. African Americans now represent 12.6 percent of the population, Asians 4.8 percent, Native Americans 0.9 percent, and Native Hawaiians/Pacific Islanders 0.2 percent. Many immigrants, especially those of color, become members of ethnic minorities when they relocate to North America. As such, they may experience racial discrimination or may be further viewed as inferior by the nonminority community due to their lack of political power or lack of adaptive skills arising from their difficulties in acculturation (Green, 2009; Hays, 2008).

To fairly and successfully treat such individuals, the ethics code of the American Psychological Association (2002) recommends that psychologists consider various test factors, test-taking abilities, and other characteristics of the person being assessed, such as situational, linguistic, and cultural differences, that might affect his or her judgments or reduce the accuracy of his or her interpretations. Thus, psychologists who use tests in a culturally competent manner must bear in mind a range of issues and factors involved with culturally and linguistically diverse clients. These issues involve the importance of ensuring that the characteristics of the test being employed are appropriate across cultures and that potential biasing factors do not interfere with critical thinking in the overall assessment process.

The challenges of understanding clients when performing multicultural assessments have been described (Butcher et al., 2006; Hays, 2008) and involve both test instrument characteristics and sociocultural factors such as the relationships among culture, behavior, and psychopathology. Psychologists need to ensure that the test procedures they employ are appropriate for the particular client. For example, the psychological equivalence of a test for use with a particular population should be determined. The meaning or cultural significance of test items should be similar across cultural groups (Butcher & Han, 1996), and the norms used to compare the client should be appropriate. In using Western-developed tests, users need to take into account the dominant language, socioeconomic status, ethnicity, and gender of their clients. For example, clients from non–English-speaking countries might have insufficient English language skills, which will influence their test performance. When using a translated version of a test, interpreters need to be aware of the possible differences that can arise when using an adapted version. Thus, psychologists need to be aware of the available research on the instrument's use with the target population in order to assess whether the adapted version measures the same variables in the new cultures. Finally, test users need to be concerned with the impact and fairness of the instruments they employ with clients from diverse groups—for example, whether there are any possible performance differences on the scales between groups.

The most widely used personality measure, the Minnesota Multiphasic Personality Inventory (MMPI-2) (discussed later in this chapter), has been widely evaluated both in international applications with translated versions (Butcher & Williams, 2009) and in diverse subcultural groups in the United States (Butcher et al., 2007). Spanish-language versions of the test have been developed. Recent research has provided support for the use of the MMPI-2 with minorities (Robin et al., 2003), and the analyses provided by Hall and colleagues (1999) support the use of the MMPI-2 with Hispanic clients.

The Influence of Professional Orientation

How clinicians go about the assessment process often depends on their basic treatment orientations. For example, a biologically oriented clinician—typically a psychiatrist or other medical practitioner—is likely to focus on biological assessment methods aimed at determining any underlying organic malfunctioning that may be causing the maladaptive behavior. A psychodynamic or psychoanalytically oriented clinician may choose unstructured personality assessment techniques, such as the Rorschach inkblots or the Thematic Apperception Test (described later in this chapter), to identify intrapsychic conflicts or may simply proceed with therapy, expecting these conflicts to emerge naturally as part of the treatment process. A behaviorally oriented clinician, in an effort to determine the functional relationships between environmental events or reinforcements and the abnormal behavior, will rely on such techniques as behavioral observation and self-monitoring to identify learned maladaptive patterns; for a cognitively oriented behaviorist, the focus would shift to the dysfunctional thoughts supposedly mediating those patterns.

The preceding examples represent general trends and are in no way meant to imply that clinicians of a particular orientation limit themselves to a particular assessment method or that each assessment technique is limited to a particular theoretical orientation. Such trends are instead a matter of emphasis and point to the fact that certain types of assessments are more conducive than others to uncovering particular causal factors or for eliciting information about symptomatic behavior central to understanding and treating a disorder within a given conceptual framework.

As you will see in what follows, both physical and psychosocial data can be extremely important to understanding a patient. In the sections that follow, we discuss several assessment instruments and examine in some detail an actual psychological study of a woman who experienced a traumatic situation in the workplace that resulted in severe emotional adjustment problems.

Reliability, Validity, and Standardization

Three measurement concepts that are important in understanding clinical assessment and the utility of psychological tests are reliability, validity, and standardization. These concepts are briefly described here and then illustrated throughout the chapter. A psychological test or measurement construct needs to show reliability in order to be effective. **Reliability** is a term describing the degree to which an assessment measure produces the same result each time it is used to evaluate the same thing. If, for example, your scale showed a significantly different weight each time you stepped on it over a brief period of time, you would consider it a fairly unreliable measure of your body mass. In the context of assessment or classification, reliability is an index of the extent to which a measurement instrument can agree that a person's behavior fits a given diagnostic class. If the observations are different, it may mean that the classification criteria are not precise enough to determine whether the suspected disorder is present.

The psychological test or classification system must also be valid. **Validity** is the extent to which a measuring instrument actually measures what it is supposed to measure. In the context of testing or classification, validity is the degree to which a measure accurately conveys to us something clinically important about the person whose behavior fits the category, such as helping to predict the future course of the disorder. If, for example, a person is predicted to have or is diagnosed as having schizophrenia, we should be able to infer the presence of some fairly precise characteristics that differentiate the person from individuals who are considered normal or from those with other types of mental disorder. The classification or diagnosis of schizophrenia, for example, implies a disorder of unusually stubborn persistence, with recurrent episodes being common.

Normally, the validity of a mental health measure or classification presupposes reliability. If clinicians can't agree on the class to which a person with a disorder's behavior belongs, then the question of the validity of the diagnostic classifications under consideration becomes irrelevant. To put it another way, if we can't confidently pin down what the diagnosis is, then whatever useful information a given diagnosis might convey about the person being evaluated is lost. On the other hand, good reliability does not in itself guarantee validity. For example, handedness (left, right, ambidextrous) can be assessed with a high degree of reliability, but handedness accurately predicts neither mental health status nor countless other behavioral qualities on which people vary; that is, it is not a valid index of these qualities (although it may be a valid index for success in certain situations involving the game of baseball, for example). In like manner, reliable assignment of a person's behavior to a given class of mental disorder will prove useful only to the extent that the validity of that class has been established through research.

Standardization is a process by which a psychological test is administered, scored, and interpreted in a consistent or "standard" manner. Standardized tests are considered to be more fair than nonstandardized tests in that they are applied consistently and in the same manner to all persons taking them. Many psychological tests are standardized to allow the test user to compare a particular individual's score on the test with a reference population, often referred to as a normative sample. For example, comparing a particular individual's test score on a distribution of test scores from a large normative population can enable the user to evaluate whether the individual's score is low, average, or high along the distribution of scores (referred to as a **T score distribution**).

Trust and Rapport Between the Clinician and the Client

In order for psychological assessment to proceed effectively and to provide a clear understanding of behavior and symptoms, the client being evaluated must feel comfortable with the clinician. In a clinical assessment situation, this means that a client must feel that the testing will help the practitioner gain a clear understanding of her or his problems and must understand how the tests will be used and how the psychologist will incorporate them into the clinical evaluation. The clinician should explain what will happen during assessment and how the information gathered will help provide a clearer picture of the problems the client is facing.

Clients need to be assured that the feelings, beliefs, attitudes, and personal history that they are disclosing will be used appropriately, will be kept in strict confidence, and will be made available only to therapists or others involved in the case. An important aspect of confidentiality is that the test results are released to a third party only if the client signs an appropriate release form. In cases in which the person is being tested for a third party such as the court system, the client in effect is the referring source—for example, the judge ordering the evaluation—not the individual being tested. In these cases the testing relationship is likely to be strained and developing rapport is likely to be difficult. Of course, in a court-ordered evaluation, the person's test-taking behavior is likely to be very different from what it would be otherwise, and interpretation of the test needs to reflect this different motivational set created by the person's unwillingness to cooperate.

People being tested in a clinical situation are usually highly motivated to be evaluated and like to know the results of the testing. They generally are eager for some definition of their discomfort. Moreover, providing test feedback in a clinical setting can be an important element in the treatment process (Harwood & Beutler, 2009). Interestingly, when patients are given appropriate feedback on test results, they tend to improve—just from gaining a perspective on their problems as a result of the testing. The test feedback process itself can be a powerful clinical intervention (Finn & Kamphuis, 2006). When persons who were not provided psychological test feedback were compared with those who were provided with feedback, the latter group showed a significant decline in reported symptoms and an increase in measured self-esteem as a result of having a clearer understanding of their own resources.

in review

- What is the difference between clinical diagnosis and psychological assessment? What components must be integrated into a dynamic formulation?
- Describe the important elements in a social or behavioral history.
- What does it mean to use culturally fair assessments?
- What is the impact of professional orientation on the structure and form of a psychological evaluation?
- Does providing test feedback to clients aid them in their adjustment?

Assessment of the Physical Organism

4.2 **Describe the factors involved in the assessment of the physical organism.**

In some situations and with certain psychological problems, a medical evaluation is necessary to rule out the possibility that physical abnormalities may be causing or contributing to the problem. The medical evaluation may include both a general physical examination and special examinations aimed at assessing the structural (anatomical) and functional (physiological) integrity of the brain as a behaviorally significant physical system (Swartz, 2014).

The General Physical Examination

In cases in which physical symptoms are part of the presenting clinical picture, a referral for a medical evaluation is recommended. A physical examination consists of the kinds of procedures most of us have experienced when getting a "medical checkup." Typically, a medical history is obtained, and the major systems of the body are checked (LeBlond et al., 2004; Swartz, 2014). This part of the assessment procedure is of obvious importance for disorders that entail physical problems, such as a psychologically based physical condition, addictive disorders, and organic brain syndromes. In addition, a variety of organic conditions, including various hormonal irregularities, can produce behavioral symptoms that closely mimic those of mental disorders usually considered to have predominantly psychosocial origins. Although some long-lasting pain can be related to actual organic conditions, other such pain can result from strictly emotional factors. A case in point is chronic back pain, in which psychological factors may sometimes play an important part. A diagnostic error in this type of situation could result in costly and ineffective surgery; hence, in equivocal cases, most clinicians insist on a medical clearance before initiating psychosocially based interventions.

The Neurological Examination

Because brain pathology is sometimes involved in some mental disorders (e.g., unusual memory deficits or motor impairments), a specialized neurological examination can be administered in addition to a general medical examination. This may involve the client's getting an **electroencephalogram (EEG)** to assess brain wave patterns in awake and sleeping states. An EEG is a graphical record of the brain's electrical activity (Yamada & Meng, 2011). It is obtained by placing electrodes on the scalp and amplifying the minute brain wave impulses from various brain areas; these amplified impulses drive oscillating pens whose deviations are traced on a strip of paper moving at a constant speed. Much is known about the normal pattern of brain impulses in waking and sleeping states and under various conditions of sensory stimulation. Significant divergences from the normal pattern can thus reflect abnormalities of brain function such as might be caused by a brain tumor or other lesion. An EEG may reveal a **dysrhythmia**, or irregular pattern, in the brain's electrical activity. For example, recent research has supported a link between resting frontal EEG asymmetry and depression (see Stewart et al., 2010) and anxiety (see Thibodeau et al., 2006). When an EEG reveals an irregular pattern, other specialized techniques may be used in an attempt to arrive at a more precise diagnosis of the problem.

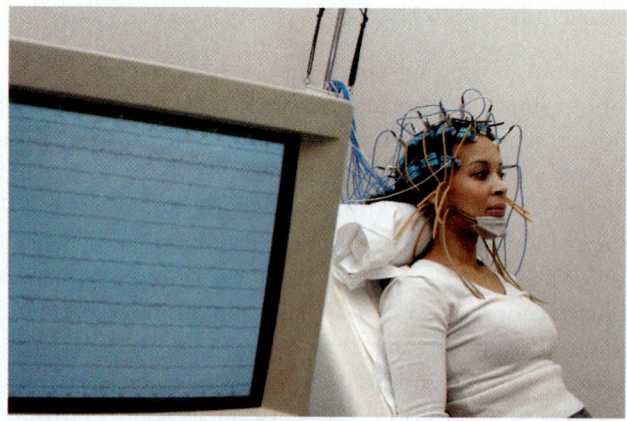

An EEG is a graphical record of the brain's electrical activity. Electrodes are placed on the scalp, and brain wave impulses are amplified. The amplified impulses drive oscillating pens whose deviations are traced on a strip of paper moving at a constant speed. Significant differences from the normal pattern can reflect abnormalities of brain function.

ANATOMICAL BRAIN SCANS   Radiological technology, such as a **computerized axial tomography (CAT) scan**, is one of these specialized techniques (Mishra & Singh, 2010). Through the use of X-rays, a CAT scan reveals images of parts of the brain that might be diseased. This procedure has aided neurological study in recent years by providing rapid access, without surgery, to accurate information about the localization and extent of anomalies in the brain's structural characteristics. The procedure involves the use of computer analysis applied to X-ray beams across sections of a patient's brain to produce images that a neurologist can then interpret.

CAT scans have been increasingly replaced by **magnetic resonance imaging (MRI)**. The images of the interior of the brain are frequently sharper with MRI because of its superior ability to differentiate subtle variations in soft tissue. In addition, the MRI procedure is normally far less complicated to administer than a CAT scan and does not subject the patient to ionizing radiation.

Essentially, MRI involves the precise measurement of variations in magnetic fields that are caused by the varying amounts of water content of various organs and parts of organs. In this manner the anatomical structure of a cross section at any given plane through an organ such as the brain can be computed and graphically depicted with astonishing structural differentiation and clarity. MRI thus makes possible, by noninvasive means, visualization of all but the most minute abnormalities of brain structure. It has been particularly useful in confirming degenerative brain processes as shown, for example, in enlarged areas of the brain. Therefore, MRI studies have considerable potential to illuminate the contribution of brain anomalies to nonorganic psychoses such as schizophrenia, and some progress in this area has already been made (Mathalondolf et al., 2001).

Still, the MRI can be problematic. For example, some patients have a claustrophobic reaction to being placed into the narrow cylinder of the MRI machine that is necessary to contain the magnetic field and block out external radio signals. In addition, an evaluation and critique of the MRI approach in medicine was published by Joyce (2008), who interviewed physicians and MRI technologists and also conducted ethnographic research at imaging sites and attended radiology conferences. In her critique, she demonstrated that current beliefs about MRI draw on cultural ideas about technology and are reinforced by health care policies and insurance reimbursement practices. However, her review raises questions about the work practices of many physicians and technologists and suggests that MRI scans do not reveal the truth about the body that many medical practices often hold. For example, she concludes that MRI studies do not always lead to better outcomes for patients.

Watch   MRI Research

PET SCANS: A METABOLIC PORTRAIT   Another scanning technique is the **positron emission tomography (PET) scan**. Whereas a CAT scan is limited to distinguishing anatomical features such as the shape of a particular internal structure, a PET scan allows for an appraisal of how an organ is functioning (Meyer et al., 2012). The PET scan provides metabolic portraits by tracking natural compounds, such as glucose, as they are metabolized by the brain or other organs. By revealing areas of differential metabolic activity, the PET scan enables a medical specialist to obtain more clear-cut diagnoses of brain pathology by, for example, pinpointing sites responsible for epileptic seizures, trauma from head injury or stroke, and brain tumors. Thus, the PET scan may be able to reveal problems that are not immediately apparent anatomically. Moreover, the use of PET scans in research on brain pathology that occurs in abnormal conditions such as Alzheimer's disease may lead to important discoveries about the organic processes underlying these disorders and aid in the treatment of dementia (Saykin et al., 2006). PET scans have, however, been of somewhat limited value thus far because of the low-fidelity pictures obtained (Fletcher, 2004) and their cost, since they require a very expensive instrument nearby to produce the short-lived radioactive atoms required for the procedure. Although PET scans are admitted into court cases to illustrate potential brain damage, some investigators recommend questioning their use in forensic evaluations (Moriarty et al., 2013).

THE FUNCTIONAL MRI The technique known as **functional MRI (fMRI)** has been used in the study of psychopathology for a number of years. As originally developed and employed, the MRI could reveal brain structure but not brain activity. For the latter, clinicians and investigators remained dependent on PET scans. Improving on these techniques, fMRI most often measures changes in local oxygenation (i.e., blood flow) of specific areas of brain tissue that in turn depend on neuronal activity in those specific regions (Bandettini, 2007; Ulmer & Jansen, 2010). Ongoing psychological activity, such as sensations, images, and thoughts, can thus be "mapped," at least in principle, revealing the specific areas of the brain that appear to be involved in their neurophysiological processes. For example, one study (Wright & Jackson, 2007) examined the task of judgment of serve direction among tennis players and found that different patterns produce different responses in the brain.

Because the measurement of change in this context is critically time dependent, the emergence of fMRI required the development of high-speed devices for enhancing the recording process, as well as the computerized analysis of incoming data. These improvements are now widely available and will likely lead to a marked increase in studying people with disorders using functional imaging. Optimism about the ultimate value of fMRI in mapping cognitive processes in mental disorders is still strong. The fMRI is thought by some to hold more promise for depicting brain abnormalities than currently used procedures such as the neuropsychological examination (see next section).

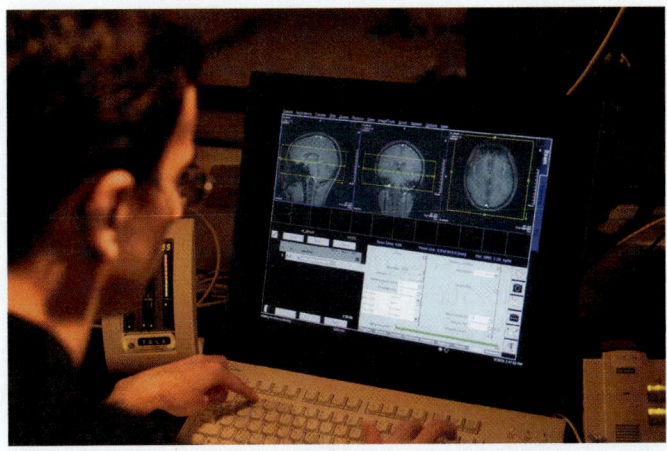

The functional MRI (fMRI), like the MRI, allows clinicians to "map" brain structure. The exciting breakthrough in fMRI technology gives clinicians the ability to measure brain activities underlying such things as sensations, images, and thoughts, revealing the specific areas of the brain involved.

A number of studies have provided support for this optimism (MacDonald & Jones, 2009). Research using fMRI has explored the cortical functioning that underlies various psychological processes; for example, one study showed that psychological factors or environmental events can affect brain processes as measured by fMRI. Eisenberger, Lieberman, and Williams (2003) found that participants who were excluded from social participation showed a similar pattern of brain activation (in the right ventral prefrontal cortex) as participants experiencing physical pain. Joseph and colleagues (2014) studied differences between alcohol users and problem drinkers and found that individuals who report problematic drinking, but who are not alcohol dependent, may show patterns that are consistent with findings in individuals who are alcohol dependent; and Dager et al. (2014) reported that heavy drinkers differed from light drinkers in the ways their brains compensated during memory tasks. Longe and colleagues (2010) found that fMRI was effective at detecting neural correlates for self-critical thinking. Some researchers have pointed out that fMRI has a high potential for contributing to a treatment approach in mental health care (Schneider et al., 2009). Although some research has suggested that fMRI can be an effective procedure for detecting malingering or lying (Langleben et al., 2005), one court has recently ruled against the use of fMRI as a lie detector (Couzin-Frankel, 2010).

Other studies have addressed problems in abnormal behavior. One study showed that the impaired time estimation found in people with schizophrenia might result from dysfunction in specific areas of the brain, thalamus, and prefrontal cortex (Suzuki et al., 2004), while others addressed cortical functioning in auditory hallucinations in schizophrenia (Shergill et al., 2000); effects of neuroleptic medication in people with schizophrenia (Braus et al., 1999); and the neuroanatomy of anxiety (Paulesu et al. 2010) and depression (Brody et al., 2001). Finally, Whalley and colleagues (2004) found that the fMRI technique has the potential of adding to our understanding of the early development of psychological disorder. One study of treatment for **aphasia**, a disorder in which there is a loss of ability to communicate verbally (Meinzer et al., 2007), showed that changes in behavioral performance and the brain activation pattern were disclosed as affecting the brain's reorganization.

There are some clear methodological limitations that can influence fMRI results. For example, both MRI and fMRI are quite sensitive to instrument errors or inaccurate observations as a result of slight movements of the person being evaluated (Davidson et al., 2003; Shulman, 2013). Additionally, the results of fMRI studies are often difficult to interpret. Even though group differences emerge between a cognitively impaired group and a control sample, the results usually do not provide much specific information about the processes studied. Fletcher (2004) provides a somewhat sobering analysis of the current status of fMRI in contemporary psychiatry, noting that many professionals who had hoped for intricate and unambiguous results might be disappointed with the overall lack of effective, pragmatic methodology in fMRI assessment of cognitive processes. At this point the fMRI is not considered to be a valid or useful diagnostic tool for mental disorders or for use in forensic evaluations (Buckholtz & Faigman, 2014); however, investigators are optimistic that this procedure shows great promise for understanding brain functioning (MacDonald & Jones, 2009). The primary value of this procedure continues to be research into cortical activity and cognitive processes.

The Neuropsychological Examination

The techniques described so far have shown success in identifying brain abnormalities that are very often accompanied by gross impairments in behavior and varied psychological deficits. However, behavioral and psychological impairments due to organic brain abnormalities may manifest before any organic brain lesion is detectable by scanning or other means. In these instances, reliable techniques are needed to measure any alteration in behavioral or psychological functioning that has occurred because of the organic brain pathology. This need is met by a growing cadre of psychologists specializing in **neuropsychological assessment**, which involves the use of various testing devices to measure a person's cognitive, perceptual, and motor performance as clues to the extent and location of brain damage (Snyder et al., 2006).

In many instances of known or suspected organic brain involvement, a clinical neuropsychologist administers a test battery to a patient. The person's performance on standardized tasks, particularly perceptual-motor tasks, can give valuable clues about any cognitive and intellectual impairment following brain damage (Horton, 2008; Lezak et al., 2004; Reitan & Wolfson, 1985). Such testing can even provide clues to the probable location of the brain damage, although PET scans, MRIs, and other physical tests may be more effective in determining the exact location of the injury.

Many neuropsychologists prefer to administer a highly individualized array of tests, depending on a patient's case history and other available information. Others administer a standard set of tests that have been preselected to sample, in a systematic and comprehensive manner, a broad range of psychological competencies known to be adversely affected by various types of brain injury (Gass, 2009). The use of a constant set of tests has many research and clinical advantages, although it may compromise flexibility. Consider the components of one such standard procedure, the Halstead-Reitan neuropsychological test battery. The Halstead-Reitan battery is composed of several tests and variables from which an "index of impairment" can be computed (Preiss & Preiss, 2013; Reitan & Wolfson, 1985). In addition, it provides specific information about a subject's functioning in several skill areas. The Halstead-Reitan battery for adults is made up of a group of tests such as the following:

1. **Halstead category test:** Measures a subject's ability to learn and remember material and can provide clues as to his or her judgment and impulsivity. The subject is presented with a stimulus (on a screen) that suggests a number between 1 and 4. The subject presses a button indicating the number she or he believes was suggested. A correct choice is followed by the sound of a pleasant doorbell, an incorrect choice by a loud buzzer. The person is required to determine from the pattern of buzzers and bells what the underlying principle of the correct choice is.

2. **Tactual performance test:** Measures a subject's motor speed, response to the unfamiliar, and ability to learn and use tactile and kinesthetic cues. The test surface is a board that has spaces for 10 blocks of varied shapes. The subject is blindfolded (never actually seeing the board) and asked to place the blocks into the correct grooves in the board. Later, the subject is asked to draw the blocks and the board from tactile memory.

3. **Rhythm test:** Measures attention and sustained concentration through an auditory perception task. It includes 30 pairs of rhythmic beats that are presented on a tape recorder. The subject is asked whether the pairs are the same or different.

4. **Speech sounds perception test:** Determines whether an individual can identify spoken words. Nonsense words are presented on a tape recorder, and the subject

is asked to identify the presented word in a list of four printed words. This task measures the subject's concentration, attention, and comprehension.

5. **Finger oscillation task:** Measures the speed at which an individual can depress a lever with the index finger. Several trials are given for each hand.

In summary, the medical and neuropsychological sciences are developing many new procedures to assess brain functioning and behavioral manifestations of organic disorder. Medical procedures to assess organic brain damage include EEGs and CAT, PET, and MRI scans. The new technology holds great promise for detecting and evaluating organic brain dysfunction and increasing our understanding of brain function. Neuropsychological testing provides a clinician with important behavioral information on how organic brain damage is affecting a person's present functioning. However, in cases where the psychological difficulty is thought to result from nonorganic causes, psychosocial assessment is used.

in review

- Compare and contrast five important neurological procedures. What makes each one particularly valuable?
- What is the difference between a PET scan and an fMRI?
- Describe the use of neuropsychological tests in evaluating the behavioral effects of organic brain disorders.

Psychosocial Assessment

4.3 Explain the interview process, clinical observation, and testing in psychosocial assessment.

Psychosocial assessment attempts to provide a realistic picture of an individual in interaction with his or her social environment. This picture includes relevant information about the individual's personality makeup and present level of functioning, as well as information about the stressors and resources in her or his life situation. For example, early in the process, clinicians may act as puzzle solvers, absorbing as much information about the client as possible—present feelings, attitudes, memories, demographic facts—and trying to fit the pieces together into a meaningful pattern. Clinicians typically formulate hypotheses and discard or confirm them as they proceed. Starting with a global technique such as a clinical interview, clinicians may later select more specific assessment tasks or tests. The following are some of the psychosocial procedures that may be used.

Assessment Interviews

An assessment interview, often considered the central element of the assessment process, usually involves a face-to-face interaction in which a clinician obtains information about various aspects of a client's situation, behavior, and personality (Berthold & Ellinger, 2009; Craig, 2009; Sharp et al., 2013). The interview may vary from a simple set of questions or prompts to a more extended and detailed format (Kici & Westhoff, 2004). It may be relatively open in character, with an interviewer making moment-to-moment decisions about his or her next question on the basis of responses to previous ones, or it may be more tightly controlled and structured so as to ensure that a particular set of questions is covered. In the latter case, the interviewer may choose from a number of highly structured, standardized interview formats whose reliability has been established in prior research.

STRUCTURED AND UNSTRUCTURED INTERVIEWS Although many clinicians prefer the freedom to explore as they feel responses merit, research data show that the more controlled and **structured assessment interview** yields far more reliable results than the flexible format. There appears to be widespread overconfidence among clinicians in the accuracy of their own methods and judgments (Taylor & Meux, 1997). Every rule has exceptions, but in most instances, an assessor is wise to conduct an interview that is carefully structured in terms of goals, comprehensive symptom review, other content to be explored, and the type of relationship the interviewer attempts to establish with the person.

Structured interviews follow a predetermined set of questions throughout the interview, for example, "Have you ever had periods in which you could not sleep lately?" and "Have you experienced feeling very nervous about being in public?" The beginning statements and introduction to the interview follow set procedures. The themes and questions are predetermined to obtain particular responses for all items. The interviewer cannot deviate from the question lists and procedures. All questions are asked of each client in a preset way. Each question is structured in a manner so as to allow responses to be quantified or clearly determined. On the negative side, structured interviews typically take longer to administer than unstructured interviews and may include some seemingly tangential questions. Clients can sometimes be frustrated by the overly detailed questions in areas that are of no concern to them.

Unstructured assessment interviews are typically subjective and do not follow a predetermined set of questions. The beginning statements in the interview are usually general, and follow-up questions are tailored for each client. The content of the interview questions is influenced by the habits or theoretical views of the interviewer. The interviewer does not ask the same questions of all clients; rather, he or she subjectively decides what to ask based on the client's response to previous questions. Because the questions are asked in an unplanned way, important criteria needed for a *DSM-5* diagnosis might be skipped. Responses based on unstructured interviews are difficult to quantify or compare with responses of clients from other interviews. Thus, the use of unstructured interviews in mental health research is limited. On the positive side, clients may view unstructured interviews as being more sensitive to their needs or problems than more structured procedures. Moreover, the spontaneous follow-up questions that emerge in an unstructured interview can, at times, provide valuable information that would not emerge in a structured interview.

During an assessment interview, a clinician obtains information about various aspects of a patient's situation, behavior, and personality makeup. The interview is usually conducted face to face and may have a relatively open structure or be more tightly controlled, depending on the goals and style of the clinician.

The reliability of an assessment interview may be enhanced by the use of **rating scales** that help focus inquiry and quantify the interview data. For example, an individual may be rated on a 3-, 5-, or 7-point scale with respect to self-esteem, anxiety, and various other characteristics. Such a structured and preselected format is particularly effective in obtaining a comprehensive impression, or "profile," of the subject and her or his life situation and in revealing specific problems or crises—such as marital difficulties, drug dependence, or suicidal fantasies—that may require immediate therapeutic intervention.

Clinical interviews can be subject to error because they rely on human judgment to choose the questions and process the information. Evidence of this unreliability includes the fact that different clinicians have often arrived at different formal diagnoses on the basis of the interview data they elicited from a particular client. It is chiefly for this reason that recent versions of the *DSM* have emphasized an "operational" assessment approach, one that specifies

observable criteria for diagnosis and provides specific guidelines for making diagnostic judgments. "Winging it" has limited use in this type of assessment process. The operational approach leads to more reliable psychiatric diagnoses, perhaps at some cost in reduced interviewer flexibility. It is also important to consider racial or ethnic factors when conducting diagnostic interviews. Recent research indicates (Alcántara & Gone, 2014) that the interview process and outcome can be substantially influenced by the ethnicity of the interviewer and the client.

The Clinical Observation of Behavior

One of the traditional and most useful assessment tools that a clinician has available is direct observation of a client's characteristic behavior (Hartmann et al., 2004). The main purpose of direct observation is to learn more about the person's psychological functioning by attending to his or her appearance and behavior in various contexts. In clinical observation the clinician provides an objective description of the person's appearance and behavior—her or his personal hygiene and emotional responses and any depression, anxiety, aggression, hallucinations, or delusions she or he may manifest. Ideally, clinical observation takes place in a natural environment (such as observing a child's behavior in a classroom or at home), but it is more likely to take place upon admission to a clinic or hospital (Leichtman, 2009). For example, a brief description is usually made of a subject's behavior upon hospital admission, and more detailed observations are made periodically on the ward.

Some practitioners and researchers use a more controlled, rather than a naturalistic, behavioral setting for conducting observations in contrived situations. These *analogue situations*, which are designed to yield information about the person's adaptive strategies, might involve such tasks as staged **role-playing**, event reenactment, family interaction assignments, or think-aloud procedures (Haynes et al., 2009).

In addition to making their own observations, many clinicians enlist their clients' help by providing them instruction in **self-monitoring**: self-observation and objective reporting of behavior, thoughts, and feelings as they occur in various natural settings. This method can be a valuable aid in determining the kinds of situations in which maladaptive behavior is likely to be evoked, and numerous studies also show it to have therapeutic benefits in its own right. Alternatively, a client may be asked to fill out a more or less formal self-report or a checklist concerning problematic reactions experienced in various situations. Many instruments have been published in the professional literature and are commercially available to clinicians. These approaches recognize that people are excellent sources of information about themselves. Assuming that the right questions are asked and that people are willing to disclose information about themselves, the results can have a crucial bearing on treatment planning.

RATING SCALES   As in the case of interviews, the use of rating scales in clinical observation and in self-reports helps both to organize information and to encourage reliability and objectivity (Aiken, 1996; Garb, 2007). That is, the formal structure of a scale is likely to keep observer inferences to a minimum. The most useful rating scales are those that enable a rater to indicate not only the presence or absence of a trait or behavior but also its prominence or degree. The following item is an example from such a rating scale; the observer would check the most appropriate description.

Sexual Behavior

_____ 1.   Sexually assaultive: aggressively approaches males or females with sexual intent.

_____ 2.   Sexually soliciting: exposes genitals with sexual intent, makes overt sexual advances to other patients or staff, and masturbates openly.

_____ 3.   No overt sexual behavior: not preoccupied with discussion of sexual matters.

_____ 4.   Avoids sex topics: made uneasy by discussion of sex, becomes disturbed if approached sexually by others.

_____ 5.   Excessive prudishness about sex: considers sex filthy, condemns sexual behavior in others, becomes panic-stricken if approached sexually.

Ratings like these may be made not only as part of an initial evaluation but also to check on the course or outcome of treatment. One of the rating scales most widely used for recording observations in clinical practice and in psychiatric research is the **Brief Psychiatric Rating Scale (BPRS)** (Leucht, 2014; Overall & Hollister, 1982). The BPRS provides a structured and quantifiable format for rating clinical symptoms such as overconcern with physical symptoms, anxiety, emotional withdrawal, guilt feelings, hostility, suspiciousness, and unusual thought patterns. It contains 24 scales that are scored from ratings made by a clinician following an interview with a patient. The distinct patterns of behavior reflected in the BPRS ratings enable clinicians to make a standardized comparison of their patients' symptoms with the behavior of other patients in mental health settings. The BPRS has been found to be an extremely useful instrument in clinical research (e.g., see Davidson et al., 2004), especially for the purpose of assigning patients to treatment groups on the basis of similarity in symptoms. However, it is not widely used for making treatment or diagnostic decisions in clinical practice. The Hamilton Rating Scale for Depression (HRSD), a similar but more specifically targeted instrument, is one of the most widely used procedures for selecting research subjects who are clinically depressed and also for assessing the response of such subjects to various treatments (see Beevers & Miller, 2004; Brown et al., 2007).

Rating scales based on contemporary diagnostic systems, the *ICD-10* and *DSM-5*, are available. The *DSM-5* (American Psychiatric Association, 2013) provides several rating scales, called "Cross-Cutting Symptom Measures," that clinicians can use to obtain the symptom experiences of clients and for follow-up evaluations of symptoms over time. The rating scales are completed by the client (or some by the practitioner) or by the parent/custodian if the patient is a child or adolescent. The WHO provides a widely used rating scale for mental health and health problems, called the WHODAS 2.0 (WHO, 2014b).

Psychological Tests

Interviews and behavioral observation are relatively direct attempts to determine a person's beliefs, attitudes, and problems. Psychological tests are a more indirect means of assessing psychological characteristics. Scientifically developed psychological tests (as opposed to the recreational ones sometimes appearing in magazines or on the Internet) are standardized sets of procedures or tasks for obtaining samples of behavior (see American Psychological Association, 2014; Kolen & Hendrickson, 2013). A subject's responses to the standardized stimuli are compared with those of other people who have comparable demographic characteristics, usually determined through established

A wide variety of psychological tests have been developed that measure the intellectual abilities of children. The researcher in this photo is measuring this child's cognitive development by evaluating how she classifies and sorts the candy.

test norms or test score distributions. From these comparisons, a clinician can then draw inferences about how much the person's psychological qualities differ from those of a reference group, typically a psychologically normal one. Among the characteristics that these tests can measure are coping patterns, motive patterns, personality characteristics, role behaviors, values, levels of depression or anxiety, and intellectual functioning. Impressive advances in the technology of test development have made it possible to create instruments of acceptable reliability and validity to measure almost any conceivable psychological characteristic on which people may vary. Moreover, many procedures are available in a computer-administered and computer-interpreted format (see the Developments in Practice box).

Although psychological tests are more precise and often more reliable than interviews or some observational techniques, they are far from perfect tools. Their value often depends on the competence of the clinician who interprets them. In general, they are useful diagnostic tools for psychologists in much the same way that blood tests, X-ray films, and MRI scans are useful to physicians. In all these cases, pathology may be revealed in people who appear to be normal, or a general impression of "something wrong" can be checked against more precise information. Two general categories of psychological tests for use in clinical practice are intelligence tests and personality tests (projective and objective).

INTELLIGENCE TESTS A clinician can choose from a wide range of **intelligence tests**. The Wechsler Intelligence Scale for Children–Revised (WISC-IV) (see Weiss et al., 2006) and the current edition of the Stanford-Binet Intelligence Scale (Kamphaus & Kroncke, 2004) are widely used in clinical settings for measuring the intellectual abilities of children (Wasserman, 2003). Probably the most commonly used test for measuring adult intelligence is the Wechsler Adult Intelligence Scale–Revised (WAIS-IV) (Lichtenberger & Kaufman, 2009; Weiss et al., 2013). It includes both verbal and performance material and consists of 15 subtests. A brief description of two of the subtests will serve to illustrate the types of functions the WAIS-IV measures.

- **Vocabulary (verbal):** This subtest consists of a list of words to define that are presented orally to the individual. This task is designed to evaluate knowledge of vocabulary, which has been shown to be highly related to general intelligence.

- **Digit span (performance):** In this test of short-term memory, a sequence of numbers is administered orally. The individual is asked to repeat the digits in the order administered. Another task in this subtest involves the individual remembering the numbers, holding them in memory, and reversing the order sequence—that is, the individual is instructed to say them backward (Lichtenberger & Kaufman, 2009).

Developments in Practice

The Automated Practice: Use of the Computer in Psychological Testing

Perhaps the most dramatic innovation in clinical assessment during the past 40 years has been the increasing use of computers in individual assessment. Computers are effectively used in assessment both to gather information directly from an individual and to assemble and evaluate all the information that has been gathered previously through interviews, tests, and other assessment procedures. By comparing the incoming information with data previously stored in its memory banks, a computer can perform a wide range of assessment tasks (Butcher et al., 2009; Butcher, 2013). It can supply a probable diagnosis, indicate the likelihood of certain kinds of behavior, suggest the most appropriate form of treatment, predict the outcome, and print a summary report concerning the subject. In many of these functions, a computer is actually superior to a clinician because it is more efficient and accurate in recalling stored material (Epstein & Klinkenberg, 2001; Olson, 2001).

With the increased efficiency and reliability of computers one might expect a nearly unanimous welcoming of them into clinical practice. Luxton, Pruitt, and Osenbach (2014) have noted a broad acceptance of automated assessment through "telehealth technologies" that can be used to conduct psychological evaluations. However, new technologies are not always accepted or readily applied; a few hold-outs continue to resist using such "modern" techniques as e-mail, fax machines, and computerized billing in their practices (McMinn et al., 1999). Some clinicians are reluctant to use computer-based test interpretations (Rabin et al., 2014) in spite of their demonstrated utility and low cost. Even though most clinics and independent practitioners use microcomputers for record keeping and billing purposes, a smaller number incorporate computer-based clinical assessment procedures into their practice. Possible reasons for the underutilization of computer-based assessment procedures include the following: (1) Practitioners who were trained before the widespread use of computers may feel uncomfortable with them or may not have time to get acquainted with their use; (2) they may limit their practice to psychological treatment and do not use extensive pretreatment assessments in their practice; (3) they may have little interest in, or time for, the systematic evaluation of treatment efficacy that periodic formal assessments facilitate; or (4) they may feel that the impersonal and mechanized look of the keyboard or booklets and answer sheets common to much computerized assessment is inconsistent with the image and style of warm and personal engagement they hope to convey to clients.

Individually administered intelligence tests—such as the WISC-IV, the WAIS-IV, and the Stanford-Binet—typically require 2 to 3 hours to administer, score, and interpret. In many clinical situations, there is not enough time or funding to use these tests. In cases where intellectual impairment or organic brain damage is thought to be central to a patient's problem, however, intelligence testing may be the most crucial diagnostic procedure in the test battery. Moreover, information about cognitive functioning or deterioration can provide valuable clues to a person's intellectual resources in dealing with problems (Kihlstrom, 2002). Yet in many clinical settings and for many clinical cases, gaining a thorough understanding of a client's problems and initiating a treatment program do not require knowing the kind of detailed information about intellectual functioning that these instruments provide. In these cases, intelligence testing is not recommended.

Watch Intelligence Testing: Then and Now

David Wechsler (1896–1981) served in the military, testing army recruits during World War I. He came to believe that the ways in which psychologists viewed and measured "intelligence" was inadequate. In 1934 he began construction of the most widely used adult intelligence test battery, the Wechsler Adult Intelligence Scale (WAIS), which set the standard for practical measurement of intelligence.

PROJECTIVE PERSONALITY TESTS A great many tests have been designed to measure personal characteristics other than intellectual ability. It is customary to group these **personality tests** into projective and objective measures. **Projective personality tests** are unstructured in that they rely on various ambiguous stimuli such as inkblots or vague pictures rather than on explicit verbal questions, and in that the person's responses are not limited to the "true," "false," or "cannot say" variety. Through their interpretations of these ambiguous materials, people reveal a good deal about their personal preoccupations, conflicts, motives, coping techniques, and other personality characteristics. An assumption underlying the use of projective techniques is that in trying to make sense out of vague, unstructured stimuli, individuals "project" their own problems, motives, and wishes into the situation. Such responses are akin to the childhood pastime of seeing objects or scenes in cloud formations, with the important exception that the stimuli are in this case fixed and largely the same for all subjects. It is the latter circumstance that permits determination of the normative range of responses to the test materials, which in turn can be used to identify objectively deviant responding. Thus, projective tests are aimed at discovering the ways in which an individual's past learning and personality structure may lead him or her to organize and perceive ambiguous information from the environment. Prominent among the several projective tests in common use are the Rorschach Inkblot Test, the Thematic Apperception Test (TAT), and sentence completion tests.

The Rorschach The **Rorschach Inkblot Test** is named after the Swiss psychiatrist Hermann Rorschach (1884–1922), who initiated the experimental use of inkblots in personality assessment in 1911. And, even though the Rorschach test was developed over a century ago, it is still widely used in evaluating people with mental health problems. The test uses 10 inkblot pictures, to which a subject responds in succession after being instructed as follows (Exner, 1993):

> People may see many different things in these inkblot pictures; now tell me what you see, what it makes you think of, what it means to you.

The following excerpts are taken from a subject's responses to one of the actual blots:

> This looks like two men with genital organs exposed. They have had a terrible fight and blood has splashed up against the wall. They have knives or sharp instruments in their hands and have just cut up a body. They have already taken out the lungs and other organs. The body is dismembered . . . nothing remains but a shell . . . the pelvic region. They were fighting as to who will complete the final dismemberment . . . like two vultures swooping down . . . .

The extremely violent content of this response was not common for this particular blot or for any other blot in the series. Although no responsible examiner would base conclusions on a single instance, such content was consistent with other data from this subject, who was diagnosed as an antisocial personality with strong hostility.

Use of the Rorschach in clinical assessment is complicated and requires considerable training (Exner & Erdberg, 2002; Weiner & Meyer, 2009). Methods of administering the test vary; some approaches can take several hours and hence must compete for time with other essential clinical services. Furthermore, the results of the Rorschach can be unreliable because of the subjective nature of test interpretations. For example, interpreters might disagree on the symbolic significance of the response "a house in flames." One person might interpret this particular response as suggesting great feelings of anxiety, whereas another interpreter might see it as suggesting a desire on the part of the patient to set fires. One reason for the diminished use of the Rorschach in projective testing today comes from the fact that many clinical treatments used in today's mental health facilities generally require specific behavioral descriptions rather than descriptions of deep-seated personality dynamics, such as those that typically result from interpretation of the Rorschach test.

In the hands of a skilled interpreter, however, the Rorschach can be useful in uncovering certain psychodynamic issues, such as the impact of unconscious motivations on current perceptions of others (Weiner, 2013). Furthermore, attempts have been made to objectify Rorschach interpretations by clearly specifying test variables and empirically exploring their relationship to external criteria such as clinical diagnoses (Exner, 1995). The Rorschach, although generally considered an open-ended, subjective instrument, has been adapted for computer interpretation (Exner, 1987). In a study of the reliability of conclusions drawn from the computer interpretation system, Meyer and colleagues (2005) found that clinicians tended to draw the same conclusions from Rorschach responses as the computer system did.

Some researchers, however, have raised questions about the norms on which the Exner Rorschach Comprehensive System, a scoring and interpretation system, is based (Shaffer et al., 1999; Wood et al., 2001) or on the validity of some of the measures (Wood et al., 2015). The Rorschach was shown to "overpathologize" persons taking the test—that is, the test appears to show psychopathology even when the person is a "normal" person randomly drawn from the community. The extent to which the Rorschach provides valid information beyond what is available from other, more economical instruments has not been demonstrated. Although some researchers have rallied support for the comprehensive system (Hibbard, 2003; Mihura et al., 2013, 2015; Weiner &

Meyer, 2009), the Rorschach test has also been widely criticized as an instrument with low or negligible validity (Garb et al., 1998; Hunsley & Bailey, 1999). A new interpretive system has recently been developed in an effort to provide a more effective system than the Exner Rorschach Comprehensive System (see Meyer et al., 2011).

The use of the Rorschach in clinical assessment has diminished somewhat (Butcher et al., 2013; Piotrowski et al., 1998), in part because insurance companies do not pay for the considerable amount of time needed to administer, score, and interpret the test. However, the Rorschach remains one of the most frequently used instruments in personality assessment (see Choca, 2012, for an introduction).

The Thematic Apperception Test   The **Thematic Apperception Test (TAT)** was introduced in 1935 by its authors, C. D. Morgan and Henry Murray of the Harvard Psychological Clinic. It still is widely used in clinical practice (Rossini & Moretti, 1997) and personality research (Teglasi, 2010). The TAT uses a series of simple pictures, some highly representational and others quite abstract, about which a subject is instructed to make up stories. The content of the pictures, much of them depicting people in various contexts, is highly ambiguous as to actions and motives, so subjects tend to project their own conflicts and worries onto it (see Morgan, 2002, for a historical description of the test stimuli).

Several scoring and interpretation systems have been developed to focus on different aspects of a subject's stories such as expressions of needs (Atkinson, 1992), the person's perception of reality (Arnold, 1962), and the person's fantasies (Klinger, 1979). It is time consuming to apply these systems, and there is little evidence that they make a clinically significant contribution. Hence, most often a clinician simply makes a qualitative and subjective determination of how the story content reflects the person's underlying traits, motives, and preoccupations. Such interpretations often depend as much on "art" as on "science," and there is much room for error in such an informal procedure.

An example of the way a subject's problems may be reflected in TAT stories is shown in the following case, which is based on Card 1 (a picture of a boy staring at a violin on a table in front of him). The client, David, was a 15-year-old boy who had been referred to the clinic by his parents because of their concern about his withdrawal and poor work at school.

David's TAT Response

David was generally cooperative during the testing, although he remained rather unemotional and unenthusiastic throughout. When he was given Card 1 of the TAT, he paused for over a minute, carefully scrutinizing the card.

"I think this is a . . . uh . . . machine gun . . . yeah, it's a machine gun. The guy is staring at it. Maybe he got it for his birthday or stole it or something." [Pause. The examiner reminded him that he was to make up a story about the picture.]

"OK. This boy, I'll call him Karl, found this machine gun . . . a Browning automatic rifle . . . in his garage. He kept it in his room for protection. One day he decided to take it to school to quiet down the jocks that lord it over everyone. When he walked into the locker hall, he cut loose on the top jock, Amos, and wasted him. Nobody bothered him after that because they knew he kept the BAR in his locker."

It was inferred from this story that David was experiencing a high level of frustration and anger in his life. The extent of this anger was reflected in his perception of the violin in the picture as a machine gun—an instrument of violence. The clinician concluded that David was feeling threatened not only by people at school but even in his own home, where he needed "protection."

This example shows how stories based on TAT cards may provide a clinician with information about a person's conflicts and worries as well as clues as to how the person is handling these problems.

The TAT has been criticized on several grounds (Lilienfeld et al., 2001). There is a "dated" quality to the test stimuli: The pictures, developed in the 1930s, appear quaint to many contemporary subjects, who have difficulty identifying with the characters in the pictures. Subjects often preface their stories with statements like "This is something from a movie I saw on the late-night movies." Additionally, the TAT can require a great deal of time to administer and interpret. As with the Rorschach, interpretation of responses to the TAT is generally subjective, which limits the reliability and validity of the test.

A review (Rossini & Moretti, 1997) pointed out an interesting paradox: Even though the TAT remains popular among practicing clinicians, clinical training programs have reduced the amount of time devoted to teaching graduate students about the TAT, and relatively few contemporary training resources (such as books and manuals) exist. Again, we must note that some examiners, notably those who have long experience in the instrument's use, are capable of making astonishingly accurate interpretations with TAT stories. Typically, however, they have difficulty teaching these skills to others. On reflection, such an observation should not be unduly surprising, but it does point to the essentially "artistic" element involved at this skill level.

Sentence Completion Test   Another projective procedure that has proved useful in personality assessment is the **sentence completion test** (Fernald & Fernald, 2010). A number of such tests have been designed for children, adolescents, and adults. Such tests consist of the beginnings of sentences that an adult might be asked to complete, as in these examples:

1. I wish _____
2. My mother _____
3. Sex _____
4. I hate _____
5. People _____

Sentence completion tests, which are related to the free-association method, a procedure in which a client is asked to respond freely, are somewhat more structured than the Rorschach and most other projective tests. They help examiners pinpoint important clues to an individual's problems, attitudes, and symptoms through the content of her or his responses. Interpretation of the item responses, however, is generally subjective and unreliable. Despite the fact that the test stimuli (the sentence stems) are standard, interpretation is usually done in an ad hoc manner and without benefit of normative comparisons.

In sum, projective tests have an important place in many clinical settings, particularly those that attempt to obtain a comprehensive picture of a person's psychodynamic functioning and those that have the necessary trained staff to conduct extensive individual psychological evaluations. The great strengths of projective techniques—their unstructured nature and their focus on the unique aspects of personality—are at the same time their weaknesses because they make interpretation subjective, unreliable, and difficult to validate. Moreover, projective tests typically require a great deal of time to administer and advanced skill to interpret—both scarce quantities in many clinical settings.

OBJECTIVE PERSONALITY TESTS   **Objective personality tests** are structured—that is, they typically use questionnaires, self-report inventories, or rating scales in which questions or items are carefully phrased and alternative responses are specified as choices. They therefore involve a far more controlled format than projective devices and thus are more amenable to objectively based quantification. One virtue of such quantification is its precision, which in turn enhances the reliability of test outcomes.

A large number of personality assessment measures are available for use in personality and clinical assessment. For example, the NEO-PI (Neuroticism-Extroversion-Openness Personality Inventory) provides information on the major dimensions in personality and is widely used in evaluating personality factors in normal-range populations (Costa & Widiger, 2002). In addition, many objective assessment instruments have been developed to assess focused clinical problems. For example, the Millon Clinical Multiaxial Inventory (MCMI-III; see Choca, 2004) was developed to evaluate the underlying personality dimensions among clients in psychological treatment or prior to the beginning of therapy. In this chapter, we focus primarily on the most widely used personality assessment instrument, the MMPI-2.

The MMPI One of the major structured inventories for personality assessment is the **Minnesota Multiphasic Personality Inventory (MMPI)**, now called the MMPI-2 for adults after a revision in 1989 (Butcher, 2011; Friedman et al., 2015). We focus on it here because in many ways it is the prototype and the standard for this class of instruments.

Several years in development, the MMPI was introduced for general use in 1943 by Starke Hathaway and J. C. McKinley; it is today the most widely used personality test for clinical and **forensic** (court-related) assessment and for psychopathology research in the United States (Archer et al., 2006; Lally, 2003). (For a comprehensive discussion of the use of the MMPI-2 in court testimony, see Butcher et al., 2015.) The MMPI-2 is also the personality assessment instrument most frequently taught in graduate clinical psychology programs (Ready & Veague, 2014). Over 19,000 books and articles on the MMPI instruments have been published since the test was introduced. Moreover, translated versions of the inventory are widely used internationally. (The original MMPI was translated over 150 times and used in over 46 countries; Butcher, 2010.) International use of the revised inventory is increasing rapidly; over 32 translations have been made since it was published in 1989 (Butcher & Williams, 2009).

The Validity and Clinical Scales of the MMPI The original MMPI, a self-report questionnaire, consisted of 550 items covering topics ranging from physical condition and psychological states to moral and social attitudes. Typically, clients are encouraged to answer all of the items either "true" or "false." The pool of items was originally administered to a large group of normal individuals (affectionately called the "Minnesota normals") and several quite homogeneous groups of patients with particular psychiatric diagnoses. Answers to all the items were then item-analyzed to see which ones differentiated the various groups. On the basis of the findings, the 10 clinical scales were constructed, each consisting of the items that were answered by one of the patient groups in the direction opposite to the predominant response of the normal group. This rather ingenious method of selecting scorable items, known as "empirical keying," originated with the MMPI and doubtless accounts for much of the instrument's power. Note that it involves no subjective prejudgment about the "meaning" of a true or false answer to any item; that meaning resides entirely in whether the answer is the same as the answer deviantly given by patients of varying diagnoses. Should an examinee's pattern of true and false responses closely approximate that of a particular pathological group, it is a reasonable inference that he or she shares other psychiatrically significant characteristics with that group—and may in fact "psychologically" be a member of that group. (See the MMPI-2 profile in Table 4.1.)

Each of these 10 clinical scales thus measures tendencies to respond in psychologically deviant ways. Raw scores on these scales are compared with the corresponding scores of the normal population, many of whom did (and do) answer a few items in the critical direction (suggesting psychological problems), and the results are plotted on the standard MMPI profile form. By drawing a line connecting the scores for the different scales, a clinician can construct a profile that shows how far from normal a patient's performance is on each of the scales. To reiterate the basic strategy with an example, the Schizophrenia scale is made up of the items that patients diagnosed with schizophrenia consistently answered in a way that differentiated

Starke R. Hathaway (1903–1984), clinical psychologist, was a pioneer in physiological psychology and personality assessment. In 1940, he and J. C. McKinley published the Minnesota Multiphasic Personality Inventory for evaluating the symptoms and behavior of psychiatric and medical patients. The MMPI became the most widely used personality assessment instrument in use, and its revised version (MMPI-2) is the most frequently used personality measure today.

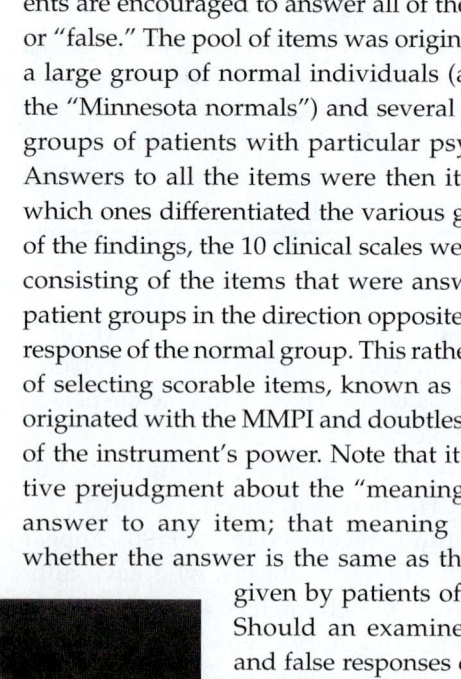

J. C. McKinley (1891–1950), a neuropsychiatrist at the University of Minnesota Hospital, coauthored the MMPI with Starke Hathaway and conducted research on the MMPI with both medical and psychiatric populations.

Table 4.1 The Scales of the MMPI-2

Validity Scales	
Cannot say score (?)	Measures the total number of unanswered items
Infrequency scale (F)	Measures the tendency to falsely claim or exaggerate psychological problems in the first part of the booklet; alternatively, detects random responding
Infrequency scale (FB)	Measures the tendency to falsely claim or exaggerate psychological problems on items toward the end of the booklet
Infrequency scale (Fp)	Measures the tendency to exaggerate psychological problems among psychiatric inpatients
Lie scale (L)	Measures the tendency to claim excessive virtue or to try to present an overall favorable image
Defensiveness scale (K)	Measures the tendency to see oneself in an unrealistically positive way
Superlative Self-Presentation scale (S)	Measures the tendency for some people to present themselves in a highly positive manner or superlative manner. The S scale contains five subscales that address ways in which the person presents in an overly positive manner
Response Inconsistency scale (VRIN)	Measures the tendency to endorse items in an inconsistent or random manner
Response Inconsistency scale (TRIN)	Measures the tendency to endorse items in an inconsistently true or false manner
Clinical Scales	
Scale 1 Hypochondriasis (Hs)	Measures excessive somatic concern and physical complaints
Scale 2 Depression (D)	Measures symptomatic depression
Scale 3 Hysteria (Hy)	Measures hysteroid personality features such as a "rose-colored glasses" view of the world and the tendency to develop physical problems under stress
Scale 4 Psychopathic deviate (Pd)	Measures antisocial tendencies
Scale 5 Masculinity-femininity (Mf)	Measures gender-role reversal
Scale 6 Paranoia (Pa)	Measures suspicious, paranoid ideation
Scale 7 Psychasthenia (Pt)	Measures anxiety and obsessive, worrying behavior
Scale 8 Schizophrenia (Sc)	Measures peculiarities in thinking, feeling, and social behavior
Scale 9 Hypomania (Ma)	Measures unrealistically elated mood state and tendencies to yield to impulses
Scale 0 Social introversion (Si)	Measures social anxiety, withdrawal, and overcontrol
Special Scales	
Scale APS Addiction Proneness scale	Assesses the extent to which the person matches personality features of people in substance use treatment
Scale AAS Addiction Acknowledgment scale	Assesses the extent to which the person has acknowledged substance abuse problems
Scale MAC-R MacAndrew Addiction scale	An empirical scale measuring proneness to become addicted to various substances
Scale MDS Marital Distress scale	Assesses perceived marital relationship problems
Hostility scale (Ho)	Addresses hostility or anger control problems
Posttraumatic Stress scale (Pk)	Assesses a number of symptoms and attitudes that are found among people who are experiencing posttraumatic stress problems

them from normal individuals. People who score high (relative to norms) on this scale, though not necessarily schizophrenic, often show characteristics typical of that clinical population. For instance, high scorers on this scale may be socially inept, may be withdrawn, and may have peculiar thought processes; they may have diminished contact with reality and, in severe cases, may have delusions and hallucinations.

The MMPI also includes a number of validity scales to detect whether a patient has answered the questions in a straightforward, honest manner. For example, there is one scale that detects lying by one's claiming of extreme virtue and several scales that detect possible malingering or faking of symptoms. Extreme endorsement of the items on any of these scales may invalidate the test, whereas lesser endorsements frequently contribute important interpretive insights. In addition to the validity scales and the 10 clinical scales, a number of additional scales have been devised—for example, to detect substance abuse, marital distress, and posttraumatic stress disorder.

Clinically, the MMPI is used in several ways to evaluate a patient's personality characteristics and clinical problems. Perhaps the most typical use of the MMPI is as a diagnostic standard. As we have seen, the individual's profile pattern is compared with profiles of known patient groups. If the profile matches a group, information about patients in this group can suggest a broad descriptive diagnosis for the patient under study.

Revision of the Original MMPI The original MMPI, in spite of being the most widely used personality measure, has not been without its critics. Some psychodynamically oriented clinicians felt that the MMPI (like other structured, objective tests) was superficial and did not adequately reflect the complexities of an individual taking the test. Some behaviorally oriented critics, on the other hand, criticized the MMPI (and in fact, the entire genre of personality tests) as being too oriented toward measuring unobservable "mentalistic" constructs such as traits. A more specific criticism was leveled at the datedness of the MMPI.

In response to these criticisms, the publisher of the MMPI sponsored a revision of the instrument. The scales listed on the standard original MMPI-2 profile form are described in Table 4.1. This revised MMPI, designated "MMPI-2" for adults, became available for general professional use in mid-1989 (Butcher, 2011; Butcher et al., 2001), and the MMPI-A for adolescents (see Williams & Butcher, 2011) was published in 1992. The original 10 clinical scales were kept on the revised version. The revised versions of the MMPI have been validated in many clinical studies (Greene, 2011).

Research has provided strong support for the revised versions of the MMPI (Friedman et al., 2015; Greene et al., 2003). The clinical scales, which, apart from minimal item deletion or rewording, have been retained in their original form, seem to measure the same properties of personality organization and functioning as they always have. A comparable stability of meaning is observed for the standard validity scales (also essentially unchanged), which have been reinforced with three additional scales to detect tendencies to respond untruthfully to some items.

Advantages and Limitations of Objective Personality Tests Self-report inventories such as the MMPI have a number of advantages over other types of personality tests. They are cost effective, highly reliable, and objective; they also can be scored and interpreted (and, if desired, even administered) by computer. A number of general criticisms, however, have been leveled against the use of self-report inventories. As we have seen, some clinicians consider them too mechanistic to portray the complexity of human beings and their problems accurately. Also, because these tests require the subject to read, comprehend, and answer verbal material, patients who are illiterate or confused cannot take the tests. Furthermore, the individual's cooperation is required in self-report inventories, and it is possible that the person might distort his or her answers to create a particular impression. The validity scales of the MMPI-2 are a direct attempt to deal with this last criticism.

Because of their scoring formats and emphasis on test validation, scientifically constructed objective personality inventories lend themselves particularly well to automated interpretation. The earliest practical applications of computer technology to test scoring and interpretation

involved the MMPI. Over 50 years ago, psychologists at the Mayo Clinic programmed a computer to score and interpret clinical profiles. Computerized personality assessment has evolved substantially during the past few years, and other highly sophisticated MMPI and MMPI-2 interpretation systems have been developed (Butcher et al., 2004). Computer-based MMPI interpretation systems typically employ powerful **actuarial procedures** (Grove et al., 2000). In such systems, descriptions of the actual behavior or other established characteristics of many subjects with particular patterns of test scores have been stored in the computer. Whenever a person has one of these test score patterns, the appropriate description is printed out in the computer's evaluation. Such descriptions have been written and stored for a number of different test score patterns, most of them based on MMPI-2 scores.

The accumulation of precise actuarial data for an instrument like the MMPI-2 is difficult, time consuming, and expensive. This is in part because of the complexity of the instrument itself; the potential number of significantly different MMPI-2 profile patterns is legion. The profiles of many subjects therefore do not "fit" the profile types for which actuarial data are available. Problems of actuarial data acquisition also arise at the other end: the behaviors or problems that are to be detected or predicted by the instrument. Many conditions that are of vital clinical importance are relatively rare (for example, suicide) or are psychologically complex (for example, possible psychogenic components in a patient's physical illness). Thus, it is difficult to accumulate enough cases to serve as an adequate actuarial database. In these situations, the interpretive program writer is forced to fall back on general clinical lore and practical experience to formulate clinical descriptions appropriate to the types of profiles actually obtained.

Sometimes the different paragraphs generated by the computer have inconsistencies resulting from the fact that different parts of a subject's test pattern call up different paragraphs from the computer. The computer simply prints out blindly what has been found to be typical for people making similar scores on the various clinical scales and cannot integrate the descriptions it picks up. At this point the human element comes in: In the clinical use of computers, it is always essential that a trained professional further interpret and monitor the assessment data (Atlis et al., 2006).

Computerized personality assessment is no longer a novelty but an important, dependable adjunct to clinical assessment. Computerized psychological evaluations are a quick and efficient means of providing a clinician with needed information early in the decision-making process. Examples of computer-generated descriptions for the case of Andrea C., presented in the next section, appear in the evaluations reprinted in the Developments in Practice box.

The Case of Andrea C.: Experiencing Violence in the Workplace

4.4 **Evaluate the case study of a woman who experienced violence in the workplace.**

Andrea C., a 49-year-old divorced woman, was employed as a manager in a firm whose office was located in a somewhat isolated section of the community. Her responsibilities included opening the office building at 6:00 a.m. and preparing the office activities for the day. She felt somewhat unsafe in opening up the office alone and had complained to upper management about the lack of security in the building. One morning, as she was opening the office door, she was accosted by a stranger who hit her on the head, knocking her unconscious, breaking her nose, and cutting her face and neck. The assailant stabbed her several times in her leg and attempted to sexually assault her, but ran away with her purse as car lights came on the street.

Andrea suffered a number of physical injuries and recurring symptoms from the assault and was hospitalized for 8 days following the attack. Her symptoms included a fractured skull, fractured nose, multiple stab wounds on her body, facial injuries, dizziness, impaired balance, wrist pain, residual cognitive symptoms from being unconscious, poor memory, intense anxiety, and symptoms of posttraumatic stress. After recovery from the physical injuries she was fearful to return to work, and she applied for disability as a result of her injuries. The company for which she worked rejected her request, and she filed a lawsuit for personal injury disability.

A psychological evaluation was requested by the company's insurer to determine the legitimacy of Andrea's disability claim. As a central part of the evaluation, the MMPI-2 was administered by the psychologist hired by the defense to appraise Andrea's personality and symptoms (see the validity, clinical, and supplementary profiles shown in Figures 4.1 and 4.2). The MMPI-2 clinical scale pattern shows clear mental health problems. Her clinical scale pattern with the high scores on the D (Depression), Hs (Hypochondriasis), and Pt (Anxiety)

Figure 4.1 Profile of the MMPI-2 validity scales for Andrea C.

(Excerpted from *The Minnesota Report™: Adult Clinical System-Revised*, 4th Edition, by James N. Butcher.)

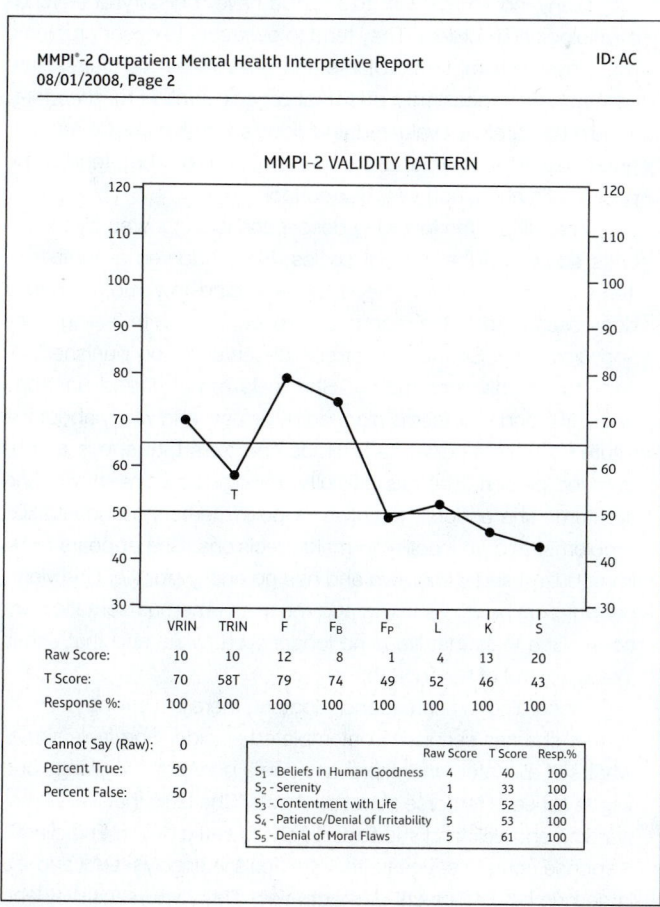

Figure 4.2 Profile of the MMPI-2 clinical scales and supplementary scales for Andrea C.

(Excerpted from *The Minnesota Report™: Adult Clinical System-Revised*, 4th Edition, by James N. Butcher.)

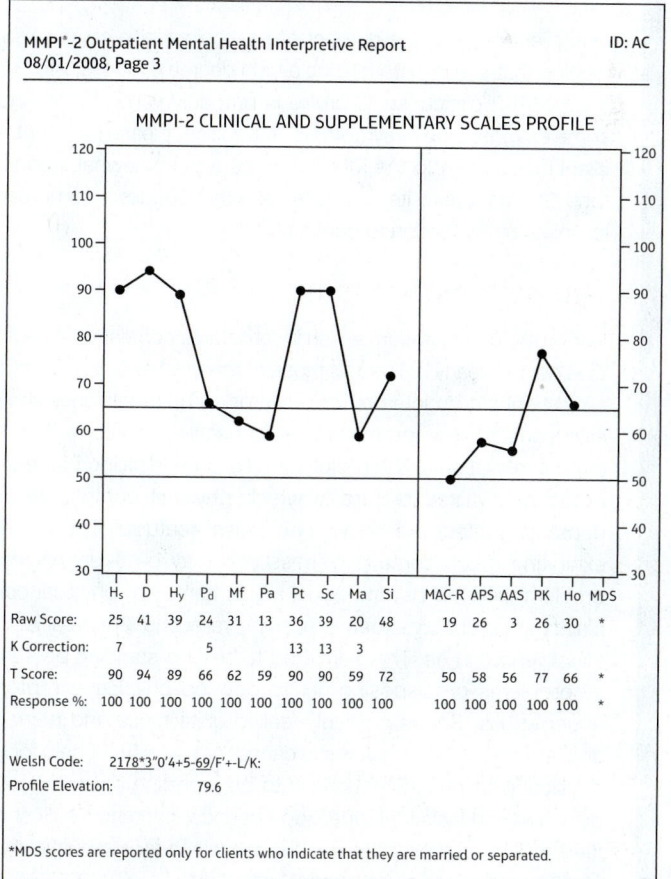

scales, along with the high score obtained on the PTSD scale, indicate that she is experiencing mental health symptoms related to stressful life events. A full description of this symptom picture is presented in the computer-based interpretive report shown in the Developments in Practice box.

Interestingly, the insurance company's psychological expert recommended against Andrea's receiving compensation based on his interpretation of a controversial psychological scale (referred to as the Fake Bad Scale, or FBS) that was designed to assess "malingering." After an initial hearing to examine the validity and acceptability of the FBS, the judge in the case prohibited the use of the scale as a measure of effort, malingering, or overreporting of symptoms to bolster his opinion.

The case went to trial, and Andrea's attorneys relied on the medical evidence and results of the MMPI-2 to support her claim of physical damages and posttraumatic adjustment problems. The jury awarded Andrea substantial damages as a result of the injuries and the trauma that she experienced from the assault.

EVALUATING ANDREA'S COMPUTER-GENERATED MMPI-2 REPORT   The narrative report of the computer-based MMPI-2 interpretation contains technical test information to assist the assessment psychologist in interpreting the test results. The report is considered a professional-to-professional consultation and is not recommended for release to patients. The computer report for Andrea contains detailed data about the relative frequency of the test pattern's occurrence in relevant clinical settings and in the normative or standardized population. For example, the report provides information as to how Andrea's elevated clinical scale scores compare with persons being evaluated in an outpatient clinical setting as well as the frequency of the score in the MMPI-2 general normative sample of women. Her test results indicated that her highest score, the Depression scale score, typically occurs in 18.7 percent of the outpatient women. Moreover, only 4.4 percent of women in the normative sample obtain this high elevation on the Depression scale. Thus, this high Depression scale elevation is considered to be a relatively common symptom among women seeking outpatient mental health services.

Developments in Practice
Computer-Based MMPI-2 Report for Andrea C.

Profile Validity

This client endorsed a number of psychological problems, suggesting that she is experiencing a high degree of stress. Although the MMPI-2 clinical scale profile is probably valid, it may show some exaggeration of symptoms. In addition, please note that the client's approach to the MMPI-2 items was somewhat inconsistent. She endorsed items in a pattern that suggests some carelessness or inattention to content.

Symptomatic Patterns

Her profile configuration, which incorporates correlates of Hs and D, is not as clearly defined as those of many other clients from this clinical setting. In interpreting the profile, the practitioner should also consider any prominent clinical scale elevations that are close in elevation to the prototype. This client's profile presents a broad and mixed picture in which physical complaints and depressed affect are likely to be salient features. The client is exhibiting much somatic distress and may be experiencing a problem with her psychological adjustment. Her physical complaints are probably extreme, possibly reflecting a general lack of effectiveness in life. There are likely to be long-standing personality problems predisposing her to develop physical symptoms under stress. She is probably feeling quite tense and nervous, and she may be feeling that she cannot get by without help for her physical problems. She is likely to be reporting a great deal of pain, and she feels that others do not understand how sick she is feeling. She may be quite irritable and may become hostile if her symptoms are not given "proper" attention.

Many individuals with this profile have a history of psychophysiological disorders. They tend to overreact to minor problems with physical symptoms. Ulcers and gastrointestinal distress are common. The possibility of actual organic problems, therefore, should be carefully evaluated. Individuals with this profile report a great deal of tension and a depressed mood. They tend to be pessimistic and gloomy in their outlook.

In addition, the following description is suggested by the client's scores on the content scales. She endorsed a number of items suggesting that she is experiencing low morale and a depressed mood. She reports a preoccupation with feeling guilty and unworthy. She feels that she deserves to be punished for wrongs she has committed. She feels regretful and unhappy about life, and she seems plagued by anxiety and worry about the future. She feels hopeless at times and feels that she is a condemned person. She has difficulty managing routine affairs, and the items she endorsed suggest a poor memory, concentration problems, and an inability to make decisions. She appears to be immobilized and withdrawn and has no energy for life. She views her physical health as failing and reports numerous somatic concerns. She feels that life is no longer worthwhile and that she is losing control of her thought processes.

According to her response content, there is a strong possibility that she has seriously contemplated suicide. She feels somewhat self-alienated and expresses some personal misgivings or a vague sense of remorse about past acts. She feels that life is unrewarding and dull, and she finds it hard to settle down. The client's response content suggests that she feels intensely fearful about a large number of objects and activities. This hypersensitivity and fearfulness appear to be generalized at this point and may be debilitating to her in social and work situations.

Long-term personality factors identified by other scale elevations may help provide a clinical context for the symptoms she is presently experiencing. She apparently holds some unusual beliefs that appear to be disconnected from reality. Her high score on one MMPI-2 scale, the PSYC (Psychoticism) scale, suggests that she often feels alienated from others and might experience unusual symptoms such as delusional beliefs, circumstantial and tangential thinking, and loose associations. She also shows a meager capacity to experience pleasure in life. Persons with high scores on another MMPI-2 scale, the INTR (Introversion/Low Positive Emotionality), tend to be pessimistic.

Profile Frequency

Profile interpretation can be greatly facilitated by examining the relative frequency of clinical scale patterns in various settings. The client's high-point clinical scale score (D) occurred in 7.0 percent of the MMPI-2 normative sample of women. However, only 4.4 percent of the women had D scale peak scores at or above a T score of 65, and only 2.1 percent had well-defined D spikes. Her elevated MMPI-2 profile configuration (1-2/2-1) is rare in samples of normals, occurring in 1.0 percent of the MMPI-2 normative sample of women.

This high-point MMPI-2 score is the most frequent clinical scale score in various samples of outpatient women. In the Pearson outpatient sample, the high-point clinical scale score on D occurred in 18.7 percent of the women. Moreover, 17.1 percent of the outpatient women had the D scale spike at or above a T score of 65, and 9.0 percent had well-defined D spikes. Her elevated MMPI-2 profile configuration (1-2/2-1) occurred in 2.9 percent of the women in the Pearson outpatient sample.

Profile Stability

The relative elevation of her clinical scale scores suggests that her profile is not as well defined as many other profiles. There was no difference between the profile type used to develop the present report (involving Hs and D) and the next highest scale in the profile code. Therefore, behavioral elements related to elevations on Pt should be considered as well. For example, intensification of anxiety, negative self-image, and unproductive rumination could be important in her symptom pattern.

Interpersonal Relations

She appears to be somewhat passive-dependent in relationships. She may manipulate others through her physical symptoms, and she may become hostile if sufficient attention is not paid to her complaints.

She is a very introverted person who has difficulty meeting and interacting with other people. She is shy and emotionally distant. She tends to be very uneasy, rigid, and overcontrolled in social situations. Her shyness is probably symptomatic of a broader pattern of social withdrawal. Personality characteristics related to social introversion tend to be stable over time. Her generally reclusive behavior, introverted lifestyle, and tendency toward interpersonal avoidance may be prominent in any future test results.

The client's scores on the content scales suggest the following additional information concerning her interpersonal relations. She appears to be an individual who has rather cynical views about life. Any efforts to initiate new behaviors may be colored by her negativism. She may view relationships with others as threatening and harmful.

Diagnostic Considerations

Individuals with this profile type are often seen as neurotic and may receive a diagnosis of somatoform disorder. Actual organic problems such as ulcers or hypertension might be part of the clinical picture. Some individuals with this profile have problems with abuse of pain medication or other prescription drugs.

Treatment Considerations

Her view of herself as physically disabled needs to be considered in any treatment planning. She tends to somatize her difficulties and to seek medical solutions rather than deal with them psychologically. She seems to tolerate a high level of psychological conflict and may not be motivated to deal with her problems directly. She is probably not a strong candidate for psychotherapy treatment approaches that require self-scrutiny, insight development, and high motivation for change. Psychological treatment may progress more rapidly if her symptoms are dealt with through behavior modification techniques. However, with her generally pessimistic attitude and low energy resources, she seems to have little hope of getting better.

The client's scores on the content scales seem to indicate low potential for change. She may feel that her problems are not addressable through therapy and that she is not likely to benefit much from psychological treatment at this time. Her apparently negative treatment attitudes may need to be explored early in therapy if treatment is to be successful.

She harbors many negative work attitudes that could limit her adaptability in the workplace. Her low morale and lack of interest in work could impair future adjustment to employment, a factor that should be taken into consideration in treatment.

Source: Excerpted from *The Minnesota Report™: Adult Clinical System-Revised*, 4th Edition, by James N. Butcher.

The reader should also note that some of the scales mentioned in the computer narrative report for Andrea are not listed in Table 4.1. There are a number of other MMPI-2 scales in the literature and in common use with the MMPI-2 that are not listed due to space restrictions in this book. For example, the MMPI-2 has 15 content-based scales, that is, scales that are comprised of homogeneous content themes (such as Negative Work Attitudes, Family Problems, and Type-A Behavior). These scales address specific problem themes in patients with mental health challenges. Five additional scales, referred to as the Psychopathology Five (PSY-5) scales, address the personality disorder content domains that are referred to as the "Big 5" personality dimensions. These personality dimensions include Aggressiveness, Psychoticism, Disconstraint, Negative Emotionality/Neuroticism, and Introversion/Low Positive Emotionality.

in review

- Distinguish between structured and unstructured clinical assessment interviews.
- What are the assumptions behind the use of projective personality tests? How do they differ from objective tests?
- What advantages do objective personality tests offer over less structured tests?
- What is the Minnesota Multiphasic Personality Inventory (MMPI-2)? Describe how the MMPI-2 scales work.

The Integration of Assessment Data

4.5 **Discuss how practitioners integrate assessment data in treatment planning.**

As assessment data are collected, their significance must be interpreted so that they can be integrated into a coherent working model for use in planning. Clinicians in individual private practice normally assume this complicated task on their own. In a clinic or hospital setting, assessment data are often evaluated in a staff conference attended by members of an interdisciplinary team (perhaps consisting of a clinical psychologist, a psychiatrist, a social worker, and other mental health personnel) who are concerned

In a clinic or hospital setting, assessment data are usually evaluated in a staff conference attended by members of an interdisciplinary team—including, for example, a clinical psychologist, a psychiatrist, a social worker, and a psychiatric nurse. A staff decision may determine whether a person with severe depression will be hospitalized or remain with his or her family or whether an accused person will be declared competent to stand trial. Because these decisions can have such great impact on the lives of the clients, it is critical that clinicians be well aware of the limitations of assessment.

with the decisions to be made regarding treatment. By putting together all the information they have gathered, they can see whether the findings complement each other and form a definitive clinical picture or whether gaps or discrepancies exist that necessitate further investigation.

This integration of all the data gathered at the time of an original assessment may lead to agreement on a tentative diagnostic classification for a patient. In any case, the findings of each member of the team, as well as the recommendations for treatment, are entered into the case record so that it will always be possible to check back and see why a certain course of therapy was undertaken, how accurate the clinical assessment was, and how valid the treatment decision turned out to be.

New assessment data collected during the course of therapy provide feedback on the therapy's effectiveness and serve as a basis for making needed modifications in an ongoing treatment program. As we have noted, clinical assessment data are also commonly used in evaluating the progress of therapy and in comparing the effectiveness of different therapeutic and preventive approaches.

Ethical Issues in Assessment

The decisions made on the basis of assessment data may have far-reaching implications for the people involved. A staff decision may determine whether a person with severe depression will be hospitalized or remain with her or his family, or whether an accused person will be declared competent to stand trial. Thus, a valid decision, based on accurate assessment data, is of far more than theoretical importance. Because of the impact that assessment can have on the lives of others, it is important that those involved keep several factors in mind when evaluating test results:

1. **Potential cultural bias of the instrument or the clinician:** Some psychological tests may not elicit valid information for a patient from a minority group (Gray-Little, 2009; Wen-Shing & Streltzer, 2008). A clinician from one sociocultural background may have trouble assessing objectively the behavior of someone from another background. It is important to ensure—as Greene and colleagues (2003) and Zapata-Sola and colleagues (2009) have shown with the MMPI-2—that the instrument can be confidently used with persons from minority groups.

2. **Theoretical orientation of the clinician:** Assessment is inevitably influenced by a clinician's assumptions, perceptions, and theoretical orientation. For example, a psychoanalyst and a behaviorist might assess the same behaviors quite differently. The psychoanalytically oriented professional is likely to view behaviors as reflecting underlying motives, whereas the behavioral clinician is likely to view the behaviors in the context of the immediate or preceding stimulus situations. Different treatment recommendations are likely to result.

3. **Underemphasis on the external situation:** Many clinicians overemphasize personality traits as the cause of patients' problems without paying enough attention to the possible role of stressors and other circumstances in the patients' life situations. An undue focus on a patient's personality, which some assessment techniques encourage, can divert attention from potentially critical environmental factors.

4. **Insufficient validation:** Some psychological assessment procedures in use today have not been sufficiently validated. For example, unlike many of the personality scales, widely used procedures for behavioral observation and behavioral self-report and the projective techniques have not been subjected to strict psychometric validation.

5. **Inaccurate data or premature evaluation:** There is always the possibility that some assessment data—and any diagnostic label or treatment based on them—may be inaccurate or that the team leader (usually a psychiatrist) might choose to ignore test data in favor of other information. Some risk is always involved in making predictions for an individual on the basis of group data or averages. Inaccurate data or premature conclusions may not only lead to a misunderstanding of a patient's problem but also close off attempts to get further information, with possibly grave consequences for the patient.

in review

- What are some ethical issues that clinicians should be aware of when evaluating a patient's test results?
- Are there concerns over cultural biases in some psychological tests?
- What is test validity?

Classifying Abnormal Behavior

4.6 Explain the process for classifying abnormal behavior.

Classification is important in any science, whether we are studying chemical elements, plants, planets, or people. With an agreed-on classification system we can be confident that we are communicating clearly. If someone says to you, "I saw a dog running down the street," you can probably produce a mental image broadly approximating the appearance of that dog—not from seeing it but rather from your knowledge of animal classifications. There are of course many breeds of dogs, which vary widely in size, color, muzzle length, and so on, and yet we have little difficulty in recognizing the essential features of "dogness." "Dogness" is an example of what psychologists refer to as a "cognitive prototype" or "pattern."

In abnormal psychology, classification involves the attempt to delineate meaningful subvarieties of maladaptive behavior. Like defining abnormal behavior, classification of some kind is a necessary first step toward introducing order into our discussion of the nature, causes, and treatment of such behavior. Classification makes it possible to communicate about particular clusters of abnormal behavior in agreed-on and relatively precise ways. For example, we cannot conduct research on what might cause eating disorders unless we begin with a more or less clear definition of the behavior under examination; otherwise, we would be unable to select, for intensive study, persons whose behavior displays the aberrant eating patterns we hope to understand. There are other reasons for diagnostic classifications, too, such as gathering statistics on how common the various types of disorders are and meeting the needs of medical insurance companies (which insist on having formal diagnoses before they will authorize payment of claims).

Keep in mind that, just as with the process of defining abnormality itself, all classification is the product of human invention—it is, in essence, a matter of making generalizations based on what has been observed. Even when observations are precise and carefully made, the generalizations we arrive at go beyond those observations and enable us to make inferences about underlying similarities and differences. For example, it is common for people experiencing episodes of panic to feel they are about to die. When "panic" is carefully delineated, we find that it is not in fact associated with any enhanced risk of death but, rather, that the people experiencing such episodes tend to share certain other characteristics, such as recent exposure to highly stressful events.

It is not unusual for a classification system to be an ongoing work in progress as new knowledge demonstrates an earlier generalization to be incomplete or flawed. It is important to bear in mind, too, that formal classification is successfully accomplished only through precise techniques of psychological, or clinical, assessment—techniques that have been increasingly refined over the years.

Differing Models of Classification

Three basic approaches are currently used to classify abnormal behavior: the categorical, the dimensional, and the prototypal (Widiger & Boyd, 2009).

THE CATEGORICAL APPROACH The categorical approach, like the diagnostic system of general medical diseases, assumes (1) that all human behavior can be divided into the categories of "healthy" and "disordered," and (2) that within the latter there exist discrete, nonoverlapping classes or types of disorder that have a high degree of within-class homogeneity in both symptoms displayed and the underlying organization of the disorder identified.

THE DIMENSIONAL APPROACH The dimensional and prototypal approaches differ fundamentally in the assumptions they make, particularly with respect to the requirement of discrete and internally homogeneous classes of behavior. In the dimensional approach, it is assumed that a person's typical behavior is the product of differing strengths or intensities of behavior along several definable dimensions such as mood, emotional stability, aggressiveness, gender identity, anxiousness, interpersonal trust, clarity of thinking and communication, social introversion, and so on. The important dimensions, once established, are the same for everyone. People are assumed to differ from one another in their configuration or profile of these dimensional traits (each ranging from very low to very high), not in terms of behavioral indications of a corresponding "dysfunctional" entity presumed to underlie and give rise to the disordered pattern of behavior (Miller et al., 2004; Widiger et al., 2012). "Normal" is discriminated from "abnormal," then, in terms of precise statistical criteria derived from dimensional intensities among unselected people in general, most of whom may be presumed to be close to average, or mentally "normal." We could decide, for example, that anything above the 97th normative percentile on aggressiveness and anything below the 3rd normative percentile on sociability would be considered "abnormal" findings.

Dimensionally based diagnosis has the incidental benefit of directly addressing treatment options. Because the patient's profile of psychological characteristics will normally consist of deviantly high and low points, therapies can be designed to moderate those of excessive intensity (e.g., anxiety) and to enhance those that constitute deficit status (e.g., inhibited self-assertiveness).

Of course, in taking a dimensional approach, it would be possible (perhaps even probable) to discover that such profiles tend to cluster together in types—and even that some of these types are correlated, though imperfectly, with recognizable sorts of gross behavioral malfunctions such as anxiety disorders or depression. It is highly unlikely, however, that any individual's profile will exactly fit a narrowly defined type or that the types identified will not have some overlapping features. This brings us to the prototypal approach.

THE PROTOTYPAL APPROACH A *prototype* (as the term is used here) is a conceptual entity (e.g., personality disorder) depicting an idealized combination of characteristics that more or less regularly occur together in a less-than-perfect or standard way at the level of actual observation. Westen, Shedler, and Bradley (2006), for example, suggest that the *DSM* should provide a narrative description of a

prototypical case of each personality disorder rather than having a listing of diagnostic criteria as it now has. The diagnostician could indicate on a 5-point scale the extent to which a patient matches this description. The clinician would simply rate the overall similarity or "match" between a patient and the prototype.

As we shall see, the official diagnostic criteria defining the various recognized classes of mental disorder, although explicitly intended to create categorical entities, more often than not result in prototypal ones. The central features of the various identified disorders are often somewhat vague, as are the boundaries purporting to separate one disorder from another. Much evidence suggests that a strict categorical approach to identifying differences among types of human behavior, whether normal or abnormal, may well be an unattainable goal. Bearing this in mind as we proceed may help you avoid some confusion. For example, we commonly find that two or more identified disorders regularly occur together in the same individual—a situation known as **comorbidity**. Does this really mean that such a person has two or more entirely separate and distinct disorders? In the typical instance, probably not.

Formal Diagnostic Classification of Mental Disorders

Today, two major psychiatric classification systems are in use: the *International Classification of Diseases* (*ICD-10*) system, published by the WHO, and the *Diagnostic and Statistical Manual of Mental Disorders* (*DSM-5*), published by the American Psychiatric Association. The *ICD-10* system is widely used in Europe and many other countries, whereas the *DSM* system is the standard guide for the United States. Both systems are similar in many respects, such as in using symptoms as the focus of classification and in dividing problems into different facets (to be described in the section that follows).

Certain differences in the way symptoms are grouped in these two systems can sometimes result in a different classification on the *DSM* than on the *ICD-10*. We will focus on the *DSM* system in our discussion of what is to be considered a mental disorder. The *DSM* specifies what subtypes of mental disorders are currently officially recognized and provides, for each, a set of defining criteria in the United States and some other countries. As already noted, the system purports to be a categorical one with sharp boundaries separating the various disorders from one another, but it is in fact a prototypal one with much fuzziness of boundaries and considerable interpenetration, or overlap, of the various "categories" of disorder it identifies.

The criteria that define the recognized categories of disorder consist for the most part of symptoms and signs. The term **symptoms** generally refers to the patient's subjective description, the complaints she or he presents about what is wrong. **Signs**, on the other hand, are objective observations that the diagnostician may make either directly (such as the patient's inability to look another person in the eye) or indirectly (such as the results of pertinent tests administered by a psychological examiner). To make any given diagnosis, the diagnostician must observe the particular criteria—the symptoms and signs that the *DSM* indicates must be met (see Black & Andreasen, 2014).

THE EVOLUTION OF THE *DSM* The *DSM* is currently in its fifth edition (*DSM-5*), published in 2013 after considerable debate and controversy. This system is the product of more than a six-decade evolution involving increasing refinement and precision in the identification and description of mental disorders. The first edition of the manual (*DSM-I*) appeared in 1952 and was largely an outgrowth of attempts to standardize diagnostic practices in use among military personnel during World War II. The 1968 *DSM-II* reflected the additional insights gleaned from a markedly expanded postwar research effort in mental health sponsored by the federal government. Over time, practitioners recognized a defect in both these early efforts: The various types of disorders identified were described in narrative and jargon-laden terms that proved too vague for mental health professionals to agree on their meaning. The result was a serious limitation of diagnostic reliability; that is, two professionals examining the same patient might very well come up with completely different impressions of what disorder(s) the patient had. *DSM-III* (1980) and *DSM-IV-TR* (2000) provided further modification and elaboration of disorders with efforts to make the diagnostic classification clearer. *DSM-5* incorporated more theoretical shifts in diagnostic thinking for many years and has been the most controversial alteration to diagnostic thinking to date. (See the Unresolved Issues at the end of this chapter.)

To address this clinical and scientific impasse, the *DSM-III* of 1980 introduced a radically different approach, one intended to remove, as much as possible, the element of subjective judgment from the diagnostic process. It did so by adopting an "operational" method of defining the various disorders that would officially be recognized. This innovation meant that the *DSM* system would now specify the exact observations that must be made for a given diagnostic label to be applied. In a typical case, a specific number of signs or symptoms from a designated list must be present before a diagnosis can properly be assigned. The new approach, continued in the *DSM-III*'s revised version of 1987 (*DSM-III-R*) and in the 1994 *DSM-IV*, clearly enhanced diagnostic reliability and made efforts to incorporate cultural and ethnic considerations. As an example of the operational approach to diagnosis in *DSM-5*, see the diagnostic criteria for Persistent Depressive Disorder (Dysthemia) in Chapter 7. Note that the revised diagnostic system combines diagnostic criteria from two diagnoses from *DSM-IV*: Chronic Major Depression and Dysthymic Disorder.

The number of recognized mental disorders has increased enormously from *DSM-I* to *DSM-5* due both to the addition of new diagnoses and to the elaborate subdivision of older ones. Because it is unlikely that the nature of the American psyche has changed much in the interim period, it seems more reasonable to assume that mental health professionals view their field in a different light than they did 50 years ago. The *DSM* system is now both more comprehensive and more finely differentiated into subsets of disorders. Most diagnostic categories in *DSM-5* contain a listing of subtypes and specifiers that allow the diagnostician to further refine the diagnosis in order to provide more specific subgroupings of patients.

GENDER DIFFERENCES IN DIAGNOSIS In the origin and manifestation of mental health symptoms, gender differences have long been noted for some disorders. Some disorders show a higher prevalence rate for male patients (such as antisocial personality) than females; other disorders (such as anorexia) are more prominently found in females. Moreover, males and females who are diagnosed with the same disorder (such as conduct disorder) often show different symptom patterns. Males have a higher rate of fighting and aggression, and females have a greater tendency to lie and be truant from school and they tend to run away from home. The *DSM-5* allows for gender-related differences to be incorporated into the diagnosis.

APPRAISAL OF CULTURAL BACKGROUND IN *DSM-5* The United States is a highly diverse society that is comprised of people from multiple language and cultural backgrounds. Increasingly today, mental health practitioners find themselves engaged in a diagnostic evaluation of a client from a diverse background and with marginal or limited English language skills. The client's ethnicity and cultural background, level of English language comprehension, religious background, and extent of their acclimation to the United States can result in incorrect appraisal of mental health symptoms. People who have not been acculturated to the environment in which they live can appear more psychologically disturbed on tests and interviews than they actually are (Okazaki et al., 2009). It is extremely important for the clinician to carefully appraise the client's background, including the values and attitudes they might bring to the interview, in order to reduce negative impact on the decision-making process.

The *DSM-5* provides a structured interview that focuses on the patient's approach to problems. The Cultural Formulation Interview (CFI) contains 16 questions that the practitioner can use to obtain information during a mental health assessment about the potential impact the client's culture can have on mental health care. The interview questions inquire about patients' perspectives on their present problems, how they perceive the influence of others in influencing their problems, and ways in which their cultural background can influence their adjustment. Moreover, the interview inquires about patients' previous experiences when seeking treatment for their problems. The interview questions attempt to obtain clients' perspectives without typecasting their problems.

THE PROBLEM OF LABELING The psychiatric diagnoses of the sort typified by the *DSM* system are not uniformly revered among mental health professionals (e.g., MacCulloch, 2010; Sarbin, 1997). One important criticism is that a psychiatric diagnosis is little more than a label applied to a defined category of socially disapproved or otherwise problematic behavior.

The diagnostic label describes neither a person nor any underlying pathological condition ("dysfunction") the person necessarily harbors but, rather, some behavioral pattern associated with that person's current level of functioning. Yet once a label has been assigned, it may close off further inquiry. It is all too easy—even for professionals—to accept a label as an accurate and complete description of an individual rather than of that person's current behavior. When a person is labeled "depressed" or "schizophrenic," others are more likely to make certain assumptions about that person that may or may not be accurate. In fact, a diagnostic label can make it hard to look at the person's behavior objectively, without preconceptions about how he or she will act. These expectations can influence even clinically important interactions and treatment choices. For example, arrival at the diagnosis "persistent depressive disorder" may cut off any further inquiry about the patient's life situation and lead abruptly to a prescription for antidepressant medication (Tucker, 1998), or the application of a label such as "borderline personality" might cause the mental health treatment staff to be less optimistic about the patient's prognosis (Markham, 2003).

Once an individual is labeled, he or she may accept a redefined identity and play out the expectations of that role. ("I'm nothing but a substance abuser. I might as well do drugs—everyone expects me to anyway. Also, this is a condition deemed out of my control, so it is pointless for me to be an active participant in my treatment.") This acquisition of a new social identity can be harmful for a variety of reasons. The pejorative and stigmatizing implications of many psychiatric labels can mark people as second-class citizens with severe limitations that are often presumed to be permanent (Link, 2001; Slovenko, 2001). They can also have devastating effects on a person's morale, self-esteem, and relationships with others. The person so labeled may decide that he or she "is" the diagnosis and may thus adopt it as a life "career."

Clearly, it is in the person with the disorder's best interests for mental health professionals to be circumspect in the diagnostic process, in their use of labels, and in ensuring confidentiality with respect to both. A related

change has developed during the past 50 years: For years the traditional term for a person who goes to see a mental health professional was *patient*, a term that is closely associated with medical sickness and a passive stance, waiting (patiently) for the doctor's cure. Today many mental health professionals, especially those trained in nonmedical settings, prefer the term *client* because it implies greater participation on the part of an individual and more responsibility for bringing about his or her own recovery. We use these terms interchangeably in this text.

LIMITED USEFULNESS OF DIAGNOSIS Keep in mind that a *DSM* diagnosis per se may be of limited usefulness. Arriving at a diagnosis is usually required, at least in the form of a "diagnostic impression," before the commencement of clinical services. This is necessitated, perhaps unwisely, by medical insurance requirements and long-standing clinical administrative tradition. The additional information required for adequate clinical assessment may be extensive and extremely difficult to unearth. For the most part, in keeping with psychiatric tradition, that process is interview based. That is, the examiner engages the patient (or perhaps a family member of the patient) in a conversation designed to elicit the information necessary to place the patient in one or more *DSM* diagnostic categories. The interviewer introduces various questions and probes, typically becoming increasingly specific as she or he develops diagnostic hypotheses and checks them out with additional probes related to the criteria for particular *DSM* diagnoses. Physicians in general medical practice do something similar in the course of an examination.

UNSTRUCTURED DIAGNOSTIC INTERVIEWS Like the assessment interviews described earlier, diagnostic interviews are of two general types: unstructured and structured. In the unstructured interview, the examiner follows no preexisting plan with respect to content and sequence of the probes introduced. Unstructured interviews, as their name implies, are somewhat freewheeling. The therapist/clinician asks questions as they occur to him or her, in part on the basis of the responses to previous questions. For example, if the patient/client mentions a father who traveled a lot when he or she was a child, the clinician is free to ask, "Did you miss your father?" or (pursuing a different tack), "How did your mother handle that?" rather than being required to ask the next question in a predetermined list. Many clinical examiners prefer this unfettered approach because it enables them to follow perhaps idiosyncratic "leads." In the preceding example, the clinician might have chosen to ask about the mother's reaction on the basis of a developing suspicion that the mother may have been depressed during the client's childhood years. There is one serious drawback to the freewheeling style, however: The information that an interview yields is limited to the content of that interview. Should another clinician conduct another unstructured interview of the same patient, he or she might come up with a different clinical picture.

STRUCTURED DIAGNOSTIC INTERVIEWS The structured interview probes the client in a manner that is highly controlled (Daniel & Gurczynski, 2010; Mestre et al., 2013). Guided by a sort of master plan (sometimes to the extent of specifying the examiner's exact wording), the clinician using a structured interview typically seeks to discover whether the person's symptoms and signs "fit" diagnostic criteria that are more precise and "operational" than in the past. The use of more precise criteria and of highly structured diagnostic interviewing has substantially improved diagnostic reliability, but the structured interview format is still used only sporadically in routine clinical work. Nevertheless, the precision of clinical research, including epidemiological research to be discussed later, has profited enormously from these developments. A number of structured diagnostic interviews have been developed that can be used in various contexts. In clinical and research situations, a popular instrument has been the Schedules for Clinical Assessment in Neuropsychiatry (SCAN), published by the WHO (1994), which enables the diagnostician to arrive at an *ICD-10* diagnosis.

in review

- Why is a classification system needed in abnormal psychology?
- What is the meaning of reliability and validity in the context of such a classification system?
- What is the difference between dimensional and prototypal classification strategies?
- Describe the differences between structured and unstructured diagnostic interviews.

Unresolved Issues

The *DSM-5*: Issues in Acceptance of Changed Diagnostic Criteria

Change is a part of life, and complex criteria such as those contained in the *Diagnostic and Statistical Manual* can become obsolete or inadequate as a result of new research developments or changes in clinical practice requirements. As noted in Chapter 1, periodic updating of the diagnostic criteria is required to make them more effective and acceptable to the professional community. The revision of the diagnostic system that resulted in *DSM-5* was an arduous task that was initiated in 2007 by the American Psychiatric Association. The revision program involved obtaining substantial input from numerous mental health professionals, both practitioners and researchers, before it was completed. Although many aspects of the *DSM-IV-TR* version were continued in the *DSM-5* because of their clarity and broad acceptance, some categories were modified, moved to different locations in the system, or even dropped. Moreover, a number of new diagnostic criteria were added. The revision process for the *DSM* generated substantial controversy, and a number of critics have expressed their concerns over various changes (see the Thinking Critically box in Chapter 1 as well as discussions by Alarcón et al., 2009; Batstra & Frances, 2012a, 2012b; Jones, 2012; Kornstein, 2010).

One of the most widely discussed problems with the earlier diagnostic manuals was the manner in which personality disorders were classified, that is, in a categorical rather than dimensional system. Earlier in this chapter, we described the differing approaches to categorizing personality disorders from the dimensional versus the prototypal perspective. (This topic will be considered in greater detail in Chapter 10.) The debates between the proponents of each classification are likely to continue (see also the comprehensive discussion provided by O'Donohue et al., 2007). The *DSM-5* system will likely require substantial time and effort to overcome issues and various viewpoints on conceptualizing personality disorders in order to produce a model that will be useful both in clinical diagnosis and in guiding research.

Personality disorders are not the only diagnostic categories that required significant rethinking. Other categories, such as posttraumatic stress disorder (PTSD), have been found to be unclear in many respects and limited or overly narrow in others (see Chapter 5). The earlier diagnostic manuals required direct involvement in an experienced trauma in order for the PTSD diagnosis to be applied. However, as a result of experiences following the World Trade Center terrorist attack in 2001, many people who were "traumatized" by the unfolding saga through the constant media coverage of the events also experienced PTSD as a result of indirect exposure. Under the *DSM-IV-TR*, these circumstances would not apply, so the diagnostic classification of PTSD would be considered inappropriate. This requirement resulted in many authorities proposing a modification of the criteria to reduce this limitation (Marshall et al., 2007), while others remain concerned that such changes could result in a problematic expansion of the diagnosis of PTSD. For example, there is concern that the broadened classification would label people who might be experiencing "normal" grief as having a major depressive disorder (Frances, 2010b). This could result from a "medicalization of normal emotion" and could prompt some drug companies to "quickly and greedily" pounce on the opportunity to mount a marketing campaign for people who are bereaved (Frances, 2010b).

The diagnostic criteria for mental disorders in the DSM are not viewed by most mental health professionals as fixed-component systems but as workable criteria that evolve and develop to accommodate new research and practical developments. The periodic remaking of the *DSM* is never a smooth transition, but the resulting system is, nevertheless, a valuable conceptual guide that provides an agreed-on language that students, practitioners, and researchers can employ to enable clear communication about mental disorders. Frances and Widiger (2012) pointed out that the *DSM* system is "imperfect, but it is indispensable" (p. 111).

Summary

4.1 Identify the basic elements in assessment.

- Clinical assessment is one of the most important and complex responsibilities of mental health professionals. The extent to which a person's problems are understood and appropriately treated depends largely on the adequacy of the psychological assessment.

- The goals of psychological assessment include identifying and describing the individual's symptoms; determining the chronicity and severity of the problems; evaluating the potential causal factors in the person's background; and exploring the individual's personal resources that might be an asset in his or her treatment program.

4.2 Describe the factors involved in the assessment of the physical organism.

- Because many psychological problems have physical components, either as underlying causal factors or as symptom patterns, it is often important to include a medical examination in the psychological assessment.

- In cases where organic brain damage is suspected, it is important to conduct neurological tests—such as an EEG; a CAT, PET, or MRI scan; or an fMRI—to help determine the site and extent of organic brain disorder.

- For someone with suspected organic brain damage, a battery of neuropsychological tests might be recommended to determine whether or in what manner the underlying brain disorder is affecting her or his mental and behavioral capabilities.

4.3 Explain the interview process, clinical observation, and testing in psychosocial assessment.

- The most widely used and flexible psychosocial assessment methods are the clinical interview and behavior observation. There are two basic strategies in assessment by interview: structured and unstructured interview procedures. Clinical observation involves the clinician's development of an objective description of the person's appearance and behavior including emotional responses and mental health symptoms he or she may manifest.

- Psychological tests include standardized stimuli for collecting behavior samples that can be compared with other individuals' behavior via test norms. Examples include intelligence and personality tests.

- Two different personality-testing approaches have evolved: (1) projective tests, such as the Rorschach or the TAT, in which unstructured stimuli are presented to a subject, who then "projects" meaning or structure onto the stimulus, thereby revealing "hidden" motives, feelings, and so on; and (2) objective tests, or personality inventories, in which a subject is required to read and respond to itemized statements or questions.

- Objectively scored personality tests, such as the MMPI-2 and MMPI-A, provide a cost-effective means of collecting a great deal of personality information rapidly.

4.4 Evaluate the case study of a woman who experienced violence in the workplace.

- Andrea C.'s case, involving a computer interpretation of the MMPI-2, illustrates the use of psychological assessment in describing mental health problems.

4.5 Discuss how practitioners integrate assessment data in treatment planning.

- Clinicians in individual private practice normally interpret assessment data and integrate it into a working model for use in planning on their own.

- In a clinic or hospital setting, assessment data are often evaluated in a staff conference attended by members of an interdisciplinary team. By putting together all the information that has been gathered, the team can see whether the findings complement each other and form a clinical picture along with recommendations for treatment. Because of the impact such an assessment can have on the lives of others, it is important for those involved to keep several ethical factors in mind when evaluating test results.

4.6 Explain the process for classifying abnormal behavior.

- Three basic approaches are currently used for classifying abnormal behavior: the categorical, the dimensional, and the prototypal.

- Two major psychiatric classification systems are in use: the *International Classification of Diseases* (*ICD-10*) system, published by the WHO, and the *Diagnostic and Statistical Manual of Mental Disorders* (*DSM-5*), published by the American Psychiatric Association.

- The client's gender, ethnicity, and cultural background are taken into consideration in the appraisal of mental health symptoms for a *DSM* diagnosis. Arriving at a diagnosis is usually required in mental health settings, at least in the form of a "diagnostic impression," before the commencement of clinical services.

Key Terms

actuarial procedures, p. 124

aphasia, p. 114

Brief Psychiatric Rating Scale (BPRS), p. 117

clinical diagnosis, p. 107

comorbidity, p. 130

computerized axial tomography (CAT) scan, p. 112

cultural competence, p. 109

dysrhythmia, p. 112

electroencephalogram (EEG), p. 111

forensic, p. 122

functional MRI (fMRI), p. 113

intelligence test, p. 118

magnetic resonance imaging (MRI), p. 112

Minnesota Multiphasic Personality Inventory (MMPI), p. 122

neuropsychological assessment, p. 114

objective personality tests, p. 121

personality tests, p. 119

positron emission tomography (PET) scan, p. 112

presenting problem, p. 107

projective personality tests, p. 119

psychological assessment, p. 114

rating scales, p. 116

reliability, p. 110

role-playing, p. 116

Rorschach Inkblot Test, p. 119

self-monitoring, p. 116

sentence completion test, p. 121

signs, p. 130

standardization, p. 110

structured assessment interview, p. 115

symptoms, p. 130

T score distribution, p. 110

Thematic Apperception Test (TAT), p. 120

unstructured assessment interviews, p. 115

validity, p. 110

Chapter 5
Stress and Physical and Mental Health

Learning Objectives

5.1 Explain the factors that make people more stress sensitive and the characteristics of stressors that make them hardest to cope with.

5.2 Summarize how the body responds to stress.

5.3 Discuss how stress causes dysregulation in the immune system.

5.4 Describe the role that emotions play in physical health and identify helpful and harmful emotions.

5.5 Explain the psychological interventions that can be used to reduce stress and treat stress-related disorders.

5.6 Identify the similarities and differences between adjustment disorder, posttraumatic stress disorder, and acute stress disorder.

5.7 Describe the clinical features of and risk factors for posttraumatic stress disorder.

5.8 Explain the treatment approaches that are used to help people with PTSD.

With its deadlines, interpersonal tensions, financial pressures, and everyday hassles, daily life places many demands on us. We are all exposed to stress, and this exposure affects our physical and our psychological well-being. Sometimes even leisure activities can be stressful. For example, a loss in the Superbowl is followed by an increase in heart attacks and deaths over the following 2 weeks in the losing team's city (Kloner et al., 2011). And watching a stressful soccer match more than doubles the risk of having acute cardiovascular problems (Wilbert-Lampen et al., 2008). How are you affected by stress? Does it make you anxious? Does it give you migraines?

After a Superbowl loss, heart attacks and deaths increase in the losing team's city.

The field of **health psychology** is concerned with the effects of stress and other psychological factors in the development and maintenance of physical problems. Health psychology is a subspecialty within **behavioral medicine**. A behavioral medicine approach to physical illness is concerned with psychological factors that may predispose an individual to medical problems. These may include such factors as stressful life events, certain personality traits, particular coping styles, and lack of social support. Within behavioral medicine there is also a focus on the effects of stress on the body, including the immune, endocrine, gastrointestinal, and cardiovascular systems.

But stress affects the mind as well as the body. As we discussed in Chapter 3, the role that stress can play in triggering the onset of mental disorders in vulnerable people is explicitly acknowledged in the diathesis-stress model. Moreover, exposure to extreme and traumatic stress may overwhelm the coping resources of otherwise apparently healthy people, leading to mental disorders such as **posttraumatic stress disorder (PTSD)**, as in the following example.

Posttraumatic Stress in a Military Nurse

Jennifer developed PTSD after she served as a nurse in Iraq. During her deployment she worked 12- to 14-hour shifts in 120-degree temperatures. Sleep was hard to come by and disaster was routine.

Day in and day out there was a never-ending flow of mangled bodies of young soldiers. Jennifer recalled one especially traumatic event:

> I was working one evening. We received information that a vehicle, on a routine convoy mission, had been hit by an improvised explosive device (IED). Three wounded men and one dead soldier were on their way to our hospital. Two medics in the back room were processing the dead soldier for Mortuary Affairs. The dead soldier was lying on a cot. The air was strong with the smell of burned flesh. I was staring at the body and trying to grasp what was different about this particular body. After a while I realized. The upper chest and head of the dead soldier were completely missing. We received his head about an hour later. (Based on Feczer & Bjorklund, 2009).

In this chapter we consider the role that stress plays in the development of physical and mental disorders. We discuss both physical and mental problems because the mind and the body are powerfully connected and because stress takes its toll on both. Although the problems that are linked to stress are many, we focus particularly on the most severe stress-related physical and mental disorders. In the physical realm, we place an emphasis on heart disease. For mental disorders, we concern ourselves primarily with PTSD.

What Is Stress?

5.1 **Explain the factors that make people more stress sensitive and the characteristics of stressors that make them hardest to cope with.**

Life would be very simple if all of our needs were automatically satisfied. In reality, however, many obstacles, both personal and environmental, get in the way. A promising athletic career may be brought to an end by injury; we may have less money than we need; we may be rejected by the person we love. The demands of life require that we adjust. When we experience or perceive challenges to our physical or emotional well-being that exceed our coping resources and abilities, the psychological condition that results is typically referred to as stress (see Shalev, 2009). To avoid confusion, we will refer to external demands as **stressors**, to the effects they create within the organism as **stress**, and to efforts to deal with stress as **coping strategies**. It is also important to note that stress is fundamentally an interactive and dynamic construct because it reflects the interaction between the organism and the environment over time (Monroe, 2008).

All situations that require adjustment can be regarded as potentially stressful. Prior to the influential work of Canadian physician and endocrinologist Hans Selye (1956, 1976), *stress* was a term used by engineers. Selye took the word and used it to describe the difficulties and strains experienced by living organisms as they struggled to cope with and adapt to changing environmental conditions. His work provided the foundation for current stress research. Selye also noted that stress could occur not only in negative situations (such as taking an examination) but also in positive situations (such as a wedding). Both kinds of stress can tax a person's resources and coping skills, although bad stress (**distress**) typically has the potential to do more damage. Stress can also occur in more than one form—not just as a simple catastrophe but also as a continuous force that exceeds a person's ability to manage it.

Stress can result from both negative and positive events. Both types of stress can tax a person's resources and coping skills, although distress (negative stress) typically has the potential to do more damage.

Stress and the *DSM*

The relationship between stress and psychopathology is considered so important that the role of stress is recognized in diagnostic formulations. Nowhere is this more apparent than in the diagnosis of PTSD—a severe disorder that we will discuss in detail later. PTSD was classified as an anxiety disorder in *DSM-IV-TR*. However, *DSM-5* introduced a new diagnostic category called trauma- and stressor-related disorders. PTSD is now included there. Some other disorders in this new category are adjustment disorder and acute stress disorder. These disorders involve patterns of psychological and behavioral disturbances that occur in response to identifiable stressors. The key differences among them lie not only in the severity of the disturbances but also in the nature of the stressors and the time frame during which the disorders occur.

Factors Predisposing a Person to Stress

Everyone faces a unique pattern of demands to which he or she must adjust. This is because people perceive and interpret similar situations differently and also because, objectively, no two people are faced with exactly the same pattern of stressors. Some individuals are also more likely to develop long-term problems under stress than

others. This may be linked, in part, to coping skills and the presence—or absence—of particular resources. Children, for example, are particularly vulnerable to severe stressors such as war and terrorism (Petrovic, 2004). Research also suggests that adolescents with parents who are depressed are more sensitive to stressful events; these adolescents are also more likely to have problems with depression themselves after experiencing stressful life events than those who do not have parents with depression (Bouma et al., 2008).

Individual characteristics that have been identified as improving a person's ability to handle life stress include higher levels of optimism, greater psychological control or mastery, increased self-esteem, and better social support (Declercq et al., 2007; Taylor & Stanton, 2007). These stable factors are linked to reduced levels of distress in the face of life events as well as more favorable health outcomes. There is also some evidence from twin studies that differences in coping styles may be linked to underlying genetic differences (Jang et al., 2007).

More generally, it is now widely accepted that our genetic makeup can render us more or less "stress sensitive." Researchers are exploring genes that may play a role in determining how reactive to stress we are (Alexander et al., 2009; Armbruster et al., 2012). A major development in stress research was the discovery that a particular form of a particular gene (the *5HTTLPR* gene) was linked to how likely it was that people would become depressed in the face of life stress. Caspi and colleagues (2003) found that people who had two "short" forms of this gene (the *s/s* genotype) were more likely to develop depression when they experienced four or more stressful life events than were people who had two "long" forms of this gene (the *l/l* genotype). Although this specific finding was controversial for a while, there is now clear support for the original result (Karg et al., 2011). Even more recent research has clarified that the interaction between the *s* carrier genotype (one or two *s* alleles) and life events is most marked for interpersonal events (such as those involving loss or rejection) rather than for noninterpersonal life events that do not involve relationships (Vrshek-Schallhorn et al., 2013).

The amount of stress we experience early in life may also make us more sensitive to stress later on (Gillespie & Nemeroff, 2007; Lupien et al., 2009). The effects of stress may be cumulative, with each stressful experience serving to make the system more reactive. Evidence from animal studies shows that being exposed to a single stressful experience can enhance responsiveness to stressful events that occur later (Johnson, O'Connor, et al., 2002). Rats that were exposed to stressful tail shocks produced more of the stress hormone cortisol when they were later exposed to another stressful experience (being placed on a platform). Other biological changes associated with stress were also more pronounced in these rats. These results suggest that prior stressful experiences may sensitize us biologically, making us more reactive to later stressful experiences. The term **stress tolerance** refers to a person's ability to withstand stress without becoming seriously impaired.

Stressful experiences may also create a self-perpetuating cycle by changing how we think about, or appraise, the things that happen to us. Studies have shown that stressful situations may be related to or intensified by a person's cognitions (Nixon & Bryant, 2005). This may explain why people with a history of depression tend to experience negative events as more stressful than other people do (Havermans et al., 2007). For example, if you're feeling depressed or anxious already, you may perceive a friend's canceling a movie date as an indication that she doesn't want to spend time with you. Even though the reality may be that a demand in her own life has kept her from keeping your date, when you feel bad you will be much more inclined to come to a negative conclusion about what just happened rather than see the situation in a more balanced or more optimistic way. Can you think of an example in your own life when something like this has happened to you?

Characteristics of Stressors

Why is misplacing our keys so much less stressful than being in an unhappy marriage or being fired from a job? At some level we all intuitively understand what makes one stressor more serious than another. The key factors involve (1) the severity of the stressor, (2) its chronicity (i.e., how long it lasts), (3) its timing, (4) how closely it affects our own lives, (5) how expected it is, and (6) how controllable it is.

Stressors that involve the more important aspects of a person's life—such as the death of a loved one, a divorce, a job loss, a serious illness, or negative social exchanges—tend to be highly stressful for most people (Aldwin, 2007; Newsom et al., 2008). Furthermore, the longer a stressor operates, such as might be the case with abuse and emotional neglect, or with living in poverty, the more severe its effects. Encountering a number of stressors at the same time also makes a difference. If a man loses his job, learns that his wife is seriously ill, and receives news that his son has been arrested for selling drugs, all at the same time, the resulting stress will be more severe than if these events had occurred separately over an extended period. Symptoms of stress also intensify when a person is more closely involved in an immediately traumatic situation. Learning that the uncle of a close friend was injured in a car accident is not as stressful as being in an accident oneself.

Extensive research has shown that events that are unpredictable and unanticipated (and for which no previously developed coping strategies are available) are likely to place a person under severe stress. A devastating house fire and the damage it brings are not occurrences with

which anyone has learned to cope. Likewise, recovery from the stress created by major surgery can be improved when a patient is given realistic expectations beforehand; knowing what to expect adds predictability to the situation. In one study, patients who were about to undergo hip replacement surgery watched a 12-minute film the evening before they had the operation. The film described the entire procedure from the patient's perspective. Compared to controls who did not see the film, patients who saw the video were less anxious on the morning of the surgery, were less anxious after the surgery, and needed less pain medication (Doering et al., 2000).

A devastating house fire is not an event we can anticipate. It is almost impossible to be psychologically prepared to experience a stressor such as this.

Finally, with an uncontrollable stressor, there is no way to reduce its impact, such as by escape or avoidance. In general, both people and animals are more stressed by unpredictable and uncontrollable stressors than by stressors that are of equal physical magnitude but are either predictable or controllable or both (e.g., Evans & Stecker, 2004; Maier & Watkins, 2010).

Unpredictable and uncontrollable events cause the greatest stress. These people are reacting to the collapse of the World Trade Center towers after the terrorist attacks of September 11, 2001.

Most of us experience occasional periods of especially acute (sudden and intense) stress. The term **crisis** is used to refer to times when a stressful situation threatens to exceed or exceeds the adaptive capacities of a person or a group. Crises are often especially stressful, because the stressors are so potent that the coping techniques we typically use do not work. Stress can be distinguished from crisis in this way: A traumatic situation or crisis overwhelms a person's ability to cope, whereas stress does not necessarily overwhelm the person.

Measuring Life Stress

Life changes, even positive ones such as being promoted or getting married, place new demands on us and may therefore be stressful. And the faster life changes occur, the greater the stress that is experienced.

A major focus of research on life changes has concerned the measurement of life stress. Years ago, Holmes and Rahe (1967) developed the Social Readjustment Rating Scale. This is a self-report checklist of fairly common, stressful life experiences (see also Chung et al., 2010; Cooper & Dewe, 2007). A version of this scale, developed specifically to assess life stress in college students, is shown in Figure 5.1.

Although easy to use, limitations of the checklist method later led to the development of interview-based approaches such as the Life Events and Difficulties Schedule (LEDS; Brown & Harris, 1978). One advantage of the LEDS is that it includes an extensive manual that provides rules for rating both acute and chronic forms of stress. The LEDS system also allows raters to consider the context in which a life event occurs and take into account a person's unique circumstances when rating each life event. For example, if a woman who is happily married and in good financial circumstances learns that she is going to have a baby, she may experience this news in a way that is quite different from that of an unmarried teenager who is faced with the prospect of having to tell her parents that she is pregnant. Although interview-based approaches are more time consuming and costly to administer, they are considered more reliable than checklist methods and are preferred for research in this area (see Monroe, 2008).

Resilience

After experiencing a potentially traumatic event, some people function well and experience very few symptoms in the following weeks and months. This kind of healthy psychological and physical functioning after a potentially traumatic event is called **resilience**. You might be surprised to learn that resilience is not rare. In fact, resilience is the most common reaction following loss or trauma (Bonanno et al., 2011; Quale & Schanke, 2010).

Figure 5.1 How Stressed Are You?

Sum all your ratings to get a total score of your life stress in the past year. In a large sample of undergraduates, the average score was 1,247, with a range from 182 to 2,571 (Renner & Mackin, 1998). Where does your stress score fall?

College Life Stress Inventory

Copy the "stress rating" number into the last column for any item that has happened to you in the last year, then add these.

Event	Stress Ratings	Your Items
Being raped	100	
Finding out that you are HIV-positive	100	
Being accused of rape	98	
Death of a close friend	97	
Death of a close family member	96	
Contracting a sexually transmitted disease (other than AIDS)	94	
Concerns about being pregnant	91	
Finals week	90	
Concerns about your partner being pregnant	90	
Oversleeping for an exam	89	
Flunking a class	89	
Having a boyfriend or girlfriend cheat on you	85	
Ending a steady dating relationship	85	
Serious illness in a close friend or family member	85	
Financial difficulties	84	
Writing a major term paper	83	
Being caught cheating on a test	83	
Drunk driving	82	
Sense of overload in school or work	82	
Two exams in one day	80	
Cheating on your boyfriend or girlfriend	77	
Getting married	76	
Negative consequences of drinking or drug use	75	
Depression or crisis in your best friend	73	
Difficulties with parents	73	
Talking in front of a class	72	
Lack of sleep	69	
Change in housing situation (hassles, moves)	69	
Competing or performing in public	69	
Getting in a physical fight	66	
Difficulties with a roommate	66	
Job changes (applying, new job, work hassles)	65	
Declaring a major or concerns about future plans	65	
A class you hate	62	
Drinking or use of drugs	61	
Confrontations with professors	60	
Starting a new semester	58	
Going on a first date	57	
Registration	55	
Maintaining a steady dating relationship	55	
Commuting to campus or work, or both	54	
Peer pressures	53	
Being away from home for the first time	53	
Getting sick	52	
Concerns about your appearance	52	
Getting straight A's	51	
A difficult class that you love	48	
Making new friends; getting along with friends	47	
Fraternity or Sorority rush	47	
Falling asleep in class	40	
Attending an athletic event (e.g., football game)	20	
Total		

But why are some people more resilient than others? Research suggests that no single factor predicts resilience. Rather, resilience is linked to a variety of different characteristics and resources. Factors that increase resilience include being male, being older, and being well educated. Having more economic resources is also beneficial. Some earlier studies suggested that, after the 9/11 attacks in New York, African Americans and members of some Latino groups fared more poorly and showed lower levels of resilience compared to whites. However, race and ethnicity are often confounded with social class. Importantly, when social class is controlled for, statistics show that race and ethnicity are no longer predictive of reduced resiliency.

It also helps to be a positive person. Research shows that people who can still show genuine positive emotions when talking about their recent loss also tend to adjust better after bereavement (see Bonanno et al., 2011). In contrast, having more negative affect, being more inclined to ruminate, and trying to find meaning in what has happened is associated with people doing less well after a traumatic event.

Resilience is the most common response to a potentially traumatic event. Optimism, positive emotions, and having more economic resources are all predictive of resilience.

The importance of positive and negative emotions is nicely illustrated in a study of 80 people who were being treated in a specialized rehabilitation hospital (Quale & Schanke, 2010). All had multiple traumatic injuries or severe spinal cord injuries, usually caused by accidents. The people who showed most resilience in the months after their injuries were those who, when interviewed shortly after arriving in the hospital, reported that they generally had an optimistic approach to life. In addition to optimism, being generally high on positive affect and low on negative affect also predicted having a more resilient trajectory (as opposed to a distress trajectory) over the period of rehabilitation treatment.

Finally, it is interesting to note that people who are very self-confident and who view themselves in an overly positive light also tend to cope remarkably well in the face

of trauma. Although people with this kind of self-enhancing style are sometimes unpleasant to interact with, such a style may serve them well in times of crisis. For example, in a prospective study, Gupta and Bonanno (2010) showed that college students with this self-enhancing style coped much better over a 4-year period than people who did not.

---

in review

- What factors play a role in determining a person's stress tolerance?
- What characteristics of stressors make them more serious and more difficult to adapt to?
- Describe two methods that can be used to measure life stress.
- What is resilience? Describe three factors that increase resilience and three factors that are associated with reduced resilience.

Stress and Physical Health

5.2   **Summarize how the body responds to stress.**

The biological cost of adapting to stress is called the **allostatic load** (Oken et al., 2015). When we are relaxed and not experiencing stress, our allostatic load is low. When we are stressed and feeling pressured, our allostatic load is higher. Although efforts to relate specific stressors to specific medical problems have not generally been successful, stress is becoming a key underlying theme in our understanding of the development and course of virtually all physical illness. For example, a person with allergies may find his or her resistance further lowered by emotional tension. Similarly, when a virus has already entered a person's body—as is thought to be the case in multiple sclerosis—emotional stress may interfere with the body's normal defensive forces or immune system. In like manner, any stress may tend to aggravate and maintain certain disorders, such as migraine headaches (Milde-Busch et al., 2011) and rheumatoid arthritis (Cutolo & Straub, 2006).

When we are relaxed and calm, our allostatic load is low.

When our allostatic load is high, we experience the biological signs of stress including high heart rate and increased levels of cortisol.

At the less severe end of the physical health spectrum, stress increases our susceptibility to catching a cold (Cohen, 2005). More dangerously, stress also increases the risk of having a heart attack. Several researchers have documented that deaths from coronary heart disease (CHD) rise in the days and weeks following a severe earthquake (see Leor et al., 1996). As Figure 5.2 shows, after the Northridge earthquake in Los Angeles in 1994, the number of sudden deaths due to CHD rose from an average of 4.6 (in the days preceding the earthquake) to 24 on the day of the earthquake (Kloner et al., 1997). There was also an increase in sudden death from cardiac events after the Hanshin-Awaji earthquake in Japan (Kario & Ohashi, 1997).

Figure 5.2 Cardiac Deaths and Earthquakes
On the day of the Northridge earthquake in California (January 17, 1994), cardiac deaths showed a sharp increase.

(Adapted from Leor et al., 1996. *The New England Journal of Medicine*, 334(7), February 15, 1996, p. 415.)

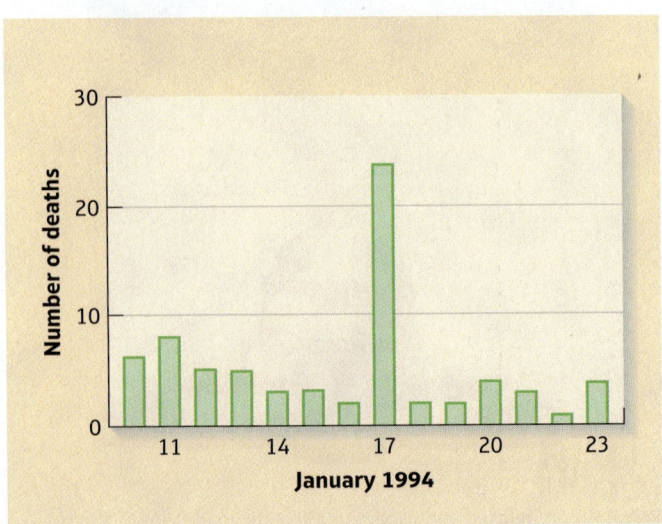

Everyday forms of stress can also elevate risk for heart disease and death (Matthews & Gump, 2002; Smith & Ruiz, 2002). A good example is work-related stress. Here the key factors appear to be having a highly demanding job and having little control over decision making. Both of these types of job stress increase risk for future heart disease. Moreover, this association still holds when other negative health behaviors (such as smoking) are controlled (see Peter & Siegrist, 2000). It is also interesting to note that, in people who work, most heart attacks occur on a Monday. The stress of returning to work after the weekend is thought to play a role in this (Kloner, 2006).

Finally, simply being asked to give a 5-minute speech about an assigned topic to a small (but evaluative) audience was enough to produce detectable changes in cardiac function in about 20 percent of patients with existing coronary artery disease (see Sheps et al., 2002). Furthermore, those patients who were most reactive to this form of mental stress were almost three times more likely (compared to the less reactive patients) to die in the next 5 to 6 years. Mental stress is known to raise blood pressure and also to cause an elevation in epinephrine. Mental stress may also reduce the oxygen supply to the heart muscle (Yeung et al., 1991). What the results of the Sheps study illustrate, however, is that stress does not have to be extreme or severe to be associated with lethal consequences later.

The Stress Response

To understand why stress can lead to physical and psychological problems, we need to know what happens to our bodies when we experience stress. Faced with the threat of a perceived stressor, the body undergoes a cascade of biological changes. Two distinct systems are involved here. The **sympathetic-adrenomedullary (SAM) system** (see Gunnar & Quevedo, 2007) is designed to mobilize resources and prepare for a fight-or-flight response. The stress response begins in the hypothalamus, which stimulates the sympathetic nervous system (SNS). This, in turn, causes the inner portion of the adrenal glands (the adrenal medulla) to secrete adrenaline (also known as epinephrine) and noradrenaline (norepinephrine). As these circulate through the blood, they cause an increase in heart rate (familiar to all of us). They also get the body to metabolize glucose more rapidly. The second system involved in the stress response is called the **hypothalamus-pituitary-adrenal (HPA) system** (which we introduced in Chapter 3; also see Figure 5.3). In addition to stimulating the SNS, the hypothalamus releases a hormone called *corticotropin-releasing hormone* (CRH). Traveling in the blood, this hormone stimulates the pituitary gland. The pituitary then secretes adrenocorticotropic hormone (ACTH). This

Figure 5.3 The Hypothalamic-Pituitary-Adrenal (HPA) Axis
Prolonged stress leads to secretion of the adrenal hormone cortisol, which elevates blood sugar and increases metabolism. These changes help the body sustain prolonged activity but at the expense of decreased immune system activity.

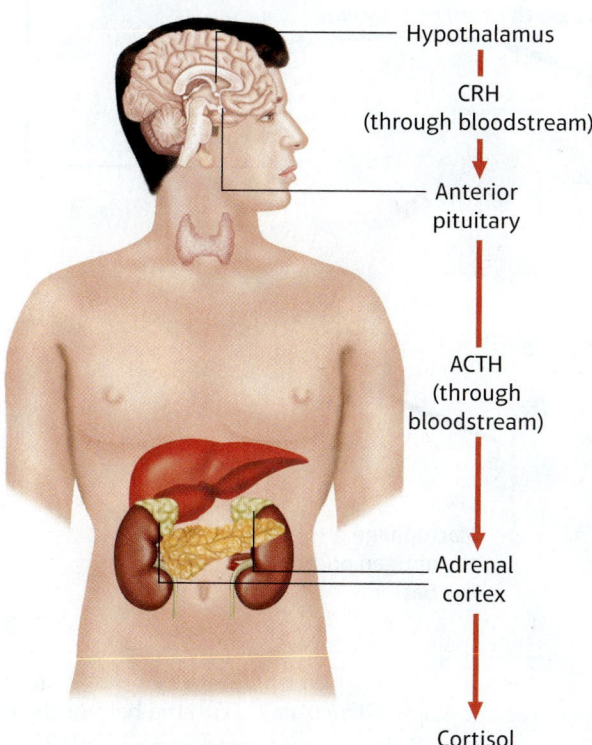

Hypothalamus

CRH
(through bloodstream)

Anterior
pituitary

ACTH
(through
bloodstream)

Adrenal
cortex

Cortisol

induces the adrenal cortex (the outer portion of the adrenal gland) to produce the stress hormones called glucocorticoids. In humans, the stress glucocorticoid that is produced is called **cortisol**. Figure 5.3 illustrates this sequence of events.

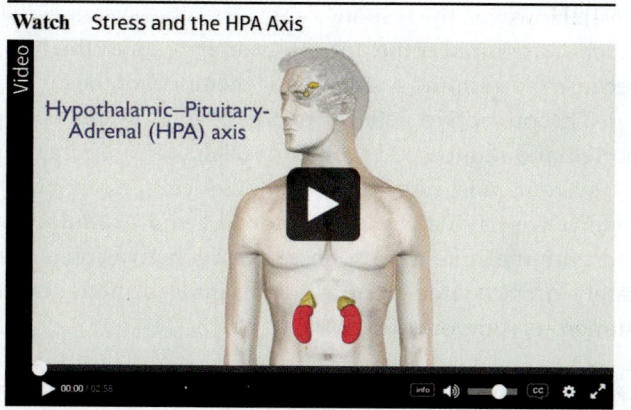

Watch Stress and the HPA Axis

Hypothalamic–Pituitary–Adrenal (HPA) axis

Cortisol is a good hormone to have around in an emergency. It prepares the body for fight or flight. It also inhibits the innate immune response. This means that if an injury does occur, the body's inflammatory response to it is delayed. In other words, escape has priority over healing, and tissue repair is secondary to staying alive. This obviously

has survival value if you need to run away from a bear that has just attacked you. It also explains why cortisone injections are sometimes used to reduce inflammation in damaged joints.

But there is also a downside to cortisol. If the cortisol response is not shut off, cortisol can damage brain cells, especially in the hippocampus (see Sapolsky, 2000). At a very fundamental level, stress is bad for your brain. It may even stunt growth (babies who are stressed don't gain weight in the normal way and "fail to thrive"). Accordingly, the brain has receptors to detect cortisol. When these are activated, they send a feedback message that is designed to dampen the activity of the glands involved in the stress response. But if the stressor remains, the HPA axis stays active and cortisol release continues. Although short-term cortisol production is highly adaptive, a chronically overactive HPA axis, with high levels of circulating cortisol, may be problematic.

The Mind–Body Connection

The link between stress and physical illness involves diseases (like colds) that are not directly related to nervous system activity. This suggests that stress may cause an overall vulnerability to disease by compromising immune functioning. **Psychoneuroimmunology** is the study of the interactions between the nervous system and the immune system. Although it was once thought that the immune system was essentially "closed" and responsive only to challenges from foreign substances, we now know that this is not the case. The nervous system and the immune system communicate in ways that we are now beginning to understand.

Evidence continues to grow that the brain influences the immune system and that the immune system influences the brain. In other words, a person's behavior and psychological state can affect immune functioning. The status of the immune system also influences current mental states and behavioral dispositions by affecting the blood levels of circulating neurochemicals; these, in turn, modify brain states. For example, we have already seen that glucocorticoids can cause stress-induced **immunosuppression**. In the short term, this can be adaptive (escape first, heal later). However, it makes sense that longer-term stress might create problems for the immune system. To appreciate why this might be, we need to describe briefly the basics of immune functioning.

Understanding the Immune System

The word *immune* comes from the Latin *immunis*, which means "exempt." The **immune system** protects the body from such things as viruses and bacteria. In many ways it can be likened to a police force. If it is too weak, it cannot function effectively, and the body succumbs to damage from invading viruses and bacteria. Conversely, if the

Figure 5.4 Immune System Responses to a Bacterial Infection

(Adapted from J. W. Kalat, 2001, *Biological Psychology*, 7th ed. Belmont, CA: Wadsworth.)

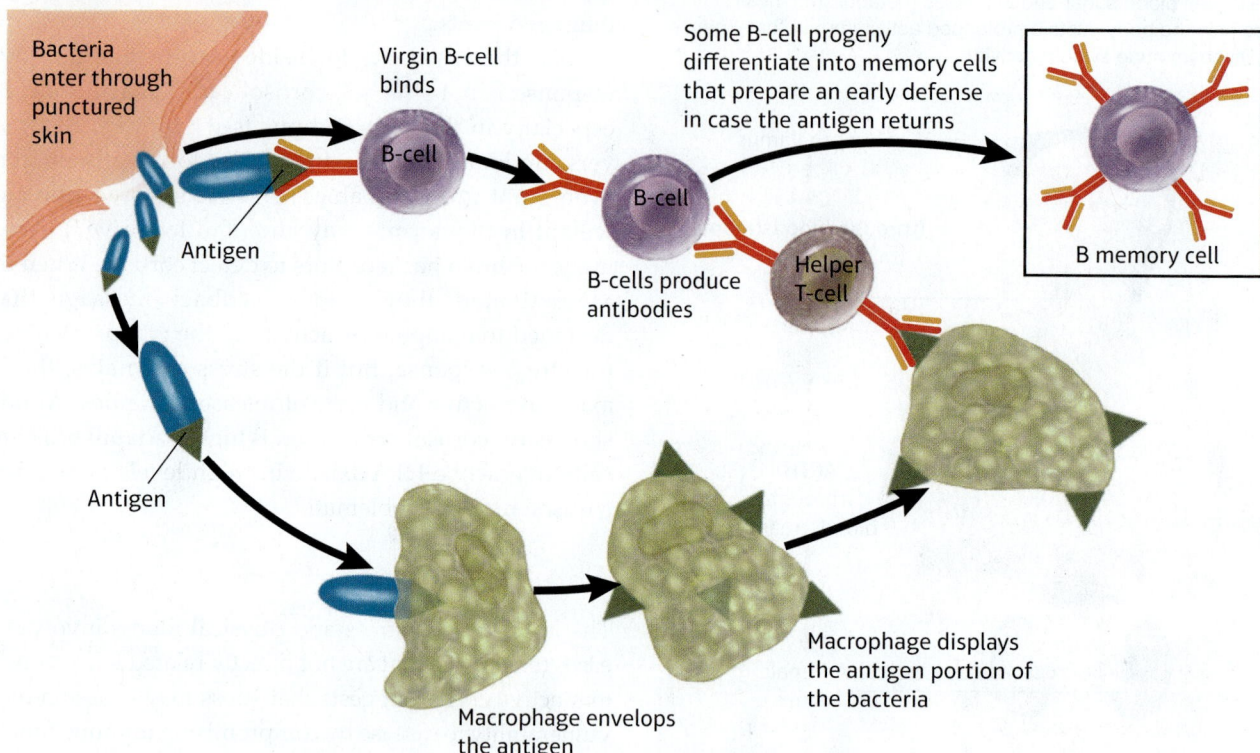

immune system is too strong and unselective, it can turn on the body's own healthy cells. This is what may happen in the case of autoimmune diseases such as rheumatoid arthritis and lupus.

The front line of defense in the immune system is the white blood cells. These **leukocytes** (or **lymphocytes**) are produced in the bone marrow and then stored in various places throughout the body, such as the spleen and the lymph nodes. There are two important types of leukocytes. One type, called a **B-cell** (because it matures in the bone marrow), produces specific antibodies that are designed to respond to specific antigens. **Antigens** (the word is a contraction of *antibody generator*) are foreign bodies such as viruses and bacteria, as well as internal invaders such as tumors and cancer cells. The second important type of leukocyte is the **T-cell** (so named because it matures in the thymus, which is an important endocrine gland). When the immune system is stimulated, B-cells and T-cells become activated and multiply rapidly, mounting various forms of counterattack (see Figure 5.4). If this did not happen, you would inevitably die of infection.

T-cells circulate through the blood and lymph systems in an inactive form. Each T-cell has receptors on its surface that recognize one specific type of antigen. However, the T-cells are unable to recognize antigens by themselves. They become activated when immune cells called *macrophages* (the word means "big eater") detect antigens and start to engulf and digest them. To activate the T-cells, the macrophages release

a chemical known as *interleukin-1*. With the help of the macrophages, the T-cells become activated and are able to begin to destroy antigens (Maier et al., 1994).

B-cells are different in structure from T-cells. When a B-cell recognizes an antigen, it begins to divide and to produce antibodies that circulate in the blood. This process is facilitated by cytokines (like interleukin-1) that are released by the T-cells. We will tell you more about cytokines shortly. Production of antibodies takes 5 days or more (Maier et al., 1994). However, the response of the immune system will be much more rapid if the antigen ever appears in the future because the immune system has a "memory" of the invader.

The protective activity of the B- and T-cells is supported and reinforced by other specialized components of the system, most notably natural killer cells, macrophages (which we have already mentioned), and granulocytes. The immune system's response to antigen invasion is intricately orchestrated, requiring the intact functioning of numerous components.

in review

- What is the evidence that stress is linked to physical health problems?
- What is meant by the term *allostatic load*?
- What is cortisol? Is cortisol beneficial or harmful?
- Describe the biological changes that occur when we are under stress.

Stress and Immune System Functioning

5.3   **Explain how stress causes dysregulation in the immune system.**

Would you be surprised to learn that stress slows the healing of wounds by as much as 24 to 40 percent (Gouin & Kiecolt-Glaser, 2011)? This is because stress is linked to suppression of the immune system (Segerstrom & Miller, 2004). In one study, 11 dental student volunteers had a punch biopsy wound performed on their hard palate (roof of the mouth) on two separate occasions. The first biopsy was performed in mid-August when the students were on summer vacation. The second occurred 6 weeks later, just 3 days before a major examination. On average, the wounds healed 40 percent more slowly during the stressful period before the examination than they did when the students were on vacation (Marucha et al., 1998). Indeed, for every person in this study, healing time was longer when the wound occurred during the time of high versus low stress (see Figure 5.5).

Although short-term stress (such as occurs when we take an examination) compromises the immune system, it is the more enduring stressors such as unemployment or interpersonal problems with family or friends that are associated with the most global immunosuppression. People who are unemployed have lower levels of immune functioning than people who are employed. The good news, however, is that immune functioning returns to normal again once people find another job (Cohen et al., 2007).

Stress causes our immune system to function less efficiently.

Stress and Cytokines

You now know that stress causes a dysregulation in the immune system, slowing down healing and making us more susceptible to illness. But how does this happen? To understand more, you need to know a little about **cytokines**. Cytokines are small protein molecules and they are an important component of the immune system. Cytokines serve as chemical messengers and allow immune cells to communicate with each other. One cytokine that you may have heard about is interferon, which is given to patients with cancer, multiple sclerosis, and hepatitis C.

What makes cytokines especially interesting is that in addition to communicating with the immune system, they also have broader effects. Importantly, they influence the brain. Researchers used to believe that the immune system was a self-contained entity. We now know this is not the case. Instead, the brain and the body work together to

Figure 5.5 Wound Healing and Stress

Healing time is shown for each of the 11 subjects for the two time periods, summer vacation (low stress) and examinations (high stress).

(Adapted from P. T. Marucha et al., *Psychosomatic Medicine*, 60:362–365 (1998).)

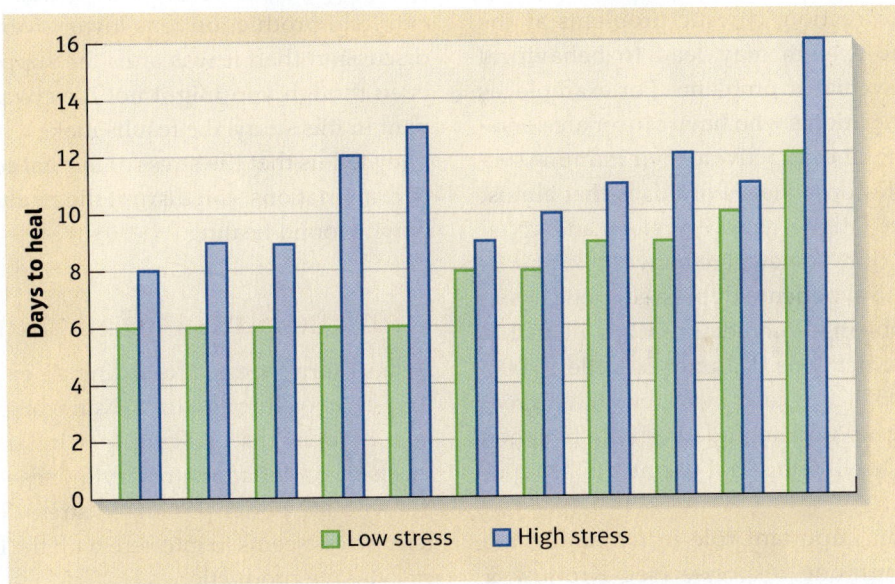

coordinate a response to sickness. For example, when you are ill you tend to feel tired, to sleep more, and to have very little appetite. This is classic sickness behavior and it is familiar to us all. What you may not know, however, is that these symptoms of illness result, at least in part, from the effects of specific cytokines. These cytokines act on the brain and this is the reason we feel so unwell (Dantzer & Kelley, 2007). Although unpleasant, feeling this way is highly adaptive, causing us to withdraw from our usual routines, rest, and take care of ourselves until we get better.

Cytokines, which are produced by the immune system, have effects on the brain, making us feel unwell.

Not only is the brain influenced by products of the immune system (such as cytokines), but the close communication between the brain and the immune system also means that the brain is capable of influencing immune processes. With this in mind, some of the findings discussed later in this chapter (the link between depression and physical disease, for example, and the health benefits of optimism and social support) make much more sense.

In the opposite direction, chronic problems at the level of the immune system may lead to behavioral changes or even to psychiatric problems. For example, as we mentioned earlier, patients who have cancer are sometimes treated with cytokines to activate their immune systems. One unfortunate consequence of this is that almost all patients experience fatigue, as well as sleep and appetite problems. In addition, somewhere between 30 and 50 percent of patients also experience depressed mood, anxiety, and cognitive problems—problems that are alleviated by antidepressant medications (Dantzer & Kelley, 2007; Musselman et al., 2001). In short, cytokines have great potential for helping us understand the links between physical and mental well-being that are at the heart of behavioral medicine.

Cytokines play an important role in mediating the inflammatory and immune response (see Kronfol &

Remick, 2000, for a review). They can be divided into two main categories: proinflammatory cytokines and anti-inflammatory cytokines. Proinflammatory cytokines such as interleukin-1 (IL-1), IL-6, or tumor necrosis factor (TNF) help us deal with challenges to our immune system by augmenting the immune response. In contrast, anti-inflammatory cytokines such as IL-4, IL-10, and IL-13 decrease or dampen the response that the immune system makes. Sometimes they accomplish this by blocking the synthesis of other cytokines.

Under conditions of stress, the production of proinflammatory cytokines is disrupted. This affects the healing of wounds. In a compelling demonstration of this, Kiecolt-Glaser and her colleagues (2005) recruited a sample of married couples and admitted them for 24 hours to a hospital research unit. In the pursuit of science, the researchers then gave each member of the couple a blister wound to the arm. Following this, each couple was asked to engage in a supportive discussion. At various point after the discussion, fluid was taken from the blisters and analyzed for the presence of cytokines. Then, approximately 2 months later, the couples came back, went through exactly the same procedures, but this time the discussion they were asked to have was designed to provoke marital conflict.

What were the findings? One result was that the blister wounds took 1 day longer to heal when couples had engaged in the conflict discussion compared to the supportive discussion. In other words, the stress of the conflict slowed down the healing process. This is similar to the findings of the study involving the dental students that we told you about earlier. What Kiecolt-Glaser and her colleagues were also able to shed light on, however, was *why* wound healing was delayed. Although proinflammatory cytokine production (IL-1, IL-6, and TNF) increased in the blisters regardless of the nature of the discussion the couple had had (reflecting the start of the healing process), cytokine production was lower overall after the conflict discussion than it was after the supportive exchange. So, even though you might not have wanted to be a participant in this study, the results make a very important point. They tell us that the stress of marital conflict, like the stress of examinations, can disrupt the immune system and slow down wound healing.

Chronic Stress and Inflammation

If short-term stress (like taking an examination) is bad, is long-term or chronic stress even worse? The answer here is yes. Evidence is growing that inflammation—increased levels of proinflammatory cytokines—is increased in people who are under prolonged stress. This is because long-term stress seems to interfere with the body's ability to *turn off* cytokine production.

Under ordinary conditions, IL-1 and other cytokines stimulate the HPA axis (refer back to Figure 5.3), leading to an increase in cortisol. Cortisol (which you will recall is a stress hormone) is supposed to regulate (turn off) cytokine production. In other words, cytokine production sets off a negative feedback loop that is designed to prevent an excessive or exaggerated immune or inflammatory response. Chronic stress, however, seems to impair the body's ability to respond to the signals that will terminate immune system reactivity. The result is *inflammation*.

Chronic inflammation is a risk factor for a wide range of health problems and diseases. These include cardiovascular disease, type 2 diabetes, asthma, osteoporosis, rheumatoid arthritis, and many others (Ershler & Keller, 2000; Jaremka et al., 2013). This is why doctors now test for the presence of C-reactive protein (CRP)—a molecule produced by the liver in response to IL-6—when they want to assess a person's risk for heart disease.

Chronic stress can take many forms. One ***correlational research*** study showed that women who were caring for a family member with Alzheimer's disease had higher levels of IL-6 than women who were either anticipating the stress of relocation or who were experiencing neither of these stressors (Lutgendorf et al., 1999). This difference was found even though the women who were caregivers were 6 to 9 years younger than the women in the other two groups and even though IL-6 levels are known to increase with age. Other research links discrimination—another form of chronic stress—to elevated levels of CRP in African Americans (see the World Around Us box).

Research Close-Up
Correlational Research

In contrast to experimental research (which involves manipulating variables in some way and seeing what happens), in correlational research the researcher observes or assesses the characteristics of different groups, learning much about them without manipulating the conditions to which they are exposed.

Stress and Premature Aging

Much of our discussion so far has concerned fairly common forms of acute (e.g., examinations, disagreements) and chronic (discrimination, unemployment, caring for a spouse with dementia) forms of stress. But what about chronic and severe stress that occurs early in life? Researchers have begun to explore this issue and the results are very worrisome. Traumatic stressors that are experienced during childhood seem to increase risk of premature death in later life.

In the first study of this kind, Brown and colleagues (2009) collected information about adverse childhood experiences from over 17,000 adults who attended a primary

The World Around Us
Racial Discrimination and Cardiovascular Health in African Americans

Experiences of discrimination have been linked to a number of bad health outcomes, including increased blood pressure and signs of cardiovascular disease. But how might this association arise? An important mediator in this relationship may be C-reactive protein, or CRP.

CRP is a protein synthesized in the liver. High levels of CRP signal widespread inflammation in the body. In an interesting study, Lewis and colleagues (2010) measured levels of CRP in blood samples taken from 296 older African Americans, whose average age was 73. These research participants also completed a questionnaire that asked about their experiences of everyday discrimination. Items on the questionnaire included being treated with disrespect, getting poorer service in restaurants or stores, as well as experiences of being insulted or harassed.

The findings revealed a significant correlation between everyday discrimination and CRP, where more experiences of discrimination were associated with higher levels of CRP. The association also remained even after factors such as smoking, high blood pressure, depression, and other health problems were considered. Although much more remains to be learned, these preliminary findings are very exciting. They provide a clue about a

potential pathway through which experiences of racial bias might ultimately play a role in the poor cardiovascular health of older African Americans.

What is stressful about discrimination? Is this something you have experienced? If so, how did it affect you?

care clinic from 1995 to 1997. Adverse childhood experiences included such things as emotional, physical, or sexual abuse, domestic violence, having a family member incarcerated, and parental separation or divorce during the person's first 18 years of life. Then, approximately 10 years later, the researchers identified people who had died in the intervening period. The findings were sobering. People who had reported six or more adverse events during their childhood died much earlier (in fact, almost 20 years earlier) than would have been expected based on estimates of standard life expectancy. The top two leading causes of death were heart disease (or stroke) and cancer.

Of course, interpreting data from a study such as this is complicated. However, a more recent study, using a prospective longitudinal design has reported that the risk of death was 57 percent higher in men who experienced two or more adverse childhood experiences compared to men who had not experienced any childhood adversity. For women, the corresponding figure was 80 percent increased risk. Moreover, lifestyle factors in adulthood did not provide a very satisfactory explanation of the premature mortality that was found (Kelly-Irving et al., 2013).

What might this mean? Although we cannot yet be certain, there is reason to suspect that early life stress may have biological consequences that advance aging, making it more likely that people will die earlier from the kinds of diseases (cancer, heart disease) that are associated with increased age. But how could this come about? Telomeres may be part of the answer.

Telomeres (from the Greek words *telos*, meaning "end," and *meros*, meaning "part") are the protective end parts of chromosomes. You can think of them as being rather like the ends of shoelaces in this respect. Unfortunately, telomeres shorten with age. And if they get too short, cells do not function correctly and the risk of disease is increased.

The reason all of this is so important is that *stress shortens the length of telomeres*. In the first study of this kind, Epel and her colleagues (2004) compared telomere lengths in the blood cells of two groups of mothers: mothers caring for a child with a chronic illness and mothers of children who were healthy. The longer the mothers had been caring for their ill child the shorter their telomeres were. And in both groups of mothers, telomere length was also related to how much stress the mothers reported being under. The differences were also not trivial. The reduction in telomere length in the mothers who felt most stressed was equivalent to 10 years of aging!

Research in this exciting area is now expanding rapidly and we have already learned a lot. We know that telomere length is maintained by an enzyme called telomerase and that the stress hormone cortisol can reduce the activity of this enzyme (Price et al., 2013). In other words, we are beginning to understand how experiencing stress can start to bring about an array of changes that, if left unchecked, can compromise the immune system, create conditions of chronic inflammation, and shorten the length of our telomeres. We are also learning that drinking too much sugar-sweetened soda might shorten telomeres (Leung et al., 2014),

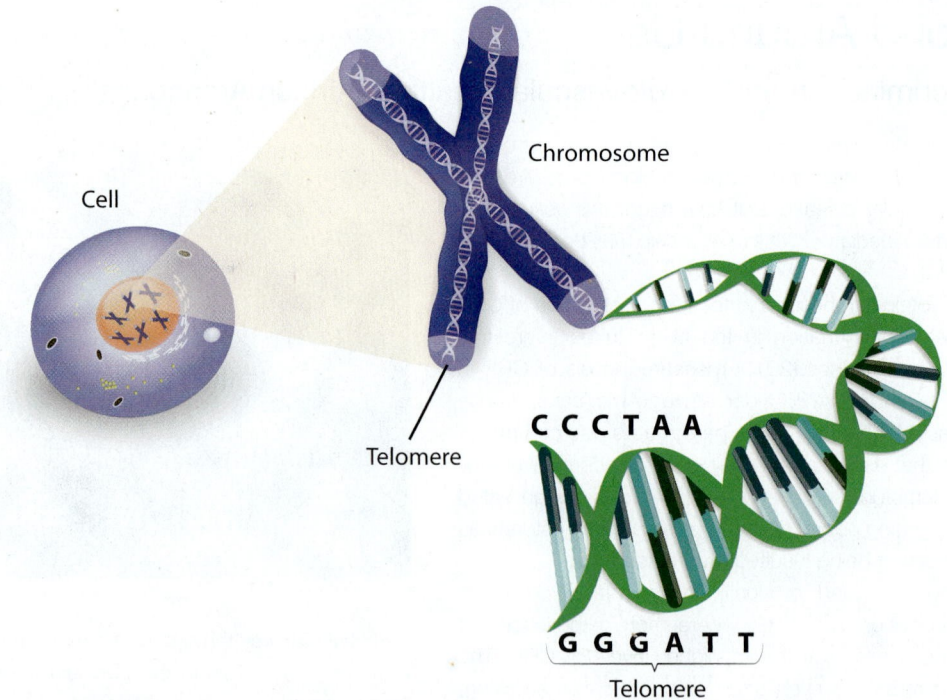

Cell

Chromosome

Telomere

C C C T A A

G G G A T T

Telomere

Telomeres are the protective end parts of chromosomes. Telomeres shorten with age, increasing the risk of disease. Stress also shortens telomeres. Telomere length is maintained by an enzyme called telomerase and the activity of telomerase is reduced by the stress hormone cortisol. If you needed a reason to reduce the amount of stress in your life, you have a good one now!

pessimism may accelerate the rate of telomere shortening (O'Donovan et al., 2009), and meditation may promote telomerase activity (Jacobs et al., 2011). And just in case you are inclined to blow off the gym, you should also know that exercise seems to act as a buffer against the bad effects of stress on telomeres (Puterman et al., 2010). In essence, science is now explaining exactly why we should be striving to live in a happy, healthy, and more relaxed manner.

in review

- How can acute stress lead to immunosuppression?
- How can chronic stress lead to inflammation?
- In what way might chronic stress lead to premature aging and disease?
- What is the difference between a cytokine and a telomere?
- How might racial bias play a role in the development of cardiovascular disease?

Emotions and Health

5.4 **Describe the role that emotions play in physical health and identify helpful and harmful emotions.**

We have already described how stress can result in the immune system going out of balance in ways that may compromise health. But stress is not the whole story. The same also seems to be true for negative emotions. Because the brain influences the immune system, psychological factors are of great importance to our health and well-being. How you view problems and cope with challenges, and even your temperament, may directly affect your underlying physical health.

Personality

Attempts to explore the psychological contribution to the development of heart disease date back to the identification of the **Type A behavior pattern** (Friedman & Rosenman, 1959). Type A behavior is characterized by excessive competitive drive, extreme commitment to work, impatience or time urgency, and hostility. Many of us know people who are like this, and the term *Type A* is commonly used in everyday language.

Early findings suggested that Type A personality in otherwise healthy men ages 35 to 59 was associated with a twofold increased risk for coronary artery disease and an eightfold increased risk of having a heart attack over the course of an 8.5-year follow-up (Rosenman et al., 1975). A subsequent major study called the Framingham Heart Study not only confirmed the findings of the earlier (Western Collaborative Group) study but extended them to women as well (see Kannel et al., 1987). However, as research with the construct has continued, it has become clear that it is the hostility component of the Type A construct (including anger, contempt, scorn, cynicism, and mistrust) that is most closely correlated with coronary artery deterioration (Chida & Steptoe, 2009; Wong et al., 2013).

A more recent development is the identification of the "distressed" or **Type D personality** type (Denollet et al., 2000). People with Type D personality have a tendency to experience negative emotions and also to feel insecure and anxious. Men with CHD who scored high on measures of chronic emotional distress were more likely to have fatal and nonfatal heart attacks over the 5-year follow-up period than were men who did not have these Type D personality traits (Denollet et al., 2000). People with higher scores on the negative affectivity component of Type D personality (see Figure 5.6) are also at increased risk of having more problems after cardiac surgery (Tully et al., 2011).

Figure 5.6 Characteristics of the Type D Personality

(Adapted from Johan Denollet, 1998, Personality and coronary heart disease: The type-D Scale-16 (DS16). *Annals of Behavioral Medicine, 20*(3) 209–215, and N. Kupper and J. Denollet, 2007. Type D Personality as a prognostic factor in heart disease: Assessment and mediating mechanisms. *Journal of Personality Assessment, 89*(3) 265–276.)

TEST: ARE YOU A TYPE D?

The social and emotional problems associated with Type D personality can increase your chances of developing heart disease. Read each statement and circle the appropriate number to indicate your answer. There are no right or wrong answers: your own impression is the only thing that matters.

1 TAKE THE TEST
Circle your answers:

	False	Less false	Neutral	Less true	True
1. I make contact easily when I meet people	4	3	2	1	0
2. I often make a fuss about unimportant things	0	1	2	3	4
3. I often talk to strangers	4	3	2	1	0
4. I often feel unhappy	0	1	2	3	4
5. I am often irritated	0	1	2	3	4
6. I often feel inhibited in social interactions	0	1	2	3	4
7. I take a gloomy view of things	0	1	2	3	4
8. I find it hard to start a conversation	0	1	2	3	4
9. I am often in a bad mood	0	1	2	3	4
10. I am a closed kind of person	0	1	2	3	4
11. I would rather keep people at a distance	0	1	2	3	4
12. I often find myself worrying about something	0	1	2	3	4
13. I am often down in the dumps	0	1	2	3	4
14. When socializing, I don't find the right things to talk about	0	1	2	3	4

2 ADD YOUR ANSWERS
Negative Affectivity:
Add scores for questions 2, 4, 5, 7, 9, 12 and 13

Social Inhibition:
Add scores for questions 1, 3, 6, 8, 10, 11, and 14

3 SCORE THE RESULTS
You qualify as a Type D personality if your Negative Affectivity is 10 or higher and your Social Inhibition is 10 or higher.

Depression

Like stress, depression is associated with disrupted immune function (Kiecolt-Glaser et al., 2002). Moreover, the relationship between depression and suppression of the immune system is at least partially independent of specific situations or events that may have provoked depressed feelings. In other words, the state of being depressed adds something beyond any negative effects of the stressors precipitating the depressed mood.

Depression is also a factor in heart disease. People with heart disease are approximately three times more likely than healthy people to be depressed (Chesney, 1996; Shapiro, 1996). This may not strike you as especially surprising. If you had heart disease, perhaps you would be depressed too. However, depression is much more commonly found in people who have heart disease than it is in people who have other serious medical problems, like cancer (Miller & Blackwell, 2006). Furthermore, heart attack patients with high levels of depressive symptoms after having a heart attack are three times more likely to die during the next 5 years than patients who do not show high levels of depression (Glassman, 2007; Lesperance et al., 2002). Research also suggests that anhedonia (which is a symptom of depression characterized by profound loss of interest or pleasure) may be especially predictive of increased mortality after a heart attack (Davidson et al., 2010).

Depression also appears to be a *risk factor* for the *development* of CHD. A recent meta-analysis of prospective studies involving almost 900,000 participants has shown that depression is associated with a 30 percent increased risk for developing heart disease or having a heart attack in the future (Gan et al., 2014). The link between depression and future heart problems also remained even when other potential confounding variables such as lifestyle were taken into account.

Research Close-Up

Risk Factor

A risk factor is a variable that increases the likelihood of a specific (and usually negative) outcome occurring at a later time. For example, obesity is a risk factor for heart disease; perfectionism is a risk factor for eating disorders.

Watch   Risk Factor

Why are depression and heart disease so closely linked? Current thinking is that this is another example of the mind–body connection. As mentioned earlier, stress is thought to activate the immune system, triggering the production of proinflammatory cytokines such as IL-1, IL-6, and tumor necrosis factor by the white blood cells. Long-term exposure to these proinflammatory cytokines is thought to lead to changes in the brain that manifest themselves as symptoms of depression. Depression may then interact with stress to further enhance the inflammatory responses that are naturally triggered by stress exposure, rather like putting gasoline on a fire (Fagundes et al., 2013). Proinflammatory cytokines also trigger the growth of plaques in the blood vessels as well as making it more likely that those plaques will rupture and cause a heart attack. In other words, as illustrated in Figure 5.7, the link between heart disease and depression is due to inflammation and the presence of inflammatory cytokines (see Miller & Blackwell, 2006; Robles et al., 2005).

New findings also suggest that people who are depressed have shorter telomeres

---

Figure 5.7 Stress, Inflammation, Depression, and Heart Disease

Model of how inflammatory processes mediate the relations among chronic stressors, depressive symptoms, and cardiac disease. Stressors activate the immune system in a way that leads to persistent inflammation. With long-term exposure to the molecular products of inflammation, people are expected to develop symptoms of depression and experience progression of cardiac disease.

(Adapted from Miller & Blackwell, 2006. Turning up the heat: Inflammation as a mechanism linking chronic stress, depression and heart disease. *Current Directions in Psychological Science, 15*(6), 269–272(4). Copyright © 2006. Reproduced with permission of Blackwell Publishing Ltd.)

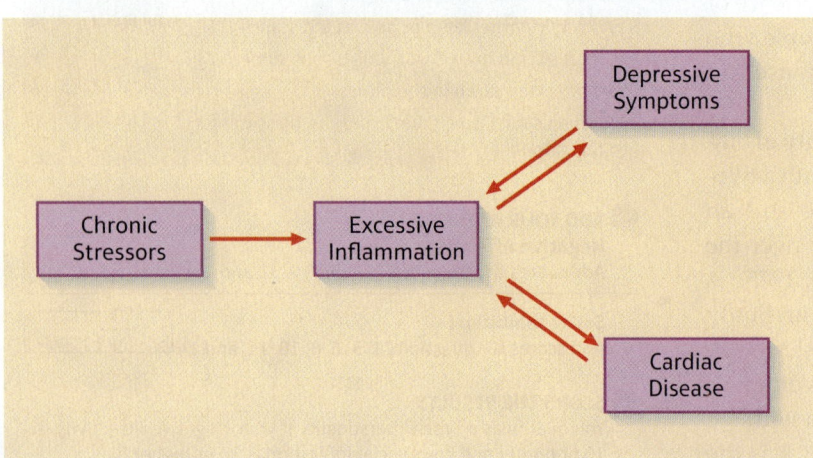

than never depressed controls, even after controlling for other health and lifestyle variables (Verhoeven et al., 2014). In the study by Verhoeven and colleagues, the reduction in telomere length in the participants with depression was equivalent to 4 to 6 years of accelerated aging (that is, the depressed people had telomeres about the length of people 4 to 6 years older). There was also a *dose–response relationship*, meaning that the more chronic and severe the depression, the shorter people's telomeres were. Of course, one limitation of this study is that it was cross sectional. Without longitudinal data we cannot say conclusively that depression causes a reduction in telomere length. Nonetheless, the results give us pause for thought. One implication of these findings is that depression is an emotionally stressful condition that may have an impact on how much physical wear and tear can be detected in the body. And the older our bodies are, the more liable we are to have the kinds of serious health problems that often accompany aging.

Anxiety

Depression is not the only form of negative affect that is linked to CHD. Research has also demonstrated a relationship between phobic anxiety and increased risk for sudden cardiac death. In a classic early study, Kawachi, Colditz, and colleagues (1994) examined nearly 34,000 male professionals who had been assessed for panic disorder, agoraphobia, and generalized anxiety. Over the course of the 2-year follow-up study, sudden cardiac death was six times higher in the men with the highest levels of anxiety. The findings were replicated in a second study of nearly 2,300 men who were participating in a normative aging study (Kawachi, Sparrow, et al., 1994, 1995). Prospective studies of women who were free of cardiac disease at the start of the study have also linked phobic anxiety with a higher risk of sudden cardiac death (Albert et al., 2005).

Social Isolation and Lack of Social Support

How we live—and our feelings of social isolation—also make a difference. Studies point to the strong link between social factors and the development of CHD. Monkeys housed alone have four times more atherosclerosis (fatty deposits in blood vessels that eventually create a blockage) than monkeys housed in social groups (Shively et al., 1989). Lonely people are also at increased risk of developing heart disease. Loneliness is a different construct from social support or depression, and it is not closely related to any objective measures of a person's social network size. In one study, 3,000 men and women who were free of cardiovascular problems were followed up for a period of more than 19 years. Women who reported higher levels of loneliness on two separate assessment occasions were 76 percent

more likely to develop heart disease in the subsequent years. This association also held when other variables such as age, smoking, physical activity, and depression were accounted for statistically. Interestingly, no association between loneliness and depression was found for men (Thurston & Kubzansky, 2009). This may be because women were much more likely to report feelings of loneliness than men were.

Loneliness is a risk factor for the development of later heart disease in women.

For people who already have CHD, there is similar evidence that feelings of being emotionally supported make a difference. In one study of people who had already suffered a heart attack, those who reported that they had low levels of emotional support were almost three times more likely to experience another cardiac event (Berkman et al., 1992). In another study, death in patients with CHD was three times more likely during the next 5 years if they were unmarried or had no one to confide in (Williams et al., 1992). Echoing these findings, Coyne and colleagues (2001) have shown that the quality of the marital relationship predicts 4-year survival rates in patients with congestive heart failure. Although uncertain at this time, it may be that the stress that comes from marital tension or from a lack of social support triggers an inflammatory response in the immune system, causing depression and heart problems as a result. It may also be that depression, which is linked to relationship problems, could trigger an inflammatory response in its own right.

Positive Emotions

Negative emotions such as depression, anxiety, and anger may be especially important to avoid because they are associated with poor health (see Kiecolt-Glaser et al., 2002). On the other hand, an optimistic outlook on life, as well as an absence of negative emotions, may have some beneficial health consequences (see Rasmussen et al., 2009).

Perhaps you are familiar with the term **positive psychology**. This school of psychology focuses on human traits and resources such as humor, gratitude, and compassion that might have direct implications for our physical and mental well-being. An illustration of this comes from a study by Witvliet and colleagues (2001). These researchers asked college students to select a real-life interpersonal offense (such as rejection, betrayals of trust, and personal insults) that they had experienced in the past. The researchers then collected self-reports as well as heart rate, blood pressure, and facial muscle tension data from the students while they were imagining responding to the real-life transgression in a way that was either forgiving or unforgiving. In the forgiving condition, the students were asked to think about granting forgiveness or developing feelings of empathy for the perpetrator. In the unforgiving condition, they were asked to stay in the victim role, to go over the hurt in their minds, and to nurse a grudge.

The findings showed that when they were asked to be forgiving, participants did indeed report more feelings of empathy and forgiveness. And, when asked to ruminate and be unforgiving, participants reported that they felt more negative, angry, sad, aroused, and out of control. They also showed greater tension in their brows. Importantly,

Forgiving those who have wronged us may lower our stress levels and enhance overall well-being.

their heart rates went up, their blood pressures increased, and their skin conductance (a measure of SNS arousal) revealed more arousal. Even more striking was the finding that even after the grudge-harboring imagery was over and the subjects were told to relax, they were unable to do so. In other words, the high state of physiological arousal that had been triggered by dwelling on the past hurt could not easily be turned off.

What are the implications of these findings? Although fleeting feelings of anger probably do us no real harm, people who have a tendency to brood about the wrongs that other people have done to them may be doing themselves a major disservice. To the extent that perpetuating feelings of anger and increasing cardiovascular reactivity have consequences for heart disease and immune system functioning, harboring grudges may be hazardous to our health. Indeed, recent research shows that college-age adults who score high on a measure of forgivingness have fewer symptoms of both physical and mental health problems (Toussaint et al., 2015). Being forgiving also acts as a buffer against the effects of stress on mental health, although no similar association was found for physical health. Although the study just described was a cross-sectional one, longitudinal research has shown that more forgiveness predicts fewer health symptoms, but that having fewer health symptoms does not predict being more forgiving (Seawell et al., 2014). In other words, it is most likely that it is forgiveness that is making a difference to health, rather than healthy people being more forgiving. If this is true, there is an important take-home message. Although it is not always easy, forgiving those who have offended us may lower our stress levels and enhance our physical and emotional well-being.

Now that you understand the importance of positive and negative emotions in physical health, consider the case of Dr. M.

The Angry Physician

Dr. M was a 44-year-old physician. The middle son of parents who had emigrated from Italy, he was ambitious and determined to make a successful life for himself and his family. He worked long hours helping patients with cancer, and he was caring and compassionate. His patients loved him. But his job was also very stressful. Added to the many demands of maintaining a busy medical practice was the great sadness that he felt when (inevitably) many of his terminally ill patients died.

At home Dr. M was a loyal husband and devoted father to his three children. But he was not an easy person to live with. He found it hard to relax, and he had a very volatile disposition. He was frequently angry and would shout at everyone whenever he had had a bad day. Often his moods were caused by his feeling that he was not fully appreciated by the other doctors with whom he worked. Although his wife realized that he "just needed to vent," his moods took a toll on the family. His children distanced themselves from him much of the time, and his wife became less and less happy in the marriage.

One day at work, Dr. M started to feel unwell. He began to sweat and experienced a heavy pressure in his chest. It was difficult for him to breathe. Dr. M recognized the severity of his symptoms and called out for medical help. He had a sudden and severe heart attack and survived only because he was working in a hospital at the time of the attack. If he had not received prompt medical attention, he almost certainly would have died.

After his heart attack Dr. M became very depressed. It was almost as though he could not accept that he, a physician, had a severe medical problem. Although he lived in fear of having another heart attack, his efforts to lose weight (which his doctor had told him to do) were sabotaged by his unwillingness to follow any diet. He would try and then give up, coming back from the Italian bakery with bags of pastries. Making the problem worse was the fact that because he was a doctor, his own doctors were somewhat reticent about telling him what he had to do to manage his illness. He went back to work, and his family walked on eggshells, afraid to do or say anything that might stress him. His wife tried to encourage him to follow the doctors' recommendations. However, Dr. M's attitude was that if he was going to die anyway, he might as well enjoy himself until he did.

The Importance of Emotion Regulation

If hostility, depression, and anxiety are all predictive of developing coronary heart disease, is it beneficial to be able to regulate one's emotions? Research suggests that it is. In one study of men and women without a history of heart disease, it was found that it was the people who were *least* able to control their anger who developed more heart problems during the next 10 to 15 years (Haukkala et al., 2010). In another study of 1,122 men who were followed for an average of 13 years, it was again those with the best emotion regulation skills who were the least likely to develop cardiac disease (Kubzansky et al., 2011). Taken together these findings suggest that self-regulation skills may be very important—not only for our psychological well-being but for our physical health as well. Although regulating our emotions is not easy, learning how to stay in emotional control is well worth the effort.

---

in review

- What emotional risk factors are associated with coronary heart disease?
- What is Type A personality?
- What is Type D personality?
- How might positive emotions be beneficial for our physical health?

Treatment of Stress-Related Physical Disorders

5.5   Explain the psychological interventions that can be used to reduce stress and treat stress-related disorders.

As you have learned, environmental stressors are often closely linked to the development of a physical illness. Unfortunately, once an illness has developed and physical changes have taken place, removal of the stressor may not be enough to bring about recovery and restore health. This emphasizes the value of prevention and highlights the importance of stress management.

Biological Interventions

People who have serious physical diseases obviously require medical treatment for their problems. For patients with CHD, such treatments might include surgical procedures as well as medications to lower cholesterol or reduce the risk of blood clots. However, in light of the strong associations between depression and risk for CHD, treating depression is also of the utmost importance. Unfortunately, most people with clinical depression go untreated, resulting in an unnecessary added risk for CHD. Moreover, even though there is no medical risk factor that is more important in predicting mortality for patients who have already had a heart attack (Welin et al., 2000), physicians often fail to treat depression in their cardiac patients. Instead, they dismiss it as an understandable consequence of having had a life-threatening medical scare (Glassman, 2005). Of those with major depression at the time of a heart attack, approximately one-half of those who have gone without treatment remain depressed or else have relapsed again 1 year later (Hance et al., 1996). However, research shows that thousands of lives can be saved each year by giving antidepressant medications to patients who have suffered a myocardial infarction and who are depressed. In one study, patients treated with selective serotonin reuptake inhibitors (SSRIs) were much less likely to die or have another heart attack than patients who were not taking antidepressant medications (Taylor et al., 2005). It is also worth noting that, in this study, treatment with cognitive-behavior therapy (CBT; see Chapter 16 for more about this approach) was not associated with reduced mortality in the patients, although CBT treatment did help alleviate depression (see Berkman et al., 2003; Glassman, 2005).

Psychological Interventions

How can we help ourselves stay healthy in the face of stress? As we have already mentioned, developing effective emotion regulation skills is probably beneficial. Evidence suggests that the following approaches are also helpful.

EMOTIONAL DISCLOSURE "Opening up" and writing expressively about life problems in a systematic way does seem to be an effective therapy for many people with illnesses (Frattaroli, 2006; Pennebaker, 1997). It may also speed up wound healing. In one recent study, healthy older adults (average age 79 years) were asked to write for 20 minutes each day over a period of 3 consecutive days. One group wrote about their most traumatically stressful life experience, delving into their most private and deep thoughts and emotions. Another group simply wrote about their planned activities for the following day. Two weeks later, all participants were given a punch biopsy wound on their arm. Wound healing was significantly faster in the participants who had been asked to write about upsetting life events (Koschwanez et al., 2013). This is potentially very important because wound healing slows down as we get older. Simple interventions of this kind could therefore have great practical importance for seniors about to undergo surgery, for example.

Expressive writing also seems to provide some modest benefits (reduced fatigue at a 3-month follow-up assessment) for people who have been diagnosed with autoimmune illnesses such as lupus and rheumatoid arthritis (Danoff-Burg et al., 2006). However, findings suggest that expressive writing does not seem to improve sleep problems, depression, or overall quality of life in people being treated for cancer (Lepore et al., 2015). There is also some evidence that expressive writing may even get in the way of emotional recovery in people who have experienced a marital separation (Sbarra et al., 2013). In other words, the findings are often mixed and expressive writing is far from a cure-all.

In studies that involve emotional disclosure, patients often experience initial increases in emotional distress during the writing phase but then show improvement in their medical status over follow-up. Why emotional disclosure provides clinical benefits for some patients is still not clear, however. One reason could be that patients are given an opportunity for emotional catharsis, or "blowing off steam." Another possibility is that writing gives people an opportunity to rethink their problems or reduce how threatening these problems seem. This is known as reframing. But depending on the problem and the timing of when it occurred, there is perhaps the risk that expressive writing could sometimes lead to rumination ("Why did he leave me?") rather than reframing ("That was a bad relationship and I am better off on my own"). If this is the case, expressive writing too soon after an upsetting life event may make things worse rather than better. For events that are more in the past, however, it is not unreasonable to speculate that both emotional catharsis and rethinking problems could help improve immune function or perhaps decrease levels of circulating stress hormones. As research progresses we will understand more about the factors that determine whether or not expressive writing is helpful (moderator variables) as well as the mechanisms (mediating variables) through which expressive writing might work.

BIOFEEDBACK Biofeedback procedures aim to make patients more aware of such things as their heart rate, level of muscle tension, or blood pressure. This is done by connecting the patient to monitoring equipment and then providing a cue (for example, an audible tone) to the patient when he or she is successful at making a desired response (e.g., lowering blood pressure or decreasing tension in a facial muscle). Over time, patients become more consciously aware of their internal responses and are able to modify them when necessary.

Biofeedback seems to be helpful in treating some conditions, such as headaches (Nestoriuc et al., 2008). After an average of 11 sessions, patients report improvement in their symptoms and a decrease in the frequency of their headaches. Moreover, these treatment effects tend to be stable over time. Although it is especially helpful for children and adolescents, adults who have experienced headaches for a long time are also helped by biofeedback.

RELAXATION AND MEDITATION Researchers have examined the effects of various behavioral relaxation techniques on selected stress-related illnesses. The results have been variable, though generally encouraging. For example, evidence suggests that relaxation techniques can help patients with essential hypertension (see Blumenthal et al., 2002). Relaxation training can also help patients who experience tension headaches (Holroyd, 2002). However, in general, people with headaches who are treated with biofeedback appear to do better than those treated only with relaxation, and the best clinical results occur when these two treatments are combined (Nestoriuc et al., 2008).

A current focus of interest is meditation. Schneider and colleagues (2005) have shown that the daily practice of Transcendental Meditation may be helpful in reducing blood pressure. In this study, 194 African American

Watch Managing Stress

patients with chronic hypertension were randomly assigned to receive training in either Transcendental Meditation or progressive muscle relaxation (which involves tensing and relaxing various muscle groups in a systematic way) or else to receive general information about lifestyle changes that would be helpful to them. Patients who practiced Transcendental Meditation for 20 minutes twice a day reduced their diastolic blood pressure significantly more than did patients who practiced muscle relaxation or who received sound health care advice.

COGNITIVE-BEHAVIOR THERAPY CBT has been shown to be an effective intervention for headache (Martin, Forsyth, & Reece, 2007), as well as for other types of pain. CBT-oriented family therapy was markedly more successful than routine pediatric care in alleviating children's complaints of recurrent abdominal pain (Robins et al., 2005). Some CBT techniques have also been used for patients with rheumatoid arthritis. Compared to those receiving standard medical care, patients who received CBT showed better physical, social, and psychological functioning (Evers et al., 2002).

Finally, we note that making a conscious effort to slow down and enjoy life seems to be a prescription for better health. Meyer Friedman, who was the co-discoverer of the link between Type A behavior and heart disease, had a heart attack at age 55. A self-described Type-A personality, he made a conscious choice to change his ways in accordance with his own discoveries. To get more in touch with his slow, patient, and creative side, he read Proust's languid seven-volume opus *Remembrance of Things Past* three times. In short, he trained himself to relax and to enjoy life. He had the last laugh at stress by living to the ripe old age of 90 (Wargo, 2007).

Making an effort to slow down and relax may provide many health benefits.

in review
- Why is it so important to screen people with heart disease for depression?
- What clinical approaches have been used to treat stress-related disorders?

Stress and Mental Health

5.6 Identify the similarities and differences between adjustment disorder, posttraumatic stress disorder, and acute stress disorder.

Our focus thus far has been on describing the nature of stress, highlighting the role it plays in physical disorders. But, as we have noted repeatedly throughout this chapter, when we experience stress, we pay a price not only in our bodies but also in our minds. In the sections that follow, we discuss the psychological consequences of experiencing the kind of stress that overwhelms our abilities to adjust and to cope. More specifically, we focus on three *DSM* disorders, **adjustment disorder**, **acute stress disorder**, and PTSD. All of these are precipitated by exposure to stress. There are important differences between them, however. In adjustment disorder, the stressor is something that is commonly experienced, and the nature of the psychological reaction is much less severe. In contrast, both acute stress disorder and PTSD involve exposure to a more traumatic stressor. This can lead to short term problems (acute stress disorder) or more long-term and intense difficulties that can be debilitating (PTSD).

Adjustment Disorder

An adjustment disorder is a psychological response to a common stressor (e.g., divorce, death of a loved one, loss of a job) that results in clinically significant behavioral or emotional symptoms. The stressor can be a single event, such as going away to college, or involve multiple stressors, such as a business failure and marital problems. People undergoing severe stress that exceeds their coping resources may warrant the diagnosis of adjustment disorder (Strain & Newcorn, 2007). For the diagnosis to be given, symptoms must begin within 3 months of the onset of the stressor. In addition, the person must experience more distress than would be expected given the circumstances or be unable to function as usual.

In adjustment disorder, the person's symptoms lessen or disappear when the stressor ends or when the person learns to adapt to the stressor. In cases where the symptoms continue beyond 6 months, the diagnosis is usually changed to some other mental disorder. Adjustment disorder is probably the least stigmatizing and mildest diagnosis a therapist can assign to a client.

Adjustment Disorder Caused by Unemployment

Work-related problems can produce great stress in employees (Lennon & Limonic, 2010). But being unemployed can be even more stressful. As a result of the recent recession, millions of Americans have had to cope with chronic unemployment. Tony is one of them.

Maybe Today Will Be the Day

Tony wakes up at 5:30 every morning and makes coffee. He arranges his laptop, phone, and notepad on the kitchen table. And then he waits for the phone to ring. Unemployed for the last 16 months after losing his job as a transportation sales manager, Tony spends the day sending out resumes and cover letters. But most days nothing happens. "The worst moment is at the end of the day when it's 4:30 and you did everything you could, and the phone hasn't rung, the emails haven't come through," says Tony. He asks himself what he is doing wrong. Tony misses his old routine of getting dressed in the morning and going out to work. But he tries to stay optimistic. "You always have to hope that that morning when you get up, it's going to be the day." (Based on Kwoh, 2010)

During the recent recession, unemployment reached a peak of 10.6 percent of the labor force in January 2010. Although things have improved since then, in almost every community, one can find workers who have been laid off from jobs they had held for many years and who are facing the end of their unemployment compensation. Unemployment is an especially severe problem for young minority males, many of whom live in a permanent economic depression with few job prospects. Rates of unemployment for blacks are twice as high as they are for whites (Bureau of Labor Statistics, 2013).

Managing the stress associated with unemployment requires great coping strength, especially for people who have previously earned an adequate living. Some people (like Tony in the case example above) find ways to stay focused and motivated, even though this can be very difficult at times. For others, however, unemployment can have serious long-term effects. One of the most disturbing findings is that unemployment, especially if it is prolonged, increases the risk of suicide (Borges et al., 2010; Classen & Dunn, 2011). Unemployment also takes its toll on other family members, especially children. When children live in families where a parent has lost a job, they are 15 percent more likely to have to repeat a grade at school (Stevens & Schaller, 2009).

Posttraumatic Stress Disorder

In *DSM-5* posttraumatic stress disorder is grouped with other disorders in a new diagnostic category called trauma- and stressor-related disorders. Adjustment disorder, which

we have just discussed, and acute stress disorder (see next section) are also part of this new diagnostic category. This is because the experience of major stress is central to the development of all of these conditions.

Watch   Bonnie: Posttraumatic Stress Disorder

The diagnosis of PTSD first entered the *DSM* in 1980 (see the Criteria for Posttraumatic Stress Disorder box later in this chapter for current clinical criteria). At this time, psychiatry began to realize that many veterans were emotionally scarred and unable to return to normal civilian life after their military service in Vietnam. The proposal to include PTSD in the diagnostic system was initially opposed, not least because including a disorder that had a clear and explicit cause (trauma) was inconsistent with the atheoretical nature of the *DSM*. Nonetheless, a consensus emerged that any extreme, terrifying, and stressful event

Traumatic stressors include combat, rape, and experiencing a natural disaster such as an earthquake, flood, tornado, or hurricane.

that was life threatening and outside the ordinary bounds of everyday experience could lead to psychological symptoms similar to those experienced by the Vietnam veterans. In other words, at the time of its entry into the *DSM* (which is after all a manual of mental disorders), PTSD was viewed as a *normal* response to an *abnormal* stressor (see McNally, 2008). In the Thinking Critically about *DSM-5* box we describe how changes to the diagnostic criteria for PTSD have changed over time.

Traumatic stressors include combat, rape, being confined in a concentration camp, and experiencing a natural disaster such as a tsunami, earthquake, or tornado. These are all terrible experiences and, as would be expected, stress symptoms are very common in the immediate aftermath of a traumatic event. However, for most people, these symptoms decrease with time. Rothbaum and Foa (1993) reported that 95 percent of women who had been raped

met the symptom criteria for PTSD within 2 weeks of the assault. One month after the rape, this figure had declined to 63.3 percent of women, and after 3 months, 45.9 percent of the women were diagnosed with PTSD. Natural recovery with time is therefore a common pattern.

In the case of PTSD, however, the stress symptoms fail to abate even when the traumatic event has passed and the danger is over. Instead, what becomes established is a memory of the traumatic event that results in the traumatic event being reexperienced involuntarily and with the same full emotional force that characterized the original experience (McNally, 2015). Although being able to remember potentially life-threatening experiences is highly adaptive for our overall survival, having prolonged, intense, and intrusive memories that cause extreme stress symptoms is not. This is why PTSD is considered to be a mental disorder.

DSM-5 Thinking Critically about *DSM-5*

Changes to the Diagnostic Criteria for PTSD

When PTSD was first introduced into the *DSM*, the diagnostic criteria required exposure to a traumatic event that was "outside the range of usual human experience" and that would cause "significant symptoms of distress in almost anyone." The exemplars provided included rape, earthquakes, torture, and military combat. In other words, the emphasis was on the nature of the stressor itself and not on the emotional response of the victim (Breslau & Kessler, 2001; McNally, 2008; Shalev, 2009).

A major change occurred with *DSM-IV*. Not only was there a broadening of the range of experiences that could now be used to diagnose PTSD, but it was also required that the person's response involve "intense fear, helplessness or horror." Qualifying events could now include learning about the death of a close friend or relative (as long as the death was sudden and unexpected), being diagnosed with a life-threatening illness, or learning about traumatic events experienced by others. In short, there was a change in emphasis from the characteristics of the stressor to the experience of the victim. Rather than conceptualizing PTSD as a normal response to an *abnormal stressor*, in *DSM-IV*, PTSD was viewed as a *pathological response* to an extreme form of stress (McNally, 2008).

The implications of these changes were not trivial. Using the wider variety of stressors permitted in *DSM-IV*, a survey of community residents revealed that the vast majority (89.6 percent) reported that they had been exposed to a traumatic event that (given also the required level of emotional response and presence of other symptoms) would potentially qualify them for PTSD diagnosis (Breslau & Kessler, 2001). In most cases, the traumatic event was learning of the sudden and unexpected death of a loved one. Moreover, females who reported

traumatic events were much more likely than males to also report that they had had an emotional reaction that was severe enough for them to qualify for the PTSD diagnosis. So not only was the definition of a traumatic event broadened, but the kind of emotional response that qualifies for PTSD was much more likely to be reported by women than by men (Pratchett et al., 2010).

In *DSM-5*, the diagnostic criteria for PTSD have been tightened. The traumatic event must now be experienced by the person directly, either because the event happens to you or because you witness, in person, something traumatic happening to someone else. No longer is it possible to experience trauma indirectly through electronic media (which could occur when someone watches television footage of a terrible event). As before, there is also a provision for experiencing trauma by learning of the death of another person. However, the person must be a close friend or relative and their death must have been violent or accidental. Yet another change is the removal of the requirement that the person respond in a particular way (i.e., with fear, helplessness, or horror) because this confounds the response with the event itself (McNally, 2009) and also makes it more likely that women will receive the diagnosis. Defining trauma exposure is difficult to do. Nonetheless, we believe that the modifications that have been made to the *DSM* criteria are good overall. Tightening the diagnostic criteria in these ways means that PTSD is more likely to remain a distinct diagnosis reserved for people who have experienced devastating life events. No longer will it be possible to diagnose PTSD in people who merely watch traumatic events on their computer or television screens and are very distressed by what they see.

Acute Stress Disorder

The diagnosis of PTSD requires that symptoms must last for at least 1 month. What this means is that, in the study just described, the women who had symptoms within 2 weeks of the assault would not be diagnosed with PTSD. Instead, the diagnosis would be **acute stress disorder**. Acute stress disorder is a diagnostic category that can be used when symptoms develop shortly after experiencing a traumatic event and last for at least 2 days. The existence of this diagnosis means that people with symptoms do not have to wait a whole month to be diagnosed with PTSD. Instead they can receive treatment as soon as they experience symptoms (Cardeña & Carlson, 2011). Moreover, if symptoms persist beyond 4 weeks, the diagnosis can be changed from acute stress disorder to posttraumatic stress disorder. Studies show that people who develop an acute stress disorder shortly after traumatic event are indeed at increased risk of developing PTSD (Kleim et al., 2007). This highlights the importance of early intervention.

Of course, PTSD is not the only disorder that can develop after a traumatic experience. Bryant and colleagues (2010) conducted a prospective study of a large sample of people who were injured in accidents. They were assessed at the time of their injury and then followed up 3 and 12 months later. The investigators found that, 12 months after injury, 31 percent of patients reported a psychiatric disorder, and 22 percent of them had a disorder they had never experienced before. The most common disorders were depression (9 percent), generalized anxiety disorder (9 percent), and PTSD (6 percent).

in review

- What is an adjustment disorder?
- What kinds of stressors are potential triggers for the development of an adjustment disorder?
- What is the main difference between acute stress disorder and PTSD?

Posttraumatic Stress Disorder: Causes and Risk Factors

5.7 **Describe the clinical features of and risk factors for posttraumatic stress disorder.**

In PTSD a traumatic event is thought to cause a *pathological memory* that is at the center of the characteristic clinical symptoms associated with the disorder (McNally, 2013). These memories are often brief fragments of the experience and typically concern events that happened just before the moment with the largest emotional impact (e.g., "Perpetrator standing at the window with the knife"; Hackmann et al., 2004). The clinical symptoms of PTSD are shown in the Criteria for Posttraumatic Stress Disorder box. Note that these symptoms are grouped into four main areas and concern the following:

1. **Intrusion:** Recurrent reexperiencing of the traumatic event through nightmares, intrusive images, and physiological reactivity to reminders of the trauma. (In *DSM-IV* ruminative thoughts about the trauma were also considered to reflect intrusion. This is not the case in *DSM-5*.)

2. **Avoidance:** Efforts to avoid thoughts, feelings, or reminders of the trauma.

3. **Negative alterations in cognitions and mood:** This includes such symptoms as feelings of detachment as well as negative emotional states such as shame or anger, or distorted blame of oneself or others.

4. **Arousal and reactivity:** Hypervigilance, excessive response when startled, aggression, and reckless behavior.

The symptoms are illustrated in the following case.

Abducted and Terrorized

Mr. A. was a married accountant, the father of two, in his early 30s. One night, while out running an errand, he was attacked by a group of young men. They forced him into their car and took him to a deserted country road. There they pulled him from the car and began beating and kicking him. They took his wallet, began taunting him about its contents (they had learned his name, his occupation, and the names of his wife and children), and threatened to go to his home and harm his family. Finally, after brutalizing him for several hours, they tied him to a tree. One man held a gun to his head. Mr. A. begged and pleaded for his life; then the armed assailant pulled the trigger. The gun was empty, but at the moment the trigger was pulled, Mr. A. defecated and urinated in his pants. Then the men untied him and left him on the road.

Mr. A. slowly made his way to a gas station and called the police. [One of the authors] was called to examine him and did so at intervals for the next 2 years. The diagnosis was PTSD. Mr. A. had clearly experienced an event outside the range of normal human experience and was reexperiencing the event in various ways: intrusive recollections, nightmares, flashbacks, and extreme fear upon seeing groups of tough-looking young men. He was initially remarkably numb in other respects: He felt estranged and detached. He withdrew from his family, lost interest in his job, and expected to die in the near future. Mr. A. also showed symptoms of increased physiological arousal. His sleep was poor, he had difficulty concentrating, and he was easily startled. When Mr. A. first spoke about his abduction in detail he actually soiled himself at the moment he described doing so during the original traumatic experience.

Mr. A. received treatment from a psychiatrist for the next 2 years. This consisted of twice-weekly individual psychotherapy as

DSM-5 *Criteria for. . .*

Posttraumatic Stress Disorder

Note: The following criteria apply to adults, adolescents, and children older than 6 years.

A. Exposure to actual or threatened death, serious injury, or sexual violence in one (or more) of the following ways:

1. Directly experiencing the traumatic event(s).
2. Witnessing, in person, the event(s) as it occurred to others.
3. Learning that the traumatic event(s) occurred to a close family member or close friend. In cases of actual or threatened death of a family member or friend, the event(s) must have been violent or accidental.
4. Experiencing repeated or extreme exposure to aversive details of the traumatic event(s) (e.g., first responders collecting human remains; police officers repeatedly exposed to details of child abuse).

    Note: Criterion A4 does not apply to exposure through electronic media, television, movies, or pictures, unless this exposure is work related.

B. Presence of one (or more) of the following intrusion symptoms associated with the traumatic event(s), beginning after the traumatic event(s) occurred:

1. Recurrent, involuntary, and intrusive distressing memories of the traumatic event(s).

    Note: In children older than 6 years, repetitive play may occur in which themes or aspects of the traumatic event(s) are expressed.
2. Recurrent distressing dreams in which the content and/or affect of the dream are related to the traumatic event(s).

    Note: In children, there may be frightening dreams without recognizable content.
3. Dissociative reactions (e.g., flashbacks) in which the individual feels or acts as if the traumatic event(s) were recurring. (Such reactions may occur on a continuum, with the most extreme expression being a complete loss of awareness of present surroundings.)

    Note: In children, trauma-specific reenactment may occur in play.
4. Intense or prolonged psychological distress at exposure to internal or external cues that symbolize or resemble an aspect of the traumatic event(s).
5. Marked physiological reactions to internal or external cues that symbolize or resemble an aspect of the traumatic event(s).

C. Persistent avoidance of stimuli associated with the traumatic event(s), beginning after the traumatic event(s) occurred, as evidenced by one or both of the following:

1. Avoidance of or efforts to avoid distressing memories, thoughts, or feelings about or closely associated with the traumatic event(s).
2. Avoidance of or efforts to avoid external reminders (people, places, conversations, activities, objects, situations) that arouse distressing memories, thoughts, or feelings about or closely associated with the traumatic event(s).

D. Negative alterations in cognitions and mood associated with the traumatic event(s), beginning or worsening after the traumatic event(s) occurred, as evidenced by two (or more) of the following:

1. Inability to remember an important aspect of the traumatic event(s) (typically due to dissociative amnesia and not to other factors such as head injury, alcohol, or drugs).
2. Persistent and exaggerated negative beliefs or expectations about oneself, others, or the world (e.g., "I am bad," "No one can be trusted," "The world is completely dangerous," "My whole nervous system is permanently ruined").
3. Persistent, distorted cognitions about the cause or consequences of the traumatic event(s) that lead the individual to blame himself/herself or others.
4. Persistent negative emotional state (e.g., fear, horror, anger, guilt, or shame).
5. Markedly diminished interest or participation in significant activities.
6. Feelings of detachment or estrangement from others.
7. Persistent inability to experience positive emotions (e.g., inability to experience happiness, satisfaction, or loving feelings).

E. Marked alterations in arousal and reactivity associated with the traumatic event(s), beginning or worsening after the traumatic event(s) occurred, as evidenced by two (or more) of the following:

1. Irritable behavior and angry outbursts (with little or no provocation) typically expressed as verbal or physical aggression toward people or objects.
2. Reckless or self-destructive behavior.
3. Hypervigilance.
4. Exaggerated startle response.
5. Problems with concentration.
6. Sleep disturbance (e.g., difficulty falling or staying asleep or restless sleep).

F. Duration of the disturbance (Criteria B, C, D, and E) is more than 1 month.

G. The disturbance causes clinically significant distress or impairment in social, occupational, or other important areas of functioning.

H. The disturbance is not attributable to the physiological effects of a substance (e.g., medication, alcohol) or another medical condition.

Source: Reprinted with permission from the *Diagnostic and Statistical Manual of Mental Disorders*, Fifth Edition (Copyright 2013). American Psychiatric Association.

well as antidepressant medications. A focus of the therapy was the sense of shame and guilt Mr. A. felt over his behavior during his abduction. He wished he had been more stoic and had not pleaded for his life. With the help of his therapist, Mr. A. came to see that his murderous rage at his abductors was understandable, as was his desire for revenge. He was also able to accept that his response to his experience was likely similar to how others might have responded if faced with the same circumstances. By the end of treatment Mr. A. was almost without symptoms, although he still became somewhat anxious when he saw some groups of young men. Most important, his relationship with his wife and children was warm and close, and he was again interested in his work.

Prevalence of PTSD in the General Population

Estimates from the National Comorbidity Survey Replication (NCS-R) suggest that the lifetime prevalence of PTSD in the United States is 6.8 percent (Kessler, Berglund, Demler, et al., 2005). However, this figure obscures the gender difference in the prevalence of PTSD. The NCS-R data show that the lifetime prevalence of PTSD is higher in women. Over the course of their lives, 9.7 percent of women and 3.6 percent of men will develop this disorder.

The difference in the prevalence of PTSD in men and women is interesting, not least because studies show that men are much more likely to be exposed to traumatic events (Tolin & Foa, 2006). Some have suggested that the gender difference reflects the fact that women are more likely to be exposed to certain kinds of traumatic experiences, such as rape, that may be inherently more traumatic (Cortina & Kubiak, 2006). However, even when the type of traumatic event is controlled for, women still show higher rates of PTSD and tend to have more severe symptoms (Tolin & Foa, 2006). This suggests that there are differences between men and women that may determine their risk of developing PTSD after experiencing trauma.

Rates of PTSD after Traumatic Experiences

Disasters, both naturally occurring and human caused, are far from rare occurrences. In a typical year countless people are exposed to the kinds of traumatic events that can cause PTSD. For example, more than 900 earthquakes with a magnitude between 5 and 8 on the Richter scale occur annually throughout the world (Naeem et al., 2011). Tsunamis also devastate coastal villages, and hurricanes, tornadoes, and floods destroy lives and livelihoods. Of course, some places are safer than others. Not surprisingly, rates of PTSD throughout the world tend to be lower in areas where people experience fewer natural disasters and where wars and organized violence are less common.

Estimates of the prevalence of PTSD vary widely across different studies (Sundin et al., 2010). One reason for this is that rates of PTSD seem to differ according to the type of trauma that is experienced. More specifically, traumatic events that result from human intent (such as rape, as noted above) are more likely to cause PTSD than are traumatic events (such as accidents and natural disasters) that are not personal in nature (see Charuvastra & Cloitre, 2008). For example, Shalev and Freedman (2005) compared rates of PTSD after car accidents and after terrorist attacks in the same community in the Middle East. Interviews were conducted 1 week and 4 months after the traumatic event had occurred. Although there were no differences in the symptoms that people reported at the 1-week interview, at 4 months, rates of PTSD were much higher in the terrorist attack survivors than in those who had survived the car accidents. Traumatic events involving humans who do terrible things are perhaps even more difficult to come to terms with because they can destroy the sense of safety we often assume comes from being a member of a rule-abiding and lawful social group.

Another factor that is crucially important with respect to the development of PTSD is the degree of direct exposure to the traumatic event. After reviewing all published disaster research over a 25-year period, Neria, Nandi, and Galea (2008) have estimated that rates of PTSD range between 30 and 40 percent for adults who are directly exposed to disasters. The prevalence of PTSD in rescue workers, on the other hand, tends to be lower (5–10 percent), probably because they are not directly exposed to the traumatic event when it is happening. Nonetheless, these figures highlight the risk of PTSD in rescue workers. They also show that disasters leave large numbers of traumatized people in their wakes.

Finally, we should point out that differences in rates of PTSD across different studies may sometimes be linked to the way that PTSD is defined and the manner in which it is assessed. Estimates based on questionnaires tend to be higher than those based on clinical interviews. For example, in a study of Dutch veterans of the Iraq War, questionnaire assessments yielded rates of PTSD of 21 percent. However, when structured diagnostic interviews were used, only 4 percent of veterans met the criteria for PTSD (Engelhard et al., 2007). Reasons for the overestimates when questionnaire measures are used include misunderstanding the meaning of items on the questionnaire, presence of symptoms that cause little impairment in functioning, and inclusion of symptoms that began at times other than during or after a traumatic event.

THE TRAUMA OF MILITARY COMBAT In a combat situation, with the continual threat of injury or death and repeated narrow escapes, a person's ordinary coping methods are relatively useless. The adequacy and security the person has known in the relatively safe and dependable civilian world are completely undermined. Combat brings with it constant fear, unpredictability, many uncontrollable circumstances, and the necessity of killing. Other factors may further contribute to the overall stress experienced by soldiers. These include separation from loved ones, reductions in personal freedom, sleep deprivation, extreme and harsh climate conditions, and increased risk for disease.

Many people who have been involved in the turmoil of war experience devastating psychological problems for months or even years afterward (Garakani et al., 2004). During World War I, traumatic reactions to combat conditions were called "shell shock," a term coined by a British pathologist, Col. Frederick Mott (1919), who regarded these reactions as organic conditions produced by minute brain hemorrhages. It was gradually realized, however, that only a small percentage of such cases represented physical injury. Most victims were suffering instead from the general combat situation, with its physical fatigue, ever-present threat of death or mutilation, and severe psychological shocks. During World War II, traumatic reactions to combat were known as *operational fatigue* and *war neuroses*, before finally being termed *combat fatigue* or *combat exhaustion* in the Korean and Vietnam Wars. Even the latter terms were none too aptly chosen because they implied that physical exhaustion played a more important role than was usually the case.

It has been estimated that in World War II, 10 percent of Americans in combat developed combat exhaustion. However, the actual incidence is not known because many soldiers received supportive therapy at their battalion aid stations and were returned to combat within a few hours. Recent evaluations of World War II psychiatric casualty files concluded that this practice of "forward psychiatry" was not effective at returning soldiers with shell shock to combat, but their improved mood and adjustment allowed them to be reassigned to noncombat roles, resulting in reduced manpower losses overall (Jones et al., 2007). In World War II, combat exhaustion was the greatest single cause of loss of personnel (Bloch, 1969).

MENTAL HEALTH CONSEQUENCES OF DEPLOYMENT TO IRAQ AND AFGHANISTAN   Around 2.5 million members of the armed forces were deployed for operations in Iraq and Afghanistan according to U.S. Department of Defense figures. During these deployments these veterans were exposed to many traumatic experiences and had to function under conditions of sustained threat. In one study, the overwhelming majority (92 percent) of Army soldiers and Marines in Iraq reported that they had been attacked or ambushed, and 86 percent reported knowing someone who was killed or seriously injured (Hoge et al., 2004). We should also keep in mind that some brigade combat teams were deployed multiple times (Thomas et al., 2010). Not

surprisingly, this has taken a toll on the mental health of those team members.

The high prevalence of postdeployment mental disorders in these military personnel continues to be a major source of concern. A recent meta-analysis has reported rates of PTSD of 12.9 percent in military personnel following deployment to Iraq and a rate of 7.1 percent for those who served in Afghanistan (Hines et al., 2014). The figures for Iraq veterans are comparable to the rates of PTSD reported for veterans of the Vietnam War (12–16 percent; Thompson et al., 2006) and Gulf War (12 percent; Kang et al., 2003), but higher than rates of PTSD in U.K. military personnel following deployment to Iraq or Afghanistan (4.8 percent; see Iversen et al., 2009). In addition to PTSD, rates of depression, aggression, and problems with postdeployment alcohol misuse are also elevated (Seal et al., 2009; Thomas et al., 2010).

As might be expected, rates of PTSD tend to be higher in military personnel who were deployed into a combat role versus a support role (12.4 versus 4.9 percent). Reflecting this, army and marine personnel had higher rates of PTSD (13 and 10 percent, respectively) than those who had served in the navy (7 percent) or air force (3 percent; Hines et al., 2014). There is also evidence that theater-specific duties may shape some of the symptoms that veterans have. In addition to PTSD, clinicians are seeing veterans with compulsive checking behaviors.

The military is also trying to cope with another serious problem—soldier suicide. During 2013, according to the most recent figures, 259 members of the armed forces took their own lives and many more made suicide attempts (U.S. Department of Defense, 2014). Most of these suicides resulted from self-inflicted gunshot wounds. Suicide rates in the U.S. Army are especially high. Clay's story serves as a tragic reminder of how destructive and invisible some of the wounds of war can be.

A Warrior Takes His Own Life

Clay was a handsome and friendly 28-year-old. A former Marine corporal, he received a Purple Heart after taking a bullet in Iraq and later returned to combat in Afghanistan. After his deployment was over Clay became involved in humanitarian work in Chile and Haiti. He lobbied in Washington to improve the disability claims process for veterans and was chosen to appear in a public service announcement to remind veterans that they were not alone. But Clay's smiles and boundless energy were masks covering the emotional pain he lived with every day. Clay suffered from PTSD and depression. He also experienced survivor guilt, asking himself why he had survived when many people he had served with had died. One day in the early spring, Clay locked the door of his apartment and shot himself. His death leaves a void in the lives of his family and friends. It also highlights the need for continued efforts within the military to address the problem of suicide by members of the armed forces. (Based on Helfling, 2011)

Causal Factors in Posttraumatic Stress Disorder

The study of causal risk factors that might be involved in the development of PTSD has been a controversial area (McNally, 2008). There are two major reasons for this. First, the very notion of PTSD makes it explicit that PTSD is caused by experiencing trauma. So why should we look any further if we wish to know what causes PTSD? The second concern is that, if some people are more likely to develop PTSD in the face of severe stress than other people are, might this not lead to double victimization, with victims of trauma also being stigmatized and being blamed for the troubles that they have?

On the other side of the issue, we know that not everyone who is exposed to a traumatic event will develop PTSD. This suggests that some people may be more vulnerable to developing PTSD than others. To prevent and better treat this disorder, we therefore need to understand more about the factors that are involved in its development.

As we have already noted, the nature of the traumatic stressor and how directly it was experienced can account for much of the differences in stress response (see Dohrenwend et al., 2013). For example, there is a close relationship between the total number of people killed and wounded and the number of psychiatric casualties in war (Jones & Wessely, 2002). Soldiers who report killing or being responsible for killing during their deployment are also more vulnerable to developing PTSD (Maguen et al., 2010).

If the level of stress is high enough, then, the average person can be expected to develop some psychological difficulties (which may be either short lived or long term) following a traumatic event. But why is the breaking point of one person different from the breaking point of another? In the sections below, we highlight some areas that appear to be important.

Individual Risk Factors

When it comes to risk for PTSD, we need to keep two things in mind: As has been noted by researchers in this field, there is *risk for experiencing trauma* and there is also *risk for PTSD* given that there has been exposure to trauma (see McNally, 2013). Not everyone is at equal risk when it comes to the likelihood that she or he will experience a traumatic event. Certain occupations, such as being a soldier or a firefighter, carry more risk than others, such as being a librarian. Risk factors that increase the likelihood of being exposed to trauma include being male, having less than a college education, having had conduct problems in childhood, having a family history of psychiatric disorder, and scoring high on measures of extraversion and neuroticism (Breslau et al., 1991, 1995). Rates of exposure to traumatic events are also higher for black Americans than they are for white Americans.

Certain occupations place people at higher risk of experiencing a traumatic event.

Given that someone has been exposed to a traumatic event, what factors increase risk for *developing* PTSD? As we have already noted, being female is a risk factor. Other individual risk factors that have been identified by researchers include higher levels of neuroticism (having a tendency to experience negative affect), having preexisting problems with depression and anxiety, and having a family history of depression, anxiety, and substance abuse (see McNally, 2015; Wilk et al., 2010). Reflecting this, a prospective longitudinal study of military personnel has confirmed that psychiatric problems measured predeployment significantly increase the risk of developing PTSD postdeployment (Sandweiss et al., 2011). This highlights the importance of mental health screening prior to deployment and the need to provide additional resources and support for soldiers who may be most vulnerable.

Low levels of social support have also been noted as a risk factor. One problem here, however, is that social support is typically assessed after people have developed PTSD. This makes it difficult to separate cause from consequence. Do the emerging symptoms of PTSD alienate people and so reduce the available level of social support? Or is a lack of adequate social support causally implicated in the development of PTSD? It is also possible that both processes are operating. Also relevant are the appraisals people make of their own stress symptoms shortly after the trauma. If people believe that their symptoms are a sign of personal weakness or if they believe that others will be ashamed of them because they are experiencing symptoms, they are at increased risk for developing PTSD, even when the level of initial symptoms is statistically controlled (Dunmore et al., 2001).

There is even some very new evidence suggesting that people who have disturbing thoughts or images about traumatic events that could happen *in the future* may be at elevated risk of developing PTSD later. Bertsen and Rubin (2015) asked Danish soldiers who were about to be deployed to Afghanistan to complete a measure of what they called pretraumatic stress reactions. This asked about how much people had been bothered by thoughts or images of possible future stressful experiences, or whether they had strong physical reactions when something reminded them of a stressful event they might experience at a later time. The measure of pretraumatic stress that the soldiers completed before deployment predicted their level of PTSD symptoms both during and after their service in Afghanistan, even after such factors as combat exposure and baseline PTSD symptoms were accounted for. This finding is potentially very important. It challenges our understanding of PTSD as a disorder that is solely related to past experiences. Instead the results appear to highlight the importance of mental imagery, suggesting that pre- and posttraumatic stress reactions might have much in common.

On the other side of the coin, are there factors that may be *protective* and buffer against PTSD? Good cognitive ability seems to be important here. Breslau, Lucia, and Alvarado (2006) collected IQ data from 6-year-old children who lived in and around Detroit. When these children reached the age of 17, they were interviewed and assessed both for exposure to trauma and for PTSD. The children who at age 6 had IQ scores above 115 were less likely to have experienced a traumatic event by age 17; furthermore, if they *had* been exposed to trauma, they were at lower risk for developing PTSD. These findings suggest that having a higher IQ may be protective against experiencing trauma and developing PTSD because children who had average or below-average IQ scores were at similar risk for PTSD.

Similar findings have also been reported for Vietnam veterans. Kremen and colleagues (2007) collected information from a large sample of twins and also obtained information about the twins' cognitive ability scores before they went to serve in Vietnam. All of the men involved in the study were subsequently exposed to traumatic events during their military service. Compared with men who had scored in the lowest quartile on the Armed Forces Qualification Test (a measure of cognitive ability), men who had scored in the highest quartile had a 48 percent *lower risk* of developing PTSD.

Why might higher pretrauma cognitive abilities provide protection against PTSD? One possibility is that individuals with more intellectual resources might be better able to create some meaning from their traumatic experiences and translate them into a personal narrative of some kind. Earlier in this chapter, we discussed the therapeutic benefits of systematically writing about distressing events (Pennebaker, 1997). Perhaps people with higher cognitive abilities are more naturally able to incorporate their traumatic experiences into their life narratives in ways that are ultimately adaptive and emotionally protective.

Biological Factors

Given that PTSD is a stress disorder, you might expect people with this disorder would have high levels of hormones such as cortisol. However, this does not seem to be the case (Pittman et al., 2012; Young & Breslau, 2004). Under conditions of imposed experimental stress (trauma reminders, cognitive challenges), people with PTSD do seem to show an exaggerated cortisol response (de Kloet et al., 2006). However, baseline levels of cortisol are often very similar in people with PTSD when they are compared to those of healthy controls (Meewisse et al., 2007).

Gender may be an important factor here, however. Women with PTSD do seem to have higher levels of baseline cortisol than women without PTSD. This is not so for men with and without PTSD. Another interesting finding is that levels of cortisol tend to be lower in people with PTSD who have experienced physical or sexual abuse. In other words, the type of trauma may be an important factor (Meewisse et al., 2007). Although many of the findings in this area are confusing, researchers are still exploring biological dysregulations in PTSD.

Another focus of research interest is gene–environment interactions. Earlier we discussed how people with a particular form of a particular gene (the *5HTTLPR*, or serotonin transporter gene) seem to be more at risk for developing depression in the face of four or more life events. Data now suggest that this gene may also be a risk factor for the development of PTSD. Kilpatrick and colleagues (2007) collected DNA data and interviewed 589 adults from Florida 6 to 9 months after the 2004 hurricane season. The prevalence of post-hurricane PTSD in the sample overall was 3.2 percent. Risk factors for developing PTSD were a high level of exposure to the hurricanes and low levels of social support. However, people who had the high-risk (*s/s*) genotype of the serotonin-transporter gene were at especially high risk for the development of PTSD if they *also* had high hurricane exposure *and* low social support. For those in this group, the rate of PTSD was 14.8 percent— 4.5 times higher. People with the *s/s* genotype were also more likely to develop depression if they had high hurricane exposure and low social support. These findings suggest that having the *s/s* form of the serotonin-transporter gene makes a bad situation worse. People with this genotype may be especially susceptible to the effects of traumatic stress, particularly if they also have low levels of social support.

A recent study sheds some light on why this might be. Disner and colleagues (2013) have reported that soldiers with two short alleles of the serotonin transporter gene (*s/s* genotype) were more likely to develop a bias toward looking longer at fearful facial stimuli after they had been deployed to Iraq versus before deployment. This gaze bias was found, even after other relevant factors (such as PTSD symptoms and depression) had been controlled. What these findings suggest is that people with the *s/s* form of the serotonin-transporter gene may be especially sensitive to certain environmental experiences such as war zone stress, and that one consequence of this is that they become more attentive to negative stimuli. In other words, the interaction between certain genes and certain environmental experiences may prime the attentional system to develop cognitive biases toward negative stimuli. Although this might possibly be adaptive in combat settings, it could contribute to the development of psychopathology at a later time.

What do we know about the brains of people with PTSD? Studies show that a brain area called the hippocampus seems to be reduced in size in people with PTSD (Pittman et al., 2012). The hippocampus is a brain area known to be involved in memory. It is also a brain area known to be responsive to stress. In a landmark study, Gilbertson and colleagues (2002) measured the volume of the hippocampus in combat veterans with and without PTSD. The results showed that the veterans with PTSD had smaller hippocampal volumes than did the veterans without PTSD. The reason this study is so important, however, is that all the men were MZ (identical) twins. And when Gilbertson and colleagues looked at the volume of the hippocampus in the healthy co-twins of the combat veterans with PTSD, they found that these men *also had small hippocampal volumes*, just like their brothers. In contrast, the combat veterans who did not have PTSD, as well as their twins (who had not been involved in combat), had similar (and larger) hippocampal volumes. What these findings suggest, then, is that for reasons we do not yet understand, small hippocampal volume may be a vulnerability factor for developing PTSD in people who are exposed to trauma. There is also a possibility that trauma reduces the size of the hippocampus to some extent. A meta-analysis shows that people who have been exposed to trauma (but who do not have PTSD) have smaller hippocampi than people who have not been exposed to trauma (Woon et al., 2010). In other words, reduced hippocampal size could be both a risk factor for PTSD and also be a consequence of trauma exposure.

A major problem with research in this area is that many of the brain abnormalities associated with PTSD (including reduced hippocampal size) are also found in people who are depressed. Because PTSD and depression are highly comorbid and co-occurring disorders, it is therefore hard for researchers to be sure which brain abnormalities are specific to PTSD and which might stem from depression (Kroes et al., 2011). But perhaps it is a bit naïve to expect that PTSD would be associated with brain abnormalities that are completely unique and distinct and that are not shared with any other disorders. We know that stress plays a role in the development of depression and the development of PTSD. We also know that stress (via glucocorticoids) has a negative impact on brain areas (like the hippocampus) that are important for healthy emotional functioning. Why then should we not expect to see some commonalities when we look at people who have disorders in which stress is implicated?

Sociocultural Factors

Being a member of a minority group seems to place people at higher risk for developing PTSD. DiGrande and colleagues (2011) studied 3,271 civilians who were evacuated from the World Trade Center towers on September 11, 2001. Two to three years after the attacks, 15 percent of people were assessed as having PTSD. Compared with whites, African American and Hispanic survivors were more likely to have PTSD. Echoing the discussion of resilience earlier in this chapter, being more educated and having a higher annual income were also factors associated with lower rates of PTSD overall.

Returning to a negative and unsupportive social environment can also increase vulnerability to posttraumatic stress (Charuvastra & Cloitre, 2008). For example, in a 1-year follow-up of Israeli men who had been psychiatric war casualties during the Yom Kippur War, Merbaum (1977) found that not only did these men continue to show extreme anxiety, depression, and extensive physical complaints, but (in many instances) they also appeared to become more disturbed over time. Merbaum hypothesized that the men's further psychological deterioration was due to the negative attitudes of the community. In a country so reliant on the strength of its army for its survival, considerable stigma is attached to psychological breakdown in combat. Because of this stigma, many of the men were experiencing not only isolation within their communities but also self-recrimination about what they perceived as their own failure. These feelings exacerbated the soldiers' already stressful situations.

Sociocultural variables also appear to play a role in determining a person's adjustment to combat. Important

Group cohesiveness and good leadership can help soldiers cope better with the inevitable stress of combat.

factors include justification for the combat and how clear and acceptable the war's goals are to the person whose life is being put in harm's way (Hoge et al., 2004). Identification with the combat unit and the quality of leadership also make a difference (Jones & Wessely, 2007).

Today, military psychiatrists apply techniques that have been learned during the past century to help reduce psychological casualties. Interventions that promote morale and encourage cohesion that were developed during World War II and the Korean and Vietnam Wars have proved effective at reducing psychological casualties occurring among U.S. troops during their deployments to the Afghanistan and Iraqi war zones (Ritchie, 2007). Strategically placed combat stress control teams deploy as soon as is practical after combat engagements to provide timely counseling to troops. To improve the morale of troops, the military also makes an effort to provide breaks from long engagements by providing "safe" zones that include such improvements as air conditioning, regular mail delivery, and good food. One of the most effective morale builders among troops has been the availability of the Internet at most established facilities in both Iraq and Afghanistan.

Having access to the Internet improves the morale of soldiers during long deployments.

Long-Term Effects of Posttraumatic Stress

As we have already noted, soldiers who have experienced combat exhaustion may show symptoms of posttraumatic stress for sustained periods of time (Shalev, 2009; Solomon & Mikulincer, 2007). If it develops, PTSD can be a severe and chronic condition. Moreover, in some cases, soldiers who stood up exceptionally well during their deployments have experienced delayed PTSD on their return home. The difficulties readjusting to life as a civilian after extended periods away from home cannot be underestimated. Feelings of responsibility associated with killing, as well as feelings of guilt for having survived when friends and unit peers did not, may also play a role here.

The nature and extent of PTSD are somewhat controversial, however (McNally, 2015). The delayed version of PTSD is less well defined and more difficult to diagnose than disorders that emerge shortly after the precipitating incident (Andrews et al., 2007). Moreover, with the exception of Vietnam veterans, cases of delayed-onset PTSD are exceedingly rare, with only one case of delayed PTSD being reported in a civilian study (Breslau et al., 1991). Reports of delayed stress syndrome among Vietnam combat veterans are often difficult to relate explicitly to combat stress because these people may also have other significant adjustment problems. Some authorities have questioned whether a delayed reaction should be diagnosed as PTSD at all; instead, some would categorize such a reaction as another type of disorder. For example, people with adjustment difficulties may erroneously attribute their present problems to specific incidents from their past, such as experiences in combat.

Also troubling are findings that show that 7 percent of men seeking treatment for combat-related PTSD had either never served in Vietnam or had not been in the military at all (Frueh et al., 2005). The wide publicity given to delayed PTSD and the potential for receiving service-connected disability payments may be relevant factors here. Based on their analysis of a large federal database, a group of labor economists has concluded that the enormous increase in PTSD disability claims made by Vietnam veterans results more from financial need than it does from psychiatric disorder (Agrist et al., 2010).

in review

- What risk factors are associated with experiencing trauma?
- What risk factors are implicated in the development of PTSD?
- Why might high IQ be protective against PTSD?
- How might genetic factors play a role in the development of PTSD?
- What is controversial about the diagnosis of delayed PTSD?

Prevention and Treatment of Stress Disorders

5.8 Explain the treatment approaches that are used to help people with PTSD.

Prevention

One way to prevent PTSD is to reduce the frequency of traumatic events. Although natural disasters are inevitable, efforts could be made to lessen the access that adolescents have to firearms. This could reduce the frequency of school violence and shootings. Other changes in the law and in social policy might also yield beneficial effects.

It is also worth considering whether it is possible to prevent maladaptive responses to stress by preparing people in advance and providing them with information and coping skills. As we noted earlier, this approach has been helpful for people experiencing the stress of major surgery. Other research further supports the idea that psychological preparedness can foster resilience in political activists who are arrested and tortured (Basoglu et al., 1997). Adequate training and preparation for extreme stressors may also help soldiers, firefighters, and others for whom exposure to traumatic events is highly likely. Findings from a study that examined PTSD in rescue and recovery workers at the World Trade Center site are consistent with this (Perrin, DiGrande, et al., 2007). Rates of PTSD differed markedly across occupations, with lower rates being reported in police (6.2 percent) and the highest rates being found in volunteers (21.2 percent) who had occupations that were completely unrelated to rescue and recovery work (e.g., finance or real estate).

The use of cognitive-behavioral techniques to help people manage potentially stressful situations or difficult events has been widely explored (Brewin & Holmes, 2003). This preventive strategy, often referred to as **stress-inoculation training**, prepares people to tolerate an anticipated threat by changing the things they say to themselves before or during a stressful event. As helpful as these approaches are, however, it is almost impossible to be prepared psychologically for most disasters or traumatic situations, which by their nature are often unpredictable and uncontrollable.

Given this, what might be done to help people who have just experienced a traumatic event? How might we reduce risk for PTSD? Strange as it may seem, there is reason to believe that playing Tetris might have some benefits (see the World Around Us box).

The World Around Us

Does Playing Tetris After a Traumatic Event Reduce Flashbacks?

"Flashbacks," or intrusive memories, are a hallmark feature of PTSD. They often involve visual experiences where the person reexperiences the traumatic event. Because of this flashbacks can be very frightening. But can flashbacks be prevented?

In a clever and creative study, Holmes and colleagues (2009) exposed a group of research participants to 12 minutes of graphic film footage depicting scenes of injury and death. Thirty minutes after seeing the footage, some participants played Tetris for 10 minutes while others (control condition) sat quietly for the same period of time. All participants then used a diary to record the number of flashbacks they experienced over the course of the following week. Compared to the participants in the control condition, those people who played Tetris after viewing the trauma film reported significantly fewer involuntary flashbacks (4.6 versus 12.8 for controls).

But why should this be? Forming a memory involves a neurobiological process. But in the early stages of this process (within the first 6 hours), the memory consolidation process can be disrupted. The brain also has a limited capacity. Because Tetris is a visuospatial task, playing Tetris shortly after the traumatic experience may disrupt the consolidation of traumatic visual memories. In other words, the new images of Tetris compete with the earlier visual images from the film, making the visual memories of the film less strong.

In other work, this same group of researchers has shown that simply being distracted after viewing the traumatic film does not reduce the frequency of later flashbacks (Holmes et al., 2010). In fact, participants who were assigned to a verbal task condition (playing Pub Quiz—a general knowledge, verbal computer game) showed an *increased* number of flashbacks compared to both the group that played Tetris and the group that did nothing.

Taken together, the results of these interesting studies support the possibility that simple visuospatial tasks such as Tetris might have promise as a "cognitive vaccine" if they can be administered early enough. Importantly, although they experienced fewer intrusive flashbacks, people who played Tetris were still

People who played Tetris after viewing a traumatic film reported fewer involuntary flashbacks the following week.

able to recall as many details from the film as people in the control group. In other words, their factual memories of the film remained intact. This is obviously important from the perspective of legal proceedings, where victims of trauma might need to testify about the events that they had experienced.

The researchers conducted a second study where the control condition was playing Pub Quiz, a verbal computer game. Why was it important for the researchers to conduct a second study and why was using a verbal game a good choice for the control condition?

Treatment for Stress Disorders

As we have already discussed, many people who are exposed to a traumatic stressor will experience symptoms and then gradually begin to recover without any professional help. After the terrorist attacks at the World Trade Center, grief and crisis counselors flocked to New York City because it was expected that countless numbers of people would be seeking psychological assistance. Relatively few people sought professional help, however, and millions of dollars that had been allocated to cover the costs of providing free counseling went unspent (McNally et al., 2003). With time, and with the help of friends and family, it is quite typical for traumatized people to recover naturally.

TELEPHONE HOTLINES National and local telephone hotlines provide help for people under severe stress and for people who are suicidal. In addition, there are specific hotlines for victims of rape and sexual assault and for runaways who need help. Many of these hotlines are staffed by volunteers. How skilled and knowledgeable the volunteer is plays an important role in how satisfied users are with the hotline (Finn et al., 2010). Studies also suggest that the most positive outcomes are seen when helpers show empathy and respect for callers (Mishara et al., 2007).

CRISIS INTERVENTION **Crisis intervention** has emerged in response to especially stressful situations, be they disasters or family situations that have become intolerable (Brown et al., 2013; Callahan, 2009; Krippner et al., 2012). Short-term crisis therapy is of brief duration and focuses on the immediate problem with which an individual or family is having difficulty (Scott & Stradling, 2006). Although medical problems may also require emergency treatment, therapists are concerned here with problems of an emotional nature. A central assumption in crisis-oriented therapy is that the individual was functioning well psychologically before the trauma. Thus therapy is focused only on helping the person through the immediate crisis, not on "remaking" her or his personality.

In such crisis situations, a therapist is usually very active, helping to clarify the problem, suggesting plans of action, providing reassurance, and otherwise providing needed information and support. A single-session behavioral treatment has been shown to lower fears and provide an increased sense of control among earthquake trauma victims (Basoglu et al., 2007). Although people are far from better after this single session, they receive knowledge and learn skills that will help them gain better control over their lives in the ensuing weeks and months.

PSYCHOLOGICAL DEBRIEFING Psychological debriefing approaches are designed to help and speed up the healing process in people who have experienced disasters or been exposed to other traumatic situations (Day, 2007). As a central strategy, traumatized victims are provided with emotional support and encouraged to talk about their experiences during the crisis (Dattilio & Freeman, 2007). The discussion is usually quite structured, and common reactions to the trauma are normalized. Some believe that this form of counseling (much of which is conducted by people who are not mental health professionals) should be mandated for disaster victims in order to prevent PTSD (Conlon & Fahy, 2001). Indeed, a small industry has sprung up to provide debriefing services, and disaster scenes are often swarmed by well-intentioned service providers—many of whom have little or no mental health training.

One form of psychological debriefing is Critical Incident Stress Debriefing (CISD; see McNally et al., 2003). A single session of CISD lasts between 3 and 4 hours and is conducted in a group format, usually 2 to 10 days after a "critical incident" or trauma.

Psychological debriefing is currently quite controversial. Reviews of the literature have generally failed to support the clinical effectiveness of the approach (Bisson et al., 2009; Devilly et al., 2006; McNally et al., 2003). Although those who experience the debriefing sessions often report satisfaction with the procedure and with the organization's desire to provide assistance, no well-controlled study has shown that it reduces symptoms of PTSD or hastens recovery in civilians (see Adler et al., 2008).

Clearly, trauma survivors should not be left alone to pick up the pieces of their lives. As we noted earlier, lack of social support is a risk factor for the development of PTSD. Moreover, providing the right kind of social support may facilitate recovery. The most appropriate crisis intervention methods may not be those that follow an explicit protocol and urge emotional expression even when the trauma survivor is not ready. Rather, the most beneficial interventions may be those that focus explicitly on the needs of the individual and time their approaches accordingly. As Foa (cited in McNally et al., 2003) has wisely suggested, in the aftermath of a trauma, survivors should follow their own natural inclination and talk (or not talk) with the people they want to talk to. In a related vein, therapists should take their lead from the trauma survivor, engaging in active listening, being supportive, but not directing or pushing for more information than the survivor wishes to provide. Caring, kindness, and common sense can go a long way to helping trauma survivors along the path to healing.

MEDICATIONS As we have seen, persons experiencing traumatic situations usually report intense feelings of anxiety or depression, numbing, intrusive thoughts, and sleep disturbance. To help with these problems, patients are often treated with antidepressants. Antipsychotic medications like those used to treat disorders such as schizophrenia are also sometimes used (Bartzokis et al., 2005; David et al., 2004). Unfortunately, evidence for the effectiveness many of these medications is slim. Antidepressants (particularly SSRIs such as fluoxetine [Prozac], paroxetine [Paxil], and venlafaxine [Effexor]) provide modest benefits compared to placebo. However, there is little evidence that most other medications provide significant benefits (Hoskins et al., 2015).

COGNITIVE-BEHAVIORAL TREATMENTS If you watch a scary movie over and over again what happens? Over time, the fear decreases and the movie becomes less frightening to you. One behaviorally oriented treatment strategy that is now being used for PTSD is **prolonged exposure** (Cloitre, 2009). It operates on exactly the same principle. The patient is asked to vividly recount the traumatic event over and over until there is a decrease in his or her emotional responses. This procedure also involves repeated or extended exposure, either in vivo or in the imagination, to feared (but objectively harmless) stimuli that the patient is avoiding because of trauma-related fear (Foa & Rauch, 2004; Powers et al., 2010). Prolonged exposure can also be supplemented by other behavioral techniques (Taylor, 2010). For example, relaxation training might also be used to help the person manage anxiety following a traumatic event.

Because prolonged exposure therapy involves persuading clients to confront the traumatic memories they fear, the therapeutic relationship may be of great importance in this kind of clinical intervention (Charuvastra & Cloitre, 2008). The client has to trust in the therapist enough to engage in the exposure treatment. In all clinical work, the therapist needs to provide a safe, warm, and supportive environment that can facilitate clinical change. For those who have been traumatized, and who may have extreme issues with trust, having a capable, understanding, and caring therapist may be especially necessary.

Prolonged exposure is an effective treatment for PTSD (Doane et al., 2010; Powers et al., 2010). In a recent study involving women who had served in the military, ten 90-minute treatment sessions led to a reduction of symptoms and a decrease in the number of women meeting diagnostic criteria for PTSD compared to a sample of women who had received a form of treatment that focused on their current life problems (Schnurr et al., 2007). However, one problem with prolonged exposure therapy is that it tends to have a higher dropout rate than other approaches. This no doubt is because it is difficult for people with PTSD to be exposed to their traumatic memories. Another current issue of concern is how long the treatment effects last. In the study just described, the longer-term

effects of the prolonged exposure treatment were less robust than expected.

Recognizing the need for improvements in the treatment of PTSD, other approaches are now being developed and refined. Ehlers and colleagues (2005) have developed a treatment for PTSD that is based on a cognitive model of the disorder. More specifically, it is thought that PTSD becomes persistent when people who have experienced trauma make excessively negative and idiosyncratic appraisals of what has happened to them in a way that creates a sense of a serious, current threat. For example, a bus driver who was assaulted by one of his passengers believed he was a terrible father who had failed his children because he had asked the passenger to buy a ticket before the passenger attacked him (Ehlers & Clark, 2008). Cognitive therapy for PTSD is designed to modify excessively negative appraisals of the trauma or its consequences, decrease the threat that patients experience when they have memories of the traumatic event, and remove problematic cognitive and behavioral strategies.

Evidence suggests that this treatment approach is very effective. In three different studies comparing patients who received cognitive therapy with patients assigned to a waiting list control group, rates of recovery were significantly higher in the cognitive therapy group and ranged from 71 to 89 percent. The drop-out rate was also very low. In fact, the only patient who dropped out of the treatment was a woman who moved abroad (Ehlers & Clark, 2008). Moreover, these treatment gains appear to continue after treatment has ended. Evidence further suggests that improvements in symptoms come as a result of changes in negative appraisals, just as predicted by the cognitive model (Kleim et al., 2013).

Another exciting treatment development that seems to be well received by clients is virtual reality exposure therapy (see the World Around Us box). There is also preliminary evidence that expressive writing, which we described earlier, may be beneficial (Sloan et al., 2013).

Trauma and Physical Health

If stress is linked to problems with physical health, what role does psychological trauma play in our physical well-being? In asking this question we come full circle, again recognizing the importance of the mind–body connection. Although questions like this have only recently begun to attract empirical attention, the findings give cause for concern. For example, in a sample of men and women who were HIV positive, previous trauma (occurring years before the study and usually during childhood) was highly predictive of death from HIV and also

The World Around Us

Virtual Reality Exposure Treatment for PTSD in Military Personnel

Large numbers of military personnel begin showing signs of PTSD within 6 months of deploying (Milliken et al., 2007). However, because of stigma, many soldiers are reluctant to seek help. As one marine explained, "I didn't want it put on my military record that I was crazy" (Halpern, 2008).

A much-needed development in this regard is the use of computer simulations and virtual reality to provide a form of exposure therapy. Although such approaches are not new, technological advances now allow for the virtual reality programs to be customized to reflect the individual soldier's traumatic experience as closely as possible. With the click of a mouse, the therapist can add such trauma-related cues as vibrations of the ground, the smell of smoke, and the sound of AK-47 fire. Treatment is typically short term (4 weeks), consisting of four to six 90-minute individual sessions. The first session is devoted to obtaining sufficient details of the trauma (time of day, weather conditions, location, sounds, smells, etc.) to make the virtual reality experience as realistic as possible. As the therapy progresses, new cues may be added to the program to provide further exposure experiences.

Early reports suggest that virtual reality exposure treatment is associated with substantial decreases in PTSD symptoms and improvements in overall functioning (Gerardi et al., 2008; Reger & Gahm, 2008). Importantly, virtual reality treatment approaches are also well received by soldiers and preferred over traditional

Virtual reality treatment is well received by soldiers.

talk therapy (Wilson et al., 2008). As one soldier put it, virtual reality "sounded pretty cool" (see Halpern, 2008). Given the growing numbers of veterans now being diagnosed with PTSD, any form of treatment that is well received by soldiers and provides relief from debilitating symptoms cannot come a moment too soon.

What makes virtual reality therapy an acceptable form of treatment for many military personnel? And why do you think this approach is successful in helping reduce symptoms? How might it work?

from other causes (Leserman et al., 2007). In a more recent study, female political prisoners who had experienced torture during their detentions had high rates of both PTSD and cardiovascular problems when assessed one or two decades after their release (Ghaddar et al., 2014). In other words, traumatic events are not only bad for the mind, they also damage the body. Although the mechanisms for this are still being explored (recall the research on stress and telomeres we described earlier), these findings again highlight the role that stress and trauma play in both physical health and psychological well-being. So now that you have finished this chapter, go and relax!

in review

- What strategies are useful for preventing or reducing maladaptive responses to stress?
- Describe crisis intervention therapy. How is this treatment approach different from psychotherapy for other mental health conditions?
- In what ways are medications used to treat individuals in crisis?
- Describe the controversy surrounding the use of "debriefing interventions."
- What forms of cognitive-behavioral treatments are effective for patients with PTSD?
- Why is the therapeutic relationship so important in the treatment of chronic PTSD?

Unresolved Issues

Why Is the Study of Trauma So Contentious?

Unlike other research topics, the field of traumatic stress study is characterized by passionate and highly divisive argument. For example, although researchers routinely seek to identify risk factors for the development of various disorders such as depression or eating disorders, the idea that there could be individual risk factors for PTSD (apart from exposure to the traumatic event itself) was a taboo topic for many years. The reason it was unacceptable was because it was viewed as "blaming the victim." There were also concerns that the study of vulnerability factors might provide the federal government with an excuse to deny treatment and benefits to Vietnam veterans. In other words, advocacy—rather than science—was the priority.

Now, of course, the study of individual vulnerability factors for PTSD is an active area of research. Nonetheless, individual scientists in this area are still subjected to attacks when they present findings that some in the trauma field do not want to hear (Satel, 2007). A case in point is the reanalysis of data from the National Vietnam Veterans Readjustment Study. This suggested that the originally reported estimates of PTSD might have been too high. Rather than engage in discourse about the methodology of the study or the statistical analysis used, prominent members of the audience instead chose to attack the presenter, coming close to accusing him of lying (Satel, 2007).

This is not an isolated example. After scholars published a meta-analysis that revealed that there was only a weak association between childhood sexual abuse and later psychopathology (Rind et al., 1998) there was a huge outcry from experts in the trauma field. The American Psychological Association made efforts to distance itself from the conclusions made by the authors and eventually Congress weighed in, issuing a formal condemnation of the article (see Lilienfeld, 2002). In another case, some scholars were accused of "minimization or outright denial of human suffering" (Marshall, 2006, p. 629) after they referred to the transient rise in stress reactions following the 9/11 terrorist attacks as normal emotional responses (see McNally, 2013).

Science searches for truth. And, as McNally (2013) notes, advocacy for victims of trauma is best served by scientific inquiry that is free of ideology. If certain assumptions are off-limits to investigation or critique, no one is well served. Advocates for trauma victims are no doubt well intentioned. But when advocacy determines what scientific findings are or are not acceptable, do we not all lose?

Summary

5.1   Explain the factors that make people more stress sensitive and the characteristics of stressors that make them hardest to cope with.

- When challenges to our physical or emotional well-being exceed our coping abilities or resources, we experience stress. Stress can result from negative or positive situations.

- How we deal with stress is linked to our coping skills and resources. For this reason children may be especially vulnerable. People with the *s/s* genotype of the serotonin promoter (*5HTTLPR*) gene also seem to be more stress sensitive. Past experiences of stress may also make us more sensitive to stress later on. In contrast, people who are optimistic, have higher self-esteem, better social support, and a greater sense of control or mastery in their own lives tend to handle life stress better overall.

- Key factors involved in making one situation more stressful than another include how severe the stressor is, how long it lasts, when it occurs, how much it impacts our lives, how expected it is, and how much control we have over the situation.

5.2   Summarize how the body responds to stress.

- Stress takes its toll on our physical and psychological well-being.

- When we are stressed, the autonomic nervous system responds in a variety of ways. The hypothalamus stimulates the sympathetic nervous system, and hormones such as adrenaline (epinephrine) and noradrenaline (norepinephrine) are released from the adrenal medulla. These hormones circulate in the bloodstream and prepare the body for fight or flight. Heart rate increases, and the body metabolizes glucose more rapidly to provide energy.

- Stress also activates the hypothalamus-pituitary-adrenal (HPA) system. A hormone called cortisol-releasing hormone is released from the hypothalamus, stimulating the pituitary gland and causing it to secrete ACTH. This stimulates the adrenal cortex to produce stress hormones such as cortisol. High levels of cortisol may be beneficial in the short term but problematic over the longer term.

5.3   Discuss how stress causes dysregulation in the immune system.

- Stress compromises immune functioning, slowing down wound healing. Psychoneuroimmunology is a developing field concerned with the interactions between the nervous system and the immune system.

- In the immune system, specialized white blood cells called B-cells and T-cells respond to antigens such as viruses and bacteria. They are assisted by natural killer cells, granulocytes, and macrophages.

- Activation of the immune system stimulates the production of cytokines. Cytokines are chemical messengers that allow the brain and the immune system to communicate with each other. Some cytokines respond to a challenge to the immune system by causing an inflammatory response. Other cytokines, called anti-inflammatory cytokines, dampen the response that the immune system makes when it is challenged.

- Long-term stress seems to interfere with the body's ability to turn off cytokine production, leading to inflammation.

5.4   Describe the role that emotions play in physical health and identify helpful and harmful emotions.

- Because the brain can influence the immune system, psychological factors are important to our physical well-being.

- Negative emotional states, such as depression, hostility, anger, anxiety, or feelings of loneliness, have all been linked to the development of cardiovascular disease. This may be because negative emotions function as a source of stress.

- In contrast, having a more optimistic attitude toward life, or being more forgiving, may have beneficial health consequences.

5.5   Explain the psychological interventions that can be used to reduce stress and treat stress-related disorders.

- Expressive writing, in which people write down their innermost thoughts about their most traumatically stressful experiences, speeds up wound healing and may be a valuable approach for individuals with some stress-related illnesses. This approach may work because it allows people to vent and/or because it also permits them to think about their problems in a different way (reframing).

- Biofeedback, in which people are helped via monitoring equipment to become more aware of their heart rate, muscle tension, or blood pressure, is another approach for some stress-related problems such as headaches.

- Another widely used treatment is relaxation training. This can be combined with other approaches such as biofeedback.

- Meditation and other stress-reducing approaches that facilitate nonjudgmental awareness are now an active focus of research interest.

- Cognitive-behavioral therapy is also widely used. CBT can be helpful in reducing pain from headaches or stomach problems as well as providing techniques to help people cope with stress.

5.6   Identify the similarities and differences between adjustment disorder, posttraumatic stress disorder, and acute stress disorder.

- An adjustment disorder is a much less severe disorder than PTSD or acute stress disorder. Although all of these disorders result from stress, adjustment disorder is a response to a more common stressor such as unemployment or marital problems. In the case of PTSD and acute stress disorder, the stressor is much more severe and traumatic.

- Both PTSD and acute stress disorder have similar symptoms. The key difference between them involves the duration of symptoms. PTSD is diagnosed when symptoms have lasted for more than 1 month. If symptoms have only recently developed and have not lasted more than a month, the diagnosis is acute stress disorder. Also, because natural recovery with time is a common pattern, not everyone diagnosed with an acute stress disorder will go on to be diagnosed with PTSD.

5.7   Describe the clinical features of and risk factors for posttraumatic stress disorder.

- In PTSD, experiencing a traumatic event is thought to create a pathological memory. This memory does not abate over time. When it intrudes, the person reexperiences the traumatic event with full emotional force even when there is no longer any danger.

- PTSD can involve a variety of symptoms, including intrusive memories or recurrent and distressing dreams about the event, avoidance of stimuli associated with the trauma, negative cognitions or impaired memory about aspects of the traumatic event, and increased arousal or reactivity.

- Many factors influence a person's response to stressful situations. The impact of stress depends not only on its severity but also on the person's preexisting vulnerabilities. Resilience is the most common long-term trajectory.

- Although it is very common to experience psychological symptoms after a traumatic event, these often fade with time. Most people exposed to traumatic events do not develop PTSD. The prevalence of PTSD in the general population is 6.8 percent.

- Factors that increase a person's risk of experiencing traumatic events include certain occupations (e.g., firefighter), being male, not having a college education, conduct problems in childhood, high levels of extraversion and neuroticism, as well as a family history of psychiatric problems.

- Factors that increase the risk of developing PTSD include being female and having low levels of social support; higher levels of neuroticism; a family history of depression, anxiety, and substance abuse; as well as preexisting problems with anxiety and depression. A tendency to have thoughts or images about traumatic events that could happen in the future has also been identified as a risk factor.

- Women with PTSD have higher baseline cortisol levels than women who do not have PTSD. This is not the case for men with PTSD. Under conditions of stress, people with PTSD show an exaggerated cortisol response.

- Having the *s/s* genotype of the serotonin-transporter gene may increase vulnerability to PTSD in the face of trauma exposure. Smaller hippocampal volume is also a biological vulnerability factor.

5.8 **Explain the treatment approaches that are used to help people with PTSD.**

- Medications are sometimes used in the treatment of PTSD, although they are not especially effective. Some SSRIs provide modest benefits.

- Psychological treatments include prolonged exposure therapy and cognitive therapy. A new approach that appears promising is the use of virtual reality exposure therapy.

Key Terms

acute stress disorder, p. 158
adjustment disorder, p. 158
allostatic load, p. 141
antigens, p. 144
B-cell, p. 144
behavioral medicine, p. 137
coping strategies, p. 137
correlational research, p. 147
cortisol, p. 143
crisis, p. 140
crisis intervention, p. 167
cytokines, p. 145
debriefing sessions, p. 167

distress, p. 138
health psychology, p. 137
hypothalamus-pituitary-adrenal (HPA) system, p. 142
immune system, p. 143
immunosuppression, p. 143
leukocytes, p. 144
lymphocytes, p. 144
positive psychology, p. 152
posttraumatic stress disorder (PTSD), p. 137
prolonged exposure, p. 168
psychoneuroimmunology, p. 143

resilience, p. 140
stress, p. 137
stress-inoculation training, p. 166
stress tolerance, p. 139
stressors, p. 137
sympathetic-adrenomedullary (SAM) system, p. 142
T-cell, p. 144
telomere, p. 148
Type A behavior pattern, p. 149
Type D personality, p. 149

Chapter 6
Panic, Anxiety, Obsessions, and Their Disorders

Learning Objectives

6.1 Distinguish between fear and anxiety.

6.2 Describe the essential features of anxiety disorders.

6.3 Explain the clinical features of specific phobias.

6.4 Discuss the clinical features of social phobia.

6.5 Describe the clinical features of panic disorder.

6.6 Explain the clinical aspects of generalized anxiety disorder.

6.7 Describe the clinical features of obsessive-compulsive disorder and how it is treated.

6.8 Summarize some examples of cultural differences in sources of worry.

Jeni: Worried about Worrying So Much

Jeni is a 21-year-old college student. Although she is doing exceptionally well in school, for the past year she has worried constantly that she will fail and be thrown out. When her fellow students and professors try to reassure her, Jeni worries that they are just pretending to be nice to her because she is such a weak student. Jeni also worries about her mother becoming ill and about whether she is really liked by her friends. Although Jeni is able to acknowledge that her fears are excessive (she has supportive friends, her mother is in good health, and, based on her grades, Jeni is one of the top students in her school), she still struggles to control her worrying. Jeni has difficulty sleeping, often feels nervous and on edge, and experiences a great deal of muscle tension. When her friends suggested she take a yoga class to try and relax, Jeni even began to worry about that, fearing that she would be the worst student in the class. "I know it makes no sense," she says, "But that's how I am. I've always been a worrier. I even worry about worrying so much!"

Anxiety involves a general feeling of apprehension about *possible future danger*, whereas **fear** is an alarm reaction that occurs in response to *immediate danger*. The *DSM* has identified a group of disorders—known as the *anxiety disorders*—that share symptoms of clinically significant anxiety or fear. Anxiety disorders affect approximately 29 percent of the U.S. population at some point in their lives and are the most common category of disorders for women and the second most common for men (Kessler, Berglund, Delmar, et al., 2005). In any 12-month period, about 18 percent of the adult population suffers from at least one anxiety disorder (Kessler, Chiu, et al., 2005). Anxiety disorders create enormous personal, economic, and health care problems for those affected and for society more generally. Anxiety disorders have the earliest age of onset of all mental disorders (Kessler, Aguilar-Gaxiola, et al., 2009) and are associated with an increased prevalence of a number of medical conditions including asthma, chronic pain, hypertension, arthritis, cardiovascular disease, and irritable bowel syndrome (Roy-Byrne et al., 2008). People with anxiety disorders are very high users of medical services (Chavira et al., 2009).

Historically, anxiety disorders were considered to be classic neurotic disorders. Although individuals with **neurotic disorders** show maladaptive and self-defeating behaviors, they are not incoherent, dangerous, or out of touch with reality. To Freud, these neurotic disorders developed when intrapsychic conflict produced significant anxiety. Anxiety was, in Freud's formulation, a sign of an inner battle or conflict between some primitive desire (from the id) and prohibitions against its expression (from the ego and superego). Sometimes this anxiety was overtly expressed (as in those disorders known today as the anxiety disorders). In certain other neurotic disorders, however, he believed that the anxiety might not be obvious, either to the person involved or to

others, if psychological defense mechanisms were able to deflect or mask it. The term *neurosis* was dropped from the *DSM* in 1980. In addition, in *DSM-III*, some disorders that did not involve obvious anxiety symptoms were reclassified as either dissociative or somatoform disorders. (Some neurotic disorders were absorbed into the mood disorders category as well—see Chapters 7 and 8.) In *DSM-5* this trend has gone a step further. **Obsessive-compulsive disorder (OCD)** is no longer classified as an anxiety disorder. Instead, it is now listed in its own category of obsessive-compulsive and related disorders (see the Thinking Critically about *DSM-5* box later in this chapter).

We begin by discussing the nature of fear and anxiety as emotional and cognitive states and patterns of responding, each of which has an extremely important adaptive value but to which humans at times seem all too vulnerable. We will then move to a discussion of the anxiety disorders. Finally, we consider OCD and other disorders from the new obsessive-compulsive and related disorders category.

The Fear and Anxiety Response Patterns

6.1   Distinguish between fear and anxiety.

There has never been complete agreement about how distinct the two emotions of fear and anxiety are from each other. Historically, the most common way of distinguishing between the fear and anxiety response patterns has been to determine whether a clear and obvious source of danger is present that would be regarded as real by most people. When the source of danger is obvious, the experienced emotion has been called fear (e.g., "I'm afraid of snakes"). With anxiety, however, we frequently cannot specify clearly what the danger is (e.g., "I'm anxious about my parents' health").

Fear

In recent years, many prominent researchers have proposed a more fundamental distinction between the fear and anxiety response patterns (e.g., Barlow, 2002; Bouton, 2005; McNaughton, 2008). According to these theorists, fear is a basic emotion (shared by many animals) that involves activation of the "fight-or-flight" response of the autonomic nervous system. This is an almost instantaneous reaction to any imminent threat such as a dangerous predator or someone pointing a loaded gun.

Its adaptive value as a primitive alarm response to imminent danger is that it allows us to escape. When the fear response occurs in the absence of any obvious external danger, we say the person has had a spontaneous or uncued **panic attack**. The symptoms of a panic attack are nearly identical to those experienced during a state of fear except that panic attacks are often accompanied by a subjective sense of impending doom, including fears of dying, going crazy, or losing control. These latter cognitive symptoms do not generally occur during fear states. Thus, fear and panic have three components:

1. cognitive/subjective components (e.g., "I'm going to die")

2. physiological components (e.g., increased heart rate and heavy breathing)

3. behavioral components (e.g., a strong urge to escape or flee).

These components are only "loosely coupled" (Lang, 1985), which means that someone might show, for example, physiological and behavioral indications of fear or panic without much of the subjective component, or vice versa.

Fear or panic is a basic emotion that is shared by many animals, including humans, and may activate the fight-or-flight response of the sympathetic nervous system. This allows us to respond rapidly when faced with a dangerous situation, such as being threatened by a predator. In humans who are having a panic attack, there is no external threat; panic occurs because of some misfiring of this response system.

Anxiety

In contrast to fear and panic, the anxiety response pattern is a complex blend of unpleasant emotions and cognitions that is both more oriented to the future and much more diffuse than fear (Barlow, 2002). But like fear, it has not only cognitive/subjective components but also physiological and behavioral components. At the cognitive/subjective level, anxiety involves negative mood, worry about possible future threats or danger, self-preoccupation, and a sense of being unable to predict the future threat or to control it if it occurs. At a physiological level, anxiety often creates a state of tension and chronic overarousal, which may reflect risk assessment and readiness for dealing with danger should it occur ("Something awful may happen, and I had better be ready for it if it does"). Although there is no activation of the fight-or-flight response as there is with fear, anxiety does prepare or prime a person for the fight-or-flight response should the

anticipated danger occur. At a behavioral level, anxiety may create a strong tendency to avoid situations where danger might be encountered, but the immediate behavioral urge to flee is not present with anxiety as it is with fear (Barlow, 2002). Support for the idea that anxiety is descriptively and functionally distinct from fear or panic comes both from statistical analyses of subjective reports of panic and anxiety and from a great deal of neurobiological evidence (e.g., Bouton, 2005; Davis, 2006; Grillon, 2008). Table 6.1 compares and contrasts the components of fear and anxiety.

Table 6.1 Components of Fear and Anxiety

Component	Fear	Anxiety
1. Cognitive/subjective	"I am in danger!"	"I am worried about what might happen."
2. Physiological	Increased heart rate, sweating	Tension, chronic overarousal
3. Behavioral	Desire to escape or run	General avoidance

The adaptive value of anxiety may be that it helps us plan and prepare for a possible threat. In mild to moderate degrees, anxiety actually enhances learning and performance. For example, a mild amount of anxiety about how you are going to do on your next exam, or in your next tennis match, can actually be helpful. But, although anxiety is often adaptive in mild or moderate degrees, it is maladaptive when it becomes chronic and severe, as we see in people diagnosed with anxiety disorders.

Although many threatening situations can occur that provoke fear or anxiety unconditionally, many of our sources of fear and anxiety are learned. Years of human and nonhuman animal experimentation have established that the basic fear and anxiety response patterns are highly conditionable (Fanselow & Ponnusamy, 2008; Lipp, 2006). That is, previously neutral and novel stimuli (conditioned stimuli) that are repeatedly paired with, and reliably predict, frightening or unpleasant events such as various kinds of physical or psychological trauma (unconditioned stimulus) can acquire the capacity to elicit fear or anxiety themselves (conditioned response). Such conditioning is a completely normal and adaptive process that allows all of us to learn to anticipate upcoming frightening events if they are reliably preceded by a signal. Yet this normal and adaptive process can also lead in some cases to the development of clinically significant fears and anxieties, as we will see.

For example, a girl named Angela sometimes saw and heard her father physically abuse her mother in the evening. After this happened four or five times, Angela started to become anxious as soon as she heard her father's car arrive in the driveway at the end of the day. In such situations a wide variety of initially neutral stimuli may accidentally come to serve as cues that something threatening and unpleasant is about to happen—and thereby come to elicit fear or anxiety themselves. Our thoughts and images can also serve as conditioned stimuli capable of eliciting the fear or anxiety response pattern. For example, Angela came to feel anxious even when thinking about her father.

in review

- Compare and contrast fear or panic with anxiety, making sure to note that both emotions involve three response systems.
- Explain the significance of the fact that both fear and anxiety can be classically conditioned.

Overview of the Anxiety Disorders and Their Commonalities

6.2 Describe the essential features of anxiety disorders.

Anxiety disorders are characterized by unrealistic, irrational fears or anxieties that cause significant distress and/or impairments in functioning. Among the disorders recognized in *DSM-5* are:

1. specific phobia
2. social anxiety disorder (social phobia)
3. panic disorder
4. agoraphobia
5. generalized anxiety disorder.

People with these varied disorders differ from one another both in terms of the amount of fear or panic versus anxiety symptoms that they experience and in the kinds of objects or situations that most concern them. For example, people with *specific* or *social* phobias experience a fear or panic response not only when they encounter the object or situation that they fear, but also in response to even the possibility of encountering their phobic situation. People with *panic disorder* experience both frequent panic attacks and intense anxiety focused on the possibility of having another one. People with *agoraphobia* go to great lengths to avoid a variety of feared situations, ranging from open streets and bridges to crowded public places. By contrast, people with *generalized anxiety disorder* (like Jeni in the case study that opened this chapter) mostly experience a general sense of diffuse anxiety and worry about many potentially bad things that may happen; some may also experience an occasional panic attack, but it is not a focus of their anxiety. It is also important to note that many people with one anxiety disorder will experience at least one more anxiety disorder and/or depression either concurrently or at a different point in their lives (Brown & Barlow, 2009; Kessler, Berglund, Demler, et al., 2005).

Given these commonalities across the anxiety disorders, it should come as no surprise that there are some important similarities in the basic causes of these disorders (as well as many differences). Among biological causal factors, we will see that genetics contributes to each of these disorders and that at least part of the genetic vulnerability may be nonspecific, or common across the disorders (Shimada-Sugimoto et al., 2015). In adults, the common genetic vulnerability is manifested at a psychological level at least in part by the important personality trait called *neuroticism*—a proneness or disposition to experience negative mood states that is a common risk factor for both anxiety and mood disorders (Klein et al., 2009). The brain structures most centrally involved in most disorders are generally in the limbic system (often known as the "emotional brain") and certain parts of the cortex, and the neurotransmitter substances that are most centrally involved are gamma aminobutyric acid (GABA), norepinephrine, and serotonin (see Chapter 3).

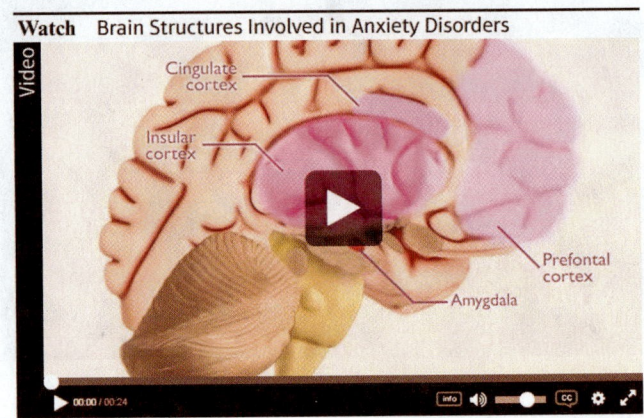

Watch Brain Structures Involved in Anxiety Disorders

Among common psychological causal factors, we will see that classical conditioning of fear, panic, or anxiety to a range of stimuli plays an important role in many of these disorders (Mineka & Oehlberg, 2008; Mineka & Zinbarg, 2006). In addition, people who have perceptions of a lack of control over either their environments or their own emotions (or both) seem more vulnerable to developing anxiety disorders. The development of such perceptions of uncontrollability depends heavily on the social environment people are raised in, including parenting styles (Hudson & Rapee, 2009; Mineka & Zinbarg, 2006). For certain disorders, faulty or distorted patterns of cognition also may play an important role. Finally, the sociocultural environment in which people are raised also has prominent effects on the kinds of objects and experiences people become anxious about or come to fear. As with the other disorders described in this book, a biopsychosocial approach is best suited for understanding how all different types of causal factors interact with one another in the development of these disorders.

Finally, as we will see, many commonalities are seen across the effective treatments for the various anxiety disorders (Barlow, 2004; Campbell-Sills & Barlow, 2007). For each disorder, graduated exposure to feared cues, objects, and situations—until fear or anxiety begins to habituate—constitutes the single most powerful therapeutic ingredient. For certain disorders the addition of cognitive restructuring techniques can provide added benefit by helping the individual to understand his or her distorted patterns of thinking about anxiety-related situations and how these patterns can be changed. Medications also can be useful in treating all disorders except specific phobias, and nearly all tend to fall into two primary medication categories: antianxiety medications (anxiolytics) and antidepressant medications.

We now turn to a more detailed discussion of each disorder, highlighting their common and their distinct features as well as what is known about their causes. We start with phobic disorders—the most common anxiety disorders. A **phobia** is a persistent and disproportionate fear of some specific object or situation that presents little or no actual danger and yet leads to a great deal of avoidance of these feared situations. As we will see, the three main categories of phobias are (1) specific phobia, (2) social phobia, and (3) agoraphobia.

in review

- What is the central feature of all anxiety disorders? That is, what do they have in common?
- What differentiates the anxiety disorders from one another?
- What are some common kinds of biological and psychosocial causes of the different anxiety disorders?
- What is the most important ingredient across effective psychosocial treatments for the anxiety disorders?

Specific Phobias

6.3   Explain the clinical features of specific phobias.

We all have things that we are afraid of: scary movies, tigers, clowns, scary movies about tiger-riding clowns. Having such fears is normal. However, a **specific phobia** is said to be present if a person shows strong and persistent fear that is triggered by the presence of a specific object or situation and leads to significant distress and/or impairment in a person's ability to function (see *DSM-5* box for diagnostic criteria). When people with specific phobias encounter a phobic stimulus, they often show an immediate fear response that often resembles a panic attack except for the existence of a clear external trigger (APA, 2013). Not surprisingly, such individuals also experience anxiety if they anticipate they may encounter a phobic object or situation and so go to great lengths to avoid encounters with their phobic stimulus. Indeed, they often even avoid seemingly harmless representations of it such as photographs or television images. For example, claustrophobic persons may go to great lengths to avoid entering a closet or an elevator, even if this means climbing many flights of stairs or turning down jobs that might require them to take an elevator. Generally, people with specific phobias recognize that their fear is somewhat excessive or unreasonable although occasionally they may not have this insight.

This avoidance is a cardinal characteristic of phobias; it occurs both because the phobic response itself is so unpleasant and because of the phobic person's irrational appraisal of the likelihood that something terrible will happen. Table 6.2 lists the five subtypes of specific phobias recognized in *DSM-5*.

DSM-5 *Criteria for. . .*

Specific Phobia

A. Marked fear or anxiety about a specific object or situation (e.g., flying, heights, animals, receiving an injection, seeing blood).
   Note: In children, the fear or anxiety may be expressed by crying, tantrums, freezing, or clinging.

B. The phobic object or situation almost always provokes immediate fear or anxiety.

C. The phobic object or situation is actively avoided or endured with intense fear or anxiety.

D. The fear or anxiety is out of proportion to the actual danger posed by the specific object or situation and to the sociocultural context.

E. The fear, anxiety, or avoidance is persistent, typically lasting for 6 months or more.

F. The fear, anxiety, or avoidance causes clinically significant distress or impairment in social, occupational, or other important areas of functioning.

G. The disturbance is not better explained by the symptoms of another mental disorder, including fear, anxiety, and avoidance of situations associated with panic-like symptoms or other incapacitating symptoms (as in agoraphobia); objects or situations related to obsessions (as in obsessive-compulsive disorder); reminders of traumatic events (as in posttraumatic stress disorder); separation from home or attachment figures (as in separation anxiety disorder); or social situations (as in social anxiety disorder).

Source: Reprinted with permission from the *Diagnostic and Statistical Manual of Mental Disorders*, Fifth Edition (Copyright 2013). American Psychiatric Association.

Table 6.2 Subtypes of Specific Phobias in *DSM-5*

Phobia Type	Examples
Animal	Snakes, spiders, dogs, insects, birds
Natural environment	Storms, heights, water
Blood-injection-injury	Seeing blood or an injury, receiving an injection, seeing a person in a wheelchair
Situational	Public transportation, tunnels, bridges, elevators, flying, driving, enclosed spaces
Other	Choking, vomiting, "space phobia" (fear of falling down if away from walls or other support)

Data from the Diagnostic and Statistical Manual of Mental Disorders, Fifth Edition, (Copyright 2013). American Psychiatric Association.

The following case is typical of specific phobia.

A Mother's Fears

Mary, a married mother of three, was 47 at the time she first sought treatment for anxiety. She reported being intensely afraid of enclosed spaces (claustrophobia) and of heights (acrophobia) since her teens. She said that as a child, her older siblings used to lock her in closets and hold her down under blankets while saying things to scare her. She traced the onset of her claustrophobia to those traumatic incidents, but she had no idea why she was afraid of heights. While her children had been growing up, she had been a housewife and had managed to live a fairly normal life in spite of her two specific phobias. However, her children were now grown, and she wanted to find a job outside her home. This was proving to be very difficult because she could not take elevators and was terrified of being any higher than the first floor of an office building. Moreover, her husband had for some years been working for an airline, which entitled him to free airline tickets. The fact that Mary could not fly (due to her phobias) had become a sore point in her marriage because they both wanted to be able to take advantage of these free tickets to travel to distant places. Thus, although she had had these phobias for many years, they had become truly disabling only in recent years as her life circumstances had changed and she could no longer easily avoid heights or enclosed spaces.

If people who suffer from phobias attempt to approach the object of their phobia, they are overcome with fear or anxiety, which may vary from mild feelings of apprehension and distress (usually while still at some distance) to full-fledged activation of the fight-or-flight response. Regardless of how it begins, phobic behavior tends to be reinforced because every time the person with a phobia avoids a feared situation, his or her anxiety decreases. In addition, the secondary benefits derived from being disabled, such as increased attention, sympathy, and some control over the behavior of others, can also sometimes reinforce a phobia.

One category of specific phobias that has a number of interesting and unique characteristics is **blood-injection-injury phobia**. It occurs in approximately 3 to 4 percent of the population (Ayala et al., 2009). People afflicted with

People with acrophobia (fear of heights) are so frightened of being in high places like airplanes, tall buildings, or even upper levels of shopping malls that they go through great lengths to avoid them. If for some reason they must be in a high place, people with acrophobia will be extremely frightened and may have thoughts about falling or being injured in some way. We are pretty sure that this climber does not suffer from acrophobia.

this phobia typically experience at least as much (if not more) disgust as fear (Teachman & Saporito, 2009). They also show a unique physiological response when confronted with the sight of blood or injury. Rather than showing the simple increase in heart rate and blood pressure seen when most people with phobias encounter their phobic object, these people show an initial acceleration, followed by a

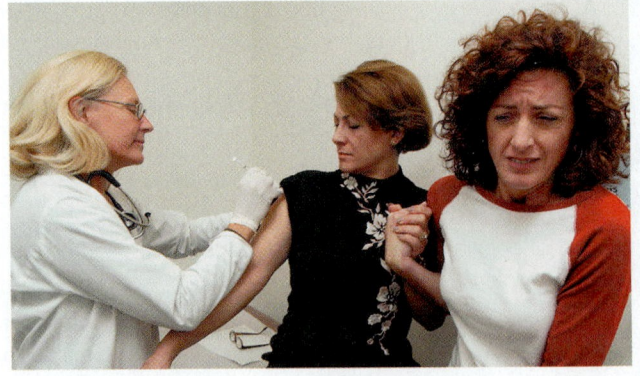

In blood-injection-injury phobia, the afflicted person experiences disgust and fear at the sight of someone receiving an injection. When confronted with the sight of blood or injury, people with this phobic disorder often experience nausea, dizziness, or fainting.

dramatic drop in both heart rate and blood pressure. This is very frequently accompanied by nausea, dizziness, or fainting, which does not occur with other specific phobias (Öst & Hellström, 1997; Page & Tan, 2009).

Interestingly, people with this phobia demonstrate this unique physiological response pattern only in the presence of blood and injury stimuli; they exhibit the more typical physiological response pattern characteristic of the fight-or-flight response to their other feared objects (Dahllöf & Öst, 1998). From an evolutionary and functional standpoint, this unique physiological response pattern may have evolved for a specific purpose: By fainting, the person being attacked might inhibit further attack, and if an attack did occur, the drop in blood pressure would minimize blood loss (Craske, 1999; Marks & Nesse, 1991). This type of phobia appears to be highly heritable (Czajkowski et al., 2011).

Prevalence, Age of Onset, and Gender Differences

Specific phobias are common, occurring in about 12 percent of people at some point in their lifetime (Kessler, Chiu, et al., 2005). Phobias are much more common in women than in men, although the gender ratio varies by type of phobia. For example, about 90 to 95 percent of people with animal phobias are women, but the gender ratio is less than 2:1 for blood-injection-injury phobia. Animal phobias usually begin in childhood, as do blood-injection-injury phobias and dental phobias. However, other phobias such as claustrophobia and driving phobia tend to begin in adolescence or early adulthood (Barlow, 2002; Öst, 1987).

Psychological Causal Factors

A variety of psychological causal factors have been implicated in the origins of specific phobias, ranging from deep-seated psychodynamic conflicts to relatively straightforward traumatic conditioning of fear and a multitude of individual differences in who is at risk for such conditioning.

PSYCHOANALYTIC VIEWPOINT According to the psychoanalytic view, phobias represent a defense against anxiety that stems from repressed impulses from the id. Because it is too dangerous to "know" the repressed id impulse, the anxiety is displaced onto some external object or situation that has some symbolic relationship to the real object of the anxiety (Freud, 1909). However, this prototypical psychodynamic account of how phobias are acquired was long criticized as being far too speculative, and an alternative, simpler account from learning theory was first proposed by Wolpe and Rachman (1960), which has now been further refined and expanded as discussed below.

PHOBIAS AS LEARNED BEHAVIOR Wolpe and Rachman (1960) developed an account based on learning theory,

which sought to explain the development of phobic behavior through classical conditioning. The fear response can readily be conditioned to previously neutral stimuli when these stimuli are paired with traumatic or painful events. We would also expect that, once acquired, phobic fears would generalize to other, similar objects or situations. Recall, for example, that Mary's claustrophobia had probably been caused by multiple incidents as a child when her siblings locked her in closets and confined her under blankets to scare her. But as an adult, Mary feared elevators and caves as well as other enclosed places.

Monkeys who watch a model monkey (such as the one illustrated here) behaving fearfully with a live boa constrictor will rapidly acquire an intense fear of snakes themselves. Fears can thus be learned vicariously without any direct traumatic experience.

Vicarious Conditioning Direct traumatic conditioning in which a person has a terrifying experience in the presence of a neutral object or situation is not the only way that people can learn irrational, phobic fears. Simply watching a phobic person behaving fearfully with his or her phobic object can be distressing to the observer and can result in fear being transmitted from one person to another through vicarious or observational classical conditioning. In addition, watching a nonfearful person undergoing a frightening experience can also lead to vicarious conditioning. For example, one man, as a boy, had witnessed his grandfather vomit while dying. Shortly after this traumatic event (his grandfather's distress while dying) the boy had developed a strong and persistent vomiting phobia. Indeed, when this man was in middle age he even contemplated suicide one time when he was nauseated and feared vomiting (Mineka & Zinbarg, 2006). Related experimental findings have been observed in laboratory analogue studies of human children. For example, two studies showed that 7- to 9-year-old children who saw pictures of an unfamiliar animal (an

Australian marsupial) paired 10 times with fearful facial expressions showed increased fear beliefs and behavioral avoidance of this conditioned stimulus (CS) relative to children who saw the unfamiliar animal paired with happy facial expressions. These effects persisted for at least 1 week (Askew & Field, 2007; 2008).

Individual Differences in Learning Given all the traumas that people undergo and watch others experience, why don't more people develop phobias (Mineka & Oehlberg, 2008)? One reason is that individual differences in life experiences strongly affect whether conditioned fears or phobias actually develop. Importantly, some life experiences may serve as *risk factors* and make certain people more vulnerable to phobias than others, whereas others experiences may serve as *protective factors* for the development of phobias (Mineka & Sutton, 2006). For example, children who have had more previous nontraumatic experiences with a dentist are less likely to develop dental anxiety after a bad and painful experience than are children with fewer previous nontraumatic experiences (Ten Berge et al., 2002). This is true for vicarious learning as well. For instance, toddlers who watch their mothers reacting positively to a snake or spider later show less fear in response to snake or spider exposure than toddlers who didn't see their mothers having positive experiences with the snake or spider (Egliston & Rapee, 2007). Results like these illustrate how parents and others close to a child can help to influence the child's later experience of fear and anxiety.

A person who has had good experiences with a potentially phobic stimulus, such as the little girl playing here with her dog, is likely to be immunized from later acquiring a fear of dogs even if she has a traumatic encounter with one.

Certain aspects of the conditioning experience, and our response to it, also are important in determining the level of fear that is conditioned. For example, experiencing an inescapable and uncontrollable event, such as being attacked by a dog that one cannot escape from after being bitten, is expected to condition fear much more powerfully than experiencing the same intensity of trauma that is escapable

or to some extent controllable (e.g., by running away after the attack; Mineka, 1985; Mineka & Zinbarg, 1996, 2006). It has also been shown that our cognitions, or thoughts, can help maintain our phobias once they have been acquired. For example, people with phobias are constantly on the alert for their phobic objects or situations and for other stimuli relevant to their phobia (McNally & Reese, 2009). Nonphobic persons, by contrast, tend to direct their attention away from threatening stimuli (Mineka et al., 2003). In addition, phobics also markedly overestimate the probability that feared objects have been, or will be, followed by frightening events. This cognitive bias may help maintain or strengthen phobic fears with the passage of time (Muhlberger et al., 2006; Öhman & Mineka, 2001).

Evolutionary Preparedness for Learning Certain Fears and Phobias Have you noticed that people are much more likely to have phobias of snakes, water, heights, and enclosed spaces than of motorcycles, guns, and chainsaws even though the latter objects may be at least as likely to be associated with trauma? This is because our evolutionary history has affected which stimuli we are most likely to come to fear. Primates and humans seem to be *evolutionarily prepared* to rapidly associate certain objects—such as snakes, spiders, water, and enclosed spaces—with frightening or unpleasant events (Mineka & Öhman, 2002; Öhman, 1996; Seligman, 1971). This **prepared learning** occurs because, over the course of evolution, those primates and humans who rapidly acquired fears of certain objects or situations that posed real threats to our early ancestors may have enjoyed a selective advantage (meaning, they survived more often than those who had no fear of such things). Thus, "prepared" fears are not inborn or innate but rather are easily acquired or especially resistant to extinction. Guns, motorcycles, and chainsaws, by contrast, were not present in our early evolutionary history and so did not convey any such selective advantage.

Experimental evidence strongly supports the preparedness theory of phobias. In one important series of experiments using human subjects, Öhman and his colleagues (see Öhman, 1996, 2009; Öhman & Mineka, 2001, for reviews) found that fear is conditioned more effectively to fear-relevant stimuli (slides of snakes and spiders) than to fear-irrelevant stimuli (slides of flowers and mushrooms). Moreover, once the individuals acquired the conditioned responses to fear-relevant stimuli, these responses (including activation of the relevant brain area, the amygdala) could be elicited even when the fear-relevant stimuli (but not the fear-irrelevant stimuli) were presented subliminally (i.e., presentation was so brief that the stimuli were not consciously perceived; e.g., Carlsson et al., 2004; Öhman et al., 2007). This subliminal activation of responses to phobic stimuli may help to account for certain aspects of the irrationality of phobias. That is, people with phobias may not be able to control their fear because the fear may arise from cognitive structures that are not under conscious control (Öhman & Mineka, 2001; Öhman & Soares, 1993).

Another series of experiments showed that lab-reared monkeys in a vicarious conditioning paradigm can easily acquire fears of fear-relevant stimuli such as toy snakes and toy crocodiles but not of fear-irrelevant stimuli such as flowers and a toy rabbit (Cook & Mineka, 1989, 1990). Thus, both monkeys and humans seem selectively to associate certain fear-relevant stimuli with threat or danger. Importantly, these lab-reared monkeys had no prior exposure to any of the stimuli involved (e.g., snakes or flowers), supporting the evolutionarily based preparedness hypothesis even more strongly than the human experiments. For example, human subjects (unlike the lab-reared monkeys) might show superior conditioning to snakes or spiders because of preexisting negative associations to snakes or spiders rather than because of evolutionary factors (Mineka & Öhman, 2002).

Biological Causal Factors

Genetic and temperamental variables also affect the speed and strength of conditioning of fear (Gray, 1987; Hettema et al., 2003; Oehlberg & Mineka, 2011). For example, Lonsdorf and colleagues (2009) found that individuals who are carriers of one of the two variants of the serotonin-transporter gene (the *s* allele, which has been linked to heightened neuroticism) show superior fear conditioning than those without the *s* allele. However, those with one of two variants of a different gene (the COMT met/met genotype) did not show superior conditioning but did show enhanced resistance to extinction (see also Lonsdorf & Kalisch, 2011). Relatedly, Kagan and his colleagues (2001) found that *behaviorally inhibited* toddlers (who are excessively timid, shy, easily distressed, etc.) at 21 months of age were at higher risk of developing multiple specific phobias by 7 to 8 years of age than were uninhibited children (32 versus 5 percent).

Several behavior genetic studies also suggest a modest genetic contribution to the development of specific phobias. For example, large twin studies show that monozygotic (identical) twins are more likely to share animal phobias and situational phobias (such as of heights or water) than were dizygotic (nonidentical) twins (Hettema, Prescott, et al., 2005; Kendler et al., 1999b). However, the same studies also found that nonshared environmental factors (i.e., individual specific experiences not shared by twins) play a substantial role in the origins of specific phobias, a result that supports the idea that phobias are learned behaviors. Another study found that the heritability of animal phobias was separate from the heritability of complex phobias such as social phobia and agoraphobia (Czajkowski et al., 2011).

Treatments

An enormous body of literature has shown that the most effective treatment for specific phobias is **exposure therapy**—a form of behavior therapy that involves controlled exposure to the stimuli or situations that elicit phobic fear (Choy et al., 2007; Craske & Mystkowski, 2006). In exposure therapy, clients are encouraged to gradually expose themselves (either alone or with the aid of a clinician or friend) to their feared situations for long enough periods of time so that their fear begins to subside. One variant on this procedure, known as *participant modeling,* is often more effective than exposure alone. Here the therapist calmly models ways of interacting with the phobic stimulus or situation (Bandura, 1977, 1997). These techniques enable clients to learn that these situations are not as frightening as they had thought and that their anxiety, while unpleasant, is not harmful and will gradually dissipate (Craske & Mystkowski, 2006; Craske & Rowe, 1997). The new learning is believed to be mediated by changes in brain activation in the amygdala, which is centrally involved in the emotion of fear.

For certain phobias such as small-animal phobias, flying phobia, claustrophobia, and blood-injury phobia, exposure therapy is often highly effective when administered in a single long session (of up to 3 hours) (Öst, 1997; Öst et al., 2001). This can be an advantage because some people are more likely to seek treatment if they have to go only once. This treatment has also been shown to be highly effective in youth with specific phobias (Ollendick et al., 2009).

An example of the use of exposure therapy comes from the treatment of Mary, the housewife whose acrophobia and claustrophobia we described earlier.

Mary's Treatment

Mary participated in 13 sessions of graduated exposure exercises in which her clinician accompanied Mary first into mildly fear-provoking situations and then gradually into more and more fear-provoking situations. Mary also engaged in homework, doing these exposure exercises by herself. The prolonged *in vivo* ("real-life") exposure sessions lasted as long as necessary for her anxiety to subside. Initial sessions focused on Mary's claustrophobia and on getting her to be able to ride for a few floors in an elevator, first with the therapist and then alone. Later she took longer elevator rides in taller buildings. Exposure for the acrophobia consisted of walking around the periphery of the inner atrium on the top floor of a tall hotel and, later, spending time at a mountain vista overlook spot. The top step of Mary's claustrophobia hierarchy consisted of taking a tour of an underground cave. After 13 sessions, Mary successfully took a flight with her husband to Europe and climbed to the top of many tall tourist attractions there.

Several recent advances have boosted the feasibility and effectiveness of exposure therapy even further. Exposure to things like height and airplanes is not always feasible (e.g., for clients or clinicians who don't live near

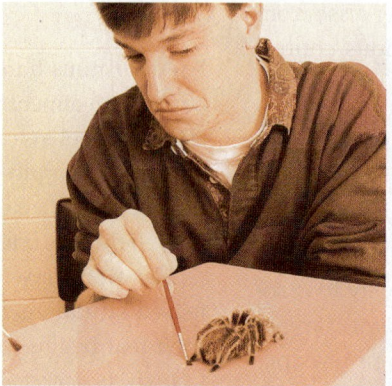

One variation on exposure therapy is called participant modeling. Here the therapist models how to touch and pick up a live tarantula and encourages the spider-phobic client to imitate her behavior. This treatment is graduated, with the client's first task being simply to touch the tarantula from the outside of the cage, then to touch the tarantula with a stick, then with a gloved hand, then with a bare hand, and finally to let the tarantula crawl over his hand. This is a highly effective treatment, with the most spider-phobic clients being able to reach the top of the hierarchy within 60 to 90 minutes.

an airport). To address this problem, psychologists have begun to use virtual reality to simulate different kinds of phobic situations. Controlled studies have yielded very promising results and show results comparable to those seen with live exposure (Choy et al., 2007; Parsons & Rizzo, 2008; Rothbaum et al., 2006).

New treatments using virtual reality environments allow therapists to simulate certain kinds of phobic situations, such as standing at heights or sitting in airplanes, in a contrived setting.

Researchers have tried several other ways of increasing the effectiveness of exposure therapy. The use of cognitive restructuring techniques alone has not produced results as good as those using exposure-based techniques, and the addition of cognitive techniques to exposure therapy has generally not added much (Craske & Mystkowski, 2006; Wolitzky-Taylor et al., 2008). Similarly, medication treatments are ineffective by themselves, and there is even some evidence that antianxiety medications may interfere with the beneficial effects of exposure therapy (Antony & Barlow, 2002; Choy et al., 2007). Recently, however, studies have shown that a drug called D-*cycloserine*, which is known to facilitate extinction of conditioned fear in animals (e.g., Davis et al., 2005, 2006), can enhance the effectiveness of exposure therapy for fear of heights in a virtual reality environment (Norberg et al., 2008, Ressler et al., 2004). D-Cycloserine by itself, however, has no effect.

in review

- What are the five subtypes of specific phobias?
- Describe the original classical conditioning explanation for the origins of specific phobias as well as how vicarious conditioning may be involved.
- Explain several sources of individual differences in learning that have improved and expanded the basic conditioning hypothesis of phobia acquisition.

- Explain how evolutionary factors have influenced which objects and situations we are most likely to learn to fear.
- Describe the most effective treatment for specific phobias.

Social Phobia

6.4 Discuss the clinical features of social phobia.

Social phobia (or social anxiety disorder) is characterized by disabling fears of one or more specific social situations (such as public speaking, urinating in a public bathroom, or eating or writing in public; see the *DSM-5* box). In these situations, a person fears that she or he may be exposed to the scrutiny and potential negative evaluation of others or that she or he may act in an embarrassing or humiliating manner. Because of their fears, people with social phobia either avoid these situations or endure them with great distress. Intense fear of public speaking is the single most common type of social phobia. *DSM-5* also identifies two subtypes of social phobia, one of which centers on performance situations such as public speaking and one of which is more general and includes nonperformance situations (such as eating in public). People with the more general subtype of social phobia often have significant fears of most social situations (rather than simply a few) and often also have a diagnosis of avoidant personality disorder (see Chapter 10; Stein & Stein, 2008).

Watch Steve: Social Anxiety Disorder

Intense fear of public speaking is the single most common social phobia.

Prevalence, Age of Onset, and Gender Differences

Approximately 12 percent of the population meets the diagnostic criteria for social phobia at some point in their lives (Kessler, Berglund, Demler, et al., 2005; Ruscio et al., 2008). Social phobia is more common among women (about 60 percent of sufferers are women), and it typically begins during adolescence or early adulthood (Bruce et al., 2005; Ruscio et al., 2008). Nearly two-thirds of people with social phobia suffer from one or more additional anxiety disorders at some point in their lives, and about 50 percent also suffer from a depressive disorder at the same time (Kessler, Chiu, et al., 2005; Ruscio et al., 2008). Approximately one-third abuse alcohol to reduce their anxiety and help them face the situations they fear (for example, drinking before going to a party; Magee et al., 1996). Moreover, because of their distress and avoidance of social situations, people with social phobia, on average, have lower employment rates and lower socioeconomic status, and approximately one-third have severe impairment in one or more domains of their life (Harvey et al., 2005; Ruscio et al., 2008). Finally, the disorder is remarkably persistent, with one study finding that only about a third recover spontaneously over a 12-year period (Bruce et al., 2005).

The case of Paul is typical of social phobia.

A Surgeon's Social Phobia

Paul was a single, white male in his mid-30s when he first presented for treatment. He was a surgeon who reported a 13-year history of social phobia. He had very few social outlets because of his persistent concerns that people would notice how nervous he was in social situations, and he had not dated in many years. Convinced that people would perceive him as foolish or crazy, he particularly worried that people would notice how his jaw tensed up when around other people. Paul frequently chewed gum in public situations, believing that this kept his face from looking distorted. Notably, he had no particular problems talking with people in professional situations. For example, he was quite calm talking with patients before and after surgery. During surgery, when his face was covered with a mask, he also had no trouble carrying out surgical tasks or interacting with the other surgeons and nurses in the room. The trouble began when he left the operating room and had to make small talk—and eye contact—with the other doctors and nurses or with the patient's family. He frequently had panic attacks in these social situations. During the panic attacks he experienced heart palpitations, fears of "going crazy," and a sense of his mind "shutting down." Because the panic attacks occurred only in social situations, he was diagnosed as having social phobia rather than panic disorder.

Paul's social phobia and panic had begun about 13 years earlier when he was under a great deal of stress. His family's business had failed, his parents had divorced, and his mother had had a heart attack. It was in this context of multiple stressors that a personally traumatic incident probably triggered the onset of his social phobia. One day he had come home from medical school to find his best friend in bed with his fiancée. About a month later he had his first panic attack and started avoiding social situations.

Psychological Causal Factors

Like specific phobias, social phobia generally involves learned behaviors that have been shaped by evolutionary factors. Such learning is most likely to occur in people who are genetically or temperamentally at risk.

SOCIAL PHOBIA AS LEARNED BEHAVIOR As with specific phobias, social phobia often seems to originate from simple instances of direct or vicarious classical conditioning such as experiencing or witnessing a perceived social defeat or humiliation, or being or witnessing the target of anger or criticism (Harvey et al., 2005; Mineka & Zinbarg, 1995, 2006; Tillfors, 2004). In two studies, 56 to 58 percent of people with social phobia recalled and identified direct traumatic experiences as having been involved in the origin of their social phobias (Öst & Hugdahl, 1981; Townsley et al., 1995). Another study reported that 92 percent of an adult sample of people with social phobia reported a history of severe teasing in childhood, compared to only 35 percent in a group of people with obsessive-compulsive disorder (McCabe et al., 2003). Moreover, a laboratory study of people with social phobia revealed that they showed especially robust conditioning of fear when the unconditioned stimulus was socially relevant (critical facial expressions and verbal insults) as opposed to more nonspecifically negative stimuli (such as unpleasant odors and painful pressure) (Lissek et al., 2008).

Öst and Hugdahl (1981) reported that another 13 percent of their subjects recalled vicarious conditioning experiences of some sort. One study interviewed a group of people with social phobia about their images of themselves in socially phobic situations and asked where those images had originated (Hackmann et al., 2000). Ninety-six percent of these people remembered some socially traumatic experience that was linked to their own current image of themselves in socially phobic situations. The themes of these memories included having been "criticized for having an anxiety symptom" (e.g., being red or blushing), and having felt "self-conscious and uncomfortable in public as a consequence of past criticism" such as "having previously been bullied and called a 'nothing'" (Hackmann et al., 2000, p. 606). It is important to keep in mind that, as with specific phobias, not everyone who experiences direct or vicarious conditioning in social situations develops social phobia. Individual differences in experiences play an important role in who develops social phobia, as is the case with specific phobias.

SOCIAL FEARS AND PHOBIA IN AN EVOLUTIONARY CONTEXT Social fears and phobia by definition involve fears of members of one's own species. By contrast, animal fears and phobias usually involve fear of potential predators. Although animal fears probably evolved to trigger

---

DSM-5 *Criteria for. . .*

Social Anxiety Disorder (Social Phobia)

A. Marked fear or anxiety about one or more social situations in which the individual is exposed to possible scrutiny by others. Examples include social interactions (e.g., having a conversation, meeting unfamiliar people), being observed (e.g., eating or drinking), and performing in front of others (e.g., giving a speech).
   Note: In children, the anxiety must occur in peer settings and not just during interactions with adults.

B. The individual fears that he or she will act in a way or show anxiety symptoms that will be negatively evaluated (i.e., will be humiliating or embarrassing; will lead to rejection or offend others).

C. The social situations almost always provoke fear or anxiety.
   Note: In children, the fear or anxiety may be expressed by crying, tantrums, freezing, clinging, shrinking, or failing to speak in social situations.

D. The social situations are avoided or endured with intense fear or anxiety.

E. The fear or anxiety is out of proportion to the actual threat posed by the social situation and to the sociocultural context.

F. The fear, anxiety, or avoidance is persistent, typically lasting for 6 months or more.

G. The fear, anxiety, or avoidance causes clinically significant distress or impairment in social, occupational, or other important areas of functioning.

H. The fear, anxiety, or avoidance is not attributable to the physiological effects of a substance (e.g., a drug of abuse, a medication) or another medical condition.

I. The fear, anxiety, or avoidance is not better explained by the symptoms of another mental disorder, such as panic disorder, body dysmorphic disorder, or autism spectrum disorder.

J. If another medical condition (e.g., Parkinson's disease, obesity, disfigurement from burns or injury) is present, the fear, anxiety, or avoidance is clearly unrelated or is excessive.

Source: Reprinted with permission from the *Diagnostic and Statistical Manual of Mental Disorders*, Fifth Edition (Copyright 2013). American Psychiatric Association.

activation of the fight-or-flight response to potential predators, it has been proposed that social fears and phobia evolved as a by-product of dominance hierarchies that are a common social arrangement among animals such as primates (Dimberg & Öhman, 1996; Öhman et al., 1985). Dominance hierarchies are established through aggressive encounters between members of a social group, and a defeated individual typically displays fear and submissive behavior but only rarely attempts to escape the situation completely. Thus, these investigators argued, it is not surprising that people with social phobia endure being in their feared situations rather than running away and escaping them, as people with animal phobias often do (Longin et al., 2010; Öhman, 2009).

If social phobia evolved as a by-product of dominance hierarchies, it is not surprising that humans have an evolutionarily based predisposition to acquire fears of social stimuli that signal dominance and aggression from other humans. These social stimuli include facial expressions of anger or contempt, which on average all humans seem to process more quickly and readily than happy or neutral facial expressions (Öhman, 2009; Schupp et al., 2004). In a series of experiments that paralleled ones for specific phobias, Öhman and colleagues demonstrated that subjects develop stronger conditioned responses when slides of angry faces are paired with mild electric shocks than when happy or neutral faces are paired with the same shocks (Dimberg & Öhman, 1996). Indeed, even very brief subliminal (not consciously perceived) presentations of the angry face that had been paired with shock were sufficient to activate the conditioned responses (Parra et al., 1997), probably because even these subliminal angry faces activate the amygdala—the central structure involved in fear learning (Öhman et al., 2007). Relatedly, people who have social phobia show greater activation of the amygdala (and other brain areas involved in emotion processing) in response to negative facial expressions (such as angry faces) than do normal controls (Goldin et al., 2009; Phan et al., 2006). Such results may help explain the seemingly irrational quality of social phobia, in that the angry faces are processed very quickly and an emotional reaction can be activated without a person's awareness of any threat. The hyperactivity to negative facial expressions is paralleled by heightened neural responses to criticism (Blair et al., 2008; Shin & Liberzon, 2009).

PERCEPTIONS OF UNCONTROLLABILITY AND UNPREDICTABILITY Being exposed to uncontrollable and unpredictable stressful events (such as parental separation and divorce, family conflict, or sexual abuse) may play an important role in the development of social phobia (Mathew et al., 2001; Mineka & Zinbarg, 2006). In the case of Paul, the precipitating event seemed to be finding his fiancée in bed with his best friend. Perceptions of uncontrollability and unpredictability often lead to submissive and unassertive behavior, which is characteristic of people who are socially anxious or phobic. This kind of behavior is especially likely if the perceptions of uncontrollability stem from an actual social defeat, which is known in animals to lead to both increased submissive behavior and increased fear (Mineka & Zinbarg, 1995, 2006). Consistent with this, people with social phobia have a diminished sense of personal control over events in their lives (Leung & Heimberg, 1996). This diminished expectation of personal control may develop, at least in part, as a function of having been raised in families with somewhat overprotective (and sometimes rejecting) parents (Lieb et al., 2000).

COGNITIVE BIASES Cognitive factors also play a role in the onset and maintenance of social phobia. Beck and colleagues (1985) suggested that people with social phobia tend to expect that other people will reject or negatively evaluate them. They argued that this leads to a sense of vulnerability when they are around people who might pose a threat. Clark and Wells (1995; Wells & Clark, 1997) later further proposed that these danger schemas of socially anxious people lead them to expect that they will behave in an awkward and unacceptable fashion, resulting in rejection and loss of status. Such negative expectations lead to their being preoccupied with bodily responses and with stereotyped, negative self-images in social situations; to their overestimating how easily others will detect their anxiety; and to their misunderstanding how well they come across to others (Hirsch et al., 2004). Such intense self-preoccupation during social situations, even to the point of attending to their own heart rate, interferes with their ability to interact skillfully (Hirsch et al., 2003; Pineles & Mineka, 2005). A vicious cycle may evolve: The inward attention and potentially awkward interactions of someone with social phobia may lead others to react to them in a less friendly fashion, confirming their expectations (D. M. Clark, 1997; Clark & McManus, 2002).

Another cognitive bias seen in social phobia is a tendency to interpret ambiguous social information in a negative rather than a benign manner (e.g., when someone smiles at you, does it mean they like you or that they think you're foolish?). Moreover, it is the negatively biased interpretations that socially anxious people make that are remembered (Hertel et al., 2008). It has also been suggested that these biased cognitive processes combine to maintain social phobia and possibly even contribute to its development (Hirsch et al., 2006).

Biological Causal Factors

The most important temperamental variable is *behavioral inhibition*, which shares characteristics with both neuroticism and introversion (Bienvenu et al., 2007). Behaviorally inhibited infants who are easily distressed by unfamiliar

Infants and young children who are fearful and easily distressed by novel people or situations are sometimes high on the temperamental variable called behavioral inhibition. Such children show an increased risk of developing social phobia in adolescence.

stimuli and who are shy and avoidant are more likely to become fearful during childhood and, by adolescence, to show increased risk of developing social phobia (Hayward et al., 1998; Kagan, 1997). For example, one classic study was conducted on behavioral inhibition as a risk factor in a large group of children, most of whom were already known to be at risk for anxiety because their parents had an emotional disorder. Among these children, those who had been assessed as being high on behavioral inhibition between 2 and 6 years of age were nearly three times more likely to be diagnosed with social phobia (22 percent) even in middle childhood (average age of 10) than were children who were low on behavioral inhibition at 2 to 6 years (8 percent; Hirshfeld-Becker et al., 2007). Results from twin studies have shown that there is a modest genetic contribution to social phobia; estimates are that about 30 percent of the variance in liability to social phobia is due to genetic factors (Hettema, Prescott, et al., 2005; Smoller et al., 2008). Nevertheless, these studies suggest that an even larger proportion of variance in who develops social phobia is due to nonshared environmental factors, which is consistent with a strong role for learning.

Treatments

Treatment for social phobia is centered around both cognitive and behavior therapies and sometimes involves medication.

COGNITIVE AND BEHAVIORAL THERAPIES   As with specific phobias, prolonged and graduated exposure to the feared situation (in this case, social situations), has proven to be a very effective treatment. As research has revealed the underlying distorted cognitions that characterize social phobia, **cognitive restructuring** techniques have been added to the behavioral techniques, generating a form of cognitive-behavioral therapy (Barlow et al., 2007). In cognitive

restructuring the therapist attempts to help clients with social phobia identify their underlying negative, automatic thoughts ("I've got nothing interesting to say" or "No one is interested in me"). After helping clients understand that such automatic thoughts (which usually occur just below the surface of awareness but can be accessed) often involve cognitive distortions, the therapist helps the clients change these inner thoughts and beliefs through logical reanalysis. The process of logical reanalysis might involve asking oneself questions to challenge the automatic thoughts: "Do I know for certain that I won't have anything to say?" "Does being nervous have to lead to or equal looking stupid?"

In one highly effective version of such treatments, clients may be assigned exercises in which they manipulate their focus of attention (internally versus externally) to demonstrate to themselves the adverse effects of internal self-focus. They may also receive videotaped feedback to help them modify their distorted self-images. Such techniques have been very successfully applied to the treatment of social phobia (Clark et al., 2006; Heimberg, 2002; Mörtberg et al., 2007). Many studies over the years have shown that exposure therapy and cognitive-behavioral therapy produce comparable results. However, one study suggests that this new, very effective variant on cognitive treatment may be more effective than exposure therapy (Clark et al., 2006). Moreover, at least one study has now shown that simply training individuals with social phobia to disengage from negative social cues during a 15-minute lab task that is repeated eight times over 4 to 6 weeks produced such remarkable reductions in social anxiety symptoms that nearly three out of four of the participants no longer met the criteria for social phobia (Schmidt et al., 2009).

An example of successful combined treatment can be seen in the case of Paul, the surgeon described earlier who had social phobia.

Paul's Treatment

Since the onset of his social phobia 13 years earlier, Paul had taken an antidepressant at one point. The drug had helped stop his panic attacks, but he continued to fear them intensely and still avoided social situations. Thus, he had little relief from his social phobia. He had also been in supportive psychotherapy, which had helped his depression at the time but not his social phobia or his panic. When he went for treatment at a clinic that specialized in the treatment of anxiety disorders, he was not on any medication or in any other form of treatment. Treatment consisted of 14 weeks of cognitive-behavioral therapy. By the end of treatment, Paul was not panicking at all and was quite comfortable in most social situations that he had previously avoided. He was seeing old friends whom he had avoided for years because of his anxiety, and he was beginning to date. Indeed, he even asked his female therapist for a date during the last treatment session! Although such a request was clearly inappropriate, it did indicate how much progress he had made.

MEDICATIONS Unlike specific phobias, social phobia can sometimes be effectively treated with medications. The most effective and widely used medications are several categories of antidepressants (including the monoamine oxidase inhibitors and the selective serotonin reuptake inhibitors discussed extensively in Chapters 7 and 16; Ipser et al., 2008; Roy-Byrne & Cowley, 2007). In some studies, the effects of these antidepressant medications have been comparable to those seen with cognitive-behavioral treatments. However, in several studies, the newer version of cognitive-behavior therapy discussed earlier produced much more substantial improvement than did medication (Clark, Ehlers, et al., 2003). Moreover, the medications must be taken over a long period of time to help ensure that relapse does not occur (Stein & Stein, 2008). A distinct advantage of behavioral and cognitive-behavioral therapies over medications, then, is that they generally produce more long-lasting improvement with very low relapse rates; indeed, clients often continue to improve after treatment is over. Finally, several studies have also suggested that when D-cycloserine (discussed with treatment of specific phobias) is added to exposure therapy, the treatment gains occur more quickly and are more substantial (Guastella et al., 2008).

in review

- What are the primary diagnostic criteria for social phobia and its two subtypes?
- Identify three of the psychological causal factors for social phobia and two of the biological causal factors.
- Describe the major treatment approaches used for social phobia.

Panic Disorder

6.5 Describe the clinical features of panic disorder.

Panic disorder is defined and characterized by the occurrence of panic attacks that often seem to come "out of the blue." According to the *DSM-5* criteria for panic disorder, the person must have experienced recurrent, unexpected attacks and must have been persistently concerned about having another attack or worried about the consequences of having an attack for at least a month (often referred to as anticipatory anxiety). For such an event to qualify as a full-blown panic attack, there must be abrupt onset of at least 4 of 13 symptoms. Most of these symptoms are physical, although three are cognitive (see the last three items in the *DSM-5* box). Panic attacks are fairly brief but intense, with symptoms developing abruptly and usually reaching peak intensity within 10 minutes; the attacks often subside in 20 to 30 minutes and rarely last more than an hour. Periods of anxiety, by contrast, do not typically have such an abrupt onset and are more long lasting.

Panic attacks often are "unexpected" or "uncued" in the sense that they do not appear to be provoked by identifiable aspects of the immediate situation. Indeed, they sometimes occur in situations in which they might be least expected, such as during relaxation or during sleep (known as *nocturnal panic*). In other cases, however, panic attacks are said to be situationally predisposed, occurring only sometimes while the person is in a particular situation such as while driving a car or being in a crowd.

Because most symptoms of a panic attack are physical, it is not surprising that as many as 85 percent of people having a panic attack may show up repeatedly at emergency departments or physicians' offices for what they are convinced is a medical problem—usually cardiac, respiratory, or neurological (Korczak et al., 2007; White & Barlow, 2002).

Unfortunately, a correct diagnosis is often not made for years due to the normal results on numerous costly medical tests. Further complications arise because patients with cardiac problems are at a nearly twofold elevated risk for developing panic disorder (Korczak et al., 2007). Prompt diagnosis and treatment are also important because panic disorder causes approximately as much impairment in social and occupational functioning as that caused by major depressive disorder (Roy-Byrne et al., 2008) and because panic disorder can contribute to the development or worsening of a variety of medical problems (White & Barlow, 2002).

The case of Jackson is typical.

A Student's Struggle with Panic

Jackson is a 21-year-old college student who came to his university's mental health clinic complaining of unexplainable panic attacks. He reports experiencing these attacks for about a year, and is coming for treatment now because they have been increasing in frequency and have gotten to the point of interfering significantly with his ability to pay attention in class and to interact with his friends socially. Jackson describes his panic attacks as coming on completely out of the blue. They are typically characterized by feelings of derealization, extreme panic, and a strong desire to leave whatever situation he is in, and physical symptoms of racing heart, dizziness, sweating, chest pains, and shortness of breath. Jackson has these panic attacks at seemingly random times, but they occur most often in the shower, during his morning classes, and in the dining hall. Because of the distress experienced during these attacks and out of fear of having more attacks, Jackson has been showering less frequently, leaving class whenever he thinks a panic attack may be coming, and he no longer eats in the dining hall. He also has begun drinking alcohol earlier and earlier each evening because he has noticed that alcohol calms his anxiety and seems to decrease the amount of panic he experiences during the evening.

DSM-5 *Criteria for. . .*

Panic Disorder

A. Recurrent unexpected panic attacks. A panic attack is an abrupt surge of intense fear or intense discomfort that reaches a peak within minutes, and during which time four (or more) of the following symptoms occur:

Note: The abrupt surge can occur from a calm state or an anxious state.

1. Palpitations, pounding heart, or accelerated heart rate.
2. Sweating.
3. Trembling or shaking.
4. Sensations of shortness of breath or smothering.
5. Feelings of choking.
6. Chest pain or discomfort.
7. Nausea or abdominal distress.
8. Feeling dizzy, unsteady, light-headed, or faint.
9. Chills or heat sensations.
10. Paresthesias (numbness or tingling sensations).
11. Derealization (feelings of unreality) or depersonalization (being detached from oneself).
12. Fear of losing control or "going crazy."
13. Fear of dying.

Note: Culture-specific symptoms (e.g., tinnitus, neck soreness, headache, uncontrollable screaming or crying) may be seen. Such symptoms should not count as one of the four required symptoms.

B. At least one of the attacks has been followed by 1 month (or more) of one or both of the following:

1. Persistent concern or worry about additional panic attacks or their consequences (e.g., losing control, having a heart attack, "going crazy").
2. A significant maladaptive change in behavior related to the attacks (e.g., behaviors designed to avoid having panic attacks, such as avoidance of exercise or unfamiliar situations).

C. The disturbance is not attributable to the physiological effects of a substance (e.g., a drug of abuse, a medication) or another medical condition (e.g., hyperthyroidism, cardiopulmonary disorders).

D. The disturbance is not better explained by another mental disorder (e.g., the panic attacks do not occur only in response to feared social situations, as in social anxiety disorder; in response to circumscribed phobic objects or situations, as in specific phobia; in response to obsessions, as in obsessive-compulsive disorder; in response to reminders of traumatic events, as in posttraumatic stress disorder; or in response to separation from attachment figures, as in separation anxiety disorder).

Source: Reprinted with permission from the *Diagnostic and Statistical Manual of Mental Disorders*, Fifth Edition (Copyright 2013). American Psychiatric Association.

Agoraphobia

Historically, agoraphobia was thought to involve a fear of the *agora*—the Greek word for "open gathering place." In **agoraphobia** the most commonly feared and avoided situations include streets and crowded places such as shopping malls, movie theaters, and stores. Standing in line can be particularly difficult. Sometimes, agoraphobia develops as a complication of having panic attacks in one or more such situations. Concerned that they may have a panic attack or get sick, people with agoraphobia are anxious about being in places or situations from which escape would be difficult or embarrassing, or in which immediate help would be unavailable if something bad happened (see the *DSM-5* box for diagnostic criteria). Typically people with agoraphobia are also frightened by their own bodily sensations, so they also avoid activities that will create arousal such as exercising, watching scary movies, drinking caffeine, and even engaging in sexual activity.

As agoraphobia first develops, people tend to avoid situations in which attacks have occurred, but usually the avoidance gradually spreads to other situations where attacks might occur. In moderately severe cases, people with agoraphobia may be anxious even when venturing outside their homes alone. In very severe cases, agoraphobia is an utterly disabling disorder in which a person cannot go beyond the narrow confines of home—or even particular parts of the home.

The case of John D. is typical of someone with both panic disorder and agoraphobia.

John D.

John D. was a 45-year-old married European American man with three sons. Although well-educated and successful . . . John had been experiencing difficulties with panic attacks for 15 years . . . experiencing two to five panic attacks per month. The previous week John had had a panic attack while driving with his family to a computer store. He recollected that before the panic attack he might have been "keyed up" over the kids making a lot of noise in the back seat; the attack began right after he had quickly turned around to tell the kids to "settle down." Immediately after he turned back to look at the road, John felt dizzy. As soon as he noticed this, John experienced a rapid and intense surge of other sensations including sweating, accelerated heart rate, hot flushes, and trembling. Fearing that he was going to crash the car, John quickly pulled to the side of the road. . . .

John was having only a few panic attacks per month, but he was experiencing a high level of anxiety every day, focused on the possibility that he might have another panic attack at any time.

Indeed, John had developed extensive apprehension or avoidance of driving, air travel, elevators, wide-open spaces, taking long walks alone, movie theaters, and being out of town.

[His] first panic attack had occurred 15 years ago. John had fallen asleep on the living room sofa at around 1:00 A.M. after returning from a night of drinking with some of his friends. Just after awakening at 4:30, John felt stomach pains and a pulsating sensation in the back of his neck. All of a sudden, John noticed that his heart was racing, too. . . . Although he did not know what he was suffering from, John was certain that he was dying.

John remembered having a second panic attack about a month later. From then on, the panic attacks began to occur more regularly. When the panic attacks became recurrent, John started to avoid situations in which the panic attacks had occurred as well as situations in which he feared a panic attack was likely to occur. On three occasions during the first few years of his panic attacks, John went to the emergency department of his local hospital because he was sure that his symptoms were a sign of a heart attack.

Source: Adapted from Brown & Barlow, 2001, pp. 19–22.

Agoraphobia is a frequent complication of panic disorder. As noted, the case of John D. is typical. However, many patients with agoraphobia do not experience panic. Recognizing this, in *DSM-5* agoraphobia is now listed as a distinct disorder. As agoraphobia develops, there is often a gradually spreading fearfulness in which more and more aspects of the environment outside the home become threatening. The most recent estimate of the lifetime prevalence of agoraphobia without panic is 1.4 percent (Kessler, Chiu, et al., 2006).

Prevalence, Age of Onset, and Gender Differences

Approximately 4.7 percent of the adult population has had panic disorder with or without agoraphobia at some time in their lives, with panic disorder without agoraphobia being more common (Kessler, Chiu, et al., 2005). Panic disorder with or without agoraphobia typically begins in the 20s to the 40s, but sometimes begins in the late teen years (Kessler, Chiu, et al., 2006). Once panic disorder develops, it tends to have a chronic and disabling course, although the intensity of symptoms often waxes and wanes over time (White & Barlow, 2002). Indeed, one 12-year longitudinal study found that less than 50 percent of patients with panic disorder with agoraphobia had recovered in 12 years, and 58 percent of those who had recovered at some point had had a recurrence (new onset; Bruce et al., 2005). Panic disorder is about twice as prevalent in women as in men (Eaton et al., 1994; White & Barlow, 2002). Agoraphobia also occurs much more frequently in women than in men, and the percentage of women

---

DSM-5 *Criteria for. . .*

Agoraphobia

A. Marked fear or anxiety about two (or more) of the following five situations:

1. Using public transportation (e.g., automobiles, buses, trains, ships, planes).
2. Being in open spaces (e.g., parking lots, marketplaces, bridges).
3. Being in enclosed places (e.g., shops, theaters, cinemas).
4. Standing in line or being in a crowd.
5. Being outside of the home alone.

B. The individual fears or avoids these situations because of thoughts that escape might be difficult or help might not be available in the event of developing panic-like symptoms or other incapacitating or embarrassing symptoms (e.g., fear of falling in the elderly; fear of incontinence).

C. The agoraphobic situations almost always provoke fear or anxiety.

D. The agoraphobic situations are actively avoided, require the presence of a companion, or are endured with intense fear or anxiety.

E. The fear or anxiety is out of proportion to the actual danger posed by the agoraphobic situations and to the sociocultural context.

F. The fear, anxiety, or avoidance is persistent, typically lasting for 6 months or more.

G. The fear, anxiety, or avoidance causes clinically significant distress or impairment in social, occupational, or other important areas of functioning.

H. If another medical condition (e.g., inflammatory bowel disease, Parkinson's disease) is present, the fear, anxiety, or avoidance is clearly excessive.

I. The fear, anxiety, or avoidance is not better explained by the symptoms of another mental disorder—for example, the symptoms are not confined to specific phobia, situational type; do not involve only social situations (as in social anxiety disorder); and are not related exclusively to obsessions (as in obsessive-compulsive disorder), perceived defects or flaws in physical appearance (as in body dysmorphic disorder), reminders of traumatic events (as in posttraumatic stress disorder), or fear of separation (as in separation anxiety disorder).

Note: Agoraphobia is diagnosed irrespective of the presence of panic disorder. If an individual's presentation meets criteria for panic disorder and agoraphobia, both diagnoses should be assigned.

Source: Reprinted with permission from the *Diagnostic and Statistical Manual of Mental Disorders*, Fifth Edition (Copyright 2013). American Psychiatric Association.

increases as the extent of agoraphobic avoidance increases. Among people with severe agoraphobia, approximately 80 to 90 percent are female (Bekker, 1996; White & Barlow, 2002). Table 6.3 outlines gender differences in the prevalence of other anxiety disorders for comparison purposes.

Table 6.3 Association Between Gender and Lifetime Risk of Anxiety Disorders: Results from a Study of 15 Countries

Disorder	Odds Ratio
Agoraphobia	2.0
Specific phobia	2.0
Panic disorder	1.9
Generalized anxiety disorder	1.7
Social phobia	1.3

NOTE: Odds ratios represent the increase in the odds of anxiety disorders associated with female (vs. male) gender. Source: WHO World Mental Health Survey Initiative (Seedat et al. [2009]. Cross-national associations between gender and mental disorders in the World Health Organization World Mental Health Surveys. *Archives of General Psychiatry, 66*, 785–95.).

The most common explanation of the pronounced gender difference in agoraphobia is a sociocultural one (McLean & Anderson, 2009). In our culture (and many others as well), it is more acceptable for women who experience panic to avoid the situations they fear and to need a trusted companion to accompany them when they enter feared situations. Men who experience panic are more prone to "tough it out" because of societal expectations and their more assertive, instrumental approach to life (Bekker, 1996). Some evidence indicates that men with panic disorder may be more likely to self-medicate with nicotine or alcohol as a way of coping with and enduring panic attacks rather than developing agoraphobic avoidance (Starcevic et al., 2008).

Comorbidity with Other Disorders

The vast majority of people with panic disorder (83 percent) have at least one comorbid disorder, most often generalized anxiety disorder, social phobia, specific phobia, PTSD, depression, and substance-use disorders (especially smoking and alcohol dependence; Bernstein et al., 2006; Kessler, Chiu, et al., 2006; Zvolensky & Bernstein, 2005). Depression is especially common among those with panic disorder, with approximately 50 to 70 percent of people with panic disorder experiencing serious depression at some point in their lives (Kessler, Chiu, et al., 2006). Perhaps related to the fear of having a panic attack, they may also meet criteria for dependent or avoidant personality disorder (see Chapter 10).

Although people often think of suicide as being especially associated with depression, a major study in the 1980s reported that panic disorder is a strong predictor of suicidal behavior (Weissman et al., 1989). Subsequent research suggested that the link between panic and suicidal behavior is largely explained by the presence of comorbid disorders such as depression and substance abuse, leading researchers to conclude that panic itself doesn't increase the risk of suicidal behavior (e.g., Vickers & McNally, 2004). However, two recent, very large epidemiological studies (one with 10,000 people from the United States and one with over 100,000 people from 21 countries) have found that panic disorder is indeed associated with increased risk for suicidal ideation and attempts independent of its relationship with comorbid disorders (Nock et al., 2009, 2010).

The Timing of a First Panic Attack

Although panic attacks themselves appear to come "out of the blue," the first one frequently occurs following feelings of distress or some highly stressful life circumstance such as loss of a loved one, loss of an important relationship, loss of a job, or criminal victimization (Barlow, 2002; Klauke et al., 2010). Although not all studies have found this, some have estimated that approximately 80 to 90 percent of people report that their first panic attack occurred after one or more negative life events.

People with severe agoraphobia are often fearful of venturing out of their homes into public places, in part because of their fear of having a panic attack in a place in which escape might prove physically difficult or psychologically embarrassing. They may even become housebound unless accompanied by a spouse or trusted companion.

Nevertheless, not all people who have a panic attack following a stressful event go on to develop full-blown panic disorder. Current estimates are that nearly 23 percent of adults have experienced at least one panic attack in their lifetimes, but most do not go on to develop full-blown panic disorder (Kessler, Chiu, et al., 2006). Given that panic attacks are much more frequent than panic disorder, what causes full-blown panic disorder to develop in only a subset of these people? Several different prominent theories about the causes of panic disorder have addressed this question.

Biological Causal Factors

The biological causal factors of panic disorder include genetics, brain activity, and biochemical abnormalities.

GENETIC FACTORS   According to family and twin studies, panic disorder has a moderate heritable component (Maron et al., 2010; Norrholm & Ressler, 2009). In a large twin study, López-Solà and colleagues (2014) estimated that 30 to 34 percent of the variance in liability to panic symptoms is due to genetic factors. As noted earlier, this genetic vulnerability is manifested at a psychological level at least in part by the important personality trait called neuroticism (which is in turn related to the temperamental construct of behavioral inhibition). Several studies have begun to identify which specific genetic polymorphisms are responsible for this moderate heritability (Strug et al., 2010), either alone or in interaction with certain types of stressful life events (Klauke et al., 2010).

Some studies have suggested that this heritability is at least partly specific for panic disorder (rather than for all anxiety disorders), but twin studies suggest that there is overlap in the genetic vulnerability factors for panic disorder and both phobias and separation anxiety (Battaglia et al., 2009; Kendler, Walters, et al., 1995). This would be consistent with some preliminary evidence that people with a history of phobia are at heightened risk for developing panic disorder (Biederman et al., 2006). However, another study suggests overlap in the genetic vulnerability for panic disorder, generalized anxiety disorder, and agoraphobia (Hettema, Prescott, et al., 2005). Only further research can resolve these inconsistencies in findings (Norrholm & Ressler, 2009).

PANIC AND THE BRAIN   One relatively early prominent theory about the neurobiology of panic attacks implicated the *locus coeruleus* in the brain stem (see Figure 6.1) and a particular neurotransmitter—norepinephrine—that is centrally involved in brain activity in this area (Goddard et al., 1996). However, today it is recognized that it is increased activity in the amygdala that plays a more central role in panic attacks than does activity in the locus coeruleus. The **amygdala** is a collection of nuclei in front of the hippocampus in the limbic system of the brain that is critically involved in the emotion of fear. Stimulation of the central nucleus of the amygdala is known to stimulate the locus coeruleus as well as the other autonomic, neuroendocrine, and behavioral responses that occur during panic attacks (e.g., Gorman et al., 2000; LeDoux, 2000). Other recent research has also implicated the periaqueductal gray area in the midbrain (Del-Ben & Graeff, 2009; Graeff & Del-Ben, 2008).

Figure 6.1 A Biological Theory of Panic, Anxiety, and Agoraphobia

According to one theory, panic attacks may arise from abnormal activity in the amygdala, a collection of nuclei in front of the hippocampus in the limbic system. The anticipatory anxiety that people develop about having another panic attack is thought to arise from activity in the hippocampus of the limbic system, which is known to be involved in the learning of emotional responses. Agoraphobic avoidance, also a learned response, may also involve activity of the hippocampus and higher cortical centers (Gorman et al., 2000).

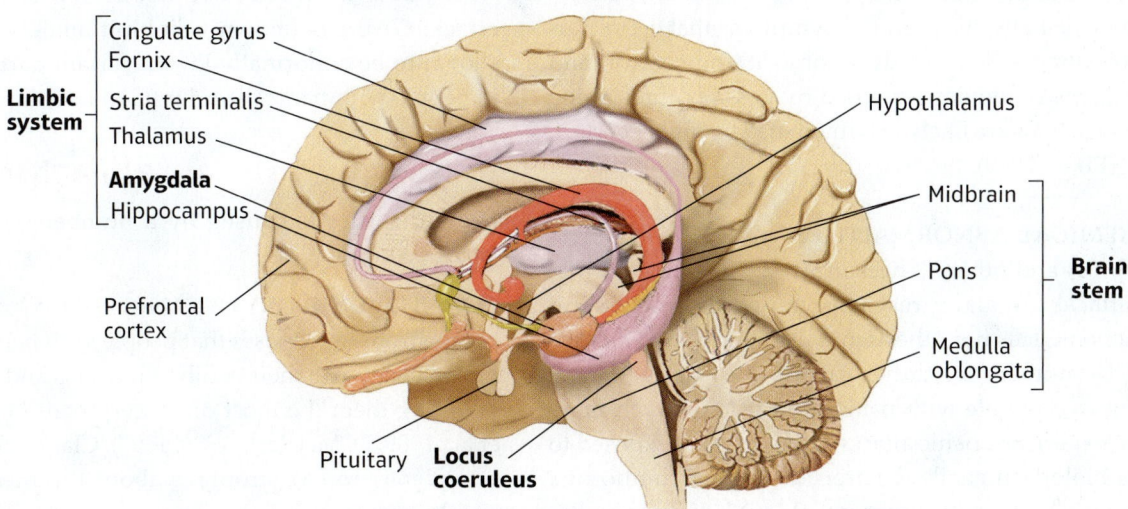

Some research has suggested that the amygdala is the central area involved in what has been called a "fear network," with connections not only to lower areas in the brain like the locus coeruleus but also to higher brain areas like the *prefrontal cortex* (Gorman et al., 2000). According to this view, panic attacks occur when the fear network is activated, either by cortical inputs or by inputs from lower brain areas. So according to this influential theory, panic disorder is likely to develop in people who have abnormally sensitive fear networks that get activated too readily to be adaptive. This theory about abnormally sensitive fear networks is also consistent with findings that individuals with panic disorder showed heightened startle responses to loud noise stimuli as well as slower habituation of such responding (Ludewig et al., 2005; see also Shin & Liberzon, 2009). Sakai and colleagues (2005), using functional neuroimaging techniques, also found support for this neuroanatomical hypothesis. Abnormally sensitive fear networks may have a partially heritable basis but may also develop as a result of repeated stressful life experiences, particularly early in life (Ladd et al., 2000).

But panic attacks are only one component of panic disorder. People with panic disorder also become anxious about the possibility of another attack, and those with agoraphobia also engage in phobic avoidance behavior (Gorman et al., 2000). Different brain areas are probably involved in these different aspects of panic disorder. The panic attacks themselves arise from activity in the amygdala, either by cortical inputs (e.g., evaluating a stimulus as highly threatening) or by activity coming from more downstream areas like the locus coeruleus. For people who have one or more panic attacks and who go on to develop significant conditioned anxiety about having another one in particular contexts, the *hippocampus* (also a part of the *limbic system*, below the cortex, which is very involved in the learning of emotional responses; see Figure 6.1) is thought to generate this conditioned anxiety (Charney et al., 1998; Gray & McNaughton, 2000) and is probably also involved in the learned avoidance associated with agoraphobia (Gorman et al., 2000). Finally, the cognitive symptoms that occur during panic attacks (fears of dying or of losing control) and overreactions to the danger posed by possibly threatening bodily sensations are likely to be mediated by higher cortical centers (Etkin, 2010).

BIOCHEMICAL ABNORMALITIES Over 30 years ago, Klein (1981) and others (Sheehan, 1982, 1983) argued that panic attacks are alarm reactions caused by biochemical dysfunctions. This hypothesis initially appeared to be supported by numerous studies during the past 40 years, showing that people with panic disorder are much more likely to experience panic attacks when they are exposed to various biological challenge procedures than are normal people or people with other psychiatric disorders. For example, some of these laboratory tests involve infusions of sodium lactate (a substance resembling the lactate our bodies produce during exercise; Gorman et al., 1989), inhaling air with altered amounts of carbon dioxide (Woods et al., 1987), or ingesting large amounts of caffeine (Uhde, 1990). In each case, such procedures produce panic attacks in panic disorder clients at a much higher rate than in normal subjects (Barlow, 2002). There is a broad range of these so-called **panic provocation procedures**, and some of them are associated with quite different and even mutually exclusive neurobiological processes. Thus, no single neurobiological mechanism could possibly be implicated (Barlow, 2002; Roy-Byrne et al., 2006). However, as explained later in the section on causal factors, simpler biological and psychological explanations can account for this pattern of results. These alternative explanations stem from the observation that what all these biological challenge procedures have in common is that they put stress on certain neurobiological systems, which in turn produce intense physical symptoms of arousal (such as increased heart rate, respiration, and blood pressure).

At present, two primary neurotransmitter systems are most implicated in panic attacks: the noradrenergic and the serotonergic systems (Graeff & Del-Ben, 2008; Neumeister et al., 2004). Noradrenergic activity in certain brain areas can stimulate cardiovascular symptoms associated with panic (Gorman et al., 2000). Increased serotonergic activity also decreases noradrenergic activity. This fits with results showing that the medications most widely used to treat panic disorder today—the selective serotonin reuptake inhibitors (SSRIs)—seem to increase serotonergic activity in the brain but also to decrease noradrenergic activity. By decreasing noradrenergic activity, these medications decrease many of the cardiovascular symptoms associated with panic that are ordinarily stimulated by noradrenergic activity (Gorman et al., 2000).

The inhibitory neurotransmitter GABA has also been implicated in the anticipatory anxiety that many people with panic disorder have about experiencing another attack. GABA is known to inhibit anxiety and has been shown to be abnormally low in certain parts of the cortex in people with panic disorder (Goddard et al., 2001, 2004).

Psychological Causal Factors

Panic disorder is caused by a number of psychological factors.

COGNITIVE THEORY OF PANIC The cognitive theory of panic disorder proposes that people with panic disorder are hypersensitive to their bodily sensations and are very prone to giving them the most dire interpretation possible (Beck et al., 1985; D. M. Clark, 1986, 1997). Clark referred to this as a tendency to catastrophize about the meaning of their bodily sensations. For example, a person who develops panic disorder might notice that his heart is racing and conclude that he is having a heart attack, or notice that he is dizzy, which may lead to fainting or to the thought that he may have a brain tumor. These very frightening thoughts may cause many more physical symptoms of anxiety, which further fuel the catastrophic thoughts, leading to a vicious circle culminating in a panic attack (see Figure 6.2). The person is not necessarily aware of making these catastrophic interpretations; rather, the thoughts are often just barely out of the realm of awareness (Rapee, 1996). These *automatic thoughts*, as Beck calls them, are in a sense the triggers of panic. Although it is not yet clear how the tendency to catastrophize develops, the cognitive model proposes that only people with this tendency to catastrophize go on to develop panic disorder (D. M. Clark, 1997).

Several lines of evidence are consistent with the cognitive theory of panic disorder. For example, people with panic disorder are much more likely to interpret their

---

Figure 6.2 The Panic Circle

Any kind of perceived threat may lead to apprehension or worry, which is accompanied by various bodily sensations. According to the cognitive model of panic, if a person then catastrophizes about the meaning of his or her bodily sensations, this will raise the level of perceived threat, thus creating more apprehension and worry as well as more physical symptoms, which fuel further catastrophic thoughts. This vicious circle can culminate in a panic attack. The initial physical sensations need not arise from the perceived threat (as shown at the top of the circle) but may come from other sources (exercise, anger, psychoactive drugs, etc., as shown at the bottom of the circle).

(Adapted from D. M. Clark, 1986, 1997.)

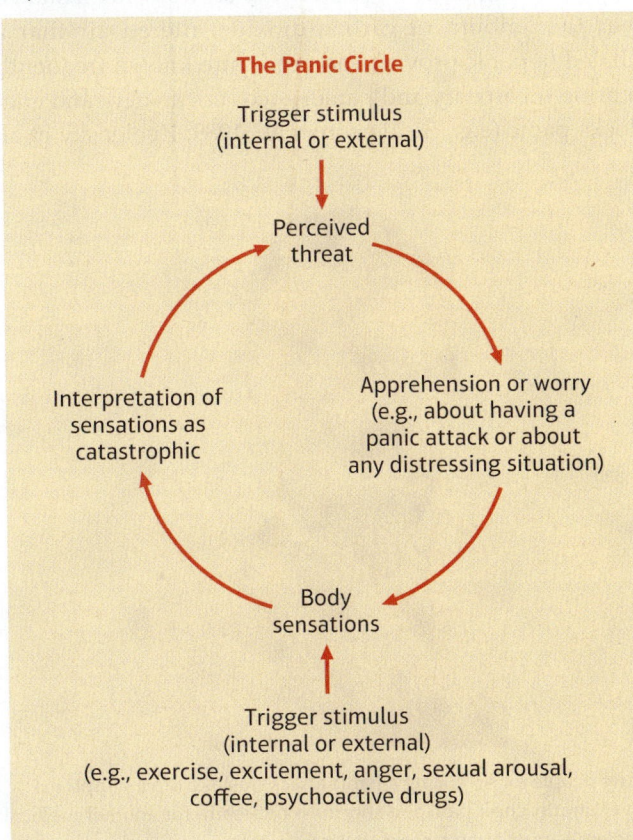

bodily sensations in a catastrophic manner (Teachman et al., 2007), and the greater the tendency to do so, the greater the severity of panic (Casey et al., 2005). The model also predicts that changing their cognitions about their bodily symptoms should reduce or prevent panic. Evidence that cognitive therapy for panic works is consistent with this prediction (D. M. Clark et al., 1994, 1999). In addition, a brief explanation of what to expect in a panic provocation study can prevent or reduce panic symptoms (D. M. Clark, 1997; Schmidt et al., 2006, for related results).

COMPREHENSIVE LEARNING THEORY OF PANIC DISORDER   A comprehensive learning theory of panic disorder developed during the past few decades suggests that initial panic attacks become associated with initially neutral internal (interoceptive) and external (exteroceptive) cues through an **interoceptive conditioning** (or **exteroceptive conditioning**) process, which leads anxiety to become conditioned to these CSs, and the more intense the panic attack, the more robust the conditioning that will occur. Other types of instrumental and avoidance learning are also involved but will not be explained here (see Bouton, 2005; Bouton et al., 2001; Mineka & Zinbarg, 2006).

This conditioning of anxiety to the internal or external cues associated with panic thus sets the stage for the development of two of the three components of panic disorder: anticipatory anxiety and, sometimes, agoraphobic fears. Specifically, when people experience their initial panic attacks (which are terrifying emotional events replete with strong internal bodily sensations), interoceptive and exteroceptive conditioning can occur to different kinds of cues, ranging from heart palpitations and dizziness to shopping malls. Because anxiety becomes conditioned to these CSs, anxious apprehension about having another attack, particularly in certain contexts, may develop, as may agoraphobic avoidance of contexts in which panic attacks might occur in a subset of individuals. Moreover, a recent study demonstrated that once an individual has developed panic disorder, that person shows greater generalization of conditioned responding to other similar cues than do controls without panic disorder (Lissek et al., 2010). In individuals who have panic disorder, extinction of conditioned anxiety responses occurs more slowly than in normal controls (Michael et al., 2007). Because extinction involves inhibitory learning, which seems to be impaired in panic disorder, it is not surprising that individuals with panic disorder also show impaired discriminative conditioning because of their deficits in learning that a CS is a safety cue (Lissek et al., 2009).

However, another important effect is that panic attacks themselves (the third component of panic disorder) are also likely to be conditioned to certain internal cues. This leads to the occurrence of panic attacks that seemingly

Developments in Research

Nocturnal Panic Attacks

Although the majority of panic attacks experienced by people with panic disorder occur during waking hours, approximately 50 to 60 percent of people report that they have experienced a panic attack during sleep at least once (Barlow, 2002; O'Mahony & Ward, 2003). Nocturnal panic refers to waking from sleep in a state of panic. It seems to occur with some regularity in about 20 to 40 percent of people with panic disorder and is frequently associated with insomnia and frequent awakenings during sleep (Craske et al., 2002; Overbeek et al., 2005; Papadimitriou & Linkowski, 2005). Although one might think that such panic attacks occur in response to nightmares, considerable research shows that this is not the case. Sleep has five stages that occur in a fairly invariant sequence multiple times throughout the night: one stage called REM sleep (rapid eye movement sleep) during which vivid dreaming occurs, and four stages of non-REM sleep (Stages 1–4) when vivid dreams do not occur. If nocturnal panic attacks occurred in response

to dreams, we would expect them to occur during REM sleep (when nightmares usually occur), but in fact they occur during Stage 2 and early Stage 3 sleep, usually a few hours after falling asleep.

It is important to note that nocturnal panic attacks are different from "sleep terrors" or "night terrors," which usually occur during Stage 4 sleep. Night terrors are usually experienced by children, who often scream and then fear that someone or something is chasing them around the room; however, they do not wake up (Barlow, 2002). Nocturnal panic attacks also differ from isolated sleep paralysis, which can sometimes occur during the transition from sleep to waking. Sleep paralysis involves awareness of one's surroundings accompanied by a stark sense of terror (resembling that during a panic attack) and an inability to move, which seems to occur because the individuals are waking from REM (dream) sleep, when muscle activity below the neck is suppressed (Hinton et al., 2005).

---

come out of the blue when people unconsciously experience certain internal bodily sensations (CSs). For example, one young man with panic disorder who was particularly frightened of signs that his heart was racing experienced a surprising and unexpected panic attack after hearing that his favorite presidential candidate had won. The panic attack thus occurred when he was happy and excited (which is what made it so surprising for him). However, from the standpoint of this theory, the attack was actually not surprising. Because the man was excited, his heart was racing, which probably served as an internal CS that triggered the panic (Mineka & Zinbarg, 2006). Notably, some people even have panic attacks while not consciously focused on their internal state at all—that is, while sleeping (see the Developments in Research box). This theory also underscores why not everyone who experiences an occasional panic attack goes on to develop panic disorder. Instead, people with certain genetic, temperamental or personality, or cognitive-behavioral vulnerabilities will show stronger conditioning of both anxiety and panic (Barlow, 2002; Bouton et al., 2001; Mineka & Zinbarg, 2006).

ANXIETY SENSITIVITY AND PERCEIVED CONTROL Cognitive and learning explanations of panic and agoraphobia have looked at a number of different factors that can generally be explained within either the cognitive or learning perspective. For example, people who have high levels of **anxiety sensitivity**—a trait-like belief that certain bodily symptoms may have harmful consequences—are more prone to developing panic attacks and perhaps panic disorder (McNally, 2002; Pagura et al., 2009). People with anxiety sensitivity endorse statements such as

"When I notice that my heart is beating rapidly, I worry that I might have a heart attack." Anxiety sensitivity has been shown to predict the development of panic attacks (Li & Zinbarg, 2007; Schmidt et al., 1997), as well as the onset of other anxiety disorders (Schmidt et al., 2006).

In addition, several important studies have shown that simply having a sense of *perceived control*—for instance, over the amount of carbon-dioxide–altered air that is inhaled (a panic provocation procedure known frequently to bring on anxiety and panic)—reduces anxiety and even blocks panic (e.g., Sanderson et al., 1989; Zvolensky et al.,

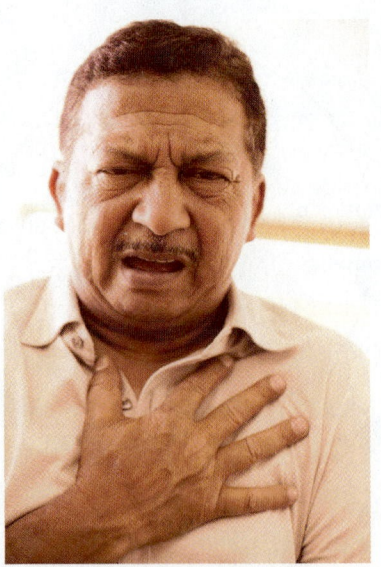

Many people experiencing a panic attack mistake their symptoms (for example, chest pain and shortness of breath) for another medical problem—most often a heart attack.

1998, 1999). In addition, if a person with panic disorder is accompanied by a "safe" person when undergoing a panic provocation procedure, that person is likely to show reduced distress, lowered physiological arousal, and reduced likelihood of panic relative to someone who came alone (without a "safe" person; Carter et al., 1995). Moreover, anxiety sensitivity has a greater effect on panic symptoms in people with low perceived control (Bentley et al., 2013). Finally, individuals with panic disorder may also be protected against the development of agoraphobic avoidance if they have relatively high levels of perceived control over their emotions and threatening situations (Suárez et al., 2009; White, Brown, et al., 2006).

SAFETY BEHAVIORS AND THE PERSISTENCE OF PANIC Why do people who have developed panic disorder continue to have panic attacks in spite of the fact that their predictions of heart attacks, death, and insanity rarely, if ever, come true? Some people with panic disorder may, for example, have three or four panic attacks a week for 20 years; each time they may believe they are having a heart attack, and yet they never do. After experiencing hundreds or thousands of panic attacks without having a heart attack, one would think, from the cognitive perspective, that this catastrophic thought would have been proved wrong so many times that it would finally go away. However, evidence suggests that such disconfirmation does not occur because people with panic disorder frequently engage in safety behaviors (such as breathing slowly or carrying a bottle with anxiolytic medication) before or during an attack. They then mistakenly tend to attribute the lack of catastrophe to their having engaged in this safety behavior rather than to the idea that panic attacks actually do not lead to heart attacks. Similarly, people who think they may faint will tend to lean against solid objects (D. A. Clark, 1997; Salkovskis et al., 1996). Research suggests that it is important during treatment to identify these safety behaviors so that the person can learn to give them up and finally see that the feared catastrophe still does not occur. Indeed, a good number of studies have found that asking people to drop their safety behaviors during cognitive-behavioral treatment can increase the effectiveness of the treatment (Rachman et al., 2008).

COGNITIVE BIASES AND THE MAINTENANCE OF PANIC Finally, many studies have shown that people with panic disorder are biased in the way they process threatening information. Such people not only interpret ambiguous bodily sensations as threatening (D. A. Clark, 1997; Teachman et al., 2006), but they also interpret other ambiguous situations as more threatening than do controls. People with panic disorder also seem to have their attention automatically drawn to threatening information in their environment such as words that represent things they fear, such as *palpitations*, *numbness*, or *faint* (see Lim &

Kim, 2005; Mathews & MacLeod, 2005; Mineka et al., 2003, for reviews). One study using fMRI techniques demonstrated that people with panic disorder showed greater activation to threat words than did normal people in brain areas involved in memory processing of threatening material (Maddock et al., 2003). Whether these information-processing biases are present before the disorder begins and help to cause it is as yet unclear, but these biases are certainly likely to help maintain the disorder once it has begun. For example, having one's attention automatically drawn to threatening cues in the environment is likely to provoke more attacks.

In summary, research into both biological and psychosocial factors involved in panic disorder has provided important insights into this disorder since it was first identified as a distinct disorder in 1980. It seems unlikely that research from either tradition alone will ever provide a complete account of this disorder, and more research is needed to synthesize these findings into a biopsychosocial theory.

Treatments

Treatment for panic disorder includes behavioral and cognitive-behavioral approaches and different categories of medication.

BEHAVIORAL AND COGNITIVE-BEHAVIORAL TREATMENTS The original behavioral treatment for agoraphobia from the early 1970s involved prolonged exposure to feared situations, often with the help of a therapist or family member. Similar to what is done with specific and social phobias, the idea was to make people gradually face the situations they feared and learn that there was nothing to fear. Such exposure-based treatments were quite effective and helped about 60 to 75 percent of people with agoraphobia show clinically significant improvement (Barlow et al., 2007). These effects were generally well maintained at 2- to 4-year follow-up. But this left approximately 25 to 40 percent not improved to a *clinically significant* degree (Barlow et al., 2002).

One limitation of these original treatments was that they did not specifically target panic attacks. In the mid-1980s, two new techniques were developed as clinical researchers increasingly recognized the importance of panic attacks to most people with agoraphobia. One technique involves the variant on exposure known as *interoceptive exposure*, meaning deliberate exposure to feared *internal* sensations. The idea was that fear of these internal sensations should be treated in the same way that fear of external agoraphobic situations is treated—namely, through prolonged exposure to those internal sensations so that the fear may extinguish. For example, people are asked to engage in various exercises that bring on various internal sensations (e.g., spinning in a chair, hyperventilating, running in place) and to stick with those sensations until they subside, thereby allowing habituation of their fears of these sensations.

The second set of techniques that were developed is cognitive restructuring techniques, in recognition that catastrophic automatic thoughts may help maintain panic attacks. One kind of integrative cognitive-behavioral treatment for panic disorder—*panic control treatment* (PCT)—targets both agoraphobic avoidance and panic attacks. PCT has several aspects. First, clients are educated about the nature of anxiety and panic and how the capacity to experience both is adaptive. A second part of the treatment involves teaching people with panic disorder to control their breathing. Third, clients are taught about the logical errors that people who have panic disorders are prone to making and learn to subject their own automatic thoughts to a logical reanalysis. Finally, they are exposed to feared situations and feared bodily sensations to build up a tolerance to the discomfort. Generally, this integrative treatment produces better results than the original exposure-based techniques that focused exclusively on exposure to external situations (Arch & Craske, 2009; D. M. Clark, 1997). In many of the studies conducted using one of the variants on these treatments, 70 to 90 percent of people with panic disorder were panic free at the end of 8 to 14 weeks of treatment, and gains were well maintained at 1- to 2-year follow-ups (Arch & Craske, 2008; McCabe & Gifford, 2009). Overall, the magnitude of improvement is often greater with these cognitive and behavioral treatments than with medications (Arch & Craske, 2009; Barlow et al., 2002). Moreover, these treatments have been extended and shown to be very useful in treating people who also have nocturnal panic (Arch & Craske, 2008).

Research Close-Up

Clinically Significant

Not all statistically significant changes are of sufficient magnitude to be clinically significant. Clinical significance reflects how large the effects of a particular treatment or intervention are with respect to how much meaningful change they provide in a person's level of functioning or well-being.

Watch   **Clinically Significant**

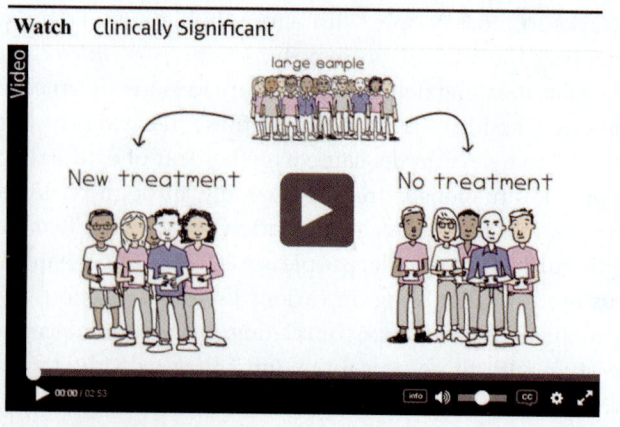

MEDICATIONS Many people with panic disorder are prescribed *anxiolytics* (antianxiety medications) from the benzodiazepine category such as alprazolam (Xanax) or clonazepam (Klonopin). One major advantage of these drugs is that they act very quickly (30–60 minutes) and so can be useful in acute situations of intense panic or anxiety. However, these anxiolytic medications can also have undesirable side effects such as drowsiness and sedation, which can lead to impaired cognitive and motor performance. Also, with prolonged use, most people using moderate to high doses develop physiological dependence on the drug, which results in withdrawal symptoms when the drug is discontinued (e.g., nervousness, sleep disturbance, dizziness, and further panic attacks). Withdrawal from these drugs can be very slow and difficult, and it leads to relapse in a high percentage of cases (Pollack & Simon, 2009; Roy-Byrne & Cowley, 2007). These are the reasons why benzodiazepines are no longer considered as a first-choice treatment (Katon, 2006).

The other category of medication that is useful in the treatment of panic disorder and agoraphobia is the antidepressants (including primarily the tricyclics, the SSRIs, and most recently the serotonin-norepinephrine reuptake inhibitors). These medications have both advantages and disadvantages compared with anxiolytics. One major advantage is that they do not create physiological dependence in the way benzodiazepines can, and they also can alleviate any comorbid depressive symptoms or disorders (Pollack & Simon, 2009; Roy-Byrne & Cowley, 2007). However, it takes about 4 weeks before they have any beneficial effects, so they are not useful in an acute situation where a person is having a panic attack. Troublesome side effects (such as dry mouth, constipation, and blurred vision with the tricyclics, and interference with sexual arousal with the SSRIs) mean that large numbers of people refuse to take the medications or discontinue their use. Moreover, relapse rates when the drugs are discontinued are quite high (although not as high as with the benzodiazepines; Roy-Byrne & Cowley, 2007).

Today the SSRIs are more widely prescribed than the tricyclics because the SSRIs are generally better tolerated by most patients. Moreover, both are generally preferred by physicians to benzodiazepines because of the risks associated with the latter (Roy-Byrne & Cowley, 2007).

What about the combination of antianxiety medication and cognitive-behavioral therapy (CBT)? In the short term, such combined treatment sometimes produces a slightly superior result compared to either type of treatment alone (Barlow et al., 2007; Mitte, 2005). In addition, one study showed that those individuals who had received combined treatment showed fewer medication side effects and fewer dropouts than those who had used medication alone (S. M. Marcus et al., 2007). However, in the long term, after medication has been tapered (especially benzodiazepine medications), clients who have been on medication with or without cognitive or behavioral treatment seem to show a greater likelihood of relapse (Arch & Craske, 2008; Barlow et al., 2002; Marks et al., 1993). Perhaps this is because they have attributed their gains to the medication rather than to their personal efforts (Başoğlu et al., 1994; Mitte, 2005). The one medication that has shown promise for enhancing responsiveness of panic disorder to CBT is D-cycloserine—the same medication discussed earlier that can enhance the speed of treating specific and social phobias (Hofmann et al., 2015).

in review

- You are experiencing a panic attack. What are your symptoms?
- Describe the major diagnostic features of both panic disorder and agoraphobia. Why do the two disorders often occur together?
- What biological causal factors have been implicated in panic disorder?
- Compare and contrast the learning or conditioning theory and cognitive models of panic disorder.
- Describe the major treatment approaches for panic disorder and their relative advantages and disadvantages.

Generalized Anxiety Disorder

6.6 **Explain the clinical aspects of generalized anxiety disorder.**

Everyone experiences worry—a state of anxiety and uncertainty about something in the future. Indeed, this is an adaptive emotional state that helps us plan and prepare for possible threats. But for some people, worry about many different aspects of life (including minor events) becomes chronic, excessive, and unreasonable. In these cases, **generalized anxiety disorder (GAD)** may be diagnosed. *DSM-5* criteria specify that the worry must occur on more days than not for at least 6 months and that it must be experienced as difficult to control (see *DSM-5* criteria box). The worry must be about a number of different events or activities, and its content cannot be exclusively related to the worry associated with another concurrent disorder, such as the possibility of having a panic attack. The subjective experience of excessive worry must also be accompanied by at least three of six other symptoms, as listed in the *DSM-5* box, such as muscle tension or being easily fatigued. There was discussion leading up to *DSM-5* as to whether this is the optimal set of criteria for GAD (e.g., the 6-month duration requirement and the excessive worry requirement; Lee et al., 2009; Ruscio et al., 2005) and whether this is the optimal name for the disorder (versus generalized worry disorder or pathological worry disorder; Andrews et al., 2010). However, ultimately a conservative approach was taken and no changes were made to this diagnosis.

Muscle tension, restlessness, and difficulty concentrating are all symptoms that people with generalized anxiety disorder may have. Such individuals also worry excessively and are hypervigilant for possible signs of threat in their environment.

People suffering from GAD live in a relatively constant, future-oriented mood state of anxious apprehension, chronic tension, worry, and diffuse uneasiness that they cannot control. They also show marked vigilance for possible signs of threat in the environment and frequently engage in subtle avoidance activities such as procrastination, checking, or calling a loved one frequently to see if he or she is safe (Barlow, 2002). Such anxious apprehension also occurs in other anxiety disorders (for example, the person with agoraphobia shows anticipatory anxiety about future panic attacks and about dying, and the person with social phobia is anxious about possible negative social evaluation). But this apprehension is the essence of GAD, leading Barlow and others to refer to GAD as the "basic" anxiety disorder (Roemer et al., 2002; Wells & Butler, 1997).

Watch Philip: Generalized Anxiety Disorder

The nearly constant worries of people with generalized anxiety disorder leave them continually upset and discouraged. The most common areas of worry tend to be

DSM-5 *Criteria for. . .*

Generalized Anxiety Disorder

A. Excessive anxiety and worry (apprehensive expectation), occurring more days than not for at least 6 months, about a number of events or activities (such as work or school performance).

B. The individual finds it difficult to control the worry.

C. The anxiety and worry are associated with three (or more) of the following six symptoms (with at least some symptoms having been present for more days than not for the past 6 months):
Note: Only one item is required in children.

1. Restlessness or feeling keyed up or on edge.
2. Being easily fatigued.
3. Difficulty concentrating or mind going blank.
4. Irritability.
5. Muscle tension.
6. Sleep disturbance (difficulty falling or staying asleep, or restless, unsatisfying sleep).

D. The anxiety, worry, or physical symptoms cause clinically significant distress or impairment in social, occupational, or other important areas of functioning.

E. The disturbance is not attributable to the physiological effects of a substance (e.g., a drug of abuse, a medication) or another medical condition (e.g., hyperthyroidism).

F. The disturbance is not better explained by another mental disorder (e.g., anxiety or worry about having panic attacks in panic disorder, negative evaluation in social anxiety disorder [social phobia], contamination or other obsessions in obsessive-compulsive disorder, separation from attachment figures in separation anxiety disorder, reminders of traumatic events in posttraumatic stress disorder, gaining weight in anorexia nervosa, physical complaints in somatic symptom disorder, perceived appearance flaws in body dysmorphic disorder, having a serious illness in illness anxiety disorder, or the content of delusional beliefs in schizophrenia or delusional disorder).

Source: Reprinted with permission from the *Diagnostic and Statistical Manual of Mental Disorders*, Fifth Edition (Copyright 2013). American Psychiatric Association.

family, work, finances, and personal illness (Roemer et al., 1997). Not only do those with GAD have difficulty making decisions, but after they have managed to make a decision they worry endlessly, even after going to bed, over possible errors and unforeseen circumstances that may prove the decision wrong and lead to disaster. They have no appreciation of the logic by which most of us conclude that it is pointless to torment ourselves about possible outcomes over which we have no control. As two researchers in this area put it, "The result is that they fail to escape the illusory world created in their thoughts and images and rarely experience the present moment that possesses the potential to bring them joy" (Behar & Borkovec, 2006, p. 184). It is not surprising then that those with GAD experience a similar amount of role impairment and lessened quality of life to those with major depression (Hoffman et al., 2008).

The next case is fairly typical of generalized anxiety disorder.

A Graduate Student with GAD

Rodney was a 26-year-old, single graduate student in the social sciences at a prestigious university. He reported that he had had problems with anxiety nearly all his life, but they had become worse since he had left home and gone to an Ivy League college. During the past year his anxiety had seriously interfered with his functioning, and he worried about several different spheres of his life such as his own and his parents' health. During one incident a few months earlier, he had thought that his heart was beating more slowly than usual, and he had experienced some tingling sensations; this led him to worry that he might die. In another incident he had heard his name spoken over a loudspeaker in an airport and had worried that someone at home must be dying. He was also very worried about his future because his anxiety had kept him from completing his master's thesis on time. Rodney also worried excessively about getting a bad grade even though he had never had one either in college or in graduate school. In classes he worried excessively about what the professor and other students thought of him. Although he had a number of friends, he had never had a girlfriend because of his shyness about dating. He had no problem talking or socializing with women as long as it was not defined as a dating situation. He worried that he should date a woman only if he was quite sure, from the outset, that it could be a serious relationship. He also worried excessively that if a woman did not want to date him, it meant that he was boring.

In addition to his worries, which he perceived as uncontrollable, Rodney reported muscle tension and becoming easily fatigued. He also reported great difficulty concentrating and a considerable amount of restlessness and pacing. At times he had difficulty falling asleep if he was particularly anxious, but at other times he slept excessively, in part to escape from his worries. He frequently experienced dizziness and palpitations, and in the past he had had full-blown panic attacks.

Rodney's mother was also quite anxious and had been treated for panic disorder. Rodney was obviously extremely bright and had managed to do very well in school in spite of his lifelong problems with anxiety. But as the pressures of finishing graduate school and starting his career loomed before him, and as he got older and had still never dated, the anxiety became so severe that he sought treatment.

Prevalence, Age of Onset, and Gender Differences

Approximately 3 percent of the population suffers from GAD in any 1-year period and 5.7 percent at some point in their lives (Kessler et al., 1994; Kessler, Berglund, Demler, et al., 2005; Kessler, Chiu, et al., 2005). It also tends to be chronic. One 12-year follow-up study of people diagnosed with GAD found that 42 percent had not remitted 13 years later and of those who had remitted, nearly half had had a recurrence (Bruce et al., 2005; see also Hoffman et al., 2008). After age 50 the disorder seems to disappear for many people (Rubio & Lopez-Ibor, 2007); however, it often tends to be replaced by a somatic symptom disorder and characterized by physical symptoms and health concerns.

GAD is approximately twice as common in women as in men (see Table 6.3 for summaries of gender differences in the different anxiety disorders). Although GAD is quite common, most people with this disorder manage to function (albeit with some role impairment) in spite of their high levels of worry and low perceived well-being (Stein, 2004). They are less likely to go to clinics for psychological treatment than are people with panic disorder or major depressive disorder. However, people with GAD do frequently show up in physicians' offices with medical complaints (such as muscle tension or gastrointestinal and/or cardiac symptoms) and are known to be overusers of health care resources (similar to people with panic disorder; Greenberg et al., 1999; Katon et al., 2002).

Age of onset is often difficult to determine because 60 to 80 percent of people with GAD remember having been anxious nearly all their lives, and many others report a slow and insidious onset (Roemer et al., 2002; Wells & Butler, 1997). However, research has also documented that GAD often develops in older adults, for whom it is the most common anxiety disorder (e.g., Mackenzie et al., 2011; Stein, 2004).

Comorbidity with Other Disorders

Generalized anxiety disorder often co-occurs with other disorders, especially other anxiety and mood disorders such as

Watch   Christy: Generalized Anxiety Disorder with Insomnia

panic disorder, social phobia, specific phobia, PTSD, and major depressive disorder (Kessler, Chiu, et al., 2005; Tyrer & Baldwin, 2006). In addition, many people with GAD (like Rodney) experience occasional panic attacks without qualifying for a diagnosis of panic disorder (Barlow, 2002).

Psychological Causal Factors

A number of psychological factors cause GAD.

THE PSYCHOANALYTIC VIEWPOINT   According to this viewpoint, generalized or free-floating anxiety results from an unconscious conflict between ego and id impulses that is not adequately dealt with because the person's defense mechanisms have either broken down or have never developed. Freud believed that it was primarily sexual and aggressive impulses that had been either blocked from expression or punished upon expression that led to free-floating anxiety. Defense mechanisms may become overwhelmed when a person experiences frequent and extreme levels of anxiety, as might happen if id impulses are frequently blocked from expression (e.g., under periods of prolonged sexual deprivation). According to this view, the primary difference between specific phobias and free-floating anxiety is that in phobias, the defense mechanisms of repression and displacement of an external object or situation actually work, whereas in free-floating anxiety these defense mechanisms do not work, leaving the person anxious nearly all the time. Unfortunately, this viewpoint is not testable and therefore has been largely abandoned among clinical researchers.

PERCEPTIONS OF UNCONTROLLABILITY AND UNPREDICTABILITY   Uncontrollable and unpredictable aversive events are much more stressful than controllable and predictable aversive events, so it is perhaps not surprising that the former create more fear and anxiety, as we discussed with specific and social phobias (Barlow, 2002; Craske & Waters, 2005; Mineka & Oehlberg, 2008). This has led researchers to hypothesize that people with GAD may have a history of experiencing many important events in their lives as unpredictable or uncontrollable. For example, having a boss or spouse who has unpredictable bad moods or outbursts of temper for seemingly trivial reasons might keep a person in a chronic state of anxiety.

Although the unpredictable and uncontrollable events involved in GAD are generally not as severe and traumatic as those involved in the origins of posttraumatic stress disorder (PTSD), some evidence indicates that people with GAD may be more likely to have had a history of trauma in childhood than individuals with several other anxiety disorders (Borkovec et al., 2004; Kendler, Hettema, et al., 2003). Moreover, people with GAD have far less tolerance for uncertainty than nonanxious controls and even people with panic disorder (Dugas et al., 2004, 2005; Koerner & Dugas,

2008). This low tolerance for uncertainty in people with GAD suggests that they are especially disturbed by not being able to predict the future (as none of us can; Roemer et al., 2002). Moreover, the greater the intolerance of uncertainty, the more severe the GAD (Dugas et al., 2007). A similar intolerance for uncertainty also seems to be elevated in people with obsessive-compulsive disorder (e.g., Behar et al., 2008), as discussed later in a section on that topic.

A SENSE OF MASTERY: THE POSSIBILITY OF IMMUNIZING AGAINST ANXIETY   A person's history of control over important aspects of his or her environment is another significant experiential variable strongly affecting reactions to anxiety-provoking situations. Although we cannot study this experimentally in humans, we can learn a lot from laboratory analogue studies in animals. For example, one longitudinal experiment with infant rhesus monkeys found that infant monkeys reared with a sense of mastery and control over their environments for 7 to 10 months later adapted more readily to frightening events and novel anxiety-provoking situations than did monkeys reared in environments that were identical except for the experiences with control (Mineka et al., 1986; see also Craske & Waters, 2005; Mineka & Zinbarg, 2006). In human children, experiences with control and mastery often also occur in the context of the parent–child relationship and so parents' responsiveness to their children's needs directly influences their children's developing sense of mastery (Chorpita, 2001; Craske & Waters, 2005; Mineka & Zinbarg, 2006). Unfortunately, parents of anxious children often have an intrusive, overcontrolling parenting style, which may serve only to promote their children's anxious behaviors by making them think of the world as an unsafe place in which they require protection and have little control themselves (Craske & Waters, 2005).

THE REINFORCING PROPERTIES OF WORRY   The worry process is now considered the central feature of GAD and has been the focus of much research in the past 20 years. One question that researchers have puzzled over is this: If worrying is so anxiety-provoking and distressing, why do people keep doing it? Borkovec and colleagues (Behar & Borkovec, 2006; Borkovec, 1994; Borkovec et al., 2004) investigated both what people with GAD think the benefits of worrying are and what actual functions worry serves. Several of the benefits that people with GAD most commonly think derive from worrying are:

- Superstitious avoidance of catastrophe ("Worrying makes it less likely that the feared event will occur")
- Avoidance of deeper emotional topics ("Worrying about most of the things I worry about is a way to distract myself from worrying about even more emotional things, things that I don't want to think about")

- Coping and preparation ("Worrying about a predicted negative event helps me to prepare for its occurrence"; Borkovec, 1994, pp. 16–17; Borkovec et al., 2004).

Some evidence suggests that for a subset of people with GAD, these positive beliefs about worry play a key role in maintaining high levels of anxiety and worry, especially in the early phases of the development of GAD (Dugas et al., 2007). In addition, exciting new discoveries about the functions that worry actually serves help reveal why the worry process is so self-sustaining. When people with GAD worry, their emotional and physiological responses to aversive imagery are actually suppressed. This suppression of aversive emotional physiological responding may serve to reinforce the process of worry (that is, to increase its probability; Borkovec et al., 2004; McLaughlin et al., 2007). Because worry suppresses physiological responding, it also insulates the person from fully experiencing or processing the topic that she or he is worrying about, and it is known that such full processing is necessary if extinction of that anxiety is to occur. Thus, the threatening meaning of the topic being worried about is maintained (Borkovec et al., 2004; Sibrava & Borkovec, 2006).

THE NEGATIVE CONSEQUENCES OF WORRY Although worry can be reinforcing, some of its effects are clearly negative (Mineka, 2004). For example, worry itself is certainly not an enjoyable activity and can actually lead to a greater sense of danger and anxiety (and lower positive mood) because of all the possible catastrophic outcomes that the worrier envisions (McLaughlin et al., 2007). In addition, people who worry about something tend subsequently to have more negative intrusive thoughts than people who do not worry. For example, in one study in which people were showed a gruesome film, participants later told to worry in verbal form about the film experienced more intrusive images from the film relative to people told to imagine the events from the film (Wells & Papageorgiou, 1995). Perhaps not surprisingly then, people with GAD tend to experience more intense negative emotions when reacting to a sad film (McLaughlin et al., 2007).

Finally, there is now considerable evidence that attempts to control thoughts and worry may paradoxically lead to increased experience of intrusive thoughts and enhanced perception of being unable to control them (Abramowitz et al., 2001; Wells, 1999; Wells & Butler, 1997). Somewhat paradoxically, these intrusive thoughts can serve as further trigger topics for more worry, and a sense of uncontrollability over worry may develop in people caught in this cycle that occurs in GAD. As we have noted, perceptions of uncontrollability are also known to be associated with increased anxiety, so a vicious circle of anxiety, worry, and intrusive thoughts may develop (Mineka, 2004; Mineka & Zinbarg, 2006).

COGNITIVE BIASES FOR THREATENING INFORMATION Not only do people with GAD have frequent frightening thoughts, they also process threatening information in a biased way, perhaps because they have prominent danger schemas. Anxious people tend to preferentially allocate their attention toward threatening cues when both threat and nonthreat cues are present in the environment. Nonanxious people do not show a bias except under limited circumstances, in which they actually may show the opposite bias (MacLeod & Mathews, 2012; Mathews & MacLeod, 2005). Further, this attentional vigilance for threat cues can occur at a very early stage of information processing, even before the information has entered the person's conscious awareness. If a person is already anxious, having her or his attention automatically focused on threat cues in the environment would seem only to maintain the anxiety or even make it worse. Moreover, recent evidence also strongly supports the idea that such attentional biases play a causal role in anxiety as well (MacLeod & Mathews, 2012; Mathews & MacLeod, 2002). For example, several studies have shown that training nonanxious individuals to show an attentional bias toward threat leads to their showing a greater increase in anxiety in stressful situations (MacLeod et al., 2002). Conversely, training anxious people to attend away from threat leads to a decrease in their anxiety symptoms (MacLeod & Mathews, 2012).

Anxious people are also more likely than nonanxious people to think that bad things are likely to happen in the future (MacLeod, 1999), and they have a much stronger tendency to interpret ambiguous information in a threatening way. For example, when clinically anxious subjects read a series of ambiguous sentences (e.g., "The doctor examined little Emma's growth" or "They discussed the priest's convictions"), they are more likely than nonanxious controls to remember the threatening interpretation of each sentence (Eysenck et al., 1991; see also MacLeod et al., 2004; Mathews & MacLeod, 2005; Ouimet et al., 2009). This tendency to interpret ambiguous information negatively has actually been shown to increase anxiety in several situations, including watching a stressful video (Wilson et al., 2006).

In summary, several psychosocial variables seem to promote the onset of generalized anxiety as well as its maintenance. Experience with unpredictable and/or uncontrollable life events may create a vulnerability to anxiety and promote current anxiety. People also believe that worry serves a number of important functions, and it may actually be reinforced because it dampens physiological arousal. But worry also has some negative consequences, including the fact that worry begets further worry and creates a sense of perceived uncontrollability over the worry process, which further enhances anxiety. Finally, anxiety is associated with an automatic attentional and interpretive bias toward threatening information.

Biological Causal Factors

The biological factors involved in GAD can be attributed to genetics, neurotransmitter abnormalities, and neurobiological differences.

GENETIC FACTORS Evidence for genetic factors in GAD is mixed, but there does seem to be a modest heritability, although perhaps smaller than that for most other anxiety disorders except phobias (Hettema, Prescott, & Kendler, 2001). Part of the problem for research in this area has been the evolving nature of our understanding of GAD and what its diagnostic criteria should be. Several large twin studies have revealed that heritability estimates vary as a function of one's definition of GAD, and indicate that 15 to 20 percent of the variance in liability to GAD is due to genetic factors (Hettema, Neale, & Kendler, 2001; Kendler et al., 1992).

The evidence is increasingly strong that GAD and major depressive disorder have a common underlying genetic predisposition (Kendler, Gardner, et al., 2007). What determines whether individuals with a genetic risk for GAD and/or major depression develop one or the other disorder seems to depend entirely on the specific environmental experiences they have (nonshared environment). At least part of this common genetic predisposition for GAD and major depression is best conceptualized as the basic personality trait commonly known as neuroticism (Hettema et al., 2004; Kendler, Gardner, et al., 2007).

NEUROTRANSMITTER AND NEUROHORMONAL ABNORMALITIES

A Functional Deficiency in GABA   In the 1950s, the benzodiazepine category of medications was found to reduce anxiety. This discovery was followed in the 1970s by the finding that these drugs probably exert their effects by stimulating the action of GABA, a neurotransmitter now strongly implicated in generalized anxiety (Davis, 2002; LeDoux, 2002; Nutt et al., 2006). It appears that highly anxious people have a kind of functional deficiency in GABA, which ordinarily plays an important role in the way our brain inhibits anxiety in stressful situations. The benzodiazepine drugs appear to reduce anxiety by increasing GABA activity in certain parts of the brain implicated in anxiety, such as the limbic system, and by suppressing the stress hormone cortisol. Whether the functional deficiency in GABA in anxious people causes their anxiety or occurs as a consequence of it is not yet known, but it does appear that this functional deficiency promotes the maintenance of anxiety.

More recently, researchers have discovered that another neurotransmitter—serotonin—is also involved in modulating generalized anxiety (Goodman, 2004; Nutt et al., 2006). At present, it seems that GABA, serotonin, and perhaps norepinephrine all play a role in anxiety, but the ways in which they interact remain largely unknown (LeDoux, 2002).

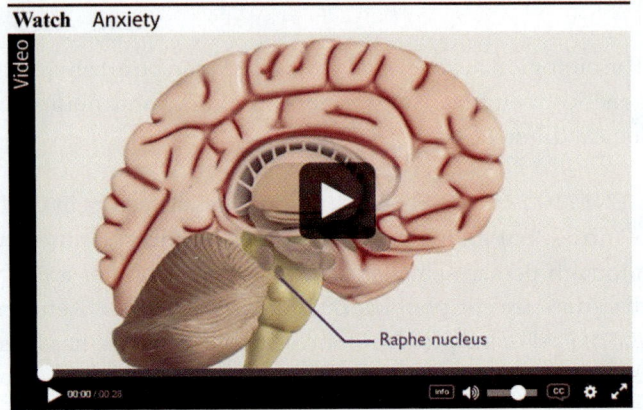

Watch Anxiety

Raphe nucleus

The Corticotropin-Releasing Hormone System and Anxiety
An anxiety-producing hormone called corticotropin-releasing hormone (CRH) has also been strongly implicated as playing an important role in generalized anxiety (and depression; Leonardo & Hen, 2006; Maier & Watkins, 2005). When activated by stress or perceived threat, CRH stimulates the release of ACTH (adrenocorticotropic hormone) from the pituitary gland, which in turn causes release of the stress hormone cortisol from the adrenal gland (Leonardo & Hen, 2006); cortisol helps the body deal with stress. CRH may play an important role in generalized anxiety through its effects on the bed nucleus of the *stria terminalis* (an extension of the amygdala; see Figure 6.1), which is now believed to be an important brain area mediating generalized anxiety (Davis, 2006; Lang et al., 2000).

NEUROBIOLOGICAL DIFFERENCES BETWEEN ANXIETY AND PANIC As we noted at the beginning of this chapter, contemporary theorists are drawing several fundamental distinctions between fear, panic, and anxiety, including their neurobiological bases. Fear and panic involve activation of the fight-or-flight response, and the brain areas and neurotransmitters that seem most strongly implicated in these emotional responses are the amygdala (and locus coeruleus) and the neurotransmitters norepinephrine and serotonin. Generalized anxiety (or anxious apprehension) is a more diffuse emotional state than acute fear or phobia that involves arousal and a preparation for possible impending threat; and the brain area, neurotransmitters, and hormones that seem most strongly implicated are the limbic system (especially the bed nucleus of the stria terminalis, an extension of the amygdala), GABA, and CRH (Davis, 2006; Lang et al., 2000). Although serotonin may play a role in both anxiety and panic, it probably does so in somewhat different ways. Recently, people with GAD have been found to have a smaller left hippocampal region similar to what is seen with major depression (Hettema et al., 2012); this may represent a common risk factor for the two disorders.

Treatments

As noted earlier, most treatment for GAD involves medication or cognitive-behavioral approaches.

MEDICATIONS Many clients with generalized anxiety disorder consult family physicians, seeking relief from their "nerves" or anxieties or their various functional (psychogenic) physical problems. Most often in such cases, medications from the benzodiazepine (anxiolytic) category such as Xanax or Klonopin are used—and misused—for tension relief, reduction of other somatic symptoms, and relaxation. Their effects on worry and other psychological symptoms are not as great. Moreover, they can create physiological and psychological dependence and withdrawal and are therefore difficult to taper. A newer medication called buspirone (from a different medication category) is also effective, and it is neither sedating nor does it lead to physiological dependence. It also has greater effects on psychic anxiety than do the benzodiazepines. However, it may take 2 to 4 weeks to show results (Roy-Byrne & Cowley, 2002, 2007). Several categories of antidepressant medications like those used in the treatment of panic disorder are also useful in the treatment of GAD, and they also seem to have a greater effect on the psychological symptoms of GAD than do the benzodiazepines (Goodman, 2004; Roy-Byrne & Cowley, 2002, 2007). However, they also take several weeks before their effects are apparent.

COGNITIVE-BEHAVIORAL TREATMENT CBT for generalized anxiety disorder has become increasingly effective as clinical researchers have refined the techniques used. It usually involves a combination of behavioral techniques, such as training in applied muscle relaxation, and cognitive restructuring techniques aimed at reducing distorted cognitions and information-processing biases associated with GAD as well as reducing catastrophizing about minor events (Barlow et al., 2007; Borkovec, 2006). GAD initially appeared to be among the most difficult of the anxiety disorders to treat, and to some extent this is still true. However, advances have been made, and a quantitative review of many controlled studies showed that CBT approaches resulted in large changes on most symptoms measured (Mitte, 2005). The magnitude of the changes seen with cognitive-behavioral treatment was at least as large as those seen with benzodiazepines, and it led to fewer dropouts (i.e., it was better tolerated). Finally, CBT has also been found to be useful in helping people who have used benzodiazepines for over a year to successfully taper their medications (Gosselin et al., 2006).

CBT for Rodney's GAD

The case of Rodney, the graduate student with GAD discussed earlier, serves as an example of the success of cognitive-behavioral therapy with this condition. Before receiving CBT, Rodney had seen someone at a student counseling center for several months, but he hadn't found the "talk therapy" very useful. He had heard that CBT might be useful and had sought such treatment. He was in treatment for about 6 months, during which time he found training in deep muscle relaxation helpful in reducing his overall level of tension. Cognitive restructuring helped reduce his worry levels about all spheres of his life. He still had problems with procrastinating when he had deadlines, but this too was improving. He also began socializing more frequently and had tentatively begun dating when treatment ended for financial reasons. He could now see that if a woman didn't want to go out with him again, this did not mean that he was boring but simply that they might not be a good match.

in review

- What are the key characteristics of GAD, and what is its typical age of onset?
- Describe the various psychosocial causal factors that may be involved in GAD, and indicate what functions worry may serve for those with GAD.
- What are the major biological causal factors in GAD?
- Compare and contrast the biological and cognitive-behavioral treatments for GAD.

Obsessive-Compulsive and Related Disorders

6.7   **Describe the clinical features of obsessive-compulsive disorder and how it is treated.**

Obsessive-compulsive and related disorders used to be classified in the *DSM* as anxiety disorders; however, as of *DSM-5* they have been classified separately as their own type of disorder (see the box on Thinking Critically about

DSM-5). This new category includes not only OCD but also body dysmorphic disorder, **hoarding disorder**, excoriation (skin-picking) disorder, and trichotillomania (compulsive hair pulling).

Obsessive-Compulsive Disorder

Obsessive-compulsive disorder is defined by the occurrence of both obsessive thoughts and compulsive behaviors performed in an attempt to neutralize such thoughts (see the *DSM-5* box for diagnostic criteria). **Obsessions** are persistent and recurrent intrusive thoughts, images, or impulses that are experienced as disturbing, inappropriate, and uncontrollable. People who have such obsessions actively try to resist or suppress them or to neutralize them with some other thought or action. **Compulsions** involve overt repetitive behaviors that are performed as lengthy rituals (such as hand washing, checking, putting things in order over and over again). Compulsions may also involve more covert mental rituals (such as counting, praying, or saying certain words silently over and over again). A person with OCD usually feels driven to perform this compulsive, ritualistic behavior in response to an obsession, and there are often very rigid rules regarding exactly how the compulsive behavior should be performed. The compulsive behaviors are performed with the goal of preventing or reducing distress or preventing some dreaded event or situation. OCD is often one of the most disabling mental disorders in that it leads to a lower quality of life and a great deal of functional impairment (Stein et al., 2009).

DSM-5   Thinking Critically about *DSM-5*

Why Is OCD No Longer Considered to Be an Anxiety Disorder?

In *DSM-5*, obsessive-compulsive disorder was removed from the anxiety disorders category and placed into a new category called "obsessive-compulsive and related disorders." (As you already know from Chapter 5, PTSD was also removed and put into a new category called "trauma and stressor-related disorders.")

One reason for moving OCD into the new category was that anxiety is not generally used as an indicator of OCD severity. Indeed, for people with certain forms of OCD such as symmetry-related obsessions and compulsions, anxiety is not even a prominent symptom. It was also noted that anxiety occurs in a wide range of disorders, so the presence of some anxiety is not a valid reason to regard OCD as an anxiety disorder. Indeed D. J. Stein et al. (2010) wrote that "the highly stereotyped, driven, repetitive, and nonfunctional quality of compulsive behaviors differentiate OCD from normal acts and from the types of avoidance that occur in other anxiety disorders" (p. 497).

,   Yet another reason is that the neurobiological underpinnings of OCD appear to be rather different from those of other anxiety disorders, focusing on frontal-striatal neural circuitry including the orbitofrontal cortex, anterior cingulate cortex, and striatum (especially the caudate nucleus). Studies examining the "OCD-related disorders" such as body dysmorphic disorder (obsessing about perceived or imagined flaws in physical appearance) and trichotillomania (chronic hair pulling) also suggest shared involvement of frontal-striatal neural circuitry. Finally, other anxiety disorders respond to a wider range of medication treatments than does OCD, which seems to respond selectively to SSRIs.

How compelling do these reasons sound to you? What kinds of research findings might further support the grouping of OCD with related disorders such as hoarding or trichotillomania? On the contrary, what research findings might incline you to think that it was wrong to remove OCD from the anxiety disorders category?

Watch   Dave: Obsessive-Compulsive -Disorder

In addition, the person must recognize that the obsession is the product of his or her own mind rather than being imposed from without (as might occur in schizophrenia). However, there is a continuum of "insight" among persons with OCD about exactly how senseless and excessive their obsessions and compulsions are (Ruscio et al., 2010). In a minority of cases, this insight is absent most of the time. Most of us have experienced minor obsessive thoughts, such as whether we remembered to lock the door or turn the stove off. In addition, most of us occasionally engage in repetitive or stereotyped behavior, such as checking the stove or the lock on the door or stepping over cracks on a sidewalk. One recent study found that more than 25 percent of people in the United States report experiencing obsessions or compulsions at some time in their lives (Ruscio et al., 2010). With OCD, however, the thoughts are excessive and much more persistent and distressing, and the associated compulsive acts interfere with everyday activities. Diagnosis requires that obsessions and compulsions take at least 1 hour per day, and in severe cases they may take most of the person's waking hours. It is important to note that normal and abnormal obsessions and compulsive behaviors exist on a continuum, differing in the frequency and intensity of the obsessions and in the degrees to which the obsessions and compulsions are resisted and are troubling (Steketee & Barlow, 2002).

Many *obsessive thoughts* involve contamination fears, fears of harming oneself or others, and pathological doubt. Other fairly common themes are concerns about or need for symmetry (e.g., having magazines on a table arranged in a way that is "exactly right"), sexual obsessions, and obsessions concerning religion or aggression. These themes are quite consistent cross-culturally and across the life span (Steketee & Barlow, 2002). Obsessive thoughts involving themes of violence or aggression might include a wife being obsessed with the idea that she might poison her husband or child, or a daughter constantly imagining pushing her mother down a flight of stairs. Even though such obsessive thoughts are very rarely acted on, they remain a source of often excruciating torment to a person plagued with them. The following case of Mark is fairly typical of severe OCD.

Obsessions about Confessing and Compulsive Checking

Mark was a 28-year-old single male who, at the time he entered treatment, suffered from severe obsessive thoughts and images about causing harm to others such as running over pedestrians while he was driving. He also had severe obsessions that he would commit a crime such as robbing a store of a large amount of money or poisoning family members or friends. These obsessions were accompanied by lengthy and excessive checking rituals. For example, one day when he drove, he began obsessing that he had caused an accident and hit a pedestrian at an intersection, and he felt compelled to spend several hours driving and walking around all parts of that intersection to find evidence of the accident.

At the time Mark went to an anxiety disorder clinic, he was no longer able to live by himself after having lived alone for several years since college. He was a very bright young man with considerable artistic talent. He had finished college at a prestigious school for the arts and had launched a successful career as a young artist when the obsessions began in his early 20s. At first, they were focused on the possibility that he would be implicated in some crime that he had not committed; later, they evolved to the point where he was afraid that he might actually commit a crime and confess to it. The checking rituals and avoidance of all places where such confessions might occur eventually led to his having to give up his career and his own apartment and move back in with his family.

At the time he presented for treatment, Mark's obsessions about harming others and confessing to crimes (whether or not he had committed them) were so severe that he had virtually confined himself to his room at his parents' house. Indeed, he could leave his room only if he had a tape recorder with him so that he would have a record of any crimes he confessed to out loud because he did not trust his own memory. The clinic was several hours' drive from his home; his mother usually had to drive because of his obsessions about causing accidents with pedestrians or moving vehicles and because the associated checking rituals could punctuate any trip with several very long stops. He also could not speak at all on the phone for fear of confessing some crime that he had (or had not) committed, and he could not mail a letter for the same reason. He also could not go into a store alone or into public bathrooms, where he feared he might write a confession on the wall and be caught and punished.

As we have noted, people with OCD feel compelled to perform acts repeatedly that often seem pointless and absurd even to them and that they in some sense do not want to perform. There are five primary types of compulsive rituals: cleaning (hand washing and showering), checking, repeating, ordering or arranging, and counting (Antony et al., 1998; Mathews, 2009), and many people exhibit multiple kinds of rituals. For a smaller number of people, the compulsions are to perform various everyday acts (such as eating or dressing) extremely slowly (primary obsessional slowness), and for others the compulsions are to have things exactly symmetrical or "evened up" (Mathews, 2009; Steketee & Barlow, 2002).

DSM-5 *Criteria for. . .*

Obsessive-Compulsive Disorder

A. Presence of obsessions, compulsions, or both: Obsessions are defined by (1) and (2):

1. Recurrent and persistent thoughts, urges, or images that are experienced, at some time during the disturbance, as intrusive and unwanted, and that in most individuals cause marked anxiety or distress.

2. The individual attempts to ignore or suppress such thoughts, urges, or images, or to neutralize them with some other thought or action (i.e., by performing a compulsion).

Compulsions are defined by (1) and (2):

1. Repetitive behaviors (e.g., hand washing, ordering, checking) or mental acts (e.g., praying, counting, repeating words silently) that the individual feels driven to perform in response to an obsession or according to rules that must be applied rigidly.

2. The behaviors or mental acts are aimed at preventing or reducing anxiety or distress, or preventing some dreaded event or situation; however, these behaviors or mental acts are not connected in a realistic way with what they are designed to neutralize or prevent, or are clearly excessive.

Note: Young children may not be able to articulate the aims of these behaviors or mental acts.

B. The obsessions or compulsions are time-consuming (e.g., take more than 1 hour per day) or cause clinically significant distress or impairment in social, occupational, or other important areas of functioning.

C. The obsessive-compulsive symptoms are not attributable to the physiological effects of a substance (e.g., a drug of abuse, a medication) or another medical condition.

D. The disturbance is not better explained by the symptoms of another mental disorder (e.g., excessive worries, as in generalized anxiety disorder; preoccupation with appearance, as in body dysmorphic disorder; difficulty discarding or parting with possessions, as in hoarding disorder; hair pulling, as in trichotillomania [hair-pulling disorder]; skin picking, as in excoriation [skin-picking] disorder; stereotypies, as in stereotypic movement disorder; ritualized eating behavior, as in eating disorders; preoccupation with substances or gambling, as in substance-related and addictive disorders; preoccupation with having an illness, as in illness anxiety disorder; sexual urges or fantasies, as in paraphilic disorders; impulses, as in disruptive, impulse-control, and conduct disorders; guilty ruminations, as in major depressive disorder; thought insertion or delusional preoccupations, as in schizophrenia spectrum and other psychotic disorders; or repetitive patterns of behavior, as in autism spectrum disorder).

Source: Reprinted with permission from the *Diagnostic and Statistical Manual of Mental Disorders*, Fifth Edition (Copyright 2013). American Psychiatric Association.

People who suffer from OCD often exhibit repetitive behaviors that are structured around rigid rules for performance. For example, this person turns the key in the lock a set number of times every time she leaves the house.

Washing or cleaning rituals vary from relatively mild ritual-like behavior such as spending 15 to 20 minutes washing one's hands after going to the bathroom, to more extreme behavior such as washing one's hands with disinfectants for hours every day to the point where the hands bleed. Checking rituals also vary in severity from relatively mild (such as checking all the lights, appliances, and locks two or three times before leaving the house) to very extreme (such as going back to an intersection where one thinks one may have run over a pedestrian and spending hours checking for any sign of the imagined accident, much as Mark does in the case study). Both cleaning and checking rituals are often performed a specific number of times and thus also involve repetitive counting. The performance of the compulsive act or the ritualized series of acts usually brings a feeling of reduced tension and satisfaction, as well as a sense of control, although this anxiety relief is typically fleeting. This is why the same rituals need to be repeated over and over (Purdon, 2009; Steketee & Barlow, 2002).

Prevalence, Age of Onset, and Gender Differences

Approximately 2 to 3 percent of people meet criteria for OCD at some point in their lifetime, and approximately 1 percent meet criteria in a given year (Ruscio et al., 2010). Over 90 percent of treatment-seeking people with OCD experience both obsessions and compulsions (Foa & Kozak, 1995; Franklin & Foa, 2007). When mental rituals and compulsions such as counting are included as compulsive behaviors, this figure jumps to 98 percent.

Howard Stern, a famous radio personality and author, as with other people who have suffered from OCD, found relief in a compulsive act or ritualized series of acts to bring about a feeling of reduced tension and a sense of control. In his book *Miss America*, Stern describes behaviors such as turning pages in magazines only with his pinky finger, walking through doors with the right side of his body leading, and flipping through television stations in a particular order before turning the set off.

Divorced (or separated) and unemployed people are somewhat overrepresented among people with OCD (Torres et al., 2006), which is not surprising given the great difficulties this disorder creates for interpersonal and occupational functioning. Some studies showed little or no gender difference in adults, which would make OCD quite different from most of the rest of the anxiety disorders. However, one British epidemiological study found a gender ratio of 1.4 to 1 (women to men; Torres et al., 2006). OCD typically begins in late adolescence or early adulthood, but also can occur in children, where its symptoms are strikingly similar to those of adults (Poulton et al., 2009; Torres et al., 2006). Childhood or early adolescent onset is more common in boys than in girls and is often associated with greater severity (Lomax et al., 2009) and greater heritability (Grisham et al., 2008). In most cases the

disorder has a gradual onset, and once it becomes a serious condition, it tends to be chronic, although the severity of symptoms sometimes waxes and wanes over time (Mataix-Cols et al., 2002).

Many of us show some compulsive behavior, but people with OCD feel compelled to perform repeatedly some action in response to an obsession, in order to reduce the anxiety or discomfort created by the obsession. Although the person may realize that the behavior is excessive or unreasonable, he or she does not feel able to control the urge. Obsessive-compulsive hand washers may spend hours a day washing and may even use abrasive cleansers to the point that their hands bleed.

Comorbidity with Other Disorders

OCD frequently co-occurs with other anxiety disorders, most commonly social phobia, panic disorder, GAD, and PTSD (Kessler, Chiu, Demler, et al., 2005; Mathews, 2009). Moreover, approximately 25 to 50 percent of people with OCD experience major depression at some time in their lives and as many as 80 percent experience significant depressive symptoms (Steketee & Barlow, 2002; Torres et al., 2006), often at least partly in response to having OCD.

Psychological Causal Factors

The following psychological factors may cause obsessive-compulsive disorder.

OCD AS LEARNED BEHAVIOR The dominant behavioral or learning view of obsessive-compulsive disorder is derived from Mowrer's two-process theory of avoidance learning (1947). According to this theory, neutral stimuli become associated with frightening thoughts or experiences through classical conditioning and come to elicit anxiety. For example, touching a doorknob or shaking hands might become associated with the "scary" idea of contamination. Once having made this association, the person may discover that the anxiety produced by shaking hands or touching a doorknob can be reduced by hand washing.

Washing his or her hands extensively reduces the anxiety, and so the washing response is reinforced, which makes it more likely to occur again in the future when other situations evoke anxiety about contamination (Rachman & Shafran, 1998). Once learned, such avoidance responses are extremely resistant to extinction (Mineka & Zinbarg, 2006). Moreover, any stressors that raise anxiety levels can lead to a heightened frequency of avoidance responses in animals or compulsive rituals in humans (Cromer et al., 2007).

Several classic experiments conducted by Rachman and Hodgson (1980) supported this theory. They found that for most people with OCD, exposure to a situation that provoked their obsession (e.g., a doorknob or toilet seat for someone with obsessions about contamination) did indeed produce distress, which would continue for a moderate amount of time and then gradually dissipate. If the person was allowed to engage in the compulsive ritual immediately after the provocation, however, her or his anxiety would generally decrease rapidly (although only temporarily) and therefore reinforce the compulsive ritual.

This model predicts, then, that exposure to feared objects or situations should be useful in treating OCD if the exposure is followed by prevention of the ritual, enabling the person to see that the anxiety will subside naturally in time without the ritual (see also Rachman & Shafran, 1998). This is indeed the core of the most effective form of behavior therapy for OCD, as discussed later. Thus, the early behavioral model has been very useful in helping us understand what factors maintain obsessive-compulsive behavior, and it has also generated an effective form of treatment. However, it has not been so helpful in explaining why people with OCD develop obsessions in the first place and why some people never develop compulsive behaviors.

OCD AND PREPAREDNESS The preparedness concept described earlier that considers the evolutionarily adaptive nature of fear and anxiety for our early ancestors also can help us to understand the occurrence and persistence of OCD (De Silva, Rachman, & Seligman, 1977; Rapoport, 1989). The fact that many people with OCD have obsessions and compulsions focused on dirt, contamination, and other potentially dangerous situations has led many researchers to conclude that these features of the disorder likely have deep evolutionary roots (Mineka & Zinbarg, 1996, 2006). In addition, some theorists have argued that the displacement activities that many species of animals engage in under situations of conflict or high arousal resemble the compulsive rituals seen in obsessive-compulsive disorder (Craske, 1999; Mineka & Zinbarg, 1996; Rapoport, 1989; Winslow & Insel, 1991). Displacement activities often involve grooming (such as a bird preening its feathers) or nesting under conditions of high conflict or frustration. They may therefore be related to the distress-induced grooming (such as washing) or tidying rituals seen in people with OCD, which are often provoked by obsessive thoughts that elicit anxiety.

COGNITIVE CAUSAL FACTORS

The Effects of Attempting to Suppress Obsessive Thoughts Quick, don't think about a white bear! Gotcha. When most people attempt to suppress unwanted thoughts they sometimes experience a paradoxical increase in those thoughts later (Wegner, 1994). As already noted, people with normal and abnormal obsessions differ primarily in the degree to which they resist their own thoughts and find them unacceptable. Thus, one factor contributing to the frequency of obsessive thoughts, and the negative moods with which they are often associated, may be these attempts to suppress them (similar to what was discussed earlier about the effects of attempts to control worry in people with GAD). For example, when people with OCD are asked to record intrusive thoughts in a diary, both on days when they were told to try to suppress those thoughts and on days without instructions to suppress, they reported approximately twice as many intrusive thoughts on the days when they were attempting to suppress them (Salkovskis & Kirk, 1997). In addition, thought suppression leads to a more general increase in obsessive-compulsive symptoms beyond just the frequency of obsessions (Purdon, 2004). Finally, naturalistic diary studies of people with OCD reveal that they engage in frequent, strenuous, and time-consuming attempts to control the intrusive thoughts, although they are generally not effective in doing so (Purdon et al., 2007).

Quick, don't think about a white bear!

Appraisals of Responsibility for Intrusive Thoughts Salkovskis (e.g., 1989), Rachman (1997), and other cognitive theorists have distinguished between obsessive or intrusive thoughts per se and the negative automatic thoughts and catastrophic appraisals that people have about experiencing such thoughts. For example, people with OCD often seem to have an inflated sense of responsibility. In turn, in some vulnerable people, this inflated sense of responsibility can be associated with beliefs that simply having a thought about doing something (e.g., a mother's thought about harming her infant) is morally equivalent to actually having done it, or that thinking about the behavior increases the chances of actually doing so. This is known as *thought–action fusion* (Berle & Starcevic, 2005; Rachman et al., 2006). This inflated sense of responsibility for the harm they may cause can motivate compulsive behaviors to try to reduce the likelihood of anything harmful happening (Rachman et al., 2006). Thus, part of what differentiates normal people who have obsessions and can ordinarily dismiss them from people with OCD is this sense of responsibility that makes the thought so concerning to them.

Cognitive Biases and Distortions   Cognitive factors have also been implicated in OCD. More specifically, people with OCD have an attentional bias toward disturbing material relevant to their obsessive concerns, much as occurs in the other anxiety disorders (McNally, 2000; Mineka et al., 2003). They also have difficulty blocking out negative, irrelevant input or distracting information, so they may attempt to suppress negative thoughts stimulated by this information (McNally, 2000). As we have noted, trying to suppress negative thoughts may paradoxically increase their frequency. Moreover, those with OCD have low confidence in their memory ability (especially for situations they feel responsible for), which may contribute to their repeating their ritualistic behaviors over and over again (Cougle et al., 2007; Dar et al., 2000). An additional factor contributing to their repetitive behavior is that people with OCD have deficits in their ability to inhibit both motor responses (Morein-Zamir et al., 2010) and irrelevant information (Bannon et al., 2008).

Biological Causal Factors

In recent years there has been an increase in research on the possible biological basis for OCD, ranging from studies about its genetic basis to studies of abnormalities in brain function and neurotransmitter abnormalities. The evidence accumulating from all three kinds of studies suggests that biological causal factors may play a stronger causal role for OCD relative to the other disorders discussed in this chapter.

GENETIC FACTORS   Evidence from twin studies reveals a moderately high concordance rate for OCD for monozygotic twins and a lower rate for dizygotic twins. One review of 14 published studies included 80 monozygotic pairs of twins, of whom 54 were concordant for the diagnosis of OCD, and 29 pairs of dizygotic twins, of whom 9 were concordant. This is consistent with a moderate genetic

heritability, although it may be at least partially a nonspecific "neurotic" predisposition (Hanna, 2000; van Grootheest et al., 2007). Consistent with twin studies, most family studies have found 3 to 12 times higher rates of OCD in first-degree relatives of OCD clients than would be expected from current estimates of the prevalence of OCD (Grabe et al., 2006; Hettema, Prescott, & Kendler, 2001). Finally, evidence also shows that early-onset OCD has a higher genetic loading than later-onset OCD (Grisham et al., 2008; Mundo et al., 2006).

Further compelling evidence of a genetic contribution to some forms of OCD concerns a type of OCD that often starts in childhood and is characterized by chronic motor tics (Lochner & Stein, 2003). This form of tic-related OCD is linked to Tourette's syndrome, a disorder characterized by severe chronic motor and vocal tics that is known to have a substantial genetic basis (see Chapter 15). For example, one study found that 23 percent of first-degree relatives of people with Tourette's syndrome had diagnosable OCD even though Tourette's syndrome itself is very rare (Pauls et al., 1986, 1991, 1995).

Finally, in recent years a number of molecular genetic studies have begun to examine the association of OCD with specific genetic polymorphisms (naturally occurring variations of genes; Grisham et al., 2008; Mundo et al., 2006; Stewart et al., 2007). Preliminary findings indicate that different genetic polymorphisms are implicated in OCD with Tourette's syndrome and in OCD without Tourette's syndrome, suggesting that these two forms of OCD are at least partially distinguishable at a genetic level (Stewart et al., 2007).

OCD AND THE BRAIN   The search for brain abnormalities in OCD has been intense in the past 30 years as advances have been made in brain-imaging techniques. This research has revealed that abnormalities occur primarily in certain cortical and subcortical structures such as the *basal ganglia*. The basal ganglia are in turn linked at the amygdala to the limbic system, which controls emotional behaviors. Findings from a good number of studies using PET scans have shown that people with OCD have abnormally high levels of activity in two parts of the frontal cortex (the orbital frontal cortex and the cingulate cortex/gyrus), which are also linked to the limbic area. People with OCD also have abnormally high levels of activity in the subcortical caudate nucleus, which is part of the basal ganglia (see the three-dimensional depiction of the relevant brain parts in Figure 6.3). These primitive brain circuits are involved in executing primitive patterns of behavior such as those involved in sex, aggression, and hygiene concerns. Indeed, activity in some of these areas is further increased when symptoms are provoked by relevant stimuli that activate obsessive thoughts (e.g., dirt; Evans, Lewis, & Iobst, 2004; Rauch & Savage, 2000). Studies have also shown partial normalization of at least some of these abnormalities

Figure 6.3 Neurophysiological Mechanisms for Obsessive-Compulsive Disorder

This three-dimensional view illustrates parts of the brain implicated in OCD. The overlying cerebral cortex has been made transparent so that the underlying areas can be seen. The orbital frontal cortex, cingulate gyrus/cortex, and basal ganglia (especially the caudate nucleus) are the brain structures most often implicated in OCD. Increased metabolic activity has been found in each of these three areas in people with OCD.

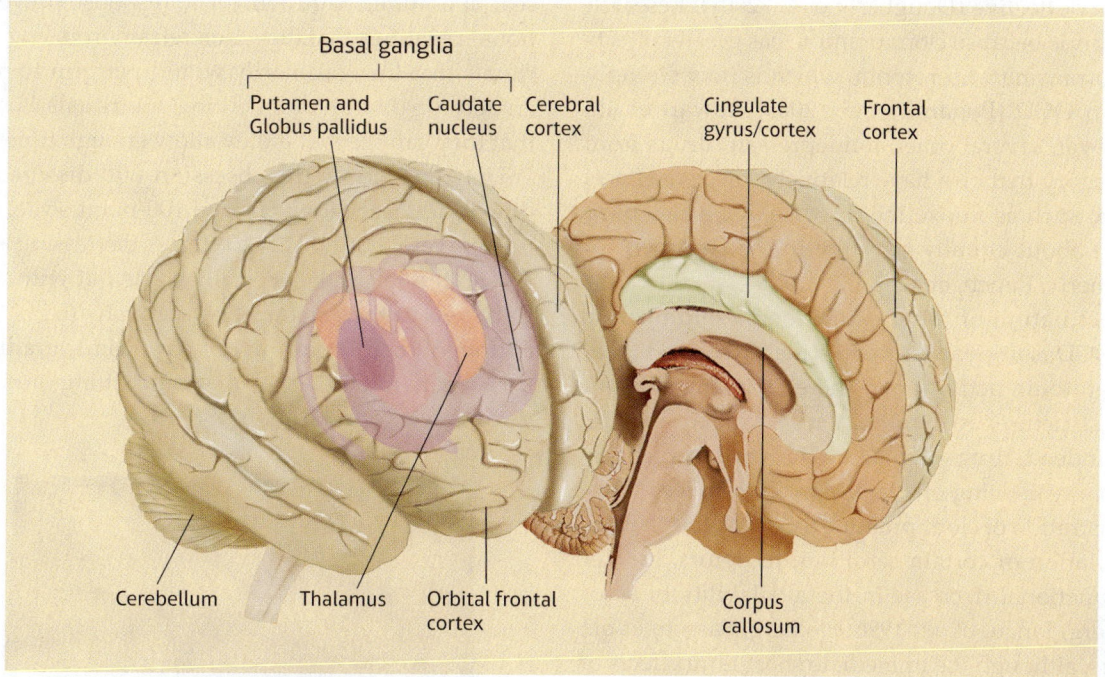

with successful treatment through either medication or behavior therapy (Baxter et al., 2000; Saxena et al., 2002, 2009).

The orbital frontal cortex seems to be where primitive urges regarding sex, aggression, hygiene, and danger come from (the "stuff of obsessions"; Baxter et al., 1991, p. 116). These urges are ordinarily filtered by the caudate nucleus as they travel through the cortico–basal–ganglionic–thalamic circuit, allowing only the strongest to pass on to the thalamus. The caudate nucleus or corpus striatum (part of the set of structures called the basal ganglia, which are involved in the execution of voluntary, goal-directed movements) is part of an important neural circuit linking the orbital frontal cortex to the thalamus. The basal ganglia also include two other structures—the globus pallidus and the substantia nigra—that are also involved in this cortico–basal–ganglionic–thalamic circuit. The thalamus is an important relay station that receives nearly all sensory input and passes it back to the cerebral cortex.

This cortico–basal–ganglionic–thalamic circuit is normally involved in the preparation of complex sets of interrelated behavioral responses used in specific situations such as those involved in territorial or social concerns. Several theories have been proposed regarding what the sources of dysfunction in this circuit are. For example, Baxter and colleagues (1991, 2000) cited evidence that when this circuit is not functioning properly, inappropriate behavioral responses may occur, including repeated sets of behaviors stemming from territorial and social concerns (e.g., checking and aggressive

behavior) and from hygiene concerns (e.g., cleaning). Thus, the overactivation of the orbital frontal cortex, which stimulates the "stuff of obsessions," combined with a dysfunctional interaction among the orbital frontal cortex, the corpus striatum or caudate nucleus, and the thalamus (which is downstream from the corpus striatum) may be the central component of the brain dysfunction in OCD. According to Baxter's theory, the dysfunctions in this circuit in turn prevent people with OCD from showing the normal inhibition of sensations, thoughts, and behaviors that would occur if the circuit were functioning properly. In this case, impulses toward aggression, sex, hygiene, and danger that most people keep under control with relative ease "leak through" as obsessions and distract people with OCD from ordinary goal-directed behavior. Evidence suggests that at least part of the reason that this circuit does not function properly may be due to abnormalities in white matter in some of these brain areas; white matter is involved in connectivity among various brain structures (Szeszko et al., 2004; Yoo et al., 2007).

Considering these problems, Baxter and colleagues proposed that we can begin to understand how the prolonged and repeated bouts of obsessive-compulsive behavior in people with OCD may occur (Baxter et al., 1991, 1992, 2000). Several other slightly different theories have also been proposed as to the exact nature or source of the dysfunctions, but there seems to be general agreement about most of the brain areas involved (Friedlander & Desrocher, 2006; Harrison et al., 2009; Saxena & Rauch, 2000).

NEUROTRANSMITTER ABNORMALITIES Pharmacological studies of causal factors in OCD intensified with the discovery in the 1970s that a tricyclic drug called clomipramine (Anafranil) is often effective in the treatment of OCD even though other tricyclic antidepressants are generally not very effective (Dougherty et al., 2007). Research shows that this is because clomipramine has greater effects on the neurotransmitter serotonin, which is now strongly implicated in OCD (Pogarell et al., 2003; Stewart et al., 2009). Moreover, several other antidepressant drugs from the SSRI category that also have relatively selective effects on serotonin, such as fluoxetine (Prozac), have also been shown to be about equally effective in the treatment of OCD (Dougherty, Rauch, et al., 2002, 2007).

The exact nature of the dysfunction in serotonergic systems in OCD is unclear. Current evidence suggests that increased serotonin activity and increased sensitivity of some brain structures to serotonin are involved in OCD symptoms. Indeed, drugs that stimulate serotonergic systems lead to a worsening of symptoms. In this view, long-term administration of clomipramine (or fluoxetine) causes a downregulation of certain serotonin receptors, further causing a functional decrease in the availability of serotonin (Dolberg, Iancu, et al., 1996; Dolberg, Sasson, et al., 1996). That is, although the immediate short-term effects of clomipramine or fluoxetine may be to increase serotonin levels (and exacerbate OCD symptoms too), the long-term effects are quite different. This is consistent with the finding that these drugs must be taken for at least 6 to 12 weeks before significant improvement in OCD symptoms occurs (Baxter et al., 2000; Dougherty, Rauch, et al., 2002, 2007). However, it is also becoming clear that dysfunction in serotonergic systems cannot by itself fully explain this complex disorder. Other neurotransmitter systems (such as the dopaminergic, GABA, and glutamate systems) also seem to be involved, although their role is not yet well understood (Dougherty et al., 2007; Stewart et al., 2009).

In summary, a substantial body of evidence now implicates biological causal factors in OCD. This evidence comes from genetic studies, from studies of abnormalities in brain function, and from studies of neurotransmitter abnormalities. Although the exact nature of these factors and how they are interrelated is not yet fully understood, major research efforts that are currently under way are sure to enhance our understanding of this disorder, which is often very serious and disabling.

Treatments

Treatment for OCD includes behavioral and cognitive-behavioral approaches as well as medication.

BEHAVIORAL AND COGNITIVE-BEHAVIORAL TREATMENTS The most effective treatment for OCD is a behavioral treatment called **exposure and response prevention** (Franklin & Foa, 2007; Stein et al., 2009). The exposure component involves having individuals with OCD repeatedly expose themselves (either in guided fantasy or directly) to stimuli that provoke their obsessions (e.g., for someone with contamination fears this may involve touching a toilet seat in a public bathroom). The response prevention component requires that they then refrain from engaging in the rituals that they ordinarily would perform to reduce their anxiety or distress. Preventing the rituals is essential so that they can see that if they allow enough time to pass, the anxiety created by the obsession will dissipate naturally down to at least 40 to 50 on a 100-point scale, even if this takes several hours. This is often as distressing as it sounds, and so the treatment typically starts out with manageable first steps in the person's fear hierarchy (e.g., touching the bottom of their shoe) and only over time, gradually works up to more intense exposures (e.g., sitting on the floor of a dirty public restroom).

Exposure and response prevention treatment for OCD involves having the patient encounter the source of their obsessions, such as the germs imagined to lurk in a dirty bathroom, and preventing them from engaging in compulsive behaviors, such as repetitive cleaning. The treatment is often not fun for the patient, but can be very effective in decreasing OCD symptoms.

In intensive versions of this treatment, clients who, for example, are used to spending 2 to 3 hours a day showering and hand washing may be asked to not shower at all for 3 days at a time (and when they finally do, to spend no more than 10 minutes in the shower). Later in treatment they are encouraged to shower for only 10 minutes a day, with no more than five 30-second hand washings at meal-times, after bathroom use, and after touching clearly soiled objects. In addition to the exposures conducted during therapy sessions, "homework" is liberally assigned. For example, on one occasion well into treatment, a therapist drove a patient who was terrified of being contaminated by "dog dirt," bathroom germs, garbage, and dead animals in the road to a place where she had observed a dead cat on the roadside. The therapist insisted that the patient approach the "smelly" corpse, touch it with the sole of her shoe, and then touch her shoe. A pebble lying close by and a stick with which she had touched the cat were presented to the patient with the instruction that she keep them in her pocket and touch them frequently throughout the day. (Franklin & Foa, 2008, pp. 192–205).

Although some people refuse such treatment or drop out early, most who stick with it show a 50 to 70 percent reduction in symptoms (Abramowitz et al., 2009; Steketee, 1993), as well as improvement in quality of life (Diefenbach et al., 2007). Approximately 50 percent are much improved or very much improved, and another 25 percent are moderately improved; about 76 percent maintain their gains at several-year follow-ups. These results are superior to those obtained with medication (Abramowitz et al., 2009; Franklin & Foa, 2008). There is also evidence that D-cycloserine (the drug known to facilitate extinction of fear) enhances the effectiveness of CBT; however, this enhancement is blocked if the person is also taking an antidepressant (Andersson et al., 2015). Finally, during the past 20 years a form of cognitive-behavioral therapy has also been developed by Salkovskis and colleagues (Salkovskis & Wahl, 2003). Some of the goals were to determine whether it might help a higher percentage of people with OCD, or help increase the degree of symptom improvement, or decrease dropout rates. Current evidence suggests that this form of treatment can also be quite effective, but unfortunately it has not been shown to be superior to exposure and response prevention therapy in any of the predicted ways (Abramowitz et al., 2009; D. A. Clark, 2005). Moreover, some researchers have concluded that exposure and response prevention treatment might be enhanced by the addition of cognitive therapy (Abramowitz et al., 2009). Given that OCD rarely remits completely, leaving the client with some residual obsessional problems or rituals (Abramowitz et al., 2009; Franklin & Foa, 2007), there is clearly a need to improve further the efficacy of these treatments.

The successful use of this exposure and response prevention treatment in the case of Mark, the young artist with severe OCD, is described here briefly.

Mark's Treatment

Mark was initially treated with medication and with exposure and response prevention. He found the side effects of the medication

(clomipramine) intolerable and gave it up within a few weeks. For the behavioral treatment, he was directed to get rid of the tape recorder and was given a series of exercises in which he exposed himself to feared situations where he might confess to a crime or cause harm to others, including making phone calls, mailing letters, and entering stores and public bathrooms (all things he had been unable to do). Checking rituals (including the tape recorder) were prevented. Although the initial round of treatment was not especially helpful, in part because of difficulty in getting to treatment, he did eventually make a commitment to more intensive treatment by moving to a small apartment closer to the clinic. Thereafter, he did quite well.

MEDICATIONS Whereas the other anxiety disorders respond to a range of drugs, OCD seems to respond best to medications that affect the serotonin system. These medications, such as clomipramine (Anafranil) and fluoxetine (Prozac) reduce the intensity of OCD symptoms, with approximately 40 to 60 percent of people showing at least a 25 to 35 percent reduction in symptoms (relative to 4 to 5 percent on placebo; Dougherty et al., 2007; Iancu et al., 2000). Some clients show greater improvement than this, but about 30 to 50 percent do not show any clinically significant improvement (Mancebo et al., 2006). In approximately one-third of people who fail to respond to these serotonergic medications, small doses of certain antipsychotic medications may produce significantly greater improvement (Bloch et al., 2006).

A major disadvantage of medication treatment for OCD, as for other anxiety disorders, is that when the medication is discontinued relapse rates are generally very high (as high as 50 to 90 percent; Dougherty et al., 2007; Simpson & Liebowitz, 2006). Thus, many people who do not seek alternative forms of behavior therapy that have more long-lasting benefits may have to stay on these medications indefinitely. Studies in adults have generally not found that combining medication with exposure and response prevention is much more effective than behavior therapy alone (Foa et al., 2005; Franklin & Foa, 2002, 2007), although one large study showed that a combination treatment was superior in the treatment of children and adolescents with OCD (March & Franklin, 2006; Pediatric OCD Treatment Study, 2004).

Finally, because OCD in its most severe form is such a crippling and disabling disorder, psychiatrists have begun to examine the usefulness of certain neurosurgical techniques for the treatment of severe, intractable OCD (which may afflict as many as 10 percent of people diagnosed with OCD; Mindus et al., 1994). Given the invasiveness of this intervention, before such surgery is even contemplated, the person must have had severe OCD for at least 5 years and must not have responded to any of the known treatments discussed so far (medication or behavior therapy). Several studies have shown that approximately 35 to 45 percent of these intractable cases respond quite well (at least a one-third reduction in symptoms) to neurosurgery designed to destroy brain tissue in one of the areas implicated in this condition (Dougherty, Baer, et al., 2002; Jenike, 2000; Rück et al., 2008). However, a significant number of these have adverse side effects. The results of these techniques are discussed in greater detail in Chapter 16.

Body Dysmorphic Disorder

Body dysmorphic disorder (BDD) was classified as a somatoform disorder in *DSM-IV-TR* because it involves preoccupation with certain aspects of the body. However, because of its very strong similarities with OCD, it was moved out of the somatoform category and into the OCD and related disorders category in *DSM-5*. People with BDD are obsessed with some *perceived* or *imagined flaw* or flaws in their appearance to the point they firmly believe they are disfigured or ugly (see *DSM-5* criteria). This preoccupation is so intense that it causes clinically significant distress and impairment in social or occupational functioning. Although it is not considered necessary for the diagnosis, most people with BDD have compulsive checking behaviors (such as checking their appearance in the mirror excessively or hiding or repairing a perceived flaw). Another very common symptom is avoidance of usual activities because of fear that other people will see the imaginary defect and be repulsed. In severe cases, they may become so isolated that they lock themselves up in their houses and never go out, even to work, with the average employment rate estimated at only about 50 percent (Neziroglu et al., 2004). Not surprisingly, their average quality of life is quite poor (IsHak et al., 2012). Table 6.4 illustrates the range of activities with which BDD interferes.

People with body dysmorphic disorder are preoccupied with perceived defects in certain aspects of their body and frequently spend an inordinate amount of time obsessively checking their appearance in the mirror.

Table 6.4 BDD Interference in Functioning

Problem	Percentage of People with BDD Who Experienced the Problem
Interference with social functioning (e.g., with friends, family, or intimate relationships) due to BDD	99
Periods of avoidance of nearly all social interactions because of BDD	95
Ever felt depressed because of BDD	94
Interference with work or academic functioning because of BDD	90
Ever thought about suicide because of BDD*	63
Completely housebound for at least 1 week because of BDD	29
Psychiatrically hospitalized at least once because of BDD	26
Ever attempted suicide	25
Ever attempted suicide because of BDD	14
Average Number of Days Missed	
Days of work missed because of BDD*	52 days
Days of school missed because of BDD*	49 days

*Since BDD began.

SOURCE: Adapted from Katherine A. Phillips. *The Broken Mirror: Understanding and Treating Dysmorphic Disorder.* © 2005 Oxford University Press. Reprinted with permission.

People with BDD may focus on almost any body part: Their skin has blemishes, their breasts are too small, their face is too thin (or too fat) or disfigured by visible blood vessels that others find repulsive, and so on. Some of the more common locations for perceived defects include skin (73 percent), hair (56 percent), nose (37 percent), eyes (20 percent), breasts/chest/nipples (21 percent), stomach (22 percent), and face size/shape (12 percent) (Phillips, 2005). Many sufferers have perceived defects in more than one body part. It is very important to remember that these are not the ordinary concerns that most of us have about our appearance; they are far more extreme, leading in many cases to complete preoccupation and significant emotional pain. Some researchers estimate that about half the people with BDD have concerns about their appearance that are of delusional intensity (Allen & Hollander, 2004). It is important to remember that others do not even see the defects that the person with BDD believes she or he has, or if they do, they see only a very minor defect within the normal range.

Another common feature of BDD is that people with this condition frequently seek reassurance from friends and family about their defects, but the reassurances almost never provide more than very temporary relief. They also frequently seek reassurance for themselves by checking their appearance in the mirror countless times in a day (although some avoid mirrors completely). They are usually driven by the hope that they will look different, and sometimes they may think their perceived defect does not look as bad as it has at other times. However, much more commonly they feel worse after mirror gazing (Veale & Riley, 2001). They frequently engage in excessive grooming behavior, often trying to camouflage their perceived defect through their hairstyle, clothing, or makeup (Sarwer et al., 2004).

The following case illustrates the primary features of this disorder.

Seeing Spots

Steve is a 24-year-old engineer who presented for treatment at the request of his wife. He was recently fired from his job after refusing to go into work for a 2-week period because of his extreme concerns about his appearance. He explains that he could no longer tolerate the enormous birth marks that cover his face, and so he has begun trying to pluck them off his face with nail clippers. This led to noticeable cuts and scabs on his face, which embarrassed him further and prevented him from going to work. Steve's wife reports that although he does have a few very small and hardly noticeable freckles on this face, Steve has never had any significant birth marks or detectable skin discoloration.

Steve explained that ever since he can remember he has "not been thrilled" with the beauty marks on his face, but in the past year that have really bothered him to the point of thinking about them constantly and wishing they were gone. His wife said that Steve spends at least an hour in the mirror each morning and evening looking at the marks, asking her if she really loves him despite their presence, and researching ways to eliminate them via facial plastic surgery, bleaching, or some other cosmetic procedure. His job loss and facial lacerations were enough to push Steve's wife to insist that he see a psychologist for treatment, and Steve has agreed to do so.

DSM-5 *Criteria for. . .*

Body Dysmorphic Disorder

A. Preoccupation with one or more perceived defects or flaws in physical appearance that are not observable or appear slight to others.

B. At some point during the course of the disorder, the individual has performed repetitive behaviors (e.g., mirror checking, excessive grooming, skin picking, reassurance seeking) or mental acts (e.g., comparing his or her appearance with that of others) in response to the appearance concerns.

C. The preoccupation causes clinically significant distress or impairment in social, occupational, or other important areas of functioning.

D. The appearance preoccupation is not better explained by concerns with body fat or weight in an individual whose symptoms meet diagnostic criteria for an eating disorder.

Source: Reprinted with permission from the *Diagnostic and Statistical Manual of Mental Disorders,* Fifth Edition (Copyright 2013). American Psychiatric Association.

PREVALENCE, AGE OF ONSET, AND GENDER DIFFERENCES Good estimates of the prevalence of BDD are difficult to obtain because of the great secrecy that usually surrounds this disorder. Some leading researchers estimate that it is not a rare disorder, affecting perhaps 1 to 2 percent of the general population and up to 8 percent of people with depression (Buhlmann et al., 2010; Phillips, 2005; Rief et al., 2006). The prevalence seems to be approximately equal in men and women, although the primary body parts that are focused on tend to differ in men and women (Phillips, 2005; Phillips & Diaz, 1997). Men are more likely to obsess about their genitals, body build, and balding, whereas women tend to obsess more about their skin, stomach, breasts, buttocks, hips, and legs (Phillips, Menard, & Fay, 2006). The age of onset is usually in adolescence, when many people start to become preoccupied with their appearance. People with BDD very commonly also have a depressive diagnosis (with most estimates being over 50 percent; Allen & Hollander, 2004), and it can even lead to suicide attempts or death (Neziroglu et al., 2004; Phillips & Menard, 2006). Indeed, of nearly 200 patients with BDD, Phillips and Menard (2006) found that 80 percent reported a history of suicidal ideation, and 28 percent had a history of a suicide attempt. Rates of comorbid social phobia and obsessive-compulsive disorder are also quite substantial, although not as high as for depression (Allen & Hollander, 2004; Coles et al., 2006). Not surprisingly, BDD, like OCD, is often associated with a poor quality of life (IsHak et al., 2012).

Sufferers of BDD commonly make their way into the office of a dermatologist or plastic surgeon, one estimate being that over 75 percent seek nonpsychiatric treatment (Phillips et al., 2001). One study found that 8 percent of those seeking cosmetic medical treatments met criteria for BDD (Crerand et al., 2004), although other studies have estimated this to be as high as 20 percent (Phillips, 2005). An astute doctor will not do the requested procedures and may instead make a referral to a psychologist or psychiatrist. All too often, though, the patient does get what he or she requests—and unfortunately is almost never satisfied with the outcome. Even if they are satisfied with the outcome, such patients still tend to retain their diagnosis of BDD (Tignol et al., 2007).

RELATIONSHIP TO OCD AND EATING DISORDERS People with BDD, like those with OCD, have prominent obsessions, and they engage in a variety of ritualistic behaviors such as reassurance seeking, mirror checking, comparing themselves to others, and camouflage. Moreover, they are even more convinced that their obsessive beliefs are accurate than are people with OCD (Eisen et al., 2003). In addition to these similarities in symptoms, there is overlap in the potential causes. For example, the same neurotransmitter (serotonin) and the same sets of brain structures are implicated in the two disorders (Rauch et al., 2003; Saxena & Feusner, 2006), and the same kinds of treatments that work for OCD are also the treatments of choice for BDD (Phillips, 2005).

Some researchers have noted similarities between BDD and eating disorders, especially anorexia nervosa. Perhaps the most striking similarities between these disorders are the excessive concern and preoccupation about physical appearance, dissatisfaction with one's body, and a distorted image of certain features of one's body (Allen & Hollander, 2004; Cororve & Gleaves, 2001). It is important to remember, however, that people with BDD look normal and yet are terribly obsessed and distressed about some aspect of their appearance. By contrast, people with anorexia are emaciated and generally satisfied with this aspect of their appearance (Phillips, 2005).

WHY NOW?   BDD has existed for centuries and seems to be a universal disorder, occurring in all European countries, the Middle East, China, Japan, and Africa (Phillips, 2005). Why, then, did its examination in the literature begin only recently? One possible reason is that its prevalence may actually have increased in recent years as contemporary Western culture has become increasingly focused on "looks as everything," with billions of dollars spent each year on enhancing appearance through makeup, clothes, plastic surgery, and other means (Fawcett, 2004). A second reason BDD has been understudied is that most people with this condition never seek psychological or psychiatric treatment. Rather, they suffer silently or go to dermatologists or plastic surgeons (Crerand et al., 2004; Phillips, 2001; Tignol et al., 2007). Reasons for this secrecy and shame include worries that others will think they are superficial, silly, or vain and that if they mention their perceived defect, others will notice it and focus more on it. Part of the reason why more people are now seeking treatment is that starting in the past 15 years the disorder has received a good deal of media attention. It has even been discussed on some daily talk shows, where it is sometimes called "imaginary defect disorder." As increasing attention is focused on this disorder, the secrecy and shame often surrounding it should decrease, and more people will seek treatment.

CAUSAL FACTORS: A BIOPSYCHOSOCIAL APPROACH TO BDD   Our understanding of what causes BDD is still at a preliminary stage, but recent research seems to suggest that a biopsychosocial approach offers some reasonable hypotheses. First, one recent twin study found that over-concern with a perceived or slight defect in physical appearance is a moderately heritable trait (Monzani et al., 2012). Second, BDD seems to be occurring, at least today, in a sociocultural context that places great value on attractiveness and beauty, and people who develop BDD often hold attractiveness as their primary value. This means that their self-schemas are heavily focused around such ideas as "If my appearance is defective, then I am worthless" (endorsed

by 60 percent in one study) (Buhlmann & Wilhelm, 2004, p. 924). One possibility why this occurs is that, in many cases, people with BDD were reinforced as children for their overall appearance more than for their behavior (Neziroglu et al., 2004). Another possibility is that they were teased or criticized for their appearance, which caused conditioning of disgust, shame, or anxiety to their own image of some part of their body. For example, one study of individuals with BDD found that 56 to 68 percent reported a history of emotional neglect or emotional abuse, and approximately 30 percent reported a history of physical or sexual abuse or physical neglect (Didie et al., 2006).

In addition, substantial empirical evidence now demonstrates that people with BDD show biased attention and interpretation of information relating to attractiveness (Buhlmann & Wilhelm, 2004). They selectively attend to positive or negative words such as *ugly* or *beautiful* more than to other emotional words not related to appearance, and they tend to interpret ambiguous facial expressions as contemptuous or angry more than do controls. When they are shown pictures of their own face that have been manipulated to be more or less symmetrical than in reality, they show a greater discrepancy than controls between judgments of their "actual" face and their "ideal" face. Asked to choose the pictures that best matched their faces, controls' choices were more symmetrical than their real faces, while patients with BDD lacked this bias (Lambrou et al., 2011). Moreover, several fMRI studies have found that patients with BDD showed fundamental differences in visually processing other people's faces relative to controls. Specifically, they showed a bias for extracting local, detailed features rather than the more global or holistic processing of faces seen in controls (Feusner et al., 2007). A second study showed that when patients with BDD are shown a picture of their own face, they demonstrate greater activation than do healthy controls in brain regions associated with inhibitory processes and the rigidity of behavior and thinking (the orbitofrontal cortex and the caudate) (Feusner et al., 2010). Similarly, compared to controls, patients with BDD demonstrate performance deficits on tasks that measure executive functioning (e.g., manipulating information, planning, and organization), which is thought to be guided by prefrontal brain regions (Dunai et al., 2010). Whether or not these factors play a causal role is not yet known, but certainly having such biases and deficits in processing information would, at a minimum, serve to perpetuate the disorder once it has developed.

TREATMENT OF BODY DYSMORPHIC DISORDER   The treatments that are effective for BDD are closely related to those used in the effective treatment of OCD. Some evidence indicates that antidepressant medications from the SSRI category often produce moderate improvement in patients with BDD, but many are not helped or show only a modest improvement (Phillips, 2004, 2005; Phillips,

Pagano, & Menard, 2006). However, in some cases showing only limited improvement, it is possible that inadequate doses of the medication were used, thus leading to an underestimation of their true potential effects. In general, it seems that higher doses of these medications are needed to effectively treat BDD relative to OCD (Hadley et al., 2006). In addition, a form of cognitive-behavioral treatment emphasizing exposure and response prevention has been shown to produce marked improvement in 50 to 80 percent of treated patients (Sarwer et al., 2004; Simon, 2002). These treatment approaches focus on getting the patient to identify and change distorted perceptions of his or her body during exposure to anxiety-provoking situations (e.g., when wearing something that highlights rather than disguises the "defect") and on prevention of checking responses (e.g., mirror checking, reassurance seeking, and repeated examination of the imaginary defect). The treatment gains are generally well maintained at follow-up (Looper & Kirmayer, 2002; Sarwer et al., 2004).

Hoarding Disorder

Hoarding is a condition that had received very little research attention until the past 15 to 20 years. It has been brought into public awareness recently through several TV series such as A&E's *Hoarders* or TLC's *Hoarding: Buried Alive*. Traditionally, hoarding was thought of as one particular symptom of OCD, but this categorization was increasingly questioned (Mataix-Cols et al., 2010) and hoarding was added as a new disorder in *DSM-5*. Compulsive hoarding (as a symptom) occurs in approximately 3 to 5 percent of the adult population, and in 10 to 40 percent of people diagnosed with OCD (Mataix-Cols et al., 2010; Steketee & Frost, 2004). People with hoarding disorder both acquire and fail to discard many possessions that seem useless or of very limited value, in part because of the emotional attachment they develop to their possessions. In addition, their living spaces are extremely cluttered and disorganized to the point of interfering with normal activities that would otherwise occur in those spaces, such as cleaning, cooking, and walking through the house. In severe cases people have literally been buried alive in their own home by their hoarded possessions.

Recent neuroimaging research has found that people diagnosed with OCD who have compulsive hoarding symptoms also show patterns of activation in certain brain areas when their symptoms are provoked. These brain activation patterns are different from those of people diagnosed with OCD who do not have hoarding symptoms (Mataix-Cols et al., 2004, 2010; Pertusa et al., 2010). This has led some to suggest that people with compulsive hoarding may be neurologically distinct from people with OCD (Mataix-Cols et al., 2010; Saxena, 2008). This conclusion would also be consistent with some findings of a relative lack of responsiveness to the same medications that are often successful in reducing the severity of other forms of OCD and with recent findings that different genes seem to be implicated in OCD without hoarding versus OCD with hoarding (Pertusa et al., 2010; Samuels et al., 2007).

Part of the reason compulsive hoarding has become a focus of significant research attention stems from the realization that, on average, compulsive hoarders are significantly more disabled (both occupationally and socially) than people with OCD but without compulsive hoarding symptoms (Mataix-Cols et al., 2010; Pertusa et al., 2010). They are also at high risk for fire, falling, poor sanitation, and serious health problems (Saxena et al., 2011; Steketee & Frost, 2004). In addition, these individuals have a poorer prognosis for treatment than do people without hoarding symptoms. Notably, although the medications typically used to treat OCD are generally not effective in treating people with compulsive hoarding symptoms, some studies have suggested that one antidepressant can be somewhat effective (Saxena, 2007). Traditional behavioral therapy using exposure and response prevention is also less effective than for traditional OCD (Saxena, 2007), although there are some promising, new intensive and prolonged behavioral treatments that include home visits, which seem to be more effective (2008).

Trichotillomania

Trichotillomania (also known as compulsive hair pulling) has as its primary symptom the urge to pull out one's hair from anywhere on the body (most often the scalp, eyebrows, or arms), resulting in noticeable hair loss. In earlier editions of the *DSM*, trichotillomania was categorized as an impulse-control disorder. However, reflecting its relationship to OCD, in *DSM-5* it is now placed in the obsessive-compulsive and related disorders category. The hair pulling is usually preceded by an increasing sense of tension, followed by pleasure, gratification, or relief when the hair is pulled out. The symptoms must cause clinically significant distress or impairment in some important areas of functioning. It usually occurs when the person is alone (or with immediate family members) and the person often examines the hair root, twirls it off, and sometimes pulls the strand between their teeth and/or eats it. The onset can be in childhood or later, with onset post-puberty being associated with a more severe course (Odlaug & Grant, 2012). Research on trichotillomania is in very early stages and much remains to be learned about this condition.

---

in review

- Summarize the major symptoms of obsessive-compulsive disorder.
- How have conditioning and cognitive factors been implicated in OCD?

- What are the major biological causal factors for OCD?
- What are the primary symptoms of body dysmorphic disorder, and how are they related to obsessive-compulsive disorder?
- What are the primary symptoms of hoarding disorder and why is it often so debilitating?
- What are the primary symptoms of trichotillomania?

Cultural Perspectives

6.8   Summarize some examples of cultural differences in sources of worry.

Cross-cultural research suggests that although anxiety is a universal emotion, and anxiety disorders probably exist in all human societies, there are some differences in prevalence and in the form in which the different disorders are expressed in different cultures (Barlow, 2002; Good & Kleinman, 1985; Kirmayer et al., 1995). Within the United States, lifetime prevalence rates of several anxiety disorders vary in somewhat surprising ways across different racial and ethnic groups (Breslau et al., 2006). Specifically, lifetime risk for social phobia, generalized anxiety disorder, and panic disorder is somewhat lower among ethnic minority groups than among the non-Hispanic whites.

These differences were slightly larger for people under age 45 and from lower socioeconomic classes. However, once a disorder has developed, the disorders are equally persistent across ethnic groups.

Latin Americans from the Caribbean (especially those from Puerto Rico), and other people from the Caribbean, do show higher rates of a variant of panic disorder called *ataque de nervios* (Guarnaccia et al., 2010; Hinton et al., 2008; Hinton, Lewis-Fernandez, & Pollack, 2009) than do other groups. Most of the symptoms of *ataque de nervios* are the same as in a panic attack, but they may also include bursting into tears, anger, and uncontrollable shouting. Other symptoms can include shakiness, verbal or physical aggression, dissociative experiences, and seizure-like or fainting episodes. Such attacks are often associated with a stressful event relating to the family (e.g., news of a death), and the person may have amnesia for the episode. At least in Puerto Rico, this disorder is quite common in children and adolescents as well, affecting about 9 percent (Guarnaccia et al., 2005). Individuals who experience *ataque de nervios* also seem to be vulnerable to a wider range of other anxiety and mood disorders (Guarnaccia et al., 2010).

Looking at anxiety disorders from a cross-national perspective, one very large study of more than 60,000 people across 14 countries (8 developed and 6 less developed)

The World Around Us

Taijin Kyofusho

Some evidence indicates that the form that certain anxiety disorders take has actually evolved to fit certain cultural patterns (Hinton, Park, et al., 2009). A good example is the Japanese disorder *taijin kyofusho*, which is related to the Western diagnosis of social phobia. Like social phobia, it is a fear of interpersonal relations or of social situations (Kim et al., 2008; Kirmayer, 1991). However, Westerners with social phobia are afraid of social situations where they may be the object of scrutiny or criticism. By contrast, most people with *taijin kyofusho* are concerned about doing something that will embarrass or offend others (Kim et al., 2008). For example, they may fear offending others by blushing, emitting an offensive odor, staring inappropriately into the eyes of another person, or through their perceived physical defects or imagined deformities (which can reach delusional levels; Kim et al., 2008). This fear of bringing shame on others or offending them is what leads to social avoidance (Kleinknecht et al., 1997). Body dysmorphic disorder, described earlier, also commonly occurs in people with *taijin kyofusho* (Nagata et al., 2006).

Kirmayer (1991) and colleagues (1995) have argued that the pattern of symptoms that occurs in *taijin kyofusho* has clearly been shaped by cultural factors. Japanese children are raised to be highly dependent on their mothers and to have a fear of the outside world, especially strangers. As babies and young children,

they are praised for being obedient and docile. A great deal of emphasis is also placed on implicit communication—being able to guess another's thoughts and feelings and being sensitive to them. People who make too much eye contact are likely to be considered aggressive and insensitive, and children are taught to look at the throat of people with whom they are conversing rather than into their eyes. The society is also very hierarchical and structured, and many subtleties in language and facial communication are used to communicate one's response to social status.

At a more general level, cross-cultural researchers have noted that recognition of the cognitive component of most anxiety disorders leads one to expect many cross-cultural variations in the form that different anxiety disorders take. Anxiety disorders can be considered, at least in part, disorders of the interpretive process. Because cultures influence the categories and schemas that we use to interpret our symptoms of distress, there are bound to be significant differences in the form that anxiety disorders take in different cultures (Barlow, 2002; Good & Kleinman, 1985; Kirmayer et al., 1995).

Should different manifestations of anxiety seen in different cultures be considered different disorders, or simply different manifestations of the same underlying condition?

by the World Health Organization (WHO World Mental Health Survey Consortium, 2004) showed that anxiety disorders were the most common category of disorder reported in all but one country (Ukraine). However, reported prevalence rates for all the anxiety disorders combined varied from 2.4 percent (Shanghai, China) to 18.2 percent (United States). Other countries with moderately high rates of reported anxiety disorders were Colombia, France, and Lebanon, and other countries with moderately low rates were China, Japan, Nigeria, and Spain. We now turn to several examples of cultural variants on anxiety disorders that illustrate the range of expressions of anxiety that are exhibited worldwide.

In the Yoruba culture of Nigeria, three primary clusters of symptoms are associated with generalized anxiety: worry, dreams, and bodily complaints. However, the sources of worry are very different than those in Western society; they focus on creating and maintaining a large family and on fertility. Dreams are a major source of anxiety because they are thought to indicate that one may be bewitched. The common somatic complaints are also unusual from a Western standpoint: "I have the feeling of something like water in my brain," "Things like ants keep on creeping in various parts of my brain," and "I am convinced some types of worms are in my head" (Ebigbo, 1982; Good & Kleinman, 1985). Nigerians with this syndrome often have paranoid fears of malevolent attack by witchcraft (Kirmayer et al., 1995). In India also there are many more worries about being possessed by spirits and about sexual inadequacy than are seen in generalized anxiety in Western cultures (Carstairs & Kapur, 1976; Good & Kleinman, 1985).

Another culture-related syndrome that occurs in places like China and other Southeast Asian countries is *koro*, which for men involves intense, acute fear that the penis is retracting into the body and that when this process is complete the sufferer will die. *Koro* occurs less frequently in women, for whom the fear is that their nipples are retracting and their breasts shrinking. *Koro* tends to occur in epidemics (sometimes referred to as a form of mass hysteria; Sinha, 2011)—especially in cultural minority groups when their survival is threatened—and it is often attributed to either malicious spirits or contaminated food. A variant on this syndrome also occurs in West African nations, where afflicted individuals report shrinking of the penis or breasts (but not retraction), which they fear will lead to loss of sexual functioning and reproductive capacity (but not death). Frequently, another person who was present at the time is blamed and often severely beaten or otherwise punished (Dzokoto & Adams, 2005). They both occur in a cultural context where there are serious concerns about male sexual potency (Barlow, 2002; Kirmayer et al., 1995).

in review

- What are some examples of cultural differences in sources of worry?

Unresolved Issues

The Choice of Treatments: Medications or Cognitive-Behavior Therapy?

Many people with anxiety or obsessive-compulsive disorders are unaware of the treatment options that are available to them. They also know little about the pros and cons of different types of treatment. Many mental health professionals are similarly uninformed or lack the training to conduct some of the more specialized treatments. For these reasons they may not recommend referral to what could be a more effective form of treatment. For example, in the United States specialized training in exposure and response prevention treatment for OCD is often not given to therapists in training. Many graduate programs in clinical psychology are also not very scientifically based (Baker et al., 2008).

Some people prefer treatment with medications because they believe it is easier to take pills than to engage in cognitive-behavior therapy (which might be more costly or involve homework assignments). On the other hand, therapy (unlike medications) does not typically lead to unpleasant side effects other than briefly elicited fear or anxiety. Over the longer term, therapy can also be more cost effective because people treated with medications routinely stay on them indefinitely, but therapy usually has very long-lasting effects that do not wear off with time. Medications sometimes also have limited effectiveness relative to the treatment effects that are seen with properly administered cognitive-behavior therapy.

Finding a well-trained cognitive-behavior therapist, however, is far from easy. And even trained therapists are frequently limited in the range of disorders they have been trained to treat. One solution is to provide therapists in training with proficiency in treating a broader range of disorders. The Association for Psychological Science is trying to improve this situation by developing a new system for accrediting clinical training programs that teach their students well-validated forms of effective treatments. Although progress is being made, the pace of change is much slower than would be desirable.

Summary

6.1 Distinguish between fear and anxiety.

- The anxiety disorders have anxiety or panic or both at their core. They were initially considered a subset of the neuroses, but this term was largely abandoned after *DSM-III*.

- Fear or panic is a basic emotion that involves activation of the fight-or-flight response of the autonomic nervous system; it occurs in response to imminent danger.

- Anxiety is a more diffuse blend of emotions that includes high levels of negative affect, worry about possible threat or danger, and the sense of being unable to predict threat or to control it if it occurs.

6.2 Describe the essential features of anxiety disorders.

- Anxiety disorders all are characterized by unrealistic, irrational fears or anxieties that cause significant distress and/or impairments in functioning.

- Among the anxiety disorders recognized in *DSM-5* are specific phobia, social phobia (social anxiety disorder), panic disorder, agoraphobia, and generalized anxiety disorder.

- People with these varied disorders differ from one another both in terms of the amount of fear or panic versus anxiety symptoms that they experience and in the kinds of objects or situations that most concern them.

6.3 Explain the clinical features of specific phobias.

- With *specific phobias*, an individual has an intense and irrational fear of specific objects or situations that leads to a great deal of avoidance behavior; when confronted with a feared object, the person with a phobia often shows activation of the fight-or-flight response, which is also associated with panic.

6.4 Discuss the clinical features of social phobia.

- In *social phobia*, a person has disabling fears of one or more social situations, usually because of fears of negative evaluation by others or of acting in an embarrassing or humiliating manner; in some cases a person with social phobia may actually experience panic attacks in social situations.

- People with social phobia also have prominent perceptions of unpredictability and uncontrollability and are preoccupied with negative self-evaluative thoughts that tend to interfere with their ability to interact in a socially skillful fashion.

6.5 Describe the clinical features of panic disorder.

- In *panic disorder*, a person experiences recurrent, unexpected panic attacks that often create a sense of stark terror and numerous other physical symptoms of the fight-or-flight response; panic attacks usually subside in a matter of minutes.

- Many people who experience panic attacks develop anxious apprehension about experiencing another attack; this apprehension is required for a diagnosis of panic disorder.

- Many people with panic disorder also develop agoraphobic avoidance of situations in which they fear that they might have an attack.

- Biological theories of panic disorder emphasize that the disorder may result from biochemical abnormalities in the brain as well as abnormal activity of the neurotransmitters norepinephrine and serotonin.

- Panic attacks may arise primarily from the brain area called the amygdala, although many other areas are also involved in panic disorder.

- The learning theory of panic disorder proposes that panic attacks cause the conditioning of anxiety primarily to external cues associated with the attacks and conditioning of panic itself primarily to interoceptive cues associated with the early stages of the attacks.

- The cognitive theory of panic disorder holds that this condition may develop in people who are prone to making catastrophic misinterpretations of their bodily sensations, a tendency that may be related to preexisting high levels of anxiety sensitivity.

6.6 Explain the clinical aspects of generalized anxiety disorder.

- In *generalized anxiety disorder*, a person has chronic and excessively high levels of worry about a number of events or activities and responds to stress with high levels of psychic and muscle tension.

- Generalized anxiety disorder may occur in people who have had extensive experience with unpredictable or uncontrollable life events.

- People with generalized anxiety seem to have danger schemas about their inability to cope with strange and dangerous situations that promote worries focused on possible future threats.

- The neurobiological factor most implicated in generalized anxiety is a functional deficiency in the neurotransmitter GABA, which is involved in inhibiting anxiety in stressful situations; the limbic system is the brain area most involved.

- Once a person has an anxiety disorder, mood-congruent information processing, such as attentional and interpretive biases, seems to help maintain it. This explains why, without treatment, anxiety disorders are often chronic conditions.

- Many people with anxiety disorders are treated by physicians, often with medications designed to allay anxiety or with antidepressant medications that also have antianxiety effects when taken for at least 3 to 4 weeks. Such treatment focuses on suppressing the symptoms, and some anxiolytic medications have the potential to cause physiological dependence. Once the medications are discontinued, relapse rates tend to be high.

- Behavioral and cognitive therapies have a very good track record with regard to treatment of the anxiety disorders. A key ingredient of effective treatment is prolonged exposure to feared situations.

- Cognitive therapies focus on helping clients understand their underlying automatic thoughts, which often involve cognitive distortions such as unrealistic predictions of catastrophes that in reality are very unlikely to occur. Then they learn to change these inner thoughts and beliefs through a process of logical reanalysis known as cognitive restructuring.

6.7 Describe the clinical features of obsessive-compulsive disorder and how it is treated.

- In *obsessive-compulsive disorder*, a person experiences unwanted and intrusive distressing thoughts or images that are usually accompanied by compulsive behaviors performed to neutralize those thoughts or images. Checking and cleaning rituals are most common.

- Biological causal factors are also involved in obsessive-compulsive disorder, with evidence coming from genetic studies, studies of brain functioning, and psychopharmacological studies.

- Once this disorder begins, the anxiety-reducing qualities of the compulsive behaviors may help to maintain the disorder.

- Behavior therapies that involve exposure are effective in the treatment of OCD. Rituals must also must be prevented following exposure to the feared situations.

6.8 Summarize some examples of cultural differences in sources of worry.

- In Nigeria, sources of worry center on creating and maintaining a large family, being bewitched in one's dreams, and having problems with one's brain (such as experiencing insects or worms crawling in the brain).

- In China and other Southeast Asian countries that have cultural concerns about male sexual potency, a common source of worry is the penis retracting into the body.

Key Terms

agoraphobia, p. 188
amygdala, p. 191
anxiety, p. 174
anxiety disorders, p. 176
anxiety sensitivity, p. 194
blood-injection-injury
    phobia, p. 178
body dysmorphic disorder
    (BDD), p. 212
cognitive restructuring, p. 186
compulsions, p. 203

exposure and response
    prevention, p. 210
exposure therapy, p. 181
exteroceptive conditioning, p. 193
fear, p. 174
generalized anxiety disorder
    (GAD), p. 197
hoarding disorder, p. 203
interoceptive conditioning, p. 193
neurotic disorders, p. 174
obsessions, p. 203

obsessive-compulsive disorder
    (OCD), p. 174
panic attack, p. 174
panic disorder, p. 187
panic provocation procedures, p. 192
phobia, p. 177
prepared learning, p. 180
social phobia, p. 183
specific phobia, p. 177
trichotillomania, p. 215

Chapter 7
Mood Disorders and Suicide

Learning Objectives

7.1 Describe the types of mood disorders, their primary symptoms, and their prevalence.

7.2 Distinguish between the different types of depressive disorders.

7.3 Describe the factors believed to cause unipolar mood disorders.

7.4 List and distinguish between different types of bipolar disorders.

7.5 Describe the causal factors influencing the development and maintenance of bipolar disorders.

7.6 Explain how cultural factors can influence the expression of mood disorders.

7.7 Describe and distinguish between different treatments for mood disorders.

7.8 Describe the prevalence and clinical picture of suicidal behaviors.

7.9 Explain the efforts currently used to prevent and treat suicidal behaviors.

A Successful "Total Failure"

Sophie, a junior in college, was getting all A's in her classes, working in her spare time as a research assistant in a psychology laboratory, and had a lot of great friends and a 2-year relationship with the guy of her dreams. Things soon changed, however, when her boyfriend unexpectedly told her that he was leaving her for someone else. Following her initial shock and rage, she began to have uncontrollable crying spells and doubts about her other relationships and even about her abilities in the classroom and research lab. Decision making became an ordeal. Her spirits rapidly sank, and she began to spend more and more time in bed, refusing to talk with anyone. Her alcohol consumption increased to the point where she was seldom entirely sober. Within a period of weeks, her grades plummeted due to her inability, or refusal, to attend class or complete any assignments. She felt she was a "total failure," even when her friends reminded her of her considerable achievements; indeed, her self-criticism gradually spread to all aspects of her life and her personal history. Finally, her parents intervened and forced her to accept an appointment with a clinical psychologist.

Was something "wrong" with Sophie, or was she merely experiencing normal human emotions because of her boyfriend having deserted her? The psychologist concluded that she was suffering from a serious mood disorder and initiated treatment. The diagnosis, based on the severity of the symptoms and the degree of impairment, was major depressive disorder. Secondarily, she had also developed a serious drinking problem—a condition that frequently co-occurs with major depressive disorder.

Most of us feel depressed from time to time. Failing an exam, arguing with a friend, not being accepted into one's first choice of college or job, and breaking up with a romantic partner are all examples of events that can cause a depressed mood in many people. However, **mood disorders** involve much more severe alterations in mood for much longer periods of time. In such cases the disturbances of mood are intense and persistent enough to lead to serious problems in relationships and work performance.

Mood disorders are diverse in nature, as is illustrated by the many types of depression recognized in the *DSM-5* that we will discuss. Nevertheless, in all mood disorders (formerly called *affective disorders*), extremes of emotion or *affect*—soaring elation or deep depression—dominate the clinical picture. Other symptoms are also present, but abnormal mood is the defining feature.

Mood Disorders: An Overview

7.1 **Describe the types of mood disorders, their primary symptoms, and their prevalence.**

The two key moods involved in mood disorders are **depression**, which usually involves feelings of extraordinary sadness and dejection, and **mania**, often characterized by intense and unrealistic feelings of excitement and euphoria. Some people with mood disorders experience only time periods or episodes characterized by depressed moods. However, other people experience manic episodes at certain time points and depressive episodes at other time points. Normal mood states can occur between both types of episodes. Manic and depressive mood states are often conceived to be at opposite ends of a mood continuum, with normal mood in the middle. Although this concept is accurate to a degree, sometimes an individual may have symptoms of mania and depression during the same time period. In these *mixed-episode* cases, the person experiences rapidly alternating moods such as sadness, euphoria, and irritability, all within the same episode of illness.

Types of Mood Disorders

We will first discuss **unipolar depressive disorders**, in which a person experiences only depressive episodes, and then move onto **bipolar and related disorders**, in which a person experiences both depressive *and* manic episodes.

The most common form of mood disturbance involves a **depressive episode**, in which a person is markedly depressed or loses interest in formerly pleasurable activities (or both) for at least 2 weeks, as well as other symptoms such as changes in sleep or appetite, or feelings of worthlessness (see the *DSM-5* box for diagnostic criteria).

The other primary kind of mood episode is a **manic episode**, in which a person shows a markedly elevated, euphoric, or expansive mood, often interrupted by occasional outbursts of intense irritability or even violence—particularly when others refuse to go along with the manic person's wishes and schemes. These extreme moods must persist for at least a week for this diagnosis to be made. In addition, three or more additional symptoms must occur in the same time period, ranging from behavioral symptoms (such as a notable increase in goal-directed activity), to mental symptoms where self-esteem becomes grossly inflated and mental activity may speed up (such as a "flight of ideas" or "racing thoughts"), to physical symptoms (such as a decreased need for sleep or psychomotor agitation). (See the Criteria for Manic Episode *DSM-5* box.)

In milder forms, similar kinds of symptoms can lead to a diagnosis of **hypomanic episode**, in which a person experiences abnormally elevated, expansive, or irritable mood for at least 4 days. In addition, the person must have at least three other symptoms similar to those involved in mania but to a lesser degree (inflated self-esteem, decreased need for sleep, flights of ideas, pressured speech, etc.). Although the symptoms listed are the same for manic and hypomanic episodes, there is much less impairment in social and occupational functioning in hypomania, and hospitalization is not required.

DSM-5 *Criteria for...*

Major Depressive Disorder

A. Five (or more) of the following symptoms have been present during the same 2-week period and represent a change from previous functioning; at least one of the symptoms is either (1) depressed mood or (2) loss of interest or pleasure.

Note: Do not include symptoms that are clearly attributable to another medical condition.

1. Depressed mood most of the day, nearly every day, as indicated by either subjective report (e.g., feels sad, empty, or hopeless) or observation made by others (e.g., appears tearful). (**Note:** In children and adolescents, can be irritable mood.)

2. Markedly diminished interest or pleasure in all, or almost all, activities most of the day, nearly every day (as indicated by either subjective account or observation).

3. Significant weight loss when not dieting or weight gain (e.g., a change of more than 5% of body weight in a month), or decrease or increase in appetite nearly every day. (**Note:** In children, consider failure to make expected weight gain.)

4. Insomnia or hypersomnia nearly every day.

5. Psychomotor agitation or retardation nearly every day (observable by others; not merely subjective feelings of restlessness or being slowed down).

6. Fatigue or loss of energy nearly every day.

7. Feelings of worthlessness or excessive or inappropriate guilt (which may be delusional) nearly every day (not merely self-reproach or guilt about being sick).

8. Diminished ability to think or concentrate, or indecisiveness, nearly every day (either by subjective account or as observed by others).

9. Recurrent thoughts of death (not just fear of dying), recurrent suicidal ideation without a specific plan, or a suicide attempt or a specific plan for committing suicide.

B. The symptoms cause clinically significant distress or impairment in social, occupational, or other important areas of functioning.

C. The episode is not attributable to the physiological effects of a substance or another medical condition.

Note: Criteria A–C constitute a major depressive episode. Major depressive episodes are common in bipolar I disorder but are not required for the diagnosis of bipolar I disorder.

Note: Responses to a significant loss (e.g., bereavement, financial ruin, losses from a natural disaster, a serious medical illness or disability) may include the feelings of intense sadness, rumination about the loss, insomnia, poor appetite, and weight loss noted in Criterion A, which may resemble a depressive episode. Although such symptoms may be understandable or considered appropriate to the loss, the presence of a major depressive episode in addition to the normal response to a significant loss should also be carefully considered. This decision inevitably requires the exercise of clinical judgment based on the individual's history and the cultural norms for the expression of distress in the context of loss.

D. The occurrence of the major depressive episode is not better explained by schizoaffective disorder, schizophrenia, schizophreniform disorder, delusional disorder, or other specified and unspecified schizophrenia spectrum and other psychotic disorders.

E. There has never been a manic episode or a hypomanic episode.

Note: This exclusion does not apply if all of the manic-like or hypomanic-like episodes are substance-induced or are attributable to the physiological effects of another medical condition.

Source: Reprinted with permission from the *Diagnostic and Statistical Manual of Mental Disorders*, Fifth Edition (Copyright 2013). American Psychiatric Association.

The Prevalence of Mood Disorders

Major mood disorders occur with alarming frequency—at least 15 to 20 times more frequently than schizophrenia, for example, and at almost the same rate as all the anxiety disorders taken together. Of the two types of serious mood disorders, *major depressive disorder* (MDD), in which only **major depressive episodes** occur (also known as *unipolar major depression*), is the most common, and its occurrence has apparently increased in recent decades (Kessler et al., 2003). The most recent epidemiological results from the National Comorbidity Survey Replication (NCS-R) found lifetime prevalence rates of unipolar major depression at nearly 17 percent (12-month prevalence rates were nearly 7 percent; Kessler, Chiu, et al., 2005). Worldwide, mood disorders are the second most prevalent type of disorder (following anxiety disorders), with a 12-month prevalence ranging from 1 to 10 percent across different countries (WHO World Mental Health Survey Consortium, 2004) (see Figure 7.1).

Moreover, rates for unipolar major depression are always much higher for women than for men (usually about 2:1), similar to the sex differences for most anxiety disorders (see Chapter 6) (Hasin et al., 2005; Nolen-Hoeksema, 2012; Nolen-Hoeksema & Hilt, 2009). These differences occur in most countries around the world. In the United States, this sex difference starts in adolescence and continues until about age 65, when it seems to disappear. Yet among schoolchildren, boys are equally likely or slightly more likely to be diagnosed with depression.

The other type of major mood disorder, *bipolar disorder* (in which both manic and depressive episodes occur), is

DSM-5 *Criteria for...*

Manic Episode

A. A distinct period of abnormally and persistently elevated, expansive, or irritable mood and abnormally and persistently increased goal-directed activity or energy, lasting at least 1 week and present most of the day, nearly every day (or any duration if hospitalization is necessary).

B. During the period of mood disturbance and increased energy or activity, three (or more) of the following symptoms (four if the mood is only irritable) are present to a significant degree and represent a noticeable change from usual behavior:

1. Inflated self-esteem or grandiosity.
2. Decreased need for sleep (e.g., feels rested after only 3 hours of sleep).
3. More talkative than usual or pressure to keep talking.
4. Flight of ideas or subjective experience that thoughts are racing.
5. Distractibility (i.e., attention too easily drawn to unimportant or irrelevant external stimuli), as reported or observed.
6. Increase in goal-directed activity (either socially, at work or school, or sexually) or psychomotor agitation (i.e., purposeless non-goal-directed activity).

7. Excessive involvement in activities that have a high potential for painful consequences (e.g., engaging in unrestrained buying sprees, sexual indiscretions, or foolish business investments).

C. The mood disturbance is sufficiently severe to cause marked impairment in social or occupational functioning or to necessitate hospitalization to prevent harm to self or others, or there are psychotic features.

D. The episode is not attributable to the physiological effects of a substance (e.g., a drug of abuse, a medication, other treatment) or to another medical condition.

Note: A full manic episode that emerges during antidepressant treatment (e.g., medication, electroconvulsive therapy) but persists at a fully syndromal level beyond the physiological effect of that treatment is sufficient evidence for a manic episode and, therefore, a bipolar I diagnosis.

Note: Criteria A–D constitute a manic episode. At least one lifetime manic episode is required for the diagnosis of bipolar I disorder.

Source: Reprinted with permission from the *Diagnostic and Statistical Manual of Mental Disorders*, Fifth Edition (Copyright 2013). American Psychiatric Association.

much less common. The NCS-R estimated that the lifetime risk of developing the classic form of this disorder is about 1 percent (see also Goodwin & Jamison, 2007), and there is no discernible difference in the prevalence rates between the sexes.

Nationally representative surveys of U.S. residents suggest that mood disorders occur less frequently among African Americans than among European white Americans and Hispanics, whose rates are comparable (Kessler, Chiu, et al., 2005; Williams et al., 2007). Native Americans, by contrast, have significantly elevated rates compared to white Americans (Hasin et al., 2005). There are no significant differences among such groups for bipolar disorder.

Figure 7.1   Annual Prevalence of Mood Disorders Around the World

This figure shows the annual (12-month) prevalence of mood disorders using data collected via household surveys in 17 different countries as part of the WHO World Mental Health Survey Initiative

(Adapted from WHO World Mental Health Survey Consortium, 2004.)

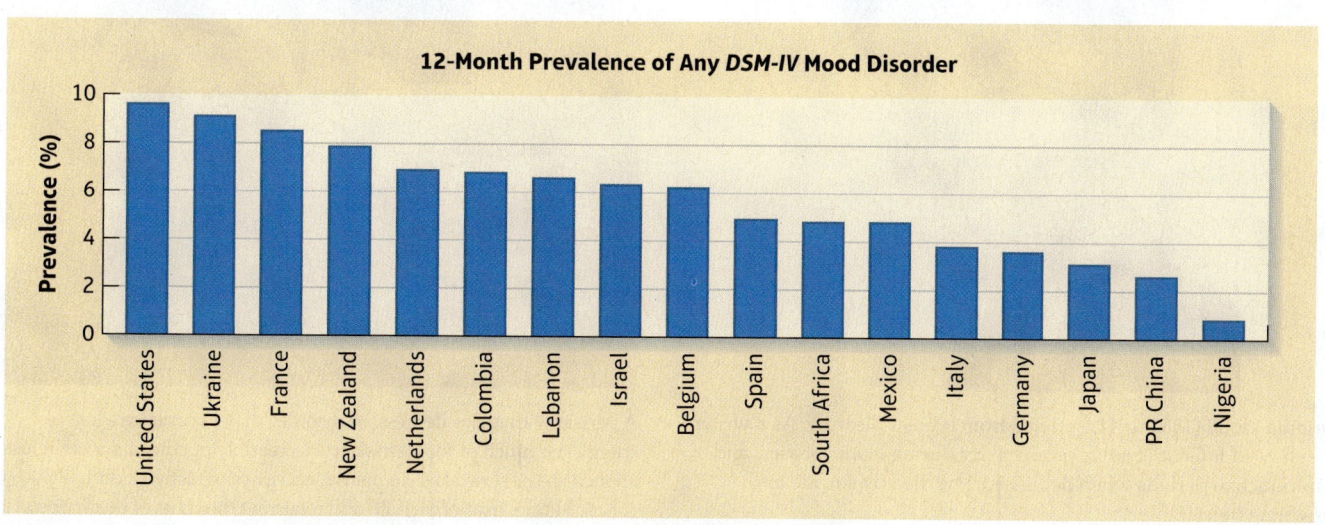

Other epidemiologic research indicates that rates of unipolar depression are inversely related to socioeconomic status (SES); that is, higher rates occur in lower socioeconomic groups (Kessler, Chiu, et al., 2005; Monroe et al., 2009). This may be because low SES leads to adversity and life stress (Dohrenwend, 2000; Monroe & Hadjiyannakis, 2002). However, in spite of earlier indications that rates of bipolar disorder are *elevated* among those in higher socioeconomic groups, current evidence from carefully controlled studies has not found bipolar disorder to be related to socioeconomic class (Goodwin & Jamison, 2007).

Another group that has elevated rates of mood disorders consists of individuals who have high levels of accomplishments in the arts. Indeed, a good deal of evidence has shown that both unipolar and bipolar disorder, but especially bipolar disorder, occur with alarming frequency in poets, writers, composers, and artists (Jamison, 1993; Murray & Johnson, 2010). Jamison has also documented for a number of such famous creative individuals how their periods of productivity co-vary with the manic, or hypomanic, and depressive phases of their illnesses. One possible hypothesis to explain this relationship is that mania or hypomania actually facilitates the creative process and/or that the intense negative emotional experiences of depression provide material for creative activity. A study of the eminent nineteenth-century American poet Emily Dickinson provides support for the latter part of this hypothesis—that is, evidence supports the idea that Dickinson's painful experiences with panic disorder and depression provided ideas for her especially high-quality work during those times. However, a detailed analysis of her hypomanic periods suggests that her hypomanic symptoms increased her motivation and output but not her creativity per se (Ramey & Weisberg, 2004).

Virginia Woolf (1882–1941) suffered from bipolar disorder. As a writer, she showed intense creative productivity during manic phases, and unproductive periods when depressed. She died by suicide by drowning herself.

in review

- What are the primary distinctions between depressive disorders and bipolar disorders?
- How prevalent are the two types of mood disorders?
- How do the prevalence rates of depressive and bipolar disorders differ between the sexes?
- What are some of the basic demographic differences in the United States influencing rates of unipolar and bipolar disorders?

Unipolar Depressive Disorders

7.2 Distinguish between the different types of depressive disorders.

Sadness, discouragement, pessimism, and hopelessness about matters improving are familiar feelings to most people. Feelings of depression are unpleasant when we are experiencing them, but they usually do not last long, dissipating on their own after a period of days or weeks or after they have reached a certain intensity level. Indeed, mild and brief depression may actually be "normal" and adaptive in the long run. By slowing us down, mild depression sometimes saves us from wasting a lot of energy in the futile pursuit of unobtainable goals (Keller & Nesse, 2005; Nesse, 2000). Usually, normal depressions would be expected to occur in people undergoing painful but common life events such as significant personal, interpersonal, or economic losses.

Major Depressive Disorder

The diagnostic criteria for **major depressive disorder** (MDD; also known as "major depression") require that a

A person with major depressive disorder may experience a loss of energy, too much or too little sleep, decreased appetite and weight loss, an increase or slowdown in mental and physical activity, difficulty concentrating, irrational guilt, and recurrent thoughts of death or suicide.

person must be in a *major depressive episode* and never have had a manic, hypomanic, or mixed episode.

The following account illustrates a moderately severe case of MDD.

Jennifer

Jennifer is a 35-year-old graphic designer who is married and has three young children at home. She has been running a successful, and growing, business out of her home office, which she has really enjoyed because working from home allows her the time and flexibility to be with her children when they are not in school. Jennifer experienced a major life stressor 6 months ago when her husband of 15 years, Michael, told her that he is leaving her for a younger woman he met at his job. Jennifer was totally blindsided by this news. After an initial period of trying to work things out, Michael moved out of the house. Jennifer continued on with her business and managing of her household for several weeks, but then things started to change. She felt increasingly sad and would have long periods of crying throughout the day several times per week. Whereas she used to enjoy work, time with her children, and going out with her girlfriends, none of that seemed fun anymore. Even "movie nights" at home with the kids, which was one of her favorite times of the week, just wasn't enjoyable to her anymore. Her body felt heavier and heavier and she lacked the energy to keep up appointments, leading her business to decline—she began losing even her most loyal clients. Jennifer also had difficulties managing her household, on several occasions forgetting to pick up her children from school and not remembering to make dinner for the family. Her eating and sleeping both declined drastically, and she spent hours lying in bed feeling like she had let down her husband, her children, and her friends. In addition to her extreme sadness, Jennifer began to experience extreme anxiety and worry in multiple domains. How would her business succeed? If she lost her business, wouldn't she lose her house? Would she lose her children as well? Who would take care of them? She wanted to address all of these things but felt paralyzed and unable to take action. This led her to feel even more like a failure. She believed she was completely worthless and began contemplating whether everyone wouldn't be better off if she was dead, which increased to explicit and frequent thoughts of suicide.

Jennifer's case illustrates that a person with MDD shows not only mood symptoms of sadness but also a variety of symptoms that are more severe than those in milder forms of depression. Jennifer lacks energy and the ability to carry out her activities of daily life. Her physical symptoms include loss of appetite and sleep disturbance. She also shows cognitive symptoms of worthlessness and thoughts of death and suicide.

Note also that few if any depressions—including milder ones—occur in the absence of significant anxiety (e.g., Merikangas et al., 2003; Mineka et al., 1998; Watson, 2005). Indeed, there is a high degree of overlap between measures of depressive and anxious symptoms in self-reports and in clinician ratings. At the diagnostic level, there are very high levels of comorbidity between depressive and anxiety disorders (e.g., Kessler et al., 2007; Watson, 2005). The issues surrounding the co-occurrence of depression and anxiety, which have received a great deal of attention in recent years, are very complex.

DEPRESSION AS A RECURRENT DISORDER When a diagnosis of MDD is made, it is usually also specified whether this is a first, and therefore *single* (initial), episode or a *recurrent* episode (preceded by one or more previous episodes). Depressive episodes typically last about 6 to 9 months if untreated. In approximately 10 to 20 percent of people with MDD, the symptoms do not remit for over 2 years, in which case persistent depressive disorder is diagnosed (Boland & Keller, 2009; Gilmer et al., 2005). Chronic major depression has been associated with serious childhood family problems and an anxious personality in childhood (Angst et al., 2011).

Although most depressive episodes remit (which is not said to occur until symptoms have largely been gone for at least 2 months), depressive episodes often return at some future point. This return of symptoms is of one of two types: **relapse** and **recurrence**. Relapse refers to the return of symptoms within a fairly short period of time, a situation that probably reflects the fact that the underlying episode of depression has not yet run its course (Boland & Keller, 2002; Frank et al., 1991). For example, relapse may commonly occur when pharmacotherapy is terminated prematurely—after symptoms have remitted but before the underlying episode is really over (Hollon & Dimidjian, 2009).

Recurrence, which refers to the onset of a new episode of depression, occurs in approximately 40 to 50 percent of people who experience a depressive episode (Monroe & Harkness, 2011). The probability of recurrence increases with the number of prior episodes and also when the person has comorbid disorders. Unfortunately, people who experience multiple depressive episodes often are not symptom-free in between episodes, but instead have some depressive symptoms half to two-thirds of the time (Judd et al., 1998). Moreover, people with some residual symptoms, or with significant psychosocial impairment, following an initial depressive episode are more likely to have recurrences than those whose symptoms remit completely (Judd et al., 1999; Solomon et al., 2004).

DEPRESSION THROUGHOUT THE LIFE CYCLE Although the onset of unipolar depressive disorders most often occurs during late adolescence up to middle adulthood, such reactions may begin at any time from early childhood to old age. Depression was once thought not to occur in childhood, but more recent research has estimated that about 1 to 3 percent of school-age children meet the criteria for some form of unipolar depressive disorder, with a smaller percentage exhibiting dysthymic disorder (discussed later) than major depression (see Avenevoli et al., 2008; Garber et al., 2009). As in adults, recurrence rates are high in children.

The incidence of depression rises sharply during adolescence—a period of great turmoil for many people. Indeed, approximately 15 to 20 percent of adolescents experience major depressive disorder at some point, and subclinical levels of depression affect a further 10 to 20 percent (Avenevoli et al., 2008; Lewinsohn & Essau, 2002). It is during this time period that sex differences in rates of depression first emerge (Hankin et al., 2008; Nolen-Hoeksema, 2012). The Developments in Research box later in the chapter provides some insights into why this might be. The long-term effects of major depressive disorder in adolescence can last at least through young adulthood, when such individuals show small but significant psychosocial impairments in many domains, including their occupational lives, interpersonal relationships, and general quality of life (e.g., Lewinsohn et al., 2003; Rudolph, 2008). Moreover, major depression that occurs in adolescence is very likely to recur in adulthood (Avenevoli et al., 2008; Rudolph, 2008).

The occurrence of major depression continues into later life. Although the prevalence of major depression is significantly lower in people over age 65 than in younger adults (Kessler et al., 2010), MDD in older adults is still considered a major public health problem (Blazer & Hybels, 2009; Kessler, Berglund, Demler, et al., 2005). Unfortunately, depression in later life can be difficult to diagnose because many of the symptoms overlap with those of several medical illnesses and dementia (Alexopoulos et al., 2002; Harvey et al., 2006). Yet it is very important to try and diagnose it reliably because depression in later life has many adverse consequences for a person's health, including doubling the risk of death in people who have had a heart attack or stroke (e.g., Davidson et al., 2010; Schulz et al., 2002).

SPECIFIERS FOR MAJOR DEPRESSIVE EPISODES Some individuals who meet the basic criteria for diagnosis of a major depressive episode also have additional patterns of symptoms or features that are important to note when making a diagnosis because these patterns have implications for understanding more about the course of the disorder and its most effective treatment. These different patterns of symptoms or features are called **specifiers** in *DSM-5* (see Table 7.1 for a summary of the major specifiers). One such specifier is **major depressive episode with melancholic features**. This designation is applied when, in addition to meeting the criteria for a major depressive episode, a patient either has lost interest or pleasure in almost all activities or does not react to usually pleasurable stimuli or desired events. This subtype of depression is more heritable than most other forms of depression and is more often associated with a history of childhood trauma (Harkness & Monroe, 2002; Kendler, 1997).

Table 7.1 Specifiers of Major Depressive Episodes

Specifier	Characteristic Symptoms
With Melancholic Features	Three of the following: early morning awakening, depression worse in the morning, marked psychomotor agitation or retardation, loss of appetite or weight, excessive guilt, qualitatively different depressed mood
With Psychotic Features	Delusions or hallucinations (usually mood congruent); feelings of guilt and worthlessness common
With Atypical Features	Mood reactivity—brightens to positive events; two of the four following symptoms: weight gain or increase in appetite, hypersomnia, leaden paralysis (arms and legs feel as heavy as lead), being acutely sensitive to interpersonal rejection
With Catatonic Features	A range of psychomotor symptoms from motoric immobility to extensive psychomotor activity, as well as mutism and rigidity
With Seasonal Pattern	At least two or more episodes in past 2 years that have occurred at the same time (usually fall or winter), and full remission at the same time (usually spring). No other nonseasonal episodes in the same 2-year period

Psychotic symptoms, characterized by loss of contact with reality and delusions (false beliefs) or hallucinations (false sensory perceptions), may sometimes accompany other symptoms of major depression. In such cases the diagnosis is **severe major depressive episode with psychotic features**. Ordinarily, any delusions or hallucinations present are **mood congruent**—that is, they seem in some sense appropriate to serious depression because the content is negative in tone, such as themes of personal inadequacy, guilt, deserved punishment, death, or disease. For example, some people with severe depression hold the delusional idea that their internal organs have totally deteriorated. Individuals who are psychotically depressed are likely to have longer episodes, more cognitive impairment, and a poorer long-term prognosis than those suffering from depression without psychotic features (Bora et al., 2010; Flores & Schatzberg, 2006), and any recurrent episodes are also likely to be characterized by psychotic symptoms (Fleming et al., 2004). Treatment generally involves an antipsychotic medication as well as an antidepressant (Keller et al., 2007).

A third important specifier is used when the individual shows "atypical features." **Major depressive episode with atypical features** includes a pattern of symptoms characterized by mood reactivity; that is, the person's mood brightens in response to potential positive events. In addition, the person must show two or more of the four symptoms listed in Table 7.1. A disproportionate number of individuals who have atypical features are females, who have an earlier-than-average age of onset and who are more likely to show suicidal thoughts (Matza et al., 2003). Research has also shown that atypical depression is linked to a mild form of bipolar disorder that is associated with hypomanic rather than manic episodes (Akiskal & Benazzi, 2005). This is also an important specifier because there are indications that individuals with atypical features may preferentially respond to a different class of antidepressants—the monoamine oxidase inhibitors—than do most other individuals with depression.

A fourth specifier is used when the individual shows marked psychomotor disturbances. **Major depressive episode with catatonic features** includes a range of psychomotor symptoms, from motoric immobility (*catalepsy*—a stuporous state) to extensive psychomotor activity, as well as mutism and rigidity. Catatonia is known more as a subtype of schizophrenia, but it is actually more frequently associated with certain forms of depression and mania than with schizophrenia (Fink & Taylor, 2006).

A fifth specifier is used when individuals who experience recurrent depressive episodes show a seasonal pattern, **recurrent major depressive episode with a seasonal pattern**, also commonly known as **seasonal affective disorder**. To meet *DSM-5* criteria for this specifier, the person must have had at least two episodes of depression in the past 2 years occurring at the same time of the year (most commonly fall or winter), and full remission must also have occurred at the same time of the year (most commonly spring). In addition, the person cannot have had other, nonseasonal depressive episodes in the same 2-year period, and most of the person's lifetime depressive episodes must have been of the seasonal variety. Prevalence rates suggest that winter seasonal affective disorder is more common in people living at higher latitudes (northern climates) and in younger people.

Watch   Martha: Major Depressive Disorder (MDD)

Persistent Depressive Disorder

Persistent depressive disorder (formerly called *dysthymic disorder* or *dysthymia*) is a disorder characterized by persistently depressed mood most of the day, for more days than not, for at least 2 years (1 year for children and adolescents). In addition, individuals must have at least two of six additional symptoms when depressed (see the *DSM-5* box for diagnostic criteria). Periods of normal mood may occur briefly, but they usually last for only a few days to a

few weeks (and for a maximum of 2 months). These intermittently normal moods are one of the most important characteristics distinguishing persistent depressive disorder from MDD. Nevertheless, in spite of the intermittently normal moods, because of its chronic course people with persistent depressive disorder show poorer outcomes and as much impairment as those with MDD (Klein, 2008, 2010).

Although persistent depressive disorder is distinct from MDD, the two disorders sometimes co-occur in the same person, a condition given the designation **double depression** (Boland & Keller, 2009; Klein, 2010). People with double depression are moderately depressed on a chronic basis (meeting symptom criteria for persistent depressive disorder) but undergo increased problems from time to time, during which they also meet criteria for a major depressive episode. One clinical sample of nearly 100 individuals with early-onset dysthymia (onset before age 21) was followed for 10 years, during which time 84 percent experienced at least one major depressive episode (Klein et al., 2006; see also Keller et al., 1997). Although nearly all individuals with double depression appear to recover from their major depressive episodes (although usually just to their previous level of dysthymia), recurrence is common (Boland & Keller, 2002; Klein, 2008, 2010; Klein et al., 2006). In *DSM-5*, double depression is classified as a form of persistent depressive disorder.

Persistent depressive disorder is quite common, with a lifetime prevalence estimated at between 2.5 and 6 percent (Kessler, Berglund, Demler, et al., 2005). The average duration of persistent depressive disorder is 4 to 5 years, but it can last for 20 years or more (Klein et al., 2006). Chronic stress has been shown to increase the severity of symptoms over a 7.5-year follow-up period (Dougherty et al., 2004). Persistent depressive disorder often begins during adolescence, and over 50 percent of those who present for treatment have an onset before age 21. One 10-year prospective study of 97 individuals with early-onset dysthymia found that 74 percent recovered within 10 years but that, among those who recovered, 71 percent relapsed, with most relapses occurring within approximately 3 years of follow-up (Klein et al., 2006; see also Klein, 2010).

The following case is typical of this disorder.

A Persistently Depressed Student

Rosa, a 20-year-old college student, came into the university clinic for an evaluation at the encouragement of her roommate. She reports that "ever since high school" she has "felt sad, like, all of the time . . . it doesn't seem normal and I don't know why." Rosa notes that there was no major stressor that she can remember that triggered her feelings of sadness, "just the normal high school stuff." But her feelings of sadness have persisted for nearly 4 years now. When asked about what her sadness is like, she tells the psychologist that she just feels like she is not as good as everyone else—not as smart as the other students, not as attractive as the other girls, and can't

DSM-5 *Criteria for...*

Persistent Depressive Disorder

A. Depressed mood for most of the day, for more days than not, as indicated by either subjective account or observation by others, for at least 2 years.

Note: In children and adolescents, mood can be irritable and duration must be at least 1 year.

B. Presence, while depressed, of two (or more) of the following:

1. Poor appetite or overeating.
2. Insomnia or hypersomnia.
3. Low energy or fatigue.
4. Low self-esteem.
5. Poor concentration or difficulty making decisions.
6. Feelings of hopelessness.

C. During the 2-year period (1 year for children or adolescents) of the disturbance, the individual has never been without the symptoms in Criteria A and B for more than 2 months at a time.

D. Criteria for a major depressive disorder may be continuously present for 2 years.

E. There has never been a manic episode or a hypomanic episode, and criteria have never been met for cyclothymic disorder.

F. The disturbance is not better explained by a persistent schizo-affective disorder, schizophrenia, delusional disorder, or other specified or unspecified schizophrenia spectrum and other psychotic disorder.

G. The symptoms are not attributable to the physiological effects of a substance (e.g., a drug of abuse, a medication) or another medical condition (e.g., hypothyroidism).

H. The symptoms cause clinically significant distress or impairment in social, occupational, or other important areas of functioning.

Note: Because the criteria for a major depressive episode include four symptoms that are absent from the symptom list for persistent depressive disorder (dysthymia), a very limited number of individuals will have depressive symptoms that have persisted longer than 2 years but will not meet criteria for persistent depressive disorder. If full criteria for a major depressive episode have been met at some point during the current episode of illness, they should be given a diagnosis of major depressive disorder. Otherwise, a diagnosis of other specified depressive disorder or unspecified depressive disorder is warranted.

Source: Reprinted with permission from the *Diagnostic and Statistical Manual of Mental Disorders*, Fifth Edition (Copyright 2013). American Psychiatric Association.

---

seem to have fun and enjoy college like everyone else seems to be doing. Rosa was very active and popular early in high school: She was a member of the track team, in honors classes and an A student, and had a wonderful and supportive network of friends. However, during her junior and senior years, she lost interest in track and school, and just didn't feel close to her friends anymore and so over time stopped hanging out with them. No one seemed to care or try to change things, which really affected Rosa's self-esteem and to this day causes her to think that no one "really" cares about her. In addition to her feelings of sadness, Rosa has been having trouble sleeping several nights per week, tossing and turning throughout the night. She also weighs about 20 pounds less than she did in high school, not because of diet or exercise but because she "doesn't really enjoy food much anymore." All of this has led to problems with Rosa's ability to care about school or to be motivated to apply herself in class, and so this once A student is now barely passing her classes. Rosa's roommate has been asking her to come in to talk with someone about all of this for months, and Rosa's declining attendance at school and decreasing contact with her family and friends led her roommate to walk her to the clinic for an evaluation today—to make sure she came in for help.

Other Forms of Depression

Depressions are nearly always precipitated by stressful life events. Some of the most stressful events possible are those involving the loss of life, as well as the creation of new life. Indeed, these dramatic events often can push a person into a depressive episode, and psychologists have struggled with how to appropriately diagnose (or not) a person's response to them.

LOSS AND THE GRIEVING PROCESS We usually think of grief as the psychological process one goes through following the death of a loved one—a process that appears to be more difficult for men than for women (Bonanno & Kaltman, 1999). Grief often has certain characteristics. Bowlby's (1980) classic observations revealed that there are usually four phases of *normal response* to the loss of a spouse or close family member: (1) numbing and disbelief, (2) yearning and searching for the dead person, (3) disorganization and despair that sets in when the person accepts the loss as permanent, and (4) some reorganization as the person gradually begins to rebuild his or her life.

For decades this was generally considered as a normal pattern, and in 2007 a careful study of over 200 individuals who had lost a loved one due to natural causes documented that this is indeed the typical sequence (Maciejewski et al., 2007). The normal nature of exhibiting a certain number of grief symptoms led *DSM-IV-TR* to suggest that a major depressive disorder usually should not be diagnosed for the first 2 months following the loss, even if all the symptom criteria are met. However, in a controversial move, this 2-month bereavement exclusion was dropped in *DSM-5* (see the Thinking Critically about *DSM-5* box). Another controversial change is described in the Developments in Thinking box.

DSM-5 Thinking Critically about *DSM-5*

Was It Wise to Drop the Bereavement Exclusion for Major Depression?

One feature of *DSM-IV-TR* was that it contained a bereavement exclusion criterion for major depression. This stipulated that people who had recently been bereaved, but who otherwise meet diagnostic criteria for a major depressive episode, could be excluded from being diagnosed with clinical depression for up to 2 months post-loss. This criterion was designed to distinguish true disorder from normal sadness, thus reducing diagnostic false-positives, unnecessary treatment, potential stigmatization, and inflated prevalence rates (Wakefield et al., 2007).

However, no exclusion was made for other types of loss. This raised the issue of whether it was justifiable to consider depression in response to the loss of a loved one as normal, and depression in response to other losses as a form of mental disorder. In an examination of this Wakefield and colleagues (2007) found that bereavement-triggered depression and depression triggered by other forms of loss were very similar on eight of nine symptoms of depression (the exception being that bereaved individuals, not surprisingly, thought about death more). There was therefore no evidence to support granting bereavement special status.

In *DSM-5*, many people expected that the specific bereavement exclusion would be dropped and replaced by an expanded exclusion that included other types of loss (loss of a job, divorce) as well as death of a loved one. However, in a controversial decision, the bereavement exclusion has not only *not been expanded*, but it has been *removed completely* from *DSM-5*.

What are the issues here? Dropping the bereavement exclusion may now create the risk that a normal grief reaction becomes misdiagnosed as a major depressive episode leading to unnecessary treatment, stigmatization, or other negative consequences. On the other hand, the assumption that any depressive response to the loss of a love one is "normal" could lead to delays in receiving needed treatment. One finding in support of keeping the bereavement criterion as it was in *DSM-IV-TR* is that people who experience symptoms of major depression following death of a loved one are not at elevated risk for a recurrence of later major depression the way people who have major depressive episodes under other conditions are. So they may indeed be a special group. What do you think? Is grief normal? How is grief different from depression? Does the removal of the bereavement criterion in *DSM-5* now pathologize grief? Going forward, what do you think some of the consequences of this change in *DSM-5* might be?

It is important to note that not all loss is followed by depression. Recent studies of those experiencing the loss of a spouse, life partner, or parent reveal that about 50 percent exhibit genuine resilience in the face of loss, with minimal, very short-lived symptoms of depression or bereavement. Also, in contrast to what was previously thought, these resilient individuals are not emotionally maladjusted or unattached to their spouses (e.g., Bonanno et al., 2004, 2005).

POSTPARTUM "BLUES" Although you might think the birth of a child is always a happy event, postpartum depression sometimes occurs in new mothers (and occasionally fathers) and it is known to have adverse effects on child outcomes (e.g., Ramchandani et al., 2005). In the past it was believed that postpartum major depression in mothers was relatively common, but more recent evidence suggests that only "postpartum blues" are very common. The

Developments in Thinking

A New *DSM-5* Diagnosis: Premenstrual Dysphoric Disorder

After years of study, surrounded by some controversy, a new disorder called premenstrual dysphoric disorder has been added to the depressive disorders category in *DSM-5*. This disorder is diagnosed if a woman has had a certain set of symptoms in the majority of her menstrual cycles for the past year. In particular, she must have at least one of the following four symptoms in the final week before the onset of menses; these symptoms must start to improve within a few days after the onset of menses, and become minimal or absent in the week post-menses. The four symptoms of which one must occur include (1) marked affective lability such as mood swings; (2) marked irritability or anger or increased interpersonal conflicts; (3) marked depressed mood, or feelings of hopelessness or self-deprecating thoughts; or (4) marked anxiety, tension, or feelings of being "keyed up" or "on edge." Seven other symptoms are listed and a total of five symptoms must be experienced. These other symptoms include (1) decreased interest in usual activities; (2) subjective sense of difficulties in concentration; (3) lethargy, easy fatigability, or lack of energy; (4) marked changes in appetite or overeating; (5) hypersomnia or insomnia; (6) a sense of being overwhelmed or out of control; and (7) physical symptoms such as breast tenderness or swelling, a sense of bloating, weight gain, etc. This is one form of depression where hormones clearly play an important role.

symptoms of postpartum blues typically include changeable mood, crying easily, sadness, and irritability, often liberally intermixed with happy feelings (Miller, 2002; Reck et al., 2009). Such symptoms occur in as many as 50 to 70 percent of women within 10 days of the birth of their child and usually subside on their own (Miller, 2002; Nolen-Hoeksema & Hilt, 2009). Hypomanic symptoms are also frequently observed, intermixed with the more depression-like symptoms (Sharma et al., 2009).

Actress Brook Shields describes her experience with postpartum depression in her popular book *Down Came the Rain*. In it, she writes, "I wasn't simply emotional or weepy, like I had been told I might be. This was something quite different. This was sadness of a shockingly different magnitude. It felt as if it would never go away."

It appears that major depression in women occurs no more frequently in the postpartum period than would be expected in women of the same age and socioeconomic status who have not just given birth (Hobfoll et al., 1995; O'Hara & Swain, 1996). Thus, the once firmly held notion that women are at especially high risk for major depression in the postpartum period has not been upheld. There is, however, a greater likelihood of developing major depression after the postpartum blues—especially if they are severe (Henshaw et al., 2004; Reck et al., 2009).

Hormonal readjustments (Miller, 2002; O'Hara et al., 1991) and alterations in serotonergic and noradrenergic functioning (Doornbos et al., 2008) may play a role in postpartum blues and depression, although the evidence on this issue is mixed. It is obvious that a psychological component is present as well. Postpartum blues or depression may be especially likely to occur if the new mother has lack of social support or has difficulty in adjusting to her new identity and responsibilities, or if the woman has a personal or family history of depression that leads to heightened sensitivity to the stress of childbirth (Collins et al., 2004; Miller, 2002; O'Hara & Gorman, 2004).

in review
- What are the major features that differentiate dysthymic disorder and major depressive disorder?
- Distinguish between recurrence and relapse.
- What are three common specifiers of major depressive disorder?

Causal Factors in Unipolar Mood Disorders

7.3 **Describe the factors believed to cause unipolar mood disorders.**

In considering the development of unipolar mood disorders, researchers have focused on the possible roles of biological, psychological, and sociocultural factors. Although each set of factors has usually been studied separately, ultimately the goal should be to understand how these different kinds of causal factors are interrelated in order to develop a biopsychosocial model.

Biological Causal Factors

It has long been known that a variety of diseases and drugs can affect mood, leading sometimes to depression and sometimes to elation or even mania. Indeed, this idea goes back to Hippocrates (c. 400 B.C.), who hypothesized that depression was caused by an excess of "black bile" in the system. As we will discuss, in the past half century investigators attempting to establish a biological basis for unipolar disorders have considered a wide range of factors.

GENETIC INFLUENCES *Family studies* have shown that the prevalence of mood disorders is approximately two to three times higher among blood relatives of persons with clinically diagnosed unipolar depression than it is in the population at large (e.g., Levinson, 2006, 2009; Wallace et al., 2002). *Twin studies*, which can provide much more conclusive evidence of genetic influences on a disorder, also suggest a moderate genetic contribution to MDD. Monozygotic co-twins of a twin with MDD are about twice as likely to develop the disorder as are dizygotic co-twins, with about 31 to 42 percent of the variance in liability due to genetic influences (Sullivan, Neale, & Kendler, 2000). The estimate is substantially higher (70 to 80 percent) for more severe, early-onset, or recurrent depressions (see also Levinson, 2009; McGuffin et al., 2007). Notably, however, even more variance in the liability to most forms of MDD is due to nonshared environmental influences (i.e., experiences that family members do not share) than to genetic factors.

Taken together, the results from family and twin studies make a strong case for a moderate genetic contribution to the causal patterns of MDD, although not as large a genetic contribution as for bipolar disorder (Farmer et al., 2005; Goodwin & Jamison, 2007). Unfortunately, the evidence for a genetic contribution to persistent depressive disorder is slim because there has been very little research on the topic (Klein, 2008).

Attempts to identify specific genes that may be responsible for these genetic influences have not yet been successful, although there are some promising leads (Levinson, 2006, 2009; Wallace et al., 2002). As discussed in Chapter 3, one candidate for a specific gene that might be implicated is the *serotonin-transporter gene*—a gene involved in the transmission and reuptake of serotonin, one of the key neurotransmitters involved in depression. Two different kinds of versions or alleles are involved: the short allele (*s*) and the long allele (*l*). People either have two short alleles (*s/s*), two long alleles (*l/l*), or one of each (*s/l*). Previous work with animals had suggested that having *ss* alleles might predispose a person to depression relative to a person having *l/l* alleles, but human work on this issue provided mixed results. In 2003, Caspi and colleagues published a landmark study in which they tested for the possibility of a *genotype–environment interaction* involving these two alleles of the serotonin-transporter gene. They studied 847 people in New Zealand who had been followed from birth to 26 years of age, at which time the researchers assessed diagnoses of major depressive episodes in the past year and the occurrence of stressful life events in the previous 5 years. Their results were very striking: As illustrated in Figure 7.2, individuals who possessed the genotype with the *s/s* alleles were twice as likely to develop a major depressive episode following four or more stressful life events in the past 5 years as those who possessed the genotype with the *l/l* alleles and had experienced four or more stressful events (those with the *s/l* alleles were intermediate). Moreover, they found that those who had the *ss* alleles and had experienced severe maltreatment as children were also twice as likely to develop a major depressive episode as those with the *l/l* alleles who had had severe maltreatment and also as compared to those with the *ss* alleles who had not been maltreated as children. These findings strongly support a diathesis–stress model; many other (but not all) studies being conducted have found similar results (e.g., Kendler et al., 2005; Uher & McGuffin, 2010). However, in 2009 a quantitative review by Risch and colleagues (2009) challenged these results; this led to a major controversy in the field. Fortunately by 2011 other quantitative reviews had demonstrated that the gene–environment result is robust if the studies use sensitive interview-based measures of life stress (Uher &

Figure 7.2 Number of Stressful Life Events Versus Probability of Major Depressive Episode

Results demonstrate the association between the number of stressful life events (between ages 21 and 26 years) and probability of a major depressive episode at age 26 as a function of the 5-HTT genotype. Life events predicted a diagnosis of major depression among carriers of the *s* allele (*s/s* or *s/l*), but not among carriers of two *l* alleles (*l/l*).

(Adapted from Caspi et al., 2003. Influence of life stress on depression: Moderation by a polymorphism in the 5-HTT gene. *Science, 301*, 386–89. Reprinted with permission from *Science*, 18 July 2003, Vol. 301. Copyright © 2003 AAAS.)

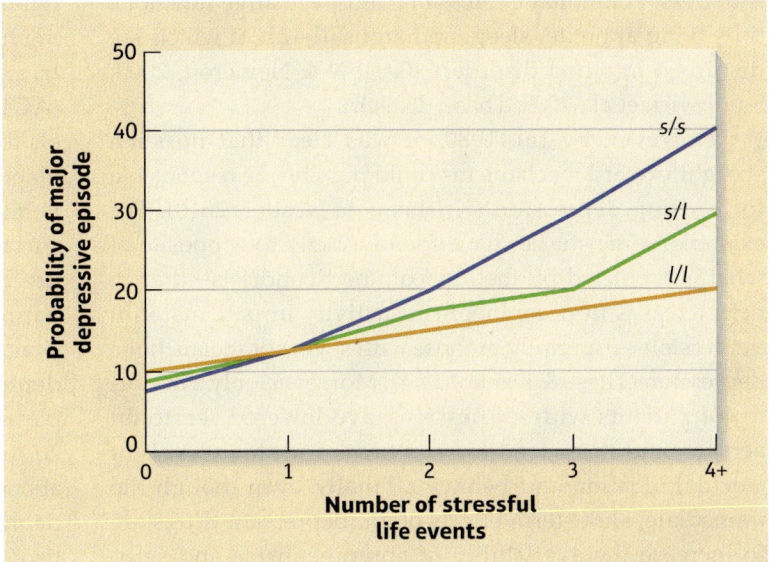

McGuffin, 2010; see also Karg et al., 2011). Such results suggest that the search for candidate genes that are likely to be involved in the etiology of major depression is likely to be much more fruitful if researchers also test for genotype–environment interactions, beyond examining the effects of a genotype itself (see Moffitt et al., 2005).

NEUROCHEMICAL FACTORS Ever since the 1960s, the view that depression may arise from disruptions in the delicate balance of neurotransmitter substances that regulate and mediate the activity of the brain's nerve cells has received a great deal of attention. A large body of evidence suggested that various biological therapies (discussed later in this chapter) that are often used to treat severe mood disorders—such as electroconvulsive therapy and antidepressant medications—affect the concentrations or activity of neurotransmitters at the synapse. Such early findings encouraged the development of neurochemical theories of the etiology of major depression.

Early attention in the 1960s and 1970s focused primarily on two neurotransmitters of the monoamine class—norepinephrine and serotonin—because researchers observed that antidepressant medications seemed to have the effect of increasing these neurotransmitters' availability at synaptic junctions (Thase & Denko, 2008). This observation led to the once influential *monoamine theory of depression*—that depression was at least sometimes due to an absolute or relative depletion of one or both of these neurotransmitters at important receptor sites in the brain (Schildkraut, 1965). This depletion could come about through impaired synthesis of these neurotransmitters in the presynaptic neuron, through increased degradation of the neurotransmitters once they were released into the synapse, or through altered functioning of postsynaptic receptors (Thase, 2009a). Collectively, these neurotransmitters are now known to be involved in the regulation of behavioral activity, stress, emotional expression, and vegetative functions (involving appetite, sleep, and arousal)—all of which are disturbed in mood disorders (Garlow & Nemeroff, 2003; Southwick et al., 2005; Thase, 2009a).

However, by the 1980s it was clear that no such straightforward mechanisms could possibly be responsible for causing depression (Krishnan & Nestler, 2010). For example, some studies have found exactly the opposite of what is predicted by the monoamine hypothesis—that is, net increases in norepinephrine activity in patients with depression—especially in those with severe or melancholic depression (Thase & Denko, 2008). Moreover, only a minority of patients with depression have lowered serotonin activity, and these tend to be patients with high levels of suicidal ideation and behavior. Finally, even though the immediate, short-term effects of antidepressant drugs are to increase the availability of norepinephrine and serotonin, the long-term clinical effects of these drugs do not emerge until 2 to 4 weeks later, when neurotransmitter levels may have normalized.

Other more recent research suggests that dopamine dysfunction (especially reduced dopaminergic activity) plays a significant role in at least some forms of depression, including depression with atypical features and bipolar depression (Krishnan & Nestler, 2010; Thase, 2009a). Because dopamine is so prominently involved in the experience of pleasure and reward, such findings are in keeping with the prominence of anhedonia, the inability to experience pleasure, which is such an important symptom of depression.

Unfortunately, the early monoamine theory has not been replaced by a compelling alternative. Altered neurotransmitter activity in several systems is clearly associated with major depression, but research for the past 20 to 25 years has focused on complex interactions of neurotransmitters (Treadway & Pizzagalli, 2014). A number of integrative theories have been proposed that include a role for neurotransmitters, not alone but rather as they interact with other disturbed hormonal and neurophysiological patterns and biological rhythms (Garlow & Nemeroff, 2003; Thase, 2009a).

ABNORMALITIES OF HORMONAL REGULATORY AND IMMUNE SYSTEMS Research interest has focused on possible hormonal causes or correlates of some forms of

mood disorder (Southwick et al., 2005; Thase, 2009a). The majority of attention has been focused on the *hypothalamic-pituitary-adrenal (HPA) axis*, and in particular on the hormone cortisol, which is excreted by the outermost portion of the adrenal glands and is regulated through a complex feedback loop. The human stress response is associated with elevated activity of the HPA axis, which is partly controlled by norepinephrine and serotonin. The perception of stress or threat can lead to norepinephrine activity in the hypothalamus, causing the release of corticotrophin-releasing hormone (CRH) from the hypothalamus, which in turn triggers the release of adrenocorticotropic hormone (ACTH) from the pituitary. The ACTH then typically travels through the blood to the adrenal cortex of the adrenal glands, where cortisol is released. Elevated cortisol activity is highly adaptive in the short term because it promotes survival in response to life-threatening or overwhelming life circumstances. However, sustained elevations are harmful to the organism, including promoting hypertension, heart disease, and obesity (which are all elevated in depression) (Stetler & Miller, 2011; Thase, 2009a). Blood plasma levels of cortisol are known to be elevated in some 20 to 40 percent of outpatients with depression and in about 60 to 80 percent of hospitalized patients with severe depression (Thase et al., 2002). Sustained elevations in cortisol—a "hallmark of mammalian stress responses"—can result from increased CRH activation (for example, during sustained stress or threat), increased secretion of ACTH, or the failure of feedback mechanisms.

One line of evidence that implicates the failure of feedback mechanisms in some patients with depression comes from robust findings that in about 45 percent of patients with serious depression, *dexamethasone*, a potent suppressor of plasma cortisol in normal individuals, either fails entirely to suppress cortisol or fails to sustain its suppression (Carroll, 2009; Thase et al., 2002). This means that the HPA axis is not operating properly in these "dexamethasone nonsuppressors." It was initially thought that dexamethasone nonsuppressor patients constituted a distinct subgroup of people with severe or melancholic depression (Holsboer, 1992). However, subsequent research has shown that several other groups of psychiatric patients, such as those with panic disorder, also exhibit high rates of nonsuppression, suggesting that nonsuppression may merely be a nonspecific indicator of generalized mental distress.

Research also has revealed that patients having depression with elevated cortisol also tend to show memory impairments and problems with abstract thinking and complex problem solving (Belanoff et al., 2001). Some of these cognitive problems may be related to other findings showing that prolonged elevations in cortisol result in cell death in the hippocampus—a part of the limbic system heavily involved in memory functioning (e.g., Southwick et al., 2005; Thase, 2009a). Other research has shown that stress in infancy and early childhood can promote long-term changes that increase the reactivity of the HPA axis, which may in turn help explain why children reared in environments with early adversity are at higher risk for developing depression later in life when they are exposed to acute stressors (e.g., Southwick et al., 2005).

The other endocrine axis that has relevance to depression is the *hypothalamic-pituitary-thyroid axis* (Garlow & Nemeroff, 2003; Thase, 2009a; Thase et al., 2002). People with low thyroid levels (*hypothyroidism*) often become depressed, and approximately 20 to 30 percent of patients with depression who have normal thyroid levels nevertheless show dysregulation of this axis. Moreover, some patients who do not respond to traditional antidepressant treatments show improvement when administered thyrotropin-releasing hormone, which leads to increased thyroid hormone levels (Garlow & Nemeroff, 2003; Thase, 2009b).

Finally, in recent years many studies have shown that depression is also accompanied by dysregulation of the *immune system* (Dantzer et al., 2009). Specifically, depression is associated with activation of the inflammatory response system as evidenced by increased production of proinflammatory cytokines such as interleukin and interferon (Dowlati et al., 2010). Both of these can contribute directly to the development of depressive symptoms.

NEUROPHYSIOLOGICAL AND NEUROANATOMICAL INFLUENCES Exciting neurophysiological research in recent years has followed up on earlier neurological findings that damage (for example, from a stroke) to the left, but not the right, *anterior prefrontal cortex* often leads to depression (Davidson et al., 2009; Robinson & Downhill, 1995). This led to the idea that depression in people without brain damage may nonetheless be linked to lowered levels of brain activity in this same region. A number of studies have supported this idea. Studies measuring the electroencephalographic (EEG) activity of both cerebral hemispheres in people who are depressed reveals an asymmetry or imbalance in the EEG activity of the two sides of the prefrontal regions of the brain. People with depression show lower activity in the left hemisphere in these regions and higher activity in the right hemisphere (Davidson et al., 2009; Stewart et al., 2010, 2011). Similar findings have been reported using positron emission tomography (PET) neuroimaging techniques (Davidson et al., 2009; Phillips et al., 2003). Notably, patients in remission show the same pattern (Henriques & Davidson, 1990; Stewart et al., 2010, 2011), as do children at risk for depression (Bruder et al., 2007). These latter findings hold promise as a way of identifying persons at risk both for an initial episode and for recurrent episodes. Indeed, a recent study found that left frontal asymmetry in never-depressed individuals predicted onset of major and minor depressive episodes over a 3-year period (Nusslock et al., 2011). The relatively lower

activity on the left side of the prefrontal cortex in depression is thought to be related to symptoms of reduced positive affect and approach behaviors to rewarding stimuli, and increased right-side activity is thought to underlie increased anxiety symptoms and increased negative affect associated with increased vigilance for threatening information (Pizzagalli et al., 2002).

Abnormalities also have been detected in several other brain areas in patients with depression, as illustrated in Figure 7.3 (Davidson et al., 2009; Koolschijn et al., 2009). For example, several regions of the prefrontal cortex, including the *orbital prefrontal cortex*, which is involved in responsivity to reward (Haber & Knutson, 2010), show decreased volume in individuals with recurrent depression relative to normal controls (Koolschijn et al., 2009; Phillips et al., 2003). Lower levels of activity in the *dorsolateral prefrontal cortex*, which are associated with decreased cognitive control, have also been observed in individuals with depression compared to controls (Disner et al., 2011; see also Chang et al., 2011), and seem to normalize following treatment with antidepressant medication (Fales et al., 2009). Another area involved is the *hippocampus*, which is critical to learning and memory and regulation of adrenocorticotropic hormone. As noted earlier, prolonged depression can lead to decreased hippocampal volume, which could be due to cell atrophy or cell death (e.g., Koolschijn et al., 2009; Sapolsky, 2000). In addition, evidence of decreased hippocampal volume in never-depressed individuals who are at high (versus low) risk for depression suggests that reductions in hippocampal volume may precede the onset of depression (Chen et al., 2010).

A third such area is the *anterior cingulate cortex*, which shows both decreased volume and abnormally low levels of activation in patients with depression (Koolschijn et al., 2009). This area is involved in selective attention, which is important in prioritizing the most important information available, and therefore in self-regulation and adaptability—all important processes that are disrupted in depression.

Finally, the *amygdala*, which is involved in the perception of threat and in directing attention, tends to show increased activation in individuals with depression (and anxiety disorders), which may be related to their biased attention to negative emotional information (Davidson et al., 2009; Disner et al., 2011; Phillips et al., 2003).

SLEEP AND OTHER BIOLOGICAL RHYTHMS Although findings of sleep disturbances in patients with depression have existed as long as depression has been studied, only recently have some of these findings been linked to more general disturbances in biological rhythms.

Sleep Sleep is characterized by five stages that occur in a relatively invariant sequence throughout the night (Stages 1–4 of non-REM sleep and REM sleep make up a sleep

Figure 7.3 The key brain regions involved in affect and mood disorders are the (A) orbital prefrontal cortex and ventromedial prefrontal cortex, (B) dorsolateral prefrontal cortex, (C) hippocampus and amygdala, and (D) anterior cingulate cortex

(Adapted from R. J. Davidson, Diego Pizzagalli, and Jack Nitschke. (2002). The representation and regulation of emotion in depression. In I. H. Gotlib and C. L. Hammen (Eds.), *Handbook of Depression* (pp. 219–244). New York: Guilford.)

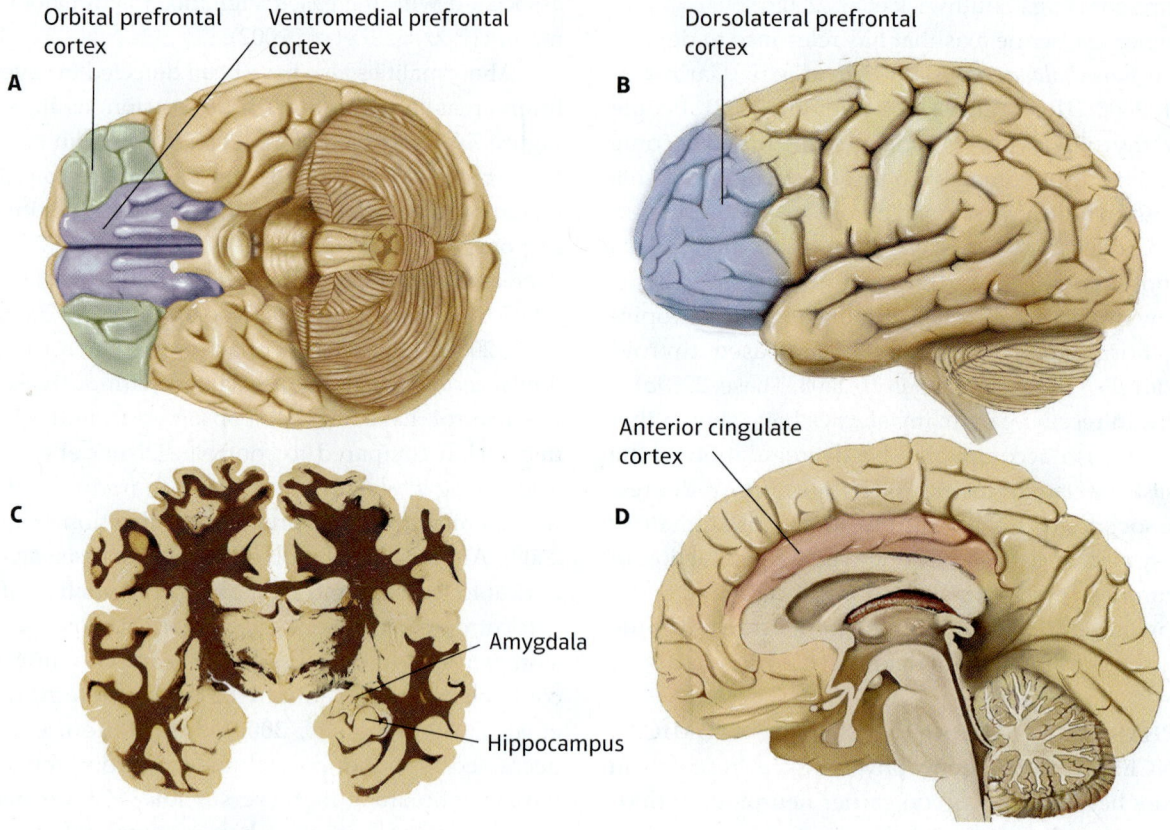

cycle). REM sleep (rapid eye movement sleep) is characterized by rapid eye movements and dreaming as well as other bodily changes; the first REM period does not usually begin until near the end of the first sleep cycle, about 75 to 80 minutes into sleep. This normal sleep–wake cycle is thought to be regulated by the *suprachiasmatic nucleus* of the hypothalamus (Steiger, 2007; Thase, 2009a). People who are depressed often show one or more of a variety of sleep problems, ranging from difficulty falling asleep, to periodic awakening during the night (poor sleep maintenance), to early morning awakening. Such changes occur in about 80 percent of hospitalized patients with depression and in about 50 percent of outpatients with depression, and are particularly pronounced in patients with melancholic features.

Moreover, research using EEG recordings has found that many patients with depression enter the first period of REM sleep after only 60 minutes or less of sleep (15 to 20 minutes sooner than nondepressed patients), show greater amounts of REM sleep during the early cycles, and have more intense and frequent rapid eye movements (Tsuno et al., 2005). Most deep sleep occurs during Stages 3 and 4, and people with depression also appear to get a lower-than-normal amount of deep sleep. Both the reduced latency to enter REM sleep and the decreased amount of deep sleep often precede the onset of depression and persist following recovery, which suggests that they may be vulnerability markers for certain forms of major depression (Hasler et al., 2004; Thase et al., 2002).

Circadian Rhythms   Humans have many circadian (24-hour, or daily) cycles that the body uses to respond appropriately to the changing environment (e.g., sleep–wake cycle, locomotor activity cycle). These circadian rhythms are controlled by two related central "oscillators," which act as internal biological clocks. Research has found some abnormalities in all of these rhythms in patients with depression including drastic changes in mood, sleep, appetite, and social interactions. Although psychologists are still working to figure out exactly how circadian rhythm abnormalities might contribute to the symptoms of depression, it is clear that circadian rhythms, the human stress response, and disorders such as depression are closely related (Landgraf et al., 2014).

Sunlight and Seasons   Another, rather different kind of rhythm abnormality or disturbance is seen in people with *seasonal affective disorder*, in which most of those affected seem to be responsive to the total quantity of available light in the environment (Oren & Rosenthal, 1992). A majority (but not all) of people with seasonal affective disorder become depressed in the fall/winter and normalize in the spring/summer (Goodwin & Jamison, 2007). Research in animals also has documented that many seasonal variations in basic functions such as sleep, activity, and appetite are related to the amount of light in a day (which, except near the equator, is much greater in summer than in winter). A good deal of research on patients with seasonal affective disorder supports the therapeutic use of controlled exposure to light, even artificial light, which may work by reestablishing normal biological rhythms (Fava & Rosenbaum, 1995; Goodwin & Jamison, 2007). Although antidepressant medications can also be useful, the use of light therapy is more cost efficient in the long term (Cheung et al., 2012).

People who live in higher latitudes (northern climates for those in the Northern Hemisphere) are more likely to exhibit seasonal affective disorder, in which depression occurs primarily in the fall and winter months and tends to remit in the spring or summer months.

BIOLOGICAL EXPLANATIONS FOR SEX DIFFERENCES

Before we leave the topic of possible biological causal factors for depression, we should note that it has been suggested that hormonal factors such as normal fluctuations in ovarian hormones account for sex differences in depression (Deecher et al., 2008). However, studies examining this hypothesis have yielded inconsistent results and overall are not very supportive (Nolen-Hoeksema & Hilt, 2009). It seems that for the majority of women, hormonal changes occurring at various points (e.g., at the onset of puberty, before menstruation, in the postpartum period, and at menopause) do not play a significant role in causing depression. However, it remains possible that there is a causal association that has not yet been discovered because of real methodological difficulties in conducting conclusive research on this topic (Naninck et al., 2011; Sanborn & Hayward, 2003). Moreover, for a small minority of women

who are already at high risk (for example, by being at high genetic risk), hormonal fluctuations may trigger depressive episodes, possibly by causing changes in the normal processes that regulate neurotransmitter systems (Deecher et al., 2008; Naninck et al., 2011). Some studies have suggested that women have a greater genetic vulnerability to depression than men, but many other studies have not supported this idea (e.g., Nolen-Hoeksema & Hilt, 2009; Wallace et al., 2002).

Psychological Causal Factors

The evidence for important psychological causal factors in most unipolar mood disorders is at least as strong as the evidence for biological factors. However, it is likely that the effects of some psychological factors such as stressful life events are mediated by a cascade of underlying biological changes that they initiate. One way in which stressors may act is through their effects on biochemical and hormonal balances and on biological rhythms (Hammen, 2005; Monroe, 2008).

STRESSFUL LIFE EVENTS AS CAUSAL FACTORS Environmental stressors are known to be involved in the onset of a variety of disorders, ranging from some of the anxiety disorders to schizophrenia, but nowhere has their role been more carefully studied than in the case of unipolar major depression. Many studies have shown that severely stressful life events often serve as precipitating factors for unipolar depression (e.g., Hammen, 2005; Monroe et al., 2009). This is especially true for young female adults for whom stressful life events are more likely to show a stronger stress–depression relationship than is the case for men (Harkness et al., 2010).

Most of the episodic stressful life events involved in precipitating depression concern loss of a loved one, serious threats to important close relationships or to one's occupation, or severe economic or serious health problems (Monroe et al., 2009). The stress of being the caregiver to a spouse with a debilitating disease such as Alzheimer's is also known to be associated with the onset of both major depression and generalized anxiety disorder in the caregiver (e.g., Russo et al., 1995).

An important distinction has been made between stressful life events that are independent of the person's behavior and personality (*independent life events*, such as losing a job because one's company is shutting down or having one's house hit by a hurricane) and events that may have been at least partly generated by the depressed person's behavior or personality (*dependent life events*). For example, people with depression sometimes generate stressful life events through their poor interpersonal problem solving (such as being unable to resolve conflicts with a spouse), which is often associated with depression. The poor problem solving in turn leads to higher levels of interpersonal stress, which in turn leads to further symptoms of depression. Another example of a dependent life event is failing to keep up with routine tasks such as paying bills, which may lead to a variety of troubles. Evidence to date suggests that dependent life events play an even stronger role in the onset of major depression than do independent life events (Hammen, 2005; Kendler et al., 1999a).

Research on stress and the onset of depression is complicated by the fact that people with depression have a distinctly negative view of themselves and the world around them (Beck, 1967; Clark, Beck, & Alford, 1999). Thus, their own perceptions of stress may result—at least to some extent—from the cognitive symptoms of their disorder rather than cause their disorder (Dohrenwend, 2006; Monroe, 2008; Monroe & Hadjiyannakis, 2002). That is, their pessimistic outlook may lead them to evaluate events as stressful that other nondepressed people would not. Therefore, researchers have developed more sophisticated interview-based measures of life stress that do not rely on the depressed person's self-report of how stressful an event is and that take into account the biographical context of a person's life. Trained independent raters evaluate what the impact of a particular event would be expected to be for an average person who has experienced this event in these particular life circumstances; the person's subjective evaluations of stress are not recorded or taken into account in the rating of impact (Monroe, 2008). For example, the stress value of divorce for a woman who has already begun to establish a new relationship would probably not be rated as highly as the divorce of a woman whose husband left her for a younger woman. There is widespread agreement that conclusions derived from studies using these more sophisticated interview-based techniques are more reliable and valid in predicting depressive episodes (e.g., Monroe, 2008; Uher & McGuffin, 2010).

Several recent reviews of studies that employed these sophisticated measurements of life stress suggest that severely stressful episodic life events play a causal role (most often within a month or so after the event) in about 20 to 50 percent of cases (Hammen, 2005; Monroe & Harkness, 2005). Moreover, people with depression who have experienced a stressful life event tend to show more severe depressive symptoms than those who have not experienced a stressful life event (Monroe & Hadjiyannakis, 2002). This relationship between severely stressful life events and depression is much stronger in people who are having their first onset than in those undergoing recurrent episodes (Kendler, Thornton, & Gardner, 2000). It has been estimated that about 70 percent of people with a first onset of depression have had a recent major stressful life event, whereas only about 40 percent of people with a recurrent episode have had a recent major life event (Monroe & Harkness, 2005).

Mildly Stressful Events and Chronic Stress   Whether mildly stressful events are also associated with the onset of depression is less clear, with conflicting findings in the literature. Studies applying more sophisticated strategies for assessing life stress have generally *not* found minor stressful events to be associated with the onset of clinically significant depression (Dohrenwend et al., 1995; Stueve et al., 1998). An interesting hypothesis has been raised that minor events may play more of a role in the onset of *recurrent* episodes than in the *initial* episode (Stroud et al., 2011).

A number of studies have demonstrated that *chronic stress* is associated with increased risk for the onset, maintenance, and recurrence of major depression (Hammen, 2005; Monroe et al., 2007). Chronic stress (or *chronic strain* or *difficulties*) has been defined in different ways, but usually refers to one or more forms of stress ongoing for at least several months (e.g., poverty, marital discord, medical problems, having a child with a disability).

Vulnerability and Responses to Stressors   It is important to keep in mind that there are important individual differences in how people respond to the experiences of episodic or chronic life stress. For example, women (and perhaps men) at genetic risk for depression not only experience more stressful life events but also are more sensitive to them (Kendler et al., 1999a). More specifically, those at high genetic risk for depression appear to be much more likely to respond to stressful life events with depression (an example of a gene–environment interaction) than those at low genetic risk (Caspi et al., 2003).

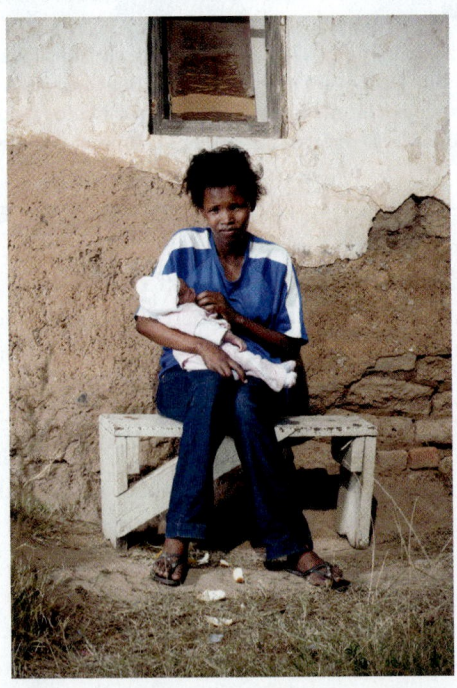

If a woman living in poverty is already genetically at risk for depression, the stresses associated with living in poverty may be especially likely to precipitate a major depression in her.

DIFFERENT TYPES OF VULNERABILITIES FOR UNIPOLAR DEPRESSION In addition to genetic variables, there are a host of other psychological and social variables that may make some people more vulnerable, and other people less vulnerable, to developing depression after experiencing one or more stressful life events.

Personality and Cognitive Diatheses Researchers have concluded that neuroticism is the primary personality variable that serves as a vulnerability factor for depression (and anxiety disorders; Klein et al., 2009; Zinbarg et al., 2011). Recall that *neuroticism*, or *negative affectivity*, refers to a stable and heritable personality trait that involves a temperamental sensitivity to negative stimuli. Thus, people who have high levels of this trait are prone to experiencing a broad range of negative moods, including not only sadness but also anxiety, guilt, and hostility. Moreover, several studies have also shown that neuroticism predicts the occurrence of more stressful life events, which frequently lead to depression (Kendler, Gardner, & Prescott, 2003; Uliaszek et al., 2012). In addition to serving as a vulnerability factor, neuroticism is associated with a worse prognosis for complete recovery from depression. Finally, some researchers attribute sex differences in depression to sex differences in neuroticism (Kendler et al., 2002; Sutin et al., 2010).

There is more limited evidence that high levels of introversion (or low positive affectivity) may also serve as vulnerability factors for depression, either alone or when combined with neuroticism (Watson et al., 2005). Positive affectivity involves a disposition to feel joyful, energetic, bold, proud, enthusiastic, and confident; people low on this disposition tend to feel unenthusiastic, unenergetic, dull, flat, and bored. It is therefore not surprising that this might make them more prone to developing clinical depression, although the evidence for this is very mixed.

The cognitive diatheses that have been studied for depression generally focus on particular negative patterns of thinking that make people who are prone to depression more likely to become depressed when faced with one or more stressful life events. For example, people who attribute negative events to internal, stable, and global causes may be more prone to becoming depressed than are people who attribute the same events to external, unstable, and specific causes (Abramson et al., 2002). A pessimistic or depressive attribution for receiving a low grade in an exam might be "I'm stupid," whereas a more optimistic attribution for the same event might be "The teacher deliberately wrote a difficult test to make us all realize we need to study harder."

Early Adversity as a Diathesis A range of adversities in the early environment (such as family turmoil, parental psychopathology, physical or sexual abuse, and other forms of intrusive, harsh, and coercive parenting) can create both a short-term and a long-term vulnerability to depression. Such factors operate, at least in part, by increasing an individual's sensitivity to stressful life events in adulthood, with similar findings having been observed in animals (Slavich et al., 2011). The long-term effects of such early environmental adversities may be mediated by both biological variables (such as alterations in the regulation of the hypothalamic-pituitary stress response system) and psychological variables (such as lower self-esteem, insecure attachment relationships, difficulty relating to peers, and pessimistic attributions; Goodman & Brand, 2009; Harkness & Lumley, 2008). However, it is also important to realize that certain individuals who have undergone early adversity remain resilient, and if the exposure to early adversity is moderate rather than severe, a form of stress inoculation may occur that makes the individual less susceptible to the effects of later stress (Parker et al., 2004). These stress-inoculation effects seem to be mediated by strengthening socioemotional and neuroendocrine resistance to subsequent stressors.

Summary As we have discussed, several different types of biological and psychological diatheses for unipolar depression have been studied, and some of these have been formulated as diathesis–stress theories, as we review in the following sections. Nevertheless it is important to keep in mind that these theories of vulnerability are not mutually exclusive, and some may simply be describing the same diathesis in different terms or at different levels of analysis. For example, there is a moderately strong genetic basis for neuroticism, and neuroticism is strongly correlated with pessimism (Clark, Watson, & Mineka, 1994), so these proposed diatheses are clearly somewhat interrelated. Moreover, dysfunctional early parenting, emotional abuse, and parental loss have been strongly implicated in the formation of some of the other cognitive diatheses (Alloy et al., 2004; Bowlby, 1980; Goodman & Brand, 2009). Thus, these two proposed diatheses may simply differ in whether they operate distally (poor early parenting) or proximally (negative thinking patterns) in contributing to vulnerability for depression.

We now turn to five major psychological theories of depression that have received much attention over the years.

PSYCHODYNAMIC THEORIES In his classic paper "Mourning and Melancholia" (1917), Freud noted the important similarity between the symptoms of clinical depression and the symptoms seen in people mourning the loss of a loved one. Freud and his colleague Karl Abraham (1927) both hypothesized that when a loved one dies the mourner regresses to the oral stage of development (when the infant cannot distinguish self from others) and introjects or incorporates the lost person, feeling all the same feelings toward the self as toward the lost person. These feelings were thought to include anger and hostility because Freud believed that we unconsciously hold negative feelings toward those we love, in part because of their power over us. This is what led to the psychodynamic idea that depression is anger turned inward. Freud hypothesized that depression could also occur in response to imagined or symbolic losses. For example, a student who fails in school or who fails at a romantic relationship may experience this symbolically as a loss of his or her parents' love.

Later psychodynamic theorists proposed a number of variants on Freud and Abraham's early psychodynamic theories (Levy & Wasserman, 2009). Perhaps the most important contribution of the psychodynamic approaches to depression has been their noting the importance of loss (both real and symbolic or imagined) to the onset of depression and noting the striking similarities between the symptoms of mourning and the symptoms of depression (Bowlby, 1980).

Children who have lost a parent through death or permanent separation may become vulnerable to depression if they receive poor subsequent care from another parent or guardian and if their environment and routine are disrupted.

BEHAVIORAL THEORIES   In the 1970s and 1980s, several theorists in the behavioral tradition developed behavioral theories of depression, proposing that people become depressed either when their responses no longer produce positive reinforcement or when their rate of negative experiences increases (Ferster, 1974; Lewinsohn & Gotlib, 1995). Such theories are consistent with research showing that people with depression do indeed receive fewer positive verbal and social reinforcements from their families and friends than do people who are not depressed and also experience more negative events. Moreover, they have lower activity levels, and their moods seem to vary with both their positive and their negative experiences rates (Lewinsohn & Gotlib, 1995; Martell, 2009). Nevertheless, although such findings are consistent with behavioral theories, they do not show that depression is *caused* by these factors. Instead, it may be that some of the primary symptoms of depression, such as pessimism and low levels of

energy, cause the person with depression to experience lower rates of reinforcement, which in turn may help maintain the depression. Interestingly, exciting new research has demonstrated that a novel form of behavioral treatment inspired by these behavioral theories—behavioral activation treatment—seems to be an effective treatment for depression (Dimidjian et al., 2011; Martell, 2009).

BECK'S COGNITIVE THEORY   Since 1967 one of the most influential theories of depression has been that of Aaron Beck (b. 1921), a psychiatrist who became disenchanted with psychodynamic theories of depression early in his career and developed his own cognitive theory of depression (Beck, 1967, 2005). Whereas the most prominent symptoms of depression have generally been considered to be the affective or mood symptoms, Beck hypothesized that the cognitive symptoms of depression often precede and cause the affective or mood symptoms rather than vice versa (see Figure 7.4). For example, if you think that you are a failure or that you are ugly, it would not be surprising for those thoughts to lead to a depressed mood.

Figure 7.4 Beck's Cognitive Model of Depression
According to Beck's cognitive model of depression, certain kinds of early experiences can lead to the formation of dysfunctional assumptions that leave a person vulnerable to depression later in life if certain critical incidents (stressors) activate those assumptions. Once activated, these dysfunctional assumptions trigger automatic thoughts that in turn produce depressive symptoms, which further fuel the depressive automatic thoughts.

(Adapted from Fennell, 1989.)

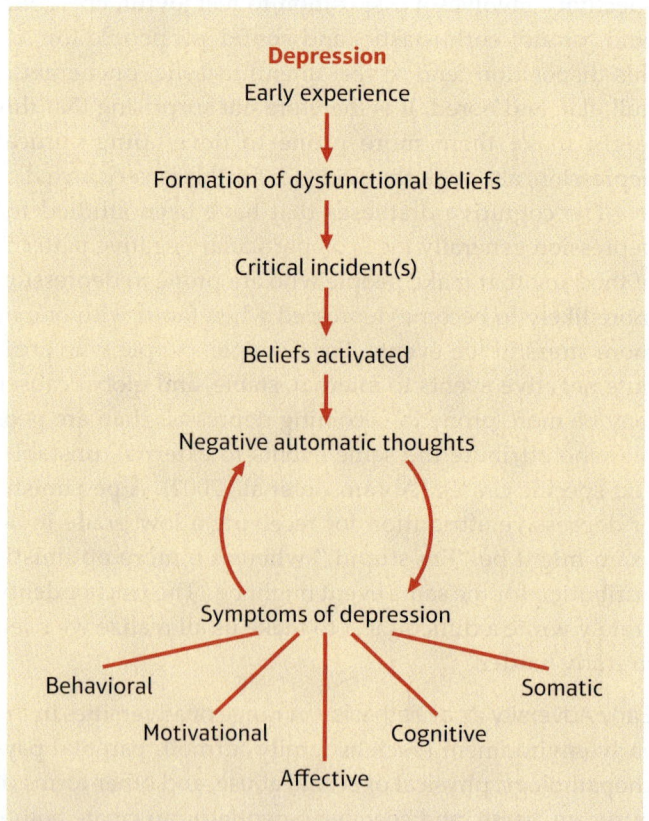

Beck's theory, a diathesis–stress theory in which negative cognitions are central, has become somewhat more elaborate over the years while still retaining its primary tenets (Beck, 1967, 2005; Clark & Beck, 2010). First, there are the underlying **dysfunctional beliefs**, known as **depressogenic schemas**, which are rigid, extreme, and counterproductive. An example of a dysfunctional belief (that a person is usually not consciously aware of) is "If everyone doesn't love me, then my life is worthless." According to cognitive theory, such a belief would predispose the person holding it to develop depression if he or she perceived social rejection. Alternatively, a person with the dysfunctional belief "If I'm not perfectly successful, then I'm a nobody" would be vulnerable to developing negative thoughts and depressed mood if she or he felt like a failure. These depression-producing beliefs or schemas are thought to develop during childhood and adolescence as a function of negative experiences with parents and significant others, and they are thought to serve as the underlying diathesis, or vulnerability, to developing depression (Beck, 1967; Ingram et al., 2006; Morley & Moran, 2011). Although they may lie dormant for years in the absence of significant stressors, when dysfunctional beliefs are activated by current stressors or depressed mood, they tend to fuel the current thinking pattern, creating a pattern of **negative automatic thoughts**—thoughts that often occur just below the surface of awareness and involve unpleasant, pessimistic predictions. These pessimistic predictions tend to center on the three themes of what Beck calls the **negative cognitive triad**, which include negative thoughts about (1) self ("I'm worthless"); (2) world ("No one loves me"); and (3) future ("It's hopeless because things will always be this way") (Clark, Beck, & Alford, 1999; see Figure 7.5).

Beck also postulated that the negative cognitive triad tends to be maintained by a variety of negative cognitive biases or errors (see also Scher et al., 2005). Each of these involves biased processing of negative self-relevant information. Examples include:

- *Dichotomous or all-or-none reasoning*, which involves a tendency to think in extremes. For example, someone might discount a less-than-perfect performance by saying, "If I can't get it 100 percent right, there's no point in doing it at all."

- *Selective abstraction*, which involves a tendency to focus on one negative detail of a situation while ignoring other elements of the situation. Someone might say, "I

Figure 7.5 Negative Cognitive Triad

Beck's cognitive model of depression describes a pattern of negative automatic thoughts. These pessimistic predictions center on three themes: the self, the world, and the future.

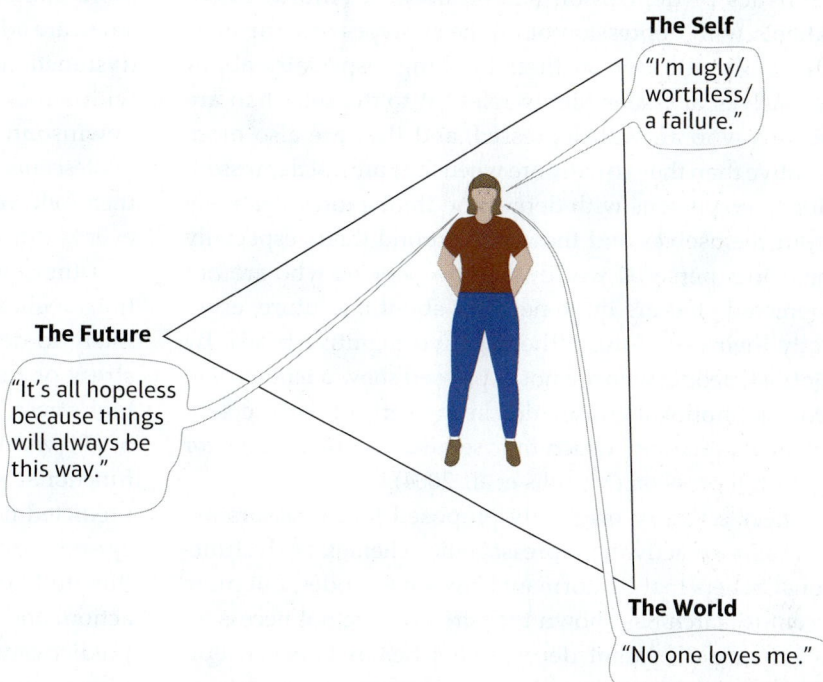

The Self
"I'm ugly/worthless/a failure."

The Future
"It's all hopeless because things will always be this way."

The World
"No one loves me."

didn't have a moment of pleasure or fun today" not because this is true but because he or she selectively remembers only the negative things that happened.

- *Arbitrary inference*, which involves jumping to a conclusion based on minimal or no evidence. A depressed person might say, after an initial homework assignment from a cognitive therapist did not work, "This therapy will never work for me." (Examples from Fennell, 1989, p. 193)

It is easy to see how each of these cognitive distortions tends to maintain the negative cognitive triad. That is, if the content of your thoughts regarding your views of yourself, your world, and your future is already negative and you tend to minimize the good things that happen to you or draw negative conclusions based on minimal evidence, those negative thoughts are not likely to disappear. In addition, just as the underlying dysfunctional beliefs (such as "If everybody doesn't love me, then my life is worthless") elicit the negative cognitive triad when activated, so too does the negative thinking produced by the negative triad serve to reinforce those underlying beliefs. Thus, each of these components of cognitive theory serves to reinforce the others, as shown in Figure 7.4. Moreover, these negative thoughts can produce some of the other symptoms of depression such as sadness, dejection, and lack of motivation.

Evaluating Beck's Theory as a Descriptive Theory An enormous amount of research has been conducted to test various aspects of Beck's theory, and it has generated a very effective form of treatment for depression known as cognitive therapy. In addition, it has been well supported as a descriptive theory that explains many prominent characteristics of depression (Clark, Beck, & Alford, 1999). Patients with depression of all the subtypes are considerably more negative in their thinking, especially about themselves or issues highly relevant to the self, than are persons who are not depressed, and they are also more negative than they usually are when they are not depressed. Moreover, persons with depression think more negatively about themselves and the world around them, especially their own personal world, than do persons who are not depressed, and are quite negative about the future, especially their own future (the negative cognitive triad). By contrast, people who are not depressed show a tendency to process emotional information in an overly optimistic, self-enhancing manner, which may serve as a protective factor against depression (Mezulis et al., 2004).

Beck's theory originally proposed that stressors are necessary to activate depressogenic schemas or dysfunctional beliefs that lie dormant between episodes, but more recent research has shown that stressors are not necessary to activate the latent depressive schemas between episodes. Indeed, simply inducing a depressed mood (e.g., through listening to sad music or recalling sad memories) in an individual who was previously depressed (that is, at risk) is generally sufficient to activate latent depressogenic schemas (e.g., Ingram et al., 2006; LeMoult et al., 2009; Scher et al., 2005).

In addition to evidence for dysfunctional beliefs and negative automatic thoughts, there is also considerable evidence for certain cognitive biases for negative self-relevant information in depression. For example, people with depression show better or biased recall of negative information and negative autobiographical memories, whereas people who are not depressed tend to show biased recall of positive emotional information and positive autobiographical memories (Gotlib & Joormann, 2010; Hertel & Brozovich, 2010; Mathews & MacLeod, 2005; Mineka et al., 2003). In addition, people with depression are more likely than people who are not depressed to draw negative conclusions that go beyond the information presented in a scenario and to underestimate the positive feedback they have received (Clark, Beck, & Alford, 1999). It is easy to see how, if one is already depressed, remembering primarily the bad things that have happened is likely to maintain or exacerbate the depression. Teasdale (1988, 1996) aptly called this the "vicious cycle of depression."

Evaluating the Causal Aspects of Beck's Theory   Although research supports most of the descriptive aspects of Beck's theory, research directed toward confirming the causal hypotheses of Beck's theory has yielded more mixed results. The causal hypotheses are usually tested with a prospective study design. People who are not depressed are tested for their cognitive vulnerability (usually, dysfunctional beliefs) at Time 1 and then are followed for 1 or more months or years, after which measurements of life stress are administered. Only some studies have found that dysfunctional beliefs or attitudes at Time 1, in interaction with stressful life events, predict depression at Time 2. Lewinsohn and colleagues (2001) assessed about 1,500 adolescents for their dysfunctional beliefs or attitudes and then followed them for 1 year, at which point stressful life events during that year were assessed. Results indicated that those who had started with high levels of dysfunctional beliefs and who experienced high stress were more likely to develop major depression than those with low stress or than those with low dysfunctional beliefs and high stress. Another study with a large community sample of 700 women (average age was 41) also found that dysfunctional beliefs at the outset of a 3-year follow-up period predicted new onsets and recurrences of major depressive episodes over the next 3 years (Otto et al., 2007). However, this study did not find evidence of a diathesis–stress interaction, and dysfunctional beliefs did not have additional predictive value beyond that afforded by knowing a prior history of the person's depressive episodes. Because of inconsistencies in results across studies, more research is still needed to fully assess the causal aspects of Beck's cognitive theory of depression.

THE HELPLESSNESS AND HOPELESSNESS THEORIES OF DEPRESSION   Whereas Beck's theory grew out of his clinical observations and research on the pervasive patterns of negative thinking seen in patients with depression, the learned helplessness theory of depression originated out of observations in an animal research laboratory. Martin Seligman (1974, 1975) first proposed that the laboratory phenomenon known as **learned helplessness** might provide a useful animal model of depression. In the late 1960s, Seligman and his colleagues (Maier et al., 1969; Overmier & Seligman, 1967) noted that laboratory dogs who were first exposed to uncontrollable shocks later acted in a passive and helpless manner when they were in a situation where they could control the shocks. In contrast, animals first exposed to equal amounts of controllable shocks had no trouble learning to control the shocks.

Seligman and his colleagues (Maier et al., 1969; Overmier & Seligman, 1967) developed the learned helplessness hypothesis to explain these effects. It states that when animals or humans find that they have no control over aversive events (such as shock), they may learn that they are helpless, which makes them unmotivated to try to respond in the future. Instead they exhibit passivity and even depressive symptoms. They are also slow to learn that any response they do make is effective, which may parallel the negative cognitive set in human depression. Seligman's observations that the animals looked depressed captured his attention and ultimately led to his proposing a learned helplessness model of depression (Seligman, 1974, 1975). Subsequent research demonstrated that helpless animals also show other depressive symptoms such as lower levels of aggression, loss of appetite and weight, and changes in monoamine neurotransmitter levels. After demonstrating that learned helplessness also occurs in humans (Hiroto & Seligman, 1975), he went on to propose that learned helplessness may underlie some types of human depression. That is, people undergoing stressful life events over which they have little or no control may develop a syndrome like the helplessness syndrome seen in animals.

The Reformulated Helplessness Theory Some of the research with humans on helplessness soon led to a major reformulation of the helplessness theory, addressing some of the complexities of what humans do when faced with uncontrollable events (Abramson et al., 1978). In particular, Abramson and colleagues proposed that when people (probably unlike animals) are exposed to uncontrollable negative events, they ask themselves why, and the kinds of **attributions** that people make are, in turn, central to whether they become depressed. These investigators proposed three critical dimensions on which attributions are made: (1) internal/external, (2) global/specific, and (3) stable/unstable. They proposed that a depressogenic or pessimistic attribution for a negative event is an internal, stable, and global one. For example, if your boyfriend treats you badly and you conclude that "It's because I'm ugly and boring," you are much more likely to become depressed than if you conclude that "It's because he's in a bad mood today and he is taking it out on me."

Abramson and colleagues (1978) proposed that people who have a relatively stable and consistent **pessimistic attributional style** have a vulnerability or diathesis for depression when faced with uncontrollable negative life events. This kind of cognitive style seems to develop, at least in part, through social learning (Alloy, Abramson, Smith, et al., 2006). For example, children may learn this cognitive style by observing and modeling inferences made by their parents. Alternatively or additionally, the parents may communicate their own inferences about negative events happening to their children, or engage in generally negative parenting practices such as high levels of negative psychological control (criticism, intrusiveness, and guilt) as well as a lack of warmth and caring.

This *reformulated helplessness theory* led to a great deal of research. Many studies demonstrated that depressed people do indeed have this kind of pessimistic attributional style, but of course this does not mean that pessimistic attributional style plays a causal role. Using prospective designs, many studies have examined the ability of a pessimistic attributional style to predict the onset of depression in

interaction with negative life events (Abramson et al., 1989; Alloy et al., 2008). Some results have supported this theory and some have not.

The helplessness theory has been used to explain sex differences in depression. This theory proposes that by virtue of their roles in society, women are more prone to experiencing a sense of lack of control over negative life events. These feelings of helplessness might stem from poverty, discrimination in the workplace, high rates of sexual and physical abuse against women (either currently or in childhood), role overload (e.g., being a working wife and mother), and less perceived control over traits that men value when choosing a long-term mate, such as beauty, thinness, and youth (Heim et al., 2000; Nolen-Hoeksema & Hilt, 2009). There is at least some evidence that each of these conditions is associated with higher-than-expected rates of depression, although whether the effects involve a sense of helplessness has not yet been established (Nolen-Hoeksema et al., 1999). Combining the neuroticism theory with the helplessness theory, it is important to note that there is evidence that people who are high on neuroticism are more sensitive to the effects of adversity relative to those low on neuroticism (a genotype–environment interaction; Kendler et al., 2004; Lahey, 2009). So given that women have higher levels of neuroticism and experience more uncontrollable stress, the increased prevalence of depression in women becomes less surprising.

The Hopelessness Theory of Depression A further revision of this theory, known as the *hopelessness theory*, was later presented (Abramson et al., 1989; see Alloy et al., 2008). Abramson and colleagues (1989) propose that having a pessimistic attributional style in conjunction with one or more negative life events was not sufficient to produce depression unless one first experienced a state of hopelessness. A hopelessness expectancy was defined by the perception that one had no control over what was going to happen and by the absolute certainty that an important bad outcome was going to occur or that a highly desired good outcome was not going to occur. They also proposed that the internal/external dimension of attributions was not important to depression. Specifically, they proposed that depression-prone individuals not only tend to make global and stable attributions for negative events but also tend to make negative inferences about other likely negative consequences of the event (e.g., that this means more bad things will also happen) and negative inferences about the implications of the event for the self-concept (e.g., that one is unworthy or deficient; Abramson et al., 2002).

Research during the past 25 years has been testing this theory. A major longitudinal prospective study of several hundred college students who were hypothesized to be at high risk for unipolar depression (because they had both a pessimistic attributional style and high levels of dysfunctional beliefs) has yielded evidence supportive of some of the major tenets of the hopelessness theory (Abramson et al., 2002; Alloy, Abramson, Whitehouse, et al., 2006; Alloy et al., 2008). For example, in a 2.5-year follow-up period, students in the high-risk group who had never previously been depressed at the outset of the study were about four times more likely (16.2 versus 3.6 percent) to develop a first episode of major depression (or comorbid depression and anxiety) than those in the low-risk group. For those who had already had a previous episode of depression prior to entry into the study, the high-risk group was about three times more likely to experience a recurrent episode of major depression in the 2.5-year follow-up period.

Additional support for the hopelessness theory has been accumulating as well. Several smaller studies have shown evidence for the interaction of cognitive vulnerability with life stress in predicting depressive symptoms and onset of depression (Hankin et al., 2004), although others have not (Alloy et al., 2008). Furthermore, research has begun to integrate hopelessness theory with a motivational theory of depression that posits that depression is associated with decreased approach behavior (Nusslock et al., 2011). Specifically, some researchers have hypothesized that cognitively vulnerable individuals are at risk for decreased approach-related behavior as a result of increased hopelessness under stress, thereby contributing to depression. There is at least initial empirical support for this notion. For example, in one investigation of undergraduate students, cognitive vulnerability interacted with life stress to predict a decrease in goal-directed behavior, which was then associated with higher levels of depressive symptoms (Haeffel et al., 2008). The relationship between cognitive vulnerability and stress with goal-directed behavior was mediated by increased feelings of hopelessness. Additional tests of the hopelessness theory and its predictions are needed, but future research on the hopelessness theory is likely to continue to provide important insights into psychosocial causes of depression.

The Ruminative Response Styles Theory of Depression Nolen-Hoeksema's ruminative response style cognitive theory of depression (1991, 2000, 2012) focuses on different kinds of responses that people have when they experience feelings and symptoms of sadness and distress, and how their differing response styles affect the course of their depression. Specifically, when some people have such feelings, they tend to focus intently on how they feel and why they feel that way—a process called **rumination**, which involves a pattern of repetitive and relatively passive mental activity. Other people, by contrast, have a more action-oriented or problem-solving response to such feelings and, for example, distract themselves with another activity or actually try to do something that will solve the problems that are leading to the sadness and distress. Research has consistently shown that there are stable individual differences in the tendency to ruminate and that people who ruminate a great deal tend to have more lengthy periods of depressive symptoms. They are also more likely to develop full-blown episodes of major depressive disorder (Nolen-Hoeksema, 2000; Nolen-Hoeksema & Hilt, 2009).

Interestingly, it seems that women are more likely than men to ruminate when they become depressed (Nolen-Hoeksema & Aldao, 2011; Nolen-Hoeksema & Corte, 2004). Moreover, self-focused rumination leads to increased recall of more negative autobiographical memories, thereby feeding a vicious circle of depression (Hertel & Brozovich, 2010; Lyubomirsky et al., 1998; Nolen-Hoeksema et al., 2008). Importantly, when gender differences in rumination are statistically controlled, gender differences in depression are no longer significant (Nolen-Hoeksema & Hilt, 2009).

Men, by contrast, are more likely to engage in a distracting activity (or consume alcohol) when they get in a depressed mood, and distraction seems to reduce depression (Nolen-Hoeksema, 2012; Nolen-Hoeksema & Corte, 2004). Distraction might include going to a movie, playing a sport, or avoiding thinking about why they are depressed. The origin of these sex differences in response to depression is unclear, but if further research supports this hypothesis it would certainly suggest that effective prevention efforts might include teaching girls to seek distraction rather than to ruminate as a response to depression.

Women are more likely than men to ruminate when they are depressed. Men, in contrast, tend to engage in distracting activities when they get into a depressed mood.

Developments in Research

Why Do Sex Differences in Unipolar Depression Emerge During Adolescence?

It is interesting to consider why the sex difference in depression starts in adolescence (Essau et al., 2010; Hankin & Abramson, 2001; Hankin et al., 2008). It begins between ages 12 and 13 and reaches its most dramatic peak between ages 14 and 16, although it is actually more tied to pubertal status than to age per se (Becker et al., 2007; Conley & Rudolph, 2009; Sanborn & Hayward, 2003). This is a time of rapid physiological, environmental, and psychological changes known to create turmoil for many adolescents, but why are adolescent females more likely to become depressed? Hankin, Abramson, and colleagues (Hankin & Abramson, 2001; Hankin et al., 2008) have proposed an intriguing cognitive vulnerability-stress model of the development of gender differences during adolescence. Building on ideas from the reformulated helplessness and hopelessness models of depression for adults, they summarize research indicating that children and adolescents, like adults, are prone to experiencing increases in depressive symptoms if they have a pessimistic attributional style and experience stressful life events (e.g., Hankin, 2006; Hankin & Abramson, 2001). Moreover, during early adolescence, gender differences in attributional style, in rumination, and in stressful life events emerge such that girls tend to have a more pessimistic attributional style, to show more rumination, and to experience more negative life events (especially interpersonal events; Rudolph, 2008). Thus, one can see how, with all three of these risk factors showing gender differences in adolescence, a synergistic effect might lead to the dramatic rise in depression in adolescent girls. Moreover, Hankin and Abramson (2001; see also Hankin et al., 2008) review evidence that the experience of negative life events may contribute to greater cognitive vulnerability, which in turn further increases susceptibility to depressive symptoms. Furthermore, depressive symptoms in adolescent girls, as in adults, are likely to result in more dependent life stress being generated, which in turn may exacerbate depression (Liu & Alloy, 2010; Rudolph, 2008). Finally, girls not only experience more negative life events than boys but also encode them in greater detail and show better memory for emotional events (though not for nonemotional events).

Hankin and Abramson (2001) also emphasized the role of negative cognitions about attractiveness and body image in the emergence of sex differences in depression during adolescence. There is evidence that the development of secondary sexual characteristics is harder psychologically for girls than for boys. Body dissatisfaction goes up for females at this time, and down for males; moreover, body dissatisfaction is more closely related to self-esteem for girls than for boys. Much of girls' dissatisfaction with their bodies comes from their realization of the discrepancy between our society's ideal of a thin, prepubescent body shape for females and the fact that they are gaining fat as they mature sexually. Hankin and Abramson (2001) summarized evidence that girls are more likely than boys to make pessimistic attributions and other negative inferences about negative events that may occur (such as negative remarks) related to the domain of physical attractiveness. Given that physical attractiveness may be more motivationally significant for girls than for boys, it becomes plausible that this may be one important factor that makes depression especially likely in adolescent girls.

The ruminative response styles theory of depression has been integrated with the two previously discussed cognitive theories of depression. For example, research reviewed recently by Alloy, Abramson, and colleagues (2008) shows that for people with high levels of dysfunctional attitudes and/or pessimistic attributional styles, their tendencies to ruminate moderated the effects of the negative cognitive styles on increasing vulnerability to depression. Specifically, those who had negative cognitive styles who also tended to ruminate a lot were most likely to develop depressive episodes. The researchers suggest that people with negative cognitive styles have a lot of negative content to their thoughts but that only if they dwell on this and brood about it (high ruminators) are they especially likely to develop clinical depression (see also Robinson & Alloy, 2003).

Comorbidity of Anxiety and Mood Disorders   The issue of whether depression and anxiety can be differentiated in a reliable and valid way has received a good deal of attention over the years. Only in the past two decades, however, have researchers begun to make significant advances in understanding the real scope of the problem. The overlap between measures of depression and anxiety occurs at all levels of analysis: patient self-report, clinician ratings, diagnosis, and family and genetic factors (Clark & Watson, 1991; Mineka et al., 1998; Watson, 2005). Just over half of the patients who receive a diagnosis of a mood disorder also receive a diagnosis of an anxiety disorder at some point in their lives, and vice versa (Hettema, 2008; Watson, 2005). Finally, there is considerable evidence from genetic and family studies of the close relationship between anxiety and unipolar depressive disorders (Garber & Weersing, 2010). The shared genetically based factor among these disorders seems to be at least in part the personality trait of neuroticism—a major risk factor for all of these disorders (Hettema, 2008; Watson et al., 2006).

Although depressed and anxious individuals cannot be differentiated on the basis of their high level of negative affect, they do differ in their reports of positive affect, which includes affective states such as excitement, delight, interest, and pride. Depressed persons tend to be characterized by low levels of positive affect, but anxious individuals usually are not (with the exception of people with social phobia; Naragon-Gainey et al., 2009; Watson et al., 2006). People with anxiety (especially those who experience panic), but not people with depression, also tend to be characterized by high levels of another mood dimension known as anxious hyperarousal, symptoms of which include racing heart, trembling, dizziness, and shortness of breath. This tripartite model of anxiety and depression thus explains what features anxiety and depression share (high negative affect) and what features they differ on (low positive affect for depression and anxious hyper-arousal for panic; Mineka et al., 1998). Each of the other anxiety disorders has its own separate and relatively unique component as well (Barlow, 2002; Prenoveau et al., 2010; Watson, 2005).

INTERPERSONAL EFFECTS OF MOOD DISORDERS

Although there is no interpersonal theory of depression that is as clearly articulated as the cognitive theories, a considerable amount of research has been done on interpersonal factors in depression. Interpersonal problems and social-skills deficits may well play a causal role in at least some cases of depression. In addition, depression creates many interpersonal difficulties—with strangers and friends as well as with family members (Hammen, 1995, 2005; Joiner & Timmons, 2009).

Lack of Social Support and Social-Skills Deficits Brown and Harris (1978), in their classic study of community women in a poor area of inner London, reported that women without a close, confiding relationship were more likely than those with at least one close confidant to become

Why are people without social support networks more prone to depression when faced with major stressors?

depressed if they experienced a severely stressful event. Many studies have since supported the idea that people who are lonely, socially isolated, or lacking social support are more vulnerable to becoming depressed and that individuals with depression have smaller and less supportive social networks, which tends to precede the onset of depression (Cacioppo et al., 2006; Gotlib & Hammen, 1992; Ibarra-Rovillard & Kuiper, 2011). In addition, some people with depression have social-skills deficits. For example, they seem to speak more slowly and monotonously and to maintain less eye contact; they are also less skilled than people without depression at solving interpersonal problems (Ingram et al., 1999; Joiner & Timmons, 2009).

The Effects of Depression on Others Not only do people with depression have interpersonal problems, but, unfortunately, their own behavior also seems to make these problems worse. For example, the behavior of someone who is depressed often places others in the position of providing sympathy, support, and care. However, positive reinforcement does not necessarily follow. Depressive behavior can elicit negative feelings (sometimes including hostility) and rejection in other people, including strangers, roommates, and spouses (Coyne, 1976; Ingram et al., 1999; Joiner & Timmons, 2009). Although these negative feelings may initially make the person who is not depressed feel guilty, which leads to sympathy and support in the short term, ultimately a downwardly spiraling relationship usually results, making the person with depression feel worse (e.g., Joiner, 2002; Joiner & Metalsky, 1995). Social rejection may be especially likely if the person with depression engages in excessive reassurance seeking (Joiner & Timmons, 2009; Prinstein et al., 2005).

Marriage and Family Life Interpersonal aspects of depression also have been carefully studied in the context of marital and family relationships. A significant proportion of couples experiencing marital distress have at least one partner with clinical depression, and there is a high correlation between marital dissatisfaction and depression for both women and men (Beach & Jones, 2002; Rehman et al., 2008; Whisman, 2007). In addition, marital distress spells a poor prognosis for a spouse with depression whose symptoms have remitted. That is, a person whose depression clears up is likely to relapse if he or she has an unsatisfying marriage, especially one characterized by high levels of critical and hostile comments from the spouse (Butzlaff & Hooley, 1998; Hooley, 2007).

Why should criticism be linked to relapse? One possibility is that criticism perturbs some of the neural circuitry that underlies depression. Moreover, *even after full recovery*, criticism may still be a powerful trigger for those who are vulnerable to depression. In a novel study,

Figure 7.6 Brain Activation in Response to Maternal Criticism

When healthy (never-depressed) participants hear criticism from their own mothers they show significantly greater activation in the dorsolateral prefrontal cortex and anterior cingulate cortex than do people who have a history of depression but who are currently fully recovered. Amygdala activation during criticism is significantly greater in formerly depressed participants than it is in controls (Hooley et al., 2009).

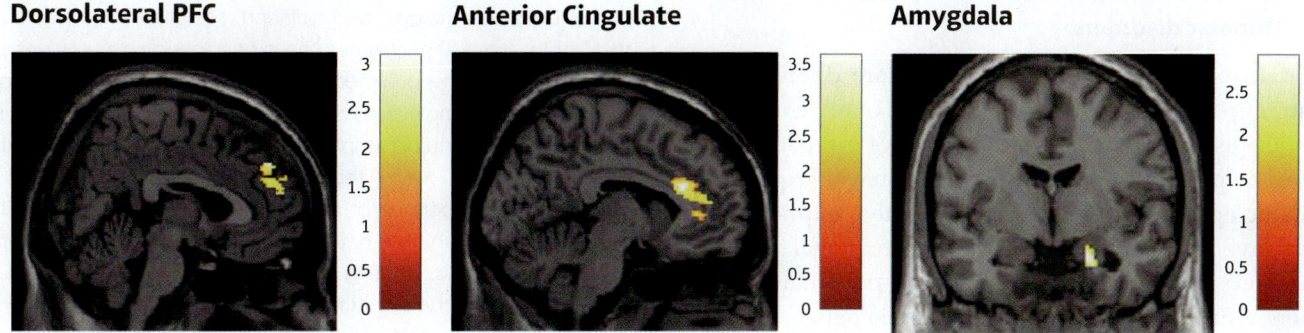

Hooley and colleagues (2009) exposed healthy (never-depressed) controls and women with a past history of depression to critical remarks from their own mothers. While they were lying in a brain scanner, each participant heard her own mother making personally relevant critical remarks. Even though all the young women in the recovered-depressed group were completely well and had no symptoms of depression, their brains still responded differently from the healthy controls when challenged by criticism. As you can see in Figure 7.6, there are differences in several brain areas that, as you have already learned, have been implicated in depression. When they heard criticism from their mothers, the recovered-depressed participants showed less brain activation in the dorsolateral prefrontal cortex and anterior cingulate cortex than the never-depressed controls did. In contrast, during criticism, brain activity in the amygdala was much higher in the recovered-depressed participants than it was in the controls. What was especially interesting was that all of this occurred without the recovered-depressed subjects being aware that they were responding differently to the criticisms. Taken together, these findings suggest that criticism might be associated with relapse in depression because it is capable of activating some of the neural circuits that are thought to be involved in the disorder. They also suggest that people who are vulnerable to depression may be especially sensitive to criticism even after they have made a full recovery.

The effects of depression in one family member can extend to children of all ages as well. Parental depression puts children at high risk for many problems, but especially for depression (Goodman, 2007; Hammen, 2009; Hammen et al., 2011). Although these effects occur with both fathers and mothers with depression, the effects of maternal depression are somewhat larger (Hammen, 2009). Children of parents with depression who become depressed themselves tend to become depressed earlier and to show a more severe and persistent course than

control children who become depressed who do not have a parent with depression (see Hammen, 2009).

Some of these effects probably occur because these children inherit a variety of traits such as temperament (including shyness, behavioral inhibition, and neuroticism), low levels of positive emotions, and poor ability to regulate emotions that are all known risk factors for depression (Durbin et al., 2005; Hammen, 2009). In addition, many studies have documented the damaging effects of negative interactional patterns between mothers with depression and their children. For example, mothers with depression show more friction and have fewer playful, mutually rewarding interactions with their children (Goodman & Gotlib, 1999). They are also less sensitively attuned to their infants and less affirming of their infants' experiences (Goodman & Brand, 2009). Furthermore, their young children are given multiple opportunities for observational learning of negative cognitions, depressive behavior, and depressed affect. Thus, although genetically determined vulnerability is clearly involved, psychosocial influences clearly also play an important role (Hammen, 2009; Natsuaki et al., 2010), and evidence is accumulating that inadequate parenting is what mediates the association between parental depression and their children's depression (Goodman, 2007).

in review

- Summarize the major biological causal factors for unipolar depression, including genetic, biochemical, neuroendocrinological, and neurophysiological factors.

- What is the role of stressful life events in unipolar depression, and what kinds of diatheses have been proposed to interact with them?

- Describe the following theories of depression: Beck's cognitive theory, the helplessness and hopelessness theories, ruminative response styles theory, and interpersonal theories.

Bipolar and Related Disorders

7.4   List and distinguish between different types of bipolar disorders.

As discussed earlier, *bipolar disorders* are distinguished from unipolar disorders by the presence of manic or hypomanic episodes, which are nearly always preceded or followed by periods of depression. A person who experiences a manic episode has a markedly elevated, euphoric, and expansive mood, often interrupted by occasional outbursts of intense irritability or even violence—particularly when others refuse to go along with the manic person's wishes and schemes. Hypomanic episodes can also occur; these involve milder versions of the same symptoms. Although the symptoms listed are the same for manic and hypomanic episodes, there is much less impairment in hypomania, and hospitalization is not required.

Cyclothymic Disorder

Some people experience cyclical mood changes that are more severe than normal, but less severe than the mood swings seen in bipolar disorder. **Cyclothymic disorder** refers to the repeated experience of hypomanic symptoms for a period of at least 2 years. This is a less serious version of full-blown bipolar disorder because it lacks the extreme mood and behavior changes, psychotic features, and marked impairment seen in bipolar disorder.

Symptoms of the hypomanic phase of cyclothymia are essentially the opposite of the symptoms of persistent depressive disorder. In this phase of the disorder, the person may become especially creative and productive because of increased physical and mental energy. There may be significant periods between episodes in which the person with cyclothymia functions in a relatively adaptive manner. For a diagnosis of cyclothymia, there must be at least a 2-year span during which there are numerous periods with hypomanic and depressed symptoms (1 year for adolescents and children), and the symptoms must cause clinically significant distress or impairment in functioning (although not as severe as in bipolar disorder). Individuals with cyclothymia are at greatly increased risk of later developing full-blown bipolar I or II disorder (Goodwin & Jamison, 2007).

In the depressed phase of cyclothymic disorder, a person's symptoms are very similar to what is seen in persistent depressive disorder but without the duration criterion. The individual's mood is dejected, and he or she experiences a distinct loss of interest or pleasure in customary activities and pastimes. In addition, the person may show other symptoms such as low energy, feelings of inadequacy, social withdrawal, and a pessimistic, brooding attitude.

The following case illustrates cyclothymia.

A Cyclothymic Chef

Kevin is a 35-year-old chef who is seeking treatment at the suggestion of both his employer and girlfriend. His presenting problem is that "for the past 10 or so years I have been having extreme ups and downs . . . pretty serious mood swings." Kevin says that he knows that some of his employees refer to him as "Dr. Jekyll and Mr. Hyde" behind his back, and his employer and girlfriend have said that they never know "which Kevin" they are going to see. He describes his mood swings as periods of ups and downs. The "ups" last 3 to 5 days during which he is happy, full of energy and creativity, often expanding his menu, creating new dishes, and experiencing "a deep love of life and everything in it." The "downs" last a little bit longer, maybe 5 to 7 days, and during those periods he feels down, lacks energy, has to really push himself to get into work and prepare his menu, and is often agitated—yelling at his cooks, occasionally so loud that customers can hear him. This pattern of ups and downs has started to have a negative impact on his work, and is putting a significant strain on his relationship.

Bipolar Disorders (I and II)

Recurrent cycles of mania and melancholia were recognized as early as the sixth century; however, it wasn't until 1899 that Kraepelin introduced the term *manic-depressive insanity* and clarified the clinical picture. Kraepelin described the disorder as a series of attacks of elation and depression, with periods of relative normality in between. Today we call this illness *bipolar disorder*, although the term *manic-depression* is still commonly used as well.

Bipolar I disorder is distinguished from MDD by the presence of mania (see Table 7.2 for a summary). A **mixed episode** is characterized by symptoms of both full-blown manic and major depressive episodes for at least 1 week, either intermixed or alternating rapidly every few days. Mixed episodes were once thought to be relatively rare, but a recent review of 18 studies found that approximately 28 percent of bipolar patients experience mixed states at least some of the time. Moreover, many patients in a manic episode have some symptoms of depressed mood, anxiety,

Table 7.2 Distinguishing Between Bipolar I and Bipolar II Disorder

Bipolar I:
- Person has full-blown mania.
- Person experiences episodes of mania and periods of depression. Even if the periods of depression do not reach the threshold for a major depressive episode, the diagnosis of bipolar I disorder is still given.

Bipolar II:
- Person experiences periods of hypomania, but his or her symptoms are below the threshold for full-blown mania.
- Person experiences periods of depressed mood that meet the criteria for major depression.

guilt, and suicidal thoughts, even if these are not severe enough to qualify as a mixed episode. People whose first episode of mania is a mixed episode have a worse long-term outcome than those originally presenting with a depressive or a manic episode (Baldessarini et al., 2010; Dodd et al., 2010).

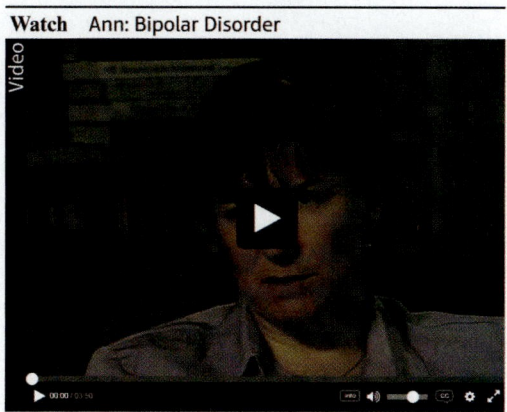

Watch Ann: Bipolar Disorder

If a person shows only manic symptoms, it is nevertheless assumed that a bipolar disorder exists and that a depressive episode will eventually occur. Although some researchers have noted the probable existence of a unipolar type of manic disorder (i.e., "pure mania"; Kessler et al., 1997; Solomon et al., 2003), critics of this diagnosis argue that such patients usually have bipolar relatives and may well have had mild depressions that went unrecognized (Goodwin & Jamison, 2007; Winokur & Tsuang, 1996).

The following case illustrates both phases of bipolar I disorder.

Sped Up and Out of Control

Tim is a 25-year-old student and aspiring poet, rapper, and musician. He was just admitted to a psychiatric hospital in an apparent manic episode. Although he has had a fairly stable life in which he lives with his girlfriend, Tessa, takes classes at the local community college, and works at a coffee shop in town, his behavior has become increasingly erratic. More specifically, his girlfriend reports that Tim has appeared to be "really sped up" the past month, talking faster than usual, expressing some pretty grandiose ideas (e.g., "I'm going to start and finish a PhD in poetry this year," "I set up a meeting with Kanye West to discuss signing with him," and "I am Tupac reincarnated!"). Tessa reports that things have gotten much worse during the past 2 weeks, during which Tim sleeps just 1 to 2 hours per night and spends the rest of his time in the evenings making music, smoking marijuana, and buying expensive items online (he has maxed out their credit cards buying multiple guitars, turntables, a new refrigerator, and a five-star trip to Paris). She also reports that Tim disappeared for the past 4 days (skipping school and work as well), only to return home this morning saying that he "has been living with another woman he just met." Tessa says that this is all very out of character for Tim. Since she has known him he has had peri-

ods of pretty severe depression during which he becomes extremely sad, stops playing or making music, sleeps most of the day, and barely leaves the house. However, she has never seen him so sped up and out of control and he has become a completely different person these past few weeks.

DSM-5 also identifies a distinct form of bipolar disorder called **bipolar II disorder**, in which the person does not experience full-blown manic (or mixed) episodes but has experienced clear-cut hypomanic episodes as well as major depressive episodes. Bipolar II disorder is equally or somewhat more common than bipolar I disorder, and, when combined, estimates are that about 2 to 3 percent of the U.S. population will suffer from one or the other disorder (Kessler et al., 2007). Bipolar II disorder evolves into bipolar I disorder in only about 5 to 15 percent of cases, suggesting that they are distinct forms of the disorder (Coryell et al., 1995; Goodwin & Jamison, 2007). Recently, a subthreshold form of bipolar II disorder also has been recognized and as many as 40 percent of individuals diagnosed with MDD have a similar number of hypomanic symptoms, although not with a sufficient number or duration to qualify for a hypomanic episode (Zimmerman et al., 2009). Findings like these are leading psychologists to recognize that MDD is a far more heterogeneous category than previously recognized.

Bipolar disorder occurs equally in males and females (although depressive episodes are more common in women than men) and usually starts in adolescence and young adulthood, with an average age of onset of 18 to 22 years (Goodwin & Jamison, 2007; Merikangas et al., 2007). Bipolar II disorder has an average age of onset approximately 5 years later than bipolar I disorder (Baldessarini et al., 2010). Both bipolar I and II are typically recurrent disorders, with people experiencing single episodes extremely rarely (Kessler et al., 2007). In about two-thirds of cases, the manic episodes either immediately precede or immediately follow a depressive episode; in other cases, the manic and depressive episodes are separated by intervals of relatively normal functioning. Figure 7.7 illustrates the different patterns of manic, hypomanic, and depressive symptoms and episodes that can be seen in bipolar-spectrum disorders. Most patients with bipolar disorder experience periods of remission during which they are relatively symptom-free, although this may occur on only about 50 percent of days (Kupka et al., 2007). Moreover, as many as 20 to 30 percent continue to experience significant impairment (occupational and/or interpersonal) and mood lability most of the time, and as many as 60 percent have chronic occupational or interpersonal problems between episodes. As with unipolar major depression, the recurrences can be seasonal in nature, in which case **bipolar disorder with a seasonal pattern** is diagnosed.

Figure 7.7 The Manic-Depressive Spectrum

There is a spectrum of bipolarity in moods. All of us have our ups and downs, which are indicated here as normal mood variation. People with a cyclothymic personality have more marked and regular mood swings, and people with cyclothymic disorder go through periods when they meet the criteria for dysthymia (except for the 2-year duration) and other periods when they meet the criteria for hypomania. People with bipolar II disorder have periods of major depression and periods of hypomania. Unipolar mania is an extremely rare condition. Finally, people with bipolar I disorder have periods of major depression and periods of mania.

(Adapted from Frederick K. Goodwin and Kay R. Jamison. (2009). *Manic Depressive Illness*. Copyright © 1990. Oxford University Press, Inc.)

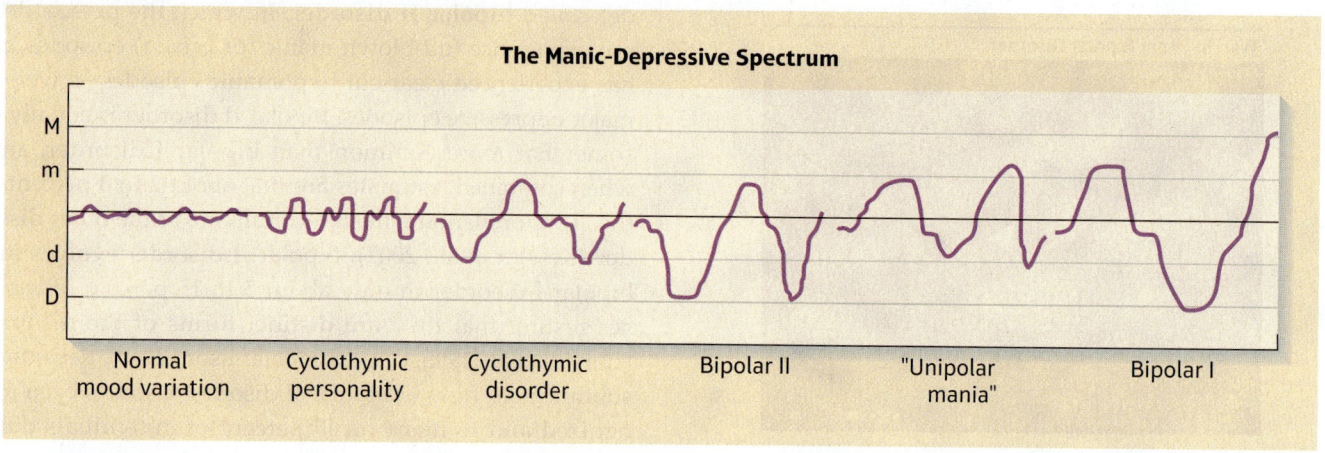

The Manic-Depressive Spectrum

Normal mood variation — Cyclothymic personality — Cyclothymic disorder — Bipolar II — "Unipolar mania" — Bipolar I

FEATURES OF BIPOLAR DISORDER The duration of manic and hypomanic episodes tends to be shorter than the duration of depressive episodes, with typically about three times as many days spent depressed as manic or hypomanic (Goodwin & Jamison, 2007). There has been controversy over whether the symptoms of the depressive episodes of bipolar disorder are clinically distinguishable from those seen in unipolar major depressive episodes (Cuellar et al., 2005; Perris, 1992). Although there is a high degree of overlap in symptoms, there are some significant differences. The most widely replicated differences are that, relative to people with a unipolar depressive episode, people with a bipolar depressive episode tend to show more mood lability, more psychotic features, more psychomotor retardation, and more substance abuse (Goodwin & Jamison, 2007). By contrast, individuals with unipolar depression, on average, show more anxiety, agitation, insomnia, physical complaints, and weight loss (Johnson et al., 2009). In spite of the high degree of similarity in symptoms, research clearly indicates that major depressive episodes in people with bipolar disorder are more severe than those seen in unipolar disorder, and, not surprisingly, they also cause more role impairment (Kessler et al., 2007).

Misdiagnoses are unfortunate because there are somewhat different treatments of choice for unipolar and bipolar depression. Moreover, there is evidence that some antidepressant drugs used to treat what is thought to be unipolar depression may actually precipitate manic episodes in patients who actually have as-yet-undetected bipolar disorder, thus worsening the course of the illness (Ghaemi et al., 2003; Whybrow, 1997).

People with bipolar disorder suffer from more episodes during their lifetimes than do persons with unipolar disorder (although these episodes tend to be somewhat shorter, averaging 3–4 months; Angst & Sellaro, 2000; Solomon et al., 2010). As many as 5 to 10 percent of persons with bipolar disorder experience at least four episodes (either manic or depressive) every year, a pattern known as **rapid cycling**. In fact, those who go through periods of rapid cycling usually experience many more than four episodes a year. People who develop rapid cycling are slightly more likely to be women, to have a history of more episodes (especially more manic or hypomanic episodes), to have an earlier average age of onset, and to make more suicide attempts (Coryell et al., 2003; Kupka et al., 2005; Nierenberg et al., 2010). Rapid cycling is sometimes precipitated by taking certain kinds of antidepressants (Goodwin & Jamison, 2007; Kilzieh & Akiskal, 1999). Fortunately, for about 50 percent of cases, rapid cycling is a temporary phenomenon and gradually disappears within about 2 years (Coryell et al., 1995, 2003).

Overall, the probabilities of "full recovery" from bipolar disorder are discouraging even with the widespread use of mood-stabilizing medications such as lithium, with one review estimating that patients with bipolar disorder spend about 20 percent of their lives in episodes (Angst & Sellaro, 2000). One 20-year prospective study in which over 200 patients were followed for an average of 17 years found that 24 percent had relapsed within 6 months of recovery; 77 percent had had at least one new episode within 4 years of recovery; and 82 percent had relapsed within 7 years (Coryell et al., 1995). Another prospective study of 146 bipolar patients found that they experienced some symptoms (mostly subsyndromal) on an average of 47 percent of the weeks during the 13-year follow-up period. During the follow-up period, depressive symptoms were three times more common than manic or hypomanic symptoms (Judd et al., 2002; see also Judd et al., 2003).

in review

- Describe the symptoms and clinical features of cyclothymia and bipolar disorder.
- Describe the typical course of bipolar I and bipolar II disorders.

Causal Factors in Bipolar Disorders

7.5 Describe the causal factors influencing the development and maintenance of bipolar disorders.

A host of causal factors for bipolar disorder have been posited during the past century. However, biological causal factors are clearly dominant, and the role of psychological causal factors has received significantly less attention. The majority of research has concentrated on bipolar I disorder, which is what we focus on here.

Biological Causal Factors

A number of biological factors are thought to play a causal role in the onset of bipolar disorder. These factors include genetic, neurochemical, hormonal, neurophysiological, neuroanatomical, and biological rhythm influences.

GENETIC INFLUENCES There is a greater genetic contribution to bipolar I disorder than to unipolar disorder. Approximately 8 to 10 percent of the first-degree relatives of a person with bipolar I illness can be expected to have bipolar disorder, compared to 1 percent in the general population (Plomin et al., 2013; Willcutt & McQueen, 2010). The first-degree relatives of a person with bipolar disorder also are at elevated risk for unipolar major depression, although the reverse is not true (Akiskal & Benazzi, 2005; Goodwin & Jamison, 2007).

Although family studies cannot by themselves establish a genetic basis for the disorder, results from twin studies dating back to the 1950s also point to a genetic basis because the concordance rates for these disorders are much higher for identical than for fraternal twins. The average concordance rate is about 60 percent for monozygotic twins and only about 12 percent for dizygotic twins (Kelsoe, 1997). This and other studies suggest that genes account for about 80 to 90 percent of the variance in the liability to develop bipolar I disorder (Goodwin & Jamison, 2007; McGuffin et al., 2003). This is higher than heritability estimates for

unipolar disorder or any of the other major adult psychiatric disorders, including schizophrenia (Torrey et al., 1994).

Efforts to locate the chromosomal site(s) of the implicated gene or genes in this genetic transmission of bipolar disorder suggest that it is polygenic (Willcutt & McQueen, 2010). Although a great deal of research has been directed at identifying candidate genes through linkage analysis and association studies, no consistent support yet exists for any specific mode of genetic transmission of bipolar disorder (Potash & DePaulo, 2000; Tsuang et al., 2004).

Another wrinkle in the story identified by recent studies is that different disorders seem to share their genetic etiology. For instance, some of the genetic polymorphisms that are seen in those with bipolar disorder are also seen in those with schizophrenia (perhaps pointing toward why people with both disorders experience psychotic features) and with depression (perhaps explaining why people with these two disorders both experience depressive symptoms) (Cross-Disorder Group of the Psychiatric Genomics Consortium, 2014).

NEUROCHEMICAL FACTORS The early monoamine hypothesis for unipolar disorder was extended to bipolar disorder, the hypothesis being that if depression is caused by deficiencies of norepinephrine or serotonin, then perhaps mania is caused by excesses of these neurotransmitters. There is good evidence for increased norepinephrine activity during manic episodes and less consistent evidence for lowered norepinephrine activity during depressive episodes (Goodwin & Jamison, 2007; Manji & Lenox, 2000). However, serotonin activity appears to be low in both depressive and manic phases.

As noted earlier, norepinephrine, serotonin, and dopamine are all involved in regulating our mood states (Howland & Thase, 1999; Southwick et al., 2005). Evidence for the role of dopamine stems in part from research showing that increased dopaminergic activity in several brain areas may be related to manic symptoms of hyperactivity, grandiosity, and euphoria (Cousins et al., 2009; Goodwin & Jamison, 2007). High doses of drugs such as cocaine and amphetamines, which are known to stimulate dopamine, also produce manic-like behavior (Cousins et al., 2009). Drugs like lithium reduce dopaminergic activity and are antimanic. In depression there appear to be decreases in both norepinephrine and dopamine functioning (Goodwin & Jamison, 2007; Manji & Lenox, 2000). Thus disturbances in the balance of these neurotransmitters seem to be one of the keys to understanding this debilitating illness.

ABNORMALITIES OF HORMONAL REGULATORY SYSTEMS Some neurohormonal research on bipolar disorder has focused on the HPA axis. Cortisol levels are elevated in bipolar depression (as they are in unipolar depression), but they are usually not elevated during manic episodes (Goodwin & Jamison, 2007). Similarly, people with bipolar disorder who are in a depressed episode show evidence of abnormalities on the dexamethasone suppression test (DST) at about the same rate as do people experiencing a unipolar depression, and these abnormalities persist even when the patients have been fully remitted and asymptomatic for at least 4 weeks (Langan & McDonald, 2009; Watson et al., 2004). During a manic episode, however, their rate of DST abnormalities generally has been found to be much lower (Goodwin & Jamison, 2007; Manji & Lenox, 2000, although see Langan & McDonald, 2009). Research also has focused on abnormalities of the hypothalamic-pituitary-thyroid axis because abnormalities of thyroid function are frequently accompanied by changes in mood. Many bipolar patients have subtle but significant abnormalities in the functioning of this axis, and administration of thyroid hormone often makes antidepressant drugs work better (Altshuler et al., 2001; Goodwin & Jamison, 2007). However, thyroid hormone can also precipitate manic episodes in patients with bipolar disorder (Goodwin & Jamison, 2007).

NEUROPHYSIOLOGICAL AND NEUROANATOMICAL INFLUENCES With PET scans, it is possible to visualize variations in brain glucose metabolic rates in depressed and manic states, although there is far less evidence regarding manic states because of the great difficulties studying patients who are actively manic. Several summaries of the evidence from studies using PET and other neuroimaging techniques show that, whereas blood flow to the left prefrontal cortex is reduced during depression, during mania it is increased in certain other parts of the prefrontal cortex (Bermpohl et al., 2010; Goodwin & Jamison, 2007). Thus, there are shifting patterns of brain activity during mania and during depressed and normal moods (see Figure 7.8).

Figure 7.8 Mood Disorders and the Brain

Brain imaging studies have revealed that people with mood disorders show abnormalities in several different brain regions, including the prefrontal cortex, basal ganglia, thalamus, anterior cingulate cortex, amygdala, and hippocampus.

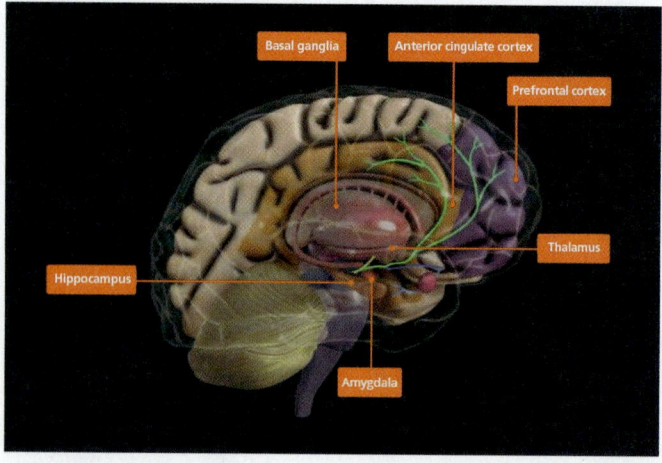

Other neurophysiological findings from patients with bipolar disorder have shown both similarities to and differences from patients with unipolar disorder and normal controls. For example, several recent reviews suggest that there are deficits in activity in the prefrontal cortex in bipolar disorder. These seem related to neuropsychological deficits that people with bipolar disorder show in problem solving, planning, working memory, shifting of attention, and sustained attention on cognitive tasks (Chen et al., 2011; Haldane & Frangou, 2004; Malhi, Ivanovski, et al., 2004). This is similar to what is seen in unipolar depression, as are deficits in the anterior cingulate cortex (Langan & McDonald, 2009). However, structural imaging studies suggest that certain subcortical structures, including the basal ganglia and amygdala, are enlarged in bipolar disorder but reduced in size in unipolar depression. The decreases in hippocampal volume that are often observed in unipolar depression are generally not found in bipolar depression (Konarski et al., 2008). Some studies using functional magnetic resonance imaging (fMRI) also find increased activation in bipolar patients in subcortical brain regions involved in emotional processing, such as the thalamus and amygdala, relative to unipolar patients and normal controls subjects (Chen et al., 2011; Malhi, Lagopoulos, et al., 2004). Overall, it is hard to draw firm conclusions in this area yet because there are so many inconsistencies in results across studies. However, there is initial meta-analytic support for dysregulation in frontal-limbic activation in individuals with bipolar disorder compared to controls (Chen et al., 2011). Hopefully more definitive findings will follow when much-needed technological innovations unfold (Goodwin & Jamison, 2007).

SLEEP AND OTHER BIOLOGICAL RHYTHMS There is considerable evidence regarding disturbances in biological rhythms such as circadian rhythms in bipolar disorder, even after symptoms have mostly remitted (Harvey, 2008; Murray & Harvey, 2010). During manic episodes, patients with bipolar disorder tend to sleep very little (seemingly by choice, not because of insomnia), and this is the most common symptom to occur prior to the onset of a manic episode. During depressive episodes, they tend toward hypersomnia (too much sleep). Even between episodes people with bipolar disorder show substantial sleep difficulties, including high rates of insomnia (Harvey, 2008; Millar et al., 2004). Bipolar disorder also sometimes shows a seasonal pattern in the same way unipolar disorder does, suggesting disturbances of seasonal biological rhythms, although these may be the result of circadian abnormalities in which the onset of the sleep–wake cycle is set ahead of the onset of other circadian rhythms. Given the cyclic nature of bipolar disorder itself, this focus on disturbances in biological rhythms holds promise for future integrative theories of the biological underpinnings of bipolar disorder.

This is particularly true because patients with bipolar disorder seem especially sensitive to, and easily disturbed by, any changes in their daily cycles that require a resetting of their biological clocks (Goodwin & Jamison, 2007; Murray & Harvey, 2010).

Psychological Causal Factors

Although biological factors play a prominent role in the onset of bipolar disorder, psychosocial factors have also been found to be involved in the etiology of the disorder. In particular, stressful life events, poor social support, and certain personality traits and cognitive styles have been identified as important psychological causal factors.

STRESSFUL LIFE EVENTS   Stressful life events appear to be as important in precipitating bipolar depressive episodes as they are in triggering unipolar depressive episodes. Both stressful life events during childhood (e.g., physical and sexual abuse) and recent life stressors during adulthood (e.g., problems with friends and partners, financial hardship) increase the likelihood of ever developing bipolar disorder as well as having recurrences (Gilman et al., 2015).

How might stressful life events operate to increase the chance of relapse? The diathesis–stress model would suggest that stressful life events influence the onset of episodes by activating the underlying vulnerability. One hypothesized mechanism is through the destabilizing effects that stressful life events may have on critical biological rhythms. Although evidence in support of this idea is still preliminary, it appears to be a promising hypothesis, especially for manic episodes (Bender & Alloy, 2011; Grandin et al., 2006).

Watch   Feliziano: Living with Bipolar Disorder

OTHER PSYCHOLOGICAL FACTORS IN BIPOLAR DISORDER   Other social environmental variables may also affect the course of bipolar disorder. For example, one study found that people with bipolar disorder who reported low social support showed more depressive recurrences over a 1-year follow-up, independent of the effects of stressful life events, which also predicted more

recurrences (Cohen et al., 2004; see also Alloy et al., 2010). There is also some evidence that personality and cognitive variables may interact with stressful life events in determining the likelihood of relapse. For example, the personality variable neuroticism has been associated with symptoms of depression and mania (Quilty et al., 2009), and two studies have found that neuroticism predicts increases in depressive symptoms in people with bipolar disorder just as it does in unipolar disorder.

Moreover, personality variables and cognitive styles that are related to goal striving, drive, and incentive motivation have been associated with bipolar disorder (Alloy et al., 2009). For example, two personality variables associated with high levels of achievement striving and increased sensitivity to rewards in the environment predicted increases in manic symptoms—especially during periods of active goal striving or goal attainment (such as studying for an important exam and then doing very well in it; Lozano & Johnson, 2001; Meyer et al., 2001). Another study found that students with a pessimistic attributional style who had also experienced negative life events showed an increase in depressive symptoms whether they had bipolar or unipolar disorder. Interestingly, however, the students with bipolar disorder who had a pessimistic attributional style and experienced negative life events also showed increases in manic symptoms at other points in time (Alloy et al., 2010; Reilly-Harrington et al., 1999).

in review

- Summarize the major biological causal factors for bipolar disorder, including genetic, biochemical, and other biological factors.
- What role do psychological factors, including stressful life events, seem to play in bipolar disorder?

Sociocultural Factors Affecting Unipolar and Bipolar Disorders

7.6   Explain how cultural factors can influence the expression of mood disorders.

Research on the association of sociocultural factors with both unipolar and bipolar mood disorders is discussed together because much of the research conducted in this area has not made clear-cut diagnostic distinctions between the two types of disorders. Although the prevalence of mood disorders seems to vary considerably among different countries, it has been difficult to provide conclusive evidence for this because of various methodological problems, including widely differing diagnostic practices in different cultures, and because the symptoms of depression appear to vary considerably across cultures (Chentsova-Dutton & Tsai, 2009; Kleinman, 2004).

Cross-Cultural Differences in Depressive Symptoms

Depression occurs in all cultures that have been studied. However, the form that it takes differs widely, as does its prevalence (Chentsova-Dutton & Tsai, 2009; Marsella, 1980). For example, in Western cultures the "psychological" symptoms of depression (e.g., guilt, worthlessness, suicidal ideation) are prominent, whereas they are not prominently reported in non-Western cultures such as China and Japan, where rates of depression are relatively low. Instead people in non-Western cultures tend to exhibit the more "physical" symptoms (e.g., sleep disturbance, loss of appetite, weight loss, and loss of sexual interest (Kleinman, 2004; Ryder et al., 2008; Tsai & Chentsova-Dutton, 2002).

Several possible reasons for these symptom differences stem from Asian beliefs in the unity of the mind and body, a lack of expressiveness about emotions more generally, and the stigma attached to mental illness in these cultures (Chentsova-Dutton & Tsai, 2009). Another reason why guilt and negative thoughts about the self may be common in Western but not in Asian cultures is that Western cultures view the individual as independent and autonomous, so when failures occur, internal attributions are made. By contrast, in many Asian cultures individuals are viewed as inherently interdependent with others. Nevertheless, as countries like China have incorporated some Western values over the course of becoming increasingly industrialized and urbanized, rates of depression have risen a good deal relative to several decades ago (Dennis, 2004; Zhou et al., 2000). Indeed, one study of adolescents

from Hong Kong and the United States found levels of depressive symptoms and hopelessness to be higher in the adolescents from Hong Kong (Stewart et al., 2004).

Cross-Cultural Differences in Prevalence

Prevalence rates for mood disorders vary a great deal across countries, as revealed by large-scale epidemiological studies. For example, the WHO World Mental Health Survey, which assesses the prevalence and characteristics of psychological disorders across more than 20 countries, reveals that the 12-month prevalence of mood disorders varies from 0.8 percent in Nigeria to 9.6 percent in the United States, as shown earlier in the chapter in Figure 7.1 (WHO World Mental Health Survey Consortium, 2004). The reasons for such wide variation are undoubtedly very complex, and much work remains to be done before we fully understand them. The ideas that are being explored include differences in willingness to report the presence of a mental disorder due to stigma, as well as different levels of important psychosocial risk variables in different cultures and different levels of stress. For example, there appear to be cross-cultural differences in hypothesized risk variables such as pessimistic attributional style, although how these differences might translate into different rates of depression is unclear because we do not yet know whether the same risk variables are operative in different cultures. However, research is beginning to explore whether psychosocial risk factors for mood disorders operate across cultures, and there is some initial evidence that factors like rumination, hopelessness, and pessimistic attributional style (Abela et al., 2011) are associated with risk for depression in other countries, such as China (Hong et al., 2010).

in review

- What kinds of cross-cultural differences are there in depressive symptoms, and what kinds of cross-cultural factors influence the prevalence of unipolar depression?

Treatments and Outcomes

7.7   Describe and distinguish between different treatments for mood disorders.

Many patients with mood disorders (especially unipolar disorders) never seek treatment. Even without formal treatment, the great majority of individuals with mania and depression will recover (often only temporarily) within less than a year. However, given the enormous amount of personal suffering and lost productivity that these individuals endure, and given the wide variety of treatments that are available today, more and more people

In some cultures the concept of depression as we know it simply does not exist. For example, Australian aborigines who are "depressed" show none of the guilt and self-abnegation commonly seen in more developed countries. They also do not show suicidal tendencies but instead are more likely to vent their hostilities onto others rather than onto themselves.

who experience these disorders are seeking treatment. There was a rapid increase in the treatment of depression from 1987 to 1997, and there has been a more modest increase since 1998 (Marcus & Olfson, 2010). Interestingly, between 1998 and 2007, there was a decline in the reported use of psychotherapy, although the use of antidepressant medication remained relatively stable. These changes are happening in an era in which there is greatly increased public awareness of the availability of effective treatments and during a time in which significantly less stigma is associated with experiencing a mood disorder. Nevertheless, only about 40 percent of people with mood disorders receive minimally adequate treatment, with the other 60 percent receiving no treatment or inadequate care (Wang, Lane, et al., 2005). Fortunately, the probability of receiving treatment is somewhat higher for people with severe unipolar depression and with bipolar disorder than for those with less severe depression (Kessler et al., 2007).

Pharmacotherapy

Antidepressant, mood-stabilizing, and antipsychotic drugs are all used in the treatment of unipolar and bipolar disorders (see Chapter 16 for further information about these medications). The first category of antidepressant medications—developed in the 1950s—is the **monoamine oxidase inhibitors (MAOIs)** because they inhibit the action of monoamine oxidase, the enzyme responsible for the breakdown of norepinephrine and serotonin once released. The MAOIs can be as effective in treating depression as other categories of medications, but they have potentially dangerous (even potentially fatal) side effects if certain foods rich in the amino acid tyramine are consumed (e.g., red wine, beer, aged cheese, salami). Thus, they are not used very often today unless other classes of medication have failed. Depression with atypical features is the one subtype of depression that seems to respond preferentially to the MAOIs.

For most patients who are moderately to seriously depressed, including those with persistent depressive disorder, the drug treatment of choice from the 1960s to the early 1990s was **tricyclic antidepressants** (TCAs; called this because of their chemical structure) such as imipramine. TCAs increase neurotransmission of the monoamines, primarily norepinephrine and to a lesser extent serotonin (Thase & Denko, 2008). The efficacy of TCAs in significantly reducing depressive symptoms has been demonstrated in hundreds of studies where the response of patients with depression who were given these drugs has been compared with the response of patients given a placebo. However, only about 50 percent show what is considered clinically significant improvement, and many of these patients still have significant residual depressive symptoms. Fortunately, about 50 percent of those who do

not respond to an initial trial of medication will show a clinically significant response when switched to a different antidepressant or to a combination of medications (Hollon, Thase, & Markowitz, 2002).

Unfortunately, TCAs have unpleasant side effects for some people (e.g., dry mouth, constipation, sexual dysfunction, and weight gain). Although these side effects often diminish over time, they are so unpleasant to many patients that they stop taking their medications before the side effects go away. In addition, because these drugs are highly toxic when taken in large doses, there is some risk in prescribing them for suicidal patients, who might use them for an overdose.

The side effects and toxicity of TCAs have led physicians to increasingly prescribe **selective serotonin reuptake inhibitors (SSRIs)** (Olfson & Marcus, 2009). SSRIs are generally no more effective than the tricyclics; indeed some findings suggest that TCAs are more effective than SSRIs for severe depression. However, the SSRIs tend to have many fewer side effects and are better tolerated by patients, as well as being less toxic in large doses. The primary negative side effects of the SSRIs are problems with orgasm and lowered interest in sexual activity, although insomnia, increased physical agitation, and gastrointestinal distress also occur in some patients (Thase, 2009b).

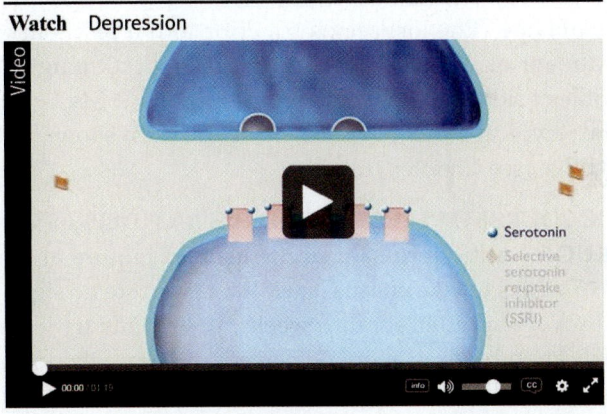

Watch   Depression

SSRIs are used not only to treat severe depression but also to treat people with mild depressive symptoms (Gitlin, 2002). Importantly, recent research has shown that antidepressant medication is superior to placebo only for patients with very severe depressive symptoms, with negligible treatment effects observed for those with less severe symptoms (Fournier et al., 2010; see Figure 7.9).

In the past decade, several new atypical antidepressants (neither tricyclics nor SSRIs) have also become increasingly popular, each with its own advantages (Marcus & Olfson, 2010). For example, bupropion (Wellbutrin) does not have as many side effects (especially sexual side effects) as the SSRIs and, because of its activating effects, is particularly good for depression involving significant weight gain, loss of energy, and oversleeping. In addition,

Figure 7.9 Effectiveness of Antidepressants Based on Severity of Depression

This figure shows the amount of change in depressive symptoms, as measured by the Hamilton Rating Scale for Depression (HRSD), from treatment intake to the end of treatment for those receiving antidepressant medication (ADM; dark circles) relative to placebo (light circles). The size of the circle represents the number of data points that contributed to that mean. The two lines represent the estimated change in depressive symptoms. Note that the circles (and lines) are overlapping for those with low and moderate depressive symptoms at intake (the left half of the figure), and a difference between ADM and placebo only emerges for those with high depressive symptoms at intake (the right half of the figure). The take-home message: Antidepressants appear to be most effective for severe depression, but are no more effective than placebo for mild or moderate depression.

(Adapted from Fournier, J.C., DeRubeis, R. J., Hollon, S. D., Dimidjian, S., Amsterdam, J.D., Shelton, R. C., & Fawcett, J. (2010). Antidepressant drug effects and depression severity: A patient-level meta-analysis. *JAMA, 303*, 47–53.)

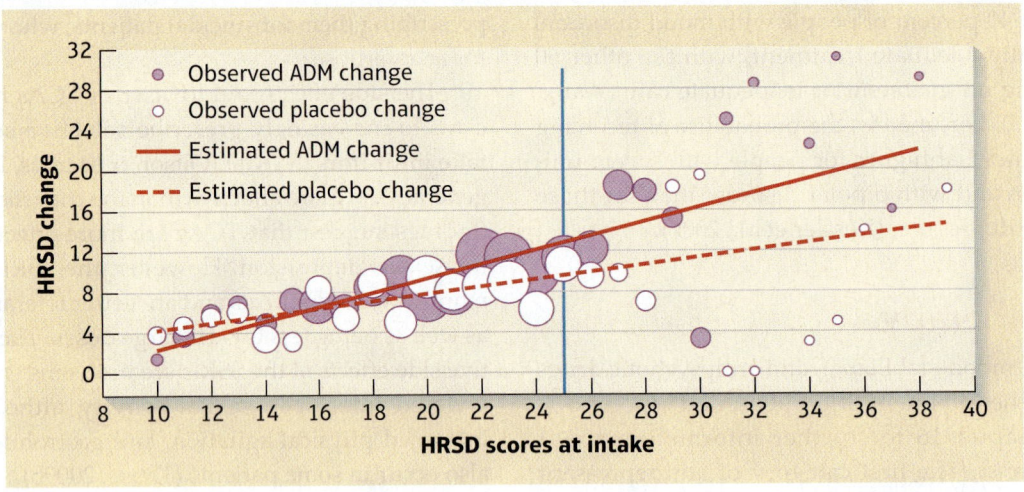

venlafaxine (Effexor) seems superior to the SSRIs in the treatment of severe or chronic depression, although the profile of side effects is similar to that for the SSRIs. Several other atypical antidepressants have also been shown to be effective (see Chapter 16).

THE COURSE OF TREATMENT WITH ANTIDEPRESSANT DRUGS Antidepressant drugs usually require at least 3 to 5 weeks to take effect. Generally, if there are no signs of improvement after about 6 weeks, physicians try a new medication because about 50 percent of those who do not respond to the first drug prescribed do respond to a second one. Also, discontinuing the drugs when symptoms have remitted may result in relapse. Recall that the natural course of an untreated depressive episode is typically 6 to 9 months. Thus, when depressed patients take drugs for 3 to 4 months and then stop because they are feeling better, they are likely to relapse because the underlying depressive episode is actually still present, and only its symptomatic expression has been suppressed (Gitlin, 2002; Hollon, Thase, & Markowitz, 2002; Hollon et al., 2006). Because depression is often a recurrent disorder, physicians have increasingly recommended that patients continue for very long periods of time on the drugs (ideally at the same dose) in order to prevent recurrence (Nutt, 2010). Thus, these medications can often be effective in prevention, as well as treatment, for patients subject to recurrent episodes (Hollon et al., 2006; Thase & Denko, 2008). Nevertheless, approximately

25 percent of patients continuing to receive medication during the maintenance phase of treatment show recurrence of MDD (Solomon et al., 2005). Patients showing residual symptoms are most likely to relapse, indicating the importance of trying to treat the patient to full remission of symptoms (Keller, 2004; Thase & Denko, 2008).

LITHIUM AND OTHER MOOD-STABILIZING DRUGS Lithium therapy has now become widely used as a mood stabilizer in the treatment of both depressive and manic episodes of bipolar disorder. The term *mood stabilizer* is often used to describe lithium and related drugs because they have both antimanic and antidepressant effects—that is, they exert mood-stabilizing effects in either direction. **Lithium** has been more widely studied as a treatment of manic episodes than of depressive episodes, and estimates are that about three-quarters of those in a manic episode show at least partial improvement. In the treatment of bipolar depression, lithium may be no more effective than traditional antidepressants (study results are inconsistent), but about three-quarters show at least partial improvement (Keck & McElroy, 2007). However, treatment with antidepressants is associated with significant risk of precipitating manic episodes or rapid cycling, although the risk of this happening is reduced if the person also takes lithium (Keck & McElroy, 2007; Thase & Denko, 2008).

Lithium is often effective in preventing cycling between manic and depressive episodes (although not necessarily for patients with rapid cycling), and patients with bipolar disorder frequently are maintained on lithium therapy over long time periods, even when not manic or depressed, simply to prevent new episodes. Unfortunately, several large studies recently have found that only about one-third of patients maintained on lithium remained free of an episode over a 5-year follow-up period. Nevertheless, patients on lithium maintenance do have fewer episodes than patients who discontinue their medication (Keck & McElroy, 2007).

Lithium therapy can have some unpleasant side effects such as lethargy, cognitive slowing, weight gain, decreased motor coordination, and gastrointestinal difficulties. Long-term use of lithium is occasionally associated with kidney malfunction and sometimes permanent kidney damage, although end-stage renal disease seems to be a very rare consequence of long-term lithium treatment (Goodwin & Jamison, 2007; Tredget et al., 2010). Not surprisingly, these side effects, combined with the fact that many patients with bipolar disorder seem to miss the highs and the abundance of energy associated with their hypomanic and manic episodes, sometimes create problems with compliance in taking the drug.

In the past several decades, evidence has emerged for the usefulness of another category of drugs known as the *anticonvulsants* (e.g., carbamazepine, divalproex, and valproate) in the treatment of bipolar disorder. These drugs are often effective in patients who do not respond well to lithium or who develop unacceptable side effects from it, and they may also be given in combination with lithium. However, a number of studies have indicated that risk for attempted and completed suicide was nearly two to three times higher for patients on anticonvulsant medications than for those on lithium (Goodwin et al., 2003; Thase & Denko, 2008), suggesting one major advantage of giving lithium to patients who can tolerate its side effects. Both people with bipolar or unipolar depression who show signs of psychosis (hallucinations and delusions) may also receive treatments with *antipsychotic medications* (see Chapters 13 and 16) in conjunction with their antidepressant or mood-stabilizing drugs (Gitlin, 2009; Keck & McElroy, 2002; Rothschild et al., 2004).

Alternative Biological Treatments

In addition to the use of pharmacotherapy, there are several other biologically oriented approaches to the treatment of mood disorders. These approaches have been the subject of empirical study in recent years, and they appear to be promising treatment options.

ELECTROCONVULSIVE THERAPY Because antidepressants often take 3 to 4 weeks to produce significant improvement, **electroconvulsive therapy (ECT)** is often used with patients who are severely depressed (especially among the elderly) and who may present an immediate and serious suicidal risk, including those with psychotic or melancholic features (Goodwin & Jamison, 2007). It is also used in patients who cannot take antidepressant medications or who are otherwise resistant to medications (Heijnen et al., 2010; Mathew et al., 2005). When selection criteria for this form of treatment are carefully observed, a complete remission of symptoms occurs for many patients after about 6 to 12 treatments (with treatments administered about every other day). This means that a majority of patients with severe depression can be vastly better in 3 to 5 weeks (George et al., 2013). The treatments, which induce seizures, are delivered under general anesthesia and with muscle relaxants. The most common immediate side effect is confusion, although there is some evidence for lasting adverse effects on cognition, such as amnesia and slowed response time (Sackeim et al., 2007). Maintenance dosages of an antidepressant and a mood-stabilizing drug such as lithium are then ordinarily used to maintain the treatment gains achieved until the depression has run its course (Mathew et al., 2005; Sackeim et al., 2009). ECT is also very useful in the treatment of manic episodes; reviews of the evidence suggest that it is associated with remission or marked improvement in 80 percent of patients with mania (Gitlin, 1996; Goodwin & Jamison, 2007). Maintenance on mood-stabilizing drugs following ECT is usually required to prevent relapse.

TRANSCRANIAL MAGNETIC STIMULATION Although transcranial magnetic stimulation (TMS) has been available as an alternative biological treatment for some time now, only in the past decade has it begun to receive significant attention. TMS is a noninvasive technique allowing focal stimulation of the brain in patients who are awake. Brief but intense pulsating magnetic fields that induce electrical activity in certain parts of the cortex are delivered (Goodwin & Jamison, 2007; Janicak et al., 2005). The procedure is painless, and thousands of stimulations are delivered in each treatment session. Treatment usually occurs 5 days a week for 2 to 6 weeks. Many studies have shown it to be quite effective—indeed in some studies quite comparable to unilateral ECT and antidepressant medications (George & Post, 2011; Janicak et al., 2005; Schulze-Rauschenbach et al., 2005). In particular, research suggests that TMS is a promising approach for the treatment of unipolar depression in patients who are moderately resistant to other treatments (George & Post, 2011). Moreover, TMS has advantages over ECT in that cognitive performance and memory are not affected adversely and sometimes even improve, as opposed to ECT, where memory-recall deficits are common (George et al., 2013). Finally, TMS appears to be safe for use with children and adolescents, with only low rates of mild and transient side effects such as headaches (12 percent) and scalp discomfort (3 percent) (Krishnan et al., 2015).

DEEP BRAIN STIMULATION In recent years, deep brain stimulation has been explored as a treatment approach for individuals with refractory depression who have not responded to other treatment approaches, such as medication, psychotherapy, and ECT. Deep brain stimulation involves implanting an electrode in the brain and then stimulating that area with electric current (Mayberg et al., 2005). Although more research on deep brain stimulation is needed, initial results suggest that it may have potential for treatment of unrelenting depression (see Chapter 16 for more details).

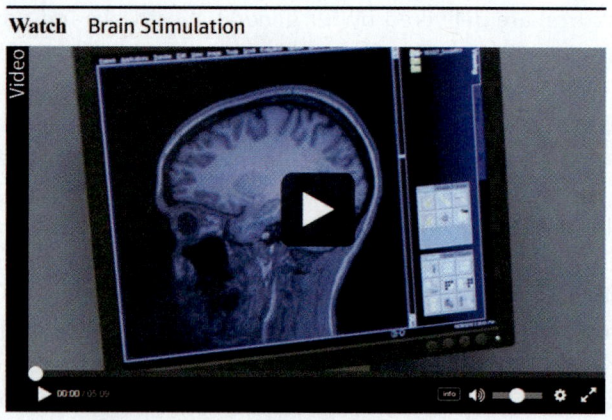

Watch Brain Stimulation

BRIGHT LIGHT THERAPY In the past decade an alternative nonpharmacological biological method has received increasing attention: *bright light therapy* (see Pail et al., 2011, for a review). This was originally used in the treatment of seasonal affective disorder, but it has now been shown to be effective in nonseasonal depressions as well (Golden et al., 2005; Lieverse et al., 2011).

Psychotherapy

Several forms of specialized psychotherapy, developed since the 1970s, have proved effective in the treatment of unipolar depression, and the magnitude of improvement of the best of these is approximately equivalent to that observed with medications. Considerable evidence also suggests that these same specialized forms of psychotherapy for depression, alone or in combination with drugs, significantly decrease the likelihood of relapse within a 2-year follow-up period (Hollon & Dimidjian, 2009; Hollon et al., 2005). Other specialized treatments have been developed to address the problems of people (and their families) with bipolar disorder.

COGNITIVE-BEHAVIORAL THERAPY One of the two best-known psychotherapies for unipolar depression with documented effectiveness is **cognitive-behavioral therapy (CBT)** (also known as **cognitive therapy**), originally developed by Beck and colleagues (Beck et al., 1979; Clark, Beck, & Alford, 1999). It is a relatively brief form of treatment (usually 10 to 20 sessions) that focuses on here-and-now

problems rather than on the more remote causal issues that psychodynamic psychotherapy often addresses. For example, cognitive therapy consists of highly structured, systematic attempts to teach people with unipolar depression to evaluate systematically their dysfunctional beliefs and negative automatic thoughts. They are also taught to identify and correct their biases or distortions in information processing and to uncover and challenge their underlying depressogenic assumptions and beliefs. Cognitive therapy relies heavily on an empirical approach in that patients are taught to treat their beliefs as hypotheses that can be tested through the use of behavioral experiments.

One example of challenging a negative automatic thought through a behavioral experiment can be seen in the following interchange between a cognitive therapist and a patient with depression.

Therapy Session: "My Husband Doesn't Love Me Anymore"

PATIENT: My husband doesn't love me anymore.

THERAPIST: That must be a very distressing thought. What makes you think that he doesn't love you?

PATIENT: Well, when he comes home in the evening, he never wants to talk to me. He just wants to sit and watch TV. Then he goes straight off to bed.

THERAPIST: OK. Now, is there any evidence, anything he does, that goes against the idea that he doesn't love you?

PATIENT: I can't think of any. Well, no, wait a minute. Actually it was my birthday a couple of weeks ago, and he gave me a watch which is really lovely. I'd seen them advertised and mentioned I liked it, and he took notice and went and got me one.

THERAPIST: Right. Now how does that fit with the idea that he doesn't love you?

PATIENT: Well, I suppose it doesn't really, does it? But then why is he like that in the evening?

THERAPIST: I suppose him not loving you any more is one possible reason. Are there any other possible reasons?

PATIENT: Well, he has been working very hard lately. I mean, he's late home most nights, and he had to go in to the office at the weekend. So I suppose it could be that.

THERAPIST: It could, couldn't it? How could you find out if that's it?

PATIENT: Well, I could say I've noticed how tired he looks and ask him how he's feeling and how the work's going. I haven't done that. I've just been getting annoyed because he doesn't pay any attention to me.

THERAPIST: That sounds like an excellent idea. How would you like to make that a homework task for this week?

(From Fennell, M. J. V. (1989). Depression. In K. Hawton, P. M. Salkovskis, J. Kirk, & D. M. Clark (Eds.), *Cognitive behaviour therapy for psychiatric problems: A practical guide*. Oxford University Press.)

The usefulness of cognitive therapy has been amply documented in dozens of studies, including several studies on hospital patients with unipolar depression and on patients diagnosed with depression with melancholic features (Craighead et al., 2007; Hollon, Haman, & Brown, 2002; Hollon et al., 2006). When compared with pharmacotherapy, it is at least as effective when delivered by well-trained cognitive therapists. It also seems to have a special advantage in preventing relapse, similar to that obtained by staying on medication (Hollon, 2011; Hollon & Ponniah, 2010). Moreover, evidence is beginning to accumulate that it can prevent recurrence several years following the episode when the treatment occurred (Craighead et al., 2007; Hollon & Dimidjian, 2009). Perhaps not surprisingly, some recent interesting brain-imaging studies have shown that the biological changes in certain brain areas that occur following effective treatment with cognitive therapy versus medications are somewhat different, suggesting that the mechanisms through which they work are also different (Clark & Beck, 2010; Hollon & Dimidjian, 2009). One possibility is that medications may target the limbic system, whereas cognitive therapy may have greater effects on cortical functions.

Recent evidence suggests that CBT and medications are equally effective in the treatment of severe depression (DeRubeis et al., 1999; Hollon et al., 2006). For example, one important two-site study of moderate to severe depression found that 58 percent responded to either cognitive therapy or medication (DeRubeis et al., 2005). However, by the end of the 2-year follow-up, when all cognitive therapy and medications had been discontinued for 1 year, only 25 percent of patients treated with cognitive therapy had had a relapse versus 50 percent in the medication group (Hollon & Dimidjian, 2009; Hollon et al., 2005). This is illustrated in Figure 7.10.

Another variant on cognitive therapy, called *mindfulness-based cognitive therapy*, has been developed in recent years to be used with people with highly recurrent depression (Segal et al., 2002, 2012; Teasdale, 2004). The logic of this treatment is based on findings that people with recurrent depression are likely to have negative thinking patterns activated when they are simply in a depressed mood. Perhaps rather than trying to alter the content of their negative thinking as in traditional cognitive therapy, it might be more useful to change the way in which these people relate to their thoughts, feelings, and bodily sensations. This group treatment involves training in mindfulness meditation techniques aimed at developing patients' awareness of their unwanted thoughts, feelings, and sensations so that they no longer automatically try to avoid them but rather learn to accept them for what they are—simply thoughts occurring in the moment rather than a reflection of reality. A recent meta-analysis of findings from six randomized controlled trials of individuals in remission from depression suggests that mindfulness-based cognitive therapy is an effective treatment for reducing risk of relapse in those with a history of three or more prior depressive episodes who have been treated with antidepressant medication (Piet & Hougaard, 2011).

Although the vast majority of research on CBT has focused on unipolar depression, recently there have been indications that a modified form of CBT may be quite useful, in combination with medication, in the treatment of bipolar disorder as well (Lam et al., 2003, 2005; Miklowitz, 2009). There is also preliminary evidence that mindfulness-based cognitive therapy may be useful in treating bipolar patients between episodes (Williams et al., 2008).

BEHAVIORAL ACTIVATION TREATMENT A relatively new and promising treatment for unipolar depression is called **behavioral activation treatment**. This treatment approach focuses intensively on getting patients to become more active and engaged with their environment and with their interpersonal relationships. These techniques include scheduling daily activities and rating pleasure and mastery while engaging in them, exploring alternative behaviors to reach goals, and role-playing to address specific deficits. Traditional cognitive therapy attends to these same issues but to a lesser extent. Behavioral activation treatment, by contrast, does not focus on implementing cognitive changes directly but rather on changing behavior. The

Figure 7.10 Survival curve illustrating how many months following the end of treatment it took patients from the two groups before they had another episode of depression (recurrence). One group had previously received cognitive therapy (CT) and the other group had received antidepressant medication (ADM)

(Adapted from From Hollon et al. (2005, April). Prevention of relapse following cognitive therapy vs. medications in moderate to severe depression. *Arch. Gen. Psychiat.*, 62(4), 417–426. © 2005 American Medical Association. Reprinted with permission.)

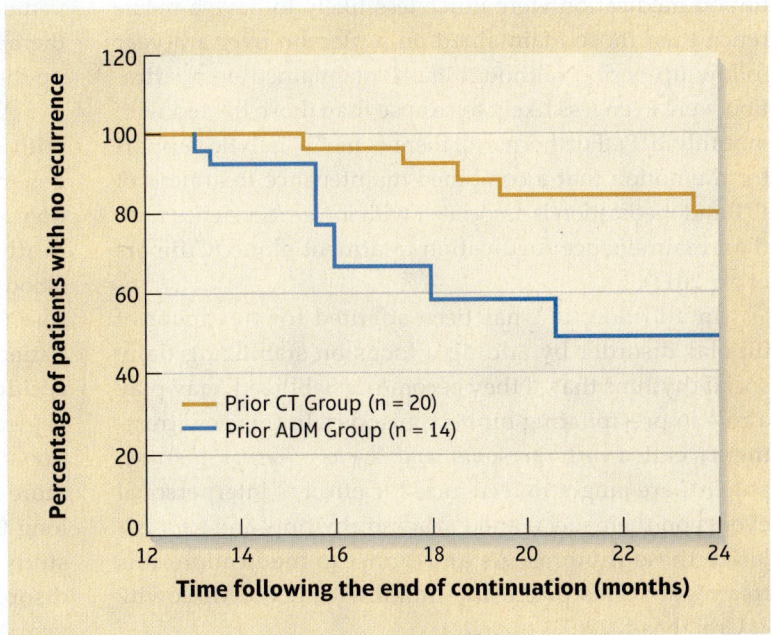

goals are to increase levels of positive reinforcement and to reduce avoidance and withdrawal (Dimidjian et al., 2011). Early results were very promising, suggesting it may be as effective as more traditional cognitive therapies (Jacobson et al., 2001), and there is now meta-analytic support for this notion (Mazzucchelli et al., 2009). Indeed, one study found that patients with moderate to severe depression who received behavioral activation treatment did as well as those on medication and even slightly better than those who received cognitive therapy (Dimidjian et al., 2006). However, the slight superiority of behavioral activation treatment relative to cognitive therapy was not maintained, with some results indicating a trend for cognitive therapy to be slightly superior at follow-up (Dobson et al., 2008). Because it is easier to train therapists to administer behavioral activation treatment than cognitive therapy, it seems likely that there will be increased attention paid to this relatively new treatment in the coming years.

INTERPERSONAL THERAPY The **interpersonal therapy (IPT)** approach has not yet been subjected to as extensive an evaluation as CBT, nor is it as widely available. However, the studies that have been completed strongly support its effectiveness for treating unipolar depression (Cuijpers et al., 2011; Hollon & Ponniah, 2010). Indeed, interpersonal therapy seems to be about as effective as medications or cognitive-behavioral treatment (Hollon, Thase, & Markowitz, 2002; Weissman & Markowitz, 2002). IPT focuses on current relationship issues, trying to help the person understand and change maladaptive interaction patterns (Bleiberg & Markowitz, 2008). Interpersonal therapy can also be useful in long-term follow-up for individuals with severe recurrent unipolar depression (Frank et al., 1990; Weissman & Markowitz, 2002). Patients who received continued IPT once a month or who received continued medication were much less likely to have a recurrence than those maintained on a placebo over a 3-year follow-up period (although those maintained on medication were even less likely to relapse than those treated with monthly IPT). Furthermore, there is meta-analytic support for the notion that a combined maintenance treatment of IPT and medication is associated with lower recurrence rates than maintenance medication treatment alone (Cuijpers et al., 2011).

In addition, IPT has been adapted for treatment of bipolar disorder by adding a focus on stabilizing daily social rhythms that, if they become destabilized, may play a role in precipitating bipolar episodes. In this new treatment, called *interpersonal and social rhythm therapy*, patients are taught to recognize the effect of interpersonal events on their social and circadian rhythms and to regularize these rhythms. As an adjunct to medication, this treatment seems promising (Miklowitz, 2009; Miklowitz & Craighead, 2007).

FAMILY AND MARITAL THERAPY In any treatment program, it is important to deal with unusual stressors in a patient's life because an unfavorable life situation may lead to a recurrence of the depression and may necessitate longer treatment. This point has been well established in studies indicating that relapse in unipolar and bipolar disorders, as in schizophrenia, is correlated with certain negative aspects of family life (Hooley, 2007; Hooley & Hiller, 2001). Behavior by a spouse that can be interpreted by a former patient as criticism seems especially likely to produce depression relapse. For example, for bipolar disorder, some types of family interventions directed at reducing the level of expressed emotion or hostility, and at increasing the information available to the family about how to cope with the disorder, have been found to be very useful in preventing relapse in these situations (Miklowitz, 2009; Miklowitz & Craighead, 2007). For married people who have unipolar depression and marital discord, marital therapy (focusing on the marital discord rather than on the depressed spouse alone) is as effective as cognitive therapy in reducing unipolar depression in the depressed spouse. Marital therapy has the further advantage of producing greater increases in marital satisfaction than cognitive therapy (Beach & Jones, 2002).

CONCLUSIONS Even without formal therapy, the great majority of patients with mania and depression recover from a given episode in less than a year. With the modern methods of treatment discussed here, the general outlook for a given episode if treatment is obtained has become increasingly favorable for many, but by no means all, diagnosed individuals. However, at least half never receive even minimally adequate treatment. Although relapses and recurrences often occur, these can now often be prevented or at least reduced in frequency by maintenance therapy—through continuation of medication and follow-up therapy sessions at regular intervals.

At the same time, the mortality rate for individuals with depression is significantly higher than that for the general population, partly because of the higher incidence of suicide but also because there is an excess of deaths due to natural causes (Coryell & Winokur, 1992; Goodwin & Jamison, 2007), including coronary heart disease (Glassman, 2005; Whang et al., 2009; see Chapter 5). Patients with mania also have a high risk of death from accidents (often with alcohol as a contributing factor), neglect of proper health precautions, or physical exhaustion (Goodwin & Jamison, 2007). Thus, the need for still-more-effective treatment methods, both immediate and long term, clearly remains. Also, a great need remains to study the factors that put people at risk for depressive disorders and to apply relevant findings to early intervention and prevention.

in review

- Evaluate the effectiveness of antidepressant medications, mood-stabilizing drugs such as lithium, and electroconvulsive therapy in the treatment of unipolar and bipolar disorders.

- Describe the three major forms of psychotherapy that have been shown to be effective for treating depression.

Suicide: The Clinical Picture and the Causal Pattern

7.8   Describe the prevalence and clinical picture of suicidal behaviors.

The risk of **suicide**—intentionally taking one's own life—is a significant factor in all types of depression. Virtually all psychological disorders increase the risk of suicidal behavior (Nock et al., 2009, 2010); indeed, approximately 90 to 95 percent of those who die by suicide have a history of at least one psychological disorder (Cavanagh et al., 2003; Nock, Borges, Bromet, Cha, et al., 2008). However, depression is the disorder that is most commonly linked with suicidal behavior. Moreover, individuals with two or more mental disorders are at even greater risk than those with only one (Nock, Borges, Bromet, Alonso, et al., 2008; Nock et al., 2010).

Suicide currently is the 15th leading cause of death in the world, accounting for 1.4 percent of all deaths (World Health Organization [WHO], 2015a). By comparison, there are more deaths each year around the world by suicide than due to all wars, genocide, and interpersonal violence combined (WHO, 2015a) (see Figure 7.11). In other words, we are each more likely to die by our own hand than someone else's. Moreover, most experts agree that the number of actual suicides is even higher than the number officially reported because many self-inflicted deaths are attributed in official records to other, less stigmatized causes (e.g., Marzuk et al., 2002). In addition to suicide death, estimates are that approximately 5 percent of Americans have made a nonlethal suicide attempt at some time in their lives and 15 percent have experienced suicidal thoughts (often referred to as "suicidal ideation") (Nock, Borges, Bromet, Alonso, et al., 2008). Thus, only about one-third of people who think about suicide go on to make a suicide attempt. Notably, the risk of transitioning from suicidal thoughts to suicide attempt is highest in the first year after onset of suicidal thinking, and the longer a person goes thinking about suicide without making a suicide attempt, the less likely that individual is to ever make an attempt (Nock, Borges, Bromet, Alonso, et al., 2008).

It is important to distinguish suicidal behavior (in which a person engages in self-harm with some intention of dying) from **nonsuicidal self-injury (NSSI)**, which refers to direct, deliberate destruction of body tissue (often taking the form of cutting or burning one's own skin) in the absence of any intent to die (Nock, 2010). Approximately 15 to 20 percent of adolescents and young adults

---

Figure 7.11 Suicide Around the World

The rate of suicide varies dramatically in different parts of the world, as shown in this figure using data from the World Health Organization. More people die each year by suicide than by all other forms of violence combined.

(Adapted from World Health Organization, http://www.who.int/mental_health/suicide-prevention/en.)

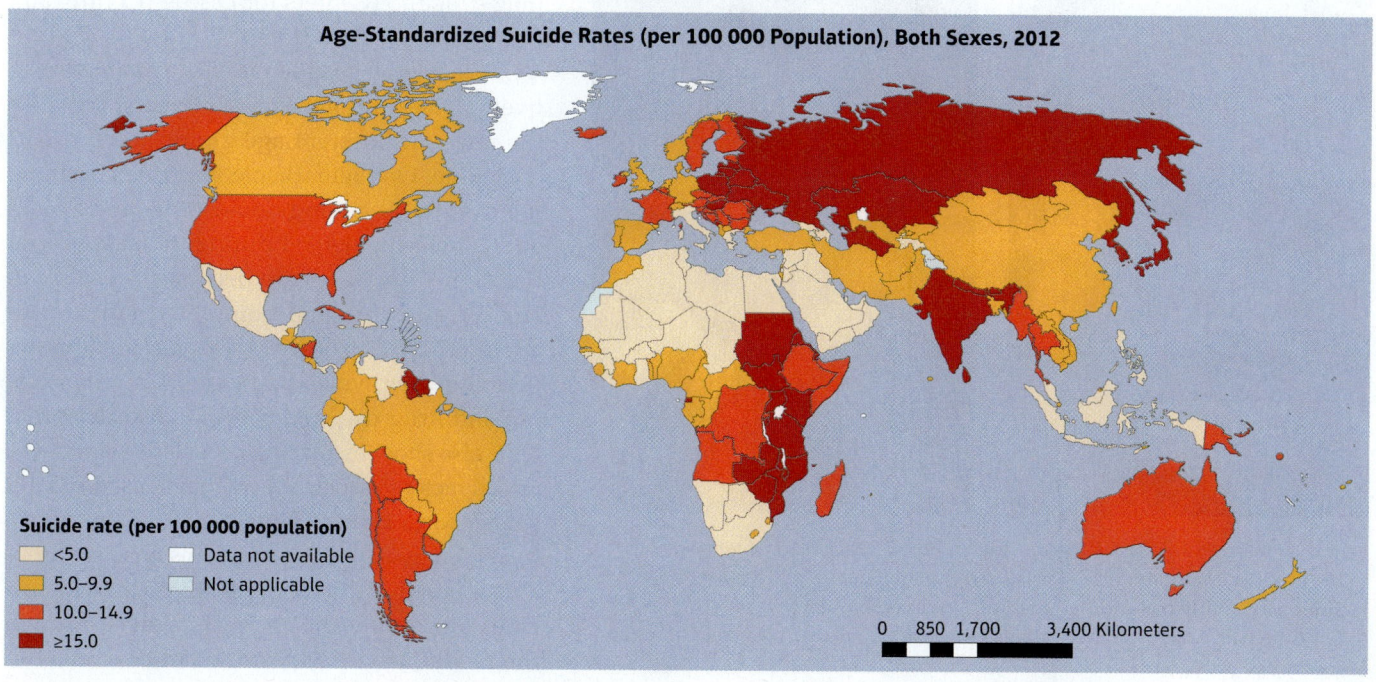

Age-Standardized Suicide Rates (per 100 000 Population), Both Sexes, 2012

Suicide rate (per 100 000 population)
- <5.0
- 5.0–9.9
- 10.0–14.9
- ≥15.0
- Data not available
- Not applicable

0   850 1,700   3,400 Kilometers

report engaging in NSSI at least once, and the primary reasons given for engaging in this behavior include that it helps both to decrease high levels of distress and to elicit help from others (Nock, 2009). Although NSSI has been reported in written history for thousands of years and in many cultures around the world, it has only been the focus of serious, systematic research for the past few decades. Psychologists are still working to understand why people engage in NSSI and how to best predict and prevent it. NSSI disorder recently was added to *DSM-5* as a condition requiring further study, and it is hoped that continued research on this condition will help to increase our understanding and ability to prevent it.

Although there is a clear distinction between suicidal and nonsuicidal self-injury, it is important to note that most people who die by suicide or make nonlethal suicide attempts are ambivalent about taking their own lives. Suicide attempts most often are made when people are alone and in a state of severe psychological distress and anguish, unable to see their problems objectively or to evaluate alternative courses of action. Thus, one tragedy is that many do not really want to die. A second tragic concern arises from the long-lasting distress among those left behind. Studies of survivors show that the loss of a loved one through suicide "is one of the greatest burdens individuals and families may endure" (Dunne, 1992, p. 222).

In the discussion that follows, we will focus on various aspects of the incidence and clinical picture of suicide, on factors that appear to be of causal significance, on degrees of intent and ways of communicating it, and on issues of treatment and prevention. Who dies by suicide? What are the motives for taking one's own life?

What general sociocultural variables appear to be relevant to an understanding of suicide?

Who Attempts and Dies by Suicide?

Although researchers are still working to understand why people engage in suicidal behavior, there are clear and consistent findings regarding which segments of the population are at higher risk. In virtually every country around the world in which suicidal behavior has been examined, women are significantly more likely than men to think about suicide and to make nonlethal suicide attempts (Nock, Borges, Bromet, Alonso, et al., 2008), but men are four times more likely than women to die by suicide (WHO, 2015). This difference in likelihood of suicide death is explained in large part by the fact that men tend to use more lethal means in their suicide attempts (e.g., firearms) than do women.

Another pattern seen consistently around the world is the dramatic increase in suicidal thoughts and behaviors (including suicide death) that occurs during childhood and young adulthood. Suicide is very rare in children—due in large part to the fact that young children do not understand the finality of death and often lack the means to act on suicidal thoughts in the unlikely event that they have them. However, suicidal thoughts and behaviors increase in prevalence starting around age 12 and continue to increase into the early to mid-20s (see Figure 7.12; Nock et al., 2013). The rate of suicide death follows a similar pattern, followed by a peaking in middle age (45–55 years) and a slight decrease and leveling off for the remainder of the life span. One notable exception to this pattern is that the suicide rate for white men in the United States shows another dramatic increase beginning at age 75 (Centers for Disease Control and Prevention [CDC], 2015c).

The overall suicide rate has remained relatively stable during the past 100 years; however, the rates for different age groups have varied over time. One remarkable trend has been the increased risk among adolescents and young adults, which emerged during the past several decades. Why has there been such a surge in suicide attempts and completed suicides in adolescence? One obvious reason is that this is a period during which depression, anxiety, alcohol and drug use, and conduct disorder problems also show increasing prevalence, and these are all factors associated with increased risk for suicide (e.g., Evans, Hawton, & Rodham, 2004). Increased availability of firearms has also probably played a role as well. Exposure to suicides (especially those of celebrities) through the media, where they are often portrayed in

Ernest Hemingway (left) died by suicide on July 2, 1961. Thirty-five years later to the day, his granddaughter Margaux (right) took her own life as well. The Hemingway family has endured five suicides over four generations—Ernest's father Clarence, Ernest and his siblings Ursula and Leicester, and granddaughter Margaux.

dramatic terms, has probably also contributed to these aggregate increases in adolescent suicide, perhaps because adolescents are highly susceptible to suggestion and imitative behavior (Hawton & Williams, 2002; Jamison, 1999). One review estimated that between 1 and 13 percent of adolescent suicides occur as a result of contagion factors (Velting & Gould, 1997). Finally, the fact that the media rarely discuss the mental disorders suffered by the suicide victims may further increase the likelihood of imitation.

Many college students also seem very vulnerable to the development of suicidal ideation and plans. The combined stressors of academic demands, social interaction problems, and career choices—perhaps interacting with challenges to their basic values—evidently make it impossible for some students to continue making the adjustments their life situations demand. For an overview of warning signs for student suicide, see the World Around Us box.

As shown in Figure 7.11, the rates of suicide death vary pretty dramatically around the world. Interestingly, geographic differences are also seen within countries. For instance, in the United States, the suicide rate is highest in the Western United States (especially Wyoming, Montana, Alaska, Colorado, and New Mexico) and lowest in the Mid-Atlantic states (such as New Jersey, New York, Maryland, and the District of Columbia) (CDC, 2015c). Racial/ethnic differences are also seen: 90 percent of suicides in the United States are classified as people who are white, 6 percent black, 3 percent Asian/Pacific Islander, and 1 percent American Indian or Alaskan Natives (CDC, 2015c).

Psychological Disorders

Beyond the demographic factors described above (e.g., sex, age, race/ethnicity), the most widely studied risk factors for suicidal behaviors are the presence of different psychological disorders. As noted earlier, the presence of virtually all disorders increases the risk of subsequent suicidal behavior, and most people who die by suicide have a prior mental disorder (Cavanagh et al., 2003).

How and why would so many different disorders be associated with suicide? Recent research has revealed that different disorders are associated with different parts of the pathway to suicide. For instance, as you might expect,

Figure 7.12 Cumulative Prevalence of Suicidal Thoughts and Behaviors During Adolescence

Data from the National Comorbidity Survey–Adolescent Supplement, a nationally representative survey of over 10,000 U.S. adolescents, show that very few people think about suicide during childhood, but then the percentage of people who have ever thought about suicide, plan suicide, or make a suicide attempt increases dramatically during adolescence. These data are from the United States (Nock et al., 2013), and a very similar pattern is observed in other countries around the world (Nock, Borges, Bromet, Alonso, et al., 2008).

(Adapted from Nock, M. K., Green, J. G., Hwang, I., McLaughlin, K. A., Sampson, N. A., Zaslavsky, A. M., & Kessler, R. C. (2013). Prevalence, correlates and treatment of lifetime suicidal behavior among adolescents: Results from the National Comorbidity Survey Replication–Adolescent Supplement (NCS-A). *JAMA Psychiatry, 70,* 300–310.)

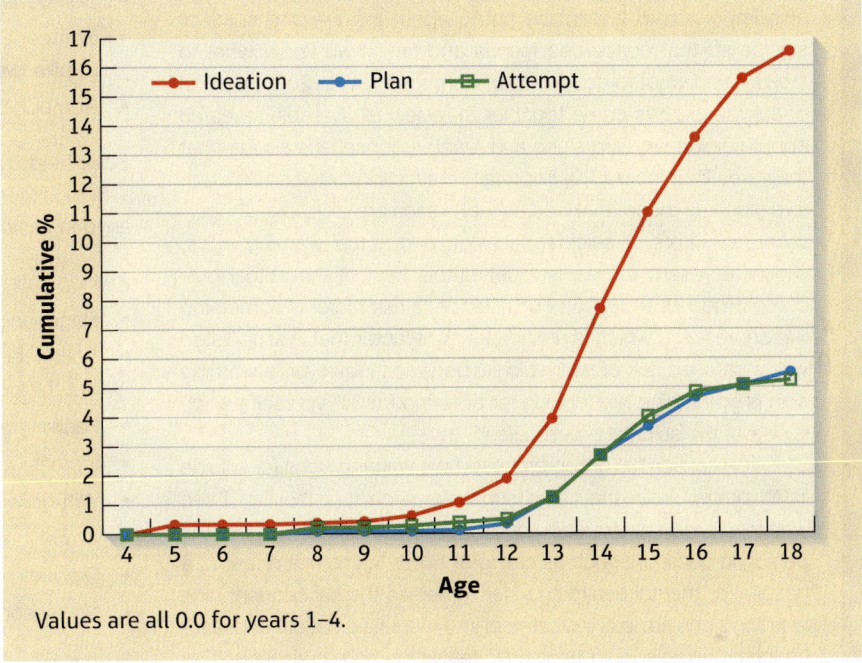

Values are all 0.0 for years 1–4.

depression is the disorder most strongly predictive of which people develop suicidal thoughts; however, it does not predict which people with suicidal thoughts go on to act on them and make suicide attempts. Instead, it is disorders characterized by agitation and aggression/impulsiveness that predict acting on one's suicidal thoughts, such as posttraumatic stress disorder, bipolar disorder, conduct disorder, and intermittent explosive disorder that predict this transition (Nock et al., 2009, 2010, 2014).

The fact that different disorders predict different parts of the pathway to suicidal behavior may help to explain the dose–response relation that is consistently observed between the number of disorders present and the risk of suicidal behavior. More specifically, a recent study of suicidal behavior across people from 17 different countries around the world revealed that compared to people with no history of psychological disorders, those with only one psychological disorder have no increased risk of suicidal thoughts or behaviors. However, those with two disorders (compared to those with none) show a doubling in their risk of suicidal behavior, whereas those with three or more disorders show a six- to ninefold increase in the risk of suicidal behavior (Nock, Borges, Bromet, Alonso, et al., 2008).

The World Around Us

Warning Signs for Suicide

Conditions like heart attacks and strokes are life threatening if not acted on immediately. For that reason, the warning signs for heart attacks and strokes have been widely disseminated. For instance, the American Heart Association lists stroke warning signs as "Spot a Stroke F.A.S.T": If you observe the signs of **F**ace drooping, **A**rm weakness, and **S**peech difficulty, it's **T**ime to call 9-1-1.

Given the life-threatening nature of suicidal behavior, it is also important to inform the public about the warning signs of suicide so that concerned friends and family will know what to look for and what to do in case of increased risk. In 2003, a panel of suicide experts came together to review all available research about suicide warning signs and reach a consensus about what they are. They noted the important distinction between *risk factors* (such as those reviewed above), which are distal (i.e., longer-term) predictors of suicidal behavior, and actual *warning signs*, which represent the earliest detectable sign of the actual outcome (Rudd et al., 2006). For instance, a risk factor is something like depression, which is an independent factor that is associated with increased risk of later suicidal behavior. However, a warning sign is something like looking for a method to kill yourself, which is part of the suicidal process itself.

The consensus group proposed the warning signs for suicide listed below. Note the tiered structure, such that the first three warning signs should lead you to immediate action to help the person in question, such as calling 9-1-1 or taking him or her to a hospital or mental health provider. Whereas the subsequent nine warning signs are less indicative of imminent risk, but still cause for concern and so should lead you to talk to the person about getting help and/or contacting a mental health professional for assistance.

Suicidal thoughts and behaviors can be scary when they occur, and it's important to know what signs to look for and how to respond in order to be able to do all you can to help yourself or those in need.

Consensus Warning Signs for Suicide

Are you or someone you love at risk for suicide? Get the facts and take action.

Call 9-1-1 or seek immediate help from a mental health provider when you hear, say, or see any one of these behaviors:

- Someone threatening to hurt or kill themselves
- Someone looking for ways to kill themselves: seeking access to pills, weapons, or other means
- Someone talking or writing about death, dying, or suicide

Seek help by contacting a mental health professional or calling 1-800-273-TALK for a referral should you witness, hear, or see anyone exhibiting any one or more of these behaviors:

- Hopelessness
- Rage, anger, seeking revenge
- Acting reckless or engaging in risky activities, seemingly without thinking
- Feeling trapped—like there's no way out
- Increasing alcohol or drug use
- Withdrawing from friends, family, or society
- Anxiety, agitation, unable to sleep, or sleeping all the time
- Dramatic changes in mood
- No reason for living; no sense of purpose in life

Source: Rudd et al., 2006

What are the pros and cons of publicizing warning signs for suicide? How might they be helpful to people? Is there a potential to do harm (and if so, how do you know)? Use data to support your argument wherever you can.

Other Psychosocial Factors Associated with Suicide

Although psychological disorders are strongly associated with suicide, most people with psychological disorders do not become suicidal. So why do some people become suicidal? Edwin Shneidman, thought of by many as the godfather of suicide research, has written extensively about the "suicidal mind" based on his extensive interviews with many suicidal people and he suggested it comes down to the experience of intense psychological pain. He wrote:

In almost every case suicide is caused by . . . psychological pain, or "psychache." . . . Suicidal death, in other words, is an escape from pain. . . . Pain is nature's great signal. Pain warns us; pain both mobilizes us and saps our strength; pain, by its very nature, makes us want to stop it or escape from it. . . . Psychache is the hurt, anguish, or ache that takes hold in the mind . . . the pain of excessively felt shame, guilt, fear, anxiety, loneliness, angst, and dread of growing old or of dying badly. . . . [I]ts introspective reality is undeniable. Suicide happens when the psychache is deemed unbearable and death is actively sought to stop the unceasing flow of painful consciousness. (Shneidman, 1996, pp. 23, 24, 29)

Research has subsequently supported the link between pain—both psychological and physical—and suicide (Hooley et al., 2014). This raises the question of why do some people experience such intense psychological pain and feel the need to die by suicide as an escape? Research suggests that the answer is not simple, and suicide may be best understood as the end product of a combination of many different factors stretching back to childhood (and beyond if we consider biological vulnerabilities).

People who become suicidal often come from backgrounds in which there was some combination of a good deal of family psychopathology, child maltreatment, and family instability (Bruffaerts et al., 2010; Gureje et al., 2011). These early experiences are thought to interact with biological vulnerabilities described below to increase the risk of personality traits such as hopelessness, impulsiveness, aggression, pessimism, and negative affectivity, which may in turn increase the risk for suicide (O'Connor & Nock, 2014; Yen et al., 2009). Other symptoms that seem to predict suicide more reliably in the short term in patients with major depression include severe anxiety, panic attacks, severe anhedonia (inability to experience pleasure), global insomnia, delusions, and alcohol abuse (Busch et al., 2003; Goodwin & Jamison, 2007). Indeed, in one study of 76 people who had committed suicide while being hospitalized, the hospital records revealed that 79 percent of these people had been severely anxious and agitated in the week prior to committing suicide (Busch et al., 2003).

Kurt Cobain, lead vocalist of the rock band Nirvana, died from a self-inflicted gunshot wound on April 8, 1994. He left behind his wife, Courtney Love, and their daughter, Frances, to deal with the emotional burden of his suicide. Forty to 60 percent of those who die by suicide are depressed.

There also is evidence that people who have a strong implicit association between the self and death or suicide are at elevated risk of future suicide attempts, even over and above the effects of other known risk factors (Nock et al., 2010). Implicit associations are mental associations that people hold between two concepts that they are unwilling or unable to report. Such associations can be measured using reaction time tests, such as the Implicit Association Test (IAT), which asks people to classify words into one of two groups (e.g., "like me" or "not like me"). Researchers have found that suicidal people are faster in classifying suicide-related words (e.g., "death," "suicide") in the "like me" group than in the "not like me" group, providing a

new method of detecting and better predicting suicidal behavior (Nock et al., 2010).

Biological Factors

There is strong evidence that suicide sometimes runs in families and that genetic factors may play a role in the risk for suicide (Brent et al., 2015). Averaging across 22 studies, the concordance rate for suicide in identical twins is about three times higher than that in fraternal twins (Baldessarini & Hennen, 2004). Moreover, this genetic vulnerability seems to be at least partly independent of the genetic vulnerability for major depression (Brezo et al., 2010).

There is also increasing evidence that this genetic vulnerability may be linked to the neurochemical correlates of suicide that have now been found in numerous studies. Specifically, suicide victims often have alterations in serotonin functioning, with reduced serotonergic activity being associated with increased suicide risk—especially for violent suicide. Such studies have been conducted not only in postmortem studies of suicide victims but also in people who have made suicide attempts and survived. This association appears to be independent of psychiatric diagnosis, including suicide victims with depression, schizophrenia, and personality disorders.

Several studies have tried to document an association between suicide and the short allele serotonin-transporter gene (which controls the uptake of serotonin from the synapse), previously discussed as being implicated in the vulnerability to depression. Although not all studies have found positive results, a quantitative review of these studies did find that people with one or two copies of the short allele are at heightened risk for suicide following stressful life events (Lin & Tsai, 2004). There is also growing support for associations between additional serotonergic gene variants and suicide attempts (Brezo et al., 2010).

Theoretical Models of Suicidal Behavior

Researchers are attempting to explain all of the prior findings about suicidal behavior with different theoretical models. Many have conceptualized suicide using diathesis–stress models in which underlying vulnerabilities (e.g., genetic, neurobiological) interact with stressful life events to produce suicidal thoughts and behaviors (Mann et al., 1999; Schotte & Clum, 1987). Others have outlined more specific models to explain suicidal behavior. For instance, Joiner's interpersonal-psychological model of suicide suggests that the psychological states of *perceived burdensomeness* (e.g., feeling like a burden to others) and *thwarted belongingness* (e.g., feeling alone) interact to produce suicidal thoughts and desires. And it is only in the presence of a third factor, the *acquired capability for suicide* (believed to be acquired through pain or provocative experiences), that a person has the desire and ability to make a lethal suicide attempt (see Figure 7.13; Joiner, 2005). No existing models have adequately explained suicidal behavior; however, researchers continue to work toward a better understanding so that we can better predict and prevent these tragic behaviors.

Figure 7.13 Joiner's Interpersonal-Psychological Model of Suicide

Joiner proposes that people desire to die by suicide when they perceive that they are a burden to others and experience a sense of thwarted belongingness. However, they cannot act on this suicidal desire unless they also have acquired the capacity for suicide. When these three factors come together, Joiner argues, a person is at high risk for suicide.

(Adapted from Joiner, 2005.)

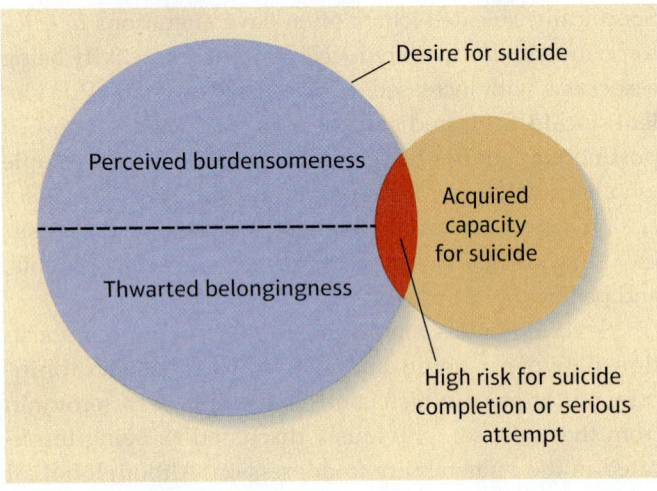

---

in review

- Which groups of people are most likely to attempt suicide, and which groups are most likely to die by suicide?
- Summarize the psychological and biological factors associated with suicide.

Suicide Prevention and Intervention

7.9 Explain the efforts currently used to prevent and treat suicidal behaviors.

Preventing suicide is extremely difficult. Most people who are depressed and contemplating suicide do not realize that their thinking is restricted and their decision making impaired and that they are in need of assistance. Indeed, only about 40 percent of people with suicidal thoughts or attempts around the world receive treatment (Bruffaerts et al., 2011). Rates of treatment receipt are much higher in high-income countries (56 percent) than low-income countries (17 percent); and this treatment is most often from a

general practitioner rather than a health care professional. The primary reasons suicidal people give for not seeking treatment is that they didn't think they needed help (58 percent said this) or that they wanted to handle the problem on their own (40 percent) (Bruffaerts et al., 2011). Currently, there are three main thrusts of preventive efforts: treatment of the person's current mental disorder(s) as noted above, crisis intervention, and working with high-risk groups.

Treatment of Mental Disorders

One way to help prevent suicide might be through treating the underlying mental disorder(s) the potentially suicidal person has. In the case of depression, such treatment is often in the form of antidepressant medications. There has been a great deal of recent controversy regarding the use of antidepressant medications and their potential for actually increasing the risk of suicidal behavior, especially among adolescents. A recent review of placebo-controlled randomized clinical trials revealed higher rates of suicidal thoughts and behaviors in those receiving antidepressants relative to those receiving placebo (Whittington et al., 2005). Findings such as these led the Food and Drug Administration (FDA) to require pharmaceutical companies to put warnings on the labels of these medications informing the public of this effect. During the past several years, numerous papers have been published on both sides of this issue, some suggesting that antidepressants increase the risk of suicidal behavior in youth, and others suggesting they are safe and effective and that the FDA warning has actually backfired and led to an increase in the suicide rate among youth due to a decrease in antidepressant use (Bridge et al., 2007, 2008). There is less argument about adults, for whom there is evidence that antidepressants can decrease suicidal thoughts and behaviors, and seem to do so via a reduction in depressive symptoms (Gibbons et al., 2012). Lithium also seems to be an especially powerful antisuicide agent over the long term (although not in acute situations; Goodwin & Jamison, 2007). Benzodiazepines are also suggested to be useful in treating the severe anxiety and panic that so often precede suicide attempts.

Crisis Intervention

The primary objective of crisis intervention is to help a person cope with an immediate life crisis. If a serious suicide attempt has been made, the first step involves emergency medical treatment, followed by referral to inpatient or outpatient mental health facilities in order to reduce the risk for future attempts (Stolberg et al., 2002).

When people contemplating suicide are willing to discuss their problems with someone at a suicide prevention center, it is often possible to avert an actual suicide attempt. Here the primary objective is to help these people regain their ability to cope with their immediate problems as quickly as possible. Emphasis is usually placed on (1) maintaining supportive and often highly directive contact with the person over a short period of time—usually one to six contacts; (2) helping the person to realize that acute distress is impairing his or her ability to assess the situation accurately and to see that there are better ways of dealing with the problem; and (3) helping the person to see that the present distress and emotional turmoil will not be endless.

Since the 1960s, the availability of competent assistance at times of suicidal crisis has been expanded through the establishment of *suicide hotlines* for suicide prevention centers. There are now more than several thousand such hotlines in the United States, but questions have been raised about the quality of care offered by the majority of them (Seeley, 1997). These centers are geared primarily toward crisis intervention, usually via the 24-hour-a-day availability of telephone contact. Suicide hotlines are usually staffed primarily by nonprofessionals who are supervised by psychologists and psychiatrists. The worker attempts to establish the seriousness of the caller's intent and simultaneously tries to show empathy and to convince the person not to attempt suicide. Efforts are also made to mobilize support from family or friends. Unfortunately, good information on the assessment of the effects of these hotlines and suicide prevention centers has not revealed much impact on suicide rates.

Focus on High-Risk Groups and Other Measures

Recent research has focused on providing treatment aimed directly at decreasing suicidal thoughts and behaviors among those already experiencing these outcomes. For instance, one recent study tested the effectiveness of cognitive therapy for reducing the risk of suicide attempt in adults who had already made at least one prior attempt. This treatment was quite beneficial in reducing further attempts (Brown et al., 2005). In the 18 months subsequent to receiving treatment, patients in the cognitive therapy group were 50 percent less likely to reattempt suicide than patients in the usual care group, and their depressive and hopelessness symptoms were also lower than those of the usual care group. Subsequent research suggests that cognitive-behavioral therapy for suicide prevention is also feasible for use with adolescents who have attempted suicide (Stanley et al., 2009).

in review

- What are three types of suicide prevention efforts, and how successful do they seem to be?

Unresolved Issues

Is There a Right to Die?

Most of us respect the preservation of human life as a worthwhile value. Thus, in our society, suicide is generally considered not only tragic but also "wrong." Efforts to prevent suicide, however, involve ethical problems. If people wish to take their own lives, what obligation—or right—do others have to interfere? Not all societies have taken the position that others should interfere when someone wishes to commit suicide. For example, the classical Greeks believed in dignity in death, and people who were extremely ill could get permission from the state to commit suicide. Officials of the state gave out hemlock (a poison) to those who received such permission (Humphry & Wickett, 1986). Today, in certain Western European countries such as the Netherlands and Belgium the law allows terminally ill people to be given access to drugs that they can use to commit suicide (Bosshard et al., 2008; Maris et al., 2000). In 1994 the state of Oregon passed the Oregon Death with Dignity Act (ODDA) allowing physician-assisted suicide for terminally ill patients who request a prescription for lethal medications that they will ingest to end their own lives (e.g., Purvis, 2012; Sears & Stanton, 2001). As of 2007 an estimated 341 people had taken their lives under the ODDA.

Passage of the ODDA was (and is) highly controversial in the United States and was challenged several times by U.S. Attorney General John Ashcroft in federal courts. So far the law remains in effect even after being reviewed by the Supreme Court, where it was upheld in January 2006. Furthermore, in 2008 Washington became the second state to pass a death with dignity act, and in Montana a court ruling made it legal as well. Nevertheless, there is still very heated debate all over the country about the right of people who are terminally ill or who suffer chronic and debilitating pain to shorten their agony. One group, the Hemlock Society, supports the rights of terminally ill people to get help in ending their own lives when they wish; the society also provides support groups for people making this decision.

Several other groups press related issues at a legislative level. One physician in Michigan, Dr. Jack Kevorkian (1928–2011), helped over 130 gravely ill people commit suicide and, in so doing, tried to get Michigan to pass laws permitting such acts. For years the state tried to block Kevorkian from assisting in any further suicides, and at several points he was even imprisoned, and his medical license revoked, because he refused to obey injunctions not to assist with any more suicides. In 1998 Kevorkian invited further attention—and prosecution—when he released a videotape to the CBS program *60 Minutes,* and millions watched him assisting in a suicide. He was later charged, and convicted in April 1999, of second-degree murder and was released and paroled for good behavior in 2007 after serving 8 years of a 10- to 25-year term in prison. In spite of Kevorkian's failure to prompt the passage of laws supporting assisted suicide for such gravely ill individuals (indeed, Michigan passed a law prohibiting assisted suicide!), substantial numbers of people, including many physicians and dying patients, have come to sympathize with this position (Curlin et al., 2008; Purvis, 2012; Wilson, Chochinov, et al., 2007; see also Szasz's 1999 book *Fatal Freedom: The Ethics and Politics of Suicide*).

Arguments against this position have included fears that the right to suicide might be abused. For example, people who are terminally ill and severely incapacitated might feel pressured to end their own lives rather than burden their families with their care or with the cost of their care in a medical facility or hospice. However, in places where assisted suicide is legal, such as the Netherlands and Oregon, this has not happened. Indeed, physicians in Oregon seem to have become more aware of and sensitive to the needs of terminally ill patients in terms of recommending hospice care and learning more about prescribing the high doses of pain medication needed to relieve suffering (Ganzini et al., 2001). Consistent with this, most patients in Oregon say they are motivated by a loss of autonomy and dignity rather than a need for help with pain control (Prokopetz & Lehmann, 2012).

But what about the rights of suicidal people who are not terminally ill and who have dependent children, parents, a spouse, or other loved ones who will be adversely affected, perhaps permanently (Lukas & Seiden, 1990; Maris et al., 2000), by their death? Here a person's "right to suicide" is not immediately obvious, and physicians are very unlikely to provide assistance in such cases (Rurup et al., 2005). The right to suicide is even less clear when we consider that, through intervention, many suicidal people regain their perspective and see alternative ways of dealing with their distress.

Rather than focusing on suicide "prevention," some have suggested suicide "intervention" both as a more appropriate term and as descriptive of a more ethically defensible professional approach to suicidal behavior. According to this perspective, suicide intervention embodies a more neutral moral stance than suicide prevention—it means interceding without the implication of preventing the act—and, in certain circumstances, such as when people are terminally ill, it may even encompass the possibility of facilitating the suicidal person's objective (e.g., Silverman & Felner, 1995).

The dilemma about the prevention concept becomes even more intense when prevention requires that a person be hospitalized involuntarily, when personal items (such as belts and sharp objects) are taken away, and when calming medication is more or less forcibly administered. Sometimes considerable restriction is needed to calm the individual. Not uncommonly, particularly in these litigious times, the responsible clinician feels trapped between threats of legal action on both sides of the issue. Moreover, preventive efforts may be fruitless; truly determined persons may find a way to commit suicide even on a "suicide watch." Indeed, about 5 percent of all completed suicides are committed by psychiatric patients while they are hospitalized in inpatient psychiatric units that are supposed to help prevent suicide (Stolberg et al., 2002).

Thus, the vexing ethical problems of whether and to what extent one should intervene in cases of threatened suicide have now been complicated by no-less-vexing legal problems. As in other areas of professional practice, clinical judgment is no longer the only consideration in intervention decisions. This is a societal problem, and the solutions—if any—will have to be societal ones.

Summary

7.1 Describe the types of mood disorders, their primary symptoms, and their prevalence.

- Mood disorders are those in which extreme variations in mood—either low or high—are the predominant feature.

- Unipolar depressive disorders are those in which a person experiences only depressive episodes; bipolar and related disorders are those in which a person experiences both depressive *and* manic episodes.

- Major mood disorders occur at almost the same rate as all the anxiety disorders taken together; rates for unipolar major depression are always much higher for women than for men, as well as individuals in lower socioeconomic groups and those who have high levels of accomplishments in the arts. Rates occur less frequently among African Americans than among European white Americans and Hispanics.

7.2 Distinguish between the different types of depressive disorders.

- Major depressive disorder (MDD; also known as *major depression*) requires that a person must be in a *major depressive episode* and never have had a manic, hypomanic, or mixed episode.

- Persistent depressive disorder (formerly called *dysthymic disorder* or *dysthymia*) is a disorder characterized by persistently depressed mood most of the day, for more days than not, for at least 2 years (1 year for children and adolescents).

- Depressions are nearly always precipitated by stressful life events. Some of the most stressful events possible are those involving the loss of life, as well as the creation of new life. Psychologists have struggled with how to appropriately diagnose (or not) a person's response to them.

7.3 **Describe the factors believed to cause unipolar mood disorders.**

- Among biological causal factors for depressive disorder, there is evidence of a moderate genetic contribution to the vulnerability for major depression and probably dysthymia as well. Moreover, major depressions are clearly associated with multiple interacting disturbances in neurochemical, neuroendocrine, and neurophysiological systems. Disruptions in circadian and seasonal rhythms are also prominent features of depression.

- Among psychosocial theories of the causes of depressive disorder are Beck's cognitive theory and the reformulated helplessness and hopelessness theories, which are formulated as diathesis–stress models; a tendency to ruminate about one's mood or problems exacerbates their effects. The diathesis is cognitive in nature (e.g., dysfunctional beliefs and pessimistic attributional style, respectively), and stressful life events are often important in determining when those diatheses actually lead to depression.

- Personality variables such as neuroticism may also serve as diatheses for depression.

- Psychodynamic and interpersonal theories of unipolar depression emphasize the importance of early experiences (especially early losses and the quality of the parent–child relationship) as setting up a predisposition for depression.

7.4 **List and distinguish between different types of bipolar disorders.**

- In the bipolar disorders (cyclothymia and bipolar I and II disorders), the person experiences episodes of both depression and hypomania or mania. During manic or hypomanic episodes, the symptoms are essentially the opposite of those experienced during a depressive episode.

- Cyclothymic disorder refers to the repeated experience of hypomanic symptoms for a period of at least 2 years.

- Bipolar I disorder is distinguished from MDD by the presence of mania. A mixed episode is characterized by symptoms of both full-blown manic and major depressive episodes for at least 1 week, either intermixed or alternating rapidly every few days.

- Bipolar II disorder is when the person does not experience full-blown manic (or mixed) episodes but has experienced clear-cut hypomanic episodes as well as major depressive episodes.

7.5 **Describe the causal factors influencing the development and maintenance of bipolar disorders.**

- Biological causal factors probably play an even more prominent role for bipolar disorders than for unipolar disorders. The genetic contribution to bipolar disorder is among the strongest of such contributions to the major psychiatric disorders. Neurochemical imbalances, abnormalities of the HPA axis, and disturbances in biological rhythms all play important roles in bipolar disorders.

- Stressful life events may be involved in precipitating manic or depressive episodes, but it is unlikely that they cause the disorder.

7.6 **Explain how cultural factors can influence the expression of mood disorders.**

Factors such as differing rates of stigma, stressors, risk factors for mood disorders, and a different manifestation of symptoms across cultures all have been suggested as possible explanations for the different rate and expression of mood disorders across cultures.

7.7 **Describe and distinguish between different treatments for mood disorders.**

Biologically based treatments such as medications or electroconvulsive therapy are often used in the treatment of the more severe major disorders. Increasingly, however, specific psychosocial treatments such as cognitive therapy, behavioral activation treatment, and interpersonal therapy are also being used to good effect in many cases of these more severe disorders as well as in the milder forms of mood disorder. Considerable evidence suggests that recurrent depression is best treated by specialized forms of psychotherapy or by maintenance on medications for prolonged periods.

7.8 **Describe the prevalence and clinical picture of suicidal behaviors.**

Suicide is one of the leading causes of death worldwide. Nearly 10 percent of adults report that they have seriously considered suicide at some point in their life, and nearly 3 percent report having made a suicide attempt at some time. The rate of suicidal thoughts and behavior increases drastically during the adolescent and young adult years, and psychological disorders such as mood and bipolar disorders are especially strong risk factors for these outcomes.

7.9 **Explain the efforts currently used to prevent and treat suicidal behaviors.**

Suicide prevention (or intervention) programs generally consist of crisis intervention in the form of suicide hotlines. Although these programs undoubtedly avert fatal suicide attempts in some cases, the long-term efficacy of treatment aimed at preventing suicide in those at high risk is much less clear at the present time.

Key Terms

attributions, p. 241

behavioral activation
   treatment, p. 257

bipolar disorder with a seasonal
   pattern, p. 247

bipolar disorders, p. 246

bipolar I disorder, p. 246

bipolar II disorder, p. 247

cognitive-behavioral therapy (CBT)
   (cognitive therapy), p. 256

cyclothymic disorder, p. 246

depression, p. 221

depressive episode, p. 221

depressogenic schemas, p. 239

double depression, p. 227

dysfunctional beliefs, p. 239

electroconvulsive therapy
   (ECT), p. 255

hypomanic episode, p. 221

interpersonal therapy (IPT), p. 258

learned helplessness, p. 240

lithium, p. 254

major depressive disorder, p. 224

major depressive episode, p. 222

major depressive episode with
   atypical features, p. 226

major depressive episode with
   catatonic features, p. 227

major depressive episode with
   melancholic features, p. 226

mania, p. 221

manic episode, p. 221

mixed episode, p. 246

monoamine oxidase inhibitors
   (MAOIs), p. 253

mood congruent, p. 226

mood disorders, p. 221

negative automatic
   thoughts, p. 239

negative cognitive triad, p. 239

nonsuicidal self-injury (NSSI), p. 259

persistent depressive disorder
   (dysthymic disorder), p. 227

pessimistic attributional
   style, p. 241

rapid cycling, p. 248

recurrence, p. 225

recurrent major depressive episode
   with a seasonal pattern, p. 227

relapse, p. 225

rumination, p. 242

seasonal affective disorder, p. 227

selective serotonin reuptake inhibitor
   (SSRI), p. 253

severe major depressive episode with
   psychotic features, p. 226

specifiers, p. 226

suicide, p. 259

tricyclic antidepressants, p. 253

unipolar depressive disorders, p. 221

Chapter 8
Somatic Symptom and Dissociative Disorders

Have you ever had the experience, particularly during a time of serious stress, when you felt like you were walking around in a daze or like you just weren't all there? What about physical symptoms? Mild dissociative or somatic symptoms are experienced at least occasionally by almost all of us. Indeed, up to 80 percent of people in the general population say that they have had somatic (physical) symptoms in the past week (Hiller et al., 2006). But when concern about these symptoms is severe and leads to significant distress or impairment, a **somatic symptom disorder** may be diagnosed. And when feelings of "being out of it" become so persistent and recurrent that the person has profound and unusual memory deficits (such as not knowing who they are), the diagnosis of a **dissociative disorder** may be warranted.

In the past both somatic symptom disorders (formerly known as **somatoform disorders**) and dissociative disorders were included with the various anxiety disorders (and neurotic depression) and considered to be forms of *neurosis*. This was because anxiety was thought to be the underlying cause of all neuroses whether or not the anxiety was experienced overtly. But in 1980, when *DSM-III* abandoned attempts to link disorders together on the basis of hypothesized underlying causes (as with neurosis) and instead focused on grouping disorders together on the basis of overt symptomatology, the anxiety, mood, somatic symptom, and dissociative disorders each became separate categories.

This approach has continued to this day. In *DSM-5* somatic symptom disorders and dissociative disorders are regarded as distinct diagnostic entities. Recognizing this, in this chapter we discuss each of these conditions separately. Let's start by taking a look at some of the diagnoses listed in the category of somatic symptom and related disorders.

Somatic Symptom and Related Disorders: An Overview

8.1 List four disorders included in the *DSM-5* category of somatic symptom and related disorders.

Somatic symptom and related disorders is a new category in *DSM-5*. The disorders in it lie at the interface between abnormal psychology and medicine. Included in this category are conditions that involve physical symptoms combined with abnormal thoughts, feelings, and behaviors in response to those symptoms (American Psychiatric Association [APA], 2013). **Soma** means "body." People with somatic symptom disorders experience bodily symptoms that cause them significant psychological distress and impairment. Richard is a good example.

I Know Something Is Wrong

Richard is a 46-year-old software engineer who reports a long history of many somatic complaints. His problems began in high school when he started to have headaches and pain in his chest. As time has progressed he has developed a broad range of symptoms all over his body including back pain, abdominal pain and discomfort, joint pain, feelings of dizziness, and a general sense of weakness and fatigue. During the past 20 years, Richard has seen many doctors and received numerous medical examinations. Although he has received several descriptive diagnoses that do little more than describe his symptoms, no medical explanation for his problems has been found. Richard worries constantly that something is being missed and that, on the days the tests were done, the underlying problem was somehow unable to be detected. Richard subscribes to several health newsletters and frequently uses the Internet to learn more about the possible causes of his symptoms. He realizes his current doctor is getting annoyed with his frequent visits, but he continues to worry constantly about his health.

As we have already noted, experiencing bodily sensations or symptoms is very common. In most cases, these symptoms go away spontaneously. But in about 25 percent of cases, the symptoms persist for a longer period, prompting people to visit their doctors. Studies conducted throughout the world show that somewhere between 20 and 50 percent of the physical symptoms that cause people to seek medical care are medically unexplained. In other words, no medical cause can be found (Kroenke, 2003). For many people that is the end of it. They are satisfied when told that all the tests that they have had are negative. But a subset of patients (like Richard) will continue to be very worried that something is seriously wrong—that they have a not-yet-diagnosed disease. These people tend to continue to seek help for their physical problems, asking for and undergoing more and more tests. In other words, they become preoccupied with some aspect of their health to the extent that they show significant impairments in functioning.

Some people become preoccupied with their health and continue to seek help for their medical problems even when no specific problem can be detected.

As you might expect, such patients are much more commonly found in medical settings than in mental health clinics. It is estimated that about 20 percent of doctor visits are caused by complaints of this sort (Steinbrecher et al., 2011). In the United States, almost every family doctor reports seeing these patients frequently (Dimsdale, 2011).

In *DSM-IV* a great deal of emphasis was placed on the idea that the symptoms were medically unexplained. In other words, although the patient's complaints suggested the presence of a medical condition, no physical pathology could be found to account for them (Allen & Woolfolk, 2012; Witthöft & Hiller, 2010). An important change in *DSM-5* is that no distinction is now made between medically explained and medically unexplained symptoms. This idea is less prominent, because it is recognized that medicine is fallible and that a medical explanation for symptoms cannot always be provided. Whether symptoms are deemed to have a medical cause or not could also depend on the personality of the doctor or on his or her predominant cultural beliefs (Klaus et al., 2013). Nonetheless, medically unexplained symptoms are still a key part of some disorders (such as conversion disorder) that we will describe later.

Equally key to these disorders is the fact that the affected patients have no control over their symptoms. They are also not intentionally faking symptoms or attempting to deceive others. For the most part, they genuinely believe something is terribly wrong with them. In our discussion, we focus specifically on the four most important disorders in the somatic symptom and related disorders category. These are (1) somatic symptom disorder, (2) illness anxiety disorder, (3) conversion disorder, and (4) factitious disorder.

Somatic Symptom Disorder

8.2 Explain the causes of and treatments for somatic symptom disorder.

Somatic symptom disorder is regarded as the most major diagnosis in its category. This new diagnosis includes several disorders that were previously considered to be separate diagnoses in *DSM-IV*. The old disorders of (1) hypochondriasis, (2) somatization disorder, and (3) pain disorder have all now disappeared. Most of the people who would in the past have been diagnosed with any one of these disorders will now be diagnosed with somatic symptom disorder. For example, it is estimated that approximately 75 percent of people previously diagnosed with hypochondriasis (where individuals are preoccupied either with fears of contracting a serious disease or with the idea that they have a disease even though they do not) will now be diagnosed with somatic symptom disorder in *DSM-5* (APA, 2013).

The diagnosis of somatic symptom disorder is a descriptive one. It contains no assumptions about cause. The name of the diagnosis was chosen to reduce some of the negative connotations associated with older diagnostic terms such as hypochondriasis, as well as ideas that disorders such as these were "all in the mind." As you know from Chapter 5, we are now beginning to understand just how closely the mind and the body affect each other.

For the diagnosis of somatic symptom disorder to be made, individuals must be experiencing chronic somatic symptoms that are distressing to them. They must also be experiencing dysfunctional thoughts, feelings, and/or behaviors. The addition of this psychological component is new. In *DSM-IV* all that was required was that people be experiencing somatic symptoms that were medically unexplained. In other words, no psychological features were required. This was a rather strange omission because a common characteristic of *DSM* mental disorders is that there are psychological features in addition to other signs and symptoms (Rief & Martin, 2014). Another radical change is that, as we noted earlier, the physical symptoms no longer need to be medically unexplained. The *DSM-5* criteria for somatic symptom disorder are shown in the *DSM-5* box.

DSM-5 *Criteria for. . .*

Somatic Symptom Disorder

A. One or more somatic symptoms that are distressing or result in significant disruption of daily life.

B. Excessive thoughts, feelings, or behaviors related to the somatic symptoms or associated health concerns as manifested by at least one of the following:

1. Disproportionate and persistent thoughts about the seriousness of one's symptoms.
2. Persistently high level of anxiety about health or symptoms.
3. Excessive time and energy devoted to these symptoms or health concerns.

C. Although any one somatic symptom may not be continuously present, the state of being symptomatic is persistent (typically more than 6 months).

Source: Reprinted with permission from the *Diagnostic and Statistical Manual of Mental Disorders*, Fifth Edition (Copyright 2013). American Psychiatric Association.

Another diagnostic change that has occurred is that, in *DSM-5* only one somatic symptom is required. In other words, if a person has *any* physical problem that they find distressing (even if it involves only a single symptom and is medically explained), the diagnosis of somatic symptom disorder is possible. Of course most patients, like Richard, have many physical complaints. It is also the case that people can suffer a great deal, even if they only have one symptom. But it is important to note that the new *DSM-5* criteria will likely lead to an increase in the diagnosis of somatic symptom disorder for this reason. Estimates are that the prevalence of somatic symptom disorder in the general population will be around 5 to 7 percent (APA, 2013). However, there has been much criticism that the new diagnostic criteria are far too loose and will lead to many people being mislabeled as having a mental disorder (Frances, 2013b). It has also been suggested that women will be disproportionately affected because they are more frequent users of medical services and because they are most at risk of being dismissed by their doctors as "catastrophizers" (Frances & Chapman, 2013).

Another concern is that people diagnosed with somatic symptom disorder might look very different from a clinical perspective (Rief & Martin, 2014). For example, Richard would be diagnosed with somatic symptom disorder. And so would Jane, who suffers from migraines and is very upset and anxious about the effect her headaches have on her life. Yet another person who would qualify for the somatic symptom disorder diagnosis is Ellen. Ellen developed breast cancer when she was 41. After surgery, radiation, and chemotherapy, her breast cancer is in remission. Nonetheless, Ellen is very fearful that it might come back. Now age 44, Ellen has physical symptoms and headaches. These could be attributed to side effects of the medications she has to take. But because the fear that the cancer could recur is always on Ellen's mind, she too would get the same diagnosis as Richard who worries constantly about his health even though he has not been diagnosed with a specific medical problem.

It is very likely that the diagnostic criteria for somatic symptoms disorder will be modified over time. This is to be expected. As we mentioned in Chapter 1, the *DSM* must always be considered a work in progress. In their revision efforts, the *DSM-5* work group may have loosened the diagnostic criteria too much. Indeed, Alan Frances, who served as the chair of the task force that developed *DSM-IV*, has called the *DSM-5* somatic symptom disorder a "loosely defined and fatally flawed" diagnosis and recommended that clinicians not use it (Frances, 2013a, p. 531). Frances has even offered revised diagnostic criteria for this disorder. These are shown in Table 8.1. Compare them to the *DSM-5* criteria. In what ways are they different? Do you think they provide any improvements?

As they now stand, the current *DSM-5* criteria may result in a wide range of patients being assigned the same diagnosis (Rief & Martin, 2014). Some will have many symptoms and some will have very few. Some will have symptoms that have a medical cause; others will not. Unknown at this time is whether this broad grouping of clinical conditions will impede the successful development

Table 8.1 Suggested Revised Diagnostic Criteria for Somatic Symptom Disorder

A: One or more prominent physical symptoms.

B: Excessive and maladaptive thoughts, feelings and behaviors related to the physical symptoms. All three of the following must be present: (a) clearly disproportionate and intrusive worries about the seriousness of the symptoms, (b) extreme anxiety about the symptoms, and (c) excessive time and energy devoted to the symptoms or health concerns.

C: The excessive concerns have persisted at a clearly problematic level for at least 6 months.

D: The excessive concerns about physical symptoms are pervasive and cause significant disruption and impairment in daily life.

E: If a diagnosed medical condition is present, the thoughts, feelings, and behaviors are grossly in excess of what would be expected, given the nature of the medical condition.

F: If no medical diagnosis has been made, a thorough medical workup has been performed to rule out possible causes and is repeated at suitable intervals to uncover medical conditions that may declare themselves with the passage of time.

G: The physical symptom or concern is not better accounted for by another mental disorder (e.g., anxiety, depressive, or psychotic disorder).

SOURCE: Frances, A. (2013a). DSM-5 somatic symptom disorder. *Journal of Nervous and Mental Disease, 2013,* 530–531.

of new treatments. Should patients with medically explained symptoms (like Ellen or Jane) be treated with the same approaches used for patients who have medically unexplained symptoms (like Richard)? Can we assume that there are similar mechanisms at work in both cases? For those who seek to develop new treatments, the changes in *DSM-5* may present some interesting challenges.

Causes of Somatic Symptom Disorder

Why do people develop somatic symptom disorders? The historical roots of the *DSM-IV* category of somatoform disorders date back to the psychoanalytic concept of hysteria and the work of Freud, Breuer, and Janet (see Chapter 2). It was long thought that symptoms developed as a defense mechanism against unresolved or unacceptable unconscious conflicts. Rather than being expressed directly, psychic energy was instead channeled into more acceptable physical problems.

Current views take a much more cognitive-behavioral approach. Of course, somatic symptom disorder is a new disorder in *DSM-5* and so has not yet been investigated much in its own right. Nonetheless, cognitive-behavioral perspectives on disorders such as hypochondriasis and somatoform disorders (which are now subsumed within the new diagnosis) are likely still valid and informative. Although several different models exist (Brown, 2004; Kirmayer & Taillefer, 1997; Rief & Barsky, 2005), their core features tend to be quite similar. First, there is a focus of attention on the body. In other words, the person is hypervigilant and has an increased awareness of bodily changes. Second, the person tends to see bodily *sensations* as somatic

Figure 8.1 Simplified Model of Somatic Symptom Disorder

People with somatic symptom disorder tend to have a cognitive style that leads them to be hypersensitive to their bodily sensations. They also experience these sensations as intense, disturbing, and highly aversive. Another characteristic of such patients is that they tend to think catastrophically about their symptoms, often overestimating the medical severity of their condition.

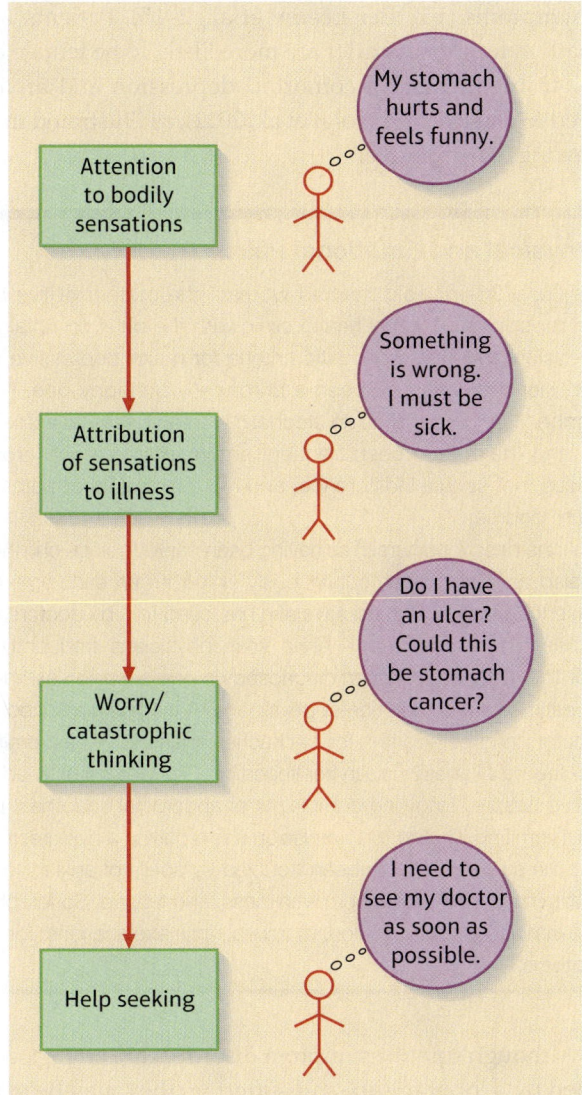

and sensitive to what is happening in their bodies. But this does not seem to be the case. Rather, experimental studies show that these individuals have an attentional bias for illness-related information (Gropalis et al., 2013; see also Jasper & Witthöft, 2011). In other words, top-down (cognitive) processes, rather than bottom-up processes (such as differences in bodily sensations), seem to account for the problems that they have. Although their physical sensations probably do not differ from those of normal controls (Marcus, Gurley, et al., 2007), people with somatic symptoms disorders seem to focus excessive attention on their physical experiences, labelling physical sensations as symptoms. They also perceive their symptoms as more dangerous than they really are and judge a particular disease to be more likely or dangerous than it really is. Once they have misinterpreted a symptom, they tend to look for confirming evidence and to discount evidence that they are in good health; in fact, they seem to believe that being healthy means being completely symptom free (Rief et al., 1998). They also perceive their probability of being able to cope with the illness as extremely low (Salkovskis & Bass, 1997) and see themselves as physically weak and unable to tolerate physical effort or exercise (Riebel et al., 2013; Wollburg et al., 2013). All this tends to create a vicious cycle in which their anxiety about illness and symptoms results in physiological symptoms of anxiety, which then provide further fuel for their convictions that they are ill.

It is also believed that an individual's past experiences with illnesses (in both him- or herself and others, and also as observed in the media) contribute to the development of a set of dysfunctional assumptions about symptoms and diseases that may predispose a person to developing a somatic symptom disorder (Marcus, Gurley, et al., 2007; Salkovskis & Warwick, 2001). These dysfunctional assumptions might include notions such as, "Bodily changes are usually a sign of serious disease, because every symptom has to have an identifiable physical cause" or "If you don't go to the doctor as soon as you notice anything unusual, then it will be too late" (Salkovskis & Bass, 1997, p. 318; see also Marcus, Gurley, et al., 2007). This is another example of top-down cognitive processes at work.

Negative affect is regarded as a risk factor for developing somatic symptom disorder. However, negative affect alone is not sufficient. Many people tend to be rather gloomy in their personalities, but only a subset of these people will also be habitual reporters of physical symptoms. Other characteristics that may be important are absorption and alexithymia. Absorption is a tendency to become absorbed in one's experiences and is often associated with being highly hypnotizable. Alexithymia, on the other hand, refers to having difficulties identifying one's feelings. People who report many symptoms but who do

symptoms, meaning that physical sensations are attributed to illness. Third, the person tends to worry excessively about what the symptoms mean and has catastrophizing cognitions. Fourth, because of this worry, the person is very distressed and seeks medical attention for his or her perceived physical problems. Figure 8.1 illustrates the basic model.

According to this formulation, somatic symptom disorder can be viewed as disorder of both perception (noticing benign sensations such as one's heart skipping a beat) and cognition ("Does this mean I have a serious heart problem?"). Individuals who are especially anxious about their health tend to believe that they are very aware of

Some individuals with somatic symptom disorder are preoccupied with unrealistic fears of disease. They are convinced that they have symptoms of physical illness, but their complaints typically do not conform to any coherent symptom pattern, and they usually have trouble giving a precise description of their symptoms.

not have any medical conditions tend to score high on all of these three traits (Bogaerts et al., 2015).

Research is also showing that when people who report a lot of physical problems are put into a negative mood (by viewing negative pictures, for example), their reporting of physical symptoms increases (Bogaerts et al., 2015; Constaninou et al., 2013). So what may be happening? People who have difficulty identifying their feelings and who are also highly susceptible to being absorbed in their own experiences may be especially sensitive to having certain attentional (top-down) processes activated when they experience negative events. These alterations in the attentional system may trigger memories or past representations of symptoms (cognitive schemas) that were formed as a result of prior experiences with illness. Once these schemas become active, they may cause the person to become aware of minor physical sensations or even trigger experiences of symptoms that are as "real" as they would be if they resulted from a known medical cause. Because all of this is thought to happen automatically, the person has no insight into or control over the process.

As we have already told you, patients with somatic symptom disorder are usually seen in medical clinics. Because they repeatedly seek medical advice (e.g., Bleichhardt & Hiller, 2006; Fink et al., 2004), their annual medical costs are much higher than average (e.g., Fink et al., 2010; Hiller et al., 2004). High levels of functional impairment are also common and many patients are severely disabled by their physical symptoms (van der Leeuw et al., 2015). Patients with somatic symptom disorder are more likely to be female and to have high levels of comorbid depression and anxiety (Creed & Barsky, 2004; Voigt et al., 2012), as illustrated in the following case example.

In Physical and Emotional Pain

Anna G., a 38-year-old married woman, the mother of five children, reports to a mental health clinic with the chief complaint of depression, meeting diagnostic criteria for major depressive disorder. Her marriage has been a chronically unhappy one. Anna describes her husband as an alcoholic with an unstable work history, and there have been frequent arguments revolving around finances, her sexual indifference, and her complaints of pain during intercourse.

Anna describes herself as having been nervous since childhood and also as having been continuously sick from an early age. She experiences chest pain and says she has been told by doctors that she has a "nervous heart." Anna sees physicians frequently for abdominal pain, having been diagnosed on one occasion as having a "spastic colon." In addition to physicians, Anna has consulted chiropractors and osteopaths for backaches, pains in her extremities, and a feeling of anesthesia in her fingertips. She was recently admitted to a hospital following complaints of abdominal and chest pain and of vomiting. During this admission she received a hysterectomy. Since the surgery she has been troubled by spells of anxiety, fainting, vomiting, food intolerance, weakness, and fatigue. So far, physical examinations have failed to reveal any explanations for her symptoms.

Although somatic symptom disorders are often accompanied by a lot of misery and suffering, they may be maintained to some degree by secondary reinforcements. Most of us learn as children that when we are sick we get special comforts and attention, as well as being excused from school or other responsibilities. In the case of the *DSM-IV* disorder of hypochondriasis, Barsky and colleagues (1994) found that their patients reported much childhood sickness and missed a lot of school. People with hypochondriasis also tend to have an excessive amount of illness in their families while growing up, which may lead to strong memories of being sick or in pain (Pauli & Alpers, 2002) and perhaps of having observed some of the secondary benefits that sick people sometimes get (Cote et al., 1996; Kellner, 1985).

Having said this, it is important to keep in mind that people with somatic symptom disorders are not *malingering*—

consciously faking symptoms to achieve a specific goal such as winning a personal injury lawsuit. They experience physical problems that cause them great concern. As described earlier, these symptoms may be caused by brain processes that occur below the radar of the person's conscious awareness.

Treatment of Somatic Symptom Disorder

The cognitive-behavioral model provides a good explanation of the causes of somatic symptom disorders. It should therefore come as little surprise that cognitive-behavioral treatments are widely used to treat these disorders (e.g., Barsky & Ahern, 2004; Tyrer, 2011; see also Hedman et al., 2011, for an example of Internet-based cognitive-behavioral therapy [CBT]). In the case of Richard, the patient you met at the beginning of this chapter, for example, the cognitive components of this treatment approach might focus on assessing his beliefs about illness and modifying misinterpretations of his bodily sensations. Behavioral techniques might include having Richard induce innocuous symptoms by intentionally focusing on parts of his body so that he could learn that selective perception of his own bodily sensations could play a major role in his symptoms. Sometimes patients treated with CBT are also directed to engage in response prevention by not checking their bodies as they usually do and by stopping their constant seeking of reassurance. Generally, the duration of CBT is relatively brief (6 to 16 sessions). Sessions can also be delivered in a group format (Weck et al., 2015). In addition to helping reduce physical symptoms and anxiety about symptoms, CBT approaches can also reduce levels of anxiety and depression more generally (Olatunji et al., 2014). Not surprisingly, patients do better if they receive more sessions of treatment. In a recent study, patients also reported that considering alternative reasons for the presence of their bodily symptoms (for example, a headache doesn't necessarily signal the presence of a brain tumor) was the most valuable aspect of CBT (Weck et al., 2015).

In addition to CBT, a certain type of medical management may provide some further benefits. General practitioners can be educated in how to better manage and treat patients with these disorders so that they are less frustrated by them (Rosendal et al., 2005; see also Edwards & Edwards, 2010). One moderately effective treatment involves identifying one physician who will integrate the patient's care by seeing the patient at regular visits (thereby trying to anticipate the appearance of new problems) and by providing physical exams focused on new complaints (thereby accepting all symptoms as valid). At the same time, however, the physician avoids unnecessary diagnostic testing and makes minimal use of medications or other therapies (Looper & Kirmayer, 2002; Mai, 2004). Several studies have found that patients show substantial decreases in health care expenditures over subsequent months and sometimes an improvement in physical functioning (although not necessarily in psychological distress; e.g., Rost et al., 1994). That is why this approach is best combined with CBT (e.g., Bleichhardt et al., 2004; Mai, 2004).

Cognitive-behavioral techniques are also widely used in the treatment of somatic symptom disorder that involves pain. Treatment programs generally include relaxation training, support and validation that the pain is real, scheduling of daily activities, cognitive restructuring, and reinforcement of "no-pain" behaviors (Simon, 2002). Patients receiving such treatments tend to show substantial reductions in disability and distress, although changes in the intensity of their pain tend to be smaller in magnitude. In addition, antidepressant medications (especially the tricyclic antidepressants) and certain selective serotonin reuptake inhibitors have been shown to reduce pain intensity in a manner independent of the effects the medications may have on mood (Aragona et al., 2005; Simon, 2002).

When one physician integrates a patient's care, the physical functioning of patients with somatic symptom disorder may improve. Why should this be?

in review

- What are the primary clinical characteristics of somatic symptom disorder?
- How does the cognitive-behavioral viewpoint help us understand somatic symptom disorder?
- What role might absorption and alexithymia play in somatic symptom disorder?
- Describe the treatment approaches that are used to help people with somatic symptom disorder.

Illness Anxiety Disorder

8.3 Identify the key difference between illness anxiety disorder and somatic symptom disorder.

Illness anxiety disorder is new to *DSM-5*. In this newly identified disorder, people have high anxiety about having or developing a serious illness. This anxiety is distressing and/or disruptive, but there are very few (or very mild) somatic symptoms (see the *DSM-5* criteria box).

DSM-5 *Criteria for...*

Illness Anxiety Disorder

A. Preoccupation with having or acquiring a serious illness.

B. Somatic symptoms are not present or, if present, are only mild in intensity. If another medical condition is present or there is a high risk for developing a medical condition (e.g., strong family history is present), the preoccupation is clearly excessive or disproportionate.

C. There is a high level of anxiety about health, and the individual is easily alarmed about personal health status.

D. The individual performs excessive health-related behaviors (e.g., repeatedly checks his or her body for signs of illness) or exhibits maladaptive avoidance (e.g., avoids doctor appointments and hospitals).

E. Illness preoccupation has been present for at least 6 months, but the specific illness that is feared may change over that period of time.

F. The illness-related preoccupation is not better explained by another mental disorder, such as somatic symptom disorder, panic disorder, generalized anxiety disorder, body dysmorphic disorder, obsessive-compulsive disorder, or delusional disorder, somatic type.

Source: Reprinted with permission from the *Diagnostic and Statistical Manual of Mental Disorders*, Fifth Edition (Copyright 2013). American Psychiatric Association.

It is estimated that around 25 percent of people who would have been diagnosed with hypochondriasis in *DSM-IV* will be diagnosed with illness anxiety disorder in *DSM-5* (APA, 2013). The remaining 75 percent will be diagnosed as having somatic symptom disorder. When hypochondriasis is accompanied by significant physical symptoms, the diagnosis will be somatic symptom disorder. When there is hypochondriasis without any physical symptoms (or with very mild ones), the diagnosis will be illness anxiety disorder.

---

in review

- What are the primary characteristics of illness anxiety disorder?
- Explain why hypochondriasis can sometimes be diagnosed as a somatic symptom disorder and sometimes as an illness anxiety disorder.

Conversion Disorder (Functional Neurological Symptom Disorder)

8.4 Summarize the clinical features of conversion disorder, also noting its prevalence, causes, and treatment.

Another disorder within the diagnostic category of somatic symptom and related disorders is **conversion disorder**. The term *conversion disorder* is relatively recent. Historically this disorder was one of several disorders that were grouped together under the term **hysteria**.

Conversion disorder is one of the most intriguing and baffling patterns in psychopathology, and we still have much to learn about it. It is characterized by the presence of neurological symptoms in the absence of a neurological diagnosis (see Feinstein, 2011). In other words, the patient has symptoms or deficits affecting the senses or motor behavior that strongly suggest a medical or neurological condition. However, the pattern of symptoms or deficits is not consistent with any neurological disease or medical problem. A few typical examples include partial paralysis, blindness, deafness, and episodes of limb shaking accompanied by impairment or loss of consciousness that resemble seizures. Of course, the diagnosis can only be made after a full medical and neurological workup has been conducted. It is also important to emphasize that the person is not intentionally producing or faking the symptoms. Rather, psychological factors are often judged to play an important role because symptoms usually either start or are exacerbated by preceding emotional or interpersonal conflicts or stressors, as in the following case example.

Unable to See for Seven Days

The patient, a 21-year-old university student in Ethiopia, came to the hospital, accompanied by her mother. She said that she had not

Watch Henry: Illness Anxiety Disorder

been able to see for the past week. An ophthalmologic exam was done, followed by a neurological examination. Both failed to reveal any specific problems. The patient was cooperative during all the testing, with normal concentration and attention. Apart from reporting severe visual impairment, the patient was smiling and reported feeling nothing unusual.

Questioning by clinic staff revealed that, 1 month earlier, the patient had been unable to speak for 2 weeks. Her inability to speak developed during a time when she had been experiencing difficulties in her studies and a few hours after her mother told her that her father had a life-threatening illness. With the assistance of friends, who helped train her to speak again, the patient recovered. A week later, while preparing for an examination, she became completely unable to see.

Eight months before her current presentation at the clinic, the patient had been voiceless for another period of 6 weeks. At that time, she had received a laryngoscopy, which revealed nothing abnormal. The patient was treated with valium and also given some therapy to help her manage her stress and anxiety. After 3 days of relaxation therapy and slow-breathing training, she began to be able to produce a coughing sound. The following day she was able to say a few words and the next day she became fully communicative again.

These same stress management techniques were used this time to help the patient with her loss of vision. She was also offered materials suitable for a blind person and asked to complete tactile tasks, making patterns with different shapes. A little later she was given painting materials. Although the patient said that she could not see what she was doing, she was able to reproduce shapes and wrap paper around pieces of wood to make pearls for a necklace. All the while, the clinic staff were encouraging and supportive, praising the patient for her skills. Then, after about a week, the patient started to see flashes of light. A short while later she began to recognize several people. Finally, after 3 weeks, she was able to see normally again. (Taken from Mulugeta et al., 2015.)

Early observations dating back to Freud suggested that most people with conversion disorder showed very little of the anxiety and fear that would be expected in a person with a paralyzed arm or loss of sight. This seeming lack of concern was known as *la belle indifférence*—French for "the beautiful indifference." For a long time it was thought to be an important diagnostic criterion for conversion disorder. However, *la belle indifférence* occurs only in about 20 percent of patients. Lack of concern about symptoms or their implications is also not specific to conversion disorder. For these reasons, this phenomenon has become de-emphasized in more recent editions of the *DSM* (Stone et al., 2006, 2011).

Authors of *DSM-5* had many suggestions for changing the term used to describe the disorder (e.g., to psychogenic, functional, and dissociative). In the end, a conservative approach was taken and the term *conversion disorder* was retained, although this is now followed in parentheses by "functional neurological symptom disorder" (Stone et al., 2011). The *DSM-5* criteria for conversion disorder are shown in the *DSM* box.

DSM-5 *Criteria for. . .*

Conversion Disorder

A. One or more symptoms of altered voluntary motor or sensory function.

B. Clinical findings provide evidence of incompatibility between the symptom and recognized neurological or medical conditions.

C. The symptom or deficit is not better explained by another medical or mental disorder.

D. The symptom or deficit causes clinically significant distress or impairment in social, occupational, or other important areas of functioning or warrants medical evaluation.

Source: Reprinted with permission from the *Diagnostic and Statistical Manual of Mental Disorders*, Fifth Edition (Copyright 2013). American Psychiatric Association.

Range of Conversion Disorder Symptoms

The range of symptoms for conversion disorder is practically as diverse as it is for physically based ailments. In describing the clinical picture in conversion disorder, it is useful to think in terms of four categories of symptoms: (1) sensory, (2) motor, (3) seizures, and (4) a mixed presentation of the first three categories (APA, 2013).

SENSORY SYMPTOMS OR DEFICITS Conversion disorder can involve almost any sensory modality, and it can often be diagnosed as conversion disorder because symptoms in the affected area are inconsistent with how known anatomical sensory pathways operate. Today the sensory symptoms or deficits are most often in the visual system (especially blindness and tunnel vision), in the auditory system (especially deafness), or in the sensitivity to feeling (especially the anesthesias). In the *anesthesias*, the person loses her or his sense of feeling in a part of the body. One of the most common is *glove anesthesia*, in which the person cannot feel anything on the hand in the area where gloves are worn, although the loss of sensation usually makes no anatomical sense.

With conversion blindness, the person reports that he or she cannot see and yet can often navigate about a room without bumping into furniture or other objects. With conversion deafness, the person reports not being able to hear and yet orients appropriately upon "hearing" his or her own name. Such observations lead to obvious questions: In conversion blindness (and deafness), can affected people actually not see (or hear), or is the sensory information received but screened from consciousness? In general, the evidence supports the idea that the sensory input is registered but is somehow screened from explicit conscious recognition (explicit perception).

MOTOR SYMPTOMS OR DEFICITS   Motor conversion reactions also cover a wide range of symptoms (e.g., Maldonado & Spiegel, 2001; see also Stone et al., 2011). For example, conversion paralysis is usually confined to a single limb such as an arm or a leg, and the loss of function is usually selective for certain functions. For example, a person may not be able to write but may be able to use the same muscles for scratching, or a person may not be able to walk most of the time but may be able to walk in an emergency such as a fire where escape is important. The most common speech-related conversion disturbance is *aphonia*, in which a person is able to talk only in a whisper although he or she can usually cough in a normal manner. (In true, organic laryngeal paralysis, both the cough and the voice are affected.) Another common motor symptom, called *globus*, involves the sensation of a lump in the throat (Finkenbine & Miele, 2004).

SEIZURES   Another relatively common form of conversion symptom involves seizures. These resemble epileptic seizures, although they are not true seizures (Bowman & Markand, 2005; Stonnington et al., 2006). For example, patients do not show any EEG abnormalities and do not show confusion and loss of memory afterward, as patients with true epileptic seizures do. Moreover, patients with conversion seizures often show excessive thrashing about and writhing not seen with true seizures, and they rarely injure themselves in falls or lose bowel or bladder control as patients with true seizures frequently do.

Important Issues in Diagnosing Conversion Disorder

Because the symptoms in conversion disorder can simulate a variety of medical conditions, accurate diagnosis can be extremely difficult. It is crucial that a person with suspected conversion symptoms receive a thorough medical and neurological examination. Unfortunately, however, misdiagnoses can still occur. Nevertheless, as medical tests (especially brain imaging) have become increasingly sophisticated, the rate of misdiagnoses has declined substantially from in the past, with estimates of misdiagnoses in the 1990s at only 4 percent, down from nearly 30 percent in the 1950s (e.g., Stone et al., 2005).

Several other criteria are also commonly used for distinguishing between conversion disorders and true neurological disturbances:

- The frequent failure of the dysfunction to conform clearly to the symptoms of the particular disease or disorder simulated. For example, little or no wasting away or atrophy of a "paralyzed" limb occurs in conversion paralyses, except in rare and long-standing cases.
- The nature of the dysfunction is highly selective. As already noted, in conversion blindness the affected

individual does not usually bump into people or objects, and "paralyzed" muscles can be used for some activities but not others.

- Under hypnosis or narcosis (a sleeplike state induced by drugs), the symptoms can usually be removed, shifted, or reinduced at the suggestion of the therapist. Similarly, a person abruptly awakened from a sound sleep may suddenly be able to use a "paralyzed" limb.

Prevalence and Demographic Characteristics

Conversion disorders were once relatively common in civilian and (especially) military life. In World War I, conversion disorder was the most frequently diagnosed psychiatric syndrome among soldiers; it was also relatively common during World War II. Conversion disorder typically occurred under highly stressful combat conditions and involved men who would ordinarily be considered stable. Here, conversion symptoms—such as paralysis of the legs—enabled a soldier to avoid an anxiety-arousing combat situation without being labeled a coward or being subject to court-martial.

Conversion disorders were fairly common during World War I and World War II. The disorder typically occurred in otherwise "normal" men during stressful combat conditions. The symptoms of conversion disorder (e.g., paralysis of the legs) enabled a soldier to avoid high-anxiety combat situations without being labeled a coward or being court-martialed.

Conversion disorders are found in approximately 5 percent of people referred for treatment at neurology clinics. The prevalence in the general population is unknown, but even the highest estimates have been around only 0.005 percent (APA, 2013). Interestingly, this decreased prevalence seems to be closely related to our growing sophistication about medical and psychological disorders: A conversion disorder apparently loses its defensive function if it can be readily shown to lack a medical basis. When it does occur today, it is most likely to occur in people who are medically unsophisticated. For example, a highly unusual "outbreak" of cases of severe conversion disorder involving serious motor weakness and wasting symptoms was reported in five 9- to 13-year-old girls living in a small, poor, rural Amish community. Each of these girls had experienced substantial psychosocial stressors including behavioral problems, dysfunctional family dynamics, and significant community stress from a serious local church crisis (see Cassady et al., 2005). Fortunately, after the caregivers of these girls were educated regarding the psychological nature of the symptoms and given advice to stick with one doctor, minimize stress, and avoid reinforcement of the "sick role," four of the five girls showed significant improvement over the next 3 months. In the fifth case, the family refused to acknowledge the psychological component of the illness, holding to the belief that the symptoms were caused by parasites.

Conversion disorder occurs two to three times more often in women than in men (APA, 2013). It can develop at any age but most commonly occurs between early adolescence and early adulthood (Maldonado & Spiegel, 2001). It generally has a rapid onset after a significant stressor and often resolves within 2 weeks if the stressor is removed, although it commonly recurs (Merkler et al., 2015). Like most other somatic symptom disorders, conversion disorder frequently occurs along with other disorders, especially major depression, anxiety disorders, and other forms of somatic symptom or dissociative conditions.

Causes of Conversion Disorders

Conversion disorders are thought to develop as a result of stress or internal conflicts of some kind. Freud used the term *conversion hysteria* for these disorders (which were fairly common in his practice) because he believed that the symptoms were an expression of repressed sexual energy—that is, the *unconscious conflict* that a person felt about his or her repressed sexual desires. However, in Freud's view, the repressed anxiety threatens to become conscious, so it is unconsciously *converted* into a bodily disturbance, thereby allowing the person to avoid having to deal with the conflict. This is not done consciously, of course, and the person is not aware of the origin or meaning of the physical symptom. Freud also thought that the

reduction in anxiety and intrapsychic conflict was the "**primary gain**" that maintained the condition, but he noted that patients often had many sources of "**secondary gain**" as well, such as receiving sympathy and attention from loved ones.

Freud's theory that conversion symptoms are caused by the conversion of sexual conflicts or other psychological problems into physical symptoms is no longer accepted outside psychodynamic circles. However, many of Freud's astute clinical observations about primary and secondary gain are still incorporated into contemporary views of conversion disorder. For example, when cast in terms of learning theory, the physical symptoms can be seen as providing negative reinforcement (relief or removal of an aversive stimulus) because being incapacitated in some way may enable the individual to escape or avoid an intolerably stressful situation without having to take responsibility for doing so. In addition, they may provide positive reinforcement in the form of care, concern, and attention from others. It is the case that, in some cultures, expressing intense emotions is not socially acceptable. When viewed through a sociocultural lens, a diagnosis of conversion disorder can therefore be seen as a more socially sanctioned way of expressing distress and escaping an unpleasant situation. However, although becoming sick or disabled is more socially acceptable, it is important to keep in mind that the person is not deliberately choosing to lose his or her sight or become unable to walk. Instead, unconscious processes are thought to be at work.

Given the important role often attributed to stressful life events in precipitating the onset of conversion disorder, it is unfortunate that little is actually known about the exact nature and timing of these psychological stress factors (Roelofs et al., 2005). One study compared the frequency of stressful life events in the recent past in patients with conversion disorder and depressed controls and did not find a difference in frequency between them. However, the greater the negative impact of the preceding life events, the greater the severity of the conversion disorder symptoms (Roelofs et al., 2005). Another study compared levels of a neurobiological marker of stress (lower levels of brain-derived neurotropic factor) in individuals with conversion disorder versus major depression versus no disorder. Both those with depression and those with conversion disorder showed reduced levels of this marker relative to the nondisordered controls (Deveci et al., 2007). This also provides support for the link between stress and the onset of conversion disorder.

Neuroimaging studies of conversion disorder are still, like the disorder itself, relatively rare. Many are case studies or involve only small numbers of patients. Nonetheless, although research in this area is still in its infancy, provocative findings are emerging. Some of these are described in the Developments in Research box.

Developments in Research

What Can Neuroimaging Tell Us about Conversion Disorder?

Functioning neuroimaging approaches to the study of conversion disorder hold the potential to provide insights into what is happening in the brain when people with sensory or motor deficits are asked to move a paralyzed limb or receive stimulation to a numb body part. In one interesting study, three patients with sensory loss (involving numbness in the hand or foot) received brain scans while a vibrating stimulus was applied to their right and left hands (or feet). When the stimulus was applied to the side that had sensation and was unaffected, the brain scans revealed the expected findings. In other words, there was activation in somatosensory areas of the brain on the opposite side to the side being stimulated. (This is because most human motor and sensory fibers cross the midline and so stimulation of the right side of the body affects the left side of the brain.) However, when tactile stimulation was applied to the affected (numb) body part, there was no activation in the contralateral area of the sensory cortex. Figure 8.2 provides an illustration of this. Instead, the tactile stimulus activated regions in the orbitofrontal cortex and the anterior cingulate cortex (Ghaffar et al., 2006). This is interesting because both of these brain regions are involved in neural networks that are thought to regulate emotion and the expression of emotion.

Similar results were found in another study involving two patients with conversion paralysis in the legs (Saj et al., 2014). When the patients were asked to slightly move their arms (or to imagine doing so), there was activation in the motor cortex, as expected. However, when asked to move their legs, there was activation in the insula cortex—a part of the limbic system that is thought to mediate emotional responses. What was also interesting was that when the patients were asked to imagine mentally rotating a paralyzed limb, there was activation in the anterior cingulate cortex.

To date, the largest functional neuroimaging study of sensory conversion disorder involves 10 female patients (Burke et al., 2014). Again, the findings suggest that when the anesthetic body part is stimulated, there is decreased activation in the somatosensory

Figure 8.2 This functional magnetic resonance image shows somatosensory activity evoked by stimulation in a patient with sensory conversion disorder affecting the left hand. When the patient's left hand was stimulated, no activity was seen in the primary somatosensory cortex (arrow). However, increased activity was seen in this area of the brain when the patient's right hand was stimulated (circle)

(From Feinstein, 2011.)

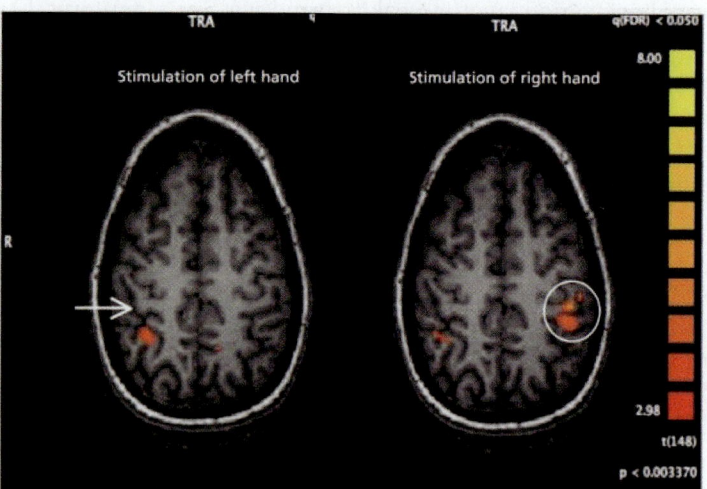

cortex but increased activation in areas such as the anterior cingulate cortex, insula, and other brain areas implicated in emotion processing. All of this is consistent with the idea that sensory areas may perhaps be being inhibited by overactive emotion-based processing. Strange as it may seem, what may be happening in patients with conversion disorders is that abnormal activation in limbic areas (or areas connected to them) might be overriding activation in motor or sensory areas, shutting off the person's ability to detect stimuli (in the case of anesthesia) or move a limb (in the case of paralysis). Although much more needs to be learned, there is some possibility that neuroimaging research may actually be supporting some of Freud's thinking about the origins of conversion disorders!

Treatment of Conversion Disorder

Our knowledge of how best to treat conversion disorder is very limited because few well-controlled studies have been conducted (e.g., Bowman & Markand, 2005; Looper & Kirmayer, 2002). However, approaches similar to those used to help the patient who suddenly became unable to see (described in the earlier case study) are often helpful. The Developments in Practice box provides another example involving treatment of a patient who was mute.

Some hospitalized patients with motor conversion symptoms have been successfully treated with a behavioral approach in which specific exercises are prescribed in order to increase movement or walking, and then reinforcements (e.g., praise and gaining privileges) are provided when patients show improvements. Any reinforcements of abnormal motor behaviors are removed in order to eliminate any sources of secondary gain. In one small study using this kind of treatment for 10 patients, all had regained their ability to move or walk in an average of 12 days, and for seven of the nine patients available at an approximately 2-year follow-up, the improvements had been maintained (Speed, 1996). At least one study has also used cognitive-

Developments in Practice
Treatment of a Patient Who Was Mute

Bryant and Das (2012) describe a creative treatment that was used to help a 51-year old Australian woman who had been mute for 4 years. Although she was unable to speak, she was, rather surprisingly, able to sing. As part of the treatment the therapist used a form of karaoke, asking the patient to imagine singing along to her favorite songs when they were played on a CD player in the therapist's office. After two sessions, the patient was not only able to sing along, but she also began to speak to the therapist. The following week her voice returned in contexts outside the therapist's office as well.

What makes this case even more interesting is that the researchers also collected brain imaging data on the patient before and after treatment. In the initial brain scan, the patient was asked to keep her lips and teeth together (to avoid any movement that would make the scan unusable) and try to vocalize the letters of the alphabet as loudly as possible. For the second scan, conducted 4 weeks after her speech returned, the patient was asked to do the same thing. Although no sounds were detected during the initial scan, the patient made audible sounds during the second scan.

When neural activation before and after treatment was examined, some interesting observations were made. One rather surprising finding was that there was a similar amount of activation in speech-related brain networks during the period when the patient was mute and after recovery. Specifically, a brain area called the inferior frontal gyrus or IFG (which contains Broca's area—an area known to be associated with speech production) showed an increase in activation during both brain scans. The major finding from the study, however, was that, after recovery, the patient had *increased* positive connectivity between the IFG and the anterior cingulate and *decreased* connectivity between the IFG and the amygdala. In other words, after recovery, the patient's speech areas were more linked to brain regions involved in emotion regulation (anterior cingulate) and less linked to brain regions associated with anxiety (amygdala). This case study provides the first demonstration that recovery from conversion disorder is associated with enhanced connectivity between the area of the brain that was implicated in the conversion disorder symptoms (in this case speech production) and neural networks that play a role in emotion regulation.

behavior therapy to successfully treat conversion seizures (LaFrance et al., 2009). Some studies have used hypnosis combined with other problem-solving therapies, and there are suggestions that hypnosis, or adding hypnosis to other therapeutic techniques, can be useful (Looper & Kirmayer, 2002; Moene et al., 2003).

Virtually all the symptoms of conversion disorder can be temporarily reduced or reproduced by hypnotic suggestion.

in review
- What makes conversion disorders so unusual from a clinical perspective?
- What factors increase a person's risk of developing a conversion disorder?
- How is emotion thought to play a role in conversion disorder?

Factitious Disorder

8.5 **Explain the difference between factitious disorder and malingering.**

The disorders we have discussed so far all assume that the people who are experiencing symptoms are reporting their problems as accurately and as truthfully as possible. But sometimes people do deliberately and consciously feign disability or illness. Also placed in the somatic symptoms and related disorders category in *DSM-5* is **factitious disorder**. In factitious disorder the person intentionally produces psychological or physical symptoms (or both). Although this may strike you as strange, the person's goal is to obtain and maintain the benefits that playing the "sick role" (even to the extent of undergoing repeated hospitalizations) may provide, including the attention and concern of family and medical personnel. The *DSM-5* criteria for factitious disorder are shown in the *DSM-5* box.

In *DSM-IV*, factitious disorder was in a category of its own. In *DSM-5* it has been moved into the category of somatic symptom and related disorders. The reason for the move is because in most cases of factitious disorder, the person presents with somatic symptoms and with expressed belief that he or she is ill. However, many regard the inclusion of factitious disorder in the somatic symptom and related disorders category as very unfortunate (Rief & Martin, 2014). These disorders have a history of being stigmatized and many doctors do not take them very seriously. To group them now with a disorder that is characterized by deliberately feigning illness runs the risk of further perpetuating these negative stereotypes.

What is the difference between factious disorder and **malingering**? The key difference is that, in factitious disorder, the person receives no tangible external rewards. In contrast, the person who is malingering is intentionally producing or grossly exaggerating his or her physical symptoms and is motivated by external incentives such as avoiding work or military service or evading criminal prosecution (APA, 2013; Maldonado & Spiegel, 2001).

DSM-5 *Criteria for. . .*

Factitious Disorder

Factitious Disorder Imposed on Self

A. Falsification of physical or psychological signs or symptoms, or induction of injury or disease, associated with identified deception.

B. The individual presents himself or herself to others as ill, impaired, or injured.

C. The deceptive behavior is evident even in the absence of obvious external rewards.

D. The behavior is not better explained by another mental disorder, such as delusional disorder or another psychotic disorder.

Source: Reprinted with permission from the *Diagnostic and Statistical Manual of Mental Disorders*, Fifth Edition (Copyright 2013). American Psychiatric Association.

In factitious disorder, patients may surreptitiously alter their own physiology—for example, by taking drugs—in order to simulate various real illnesses. Indeed, they may be at risk for serious injury or death and may even need to be committed to an institution for their own protection.

The prevalence of factitious disorder is not well established, although it is probably in the region of 0.5 to 0.8 percent of patients in general hospital settings (Bouman, 2015). The disorder is also thought to be more common in women than it is in men. Systematic research on this disorder is lacking and there is currently no theoretical model of why it develops. Some of the social gains that come from being in a patient role are thought to be involved, however.

A dangerous variant of factitious disorder is **factitious disorder imposed on another** (sometimes referred to as *Munchausen's syndrome by proxy*). Here, the person seeking medical help has intentionally produced a medical or psychiatric illness (or the appearance of an illness) in another person. This person is usually someone (such as a child) who is under his or her care (e.g., Pankratz, 2006). In a typical instance, a mother presents her own child for treatment of a medical condition she has deliberately caused. To produce symptoms, the mother might withhold food from the child, add blood to the child's urine, give the child drugs to make him or her throw up, or heat up thermometers to make it seem as if the child has a fever. If the child is hospitalized, the mother might deliberately infect an intravenous (IV) line to make the child more ill. Of course, the health of the victims is often seriously endangered by this form of child abuse and the intervention of social service agencies or law enforcement is sometimes necessary. In as many as 10 percent of cases, the actions of the mother may lead to a child's death (Hall et al., 2000).

This disorder may be suspected when the victim's clinical presentation is atypical, when lab results are inconsistent with each other or with recognized diseases, or when there are many frequent returns or increasingly urgent visits to the same hospital or clinic. The perpetrators (who often have extensive medical knowledge) tend to be highly resistant to admitting the truth about what they are doing (McCann, 1999). They also appear to be devoted to their child, making it hard for health care providers to suspect that they are the cause of the child's problems. It has been estimated that the average length of time to confirm the diagnosis is 14 months (Rogers, 2004). If the perpetrator senses that the medical staff is suspicious, he or she may abruptly terminate contact with that facility, only to show up at another one to begin the entire process anew. Compounding the problem of detection is the fact that health care professionals who realize they have been duped

Lacey Spears is currently serving a 20-year prison term for causing the death of her 5-year-old son, Garnett. According to prosecutors, ever since her son was an infant, Spears had administered salt into his feeding tube to make him sick. She had told doctors that her son could not keep food down and so needed to have a feeding tube inserted. Prosecutors alleged that Spears made her son sick because she craved social media attention, even posting pictures of her dying son on Facebook. Although she denied any mental illness, the judge in the case said that Spears had a diagnosis of Munchausen's by proxy.

may be reluctant to acknowledge their fallibility for fear of legal action. Misdiagnosing the disorder when the parent is in fact innocent can also lead to legal difficulties for the health care professionals (McNicholas et al., 2000; Pankratz, 2006). One technique that has been used with considerable success is covert video surveillance of the mother and child during hospitalizations. In one study, 23 of 41 suspected cases were finally determined to have factitious disorder by proxy, and in 56 percent of those cases video surveillance was essential to the diagnosis (Hall et al., 2000).

Distinguishing Between Different Types of Somatic Symptom and Related Disorders

Given that all the diagnoses we have discussed so far involve the presentation of physical symptoms, how can we distinguish between them? It is sometimes possible to distinguish between a conversion (or other somatic symptom) disorder and malingering, or factitiously "sick-role-playing," with a fair degree of confidence, but in other cases it is more difficult to make the correct diagnosis. Persons engaged in malingering (for which there are no formal diagnostic criteria) and those who have factitious disorder are consciously perpetrating frauds by faking the symptoms of diseases or disabilities, and this fact is often reflected in their demeanor. In contrast, individuals with conversion disorders (as well as with other somatic symptom disorders) are not consciously producing their symptoms, feel themselves to be the "victims of their symptoms," and are very willing to discuss them, often in excruciating detail (Maldonado & Spiegel, 2001, p. 109). When inconsistencies in their behaviors are pointed out, they are usually unperturbed. Any secondary gains they experience are by-products of the conversion symptoms themselves and are not involved in motivating the symptoms. On the other hand, persons who are feigning symptoms are inclined to be defensive, evasive, and suspicious when asked about them; they are usually reluctant to be examined and slow to talk about their symptoms lest the pretense be discovered. Should inconsistencies in their behaviors be pointed out, deliberate deceivers as a rule immediately become more defensive.

in review

- How is conversion disorder distinguished from malingering and from factitious disorder?
- For what reasons might some people deliberately pretend to have medical problems?
- Explain what the diagnosis of factitious disorder imposed on another involves.

Dissociative Disorders: An Overview

8.6 List three *DSM-5* dissociative disorders.

Dissociative disorders are a group of conditions involving disruptions in a person's normally integrated functions of consciousness, memory, identity, or perception (APA, 2013; Spiegel et al., 2013). Included here are some of the more dramatic phenomena in the entire domain of psychopathology: people who cannot recall who they are or where they may have come from, and people who have two or more distinct identities or personality states that alternately take control of the individual's behavior.

The concept of **dissociation** was first promoted over a century ago by the French neurologist Pierre Janet (1859–1947). Dissociation can be defined as "a disruption of and/or discontinuity in the normal, subjective integration of one or more aspects of psychological functioning, including—but not limited to—memory, identity, consciousness, perception and motor control" (Spiegel et al., 2011a, p. 826). We all dissociate to a degree some of the time. Mild dissociative symptoms occur when we daydream or lose track of what is going on around us, when we drive miles beyond our destination without realizing how we got there, or when we miss part of a conversation we are engaged in. (Figure 8.3 provides examples of items from the Dissociative Experiences Scales, a self-report measure of dissociation.) As these everyday examples suggest, there is nothing inherently pathological about dissociation itself. Dissociation only becomes pathological when the dissociative symptoms are "perceived as disruptive, invoking a loss of needed information, as producing discontinuity of experience" or as "recurrent, jarring involuntary intrusions into executive functioning and sense of self" (Spiegel et al., 2011b, p. E19).

Much of our mental life involves automatic nonconscious processes that occur below the radar of deliberate, self-awareness and monitoring. Such unaware processing extends to the areas of implicit memory and implicit perception; all people routinely show indirect evidence of remembering things they cannot consciously recall (**implicit memory**) and respond to sights or sounds as if they had perceived them even though they cannot report that they have seen or heard them (**implicit perception**; Kihlstrom, 2001, 2005; Kihlstrom et al., 1993). This type of responding also occurs in conversion disorders where people who say that they cannot see nonetheless are able to respond to some visual stimuli. As we learned in Chapter 3, the general idea of unconscious mental processes has been embraced by psychodynamically oriented clinicians for many years. Now this is a major research area in the field of cognitive psychology (though

Figure 8.3 Dissociative Experiences Scales

This figure shows sample items from the Dissociative Experiences Scales (DES), a 28-question test often used to screen for dissociative symptoms. The higher the DES score, the more likely it is that the individual has a dissociative disorder.

(Adapted from Serenity Programme™, www.serene.me.uk.)

Dissociative Experiences Scales (DES)

Identifier [   ]   Date [   ]

This questionnaire consists of twenty-eight questions about experiences that you may have in your daily life. We are interested in how often you have these experiences. It is important, however, that your answers show how often these experiences happen to you when you are not under the influence of alcohol or drugs. To answer the questions, please determine to what degree the experience described in the question applies to you and select the number to show what percentage of the time you have the experience. 100% means 'always', 0% means 'never' with 10% increments in between. This assessment is not intended to be a diagnosis. If you are concerned about your results in any way, please speak with a qualified health professional.

Never 0% | 10% | 20% | 30% | 40% | 50% | 60% | 70% | 80% | 90% | 100% Always

1 Some people have the experience of driving a car and suddenly realizing that they don't remember what has happened during all or part of the trip. Select a number to show what percentage of the time this happens to you   [0% ▾]

2 Some people find that sometimes they are listening to someone talk and they suddenly realize that they did not hear all or part of what was said. Select a number to show what percentage of the time this happens to you   [0% ▾]

3 Some people have the experience of finding themselves in a place and having no idea how they got there. Select a number to show what percentage of the time this happens to you   [0% ▾]

4 Some people have the experience of finding themselves dressed in clothes that they don't remember putting on. Select a number to show what percentage of the time this happens to you   [0% ▾]

without any of the psychodynamic implications for why so much of our mental activity is unconscious).

In people with dissociative disorders, this normally integrated and well-coordinated multichannel quality of human cognition becomes much less coordinated and integrated. When this happens, the affected person may be unable to access information that is normally in the forefront of consciousness, such as his or her own personal identity or details of an important period of time in the recent past. That is, the normally useful capacity of maintaining ongoing mental activity outside of awareness appears to be subverted, sometimes for the purpose of managing severe psychological threat. When that happens, we observe the pathological symptoms that are the cardinal characteristic of dissociative disorders. Like somatic symptom disorders, dissociative disorders appear mainly to be ways of avoiding anxiety and stress and of managing life problems that have overwhelmed the person's usual coping resources. Both types of disorders also enable the individual to deny personal responsibility for his or her "unacceptable" wishes or behavior. In the case

of *DSM*-defined dissociative disorders, the person avoids the stress by pathologically dissociating—in essence, by escaping from his or her own autobiographical memory or personal identity. The *DSM-5* recognizes several types of pathological dissociation. These include depersonalization/derealization disorder, dissociative amnesia, and dissociative identity disorder. The dissociative disorders are placed in *DSM-5* immediately after trauma and stressor-related disorders, to reflect the close relationship that exists between them.

Depersonalization/ Derealization Disorder

8.7 Summarize the clinical features of depersonalization/derealization disorder.

Two of the more common kinds of dissociative symptoms are derealization and depersonalization. We mentioned these in Chapter 6 because they sometimes occur during panic attacks. In **derealization** one's sense of the reality of the outside world is temporarily lost, and in **depersonalization** one's sense of one's own self and one's own reality is temporarily lost. As many as 50 to 74 percent of us have such experiences in mild form at least once in our lives, usually during or after periods of severe stress, sleep deprivation, or sensory deprivation (e.g., Khazaal et al., 2005; Reutens et al., 2010). But when episodes of depersonalization or derealization become persistent and recurrent and interfere with normal functioning, **depersonalization/derealization disorder** may be diagnosed, as in the following case example.

Living in a Dream

The patient, a 22-year-old man employed as a mail carrier in India, came to the outpatient clinic reporting feelings of unreality, a heaviness in his head, and a sense that his surroundings had changed. He told the doctors that his problems had begun suddenly, 6 months earlier when he was with his friends. According to the patient, he felt that his friends had changed—that they were no longer his friends but more like ghosts or devils. Scared, the patient hurried home, but when he got home and saw his mother, he felt that she, too, had changed. These feelings continued and it became hard for the patient to tell the difference between the real and the unreal. Although he continued to work in his job, he no longer had any interest in social activities. When he went into a crowded place, he felt as if he was in a dream or somehow roaming in a different kind of a world. He realized that these feelings were his own and he sometimes pinched himself to feel the pain and try and get rid of the feelings of unreality. (Based on Ghosh et al., 2007.)

In this disorder, people have persistent or recurrent experiences of feeling detached from (and like an outside observer of) their own bodies and mental processes. They may even feel they are, for a time, floating above their physical bodies, which may suddenly feel very different—as if drastically changed or unreal. During periods of depersonalization, unlike during psychotic states, reality testing remains intact. The related experience of derealization, in which the external world is perceived as strange and new in various ways, may also occur. As one leader in the field described it, in both states "the feeling puzzles the experiencers: the changed condition is perceived as unreal, and as discontinuous with his or her previous ego-states. The object of the experience, self (in depersonalization) or world (in derealization), is commonly described as isolated, lifeless, strange, and unfamiliar; oneself and others are perceived as 'automatons,' behaving mechanically, without initiative or self-control" (Kihlstrom, 2001, p. 267). Often people, like the man in the case study you just read, report feeling as though they are living in a dream or movie (Maldonado et al., 2002).

People with derealization symptoms experience the world as hazy and indistinct.

In keeping with such reports, research has shown that emotional experiences are attenuated or reduced during depersonalization—both at the subjective level and at the level of neural and autonomic activity that normally accompanies emotional responses to threatening or unpleasant emotional stimuli (Lemche et al., 2007; Phillips & Sierra, 2003; Stein & Simeon, 2009). After viewing an emotional video clip, participants with depersonalization showed higher levels of subjective and objective memory fragmentation than controls (Giesbrecht et al., 2010).

Adam Duritz, Counting Crows frontman, has talked about his experiences and struggles with depersonalization/derealization disorder.

Memory fragmentation is marked by difficulties forming an accurate or coherent narrative sequence of events, which is consistent with earlier research suggesting that time distortion is a key element of the depersonalization experience (Simeon et al., 2008).

In *DSM-IV*, derealization and depersonalization were treated as two distinct conditions. In *DSM-5* they have been combined. This is because research suggests that people who have prominent derealization or prominent depersonalization look rather similar in terms of demographic characteristics, the course and severity of their problems, and their comorbid conditions (see Lynn et al., 2015). The current *DSM-5* criteria for depersonalization/derealization disorder are shown in the *DSM* box.

As we noted earlier, transient symptoms of depersonalization or derealization are very common in the general population. This is why, to qualify for a diagnosis, episodes of depersonalization or derealization must be persistent or recurrent. Occasional depersonalization/derealization symptoms are also sometimes reported by people with schizophrenia, borderline personality disorder, panic disorder, acute stress disorder, and posttraumatic stress disorder (Hunter et al., 2003).

Dissociative disorders have not been included in the major epidemiological surveys that have been conducted to date, so we have no exact prevalence data. It is estimated that the lifetime prevalence of depersonalization/derealization disorder is around 1 to 2 percent of the population with equal numbers of males and females being affected ... Reutens et al., 2010). Although the disorder ... ldhood, the mean age of onset is around age ... a minority of people developing it after age ...3). Moreover, in nearly 80 percent of cases, the ... a fairly chronic course with little or no fluctu... nsity (Baker et al., 2003). Comorbid conditions

can include mood or anxiety disorders. Avoidant, borderline, and obsessive-compulsive personality disorders are also elevated in people with depersonalization and derealization experiences (e.g., Hunter et al., 2003; Mula et al., 2007; Reutens et al., 2010).

Although severe depersonalization/derealization symptoms can be quite frightening and may make the person fear imminent mental collapse, such fears are usually unfounded. Sometimes, however, feelings of depersonalization can be early manifestations of the development of psychotic states (see Chapter 13). In either case, professional assistance in dealing with the precipitating stressors and in reducing anxiety may be helpful. Unfortunately, however, as of yet there are no clearly effective treatments—either through medication or psychotherapy.

in review

- Explain the difference between depersonalization and derealization.

- In addition to depersonalization/derealization disorder, what other disorders sometimes involve these symptoms?

- At around what age do symptoms of depersonalization or derealization often begin? Is the disorder any more common in males than it is in females?

Dissociative Amnesia

8.8 Describe the clinical features of dissociative amnesia.

Retrograde amnesia is the partial or total inability to recall or identify previously acquired information or past experiences; by contrast, *anterograde amnesia* is the partial or total inability to retain new information (Gilboa et al., 2006;

Kapur, 1999). Persistent amnesia may occur in dissociative amnesia. It may also result from traumatic brain injury or diseases of the central nervous system. If the amnesia is caused by *brain pathology*, it most often involves failure to retain new information and experiences (anterograde amnesia). That is, the information contained in experience is not registered and does not enter memory storage (Kapur, 1999).

On the other hand, **dissociative amnesia** is usually limited to a failure to recall previously stored personal information (retrograde amnesia) when that failure cannot be accounted for by ordinary forgetting (see the *DSM-5* box for the current diagnostic criteria). The gaps in memory most often occur following intolerably stressful circumstances—wartime combat conditions, for example, or catastrophic events such as serious car accidents, suicide attempts, or traumatic experiences (Maldonado & Spiegel, 2007; Spiegel et al., 2011a). In this disorder, apparently forgotten personal information is still there beneath the level of consciousness. It sometimes becomes apparent in interviews conducted under hypnosis or narcosis (induced by sodium amytal, or so-called truth serum) and (obviously) in cases where the amnesia spontaneously clears up.

Watch Sharon: Dissociative Amnesia

Amnesic episodes usually last between a few days and a few years. Although many people experience only one such episode, some people have multiple episodes in their lifetimes (Maldonado & Spiegel, 2007; Staniloiu & Markowitsch, 2010). In typical dissociative amnesic reactions, individuals cannot remember certain aspects of their personal life history or important facts about their identity. Yet their basic habit patterns—such as their abilities to read, talk, perform skilled work, and so on—remain intact, and they seem normal aside from the memory deficit (Kihlstrom, 2005; Kihlstrom & Schacter, 2000). Thus, the only type of memory that is affected is *episodic* (pertaining to events experienced) or *autobiographical memory* (pertaining to personal events experienced). The other recognized forms of memory—semantic

(pertaining to language and concepts), procedural (how to do things), and short-term storage—seem usually to remain intact, although there is very little research on this topic (Kihlstrom, 2005; Kihlstrom & Schacter, 2000). Usually there is no difficulty encoding new information (Maldonado & Spiegel, 2007).

In rare cases a person may retreat still further from real-life problems by going into an amnesic state called a **dissociative fugue**, which, as the term implies (the French word *fugue* means "flight"), is a defense by actual flight—a person is not only amnesic for some or all aspects of his or her past but also departs from home surroundings. This is accompanied by confusion about personal identity or even the assumption of a new identity (although the identities do not alternate as they do in dissociative identity disorder). During the fugue, such individuals are unaware of memory loss for prior stages of their life, but their memory for what happens during the fugue state itself is intact (Kihlstrom, 2005; Kihlstrom & Schacter, 2000). Their behavior during the fugue state is usually quite normal and unlikely to arouse suspicion that something is wrong. However, behavior during the fugue state often reflects a rather different lifestyle from the previous one (the rejection of which is sometimes fairly obvious). Days, weeks, or sometimes even years later, such people

The celebrated English mystery writer Agatha Christie vanished suddenly in December 1926. Her mother had died a few months earlier and her husband was having an affair that he made little effort to conceal. The writer was eventually found in a health resort in Harrogate, Yorkshire, where she had checked in calling herself Teresa Noel. She had told people she was a mother from Cape Town, who was grieving the loss of her child. When her husband arrived and identified her, she simply remarked, "Fancy, my brother just arrived."

may suddenly emerge from the fugue state and find themselves in a strange place, working in a new occupation, with no idea how they got there. In other cases, recovery from the fugue state occurs only after repeated questioning and reminders of who they are. In either case, as the fugue state remits, their initial amnesia remits—but a new, apparently complete amnesia for their fugue period occurs. In *DSM-5* dissociative fugue is considered to be a subtype of dissociative amnesia rather than a separate disorder as it was in *DSM-IV*.

DSM-5 *Criteria for. . .*

Dissociative Amnesia

A. An inability to recall important autobiographical information, usually of a traumatic or stressful nature, that is inconsistent with ordinary forgetting.

   Note: Dissociative amnesia most often consists of localized or selective amnesia for a specific event or events; or generalized amnesia for identity and life history.

B. The symptoms cause clinically significant distress or impairment in social, occupational, or other important areas of functioning.

C. The disturbance is not attributable to the physiological effects of a substance (e.g., alcohol or other drug of abuse, a medication) or a neurological or other medical condition (e.g., partial complex seizures, transient global amnesia, sequelae of a closed head injury/traumatic brain injury, other neurological condition).

D. The disturbance is not better explained by dissociative identity disorder, posttraumatic stress disorder, acute stress disorder, somatic symptom disorder, or major or mild neurocognitive disorder.

Source: Reprinted with permission from the *Diagnostic and Statistical Manual of Mental Disorders*, Fifth Edition (Copyright 2013). American Psychiatric Association.

The pattern in dissociative amnesia is essentially similar to that in conversion symptoms, except that instead of avoiding some unpleasant situation by becoming physically dysfunctional, a person unconsciously avoids thoughts about the situation or, in the extreme, leaves the scene (Maldonado & Spiegel, 2007; Maldonado et al., 2002). Thus, people experiencing dissociative amnesia are typically faced with extremely unpleasant situations from which they see no acceptable way to escape. Eventually the stress becomes so intolerable that large segments of their personalities and all memory of the stressful situations are suppressed.

Several of these aspects are illustrated in the following case example of dissociative amnesia with dissociative fugue.

How Did I Get Here?

The patient is a 28-year-old medical student from Nigeria. He had been declared missing several days earlier after he disappeared from his room. While studying late one night, the patient says that he suddenly saw a human skeleton sitting and reading across the table from him. He said that the whole room started to turn and everything inside it became unstable and unreal. The patient remembers being very afraid but denies knowing anything about what happened after this and has no idea when he left his room. However, 2 days later, the patient was found at his younger brother's house, almost 400 miles away. The patient said he had no idea how he got there, how he found the money for the journey, or what transportation or roads he took. He simply had no memory of anything that happened before he arrived, exhausted and looking very disheveled, at his brother's home.

The amnesic episode appears to have been triggered by academic and financial stressors. After other academic failures, the patient was in serious danger of failing the final examinations that he was due to take in 3 months. Because of his problems in school, his family was also threatening to no longer help him financially. All of this had made the patient feel depressed and unable to cope.

While he was at the clinic, the young medical student was treated with antidepressant medication combined with psychotherapy. He responded well. However, even after recovering enough to take his final examinations (which he did not pass), the patient was still unable to recall what happened in the period after he left his room and traveled 400 miles to his brother's house. (Based on Igwe, 2013.)

Little systematic research has been conducted on individuals with dissociative amnesia and fugue. What is known comes largely from intensive studies of the memory and intellectual functioning of isolated cases with these disorders, so any conclusions should be considered tentative pending further study of larger samples with appropriate control groups. What can be gathered from a handful of such case studies is that these individuals' semantic knowledge (assessed via the vocabulary subtest of an IQ test) seems to be generally intact. The primary deficit these individuals exhibit is their compromised episodic or autobiographical memory. Indeed, several studies using brain imaging techniques have confirmed that when people with dissociative amnesia are presented with autobiographical memory tasks, they show reduced activation in their right frontal and temporal brain areas relative to normal controls doing the same kinds of tasks (Kihlstrom, 2005; Markowitsch, 1999). In a review of nine cases of dissociative amnesia for which brain imaging data were available, the authors concluded there was evidence of significant changes in the brains of these patients, mostly centered on subtle loss of function in the right anterior hemisphere—changes similar to those seen in the brains of patients with organic memory loss (Staniloiu & Markowitsch, 2010).

However, several cases (some nearly a century old) have suggested that *implicit memory* is generally intact. For example, Jones (1909, as cited in Kihlstrom & Schacter, 2000) studied a patient with dense amnesia and found that although he could not remember his wife's or daughter's names, when asked to guess what names might fit them, he produced their names correctly. In a more contemporary case (Lyon, 1985, as cited in Kihlstrom & Schacter, 2000), a patient who could not retrieve any autobiographical information was asked to dial numbers on a phone randomly. Without realizing what he was doing, he dialed his mother's phone number, which then led to her identifying him. In one particularly fascinating contemporary case of dissociative fugue, Glisky and colleagues (2004) describe a German man who had come to work in the United States. Several months before he had experienced a traumatic incident in which he had been robbed and shot. After the trauma, he wandered along unfamiliar streets for an unknown period of time. Finally, he stopped at a motel and asked if the police could be called because he did not know who he was (he had no ID because he had been robbed) and could not recall any personal details of his life. He spoke English (with a German accent) but could not speak German and did not respond to instructions in German (which he denied that he spoke). In spite of his extensive loss of autobiographical memory (and the German language), when given a variety of memory tasks, he showed intact implicit memory. Especially striking was his ability to learn German–English word pairs, which he learned much faster than did normal controls, suggesting implicit knowledge of German even though he had no conscious knowledge of it.

Some of the memory deficits in dissociative amnesia and fugue have been compared to related deficits in explicit perception that occur in conversion disorders. This has convinced many people that conversion disorder should be classified with dissociative disorders rather than with somatic symptom disorders. This issue is discussed in more detail in the Thinking Critically about *DSM-5* box.

DSM-5   Thinking Critically about *DSM-5*

Where Does Conversion Disorder Belong?

Starting with Freud and Janet, and for a large portion of the twentieth century prior to the publication of *DSM-III* in 1980, conversion disorders were classified together with dissociative disorders as subtypes of hysteria. When it was determined that *DSM-III* would rely heavily on overt behavioral symptoms rather than on ideas about underlying etiology (in this case, repressed anxiety) for classifying disorders, the decision was made to include conversion disorder with the other somatic symptom disorders. This was because its symptoms were physical ones with no demonstrable medical basis. However, as Kihlstrom (2005) and others have pointed out, this ignores some very important differences between conversion disorders and other somatic symptom disorders. The most important overall difference is that conversion symptoms (but not those of the other somatoform disorders) nearly always resemble neurological problems in their clinical presentation (such as blindness, paralysis, anesthesias, deafness, and seizures). In other words, they mimic true neurological syndromes, just as most of the dissociative disorders do.

The disorders we currently classify as dissociative disorders (such as dissociative amnesia and dissociative identity disorder) involve disruptions in explicit memory (which concerns the kind of events we can intentionally remember). The person may be unable to recall events that have occurred, or there may be disruptions in knowledge of one's identity, or both. However, events occurring during a period of amnesia or in the presence of one identity are indeed registered in the nervous system because they influence behavior indirectly even when the person cannot consciously recollect them (i.e., *implicit memory* remains at least partially intact in dissociative disorders). Similarly, Kihlstrom and others have argued that the conversion disorders involve disruptions in *explicit perception* and *action*. That is, people with conversion disorders have no conscious recognition that they can see or hear or feel, or no conscious knowledge that they can walk or talk or feel. However, patients with conversion disorder *can* see, hear, feel, or move when tricked into doing so or when indirect physiological or behavioral measures are used (see Janet, 1901, 1907; Kihlstrom, 2001, 2005). Thus, an argument can be made that, in future editions of the *DSM*, the term *conversion disorder* should be dropped and the sensory and motor types of the syndrome should be reclassified as forms of dissociative disorders. This way, the central feature of all dissociative disorders would be a disruption of the normally integrated functions of consciousness (memory, perception, and action). Such a proposal is also consistent with observations that dissociative symptoms and disorders are quite common in patients with conversion disorder (e.g., Sar et al., 2004), as well as with the neuroimaging findings we described earlier. This proposal was seriously considered and heavily debated by the *DSM-5* task force. For now, however, conversion disorder remains in the category of somatic symptom disorder and related disorders.

Watch Sharon: Living with Dissociative Amnesia

in review

- Describe dissociative amnesia and indicate what aspects of memory are affected.

- What role is stress thought to play in the development of dissociative amnesia?

- What does dissociative amnesia with fugue involve?

Dissociative Identity Disorder

8.9 Describe the clinical features of dissociative identity disorder and explain why this disorder is so controversial.

Dissociative identity disorder (DID), formerly known as *multiple personality disorder*, is a dramatic dissociative disorder. It has long provided a melodramatic focus in movies (*Sybil, Mr. Brooks, Raising Cain, Dressed to Kill*), as well as in the media. In *DSM-IV*, it was required that the person manifest two or more distinct identities (or personality states) that alternated in some way in taking control of behavior. This was accompanied by an inability to recall important personal information that could not be explained by ordinary forgetting.

In *DSM-5* there has been a subtle shift of emphasis. What is now required is that there be a disruption of identity characterized by two or more distinct personality states as well as recurrent episodes of amnesia. Importantly, this disruption in identity can either be self-reported or observed by others. In other words, DID can now be diagnosed without other people witnessing the different personalities.

Another change in *DSM-5* is the inclusion of pathological possession in the diagnostic criteria for DID. A *trance* is said to occur when someone experiences a temporary marked alteration in state of consciousness or identity. It is usually associated with either a narrowing of awareness of the immediate surroundings, or stereotyped

behaviors or movements that are experienced as beyond one's control. A *possession trance* is similar except that the alteration of consciousness or identity is replaced by a new identity that is attributed to the influence of a spirit, deity, or other power. In both cases amnesia is typically present for the trance state. When entered into voluntarily for religious or spiritual reasons, trance and possession states are not considered pathological. However, when they occur involuntarily, outside accepted cultural contexts, and cause distress, this is a serious problem. In *DSM-5*, the diagnostic criteria for DID have been modified to include pathological possession. Pathological possession is a common form of DID in Africa, Asia, and many other non-Western cultures (Spiegel et al., 2013). This important change makes the diagnosis of DID more inclusive and applicable to a broader range of cultural groups.

Chris Sizemore was the inspiration for the book and movie *Three Faces of Eve*, which explored her multiple personality disorder (now known as DID). After her recovery, Sizemore worked as an advocate for the mentally ill.

In the prototypical case of DID, however, there are different personalities that emerge and are apparent to an outside observer. Each identity may appear to have a different personal history, self-image, and name, although there may be some identities that are only partially distinct and independent from other identities. In most cases the one identity that is most frequently encountered and carries the person's real name is the **host identity**. Also in most cases, the host is not the original identity, and it may or may not be the best-adjusted identity. The **alter identities** may differ in striking ways involving gender, age, handedness, handwriting, sexual orientation, prescription for eyeglasses, predominant affect, foreign languages spoken, and general knowledge. For example, one alter may be carefree, fun loving, and sexually provocative, and another alter quiet, studious, serious, and prudish. Needs and behaviors inhibited in the primary or host identity are usually liberally displayed by one or more alter identities. Certain roles such as a child and someone of the opposite sex are extremely common.

Much of the reason for abandoning the older diagnostic term *multiple personality disorder* in favor of DID was the growing recognition that it had misleading connotations, suggesting multiple occupancy of space, time, and people's bodies by differing, but fully organized and coherent, "personalities." In fact, alters are not in any meaningful sense personalities but rather reflect a failure to integrate various aspects of a person's identity, consciousness, and memory (Spiegel, 2006). The term *DID* better captures this, as do the revised *DSM-5* criteria (see the *DSM-5* box). Indeed Spiegel (one prominent theorist in this area) has argued that "the problem is not having more than one personality, it is having less than one" (Spiegel, 2006, p. 567).

Alter identities take control at different points in time, and the switches typically occur very quickly (in a matter of seconds), although more gradual switches can also occur. When switches occur in people with DID, it is often easy to observe the gaps in memories for things that have happened—often for things that have happened to other identities. But this amnesia is not always symmetrical; that is, some identities may know more about certain alters than do other identities. In sum, DID is a condition in which normally integrated aspects of memory, identity, and consciousness are no longer integrated. Additional symptoms of DID include depression, self-injurious behavior, frequent suicidal ideation and attempts, erratic behavior, headaches, hallucinations, posttraumatic symptoms, and other amnesic and fugue symptoms (APA, 2013; Maldonado et al., 2002). Depressive disorders, PTSD, substance-use disorders, and borderline personality disorder are the most common comorbid diagnoses (Maldonado & Spiegel, 2007). One recent study found that among patients with diagnoses of DID, the average number of comorbid diagnoses (based on structured diagnostic interviews) was five, with PTSD being the most common (Rodewald et al., 2011).

DID usually starts in childhood, although most patients are in their teens, 20s, or 30s at the time of diagnosis. Approximately three to nine times more females than males are diagnosed as having the disorder, and females tend to have a larger number of alters than do males (Maldonado & Spiegel, 2007). Some believe that this pronounced gender discrepancy is due to the much greater proportion of childhood sexual abuse among females than among males, but this is a highly controversial point.

The number of alter identities in DID varies tremendously and has increased over time (Maldonado & Spiegel, 2007). One early review of 76 classic cases reported that two-thirds of these cases had only two personalities and most of the rest had three (Taylor & Martin, 1944). More recent estimates are that about 50 percent now show over 10 identities with some respondents claiming as many as a hundred. This historical trend of increasing multiplicity suggests the operation of social factors, perhaps through the encouragement of therapists, as we discuss below (e.g., Kihlstrom, 2005; Lilienfeld et al., 1999; Piper & Merskey, 2004a, 2004b). Another recent trend is that many of the reported cases of DID now include more unusual and even bizarre identities than in the past (such as being an animal) and more highly implausible backgrounds (e.g., ritualized satanic abuse in childhood).

DSM-5 *Criteria for. . .*

Dissociative Identity Disorder

A. Disruption of identity characterized by two or more distinct personality states, which may be described in some cultures as an experience of possession. The disruption in identity involves marked discontinuity in sense of self and sense of agency, accompanied by related alterations in affect, behavior, consciousness, memory, perception, cognition, and/or sensory-motor functioning. These signs and symptoms may be observed by others or reported by the individual.

B. Recurrent gaps in the recall of everyday events, important personal information, and/ or traumatic events that are inconsistent with ordinary forgetting.

C. The symptoms cause clinically significant distress or impairment in social, occupational, or other important areas of functioning.

D. The disturbance is not a normal part of a broadly accepted cultural or religious practice.
Note: In children, the symptoms are not better explained by imaginary playmates or other fantasy play.

E. The symptoms are not attributable to the physiological effects of a substance (e.g., blackouts or chaotic behavior during alcohol intoxication) or another medical condition (e.g., complex partial seizures).

Source: Reprinted with permission from the *Diagnostic and Statistical Manual of Mental Disorders*, Fifth Edition (Copyright 2013). American Psychiatric Association.

The World Around Us

DID, Schizophrenia, and Split Personality: Clearing Up the Confusion

The general public has long been confused by the distinction between DID and schizophrenia. It is not uncommon for people diagnosed with schizophrenia to be referred to as having a "split personality." You might also have heard people say such things as "I'm a bit schizophrenic on this issue" when they mean that they have more than one opinion about it. Although this misuse of the term *split personality* actually began among psychiatric professionals, today it reflects the public's general misunderstanding of schizophrenia, which does not involve a "split" or "Jekyll and Hyde" personality at all. The original confusion may have stemmed from the term *schizophrenia*, which was first coined by a Swiss psychiatrist named Bleuler. The word comes from the Greek root *sxizo* meaning "to split or crack," and *phren,* which is the Greek root for "mind." The notion that schizophrenia is characterized by a split mind or split personality may have arisen this way (see McNally, 2007, for a historical review of how this confusion arose).

However, this is not at all what Bleuler intended the word *schizophrenia* to mean. Rather, Bleuler was referring to the splitting of the normally integrated *associative threads* of the mind—

links between words, thoughts, emotions, and behavior. Splits of this kind result in thinking that is not goal directed or efficient, which in turn leads to the host of other difficulties known to be associated with schizophrenia.

It is very important to remember that people diagnosed with schizophrenia do *not* have multiple distinct identities that alternately take control over their mind and behavior. They may have a delusion and believe they are someone else, but they do not show the changes in identity accompanied by changes in tone of voice, vocabulary, and physical appearance that are often seen when identities "switch" in DID. Furthermore, people with DID (who are probably closer to the general public's notion of "split personality") do not exhibit such characteristics of schizophrenia as disorganized behavior, hallucinations coming from outside the head, and delusions, or incoherent and loose associations (e.g., Kluft, 2005).

Have you ever confused these terms or heard other people do so? In what ways does "split personality" in the context of schizophrenia differ from "split personality" in the context of dissociative identity disorder?

Causal Factors and Controversies about DID

There are at least four serious, interrelated controversies surrounding DID and how it develops. The first is whether DID is a real disorder or is faked, and whether, even if it is real, it can be faked. The second major controversy is about how DID develops. Specifically, is DID caused by early childhood trauma, or does the development of DID involve some kind of social enactment of multiple different roles that have been inadvertently encouraged by careless clinicians? Third, those who maintain that DID is caused by childhood trauma cite evidence that the vast majority of individuals diagnosed with DID report memories of an early history of abuse. But are these memories of early abuse real or false? Finally, if abuse has occurred in most individuals with DID, did the abuse play a *causal role*, or was something else correlated with the abuse actually the cause? In the following sections, we discuss each of these issues in turn.

IS DID REAL OR FAKED?   The issue of possible factitious or malingering origins of DID has dogged the diagnosis of DID for at least a century. One obvious situation in which this issue becomes critical is when it has been used by defendants and their attorneys to try to escape punishment for crimes ("My other personality did it"). For example, this defense was used, ultimately unsuccessfully, in the

famous case of the Hillside Strangler, Kenneth Bianchi (Orne et al., 1984). Bianchi was accused of brutally raping and murdering 10 young women in the Los Angeles area. Although there was a great deal of evidence that he had committed these crimes, he steadfastly denied it, and some lawyers thought perhaps he had DID. He was subsequently interviewed by a clinical psychologist, and under hypnosis a second personality, "Steve," emerged. Steve confessed to the crimes, thereby creating the basis for a plea of "not guilty by reason of insanity" (see Chapter 17). However, Bianchi was later examined even more closely by a renowned psychologist and psychiatrist specializing in this area, the late Martin Orne. Upon closer examination, Orne determined that Bianchi was faking the condition. Orne drew this conclusion in part because when he suggested to Bianchi that most people with DID have more than two identities, Bianchi suddenly produced a third (Orne et al., 1984). Moreover, there was no evidence of multiple identities existing prior to the trial. When Bianchi's faking of the disorder was discovered, he was convicted of the murders. In other words, some cases of DID may involve complete fabrication orchestrated by criminal or other unscrupulous persons seeking unfair advantages, and not all prosecutors have as clever and knowledgeable an expert witness as Martin Orne to help detect this. Nevertheless, most researchers think that factitious and malingering cases of DID (such as the Bianchi case or cases in which the person has a need to be a patient) are relatively rare.

Kenneth Bianchi, known as the "Hillside Strangler," brutally raped and murdered 10 women in the Los Angeles area. Hoping to create a plea of "not guilty by reason of insanity," Bianchi fabricated a second personality—"Steve"—who "emerged" while Kenneth was under hypnosis. A psychologist and psychiatrist specializing in DID determined he was faking the diagnosis, and Bianchi was subsequently convicted of the murders.

Figure 8.4 Reported childhood abuse in four separate studies of patients with DID (total *n* = 488).

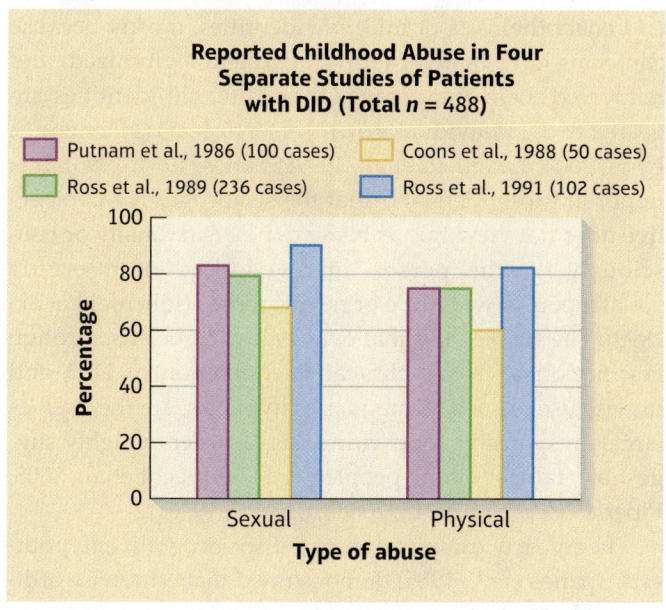

IF DID IS NOT FAKED, HOW DOES IT DEVELOP: POST-TRAUMATIC THEORY OR SOCIOCOGNITIVE THEORY?

Many professionals acknowledge that, in most cases, DID is a real syndrome (not consciously faked), but there is marked disagreement about how it develops and how it is maintained. In contemporary literature, the original major theory of how DID develops is **posttraumatic theory** (Gleaves, 1996; Maldonado & Spiegel, 2007; Ross, 1997, 1999). The vast majority of patients with DID (over 95 percent by some estimates) report memories of severe and horrific childhood abuse. Figure 8.4 shows results from several early studies. More recent investigations report similar findings (Dorahy et al., 2015).

According to posttraumatic theory, DID starts from the child's attempt to cope with an overwhelming sense of hopelessness and powerlessness in the face of repeated traumatic abuse. Lacking other resources or routes of escape, the child may dissociate and escape into a fantasy, becoming someone else. This escape may occur through a process like self-hypnosis (Butler et al., 1996), and if it helps to alleviate some of the pain caused by the abuse it will be reinforced and occur again in the future. Sometimes the child simply imagines the abuse is happening to someone else. If the child is fantasy prone, and continues to stay fantasy prone over time, the child may unknowingly create different selves at different points in time, possibly laying the foundation for dissociated identities.

But only a subset of children who undergo traumatic experiences are prone to fantasy or self-hypnosis, which leads to the idea that a diathesis–stress model may be appropriate here. That is, children who are prone to fantasy and those who are easily hypnotizable may have a diathesis for developing DID (or other dissociative disorders) when severe abuse occurs (e.g., Butler et al., 1996; Kihlstrom et al., 1993). However, it should be noted that there is nothing inherently pathological about being prone to fantasy or readily hypnotizable (Kihlstrom et al., 1994).

Increasingly, those who view childhood abuse as playing a critical role in the development of DID are beginning to see DID as perhaps a complex and chronic variant of posttraumatic stress disorder, which by definition is caused by exposure to some kind of highly traumatic event(s), including abuse (e.g., Brown, 1994; Maldonado & Spiegel, 2007; Maldonado et al., 2002). Anxiety symptoms are more prominent in PTSD than in DID, and dissociative symptoms are more prominent in DID than in PTSD. Nevertheless, both kinds of symptoms are present in both disorders (Putnam, 1997). Moreover, some (but not all) investigators have estimated that a very high percentage of individuals diagnosed with DID have a comorbid diagnosis of PTSD, suggesting the likelihood of some important common causal factors (Vermetten et al., 2006; see also Rodewald et al., 2011). Recognizing this, *DSM-5* now includes PTSD with dissociative symptoms as a new subtype.

At the other extreme from posttraumatic theory is **sociocognitive theory**. According to this theory, DID develops when a highly suggestible person learns to adopt and enact the roles of multiple identities, mostly because clinicians have inadvertently suggested, legitimized, and reinforced them and because these different identities are geared to the individual's own personal goals (Lilienfeld & Lynn, 2003; Lilienfeld et al., 1999; Spanos, 1994, 1996). It is important to understand that the sociocognitive perspective does not view this as being done intentionally or consciously by the person involved. Rather, it occurs spontaneously with little or no awareness (Lilienfeld et al., 1999). The suspicion is that overzealous clinicians, through fascination with the clinical phenomenon of DID and unwise use of such techniques as hypnosis, are themselves largely responsible for eliciting this disorder in highly suggestible, fantasy-prone people (e.g., Giesbrecht et al., 2008; Piper & Merskey, 2004a, 2004b; Spanos, 1996).

In an early examination of the sociocognitive hypothesis, Spanos et al. (1985) demonstrated that otherwise ordinary college students can be induced by suggestion under hypnosis to exhibit some of the phenomena seen in DID. These included the adoption of a second identity with a different name that showed a different profile on a personality inventory. Spanos and colleagues thus demonstrated that people can enact a second identity when situational forces encourage it. Related situational forces that may affect the individual outside the therapist's office include memories of one's past behavior (e.g., as a child), observations of other people's behavior (e.g., others being assertive and independent, or sexy and flirtatious), and media portrayals of DID (Lilienfeld et al., 1999; Piper & Merskey, 2004b; Spanos, 1994).

Sociocognitive theory is also consistent with evidence that most DID patients do not show unambiguous signs of the disorder before they enter therapy and with evidence that the number of identities often increases (sometimes dramatically) with time spent in therapy (Boysen & VanBergen, 2013; Piper & Merskey, 2004b).

Also consistent with the sociocultural perspective are changes in the prevalence of DID. Owing to their dramatic nature, cases of DID receive a great deal of attention and publicity in fiction, television, and movies. But until relatively recently, however, DID was extremely rare—or at least rarely diagnosed—in clinical practice. The number of cases began to rise in the 1970s after the publication of Flora Rhea Schreiber's book *Sybil* (1973). Ironically, as described in the World Around Us box, the case that made people much more aware of the condition and triggered an epidemic of DID has now been thoroughly discredited (see Borch-Jacobsen, 2009; Nathan, 2011; Paris, 2012c; Rieber, 2006). At about the same time, the diagnostic criteria for DID (then called multiple personality disorder) were clearly specified for the first time with the publication of

DSM-III in 1980. This seems to have led to increased acceptance of the diagnosis by clinicians, which may have encouraged reporting of it in the literature.

In addition, beginning in about 1980, prior scattered reports of instances of childhood abuse in the histories of adult patients began building into what would become a crescendo. As we will see later, many controversies arose regarding how to interpret such findings, but it is definitely true that these reports of abuse in patients with DID attracted a great deal of attention to this disorder, which in turn may have increased the rate at which it was being diagnosed. Prior to 1979, only about 200 cases could be found in the entire psychological and psychiatric literature worldwide. By 1999, however, over 30,000 cases had been reported in North America alone (Ross, 1999), although many researchers believe that this is a gross overestimate (e.g., Piper & Merskey, 2004b). Prevalence estimates in the general population are hard to come by and it is possible that no such estimates are valid, given how hard it is to make this diagnosis reliably. However, one study of 658 people in upstate New York has estimated a 1.5 percent prevalence (Johnson et al., 2006).

Many factors probably have contributed to the drastic increase in the reported prevalence of DID (although in an absolute sense it is still very rare, and most practicing psychotherapists, ourselves included, have never treated a person with DID). However, it is almost certain that some of the increase in the prevalence of DID is *artifactual* and has occurred because some therapists looking for evidence of DID in certain patients may suggest the existence of alter identities (especially when the person is under hypnosis and very suggestible; e.g., Kihlstrom, 2005; Piper & Merskey, 2004b). The therapist may also subtly reinforce the emergence of new identities by showing great interest in these new identities. Nevertheless, such factors probably cannot account for all cases of diagnosed DID, which has been observed in most parts of the world, even where there is virtually no personal or professional knowledge of DID, including rural Turkey (Akyuz et al., 1999; see also Maldonado & Spiegel, 2007) and Shanghai, China (Xiao et al., 2006).

There are also many criticisms of sociocognitive theory. For example, Spanos and colleagues' demonstration of role-playing in hypnotized college students is interesting, but it does not show that this is the way DID is actually caused in real life. For example, someone might be able to give a convincing portrayal of a person with a broken leg, but this would not establish how legs are usually broken. Moreover, the hypnotized participants in this and other experiments showed only a few of the most obvious symptoms of DID (such as more than one identity) and showed them only under short-lived, contrived laboratory conditions. Thus, although some of the *symptoms* of DID could be created by social enactment, this is not the same thing as demonstrating that the *disorder* can be created this way (e.g., Gleaves, 1996).

Former Georgia football star Herschel Walker has written a book, *Breaking Free: My Life with Dissociative Identity Disorder* (2008), in which he tells about his struggle with this disorder.

ARE RECOVERED MEMORIES OF ABUSE IN DID REAL OR FALSE? Case reports of the cruelty and torture that some patients with DID experienced as children are heartbreaking to read or hear. However, the accuracy and trustworthiness of these reports of widespread sexual and other forms of childhood abuse in DID have become a matter of major controversy. Critics (who are often proponents of sociocognitive theory) argue that many of these reports of patients with DID, which generally come up in the course of therapy, may be the result of false memories, which are in turn a product of highly leading questions and suggestive techniques applied by well-meaning but inadequately skilled and careless psychotherapists (Lilienfeld et al., 1999; Loftus & Davis, 2006; Yapko, 1994). It seems quite clear to many investigators that this sort of thing has happened, often with tragic consequences. Innocent family members have been falsely accused by patients with DID and have sometimes been convicted and imprisoned. But it is also true that brutal abuse of children occurs far too often and that it can have very adverse effects on development, perhaps encouraging pathological dissociation (e.g., Maldonado & Spiegel, 2007; Nash et al., 1993). In such cases, prosecution of the perpetrators of the abuse is indeed appropriate. Of course, the real difficulty here is in determining when the recovered memories of abuse are real and when they are false (or some combination of the two). This bitter controversy about the issue of false memory is more extensively considered in the Unresolved Issues section at the end of this chapter.

One way to document that particular recovered memories are real might be if some reliable physiological test could be developed to distinguish between them. Researchers are currently trying to determine whether there are different neural correlates of real and false memories that could be used to make this determination reliably. Another somewhat easier way to document whether

a particular recovered memory is real would be to have independent verification that the abuse had actually occurred, such as through physician, hospital, and police records. A number of studies have indeed reported that they have confirmed the reported cases of abuse, but critics have shown that the criteria used for corroborating evidence are almost invariably very loose and suspect as to their validity. For example, Chu and colleagues (1999) simply asked their subjects, "Have you had anyone confirm these events?" (p. 751) but did not specify what constituted confirmation and had no way of determining if subjects were exaggerating or distorting the information they provided as confirming evidence (Loftus & Davis, 2006; Piper & Merskey, 2004a).

In another example of a flawed study, Lewis and colleagues (1997) studied 12 convicted murderers with DID and then confirmed through medical, social service, and prison records that all 12 had been severely abused as children. Unfortunately, this study did not include a control group of otherwise comparable murderers who did not exhibit DID symptoms. Hence, we cannot be certain that the childhood abuse of these subjects is not as much (or more) associated with violence or conviction for murder as with the development of DID specifically. Moreover, Lewis and colleagues should have carefully assessed for the possibility that some of the murderers might have been malingering (i.e., faking DID; Lilienfeld et al., 1999). Thus, although this study may have been one of the most impressive attempts yet to document abuse independently in people with DID, it was significantly flawed and therefore highly inconclusive.

IF ABUSE HAS OCCURRED, DOES IT PLAY A CAUSAL ROLE IN DID? Let us put the previous controversy about the reality of recovered memories of abuse aside for a moment and assume that severe abuse has occurred in the early childhood backgrounds of many people with DID. How can we determine whether this abuse has played a critical *causal role* in the development of DID (e.g., Piper & Merskey, 2004a)? Unfortunately, many difficulties arise in answering this question. For example, child abuse usually happens in family environments plagued by many other sources of adversity and trauma (such as psychopathology, extreme neglect, and poverty). One or more of these other, correlated sources of adversity could actually be playing the causal role (e.g., Lilienfeld et al., 1999; Nash et al., 1993).

Another difficulty of determining the role of abuse is that people who have experienced child abuse as well as symptoms of DID may be more likely to seek treatment than people with symptoms of DID who did not experience abuse. Thus, the individuals in most studies on the prevalence of child abuse in DID may not be representative of the population of all people who suffer from DID. Finally, childhood abuse has been claimed by some to lead to many different forms of psychopathology including depression, PTSD, eating disorders, somatic symptom disorder, and borderline personality disorder, to name just a few. Perhaps the most we will ever be able to say is that childhood abuse may play a *nonspecific* role for many disorders, with other, more specific factors determining which disorder develops (see Chapters 10 and 12).

Current Perspectives

There are now around 20 studies that have compared the behavior of people diagnosed with DID with the behavior of people who are asked (after appropriate training) to simulate DID (see Boysen & VanBergen, 2014). The findings suggest some important similarities as well as some key differences. Overall, however, they provide somewhat more support for the sociocognitive model than for the trauma model.

One way in which simulators and diagnosed patients differ is that diagnosed patients show more symptoms of DID than simulators do. This, of course, could be related to the quality of training the simulators had. Another potentially more important difference is that, compared to simulators, patients with DID show more cognitive processing problems. Deficits in performance are apparent on tasks involving recognition of previously seen material, as well as on recall and reaction time tasks. However, cognitive problems (compared to healthy controls) are seen in patients with many types of disorders (including anxiety disorders, mood disorders, and schizophrenia). So they could be a result of psychopathology in general rather than DID in particular. We also have no way of knowing whether these cognitive problems resulted from the DID or predated it, perhaps functioning as a preexisting vulnerability factor.

There are also many similarities between simulators and diagnosed patients with DID. Of these, perhaps the most important concerns the transfer of memory across personalities. Interidentity amnesia is a key feature of DID. Most people with DID have at least some identities that seem completely unaware of the existence and experiences of certain other identities. This then raises the question of what happens when information is presented to one identity and the person switches to another identity—one who is not supposed to have any knowledge of the other identity. Does any information transfer from one identity to another? In a recent review Boysen and Van Bergen (2014) describe the results of all available studies to date and conclude that the self-reported amnesia across identities is incomplete. In other words, when information is given to Identity 1 and then the person switches to Identity 2, Identity 2 performs better on the memory task than would be

the case if there were complete amnesia across the two identities. This is true regardless of whether explicit or implicit memory tasks are used. What is also important is that the transfer of information on implicit tasks (which do not require the intentional or conscious processing of information) is similar for diagnosed patients as well as for simulators.

By way of an example, Huntjens and colleagues (2005) had 22 DID patients in Identity 1 learn to reevaluate a neutral word in a positive or negative manner through a simple evaluative conditioning procedure in which neutral words are simply paired with positive or negative words; the neutral words then come to take on positive or negative connotations. When Identity 2 was later asked to emerge, he or she also categorized the formerly neutral word in the same positive or negative manner as learned by Identity 1, showing implicit memory for the reevaluation of the word learned by Identity 1 (although complete subjective amnesia was reported by Identity 2).

What does the lack of evidence of complete amnesia in DID mean for our understanding of the disorder? The fact that simulators and diagnosed patients are similar in this regard might argue against the validity of the DID diagnosis. However, we know little about how the memories of people with DID can or should function. As Boysen and VanBergen (2014) note, in DID memory may be available but not be *subjectively* accessible. Our brains naturally integrate and incorporate new material. But there may be an important difference between what our brains know and what we are aware that we know.

Controversies concerning DID are routinely stated in a dichotomous way: Is DID real or faked? What causes DID—spontaneous social enactment of roles or repeated childhood trauma? Are recovered memories of abuse real or false? If abuse occurs, does it play a primary causal role? Yet dichotomously stated questions encourage oversimplified answers as well as needless divisiveness. Fortunately, theorists on both sides are now softening their positions and acknowledging that multiple different causal pathways are likely to be involved. Advocates of posttraumatic theory are acknowledging that some cases are faked and that some may be inadvertently caused by unskilled therapists in the course of treatment. There is also a growing appreciation that both real and false memories do occur in these patients, combined with a recognition of the critical need for new methods to be developed to help determine which is which (e.g., Gleaves & Williams, 2005; Gleaves et al., 2004). On the other side, advocates of sociocognitive theory have acknowledged that some people with DID may have undergone real abuse, although they believe it occurs far less often, and is less likely to play a real causal role, than the trauma theorists maintain (see Kihlstrom, 2005).

Cultural Factors, Treatments, and Outcomes in Dissociative Disorders

8.10 Describe the cultural factors, treatments, and outcomes in dissociative disorders.

All disorders occur within a cultural context and DID is no exception. In the following sections we discuss the role of culture in DID and also describe some approaches that are used to treat these challenging clinical conditions.

Cultural Factors in Dissociative Disorders

There seems little doubt that the prevalence of dissociative disorders, especially their more dramatic forms such as DID, is influenced by the degree to which such phenomena are accepted or tolerated either as normal or as legitimate mental disorders by the surrounding cultural context. Indeed, in our own society, the acceptance and tolerance of DID as a legitimate disorder have varied tremendously over time.

Many related phenomena, such as spirit possession and dissociative trances, occur frequently in many different parts of the world where the local cultures sanction them (Krippner, 1994; Spiegel et al., 2013). Such experi-

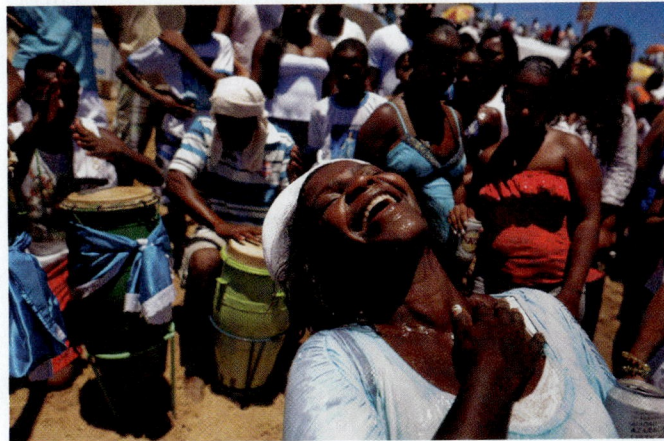

When they occur as part of a religious or spiritual ceremony, possession trances are not pathological. However, when they occur spontaneously and cause distress, possession states are regarded in *DSM-5* as a cultural variant of dissociative identity disorder.

ences are not necessarily problematic when they are volitional, transient, and occur as a normal part of religious or spiritual practices. However, when they are involuntary and cause distress, possession states are considered to be pathological.

The features of pathological possession are very similar to DID. They include distinct changes in identity as well as full or partial amnesia for the event. In pathological possession, however, the other identity is not experienced as another internal personality state but as an external spirit, power, or deity. The inclusion of pathological possession into the diagnostic criteria for DID in *DSM-5* has made the diagnosis more applicable to people from a wide range of cultural backgrounds. The inclusion of pathological possession also acknowledges that DID can present in two different forms: a possession form and a nonpossession form. In other words, how the disorder presents may be very much determined by cultural factors (Spiegel et al., 2013).

Understanding how pathological possession is treated by indigenous healers may also provide new perspectives that could be valuable overall. Interestingly, treatments by indigenous healers and therapists operating within Western culture have many similarities. Both, for example, emphasize addressing different aspects of the person's identities, allowing each to have a voice through which that identity's point of view and distress can be clarified. In contrast, however, in the majority of cases, culturally sanctioned attempts to remove or exorcise the alternate identity typically lead to poor outcomes.

There are also cross-cultural variants on dissociative disorders, such as *amok*, which is often thought of as a rage disorder. Amok occurs when a dissociative episode leads to violent, aggressive, or homicidal behavior directed at other people and objects. It occurs mostly in men and is often precipitated by a perceived slight or insult. The person often has ideas of persecution, anger, and amnesia, often followed by a period of exhaustion and depression. Amok occurs in places such as Malaysia, Laos, the Philippines, Papua New Guinea, Puerto Rico, and among Navajo Indians.

Treatment and Outcomes in Dissociative Disorders

Unfortunately, virtually no systematic, controlled research has been conducted on treatment of depersonalization disorder and dissociative amnesia. The absence of randomized controlled trials means that very little is known about how to treat these two disorders successfully. Numerous case histories, sometimes presented in small sets of cases, are available, but without control groups who are assessed at the same time or who receive nonspecific treatments, it is impossible to know the effectiveness of the varied treatments that have been attempted (Kihlstrom, 2005).

Watch   Randomized Controlled Trial

In general, depersonalization/derealization disorder may be fairly resistant to treatment, although treatment may be useful for associated problems such as anxiety and depressive disorders. Some think that hypnosis, including training in self-hypnosis techniques, may be useful because patients with depersonalization disorder can learn to dissociate and then "reassociate," thereby gaining some sense of control over their depersonalization and derealization experiences (Maldonado & Spiegel, 2007; Maldonado et al., 2002). Many types of antidepressant, antianxiety, and antipsychotic drugs have also been tried and some have had modest effects. However, one randomized controlled study showed no difference between treatment with Prozac versus with placebo (Simeon et al., 2004). A recent treatment showing some promise for the treatment of dissociative disorders involves administering rTMS (repetitive transcranial magnetic stimulation) to the temporoparietal junction, an area of the brain highly involved in the experience of a unified self and body (Mantovani et al., 2011). After 3 weeks of treatment, half of the subjects showed significant reductions in depersonalization, with nonresponders showing symptom reduction after an additional 3 weeks of treatment.

In dissociative amnesia, it is important for the person to be in a safe environment, and simply removing her or him from what he or she perceives as a threatening situation sometimes allows for spontaneous recovery of memory. Hypnosis, as well as drugs such as benzodiazepines, barbiturates, sodium pentobarbital, and sodium amobarbital, is often used to facilitate recall of repressed and dissociated memories (Maldonado & Spiegel, 2007; Maldonado et al., 2002). After memories are recalled, it is important for the patient to work through the memories with the therapist so that the experiences can be reframed in new ways. However, unless the memories can be independently corroborated, they should not be taken at their face value (Kihlstrom, 2005).

For people diagnosed with DID, most current therapeutic approaches are based on the assumption of posttraumatic theory that the disorder was caused by abuse (Kihlstrom, 2005). Most therapists set integration of the previously separate alters, together with their collective merging into the host personality, as the ultimate goal of treatment (e.g., Maldonado & Spiegel, 2007). There is often considerable resistance to this process by patients with DID, who consider dissociation as a protective device (e.g., "I knew my father could get some of me, but he couldn't get all of me"; Maldonado & Spiegel, 2007, p. 781). If successful integration occurs, the patient eventually develops a unified personality, although it is not uncommon for only partial integration to be achieved. But it is also very important to assess whether improvement in other symptoms of DID and associated disorders has occurred. Indeed, it seems that treatment is more likely to produce symptom improvement, as well as associated improvements in functioning, than to achieve full and stable integration of the different alter identities (Maldonado & Spiegel, 2007; Maldonado et al., 2002).

Typically the treatment for DID is psychodynamic and insight oriented, focused on uncovering and working through the trauma and other conflicts that are thought to have led to the disorder (Kihlstrom, 2005). One of the primary techniques used in most treatments of DID is hypnosis (e.g., Kluft, 1993; Maldonado & Spiegel, 2007; Maldonado et al., 2002). Most patients with DID are hypnotizable and when hypnotized are able to recover past unconscious and frequently traumatic memories, often from childhood. Then these memories can be processed, and the patient can become aware that the dangers once present are no longer there. (One problem here is that such patients are suggestible under hypnosis, so much of what is recalled may not be accurate; see Kihlstrom, 2005; Loftus & Davis, 2006). Through the use of hypnosis, therapists are often able to make contact with different identities and reestablish connections between distinct, seemingly separate identity states. An important goal is to integrate the personalities into one identity that is better able to cope with current stressors. Clearly, successful negotiation of this critical phase of treatment requires therapeutic skills of the highest order; that is, the therapist must be strongly committed as well as professionally competent. Regrettably, this is not always the case.

Most reports in the literature are treatment summaries of single cases. Reports of successful cases should always be considered with caution, especially given the large bias in favor of publishing positive rather than negative results. Treatment outcome data for large groups of patients with DID are seldom reported and control groups are lacking. Nonetheless, it is clear that DID does not spontaneously remit simply with the passage of time, or if a therapist chooses to ignore DID-related issues (Kluft, 1999; Maldonado et al., 2002). For example, Ellason and Ross (1997) reported on a 2-year postdischarge follow-up of patients with DID who were originally treated in a specialized inpatient unit. Of the original 135 patients,

54 were located and systematically assessed. All of them, especially those who had achieved full integration, generally showed marked improvements in various aspects of their lives. However, only 12 of the 54 had achieved full integration of their identities. Such results are encouraging, although we must wonder about the clinical status of the 81 "lost" patients who may likely have done less well. Another 10-year follow-up study reported similar results in a smaller sample of 25 patients with DID who received treatment. Only 12 were located 10 years later; of these, 6 had achieved full integration, but 2 of those had partially relapsed (Coons & Bowman, 2001). In general, it has been

found that (1) for treatment to be successful, it must be prolonged, often lasting many years, and (2) the more severe the case, the longer that treatment is needed (Maldonado & Spiegel, 2007; Maldonado et al., 2002).

in review

- Explain how cultural factors might shape the form that dissociative conditions take in different parts of the world.
- How are dissociative disorders typically treated? How effective are these approaches?

Unresolved Issues

DID and the Reality of "Recovered Memories"

Posttraumatic theorists assert that the major causal factor in the development of DID is childhood abuse, particularly sexual abuse. In many cases, these memories of abuse are "recovered" during therapy, meaning that the person was unaware of these experiences before entering therapy. This has raised questions about the validity or accuracy of recovered memories of abuse and led to intense and often bitter debate (see Loftus & Davis, 2006, for a review).

Over time, these controversies have moved beyond professional debate and have become major public issues, leading to countless legal proceedings. For example, patients with DID who have recovered memories of abuse have sued their parents for having inflicted abuse. Ironically, therapists and institutions have also been sued for implanting memories of abuse in patients who later came to believe abuse had not actually occurred. An international support organization—the False Memory Syndrome Foundation—was created by some parents who asserted they had been falsely accused. In some instances, parents have sued therapists for damages, alleging that the therapists induced false memories of parental abuse in their children. Within such a climate of suspicion, accusation, litigation, and unrelenting hostility, many families have been torn apart.

Whether DID originates in childhood abuse and whether recovered memories of abuse are accurate are basically separate issues. Nonetheless, they have tended to become fused in the course of the debate. Hence, those who doubt the validity of memories of abuse are also likely to regard the phenomenon of DID as stemming from the social enactment of roles encouraged or induced—like the memories of abuse themselves—by misguided therapy (e.g., see Bjorklund, 2000; Lilienfeld et al., 1999; Lynn et al., 2004; Piper & Merskey, 2004a, 2004b). Believers, on the other hand, have usually taken both DID and the idea that abuse is its cause to be established beyond doubt (e.g., see Gleaves, 1996; Gleaves et al., 2001; Ross, 1997, 1999).

Much of the controversy about the validity of recovered memories is rooted in disagreements about the nature, reliability, and malleability of human autobiographical memory. With some exceptions, evidence for childhood abuse as a cause of DID is restricted to the "recovered memories" (memories not originally accessible) of adults being treated for dissociative experiences. Believers argue that before treatment such memories had been "repressed" because of their traumatic nature or had been available only to certain alter identities that the host identity was generally not aware of. Treatment, according to this view of believers, dismantles the repressive defense and thus makes available to awareness an essentially accurate memory recording of the past abuse.

Disbelievers counter with several scientifically well-supported arguments. For example, scientific evidence in support of the repression concept is quite weak (e.g., Kihlstrom, 2005; Loftus & Davis, 2006; Piper, 1998). In many alleged cases of repression, the event may have been lost to memory in the course of ordinary forgetting rather than repression, or it may have occurred in the first 3 to 4 years of life, before memories can be recorded for retrieval in adulthood. In many other cases, evidence for repression has been claimed in studies where people may simply have failed to report a previously remembered event, often because they were never asked or were reluctant to disclose such very personal information (Kihlstrom, 2005; Loftus & Davis, 2006; Pope et al., 1998).

Even if memories can be repressed, there are very serious questions about the accuracy of recovered memories. Human memory does not operate in a computer-like manner, retrieving with perfect accuracy a record of information previously stored and then repressed. Rather, human memory is malleable, constructive, and very much subject to modification on the basis of events happening after any original memory trace is established (Loftus & Bernstein, 2005; Loftus & Davis, 2006; Schacter et al., 2000).

Indeed, research shows that in certain circumstances, people are sometimes very prone to the development of false memories (see Wade et al., 2007, for a review). Studies have shown that when healthy adults are asked to imagine repeatedly events that they were sure had not happened to them as children, they later increased their estimate of how likely it was that these events *had actually happened* to them (e.g., Tsai et al., 2000). Moreover, even in a relatively short time frame, adult research subjects sometimes come to believe they have performed somewhat strange acts (such as kissing a magnifying glass), as well as common acts (such as flipping a coin), after simply having imagined they had engaged in these acts several times 2 weeks earlier (Thomas & Loftus, 2002). These and other studies clearly show that when we repeatedly imagine experiencing certain events (even somewhat bizarre ones) this can lead us to have false memories of events that never happened (Loftus & Bernstein, 2005; Loftus & Davis, 2006).

One fascinating study compared a group of people who had continuous memories of childhood abuse with two groups who had recovered memories of abuse. In one of the latter groups the memories had been recovered during therapy; in the other group the memories had been recovered outside of the context of therapy. The researchers then attempted to corroborate these recovered memories. They found corroborative evidence for over half of those who had recovered memories outside of therapy. But for those who recovered their memories during therapy, no corroborating evidence was found (Geraerts et al., 2007).

McNally and Geraerts (2009) have offered a different perspective on recovered memories, one that attempts to bridge the gap between the conviction that repression underlies recovered memories and the alternate conviction that all recovered memories are false. Their third perspective suggests that some recovered memories are genuine but were never actually repressed. Instead, some abuse victims may simply not have thought about their abuse for a long period of time, have been deliberately attempting to forget the abuse (suppression rather than repression), or may have forgotten prior instances when they did recall the abuse, resulting in the false impression that a recently surfaced memory had been repressed for years. In other words, we may be getting closer to being able to reconcile some widely disparate perspectives about trauma and memory that have been so contentious for so long.

Summary

8.1   List four disorders included in the *DSM-5* category of somatic symptom and related disorders.

- Somatic symptom disorder and related disorders lie at the interface of abnormal psychology and medicine. These are disorders in which psychological problems are manifested in physical symptoms. In response to the symptoms the person also experiences abnormal thoughts, feelings, and behaviors.

- Included in the category of somatic symptom and related disorders are somatic symptom disorder, illness anxiety disorder, conversion disorder, and factitious disorder.

8.2   Explain the causes of and treatments for somatic symptom disorder.

- Somatic symptom disorder occurs in individuals who have multiple somatic complaints lasting at least 6 months. Even if the symptoms do not seem to have a medical explanation, the person's suffering is regarded as authentic.

- The psychoanalytic perspective on somatic symptom disorder views physical symptoms as resulting from unresolved or unacceptable unconscious conflicts. Instead of being expressed directly, psychic energy is channeled into physical problems, which are more socially acceptable.

- A more current perspective is cognitive-behavioral. According to this formulation, people with somatic symptom disorder are hypervigilant, focusing a great deal of attention on their bodies and on bodily changes. They also have a tendency to label bodily *sensations* as somatic *symptoms*, attributing physical sensations to illness. This is combined with excessive worry about what the symptoms mean, leading to catastrophizing cognitions. Because of their worries, people become very distressed and seek medical attention for their perceived physical problems.

- Cognitive-behavioral therapy is helpful for patients with somatic symptom disorder and related disorders. Cognitive aspects of the treatment focus on assessing beliefs about illness and modifying misinterpretations of bodily sensations. Behavioral techniques might include having the patient induce innocuous symptoms by intentionally focusing on parts of the body to learn the role that selective perception and hypervigilance play. Patients might also be directed to engage in response prevention and told not to check their bodies as they usually do.

- In addition to CBT, medical management may provide some further benefits. Having one physician who integrates the patient's care, sees the patient regularly, and accepts all symptoms as valid, but who also avoids unnecessary diagnostic testing can be helpful in some cases.

- For somatic symptom disorder that involves pain, treatment generally includes relaxation training, support and validation that the pain is real, scheduling of daily activities, cognitive restructuring, and reinforcement of "no-pain" behaviors. Antidepressant medications are also sometimes used.

8.3 Identify the key difference between illness anxiety disorder and somatic symptom disorder.

Illness anxiety disorder and somatic symptom disorder are similar in many ways. However, in somatic symptom disorder symptoms must be present. In contrast, illness anxiety disorder is a diagnosis that can be used for individuals who are very anxious about having an illness even though they may have no symptoms.

8.4 Summarize the clinical features of conversion disorder, also noting its prevalence, causes, and treatment.

- Conversion disorder involves patterns of symptoms or deficits (such as loss of vision or paralysis) that affect sensory or voluntary motor functions. Although the clinical problem suggests a medical or neurological condition, medical examination reveals no physical basis for the symptoms.

- Approximately 20 percent of patients with conversion disorder show very little of the anxiety or concern that might be expected given their symptoms. This is known as *la belle indifférence.*

- Conversion disorders are found in approximately 5 percent of people treated at neurology clinics. The prevalence in the general population is thought to be very low (no more than 0.005 percent), although the exact prevalence is unknown. Conversion disorders are thought to develop in response to extreme stress that the person is unable to cope with. They are more prevalent in women, and most commonly occur between early adolescence and early adulthood. The physical problems often resolve if the stressor is removed and the person receives support and encouragement, although recurrence is quite typical.

8.5 Explain the difference between factitious disorder and malingering.

- Individuals with factitious disorder intentionally produce medical or psychological symptoms (or both). They do this in the absence of external rewards in order to take on an illness role.

- Malingering involves the intentional production of symptoms or the exaggeration of symptoms. This is motivated by external factors such as a wish to claim insurance money, avoid work or military service, or to get leniency in a criminal prosecution.

8.6 List three *DSM-5* dissociative disorders.

- Dissociative disorders occur when the processes that normally regulate awareness and the multichannel capacities of the mind apparently become disorganized, leading to various anomalies of consciousness and personal identity.

- Three dissociative disorders included in *DSM-5* are depersonalization/derealization, dissociative amnesia, and dissociative identity disorder.

8.7 Summarize the clinical features of depersonalization/derealization disorder.

- Depersonalization/derealization disorder occurs in people who experience persistent and recurrent episodes of derealization (losing one's sense of reality of the outside world) and/or depersonalization (losing one's sense of oneself and one's own reality). Despite this, reality testing overall remains intact and the person has good awareness of what is happening to her or him.

- In *DSM-IV*, derealization and depersonalization were treated as two distinct conditions. In *DSM-5* they have been combined.

- The lifetime prevalence of depersonalization/derealization disorder is 1 to 2 percent. Equal numbers of males and females are affected. The disorder can start in childhood. However, the typical age of onset is around age 16 with only a minority of people over age 25 developing the disorder.

- There are no established and effective treatments for depersonalization/derealization disorder. The disorder usually has a fairly chronic course with little or no fluctuation in intensity. Comorbid conditions include mood or anxiety disorders. Rates of avoidant, borderline, and obsessive-compulsive personality disorders are also higher in people with depersonalization and derealization experiences.

8.8 Describe the clinical features of dissociative amnesia.

- Dissociative amnesia involves an inability to recall previously stored information that cannot be accounted for by ordinary forgetting. It is thought to be a reaction to extremely stressful circumstances. The memory loss is primarily for episodic or autobiographical memory. Other aspects of memory generally remain intact.

- In rare cases a person may retreat from real-life problems by going into an amnesic state called a dissociative fugue, in which a person is not only amnesic for some or all aspects of his or her past but also departs from home surroundings. Dissociative fugue is a subtype of dissociative amnesia.

8.9 Describe the clinical features of dissociative identity disorder and explain why this disorder is so controversial.

- In dissociative identity disorder, the person manifests at least two or more distinct identities that alternate in some way in taking control of behavior. Alter identities may differ in many ways from the host identity.

- DID is controversial for many reasons. Not everyone believes it is a real disorder. Some famous cases of DID have been faked and the disorder has been used as a defense by people accused of serious crimes. Currently, there is no way of detecting "true" DID from simulated DID. Of course, this does not mean we can conclude that genuine cases of DID do not exist.

- There is also controversy about how DID develops. According to posttraumatic theory, DID develops as a result of severe childhood trauma. Sociocultural theory, in contrast, maintains that the disorder gets shaped by clinicians who inadvertently encourage patients to adopt multiple different roles. These then become reinforced with increased attention.

8.10 Describe the cultural factors, treatments, and outcomes in dissociative disorders.

- By adding pathological possession to the diagnostic criteria for DID, *DSM-5* now acknowledges the role of cultural factors more explicitly. It is recognized that culture may shape how DID presents clinically. Including possession and nonpossession forms of DID makes the diagnosis more culturally inclusive. Other culturally influenced conditions, such as amok, also have a dissociative component.

- The treatment for DID is typically psychodynamic and insight oriented. Hypnosis is also often used. The focus is on uncovering and working through the trauma and other conflicts that are thought to have led to the disorder. Little is known about how to treat derealization/depersonalization disorders. In the case of dissociative amnesia, removing the person from what he or she perceives as a threatening situation sometimes allows for spontaneous recovery of memory.

Key Terms

alter identities, p. 290
conversion disorder, p. 276
depersonalization, p. 285
depersonalization/derealization
   disorder, p. 285
derealization, p. 285
dissociation, p. 283
dissociative amnesia, p. 287
dissociative disorders, p. 270

dissociative fugue, p. 287
dissociative identity
   disorder (DID), p. 290
factitious disorder, p. 281
factitious disorder imposed on
   another, p. 282
host identity, p. 290
hysteria, p. 276
implicit memory, p. 283

implicit perception, p. 283
malingering, p. 282
posttraumatic theory (of DID), p. 293
primary gain, p. 279
secondary gain, p. 279
sociocognitive theory (of DID), p. 294
soma, p. 270
somatic symptom disorder, p. 270
somatoform disorders, p. 270

Chapter 9
Eating Disorders and Obesity

Learning Objectives

9.1 Identify the clinical aspects of eating disorders.

9.2 Explain the risk and causal factors in eating disorders.

9.3 Discuss how eating disorders are treated.

9.4 Define obesity and explain why it is a worldwide problem.

9.5 Describe who is most at risk for obesity

9.6 Explain current treatments for obesity.

Weighing a mere 88 pounds on her 5-foot-8 frame, Brazilian model Ana Carolina Reston succumbed to a generalized infection on November 15, 2006, while battling anorexia nervosa. She was 21 years old. Having modeled for Armani and Versace and in numerous countries around the world, Ana Carolina was initially hospitalized for kidney failure. Ana Carolina's anorexia nervosa apparently began after she was criticized for being "too fat" during a casting call in China. At the height of her illness her diet consisted only of tomatoes and apples. Her death highlights the health risks associated with eating disorders.

This model's struggles with anorexia nervosa also reveal the extent to which ideals of beauty are intertwined with thinness. Looking good often means being slim, especially for those in the public eye. Not surprisingly, many celebrities, including Nicole Richie, Mary-Kate Olsen, Victoria Beckham, and the late Princess Diana, have also struggled with eating disorders.

In the same year that Ana Carolina Reston died, model Luisel Ramos from Uruguay, who was also starving herself, collapsed during a fashion show and died of heart failure. She was 5 feet 9 inches and weighed 97 pounds. Her death heralded the beginning of efforts by the fashion industry to address the situation. The organizers of the Madrid Fashion Week decided to ban models who did not have a body mass index (a measure of a person's weight relative to height) in the healthy range. In 2010, Victoria Beckham reportedly deemed 23 models "too skinny" and refused to have them be part of her New York Fashion Week runway show. And in 2015 in France, a new law was passed banning excessively thin models.

Those who hire them are now subject to heavy fines and even jail. Websites that promote excessive thinness or that encourage restricted eating will also experience penalties. What do you think? Should models be required to get a certificate from their doctors stating that they are not malnourished (this is now required in Israel) before being allowed on the catwalks? Should we expect the fashion industry to police itself, or should legislation be involved, as in France? Are you ready to see healthier-looking models in the pages of *Vogue*, or does ultrathin still mean ultrafashionable to you?

According to the *DSM-5* (APA, 2013), **eating disorders** are characterized by a persistent disturbance in eating behavior. In this chapter we focus on three of the most important adult eating disorders in *DSM-5*. We also examine obesity. Obesity is not considered to be an eating disorder or a psychiatric condition in the *DSM*; however, its prevalence is rising at an alarming rate. Obesity also accounts for more morbidity and mortality than all other eating disorders combined. Because obesity clearly involves disordered eating patterns, we discuss it in detail in this chapter.

Clinical Aspects of Eating Disorders

9.1 Identify the clinical aspects of eating disorders.

Food is essential for our existence. But for many people with adequate access to food, eating is not a straightforward and simple activity. People with eating disorders show disturbed patterns of eating that impair their health or ability to function well. In the sections that follow we describe three *DSM-5* eating disorders—anorexia nervosa, bulimia nervosa, and binge-eating disorder—in some detail.

Anorexia Nervosa

The term *anorexia nervosa* literally means "lack of appetite induced by nervousness." This definition is something of a misnomer, however, as a lack of appetite is neither the core difficulty nor necessarily even true. At the heart of **anorexia nervosa** is a pursuit of thinness that is relentless and that involves behaviors that result in a significantly low body weight. The *DSM-5*

Model Ana Carolina Reston weighed just 88 pounds when she died from medical complications of anorexia nervosa.

The late Princess Diana's courage in discussing her own struggles with bulimia nervosa helped many other individuals with the same problem to seek treatment.

criteria for anorexia nervosa are shown in the *DSM* criteria box. An important change from *DSM-IV* to *DSM-5* is that in *DSM-5* amenorrhea (cessation of menstruation) is no longer required for a person to be given the diagnosis. Studies have suggested that women who continue to menstruate but meet all the other diagnostic criteria for anorexia nervosa are very similar psychologically to women who have amenorrhea and have ceased menstruating (Attia & Roberto, 2009). Amenorrhea is also not a criterion that can be used for males, nor can it be assessed in prepubescent girls or in women who use hormonal contraceptives.

Watch   Natasha: Anorexia

Although we may think of anorexia nervosa as a modern problem, it is centuries old. Descriptions of extreme fasting that were probably signs of anorexia nervosa can be found in early religious literature (Vandereycken, 2002). The first known medical account of anorexia nervosa, however, was published in 1689 by Richard Morton (see Silverman, 1997, for a good general historical overview). Morton described two patients, an 18-year-old girl and a 16-year-old boy, who suffered from a "nervous consumption" that resulted in wasting of body tissue. The female patient eventually died because she refused treatment.

The disorder did not receive its current name until 1873, when Charles Lasègue in Paris and Sir William Gull in London independently described the clinical syndrome. In his last publication on the condition, Gull (1888) described a 14-year-old girl who began "without apparent cause, to evince a repugnance to food; and soon afterwards declined to take any whatever, except half a cup of tea or coffee." After being prescribed to eat light food every few hours, the patient made a good recovery. Gull's illustrations of the patient before and after treatment appear in Figure 9.1.

Even though they may look painfully thin or even emaciated, many patients with anorexia nervosa deny having any problem. Indeed, they may come to feel fulfilled by their weight loss. Despite this quiet satisfaction, however, they may feel ambivalent about their weight. Efforts are often made to conceal their thinness by wearing baggy clothes or carrying hidden bulky objects so that they will

Figure 9.1 Gull's patient with anorexia nervosa. (A) Before treatment. (B) After treatment.

(Adapted from Gull, W. (1888). Anorexia nervosa. *Lancet*, pp. i, 516–517.)

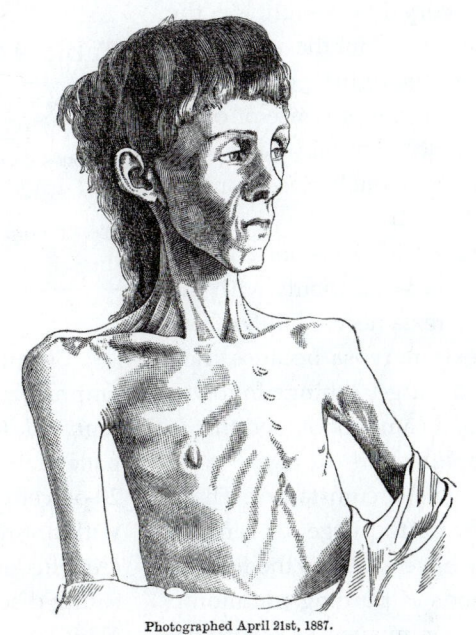

Photographed April 21st, 1887.

(A)

Photographed June 14th, 1887.

(B)

weigh more when measured by others. Patients with anorexia nervosa may even resort to drinking large amounts of water to increase their weight temporarily.

Patients with anorexia nervosa may be emaciated while still denying that they have any problems with their weight. They will go to great lengths to conceal their thinness by wearing baggy clothes, or by drinking massive amounts of water prior to being weighed (in a hospital setting, for instance).

There are two types of anorexia nervosa: the restricting type and the binge-eating/purging type. The central difference between these two subtypes concerns the way in which patients maintain their very low weight. In the restricting type, every effort is made to limit the quantity of food consumed. Caloric intake is tightly controlled. Patients often try to avoid eating in the presence of other people. When they are at the table, they may eat excessively slowly, cut their food into very small pieces, or dispose of food secretly (Beaumont, 2002).

The relentless restriction of food intake is not possible for all patients with anorexia nervosa. Patients with the binge-eating/purging type of anorexia nervosa differ from patients with restricting anorexia nervosa because they either binge, purge, or binge and purge. A **binge** involves an out-of-control consumption of an amount of food that is far greater than what most people would eat in the same amount of time and under the same circumstances. These binges may be followed by efforts to **purge**, or remove from their bodies, the food they have eaten, as the following case example shows. Methods of purging commonly include self-induced vomiting or misuse of laxatives, diuretics, and enemas. Other compensatory behaviors that do not involve purging are excessive exercise or fasting. Even purging strategies, however, do not prevent the absorption of all calories from food.

Eisha

Eisha was 22 years old and in her fourth year of graduate study at a university in the United States when she first sought treatment. Her eating disorder, however, had begun many years earlier. When she was 14 and at school in her home country of India, she reported being bullied by her classmates who told her she looked fat in her new school dress. After this incident, she started to feel that she had become fat and she began to starve herself to lose weight. By the time she was 18 she was in a physically weak state. She ate only once a day. The rest of the time she exercised, and refused all other requests to eat food. Occasionally, her restraint would break down and she would binge eat. After each binge-eating episode she would starve herself for 3 or 4 days to compensate. Eventually she began to purge routinely after eating any food to make sure she did not gain any weight. She believed that "to be beautiful you need to be thin" and that eating was bad. After eating, she would tell herself "you are good for nothing." (Based on Roy, 2014.)

Indicative of the distorted values of patients with eating disorders (see Table 9.1 for personal comments that provide examples of this), those with the restricting type of anorexia nervosa are often greatly admired by others with eating disorders. One patient reported that she had not been "successful" in her anorexia nervosa because of her failure to reach an extremely low weight. Her belief was that the hallmark of a truly successful person with anorexia nervosa was death from starvation, and that patients who were able to accomplish this should somehow be revered (see Bulik & Kendler, 2000).

Table 9.1 Distorted Thinking in Anorexia Nervosa

"I have a rule when I weigh myself. If I've gained then I starve the rest of the day. But if I've lost, then I starve too."
"Bones define who we really are, let them show."
"An imperfect body reflects an imperfect person."
"Anorexia is not a self-inflicted disease, it's a self-controlled lifestyle."
"It's not deprivation, it's liberation."

Because the artistic standards of their profession emphasize a slender physique, dancers are at especially high risk for eating disorders. This is particularly true for ballet dancers. A recent study has estimated that just under 20 percent of ballet students suffer from an eating disorder, with anorexia nervosa being the most common problem (Arcelus et al., 2014). Gelsey Kirkland, who developed an eating disorder while she was a premier ballerina with the New York City Ballet, described the existence of a "concentration camp aesthetic" within the company. This was no doubt fostered by the famous choreographer George Balanchine, who, as described by Kirkland in her autobiography, tapped her on the ribs and sternum after one event and exhorted that he "must see the bones" (Kirkland, 1986, pp. 55–56).

Ballet dancers are at very high risk for developing eating disorders. According to Gelsey Kirkland, once the premier ballerina at the New York City Ballet, the value placed on being thin can create a "concentration camp aesthetic" supported and encouraged by the dance company.

Bulimia Nervosa

Bulimia nervosa is characterized by uncontrollable binge eating and efforts to prevent resulting weight gain by using inappropriate behaviors such as self-induced vomiting and excessive exercise. Bulimia nervosa was recognized as a psychiatric syndrome relatively recently. The British psychiatrist G. F. M. Russell (1997) proposed the term in 1979,

and it was adopted into the *DSM* in 1987. The word *bulimia* comes from the Greek *bous* (which means "ox"), and *limos* ("hunger"). It is meant to denote a hunger of such proportions that the person "could eat an ox."

The *DSM-5* criteria for bulimia nervosa are shown in the *DSM* box. Compared to *DSM-IV*, the diagnostic criteria for bulimia nervosa have been relaxed. Binge eating and purging now have to occur on average once a week (instead of twice a week) over a 3-month period. This change was made after research showed that people with subthreshold bulimia nervosa were remarkably similar to those who had the full syndrome (Eddy, Doyle, et al., 2008; Fairburn et al., 2007).

The clinical picture of the binge-eating/purging type of anorexia nervosa has much in common with bulimia nervosa. Indeed, some researchers have argued that the bulimic type of anorexia nervosa should really be considered another form of bulimia nervosa. The difference between a person with bulimia nervosa and a person with the binge-eating/purging type of anorexia nervosa is weight. By definition, the person with anorexia nervosa is severely underweight. This is not true of the person with bulimia nervosa. Consequently, if the person who binges or purges also meets criteria for anorexia nervosa, the diagnosis is anorexia nervosa (binge-eating/purging type) and not bulimia nervosa. In other words, the anorexia nervosa diagnosis "trumps" the bulimia nervosa diagnosis. This is because there is a far greater mortality rate associated with anorexia nervosa than with bulimia nervosa. Recognizing this, the *DSM* requires that the more severe form of eating pathology take precedence diagnostically.

People with anorexia nervosa and bulimia nervosa share a common preoccupation with their shape and their weight. However, unlike patients with anorexia nervosa, those with bulimia nervosa are typically of normal weight or sometimes even slightly overweight. Bulimia typically

DSM-5 *Criteria for. . .*

Bulimia Nervosa

A. Recurrent episodes of binge eating. An episode of binge eating is characterized by both of the following:

1. Eating, in a discrete period of time (e.g., within any 2-hour period), an amount of food that is definitely larger than what most individuals would eat in a similar period of time under similar circumstances.

2. A sense of lack of control over eating during the episode (e.g., a feeling that one cannot stop eating or control what or how much one is eating).

B. Recurrent inappropriate compensatory behaviors in order to prevent weight gain, such as self-induced vomiting; misuse of

laxatives, diuretics, or other medications; fasting; or excessive exercise.

C. The binge eating and inappropriate compensatory behaviors both occur, on average, at least once a week for 3 months.

D. Self-evaluation is unduly influenced by body shape and weight.

E. The disturbance does not occur exclusively during episodes of anorexia nervosa.

Source: Reprinted with permission from the *Diagnostic and Statistical Manual of Mental Disorders*, Fifth Edition (Copyright 2013). American Psychiatric Association.

begins with restricted eating motivated by the desire to be slender. During these early stages, the person diets and eats low-calorie foods. Over time, however, the early resolve to restrict gradually erodes, and the person starts to eat "forbidden foods" such as potato chips, pizza, cake, ice cream, and chocolate. Of course, some patients binge on whatever food is available, including such things as raw cookie dough. During an average binge, someone with bulimia nervosa may consume as many as 4,800 calories (Johnson et al., 1982). After the binge, in an effort to manage the breakdown of self-control, the person begins to vomit, fast, exercise excessively, or abuse laxatives. This pattern then persists because, even though those with bulimia nervosa are disgusted by their behavior, the purging alleviates the fear of gaining weight that comes from eating.

Whereas people with anorexia nervosa often deny the seriousness of their disorder and are surprised by the shock and concern with which others view their emaciated conditions, those with bulimia nervosa are often preoccupied with shame, guilt, and self-deprecation. They make efforts to conceal their behavior as they struggle (often unsuccessfully) to master their urges to binge. The case described next depicts a typical pattern.

Catherine: Distressed by Her Weight

Catherine is 20 years old. Catherine has been concerned about her weight and shape for several years. As a teenager she felt plump and was frequently on a diet, even though she was within the normal weight range for her age and height. As she became older, these concerns became more serious. She severely restricted her food intake and started punishing exercise regimens. At one stage she became significantly underweight. Medical help led to weight gain, which was quickly followed by more dieting and, for the first time, she started binge eating. Distressed by the increase in her weight and by increasingly frequent binge eating, Catherine began vomiting in a desperate attempt to lose weight.

Over the past 6 months Catherine has skipped breakfast and lunch, eaten a normal evening meal with her family, but gone on to binge eat in the late evening usually two or three times a week. She binges in response to feeling upset and worried. In a recent typical binge she ate four slices of toast with butter and jam, six packets of potato chips, three large bars of chocolate, half a box of cereal, and a large bowl of ice cream. She had been feeling rejected by a friend. Catherine drinks large quantities of water to help her induce vomiting after binging. More recently she has started to take 30 to 40 laxatives, as well as vomiting. She has a strenuous exercise regime, including 500 daily sit-ups and an aerobic workout. Food is divided rigidly into good and bad categories; food in the bad category (such as cookies, chocolate, and cheese) is not allowed.

Catherine has become increasingly self-conscious. She refuses to weigh herself, has given up swimming (she used to swim on her school team), and if she goes shopping she will not try on clothes unless she has privacy. Catherine dislikes her body. She is preoccupied with her shape and reports that a little voice in her head constantly says, "You're fat and ugly, I can't stand the way you look." Catherine worries that her friends will think less of her if she does not lose weight (when out with friends she avoids eating and sucks her tummy in to the point of pain in order to appear thinner). She feels very bad about herself if she thinks she has gained weight. (Adapted from Cooper, Todd, & Wells (2000). *Bulimia Nervosa: A Cognitive Therapy Programme.* London: Jessica Kingsley Publishers.)

Binge-Eating Disorder

A new addition to *DSM-5* is the diagnosis of **binge-eating disorder (BED)**. Previously, in *DSM-IV*, binge eating was given provisional status. This encouraged researchers to study it. Research has now supported the idea that BED is a distinct clinical syndrome (Wonderlich et al., 2009). It has therefore entered the *DSM* as a new formal diagnosis.

Watch   Stacy: Binge-Eating Disorder

Although BED has some clinical features in common with bulimia nervosa, there is an important difference.

Competitive eating contests, such as the hot dog eating contest that is held every year in Coney Island, New York, attract many spectators. During a 10-minute time span, some competitors are able to eat 60 or more hot dogs. Do you think this is a healthy sport? What messages does it send about food? In what ways is competitive eating different from binge-eating disorder?

DSM-5 *Criteria for. . .*

Binge-Eating Disorder

A. Recurrent episodes of binge eating. An episode of binge eating is characterized by both of the following:

 1. Eating, in a discrete period of time (e.g., within any 2-hour period), an amount of food that is definitely larger than what most people would eat in a similar period of time under similar circumstances.

 2. A sense of lack of control over eating during the episode (e.g., a feeling that one cannot stop eating or control what or how much one is eating).

B. The binge-eating episodes are associated with three (or more) of the following:

 1. Eating much more rapidly than normal.
 2. Eating until feeling uncomfortably full.
 3. Eating large amounts of food when not feeling physically hungry.

 4. Eating alone because of feeling embarrassed by how much one is eating.

 5. Feeling disgusted with oneself, depressed, or very guilty afterward.

C. Marked distress regarding binge eating is present.

D. The binge eating occurs, on average, at least once a week for 3 months.

E. The binge eating is not associated with the recurrent use of inappropriate compensatory behavior as in bulimia nervosa and does not occur exclusively during the course of bulimia nervosa or anorexia nervosa.

Source: Reprinted with permission from the *Diagnostic and Statistical Manual of Mental Disorders*, Fifth Edition (Copyright 2013). American Psychiatric Association.

After a binge the person with BED does not engage in any form of inappropriate "compensatory" behavior such as purging, using laxatives, or even exercising to limit weight gain. (Table 9.2 summarizes the similarities and differences between different types of eating disorders.) There is also much less dietary restraint in BED than is typical of either bulimia nervosa or anorexia nervosa (Wilfley et al., 2000). A typical binge averages around 1,900 calories (Bartholme et al., 2006). Not surprisingly, binge eating disorder is associated with being overweight or even obese (Hudson et al., 2007; Pike et al., 2001), although, as with bulimia nervosa, weight is not a factor involved in making the diagnosis. The case of Jenna provides an example. Interestingly, individuals with binge-eating disorder are more likely to have overvalued ideas about the importance of weight and shape than patients who are overweight or obese and who do not have BED. In this respect, they also resemble people with bulimia nervosa (Allison et al., 2005).

Jenna

Jenna is a 33-year-old single woman who lives alone. She works as a therapist in a school for children with learning difficulties. She came to the clinic for help with chronic feelings of depression. She also acknowledged a history of obesity and binge eating dating back to her adolescent years. By the time of her initial consultation she weighed 260 pounds and had a BMI of 39.5. She was afraid that her

Table 9.2 Comparing Anorexia Nervosa, Bulimia Nervosa, and Binge-Eating Disorder

Symptom	Anorexia Nervosa		Bulimia Nervosa		Binge-Eating Disorder
	Restricting	**Binge/Purge**	**Purging**	**Nonpurging**	
Body weight	Markedly low	Markedly low	Normal weight or slightly overweight	Normal weight or slightly overweight	Typically overweight or obese
Fear of weight gain, becoming fat	Yes	Yes	Yes	Yes	No
Body image	Distorted perception	Distorted perception	Overconcerned with weight	Overconcerned with weight	May be unhappy with body and weight
Binge eating	No	Yes	Yes	Yes	Yes
Purging	No	Yes	Yes	No	No
Use of nonpurging methods to avoid weight gain	Yes	Yes	Yes	Yes	No
Feeling of lack of control over eating	No	During binges	Yes	Yes	Yes

weight would continue to increase unless she found ways to control her eating.

Jenna told the therapist that she had "always been fat." She was extremely reluctant to talk about her eating habits because to do so made her feel embarrassed and ashamed. She said that, in addition to eating three substantial meals every day, she snacked constantly because there were always cookies and cakes available in the teachers' room at school. She also had eating binges. These occurred approximately twice a week and were invariably triggered by anything that made her feel sad, disappointed, or upset. If she had a difficult day at work, she would stop at a convenience store on her way home, buy candy and cookies, and eat quickly in the car. She would then feel disgusted with herself, setting the stage for another binge eating episode when she was alone at home. She would prepare large amounts of food for herself and eat as rapidly as she could until she was so full she was uncomfortable. Jenna longed to be able to "eat normally" but also acknowledged how reliant she was on food to help her cope with all the sadness in her life. There was no evidence of any purging, fasting, or misuse of laxatives. Occasionally, Jenna did try to exercise, although she regarded herself as "too fat to go to the gym."

Age of Onset and Gender Differences

Eating disorders are often considered to be "modern" disorders, yet pathological patterns of eating date back several centuries (Silverman, 1997). St. Catherine of Sienna began to starve herself when she was around 16 years of age. She died in 1380 (at the age of 32 or 33) because she refused to consume either food or water (Keel & Klump, 2003). Moreover, as far back as the second century, the Greek physician Galen referred to a syndrome characterized by overeating, vomiting, and fainting, which he termed *bulimos* (see Ziolko, 1996). It was not until the 1970s and 1980s, however, that eating disorders began to attract significant attention. Clinicians began seeing more and more patients with pathological eating patterns. It soon became apparent that this was an important clinical problem.

Anorexia nervosa and bulimia nervosa do not occur in appreciable numbers before adolescence. Children as young as age 7, though, have been known to develop eating disorders, especially anorexia nervosa (Bryant-Waugh & Lask, 2002). Anorexia nervosa is most likely to develop in 16- to 20-year-olds. For bulimia nervosa, the age group at highest risk is young women the age range of 21 to 24 (Zerwas et al., 2014). Most patients with binge eating disorder are older than those with anorexia nervosa or bulimia nervosa, generally between 30 and 50 years of age.

Eating disorders have long been regarded as occurring primarily in women. Although in the past it was thought that the gender ratio was as high as 10:1, more recent estimates suggest that there are three females for every male with an eating disorder (Jones & Morgan, 2010). This downward revision of the gender ratio reflects the fact that eating disorders in men may have been underdiagnosed in the past because of the stereotype that they are female disorders. Another reason for the underdiagnosis of eating disorders in men is the gender bias in the *DSM* criteria. These emphasize the type of weight and shape concerns (e.g., desire to be thin) and methods of weight control (dieting) that are more typical of women. For men, body dissatisfaction often involves a wish to be more muscular. Overexercising as a means of weight control is also more common in men. As a result, men are less likely to recognize that they have an eating disorder, are more likely to be misdiagnosed when they do, and are less likely to receive specialist treatment (Jones & Morgan, 2010).

Men are now experiencing sociocultural pressures to have toned and muscular bodies. For many men, body dissatisfaction takes the form of wanting to have a more muscular upper torso.

One established risk factor for eating disorders in men is homosexuality. Gay and bisexual men have higher rates of eating disorders than heterosexual men do (Feldman & Meyer, 2007). Gay men (like heterosexual men) value attractiveness and youth in their romantic partners. Because gay men (like women) are seeking to be sexually attractive to men, body dissatisfaction may therefore be more of an issue for gay men than it is for heterosexual men. In support of this idea, Smith and colleagues (2011) found that gay men were more dissatisfied with their bodies and had higher levels of disordered eating than heterosexual men did. Moreover, gay men tended to believe that a potential mate would want them to be leaner than they themselves wanted to be. Other specific subgroups of men who are at higher risk of eating disorders are wrestlers and jockeys, who need to "make weight" in order to compete or work (Carlat et al., 1997).

DSM-5 Thinking Critically about *DSM-5*

Other Forms of Eating Disorders

The old *DSM-IV* category of eating disorders has been renamed. In *DSM-5* it is now called feeding and eating disorders. This reflects the fact that, in addition to the major diagnoses of anorexia nervosa, bulimia nervosa, and binge-eating disorder, the *DSM-5* also recognizes several other types of eating and feeding problems. One of these is purging disorder. Purging disorder, as its name suggests, involves purging in normal weight people who have not eaten large amounts of food. Obviously, because the *DSM* includes so many disorders, we can only focus on the most serious and the most common ones in this text.

But why were new disorders added and why were changes made to the diagnostic criteria for anorexia nervosa and bulimia nervosa? One important reason is that, prior to *DSM-5*, there was a diagnosis in *DSM-IV* called eating disorder not otherwise specified (EDNOS). This was designed to be a catch-all category. However, it ended up being used for a *majority* of patients—around 60 percent of adolescents and adults who sought treatment in outpatient settings (Eddy, Doyle, et al., 2008; Fairburn & Bohn, 2005). This was hardly a desirable situation. To address the problem, changes were made to the diagnostic criteria for anorexia nervosa and bulimia nervosa, and BED was also included as a formal diagnosis. As a result of these changes, it is expected that the catch-all diagnostic category of EDNOS will not be necessary and it no longer appears in *DSM-5*.

Prevalence of Eating Disorders

The most common form of eating disorder is binge eating disorder. Worldwide, and based on the most recent data, the lifetime prevalence of binge-eating disorder is around 2 percent (Kessler et al., 2013). In the United States, community-based estimates from the National Comorbidity Survey indicate a lifetime prevalence of around 3.5 percent in women and 2 percent in men (Hudson et al., 2007). It is also worth noting that the prevalence of binge-eating disorder is higher in obese people and in the range of 6.5 to 8 percent (Grilo, 2002; Sansone et al., 2008).

Worldwide, the prevalence of bulimia nervosa is estimated at 1 percent (Kessler et al., 2013). Data from the National Comorbidity Survey further show that the lifetime prevalence of bulimia nervosa in the United States is around 1.5 percent for women and 0.5 percent for men (Hudson et al., 2007). Somewhat less frequent is anorexia nervosa. Estimates from the United States suggest that this disorder has a lifetime prevalence of 0.9 percent in women and 0.3 percent in men (Hudson et al., 2007). These figures are comparable to prevalence estimates from Sweden, where the rate of anorexia nervosa is 1.2 percent in women and 0.29 percent in men (Bulik et al., 2006). Although anorexia nervosa is sometimes viewed as a very rare disorder, in its severe form it is about as common as schizophrenia.

The risk of developing anorexia nervosa seemed to increase during the twentieth century. In one study, lifetime rates of this disorder were higher in people born after 1945 than before this time (Klump et al., 2007). This is true for both males and females. This increase is not fully explained by increased awareness of the disorder and better detection by clinicians. There was also a rise in the number of new cases of bulimia nervosa from 1970 to 1993 (Keel & Klump, 2003). However, much of this increase may have occurred in the time period up to 1982. A more recent analysis has indicated that the prevalence of bulimia nervosa decreased from 1982 to 1992 and remained stable from 1992 to 2002 (Keel et al., 2006). Stable rates of bulimia nervosa from 1990 to 2004 have also been reported (Crowther et al., 2008).

Despite the encouraging news of a decrease in the prevalence of bulimia nervosa during the past few decades, many young people, particularly girls and young women in their adolescence and early adulthood, show some evidence of disturbed eating patterns or have distorted self-perceptions about their bodies. For example, in a sample of 4,746 middle and high school students, 41.5 percent of girls and 24.9 percent of boys reported problems with body image, and more than a third of the girls and almost a quarter of the boys said they placed a lot of importance on weight and shape with regard to their self-esteem (Ackard et al., 2007). Questionnaire studies further suggest that up to 19 percent of students report some bulimic symptoms (Hoek, 2002). Also of concern are findings from a survey of adults in Australia showing a twofold increase in binge eating, purging, and strict dieting or fasting in the period from 1995 to 2005 (Hay et al., 2008). Disordered eating behaviors that do not meet criteria for an eating disorder diagnosis are of concern because, in some cases, they may worsen over time, eventually leading to clinically significant problems. Table 9.3 shows some sample items from the Eating Disorders Inventory, a questionnaire measure that is often used in research.

Table 9.3 Sample Items from the Eating Disorders Inventory

Sample Statement
I am terrified of gaining weight.
I eat or drink in secrecy.
I think my hips are too big.

SOURCE: Reproduced by special permission of the Publisher, Psychological Assessment Resources, Inc., 16204 North Florida Avenue, Lutz, Florida 33549, from the *Eating Disorder Inventory-3* by David M. Garner, PhD, Copyright 1984, 1991, 2004, by Psychological Assessment Resources, Inc. (PAR). Further reproduction is prohibited without permission of PAR.

Medical Complications of Eating Disorders

The tragic deaths of Ana Carolina Reston and Luisel Ramos and the more recent death of French model Isobel Caro (who died at age 28 in 2010) serve as sad reminders of just how lethal a disorder anorexia nervosa can be. The mortality rate for people with anorexia nervosa (most of whom are females) is more than five times higher than the mortality rate for young females ages 15 to 34 in the general U.S. population (Keshavia et al., 2014). When patients with this disorder die, it is most often because of medical complications. Overall, approximately 3 percent of people with anorexia nervosa die from the consequences of their self-imposed starvation (Signorini et al., 2007).

Malnutrition also takes its toll in other ways (see Mitchell & Crow, 2010). Many patients with anorexia nervosa disorder look extremely unwell. Their hair on the scalp thins and becomes brittle, as do their nails. Their skin becomes very dry, and downy hair (called "lanugo") starts to grow on the face, neck, arms, back, and legs. Many patients also develop a yellowish tinge to their skin, especially on the palms of their hands and bottoms of their feet. Some of these problems are illustrated in Figure 9.2.

Because they are so undernourished, people with this disorder have a difficult time coping with cold temperatures. Their hands and feet are often cold to the touch and have a purplish-blue tinge due to problems with temperature regulation and lack of oxygen to the extremities. As a consequence of chronically low blood pressure, patients often feel tired, weak, dizzy, and faint. Thiamin (vitamin B_1) deficiency may also be present; this could account for some of the depression and cognitive changes documented in low-weight anorexia patients (Winston et al., 2000). Although many of these problems resolve when patients gain weight, anorexia nervosa may result in increased risk for osteoporosis in later life. This is because peak bone density is normally attained during the years of early adulthood. The failure to eat healthily during this time may result in more brittle and fragile bones forever (Attia & Walsh, 2007).

People with anorexia nervosa can die from heart arrhythmias (irregular heartbeats). Sometimes this is caused by major imbalances in key electrolytes such as potassium (Mitchell & Crow, 2010). Chronically low levels of potassium (hypokalemia) can also result in kidney damage and renal failure severe enough to require dialysis.

Abuse of laxatives, which occurs in 10 to 60 percent of patients with eating disorders (Roerrig et al., 2010) makes all of these problems much worse. Laxatives are used to induce diarrhea so that the person feels thinner or to remove unwanted calories from the body. Laxative abuse can lead to dehydration, electrolyte imbalances, and kidney disease as well as damage to the bowels and gastrointestinal tract.

Bulimia nervosa is much less lethal than anorexia nervosa, although it is still associated with a mortality rate that is approximately twice that found in people of comparable age in the general population (Arcelus et al., 2011). Bulimia nervosa also creates a number of medical concerns (Mitchell & Crow, 2010). Purging can cause electrolyte imbalances and low potassium, which, as we have already mentioned, puts the patient at risk for heart abnormalities. Another complication is damage to the heart muscle, which may be due to the

Figure 9.2 Anorexia nervosa takes its toll on the body and causes many medical problems. When starved, the body turns on itself in an effort to provide energy. Fat is burned first, then muscle. Eventually, organs are destroyed in the body's struggle to find fuel.

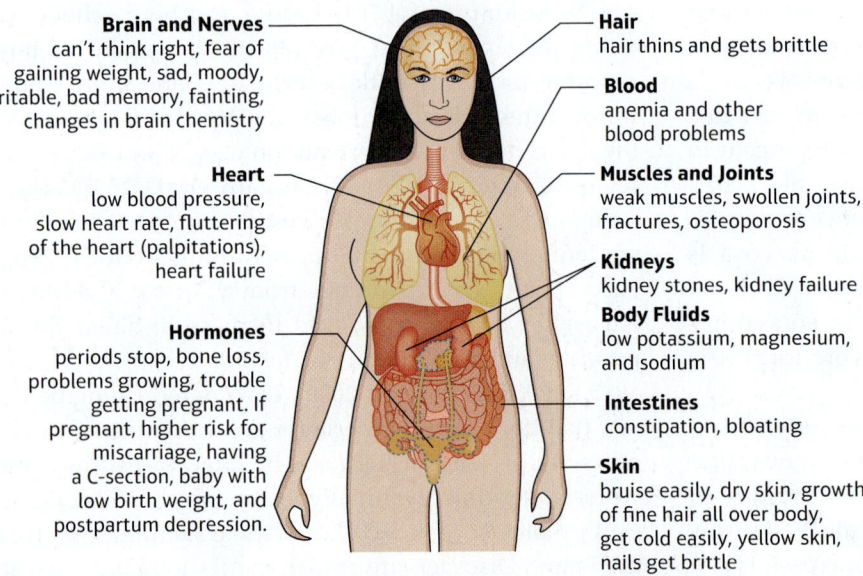

Anorexia affects your whole body

Brain and Nerves
can't think right, fear of gaining weight, sad, moody, irritable, bad memory, fainting, changes in brain chemistry

Heart
low blood pressure, slow heart rate, fluttering of the heart (palpitations), heart failure

Hormones
periods stop, bone loss, problems growing, trouble getting pregnant. If pregnant, higher risk for miscarriage, having a C-section, baby with low birth weight, and postpartum depression.

Hair
hair thins and gets brittle

Blood
anemia and other blood problems

Muscles and Joints
weak muscles, swollen joints, fractures, osteoporosis

Kidneys
kidney stones, kidney failure

Body Fluids
low potassium, magnesium, and sodium

Intestines
constipation, bloating

Skin
bruise easily, dry skin, growth of fine hair all over body, get cold easily, yellow skin, nails get brittle

············· Dash line indicates that organ is behind other main organs.

use of ipecac syrup, a poison that causes vomiting. More typically, however, patients develop calluses on their hands from sticking their fingers down their throats to make themselves sick. In extreme cases, where objects such as a toothbrush are used to induce vomiting, tears to the throat can occur.

Because the contents of the stomach are acidic, patients damage their teeth when they throw up repeatedly. Brushing the teeth immediately after vomiting damages them even more. Mouth ulcers and dental cavities are a common consequence of repeated purging, as are small red dots around the eyes that are caused by the pressure of throwing up. Finally, patients with bulimia very often have swollen parotid (salivary) glands caused by repeatedly vomiting. These are known as "puffy cheeks" or "chipmunk cheeks" by many people with bulimia. Although such swellings are not painful, they are often quite noticeable to others.

Course and Outcome

After medical complications, the second most common cause of death in those who suffer from anorexia nervosa is suicide. The most recent estimate from a meta-analysis suggests that individuals with anorexia nervosa are 18 times more likely to die by suicide than comparably aged women in the general population (Keshavia et al., 2014). It has been suggested that patients who have lost their ability to maintain an "emotionally protective" low body weight are at particularly high risk of suicide (Crisp et al., 2006). Patients who are older when they first receive clinical attention for their disorder are also more likely to have a premature death (Arcelus et al., 2011). Bulimia nervosa is not associated with increased risk of completed suicide, although suicide attempts are made in 25 to 30 percent of cases (Franko & Keel, 2006).

Although the clinical outcome for some patients is tragic, over the very long term recovery is possible. Löwe and colleagues (2001) examined what happened to patients with anorexia nervosa 21 years after they had first sought treatment. Reflecting the high morbidity associated with anorexia nervosa, 16 percent of the patients (all of whom were women) were no longer alive, having died primarily from complications of starvation or from suicide. Another 10 percent were still suffering from the disorder, and a further 21 percent had partially recovered. On the positive side, however, 51 percent of the individuals were fully recovered at the time of the follow-up. In another 6-year follow-up study, 52.1 percent of patients who had received outpatient cognitive-behavior therapy for their anorexia nervosa eventually recovered (Castellini et al., 2011). These findings provide grounds for optimism for those who suffer from this disorder. They indicate that even after a series of treatment failures it is still possible for women with anorexia nervosa to become well again.

With regard to bulimia nervosa, in the long term, prognosis tends to be quite good. Two outcome studies have shown that around 70 percent of women initially diagnosed with this disorder will be in remission and will no longer meet diagnostic criteria for any eating disorder by the end of an 11- to 12-year follow-up (Keel et al., 1999; Fichter & Quadflieg, 2007). The remaining 30 percent, however, will continue to experience significant difficulties with their eating. Substance-abuse problems, more frequent binges, more shape concerns, as well as a longer duration of illness predict worse outcomes over time (Castellini et al., 2011; Keel et al., 1999).

Finally, like patients with bulimia nervosa, patients with binge eating disorder also have high rates of clinical remission. Following a period of intensive treatment, two-thirds of a sample of 60 patients no longer had any form of eating disorder (Fichter & Quadflieg, 2007). In a larger study involving 137 Italian patients who received individual cognitive-behavior therapy, 60 percent were found to be recovered when they were assessed 6 years after the end of treatment (Castellini et al., 2011).

It is worth noting that, even when well, many individuals who recover from anorexia nervosa and bulimia nervosa still harbor residual food issues. They may be excessively concerned about shape and weight, restrict their dietary intakes, and overeat and purge in response to negative mood states (Sullivan, 2002). In other words, the idea of recovery is relative. Someone who no longer meets all of the diagnostic criteria for an eating disorder may still have issues with food and body image.

Diagnostic Crossover

One way in which eating disorders differ from other types of disorders is that there is a lot of diagnostic crossover. What this means is that it is quite common for someone who is diagnosed with one form of eating disorder to be later diagnosed with another eating disorder. Over a 7-year period, Eddy, Dorer, and colleagues (2008) report that the majority of women in their study experienced diagnostic crossover. Bidirectional transitions between the two subtypes of anorexia nervosa (restricting and binge-eating/purging) were especially common.

Shifts from anorexia nervosa to bulimia nervosa also occurred in about a third of patients. Interestingly, however, there were no cases of direct transition from the restricting type of anorexia nervosa directly into bulimia nervosa. Instead, the transition to bulimia nervosa seems to occur after an earlier transition to the binge-eating/purging subtype of anorexia nervosa. You may also recall that the main difference between patients with the binge-eating/purging subtype of anorexia nervosa and bulimia nervosa is weight (and associated amenorrhea). So if someone with anorexia nervosa (binge-eating/purging subtype) gains weight, the diagnosis will change to bulimia nervosa to reflect this fact, even though there may not be a big clinical change in the illness itself. Moreover, even after they have crossed over into bulimia nervosa, these women remain vulnerable to relapsing back into anorexia nervosa. This suggests that clinicians should pay attention to a past history of anorexia nervosa even when patients no longer meet the low-weight criterion necessary for its diagnosis.

Only a minority of patients with bulimia nervosa transition into anorexia nervosa. In one study the figure was 14 percent (Eddy, Dorer, et al., 2008). In another it was 9.2 percent (Castellini et al., 2011). Crossovers from the restricting subtype of anorexia nervosa into binge-eating disorder do not seem to occur at all. Diagnostic crossover from bulimia nervosa into binge-eating disorder occurs in about 10.9 percent of cases (Castellini et al., 2011).

Finally, we note that binge-eating disorder and anorexia nervosa appear to be quite distinct disorders. Over the course of a 12-year follow-up, no patient with binge-eating disorder developed anorexia nervosa and no patient with anorexia nervosa developed binge-eating disorder (Fichter & Quadflieg, 2007). In other words, there was no diagnostic crossover between these diagnoses. However, around 10 percent of patients who previously had binge-eating disorder transitioned into bulimia nervosa during this time. Figure 9.3 illustrates some of these trends.

Figure 9.3 Diagnostic Crossover in Eating Disorders

Diagnostic crossover is common in eating disorders with transitions between the two subtypes of anorexia nervosa being very common. Transitions from the binge-eating/purging subtype of anorexia nervosa to bulimia nervosa also often occur. In the figure, the width of the arrow denotes the relative likelihood of any transition.

(Adapted from Fichter & Quadflieg, 2007, and Eddy, Dorer, et al., 2008.)

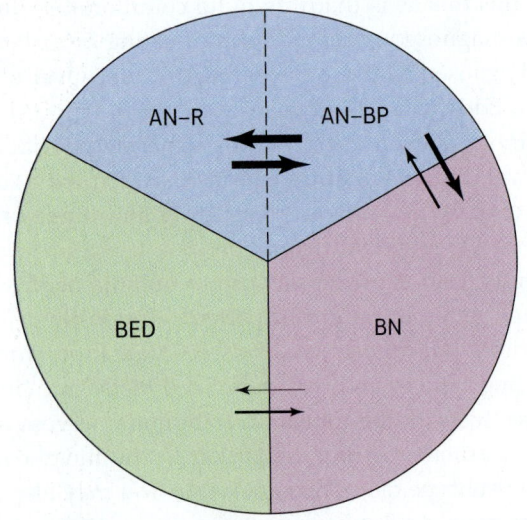

AN–R = Anorexia nervosa–restricting subtype
AN–BP = Anorexia nervosa–binge-eating/purging subtype
BN = Bulimia nervosa
BED = Binge-eating disorder

Association of Eating Disorders with Other Forms of Psychopathology

Eating disorder diagnoses are commonly associated with other diagnosable psychiatric conditions. In fact, comorbidity is the rule rather than the exception (Hudson et al., 2007). For instance, approximately 68 percent of patients with anorexia nervosa, 63 percent of patients with bulimia nervosa, and almost 50 percent of people with binge-eating disorder are also diagnosed with depression (Brewerton et al., 1995; Halmi, et al., 1991; Hudson et al., 2007; O'Brien & Vincent, 2003). Obsessive-compulsive disorder is often found in patients with anorexia nervosa and bulimia nervosa (Kaye et al., 2004; Milos et al., 2002; O'Brien & Vincent, 2003). In addition, there is frequent co-occurrence of substance abuse disorders in the binge-eating/purging subtype of anorexia nervosa as well as in bulimia nervosa. The restrictive type of anorexia nervosa, however, tends not to be associated with higher rates of substance abuse (Halmi, 2010).

Comorbid personality disorders are frequently diagnosed in people with eating disorders (Cassin & von Ranson, 2005; Rø et al., 2005). Indeed, about 58 percent of women with eating disorders may have a personality disorder (Rosenvinge et al., 2000). Personality disorders in the anxious-avoidant cluster (Cluster C) are found in those with anorexia nervosa as well as those with bulimia nervosa. However, dramatic, emotional, or erratic (Cluster B) problems, including borderline personality disorder, are more typically associated with bulimia nervosa (Halmi, 2010; Rosenvinge et al., 2000). Consistent with this, more than a third of patients with eating disorders have engaged in the kinds of self-harming behaviors (cutting or burning themselves, for example) that are symptomatic of borderline personality disorder (Paul et al., 2002).

Personality disorders are similarly reported in around 30 percent of patients with BED, with avoidant, obsessive-compulsive, and borderline personality disorders being the most common (Friborg et al., 2014). People with BED also have high rates of anxiety disorders (65 percent), mood disorders (46 percent), and substance use disorders (23 percent; see Hudson et al., 2007).

One problem with simple examinations of personality disorders in patients with eating disorders is that some of the disturbances found in these patients could reflect the consequences of malnourishment. Starvation is known to increase both irritability and obsessionality (Keys et al., 1950). We must therefore be cautious in our conclusions.

Even though the physiological consequences of eating disorders may exacerbate personality disturbances, they may only be enhancing traits that were present prior to the development of the illness. Research suggests that some personality traits in patients with eating disorders might both predate the onset of the disorder and remain even when the eating disorder remits and the patient has recovered (Kaye et al., 2004; Klump et al., 2004). Consistent with this, around two-thirds of a sample of patients with anorexia nervosa reported that they were rigid and perfectionistic, even as children (Anderluh et al., 2003).

Eating Disorders Across Cultures

Although the majority of research on eating disorders is conducted in the United States and Europe, eating disorders are not confined to these areas. Widespread eating disorder difficulties have been reported among both Caucasian and black South African college students (le Grange et al., 1998). Anorexia nervosa and bulimia nervosa are also clinical problems in Japan, Hong Kong, Taiwan, Singapore, and Korea (Lee & Katzman, 2002).

Cases of eating disorders have also been documented in India and Africa. The prevalence of eating disorders in Iran is comparable to that in the United States (Nobakht & Dezhkam, 2000). And a few years ago, the first published report of five men in central China who were diagnosed with eating disorders appeared (Tong et al., 2005). Far from being confined to industrialized Western countries, eating disorders are becoming a problem worldwide.

Being Caucasian, however, does appear to be associated with subclinical problems that may place individuals at higher risk for developing eating disorders. Examples of such problems include body dissatisfaction, dietary restraint, and a drive for thinness. A *meta-analysis* involving a total of 17,781 participants has shown that such attitudes and behaviors are significantly more prevalent in whites than in nonwhites (Wildes et al., 2001).

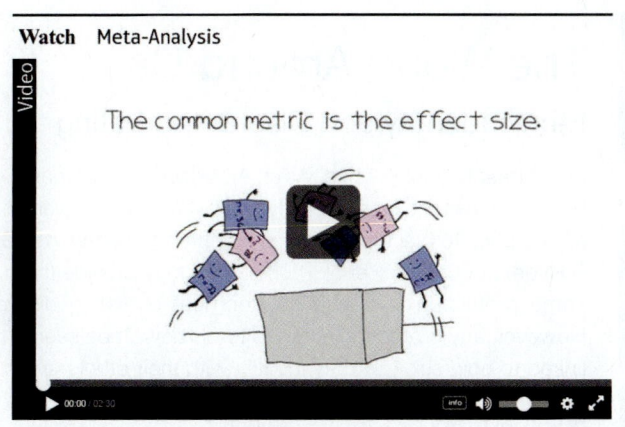

Watch Meta-Analysis

The common metric is the effect size.

in one sample of 1,061 black women, no case of anorexia nervosa was found. In contrast, out of a sample of 985 white women, 15 (1.5 percent) met clinical criteria for this disorder. Fewer black than white women also had bulimia nervosa (0.4 versus 2.3 percent; see Striegel-Moore et al., 2003).

However, as minorities become more and more integrated and internalize white, middle-class societal values about the desirability of thinness, we should expect to see increases in the rates of eating disorders in minorities. As an example of this, Alegria and colleagues (2007) have demonstrated that rates of eating disorders were higher in Latinos who were born in the United States compared with those who were not. In the World Around Us box we discuss the protective role of ethnic identity in African American women.

A select number of the clinical features of diagnosed forms of eating disorders may also vary according to culture. For instance, about 58 percent of patients with anorexia nervosa in Hong Kong are not excessively concerned about fatness. The reason they give for refusing food is fear of stomach bloating (Lee et al., 1993). Patients with anorexia nervosa who were living in Britain but who had South Asian (Indian, Pakistani, Bangladeshi) ethnic origins also were less likely than patients with English ethnic origins to show evidence of fat phobia (Tareen et al., 2005).

In yet another study, young women in Ghana who had anorexia nervosa were also not especially concerned about their weight or shape. Rather, they emphasized religious ideas of self-control and denial of hunger as the motivation for their self-starvation (Bennett et al., 2004). In a final example, Japanese women with eating disorders reported significantly lower levels of perfectionism and less of a drive for thinness than did American women with eating disorders (Pike & Mizushima, 2005). Findings such as these highlight the considerable role played by culture in the clinical presentation of eating disorders.

As noted, cases of anorexia nervosa have been reported throughout history. They have furthermore been shown to occur all over the world. In light of this reality, Keel and

---

Research Close-Up

Meta-Analysis

A meta-analysis is a statistical method used to combine the results of a number of similar research studies. The data from each separate study are transformed into a common metric called the effect size. Doing this allows data from the various studies to be combined and then analyzed. You can think of a meta-analysis as being just like the research with which you are already familiar, except that the "participants" are individual research studies, not individual people!

Although Asian women exhibit levels of pathological eating similar to those of white women (Wildes et al., 2001), it has long been held that African Americans are less susceptible to subclinical types of eating problems and body image concerns than Caucasians are. For example,

The World Around Us

Ethnic Identity and Disordered Eating

In contrast to young white, Asian American, and Hispanic girls, black adolescent girls seem less inclined to use weight and appearance to fuel their sense of identity and self-worth (Grabe & Hyde, 2006; Polivy et al., 2005). This may provide them with some protection from the development of eating disorders. However, any protection afforded to black women seems to be linked to how strongly they identify with their ethnic group and how much they receive culturally consistent messages that value what their bodies naturally look like and support who they are.

In a study of 322 African American female college students, Rogers Wood and Petrie (2010) found that women who had stronger ethnic identities were less likely to have internalized U.S. societal beauty ideals about the importance of being thin and attractive. This is an important finding because, in the same study, internalization of these ideals was found to be linked to disordered eating. An important factor in the ethnic distribution and occurrence of eating disorders is therefore the extent to which minority women are both exposed to and willing to internalize the same kind of white, middle-class values that have been linked to increased risk for eating disorders. We already have some evidence that the body dissatisfaction difference between blacks and whites is getting smaller over time (Grabe & Hyde, 2006). This highlights the importance of healthy role models for young black girls. Without these, black women will no longer

African American women who have a strong identification with their ethnicity and cultural heritage have less risk of developing eating disorders than African American women who have internalized white middle-class values about the desirability of thinness.

remain unique among American ethnic groups in their lower levels of body dissatisfaction.

Consider your own background and heritage. What role does food play? What messages about body size and attractiveness did you learn growing up? Where did these messages come from?

Klump (2003) have concluded that anorexia nervosa is not a culture-bound syndrome. Of course, as we have just stated, culture may influence the disorder's clinical manifestation. The more important point, however, is that anorexia nervosa is not a disorder that occurs simply because of exposure to Western ideals and the modern emphasis on thinness.

A good illustration of this is provided by Davis and Nguyen (2014), who describe the case of a young girl from Chicago called Jane. A pious Catholic, who joined a convent at the age of 13, Jane fasted for Lent and then kept fasting. She continued to restrict her food intake, encouraged by the nuns who told her that she could eat a smaller cookie and "make a sacrifice" or be perfect and have no cookie at all. Because she was in a convent, Jane had no access to scales or to mirrors. Her anorexia nervosa was not motivated by any desire to be thin. Rather she wished to be more pious and to become a saint. At the age of 21, she was asked to leave the convent because of concerns about her weight. Her supervisors told her that her practices were "too extreme" and it was "God's will" that she leave. She was 5 feet tall and weighed 75 pounds.

In contrast, bulimia nervosa does seem to be a culture-bound syndrome. More specifically, it seems to occur in people who have had some exposure to Western ideals about thinness, who have access to large amounts of food, and who, because of modern plumbing, can purge in private (Keel, 2010).

in review

- What are the major clinical differences between patients with anorexia nervosa and patients with bulimia nervosa? What clinical features do these two forms of eating disorders have in common?

- How do the prevalence rates for eating disorders vary according to gender, sexual orientation, and ethnicity?

- What kinds of medical problems do patients with eating disorders experience?

- What is the long-term outcome for patients with anorexia nervosa? In what ways is the clinical outcome of patients with anorexia nervosa different from the clinical outcome of patients with bulimia nervosa?

- Why is bulimia nervosa viewed as a culture-bound syndrome when anorexia nervosa is not?

Risk and Causal Factors in Eating Disorders

9.2 **Explain the risk and causal factors in eating disorders.**

There is no single cause of eating disorders. In all probability, they reflect the complex interaction between genetic and environmental factors. Biological, sociocultural, family, and individual variables likely all play a role. However, it is important not to regard these areas as distinct and in competition with each other. The question of whether eating disorders are caused by biological factors or by cultural pressures is not an appropriate one. Biological and cultural explanations are interlinked. For example, being exposed to cultural attitudes that emphasize thinness is significant in the development of eating disorders. However, only a small number of people who are exposed to such attitudes actually develop eating disorders. Genetic factors may give rise to individual differences that help explain why certain people are more sensitive than others to cultural attitudes and other environmental risk factors. In other words, eating disorders are best conceptualized in terms of the diathesis–stress model, where genes render some people more susceptible to environmental pressures and hence to the development of problematic eating attitudes and behaviors.

Biological Factors

GENETICS Much research attention is now being devoted to the study of genetic factors in eating disorders. This is because the tendency to develop an eating disorder has been shown to run in families (Wade, 2010). The biological relatives of people with anorexia nervosa or bulimia nervosa have elevated rates of anorexia nervosa and bulimia nervosa themselves. In one large family study of eating disorders, the risk of anorexia nervosa for the relatives of individuals with anorexia nervosa was 11.4 times greater than for the relatives of the healthy controls (Strober et al., 2000).

For the relatives of people with bulimia nervosa, the risk of bulimia nervosa was 3.7 times higher than it was for the relatives of the healthy controls (Strober et al., 2000). It is of additional interest that the relatives of patients with eating disorders are more likely to suffer from a variety of other disorders as well as eating disorders. For example, high rates of major depressive disorder are found in the relatives of patients with anorexia nervosa, bulimia nervosa, and binge-eating disorder (Lilenfeld et al., 1998, 2006; Mangweth et al., 2003). The relatives of people suffering from bulimia nervosa also have an increased likelihood of having problems with alcohol and drug dependence, while the relatives of those diagnosed with anorexia nervosa are at increased risk of obsessive-compulsive disorder and obsessive-compulsive personality disorder (Lilenfeld et al., 1998).

As you know, family studies do not allow for the untangling of the different contributions of genetic and environmental influences. These kinds of questions are best resolved by twin and adoption studies. Presently, we have none of the latter. Fortunately, a number of twin studies do exist. Considered together, these studies suggest that both anorexia nervosa and bulimia nervosa are heritable disorders (Fairburn & Harrison, 2003; Wade, 2010). Indeed, it has been suggested that the contribution of genetic factors to the development of eating disorders may be about as strong as the contribution of genetic factors to bipolar disorder and schizophrenia (Kaye, 2008).

Although genes undoubtedly play a role in the etiology of eating disorders, there is little that can be said specifically at this point. Several candidate genes studies have been conducted (candidate genes are genes that are thought to affect risk for eating disorders), but no convincing findings have so far emerged. A recent study failed to find any links between 182 different candidate genes and various aspects of eating disorders such as lowest body mass index, drive for thinness, or body dissatisfaction (Root et al., 2011). To cast the net more widely, researchers are now using genome-wide association studies (GWAS; described more in Chapter 13).

A large international team of researchers has recently published data from the largest genome-wide association study of anorexia nervosa ever conducted (Boraska et al., 2014). Although no highly significant findings emerged, a few small leads did appear. Again, however, we must wait for future research to provide us with more definitive answers. Although it is frustrating not to know more, this should be expected at this stage. We are not naïve enough to assume that there would be a gene for anorexia nervosa, a gene for bulimia nervosa, or a gene that creates risk for binge-eating disorder. Eating disorders involve dysregulations in complex biological systems that control appetite and energy regulation, as well as food intake. Despite the many challenges, we expect that some important findings will emerge within the next several years.

BRAIN ABNORMALITIES One brain area that plays an important role in eating is the **hypothalamus**. Animal studies have demonstrated that lesions in a part of the hypothalamus called the ventromedial hypothalamus (VMH) cause the animal to behave as if starved. Such animals eat voraciously and rapidly become obese (Ravussin et al., 2014). In contrast, when the VMH is stimulated electrically, food intake is inhibited and the animal loses weight. Stimulating another area of the hypothalamus (the lateral hypothalamus) triggers eating. Animals with lesions to this area, in contrast, will stop eating.

There is no good evidence that obvious abnormalities in the hypothalamus play a central role in eating disorders, however. Uher and Treasure (2005) reviewed a series of case reports of patients with tumors in the hypothalamus. Although these were sometimes associated with an increase or loss of appetite, there was no evidence that they resulted in specific eating disorders. In contrast, damage to the frontal and the temporal cortex did seem to be linked to the development of anorexia nervosa in some cases and bulimia nervosa in others. This is interesting because the temporal cortex is known to be involved in body image perception. Parts of the frontal cortex (particularly an area called the orbitofrontal cortex) also play a role in monitoring the pleasantness of stimuli such as smell and taste (van Kuyck et al., 2009).

Although still speculative at this time, it is reasonable to suggest that the hypothalamus "senses" weight in some way and keeps things in balance with the ventromedial hypothalamus acting as a "satiety center" and the lateral hypothalamus serving as an "appetite center." It is also reasonable to think that the lateral hypothalamus acts as a site that integrates other information relevant for regulating food intake. The lateral hypothalamus receives information from many parts of the brain, including the frontal cortex and the amygdala (which is a part of the brain involved in emotion and fear learning). Animal research suggests that a network involving these (and other) brain areas may be important not only for overeating in response to environmental cues but for suppressing eating in response to fear (Petrovich, 2011). As research progresses we will learn more about how the pieces of the puzzle fit together to result in different types of eating disorders.

SET POINTS There is a well-established tendency for our bodies to resist marked variation from some sort of biologically determined **set point** or weight that our individual bodies try to "defend" (Garner, 1997; Ravussin et al., 2014). Anyone intent on achieving and maintaining a significant decrease in body mass below his or her individual set point may be trying to do this in the face of internal physiological opposition, which is aimed at trying to get the body back close to its original set-point weight.

One important kind of physiological opposition designed to prevent us from moving far from our set point is hunger. As we lose more and more weight, hunger may rise to extreme levels, encouraging eating, weight gain, and a return to a state of equilibrium. Far from having little or no appetite, patients with anorexia nervosa may think about food constantly and make intense efforts to suppress their increasing hunger. Accordingly, chronic dieting may well enhance the likelihood that a person will encounter periods of seemingly irresistible impulses to gorge on large amounts of high-calorie food. For patients with bulimia nervosa, these hunger-driven impulses may escalate into uncontrollable binge eating.

SEROTONIN Serotonin is a neurotransmitter that has been implicated in obsessionality, mood disorders, and impulsivity. It also modulates appetite and feeding behavior. Because many patients with eating disorders respond well to treatment with antidepressants (which target serotonin), some researchers have concluded that eating disorders involve a disruption in the serotonergic system (Bailer & Kaye, 2011).

Serotonin is made from an essential amino acid called tryptophan. This can only be obtained from food. After tryptophan is consumed, it is converted to serotonin via a series of chemical reactions. People with anorexia nervosa have low levels of 5-HIAA, which is a major metabolite of serotonin. This may be because they are eating so little food. In contrast, levels of 5-HIAA are normal in people with bulimia nervosa. What is interesting is that, after recovery, both of these patient groups have higher levels of 5-HIAA than control women do; they also have higher levels of 5-HIAA than they had when they were in the ill state (Kaye, 2008). Although the finding of higher levels of 5-HIAA in recovered patients compared to controls seems counterintuitive, it has been suggested that resuming normal eating makes it possible to detect abnormalities in the serotonin system (such as higher levels of serotonin in several different brain areas) that might be involved in risk for eating disorders. Kaye and colleagues have further suggested that people with serotonin overactivity may use dieting as a way to regulate this by decreasing the amount of tryptophan that is available to make serotonin (Bailer & Kaye, 2011).

Of course, it is important to remember that neurotransmitters like serotonin do not work in isolation. A change in the serotonin system will have implications for other neurotransmitter systems too (e.g., dopamine, norepinephrine). So the situation is undoubtedly complex. Nonetheless, investigating the role of serotonin in eating disorders is still an active area of research.

Sociocultural Factors

What is the ideal body shape for women in Western culture? Next time you glance at a glossy fashion magazine, take a moment to consider the messages contained in its pages. The overall body size of the models that appear on the covers of such magazines as *Vogue* and *Cosmopolitan* has become increasingly thinner over the years (Sypeck et al., 2004). Young women are avid consumers of such magazines and are bombarded with images of unrealistically thin models. These magazines are also widely available all over the world. *British Vogue* is published in 40 or more countries and can be found in India, Argentina, and Kenya among other places (see Gordon, 2000). Moreover, social pressures toward thinness may be particularly powerful in higher socioeconomic backgrounds, from which a majority of girls and women with anorexia nervosa appear to come (McClelland & Crisp, 2001).

It is likely that thinness became deeply rooted as a cultural ideal in the 1960s, although prior to this time women had certainly been concerned with their weight and appearance. However, the type of body that was regarded as glamorous and attractive (e.g., Marilyn Monroe) was more curvaceous. One landmark event was the arrival of Twiggy on the fashion scene. Twiggy was the first super-thin supermodel. Although her appearance was initially regarded as shocking, it did not take long for the fashion industry to embrace the look she exemplified.

British supermodel Kate Moss has said that one of her mottos is "Nothing tastes as good as skinny feels."

British model Twiggy was the first superthin model to achieve international fame.

The emphasis on thinness in the fashion industry continues. Although, as we noted earlier, some efforts are being made to exclude excessively thin models from the runways, these changes are still being resisted by many designers. In an example of the glamorization of anorexia, British supermodel Kate Moss has even made up a new word to describe herself. The word is "rexy," a hybrid term that combines "anorexic" and "sexy."

A provocative illustration of the importance of the media in creating pressures to be thin comes from a now classic study that was done by Anne Becker and her colleagues (2002). When Becker first began conducting research in Fiji in the 1990s, she was struck by the considerable percentage of Fijians (especially women) who were overweight with respect to their Western counterparts. From a cultural perspective, however, this made sense. Within Fijian culture, being fat was associated with qualities that were highly valued such as being strong, able to work, and kind and generous. Being thin, in contrast, was regarded negatively because it was thought to reflect being sickly, incompetent, or having somehow received poor treatment. Culturally, fatness

was preferred over thinness, and dieting was viewed as offensive. What was also striking was the total absence of any condition that could be considered an eating disorder.

After television came to Fiji, however, the cultural climate changed. Not only were Fijians able to see programs such as *Beverly Hills 90210* and *Melrose Place* that were popular at that time, but many young women also began to express concerns about their weight and dislike of their bodies. For the first time, women in Fiji started to diet in earnest. The young Fijian women studied by Becker also made comments that suggested that their body dissatisfaction and wish to lose weight were motivated by a desire to emulate the actors they had seen on television.

Although Becker did not collect information about eating disorders themselves (she measured attitudes toward eating), this "natural experiment" provides us with some anecdotal information as to the way in which Western values about thinness may begin to insert themselves into foreign cultural environments. Indeed, a subsequent research study involving participants in 26 countries has now confirmed that the more women are exposed to Western media (via TV, movies, magazines or music), the more dissatisfied they are with their bodies (Swami et al., 2010). In another illustration of the strong link between attractiveness and the thin ideal in Western culture, after 51 years of Nigeria being unsuccessful in the Miss World beauty pageant, a 19-year-old Nigerian contestant finally won the coveted crown in 2001. Her success was later attributed to the fact that, for the first time, Nigerians had selected a contestant to represent them who was not considered to be beautiful by local standards on account of being too thin (Onishi, 2002).

In her home country of Nigeria, Agbani Darego was considered too thin to be beautiful. Nonetheless, she was selected to represent the country in the 2001 Miss World contest and won the coveted crown.

Family Influences

Clinicians have long been aware that certain problems seem to regularly characterize the families of patients with anorexia nervosa, prompting many clinicians to advocate a family therapy approach to treatment intervention (Lock et al., 2001). Echoing this sentiment, more than one-third of patients with anorexia nervosa reported that family dysfunction was a factor that contributed to the development of their eating disorder (Tozzi et al., 2003). Patients with anorexia nervosa perceive their families as more rigid, less cohesive, and as having poorer communication than healthy control participants do (Vidovic et al., 2005).

In addition, many of the parents of patients with eating disorders have long-standing preoccupations regarding the desirability of thinness, dieting, and good physical appearance (Garner & Garfinkel, 1997). Like their children, they have perfectionistic tendencies (Woodside et al., 2002).

Family factors have also been studied in connection with bulimia nervosa. Both white and ethnic minority (black, Hispanic, and biracial) adolescents with bulimia nervosa perceive their families to be less cohesive than their parents do (Hoste et al., 2007). Fairburn and colleagues (1997) have also noted that women with bulimia nervosa could be differentiated from both a general psychiatric control group and a healthy control group on such risk factors as high parental expectations, other family members' dieting, and degree of critical comments from other family members about shape, weight, or eating. In a large sample of college-age women, the strongest predictor of bulimic symptoms was the extent to which family members made disparaging comments about the woman's appearance and focused on her need to diet (Crowther et al., 2002).

Still, when attempting to depict family characteristics associated with eating disorders, we must remember that having an individual with an eating disorder in the family is likely to affect family functioning in a negative way. That is, the causal connection, if any, might be in the other direction. In fact, recent longitudinal data from a twin study suggest that disordered eating attitudes may predate parent–child conflict (Spanos et al., 2010). If this finding is replicated in future studies, we may need to reconsider the role of family conflict as a risk factor for the development of eating problems.

Individual Risk Factors

Not everyone who lives in a society that places excessive emphasis on being thin goes on to develop an eating disorder. If that were the case, eating disorders would be much more prevalent than they are. There must be other factors that increase a given person's susceptibility to the development of disordered eating. As we noted earlier, some of these factors may be biological, while others may be more psychological in nature. In a further reflection of gene–environment interaction, genetic factors may actually influence some of the traits (e.g., perfectionism, obsessiveness, anxiety) that may make some people more likely to respond to cultural pressures with disturbed eating patterns.

GENDER As you have already learned, eating disorders are much more frequently found in women than in men. Being female is a strong risk factor for developing eating disorders, particularly anorexia nervosa and bulimia nervosa (Jacobi et al., 2004). Moreover, the greatest period of risk for these disorders occurs in adolescence. Binge-eating disorder does not follow this pattern, however. The onset of binge-eating disorder is typically well after adolescence. Binge-eating disorder is also much more likely to be found in males as well as in females.

For men (but not for women) sexual orientation is a risk factor for disordered eating. As we noted earlier, this may be because gay and bisexual men are trying to be attractive to men, who (regardless of sexual orientation) typically place great emphasis on physical appearance. However, being in a relationship may moderate the risk for disordered eating. Brown and Keel (2012a) have recently shown that gay and bisexual men in their 30s and 40s who were in relationships reported less of a drive for thinness and dieted less frequently than men of the same age who were single and without a partner.

INTERNALIZING THE THIN IDEAL   The Duchess of Windsor once said that you could never be too rich or too thin. Clearly she had internalized the thin ideal, buying into the notion that being thin is highly desirable. Think for a moment about the extent to which you think this way. Do you regard thin people as unhealthy and weak? Or do you associate being thin with feeling attractive, being popular, and being happy? The extent to which people internalize the thin ideal is associated with a range of problems that are thought to be risk factors for eating disorders. These include body dissatisfaction, dieting, and negative affect (Stice, 2002). In fact, empirical evidence suggests that internalizing the thin ideal may be an early component of the causal chain that culminates in disordered eating (McKnight Investigators, 2003; Stice, 2001).

PERFECTIONISM   Perfectionism (defined as the pursuit of unattainably high standards combined with an intolerance of mistakes) has long been regarded as an important risk factor for eating disorders (Bruch, 1973). This is because people who are perfectionistic may be much more likely to subscribe to the thin ideal and relentlessly pursue the "perfect body." It has also been suggested that perfectionism helps maintain bulimic pathology through the rigid adherence to dieting that then drives the binge/purge cycle (Fairburn et al., 1997).

Research supports the association of perfectionism and eating disorders (Bardone-Cone et al., 2007). This is especially true for anorexia nervosa. In a study of 322 women, Halmi and colleagues (2000) found that women with anorexia nervosa scored higher on a measure of perfectionism than did a sample of controls without an eating disorder. The women with anorexia nervosa scored higher on perfectionism regardless of whether they had the restricting subtype of anorexia nervosa or subtypes that involved either purging or binge eating and purging. A large proportion of bulimia nervosa patients also demonstrate a long-standing pattern of excessive perfectionism (Anderluh et al., 2003; Garner & Garfinkel, 1997).

Of course, any personality characteristics found in patients with eating disorders could be the result of the eating disorder itself rather than contributory in a causal sense. But if this were the case, recovery from anorexia nervosa would be followed by a reduction in perfectionism. Yet this does not seem to happen (Bardone-Cone et al., 2007). Perfectionism also seems to predate disordered eating in those with anorexia nervosa (Halmi et al., 2012),

again suggesting that perfectionism is not a simple correlate of eating problems. Overall, the research findings support the idea that perfectionism is an enduring personality trait that places people at higher risk for the development of eating disorders (Lilenfeld et al., 2006; Stice, 2002). Perfectionism may also have a genetic basis. In a twin study, high levels of perfectionism were found in the twins with anorexia nervosa, as expected. However, high levels of perfectionism were also found in the co-twins who did not suffer from eating disorders (Wade et al., 2008).

Interestingly, men with eating disorders are less perfectionistic than are women with eating disorders (Woodside et al., 2004). If men are generally less perfectionistic than women, this might help them avoid having some of the weight and shape concerns that seem to be a stepping stone to the development of eating disorders.

NEGATIVE BODY IMAGE   One consequence of sociocultural pressure to be thin is that some young girls and women develop highly intrusive and pervasive perceptual biases regarding how "fat" they are (e.g., Fallon & Rozin, 1985; Rodin, 1993; Wiseman et al., 1992; Zellner et al., 1989). In sharp contrast, young Amish people (who live radically separated from the modern world) do not display such body image distortions (Platte et al., 2000). This supports the notion that sociocultural influences are implicated in the discrepancy between the way many young girls and women perceive their own bodies and the "ideal" female form as represented in the media. Such perceptual biases lead girls and women to believe that men prefer more slender shapes than they in fact do (Swami et al., 2010). Many women also feel evaluated by other women, believing that their female peers have even more stringent standards of weight and shape than they do themselves.

Body dissatisfaction is a risk factor for disordered eating.

It would be one thing if women had a reasonable chance of attaining their "ideal" bodies simply by not exceeding an average caloric intake or by maintaining a healthy weight. Quite simply, this is not possible for most people. As a society we are all (men, women, and children) getting heavier. In 2002, the average American woman aged 20–29 weighed 29 pounds more than her counterpart did in 1960 (Ogden et al., 2004). Some of this increase probably reflects general improvements in nutrition and pediatric health care. But other factors such as the widespread availability of high-calorie foods are also involved. Yet, as women's average weight has been increasing since the late 1950s, the weight of such cultural icons of attractiveness as *Playboy* centerfolds and Miss America contestants has decreased at a roughly comparable rate. In the name of science, two researchers (who no doubt had students lining up to help them with the study) calculated that 70 percent of *Playboy* centerfolds have a body mass index (see Table 9.4) below 18.5 (Katzmarzyk & Davis, 2001).

Table 9.4 Calculating Body Mass Index

$\dfrac{\text{weight (lb.)}}{\text{height (in.)}^2} \times 703 = \text{BMI}$	
	BMI
Healthy	18.5–24.9
Overweight	25–29.9
Obese	30–39.9
Morbidly obese	40

Even children's toys promote unrealistically slender ideals. Consider, for instance, the size and shape of the Barbie doll. For an average woman to achieve Barbie's proportions she would have to be 7 feet 2 inches tall, lose 10 inches from her waist, and add 12 inches to her bust (Moser, 1989). Yet

Valeria Lukyanova, a young Ukrainian woman, has had many surgeries to make her look like a real-life Barbie doll.

this has not stopped Valeria Lukyanova, a young Ukrainian woman, from undergoing extensive cosmetic surgery in her quest to look like a real-life Barbie doll. Up close, Lukyanova, who has a 17-inch waist and enormous breast implants, almost looks as if she is made of plastic. Rounding out the total package, Ms. Lukyanova who currently subsists on a liquid diet, says she is training herself to live off light and air.

The research literature strongly implicates body dissatisfaction as an important risk factor for pathological eating (McKnight Investigators, 2003). Indeed, in a recent prospective longitudinal study, body dissatisfaction emerged as the most powerful predictor of the onset of eating disorders in a sample of almost 500 adolescent girls (Stice et al., 2011). Body dissatisfaction is also associated with dieting and with negative affect. Pointedly, if we don't like how we look, we are likely to feel bad about ourselves. We may also try to lose weight in order to look better.

DIETING When people wish to be thinner, they typically go on a diet. Nearly all instances of eating disorders begin with the "normal" dieting that is routine in our culture. Have you ever dieted? Most people have, at some point in their lives (Jeffrey et al., 1991). Estimates are that, at any one time, approximately 39 percent of women and 21 percent of men are trying to lose weight (Hill, 2002).

Dieting is a risk factor for the development or worsening of eating disorders (Jacobi et al., 2004; Striegel-Moore & Bulik, 2007). In a large sample of adolescent girls, body dissatisfaction and dieting predicted symptoms of bulimia nervosa at a 1-year follow-up (Johnson & Wardle, 2005). In another large-scale longitudinal study, it was found that the majority of adolescent girls who went on to develop anorexia nervosa had been dieters (Patton et al., 1990).

As we all know, however, not everyone who diets develops an eating disorder. And in some cases diets can be helpful. For example, when overweight women were randomly assigned to either a low-calorie diet or a waiting list control group (that did not involve a diet), those who received the diet lost weight and showed a decrease in bulimic symptoms (Presnell & Stice, 2003). So why has dieting been linked to eating disorders?

Findings from a large longitudinal study provide some clarification. More than 1,800 young people were assessed and then followed up over a 10-year period (Goldschmidt et al., 2012). At each time point they were asked whether they had been dieting. Results indicated that going on a diet was indeed predictive of future binge eating. However, the results also highlighted the importance of other factors. More specifically, it was the people who dieted and who also reported more symptoms of depression or who had low self-esteem who were most likely to develop problems with binge eating later. In other words, although dieting itself was a risk factor for future binge eating, low self-esteem and symptoms of depression created additional risk.

Dieting is a risk factor for the development or worsening of eating disorders.

Although not included in the study just described, factors such as perfectionism, may also play a role. Those who have the highest expectations of themselves may be the people who are most likely to feel bad when they fail to meet their own self-imposed high standards. This highlights the importance of individual risk factors that might make dieting more problematic for some people as opposed to others.

NEGATIVE EMOTIONALITY   Negative affect (feeling bad) is a causal risk factor for body dissatisfaction (Stice, 2002). When we feel bad, we tend to become very self-critical. We may focus on our limitations and shortcomings while magnifying our flaws and defects. This seems to be especially true of individuals with eating disorders, who, like people with depression, tend to show distorted ways of thinking and of processing information received from the environment (e.g., Butow et al., 1993; Garner et al., 1997). In many cases, there is widespread negative self-evaluation (e.g., Fairburn et al., 1997). These cognitive distortions ("I'm fat; I'm a failure; I'm useless") have the potential to make people feel even worse about themselves.

Longitudinal studies have confirmed that depression and general negative affect are predictive of a high risk for later developing an eating disorder (Johnson, Cohen, et al., 2002; Leon et al., 1997). Moreover, evidence suggests that negative affect may work to maintain binge eating (see Stice, 2002). Patients often report that they engage in binges when they feel stressed, down, or bad about themselves. They further indicate that in the very short term, eating provides much-needed comfort. These reports are highly consistent with affect-regulation models that view binge eating as a distraction from negative feelings (see Vögele & Gibson, 2010). Of course, a major problem is that after binges patients feel disappointed or even disgusted with themselves. In short, a difficult situation leads to behavior that makes circumstances even worse.

Negative affect also predicts dietary restraint in anorexia nervosa. In one study 118 women with anorexia nervosa were asked to report on their mood and behaviors several times each day in response to a signal from a palm-top device. Being in a more negative mood on one day was associated with more restrictive eating the following day. Importantly, the opposite relationship was not found. More negative affect was not reported by participants on the day after a dietary restriction. This suggests that negative affect is more likely to be the trigger for dietary restriction, rather than the other way around (Engel et al., 2013).

CHILDHOOD SEXUAL ABUSE   Childhood sexual abuse has been implicated in the development of eating disorders (Jacobi et al., 2004). However, there is some debate about whether sexual abuse is truly a risk factor for eating disorders (see Stice, 2002). In one prospective study, Vogeltanz-Holm and colleagues (2000) failed to find that early sexual abuse predicted the later onset of binge eating. However, another prospective study found that children who had been sexually abused or physically neglected had higher rates of eating disorders and eating problems in adolescence and adulthood (Johnson, Cohen, et al., 2002). A meta-analysis of 53 studies also revealed a weak—but positive—association between childhood sexual abuse and eating pathology (Smolak & Murnen, 2002).

This suggests that the two variables are linked in some way, although the precise nature of the link is not yet clear. One possibility is that being sexually abused increases the risk of developing other disorders that are comorbid with eating disorders. This would mean that abuse is a general risk factor for psychopathology rather than a specific risk factor. Abuse may also increase other known risk factors for eating disorders, such as having a negative body image or high levels of negative affect. In other words, the causal pathway from early abuse to a later eating disorder may be an indirect one (rather than a direct one) that involves an array of other intervening variables.

in review

- What evidence suggests that genetic factors may play a role in the development of eating disorders?
- What brain areas are implicated in eating and eating disorders?
- What neurotransmitter has been implicated (and most well studied) in eating disorders?
- What individual characteristics are associated with increased risk for eating disorders?
- How might a diathesis–stress model be used to explain the development of eating disorders?

Treatment of Eating Disorders

9.3 Discuss how eating disorders are treated.

Patients with eating disorders are often very conflicted about getting well. Approximately 17 percent of patients with severe eating disorders have to be committed to a hospital for treatment against their will (Watson, Bowers, & Andersen, 2000). Suicide attempts are often made, and clinicians need to be mindful of this risk, even when patients have received a great deal of treatment (Franko et al., 2004).

This ambivalence toward recovery is apparent in the behavior of individuals admitted to inpatient units. Hospitalization also often means that those with anorexia nervosa will be exposed to other patients who are thinner and more experienced than they are. This can lead to competitive pressure to be the "best anorexic" patient on the unit (Wilson, Grilo, & Vitousek, 2007).

Some "pro-ana" (short for "pro-anorexia") or "pro-mia" ("pro-bulimia") websites actively support anorexic or bulimic behavior, creating much concern in the treatment community. These sites are often visited by young people (Custers & Van den Bulck, 2009). An experimental study has also shown that exposure to the material on these websites has significant negative consequences for young women. After viewing material on a pro-anorexia website, undergraduate participants reported more negative affect and felt less positive about themselves and their bodies than did participants assigned to view other websites that concerned fashion or home décor (Bardone-Cone & Cass, 2007).

Treatment of Anorexia Nervosa

Individuals with anorexia nervosa view the disorder as a chronic condition and are generally pessimistic about their potential for recovery (Holliday et al., 2005). They have a high dropout rate from therapy, and patients with the binge-eating/purging subtype of anorexia nervosa are especially likely to terminate inpatient treatment prematurely (Steinhausen, 2002; Woodside et al., 2004). Making the situation even worse, there have been surprisingly few controlled studies on which to base an informed judgment about which treatment modality will work best (le Grange & Lock, 2005; Wilson, Grilo, & Vitousek, 2007). In part, this is due to the fact that the disorder is rare. However, patients who suffer from anorexia nervosa are also often extremely reluctant to seek treatment. And when they do, taking part in research studies is unlikely to be a priority for them. These factors combine to make treatment research extremely difficult.

The most immediate concern with patients who have anorexia nervosa is to restore their weight to a level that is no longer life threatening. In severe cases, this requires hospitalization and extreme measures such as intravenous feeding. This is followed by rigorous control of the patient's caloric intake so as to progress toward a targeted range of weight gain. Normally, this short-term effort is successful. However, without treatment designed to address the psychological issues that fuel the anorexic behavior, any weight gain will be temporary and the patient will soon need medical attention again. In some cases aggressive treatment efforts can backfire (Strober, 2004).

MEDICATIONS   Antidepressants are sometimes used in the treatment of anorexia nervosa, although there is no evidence that they are especially effective (Brown & Keel, 2012b). In contrast, research suggests that treatment with an antipsychotic medication called olanzapine may be beneficial. Antipsychotic medications (which help with disturbed thinking) are routinely used in the treatment of schizophrenia (see Chapter 13). These medications also provide benefits in the treatment of anorexia nervosa, which is characterized by distorted beliefs about body shape and size. More importantly, one side effect of olanzapine is weight gain. Although this is a problem for patients with schizophrenia, in the treatment of anorexia nervosa weight gain is obviously much more desirable.

FAMILY THERAPY   For adolescents with anorexia nervosa, family therapy is considered to be the treatment of choice. The best-studied approach, which (very importantly) blames neither the parents nor the child for the anorexia nervosa, is known as the Maudsley model (le Grange & Lock, 2005). A typical treatment program involves 10 to 20 sessions spaced over 6 to 12 months. The treatment has three phases. In the refeeding phase, the therapist works with the parents and supports their efforts to help their child (typically a daughter) to eat healthily once more. Family meals are observed by the therapist, and efforts are made to guide the parents as a functioning support team for their daughter's recovery. After the patient starts to gain weight, the negotiations for a new pattern of relationships phase begins, and family issues and problems begin to be addressed. Later, in the termination phase of treatment, the focus is on the development of more healthy relationships between the patient and her parents (see Lock et al., 2001).

Randomized controlled trials have shown that patients treated with family therapy for 1 year do better than patients who are assigned to a control treatment (where they receive supportive counseling on an individual basis). Five years after treatment, 75 to 90 percent of patients show full recovery (le Grange & Lock, 2005). In a more recent study, 121 adolescents were randomly assigned to receive either family-based treatment or individual therapy. Both treatments involved a total of 24 hours of treatment spaced over the course of a year. At the end of treatment, 42 percent of patients who received family treatment were in full remission. For those who received individual therapy, the corresponding figure was 23 percent. When followed up another year later, 49 percent of the patients who had received family-based therapy were well, compared with 23 percent of those who had been treated with individual therapy (Lock et al., 2010). What is encouraging about these findings is that an overwhelming majority of adolescents completed the treatments and did not drop out. This suggests that, although individual therapy (which encouraged weight gain, the development of autonomy, and accepting responsibility for food-related issues) was slightly less efficacious overall than family treatment, it was still very acceptable to the adolescents who received it and it still provided some benefit. This is good news, especially for adolescents whose family members are unable or unwilling to participate in family treatment.

Family therapy is now regarded as the treatment of choice for adolescents with anorexia nervosa. The therapy is most effective for those in the earlier stages of the illness.

Not surprisingly, family treatment is more helpful for some patients than it is for others. Patients who develop anorexia nervosa before age 19 and have been ill for fewer than 3 years seem to do better than patients who have been ill for longer or who have bulimia nervosa (Dare & Eisler, 2002). This highlights the importance of early treatment, which may save some patients from a lifetime of suffering. For patients who are older or who have a long history of anorexia nervosa, the Maudsley approach unfortunately provides little clinical benefit (Wilson, Grilo, & Vitousek, 2007).

Research Close-Up
Randomized Controlled Trials

A randomized controlled trial involves a specific treatment group (which is the group the researchers are most interested in) as well as a control treatment group (against which the treatment group will be compared). Participants have an equal chance of being placed in either group because which group they go into is randomly determined.

COGNITIVE-BEHAVIOR THERAPY Cognitive-behavior **therapy (CBT)**, which involves changing behavior and maladaptive styles of thinking, has proved to be very effective in treating bulimia nervosa. Because anorexia nervosa shares many features with bulimia nervosa, CBT is often used with patients with anorexia nervosa as well (Vitousek, 2002). The recommended length of treatment is 1 to 2 years. A major focus of the treatment involves modifying distorted beliefs concerning weight and food, as well as distorted beliefs about the self that may have contributed to the disorder (e.g., "People will reject me unless I am thin").

Pike and colleagues (2003) treated a sample of 33 women who had anorexia nervosa, after they had been discharged from the hospital. Over the course of 1 year, the women received either 50 sessions of CBT or nutritional counseling. Despite this, only 17 percent of patients who received CBT showed full recovery. None of the women who received nutritional counseling was fully well (i.e., normal weight, no binge eating or purging, and with eating attitudes and concerns about weight within normal limits) at the end of treatment. The limited success of CBT for patients with anorexia nervosa may be due to the extreme cognitive rigidity that is characteristic of those with this disorder (Brown & Keel, 2012a). There is clearly a need for new treatment developments, particularly for older patients with more long-standing problems. As the Developments in Practice box illustrates, however, there are some promising new approaches.

Treatment of Bulimia Nervosa

MEDICATIONS It is quite common for patients with bulimia nervosa to be treated with antidepressant medications. Researchers became interested in using these medications after it became clear that many patients with bulimia nervosa also suffer from mood disorders. Generally speaking

Developments in Practice

New Options for Adults with Anorexia Nervosa

Anorexia nervosa is a challenging disorder to treat, especially in adults. Psychotherapy remains the preferred treatment, although the results are often disappointing. There is also no leading treatment.

A recent randomized controlled trial involving 242 patients who received one of three very different treatments has provided further confirmation of this (Zipfel et al., 2014). The results showed that CBT, a psychodynamic type of therapy, and an improved version of treatment as usual all provided patients with some clinical benefit. Importantly, no approach was superior to any other. Similar findings have also been reported by Schmidt and colleagues (2015). These researchers compared a treatment that targeted both cognitive and interpersonal factors with a treatment that was more supportive in nature and gave patients information, advice, and encouragement. Although patients tended to prefer the cognitive–interpersonal treatment

(which addressed rigid thinking, perfectionism, unhealthy positive beliefs about anorexia nervosa, as well as emotional issues), there were no overall differences between the two treatments with regard to how well patients did. By the 12-month follow-up assessment, 84 percent of patients in the cognitive–interpersonal group were partially or fully recovered. For the supportive treatment group, the corresponding figure was 82 percent. For both treatments, partial recovery was much more common than full recovery.

Rather than lamenting the fact that we have no leading treatment for adults with anorexia nervosa, we view these findings in a more positive light. No single treatment seems to be best at this time. Instead, a number of different approaches appear to have promise. This provides a range of potential treatment options for patients, allowing their preferences, as well as the expertise of the clinician, to be fully considered.

(and in contrast to patients with anorexia nervosa), patients taking antidepressants do better than patients who are given inert, placebo medications. A positive response is usually apparent within the first 3 weeks. People who do not show early improvement are unlikely to benefit from further treatment with the same medication (Sysko et al., 2010). Perhaps surprisingly, antidepressants seem to decrease the frequency of binges as well as improve patients' mood and preoccupation with shape and weight (McElroy et al., 2010).

COGNITIVE-BEHAVIORAL THERAPY   The leading treatment for bulimia nervosa is CBT. Most of the current treatment approaches are based on the work of Fairburn and colleagues in Oxford, England. Multiple controlled studies that include posttreatment and long-term follow-up outcomes attest to the clinical benefits of CBT for bulimia (Fairburn et al., 1993; Wilson, 2010). Such studies have included comparisons with medication therapy (chiefly antidepressants) and with interpersonal psychotherapy (see Agras et al., 2000). They generally reveal CBT to be superior. In fact, combining CBT and medications produces only a modest increment in effectiveness over that attainable with CBT alone.

The "behavioral" component of CBT for bulimia nervosa focuses on normalizing eating patterns. This includes meal planning, nutritional education, and ending binging and purging cycles by teaching the person to eat small amounts of food more regularly. The "cognitive" element of the treatment is aimed at changing the cognitions and behaviors that initiate or perpetuate a binge cycle. This is accomplished by challenging the dysfunctional thought

patterns typically present in bulimia nervosa, such as the "all-or-nothing" or dichotomous thinking described earlier. For instance, CBT challenges the tendency to divide all foods into "good" and "bad" categories. This is done by providing factual information, as well as by arranging for the patients to demonstrate to themselves that ingesting "bad" food does not inevitably lead to a total loss of control over eating. Figure 9.4 shows a cognitive worksheet that was completed by a patient. It provides a good example of the kind of "hot thought" that can facilitate a binge.

Treatment with CBT clearly helps to reduce the severity of symptoms in patients with bulimia nervosa. Still, patients with the disorder are rarely entirely well at the end of treatment (Lundgren et al., 2004). Binging and purging is eliminated in around 30 to 50 percent of cases (Wilson, 2010). Even after treatment, weight and shape concerns may remain. In an effort to improve treatment efficacy, new approaches such as dialectical behavior therapy (which is a treatment for borderline personality disorder; see Chapter 10) are now being explored, with some success (Chen & Safer, 2010, Safer et al., 2001). Another promising development involves using more individualized CBT approaches that are specifically tailored to the needs of the patient as opposed to a more standardized treatment format (Ghaderi, 2006).

One of the newest developments in the treatment of eating disorders is to adopt a transdiagnostic approach to treatment. As we have already mentioned, the majority of patients with eating disorders have a mixed clinical picture. What this means is that they show some symptoms of anorexia and some symptoms of bulimia, combined in a

Figure 9.4

Ellie's completed worksheet: Identifying dysfunctional thoughts

Situation	Emotions and feelings	Dysfunctional thoughts
At home, alone.	Restless	If I don't eat it now, I'll never get it again.
Didn't go to the gym.	Tired	I'll just have one
Feeling bad about overeating yesterday.	Angry at self	I'm alone. No one will know
		You'll never be able to sustain any progress anyway, so why not just eat?

- What is the situation?
- Who is there?
- What are you doing?
- What are you thinking about?

- What emotions or feelings are you having?

- What are you saying to yourself that gives you permission to start eating or keep eating?
- Can you identify the "hot thought" that makes it likely you will binge?

variety of ways. Fairburn and colleagues (2009) have now reformulated cognitive behavior therapy for bulimia nervosa in an effort to increase its potency and also to make it a relevant treatment for pathological eating, no matter what the diagnosis is. The new treatment is called enhanced cognitive-behavior therapy, or CBT-E. One form of the treatment (the default treatment) is quite focused, targeting eating issues as well as concerns about shape and weight, extreme dieting, purging, and binge eating. The other form of the treatment is broader and also addresses such things as perfectionism, low self-esteem, and relationship problems.

In a recent evaluation of the default form of enhanced cognitive-behavior therapy, 130 patients with eating disorders were randomly assigned to receive either CBT-E or another treatment called interpersonal psychotherapy (IPT). IPT, which seeks to improve interpersonal functioning, is often used in the treatment of mood disorders (see Chapter 7) and is also the leading alternative treatment for eating disorders. All patients received 20 sessions of their assigned treatment and were then followed up for more than a year. At the end of treatment, 66 percent of the patients who received CBT-E were in remission compared to 33 percent of those who received IPT (Fairburn et al., 2015). Moreover, at the end of the 1-year follow-up, patients who had been treated with CBT-E were still doing better, although the IPT group had caught up somewhat (69 versus 49 percent remitted). Overall, these findings show that, as a transdiagnostic treatment, CBT-E is very beneficial. The results also suggest that although IPT is a viable alternative treatment, CBT-E works more quickly. All of this is very welcome news for people struggling to cope with eating disorders.

Watch   In the Real World: Eating Disorders

Treatment of Binge-Eating Disorder

BED has attracted a lot of attention from researchers, and a number of different treatment approaches have been suggested. Due to the high level of comorbidity between binge-eating disorder and depression, antidepressant medications are sometimes used to treat this disorder. Other categories of medications, such as appetite suppressants and anticonvulsant medications, have also been a focus of interest (McElroy et al., 2010).

In one of the largest and most scientifically rigorous studies to date, Wilson and colleagues (2010) randomly assigned 205 men and women who were overweight or obese and who met diagnostic criteria for BED to one of three different treatments. Some people received interpersonal psychotherapy, which we mentioned earlier. Others received CBT in the form of a self-help book (*Overcoming Binge Eating*, Fairburn, 1995), guided by a therapist. People in the third group were assigned to a behavioral weight loss treatment that involved exercise and moderate restriction of calories. So how did everyone do? At the end of 6 months of treatment, there were no significant differences between the groups with regard to remission from binge eating. However, at 2-year follow-up, people who had received either IPT or guided CBT were doing better than those in the behavioral weight loss group. What is also noteworthy is that the dropout rate was much lower for people in the IPT group (7 percent dropped out) than it was in the guided CBT (30 percent) or behavioral weight loss groups (28 percent). This is important because, overall, the dropout rate for minorities in this study was very high (approximately one-third). The findings therefore suggest that for racial and ethnic minorities with BED, interpersonal psychotherapy might be a particularly suitable treatment approach.

in review

- What factors make eating disorders (especially anorexia nervosa) so difficult to treat?
- Describe the main features of the Maudsley approach for the treatment of anorexia nervosa. For what kind of patients does this approach yield better results?
- What treatment approaches have been shown to be helpful for binge-eating disorder?
- Why do you think cognitive-behavior therapy is so beneficial for patients with bulimia nervosa?
- What is a transdiagnostic treatment approach?

The Problem of Obesity

9.4   **Define obesity and explain why it is a worldwide problem.**

Humans have evolved to be able to store surplus energy as fat. This has obvious advantages: It serves as a hedge against periods of food shortage and makes survival more likely during times of famine. But in our modern world, access to food is no longer a problem for millions of people. The food supply is stable, and large amounts of energy-dense foods are readily available. Not surprisingly, most of us are getting heavier. For some people, the problem becomes even more extreme and results in obesity. Considered in this way, obesity can be regarded as a state of excessive, chronic fat storage (Berthoud & Morrison, 2008).

Worldwide, obesity is now a major public health problem. The statistics are alarming. Since 1980, the prevalence of obesity has more than doubled (World Health Organization, 2015c). More than 1.9 billion adults are overweight and 600 million are obese. In the United States, the most recent estimates show that 35 percent of adults are obese and another 34 percent are overweight (Ogden et al., 2014). In other words, less than a third of the population is at a normal or healthy weight. Figure 9.5 illustrates the prevalence and distribution of obesity in adults across America.

Figure 9.5   Prevalence* of Self-Reported Obesity Among U.S. Adults by State and Territory, BRFSS, 2013

Obesity has increased dramatically in the United States during the past 20 years.

(Adapted from Behavioral Risk Factor Surveillance Systems (BRFSS), Centers for Disease Control and Prevention.)

*Prevalence estimates reflect BRFSS methodological changes started in 2011. These estimates should not be compared to prevalence estimates before 2011.

+Guam and Puerto Rico were the only U.S. territories with obesity data available on the 2013 BRFSS.

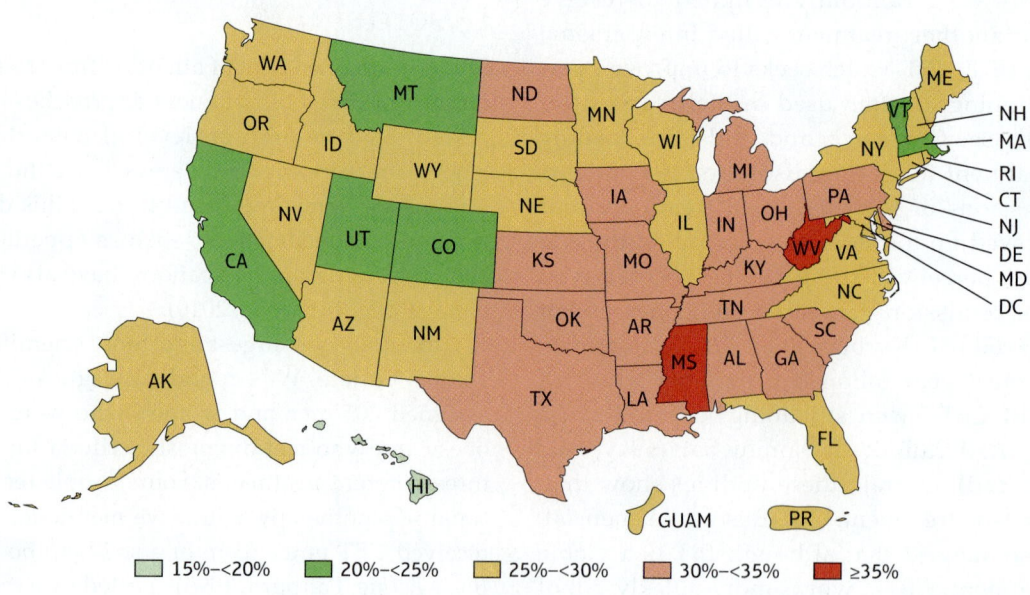

15%–<20%   20%–<25%   25%–<30%   30%–<35%   ≥35%

Medical Issues

Obesity brings with it increased risk for many health problems. These include high cholesterol, hypertension, heart disease, arthritis, diabetes, and cancer (Malnick & Knobler, 2006). It has been estimated that, by 2030, the cost of treating these problems in the United States alone will exceed $850 billion annually (Wang et al., 2008). In addition, people who are obese have a reduced life expectancy of 5 to 20 years (Fontaine et al., 2003). It should therefore come as no surprise that the World Health Organization recognizes obesity as one of the top 10 global health problems.

Definition and Prevalence

Obesity is defined on the basis of a statistic called the **body mass index (BMI)**. This is a measure of a person's weight relative to height and is calculated using the formula shown earlier in Table 9.4. Generally speaking, people with a BMI below 18.5 are considered underweight; 18.5 to 24.9 is considered normal; 25.0 to 29.9 is overweight; and obesity is defined as having a BMI above 30. Having a BMI above 40 or being more than 100 pounds overweight is called morbid obesity. This is the point at which excess weight begins to interfere with basic activities such as walking and creates many health problems.

Table 9.5 shows current prevalence rates of overweight and obesity for different groups of adults in the United States. As we have already mentioned, the majority of us (68.5 percent) weigh more than we should. But gender and ethnicity are also very important. With the exception of Asians, obesity is more prevalent in ethnic minorities. In general, rates of obesity are also somewhat higher in men than they are in women. The notable exception here involves African Americans. One in every two black women is obese. This is the highest rate of obesity found for any group (Ogden et al., 2014).

Table 9.5 Prevalence of Overweight and Obesity in U.S. Adults

Group	Overweight or Obese (%)	Obese (%)
All	68.5	34.9
Non-Hispanic White	67.2	32.6
Hispanic	77.9	42.5
Non-Hispanic Asian	38.6	10.8
Non-Hispanic Black	76.2	47.8

NOTE: Figures based on BMI of 25 or above for overweight and 30 or above for obesity.

SOURCE: Ogden et al. (2014).

Weight Stigma

People who are obese are often judged harshly by others. They are routinely ridiculed, discriminated against, and stigmatized (Carr & Friedman, 2005). A powerful source of this is the media, which perpetuates weight-based stereotypes and often depicts people who are overweight or obese in a very negative light. Compared to thin television characters, those who are overweight or obese are more likely to be shown when eating, are less likely to be depicted as being involved in romantic relationships, and are more likely to be the target of derisive comments (see Schvey et al., 2011). Audiences also laugh more when negative comments are directed toward overweight characters, especially female ones.

Juror perceptions may also be biased against women with obesity. In a novel study, participants were asked to read a vignette describing a case of check fraud. At the same time, they were also shown an image (mug shot) of the alleged defendant. The mug shots were either of a lean man, a lean woman, or (thanks to digital alteration software) the same man or woman who now looked obese. All participants read the same case vignette and saw one of the four mug shots. They were then asked to rate the defendant's guilt on a 5-point scale (Schvey et al., 2013). So what difference did the weight of the defendant make? When the defendant was male, his weight made no difference at all. However, when the defendant was female, male participants (but not female participants) were much more likely to rate her as guilty if she was obese rather than lean. They also rated her as more likely to be a repeat offender. These results are important because they illustrate how gender and weight may have an impact on perceptions of guilt and culpability in a simulated jury study. They also raise the possibility that weight-based discrimination could operate against women who are visibly obese in legal situations.

Weight bias is even found in health care professionals who may blame patients who are obese for being overweight and having weight-related health problems (Mold & Forbes, 2011). The World Around Us box describes some of the consequences that stigma has on people who are overweight.

But being obese may not be the personal choice that many people believe it is. The more research progresses, the more we are learning about how important genes and other biological factors are in determining the drive to eat and the way our bodies respond when we eat less. We are also learning how powerful environmental factors can be. In short, the idea that we can simply decide to control our weight by eating less and exercising more does not always fit with the scientific facts.

The World Around Us

Do Negative Messages about Being Overweight Encourage Overweight People to Eat More or Less?

In our society many people still consider it acceptable to make fun of those who are overweight or obese. But what effect does this have on the people who receive such stigmatizing messages? To address this question, Schvey and colleagues (2011) asked overweight and normal-weight women to view one of two videos. One video depicted clips from neutral scenes such as insurance commercials. The other video contained clips from televisions shows and movies that depicted women who were overweight and obese in negative ways (e.g., as clumsy, lazy, and loud). After watching the videos, all the women were given questionnaires to complete in private. The room also contained three different bowls of snack foods, which the women were invited to eat.

The variable that the researchers were most interested in was how much the women ate after being exposed to the different types of films. After seeing the stigmatizing videos the overweight women consumed 303 calories of snack food. This is more than three times as much as the 89 calories consumed by the overweight women who had watched the neutral film. The overweight women who had watched the stigmatizing videos also ate significantly more calories than the normal-weight women who watched either type of film.

Television is a powerful source of weight-based stereotypes. The average American watches around 150 hours of television a month. Far from motivating people who are overweight and obese to lose weight, the negatively biased portrayals of obesity that we routinely see on TV may actually lead people to eat more rather than less.

Next time you watch TV, be on the lookout for biased portrayals of obesity. How is obesity treated in the media? Why do you think it is still acceptable to many people to make jokes at the expense of people who are obese?

Obesity and the *DSM*

From a diagnostic perspective, obesity is not an eating disorder, and it is not included in *DSM-5*. However, Volkow and O'Brien (2007) suggest that some forms of obesity are driven by an excessive motivational desire for food. They liken such symptoms as the compulsive consumption of food and the inability to restrain eating despite the wish to do so to symptoms of substance abuse and drug dependence. This parallels the view, offered by some, that obesity is a "food addiction" (see Cota et al., 2006). It has also been suggested that obesity and addiction may both concern problems in key brain regions involved in motivation, reward, and inhibitory control. Of course, the idea that obesity is a brain disorder is very controversial. Nonetheless, it does illustrate how much ideas about obesity are beginning to change.

in review

- Why is the increase in the prevalence of obesity such a public health concern?
- Explain the importance of the body mass index in the definition of obesity.
- How are ethnicity, gender, and social class related to rates of obesity?
- How do the media portray people who are overweight and obese? What are some of the consequences of this?
- On what grounds is the argument being made that obesity might be a brain disorder? What effect might this have on stigma?

Risk and Causal Factors in Obesity

9.5 **Describe who is most at risk for obesity.**

Many factors contribute to the development of obesity. They include genes, hormones involved in regulating appetite or energy balance, as well as lifestyle factors and family influences.

The Role of Genes

Are you the kind of person who can eat high-calorie foods without significant weight gain? Or does it seem as though you need only to look at a piece of chocolate cake to gain a few pounds? In all probability our genetic makeup plays an important role in determining how predisposed we are to becoming obese in the modern environment of increased food availability. Some of the genes that may, in our ancestral past, have been advantageous and helped us survive in times of famine may predispose those who carry them to readily gain weight when food is plentiful. Interestingly, population groups that were most susceptible to starvation throughout history (e.g., Pima Indians, Pacific Islanders) are those that are most inclined to become obese when they have a sedentary lifestyle and a Western diet (see Friedman, 2003).

Thinness seems to run in families (Bulik & Allison, 2002). Genes associated with thinness and leanness have been found in certain animals, and a special type of rat has now been bred that does not become obese even when fed a high-fat diet. Twin studies further suggest that genes play a role both in the development of obesity and in the tendency to binge (Bulik, Sullivan, et al., 2003; Javaras et al., 2008).

Indeed, a genetic mutation has been discovered that is specifically associated with binge eating (Branson et al., 2003). Although this mutation was found only in a minority (5 percent) of the people with obesity in the study, all of the obese people with the gene reported problems with binge eating. In contrast, only 14 percent of people with obesity who did not have the genetic mutation displayed a pattern of binge eating.

Although we often seek simplicity and hope to find small numbers of genes that have powerful effects, the available evidence suggests that BMI is polygenic and likely is very much influenced by a large number of common genes. Using GWAS approaches, researchers have now identified 97 genetic regions that are associated with body mass index and body fat distribution (Locke et al., 2015). Many more will likely be found in the future. The genes that have been identified thus far play a role in a broad range of functions highlighting the complexity of the biological pathways that influence obesity.

Hormones Involved in Appetite and Weight Regulation

In the course of a year, the average person will consume 1 million calories or more and yet keep a reasonably stable weight. How do we accomplish this? The answers lie in the remarkable ability of our bodies to regulate the daily quantity of food consumed and to balance this with our energy output over the longer term. This is relevant to the concept of a set point that we described earlier. Remarkably, we are able to regulate our energy balance with a precision of more than 99.5 percent. This is far in excess of what we could monitor in any conscious or mindful way (Friedman, 2004).

One key element of this homeostatic system is a hormone called **leptin**. Leptin (the name comes from the Greek word *leptos*, meaning "thin") is produced by fat cells. It provides a key metabolic signal that informs the central nervous system about the state of the body's fat reserves. When body fat levels decrease, leptin production decreases and food intake is stimulated (Ravussin et al., 2014). Rare genetic mutations that result in an inability to produce leptin cause people to have an insatiable appetite and result in morbid obesity. One 9-year-old girl in England weighed 200 pounds. She could hardly walk because of her extreme weight. When it was discovered that she was lacking leptin, she was treated with injections of the hormone, and her weight consequently returned to normal (Farooqi et al., 2002; Montague et al., 1997).

Unfortunately, when leptin is given to individuals who are overweight, in the majority of cases it has little effect. People who are overweight generally have high levels of leptin in their bloodstream. The problem is that they are resistant to its effects. In fact, it has been suggested that obesity may result from a person's being resistant to leptin (Friedman, 2004). However, this is not an adequate explanation because even lean individuals show resistance to high concentrations of leptin (Ravussin et al., 2014). Despite this complication, the leptin system is still a major focus of interest in the search for antiobesity drugs.

Why do we get hungry at regular times during the day even if we do not even see or smell food? The reason may lie in a hormone called **ghrelin**. Ghrelin (the name comes from a Hindu word meaning "growth") is a hormone that is produced by the stomach. It is a powerful appetite stimulator. Under normal circumstances, ghrelin levels rise before a meal and fall after we have eaten. When ghrelin is injected into human volunteers, it makes them very hungry. This suggests that ghrelin is a key contributor to the appetite control system.

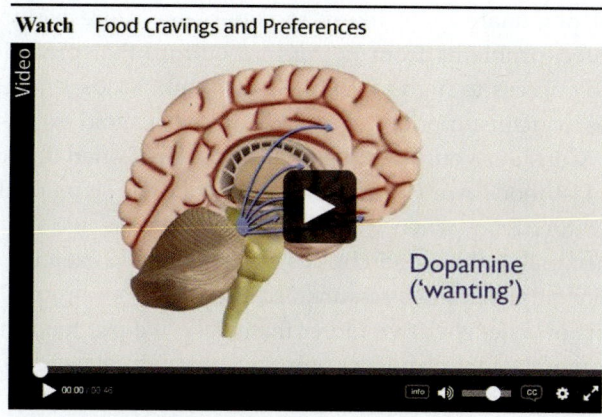

People with a rare condition called Prader–Willi syndrome have chromosomal abnormalities that create many problems, one of which is very high levels of ghrelin. Sufferers are extremely obese and often die before

This woman suffers from Prader–Willi syndrome, a rare genetic disorder that makes people insatiably hungry. After a year in a group home with rigid dietary rules, she lost 80 pounds.

age 30 from obesity-related causes. The food cravings experienced by people with Prader–Willi syndrome can be so extreme that food has to be kept locked away so that they cannot binge. Although this genetic disorder is very unusual, findings such as this highlight the role of genetics in the regulation of eating behavior and weight. They also illustrate how the biological drive to eat can be so powerful that willpower is no match for it.

Sociocultural Influences

The examples of Prader–Willi syndrome and mutations of the leptin gene tell us that genes alone can sometimes explain why people differ in their weight and eating patterns. However, in most cases environmental factors also play an important role. As with other disorders we have discussed in this text, a diathesis–stress perspective is most appropriate. Some of us, by virtue of our genetic makeup and personality, are likely to experience more weight-related problems from living in a culture that provides ready access to high-fat, high-sugar (junk) foods, encourages overconsumption, and makes it easy to avoid exercise.

Consider your own lifestyle issues. How often do you eat fast food? Are you more likely to take the stairs or the elevator? Even when we have good intentions, we sometimes make poor food choices or get too little exercise. A major culprit is time pressure. Because we are so chronically short of time, we drive rather than walk. We put food into our mouths far too quickly, outpacing our natural feelings of fullness. This leads us to keep eating. Finally, as the pace of life gets faster, we have less time to prepare food. So we eat out more often or buy more prepackaged or fast food. Which of these behaviors do you recognize in yourself?

As Brownell and his colleagues (Brownell, 2003; Gearhardt et al., 2011) have pointed out, the food industry is also highly skilled at getting us to maximize our food intake. The original bottle of Coco-Cola was 6.5 oz. Many individually sized bottles are now three times that big (Pomeranz & Brownell, 2014). And restaurants in the United States serve large portions of foods that are specifically engineered to be hyperpalatable (especially tasty and rewarding) because they contain so much sugar or fat. Some examples of commonly eaten foods are shown in Table 9.6. One comparison of the same fast-food chains and eateries in Philadelphia and Paris found that the average portion sizes in Paris were 25 percent smaller (Rozin et al., 2003). In addition, the culture of supersizing tempts us to buy more than we might choose to buy otherwise simply because it costs only a little bit more (Brownell, 2003). And when people are given free access to food, the amount they eat each day is around 150 percent of what they actually need for their energy requirements (Ravussin et al., 2014). What do you think the implications of this are for people who go on a cruise vacation or stay at an "all-inclusive" resort?

When people are given free access to food, they eat much more than they need to fulfill their basic energy requirements. If you have ever been on a cruise, or helped yourself from an all-you-can-eat buffet, you probably already know this!

Table 9.6 Sugar and Fat in Traditional and Hyperpalatable Foods

Food	Portion Size	Type	Sugar (g)	Fat (g)
Apple	1 medium	T	19	0
Tomato	1 medium	T	3	0
Orange	1 cup, sections	T	17	0
Chicken breast	3 ounces	T	0	3
Coca-Cola	1 can	H	39	0
McDonald's fries	1 medium	H	0	19
Dairy Queen	1 medium ice cream	H	34	10

NOTE: T = traditional food; H = hyperpalatable food. Dairy Queen ice cream cone is chocolate flavor.

SOURCE: Gearhardt et al. (2011).

Ultraprocessed foods that are high in sugar, fat, and salt may be capable of triggering an addictive process. When rats were given extended access to a "cafeteria" diet of foods such as chocolate, cheesecake, sausage, and bacon (as well as to standard rat chow), they rapidly gained weight. They also began to consume these foods almost exclusively, eating very little of the rat chow. What was especially noteworthy was that the rats with extended access to the cafeteria diet were also insensitive to cues that signaled the delivery of electric foot shocks. Even under conditions of punishment, these rats did not decrease their intake of the foods they desired (Johnson & Kenny, 2010). There was also evidence that extended access to the high-fat, high-sugar foods resulted in a downregulation of activity in brain reward circuits, perhaps because the brain reward systems had been overstimulated by the excessive consumption of the palatable foods. If this is true, overconsumption of ultraprocessed foods could contribute to the development and maintenance of compulsive eating because eating these foods becomes less and less rewarding over time and more and more food is required to obtain the same amount of "reward."

Rats given extended access to high-fat, high-sugar foods quickly gain weight. They also show decreases in brain reward circuits. If food becomes less rewarding, this could potentially drive the development of compulsive eating.

Consider also the issue of accessibility. Foods with low nutritional value (high fat, high sugar) are less expensive and also much easier to find than foods with high nutritional value. Next time you go to a gas station or go out to see a movie, look at the food choices that are available. How much healthy food is on offer? Is it easier to find an apple or a candy bar? Notice how easy it is to mindlessly pick up a cheap high-calorie item that provides little nutrition.

If you like to snack in front of the TV you should also be aware of how powerful food advertising can be. Food advertising seems to trigger the kind of automatic and unconscious eating that is not related to being hungry. In one study, children ate 45 percent more after watching a TV cartoon that contained food advertisements than they did if the cartoon contained advertising for other products (Harris et al., 2009). This is a worrying finding given that children ages 2 to 11 see about a dozen television ads each day for products high in fat, salt, or sugar (Powell et al., 2013). A recent fMRI study has also demonstrated a link between food commercials and weight gain in adolescents.

Food advertising leads us to eat more even when we are not hungry. In one study, children ate 45 percent more when they watched a cartoon that contained food advertising.

Compared to those whose brains showed less activation, adolescents who showed greater activity in the striatum (a brain region involved in reward processing) in response to food commercials gained more weight over the following year (Yokum et al., 2014).

Continued exposure to a culture that provides easy access to highly palatable foods, offers large portions, and bombards people with endless food advertisements may explain why rates of obesity increase in immigrants after they have lived in the United States for a while. Although recent immigrants are less likely to be overweight and obese than people born in the United States, after they have lived in the country for 10 years or longer they have a significant increase in their body mass index (Goel et al., 2004). This suggests that sociocultural factors are likely to be playing a major role. In addition to the emphasis on food, what other aspects of American culture do you think might be exerting an influence here?

Family Influences

Family behavior patterns may also play a role in the development of excessive eating and obesity. In some families, a high-fat, high-calorie diet (or an overemphasis on food) may lead to obesity in many or all family members, including the family pet. In other families, eating (or overeating) becomes a habitual means of alleviating emotional distress or showing love (Musante et al., 1998). Children whose mothers smoked during pregnancy or whose mothers gained a lot of weight during the pregnancy are also at a higher risk of being overweight at age 3 (Gillman et al., 2008).

Family attitudes toward food are important because their consequences are likely to remain with us for a long time. Obesity is related to the number and size of fat (adipose) cells in the body (Heymsfield et al., 1995). People who are obese have markedly more adipose cells than people of normal weight (Peeke & Chrousos, 1995). When people with obesity lose weight, the size of the cells is reduced but not their number. Some evidence suggests that the total number of adipose cells stays the same from childhood onward (Crisp et al., 1970).

It is possible that overfeeding infants and young children causes them to develop more adipose cells and may thus predispose them to weight problems in adulthood. Consistent with this, DiPietro and colleagues (1994) found that, in a 40-year follow-up study, the majority of a sample of 504 overweight children became overweight adults.

Finally, there is some evidence that obesity might be "socially contagious." Provocative research findings have shown that if someone close to us (e.g., a spouse, sibling, or friend) becomes obese, the chance that we ourselves will later become obese can increase by as much as 57 percent. The effect is most marked within same-sex versus opposite-sex relationships, suggesting that social influences might be playing a key role. In contrast, weight gain in neighbors was not associated with later weight gain in those who lived close by, again suggesting that it is the closeness of the relationship, rather than exposure to common environmental factors, that might be important (Christakis & Fowler, 2007). Although the mechanisms of this social transmission are far from clear, it is possible that obesity in our close friends and family members could lead us to change our attitudes about weight or perhaps could influence our eating patterns.

Research suggests that obesity can be socially contagious. If someone close to us becomes obese, the chance that we will later become obese can increase by as much as 57 percent.

Stress and "Comfort Food"

Do you eat when you are stressed or unhappy? If you do, what kinds of food do you crave? Foods that are high in fat or carbohydrates are the foods that console most of us when we are feeling troubled (Canetti et al., 2002). Workers who say that they are under a lot of stress report that they eat less healthy foods, and foods that are higher in fat, relative to their less stressed counterparts (Ng & Jeffery, 2003).

Eating for comfort is found in rats too. When rats were placed under chronic stress (being subjected to cold temperatures), they selected diets that were higher in fat and sugar (Dallman et al., 2003). What is also interesting in this study is that the rats that ate the comfort food gained weight in their bellies and became calmer in the face of new acute stress. This prompted the researchers to speculate that the sugary and fatty foods helped to reduce activation in the stress response system.

Might overeating function as a means of reducing feelings of distress or depression? Certainly many people with obesity experience psychological problems such as depression. In a large community sample of more than 40,000 people, lifetime rates of mood disorders were higher in people who were obese than in people whose weight was in the normal range (Petry et al., 2008). Other research has found that a striking percentage of people with an eating disorder binge eat in response to aversive emotional states, such as feeling depressed or anxious (Kenardy et al., 1996).

In light of Dallman's data on the stressed rats, it is easy to grasp how weight gain (or a tendency to maintain excessive weight) may be explained quite simply in terms of learning principles. We are all conditioned to eat in response to a wide range of environmental stimuli (at parties, during movies, while watching TV). Individuals who are obese have been shown to be conditioned to more cues—both internal and external—than others of normal weight. Anxiety, anger, boredom, and depression may lead to overeating. Eating in response to such cues is then reinforced because the taste of good food is pleasurable and because the individual's emotional tension is reduced.

Pathways to Obesity

Understanding the causes of obesity is complex because it results from a combination of genetic, environmental, and sociocultural influences. An important step along the pathway to obesity, however, may be binge eating. In a prospective study of 231 adolescent girls, Stice and colleagues (2002) established that binge eating is a predictor of later obesity. This suggests that we should pay close attention to the causes of binge eating.

Animal studies show that, in rats, any genetic differences that exist in the tendency to binge eat only start to emerge during puberty (Klump et al., 2011). Biological risk factors may thus become more important as we enter adolescence. Unfortunately, this is also the developmental period when sociocultural pressures may be most intense.

Relevant here is research suggesting that one pathway to binge eating may be through social pressure to conform to the thin ideal, as ironic as this may seem (Stice et al., 2002). Being heavy often leads to dieting, which may lead to binge eating when willpower wanes (see Figure 9.6). Another pathway to binge eating may operate through depression and low self-esteem. In Stice and colleagues' prospective study, low levels of support from peers, as well as depression, made girls more at risk for binging. We further have confirmation that when children are overweight, they are more likely to be rejected by their peers (Latner & Stunkard, 2003; Strauss & Pollack, 2003), consequently increasing their negative affect. As Figure 9.6 shows, a pattern of binge eating in response to negative emotions may make a bad situation much worse—increasing weight, depression, and fostering alienation from peers in a vicious cycle.

Figure 9.6 Pathways to Obesity

(A) One pathway to obesity is through social pressures to be thin.
(B) Another pathway may operate via depression and low self-esteem.

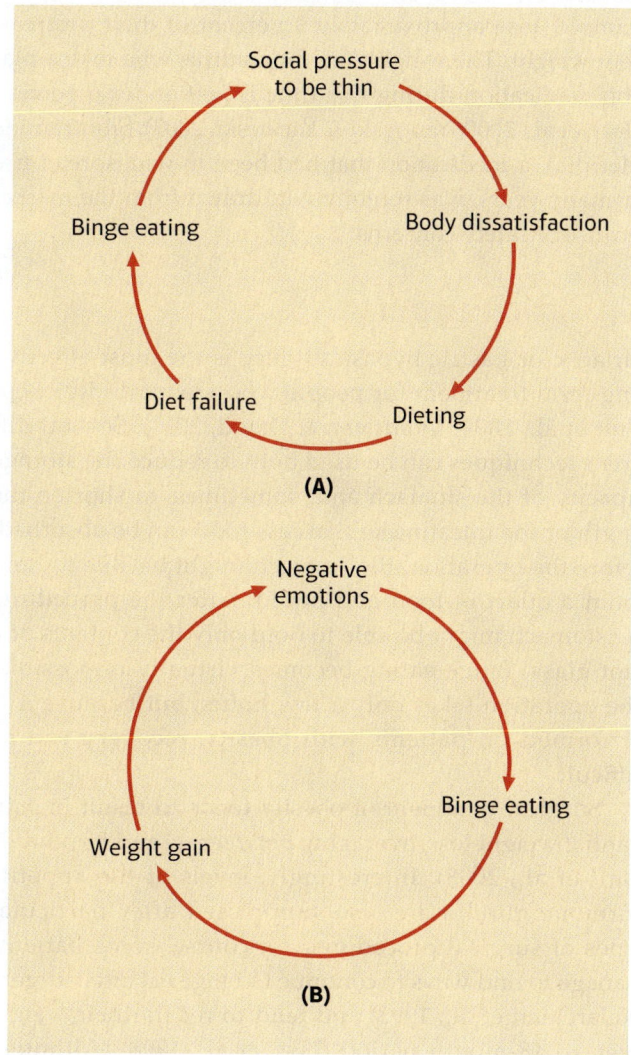

Lifestyle Modifications

A first step in the treatment of obesity is a clinical approach that, ideally, involves a low-calorie diet, exercise, and some form of behavioral intervention. Several research trials have now demonstrated that lifestyle modification approaches yield positive benefits for patients, although the results are far from dramatic. Sustained weight loss of around 7 pounds (3.2 kilograms) is quite typical (Powell et al., 2007). However, it is important to keep in mind that for people who are overweight, even small amounts of weight loss may yield some health benefits. Using meal-replacement products (e.g., calorie-controlled shakes), continuing a relationship with a treatment provider, and maintaining a high level of physical activity all help improve efforts at long-term weight control (Fabricatore & Wadden, 2006).

Sustained weight loss of around 7 pounds is typical for people who exercise and reduce their intake of calories. Even modest weight loss can lead to health benefits.

What about popular diets? Gardner, Kiazand, and colleagues (2007) compared the Atkins diet, the Zone diet, the Ornish diet, and a more traditional diet approach in a sample of women ages 25 to 50 who were overweight and obese. At the end of a year, those who had followed the Atkins diet had lost the most weight (10.4 pounds or 4.7 kilograms) compared with a weight loss of 3.5 pounds (1.6 kilograms) for the Zone, 5.7 pounds (2.6 kilograms) for the Ornish, and 4.8 pounds (2.2 kilograms) for the traditional approach. Nonetheless, even for the most successful dieters, the amount of weight loss was not especially large.

Weight Watchers is the only commercial weight loss program with demonstrated efficacy in a randomized controlled trial. Over the course of 6 months, overweight and obese people who attended Weight Watchers lost more weight (10.5 versus 3 pounds) than did people who received self-help materials and two brief sessions with a nutritionist (Heshka et al., 2000). At a later follow-up, those who had attended Weight Watchers were still doing better

in review

- What role do genetic factors play in obesity?
- How do hormones such as leptin and ghrelin help regulate appetite?
- In what ways might negative emotional states contribute to the development of obesity?
- In what ways is the food industry implicated in the obesity epidemic?
- Why is understanding binge eating important for understanding obesity?

Treatment of Obesity

9.6 **Explain current treatments for obesity.**

Three main treatment options are used with people who are overweight or obese: (1) lifestyle modifications (diet, exercise, and behavior therapy), (2) medications, and (3) bariatric surgery.

than the people who had been assigned to the self-help group (Heshka et al., 2003).

"Crash" diets and extreme treatments to bring about dramatic weight loss (including starvation of patients in a hospital setting) are now considered to be outmoded and ineffective approaches. Although they lead to weight loss in the short term, the weight loss is not maintained. Indeed, at follow-up, people who have been subjected to these procedures usually weigh more than they did before the treatment started (Mann et al., 2007).

Although we may be tempted by every new diet or weight loss fad that comes along, in the long run it is the calories that matter. Recent research has shown that focusing on the proportion of fat, protein, or carbohydrates in the diet is far less important than just eating less (Sacks et al., 2009). If you are able to do this, regardless of what kind of diet you choose, you will have some success.

But the harsh reality is that losing weight is difficult for most people. And for those who are obese, losing weight and maintaining the weight loss present a truly formidable challenge. As we mentioned earlier, our bodies try to defend a set-point weight. When we try to go below this, marked metabolic and hormonal changes occur. The body goes into "starvation mode" and hunger is increased, the metabolic rate slows, and we also feel less full after eating (Goldsmith et al., 2010). It is also the case that energy expenditure decreases significantly following weight loss. This means that if a person with obesity loses 100 pounds, decreasing in weight from 300 pounds to 200 pounds, the person has to consume far fewer calories to maintain this new weight than a person who already weighed 200 pounds would (Friedman, 2004). It is hardly surprising, therefore, that relapse rates are so high after weight loss and that people who attempt to lose weight often feel so discouraged. Indeed, some researchers now maintain that obesity is resistant to psychological methods of treatment (Cooper et al., 2010). This makes prevention all the more important.

Medications

Several medications are approved by the FDA for use in conjunction with a reduced-calorie diet. Orlistat (Xenical) works by reducing the amount of fat in the diet that can be absorbed once it enters the gut. Other drugs such as lorcaserin (Belviq) work in different ways and target serotonin or other neurotransmitters. The newest medication to receive FDA approval is Contrave. This is a combination of naltrexone (used to treat drug and alcohol addiction) and bupropion (used to treat depression and to help smokers quit).

All of these medications provide modest clinical benefits and lead to more weight loss than placebo (Fabricatore

& Wadden, 2006). However, the differences are not especially impressive and typically are much less (around 3–9 percent of initial weight) than patients are seeking (Pucci & Finer, 2015). Patients who take Orlistat for 1 year, for example, lose approximately 9 percent of their pretreatment weight. The weight loss for controls who take a placebo medication during this time is just under 6 percent (Heck et al., 2000; Yanovski & Yanovski, 2002). Sibutramine (Meridia), a medication that had been in widespread use for many years, was recently withdrawn from the market because of safety concerns.

Bariatric Surgery

Bariatric or gastric bypass surgery is the most effective long-term treatment for people who are morbidly obese (Bult et al., 2008; Moldovan & David, 2011). Several different techniques can be used both to reduce the storage capacity of the stomach and, sometimes, to shorten the length of the intestine so that less food can be absorbed. Before the operation, the stomach might be able to hold about a quart of food and liquid. After the procedure, the stomach might be able to hold only the contents of a shot glass. Binge eating becomes virtually impossible. The operation takes only a few hours, but because it is performed on patients with obesity, recovery can be difficult.

Surgical treatment of obesity tends to result in substantial weight loss, averaging between 44 and 88 pounds (Bult et al., 2008). Interestingly, levels of the appetite hormone ghrelin are also suppressed after particular types of surgical procedures. Of course, some patients manage to find ways to continue to binge eat after surgery (Kalarchian et al., 1998) and tend to regain their weight over an 18-month period (Hsu et al., 1998). Although bariatric surgery is not without risk (mortality rates hover around 1 percent), the risk of the surgery should be evaluated against the health risks that accompany untreated obesity. The case study that follows describes a successful outcome from the procedure.

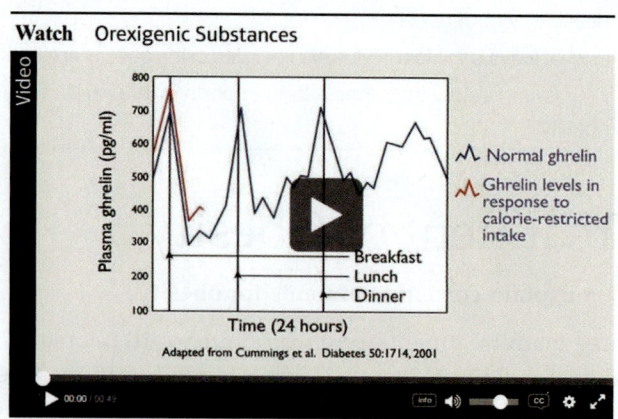

Watch   Orexigenic Substances

People Hardly Recognize Him

Stanley's weight problems began when he was 19. He gained weight and then kept on gaining. A big man with a fun-loving personality, he tried dieting from time to time. But nothing really worked for him. Part of the problem was that he hated to exercise. By the time he was 59 years old he weighed close to 400 pounds. He had mobility issues. He also had diabetes.

Stanley knew he had to do something. Although he was comfortable with who he was, he was concerned about the impact his obesity was having on his health and long-term longevity. His doctor recommended gastric bypass surgery. Stanley agreed.

There was much to be done before the surgery itself. To ensure that he was physically able to cope with the procedure, Stanley was evaluated by a staff physician. Other members of the team included a dietitian, who explained the many changes Stanley would need to make before and after the surgery. A psychologist also explored Stanley's readiness to commit to what was ahead. Finally, Stanley's surgeon carefully explained the details of the procedure and what would be involved. Stanley was then placed on a diet and told to lose weight before a surgery date could be arranged.

On the day of the surgery, Stanley arrived—already 13 pounds lighter as a result of following the prescribed diet. Then, during a procedure that lasted 5 hours, part of Stanley's stomach was permanently closed off with staples. His stomach was reduced from the size of a football to the size of an egg. In addition, a piece of his intestine was rerouted so that food from the newly created stomach pouch bypassed the early sections of the intestines (where nutrients and calories are typically absorbed after eating). Following the surgery, Stanley spent 5 days in the hospital recovering.

Almost immediately after the surgery, Stanley's diabetes disappeared. He was put on a liquid diet for the first few weeks and told to drink a lot of water. Then he graduated to eating soft foods like boiled eggs. Eventually, he began to eat more normal foods, although Stanley was surprised by how little he could actually tolerate.

Now, 1 year after the surgery, Stanley still has to be careful about what he eats. Carbonated beverages and spicy foods no longer agree with him and he has become intolerant of lactose. The amount of food he can eat without discomfort is very small. But Stanley has already lost 140 pounds and he is still losing weight. He talks about a fellow patient who had the same procedure. "He was telling me that he had figured out a way to get around the eating restrictions," says Stanley. "I don't get it. Why would anyone go through this procedure and then do that?" In contrast, Stanley feels that the gastric bypass he received has given him a tremendous opportunity. He feels better. He has more energy. And he knows he has improved his chances of living a longer life. He is especially amused when people he knows hardly recognize him. "I like that," he says.

The Importance of Prevention

Reducing the prevalence of obesity is now a top priority. But if obesity is to be prevented, it must first be recognized. Astonishingly, in a recent study conducted in Finland, 57 percent of parents who had a 7-year-old child who was overweight or obese failed to recognize that their child was overweight (Vanhala et al., 2009). In this Finnish study, childhood obesity was predicted by having a parent with obesity, skipping breakfast, habitual overeating, and not being physically active. Because we know that childhood obesity predicts adult obesity, parental education is clearly very important.

Losing weight is difficult because it is a battle against biological mechanisms designed to keep us at

Al Roker, the NBC weatherman on the *Today* show, had gastric bypass surgery, one form of bariatric surgery. He weighed 320 pounds at the time of his surgery. A year later, Roker had shed 100 pounds.

It has been estimated that increasing the tax on sugar-sweetened beverages by 20 percent could lead to an average weight loss of almost 4 pounds a year for adults.

our current weight. This highlights the importance of not gaining weight in the first place. Over an 8-year period, the average adult (in the 20–40 age range) will gain about 14 to 16 pounds (Hill et al., 2003). How can this be avoided? Most of the weight gain that people often regard as inevitable could be prevented through a combination of increased energy expenditure and reduced food intake. And this may be easier to do than we might imagine. Hill and colleagues have calculated that all that we need to do is cut back on our intake of calories by a mere 100 calories per day or walk an extra mile each day. Here are some simple ways to accomplish this:

- Eat three fewer bites of food when you eat a meal. Three bites of hamburger, for example, equal 100 calories.
- Take the stairs, combine a meeting with a walk, or park a little farther from your destination. A mile of walking is only 2,000 to 2,500 extra steps, and we can add these in small increments throughout the day.

- Sleep more. Research is showing that babies who sleep fewer than 12 hours a day are more likely to be overweight at age 3 (Taveras et al., 2008). And adults who sleep only 5 to 6 hours a night gain more weight over time than those who sleep 7 to 8 hours a night (Chaput et al., 2008).

By making these habits part of your daily routine, you will be able to prevent weight gain as you age, improving your overall health.

in review

- Why is losing weight so difficult for most people?
- What is the most effective treatment for people who are morbidly obese?
- What are the elements of a lifestyle modification treatment for obesity?
- What social policy changes might reduce or prevent obesity?

Unresolved Issues

The Role of Public Policy in the Prevention of Obesity

The prevalence of childhood obesity has tripled since 1980. Almost 32 percent of children and teens are now overweight or obese (Ogden et al., 2014). Once people become obese, treatment is very difficult. Preventing obesity, both in children and adults, is therefore a major priority.

At the national level the problem of obesity is unlikely to be solved without changes in public policy. We are all aware that rates of lung cancer have decreased as a result of increased taxes on cigarettes. Can we reduce obesity by changing the environmental conditions that encourage unhealthy eating or limit physical activity? And are we, as a society, ready for this?

In 2008, much to the dismay of the restaurant industry, New York City became the first place to require chain restaurants to post calorie information on their menu boards. This was an important move because most people consistently underestimate the calories in the food they eat outside the home. One study suggests that when people order from a menu that includes calorie information, they consume 14 percent fewer calories than people who order from a menu that contains no calorie information (Roberto et al., 2010). In 2012 the New York City Board of Health voted to ban the sale of sugary drinks over 16 ounces in size. Although many medical professionals applauded this ban, others were angry that their choices were being limited. The ban became a focus of legal action and was subsequently struck down.

Children consume 35 to 50 percent of their daily calories while they are at school. Many of these calories come from foods purchased from vending machines, school stores, or a la carte cafeteria offerings (Weir, 2012). However, this is changing. In 2010 Congress passed the Healthy, Hunger-Free Kids Act. This puts in place new policies for food in schools via the School Lunch Program. The new law requires the development of nutritional standards for all of the foods sold in schools. This could be very beneficial. Evidence suggests that children who live in states where there are stringent laws governing the sale of junk food gain less weight between the fifth and eighth grades than those who live in states with more lax soda and snack food regulations (Taber et al., 2012).

Other approaches that have been suggested include improving opportunities for physical activity, better regulation of food advertising aimed at children, subsidizing the sale of healthful foods, and increasing taxes on sugar-sweetened beverages like soda (Gearhardt et al., 2012; Novak & Brownell, 2011). Needless to say, many of these ideas are being strenuously opposed by some citizen's groups and by the food industry.

What do you think? Have you seen calorie information on menus? Does it affect what you decided to order? Is being able to buy a supersized beverage important to you? Do you support increased taxes on unhealthy foods? What do you think needs to be done to stop the nationwide problem of obesity from escalating even further out of control?

Summary

9.1 Identify the clinical aspects of eating disorders.

- Included in *DSM-5* are three different eating disorders: anorexia nervosa, bulimia nervosa, and binge-eating disorder. Binge-eating disorder is a new disorder that was officially recognized for the first time in *DSM-5*.

- Anorexia nervosa is characterized by a relentless pursuit of thinness as well as behaviors designed to accomplish this goal. Patients with anorexia nervosa are severely underweight.

- Bulimia nervosa is characterized by recurrent episodes of binge eating combined with efforts to minimize (by purging, using laxatives or excessive exercise) the weight gain that might come from this. People with bulimia nervosa are usually of normal weight or overweight.

- Binges are also a key clinical feature of binge-eating disorder. However, no effort is made to compensate for the effects of consuming so much food. As a result, people with binge-eating disorder are commonly overweight or obese.

- Eating disorders are more common in women than in men (3:1 ratio). They can develop at any age, although they typically emerge in adolescence or early adulthood. Anorexia nervosa usually begins at an earlier age (16–20) than bulimia nervosa (21–24) or binge-eating disorder (30–50).

- Anorexia nervosa has a lifetime prevalence of approximately 0.9 percent in women and 0.3 percent in men. Bulimia nervosa is more common, with a lifetime prevalence of 1.5 percent in women and 0.5 percent in men. Binge-eating disorder is the most common eating disorder with a prevalence of 3.5 percent in women and 2.0 percent in men. Many more people suffer from less severe forms of disturbed eating patterns

9.2 Explain the risk and causal factors in eating disorders.

- Genetic factors play an important role in eating disorders, although specific genes have not yet been reliably identified. Genes may make some people more susceptible to binge eating or to sociocultural influences, or may underlie personality styles (e.g., perfectionism) that increase risk for eating disorders.

- The neurotransmitter serotonin has been implicated in eating disorders. This neurotransmitter is also involved in mood disorders, which are highly comorbid with eating disorders.

- Sociocultural influences are integral in the development of eating disorders. Our society places great value on being thin. Western values concerning thinness may be spreading. This may help explain why eating disorders are now found throughout the world.

- Individual risk factors such as internalizing the thin ideal, body dissatisfaction, dieting, negative affect, and perfectionism have been implicated in the development of eating disorders.

9.3 Discuss how eating disorders are treated.

- Anorexia nervosa is very difficult to treat. Treatment is long term, and many patients resist getting well. For younger patients, family therapy appears to be very beneficial. Olanzapine is also helpful.

- The treatment of choice for bulimia nervosa is cognitive-behavior therapy. CBT is also helpful for binge-eating disorder. Interpersonal therapy seems to be helpful for binge-eating disorder and may be especially acceptable to minorities.

- A new development in the treatment of eating disorders is to use a transdiagnostic approach. Enhanced cognitive behavior therapy is an example of this. The treatment targets eating issues as well as concerns about shape and weight, extreme dieting, purging, and binge eating.

9.4 Define obesity and explain why it is a worldwide problem.

- Obesity is defined as having a body mass index of 30 or above.

- Obesity is associated with many medical problems and increased mortality. Obesity is not currently viewed as an eating disorder or as a psychiatric condition in the *DSM*.

9.5 Describe who is most at risk for obesity.

- A tendency toward being thin or heavy may be inherited. Our genetic makeup may make us more or less likely to gain weight in a cultural environment that promotes overconsumption of food and a sedentary lifestyle.

- Minorities (with the exception of Asians) are at especially high risk for obesity. Obesity rates are highest (50 percent) in black women. Overall, however, men are slightly more likely to be obese than women are.

9.6   **Explain current treatments for obesity.**

- Obesity is a chronic problem. Lifestyle modifications and medications help patients to lose small amounts of weight. Drastic weight loss, however, usually requires bariatric surgery.

- Because obesity tends to be a lifelong problem and because treating obesity is so difficult, there is now a focus on trying to prevent people from becoming obese in the first place. Implementing many of the approaches that have been recommended will require changes in social policy.

Key Terms

anorexia nervosa, p. 304
binge, p. 306
binge-eating disorder (BED), p. 308
body mass index (BMI), p. 329
bulimia nervosa, p. 307
cognitive-behavior therapy (CBT), p. 325

eating disorder, p. 304
ghrelin, p. 331
hypothalamus, p. 317
leptin, p. 331
negative affect, p. 323
obesity, p. 329

perfectionism, p. 321
purge, p. 306
randomized controlled
   trials, p. 324
serotonin, p. 318
set point, p. 318

Chapter 10
Personality Disorders

10.1 Describe the general features of personality disorders.

10.2 Summarize the challenges of doing research on personality disorders.

10.3 List the three Cluster A personality disorders and describe the key clinical features of each.

10.4 Describe the four Cluster B personality disorders and explain what common features they share.

10.5 List the three Cluster C personality disorders and describe the clinical features that are central to each.

10.6 Explain the role that sociocultural factors might play in the prevalence of personality disorders.

10.7 Discuss the challenges associated with treating personality disorders and summarize the approaches that are used.

10.8 Describe the clinical features of psychopathy and explain how it is similar to and different from antisocial personality disorder.

How would you describe yourself? Are you extraverted or more withdrawn? Can people rely on you or are you unpredictable? Are you calm under pressure or easily stressed? A person's characteristic traits, coping styles, and ways of interacting in the social environment emerge during childhood and normally crystallize into established patterns by the end of adolescence or early adulthood. These patterns constitute the individual's *personality*—the set of unique traits and behaviors that characterize the individual. Today there is reasonably broad agreement among personality researchers that about five basic personality trait dimensions can be used to characterize normal personality. The five traits that are at the center of the five-factor model of personality are neuroticism (emotional instability), extraversion/introversion, openness to experience (unconventionality), agreeableness/antagonism, and conscientiousness (e.g., Goldberg, 1990; John & Naumann, 2008; McCrae & Costa, 2008).

Clinical Features of Personality Disorders

10.1 **Describe the general features of personality disorders.**

By the time we are adults, most of us have a personality that is attuned to the demands of society. In other words, we readily comply with most societal expectations. We go to school or work, we honor our financial obligations, and we develop and try to sustain relationships. We also have a sense of who we are. In contrast, there are certain people who, although they do not necessarily display obvious symptoms of most of the disorders discussed in this book, nevertheless have certain traits that are so inflexible and maladaptive that they are unable to function effectively or meet the demands of their society. In such cases we may say the person has a **personality disorder**. The general features that characterize most personality disorders are chronic interpersonal difficulties, problems with one's identity or sense of self, and an inability to function adequately in society (Livesley & Jang, 2000).

In the following case, many of the varied characteristics of someone with a personality disorder are illustrated.

Narcissistic Personality Disorder

Alan is a 25-year-old student enrolled in a graduate program. Although he is quick to tell his professors how motivated and excited he is about his academic work, Alan rarely bothers to read the assigned material and hands in papers that are little more than unfinished drafts. When he receives mediocre grades in his classes, Alan is quick to complain to other students that he is not being treated well by his professors and says he is being singled out for unnecessary criticism. He believes he is much more talented than his grades suggest and blames his professors for not recognizing this. Alan also resents being told how he can improve his work. Although he writes detailed notes in feedback meetings with his professors and tells them how eager he is to improve, in reality he sees any efforts to help him as demeaning and unnecessary. And even though his fellow students try to help him understand why he is having problems, Alan refuses to acknowledge any responsibility for his situation. Instead he claims that his professors use lower standards when they evaluate other students in the program and that this is the reason why his fellow students are receiving better grades than he is. Eventually, Alan starts to spread malicious rumors about various faculty members to "make them pay" for not treating him better.

For a personality disorder to be diagnosed, the person's enduring pattern of behavior must be *pervasive* and *inflexible*, as well as *stable* and of *long duration*. It must also cause either *clinically significant distress* or *impairment in*

functioning and be manifested in at least two of the following areas: cognition, affectivity, interpersonal functioning, or impulse control. From a clinical standpoint, people with personality disorders often cause at least as much difficulty in the lives of others as they do in their own lives. Other people tend to find the behavior of individuals with personality disorders confusing, exasperating, unpredictable, and, to varying degrees, unacceptable. Whatever the particular trait patterns affected individuals have developed (obstinacy, covert hostility, suspiciousness, or fear of rejection, for example), these patterns color their reactions to each new situation and lead to a repetition of the same maladaptive behaviors because they do not learn from previous mistakes or troubles. For example, a dependent person may wear out a relationship with someone such as a spouse by incessant and extraordinary demands such as never being left alone. After that partner leaves, the person may go almost immediately into another equally dependent relationship without choosing the new partner carefully.

Personality disorders typically do not stem from debilitating reactions to stress in the recent past, as does post-traumatic stress disorder (PTSD) or many cases of major depression. Rather, these disorders stem largely from the gradual development of inflexible and distorted personality and behavioral patterns that result in persistently maladaptive ways of perceiving, thinking about, and relating to the world. Nonetheless, stressful events early in life may help set the stage for the development of these inflexible and distorted personality patterns.

The category of personality disorders is broad, encompassing behavioral problems that differ greatly in form and severity. In the milder cases we find people who generally function adequately but who would be described by their relatives, friends, or associates as troublesome, eccentric, or hard to get to know. They may have difficulties developing close relationships with others or getting along with those with whom they do have close relationships. One severe form of personality disorder (called *antisocial personality disorder*) results in extreme and often unethical "acting out" against society. Many such individuals are incarcerated in prisons, although some are able to manipulate others and keep from getting caught.

The *DSM-5* personality disorders are grouped into three clusters. These were derived on the basis of what were originally thought to be important similarities of features among the disorders within a given cluster. Table 10.1 provides a summary.

- **Cluster A:** *Includes paranoid, schizoid, and schizotypal personality disorders.* People with these disorders often seem odd or eccentric, with unusual behavior ranging from distrust and suspiciousness to social detachment.

Table 10.1 Summary of Personality Disorders

Personality Disorder	Characteristics	Point Prevalence in General Population	Gender Ratio Estimate
CLUSTER A			
Paranoid	Suspiciousness and mistrust of others; tendency to see self as blameless; on guard for perceived attacks by others	1.5%	Males = females
Schizoid	Impaired social relationships; inability and lack of desire to form attachments to others	1.2%	Males > females
Schizotypal	Peculiar thought patterns; oddities of perception and speech that interfere with communication and social interaction	1.1%	Males > females
CLUSTER B			
Histrionic	Self-dramatization; overconcern with attractiveness; tendency to irritability and temper outbursts if attention seeking is frustrated	1.2%	Females > males
Narcissistic	Grandiosity; preoccupation with receiving attention; self-promoting; lack of empathy	<1%	Males > females
Antisocial	Lack of moral or ethical development; inability to follow approved models of behavior; deceitfulness; shameless manipulation of others; history of conduct problems as a child	1% females, 3% males	Males > females
Borderline	Impulsiveness; inappropriate anger; drastic mood shifts; chronic feelings of boredom; attempts at self-mutilation or suicide	1.4%	Females = males
CLUSTER C			
Avoidant	Hypersensitivity to rejection or social derogation; shyness; insecurity in social interaction and initiating relationships	2.5%	Females > males
Dependent	Difficulty in separating in relationships; discomfort at being alone; subordination of needs in order to keep others involved in a relationship; indecisiveness	1%	Females > males
Obsessive-Compulsive	Excessive concern with order, rules, and trivial details; perfectionistic; lack of expressiveness and warmth; difficulty in relaxing and having fun	2.1%	Males > females

SOURCE: Torgersen (2012).

Figures are point prevalence means based on 11 different epidemiological studies. Lifetime prevalence rates are around three times higher. Personality disorders are more common in clinical populations than in community samples.

- **Cluster B:** *Includes histrionic, narcissistic, antisocial, and borderline personality disorders.* Individuals with these disorders share a tendency to be dramatic, emotional, and erratic.
- **Cluster C:** *Includes avoidant, dependent, and obsessive-compulsive personality disorders.* In contrast to the other two clusters, people with these disorders often show anxiety and fearfulness.

Personality disorders first appeared in the *DSM* in 1980 (in *DSM-III*). Although the use of clusters has continued since then, research has raised many questions about their validity. As will be discussed later in this chapter (see "Unresolved Issues"), there are substantial limitations to the category and cluster designations. Indeed, several proposals carefully considered by the *DSM-5* task force involved removing four personality disorders entirely and abandoning the cluster organization. One of the primary issues is that there are simply too many overlapping features across both categories and clusters (Krueger & Eaton, 2010; Sheets & Craighead, 2007; Widiger & Mullins-Sweatt, 2005). Nevertheless, because these clusters are still used as an organizing structure in *DSM-5*, we continue to mention them here.

In recent years, several **epidemiological studies** have assessed the prevalence of the personality disorders. Some of the studies were conducted in the United States and others were conducted in Europe. The studies also often used different assessment interviews. Despite these concerns, the overall prevalence estimates tend to be remarkably similar. They suggest that somewhere between 10 and 12 percent of people meet criteria for at least one personality disorder when the time period being asked about is the person's behavior over the last 2 to 5 years (Lenzenweger, 2008; Torgersen, 2012). In other words, approximately 1 person in 10 has a diagnosable personality disorder of some kind. When we consider the *DSM* clusters, we find that Cluster C disorders are most common, with a prevalence of around 7 percent. Cluster A disorders are next, with a prevalence of approximately 4 percent. Finally, the prevalence of Cluster B disorders is slightly lower, in the range of 3.5 to 4 percent (Torgersen, 2012). Due to the high comorbidity between clusters, some individuals meet criteria for personality disorders in more than one cluster, so the percentage of people in each cluster adds up to more than 10 to 12 percent.

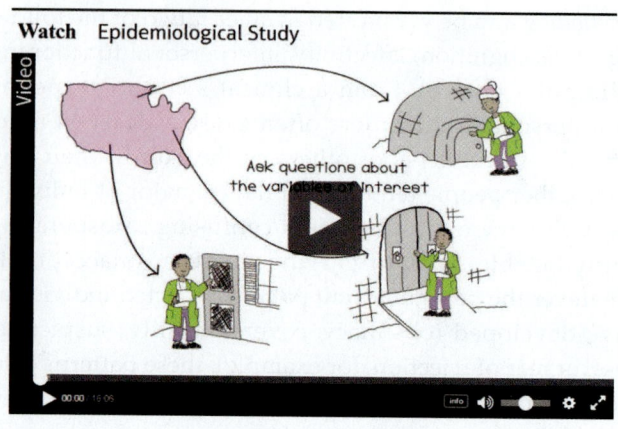

Watch Epidemiological Study

From their initial entry into the *DSM* in 1980 and through to *DSM-IV-TR*, the personality disorders were coded on a separate axis, Axis II. This was because they were regarded as different enough from the standard psychiatric syndromes (which were coded on Axis I) to warrant separate classification. However, in *DSM-5*, the multiaxial system was abandoned. Personality disorders are now included with the rest of the disorders we discuss in this book. Personality disorders are often associated with (or comorbid with) anxiety disorders (Chapters 5 and 6), mood disorders (Chapter 7), substance use problems (Chapter 11), and sexual difficulties and disorders (Chapter 12). (See, for example, L. A. Clark, 2005, 2007; Links et al., 2012; Mattia & Zimmerman, 2001.) One summary of evidence estimated that about three-quarters of people diagnosed with a personality disorder also have another disorder as well (Dolan-Sewell et al., 2001).

in review

- What is the definition of a personality disorder?
- What are the general *DSM* criteria for diagnosing personality disorders?
- What is the approximate prevalence of personality disorders in the general population?

Challenges in Personality Disorders Research

10.2 Summarize the challenges of doing research on personality disorders.

Before we discuss the clinical features and causes of personality disorders, we should note that several important aspects of doing research in this area have hindered progress relative to what is known about many other disorders. Two major categories of difficulties are briefly described.

Research Close-Up

Epidemiological Study

Epidemiological studies are designed to establish the prevalence (number of cases) of a particular disorder in a very large sample (usually many thousands) of people living in the community.

Difficulties in Diagnosing Personality Disorders

Special caution is in order regarding the diagnosis of personality disorders because more misdiagnoses probably occur here than in any other category of disorder. There are a number of reasons for this. One problem is that diagnostic criteria for personality disorders are not as sharply defined as they are for most other diagnostic categories, so they are often not very precise or easy to follow in practice. For example, it may be difficult to diagnose reliably whether someone meets a given criterion for dependent personality disorder such as "goes to excessive lengths to obtain nurturance and support from others" or "has difficulty making everyday decisions without an excessive amount of advice and reassurance from others." Because the criteria for personality disorders are defined by inferred traits or consistent patterns of behavior rather than by more objective behavioral standards (such as having a panic attack or a prolonged and persistent depressed mood), the clinician must exercise more judgment in making the diagnosis than is the case for many other disorders.

With the development of semistructured interviews and self-report inventories for the diagnosis of personality disorders, certain aspects of diagnostic reliability increased substantially. However, because the agreement between the diagnoses made on the basis of different structured interviews or self-report inventories is often rather low, there are still substantial problems with the reliability and validity of these diagnoses (Clark & Harrison, 2001; Livesley, 2003; Trull & Durrett, 2005). This means, for example, that three different researchers using three different assessment instruments may identify groups of individuals with substantially different characteristics as having a particular diagnosis such as borderline or narcissistic personality disorder. Of course, this virtually ensures that few obtained research results will be replicated by other researchers even though the groups studied by the different researchers have the same diagnostic label (e.g., Clark & Harrison, 2001).

Given problems with the unreliability of diagnoses (e.g., Clark, 2007; Livesley, 2003; Trull & Durrett, 2005), a great deal of work during the past 20 years has been directed toward developing a more reliable and accurate way of assessing personality disorders. Several theorists have attempted to deal with the problems inherent in a categorical approach to personality disorders (where disorders are considered to be distinct and separate) by adopting a dimensional approach. This assumes that personality (and personality disorder) is more on a continuum. Accordingly, efforts have been made to develop dimensional systems of assessment for the symptoms and traits involved in personality disorders (e.g., Clark, 2007; Krueger & Eaton, 2010; Trull & Durrett, 2005; Widiger et al., 2009). However,

a unified dimensional classification of personality disorders has been slow to emerge, and a number of researchers have been trying to develop an approach that will integrate the many different existing approaches (e.g., Krueger, Eaton, Clark et al., 2011a; Markon et al., 2005; Widiger et al., 2009, 2012).

The model that has perhaps been most influential is the five-factor model. This builds on the five-factor model of normal personality mentioned earlier to help researchers understand the commonalities and distinctions among the different personality disorders by assessing how these individuals score on the five basic personality traits (e.g., Clark, 2007; Widiger & Trull, 2007; Widiger et al., 2009, 2012). To fully account for the myriad ways in which people differ, each of these five basic personality traits also has subcomponents or facets. For example, the trait of neuroticism is comprised of the following six facets: anxiety, angry-hostility, depression, self-consciousness, impulsiveness, and vulnerability. Different individuals who all have high levels of neuroticism may vary widely in which facets are most prominent; for example, some might show more prominent anxious and depressive thoughts, others might show more self-consciousness and vulnerability, and yet others might show more angry-hostility and impulsivity. And the trait of extraversion is composed of the following six facets: warmth, gregariousness, assertiveness, activity, excitement seeking, and positive emotions. (All the facets of each of the five basic trait dimensions and how they differ across people with different personality disorders are explained in Table 10.2.) By assessing whether a person scores low, high, or somewhere in between on each of these 30 facets, it is easy to see how this system can account for an enormous range of different personality patterns—far more than the 10 personality disorders currently classified in the *DSM*.

Within a dimensional approach, normal personality trait dimensions can be recast into corresponding domains that represent more pathological extremes of these dimensions: negative affectivity (neuroticism); detachment (extreme introversion); antagonism (extremely low agreeableness); and disinhibition (extremely low conscientiousness). A fifth dimension, psychoticism, does not appear to be a pathological extreme of the final dimension of normal personality (openness)—rather, as we will discuss later in the chapter in the section on schizotypal personality disorder, it reflects traits similar to the symptoms of psychotic disorders (e.g., schizophrenia) (Watson et al., 2008).

With these cautions and caveats in mind, we will look at the clinical features of the personality disorders. It is important to bear in mind, however, that what we are describing is merely the prototype for each personality disorder. In reality, as would be expected from the standpoint

Table 10.2 *DSM-5* Personality Disorders and the Five-Factor Model

NEO-PI-R Domains and Facets	PAR	SZD	SZT	ATS	BDL	HST	NAR	AVD	DEP	OBC
Neuroticism										
Anxiety			H		H			H	H	
Angry-hostility	H			H	H		H			
Depression					H	H		H		
Self-consciousness			H			H	H	H	H	
Impulsiveness					H					
Vulnerability					H			H	H	
Extraversion										
Warmth		L	L			H			H	
Gregarious		L	L			H		L		
Assertiveness								L	L	H
Activity										
Excitement seeking				H		H		L		
Positive emotions		L	L			H				
Openness to Experience										
Fantasy		H			H	H				
Aesthetics										
Feelings		L				H				
Actions			H							
Ideas			H							
Values										L
Agreeableness										
Trust	L		L		L	H			H	
Straightforwardness	L			L						
Altruism				L			L		H	
Compliance	L			L	L				H	L
Modesty							L		H	
Tender mindedness				L			L			
Conscientiousness										
Competence					L					
Order										H
Dutifulness				L						H
Achievement striving							H			H
Self-discipline				L						H
Deliberation				L						

Note: NEO-PI-R = Revised NEO Personality Inventory. H, L = high, low, respectively, based on the fourth edition of the *Diagnostic and Statistical Manual of Mental Disorders* (*DSM-IV*; American Psychiatric Association, 1994) diagnostic criteria. The diagnostic criteria for personality disorders remain unchanged in *DSM-5*. Personality disorders: PAR = paranoid; SZD = schizoid; SZT = schizotypal; ATS = antisocial; BDL = borderline; HST = histrionic; NAR = narcissistic; AVD = avoidant; DEP = dependent; OBC = obsessive-compulsive.

SOURCE: Adapted from Widiger et al. (2002). A description of the DSM-IV personality disorders with the five-factor model of personality. In P. T. Costa & T. A. Widiger (Eds.), *Personality disorders and the five-factor model of personality* (2nd ed., p. 90). Washington, DC: APA Books.

of the five-factor model of personality disorders, it is rare for any individual to fit these "ideal" descriptions. And, as the Thinking Critically about *DSM-5* box illustrates, this situation remains unchanged in *DSM-5*.

Difficulties in Studying the Causes of Personality Disorders

Relatively little is known about the causal factors involved in the development of most personality disorders. One reason for this is that personality disorders only began to receive consistent attention from researchers after they entered the *DSM* in 1980. Another problem stems from the high level of comorbidity among them. For example, in an early review of four studies, Widiger and colleagues found that 85 percent of patients who qualified for one personality disorder diagnosis also qualified for at least one more, and many qualified for several more (Widiger & Rogers, 1989; Widiger et al., 1991). A study of nearly 900 psychiatric outpatients reported that 45 percent qualified for at least one personality disorder diagnosis and, among those with one, 60 percent had more than one and 25 percent had two or more (Zimmerman et al., 2005). Even in a nonpatient sample, Zimmerman and Coryell (1989) found that of those with one personality disorder, almost 25 percent had at least one more (see also Mattia & Zimmerman, 2001; Trull et al., 2012). This substantial comorbidity adds to the difficulty of untangling which causal factors are associated with which personality disorder.

DSM-5   Thinking Critically about *DSM-5*

Why Were No Changes Made to the Way Personality Disorders Are Diagnosed?

Many new and innovative proposals were offered for inclusion in the personality disorders section of *DSM-5*. Indeed, the proposed revisions were among the most radical for any of the disorders covered in this text. The details were hotly debated, although the general goal was to incorporate a more dimensional approach to the assessment and diagnosis of personality pathology (Livesley, 2011; Skodol et al., 2011; Widiger et al., 2009).

In the end, the *DSM-5* task force proposed revisions that reflected a *hybrid dimensional–categorical* model. This consisted of both categorical components and dimensional components. This model includes a set of general criteria for all personality disorders, an overall dimensional measure of the severity of personality dysfunction, a limited set of personality disorder types, and a set of pathological personality traits that could be specified in the absence of one of the personality disorder types. The proposed categorical component also retained 6 of the original 10 specific personality disorder types (antisocial, avoidant, borderline, narcissistic, obsessive-compulsive, and schizotypal).

The greatest change to the status quo came from the incorporation of dimensional components. The new personality domain was intended to describe personality characteristics of *all* patients, even those without a specific personality disorder. The proposals would have allowed clinicians to rate the level of impairment in personality functioning, reflecting aspects of both identity (having a stable and coherent sense of self and the ability to pursue meaningful life goals) and interpersonal functioning (the capacity for empathy and intimacy). In addition, diagnosticians could indicate the degree to which the patient showed substantial abnormality on five trait domains (negative affectivity, detachment, antagonism, disinhibition, and psychoticism), which are based primarily on the five-factor trait model discussed earlier.

Ultimately, however, the Board of Trustees of the American Psychiatric Association vetoed all of the proposed changes and decided to retain the old categories of personality disorders. In other words, personality disorders in *DSM-5* are the same as they were in *DSM-IV-TR*. Why were no changes accepted? We cannot be sure. But, as you may have gathered from our description above, the new system was very complicated. Although it may have led to a better classification system, the fact that it was not very intuitive or user-friendly may have been a problem. The primary audience for the *DSM* is clinicians who diagnose and treat people with mental disorders. We suspect that the new proposed system was rejected because it was quite cumbersome and judged too time consuming for overworked clinicians to learn and use. Moreover clinicians probably would not have found the proposed system to be user-friendly in part because the idea of rating people on dimensions is foreign to the way clinicians have been taught to think. The new proposals were not dismissed entirely, however. They now appear in Section III of *DSM-5* as an alternative model in need of further study. This may have been a wise course of action. Perhaps with more time and more research, it will become apparent whether or not the new approach provides enough benefits to make people willing to accept the challenges learning to use it will require.

One of the problems with the diagnostic categories of personality disorders is that the exact same observable behaviors may be associated with different personality disorders and yet have different meanings with each disorder. For example, this woman's behavior and expression could suggest the suspiciousness and avoidance of blame seen in paranoid personality disorder. Or they could indicate the social withdrawal and absence of friends that characterize schizoid personality disorder. Or they could indicate the social anxiety about interacting with others because of fear of being rejected or negatively evaluated that is seen in avoidant personality disorder.

Another problem in drawing conclusions about causes occurs because researchers have more confidence in prospective studies. In prospective studies groups of people are observed before a disorder appears and are followed over a period of time to see which individuals develop problems and what causal factors have been present. Although this has begun to change, to date, relatively little prospective research has been conducted with most of the personality disorders. Instead, the vast majority of research has been conducted on people who already have the disorders; some of it relies on retrospective recall of prior events, and some of it relies on observing current biological, cognitive, emotional, and interpersonal functioning. Thus, any conclusions about causes that are suggested must be considered tentative.

Of possible biological factors, it has been suggested that infants' temperament (an inborn disposition to react affectively to environmental stimuli; see Chapter 3) may predispose them to the development of particular personality traits and disorders (e.g., L. A. Clark, 2005; Mervielde et al., 2005; Paris, 2012b). Some of the most important dimensions of temperament are negative emotionality, sociability versus social inhibition or shyness, and activity level. One way of thinking about temperament is that it lays the early foundation for the development of the adult personality, but it is not the sole determinant of adult personality. Given that most temperamental and personality traits have been found to be moderately heritable (e.g., Bouchard & Loehlin, 2001; Livesley, 2005), it is not surprising that there is increasing evidence for genetic contributions to certain personality disorders (e.g., Kendler et al., 2008, 2011; Livesley, 2005, 2008; Livesley & Jang, 2008; South et al., 2012; Torgersen et al., 2000). However, for at least most disorders, the genetic contribution appears to be mediated by the genetic contributions to the primary trait dimensions most implicated in each disorder rather than to the disorders themselves (Kendler et al., 2008; Livesley, 2005). In addition, some progress is being made in understanding the psychobiological substrate of at least some of the traits prominently involved in the personality disorders (e.g., Depue, 2009; Depue & Lenzenweger, 2001, 2006; Livesley, 2008; Paris, 2005, 2007; Roussos & Siever, 2012).

Among psychological factors, psychodynamic theorists originally attributed great importance in the development of character disorders to an infant's getting excessive versus insufficient gratification of his or her impulses in the first few years of life (Fonagy & Luyten, 2012). More recently, learning-based habit patterns and maladaptive cognitive styles have received more attention as possible causal factors (e.g., Beck et al., 1990, 2004; Lobbestael & Arntz, 2012). Many of these maladaptive habits and cognitive styles that have been hypothesized to play important roles for certain disorders may originate in disturbed parent–child attachment relationships rather than derive simply from differences in temperament (e.g., L. S. Benjamin, 2005; Fraley &

Genetic propensities and temperament may be important predisposing factors for the development of particular personality traits and disorders. Parental influences, including emotional, physical, and sexual abuse, may also play a big role in the development of personality disorders.

Shaver, 2008; Meyer & Pilkonis, 2005; Shiner, 2009). Parental psychopathology and ineffective parenting practices have also been implicated in certain disorders (e.g., Farrington, 2006; Paris, 2001, 2007). Many studies have also suggested that early emotional, physical, and sexual abuse may be important factors in a subset of cases for several different personality disorders (Battle et al., 2004; Grover et al., 2007).

Various kinds of social stressors, societal changes, and cultural values have also been implicated as sociocultural causal factors (Paris, 2001). Ultimately, of course, the goal is to achieve a biopsychosocial perspective on the origins of each personality disorder. As of now, we are a considerable distance away from reaching that goal.

in review

- What are three reasons for the high frequency of misdiagnoses of personality disorders?
- What are two reasons why it is difficult to conduct research on personality disorders?

Cluster A Personality Disorders

10.3 List the three Cluster A personality disorders and describe the key clinical features of each.

People with Cluster A personality disorders display unusual behaviors such as distrust, suspiciousness, and social detachment and often come across as odd or eccentric. In the following subsections, we look at paranoid, schizoid, and schizotypal personality disorders.

Paranoid Personality Disorder

Individuals with **paranoid personality disorder** are suspicious and distrustful of others, often reading hidden meanings into ordinary remarks. They tend to see themselves as blameless, instead blaming others for their own mistakes and failures—even to the point of ascribing evil motives to others. Such people are chronically tense and "on guard," constantly expecting trickery and looking for clues to validate their expectations while disregarding all evidence to the contrary. They are often preoccupied with doubts about the loyalty of friends and hence are reluctant to confide in others. They commonly bear grudges, refuse to forgive perceived insults and slights, and are quick to react with anger and sometimes violent behavior (Bernstein & Useda, 2007; Oltmanns & Okada, 2006). All of this leads them to have to numerous interpersonal difficulties. The prevalence of paranoid personality disorder in the community is around 1 to 2 percent with equal numbers of men and women being affected (Torgersen, 2012).

DSM-5 *Criteria for. . .*

Paranoid Personality Disorder

A. A pervasive distrust and suspiciousness of others such that their motives are interpreted as malevolent, beginning by early adulthood and present in a variety of contexts, as indicated by four (or more) of the following:

1. Suspects, without sufficient basis, that others are exploiting, harming, or deceiving him or her.
2. Is preoccupied with unjustified doubts about the loyalty or trustworthiness of friends or associates.
3. Is reluctant to confide in others because of unwarranted fear that the information will be used maliciously against him or her.
4. Reads hidden demeaning or threatening meanings into benign remarks or events.
5. Persistently bears grudges (i.e., is unforgiving of insults, injuries, or slights).

6. Perceives attacks on his or her character or reputation that are not apparent to others and is quick to react angrily or to counterattack.
7. Has recurrent suspicions, without justification, regarding fidelity of spouse or sexual partner.

B. Does not occur exclusively during the course of schizophrenia, a bipolar disorder or depressive disorder with psychotic features, or another psychotic disorder and is not attributable to the physiological effects of another medical condition.

Note: If criteria are met prior to the onset of schizophrenia, add "premorbid," i.e., "paranoid personality disorder (premorbid)."

Source: Reprinted with permission from the *Diagnostic and Statistical Manual of Mental Disorders,* Fifth Edition (Copyright © 2013). American Psychiatric Association.

It is important to keep in mind that people with paranoid personalities are not usually psychotic. Most of the time they are in clear contact with reality. During periods of high stress, however, they may experience transient psychotic symptoms that last from a few minutes to a few hours (APA, 2013). People with schizophrenia share some symptoms found in paranoid personality, but they have many additional problems including more persistent loss of contact with reality, delusions, and hallucinations. Nevertheless, individuals with paranoid personality disorder do appear to be at elevated liability for schizophrenia (Lenzenweger, 2009).

CAUSAL FACTORS   As a disorder, paranoid personality disorder is not very well studied. One reason for this is that people who are highly suspicious and lacking in trust tend not to want to participate in research studies. Some have argued for partial genetic transmission that may link the disorder to schizophrenia, but results examining this issue are inconsistent, and if there is a significant relationship it is not a strong one (Kendler et al., 2006; Miller, Useda, et al., 2001). Nonetheless, there is evidence of modest genetic liability to paranoid personality disorder itself (Kendler, Myers, et al., 2007). This may occur through the heritability of high levels of antagonism (low agreeableness) and neuroticism (angry-hostility), which are among the primary traits in paranoid personality disorder (Hopwood & Thomas, 2012; Widiger et al., 2002). Psychosocial causal factors that are suspected to play a role include parental neglect or abuse and exposure to violent adults, although any links between early adverse experiences and adult paranoid personality disorder are clearly not specific to this one personality disorder and may play a role in other

disorders as well (Battle et al., 2004; Grover et al., 2007; Natsuaki et al., 2009). Symptoms of paranoid personality disorder also seem to increase after traumatic brain injury and are often found in chronic cocaine users (see Hopwood & Thomas, 2012). In the case below, head trauma and alcohol abuse are both suggested as possible causal factors.

Paranoid Personality Disorder

The patient, a 46-year-old male who worked in a blue collar job, was admitted to the psychiatric hospital after he made a suicide attempt. In his teenage years, he had been involved in a car accident and was hospitalized for head trauma and brain concussion. He also had a long history of abusing alcohol. Those who knew him described him as hypersensitive, touchy, suspicious, and mistrustful. His most prominent feature, however, was concern about his wife's fidelity. He repeatedly accused her of being unfaithful and "interrogated" her frequently about a wide range of matters. When he drank, his paranoia became even more marked. (Taken from Birkeland, 2013.)

Schizoid Personality Disorder

Individuals with **schizoid personality disorder** have difficulties forming social relationships and usually lack much interest in doing so. Consequently, they tend not to have good friends, with the possible exception of a close relative. Such people are unable to express their feelings and are seen by others as cold and distant. They often lack social skills and can be classified as loners or introverts, with solitary interests and occupations, although not all loners or introverts have schizoid personality disorder

(Bernstein et al., 2009; Miller, Useda, et al., 2001). People with this disorder tend not to take pleasure in many activities, including sexual activity, and rarely marry. More generally, they are not very emotionally reactive, rarely experiencing strong positive or negative emotions, but rather show a generally apathetic mood. These deficits contribute to their appearing cold and aloof (Miller, Useda, et al., 2001; Mittal et al., 2007). The prevalence of schizoid personality disorder, which is more common in males than females, is a little over 1 percent (Torgersen, 2012).

People with schizoid personality disorder have little interest in developing close social relationships.

In terms of the five-factor model, people with schizoid personality disorder show extremely high levels of introversion (especially low on warmth, gregariousness, and positive emotions). They are also low on openness to feelings (one facet of openness to experience) and on achievement striving (e.g., Hopwood & Thomas, 2012). The case of Bill provides an example.

The Introverted Computer Analyst

Bill, a highly intelligent but quite introverted and withdrawn 33-year-old computer analyst, was referred for psychological evaluation by his physician, who was concerned that Bill might be depressed and unhappy. Bill had virtually no contact with other people. He lived alone in his apartment, worked in a small office by himself, and usually saw no one at work except his supervisor, who occasionally visited to give him new work and pick up completed projects. He ate lunch by himself, and about once a week, on nice days, went to the zoo for his lunch break.

Bill was a lifelong loner; as a child he had had few friends and had always preferred solitary activities over family outings (he was the oldest of five children). In high school he had never dated and in college had gone out with a woman only once—and that was with a group of students after a game. He had been active in sports, however, and had played varsity football in both high school and college. In college he had spent a lot of time with one relatively close friend—mostly drinking. However, this friend now lived in another city.

Bill reported rather matter-of-factly that he had a hard time making friends; he never knew what to say in a conversation. On a number of occasions he had thought of becoming friends with other people but simply couldn't think of the right words, so "the conversation just died." He reported that he had given some thought lately to changing his life in an attempt to be more "positive," but it had never seemed worth the trouble. It was easier for him not to make the effort because he became embarrassed when someone tried to talk with him. He was happiest when he was alone.

CAUSAL FACTORS Like paranoid personality disorder, schizoid personality disorder has not been the focus of much research attention. Again, this is hardly surprising since people with schizoid personality disorder are not exactly the people we might expect to volunteer for a research study. Schizoid personality traits have been shown to have fairly high heritability of around 55 percent

---

DSM-5 *Criteria for...*

Schizoid Personality Disorder

A. A pervasive pattern of detachment from social relationships and a restricted range of expression of emotions in interpersonal settings, beginning by early adulthood and present in a variety of contexts, as indicated by four (or more) of the following:

  1. Neither desires nor enjoys close relationships, including being part of a family.
  2. Almost always chooses solitary activities.
  3. Has little, if any, interest in having sexual experiences with another person.
  4. Takes pleasure in few, if any, activities.
  5. Lacks close friends or confidants other than first-degree relatives.
  6. Appears indifferent to the praise or criticism of others.
  7. Shows emotional coldness, detachment, or flattened affectivity.

B. Does not occur exclusively during the course of schizophrenia, a bipolar disorder or depressive disorder with psychotic features, another psychotic disorder, or autism spectrum disorder and is not attributable to the physiological effects of another medical condition.

Note: If criteria are met prior to the onset of schizophrenia, add "premorbid," i.e., "schizoid personality disorder (premorbid)."

Source: Reprinted with permission from the *Diagnostic and Statistical Manual of Mental Disorders,* Fifth Edition (Copyright © 2013). American Psychiatric Association.

(Kendler et al., 2006). Consistent with the ideas of early theorists, there is also evidence that symptoms of schizoid personality disorder do precede psychotic illness in some cases (Bolinskey et al., 2015; Hopwood & Thomas, 2012). There is also some link between schizoid personality and autism spectrum disorders. This is interesting in light of recent research suggesting that schizophrenia and autism may have some common genetic basis (see Chapter 13 for more about this).

Some theorists have suggested that the severe disruption in sociability seen in schizoid personality disorder may be due to severe impairment in an underlying affiliative system (Depue & Lenzenweger, 2005, 2006). Cognitive theorists propose that individuals with schizoid personality disorder exhibit cool and aloof behavior because of maladaptive underlying schemas that lead them to view themselves as self-sufficient loners and to view others as intrusive. Their core dysfunctional belief might be "I am basically alone" (Beck et al., 1990, p. 51) or "Relationships are messy [and] undesirable" (Pretzer & Beck, 1996, p. 60; see also Beck et al., 2004). Unfortunately, we do not know why or how some people might develop such dysfunctional beliefs.

Schizotypal Personality Disorder

Like people with schizoid personality disorder, individuals with **schizotypal personality disorder** are also excessively introverted and have pervasive social and interpersonal deficits. But in addition they have cognitive and perceptual distortions, as well as oddities and eccentricities in their communication and behavior (Kwapil & Barrantes-Vidal, 2012; Raine, 2006). Although contact with reality is usually maintained, highly personalized and superstitious thinking is characteristic of people with schizotypal personality, and under extreme stress they may experience transient psychotic symptoms (APA, 2013; Widiger & Frances, 1994). Indeed, they often believe that they have magical powers and may engage in magical rituals. Other cognitive–

Magical thinking is a symptom of schizoid personality disorder.

perceptual problems include ideas of reference (the belief that conversations or gestures of others have special meaning or personal significance), odd speech, and paranoid beliefs.

Oddities in thinking, speech, and other behaviors are the most stable characteristics of schizotypal personality disorder (McGlashan et al., 2005) and are similar to those often seen in patients with schizophrenia. In fact, many researchers conceptualize schizotypal personality disorder as an attenuated form of schizophrenia (Lenzenweger, 2010; Raine, 2006). Interestingly, although some aspects of schizotypy appear related to the five-factor model of normal personality (specifically facets of introversion and neuroticism), the other aspects related to cognitive and perceptual distortions are *not* adequately explained by the five-factor model of normal personality (Watson et al., 2008). Indeed, these core symptoms of schizotypy form the basis of the only proposed trait that does not map neatly onto the five factors of normal personality. This pathological trait is psychoticism, which consists of three facets: unusual beliefs and experiences, eccentricity, and cognitive and perceptual dysregulation (Krueger, Eaton, Derringer, et al., 2011).

CAUSAL FACTORS Unlike schizoid and paranoid personality disorders, there has been a significant amount of research on schizotypal personality disorder (Esterberg et al., 2010). In fact, in the original proposal for the *DSM-5*, schizotypal personality was the only categorical disorder retained from Cluster A. The prevalence of this disorder in the general population is estimated to be around 1 percent, with more males affected than females (Torgersen, 2012).

Schizotypal personality disorder has moderate heritability (Kwapil & Barrantes-Vidal, 2012; Lin et al., 2006, 2007; Raine, 2006). A genetic relationship to schizophrenia has also long been suspected. In fact, this disorder appears to be part of a spectrum of liability for schizophrenia and often occurs in some of the first-degree relatives of people with schizophrenia (Kendler & Gardner, 1997; Kwapil & Barrantes-Vidal, 2012; Raine, 2006; Tienari et al., 2003). The biological associations of schizotypal personality disorder with schizophrenia are remarkable (Cannon et al., 2008; Jang et al., 2005; Siever & Davis, 2004; Yung et al., 2004). A number of studies on patients, as well as on college students with schizotypal personality disorder (e.g., Raine, 2006; Siever et al., 1995), have shown the same deficit in the ability to track a moving target visually that is found in schizophrenia (Coccaro, 2001; see also Chapter 13). They also show numerous other mild impairments in cognitive functioning (Voglmaier et al., 2005), including deficits in their ability to sustain attention (Lees-Roitman et al., 1997; Raine, 2006) and deficits in working memory (e.g., being able to remember a span of digits), both of which are common in schizophrenia. In addition, individuals with schizotypal

DSM-5 *Criteria for. . .*

Schizotypal Personality Disorder

A. A pervasive pattern of social and interpersonal deficits marked by acute discomfort with, and reduced capacity for, close relationships as well as by cognitive or perceptual distortions and eccentricities of behavior, beginning by early adulthood and present in a variety of contexts, as indicated by five (or more) of the following:

1. Ideas of reference (excluding delusions of reference).
2. Odd beliefs or magical thinking that influences behavior and is inconsistent with subcultural norms (e.g., superstitiousness, belief in clairvoyance, telepathy, or "sixth sense"; in children and adolescents, bizarre fantasies or preoccupations).
3. Unusual perceptual experiences, including bodily illusions.
4. Odd thinking and speech (e.g., vague, circumstantial, metaphorical, overelaborate, or stereotyped).
5. Suspiciousness or paranoid ideation.
6. Inappropriate or constricted affect.
7. Behavior or appearance that is odd, eccentric, or peculiar.
8. Lack of close friends or confidants other than first-degree relatives.
9. Excessive social anxiety that does not diminish with familiarity and tends to be associated with paranoid fears rather than negative judgments about self.

B. Does not occur exclusively during the course of schizophrenia, a bipolar disorder or depressive disorder with psychotic features, another psychotic disorder, or autism spectrum disorder.

Note: If criteria are met prior to the onset of schizophrenia, add "premorbid," e.g., "schizotypal personality disorder (premorbid)."

Source: Reprinted with permission from the *Diagnostic and Statistical Manual of Mental Disorders,* Fifth Edition (Copyright © 2013). American Psychiatric Association.

---

personality disorder, like patients with schizophrenia, show deficits in their ability to inhibit attention to a second stimulus that rapidly follows presentation of a first stimulus. For example, if healthy individuals are presented with a weak auditory stimulus about 0.1 second before they hear a loud sound (the kind of sound that elicits a startle response) they show a smaller startle response than they would have done if they had not heard the weak auditory stimulus first (Cadenhead, Light, et al., 2000; Cadenhead, Swerdlow, et al., 2000). This normal inhibitory effect is reduced in people with schizophrenia and as well as in people with schizotypal personality disorder. It may be related to their high levels of distractibility and difficulty staying focused (see also Hazlett et al., 2003; Raine, 2006). Finally, people with schizotypal personality disorder also show language abnormalities that may be related to abnormalities in their auditory processing (Dickey et al., 2008).

In light of such findings, you may not be too surprised to learn that teenagers who have schizotypal personality disorder have been shown to be at increased risk for developing schizophrenia and schizophrenia-spectrum disorders in adulthood (Asarnow, 2005; Cannon et al., 2008; Raine, 2006; Tyrka et al., 1995). Nevertheless, it has also been proposed that there is a second subtype of schizotypal personality disorder that is not genetically linked to schizophrenia. This subtype is characterized by cognitive and perceptual deficits and is instead linked to a history of childhood abuse and early trauma (Berenbaum et al., 2008; Raine, 2006). Schizotypal personality disorder in adolescence has been associated with elevated exposure to stressful life events (Anglin et al., 2008; Tessner et al., 2011) and low family socioeconomic status (Cohen et al., 2008).

in review

- Describe and differentiate among the following Cluster A personality disorders: paranoid, schizoid, and schizotypal.

Cluster B Personality Disorders

10.4 **Describe the four Cluster B personality disorders and explain what common features they share.**

In the following subsections, we look closely at histrionic, narcissistic, antisocial, and borderline personality disorders. Remember that people with Cluster B personality disorders share a tendency to be dramatic, emotional, and erratic.

Histrionic Personality Disorder

Excessive attention-seeking behavior and emotionality are the key characteristics of individuals with **histrionic personality disorder**. As you can see from the *DSM-5* criteria box, these individuals tend to feel unappreciated if they are not the center of attention; their lively, dramatic, and excessively extraverted styles often ensure that they can charm others into attending to them. But these qualities do not lead to stable and satisfying relationships because others tire of providing this level of attention. In craving stimulation and attention, their appearance and behavior are often quite theatrical and emotional as well as sexually provocative (Freeman et al., 2005). They may attempt to control their partners through seductive behavior and emotional manipulation, but they also show a good deal of dependence (e.g., Blagov et al., 2007; Bornstein & Malka, 2009; Rasmussen, 2005a). Their speech is often vague and impressionistic, and they are usually considered self-centered, vain, and excessively concerned about the approval of others, who see them as overly reactive, shallow, and insincere.

DSM-5 *Criteria for. . .*

Histrionic Personality Disorder

A pervasive pattern of excessive emotionality and attention seeking, beginning by early adulthood and present in a variety of contexts, as indicated by five (or more) of the following:

1. Is uncomfortable in situations in which he or she is not the center of attention.

2. Interaction with others is often characterized by inappropriate sexually seductive or provocative behavior.

3. Displays rapidly shifting and shallow expression of emotions.

4. Consistently uses physical appearance to draw attention to self.

5. Has a style of speech that is excessively impressionistic and lacking in detail.

6. Shows self-dramatization, theatricality, and exaggerated expression of emotion.

7. Is suggestible (i.e., easily influenced by others or circumstances).

8. Considers relationships to be more intimate than they actually are.

Source: Reprinted with permission from the *Diagnostic and Statistical Manual of Mental Disorders*, Fifth Edition (Copyright © 2013). American Psychiatric Association.

The prevalence of histrionic personality disorder in the general population is a little over 1 percent, although some believe rates of the disorder may be decreasing (Blashfield et al., 2012; Torgersen, 2012). Some studies suggest that this disorder occurs more often in women than in men (Lynam & Widiger, 2007; Widiger & Bornstein, 2001). Reasons for the possible sex difference have been very controversial. One review suggested that this sex difference is not surprising, given the number of traits that occur more often in females that are involved in the diagnostic criteria. For example, many of the criteria for histrionic personality disorder (as well as for several other personality disorders such as dependent) involve maladaptive variants of female-related traits (e.g., Widiger & Bornstein, 2001) such as overdramatization, vanity, seductiveness, and overconcern with physical appearance. However, other personality traits prominent in histrionic personality disorder are actually more common in men than in women (e.g., high excitement

seeking and low self-consciousness). A recent careful analysis of the issue suggests that the higher prevalence of histrionic personality in women actually would not be predicted based on known sex differences in the personality traits prominent in the disorder. This does indeed suggest the influence of some form of sex bias in the diagnosis of this disorder (Lynam & Widiger, 2007).

This woman could be just "clowning around" one night with friends. But if she frequently seeks opportunities to engage in seductive and attention-seeking behavior, she could have histrionic personality disorder.

CAUSAL FACTORS Very little systematic research has been conducted on histrionic personality disorder, perhaps as a result of the difficulty researchers have had in differentiating it from other personality disorders (Bornstein & Malka, 2009) and/or because many do not believe it is a valid diagnosis (Blashfield et al., 2012). Reflecting this, histrionic personality disorder was one of the four diagnoses recommended for removal in *DSM-5*. Histrionic personality disorder is highly comorbid with borderline, antisocial, narcissistic, and dependent personality disorder diagnoses (Bakkevig & Karterud, 2010; Blagov & Westen, 2008; Bornstein & Malka, 2009).

A Histrionic Housewife

Lulu, a 24-year-old housewife, was seen in an inpatient unit several days after she had been picked up for "vagrancy" after her husband had left her at the bus station to return her to her own family because he was tired of her behavior and of taking care of her. Lulu showed up for the interview all made-up and in a very feminine robe, with her hair done in a very special way. Throughout the interview with a male psychiatrist, she showed flirtatious and somewhat childlike seductive gestures and talked in a rather vague way about her problems and her life. Her chief complaints were that her husband had deserted her and that she couldn't return to her family because two of her brothers had abused her. Moreover, she had no friends to turn to and wasn't sure how she was going to get along. Indeed, she complained that she had never had female friends, whom she felt just didn't like her, although she wasn't quite sure why, assuring the interviewer that she was a very nice and kind person.

Recently she and her husband had been out driving with a couple who were friends of her husband's. The wife had accused Lulu of being overly seductive toward the wife's husband, and Lulu had been hurt, thinking her behavior was perfectly innocent and not at all out of line. This incident led to a big argument with her own husband, one in a long series during the past 6 months in which he complained about her inappropriate behavior around other men and about how vain and needing of attention she was. These arguments and her failure to change her behavior had ultimately led her husband to desert her.

There is some evidence for a genetic link with antisocial personality disorder, the idea being that there may be some common underlying predisposition that is more likely to be manifested in women as histrionic personality disorder and in men as antisocial personality disorder (e.g., Cale & Lilienfeld, 2002a, 2002b). The suggestion of some genetic propensity to develop this disorder is also supported by findings that histrionic personality disorder may be characterized as involving extreme versions of two common, normal personality traits, extraversion and, to a lesser extent, neuroticism—two normal personality traits known to have a partial genetic basis (Widiger & Bornstein, 2001). In terms of the five-factor model (refer back to Table 10.2), the very high levels of extraversion of patients with histrionic personality disorder include high levels of gregariousness, excitement seeking, and positive emotions. Their high levels of neuroticism particularly involve the depression and self-consciousness facets; they are also high on openness to fantasies (Widiger et al., 2002).

Cognitive theorists emphasize the importance of maladaptive schemas revolving around the need for attention to validate self-worth. Core dysfunctional beliefs might include "Unless I captivate people, I am nothing" and "If I can't entertain people, they will abandon me" (Beck et al., 1990, p. 50). No systematic research has yet explored how these dysfunctional beliefs might develop.

Narcissistic Personality Disorder

Individuals with **narcissistic personality disorder** show an exaggerated sense of self-importance, a preoccupation with being admired, and a lack of empathy for the feelings of others (Pincus & Lukowitsky, 2010; Ronningstam, 2005, 2009, 2012). Numerous studies support the notion of two subtypes of narcissism: grandiose and vulnerable narcissism (Cain et al., 2008; Ronningstam, 2005, 2012). The grandiose presentation of narcissism, highlighted in the *DSM-5* criteria, is manifested by traits related to grandiosity, aggression, and dominance. These are reflected in a strong tendency to overestimate their abilities and accomplishments while underestimating the abilities and accomplishments of others. Their sense of entitlement is frequently a source of astonishment to others, although they themselves seem to regard their lavish expectations as merely what they deserve. They behave in stereotypical ways (e.g., with constant self-references and bragging) to gain the acclaim and recognition they crave. Because they believe they are so special, they often think they can be understood only by other high-status people or that they should associate only with such people. Finally, as was illustrated in the case of Alan at the beginning of this chapter, their sense of entitlement is also associated with their unwillingness to forgive others for perceived slights, and they easily take offense (Exline et al., 2004).

DSM-5 *Criteria for. . .*
Narcissistic Personality Disorder

A pervasive pattern of grandiosity (in fantasy or behavior), need for admiration, and lack of empathy, beginning by early adulthood and present in a variety of contexts, as indicated by five (or more) of the following:

1. Has a grandiose sense of self-importance (e.g., exaggerates achievements and talents, expects to be recognized as superior without commensurate achievements).
2. Is preoccupied with fantasies of unlimited success, power, brilliance, beauty, or ideal love.
3. Believes that he or she is "special" and unique and can only be understood by, or should associate with, other special or high-status people (or institutions).
4. Requires excessive admiration.
5. Has a sense of entitlement (i.e., unreasonable expectations of especially favorable treatment or automatic compliance with his or her expectations).
6. Is interpersonally exploitative (i.e., takes advantage of others to achieve his or her own ends).
7. Lacks empathy: is unwilling to recognize or identify with the feelings and needs of others.
8. Is often envious of others or believes that others are envious of him or her.
9. Shows arrogant, haughty behaviors or attitudes.

Source: Reprinted with permission from the *Diagnostic and Statistical Manual of Mental Disorders*, Fifth Edition (Copyright © 2013). American Psychiatric Association.

The vulnerable presentation of narcissism is not as clearly reflected in the *DSM* criteria but nevertheless represents a subtype long observed by researchers and clinicians. Vulnerable narcissists have a very fragile and unstable sense of self-esteem, and for these individuals, arrogance and condescension is merely a façade for intense shame and hypersensitivity to rejection and criticism (Cain et al., 2008; Miller et al., 2010; Pincus & Lukowitsky, 2010; Ronningstam, 2005, 2012). Vulnerable narcissists may become completely absorbed and preoccupied with fantasies of outstanding achievement but at the same time experience profound shame about their ambitions. They may avoid interpersonal relationships due to fear of rejection or criticism.

There is increasing evidence that the grandiose and vulnerable presentations of narcissism are related but distinct in important ways. In terms of the five-factor model, both subtypes are associated with high levels of interpersonal antagonism/low agreeableness (which includes traits of low modesty, arrogance, grandiosity, and superiority), low altruism (expecting favorable treatment and exploiting others), and tough-mindedness (lack of empathy). However, the person with a more grandiose form of narcissism is exceptionally low in certain facets of neuroticism and high in extraversion. When the narcissism involves more grandiosity, close friends and relatives may be more distressed about his or her behavior than is the narcissist him- or herself. One study concluded, "The strongest impairment associated with narcissistic personality disorder is the distress of 'pain and suffering' experienced not by the narcissist but by his or her significant others" (Miller, 2007, p. 176). However, the case is quite different for the vulnerable narcissist, who has very *high* levels of negative affectivity/neuroticism (Cain et al., 2008; Miller et al., 2010). Thus, spouses describe patients with either grandiosity or vulnerability as being "bossy, intolerant, cruel, argumentative, dishonest, opportunistic, con-

ceited, arrogant, and demanding," but only those high on grandiosity were additionally described as being "aggressive, hardheaded, outspoken, assertive, and determined," while those high on vulnerability were described as "worrying, emotional, defensive, anxious, bitter, tense, and complaining" (Wink, 1991, p. 595). Importantly, some individuals with narcissistic personality disorder may fluctuate between grandiosity and vulnerability (Pincus & Lukowitsky, 2010; Ronningstam, 2009).

People with narcissistic personalities also share another central trait—they are unwilling or unable to take the perspective of others, to see things other than "through their own eyes." Moreover, if they do not receive the validation or assistance they desire, they are inclined to be hypercritical and retaliatory (Rasmussen, 2005b). Indeed, one study of male students with high levels of narcissistic traits showed that they had greater tendencies toward sexual coercion when they were rejected by the target of their sexual desires than did men with lower levels of narcissistic traits. They also rated filmed depictions of rape less unfavorably and as more enjoyable and sexually arousing than did the men with low levels of narcissistic traits (Bushman et al., 2003).

In community samples, slightly under 1 percent of people meet the diagnostic threshold for narcissistic personality disorder, with the disorder probably being more common in men than women (Torgersen, 2012). This gender difference is to be expected, based on known sex differences in the personality traits most prominent in narcissistic personality disorder (Lynam & Widiger, 2007).

CAUSAL FACTORS For a long time there was a great deal of theory but precious little empirical data on the environmental and genetic factors involved in the etiology of narcissistic personality disorder (Kohut & Wolff, 1978; Millon & Davis, 1995; Widiger & Bornstein, 2001). Fortunately, a number of researchers are now actively trying to understand the causes of this fascinating disorder. A key finding has been that the grandiose and vulnerable forms of narcissism are associated with different causal factors. Grandiose narcissism has not generally been associated with childhood abuse, neglect, or poor parenting. Indeed, there is some evidence that grandiose narcissism is associated with parental overvaluation. By contrast, vulnerable narcissism has been associated with emotional, physical, and sexual abuse, as well parenting styles characterized as intrusive, controlling, and cold (Horton et al., 2006; Miller, 2011; Miller & Campbell, 2008; Otway & Vignoles, 2006).

Antisocial Personality Disorder

The outstanding characteristic of people with **antisocial personality disorder (ASPD)** is their tendency to persistently disregard and violate the rights of others. They do this through a combination of deceitful, aggressive, and antisocial behaviors. These people have a lifelong pattern of unsocialized and irresponsible behavior with little regard for safety—either their own or that of others. These characteristics bring them into repeated conflict with society, and a high proportion end up becoming incarcerated. Only individuals ages 18 or over can be diagnosed with ASPD. For the diagnosis to be made, the person must have shown symptoms of conduct disorder before age 15 (see Chapter 15). After age 15, there must also be evidence of such things as repeated unlawful behavior, deceitfulness, impulsivity, aggressiveness, or consistent irresponsibility in work or financial matters. The case of Mark provides an example.

A Thief with Antisocial Personality Disorder

Mark, a 22-year-old, was awaiting trial for car theft and armed robbery. His case records included a long history of arrests beginning at age 9, when he had been picked up for vandalism. He had been expelled from high school for truancy and disruptive behavior. On a number of occasions he had run away from home for days or weeks at a time—always returning in a disheveled and "rundown" condition. To date he had not held a job for more than a few days at a time even though his generally charming manner enabled him to obtain work readily. He was described as a loner with few friends. Although initially charming, Mark usually soon antagonized those he met with his aggressive, self-oriented behavior. Shortly after his first therapy session, he skipped bail and presumably left town to avoid his trial. His therapist never saw him again.

The prevalence of antisocial personality disorder in the general population is around 2 to 3 percent (Glenn et al., 2013). The disorder is more common in men (approximately 3 percent) than in women (approximately 1 percent), although some studies suggest that the preponderance of men is even greater and closer to 5 to 1 (Hare et al., 2012). As you might expect having seen the diagnostic criteria, ASPD is very common in prison samples. Around 47 percent of incarcerated men and 21 percent of incarcerated women qualify for the diagnosis (see Glenn et al., 2013).

The term *antisocial personality disorder* is often used interchangeably with *psychopathy*. But this is a mistake. Although there is some overlap between ASPD and psychopathy, they are not the same thing. The current *DSM* criteria for antisocial personality disorder place a heavy emphasis on observable behaviors such as lying, getting into fights, or failing to honor financial obligations. In contrast, in the construct of psychopathy, more attention is paid to personality characteristics such as superficial charm, lack of empathy, and manipulativeness. Because there is so much confusion about ASPD and psychopathy, and because ASPD and psychopathy place a heavy burden on our society, we discuss them again in some detail in a later part of this chapter.

CAUSAL FACTORS Research suggests that genes play a role in antisocial personality disorder and criminality. Many studies have compared concordance rates between monozygotic and dizygotic twins. Others have used the adoption method, comparing rates of criminal behavior in the adopted-away children of criminals with rates of criminal behavior in the adopted-away children of ordinary (noncriminal) parents. The results of both kinds of studies show a moderate heritability for antisocial or criminal behavior (Carey & Goldman, 1997; Hare et al., 2012; Sutker & Allain, 2001) and for ASPD (Waldman & Rhee, 2006). What is inherited, however, is far from clear. It could be impulsivity, low levels of anxiousness, aggressive tendencies, or a combination of these and other dispositions.

DSM-5 *Criteria for. . .*

Antisocial Personality Disorder

A. A pervasive pattern of disregard for and violation of the rights of others, occurring since age 15 years, as indicated by three (or more) of the following:

1. Failure to conform to social norms with respect to lawful behaviors, as indicated by repeatedly performing acts that are grounds for arrest.
2. Deceitfulness, as indicated by repeated lying, use of aliases, or conning others for personal profit or pleasure.
3. Impulsivity or failure to plan ahead.
4. Irritability and aggressiveness, as indicated by repeated physical fights or assaults.
5. Reckless disregard for safety of self or others.
6. Consistent irresponsibility, as indicated by repeated failure to sustain consistent work behavior or honor financial obligations.
7. Lack of remorse, as indicated by being indifferent to or rationalizing having hurt, mistreated, or stolen from another.

B. The individual is at least age 18 years.

C. There is evidence of conduct disorder with onset before age 15 years.

D. The occurrence of antisocial behavior is not exclusively during the course of schizophrenia or bipolar disorder.

Source: Reprinted with permission from the *Diagnostic and Statistical Manual of Mental Disorders*, Fifth Edition (Copyright © 2013). American Psychiatric Association.

Many environmental factors have also been implicated in the development of antisocial personality disorder. These include low family income, inner-city living, poor supervision by parents, having a young mother, being raised in a single-parent family, conflict between parents, having a delinquent sibling, neglect, large family size, and also harsh discipline from parents (Farrington, 2006; Granic & Patterson, 2006). Other nonshared environmental factors (nonshared because they are not necessarily experienced by all children in the family) that are important are having delinquent peers, physical or sexual abuse, and various academic or social experiences. Researchers also note that these environmental influences interact with genetic predispositions (a genotype–environment interaction) to determine which individuals become criminals or antisocial personalities (Carey & Goldman, 1997; Hare et al., 2012; Moffitt, 2005). Indeed, this must be the case, given the dramatic increases in crime that have occurred in the United States and the United Kingdom since 1960, as well as the tenfold-higher murder rate in the United States than in the United Kingdom (Rutter, 1996)—such findings cannot be accounted for by genetic factors alone but must involve psychosocial or sociocultural causal factors.

One excellent study by Cadoret and colleagues (1995; see also Riggins-Caspers et al., 2003) found that adopted-away children of biological parents with ASPD were more likely to develop antisocial personalities if their adoptive parents exposed them to an adverse environment than if their adoptive parents exposed them to a more normal environment. Adverse environments were characterized by some of the following: marital conflict or divorce, legal problems, and parental psychopathology. Similar findings of a gene–environment interaction were also found in twins who were at high or low risk for conduct disorder (typically a childhood precursor of ASPD); in this study, the environmental risk factor was physical maltreatment (Jaffee et al., 2005).

One very influential study on gene–environment interactions and ASPD identified a candidate gene that seems to be important (Caspi et al., 2002). This gene, known as the monoamine oxidase A gene (*MAOA* gene), is involved in the breakdown of neurotransmitters like norepinephrine, dopamine, and serotonin—all neurotransmitters affected by the stress of maltreatment that can lead to aggressive behavior (see Figure 10.1). In this study, over a thousand children from New Zealand were followed from birth to age 26. Researchers found that individuals with low MAOA activity were far more likely to develop ASPD if they had experienced early maltreatment than were individuals with high MAOA activity and early maltreatment and individuals with low levels of MAOA activity without early maltreatment. The basic finding of MAOA gene–environment interaction has now been replicated in a large number studies (see Foley et al., 2004; Kim-Cohen et al., 2006).

Figure 10.1 Means on the composite index of antisocial behavior as a function of high or low *MAOA* gene activity and a childhood history of maltreatment.

(Reprinted with permission from Caspi et al. (2002), *Science*, 297, 851–854. Copyright © 2002 AAAS.)

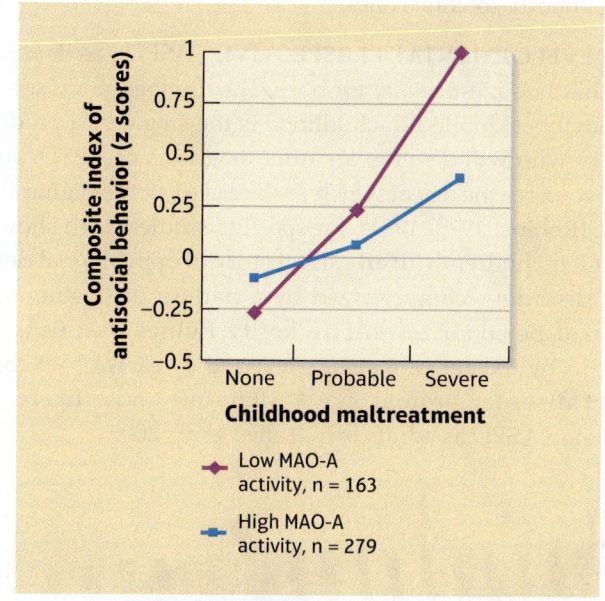

The relationship between antisocial behavior and substance abuse is sufficiently strong that some have questioned whether there may be a common factor leading to both alcoholism and antisocial personality. In support of this, research suggests that there is significant genetic involvement in their high level of comorbidity (e.g., Krueger et al., 2002; Slutske et al., 1998; Taylor & Lang, 2006). Moreover, one study found that ASPD and other externalizing disorders (like alcohol and drug dependence and conduct disorder) all share a strong common genetic vulnerability; environmental factors were more important in determining which disorder a particular person developed (Hicks et al., 2004; Krueger et al., 2007).

Of course it is difficult to separate out the relative contributions of genetic and environmental influences in antisocial personality disorder for many reasons. Antisocial individuals may receive their genes from antisocial parents. In such cases, these parents will likely also expose the child to a home environment that may provide a model for criminality, or contain risk factors such as abuse, neglect, parental separations, violence, and a host of other factors. A child with a genetic liability to antisocial behavior may also elicit problems in others because of his or her behavior (this is known as evocative gene–environment correlation). Such child-driven environmental factors here might include marital conflict, increased mental health problems in parents, or harsh discipline from parents (Jackson & Beaver, 2015). In other words, the links between the family environment and antisocial behavior are complex. Genetic and environmental effects are hard to disentangle. Their relative importance may also change over the course of development. Just as parents influence their children, children, in turn, should also be viewed as agents capable of shaping family dynamics. In other words, bidirectional causal models are now replacing simple unidirectional (e.g., family-to-child) ones.

A DEVELOPMENTAL PERSPECTIVE ASPD has its roots in childhood, especially for boys. The number of antisocial behaviors exhibited in childhood is the single best predictor of who will develop an adult diagnosis of ASPD, and the younger the age at which problems start, the higher the risk (Robins, 1978, 1991). Prospective studies have shown that it is children with an early history of oppositional defiant disorder—characterized by a pattern of hostile and defiant behavior toward authority figures that usually begins by the age of 6 years, followed by early-onset conduct disorder around age 9—who are most likely to develop ASPD as adults (e.g., Lahey et al., 2005).

Children and adolescents who show persistent patterns of aggression toward people or animals, destruction of property, deceitfulness or theft, and serious violation of rules at home or in school may be at risk for developing conduct disorder and antisocial personality disorder.

The second early diagnosis that is often a precursor to adult ASPD is attention-deficit/hyperactivity disorder (ADHD). ADHD is characterized by restless, inattentive, and impulsive behavior, a short attention span, and high distractibility (see Chapter 15). When ADHD co-occurs with conduct disorder (which happens in at least 30 to 50 percent of cases), this leads to a high likelihood that the person will develop a severely aggressive form of ASPD and possibly psychopathy, which we discuss shortly (Abramowitz et al., 2004; Lahey et al., 2005; Patterson et al., 2000).

To summarize, there is increasing evidence that genetic propensities to mild neuropsychological problems such as those leading to hyperactivity or attentional difficulties, along with a difficult temperament, may be important predisposing factors for early-onset conduct disorder, which often leads to life-course-persistent adult ASPD. The behavioral problems that these predisposing factors create have a cascade of pervasive effects over time. For example, on the basis of extensive longitudinal prospective research, Moffitt, Caspi, and colleagues (2002; Moffitt, 2006) have suggested that

> *"Life-course-persistent" antisocial behavior originates early in life, when the difficult behavior of a high-risk young child is exacerbated by a high-risk social environment. According to the theory, the child's risk emerges from inherited or acquired neuropsychological variation, initially manifested as subtle cognitive deficits, difficult temperament, or hyperactivity. The environment's risk comprises factors such as inadequate parenting, disrupted family bonds, and poverty. The environmental risk domain expands beyond the family as the child ages, to include poor relations with people such as peers and teachers, then later with partners and employers. Over the first 2 decades of development, transactions between individual and environment gradually construct a disordered personality with hallmark features of physical aggression, and antisocial behavior persisting to midlife. (Moffit et al., 2002, p. 180)*

A general mediational model for how all this occurs is shown in Figure 10.2. But how exactly does genetic variability interact with environmental stress to set the stage for later problems? It is too early to draw any strong conclusions. However, it is very likely that problems in brain development play a role. For example, it has been suggested that variability in *MAOA*, the gene we discussed earlier, may alter serotonin levels during the course of development. This in turn, may compromise the structure, function, and connectivity of the brain as the person matures (Buckholtz & Meyer-Lindenberg, 2014). It is also known that antisocial individuals show abnormalities in both the structure and function of the prefrontal cortex (Yang & Raine, 2009), although the origins of these abnormalities are still unclear. Regardless, given the role that this key brain area plays in decision making as well as in behavioral and emotional control, we might expect that people with dysfunctions in this region might engage in a whole range of unwise and antisocial behaviors (see Buckholtz, 2015). Of course, we are a long way from putting all of the pieces of the puzzle together at this time. Nonetheless, the links between genes, adverse environmental

Figure 10.2 A model for the association of family context and antisocial behavior. Each of the contextual variables in this model has been shown to be related to antisocial behavior in boys, which in turn is related to antisocial behavior in adults. Antisocial behavior in girls is far less common and has also been found to be less stable over time, making it more difficult to predict.

(Capaldi & Patterson, 1994. Interrelated influences of contextual factors on antisocial behavior. In D. C. Fowles et al. (Eds.), *Progress in Experimental Personality and Psychopathology Research*. Springer Publishing Company.)

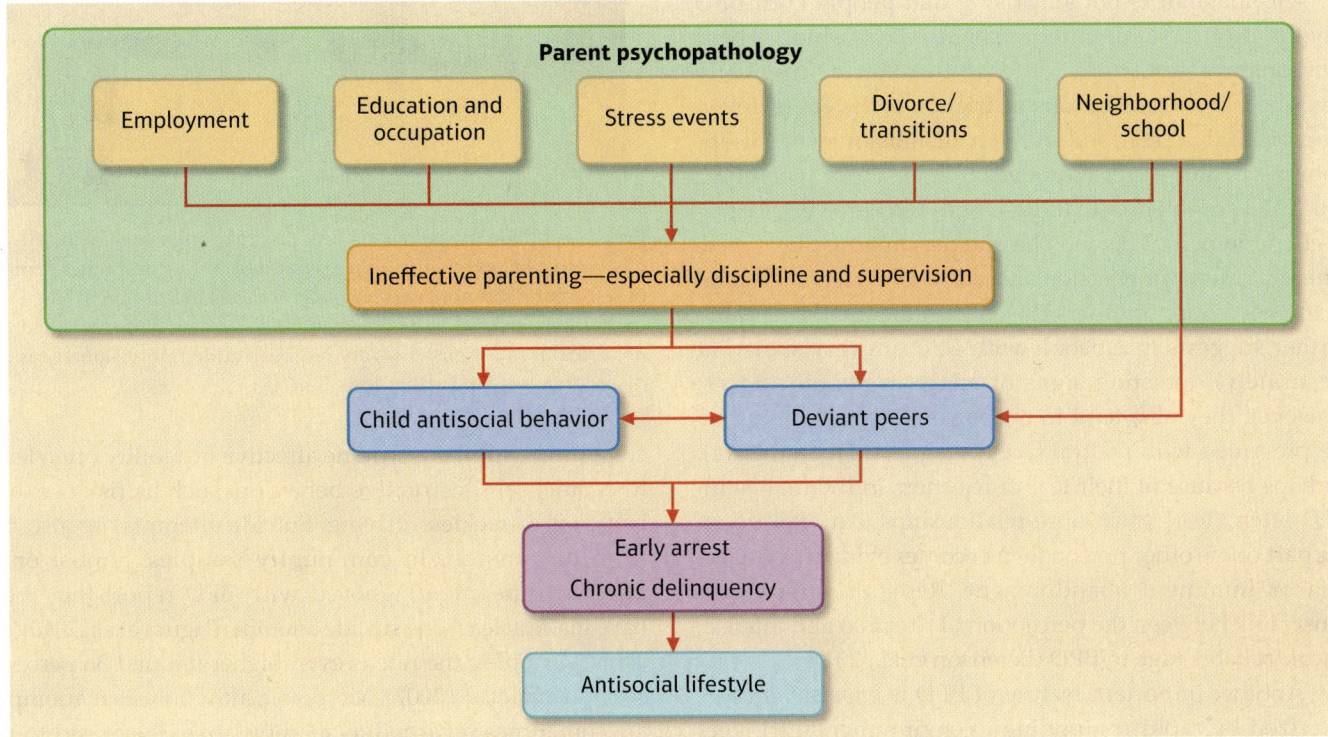

experiences, brain development, and a person's capacity for prosocial or antisocial behavior offer intriguing avenues for future research.

Borderline Personality Disorder

The term *borderline personality* has a long and rather confusing history (Hooley et al., 2012). Originally it was used to refer to patients who were very challenging to deal with and who were thought to have a condition that was on the "border" between neurosis and psychosis. Later, the word was used to describe patients who had some features of schizophrenia (as in *borderline schizophrenia*). By 1980, however, the key clinical aspects of **borderline personality disorder (BPD)** had been clarified sufficiently to permit entry into the *DSM* as a distinct diagnosis. It is now the most well-researched form of personality pathology. Although we acknowledge that the name of the disorder itself is not especially informative (the term *emotionally unstable disorder* is used in *ICD-10*), borderline personality disorder is a fascinating clinical condition. It is characterized by great suffering on the part of the patients themselves. It is also often misunderstood and stigmatized by clinical professionals.

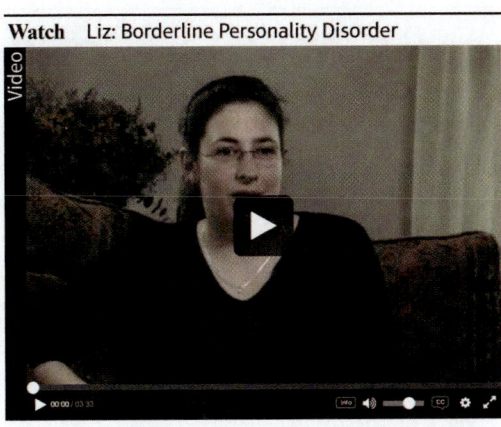

Watch Liz: Borderline Personality Disorder

People with borderline personality disorder (BPD) show a pattern of behavior characterized by impulsivity and instability in their interpersonal relationships, their self-image, and their moods. A central characteristic is *affective instability*. This shows itself in unusually intense emotional responses to environmental triggers, and a slow return to a baseline emotional state. Affective instability is also characterized by drastic and rapid shifts from one emotion to another (Livesley, 2008; Paris, 2007). This is combined with a *highly unstable self-image* or sense of self.

People with BPD often have chronic feelings of emptiness and have difficulty forming a sense of who they really are. They also struggle to cope with a highly negative self-concept and find it hard to tolerate being alone.

Given their affective instability combined with unstable self-image, it is not surprising that people with BPD have highly unstable interpersonal relationships. These relationships tend to be intense but stormy, typically involving overidealizations of friends or lovers (or even therapists) that later end in bitter disillusionment, disappointment, and anger (Gunderson et al., 1995; Lieb et al., 2004). One problem is that those with BPD are very fearful of abandonment. This may be one reason why they are so attuned to signs of rejection and quick to perceive rejection in the behaviors of others (Staebler et al., 2011). Research further suggests that people with BPD are very skilled at (accurately) detecting signs of anger in people's faces. However, they also tend to misperceive anger when they are presented with neutral faces (Veague & Hooley, 2014). Perhaps because of their fear of rejection, individuals with BPD often "test" their close relationships. Any failure on the part of the other person then becomes evidence of rejection or imminent abandonment. Research supports a causal link between the perception of rejection and intense, uncontrollable rage in BPD (Berenson et al., 2011).

Another important feature of BPD is *impulsivity* characterized by rapid responding to environmental triggers without thinking (or caring) about long-term consequences (Paris, 2007). These individuals' high levels of impulsivity

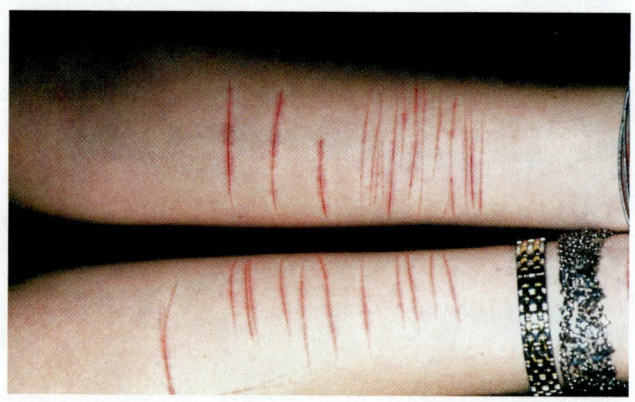

People with borderline personality disorder often engage in self-destructive behaviors including repetitive cutting and other forms of self-injury. But not everyone who engages in self-injury has borderline personality disorder. In *DSM-5* a new disorder called nonsuicidal self-injury disorder has been added provisionally as a disorder in need of further research.

combined with their extreme affective instability often lead to erratic, self-destructive behaviors such as risky sexual behavior or reckless driving. Suicide attempts are also far from uncommon. In community samples, almost one-quarter of people diagnosed with BPD report that they have made at least one suicide attempt (Pagura et al., 2010). In clinical samples, the rate is even higher (around 35 percent; see Asnaani et al., 2007). Moreover, although such attempts are sometimes regarded as manipulative, they need to be taken very seriously because approximately 8 to 10 percent of people with BPD will end their lives by suicide (Oldham,

---

DSM-5 Thinking Critically about *DSM-5*

Nonsuicidal Self-Injury: Distinct Disorder or Symptom of Borderline Personality Disorder?

Nonsuicidal self-injury (NSSI) involves deliberate damage to body tissue such as might occur with skin cutting or burning (Nock, 2009). This behavior (which is sometimes called self-mutilation) occurs in the absence of an intent to die (hence the term *nonsuicidal*). Self-mutilating behavior has long been listed in the *DSM* as a symptom of BPD. However, many people who engage in self-injury do not have BPD, although they do report high levels of depressive symptoms, anxiety, suicidality, and generally low levels of functioning (Selby et al., 2012). Of great concern, people who engage in NSSI are at elevated risk for later suicide (Wilkinson et al., 2011). For these reasons, the *DSM-5* task force was charged with determining whether people who display a significant amount of nonsuicidal self-injurious behavior should be diagnosed with a new disorder that would be called *nonsuicidal self-injury disorder*.

NSSI is found in males and females, as well as in people of all ethnicities and economic backgrounds. The risk for NSSI seems to be greatest in the adolescent years, with lifetime prevalence rates around 17 percent (Swannell et al., 2014). However, prevalence rates are also high in young adults (13 percent) as

well as in adults, where community prevalence rates are around 5 percent.

Why do people hurt themselves by cutting or burning? Tension relief is one reason that many people give. NSSI is often used to regulate intense or extreme negative emotions. Hooley, Ho, et al. (2010) have also found that people who engage in NSSI tend to have higher pain endurances than the rest of us. In addition, they have a highly self-critical cognitive style and "may regard suffering and pain as something they deserve" (Hooley, Ho, et al., 2010, p. 170). This may help explain why such people choose to regulate their emotions by engaging in behaviors that are self-damaging and painful rather than using other more healthy coping strategies such as talking to a friend or going for a run.

NSSI is a growing problem. Recognizing this, it has now been added to *DSM-5*. NSSI disorder is listed in Section III as a condition in need of further study. This move is likely to stimulate research. As we learn more we may be in a better position to understand, treat, and perhaps even prevent this increasingly prevalent condition.

2006; Skodol, Gunderson, et al., 2002). *Self-mutilation* (such as repetitive cutting behavior) is another characteristic feature of borderline personality. However, as illustrated in the Thinking Critically about *DSM-5* box, many people who engage in self-injury do not have BPD. The diagnostic criteria for borderline personality disorder are shown in the *DSM-5* box. They are also well illustrated in the case of Ms. R.

Ms. R: Borderline Personality Disorder

Ms. R. is 19 years old. Although she has no formal history of psychiatric treatment, she reports a long history of mood instability, suicidal gestures, and skin cutting. She also has had many stormy relationships, including a history of physical abuse, as well as three abortions. She was admitted to the hospital for the first time after she threatened to kill herself following a physical fight with her boyfriend and crashing the family car. The patient says that she recently moved out of her family home and went to live with her boyfriend. After a fight with her boyfriend that left her with a bloody lip, she was feeling "depressed." She returned home and began to fight with her mother. She then stole the family car and crashed into a pole. When a neighbor found her, she stated she was going to kill herself. Her mother subsequently brought her to the hospital. On admission, Ms. R said she was "depressed" and suicidal. She was described as angry, entitled, manipulative, and "regressed." She was diagnosed with borderline personality. The presence of narcissistic traits was also noted. (From Avery et al., 2012.)

In addition to having affective and impulsive behavioral symptoms, as many as 75 percent of people with BPD have cognitive symptoms. These include relatively short or transient episodes in which they appear to be out of contact with reality and experience psychotic-like symptoms such as hallucinations, paranoid ideas, or severe dissociative symptoms (Lieb et al., 2004; Skodol, Gunderson, et al., 2002). These brief psychotic episodes are most likely to occur during times of stress, although they are also present at other times as well (Stiglmayr et al., 2008). Given the many and varied symptoms of BPD, it is not surprising that this personality disorder produces significant impairment in social, academic, and occupational functioning (Bagge et al., 2004; Grant et al., 2008).

Estimates are that around 1 to 2 percent of the population may qualify for the diagnosis of BPD (Lenzenweger et al., 2007). However, BPD is very common in clinical settings and is found in about 10 percent of outpatients and 15 to 20 percent of psychiatric inpatients (Asnaani et al., 2007; Hooley et al., 2012; Trull, 2015). Although early research

---

DSM-5 *Criteria for. . .*

Borderline Personality Disorder

A pervasive pattern of instability of interpersonal relationships, self-image, and affects, and marked impulsivity, beginning by early adulthood and present in a variety of contexts, as indicated by five (or more) of the following:

1. Frantic efforts to avoid real or imagined abandonment. (**Note:** Do not include suicidal or self-mutilating behavior covered in Criterion 5.)

2. A pattern of unstable and intense interpersonal relationships characterized by alternating between extremes of idealization and devaluation.

3. Identity disturbance: markedly and persistently unstable self-image or sense of self.

4. Impulsivity in at least two areas that are potentially self-damaging (e.g., spending, sex, substance abuse, reckless driving, binge eating). (**Note:** Do not include suicidal or self-mutilating behavior covered in Criterion 5.)

5. Recurrent suicidal behavior, gestures, or threats, or self-mutilating behavior.

6. Affective instability due to a marked reactivity of mood (e.g., intense episodic dysphoria, irritability, or anxiety usually lasting a few hours and only rarely more than a few days).

7. Chronic feelings of emptiness.

8. Inappropriate, intense anger or difficulty controlling anger (e.g., frequent displays of temper, constant anger, recurrent physical fights).

9. Transient, stress-related paranoid ideation or severe dissociative symptoms.

Source: Reprinted with permission from the *Diagnostic and Statistical Manual of Mental Disorders,* Fifth Edition (Copyright © 2013). American Psychiatric Association.

found that approximately 75 percent of individuals receiving this diagnosis in clinical settings are women, such findings likely arise from a gender imbalance in treatment seeking rather than prevalence of the disorder. Consistent with this, more recent epidemiological studies of community residents suggest an equal gender ratio (Coid et al., 2009; Grant et al., 2008).

COMORBIDITY WITH OTHER DISORDERS BPD is rarely diagnosed alone. It commonly co-occurs with a variety of other disorders. What makes BPD unusual, however, is that it tends to be comorbid with both internalizing disorders (such as mood and anxiety disorders), as well as externalizing disorders (such as substance use disorders; Eaton et al., 2011). In a large sample of community residents, BPD was most strongly associated with major depressive disorder and mania, as well as with panic disorder, agoraphobia, generalized anxiety disorder, and post-traumatic stress disorder (Tomko et al., 2014). Remarkably, in this study, of those diagnosed with BPD, 85 percent also met criteria for a current or past anxiety disorder, 83 percent had had a lifetime mood disorder or episode of depression, and 78 percent met criteria for a current or past substance abuse disorder. Although it was once suggested that BPD be regarded as a variant of mood disorder because of the high comorbidity between BPD and depression, the broad scope of other disorders that are comorbid with BPD suggests otherwise. Moreover, neuroimaging data indicate that BPD individuals show different neural responses to emotional stimuli than do individuals with chronic depression (Hooley, Gruber, et al., 2010).

There is also substantial co-occurrence of BPD and other personality disorders. BPD can be comorbid with the full range of other personality disorders, although comorbidity with schizotypal, narcissistic, and dependent disorder is particularly high (Tomko et al., 2014). Despite being viewed as a categorical diagnosis in *DSM-5* (that is, as a specific diagnostic entity), BPD appears to be very amenable to being described using a pathological trait approach (Few et al., 2015). In terms of the five-factor model, BPD is conceptualized as involving high neuroticism, low agreeableness, low conscientiousness, and high openness to feelings and actions (refer back to Table 10.2).

CAUSAL FACTORS BPD runs in families. In the most methodologically rigorous study to date, the risk of having a BPD diagnosis was found to be four times higher in the biological relatives of patients with BPD than it was in the relatives of people who did not have a diagnosis of BPD (Gunderson et al., 2011). Of course, we must keep in mind that just because a disorder runs in families does not invariably mean that this must be because of genes. However, in the case of BPD, we have many reasons to believe that genes are important. Indeed, they may account for 40 percent of the variance in the disorder (Amad et al., 2014). But

do not take this to mean that BPD, as a disorder, is inherited. Rather, what is most likely inherited are genes that confer susceptibility to certain personality traits—traits such as neuroticism or impulsivity that are prominent aspects of BPD (Hooley et al., 2012; Paris, 2007). These inherited traits are also not specific to BPD but instead confer risk for a range of other psychopathological conditions as well. Once you appreciate this, it becomes easier to understand why BPD is so often comorbid with other disorders. It also helps explain why we see mood and anxiety disorders, impulse control disorders, and other personality disorders in the family members of people diagnosed with BPD (Zanarini et al., 2009).

But which genes are involved? As of now we cannot be certain. Research to date has largely focused on candidate genes related to the serotonin system (serotonin is a neurotransmitter that is implicated in mood and impulsivity) and the dopamine system (dopamine is involved in impulse control, cognition, and sensitivity to reward, among other things). Two genome-wide association studies (GWASs) have also been published (Lubke et al., 2014; Witt et al., 2014). To date, however, the results have been disappointing and we do not have any consistent or conclusive findings (Amad et al., 2014, for a recent review). In part this may be because the studies that have been conducted so far involve relatively small sample sizes (for genetic research). Another problem is that BPD is a very complicated and clinically heterogeneous disorder and may involve a very large number of genes. Yet another reason is that the influence of environmental factors is very rarely taken into account.

This is important because environmental factors are thought to account for the largest proportion (55 percent) of variance in borderline traits. We also know that genes influence sensitivity to environmental stressors (Caspi et al., 2010). It is likely that such experiences as well as other environmental influences interact with genes to determine who will develop problems at a later point (see Figure 10.3 for an illustration of a possible diathesis–stress model). In other words, rather than looking for genes that are linked to specific disorders, we should perhaps be looking for genes that might play a role in making us more or less susceptible to the positive and negative aspects of our environments (Amad et al., 2014).

With regard to the latter, child maltreatment and other extreme early life experiences have long been linked to BPD. Importantly, two prospective community-based studies have shown that childhood adversity and maltreatment increases the risk of developing BPD in adulthood (Johnson et al., 1999; Widom et al., 2009). These studies are consistent with a wealth of retrospective research showing that people with this disorder usually report a large number of negative and sometimes traumatic events in childhood. For example, in one large study on abuse and

Figure 10.3 Multidimensional Diathesis–Stress Theory of Borderline Personality Disorder

(Adapted from Paris (1999).)

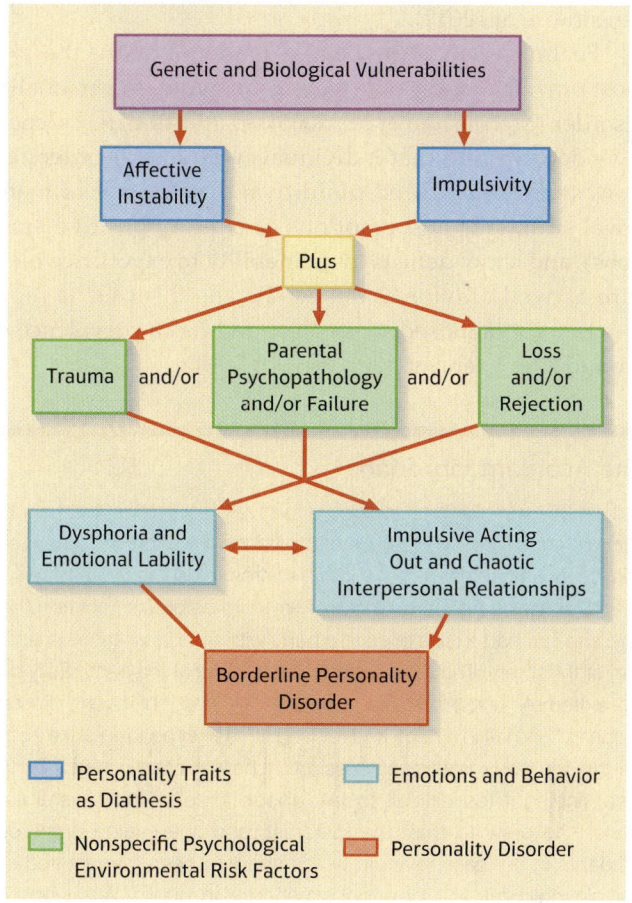

Personality Traits as Diathesis

Nonspecific Psychological Environmental Risk Factors

Emotions and Behavior

Personality Disorder

Many studies have shown that people with borderline personality disorder report a large number of negative, even traumatic, events in childhood. These include abuse and neglect, and separation and loss.

neglect, Zanarini and colleagues (1997) reported on the results of detailed interviews of over 350 patients with BPD and over 100 patients with other personality disorders. Patients with BPD reported significantly higher rates of abuse than did patients with other personality disorders (which were also quite high): emotional abuse (73 versus 51 percent), physical abuse (59 versus 34 percent), and sexual abuse (61 versus 32 percent). Overall, about 90 percent of patients with BPD reported some type of childhood abuse or neglect.

Although these figures are striking, childhood adversity cannot be regarded as a specific risk factor only for borderline pathology. It is reported at relatively high rates by people with all of the other personality disorders as well (Hengartner et al., 2013; Moran et al., 2010). It is also associated with more subtle forms of personality disturbance. For example, emotional abuse has been linked to all of the Big Five traits and is associated with increased neuroticism and greater openness, as well as less extroversion, agreeableness, and conscientiousness (Hengartner et al., 2015). We should also keep in mind that childhood abuse nearly always occurs in families with various other problems

including poverty, marital discord, parental separations, parental substance abuse, and family violence. Of course, none of this takes away from the findings that childhood adversity is commonly found in people with BPD. Rather than looking at specific types of childhood maltreatment, however, we should perhaps simply acknowledge that bad childhood experiences increase the risk of a wide array of personality problems including, but not limited to, borderline personality disorder.

So how can we best understand the causes of BPD? At the present time, it is reasonable to suggest that some people, by virtue of their genetic predispositions, may be highly sensitive to the effects of negative early life experiences. These stressful early experiences may create long-term dysregulation of the HPA axis (which you learned about in Chapter 5) and shape brain development, perhaps compromising key brain circuits that are involved in emotion regulation (see Hooley et al., 2012). Neuroimaging studies suggest that BPD is associated with increased amygdala activation in emotion-inducing situations, as well as with reduced prefrontal regulation (Leichsenring et al., 2011). But why these problems in brain functioning develop is still unknown. Although still speculative at this stage, we suggest that genetic factors may interact with negative childhood experiences to create problems in the neural circuits that are involved in regulating mood, thinking, and behavior. This helps explain why so many areas of functioning are affected in BPD and why people with this disorder find their emotions so difficult to control.

in review

- Describe and differentiate among the following Cluster B personality disorders: histrionic, narcissistic, antisocial, and borderline.

Cluster C Personality Disorders

10.5 List the three Cluster C personality disorders and describe the clinical features that are central to each.

People with Cluster C personality disorders often show anxiety and fearfulness. These are characteristics that we do not see in the other two clusters. In the following subsections, we examine avoidant, dependent, and obsessive-compulsive personality disorders.

Avoidant Personality Disorder

Individuals with **avoidant personality disorder** show extreme social inhibition and introversion, leading to lifelong patterns of limited social relationships and reluctance to enter into social interactions. Because of their hypersensitivity to, and fear of, criticism and disapproval, they do not seek out other people, yet they desire affection and are often lonely and bored. Unlike schizoid personalities, people with avoidant personality disorder do not enjoy their aloneness. Avoidant individuals want contact with other people. However, their inability to relate comfortably to

The person with avoidant personality desires social contact but avoids it because of a fear of rejection.

other people causes them acute anxiety. They are painfully self-conscious in social settings and highly critical of themselves. Not surprisingly, avoidant personality disorder is often associated with depression (Grant, Hasin, et al., 2005; Sanislow et al., 2012).

Feeling inept and socially inadequate are the two most prevalent and stable features of avoidant personality disorder (McGlashan et al., 2005). In addition, researchers have documented that individuals with this disorder also show more generalized timidity and avoidance of many novel situations and emotions (including positive emotions), and show deficits in their ability to experience pleasure as well (Taylor et al., 2004). The disorder is more commonly diagnosed in women, and has a prevalence of around 2 to 3 percent.

The Avoidant Librarian

Sally, a 35-year-old librarian, lived a relatively isolated life and had few acquaintances and no close personal friends. From childhood on, she had been very shy and had withdrawn from close ties with others to keep from being hurt or criticized. Two years before she entered therapy, she had had a date to go to a party with an acquaintance she had met at the library. The moment they had arrived at the party, Sally had felt extremely uncomfortable because she had not been "dressed properly." She left in a hurry and refused to see her acquaintance again.

In the early treatment sessions, she sat silently much of the time, finding it too difficult to talk about herself. After several sessions, she grew to trust the therapist, and she related numerous incidents in her early years in which she had been "devastated" by her alcoholic father's obnoxious behavior in public. Although she had tried to keep her school friends from knowing about her family problems, when this had become impossible, she instead had limited her friendships, thus protecting herself from possible embarrassment or criticism.

When Sally first began therapy, she avoided meeting people unless she could be assured that they would "like her." With therapy that focused on enhancing her assertiveness and social skills, she made some progress in her ability to approach people and talk with them.

From a clinical perspective, avoidant personality disorder looks a lot like schizoid personality disorder. Both types of people are socially isolated. The key difference is that the person with schizoid personality disorder has little desire to form close relationships. Such people tend to be rather aloof, cold, and relatively indifferent to criticism (Millon & Martinez, 1995). In contrast, the person with avoidant personality disorder wants interpersonal contact but is shy, insecure, and hypersensitive to criticism. A much less clear distinction is that between avoidant personality disorder and generalized social phobia (Chapter 6). Numerous studies have found substantial overlap between these two disorders, leading some investigators to conclude that avoidant personality disorder may simply be a somewhat more severe manifestation of generalized social phobia (Alpert et al., 1997; Carter & Wu, 2010; Tillfors et al., 2004) that does not warrant a separate diagnosis (Chambless et al., 2008). This is consistent with the finding that there are cases of generalized social phobia without avoidant personality disorder but very few cases of avoidant personality disorder without generalized social phobia. Somewhat higher levels of dysfunction and distress are also found in the individuals with avoidant personality disorder, including more consistent feelings of low self-esteem (Hummelen et al., 2007; Millon & Martinez, 1995; Tillfors et al., 2004).

DSM-5 *Criteria for. . .*

Avoidant Personality Disorder

A pervasive pattern of social inhibition, feelings of inadequacy, and hypersensitivity to negative evaluation, beginning by early adulthood and present in a variety of contexts, as indicated by four (or more) of the following:

1. Avoids occupational activities that involve significant interpersonal contact because of fears of criticism, disapproval, or rejection.

2. Is unwilling to get involved with people unless certain of being liked.

3. Shows restraint within intimate relationships because of the fear of being shamed or ridiculed.

4. Is preoccupied with being criticized or rejected in social situations.

5. Is inhibited in new interpersonal situations because of feelings of inadequacy.

6. Views self as socially inept, personally unappealing, or inferior to others.

7. Is unusually reluctant to take personal risks or to engage in any new activities because they may prove embarrassing.

Source: Reprinted with permission from the *Diagnostic and Statistical Manual of Mental Disorders,* Fifth Edition (Copyright © 2013). American Psychiatric Association.

CAUSAL FACTORS   Some research suggests that avoidant personality may have its origins in an innate "inhibited" temperament that leaves the infant and child shy and inhibited in novel and ambiguous situations. A large twin study in Norway has shown that traits prominent in avoidant personality disorder show a modest genetic influence, and that the genetic vulnerability for avoidant personality disorder is at least partially shared with that for social phobia (Reichborn-Kjennerud, Czajkowski, Torgersen, et al., 2007). Moreover, there is also evidence that the fear of being negatively evaluated, which is prominent in avoidant personality disorder, is moderately heritable (Stein et al., 2002); introversion and neuroticism are also both elevated (refer back to Table 10.2), and they too are moderately heritable.

This genetically and biologically based inhibited temperament may often serve as the diathesis that leads to avoidant personality disorder in some children who experience emotional abuse, rejection, or humiliation from parents who are not particularly affectionate (Alden et al., 2002; Bernstein & Travaglini, 1999; Kagan, 1997). Such abuse and rejection would be especially likely to lead to anxious and fearful attachment patterns in temperamentally inhibited children (Bartholomew et al., 2001).

Dependent Personality Disorder

Individuals with **dependent personality disorder** show an extreme need to be taken care of, which leads to clinging and submissive behavior. They also show acute fear at the possibility of separation or sometimes of simply having to be alone because they see themselves as inept (Bornstein et al., 2015; Widiger & Bornstein, 2001). Such individuals usually build their lives around other people and subordinate their own needs and views to keep these people involved with them. Accordingly, they may be indiscriminate in their selection of mates. They often fail to get appropriately angry with others because of a fear of losing their support, which means that people with dependent personalities may remain in psychologically or physically abusive relationships. They have great difficulty making even simple, everyday decisions without a great deal of advice and reassurance because they lack self-confidence and feel helpless even when they have actually developed good work skills or other competencies. They may function well as long as they are not required to be on their own.

The Dependent Wife

Sarah, a 32-year-old mother of two and a part-time tax accountant, came to a crisis center late one evening after Michael, her husband of a year and a half, had abused her physically and then left home. Although he never physically harmed the children, he frequently threatened to do so when he was drunk. Sarah appeared acutely anxious and worried about the future and "needed to be told what to do." She wanted her husband to come back and seemed rather unconcerned about his regular pattern of physical abuse. At the time, Michael was an unemployed resident in a day treatment program at a halfway house for paroled drug abusers. He was almost always in a surly mood and "ready to explode."

Although Sarah had a well-paying job, she voiced great concern about being able to make it on her own. She realized that it was foolish to be "dependent" on her husband, whom she referred to as a "real loser." (She had had a similar relationship with her first husband, who had left her and her oldest child when she was 18.) Several times in the past few months, Sarah had made up her mind to get out of the marriage but couldn't bring herself to break away. She would threaten to leave, but when the time came to do so, she would "freeze in the door" with a numbness in her body and a sinking feeling in her stomach at the thought of "not being with Michael."

Estimates are that dependent personality disorder occurs in slightly under 1 percent of the population and is more common in women than in men (Bornstein et al., 2015; Torgersen, 2012). This gender difference is not due to a sex bias in making the diagnosis but rather to the higher prevalence in women of certain personality traits such as neuroticism and agreeableness, which are prominent in dependent personality disorder (Lynam & Widiger, 2007). Dependent personality disorder is often comorbid with other disorders including mood disorders, anxiety disorders, eating disorders, and somatic symptom disorders. Comorbidity is also high between dependent personality disorder and other personality disorders, especially schizoid, avoidant, borderline, and histrionic personality disorder (Bornstein et al., 2015).

Some of this comorbidity may stem from overlap between the features of dependent personality disorder and those of borderline, histrionic, and avoidant personality disorders. However, at the clinical level, there are key differences as well (refer back to Table 10.2). For example, both borderline personalities and dependent personalities fear abandonment. However, the borderline personality, who usually has intense and stormy relationships, reacts with feelings of emptiness or rage if abandonment occurs, whereas the dependent personality reacts initially with submissiveness and appeasement and then finally with an urgent seeking of a new relationship. Histrionic and dependent personalities both have strong needs for reassurance and approval, but the histrionic personality is much more gregarious, flamboyant, and actively demanding of attention, whereas the dependent personality is more docile and self-effacing. It can also be hard to distinguish between dependent and avoidant personalities. As noted, dependent personalities have great difficulty separating

in relationships because they feel incompetent on their own and have a need to be taken care of, whereas avoidant personalities have trouble initiating relationships because they fear the humiliation they will experience if they are criticized or rejected (Millon & Martinez, 1995). Even so, we should remember that avoidant personality co-occurs with dependent personality disorder rather frequently (Arntz et al., 2009; Bernstein & Travaglini, 1999; Bornstein et al., 2015). This fits with the observation that people with avoidant personality disorder do not avoid absolutely everyone and that their dependent personality disorder characteristics are focused on the one or few individuals whom they do not avoid (Alden et al., 2002). In terms of the five-factor model, dependent personality disorder is associated with high levels of neuroticism and agreeableness (Lowe et al., 2009).

CAUSAL FACTORS Estimates are that somewhere between 30 and 60 percent of the variance in dependent personality disorder symptoms might be attributable to genetic factors (Bornstein et al., 2015; Gjerde et al., 2012). Moreover, several other personality traits such as neuroticism and agreeableness that are prominent in dependent personality disorder also have a genetic component (Widiger & Bornstein, 2001). It is possible that people with these partially genetically based predispositions to dependence and anxiousness may be especially prone to the adverse effects of parents who are authoritarian and overprotective (not promoting autonomy and individuation in their child but instead reinforcing dependent behavior). This might lead children to believe that they must rely on others for their own well-being and are incompetent on their own (Widiger & Bornstein, 2001). Cognitive theorists describe the underlying maladaptive schemas for these individuals

DSM-5 *Criteria for...*

Dependent Personality Disorder

A pervasive and excessive need to be taken care of that leads to submissive and clinging behavior and fears of separation, beginning by early adulthood and present in a variety of contexts, as indicated by five (or more) of the following:

1. Has difficulty making everyday decisions without an excessive amount of advice and reassurance from others.

2. Needs others to assume responsibility for most major areas of his or her life.

3. Has difficulty expressing disagreement with others because of fear of loss of support or approval. (**Note:** Do not include realistic fears of retribution.)

4. Has difficulty initiating projects or doing things on his or her own (because of a lack of self-confidence in

judgment or abilities rather than a lack of motivation or energy).

5. Goes to excessive lengths to obtain nurturance and support from others, to the point of volunteering to do things that are unpleasant.

6. Feels uncomfortable or helpless when alone because of exaggerated fears of being unable to care for himself or herself.

7. Urgently seeks another relationship as a source of care and support when a close relationship ends.

8. Is unrealistically preoccupied with fears of being left to take care of himself or herself.

as involving core beliefs about weakness and competence and needing others to survive, such as "I am completely helpless" and "I can function only if I have access to somebody competent" (Beck et al., 1990, p. 60; Beck et al., 2004). Recent research supports the hypothesis that these beliefs characterize those with dependent personality disorder (Arntz et al., 2011).

Obsessive-Compulsive Personality Disorder

Perfectionism and an excessive concern with orderliness and control characterize individuals with **obsessive-compulsive personality disorder (OCPD)**. Do not move anything on their neat desks! Their preoccupation with maintaining mental and interpersonal control occurs in part through careful attention to rules, order, and schedules. They are very careful in what they do so as not to make mistakes, but because the details they are preoccupied with are often trivial they use their time poorly and have a difficult time seeing the larger picture (Aycicegi-Dinn et al., 2009; Yovel et al., 2005). Their perfectionism is also often quite dysfunctional in that it can result in them never finishing projects. They also tend to be devoted to work to the exclusion of leisure activities and may have difficulty taking vacations, relaxing, or doing anything just for fun (Widiger & Frances, 1994). Even hobbies are serious activities that require perfection. At an interpersonal level, people with OCPD have difficulty delegating tasks to others ("They will not do it exactly right and exactly how I want them to do it"). They are also seen by others as being rigid, stubborn, and cold. Research indicates that rigidity,

Individuals with obsessive-compulsive personality disorder are highly perfectionistic. They experience difficulties delegating tasks and have problems finishing projects. Excessively devoted to work and inflexible about moral and ethical issues, they are also inclined to be ungenerous with themselves and others.

stubbornness, and perfectionism, as well as reluctance to delegate, are the most prevalent and stable features of OCPD (Ansell et al., 2008; Grilo et al., 2004; McGlashan et al., 2005; Samuel & Widiger, 2011).

Although the name sounds similar, people with OCPD do not have true obsessions or compulsive rituals as is the case with obsessive-compulsive disorder (OCD; see Chapter 6). Indeed, only about 20 percent of patients with OCD have a comorbid diagnosis of OCPD. This is not significantly different from the rate of OCPD in patients with panic disorder (Albert et al., 2004). Interestingly, somewhere between 20 and 61 percent of people with anorexia nervosa have a comorbid diagnosis of OCPD (Samuels & Costa, 2012). This makes sense, given that perfectionism and rigidity are major features of both conditions. There is also significant comorbidity between OCPD and the usual suspects, namely, mood and anxiety disorders (Reichborn-Kjennerud & Knudsen, 2015).

The Perfectionist Train Dispatcher

Alan appeared to be well suited to his work as a train dispatcher. He was conscientious, perfectionistic, and attended to minute details. However, he was not close to his coworkers, and they reportedly thought him "off." He would get quite upset if even minor variations to his daily routine occurred. For example, he would become tense and irritable if coworkers did not follow exactly his elaborately constructed schedules and plans. Alan also had difficulty when his coworkers suggested other ways to accomplish work-related tasks. He was unable to acknowledge that there might be other equally good ways to do things, and he quickly dismissed all suggestions and ideas from his colleagues and coworkers.

In short, Alan got little pleasure out of life and worried constantly about minor problems. His rigid routines were impossible to maintain, and he often developed tension headaches or stomachaches when he couldn't keep his complicated plans in order. His physician, noting the frequency of his physical complaints and his generally perfectionistic approach to life, referred him for a psychological evaluation. Psychotherapy was recommended, but he did not follow up on the treatment recommendations because he felt that he could not afford the time away from work.

In community samples, the point prevalence of OCPD is around 2 percent. The disorder is thought to be slightly more common in men than women (Torgersen, 2012). Some features of OCPD overlap with some features of narcissistic, antisocial, and schizoid personality disorders, although there are also distinguishing features. For example, individuals with narcissistic and ASPDs may share the lack of generosity toward others that characterizes OCPD. However, the former tend to be willing to indulge themselves, whereas those with OCPD are equally unwilling to be generous with themselves. In addition, both the schizoid and the obsessive-compulsive

DSM-5 *Criteria for. . .*

Obsessive-Compulsive Personality Disorder

A pervasive pattern of preoccupation with orderliness, perfectionism, and mental and interpersonal control, at the expense of flexibility, openness, and efficiency, beginning by early adulthood and present in a variety of contexts, as indicated by four (or more) of the following:

1. Is preoccupied with details, rules, lists, order, organization, or schedules to the extent that the major point of the activity is lost.

2. Shows perfectionism that interferes with task completion (e.g., is unable to complete a project because his or her own overly strict standards are not met).

3. Is excessively devoted to work and productivity to the exclusion of leisure activities and friendships (not accounted for by obvious economic necessity).

4. Is overconscientious, scrupulous, and inflexible about matters of morality, ethics, or values (not accounted for by cultural or religious identification).

5. Is unable to discard worn-out or worthless objects even when they have no sentimental value.

6. Is reluctant to delegate tasks or to work with others unless they submit to exactly his or her way of doing things.

7. Adopts a miserly spending style toward both self and others; money is viewed as something to be hoarded for future catastrophes.

8. Shows rigidity and stubbornness.

Source: Reprinted with permission from the *Diagnostic and Statistical Manual of Mental Disorders,* Fifth Edition (Copyright © 2013). American Psychiatric Association.

---

personalities may have a certain amount of formality and social detachment, but only the schizoid personality lacks the capacity for close relationships. The person with OCPD has difficulty in interpersonal relationships because of excessive devotion to work and great difficulty expressing emotions.

CAUSAL FACTORS Theorists who take a five-factor dimensional approach to understanding OCPD note that these individuals have excessively high levels of conscientiousness (Samuel & Widiger, 2011). This leads to extreme devotion to work, perfectionism, and excessive controlling behavior. They are also high on assertiveness (a facet of extraversion) and low on compliance (a facet of agreeableness). Another influential biological dimensional approach—that of Cloninger (1987)—posits three primary dimensions of personality: novelty seeking, reward dependence, and harm avoidance. Individuals with obsessive-compulsive personalities have low levels of novelty seeking (i.e., they avoid change) and reward dependence (i.e., they work excessively at the expense of pleasurable pursuits) but high levels of harm avoidance (i.e., they respond strongly to aversive stimuli and try to avoid them). Research has also demonstrated that the OCPD traits show a modest genetic influence (Calvo et al., 2009; Reichborn-Kjennerud, Czajkowski, Neale, et al., 2007).

in review

- Describe and differentiate among the following Cluster C personality disorders: avoidant, dependent, and obsessive-compulsive.

General Sociocultural Causal Factors for Personality Disorders

10.6 Explain the role that sociocultural factors might play in the prevalence of personality disorders.

The sociocultural factors that contribute to personality disorders are not well understood. As with other forms of psychopathology, the incidence and particular features of personality disorders vary somewhat with time and place, although not as much as one might guess (Allik, 2005; Rigozzi et al., 2009). Indeed, there is less variance across cultures than within cultures. This may be related to findings that all cultures (both Western and non-Western, including Africa and Asia) share the same five basic personality traits discussed earlier, and their patterns of covariation also seem universal (see Allik, 2005, for a review).

Some researchers believe that certain personality disorders have increased in American society in recent years (e.g., Paris, 2001). If this claim is true, we can expect to find the increase related to changes in our culture's general priorities and activities. Is our emphasis on impulse gratification, instant solutions, and pain-free benefits leading more people to develop the self-centered lifestyles that we see in more extreme forms of the personality disorders? For example, there is some evidence that narcissistic personality disorder is more common in Western cultures, where personal ambition and success are encouraged and reinforced (e.g., Widiger & Bornstein, 2001). There is also some evidence that histrionic personality might be expected to be (and is) less common in Asian cultures, where sexual seductiveness and drawing attention to oneself are frowned on; by contrast, it may be higher in Hispanic cultures, where such tendencies are common and well tolerated (e.g., Bornstein et al., 2015). One study in the United States has found higher rates of histrionic personality disorder in African American women relative to Caucasian women (Grant, Hasin, et al., 2004). Again within the United States, rates of BPD are higher in Hispanic Americans than they are in African Americans and Caucasians, but rates of schizotypal personality disorder are higher in African Americans than in Caucasians (Chavira et al., 2003).

It has also been suggested that known increases over the 70 years since World War II in emotional dysregulation (e.g., depression, self-injurious behavior, and suicide) and impulsive behaviors (substance abuse and criminal behavior) may be related to increases in the prevalence of borderline and ASPDs over the same time period. This could stem from increased breakdown of the family and other traditional social structures (Paris, 2001, 2007) and may vary across cultures depending on whether similar breakdowns have occurred.

---

in review

- Describe the role played by sociocultural factors in explaining the prevalence of personality disorders.

Treatments and Outcomes for Personality Disorders

10.7 **Discuss the challenges associated with treating personality disorders and summarize the approaches that are used.**

Personality disorders are generally very difficult to treat, in part because they are, by definition, relatively enduring, pervasive, and inflexible patterns of behavior and inner experience. Moreover, many different goals of treatment can be formulated, and some are more difficult to achieve than others. Goals might include reducing subjective distress, changing specific dysfunctional behaviors, and changing whole patterns of behavior or the entire structure of the personality.

In many cases, people with personality disorders enter treatment only at someone else's insistence, and they often do not believe that they need to change. Moreover, those from the odd/eccentric Cluster A and the erratic/dramatic Cluster B have general difficulties in forming and maintaining good relationships, including with a therapist. For those from the erratic/dramatic Cluster B, the pattern of acting out typical in their other relationships is carried into the therapy situation. Instead of dealing with their problems at the verbal level, they may become angry at their

therapist and create conflict during sessions. Noncompletion of treatment is a particular problem in the treatment of personality disorders; one review reported that an average of 37 percent of patients with personality disorders drop out of therapy prematurely (McMurran et al., 2010).

In addition, when people have a personality disorder as well as another disorder (such as depression or an eating disorder) they tend to do less well than comparable patients without comorbid personality disorders (Crits-Christoph & Barber, 2002, 2007; Pilkonis, 2001). This is partly because people with personality disorders have rigid, ingrained personality traits that often lead to poor therapeutic relationships and additionally make them resist doing the things that would help improve their other conditions.

Adapting Therapeutic Techniques to Specific Personality Disorders

Therapeutic techniques must often be modified. For example, recognizing that traditional individual psychotherapy tends to encourage dependence in people who are already too dependent (as in dependent, histrionic, and BPDs), it is often useful to develop treatment strategies specifically aimed at altering these traits. Patients from the anxious/fearful Cluster C, such as those with dependent and avoidant personalities, may also be hypersensitive to any criticism they may perceive from the therapist, so therapists need to be extremely careful to make sure that they do not come across in this way.

For people with severe personality disorders, therapy may be more effective in situations where acting-out behavior can be constrained. For example, many patients with BPD are hospitalized at times, for safety reasons, because of their frequent suicidal behavior. However, partial-hospitalization programs are increasingly being used as intermediate and less expensive alternatives to inpatient treatment (Azim, 2001). In these programs, patients live at home and receive extensive individual and group treatment on weekdays. Several studies conducted in the Netherlands suggest that short-term inpatient treatment is more effective than outpatient treatment for both Cluster B and Cluster C personality disorders (Bartak et al., 2010, 2011).

Cognitive approaches are also increasingly used. Cognitive therapy for personality disorders assumes that the dysfunctional feelings and behaviors associated with the personality disorders are largely the result of schemas (styles of thinking) that tend to produce consistently biased judgments, as well as tendencies to make cognitive errors (e.g., Beck et al., 2003; Cottraux & Blackburn, 2001; Leahy & McGinn, 2012; Pretzer & Beck, 2005). Changing these underlying dysfunctional schemas is difficult but is at the heart of cognitive therapy for personality disorders.

gnitive approaches use techniques such as monitoring omatic thoughts, challenging faulty logic, and assign- g behavioral tasks in an effort to challenge the patient's dysfunctional beliefs. Table 10.3 provides examples of some of the central beliefs associated with different personality disorders.

Table 10.3 Beliefs Associated with Specific Personality Disorders

Personality Disorder	Core Belief
Paranoid	I cannot trust people.
Schizoid	Relationships are messy, undesirable.
Schizotypal	It's better to be isolated from others.
Histrionic	People are there to serve or admire me.
Narcissistic	Since I am special, I deserve special rules.
Antisocial	I am entitled to break rules.
Borderline	I deserve to be punished.
Avoidant	If people know the "real" me, they will reject me.
Dependent	I need people to survive, be happy.
Obsessive-Compulsive	People should do better, try harder.

SOURCE: Beck, Freeman, & Davis (2004). *Cognitive Therapy of Personality Disorders*, New York: Guildford Press.

Treating Borderline Personality Disorder

Of all personality disorders, most clinical and research attention has been paid to the treatment of BPD. This is due to the severity of this disorder and the high risk of suicide that is associated with it. Psychological treatment is considered essential. Medications are also used, although most appropriately in a time-limited way and as an adjunct to psychological treatment approaches (Bateman et al., 2015).

PSYCHOSOCIAL TREATMENTS   Clinical trials suggest that several types of psychotherapy may be effective for BPD. As discussed below, however, these treatments share two common weaknesses: their relative complexity and long duration, both of which make them challenging to disseminate to the broader population (Paris, 2009).

Dialectical behavior therapy (DBT), developed by Marsha Linehan, is a unique kind of cognitive and behavioral therapy specifically adapted for BPD (Linehan, 1993; Lynch & Cuper, 2012; Neacsiu & Linehan, 2014). Linehan (who, as described in the World Around Us box, once struggled with BPD herself) believes that patients' inability to tolerate strong states of negative affect is central to this disorder. One of the primary goals of treatment is to encourage patients to accept this negative affect without engaging in self-destructive or other maladaptive behaviors. Accordingly, Linehan has developed a problem-focused treatment based on a clear hierarchy of goals, which prioritizes decreasing suicidal and self-injurious

behavior and increasing coping skills. The therapy combines individual and group components as well as phone coaching. In the group setting, patients learn interpersonal effectiveness, emotion regulation, and distress tolerance skills. The individual therapist, in turn, uses therapy sessions and phone coaching to help the patient identify and change problematic behavior patterns and apply newly learned skills effectively.

Dialectical behavior therapy (DBT) appears to be an efficacious treatment for BPD (Binks et al., 2006; Neacsiu & Linehan, 2014). However, there are still not enough randomized controlled trials to say whether it works as well in men as in women, and whether it works well with minority patients (Lynch & Cuper, 2012). Patients receiving DBT show reductions in self-destructive and suicidal behaviors as well as in levels of anger (Linehan et al., 2006; Lynch et al., 2007). Evidence also suggests that these gains are sustainable (Zanarini et al., 2005). As a result of Linehan's many efforts to help clinicians learn her methods, DBT is increasingly available to patients. Briefer versions of the treatment are also being developed (see Neacsiu & Linehan, 2014; Stanley et al., 2007).

Another psychosocial treatment for BPD involves a variant of psychodynamic psychotherapy. Kernberg (1985, 1996) and his colleagues (Koenigsberg et al., 2000; see also Clarkin et al., 2004) have developed a form of psychodynamic psychotherapy that is much more directive than is typical of psychodynamic treatment. The approach is called transference-focused psychotherapy (Yeomans et al., 2013). The primary goal is seen as strengthening the weak egos of these individuals, with a particular focus on their primary primitive defense mechanism of splitting. This leads them to black-and-white, all-or-none thinking, as well as to rapid shifts in their reactions to themselves and to other people (including the therapist) as "all good" or "all bad." One major goal is to help patients see the shades of gray between these extremes and integrate positive and negative views of themselves and others into more nuanced views. Although this treatment is often expensive and time consuming (often lasting a number of years), it has been shown in at least one study to be as effective as DBT, which is now regarded as the most established, effective treatment (Clarkin et al., 2007). We now await replications of these findings in other treatment centers to further support the usefulness of this approach.

Finally, we note that one other promising treatment approach deserves mention. Bateman and Fonagy (2010) have developed a new therapeutic approach called mentalization. This uses the therapeutic relationship to help patients develop the skills they need to accurately understand their own feelings and emotions, as well as the feelings and emotions of others. Randomized controlled trials of mentalization-based therapy have revealed it to be an efficacious treatment for BPD. Moreover, many clinical

The World Around Us

Marsha Linehan Reveals Her Own Struggle with Borderline Personality Disorder

In a bold and courageous move, Marsha Linehan, the developer of dialectical behavior therapy, has acknowledged her own experiences with mental illness (see Carey, 2011). When she was 17, Linehan was hospitalized for 26 months. During that time she was given a diagnosis of schizophrenia, treated with powerful antipsychotic medications as well as other drugs, placed in seclusion on a locked ward, given a total of 30 electroshock treatments, and psychoanalyzed. But nothing seemed to work. No one understood what Linehan, who was considered one of the most disturbed patients in the hospital, really needed. She burned herself with cigarettes, she slashed her arms, legs, and midsection with any sharp object she could find, and eventually, when she was hospitalized and in seclusion, she banged her head against the wall of her locked room. "I was in hell," she said. "I felt totally empty, like the Tin Man."

After she left the hospital, Linehan still continued to struggle. She made a suicide attempt when she first arrived home and then moved away to try and start over. Many ups and downs followed. But Linehan was slowly starting on a new path. She began to accept herself and her life, coming to terms with the gulf between who she wanted to be and who she was. She enrolled in graduate school and earned her Ph.D. in psychology. And she began to use her experiences to help people who were struggling with borderline personality disorder—the diagnosis she now says that she would have given to her younger self. Over time she developed, refined, and tested a powerful and innovative treatment she called DBT—a treatment designed to give patients the kind of help she herself had so desperately needed at an earlier point in her life. Her treatment has saved lives and provided countless numbers of people with a brighter future. But Linehan's personal story has done something else. Because of her courageous disclosure, Linehan has become a real-life of example of how BPD can be overcome. In revealing her own fight with mental illness, she has given all patients with BPD a new reason to have hope.

How important do you think it is when someone like Marsha Linehan acknowledges a personal history of mental illness? Why do you think it took her so many years to reveal her story? If you were in her position, what would you have done? Why?

---

improvements seem to be maintained even after an 8-year follow-up (Bateman & Fonagy, 2008). Although DBT is still a very popular treatment, it is encouraging that people with BPD now have other treatment options available to them.

BIOLOGICAL TREATMENTS   Drugs are often used in the treatment of BPD. Indeed, many patients with BPD are taking multiple medications. Yet there is little evidence to support their use (Bateman et al., 2015). Antidepressant medications (most often from the selective serotonin reuptake inhibitors [SSRI] category) are widely used, although there is no compelling evidence that they are effective. They are most appropriate only when patients have a comorbid mood disorder (Silk & Feurino, 2012). Some second-generation antipsychotic medications (such as aripiprazole and olanzapine) and mood stabilizers (such as topiramate, valproate, and lamotrigine) may slightly reduce symptoms over the short term. However, as with all medications, the risks and benefits need to be weighed carefully.

Treating Other Personality Disorders

Treatment of Cluster A and other Cluster B personality disorders is not, so far, as promising as some of the recent advances that have been made in the treatment of BPD. In schizotypal personality disorder, low doses of antipsychotic drugs (including the newer, atypical antipsychotics; e.g., Keshavan et al., 2004; Koenigsberg et al., 2007; Raine, 2006) may result in modest improvements. Antidepressants

from the SSRI category may also be useful. However, no treatment has yet produced anything approaching a cure for most people with this disorder (Koenigsberg et al., 2002, 2007; Markovitz, 2001, 2004; Silk & Feurino, 2012). Other than uncontrolled studies or single cases, no systematic, controlled studies of treating people with either medication or psychotherapy yet exist for paranoid, schizoid, narcissistic, or histrionic disorder (Beck et al., 2003; Crits-Christoph & Barber, 2007). One reason for this is that these people (because of the nature of their personality pathology) rarely seek treatment.

Although not extensively studied, treatment of some Cluster C disorders, such as dependent and avoidant personality disorder, appears somewhat more promising. Winston and colleagues (1994) found significant improvement in patients with Cluster C disorders using a form of short-term psychotherapy that is active and confrontational (see also Pretzer & Beck, 1996). Several studies using cognitive-behavior treatment with avoidant personality disorder have also reported significant gains (see Crits-Christoph & Barber, 2007), and a recent meta-analysis concluded both cognitive-behavior and psychodynamic therapies resulted in significant and lasting treatment gains (Simon, 2009). Another study in the Netherlands found that short-term inpatient treatment for Cluster C personality disorders is even more effective than long-term inpatient or outpatient therapy (Bartak et al., 2011). Antidepressants from the monoamine oxidase inhibitor (MAOI) and SSRI categories may also sometimes help in the treatment of avoidant personality disorder, just as they do in closely related social phobia (Koenigsberg et al., 2007; Markovitz, 2001).

in review

- Why are personality disorders especially resistant to therapy?
- Under what circumstances do individuals with personality disorders generally get involved in psychotherapy?
- What is known about the effectiveness of treatments for borderline personality disorder?

Psychopathy

10.8 Describe the clinical features of psychopathy and explain how it is similar to and different from antisocial personality disorder.

The use of the term *antisocial personality disorder* dates back to 1980 when personality disorders first entered the *DSM* (in *DSM-III*). However, prior to that time, clinicians and researchers had been interested in a syndrome that was initially called sociopathic personality but is now usually referred to as **psychopathy**. This syndrome was first identified in the nineteenth century when terms such as *manie sans delire* (insanity without delirium), *moral weakness*, or *moral insanity* were used to describe it (see Patrick & Drislane, 2015). However, the most comprehensive early description of psychopathy was made by Cleckley in the 1940s. In his book, *The Mask of Sanity*, Cleckley (1941) provided detailed case studies of people he identified as psychopaths. He also outlined 21 core traits of psychopathy. Over time, these were revised and reduced to 16 traits (Cleckley, 1988), as listed in Table 10.4.

Table 10.4 Cleckley's Criteria for Psychopathy

Superficial charm and good "intelligence"
Absence of delusions and other signs of irrational thinking
Absence of nervousness or psychoneurotic manifestations
Unreliability
Untruthfulness and insincerity
Lack of remorse or shame
Inadequately motivated antisocial behavior
Poor judgement and failure to learn from experience
Pathological egocentricity and incapacity for love
General poverty in major affective reactions
Specific loss of insight
Unresponsiveness in general interpersonal relations
Fantastic and uninviting behavior with drink and sometimes without
Suicide rarely carried out
Sex life impersonal, trivial, and poorly integrated
Failure to follow any life plan

SOURCE: Cleckley, H. (1988). *The Mask of Sanity*, 5th ed., Augusta, GA: Emily S. Cleckley, pp. 337–338.

The prevalence of psychopathy is unknown because no epidemiological studies have assessed this. However, for males in North America, the prevalence is estimated to be about 1 to 2 percent (Patrick & Drislane, 2015). Rates for women are estimated to be much lower (well under 1 percent). You should also note that, with their strong emphasis on behavioral criteria that can be measured reasonably objectively, the features of *DSM-5* antisocial personality disorder do not fully map onto the construct of psychopathy as originally described. This was done deliberately in an attempt to increase the reliability of the ASPD diagnosis (i.e., the level of agreement between clinicians on the diagnosis). However, many researchers expressed concern that reliability was being emphasized at the expense of validity and that many key features of psychopathy were not included in the diagnostic criteria. This has raised questions about whether the ASPD construct is the same as psychopathy. It is generally accepted that there is a good deal of overlap, although the diagnosis of ASPD is more inclusive and reflects a lot of criminality, whereas the diagnosis of psychopathy is more narrow and much more focused on personality structure.

Dimensions of Psychopathy

Recognizing the need for a reliable and valid assessment tool, Robert Hare (1980, 1991, 2003) made a major contribution by developing the 20-item Psychopathy Checklist–Revised (PCL-R). This provides a way for clinicians and researchers to diagnose psychopathy on the basis of the Cleckley criteria following a detailed interview and careful checking of past school, police, and prison records. The measure is widely used in forensic assessments.

Extensive research with this checklist has shown that psychopathy can best be understood by considering the following four dimensions (Hare et al., 2012). Note that in much of the earlier research, the Interpersonal and Affective dimensions were combined and referred to as Factor 1. Similarly, the Lifestyle and Antisocial dimensions together are referred to as Factor 2. For this reason, we label the four dimensions as 1a, 1b, 2a, and 2b.

1a. The *interpersonal* dimension reflects a personality style that is characterized by glibness/superficial charm, a grandiose sense of self-worth, pathological lying, and the conning manipulation of others.

1b. The *affective* dimension reflects traits such as lack of remorse or guilt, callousness/lack of empathy, shallow affect, and a failure to accept responsibility for one's behavior.

2a. The *lifestyle* dimension reflects a need for stimulation, a tendency to be easily bored, impulsivity, irresponsibility, a lack of reasonable long-term goals, as well as a parasitic lifestyle.

2b. Finally, the *antisocial* dimension reflects the aspects of psychopathy that involve poor behavior controls, early behavior problems, delinquency, and criminality.

The lifestyle and antisocial dimensions are much more closely related to the *DSM* diagnosis of ASPD than the interpersonal and affective dimensions are (Widiger, 2006). Not surprisingly, therefore, when comparisons have been made in prison settings to determine what percentage of prison inmates qualify for a diagnosis of psychopathy versus ASPD, it is typically found that about 70 to 80 percent qualify for a diagnosis of ASPD but that only about 25 to 30 percent meet the criteria for psychopathy (Patrick, 2005). Put somewhat differently, a significant number of inmates show the antisocial and aggressive behaviors necessary for a diagnosis of ASPD but do not show enough selfish, callous, and exploitative behaviors to qualify for a diagnosis of psychopathy.

The issues surrounding these diagnoses remain highly controversial. There was considerable discussion by the *DSM-5* task force about expanding the diagnostic criteria for ASPD to include more of the features of psychopathy. However, in the end no official changes were made. An alternative approach to the diagnosis of ASPD (which places more emphasis on pathological personality traits) now appears in Section III of the *DSM-5* manual and will likely receive increased attention in the future. Making matters more complicated, many researchers continue to use the Cleckley/Hare psychopathy diagnosis rather than the *DSM* ASPD diagnosis, not only because of the long and rich research tradition on psychopathy but also because the psychopathy diagnosis has been shown to be a better predictor of a variety of important facets of criminal behavior than the ASPD diagnosis (Hare et al., 2012). Overall, a diagnosis of psychopathy appears to be the single best predictor of violence and recidivism (offending again after imprisonment; Douglas et al., 2006; Gretton et al., 2004; see also Leistico et al., 2008). Moreover, as illustrated in Figure 10.4, adolescents with higher psychopathy scores are not only more likely to show violent reoffending but are also more likely to reoffend more quickly (Gretton et al., 2004).

What about people who do not get caught? An additional concern about the current conceptualization of ASPD is that it fails to include people who show many of the features of the affective and interpersonal dimensions of psychopathy but not as many features of the lifestyle and antisocial dimensions, or at least few enough that these individuals do not generally get into trouble with the law. This group might include, for example, unprincipled and predatory business or financial professionals, manipulative lawyers, high-pressure evangelists, and crooked politicians (Hall & Benning, 2006). Certainly,

Cleckley did not believe that aggressive behavior was central to the concept of psychopathy (Patrick, 2006). Years ago, one researcher (Widom, 1977) who wanted to study psychopathic people who managed to stay out of correctional institutions ran an ingenious ad in a Boston underground newspaper:

> *Are you adventurous? Psychologist studying adventurous, carefree people who've led exciting, impulsive lives. If you're the kind of person who'd do almost anything for a dare and want to participate in a paid experiment, send name, address, phone, and short biography proving how interesting you are to . . . (p. 675)*

A later version of the ad read:

> *Wanted charming aggressive carefree people who are impulsively irresponsible but are good at handling people and at looking after number one. Send name, address. . .*

Widom received responses from a fairly limited number of individuals. And one person actually wrote: "Are you looking for hookers or trying to make a listing of all the sociopaths in Boston?" (p. 675). But when those who did respond were given a battery of tests, they turned out to be similar in personality makeup to that of institutionalized psychopaths. Several further studies on people with noncriminal psychopathy (these people are often called successful psychopaths) confirmed this finding (Hall & Benning, 2006; Hare et al., 1999). Nonetheless, there are reasons to think that these two groups may differ biologically in some significant ways.

Raine and his colleagues had the clever idea of recruiting successful and unsuccessful criminal psychopaths living in the community as well as control subjects from temporary employment agencies (Ishikawa et al., 2001). In one study, each hired research participant was told to give a short speech about his personal faults and weaknesses, during which time he was observed and videotaped. While subjects were preparing for and giving the speech, their heart rate was monitored. The results indicated that successful psychopaths (who had committed approximately the same number and type of crimes as the unsuccessful psychopaths, although they had never been convicted) showed greater heart rate reactivity under stress than the controls or the unsuccessful psychopaths did. One possibility raised by these findings is that the increased cardiac reactivity of the successful psychopaths may serve them well in processing what is going on in risky situations and perhaps facilitate them making decisions that may prevent their being caught. As the Developments in Research box shows, researchers are now studying the prevalence of psychopathy in corporate settings.

Other differences in brain structure and function have also been reported. Deficits in the prefrontal cortex (which is involved in behavioral control and decision

Figure 10.4 Survival curve of months free in the community until first violent reoffense plotted by score on the Hare Psychopathy Checklist: Youth Version (PCL:YV) group. The survival curve illustrates the percentage of individuals in each group who have not shown a violent reoffense at 12-month intervals. Those in the High-PCL-YV group are more likely to have violent reoffenses than those in the other two groups (lower probability of survival) and are more likely to have them sooner after release (indicated by the steeper slope).

(From Gretton et al. (2004). Psychopathy and offending from adolescence to adulthood: A 10-year follow-up. *Journal of Consulting and Clinical Psychology*, 72, 636–645. Copyright © 2004 by the American Psychological Association. Reproduced with permission.)

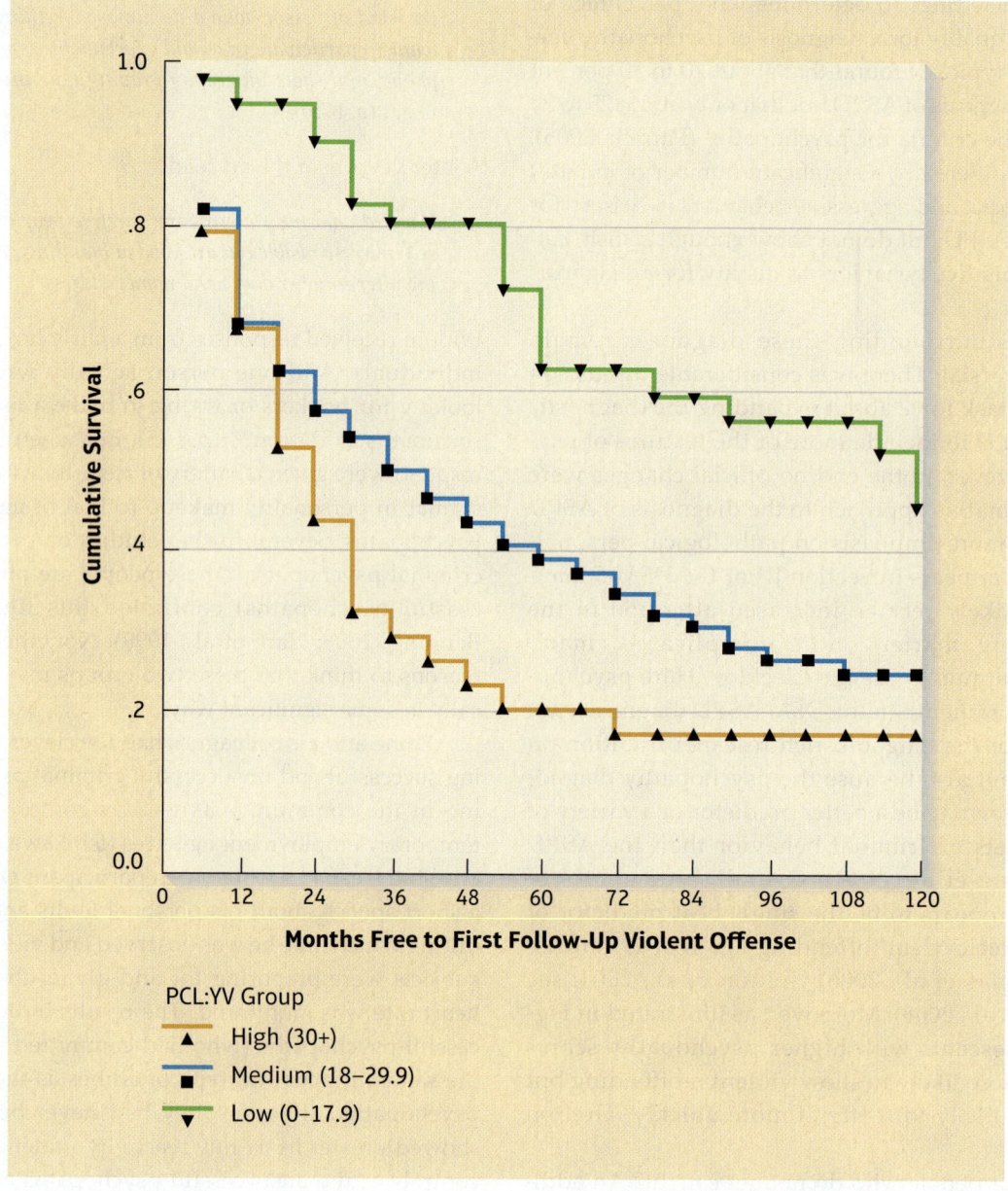

making) as well as the amygdala (which is a key brain area for emotion and fear conditioning) are thought to play a role in some of the behavioral and emotional disturbances linked to psychopathy (Kiehl, 2006; Yang & Raine, 2009). Unsuccessful psychopaths, however, seem to have more pronounced defects in these areas than successful psychopaths or healthy controls (Yang et al., 2010). For example, as illustrated in Figure 10.5, it is the unsuccessful psychopaths who have the most marked reduction in amygdala volume compared to normal controls. In contrast, the reduction in amygdala volumes of the successful psychopaths is much less marked and not significantly different from the controls. Deficits in the amygdala may be linked to problems with fear conditioning (which as you will soon learn, is impaired in psychopaths), as well as disruptions in moral development and socialization.

Developments in Research

Are You Working for a Psychopath?

Media headlines and TV crime shows tend to reinforce the public perception that psychopathy is invariably associated with violence and criminality. But as Robert Hare once casually remarked, "Not all psychopaths are in prison. Some are in the Boardroom" (see Babiak et al., 2010, p. 174). Research suggests he is right. Babiak and colleagues studied 203 corporate professionals who were employed in companies in the United States. As part of an assessment for participation in a management development program, all individuals completed the PCL-R. They were also rated by 5 to 10 of their colleagues as part of a 360-degree feedback assessment (so-called because data are collected from individuals "all around" the target individual).

As might be expected, most people scored in the low range on the PCL-R. Four percent of participants, however, had scores that were above the threshold for psychopathy. Moreover, of those who scored in the high range, two were company vice presidents, two were directors, and two were managers or supervisors! In other words, they had attained considerable status in their respective companies. The findings also revealed that higher psychopathy scores were correlated with colleagues rating the person as having good communication and strategic thinking skills, as well as being creative and innovative. However, psychopathy was also associated with the perception the person was not a team player and had a poor style of management. Consistent with this, people who scored higher on psychopathy tended to receive lower performance appraisal ratings.

Taken together, the results of this study suggest that rates of psychopathy may be higher in corporate samples (4 percent) than

they are in community samples (1 percent) although not as high as they are in male offenders (15 percent). They further suggest that some psychopathic individuals are able to rise high in the corporate world even in the face of negative performance reviews and poor management skills. Babiak and colleagues (2010) speculate that psychopathic traits such as charm and grandiosity might be mistaken for leadership skills and vision. Similarly, lack of empathy or remorse, could be viewed as being cool under fire or able to make tough and unpopular decisions. Regardless, it would seem that, at least in some work settings, having psychopathic traits is not necessarily an impediment to advancing up the corporate ladder.

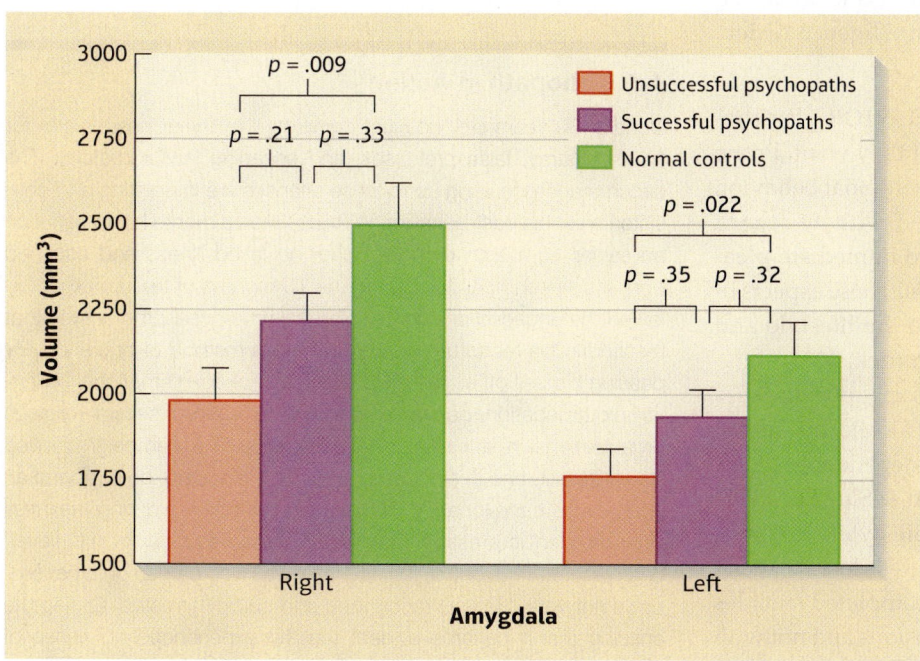

Figure 10.5 Amygdala volumes on both the left and right sides (i.e., bilaterally) are reduced in unsuccessful psychopaths relative to successful psychopaths and healthy controls. Although somewhat reduced, the amygdala volumes of successful psychopaths are not significantly different from those of controls. The amygdala is a brain area involved in fear conditioning. Fear helps keep us out of trouble. Having a relatively larger amygdala volume may help explain why "successful" psychopaths have avoided criminal conviction while "unsuccessful" psychopaths have not.

(**SOURCE:** Yang et al., 2010.)

The Clinical Picture in Psychopathy

Often charming, spontaneous, and likable on first acquaintance, psychopaths are deceitful and manipulative, callously using others to achieve their own ends. Unencumbered by feelings for others, they are free to be social predators, taking what they want and doing what they please, sometimes for no better reason than because they are bored. This makes them extremely dangerous to others and highly destructive to society.

Next we summarize the major characteristics of psychopaths and then describe a case that illustrates the wide range of behavioral patterns that may be involved. Although all the characteristics examined in the following subsections are not usually found in any one particular case, they are typical of psychopaths as first described by Cleckley (1941). A subset of these characteristics occurs in ASPD as well.

INADEQUATE CONSCIENCE DEVELOPMENT Psychopaths appear unable to understand and accept ethical values except on a verbal level. They may glibly claim to adhere to high moral standards that have no apparent connection with their behavior. In short, their conscience development is severely retarded or nonexistent, and they behave as though social regulations and laws do not apply to them (Frick & Marsee, 2006; Salekin, 2006). These characteristics are most strongly related to the interpersonal and affective core of psychopathy (Fowles & Dindo, 2006). In spite of their stunted conscience development, their intellectual development is typically normal. Nevertheless, intelligence is one trait that has different relationships with the various dimensions of psychopathy. The affective and interpersonal dimensions are positively related to verbal intelligence (Salekin et al., 2004); the lifestyle and antisocial dimensions are negatively related to intelligence (Frick, 1998; Hare et al., 1999).

IRRESPONSIBLE AND IMPULSIVE BEHAVIOR Psychopaths learn to take rather than earn what they want. Prone to thrill seeking and deviant and unconventional behavior, they often break the law impulsively and without regard for the consequences. They seldom forgo immediate pleasure for future gains and long-range goals. These aspects of psychopathy are most closely related to the lifestyle and antisocial dimensions of psychopathy (Patrick, 2005).

Many studies have shown that antisocial personalities and some psychopaths have high rates of alcohol abuse and dependence and other substance abuse/dependence disorders (e.g., Taylor & Lang, 2006; Waldman & Slutske, 2000). Alcohol abuse is related only to the lifestyle/antisocial dimensions of the PCL-R (Patrick, 2005; Reardon al., 2002). Elevated rates of suicide attempts and completed suicides are also only associated with these dimensions and not with the interpersonal-affective dimensions (Verona et al., 2001).

ABILITY TO IMPRESS AND EXPLOIT OTHERS Some psychopaths are superficially charming and likable, with a disarming manner that easily wins them new friends (Cleckley, 1941, 1976; Patrick, 2006). They seem to have good insight into other people's needs and weaknesses and they are highly adept at exploiting them. These frequent liars usually seem sincerely sorry if caught in a lie. They promise to make amends. But they do not do so. Not surprisingly, then, psychopaths are seldom able to keep close friends. They seemingly cannot understand love in others or give it in return. Manipulative, exploitative, and sometimes coercive in sexual relationships, psychopaths are irresponsible and unfaithful partners.

Hare, a highly influential researcher in this area, summarized the prototypic psychopath in the following manner:

> *Conceptualizing psychopaths as remorseless predators helped me to make sense of what often appears to be senseless behavior. These are individuals who, lacking in conscience and feelings for others, find it easy to use charm, manipulation, intimidation, and violence to control others and to satisfy their own social needs . . . without the slightest sense of guilt or regret . . . they form a significant proportion of persistent criminals, drug dealers, spouse and child abusers, swindlers and con men . . . . They are well represented in the business and corporate world, particularly during chaotic restructuring, where the rules and their enforcement are lax. . . . Many psychopaths emerge as "patriots" and "saviors" in societies experiencing social, economic, and political upheaval (e.g., Rwanda, the former Yugoslavia, and the former Soviet Union) . . . by callously exploiting ethnic, cultural, or racial tensions and grievances. (Hare, 1998, pp. 128–129)*

Psychopathy is well illustrated in the following classic case study published by Hare (1970).

A Psychopath in Action

Donald, 30 years old, has just completed a 3-year prison term for fraud, bigamy, false pretenses, and escaping lawful custody. The circumstances leading up to these offenses are interesting and consistent with his past behavior. With less than a month left to serve on an earlier 18-month term for fraud, he faked illness and escaped from the prison hospital. During the 10 months of freedom that followed, he engaged in a variety of illegal enterprises; the activity that resulted in his recapture was typical of his method of operation. By passing himself off as the "field executive" of an international philanthropic foundation, he was able to enlist the aid of several religious organizations in a fund-raising campaign. The campaign moved slowly at first, and in an attempt to speed things up, he arranged an interview with the local TV station. His performance during the interview was so impressive that funds started to pour in. However, unfortunately for Donald, the interview was also carried on a national news network. He was recognized and quickly arrested. During the ensuing trial it became evident that he experienced no sense of wrongdoing for his activities. . . . At the same time, he stated that most donations to charity are made by those who feel guilty about something and who therefore deserve to be bilked.

While in prison he was used as a subject in some of the author's research. On his release he applied for admission to a university and, by way of reference, told the registrar that he had been one of the author's research colleagues! Several months later the author received a letter from him requesting a letter of recommendation on behalf of Donald's application for a job.

Background. Donald was the youngest of three boys born to middle-class parents. Both of his brothers led normal, productive lives. His father spent a great deal of time with his business; when he was home he tended to be moody and to drink heavily when things were not going right. Donald's mother was a gentle, timid woman who tried to please her husband and to maintain a semblance of family harmony. . . . However, . . . on some occasions [the father] would fly into a rage and beat the children, and on others he would administer a verbal reprimand, sometimes mild and sometimes severe.

By all accounts Donald was considered a willful and difficult child. When his desire for candy or toys was frustrated he would begin with a show of affection, and if this failed he would throw a temper tantrum; the latter was seldom necessary because his angelic appearance and artful ways usually got him what he wanted. . . . Although he was obviously very intelligent, his school years were academically undistinguished. He was restless, easily bored, and frequently truant . . . when he was on his own he generally got himself or others into trouble. Although he was often suspected of being the culprit, he was adept at talking his way out of difficulty.

Donald's misbehavior as a child took many forms including lying, cheating, petty theft, and the bullying of smaller children. As he grew older he became more and more interested in sex, gambling, and alcohol. When he was 14 he made crude sexual advances toward a younger girl, and when she threatened to tell her parents he locked her in a shed. It was about 16 hours before she was found. Donald at first denied knowledge of the incident, later stating that she had seduced him and that the door must have locked itself. . . . His parents were able to prevent charges being brought against him. . . .

When he was 17, Donald . . . forged his father's name to a large check and spent about a year traveling around the world. He apparently lived well, using a combination of charm, physical attractiveness, and false pretenses to finance his way. During subsequent years he held a succession of jobs, never . . . for more than a few months. Throughout this period he was charged with a variety of crimes, including theft, drunkenness in a public place, assault, and many traffic violations. In most cases he was either fined or given a light sentence.

A Ladies' Man. His sexual experiences were frequent, casual, and callous. When he was 22, he married a 41-year-old woman whom he had met in a bar. Several other marriages followed, all bigamous. . . . The pattern was the same: He would marry someone on impulse, let her support him for several months, and then leave. One marriage was particularly interesting. After being charged with fraud Donald was sent to a psychiatric institution for a period of observation. While there he came to the attention of a female member of the professional staff. His charm, physical attractiveness, and convincing promises to reform led her to intervene on his behalf. He was given a suspended sentence, and they were married a week later. At first things went reasonably well, but when she refused to pay some of his gambling debts he forged her name to a check and left. He was soon caught and given an 18-month prison term. . . . He escaped with less than a month left to serve.

It is interesting to note that Donald sees nothing particularly wrong with his behavior, nor does he express remorse or guilt for using others and causing them grief. Although his behavior is self-defeating in the long run, he considers it to be practical and possessed of good sense. Periodic punishments do nothing to decrease his egotism and confidence in his own abilities. . . . His behavior is entirely egocentric, and his needs are satisfied without any concern for the feelings and welfare of others. (Reprinted with permission of Robert P. Hare, University of British Columbia, rhare@interchange.ubc.ca.)

Causal Factors in Psychopathy

The causes of psychopathy are complex and involve many factors. Genetics, temperamental characteristics, deficiencies in fear and anxiety, more general emotional deficits, hypersensitivity to reward, the early learning of antisocial behavior as a coping style, as well as particular family and environmental factors are thought to be involved.

GENETIC INFLUENCES Until fairly recently, most behavior genetic research focused on genetic and environmental influences on antisocial behavior or criminality rather than on psychopathy itself. However, several strong studies have now demonstrated that psychopathy and some of its important features also show considerable heritability (e.g., Blonigen et al., 2003, 2006; see Hare et al., 2012; Waldman & Rhee, 2006, for reviews). For example, a twin study of 3,687 twin pairs at age 7 found that the early signs of callous/unemotional traits in these children were highly heritable (Viding et al., 2005). Moreover, children with these disturbing traits also receive high levels of negative parenting (such as parental anger and frustration). This suggests the possibility that callous and emotional traits in young children may provoke the kind of reactions

Parents may react to callous and unemotional personality traits in children by adopting a harsh discipline style.

in parents that may further increase risk for future antisocial behavior (Larsson et al., 2008). Based on a study of over 1,000 twins, it has been estimated that between 43 and 56 percent of the variance in the dimensions of psychopathy is attributable to genetic factors, with the remaining variance being explained more by nonshared environmental influences rather than by shared environmental factors (Larsson et al., 2006).

LOW-FEAR AND IMPAIRED FEAR CONDITIONING
Research indicates that psychopaths who are high on the dimensions of the first factor and who are egocentric, callous, and exploitative have low trait anxiety and show poor conditioning of fear (Fowles & Dindo, 2006; Lykken, 1995; Patrick, 2005). This is consistent with the amygdala deficits described earlier. In an early classic study, Lykken (1957) found that psychopaths showed deficient conditioning of skin conductance responses (reflecting activation of the sympathetic nervous system) when anticipating an unpleasant or painful event and that they were slow at learning to stop responding in order to avoid punishment. As a result, psychopaths presumably fail to acquire many of the conditioned reactions essential to normal passive avoidance of punishment, to conscience development, and to socialization. Hare (1998) aptly summarized work on this issue: "It is the emotionally charged thought, images, and internal dialogue that give the 'bite' to conscience, account for its powerful control over behavior, and generate guilt and remorse for transgressions. This is something that psychopaths cannot understand. For them conscience is little more than an intellectual awareness of rules others make up—empty words" (p. 112).

Serial killer Ted Bundy exhibited antisocial behavior at its most extreme and dangerous. Bundy used his clean-cut image to get close to his victims—mainly young university women—whom he sexually assaulted and then savagely murdered. From all outward appearances, Bundy was a fine, upstanding citizen.

An impressive array of studies since the early work of Lykken has confirmed that psychopaths are deficient in the conditioning of at least subjective and certain physiological

components of fear (e.g., Birbaumer et al., 2005; Flor et al., 2002; Fowles, 2001; Lykken, 1995), although they do learn at a purely cognitive level that the conditioned stimulus predicts the unconditioned stimulus (Birbaumer et al., 2005). Because such conditioning may underlie successful avoidance of punishment, this may also explain why their impulsive behavior goes unchecked.

Other interesting work concerns the startle response. Both humans and animals show a larger startle response if a startle probe stimulus (such as a loud noise) is presented when the subject is already in an anxious state. This is known as fear-potentiated startle. Comparing psychopathic and nonpsychopathic prisoners, Patrick and colleagues (1993) found that the psychopaths did not show this effect, although nonpsychopathic prisoners did. Indeed, the psychopaths showed smaller rather than larger startle responses when viewing unpleasant and pleasant slides than when watching neutral slides (see also Patrick, 1994, and Sutton et al., 2002, for related results). These deficits in fear-potentiated startle responding are related only to the first, affective dimension of psychopathy and not to the second, antisocial dimension (Patrick, 2005). Newman and colleagues (e.g., Baskin-Sommers et al., 2010; Newman & Lorenz, 2003) have also conducted research suggesting that people with psychopathy have an excessive focus on reward. This may interfere with their ability to use punishment or other contextual cues or information to modulate their behavior. Moreover, when they are engaged in goal-directed behavior, Newman and colleagues have hypothesized that psychopaths have a deficient ability to modulate their attention, developing something akin to tunnel vision in their single-minded pursuit of their goal. One consequence of this is that they are less likely to attend to more peripheral information, such as affective information (such as fear), or other cues that might provide greater perspective and allow them to evaluate situations more fully. Newman and colleagues believe that this response modulation deficit is more central to psychopathy than is a fear deficit (or even a general emotional deficit). A number of interesting studies have produced findings consistent with this idea and Newman's perspective is becoming increasingly influential (Hare et al., 2012). However, there is still controversy over whether this response modulation deficit hypothesis can account for the wide array of findings with regard to low fear and other emotional deficits.

MORE GENERAL EMOTIONAL DEFICITS Psychopaths appear to have more general emotional deficits than simple deficits in the conditioning of anxiety. Brain imaging studies show that individuals with psychopathy show less activity in the amygdala (relative to controls) not only during fear conditioning but also when viewing sad or frightened faces (see Marsh & Blair, 2008, for a quantitative review). Psychopaths also show less significant physiological reactivity to images of distress (slides of people crying) than do nonpsychopaths. This is consistent with the idea that psychopaths are low on empathy (Blair, 2006; Blair et al., 1997), in addition to being low on fear.

In a nice demonstration of this, Decety and colleagues (2013) collected brain scan data from 37 incarcerated men who scored high on psychopathy while they were watching slides of painful (trapping one's finger in a door) and nonpainful situations (putting one's hand on a drawer handle). Other volunteers with low or medium psychopathy scores also completed the same procedures. When they were viewing the pictures, participants were sometimes asked to imagine that the situation was happening to them personally. On other trials they were told to imagine the situation (e.g., a trapped finger) was happening to someone else. When they imagined pain in themselves, the inmates who scored high on psychopathy showed a typical response in brain areas involved in empathy for pain processing including the anterior insula and the amygdala. In contrast, when they imagined the pain of another person, activation in these areas was diminished. What was also interesting (and rather chilling) was that the psychopaths who scored highest on Factor 1 of the PCL (interpersonal and affective dimensions) actually showed an increase in activation in the ventral striatum when they were asked to take the imagine-other (as opposed to the imagine-self) perspective. This is a brain area involved in the anticipation of reward. One interpretation of these findings is that psychopaths are not only less affected by distress in others but that they find the idea of others experiencing pain to be pleasing in some way. Such deficits in turn may be closely linked to the deficits in moral reasoning and behavior seen in people with psychopathy because to reason about moral issues requires that an individual has concern about the rights and welfare of other people (Blair, 2007).

EARLY PARENTAL LOSS, PARENTAL REJECTION, AND INCONSISTENCY In addition to genetic factors and emotional deficits, slow conscience development and high levels of both reactive and instrumental aggression are influenced by the damaging effects of parental rejection, abuse, and neglect accompanied by inconsistent discipline (e.g., Farrington, 2006; Luntz & Widom, 1994). However, studies of gene–environment interactions reviewed earlier clearly indicate that these kinds of disturbances are not sufficient explanations for the origins of psychopathy or antisocial personality because some people are clearly more susceptible to these effects than others. Moreover, these same conditions have been implicated in a wide range of later maladaptive behaviors. In the following section, we present an integrated developmental perspective using a biopsychosocial approach with multiple interacting causal pathways.

A Developmental Perspective on Psychopathy

In the past decade, Frick and colleagues have developed a way of assessing children's callous and unemotional traits, which seem to represent early manifestations of this first dimension of psychopathy (e.g., Frick & Marsee, 2006; Frick & Morris, 2004; Frick, Cornell, Barry, et al., 2003; Frick, Cornell, Bodin, et al., 2003). They have noted that there are at least two different dimensions of children's difficult temperament that seem to lead to different developmental outcomes. Some children have great difficulty learning to regulate their emotions and show high levels of emotional reactivity, including aggressive and antisocial behaviors when responding to stressful demands and negative emotions like frustration and anger. Such children are at increased risk for developing ASPD and high scores on the antisocial dimension of psychopathy. But other children may have few problems regulating negative emotions, instead showing fearlessness and low anxiety as well as callous/unemotional traits and reduced amygdala activation while responding to fearful facial expressions (e.g., Marsh et al., 2008). These are the children most likely to show poor development of conscience, and their aggressive behaviors are more instrumental and premeditated rather than reactive as seen with those children who have emotional regulation difficulties. These latter children are likely to develop high scores on the first, interpersonal affective core of psychopathy, leading to the cold, remorseless psychopaths who show low fear and lack of empathy.

SOCIOCULTURAL CAUSAL FACTORS Psychopaths have existed throughout history. They are found in all socioeconomic groups, races, ethnicities, and cultures. People with psychopathic traits are called *kunlangeta* by Native Alaskans. When the anthropologist Jane Murphy asked an Inuit man how *kunlangeta* would be dealt with in Native Alaskan society, he told her, "Somebody would have pushed him off the ice when nobody else was looking." Nevertheless, the exact manifestations of the disorder are influenced by cultural factors, and the prevalence of the disorder also seems to vary with sociocultural influences that encourage or discourage its development (Cooke et al., 2005; Hare et al., 1999; Sullivan & Kosson, 2006).

Regarding different cross-cultural manifestations of the disorder, one of the primary symptoms where cultural variations occur is the frequency of aggressive and violent behavior. Socialization forces have an enormous impact on the expression of aggressive impulses. Thus, it is not surprising that in some cultures, such as China, psychopaths may be much less likely to engage in aggressive, especially violent, behavior than they are in most Western cultures (Cooke, 1996). By contrast, cross-cultural studies have indicated that the affective-interpersonal dimension of psychopathy is the most consistent across cultures (Cooke et al., 2005).

Moreover, cultures can be classified according to how individualistic or collectivist they are. Competitiveness, self-confidence, and independence from others are emphasized in relatively individualistic societies, whereas contributions and subservience to the social group, acceptance of authority, and stability of relationships are encouraged in relatively collectivist societies (Cooke, 1996; Cooke & Michie, 1999). Thus, we would expect individualistic societies (such as in the United States) to be more likely to promote some of the behavioral characteristics that, carried to the extreme, result in psychopathy. These characteristics include "grandiosity, glibness and superficiality, promiscuity . . . as well as a lack of responsibility for others. . . . The competitiveness ... not only produces higher rates of criminal behavior but also leads to an increased use of . . . deceptive, manipulative, and parasitic behavior" (Cooke & Michie, 1999, p. 65). Although the evidence bearing on this is minimal, it is interesting to note that estimates of the prevalence of ASPD are much lower in Taiwan, a relatively collectivist society, than they are in the United States (approximately 0.1–0.2 percent versus 1.5–4 percent).

Treatments and Outcomes in Psychopathic Personality

Psychopaths experience little personal distress and do not believe they need treatment. For reasons discussed earlier, punishment is also generally ineffective. Those who get into trouble with the law may participate in rehabilitation programs when it is in their best interests to do so (such as when seeking a lighter sentence or requesting parole). But they are rarely changed by them. Alarmingly, a few studies have found that treatments that work for other criminal offenders can actually be harmful for psychopaths in that rates of reoffending increase rather than decrease (Harris & Rice, 2006). This may be especially likely to occur if the treatment program emphasizes training in social skills or empathy because such skills may simply make them better at charming or conning future victims (Vitale & Newman, 2013). In light of this, some researchers suggest that treatment efforts should focus more on convincing psychopaths that they should use their abilities and talents to get their needs met in more prosocial ways (Hare et al., 2012).

Biological treatments for antisocial and psychopathic personalities have not been systematically studied, partly because there is little evidence that such approaches have any substantial impact. Moreover, even if effective pharmacological treatments were found, the problem of these individuals generally having little motivation to take their medications would remain (Markovitz, 2001).

Cognitive-behavior treatments have been thought to offer the greatest promise of more effective treatment (Hare et al., 2012; Harris & Rice, 2006). Common targets of these interventions include the following: (1) increasing self-control, self-critical thinking, and social perspective taking; (2) increasing victim awareness; (3) teaching anger management; (4) changing antisocial attitudes; and (5) curing drug addiction. Such interventions require a controlled situation in which the therapist can administer or withhold reinforcement and the individual cannot leave treatment (such as an inpatient or prison setting) because when treating antisocial behavior, we are dealing with a total lifestyle rather than a few specific, maladaptive behaviors (e.g., Hare et al., 2012). Even the best of these multifaceted, cognitive-behaviorally oriented treatment programs generally produce only modest changes, although they are somewhat more effective in treating young offenders (teenagers) than older offenders, who are often hard-core, lifelong psychopaths. Moreover, although such treatments may be useful in reducing inmates' antisocial behavior while in a prison or other forensic setting, the results do not usually generalize to the real world if the person is released (Harris & Rice, 2006).

All of this highlights the importance of early intervention. As described in Chapter 15, there are now well-established treatment approaches that can be used with young children and their families. These offer some rays of hope. Also, fortunately, the criminal activities of many psychopathic and antisocial personalities seem to decline after the age of 40 even without treatment, possibly because of weaker biological drives, better insight into self-defeating behaviors, and the cumulative effects of social conditioning. Such individuals are often referred to as "burned-out psychopaths." Although there is not a great deal of evidence on this issue (Douglas et al., 2006), one important study that followed a group of male psychopaths over many years found a clear and dramatic reduction in levels of criminal behavior after age 40. However, over 50 percent of these people continued to be arrested after age 40 (Hare et al., 1988). Moreover, it is only the antisocial behavioral dimension of psychopathy that seems to diminish with age; the egocentric, callous, and exploitative affective and interpersonal dimension persists (Cloninger et al., 1997; Hare et al., 1999). Simply stated, the personality of psychopaths may endure over time. But criminal activities take energy. As psychopaths age, they may be less inclined to engage in antisocial activities for this reason.

---

in review

- In what ways is psychopathy different from antisocial personality? What are the key features of psychopathy?

- What are several reasons why many researchers believe psychopathy is a more valid construct than ASPD?

- What biological factors contribute to these disorders?

- What are the primary features of a developmental perspective on these disorders?

Unresolved Issues

DSM-5: How Can We Improve the Classification of Personality Disorders?

Reading this chapter will have given you an understanding of some of the difficulties associated with the use of an exclusively categorical diagnostic system for personality disorders. For instance, you may have had some difficulty in developing a clear, distinctive picture of each of the personality disorders. You may also have recognized that the characteristics and attributes of some disorders, such as schizoid personality disorder, seemed to blend with other conditions, such as the schizotypal or the avoidant personality disorders. It is also the case that people frequently do not fit neatly into any one specific diagnostic category. They may also qualify for a diagnosis of more than one personality disorder (e.g., Clark, 2007; Grant, Stinson, et al., 2005; Widiger et al., 1991). Indeed, a common diagnosis is "personality disorder not otherwise specified" (e.g., Krueger & Eaton, 2010; Verheul & Widiger, 2004; Verheul et al., 2007), a category reserved for people who exhibit features from several different categories but do not cleanly fit within any of them.

In the past, many studies of personality disorder categories were conducted in an effort to find discrete breaks in such personality dimensions—that is, points at which normal behavior becomes clearly distinct from pathological behavior. None were found (Livesley, 2001; Widiger & Sanderson, 1995). Moreover, changes in the cut-points, or thresholds for diagnosis of a personality disorder, can have drastic and unacceptable effects on the apparent prevalence rates of a particular personality disorder diagnosis (Widiger & Trull, 2007). For instance, when the *DSM-III* was revised to the *DSM-III-R*, it was noted that the rate of schizoid personality disorder increased by 800 percent and narcissistic personality disorder by 350 percent (Morey, 1988).

Such issues are much less problematic when a dimensional (or continuous rating) system is used because it is expected that across individuals there will be many different patterns of elevation of scores on different facets of different traits. As noted earlier, the personality traits classified for the personality disorders are dimensional in nature. For example, everyone is suspicious at times, but the degree to which this trait exists in someone with paranoid personality disorder is extreme. A dimensional system would allow people to be rated on the degree to which they exhibit each facet and trait dimension—not on whether they do or do not have a given personality disorder. Each individual would also be rated on numerous dimensions, and highly personalized patterns of scores would thus be expected rather than problematic.

There has been serious debate among psychologists and psychiatrists over the best way to design a more dimensional system (Clark, 2007; Livesley, 2011; Skodol et al., 2011). Although it has long been clear that a more dimensional system is needed, actually implementing this has proven very difficult. A major challenge has been creating a scientifically valid diagnostic system that is not overly complicated and does not render the substantial research on existing categories useless. As we noted earlier, the proposal that was offered for inclusion in *DSM-5* was not accepted. Although moving to a dimensional system makes a lot of sense for many reasons, the complexity of the model that was proposed was no doubt a major issue. All of this speaks to the difficulty of creating a valid yet utilitarian diagnostic system that satisfies the different needs of both clinicians and researchers.

Summary

10.1 Describe the general features of personality disorders.

- People with personality disorders have inflexible and maladaptive traits that are pervasive and stable. Their ways of perceiving, thinking, and behaving compromise their ability to function effectively and relate to other people and the environment. They experience chronic interpersonal difficulties, problems with identity or sense of self, and are unable to function in an adaptive manner.

- People with mild personality disorders may function adequately but would be described by others as difficult, eccentric, or hard to get to know. At the other end

of the severity spectrum, many people with antisocial personality disorder end up in prison.

- Three general clusters of personality disorders (Clusters A, B, and C) have been described in the *DSM*, although researchers have increasingly questioned the validity of these clusters.

- Somewhere between 10 and 12 percent of people in the general population likely meet criteria for at least one personality disorder.

10.2 Summarize the challenges of doing research on personality disorders.

- Even with structured interviews, the reliability of diagnosing personality disorders typically is less than ideal. This is because many of the symptoms of specific personality disorders are not very precisely defined. A great deal of judgment is needed to know if a person's behavior meets the standard in each case.

- Many different interviews and self-report measures can be used to assess personality and personality disorders. There is not always high agreement between the diagnoses made with one instrument versus another.

- Classifying personality disorders in a categorical manner may not be the best approach. Most researchers today agree that a dimensional approach for assessing personality disorders has many advantages and would be preferable.

- It is difficult to determine the causes of personality disorders because most studies to date are retrospective.

- Most people with one personality disorder have at least one more personality disorder as well. This complicates research.

10.3 **List the three Cluster A personality disorders and describe the key clinical features of each.**

- The Cluster A personality disorders are paranoid, schizoid, and schizotypal personality disorder. Individuals with Cluster A disorders seem odd or eccentric.

- Paranoid personality disorder is characterized by suspiciousness and mistrust. It is equally common in men and women and has a prevalence of around 1 to 2 percent. Little is known about the causes of paranoid personality disorder although people with this disorder are at increased risk for schizophrenia.

- People with schizoid personality disorder have little interest in developing social relationships. They are not emotionally expressive. They are viewed by others as being cold and aloof. The lifetime prevalence of schizoid personality disorder is around 1 percent and the disorder is more common in men than women. Not much is known about the causes of schizoid personality disorder, in part because such people have little interest in taking part in research.

- Schizotypal personality disorder has a lifetime prevalence of around 1 percent. It is thought to be more common in males than females. People with this personality disorder show oddities in their thinking, speech, or behavior. They may have magical thinking or express odd beliefs. Genetic and other biological factors are implicated in schizotypal personality disorder, which is thought to be part of the schizophrenia spectrum.

10.4 **Describe the four Cluster B personality disorders and explain what common features they share.**

- Cluster B includes histrionic, narcissistic, antisocial, and borderline personality disorders; individuals with these disorders share a tendency to be dramatic, emotional,

and erratic. Little is known about the causes of histrionic and narcissistic personality disorders.

- Histrionic personality is characterized by excessive attention seeking and high levels of extraversion, as well as theatrical and sometimes seductive behavior. The lifetime prevalence of the disorder is slightly more than 1 percent and it is more common in women than men. This disorder was recommended for deletion in *DSM-5*, although this did not happen. Many question whether it is a meaningful diagnosis.

- Narcissistic personality disorder involves an exaggerated sense of self-importance, a need for admiration, and lack of empathy for the feelings of other people. Such people act in very entitled ways. The disorder is thought to be more common in men than women, with a prevalence of just under 1 percent.

- Antisocial personality disorder is characterized by deceitful, aggressive, and irresponsible behavior and a lack of regard for the rights of others. It is much more prevalent in men (around 3 percent) than women (around 1 percent). Many incarcerated people have antisocial personality disorder. Antisocial behavior has its roots in childhood and antisocial traits are thought to be heritable. Many adverse environmental factors (such as low family income, poor parental supervision, or neglect) are also implicated.

- Borderline personality disorder is characterized by emotional instability, fears of abandonment, impulsivity, self-mutilating behavior, and an unstable sense of self. People with BPD have intense and stormy personal relationships. The disorder has a lifetime prevalence of around 1 to 2 percent. Although many people are taught that borderline personality disorder is more common in women, researchers now believe it is equally common in men and women. Psychosocial causal factors (e.g., childhood adversity) have been identified as increasing the likelihood of developing borderline personality disorder. People with susceptible temperaments or those who are more impulsive and emotional are thought to be most at risk when they experience early maltreatment.

10.5 **List the three Cluster C personality disorders and describe the clinical features that are central to each.**

- Cluster C disorders are avoidant, dependent, and obsessive-compulsive personality disorder. People with these disorders show fearfulness or tension, as in anxiety-based disorders.

- Children with an inhibited temperament may be at heightened risk for avoidant personality disorder. The disorder is characterized by introversion, social anxiety, and hypersensitivity to criticism or disapproval. Avoidant personality disorder is more common in women than men and has a prevalence of around 2 to 3 percent. There is substantial overlap between avoidant personality disorder and generalized social phobia.

- People with dependent personality disorder are fearful of being alone and believe they need other people to take care of them. They have difficulty making decisions and need a lot of reassurance from others. The disorder is more common in women than men with a prevalence slightly under 1 percent. Individuals high on neuroticism and agreeableness, with authoritarian and overprotective parents, may be at heightened risk for dependent personality disorder.

- Obsessive-compulsive personality disorder involves an excessive concern with orderliness and maintaining control. People with this disorder are often perfectionists and this interferes with their ability to complete projects. They may also be very rigid and have difficulty delegating tasks or relaxing in any way. OCD is more common in men than women, with a prevalence of around 2 percent.

10.6 Explain the role that sociocultural factors might play in the prevalence of personality disorders.

- All cultures seem to share the same five basic personality traits.

- Some researchers believe that certain personality disorders have increased in the United States in recent years. This may be due to our culture's emphasis on instant gratification, personal ambition, and the breakdown of some traditional social structures.

- Disorders such as histrionic personality disorder are less common in cultures where drawing attention to oneself is frowned upon.

10.7 Discuss the challenges associated with treating personality disorders and summarize the approaches that are used.

- Personality disorders are generally difficult to treat because, by definition, they reflect enduring and pervasive styles of thinking and patterns of behavior.

- Many people with personality disorders do not believe they need treatment. Therapy is also complicated by the fact that personality disorders typically involve problems with interpersonal relationships. These problems are brought into the therapeutic relationship as well.

- Cognitive treatments for personality disorders aim to target the core dysfunctional beliefs that are thought to be so central to how the person sees the world and behaves in it.

- A form of behavior therapy called dialectical behavior therapy (DBT) is beneficial for people with BPD. DBT helps patients learn to manage their emotions and develop new coping skills. Other recently developed forms of therapy for BPD include transference-focused psychotherapy and mentalization-based treatment. A wide range of medications (antidepressants, antipsychotic medications, and mood-stabilizing medications) are also sometimes used.

10.8 Describe the clinical features of psychopathy and explain how it is similar to and different from antisocial personality disorder.

- Psychopathy is best thought of as involving elevated levels of four different dimensions of traits that can be summarized within two factors: (1) an affective-interpersonal set of traits reflecting lack of remorse or guilt, callousness/lack of empathy, glibness/superficial charm, grandiose sense of self-worth, and pathological lying; and (2) antisocial, impulsive, and socially deviant behavior; irresponsibility; and a parasitic lifestyle. A person diagnosed with ASPD is characterized primarily by antisocial and deviant lifestyle traits (Factor 2).

- Genetic and temperament, learning, and adverse environmental factors seem to be important in the development of psychopathy and ASPD.

- Psychopaths also show deficiencies in fear and anxiety as well as more general emotional deficits such as lack of empathy. They also seem to be characterized by abnormalities in limbic (amygdala) and prefrontal brain areas.

- Treatment of individuals with psychopathy is difficult, partly because they rarely see any need to change and tend to blame other people for their problems. In some cases, psychopaths may learn new skills from therapy that will allow them to be even better at manipulating other people.

Key Terms

Chapter 11
Substance-Related Disorders

Learning Objectives

11.1 Describe the characteristics of alcohol abuse and dependence.

11.2 Explain the biological, psychosocial, and sociocultural factors involved in alcohol abuse and dependence.

11.3 Discuss the treatment of alcohol-related disorders.

11.4 List the psychoactive drugs most commonly associated with abuse and dependence.

11.5 Describe the commonly used opiates and their effects on the body.

11.6 Discuss the different types of stimulants and their effects.

11.7 Describe the effects of sedatives on the brain.

11.8 List four different types of hallucinogens.

11.9 Explain whether there are addictive disorders other than alcohol and drugs.

The Cost of Alcohol and Substance Use

Lindsay Lohan became a child star at age 11, when she played the lead actress in the Disney remake of a family movie, *The Parent Trap*. Lohan went on to make several other Disney movies like *Freaky Friday* and *Herbie: Fully Loaded*, followed by the instant classic *Mean Girls* in 2004. Lohan had become an award-winning leading actress, and in addition had a budding career as a singer, designer, and model. However, shortly after achieving this success, Lohan began to experience problems with alcohol and drugs. She was arrested in 2007 for driving under the influence of alcohol, which led to 45 days in a rehabilitation facility. Unfortunately, within 2 weeks of being released Lohan was arrested again for driving under the influence in addition to possession of cocaine. This led her to lose a movie role, and was followed by ongoing difficulties, including being unable to work at the same level she had previously. Lohan continued to struggle with alcohol and substance use, including several arrests, stints in jail, and time in rehabilitation facilities.

Alcohol and drugs cause short-term pleasurable feelings; however, they are also addictive substances that can have extremely costly and damaging consequences. Some people are able to consume small amounts of alcohol and drugs and not experience any negative consequences at school, work, or in their relationships. However, others are not as lucky and can lose control of their drinking and drug use.

 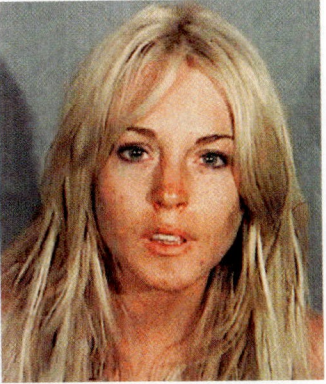

Lindsay Lohan's first film, *The Parent Trap*, launched her career in 1998. Nearly 10 years later, she was arrested for the first time on July 24, 2007, and charged with driving under the influence and cocaine possession.

Most people have used alcohol at least once, and many have tried other drugs such as tobacco, cannabis, or cocaine (Degenhardt et al., 2008). Using substances like alcohol and tobacco is therefore statistically normal and not considered pathological. However, their use is considered to be disordered when consumed in excessive amounts leading to impairment and other negative consequences. **Substance-related disorders** can be seen all around us: in extremely high rates of alcohol abuse and dependence, and in tragic exposés of cocaine abuse among star athletes and entertainers. **Addictive behavior**—behavior based on the pathological need for a substance—may involve the abuse of substances such as nicotine, alcohol, Ecstasy, or cocaine.

Addictive behavior is one of the most prevalent and difficult-to-treat mental health problems facing our society today.

The most commonly used problem substances are those that affect mental functioning in the central nervous system (CNS)—**psychoactive substances**: alcohol, nicotine, barbiturates, tranquilizers, amphetamines, heroin, Ecstasy, and marijuana. Some of these substances, such as alcohol and nicotine, can be purchased legally by adults; others, such as barbiturates or pain medications like Oxy-Contin, can be used legally under medical supervision; still others, such as heroin, Ecstasy, and methamphetamine, are illegal.

In this chapter, we cover the causes and consequences of **substance-related disorders** as well as their treatment. The material described provides both a historic and contemporary view of important research and theoretical strategies in understanding addictive disorders, thus we will, in places, refer to the substance abuse versus substance dependence distinction. The following distinctions are important to understanding and diagnosing substance-related disorders:

- **Substance abuse** generally involves an excessive use of a substance resulting in (1) potentially hazardous behavior such as driving while intoxicated or (2) continued use despite a persistent social, psychological, occupational, or health problem.
- **Substance dependence** includes more severe forms of substance use disorders and usually involves a marked physiological need for increasing amounts of a substance to achieve the desired effects. Dependence in these disorders means that an individual will show a tolerance for a drug and/or experience withdrawal symptoms when the drug is unavailable.
- **Tolerance**—the need for increased amounts of a substance to achieve the desired effects—results from biochemical changes in the body that affect the rate of metabolism and elimination of the substance from the body.
- **Withdrawal** refers to physical symptoms such as sweating, tremors, and tension that accompany abstinence from a drug.

Alcohol-Related Disorders

11.1 Describe the characteristics of alcohol abuse and dependence.

The terms *alcoholic* and *alcoholism* have been subject to some controversy and have been used differently by various groups in the past. The World Health Organization (WHO) no longer recommends the term *alcoholism* but refers instead to the *harmful use of alcohol*—"drinking that causes detrimental health and social consequences for the drinker, the people around the drinker and society at large, as well as the patterns of drinking that are associated with increased risk of adverse health outcomes" (2014a, p. 2). The WHO, as well as researchers in this area, also refer to *heavy episodic drinking* as the consumption of six or more alcoholic drinks on at least one occasion at least once per month (WHO, 2014a). However, because the terms *alcoholic* and *alcoholism* are still widely used in practice, in scientific journals, and in government agencies and publications, we will sometimes use them in this book.

People of many ancient cultures, including the Egyptians, Greeks, Romans, and Israelites, made extensive and often excessive use of alcohol (and other substances). Beer was first made in Egypt around 3000 b.c.e. The oldest surviving wine-making formulas were recorded by Marcus Cato in Italy almost a century and a half before the birth of Christ. About a.d. 800, the process of distillation was developed by an Arabian alchemist, thus making possible an increase in both the range and the potency of alcoholic beverages. Problems with excessive use of alcohol were observed almost as early as its use began. Cambyses, King of Persia in the sixth century b.c.e., has the dubious distinction of being one of the early alcohol abusers on record.

Since we've had alcohol, people have consumed it to the point of dysfunction. This picture shows an 1891 "stale beer dive" on Mulberry Street Bend, New York City, with several drunk people from the neighborhood and includes beers being served by a young girl (Campbell et al., 1892).

The Prevalence, Comorbidity, and Demographics of Alcohol Abuse and Dependence

Alcohol abuse and alcohol dependence are major problems around the world and are among the most destructive of the psychiatric disorders because of the impact excessive alcohol use can have on users' lives and those of their families and friends. Approximately 13 percent of people in the United States meet *DSM* criteria for alcohol abuse at some

point in their lifetime and about 5 percent meet criteria for alcohol dependence (Kessler, Berglund, Demler, et al., 2005). Of course, a much higher proportion of people drink alcohol, and many do so at very high volumes. Specifically, in 2013, more than half (52.2 percent) of Americans ages 12 or older reported that they currently (i.e., in the past 30 days) drink alcohol, approximately a quarter (22.9 percent) report binge drinking (i.e., having at least five drinks on one occasion in the past month), and 6.3 percent report being heavy drinkers (i.e., having at least five drinks at least five times in the past month) (Substance Abuse and Mental Health Services Administration [SAMHSA], 2014).

The potentially detrimental effects of excessive alcohol use are enormous. Heavy drinking is associated with vulnerability to injury (Cherpitel, 1997), marital discord (Hornish & Leonard, 2007), and becoming involved in intimate partner violence (Eckhardt, 2007). The life span of the average person with alcohol dependence is about 12 years shorter than that of the average person without this disorder. Alcohol significantly lowers performance on cognitive tasks such as problem solving—and the more complex the task, the more the impairment (Pickworth et al., 1997). Organic impairment, including brain shrinkage, occurs in a high proportion of people with alcohol dependence (Gazdzinski et al., 2005), and alcohol abuse is associated with increased risk of a wide range of other negative health outcomes such as diabetes, stroke, and cardiovascular disease (Molina et al., 2014).

Alcohol abuse is associated with over 40 percent of the deaths suffered in automobile accidents each year (Chou et al., 2006) and with about 40 to 50 percent of all murders (Bennett & Lehman, 1996), 40 percent of all assaults, and over 50 percent of all rapes (Abbey et al., 2001). About one of every three arrests in the United States is related to alcohol abuse, and over 43 percent of violent encounters with the police involve alcohol (McClelland & Teplin, 2001). Alcohol is more frequently associated with both violent and

Alcohol is associated with over 40 percent of deaths and serious injuries suffered in automobile accidents in the United States each year (see Chou et al., 2006).

nonviolent crime than drugs such as marijuana, and people with violence-related injuries are more likely to have a positive Breathalyzer test (Cherpitel, 1997; Dawkins, 1997).

Alcohol abuse and alcohol dependence in the United States cut across all age, educational, occupational, and socioeconomic boundaries. Alcohol abuse is found in priests, politicians, surgeons, law enforcement officers, and teenagers; the image of the alcohol-abusing person as an unkempt resident of skid row is clearly inaccurate. Recent research has shown that alcohol abuse has a strong presence in the workplace, with 15 percent of employees showing problem behaviors; many (1.7 percent, or 2.1 million people) actually drinking on the job; and 1.8 percent, or 2.3 million workers, drinking before they go to work (Frone, 2006). Some myths about alcoholism are noted in Table 11.1.

Historically, most problem drinkers—people experiencing life problems as a result of alcohol abuse—have been men; for example, men become problem drinkers at about five times the frequency of women (Helzer et al., 1990). Recent epidemiological research has suggested that the traditional gap between men and women has narrowed when it comes to the development of substance abuse disorders (Greenfield et al., 2010). There do not seem to be important differences in rates of alcohol abuse between black and white Americans, although Native Americans tend to have higher rates of alcohol abuse, and Asian Americans tend to have lower usage. It appears that problem drinking may develop during any life period from early childhood through old age. About 10 percent of men over age 65 are found to be heavy drinkers (Breslow et al., 2003). Surveys of alcoholism rates across different cultural groups around the world have found varying rates of the disorder across diverse cultural samples (Hibell et al., 2000).

Over 37 percent of people who abuse alcohol experience at least one coexisting mental disorder (Lapham et al., 2001). Not surprisingly, given that alcohol is a depressant, depression ranks high among the mental disorders often comorbid with alcoholism. There is a high comorbidity of substance abuse disorders and eating disorders (Harrop & Marlatt, 2009). It is also no surprise that many alcoholics die by suicide (McCloud et al., 2004). In addition to the serious problems that excessive drinkers create for themselves, they also pose serious difficulties for others (Gortner et al., 1997). Alcohol abuse co-occurs with high frequency with personality disorder as well (Grant, Stinson, et al., 2004).

The diagnosis of substance use disorder in *DSM-5* is based on a pathological pattern of behaviors that are

Table 11.1 Some Common Misconceptions about Alcohol and Alcohol Abuse

Fiction	Fact
Alcohol is a stimulant.	Alcohol is actually both a nervous system stimulant and a depressant.
You can always detect alcohol on the breath of a person who has been drinking.	It is not always possible to detect the presence of alcohol. Some individuals successfully cover up their alcohol use for years.
One ounce of 86-proof liquor contains more alcohol than two 12-ounce cans of beer.	Two 12-ounce cans of beer contain more than an ounce of alcohol.
Alcohol can help a person sleep more soundly.	Alcohol may interfere with sleep.
Impaired judgment does not occur before there are obvious signs of intoxication.	Impaired judgment can occur long before motor signs of intoxication are apparent.
An individual will get more intoxicated by mixing liquors than by taking comparable amounts of one kind, e.g., bourbon, scotch, or vodka.	It is the actual amount of alcohol in the bloodstream rather than the mix that determines intoxication.
Drinking several cups of coffee can counteract the effects of alcohol and enable a drinker to "sober up."	Drinking coffee does not affect the level of intoxication.
Exercise or a cold shower helps speed up the metabolism of alcohol.	Exercise and cold showers are futile attempts to increase alcohol metabolism.
People with "strong wills" need not be concerned about becoming substance abusers.	Alcohol is seductive and can lower the resistance of even the "strongest will."
Alcohol cannot produce a true addiction in the same sense that heroin can.	Alcohol has strong addictive properties.
One cannot become a substance abuser by drinking just beer.	One can consume a considerable amount of alcohol by drinking beer. It is, of course, the amount of alcohol that determines whether one becomes a substance abuser.
Alcohol is far less dangerous than marijuana.	There are considerably more individuals in treatment programs for alcohol problems than for marijuana abuse.
In a heavy drinker, damage to the liver shows up long before brain damage appears.	Heavy alcohol use can be manifested in organic brain damage before liver damage is detected.
The physiological withdrawal reaction from heroin is considered more dangerous than is withdrawal from alcohol.	The physiological symptoms accompanying withdrawal from heroin are no more frightening or traumatic to an individual than alcohol withdrawal. Actually, alcohol withdrawal is potentially more lethal than opiate withdrawal.
Everybody drinks.	Actually, 28 percent of men and 50 percent of women in the United States are abstainers.

DSM-5 *Criteria for...*

Alcohol Use Disorder

A. A problematic pattern of alcohol use leading to clinically significant impairment or distress, as manifested by at least two of the following, occurring within a 12-month period:

1. Alcohol is often taken in larger amounts or over a longer period than was intended.
2. There is a persistent desire or unsuccessful efforts to cut down or control alcohol use.
3. A great deal of time is spent in activities necessary to obtain alcohol, use alcohol, or recover from its effects.
4. Craving, or a strong desire or urge to use alcohol.
5. Recurrent alcohol use resulting in a failure to fulfill major role obligations at work, school, or home.
6. Continued alcohol use despite having persistent or recurrent social or interpersonal problems caused or exacerbated by the effects of alcohol.
7. Important social, occupational, or recreational activities are given up or reduced because of alcohol use.
8. Recurrent alcohol use in situations in which it is physically hazardous.
9. Alcohol use is continued despite knowledge of having a persistent or recurrent physical or psychological problem that is likely to have been caused or exacerbated by alcohol.
10. Tolerance, as defined by either of the following:
    a. A need for markedly increased amounts of alcohol to achieve intoxication or desired effect.
    b. A markedly diminished effect with continued use of the same amount of alcohol.
11. Withdrawal, as manifested by either of the following:
    a. The characteristic withdrawal syndrome for alcohol (refer to Criteria A and B of the criteria set for alcohol withdrawal, pp. 499–500).
    b. Alcohol (or a closely related substance, such as a benzodiazepine) is taken to relieve or avoid withdrawal symptoms.

Source: Reprinted with permission from the *Diagnostic and Statistical Manual of Mental Disorders*, Fifth Edition (Copyright © 2013). American Psychiatric Association.

related to the use of a particular substance, for example, alcohol. The *DSM* criteria for alcohol use disorder are reproduced in the *DSM-5* box as an illustration.

The Clinical Picture of Alcohol-Related Disorders

A great deal of progress has been made in understanding the physiological effects of alcohol on the brain, and the resulting symptoms that are experienced by the drinker (see, e.g., Table 11.2). For instance, alcohol consumption decreases behavioral inhibition, impairs learning and memory, and negatively impacts judgment, decision making, and motor coordination.

ALCOHOL'S EFFECTS ON THE BRAIN Alcohol has complex effects on the brain. At lower levels, alcohol activates the brain's "pleasure areas," which release endogenous opioids that are stored in the body (Braun, 1996). At higher levels, alcohol depresses brain functioning, inhibiting one of the brain's excitatory neurotransmitters, glutamate, which in turn slows down activity in parts of the brain (Koob et al., 2002). Inhibition of glutamate in the brain impairs the ability to learn and affects the higher brain centers, impairing judgment and other rational processes and lowering self-control. As behavioral restraints decline, a drinker may indulge in the satisfaction of impulses ordinarily held in check. A lack of motor coordination soon becomes apparent, and the drinker's discrimination and perception of cold, pain, and other discomforts are dulled. Typically the drinker experiences a sense of warmth, expansiveness, and well-being. In such a mood, unpleasant realities are screened out and the drinker's feelings of self-esteem and adequacy rise. Casual acquaintances become the best and most understanding of friends and the drinker enters a generally pleasant world of unreality in which worries are temporarily left behind.

In most U.S. states, when the alcohol content of the bloodstream reaches 0.08 percent, the individual is considered intoxicated, at least with respect to driving a vehicle. Muscular coordination, speech, and vision are impaired and thought processes are confused. Even before this level

---

Table 11.2 Top 10 Alcohol-Related Consequences Among Dutch Students

1	Hangover	74.3%
2*	Less energy or felt tired.	63.9%
3	While drinking, I have said or done embarrassing things.	38.0%
4*	Felt very sick to my stomach or thrown up after drinking.	34.1%
5	Ended up drinking on nights when I had planned not to drink.	29.2%
6*	Not gone to work or missed classes at school.	28.0%
7	Blackouts.	26.8%
8	Taken foolish risks when I have been drinking.	24.7%
9*	Quality of work or school has suffered because of my drinking.	21.7%
10	When drinking, I have done impulsive things I regretted later.	21.4%

SOURCE: Verster, J. C., Van Herwijnen, J., Olivier, B., & Kahler, C. W. (2009). Validation of the Dutch Brief Young Adult Alcohol Consequences Questionnaire (B-YAACQ). *Addict Behav., 34*, 411–414.

*Events that may be related to alcohol hangover.

of intoxication is reached, however, judgment becomes impaired to such an extent that the person misjudges his or her condition. For example, drinkers tend to express confidence in their ability to drive safely long after such actions are in fact quite unsafe. When the blood alcohol level reaches approximately 0.5 percent (the level differs somewhat among individuals), the entire neural balance is upset and the individual passes out. Unconsciousness apparently acts as a safety device because concentrations above 0.55 percent are usually lethal.

In general, it is the amount of alcohol actually concentrated in the bodily fluids, not the amount consumed, that determines intoxication. The effects of alcohol vary for different drinkers, depending on their physical condition, the amount of food in their stomach, and the duration of their drinking. In addition, alcohol users may gradually build up a tolerance for the drug so that ever-increasing amounts may be needed to produce the desired effects. Women metabolize alcohol less effectively than men and thus become intoxicated on lesser amounts (Gordis et al., 1995).

The effects of alcohol do not stop at intoxication—a state of being affected by one or more psychoactive drugs. Another phenomenon associated with excessive alcohol consumption is the alcohol "hangover," in which a person experiences symptoms of headache, nausea, fatigue and cognitive impairment for 8 to 24 hours after consuming alcohol (Verster et al., 2010; see Figure 11.1). Researchers are still trying to understand what causes alcohol hangovers, with leading theories focusing on dehydration along with the buildup of alcohol metabolites such as acetaldehyde, and the triggering of the body's immune response (Penning et al., 2010). Despite the lack of understanding of the causes

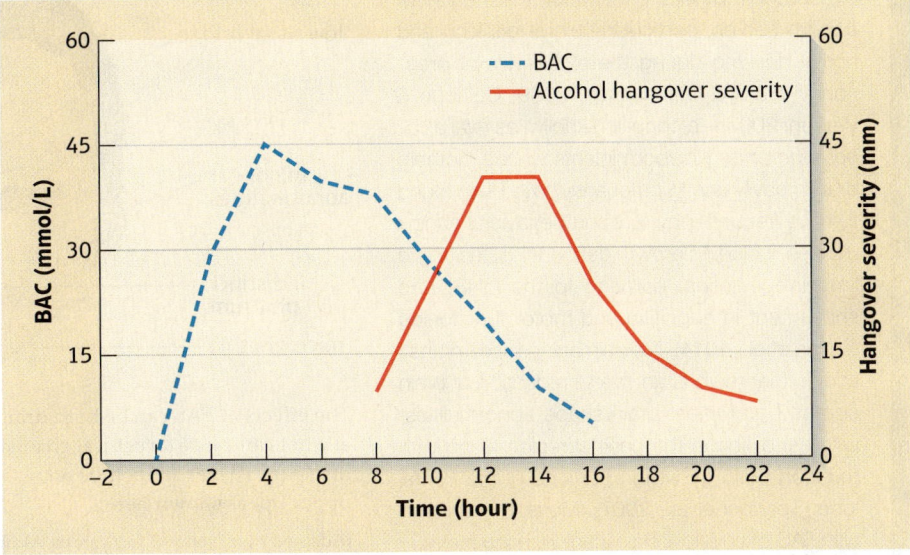

Figure 11.1 Commonly observed changes over time in blood alcohol concentration (BAC, dashed line) and alcohol hangover severity. Hangover severity is most pronounced when blood alcohol concentration reaches 0 (in this example at 12–14 hours after the start of alcohol consumption).

(Adapted from Verster et al., 2010.)

of hangovers, it is clear that beyond being unpleasant, they can be dangerous, leading to problems like impairment while driving an automobile (Hoiseth et al., 2015).

DEVELOPMENT OF ALCOHOL DEPENDENCE Excessive drinking can be viewed as progressing insidiously from early- to middle- to late-stage alcohol-related disorder, although some abusers do not follow this pattern. Many investigators have maintained that alcohol is a dangerous poison even in small amounts, but others believe that in moderate amounts it is not harmful to most people. For pregnant women, however, even moderate amounts are believed to be dangerous; in fact, no safe level has been established, as is discussed in the Developments in Research box. The accompanying photos show the differences between the brain of a normal teenager and those born with fetal alcohol syndrome (FAS), a condition that is caused by excessive alcohol consumption

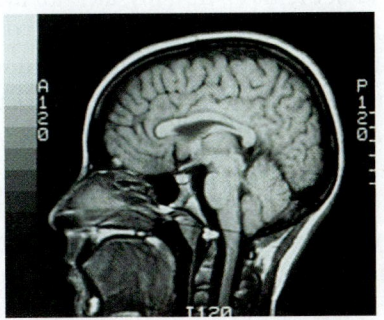 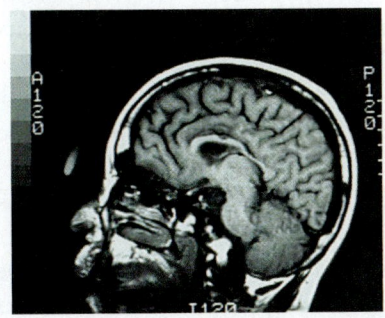 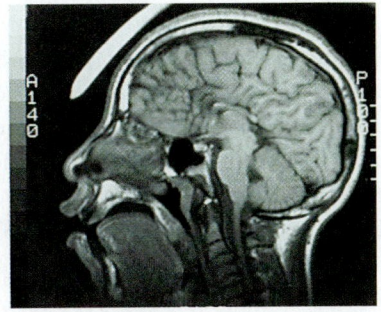

MRIs of three teenagers: (left) normal control, 13-year-old female; (center) FAS, 13-year-old male with focal thinning of the corpus callosum; (right) FAS, 14-year-old male with complete agenesis (nondevelopment) of the corpus callosum.

Developments in Research

Fetal Alcohol Syndrome: How Much Drinking Is Too Much?

Research indicates that heavy drinking by expectant mothers can affect the health of unborn babies, particularly binge drinking and heavy drinking during the early days of pregnancy (Burd & Christensen, 2009; Calhoun & Warren, 2007)—a condition known as *fetal alcohol syndrome*. Newborn infants whose mothers drank heavily during pregnancy have been found to have frequent physical and behavioral abnormalities, including growth deficiencies, facial and limb irregularities, damage to the CNS, and impairment in cognitive and motor functioning (Lucas et al., 2014). Neuroimaging research has shown that there is an overall reduction of brain size and prominent brain shape abnormalities, with narrowing in the parietal region along with reduced brain growth in portions of the frontal lobe (Spadoni et al., 2007). Moreover, children with FAS often show significant working memory deficits and altered activation patterns in some brain regions (Astley et al., 2009).

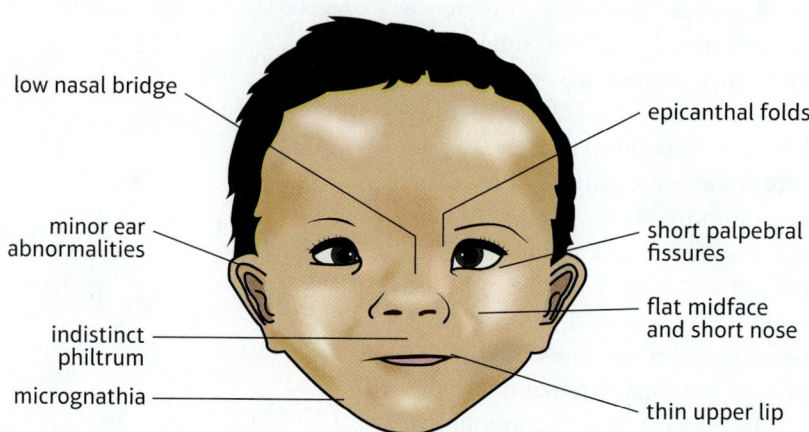

The effects of FAS can be both dramatic and long lasting. Prenatal exposure to alcohol can cause structural changes in facial features that persist throughout the life span. These can include a lowered nasal bridge, ear abnormalities, and a thin upper lip, as shown here.

(Adapted from National Institute on Alcohol Abuse and Alcoholism http://pubs.niaaa.nih.gov/publications/AA82/AA82.htm)

How much drinking endangers a newborn's health? The U.S. Centers for Disease Control and Prevention (CDC) takes the stance that "There is no safe amount of alcohol use during pregnancy or while trying to get pregnant. . . . When a pregnant woman drinks alcohol, so does her baby" (CDC, 2015a). The U.S. Surgeon General and many medical experts also have concurred that pregnant women should abstain from using alcohol during pregnancy (Carmona, 2005).

---

during pregnancy and results in birth defects such as mental retardation.

THE PHYSICAL EFFECTS OF CHRONIC ALCOHOL USE

For individuals who drink to excess, the clinical picture is highly unfavorable (Turner et al., 2006). Alcohol that is taken in must be assimilated by the body, except for the approximately 5 to 10 percent that is eliminated through breath, urine, and perspiration. The work of alcohol metabolism is done by the liver, but when large amounts of alcohol are ingested, the liver may be seriously overworked and eventually suffer irreversible damage (Lucey et al., 2009). In fact, from 15 to 30 percent of heavy drinkers develop cirrhosis of the liver, a disorder that involves extensive stiffening of the blood vessels. Many of the 36,000 annual cirrhosis deaths every year are alcohol related (Centers for Disease Control and Prevention (CDC), 2015b). Some countries, for example Britain and Scotland, have shown an increase in cirrhosis-related deaths in the past two decades because of the increased use of alcohol in their populations (Leon & McCambridge, 2006).

Alcohol is also a high-calorie drug. A pint of whiskey—enough to make about 8 to 10 ordinary cocktails—provides about 1,200 calories, which is approximately half the ordinary caloric requirement for a day (Flier et al., 1995). Thus, consumption of alcohol reduces a drinker's appetite for other food. Because alcohol has no nutritional value, the excessive drinker can suffer from malnutrition (Derr & Gutmann, 1994). Furthermore, heavy drinking impairs the body's ability to utilize nutrients, so the nutritional deficiency cannot be made up by popping vitamins. Many people who abuse alcohol also experience increased gastrointestinal symptoms such as stomach pains (Fields et al., 1994).

PSYCHOSOCIAL EFFECTS OF ALCOHOL ABUSE AND DEPENDENCE

In addition to physical and medical problems, heavy drinkers often suffer from chronic fatigue, oversensitivity, and depression. Initially, alcohol may seem to provide a useful crutch for dealing with the stresses of life, especially during periods of acute stress, by helping screen out intolerable realities and enhance the drinker's feelings of adequacy and worth. The excessive use of alcohol eventually becomes counterproductive, however, and can result in impaired reasoning, poor judgment, and gradual personality deterioration. Behavior typically becomes coarse and inappropriate, and the drinker often assumes increasingly less responsibility, loses pride in personal appearance, neglects spouse and family, and becomes irritable and unwilling to discuss the problem.

As judgment becomes impaired, an excessive drinker may be unable to hold a job and generally becomes unqualified to cope with new demands that arise (Frone, 2003). General personality disorganization and deterioration may be reflected in loss of employment and marital breakup. The drinker's general health will eventually deteriorate, and brain and liver damage will occur. For example, there is evidence that an alcoholic's brain is accumulating diffuse organic damage even when no extreme organic symptoms are present (Sullivan, Deshmukh, et al., 2000), and even mild to moderate drinking can adversely affect memory and problem solving (Gordis, 2001). Other researchers have found extensive alcohol consumption to be associated with an increased amount of organic damage in later life (Lyvers, 2000); however, recent research using fMRI has shown that this damage is partially reversible if the person abstains from alcohol use (Wobrock et al., 2009).

PSYCHOSES ASSOCIATED WITH SEVERE ALCOHOL ABUSE Excessive use of alcohol also can result in severe mental health problems. Several acute psychotic reactions fit the diagnostic classification of substance-induced disorders. These reactions may develop in people who have been drinking excessively over long periods of time. Such acute reactions usually last only a short time and generally consist of confusion, excitement, and delirium. These disorders are often called *alcohol-induced psychotic disorders* because they are marked by a temporary loss of contact with reality (Jordaan & Emsley, 2014).

Among those who drink excessively for a long time, a reaction called **alcohol withdrawal delirium** (formerly known as **delirium tremens**) may occur. This reaction usually happens following a prolonged drinking spree when the person enters a state of withdrawal. Slight noises or suddenly moving objects may cause considerable excitement and agitation. The full-blown symptoms include (1) disorientation for time and place, in which, for example, a person may mistake the hospital for a church or jail, no longer recognize friends, or identify hospital attendants as old acquaintances; (2) vivid hallucinations, particularly of small, fast-moving animals like snakes, rats, and roaches; (3) acute fear, in which these animals may change in form, size, or color in terrifying ways; (4) extreme suggestibility, in which a person can be made to see almost any animal if its presence is merely suggested; (5) marked tremors of the hands, tongue, and lips; and (6) other symptoms including perspiration, fever, a rapid and weak heartbeat, a coated tongue, and foul breath.

The delirium typically lasts from 3 to 6 days and is generally followed by a deep sleep. When a person awakens, few symptoms remain, but frequently the individual is scared and may not resume drinking for several weeks or months. It has been estimated that 5 to 25 percent of patients with alcohol withdrawal delirium die as a result of convulsions, heart failure, and other complications (Trevisan et al., 1998). Drugs such as chlordiazepoxide (Librium), however, have demonstrated the ability to decrease withdrawal symptoms and with it the risk of death as a result of withdrawal (Kumar et al., 2015).

A second alcohol-related psychosis is **alcohol amnestic disorder** (formerly known as Korsakoff's syndrome). This condition was first described by the Russian psychiatrist Korsakoff in 1887 and is one of the most severe alcohol-related disorders (d'Ydewalle & Van Damme, 2007). The primary symptom is a memory defect (particularly with regard to recent events), which is sometimes accompanied by falsification of events (confabulation). People with this disorder may not recognize pictures, faces, rooms, and other objects that they have just seen, although they may feel that these people or objects are familiar. Such people increasingly tend to fill in their memory gaps with confabulations that lead to unconnected and distorted associations. These individuals may appear to be delirious, delusional, and disoriented for time and place, but ordinarily their confusion and disordered actions are closely related to their attempts to fill in memory gaps. The memory disturbance itself seems related to an inability to form new associations in a manner that renders them readily retrievable. Such a reaction usually occurs in long-time alcohol abusers after many years of excessive drinking. These patients have also been observed to show other cognitive impairments such as planning deficits (Brokate et al., 2003), intellectual decline, emotional deficits (Snitz et al., 2002), judgment deficits (Brand et al., 2003), and cortical lesions (Estruch et al., 1998).

The symptoms of alcohol amnestic disorder result from malnutrition, specifically the lack of vitamin B (thiamine). If symptoms are correctly diagnosed within the first 48 to 72 hours, treatment with thiamine leads to a reversal of this condition and memory functioning appears to be restored with prolonged abstinence. However, if undiagnosed and with disease progression beyond several days, the brain damage causing this condition becomes irreversible (Latt & Dore, 2014).

Alcohol Amnestic Disorder

Brendan was brought into the detoxification unit of a local county hospital by the police after an incident at a crowded city park. He was arrested because of his assaultive behavior toward others (he was walking through the crowded groups of sunbathers muttering to himself, kicking at people). At admission to the hospital, Brendan was disoriented (did not know where he was), incoherent, and confused. When asked his name, he paused a moment, scratched his head, and said, "George Washington." When asked about what he was doing at the park, he indicated that he was "marching in a parade in his honor."

in review

- What is the difference between alcohol abuse and alcohol dependence?
- What are the major physiological effects of alcohol?
- Identify the physical, interpersonal, and social/occupational problems that can result from chronic alcohol use.

Causal Factors in the Abuse of and Dependence on Alcohol

11.2 Explain the biological, psychosocial, and sociocultural factors involved in alcohol abuse and dependence.

In trying to identify the causes of problem drinking, some researchers have stressed the role of genetic and biochemical factors (Hartz & Bierut, 2010); others have pointed to psychosocial factors, viewing problem drinking as a maladaptive pattern of adjustment to the stress of life; and still others have emphasized sociocultural factors such as the availability of alcohol and social approval of excessive drinking. As we will see, some combination of all of these factors seems to influence risk for developing alcohol abuse or alcohol dependency. As with most other forms of maladaptive behavior, there may be several types of alcohol abuse and dependency, each with somewhat different patterns of biological, psychosocial, and sociocultural causal factors.

Biological Causal Factors in Alcohol Abuse and Dependence

How do substances such as alcohol, cocaine, and opium (discussed later in the chapter) come to have such powerful effects—an overpowering hold that occurs in some people after only a few uses of the drug? Although the exact mechanisms are not fully agreed on by experts in the field,

two important factors are clearly involved. The first is the ability of most, if not all, addictive substances to activate areas of the brain that produce intrinsic pleasure and sometimes immediate, powerful reward. The second factor involves the person's biological makeup, or constitution, including his or her genetic inheritance and the environmental influences (learning factors) that enter into the need to seek mind-altering substances to an increasing degree as use continues. The development of an alcohol addiction is a complex process involving many elements: constitutional vulnerability and environmental encouragement, as well as the unique biochemical properties of certain psychoactive substances. Let's examine each of these elements in more detail.

THE NEUROBIOLOGY OF ADDICTION Psychoactive drugs differ in their biochemical properties as well as in how rapidly they enter the brain. There are several routes of administration, including oral, nasal, and intravenous. Alcohol is usually drunk, the slowest route, whereas cocaine is often self-administered nasally or by injection. Central to the neurochemical process underlying addiction is the role the drug plays in activating the "pleasure pathway." The **mesocorticolimbic dopamine pathway (MCLP)** is the center of psychoactive drug activation in the brain. The MCLP is made up of neuronal cells in the middle portion of the brain known as the ventral tegmental area (see Figure 11.2) and connects to other brain centers such as the nucleus accumbens and then to the prefrontal cortex. This neuronal system is involved in such functions as control of

Figure 11.2 The Mesocorticolimbic Pathway

The MCLP, running from the ventral tegmental area to the nucleus accumbens to the prefrontal cortex, is central to the release of the neurotransmitter dopamine and in mediating the rewarding properties of drugs.

(Adapted from Office of Technology Assessment, 1993.)

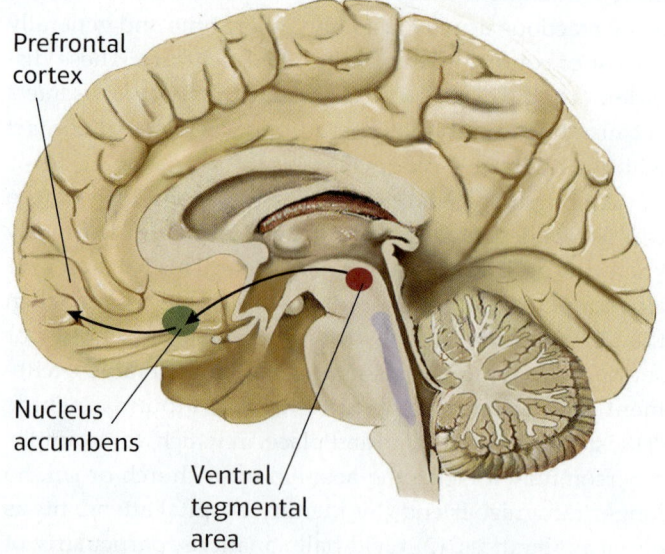

emotions, memory, and gratification. Alcohol produces euphoria by stimulating this area in the brain. Research has shown that direct electrical stimulation of the MCLP produces great pleasure and has strong reinforcing properties (Littrell, 2001). Other psychoactive drugs also operate to change the brain's normal functioning and to activate the pleasure pathway, as we discuss in more detail later. Drug ingestion or behaviors that lead to activation of the brain reward system are reinforced, so further use is promoted. The exposure of the brain to an addictive drug alters its neurochemical structure and results in a number of behavioral effects. With continued use of the drug, neuroadaptation to or tolerance and dependence on the substance develop.

GENETIC VULNERABILITY The possibility of a genetic predisposition to developing alcohol abuse problems has been widely researched. Many experts agree that heredity plays an important role in a person's developing sensitivity to the addictive power of drugs like alcohol (Plomin & DeFries, 2003; Volk et al., 2007). Several lines of research point to the importance of genetic factors in substance-related disorders.

A review of 39 studies of the families of 6,251 alcoholics and of 4,083 nonalcoholics who had been followed over 40 years reported that almost one-third of alcoholics had at least one parent with an alcohol problem (Cotton, 1979). Likewise, a study of children of alcoholics found that for males, having one alcoholic parent increased the rate of alcoholism from 12.4 percent to 29.5 percent and having two alcoholic parents increased the rate to 41.2 percent. For females with no alcoholic parents, the rate was 5.0 percent; for those with one alcoholic parent, the rate was 9.5 percent; and for those with two alcoholic parents, it was 25.0 percent (Cloninger et al., 1986).

Adoption studies also provide evidence for a genetic vulnerability for alcohol problems. In these studies, researchers followed up with children of alcoholics and children of nonalcoholics who were all adopted by nonalcoholic families. Such studies have shown that the children of alcoholic parents who had been adopted by nonalcoholic foster parents were nearly twice as likely to have alcohol problems by their late 20s as the control group of adopted children whose biological parents were not alcoholics (Goodwin et al.,1973). In another study, the same researchers compared alcoholic parents' sons who were adopted in infancy by nonalcoholic parents and sons raised by their alcoholic parents. Both adopted and nonadopted sons later evidenced high rates of alcoholism—25 percent and 17 percent, respectively (Goodwin et al.,1974). Thus, being born to an alcoholic parent significantly increases the risk of becoming an alcoholic.

Another approach to understanding the precursors to alcohol-related disorders is to study prealcoholic personalities—individuals who are at high risk for substance abuse but who are not yet affected by alcohol. An alcohol-risk personality has been described as an individual who has an inherited predisposition toward alcohol abuse and who is impulsive, prefers taking high risks, and is emotionally unstable.

Research has shown that those who are genetically predisposed to developing drug or alcohol problems but who have not yet acquired the problem show different physiological patterns than nonalcoholic men in several respects. Those at risk tend to experience greater decreases in stress following alcohol ingestion (Finn et al., 1997), show different alpha wave patterns on EEGs (Stewart et al., 1990), and have larger conditioned physiological responses to alcohol cues than individuals who were considered to have a low risk for alcoholism (Earleywine & Finn, 1990).

Some research suggests that certain ethnic groups, particularly Asians and Native Americans, have abnormal physiological reactions to alcohol—a phenomenon referred to as "alcohol flush reaction." Asian and Eskimo subjects have shown a tendency to have a hypersensitive reaction including flushing of the skin, a drop in blood pressure, heart palpitations, and nausea following the ingestion of alcohol (Gill et al., 1999). This physiological reaction is found in roughly half of all Asians (Chen & Yeh, 1997) and results from a mutant enzyme that fails to break down alcohol molecules in the liver during the metabolic process (Takeshita et al., 1993). Although cultural factors may also play a role, the relatively lower rates of alcoholism among Asian groups might be related to the extreme discomfort associated with the alcohol flush reaction (Higuci et al., 1994).

GENETICS—THE WHOLE STORY? As with the other disorders described in this book, genetics alone is not the whole story, and the exact role it plays in the development of alcohol-related disorders remains unclear. This issue continues to be debated, and some experts are not convinced of the primary role of genetics in substance abuse disorders. Genetic transmission in the case of alcohol-related disorders does not follow the hereditary pattern found in strictly genetic disorders. Importantly, the majority of children who have parents with alcohol-related problems do not themselves develop substance abuse disorders—whether or not they are raised by their biological parents. Overall, although much evidence implicates genetic factors in the etiology of alcoholism, we do not know what precise role they play. At present, it appears that the genetic interpretation of alcoholism remains an attractive hypothesis; however, additional research is needed for us to hold this view with confidence. It is not likely that genetics alone will account for the full range of alcohol and drug problems. Social circumstances are still considered powerful forces in providing both the availability and the motivation to use alcohol and other drugs.

GENETIC INFLUENCES AND LEARNING When we talk about familial or constitutional differences, we are not strictly limiting our explanation to genetic inheritance. Rather, learning factors appear to play an important part in the development of predetermined tendencies to behave in particular ways. Having a genetic predisposition or biological vulnerability to substance abuse, of course, is not a sufficient cause of the disorder. The person must be exposed to the substance to a sufficient degree for the addictive behavior to appear. In the case of alcohol, almost everyone in America is exposed to the drug to some extent—in most cases through peer pressure, parental example, and advertising (Andrews & Hops, 2010). The development of alcohol-related problems involves living in an environment that promotes initial as well as continuing use of the substance. People become conditioned to stimuli and tend to respond in particular ways as a result of learning. Learning appears to play an important part in the development of substance abuse and antisocial personality disorders. There clearly are numerous reinforcements for using alcohol in our everyday lives. However, research has also shown that psychoactive drugs such as alcohol contain intrinsic rewarding properties—apart from the social context or the drug's operation to diminish worry or frustration.

Psychosocial Causal Factors in Alcohol Abuse and Dependence

Not only do people who abuse alcohol become physiologically dependent on it, they develop a powerful psychological dependence as well—they become socially dependent on the drug to help them enjoy social situations.

FAILURES IN PARENTAL GUIDANCE Stable family relationships and parental guidance are extremely important molding influences for children (Hasin & Katz, 2010), and this stability is often lacking in families of substance

Parent substance use is associated with early adolescent substance use, and negative parental models can have longer-range negative consequences once children leave home.

abusers. Children who have parents who are extensive alcohol or drug abusers are vulnerable to developing substance abuse and related problems (Erblich et al., 2001). The experiences and lessons we learn from important figures in our early years have a significant impact on us as adults. Children who are exposed to negative role models and family dysfunction early in their lives or experience other negative circumstances because the adults around them provide limited guidance often falter on the difficult steps they must take in life (Fischer et al., 2005). These formative experiences can have a direct influence on whether a young person becomes involved in maladaptive behavior such as alcohol or drug abuse.

In one sophisticated program of research aimed at evaluating the possibility that negative socialization factors influence alcohol use, Chassin and colleagues (1993; Trim & Chassin, 2004) replicated findings that alcohol abuse in parents is associated with substance use in adolescents. They then evaluated several possible mediating factors that can affect whether adolescents start using alcohol. They found that parenting skills or parental behavior was associated with substance use in adolescents. Specifically, alcohol-abusing parents are less likely to keep track of what their children are doing, and this lack of monitoring often leads to the adolescents' affiliation with drug-using peers. In addition, stress and negative affect (more prevalent in families with an alcoholic parent) are associated with alcohol use in adolescents (Chassin et al., 1993). Extremely stressful childhood experiences such as physical abuse (Douglas et al., 2010; Kaufman et al., 2007) or child sexual abuse might also make a person vulnerable to later problems.

PSYCHOLOGICAL VULNERABILITY In recent years, substantial research has focused on the link between alcohol-related disorders and such other disorders as antisocial personality, depression, and schizophrenia to determine whether some individuals are more vulnerable to substance abuse disorders. About half of those with schizophrenia have either alcohol or drug abuse or dependence as well (Kosten, 1997). In addition, antisocial personality disorder, alcohol, and aggression are strongly associated (Moeller & Dougherty, 2001), and in a survey of eight alcohol treatment programs, Morganstern and colleagues (1997) found that 57.9 percent of those in treatment had a personality disorder, with 22.7 percent meeting the criteria for antisocial personality disorder. Considerable research also has suggested that there is a relationship between depressive disorders and alcohol abuse, and there may be gender differences in the association between these disorders (Kranzler et al., 1997). For whatever reason they co-occur, the presence of other mental disorders in patients who abuse alcohol or drugs is a very important consideration when it comes to treatment, as discussed later in this chapter.

STRESS, TENSION REDUCTION, AND REINFORCEMENT
Studies on patients undergoing substance abuse treatment have shown high levels of trauma in their prior histories—about 25 to 50 percent of PTSD patients also have substance abuse disorders (Schafer & Najavits, 2007). In one study, Deters and colleagues (2006) found that 98 percent of the American Indian adolescents in their substance abuse study reported having a history of trauma such as threat of personal injury, witnessing of injury, or sexual abuse. One recent controlled-treatment study of disaster workers who experienced PTSD following the September 11, 2001, terrorist attacks found that excessive alcohol use was associated with dropout from treatment (Difede et al., 2007). In addition, high exposure to threatening situations and atrocities among Iraq War veterans has been associated with a positive screen for alcohol abuse (Wilk et al., 2010).

A number of investigators have pointed out that the typical individual who abuses alcohol is discontented with his or her life and is unable or unwilling to tolerate tension and stress (Rutledge & Sher, 2001). Hussong and colleagues (2001) reported a high degree of association between alcohol consumption and negative affectivity such as anxiety and somatic complaints. In other words, many alcoholics drink to relax. In this view, anyone who finds alcohol tension reducing is in danger of abusing alcohol, even without an especially stressful life situation. However, the tension-reduction causal model is difficult to accept as a sole explanatory hypothesis. If this process were a main cause, we would expect substance abuse disorder to be far more common than it is because alcohol tends to reduce tension for most people who use it. In addition, this model does not explain why some excessive drinkers are able to maintain control over their drinking and continue to function in society, whereas others are not.

EXPECTATIONS OF SOCIAL SUCCESS   Some research has explored the idea that cognitive expectation may play an important role both in the initiation of drinking and in the maintenance of drinking behavior once the person has begun to use alcohol (Marlatt et al., 1998). According to the reciprocal-influence model, adolescents begin drinking as a result of expectations that using alcohol will increase their popularity and acceptance by their peers.

This view gives professionals an important and potentially powerful means of deterring drinking among young people or at least delaying its onset. From this perspective, alcohol use in teenagers can be countered by providing young people with more effective social tools and with ways of altering these expectancies before drinking begins. Some researchers have suggested that prevention efforts should be targeted at children before they begin to drink so that the positive feedback cycle of reciprocal reinforcement between expectancy and drinking will never be established (Smith et al., 1995).

Time and experience do have *moderating* influences on these alcohol expectancies, although heavy drinking in early college years can result in risky behavior and low academic motivation (Hoeppner et al., 2012). In a longitudinal study of college drinking, Sher and colleagues (1996) found that there was a significant decrease in outcome expectancy over time. That is, older students showed less expectation of the benefits of alcohol than beginning students (see the World Around Us box).

Research Close-Up
Moderating

A moderating variable is a variable that influences the association between two other variables. For example, depression is common after bereavement. However, men who have lost a spouse tend to be more likely to be depressed than women who have lost a spouse. In this case, gender is a key moderating variable for the bereavement–depression relationship.

Watch   **Moderating Variable**

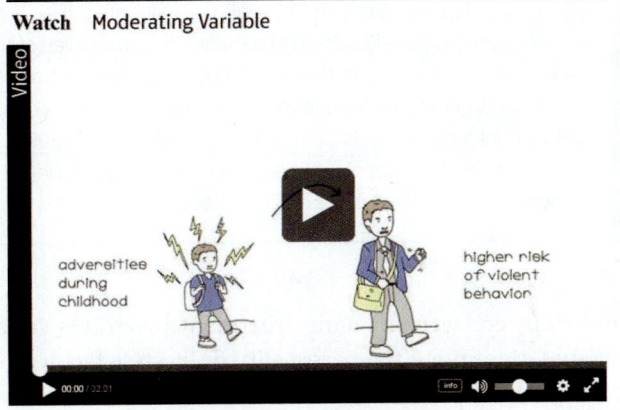

MARITAL AND OTHER INTIMATE RELATIONSHIPS
Adults with less supportive relationships tend to show greater drinking following sadness or hostility than those with close peers and with more positive relationships (Hussong et al., 2001). Excessive drinking often begins during crisis periods in marital or other intimate personal relationships, particularly crises that lead to hurt and self-devaluation. The marital relationship may actually serve to maintain the pattern of excessive drinking. Marital partners may behave toward each other in ways that promote or enable a spouse's excessive drinking. For example, a husband who lives with a wife who abuses alcohol is often unaware of the fact that, gradually and inevitably, many of the decisions he makes every day are based on the expectation that his wife will be drinking. These expectations, in turn, may make the drinking behavior more likely. Eventually an entire marriage may center on the drinking of a substance-abusing spouse. In some instances, the husband or wife may also begin to drink excessively. Thus, one

The World Around Us

Binge Drinking in College

Two alcohol-related student deaths shocked the Colorado college community in the fall of 2004. Lynn B., an entering freshman at the University of Colorado, drank so much whiskey and wine during a fraternity initiation that he became unconscious and died as a result of alcohol poisoning. This tragic incident occurred just 2 weeks after a 19-year-old sophomore at Colorado State University, Samantha S., died of alcohol poisoning after a party at which she had consumed an estimated 40 drinks (Sink, 2004).

How extensive is college binge drinking? In spite of the fact that alcohol use is illegal for most undergraduates, the National Institute on Alcohol Abuse and Alcoholism (NIAAA) indicates that approximately four out of five college students drink alcohol and half of students who drink engage in binge drinking (NIAAA, 2015). Moreover, approximately 25 percent of college students experience academic problems as a result of drinking such as missing classes and receiving poor grades (NIAAA, 2015).

What are the reasons for the widespread problem of binge drinking in college? Many factors can be cited, such as students' expressing independence from parental influence (Turrisi et al., 2000); peer group and situational influences (Read et al., 2003); developing and asserting gender roles, particularly for men adopting a "macho" role (Capraro, 2000); and holding beliefs that alcohol can help make positive transformations, such as "having a few drinks to celebrate special occasions" (Turrisi, 1999).

One study suggests that extensive drinking in college, even among the heaviest drinkers from sororities and fraternities, might be determined to a great extent by situational events, factors that change with graduation. In a follow-up study of drinking behavior a year after graduation, Sher, Bartholow, and Nanda (2001) reported that being a member of a fraternity or sorority did not predict postcollege drinking. Interestingly, a long-term follow-up of over 11 years has shown that the heavy drinking during college did not translate to heavy drinking during later years (Bartholow et al., 2003). These investigators found that heavy drinking that is associated with Greek society involvement does not generally lead to sustained heavy drinking in later life.

Some institutions provide a psychological intervention in an effort to reduce the extent of drinking among college students. One recent study reported that a procedure referred to as Brief Motivational Intervention, or BMI, produced greater self-regulation among a sample of binging college students by providing skills for them to moderate their drinking behavior (Carey et al., 2007). This procedure was more effective among students who also showed, in their pretreatment assessment, a readiness to change.

We know that most college students drink, that many binge drink, and that the consequences of doing so can be negative and even fatal. Given this, what can or should college students do to decrease the likelihood of negative (or fatal) outcomes while drinking?

---

important concern in many treatment programs today involves identifying the personality or lifestyle factors in a relationship that tend to foster the drinking in the alcohol-abusing person. Of course, such relationships are not restricted to marital partners but may also occur in those involved in love affairs or close friendships.

The Drunken Wife and Mother

Evelyn C., a 36-year-old homemaker and mother of two school-age children (from a previous marriage), began to drink to excess following intense disagreements with her husband, John, a manager of a retail business. For several months, she had been drinking during the day when her children were at school and on two occasions was inebriated when they came home. On one recent occasion, Evelyn failed to pick up her older daughter after an after-school event. Her daughter called John's cell phone (he was out of town on a business trip), and he had an assistant pick her up. When they arrived home, Evelyn (apparently unaware of the problem she had caused) created a scene and was verbally abusive toward the assistant. Her out-of-control drinking increased when her husband of 3 years began staying out all night. These emotionally charged encounters resulted in John's physically abusing her one morning when he came back home after a night away. John moved out of the house and filed for divorce.

Excessive use of alcohol is one of the most frequent causes of divorce in the United States (Perreira & Sloan, 2001) and is often a hidden factor in the two most common causes—financial and sexual problems. The deterioration in interpersonal relationships of the alcohol abuser or dependent, of course, further augments the stress and disorganization in her or his life. The breakdown of marital relationships can be a highly stressful situation for many people. The stress of divorce and the often erratic adjustment period that follows can lead to increased substance abuse.

Family relationship problems have also been found to be central to the development of alcoholism (Dooley & Prause, 2007). In a classic longitudinal study of possible etiologic factors in alcohol abuse, Vaillant and colleagues (1982) described six family relationship factors that were significantly associated with the development of alcoholism in the individuals they studied. The most important family variables that were considered to predispose an individual to substance use problems were the presence of an alcoholic father, acute marital conflict, lax maternal supervision and inconsistent discipline, many moves during the family's early years, lack of "attachment" to the father, and lack of family cohesiveness.

Sociocultural Causal Factors

Alcohol use is a pervasive component in the social life of Western civilization. Social events often revolve around it, and alcohol use before and during meals is commonplace. Alcohol is often seen as a "social lubricant" or tension reducer that enhances social events. Thus, investigators have pointed to the role of sociocultural as well as biological and psychological factors in the high rate of alcohol abuse and dependence among Americans.

The effect of cultural attitudes toward drinking is well illustrated by Muslims and Mormons, whose religious values prohibit the use of alcohol, and by orthodox Jews, who have traditionally limited its use largely to religious rituals. The incidence of alcoholism among these groups is minimal. In comparison, the incidence of alcoholism is high among Europeans. For example, one survey showed the highest alcohol-use rates among young people to be in Denmark and Malta, where one in five students reported having drunk alcohol 10 times within the past 30 days (ESPAD, 2000). Interestingly, Europe and six countries that have been influenced by European culture—Argentina, Canada, Chile, Japan, New Zealand, and the United States—make up less than 20 percent of the world's population and yet consume 80 percent of the alcohol (Barry, 1982).

The behavior that is manifested under the influence of alcohol also seems to be influenced by cultural factors. Lindman and Lang (1994), in a study of alcohol-related behavior in eight countries, found that most people expressed the view that aggressive behavior frequently follows their drinking "many" drinks. However, the expectation that alcohol leads to aggression is related to cultural traditions and early exposure to violent or aggressive behavior.

In sum, we can identify many reasons why people drink—as well as many conditions that can predispose them to do so and reinforce their drinking behavior—but the exact combination of factors that results in a person's becoming an alcoholic is still unknown.

in review

- What neurobiological processes underlie addiction?
- What are the five major psychosocial causal factors that may contribute to alcohol abuse and dependence?

Treatment of Alcohol-Related Disorders

11.3 Discuss the treatment of alcohol-related disorders.

Alcohol abuse and dependence are difficult to treat because many people who abuse alcohol refuse to admit that they have a problem before they "hit bottom," and many who do go into treatment leave before therapy is completed. Addictions have been described as "diseases of denial" (DiClemente, 1993). Overall, less than one-third of those with alcohol use disorders receive treatment, and available treatments for alcohol-related disorders show modest effects (Hasin et al., 2007; Magill & Ray, 2009). In general, a multidisciplinary approach to the treatment of drinking problems appears to be most effective because the problems are often complex, requiring flexibility and individualization of treatment procedures (Margolis & Zweben, 1998). Also, a substance abuser's needs change as treatment progresses. Treatment objectives usually include detoxification, physical rehabilitation, control over alcohol abuse behavior, and the individual's realizing that he or she can cope with the problems of living and lead a much more rewarding life without alcohol.

Traditional treatment programs usually have as their goal abstinence from alcohol (Ambrogne, 2002). However, some programs attempt to promote controlled drinking as a treatment goal for problem drinkers. For example, the BMI procedure discussed earlier attempts to modify clients' behavior through providing information and advice about the consequences of the substance use in an effort to challenge the users about their use—but leaves the responsibility to the individual (Carey et al., 2007; Miller & Rollnik, 2002; Peterson et al., 2006). No matter what the treatment method, relapse is common, and many in the field see relapse as a factor that must be addressed in the treatment and recovery process.

Use of Medications in Treating Alcohol Abuse and Dependency

Biological approaches include a variety of treatment measures such as medications to reduce cravings, to ease the detoxification process, and to treat co-occurring health (National Institutes of Health, 2001) and mental health problems that may underlie the drinking behavior.

MEDICATIONS TO BLOCK THE DESIRE TO DRINK Disulfiram (Antabuse), a drug that causes violent vomiting when followed by ingestion of alcohol, may be administered to prevent an immediate return to drinking (Grossman & Ruiz, 2004). However, such deterrent therapy is seldom advocated as the sole approach because an alcohol-dependent person may simply discontinue the use of Antabuse when he or she is released from a hospital or clinic and begins to drink again. In fact, the primary value of drugs of this type seems to be their ability to interrupt the alcohol abuse cycle for a period of time during which therapy may be undertaken. Uncomfortable side effects may accompany the use of Antabuse; for example, alcohol-based aftershave lotion can be absorbed through the skin, resulting in illness. Moreover, the cost of Antabuse treatment, which requires careful medical maintenance, is higher than that for many other, more effective treatments.

Other medications used to treat alcohol use are naltrexone, an opiate antagonist that helps reduce the craving for alcohol by blocking the pleasure-producing effects of alcohol, and acamprosate, a drug whose properties are still being studied (Gueorguieva et al., 2007; Lee et al., 2010). A recent large-scale review of 122 randomized controlled trials testing the effects of medications for alcohol use disorders found that both naltrexone and acamprosate are effective at decreasing drinking and heavy drinking (Jonas et al., 2014).

MEDICATIONS TO REDUCE THE SIDE EFFECTS OF ACUTE WITHDRAWAL In cases of acute intoxication, the initial focus is on detoxification (the elimination of alcoholic substances from an individual's body), on treatment of the withdrawal symptoms described earlier, and on a medical regimen for physical rehabilitation. One of the primary goals in treatment of withdrawal symptoms is to reduce the physical symptoms characteristic of withdrawal such as insomnia, headache, gastrointestinal distress, and tremulousness. Central to the medical treatment approaches are the prevention of heart arrhythmias, seizures, delirium, and death. These steps can usually best be handled in a hospital or clinic, where drugs such as Valium have largely revolutionized the treatment of withdrawal symptoms. Such drugs overcome motor excitement, nausea, and vomiting; prevent withdrawal delirium and convulsions; and help alleviate the tension and anxiety associated with withdrawal. Pharmacological treatments with long-lasting benzodiazepines, such as diazepam, which reduce the severity of withdrawal symptoms, have been shown to be effective (Malcolm, 2003).

Concern is growing, however, that the use of tranquilizers—drugs that depress the CNS, resulting in calmness, relaxation, reduction of anxiety, and sleeping—does not promote long-term recovery and may simply transfer the addiction to another substance. Accordingly, some detoxification clinics are exploring alternative approaches including a gradual weaning from alcohol instead of a sudden cutoff. Maintenance doses of mild tranquilizers are sometimes given to patients withdrawing from alcohol to reduce anxiety and help them sleep. Such use of medications may be less effective than no treatment at all, however. Usually patients must learn to abstain from tranquilizers as well as from alcohol because they tend to misuse both. Further, under the influence of medications, patients may even return to alcohol use.

Psychological Treatment Approaches

Once the patient has her or his drinking under control, detoxification is optimally followed by psychological treatment, including family counseling and the use of community resources related to employment and other aspects of a person's social readjustment. Although individual psychotherapy is sometimes effective, the focus of psychosocial measures in the treatment of alcohol-related problems often involves group therapy, environmental intervention, behavior therapy, and the approach used by Alcoholics Anonymous and family groups such as Al-Anon and Alateen.

GROUP THERAPY Group therapy has been shown to be effective for many clinical problems (Galanter et al., 2005), especially substance-related disorders (Velasquez et al., 2001). In the confrontational give-and-take of group therapy, people who abuse alcohol are often forced (perhaps for the first time) to face their problems and their tendencies to deny or minimize them. These group situations can be extremely difficult for those who have been engrossed in denial of their own responsibilities, but such treatment also helps them see new possibilities for coping with circumstances that have led to their difficulties. Often this paves the way for them to learn more effective ways of coping and other positive steps toward dealing with their drinking problem.

In some instances, the spouses of people who abuse alcohol and even their children may be invited to join in group therapy meetings. In other situations, family treatment is itself the central focus of therapeutic efforts. Given that alcohol abuse and dependence can cause significant strains on family relationships, family therapy in such cases involves a delicate balance of educating the drinker about the familial consequences of her or his drinking, discussing any role that the family may have played in facilitating the drinking behavior (if any), and making plans for how the family can function most adaptively in the future.

ENVIRONMENTAL INTERVENTION As with other serious maladaptive behaviors, a total treatment program for alcohol abuse or dependency usually requires measures to alleviate a patient's aversive life situation. Environmental support has been shown to be an important ingredient of an alcohol abuser's recovery. People often become estranged from family and friends because of their drinking and either lose or jeopardize their jobs. As a result, they are often lonely and live in impoverished neighborhoods. Typically, the reaction of those around them is not as understanding or as supportive as it would be if the individual who abuses alcohol had a physical illness of comparable magnitude. Simply helping people with alcohol abuse problems learn more effective coping techniques may not be enough if their social environment remains hostile and threatening. For those who have been hospitalized, halfway houses—designed to assist them in their return to family and community—are often important adjuncts to their total treatment program.

BEHAVIORAL AND COGNITIVE-BEHAVIORAL THERAPY

An interesting and often effective form of treatment for alcohol-related disorders is behavioral therapy, of which several types exist. One is aversive conditioning therapy, which involves the presentation of a wide range of noxious stimuli with alcohol consumption in order to suppress drinking behavior. For example, the ingestion of alcohol might be paired with an electric shock or a drug that produces nausea. A variety of pharmacological and other deterrent measures can be used in behavioral therapy after detoxification. One approach involves an intramuscular injection of emetine hydrochloride, an emetic. Before experiencing the nausea that results from the injection, a patient is given alcohol, so that the sight, smell, and taste of the beverage become associated with severe retching and vomiting. That is, a conditioned aversion to the taste and smell of alcohol develops. With repetition, this classical conditioning procedure acts as a strong deterrent to further drinking—probably in part because it adds an immediate and unpleasant physiological consequence to the more general socially aversive consequences of excessive drinking.

Cognitive-behavioral therapy (CBT) is commonly used to treat alcohol-related problems (Marlatt, 1985; Witkiewitz & Marlatt, 2004). This approach combines cognitive-behavioral strategies of intervention with social-learning theory and modeling of behavior. The approach, often referred to as a "skills training procedure," is usually aimed at younger problem drinkers who are considered to be at risk for developing more severe drinking problems because of an alcohol abuse history in their family or their current heavy consumption. This approach relies on such techniques as imparting specific knowledge about alcohol, developing coping skills in situations associated with increased risk of alcohol use, modifying cognitions and expectancies, acquiring stress management skills, and providing training in life skills (Connors & Walitzer, 2001). Although CBT is a widely used treatment for many psychological conditions, it has so far shown only modest effects in the treatment of alcohol problems (Magill & Ray, 2009).

Self-control training techniques, such as the BMI procedure noted earlier, in which the goal of therapy is to get alcoholics to reduce alcohol intake without necessarily abstaining altogether, have a great deal of appeal for some drinkers. For example, one approach to improve drinking outcomes by altering the drinker's social networks was found to be successful (Litt et al., 2007), and motivational interviewing with adolescents was found to be promising in decreasing substance use (Macgowan & Engle, 2010). There is now even a computer-based self-control training program available that has been shown to reduce problem drinking in a controlled study (Fals-Stewart & Lam, 2010; Neighbors et al., 2004). It is difficult, of course, for individuals who are extremely dependent on the effects of alcohol to abstain totally from drinking. Thus, many alcoholics fail to complete traditional treatment programs.

Controlled Drinking versus Abstinence

Although many people believe that abstinence is the only effective treatment of alcohol dependence, some feel that problem drinkers need not give up drinking altogether but rather can learn to drink moderately (Miller, Walters, & Bennett, 2001; Sobell & Sobell, 1995). Several approaches to learning controlled drinking have been attempted, and research has suggested that some alcoholics can learn to control their alcohol intake (Senft et al., 1997). Miller and colleagues (1986) evaluated the results of four long-term follow-up studies of controlled-drinking treatment programs. Although they found a clear trend of increased numbers of abstainers and relapsed cases at long-term follow-up, they also found that a consistent percentage (15 percent) of subjects across the four studies controlled their drinking. The researchers concluded that controlled drinking was more likely to be successful in persons with less severe alcohol problems. The finding that some individuals are able to maintain some control over their drinking after treatment (without remaining totally abstinent) was also reported in a classic study by Polich et al. (1981). These researchers found that 18 percent of the alcoholics they studied had reportedly been able to drink socially without problems during the 6-month follow-up of treatment. Many people in the field have rejected the idea that people who abuse alcohol can learn to control their drinking, and some groups, such as Alcoholics Anonymous, are adamant in their opposition to programs aimed at controlled drinking for alcohol-dependent individuals.

Alcoholics Anonymous

A practical approach to alcoholism that has become very popular around the world is that of Alcoholics Anonymous (AA). This organization was started in 1935 by two men, Dr. Bob and Bill W., in Akron, Ohio. Bill W. recovered from alcoholism through a "fundamental spiritual change" and immediately sought out Dr. Bob, who, with Bill's assistance, also achieved recovery. They in turn began to help other alcoholics. Since that time, AA has grown to over 2 million members participating in more than 100,000 AA groups around the world (Alcoholics Anonymous, 2015).

Alcoholics Anonymous operates primarily as a self-help counseling program in which both person-to-person and group relationships are emphasized. AA accepts both teenagers and adults with drinking problems, has no dues or fees, does not keep records or case histories, does not participate in political causes, and is not affiliated with any religious sect, although spiritual development is a key aspect of its treatment approach. To ensure anonymity, only first names are used. Meetings are devoted partly to social activities, but they consist mainly of discussions of the participants' problems with alcohol, often with testimonials from those who have stopped drinking. Such members usually contrast their lives before they broke their alcohol dependence with the lives they now live without alcohol. We should point out here that the term *alcoholic* is used by AA and its affiliates to refer either to persons who currently are drinking excessively or to people who have stopped drinking but must, according to AA philosophy, continue to abstain from alcohol consumption in the future. That is, in the AA view, one is an alcoholic for life, whether or not one is drinking; one is never "cured" of alcoholism but is instead "in recovery."

An important aspect of AA's rehabilitation program is that it appears to lift the burden of personal responsibility by helping alcoholics accept that alcoholism, like many other problems, is bigger than they are. Henceforth, they can see themselves not as weak willed or lacking in moral strength but rather simply as having an affliction—they cannot drink—just as other people may not be able to tolerate certain types of medication. Through mutual help and

These people are participating in an Alcoholics Anonymous meeting. AA accepts both teenagers and adults, has no dues or fees, does not keep records or case histories, does not participate in political causes, and is not affiliated with any religious sect, although spiritual development is a key aspect of its treatment approach. To ensure anonymity, only first names are used at meetings. AA is one of the most popular alcohol treatment programs, promoting total abstinence rather than controlled drinking.

reassurance from group members who have had similar experiences, many alcoholics acquire insight into their problems, a new sense of purpose, greater ego strength, and more effective coping techniques. Continued participation in the group, of course, can help prevent the crisis of a relapse. Affiliated movements such as Al-Anon family groups and Alateen are designed to bring family members together to share experiences and problems, to gain understanding of the nature of alcoholism, and to learn techniques for dealing with their own problems living in a family with one or more affected individuals.

The reported success of Alcoholics Anonymous is based primarily on anecdotal information rather than on objective study of treatment outcomes because AA does not directly participate in external comparative research efforts. Comprehensive reviews aimed at determining the effectiveness of AA's 12-step approach have been inconclusive. AA has not been shown to be any more effective than other treatment approaches, and more studies are needed that carefully evaluate the effectiveness of this approach (Ferri et al., 2006).

Outcome Studies and Issues in Treatment

The outcome of treatment for alcohol-related disorders varies considerably, depending on the population studied and on the treatment facilities and procedures employed. Results range from low rates of success for hard-core substance abusers to recovery rates of 70 to 90 percent when modern treatment and aftercare procedures are used. Treatment is most likely to be effective when an individual realizes that she or he needs help, when adequate treatment facilities are available, and when the individual attends treatment regularly.

Back in the 1940s and 1950s, psychologists used psychoanalytic and psychodynamic approaches as well as aversion therapies to try to explain and treat alcohol use disorders. More recently, however, brief interventions like "motivational interviewing" have received much more attention and support (McCrady et al., 2014). Motivational interviewing (MI) is a brief intervention that was designed to be a major departure from earlier confrontational approaches in which a clinician suggested that the drinker stop consuming so much alcohol. Instead, in MI the clinician guides the patient through a collaborative conversation in which the patient articulates the pros and cons of drinking and ultimately makes a decision about whether she or he is motivated to change (Miller & Rollnick, 2012). One great strength of MI is that it can administered in one brief (35-minute) session, and still have positive effects. For instance, one recent study found that adolescents visiting an emergency department (ED) with alcohol problems and aggression who were randomly assigned to receive a brief MI-focused intervention via a clinician or computer (compared to those who received no such intervention) showed significant reductions in their drinking and aggression up to 6 months after this brief intervention (Walton et al., 2010)

Some researchers have maintained that treatment for alcohol use and abuse disorders would be more effective if important patient characteristics (e.g., personality characteristics, degrees of severity) were considered. This view was evaluated in a study of patient–treatment matching (referred to as "Project MATCH") that was sponsored by the NIAAA (1997). This extensive study, initiated in 1989, involved 1,726 patients who were treated in 26 alcohol treatment programs in the United States by 80 different therapists representing three treatment approaches. The research design included both inpatient and outpatient treatment components. The results of this study were unexpected: Matching the patients to particular treatments did not appear to be important to having an effective outcome because the treatments studied all had equal outcomes. Gordis (1997) concludes that patients from competently run alcoholism treatment programs will do as well in any of the three treatments studied.

Relapse Prevention

One of the greatest problems in the treatment of addictive disorders is maintaining abstinence or self-control once the behavioral excesses have been checked. Most alcohol treatment programs show high success rates in getting people to stop drinking for the time being, but many programs show lessening rates of abstinence or controlled drinking at various follow-up periods. That is, it is one thing to get someone to stop drinking for 30 days, but some have argued that many treatment programs do not pay enough attention to maintaining effective behavior and preventing relapse into previous maladaptive patterns (Miller & Rollnick, 2012). Given that alcohol-dependent people are highly vulnerable to relapse, some researchers have focused on the need to help them remain abstinent. In one cognitive-behavioral approach, relapse behavior is a key factor in alcohol treatment (Witkiewitz & Marlatt, 2007). One recent study (Nattala et al., 2010) found that relapse prevention treatment worked most effectively when family members were involved in the treatment.

The behaviors underlying relapse are seen as "indulgent behaviors" that are based on an individual's learning history. When an individual is abstinent or has an addiction under control, she or he gains a sense of personal control over the indulgent behavior. The longer the person is able to maintain this control, the greater the sense of achievement—the self-efficacy or confidence—and the greater the chance that she or he will be able to cope with the addiction and maintain control. However, a person may violate this rule of abstinence through a gradual, perhaps unconscious, process rather than through the sudden "falling off the wagon" that constitutes the traditional view of craving and relapse. In the cognitive-behavioral view, a person may, even while maintaining abstinence, inadvertently make a series of mini-decisions that begin a chain of behaviors that render relapse inevitable. For example, an abstinent alcohol abuser who buys a quart of bourbon just in case his friends drop by is unconsciously preparing the way for relapse.

Appealing advertisements and displays that encourage drinking can make abstinence particularly difficult and can contribute, at the very least on a subconscious level, to a relapse.

Another type of relapse behavior involves the "abstinence violation effect," in which even minor transgressions are seen by the abstainer as having drastic significance. The effect works this way: An abstinent person may hold that she or he should not, under any circumstance, transgress or give in to the old habit. Abstinence-oriented treatment programs are particularly guided by this prohibitive rule. What happens, then, when an abstinent person becomes somewhat self-indulgent and takes a drink offered by an old friend or joins in a wedding toast? He or she may lose some of the sense of self-efficacy—confidence—needed to control his or her drinking. Feeling guilty about having technically violated the vow of abstinence, the person may rationalize that he or she "has blown it and become a drunk again, so why not go all the way?"

In *relapse prevention treatment*, clients are taught to recognize the apparently irrelevant decisions that serve as early warning signals of the possibility of relapse. High-risk situations such as parties or sports events are targeted, and the individuals learn to assess their own vulnerability to relapse. Clients are also trained not to become so discouraged that if they do relapse they lose their confidence. Some cognitive-behavioral therapists have even incorporated a "planned relapse" phase into the treatment. Research with relapse prevention strategies has shown them to be effective in providing continuing improvement over time (Rawson et al., 2002). In other words, when patients are taught to expect a relapse, they are better able to handle it.

in review

- Describe four psychosocial interventions used to treat alcohol dependence.

Drug Abuse and Dependence

11.4 List the psychoactive drugs most commonly associated with abuse and dependence.

Following alcohol, the psychoactive drugs most commonly associated with abuse and dependence in our society appear to be (1) opiates, including opium and heroin; (2) stimulants such as cocaine and amphetamines as well as caffeine and nicotine (disorders associated with tobacco withdrawal and caffeine intoxication are included in the *DSM-5* diagnostic classification system); (3) sedatives such as barbiturates; (4) hallucinogens such as LSD; (5) antianxiety drugs such as benzodiazepines; and (6) pain medications such as OxyContin (Whoriskey, 2013); The effects of these and other drugs are summarized in Table 11.3.

An estimated 21.6 million Americans ages 12 years or older report using at least one illicit drug during the past year (SAMHSA, 2014). According to the *Monitoring the Future* study, the annual prevalence rate of using any illicit drug is 37 percent for 12th graders, 35 percent for college students, and 34 percent for 19- to 28-year-olds (Johnston et al., 2009). Although they may occur at any age, drug abuse and dependence are most common during adolescence and young adulthood (Campbell, 2010).

The impact of drug use among employed people is significant. In an extensive survey of illegal drug use among 40,000 currently employed workers, researchers found the following rates of illicit drug use within the month prior to the survey: 19 percent for those 18 years of age or younger, 10.3 percent for those between 18 and 25 years, 7 percent for those between 26 and 34 years, 7 percent for those between 35 and 49 years, and 2.6 percent for those between 50 and 64 years (Larson et al., 2007). The overall frequency of illegal drug use in this work sample was 8.2 percent. The high rate of drug use in this population (many reported actually using drugs on the job) is problematic. For example, among those workers who reported current illicit drug use, 12.3 percent reported that they had worked for three or more employers in the past year, compared with 5.1 percent for nonabusing workers.

Among people who abuse drugs, behavior patterns vary markedly depending on the type, amount, and duration of drug use; on the physiological and psychological makeup of the individual; and, in some instances, on the

Table 11.3 Psychoactive Drugs Commonly Involved in Drug Abuse

Classification	Drug	Effect
Sedatives	Alcohol (ethanol)	Reduces tension Facilitates social interaction "Blots out" feelings or events
	Barbiturates 　Nembutal (pentobarbital) 　Seconal (secobarbital) 　Veronal (barbital) 　Tuinal (secobarbital and amobarbital)	Reduce tension
Stimulants	Amphetamines 　Benzedrine (amphetamine) 　Dexedrine (dextroamphetamine) 　Methedrine (methamphetamine) 　Cocaine (coca)	Increase feelings of alertness and confidence Decrease feelings of fatigue Stay awake for long periods Increase endurance Stimulate sex drive
Opiates	Opium and its derivatives 　Opium 　Morphine 　Codeine 　Heroin Methadone (synthetic narcotic)	Alleviate physical pain Induce relaxation and pleasant reverie Alleviate anxiety and tension Treatment of heroin dependence
Hallucinogens	Cannabis 　Marijuana 　Hashish Mescaline (peyote) 　Psilocybin (psychotogenic mushrooms) 　LSD (lysergic acid diethylamide-25) 　PCP (phencyclidine)	Induce changes in mood, thought, and behavior "Expand" one's mind Induce stupor
Antianxiety drugs (minor tranquilizers)	Librium (chlordiazepoxide) Miltown (meprobamate) Valium (diazepam) Xanax	Alleviate tension and anxiety Induce relaxation and sleep

Note: This list is by no means complete; for example, it does not include drugs such as Ritalin, which are designed to produce multiple effects; it does not include the less commonly used volatile hydrocarbons such as glue, paint thinner, gasoline, cleaning fluid, and nail polish remover, which are highly dangerous when sniffed for their psychoactive effects; and it does not include the antipsychotic and antidepressant drugs, which are abused, but relatively rarely. We discuss these and the antianxiety drugs in our discussion of drug therapy in Chapter 16.

social setting in which the drug experience occurs. Thus, it appears most useful to deal separately with some of the drugs that are more commonly associated with abuse and dependence in contemporary society.

Opium and Its Derivatives

11.5 Describe the commonly used opiates and their effects on the body.

People have used opium and its derivatives for centuries. Galen (A.D. 130–201) considered theriac, whose principal ingredient was opium, to be a panacea:

> It resists poison and venomous bites, cures inveterate headache, vertigo, deafness, epilepsy, apoplexy, dimness of sight, loss of voice, asthma, coughs of all kinds, spitting of blood, tightness of breath, colic, the iliac poisons, jaundice, hardness of the spleen, stone, urinary complaints, fevers, dropsies, leprosies, the trouble to which women are subject, melancholy and all pestilences. (See Brock, 1979, for a discussion of Galen.)

Even today, opiates are still used for some of the conditions Galen mentioned.

Opium is a mixture of about 18 chemical substances known as alkaloids. In 1805, the alkaloid present in the largest amount (10–15 percent) was found to be a bitter-tasting powder that could serve as a powerful sedative and pain reliever; it was named **morphine** after Morpheus, the god of sleep in Greek mythology. The hypodermic needle was introduced in America around 1856, allowing morphine to be widely administered to soldiers during the Civil War—not only to those wounded in battle but also to those suffering from dysentery (an illness with symptoms including abdominal pain and diarrhea with blood). As a consequence, many Civil War veterans returned to civilian life addicted to the drug, a condition euphemistically referred to as "soldier's illness."

Scientists concerned with the addictive properties of morphine hypothesized that one part of the morphine molecule might be responsible for its analgesic properties (that is, its ability to eliminate pain without a loss of consciousness) and another for its addictiveness. At about the turn of the century, it was discovered that if morphine was treated with an inexpensive and readily available chemical called acetic anhydride, it would be converted into another powerful analgesic called **heroin**. Heroin was hailed enthusiastically by its discoverer, Heinrich Dreser (Boehm, 1968). Leading scientists of his time agreed on the merits of heroin, and the drug came to be widely prescribed in place of morphine for pain relief and related medicinal purposes. Unfortunately, heroin proved to be an even more dangerous drug than morphine, acting more rapidly and more intensely and being equally, if not more, addictive. Eventually, heroin was removed from use in medical practice.

As it became apparent that opium and its derivatives—including codeine, which is used in some cough syrups—were extremely addictive, the U.S. Congress enacted the Harrison Act in 1914. Under this and later legislation, the unauthorized sale and distribution of certain drugs became a federal offense; physicians and pharmacists were held accountable for each dose they dispensed. Thus, overnight, the role of a chronic narcotic user changed from that of addict—whose addiction was considered a vice, but was tolerated—to that of criminal. Unable to obtain drugs through legal sources, many turned to illegal channels, and eventually to other criminal acts, as a means of maintaining their suddenly expensive drug supply. In 2011, heroin use accounted for approximately 20 percent of all drug-abuse-related ED admissions (SAMHSA, 2013).

The adolescent shown here is injecting the drug heroin—a dangerous and highly addictive substance that is widely available to adolescents today.

Biological Effects of Morphine and Heroin

Morphine and heroin are commonly introduced into the body by smoking, snorting (inhaling the powder), eating, "skin popping," or "mainlining," the last two being methods of introducing the drug via hypodermic injection. Skin popping is injecting the liquefied drug just beneath the skin, while mainlining is injecting the drug directly into the bloodstream.

Among the immediate effects of mainlined or snorted heroin is an intense feeling of euphoria (the rush) lasting 60 seconds or so, which many addicts compare to a sexual orgasm. However, vomiting and nausea have also been known to be part of the immediate effects of heroin and morphine use. This rush is followed by a high, during which an addict typically is in a lethargic, withdrawn state in which bodily needs, including needs for food and sex, are markedly diminished; pleasant feelings of relaxation and euphoria tend to dominate. These effects last from 4 to 6 hours and are followed—in addicts—by a negative phase that produces a desire for more of the drug.

The use of opiates over a period of time generally results in a physiological craving for the drug. The time required to establish the drug habit varies, but it has been estimated that continual use over a period of 30 days is sufficient. Users then find that they have become physiologically dependent on the drug in the sense that they feel physically ill when they do not take it. In addition, users of opiates gradually build up a tolerance to the drug so increasingly larger amounts are needed to achieve the desired effects.

When people addicted to opiates do not get another dose of the drug within approximately 8 hours of their last dose, they start to experience withdrawal symptoms. The character and severity of these reactions depend on many factors including the amount of the narcotic habitually used, the intervals between doses, the duration of the addiction, and especially the addict's health and personality.

Withdrawal from heroin is not always dangerous or even very painful. Many addicted people withdraw without assistance. Withdrawal can, however, be an agonizing experience for some people, with symptoms including runny nose, tearing eyes, perspiration, restlessness, increased respiration rate, and an intensified desire for the drug. As time passes, the symptoms may become more severe. Typically, a feeling of chilliness alternates with flushing and excessive sweating, vomiting, diarrhea, abdominal cramps, pains in the back and extremities, severe headache, marked tremors, and varying degrees of insomnia. Beset by these discomforts, an individual refuses food and water, and this, coupled with the vomiting, sweating, and diarrhea, results in dehydration and weight loss. Occasionally, symptoms include delirium, hallucinations, and manic activity. Cardiovascular collapse may also occur and can result in death. If morphine is administered, the subjective distress experienced by an addict temporarily ends and physiological balance is quickly restored.

Withdrawal symptoms usually decline by the third or fourth day and by the seventh or eighth day have disappeared. As the symptoms subside, the person resumes normal eating and drinking and rapidly regains lost weight. After withdrawal symptoms have ceased, the individual's former tolerance for the drug is reduced; as a result, there is a risk that taking the former large dosage might result in overdose.

Social Effects of Morphine and Heroin

Typically, the life of a person addicted to opiates becomes increasingly centered on obtaining and using drugs, so the addiction usually leads to socially maladaptive behavior as the individual does whatever he or she can (e.g., lying, stealing) to maintain a supply of drugs. Many addicts resort to petty theft to support their habits, and some turn to prostitution as a means of financing their addictions.

Along with the lowering of ethical and moral restraints, addiction has adverse physical effects on an individual's well-being—for example, disruption of the immune system (Theodorou & Haber, 2005). Lifestyle factors can lead to further problems; an inadequate diet, for example, may lead to ill health and increased susceptibility to a variety of physical ailments. The use of unsterile equipment may also lead to various problems including liver damage from hepatitis (Lucey et al., 2009) and transmission of the AIDS virus. In addition, the use of such a potent drug without medical supervision and government controls to ensure its strength and purity can result in fatal overdose. Injection of too much heroin can cause coma and death. In fact, heroin-related deaths have shown an increase in cities where data are collected (SAMHSA, 2013). The most common drug-related deaths in the United States involve combinations of heroin, cocaine, and alcohol. Women who use heroin during pregnancy subject their unborn children to the risk of dire consequences. One tragic outcome is premature babies who are themselves addicted to heroin and vulnerable to a number of diseases.

Heroin is a dangerous substance on its own, but becomes especially harmful in combination with other drugs. The combination of heroin with substances like cocaine and alcohol can be lethal, and sadly led to the recent deaths of actors Philip Seymour Hoffman and Corey Monteith.

Addiction to opiates usually leads to a gradual deterioration of well-being (Brown & Lo, 2000). For example, some research has shown that opiates actively alter the immune system, rendering the person vulnerable to organ damage (McHugh & Kreek, 2004). The ill health and general personality degeneration often found in opiate addiction do not always result directly from the pharmacological effects of the drug, however; rather, they are often products of the sacrifices of money, proper diet, social position, and self-respect as an addict becomes more desperate to procure the required daily dosage.

Causal Factors in Opiate Abuse and Dependence

No single causal pattern fits all addictions to opiates, and both genetic and environmental influences seem to play a role (Kendler, Sundquist, et al., 2012). The three most frequently cited reasons that people given for beginning to use heroin are pleasure, curiosity, and peer pressure (e.g., Fulmer & Lapidus, 1980). Pleasure is, by far, the single most widespread reason—given by 81 percent of addicts. Other reasons such as a desire to escape life stress, personal maladjustment, and sociocultural conditions also play a part. It also has been suggested that various forms of substance abuse such as smoking, drinking, and the use of drugs are all related to a personality characteristic referred to as "sensation seeking," which is itself thought to be mediated through genetic and biological mechanisms as well as through peer influences (Zuckerman, 2007).

Neural Bases for Physiological Addiction

Drugs of abuse work by acting on different neural receptors in the brain. Receptor sites are found on specific nerve cells into which given psychoactive drugs fit like keys into locks. Opiate drugs work by binding to opiate receptors in specific parts of the brain that are involved in the regulation of pleasure, pain, and breathing (Lukas, 2015). The human body produces its own opium-like substances, called **endorphins**, in the central nervous system and pituitary gland. Heroin plugs into opiate receptors (taking the place of endorphins), but works much more quickly and intensely, producing the extreme euphoria described above. This intensely positive feeling leads some people to use heroin over and over again, sometimes multiple times per day, in order to reexperience that euphoric feeling. Over time, people build up tolerance in which more and more of the drug is required to produce the same high. Over repeated administrations, a person will also begin to experience withdrawal symptoms when the drug wears off, and so must either suffer through those symptoms or readminister the drug in order to stop the withdrawal symptoms and reexperience euphoria yet again. This can develop into a vicious cycle that is difficult for many to escape.

Not all drugs work by binding to opiate receptors; however, there does seem to be a common pathway for all addictions, both drug (e.g., alcohol, opiates, cocaine) and nondrug (e.g., gambling) related. The **dopamine theory of addiction** suggests that addiction is the result of a dysfunction of the dopamine reward pathway (Diana, 2011; Wise, 1980). This pathway, also called the "pleasure pathway," as mentioned earlier in our discussion of alcohol addiction, was first discovered in seminal work by Olds and Milner (1954), who found that rats would repeatedly press a lever to self-stimulate certain areas of their brain (via electrodes placed there)

instead of engaging in any other activity. Researchers later realized that what Olds and Milner had stumbled upon was the dopamine reward pathway, which stretches from the ventral tegmental area to the nucleus accumbens (see Figure 11.2 earlier in this chapter), which in turn connects with other parts of the brain such as the amygdala and prefrontal cortex. Early versions of the dopamine theory of addiction suggested that all addictive drugs (e.g., alcohol, opiates, cocaine) and behaviors (e.g., gambling) activate the dopamine reward pathway, thus causing pleasure and increasing the likelihood of drug use and engagement in addictive behavior.

Several decades of research, however, have demonstrated that the picture appears to be much more complex than that, and the pleasure experienced in response to drug use is not simply the result of elevated levels of dopamine (Berridge & Kringelbach, 2015; Nutt et al., 2015). Although much remains to be learned about the addiction process, several additional pieces of the puzzle have been recently discovered and are fairly well agreed on by researchers. First, if substances and experiences that lead to pleasurable internal states were the whole story, then exposure to these things would explain addiction. However, it is clear that people differ in their vulnerability to addiction—some of us can have one drink and then stop, whereas others of us have a strong urge to keep drinking over and over again. The **reward deficiency syndrome** hypothesis suggests that addiction is much more likely to occur in individuals who have genetic deviations in components of the reward pathway, which leads them to be less satisfied by natural rewards (e.g., from food, sex, drugs, and other pleasurable activities), which in turn leads them to overuse drugs and related experiences as a way to adequately stimulate their reward pathway (Blum et al., 1996; 2015). Significant evidence has emerged to support the reward deficiency syndrome hypothesis during the past several decades; however, with this supportive evidence has come the further realization that understanding addiction does not come down to pinpointing a specific, deficient gene, but in understanding how genetic, neural, and environmental factors interact to lead to addictive behavior (Blum et al., 2015).

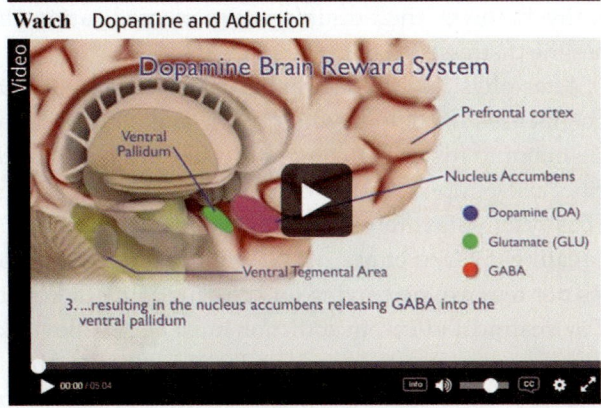

Watch Dopamine and Addiction

Second, researchers have come to understand that there is not a simple, single "pleasure pathway" in the brain. For instance, although dopaminergic pathways play a primary role in the "wanting" or anticipation of reward, it is the opioid system that seems to play a primary role in the "liking" or consumption of rewarding stimuli (Smith & Berridge, 2007). Findings such as these highlight that dopamine plays an important role in the neural understanding of addiction, but that other neurotransmitters, and other explanations altogether, may be needed to fully understand how and why people become addicted to substance use and other behaviors.

Addiction Associated with Psychopathology

Opioid abuse is associated with a dramatically increased risk of other forms of psychopathology, as well as a range of other negative outcomes. More specifically, approximately 70 percent of people who abuse opioids have other psychological diagnoses, 50 percent have other forms of substance abuse, and 36 percent have a history of trauma (White et al., 2005). Moreover, people who abuse opioids are significantly more likely than nonabusers to use the full range of medical services (e.g., mental health visits, ED visits, hospital stays; White et al., 2005). The direction and causal associations of these comorbidities are not yet clear. It may be that psychological disorders like depression and anxiety lead people to use opiates as a way to escape from their negative thoughts and feelings. But it is also possible that the negative consequences of opiate use lead people to be depressed and anxious, or both. Either way, it is clear that opiate addiction is associated with a host of other problems that must be understood, assessed, and addressed in each case.

Treatments and Outcomes

Treatment for opiate addiction is initially similar to that for alcoholism in that it involves restoring physical and psychological health and providing help through the withdrawal period. Addicts often dread the discomfort of withdrawal, but in a hospital setting it is less abrupt and usually involves the administration of medication that eases the distress.

After physical withdrawal has been completed, treatment focuses on helping the person make an adequate adjustment to his or her community and abstain from the further use of opiates. Traditionally, however, the prognosis has been unfavorable, with many clients dropping out of treatment (Katz et al., 2004). Withdrawal from heroin does not remove the craving for the drug. Thus, a key target in treatment of heroin addiction must be the alleviation of this craving. One approach to dealing with the physiological craving for heroin was pioneered by a research

team at Rockefeller University in New York. It involved the use of the drug **methadone** in conjunction with a rehabilitation program (counseling, group therapy, and other procedures) directed toward the "total resocialization" of addicts. Methadone hydrochloride is a synthetic narcotic that is related to heroin and is equally addictive physiologically. Its usefulness in treatment lies in the fact that it satisfies an addict's craving for heroin without producing serious psychological impairment, if only because it is administered as a "treatment" in a formal clinical context and can result in reduced drug use and improved cognitive performance (Gruber et al., 2006; Kreek et al., 2010). (See the Unresolved Issues section at the end of this chapter.)

Other medications, such as buprenorphine, have also been used to treat heroin addiction (Meier & Patkar, 2007). Buprenorphine promises to be as effective a substitute for heroin as methadone but with fewer side effects (Ling et al., 2010). It operates as a partial antagonist to heroin and produces the feelings of contentment associated with heroin use (Mendelson & Mello, 1992). Yet the drug does not produce the physical dependence that is characteristic of heroin (Grant & Sonti, 1994) and can be discontinued without severe withdrawal symptoms. Like methadone, buprenorphine appears to work best at maintaining abstinence if it is provided along with behavior therapy (Bickel et al., 1997).

---

in review

- What are the major biological and psychological effects of using opiates such as morphine and heroin?
- What are the three major causal factors in the development of opiate abuse and dependence?

Stimulants

11.6 Discuss the different types of stimulants and their effects.

In contrast to opiates, which depress (slow down) the action of the CNS, cocaine, amphetamines, methamphetamine, caffeine, and nicotine stimulate it (speed it up).

Cocaine

Like opium, **cocaine** is a plant product discovered in ancient times and used ever since. It was widely used in the pre-Columbian world of Mexico and Peru, where leaves of the coca plant were wrapped around lime and placed inside the cheek to provide a slow release— allowing workers to decrease their hunger and elevate their mood and energy so they could work long hours (Guerra, 1971). Cocaine later gained popularity in the 1880s when Sigmund Freud came to see it as a wonderful treatment for depression, indigestion, and a range of other maladies.

Arthur Conan Doyle described how his fictional character—Sherlock Holmes—enjoyed the drug, and entrepreneur John Pemberton included it as a key ingredient in his new soft drink: Coca-Cola™ (Markel, 2011). As the dangers of cocaine became apparent in the early 1900s, it was made illegal and its use decreased dramatically. When banned in the United States, it became very costly to obtain and was considered as the "high" for the affluent. However, with more widespread availability and lowering of prices, the drug's use increased significantly in the United States during the 1980s and 1990s—to the point where its use was considered epidemic, especially among middle- and upper-income groups. "Crack" is the street name that is applied to cocaine that has been processed from cocaine hydrochloride to a free base for smoking. The name refers to the crackling sound emitted when the mixture is heated. Cocaine is still illegal; however, approximately 0.6 percent of those 12 years or older report having used cocaine in the past month (SAMHSA, 2013).

Like the opiates, cocaine may be ingested by sniffing, swallowing, or injecting. However, cocaine affects the brain in a different way than alcohol or opioids. Cocaine has its primary effect by blocking the presynaptic dopamine transporter (whose job it is to retrieve excess dopamine from the synapse), thus increasing the availability of dopamine in the synapse and increasing the activation of the receiving cells. The increase of dopamine activity in the nucleus accumbens is believed to be especially important in cocaine addiction, because specific parts of this brain region have been suggested to be "hedonic hot spots" that have been consistently associated with the experience of reward and pleasure (Berridge & Kringelbach, 2015).

Watch Dopamine and Cocaine

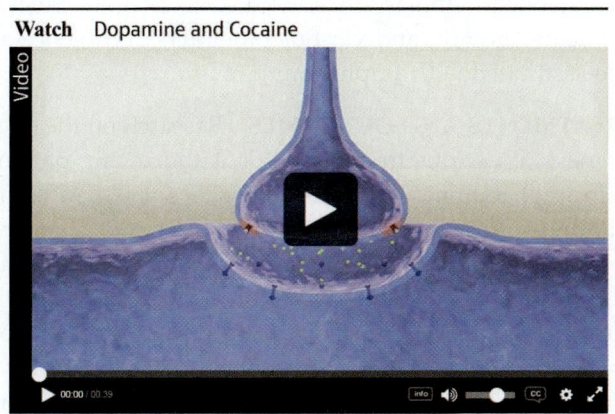

Also like the opiates, the euphoric state resulting from cocaine use lasts for 4 to 6 hours, during which a user experiences feelings of confidence and contentment. However, this blissful state may be followed by headache, dizziness, and restlessness. When cocaine is chronically abused, acute toxic psychotic symptoms may occur, including frightening visual, auditory, and tactile hallucinations similar to those in acute schizophrenia.

Many people develop both acute and chronic tolerance to cocaine over time. Moreover, cognitive impairment associated with cocaine abuse is likely to be an important consideration in long-term effects of the drug (Abi-Saab et al., 2005; Mann, 2004). The psychological and life problems experienced by cocaine users are often great. Employment, family, psychological, and legal problems are all more likely to occur among cocaine and crack users than among nonusers. Many life problems experienced by cocaine abusers result in part from the considerable amounts of money that are required to support their habits.

Women who use cocaine when they are pregnant place their babies at risk for both health and psychological problems. Although research has suggested that there is no "fetal crack syndrome" similar to the syndrome associated with mothers who abuse alcohol (Azar, 1997), children of crack-using mothers are at risk of being maltreated as infants as well as of losing their mothers during infancy. Wasserman and Leventhal (1993) studied a group of cocaine-exposed children and a control sample of nonexposed children for a 24-month period following their birth. They found that children who were regularly exposed to cocaine *in utero* were more likely to be mistreated (23 percent compared with only 4 percent of controls).

TREATMENTS AND OUTCOMES   Treatment for cocaine dependence is similar in many ways to that for other drugs that involve physiological dependence (Schmitz et al., 2004). To reduce cravings as part of psychological therapy and to ensure treatment compliance, drugs such as naltrexone and methadone have been used to reduce cocaine use (Carroll et al., 2004; Weinstock et al., 2010). The feelings of tension and depression that accompany absence of the drug have to be dealt with during the immediate withdrawal period.

Despite cocaine's addictive potential, psychological interventions have proven to be quite effective in successfully treating cocaine dependence. A recent review of 34 studies testing psychological treatments for substance use disorders evaluated in randomized controlled trials reported that both CBT (described earlier) and contingency management (CM) approaches are effective treatments for substance use disorders (Dutra et al., 2008). CBT for cocaine dependence focuses on teaching patients cognitive and behavioral skills intended to help them navigate daily life and difficult situations without engaging in drug use. It has proven to be an effective method of decreasing cocaine use in those meeting the criteria for cocaine dependence, even when administered in a fully computerized form (Carroll et al., 2014). CM is based on the principles of operant conditioning and offers rewards or financial incentives for meeting agreed-on treatment targets (e.g., drug-free urine). CM has been shown to be slightly more effective than CBT for cocaine dependence

(Dutra et al., 2008; Farronato et al., 2013). Recent research has shown that CM is just as effective when it uses relatively low-cost reinforcers (Petry et al., 2014). Importantly, recent research has shown that psychological treatments for cocaine dependence are associated with decreases not just in cocaine use but in a range of other problems (Kiluk et al., 2014), are effective in both men and women (DeVito et al., 2014), and are no less effective in patients who are referred for treatment by the criminal justice system (Kiluk et al., 2015).

Amphetamines

The earliest **amphetamine** to be introduced—Benzedrine, or amphetamine sulfate—was first synthesized in 1927 and became available in drugstores in the early 1930s as an inhalant to relieve stuffy noses. However, the manufacturers soon learned that some customers were chewing the wicks in the inhalers for "kicks." Thus, the stimulating effects of amphetamine sulfate were discovered by the public before the drug was formally prescribed as a stimulant by physicians. In the late 1930s, two newer amphetamines were introduced: Dexedrine (dextroamphetamine) and Methedrine (methamphetamine hydrochloride, also known as "speed"). The latter preparation is a far more potent stimulant of the CNS than either Benzedrine or Dexedrine and hence is considered more dangerous. In fact, its abuse can be lethal.

Initially these preparations were considered to be "wonder pills" that helped people stay alert and awake and function temporarily at a level beyond normal. During World War II, the military became interested in the stimulating effects of these drugs and they were used by soldiers to ward off fatigue (Jarvik, 1967). Similarly, among civilians, amphetamines came to be widely used by night workers, long-distance truck drivers, students cramming for exams, and athletes striving to improve their performance. It was also discovered that amphetamines tend to suppress appetite, and they became popular with people trying to lose weight. In addition, they were often used to counteract the effects of barbiturates or other sleeping pills that had been taken the night before. As a result of their many uses, amphetamines were widely prescribed by doctors.

Today amphetamines are occasionally used medically for curbing appetite when weight reduction is desirable; for treating individuals suffering from narcolepsy, a disorder in which people cannot prevent themselves from continually falling asleep during the day; and for treating hyperactive children. Curiously enough, amphetamines have a calming rather than a stimulating effect on those with ADHD. Amphetamines also are sometimes prescribed for alleviating mild feelings of depression, relieving fatigue, and maintaining alertness for sustained periods of time.

Since the passage of the Controlled Substance Act of 1970 (Drug Enforcement Administration, 1979), amphetamines have been classified as Schedule II controlled substances—that is, drugs with high abuse potential that require a prescription for each purchase. As a result, medical use of amphetamines has declined in the United States in recent years and they are more difficult to obtain legally. However, it is often possible to find illegal sources of amphetamines, which thus remain among the most widely abused drugs. Amphetamines are among the most widely used illicit drugs in other countries as well (Lintzeris et al., 1996). Approximately 7 percent of drug-related ED visits involve amphetamines or methamphetamines (SAMHSA, 2013).

EFFECTS OF AMPHETAMINE ABUSE Despite their legitimate medical uses, amphetamines are not a source of extra mental or physical energy. Instead, they push users toward greater expenditures of their own resources—often to the point of hazardous fatigue. Amphetamines are psychologically and physically addictive, and the body rapidly builds up tolerance to them (Wise, 1996). Thus, habituated abusers may use the drugs in amounts that would be lethal to nonusers. In some instances, users inject the drug to get faster and more intense results.

For a person who exceeds prescribed dosages, amphetamine consumption results in heightened blood pressure, enlarged pupils, unclear or rapid speech, profuse sweating, tremors, excitability, loss of appetite, confusion, and sleeplessness. Injected in large quantities, Methedrine can raise blood pressure enough to cause immediate death. In addition, chronic abuse of amphetamines can result in brain damage and a wide range of psychopathology, including a disorder known as "amphetamine psychosis," which appears similar to paranoid schizophrenia. Suicide, homicide, assault, and various other acts of violence are also associated with amphetamine abuse.

TREATMENTS AND OUTCOMES Research on the effectiveness of various treatments for withdrawing patients from amphetamines is scarce (Baker & Lee, 2003). Although withdrawal from amphetamines is usually safe, some evidence suggests that physiological dependence on the drug is an important factor to consider in treatment (Wise & Munn, 1995). In some instances, abrupt withdrawal from the chronic, excessive use of amphetamines can result in cramping, nausea, diarrhea, and even convulsions. Moreover, abrupt abstinence commonly results in feelings of weariness and depression. The depression usually peaks in 48 to 72 hours, often remains intense for a day or two, and then tends to lessen gradually over a period of several days. Mild feelings of depression and lassitude may persist for weeks or even months. If brain damage has occurred, the residual effects may include impaired ability to concentrate, learn, and remember, with resulting social, economic, and personality deterioration.

Methamphetamine

Methamphetamine, referred to on the streets as "crystal meth" or "ice" because of its appearance, is a highly addictive stimulant drug that can provide an immediate and long-lasting "high." However, it is one of the most dangerous illegal drugs (Covey, 2007). Methamphetamine is a form of amphetamine that can be "cooked" in large quantities in makeshift laboratories (e.g., within peoples' own homes). It can be manufactured, for example, in a portable cooler with ingredients that can be legally obtained from any drugstore. This drug is relatively cheap to manufacture and is sometimes referred to as "poor people's cocaine." Like cocaine and heroin, it can be ingested in a variety of ways, through smoking, snorting, swallowing, or injecting.

Methamphetamine operates by increasing the level of dopamine in the brain, but is metabolized more slowly than other drugs such as cocaine and produces a high for a longer

Methamphetamine, known as "crystal" or "ice," can be "cooked" in large quantities in makeshift laboratories. The man shown in this photo was arrested in a police raid on one such laboratory.

period of time. Prolonged use of methamphetamine produces structural changes in the brain (Chang, Alicata, et al., 2007), and the severity of psychiatric symptoms associated with the drug is related to the duration of use (Yoshimoto et al., 2002). Moreover, discontinuing the drug after the person has become habituated can result in problems with learning, memory, and cognitive dysfunction (Cretzmeyer et al., 2003; Rothman et al., 2000) and severe mental health problems such as paranoid thinking and hallucinations (Brecht et al., 2004; Srisurapanont et al., 2003). When the drug wears off or when users "come down from the high," they are likely to feel extremely weak, lethargic, sleepy, and depressed.

There is some evidence that people become more quickly addicted to methamphetamine and require treatment sooner than those using cocaine (Castro et al., 2000). People who are addicted to methamphetamine are highly resistant to treatment, and posttreatment relapse is common, with approximately one-third relapsing within 6 months after treatment and half relapsing during the next 3 years (Brecht et al., 2000).

Caffeine and Nicotine

DSM-5 includes addictions to two legally available and widely used substances: **caffeine** and **nicotine**. Although these substances do not involve the extensive and self-destructive problems found in alcohol and drug use disorders, they can create important physical and mental health problems in our society for several reasons:

- These drugs are easy to abuse. It is easy to become addicted to them because they are widely used and most people are exposed to them early in life.

DSM-5 Thinking Critically about *DSM-5*

Can Changes to the Diagnostic Criteria Result in Increased Drug Use?

A number of modifications have been made to the way some disorders are diagnosed in *DSM-5*. These changes will likely influence medical treatment with many more patients being treated with stimulant drugs. One of these modified disorders, attention-deficit/hyperactivity disorder or ADHD (see Chapter 15 for details), results in an expanded population of patients who can receive this diagnosis across the adult years. Although, the diagnostic criteria for ADHD in *DSM-5* are similar to those in *DSM-IV* for young people, several changes have been introduced in *DSM-5* that expands the application among adults. This change will likely result in many more adults being treated with prescription drugs for ADHD symptoms.

One of the most popular treatments for ADHD in children and adolescents is the drug methylphenidate (Morton et al., 2000), which is classified as a CNS stimulant. Methylphenidate,

when used intranasally, has receptor effects similar to those of cocaine. These frequently prescribed drugs (Ritalin, Adderall, and Quillivant) are also FDA approved for treatment of adults. The side effects of these medications can result in long-term problems such as sleep problems, headaches, decreased appetite, and jitteriness. Moreover, methylphenidate drugs are addicting and can result in long-term use.

The concern over expanded medication use and potential for abuse has been raised by Batstra and Frances (2012b) in their review of the *DSM-5* committee's changes. They pointed out that *DSM-5* will likely trigger a fad of diagnosing adult attention-deficit disorder and lead to widespread misuse of stimulant drugs for performance enhancement and recreation use and will contribute substantially to the already extensive problem of stimulant abuse.

- These drugs are readily available to anyone who wants to use them; in fact, because of peer pressure, it is usually difficult to avoid using them in our society.

- Both caffeine and nicotine have clearly addictive properties; use of them promotes further use, until one craves a regular "fix" in one's daily life.

- It is difficult to quit using these drugs both because of their addictive properties and because they are so embedded in the social context. (Nicotine use, however, is falling out of favor in many settings.)

- The extreme difficulty most people have in dealing with the withdrawal symptoms when trying to "break the habit" often produces considerable frustration.

- The health problems and side effects of these drugs, particularly nicotine, have been widely noted for many years (U.S. Department of Health and Human Services, 1994). One in seven deaths in the United States is associated with cigarette consumption.

Because of their tenacity as habits and their contributions to many major health problems, we will examine each of these addictions in more detail.

Because they are socially acceptable and readily available, caffeine and nicotine can be insidiously addictive substances. Though they do not result in the same kind of extensive, self-destructive problems as alcohol and drug disorders, caffeine and nicotine addiction can cause a myriad of health problems and are now included in the *DSM-5*.

CAFFEINE   The chemical compound caffeine is found in many commonly available drinks and foods. Although the consumption of caffeine is widely practiced and socially promoted in contemporary society, problems can result from excessive caffeine intake. The negative effects of caffeine involve intoxication rather than withdrawal. Unlike addiction to drugs such as alcohol or nicotine, withdrawal from caffeine does not produce severe symptoms, except for headache, which is usually mild.

As described in *DSM-5* caffeine-related disorder involves symptoms of restlessness, nervousness, excitement, insomnia, muscle twitching, and gastrointestinal complaints. It follows the ingestion of caffeine-containing substances such as coffee, tea, cola, and chocolate. The amount of caffeine that results in intoxication differs among individuals.

NICOTINE   The poisonous alkaloid nicotine is the chief active ingredient in tobacco; it is found in such items as cigarettes, chewing tobacco, and cigars, and it is even used as an insecticide. The use of tobacco is a significant problem in the general population. The number of Americans ages 12 and older who use some form of tobacco is estimated at 70.9 million people, or about 28.4 percent of the population (SAMHSA, 2009). However, an estimated 63 percent of women and 53 percent of men have never smoked (Pleis et al., 2009). The *DSM-5* contains a diagnostic category for nicotine abuse. The criteria for tobacco use disorder are the same for other addictive disorders.

Strong evidence exists for a nicotine-dependence syndrome (Malin, 2001; Watkins et al., 2000), which nearly always begins during the adolescent years and may continue into adult life as a difficult-to-break and health-endangering habit. Supporting the finding that nicotine may have an antianxiety property, nicotine use has been observed as being highly prevalent among those with anxiety disorders (Morissette et al., 2007). Recent evidence from stroke-related brain injury suggests that nicotine addiction might be controlled by a portion of the brain near the ear called the insula (Naqvi et al., 2007). A stroke patient with damage to that area of the brain reported that his craving for cigarettes vanished. This result suggests that the insula might be an important center for addiction to smoking, but more research is needed to support this conclusion.

The "tobacco withdrawal disorder," as it is called in *DSM-5*, results from ceasing or reducing the intake of nicotine-containing substances after an individual has developed physical dependence on them. The diagnostic criteria for nicotine withdrawal include (1) the daily use of nicotine for at least several weeks, and (2) the presence of the following symptoms after nicotine ingestion is stopped or reduced: craving for nicotine; irritability, frustration, or anger; anxiety; difficulty concentrating; restlessness; decreased heart rate; and increased appetite or weight gain. Several other physical concomitants are associated with withdrawal from nicotine including decreased metabolic rate, headaches, insomnia, tremors, increased coughing, and impairment of performance on tasks requiring attention.

These withdrawal symptoms usually continue for several days to several weeks, depending on the extent of the nicotine habit. Some individuals report a desire for nicotine continuing for several months after they quit smoking. In general, nicotine withdrawal symptoms operate in a manner similar to those of withdrawal from other addictions—they are time limited and are reduced over time as the drug intake stops (Hughes, 2007).

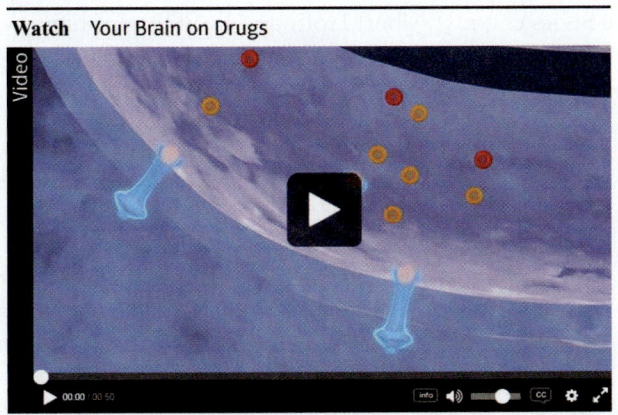

Watch Your Brain on Drugs

Treatment of Nicotine Withdrawal   During the past three decades, numerous treatment programs have been developed to help smokers quit (Hughes, 2007). Available programs use many different methods including social support groups; various pharmacological agents that replace cigarette consumption with safer forms of nicotine such as candy, gum, or patches; self-directed change that involves giving individuals guidance in changing their own behaviors; and professional treatment using psychological procedures such as behavioral or cognitive-behavioral interventions. One recent study provided smokers with ultrasound photographs of their carotid and femoral arteries along with quit-smoking counseling. This group showed higher quit rates than controls (Bovet et al., 2002).

In general, tobacco dependence can be successfully treated, and most of the quit-smoking programs enjoy some success. They average only about a 20 to 25 percent success rate, however, although rates have been reported to be higher with treatment (Hays et al., 2001). This same level of success appears to result from the use of nicotine replacement therapy (NRT). Shiffman and colleagues (2006) point out that high-dose NRT reduces withdrawal symptoms. Treatment with active patches reduced withdrawal and craving during cessation and completely eliminated deprivation-related changes in affect or concentration. Recently, encouraging results have been

reported on the use of the drug bupropion (Zyban) in preventing relapse for smokers trying to quit. The drug reduced relapse as long as the person was taking it, but relapse rates were similar to those of other treatments once the drug was discontinued (Barringer & Weaver, 2002). The highest self-reported quit rates for smokers were reportedly among patients who were hospitalized for cancer (63 percent), cardiovascular disease (57 percent), or pulmonary disease (46 percent; Smith, Reilly, et al., 2002).

in review

- What is methamphetamine? What are the major health factors related to methamphetamine use?
- Describe the effects of nicotine and caffeine use, and explain why these commonly available substances are included in this chapter on substance abuse.

Sedatives

11.7   Describe the effects of sedatives on the brain.

For over a hundred years, powerful sedatives called **barbiturates** have been available as an aid to falling asleep (López-Munoz et al., 2005). Although barbiturates have legitimate medical uses, they are extremely dangerous drugs commonly associated with both physiological and psychological dependence and lethal overdoses.

Effects of Barbiturates

Barbiturates were once widely used by physicians to calm patients and induce sleep. They act as depressants—somewhat like alcohol—to slow down the action of the CNS (Nemeroff, 2003) and significantly reduce performance on cognitive tasks (Pickworth et al., 1997). Shortly after taking a barbiturate, or "downer," an individual experiences a feeling of relaxation in which tensions seem to disappear, followed by a physical and intellectual lassitude and a tendency toward drowsiness and sleep—the intensity of such feelings depends on the type and amount of barbiturate taken. Strong doses produce sleep almost immediately; excessive doses are lethal because they result in paralysis of the brain's respiratory centers. Impaired decision making and problem solving, sluggishness, slow speech, and sudden mood shifts are also common effects of barbiturates (Lemmer, 2007).

Excessive use of barbiturates leads to increased tolerance as well as to physiological and psychological dependence. It can also lead to brain damage and personality deterioration. Unlike tolerance for opiates, tolerance for barbiturates does not increase the amount needed to cause death. This means that users can easily ingest fatal overdoses, either intentionally or accidentally.

Causal Factors in Barbiturate Abuse and Dependence

Although many young people experiment with barbiturates, most do not become dependent. In fact, the people who do become dependent on barbiturates tend to be middle-aged and older people who often rely on them as "sleeping pills" and who do not commonly use other classes of drugs (except possibly alcohol and minor tranquilizers). These people have been referred to as "silent abusers" because they take the drugs in the privacy of their homes and ordinarily do not become public nuisances. Barbiturates are often used with alcohol. Some users claim they can achieve an intense high by combining barbiturates, amphetamines, and alcohol. However, one possible effect of combining barbiturates and alcohol is death because each drug potentiates (increases the action of) the other.

Treatments and Outcomes

As with many other drugs, it is often essential in treatment to distinguish between barbiturate intoxication, which results from the toxic effects of overdose, and the symptoms associated with drug withdrawal, because different procedures are required. With barbiturates, withdrawal symptoms are more dangerous, severe, and long lasting than in opiate withdrawal. A patient going through barbiturate withdrawal becomes anxious and apprehensive and manifests coarse tremors of the hands and face; additional symptoms commonly include insomnia, weakness, nausea, vomiting, abdominal cramps, rapid heart rate, elevated blood pressure, and loss of weight. An acute delirious psychosis may develop.

For persons accustomed to taking large dosages, withdrawal symptoms may last for as long as a month, but usually they tend to abate by the end of the first week. Fortunately, the withdrawal symptoms in barbiturate addiction can be minimized by administering increasingly smaller doses of the barbiturate itself or another drug that produces similar effects. The withdrawal program is still a dangerous one, however, especially if barbiturate addiction is complicated by alcoholism or dependence on other drugs.

in review

- How do sedatives act on the nervous system?
- Who is most at risk of developing sedative dependence?

Hallucinogens

11.8 List four different types of hallucinogens.

The **hallucinogens** are drugs that are thought to induce hallucinations. However, these preparations usually do not in fact "create" sensory images but distort them so that an individual sees or hears things in different and unusual ways. These drugs are often referred to as psychedelics. The major drugs in this category are LSD (lysergic acid diethylamide) or "acid," mescaline, psilocybin, Ecstasy, and marijuana.

LSD

The most potent of the hallucinogens, the odorless, colorless, and tasteless drug **LSD** can produce intoxication with an amount smaller than a grain of salt. It is most often sold and consumed via tiny sheets of blotter paper containing a few micrograms of the drug, which is ingested by letting the paper dissolve on the tongue. It is a chemically synthesized substance first discovered by the Swiss chemist Albert Hofmann in 1938. Hofmann was not aware of the potent hallucinatory qualities of LSD until he swallowed a small amount. This is his report of the experience:

> Last Friday, April 16, 1943, I was forced to stop my work in the laboratory in the middle of the afternoon and to go home, as I was seized by a peculiar restlessness associated with a sensation of mild dizziness. On arriving home, I lay down and sank into a kind of drunkenness which was not unpleasant and which was characterized by extreme activity of imagination. As I lay in a dazed condition with my eyes closed (I experienced daylight as disagreeably bright) there surged upon me an uninterrupted stream of fantastic images of extraordinary plasticity and vividness and accompanied by an intense kaleidoscope-like play of colors. This condition gradually passed off after about 2 hours. (Hofmann, 1971, p. 23)

Hofmann followed up this experience with a series of planned self-observations with LSD, some of which he described as "harrowing." Researchers thought LSD might be useful for the induction and study of hallucinogenic states or "model psychoses," which were thought to be related to schizophrenia. About 1950, LSD was introduced into the United States for the purposes of such research and to ascertain whether it might have medical or therapeutic uses. Despite considerable research, however, LSD did not prove to be therapeutically useful.

After taking LSD, a person typically goes through about 8 hours of changes in sensory perception, mood swings, and feelings of depersonalization and detachment. The LSD experience is not always pleasant. It can be extremely traumatic, and the distorted objects and sounds, the illusory colors, and the new thoughts can be menacing and terrifying. For example, while under the influence of LSD, a British law student tried to continue time by using a dental drill to bore a hole in his head (Rorvik, 1970). In other instances, people undergoing bad trips have set themselves aflame, jumped from high places, and taken other drugs that proved lethal in combination with LSD.

An interesting and unusual phenomenon that may occur sometime following the use of LSD is the **flashback**, an involuntary recurrence of perceptual distortions or hallucinations weeks or even months after an individual has taken the drug. Flashbacks appear to be relatively rare among people who have taken LSD only once—although they do sometimes occur. Even if no flashbacks occur, one study found that continued effects on visual function were apparent at least 2 years after LSD use. In this study, Abraham and Wolf (1988) reported that individuals who had used LSD for a week had reduced visual sensitivity to light during dark adaptation and showed other visual problems compared with controls.

Although the widespread use of LSD during the 1960s and 1970s has waned in recent years with the availability of other drugs, it is still used among young people associated with the "rave culture" or club scene. One study reported that in a sample of 782 youths in treatment for substance abuse, 42 percent had used LSD (Hopfer et al., 2006).

Mescaline and Psilocybin

Two other hallucinogens are **mescaline**, which is derived from the small, disk-like growths (mescal buttons) at the top of the peyote cactus, and **psilocybin**, which is obtained from a variety of "sacred" Mexican mushrooms known as *Psilocybe mexicana*. These drugs have been used for centuries in the ceremonial rites of Native peoples living in Mexico, the American Southwest, and Central and South America. In fact, they were used by the Aztecs for such purposes long before the Spanish invasion. Both drugs have mind-altering and hallucinogenic properties, but their principal effect appears to be enabling an individual to see, hear, and otherwise experience events in unaccustomed ways—transporting him or her into a realm of "nonordinary reality." As with LSD, no definite evidence shows that mescaline and psilocybin actually "expand consciousness" or create new ideas; rather, they mainly alter or distort experience.

Ecstasy

The drug **Ecstasy**, or MDMA (3,4-methylenedioxymethylamphetamine), is both a hallucinogen and a stimulant that is popular as a party drug among young adults. The drug was originally patented in 1914 by the pharmaceutical company Merck, supposedly to be sold as a diet pill, but the company decided against marketing the drug because of its side effects. The drug was further evaluated and tested during the 1970s and 1980s as a potential medication for use in psychological treatment for a wide range of conditions such as posttraumatic stress, phobias, psychosomatic disorders, depression, suicidality,

drug addiction, and relationship difficulties (Grob, 2000). However, its value in this capacity was not supported. At present, this drug is considered a "dangerous" drug and is listed in the most restricted category by the U. S. Drug Enforcement Administration (DEA) (Murray, 2001). It is currently available in the United States only through illicit means.

The Ecstasy drug (MDMA—3,4-methylenedioxymethylamphetamine) is taken in pill form and is often used at "raves" or nightclubs to enhance mood. Ecstasy is an illegal substance, and manufacturers do not follow regulation and quality control.

Ecstasy is chemically similar to methamphetamine and to the hallucinogen mescaline and produces effects similar to those of other stimulants. Usually about 20 minutes after ingesting Ecstasy (typically in pill form), the person experiences a "rush" sensation followed by a feeling of calmness, energy, and well-being. The effects of Ecstasy can last for several hours. People who take the drug often report an intense experience of color and sound and mild hallucinations (Fox et al., 2001; Lieb et al., 2002; Soar et al., 2001) in addition to the high levels of energy and excitement that are produced. The drug MDMA is an addictive substance, but it is not thought to be as addictive as cocaine (Degenhardt et al., 2010). Use of the drug is accompanied by a number of adverse consequences such as nausea, sweating, clenching of teeth, muscle cramps, blurred vision, and hallucinations (Parrott, 2001).

Ecstasy has been used increasingly among college students and young adults as a party enhancement or "rave" drug at dances (Hopfer et al., 2006). In a survey of 14,000 college students, Strote and colleagues (2002) found that between 1997 and 1999, Ecstasy use increased 69 percent, from 2.8 to 4.7 percent. Ecstasy reportedly grew in use among 8th, 10th, and 12th graders, as noted by the *Monitoring the Future* study, in which nearly 5 percent of 10th and 12th graders and about 2 percent of 8th graders reportedly had used MDMA in the past year (Johnston et al., 2009).

As with many other illicit drugs, the recreational use of Ecstasy has been associated with personality characteristics of impulsivity and poor judgment (Morgan, 1998). Ecstasy users have been found to be more likely to use marijuana, engage in binge drinking, smoke cigarettes, and have multiple sexual partners (Strote et al., 2002). However, Ecstasy use is also found among naïve partygoers who are provided the drug as a means of staying awake while socializing (Boys et al., 2001).

The negative psychological and health consequences (including death) of using Ecstasy have been widely reported in the literature. One study reported on the case of a 21-year-old man who developed panic disorder after taking Ecstasy (Windhaber et al., 1998); in another case study, an 18-year-old woman reportedly developed a prolonged psychosis after a single recreational use of Ecstasy (Van Kampen & Katz, 2001). The use of Ecstasy has also been found to be associated with memory impairment (Parrott et al., 1998) and obstructive sleep apnea (Chamberlin & Saper, 2009; McCann et al. 2009). Severe organic brain problems have also been reported. Granato and colleagues (1997) describe a case in which a 20-year-old male suffered from cerebrovascular injury after taking Ecstasy. The youth went into a coma about a minute or so after taking the drug. Upon awakening, he was found to have dissociation, delirium, visual hallucinations, and poor memory for past events. Subsequent examination showed damage to his frontal lobes and his right temporal lobe. Ecstasy users have consistently shown memory deficits (Roberts et al., 2009). A recent study by Schilt and colleagues (2010) found long-term harmful neurological effects in middle-aged Ecstasy users. Moderate to heavy Ecstasy users showed moderate memory loss compared to controls.

Marijuana

Marijuana comes from the leaves and flowering tops of the hemp plant, *Cannabis sativa*, which grows in mild climates throughout the world. In its prepared state, marijuana consists chiefly of dried green leaves—hence, the colloquial name "grass." It is ordinarily smoked in the form of cigarettes (variously referred to as "pot," "reefers," "joints," "weed," etc.) or in pipes. In some cultures the leaves are steeped in hot water and the liquid is drunk, much as one might drink tea. Marijuana is related to a stronger drug, **hashish**, which is derived from the resin exuded by the cannabis plant and made into a gummy powder. Hashish, like marijuana, is usually smoked. Although marijuana can be considered a mild hallucinogen, there are significant differences between the nature, intensity, and duration of its effects and those induced by drugs like LSD, mescaline, and other major hallucinogens.

Both marijuana use and hashish use can be traced far back into history. Cannabis was apparently known in ancient China (Blum, 1969) and was listed in the herbal compendiums of the Chinese Emperor Shen Nung, written about 2737 B.C.E. Today, marijuana is the most frequently used illicit drug. In the United States, 7.5 percent of those 12 years and older report having used marijuana in the past month (SAMHSA, 2014). Marijuana use is likely to show an increase in the future, given that it has been legalized in some states even though it is illegal according to federal legal standards. In a recent survey of drug-related visits to the ED, 18.5 percent were for marijuana abuse (SAMHSA, 2013).

EFFECTS OF MARIJUANA   The specific effects of marijuana vary greatly, depending on the quality and dosage of the drug, the personality and mood of the user, the user's past experiences with the drug, the social setting, and the user's expectations. However, considerable consensus exists among regular users that when marijuana is smoked and inhaled, a state of slight intoxication results. This state is one of mild euphoria distinguished by increased feelings of well-being, heightened perceptual acuity, and pleasant relaxation, often accompanied by a sensation of drifting or floating away. Sensory inputs are intensified. Marijuana has the effect on the brain of altering one's internal clock (O'Leary et al., 2003). Often a person's sense of time is stretched or distorted so that an event that lasts only a few seconds may seem to cover a much longer span. Short-term memory may also be affected, as when one notices that a bite has been taken out of a sandwich but does not remember having taken it. For most users, pleasurable experiences, including sexual intercourse, are reportedly enhanced. When smoked, marijuana is rapidly absorbed, and its effects appear within seconds to minutes but seldom last more than 2 to 3 hours. Marijuana has also been used to relieve pain or nausea; see the World around Us box for a discussion of the controversy over medical marijuana.

Marijuana can produce extreme euphoria, hilarity, and hyper-talkativeness, but it can also produce intense anxiety and depression as well as delusions, hallucinations, and other psychotic-like behavior.

The World Around Us

Should Marijuana Be Marketed and Sold Openly as a Medication?

Marijuana is a Schedule I drug according to the 1970 Controlled Substances Act, and U.S. government drug control agencies have strongly opposed legalization of the drug (Walters, 2006); however, substantial efforts have been made to broaden its use and availability. In recent years marijuana has been distributed for pain or nausea relief from medical conditions such as cancer, AIDS, glaucoma, multiple sclerosis, migraines, and epilepsy. Proponents of medical marijuana cite its value in the treatment of these conditions, and some have pointed out that medical marijuana treatment is consistent with participation in other forms of drug treatment and may not adversely affect the outcome (Swartz, 2010). Marijuana does not cure any illness; it only reduces pain for which other medications exist (Watson, Benson, & Joy, 2000).

Proponents of medical marijuana have made considerable inroads in securing legalization of marijuana as a treatment in 23 states and the District of Columbia. Although many professional researchers and practitioners discourage the use of marijuana because of the ill effects, others, including mental health professionals, politicians, and laypersons, press society to change the rigid control over the drug and make it legal.

States vary in how medical marijuana is made available to the public. Some locations, such as the District of Columbia, have approved medical marijuana use by a limited and controlled number of dispensaries (Southall, 2010), while others have allowed a broad and less controlled environment to develop. The ready access to marijuana has heightened concerns over the drug serving as an "entry-level" drug for more addictive and dangerous illicit substances. This problem has been a focus of the U.S. government's opposition to legalizing marijuana since it has become more widely available (Walters, 2006). In 2012, the Los Angeles City Council rescinded its early approval of the sale of medical marijuana and closed down the numerous "clinics" that provided open access to the drug (Zahniser, 2012). It is uncertain as to what the future access to medical marijuana will be as various states may change their positions on marijuana use and availability.

A number of problems with the use of medical marijuana have been reported, in part because of the unregulated availability of the drug; for example, one can get a "prescription" for the drug by walking into one of the many "treatment centers" and talking with a salesperson. An article by Moore (2009) describes the sentencing of an owner of a marijuana dispensary to a year in prison for distributing marijuana. Thus, providers of medical marijuana to the public can still face the possibility of jail time in some situations. Yardley (2010) pointed out a number of crimes that resulted from medical marijuana users having had large amounts of marijuana in their homes. Mascia (2010) highlighted another problem in using medical marijuana in employment settings. A number of people have lost jobs or have not been offered a position as a result of drug screening—a requirement for employment in many positions such as security personnel, police applicants, pilots, and even some corporations such as Walmart.

Marijuana's short-range physiological effects include a moderate increase in heart rate, a slowing of reaction time, a slight contraction of pupil size, bloodshot and itchy eyes, a dry mouth, and increased appetite. Furthermore, marijuana induces memory dysfunction and a slowing of information processing (Pope et al., 2001). Continued use of high dosages over time tends to produce lethargy and passivity along with reduced life success (Lane et al., 2005). In such cases marijuana appears to have a depressant and a hallucinogenic effect. The effects of long-term and habitual marijuana use are still under investigation, although a number of possible adverse side effects have been found to be related to the prolonged, heavy use of marijuana (Earleywine, 2002). With higher dosages marijuana can produce extreme euphoria, hilarity, and overtalkativeness, but it can also produce intense anxiety (Zvolensky et al., 2010) and depression as well as delusions, hallucinations, and other psychotic-like experiences. Evidence suggests a strong relationship between daily marijuana use and the occurrence of psychotic symptoms (Raphael et al., 2005).

Should medical marijuana be considered a legitimate pharmaceutical treatment, or does its potential as an entry-level drug and its negative consequences counter its value as a treatment?

TREATMENT When abstaining from marijuana use, some users report having uncomfortable withdrawal-like symptoms such as nervousness, tension, sleep problems, and appetite change (Budney et al., 2003; Zickler, 2002). Psychological treatment methods have been shown to be effective in reducing marijuana use in adults who are dependent on the drug (Marijuana Treatment Project Research Group, 2004), and no specific treatment approach has been found to be more effective than the others (Nordstrom & Levin, 2007). No pharmacotherapy treatment for cannabis dependency has been shown to be very effective (Nordstrom & Levin, 2007); however, one recent study using buspirone for treatment of marijuana dependency showed slight improvement over a placebo group (McRae-Clark et al., 2009).

SYNTHETIC CANNABINOIDS AND CATHINONES During the past several years, drug developers have attempted to make and sell synthetic psychoactive substances that produce the same effects as naturally occurring drugs such as marijuana and cocaine, but do not contain the legally banned substance and so are not subject to prosecution. Two examples of this are synthetic cannabinoids and synthetic cathinones. **Synthetic cannabinoids** are substances that mimic the effects of tetrahydrocannabinol (THC), the active plant-derived substance in marijuana, and activate the human endocannabinoid system (Baumann et al., 2014). Synthetic cannabinoids, sold under the names "Spice," "K2," "Blaze," and others, do contain some actual plants/herbs, but it is the synthetic chemical additive that causes the marijuana-like effects. Specifically, synthetic cannabinoids bind with CB_1 receptors and produce marijuana-like intoxication. However, synthetic cannabinoids are much more likely than marijuana to have serious adverse side effects such as anxiety, tachycardia, hypertension, heart palpitations, seizures, and psychosis-like effects (van Amsterdam et al., 2015; Wells & Ott, 2011). In response to the recent rise in synthetic cannabinoids, and their dangerous side effects, in 2011 the DEA declared these chemicals to be illegal substances (Kraft, 2011).

Synthetic cathinones are substances that mimic the effects of amphetamines and cocaine by activating the body's monoamine system (Baumann et al., 2014). Synthetic cathinones, sold under the name "bath salts," first appeared in the illegal drug scene in 2010. Since then they have been examined in human epidemiologic and laboratory animal studies, and have been found to produce increased motor activity, agitation, violence, psychosis-like effects, and heart problems (Baumann et al., 2014).

Bath salts are becoming a widely used and dangerous stimulant drug and are now considered an illegal substance even though they are often available in bath products or fertilizers. The drug's effects are very similar to those of Ecstasy or cocaine. Bath salts contain amphetamine- or cocaine-like chemicals, such as methylenedioxypyrovalerone (MDPV). They tend to cause intense euphoria and make the user very talkative and sexually aroused and often produce bizarre results.

in review

- What are the physical risks of taking Ecstasy?
- Describe the effects of cannabis.

Gambling Disorder

11.9 **Explain whether there are addictive disorders other than alcohol and drugs.**

Although **pathological gambling** does not involve a chemically addictive substance, it is considered by many to be an addictive disorder because of the personality factors that tend to characterize compulsive gamblers (Petry & Madden, 2010). Like the substance abuse disorders, pathological gambling involves behavior maintained by short-term gains despite long-term disruption of an individual's life. There is a high comorbidity between pathological gambling and alcohol abuse disorders (Blanco et al., 2010) and with personality disorders (Sacco et al., 2008). Pathological gambling, also known as "compulsive gambling" or disordered gambling, is a progressive disorder characterized by continuous loss of control over gambling, a preoccupation with gambling and with obtaining money for gambling, and continuation of the gambling behavior in spite of adverse consequences.

Estimates place the number of pathological gamblers worldwide at between 1 and 2 percent of the adult population (Petry, 2005). Both men and women appear to be vulnerable to pathological gambling (Hing & Breen, 2001). However, rates differ by subpopulation; for example, in some high-risk populations, such as alcoholics, the rates are higher. One study of elderly African Americans from two senior citizen centers documented the extent of gambling problems in this population; 17 percent were found to be people with gambling disorders (Bazargan et al., 2001). Pietrzak and colleagues (2007) found that older, disordered gamblers were significantly more likely than non-gambling older adults to have alcohol abuse problems, nicotine addiction, and health problems.

Cultural factors also appear to be important in the development of gambling problems. Pathological gambling is a particular problem among some cultural groups (e.g., Chinese, Jewish) and among ethnic minorities and indigenous groups (e.g., Native Americans), perhaps due to the availability and acceptability of gambling behavior (Alegria et al., 2009; Raylu & Oei, 2004). Gambling in our society takes many forms including casino gambling, betting on horse races or sports (legally or otherwise), Internet gaming, numbers games, lotteries, dice, bingo, and cards. Whatever an individual gambler's situation, compulsive gambling significantly affects the social, psychological, and economic well-being of the gambler's family. In fact, studies have found that a high proportion of pathological gamblers commit crimes that are related to gambling (Blaszczynski et al., 1989), family violence (Afifi et al., 2010), and other crimes of aggression (Folino & Abait, 2009).

Pathological gambling seems to be a learned pattern that is highly resistant to extinction. Some research suggests

DSM-5 *Criteria for. . .*

Gambling Disorder

A. Persistent and recurrent problematic gambling behavior leading to clinically significant impairment or distress, as indicated by the individual exhibiting four (or more) of the following in a 12-month period:

1. Needs to gamble with increasing amounts of money in order to achieve the desired excitement.
2. Is restless or irritable when attempting to cut down or stop gambling.
3. Has made repeated unsuccessful efforts to control, cut back, or stop gambling.
4. Is often preoccupied with gambling (e.g., having persistent thoughts of reliving past gambling experiences, handicapping or planning the next venture, thinking of ways to get money with which to gamble).

5. Often gambles when feeling distressed (e.g., helpless, guilty, anxious, depressed).
6. After losing money gambling, often returns another day to get even ("chasing" one's losses).
7. Lies to conceal the extent of involvement with gambling.
8. Has jeopardized or lost a significant relationship, job, or educational or career opportunity because of gambling.
9. Relies on others to provide money to relieve desperate financial situations caused by gambling.

B. The gambling behavior is not better explained by a manic episode.

Source: Reprinted with permission from the *Diagnostic and Statistical Manual of Mental Disorders*, Fifth Edition (Copyright © 2013). American Psychiatric Association.

---

that control over gambling is related to duration and frequency of playing (Scannell et al., 2000). However, many people who become pathological gamblers won a substantial sum of money the first time they gambled; chance alone would dictate that a certain percentage of people would have such "beginner's luck." The reinforcement a person receives during this introductory phase may be a significant factor in later pathological gambling. Because everyone is likely to win from time to time, the principles of intermittent reinforcement—the most potent reinforcement schedule for operant conditioning—could explain an addict's continued gambling despite excessive losses.

Research has shown that pathological gambling frequently co-occurs with other disorders, particularly substance abuse such as alcohol and cocaine dependence (Kausch, 2003; Welte et al., 2004) and impulse disorders (Grant & Potenza, 2010). Those with co-occurring substance abuse disorders typically have the most severe gambling problems (Ladd & Petry, 2003).

The causes of impulse-driven behavior in pathological gambling are complex. Some research has suggested that early trauma might contribute to the development of compulsive gambling (Scherrer et al., 2007). Although learning undoubtedly plays an important part in the development of personality factors underlying the "compulsive" gambler, recent research on brain mechanisms that are involved in motivation, reward, and decision making indicates that these mechanisms could influence the underlying impulsivity in personality (Chambers & Potenza, 2003). These investigators have suggested that important neurodevelopmental events during adolescence occur in brain regions associated

with motivation and impulsive behavior. Recent research has also suggested that genetic factors might play a part in developing pathological gambling habits (Slutske et al., 2010).

Treatment of pathological gamblers has tended to parallel that of other addictive disorders. The most extensive treatment approach used with pathological gamblers is cognitive-behavioral therapy (Okuda et al., 2009). For example, Sylvain, Ladouceur, and Boisvert (1997) provided CBT for 58 pathological gamblers. Although 18 participants dropped out at the start and 11 quit during therapy, those who remained in treatment showed significant improvement. Of those who completed therapy, 86 percent were considered "no longer" pathological gamblers at a 1-year follow-up. However, one study (Hodgins & el-Guebaly, 2004) reported very high relapse rates among pathological gamblers—only 8 percent were free of gambling 12 months after treatment. Even studies that show improvement during treatment also report participants' difficulty remaining abstinent. In a study of 231 gamblers (Petry et al., 2006), some improved when receiving CBT and when attending Gambler's Anonymous (GA) meetings, an organization modeled after Alcoholics Anonymous, or when attending GA and receiving a workbook. The patients tended not to remain abstinent, although incidents were fewer than they usually reported. Most participants reported some gambling during the follow-up period. More positive outcomes in treating pathological gambling have been found when family relationship problems are addressed in the treatment (McComb et al., 2009).

Pathological gambling is on the increase in the United States (Potenza, 2002), particularly with the widely available gambling opportunities on the Internet (Griffiths, 2003). Liberalized gambling legislation has permitted state-operated lotteries, horse racing, and gambling casinos in an effort to increase state tax revenues. In the context of this apparent environmental support and "official" sanction for gambling, it is likely that pathological gambling will increase substantially as more and more people "try their luck." Given that pathological gamblers are resistant to treatment, future efforts to develop more effective preventive and treatment approaches will need to be increased as this problem continues to grow.

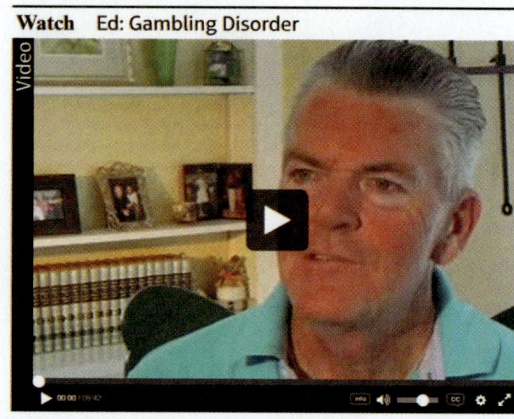

Watch   Ed: Gambling Disorder

Unresolved Issues

Exchanging Addictions: Is This an Effective Treatment Approach?

Withdrawal from heroin can be extremely difficult because of the intense craving that develops for the drug. Wouldn't it be great if we had a magic bullet—a medication—that would allow people who are addicted to heroin to withdraw from it painlessly? One approach that has been used for several decades involves the administration of methadone (methadone hydrochloride, a synthetic narcotic that is as addictive as heroin), often in conjunction with a psychological or social rehabilitation program that is aimed at resocialization of the abuser. The value of this treatment comes from the fact that methadone satisfies an addict's craving for heroin without producing serious psychological impairment.

Many researchers have concluded that in addition to facilitating psychological or social rehabilitation, this drug is effective at reducing the dependence on heroin (Kreek et al., 2010). Thus, it enables many people to experience reduced craving, allowing them to alter somewhat the often desperate life circumstances they find themselves in through trying to support their expensive and all-consuming habit. In addition, opiate addicts who remain on methadone have a substantially lower death rate than those discharged from methadone maintenance programs (Fugelstad et al., 2007).

The idea that addicts may need to be maintained for life on methadone, itself a powerful and addicting drug, has been questioned both on moral and practical grounds. Methadone advocates, however, point out that people using methadone can function normally and hold jobs, which is not possible for most heroin addicts. In addition, methadone is available legally, and its quality is controlled by government standards. Advocates for methadone programs point out that it is not necessary to increase the dosage over time as it is with heroin use. In fact, some patients can eventually stop taking methadone without danger of relapse to heroin addiction.

However, negative consequences are sometimes associated with the use of methadone (Miller & Lyon, 2003). Methadone patients are at increased risk for health problems such as hepatitis (McCarthy & Flynn, 2001) and cognitive impairment (Scheurich, 2005; Verdejo et al., 2005). In addition, many social problems, such as trading sex for drugs, persist (El-Bassel et al., 2001); some addicts get involved with other drugs such as cocaine (Avants et al., 1998; Silverman et al., 1996); suicide attempts are common (Darke & Ross, 2001); and violent deaths and drug overdoses are common among methadone patients (Sunjic & Zabor, 1999).

Summary

11.1 Describe the characteristics of alcohol abuse and dependence.

- Substance-related disorders such as alcohol or drug abuse and dependency are among the most widespread and intransigent mental health problems facing us today.

- Many problems of alcohol or drug use involve difficulties that stem solely from the intoxicating effects of the substances.

- Dependence occurs when an individual develops a tolerance for the substance or exhibits withdrawal symptoms when the substance is not available.

- Several psychoses related to alcoholism have been identified: withdrawal delirium, alcohol-induced psychotic disorder, and dementia associated with alcoholism.

11.2 Explain the biological, psychosocial, and sociocultural factors involved in alcohol abuse and dependence.

- It is widely believed that genetic factors play some role in causing susceptibility to alcohol abuse problems through such biological avenues as metabolic rates and sensitivity to alcohol.
- Psychological factors—such as psychological vulnerability, stress, and the desire for tension reduction—and disturbed marital relationships or failure in parental guidance are also seen as important etiologic elements in substance use disorders.
- Although the existence of an "alcoholic personality type" has been disavowed by most theorists, a variety of personality factors apparently play an important role in the development and expression of addictive disorders.
- Sociocultural factors such as attitudes toward alcohol may predispose individuals to alcohol-related disorders.

11.3 Discuss the treatment of alcohol-related disorders.

- Less than one-third of those with alcohol use disorders receive treatment, because many people with these disorders deny that the problems exist and so may not be motivated to work on them.
- Several approaches to the treatment of chronic substance-related disorders have been developed—for example, medication to deal with withdrawal symptoms and withdrawal delirium, and dietary evaluation and treatment for malnutrition.
- Psychological therapies such as group therapy and behavioral interventions may be effective for some people with alcohol use disorders. Another source of help is Alcoholics Anonymous; however, the extent of successful outcomes with this program has not been sufficiently studied.
- Most treatment programs require abstinence; however, some research has suggested that some people with alcohol use disorders can learn to control their drinking while continuing to drink socially. The controversy surrounding controlled drinking continues.

11.4 List the psychoactive drugs most commonly associated with abuse and dependence.

- Drug use disorders may involve physiological dependence on substances such as opiates—particularly heroin—or barbiturates; however, psychological dependence may also occur with any of the drugs that are commonly used today, for example, marijuana.
- A number of factors are considered important in the etiology of drug use disorders. Some substances, such as alcohol and opiates, stimulate brain centers that produce euphoria—which then becomes a desired goal.

11.5 Describe the commonly used opiates and their effects on the body.

- Opium is a powerful sedative and pain reliever that depresses or slows down the central nervous system. It also causes a state of euphoria and is highly addictive, and has been used for centuries. It is known to activate the dopamine reward pathway, or "pleasure pathway," often leading to addiction and unfortunately—at times—to fatal outcomes.
- Opium appears most commonly today in pain relievers such as morphine and codeine, and in illicit drugs like heroin. Methadone is a synthetic narcotic that is often used to treat heroin addiction; it is similarly addictive, but does not produce the same euphoria or impairments.

11.6 Discuss the different types of stimulants and their effects.

- Stimulants stimulate (hence, their name) the action of the central nervous system. As a result, people taking stimulants are "sped up" in their thoughts and behaviors.
- Commonly used stimulants include several illicit drugs, such as cocaine, amphetamines, and methamphetamine, as well as several legal ones, such as caffeine and nicotine.

11.7 Describe the effects of sedatives on the brain.

- Like opiates, sedatives also depress, or slow down, the activity of the central nervous system. A major difference is that they produce more sedation and less euphoria, and as such they are commonly used for medicinal purposes to help people to sleep.
- Strong doses of sedatives produce sleep almost immediately, and higher doses can lead to paralysis and even death.

11.8 List four different types of hallucinogens.

- Hallucinogens cause people to see or hear things differently. Some of the most commonly used hallucinogens include LSD, mescaline, psilocybin, Ecstasy/MDMA, and marijuana.
- Recent years have seen an increase in the prevalence of synthetic cannabinoids (which mimic the active ingredient in marijuana) and cathinones (which mimic the active ingredients in amphetamines and cocaine).

11.9 Explain whether there are addictive disorders other than alcohol and drugs.

- Although pathological gambling does not involve a chemically addictive substance, it is considered by many to be an addictive disorder because of the personality factors that tend to characterize compulsive gamblers. Like the substance abuse disorders, pathological gambling involves behavior maintained by short-term gains despite long-term disruption of an individual's life.

Key Terms

addictive behavior, p. 385
alcohol amnestic disorder, p. 391
alcohol withdrawal delirium, p. 391
amphetamine, p. 408
barbiturates, p. 411
caffeine, p. 409
cocaine, p. 406
delirium tremens, p. 391
dopamine theory of addiction, p. 405
Ecstasy, p. 413
endorphins, p. 405

flashback, p. 413
hallucinogens, p. 412
hashish, p. 414
heroin, p. 403
LSD, p. 412
marijuana, p. 414
mescaline, p. 413
mesocorticolimbic dopamine pathway (MCLP), p. 392
methadone, p. 406
morphine, p. 403
nicotine, p. 409

opium, p. 403
pathological gambling, p. 416
psilocybin, p. 413
psychoactive substances, p. 385
reward deficiency syndrome, p. 405
substance abuse, p. 385
substance dependence, p. 385
substance-related disorders, p. 385
synthetic cannabinoids, p. 416
synthetic cathinones, p. 416
tolerance, p. 385
withdrawal, p. 385

Chapter 12
Sexual Variants, Abuse, and Dysfunctions

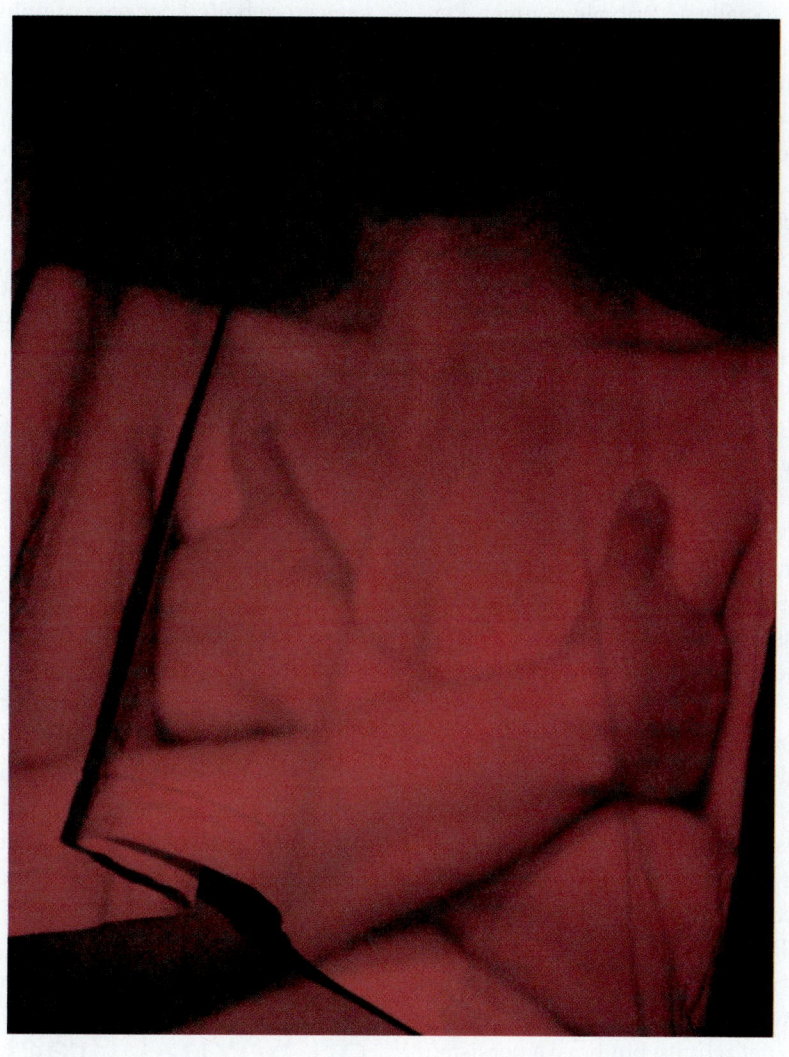

Learning Objectives

12.1 Explain why it is difficult to define boundaries between normality and psychopathology in the area of variant sexuality.

12.2 List and describe four types of paraphilia.

12.3 Explain the key characteristics of gender dysphoria.

12.4 Describe three primary types of sexual abuse.

12.5 Define sexual dysfunction and name three sexual dysfunction disorders.

Loving and sexually satisfying relationships contribute a great deal to our happiness. When we are not in such relationships, we often spend a great deal of time and energy looking for them. Sexuality is one of the most central concerns of our lives, influencing our choice of romantic partners and spouses and determining how happy we are with our life partners and with ourselves.

In this chapter we first look at the psychological problems that make sexual fulfillment especially difficult for some people, who develop unusual sexual interests that are difficult to satisfy in a socially acceptable manner. Perhaps no other area covered in this text highlights the difficulties in defining boundaries between normality and psychopathology as much as this area does. For example, different people are turned on by different things; however, exhibitionists are sexually aroused by showing their genitals to strangers, which most other members of society find to be inappropriate (and criminal). Other sexual or gender variants may be problematic primarily to the individual: Transsexualism, for example, is a disorder involving discomfort with one's biological sex and a strong desire to be of the opposite sex. Still other variants such as fetishism, in which sexual interest centers on some inanimate object or body part, involve behaviors that, although bizarre and unusual, do not clearly harm anyone.

The second issue we consider is sexual abuse, a pattern of pressured, forced, or inappropriate sexual contact with another person. During the past few decades, there has been a tremendous increase in attention to the problem of sexual abuse of both children and adults. A great deal of research has addressed its causes and consequences. As we shall see, some related issues, such as the reality of recovered memories of sexual abuse, are extremely controversial.

The third category of sexual difficulties examined in this chapter is sexual dysfunctions, which include problems that impede the performance of sexual acts. People who have sexual dysfunctions (or their partners) typically view them as problems. Premature ejaculation, for example, causes men to reach orgasm much earlier than expected or desired. And women with orgasmic disorder get sexually aroused and enjoy sexual activity but have a persistent delay, or absence, of orgasm following a normal sexual **excitement (arousal) phase**.

Much less is known about sexual deviations, abuse, and dysfunctions than is known about many of the other disorders we have considered thus far in this text. There also are fewer sex researchers than researchers for many other disorders, so fewer articles related to research on sexual deviations and dysfunctions are published compared with the number of articles on anxiety and mood disorders or schizophrenia. One major reason is the sex taboo. Although sex is an important concern for most people, many have difficulty talking about it openly—especially when the relevant behavior is socially stigmatized, as

homosexuality has been historically. This makes it hard to obtain knowledge about even the most basic facts, such as the frequency of various sexual practices, feelings, and attitudes.

A second reason sex research has progressed less rapidly is that many issues related to sexuality—including homosexuality, teenage sexuality, abortion, and childhood sexual abuse—are among the most divisive and controversial in our society. In fact, sex research is itself controversial and not well funded. In the 1990s, two large-scale sex surveys were halted because of political opposition even after the surveys had been officially approved and deemed scientifically meritorious (Udry, 1993). A conservative senator at the time, Jesse Helms, and others, argued that sex researchers tended to approve of premarital sex (the horror!) and that this would likely bias the results of the surveys. Fortunately, one of these surveys was funded privately, though on a much smaller scale, and it is still considered definitive—even though it was conducted two decades ago (Laumann et al., 1994, 1999). Another attack led by conservatives occurred in 2003, when several federal grants were criticized because they focused on sex (Kempner, 2008). A legislative attempt to defund five of the grants barely failed.

When considering the lack of information on these topics, it is important to know that this is a relatively new area of scientific research. The contemporary era of sex research was first launched by Alfred Kinsey in the early 1950s (Kinsey et al., 1948, 1953). Kinsey and his pioneering work are portrayed in the 2004 award-winning movie, creatively titled *Kinsey*. Before discussing recent progress in understanding of sexual variants and related topics, we first consider sociocultural influences on sexual behavior and attitudes in order to provide some perspective about cross-cultural variability in standards of sexual conduct and how these perspectives have changed over time.

Sociocultural Influences on Sexual Practices and Standards

12.1 **Explain why it is difficult to define boundaries between normality and psychopathology in the area of variant sexuality.**

Although some aspects of sexuality and mating are cross-culturally universal, such as men's greater emphasis (than women's) on their partner's attractiveness (Buss, 1989), others are quite variable. For example, all known cultures have taboos against sex between close relatives, but attitudes toward premarital sex vary considerably across history and around the world. Views about what is acceptable sexual behavior also change over time. Less than 100 years ago, sexual modesty in Western cultures was such that women's arms and legs were always hidden in public. Today, Miley Cyrus swings naked on a wrecking ball in a music video shown on television. In many Muslim countries, women's arms and legs are still covered today. In this context, it is difficult to say what kind of behavior should be considered "abnormal." Because the influences of time and place are so important in shaping sexual behavior and attitudes, we begin by exploring three cases that illustrate how opinions about "acceptable" and "normal" sexual behavior may change dramatically over time and may differ dramatically from one culture to another.

Loving, sexually satisfying relationships contribute a great deal to our happiness, but our understanding of them has advanced slowly, largely because they are so difficult for people to talk about openly and because funding for research is often hard to come by.

Case 1: Degeneracy and Abstinence Theory

During the 1750s, Swiss physician Simon Tissot developed *degeneracy theory*, the central belief of which was that semen is necessary for physical and sexual vigor in men and for masculine characteristics such as beard growth (Money, 1985, 1986). He based this theory on observations about castrated men and animals. We now know, of course, that loss of the male hormone testosterone, and not semen, is responsible for the relevant characteristics of those who have been castrated. On the basis of his theory, however, Tissot asserted that two practices were especially harmful: masturbation and patronizing prostitutes. Both of these practices wasted the vital fluid, semen, as well as (in his view) overstimulated and exhausted the nervous system. Tissot also recommended that married people engage solely in procreative sex to avoid the waste of semen.

A descendant of degeneracy theory, abstinence theory was advocated in America during the 1830s by the Reverend Sylvester Graham (Money, 1985, 1986). The three cornerstones of his crusade for public health were healthy

food (*Note:* He invented the graham cracker with the belief that eating bland foods would decrease sexual urges), physical fitness, and sexual abstinence. In the 1870s Graham's most famous successor, Dr. John Harvey Kellogg, published a paper in which he ardently disapproved of masturbation and urged parents to be wary of signs that their children were indulging in it. He wrote about the 39 signs of "the secret vice," which included weakness, dullness of the eyes, sleeplessness, untrustworthiness, bashfulness, love of solitude, unnatural boldness, mock piety, and round shoulders.

As a physician, Kellogg was professionally admired and publicly influential, and he earned a fortune publishing books discouraging masturbation. His recommended treatments for "the secret vice" were quite extreme. For example, he advocated that persistent masturbation in boys be treated by sewing the foreskin with silver wire or, as a last resort, by circumcision without anesthesia. Female masturbation was to be treated by burning the clitoris with carbolic acid. Kellogg, like Graham, was also very concerned with dietary health—especially with the idea that consumption of meat increased sexual desire. Thus, he urged people to eat more cereal and invented Kellogg's cornflakes "almost literally, as anti-masturbation food" (1986, p. 186).

Unwanted sexual urges? Have a graham cracker and calm yourself down.

Given the influence of physicians like Kellogg, it should come as no surprise that many people believed that masturbation caused insanity (Hare, 1962). This hypothesis had started with the anonymous publication in the early eighteenth century in London of a book entitled *Onania*, or the *Heinous Sin of Self-Pollution*. It asserted that masturbation was a common cause of insanity. This idea probably arose from observations that many patients in mental asylums masturbated openly (unlike sane people, who are more likely to do it in private) and that the age at which masturbation tends to begin (at puberty in adolescence) precedes by several years the age when the first signs of insanity often appear (in late adolescence and young adulthood) (Abramson & Seligman, 1977). The idea that masturbation may cause insanity appeared in some psychiatry textbooks as late as the 1940s.

Although abstinence theory and associated attitudes seem highly puritanical by today's standards, they have had a long-lasting influence on attitudes toward sex in American and other Western cultures. It was not until 1972 that the American Medical Association (AMA) declared, "Masturbation is a normal part of adolescent sexual development and requires no medical management" (American Medical Association Committee on Human Sexuality, 1972, p. 40). Around the same time, the Boy Scout manual dropped its antimasturbation warnings. Nonetheless, in 1994 Jocelyn Elders was fired as U.S. Surgeon General for suggesting publicly that sex education courses should include discussion of masturbation. Moreover, the Roman Catholic Church still holds that masturbation is sinful.

Case 2: Ritualized Homosexuality in Melanesia

Melanesia is a group of islands in the South Pacific that has been intensively studied by anthropologists, who have uncovered cultural influences on sexuality unlike any known in the West. Up until several decades ago, some Melanesian societies practiced a form of homosexuality within the context of male initiation rituals, which all male members of society had to experience.

The best-studied society has been the Sambia of Papua New Guinea (Herdt, 2000; Herdt & Stoller, 1990). Two beliefs reflected in Sambian sexual practices are semen conservation and female pollution. Like Tissot, the Sambians believed that semen is important for many things including physical growth, strength, and spirituality. They believed that it takes many inseminations (and much semen) to impregnate a woman, and also that semen could not easily be replenished by the body and so had to be conserved or obtained elsewhere. The female pollution doctrine is the belief that the female body is unhealthy to males, primarily because of menstrual fluids. At menarche, Sambian women were secretly initiated in the menstrual hut forbidden to all males.

To obtain or maintain adequate amounts of semen, young Sambian males practiced semen exchange with each other. Beginning as boys, they learned to practice fellatio (oral sex) in order to ingest sperm, but after puberty they could also take the penetrative role, inseminating younger boys. Ritualized homosexuality among the young Sambian men was seen as an exchange of sexual pleasure for vital semen. Notably, both the Sambians and the Victorian-era Americans believed in semen conservation, but their solutions to the problem were radically different. When Sambian males were well past puberty, they began the transition to heterosexuality. At this time the female body was thought to be less dangerous because the males had ingested protective semen over the previous years. For a time, they began having sex with women and still participated in fellatio with younger boys, but homosexual behavior stopped after the birth of a man's first child.

Ritualized homosexuality among the Melanesians is an example of the influence of culture on sexual attitudes and behavior. A Melanesian adolescent who refuses to practice homosexuality would have been viewed as abnormal, and such adolescents were apparently absent or rare. In the United States ritualized homosexuality of this type would be stigmatized as homosexual pedophilia, but Melanesian boys who practiced it appeared neither to have strong objections nor to be derailed from eventual heterosexuality.

Case 3: Homosexuality and American Psychiatry

During the past half-century, the status of homosexuality has changed enormously, both within psychiatry and psychology and for many Western societies in general. In the not-too-distant past, homosexuality was a taboo topic. Now, books, movies, and television shows address the topic explicitly by including gay men and lesbians in leading roles. Developments in psychiatry and psychology have played an important part in these changes. Homosexuality was considered a mental disorder for some time, before being officially removed from the *DSM* (where it had previously been classified as a sexual deviation) in 1974. A brief review of attitudes toward homosexuality within the mental health field itself provides another illustration of how attitudes toward various expressions of human sexuality may change over time.

HOMOSEXUALITY AS SICKNESS Reading the medical and psychological literature on homosexuality written before 1970 can be a jarring experience. Relevant articles included "Effeminate Homosexuality: A Disease of Childhood" and "On the Cure of Homosexuality." It is only fair to note, however, that the view that homosexual people are mentally ill was relatively tolerant compared with some earlier views—for example, the idea that homosexual people are criminals in need of incarceration (Bayer, 1981). British and American cultures had long taken punitive approaches to homosexual behavior. In the sixteenth century, King Henry VIII of England declared "the detestable and abominable vice of buggery [anal sex]" a felony punishable by death, and it was not until 1861 that the maximum penalty was reduced to 10 years' imprisonment. Similarly, laws in the United States were very repressive until recently, with homosexual behavior continuing to be a criminal offense in some states (Eskridge, 2008) until the 2003 Supreme Court ruling that struck down a Texas state law banning sexual behavior between two people of the same sex (*Lawrence & Garner v. Texas*). For the first time, this ruling established a broad constitutional right to sexual privacy in the United States.

During the late nineteenth and early twentieth centuries, several prominent sexologists such as Havelock Ellis and Magnus Hirschfeld suggested that homosexuality is natural and consistent with psychological normality. Freud's own attitude toward homosexual people was also remarkably progressive for his time and is well expressed in his touching "Letter to an American Mother" (1935).

Dear Mrs. . . .

I gather from your letter that your son is a homosexual. I am most impressed by the fact that you do not mention this term yourself in your information about him. May I question you, why you avoid it? Homosexuality is assuredly no advantage, but it is nothing to be ashamed of, no vice, no degradation, it cannot be classified as an illness. . . . Many highly respectable individuals of ancient and modern times have been homosexuals, several of the greatest men among them (Plato, Michelangelo, Leonardo da Vinci, etc.). It is a great injustice to persecute homosexuality as a crime, and cruelty too. . . .

By asking me if I can help, you mean, I suppose, if I can abolish homosexuality and make normal heterosexuality take its place. The answer is, in a general way, we cannot promise to achieve it. . . .

Sincerely yours with kind wishes,
Freud

Beginning in the 1940s, however, other psychoanalysts, led by Sandor Rado, began to take a more pessimistic view of the mental health of homosexual people—and a more optimistic view of the possible success of therapy to induce heterosexuality (Herek, 2010). Rado (1962) believed that homosexuality develops in people whose heterosexual desires are too psychologically threatening; thus, in this view, homosexuality is an escape from heterosexuality and therefore incompatible with mental health (see also Bieber et al., 1962). In the case of male homosexuality, one argument was that domineering, emotionally smothering mothers and detached, hostile fathers played a causal role. Unfortunately, these psychoanalysts based their opinions primarily on their experiences seeing gay men in therapy, who are obviously more likely than other gay men to be psychologically troubled (Herek, 2010).

HOMOSEXUALITY AS NONPATHOLOGICAL VARIATION Around 1950, the view of homosexuality as sickness began to be challenged by both scientists and homosexual people themselves (Herek, 2010). Scientific blows to the pathology position included Kinsey's finding that homosexual behavior was more common than had been previously believed (Kinsey et al., 1948, 1953). Influential studies also demonstrated that trained psychologists could not distinguish the psychological test results of homosexual subjects from those of heterosexual subjects (Hooker, 1957).

Gay men and lesbians also began to challenge the psychiatric orthodoxy that homosexuality is a mental disorder. The 1960s saw the birth of the radical gay liberation movement, which took the more uncompromising stance that "gay is good." The decade closed with the famous Stonewall riot in New York City, sparked by police mistreatment of gay men, which sent a clear signal that homosexual people would no longer tolerate being treated as second-class citizens. By the 1970s, openly gay psychiatrists and psychologists were working from within the mental health profession to have homosexuality removed from *DSM-II* (American Psychiatric Association, 1968). After acrimonious debate in 1973 and 1974, the American Psychiatric Association voted in 1974 by a vote of 5,854 to 3,810 to remove homosexuality from *DSM-II*.

At that point, research in this area shifted to begin to address mental health concerns of gay men and lesbians. Several large surveys examined rates of mental problems in people with and without homosexual feelings or behavior (Chakraborty et al., 2011; Sandfort et al., 2001; see Herek & Garnets, 2007, for a review). Homosexual people do appear to have elevated risk for some mental problems. For example, compared with heterosexual men and women, gay-identified men and lesbian-identified women have higher rates of anxiety disorders and depression (Bostwick et al., 2010). Whether gay and lesbian people are at increased risk for suicide remains controversial (Savin-Williams, 2006), with a recent population study finding no increased risk for gay men (Cochran & Mays, 2011). Lesbians also have a higher rate of substance abuse (Herek & Garnets, 2007; Sandfort et al., 2001). Although it remains unclear why homosexual people have higher rates of certain problems (Bailey, 1999; Cochran, 2012), one plausible explanation is that such problems result from stressful life events related to societal stigmatizing of homosexuality (Herek & Garnets, 2007).

The past 50 years have brought momentous progress toward legal rights and social acceptance in much of the developed world. For example, in 2010 for the first time a majority of Americans viewed homosexual relations between adults as morally acceptable (Gallup, 2010). Many Americans now support marriage for same-sex couples, and in June 2015 the U.S. Supreme Court ruled that same-sex couples can be legally married in all 50 U.S. states. In some parts of the world, however, progress toward equal rights and acceptance has lagged far behind. In some countries in Africa and the Middle East, large majorities disapprove of homosexuality (Pew Research Center, 2013), and in a few of those countries homosexual people may be subject to capital punishment. The marked cross-cultural and historical variation in treatment of homosexual people should remind us to be cautious in assuming that a currently unpopular or uncommon trait is pathological without careful and persuasive analysis. Sometimes it is culture that is the problem.

in review

- What does each of the three examples of sociocultural influences on sexual practices and standards reveal about cultural differences and historical changes in what is considered acceptable and normal sexual behavior?

- How has the psychiatric view of homosexuality changed over time? Identify a few key historical events that propelled this change.

Paraphilic Disorders

12.2 List and describe four types of paraphilia.

Paraphilic disorders are characterized by recurrent, intense sexually arousing fantasies, sexual urges, or behaviors that generally involve (1) abnormal targets of sexual attraction (e.g., shoes, children), (2) unusual courtship behaviors (e.g., watching others undress without their knowledge, or exposing oneself to others against their wishes), or (3) the desire for pain and suffering of oneself or others.

Paraphilias have challenged authors of past *DSM* editions for two main reasons. First, some paraphilias—especially pedophilia—are widely considered pathological even if the paraphilic individual does not experience distress. For example, consider a pedophile who has molested children but does not feel guilty. Most people believe that such a man has a mental disorder. In the past, pedophilia has been diagnosed even in the absence of distress; so have frotteurism and exhibitionism, both of which typically involve nonconsenting individuals in sexual acts. A second challenge has been that some other categories of paraphilias may be compatible with psychological health and happiness. For example, some men who have a foot fetish are comfortable with their sexual interest and even find willing partners who happily indulge them, while others feel substantial shame and guilt (Bergner, 2009). In the past, only foot fetishists with intense shame and guilt (or other problems related to their fetish) would be diagnosed as paraphilic. A useful distinction included in *DSM-5* is that between paraphilias and paraphilic disorders (Blanchard, 2010). Paraphilias are unusual sexual interests, but they need not cause harm either to the individual or to others. Only if they cause such harm do they become paraphilic disorders. Thus, foot fetishists have a paraphilia, but only those who suffer due to their sexual interest have a paraphilic disorder.

Although mild forms of these conditions probably occur in the lives of many normal people, a paraphilic person is distinguished by the insistence, and in some cases the relative exclusivity, with which his sexuality focuses on the acts or objects in question—without which orgasm is sometimes impossible. Paraphilias also frequently have a compulsive quality, and some individuals with paraphilias require orgasmic release as often as 4 to 10 times per day (Garcia & Thibaut, 2010). Individuals with paraphilias may or may not have persistent desires to change their sexual preferences. Because nearly all such persons are male (a fact whose etiologic implications we consider later), we use masculine pronouns to refer to them (see Fedoroff et al., 1999, for some possible examples of women with paraphilias).

It is difficult to estimate the prevalence of paraphilias because many people are reluctant to disclose such deviant behavior (Griffifths, 2012). The *DSM-5* recognizes eight specific paraphilias: (1) fetishism, (2) transvestic fetishism, (3) pedophilia, (4) voyeurism, (5) exhibitionism, (6) frotteurism, (7) sexual sadism, and (8) sexual masochism. An additional category, paraphilias not otherwise specified, includes several rarer disorders such as telephone scatologia (obscene phone calls), necrophilia (sexual desire for corpses), zoophilia (sexual interest in animals), apotemnophilia (sexual excitement and desire about having a limb amputated), and coprophilia (sexual arousal to feces). Although some of the different paraphilias tend to co-occur together, we discuss each of them separately. In addition, our discussion of pedophilia is postponed until a later section concerning sexual abuse.

Fetishistic Disorder

In **fetishism**, the individual has recurrent, intense sexually arousing fantasies, urges, and behaviors involving the use of some inanimate object or a part of the body not typically found erotic (e.g., feet) to obtain sexual gratification (see the *DSM-5* Criteria for Several Different Paraphilic Disorders box). As is generally true for the paraphilias, reported cases of female fetishists are extremely rare (Mason, 1997). Usually the fetishistic object is required or strongly preferred during sexual arousal and activity. Many men have a strong sexual fascination for paraphernalia such as bras, garter belts, pantyhose, and high heels, but most do not typically meet diagnostic criteria for fetishism because the paraphernalia are not necessary or strongly preferred for sexual arousal. Nevertheless, they do illustrate the relatively high frequency of fetish-like preferences among men. Fetishism occurs frequently in the context of sadomasochistic activity but is relatively rare among sexual offenders (Kafka, 2010).

The mode of using these objects to achieve sexual excitation and gratification varies considerably, but it commonly involves masturbating while kissing, fondling, tasting, or smelling the objects. In the context of consensual sexual relationships, fetishism does not normally interfere with the rights of others. However, some partners who do

DSM-5 *Criteria for...*

Several Different Paraphilic Disorders

Fetishistic Disorder

A. Over a period of at least 6 months, recurrent and intense sexual arousal from either the use of nonliving objects or a highly specific focus on nongenital body part(s), as manifested by fantasies, urges, or behaviors.

B. The fantasies, sexual urges, or behaviors cause clinically significant distress or impairment in social, occupational, or other important areas of functioning.

C. The fetish objects are not limited to articles of clothing used in cross-dressing (as in transvestic disorder) or devices specifically designed for the purpose of tactile genital stimulation (e.g., vibrator).

Transvestic Disorder

A. Over a period of at least 6 months, recurrent and intense sexual arousal from cross-dressing, as manifested by fantasies, urges, or behaviors.

B. The fantasies, sexual urges, or behaviors cause clinically significant distress or impairment in social, occupational, or other important areas of functioning.

Pedophilic Disorder

A. Over a period of at least 6 months, recurrent, intense sexually arousing fantasies, sexual urges, or behaviors involving sexual activity with a prepubescent child or children (generally age 13 years or younger).

B. The individual has acted on these sexual urges, or the sexual urges or fantasies cause marked distress or interpersonal difficulty.

C. The individual is at least age 16 years and at least 5 years older than the child or children in Criterion A.
   Note: Do not include an individual in late adolescence involved in an ongoing sexual relationship with a 12- or 13-year-old.

Voyeuristic Disorder

A. Over a period of at least 6 months, recurrent and intense sexual arousal from observing an unsuspecting person who is naked, in the process of disrobing, or engaging in sexual activity, as manifested by fantasies, urges, or behaviors.

B. The individual has acted on these sexual urges with a nonconsenting person, or the sexual urges or fantasies cause clinically

significant distress or impairment in social, occupational, or other important areas of functioning.

C. The individual experiencing the arousal and/or acting on the urges is at least 18 years of age.

Exhibitionistic Disorder

A. Over a period of at least 6 months, recurrent and intense sexual arousal from the exposure of one's genitals to an unsuspecting person, as manifested by fantasies, urges, or behaviors.

B. The individual has acted on these sexual urges with a nonconsenting person, or the sexual urges or fantasies cause clinically significant distress or impairment in social, occupational, or other important areas of functioning.

Frotteuristic Disorder

A. Over a period of at least 6 months, recurrent and intense sexual arousal from touching or rubbing against a nonconsenting person, as manifested by fantasies, urges, or behaviors.

B. The individual has acted on these sexual urges with a nonconsenting person, or the sexual urges or fantasies cause clinically significant distress or impairment in social, occupational, or other important areas of functioning.

Sexual Sadism Disorder

A. Over a period of at least 6 months, recurrent and intense sexual arousal from the physical or psychological suffering of another person, as manifested by fantasies, urges, or behaviors.

B. The individual has acted on these sexual urges with a nonconsenting person, or the sexual urges or fantasies cause clinically significant distress or impairment in social, occupational, or other important areas of functioning.

Sexual Masochism Disorder

A. Over a period of at least 6 months, recurrent and intense sexual arousal from the act of being humiliated, beaten, bound, or otherwise made to suffer, as manifested by fantasies, urges, or behaviors.

B. The fantasies, sexual urges, or behaviors cause clinically significant distress or impairment in social, occupational, or other important areas of functioning.

Source: Reprinted with permission from the *Diagnostic and Statistical Manual of Mental Disorders*, Fifth Edition (Copyright 2013). American Psychiatric Association.

---

not share an erotic fascination with a fetishistic object may understandably object to participating. Some paraphilic men are so ashamed of their desires that they cannot bring themselves to ask partners. Bergner (2009) related the case of a foot fetishist who chose chemical castration to suppress his desire rather than tell his wife. As depicted in the case study below, people with fetishes often try very hard to keep them concealed.

The Secret

William was a 45-year-old, single financial consultant who came into a university clinic for an evaluation and potential treatment for "relationship concerns." During his initial evaluation with a graduate student therapist, he revealed that his primary concern is a "secret" that he has been keeping from his girlfriend. William reported that since he was a young child, he has been "obsessed with women's panties and stockings." He indicated that he is attracted to women, but since adolescence has had a difficult time becoming sexually aroused without the sight of panties and/or stockings. He reports that he watches pornographic movies every day that center around women putting on and taking off their panties and stockings, and that on many occasions he has stolen these garments from stores and from women he has dated and/or had sexual encounters with. He also notes that he has a collection of these stolen items hidden in his bedroom and sometimes masturbates while wearing the garments himself. This "hobby" brings him great pleasure, but also causes him to feel extremely ashamed and guilty at times. He is coming in for treatment now because he has gotten much closer with his current girlfriend but is afraid of how she will respond if and when she learns about his 'hobby.'

One common hypothesis regarding the etiology of fetishism emphasizes the importance of classical conditioning and social learning (Hoffmann, 2012). For example, it is not difficult to imagine how women's underwear might become eroticized via its close association with sex and the female body. But only a small number of men develop fetishes, so even if the hypothesis has merit there must be individual differences in conditionability of sexual responses (just as there are differences in the conditionability of fear and anxiety responses, as discussed in Chapter 6). Men high in sexual conditionability would be prone to developing one or more fetishes. We will return later to the role of conditioning in the development of paraphilias more generally.

Transvestic Disorder

According to *DSM-5*, heterosexual men who experience recurrent, intense sexually arousing fantasies, urges, or behaviors that involve cross-dressing as a female may be diagnosed with **transvestic disorder**, if they experience significant distress or impairment due to the condition (see the earlier *DSM-5* criteria box). Although some gay men dress "in drag" on occasion, they do not typically do this for sexual pleasure and hence do not have the paraphilia transvestism. Typically, the onset of transvestism is during adolescence and involves masturbation while wearing female clothing or undergarments. Blanchard (2010) has hypothesized that the psychological motivation of most heterosexual transvestites includes *autogynephilia:* paraphilic sexual arousal by the thought or fantasy of being a woman (Blanchard, 1993; Lawrence, 2013). The sexologist Magnus Hirschfeld (1984) first identified a class of cross-dressing men who are sexually aroused by the image of themselves as women: "They feel attracted not by the women outside them, but by the woman inside them" (p. 167). Not all men with transvestic fetishism show clear evidence of autogynephilia (Blanchard, 2010). Some men seem quite similar to typical fetishists, focusing on specifics of their preferred female clothing and without having clearly

apparent fantasies of becoming women. Among transvestic fetishists, the strength of autogynephilic fantasies strongly predicts gender dysphoria, which refers to discomfort with one's sex-relevant physical characteristics or with one's assigned gender (see the next section for more on this topic; Blanchard, 2010). Like other kinds of fetishism, transvestic fetishism causes overt harm to others only when accompanied by such an illegal act as theft or destruction of property. Such acts are rare, and the vast majority of transvestites are harmless.

One large survey of over 2,400 men and women in Sweden estimated that almost 3 percent of the men and 0.4 percent of the women reported having engaged in at least one episode of erotic cross-dressing, but the actual prevalence of the disorder is likely much lower (Langstrom & Zucker, 2005). This same study reported on various demographic and experiential differences between the men who had cross-dressed and those who had not. Among the most interesting findings were that the men who had cross-dressed had experienced more sexual abuse before age 10, were more easily sexually aroused, had a higher frequency of masturbation, made greater use of pornography, and had other paraphilias. An earlier survey of over 1,000 men who frequently crossed-dressed reported that the vast majority (87 percent) were heterosexual, 83 percent had married, and 60 percent were married at the time of the survey (Docter & Prince, 1997). Many managed to keep their cross-dressing a secret, at least for a while. However, wives often found out and had a wide range of reactions, from accepting to being extremely disturbed. The following case illustrates both the typical early onset of transvestic fetishism and the difficulties the condition may raise in a marriage.

A Transvestite's Dilemma

Edward is a 57-year-old married father of three who has worked as a fireman for the past 35 years. When he was in the sixth grade, he became sexually aroused while handling his older sister's underwear while folding the laundry. Over a period of weeks, he began secretly wearing her underwear for longer and longer periods of time, and eventually to masturbating while wearing her underwear. Although he enjoyed this practice, he had a sense that it was unusual and so he did not tell anyone about it. When he moved out of his parents' house at age 21 and into his own apartment, he began wearing women's underwear under his clothes and sleeping in women's nightgowns whenever he was home. Edward has always been attracted only to women, and married his high school sweetheart while in his early 20s. He eventually revealed his fondness for dressing in women's undergarments during their first years of marriage, and she responded supportively telling him that it was okay that he did it, as long as he did not do so outside of the home, and to the extent possible, she did not want to see him in women's clothing. This arrangement worked for a long time and they had, and raised, three children. Now that the children are all grown and out of the home, Edward is having increasing thoughts and urges about dressing in women's clothing full time. However, he understands that this may upset his wife, and almost certainly will not go over well at the firehouse. This dilemma is causing him a lot of stress and he is not sure what he should do, so he came into the clinic for an evaluation and course of therapy.

Voyeuristic Disorder

A person is diagnosed with **voyeuristic disorder** if he has recurrent, intense sexually arousing fantasies, urges, or behaviors involving the observation of unsuspecting females who are undressing or of couples engaging in sexual activity (see the earlier *DSM-5* criteria box). Frequently, such individuals masturbate during their peeping activity. "Peeping Toms," as they are commonly called, commit these offenses primarily as young men. Voyeurism often co-occurs with exhibitionism, and it is also associated with interest in sadomasochism and cross-dressing (Langstrom & Seto, 2006). Voyeurism is believed to be the most common illegal sexual activity (Langstrom, 2010).

How do some young men develop this pattern? Viewing the body of an attractive female is sexually stimulating for most heterosexual men. In addition, the privacy and mystery that have traditionally surrounded sexual activities tend to increase curiosity about them. Moreover, if a young man with such curiosity feels shy and inadequate in his relations with the opposite sex, he may accept the substitute of voyeurism, which satisfies his curiosity and to some extent meets his sexual needs without the trauma of actually approaching a female. He thus avoids the rejection and lowered self-status that such an approach might bring. In fact, voyeuristic activities often provide important compensatory feelings of power and secret domination over an unsuspecting victim, which may contribute to the maintenance of this pattern. If a voyeur manages to find a wife in spite of his interpersonal difficulties, as many do, he is rarely well-adjusted sexually in his relationship with his wife, as the following case illustrates.

A Peeping Tom

John was a young, married graduate student who lived with his wife in an apartment just across the street from the undergraduate campus. John's wife worked as a lawyer and typically came home at night tired, irritable, and not in the mood for sexual relations. In order "to obtain some sexual gratification" after his wife went to sleep, John would take a pair of binoculars into the living room and look into the 12-story dormitory building across the street in order to watch female students undress and occasionally to observe young couples engaged in sexual activities. This stimulated him greatly, and he decided to extend his peeping to other dormitories on campus, as well as to campus sorority houses. While out looking into sorority houses one night, he was spotted, reported, and apprehended by the university police.

More permissive laws concerning pornographic movies, videos, and magazines in recent years have removed some of the secrecy about sexual behavior and also have provided an alternative source of gratification for would-be voyeurs. However, for many voyeurs, these movies and magazines probably do not provide an adequate substitute for secretly watching the sexual behavior of an unsuspecting couple or the "real-life" nudity of a woman who mistakenly believes she enjoys privacy. Moreover, the actual effect of pornographic material on voyeurism is a matter of speculation because there never have been good epidemiologic data on the prevalence of this paraphilia, although it is thought to be one of the most common (Langstrom, 2010). The large Swedish survey mentioned earlier that was conducted with over 2,400 men and women found that 11.5 percent of the men and 3.0 percent of the women had at some time engaged in voyeuristic activity (Langstrom & Seto, 2006). Among those who did report such activity, they also reported more psychological problems, less satisfaction with life, higher rates of masturbation, greater use of pornography, and greater ease of sexual arousability.

Although a voyeur may become reckless in his behavior and thus may be detected or even apprehended by the police, voyeurism does not ordinarily have any other serious criminal or antisocial behaviors associated with it. In fact, many people probably have some voyeuristic inclinations, which are checked by practical considerations such as the possibility of being caught and by ethical attitudes concerning the right to privacy.

Exhibitionistic Disorder

Exhibitionistic disorder (*indecent exposure* in legal terms) is diagnosed in a person with recurrent, intense urges, fantasies, or behaviors that involve exposing his genitals to others (usually strangers) in inappropriate circumstances and without their consent (see the earlier *DSM-5* criteria box). Frequently the element of shock in the victim is highly arousing to these individuals. The exposure may take place in some secluded location such as a park or in a more public place such as a department store, church, theater, or bus. In cities, an exhibitionist (also known as a flasher) often drives by schools or bus stops, exhibits himself while in the car, and then drives rapidly away. In many instances the exposure is repeated under fairly constant conditions, such as only in churches or buses or in the same general vicinity and at the same time of day. In one case, a youth exhibited himself only at the top of an escalator in a large department store. For a male offender, the typical victim is ordinarily a young or middle-aged female who is not known to the offender, although children and adolescents may also be targeted (Murphy, 1997).

Men who engage in exhibitionism often cause emotional distress in the viewers because of the intrusive quality of the act, along with its explicit violation of propriety norms.

Exhibitionism, which usually begins in adolescence or young adulthood, is the most common sexual offense reported to the police in the United States, Canada, and Europe, accounting for about one-third of all sexual offenses (McAnulty et al., 2001). According to some estimates, as many as 20 percent of women have been the target of either exhibitionism or voyeurism (Kaplan & Krueger, 1997; Meyer, 1995). Although there are no good epidemiologic data on the prevalence of this paraphilia, the large Swedish survey of over 2,400 people mentioned earlier reported that 4.1 percent of the men and 2.1 percent of the women had had at least one episode of exhibitionistic behavior (Langstrom & Seto, 2006). It commonly co-occurs with voyeurism and also tends to co-occur with sadomasochistic interests and cross-dressing (Langstrom, 2010). Exhibitionism is associated with greater psychological problems, lower life satisfaction, greater use of pornography, and more frequent masturbation.

In some instances, exposure of the genitals is accompanied by suggestive gestures or masturbation, but more often there is only exposure. A significant minority of exhibitionists commit aggressive acts, sometimes including coercive sex crimes against adults or children. Some men who expose themselves may do so because they have antisocial personality disorder, as described in Chapter 10, rather than a paraphilia (Langstrom, 2010).

Despite the rarity of aggressive or assaultive behavior in these cases, an exhibitionistic act nevertheless takes place without the viewer's consent and may be emotionally upsetting, as is indeed the perpetrator's intent. This intrusive quality of the act, together with its explicit violation of propriety norms about "private parts," ensures condemnation. Thus, society considers exhibitionism a criminal offense.

Frotteuristic Disorder

Frotteurism is sexual excitement at rubbing one's genitals against, or touching, the body of a nonconsenting person. As with voyeurism, frotteurism reflects inappropriate and persistent interest in something that many people enjoy in a consensual context. Frotteurism commonly co-occurs with voyeurism and exhibitionism (Langstrom, 2010). Being the victim of a frotteuristic act often occurs among regular riders of crowded buses or subway trains. Some have speculated that frotteurs' willingness to touch others sexually without their consent means that they are at risk for more serious sexual offending, but there is currently no evidence to support this concern (Langstrom, 2010). Because frotteurism typically requires the unwilling participation of others, frotteuristic disorder is diagnosed if frotteuristic acts occur, whether or not the frotteurer is, himself, bothered by his urges.

Sexual Sadism Disorder

The term *sadism* is derived from the name of the Marquis de Sade (1740–1814), who, for sexual purposes, inflicted such cruelty on his victims that he was eventually involuntarily committed to a psychiatric hospital. For a diagnosis of **sexual sadism disorder**, a person must have recurrent, intense sexually arousing fantasies, urges, or behaviors that involve inflicting psychological or physical pain on another individual (see the earlier *DSM-5* criteria box). Sadistic fantasies often include themes of dominance, control, and humiliation (Kirsch & Becker, 2007). A closely related, but less severe, pattern is the practice of "bondage and discipline" (B&D), which may include tying a person up, hitting or spanking, and so on to enhance sexual excitement. The large majority of sexually sadistic acts probably occur in the context of a consensual sexual relationship without any evident harm. In large urban communities, there is often a "BDSM" subculture consisting of individuals who enjoy mild bondage and discipline, as well as sadism and masochism. It is thus important to distinguish transient or occasional interest in sadomasochistic practices from sadism as a paraphilia. Surveys have found that perhaps 5 to 15 percent of men and women enjoy sadistic and/or masochistic activities voluntarily on occasion (Baumeister & Butler, 1997; Hucker, 1997).

A small minority of men with sexual sadism, in contrast, enjoy inflicting sadistic acts that are nonconsensual, serious, and sometimes fatal (Dietz et al., 1990; Krueger, 2010). In some cases, sadistic activities lead up to or terminate in actual sexual relations; in others, full sexual gratification is obtained from the sadistic practice alone. A sadist, for example, might slash a woman with a razor or stick her with a needle, experiencing an orgasm in the process. The pain inflicted by sadists may come from whipping, biting, cutting, or burning; the act may vary in intensity, from fantasy to severe mutilation and even murder. Paraphilic sadism and masochism, in which sadomasochistic activities are the preferred or exclusive means to sexual gratification, are much rarer; not uncommonly, they co-occur in the same individual (Kirsch & Becker, 2007). *DSM-5* requires that the diagnosis of sadism be reserved for cases either in which the victim is nonconsenting or in which the sadistic experience is marked by distress or interpersonal difficulties. Many cases of sexual sadism have comorbid disorders—especially the narcissistic, schizoid, or antisocial personality disorders (Kirsch & Becker, 2007). Sexual sadists with these personality disorders may be especially nonempathic and thus likely to act on their sexual urges.

Extreme sexual sadists may mentally replay their torture scenes later while masturbating. Serial killers, who tend to be sexual sadists, sometimes record or videotape their sadistic acts. One study characterized 20 sexually sadistic serial killers who were responsible for 149 murders throughout the United States and Canada (Warren et al., 1996). Most were white males in their late 20s or early 30s. Their murders were remarkably consistent over time, reflecting sexual arousal to the pain, fear, and panic of their victims. Choreographed assaults allowed them to carefully control their victims' deaths. Some of the men reported that the God-like sense of being in control of the life and death of another human being was especially exhilarating. Eighty-five percent of the sample reported consistent violent sexual fantasies, and 75 percent collected materials with a violent theme including audiotapes, videotapes, pictures, or sketches of their sadistic acts or sexually sadistic pornography.

Notorious serial killers include Ted Bundy, who was executed in 1989. Bundy confessed to the murder of over 30 young women, nearly all of whom fit a targeted type: women with long hair parted in the middle. Bundy admitted that he used his victims to re-create the covers of detective magazines or scenes from "slasher movies." Jeffrey Dahmer was convicted in 1992 of having mutilated and murdered 15 boys and young men, generally having sex with them after death. (He was subsequently murdered in prison.) Dennis Rader, the BTK Killer (for Bind, Torture, Kill), was captured in 2005 after committing 10 murders over 30 years in Wichita, Kansas. Rader exemplifies several interesting phenomena associated with homicidal sexual sadism. As a child he tortured animals and fantasized about tying up and torturing attractive children he watched on television. When he began enacting his fantasies, he stalked his victims for weeks to learn their habits before he attacked them. He enjoyed tying them up and then strangled them. Only after they were dead would he gratify himself sexually through masturbation. He often retained the clothing of his victims, which he would sometimes wear. Sometimes in private he would practice bondage on himself because he found this erotic.

Dennis Rader was married with two children, an active member in his church, and a respected member of the community; he was also a serial killer known as the BTK Killer.

What causes some men to be sexually sadistic killers? Although many sadists have had chaotic childhoods, Bundy, Dahmer, and Rader all came from apparently stable and loving families. Unfortunately, we do not have a good understanding of the causal factors involved in these extreme cases of sadism.

Sexual sadism is understandably an important concern of criminologists, law enforcement officers, and forensic mental health professionals. Unfortunately, the diagnosis of sexual sadism is not very reliable (Marshall & Hucker, 2006) or valid (Kingston et al., 2010), perhaps due to the sadist's unwillingness to discuss his sometimes appallingly violent sexual fantasies (Nitschke et al., 2012). This is concerning, given how important it is to detect dangerous sexual sadists and how stigmatizing a diagnosis of sexual sadism might be to someone whose sexual desires are harmless. One promising modification currently being considered is a dimensional approach that could distinguish sexual sadists who are dangerous from those who are not (Krueger, 2010; Marshall & Hucker, 2006). Another is to focus on behavioral indicators of sadism, which are sometimes more apparent (Nitschke et al., 2012).

Sexual Masochism Disorder

The term **masochism** is derived from the name of the Austrian novelist Leopold V. Sacher-Masoch (1836–1895), whose fictional characters derived sexual pleasure from being dominated and made to experience pain. In sexual masochism, a person experiences sexual stimulation and gratification from the experience of pain and degradation in relating to a lover. According to *DSM-5* (see the earlier *DSM-5* criteria box), the person must have experienced recurrent, intense sexually arousing fantasies, urges, or behaviors involving the act of being humiliated, beaten, bound, or otherwise made to suffer.

Sadomasochistic activities, including bondage and discipline, are often performed communally within "dungeons" popular in major cities.

Consensual sadomasochistic relationships, involving a dominant, sadistic "master" and a submissive, masochistic "slave" are not uncommon in either heterosexual or homosexual relationships. Such masochists do not usually want, or cooperate with, true sexual sadists and prefer individuals willing to hurt or humiliate them within preset limits. Masochism appears to be more common than sadism and occurs in both men and women (Baumeister & Butler, 1997; Sandnabba et al., 2002). Sadomasochistic activities, including bondage and discipline, are often performed communally within "dungeons" popular in major cities. Such activities might involve men being bound and whipped by women called "dominatrixes," who wear tight leather or rubber outfits and are paid to inflict pain and humiliation in a sexually charged sense. Most members of this sadomasochistic community are high functioning and do not appear to suffer because of their sexual interests (Krueger, 2010).

Some rare forms of masochism are more problematic, however. One particularly dangerous form of masochism, called *autoerotic asphyxia*, involves self-strangulation. Although some writers have speculated that loss of oxygen to the brain intensifies orgasm, there is little evidence that this motivates practitioners of autoerotic asphyxia. In contrast, studies of such practitioners have found that their sexual fantasies are strongly masochistic (Hucker, 2011). Coroners in most major U.S. cities are familiar with cases in which the deceased is found hanged next to masochistic pornographic literature or other sexual paraphernalia. Accidental deaths attributable to this practice have been estimated to range between 500 and 1,000 per year in the United States (LeVay & Baldwin, 2012). Although autoerotic asphyxia is much more common in men, it can occur in women too, and it has occurred across many cultures going back hundreds of years. In some cases it occurs in a consensual or nonconsensual sadomasochistic act between two or more people (McGrath & Turvey, 2008).

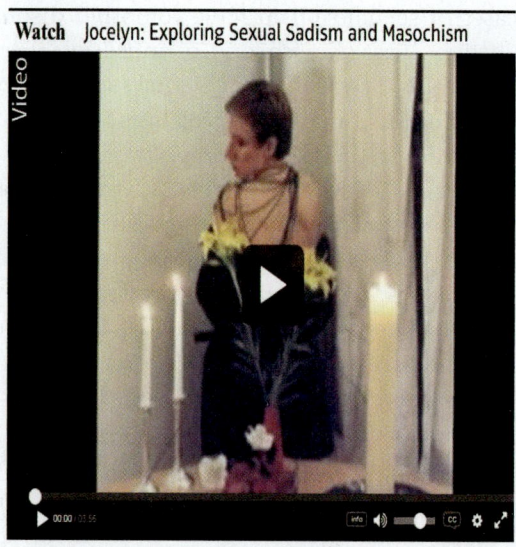

Watch Jocelyn: Exploring Sexual Sadism and Masochism

Causal Factors and Treatments for Paraphilias

Many individuals with paraphilias have explanations for their unusual sexual preferences. For example, one amputee paraphilic (whose preference was a partner with a missing limb) recalled that his fascination with female amputees originated during adolescence. He was neglected emotionally by his cold family but heard a family member express sympathetic feelings for an amputee. He developed the wish that he would become an amputee and thus earn their sympathy (see First, 2005, for a discussion of this paraphilia, known as *apotemnophilia*). This story raises many questions. Emotionally cold families are not uncommon, and sympathy for amputees is nearly universal. Certainly not every male in a cold family who detects sympathy for amputees develops an amputee paraphilia. Such stories do not necessarily have any validity because we are often unaware of the forces that shape us (Nisbett & Wilson, 1977; Wilson, 2009).

Several facts about paraphilia are likely to be important in their development. First, as we have already noted, nearly all persons with paraphilias are male; females with most paraphilias are so rare that they are found in the literature only as case reports or a series of case reports (Fedoroff et al., 1999). Second, paraphilias usually begin around the time of puberty or early adolescence. Third, people with paraphilias often have a strong sex drive, with some men often masturbating many times a day. Fourth, people with paraphilias frequently have more than one. For example, men who died accidentally in the course of autoerotic asphyxia were partially or fully cross-dressed in 25 to 33 percent of cases (Blanchard & Hucker, 1991). There is no obvious reason for the association between sexual masochism and transvestism. Why should it be so?

Money (1986) and others have suggested that male vulnerability to paraphilias is closely linked to their greater dependence on visual sexual imagery. Perhaps sexual arousal in men depends on physical stimulus features to a greater degree than in women, whose arousal may depend more on emotional context such as being in love with a partner. If so, men may be more vulnerable to forming sexual associations to nonsexual stimuli, which may be most likely to occur after puberty, when the sexual drive is high. Many believe that these associations arise as a result of classical and instrumental conditioning and/or social learning that occurs through observation and modeling. When observing paraphilic stimuli (e.g., photographs of models in their underwear), or when fantasies about paraphilic stimuli occur, boys may masturbate, and the reinforcement gained from orgasm release may serve to condition an intense attraction to paraphilic stimuli (Kaplan & Krueger, 1997; LeVay & Baldwin, 2012). This hypothesis cannot explain, however, why only a small minority of males develop fetishes for panties and bras, despite the nearly universal experience of masturbating to pictures or videos of women wearing them.

The vast majority of studies concerning the treatment of paraphilias have been conducted with sex offenders. The literature concerning treatment of men with paraphilias who have not committed any offense, or who have victimless paraphilias (e.g., masochism), consists primarily of case reports because most people with paraphilias do not seek treatment for these conditions. Thus, we defer discussion of the treatment of paraphilias until we discuss the treatment of sex offenders, many of whom have paraphilias.

---

in review

- Define *paraphilia*, and cite four paraphilias recognized in the *DSM*, along with their associated features.

Gender Dysphoria

12.3 **Explain the key characteristics of gender dysphoria.**

Gender dysphoria is discomfort with one's sex-relevant physical characteristics or with one's assigned gender. *Gender dysphoria* is a new term used in *DSM-5*, in place of the previous *gender identity disorder.* The change in terminology is both usefully descriptive and theoretically neutral. That is, individuals who have been previously diagnosed with gender identity disorder certainly experience gender dysphoria, but whether or not this is always due to atypical gender identity development is less clear. Gender dysphoria also is consistent with a dimensional approach (the degree of dysphoria can vary) and may fluctuate over time within the same individual (Cohen-Kettenis & Pfafflin, 2010). Gender dysphoria can be diagnosed at two different life stages, either during childhood (gender dysphoria in children) or adolescence or adulthood (i.e., gender dysphoria in adolescents and adults).

Boys with gender dysphoria often show a preoccupation with traditionally feminine activities (Cohen-Kettenis & Klink, 2015). They may prefer to dress in female clothing.

DSM-5 *Criteria for. . .*

Gender Dysphoria in Children

A. A marked incongruence between one's experienced/expressed gender and assigned gender, of at least 6 months' duration, as manifested by at least six of the following (one of which must be Criterion A1):

1. A strong desire to be of the other gender or an insistence that one is the other gender (or some alternative gender different from one's assigned gender).

2. In boys (assigned gender), a strong preference for cross-dressing or simulating female attire; or in girls (assigned gender), a strong preference for wearing only typical masculine clothing and a strong resistance to the wearing of typical feminine clothing.

3. A strong preference for cross-gender roles in make-believe play or fantasy play.

4. A strong preference for the toys, games, or activities stereotypically used or engaged in by the other gender.

5. A strong preference for playmates of the other gender.

6. In boys (assigned gender), a strong rejection of typically masculine toys, games, and activities and a strong avoidance of rough-and-tumble play; or in girls (assigned gender), a strong rejection of typically feminine toys, games, and activities.

7. A strong dislike of one's sexual anatomy.

8. A strong desire for the primary and/or secondary sex characteristics that match one's experienced gender.

B. The condition is associated with clinically significant distress or impairment in social, school, or other important areas of functioning.

Source: Reprinted with permission from the *Diagnostic and Statistical Manual of Mental Disorders*, Fifth Edition (Copyright 2013). American Psychiatric Association.

They enjoy stereotypical girls' activities such as playing dolls and playing house. They usually avoid rough-and-tumble play and often express the desire to be a girl.

Girls with gender dysphoria typically prefer traditional boys' clothing and short hair. Fantasy heroes often include powerful male figures like Batman and Superman. They show little interest in dolls and increased interest in sports. Although many girls considered to be "tomboys" frequently have many or most of these traits, girls with gender dysphoria are distinguished by their desire to actually be a boy or to grow up as a man. Young girls with gender dysphoria are treated better by their peers than are boys with gender dysphoria because cross-gender behavior in girls is better tolerated (Cohen-Kettenis et al., 2003). In clinic-referred gender dysphoria, boys outnumbered girls five to one in one study (Cohen-Kettenis et al., 2003) and three to one in another study (Cohen-Kettenis et al., 2006). An appreciable percentage of that imbalance may reflect greater parental concern about femininity in boys than about masculinity in girls.

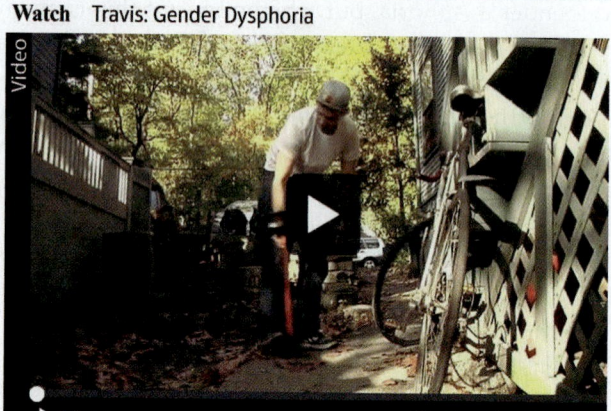

Watch Travis: Gender Dysphoria

The most common adult outcome of boys with gender dysphoria has been homosexuality rather than transsexualism (Zucker, 2005). In Richard Green's (1987) prospective study of 44 very feminine boys from the community, only 1 had sought sex change surgery by age 18. About three-quarters became gay or bisexual men who were evidently satisfied with their biological sex. However, several later studies of clinic-referred children have found that 10 to 20 percent of boys with gender dysphoria were transsexual by age 16 or 18, and about 40 to 60 percent identified themselves as homosexual or bisexual, a percentage that may have increased by the time they were older (Zucker, 2005). Several smaller prospective studies of girls with gender dysphoria have shown that 35 to 45 percent may show persistent gender dysphoria (leading to a desire for sex reassignment surgery in many), and approximately half had a homosexual orientation. However, the largest prospective study to date, which followed 25 girls with gender dysphoria (ages 3–12) into young adulthood (average age 23), found somewhat lower rates of persistent gender dysphoria and homosexuality. At follow-up, three were classified as being dissatisfied with their gender, and two of these three wanted to have sex reassignment surgery. However, 32 percent had homosexual or bisexual fantasies, and 24 percent engaged in homosexual or bisexual behavior. These rates are clearly much higher than expected from base rates of gender dysphoria in the population but not as high as in boys with gender dysphoria (Drummond et al., 2008).

Given that many such children typically adjust well in adulthood, should they be considered to have a mental disorder as children? Some have argued that such children should not be considered "disordered" because the primary obstacle to their happiness may be a society that is intolerant of cross-gender behavior. However, many

DSM-5 *Criteria for. . .*

Gender Dysphoria in Adolescents and Adults

A. A marked incongruence between one's experienced/expressed gender and assigned gender, of at least 6 months' duration, as manifested by at least two of the following:

1. A marked incongruence between one's experienced/expressed gender and primary and/or secondary sex characteristics (or in young adolescents, the anticipated secondary sex characteristics).
2. A strong desire to be rid of one's primary and/or secondary sex characteristics because of a marked incongruence with one's experienced/expressed gender (or in young adolescents, a desire to prevent the development of the anticipated secondary sex characteristics).
3. A strong desire for the primary and/or secondary sex characteristics of the other gender.

4. A strong desire to be of the other gender (or some alternative gender different from one's assigned gender).
5. A strong desire to be treated as the other gender (or some alternative gender different from one's assigned gender).
6. A strong conviction that one has the typical feelings and reactions of the other gender (or some alternative gender different from one's assigned gender).

B. The condition is associated with clinically significant distress or impairment in social, occupational, or other important areas of functioning.

Source: Reprinted with permission from the *Diagnostic and Statistical Manual of Mental Disorders*, Fifth Edition (Copyright 2013). American Psychiatric Association.

researchers who work with these children maintain that the distress and unhappiness these children and adolescents have about the discrepancy between their biological sex and their psychological gender are consistent with this being called a mental disorder (Zucker, 2005, 2010). Moreover, these children are frequently mistreated by their peers and have strained relations with their parents even though their cross-gender behavior harms no one.

Research from non-Western cultures shows that stigmatization of gender-nonconforming children is not universal (Vasey & Bartlett, 2007). In Samoa, very feminine males are often considered "fa'afafine" (roughly meaning "in the manner of women"), a kind of third gender, neither male nor female. Fa'afafine are identified as young children by their behavior and usually are accepted by their families and culture. As adults these individuals are sexually attracted to other men and typically have sexual relations with heterosexual men. They generally do not recall that their childhood gender nonconformity was associated with distress. Because of this, some have argued that childhood gender dysphoria should not appear in *DSM-5* (Vasey & Bartlett, 2007). Despite these objections, the diagnosis has been retained as gender dysphoria in children (Zucker, 2010).

Treatment for Gender Dysphoria

Children and adolescents with gender dysphoria are often brought in by their parents for psychotherapy (Zucker et al., 2008). Specialists attempt both to treat the child's unhappiness with his or her biological sex and to ease strained relations with parents and peers. Children with gender dysphoria often have other general psychological and behavioral problems such as anxiety and mood disorders that also need therapeutic attention (Zucker et al., 2002). Therapists try to improve peer and parental relations by teaching such children how to reduce their cross-gender behavior, especially in situations where it might cause interpersonal problems. Gender dysphoria is typically treated psychodynamically—that is, by examining inner conflicts. Controlled studies evaluating such treatment remain to be conducted (Zucker, 2005). If a child will eventually transition into the other sex, it is beneficial to prevent full sexual maturity from occurring in the original, unwanted sex. Thus, in the progressive Netherlands, under some circumstances, early adolescents with gender dysphoria are given hormonal treatment to delay puberty while they decide how to proceed (Cohen-Kettenis, 2010).

Two related facts about gender dysphoria in children are especially important clinically. First, as we have noted, most children with gender dysphoria do not become adults with gender dysphoria. The problem generally remits during childhood (Wallien & Cohen-Kettenis, 2008). Second, individuals who are still gender dysphoric into adolescence are likely to remain so into adulthood, and they are also likely to take medical steps to transform their bodies. The crucial period at which many children with gender dysphoria desist or persist appears to be ages 10 to 13 (Steensma et al., 2011). Increasing numbers of parents of children with gender dysphoria are cooperating with their children's wishes and allowing them socially to assume an identity opposite their birth sex (Rosin, 2008).

Transsexualism

Transsexualism occurs in adults with gender dysphoria who desire to change their sex, and surgical advances have made this goal, although expensive, partially feasible. Transsexualism represents the extreme on a continuum of transgenderism, or the degree to which one identifies as the other sex (Cohen-Kettenis & Pfafflin, 2010). Transsexualism is apparently a very rare disorder. In the past, European studies suggested that approximately 1 in 30,000 adult males and 1 in 100,000 adult females seek sex reassignment surgery. However, more recent estimates suggest that about 1 in 12,000 men in Western countries has actually undergone the surgery (Lawrence, 2007). Until fairly recently, most researchers assumed that transsexualism was the adult version of childhood gender dysphoria, and indeed this is often the case. That is, many transsexuals had gender dysphoria as children (despite the fact that most children with gender dysphoria do not become transsexual), and their adult behavior is analogous. This appears to be the case for the large majority of female-to-male transsexuals (individuals born female who become male). Virtually all such individuals recall being extremely tomboyish, with masculinity persisting unabated into adulthood. Most, but not all, female-to-male transsexuals are sexually attracted to women.

In contrast to female-to-male transsexuals, there are at least two kinds of male-to-female transsexuals, with very different causes and developmental courses: *homosexual* and *autogynephilic transsexuals* (Bailey, 2003; Blanchard, 1989). Homosexual transsexual men are generally very feminine and have the same sexual orientation as gay men: They are sexually attracted to biological males (their preoperative biological sex). However, because these transsexual men experience their gender identity as female, they often define their sexual orientation as heterosexual and resent being labeled gay. Thus, what is referred to in the research literature as a homosexual male-to-female transsexual is a genetic male seeking a sex change operation who describes himself as a woman trapped in a man's body and who is sexually attracted to heterosexual male partners (Bailey, 2003). In contrast, autogynephilic transsexuals are motivated by **autogynephilia**—a paraphilia in which their attraction is to thoughts, images, or fantasies of themselves as a woman (Blanchard, 1991, 1993). Although it may not be relevant for treatment purposes (both types of transsexuals are appropriate candidates for sex reassignment surgery), this distinction is fundamental to understanding the diverse psychology of male-to-female transsexualism. Moreover, estimates show an increased prevalence in Western countries of male-to-female transsexualism in recent years, and most of this increase is in autogynephilic transsexualism (Lawrence, 2007).

One important finding is that homosexual transsexuals generally have had gender dysphoria since childhood, paralleling what is found in female-to-male transsexuals, as discussed above. However, because most boys with gender dysphoria do not become transsexual adults (but instead become gay or bisexual men), there must be other important determinants of transsexualism. One hypothesis is that some prenatal hormonal influences affect which children who develop gender dysphoria later become transsexuals (Meyer-Bahlburg, 2011). Another is that some families are more systematic in their support of boys' defeminization compared with other families.

 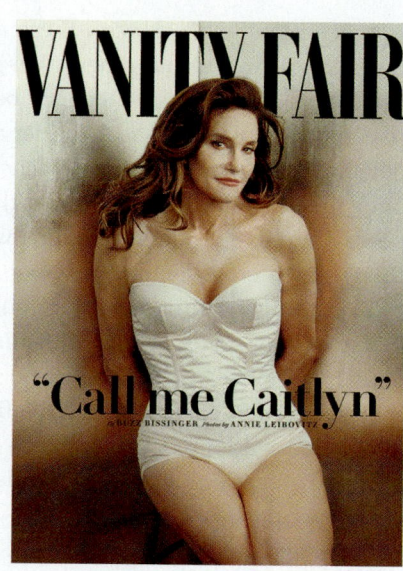

Bruce Jenner won the 1976 Olympic men's decathlon and was subsequently named the "World's Greatest Athlete." For decades Jenner was a symbol of masculinity. However, in 2015, Jenner revealed that he had experienced gender dysphoria since childhood and considers himself to be a woman who goes by the name of Caitlyn Jenner. Jenner reports that she has always been attracted to women, and has long identified as a woman and has now decided to live publicly as a woman.

Autogynephilic (sometimes called heterosexual) transsexualism almost always occurs in genetic males who usually report a history of transvestic fetishism. However, unlike other transvestites, autogynephilic transsexuals fantasize that they have female genitalia, which can lead to acute gender dysphoria, motivating their desire for sex reassignment surgery. Autogynephilic transsexuals may report sexual attraction to women, to both men and women, or to neither. Research has shown that these subtypes of autogynephilic transsexuals (varying in sexual orientation) are very similar to each other and differ from homosexual transsexuals in other important respects (Bailey, 2003; Blanchard, 1991). For example, relative to homosexual transsexuals, the autogynephilic transsexuals have more fetishistic and masochistic tendencies, a stronger preference for younger and more attractive partners, and a stronger interest in uncommitted sex (Veale et al., 2008). Unlike homosexual transsexuals, autogynephilic transsexuals do not appear to have been especially feminine in childhood or adulthood, and they typically seek sex reassignment surgery much later in life than do homosexual transsexuals (Blanchard, 1994). The causes of autogynephilic transsexualism thus probably overlap etiologically with the causes of other paraphilias (with which they often co-occur) but are not yet well understood (Veale et al., 2008).

Autogynephilia remains a controversial concept among some transgender individuals, who object that autogynephilia is inconsistent with their experiences and that their motivation to change their sex is not sexual. Some supporters of the theory of autogynephilia attribute the denial of autogynephilia to factors including sexual shame and stigmatization (Bailey & Triea, 2007). In *DSM-IV* adult gender identity disorder, the distinction between homosexual and autogynephilic transsexualism was recorded as a specifier: the patient's sexual orientation. This practice was intended to facilitate data collection regarding possible important clinical differences between the two types. However, some transsexuals vehemently dislike the idea that there are two different kinds of male-to-female transsexuals; they are especially hostile to the notion of autogynephilia (Dreger, 2008). For this reason, the specifier of sexual orientation has been removed from adult gender dysphoria in *DSM-5*.

Treatment for Transsexualism

Psychotherapy is usually not effective in helping adolescents or adults to resolve their gender dysphoria (Cohen-Kettenis et al., 2000; Zucker & Bradley, 1995). The only treatment that has been shown to be effective is surgical sex reassignment. Initially, transsexuals who want and are awaiting surgery are given hormone treatment. Biological men are given estrogens to facilitate breast growth, skin softening, and shrinking of muscles. Biological women are given testosterone, which suppresses menstruation, increases facial and body hair, and deepens the voice. Before they are eligible for surgery, transsexuals typically must live for many months with hormonal therapy, and they generally must live at least a year as the gender they wish to become. If they successfully complete the trial period, they undergo surgery and continue to take hormones indefinitely. In male-to-female transsexuals, this entails removal of the penis and testes and the creation of an artificial vagina. One fascinating study of 11 male-to-female transsexuals found that the artificial vaginal tissue created from penile tissue showed signs of sexual arousal to male erotic stimuli if the person was a homosexual male-to-female transsexual, and to female erotic stimuli if the person was an autogynephilic transsexual (Lawrence et al., 2005). In general, the transsexual neo-vagina is sexually functional. Male-to-female transsexuals usually also undergo extensive electrolysis to remove their beards and body hair. They also learn to raise the pitch of their voice.

Female-to-male transsexuals typically are given mastectomies and hysterectomies and often have other plastic surgery to alter various facial features (such as the Adam's apple). Only a subset of female-to-male transsexuals seeks an artificial penis because relevant surgical techniques are still somewhat primitive and very expensive. Moreover, the artificial penis is not capable of normal erection, so those who have this surgery must rely on artificial supports to have intercourse anyway. The others function sexually without any penis.

Does sex reassignment surgery help transsexuals lead satisfying lives? In 1990 a review of the outcome literature found that 87 percent of 220 male-to-female transsexuals had satisfactory outcomes (meaning that they did not regret their decisions) and that 97 percent of 130 female-to-male transsexuals had successful outcomes (Green & Fleming, 1990). More recent studies have reported similar findings. Thus, the majority of transsexuals are satisfied with the outcome of sex reassignment surgery, although there is variability in the degree of satisfaction (Cohen-Kettenis & Gooren, 1999; Lawrence, 2006). The Lawrence study (2006) of 232 male-to-female transsexuals all operated on by the same surgeon found the participants to be least satisfied with vaginal lubrication and vaginal touch sensations, although overall level of satisfaction was still high. Regarding psychological adjustment, a recent follow-up showed that transsexuals who had sex reassignment surgery were less well adjusted compared with normal controls (Dhejne et al., 2011). The optimal comparison, however, is not with normal controls but with transsexuals desiring but not given sex reassignment surgery. In spite of the reasonably good success record for transsexual patients who are carefully chosen, such surgery remains controversial because some professionals continue to maintain that it is inappropriate to treat psychological disorders through drastic anatomical changes.

in review

- What two components characterize gender dysphoria?
- Identify the two types of male-to-female transsexuals, and describe their developmental course as well as that of female-to-male transsexuals.
- What are the most effective treatments for childhood gender dysphoria and adult transsexualism?

Sexual Abuse

12.4 Describe three primary types of sexual abuse.

Sexual abuse is sexual contact that involves physical or psychological coercion of at least one individual who cannot reasonably consent to the contact (e.g., a child). Such abuse includes pedophilia, incest, and rape, and it concerns society much more than any other sexual problem. It is somewhat ironic, then, that of these three forms of abuse, only pedophilia is included in *DSM-5*. This partly reflects the seriousness with which society views these offenses and its preference for treating coercive sex offenders as criminals rather than as having a mental disorder (although many criminals also have mental disorders).

Childhood Sexual Abuse

The past few decades have seen intense concern about childhood sexual abuse, with an accompanying increase in relevant research. There are at least three reasons for including some discussion of this here. First, as noted in previous chapters, there are possible links between childhood sexual abuse and some mental disorders, so such abuse may be important in the etiology of some disorders (see especially Chapters 3, 5, 8, and 10). Second, much evidence suggests that, broadly defined, childhood sexual abuse is more common than was once assumed, and it is important to understand some of its causes. Third, some dramatic and well-publicized cases involving allegations of childhood sexual abuse have raised very controversial issues such as the validity of children's testimony and the accuracy of recovered memories of sexual abuse. We consider all three of these issues in turn.

PREVALENCE OF CHILDHOOD SEXUAL ABUSE Nationally representative surveys from 21 different countries around the world reveal that 1.6 percent of people report having been the victim of sexual abuse during childhood (Kessler, McLaughlin, et al., 2010). The prevalence of childhood sexual abuse is even higher in the United States, where 4 to 6 percent of people report such a history (Green et al., 2010; McLaughlin, Green, et al., 2012). In reading and understanding studies on this topic, it is important to keep in mind that reports of the prevalence of childhood sexual abuse vary in the definition used. For example, different studies use different definitions of "childhood," with the upper age limit ranging from 12 to as high as 19 years. Some studies have counted any kind of sexual interaction, even that which does not include physical contact (e.g., exhibitionism); others have counted only physical contact; others have counted only genital contact; and still others have counted consensual sexual contact with a minor.

CONSEQUENCES OF CHILDHOOD SEXUAL ABUSE

People who are sexually abused during childhood are approximately twice as likely as children who were not sexually abused to develop a later mental disorder (Kessler, McLaughlin, et al., 2010), with the highest risk being for fear/anxiety and substance use disorders (McLaughlin, Green, et al., 2012). Children who are the victims of sexual abuse also have a significantly increased risk of later suicidal thoughts and behaviors (Bruffaerts et al., 2010).

A wide variety of sexual symptoms have also been alleged to result from early sexual abuse (e.g., Leonard & Follette, 2002; Loeb et al., 2002; see review in Maniglio, 2009), ranging, for example, from sexual aversion to sexual promiscuity. A similar range of negative consequences has also been reported in a sample of about 3,000 male and female adults in China, although the rate of childhood sexual abuse in China is lower than in Western countries (Luo et al., 2008). Unfortunately, as discussed in Chapters 8 and 10, knowledge about these hypothesized associations is very limited because of difficulties in establishing causal links between early experiences and adult behavior (see also the Unresolved Issues section at the end of the chapter).

CONTROVERSIES CONCERNING CHILDHOOD SEXUAL ABUSE Several types of high-profile criminal trials have highlighted the limitations of our knowledge concerning questions of great scientific and practical importance. In one type of case, children have accused adults working in day care settings of extensive, often bizarre sexual abuse, and controversial issues have been raised about the degree to which children's accusations can be trusted. In a second type of case, adults claim to have repressed and completely forgotten memories of early sexual abuse and then to have "recovered" the memories during adulthood, typically while seeing a therapist who believes that repressed memories of childhood sexual abuse are a very common cause of adult psychopathology. Many issues have been raised about the validity of these "recovered" memories.

Children's Testimony Several cases of alleged sexual abuse in day care settings shocked the country in the 1980s and 1990s. The most notorious was the McMartin Preschool case in California. In 1983, Judy Johnson complained to police that her son had been molested by Raymond Buckey, who helped run the McMartin Preschool. Johnson's complaints grew increasingly bizarre. For example,

she accused Buckey of sodomizing her son while he stuck the boy's head in a toilet and of making him ride naked on a horse. Johnson was later diagnosed with acute paranoid schizophrenia, and she died of alcohol-related liver disease in 1986. Before she died, however, other children at the preschool who were interviewed began to tell fantastically lurid stories—for example, that they were forced to dig up dead bodies at cemeteries, jump out of airplanes, and kill animals with bats. Despite the unbelievable nature of these reports, prosecutors and many McMartin parents believed the children. Buckey and his mother (who owned the day care facility) were tried in a trial that took two and a half years and cost $15 million. The jury acquitted Ms. Buckey on all counts and failed to convict Raymond Buckey on any; however, he was freed only after retrial, after having spent 5 years in jail. The jurors' principal reason for not finding the defendants guilty was their concern that interviewers had used leading questions or coercive methods of questioning. Moreover, subsequent research on children who reported satanic abuse found no evidence (including physical evidence) that such abuse had occurred (London et al., 2005). Despite these concerns, some day care workers accused of satanic sexual abuse have served years in prison.

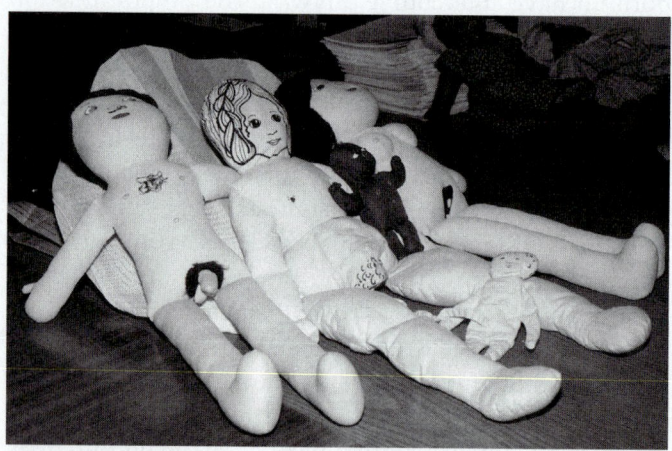

Evidence has suggested that the use of anatomically correct dolls to question young children about where they may have been touched in alleged incidents of sexual abuse does not improve the accuracy of their testimony relative to verbal interviews alone.

Recovered Memories of Sexual Abuse In 1990, a young woman named Eileen Franklin testified in court that she had seen her father rape and murder an 8-year-old playmate 20 years earlier. Remarkably, despite her claim to have witnessed the murder, she never had any memory of the event until she "recovered" it by accident in adulthood (MacLean, 1992). Franklin's father was convicted and given a life sentence, although in 1995 the conviction was overturned because of two serious constitutional errors made during the original trial that might have affected the jury's verdict. In another case, Patricia Burgus sued her two psychiatrists in Chicago for false-memory implantation, claiming the doctors had persuaded her through hypnosis and other therapeutic techniques "to believe that she was a member of a satanic cult, that she was sexually abused by multiple men, and that she engaged in cannibalism and abused her own children" (Brown et al., 2000, p. 3). In 1997 she was awarded $10.6 million.

As discussed in some detail in Chapter 8, whether traumatic experiences can be utterly forgotten and then somehow recovered intact years later has been heatedly debated during the past several decades. Some have argued that repressed memories are common (Herman, 1993) and are responsible for a great deal of psychopathology. In the controversial but very popular book *The Courage to Heal*, journalists Ellen Bass and Laura Davis assert, "If you are unable to remember any specific instances [of sexual abuse] . . . but still have the feeling that something abusive happened to you, it probably did" (1988, p. 21). Yet as researchers have pointed out, there is absolutely no evidence that this statement is true. Some therapists still routinely give this book to their clients, and those clients often do report "recovering" such memories. Those skeptical about recovery of repressed memories point out that even normal, unrepressed memories can be highly inaccurate and that false memories can be induced experimentally (Davis & Loftus, 2009; Loftus et al., 1995) (see Chapter 8). The debate about the validity of memories of childhood sexual abuse that arise during therapy remains extremely heated. Most researchers maintain that the concept of repressed memory is wholly or largely invalid and that all "recovered memories" are false (Crews, 1995; Davis & Loftus, 2009; Thomas & Loftus, 2002). Many believe that valid recovered memories are simply the remembering of events forgotten because, at the time, they were not traumatic (McNally & Geraerts, 2009). Despite the continuing controversy among scientists, cases of recovered memories of sexual abuse appear to have become much rarer. A survey conducted of the False Memory Syndrome Foundation—largely parents who say they have been accused by their children of sexual abuse based on recovered memories—showed that accusations peaked in 1991 and 1992, with 579 made during that time. In 1999 and 2000 only 36 accusations were made (McHugh & Kreek, 2004).

Pedophilic Disorder

According to *DSM-5*, **pedophilic disorder** is diagnosed when an adult has recurrent, intense sexual urges or fantasies about sexual activity with a prepubertal child; acting on these desires is not necessary for the diagnosis if they cause the pedophile distress (see the earlier *DSM-5* criteria box). *DSM-5* indicates that a child is someone who is "generally age 13 or younger." In doing so, the *DSM-5* rejected

two potentially important suggestions from the *DSM-5* subcommittee on paraphilias: first, that pedophilia be diagnosed according to the degree of physical maturity of the child (as rated by Tanner scores, which index degree of pubertal maturation) and, second, that diagnostic criteria for pedophilia (attraction to prepubescent children) be changed to include men with hebephilia (attraction to pubescent children—children in the early stages of puberty). The debate over these proposals was heated. Read the Thinking Critically about *DSM-5* box to see where you stand on these issues.

Pedophiles' sexual interaction with children frequently involves manual or oral contact with a child's genitals; penetrative anal or vaginal sex is much rarer. Although penetration and associated force are often injurious to the child, injuries are usually a by-product rather than the goal, as they would be with a sadist (although a minority of men diagnosed with pedophilic disorder are also sexual sadists; Cohen & Galynker, 2002).

Nearly all individuals with pedophilia are male, and about two-thirds of pedophilic offenders' victims are girls, typically between the ages of 8 and 11 (Cohen & Galynker, 2002). The rate of homosexuality among pedophiles is much higher than the analogous rate among normal adult-attracted men (Seto, 2004). Although some social conservatives have argued that this shows that gay men tend to commit pedophilic acts, this is an incorrect inference. Gay men are no more interested in male children than heterosexual men are in female children. Homosexual pedophilia is an entirely different erotic preference from normal male homosexuality (Seto, 2012). Homosexual pedophilic sex offenders tend to have more victims than heterosexual pedophilic sex offenders (Blanchard et al., 2000; Cohen & Galynker, 2002). One survey of pedophiles found that a majority have used childhood pornography (Seto, 2004).

Studies investigating the sexual responses of men with pedophilia have revealed several patterns of results (Barbaree & Seto, 1997; Seto et al., 2006). Such studies typically use a *penile plethysmograph* to measure erectile responses to sexual stimuli directly rather than relying on self-report. (A plethysmograph consists of an expandable band placed around the penis that is connected to a recording device.) Men with pedophilia typically show greater sexual arousal than matched nonoffenders in response to pictures of nude or partially clad girls—and greater arousal to such pictures than to pictures of adult women. Some men with pedophilia respond to children as well as to adolescents and/or adults (Seto, 2004; Seto et al., 1999).

Child molesters are more likely than nonoffenders to engage in self-justifying cognitive distortions, including the beliefs that children will benefit from sexual contact with adults and that children often initiate such contact

DSM-5   Thinking Critically about *DSM-5*

Pedophilia and Hebephilia

Pedophilia has been understood and defined as attraction to pre-pubertal children, that is, children without any signs of puberty (e.g., no pubic hair, breast growth, or penis growth). However, studies of sex offenders, both of victim characteristics and of offender sexual arousal patterns, have unequivocally demonstrated the existence of a subgroup who are most aroused not to prepubescent children, but to pubescent children (children in the early stages of puberty). Scientists have called such men *hebephiles*. Pubescent children are not fully sexually mature, despite showing some signs of pubertal development. Pedophilia and hebephilia appear to be closely related, because it is not uncommon for pedophiles also to be attracted to pubescent children and hebephiles to prepubescent children. The *DSM-5* paraphilias subcommittee proposed that the definition of pedophilia be expanded to include attraction to pubescent children. Furthermore, instead of diagnosing pedophilia based on the age of children to whom a man is sexually attracted (i.e., 13 years old and younger), the committee proposed that diagnosis be made based on the physical maturity of the children. They proposed that this be done on the basis of well-known developmental markers. (These markers, called *Tanner scores*, represent the degree of pubertal maturation and range from "none" to "completed.") This would be more diagnostically accurate than relying on children's ages because children mature at variable rates. A 12-year-old girl might be prepubescent, but in this day and age she is more likely to be pubescent because most girls in the United States have begun puberty by that age (Razzak, 2012).

The proposed changes proved highly controversial because of the proposed expansion of pedophilia to include attraction to pubescent children. Opponents of its inclusion asserted that attraction to pubescent girls is characteristic of normal men (e.g., Rind & Yuill, 2012; Wakefield, 2012). However, the idea that normal men are attracted to pubescent children is largely mistaken, and represents a failure to appreciate the physical immaturity of children in the early stages of puberty, compared with children or adolescents who have completed puberty. In the end, the *DSM-5* rejected both the expansion of the definition of pedophilia to include attraction to pubescent children and diagnosing pedophilia on the basis of desired children's degree of sexual maturity (focusing on developmental markers of prepubescence and pubescence). Instead, *DSM-5* retains the internally contradictory criteria of *DSM-IV-TR*, namely, that pedophilia is attraction to prepubescent children, and that prepubescence is understood as "younger than age 13" even though many such children are not prepubescent. Many people working in the area are not pleased that *DSM-5* did not make the proposed changes. What do you think?

(Marziano et al., 2006). Motivationally, many pedophilic child molesters appear to be shy and introverted yet still desire mastery or dominance over another individual. Some also idealize aspects of childhood such as innocence, unconditional love, or simplicity (Cohen & Galynker, 2002).

Pedophilia usually is first recognized in adolescence and persists over a person's life. Many pedophiles engage in work with children or youth so that they have extensive access to children. Some pedophiles never act on their preferences, but many do. It is currently impossible to estimate the proportion of men with pedophilia who remain child-celibate. Several studies show that adolescent and adult men with pedophilia are much more likely to have been sexually or physically abused as children than are adults who sexually abuse other adults (Daversa & Knight, 2007; Lee & Katzman, 2002).

Recent research suggests that pedophilia may involve certain perturbations of early neurodevelopment that create a vulnerability to the disorder. For instance, compared with nonpedophilic sex offenders, men with pedophilia have lower IQs (Cantor, Blanchard, et al., 2005; Seto, 2004), threefold higher rates of non-right-handedness (Cantor, Klassen, et al., 2005; Seto, 2004), higher rates of head injuries resulting in loss of consciousness, and differences in brain structure (detected by brain-imaging techniques), at least some of which are critical for normal sexual development (Cantor et al., 2008; Schiltz et al., 2007).

Not all men with pedophilia molest children. In a confidential study of German men who sought mental health services because of their pedophilic feelings, 30 percent reported that they had never had sexual contact with a child. Most of those, however, had viewed child pornography (Neutze et al., 2011). The organization B4UAct (Before You Act) is intended to support law-abiding men with pedophilic feelings and to raise awareness that such men exist and that they experience societal prejudice (Clarke-Flory, 2012). Another organization, called Virtuous Pedophiles, is intended to reduce stigma toward law-abiding pedophiles by raising consciousness about their existence (Clarke-Flory, 2012).

Incest

Incest refers to culturally prohibited sexual relations between family members such as a brother and sister or a parent and child. Although a few societies have sanctioned certain incestuous relationships—at one time it was the established practice for Egyptian pharaohs to marry their sisters to prevent the royal blood from being "contaminated"—the incest taboo is virtually universal among human societies. Incest often produces children with mental and physical problems because close genetic relatives are much more likely than nonrelatives to share the same recessive genes (which often have negative biological effects) and hence to produce children with two sets of recessive genes. Presumably for this reason, many nonhuman animal species, and all known primates, have an evolved tendency to avoid mating between close relatives. The mechanism for human incest avoidance appears to be lack of sexual interest in people to whom one is continuously exposed from an early age. For example, biologically unrelated children who are raised together in Israeli kibbutzim rarely marry or have affairs with others from their rearing group when they become adults (Kenrick & Luce, 2004). Evolutionarily, this makes sense. In most cultures, children reared together are biologically related.

In our own society, the actual incidence of incest is difficult to estimate because it usually comes to light only when reported to law enforcement or other agencies. It is almost certainly more common than is generally believed, in part because many victims are reluctant to report the incest or do not consider themselves victimized. Brother–sister incest is the most common form of incest even though it is rarely reported (LeVay & Baldwin, 2012). The second most common pattern is father–daughter incest. Mother–son incest is thought to be relatively rare. Frequently, incest offenders do not stop with one child in a family (Wilson, 2004), and some incestuous fathers involve all of their daughters serially as they become pubescent.

Some incestuous child molesters have pedophilic arousal patterns (Barsetti et al., 1998; Seto et al., 1999), suggesting that they are at least partly motivated by sexual attraction to children, although they also show arousal to adult women. However, they differ from extra-familial child molesters in at least two respects (Quinsey et al., 1995). First, the large majority of incest offenses are against girls, whereas extra-familial offenses show a more equal distribution between boys and girls. Second, incest offenders are more likely to offend with only one or a few children in the family, whereas pedophilic child molesters are likely to have more victims (LeVay & Baldwin, 2012).

In 2007 the world was shocked at revelations concerning the case of an Austrian incest perpetrator named Josef Fritzl. Years earlier Fritzl had kidnapped his own daughter Elisabeth when she was age 18 and incarcerated her in a soundproof compartment he had built in his own basement. He forced her to write a note saying that she had joined a cult and that she wanted no further contact with the family. She lived there for 24 years without the knowledge of her mother and other family members who lived upstairs. During her long incarceration, her father repeatedly forced her to have sex. During those years she bore seven children (one of whom died in infancy). Three of the children were reared by the family upstairs, ostensibly having been left for the family by Elisabeth. The other three lived in the basement with her. It was due to a medical problem in one of the latter children that the ordeal finally ended. She begged Josef to let her take the child to the hospital, and he agreed. Hospital staff thought the Fritzls' cover story to be suspicious and alerted police, who successfully investigated (Dahlkamp et al., 2008).

Rape

The term **rape** describes sexual intercourse that occurs under actual or threatened forcible coercion of one person by another (see Figure 12.1). In most states, legal definitions restrict forcible rape to forced intercourse or penetration of a bodily orifice by a penis or other object. *Statutory rape* is sexual activity with a person who is legally defined (by statute or law) to be under the age of consent (18 in most states) even if the underage person consents. In the vast majority of cases, rape is a crime of men against women, although especially in prison settings, it is often committed by men against men. Forced sex is not unique to humans and occurs in many species of other animals, where it has often evolved as a reproductive strategy by males to produce more offspring. It also has existed in most human societies (including preliterate ones) (Lalumière et al., 2005a). The term **sexual assault** refers to acts, separate from rape, that involve unwanted sexual contact, such as groping or fondling another person without their consent.

Figure 12.1 Statistics on Sexual Assault

These data from the U.S. Department of Justice outline some of the statistics about women who were raped from 2005 to 2010.

(Based on Planty et al., 2013.)

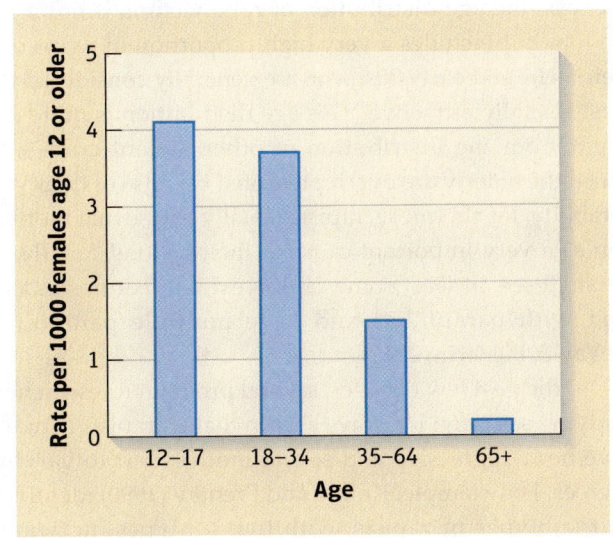

PREVALENCE Estimates of the prevalence of rape have varied widely. This is, at least in part, because of differences across studies in the precise definition of rape and the way information is gathered (direct or indirect questions, for example). The U.S. Department of Justice census-based survey indicates that the rate of rape and sexual assault victimization has been falling in recent years, dropping from a rate of 0.5 percent of women per year in 1995 to 0.2 percent per year in 2010 (Planty et al., 2013). Those percentages may seem low, but they mean that 1 out of every 200 to 500 women over age 12 is raped or sexually assaulted each year, which is an unacceptably high number. The risk of rape and sexual assault is highest in women under age 34 who live in low-income and rural areas. In addition, most instances of sexual violence involve a perpetrator who was known to the victim (78 percent), which may be why only a minority of such assaults involve the use of a weapon such as a gun or knife (11 percent) (Planty et al., 2013). See Figure 12.1 for some statistics about who is at risk for sexual assault.

IS RAPE MOTIVATED BY SEX OR AGGRESSION? Traditionally, rape has been classified as a sex crime, and society has assumed that a rapist is motivated by lust. However, in the 1970s some feminist scholars began to challenge this view, arguing that rape is motivated by the need to dominate, to assert power, and to humiliate a victim rather than by sexual desire for her (Brownmiller, 1975). Certainly from the perspective of the victim, rape—which is among women's greatest fears—is always an act of violence and is certainly not a sexually pleasurable experience, whatever the rapist's motivation.

Although much of the motivation for rape may stem from a desire to dominate or humiliate others, there are many compelling reasons why sexual motivation is often, if not always, a very important factor too (Bryden & Grier, 2013; Ellis, 1989; Thornhill & Palmer, 2000). Although rape victims include females of all degrees of physical attractiveness, the age distribution of rape victims is not at all random but includes a very high proportion of women in their teens and early 20s, who are generally considered the most sexually attractive. This age distribution is quite different from the distribution of other violent crimes, in which the elderly are overrepresented because of their vulnerability. Furthermore, rapists usually cite sexual motivation as a very important cause of their actions. Finally, as we shall see, at least some rapists exhibit features associated with paraphilias and have multiple paraphilias (LeVay & Baldwin, 2012).

In the past few decades, several prominent researchers studying sex offenders have shown that all rapists actually have both aggressive and sexual motives but to varying degrees. For example, Knight and Prentky (1990) identified four subtypes of rapists, with two subtypes motivated primarily by aggression and two subtypes motivated primarily by distorted sexual motives (see also Knight et al., 1994). More recently, McCabe and Wauchope (2005) provided empirical support for a somewhat different classification system that also has four subtypes of rapists with differing amounts of sexual and aggressive motives. At present it is not clear which scheme of classification is best, and some rapists cannot readily be characterized (LeVay & Baldwin, 2012).

RAPE AND ITS AFTERMATH In addition to the physical trauma inflicted on a victim, the psychological trauma may be severe, leading in a substantial number of female victims to PTSD (see Chapter 5). A rape may also have a negative impact on a victim's sexual functioning and on her marriage or other intimate relationships. Although there has been little systematic study of men who have been raped, one study of 40 male rape victims revealed that nearly all experienced some long-term psychological distress following rape, including anxiety, depression, increased feelings of anger, and loss of self-image (Walker et al., 2005).

Although there is a clear perpetrator in all instances of rape and sexual assault, there remains an unfortunate myth of "victim-precipitated" rape—a position often invoked by defense attorneys trying to prevent the perpetrator from being charged with rape. According to this view, a victim (especially a repeat victim), though often bruised both psychologically and physically, is regarded as the cause of the crime, often on such grounds as the alleged provocativeness of her clothing, her past sexual behavior, or her presence in a location considered risky (LeVay & Baldwin, 2012; Stermac et al., 1990). The attacker, on the other hand, is regarded as unable to quell his lust in the face of such irresistible provocation—and therefore is not legally responsible for the act. Fortunately, *rape shield laws* began to be introduced in the 1970s. These laws protect rape victims by, for example, preventing the prosecutor from using evidence of a victim's prior sex history; however, many problems in these laws still remain (LeVay & Baldwin, 2012).

A recent example of the complexity inherent in the legal situation of rape prosecution is that of Dominique Strauss-Kahn (DSK), who was managing director of the International Monetary Fund and an aspiring French politician. In May 2011, he was accused by a New York City hotel worker of sexually assaulting her when she entered his hotel room to clean it. A police investigation confirmed that sexual contact had occurred, but DSK insisted that it was consensual. Subsequently, another woman came forward accusing him of raping her years earlier in France. However, the 2011 case unraveled when prosecutors learned that DSK's accuser had lied about other matters, including the claim that she had been raped in her country of origin. The charges were dropped. It is possible that DSK got away with rape. It is also possible that he was falsely accused. Cases such as the accusations against DSK highlight both barriers to prosecuting rape cases and the need for adequate protections for the accused.

RAPISTS AND CAUSAL CONSIDERATIONS According to the FBI's Uniform Crime Reports, about 60 percent of all rapists arrested are under 25 years old. Of the rapists who get into police records, about 30 to 50 percent are married and living with their wives at the time of the crime. As a group, they come from the low end of the socioeconomic ladder and commonly have a prior criminal record (Ward et al., 1997). They are also quite likely to have experienced sexual abuse, a violent home environment, and inconsistent caregiving in childhood (Hudson & Ward, 1997).

One subset of rapists, date rapists (i.e., an acquaintance who rapes a woman in the context of a date or other social interaction), have a somewhat different demographic profile in that they are often middle- to upperclass young men who rarely have criminal records. However, these men, like incarcerated rapists, are characterized by promiscuity, hostile masculinity, and an emotionally detached, predatory personality (LeVay & Baldwin, 2012). Their victims are often highly intoxicated (Mohler-Kuo et al., 2004; Testa et al., 2003). What distinguishes them, primarily, is that incarcerated rapists show much higher levels of impulsive, antisocial behavior than date rapists.

As suggested earlier, there is evidence that some rapists are afflicted by a paraphilia (Abel & Rouleau, 1990; Freund & Seto, 1998). For example, rapists often report having recurrent, repetitive, and compulsive urges to rape. Although they typically try to control these urges, the urges sometimes become so strong that they act on them. Many rapists also have other paraphilias such as exhibitionism and voyeurism. They also frequently have

a characteristic pattern of sexual arousal (Abel & Rouleau, 1990; Lohr et al., 1997). Most rapists are similar to normal, nonoffending men in being sexually aroused by depictions of mutually satisfying, consensual intercourse, but many rapists are also sexually aroused by depictions of sexual assaults involving an unwilling victim (Clegg & Fremouw, 2009; Lalumière et al., 2005b). A small minority of rapists are sexual sadists, characterized by very violent assaults and aroused more by the assault than by sexual stimuli.

In terms of personality, rapists are very often characterized by impulsivity, quick loss of temper, lack of personally intimate relationships, and insensitivity to social cues or pressures (Giotakos et al., 2004), and a subset qualify for a diagnosis of psychopathy (Knight & Guay, 2006). Many rapists also show some deficits in social and communication skills (Emmers-Sommer et al., 2004), as well as in their cognitive appraisals of women's feelings and intentions (Ward et al., 1997). For example, they are particularly deficient in skills required for successful conversation, which is necessary for developing consenting relationships with women. In addition, they have difficulty decoding women's negative cues during social interactions and often interpret friendly behavior as flirtatious or sexually provocative (Emmers-Sommer et al., 2004). This can lead to inappropriate behaviors that women would experience as sexually intrusive.

Estimates are that only 20 to 28 percent of rapes are ever reported, compared to 60 percent of robberies, but the proportion of rapes being reported has increased during the past several decades (Magid et al., 2004). Among men who are arrested, only about half are convicted; of these, only about two-thirds serve a jail term (LeVay & Baldwin, 2012). Convictions often bring light sentences, and a jail term does not dissuade a substantial number of offenders from repeating their crimes. Consequently, the large majority of rapists are not in prison but out among us.

Which scenario do you think is more likely to lead to rape? It is difficult to guess because date rape is increasingly common, and rapes by casual acquaintances usually occur in dark, lonely places.

Treatment and Recidivism of Sex Offenders

For several decades in the United States there has been extreme concern about, and intolerance of, sex offenders who repeat their crimes. Soon after his release from prison, convicted sex offender Earl Shriner forced a 7-year-old boy off his bike in the woods near Tacoma, Washington, and then raped and stabbed him before cutting off the boy's penis. Just before his release from prison, Shriner had confided to a cellmate that he still had fantasies of molesting and murdering children (Popkin, 1994). In a similar case, 7-year-old Megan Kanka was sexually molested and murdered by a convicted child molester living in her neighborhood. Cases such as these have inspired a number of measures to protect society from sexual predators (see the World Around Us box).

But are such stories representative? Are sex offenders typically incurable? Should they receive life sentences on the presumption that they are bound to offend again? Or have they been unfairly singled out by media sensationalism even though they really are responsive to treatment? The efficacy of treatment for sex offenders is controversial, and this is the topic to which we now turn (Fedoroff, 2009).

In general, sex offender recidivism is actually markedly lower than for many other kinds of crimes. However, sex offenders with deviant sexual preferences (e.g., exhibitionists, severe sadists, and those who are most attracted to children) have particularly high rates of sexual recidivism (Dickey et al., 2002; Langevin et al., 2004). One follow-up study of more than 300 sex offenders over 25 years found that over half were charged with at least one additional sexual offense (Langevin et al., 2004). A recent review found that sexualized violence—a preference for sadistic or coercive sex—was the strongest predictor of recidivism. Other predictors included negative social influences, poor cognitive problem solving, and loneliness (Mann et al., 2010). The recidivism rate for rapists steadily decreases with age, as does performance of sexually deviant behavior more generally (Barbaree & Blanchard, 2008).

The World Around Us

Megan's Law

On July 29, 1994, 7-year-old Megan Kanka, from Hamilton Township, New Jersey, was walking home from her friend's house when a neighbor invited her to his house to see his new puppy. The neighbor, Jesse Timmendequas, 33, was a landscaper who had lived across the street for about a year. Unknown to Megan, to Megan's parents, or to anyone else in the neighborhood, he was also a twice-convicted child molester (who lived with two other convicted sex offenders). When Megan followed him inside, he led her to an upstairs bedroom, strangled her unconscious with his belt, raped her, and asphyxiated her with a plastic bag. Timmendequas then placed Megan's body in a toolbox, drove to a soccer field, and dumped it near a portable toilet. Timmendequas was subsequently apprehended, convicted, and sentenced to death; however, because New Jersey abolished the death penalty in 2007, he will serve a life term in prison.

Megan's murder sparked outrage at the fact that dangerous sex offenders could move into a neighborhood without notifying the community of their presence. In response, the New Jersey state legislature passed Megan's Law, which mandates that upon release, convicted sex offenders register with police and that authorities notify neighbors that convicted sex offenders have moved in by distributing fliers, alerting local organizations, and canvassing door-to-door. Similar laws have been passed in many other states, and it is now possible in several states to visit a website containing pictures and addresses of convicted sex offenders, subject to that state's Megan's Law. Although Megan's Laws have been enormously popular with state legislators and citizens, they have not been uncontroversial.

Civil libertarians have objected to community notification requirements, which, they argue, endanger released offenders (who have arguably paid their debts to society) and also prevent them from integrating successfully back into society. Although the various Megan's Laws are intended to protect potential victims rather than to encourage harassment of sex offenders, the latter has occurred, with up to one-third to one-half of registered offenders in some states experiencing one or more of the following: loss of a job or home, threats, harassment, property damage, and/ or harm to family members (Levenson et al., 2007). In addition, the limited amount of relevant data has brought the effectiveness of Megan's Laws into question. For example, since 1995 a number of studies have compared recidivism rates from the period before which registration as a sex offender was required to rates after these laws were passed. Unfortunately, the results have not really provided any reassuring evidence that notifying communities has enhanced community safety (Levenson et al., 2007). A recent analysis in New Jersey, where Megan Kanka lived and died, found that Megan's Law had made no difference (Zgoba & Levenson, 2008).

Megan's Law mandates that convicted sex offenders must register with their local police department so that neighbors know about the potential risk to them and others. There are potential benefits to this, as well as potential costs (e.g., harassment of the sex offender by members of the community). If you could propose a change to this law, what would it be?

PSYCHOTHERAPIES AND THEIR EFFECTIVENESS

Therapies for sex offenders typically have at least one of the following four goals: to modify patterns of sexual arousal and attraction, to modify cognitions and social skills in order to allow more appropriate sexual interactions with adult partners, to change habits or behavior that increases the chance of reoffending, or to reduce sexual drive. Attempts to modify sexual arousal patterns usually involve *aversion therapy*, in which a paraphilic stimulus such as a slide of a nude prepubescent girl for a man with pedophilia is paired with an aversive event such as forced inhalation of noxious odors or a shock to the arm. An alternative to electric aversion therapy is *covert sensitization*, in which the patient imagines a highly aversive event while viewing or imagining a paraphilic stimulus, or *assisted covert sensitization*, in which a foul odor is introduced to induce nausea at the point of peak arousal (Beech & Harkins, 2012).

Deviant arousal patterns also need to be replaced by arousal to acceptable stimuli (Maletzky, 2002). Most often, investigators have attempted to pair the pleasurable stimuli of orgasm with sexual fantasies involving sex between consenting adults. For example, sex offenders are asked to masturbate while thinking of deviant fantasies. At the moment of ejaculatory inevitability, the patient switches his fantasy to a more appropriate theme. Although aversion therapy has been shown to be somewhat effective in the laboratory (Maletzky, 1998; Quinsey & Earls, 1990), how well this therapeutic change generalizes to the patient's outside world is uncertain if his motivation wanes. Further, although aversion therapy is still widely used for sex offenders, it is no longer used as a sole form of treatment (Marshall, 1998).

The remaining psychological treatments are aimed at reducing the chances of sexual reoffending. *Cognitive restructuring* attempts to eliminate sex offenders' cognitive distortions because these may play a role in sexual abuse (Maletzky, 2002). For example, an incest offender who maintained that "If my ten-year-old daughter had said no, I would have stopped" might be challenged about a number of implied distortions: that a child has the capacity to consent to have sex with an adult; that if a child does not say no, she has consented; and that it is the child's responsibility to stop sexual contact. In addition, *social-skills training* aims to help sex offenders (especially rapists) learn to process social information from women more effectively and to interact with them more appropriately (Beech & Harkins, 2012; Maletzky, 2002; McFall, 1990). For example, some men read positive sexual connotations into women's neutral or negative messages or believe that women's refusals of sexual advances reflect "playing hard to get." Training typically involves interaction of perpetrators with female partners, who can give the offenders feedback on their response to the interactions.

Although some studies in the treatment literature have reached positive conclusions (Maletzky, 2002), other studies have found essentially no differences between treated and untreated offenders (Emmelkamp, 1994; Rice et al., 1991). A recent meta-analysis of 23 recidivism outcome studies revealed an advantage for treatment: 10.9 percent of treated sex offenders versus 19.2 percent of untreated offenders committed another sex crime (Hanson et al., 2009). The most effective treatment programs followed the Canadian "Risk-Need-Responsiveness" model, in which an offender's risk is first assessed to determine who should get the most intensive treatment. Second, there is a focus on factors that directly increase chance of reoffending such as paraphilic desire or impulsivity. Third, correctional programs should be matched to offender characteristics such as learning style, level of motivation, and the offender's individual characteristics. Such multifaceted cognitive-behavioral techniques appear to be more effective than older techniques such as aversion therapy. There are also indications in the literature that certain paraphilias respond better to treatment than others (Laws & O'Donohue, 2008). For example, one very long-term follow-up (5 to 15 years) of over 2,000 sex offenders who had entered a cognitive-behavioral treatment program found that nonpedophilic child molesters and exhibitionists achieved better overall success rates than pedophilic offenders and rapists (Maletzky & Steinhauser, 2002).

BIOLOGICAL AND SURGICAL TREATMENTS In recent years, antidepressants from the SSRI (selective serotonin reuptake inhibitor) category have been found to be useful in treating a variety of paraphilias by reducing paraphilic desire and behavior. However, they are not useful in the treatment of sexual offenders. The most controversial treatment for sex offenders involves castration—either surgical removal of the testes or the hormonal treatment sometimes called "chemical castration" (Berlin, 2003; Bradford & Greenberg, 1996; Weinberger et al., 2005). Both surgical and chemical castration lower the testosterone level, which in turn lowers the sex drive, allowing the offender to resist any inappropriate impulses. Chemical castration has most often involved the administration of antiandrogen steroid hormones such as Depo-Provera and Lupron, both of which can have serious side effects. One uncontrolled study of the drug Lupron yielded dramatic results: Thirty men with paraphilias reported an average of 48 deviant fantasies per week prior to therapy, and no such fantasies during treatment (Rosler & Witztum, 1998; Maletzky & Field, 2003). However, relapse rates upon discontinuation of the drug were very high (Maletzky, 2002).

Studies of surgical castration of repeat sex offenders with violent tendencies conducted in Europe and more recently in the United States had similar results (but without high rates of relapse; Weinberger et al., 2005). These studies have typically included diverse categories of offenders, from child molesters to rapists of adult women. Follow-up has sometimes exceeded 10 years. Recidivism rates for castrated offenders are typically less than 3 percent, compared with greater than 50 percent for uncastrated offenders (Berlin, 1994; Green, 1992; Prentky, 1997). Despite the apparently high success rates, many feel that the treatment is brutal, unethical, and dehumanizing (Farkas & Stichman, 2002; Gunn, 1993), although this assumption has been challenged (Bailey & Greenberg, 1998).

Interestingly, some recent cases have involved a request by the sex offender himself to be castrated in exchange for a lighter sentence (LeVay & Baldwin, 2012). In some states such as California, a repeat offender's eligibility for probation or parole following childhood molestation is linked to his acceptance of mandated hormonal therapy (Scott & Holmberg, 2003). Oregon evaluated the success of requiring such treatment and found that those receiving chemical castration fared better in terms of committing fewer new offenses and fewer parole violations, and were less likely to return to prison (Maletzky et al., 2006). Nevertheless, civil libertarians, exemplified by the American Civil Liberties Union (ACLU), have argued that because of potentially severe side effects, such requirements violate the Constitution's ban on cruel and unusual punishment. More research is desirable to determine whether, and under what conditions, such biological treatments should be used with some sex offenders (Rice & Harris, 2011). Such research should be a priority.

COMBINING PSYCHOLOGICAL AND BIOLOGICAL TREATMENTS Not surprisingly, many treatment programs now use a combination of hormone therapy and cognitive-behavioral treatments, the hope being that the hormone treatment can be tapered off after the offender has learned techniques for impulse control (Maletzky, 2002). However, the single most important defect of nearly all available studies is the lack of randomly assigned controls who are equally motivated for treatment. Some have argued that denying treatment to sex offenders is unethical (Marshall et al., 1991). However, this would be true only if the treatment were effective, and it is not clear at this point whether it is. Thus, others have argued that randomized controlled trials are crucial for making progress in his area (Seto et al., 2008). Research on this subject is further complicated by the fact that the outcome variable in most studies is whether the man is convicted for another sex offense during the follow-up period. The fact that most sex offenses go unpunished (the offender is often never even caught, let alone convicted) might exaggerate the apparent effectiveness of treatment and underestimate the dangerousness of sex offenders. Given the social importance of determining whether sex offenders can be helped and how likely they

are to reoffend, it is crucial that society devote the resources necessary to answering these questions.

SUMMARY It is possible both to acknowledge that sex offenders cause immense human suffering and to feel sympathy for the plight of the many offenders who have been burdened with a deviant sexual arousal pattern that has caused them great personal and legal trouble. Society cannot allow these people to act on their sexual preference, nor can their past crimes be forgotten. Nevertheless, in deciding how to treat these people, it is important and humane to remember that many of them have a tormented inner life.

---

in review

- What are the short-term consequences of childhood sexual abuse, and why are we less certain about its long-term consequences?
- What are the major issues surrounding children's testimony about sexual abuse and adults' recovered memories of sexual abuse?
- Define pedophilia, incest, and rape, and summarize the major clinical features of the perpetrators of these crimes.
- Identify the main goals of treatment of sex offenders, and describe the different treatment approaches.

Sexual Dysfunctions

12.5 **Define sexual dysfunction and name three sexual dysfunction disorders.**

The term **sexual dysfunction** refers to impairment either in the desire for sexual gratification or in the ability to achieve it. The impairment varies markedly in degree, but regardless of which partner is alleged to be dysfunctional, the enjoyment of sex by both parties in a relationship is typically adversely affected. Sexual dysfunctions occur in both heterosexual and homosexual couples. In some cases, sexual dysfunctions are caused primarily by psychological or interpersonal factors. In others, physical factors are most important, including many cases of sexual dysfunction that are secondary consequences of medications people may be taking for other, unrelated medical conditions (Baron-Kuhn & Segraves, 2007). Several different psychological interventions for sexual dysfunctions are not *evidence-based treatments*.

Research Close-Up
Evidence-Based Treatments

Evidence-based treatments are treatments that have been determined to be helpful based on well-designed, scientific research by more than just one group of researchers.

Researchers and clinicians typically identify four different phases of the human sexual response as originally proposed by Masters and Johnson (1966, 1970, 1975) and Kaplan (1979). According to *DSM-5*, disorders can occur in any of the first three phases:

- The first phase is the **desire phase**, which consists of fantasies about sexual activity or a sense of desire to have sexual activity.

- The second phase is the excitement, or arousal, phase. It is characterized both by a subjective sense of sexual pleasure and by physiological changes that accompany this subjective pleasure, including penile erection in the male and vaginal lubrication and clitoral enlargement in the female.

- The third phase is **orgasm**, during which there is a release of sexual tension and a peaking of sexual pleasure.

- The final phase is **resolution**, during which the person has a sense of relaxation and well-being.

Although these four phases are described as if they were distinct, it is important to remember that they are experienced by an individual as a continuous set of feelings and biological and behavioral reactions. There are other conceivable ways to discuss and organize the sequence that occurs. Indeed, in *DSM-5*, **female sexual interest/arousal disorder** replaces two separate disorders in *DSM-IV-TR*, because research has not adequately demonstrated that sexual interest and arousal are distinguishable in women (Brotto, 2010; Graham, 2010).

How common are sexual dysfunctions? It is obviously difficult to do large-scale research on such a sensitive topic. Nevertheless, the National Health and Social Life Survey (Laumann et al., 1999) assessed sexual problems in 3,159 randomly selected Americans by asking them if they had experienced the symptoms of any of the different sexual dysfunctions in the past 12 months. Sexual problems were very common, with 43 percent of women and 31 percent of men reporting having experienced at least one of these problems in the previous 12 months. For women, the

reported rate of sexual problems decreased with age; for men it increased. Married men and women, and those with higher educational attainment, had lower rates of problems. For women, the most common complaints were lack of sexual desire (22 percent) and sexual arousal problems (14 percent). For men, climaxing too early (21 percent), erectile dysfunction (5 percent), and lack of sexual interest (5 percent) were reported most frequently. However, this study was criticized by Bancroft et al. (2003), who believe that these numbers overestimate how many people have true sexual dysfunctions. Although the Laumann and colleagues' results are often referred to as being about sexual *dysfunction*, in fact, the investigators never asked people about whether the problems caused them distress or impairment in any way; yet these are necessary criteria for making a diagnosis in *DSM-5*. When Bancroft et al. (2003) did a related survey (although just in women), they found very similar percentages to those found by Laumann and colleagues. However, Bancroft and colleagues found that only about half as many reported that the problem caused them "severe distress." Nevertheless, this is still a relatively high percentage of people experiencing sexual dysfunction at some point in their lives.

Interestingly, a later study of 27,500 people across 29 countries all over the world revealed fairly similar results (Laumann et al., 2005). East Asian and Southeast Asian countries reported slightly higher rates of sexual problems than most other countries. The *DSM-5* criteria box summarizes each of the dysfunctions covered here.

Sexual Dysfunctions in Men

For cultural reasons, and possibly also for biological reasons, sex is thought to be especially important to men. Certainly the pharmaceutical industry has capitalized on men's distress about sexual dysfunction, earning billions of dollars from sales of treatments for male sexual dysfunction, primarily **erectile disorder**. Whether men are actually more upset than women by sexual dysfunction or this is simply one more domain where women's feelings have been ignored until recently, there is no dispute that we know far more about men's sexual dysfunctions than women's.

MALE HYPOACTIVE SEXUAL DESIRE DISORDER Hypoactive sexual desire disorder is diagnosed in men who have for at least 6 months been distressed or impaired due to low levels of sexual thoughts, desires, or fantasies. Men given this diagnosis are also assessed for the course of the dysfunction (i.e., lifelong or acquired) and possible causal factors, including problems emanating from partners, relationships, cultural beliefs or attitudes, personal vulnerabilities (e.g., poor body image), or medical conditions. Despite the historically higher level of attention to

DSM-5 *Criteria for. . .*

Different Sexual Dysfunctions

Men

Male Hypoactive Sexual Desire Disorder

A. Persistently or recurrently deficient (or absent) sexual/erotic thoughts or fantasies and desire for sexual activity. The judgment of deficiency is made by the clinician, taking into account factors that affect sexual functioning, such as age and general and sociocultural contexts of the individual's life.

B. The symptoms in Criterion A have persisted for a minimum duration of approximately 6 months.

C. The symptoms in Criterion A cause clinically significant distress in the individual.

D. The sexual dysfunction is not better explained by a nonsexual mental disorder or as a consequence of severe relationship distress or other significant stressors and is not attributable to the effects of a substance/medication or another medical condition.

Erectile Disorder

A. At least one of the three following symptoms must be experienced on almost all or all (approximately 75%–100%) occasions of sexual activity (in identified situational contexts or, if generalized, in all contexts):

1. Marked difficulty in obtaining an erection during sexual activity.
2. Marked difficulty in maintaining an erection until the completion of sexual activity.
3. Marked decrease in erectile rigidity.

B. The symptoms in Criterion A have persisted for a minimum duration of approximately 6 months.

C. The symptoms in Criterion A cause clinically significant distress in the individual.

D. The sexual dysfunction is not better explained by a nonsexual mental disorder or as a consequence of severe relationship distress or other significant stressors and is not attributable to the effects of a substance/medication or another medical condition.

Premature (Early) Ejaculation

A. A persistent or recurrent pattern of ejaculation occurring during partnered sexual activity within approximately 1 minute following vaginal penetration and before the individual wishes it. **Note:** Although the diagnosis of premature (early) ejaculation may be applied to individuals engaged in nonvaginal sexual activities, specific duration criteria have not been established for these activities.

B. The symptom in Criterion A must have been present for at least 6 months and must be experienced on almost all or all (approximately 75%–100%) occasions of sexual activity (in identified situational contexts or, if generalized, in all contexts).

C. The symptom in Criterion A causes clinically significant distress in the individual.

D. The sexual dysfunction is not better explained by a nonsexual mental disorder or as a consequence of severe relationship distress or other significant stressors and is not attributable to the effects of a substance/medication or another medical condition.

Delayed Ejaculation

A. Either of the following symptoms must be experienced on almost all or all occasions (approximately 75%–100%) of partnered sexual activity (in identified situational contexts or, if generalized, in all contexts), and without the individual desiring delay:

1. Marked delay in ejaculation.
2. Marked infrequency or absence of ejaculation

B. The symptoms in Criterion A have persisted for a minimum duration of approximately 6 months.

C. The symptoms in Criterion A cause clinically significant distress in the individual.

D. The sexual dysfunction is not better explained by a nonsexual mental disorder or as a consequence of severe relationship distress or other significant stressors and is not attributable to the effects of a substance/medication or another medical condition.

Women

Female Sexual Interest/Arousal Disorder

A. Lack of, or significantly reduced, sexual interest/arousal, as manifested by at least three of the following:

1. Absent/reduced interest in sexual activity.
2. Absent/reduced sexual/erotic thoughts or fantasies.
3. No/reduced initiation of sexual activity, and typically unreceptive to a partner's attempts to initiate.
4. Absent/reduced sexual excitement/pleasure during sexual activity in almost all or all (approximately 75%–100%) sexual encounters (in identified situational contexts or, if generalized, in all contexts).
5. Absent/reduced sexual interest/arousal in response to any internal or external sexual/erotic cues (e.g., written, verbal, visual).
6. Absent/reduced genital or nongenital sensations during sexual activity in almost all or all (approximately 75%–100%) sexual encounters (in identified situational contexts or, if generalized, in all contexts).

B. The symptoms in Criterion A have persisted for a minimum duration of approximately 6 months.

C. The symptoms in Criterion A cause clinically significant distress in the individual.

D. The sexual dysfunction is not better explained by a nonsexual mental disorder or as a consequence of severe relationship distress (e.g., partner violence) or other significant stressors and is not attributable to the effects of a substance/medication or another medical condition.

Genito-Pelvic Pain/Penetration Disorder

A. Persistent or recurrent difficulties with one (or more) of the following:

1. Vaginal penetration during intercourse.
2. Marked vulvovaginal or pelvic pain during vaginal intercourse or penetration attempts.
3. Marked fear or anxiety about vulvovaginal or pelvic pain in anticipation of, during, or as a result of vaginal penetration.
4. Marked tensing or tightening of the pelvic floor muscles during attempted vaginal penetration.

B. The symptoms in Criterion A have persisted for a minimum duration of approximately 6 months.

C. The symptoms in Criterion A cause clinically significant distress in the individual.

D. The sexual dysfunction is not better explained by a nonsexual mental disorder or as a consequence of severe relationship distress (e.g., partner violence) or other significant stressors and is not attributable to the effects of a substance/medication or another medical condition.

Female Orgasmic Disorder

A. Presence of either of the following symptoms and experienced on almost all or all (approximately 75%–100%) occasions of sexual activity (in identified situational contexts or, if generalized, in all contexts):

1. Marked delay in, marked infrequency of, or absence of orgasm.
2. Markedly reduced intensity of orgasmic sensations.

B. The symptoms in Criterion A have persisted for a minimum duration of approximately 6 months.

C. The symptoms in Criterion A cause clinically significant distress in the individual.

D. The sexual dysfunction is not better explained by a nonsexual mental disorder or as a consequence of severe relationship distress (e.g., partner violence) or other significant stressors and is not attributable to the effects of a substance/medication or another medical condition.

Men/Women

Substance/Medication-Induced Sexual Dysfunction

A. A clinically significant disturbance in sexual function is predominant in the clinical picture.

B. There is evidence from the history, physical examination, or laboratory findings of both (1) and (2):

1. The symptoms in Criterion A developed during or soon after substance intoxication or withdrawal or after exposure to a medication.
2. The involved substance/medication is capable of producing the symptoms in Criterion A.

C. The disturbance is not better explained by a sexual dysfunction that is not substance/medication-induced. Such evidence of an independent sexual dysfunction could include the following:

The symptoms precede the onset of the substance/medication use; the symptoms persist for a substantial period of time (e.g., about 1 month) after the cessation of acute withdrawal or severe intoxication; or there is other evidence suggesting the existence of an independent non-substance/medication-induced sexual dysfunction (e.g., a history of recurrent non-substance/medication-related episodes).

D. The disturbance does not occur exclusively during the course of a delirium.

E. The disturbance causes clinically significant distress in the individual.

Note: This diagnosis should be made instead of a diagnosis of substance intoxication or substance withdrawal only when the symptoms in Criterion A predominate in the clinical picture and are sufficiently severe to warrant clinical attention.

Source: Reprinted with permission from the *Diagnostic and Statistical Manual of Mental Disorders*, Fifth Edition (Copyright 2013). American Psychiatric Association.

---

male than to female sexual dysfunctions, this is one disorder in men that has received relatively little attention—and substantially less than its parallel disorder in women (Brotto, 2010). In the large American survey conducted by Laumann et al. (1999), men in the oldest cohort (50–59 years old) were three times more likely to suffer from low desire compared with men in the youngest cohort (18–29 years old). Predictors of low desire included daily alcohol use, stress, unmarried status, and poorer health. In a large British survey, complaints of low interest in sex was the most common problem reported by men (17.1 percent; Mercer et al., 2003). However, only a small minority (1.8 percent) of

the male sample had low desire for the required 6-month period to qualify for diagnosis. Most experts believe that **male hypoactive sexual desire disorder** is acquired or situational rather than lifelong. Typical situational risk factors include depression and relationship stress.

Treatment The treatment literature on low sexual desire in men is scant. In men whose testosterone levels are markedly low (including hypogonadal men whose testes make insufficient testosterone and men with HIV that diminishes their testosterone production), testosterone injections have helped (Brotto, 2010). Because psychological factors are more closely linked to low male sexual desire compared with hormonal factors, psychological treatments may be more effective for other men.

ERECTILE DISORDER Inability to achieve or maintain an erection sufficient for successful sexual intercourse was formerly called *impotence*. It is now known as male erectile disorder and can be diagnosed only when the difficulties are considered to originate from either psychogenic or a combination of psychogenic and medical factors (see the earlier *DSM-5* criteria box). In lifelong erectile disorder, a man with adequate sexual desire has never been able to sustain an erection long enough to accomplish a satisfactory duration of penetration. In acquired or situational erectile disorder, a man with adequate sexual desire has had at least one successful experience of sexual activity requiring an erection but is presently unable to produce or maintain the required level of penile rigidity. Lifelong erectile disorder is relatively rare, but most men of all ages occasionally have difficulty obtaining or maintaining an erection. A landmark study on the prevalence of sexual dysfunction estimates that 7 percent of 18- to 19-year-old men and 18 percent of 50- to 59-year-old men reported having erectile disorder (Laumann et al., 1999).

Masters and Johnson (1975; Masters et al., 1992) and Kaplan (1987) hypothesized that erectile dysfunction is primarily a function of anxiety about sexual performance. In other reviews of the accumulated evidence, however, Barlow and colleagues (Beck & Barlow, 1984; Sbrocco & Barlow, 1996) have played down the role of anxiety per se—because under some circumstances, anxiety can actually enhance sexual performance in normally functioning men and women (Barlow et al., 1983; Palace & Gorzalka, 1990; Sbrocco & Barlow, 1996). Barlow (2002) emphasizes that it is the cognitive distractions frequently associated with anxiety in dysfunctional people that seem to interfere with their sexual arousal. For example, one study found that nondysfunctional men who were distracted by material they were listening to on earphones while watching an erotic film showed less sexual arousal than men who were not distracted (Abrahamson et al., 1985). Barlow and colleagues hypothesize that sexually dysfunctional men and women get distracted by negative thoughts about their performance during a sexual encounter ("I'll never get aroused" or "She'll think I'm inadequate"). Their research suggests that this preoccupation with negative thoughts, rather than anxiety per se, is responsible for inhibiting sexual arousal (see also Weiner & Rosen, 1999; Wincze et al., 2008). Moreover, such self-defeating thoughts not only decrease pleasure but also can increase anxiety if the erection does not happen, and this in turn can fuel further negative, self-defeating thoughts (Sbrocco & Barlow, 1996). A related finding is that men with erectile dysfunction make more internal and stable causal attributions for hypothetical

negative sexual events than do men without sexual dysfunction, much as people with depression do for more general hypothetical negative events (Nobre, 2010; Scepkowski et al., 2004). Combined with Bancroft and colleagues' (2005) findings that fear of performance failure is a strong predictor of erectile dysfunction in both gay and heterosexual men, one can see how a vicious cycle develops in which fears of failure are sometimes followed by erectile dysfunction, which is then attributed to internal and stable causes, thereby perpetuating the problem.

Sexual dysfunctions can occur in the desire, excitement, or orgasm phases of the sexual response cycle. Many people, if not most, will experience some sexual dysfunction sometime during their lives. If it becomes chronic or disturbing to one or both partners, it warrants treatment.

Erectile problems occur in as many as 90 percent of men on certain antidepressant medications (especially the SSRIs) and are one of the primary reasons men cite for discontinuing these medications (Rosen & Marin, 2003). These problems are also a common consequence of aging. One large study of over 1,400 men found that 37 percent between ages 57 and 85 reported significant erectile difficulties, with the problems gradually increasing with age (Lindau et al., 2007). However, complete and permanent erectile disorder before the age of 60 is relatively rare. Moreover, studies have indicated that men and women in their 80s and 90s are often quite capable of enjoying intercourse (Masters et al., 1992; Meston & Rellini, 2008). For example, in one study of 202 healthy men and women between the ages of 80 and 102, it was found that nearly two-thirds of the men and one-third of the women were still having sexual intercourse, although this was generally not their most common form of sexual activity (Bretschneider & McCoy, 1988).

The most frequent cause of erectile disorder in older men is vascular disease, which results in decreased blood flow to the penis or in diminished ability of the penis to hold blood to maintain an erection. Thus hardening of the arteries, high blood pressure, and other diseases such as diabetes that cause vascular problems often account for erectile disorder. Smoking, obesity, and alcohol abuse are associated lifestyle factors, and lifestyle changes can improve erectile function (Gupta et al., 2011). Diseases that affect the nervous system, such as multiple sclerosis, can also cause erectile problems. For young men, one cause of erectile problems is having had priapism—that is, an erection that will not diminish even after a couple of hours, typically unaccompanied by sexual excitement. Priapism can occur as a result of prolonged sexual activity, as a consequence of disease, or as a side effect of certain medications. Untreated cases of priapism are likely to result in erectile dysfunction and thus should be regarded as a medical emergency (Morrison & Burnett, 2011).

Treatment   A variety of treatments—primarily medical—have been employed in recent years, often when cognitive-behavioral treatments have failed. These include (1) medications that promote erections like Viagra, Levitra, and Cialis; (2) injections of smooth-muscle-relaxing drugs into the penile erection chambers (corpora cavernosa); and (3) even a vacuum pump (Duterte et al., 2007; Rosen, 1996). In extreme cases, for example when erections are impossible due to nerve damage that can be a consequence of surgery for prostate cancer, penile implants may still be used. These devices can be inflated to provide erection on demand. They are made of silicone rubber or polyurethane rubber. Such treatments have generally shown success in clinical trials, although they are rather extreme interventions that often evoke bothersome side effects such as decreased penis size (Duterte et al., 2007). They were used in thousands of cases in the 1960s and 1970s before current medications were available.

In 1998 the revolutionary drug Viagra (sildenafil) was introduced on the U.S. market and was received with a great deal of attention. Viagra works by making nitric oxide, the primary neurotransmitter involved in penile erection, more available. Viagra is taken orally at least 30 to 60 minutes before sexual activity. Unlike some other biological treatments for erectile dysfunction, Viagra promotes erection only if some sexual excitation is present. Thus, contrary to some myths, Viagra does not improve libido or promote spontaneous erections (Duterte et al., 2007; Segraves & Althof, 2002). Two other related medications introduced in 2003 to treat erectile dysfunction are Levitra (vardenafil; Stark et al., 2001) and Cialis (tadalafil; Padma-Nathan et al., 2001), with the effects of Cialis being longer lasting (up to 36 hours). Clinical trials of these medications have been impressive. In one early double-blind study, over 70 percent of men receiving at least 50 mg of Viagra reported that their erections had improved, compared with fewer than 30 percent of men receiving a placebo (Carlson, 1997; see also Goldstein et al., 1998). Results with Cialis and Levitra are similar. Overall efficacy rates in

terms of ability to obtain an erection are 40 to 80 percent, but levels of satisfaction are often much lower, perhaps because these medications do not increase sexual desire or satisfaction and perhaps because sexual desire and satisfaction are more closely intertwined with psychological and relationship factors. Side effects are relatively uncommon and not serious (e.g., the most common side effects are headache and facial flushing, seen in 10 to 20 percent of men), provided that the person had no serious preexisting heart problems (Duterte et al., 2007). When heart problems do exist, these medications should be prescribed with caution because they can interact in dangerous ways with heart medications. These medications have been highly successful commercially—for example, in 2008 almost $2 billion worth of Viagra was sold. Interestingly, however, many men who fill one prescription never refill it, according to the drug companies' own statistics. The commercial success of drugs like Viagra and Cialis is an indication of both the high prevalence of sexual dysfunction in men and the importance that people attach to sexual performance. There are also a few studies showing that the usefulness of these medications may be further enhanced when used in conjunction with cognitive-behavioral treatment (Bach et al., 2004; Meston & Rellini, 2008).

EARLY EJACULATION   In *DSM-5* "premature ejaculation" is called early ejaculation disorder, the persistent and recurrent onset of orgasm and ejaculation with minimal sexual stimulation. It may occur before, on, or shortly after penetration and before the man wants it to (see the earlier *DSM-5* criteria box). The average duration of time to ejaculate in men with this problem is 15 seconds or 15 thrusts of intercourse. The consequences often include failure of the partner to achieve satisfaction and, often, acute embarrassment for the early ejaculating man, with disruptive anxiety about recurrence on future occasions. Men who have had this problem from their first sexual encounter often try to diminish sexual excitement by avoiding stimulation, by self-distracting, and by "spectatoring," or psychologically taking the role of an observer rather than a participant (Metz et al., 1997). Early ejaculation decreases sexual and relationship satisfaction both in men who have it and their partners (Graziottin & Althof, 2011).

An exact definition of prematurity is necessarily somewhat arbitrary. For example, the age of a client must be considered—the alleged "quick trigger" of the younger man being more than a mere myth (McCarthy, 1989). Indeed, perhaps half of young men complain of early ejaculation. Not surprisingly, early ejaculation is most likely after a lengthy abstinence. *DSM-5* acknowledges these many factors that may affect time to ejaculation by noting that the diagnosis is made only if ejaculation occurs before, on, or shortly after penetration and before the man wants it to. Early ejaculation is the most common male sexual dysfunction among those under 60 years of age, with erectile dysfunction becoming more common in older men (Meston & Rellini, 2008; Segraves & Althof, 2002).

In sexually normal men, the ejaculatory reflex is, to a considerable extent, under voluntary control. They monitor their sensations during sexual stimulation and are somehow able, perhaps by judicious use of distraction, to forestall the point of ejaculatory inevitability until they decide to "let go," with the average latency to ejaculation from penetration being 10 minutes for men with no sexual problems. Men with early ejaculation are for some reason unable to use this technique effectively. Explanations have ranged from psychological factors such as increased anxiety, to physiological factors such as increased penile sensitivity and higher levels of arousal to sexual stimuli. Presently, however, no explanation has received much empirical support, and it is clear that none of these possible explanations alone can account for all men with the problem (Meston & Rellini, 2008).

Treatment   For many years, most sex therapists considered early ejaculation to be psychogenically caused and highly treatable via behavioral therapy such as the pause-and-squeeze technique developed by Masters and Johnson (1970). This technique requires the man to monitor his sexual arousal during sexual activity. When arousal is intense enough that the man feels that ejaculation might occur soon, he pauses, and he or his partner squeezes the head of the penis for a few moments until the feeling of pending ejaculation passes, repeating the stopping of intercourse as many times as needed to delay ejaculation. Initial reports suggested that this technique was approximately 60 to 90 percent effective; however, more recent studies have reported a much lower overall success rate (Duterte et al., 2007; Segraves & Althof, 2002). In recent years, for men for whom behavioral treatments have not worked, there has been increasing interest in the possible use of pharmacological interventions. Antidepressants such as paroxetine (Paxil), sertraline (Zoloft), fluoxetine (Prozac), and dapoxetine (Priligy), which block serotonin reuptake, have been found to significantly prolong ejaculatory latency in men with early ejaculation (Porst, 2011). Evidence suggests, however, that the medications work only as long as they are being taken.

DELAYED EJACULATION DISORDER   Delayed ejaculation disorder refers to the persistent inability to ejaculate during intercourse (see the earlier *DSM-5* criteria box). It occurs in only about 3 to 10 percent of men. Men who are completely unable to ejaculate are rare. About 85 percent of men who have difficulty ejaculating during intercourse can nevertheless achieve orgasm by other means of stimulation, notably through solitary masturbation (Wincze et al., 2008). In milder cases a man can ejaculate in the presence of a partner but only by means of manual or oral stimulation.

In other cases, delayed ejaculation can be related to specific physical problems such as multiple sclerosis or to the use of certain medications. For example, we noted that antidepressants that block serotonin reuptake appear to be an effective treatment for early ejaculation. However, in other men, these same medications—especially the SSRIs—sometimes delay or prevent orgasm to an unpleasant extent (Ashton et al., 1997; Meston & Rellini, 2008). These side effects are common but can sometimes be treated pharmacologically with medications like Viagra (Ashton et al., 1997).

Treatment   Psychological treatments include couples therapy in which a man tries to get used to having orgasms through intercourse with a partner rather than via masturbation. Treatment may also emphasize the reduction of performance anxiety about the importance of having an orgasm versus sexual pleasure and intimacy in addition to increasing genital stimulation (Meston & Rellini, 2008; Segraves & Althof, 2002).

Sexual Dysfunctions in Women

Although more is known about sexual dysfunction in men than in women, it is clear that women also experience problems in sexual interest, arousal, and orgasm. Several forms of sexual dysfunctions in women have received increasing research attention.

FEMALE SEXUAL INTEREST/AROUSAL DISORDER Research suggests that women with low desire tend to have low levels of sexual arousal during sexual activity and vice versa. There are no common syndromes in which women with low sexual desire have normal levels of sexual arousal, or vice versa. Thus, for women, *DSM-5* has combined dysfunctionally low desire with dysfunctionally low sexual arousal in the disorder. Research on the degree to which the diminished sex drive has a biological basis remains controversial, but in many (and perhaps most) cases (and especially in women), psychological factors appear to be more important than biological factors (Meston & Bradford, 2007; Segraves & Woodard, 2006). In the past, these people usually came to the attention of clinicians primarily at the request of their partners (who typically complained of insufficient sexual interaction), but as public knowledge about the frequency of this disorder has increased, more people are presenting for treatment on their own. This fact exposes one problem with the diagnosis, because it is known that preferences for frequency of sexual contact vary widely among otherwise normal individuals. Who is to decide what is "not enough"? *DSM-5* explicitly indicates that this judgment is left to the clinician, taking into account the person's age and the context of his or her life.

Prior or current depression or anxiety disorders may contribute to many cases of sexual desire disorders (Meston & Bradford, 2007). Although sexual desire disorders typically occur in the absence of obvious physical pathology, there is evidence that physical factors sometimes play a role. For example, in both men and women, sexual desire depends in part on testosterone (Meston & Rellini, 2008). That sexual desire problems increase with age may be in part attributable to declining levels of testosterone, but testosterone replacement therapy is usually not beneficial, except in men and women who have very low testosterone levels (Meston & Rellini, 2008). In addition, medications from the SSRI category of antidepressants (see Chapters 7 and 16) not uncommonly reduce sexual desire. Different antidepressants vary considerably in their negative effect on sexual function, and psychiatrists have not always paid close enough attention to the impact that these effects have on patients' general functioning (Serretti & Chiesa, 2009). Psychological factors thought to contribute to sexual desire disorders include low relationship satisfaction, daily hassles and worries, increased disagreements and conflicts, low levels of feelings, and reduced cues of emotional bonding (Meston & Rellini, 2008). In some cases a history of unwanted sexual experiences such as rape may also contribute.

Hypoactive sexual desire disorder is the most common female sexual dysfunction in most other countries across the world (Laumann et al., 1994, 1999, 2005). Despite this fact, disorders of female sexual desire have inspired far less research into its origins and treatment than have most male dysfunctions, especially erectile disorder and early ejaculation. One main reason for this disparity may be the great importance that many men place on their ability to perform sexually. Until recently, there has also been a more general neglect of female sexuality and an implicit (though largely mistaken) societal attitude that women simply do not care much about sex.

Fortunately, this has been changing gradually in recent years (Althof et al., 2005; Basson, 2005; Meston & Bradford, 2007). One emerging finding is that it is uncommon for women to cite sexual desire as a reason or incentive for sexual activity. For many women, sexual desire is experienced only after sexual stimuli have led to subjective sexual arousal (Basson, 2003; Meston & Bradford, 2007), and for others, motivation for sexual activity may involve a desire for increasing emotional intimacy or increasing one's sense of well-being and one's self-image as an attractive female (Basson, 2003, 2005). Thus, some research suggests that the supposedly linear sequence of desire leading to arousal, leading to orgasm that was originally posited for women as well as men by Masters and Johnson (1970) and the *DSM* is not very accurate for women (Basson, 2005; Meston & Bradford, 2007).

Dysfunctionally low sexual arousal in women was formerly and somewhat pejoratively known as *frigidity*. In *DSM-IV* female sexual arousal disorder—the absence of feelings of sexual arousal and an unresponsiveness to most or all forms of erotic stimulation—was in many ways the female counterpart of erectile disorder (see the earlier *DSM-5* criteria box). Its chief physical manifestation was a failure to produce the characteristic swelling and lubrication of the vulva and vaginal tissues during sexual stimulation—a condition that may make intercourse quite uncomfortable and orgasm impossible.

Although the causes of low sexual arousal are not well understood, possible reasons range from early sexual traumatization, to excessive and distorted socialization about the "evils" of sex, to dislike of, or disgust with, a current partner's sexuality, to her partner's restricted repertoire of sexual activity. One interesting study also found that women with sexual arousal disorder show lower tactile sensitivity than is seen in other women; the lower their level of tactile sensitivity, the more severe their arousal dysfunction (Frolich & Meston, 2005). Biological causal factors include the use of SSRIs for anxiety and depression, the occurrence of certain medical illnesses (e.g., spinal cord injury, cancer treatment, diabetes), and the decreases in estrogen levels that occur during and following menopause. Some difficulties with physiological arousal and lubrication have been noted in 20 to 30 percent of sexually active women and in as many as 44 percent of postmenopausal women. Moreover, arousal problems in women very frequently co-occur with low levels of sexual desire. Indeed, having problems with sexual arousal may often lead to lack of desire (Meston & Bradford, 2007).

Treatment Although there has been interest since antiquity in the possibility that a drug to increase sexual desire might be found, no effective aphrodisiacs yet exist. As noted earlier, testosterone appears to be effective only in men and women who have very low levels of testosterone; that is, raising levels of this important sex hormone above normal levels has no beneficial effects (Meston & Rellini, 2008). Consistent with an effect of hormones, a German study showed that women using oral contraceptives, which sometimes work by raising estrogen levels, which in turn reduce testosterone levels, had somewhat lower levels of sexual desire and arousal compared with those who did not (Wallwiener et al., 2010).

Several studies have found that sustained use of bupropion (an atypical antidepressant), relative to placebo, improved sexual arousability and orgasm frequency in women who were in a committed relationship and had hypoactive sexual desire disorder (Segraves et al., 2004). Another drug, flibanserin (Addyi), has been developed to increase sexual desire in women, and was approved by the Food and Drug Administration in August 2015.

There are no well-established psychotherapies for hypoactive sexual desire. Typically therapists focus on education, communication training, cognitive restructuring of dysfunctional beliefs about sexuality, sexual fantasy training, and sensate focus training (Meston & Rellini, 2008). Sensate focus exercises are also used in the treatment of several other forms of sexual dysfunctions, as we will see. They involve teaching couples to focus on the pleasurable sensations brought about by touching without the goal of actually having intercourse or orgasm. Relationship problems often contribute importantly to low sexual desire, as do concerns related to body image (Basson, 2010). Addressing these problems may be helpful.

Few controlled treatment studies of low sexual arousal in women have been conducted (Meston & Bradford, 2007), although clinical experience suggests that psychotherapy and sex therapy may play important roles in helping women with this disorder. Typically the techniques that are used are similar to those used to increase sexual desire. The widespread use of vaginal lubricants may effectively mask and treat the symptoms of this disorder in many women, but lubricants do not enhance genital blood flow or genital sensations.

In addition, because female genital response depends in part on the same neurotransmitter systems as male genital response, there has been great interest in the possibility that Viagra, Levitra, or Cialis would have positive effects for women analogous to their positive effects for men (Meston & Rellini, 2008). Unfortunately, enough research has now been performed to make it clear that such drugs are not as useful for women as they are for men (Basson et al., 2002; Meston & Rellini, 2008). Although these medications may enhance genital arousal and perceptions of physical sensations in women, they do not affect women's psychological experiences of arousal. It is likely that women's sexual desire and arousal are more dependent on relationship satisfaction and mood than they are in men.

GENITO-PELVIC PAIN/PENETRATION DISORDER This disorder represents an important change in *DSM-5*. Earlier versions of the *DSM* distinguished two "sexual pain disorders": vaginismus and dyspareunia. The disorders have been combined in *DSM-5* because scientific research did not support their distinction (Binik, 2010a, 2010b). In particular, vaginismus has been believed to be an involuntary spasm of the muscles near the entrance of the vagina, preventing penetration and sexual intercourse. However, no scientific evidence exists that women with vaginismus have vaginal spasms or that vaginismus could be reliably diagnosed. In contrast, women diagnosed with vaginismus commonly complained of pain during penetration and anxiety before and during sexual encounters (Reissing et al., 2003). The latter symptoms made the distinction between vaginismus and dyspareunia (which is genital pain associated with sexual intercourse) unclear. That is, women with a past diagnosis of vaginismus were not

clearly distinct from those with a past diagnosis of dyspareunia. Furthermore, as noted, the hallmark "symptom" of vaginismus, does not clearly occur, while the hallmark symptom of dyspareunia, genital pain during penetration, occurs commonly in women with vaginismus as well. Thus, in *DSM-5* there is only one **genito-pelvic pain/penetration disorder**, which combines the genital pain of dyspareunia with muscle tension (not muscle spasms) and fear and anxiety related to genital pain or penetrative sexual activity.

Based on past studies of women with "sexual pain disorders" it appears that genito-pelvic pain/penetration disorder is more likely to have organic than psychological causes. Some examples of physical causes include acute or chronic infections or inflammations of the vagina or internal reproductive organs, vaginal atrophy that occurs with aging, scars from vaginal tearing, or insufficiency of sexual arousal.

Recently, some prominent sex researchers have argued against classifying sexual pain disorders as "sexual disorders" rather than as "pain disorders" (Binik, 2005; Binik et al., 2007). For example, Binik and colleagues argue that the pain in "sexual pain disorders" is qualitatively similar to the pain in other, nonsexual areas of the body and that the causes of "sexual pain disorder" are more similar to the causes of other pain disorders (e.g., lower back pain) than to the causes of other sexual dysfunctions. This concern is represented in the new name for the diagnosis (i.e., genito-pelvic pain/penetration disorder). It is also interesting to note in this regard that the disorder sometimes precedes any sexual experiences—for example, in some adolescent girls trying to use a tampon.

Treatment In past treatment studies of vaginismus and dyspareunia, cognitive-behavioral interventions have been effective in some cases. Cognitive-behavioral treatment techniques tend to include education about sexuality, identifying and correcting maladaptive cognitions, graduated vaginal dilation exercises to facilitate vaginal penetration, and progressive muscle relaxation (Bergeron et al., 2001). Medical treatments, such as surgical removal of the vulvar vestibule, a small area of the vulva between the labia minora, can be very successful (Binik, 2010a). It is likely that genito-pelvic pain/penetration disorder comprises several distinct syndromes with different etiologies and potentially different treatments. If so, the more we learn, the better our treatment options will be.

FEMALE ORGASMIC DISORDER The diagnosis of orgasmic dysfunction in women is complicated by the fact that the subjective quality of orgasm varies widely among women, within the same woman from time to time, and in regard to mode of stimulation (Graham, 2010). Nevertheless, according to *DSM-5*, **female orgasmic disorder** can be diagnosed in women who are readily sexually excitable and who otherwise enjoy sexual activity but who show persistent or recurrent delay in or absence of orgasm following a normal sexual excitement phase and who are distressed by this (see the earlier *DSM-5* criteria box). Of these women, many do not routinely experience orgasm during sexual intercourse without direct supplemental stimulation of the clitoris; indeed, this pattern is so common that it is generally not considered dysfunctional (Meston & Bradford, 2007). A small percentage of women are able to achieve orgasm only through direct mechanical stimulation of the clitoris, as in vigorous digital manipulation, oral stimulation, or the use of an electric vibrator. Even fewer are unable to have the experience under any known conditions of stimulation; this condition, which is called lifelong orgasmic dysfunction, is analogous to lifelong erectile disorder in males. More commonly, women experience difficulty having an orgasm only in certain situations or were able to achieve orgasm in the past but currently can rarely do so (Meston & Bradford, 2007). Laumann et al. (1999) found that rates of this disorder are highest in the 21- to 24-year-old age category and decline thereafter, and other studies have estimated that about one in three or four women report having had significant orgasmic difficulties in the past year (Meston & Bradford, 2007).

What causes female orgasmic disorder is not well understood, but a multitude of contributory factors have been hypothesized. For example, some women feel fearful and inadequate in sexual relations. A woman may be uncertain whether her partner finds her sexually attractive, and this may lead to anxiety and tension, which then interfere with her sexual enjoyment. Or she may feel inadequate or experience sexual guilt (especially common in those who are religious) because she is unable to have an orgasm or does so infrequently.

Possible biological causal factors sometimes contributing to orgasmic difficulties in women (as they do in men) include intake of the SSRIs and the presence of medical conditions previously mentioned with other sexual disorders (Meston & Rellini, 2008). Recent evidence suggests that differences between women's genital anatomies may allow some women to have orgasms during intercourse more easily than other women can (Wallen & Lloyd, 2011).

Treatment One important issue regarding treatment is whether women should seek it or not. Most clinicians agree that a woman with lifelong orgasmic disorder needs treatment if she is to become orgasmic. However, in the middle range of orgasmic responsiveness, our own view is that this question is best left to a woman herself to answer. If she is dissatisfied about her responsiveness, then she should seek treatment.

For those who do seek treatment, it is important to distinguish between lifelong and situational female orgasmic dysfunction. Cognitive-behavioral treatment of orgasmic dysfunction usually involves education about female sexuality and female sexual anatomy, as well as directed masturbation exercises. Later the partner may be included to explore these activities with the client. For those with lifelong orgasmic dysfunction, such programs can have nearly a 100 percent success rate in terms of the woman's ability to have an orgasm at least through masturbation, but transition to having an orgasm with a partner can be slow and difficult in some cases (Meston & Rellini, 2008). "Situational" anorgasmia (where a woman may experience orgasm in some situations, with certain kinds of stimulation, or with certain partners, but not under the precise conditions she desires) often proves more difficult to treat, perhaps in part because it is often associated with relationship problems that may also be hard to treat (Althof & Schreiner-Engel, 2000).

in review

- Compare and contrast the symptoms of the dysfunctions of sexual desire, arousal, and orgasm in men and women.
- Why have common female sexual dysfunctions been studied less than male sexual dysfunctions?
- What are the most effective treatments for male erectile disorder and premature ejaculation and for female orgasmic disorder?

Unresolved Issues

How Harmful Is Childhood Sexual Abuse?

Most contemporary Americans believe that childhood sexual abuse (CSA) is very harmful. This is reflected both in their concern for the victims of CSA and in their outrage at its perpetrators. The assumption of harmfulness is so deeply ingrained that many people find it shocking even to consider the alternative possibility that, at least sometimes, CSA is not very harmful. Surely, though, the issue of harm is answerable by empirical means. What do the results show?

In 1998 psychologist Bruce Rind of Temple University and two colleagues published, in the prestigious journal *Psychological Bulletin*, an article reviewing 49 previous studies that had asked college students about their sexual experiences during childhood (Rind et al., 1998). Furthermore, the studies assessed the students' current adjustment, enabling Rind and colleagues to examine the association between early sexual experiences and mental health in young adulthood. Here are some conclusions of this study:

- Correlations between childhood sexual abuse and later problems were of surprisingly small magnitude, suggesting that such experiences are not typically very harmful.
- After general family problems had been statistically controlled for, the small association between CSA and adult problems was reduced to essentially zero, suggesting that the negative family environment in which child sexual abuse often occurs, rather than the sexual abuse per se, might explain much of the link between CSA and later problems. Indeed, poor family environment predicted adjustment problems an average of nine times more strongly than CSA did (Rind & Tromovitch, 2007).
- Incest (sex with relatives) and forced sex were both associated with more problems than sex between nominally consenting, nonrelated individuals.
- Age at which CSA was experienced was unrelated to adult outcome.

At first, the study's provocative conclusions attracted little attention. However, after the conservative radio personality Dr. Laura Schlessinger learned of the study, she incited a firestorm of controversy. Both Dr. Laura and other critics accused Rind and his coauthors of giving comfort to child molesters and being insensitive to victims of CSA. The controversy culminated in 1999 with a resolution by the U.S. House of Representatives that condemned the study (Lilienfeld, 2002; Rind et al., 2000).

Rind's study was attacked on two general grounds: First, some argued that it is socially dangerous to make the kinds of claims that the authors make in their article (Ondersma et al., 2001). Second, some argued that the study was not strong enough, scientifically, to justify such risky conclusions. Let us examine both criticisms.

Clearly, it would be wrong to understate the harm of CSA. Victims of CSA would suffer from having their pain unappreciated, and we may well invest too little in solving problems related to CSA. But overstating the harm of CSA may also entail significant costs. For example, people who are led to believe that they have been gravely and permanently harmed by CSA may suffer unnecessarily if CSA actually does not invariably have grave and permanent consequences. If CSA is often not very harmful, we need to know that.

Assessing the validity of Rind's study is a scientific matter. *Psychological Bulletin* published a lengthy scientific critique of Rind's study (Dallam et al., 2001) along with a reply by Rind and his coauthors (2001). One criticism of the original study was that it relied on college students, who may be unrepresentative. Perhaps they were able to attend college despite CSA because they were especially resilient. However, in another study, Rind analyzed data from community samples (samples not selected on the basis of educational attainment) and got virtually identical results (Rind & Tromovitch, 1997). Some of Rind's statistical decisions and analyses have also been criticized, but he has shown that his results do not change much when he analyzes the data the way his critics would.

A later meta-analysis of a large representative group of nearly 1,800 adult Australians (ages 18 to 59) reported that CSA in women is associated with their having more symptoms of sexual dysfunction in adulthood (Najman et al., 2005). However, a later reanalysis of these data by Rind and Tromovitch (2007) showed that the magnitude of this relationship was quite small (similar to that in Rind et al.'s 1998 study). Moreover, Najman and colleagues did not statistically control for other important factors, such as poor family environment, that were shown to be even more important in Rind et al.'s 1998 study. Rind (2003, 2004) also extended his discussion to the issue of how harmful *adult–adolescent* sexual relationships are. The current American view, which has spread throughout the Western world, is that such relations are by definition also "childhood sexual abuse" even though marriages involving young teenagers were common in previous centuries. He reviewed evidence showing that current views on this topic are driven by ideology and moral panic rather than by any empirical research showing these experiences to be harmful—especially those between adolescent boys and adult females, where considerable evidence suggests that many teenage boys see perceived benefits from such relationships regarding their sexual confidence and self-acceptance. These are obviously controversial issues that deserve additional careful research in the future.

Clearly these studies do not yet definitively answer the question of "How harmful is CSA?" but future research must contend with their findings and pay close attention to the relative importance of other negative family factors that are usually highly correlated with CSA.

Summary

12.1 Explain why it is difficult to define boundaries between normality and psychopathology in the area of variant sexuality.

- Defining boundaries between normality and psychopathology in the area of variant sexuality is very

difficult, in part because sociocultural influences on what have been viewed as normal or aberrant sexual practices abound.

- Degeneracy theory and abstinence theory both maintained that sexual activity should only occur for purposes of procreation because wasting semen was harmful; both were very influential for long periods of time in the United States and many other Western cultures and led to very conservative views on heterosexual sexuality.

- In contrast to Western cultures, in the Sambia tribe in Melanesia, homosexuality is practiced by all adolescent males in the context of male sexual initiation rites; these males transition to heterosexuality in young adulthood.

- Until rather recently in many Western cultures, homosexuality was viewed either as criminal behavior or as a form of mental illness. However, since 1974 homosexuality has been considered by mental health professionals to be a normal sexual variant.

12.2 List and describe four types of paraphilia.

- Paraphilias involve persistent and recurrent patterns of sexual behavior and arousal, lasting at least 6 months, in which unusual objects, rituals, or situations are required for full sexual satisfaction. They occur almost exclusively in males, who often have more than one of them.

- Paraphilias include fetishes (sexual arousal from a nonliving object), transvestic fetishism (sexual arousal from cross-dressing), pedophilia (sexual arousal from children), voyeurism (sexual arousal from observing others naked, undressing, or engaged in sexual activities), exhibitionism (sexual arousal from exposing one's genitals), frotteurism (sexual arousal from touching or rubbing against a nonconsenting person), sadism (sexual arousal from the physical or psychological suffering of another person), and masochism (sexual arousal from suffering at the hands of someone else).

12.3 Explain the key characteristics of gender dysphoria.

- Gender dysphoria occurs in children and adults. Childhood gender dysphoria occurs in children who have dysphoria/distress about their biological sex. Most boys who have this disorder grow up to have a homosexual orientation; a much smaller number become transsexuals. Prospective studies of girls who have this disorder have reported similar results.

- Transsexualism is a very rare disorder in which the person believes that he or she is trapped in the body of the wrong sex and goes through elaborate steps necessary to change his or her sex. It is now recognized that there are two distinct types of male-to-female transsexuals: homosexual transsexuals and autogynephilic transsexuals, each with different characteristics and developmental antecedents. The only known effective treatment for transsexuals is a sex change operation.

Although its use remains highly controversial, it does appear to have fairly high success rates when the people are carefully diagnosed before the surgery as being true transsexuals.

12.4 Describe three primary types of sexual abuse.

- There are three overlapping categories of sexual abuse: pedophilia, incest, and rape. All three kinds of abuse occur at alarming rates today.

- Pedophilia is defined as sexual interest in prepubertal children.

- Incest involves sexual activity between blood relatives.

- Rape describes sexual activity that occurs under actual or threatened forcible coercion by one person on another.

- Treatment of sex offenders has not as yet proved highly effective in most cases, although promising research in this area is being conducted.

12.5 Define sexual dysfunction and name three sexual dysfunction disorders.

- Sexual dysfunction involves impairment either in the desire for sexual gratification or in the ability to achieve it. Dysfunction can occur in the first three of the four phases of the human sexual response: the desire phase, the excitement phase, and orgasm.

- Male hypoactive sexual desire disorder is diagnosed in men when they have little or no interest in sex. In extreme cases they may actually have an aversion to sexual activity.

- Erectile disorder occurs in men who are unable to attain or to maintain an adequate erection until the completion of sexual activity.

- Formerly called premature ejaculation, early ejaculation occurs in men who persistently and recurrently have the onset of orgasm with ejaculation occurring after only minimal sexual stimulation.

- Delayed ejaculation refers to the persistent inability to ejaculate during intercourse.

- Female sexual interest/arousal disorder is diagnosed in women who persistently show a lack of interest in sexual activity and/or great difficulty getting adequately aroused enough to have an orgasm.

- Genito-pelvic pain/penetration disorder is diagnosed in women who have persistent or recurrent difficulties in at least one of the following four areas: (1) marked difficulty having vaginal intercourse/penetration; (2) marked vulvovaginal or pelvic pain during vaginal intercourse/penetration attempts; (3) marked fear or anxiety either about vulvovaginal or pelvic pain or vaginal penetration; (4) marked tensing or tightening of the pelvic floor muscles during attempted vaginal penetration.

Key Terms

Chapter 13
Schizophrenia and Other Psychotic Disorders

Learning Objectives

13.1 Describe the prevalence of schizophrenia and who is most affected.

13.2 Identify the symptoms of schizophrenia as described in *DSM-5*.

13.3 List four different types of psychotic disorders and state one way in which each is different from schizophrenia.

13.4 Explain the genetic and biological risk and causal factors associated with schizophrenia.

13.5 Discuss how the brain is affected in schizophrenia.

13.6 Explain the psychosocial and cultural factors associated with schizophrenia.

13.7 Describe the clinical outcome of schizophrenia and how is it treated, noting the advantages and disadvantages associated with the use of antipsychotic medications.

Emilio: "Eating Wires and Lighting Fires"

Emilio is a 40-year-old man who looks 10 years younger. He is brought to the hospital, his 12th hospitalization, by his mother because she is afraid of him. He is dressed in a ragged overcoat, bedroom slippers, and a baseball cap, and he wears several medals around his neck. His affect ranges from anger at his mother ("She feeds me shit . . . what comes out of other people's rectums") to a giggling, obsequious seductiveness toward the interviewer. His speech and manner have a childlike quality, and he walks with a mincing step and exaggerated hip movements. His mother reports that he stopped taking his medication about a month ago and has since begun to hear voices and to look and act more bizarrely. When asked what he has been doing, he says "Eating wires and lighting fires." His spontaneous speech is often incoherent and marked by frequent rhyming and clang associations (where sounds, rather than meaningful relationships, govern word choice).

Emilio's first hospitalization occurred after he dropped out of school at age 16, and since that time he has never been able to attend school or hold a job. He has been treated with neuroleptics (medications used to treat schizophrenia) during his hospitalizations, but he doesn't continue to take his medications when he leaves, so he quickly becomes disorganized again. He lives with his elderly mother, but he sometimes disappears for several months at a time and is eventually picked up by the police as he wanders the streets. (Modified from Spitzer et al., 2002, pp. 189–190.)

The internal suffering of the person with schizophrenia is often readily apparent, as are bizarre behavior and unusual appearance.

The disorder that Emilio has is called schizophrenia. Schizophrenia is a severe disorder that is often associated with considerable impairments in functioning. This chapter describes the pieces of the schizophrenia puzzle through a description of both classic studies as well as the most recent research. Keep in mind from the outset that not all of the pieces or their presumed interconnections have been found, so our puzzle is far from being solved. As you read through this chapter you will learn just how complex and challenging this disorder is—not only for patients who suffer from it and for their families who try to care for them, but also for the clinicians who attempt to treat it and the researchers who are determined to understand it.

Schizophrenia

13.1 **Describe the prevalence of schizophrenia and who is most affected.**

Schizophrenia occurs in people from all cultures and from all walks of life. The disorder is characterized by an array of diverse symptoms, including extreme oddities in perception, thinking, action, sense of self, and manner of relating to others. However, the hallmark of schizophrenia is a significant loss of contact with reality, referred to as **psychosis**. Although the clinical presentation of schizophrenia differs from one patient to another, the case of Emilio is quite typical.

Origins of the Schizophrenia Construct

The first detailed clinical description of what we now recognize to be schizophrenia was offered in 1810 by John Haslam, the apothecary at the Bethlem Hospital in London, England. Haslam described the case of a patient who appears to have suffered from a variety of symptoms—including delusions—that are typical of schizophrenia (see Carpenter, 1989). Fifty years later, the Belgian psychiatrist Benedict Morel described the case of a 13-year-old boy who had formerly been the most brilliant pupil in his school but who gradually lost interest in his studies; became increasingly withdrawn, lethargic, reclusive, and quiet; and appeared to have forgotten everything he had learned. Morel thought the boy's intellectual, moral, and physical functions had deteriorated as a result of brain degeneration of hereditary origin. He used the term *démence précoce* (mental deterioration at an early age) to describe the condition and to distinguish it from the dementing disorders associated with old age.

It is the German psychiatrist Emil Kraepelin (1856–1926) who is best known for his careful description of what we now regard as schizophrenia. Kraepelin used the Latin version of Morel's term (*dementia praecox*) to refer to a group of conditions that all seemed to feature mental deterioration beginning early in life. Kraepelin, an astute observer of clinical phenomena, described the patient with dementia praecox as someone who "becomes suspicious of those around him, sees poison in his food, is pursued by the police, feels his body is being influenced, or thinks that he is going to be shot or that the neighbours are jeering at him" (Kraepelin, 1896). Kraepelin also noted that the disorder was characterized by hallucinations, apathy and indifference, withdrawn behavior, and an incapacity for regular work.

It was a Swiss psychiatrist named Eugen Bleuler (1857–1939) who gave us the diagnostic term we still use today. In 1911, Bleuler used *schizophrenia* (from the Greek roots of *sxizo*, pronounced "schizo" and meaning "to split or crack," and *phren*, meaning "mind") because he believed the condition was characterized primarily by disorganization of thought processes, a lack of coherence between thought and emotion, and an inward orientation away (split off) from reality. Although the term is often thought to reflect a "Jekyll and Hyde" split personality, this is a major misconception. The splitting does not refer to multiple personalities (an entirely different form of disorder, now called dissociative identity disorder). Instead, in schizophrenia there is a split within the intellect, between the intellect and emotion, and between the intellect and external reality. Interestingly, the subtitle of Bleuler's monograph (Bleuler, 1911/1950) was "The Group of Schizophrenias," indicating that he believed this disorder was not a single diagnostic entity.

Epidemiology

The risk of developing schizophrenia over the course of one's lifetime is a little under 1 percent—actually around 0.7 percent (Saha et al., 2005). What this means is that approximately 1 out of every 140 people alive today who survive until at least age 55 will develop the disorder. Of course, a statistic like this does not mean that everyone has exactly the same risk. This is an average lifetime risk estimate.

As we shall see later, some people (e.g., those who have a parent with schizophrenia) have a statistically higher risk of developing the disorder than do others (e.g., people who come from families where there has never been a case of schizophrenia).

There are also other groups of people who seem to have an especially high risk of developing schizophrenia. For example, people whose fathers were older (50 years or more) at the time of their birth have an elevated risk of developing schizophrenia when they grow up (Miller et al., 2011). Having a parent who works as a dry cleaner is also a risk factor (Perrin, Opler, et al., 2007). Rates of schizophrenia are also higher than expected in first- and second-generation immigrants, particularly those from black Caribbean and black African countries who live in majority white communities (Bourque et al., 2011; Matheson et al., 2014). Although the reasons for these differences are not well understood, they are of great interest to researchers.

The vast majority of cases of schizophrenia begin in late adolescence and early adulthood, with 18 to 30 years of age being the peak time for the onset of the illness (Tandon et al., 2009). Although schizophrenia is sometimes found in children, such cases are rare (Green et al., 1992; McKenna et al., 1994). Schizophrenia can also have its initial onset in middle age or later, but again, this is not typical.

The characteristic age of onset of schizophrenia differs in men and women. In men, there is a peak in new cases of schizophrenia between ages 20 and 24. The incidence of schizophrenia in women peaks during the same age period, but the peak is less marked than it is for men (see Figure 13.1). After about age 35, the number of men developing schizophrenia falls markedly, whereas the number of women developing schizophrenia does not. Instead,

Figure 13.1 Onset of Schizophrenia

Age distribution of onset of schizophrenia (first sign of mental disorder) for men and women.

(Adapted from Haffner, H., et al. (1998). Causes and consequences of the gender difference in age at onset of schizophrenia. *Schizophrenia Bulletin, 24*(1), 99–114.)

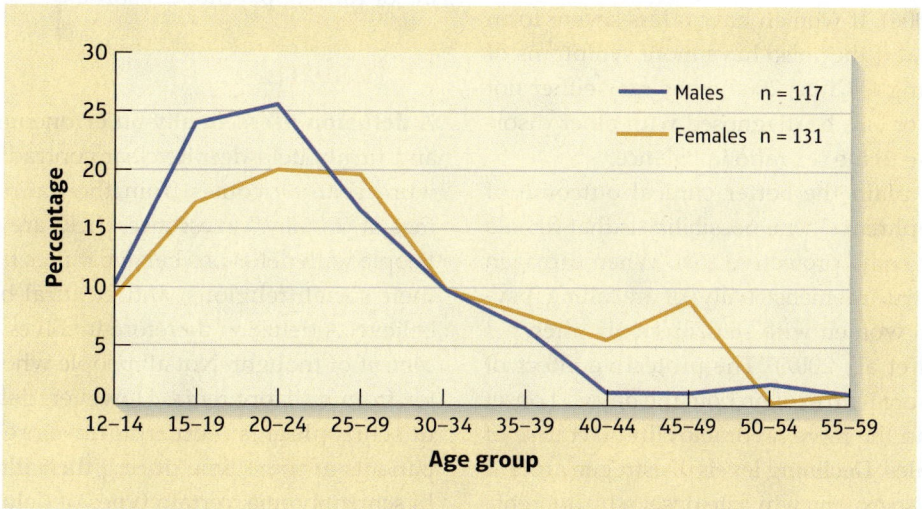

there is a second rise in new cases that begins around age 40, as well as a third spike in onset that occurs when women are in their early sixties (Abel et al., 2010).

Children whose fathers are older at the time of their birth have two to three times the normal risk of developing schizophrenia.

In addition to being more likely to have an early age of onset, males also tend to have a more severe form of schizophrenia (Leung & Chue, 2000). Brain-imaging studies show that schizophrenia-related anomalies of brain structure (discussed later) are more severe in male patients than they are in female patients. Gender-related differences in illness severity may also explain why schizophrenia is more common in males than it is in females. The male-to-female ratio is 1.4:1. So for every three men who develop the disorder, only two women do so (Aleman et al., 2003; Kirkbridge et al., 2006). If women have a less severe form of schizophrenia, and if they also have more symptoms of depression (see Leung & Chue, 2000), they may either not be diagnosed at all or else be diagnosed with other disorders, thus giving rise to the sex ratio imbalance.

What might explain the better clinical outcome of women with schizophrenia? One possibility is that female sex hormones play some protective role. When estrogen levels are low (as is true premenstrually) or are falling, psychotic symptoms in women with schizophrenia often get worse (Bergemann et al., 2007). The protective effect of estrogen may therefore help explain both the delayed onset of schizophrenia and the more favorable clinical course of the disorder in females. Declining levels of estrogen around menopause might also explain why late-onset schizophrenia

is much more likely to strike women than men. There is some evidence that this late-onset pattern in women is associated with a more severe clinical presentation (Haffner et al., 1998).

in review

- What did Kraepelin mean by the term *dementia praecox*? How accurate is this description?
- What was Bleuler's use of the term *schizophrenia* meant to convey?
- Is schizophrenia the same thing as split personality?
- What is the prevalence of schizophrenia? What groups of people show lower or higher rates of schizophrenia than expected?
- How does the age of onset of schizophrenia vary by gender?
- How does gender influence the severity of schizophrenia? Why might this be?

Clinical Picture

13.2 **Identify the symptoms of schizophrenia as described in *DSM-5*.**

As we have mentioned earlier, the *DSM* is a work in progress. Diagnostic criteria are not fixed and immutable but instead change subtly over time as new research findings become available. We show the current *DSM-5* criteria for the diagnosis of schizophrenia in the *DSM-5* box. These are broadly similar to those used in *DSM-IV-TR* and to the diagnostic criteria in the *ICD* (WHO, 2003), which is the diagnostic system used in Europe and other parts of the world. One change that occurred with *DSM-5* was the elimination of the requirement that only one other symptom had to be present if delusions were bizarre or if the auditory hallucinations were of a certain type.

In isolation, however, lists of symptoms convey little about the clinical essence of schizophrenia. In the sections that follow, we elaborate on the hallmark symptoms of this major form of psychotic disorder.

Delusions

A **delusion** is essentially an erroneous belief that is fixed and firmly held despite clear contradictory evidence. The word *delusion* comes from the Latin verb *ludere*, which means "to play." In essence, tricks are played on the mind. People with delusions believe things that others who share their social, religious, and cultural backgrounds do not believe. A delusion therefore involves a disturbance in the *content* of thought. Not all people who have delusions suffer from schizophrenia. However, delusions are common in schizophrenia, occurring in more than 90 percent of patients at some time during their illness (Cutting, 1995). In schizophrenia, certain types of delusions or false beliefs

DSM-5 *Criteria for. . .*

Schizophrenia

A. Two (or more) of the following, each present for a significant portion of time during a 1-month period (or less if successfully treated). At least one of these must be (1), (2), or (3):

  1. Delusions.
  2. Hallucinations.
  3. Disorganized speech (e.g., frequent derailment or incoherence).
  4. Grossly disorganized or catatonic behavior.
  5. Negative symptoms (i.e., diminished emotional expression or avolition).

B. For a significant portion of the time since the onset of the disturbance, level of functioning in one or more major areas, such as work, interpersonal relations, or self-care, is markedly below the level achieved prior to the onset (or when the onset is in childhood or adolescence, there is failure to achieve expected level of interpersonal, academic, or occupational functioning).

C. Continuous signs of the disturbance persist for at least 6 months. This 6-month period must include at least 1 month of symptoms (or less if successfully treated) that meet Criterion A (i.e., active-phase symptoms) and may include periods of prodromal or residual symptoms. During these prodromal or residual periods, the signs of the disturbance may be manifested by only negative symptoms or by two or more symptoms listed in Criterion A present in an attenuated form (e.g., odd beliefs, unusual perceptual experiences).

D. Schizoaffective disorder and depressive or bipolar disorder with psychotic features have been ruled out because either (1) no major depressive or manic episodes have occurred concurrently with the active-phase symptoms, or (2) if mood episodes have occurred during active-phase symptoms, they have been present for a minority of the total duration of the active and residual periods of the illness.

E. The disturbance is not attributable to the physiological effects of a substance (e.g., a drug of abuse, a medication) or another medical condition.

F. If there is a history of autism spectrum disorder or a communication disorder of childhood onset, the additional diagnosis of schizophrenia is made only if prominent delusions or hallucinations, in addition to the other required symptoms of schizophrenia, are also present for at least 1 month (or less if successfully treated).

Source: Reprinted with permission from the *Diagnostic and Statistical Manual of Mental Disorders*, Fifth Edition (Copyright 2013). American Psychiatric Association.

are quite characteristic. Prominent among these are beliefs that one's thoughts, feelings, or actions are being controlled by external agents (made feelings or impulses), that one's private thoughts are being broadcast indiscriminately to others (thought broadcasting), that thoughts are being inserted into one's brain by some external agency (thought insertion), or that some external agency has robbed one of one's thoughts (thought withdrawal). Also common are delusions of reference, where some neutral environmental event (such as a television program or a song on the radio) is believed to have special and personal meaning intended only for the person. Other strange propositions, including delusions of bodily changes (e.g., bowels do not work) or removal of organs, are also not uncommon.

Sometimes delusions are not just isolated beliefs. Instead they become elaborated into a complex delusional system. The next case study provides an example of this. This material was printed on a flier and handed to one of the authors by a man who appeared to be in his 30s. Any errors of grammar are errors in the original flier.

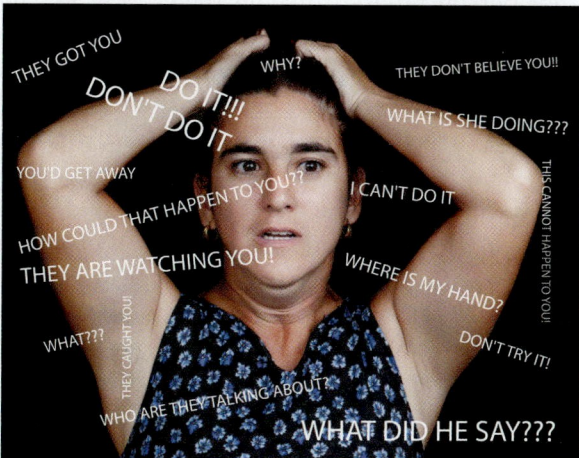

The inner world of people with schizophrenia is often confused, punctuated by alien voices, paranoia, and illogical thoughts.

Are You Being Mind Controlled?

Are you being or were you mind controlled to do something very stupid? Twenty-five percent of our population have what is called electronic hearing. This 25 percent can hear a silent radio and do not hear it. You might be one. In hearing pitch the average person hears from zero to sixteen thousand cycles. Twenty-five percent can hear up to thirty thousand cycles. The silent radio can be heard by these high hearing frequency persons. The silent radio sounds the same as thoughts in their minds.

This silent radio tricks these persons into every crime imaginable. It tricks them into bad decisions, to quit jobs, to divorce, to run away, to be sheriff saled and any stupidity possible. The broadcasters over this silent radio are government, medical, psychiatrists, religious and educational. This is an enormous budget used to destroy the innocent and helpless. The media is scared to cover this up.

This minority, which can be in any ethnic or race, has lost all rights under law because the Russians do it everywhere. It is shocking to discover very large corporations and all colleges have mind control departments. If you and your family constantly make bad decisions and have ruinous problems, you probably are mind controlled. Every year these mind controlled people are going down the economic ladder as they cannot be trusted. No company knows when one will be selected as a guinea pig. Who could risk a sizeable work force of persons with electronic hearing for your competitor could easily wipe you out?

Hallucinations

A **hallucination** is a sensory experience that seems real to the person having it, but occurs in the absence of any external perceptual stimulus. This is quite different from an illusion, which is a misperception of a stimulus that actually exists. The word comes from the Latin verb *hallucinere* or *allucinere*, meaning to "wander in mind" or "idle talk." Hallucinations can occur in any sensory modality (auditory, visual, olfactory, tactile, or gustatory). However, auditory hallucinations (e.g., hearing voices) are by far the most common. In a sample recruited from seven different countries, auditory hallucinations were found in 75 percent of patients with schizophrenia (Bauer et al., 2011). In contrast, visual hallucinations were reported less frequently (39 percent of patients), and olfactory, tactile, and gustatory hallucinations were even more rare (1–7 percent). Even deaf people who are diagnosed with schizophrenia sometimes report auditory hallucinations (Aleman & Larøi, 2008). As the World Around Us box illustrates, hallucinations can even be induced in healthy people if they are under a lot of stress and drink a lot of caffeine.

Hallucinations often have relevance for the patient at some affective, conceptual, or behavioral level. Patients can become emotionally involved in their hallucinations, often incorporating them into their delusions. In some cases, patients may even act on their hallucinations and do what the voices tell them to do. People who consider themselves to be socially inferior tend to perceive the voices they hear as being more powerful than they are and to behave accordingly (Paulik, 2011).

In a highly informative study of the phenomenology of auditory hallucinations, Nayani and David (1996) interviewed 100 hallucinating patients and asked them a series of questions about their hallucinatory voices. The majority of patients (73 percent) reported that their voices usually spoke at a normal conversational volume. Hallucinated voices were often those of people known to the patient in real life, although sometimes unfamiliar voices or the voices of God or the Devil were heard. Most patients reported that they heard more than one voice and that their hallucinations were worse when they were alone. Most commonly, the hallucinated voices uttered rude and vulgar expletives or else were critical ("You are

stupid"), bossy ("Get the milk"), or abusive ("Ugly bitch"), although some voices were pleasant and supportive ("My darling").

Watch Larry: Schizophrenia

Are patients who are hallucinating really hearing voices? Neuroimaging studies that compare hallucinating patients with nonhallucinating patients suggest that patients with speech hallucinations have a reduction in brain (gray matter) volume in the left hemisphere auditory and speech perception areas (Allen et al., 2008). Reduced brain volume in these areas could lead to a failure to correctly identify internally generated speech, erroneously tagging it as coming from an external source. PET and fMRI studies that have looked at activity in the brains of patients when they are actually experiencing auditory hallucinations provide further support for this idea. Rather than showing an increase of activity in areas of the brain involved in speech comprehension (e.g., Wernicke's area in the temporal lobe), neuroimaging studies reveal that hallucinating patients show increased activity in Broca's area—an area of the temporal lobe that is involved in speech production. In some cases, the pattern of brain activation that occurs when patients experience auditory hallucinations is very similar to that seen when healthy volunteers are asked to imagine that there is another person talking to them (Shergill et al., 2000). Indeed, if transcranial magnetic stimulation (in which a magnetic field passing through the skull temporarily disrupts activity in underlying brain areas) is used to reduce activity in speech production areas, hallucinating patients actually show a reduction in their auditory hallucinations (Hoffman et al., 2005). Such an approach could possibly have promise for the future as a novel form of treatment (Slotema et al., 2014). Overall, however, the research findings suggest that auditory hallucinations occur when patients misinterpret their own self-generated and verbally mediated thoughts (inner speech or self-talk) as coming from another source. Modern research approaches are thus supporting a very old idea: Auditory hallucinations are really a form of misperceived subvocal speech (Gould, 1949).

The World Around Us

Stress, Caffeine, and Hallucinations

Do you feel that you are under a lot of stress? Do you drink a lot of caffeinated beverages each day? If so, you may be interested in the findings from a recent study that was conducted using healthy volunteers who had no history of psychiatric disorders (Crowe et al., 2011). Ninety-two participants were recruited into what they believed was a study of auditory perception. As participants entered the testing room to begin the experiment, the song "White Christmas" by Bing Crosby was playing. After the song ended, participants were given headphones and asked to listen to white noise. They were told that the "White Christmas" song they had just heard might be embedded in the white noise at a subthreshold level. Every time they thought they heard a fragment of the song during the 3 minutes of white noise, participants were told to note this using a hand counter.

In reality, no sound fragments of "White Christmas" were embedded in the sound at all. Participants only heard white noise. However, those participants who reported that they had been under a high level of stress in the past year *and* who were high caffeine users (five or more drinks per day) reported hearing significantly more embedded song fragments than participants in the low-stress and low-caffeine group did. Moreover, it was the combination of high stress and high caffeine intake that was important. In participants who reported high stress but low caffeine intake or in participants who reported low stress but high caffeine intake, the number of false alarms or "hallucinations" (hearing a song fragment that was not there) was not elevated. The associations also remained when variables such as age, creativity, social desirability, mental imagery ability, and hallucination-proneness were taken into account.

Overall the results of this study demonstrate that, under certain conditions, the combination of high caffeine consumption

The combination of high stress levels and high caffeine intake is associated with hallucinations in psychiatrically healthy people.

and high stress can render normal people vulnerable to auditory hallucinations. Caffeine is known to increase how much cortisol is produced in response to a stressor. Caffeine consumption has also been found to correlate with hallucination proneness in other studies of healthy people (Jones & Fernyhough, 2009). It is also important to note that patients with schizophrenia typically drink a great deal of coffee. During times of high stress, this might perhaps increase their risk of having an exacerbation in hallucinatory symptoms.

Is it true that hallucinations are only found in people who have schizophrenia? If not, under what circumstances might hallucinations be induced?

Disorganized Speech

Delusions reflect a disorder of thought *content*, or in the ideas being expressed. Disorganized speech, on the other hand, is the external manifestation of a disorder in thought *form*. Basically, an affected person fails to make sense, despite seeming to using language in a conventional way and following the semantic and syntactic rules governing verbal communication. The failure is not attributable to low intelligence, poor education, or cultural deprivation. Years ago, Meehl (1962) aptly referred to the process as one of "cognitive slippage"; others have referred to it as "derailment" or "loosening" of associations or, in its most extreme form, as "incoherence."

In disorganized speech, the words and word combinations sound communicative, but the listener is left with little or no understanding of the point the speaker is trying to make. In some cases, completely new, made-up words known as *neologisms* (literally, "new words") appear in the patient's speech. An example might be the word *detone*,

which looks and sounds like a meaningful word but is a neologism. *Formal thought disorder* (a term clinicians use to refer to problems in the way that disorganized thought is expressed in disorganized speech) is well illustrated in the following example. It is taken from a letter written by a man with schizophrenia and addressed to Queen Beatrix of the Netherlands.

Disorganized Speech: A Letter to Queen Beatrix

I have also "killed" my ex-wife, [name], in a 2.5 to 3.0 hours sex bout in Devon Pennsylvania in 1976, while two Pitcairns were residing in my next room closet, hearing the event. Enclosed, please find my urology report, indicating that my male genitals, specifically my penis, are within normal size and that I'm capable of normal intercourse with any woman, signed by Dr. [name], a urologist and surgeon who performed a circumcision on me in 1982. Conclusion: I cannot be a nincompoop in a physical sense (unless Society would feed me chemicals for my picture in the nincompoop book).

Disorganized Behavior

Disorganized behavior can show itself in a variety of ways. Goal-directed activity is almost universally disrupted in schizophrenia. The impairment occurs in areas of routine daily functioning, such as work, social relations, and self-care, to the extent that observers note that the person is not himself or herself anymore. For example, the person may no longer maintain minimal standards of personal hygiene or may exhibit a profound disregard of personal safety and health. In other cases, grossly disorganized behavior appears as silliness or unusual dress (e.g., wearing an overcoat, scarf, and gloves on a hot summer day). Many researchers attribute these disruptions of "executive" behavior to impairment in the functioning of the prefrontal region of the cerebral cortex.

Catatonia is an even more striking behavioral disturbance. The patient with catatonia may show a virtual absence of all movement and speech and be in what is called a *catatonic stupor*. At other times, the patient may hold an unusual posture for an extended period of time without any seeming discomfort.

A person with catatonia may maintain an odd position for minutes or even hours.

Negative Symptoms

Since the days of Bleuler, two general symptom patterns, or syndromes, of schizophrenia have been differentiated. These are referred to as positive- and negative-syndrome schizophrenia. Researchers began to highlight the difference between positive and negative symptoms in the 1980s (Andreasen, 1985) and this distinction is still relevant today.

Positive symptoms are those that reflect an excess or distortion in a normal repertoire of behavior and experience, such as delusions and hallucinations. Disorganized thinking (as revealed by disorganized speech) is also thought of in this way. **Negative symptoms**, by contrast, reflect an absence or deficit of behaviors that are normally present.

Current thinking is that negative symptoms fall into two broad domains (Barch, 2013; Kring et al., 2013). One domain involves reduced expressive behavior—either in voice, facial expression, gestures or speech. This may show itself in the form of **blunted affect** or **flat affect** or in **alogia**, which means very little speech. The other domain concerns reductions in motivation or in the experience of pleasure. The inability to initiate or persist in goal-directed activity is called **avolition**. For example, the patient may sit for long periods of time staring into space or watching TV with little interest in any outside work or social activities. Diminished ability to experience pleasure is called *anhedonia*.

Positive, negative, and disorganized symptoms can co-occur in the same patient. This woman appears to exhibit marked social withdrawal (a negative symptom) in addition to showing bizarre behavior (a disorganized symptom).

Although most patients exhibit both positive and negative symptoms during the course of their disorders, the presence of negative symptoms in the clinical picture is not a good sign for the patient's future outcome (e.g., Malla & Payne, 2005; Milev et al., 2005).

Even though patients with negative symptoms may seem emotionally unexpressive, how they appear and how they are feeling are two different things. In an important early study, Kring and Neale (1996) studied unmedicated male patients with schizophrenia while they were watching film clips. Three different types of film clips were used, the scenes in them being very positive, very negative, or neutral in terms of the emotions they were designed to elicit in the viewers. Videotapes of how the patients looked while they were watching the films were then coded by trained raters. As might be expected, the patients with schizophrenia showed less facial expressiveness than a group of healthy controls.

What *was* surprising was that when the patients were asked about their emotional experiences during the films, they reported as many emotional feelings as the controls—and sometimes slightly more. Measures of autonomic arousal also showed that when they were watching the films, the patients exhibited more physiological reactivity than the controls did. Although the original research used only male patients, a recent study that includes women with schizophrenia has replicated the results about diminished emotional expression (Mote et al., 2014). What the findings suggest, therefore, is that even though patients with schizophrenia may sometimes appear emotionally unexpressive, they are nonetheless experiencing plenty of emotion.

Subtypes of Schizophrenia

There is a great deal of heterogeneity in the presentation of schizophrenia, and patients with this disorder often look quite different clinically. In consideration of this, the *DSM-IV-TR* recognized several subtypes of schizophrenia. The most clinically meaningful of these were **paranoid schizophrenia** (where the clinical picture is dominated by absurd and illogical beliefs that are often highly elaborated and organized into a coherent, though delusional, framework), **disorganized schizophrenia** (characterized by disorganized speech, disorganized behavior, and flat or inappropriate affect), and **catatonic schizophrenia** (which involves pronounced motor signs that reflect great excitement or stupor). Unfortunately, research using the subtyping approach did not yield major insights into the etiology or treatment of the disorder. Reflecting this, subtypes of schizophrenia are no longer included in *DSM-5*.

in review

- What are the major symptoms of schizophrenia?
- How is a hallucination different from a delusion?
- Explain the differences among positive, negative, and disorganized symptoms.
- Why were the subtypes of schizophrenia not included in *DSM-5*?

Other Psychotic Disorders

13.3 List four different types of psychotic disorders and state one way in which each is different from schizophrenia.

Schizophrenia is a form of psychotic disorder, but it is not the only one. There are a number of other types of psychotic disorders, such as schizoaffective disorder, schizophreniform disorder, delusional disorder, and brief psychotic disorder.

Schizoaffective Disorder

The *DSM-5* recognizes a diagnostic category called **schizoaffective disorder** (see the *DSM-5* box for diagnostic criteria). This diagnosis is conceptually something of a hybrid, in that it is used to describe people who have features

of schizophrenia and severe mood disorder. In other words, the person not only has psychotic symptoms that meet criteria for schizophrenia but also has marked changes in mood for a substantial amount of time. Because mood disorders can be unipolar or bipolar in type, these are recognized as subtypes of schizoaffective disorder.

The reliability of schizoaffective disorder has tended to be quite poor, and clinicians often do not agree about who meets the criteria for the diagnosis (Maj et al., 2000; Vollmer-Larsen et al., 2006). In an effort to improve this, *DSM-5* specifies that mood symptoms have to meet criteria for a full major mood episode and also have to be present for more than 50 percent of the total duration of the illness. This clarification should help improve the reliability of this diagnosis and possibly also decrease the number of people who receive it.

DSM-5 *Criteria for. . .*

Schizoaffective Disorder

A. An uninterrupted period of illness during which there is a major mood episode (major depressive or manic) concurrent with Criterion A of schizophrenia.
   Note: The major depressive episode must include Criterion A1: Depressed mood.

B. Delusions or hallucinations for 2 or more weeks in the absence of a major mood episode (depressive or manic) during the lifetime duration of the illness.

C. Symptoms that meet criteria for a major mood episode are present for the majority of the total duration of the active and residual portions of the illness.

D. The disturbance is not attributable to the effects of a substance (e.g., a drug of abuse, a medication) or another medical condition.

Source: Reprinted with permission from the *Diagnostic and Statistical Manual of Mental Disorders*, Fifth Edition (Copyright 2013). American Psychiatric Association.

In general, the prognosis for patients diagnosed with schizoaffective disorder is somewhere between that of patients with schizophrenia and that of patients with mood disorders (Walker et al., 2004). Research suggests that the long-term (10-year) outcome is much better for patients with schizoaffective disorder than it is for patients with schizophrenia (Harrow et al., 2000).

Schizophreniform Disorder

Schizophreniform disorder is a category reserved for schizophrenia-like psychoses that last at least a month but do not last for 6 months and so do not warrant a diagnosis of schizophrenia (see the *DSM-5* box for diagnostic criteria). It may include any of the symptoms described in the

---

DSM-5 *Criteria for. . .*

Schizophreniform Disorder

A. Two (or more) of the following, each present for a significant portion of time during a 1-month period (or less if successfully treated). At least one of these must be (1), (2), or (3):

    1. Delusions.
    2. Hallucinations.
    3. Disorganized speech (e.g., frequent derailment or incoherence).
    4. Grossly disorganized or catatonic behavior.
    5. Negative symptoms (i.e., diminished emotional expression or avolition).

B. An episode of the disorder lasts at least 1 month but less than 6 months. When the diagnosis must be made without waiting for recovery, it should be qualified as "provisional."

C. Schizoaffective disorder and depressive or bipolar disorder with psychotic features have been ruled out because either (1) no major depressive or manic episodes have occurred concurrently with the active-phase symptoms, or (2) if mood episodes have occurred during active-phase symptoms, they have been present for a minority of the total duration of the active and residual periods of the illness.

D. The disturbance is not attributable to the physiological effects of a substance (e.g., a drug of abuse, a medication) or another medical condition.

Source: Reprinted with permission from the *Diagnostic and Statistical Manual of Mental Disorders*, Fifth Edition (Copyright 2013). American Psychiatric Association.

---

preceding sections. Because of the possibility of an early and lasting remission after a first psychotic breakdown, the prognosis for schizophreniform disorder is better than that for established forms of schizophrenia.

Delusional Disorder

Patients with **delusional disorder**, like many people with schizophrenia, hold beliefs that are considered false and absurd by those around them. Unlike individuals with schizophrenia, however, people given the diagnosis of delusional disorder may otherwise behave quite normally. Their behavior does not show the gross disorganization and performance deficiencies characteristic of schizophrenia, and general behavioral deterioration is rarely observed in this disorder, even when it proves chronic (see the *DSM-5* box for criteria for delusional disorder). One interesting subtype of delusional disorder is *erotomania*. Here, the theme of the delusion involves great love for a person, usually of higher

status. Some evidence suggests that a significant proportion of female stalkers are diagnosed with erotomania (Purcell et al., 2001; West & Friedman, 2008).

Brief Psychotic Disorder

Brief psychotic disorder is exactly what its name suggests. It involves the sudden onset of psychotic symptoms or disorganized speech or catatonic behavior. Even though there is often great emotional turmoil, the episode usually lasts only a matter of days (too short to warrant a diagnosis of schizophreniform disorder). After this, the person returns to his or her former level of functioning and may never have another episode again (see the *DSM-5* box for criteria for brief psychotic disorder). Cases of brief psychotic disorder are infrequently seen in clinical settings, perhaps because they remit so quickly. Brief psychotic disorder is often triggered by stress, as illustrated in the following case.

DSM-5 *Criteria for. . .*

Delusional Disorder

A. The presence of one (or more) delusions with a duration of 1 month or longer.

B. Criterion A for schizophrenia has never been met.
    Note: Hallucinations, if present, are not prominent and are related to the delusional theme (e.g., the sensation of being infested with insects associated with delusions of infestation).

C. Apart from the impact of the delusion(s) or its ramifications, functioning is not markedly impaired, and behavior is not obviously bizarre or odd.

D. If manic or major depressive episodes have occurred, these have been brief relative to the duration of the delusional periods.

E. The disturbance is not attributable to the physiological effects of a substance or another medical condition and is not better explained by another mental disorder, such as body dysmorphic disorder or obsessive-compulsive disorder.

Source: Reprinted with permission from the *Diagnostic and Statistical Manual of Mental Disorders*, Fifth Edition (Copyright 2013). American Psychiatric Association.

DSM-5 *Criteria for. . .*

Brief Psychotic Disorder

A. Presence of one (or more) of the following symptoms. At least one of these must be (1), (2), or (3):

1. Delusions.
2. Hallucinations.
3. Disorganized speech (e.g., frequent derailment or incoherence).
4. Grossly disorganized or catatonic behavior.

Note: Do not include a symptom if it is a culturally sanctioned response.

B. Duration of an episode of the disturbance is at least 1 day but less than 1 month, with eventual full return to premorbid level of functioning.

C. The disturbance is not better explained by major depressive or bipolar disorder with psychotic features or another psychotic disorder such as schizophrenia or catatonia, and is not attributable to the physiological effects of a substance (e.g., a drug of abuse, a medication) or another medical condition.

Source: Reprinted with permission from the *Diagnostic and Statistical Manual of Mental Disorders*, Fifth Edition (Copyright 2013). American Psychiatric Association.

Four Days of Symptoms and Rapid Recovery

Ronald was 32 years old and had worked successfully as a lawyer for 6 years. He was married with two young children and he had many close friends. One day he returned home early from work and was shocked to find his wife in bed with his best friend. His initial reaction was anger, followed by depression. However, within 2 days he began to hear voices that called his name and that said, "Love, love, love." Ronald began to express odd ideas, speaking of fusing with God and dispensing peace on Earth. He also talked about needing to fight what he called the "giant conspiracy." During this time his affect was flat and he spoke in a slow and distinct manner. Ronald was admitted to hospital and was given medication. He and his wife also began marital therapy. Ronald showed rapid improvement of his symptoms and within 5 days of the onset of his initial symptoms he was back at work again. (Based on Janowsky et al., 1987.)

in review

- In what ways are schizophrenia and schizoaffective disorder different?
- How will the change to the criteria for schizoaffective disorder in *DSM-5* improve the reliability of this diagnosis?
- What are the major differences between schizophreniform disorder and brief psychotic disorder?

Genetic and Biological Factors

13.4 **Explain the genetic and biological risk and causal factors associated with schizophrenia.**

What causes schizophrenia? Despite enormous efforts by researchers, this question still defies a simple answer. In the sections that follow, we discuss what is currently known about the etiology of schizophrenia. What is clear is that no one factor can fully explain why schizophrenia develops. The old dichotomy of nature versus nurture is as misleading as it is simplistic. Psychiatric disorders are not the result of a single genetic switch being flipped. Rather, a complex interplay between genetic and environmental factors is responsible.

Genetic Factors

It has long been known that disorders of the schizophrenia type are "familial" and tend to "run in families." There is overwhelming evidence for higher-than-expected rates of schizophrenia among biological relatives of *index* cases; that is, the diagnosed group of people who provide the starting point for inquiry (also called *probands*). Figure 13.2 shows the percentage risk of developing schizophrenia given a specific genetic relationship with someone who has the disorder. As you can see, there is a strong association between the closeness of the blood relationship (i.e., level of gene sharing or consanguinity) and the risk for developing the disorder. For example, the prevalence of schizophrenia in the first-degree relatives (parents, siblings, and offspring) of a proband with schizophrenia is about 10 percent. For second-degree relatives who share only 25 percent of their genes with the proband (e.g., half-siblings, aunts, uncles, nieces, nephews, and grandchildren), the lifetime prevalence of schizophrenia is closer to 3 percent.

Of course, just because something runs in families does not automatically implicate genetic factors. The terms *familial* and *genetic* are not synonymous, and a disorder can run in a family for nongenetic reasons (if I am obese and my dog is also obese, the reasons for this are clearly not genetic!). As we have repeatedly emphasized, the interpretation of familial concordance patterns is never completely straightforward, in part because of the strong relationship between the sharing of genes and the sharing of the environments in which those genes express themselves. Although they are indispensable in providing a starting point for researchers, family studies cannot, by themselves, tell us why a disorder runs in families. To disentangle the contributions of genes and environment, we need twin and adoption studies.

Figure 13.2 Risk of Developing Schizophrenia by Genetic Relationship

Lifetime age-adjusted, averaged risks for the development of schizophrenia-related psychoses in classes of relatives differing in their degree of genetic relatedness.

(Compiled from family and twin studies in European populations between 1920 and 1987. From Gottesman, I. I. (1991). *Schizophrenia Genesis: The Origins of Madness* (p. 96). Copyright © 1991 by Irving I. Gottesman. Used with permission of W. H. Freeman and Company/Worth Publishers.)

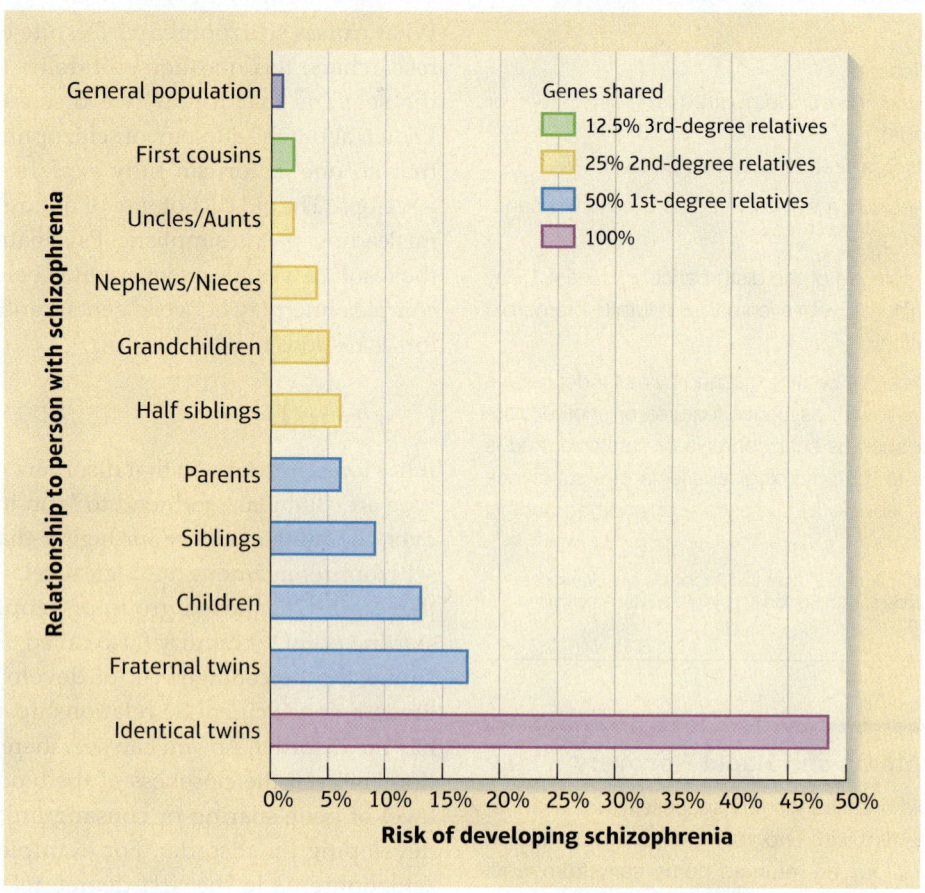

TWIN STUDIES We discussed twin studies in general in Chapter 3 and again more specifically in relation to anxiety and mood disorders. As with the mood disorders, schizophrenia concordance rates for identical twins are routinely and consistently found to be significantly higher than those for fraternal twins or ordinary siblings. The most famous case of concordance for schizophrenia involves the Genain quadruplets. Their story is summarized in the World Around Us box.

Although being a twin does not increase one's risk for developing schizophrenia (the incidence of schizophrenia among twins is no greater than it is for the general population), study after study has shown a higher concordance for schizophrenia among identical, or monozygotic (MZ), twins than among people related in any other way, including fraternal, or dizygotic (DZ), twins.

E. Fuller Torrey is a noted schizophrenia researcher who has a sister with the disorder. He and his colleagues (1994) published a review of the major literature worldwide on twin studies of schizophrenia. The overall pairwise concordance rate is 28 percent in MZ twins and 6 percent in DZ twins. This suggests that a reduction in shared genes from 100 percent to 50 percent reduces the risk of schizophrenia by nearly 80 percent. Also note that sharing 50 percent of one's genes with a co-twin with schizophrenia is associated with a lifetime risk for schizophrenia of 6 percent. Although this is low in absolute terms, it is markedly higher than the baseline risk of less than 1 percent found in the general population.

If schizophrenia were exclusively a genetic disorder, the concordance rate for identical twins would, of course, be 100 percent. Although MZ concordance rates vary from one twin study to another, and although some researchers report higher rates than the 28 percent reported by Torrey and colleagues (1994), they are never even close to 100 percent. Two conclusions can therefore be drawn: First, genes undoubtedly play a role in causing schizophrenia. Second, genes themselves are not the whole story. Twin studies provide some of the most solid evidence that the environment plays an important role in the development of schizophrenia. But why one MZ twin should develop schizophrenia when his or her co-twin does not is a fascinating question.

The World Around Us

The Genain Quadruplets

The Genain quadruplets, born sometime in the early 1930s, were rare MZ quadruplets who each developed schizophrenia, an outcome that would be expected to occur by chance only once in approximately 1.5 billion births. The genetically identical girls, given the pseudonym *Genain* (from the Greek for "dreadful gene"), were hospitalized at the National Institute of Mental Health in the mid-1950s and studied intensively by lead researcher David Rosenthal (see Rosenthal, 1963; see also Mirsky & Quinn, 1988). Rosenthal also selected first names for the girls using the initials of the institution, NIMH. Accordingly, the women are known to us as Nora (the firstborn), Iris, Myra, and Hester. They are all concordant for schizophrenia. However, they are discordant with regard to the severity of their illnesses.

Hester has been the most severely ill Genain. She was born last and had the lowest birth weight. Hester was always the slowest to develop, and was removed from school after 11th grade. She has experienced chronic and unremitting severe symptoms from the age of 18 and has never held a job outside the home. Testing at NIMH revealed that, like Nora, Hester showed a great deal of neurocognitive impairment.

Nora was always considered by the family to be the best of the four girls. She had the highest IQ and was the first to get a job. Nonetheless, after she was hospitalized at the age of 22 with hallucinations, delusions, and withdrawal, she had a long history of hospitalizations and has never been able to live independently or hold a job for an extended period of time.

In contrast, third-born Myra, despite having some problems in her 20s (when she was questionably diagnosed as having schizophrenia), does not appear to have experienced delusions and paranoia until her mid-40s. Myra was the only one of the Genains to marry and have children and her clinical picture is more suggestive of schizoaffective disorder (a blend of psychotic symptoms and mood symptoms). Although she was never psychiatrically well by any definition, Myra was able to go off medications and eventually went into remission.

Finally, there is Iris. Like Nora, Iris had her first psychiatric hospitalization at age 22. She spent 12 years in a state hospital and suffered from hallucinations, delusions, and motor abnormalities. Although neurocognitive testing did not reveal any obvious brain disturbance, she clearly has a severe form of schizophrenia.

Why do these identical quadruplets not have identical illnesses? We do not know. Did Nora and Hester, being born first and last, experience more traumatic birth complications? Did Iris do less well than might have been expected from her neurocognitive test results because her parents insisted on treating the quads as though they were two sets of twins—a superior and talented set consisting of Nora and Myra, and an inferior, problematic set consisting of Iris and Hester? Did being paired with Hester somehow compromise Iris's development? Did Myra do so well (relatively) because she was the most favored and because she did not sustain any brain damage?

And why did the quadruplets develop schizophrenia at all? It is very likely that there was a family history of the disorder. Mr. Genain's mother (the girls' grandmother) had a nervous breakdown in her teens and appears to have had some symptoms of paranoid schizophrenia. The family environment was also far from healthy and may have provided the stress that acted on the quadruplets' genetic predispositions to induce full-blown illness. Mr. Genain was a very disturbed man who spent most of his time drinking and expressing his various fears and obsessions to his family. He imposed extreme restrictions and surveillance on the girls until the time of their breakdowns. He was sexually promiscuous and was reported to have sexually molested at least two of his daughters. Mrs. Genain seems to have ignored the sexual exploitation occurring in the home. In short, nothing about the family environment can be considered to have been normal.

What insights about schizophrenia do we get from the fact that the Genain quadruplets (who were all identical genetically) did not have identical forms of the illness?

A great deal of research attention is now being directed at studying people with a known genetic liability for schizophrenia. Historically, the most important subjects to study in this regard have been MZ twins who are discordant for schizophrenia. This investigative strategy was pioneered many years ago by Fischer (1971, 1973) in an ingenious study. Fischer reasoned that genetic influences, if present, would be just as likely to show up in the offspring of the twins without schizophrenia in discordant pairs (see Figure 13.3) as they would be to show up in the offspring of the twins with schizophrenia (because they share all their genes in common). And, in a search of official records in Denmark, Fischer found exactly that. Subsequent to this, in a follow-up of Fischer's subjects, Gottesman and Bertelson (1989) reported an

age-corrected incidence rate for schizophrenia of 17.4 percent for the offspring of the MZ twins without schizophrenia (i.e., the well MZ twins). This rate, which far exceeds normal expectancy, was not significantly different from that for offspring of the twins with schizophrenia in discordant pairs or from that for offspring of DZ twins with schizophrenia. Assuming that exposure to an aunt or uncle with schizophrenia would play a limited role in the development of the same illness in their nieces or nephews, these results lend impressive support to the genetic hypothesis. They also, as the authors note, indicate that a predisposition to schizophrenia may remain "unexpressed" (as in the twins without schizophrenia in discordant pairs) unless "released" by unknown environmental factors.

Figure 13.3 Fischer's Study

Because MZ twins have identical genes, the children of the well twin will have an elevated risk of schizophrenia even if their parent did not suffer from the disorder.

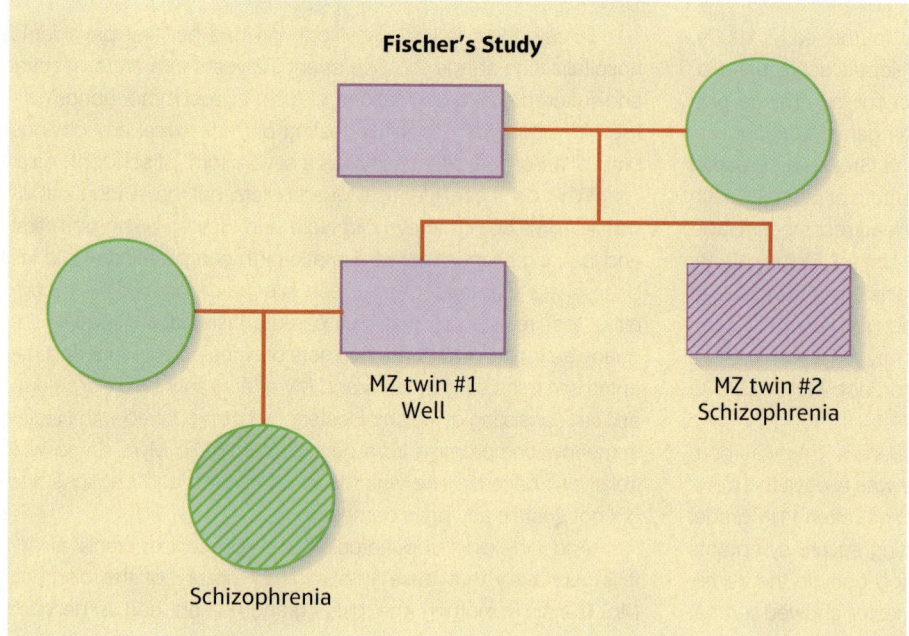

Fischer's Study

MZ twin #1
Well

MZ twin #2
Schizophrenia

Schizophrenia

Research Close-Up

Age-Corrected Incidence Rate

Incidence is the number of new cases that develop. An age-corrected incidence rate takes into account predicted breakdowns for subjects who are not yet beyond the age of risk for developing the disorder.

ADOPTION STUDIES One major assumption that twin studies make is that any differences found between MZ and DZ twins are attributable to genes. At the heart of this assumption is the idea that the environments of MZ twins are no more similar than the environments of DZ twins. But it is very reasonable to expect that, because MZ twins are identical (and always of the same gender), their environments will actually be more similar than the environments of DZ twins. To the extent that this is true, twin studies will overestimate the importance of genetic factors (because some similarities between MZ twins that actually occur for nongenetic reasons will be attributed to genetic factors). In some cases, of course, MZ twins go to a great deal of effort to try to be different from one another. The bottom line, however, is that the assumption that MZ and DZ twins have equally similar environments can create some problems when we try to interpret the findings of twin studies.

Several studies have attempted to overcome the shortcomings of the twin method in achieving a true separation of hereditary from environmental influences by using what

is called the adoption strategy. Here, concordance rates for schizophrenia are compared for the biological and the adoptive relatives of people who have been adopted out of their biological families at an early age (preferably at birth) and have subsequently developed schizophrenia. If concordance is greater among the patients' biological rather than adoptive relatives, a hereditary influence is strongly suggested; the reverse pattern would argue for environmental causation.

The first study of this kind was conducted many years ago by Heston in 1966. Heston followed up 47 children who had been born to mothers who were in a state mental hospital suffering from schizophrenia. The children had been placed with relatives or into foster homes within 72 hours of their birth. In his follow-up study, Heston found that 16.6 percent of these children were later diagnosed with schizophrenia. In contrast, none of the 50 control children (selected from among residents of the same foster homes whose biological mothers did not have schizophrenia) developed schizophrenia. In addition to the greater probability of being diagnosed with schizophrenia, the offspring whose mothers had schizophrenia were also more likely to be diagnosed as mentally retarded, neurotic, or psychopathic (i.e., antisocial). They also had been involved more frequently in criminal activities and had spent more time in penal institutions. These findings are often taken to suggest that any genetic liability conveyed by the mothers is not specific to schizophrenia but also includes a liability for other forms of psychopathology. But we must be careful about drawing such a conclusion. Heston's study provided no information about psychopathology in the fathers of the children. We therefore cannot know to what extent some of the problems the children had were due to genetic liability conveyed by their fathers.

Heston's study began by identifying mothers with schizophrenia and then traced what had happened to their adopted-away offspring. An alternative approach involves locating adult patients with schizophrenia who were adopted early in life and then looking at rates of schizophrenia in their biological and adoptive relatives. A large-scale and multi-faceted adoption study of this type was undertaken in Denmark, with Danish and American investigators working in collaboration (Kendler & Gruenberg, 1984; Kendler et al., 1994; Kety et al., 1978, 1994). As would be expected on the basis of a genetic model, the data showed a preponderance of schizophrenia and "schizophrenia-spectrum" problems (e.g., schizotypal and paranoid personality disorder) in the biological relatives of adoptees with schizophrenia. More specifically, 13.3 percent of the 105 biological relatives had schizophrenia or schizophrenia-spectrum disorders themselves. In contrast, only 1.3 percent of the 224 adoptive parents showed such problems.

THE QUALITY OF THE ADOPTIVE FAMILY The Danish adoption studies did not include independent assessments of the child-rearing adequacy of the adoptive families into which the index children (those who developed schizophrenia) and the control children (those who did not) had been placed. It remained for Tienari and colleagues (1987, 2000, 2004) to add this feature to their research design. The Finnish Adoptive Family Study of Schizophrenia, as it is known, followed up the adopted-away children of all women in Finland who were hospitalized for schizophrenia between 1960 and 1979. As they grew to adulthood, the functioning of these index children was compared with the functioning of a control sample of adoptees whose biological mothers were psychiatrically healthy. Over the course of a 21-year follow-up, the index adoptees developed more schizophrenia and schizophrenia-related disorders than did the controls (Tienari et al., 2000, 2003). What sets this study apart, however, is what it tells us about the interaction between genes and environment.

One measure of the family environment that the researchers looked at was communication deviance (Wahlberg et al., 1997). Communication deviance is a measure of how understandable and "easy to follow" the speech of a family member is. Vague, confusing, and unclear communication reflects high communication deviance. What Wahlberg and colleagues found was that it was the combination of genetic risk and high communication deviance in the adopted families that was problematic. Children who were at genetic risk and who lived in families where there was high communication deviance showed high levels of thought disorder at the time of the follow-up. In contrast,

the control adoptees who had no genetic risk for schizophrenia showed no thought disorder, regardless of whether they were raised in a high- or a low-communication-deviance family. Perhaps what was most remarkable, though, was the outcome for the high-risk children who were raised by adopted families low in communication deviance. These children were healthier at follow-up than any of the other three groups! In other words, if they are raised in a benign environment, even children who are at genetic risk for schizophrenia appear to do very well.

Tienari and colleagues (2004) have provided further evidence of a genotype–environment interaction in schizophrenia. (If you are unsure what these terms mean, check back to Chapter 3.) Using interviews, the researchers first looked at the quality of the family environment in which the adopted children were raised. They then looked at what happened to the children who were raised in healthy versus dysfunctional families. The degree of adversity in the family environment predicted later problems in the adopted children. However, only those children who were raised in dysfunctional families *and* had high genetic risk for schizophrenia went on to develop schizophrenia-related disorders themselves. Children at high genetic risk who were raised in healthy family environments did not develop problems any more frequently than did children at low genetic risk.

These findings are important because they suggest that our genetic makeup may control how sensitive we are to certain aspects of our environments. If we have no genetic risk, certain kinds of environmental influences may not affect us very much. But if we have high genetic risk, we may be much more vulnerable to certain types of environmental risks such as high communication deviance or adverse family environments. Findings such as these also raise the exciting possibility that certain kinds of environments may protect people with a genetic susceptibility to schizophrenia from ever developing the illness.

In summary, these findings indicate a strong interaction between genetic vulnerability and an unfavorable family environment in the causal pathway leading to schizophrenia. Of course, it could be argued that the children who went on to develop problems caused the disorganization of their adoptive families. However, there is little support for this alternative interpretation (see Tienari et al., 2004; Wahlberg et al., 1997). Some independent work reported by Kinney and colleagues (1997) also fails to show diminished mental health in adoptive parents raising children who later developed schizophrenia. Everything considered, the Finnish Adoptive Family Study has provided strong confirmation of the diathesis–stress model as it applies to the origins of schizophrenia.

MOLECULAR GENETICS Family studies tell us that schizophrenia runs in families, and twin and adoption studies help us explore the relative contributions of genes

Even if children are at genetic high risk for schizophrenia they are less likely to develop the disorder if they are raised in a healthy family environment.

and environment. These approaches also inform us about the genetic heterogeneity of schizophrenia. For example, in addition to higher rates of schizophrenia, higher rates of schizotypal personality disorder are also found in the relatives of patients with schizophrenia. This supports the idea of the schizophrenia spectrum and suggests that a genetic liability to schizophrenia sometimes manifests itself in a form of pathology that is "schizophrenia-like" but not exactly schizophrenia itself (see Lenzenweger, 2010).

The question now is not whether genes contribute to schizophrenia but which ones are involved. Researchers no longer believe that schizophrenia will, like Huntington's disease (see Chapter 14), be explained by one mutated gene on one specific chromosome. Current thinking is that, in most cases, schizophrenia probably involves many genes (many hundreds or more) working together to confer susceptibility to the illness. The individual's "dose" of schizophrenia genes may explain why one person develops schizophrenia and another develops a milder variant within the schizophrenia spectrum, such as schizotypal personality disorder.

Candidate genes are genes that are involved in processes that are believed to be aberrant in schizophrenia. An example is the *COMT* (catechol-O-methyltransferase) gene. This gene is located on chromosome 22 and is involved in dopamine metabolism. As you will soon learn, dopamine is a neurotransmitter that has long been implicated in psychosis (impaired reality testing). Interestingly, children who have a genetic syndrome (called *velocardiofacial syndrome*) that involves a deletion of genetic material on chromosome 22 are at high risk for developing schizophrenia as they move through adolescence (Gothelf et al., 2007). Prior to the onset of any disorder, they often report transient psychotic symptoms (such as auditory hallucinations) and have poor social functioning and reduced IQ (Debbané et al., 2006). Furthermore, as we shall see later, people with a particular variant of the *COMT* gene are much more likely to become psychotic as adults if they use cannabis during adolescence. For obvious reasons, schizophrenia researchers have been very interested in chromosome 22 and in the *COMT* gene in their search to understand the origins of the disorder. Other genes that have been implicated in schizophrenia are the *neuregulin 1* gene (located on chromosome 8), the *dysbindin* gene (on chromosome 6), the *DISC1* (which stands for "disrupted in schizophrenia") gene on chromosome 1, as well as several dopamine receptor genes (Gejman et al., 2011; Pogue-Geile & Yokley, 2010). Again, these candidate genes are involved in various neurobiological processes that are thought to have gone awry in schizophrenia.

One problem with candidate gene studies is that the findings from one study often fail to replicate in another study. But the field of molecular genetics is developing rapidly. One of the most important new tools for understanding the genetics of schizophrenia and other disorders involves the **genome-wide association study (GWAS)**.

Unlike other genetic approaches where only a few genetic regions are tested, in a GWAS the entire genome is investigated. Typically two groups of participants are tested: one group that has the disease or disorder of interest (for example, schizophrenia) and another group that does not (the control or comparison group). Study participants provide a sample of DNA and then millions of genetic variants are explored and compared across the two groups. By using such an approach, researchers can identify single nucleotide polymorphisms (SNPs—pronounced "snips"), which are sequences of DNA, or other types of genetic variants, that are more frequently found in people with the disorder than without it. Of course, there is a difference between finding a genetic locus and finding the gene itself. But a good rule of thumb is that the relevant gene maybe the one closest to the locus that has been identified. One advantage of the GWAS method, therefore, is that this approach may help us detect genes that have very small effects but that might contribute to susceptibility for schizophrenia.

Watch   Genetic Approaches to Understanding Disorders

So what are the most recent findings? A groundbreaking new study has recently been published (Schizophrenia Working Group of the Psychiatric Genomics Consortium, 2014). This combines all GWAS data from all available schizophrenia samples into one single analysis of more than 150,000 people. The study has identified 108 loci that are associated with the presence of schizophrenia, 83 of which are newly discovered genetic regions. No one believes that this number of genetic loci will be sufficient to fully explain the genetics of schizophrenia (Flint & Munafò, 2014). Nonetheless, the findings have several important implications. First, they provide further evidence that a large number of alleles (an allele is an alternative form of a gene) are involved in creating genetic susceptibility for schizophrenia. Second, many of the genes that are implicated are involved in processes that have long been thought to be important for understanding schizophrenia. For example, some dopamine-related genes (such as *DRD2*) discriminated between people who had schizophrenia and people who did not. Other genetic regions that were identified in the analysis involved glutamate, another neurotransmitter that, as we shall see soon, has been implicated in schizophrenia. Perhaps the biggest surprise, however, was that the strongest finding to emerge concerned a region on chromosome 6 that contains genes involved in immune functioning. The idea that schizophrenia could have something to do with immune function is a major new development. It is also, as you will soon learn, not as far fetched as it might appear at first glance.

Looking beyond schizophrenia itself, GWAS approaches are also telling us that some of the risk alleles that are being implicated in schizophrenia are implicated in bipolar disorder (Smoller, 2013). What this means is that, far from being distinct disorders (which is the impression one gets from reading the *DSM*), schizophrenia and bipolar disorder (at least at the genetic level) have a lot of overlap. Third, even though lots of common alleles likely work in combination to increase a person's risk for schizophrenia, rare alleles also probably play an important role (see Figure 13.4). Moreover, unlike the common alleles, these rare alleles are likely to be more specific to schizophrenia and not associated with increased risk for bipolar disorder. These rare alleles may result from mutations that compromise brain functioning in a negative way. Recent research has shown links between deletions and duplications of DNA (these are called *copy number variations* or CNVs) and schizophrenia. CNVs have also been implicated in autism, attention-deficit/hyperactivity disorder (ADHD), and intellectual disability (see Doherty et al., 2012). All of these conditions are characterized by mental challenges in various ways. Viewed in this way, schizophrenia may be one form of neurodevelopmental disorder with genetic links to autism, ADHD, and intellectual disability. Although much more remains to be learned, it is fast becoming clear that we can no longer consider schizophrenia to be a discrete disorder that (at least from a genetic perspective) is in a category of its own.

ENDOPHENOTYPES We are certain that schizophrenia has a genetic basis. But progress has been frustratingly slow because schizophrenia appears to be very complex genetically. Another impediment is that researchers are still not sure exactly what phenotype (i.e., measurable characteristic of interest) they should be looking for (remember Bleuler's idea of "the schizophrenias"?). Because genetic analysis requires that we know who is "affected" and who is not, this is a big problem.

One solution is to focus on less complex and more homogenous phenotypes (such as specific symptom clusters) that may potentially be under the control of a smaller number of genes. Researchers are also exploring **endophenotypes**—discrete, stable, and measurable traits that are thought to be under genetic control. By studying different endophenotypes, researchers hope to get closer to specific genes that might be important in

Figure 13.4 The multifactorial etiology of schizophrenia includes (1) rare genes that have a large effect, (2) common genes that have a small effect, and (3) the environmental factors and gene–environmental interactions that confer risk for schizophrenia.

(Adapted from Haller, C. S., Padmanabhan, J. L., Lizano, P., Torous, J., & Keshavan, M. (2014). Recent advances in understanding schizophrenia. *F1000Prime Reports 2014*, 6:57 (doi:10.12703/P6-57).)

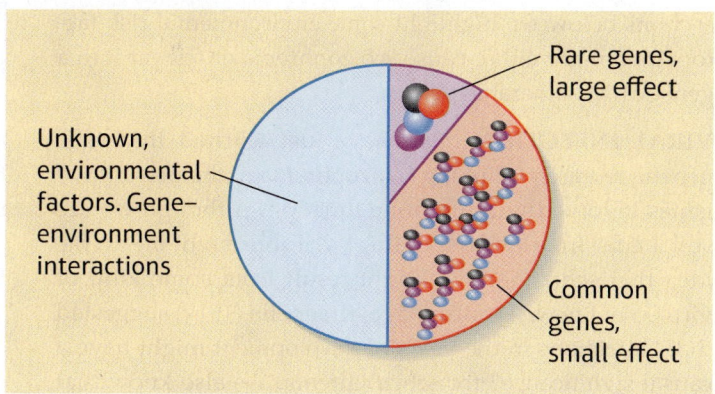

schizophrenia (Gottesman & Gould, 2003; Lenzenweger, 2010). Accordingly, researchers are interested in people who score high on certain tests or measures that are thought to reflect a predisposition to schizophrenia. One example is subjects who score high on a self-report measure of schizotypic traits involving perceptual aberrations and magical ideation (the Per-Mag Scale; see Chapman et al., 1982, 1994). Examples of items from these scales are shown in Table 13.1. Other endophenotypic risk markers for schizophrenia include abnormal performance on measures of cognitive functioning such as tests of working memory (see Barch, 2005; Lenzenweger, 2010). By studying these traits rather than the disorder itself, researchers hope to speed up progress in the search for the genes related to schizophrenia. Moreover, because many endophenotypes are not specific to schizophrenia (anhedonia is also characteristic of depression, for example) studying such traits may shed light on basic processes that have gone wrong in other disorders as well.

Table 13.1 Sample Items Measuring Psychosis-Proneness

Magical Ideation		
T	F	Things seem to be in different places when I get home, even though no one has been there.
T	F	I have sometimes felt that strangers were reading my mind.
T	F	At times, I have felt that a professor's lecture was meant especially for me.
Perceptual Aberration		
T	F	Sometimes people whom I know well begin to look like strangers.
T	F	Ordinary colors sometimes seem much too bright for me.
T	F	Now and then, when I look in the mirror, my face seems quite different than usual.

SOURCES: Chapman et al. (1978); Eckblad & Chapman (1983). Answering "true" to these items is more indicative of psychosis-proneness.

Prenatal Exposures

Whether or not a genotype is expressed depends on biological and environmental triggers. We now know that a range of environmental factors, including such things as maternal exposure to stress, are capable of influencing patterns of gene expression in the developing offspring. In the sections below we highlight some environmental risk factors that might either cause schizophrenia or trigger it in a genetically vulnerable person.

VIRAL INFECTION You have just learned that new genetic research is linking schizophrenia to the presence of genes involved with immune function. Although we are still are far from understanding what this might mean, the idea that schizophrenia might result from some kind of virus is not new. A century ago, Kraepelin (1919) suggested that "infections in the years of development might have a causal significance" for schizophrenia. We also know that in the Northern Hemisphere, more people with schizophrenia are born between January and March than would be expected by chance (Waddington et al., 1999). Could some seasonal factor, such as a virus, be implicated?

In 1957 there was a major epidemic of influenza in Finland. Studying the residents of Helsinki, Mednick and colleagues (1988) found elevated rates of schizophrenia in children born to mothers who had been in their second trimester of pregnancy at the time of the influenza epidemic. This study was the first of its kind and it was followed by several replication attempts. Some of these supported the link between maternal influenza and subsequent schizophrenia in the grown offspring. Others did not. But one problem with the design of these studies was that the researchers had no way of knowing whether the mothers actually had influenza during their pregnancies.

The first study to definitely test the maternal influenza–schizophrenia link was not done until 2004. Brown and colleagues (2004) analyzed specimens of maternal serum (serum is the clear liquid that separates out from coagulated blood). These had been routinely collected throughout the pregnancies of women in California and stored in an archive. This meant that they could be tested later for the presence of antibodies to influenza. The researchers were thus able to establish definitely which mothers had had influenza during their pregnancies. The results showed that influenza exposure during the first trimester of pregnancy was associated with a sevenfold increased risk of schizophrenia or schizophrenia spectrum disorders in the offspring. More generally, influenza exposure during the first half of pregnancy was associated with a threefold increase in risk. Because of the small sample size, neither of these results was statistically significant, although they were close ($P = 0.08$ and $P = 0.052$, respectively).

Although the size of the effect is small and influenza clearly does not account for very many cases of schizophrenia, the fact that any associations exist at all is very provocative. Other maternal infections such as rubella (German measles) and toxoplasmosis (a very common parasitic infection) that occur during pregnancy have also been linked to increased risk for the later development of schizophrenia (Brown, 2011; Khandaker et al., 2013). But how can maternal influenza set the stage for schizophrenia in a child two or three decades later? One possibility is that the mother's antibodies to the virus cross the placenta and somehow disturb brain development in the fetus. Another possibility is that influenza causes an increase in the production of inflammatory cytokines (you read about these in Chapter 5) that cause neurodevelopmental damage. Influenza could also have a direct and damaging effect on the developing brain (Brown, Begg, et al., 2004). As you will see in the Developments in Thinking box, these and other findings are making researchers more and more excited about the possible causal role of infection and immunity in schizophrenia.

RHESUS INCOMPATIBILITY Another example of how the mother's immune system might damage the developing brain of the fetus comes from a completely different source. Rhesus (Rh) incompatibility occurs when an Rh-negative mother carries an Rh-positive fetus. (Rhesus-positive or -negative is a way of typing a person's blood.) Incompatibility between the mother and the fetus is a major cause of blood disease in newborns. Interestingly, Rh incompatibility also seems to be associated with increased risk for schizophrenia. Hollister, Laing, and Mednick (1996) have shown that the rate of schizophrenia is about 2.1 percent in males who are Rh-incompatible with their mothers. For males who have no such incompatibility with their mothers, the rate of schizophrenia is 0.8 percent—very near the expected base rate found in the general population. Hollister is another example of a schizophrenia researcher who has a family member with the disorder, in this case a sister who was Rh-incompatible with her mother.

How might Rh incompatibility increase the risk for schizophrenia? One possibility is that the mechanism involves oxygen deprivation, or hypoxia. This suggestion is supported by studies that have linked the risk for schizophrenia to birth complications. Recent research also suggests that incompatibility between the blood of the mother and the blood of the fetus may increase the risk of brain abnormalities of the type known to be associated with schizophrenia (Freedman et al., 2011).

PREGNANCY AND BIRTH COMPLICATIONS Patients with schizophrenia are much more likely to have been born following a pregnancy or delivery that was complicated in some way (Cannon et al., 2002). Although the type of obstetric complication varies, many delivery problems (e.g., breech delivery, prolonged labor, or the umbilical cord around the baby's neck) affect the oxygen supply of the newborn. Although we still have much to learn, the

Developments in Thinking

Could Schizophrenia Be an Immune Disorder?

Evidence is growing that prenatal exposure to maternal infections may increase the risk of schizophrenia in offspring years later. But how could this work? The mother's inflammatory response may be a key factor. In an important new study Canetta and colleagues (2014) measured levels of C-reactive protein in stored serum samples taken from mothers during the first and second trimesters of their pregnancies. C-reactive protein (which you first encountered in Chapter 5) is a well-established marker of inflammation. What Canetta and colleagues found was that when maternal levels of C-reactive protein were high, the offspring had a nearly 60 percent higher risk of developing schizophrenia decades later.

But why was C-reactive protein elevated at all? Infections in the mother are obvious candidates. High levels of stress also increase inflammation. Researchers believe that early exposure to inflammatory processes at critical times in development might have effects on brain development. So if high levels of maternal C-reactive protein lead to high levels of C-reactive protein in the brain of the developing offspring, bad things may result. In essence the brain may be primed to develop schizophrenia later in life, especially if another "hit" is encountered. This hit could take many forms and might include some of the risk factors (obstetric complications, head injury, migration) that we describe elsewhere in the chapter.

It also warrants mention that the most current genetic research on schizophrenia is implicating genes on chromosome 6 that are involved in immune function. At first this may seem strange. But these genes also play a role in brain development. Do these genes get turned on by inflammation and so change how the brain develops? Or do some forms of these genes make a person more vulnerable to other negative effects of inflammation? It is too soon to put all the pieces together. What is interesting though is that people with schizophrenia have a 53 percent increased risk of developing autoimmune diseases such as psoriasis, Crohn's disease, and multiple sclerosis (Benros et al., 2014). And people with autoimmune diseases are at increased risk of developing schizophrenia (Eaton et al., 2010). So there is now an established link between schizophrenia and autoimmune disorders.

Taken together, all of these findings suggest we might do well to start thinking about schizophrenia as a disorder that might arise from exposure to an inflammatory state in prenatal life or early after. They also raise the possibility that a genetic vulnerability to schizophrenia could take the form of a genetic vulnerability toward dysregulation of the immune system (Cannon et al., 2014). Finally, inflammatory models of schizophrenia suggest new and exciting avenues for prevention. If we can protect pregnant women from infections or from high levels of stress, might this eventually lead to a decrease in rates of schizophrenia?

---

research again points toward damage to the brain at a critical time of development.

EARLY NUTRITIONAL DEFICIENCY Yet another piece of evidence that supports the idea that schizophrenia might be caused or triggered by environmental events that interfere with normal brain development comes from a tragedy that occurred in the Netherlands toward the end of World War II. In October 1944, a Nazi blockade resulted in a severe famine that affected people living in Amsterdam and other cities in the west of the country. The Dutch Hunger Winter (as it was known) continued until the Netherlands was liberated in May 1945. The population was severely malnourished during this time, and many died of starvation. Not surprisingly, fertility levels fell and the birth rate dropped precipitously. However, some children were born during this time. Those who were conceived at the height of the famine had a two-fold increase in their risk of later developing schizophrenia (Brown, 2011). Early prenatal nutritional deficiency appears to have been the cause. Whether the problem was general malnutrition or the lack of a specific nutrient such as folate or iron is not clear. But again, something seems to have compromised the development of the fetus during a critical stage.

MATERNAL STRESS If a mother experiences an extremely stressful event late in her first trimester of pregnancy or

early in the second trimester, the risk of schizophrenia in her child is increased (King et al., 2010). For example, in a large population study conducted in Denmark, the death of a close relative during the first trimester was associated with a 67 percent increase in the risk of schizophrenia in the child (Khashan et al., 2008). Currently, it is thought that the increase in stress hormones that pass to the fetus via the placenta might have negative effects on the developing brain, although the mechanisms through which maternal stress increases risk for schizophrenia are not yet well understood.

Genes and Environment in Schizophrenia: A Synthesis

Without question, schizophrenia has a strong genetic component. Current thinking is that genetic risk for schizophrenia emerges in one of two ways. The first is from large numbers (perhaps even thousands) of common genes. The individual contribution of each of these genes is likely very small. However, when all of these genetic variants interact together, they set the stage for the development of the illness. The other way that schizophrenia may arise is because of very rare genetic mutations. These could be highly specific to certain people or to certain families (see Crow, 2007;

McClellan, Susser, & King, 2007). These genetic events might involve microdeletions (bits of the DNA sequence that are missing in some places) or problems in the DNA sequence itself (such as repetitions of specific sections; St. Clair, 2009).

It is also possible that the focus on MZ concordance rates has caused us to overestimate the heritability of schizophrenia. This is because some MZ, and all DZ, twins do not have equally similar prenatal environments. Around two-thirds of MZ embryos are monochorionic, which means they share a placenta and blood supply. The remaining MZ twins and all DZ twins are dichorionic; they have separate placentas and separate fetal circulations. This is shown in Figure 13.5. The higher concordance rate for schizophrenia in MZ than in DZ twins might therefore be a consequence, at least in part, of the greater potential for monochorionic MZ twins to share infections. Davis, Phelps, and Bracha (1995) have found that MZ twins who are monochorionic are much more likely to be concordant for schizophrenia (around 60 percent concordance) than MZ twins who are dichorionic (around 11 percent concordance). The concordance figure for dichorionic MZ twins is very similar to that generally reported for DZ twins. Monochorionic MZ twins may therefore have inflated concordance rates in schizophrenia, which may have caused us to overattribute to genetics what might more accurately be attributed to environmental influences.

Finally, we need to keep in mind that genes get "turned on" and "turned off" in response to environmental changes. MZ twins who are discordant for schizophrenia show differences in their gene expression (Petronis et al., 2003). Perhaps some environmental "hits" turn on the genes for schizophrenia in one twin and not in the other. And perhaps some environments can keep the genes for schizophrenia from ever being turned on at all. Unfortunately, consistent with the diathesis–stress perspective, being at genetic risk does seem to make people more susceptible to environmental insults. In a study looking at the consequences of birth complications, Cannon and colleagues (1993) found that only the people who had a parent with schizophrenia and who had birth complications later showed brain abnormalities in adulthood such as enlarged ventricles (fluid-filled spaces in the brain). Moreover, for people who had two parents with schizophrenia, the problems were even worse. In contrast, people with no family history of schizophrenia did not show enlarged ventricles regardless of whether they experienced delivery complications when they were born. The message seems to be clear: A genetic liability to schizophrenia may predispose an individual to suffer more damage from environmental insults than would be the case in the absence of the genetic predisposition.

A Neurodevelopmental Perspective

Earlier in this chapter you learned that schizophrenia typically strikes people in late adolescence or early adulthood. Yet in the sections above, we saw that some of the factors thought to cause schizophrenia occur very early in life—in some cases before birth. How can this be? Current thinking is that schizophrenia is a disorder in which the development of the brain is disturbed very early on. Risk for schizophrenia may start with the presence of certain genes that, if turned on, have the potential to disrupt the normal development of the nervous system. Exposure to environmental insults in the prenatal period may turn on these genes or may create problems in other ways, independently of genotype. What this means is that the stage for schizophrenia, in the form of abnormal brain development, may be set very early in life. Nonetheless, problems may not be apparent until other triggering events take place or until the normal maturation of the brain reveals them. This may not occur until the brain is fully mature, typically late in the second decade of life (Conklin & Iacono, 2002; Weinberger, 1987).

What goes wrong? We are not yet certain. Brain development is a complex process that involves a programmed, orderly, and progressive sequence of events (Romer & Walker, 2007). For example, if brain development were disrupted during important stages of cell migration, some cells might fail to reach their target destinations, greatly affecting the "internal connectivity" of the brain. (Organic solvents used in the dry cleaning business might disrupt fetal

Figure 13.5 Chorionic Arrangements in Twins

(A) Dichorionic twins, who can be either dizygotic or monozygotic, have separate placentas and separate fetal circulation. (B) Monochorionic twins, who are always monozygotic, have a single placenta and shared circulation.

(From Davis, J. O., Phelps, J. A., & Bracha, H. S. (1995). Prenatal development of monozygotic twins and concordance for schizophrenia. *Schizophrenia Bulletin*, 21(3), 357–366.)

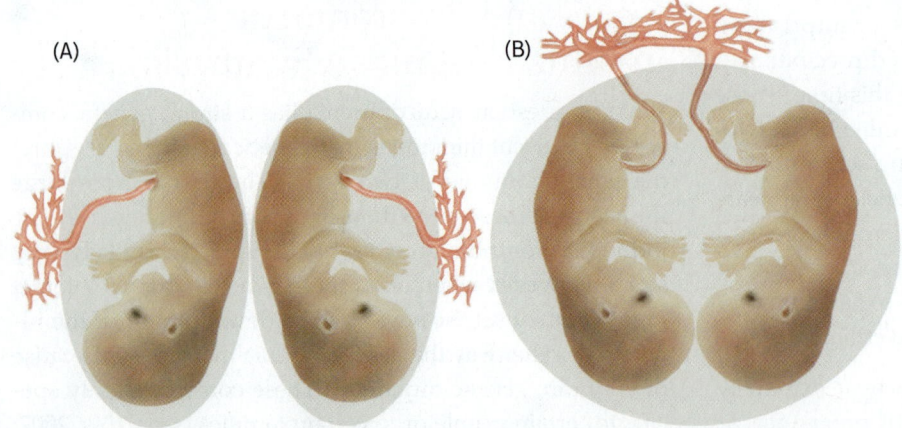

(A)　　　　　　　　(B)

neurodevelopment and so explain why having a parent who works as a dry cleaner triples the risk of schizophrenia in the offspring.) As we have already described, some of the genes that have been implicated in schizophrenia are known to play a role in brain development and neural connections. For example, earlier you learned that one region of the genome that has been linked to schizophrenia contains genes that are involved in immune functioning. This region (which is called the major histocompatibility complex (MHC) also plays an important role in brain development and neuronal function. Although very speculative at this time, it is possible genetic vulnerability to schizophrenia could be explained by greater genetic vulnerability to infection. It is also possible that infection could affect gene expression (which genes are turned on or off) and lead to changes in brain development that "prime" the brain for the later onset of schizophrenia. Although we still have much to learn about how all the facts fit together, problems in brain development and maternal inflammation or infection during pregnancy are very much implicated. In the next few years we expect some exciting new leads to emerge.

If the seeds of schizophrenia are sown so early in life, can we see early indications of vulnerability to the disorder before the illness itself strikes? An ingenious series of studies reported by Walker and colleagues nicely illustrates the association between early developmental deviation and schizophrenia risk. These investigators gathered family home movies made during the childhoods of 32 people who eventually developed schizophrenia. Trained observers made "blind" ratings (i.e., the observers were uninformed of outcomes) of certain dimensions of the emotional (Grimes & Walker, 1994) and facial expressions (Walker et al., 1993), motor skills, and neuromotor abnormalities (Walker et al., 1994) of these children and their healthy-outcome siblings from the same movie clips. The facial and emotional expressions and the motor competence of the "preschizophrenia" and the healthy-outcome children were found by the raters to differ significantly. The "preschizophrenia" children showed more motor abnormalities including unusual hand movements than their healthy siblings; they also showed less positive facial emotion and more negative facial emotion. In some instances these differences were apparent by age 2. Of course, we must keep in mind that these early problems do not characterize all children who will later develop schizophrenia. But they do tell us that subtle abnormalities can be found in children who are vulnerable to the disorder. We should also note that a major advantage of Walker's research design was that it avoided the problem of retrospective bias. Rather than asking parents or siblings what patients were like when they were growing up, the study used home movies to provide an objective behavioral record.

Another way to explore childhood indicators without the problem of retrospective bias is to use a prospective research design (see Chapter 1). Jones and colleagues (1994) and Isohanni and colleagues (2001) studied whole cohorts of children born in particular years and followed them up over time. Both groups of researchers found evidence of delayed speech and delayed motor development at age 2 in children who later went on to develop schizophrenia.

Yet another approach is to follow children who are known to be at high risk for schizophrenia by virtue of their having been born to a parent with the disorder. This strategy, pioneered decades ago by Mednick and Schulsinger (1968), has led to several other studies of high-risk children (for reviews, see Cornblatt et al., 1992; Erlenmeyer-Kimling & Cornblatt, 1992; Neale & Oltmanns, 1980; Watt et al., 1984). Obviously, research of this kind is both costly and time consuming. It also requires a great deal of patience on the part of researchers because children at risk have to be identified early in their lives and then followed into adulthood. Moreover, because the majority of people with schizophrenia do not have a parent with the disorder (in fact, 89 percent of patients have no first- or second-degree relatives with schizophrenia [Gottesman, 2001]), high-risk samples are not particularly representative. Nonetheless, they have provided us with some valuable information about what people at risk look like prior to developing the full illness.

Ratings of clips of old home movies revealed that children who went on to develop schizophrenia showed more unusual hand movements than their healthy siblings, even when they were just 2 years old.

One of the most consistent findings from high-risk research is that children with a genetic risk for schizophrenia are more deviant than control children on research tasks that measure attention (Erlenmeyer-Kimling & Cornblatt, 1992). Adolescents at risk for schizophrenia are also rated lower in social competence than adolescents at risk for affective illness (Dworkin et al., 1994; Hooley, 2010). Some of the social problems that these high-risk children have may result from underlying attentional problems (Cornblatt et al., 1992).

Echoing the findings from Walker's home movie study is evidence that early motor abnormalities might be an especially strong predictor of later schizophrenia. Using data from the New York High-Risk Study, Erlenmeyer-Kimling and colleagues (1998) reported that, of an initial group of 51 high-risk children, 10 developed schizophrenia or schizophrenia-like psychosis as adults. Of these, 80 percent had shown unusual motor behavior when they were between 7 and 12 years of age. In another study, adolescents at high risk for schizophrenia showed more movement abnormalities (e.g., facial tics, blinking, tongue thrusts) than either nonclinical controls or adolescents with personality or behavioral problems (Mittal et al., 2008). Moreover, these movement abnormalities became more marked with time and also became more strongly correlated with psychotic symptoms as the children got older. Although we might have suspected that schizophrenia would first begin to show itself via hallucinations or delusions, it may be that the first signs of the illness can instead be found in the way that children move. This could be because movement abnormalities and psychotic symptoms share some of the same neural circuitry in the brain. Problems in this neural circuitry might show themselves first via movement abnormalities. Then, as the brain matures, problems in the same neural circuits manifest themselves in psychotic symptoms (see MacManus et al., 2011; Mittal et al., 2008).

The original high-risk studies have given us many insights into the problems that characterize people at risk for schizophrenia. But researchers have now changed their strategies. A new generation of high-risk studies is focusing on young people who are at clinical (as opposed to genetic) high risk. By focusing on those who are already showing some **prodromal**, or very early, signs of schizophrenia, researchers are hoping to improve their ability to detect, and also perhaps intervene with, people who appear to be on a pathway to developing the disorder (Addington et al., 2007; Cannon et al., 2007). Recognizing this, the new diagnosis of **attenuated psychosis syndrome** (see Fusar-Poli et al., 2014) has entered *DSM-5* as a disorder in need of further study. More information about this condition is provided in the Thinking Critically about *DSM-5* box.

What kinds of problems do people with attenuated psychotic symptoms have? One of the most frequently reported difficulties involves being perplexed by reality

DSM-5 Thinking Critically about *DSM-5*

Attenuated Psychosis Syndrome

There was lively debate about whether a new diagnosis called attenuated psychosis syndrome should be added to the *DSM-5* (Carpenter & Van Os, 2011). In the end it was decided that the syndrome should be included in a provisional manner and placed in a section reserved for disorders in need of further study. But what is attenuated psychosis syndrome and why is it such a controversial diagnosis?

Attenuated psychosis syndrome is characterized by mild psychotic symptoms that are not severe enough to meet clinical criteria for another full-blown psychotic disorder. People with this syndrome are thought to be at risk for later psychosis. They are also experiencing some distress or disability and are seeking help for their problems. Proponents of including the syndrome in *DSM-5* argued that it would help clinicians identify these people and provide them with treatment at an early stage. This could, in theory, reduce distress in the short term and prevent the onset of a full-blown psychotic disorder in the long term. This is important because, once schizophrenia has developed, most patients are likely to experience recurring positive and negative symptoms, as well as persistent impairments in their work or social functioning for a large part of their lives (Jobe & Harrow, 2010).

Although these may seem like valid reasons to include the new diagnosis, there are also arguments against doing so. The potential for stigma is one problem (Yang et al., 2013). Another concern is that the majority of people who are identified as being at high risk are not on their way to developing a psychotic disorder. Addington and colleagues (2011) followed 303 young adults who were showing prodromal symptoms of schizophrenia. At the end of the follow-up period the majority of these young people (71 percent) had not made the transition into psychosis. Although the follow-up period was relatively short it seems that the false-positive rate here is very high (see also Fusar-Poli et al., 2012).

Another concern is that the existence of the diagnosis will increase the likelihood that antipsychotic medications will be used to treat it (see Weiser, 2011). But is it really appropriate and ethical to prescribe antipsychotic medications to someone who has only mild psychotic symptoms? Second-generation antipsychotic medications are not as effective as had been initially hoped. They also appear to be associated with some very undesirable changes (such as tissue loss) in the brain (Ho et al., 2011; Lewis, 2011). When used long term, they may even perpetuate psychosis (see the Unresolved Issues feature at the end of this chapter). Given this, it behooves us to be cautious with their use.

The inclusion of attenuated psychosis in Section III of the *DSM* may be a good interim solution. It will encourage more research into this new disorder. This may help us refine and improve the diagnostic criteria that are currently being used. More research may also stimulate the development of new treatment approaches capable of providing clinical benefits to patients without exposing them to unnecessary risks.

(e.g., confusing dreams with reality). People also reported losing control over the content of their thoughts or having ideas of being regarded in a negative way by others. Suspiciousness of friends or acquaintances was also characteristic, as was hearing sounds such as buzzing, hissing, knocking, or footsteps (Marshall et al., 2014). Note that these are all below the level of full-blown psychotic symptoms with regard to their severity. However, the presence of such experiences suggests that someone could be at risk of developing psychosis at a later point.

in review

- What evidence supports a genetic contribution to schizophrenia?
- Describe five environmental factors that have been shown to increase risk for schizophrenia.

Structural and Functional Brain Abnormalities

13.5 Discuss how the brain is affected in schizophrenia.

Technological developments now allow us to study the brain in ways that used to be impossible. These new approaches are revealing abnormalities in the structure and function of the brain as well as in neurotransmitter activity in people with schizophrenia. In the sections that follow we describe some of the problems in cognitive functioning that have long been known to characterize people with this disorder. We then consider what abnormalities in the structure and functioning of the brain might be responsible for these and other problems.

Neurocognition

Cognitive impairment is regarded as a core feature of schizophrenia. People with schizophrenia perform much worse (on average almost a full standard deviation worse) than healthy controls on a broad range of neuropsychological tests (see Heinrichs, 2005; Heinrichs & Zakanis, 1998). Almost all aspects of cognition (involving attention, language, and memory) are impaired. Nonetheless, we should keep in mind that not all patients show impairments in all areas and some perform within the normal range of functioning. However, even these patients may be showing significant declines from their earlier levels of cognitive functioning (Keefe, 2014).

Cognitive impairments appear early. Even before they have a diagnosable illness, young people at clinical high risk for developing psychosis perform less well than healthy controls on certain neurocognitive tests (Corigliana et al., 2014). Because cognitive difficulties can be seen right from the start of the illness (or even well before), it is unlikely that they are due to the effects of extended hospi-

talizations or medications. Indeed, very recent research suggests that having a lower IQ may itself be an independent risk factor for developing schizophrenia at a later point and that having a higher IQ may be protective in some way (Kendler et al., 2015).

Although people with lower IQs may (for reasons we do not yet understand) be more susceptible to developing schizophrenia, it is nonetheless the case that any preexisting cognitive impairments become more prominent and extensive as the illness progresses. What this means is that the cognitive impairments we see in patients experiencing their first episodes of illness are more severe and more wide ranging than the cognitive impairments found in people in the early (premorbid or prodromal) phases. It is also noteworthy that patients who have only recently become ill perform about the same on neuropsychological tests as patients who have been ill for many years (McCleery et al., 2014; Mesholam-Gately et al., 2009). For this reason researchers think that a sharp decline in cognitive ability (and IQ) occurs during the period of transition from the premorbid period into full-blown illness (Meier et al., 2014). After the first psychotic episode, the cognitive decline seems to stabilize (Nuechterlein et al., 2014). However, there may be a second period of deterioration that begins around age 65 (Harvey, 2014).

What kind of cognitive problems do people with schizophrenia show? Many examples can be given. For example, when asked to respond to a stimulus as quickly and appropriately as possible (this is a measure of reaction time), patients with schizophrenia do poorly compared with controls (see Nuechterlein, 1977). In addition, they show deficits on the Continuous Performance Test (CPT; e.g., Cornblatt et al., 1989). This task requires the subject to attend to a series of letters or numbers and then to detect an intermittently presented target stimulus that appears on the screen along with the letters or numbers (e.g., "Press when you see the number 7"). There are also problems with working memory (Barch, 2005; Park et al., 1995), which can be thought of as our "mental blackboard." When they engage in tasks of working memory, patients with schizophrenia show less prefrontal brain activity compared to healthy controls (Cannon et al., 2005).

Deficits are even apparent in the very earliest stages of visual and auditory processing. For example, somewhere between 54 and 86 percent of people with schizophrenia show eye-tracking dysfunction (see Figure 13.6) and are deficient in their ability to track a moving target such as a pendulum (Cornblatt et al., 2008). This is a skill referred to as smooth-pursuit eye movement (Levy et al., 2010). In contrast, only about 6 to 8 percent of the general population shows problems with eye tracking. Especially interesting is that around 50 percent of the first-degree relatives of patients with schizophrenia also show eye-tracking problems even though they do not have schizophrenia

Figure 13.6 Normal and Abnormal Eye Tracking of a Sinusoidal Wave

The top pattern is the target, the middle pattern is a record of normal tracking, and the lowest pattern is the kind of abnormal record produced by some patients with schizophrenia.

(Figure from Levy et al. (1993). Eye tracking dysfunction and schizophrenia: A critical perspective. *Schizophrenia Bulletin, 19*(3), 461–536. Used with permission of Oxford University Press.)

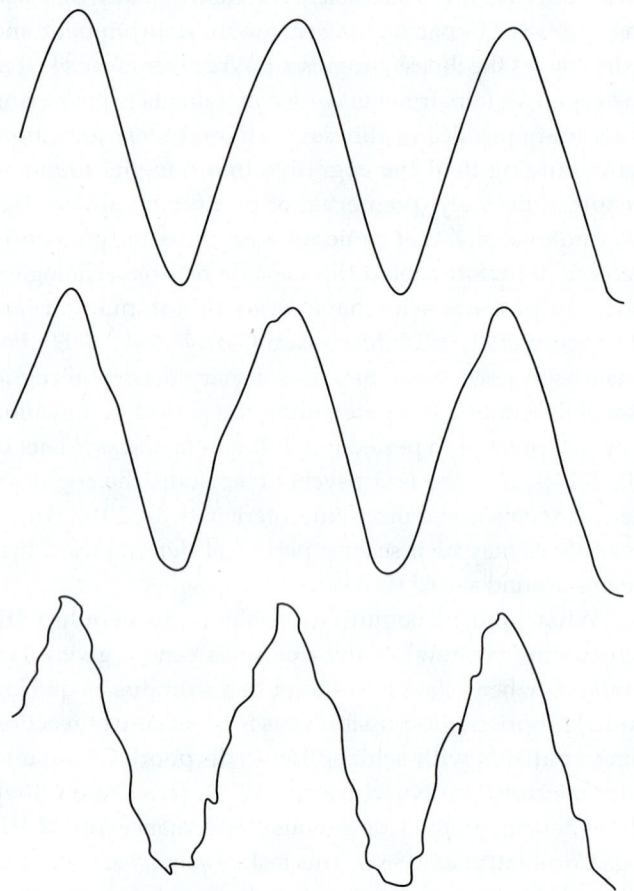

themselves (e.g., Iacono et al., 1992; Sporn et al., 2005). This suggests that disturbances in eye tracking have a genetic basis and that eye tracking may represent a viable endophenotype for genetic studies.

In the area of auditory information processing, people with schizophrenia show problems with a process called **sensory gating** (Heinrichs, 2001; Potter et al., 2006). When two clicks are heard in close succession, the brain (receiving the auditory signal) produces a positive electrical response to each click. This response is called P50 because it occurs 50 milliseconds after the click. In normal subjects, the response to the second click is less marked than the response to the first click because the normal brain dampens, or "gates," responses to repeated sensory events. If this didn't happen, habituation to a stimulus would never occur. Many patients with schizophrenia, in contrast, respond almost as strongly to the second click as to the first. This is referred to as "poor P50 suppression." First-degree family members of

patients with schizophrenia are also more likely than controls to have problems with P50 suppression (Clementz et al., 1998).

Taken together, the weight of the evidence suggests that patients with schizophrenia have problems with both basic and higher-level cognitive processing. This makes the world very difficult for them. The following comment, from a patient with schizophrenia, illustrates the struggle in a personal way:

> *I have trouble concentrating and keeping my mind on one thing at a time, especially when I'm with people. I can hear what they're saying, but I can't keep up with them and make sense of the conversation. I lose my grip on being part of the conversation and drift off. It's not so bad when I'm talking with just one other person, but if I'm trying to tune in to a conversation with several people, things come in too fast and I get lost. It's hard for me to contribute to a conversation when the ideas get blurred. (Liberman, 1982, p. 78)*

Social Cognition

If you were having dinner and your partner stared at your dessert and commented on how delicious it looked, what conclusion would you draw? You would likely assume that your partner wanted a bite of your dessert. **Social cognition** is concerned with how we recognize, think about, and respond to social information including the emotions and intentions of others. In addition to having problems with basic neurocognitive processes, people with schizophrenia show significant impairments in social cognition (Pinkham, 2014). For example, they fail to spot the kinds of subtle (or not so subtle) social hints that most of us (as in the example about the dessert) can detect without difficulty. They also have difficulties recognizing emotion in faces (Kohler et al., 2010) and emotion being conveyed in speech (Hooker & Park, 2002). Compared to healthy controls, they are also less able to recognize when someone has made a social error (a faux pas) such as forgetting that a party is supposed to be a surprise. Social cognition seems to be especially compromised for people with schizophrenia. Patients with bipolar disorder, for example, when they are not in an episode of illness, perform as well as controls on such tests (Lee et al., 2013).

Of course, intact cognitive functions are required for a person to perform well on tests of social cognition. Nonetheless, although social cognition and nonsocial (neurocognition) are related, they are largely distinct constructs (Lee et al., 2013). Both help explain how well patients are able to function in the real world. However, when it comes to predicting social skills or quality of life, social cognitive abilities (such as social perception, emotion recognition, ability to detect irony and the like) seem to play a greater role than neurocognitive skills such as attention or memory (Maat et al., 2012; Pinkham, 2014).

Loss of Brain Volume

Given the many impairments that are characteristic of schizophrenia, it is hardly surprising that we see brain abnormalities associated with the illness, both in terms of brain structure (what the brain looks like) and brain function (how the brain works). One of the most well-replicated findings concerns the brain ventricles. These are fluid-filled spaces that lie deep within the brain. Compared with controls, patients with schizophrenia have enlarged brain ventricles, with males possibly being more affected than females (Haijma et al., 2013; Lawrie & Abukmeil, 1998; Shenton et al., 2001). However, enlarged brain ventricles are not seen in all patients and are not specific to schizophrenia. They are also characteristic of patients with Alzheimer's disease, Huntington's disease, and chronic alcohol problems.

Enlarged brain ventricles are important because they are an indicator of a reduction in the amount of brain tissue. The brain normally occupies fully the rigid enclosure of the skull. Enlarged ventricles therefore imply that the brain areas that border the ventricles have somehow shrunk or decreased in volume, the ventricular space becoming larger as a result. In fact, MRI studies of patients with schizophrenia show about a 3 percent reduction in whole brain volume relative to that in controls (Hulshoff Pol & Kahn, 2008). This decrease in brain volume is present very early in the illness. Even patients with a recent onset of schizophrenia have lower overall brain volumes than controls (Steen et al., 2006; Vita et al., 2006) or else show evidence of enlarged ventricles (Cahn et al., 2002). These findings suggest that some brain abnormalities likely predate the illness rather than develop as a result of untreated psychosis or as a consequence of taking neuroleptic medications. Consistent with this, important new research shows that brain volume changes can be seen in genetically high-risk individuals as the illness is starting to develop. Indeed, it has been suggested that these changes may play a causal role in the onset of symptoms (Karlsgodt et al., 2010; Sun et al., 2009).

We also know that the brain changes that characterize people in the early stages of the illness progressively get worse with time. Cahn and colleagues (2002) measured changes in the overall volume of gray matter (which is made up of nerve cells) in patients who were experiencing their first episode of schizophrenia. Thirty-four patients and 36 matched, healthy comparison subjects received MRI brain scans at the start of the study and then again 1 year later. The results showed that the volume of gray matter declined significantly over time in the patients but not in the controls. More specifically, there was almost a 3 per-

cent decrease in the volume of gray matter in the patients in the 1-year period between the first and the second scans. Figure 13.7 illustrates the progressive loss of gray matter over a 5-year period in another sample of adolescents with schizophrenia compared to healthy controls.

Studies of more chronically ill patients suggest that decreases in brain tissue and increases in the size of the brain ventricles are not limited to the early phases of this illness. Instead, progressive brain deterioration continues for many years. Moreover, these brain changes can also be found in MZ twins where one has schizophrenia and the other does not. The fact that brain changes are present in the discordant twin (the one without schizophrenia) suggests that they cannot be explained by the influence of antipsychotic medications and may instead be under genetic control (Brans et al., 2008; Hulshoff Pol & Kahn, 2008). Overall, the research findings suggest that in addition to being a neurodevelopmental disorder, schizophrenia is also a neuroprogressive disorder characterized by a loss of brain tissue over time. Kraepelin's use of the term *dementia praecox* may have been highly appropriate after all.

Affected Brain Areas

Are there regions of the brain that are especially implicated in schizophrenia? Although much remains to be learned, there is evidence of reductions in the volume of regions in the frontal and temporal lobes. These brain areas play critical roles in memory, decision making, and in the processing of auditory information. More specifically, there is a reduction in the volume of such medial temporal areas as the amygdala, which is involved in emotion; the hippocampus, which plays a key role in memory; and the thalamus, which is a relay center that receives almost all sensory input (Adriano et al., 2012; Haijma et al., 2013; Keshavan et al., 2008; Shenton et al., 2001). But reductions in gray matter are not invariably found. Recently, Ren and colleagues (2013) used MRI to compare the brains of 100 first-episode schizophrenia patients with 100 healthy controls who were comparable in terms of sex and years of education. This is the largest sample of patients studied so far. Unexpectedly, the patient group showed *increases* in gray matter volume in multiple brain areas. One thing that was different about the patients in this study was that they had not yet been treated with medications. In other words, they were all drug naïve. Although we still do not know how best to understand the findings from this study, the results challenge our thinking about brain changes associated with schizophrenia. Clearly, brain structure is abnormal in schizophrenia. But the nature of the abnormality (increased or decreased gray matter volume) may be linked to the stage of the illness, use of medications, or other factors that we still need to identify. As always, schizophrenia continues to be a disorder that does not give up its secrets easily.

Figure 13.7 Progressive Gray Matter Loss in Schizophrenia

Compared with normal adolescents, young people with early-onset schizophrenia show a progressive loss of gray matter in their brains over time. MRI scans repeated over a 5-year period show a much greater loss of brain tissue in patients with schizophrenia than in healthy controls. Gray matter loss occurs in many brain areas, beginning in the parietal cortex and spreading to the temporal cortex and the frontal cortex.

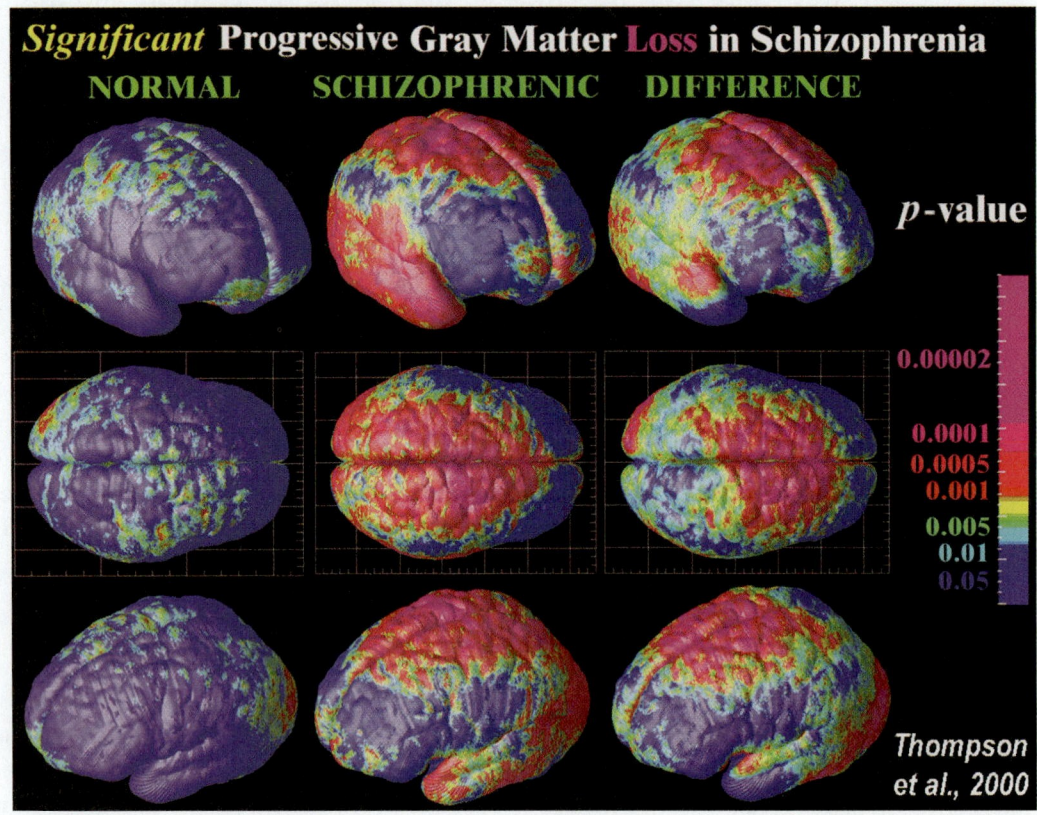

White Matter Problems

When we talk about volume loss in the brains of people with schizophrenia we are referring to the loss of brain cells or gray matter. However, evidence is growing that schizophrenia also involves problems with white matter. Nerve fibers are covered in a myelin sheath (which looks white in color in a chemically preserved brain). Myelin acts as an insulator and increases the speed and efficiency of conduction between nerve cells. White matter is therefore crucially important for the connectivity of the brain. If there are disruptions in the integrity of white matter, there will be problems in how well the cells of the nervous system can function. For example, imagine the problems you would have in a group of networked computers if the connections that linked them were damaged in some way.

Studies of patients with schizophrenia show that they have reductions in white matter volume as well as structural abnormalities in the white matter itself (Haijma et al., 2013). Interestingly, these abnormalities can be found in first-episode patients and also in people at genetic high risk for the disorder. This suggests that they are not a result of the disease itself or the effects of treatment. The fundamental problem seems to be one of dysconnectivity—abnormal integration between distinct brain regions, particularly those involving the frontal lobes (Pettersson-Yeo et al., 2011). This could help explain a lot about the clinical features of schizophrenia. For example, viewed in this way auditory hallucinations can be thought of as

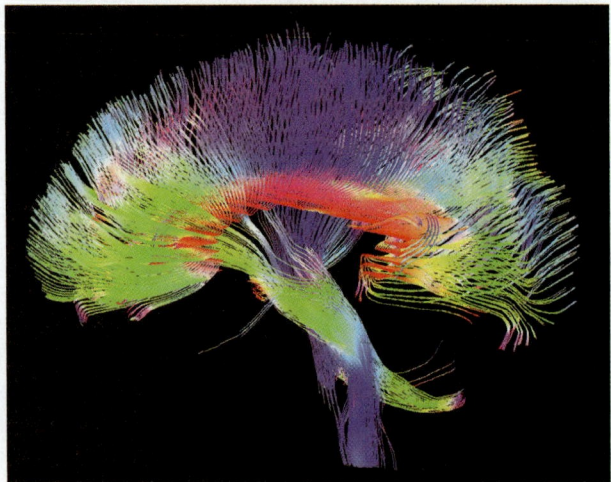

Nerve fibers are covered by a fatty myelin sheath, which looks white in a preserved brain (hence the term white matter). Myelin improves the electrical conductivity of nerve cells. This image illustrates white matter tracts (shown here in color for better clarity) and shows how interconnected the brain is.

Figure 13.8 The Brain in Schizophrenia

Many brain regions and systems operate abnormally in schizophrenia, including those highlighted here.

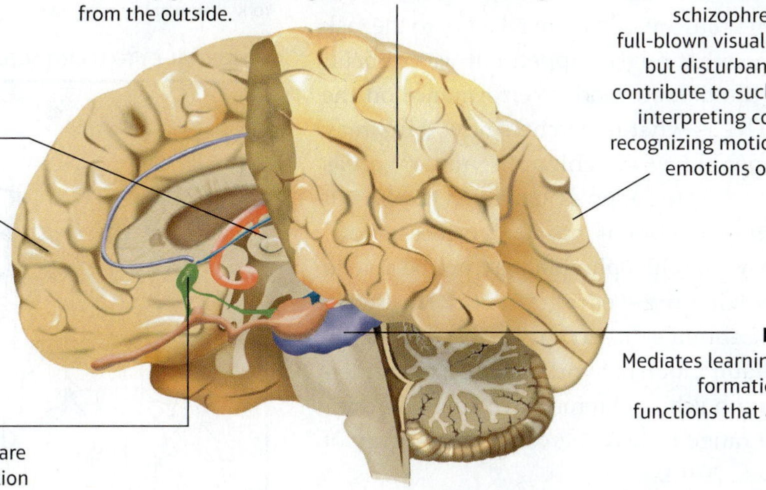

THE BRAIN IN SCHIZOPHRENIA

BASAL GANGLIA
Involved in movement and emotions and in integrating sensory information. Abnormal functioning in schizophrenia is thought to contribute to paranoia and hallucinations. (Excessive blockade of dopamine receptors in the basal ganglia by traditional antipsychotic medicines leads to motor side effects.)

AUDITORY SYSTEM
Enables humans to hear and understand speech. In schizophrenia, dysconnectivity between speech production and comprehension areas may result in auditory hallucinations—the misperception that internally generated thoughts are real voices coming from the outside.

OCCIPITAL LOBE
Processes information about the visual world. People with schizophrenia rarely have full-blown visual hallucinations, but disturbances in this area contribute to such difficulties as interpreting complex images, recognizing motion, and reading emotions on others' faces.

FRONTAL LOBE
Critical to problem solving, insight, and other high-level reasoning. Perturbations in schizophrenia lead to difficulty in planning actions and organizing thoughts.

HIPPOCAMPUS
Mediates learning and memory formation, intertwined functions that are impaired in schizophrenia.

LIMBIC SYSTEM
Involved in emotion. Disturbances are thought to contribute to the agitation frequently seen in schizophrenia.

arising from a disconnection between language production and language comprehension areas. This could make internally generated speech (self-talk) seem as if it is being "heard."

At the clinical level, white matter abnormalities have been shown to be correlated with cognitive impairments (Kubicki et al., 2007). This makes sense if the connections that various brain regions have with the frontal lobes are not what they should be. In people at high risk of developing schizophrenia, white matter changes in the temporal areas of the brain also predict later social functioning (Karlsgodt et al., 2009). Another interesting recent finding is that children of people with schizophrenia, even though they are not psychotic themselves, have a reduction in the volume of the corpus callosum—a massive tract of white matter fibers that connects the two hemispheres of the brain (Francis et al., 2011). Although much remains to be learned, it is becoming increasingly clear that abnormalities in white matter, and in white matter development, may provide us with important additional insights into what goes wrong with the brain in schizophrenia.

Brain Functioning

Studies of brain functioning tell us what is going on in the working brain, either when it is engaged in a task or at rest. You have already learned about the structural brain abnormalities associated with schizophrenia and the problems that patients with schizophrenia have on various neurocognitive tests and on tests of social cognition. Given this, you will hardly be surprised to learn that neuroimaging research is showing us just how disrupted brain functioning is in patients with this disorder.

For example, some patients show abnormally low frontal lobe activation (known as "hypofrontality") when they are involved in mentally challenging tasks such as the Wisconsin Card Sorting Test (WCST) or in other tests generally thought to require substantial frontal lobe involvement. Essentially, this brain area does not seem to be able to kick into action when patients perform complex tasks (see Figure 13.8). In other patients, hyperactivation in frontal brain areas is found, suggesting that they are having to work harder to be successful on the task. In both sets of circumstances, however, the brain is not functioning in an optimal and efficient way.

Impaired functioning of the frontal lobes during cognitive tasks is also found in patients in the early stages of schizophrenia as well as in people at high risk for developing the disorder (Fusar-Poli et al., 2007). Again, however, it is important to remember that such alterations in functioning are not characteristic of all patients (e.g., Buchsbaum et al., 1992; Heinrichs, 2001). Nonetheless, frontal lobe dysfunction is believed to account for some of the negative symptoms of schizophrenia and perhaps to be involved in some attentional-cognitive deficits (Cannon et al., 1998; Goldman-Rakic & Selemon, 1997).

Dysfunction of the temporal lobe is also found, although here the findings are often not very consistent (Keshavan et al., 2008). However, what may be most important is that there may be a problem with the way activity in different brain regions gets *coordinated*. When we are at rest or relaxing and just involved in our own thoughts, there is activation in a network of brain regions that comprise the "default mode network." You can think of this as the brain on standby. Then, when we are actively engaged in a task, activity in this network of brain areas has to be suppressed in favor of activity in brain areas that are relevant to the task at hand. But imagine what might happen if it was difficult to disengage from the default mode. Performance on the task would suffer. This is what researchers now think may be happening in people with schizophrenia. Whereas healthy people find it easy to suppress activity in the default mode network (tuning their brains into the "correct station" so to speak), people with schizophrenia may not be able to do this as efficiently (Guerrero-Pedrazza et al., 2011; Ren et al., 2013; Whitfield-Gabrieli et al., 2009). This lack of ability to disengage the default mode network may help us understand why people with schizophrenia have so many difficulties with a wide range of tasks across a broad array of areas (Karlsgodt et al., 2010).

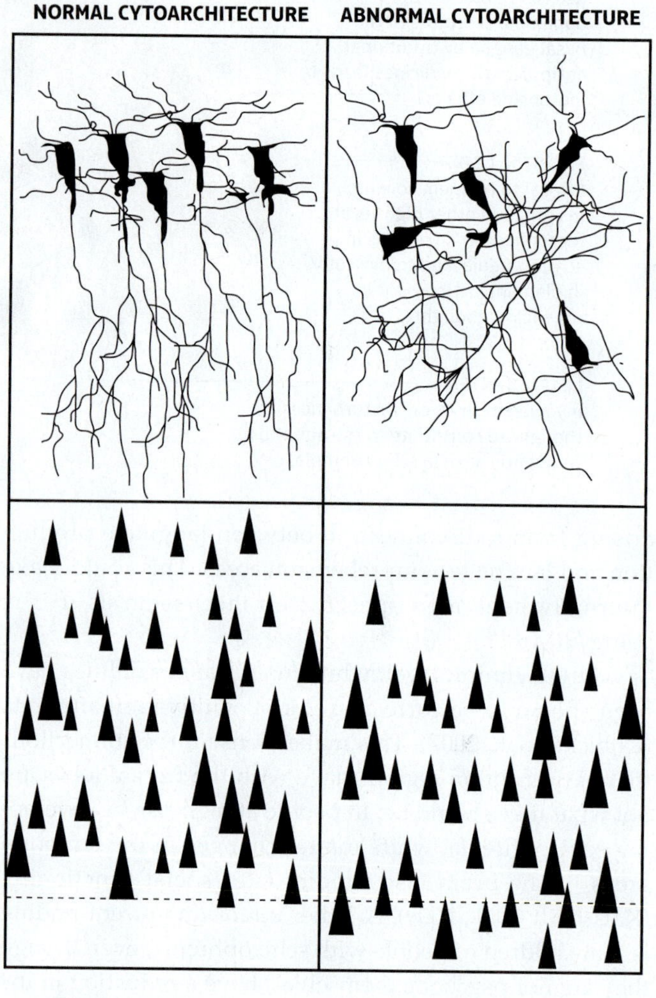

Cytoarchitecture

As we have seen, one hypothesis about schizophrenia is that genetic vulnerabilities, perhaps combined with prenatal insults, can lead to disruption of the migration of neurons in the brain. If this is true, some cells will fail to arrive at their final destinations, and the overall organization of cells in the brain (the brain's *cytoarchitecture*) will be compromised. This is illustrated in Figure 13.9.

The organization of cells in the brain appears to be disrupted in other ways as well. Using complex, three-dimensional counting techniques, researchers have reported an increase in neuronal density in some areas of the brains of patients with schizophrenia (see Selemon, 2004). There are also abnormalities in the distribution of cells in different layers of the cortex and hippocampus (Arnold, 2000; Kalus et al., 1997; Selemon et al., 1995). Of particular importance is the finding that patients with schizophrenia are missing particular types of neurons known as "inhibitory interneurons" (Benes & Berretta, 2001). These are called GABA interneurons and they are responsible for regulating the excitability of other neurons. (Essentially they tell other neurons to calm down.) Their absence may mean that bursts of activity by excitatory neurons in the brain go unchecked. Again, research suggests that the brains of patients with schizophrenia may be less able to regulate or dampen down overactivity in certain key neural circuits (see Daskalakis et al., 2002). As we will see shortly, patients with schizophrenia have difficulty

Figure 13.9 Cytoarchitecture and Neural Development
The upper diagram shows examples of normal and abnormal pyramidal cell orientation in the hippocampus. The lower diagram is a schematic representation of stained neurons and the "downward-shift" phenomenon. Premature arrest of cell migration during development may underlie the high frequency of cells in lower regions close to white matter and their relative paucity near the cortical surface.

(Figure 7.1 from Heinrichs R. W. (2001). *In search of madness: Schizophrenia and neuroscience* (p. 196). Oxford University Press. Adapted from Arnold, S. E., & Trojanowski, J. Q. (1996). Recent advances in defining the neuropathology of schizophrenia. *Acta Neuropathologie, 92*, 217–31 and Kolb, B., & Wishaw, I. Q. (1996). *Fundamentals of human neuropsychology* (4th ed.). New York: Freeman.)

NORMAL CYTOARCHITECTURE   ABNORMAL CYTOARCHITECTURE

handling even normal levels of stress. Given what we have just learned, this makes a great deal of sense.

Did you ever wonder how research of this kind gets done? This is a topic that most of us do not think about (or perhaps care to think about) very much. But researchers owe a debt of gratitude to people who have generously donated their brains for scientific study after their death. In the United States and throughout the world, psychiatric brain banks provide brain tissue samples for use in schizophrenia research, as well as research on other psychiatric and neurodegenerative disorders including Alzheimer's disease (Deep-Soboslay et al., 2011). As you can imagine, there are many methodological issues associated with using postmortem brain tissue to understand schizophrenia. These include the older age of the brains, the high level of comorbid substance abuse in patients, as well as medication effects. The scarcity of donations is also a challenge. For example, on average only 9 schizophrenia brains and 13 healthy control brains are donated to the tissue bank maintained by the National Institute of Mental Health (NIMH) each year.

Brain Development in Adolescence

Although we have every reason to believe that risk genes and early prenatal experiences compromise brain development in the fetus, the story may not end so early. The brain continues to develop and mature through adolescence and into young adulthood. For example, we all have an excess of synapses well into our late teens. However, normal processes that occur during adolescence prune (or reduce) these synapses, so decreasing "neuronal redundancy." There is also a normal reduction in gray matter volume that occurs in adolescence, as well as an increase both in white matter and in the volume of the hippocampus and the amygdala. In addition, the number of excitatory synapses decreases and the number of inhibitory synapses increases. All of these processes are thought to occur to enhance brain function overall and to make the brain more "adult" (Insel, 2010; Walker et al., 2010).

But what if these processes fail to occur in a normal way? Depending on what goes wrong and when, we might expect to see many of the differences (increased or reduced gray matter volume, less white matter, reduced volume of the hippocampus) that we do actually see in schizophrenia. In other words, we can think of schizophrenia as a disorder characterized by abnormal maturation (excessive pruning of synapses, abnormal myelination) of the brain and its networks.

Major brain changes take place during adolescence as the brain matures. If problems occur during this critical phase of development, schizophrenia may be the result.

The idea that schizophrenia involves abnormal or disrupted brain development is further supported by recent research linking schizophrenia to a history of head injury. People who have had a hospital contact for a head injury have a 65 percent increase in later risk for schizophrenia (Orlovska et al., 2014). This increased risk appears to be independent of having a family history of psychiatric illness. Furthermore, if the head injury occurs between the ages of 11 and 15, the risk of schizophrenia is increased even more (85 percent increase). All of this points to the possibility that there are sensitive periods in brain development when environmental insults might be especially damaging. Some of these probably occur very early in life, before or around the time of birth. Still others might occur much later. As we have said before, the etiology of schizophrenia is very complicated. But many of the answers undoubtedly lie in what goes wrong in the brain at critical periods of development.

Synthesis

The brain is compromised in schizophrenia, although the compromise is often very subtle. Some of the brain abnormalities that are found are likely to be genetic in origin. Others may reflect environmental insults. For example, Baaré and colleagues (2001) used MRI to study the brains of MZ and DZ twins who were discordant for schizophrenia and then compared the results for these groups to results from a group of healthy twins. What these researchers found was that the patients with schizophrenia had smaller brain volumes than their well co-twins. What was interesting, however, was that these well co-twins also had smaller brains than the healthy control twins. Baaré and colleagues propose that genetic risk for schizophrenia may be associated with reduced brain development early in life. This is why the healthy twins who had a co-twin with schizophrenia had smaller brain volumes than the healthy controls. Baaré and colleagues also hypothesize that patients who develop schizophrenia suffer additional brain abnormalities that are not genetic in origin. This explains why the twins with schizophrenia had smaller brain volumes than their discordant co-twins. In people at genetic risk for schizophrenia (but not in those without genetic risk), a history of fetal oxygen deprivation has been shown to be associated with brain abnormalities in later life (Cannon et al., 2002). In other words, what we may have here is an excellent example of how genes can create an enhanced susceptibility to potentially aversive environmental events. Moreover, even when both members of a twin pair have identical genes (as is the case for MZ twins), if only one of them experiences the environmental insult (for example, a birth cord around the neck, creating hypoxia or a perhaps a head injury), only one twin might be pushed across the threshold into illness while the co-twin remains healthy.

Finally, we emphasize that it is unlikely that schizophrenia is the result of any one problem in any one specific region of the brain. The brain is comprised of *functional circuits*—regions that are linked to other regions by a network of interconnections. If there is a problem at any point in the circuit, the circuit will not function properly. The focus now is on learning how the brain is wired and what regions are functionally linked. Research on the default mode network is an example of this. Subtle brain abnormalities in some key functional circuits (or deficiencies in the ability to switch from one functional circuit to another) may wreak havoc with normal functioning. As we gain more knowledge about how the brain does its job, we will understand more about how exactly the brain is compromised in schizophrenia.

Neurochemistry

After researchers discovered in 1943 that LSD could cause profound mental changes, those interested in schizophrenia began to consider the possible biochemical basis of the disorder. Now the idea that serious mental disorders are due to "chemical imbalances" in the brain is commonplace. This phrase is often used to provide a general explanation of why someone has a disorder like schizophrenia. But the notion of "chemical imbalance" is vague and imprecise. All it really conveys is the widely accepted notion that alterations in brain chemistry may be associated with abnormal mental states.

The most well-studied neurotransmitter implicated in schizophrenia is **dopamine**. The *dopamine hypothesis* dates back to the 1960s and was derived from three important observations. The first was the pharmacological action of the drug chlorpromazine (Thorazine). Chlorpromazine was first used in the treatment of schizophrenia in 1952. It rapidly became clear that this drug was helpful to patients. Eventually, it was learned that the therapeutic benefits of chlorpromazine were linked to its ability to block dopamine receptors.

The second piece of evidence implicating dopamine in schizophrenia came from an entirely different direction. Amphetamines are drugs that produce a functional excess of dopamine (i.e., the brain acts as if there is too much dopamine in the system). In the late 1950s and early 1960s, researchers began to see that abuse of amphetamines led, in some cases, to a form of psychosis that involved paranoia and auditory hallucinations (Connell, 1958; Kalant, 1966; Tatetsu, 1964). There was thus clinical evidence that a drug that gave rise to a functional excess of dopamine also gave rise to a psychotic state that looked a lot like schizophrenia.

The third piece of indirect evidence linking dopamine to schizophrenia came from clinical studies that actually treated patients by giving them drugs that increase the availability of dopamine in the brain. An example here is

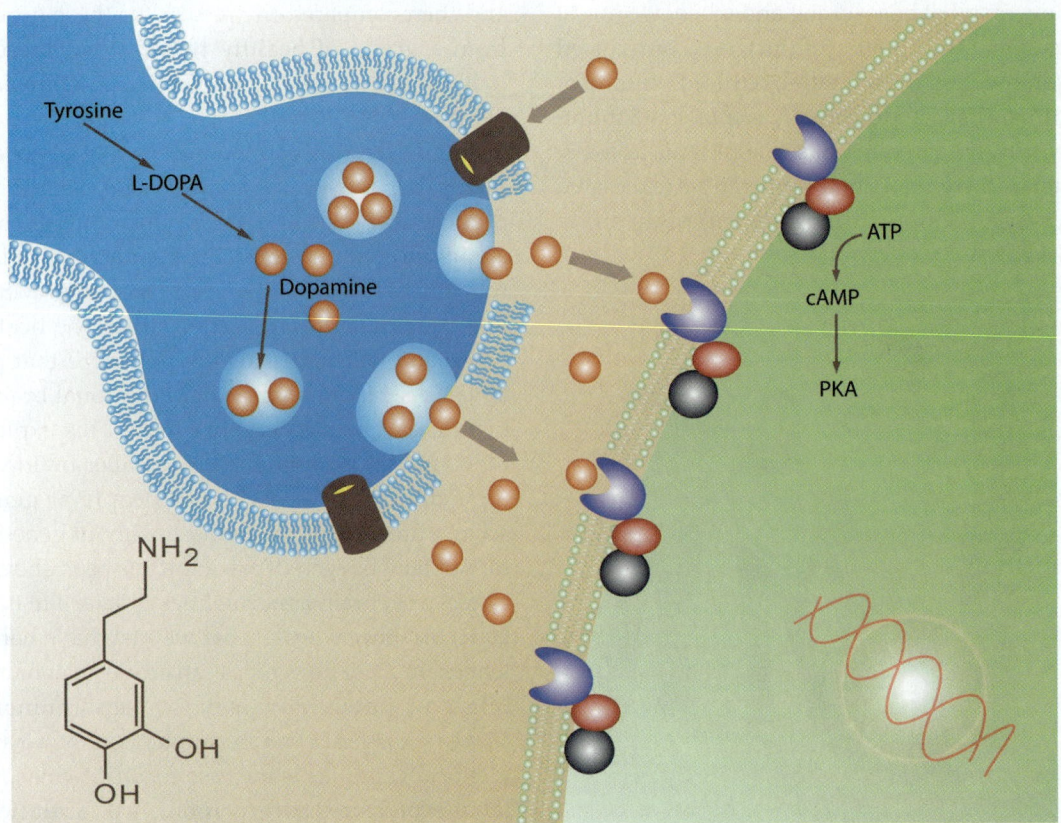

After being synthesized, dopamine is stored until it is released into the synapse. Dopamine binds to receptors on the postsynaptic neuron (shown in blue) triggering other reactions. It is then recycled back into the neuron to be used again.

Parkinson's disease, which is caused by low levels of dopamine in a specific brain area (the basal ganglia; see Figure 13.8) and is treated with a drug called L-DOPA. Psychotic symptoms are a significant complication of treatment with L-DOPA. Again, then, the circumstantial evidence pointed to the role of dopamine in inducing psychosis.

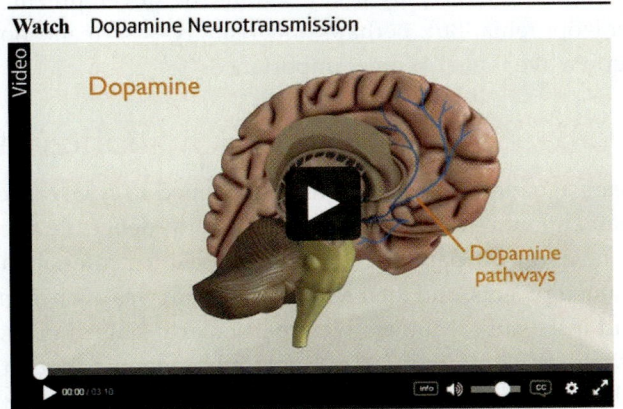

Watch Dopamine Neurotransmission

How could dopamine induce psychosis? Activity in the dopamine system may play a role in determining how much salience we give to internal and external stimuli. Dysregulated dopamine transmission may actually make us pay more attention to and give more significance to stimuli that are not especially relevant or important. This is called "aberrant salience" (see Kapur, 2003). If this is the case, it is quite easy to see why patients might develop delusions or experience hallucinations and why psychotic experiences might be so shaped by the patient's culture and history. In the early stages of their illnesses, patients often report heightened sensory awareness ("My senses were sharpened. I became fascinated by the little insignificant things around me") or increased meaning in events ("I felt that there was some overwhelming significance in this"). If dopamine creates aberrant salience, the person will struggle to make sense of everyday experiences that were previously in the background but that now have become inappropriately important and worthy of attention. In this way, the hum of a refrigerator could become a voice talking; or the arrival of a package could signal a threat, which then prompts the patient to look carefully at the subtle behaviors of others to see who could be a source of harm and persecution.

But how might a functional excess of dopamine in the system come about? One way is through too much dopamine being available in the synapse (the gap between nerve cells that has to be "bridged" by a neurotransmitter for a nerve impulse to be carried from one neuron to another). This could come about by increasing the synthesis or production of dopamine, by releasing more of it into the synapse, by slowing down the rate at which dopamine is metabolized or broken down once it is in the synapse, or by blocking neuronal reuptake (the "recycling" of dopamine back into the neuron). Any or all of these could increase the overall availability of dopamine. There are also ways in which a functional excess of dopamine could be produced or, more accurately, mimicked. If the receptors that dopamine acts on (i.e., those on the postsynaptic membrane) are especially dense and prolific or if they are especially sensitive (or both), the effects of a normal amount of dopamine being released into the synapse would be multiplied. In other words, the system acts as though there were more dopamine available even though there really isn't.

Before the development of highly sophisticated imaging techniques, researchers interested in learning about dopamine in the brains of people with schizophrenia could use one of two approaches. They could measure dopamine in the (postmortem) brains of deceased patients, or they could study dopamine indirectly by measuring its major metabolite (what most of it is converted into). The major metabolite of dopamine is homovanillic acid, or HVA. However, HVA is best collected in cerebrospinal fluid (CSF). This requires that the patient agree to a lumbar puncture, which involves a large needle being inserted into the spine to draw off fluid. Not only was this potentially dangerous, it also left the patient with a violent headache.

Research in this area has progressed rapidly in recent years thanks to technological developments, such as PET scans. These allow us to study the working brain and to look at dopamine synthesis as well as the density of dopamine receptors in living patients. There are five subtypes of dopamine receptors (D1–D5). Of these, the D2 receptor is the most relevant clinically, and most of the research has focused on this. So what do we know? The most current findings tell us that the biggest abnormality in dopamine functioning occurs presynaptically. In other words, too much dopamine (about 14 percent more) is being synthesized and released into the synapse (Fusar-Poli & Meyer-Lindberg, 2012; Howes et al., 2012). There is also some evidence that patients with schizophrenia have an increased number of D2 or D3 receptors. However, the difference is small and is not found in patients who have not taken antipsychotic medications. This suggests that elevations in dopamine receptor density are more likely linked to treatment effects rather than being integral to schizophrenia itself.

But dopamine is not the only neurotransmitter implicated in schizophrenia. Before leaving our discussion of neurochemistry, let's take a quick look at another key neurotransmitter that is attracting a lot of attention.

Glutamate is an excitatory neurotransmitter that is widespread in the brain. As was the case for dopamine, there are a number of reasons why researchers suspect that a dysfunction in glutamate transmission might be involved in schizophrenia. First, PCP, or angel dust, is known to block glutamate receptors. PCP also induces symptoms (both positive and negative) that are very similar to those of schizophrenia. Moreover, when people with schizophrenia take PCP, it exacerbates their symptoms.

Second, physicians had to stop using ketamine, which is an anesthetic, because when it is given intravenously to healthy volunteers, it produces schizophrenia-like positive and negative symptoms (see Krystal et al., 2005). When given to patients whose schizophrenia is stable and well controlled, ketamine exacerbates hallucinations, delusions, and thought disorder. But what is all the more remarkable about ketamine is that it does not cause any of these problems when it is administered to animals or to children, for whom it continues to be used as an anesthetic. This suggests that age (and brain maturity) determines whether ketamine causes psychosis.

Like PCP, ketamine blocks glutamate receptors. Researchers are now exploring concentrations of glutamate in the postmortem brains of patients with schizophrenia and finding lower levels of glutamate in both the prefrontal cortex and the hippocampus compared with the levels in control subjects (Goff & Coyle, 2001). Recent results from a meta-analysis further suggest that glutamate levels are also low in the brains of living patients who have schizophrenia (Marsman et al., 2011). This is exciting because, many years ago, Olney and Farber (1995) proposed that diminished activity at certain types of glutamate receptors (known as "NMDA" receptors) may not only trigger schizophrenia-like symptoms but may also cause the degeneration of neurons in key brain areas. In other words, if the NMDA receptors are not normally active (perhaps because glutamate levels are low), subtle brain damage may result.

For all of these reasons, the *glutamate hypothesis* of schizophrenia is now attracting a lot of research attention. It is also prompting the development of new experimental drugs that might provide additional ways to treat schizophrenia. For example, amino acids such as glycine and D-serine are now being used to enhance neurotransmission at NMDA receptor sites. This research is still in its early stages; nonetheless, the initial findings have promise (Javitt, 2012; Lane et al., 2008).

Finally, does the importance of glutamate challenge the importance of dopamine in the neurochemistry of schizophrenia? No. One action of dopamine receptors is to inhibit the release of glutamate. Simply stated, an overactive dopaminergic system could result in excessive suppression of glutamate, leading to the underactivity (hypofunction) of the NMDA receptors. The dopamine hypothesis of schizophrenia is actually made all the more credible by discoveries about glutamate.

---

in review

- What is the dopamine hypothesis? Describe the current status of this explanation for schizophrenia.
- What neuroanatomical abnormalities differentiate people with schizophrenia from people who do not suffer from this disorder?

Psychosocial and Cultural Factors

13.6 **Explain the psychosocial and cultural factors associated with schizophrenia.**

Biological factors play a key role in the development of schizophrenia. But, perhaps surprisingly, where and how people live is also of great importance.

Do Bad Families Cause Schizophrenia?

Years ago, parents were routinely assumed to have caused their children's disorders through hostility, deliberate rejection, or gross parental ineptitude. Many professionals blamed parents, and their feedback to them was often angry and insensitive. Mothers were particularly singled out for criticism. The idea of the "schizophrenogenic mother," whose cold and aloof behavior was the root cause of schizophrenia, was very influential in many clinical circles (Fromm-Reichman, 1948). This was very distressing for families. Not only were they faced with the difficulties of coping with a son or daughter who had a devastating illness, but they suffered all the more because of the blame that was directed toward them by mental health professionals.

Today, things are very different. Theories that were popular many decades ago—for example, the idea that schizophrenia was caused by destructive parental interactions (Lidz et al., 1965)—have foundered for lack of empirical support. Another idea that has not stood the test of time is the *double-bind hypothesis* (Bateson, 1959, 1960). A double bind occurs when the parent presents the child with ideas, feelings, and demands that are mutually incompatible (e.g., a mother may complain about her son's lack of affection but freeze up or punish him when he approaches her affectionately). According to Bateson's etiologic hypothesis, such a son is continually placed in situations where he cannot win, and he becomes increasingly anxious. Presumably, over time, such disorganized and contradictory communications in the family come to be reflected in his own thinking. However, no solid support for these ideas has ever been reported.

Instead, we have learned from past research that disturbances and conflict in families that include an individual with schizophrenia may well be caused by having a person with psychosis in the family (e.g., Hirsch & Leff, 1975). In other words, rather than causing the schizophrenia, family communication problems could be the result of trying to communicate with someone who is severely ill and disorganized (Liem, 1974; Mishler & Waxler, 1968). Of course, some families do show unusual communication patterns that we now refer to as "communication deviance" and which we described earlier. These amorphous and fragmented communications may actually reflect genetic susceptibility to schizophrenia on the part of the relative

(Hooley & Hiller, 2001; Miklowitz & Stackman, 1992). However, as we know from the Finnish Adoptive Family Study of Schizophrenia, adverse family environments and communication deviance probably have little pathological consequence if the child who is exposed has no genetic risk for schizophrenia (Tienari et al., 2004; Wahlberg et al., 1997).

Families and Relapse

Although schizophrenia is often a chronic disorder, its symptoms may be especially severe at some times (i.e., when there is a relapse) and less severe at other times (e.g., during a period of remission). Decades ago, George Brown and his colleagues (1958) observed that the kind of living situation patients with schizophrenia had after they left the hospital predicted how well they would fare clinically. Surprisingly, patients who returned home to live with parents or with a spouse were at higher risk of relapse than patients who left the hospital to live alone or with siblings. Brown reasoned that highly emotional family environments might be stressful to patients. He also suspected that what might be important was not the presence of markedly disturbed or pathological patient–family relationships (although those certainly existed in some families) but something much more ordinary and commonplace. Brown's hunch was that researchers should focus on "the range of feelings and emotions to be found in ordinary families" (see Brown, 1985, p. 22). This was an unusual insight at the time. But viewed today in the context of the diathesis–stress model, we see just how prescient Brown was.

In a series of studies, Brown and his colleagues went on to develop and refine the construct of **expressed emotion, or EE**. Expressed emotion is a measure of the family environment that is based on how a family member speaks about the patient during a private interview with a researcher (Hooley, 2007). It has three main elements: criticism, hostility, and emotional overinvolvement (EOI). The most important of these is criticism, which reflects dislike or disapproval of the patient. Hostility is a more extreme form of criticism that indicates a dislike or rejection of the patient as a person. Finally, EOI reflects a dramatic or overconcerned attitude on the part of the family member toward the patient's illness.

Expressed emotion is important because it has been repeatedly shown to predict relapse in patients with schizophrenia. In a meta-analysis of 27 studies, Butzlaff and Hooley (1998) demonstrated that living in a high-EE home environment more than doubled the baseline level of relapse risk for patients with schizophrenia in the 9 to 12 months after hospitalization. Moreover, even though EE predicts relapse regardless of whether the patients studied have been ill for a short, medium, or long time, EE seems to be an especially strong predictor of relapse for patients who are chronically ill.

Of course, it could be that families simply tend to be more critical of patients who are more severely ill. This

would then explain why EE and relapse are correlated. However, the literature provides no strong support for this assumption (see Hooley et al., 1995). Also, EE predicts relapse even when potentially important patient variables are controlled statistically (Nuechterlein et al., 1992). Finally, research shows that when EE levels in families are lowered (usually by clinical interventions), patients' relapse rates also decrease (Falloon et al., 1985; Hogarty et al., 1986; Leff et al., 1982; McFarlane et al., 1995). This suggests that EE may play a causal role in the relapse process.

But how might EE trigger relapse? There is a great deal of evidence that patients with schizophrenia are highly sensitive to stress. Consistent with the diathesis–stress model, environmental stress is thought to interact with preexisting biological vulnerabilities to increase the probability of relapse (Nuechterlein et al., 1992). We know, for example, that independent stressful life events occur more frequently just prior to psychotic relapse than at other times (Ventura et al., 1989, 1992) and may exert their effects over longer periods of time too. Furthermore, one of the primary manifestations of the stress response in humans is the release of cortisol (a glucocorticoid) from the adrenal cortex. Animal and human studies show that cortisol release triggers dopamine activity (McMurray et al., 1991; Rothschild et al., 1985). Glucocorticoid secretion also affects glutamate release (Walker & Diforio, 1997). In other words, two of the major neurotransmitters implicated in schizophrenia (dopamine and glutamate) are affected by cortisol, which is released when we are stressed.

Along these lines, Hooley and Gotlib (2000) have suggested that, to the extent that high-EE behaviors exhibited by family members are perceived as stressful by patients, these behaviors are likely to trigger the release of cortisol. In support of this idea, high-EE relatives have been found to be more behaviorally controlling of patients than low-EE relatives are (Hooley & Campbell, 2002). When they try to help, they seem to do so in rather intrusive ways (e.g., "She wouldn't go to sleep so I held her head down onto the pillow"). Furthermore, controlling behaviors such as these predict relapse in patients with schizophrenia. Quite possibly, relatives' well-meaning attempts to get patients to function better simply backfire. If patients are stressed by what their relatives do, this could increase cortisol levels, affect important neurotransmitter systems, and perhaps eventually lead to a return of symptoms.

At the present time, we have no direct evidence that this happens. However, one study is worthy of note. A group of researchers studied the behavior of patients with schizophrenia when they were involved in interactions with high-EE and low-EE relatives (Rosenfarb et al., 1995). The researchers observed that when patients said something strange (e.g., "If that kid bites you, you'll get rabies"), high-EE relatives tended to respond by being critical of the patient. What was interesting was that when this happened, it tended to be followed by another unusual remark from the patient. In other words, an increase in patients' unusual thinking occurred immediately after the patient was criticized by a family member. Although other interpretations of the findings are possible, the results of this study are consistent with the idea that negative (stress-inducing) behaviors by relatives can trigger increases in unusual thinking in patients with schizophrenia. Although we have no way of knowing what was happening to the cortisol levels of these patients, it is intriguing to speculate that increased cortisol release might somehow be involved.

Researchers are now using functional neuroimaging techniques (see Chapter 1) to learn more directly how EE affects the brain. Recent findings show that hearing criticism or being exposed to emotionally overinvolved comments leads to different patterns of brain activity in people who are vulnerable to psychopathology compared to healthy controls (Hooley et al., 2009; Hooley, Gruber, et al., 2010). We do not yet know if people who show this pattern of brain activation are at increased risk of relapse, although this might be expected.

Patients with schizophrenia who live in families where there is a high level of emotional tension have more than twice the risk of relapse.

Urban Living

Being raised in an urban environment seems to increase a person's risk of developing schizophrenia. Pederson and Mortensen (2001) studied a sample of 1.9 million people in Denmark, a country in which information about where people live is recorded in a national registry and people have to notify authorities when they change addresses in order to retain eligibility for benefits. The researchers found that children who had spent the first 15 years of their lives living in an urban environment were 2.75 times more likely to develop schizophrenia in adulthood than were children who had spent their childhoods in more rural settings. Other methodologically sound studies also confirm this association (Sundquist et al., 2004). It has been estimated that if this risk factor could be removed (that is, if we all lived in rela-

tively rural settings) the number of cases of schizophrenia could decrease by about 30 percent (see Brown, 2011).

Immigration

The findings showing that urban living raises a person's risk for developing schizophrenia suggest that stress or social adversity might be important factors to consider with respect to this disorder. Supporting this idea, research is also showing that recent immigrants have much higher risks of developing schizophrenia than do people who are native to the country of immigration. Looking at the results of 40 different studies involving immigrant groups from many different parts of the world, Cantor-Graae and Selten (2005) found that first-generation immigrants (i.e., those born in another country) had 2.7 times the risk of developing schizophrenia; for second-generation immigrants (i.e., those with one or both parents having been born abroad), the relative risk was even higher at 4.5. In other words, there is something about moving to another country that appears to be a risk factor for developing schizophrenia. The following case study illustrates this.

Schizophrenia in an Immigrant from China

After she lost her job, Lian, a young Chinese woman, was sent by her parents to live in Ireland. Upon arrival, Lian lived first in a boarding house. She then moved into a house that she shared with eight other young Chinese. Lian enrolled in a language school and also began to study for a degree in business administration. She made very few friends and spent most of her time on her own reading or playing games. The people who knew her described her as being a very private person who usually preferred to be alone.

Lian's difficulties began after she learned that two young Chinese students in Dublin had died under suspicious circumstances. She became exceedingly alarmed—so much so that she left the language school and moved back into the boarding house to be with her former landlady. She began to believe that her abdomen contained a "presence" that was living there. She also reported hearing multiple voices coming from the "presence." These voices, which spoke both Chinese and English, included the voices of teachers from Lian's language school, her landlady, and her family from China. Lian reported that she had received a banknote from her family and that the picture on the banknote had spoken to her saying, "You are no longer welcome here." Lian also developed a delusion that the family who had raised her were not her real family. She rapidly cut off all contact with them and talked about wanting to find her "real mother." Lian also said that the CIA was searching for her. When questioned about why this should be the case, she was unable to say. (Based on Feeney et al., 2002.)

Why should immigration be associated with an elevated risk of developing schizophrenia? One possibility is that immigrants are more likely to receive this diagnosis because of cultural misunderstandings (Sashidharan, 1993). However, there is no convincing evidence that this is the case (Harrison et al., 1999; Takei et al., 1998). Another hypothesis is that people who are genetically predisposed to develop schizophrenia are more likely to move to live in another country. However, some of the impairments associated with the early stages of schizophrenia seem incompatible with this idea because negative symptoms and frontal lobe dysfunctions may make it harder to be organized enough to emigrate (see Cantor-Graae & Selten, 2005).

Perhaps the strongest clue comes from the finding that immigrants with darker skin have a much higher risk of developing schizophrenia than do immigrants with lighter skin (Cantor-Graae & Selten, 2005). This raises the possibility that experiences of being discriminated against could lead some immigrants to develop a paranoid and suspicious outlook on the world, which could set the stage for the development of schizophrenia. In support of this idea, the results of a prospective study show that healthy people who felt discriminated against were more likely to develop psychotic symptoms over time than were healthy people who did not perceive any discrimination (Janssen et al., 2003). Another possibility suggested by animal studies is that the stress that results from social disadvantage and social defeat may have an effect on dopamine release or dopamine activity in key neural circuits (Tidey & Miczek, 1996). Moreover, some of these biological changes could make people more sensitive to the effects of using illicit substances (Miczek et al., 2004). This is especially interesting in light of evidence linking cannabis abuse to the development of schizophrenia.

Immigration has been found to be a risk factor for developing schizophrenia. People who leave their native land to live in another country have almost three times the risk of developing schizophrenia compared to people who remain living in their home country. What factors may contribute to this increased risk?

Cannabis Use and Abuse

People with schizophrenia are twice as likely as people in the general population to smoke cannabis (van Os et al., 2002). This has prompted researchers to ask whether there is a causal link between cannabis abuse and the development of psychosis. A methodologically rigorous study of conscripts to the Swedish army shows that, compared to those who had never used cannabis, young men who were heavy cannabis users by the time they were 18 were more than six times more likely to have developed schizophrenia 27 years later (Zammit et al., 2002). This association also remained even after people who had used other kinds of drugs were removed from the statistical analysis.

Other studies have now replicated this link and have highlighted early cannabis use as being particularly problematic (see van Winkel & Kuepper, 2014, for a review). For example, Arsenault and colleagues (2002) report that 10.3 percent of those who used cannabis by age 15 were diagnosed with signs of schizophrenia by age 26, compared with only 3 percent of the controls who did not use cannabis. Taken together, the research findings suggest that using cannabis during adolescence more than doubles a person's risk of developing schizophrenia at a later stage of life.

A major methodological concern in studies of this kind is whether people who are in the early stages of developing psychosis are more likely to use cannabis. If this were the case, cannabis use would simply be a correlate of schizophrenia and not a cause. However, even after childhood psychotic symptoms are considered and accounted for statistically, cannabis use has still been found to be a predictor of later schizophrenia (Fergusson et al., 2003). Moreover, a meta-analysis involving 8,167 patients with psychosis has shown that those who used cannabis (but not those who used alcohol) had an earlier onset of their symptoms compared to nonusers. These findings are consistent with the idea that cannabis use might trigger or bring forward the onset of psychosis (Large et al., 2011). This could be because one of the active ingredients of cannabis (called THC) increases dopamine in several areas of the brain (El Khoury et al., 2012). Cannabis also makes symptoms worse in patients who already have schizophrenia (D'Souza et al., 2005).

Of course, the vast majority of people who use cannabis do not develop schizophrenia. So can we predict who is at higher risk? Having a family history of schizophrenia may make people more sensitive to the psychosis-inducing effects of cannabis. And, in an early study, Caspi and colleagues (2005) reported that people carrying a particular form of the *COMT* gene (one or two copies of the valine or val allele) were at increased risk for developing psychotic symptoms (hallucinations or delusions) in adulthood if they used cannabis during adolescence. However, this link has proven difficult to replicate. Nonetheless, other gene–environment associations have been reported and a gene called *AKT1* is now a focus of interest (van Winkel & Kuepper, 2014). How everything fits together still remains to be discovered, however.

Finally, we note that there is some evidence that cannabis may actually accelerate the progressive brain changes that seem to go along with schizophrenia. Rais and colleagues (2008) collected brain scan data from 51 patients with recent-onset schizophrenia and 31 healthy controls. Nineteen of the patients were using cannabis (but not other illicit drugs) and 32 patients were not. When MRI scans were conducted again 5 years later, the patients who had continued to use cannabis during this time showed more marked decreases in brain volume relative to the patients who did not use cannabis. The changes in gray matter (brain cell) volume in the healthy controls, cannabis-using patients, and patients who did not use cannabis over the 5-year period are shown in Figure 13.10. Although both groups of patients lost more brain tissue over time than the healthy controls did, loss of brain tissue was especially pronounced in the patients who used cannabis. The conclusion is obvious. If you have schizophrenia, cannabis is probably very bad for your brain.

Figure 13.10 Brain Volume Changes over 5 Years in Patients with Schizophrenia and Healthy Comparison Subjects

Patients with schizophrenia who also use cannabis show more loss of gray matter over the course of a 5-year follow-up than patients who do not use cannabis or healthy controls.

(Adapted from *American Journal of Psychiatry*. Online by Rais. Copyright 2009 by American Psychiatric Association (Journals). Reproduced with permission of American Psychiatric Association (Journals) in the format Textbook via Copyright Clearance Center.)

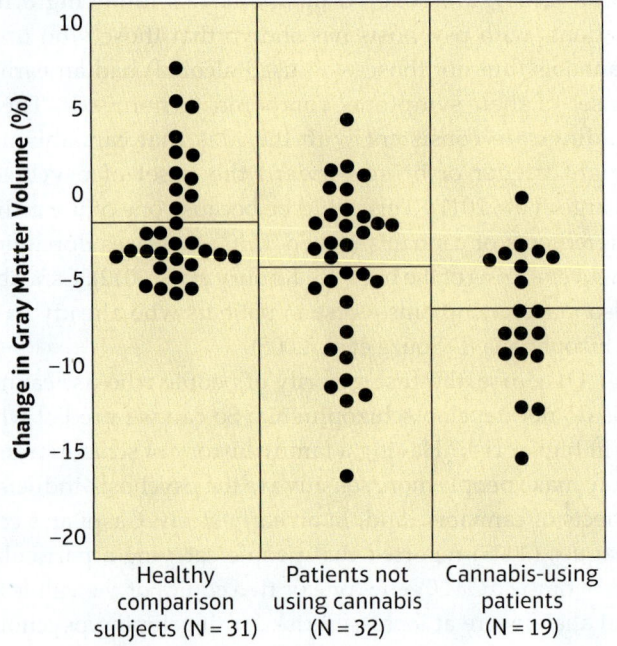

A Diathesis–Stress Model of Schizophrenia

Biological factors undoubtedly play a role in the etiology of schizophrenia. But genetic predispositions can be shaped by environmental factors such as prenatal exposures,

infections, and stressors that occur during critical periods of brain development (see Table 13.2 for a summary of nongenetic risk factors). Favorable environments may also reduce the chance that a genetic predisposition will result in schizophrenia. As we have discussed, children at genetic risk who are adopted into healthy family environments do very well (Tienari et al., 2004; Wahlberg et al., 1997). What you should take away from this chapter therefore is an understanding that schizophrenia is a genetically influenced, not a genetically determined, disorder (Gottesman, 2001).

Table 13.2 Nongenetic Risk Factors for Schizophrenia

Older father
Virus exposure
Obstetric complications
Urban upbringing
Head injury
Cannabis use
Migrant status

The diathesis–stress model, whose origins largely derive from schizophrenia research, predicts exactly these sorts of scenarios (e.g., Walker & Diforio, 1997; Zubin & Spring, 1977). Figure 13.11 provides a general summary of the interplay between genetic factors, prenatal events, brain maturational processes, and stress in the development of schizophrenia.

The bottom line is that there is no simple answer to the question of what causes schizophrenia. The etiology of this disorder (or group of related disorders) is complicated and complex. In the case of a person who develops schizophrenia, predisposing genetic factors must have combined in additive and interactive ways with multiple environmental risk factors, some known and some still unknown, that operate prenatally, perinatally, and also postnatally (see Gottesman, 2001; Walker & Tessner, 2008). The net result of this is that brain pathways develop abnormally. It is also very likely that these same pathways can be damaged in a host of different ways (in much the same way as a car engine can be damaged by lack of oil, lack of coolant, or from using the wrong kind of fuel). In other words, lots of roads may lead to the same end point, which is schizophrenia or a schizophrenia-like illness. This helps explain why past efforts to find the single cause of schizophrenia were doomed to fail, although no one could know this at the time. How we are born and how we live make major contributions. As one researcher has so aptly stated, "Schizophrenia may be the uniquely human price we pay as a species for the complexity of our brain; in the end, more or less by genetic and environmental chance, some of us get wired for psychosis" (Gilmore, 2010, p. 9).

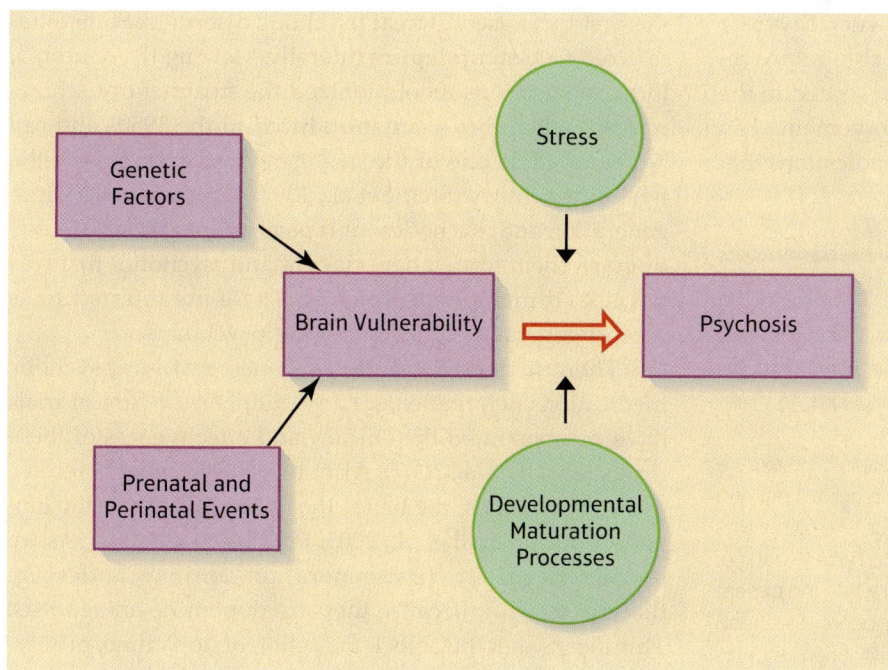

Figure 13.11 A Diathesis–Stress Model of Schizophrenia

Genetic factors and acquired constitutional factors (such as prenatal events and birth complications) combine to result in brain vulnerability. Normal maturational processes, combined with stress factors (family stress, cannabis use, urban living, immigration, etc.), may push the vulnerable person across the threshold and into schizophrenia.

in review

- What environmental factors are important in the development of schizophrenia?

- Why is avoiding cannabis so important for people with schizophrenia?

- Why do we believe that schizophrenia is both a developmental and a neuroprogressive disorder?

- Why is the diathesis–stress perspective so appropriate for understanding schizophrenia?

Treatments and Outcomes

13.7 Describe the clinical outcome of schizophrenia and how is it treated, noting the advantages and disadvantages associated with the use of antipsychotic medications.

Before the 1950s the prognosis for schizophrenia was bleak. Treatment options were very limited. Agitated patients might be put in straitjackets or treated with electroconvulsive "shock" therapy. Most lived in remote and forbidding institutions that they were expected never to leave (Deutsch, 1948).

Dramatic improvement came in the 1950s when a class of drugs known as antipsychotics was introduced. Pharmacotherapy (treatment by drugs) with these medications rapidly transformed the environment of mental hospitals by calming patients and virtually eliminating their wild, dangerous, and out-of-control behaviors. A new and more hopeful era had arrived.

Clinical Outcome

Studies of clinical outcome show that 15 to 25 years after developing schizophrenia, around 38 percent of patients have a generally favorable outcome and can be thought of as being recovered (Harrison et al., 2001). This does not mean that patients return to how they were before they became ill, however. Rather, it means that with the help of therapy and medications, patients can function quite well. For a minority of patients (around 12 percent), long-term institutionalization is necessary. And around a third of patients show continued signs of illness, usually with prominent negative symptoms.

When more stringent criteria are used to define recovery (i.e., remission of symptoms and good general social functioning with improvements in at least one of these areas lasting 2 years or more), rates of recovery are even more modest. Recent estimates suggest that they are around 14 percent (Jääskeläinen et al., 2013). What this means is that, despite many advances in treatment during the past 50 to 60 years, a "cure" for schizophrenia has not materialized.

Interestingly, patients who live in less industrialized countries tend to do better overall than patients who live in more industrialized nations (Jablensky et al., 1992). This may be because levels of EE are much lower in countries such as India than in the United States and Europe. For example, in highly industrialized cultures, more than 50 percent of families are high in EE. In contrast, studies with Mexican American and Hindi-speaking Indian samples show that only 24 and 41 percent of families, respectively, are high in EE (see Karno et al., 1987; Leff et al., 1987). These differences may help explain why the clinical outcome of patients is different in different parts of the world.

Sometimes, patients who have been very severely impaired by schizophrenia show considerable improvement late in the course of their illness. As illustrated in the case that follows, these spontaneous improvements can occur even when there is no change in the medications that patients are taking.

From Impairment to Improvement

The patient is a 46-year-old man who first became ill when he was 17 years old. At the time his illness began, he was hearing voices and he had grandiose delusions. He also had delusions of being persecuted.

By the time he was 30, he was living in the hospital. He experienced continuous symptoms including delusions, hallucinations, and incoherent speech. His self-care was also very poor. His symptoms showed only minimal improvement after he was treated with clozapine.

Spontaneous clinical improvement was noted when the patient was in his 40s. He became less isolated and he began to spend more time doing activities. Although he had previously been incoherent when he spoke, he began to speak rationally, although there was still some poverty in the content of his speech. His self-care also improved. However, hospital staff still needed to prompt him to bathe and change his clothes. (Adapted from Murray et al., 2004.)

MORTALITY The health risks of having schizophrenia cannot be understated. This is a disorder that reduces life expectancy. Recent data from the United Kingdom show that men with schizophrenia die 14.6 years earlier than would be expected based on national norms. For women with schizoaffective disorder the reduction in life span is 17.5 years (Chang et al., 2011). Some of the factors implicated in the early deaths of patients with schizophrenia and schizophrenia-related illnesses are long-term use of antipsychotic medications, obesity, smoking, poor diet, use of illicit drugs, and lack of physical activity. The risk of suicide in patients with schizophrenia is also high compared to the general population, with about 12 percent of patients ending their lives in this way (Dutta et al., 2010). In general, overall mortality is lower in patients who are treated with antipsychotic medications compared to untreated patients (Tiihonen et al., 2011). This no doubt reflects the extent to which people who are actively psychotic are a risk to themselves.

Pharmacological Approaches

Medications are widely used in the treatment of schizophrenia. Over 60 different antipsychotic drugs have been developed. The common property that they all share is their ability to block dopamine D2 receptors in the brain (Seeman, 2011).

FIRST-GENERATION ANTIPSYCHOTICS First-generation **antipsychotics** are medications like chlorpromazine (Thorazine) and haloperidol (Haldol), which were among the first to be used to treat psychotic disorders. Sometimes referred to as **neuroleptics** (literally, "seizing the neuron"), these medications revolutionized the treatment of schizophrenia when they were introduced in the 1950s and can be regarded as one of the major medical advances of the twentieth century (Sharif et al., 2007). They are called first-generation antipsychotics (or typical antipsychotics) to distinguish them from a new class of antipsychotics that was developed much more recently. These are referred to as second-generation (or atypical) antipsychotics.

There is overwhelming evidence that antipsychotic medications help patients. Large numbers of clinical trials have demonstrated the efficacy and effectiveness of these drugs (Sharif et al., 2007). Also, the earlier patients receive these medications, the better they tend to do over the longer term (Marshall et al., 2005; Perkins et al., 2004). As we discussed earlier, first-generation antipsychotics are thought to work because they are dopamine antagonists. This means that they block the action of dopamine, primarily by blocking (occupying) the D2 dopamine receptors.

Some clinical change can be seen within the first 24 hours of treatment (Kapur et al., 2005). This supports the idea that these medications work by interfering with dopamine transmission at the D2 receptors because dopamine blockade begins within hours after a patient is given the medication. However, it may take several weeks or even months for maximal clinical benefit to be achieved, although how a patient does on a particular medication in the first 2 to 4 weeks of treatment is a good predictor of how much he or she will benefit overall (Tandon et al., 2010).

First-generation antipsychotics work best for the positive symptoms of schizophrenia. In quieting the voices and diminishing delusional beliefs, these medications provide patients with significant clinical improvement (Tandon et al., 2010). This comes at a cost, however. Common side effects of these medications include drowsiness, dry mouth, and weight gain. Many patients on these antipsychotics also experience what are known as *extrapyramidal side effects* (EPS). These are involuntary movement abnormalities (muscle spasms, rigidity, shaking) that resemble Parkinson's disease.

African Americans and other ethnic minorities appear to be at increased risk of extrapyramidal side effects (Lawson, 2008). Such side effects are usually controlled by taking other medications. Some patients who have been treated with neuroleptics for long periods of time may also develop *tardive dyskinesia*. This involves marked involuntary movements of the lips and tongue (and sometimes the hands and neck). Rates of tardive dyskinesia are about 56 percent when patients have taken neuroleptics for 10 years or more, with females being especially susceptible (Bezchlibnyk-Butler & Jeffries, 2003). Finally, in very rare cases there is a toxic reaction to the medication that is called *neuroleptic malignant syndrome*

(Strawn et al., 2007). This condition is characterized by high fever and extreme muscle rigidity, and if left untreated it can be fatal.

SECOND-GENERATION ANTIPSYCHOTICS In the 1980s a new class of antipsychotic medications began to appear. The first of these to be used clinically was clozapine (Clozaril). This drug was introduced in the United States in 1989, although clinicians in Europe had been using it prior to this. Although initially reserved for use with treatment-refractory patients (those who were not helped by other medications), clozapine is now used widely.

Other examples of second-generation antipsychotic medications are risperidone (Risperdal), olanzapine (Zyprexa), quetiapine (Seroquel), and ziprasidone (Geodon). More recent additions include aripiprazole (Abilify) and lurasidone (Latuda). The reason why these medications are called "second-generation antipsychotics" is that they cause fewer extrapyramidal symptoms than the earlier antipsychotic medications such as Thorazine and Haldol. Although it was initially believed that second-generation antipsychotics were more effective at treating the symptoms of schizophrenia, recent research provides no support for this view (Lieberman & Stroup, 2011; Tandon et al., 2010). The exception here concerns clozapine, which does seem to be more valuable than other medications for treatment-refractory patients. Nonetheless, most patients are now treated with these newer (and more expensive) medications.

Although they are less likely to cause movement problems, the newer neuroleptic medications are not without other side effects. Drowsiness and considerable weight gain are very common. Diabetes is also a very serious concern (Sernyak et al., 2002). In rare cases, clozapine also causes a life-threatening drop in white blood cells known as agranulocytosis. For this reason, patients taking this medication must have regular blood tests.

The disappointing findings about the efficacy of second-generation antipsychotic treatments mean that there is an urgent need for innovative approaches and new medications that work better than the ones currently available. Antipsychotic medications work by blocking D2 receptors. But, as described earlier, researchers now believe that the most important dopamine abnormality in schizophrenia is occurring presynaptically. This means that current medications are working downstream from where the real problem may lie. Although antipsychotic medications do suppress dopamine neurotransmission overall (which is why they are helpful), future treatment developments that target the upstream abnormalities are clearly needed. This is all the more important in light of new research showing that current antipsychotic medications may actually contribute to the progressive brain tissue loss we see in schizophrenia (Ho et al., 2011). In the meantime, researchers continue to seek other ways to help patients.

OTHER APPROACHES At the beginning of the chapter, you learned that women with schizophrenia tend to do better than men. They have a later age of onset and, often, seem to have a less severe form of the illness. This has prompted some researchers to explore the potentially beneficial role of estrogen in the treatment of the disorder (Begemann et al., 2012).

In an interesting study, 102 young women with schizophrenia (all of whom were receiving antipsychotic medications) were randomly assigned to one of two conditions (Kulkarni et al., 2008). Some were given a transdermal (skin) patch containing estrogen; the others received a similar (placebo) patch that contained no active ingredient. The women's symptoms were assessed at baseline. They then wore the patches for a period of 28 days, receiving new patches twice a week. At the end of the study period, symptoms were reassessed.

What were the findings? Remarkably, the women who had worn the genuine (estrogen-containing) patches reported significantly fewer overall symptoms at the end of the 1-month study compared to the placebo group, with the difference for positive symptoms (shown in Figure 13.12) being most striking. Overall, the results suggest that estrogen has antipsychotic effects and that providing supplemental estrogen to women with schizophrenia may give them additional clinical benefits.

Figure 13.12 Estrogen Treatment and Positive Symptoms
Positive symptoms at baseline (day 0) and on days 7, 14, 21, and 28 for the estrogen and placebo groups.

(Figure 3 from Kulkarni et al. (2008). *Archives of General Psychiatry, 65*(8), 958 (Copyright © 2008). American Medical Association. Reprinted with permission.)

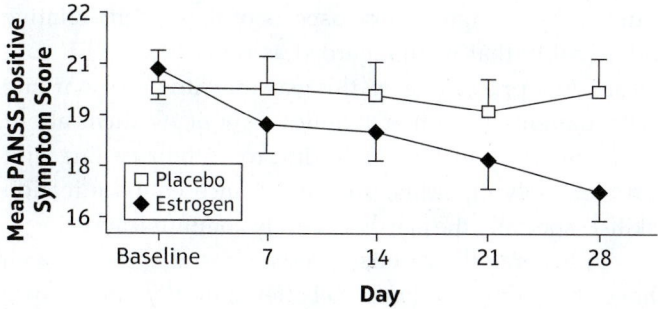

THE PATIENT'S PERSPECTIVE Not all patients benefit from antipsychotic medications, and many who do show clinical improvement will still have problems functioning without a great deal of additional help. We must also not lose sight of what it is like for patients with schizophrenia to have to take medications every day, often for years or for a lifetime. Side effects that can sound trivial to someone on the outside can be so bad for patients that they refuse to take their medications, even when those medications give them relief from their hallucinations and delusions.

Research using PET also shows that increased blockade of D2 dopamine receptors is associated with patients reporting more negative subjective experiences such as feeling tired and depressed even when other side effects (such as movement problems) are absent (Mizrahi et al., 2007). This highlights the need for better medications and for using lower dosages wherever this is clinically feasible. We also need to remember that some patients may try to avoid taking medications because, to them, needing to take medications confirms that they are mentally ill. The following comes from the mother of a daughter who suffers from schizophrenia:

> As a parent I also know that medication is not perfect and that the side effects can be distressing. When my daughter goes back on her medication, I feel bad seeing her shuffling or experiencing involuntary arm and mouth movements. These symptoms usually subside over time; but she also gains weight, and she hates being heavy. I think she hates taking medication most of all because she is, in a sense, admitting she is mentally ill, something she very much wants to deny. (From Slater, 1986.)

Psychosocial Approaches

Medications play a central role in the treatment of schizophrenia. But they are not the only treatment approaches that are available. Psychosocial treatments are also of value. Some of these approaches, which are typically used in conjunction with medication, are briefly described below.

FAMILY THERAPY The literature that links relapse in patients with schizophrenia to high family levels of EE inspired several investigators to develop family intervention programs. The idea was to reduce relapse in schizophrenia by changing those aspects of the patient–relative relationship that were regarded as central to the EE construct. At a practical level, this generally involves working with patients and their families to educate them about schizophrenia, to help them improve their coping and problem-solving skills, and to enhance communication skills, especially the clarity of family communication.

In general, the results of research studies in this area have shown that patients do better clinically and relapse rates are lower when families receive family treatment (see Pfammatter et al., 2006). Studies done in China indicate that these treatment approaches can also be used in other cultures (Xiong et al., 1994). Despite this, family treatment is still not a routine element in the accepted standard of care for patients with schizophrenia (Lehman et al., 1998). Given its clear benefits to patients and its considerable cost effectiveness (Tarrier et al. [1991] calculated that family treatment results in an average cost savings of 27 percent per patient), this seems very unfortunate. This is even more so in light of new evidence showing that extended periods of relapse predict increased loss of brain tissue over time

(Andreasen et al., 2013). Preventing relapse is therefore of paramount importance.

CASE MANAGEMENT Case managers are people who help patients find the services they need in order to function in the community. Essentially, the case manager acts as a broker, referring the patient to the people who will provide the needed service (e.g., help with housing, treatment, employment, and the like). Assertive community treatment programs are a specialized and more intensive form of case management. Typically, they involve multidisciplinary teams with limited caseloads to ensure that discharged patients don't get overlooked and "lost in the system." The multidisciplinary team delivers all the services the patient needs (see DeLuca et al., 2008; Mueser et al., 2013).

Assertive community treatment programs are cost effective because they reduce the time that patients spend in the hospital. They also enhance the stability of patients' housing arrangements. These approaches seem to be especially beneficial for patients who are already high utilizers of psychiatric and community services (see Bustillo et al., 2001).

SOCIAL-SKILLS TRAINING Even when their symptoms are controlled by medications, patients with schizophrenia often have trouble forming friendships, finding and keeping a job, or living independently. How well patients do in their everyday lives is referred to as *functional outcome*. (This is in contrast to *clinical outcome*, which is concerned with symptoms.) Improving the functional outcomes of patients with schizophrenia is now an active area of research.

One way to help improve the functional outcomes of patients with schizophrenia is through social-skills training. Patients with schizophrenia often have very poor interpersonal skills (for a review, see Hooley, 2015). Social-skills training is designed to help patients acquire the skills they need to function better on a day-to-day basis. These skills include employment skills, relationship skills, self-care skills, and skills in managing medications or symptoms. Social routines are broken down into smaller, more manageable components. For conversational skills, these components might include learning to make eye contact, speaking at a normal and moderate volume, taking one's turn in a conversation, and so on. Patients learn these skills, get corrective feedback, practice their new skills using role-playing, and then use what they have learned in natural settings (Bellack & Mueser, 1993). As Green (2001, p. 139) has noted, engaging in social-skills training is a bit like taking dance lessons. It does not resemble traditional "talk therapy" in any obvious manner.

Although the results of some early studies were mixed, the most recent research findings look more positive. Social-skills training does seem to help patients acquire new skills, be more assertive, and improve their overall levels of social functioning. These improvements also seem to be maintained over time. Importantly, patients who receive social-skills training are less likely to relapse and need hospital treatment (Kurtz & Mueser, 2008; Pfammatter et al., 2006).

An even newer treatment approach is social cognitive skills training. This is designed to improve the deficits in social cognition we described earlier. For example, patients might be trained to recognize emotion in faces or to better recognize hints. The early findings suggest that these interventions do provide benefits to patients and help them function better in the community. However, positive and negative symptoms show little change (Kurtz & Richardson, 2012).

COGNITIVE REMEDIATION Earlier we described some of the cognitive problems that go along with having schizophrenia. Researchers are now recognizing that these cognitive problems are likely to place limits on how well patients can function in the community. Because of this, the neurocognitive deficits of schizophrenia are becoming targets for treatment in their own right. The search is on to develop new medications that will enhance cognitive functioning in patients (Green, 2007; Nuechterlein et al., 2008).

A major treatment effort is also being devoted to **cognitive remediation** training. Using practice and other compensatory techniques, researchers are trying to help patients improve some of their neurocognitive deficits (e.g., problems with verbal memory, vigilance, and performance on card-sorting tasks). The hope is that these improvements will translate into better overall functioning (e.g., conversational skills, self-care, and job skills). Overall, the findings give cause for optimism. Cognitive remediation training does seem to help patients improve their attention, memory, and executive functioning skills. Patients who receive cognitive remediation training also show improvements in their social functioning. Especially encouraging is that even when patients have been ill for many years, they still seem to benefit from this treatment approach (Pfammatter et al., 2006; Wykes et al., 2007). Cognitive remediation approaches may work best when they

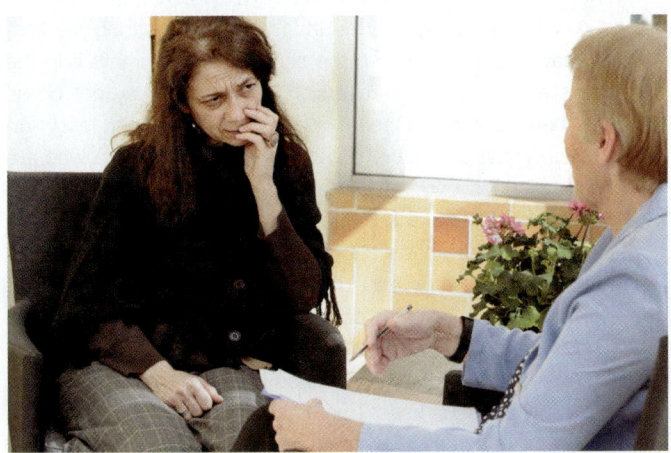

Patients with schizophrenia benefit from psychosocial treatments. These include individual therapy, case management, cognitive remediation, and family therapy.

are added to other existing rehabilitation (employment skills) strategies and offered to patients who are already clinically stable (Wykes et al., 2011).

COGNITIVE-BEHAVIOR THERAPY As you have already learned, cognitive-behavior therapy (CBT) approaches are widely used in the treatment of mood and anxiety disorders as well as many other conditions (Beck, 2005). Until fairly recently, however, researchers did not consider using them for patients with schizophrenia, no doubt because patients with schizophrenia were considered too impaired. Pioneered by researchers and clinicians in the United Kingdom, cognitive-behavior approaches have gained momentum in the treatment of schizophrenia. The goal of these treatments is to decrease the intensity of positive symptoms, reduce relapse, and decrease social disability. Working together, therapist and patient explore the subjective nature of the patient's delusions and hallucinations, examine evidence for and against their veracity or veridicality, and subject delusional beliefs to reality testing.

Although the results from the early research studies were encouraging, whether CBT is an effective treatment for schizophrenia is now the subject of some debate. Current data suggest that CBT is not very helpful for negative symptoms (Tandon et al., 2010). A recent meta-analysis also suggests that CBT is no better than control interventions (often supportive counseling) in the treatment of schizophrenia (Lynch et al., 2010). Nonetheless, the possibility that CBT works very well for some subgroups of patients is still a very real possibility.

INDIVIDUAL TREATMENT Before 1960 the optimal treatment for patients with schizophrenia was psychoanalytically oriented therapy based on a Freudian type of approach. This is what Nobel Prize–winning mathematician John Nash (who died in a car crash in 2015) received when he was a patient at McLean Hospital in Massachusetts in 1958 (the movie *A Beautiful Mind*, is based on Nash's story). By 1980, however, things had changed. Research began to suggest that in some cases, psychodynamic treatments made patients worse (see Mueser & Berenbaum, 1990). This form of individual treatment thus fell out of favor.

Individual treatment for schizophrenia now takes a different form. Hogarty and colleagues (1997a, 1997b) have reported on a controlled 3-year trial of what they call "personal therapy." Personal therapy is a nonpsychodynamic approach that equips patients with a broad range of coping techniques and skills. The therapy is staged, which means that it comprises different components that are administered at different points in the patient's recovery. For example, in the early stages, patients examine the relationship between their symptoms and their stress levels. They also learn relaxation and some cognitive techniques. Later, the focus is on social and vocational skills. Overall, this treatment appears to be very effective in enhancing the social adjustment and social role performance of discharged patients.

Educating patients about the illness and its treatment (this approach is called psychoeducation) is also helpful (Xia et al., 2011). Patients who receive psychoeducation in addition to standard treatment are less likely to relapse or be readmitted to the hospital compared to patients who receive standard treatment only. These patients also function better overall and are more satisfied with the treatment they receive. All of this highlights the importance of including patients in their own care and increasing their knowledge and understanding about their illness.

In summary, although rigorous psychoanalytic approaches may be too demanding and stressful for patients with schizophrenia, supportive forms of therapy that offer an opportunity to learn skills and yet are low key and responsive to patients' individual concerns might well be very beneficial. Just as progress in research on schizophrenia requires a partnership between scientists across many areas, progress in the treatment of schizophrenia requires balancing pharmacology with a consideration of the specific needs of the patient. For patients who are at high risk of relapse and who live with their families, family-based interventions

will be required. If patients have continuing and disturbing hallucinations and delusions, CBT may be appropriate. When patients are clinically stable, social-skills or social-cognitive training and rehabilitation efforts may be helpful. But in all of this, we must not lose sight of the need of patients (and their families) for support, validation, and respectful care. The treatment of patients with schizophrenia is not easy, and there is no "quick fix." Although many treatment advances have occurred, we still need more effective, high-quality, and clinically sensitive care.

in review

- What kinds of clinical outcomes are associated with schizophrenia? Is full recovery possible or typical?

- Why do patients with schizophrenia have increased rates of early mortality?

- In what ways are first- and second-generation (conventional and atypical) neuroleptic medications similar, and in what ways are they different? How effective are these treatments for patients with schizophrenia?

- Describe the major psychosocial approaches used in treating schizophrenia.

Unresolved Issues

Why Are Recovery Rates in Schizophrenia Not Improving?

After the introduction of the first neuroleptic medication (Thorazine) in 1955, there was great optimism that this, and other new "wonder drugs," would revolutionize the treatment of schizophrenia. Today, many decades later, clinicians have a broad array of first- and second-generation antipsychotic medications at their disposal. But if our treatment options are so much more sophisticated, why are recovery rates in schizophrenia so low?

The standard length of a clinical trial that compares a given drug against a placebo is 6 weeks. Numerous clinical studies have demonstrated that antipsychotic medications are effective for the treatment of acute symptoms. So there is little doubt that antipsychotic medications benefit patients in the short term. But what about the longer term? Does staying on antipsychotic medications provide long-term benefits for patients?

The answer may be no. Concerns are now being raised that long-term exposure to neuroleptics may set into play biological process that increase the likelihood that patients will remain chronically ill (Whitaker, 2010). This is particularly worrisome because patients who take neuroleptic medications tend to stay on them for very long periods of time.

But how could something that is clinically beneficial in the short term be potentially harmful in the longer term? Standard antipsychotic medications block D2 receptors in the brain. This is the basis of their therapeutic action. But one result of dopamine blockade is that the density of receptors on the postsynaptic neuron increases, creating a supersensitivity to dopamine. Put more simply, neuroleptics put a brake on dopamine transmission. To compensate for this, the brain responds by pressing the dopamine accelerator (in the form of extra dopamine receptors). Withdrawal of neuroleptics removes the brake and puts the system out of balance because the system is now in an "accelerator-on" mode. Moreover, any return of symptoms is taken as evidence that the drugs were working and preventing relapse. This impression gets confirmed when the patient goes back on drugs again and the psychosis abates. As one physician noted, "The use of neuroleptics is a trap. . . . It is like having a psychosis-inducing agent built into the brain." (Whitaker, 2010, pp. 107).

As you might expect, the idea that antipsychotic medications may help psychosis in the short term but create it in the longer term is highly controversial. However, it may not be as far fetched as it might seem. Data from a 20-year follow-up study show that over time, patients with schizophrenia who are not taking antipsychotic medications fare far better than those who continue to take medications (Harrow et al., 2012). Of the patients who took antipsychotic medications continuously during the follow-up study period, only 17 percent had a period of recovery at some point. In contrast, 87 percent of the patients who had gone off antipsychotic medications before the 2-year follow-up assessment were rated as being recovered at two or more or the follow-up assessments. Differences in recovery rates between the medicated and unmedicated groups began to be apparent at the 4.5-year follow-up. At that assessment, and also at all subsequent follow-up visits, the unmedicated patients were doing better.

Can we attribute the poor clinical outcomes of the medicated patients to the continued use of antipsychotics? Harrow and colleagues (2012) suggest not. Rather, they suggest that the difference between the medicated and unmedicated groups exists because the patients who go off antipsychotics have other resources and strengths that eventually lead them to have a better long-term prognosis. So the patients with the most favorable clinical outcomes stop taking medications and the patients with the least favorable clinical outcomes keep taking medications. This may be so. But it is interesting that many of the patients who stopped taking their medications did so against professional advice. So, if these patients were somehow more resilient and destined to do better, their psychiatrists apparently did not recognize it.

It is also the case that patients who stop taking medications tend not to see their psychiatrists. So clinicians don't see people who recover. This may be one reason why psychiatry as a whole has been slow to recognize that nonmedicated patients might be doing far better than expected. Also relevant here is the observation that patients in less industrialized countries tend to do better clinically than those in more developed countries. And these are the very patients who are much less likely to be maintained on antipsychotic medications.

Perhaps most provocative are the following statistics about chronic mental illness. In 1955 one in every 617 Americans was hospitalized with schizophrenia in a state or county mental hospital. These were chronic long-term patients. Today, the proportion of people with chronic schizophrenia or some other psychotic disorder is much higher—1 in every 125 people. In his efforts to understand why psychiatric medications have not improved the long-term clinical outcomes for patients with severe mental illness, Whitaker (who is an investigative reporter) has caused a storm of controversy. Nonetheless, his arguments warrant serious consideration by all mental health professionals. If the medications that are so helpful in a crisis make things worse when used long term, we need to radically rethink how we manage the treatment of patients with schizophrenia. Based on the findings of Harrow et al. (2012), perhaps the most powerful conclusion that can be drawn at this stage is that not all patients with schizophrenia need to be treated long term with medications. When patients are motivated to try a period without antipsychotics, medical professionals might do well to support this decision.

Summary

13.1 Describe the prevalence of schizophrenia and who is most affected.

Schizophrenia affects just under 1 percent of the population. Most cases begin in late adolescence or early adulthood. The disorder begins earlier in men than in women. Overall, the clinical symptoms of schizophrenia tend to be more severe in men than in women. Women also have a better long-term outcome.

13.2 Identify the symptoms of schizophrenia as described in *DSM-5*.

Schizophrenia is the most severe form of mental illness. It is characterized by impairments in many domains. Characteristic symptoms of schizophrenia include hallucinations, delusions, disorganized speech, disorganized and catatonic behavior, and negative symptoms such as flat affect or social withdrawal.

13.3 List four different types of psychotic disorders and state one way in which each is different from schizophrenia.

- Other types of psychotic disorders are schizoaffective disorder, schizophreniform disorder, delusional disorder, and brief psychotic disorder.
- Schizoaffective disorder is a mix of symptoms of schizophrenia *and* mood disorder symptoms.

- In schizophreniform disorder, the clinical picture is like that of schizophrenia apart from the fact that the symptoms have not lasted long enough (6 months) to qualify for a diagnosis of schizophrenia.
- In delusional disorder, delusions are present but the person may otherwise behave quite normally. In other words, there is no sign of the gross disorganization and performance deficiencies that are associated with schizophrenia.
- Finally, brief psychotic disorder is very short lived. It involves the sudden onset of psychotic symptoms, disorganized speech, or catatonic behavior. Although the person may be quite impaired, the duration of this impairment is very brief (and too short to allow for a diagnosis of schizophreniform disorder). The person typically returns to his or her former level of functioning within a few days.

13.4 Explain the genetic and biological risk and causal factors associated with schizophrenia.

- Genetic factors are clearly implicated in schizophrenia. Many genes, each having a small effect are likely involved, as well as some rare alleles. Having a relative with the disorder significantly raises a person's risk of developing schizophrenia.
- Other factors that have been implicated in the development of schizophrenia include prenatal exposure to

viruses, rhesus incompatibility, pregnancy and birth complications, early nutritional deficiencies, maternal stress, maternal inflammation, and head injury.

13.5   Discuss how the brain is affected in schizophrenia.

- Patients with schizophrenia have problems in many aspects of their cognitive functioning. They show a variety of attentional deficits (e.g., poor P50 suppression and deficits on the Continuous Performance Test). They also show eye-tracking dysfunctions.

- Even though schizophrenia first shows itself clinically in early adulthood, researchers believe that it is a neurodevelopmental disorder. Problems with brain development are implicated. Some of the genes implicated in schizophrenia play a role in brain development.

- Many brain areas are abnormal in schizophrenia, although abnormalities are not found in all patients. The brain abnormalities that have been found include enlarged ventricles (which reflects decreased brain volume), frontal lobe dysfunction, reduced volume of the thalamus, and abnormalities in temporal lobe areas such as the hippocampus and amygdala.

- Major changes in the brain occur during adolescence. These include synaptic pruning, decreases in the number of excitatory neurons, and increases in the number of inhibitory neurons. There is also an increase in white matter, which enhances the connectivity of the brain. Some of these changes may be abnormal in people who will later develop schizophrenia.

- The most important neurotransmitters implicated in schizophrenia are dopamine and glutamate. Research shows that the people with schizophrenia may be producing and releasing too much dopamine into the synapse.

- Some of the brain abnormalities that are characteristic of schizophrenia get worse over time. This suggests that, in addition to being a neurodevelopmental disorder, schizophrenia is also a neuroprogressive disorder. Antipsychotic medications explain some (but not all) of the brain tissue loss.

13.6   Explain the psychosocial and cultural factors associated with schizophrenia.

- Urban living, immigration, and cannabis use during adolescence have also been shown to increase the risk of developing schizophrenia.

- Current thinking about schizophrenia emphasizes the interplay between genetic and environmental factors.

13.7   Describe the clinical outcome of schizophrenia and how is it treated, noting the advantages and disadvantages associated with the use of antipsychotic medications.

- For many patients, schizophrenia is a chronic disorder requiring long-term treatment or institutionalization. However, when treated with therapy and medications, around 38 percent of patients can show a reasonable recovery. Only about 14 percent of patients recover to the extent that they have minimal symptoms and function well socially.

- Patients with schizophrenia are more likely to relapse if their relatives are high in expressed emotion (EE). High-EE environments may be stressful to patients and may trigger biological changes that cause dysregulations in the dopamine system. This could lead to a return of symptoms.

- Treatment often involves first- or second-generation antipsychotic (neuroleptic) medications. Second-generation antipsychotics are about as effective as first-generation antipsychotics but cause fewer extrapyramidal (motor abnormality) side effects. Antipsychotic drugs work by blocking dopamine receptors. Some evidence suggest antipsychotic medications may be linked to brain tissue loss.

- Psychosocial treatments for patients with schizophrenia include social-skills training, social-cognitive training, cognitive remediation training, cognitive-behavior therapy, and other forms of individual treatment, as well as case management. Family therapy provides families with communication skills and other skills that are helpful in managing the illness. Family therapy also reduces high levels of expressed emotion.

Key Terms

alogia, p. 466
antipsychotics (neuroleptics), p. 496
attenuated psychosis
    syndrome, p. 480
avolition, p. 466
blunted affect, p. 466
brief psychotic disorder, p. 468
candidate genes, p. 474
catatonic schizophrenia, p. 467
cognitive remediation, p. 499

delusion, p. 462
delusional disorder, p. 468
disorganized schizophrenia, p. 467
dopamine, p. 488
endophenotypes, p. 475
expressed emotion (EE), p. 491
flat affect, p. 466
genome-wide association
    study (GWAS), p. 474
glutamate, p. 489

hallucination, p. 464
negative symptoms, p. 466
paranoid schizophrenia, p. 467
positive symptoms, p. 466
prodromal, p. 480
psychosis, p. 460
schizoaffective disorder, p. 467
schizophrenia, p. 460
schizophreniform disorder, p. 467

Chapter 14
Neurocognitive Disorders

⌄ Learning Objectives

14.1 Describe the impairments that are associated with neurocognitive disorders and explain the presumed cause of these disorders.

14.2 Summarize the key clinical features of delirium and describe how it is treated.

14.3 Describe two permanent and three reversible causes of neurocognitive disorders.

14.4 Explain the risk factors for Alzheimer's disease and describe the changes in the brain that are found in patients with this disease.

14.5 Explain how HIV infection and vascular events can cause neurocognitive problems.

14.6 Summarize how profound impairments in memory can be caused.

14.7 Describe some of the clinical consequences of head trauma and explain the factors that are related to the degree of impairment that results.

A Simple Case of Mania?

A highly successful businessman, age 45, with no previous history of psychiatric disorder, began to act differently from his usual self. He seemed driven at work. His working hours gradually increased until finally he was sleeping only 2 to 3 hours a night; the rest of the time he worked. He became irritable and began to engage in uncharacteristic sprees of spending beyond his means.

Although he felt extremely productive and claimed he was doing the work of five men, the man's boss felt otherwise. He was worried about the quality of that work, having observed several recent examples of poor business decisions. Finally, when the man complained of headaches, his boss insisted that he seek help. (Adapted from Jamieson & Wells, 1979.)

The case you have just read concerns a man who, on first glance, looks as if he might be having an episode of mania. In fact, he is suffering from four tumorous masses in his brain. Clues that this man has a brain disorder rather than a mood disorder include the facts that he is experiencing headaches at the same time as a major change in behavior and that he has no prior history of psychopathology (see Taylor, 2000). Clinicians always need to be alert to the possibility that brain impairment itself may be directly responsible for their patients' symptoms. Failure to do so could result in serious diagnostic errors, as when a clinician falsely attributes a mood change to psychological causes and fails to consider a neuropsychological origin such as a brain tumor.

The brain is an astonishing organ. Weighing around 3 pounds and having the consistency of firm jelly, it is the most complex structure in the known universe (Thompson, 2000). It is also the only organ capable of studying and reading about itself. It is involved in every aspect of our lives from eating and sleeping to falling in love. The brain makes decisions, and it contains all the memories that make us who we are. Whether we are physically ill or mentally disturbed, the brain is involved.

Because it is so important, the brain is protected in an enclosed space and covered by a thick outer membrane called the dura mater (literally, "hard mother" in Latin). For further protection, the brain is encased by the skull. The skull is so strong that, if it were placed on the ground and weight were applied very slowly, it could support as much as 3 tons (Rolak, 2001, p. 403)! These anatomical facts alone indicate just how precious the brain is.

Even though it is highly protected, the brain is vulnerable to damage from many sources. When the brain is damaged, cognitive changes result, as you saw in the case study above. Although there may be other signs and symptoms (such as mood or personality changes) as well, changes in cognitive functioning are the most obvious signs of a damaged brain.

In this chapter we focus on disorders that arise because of changes in brain structure, function, or chemistry. In some cases, such as with Parkinson's disease or Alzheimer's disease, these are caused by internal changes that lead to destruction of brain tissue. In others, they result from damage caused by external influences such as trauma from accidents or from the repeated blows to the head that can occur in boxing, soccer, or football.

Why are neurocognitive disorders discussed at all in a text on abnormal psychology? There are several reasons. First, as their inclusion in the *DSM* indicates, these disorders are regarded as psychopathological conditions. Second, as you just saw in the **case study**, some brain disorders cause symptoms that look remarkably like other abnormal psychology disorders. Third, brain damage can cause changes in behavior, mood, and personality. Understanding what brain areas are involved when behavior, mood, and personality change after brain damage may help researchers better understand the biological underpinnings of many problems in abnormal psychology. Fourth, many people who suffer from brain disorders (e.g., people who are diagnosed as having Alzheimer's disease) react to the news of their diagnosis with depression or anxiety. Prospective studies also suggest that depressive symptoms may herald the onset of disorders such as Alzheimer's disease by several years and that episodes of depression can double the risk for Alzheimer's disease even 20 years later (Speck et al., 1995). Finally, neurocognitive disorders of the type we describe in this chapter take a heavy toll on family members, who, for many patients, must shoulder the burden of care. Again, depression and anxiety in relatives of the patients themselves are not uncommon.

Research Close-Up
Case Study

A case study is a description of one specific case. Case studies can be a useful source of information and can help researchers generate hypotheses. Because of their highly selective nature, however, they cannot be used to draw any scientific conclusions.

Brain Impairment in Adults

14.1 Describe the impairments associated with neurocognitive disorders and explain the presumed cause of these disorders.

The causes of neurocognitive disorders are often much more specific than is the case for many of the disorders we have discussed elsewhere in this text. In *DSM-5*, the disorders that used to be known as "Delirium, Dementia, and Amnestic and Other Cognitive Disorders" are now grouped into a new diagnostic category called "Neurocognitive Disorders." This term is more straightforward than

DSM-5 Thinking Critically about *DSM-5*

Is the Inclusion of Mild Neurocognitive Disorder a Good Idea?

An important addition to *DSM-5* is the new diagnosis of mild neurocognitive disorder. This change reflects an effort to recognize that cognitive problems that do not reach the level of affecting everyday functioning may still warrant clinical attention. But this new diagnostic category is not without controversy.

Some people are concerned that the use of the word *mild* trivializes the cognitive impairments that are being experienced. It may also imply that there is no need for services to be provided. On the other hand, refraining from using a term like **dementia** until the cognitive impairment is more severe may alleviate anxiety and reduce stigma.

But if minor cognitive disorder is considered to be a prodromal stage before the onset of more severe impairment, will receiving the more mild diagnosis still not be a source of anxiety? People experiencing minor cognitive impairment (MCI is a descriptive term and not a *DSM-5* diagnosis) are thought to be at increased risk for the development of Alzheimer's disease. If these people can now be formally diagnosed with a disorder (unlike MCI, mild neurocognitive disorder is now an official diagnosis) will we be alarming large numbers of people needlessly? Many people with MCI do not go on to develop more severe cognitive problems. We also have no way to treat Alzheimer's disease successfully, yet alone prevent it. So, from a practical perspective, how helpful will this new diagnosis be to those who will receive it?

Finally, how do we separate mild neurocognitive disorder from normal aging? This is all the more important because many examples of mild cognitive problems (e.g., finding that thinking is easier when not distracted by phone, TV, or other conversations or needing occasional reminders to keep track of characters in a movie or a novel) are problems that are hardly unusual for older adults. Every time we lose our keys or forget whether or not we have paid a bill should we now be worried that we have mild neurocognitive disorder?

---

its predecessor. It is also more conceptually coherent. Disorders in this category are those that involve a loss of previously attained cognitive ability and where the presumed cause is brain damage or disease. Subsections of this diagnostic category include **delirium**, **major neurocognitive disorder** (which includes the former diagnosis of dementia), and a new category of **mild neurocognitive disorder**. The distinction between major and mild neurocognitive disorder is based on severity. As the Thinking Critically about *DSM-5* box illustrates, the inclusion of a mild neurocognitive disorder in *DSM-5* raises some important issues.

Within each broad diagnostic category, the specific diagnosis is determined by what is thought to be the cause of the problem. For example, the diagnosis of major neurocognitive disorder associated with Alzheimer's disease is used for patients thought to have Alzheimer's. For patients whose brain damage is caused by a traumatic brain injury the diagnosis would be major (or mild) neurocognitive disorder associated with traumatic brain injury. In this way the diagnosis provides information about both the cause of the neurocognitive disorder as well as its degree of severity.

Clinical Signs of Brain Damage

With a few exceptions, cell bodies and neural pathways in the brain do not appear to have the power of regeneration, which means that their destruction is permanent. When brain injury occurs in an older child or adult, there is a loss in established functioning. Often, the person who has sustained this loss is painfully aware of what he or she is no longer able to do, adding a pronounced psychological burden to the physical burden of having the lesion. In other cases the impairment may extend to the loss of capacity for realistic self-appraisal (a condition called anosognosia), leaving these patients relatively unaware of their losses and hence poorly motivated for rehabilitation.

The degree of mental impairment is usually related to the degree of damage to the brain. However, this is not invariably so. Much depends on the nature and location of the damage as well as the premorbid (predisorder) competence and personality of the individual. In some cases involving relatively severe brain damage, mental change is astonishingly slight. In other cases of seemingly mild and limited damage, there may be quite marked alterations in functioning, as in the following case example.

Memory Impairment Following a Car Accident

A 68-year-old African American woman who worked as a certified nursing assistant was brought to the emergency department after being involved in a car accident. She had been a passenger in the backseat when her vehicle hit another car. As a result of the impact, she was thrown forward. She hit her head, knee, and hands on the seat in front of her. Immediately after this, she began to feel light-headed.

When she arrived at the hospital, the patient was conscious and fully oriented. She knew where she was, what day it was, and who various people were. Her memory for past events was also normal. However, it soon became apparent that she was experiencing anterograde amnesia and was not able to recall simple things that she had just been told. People who knew her said she was not acting like her usual self. Her problems got worse whenever she experienced any physical exertion.

Because of her injuries, the patient was admitted to the hospital for the next 2 days. After leaving the hospital, she continued to report headaches and dizziness. Cognitive tests conducted a month later revealed she was still experiencing memory problems although her reasoning abilities were good, her affect was appropriate, and her speech was goal directed. She also had a good recall of general information. However, in addition to her memory problems, the patient complained of difficulties concentrating or comprehending what she had read or been told. She was diagnosed with mild traumatic brain injury. (From Krishna et al., 2012.)

Diffuse Versus Focal Damage

The disorders discussed in this section are characterized by neurocognitive problems, although psychopathological problems (such as psychosis or mood change) may also be associated with them. Some of these disorders are generally well understood, with symptoms that have relatively constant features in people whose brain injuries are comparable in location and extent. For example, attention is often impaired by mild to moderate *diffuse*—or widespread—damage, such as might occur with moderate oxygen deprivation or the ingestion of toxic substances such as mercury. Such a person may complain of memory problems due to an inability to sustain focused retrieval efforts, while his or her ability to store new information remains intact.

In an illustration of this, LoSasso, Rapport, and Axelrod (2001, 2002) found that nail salon technicians reported significantly more cognitive and neurological impairments than controls did. The nail salon technicians also performed more poorly than the controls on tests of attention and information processing. This is likely due to routine exposure to (meth) acrylates and a variety of organic solvents such as toluene, acetone, and formaldehyde that are known to be potentially damaging to the central nervous system. Such findings highlight the consequences of even low-level exposure to neurotoxic substances that can be found in places where many people work and where many others routinely visit.

The brain can be damaged by exposure to solvents. Nail salons frequently use a variety of organic solvents that are known to be potentially damaging to the central nervous system.

In contrast to diffuse damage, *focal* brain lesions involve circumscribed areas of abnormal change in brain structure. This is the kind of damage that might occur with a sharply defined traumatic injury or an interruption of blood supply (a stroke) to a specific part of the brain. Figure 14.1 explains how a stroke occurs.

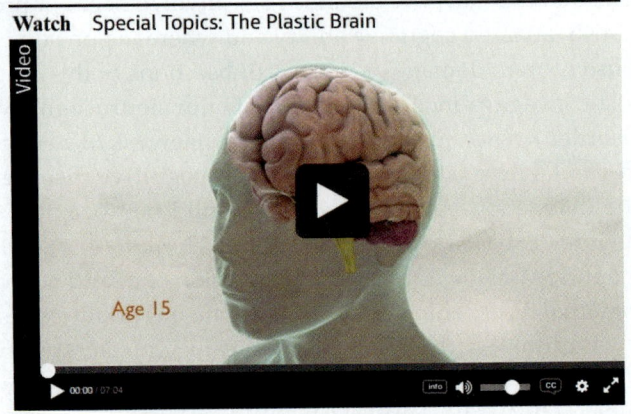

Watch Special Topics: The Plastic Brain

Age 15

Figure 14.1 How a Stroke Occurs

Most strokes occur when an artery in the brain is blocked by a clot. The others, about 13 percent of strokes, occur when a brain artery bursts. Both types can be disastrous.

(Adapted from Dr. Steven Warach, National Institute of Neurological Disorders and Stroke; American Heart Association.)

HEMORRHAGIC STROKE

1. An artery in the brain bursts and either floods the surrounding tissue with blood or floods the surface and grooves of the brain.

2. The blood irritates brain cells, disrupting their functions and causing the brain to swell with fluid.

3. If the swelling continues, the brain is stopped by the skull and squeezed through the opening in the bottom of the skull, crushing the centers for consciousness and breathing.

BURST ARTERY
Area filled by blood
BRAIN
BLOOD SUPPLY
Area deprived of blood
BLOCKAGE

ISCHEMIC STROKE

1. A blood clot forms and is swept into the brain where it blocks an artery. Clots usually form in the heart or in arteries of the neck that are damaged by atherosclerotic plaque.

2. The brain tries to protect itself by raising blood pressure, trying to clear the artery. Meanwhile, the brain cells, deprived of blood, shut down.

3. If the problem persists, brain cells swell and die.

Figure 14.2 Brain Structures and Associated Behaviors

Corpus callosum
Communication between the brain's right and left hemispheres

Motor strip
Regulation of voluntary movement

Sensory strip
Integration of sensory information from various parts of the body

Limbic system
Attention, emotions, "fight or flight," memory

Parietal lobe
Somaesthetic and motor discriminations and functions

Frontal lobe
Learning, abstracting, reasoning, inhibiting

Thalamus
Major relay station for messages from all parts of the body, important in sensations of pain

Hypothalamus
Regulation of metabolism, temperature, emotions

Occipital lobe
Visual discrimination and some aspects of visual memory

Temporal lobe
Discrimination of sounds, verbal and speech behavior

Cerebellum
Fine motor coordination, posture, and balance

Reticular formation
Arousal reactions, information screening

Medulla
Breathing, blood pressure, other vital functions

The location and extent of the damage determine what problems the patient will have. As you are aware, the brain is highly specialized. Although the two hemispheres are closely interrelated, they are involved in somewhat different types of mental processing. At the risk of oversimplifying, it is generally accepted that functions that are dependent on serial processing of familiar information, such as language and solving mathematical equations, take place mostly in the left hemisphere for nearly everyone. Conversely, the right hemisphere appears to be generally specialized for grasping overall meanings in novel situations; reasoning on a nonverbal, intuitive level; and appreciating spatial relations. Even within hemispheres, the various lobes and regions mediate specialized functions (see Figure 14.2).

Although none of these relationships between brain location and behavior can be considered universally true, it is possible to make broad generalizations about the likely effects of damage to particular parts of the brain. Damage to the frontal areas, for example, is associated with one of two contrasting clinical pictures: (1) being unmotivated and passive and with limited thoughts and ideas or (2) featuring impulsiveness and distractibility. Damage to specific areas of the right parietal lobe may produce impairment of visual-motor coordination, and damage to the left parietal area may impair certain aspects of language function, including reading and writing, as well as arithmetical abilities. Damage to certain structures within the temporal lobes disrupts an early stage of memory storage. Extensive bilateral temporal damage can produce a syndrome in which remote memory remains relatively intact but nothing new can be stored for later retrieval. Damage to other structures within the temporal lobes is associated with disturbances of eating, sexuality, and emotion. Occipital damage produces a variety of visual impairments and visual association

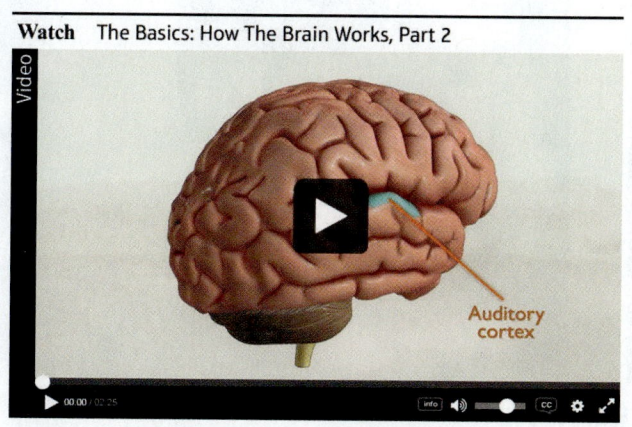

Watch The Basics: How The Brain Works, Part 2

Video

Auditory cortex

deficits, the nature of the deficit depending on the particular site of the lesion. For example, a person may be unable to recognize familiar faces. Unfortunately, many types of brain disease are general and therefore diffuse in their destructive effects, causing multiple and widespread interruptions of the brain's circuitry. Some consequences of brain disorders are described in Table 14.1.

Table 14.1 Impairments Associated with Brain Disorders

The following types of difficulties are often the consequences of brain disease, disorder, or damage.

1. *Impairment of memory.* The individual has trouble remembering recent events, although memory for past events may remain more intact. Some patients with memory problems may confabulate—that is, invent memories to fill in gaps. In severe instances, no new experience can be retained for more than a few minutes.

2. *Impairment of orientation.* The individual may not know where he or she is, what the day is, or who familiar people are.

3. *Impairment of learning, comprehension, and judgment.* The individual's thinking becomes clouded, sluggish, or inaccurate. The person may lose the ability to plan with foresight or to understand abstract concepts and hence to process complex information (described as "thought impoverishment").

4. *Impairment of emotional control or modulation.* The individual is emotionally overreactive: laughing, crying, or flying into a rage with little provocation.

5. *Apathy or emotional blunting.* The individual is emotionally underreactive and seems indifferent to people or events.

6. *Impairment in the initiation of behavior.* The individual lacks self-starting capability and may have to be reminded repeatedly about what to do next, even when the behavior involved remains well within the person's range of competence. This is sometimes referred to as "loss of executive function."

7. *Impairment of controls over matters of propriety and ethical conduct.* The individual may manifest a marked lowering of personal standards in areas such as appearance, personal hygiene, sexuality, or language.

8. *Impairment of receptive and expressive communication.* The individual may be unable to comprehend written or spoken language or may be unable to express his or her own thoughts orally or in writing.

9. *Impaired visuospatial ability.* The individual has difficulty coordinating motor activity with the characteristics of the visual environment, a deficit that affects graphomotor (handwriting and drawing) and constructional (e.g., assembling things) performance.

The Neurocognitive/Psychopathology Interaction

Most people who have a neurocognitive disorder do not develop psychopathological symptoms such as panic attacks, dissociative episodes, or delusions. However, many show at least mild deficits in cognitive processing and self-regulation. Similarly, some people who suffer from psychopathological disorders also have cognitive deficits. For example, patients with bipolar disorder have persistent cognitive deficits that can be detected even during periods of illness remission (Bora et al., 2011). This highlights the close link between psychopathological and neuropsychological conditions.

The psychopathological symptoms that do sometimes accompany brain impairment are not always predictable and can reflect individual nuances consistent with the patient's age (see Tateno et al., 2002), her or his prior personality, and the total psychological situation confronting the patient. We should also never just assume that a psychological disorder—for example, a serious depression that follows a brain injury—is always attributable to the patient's brain damage. Certainly that could be the case. However, it is also possible that the depression might be better explained by the patient's awareness of dramatically lessened competence and the loss of previous skills. After a traumatic brain injury caused by an accident or a fall, for example, around 18 percent of patients make a suicide attempt (Simpson & Tate, 2002). People who have survived a stroke are also more likely to attempt suicide, with the risk being greatest in the 2 years after the stroke (Eriksson et al., 2015).

People with more favorable life situations tend to fare better after brain injury than people whose lives are more disorganized or disadvantaged (Yeates et al., 1997). Intelligent, well-educated, mentally active people have enhanced

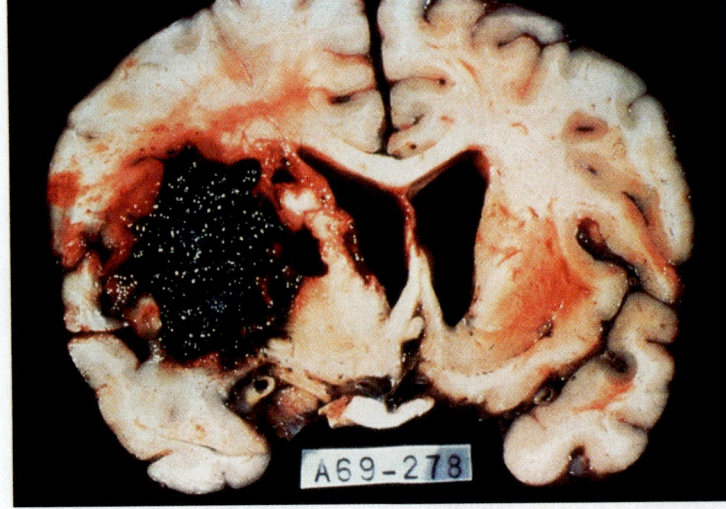 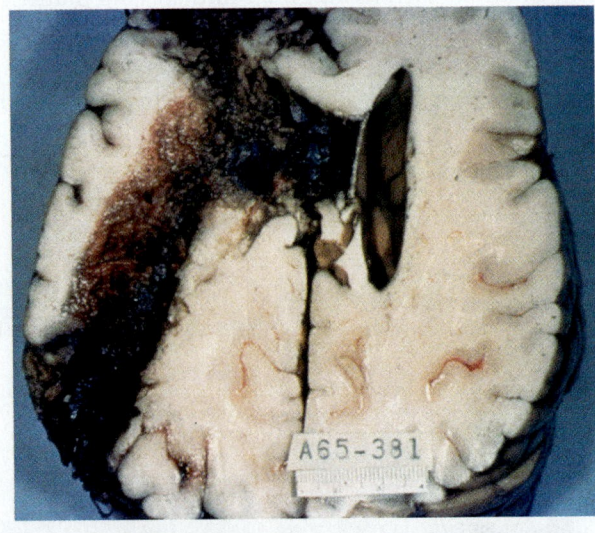

Cross sections of damaged brains. The brain on the left shows damage from a stroke. Damage from a bullet is shown on the right.

resistance to mental and behavioral deterioration following significant brain injury (e.g., see Mori et al., 1997a; Schmand et al., 1997). Because the brain is the organ responsible for the integration of behavior, however, there are limits to the amount of brain damage that anyone can tolerate or compensate for without exhibiting abnormal behavior.

in review

- Describe some of the major ways in which the brain can become damaged.
- What kinds of clinical symptoms are often associated with damage to the frontal, parietal, temporal, and occipital lobes of the brain?
- List nine impairments that are typical of focal and diffuse brain damage.

Delirium

14.2 **Summarize the key clinical features of delirium and describe how it is treated.**

Delirium is a state of acute brain failure that lies between normal wakefulness and stupor or coma (see Figure 14.3). The word comes from the Latin *delirare*, meaning "to be out of one's furrow or track."

Clinical Picture

A commonly occurring syndrome, delirium is characterized by confusion, disturbed concentration, and cognitive dysfunction (see the *DSM-5* box for diagnostic criteria). Although the *DSM-IV-TR* criteria stated that delirium involved a disturbance in consciousness, the word *consciousness* was removed in *DSM-5*. This is because the essence of delirium is better captured by the idea of a disturbance in awareness. Think of delirium as a condition with a sudden onset that involves a fluctuating state of reduced awareness. Delirium is treated as a distinct disorder in *DSM-5* (rather than as a type of major or mild neurocognitive disorder) because it can quickly fluctuate in severity. It can also coexist with a major or mild neurocognitive disorder (such as Alzheimer's disease). It therefore does not fit well with being categorized as a major or mild form of neurocognitive disorder.

In addition to a disturbance in level of awareness, delirium also involves impairments of memory and attention as well as disorganized thinking. Hallucinations and delusions are quite common (see Trzepacz et al., 2002). In addition, the syndrome often includes abnormal psychomotor activity such as wild thrashing about and disturbance of the sleep cycle. A person who is delirious is essentially unable to carry out purposeful mental activity of any kind. The intensity of the symptoms also fluctuates over the course of a 24-hour period, as described in the following case study.

Delirium Following a Routine Operation

Mrs. Patterson was 75 years old when she was admitted to the hospital. A widow who lived alone, she had broken her leg, and she needed a routine operation. The operation was successful. However, shortly afterward, Mrs. Patterson began to show signs of confusion. She had problems with awareness and attention, and she had no idea of what had happened to her or why she was in the hospital. During the day, she seemed agitated and aimlessly wandered around. She was unable to focus enough to watch television or to read. She was also unable to recognize friends and relatives who came to visit her. On several occasions, nursing staff saw her staring at an imaginary spot on the ceiling of her room and having conversations with imaginary people. Mrs. Patterson refused to take any medications. She would knock her meals onto the floor when they were brought to her. Between these outbursts, Mrs. Patterson was able to calm down, sleeping for short periods of about 30 minutes at a time. However, at night, she could hardly sleep at all. Instead, she wandered around the hospital ward. She went into the rooms of other patients, waking them up, and sometimes even trying to get into their beds. On a number of occasions, she was found in her nightdress, trying to leave the hospital. However, the staff always stopped her and carefully escorted her back to her room. (Based on Üstün et al., 1996.)

Delirium can occur in a person of any age. However, the elderly are at particularly high risk, perhaps because of brain changes caused by normal aging that lead to reduced "brain reserve." As described in the case of Mrs. Patterson, delirium is very common in the elderly after they have had surgery,

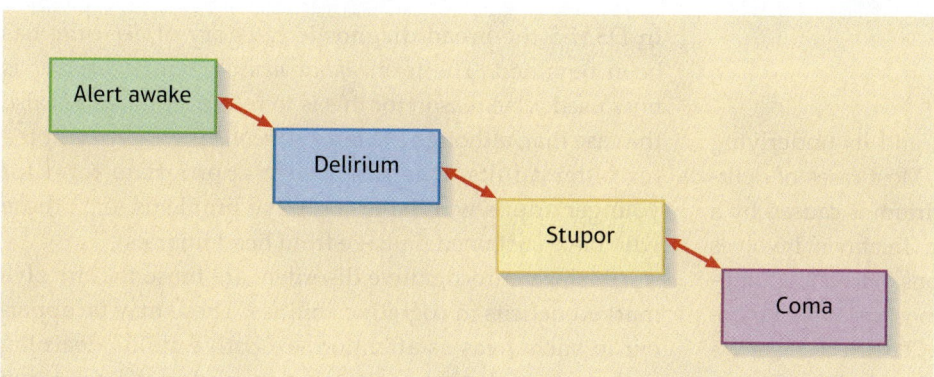

Figure 14.3 Continuum of Level of Awareness

(*American Psychiatric Publishing Textbook of Neuropsychiatry and Behavioral Neurosciences*, Fifth Edition (Copyright © 2008). American Psychiatric Publishing.)

DSM-5 *Criteria for. . .*

Delirium

A. A disturbance in attention (i.e., reduced ability to direct, focus, sustain, and shift attention) and awareness (reduced orientation to the environment).

B. The disturbance develops over a short period of time (usually hours to a few days), represents a change from baseline attention and awareness, and tends to fluctuate in severity during the course of a day.

C. An additional disturbance in cognition (e.g., memory deficit, disorientation, language, visuospatial ability, or perception).

D. The disturbances in Criteria A and C are not better explained by another preexisting, established, or evolving neurocognitive disorder and do not occur in the context of a severely reduced level of arousal, such as coma.

E. There is evidence from the history, physical examination, or laboratory findings that the disturbance is a direct physiological consequence of another medical condition, substance intoxication or withdrawal (i.e., due to a drug of abuse or to a medication), or exposure to a toxin, or is due to multiple etiologies.

Source: Reprinted with permission from the *Diagnostic and Statistical Manual of Mental Disorders*, Fifth Edition (Copyright 2013). American Psychiatric Association.

with patients over age 80 being particularly at risk (Trzepacz et al., 2002). At the other end of the age spectrum, children are also at high risk of delirium, perhaps because their brains are not yet fully developed. In addition to advanced age, other risk factors for delirium include dementia, depression, and tobacco use (Fricchione et al., 2008). A reliable and easy screening test for delirium involves asking the patient to recite the months of the year backwards (O'Regan et al., 2014). Give it a try. If you can go from December to July without error, the chances are high you do not have delirium!

Estimates of the prevalence of delirium vary widely with the age of the population studied. However, somewhere between 10 and 51 percent of patients who have had surgery will experience delirium; patients who have had cardiac surgery seem to be at especially high risk. The presence of delirium is also a bad prognostic sign. Delirium is correlated with cognitive decline, longer hospital stays, more health problems, and increased mortality; 25 percent of elderly patients with delirium die within the following 6 months (Fricchione et al., 2008; Witlox et al., 2010).

Delirium may result from several conditions including head injury and infection. However, the most common cause of delirium is drug intoxication or withdrawal. Toxicity from medications also causes many cases of delirium. This may explain why delirium is so common in the elderly after they have had surgery.

Treatments and Outcomes

Delirium is a true medical emergency, and its underlying cause must be identified and managed. Most cases of delirium are reversible, except when the delirium is caused by a terminal illness or by severe brain trauma. Treatment involves medication, environmental manipulations, and family support. The medications that are used for most cases are neuroleptics (Fricchione et al., 2008; Lee et al., 2004). These are the same drugs that are used to treat schizophrenia. For delirium caused by alcohol or drug withdrawal, benzodiazepines (such as those used in the treatment of anxiety disorders) are used (Trzepacz et al., 2002). In addition, environmental manipulations that help patients stay oriented, such as good lighting, clear signage, and easily visible calendars and clocks, can be helpful. It is also important that staff members introduce themselves when they work with patients, explain what their role is, and provide reorienting prompts whenever necessary. Some patients, however, especially elderly ones, may still have orientation problems, sleep problems, and other difficulties even months after an episode of delirium.

in review

- What clinical features characterize the syndrome of delirium?
- Describe some common causes of delirium. Who is most at risk of developing this clinical condition?
- How is delirium treated?

Major Neurocognitive Disorder

14.3 Describe two permanent and three reversible causes of neurocognitive disorders.

In *DSM-5* the broad diagnostic category of *dementia* has been renamed. The term *major neurocognitive disorder* is now used. One reason for this is to reduce stigma. It is also the case that, although the term *dementia* is widely accepted for older adults, it is not a very appropriate term for younger adults who have cognitive problems (e.g., those who have sustained damage from head injuries).

Major neurocognitive disorders are those that involve marked deficits in cognitive abilities. These may be apparent in such areas as attention, executive ability, learning and memory, language, perception, and social cognition

DSM-5 *Criteria for. . .*

Major Neurocognitive Disorder

A. Evidence of significant cognitive decline from a previous level of performance in one or more cognitive domains (complex attention, executive function, learning and memory, language, perceptual-motor, or social cognition) based on:

1. Concern of the individual, a knowledgeable informant, or the clinician that there has been a significant decline in cognitive function; and

2. Substantial impairment in cognitive performance, preferably documented by standardized neuropsychological testing or, in its absence, another quantified clinical assessment.

B. The cognitive deficits interfere with independence in everyday activities (i.e., at a minimum, requiring assistance with complex instrumental activities of daily living such as paying bills or managing medications).

C. The cognitive deficits do not occur exclusively in the context of a delirium.

D. The cognitive deficits are not better explained by another mental disorder (e.g., major depressive disorder, schizophrenia).

Source: Reprinted with permission from the *Diagnostic and Statistical Manual of Mental Disorders*, Fifth Edition (Copyright 2013). American Psychiatric Association.

(skills required for understanding, interpreting, and responding to the behavior of others). What is crucial is that there is a decline from a previously attained level of functioning (see the *DSM-5* table for diagnostic criteria for major neurocognitive disorder).

In older people the onset of cognitive deficits is typically quite gradual. Early on, the individual is alert and fairly well attuned to events in the environment. Even in the early stages, however, memory is affected, especially memory for recent events. As time goes on, patients show increasingly marked deficits in abstract thinking, the acquisition of new knowledge or skills, visuospatial comprehension, motor control, problem solving, and judgment. These are often accompanied by impairments in emotional control and in moral and ethical sensibilities; for example, the person may engage in crude solicitations for sex. Deficits may be progressive (getting worse over time) or static, but are more often the former. Occasionally a major neurocognitive disorder is reversible if it has an underlying cause that can be removed or treated (such as a vitamin deficiency). Some treatable causes of major neurocognitive disorder are listed in Table 14.2.

At least 50 different disorders are known to cause the types of cognitive deficits that are now included in the category of major neurocognitive disorders (Bondi & Lange, 2001). They include degenerative diseases such as Parkinson's disease and Huntington's disease (which are described below). Other causes are strokes (see Ivan et al., 2004); certain infectious diseases such as syphilis, meningitis, and AIDS; intracranial tumors and abscesses; certain dietary deficiencies (especially of the

Table 14.2 Some Treatable Causes of Major Neurocognitive Disorder

Medications
Clinical depression
Vitamin B_{12} deficiency
Chronic alcoholism
Certain tumors or infections of the brain
Blood clots pressing on the brain
Metabolic imbalances (including thyroid, kidney, or liver disorders)

B vitamins); severe or repeated head injury; anoxia (oxygen deprivation); and the ingestion or inhalation of toxic substances such as lead or mercury. As Figure 14.4 illustrates, the most common cause of major neurocognitive disorder is degenerative brain disease, particularly Alzheimer's disease. In this chapter we focus primarily on this greatly feared disorder. We also briefly discuss neurocognitive disorders that result from HIV infection, stroke (vascular dementia), chronic substance abuse, and traumatic brain injury.

Figure 14.4 Causes of Major Neurocognitive Disorder

Causes are presented according to the percentage of all cases they account for.

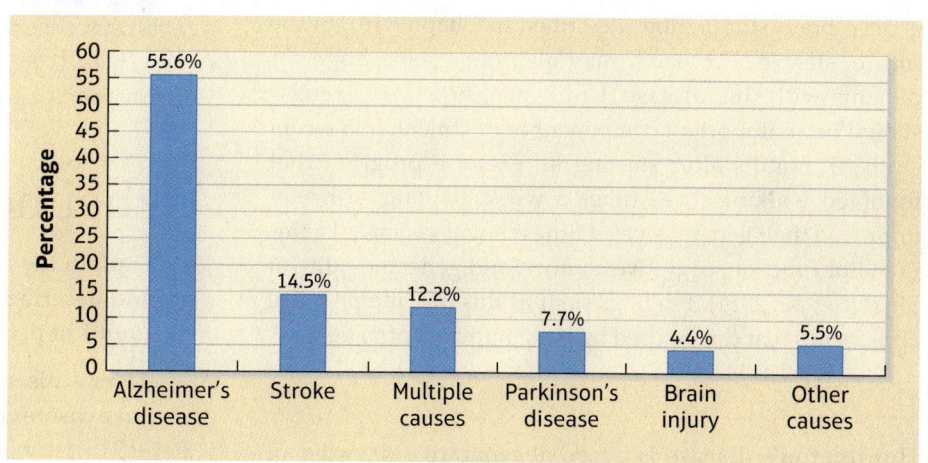

Parkinson's Disease

Named after James Parkinson, who first described it in 1817, **Parkinson's disease** is the second most common neurodegenerative disorder (after Alzheimer's disease). It is more often found in men than in women, and it affects between 0.5 and 1 percent of people between ages 65 and 69 and 1 to 3 percent of people over age 80 (Toulouse & Sullivan, 2008). However, the actor Michael J. Fox developed Parkinson's disease when he was only 30 years old. His book *Lucky Man* (2002) offers a moving personal account of his struggle with the illness and well describes some of its major symptoms.

Parkinson's disease is characterized by motor symptoms such as resting tremors or rigid movements. The underlying cause of this is loss of dopamine neurons in an area of the brain called the substantia nigra. Dopamine is a neurotransmitter that is involved in the control of movement. When dopamine neurons are lost, a person is unable to move in a controlled and fluid manner. In addition to motor symptoms, Parkinson's disease can involve psychological symptoms such as depression, anxiety, apathy, cognitive problems, and even hallucinations and delusions (Chaudhuri et al., 2011). Later on in the illness, cognitive deficits may also become apparent. Over time, 25 to 40 percent of patients with Parkinson's disease will show signs of cognitive impairment (Marsh & Margolis, 2009). The causes of Parkinson's disease are not clear, although both genetic and environmental factors are suspected. Genetic factors may be more important in cases where the Parkinson's disease develops earlier in life, and environmental factors may be more relevant in later onset cases (Wirdefeldt et al., 2011). Interestingly, smoking and drinking coffee may provide some protection against the development of Parkinson's disease, although the reasons for this remain unclear (Toulouse & Sullivan, 2008; Wirdefeldt et al., 2011).

The symptoms of Parkinson's disease can be temporarily reduced by medications, such as pramipexole (Mirapex) or levodopa/carbidopa (Sinemet), that increase the availability of dopamine in the brain either directly or indirectly. However, once the medications wear off, the symptoms return. Another treatment approach that is now being tried is deep brain stimulation (described in Chapter 16). In the future, stem cell research may also offer some hope for patients with this disease. Until then, however, exercise should be an important component of treatment. In a recent study, 6 months after starting an exercise program that involved walking three times a week, patients not only improved their general level of fitness but also showed gains in motor function, cognitive abilities, and general quality of life (Uc et al., 2014). Findings such as this provide practical approaches that can be used by large numbers of patients.

Huntington's Disease

Huntington's disease is a rare degenerative disorder of the central nervous system that afflicts about 1 in every 10,000 people (Phillips et al., 2008). It was first described in 1872 by the American neurologist George Huntington. The illness begins in midlife (the mean age of onset is around 40 years), and it affects men and women in equal numbers. Huntington's disease is characterized by a chronic, progressive chorea (involuntary and irregular movements that flow randomly from one area of the body to another). However, subtle cognitive problems often predate the onset of motor symptoms by many years. These cognitive problems are no doubt due to the progressive loss of brain tissue (detectable with brain imaging) that occurs as much as a decade before the formal onset of the illness (Shoulson & Young, 2011). Patients eventually develop dementia, and death usually occurs within 10 to 20 years of first developing the illness. There are currently no effective treatments that can restore functioning or slow down the course of this terrible and relentless disorder. American folk singer Woody Guthrie, whose song "This Land Is Your Land" is well known, died of the disease in 1967 when he was 55 years of age.

Huntington's disease is caused by a single dominant gene (the *Huntingtin* gene) on chromosome 4. (This is not a typo. The name of the gene is not the same as the name of the disease.) This genetic mutation was discovered as a result of intense research on people living in villages around Lake Maracaibo in Venezuela, where this disease is extremely common (Marsh & Margolis, 2009). Because the Huntingtin gene is a dominant gene, anyone who has a parent with the disease has a 50 percent chance of developing the disease himself or herself. A genetic test can be given to at-risk individuals to determine whether they will eventually develop the disorder. However, in the United States, only about 10 percent of people who are eligible for testing choose to know what their genetic destiny is (Shoulson & Young, 2011). If you were in this situation, what would you do? One interesting finding here is that the majority of people who have asked to be tested are women (Hayden, 2000).

in review

- What are the key clinical features of Parkinson's disease and what causes the problems associated with this disease?
- What gene is responsible for Huntington's disease? Is this a dominant or a recessive gene?

Alzheimer's Disease

14.4 Explain the risk factors for Alzheimer's disease and describe the changes in the brain that are found in patients with this disease.

Alzheimer's disease is a progressive and fatal neurodegenerative disorder. It takes its name from Alois Alzheimer (1864–1915), the German neuropathologist who first described it in 1907. It is the most common cause of dementia

(Jalbert et al., 2008). In the *DSM-5* it is officially called "major (or mild) neurocognitive disorder associated with Alzheimer's disease." Alzheimer's disease is associated with a characteristic dementia syndrome (see the case study below) that has an imperceptible onset and a usually slow but progressively deteriorating course, terminating in delirium and death.

The Forgetful Mail Carrier

At the age of 60, Harold took early retirement from his government job because, for the previous 5 years, he had been having difficulty performing his work properly. A mail carrier, he was constantly making errors and delivering mail to the wrong places. He also began to become more withdrawn, gradually giving up hobbies that had been important to him. At first, his increasing forgetfulness was not very noticeable when he was at home. Then, one day when he was 62, Harold was hiking in an area he knew well and was unable to find his way home. Since that time, his memory problems have grown increasingly worse. He loses things, forgets appointments, and can no longer find his way around his hometown. Now, at the age of 66, Harold no longer recognizes his close friends and is uninterested in reading or watching television. Things are so bad that his wife is afraid to leave him alone in the house because he is so forgetful. (Based on Üstün et al., 1996.)

Clinical Picture

The diagnosis of Alzheimer's disease is made after a thorough clinical assessment of the patient. However, the diagnosis can only be truly confirmed after the patient's death. This is because an autopsy must be performed to see the brain abnormalities that are such distinctive signs of this disease. In the living patient, the diagnosis is normally given only after all other potential causes of dementia are ruled out by medical and family history, physical examination, and laboratory tests.

Alzheimer's disease usually begins after about age 45 (Malaspina et al., 2002). Contrary to what many people believe, it is characterized by multiple cognitive deficits, not just problems with memory. There is a gradual declining course that involves slow mental deterioration. Figure 14.5 shows the performance of two men on a battery of cognitive tests repeated over a period of several years. Both men were of similar age and level of education, and both were initially free of Alzheimer's disease. However, for the man who subsequently developed Alzheimer's disease (confirmed on autopsy), a progressive, downward course in his cognitive performance is apparent (see Storandt, 2008).

In its earliest stages, Alzheimer's disease involves minor cognitive impairment. For example, the person may have difficulty recalling recent events, make more errors at work, or take longer to complete routine tasks. In the later stages, there is evidence of dementia; deficits become more severe, cover multiple domains, and result

Figure 14.5 Test Performance in a Healthy Man and a Man Who Developed Alzheimer's Disease

(Adapted from Figure 1 on page 198 from Martha Storandt. (2008). Cognitive deficits in the early stages of Alzheimer's disease. *Current Directions in Psychological Science, 17*(3), 198–202 (Copyright © 2008). Association for Psychological Science. Reproduced with permission of Blackwell Publishing Ltd.)

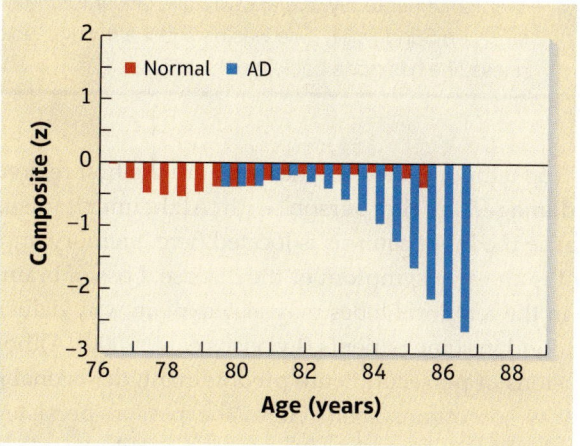

in an inability to function. For example, the person may be easily disoriented, have poor judgment, and neglect his or her personal hygiene. Because they have impaired memory for recent events, many patients have "empty" speech in which grammar and syntax remain intact, but vague and seemingly pointless expressions replace meaningful conversational exchange (e.g., "It's a nice day, but it might rain"). The case study below, which involves a man who had retired some 7 years prior to his hospitalization, is typical.

Restless and Wandering

During the past 5 years, the patient had shown a progressive loss of interest in his surroundings and during the last year had become increasingly "childish." His wife and eldest son had brought him to the hospital because they felt they could no longer care for him in their home, particularly because of the grandchildren. They stated that he had become careless in his eating and other personal habits and was restless and prone to wandering about at night. He could not seem to remember anything that had happened during the day but was garrulous concerning events of his childhood and middle years.

After admission to the hospital, the patient seemed to deteriorate rapidly. He could rarely remember what had happened a few minutes before, although his memory for remote events of his childhood remained good. When visited by his wife and children, he mistook them for old friends, and he could not recall anything about the visit a few minutes after they had departed. The following brief conversation with the patient, which took place after he had been in the hospital for 9 months (and about 3 months before his death), shows his disorientation for time and person.

DOCTOR: How are you today, Mr. _____?

PATIENT: Oh . . . hello [looks at doctor in rather puzzled way as if trying to make out who he is].

DOCTOR: Do you know where you are now?

PATIENT: Why yes . . . I am at home. I must paint the house this summer. It has needed painting for a long time but it seems like I just keep putting it off.

DOCTOR: Can you tell me the day today?

PATIENT: Isn't today Sunday . . . why, yes, the children are coming over for dinner today. We always have dinner for the whole family on Sunday. My wife was here just a minute ago but I guess she has gone back into the kitchen.

The temporal lobes of the brain are the first regions to be damaged in the person with Alzheimer's disease. Because the hippocampus is located here, memory impairment is an early symptom of the disease. Loss of brain tissue in the temporal lobes may also explain why delusions are found in some patients (Lyketsos et al., 2000). Although delusions of persecution are predominant, delusional jealousy is sometimes seen. Here, the person persistently accuses his or her partner or spouse—who is often of advanced age and physically debilitated—of being sexually unfaithful. Family members may be accused of poisoning the patient's food or of plotting to steal the patient's funds. One study of physically aggressive patients with Alzheimer's disease found that 80 percent of them were delusional (Gilley et al., 1997).

With appropriate treatment, which may include medication and the maintenance of a calm, reassuring, and unprovocative social environment, many people with Alzheimer's disease show some alleviation of symptoms. In general, however, deterioration continues its downward course over a period of months or years. Eventually, patients become oblivious to their surroundings, bedridden, and reduced to a vegetative state. Resistance to disease is lowered, and death usually results from pneumonia or some other respiratory or cardiac problem. The median time to death is 5.7 years from the time of first clinical contact (Jalbert et al., 2008).

Prevalence

Alzheimer's disease is becoming a major public health problem, straining societal and family resources. It accounts for most cases of dementia (see Yegambaram et al., 2015). Although this disease is not an inevitable consequence of aging (Betty White hosted *Saturday Night Live* when she was 89), age is a major risk factor.

It has been estimated that the rate of Alzheimer's disease doubles about every 5 years after a person reaches the age of 40 (Hendrie, 1998). Whereas fewer than 1 percent of 60- to 64-year-olds have the disease, up to 40 percent of those ages 85 and older do (Jalbert et al., 2008). In the United States, more than 5 million people are living with this disease, and someone new develops it every 67 seconds (Alzheimer's Association, 2015). Worldwide, the figure is

Cognitive difficulties are not an inevitable consequence of aging. Betty White hosted *Saturday Night Live* when she was 89 years old.

over 35 million (Selkoe, 2012). By 2030 it is expected that this number will rise to a staggering 66 million (Vreugdenhil et al., 2012). The future prospects are therefore somewhat alarming. If we have not solved the problem of preventing Alzheimer's disease (or arresting it in its early stages) by around that time, society will be faced with the overwhelming problem of caring for millions of demented senior citizens.

Watch Alvin: Alzheimer's Disease

For reasons that are not yet clear, women seem to have a slightly higher risk of developing Alzheimer's disease than men (Jalbert et al., 2008). Indeed, Alois Alzheimer's original case was a 51-year-old woman. Women tend to live longer than men, but this may not entirely explain the increased prevalence of women with Alzheimer's disease. However, a relevant factor may be loneliness. In one study of 800 elderly people (the majority of whom were female), those who reported that they felt lonely had twice the risk of developing Alzheimer's disease over the course of the 4-year follow-up. This association was independent of their scores on a measure of cognition, suggesting that loneliness is not an early sign of cognitive impairment or a consequence of impaired cognitive skill (Wilson, Krueger, et al., 2007). It is reasonable to suggest that women are more likely to experience loneliness because they live longer and so outlive their husbands. This may be important when trying to understand sex differences in the risk for Alzheimer's disease.

In addition to advanced age and being female, other risk factors for Alzheimer's disease include being a current smoker, having fewer years of formal education, having lower income, and having a lower occupational status (Jalbert et al., 2008). Recent research also suggests that long-term use of benzodiazepines (medications used to treat anxiety) increases the risk of developing Alzheimer's at a later point by about 50 percent (Billioti de Gage et al., 2014). Given how frequently these medications are prescribed, this is a serious concern. Table 14.3 provides a summary of the most well-researched risk factors to date.

Table 14.3 Summary of Risk Factors for Alzheimer's Disease

Advanced age
Female
Current smoker
Fewer years of education
Lower income
Lower occupational status
Head trauma
Obesity
Diabetes

The prevalence of Alzheimer's disease is higher in North America and Western Europe and lower in such places as Africa, India, and Southeast Asia (Ballard et al., 2011; Ferri et al., 2005). Such observations have led researchers to suspect that lifestyle factors such as diet are implicated. A Mediterranean diet consisting of a high intake of vegetables, fruit, nuts, and olive oil and a moderate intake of dairy, fish, poultry and meat seems to be beneficial for cognitive function (Ye et al., 2013). In contrast, obesity and having type 2 diabetes both increase the risk of developing Alzheimer's disease (Christensen & Pike, 2015; Sridhar et al., 2015). The association with diabetes is especially interesting because researchers have found that insulin levels are abnormally low in some of the brain areas that are most affected by Alzheimer's disease. A recent study has also demonstrated that cognitive function improves in people who are showing early signs of cognitive impairment when they are given insulin intranasally (so that it reaches the brain) for 21 days (Claxton et al., 2015). For all of these reasons, insulin-related problems are now considered to be a possible mechanism through which diet, obesity, and Alzheimer's disease might be linked.

Also now being implicated in the development of Alzheimer's disease are communities of microbes collectively termed the *microbiome* (Bhattacharjee & Lukiw, 2013; Hill et al., 2014). Although it may make you feel slightly queasy to know this, the human gut is a huge reservoir of around 100 trillion microorganisms! The role of these gut bacteria in a variety of diseases is now being explored. Remarkably, we are now learning that large amounts of amyloid (which, as you will shortly learn is a sticky protein found in large amounts in the brains of patients with Alzheimer's disease) are produced by microbes (Zhao & Lukiw, 2015). As of now, the significance of this is not clear. Because lines of inquiry involving diet and the gut microbiome are still at their earliest stages, we can say little definitive at present. Nonetheless, this is an exciting new research direction.

Causal Factors

When we picture a typical patient with Alzheimer's, we imagine a person of very advanced age. Sometimes, however, the disease begins much earlier and affects people in their 40s or 50s. In such cases, cognitive decline is often rapid. Considerable evidence suggests a substantial genetic contribution in early-onset Alzheimer's disease, although different genes may be involved in different families (see Gatz, 2007). Genes also play a role in late-onset Alzheimer's disease.

Cases of **early-onset Alzheimer's disease** (which account for only 1–2 percent of cases overall) appear to be caused by rare genetic mutations. So far, three such mutations have been identified (Guerreiro et al., 2012). One involves the *APP* (amyloid precursor protein) gene, which is located on chromosome 21. Mutations of the *APP* gene are associated with an onset of Alzheimer's disease somewhere between 55 and 60 years of age (Cruts et al., 1998). Dominant mutations of this gene account for approximately 14 percent of early-onset cases (Guerreiro et al., 2012).

The fact that a mutation of a gene on chromosome 21 has been found to be important is interesting because it has long been known that people with Down syndrome (which is caused by a tripling, or trisomy, of chromosome 21) who survive beyond about age 40 develop an Alzheimer's-like dementia (Bauer & Shea, 1986; Janicki & Dalton, 1993). They also show similar neuropathological changes (Schapiro & Rapoport, 1987). In addition, cases of Down syndrome tend to occur more frequently in the families of patients with Alzheimer's disease (Heyman et al., 1984; Schupf et al., 1994). One study has found that mothers who gave birth to a child with Down syndrome before age 35 had a 4.8 times greater risk of developing Alzheimer's disease when they were older compared to mothers of children with other types of mental retardation (Schupf et al., 2001).

Other cases of even earlier onset appear to be associated with mutations of a gene on chromosome 14 called *presenilin 1* (*PS1*) and with a mutation of the *presenilin 2* (*PS2*) gene on chromosome 1. These genes are associated with an onset of Alzheimer's disease somewhere between 30 and 50 years of age (Cruts et al., 1998). One carrier of the *PS1* mutation is even known to have developed the disorder at age 24 (Wisniewski et al., 1998). Remember, however, that these mutant genes, which are autosomal dominant genes and so nearly always cause disease in anyone who carries them, are extremely rare. The *APP*, *PS1*, and *PS2* genetic mutations probably account, together, for no more than about 5 percent of cases of Alzheimer's disease.

Most cases of Alzheimer's disease are "sporadic," meaning that they occur in patients without any family history, and develop later in life. A gene that plays an important role in cases of late-onset Alzheimer's disease is the *APOE* (*apolipoprotein*) gene on chromosome 19. This gene codes for a blood protein that helps carry cholesterol through the bloodstream. We know that differing forms (genetic alleles) of *APOE* differentially predict risk for **late-onset Alzheimer's disease**. Three such alleles have been identified, and everyone inherits two of them, one from each parent. One of these alleles, the **APOE-E4 allele**, significantly enhances risk for late-onset disease. Thus, a person may inherit zero, one, or two of the APOE-E4 alleles, and his or her risk for Alzheimer's disease increases correspondingly. For example, having one APOE-E4 allele increases risk by a factor of 3; having two APOE-E4 alleles results in an 8- to 10-fold increase in a person's chances of developing the disease (Karch et al., 2014). Another such allele, APOE-E2, seems to convey protection against late-onset Alzheimer's disease. The remaining and most common allele form (found in about 70 percent of the population) is APOE-E3, and is of neutral significance. The alleles differ in how efficient they are in clearing amyloid, with APOE-E2 being most efficient and APOE-E4 least efficient (Karran et al., 2011).

APOE-E4 has been shown to be a significant predictor of memory deterioration in older individuals with or without clinical dementia (Hofer et al., 2002). The APOE-E4 allele is relatively uncommon in Chinese people compared to its frequency in people from Europe or North America. In contrast, people of African descent are especially likely to have this allele (Waters & Nicoll, 2005). Table 14.4 summarizes the genes that have been most important in Alzheimer's disease to date. The APOE-E4 allele (which can be detected by a blood test) is overrepresented in all types of Alzheimer's disease including the early-onset and late-onset forms. Approximately 50 percent of patients have at least one copy of the APOE-E4 allele (Karch et al., 2014). Exciting as they are, however, these discoveries still do not account for all cases of Alzheimer's disease, not even all late-onset cases (e.g., Bergem et al., 1997). Genome-wide association studies are now identifying other genes that may also play a role. Currently, more than 20 new loci have been implicated, many of which (perhaps surprisingly) seem to be involved in immune functioning (Karch et al., 2014). Time will tell which of these will turn out to be real risk genes as opposed to false-positive findings.

Table 14.4 Genes Associated with Alzheimer's Disease

Gene	Chromosome	Type
Amyloid precursor protein gene (APP)	21	Mutation
Presenilin 1 (PS1)	14	Mutation
Presenilin 2 (PS2)	1	Mutation
Apolipoprotein E (APOE)	19	Susceptibility gene

It is also important to keep in mind that many people who inherit the most risky APOE pattern (two APOE-E4 alleles) do not succumb to the disorder. One study found that only 55 percent of people who had two APOE-E4 alleles had developed Alzheimer's disease by age 80 (Myers et al., 1996). And others with Alzheimer's disease have no such APOE-E4 risk factor. In addition, substantial numbers of monozygotic twins are discordant for the disease (Bergem et al., 1997; Breitner et al., 1993). Findings such as these highlight the role of other genes as well as environmental and lifestyle factors in the development of Alzheimer's disease.

Current thinking is that our genetic susceptibility interacts with other genetic factors and with environmental factors to determine whether we will succumb to any particular disorder. The role of other genes involved in the development of Alzheimer's disease still remains to be explored. We also need a better understanding of the environmental factors that may play a key role. As we have already noted, diet may be an important variable. In addition to diet and the possible role of the microbiome mentioned earlier, other environmental factors under consideration include exposure to environmental contaminants such as aluminum or copper (see Yegambaram et al., 2015) and experiencing head trauma. One prospective study has found that traumatic brain injury is associated, for up to 5 years after the injury, with a fourfold increase in the risk of developing Alzheimer's disease (see Malaspina et al., 2002). And, as the Developments in Research box highlights, depression also elevates risk of later Alzheimer's disease. On the other hand, exposure to nonsteroidal

Developments in Research

Depression Increases the Risk of Alzheimer's Disease

Having a history of depression seems to put a person at higher risk for the later development of Alzheimer's disease (Ownby et al., 2006). Although we are not yet sure why this is, researchers speculate that some of the changes in the brain that are known to be associated with depression and with stress may somehow leave the brain more vulnerable to problems down the road (Wilson et al., 2008).

Depression may also be an early warning sign of the onset of dementia. In a large, community-based prospective study of people ages 65 and older, researchers found that people who had no early (before age 50) history of depression but who developed symptoms of depression later in life were about 46 percent more likely to develop dementia over the course of the approximately 7-year follow-up period (Li et al., 2011). What this means is that late-life depression may be more than a risk factor for depression. Rather, it could be an early manifestation of the dementia itself. This raises the interesting question of whether treating depression might delay the clinical onset of dementia.

People with a genetic risk for Alzheimer's disease because they carry the APOE-E4 allele of the *APOE* gene may be especially vulnerable to developing Alzheimer's disease if they also have a history of depression. In one study, men with depression who had the APOE-E4 allele were more than seven times more likely to develop Alzheimer's disease over the course of a 6-year follow-up compared to men who had neither the allele nor a history of depression. For men who did not have the genetic risk factor but did have a history of depression, the risk of later Alzheimer's disease was also higher (1.6-fold increase), but not nearly as high as the risk for the men who had the allele *and* the history of depression (Irie et al., 2008; see also Rajan et al., 2014). Having the APOE-E4 allele does not make a person more likely to develop depression; however, when the genetic risk factor and depression occur together, the risk of later Alzheimer's disease is especially high.

---

anti-inflammatory drugs such as ibuprofen may be protective and lead to a lower risk of Alzheimer's disease (Breitner et al., 1994; in't Veld et al., 2001; Weggen et al., 2001). People with more cognitive reserve (a concept combining education, occupation, and mental engagement) also seem to be at reduced risk (Ballard et al., 2011). Recent research with mice further suggests that exposure to a more stimulating and novel environment slows down the development of Alzheimer-related changes in the brain (Li et al., 2013). In other words, it may be possible to reduce or delay the occurrence of Alzheimer's disease by deliberately limiting exposure to risks, eating a healthy diet, living a more interesting life, and taking other preventive measures.

Neuropathology

When Alois Alzheimer performed the first autopsy on his patient (she was known as Auguste D.), he identified a number of brain abnormalities that are now known to be characteristic of the disease. These are (1) amyloid plaques, (2) neurofibrillary tangles, and (3) atrophy (shrinkage) of the brain. Although plaques and tangles are also found in normal brains, they are present in much greater numbers in patients with Alzheimer's disease, particularly in the temporal lobes.

Current thinking is that, in Alzheimer's disease, neurons in the brain secrete a sticky protein substance called *beta amyloid* much faster than it can be broken down and cleared away. This beta amyloid then accumulates into **amyloid plaques** (see Figure 14.6). These are thought to interfere with synaptic functioning and to set off a cascade of events that leads to the death of brain cells. Beta amyloid has been shown to be neurotoxic (meaning it causes cell death). Amyloid plaques also trigger local chronic inflammation in the brain and release cytokines (see Chapter 5) that may further exacerbate this process. More generally, inflammation is now increasingly being viewed as a key factor, not only in the progression of Alzheimer's disease but also in its development. The fact that many inflammatory processes are upregulated by obesity again highlights the link between lifestyle factors and Alzheimer's disease.

Having the APOE-E4 form of the *APOE* gene is associated with the more rapid buildup of amyloid in the brain (Jalbert et al., 2008). Animal studies also suggest that stress makes the neurocognitive consequences of amyloid accumulation much worse (Alberini, 2009; Srivareerat et al., 2009). Insulin may also play a role in regulating amyloid. (Again, this could help explain why diet and having diabetes have been identified as risk factors.) Although some scientists believe that the accumulation of beta amyloid plays a primary role in the development of Alzheimer's disease, others suspect that it may be a defensive response rather than a causal factor. Importantly, amyloid deposits can be present as many as 10 years before clinical signs of Alzheimer's disease first show themselves (Shim & Morris, 2011). It is not yet known if symptoms become apparent when the amyloid burden in the brain crosses a certain threshold or if amyloid buildup itself triggers other destructive processes that eventually culminate in symptoms (Karran et al., 2011).

Neurofibrillary tangles are webs of abnormal filaments within a nerve cell. These filaments are made up of

Figure 14.6 Brain Damage in Alzheimer's Disease

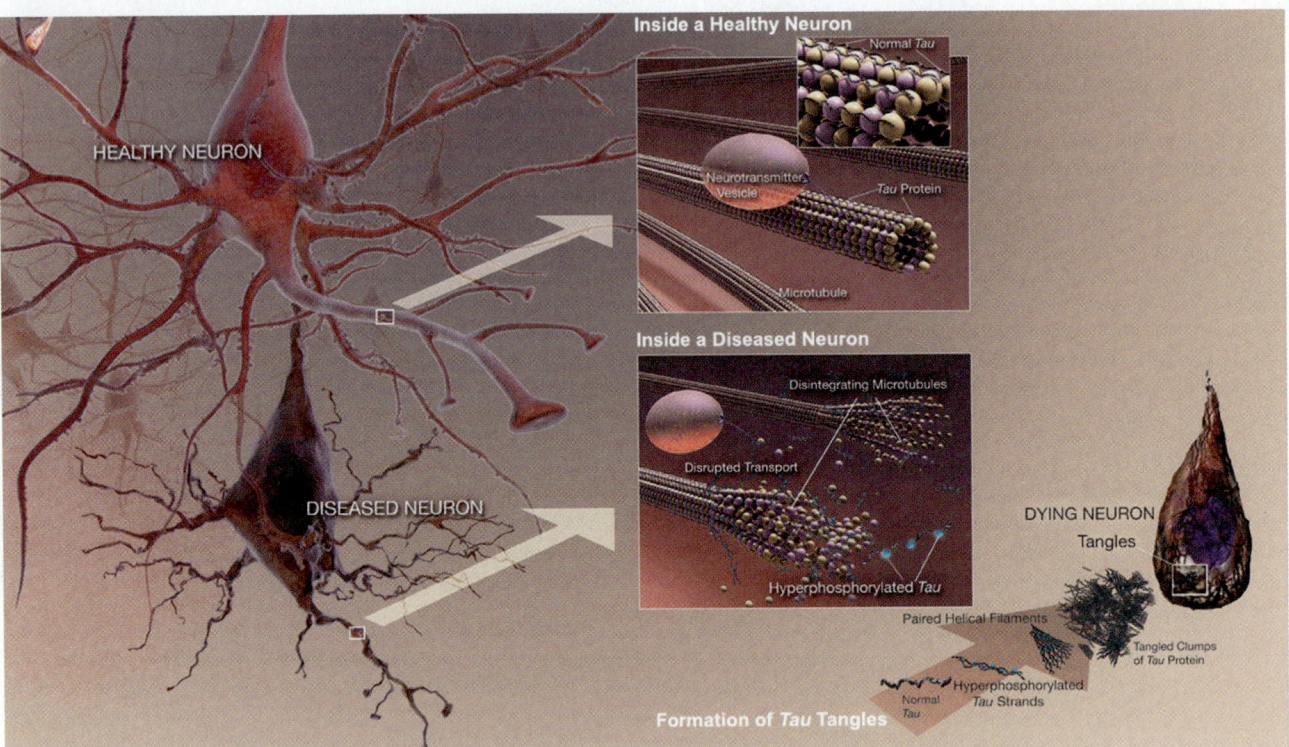

another protein called *tau*. In a normal, healthy brain, tau acts like scaffolding, supporting a tube inside neurons and allowing them to conduct nerve impulses. In Alzheimer's disease the tau is misshaped and tangled. This causes the neuron tube to collapse.

Although abnormal tau aggregation can occur independently, there is reason to believe that buildup of tau protein is accelerated by an increasing burden of amyloid in the brain (Shim & Morris, 2011). Animal studies of mice that have been genetically modified to be highly susceptible to developing Alzheimer's disease (so-called transgenic mice) support this idea (Götz et al., 2001; Lewis et al., 2001). If correct, it suggests that the most promising drug treatments for Alzheimer's disease may be those that can target and prevent amyloid buildup.

Another notable alteration in Alzheimer's disease concerns the neurotransmitter *acetylcholine* (ACh). This neurotransmitter is known to be important in the mediation of memory. Although there is widespread destruction of neurons in Alzheimer's disease, particularly in the area of the hippocampus (Adler, 1994; Mori et al., 1997b), evidence suggests that among the earliest and most severely affected structures are a cluster of cell bodies located in the basal forebrain and involved in the release of ACh (Schliebs & Arendt, 2006). The reduction in brain ACh activity in patients with Alzheimer's disease is correlated with the extent of neuronal damage (i.e., plaques, tangles) that they have sustained.

The loss of cells that produce ACh makes a bad situation much worse. Because ACh is so important in memory, its depletion contributes greatly to the cognitive and behavioral deficits that are characteristic of Alzheimer's disease. For this reason, drugs (called cholinesterase inhibitors) that inhibit the breakdown of ACh (and so increase the availability of this neurotransmitter) can be clinically beneficial for patients (Winblad et al., 2001).

This photomicrograph of a brain tissue specimen from a patient with Alzheimer's shows the characteristic plaques (dark patches) and neurofibrillary tangles (irregular pattern of strand-like fibers).

Treatment and Outcome

Despite extensive research efforts, we still have no treatment for Alzheimer's disease that will restore functions once they have been destroyed or lost. Current treatments, targeting both patients and family members, aim to diminish agitation and aggression in patients and reduce distress in caregivers as much as possible (Practice Guideline, 2007).

Some common problematic behaviors associated with dementia are wandering off, incontinence, inappropriate sexual behavior, and inadequate self-care skills. These can be somewhat controlled via behavioral approaches (see Chapter 16). Behavioral treatments need not be dependent on complex cognitive and communication abilities (which tend to be lacking in patients with dementia). For example, needed objects can be labeled. And objects needed for a specific task (such as grooming) can all be placed together in a single container. Identity bracelets can also be used for patients who tend to wander and leave the home. In general, reports of results are moderately encouraging in terms of reducing unnecessary frustration and embarrassment for the patient and difficulty for the caregiver (Brodaty & Arasratnam, 2012; Gitlin et al., 2012)

As we noted earlier, some patients with Alzheimer's disease develop psychotic symptoms and become very agitated. Antipsychotic medications (like those used in the treatment of schizophrenia) are sometimes given to alleviate these symptoms. However, these medications must be used with great caution. The U.S. Food and Drug Administration has issued a warning that patients with dementia who receive atypical antipsychotic medications are at increased risk of death (Schultz, 2008). Moreover, although antipsychotic medications may alleviate some symptoms to a very modest degree, there is no good evidence that they are better than placebo when it comes to patients' overall daily functioning and cognition (Sultzer et al., 2008).

Treatment efforts to improve cognitive functioning have focused on the consistent findings of acetylcholine depletion in Alzheimer's disease. The reasoning here is that it might be possible to improve functioning by administering drugs that enhance the availability of brain ACh. Currently, the most effective way of doing so is by inhibiting the production of acetylcholinesterase, the principal enzyme involved in the metabolic breakdown of acetylcholine. This is the rationale for administering drugs such as galantamine (Razadyne), rivastigmine (Exelon), and donepezil (Aricept). Winblad and colleagues (2001) studied 286 patients who were randomly assigned to receive either medication (donepezil) or placebo for a 1-year period. Patients' cognitive functioning and ability to perform daily activities were measured at the start of the study and again at regular intervals over the study period. Patients who received the medication did better overall than patients who received the placebo. However, all patients declined in their functioning over the course of the study. Furthermore, although donepezil does help patients a little, these gains do not mean that patients taking the drug are any less likely to avoid institutionalization than those who are not taking the medication (AD2000 Collaborative Group, 2004).

The newest medication that has been approved to treat Alzheimer's disease is memantine, which is marketed as Namenda. Unlike other approved medications, memantine is not a cholinesterase inhibitor. Instead, it appears to regulate the activity of the neurotransmitter glutamate, perhaps by protecting cells against excess glutamate by partially blocking NMDA receptors. Memantine, which can be used alone or in combination with donepezil, appears to provide patients with some cognitive benefits (Forchetti, 2005; Reisberg et al., 2003). However, when it comes to day-to-day functioning, the improvements that come from taking medications are still very small (Ballard et al., 2011; Hansen et al., 2007).

Yet another line of treatment research is focused on developing vaccines that might help clear away any accumulated amyloid plaques. Although initial findings from animal research looked promising (e.g., McLaurin et al., 2002), human clinical trials of a vaccine were terminated prematurely because of dangerous side effects. The sad reality is that no new medications have become available since Namenda was approved in 2003. Nonetheless, researchers continue to seek new approaches, as the Developments in Research box indicates.

Early Detection

Once most types of neuronal cells have died, they are permanently lost. This means that even if some new treatment could halt a patient's progressive loss of brain tissue, he or she would still be left seriously impaired. This makes the research effort to detect (and treat) Alzheimer's disease in its earliest stages all the more important.

Most researchers believe that signs of Alzheimer's disease might be detectable long before clinical symptoms appear. To explore this, they are using a range of brain-imaging techniques to study the brains of people at high risk for developing the disease. People at high risk include those who have the APOE-E4 allele as well as people who are experiencing minor cognitive impairment. MCI is thought to be on a continuum between healthy aging and the earliest signs of dementia (Risacher & Saykin, 2013). Some people with MCI report problems with memory. However, other (non-memory-related) cognitive problems are also predictive of later Alzheimer's disease (Storandt, 2008).

Brain scans of people with MCI show that, like patients with Alzheimer's disease, they have atrophy in a

Developments in Research

New Approaches to the Treatment of Alzheimer's Disease

Cholinesterase-inhibiting medications are the mainstream treatment for Alzheimer's disease, but they provide only limited benefits. New approaches are urgently needed.

Researchers are now using noninvasive brain stimulation techniques such as repetitive transcranial magnetic stimulation (rTMS) and transcranial direct current stimulation (tDCS) to try to improve cognitive functioning in patients with Alzheimer's disease. rTMS changes brain activation through the delivery of strong magnetic pulses that pass through the scalp and to the cortex beneath. In tDCS, a weak electrical current is delivered to the scalp; the type of stimulation (anodal or cathodal) determines whether excitability in the underlying cortical areas is increased or decreased. Although only a handful of studies have been conducted to date, involving a total of 200 patients, results suggest that patients perform better when they are receiving brain stimulation (Hsu et al., 2015). Unclear at this stage, however, is how durable such cognitive improvements are.

New medications also continue to be developed and tested. In early trials, one drug called a BACE inhibitor reduced amyloid levels in the brains of Alzheimer's patients. And in another small clinical trial, another drug that reduces inflammation improved cognitive functioning in patients with mild cognitive impairments. Whether these findings (which have only just been presented at a scientific meeting) will hold up as the clinical trials progress remains to be seen. When it comes to the treatment of Alzheimer's disease, disappointment has always been more routine than success. Nonetheless, researchers are doing all that they can to develop new treatment approaches and provide the types of major breakthroughs that would transform the lives of patients with Alzheimer's and their families.

number of brain areas, including the hippocampus (which you may recall is involved in memory) (Chételat et al., 2003; Devanand et al., 2007; Kubota et al., 2005). Moreover, reduction in the size of the hippocampus predicts the later development of Alzheimer's disease both in people with MCI and in elderly people who do not report any memory or cognitive impairments (De Leon et al., 2004; den Heijer et al., 2006). This suggests that atrophy of this brain area is an early sign of the disease.

Functional imaging techniques also show that the hippocampus is less active when patients with Alzheimer's disease (compared to controls) are engaged in memory tasks (Kato et al., 2001; Sperling et al., 2003). Again, this is also true of people with MCI (Chételat et al., 2003; De Santi et al., 2001). These findings are in contrast to those found in people who are cognitively normal but who are at high risk because they carry the APOE-E4 allele. These people do not show a lack of activation in the hippocampus when they are involved in memory tasks. Instead, brain-imaging studies reveal the opposite. Rather than underactivity, people who are at genetic high risk show increased activity in various parts of the brain, including the hippocampus,

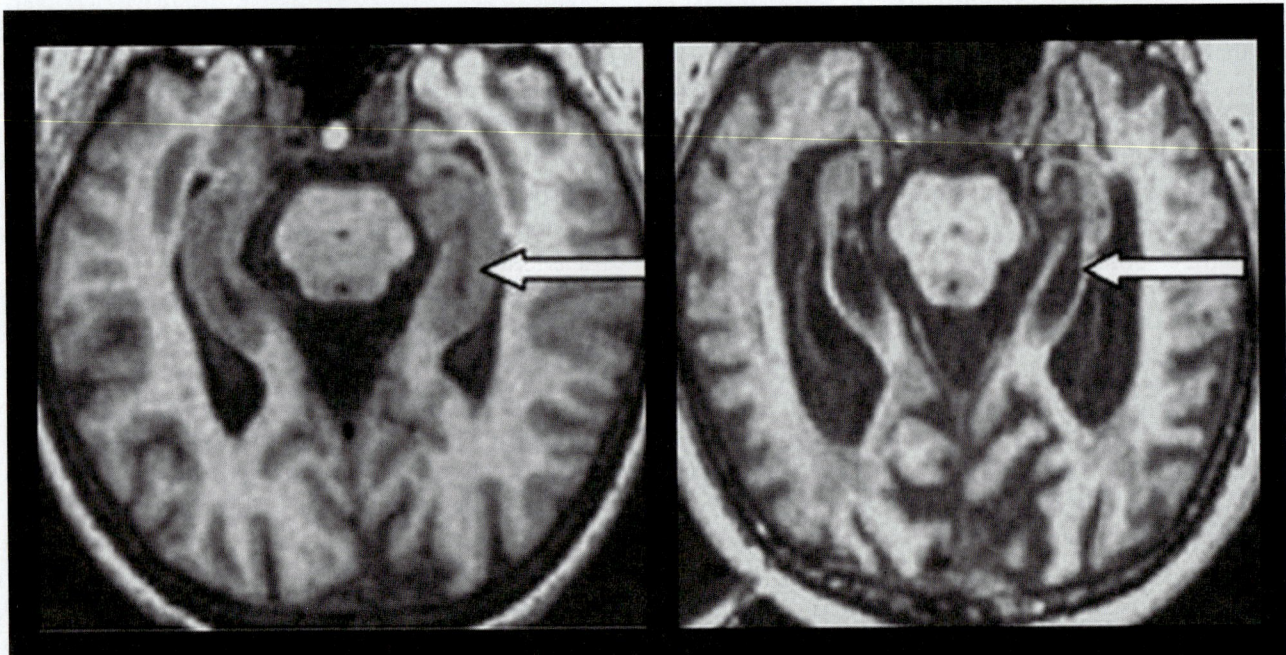

Atrophy of the hippocampus, a brain area critical for memory, is an early sign of Alzheimer' disease. In these pictures, arrows highlight the body of the hippocampus. Note the atrophy in the image on the right.

The World Around Us

Exercising Your Way to a Healthier Brain?

If you want to preserve your brain function as you age, you may be surprised to learn that one of the best things you can do is to exercise regularly. A growing amount of research suggests that exercise has considerable neurocognitive benefits. For example, in one prospective study of 299 elderly people (average age 78 years), those who walked 6 to 9 miles per week had much less loss of gray matter over time than did those who were more sedentary (Erikson et al., 2010). In another yearlong study, people ages 55 to 80 years who had no dementia were randomly assigned to a program of 40-minute walks three times a week or a program of stretching and toning that lasted the same amount of time. At the end of 1 year, those who had exercised by walking showed a 2 percent increase in the size of their hippocampus. In contrast, those in the stretching and toning control group showed a decline in their hippocampal volume (which is expected with normal aging). In other words, exercise seemed to reverse the age-related loss, whereas stretching and toning did not. What is also interesting is that increases in the volume of the hippocampus were also directly related to improvements in memory (Erikson et al., 2011).

Not surprisingly, researchers are now actively studying the effects of exercise in patients with Alzheimer's disease. Recent findings suggest that even a short program of exercise for 4 months conducted at home under the supervision of a carer or other family member can improve cognitive and physical functioning in elderly patients with Alzheimer's disease (Vreugdenhil et al., 2012). Inexpensive and easy to implement, exercise programs are now providing some much needed hope for patients and families coping with dementia.

How readily do you think that people with dementia and their carers will be able to use such findings in their own lives? Would you exercise more to preserve your brain functioning? If not, why not? What are the barriers to doing something as simple sounding as this?

---

when they engage in memory tasks (Bookheimer et al., 2000; Smith, Andersen, et al., 2002).

How can we explain these rather contradictory findings? Current thinking is that the greater degree of brain activation in people who are cognitively normal but at high risk for developing Alzheimer's disease reflects the greater effort they need to make to manage cognitive tasks. Simply put, carriers of the APOE-E4 allele may have to work harder. Because their brain tissue is still healthy (unlike in people with Alzheimer's disease or MCI), we see an *increase* in brain activation in response to a cognitive challenge rather than the decrease in activation that is more typical of patients with Alzheimer's disease or those with MCI. A similar pattern of increased brain activation in certain key areas is also found in people with MCI who are able to perform better on cognitive tests compared to those who perform worse (Clément & Belleville, 2010).

Does brain-imaging research allow us to identify people who are going to develop dementia? Not yet. None of the changes found to date are specific enough to be used to make an early diagnosis. This, however, is the goal for the future. In the meantime, if you want to preserve your brain, you might consider reading the World Around Us box. And if you think this information is just for older people, keep in mind that the brain starts to decrease in size after about age 18. By the time we reach the age of 80, our brain has lost about 15 percent of its original weight (Perl, 1999).

Supporting Caregivers

In the past few decades there has been a sharp increase in the number of dementia special care units in nursing homes. The vast majority of patients with dementia will be institutionalized before they die. Until patients reach the stage of being severely impaired, however, most live in the community, cared for by their family members. Very often, the burden of care falls on a single person.

Why must therapeutic interventions also consider the caregivers of Alzheimer's patients?

Not surprisingly, as a group, caregivers are at high risk for becoming socially isolated and for developing depression (Richards & Sweet, 2009). The stronger the bond they have with the person with Alzheimer's disease, the more likely they are to become depressed and exhausted (Wojtyna & Popiolek, 2015). Caregivers of patients with Alzheimer's disease tend to consume high quantities of medication themselves and report many stress symptoms, physical pain, and poor health (Alzheimer's Association, 2015). Providing caregivers with counseling and supportive therapy is very beneficial. It can reduce their negative reactions to patients' symptoms and also produces measurable reductions in their levels of depression (Brodaty & Arasaratnam, 2012; Mittelman et al., 2004).

in review

- What genes are implicated in Alzheimer's disease?
- Describe some of the major environmental risk factors for Alzheimer's disease.
- What kinds of neuropathological abnormalities are typical of the Alzheimer's brain?
- Summarize current treatments for Alzheimer's disease.

Neurocognitive Disorder Resulting from HIV Infection or Vascular Problems

14.5 **Explain how HIV infection and vascular events can cause neurocognitive problems.**

Neurocognitive disorders hold a unique position in *DSM-5* because the cause of the impairment is usually very clear. This is not true for most other *DSM-5* disorders. In the sections below, we consider neurocognitive disorders that result from HIV infection as well as from vascular events such as stroke.

Neurocognitive Disorder Associated with HIV-1 Infection

Infection with the human immunodeficiency virus (HIV) wreaks havoc on the immune system. Over time, this infection can lead to acquired immune deficiency syndrome, or AIDS. Worldwide, the HIV type 1 virus has infected more than 37 million people, with sub-Saharan Africa being the most affected region (World Health Organization, 2015d).

In addition to devastating the body, the HIV virus is also capable of inducing neurological disease that can result in neurocognitive problems. This can happen in two ways. First, because the immune system is weakened, people with HIV are more susceptible to rare infections caused by parasites and fungi. However, the virus also appears capable of damaging the brain more directly, resulting in

neuronal injury and destruction of brain cells (see Kaul et al., 2005; Snider et al., 1983).

The neuropathology of **HIV-associated neurocognitive impairment** involves various changes in the brain, among them generalized atrophy, edema (swelling), inflammation, and patches of demyelination (Adams & Ferraro, 1997; Sewell et al., 1994). No brain area may be entirely spared, but the damage appears to be concentrated in subcortical regions, notably the central white matter, the tissue surrounding the ventricles, and deeper gray matter structures such as the basal ganglia and thalamus. Ninety percent of patients with AIDS show evidence of such changes on autopsy (Adams & Ferraro, 1997).

The neuropsychological features of AIDS tend to appear as a late phase of HIV infection, although they often appear before the full development of AIDS itself. They begin with mild memory difficulties, psychomotor slowing, and diminished attention and concentration (see Fernandez et al., 2002, for a review). Progression is typically rapid after this point, with clear-cut dementia appearing in many cases within 1 year, although considerably longer periods have been reported. The later phases also include behavioral regression, confusion, psychotic thinking, apathy, and marked withdrawal.

Estimates from the early 1990s suggested HIV-related dementia was present in 20 to 30 percent of people with advanced HIV disease. Fortunately, the arrival of highly active antiretroviral therapy has not only resulted in infected people living longer but has also considerably reduced the prevalence of HIV-related dementia. However, although rates of frank dementia have decreased, HIV is still associated with cognitive problems. One recent study of people ages 50 and older who were HIV positive found that they had seven times the risk of being classified as having mild cognitive impairment relative to people who were HIV negative. In the HIV-positive group, the rate of MCI was 16 percent. In the HIV-negative group the rate was 2.5 percent (Sheppard et al., 2015). Importantly, all of the participants who were HIV positive were taking combination antiretroviral therapy and had undetectable levels of the virus. Even so, the findings suggest that people who are HIV positive may have brains that are aging more rapidly than normal.

As this study illustrates, treatment with antiretroviral therapy does not fully prevent the HIV virus from damaging the brain. This may be because HIV penetrates into the nervous system soon after a person becomes infected. What this means is that even though the new therapies have made HIV/AIDS a chronic but manageable condition (at least for those who have access to the necessary medications), prevention of infection remains the only certain strategy for avoiding the cognitive impairments associated with this disease.

Neurocognitive Disorder Associated with Vascular Disease

Neurocognitive disorder associated with vascular disease (**vascular dementia**) is frequently confused with Alzheimer's disease because of its similar clinical picture of progressive dementia and its increasing incidence and prevalence rates with advancing age. However, it is an entirely different disease in terms of its underlying neuropathology. In this disorder, a series of circumscribed cerebral infarcts—interruptions of the blood supply to minute areas of the brain because of arterial disease, commonly known as "small strokes"—cumulatively destroy neurons over expanding brain regions. The affected regions become soft and may degenerate over time, leaving only cavities. Although vascular cognitive impairment tends to have a more varied early clinical picture than Alzheimer's disease (Wallin & Blennow, 1993), the progressive loss of cells leads to brain atrophy and behavioral impairments that ultimately mimic those of Alzheimer's disease (Bowler et al., 1997).

Vascular cognitive impairment tends to occur after the age of 50 and affects more men than women (Askin-Edgar et al., 2002). Abnormalities of gait (e.g., being unsteady on one's feet) may be an early predictor of this condition (Verghese et al., 2002). Vascular cognitive impairment is less common than Alzheimer's disease, accounting for only 19 percent of dementia cases in a community sample of individuals age 65 years or older (Lyketsos et al., 2000). One reason for this is that these patients have a much shorter course of illness because they are vulnerable to sudden death from stroke or cardiovascular disease (Askin-Edgar et al., 2002). Accompanying mood disorders are also more common in vascular dementia than in Alzheimer's disease, perhaps because subcortical areas of the brain are more affected (Lyketsos et al., 2000).

The medical treatment of vascular dementia, though complicated, offers slightly more hope than that of Alzheimer's disease. Unlike Alzheimer's disease, the basic problem of cerebral arteriosclerosis (decreased elasticity of brain arteries) can be medically managed to some extent, perhaps decreasing the likelihood of further strokes. The daunting problems that caregivers face, however, are much the same in the two conditions, indicating the appropriateness of support groups, stress reduction techniques, and the like.

in review

- Does antiretroviral therapy prevent brain damage from HIV infection?
- What is the difference between dementia caused by vascular events and dementia that is caused by Alzheimer's disease?

Neurocognitive Disorder Characterized by Profound Memory Impairment (Amnestic Disorder)

14.6 Summarize how profound impairments in memory can be caused.

Most neurocognitive disorders involve declines in many different domains. However, the neurocognitive disorder diagnosis is also used when there is a marked decline in a single domain. This can happen when damage to the brain results in profound memory impairment.

In *DSM-IV-TR* there was a specific and distinct diagnosis called **amnestic disorder** (*amnestic* is just another way of saying *amnesia*). In *DSM-5*, patients who would have been given this diagnosis are now diagnosed as having a major neurocognitive disorder. The cause of the disorder is also listed (e.g., major neurocognitive disorder due to substance use). Unlike other forms of neurocognitive disorder, however, the substantial decline in functioning occurs in a single cognitive domain (memory).

The characteristic feature of neurocognitive disorders of this type (as a shorthand we will still call them amnestic disorders) is strikingly disturbed memory. Immediate recall (i.e., the ability to repeat what has just been heard) is not usually affected. Memory for remote past events is also usually relatively preserved. However, short-term memory is typically so impaired that the person is unable to recall events that took place only a few minutes previously. To compensate, patients sometimes confabulate, making up events to fill in the void that they have in their memories.

In contrast to patients with other forms of neurocognitive disorders, overall cognitive functioning in a patient with amnestic disorder is often quite good. The affected person may be able to execute a complex task if it provides its own distinctive cues for each stage of the sequence.

Brain damage is the root cause of amnestic disorder. This damage might be caused by strokes, injury, tumors, or infections (Andreescu & Aizenstein, 2009). However, not all brain damage is permanent. **Korsakoff's syndrome** is an amnestic disorder that is caused by a vitamin B_1 (thiamine) deficiency. Because of this, the memory problems associated with Korsakoff's syndrome can sometimes be reversed if the syndrome is detected very early and vitamin B_1 is given. Korsakoff's syndrome is often found in people with chronic alcoholism or in those who do not eat a healthy diet. It was the cause of the memory loss of the patient in the following case study.

He Forgot the Name of His Daughter

A powerfully built six-footer, Charles Jackson still showed traces of a military bearing. Before he left the army a year before, he had been demoted to buck private; this was the culmination of a string of disciplinary actions for drunkenness.

For over a year he had had monthly consultations with the current interviewer. On this occasion, the interviewer asked when they had last met. Charles replied, "Well, I just don't know. What do you think?" To the follow-up question, he said he guessed he had seen the interviewer before. "Maybe it was last week."

Asking him to remain seated, the interviewer went into the waiting room to ask Mrs. Jackson how she thought her husband was doing. She said, "Oh, he's about the same as before. He sketches some. But mostly he just sits around the house and watches TV. I come home and ask him what he's watching, but he can't even tell me."

At any rate, Charles was no longer drinking, not since they had moved to the country. It was at least 2 miles to the nearest convenience store, and he didn't walk very well anymore. "But he still talks about drinking. Sometimes he seems to think he's still in the army. He orders me to go buy him a quart of gin."

Charles remembered quite a few things, if they happened long enough ago—the gin, for example, and getting drunk with his father when he was a boy. But he couldn't remember the name of his daughter, who was two and a half. Most of the time, he just called her "the girl."

The interviewer walked back into the inner office. Charles looked up and smiled.

"Have I seen you before?" asked the interviewer.

"Well, I'm pretty sure."

"When was it?"

"It might have been last week."

(Adapted from Morrison, 1995, pp. 50–51.)

Another common cause of profound memory loss is head trauma. Stroke, surgery in the temporal lobe area of the brain, hypoxia (oxygen deprivation), and some forms of brain infections (such as encephalitis) can also lead to amnestic disorder. In these cases, depending on the nature and extent of damage to the affected neural structures and on the treatment undertaken, the disorder may remit with time. A wide range of techniques have been developed to assist the good-prognosis amnestic patient in remembering recent events (e.g., Gouvier et al., 1997). Moreover, because procedural memory (i.e., the ability to learn routines, skills, and actions) is often preserved in patients with amnesia, even patients without memory for specific personal experiences can still be taught to perform tasks that might help them reenter the workforce (Cavaco et al., 2004).

in review

- What are the most striking clinical features of amnestic disorder?
- What are some of the major causes of amnestic disorder?
- How is amnestic disorder diagnosed in *DSM-5*?

Disorders Involving Head Injury

14.7 Describe some of the clinical consequences of head trauma and explain the factors that are related to the degree of impairment that results.

Traumatic brain injury (TBI) occurs frequently, affecting just under 2 million people each year in the United States. The most common causes of TBI are falls, followed by motor vehicle accidents. Other causes include assaults and sports injuries (although the vast majority of these are probably never even reported). Children ages 0 to 4, adolescents ages 15 to 19, and adults ages 65 years and older are most likely to experience a TBI. In every age group rates of TBI are higher for males than they are for females (Faul et al., 2010). In *DSM-5* diagnostic terms such as major (or mild) neurocognitive disorder associated with head trauma are used to refer to the cognitive compromises that result from head injury.

Former Arizona Congresswoman Gabrielle Giffords is continuing her recovery from a traumatic brain injury sustained after an assailant shot her in the head in January 2011. She is receiving extensive therapy and is making considerable progress.

In recent years there has been an escalation of cases of TBI in military personnel caused by explosive blasts (Champion et al., 2009). Blasts seem to damage the brain in ways that are different from the brain damage seen in civilian cases of TBI. So many veterans have been injured by improvised explosive devices that TBI has been referred to as the signature injury of the Iraq War. Research suggests that around 15 percent of soldiers who have served in Iraq have experienced a TBI (Hoge et al., 2008). The military has made many efforts to improve screening and to increase rehabilitation services for veterans (see Munsey, 2007). However, for many, a full recovery may never be possible.

Clinical Picture

Clinicians categorize brain injuries as resulting from either a closed-head injury (where the cranium remains intact) or a penetrating head injury (where some object such as a bullet enters the brain). In closed-head injury, the damage to the brain is indirect—caused by inertial forces that cause the brain to come into violent contact with the interior skull wall or by rotational forces that twist the brain mass relative to the brain stem. Not uncommonly, closed-head injury also causes diffuse neuron damage because of the inertial force. In other words, the rapid movement of the rigid cranium is stopped on contact with an unyielding object. However, the softer brain tissue within keeps moving, and this has a shearing effect on nerve fibers and their synaptic interconnections.

Severe head injuries usually cause unconsciousness and disruption of circulatory, metabolic, and neurotransmitter regulation. Normally, if a head injury is severe enough to result in unconsciousness, the person experiences **retrograde amnesia**, or inability to recall events immediately *preceding* the injury. Apparently, the trauma interferes with the brain's capacity to consolidate into long-term storage the events that were still being processed at the time of the trauma. **Anterograde amnesia** (also called posttraumatic amnesia) is the inability to store effectively in memory events that happen during variable periods of time *after* the trauma. (If you remember that *anterograde* and *after* both begin with an "*a*" you will remember this more easily.) Anterograde amnesia is also frequently observed and is regarded by many as a negative prognostic sign.

A person rendered unconscious by a head injury usually passes through stages of stupor and confusion on the way to recovering clear consciousness. This recovery of consciousness may be complete in the course of minutes, or it may take hours or days. Following a severe injury and loss of consciousness, a person's pulse, temperature, blood pressure, and important aspects of brain metabolism are all affected, and survival may be uncertain. In rare cases, an individual may live for extended periods of time without regaining consciousness, a condition known as *coma*. The duration of the coma is generally related to the severity of the injury. If the patient survives, coma may be followed by delirium, marked by acute excitement and disorientation and hallucinations. Gradually the confusion may clear up and the individual may regain contact with reality. Individual courses of recovery are highly variable and difficult to predict (Waters & Nicoll, 2005).

Large numbers of relatively minor closed-head brain concussions and contusions (bruises) occur every year as a result of car accidents, athletic injuries, falls, and other mishaps. Even riding roller coasters that generate high G-forces may cause brain injury in some people (see Fukutake et al., 2000). It is estimated that two deaths per

Exposure to high G-forces, such as those experienced on some theme park rides, can cause neurological injury in some individuals by creating small tears in delicate blood vessels in the brain.

year can be attributed to brain hemorrhages that result from roller coaster rides (Pelletier & Gilchrist, 2005). Although these statistics are unlikely to dissuade you from heading to a theme park the next time you want to have some fun, they have prompted some calls for greater oversight of the industry.

People who play certain sports are at high risk of experiencing concussions and brain injuries. For males, the greatest risk comes from playing football; for females, the greatest risk comes from playing soccer (Lincoln et al., 2011). Moreover, because there is a critical period of brain development that occurs from ages 10 to 12, it may be especially important for boys to avoid tackle football until they have passed this stage (Stamm et al., 2015).

Avoiding tackle football until after age 12 is a wise decision because critical brain changes take place between the ages of 10 and 12. Injuries sustained during this time may be especially problematic later.

You should also know that small hits matter. Changes in the brain can result from impacts to the head that are not severe enough to cause concussions (Bazarian et al., 2014; Montenigro et al., 2015). Recent neuroimaging research also shows that college athletes who have played football—even those who have never had a concussion—have smaller hippocampal volumes than student athletes who have never played football at all (Singh et al., 2014). The reduction in the volume of the hippocampus is even more marked in the athletes who played football and had a history of concussion. These findings are illustrated in Figure 14.7. Another interesting finding from this study is that reaction times were also slower in the athletes who had played football for the longest time.

Figure 14.7 Total hippocampal volumes for healthy controls ($n = 25$), athletes with no history of concussion ($n = 25$), and athletes with a history of concussion ($n = 25$).

(Adapted from Singh et al (2014).)

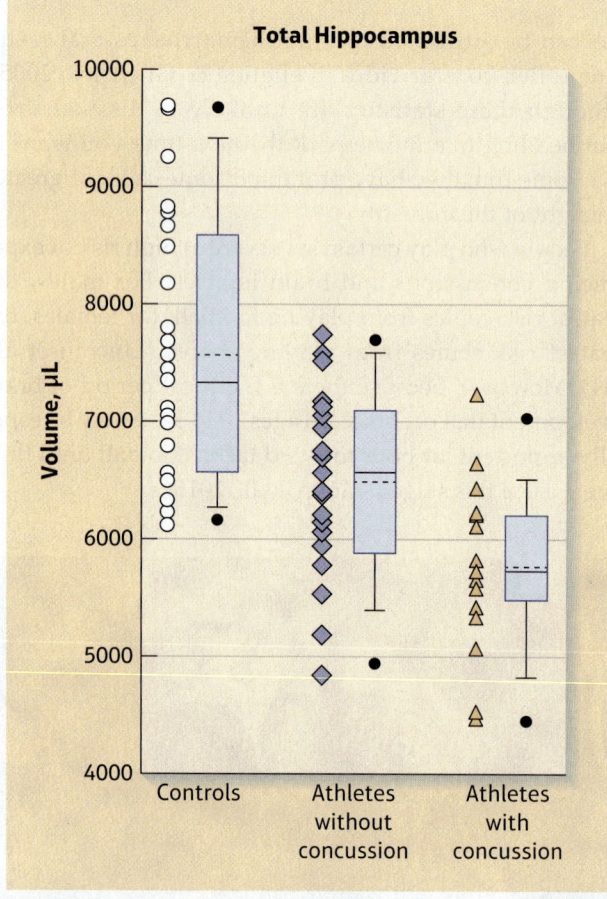

Signs of concussion are listed in Table 14.5. However, the majority of concussions do not involve a loss of consciousness. It is important to know that, after a concussion, the brain is four or five times more vulnerable to a second impact and that this increased vulnerability lasts for several weeks. As described in the World Around Us box, and as illustrated in the following case study, athletes at every level sometimes want to get back into the game without adequate recovery time, often with devastating consequences.

Table 14.5 Signs of a Concussion

Temporary loss of consciousness
Confusion or foggy feeling in the brain
Amnesia for the period surrounding the event/injury
Headache that gets worse and doesn't go away
Nausea or vomiting
Excessive drowsiness
Slurred or incoherent speech
Difficulty remembering new information
Dizziness
These symptoms may not be immediately apparent.
Some symptoms may develop several days after the injury.

Zack's Story

Zack, a gifted athlete who played both offense and defense on his junior high school football team, was injured at age 13 when his head struck the ground after tackling an opponent. The official called a time-out, and Zack was sidelined for just three plays before halftime. Despite the blow, Zack shook it off and by the start of the third quarter he was back in the game. "He always wanted to be part of the play," his father recalls.

After a hard-played second half, Zack collapsed on the field. He was airlifted to a medical facility where he underwent emergency life-saving surgery to remove the left and right side of his skull to relieve pressure from his injured and swelling brain. He experienced numerous strokes, spent 7 days on a ventilator, and was in a coma for 3 months before he awoke to a new reality. It was 9 months before Zack spoke his first word, 13 months before he could move a leg or an arm, and he spent 20 months on a feeding tube. Confined to a wheelchair, it was nearly 3 years until Zack was able to stand, with assistance, on his own two feet.

In 2009 the state of Washington passed a new law named after Zack. It requires that any young athlete who shows signs of a concussion be examined and cleared for play by a licensed health care provider. The law protects young athletes from the kind of life-threatening and potentially lifelong consequences that can be caused by shaking off an injury and returning to play. All 50 states have now followed suit and adopted return-to-play laws. (Adapted from Centers for Disease Control and Prevention, 2010.)

We are also learning something about the factors that may increase a person's susceptibility to having problems after a brain injury. One important risk factor appears to be the presence of the APOE-E4 allele that we discussed earlier (Waters & Nicoll, 2005). In one study of boxers, the presence of the APOE-E4 genetic risk factor was associated with more chronic neurological deficits (Jordan et al., 1997). A study of patients being treated in a neurosurgical unit found that having the APOE-E4 allele risk factor predicted patients doing more poorly at a 6-month follow-up. This was true even after controlling for such factors as severity of the initial injury (Teasdale et al., 1997).

Perhaps the most famous historical example of TBI is the case of Phineas Gage (Harlow, 1868). Gage, 25 years old, was the foreman of a gang of men who were building a railroad in Cavendish, Vermont. On September 13, 1848, there was an accident, and an iron rod (3 feet, 7 inches in length, about an inch in diameter, and weighing just over 13 pounds) was blown through Gage's skull, entering through his lower cheek. Gage was thrown back by the force of the explosion but started to speak a few minutes later. His men put him in an ox cart and took him to his hotel, whereupon he walked, with a little assistance, to his room, bleeding profusely. Miraculously, Gage survived the accident and eventually made a full physical recovery. However, in other respects he was a different man. What was most striking was the change in his personality. As his doctor noted, "He is fitful, irreverent, indulging at times in the grossest profanity (which was not previously his custom), manifesting but little deference for his fellows, impatient of restraint or advice when it conflicts with his desires, at times pertinaciously obstinate, yet capricious and vacillating, devising many plans of future operations, which are no sooner arranged than they are abandoned in turn for others" (Harlow, 1868, p. 327). Although some have suggested that the Phineas Gage story that is routinely told is full of mistakes and inaccuracies (see Kean, 2014), changes such as emotional dyscontrol, personality alterations, and impairment of self-awareness are fairly characteristic of severe damage to the frontal lobes (Stuss et al., 1992).

Treatments and Outcomes

As illustrated in the case of Zack, prompt medical treatment of a brain injury may be necessary to save the person's life and remove the pressure on the brain caused by intense swelling. Immediate medical treatment may also have to be supplemented by a long-range program of reeducation and rehabilitation involving many different professionals.

Although many patients with TBI show few residual effects from their injury, particularly if they have experienced only a brief loss of consciousness, other patients sustain definite and long-lasting impairment. Common symptoms of minor TBI include headaches, memory problems, sensitivity to light and sound, dizziness, anxiety, irritability, fatigue, and impaired concentration (Miller, 2011). When the brain damage is extensive, a patient's general intellectual level may be considerably reduced, especially if the temporal lobe or parietal lobes are damaged. Most people have significant delays in returning to their occupations, and many are unable to return at all (Selassie et al., 2008). Other losses of adult social role functioning are also common and are related to the severity of the injury (Rassovsky et al., 2015). Some 24 percent of TBI cases, overall, develop posttraumatic epilepsy, presumably because of the growth of scar tissue in the brain. Seizures usually develop within 2 years of the head injury. For decades after a head injury, there is also an elevated risk of depression as well as other disorders such as substance abuse, anxiety disorders, and personality disorders (Holsinger et al., 2002; Koponen et al., 2002).

Brain injury can also result in changes in personality. A relatively common change is that the person becomes more easily emotionally dysregulated. This emotional lability is frequently accompanied by irritability or disinhibition. Less commonly, apathy and paranoia may also be apparent (Max et al., 2015). Personality changes have been reported in up to 40 percent of children with severe traumatic brain injuries. In a sample of adults who had experienced severe TBI, personality change was reported by their significant others in 59 percent of cases (Norup & Mortensen, 2015).

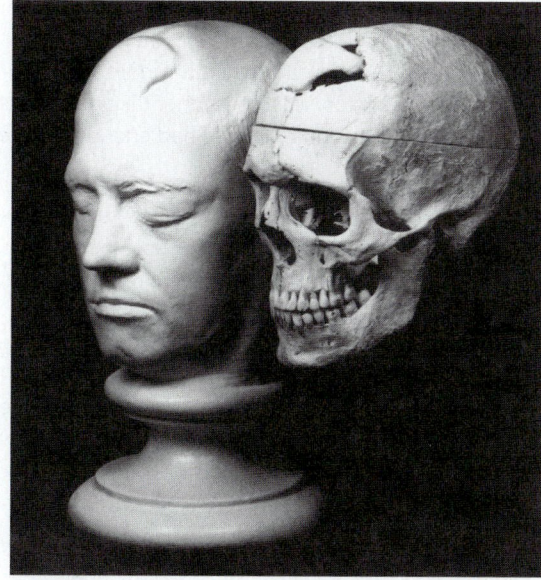 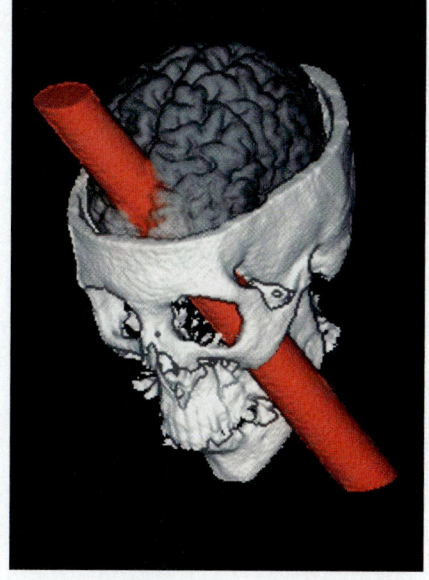

Though Phineas Gage survived when a tamping iron entered his face and shot through his head, his personality was altered such that his friends said that he was "no longer Gage."

The World Around Us

Brain Damage in Professional Athletes

For athletes, collisions are often part of the game. But new evidence is forcing many in collegiate and professional sports to consider the potential for long-term brain damage that may come from heading the ball or tackling another player. This issue first came to the attention of sports fans when Ted Johnson, a former Super Bowl champion and linebacker for the New England Patriots, went public about the crippling depressions and headaches that became routine experiences for him (MacMullan, 2007). Johnson, who has been diagnosed with a chronic postconcussion syndrome (involving fatigue, irritability, memory loss, and depression), is also showing signs of early brain damage. He believes that his problems are a direct result of the multiple hits to the head he sustained during his playing career.

Repeat concussions are very serious. After a blow to the head, the brain remains in a vulnerable state for several weeks. A second injury during this time will cause an exponential amount of damage. Johnson's cognitive functioning declined dramatically after he was involved in a serious collision during an exhibition game and had to be pulled off the field. Four days later, he was expected to engage in full contact during practice. Although he knew this was a bad idea, his pride, combined with the pressure not to appear weak, kept him from asking to be excused from the physical drills. During the practice he took a minor hit and experienced the warm and hazy sensation that signals a concussion. For Johnson, it was the beginning of the end.

Johnson decided to go public with his story after the suicide of former NFL defensive back Andre Waters. Waters, who was known to be a tough and hard-hitting player, suffered many repeat concussions during the course of his career. After his death at age 44, a neurologist examined his brain and reported that the tissue resembled that of an 85-year-old; Waters also had some signs of Alzheimer's disease. Repeat concussions were suspected to be the cause of his brain damage.

Research supports this speculation. A study of 2,552 retired professional football players showed that the majority (61 percent) had experienced at least one concussion during their playing careers. Moreover, those players who had a history of three or more concussions were five times more likely to be diagnosed with cognitive problems and had three times more memory impairment than players with no concussion history. Players who had had repeat concussions were also more likely to later be diagnosed with depression (Guskiewicz et al., 2005).

The risks associated with concussions are now being taken very seriously in the NFL. A class action lawsuit that was filed on behalf of thousands of former players in 2012 finally reached a judge-approved settlement in April 2015. In addition, several hockey players have had their careers cut short by concussions and there is now a lawsuit against the NHL. In 2011, Sidney Crosby, captain of the Pittsburgh Penguins, waited 10 months to return to the ice after experiencing two concussions, only to be sidelined again shortly afterward. He eventually returned to the ice in March 2012 and resumed his career, winning a gold medal in the 2014 Winter Olympics. As Crosby's story illustrates, after taking a hit, staying out of future games until the brain has had enough time to heal is of critical importance.

How do you think increasing awareness of the long-term consequences of concussions will change how people view football? Will players retire early, as was the case for Chris Borland, the San Francisco 49ers linebacker who left the game at age 24 because of concerns about the health risks associated with head injuries? Or will young men always be excited to play the game and be willing to take the risks that come with it? What about watching football on TV? How do you react when players take a major hit?

Sidney Crosby, captain of the Pittsburgh Penguins hockey team, experienced concussion-like symptoms for more than a year after being injured. He wisely took time to recover before returning to the ice.

Watch Head Injuries Among Athletes

The kinds of personality changes that emerge likely depend, in large measure, on the site and extent of the brain injury (Prigatano, 1992). However, even though more than half the people who sustain TBI develop psychological symptoms, and even though alleviation of such symptoms can improve rehabilitation outcome, there are currently few studies of risk factors, pathogenesis, and treatment of these disturbances (Rao & Lyketsos, 2002).

Although one might think that children would fare better after a brain injury because of brain plasticity, this is usually not the case. Children who undergo significant TBI are more likely to be adversely affected the younger they are at the time of injury and the less language, fine motor, and other competencies they have. This is because brain damage makes it harder to learn new skills and because young children have fewer developed skills to begin with. Intellectual capacity, processing speed, attention, and memory are all affected. Social competence is also compromised. The severity of their injury, limited socioeconomic resources, and family dysfunction play a role in how well children recover (Catroppa et al., 2015; Karver et al., 2012; Rosema et al., 2012). The good news is that, when the injury is mild, most children emerge without lasting negative effects. Prospective longitudinal research also suggests that, although they may still have deficits, children who have experienced a significant TBI stabilize and can make appropriate developmental gains as they get older (Anderson et al., 2012).

Treatment of TBI beyond the purely medical phase is often long, difficult, and expensive. It requires careful and

Table 14.6 Predictors of Clinical Outcome after Traumatic Brain Injury

Outcome is more favorable when there is:

- only a short period of unconsciousness or posttraumatic anterograde amnesia
- minimal cognitive impairment
- a well-functioning preinjury personality
- higher educational attainment
- a stable preinjury work history
- motivation to recover or make the most of residual capacities
- a favorable life situation to which to return
- early intervention
- an appropriate program of rehabilitation and retraining

SOURCES: Bennett et al. (1997); Dikmen et al. (1994); Diller & Gordon (1981); Mackay (1994); MacMillan et al. (2002).

continuing assessment of neuropsychological functioning and the design of interventions intended to overcome the deficits that remain. Many different treatment approaches are used including medication, rehabilitative interventions (such as occupational, physical, and speech/language therapy, cognitive therapy, behavior therapy, social skills training, vocational and recreational therapy), and individual, group, and family therapy (Hampton, 2011). Often, a treatment goal is to provide patients with new techniques to compensate for losses that may be permanent (Bennett et al., 1997). Research is also showing that patients with TBI may sometimes benefit from treatment with donepezil, an acetylcholinesterase inhibitor widely used in the treatment of Alzheimer's disease (Zhang et al., 2004). Table 14.6 shows some of the variables that are associated with patients having a more favorable outcome after a TBI.

in review

- Why is it so important to take concussions very seriously?
- What is the link between the APOE-E4 allele and problems after head injury?
- What kinds of clinical problems are associated with head injury in the short and long terms?
- What factors are associated with the degree of disability after head injury?

Unresolved Issues

Should Healthy People Use Cognitive Enhancers?

In the search for a cognitive advantage, many healthy people, young and old, are turning to drugs that may provide cognitive benefits. Many of us routinely use caffeine, which improves vigilance, working memory, and incidental learning. Others use nicotine, which, although clearly detrimental to health when smoked,

may enhance attention, working memory, and attention in the short term (Husain & Mehta, 2011; Lanni et al., 2008).

A more recent trend, however, involves the use of prescription stimulants. These include methylphenidate (Ritalin), which is used in the treatment of attention-deficit disorder, and modafinil

(Provigil), which is used as a wake-promoting agent for people with excessive daytime sleepiness. These compounds (which are not always legally prescribed) are now being used by students seeking better grades as well as by military personnel who need to remain awake during long missions. According to some studies, around 16 percent of college students acknowledge that they have used methylphenidate for recreational purposes (Babcock & Byrne, 2000; White, Becker-Blease, & Grace-Bishop, 2006).

Studies suggest that physicians are disinclined to prescribe these medications to young, cognitively healthy people (Banjo et al., 2010). In part, this reluctance stems from concerns about the safety of these compounds and beliefs that the benefits they provide are very small. Certainly, evidence suggests that the benefits of cognitive enhancers in healthy individuals are indeed very modest. But there are ethical issues, too (Hyman, 2011; Lanni et al., 2008). Should drugs developed as treatments be used as cognitive enhancers in people who do not have the disorders the drugs were designed to help? Who is most likely to have access to these cognitive enhancers? And will their use lead to a "cognitive arms race" rather like that in some professional sports where athletes who do not take steroids are highly disadvantaged? Could it be that students of the future might be required to provide a urine sample before taking a high-stakes exam?

Summary

14.1 Describe the impairments that are associated with neurocognitive disorders and explain the presumed cause of these disorders.

- The *DSM-5* recognizes major and mild forms of neurocognitive disorders. These disorders are thought to result from transient or permanent damage to the brain. Chronic neurocognitive disorders involve the permanent loss of neural cells.

- The primary clinical deficit found in neurocognitive disorders involves cognitive problems. Neurocognitive disorders are characterized by a loss or a decline in previously acquired skills.

- Depending on the cause, the onset can be slow or gradual with a deteriorating course. The most common cause of major neurocognitive disorders is Alzheimer's disease.

- There is no simple relationship between the extent of brain damage and degree of impaired functioning. Some people who have severe damage develop no severe symptoms, whereas some with slight damage have extreme reactions.

14.2 Summarize the key clinical features of delirium and describe how it is treated.

Delirium has a sudden onset. Common among the elderly, it is characterized by a state of awareness that fluctuates between wakefulness and stupor or coma. Delirium is treated with neuroleptic medications and also with benzodiazepines.

14.3 Describe two permanent and three reversible causes of neurocognitive disorders.

- There are many causes of neurocognitive disorders. In some cases the impairment is transient and can be reversed or improved with treatment. In other cases the damage is permanent.

- Potentially treatable causes of neurocognitive disorders include cognitive impairment caused by medications, vitamin B_{12} deficiency, alcoholism, infections to the brain, certain tumors, blood clots pressing on the brain, metabolic imbalances, and depression.

- Nonreversible causes of neurocognitive disorders include Alzheimer's disease, Huntington's disease, Parkinson's disease, HIV infection, oxygen deprivation, vascular events such as stroke, and brain injury.

14.4 Explain the risk factors for Alzheimer's disease and describe the changes in the brain that are found in patients with this disease.

- Age is a major risk factor for Alzheimer's disease as well as for other forms of dementia such as vascular dementia.

- Genes play a major role in susceptibility to and risk for Alzheimer's disease. Genetic mutations of the *APP*, *PS1*, and *PS2* genes are implicated in early-onset Alzheimer's disease. The APOE-E4 allele of the *APOE* gene is also a risk factor for Alzheimer's disease.

- The characteristic neuropathology of Alzheimer's disease involves cell loss, plaques, and neurofibrillary tangles. Plaques contain a sticky protein called beta amyloid. Neurofibrillary tangles contain abnormal tau protein.

- Alzheimer's disease causes the destruction of cells that make acetylcholine, a neurotransmitter important for memory. Drug treatments for Alzheimer's disease include cholinesterase inhibitors such as donepezil (Aricept). These drugs help stop ACh from being broken down and so make more of it available to the brain.

14.5 Explain how HIV infection and vascular events can cause neurocognitive problems.

- HIV virus can cause neurocognitive problems in two ways. First, because the immune system is weakened, people with HIV are more susceptible to rare infections. The virus also appears capable of damaging the brain more directly, resulting in neuronal injury and destruction of brain cells.

- Antiretroviral medication has dramatically reduced the dementia that is associated with untreated HIV infection. However, mild cognitive impairments have been noted in people taking antiretroviral medication even when no traces of the virus can be detected in their bodies. This may be because HIV penetrates into the nervous system soon after a person becomes infected and before treatment is started.

- Vascular events such as a series of small strokes cause brain damage by interrupting the blood supply to areas of the brain.

- Over time these events cumulatively destroy neurons over expanding brain regions. The affected regions become soft and may degenerate over time, leaving only cavities.

14.6 Summarize how profound impairments in memory can be caused.

- Amnestic disorders involve severe memory loss. The most common cause of severe memory impairment is chronic alcohol abuse.

- Other causes include head trauma, stroke, surgery, infections, and hypoxia.

14.7 Describe some of the clinical consequences of head trauma and explain the factors that are related to the degree of impairment that results

- Head injuries can cause amnesia as well as other cognitive impairments. Retrograde amnesia is the inability to recall events that preceded the trauma. Anterograde amnesia is the inability to remember things that follow it.

- An individual's premorbid personality and life situation are important in determining his or her reactions to brain damage. However, the reasons for these associations are not fully understood.

- The severity of the trauma, age of the person who is injured, and site of the injury play a role in the degree of impairment that results. The APOE-E4 genetic allele may also be a factor.

Key Terms

Alzheimer's disease, p. 512
amnestic disorder, p. 523
amyloid plaques, p. 517
anterograde amnesia, p. 525
APOE-E4 allele, p. 516
case study, p. 504
delirium, p. 505
dementia, p. 505

early-onset Alzheimer's disease, p. 515
HIV-associated neurocognitive impairment, p. 522
Huntington's disease, p. 512
Korsakoff's syndrome, p. 523
late-onset Alzheimer's disease, p. 516

major neurocognitive disorder, p. 505
mild neurocognitive disorder, p. 505
neurofibrillary tangles, p. 517
Parkinson's disease, p. 512
retrograde amnesia, p. 525
traumatic brain injury (TBI), p. 524
vascular dementia, p. 523

Chapter 15

Disorders of Childhood and Adolescence (Neurodevelopmental Disorders)

15.1 Explain how the understanding of psychological disorders among children and adolescents differs from that of adults.

15.2 Distinguish between developmentally normal and abnormal anxiety and mood in children and adolescents.

15.3 Describe the presentation and prevalence of oppositional defiant disorder and conduct disorder.

15.4 List and define elimination disorders.

15.5 Summarize what is known about the characteristics, course, and treatment of attention-deficit/hyperactivity disorder and autism spectrum disorder.

15.6 Describe what is currently known about the causes and treatment of learning disorders.

15.7 Define intellectual disability and name three known causal factors involved in its development.

15.8 Discuss how the treatment of youth differs from that of adults.

A Case of Adolescent Depression and Attempted Suicide

Amalia is a 14-year-old Latina girl from a middle-class background in Texas. Amalia's mother died from cancer when Amalia was 8 years old. Her mother's period of illness and subsequent death were extremely difficult for Amalia, and she has struggled with several episodes of depression during which she experiences long periods of sadness, anhedonia, worthlessness, and low self-esteem. For the past 2 years, Amalia has secretly engaged in non-suicidal self-injury (NSSI) in the form of cutting her arms and legs with a razor several times per week. She was also recently caught shoplifting and skipping school.

Amalia's father has been extremely concerned and has tried repeatedly to speak with her about her feelings and increasingly out-of-control behavior; however, this has only led to arguments and to a growing tension between them. Amalia also refused her father's request that she go with him to see a psychologist. One weekend, after a night out drinking alcohol with her friends, Amalia returned home in a very sad mood and, while alone in her room, wrote a suicide note and ingested an entire bottle of sleeping pills. Her father discovered her, called 911, and brought her to the hospital for emergency care. At the hospital, Amalia denied taking the pills or wanting to die, and even denied experiencing any symptoms of depression. The hospital staff decided to keep Amalia in the hospital for a 72-hour observation period, during which they determined that she was suffering from major depressive disorder. She received 1 week of inpatient treatment and then was referred for outpatient psychotherapy. She was also given anti-depressant medication.

Before the twentieth century, the study and treatment of mental disorders focused on adults and little attention was given to children and adolescents. It wasn't until the advent of the mental health movement and the availability of child guidance centers in the 1920s and 1930s that significant efforts were dedicated to assessing, treating, and understanding the maladaptive behavior patterns of children and adolescents. Disorders of childhood and adolescence now represent a major focus of psychological scientists and clinicians.

Nationally representative surveys designed specifically to estimate the prevalence of mental disorders among children and adolescents reveal that they occur quite frequently. Approximately half (49.5 percent) of children and adolescents meet criteria for at least one mental disorder by the age of 18 years (see Figure 15.1) (Merikangas et al., 2010). Anxiety disorders have the earliest onset (typically beginning around age 6), followed by behavior disorders (age 11), mood disorders (age 13), and substance use disorders (age 15) (Merikangas et al., 2010). Suicidal thoughts and behaviors are rare in children, but increase dramatically starting around age 12 (Nock et al., 2013). Approximately 12 percent of adolescents report having suicidal thoughts by the time they are 18 years old, and 4 percent report having made a suicide attempt (Nock et al., 2013). Given the prevalence and seriousness of these problems, efforts are being made to better understand disorders of childhood and adolescence.

Figure 15.1 Prevalence and Treatment of Psychological Disorders among Children and Adolescents

These data from the National Comorbidity Survey–Adolescent Supplement show (A) what percentage of U.S. adolescents meet *DSM* criteria for different types of mental disorders and (B) what percentage of those adolescents receive some form of treatment.

(Adapted from Merikangas et al., 2010; Merikangas, He, et al., 2011.)

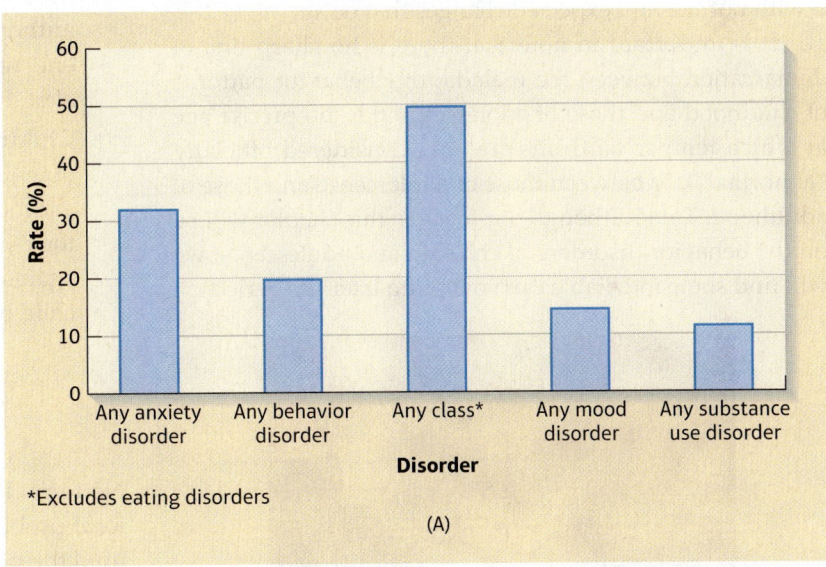

*Excludes eating disorders

(A)

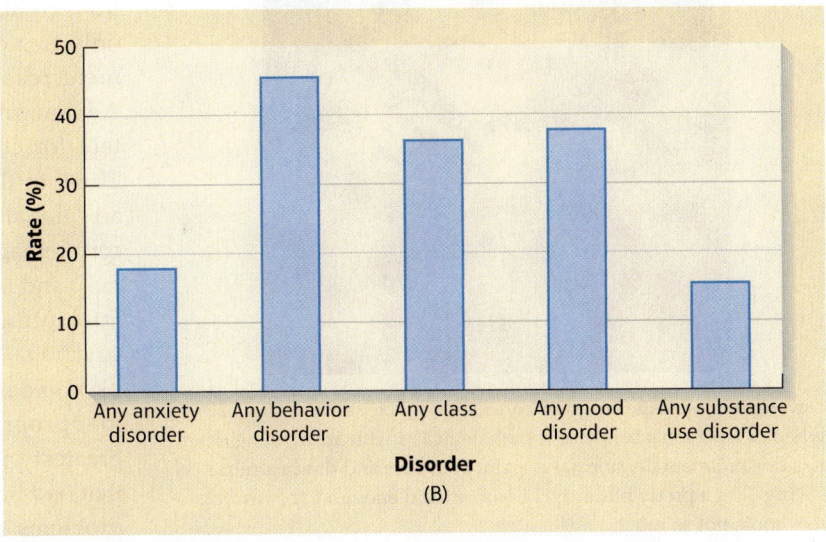

(B)

Special Considerations in Understanding Disorders of Childhood and Adolescence

15.1 Explain how the understanding of psychological disorders among children and adolescents differs from that of adults.

How do we determine which behaviors that occur during childhood and adolescence are abnormal or pathological? In short, it is important that we view a child's behavior in the context of normal childhood development (Silk et al., 2000). We cannot consider a child's behavior abnormal without determining whether the behavior in question is appropriate for the child's age. For example, eating marbles and having temper tantrums are to be expected in a 2-year-old, but would be abnormal in someone who is 17 years old. The field of **developmental psychopathology** focuses on determining what is abnormal at any point in the developmental process by comparing and contrasting it with normal and expected changes that occur.

It is important to note that there is no sharp line of demarcation between the maladaptive behavior patterns of childhood and those of adolescence (i.e., no precise age at which temper tantrums are now considered officially "abnormal"), or between those of adolescence and those of adulthood. Thus, although our focus in this chapter will be on the behavior disorders of children and adolescents, we will find some inevitable carryover into later life periods.

Developmental stage has to be considered when determining whether a person's behavior is pathological. If you are a young child, it is developmentally normal to paint your face and dance around saying "I'm a pretty butterfly!" If you are old enough to be reading this book, not so much.

Psychological Vulnerabilities of Young Children

Young children are especially vulnerable to psychological problems (Ingram & Price, 2001). In evaluating the presence or extent of mental health problems in children and adolescents, one needs to consider the following:

- They do not have as complex and realistic a view of themselves and their world as they will have later, and they have not yet developed a stable sense of identity or a clear understanding of what is expected of them and what resources they might have to deal with problems.

- Immediately perceived threats are tempered less by considerations of the past or future and thus tend to be seen as disproportionately important. As a result, children often have more difficulty than adults in coping with stressful events (Mash & Barkley, 2006).

- Children's lack of experience in dealing with adversity can make manageable problems seem insurmountable (Scott et al., 2010). For instance, one of the authors of this book thought the world would literally end when he didn't attend his junior prom. (*Spoiler alert:* It did not.)

- Children also are more dependent on other people than are adults. Although in some ways this dependency serves as a buffer against other dangers because the adults around him or her might "protect" a child against stressors in the environment, it also makes the child highly vulnerable to abuse or neglect by others.

The Classification of Childhood and Adolescent Disorders

No formal system for classifying the emotional or behavioral problems of children and adolescents was available until the publication of the *DSM-I* in 1952. Initially, the section on childhood disorders was quite limited and included only two disorders: childhood schizophrenia and adjustment reaction of childhood. In 1966, the Group for the Advancement of Psychiatry provided a classification system for children that was detailed and comprehensive. Thus, in the 1968 revision of the *DSM* (*DSM-II*), several additional categories were added. However, growing concern remained—both among clinicians attempting to diagnose and treat childhood problems and among researchers attempting to broaden our understanding of childhood psychopathology—that the then-current ways of viewing psychological disorders in children and adolescents were inappropriate and inaccurate for several reasons. The greatest problem was that the same classification system that had been developed for adults was used for childhood problems even though many childhood disorders, such as autism, learning disabilities, and school phobias, have no counterpart in adult psychopathology. The early systems also ignored the fact that in childhood disorders, environmental factors play an important part in the expression of symptoms—that is, symptoms are highly influenced by a family's acceptance or rejection of the behavior. In addition, symptoms were not considered with respect to a child's developmental level. Some behaviors that the *DSM* defined as problematic could be considered to be age-appropriate ones that would eventually be outgrown (e.g., fears, temper tantrums). All of these concerns are fully addressed in the *DSM-5*.

The *DSM-5* includes diagnoses for a large number of childhood and adolescent disorders. We don't have the space to review them all in this chapter, so we have selected several disorders that illustrate the broad range of problems that can occur in childhood and adolescence. We focus first on disorders that you learned about earlier in this book that can occur among children as well (e.g., anxiety and depression) and then turn our attention to disorders that always have their onset during childhood or adolescence such as oppositional defiant disorder, conduct disorder, and neurodevelopmental disorders.

in review

- Define developmental psychopathology.
- Discuss the special psychological vulnerabilities of children.

Anxiety and Depression in Children and Adolescents

15.2 **Distinguish between developmentally normal and abnormal anxiety and mood in children and adolescents.**

The anxiety and depressive disorders that you learned about earlier often have their onset during childhood and adolescence. Each of the disorders described earlier in this book can occur among youth; however, it is important to determine in each case whether a child's behavior reflects an underlying disorder or is normal given the child's developmental level. Here we discuss anxiety, depressive, and bipolar disorders.

Anxiety Disorders of Childhood and Adolescence

Most children are vulnerable to fear, uncertainty, and anxiety as a normal part of growing up. During childhood, many of us feared things like heights, thunder, the dark, clowns, and so on. Such fears are a normal part of human development, are not considered to be pathological in

most cases, and are outgrown over time. However, in some cases the experience of fear and anxiety are so extreme, persistent, impairing, and beyond what would be expected developmentally that the child is determined to have an anxiety disorder. Anxiety disorders of childhood and adolescence are classified similarly to anxiety disorders in adults, and as in adulthood are often comorbid with depressive disorders (Kendall et al., 2010; O'Neil et al., 2010).

Anxiety disorders are the most common mental disorder among children and adolescents, occurring at some point in the lifetime of approximately 32 percent of U.S. youth (Merikangas et al., 2010). They occur at higher rates among girls (38 percent) than boys (26 percent), and most commonly take the form of specific phobias (19 percent), social phobia (9 percent), separation anxiety disorder (8 percent), and posttraumatic stress disorder (5 percent) (see Figure 15.2). You learned about most of the anxiety disorders in Chapters 5 and 6, but not about the occurrence of separation anxiety disorder, which we now present below.

SEPARATION ANXIETY DISORDER   **Separation anxiety disorder**, classified under anxiety disorders in *DSM-5*, is characterized by excessive anxiety about separation from major attachment figures, such as mothers, and from familiar home surroundings (Bernstein & Layne, 2006). Children with separation anxiety disorder often lack self-confidence, are apprehensive in new situations, and tend to be immature for their age. Such children are described by their parents as shy, sensitive, nervous, submissive, easily discouraged, worried, and frequently moved to tears. In many cases, a clear psychosocial stressor can be identified, such as the death of a relative or a pet. The case study below illustrates the clinical picture in this disorder.

When children with separation anxiety disorder are actually separated from their attachment figures, they typically become preoccupied with morbid fears, such as the worry that their parents are going to become ill or die.

Figure 15.2 Prevalence of Anxiety Disorders in Girls and Boys

As shown in these data from the National Comorbidity Survey–Adolescent Supplement, a nationally representative sampling of 10,000 U.S. adolescents, anxiety disorders are prevalent among youth and are much more commonly seen in girls than boys.

(Adapted from Merikangas et al., 2010.)

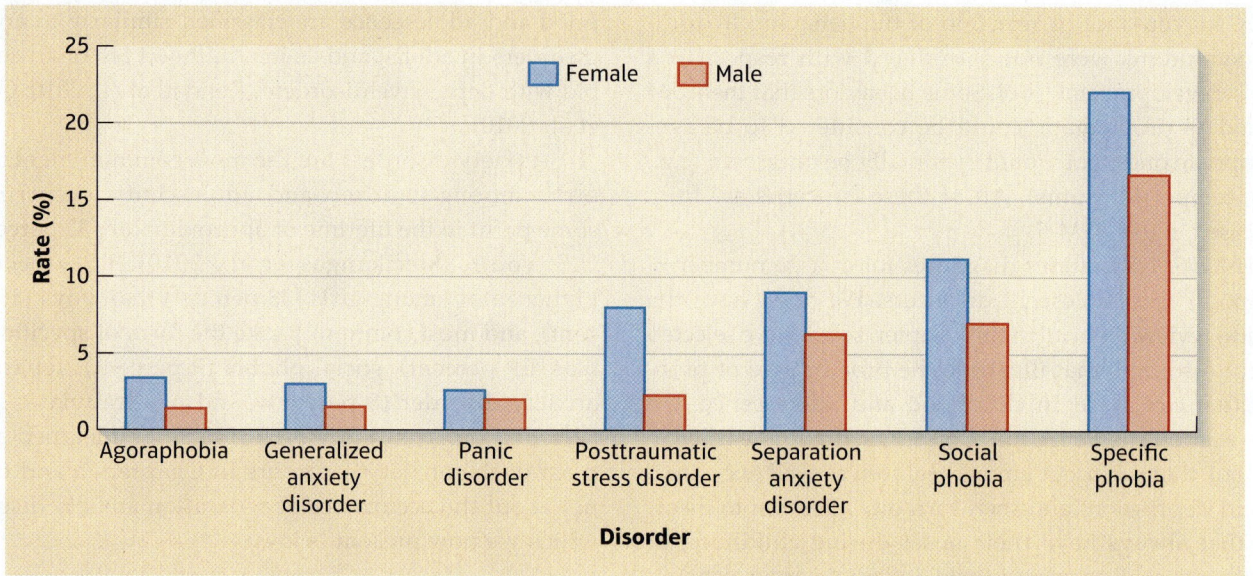

Johnny's Severe Separation Anxiety

Johnny was a highly sensitive 6-year-old who suffered from numerous fears, nightmares, and chronic anxiety. He was terrified of being separated from his mother, even for a brief period. When his mother tried to enroll him in kindergarten, he became so upset when she left the room that the principal arranged for her to remain in the classroom. After 2 weeks, however, this arrangement had to be discontinued, and Johnny had to be withdrawn from kindergarten because his mother could not leave him even for a few minutes. Later, when his mother attempted to enroll him in the first grade, Johnny displayed the same intense anxiety and unwillingness to be separated from her. At the suggestion of the school counselor, Johnny's mother took him to a community clinic for assistance with the problem. The therapist who initially saw Johnny and his mother was wearing a white clinic jacket, which led to a severe panic reaction on Johnny's part. His mother had to hold him to keep him from running away, and he did not settle down until the therapist removed his jacket. Johnny's mother explained that he was terrified of doctors and that it was almost impossible to get him to a physician even when he was sick.

When children with separation anxiety disorder are actually separated from their attachment figures, they typically become preoccupied with morbid fears, such as the worry that their parents are going to become ill or die. They cling helplessly to adults, have difficulty sleeping, and become intensely demanding. Separation anxiety is slightly more common in girls (9 percent) than boys (6 percent) (Merikangas et al., 2010). In many children with separation anxiety disorder, the disorder will go away on its own over time (Cantwell & Baker, 1989). However, some children go on to exhibit school refusal problems (a fear of leaving home and parents to attend school) and continue to have subsequent adjustment difficulties. A disproportionate number of children with separation anxiety disorder also experience a high number of other anxiety-based disorders such as phobia and obsessive-compulsive disorder (Egger et al., 2003; Kearney et al., 2003).

CAUSAL FACTORS IN ANXIETY DISORDERS A number of causal factors have been emphasized in explanations of the childhood anxiety disorders. Although genetic factors have been thought to contribute to the development of anxiety disorders, particularly obsessive-compulsive disorder, in children (Nestadt et al., 2010), social and cultural factors are likely to be influential in resulting in anxiety disorders in children. For example, some research has reported an increased risk of anxiety and depression among immigrant Latino youth (Potochnick & Perreira, 2010). Parental behavior and family stress in minority families have been particularly noted as potential influential factors in the origin of anxiety disorders in children; however, broader cultural factors are also important considerations.

Anxious children often manifest an unusual constitutional sensitivity that makes them easily conditionable by aversive stimuli. For example, they may be readily upset by even small disappointments—a lost toy or an encounter with an overeager dog. They then have a harder time calming down, a fact that can result in a buildup and generalization of surplus fear reactions.

The child can become anxious because of early illnesses, accidents, or losses that involved pain and discomfort. The traumatic effect of experiences such as hospitalizations makes such children feel insecure and inadequate. The traumatic nature of certain life changes such as moving away from friends and into a new situation can also have an intensely negative effect on a child's adjustment.

Overanxious children often have the modeling effect of an overanxious and protective parent who sensitizes a child to the dangers and threats of the outside world. Often, the parent's overprotectiveness communicates a lack of confidence in the child's ability to cope, thus reinforcing the child's feelings of inadequacy (Woodruff-Borden et al., 2002).

Indifferent or detached parents (Chartier et al., 2001) or rejecting parents (Hudson & Rapee, 2001) also foster anxiety in their children. The child may not feel adequately supported in mastering essential competencies and in gaining a positive self-concept. Repeated experiences of failure stemming from poor learning skills may lead to subsequent patterns of anxiety or withdrawal in the face of "threatening" situations. Other children may perform adequately but may be overcritical of themselves and feel intensely anxious and devalued when they perceive themselves as failing to do well enough to earn their parents' love and respect.

The role that social-environmental factors might play in the development of anxiety-based disorders, though important, is not clearly understood. A cross-cultural study of fears (Ollendick et al., 1996) found significant differences among American, Australian, Nigerian, and Chinese children and adolescents. These authors suggest that cultures that favor inhibition, compliance, and obedience appear to increase the levels of fear reported. In another study in the United States, Last and Perrin (1993) reported that there are some differences between African American and white children with respect to types of anxiety disorders. White children are more likely to present with school refusal than are African American children, who show more posttraumatic stress syndrome (PTSD) symptoms. This difference might result from differing patterns of referral for African American and white families, or it might reflect differing environmental stressors placed on the children. Several studies have also reported a strong association between exposure to violence and a reduced sense of security and psychological well-being (Cooley-Quille et al., 2001). Children who experience a sense of diminished control over negative environmental factors may become more vulnerable to the development of anxiety than those children who achieve a sense of efficacy in managing stressful circumstances.

TREATMENTS AND OUTCOMES

Biologically Based Treatments Psychopharmacological treatment of anxiety disorders in children and adolescents is becoming more common today (Vitiello & Waslick, 2010). In general, the same medications used to treat adult anxiety disorders are used in the treatment of these disorders among children and adolescents. The most commonly used medications are benzodiazepines, which rapidly inhibit the central nervous system (CNS), providing a calming effect, and selective serotonin reuptake inhibitors, which increase the availability of serotonin over time (Coffey & Zwilling, 2012).

Psychological Treatment Cognitive-behavior therapy (CBT) has been shown to be highly effective at reducing anxiety symptoms in young children (Hirshfeld-Becker et al., 2010; Legerstee et al., 2010). Kendall and colleagues have pioneered the use of CBT for child anxiety using positive reinforcement to enhance coping strategies to deal with fears (Chu & Kendall, 2004). Using this approach, the clinician tailors the treatment to a child's particular problem, and exposure to the anxiety-provoking stimuli is an especially important component of this approach (Svensson et al., 2002).

An interesting and effective cognitive-behavioral anxiety prevention and treatment study was implemented in Australia. In an effort to identify and reduce anxiousness in young adolescents, Dadds and colleagues (1997) identified 314 children who met the criteria for an anxiety disorder out of a sample of 1,786 children 7 to 14 years old in a school system in Brisbane, Australia. They contacted the parents of these anxious children to engage them in the treatment intervention, and the parents of 128 of the children agreed to participate. The treatment intervention involved holding group sessions with the children in which they were taught to recognize their anxious feelings and deal with them more effectively than they otherwise would have. In addition, the parents were taught behavioral management procedures to deal more effectively with their child's behavior. Six months after therapy was completed, significant anxiety reduction was shown for the treatment group compared with an untreated control sample.

Childhood Depression and Bipolar Disorder

Childhood depression, like depression in adults, is characterized by symptoms of sadness, withdrawal, crying, poor sleep and appetite, and in some cases thoughts of suicide or suicide attempts. In the past, childhood depression was classified according to essentially the same *DSM* diagnostic criteria used for adults. One modification used for diagnosing depression in children is that irritability is often found as a major symptom and can be substituted for depressed mood.

The Depressed Child

James is a 9-year-old African American boy who has recently has become extremely irritable, crying and throwing temper tantrums when things don't go his way. Initially his mother and teacher thought that he was doing this intentionally to try to get his way, but his mother has noticed that he is increasingly sad and isolating himself from others at home—he lies in his bed for hours at a time after school. Similarly, James' teachers have noticed that he doesn't play with the other kids at school like he used to; instead, he has been keeping to himself most of the time and even avoids eye contact with others. James hasn't been eating or sleeping very much, seems worried and on edge much of the time, and recently has started saying that he just doesn't belong anywhere and his family would be better off if he had never been born.

Childhood depression includes behaviors such as withdrawal, crying, avoiding eye contact, physical complaints, poor appetite, and in some extreme cases, aggressive behavior and suicide.

Depression in children and adolescents occurs with high frequency. Approximately 12 percent of children and adolescents meet criteria for major depression at some point in their lives, with higher rates in girls (16 percent) than boys (8 percent) (Merikangas et al., 2010). These rates have been generally consistent during the past several decades (Costello et al., 2006). Although depression can occur in children, the rates are low during childhood but increase dramatically during adolescence.

Bipolar disorder occurs less frequently (3 percent of boys and girls), but it can be diagnosed in children and adolescents (Merikangas et al., 2010). An increased use of bipolar diagnosis has been noted among children and adolescents in the United States (see the Developments in Research feature). Moreno and colleagues (2007) reported that the estimated annual number of youth office-based visits with a diagnosis of bipolar disorder

increased from 25 (1994–1995) to 1,003 (2002–2003) visits per 100,000 people, as did adult visits, with the majority of visits by males (66.5). A high percentage of these adolescents received a comorbid diagnosis, frequently attention-deficit/hyperactivity disorder.

CAUSAL FACTORS IN CHILDHOOD DEPRESSION The causal factors implicated in the childhood anxiety disorders are pertinent to the depressive disorders as well.

Biological Factors There appears to be an association between parental depression and behavioral and mood problems in children (Halligan et al., 2007; Hammen et al., 2004). Children of parents with major depression are more impaired, receive more psychological treatment, and have more psychological diagnoses than children of parents with no psychological disorders (Kramer et al., 1998). This is particularly the case when the parent's depression affects the child through less-than-optimal interactions (Carter et al., 2001). A controlled study of family history and onset of depression found that children from mood-disordered families had significantly higher rates of depression than those from nondisordered families (Kovacs et al., 1997). The suicide attempt rate has also been shown to be higher for children of parents with depression (7.8 percent) than for the offspring of nondepressed parents (Weissman et al., 1992).

Other biological factors might also make children vulnerable to psychological problems like depression. These factors include biological changes in the neonate as a result of alcohol intake by the mother during pregnancy, because prenatal exposure to alcohol is related to depression in children. M. J. O'Connor's (2001) study of children exposed to alcohol in utero reveals a continuity between alcohol use by the mother and infant negative affect and early childhood depression symptoms.

Negative Life Events and Learning Factors The experience of negative life events and the learning of maladaptive behaviors appear to be important in childhood depressive disorders. A number of studies have indicated that children's exposure to early traumatic events can increase their risk for the development of depression. Children who have experienced past stressful events are susceptible to states of depression that make them vulnerable to suicidal thinking under stress (Silberg et al., 1999). Intense or persistent sensitization of the central nervous system in response to severe stress might induce hyperreactivity and alteration of the neurotransmitter system, leaving these children vulnerable to later depression (Heim & Nemeroff, 2001).

Children who are exposed to negative parental behavior or negative emotional states may develop depressed affects themselves (Herman-Stahl & Peterson, 1999). Investigators have been evaluating the possibility that mothers who are depressed transfer their low mood to their infants through their interactions with them (Jackson & Huang,

Developments in Research

Bipolar Disorder in Children and Adolescents: Is There an Epidemic?

Bipolar disorder is characterized by extreme mood swings and aggressive, irritable behavior (Braaten, 2011). Historically, bipolar disorder has been conceptualized as an adult disorder; however, starting in the mid-1990s, psychiatrists began applying the diagnosis to children and adolescents and prescribing bipolar medication for their treatment (see Geller & DelBello, 2008). Interestingly, the application of the diagnosis to children and adolescents quickly skyrocketed, going from 25 per 100,000 people in 1994–1995 to 1,003 per 100,000 in 2002–2003 (see Figure 15.3; Moreno et al., 2007). Why such a dramatic increase in the diagnosis of bipolar disorder in children and adolescents? Is there an epidemic?

There are several potential explanations for this increase. It could reflect a true increase in the disorder in young people. Or, it could be that the rate of bipolar disorder was always high but unrecognized, and with increased awareness practitioners are now recognizing more patients with the disorder that they had "missed" in the past. A third possibility is that clinicians are using the bipolar diagnosis more liberally now than in the past and are erroneously increasing the application of the diagnosis to a wide range of behavior problems, for example, attention-deficit/hyperactivity disorder (ADHD). Many experts support this last possibility. For instance, children and adolescents diagnosed with bipolar disorder are much more likely than adults with such diagnoses to be male (67 percent versus 32 percent) and to have a comorbid diagnosis of ADHD (32 percent versus 3 percent) (Moreno et al., 2007). **Longitudinal research** studies (those in which assessments are done repeatedly over

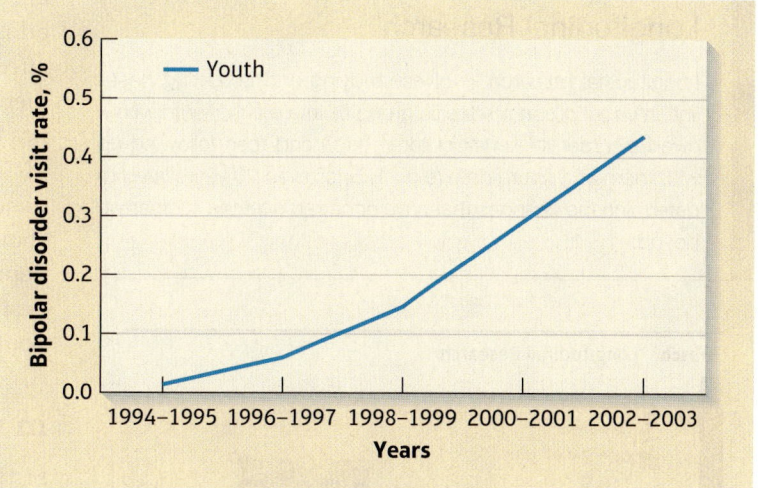

Figure 15.3 National trends in visits with a diagnosis of bipolar disorder as a percentage of total office-based visits by youth (ages 0–19 years).

(Adapted from Moreno et al., 2007.)

some period of time) that follow children and adolescents diagnosed with bipolar disorder into adulthood have documented that many of these children continue to meet criteria for this disorder in adulthood, suggesting that in many cases the diagnosis is being validly applied to youth (Geller et al., 2008). However, more research is needed to gain a better understanding of which children diagnosed with bipolar disorder really do suffer from this disorder and should receive appropriate treatment for it, and which children are inaccurately diagnosed and would be better served with a different treatment response.

2000). Depression among mothers is not uncommon and can result from several sources, such as financial or marital problems. One study found that parenting problems and depressed mood in mothers are associated with depression in children (Oldehinkel et al., 2007).

Mothers with depression often do not respond effectively to their children (Goldsmith & Rogoff, 1997) and tend to be less attuned to, and more negative toward, their infants than nondepressed mothers. Other research has shown that negative (depressed) affect and constricted mood on the part of a mother, which shows up as unresponsive facial expressions and irritable behavior, can produce similar responses in her infant (Tronick & Cohn, 1989). Interestingly, the negative impact of depressed mothers' interaction style has also been studied at the physiological level. Infants have been reported to exhibit greater frontal brain electrical activity during the expression of negative emotionality by their mothers (Dawson et al., 1997). Although many of these studies have implicated the

Mothers who are depressed may transmit their depression to their children by their lack of responsiveness to the children as a result of their own depression (Bagner et al., 2010). Unfortunately, depression among mothers is all too common. Exhaustion, marital distress as a result of the arrival of children in a couple's lives, delivery complications, and the difficulties of particular babies may all play a part.

mother–child relationship in development of the disorder, depression in fathers has also been related to depression in children (Jacob & Johnson, 2001). Overall, studies like these have shown that depression can be transmitted from one generation to the next.

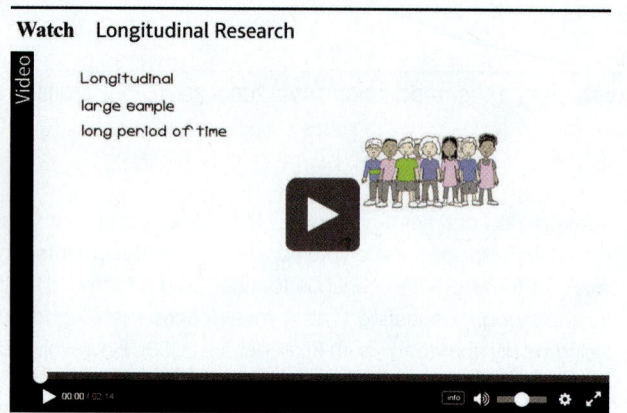

TREATMENTS AND OUTCOMES More than one-third (38 percent) of children and adolescents with depression or bipolar disorder receive mental health treatment (Merikangas, He, et al., 2011). The view that childhood and adolescent depression is like adult depression has prompted researchers to treat children displaying mood disorder with medications that have worked with adults. Antidepressants are among the most widely used drugs in treating child and adolescent mental disorders (Emslie et al., 2010). Unfortunately, research on the effectiveness of antidepressant medications with children has been mixed. Some studies of adolescents with depression have suggested that antidepressants such as fluoxetine (Prozac) are more effective than a placebo (Treatment for Adolescents with Depression Study Team, U.S., 2004). On the other hand, in addition to having some undesirable somatic side effects (nausea, headaches, nervousness, insomnia, and even seizures) in children and adolescents, some research has suggested that antidepressant medication treatment in children and adolescents is associated with an increased risk of suicidal thoughts and behaviors (Whittington et al., 2004). The association between the use of antidepressant medication and subsequent onset of

suicidal behavior remains a topic of intense debate within the field.

Psychological treatments have proven effective in the treatment of depression in children and adolescents. Controlled studies of psychological treatment of adolescents with depression have shown significantly reduced symptoms with the use of CBT (Spirito et al., 2011). Comprehensive meta-analytic studies that examine the overall effectiveness of psychological treatments for child and adolescent depression reveal that such interventions are effective, especially in the short term, and that such treatments also seem to decrease anxiety symptoms (although not behavior problems) in children receiving them (Weisz, McCarty, & Valeri, 2006). Longitudinal follow-up studies of adolescents who have been treated for depression have shown that effective treatment can reduce the recurrence of depression (Beevers et al., 2007). Overall, these studies suggest that although depression is fairly common among youth, effective treatments are available.

in review

- How do the symptoms of childhood depression compare to those seen in adult depression?
- Which type of disorder is most common in children and adolescents?
- What treatments are used to effectively treat mood and anxiety disorders in children and adolescents?

Disruptive, Impulse-Control, and Conduct Disorder

15.3 **Describe the presentation and prevalence of oppositional defiant disorder and conduct disorder.**

Anxiety and depressive disorders often are referred to as "internalizing disorders" because the focus of the symptoms is on what is happening inside the person (i.e., abnormalities in their thoughts and feelings). In contrast, disorders characterized by symptoms focused outside the person, such as engagement in disruptive and impulsive behavior, often are referred to as "externalizing disorders." Two of the most common externalizing disorders are *oppositional defiant disorder* and *conduct disorder*. Of course, many children will act out from time to time, disobeying adults and getting into fights, and so it is important to distinguish normal acting out from the more severe and persistent behaviors that can occur in those with oppositional defiant disorder and conduct disorder. It also is important to differentiate between these disorders and illegal activity among youth. **Juvenile delinquency** is the legal term used to refer to violations of the law committed by minors. Although youth with externalizing disorders may break the law, breaking the law in itself does not signal the presence of one of these disorders. (See the Unresolved Issues section at the end of this chapter.)

Oppositional Defiant Disorder

Oppositional defiant disorder (ODD) is characterized by a recurrent pattern of negativistic, defiant, disobedient, and hostile behavior toward authority figures that persists for at least 6 months. ODD is grouped into three subtypes: angry/irritable mood, argumentative/defiant behavior, and vindictiveness. This disorder usually begins by the age of 8 and has a lifetime prevalence of 10 percent, with a slightly higher rate among boys (11 percent) than girls (9 percent) (Nock et al., 2007). Prospective studies have found a developmental sequence from ODD to conduct disorder, with common risk factors for both conditions (Hinshaw, 1994). That is, virtually all cases of conduct disorder are preceded developmentally by ODD, but not all children with ODD go on to develop conduct disorder within a 3-year period (Lahey et al., 2000). The risk factors for both include family discord, socioeconomic disadvantage, and antisocial behavior in the parents.

Defiant, oppositional, and hostile behaviors are characteristics of both oppositional defiant disorder and conduct disorder, although there are important differences between these two conditions.

Conduct Disorder

Conduct disorder (CD) is characterized by a persistent, repetitive violation of rules and a disregard for the rights of others (see the *DSM* criteria box for CD). CD has a median age of onset of 12 years (meaning half of those who ever develop this disorder have it by age 12) and a lifetime prevalence of 10 percent (Nock et al., 2006). Like ODD, CD is more common among boys (12 percent) than girls (7 percent).

DSM-5 *Criteria for...*

Conduct Disorder

A. A repetitive and persistent pattern of behavior in which the basic rights of others or major age-appropriate societal norms or rules are violated, as manifested by the presence of at least three of the following 15 criteria in the past 12 months from any of the categories below, with at least one criterion present in the past 6 months:

Aggression to People and Animals

1. Often bullies, threatens, or intimidates others.
2. Often initiates physical fights.
3. Has used a weapon that can cause serious physical harm to others (e.g., a bat, brick, broken bottle, knife, gun).
4. Has been physically cruel to people.
5. Has been physically cruel to animals.
6. Has stolen while confronting a victim (e.g., mugging, purse snatching, extortion, armed robbery).
7. Has forced someone into sexual activity.

Destruction of Property

8. Has deliberately engaged in fire setting with the intention of causing serious damage.
9. Has deliberately destroyed others' property (other than by fire setting).

Deceitfulness or Theft

10. Has broken into someone else's house, building, or car.
11. Often lies to obtain goods or favors or to avoid obligations (i.e., "cons" others).
12. Has stolen items of nontrivial value without confronting a victim (e.g., shoplifting, but without breaking and entering; forgery).

Serious Violations of Rules

13. Often stays out at night despite parental prohibitions, beginning before age 13 years.
14. Has run away from home overnight at least twice while living in the parental or parental surrogate home, or once without returning for a lengthy period.
15. Is often truant from school, beginning before age 13 years.

B. The disturbance in behavior causes clinically significant impairment in social, academic, or occupational functioning.

C. If the individual is age 18 years or older, criteria are not met for antisocial personality disorder.

Source: Reprinted with permission from the *Diagnostic and Statistical Manual of Mental Disorders*, Fifth Edition (Copyright 2013). American Psychiatric Association.

Because the combination of any 3 of the 15 symptoms listed in the *DSM* criteria box can lead to a diagnosis of CD, there is a great deal of variability in the clinical presentation of this disorder. Statistical analyses that examine how symptoms cluster together have revealed the presence of five common subtypes of CD, with each made up of children engaging primarily in (1) rule violations (26 percent of those with CD), (2) deceit/theft (13 percent), (3) aggressive behavior (3 percent), (4) severe forms of subtypes 1 and 2 (29 percent), and (5) a combination of subtypes 1, 2, and 3 (29 percent) (Nock et al., 2006). Children and adolescents with CD are also frequently comorbid for other disorders such as substance abuse disorder (Goldstein et al., 2006) or depressive symptoms (O'Connor et al., 1998). CD significantly increases the risk of pregnancy and substance abuse in teenage girls (Zoccolillo et al., 1997) and of the later development of antisocial personality disorder and a range of other disorders (Goldstein et al., 2006). One study that followed more than 1,000 children for many years into adulthood revealed that between 25 and 60 percent of people who have a mental disorder during adulthood had a history of CD and/or ODD during childhood or adolescence (Kim-Cohen et al., 2003).

Causal Factors in ODD and CD

Our understanding of the factors associated with the development of conduct problems in childhood has increased tremendously in the past 20 years. Several factors are covered in the sections that follow.

A SELF-PERPETUATING CYCLE Evidence has accumulated that a genetic predisposition leading to low verbal intelligence, mild neuropsychological problems, and difficult temperament can set the stage for early-onset CD (Simonoff, 2001). Researchers also have found strong heritable effects of conduct problems and antisocial behavior across ethnically and economically diverse samples (Baker et al., 2007). The child's difficult temperament may lead to an insecure attachment because parents find it hard to engage in the good parenting that would promote a secure attachment. In addition, the low verbal intelligence and mild neuropsychological deficits that have been documented in many of these children—some of which may involve deficiencies in self-control functions such as sustaining attention, planning, self-monitoring, and inhibiting unsuccessful or impulsive behaviors—may help set the stage for a lifelong course of difficulties. In attempting to explain why the relatively mild neuropsychological deficits typically seen can have such pervasive effects, Moffitt and Lynam (1994) provided the following scenario: A preschooler has problems understanding language and tends to resist his mother's efforts to read to him. This deficit then delays the child's readiness for school. When he does enter school, the typically busy curriculum does not allow teachers to focus their attention on students at his low readiness level. Over time, and after a few years of

school failure, the child will be chronologically older than his classmates, setting the stage for social rejection. At some point, the child might be placed into remedial programs that contain other pupils who have similar behavioral disorders as well as learning disabilities. This involvement with conduct-disordered peers exposes him to delinquent behaviors that he adopts in order to gain acceptance.

AGE OF ONSET AND LINKS TO ANTISOCIAL PERSONALITY DISORDER Children who develop CD at an earlier age are much more likely to develop psychopathy or antisocial personality disorder as adults than are adolescents who develop CD suddenly in adolescence (Copeland et al., 2007). The link between CD and antisocial personality is stronger among lower-socioeconomic-class children (Lahey et al., 2005). It is the pervasiveness of the problems first associated with ODD and then with CD that forms the pattern associated with an adult diagnosis of psychopathy or antisocial personality. Although only about 25 to 40 percent of cases of early-onset CD go on to develop adult antisocial personality disorder, over 80 percent of boys with early-onset CD continue to have multiple problems of social dysfunction (in friendships, intimate relationships, and vocational activities) even if they do not meet all the criteria for antisocial personality disorder. By contrast, most individuals who develop CD in adolescence do not go on to become adult psychopaths or antisocial personalities but instead have problems limited to the adolescent years. These adolescent-onset cases also do not share the same set of risk factors that the child-onset cases have, including low verbal intelligence, neuropsychological deficits, and impulsivity and attentional problems.

PSYCHOSOCIAL FACTORS In addition to the genetic or constitutional liabilities that may predispose a person to develop CD and adult psychopathy and antisocial personality, family and social context factors also seem to exert a strong influence (Kazdin, 1995). Children who are aggressive and socially unskilled are often rejected by their peers, and such rejection can lead to a spiraling sequence of social interactions with peers that exacerbates the tendency toward antisocial behavior (Freidenfelt & Klinteberg, 2007). Severe conduct problems can lead to other mental health problems as well. For instance, children who report higher levels of conduct problems are nearly four times more likely to experience a depressive episode in early adulthood (Mason et al., 2004).

This socially rejected subgroup of aggressive children is also at the highest risk for adolescent delinquency. In addition, parents and teachers may react to aggressive children with strong negative affect such as anger (Capaldi & Patterson, 1994), and they may in turn reject these aggressive children. The combination of rejection by parents, peers, and teachers leads these children to become isolated and alienated. Not surprisingly, they often turn to deviant peer groups for companionship, at which point a good deal of imitation of the antisocial behavior of their deviant peer models may occur.

Investigators generally seem to agree that the family setting of a child with CD is typically characterized by rejection, harsh and inconsistent discipline, and parental neglect (Frick, 1998). There is some evidence that parental behavior can inadvertently "train" antisocial behavior in children—directly via coercive interchanges (e.g., mother asks child to get ready for bed → child starts whining → whining annoys mother so she walks away and lets her stay awake: here the child learns that if she whines she gets her way, whereas the mother learns that if she backs off the child stops whining; both behaviors are reinforced and the child has "learned" to misbehave) and indirectly via lack of monitoring and consistent discipline (Capaldi & Patterson, 1994). This all too often leads to association with deviant peers and the opportunity for further learning of antisocial behavior.

In addition to these familial factors, a number of broader psychosocial and sociocultural variables increase the probability that a child will develop CD and, later, adult psychopathy or antisocial personality disorder (Granic & Patterson, 2006) or depressive disorder (Boylan et al., 2010). Low socioeconomic status, poor neighborhoods, parental stress, and depression all appear to increase the likelihood that a child will become enmeshed in this cycle (Schonberg & Shaw, 2007).

Treatments and Outcomes

Approximately half of those with ODD (54 percent) and a third of those with CD (32 percent) have received treatment for their behavior problems (Merikangas, He, et al., 2011). Effective treatments for ODD and CD focus primarily on modifying the child's family and broader environment as a way of decreasing his or her problematic behavior (Behan & Carr, 2000; Milne et al., 2001).

PSYCHOLOGICAL TREATMENTS One interesting and often effective treatment strategy with CD is the cohesive family model (Granic & Patterson, 2006; Patterson et al., 1998). In this family-group-oriented approach, ODD and CD are conceptualized as being reinforced and maintained by ineffective parenting practices. For instance, parents can inadvertently reinforce inappropriate behavior such as in the example in the prior section in which the child learned to escape or avoid parental commands by escalating her negative behavior (whining). This tactic, in turn, increases parents' aversive interactions and criticism. The child observes the increased anger in his or her parents and models this aggressive pattern. The parental attention to the child's negative, aggressive behavior actually serves to reinforce that behavior instead of suppressing it. Viewing conduct problems as emerging from such interactions places the treatment focus squarely on the interaction between the child and the parents (Patterson et al., 1991).

Fortunately, during the past several decades, researchers have developed psychological treatments that have been shown to significantly decrease CD and ODD. Alan Kazdin, a pioneer in the development and evaluation of treatments for child conduct problems, has shown through a series of many studies that standard talk therapies are not effective in treating CD and ODD. However, two psychological approaches that target some of the key risk factors mentioned above do have a positive effect. Parent management training, an approach in which the clinician teaches the parents how to effectively prompt and reinforce prosocial behaviors while ignoring aggressive or antisocial behaviors, has been shown to be quite effective. In addition, a separate approach in which the clinician meets with the child to teach social problem-solving skills (such as how to generate and perform more adaptive responses to others) also has proven effective. The combination of these two approaches is especially effective at decreasing child conduct problems, with effects lasting well after treatment has ended (Kazdin, 2008b).

Given that prior research has identified many different risk factors for CD, researchers and clinicians can use this information to identify which children are at high risk of developing CD and can test prevention programs designed to decrease the likelihood of conduct problems. For instance, the Fast Track Prevention Program identified 891 first graders determined to be at high risk for developing CD and randomly assigned half of them to receive 10 years of prevention services that included training parents in effective behavior management procedures, social skills training for the children, and academic tutoring. The results showed that children assigned to the intervention were significantly less likely to develop CD (20 percent) compared to children in the control condition (42 percent) (see Figure 15.4; Conduct

Figure 15.4 The Fast Track Prevention Program has been shown to significantly decrease the risk of conduct disorder. In this 2011 study, only 20 percent of at-risk children receiving this intervention went on to develop conduct disorder by 12th grade, compared to 42 percent of those in the control condition.

(Adapted from Conduct Problems Prevention Research Group, 2011.)

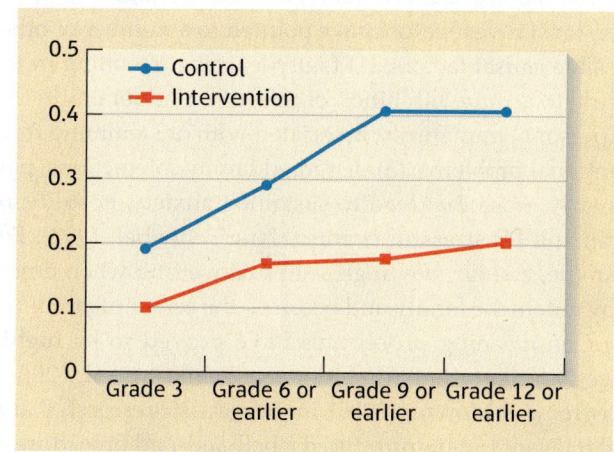

Problems Prevention Research Group, 2011). Thus, although CD is associated with significant impairment and problems later in life, such problems are treatable and even preventable.

in review

- Distinguish among oppositional defiant disorder, conduct disorder, and juvenile delinquency.
- What is known about the causes and treatment of oppositional defiant disorder and conduct disorder?

Elimination Disorders

15.4   List and define elimination disorders.

The childhood disorders we deal with in this section—"elimination disorders" (enuresis and encopresis)—involve a single outstanding symptom rather than a pervasive maladaptive pattern.

Enuresis

The term **enuresis** refers to the habitual involuntary discharge of urine, usually at night, after the age of expected continence (age 5). In the *DSM-5*, functional enuresis is an elimination disorder described as bed-wetting that is not organically caused. Children who have primary functional enuresis have never been continent; children who have secondary functional enuresis have been continent for at least a year but have regressed. Estimates of the prevalence of enuresis reported in the *DSM-5* are 5 to 10 percent among 5-year-olds, 3 to 5 percent among 10-year-olds, and 1.1 percent among children ages 15 or older.

Enuresis may result from a variety of organic conditions, such as disturbed cerebral control of the bladder (Goin, 1998), neurological dysfunction, other medical factors such as medication side effects (Took & Buck, 1996), or having a small functional bladder capacity and a weak urethral sphincter (Dahl, 1992). One group of researchers reported that 11 percent of their patients with enuresis had disorders of the urinary tract (Watanabe et al., 1994). However, most investigators have pointed to a number of other possible causal factors: (1) faulty learning, resulting in the failure to acquire inhibition of reflexive bladder emptying; (2) personal immaturity, associated with or stemming from emotional problems; (3) disturbed family interactions, particularly those that lead to sustained anxiety, hostility, or both; and (4) stressful events (Haug Schnabel, 1992). For example, a child may regress to bed-wetting when a new baby enters the family and becomes the center of attention.

Conditioning procedures have proved to be highly effective treatment for enuresis (Friman et al., 2008). Mowrer and Mowrer (1938), in their classic research that is still relevant today, introduced a bell-and-pad procedure in which a child sleeps on a pad that is wired to a battery-operated bell. At the first few drops of urine, the bell is set off, thus awakening the child. Through conditioning, the child comes to associate bladder tension with awakening.

Medical treatment of enuresis typically centers on using medications such as the antidepressant drug imipramine. The mechanism underlying the action of the drug is unclear, but it may simply lessen the deepest stages of sleep to light sleep, enabling the child to recognize bodily needs more effectively (Dahl, 1992). An intranasal desmopressin (DDAVP) has also been used to help children manage urine more effectively (Rahm et al., 2010). This medication, a hormone replacement, apparently increases urine concentration, decreases urine volume, and therefore reduces the need to urinate. The use of this medication to treat children with enuresis is no panacea, however. Disadvantages of its use include its high cost and the fact that it is effective only with a small subset of children with enuresis, and then only temporarily. Moffatt (1997) suggested that DDAVP has an important place in treating nocturnal enuresis in youngsters who have not responded well to behavioral treatment methods. Keep in mind, however, that medications by themselves do not cure enuresis and that there is frequent relapse when the drug is discontinued or the child habituates to the medication (Dahl, 1992). Some evidence suggests that a biobehavioral approach—that is, using the urine alarm along with desmopressin—is most effective (Mellon & McGrath, 2000).

With or without treatment, the incidence of enuresis tends to decrease significantly with age, but many experts still believe that enuresis should be treated in childhood because there is currently no way to identify which children will remain enuretic into adulthood (Goin, 1998). In an

When combined with medication such as desmopressin, a urine alarm (shown here) can be very effective in treating enuresis. The child sleeps with a wetness detector, which is wired to a battery-operated alarm in his or her undergarment. Through conditioning, the child comes to associate bladder tension with awakening.

evaluation of research on the treatment of bed-wetting, Houts, Berman, and Abramson (1994) concluded that treated children are more improved at follow-up than non-treated children. They also found that learning-based procedures are more effective than medications.

Encopresis

The term **encopresis** describes a symptom disorder of children who have not learned appropriate toileting for bowel movements after age 4. This condition, classified under elimination disorders in *DSM-5*, is less common than enuresis; however, *DSM*-based estimates are that about 1 percent of 5-year-olds have encopresis. A study of 102 cases of children with encopresis yielded the following list of characteristics: The average age of children with encopresis was 7, with a range of ages 4 to 13. About one-third of children with encopresis were also enuretic, and a large sex difference was found, with about six times more boys than girls in the sample. Many of the children soiled their clothing when they were under stress. A common time was in the late afternoon after school; few children actually had this problem at school. Most of the children reported that they did not know when they needed to have a bowel movement or were too shy to use the bathrooms at school.

Many children with encopresis suffer from constipation, so an important element in the diagnosis is a physical examination to determine whether physiological factors are contributing to the disorder. The treatment of encopresis usually involves both medical and psychological aspects. Several studies of the use of conditioning procedures with children with encopresis have reported moderate treatment success; that is, no additional incidents occurred within 6 months following treatment (Friman et al., 2008). However, research has shown that a minority of children (11 to 20 percent) do not respond to learning-based treatment approaches (Keeley et al., 2009).

in review

- What is functional enuresis? Describe a traditional and highly effective treatment for enuresis.
- What is encopresis? Is this condition more common among boys or girls?

Neurodevelopmental Disorders

15.5 Summarize what is known about the characteristics, course, and treatment of attention-deficit/hyperactivity disorder and autism spectrum disorder.

Neurodevelopmental disorders are a group of conditions characterized by an early onset and persistent course that are believed to be the result of disruptions to normal brain development (Andrews et al., 2009; Insel, 2014). Neurodevelopmental disorders are different from anxiety and depression in that they must have their onset during childhood. These disorders differ from ODD and CD in that they are believed to be the result of significant delays or disruptions in brain development that persist into adulthood (with a few exceptions discussed below). Although neurodevelopmental disorders are heterogeneous in nature, they often overlap and share common risk factors. In this section we review some of the most common neurodevelopmental disorders.

Attention-Deficit/Hyperactivity Disorder

Attention-deficit/hyperactivity disorder (ADHD) is characterized by a persistent pattern of difficulties sustaining attention and/or impulsiveness and excessive or exaggerated motor activity. We all have had lapses in attention or periods of excess energy during childhood; however, in order to meet criteria for ADHD these problems have to be numerous, persistent, and causing impairment at home, school, or the workplace (see the *DSM-5* criteria box for ADHD).

Perhaps due partially to their behavioral problems, children with ADHD often score approximately 7 to 15 points lower on intelligence quotient (IQ) tests (Barkley, 1997) and show deficits on neuropsychological testing that are related to poor academic functioning (Biederman et al., 2004). They often show specific learning disabilities such as difficulties in reading or learning other basic school subjects. Children and adolescents with ADHD also are at significantly higher risk of a range of school problems including suspension and repeating a grade, and these effects appear to be due in large part to disruptive behavior problems (Kessler et al., 2014). In addition to academic problems, symptoms of ADHD also can lead to significant social impairment. Hyperactive children often have great difficulty getting along with their parents because they often fail to obey rules. Their behavior problems also can result in their being viewed negatively by their peers (Hoza et al., 2005).

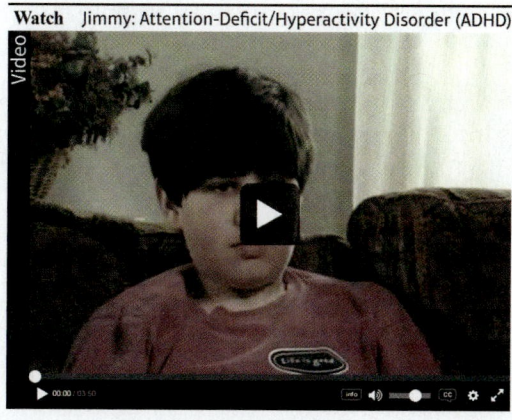

Watch Jimmy: Attention-Deficit/Hyperactivity Disorder (ADHD)

DSM-5 *Criteria for...*

Attention-Deficit/Hyperactivity Disorder

A. A persistent pattern of inattention and/or hyperactivity-impulsivity that interferes with functioning or development, as characterized by (1) and/or (2):

1. **Inattention:** Six (or more) of the following symptoms have persisted for at least 6 months to a degree that is inconsistent with developmental level and that negatively impacts directly on social and academic/occupational activities:

   Note: The symptoms are not solely a manifestation of oppositional behavior, defiance, hostility, or failure to understand tasks or instructions. For older adolescents and adults (age 17 and older), at least five symptoms are required.

   a. Often fails to give close attention to details or makes careless mistakes in schoolwork, at work, or during other activities (e.g., overlooks or misses details, work is inaccurate).

   b. Often has difficulty sustaining attention in tasks or play activities (e.g., has difficulty remaining focused during lectures, conversations, or lengthy reading).

   c. Often does not seem to listen when spoken to directly (e.g., mind seems elsewhere, even in the absence of any obvious distraction).

   d. Often does not follow through on instructions and fails to finish schoolwork, chores, or duties in the workplace (e.g., starts tasks but quickly loses focus and is easily sidetracked).

   e. Often has difficulty organizing tasks and activities (e.g., difficulty managing sequential tasks; difficulty keeping materials and belongings in order; messy, disorganized work; has poor time management; fails to meet deadlines).

   f. Often avoids, dislikes, or is reluctant to engage in tasks that require sustained mental effort (e.g., schoolwork or homework; for older adolescents and adults, preparing reports, completing forms, reviewing lengthy papers).

   g. Often loses things necessary for tasks or activities (e.g., school materials, pencils, books, tools, wallets, keys, paperwork, eyeglasses, mobile telephones).

   h. Is often easily distracted by extraneous stimuli (for older adolescents and adults, may include unrelated thoughts).

   i. Is often forgetful in daily activities (e.g., doing chores, running errands; for older adolescents and adults, returning calls, paying bills, keeping appointments).

2. **Hyperactivity and impulsivity:** Six (or more) of the following symptoms have persisted for at least 6 months to a degree that is inconsistent with developmental level and that negatively impacts directly on social and academic/occupational activities:

   Note: The symptoms are not solely a manifestation of oppositional behavior, defiance, hostility, or a failure to understand tasks or instructions. For older adolescents and adults (age 17 and older), at least five symptoms are required.

   a. Often fidgets with or taps hands or feet or squirms in seat.

   b. Often leaves seat in situations when remaining seated is expected (e.g., leaves his or her place in the classroom, in the office or other workplace, or in other situations that require remaining in place).

   c. Often runs about or climbs in situations where it is inappropriate.
   (**Note:** In adolescents or adults, may be limited to feeling restless.)

   d. Often unable to play or engage in leisure activities quietly.

   e. Is often "on the go," acting as if "driven by a motor" (e.g., is unable to be or uncomfortable being still for extended time, as in restaurants, meetings; may be experienced by others as being restless or difficult to keep up with).

   f. Often talks excessively.

   g. Often blurts out an answer before a question has been completed (e.g., completes people's sentences; cannot wait for turn in conversation).

   h. Often has difficulty waiting his or her turn (e.g., while waiting in line).

   i. Often interrupts or intrudes on others (e.g., butts into conversations, games, or activities; may start using other people's things without asking or receiving permission; for adolescents and adults, may intrude into or take over what others are doing).

B. Several inattentive or hyperactive-impulsive symptoms were present prior to age 12 years.

C. Several inattentive or hyperactive-impulsive symptoms are present in two or more settings (e.g., at home, school, or work; with friends or relatives; in other activities).

D. There is clear evidence that the symptoms interfere with, or reduce the quality of, social, academic, or occupational functioning.

E. The symptoms do not occur exclusively during the course of schizophrenia or another psychotic disorder and are not better explained by another mental disorder (e.g., mood disorder, anxiety disorder, dissociative disorder, personality disorder, substance intoxication or withdrawal).

Source: Reprinted with permission from the *Diagnostic and Statistical Manual of Mental Disorders*, Fifth Edition (Copyright 2013). American Psychiatric Association.

ADHD is fairly prevalent, occurring in approximately 9 percent of children and adolescents (Merikangas et al., 2010). Although it is not the most prevalent disorder among U.S. children and adolescents (specific phobia is seen in 19 percent of youth), it is the one that is most frequently diagnosed by health professionals (Ryan-Krause et al., 2010). The reason for this difference is that parents are much more likely to bring a child with ADHD in for treatment than they are a child with a less disruptive disorder such as specific phobia.

The rate of ADHD is much higher in boys (13 percent) than in girls (4 percent) (Merikangas et al., 2010) and is commonly comorbid with other externalizing disorders such as ODD and CD (Beauchaine et al., 2010; Frick & Nigg, 2012). ADHD is seen in cultures all around the world. For example, one study of 1,573 children from 10 European countries reported that ADHD symptoms are similarly recognized across all countries studied and that the children have significant impairments across a wide range of domains (Bauermeister et al., 2010).

Paul, a Student with ADHD

Paul was referred to a community clinic because of overactive, inattentive, and disruptive behavior. His hyperactivity and uninhibited behavior caused problems for his teachers and for other students. He would impulsively hit other children, knock things off their desks, erase material on the blackboard, and damage books and other school property. He seemed to be in perpetual motion, constantly talking and out of his seat. Although Paul was determined to be above average intelligence, he was receiving failing grades due in large part to his behavioral problems. Nevertheless, he often reported that he "felt stupid" and it was clear that he had a seriously devaluated self-image.

ADHD BEYOND ADOLESCENCE Although ADHD has long been thought of as a disorder that occurs only during childhood and adolescence, studies done in the United States and internationally suggest that approximately half of children with ADHD will continue to meet criteria in adulthood (Kessler, Green, et al., 2010; Lara et al., 2008). Interestingly, however, most cases of adult ADHD are characterized by symptoms of inattention (95 percent), whereas a much smaller percentage are characterized by hyperactivity (35 percent) (Kessler, Green, et al., 2010). It is estimated that approximately 4 percent of U.S. adults meet criteria for ADHD, with higher rates among those who are male, divorced, and unemployed (Kessler, Adler, et al., 2006). The association with unemployment may be due to trouble finding work, but may also be the result of poor work performance or absenteeism. One recent study showed that those with ADHD miss significantly more days of work (approximately 22 more days each year) than those without ADHD (de Graaf et al., 2008), highlighting the long-term impairment associated with this disorder.

Although children with ADHD are at elevated risk for employment problems later in life, most people with this disorder go on to have very happy and productive careers. For instance, the award-winning singer and actor Justin Timberlake has reported that he has struggled with ADHD, and he's doing pretty okay career-wise.

CAUSAL FACTORS IN ATTENTION-DEFICIT/HYPERACTIVITY DISORDER The specific causes of ADHD have been widely debated. As with most disorders, available evidence points to both genetic (Ilott et al., 2010; Sharp et al., 2009) and social-environmental factors (e.g., prenatal alcohol exposure; Ware et al., 2012). But how do genetic variations and social-environmental events produce the particular constellation of symptoms of ADHD that we see in children and adults? Research on the neurobiology of ADHD suggests that the answer may lie, at least in part, in the way that the brain develops in those with ADHD. Children with ADHD have smaller total brain volumes than those without ADHD (Castellanos et al., 2002), and their brains appear to mature approximately 3 years more slowly than those without ADHD (Shaw et al., 2007). Interestingly, these maturational delays are most prominent in prefrontal brain regions involved in attention and impulsiveness. Findings like these are exciting steps toward understanding this disorder, but questions remain about how and why these differences arise. Answering these questions will likely lead not just to better understanding, but to the development of more effective treatments.

TREATMENTS AND OUTCOMES Although hyperactivity in childhood was first described more than 100 years

Figure 15.5 The prevalence of stimulant use increased dramatically from the 1980s to the 1990s and remains at this higher level today. This increase is driven by prescriptions for those 6 to 18 years old. Based on the National Expenditure Survey (1987) and the Medical Expenditure Panel Survey (1996–2008).

(Adapted from Zuvekas, S. H., & Vitiello, B. (2012). Stimulant medication use in children: A 12-year perspective. *Am. J. Psychiatry, 169*(2), 160–166.)

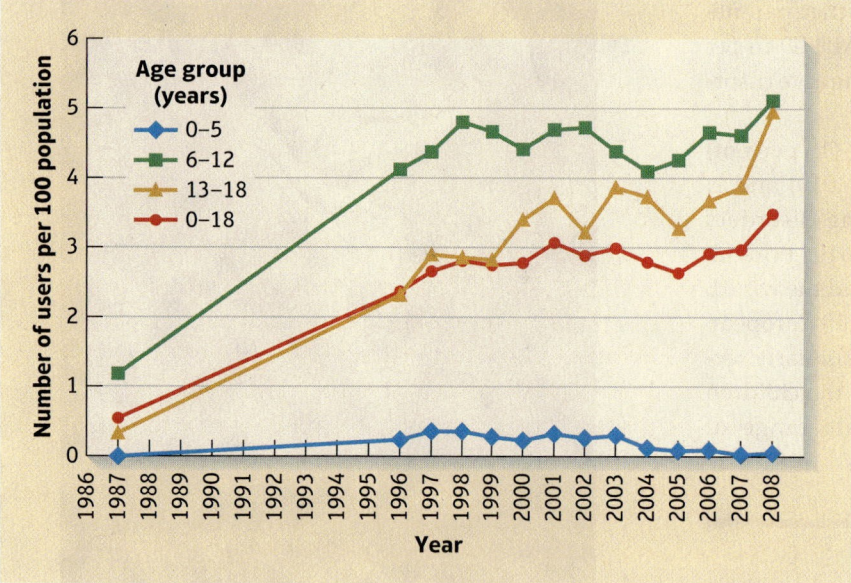

ago, disagreement over the most effective methods of treatment continues, especially regarding the use of stimulant medications such as **Ritalin** (methylphenidate) to treat young children with ADHD. Yet this approach to treating children with ADHD has great appeal in the medical community. Indeed, the use of stimulant medication to treat ADHD has risen dramatically in recent years, with this increase occurring primarily among adolescents (see Figure 15.5; Zuvekas & Vitiello, 2012).

Interestingly, research has shown that stimulants have a quieting effect on children—just the opposite of what we would expect from their effects on adults. For children with ADHD, stimulant medication decreases overactivity and distractibility and, at the same time, increases their alertness (Konrad et al., 2004). As a result, they are often able to function much better at school (Hazell, 2007; Pelham et al., 2002).

Ritalin also seems to lower the amount of aggressiveness in children with ADHD (Fava, 1997). In fact, many children whose behavior has not been acceptable in regular classes can function and progress in a relatively normal manner when they use such a drug. In a 5-year follow-up study, Charach, Ickowicz, and Schachar (2004) reported that children with ADHD on medication showed greater improvement in teacher-reported symptoms than non-treated children. The possible side effects of Ritalin, however, are numerous: decreased blood flow to the brain, which can result in impaired thinking ability and memory loss; disruption of growth hormone, leading to suppression of growth in the body and brain of the child; insomnia;

psychotic symptoms; and others. Although amphetamines do not cure ADHD, they have reduced the behavioral symptoms in about one-half to two-thirds of the cases in which medication appears warranted. Newer variants of the drug, referred to as extended-release methylphenidate (Concerta), have similar benefits and are available in doses that may better suit an adolescent's lifestyle (Mott & Leach, 2004; Spencer, 2004b).

Three other medications for treating ADHD have received attention in recent years. **Pemoline** is chemically very different from Ritalin (Faigel & Heiligenstein, 1996); it exerts beneficial effects on classroom behavior by enhancing cognitive processing and has fewer adverse side effects than Ritalin (Bostic et al., 2000; Pelham et al., 2005). **Strattera** (atomoxetine), a noncontrolled treatment option that can be obtained readily, is a U.S. Food and Drug Administration (FDA)-approved nonstimulant medication (FDA, 2002). Side effects include decreased appetite, nausea, vomiting, and fatigue. The development of jaundice has been reported, and the FDA (2004) has warned of the possibility of liver damage from using Strattera. Another drug that reduces symptoms of impulsivity and hyperactivity in children with ADHD is **Adderall**. This medication is a combination of amphetamine and dextroamphetamine; however, research has suggested that Adderall provides no advantage or improvement in results over Ritalin or Strattera (Miller-Horn et al., 2008). Although the short-term pharmacological effect of stimulants on the symptoms of hyperactive children is well established, their long-term effects are not well known (Safer, 1997a).

Although questions remain about the long-term effects of ADHD medications, recent studies have shown that adults with ADHD who take these medications show clear benefits. For instance, adults with ADHD are at significantly increased risk of outcomes such as car accidents and suicide attempts; however, the risk of these outcomes is significantly reduced when these adults are using ADHD medications (Chang et al., 2014; Chen et al., 2014).

Despite the benefits of these medications, the pharmacological similarity of Ritalin and cocaine has caused some investigators to be concerned about its use in the treatment of ADHD (Volkow et al., 1995). There have also been some reported recreational uses of Ritalin, particularly among college students. Kapner (2003) described several surveys in which Ritalin was reportedly abused on college campuses. In one survey, 16 percent of students at one university reported using Ritalin, and in another study 1.5 percent of the population surveyed reported using Ritalin for recreational purposes within the past 30 days. Some college students share the prescription medications of friends as a means of obtaining a "high" (Chutko et al., 2010).

Due to concerns about the use of stimulant medications with children, some parents and clinicians prefer using psychological interventions, which also have shown positive effects (Corcoran, 2011; Pelham & Fabiano, 2008). The behavioral intervention techniques that have been developed for ADHD include positive reinforcement of desired behaviors in the classroom (DuPaul et al., 1998) and family therapy (Everett & Everett, 2001). Van Lier and colleagues (2004) conducted a school-based behavioral intervention program using positive reinforcement aimed at preventing disruptive behavior in elementary school children. They found this program to be effective with children with ADHD with different levels of disorder but most effective with children at lower or intermediate levels.

Autism Spectrum Disorder

Autism spectrum disorder (which we refer to as "autism") is a neurodevelopmental disorder that involves a wide range of problematic behaviors including deficits in language and perceptual and motor development; defective reality testing; and impairments in social communication. The following case illustrates some of the behaviors that may be seen in a child with autism.

The Need for Routine

Matthew is 5 years old. He rarely speaks to others and almost never makes direct and sustained eye contact. Matthew's parents began to notice 3 years ago that while other children were starting to put words together into sentences and have back-and-forth conversations with their parents, he never seemed to develop these abilities. Matthew spends much of his time alone, often playing with his toys in his room. While doing so, he frequently engages in repetitive movements over and over again, such as wheeling his toy train back and forth hundreds of times in a row. Matthew doesn't like to leave his home, which his parents think has to do with him being overly sensitive to all of the sights and sounds outside. He also struggles when things deviate from his normal daily routine, which leads him to repeatedly scream at the top of his lungs several dozen times in a row.

Autism was first described in 1943 (Kanner). It afflicts tens of thousands of American children from all socioeconomic levels and is seemingly on the increase—estimates range between 30 and 60 people in 10,000 (Fombonne, 2005). A recent study by the Centers for Disease Control and Prevention (Baio, 2014) reported that the rate of autism among children is about 1 in 68. This reported increase in autism in recent years is likely due to methodological differences between studies and changes in diagnostic practice and public and professional awareness in recent years rather than an increase in prevalence (Williams et al., 2006). Autism is usually identified before a child is 30 months of age and diagnostic stability over the childhood years is quite high. Lord and colleagues (2006) report that children diagnosed with autism by age 2 tend to be similarly diagnosed at age 9. Recent research suggests that early signs of problems with social communication can be detected in the first 6 months of an infant's life (Jones & Klin, 2014). When scanning the world around them, typically developing infants from 2 to 6 months of age focus increasingly on the face and especially the eyes of others. This focus allows infants to better understand those caring for them and helps facilitate later social interaction. In contrast, children later diagnosed with autism show a significant *decline* in their focus on the eyes of others from 2 to 6 months of age and this decline continues until 24 months—at which point it is approximately half the level of focus as that seen in typically developing children (see Figure 15.6; Jones & Klin, 2014). In contrast, while their attention to other people's eyes decreases, infants later diagnosed with autism show a significant *increase* in their focus on inanimate objects, which is double the level of typically developing children by 24 months.

THE CLINICAL PICTURE IN AUTISTIC SPECTRUM DISORDER Children with autism show varying degrees of impairments and capabilities. A cardinal and typical sign is that a child seems apart or aloof from others, even in the earliest stages of life (Hillman et al., 2007). Mothers often remember such babies as not being cuddly, not reaching out when being picked up, not smiling or looking at them while being fed, and not appearing to notice the comings and goings of other people.

A Social Deficit Children with autism often do not show any need for affection or contact with others. Several studies, however, have questioned the traditional view that children with autism are emotionally flat. These studies have shown that children with autism do express emotions and should not be considered as lacking emotional reactions (Jones et al., 2001). Instead, some have characterized the seeming inability of children with autism to respond to others as a lack of social understanding—a deficit in the ability to attend to social cues from others. Indeed, neuroimaging studies have revealed that children with autism show decreased activity in the medial prefrontal cortex, a region associated with understanding the mental states of others, but increased activation in the ventral occipitotemporal regions involved in object perception (Sigman et al., 2006).

Additionally, children with autism show deficits in attention and in locating and orienting to sounds in their environment (Hillman et al., 2007). These children often show an

Figure 15.6 In a recent study by Jones and Klin (2014), the authors showed infants videos of humans and objects and found that children later diagnosed with autism showed a decline in their focus on the eyes of others (choosing instead to focus on inanimate objects). Part (A) shows eye-gaze data from a 6-month-old later diagnosed with autism, (B) shows eye-gaze data from a typically developing 6-month-old, (C) shows the pattern of decline for two children later diagnosed with autism, and (D) shows the pattern of stability for two typically developing children.

(Adapted from Jones & Klin, 2013.)

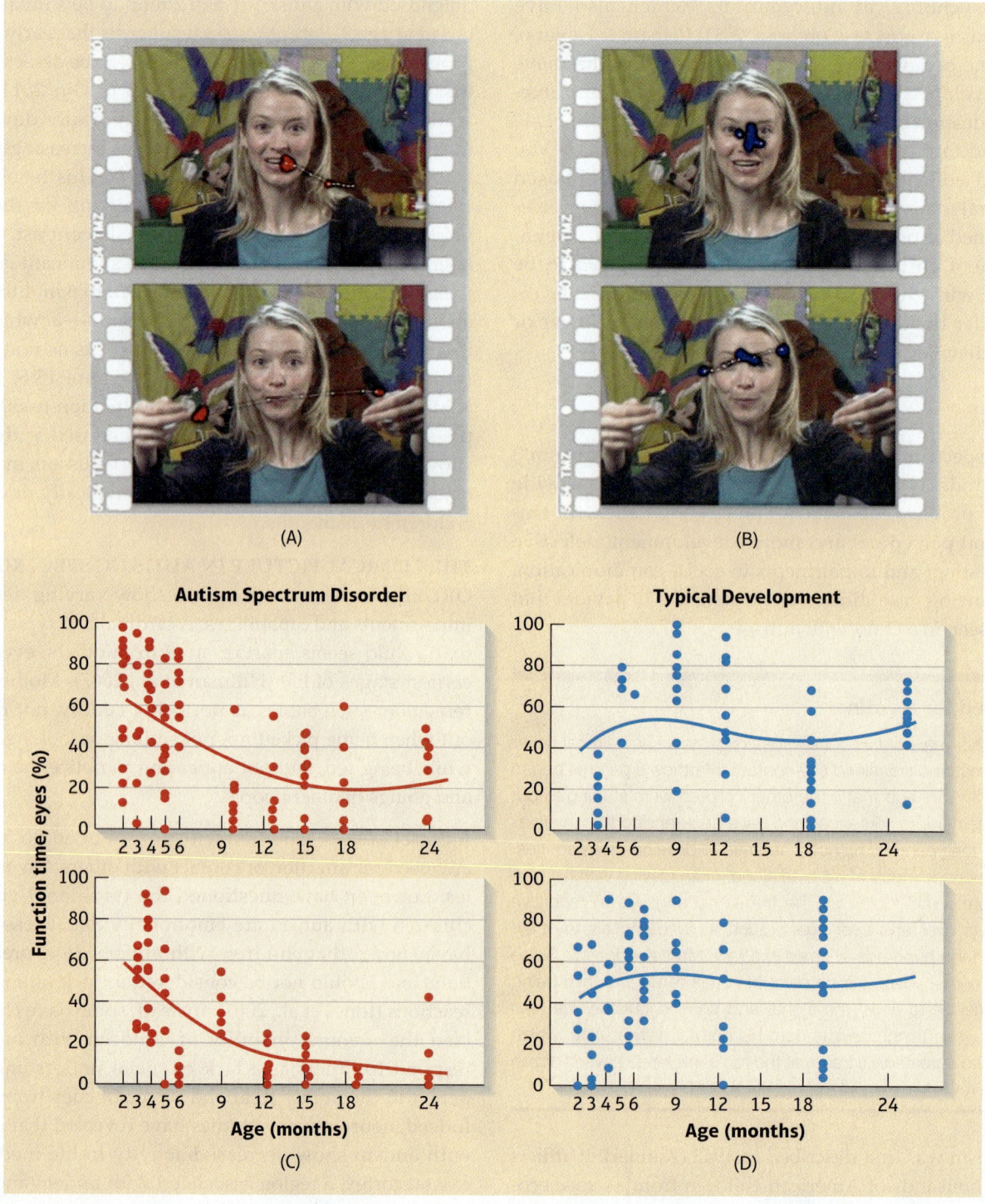

aversion to auditory stimuli, crying even at the sound of a parent's voice. The pattern is not always consistent, however; children with autism may at one moment be severely agitated or panicked by a very soft sound and at another time be totally oblivious to a loud noise.

An Absence of Speech Children with autism do not effectively learn by imitation (Smith & Bryson, 1994). This dysfunction might explain their characteristic absence or severely limited use of speech. If speech is present, it is almost never used to communicate except in the most

DSM-5 *Criteria for...*

Autism Spectrum Disorder

A. Persistent deficits in social communication and social interaction across multiple contexts, as manifested by the following, currently or by history (examples are illustrative, not exhaustive; see text):

1. Deficits in social-emotional reciprocity, ranging, for example, from abnormal social approach and failure of normal back-and-forth conversation; to reduced sharing of interests, emotions, or affect; to failure to initiate or respond to social interactions.

2. Deficits in nonverbal communicative behaviors used for social interaction, ranging, for example, from poorly integrated verbal and nonverbal communication; to abnormalities in eye contact and body language or deficits in understanding and use of gestures; to a total lack of facial expressions and nonverbal communication.

3. Deficits in developing, maintaining, and understanding relationships, ranging, for example, from difficulties adjusting behavior to suit various social contexts; to difficulties in sharing imaginative play or in making friends; to absence of interest in peers.

B. Restricted, repetitive patterns of behavior, interests, or activities, as manifested by at least two of the following, currently or by history (examples are illustrative, not exhaustive; see text):

1. Stereotyped or repetitive motor movements, use of objects, or speech (e.g., simple motor stereotypies, lining up toys or flipping objects, echolalia, idiosyncratic phrases).

2. Insistence on sameness, inflexible adherence to routines, or ritualized patterns of verbal or nonverbal behavior (e.g., extreme distress at small changes, difficulties with transitions, rigid thinking patterns, greeting rituals, need to take same route or eat same food every day).

3. Highly restricted, fixated interests that are abnormal in intensity or focus (e.g., strong attachment to or preoccupation with unusual objects, excessively circumscribed or perseverative interests).

4. Hyper- or hyporeactivity to sensory input or unusual interest in sensory aspects of the environment (e.g., apparent indifference to pain/temperature, adverse response to specific sounds or textures, excessive smelling or touching of objects, visual fascination with lights or movement).

C. Symptoms must be present in the early developmental period (but may not become fully manifest until social demands exceed limited capacities, or may be masked by learned strategies in later life).

D. Symptoms cause clinically significant impairment in social, occupational, or other important areas of current functioning.

E. These disturbances are not better explained by intellectual disability (intellectual developmental disorder) or global developmental delay. Intellectual disability and autism spectrum disorder frequently co-occur; to make comorbid diagnoses of autism spectrum disorder and intellectual disability, social communication should be below that expected for general developmental level.

Note: Individuals with a well-established DSM-IV diagnosis of autistic disorder, Asperger's disorder, or pervasive developmental disorder not otherwise specified should be given the diagnosis of autism spectrum disorder. Individuals who have marked deficits in social communication, but whose symptoms do not otherwise meet criteria for autism spectrum disorder, should be evaluated for social (pragmatic) communication disorder.

Source: Reprinted with permission from the *Diagnostic and Statistical Manual of Mental Disorders*, Fifth Edition (Copyright 2013). American Psychiatric Association.

---

rudimentary fashion, such as by saying "yes" in answer to a question or by the use of **echolalia**—the parrot-like repetition of a few words. Whereas the echoing of parents' verbal behavior is found to a small degree in normal children as they experiment with their ability to produce articulate speech, persistent echolalia is found in about 75 percent of children with autism (Prizant, 1983).

Self-Stimulation Self-stimulation is often characteristic of children with autism. It usually takes the form of such repetitive movements as head banging, spinning, and rocking, which may continue by the hour.

Maintaining Sameness Many children with autism become preoccupied with and form strong attachments to unusual objects such as rocks, light switches, or keys. When their preoccupation with the object is disturbed—for example, by its removal or by attempts to substitute something in its place—or when anything familiar in the environment is altered even slightly, these children may have a violent temper tantrum or a crying spell that continues until the familiar situation is restored. Thus children with autism are often said to be "obsessed with the maintenance of sameness."

Watch Xavier: Autism Spectrum Disorder

CAUSAL FACTORS IN AUTISM   Autism is a complex disorder and its precise causes are unknown. Twin and sibling studies have shown that there is a very strong heritable component in autism. For instance, 2 to 14 percent of siblings of children diagnosed with autism also have the disorder, and approximately 20 percent have some symptoms of the disorder (Newschaffer et al., 2007). Although there is a clear heritable component, the exact mode of genetic transmission is not yet understood. On one hand, recent research has shown that hundreds of different genes are associated with increased risk of autism, suggesting that there are many different paths to developing this disorder (Robinson et al., 2014; State & Šestan, 2012). On the other hand, research also has shown that the same genetic variants are associated with multiple disorders. For instance, some of the same genes that have been linked with an increased risk of autism also increase the risk of ADHD, schizophrenia, bipolar disorder, and depression (Smoller et al., 2013).

Given the complexity of this picture, how will we ever know what causes autism? Researchers are pursuing several different avenues of research to try to answer this question. They are trying to determine what portion of the genetic risk is inherited (52 percent) and what portion is due to *de novo* genetic mutations (3 percent). *De novo* mutations are those that occur in the egg or sperm and are passed on to every cell in the child's body, despite not appearing in the parents' DNA. It seems that much of the risk for autism is indeed inherited from one's parents (Gaugler et al., 2014). However, a significant portion of risk also arises due to *de novo* mutations. This is important to know, because as we learn about factors that increase the likelihood of genetic mutations, we can take steps to try to decrease their occurrence. For instance, genetic mutations have been reported to occur at higher rates in the sperm of older men, and there is now converging evidence that older father age at a child's birth is associated with increased risk of autism (D'Onofrio et al., 2014). Findings like these do not explain how or why such mutations increase the risk of autism, but can be useful for the purposes of family planning.

TREATMENTS AND OUTCOMES OF AUTISM   The treatment prognosis for many children with autism is poor in part because so many people with autism are insufficiently treated (Moldin & Rubenstein, 2006). Moreover, many children with autism are subjected to a range of fads and "novel" approaches that have little to no support for their effectiveness. The good news, however, is that intensive behavioral treatments have proven to be effective for many people diagnosed with autism.

Behavioral Treatment   For many years, it was generally accepted that there is no effective way to treat people diagnosed with autism. However, in 1987, Ivar Lovaas (1987) reported that an intensive behavioral intervention administered via one-on-one meetings with the child for over 40 hours per week for 2 years resulted in extremely positive results. The intervention was based on both discrimination-training strategies (reinforcement) and contingent aversive techniques (punishment). The treatment plan typically enlists parents in the process and emphasizes teaching children to learn from and interact with "normal" peers in real-world situations. Of the treated children in the study by Lovaas and colleagues, 47 percent achieved normal intellectual and educational functioning, compared with only 2 percent of children in the untreated control condition.

More recent versions of this intensive behavioral approach have continued to demonstrate success. Geraldine Dawson and colleagues (2010) recently showed that toddlers (18–30 months old) with autism who were randomly assigned to receive the Early Start Denver Model (ESDM) intervention showed significant improvements in IQ (an average of a 17-point increase), language, and adaptive behavior as well as a decrease in symptoms of autism. The ESDM intervention involves more than 20 hours per week of intensive behavioral work with the child and parent(s) focused on interpersonal exchanges, verbal and nonverbal communication, and adult sensitivity to children's cues. Children receiving the ESDM intervention also showed greater cortical activation when viewing other people's faces (compared to objects), which in turn was correlated with greater improvements in the children's social communication (Dawson et al., 2012). Although treatments like this one are extremely time consuming, their powerful results suggest that behavioral interventions can cause improvements in people diagnosed with autism. See the Developments in Practice box for other novel approaches to treating autism.

Tic Disorders

A **tic** is a persistent, intermittent muscle twitch or spasm, usually limited to a localized muscle group. The term is used broadly to include blinking the eye, twitching the mouth, licking the lips, shrugging the shoulders, clearing the throat, and grimacing, among other actions. Tic disorders are classified under motor disorders in *DSM-5*. Tics occur most frequently between the ages of 2 and 14 (Evans et al., 1996). In some instances, as in clearing the throat, an individual may be aware of the tic when it occurs, but usually he or she performs the act habitually and does not notice it. In fact, many individuals do not even realize they have a tic unless someone brings it to their attention. A cross-cultural examination of tics found a similar pattern in research and clinical case reports from other countries (Staley et al., 1997). Moreover, the age of onset (average 7 to 8 years old) and predominant gender (male) of cases were

Developments in Practice

Can Video Games Help Children with Neurodevelopmental Disorders?

Kids love video games. They are fun, provide ongoing and immediate reinforcement, and are able to engage children's attention for hours at a time. While capturing children's attention for hours at a time, many popular video games teach children how to get very good at driving cars at high speeds (*Mario Kart Wii*), shooting at people (*Call of Duty*), or both (*Grand Theft Auto*). Recently, however, psychologists have been experimenting with using video games to engage children while teaching them social, cognitive, and emotional skills. Although children with autism often have trouble with attention and disruptive behavior, they can readily become engrossed in the world of video games (Durkin, 2010). Researchers are now using new technologies, including video games, to help children with autism to improve on some of their social, cognitive, and emotional deficits. For instance, children with autism have trouble producing emotional expressions, which contributes to their social communication problems. To address this, researchers developed a Pacman-like game in which the player has to gobble up candy, but in order to get to the candy, the player must remove obstacles in his or her path by producing different facial expressions (e.g., happy, angry), which are read by computer facial recognition software (see Figure 15.7). Gordon and colleagues (2014) showed that children with autism who play this game show improvements in their facial expressions of emotion, and in fact make them indistinguishable in quality from those of typically developing children.

As part of their difficulty communicating with others, children with autism often have trouble delivering compliments appropriately. This contributes to their impairment, because compliments can increase the extent to which others like us and want to engage with us socially. To address this, Macpherson, Charlop, and Miltenberger (2014) created an iPad®-based video training that showed children how to compliment others. The use of portable technology allowed them to test this intervention in a real-world child setting: a kickball game! They showed that when kids with autism played kickball, they didn't compliment their teammates very much at all. However, when they administered the

Figure 15.7   In this "Happy" level of the game *FaceMaze*, the player (represented by the purple face) must move through the maze eating candy pieces and has to make a "happy" expression to remove the yellow faces blocking his path. Gordon and colleagues (2014) showed that playing this game significantly improves the ability to make different facial expressions in children with autism.

(From Gordon et al., 2014, *J. Autism Dev. Disord.*, Springer.)

intervention, which consisted of showing a video of someone complimenting a teammate (e.g., saying "That was a great kick!" and doing a fist pump), the children showed a significant increase in their use of verbal compliments and gestures. That is, there was a whole lotta fist pumping going on!

The use of video games and newer, portable technologies has attracted many people's interest, but also has prompted some important questions. For instance, research has shown that kids with autism tend to play video games for longer duration than other kids, and show greater sleep problems than typically developing kids as a result (Engelhardt et al., 2013), raising concerns about game overuse among those with autism. Although the available and acceptable use of computer-based learning methods show promise, there are professional issues and program research limitations that need to be more fully explored before the full potential of this methodology is reached.

---

reported to be similar across cultures (Turan & Senol, 2000). A recent study on the prevalence of tic disorder in children and adolescents reported that the lifetime prevalence of tic disorders (TDs) is 2.6 percent for transient tic disorder (TTD), 3.7 percent for chronic tic disorder (CTD), and 0.6 percent for Tourette's disorder (Stefanoff et al., 2008). The psychological impact that tics can have on an adolescent is illustrated in the following case.

A Vicious Cycle of Tics and Anxiety

An adolescent who had wanted very much to be a teacher told the school counselor that he was thinking of giving up his plans. When asked why, he explained that several friends had told him that he had a persistent twitching of the mouth muscles when he answered questions in class. He had been unaware of this muscle twitch and, even after being told about it, could not tell when it took place. However, he became acutely self-conscious and was reluctant to answer questions or enter into class discussions. As a result, his general level of tension increased, and so did the frequency of the tic, which now became apparent even when he was talking to his friends. Thus, a vicious circle had been established. Fortunately, the tic proved amenable to treatment by conditioning and assertiveness training.

Tourette's disorder, classified as a motor disorder in the neurodevelopmental disorders section of *DSM-5*, is an extreme tic disorder involving multiple motor and vocal patterns. This disorder typically involves uncontrollable head movements with accompanying sounds such as grunts, clicks, yelps, sniffs, or words. Some, possibly most, tics are preceded by an urge or sensation that seems to be relieved by execution of the tic. Tics are thus often difficult to differentiate from compulsions, and they are sometimes referred to as "compulsive tics" (Jankovic, 1997). An epidemiological study in Sweden reported the prevalence of Tourette's disorder in children and adolescents to be about 0.5 percent (Khalifa & von Knorring, 2004). Approximately one-third of individuals with Tourette's disorder manifest coprolalia, which is a complex vocal tic that involves the uttering of obscenities. Some people with Tourette's disorder also experience explosive outbursts (Budman et al., 2000). The average age of onset for Tourette's disorder is 7, and most cases have an onset before age 14. The disorder frequently persists into adulthood, and it is about three times more frequent among males than among females. Although the exact cause of Tourette's disorder is undetermined, evidence suggests a strong biological basis (Margolis et al., 2006). There are many types of tics, and many of them appear to be associated with the presence of other psychological disorders, particularly obsessive-compulsive disorder (OCD). Most tics, however, do not have a purely biological basis but stem from psychological causes such as self-consciousness or tension in social situations, and they are usually associated with severe behavioral problems (Rosenberg et al., 1995). As in the case of the adolescent boy previously described, an individual's awareness of the tic often increases tension and the occurrence of the tic.

Behavioral interventions also have been used to effectively treat tics (Woods & Miltenberger, 2001). One successful program, habit reversal training or HRT, involves several sequential elements, beginning with awareness training, relaxation training, and the development of incompatible responses, and then progressing to cognitive therapy and modification of the individual's overall style of action (Chang, Piacentina, & Walkup, 2007). Because children with Tourette's disorder can have substantial family adjustment (Wilkinson et al., 2001) and school adjustment problems (Nolan & Gadow, 1997), interventions should be designed to aid their adjustment and to modify the reactions of peers to them. School psychologists can play an effective part in the social adjustment of the child with Tourette's disorder by applying behavioral intervention strategies that help arrange the child's environment to be more accepting of such unusual behaviors.

Among medications, neuroleptics are the most predictably effective tic-suppressing drugs (Kurlan, 1997). Clonazepam, clonidine, and tiapride have all shown effectiveness in reducing motor tics; however, tiapride has shown the greatest decrease in the intensity and frequency of tics (Drtikova et al., 1996). Campbell and Cueva (1995) reported that both haloperidol and pimozide reduced the severity of tics by about 65 percent but that haloperidol seemed the more effective of the two medications.

---

in review

- Describe the symptoms of ADHD.
- What is known about the causes and treatments of autism spectrum disorder?
- How can tic disorder be effectively treated?

Specific Learning Disorders

15.6 Describe what is currently known about the causes and treatment of learning disorders.

Learning disorders are delays in cognitive development in the areas of language, speech, mathematical, or motor skills that are not necessarily due to any demonstrable physical or neurological defect. Of these types of problems, the best known and most widely researched are a variety of reading/writing difficulties known collectively as **dyslexia**. In dyslexia, the individual has problems in word recognition and reading comprehension; often he or she is markedly deficient in spelling and memory (Smith-Spark & Fisk, 2007) as well. On assessments of reading skill, these persons routinely omit, add, and distort words, and their reading is typically painfully slow.

The diagnosis of learning disorders is restricted to those cases in which there is clear impairment in school performance or (if the person is not a student) in daily living activities—impairment not due to intellectual disability or to a pervasive developmental disorder such as autism. Skill deficits due to ADHD are coded under ADHD. This coding presents another diagnostic dilemma, however, because some investigators hold that an attention deficit is basic to many learning disorders; evidence for the latter view is equivocal (see Faraone et al., 1993). Children (and adults) with these disorders are more generally said to have a learning disorder. Significantly more boys than girls are diagnosed as having a learning disorder, but estimates of the extent of this gender discrepancy have varied widely from study to study. Prevalence estimates have shown that approximately 1 in 59, or 4.6 million people, in the United States (National Institutes of Mental Health, 2007) have a learning disorder.

Children with learning disorders can experience deep emotional tension under normal learning circumstances.

Children with learning disorder are initially identified as such because of an apparent disparity between their expected academic achievement level and their actual academic performance in one or more school subjects such as math, spelling, writing, or reading. Typically, these children have overall IQs, family backgrounds, and exposure to cultural norms and symbols that are consistent with at least average achievement in school. They do not have obvious, crippling emotional problems, nor do they seem to be lacking in motivation, cooperativeness, or eagerness to please their teachers and parents—at least not at the outset of their formal education. Nevertheless, they fail, often abysmally and usually with a stubborn, puzzling persistence.

The consequences of these encounters between children with learning disabilities and rigid school systems can be disastrous to these children's self-esteem and general psychological well-being, and research indicates that these effects do not necessarily dissipate after secondary schooling ends but continue to impact these individuals' career adjustments (Morris & Turnbull, 2007). Thus, even when learning disorder difficulties are no longer a significant impediment, an individual may bear, into maturity and beyond, the scars of many painful school-related episodes of failure.

But there is also a brighter side to this picture. High levels of general talent and of motivation to overcome the obstacle of a learning disorder sometimes produce a life of extraordinary achievement. Sir Winston Churchill, British statesman, author, and inspiring World War II leader, is said to have had dyslexia as a child. The same attribution is made to Woodrow Wilson, former university professor and president of the United States, and to Nelson Rockefeller, former governor of New York and vice president of the United States. Such examples remind us that the "bad luck" and personal adversity of having a learning disorder need not be uniformly limiting—in fact, quite the contrary.

Causal Factors in Learning Disorder

Probably the most widely held view of the causes of specific learning disorders is that they are the products of subtle CNS impairments. In particular, these disabilities are thought to result from some sort of immaturity, deficiency, or dysregulation limited to those brain functions that supposedly mediate, for normal children, the cognitive skills that children with learning disorders cannot efficiently acquire. For example, many researchers believe that language-related learning disorders such as dyslexia are associated with a failure of the brain to develop in a normally asymmetrical manner with respect to the right and left hemispheres. Specifically, portions of the left hemisphere, where language function is normally mediated, for unknown reasons appear to remain relatively underdeveloped in many people with dyslexia (Beaton, 1997). Recent work with functional magnetic resonance imaging (see Chapter 4) has suggested that people with dyslexia have a deficiency of physiological activation in the cerebellum (Richards et al., 2005).

Some investigators believe that the various forms of learning disorder, or the vulnerability to develop them, may be genetically transmitted. This issue seems not to have been studied with the same intensity or methodological rigor as in other disorders, but identification of a gene region for dyslexia on chromosome 6 has been reported (Schulte-Koerne, 2001). Although it would be somewhat surprising if a single gene were identified as the causal factor in all cases of reading disorder, the hypothesis of a genetic contribution to at least the dyslexic form of learning disorder seems promising. One twin study of mathematics disability has also turned up evidence of some genetic contribution to this form of learning disorder (Alarcon et al., 1997).

Treatments and Outcomes

Because we do not yet have a confident grasp of any specific impairment that is present in most children with a learning disorder, it is important to have a clear assessment of each child's problems and abilities (Mapou, 2009) so that successful treatment can be appropriately tailored and implemented. We have had limited success

DSM-5   Thinking Critically about *DSM-5*

What Role Should Cultural Changes Have in Developing Medical Terminology?

Along with the addition of new diagnostic categories, such as gambling disorder and hoarding disorder, and the revision of other earlier diagnostic criteria resulting in disorders such as disruptive mood dysregulation disorder, there have been changes to some existing categories that are largely nominal in order to make the terminology more appropriate with contemporary language use and/or consistent with forthcoming *International Classification of Diseases (ICD-11)* system.

One noteworthy revision in *DSM-5* is the removal of the term *mental retardation*, which was used in describing individuals with intellectual impairment in previous editions of the *DSM*. However, the term *mental retardation* has come to be considered derogatory by many. The new term, *intellectual disability*, has replaced *mental retardation* and is becoming more commonly used by professionals, by the lay public, and by various advocacy groups. As noted by the *DSM-5* committee, a U.S.

legal statute (Public Law 111-256 or Rosa's Law) has replaced the term *mental retardation* with *intellectual disability*. At the Second Session of the 111 Congress of the United States in 2010 the following resolution was passed:

> (b) INDIVIDUALS WITH DISABILITIES EDUCATION ACT—
> (1) SECTION 601(c) (12)(C) of the Individuals with Disabilities Education Act (20 U.S.C. 1400(c) (12)(C) is amended by striking "having mental retardation" and inserting "having intellectual disabilities."

What role should cultural changes have in developing medical terminology? If a term for a psychiatric or medical condition takes on a negative connotation in our society, should it be changed? Or should we instead engage in public education campaigns in order to change the negative connotation and stigma? Who should make decisions about medical terminology, and what factors should they consider?

---

in treating many of these children. Many informal and single-case reports claim success with various treatment approaches, but direct instruction strategies often do not succeed in transforming these children's abilities (Gettinger & Koscik, 2001), and there are few well-designed and well-executed outcome studies on specific treatments for learning disorders.

We have only limited data on the long-term, adult adjustments of people who grew up with the personal, academic, and social problems that learning disorder generally entails. Two studies of college students with learning disorder (Gregg & Hoy, 1989) suggest that as a group they continue to have problems—academic, personal, and social—into the postsecondary education years. In a community survey of adults with learning disorder, Khan, Cowan, and Roy, (1997) found that some 50 percent of them had personality abnormalities. Cato and Rice (1982) extracted from the available literature a lengthy list of problems experienced by the typical adult with a learning disorder. These include—in addition to expected difficulties with self-confidence—continuing problems with deficits in the ordinary skills such as math that these people had trouble with as children. The authors do note, however, that there are considerable individual differences in these outcomes and that some adults with learning disorder are able to manage very well.

---

in review

- What is dyslexia?
- How long do learning disorders typically last?

Intellectual Disability

15.7   Define intellectual disability and name three known causal factors involved in its development.

Intellectual disability (also called *intellectual developmental disorder*) is characterized by deficits in general mental abilities, such as reasoning, problem solving, planning, abstract thinking, judgment, academic learning, and learning from experience (APA, 2013, p. 31). Intellectual disability is defined in terms of both intelligence and level of performance, and for the diagnosis to apply these problems must begin before the age of 18. By definition, any functional equivalent of intellectual disability that has its onset after age 17 is considered to be "dementia" rather than intellectual disability. The distinction is an important one because the psychological situation of a person who acquires a pronounced impairment of intellectual functioning after attaining maturity is vastly different from that of a person whose intellectual resources were below normal throughout all or most of his or her development.

Intellectual disability occurs among children throughout the world (Fryers, 2000). In its most severe forms, it is a source of great hardship to parents as well as an economic and social burden on a community. The prevalence of diagnosed intellectual disability in the United States is estimated to be about 1 percent, which would indicate a population estimate of some 2.6 million people. However, prevalence is extremely difficult to pin down because definitions of intellectual disability vary considerably (Roeleveld et al., 1997). Most states have laws providing that persons with IQs below 70 who show socially incompetent or persistently problematic behavior can be classified as "mentally retarded" and, if judged otherwise unmanageable, may be placed in an institution.

Initial diagnoses of intellectual disability most frequently occur at ages 5 to 6 (around the time that schooling begins for most children), peak at age 15, and drop off sharply after that. For the most part, these patterns in age of first diagnosis reflect changes in life demands. During early childhood, individuals with only a mild degree of intellectual impairment, who constitute the vast majority of those with intellectual disability, often appear to be normal. Their below-average intellectual functioning becomes apparent only when difficulties with schoolwork lead to a diagnostic evaluation. When adequate facilities are available for their education, children in this group can usually master essential school skills and achieve a satisfactory level of socially adaptive behavior. Following the school years, they usually make a more or less acceptable adjustment in the community and thus lose the identity of having an intellectual disability.

Individuals with mild intellectual disability constitute the largest number of those categorized as having an intellectual disability. With help, a great majority of these individuals can adjust socially, master simple academic and occupational skills, and become self-supporting citizens.

Levels of Intellectual Disability

The various levels of intellectual disability are described in greater detail in the following sections.

MILD INTELLECTUAL DISABILITY   Tests of human intelligence produce IQ scores that have an average of 100 and a standard deviation of 15. That means that most people (95 percent) receive a score somewhere between 70 and 130. Individuals with mild intellectual disability have IQ scores ranging from 50–55 to approximately 70 (i.e., more than two standard deviations below the mean) and constitute by far the largest number of those diagnosed with this condition (see Table 15.1). Within the educational context, people in this group are considered educable, and their intellectual levels as adults are comparable to those of

average 8- to 11-year-old children. Statements such as the latter, however, should not be taken too literally. An adult with mild disability with a mental age of, say, 10 (that is, his or her intelligence test performance is at the level of the average 10-year-old) may not in fact be comparable to the average 10-year-old in information-processing ability or speed (Weiss et al., 1986). On the other hand, he or she will normally have had far more experience in living, which would tend to raise the measured intelligence scores.

Table 15.1 Disability Severity and IQ Ranges

Diagnosed Level of Intellectual Disability	Corresponding IQ Range
Mild disability	50–55 to approximately 70
Moderate disability	35–40 to 50–55
Severe disability	20–25 to 35–40
Profound disability	Below 20–25

The social adjustment of people with mild intellectual disability often approximates that of adolescents, although they tend to lack normal adolescents' imagination, inventiveness, and judgment. Ordinarily, they do not show signs of brain pathology or other physical anomalies, but often they require some measure of supervision because of their limited abilities to foresee the consequences of their actions. With early diagnosis, parental assistance, and special educational programs, the great majority of individuals with mild intellectual disability can adjust socially, master simple academic and occupational skills, and become self-supporting citizens (Maclean, 1997).

MODERATE INTELLECTUAL DISABILITY   Individuals with moderate intellectual disability have IQ scores ranging between 35–40 and 50–55 and, even in adulthood, attain intellectual levels similar to those of average 4- to 7-year-old children. Although some can be taught to read and write a little and may manage to achieve a fair command of spoken language, their rate of learning is slow, and their level of conceptualizing is extremely limited. They usually appear clumsy and ungainly and suffer from bodily deformities and poor motor coordination. In general, with early diagnosis, parental help, and adequate opportunities for training, most individuals with moderate intellectual disability can achieve partial independence in daily self-care, acceptable behavior, and economic sustenance in a family or other sheltered environment. Many also can master routine skills such as cooking or minor janitorial work if provided specialized instruction in these activities.

SEVERE INTELLECTUAL DISABILITY   Individuals with severe intellectual disability have IQ scores ranging from 20–25 to 35–40 and commonly suffer from impaired speech development, sensory defects, and motor handicaps. They can develop limited levels of personal hygiene and self-help skills, which somewhat lessen their dependency, but they are always dependent on others for care. However, many profit to some extent from training and can perform simple occupational tasks under supervision.

PROFOUND INTELLECTUAL DISABILITY Most individuals with profound intellectual disability have IQ scores below 20–25 and are severely deficient in adaptive behavior and unable to master any but the simplest tasks. Useful speech, if it develops at all, is rudimentary. Severe physical deformities, CNS pathology, and retarded growth are typical; convulsive seizures, mutism, deafness, and other physical anomalies are also common. These individuals must remain in custodial care all their lives. Unfortunately, they also tend to have poor health and low resistance to disease and thus a short life expectancy. Severe and profound cases of intellectual disability can usually be readily diagnosed in infancy because of the presence of obvious physical malformations, grossly delayed development (e.g., in taking solid food), and other obvious symptoms of abnormality. These individuals show a marked impairment of overall intellectual functioning.

Causal Factors in Intellectual Disability

Some cases of intellectual disability occur in association with known organic brain pathology (Kaski, 2000). In these cases, the level of disability is virtually always at least moderate, and it is often severe. Profound intellectual disability, which fortunately is rare, always includes obvious organic impairment. In this section, we consider five biological conditions that may lead to intellectual disability, noting some of the possible interrelationships among them. Then we review some of the major clinical types of intellectual disability associated with these organic causes.

GENETIC-CHROMOSOMAL FACTORS Intellectual disability, especially mild disability, tends to run in families. Poverty and sociocultural deprivation, however, also tend to run in families. Early and continued exposure to such conditions, even the inheritance of average intellectual potential, may not prevent below-average intellectual functioning.

Genetic-chromosomal factors play a much clearer role in the etiology of relatively infrequent but more severe types of intellectual disability such as Down syndrome and a heritable condition known as fragile X (Huber & Tamminga, 2007; Schwarte, 2008). The gene responsible for fragile X syndrome (*FMR-1*) was identified in 1991 (Verkerk et al., 1991). In such conditions, genetic aberrations are responsible for metabolic alterations that adversely affect the brain's development. Genetic defects leading to metabolic alterations may also involve many

other developmental anomalies besides intellectual disability (e.g., autism) (Wassink et al., 2001). Intellectual disability associated with known genetic-chromosomal defects tends to be moderate to severe in nature.

INFECTIONS AND TOXIC AGENTS Intellectual disability also can result from a wide range of conditions due to infection, such as viral encephalitis or genital herpes (Kaski, 2000). If a pregnant woman is infected with syphilis or HIV-1 or if she gets German measles, her child may suffer brain damage as a result.

A number of toxic agents such as carbon monoxide and lead may cause brain damage during fetal development or after birth (Kaski, 2000). Similarly, if taken by a pregnant woman, certain drugs, including an excess of alcohol (West et al., 1998), may lead to congenital malformations. And an overdose of drugs administered to an infant may result in toxicity and cause brain damage. In rare cases, brain damage results from incompatibility in blood types between mother and fetus. Fortunately, early diagnosis and blood transfusions can minimize the effects of such incompatibility.

TRAUMA (PHYSICAL INJURY) Physical injury at birth can result in intellectual disability (Kaski, 2000). Although the fetus is normally well protected by its fluid-filled placenta during gestation, and although its skull resists delivery stressors, accidents that affect development can occur during delivery and after birth. Difficulties in labor due to malposition of the fetus or other complications may irreparably damage the infant's brain. Bleeding within the brain is probably the most common result of such birth trauma. Hypoxia—lack of sufficient oxygen to the brain stemming from delayed breathing or other causes—is another type of birth trauma that may damage the brain.

IONIZING RADIATION In recent decades, a good deal of scientific attention has focused on the damaging effects of ionizing radiation on sex cells and other bodily cells and tissues. Radiation may act directly on the fertilized ovum or may produce gene mutations in the sex cells of either or both parents, which may lead to intellectual disability among offspring. Sources of harmful radiation were once limited primarily to high-energy X-rays used in medicine for diagnosis and therapy, but the list has grown to include nuclear weapons testing and leakages at nuclear power plants, among others.

MALNUTRITION AND OTHER BIOLOGICAL FACTORS It was long thought that dietary deficiencies in protein and other essential nutrients during early development of the fetus could do irreversible physical and mental damage. However, it is currently believed that this assumption of a direct causal link may have been oversimplified. Ricciuti (1993) cited growing evidence that malnutrition may affect mental development more indirectly by altering a child's responsiveness, curiosity, and motivation to learn, which would in turn lead to intellectual disability. The implication here is that at least some malnutrition-associated intellectual deficit is a special case of psychosocial deprivation, which is also involved in disability-related outcomes, as described below.

Organic Intellectual Disability Syndromes

Intellectual disability stemming primarily from biological causes can be classified into several recognizable clinical types (Murphy et al., 1998), of which Down syndrome, phenylketonuria, and cranial anomalies are discussed here. Table 15.2 presents information on several other well-known forms.

DOWN SYNDROME   First described by Langdon Down in 1866, **Down syndrome** is the best known of the clinical conditions associated with moderate and severe intellectual disability. The prevalence of Down syndrome has been reported to be 5.9 per 10,000 of the general population (Cooper et al., 2009). It is a condition that creates irreversible limitations on intellectual achievement, competence in managing life tasks, and survivability (Bittles et al., 2007; Patterson & Lott, 2008). It also is associated with health problems in later life such as pneumonia and other respiratory infections. The availability of amniocentesis and chorionic villus sampling in expectant mothers has made it possible to detect in utero the extra genetic material involved in Down syndrome, which is most often the trisomy of chromosome 21, yielding 47 rather than the normal 46 chromosomes.

The Clinical Picture in Down Syndrome   A number of physical features are often found among children with Down syndrome, but few of these children have all of the

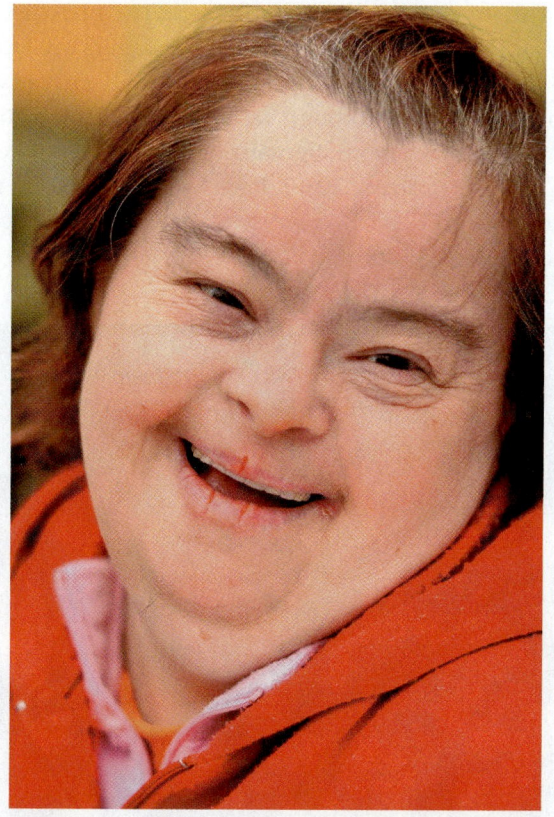

Physical features found among children with Down syndrome include almond-shaped eyes, abnormally thick skin on the eyelids, and a face and nose that are often flat and broad. The tongue may seem too big for the mouth and may show deep fissures. The iris of the eye is frequently speckled. The neck is often short and broad, as are the hands. The fingers are stubby, and the little finger is often more noticeably curved than the other fingers.

characteristics commonly thought to typify this group. The eyes appear almond shaped, and the skin of the eyelids tends to be abnormally thick. The face and nose are often flat and broad, as is the back of the head. The tongue, which seems too large for the mouth, may show deep fissures. The

Table 15.2 Other Disorders Sometimes Associated with Intellectual Disability

Clinical Type	Symptoms	Causes
No. 18 trisomy syndrome	Peculiar pattern of multiple congenital anomalies, the most common being low-set malformed ears, flexion of fingers, small jaw, and heart defects	Autosomal anomaly of chromosome 18
Tay-Sachs disease	Hypertonicity, listlessness, blindness, progressive spastic paralysis, and convulsions (death by the third year)	Disorder of lipoid metabolism, carried by a single recessive gene
Turner's syndrome	In females only; webbing of neck, increased carrying angle of forearm, and sexual infantilism; intellectual disability may occur but is infrequent	Sex chromosome anomaly (XO)
Klinefelter's syndrome	In males only; features vary from case to case, the only constant finding being the presence of small testes after puberty	Sex chromosome anomaly (XXY)
Niemann-Pick's disease	Onset usually in infancy, with loss of weight, dehydration, and progressive paralysis	Disorder of lipoid metabolism
Bilirubin encephalopathy	Abnormal levels of bilirubin (a toxic substance released by red cell destruction) in the blood; motor incoordination frequent	Often, Rh (ABO) blood group incompatibility between mother and fetus
Rubella, congenital	Visual difficulties most common, with cataracts and retinal problems often occurring together, and with deafness and anomalies in the valves and septa of the heart	The mother's contraction of rubella (German measles) during the first few months of her pregnancy

SOURCE: Based on American Psychiatric Association (2013); Harris (2006).

iris of the eye is frequently speckled. The neck is often short and broad, as are the hands. The fingers are stubby, and the little finger is often more noticeably curved than the other fingers. Although facial surgery is sometimes tried to correct the more stigmatizing features, its success is often limited (Roizen, 2007). Parents' acceptance of their Down syndrome child is inversely related to their support of such surgery (Katz et al., 1997).

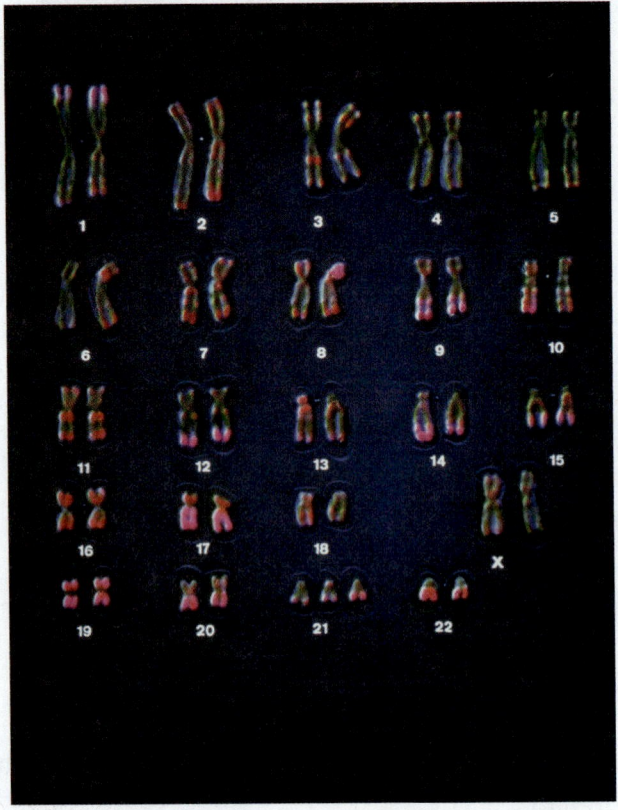

This is a reproduction (karyotype) of the chromosomes of a female patient with Down syndrome. Note the triple (rather than the normal paired) representation at chromosome 21.

SOURCE: Reproduced with permission by Custom Medical Stock Photo, Inc.

Death rates for children with Down syndrome have decreased dramatically in the past century. In 1919 the life expectancy at birth for such children was about 9 years; most of the deaths were due to gross physical problems, and a large proportion occurred in the first year of life. Thanks to antibiotics, surgical correction of lethal anatomical defects such as holes in the walls separating the heart's chambers, and better general medical care, many more of these children now live to adulthood (Hijii et al., 1997). Nevertheless, they appear as a group to experience an accelerated aging process (Hasegawa et al., 1997) and a decline in cognitive abilities (Thompson, 2003). One recent study reported that of those with Down syndrome who were age 60 and above, more than 50 percent had clinical evidence of dementia (Margallo et al., 2007).

Despite their problems, children with Down syndrome are usually able to learn self-help skills, acceptable social behavior, and routine manual skills that enable them to be of assistance in a family or institutional setting (Brown et al., 2001). The traditional view has been that children with Down syndrome are unusually placid and affectionate. However, research has called into question the validity of this generalization (Pary, 2004). These children may indeed be very docile, but probably in no greater proportion than normal children; they may also be equally (or more) difficult in various areas. In general, the quality of a child's social relationships depends on both IQ level and a supportive home environment (Alderson, 2001). Adults with Down syndrome may manifest less maladaptive behavior than comparable persons with other types of learning disabilities (Collacott et al., 1998).

Research has also suggested that the intellectual defect in Down syndrome may not be consistent across various abilities. Children with Down syndrome tend to remain relatively unimpaired in their appreciation of spatial relationships and in visual-motor coordination, although some evidence disputes this conclusion (Uecker et al., 1993). Research data are quite consistent in showing that their greatest deficits are in verbal and language-related skills (Azari et al., 1994). Because spatial functions are known to be partially localized in the right cerebral hemisphere, and language-related functions localized in the left cerebral hemisphere, some investigators speculate that the syndrome is especially crippling to the left hemisphere.

Chromosomal abnormalities other than the trisomy of chromosome 21 may occasionally be involved in the etiology of Down syndrome. However, the extra version of chromosome 21 is present in at least 94 percent of cases. As we noted earlier, it may be significant that this is the same chromosome that has been implicated in research on Alzheimer's disease, especially given that persons with Down syndrome are at extremely high risk for Alzheimer's as they get into and beyond their late 30s (Prasher & Kirshnan, 1993).

The reason for the trisomy of chromosome 21 is not clear, and research continues to address the potential causes (Korbel et al., 2009), but the defect is probably related to cognitive deficit (Kahlem, 2006) and to parental age at conception. It has been known for many years that the incidence of Down syndrome increases (from the 20s on) with increasing age of the mother. A woman in her 20s has about 1 chance in 2,000 of conceiving a Down syndrome baby, whereas the risk for a woman in her 40s is 1 in 50 (Holvey & Talbott, 1972). As in the case of all birth defects, the risk of having a baby with Down syndrome also is high for very young mothers, whose reproductive systems have not yet fully matured. Research has indicated that the father's age at conception is also implicated in Down syndrome, with higher ages conferring greater risk (Stene et al., 1981).

PHENYLKETONURIA   In **phenylketonuria (PKU)**, a baby appears normal at birth but lacks a liver enzyme needed to break down phenylalanine, an amino acid found in many foods. The genetic error results in intellectual disability only when significant quantities of phenylalanine are ingested, which is virtually certain to occur if the child's condition remains undiagnosed (Grodin & Laurie, 2000). This disorder, which occurs in about 1 in 12,000 births (Deb & Ahmed, 2000), is reversible (Embury et al., 2007); however, if it is not detected and treated, the amount of phenylalanine in the blood increases and eventually produces brain damage.

The disorder usually becomes apparent between 6 and 12 months after birth, although symptoms such as vomiting, a peculiar odor, infantile eczema, and seizures may occur during the early weeks of life. Often, the first symptoms noticed are signs of intellectual disability, which may be moderate to severe, depending on the degree to which the disease has progressed. Lack of motor coordination and other neurological problems caused by the brain damage are also common, and often the eyes, skin, and hair of untreated patients with PKU are very pale (Dyer, 1999).

The early detection of PKU by examining urine for the presence of phenylpyruvic acid is routine in developed countries, and dietary treatment (such as the elimination of phenylalanine-containing foods such as diet soda or turkey) and related procedures can be used to prevent the disorder (Sullivan & Chang, 1999). With early detection and treatment—preferably before an infant is 6 months old— the deterioration process can usually be arrested so that levels of intellectual functioning may range from borderline to normal. A few children suffer intellectual disability despite restricted phenylalanine intake and other preventive efforts, however. Dietary restriction in late-diagnosed PKU may improve the clinical picture somewhat, but there is no real substitute for early detection and prompt intervention (Pavone et al., 1993).

For a baby to inherit PKU, both parents must carry the recessive gene. Thus, when one child in a family is discovered to have PKU, it is especially critical that other children in the family be screened as well. Also, a pregnant mother with PKU whose risk status has been successfully addressed by early dietary intervention may damage her at-risk fetus unless she maintains rigorous control of phenylalanine intake.

CRANIAL ANOMALIES   Intellectual disability can occur in a number of conditions that involve alterations in head size and shape and for which the causal factors have not been firmly established (Carr et al., 2007).

Macrocephaly   In the rare condition known as **macrocephaly** ("large-headedness"), for example, there is an increase in the size and weight of the brain, an enlargement of the skull, visual impairment, convulsions, and other neurological symptoms resulting from the abnormal growth of glial cells that form the supporting structure for brain tissue.

Microcephaly   The condition known as **microcephaly** ("small-headedness") is defined by a head circumference that is more than three standard deviations below that of children of the same age and sex and is caused by decreased growth of the cerebral cortex during infancy (as skull size during infancy is determined by brain growth) (Woods, 2004). Primary microcephaly refers to decreased brain growth during pregnancy, and secondary microcephaly refers to decreased brain growth during infancy. Children with microcephaly fall within the moderate, severe, and profound categories of intellectual disability and most show little language development and are extremely limited in mental capacity.

In the condition known as microcephaly, decreased brain growth during infancy leads to smaller head circumference, as shown in the child above, and typically results in intellectual disability.

A recent review of nearly 700 cases of microcephaly revealed that the cause of the condition was identified in approximately 60 percent of cases (von der Hagen et al., 2014). Approximately half of these were caused by genetic factors, 45 percent were the result of brain damage in utero (e.g., due to factors such as maternal disease or birth complications), and 3 percent were caused by brain damage after birth. It is important to note that the cause of microcephaly is completely unknown in about 40 percent of cases, and so much additional research is needed to better understand this condition.

Hydrocephaly   The condition referred to as **hydrocephaly** is a relatively rare disorder in which the accumulation of an abnormal amount of cerebrospinal fluid within the cranium causes damage to the brain tissues and enlargement of the skull (Materro et al., 2001). In congenital cases, the head either is already enlarged at birth or begins to enlarge soon thereafter, presumably as a result of a disturbance in the formation, absorption, or circulation of the cerebrospinal fluid. The disorder can also arise in infancy or early childhood following the development of a brain tumor, subdural hematoma, meningitis, or other conditions. In these cases, the condition appears to result from a blockage of the cerebrospinal pathways and an accumulation of fluid in certain brain areas.

The clinical picture in hydrocephaly depends on the extent of neural damage, which in turn depends on the age at onset and the duration and severity of the disorder. In chronic cases, the chief symptom is the gradual enlargement of the upper part of the head out of proportion to the face and the rest of the body. Although the expansion of the skull helps minimize destructive pressure on the brain, serious brain damage occurs nonetheless. This damage leads to intellectual impairment and to such other effects as convulsions and impairment or loss of sight and hearing. The degree of intellectual impairment varies, being severe or profound in advanced cases.

Hydrocephaly can be treated by a procedure in which shunting devices are inserted to drain cerebrospinal fluid. With early diagnosis and treatment, this condition can usually be arrested before severe brain damage has occurred (Duinkerke et al., 2004). Even with significant brain damage, carefully planned and early interventions that take into account both strengths and weaknesses in intellectual functioning may minimize disability (Baron & Goldberger, 1993).

Treatments, Outcomes, and Prevention

A number of programs have demonstrated that significant changes in the adaptive capacity of children with intellectual disability are possible through special education and other rehabilitative measures (Berney, 2000). The degree of change that can be expected is related, of course, to the individual's particular condition and level of intellectual disability.

TREATMENT FACILITIES AND METHODS Parents of children with intellectual disability often find that childrearing is a significant challenge (Glidden & Schoolcraft, 2007). For example, recent research has shown that learning disability is associated with a higher incidence of mental health problems (Cooper & van der Speck, 2009). One decision that the parents of a child with an intellectual disability must make is whether to place the child in an institution (Gath, 2000). Most authorities agree that this should be considered as a last resort, in light of the unfavorable outcomes normally experienced—particularly in regard to the erosion of self-care

skills (Lynch et al., 1997). In general, children who are institutionalized fall into two groups: (1) those who, in infancy and childhood, manifest severe intellectual disability and associated physical impairment and who enter an institution at an early age; and (2) those who have no physical impairments but show relatively mild intellectual disability and a failure to adjust socially in adolescence, eventually being institutionalized chiefly because of delinquency or other problem behavior (see Stattin & Klackenberg-Larsson, 1993). In these cases, social incompetence is the main factor in the decision. The families of patients in the first group come from all socioeconomic levels, whereas a significantly higher percentage of the families of those in the second group come from lower educational and occupational strata.

For individuals with intellectual disability who do not require institutionalization, educational and training facilities have historically been woefully inadequate. It still appears that a substantial proportion of individuals with intellectual disability in the United States never get access to services appropriate to their specific needs (Luckasson et al., 1992).

This neglect is especially tragic in view of the ways that exist to help people with intellectual disability. For example, classes for individuals with mild intellectual disability, which usually emphasize reading and other basic school subjects, budgeting and money matters, and developing of occupational skills, have succeeded in helping many people become independent, productive community members. Classes for those with moderate and severe intellectual disability usually have more limited objectives, but they emphasize the development of self-care and other skills—for example, toilet habits (Wilder et al., 1997)—that enable individuals to function adequately and to be of assistance in either a family (e.g., Heller et al., 1997) or an institutional setting. Just mastering toilet training and learning to eat and dress properly may mean the difference between remaining at home or in a community residence or being institutionalized.

Currently, approximately 129,000 people with intellectual disability and other related conditions are receiving intermediate care, although many are not institutionalized. This is considerably less than the number of residents in treatment 40 years ago. These developments reflect both the new optimism that has come to prevail and, in many instances, new laws and judicial decisions upholding the rights of people with intellectual disabilities and their families. A notable example is Public Law 94–142, passed by Congress in 1975 and since modified several times (see Hayden, 1998). This statute, termed the Education for All Handicapped Children Act, asserts the right of people with intellectual disabilities to be educated at public expense in the least restrictive environment possible.

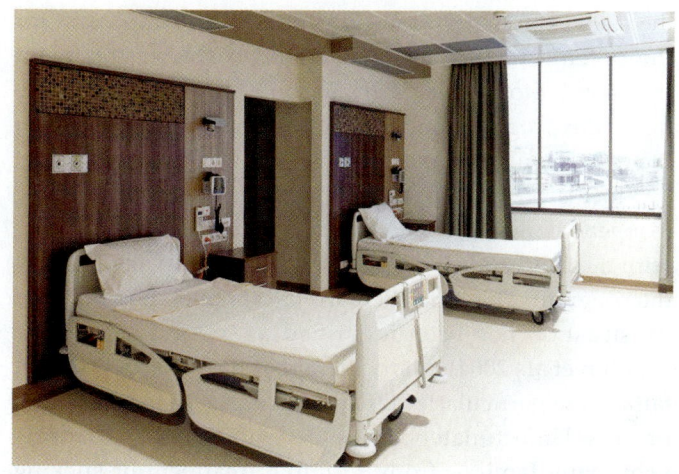

Although psychiatric hospitals typically are portrayed in movies and television shows as dark, ghost-filled haunted houses, in reality, psychiatric hospitals (or psychiatric units/floors within general hospitals) look just like modern-day general hospitals.

During the 1970s, there was a rapid increase in alternative forms of care for individuals with intellectual disability. These included the use of decentralized regional facilities for short-term evaluation and training, small private hospitals specializing in rehabilitative techniques, group homes or halfway houses integrated into the local community, nursing homes for the elderly with intellectual disability, the placement of children with severe intellectual disability in more enriched foster-home environments, varied forms of support to the family for own-home care, and employment services (Conley, 2003). The past 25 years have seen a marked enhancement in alternative modes of life for individuals with intellectual disability, rendering obsolete (and often leading to the closing of) many public institutions formerly devoted exclusively to this type of care.

EDUCATION AND INCLUSION PROGRAMMING   Typically, educational and training procedures involve mapping out target areas of improvement such as personal grooming, social behavior, basic academic skills, and simple occupational skills (see Shif, 2006). Within each area, specific skills are divided into simple components that can be learned and reinforced before more complex behaviors are required. Behavior modification that builds on a step-by-step progression can bring those with intellectual disability repeated experiences of success and lead to substantial progress even in individuals with severe impairments (Mash & Barkley, 2006).

For children with mild intellectual disability, the question of what schooling is best is likely to challenge both parents and school officials. Many such children fare better when they attend regular classes for much of the day. Of course, this type of approach—often called **mainstreaming** or "inclusion programming"—requires careful planning, a high level of teacher skill, and facilitative teacher attitudes (Wehman, 2003).

in review

- Compare and contrast mild, moderate, severe, and profound intellectual disability.
- Describe five biological conditions that may lead to intellectual disability.
- Describe some of the physical characteristics of children born with Down syndrome. What is its cause?
- What is the cause of and the preventive treatment for phenylketonuria (PKU)?
- Describe rehabilitation approaches to intellectual disability.

Special Considerations in the Treatment of Children and Adolescents

15.8   **Discuss how the treatment of youth differs from that of adults.**

In our earlier discussion of several disorders of childhood and adolescence, we noted the wide range of treatment procedures available as well as the marked differences in outcomes. In concluding this chapter, we discuss certain special factors associated with the treatment of children and adolescents that can affect the success of an intervention.

Special Factors Associated with Treatment of Children and Adolescents

There are a number of special factors to consider in relation to treatment for children and adolescents, as follows.

THE CHILD'S INABILITY TO SEEK ASSISTANCE   Most children with psychological disorders who need assistance are not in a position to ask for help themselves or to transport themselves to and from child treatment clinics. Thus, unlike an adult, who can usually seek help, a child is dependent, primarily on his or her parents. Adults should realize when a child needs professional help and take the initiative in obtaining it. Often, however, adults are unaware of the problems or neglect this responsibility.

The law identifies four areas in which treatment without parental consent is permitted: (1) in the case of mature minors (those considered capable of making decisions about themselves); (2) in the case of emancipated minors (those living independently, away from their parents); (3) in emergency situations; and (4) in situations in which a court orders treatment. Many children, of course, come to the attention of treatment agencies as a consequence of school referrals, delinquent acts, abuse by parents, or as a result of family custody court cases.

VULNERABILITIES THAT PLACE CHILDREN AT RISK FOR DEVELOPING EMOTIONAL PROBLEMS Children and youth who experience or are exposed to violence are at increased risk for developing psychological disorders (Seifert, 2003). In addition, many families provide an undesirable environment for their growing children (Ammerman et al., 1998). Studies have shown that up to a fourth of American children may be living in inadequate homes and that approximately 8 percent of youth in the United States report spending at least one night in a shelter, public place, or abandoned building (Ringwalt et al., 1998). Another study revealed that 23 percent of newly homeless men in New York City report a history of out-of-home care as children (Susser et al., 1993). Parental substance abuse also has been found to be associated with the vulnerability of children to the development of psychological disorders (Bijttebier & Goethals, 2006).

High-risk behaviors or difficult life conditions need to be recognized and taken into consideration (Harrington & Clark, 1998). For example, there are a number of behaviors such as engaging in sexual acts or delinquency and using alcohol or drugs that might place young people at greater risk for developing emotional problems. Moreover, physical or sexual abuse, parental divorce, family turbulence, and homelessness can place young people at great risk for emotional distress and subsequent maladaptive behavior (Cauce et al., 2000; Spataro et al., 2004) (see the World Around Us box). For example, children from homes with harsh discipline and physical abuse are more likely to be aggressive and to have conduct disorder than those from homes with less harsh discipline and from nonabusing families (Dodge et al., 1997).

POSSIBILITY OF USING PARENTS AS CHANGE AGENTS Although parents can, in some instances, help to create an environment that increases the risk of psychological disorders, on the flip side, they can be used as agents of positive change. Because the typical child therapist only sees the child for approximately 1 hour per week, whereas parents have access to their children the other 167 hours of the week, parents can be used as change agents by training them in techniques that enable them to modify their children's thoughts, feelings, and behaviors. Typically, such training focuses on helping the parents understand their child's psychological disorder and teaching them to reinforce adaptive behavior while withholding reinforcement for undesirable behavior. Many of the most effective treatments for children and adolescents rely heavily on such help from the child's parents or guardians.

NEED TO TREAT PARENTS AS WELL AS CHILDREN Because many of the behavior disorders specific to childhood appear to grow out of pathogenic family interactions and result from having parents with psychiatric problems themselves (Johnson et al., 2000), it is often important for the parents, as well as their child, to receive treatment (Dishion & Stormshak, 2007). In some instances, in fact, the treatment program may focus on the parents entirely, as in the case of child abuse.

Increasingly, then, the treatment of children has come to mean family therapy in which one or both parents, along with the child and siblings, may participate in all phases of the program. This is particularly important when the family situation has been identified as involving violence (Chaffin et al., 2004). Many therapists have discovered that fathers are particularly difficult to engage in the treatment process. Unfortunately, there are many barriers that prevent many families from initiating treatment or sticking with it once they start. Some of the most common barriers include concrete stressors or obstacles such as lack of transportation of child care, as well as the perception that treatment is not relevant or help and a poor relationship with one's therapist (Kazdin et al., 1997).

PROBLEM OF PLACING A CHILD OUTSIDE THE FAMILY Most communities have juvenile facilities that, day or night, will provide protective care and custody for young victims of abuse, neglect, and related conditions. Depending on the home situation and the special needs of the child, he or she will later either be returned to his or her parents or placed elsewhere. In the latter instance, four types of facilities are commonly relied on: (1) foster homes, (2) private institutions for the care of children such as group homes, (3) county or state institutions, and (4) the homes of relatives. At any one time, more than half a million children are living in foster care facilities, many of whom have been abused or neglected (Minnis et al., 2006).

The quality of a child's new home is, of course, a crucial determinant of whether the child's problems will be alleviated or made worse, and there is evidence to suggest that foster home placement has more positive effects than group home placement (Buckley & Zimmermann, 2003; Groza et al., 2003). Efforts are usually made to screen the placement facilities and maintain contact with the situation through follow-up visits, but even so, there have been cases of mistreatment in the new home (Dubner & Motta, 1999; Wilson et al., 2000). In cases of child abuse, child abandonment, or a serious childhood behavior problem that parents cannot control, it had often been assumed that the only feasible action was to take the child out of the home and find a temporary substitute. With such a child's own home so obviously inadequate, the hope was that a more stable outside placement would be better for the child. But when children are taken from their homes and placed in an institution or in a series of foster homes, they may feel rejected by their own parents, unwanted by their new caretakers, rootless, constantly insecure, lonely, and bitter. Not surprisingly, children and adolescents in foster

The World Around Us

The Impact of Child Abuse on Psychological Disorders

Child abuse and neglect continue to be enormous concerns around the world. Approximately 1 percent of children in the United States are the victims of documented cases of child abuse or neglect each year. Most of these cases involve child neglect (78 percent), whereas 18 percent involve physical abuse and 9 percent involve sexual abuse (U.S. Department of Health and Human Services, 2013). Unfortunately, most abuse and neglect goes undocumented, so the actual rates of occurrence are much higher. In a recent nationally representative survey of U.S. adolescents, 4 percent reported being physically abused and 4 percent reported being sexually abused (McLaughlin, Green, et al., 2012). Cross-national studies indicate that approximately 8 percent of people report being physically abused during childhood and 2 percent report being the victim of sexual abuse (Kessler, McLaughlin, et al., 2010). In extreme cases, the abuse and neglect of children can lead to death. Beyond the direct and intentional killing of a child (known as *filicide*), abuse and neglect can increase the risk of death via inadequate health care or poor parental supervision (Sidebotham et al., 2014).

Most cases of child abuse and neglect are not lethal, but they can still have an enormous impact on the development of psychopathology. Children who experience physical or sexual abuse show a doubling in the risk of developing a range of different psychological disorders (McLaughlin, Green, et al., 2012) as well as a doubling in the risk of suicidal behavior (Bruffaerts et al., 2010). Moreover, this elevated risk of psychopathology and suicidal behavior is seen in cultures all around the globe and extends across the life span (Bruffaerts et al., 2010; Kessler, McLaughlin, et al., 2010), suggesting that events that occur during childhood can have a broad and long-lasting impact. Indeed, children who have been abused also show long-term adjustment problems such as difficulties adjusting to college (Elliott et al., 2009) and within intimate relationships later in life (Friesen et al., 2010).

Of course, not all instances of abuse lead to psychopathology, and many people who experience abuse go on to lead happy and healthy lives (Rind et al., 1998). In some cases, those who suffered through abuse seek treatment, which often aims at addressing potential problems with social adjustment and interpersonal skills that may have been affected or hindered by the abuse. Treatment can be especially effective if it is targeted to the specific needs of the affected child (Harvey & Taylor, 2010).

Psychologists are conducting studies to try to understand why child abuse leads to psychological disorders in some people, but not in others. What factors do you think they should study to help answer this question?

---

homes tend to require more mental health services than do other children (dos Reis et al., 2001).

Accordingly, the trend today is toward permanent planning. First, every effort is made to hold a family together and to give the parents the support and guidance they need for adequate childrearing. If this is impossible, then efforts are made to free the child legally for adoption and to find an adoptive home as soon as possible. This, of course, means that the public agencies need specially trained staffs with reasonable caseloads and access to resources that they and their clients may need.

VALUE OF INTERVENING BEFORE PROBLEMS BECOME ACUTE Rather than waiting until children at risk develop acute psychological problems, psychologists increasingly are attempting to intervene before development has been seriously distorted (Schroeder & Gordon, 2002). As described in Chapter 5, one type of early intervention has been developed in response to the special vulnerability children experience in the wake of a disaster or trauma such as a hurricane, accident, hostage-taking, or shooting (Shaw, 2003). Children and adolescents often require considerable support and attention to deal with such traumatic events, which are all too frequent in today's world. Individual and small-group psychological therapy might be implemented for victims of trauma (Cohen et al., 2006); support programs might operate through school-based interventions (Klingman, 1993); or community-based programs might be implemented to reduce the posttraumatic symptoms. Early intervention has the double goal of reducing the stressors in a child's life and strengthening the child's coping mechanisms. It can often reduce the incidence and intensity of later maladjustment, thus averting problems for both the individuals concerned and the broader society.

Family Therapy as a Means of Helping Children

To address a child's problems, it is often necessary to alter pathological family interaction patterns that produce or serve to maintain the child's behavior problems (Mash & Barkley, 2006). Several family therapy approaches have been developed (Prout & Brown, 2007) that differ in some important ways—for example, in terms of how the family is defined (whether to include extended family members); what the treatment process will focus on (whether communications between the family members or the aberrant behavior of the problem family members is the focus); and what procedures will be used in treatment (analyzing and interpreting hidden messages in the family communications or altering the reward and punishment contingencies through behavioral assessment and reinforcement). But whatever their differences, all family therapies view a child's problems, at least in part, as an outgrowth of pathological interaction patterns within the family, and they attempt to bring about positive change in family members through analysis and modification of the deviant family patterns (Everett & Everett, 2001).

Child Advocacy Programs

There are over 74 million people under age 18 in the United States (U.S. Census Bureau, 2009). Children who encounter mental health problems are at substantial risk for adjustment problems in later life (Smith & Smith, 2010). Unfortunately, both treatment and preventive programs for our society's children remain inadequate for dealing with the extent of psychological problems among children and adolescents.

In the United States, one approach that has evolved in recent years is mental health child advocacy. Advocacy programs attempt to help children or others receive services that they need but often are unable to obtain for themselves. In some cases, advocacy seeks to better conditions for underserved populations by changing the system (Pithouse & Crowley, 2007). Federal programs offering services for children are fragmented in that different agencies serve different needs; thus, no government agency is charged with considering the whole child and planning comprehensively for children who need help. Consequently, child advocacy is often frustrating and difficult to implement.

Outside the federal government, advocacy efforts for children have until recently been supported largely by legal and special-interest citizen's groups such as the Children's Defense Fund, a public interest organization based in Washington, D.C. Mental health professionals were typically not involved. Today, however, there is greater interdisciplinary involvement in attempts to provide effective advocacy programs for children (Carlson, 2001; Singer & Singer, 2000).

in review

- What special factors must be considered in providing treatment for children and adolescents?

- Why is therapeutic intervention a more complicated process with children than with adults?

Unresolved Issues

How Should Society Deal with Delinquent Behavior?

One of the most troublesome and widespread problems in childhood and adolescence is delinquent behavior, especially that involving juvenile violence (Popma, 2007). This behavior includes such acts as destruction of property, violence against other people, and various behaviors that violate the rights of others and society's laws. The term *juvenile delinquency* is a legal one that refers to illegal acts committed by individuals between the ages of 8 and 18 (depending on state law). It is not recognized in the *DSM* as a disorder. The actual incidence of juvenile delinquency is difficult to determine because many delinquent acts are not reported. However, some data are available:

- In 2008, more than 2.1 million juveniles were arrested in the United States, which accounts for about 16 percent of all violent crime arrests; 1,740 juveniles were murder victims (about 11 percent of all murders) (Puzzanchera, 2009).
- Although most juvenile crime is committed by males, the rate has also risen for females. Female delinquents are commonly apprehended for drug use, sex offenses, and running away from home.
- Approximately one in five adolescents entering the juvenile justice system suffers from a mental health condition (Phillippi & DePrato, 2010). Moreover, adolescents detained in adult correctional facilities have a high rate of suicide and are likely to commit more crimes when they are released (Bath & Billick, 2010).

Causal Factors

Only a small group of "continuous" delinquents actually evolve from oppositional defiant behavior to conduct disorder and then to adult antisocial personality; most people who engage in delinquent acts as adolescents do not follow this path (Nock et al., 2007). The individuals who show adolescence-limited delinquency are thought to do so as a result of social mimicry. As they mature, they lose their motivation for delinquency and gain rewards for more socially acceptable behavior. Several key variables seem to play a part in the genesis of delinquency. They fall into the general categories of personal pathology, pathogenic family patterns, and undesirable peer relationships.

Genetic Determinants

Although the research on genetic determinants of antisocial behavior is far from conclusive, some evidence suggests possible hereditary contributions to criminality (Bailey, 2000).

Brain Damage and Learning Disability

In a distinct minority of delinquency cases (an estimated 1 percent or less), brain pathology results in lowered inhibitory controls and a tendency toward episodes of violent behavior. Such adolescents are often hyperactive, impulsive, emotionally unstable, and unable to inhibit themselves when strongly stimulated.

Psychological Disorders

Some delinquent acts appear to be directly associated with behavior disorders such as ODD, CD, or ADHD.

Antisocial Traits

Many habitual delinquents appear to share the traits typical of antisocial personalities (Bailey, 2000). They are impulsive, defiant, resentful, devoid of feelings of remorse or guilt, incapable of establishing and maintaining close interpersonal ties, and seemingly unable to profit from experience.

Drug Abuse

Many delinquent acts—particularly theft, prostitution, and assault—are directly associated with alcohol or drug use (Leukefeld et al., 1998). Many adolescents who abuse hard drugs such as heroin are forced to steal to maintain their habit. In the case of female addicts, theft may be combined with or replaced by prostitution as a means of obtaining money.

Parental Absence or Family Conflict

Delinquency appears to be much more common among youths from homes in which parents have separated or divorced than among those from homes in which a parent has died, suggesting that parental conflict may be a key element in causing delinquency.

Parental Rejection and Faulty Discipline

In many cases, one or both parents reject a child. When the father is the rejecting parent, it is difficult for a boy to identify with him and use him as a model for his own development. However, the detrimental effects of parental rejection and inconsistent discipline are by no means attributable only to fathers. Adolescents who experience alienation from both parents have been found to be more prone to delinquent behavior (Leas & Mellor, 2000).

Undesirable Peer Relationships

Delinquency tends to be an experience shared by a cultural group (O'Donnell, 2004). In a classic study, Haney and Gold (1973) found that about two-thirds of delinquent acts are committed in association with one or two other people, and most of the remainder involve three or four others. Usually the offender and the companion or companions are of the same sex. Interestingly, girls are more likely than boys to have a constant friend or companion in delinquency.

Broad social conditions may also tend to produce or support delinquency (Ward & Laughlin, 2003). An adolescent's developmental level can have a great deal of influence over how effectively he or she engages with the justice system and resolves his or her problems (Kraus & Pope, 2010). Interrelated factors that appear to be of key importance include alienation and rebellion, social rejection, and the psychological support afforded by membership in a delinquent gang. Gang activity remains a widespread problem across the United States, with prevalence rates remaining fairly stable from 1996 to 2008, and with approximately one-third of all cities and towns in the United States reporting gang problems (Egley et al., 2010). One study found that a significant number of homeless youth (32 percent of the sample) become gang members (Yoder et al., 2003). Gang membership gives them a sense of belonging and a means of gaining some measure of status and approval.

Dealing with Delinquency

If juvenile institutions have adequate facilities and personnel, they can be of great help to youth who need to be removed from aversive environments (Scott, 2010). These institutions can give adolescents a chance to further their education and develop needed skills, and to find purpose and meaning in their lives. In such settings, young people may also have the opportunity to receive psychological counseling and group therapy. The use of "boot camps" (juvenile facilities designed along the lines of army-style basic training) has received some attention as a means of intervening in the delinquency process; however, meta-analyses suggest that these programs do not improve delinquent behavior and may actually make it worse (Lilienfeld, 2007).

In contrast, some treatment approaches have shown an ability to decrease delinquent behavior in children and adolescents. For instance, multisystemic therapy (MST) is a comprehensive intervention in which the clinician attempts to make changes in several of the systems that influence delinquent behavior, including the adolescent's family, peer network, school, and community (Henggler, 2011). MST has been tested in dozens of studies and has been shown to significantly decrease delinquency, and also to improve a range of other outcomes such as psychopathology, substance use, family functioning, and the rate of out-of-home placements (van der Stouwe et al., 2014). Treatments like this one provide hope that with the right intervention, children at risk for delinquency can go on to happy and healthy lives.

Summary

15.1 **Explain how the understanding of psychological disorders among children and adolescents differs from that of adults.**

- A child's behavior is not considered abnormal without determining whether the behavior in question is appropriate for the child's age, as is done in the field of developmental psychopathology.

- Compared to adults, young children do not yet have a realistic view of themselves and their world; they may have more difficulty coping with stressful events and lack of experience in dealing with adversity. They are also more dependent on other people than are adults. Children are therefore, more psychologically vulnerable than adults.

- Many childhood disorders have no counterpart in adult psychopathology. In addition, environmental factors play an important part in the expression of symptoms in childhood disorders.

15.2 Distinguish between developmentally normal and abnormal anxiety and mood in children and adolescents.

- Most children are vulnerable to fears and anxiety; however, in some cases the experience of fear and anxiety is so extreme, persistent, impairing, and beyond what would be expected that the child is determined to have an anxiety disorder.

- Childhood depression, like depression in adults, is characterized by symptoms of sadness, withdrawal, crying, poor sleep and appetite, and in some cases thoughts of suicide or suicide attempts.

15.3 Describe the presentation and prevalence of oppositional defiant disorder and conduct disorder.

- Oppositional defiant disorder is characterized by a recurrent pattern of negativistic, defiant, disobedient, and hostile behavior toward authority figures that persists for at least 6 months. It usually begins by the age of 8 and has a lifetime prevalence of 10 percent, with a slightly higher rate among boys than girls.

- Conduct disorder is characterized by a persistent, repetitive violation of rules and a disregard for the rights of others. It has a median age of onset of 12 years (meaning half of those who ever develop this disorder have it by age 12) and a lifetime prevalence of 10 percent. Like ODD, CD is more common among boys (12 percent) than girls (7 percent).

- The risk factors for both disorders include family discord, socioeconomic disadvantage, and antisocial behavior in the parents.

15.4 List and define elimination disorders.

- Elimination disorders (enuresis and encopresis) involve a single outstanding symptom rather than a pervasive maladaptive pattern.

- Enuresis refers to the habitual involuntary discharge of urine, usually at night, after the age of expected continence (age 5). The term encopresis describes a symptom disorder of children who have not learned appropriate toileting for bowel movements after age 4.

15.5 Summarize what is known about the characteristics, course, and treatment of attention-deficit/ hyperactivity disorder and autism spectrum disorder.

- Attention-deficit/hyperactivity disorder is characterized by a persistent pattern of difficulties sustaining attention and/or impulsiveness and excessive or exaggerated motor activity that interferes with an individual's ability to accomplish tasks. Children with ADHD often show specific learning disabilities and possess behavior problems. The major approaches to treating children with ADHD have been medication and behavior therapy.

- Autism spectrum disorder is a neurodevelopmental disorder that involves a wide range of problematic behaviors, including deficits in language and perceptual and motor development; defective reality testing; and impairments in social communication. Though many children with autism have been insufficiently treated in the past, more recent intensive behavioral approaches to treatment have demonstrated some success.

15.6 Describe what is currently known about the causes and treatment of learning disorders.

- The most widely held view of the causes of specific learning disorders is that they are the products of subtle CNS impairments. In particular, these disabilities are thought to result from some sort of immaturity, deficiency, or dysregulation limited to those brain functions that supposedly mediate, for normal children, the cognitive skills that children with learning disorders cannot efficiently acquire.

- Various treatment approaches have been used for informal and single-case reports, but there are few well-designed and well-executed outcome studies on specific treatments for learning disorders.

15.7 Define intellectual disability and name three known causal factors involved in its development.

- Intellectual disability is characterized by deficits in general mental abilities, such as reasoning, problem solving, planning, abstract thinking, judgment, academic learning, and learning from experience (APA, 2013, p. 31).

- The causes for intellectual disability include genetic-chromosomal factors, infections and toxic agents during fetal development, trauma (physical injury) at birth, ionizing radiation on sex cells and other bodily cells and tissues, and malnutrition or other biological factors.

15.8 Discuss how the treatment of youth differs from that of adults.

Unlike adults who can seek help on their own, a child is dependent primarily on parents who must take the initiative in obtaining help for their child. Advocacy programs attempt to help children or others receive services that they need but often are unable to obtain for themselves. Unfortunately, the financing and resources necessary for such services are not always readily available, and the future of programs for improving psychological environments for children remains uncertain.

Key Terms

Adderall, p. 548

attention-deficit/hyperactivity disorder (ADHD), p. 545

autism spectrum disorder, p. 549

conduct disorder, p. 541

developmental psychopathology, p. 534

Down syndrome, p. 559

dyslexia, p. 554

echolalia, p. 551

encopresis, p. 545

enuresis, p. 544

hydrocephaly, p. 561

intellectual disability, p. 556

juvenile delinquency, p. 540

learning disorders, p. 554

macrocephaly, p. 561

mainstreaming, p. 563

microcephaly, p. 561

neurodevelopmental disorders, p. 545

oppositional defiant disorder (ODD), p. 541

Pemoline, p. 548

phenylketonuria (PKU), p. 561

Ritalin, p. 548

separation anxiety disorder, p. 535

Strattera, p. 548

tic, p. 552

Tourette's disorder, p. 554

Chapter 16
Psychological Treatment

⌄ Learning Objectives

16.1 Describe who seeks psychological treatment and what the most common goals are.

16.2 Explain how the success of psychological treatment is measured.

16.3 Describe some of the factors that must be considered to provide optimal treatment.

16.4 List the psychological approaches most often used to treat abnormal behavior.

16.5 Explain the roles that social values and culture play in psychological treatment.

16.6 Describe three biological approaches used to treat abnormal behavior.

Most of us have experienced a time or situation when we were dramatically helped by talking things over with a relative or friend. However, there is more to psychological treatment than just giving someone an opportunity to talk. Psychologists and other clinicians also use specific psychological treatments that are designed to promote new understandings, behaviors, or both on the client's part. The fact that these interventions are deliberately planned and systematically guided by certain theoretical preconceptions is what distinguishes professional psychological treatment from more informal helping relationships.

An Overview of Treatment

16.1 Describe who seeks psychological treatment and what the most common goals are.

The belief that people with psychological problems can change—can learn more adaptive ways of perceiving, evaluating, and behaving—is the conviction underlying all **psychotherapy** or psychological treatment. Achieving these changes is by no means easy. Sometimes a person's view of the world and her or his self-concept are distorted because of pathological early relationships that have been reinforced by years of negative life experiences. In other instances, environmental factors such as an unsatisfying job, an unhappy relationship, or financial stresses must be the focus of attention in addition to psychotherapy. Because change can be hard, people sometimes find it easier to bear their present problems than to challenge themselves to chart a different life course. Therapy also takes time and offers no magical transformations. Nevertheless, it holds promise even for the most severe mental disorders.

Psychotherapeutic interventions have been applied to a wide variety of chronic problems. Even severely disturbed clients with psychosis may profit from a therapeutic relationship that takes into account their level of functioning and maintains therapeutic subgoals that are within their capabilities (e.g., Kendler, 1999; Valmaggia et al., 2008). Moreover, contrary to common opinion, psychotherapy can be less expensive in the long run than alternative modes of intervention (Dobson et al., 2008).

Numerous therapeutic approaches have been tried throughout history (some of them cruel and unusual in hindsight), and many exist today. However, the era of managed care has prompted new and increasingly stringent demands that the efficacy of treatments be empirically demonstrated. This chapter explores some of the most widely accepted psychological and biological treatment approaches in use today. Although we recognize that different groups of mental health professionals often have their own preferences with respect to the use of the terms *client* and *patient*, in this chapter we use the terms interchangeably.

Watch History of the Treatment of Psychological Disorders

Why Do People Seek Therapy?

People who seek therapy vary widely in their problems and in their motivations to solve them. Below we explore a few such motivations.

PSYCHOLOGICAL DISORDERS AND STRESSFUL LIFE CIRCUMSTANCES Perhaps the most obvious candidates for psychological treatment are people experiencing one of the psychological disorders described in this book. Approximately 15 percent of adults in the United States receive mental health care treatment each year, with rates in other countries varying from 1 to 12 percent (see Figure 16.1; WHO World Mental Health Survey Consortium, 2004). Not surprisingly, those with psychological disorders, and especially those with serious conditions in which there is considerable impairment in daily functioning, are much more likely to receive treatment. However, most people who receive treatment do not meet full criteria for a psychological disorder (WHO World Mental Health Survey Consortium, 2004). So why would they be seeking treatment? Many people seek therapy due to sudden and highly stressful situations such as a divorce or unemployment—situations that can lead people to feel so overwhelmed by a crisis that they cannot manage on their own.

RELUCTANT CLIENTS Some people enter therapy by an indirect route. Perhaps they were court-ordered to do so by a judge because of substance abuse or domestic violence, or maybe they had consulted a physician for their headaches or stomach pains, only to be told that nothing was physically wrong with them. Motivation to enter treatment differs widely among psychotherapy clients. Reluctant clients may come from many situations—for example, a person with a substance abuse problem whose spouse threatens "either therapy or divorce," or a suspected felon whose attorney advises that things will go better at trial if it can be announced that the suspect has "entered therapy." A substantial number of angry parents bring their children to therapists with demands that their child's "problematic behavior," which they view as independent of the family context, be "fixed." These parents may be surprised and

Figure 16.1 Prevalence of Mental Health Care Treatment Around the World

This figure shows data on the percentage of people in different countries around the world who reported receiving treatment for a mental or emotional problem in the past 12 months.

(Adapted from WHO World Mental Health Survey Consortium, 2004, *JAMA*.)

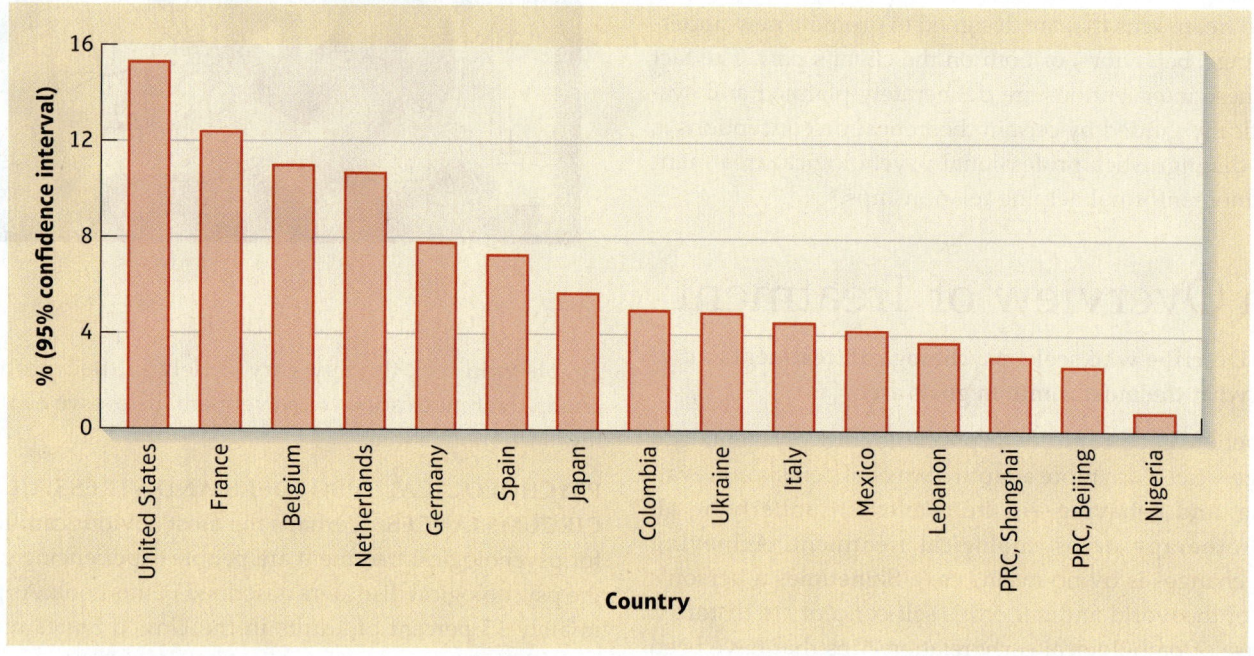

reluctant to recognize their own roles in shaping their child's behavior patterns.

In general, males are more reluctant to seek help when they are experiencing problems than are females. In the case of depression, far more men than women say that they would never consider seeing a therapist; when men are depressed they are even reluctant to seek informal help from their friends. Moreover, when men do seek professional help, they tend to ask fewer questions than women do (see Addis & Mahalik, 2003).

Why would this be? One answer is that men are less able than women to recognize and label feelings of distress and to identify these feelings as emotional problems. In addition, men who subscribe to masculine stereotypes emphasizing self-reliance and lack of emotionality also tend to experience more gender-role conflict when they consider traditional counseling, with its focus on emotions and emotional disclosure. For a man who prides himself on being emotionally stoic, seeking help for a problem like depression may present a major threat to his self-esteem. Seeking help also requires giving up some control and may run counter to the ideology that "a real man helps himself."

How can men be encouraged to seek help when they have difficulties? Part of the solution may be to develop new treatment approaches that provide a better fit for men who see little value in talking about their problems. An example here might be the use of virtual reality therapy to treat soldiers with posttraumatic stress disorder

(PTSD; see Chapter 5). Another strategy is to use more creative approaches to encourage men to seek help and support. For example, television commercials for erectile dysfunction use professional basketball players and football coaches to encourage men with similar problems to "step up to the plate" and talk to their doctors. Making men more aware of other "masculine men" who have been "man enough" to go for help when they needed it may be an important step toward educating those whose adherence to masculine gender roles makes it difficult for them to acknowledge and seek help for their problems.

PEOPLE WHO SEEK PERSONAL GROWTH A final group of people who enter therapy have problems that would be considered relatively normal. That is, they appear to have achieved success, have financial stability, have generally accepting and loving families, and have accomplished many of their life goals. They enter therapy not out of personal despair or impossible interpersonal involvements but out of a sense that they have not lived up to their own expectations and realized their own potential. These people, partly because their problems are more manageable than the problems of others, may make substantial gains in personal growth.

It should be clear from these brief descriptions that there is no typical client. Neither is there a model therapy. No currently used form of therapy is applicable to all types of clients. Most authorities agree that client variables such as motivation to change and severity of symptoms are exceedingly important to the outcome of therapy (Clarkin & Levy, 2004). As we will see, the various therapies have relatively greater success when a therapist takes the characteristics of a particular client into account in determining treatment approaches.

Who Provides Psychotherapeutic Services?

Members of many different professions have traditionally provided advice and counsel to individuals in emotional distress. Physicians, in addition to caring for their patients' physical problems, often become trusted advisers in emotional matters as well. Many physicians are trained to recognize psychological problems that are beyond their expertise and to refer patients to psychological specialists or to psychiatrists.

Another professional group that deals extensively with emotional problems is the clergy. A minister, priest, or rabbi is frequently the first professional to encounter a person experiencing an emotional crisis. Although some clergy are trained mental health counselors, most limit their counseling to religious matters and spiritual support and do not attempt to provide psychotherapy. Rather, like general-practice physicians, they are trained to recognize problems that require professional management and to refer seriously disturbed people to mental health specialists.

Often the first person that someone experiencing an emotional crisis will talk to is a trusted member of his or her religious community.

The three types of mental health professionals who most often administer psychological treatment in mental health settings are clinical psychologists, psychiatrists, and psychiatric social workers. In addition to their being able to provide psychotherapy, the medical training and licensure qualifications of psychiatrists enable them to prescribe psychoactive medications and also to administer other forms of medical treatment such as electroconvulsive therapy. In some states, appropriately supervised psychologists and other clinical specialists may prescribe medications if they have received additional training. Although mental health professionals differ with respect to their training and approach to treatment, generally, psychiatrists differ from psychologists insofar as they treat mental disorders using biological approaches (e.g., medications), whereas psychologists treat patients' problems by examining and in some cases changing their patients' behaviors and thought patterns.

In a clinic or hospital (as opposed to an individual practice), a wide range of treatment approaches may be used. These range from the use of medications, to individual or group psychotherapy, to home, school, or job visits aimed at modifying adverse conditions in a client's life—for example, helping a teacher become more understanding and supportive of a child-client's needs. Often the latter is as important as treatment directed toward modifying the client's personality, behavior, or both.

This willingness to use a variety of procedures is reflected in the frequent use of a team approach to assessment and treatment, particularly in group practice and institutional settings. This approach ideally involves the coordinated efforts of medical, psychological, social work, and other mental health personnel working together as the needs of each case warrant. Also of key importance is the current practice of providing treatment facilities in the community. Instead of considering maladjustment to be an individual's private misery, which in the past often required confinement in a distant mental hospital, this approach integrates family and community resources in a total treatment approach.

The Therapeutic Relationship

The therapeutic relationship evolves out of what both client and therapist bring to the therapeutic situation. The outcome of psychotherapy normally depends on whether the client and therapist are successful in achieving a productive working alliance. The client's major contribution is his or her motivation. Clients who are pessimistic about their chances of recovery or who are ambivalent about dealing with their problems and symptoms respond less well to treatment (Mussell et al., 2000).

Although definitions of the therapeutic alliance vary, its key elements are (1) a sense of working collaboratively on the problem, (2) agreement between patient and therapist about the goals and tasks of therapy, and (3) an affective bond between patient and therapist (Constantino et al., 2001; Martin et al., 2000). Clear communication is also important. This is no doubt facilitated by the degree of shared experience in the backgrounds of client and therapist.

What are some of the key elements of an effective therapeutic alliance between client and therapist?

Almost as important as motivation is a client's expectation of receiving help. This expectancy is often sufficient in itself to bring about substantial improvement, perhaps because patients who expect therapy to be effective engage more in the process (Meyer et al., 2002). Just as a placebo often lessens pain for someone who believes it will do so, a person who expects to be helped by therapy is more likely to benefit. The downside of this fact is that if a therapy or therapist fails for whatever reason to inspire client confidence, the effectiveness of treatment is likely to be compromised.

To the art of therapy, a therapist brings a variety of professional skills and methods intended to help people see themselves and their situations more objectively—that is, to gain a different perspective. Besides helping provide a new perspective, most therapy situations also offer a client a safe setting in which he or she is encouraged to practice new ways of feeling and acting, gradually developing both the courage and the ability to take responsibility for acting in more effective and satisfying ways.

To bring about such changes, an effective psychotherapist must help the client give up old and dysfunctional behavior patterns and replace them with new, functional ones. Because clients will present varying challenges in this regard, the therapist must be flexible enough to use a variety of interactive styles.

in review

- Why do people seek therapy?
- What kinds of professionals provide help to people in psychological distress? In what kinds of settings does treatment occur?
- What factors are important in determining how well patients do in therapy?

Measuring Success in Psychotherapy

16.2 Explain how the success of psychological treatment is measured.

Psychologists and, of course, consumers of psychological treatment have a strong interest in measuring whether treatment is successful or not. Unfortunately, evaluating treatment success is not always as easy as it might seem (Hill & Lambert, 2004). In this section we consider some key issues in the measurement of the effectiveness of psychological treatments.

Objectifying and Quantifying Change

Attempts at estimating clients' gains in therapy generally depend on one or more of the following sources of information: (1) a client's reports of change in their symptoms or functioning, (2) a clinician's ratings of changes that have occurred, (3) reports from the client's family or friends, (4) comparison of pretreatment and posttreatment scores on instruments designed to measure relevant facets of psychological functioning, and (5) measures of change in selected overt behaviors. Each of these sources has strengths, but also some important limitations.

CLIENT RATINGS In studies aimed at testing the effectiveness of different forms of therapy, and in many clinical settings, there is an emphasis on using client ratings on quantitative measures to determine how much change has occurred. For example, the Beck Depression Inventory (a self-report measure of depression severity) is widely used to measure the degree of severity of a client's depression. It has become almost standard in the pretherapy and post-therapy assessment of depression.

Unfortunately, a client is not necessarily a reliable source of information on therapeutic outcomes. Not only may clients want to believe for various personal reasons that they are getting better, but in an attempt to please the therapist they may report that they are being helped. In addition, because therapy often requires a considerable investment of time, money, and sometimes emotional distress, the idea that it has been useless is a dissonant one.

CLINICIAN RATINGS The effectiveness of therapy also is often evaluated by the treating clinician. For instance, the Hamilton Rating Scale for Depression is a rating scale used by clinicians to measure the severity of a patient's depression—similar to the Beck Depression Inventory mentioned above, but completed by the clinician rather than the client. Although the clinician may be more objective than the patient, clinicians also may not be the best judge of clients' progress because they may be biased in favor of seeing themselves as competent and successful. In addition, the clinician typically has only a limited observational sample (the client's in-session behavior) from which to make judgments of overall change. Furthermore, clinicians can inflate improvement averages by deliberately or subtly encouraging difficult clients to discontinue therapy.

THIRD-PARTY RATINGS Client change also can be evaluated by third-party raters, meaning people *not* involved in the treatment. This may include family members or trained independent evaluators. The latter are people who are trained to conduct clinical interviews and to rate the amount of clinical change that has occurred in a patient. Of course, relatives of the client may be inclined to "see" the improvement they had hoped for, although they often seem to be more realistic than either the therapist or the client in their evaluations of outcome. Because of their objectivity and consistency, independent evaluators who are blind to condition (meaning they do not know what kind of treatment a person received and so cannot be biased to say that one form of treatment is more effective than another) are used frequently in rigorous studies of treatment effectiveness.

OBJECTIVE MEASURES Another widely used objective measure of client change is performance on various psychological tests. A client evaluated in this way takes a battery of tests before and after therapy, and the differences in scores are assumed to reflect progress, or lack of progress, or occasionally even deterioration. However, some of the changes that such tests show may be artifactual, as with *regression to the mean*, wherein very high (or very low) scores tend on repeated measurement to drift toward the average of their own distributions, yielding a false impression that some real change has been documented. Also, the particular tests selected are likely to focus on the theoretical predictions of the therapist or researcher. Thus, they are not necessarily valid predictors of the changes, if any, that the therapy actually induces or of how the client will behave in real life. And without follow-up assessment, they provide little information on how enduring any change is likely to be.

In research settings, functional magnetic resonance imaging (fMRI) can be used to examine brain activity before and after treatment. For example, Nakao and colleagues (2005) studied 10 outpatients with obsessive-compulsive disorder (OCD). At the start of the study, all the patients received a brain scan while they were engaged in a task that required them to think about words (e.g., sweat, urine, feces) that triggered their obsessions and compulsions. Patients were then treated for 12 weeks either with the SSRI (selective serotonin reuptake inhibitor) fluvoxamine (Luvox) or with behavior therapy. At the end of this treatment period, the brain scanning was repeated.

The results showed that, before treatment, certain areas of the brain thought to be involved in OCD (e.g., a brain region in the frontal lobe called the orbitofrontal cortex) were activated during the symptom-provocation task. However, after therapy, these same regions showed much less activation when the patients were challenged to think about the provocative trigger words. In subsequent research these scientists have also shown that, after 12 weeks of behavior therapy, patients with OCD again show changes in several brain regions that are implicated in this disorder (Nabeyama et al., 2008). Research of this type suggests that physiological changes may indeed accompany the clinical gains that occur in psychotherapy (see Siegle et al., 2012). It is important to keep in mind, however, that changes on rating scales (or on MRI scans) do not necessarily tell us how well the patient is functioning in everyday life (Kazdin, 2008a).

OVERT BEHAVIORS Perhaps the most direct way to know if someone has improved in treatment is to observe their behavior directly. For instance, if someone is being treated for a bug phobia, the clinician can observe the client's ability to approach and hold bugs of different sizes before, during, and after treatment to see if the individual's behavior has changed. The advantage of behavioral observation is that it is objective, difficult to "fake," and often reflective of precisely the change that is intended in treatment. The downside is that it may be less appropriate for problems that are less easily observed (e.g., suicidal thoughts).

Research Close-Up

Regression to the Mean

This reflects the statistical tendency for extreme scores (e.g., very high or very low scores) on a given measure to look less extreme at a second assessment (as occurs in a repeated-measures design). Because of this statistical artifact, people whose scores are farthest away from the group mean to begin with (e.g., people who have the highest anxiety scores or the lowest scores on self-esteem) will tend to score closer to the group mean at the second assessment, even if no real clinical change has occurred.

Watch Regression to the Mean

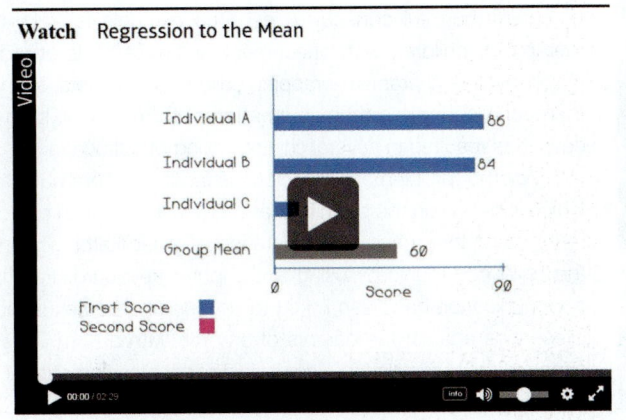

Would Change Occur Anyway?

What happens to disturbed people who do not obtain formal treatment? In view of the many ways in which people can help each other, it is not surprising that improvement often occurs without professional intervention. Moreover, some forms of psychopathology, such as depressive episodes or brief psychotic disorder, sometimes run a fairly short course with or without treatment. In other instances, disturbed people improve over time for reasons that are not apparent.

Even if many people with emotional disturbances tend to improve over time without psychotherapy, psychotherapy can often accelerate improvement or bring about desired behavior change that might not otherwise occur. Most researchers today would agree that psychotherapy is more effective than no treatment (Shadish et al., 2000), and indeed the pertinent evidence, widely cited throughout this entire text, confirms this (Lambert & Ogles, 2004). Research suggests that about 50 percent of patients show clinically significant change after 21 therapy sessions. After 40 sessions, about 75 percent of patients have improved (Lambert et al., 2001).

But *why* do patients improve? Remarkably, we know very little about the mechanisms through which therapeutic change occurs, or about the "active ingredients" of effective therapy (Hayes et al., 2011; Kazdin & Nock, 2003). We do know that progress in therapy is not always smooth and linear, however. Sudden gains can occur between one therapy session and another (Tang & DeRubeis, 1999; Tang et al., 2002). These clinical leaps appear to be triggered by cognitive changes that patients experience in critical sessions. Researchers are now actively exploring how such factors as therapist adherence (how well a therapist delivers a particular type of therapy) and therapist competence (how skillfully the therapist administers the therapy) impact how well a patient does (Strunk et al., 2010; Webb et al., 2010).

Can Therapy Be Harmful?

The outcomes of psychotherapy are not invariably either neutral (no effect) or positive. Some clients are actually harmed by their encounters with psychotherapists (see the World Around Us box). It has been estimated that between 5 and 10 percent of clients deteriorate during treatment (Lambert & Ogles, 2004). Unfortunately, clinicians are often quite bad at recognizing when their clients are not doing well (Whipple & Lambert, 2011). To address this problem, research-based measures to assess clinical deterioration are now being developed. Clinicians who use these measures in their routine clinical practice will be warned when their clients are not progressing in an expected manner. A major hurdle, however, is implementation. We would not be surprised to learn that the least effective therapists are the ones most reluctant to use such patient-monitoring methods.

A special case of therapeutic harm concerns what are called *boundary violations*. This is when the therapist

---

The World Around Us

When Therapy Harms

There are many ways in which therapy can be detrimental. For example, a particular therapy might make certain symptoms worse, make a person more concerned about the symptoms they do have, or make the client excessively dependent on the therapist in order to function. Encounters with some therapists or forms of therapy may also make a person less willing to seek therapy in the future.

Lilienfeld (2007) has developed a list of therapies that have potentially harmful consequences. One example is "rebirthing" therapy for children with attachment problems. This approach, which involves therapists wrapping children in blankets, sitting on them, and squeezing them in an attempt to mirror the birth process, has resulted in several children dying of suffocation.

Another problematic technique is facilitated communication, which is based on the premise that children with autism can communicate if they have the assistance of a facilitator who helps the child communicate using a computer keyboard. Facilitated communication has been linked to dozens of child sexual abuse allegations against the parents of children with autism. This has exposed these families to a great deal of needless emotional pain and suffering because studies show that the communications in facilitated communication do not come from the children themselves. Rather, they are unknowingly generated by the facilitators themselves as they guide the child's hands over the keyboard. Despite the fact that facilitated communication was debunked more than 20 years ago, many people still use it to this day (Lilienfeld et al., 2015).

All practicing clinicians and therapists owe it to their clients (and to the families of their clients) to educate themselves about research on potentially harmful treatments. They should also monitor their own behavior and adhere to high ethical standards of practice. In this way they can minimize the likelihood that they will cause damage to the people who come to them seeking help.

Studies suggest that many forms of treatment are not helpful, and some are even harmful. What do you think are some of the reasons that people keep using treatments that have been shown not to work? And how might we get clinicians to stop using ineffective treatments and start using more effective ones?

behaves in ways that exploit the trust of the patient or engages in behavior that is highly inappropriate (e.g., taking the patient to dinner, giving the patient gifts). One case involved a patient who had been treated by a psychiatrist for 10 years. During this time the patient gave the therapist gifts of a refrigerator and a dining table and six chairs. She also sold him her Waterford crystal, her china, and a silver service. The silver had an appraised value of $1,600. However, it was purchased by the psychiatrist for only $200. The psychiatrist also sold the patient two of his boats, without her even having seen them (Norris et al., 2003).

A sexual relationship between the patient and the therapist represents perhaps the most obvious and extreme example of a serious boundary violation. This is highly unethical conduct. Given the frequently intense and intimate quality of therapeutic relationships, it is not surprising that sexual attraction arises. However, it is the therapist's professional responsibility to maintain the appropriate boundaries at all times. When exploitive and unprofessional behavior on the part of therapists does occur, it results in great harm to patients (Norris et al., 2003). Anyone seeking therapy needs to be sufficiently aware enough to determine that the therapist she or he has chosen is committed to high ethical and professional standards. For the vast majority of therapists, this is indeed the case.

in review

- What approaches can be used to evaluate treatment success? What are the advantages and limitations of these approaches?
- Do people who receive psychological treatment always show a clinical benefit?
- What is a boundary violation? Give three examples.

What Therapeutic Approaches Should Be Used?

16.3 Describe some of the factors that must be considered to provide optimal treatment.

Before optimal treatment can be provided, a number of important decisions must be made. In the sections below we consider some of the factors that are important.

Evidence-Based Treatment

When a pharmaceutical company develops a new drug, it must obtain approval of the drug from the U.S. Food and Drug Administration (FDA) before that drug can be marketed. This involves, among other things, demonstrating

through research on human subjects that the drug has **efficacy**—that is, that the drug cures or relieves some target condition. These tests, using voluntary and informed patients as subjects, are called **randomized clinical trials (RCTs)** or, more simply, *efficacy trials*. Although these trials may become quite elaborate, the basic design is one of randomly assigning (e.g., by the flip of a coin) half the patients to the supposedly "active" drug and the other half to a visually identical but physiologically inactive placebo. Usually, neither the patient nor the clinician is informed which is to be administered; that information is recorded in code by a third party. This *double-blind study* (see Chapter 1) is an effort to ensure that expectations on the part of the patient and prescriber play no role in the study. After a predetermined treatment interval, the code is broken and the active-drug or placebo status of all subjects is revealed. If subjects on the active drug have improved in health significantly more than subjects on the placebo, the investigator has evidence of the drug's efficacy. Obviously, the same design could be modified to compare the efficacy of two or more active drugs, with the option of adding a placebo condition. Thousands of such studies are in progress daily across the country. They usually take place in academic medical settings, and many are financially supported by the pharmaceutical industry.

Watch Assessing Treatment Effectiveness

Investigators of psychotherapy outcomes have attempted to apply this research design to their own field of inquiry, with necessary modifications (see Chambless & Ollendick, 2001). A source of persistent frustration has been the difficulty of creating a placebo condition that will appear credible to patients. Most such research has thus adopted the strategy of either comparing two or more purportedly "active" therapies or using a no-treatment ("wait list") control of the same duration as the active-drug treatment. However, withholding treatment from patients in need (even temporarily) by placing them on a wait list sometimes raises ethical concerns. Another problem is that therapists, even those with the same theoretical orientations, often differ markedly in the manner in which they deliver therapy. (In contrast, pills of the same chemical compound and dosage do not vary.) To test a given therapy, it therefore becomes necessary to develop a treatment manual to specify just how the therapy under examination will be delivered. Therapists in the research trial are then trained (and monitored) to make sure that their therapy sessions do not deviate significantly from the procedures outlined in the manual (e.g., see Blum et al., 2008).

Efforts to "manualize" therapy represent one way that researchers have tried to minimize the variability in patients' clinical outcomes that might result from characteristics of the therapist themselves (such as personal charisma). Although **manualized therapies** originated principally to standardize psychosocial treatments to fit the RCT paradigm, some therapists recommend extending their use to routine clinical practice after efficacy for particular disorders has been established (see Wilson, 1998). Practicing clinicians, however, vary in their attitudes toward treatment manuals (Addis & Krasnow, 2000).

Efficacy, or RCT, studies of psychosocial treatments are increasingly common. These time-limited studies typically focus on patients who have a single *DSM* diagnosis (patients with comorbid diagnoses are sometimes excluded) and involve two or more treatment or control (e.g., wait list) conditions, where at least one of the treatment conditions is psychosocial (another could be some biological therapy, such as a particular drug). Client-participants are randomly assigned to these conditions, whose effects, if any, are evaluated systematically with a common battery of assessment instruments, usually administered both before and after treatment.

Efficacy studies of the outcomes of specific psychosocial treatment procedures are considered the most rigorous type of evaluation researchers have for establishing that a given therapy "works" for clients with a given diagnosis. Treatments that meet this standard are often described as *evidence based* or *empirically supported*.

Medication or Psychotherapy?

Advances in **psychopharmacology**—the use of medications to treat mental disorders—have allowed many people who would otherwise need hospitalization to remain with their families and function in the community. These advances have also reduced the time patients need to spend in the hospital and have made restraints and locked wards largely relics of the past. In short, medication has led to a much more favorable hospital climate for patients and staff alike.

Nevertheless, certain issues arise in the use of psychotropic drugs. Aside from possible unwanted side effects, there is the complexity of matching drug and dosage to the needs of each specific patient. It is also sometimes necessary for patients to change medication during the course of treatment. In addition, the use of medications in isolation

from other treatment methods may not be ideal for some disorders because drugs themselves generally do not cure disorders. Nonetheless, there is now a national trend toward greater use of psychiatric medications at the expense of psychotherapy. This may be problematic because, as many investigators have pointed out, drugs tend to alleviate symptoms by inducing biochemical changes, not by helping the individual understand and change the personal or situational factors that may be creating or reinforcing maladaptive behaviors. Moreover, when drugs are discontinued, patients may be at risk of relapsing (Dobson et al., 2008). For many disorders, a variety of evidence-based forms of psychotherapy may produce more long-lasting benefits than medications alone unless the medications are continued indefinitely.

Combined Treatments

The integration of medication and psychotherapy remains common in clinical practice, particularly for disorders such as schizophrenia and bipolar disorder (Olfson & Marcus, 2010). Such integrated approaches are also appreciated and regarded as essential by the patients themselves. The integrative approach is a good example of the biopsychosocial perspective that best describes current thinking about mental disorders and that is reflected throughout this book.

Medications can be combined with a broad range of psychological approaches. In some cases, they can help patients benefit more fully from psychotherapy. For example, patients with social anxiety disorder who receive exposure therapy do much better if they are given an oral dose of D-cycloserine before each session. D-cycloserine is an antibiotic used in the treatment of tuberculosis. When taken alone, it has no effect on anxiety. However, D-cycloserine activates a receptor that is critical in facilitating extinction of anxiety. By making the receptor work better, the therapeutic benefits of exposure training are enhanced in people taking D-cycloserine versus placebo (Guastella et al., 2008; Hofman et al., 2006).

Typically, psychosocial interventions are combined with psychiatric medications. This may be especially beneficial for patients with severe disorders (see Gabbard & Kay, 2001). Keller and colleagues (2000) compared the outcomes of 519 patients with depression who were treated with an antidepressant (nefazodone), with psychotherapy (cognitive-behavioral), or with a combination of both of these treatments. In the medication-alone condition, 55 percent of patients did well. In the psychotherapy-alone condition, 52 percent of patients responded to treatment. However, patients for whom the two treatments were combined did even better, with an overall positive response rate of 85 percent. Quite possibly, combined treatment is effective because medications and psychotherapy may target different symptoms and work at different rates. As Hollon and Fawcett (1995) have noted, "Pharmacotherapy appears to provide rapid, reliable relief from acute distress, and psychotherapy appears to provide broad and enduring change, with combined treatment retaining the specific benefits of each" (p. 1232).

It is important to note that combined treatments are not always superior to single treatments. Adding psychiatric medications does not generally improve the clinical efficacy of psychosocial treatments for anxiety disorders, for example. However, for people suffering from chronic or recurrent depression, combined treatments often result in better clinical outcomes (Aaronson et al., 2007).

in review

- What are the advantages and drawbacks of using a manualized therapy?
- What does it mean to describe a treatment as evidence based?
- For what kinds of disorders is combination therapy superior?

Psychosocial Approaches to Treatment

16.4 List the psychological approaches most often used to treat abnormal behavior.

Many people are fascinated by psychotherapy. As practicing therapists, we are often asked about the work that we do and the kinds of patients we see. In this section, we try to give you a sense of the different clinical approaches that therapists sometimes use. Although we have discussed treatment in earlier chapters in the context of specific disorders, our goal here is to provide you with a better sense of the different therapeutic approaches, illustrating them with case studies whenever possible.

Behavior Therapy

Behavior therapy is a direct and active treatment that recognizes the importance of behavior, acknowledges the role of learning, and includes thorough assessment and evaluation. Instead of exploring past traumatic events or inner conflicts, behavior therapists focus on the presenting problem—the problem or symptom that is causing the patient great distress. A major assumption of behavior therapy is that abnormal behavior is acquired in the same way as normal behavior—that is, by learning. A variety of behavioral techniques have therefore been developed to help patients "unlearn" maladaptive behaviors by one means or another.

EXPOSURE THERAPY   As you know, a behavior therapy technique that is widely used in the treatment of anxiety

disorders is exposure (see Chapter 6). If anxiety is learned, then, from the behavior therapy perspective, it can be unlearned. This is accomplished through guided exposure to anxiety-provoking stimuli. During exposure therapy, the patient or client is confronted with the fear-producing stimulus in a therapeutic manner. This can be accomplished in a very controlled, slow, and gradual way, as in **systematic desensitization**, or in a more extreme manner, as in **flooding**, in which the patient directly confronts the feared stimulus at full strength. (An example is a housebound patient with agoraphobia being accompanied outdoors by the therapist.) Moreover, the form of the exposure can be real (also known as *in vivo* **exposure**) or imaginary (**imaginal exposure**).

The rationale behind systematic desensitization is quite simple: Find a behavior that is incompatible with being anxious (such as being relaxed or experiencing something pleasant) and repeatedly pair this with the stimulus that provokes anxiety in the patient. Because it is difficult if not impossible to feel both pleasant and anxious at the same time, systematic desensitization is aimed at teaching a person, while in the presence (real or imagined) of the anxiety-producing stimulus, to relax or behave in some other way that is inconsistent with anxiety. It may therefore be considered a type of counterconditioning procedure. The term *systematic* refers to the carefully graduated manner in which the person is exposed to the feared stimulus.

The prototype of systematic desensitization is the classic experiment of Mary Cover Jones (1924), in which she successfully eliminated a small boy's fears of a white rabbit and other furry animals. She began by bringing the rabbit just inside the door at the far end of the room while the boy, Peter, was eating. On successive days, the rabbit was gradually brought closer until Peter could pat it with one hand while eating with the other.

Joseph Wolpe (1958; Rachman & Hodgson, 1980) elaborated on the procedure developed by Jones and coined the phrase *systematic desensitization* to refer to it. On the assumption that most anxiety-based patterns are, fundamentally, conditioned responses, Wolpe worked out a way to train a client to remain calm and relaxed in situations that formerly produced anxiety. Wolpe's approach is elegant in its simplicity, and his method is equally straightforward.

A client is first taught to enter a state of relaxation, typically by progressive concentration on relaxing various muscle groups. Meanwhile, patient and therapist collaborate in constructing an anxiety hierarchy that consists of imagined scenes graded as to their capacity to elicit anxiety. For example, for a patient with a dog phobia, a low-anxiety step might be imagining a small dog in the distance being walked on a leash by its owner. In contrast, a high-anxiety step might be imagining a large and exuberant dog running toward the patient. Therapy sessions consist of the patient's repeatedly imagining, under conditions of deep relaxation, the scenes in the hierarchy, beginning with low-anxiety images and gradually working toward those in the more extreme ranges. Treatment continues until all items in the hierarchy can be imagined without notable discomfort, at which point the client's real-life difficulties typically have shown substantial improvement.

Imaginal procedures have some limitations, an obvious one being that not everybody is capable of vividly imagining the required scenes. In an influential early study of clients with agoraphobia, Emmelkamp and Wessels (1975) concluded that prolonged exposure *in vivo* is superior to imaginal exposure. Since then, therapists have sought to use *in vivo* exposure whenever practical, encouraging clients to confront anxiety-provoking situations directly. As practicing clinicians, we sometimes receive e-mails from behavior therapists asking for instructions on making concoctions that look like vomit. In these cases the therapist is treating someone who has a vomiting phobia and has a need for something that looks realistic for an *in vivo* exposure.

Of course, *in vivo* exposure is not possible for all stimuli. In addition, occasionally a client is so fearful that he or she cannot be induced to confront the anxiety-arousing situation directly. Imaginal procedures are therefore a vital part of the therapeutic exposure repertoire. An important development in behavior therapy is the use of virtual reality to help patients overcome their fears and phobias (Rothbaum, Hodges, et al., 2000). Such approaches are obviously needed when the source of the patient's anxiety is something that is not easily reproduced in real life, such as flying. Overall, the outcome record for exposure treatments is impressive (Barlow et al., 2007; Emmelkamp, 2004). It is also encouraging that the results from virtual reality exposure are comparable to the results obtained from *in vivo* exposure (Powers & Emmelkamp, 2008).

AVERSION THERAPY   Aversion therapy involves modifying undesirable behavior by the old-fashioned method of punishment. Probably the most commonly used aversive stimuli today are drugs that have noxious effects, such as Antabuse, which induces nausea and vomiting when a person who has taken it ingests alcohol. In another variant, the client is instructed to wear a substantial elastic band on the wrist and to "snap" it when temptation arises, thus administering self-punishment.

In the past, painful electric shock was commonly employed in programs that paired it with the occurrence of the undesirable behavior, a practice that certainly contributed to aversion therapy's negative image among some segments of the public. Although aversive conditioning has been used to treat a wide range of maladaptive behaviors including smoking, drinking, overeating, drug dependence, gambling, sexual deviance, and bizarre psychotic behavior, interest in this approach has declined as other treatment options have become available (see Emmelkamp, 2004).

MODELING   As the name implies, in **modeling** the client learns new skills by imitating another person, such as a parent or therapist, who performs the behavior to be acquired. A younger client may be exposed to behaviors or roles in peers who act as assistants to the therapist and then be encouraged to imitate and practice the desired new responses. For example, modeling may be used to promote the learning of simple skills such as self-feeding for a child with profound mental retardation or more complex skills such as being more effective in social situations for a shy, withdrawn adolescent. In work with children especially, effective decision making and problem solving may be modeled when the therapist "thinks out loud" about everyday choices that present themselves in the course of therapy (Kendall, 1990; Kendall & Braswell, 1985).

Modeling and imitation are adjunctive aspects of various forms of behavior therapy as well as other types of therapy. For example, in an early classic work, Bandura (1964) found that live modeling of fearlessness, combined with instruction and guided exposure, was the most effective treatment for snake phobia, resulting in the elimination of phobic reactions in over 90 percent of the cases treated. The photographs taken during the treatment of spider phobia (see Chapter 6) provide a graphic example of a similar approach.

Exposure therapy involves confronting anxiety-provoking situations. It can be done *in vivo* (in real life) or in thoughts or imagination. *In vivo* is preferable whenever practically possible.

SYSTEMATIC REINFORCEMENT Systematic programs that use reinforcement to increase the frequency of desired behavior have achieved notable success. Often called contingency management programs, these approaches are often used in institutional settings, although this is not always the case.

Suppressing problematic behavior may be as simple as removing the reinforcements that support it, provided, of course, that they can be identified. Sometimes identification is relatively easy, as in the following case. In other instances, it may require extremely careful and detailed observation and analysis for the therapist to learn what is maintaining the maladaptive behavior.

Disrupting Class

Billy, a 6-year-old first grader, was brought to a psychological clinic by his parents because his teacher had told them that his behavior at school was inappropriate and no longer acceptable. Specifically, he had a long pattern of disrupting the class, talking back to his teacher, and being aggressive toward other children. It became apparent in observing Billy and his parents during the initial interview that both his mother and his father were uncritical and approving of everything Billy did. After further assessment, a three-phase program of therapy was undertaken: (1) Billy's parents were helped to discriminate between disruptive behavior and appropriate behavior on Billy's part (each type of behavior was defined and described in a very detailed way for the parents so they would be consistent in classifying each type of behavior). (2) They were instructed to ignore Billy when he engaged in disruptive behavior while vocally showing their approval of appropriate behavior. (3) Billy's teacher was also instructed to ignore Billy, insofar as it was feasible, when he engaged in disruptive behavior and to devote her attention at those times to children who were behaving more appropriately.

Although Billy's disruptive behavior in class increased during the first few days of this behavior therapy program, it diminished markedly after his parents and teacher no longer reinforced it. As his maladaptive behavior diminished, he was better accepted by his classmates. This helped reinforce more appropriate behavior patterns and changed Billy's negative attitude toward school.

Billy's was a case in which unwanted behavior was eliminated by eliminating its reinforcers. On other occasions, therapy is administered to establish desired behaviors that are missing. Examples of such approaches are *response shaping* and use of *token economies*. In **response shaping**, positive reinforcement is used to establish, by gradual approximation, a response that is actively resisted or is not initially in an individual's behavioral repertoire. This technique has been used extensively in working with children's behavior problems (Kazdin, 2007). For example, a child who refuses to speak in front of others (selective mutism) may be first rewarded (with praise or a more tangible treat) for making any sound. Later, only complete words, and later again only strings of words, would be rewarded.

TOKEN ECONOMIES Years ago, when behavior therapy was in its infancy, token economies based on the principles of operant conditioning were developed for use with patients experiencing long-term stays in psychiatric hospitals. When they behaved appropriately on the hospital ward, patients earned tokens that they could later use to receive rewards or privileges (Paul, 1982; Paul & Lentz, 1977).

Token economies have been used to establish adaptive behaviors ranging from elementary responses such as eating and making one's bed to the daily performance of responsible hospital jobs. In the latter instance, the **token economy** resembles the outside world, where an individual is paid for his or her work in tokens (money) that can later be exchanged for desired objects and activities. Although sometimes the subject of criticism and controversy, token economies remain a relevant treatment approach for individuals with serious mental illness and those with developmental disabilities (see Higgins et al., 2001; Le Blanc et al., 2000).

Similar reinforcement-based methods are now being used to treat substance abuse. In one study, people being treated for cocaine dependence were rewarded with vouchers worth 25 cents if their urine tests came back negative (Higgins, Wong, et al., 2000). Patients could then ask a staff member to purchase for them items from the community with the vouchers they had accumulated. Patients who received the incentive vouchers based on their abstinence from cocaine had better clinical outcomes than a comparison group of patients who also received vouchers but whose vouchers were not contingent on their abstinent behavior.

EVALUATING BEHAVIOR THERAPY Compared with some other forms of therapy, behavior therapy has some distinct advantages. Behavior therapy usually achieves results in a short period of time because it is generally directed to specific symptoms, leading to faster relief of a client's distress and to lower costs. The methods to be used are also clearly delineated, and the results can be readily evaluated. Overall, the outcomes achieved with behavior therapy compare very favorably with those of other approaches (Emmelkamp, 2004; Nathan & Gorman, 2007).

As with other approaches, behavior therapy works better with certain kinds of problems than with others. Generally, the more pervasive and vaguely defined the client's problem, the less likely behavior therapy is to be useful. For example, it appears to be only rarely employed to treat complex personality disorders, although *dialectical behavior therapy* (see Chapter 10) for patients with borderline personality disorder is an exception (Crits-Christoph & Barber, 2007). On the other hand, behavioral techniques remain central to the treatment of anxiety disorders (Barlow et al., 2007; Franklin & Foa, 2007). Because behavioral treatments are often quite straightforward, behavior therapy can be used with patients with psychosis (Kopelowicz et al., 2007). Recent research also shows that behavior therapy is an effective treatment for the vocal and motor tics that are found in people with Tourette's syndrome (Wilhelm et al., 2012). This is welcome news because the alternative treatment approach involves the use of antipsychotic medications.

A recent development in the treatment of depression is a brief and structured form of therapy called *behavioral activation* (see Chapter 7). In this treatment the patient and the therapist work together to help the patient find ways to become more active and engaged with life. The patient is encouraged to engage in activities that will help improve mood and lead to better ways of coping with specific life problems. Although this sounds quite simple, it is not always that easy to accomplish. However, evidence to date suggests that this form of therapy is very beneficial for patients and can lead to enduring change (Dimidjian et al., 2011; Dobson et al., 2008).

Cognitive and Cognitive-Behavioral Therapy

The early behavior therapists focused on observable behavior and regarded the inner thoughts of their clients as unimportant. However, starting in the 1970s, a number of behavior therapists began to reappraise the importance of "private events"—thoughts, perceptions, evaluations, and self-statements—and started to see them as processes that mediated the effects of objective stimulus conditions to determine behavior and emotions (Borkovec, 1985; Mahoney & Arnkoff, 1978).

Cognitive and *cognitive-behavioral therapy* (terms for the most part used interchangeably) stem from both cognitive psychology (with its emphasis on the effects of thoughts on behavior) and behaviorism (with its rigorous methodology and performance-oriented focus). No single set of techniques defines cognitively oriented treatment approaches. However, two main themes are important: (1) the conviction that cognitive processes influence emotion, motivation, and behavior; and (2) the use of cognitive and behavior-change techniques in a pragmatic (hypothesis-testing) manner. In the following discussion, we briefly describe the rational emotive behavior therapy of Albert Ellis and then focus in more detail on the cognitive therapy approach of Aaron Beck.

RATIONAL EMOTIVE BEHAVIOR THERAPY The first form of behaviorally oriented cognitive therapy was developed by Albert Ellis and called **rational emotive behavior therapy (REBT)** (see Ellis & Dryden, 1997). REBT attempts to change a client's maladaptive thought processes, on which maladaptive emotional responses and, thus, behavior are presumed to depend.

Ellis posited that a well-functioning individual behaves rationally and in tune with empirical reality. Unfortunately, however, many of us have learned unrealistic beliefs and perfectionistic values that cause us to expect too much of ourselves, leading us to behave irrationally and then to feel that we are worthless failures. For example, a person may continually think, "I should be able to win everyone's love and approval" or "I should be thoroughly adequate and competent in everything I do." Such unrealistic assumptions and self-demands inevitably spell problems.

The task of REBT is to restructure an individual's belief system and self-evaluation, especially with respect to the irrational "shoulds," "oughts," and "musts" that are preventing the individual from having a more positive sense of self-worth and an emotionally satisfying, fulfilling life. Several methods are used. One method is to dispute a person's false beliefs through rational confrontation ("Why should your failure to get the promotion you wanted mean that you are worthless?").

REBT therapists also use behaviorally oriented techniques. For example, homework assignments might be given to encourage clients to have new experiences and to break negative chains of behavior. Although the techniques differ dramatically, the philosophy underlying REBT has something in common with that underlying humanistic therapy (discussed later) because both take a clear stand on personal worth and human values. Rational emotive behavior therapy aims to increase an individual's feelings of self-worth and clear the way for self-actualization by removing the false beliefs that have been stumbling blocks to personal growth.

According to the cognitive model, how we think about situations is closely linked to our emotional responses to them. If this young man is having automatic thoughts such as "I'll never get to play. I'm such a loser," he is likely to be more emotionally distressed about waiting on the sideline than if he has a thought such as "There's a lot I can learn from watching how this game is going."

BECK'S COGNITIVE THERAPY Beck's cognitive therapy approach was originally developed for the treatment of depression and later for anxiety disorders. Now, however, this form of treatment is used for a broad range of conditions, including eating disorders and obesity, personality disorders, substance abuse, and even schizophrenia (Beck, 2005; Beck & Rector, 2005; Hollon & Beck, 2004). The cognitive model is basically an information-processing model of psychopathology. A fundamental assumption of the cognitive model is that problems result from biased processing of external events or internal stimuli. These biases distort the way that a person makes sense of the experiences that she or he has in the world, leading to cognitive errors.

But why do people make cognitive errors at all? According to Beck (2005), underlying these biases is a relatively stable set of cognitive structures or schemas that contain dysfunctional beliefs. When these schemas become activated (by external or internal triggers), they bias how people process information. In the case of depression, people become inclined to make negatively biased interpretations of themselves, their world, and their future.

In the initial phase of cognitive therapy, clients are made aware of the connection between their patterns of thinking and their emotional responses. They are first taught simply to identify their own automatic thoughts (such as "This event is a total disaster") and to keep records of their thought content and their emotional reactions (Wright et al., 2006). With the therapist's help, they then identify the logical errors in their thinking and learn to challenge the validity of these automatic thoughts. The errors in the logic behind their thinking lead them (1) to perceive the world selectively as harmful while ignoring evidence to the contrary; (2) to overgeneralize on the basis of limited examples—for example, seeing themselves as totally worthless because they were laid off from work; (3) to magnify the significance of undesirable events—for example, seeing the job loss as the end of the world for them; and (4) to engage in absolutistic thinking—for example, exaggerating the importance of someone's mildly critical comment and perceiving it as proof of their instant descent from goodness to worthlessness. In the case study that follows, the therapist describes some of these errors in thinking to a patient with depression.

Cognitive Therapy

THERAPIST: You have described many instances today where your interpretations led to particular feelings. You remember when you were crying a little while ago and I asked you what was going through your mind? You told me that you thought that I considered you pathetic and that I wouldn't want to see you for therapy. I said you were reading my mind and putting negative thoughts in my mind that were not, in fact,

correct. You were making an arbitrary inference, or jumping to conclusions without evidence. This is what often happens when one is depressed. One tends to put the most negative interpretations on things, even sometimes when the evidence is contrary, and this makes one even more depressed. Do you recognize what I mean?

PATIENT: You mean even my thoughts are wrong?

THERAPIST: No, not your thoughts in general, and I am not talking about right and wrong. As I was explaining before, interpretations are not facts. They can be more or less accurate, but they cannot be right or wrong. What I mean is that some of your interpretations, in particular those relating to yourself, are biased negatively. The thoughts you attributed to me could have been accurate. But there were also many other conclusions you could have reached that might have been less depressing for you, in that they would reflect less badly on you. For example, you could have thought that since I was spending time with you, that meant I was interested and that I wanted to try and help. If this had been your conclusion, how do you think that you would have felt? Do you think that you would have felt like crying?

PATIENT: Well, I guess I might have felt less depressed, more hopeful.

THERAPIST: Good. That's the point I was trying to make. We feel what we think. Unfortunately, these biased interpretations tend to occur automatically. They just pop into one's head and one believes them. What you and I will do in therapy is to try and catch these thoughts and examine them. Together we will look at the evidence and correct the biases to make the thoughts more realistic. Does this sound all right with you?

PATIENT: Yes.

Source: From I. M. Blackburn and K. M. Davidson. (1990). *Cognitive therapy for depression and anxiety: A practitioner's guide* (pp. 106–7). Copyright © 1995 Blackwell Science.

Much of the content of the therapy sessions and homework assignments is analogous to experiments in which a therapist and a client apply learning principles to alter the client's biased and dysfunctional cognitions and continuously evaluate the effects that these changes have on subsequent thoughts, feelings, and overt behavior. It is important to note, however, that in Beck's cognitive therapy, clients do not change their beliefs by debate and confrontation as is common in REBT. Rather, they are encouraged to gather information about themselves. For example, a young man who believes that he will be rejected by any attractive woman he approaches would be led to a searching analysis of the reasons why he holds this belief. The client might then be assigned the task of "testing" this dysfunctional "hypothesis" by actually approaching seemingly appropriate women whom he admires. The results of the "test" would then be discussed with the cognitive therapist, and any cognitive "errors" that may have interfered with a skillful performance would be identified and corrected.

In addition, the client is encouraged to discover the faulty assumptions or dysfunctional schemas that may be leading to problem behaviors and self-defeating tendencies

(Young et al., 2008). These generally become evident over the course of therapy as the client and the therapist examine the themes of the client's automatic thoughts. Because these dysfunctional schemas are seen as making the person vulnerable (e.g., to depression), this phase of treatment is considered essential in ensuring resistance to relapse when the client faces stressful life events in the future. That is, if the underlying cognitive vulnerability factors are not changed, the client may show only short-term improvement and will still be subject to recurrent depression.

For disorders other than depression, the general approach is quite similar. However, the nature of the patient's automatic thoughts and underlying beliefs is obviously quite different across disorders. In panic disorder, for example, the focus is on identifying the automatic thoughts about feared bodily sensations and on teaching the client to "decatastrophize" the experience of panic (Craske & Barlow, 2008). In bulimia nervosa, the cognitive approach centers on the person's overvalued ideas about body weight and shape, which are often fueled by low self-esteem and fears of being unattractive. In addition, faulty cognitions about which foods are "safe" and which are "dangerous" are explored (Fairburn et al., 2008; Wilson, 2005).

EVALUATING COGNITIVE-BEHAVIORAL THERAPIES

In spite of the widespread attention that Ellis's REBT has enjoyed, it has been less well assimilated into the mainstream than Beck's cognitive therapy (David et al., 2005). Nonetheless, REBT is still very much alive and well. In general, this approach may be most useful in helping basically healthy people to cope better with everyday stress and perhaps in preventing them from developing full-blown anxiety or depressive disorders (Haaga & Davison, 1989). With respect to controlled research studies with carefully diagnosed clinical populations, REBT appears to be inferior to exposure-based therapies in the treatment of anxiety disorders such as agoraphobia, social phobia (Haaga & Davison, 1989), and probably OCD (Franklin & Foa, 1998).

In contrast, the efficacy of Beck's cognitive treatment methods has been well documented. Research suggests that these approaches are extremely beneficial in alleviating many different types of disorders (Hollon & Beck, 2004). For all but the most severe cases of depression (e.g., psychotic depression), cognitive-behavioral therapy (CBT) is at least comparable to drug treatment. It also offers long-term advantages, especially with regard to the prevention of relapse (Craighead et al., 2007). Cognitive therapy also produces dramatic results in the treatment of panic disorder and generalized anxiety disorder (Hollon & Beck, 2004), and CBT is now the treatment of choice for bulimia (Wilson, 2010; Wilson & Fairburn, 2007). Finally, cognitive approaches have promise in the treatment of conduct disorder in children (Kazdin, 2007), substance abuse (Beck et al.,

1993), and certain personality disorders (Beck et al., 1990; Linehan, 1993).

The combined use of cognitive and behavior therapy approaches is now quite routine. Some disagreement remains about whether the effects of cognitive treatments are actually the result of cognitive changes as the cognitive theorists propose (Hollon & Beck, 2004; Jacobson et al., 1996). At least for depression and panic disorder, it does appear that cognitive change is the best predictor of long-term outcome, just as cognitive theory maintains. Exactly what the "active ingredients" of cognitive treatments really are, however, remains a source of debate and research (Garratt et al., 2007).

A recent meta-analysis that examined nearly 40 years of data on the use of CBT to treat depression yielded several very interesting findings (Johnsen & Friborg, 2015). The data showed that (1) CBT has been an effective treatment for depression since the 1970s, (2) female patients benefit more from treatment than do men, (3) more experienced clinicians have better treatment effects than less experienced ones, and (4) most alarmingly, the effectiveness of CBT seems to be *decreasing* over time. This last fact is puzzling; however, there are two leading explanations. One is that as more and more people are getting trained in using CBT over time, more inexperienced clinicians are providing the intervention, and given point (3) above, this is causing CBT to appear less effective than it used to be. Another possibility is that the novelty of CBT led to stronger expectations on the part of both clinician and client early on, but as CBT has become more common, those expectations have decreased, leading to smaller positive changes in depression. Whatever the case, it is comforting to know that CBT is still a powerful and effective treatment!

Humanistic-Experiential Therapies

The humanistic-experiential therapies emerged as significant treatment approaches after World War II. In a society dominated by self-interest, mechanization, computerization, mass deception, and mindless bureaucracy, proponents of the humanistic-experiential therapies see psychopathology as stemming in many cases from problems of alienation, depersonalization, loneliness, and a failure to find meaning and genuine fulfillment. Problems of this sort, it is held, are not likely to be solved either by delving into forgotten memories or by correcting specific maladaptive behaviors.

The humanistic-experiential therapies are based on the assumption that people have both the freedom and the responsibility to control their own behavior—that they can reflect on their problems, make choices, and take positive action. Humanistic-experiential therapists feel that a client must take most of the responsibility for the direction and success of therapy, with the therapist serving merely as counselor, guide, and facilitator. Although humanistic-experiential therapies differ in their details, their central focus is always expanding a client's "awareness."

CLIENT-CENTERED THERAPY The **client-centered** (person-centered) **therapy** of Carl Rogers (1902–1987) focuses on the natural power of the organism to heal itself (Rogers, 1951, 1961). Rogers saw therapy as a process of removing the constraints and restrictions that grow out of unrealistic demands that people tend to place on themselves when they believe, as a condition of self-worth, that they should not have certain kinds of feelings such as hostility. By denying that they do in fact have such feelings, they become unaware of their actual "gut" reactions. As they lose touch with their own genuine experience, the result is lowered integration, impaired personal relationships, and various forms of maladjustment.

The primary objective of Rogerian therapy is to resolve this incongruence—to help clients become able to accept and be themselves. To this end, client-centered therapists establish a psychological climate in which clients can feel unconditionally accepted, understood, and valued as people. Within this context, the therapist employs nondirective techniques such as empathic reflecting, or a restatement of the client's descriptions of life difficulties. If all goes well, clients begin to feel free, for perhaps the first time, to explore their real feelings and thoughts and to accept hates and angers and ugly feelings as parts of themselves. As their self-concept becomes more congruent with their actual experience, they become more self-accepting and more open to new experiences and new perspectives; in short, they become better-integrated people.

In contrast to most other forms of therapy, the client-centered therapist does not give answers, interpret what a client says, probe for unconscious conflicts, or even steer the client toward certain topics. Rather, he or she simply listens attentively and acceptingly to what the client wants to talk about, interrupting only to restate in different words what the client is saying. Such restatements, devoid of any judgment or interpretation by the therapist, help the client to clarify further the feelings and ideas that he or she is exploring—really to look at them and acknowledge them. The following excerpt from a therapist's second interview with a young woman will serve to illustrate these techniques of reflection and clarification.

Client-Centered Therapy

JENNY: I was thinking about how I always try to make people around me feel at ease. It's so important for me to make things go along smoothly.

THERAPIST: In other words, you are always trying to make other people feel better and to do all you can to keep things on an even keel and going well.

JENNY: Yes. That's right. I mean, it's not because I am such a kind person and all I want to see is other people being happy. I think the reason I do it is probably because that has always been the role that has felt the easiest for me to play. It's the role I played at home. I didn't stand up for my own convictions. And now I'm at the point where I don't really know whether I have any convictions to stand up for.

THERAPIST: So you feel this is a role you have been playing for a long time, smoothing out frictions and avoiding saying anything that might be challenging in any way.

JENNY: I think that's right.

THERAPIST: And so now you aren't sure if you even have any genuine opinions or reactions of your own. Is that right?

JENNY: That's it. Or maybe I haven't really been honest with myself and let myself even consider what I really think about things. I've just been playing a sort of a false role—being a people-pleaser. Whatever I felt other people needed me to be, that's who I was. And in the process I just got lost.

Pure client-centered psychotherapy, as originally practiced, is rarely used today in North America, although it is still relatively popular in Europe. Motivational interviewing is a new form of therapy that is based on this empathic style.

MOTIVATIONAL INTERVIEWING People tend to be ambivalent about making changes in their lives. For instance, although there are negative consequences to drinking too much alcohol, there are also some perceived benefits to drinking (e.g., experience of pleasure, social interactions). **Motivational interviewing (MI)** (Miller & Rollnick, 2012) is a brief form of therapy that can be delivered in one or two sessions. It was developed as a way to help people resolve their ambivalence about change and make a commitment to treatment (Miller, 1983). At its center is a supportive and empathic style of relating to the client that has its origins in the work of Carl Rogers. However, MI differs from client-centered counseling because it employs a more direct approach that explores the client's own reasons for wanting to change. The therapist encourages this "change talk" by asking the client to discuss his or her desire, ability, reasons, and need for change. These are reflected back by the therapist, thus exposing the client to periodic summaries of his or her own motivational statements and thoughts about change. The result is that clients can develop and strengthen their commitment to change in an active, accepting, and supportive atmosphere.

Motivational interviewing is most often used in the areas of substance abuse and addiction. When added to the beginning of a treatment program, it appears to benefit patients, perhaps because it facilitates patients' staying in treatment and following the treatment plan. A meta-analysis of the MI literature also has shown that MI has a large effect when it is used with ethnic minorities (Hettema, Steele, & Miller, 2005). In one alcoholism-treatment trial,

Native American participants did better if they received four sessions of MI than if they received 12 sessions of CBT or else participated in a 12-step program (Villanueva et al., 2003). Quite possibly, the supportive and nonconfrontational style of MI may be more congruent with the typical and culturally sanctioned communication style of Native Americans and thus represent a culturally appropriate intervention. The collaborative and nonconfrontational style of MI may also make it acceptable to adolescents. Even a very small number of sessions of MI can promote behavior change in adolescents who use drugs and alcohol (Jensen et al., 2011).

People derive pleasure and have good experiences using alcohol and drugs; however, they also can experience very negative and physically harmful consequences as well—like these three guys in the movie *The Hangover*. Rather than telling people to "just say no," motivational interviewing gets people to weigh the pros and cons of their behavior and to make a decision about future alcohol and drug use based on these factors.

GESTALT THERAPY In German, the term *gestalt* means "whole," and gestalt therapy emphasizes the unity of mind and body—placing strong emphasis on the need to integrate thought, feeling, and action. **Gestalt therapy** was developed by Frederick (Fritz) Perls (1969) as a means of teaching clients to recognize the bodily processes and emotions they had been blocking off from awareness. As with the client-centered and humanistic approaches, the main goal of gestalt therapy is to increase the individual's self-awareness and self-acceptance.

Although gestalt therapy is commonly used in a group setting, the emphasis is on one person at a time, with whom a therapist works intensively, trying to help identify aspects of the individual's self or world that are not being acknowledged in awareness. The individual may be asked to act out fantasies concerning feelings and conflicts or to represent one side of a conflict while sitting in one chair and then switch chairs to take the part of the adversary. Often the therapist or other group members will ask questions such as "What are you aware of in your body now?" and "What does it feel like in your gut when you think of that?"

In Perls' approach to therapy, a good deal of attention is also paid to dreams, but with an emphasis very different from that of classical psychoanalysis. In gestalt theory, all elements of a dream, including seemingly inconsequential, impersonal objects, are considered to be representations of unacknowledged aspects of the dreamer's self. The therapist urges the client to suspend normal critical judgment, to "be" the object in the dream, and then to report on the experience. This is illustrated in the following case study.

Gestalt Therapy

A college professor was preoccupied with his academic promotion and tenure and found himself unable to experience any joy. He sought the assistance of a friend who was a gestalt therapist. She asked him to conjure up a daydream rather than a dream. The daydream that emerged spontaneously was one of skiing. The therapist asked him to be the mountain, and he began to experience how warm he was when he was at his base. As he got closer to the top, what looked so beautiful was also very cold and frozen. The therapist asked the professor to be the snow, and he experienced how hard and icy he could be near the top. But near the bottom, people ran over him easily and wore him out. When the session was finished, the professor did not feel like crying or shouting; he felt like skiing. So he went, leaving articles and books behind. In the sparkle of the snow and sun, he realized that joy in living emerges through deeds and not through words. In his rush to succeed, he had committed one of the cardinal sins against himself—the sin of not being active.

Source: Adapted from Prochaska & Norcross, 2003, p. 183.

EVALUATING HUMANISTIC-EXPERIENTIAL THERAPIES Many of the humanistic-experiential concepts—the uniqueness of each individual, the importance of therapist genuineness, the satisfaction that comes from realizing one's potential, the importance of the search for meaning and fulfillment, and the human capacity for choice and self-direction—have had a major impact on our contemporary views of both human nature and the nature of good psychotherapy.

However, humanistic-experiential therapies have been criticized for their lack of agreed-on therapeutic procedures and their vagueness about what is supposed to happen between client and therapist. In response, proponents of such approaches argue against reducing people to abstractions, which can diminish their perceived worth and deny their uniqueness. Because people are so different, they argue, we should expect different techniques to be appropriate for different cases.

Controlled research on the outcomes achieved by many forms of humanistic-existential therapy was lacking in the past. However, research in this area is now on the increase. Evidence suggests that these treatment approaches are helpful for patients with a variety of problems including depression, anxiety, trauma, and marital difficulties (Elliot et al., 2004). And, as we have already noted, motivational interviewing is now established as an effective method for promoting behavior change in people with substance abuse problems (Ball et al., 2007; Jensen et al., 2011).

Psychodynamic Therapies

Psychodynamic therapy is a broad treatment approach that focuses on individual personality dynamics, usually from a psychoanalytic or some psychoanalytically derived perspective. Psychoanalytic therapy is the oldest form of psychological therapy and began with Sigmund Freud. The therapy is mainly practiced in two basic forms: classical psychoanalysis and psychodynamically oriented psychotherapy. As developed by Freud and his immediate followers, classical psychoanalysis is an intensive (at least three sessions per week), long-term procedure for uncovering repressed memories, thoughts, fears, and conflicts presumably stemming from problems in early psychosexual development—and helping individuals come to terms with them in light of the realities of adult life. For example, excessive orderliness and a grim and humorless focus on rigorous self-control would probably be viewed as deriving from difficulties in early toilet training.

In psychoanalytically oriented psychotherapy, the treatment and the ideas guiding it may depart substantially from the principles and procedures laid out by orthodox Freudian theory, yet the therapy is still loosely based on psychoanalytic concepts. For example, many psychodynamically oriented therapists schedule less frequent sessions (e.g., once per week) and sit face to face with the client instead of having the latter recline on a couch with the analyst out of sight behind him or her. Likewise, the relatively passive stance of the analyst (primarily listening to the client's "free associations" and rarely offering "interpretations") is replaced with an active conversational style in which the therapist attempts to clarify distortions and gaps in the client's construction of the origins and consequences of his or her problems, thus challenging client "defenses" as they present themselves. It is widely believed that this more direct approach significantly shortens total treatment time. We first examine Freud's original treatment methods, in part because of their historical significance and enormous influence; we then look briefly at some of the contemporary modifications of psychodynamic therapy, which for the most part focus on interpersonal processes. Before we do so, however, let's consider the case of Karen.

Psychodynamic Therapy

Karen was about to be terminated from her nursing program if her problems were not resolved. She had always been a competent student who seemed to get along well with peers and patients. Now, since the beginning of her rotation on 3 South, a surgical ward, she had been plagued by headaches and dizzy spells. Of more serious consequence were the two medical errors she had made when dispensing medications to patients. She realized that these errors could have proved fatal, and she was as concerned as her nursing faculty about why such problems had begun in this final year of her education. Karen knew she had many negative feelings toward the head nurse on 3 South, but she did not believe these feelings could account for her current dilemma. She entered psychotherapy.

After a few weeks of psychotherapy, the therapist realized that one of Karen's important conflicts revolved around the death of her father when she was 12 years old. Karen had just gone to live with her father after being with her mother for 7 years. She remembered how upset she was when her father had a heart attack and had to be rushed to the hospital. For a while it looked as though her father was going to pull through, and Karen began enjoying her daily visits to see him. During one of these visits, her father clutched his chest in obvious pain and told Karen to get a nurse. She remembered how helpless she felt when she could not find a nurse, although she did not recall why this was so difficult. Her search seemed endless, and by the time she finally found a nurse, her father was dead.

The therapist asked Karen the name of the ward on which her father had died. She paused and thought, and then she blurted out, "3 South." She cried at length as she told how confused she was and how angry she felt toward the nurses on the ward for not being more readily available, although she thought they might have been involved with another emergency. After weeping and shaking and expressing her resentment, Karen felt calm and relaxed for the first time in months. Her symptoms disappeared, and her problems in the nursing program were relieved.

Source: Adapted from Prochaska & Norcross, 2003, p. 28.

FREUDIAN PSYCHOANALYSIS Psychoanalysis is a system of therapy that evolved over a period of years during Freud's long career. Four basic techniques are used in this form of therapy: (1) free association, (2) analysis of dreams, (3) analysis of resistance, and (4) analysis of transference.

In classical (Freudian) psychoanalysis the technique of free association may be used to explore the contents of the preconscious.

Free Association   The basic rule of *free association* (see Chapter 2) is that an individual must say whatever comes into her or his mind regardless of how personal, painful, or seemingly irrelevant it may be. Usually a client lies in a relaxed position on a couch and gives a running account of all the thoughts, feelings, and desires that come to mind as one idea leads to another. The therapist normally takes a position behind the client so as not to disrupt the free flow of associations in any way.

Although such a running account of whatever comes into one's mind may seem random, Freud believed that associations are determined just like other events. The purpose of free association is to explore thoroughly the contents of the preconscious—that part of the mind considered subject to conscious attention but largely ignored. Analytic interpretation involves a therapist's tying together a client's often disconnected ideas, beliefs, and actions into a meaningful explanation to help the client gain insight into the relationship between his or her maladaptive behavior and the repressed (unconscious) events and fantasies that drive it.

Analysis of Dreams   Another important, related procedure for uncovering unconscious material is the analysis of dreams. When a person is asleep, repressive defenses are said to be lowered, and forbidden desires and feelings may find an outlet in dreams. For this reason, dreams have been referred to as the "royal road to the unconscious." Some motives, however, are so unacceptable to an individual that even in dreams they are not revealed openly but are expressed in disguised or symbolic form. Thus, a dream has two kinds of content: (1) **manifest content**, which is the dream as it appears to the dreamer, and (2) **latent content**, which consists of the actual motives that are seeking expression but are so painful or unacceptable that they are disguised.

It is a therapist's task, in conjunction with the associations of the patient, to uncover these disguised meanings by studying the images that appear in the manifest content of a client's dream and in the client's associations to them. For example, a client's dream of being engulfed in a tidal wave may be interpreted by a therapist as indicating that the client feels in danger of being overwhelmed by inadequately repressed fears or hostilities.

Analysis of Resistance   During the process of free association or of associating to dreams, an individual may evidence **resistance**—an unwillingness or inability to talk about certain thoughts, motives, or experiences. For example, a client may be talking about an important childhood experience and then suddenly switch topics, perhaps stating, "It really isn't that important" or "It is too absurd to discuss." Resistance may also be evidenced by the client's giving a too-glib interpretation of some association, or coming late to an appointment, or even "forgetting" an appointment altogether. Because resistance prevents painful and threatening material from entering awareness, its sources must be sought if an individual is to face the problem and learn to deal with it in a realistic manner (Horner, 2005).

Analysis of Transference   As client and therapist interact, the relationship between them may become complex and emotionally involved. Often people carry over, and unconsciously apply (or "transfer") to their therapist, attitudes and feelings that they had in their relations with a parent or other person close to them in the past, a process known as **transference**. Thus, clients may react to their analyst as they did to that earlier person and feel the same love, hostility, or rejection that they felt long ago. If the analyst is operating according to the prescribed role of maintaining an impersonal stance of detached attention, the often affect-laden reactions of the client can be interpreted, it is held, as a type of projection—inappropriate to the present situation yet highly revealing of central issues in the client's life. For example, should the client vehemently (but inaccurately) condemn the therapist for a lack of caring and attention to the client's needs, this would be seen as a "transference" to the therapist of attitudes acquired in childhood interactions with parents or other key individuals.

In helping the client to understand and acknowledge the transference relationship, a therapist may provide the client with insight into the meaning of his or her reactions to others. In doing so, the therapist may also introduce a corrective emotional experience by refusing to engage the person on the basis of his or her unwarranted assumptions about the nature of the therapeutic relationship. If the client expects rejection and criticism, for example, the therapist is careful to maintain a neutral manner. In contrast, the therapist may express positive emotions at a point where the client feels particularly vulnerable, thereby encouraging the client to reframe and rethink her or his view of the situation. In this way it may be possible for the client to recognize these assumptions and to "work through" the conflict in feelings about the real parent or perhaps to overcome feelings of hostility and self-devaluation that stem from the earlier parental rejection. In essence, the negative effects of an undesirable early relationship are counteracted by working through a similar emotional conflict with the therapist in a therapeutic setting. A person's reliving of a pathogenic past relationship in a sense re-creates the neurosis in real life, and therefore this experience is often referred to as a *transference neurosis*.

It is not possible here to consider at length the complexities of transference relationships, but a client's attitudes toward his or her therapist usually do not follow such simple patterns as our examples suggest. Often the client is ambivalent—distrusting the therapist and feeling hostile toward him or her as a symbol of authority, but at the same time seeking acceptance and love. In addition, the problems of transference are not confined to the client, for the therapist may also have a mixture of feelings toward the client. This **countertransference**, wherein the therapist reacts in accord with the client's transferred attributions rather than objectively, must be recognized and handled properly by the therapist. For this reason, it is considered important that therapists have a thorough understanding of their own motives, conflicts, and "weak spots"; in fact, all psychoanalysts undergo psychoanalysis themselves before they begin independent practice.

The resolution of the transference neurosis is said to be the key element in effecting a psychoanalytic "cure." Such resolution can occur only if an analyst successfully avoids the pitfalls of countertransference. That is, the analyst needs to keep track of his or her own transference or reaction to a client's behavior. Failure to do so risks merely repeating, in the therapy relationship, the typical relationship difficulties characterizing the client's adult life. Analysis of transference and the phenomenon of countertransference are also part of most psychodynamic derivatives of classical psychoanalysis, to which we now turn.

Psychodynamic Therapy Since Freud   The original version of psychoanalysis is practiced only rarely today. Arduous and costly in time, money, and emotional commitment, it may take several years before all major issues in the client's life have been satisfactorily resolved. In light of these heavy demands, psychoanalytic or psychodynamic therapists have worked out modifications in the procedure that are designed to shorten the time and expense required. A good review of some of these approaches can be found in the work of Prochaska and Norcross (2003).

Object Relations, Attachment-Based Approaches, and Self-Psychology   The most extensive revisions of classical psychoanalytic theory undertaken within recent decades have been related to the object-relations perspective (in psychoanalytic jargon, "objects" are other people) and, to a lesser extent, the attachment and self-psychology perspectives (Prochaska & Norcross, 2003). Whether or not psychotherapy investigators and clinicians use the term *object relations* (or *attachment* or *self-psychology*) to denote their approach, increasing numbers of them describe procedures that focus on interpersonal relationship issues, particularly as they play themselves out in the client–therapist relationship.

Interpersonally oriented psychodynamic therapists vary considerably in their time focus, whether they concentrate on remote events of the past, on current interpersonal situations and impasses (including those of the therapy itself), or on some balance of the two. Most seek to expose, bring to awareness, and modify the effects of the remote developmental sources of the difficulties the client is currently experiencing. These therapies generally retain, then, the classical psychoanalytic goal of understanding the present in terms of the past. What they ignore are the psychoanalytic notions of staged libidinal energy transformations and of entirely internal (and impersonal) drives that are channeled into psychopathological symptom formation.

EVALUATING PSYCHODYNAMIC THERAPIES The practice of classical psychoanalysis is routinely criticized for being relatively time consuming and expensive; for being based on a questionable and sometimes cult-like approach to human nature; for neglecting a client's immediate problems in the search for unconscious conflicts in the remote past; and for there being no adequate proof of its general effectiveness. Indeed, there have been no rigorous, controlled outcome studies of classical psychoanalysis. This is understandable, given the intensive and long-term nature of the treatment and the methodological difficulties inherent in testing such an approach. Nonetheless, there are some hints that this treatment approach has some value (Gabbard et al., 2002). Psychoanalysts also argue that manualized treatments unduly limit treatment for a disorder. They note that simply because a treatment cannot be standardized does not mean that it is invalid or unhelpful. Whether the clinical benefits justify the time and expense of psychoanalysis, however, remains uncertain.

In contrast, much more research has been done on some of the newer psychodynamically oriented approaches. There are signs that psychodynamic approaches may be helpful in the treatment of depression, panic disorder, PTSD, and substance abuse disorders (Gibbons et al., 2008). Recent research also supports the idea that increases in insight ("insight" is a key construct in psychodynamic theory and involves cognitive and emotional understanding of inner conflicts) must occur before there is long-term clinical change (Johansson et al., 2010).

Psychoanalytically oriented treatments are also showing promise in the treatment of borderline personality disorder. One example is *transference-focused psychotherapy*, or TFP. Developed by Kernberg and colleagues (2008), this treatment approach uses such techniques as clarification, confrontation, and interpretation to help the patient understand and correct the distortions that occur in his or her perception of other people, including the therapist. In a clinical trial, patients with borderline personality disorder who received TFP did as well as those who were assigned to receive dialectical behavior therapy (Clarkin et al., 2007). Findings such as these are creating renewed interest in psychodynamic forms of psychotherapy and energizing the field of treatment research.

Couples and Family Therapy

Many problems that therapists deal with concern distressed relationships, such as couple or marital distress. Here, the maladaptive behavior exists between the partners in the relationship. Extending the focus even further, a family systems approach reflects the assumption that the within-family behavior of any particular family member is subject to the influence of the behaviors and communication patterns of other family members. It is, in other words, the product of a "system" that may be amenable to both understanding and change. Addressing problems deriving from the existing system thus requires therapeutic techniques that focus on relationships as much as, or more than, on individuals.

COUPLES THERAPY Relationship problems are a major cause of emotional distress. The large numbers of couples seeking help with troubled relationships have made couples counseling a growing field of therapy. Typically the couple is seen together. The primary reasons that couples report for seeking treatment are communication problems and a lack of affection (Doss et al., 2004). As such, improving communication skills and developing more adaptive problem-solving styles are both major foci of clinical attention. Although it is quite routine at the start of therapy for each partner secretly to harbor the idea that only the other will have to do the changing, it is nearly always necessary for both partners to alter their reactions to the other.

Couple therapists try to help couples, like this one from the movie *Couples Retreat*, improve their communication skills and develop more adaptive ways of solving their problems.

For many years the gold standard of **couple therapy** has been **traditional behavioral couple therapy (TBCT)** (Christensen et al., 2007). TBCT is based on a social-learning model and views marital satisfaction and marital distress in terms of reinforcement. The treatment is usually short term (10 to 26 sessions) and is guided by a manual. The goal of TBCT is to increase caring behaviors in the relationship and to teach partners to resolve their conflicts in a more constructive way through training in communication skills and adaptive problem solving.

Traditional behavioral couple therapy is an empirically supported treatment for couple distress (Snyder et al., 2006). Early research established that two-thirds of couples tend to do well and to show improvement in relationship satisfaction (Jacobson et al., 1987). However, it rapidly became apparent that this form of treatment does not work for all couples (Jacobson & Addis, 1993). Moreover, even among couples who do show an improvement in relationship satisfaction, the improvement is not always maintained over time (Jacobson et al., 1987).

These limitations of TBCT led researchers to conclude that a change-focused treatment approach was not appropriate for all couples. This created the impetus for the development of **integrative behavioral couple therapy (IBCT)** (Jacobson et al., 2000; Wheeler et al., 2001). Instead of emphasizing change (which sometimes has the paradoxical effect of making people not want to change), IBCT focuses on acceptance and includes strategies that help each member of the couple come to terms with and accept some of the limitations of his or her partner. Of course, change is not forbidden. Rather, within IBCT, acceptance strategies are integrated with change strategies to provide a form of therapy that is more tailored to individual characteristics, relationship "themes" (long-standing patterns of conflicts), and the needs of the couple.

Although IBCT is a relative newcomer in the couple therapy field, findings regarding its effectiveness are quite promising. In one early study, improvement rates were 80 percent in the couples treated with IBCT versus 64 percent in couples receiving TBCT (Jacobson et al., 2000). In another, larger study, 70 percent of couples who received IBCT showed clear improvement in their relationship compared with 61 percent of couples receiving TBCT (Christensen et al., 2007). Although these differences are not statistically different from each, other data show that couples who stay together after receiving IBCT are significantly happier than couples who stay together following treatment with TBCT (Atkins et al., 2005). Most recently, ICBT has been translated into a format in which couples can work through therapy via an online self-help website (Doss et al., 2013).

FAMILY THERAPY Therapy for a family overlaps with couple and marital therapy but has somewhat different roots. Couple therapy developed in response to the large number of clients who came seeking help for relationship problems. **Family therapy** began with the finding that many people who had shown marked clinical improvement after individual treatment—often in institutional settings—had a relapse when they returned home. As you have already learned, family-based treatment approaches designed to reduce high levels of criticism and family tension have been successful in reducing relapse rates in patients with schizophrenia and mood disorders (Miklowitz & Craighead, 2007; Pfammatter et al., 2006).

Another approach to resolving family disturbances is called **structural family therapy** (Minuchin, 1974). This approach, which is based on systems theory, holds that if the family context can be changed, then the individual members will have altered experiences in the family and will behave differently in accordance with the changed requirements of the new family context. Thus, an important goal of structural family therapy is changing the organization of the family in such a way that the family members will behave more supportively and less pathogenically toward each other.

Structural family therapy is focused on present interactions and requires an active but not directive approach on the part of a therapist. Initially, the therapist gathers information about the family—a structural map of the typical family interaction patterns—by acting like one of the family members and participating in the family interactions as an insider. In this way, the therapist discovers whether the family system has rigid or flexible boundaries, who dominates the power structure, who gets blamed when things go wrong, and so on. Armed with this understanding, the therapist then operates as an agent for altering the interaction among the members, which often has transactional characteristics of enmeshment (overinvolvement), overprotectiveness, rigidity, and poor conflict resolution skills. The "identified client" is often found to play an important role in the family's mode of conflict avoidance. As discussed in Chapter 9, structural family therapy has quite a good record of success in the treatment of anorexia nervosa.

Eclecticism and Integration

The various "schools" of psychotherapy that we have just described once stood more in opposition to one another than they do now. Today, clinical practice is characterized by a relaxation of boundaries and a willingness on the part of therapists to explore differing ways of approaching clinical problems (see Castonguay et al., 2003, for a discussion), a process sometimes called *multimodal therapy* (Lazarus, 1997). When asked what their orientation is, most psychotherapists today reply "eclectic," which usually means that they try to borrow and combine concepts and techniques from various schools, depending on what seems best for the individual case. This inclusiveness extends to efforts to combine biological and psychosocial approaches as well as individual and family therapies.

One example of an eclectic form of therapy is *interpersonal psychotherapy* (IPT; see also Chapter 7). Developed by Klerman and colleagues (1984) as a treatment for depression, IPT focuses on current relationships in the patient's life and has the goals of reducing symptoms and improving functioning. Interpersonal therapy was based on the interpersonal theory of Harry Stack Sullivan as well as on Bowlby's attachment theory. Its central idea is that all of us,

at all times, involuntarily invoke schemas acquired from our earliest interactions with others, such as our parents, in interpreting what is going on in our current relationships. Although it is sometimes considered to be a form of psychodynamic psychotherapy, IPT uses techniques from several other treatment approaches. It is also focused and time limited. In addition, the emphasis in treatment is on the present, not the past (see Bleiberg & Markowitz, 2008).

IPT has shown value in the treatment of depression (de Mello et al., 2005). It has also been adapted for other disorders including bulimia nervosa (Fairburn et al., 1993), anxiety disorders (Stangier et al., 2011), and borderline personality disorder (Markowitz et al., 2006).

Rebooting Psychotherapy

Although many forms of psychotherapy look pretty similar today to how they looked decades ago (i.e., two people, one office, lots of discussion), there have been some exciting changes in recent years regarding how psychological treatment is studied and practiced. Kazdin and Blaise (2011) have referred to these (and future) changes as a "rebooting" of psychotherapy research and practice. They note that as effective as psychotherapy is, it is not able to meet the enormous demand for treatment in the United States and around the world. Instead, we need to start using advances in technology, and other areas, to become more efficient in how we make assessments and treatments available to the public.

There are many examples of how new technologies are being used to enhance the delivery of effective interventions. Effective interventions are being packaged as self-help platforms on the Internet (e.g., Doss et al., 2013). Smartphones are being equipped with programs that can record data about patients' thoughts, feelings, and behaviors in real time (Nock, Prinstein, & Sterba, 2009), as well as actually deliver interventions (Kaplan & Stone, 2013). Socially assistive robots are being used to help deliver psychological interventions to those in need (Rabbitt et al., 2015). These are just a few of the exciting developments happening in the changing landscape of psychological treatment research. It is a truly fascinating time to be learning about, and working in, this field!

---

in review

- Describe the different techniques that can be used to provide anxious patients with exposure to the stimuli they fear.
- In what ways are REBT and cognitive therapy similar? In what ways are they different?
- Explain the concepts of transference and countertransference.
- What special difficulties do clinicians face when they work with couples? How have techniques of marital therapy evolved over recent years?

Sociocultural Perspectives

16.5 Explain the roles that social values and culture play in psychological treatment.

The criticism has been raised—from both inside and outside the mental health professions—that psychotherapy can be viewed as an attempt to get people adjusted to a "sick" society rather than to encourage them to work toward its improvement. As a consequence, psychotherapy has often been considered the guardian of the status quo. This issue is perhaps easier for us to place in perspective by looking at other cultures. For example, many suggested that psychiatry was used as a means of political control in the former Soviet Union, with those in power using psychiatrists to "diagnose" political opponents with a mental disorder (Helmchen & Sartorius, 2010). Although few would claim that psychiatry in most industrialized societies is used to gain control over social critics, there is nevertheless the possibility that therapists in some ways play the role of "gatekeepers" of social values. Such charges, of course, bring us back to the question we raised in Chapter 1: What do we mean by "abnormal?" That question can be answered only in the light of our values.

Social Values and Psychotherapy

In a broader perspective, there is the complex and controversial issue of the role of values in science. Psychotherapy is not, or at least should not be, a system of ethics; it is a set of tools to be used at the discretion of a therapist in pursuit of a client's welfare. Thus, mental health professionals are confronted with the same kinds of questions that confront scientists in general: Should a physical scientist who helps develop weapons of mass destruction be morally concerned about how they are used? Similarly, should a psychologist or behavioral scientist who develops powerful techniques to influence or control how people behave be concerned about how those techniques are used?

Many psychologists and other scientists try to sidestep this issue by insisting that science is value free—that it is concerned only with gathering facts, not with how the facts are applied. Each time therapists decide that one behavior should be eliminated or substituted for another, however, they are making a value judgment. For example, is a therapist to assume that the depression of a young mother who is abused by an alcoholic husband is an internally based disorder requiring "treatment," as once would have been the routine interpretation? Or does the therapist have a larger responsibility to look beyond individual pathology and confront the abnormality of the marital relationship? Therapy takes place in a context that involves the values of the therapist, the client, and the society in which they live. There are strong pressures on a therapist—from parents, schools, courts, and other social institutions—to help people adjust to the world as it is. At the same time, there are many counterpressures, particularly from young people who are seeking support in their (sometimes overdone) attempts to become authentic people rather than blind conformists.

The dilemma in which contemporary therapists may find themselves is illustrated by the following case study.

Who Needs Therapy?

A 15-year-old high school sophomore is sent to a therapist because her parents have discovered that she has been having sex with her boyfriend. The girl tells the therapist that she feels no guilt or remorse over her behavior even though her parents strongly disapprove. In addition, she reports that she is quite aware of the danger of becoming pregnant and is careful to take contraceptive measures.

A 9-year old boy was brought into a clinic for treatment because he was "out of control" and "wouldn't listen" to his parents. When asked for examples, his parents reported that he often used the wrong detergent to clean the bathroom and he sometimes didn't tie the garbage bags correctly when he took out the trash for the family.

Watch What's In It For Me?: Finding a Therapist If You Need One

Psychotherapy and Cultural Diversity

As we have seen, the establishment and maintenance of an effective psychotherapeutic "working alliance" between client and therapist is generally regarded as a crucial and indispensable element in determining the success of the outcome. What does this mean for a client whose background is considerably different from that of the therapist?

As yet, there is little or no solid evidence that psychotherapeutic outcomes are diminished when client and therapist differ in race or ethnicity (Beutler et al., 2004; Sue et al., 1994). However, members of minority groups are seriously underrepresented in treatment research studies, and this makes it difficult to fully assess their needs and outcomes (Miranda et al., 2005; Nagayama Hall, 2001). Moreover, racial and ethnic minorities are clearly underserved by the mental health system (Snowden & Yamada, 2005; U.S. Department of Health and Human Services [USDHHS], 2001). However, the factors that are behind these disparities are complex and not well understood.

In general, minority patients tend to prefer ethnically similar therapists over European American therapists. Mexican Americans state a strong preference for therapists who share their ethnic background and express the view that such therapists are more "credible" than Anglo therapists would be (Lopez et al., 1991; Ponce & Atkinson, 1989). However, finding an ethnically matched therapist may present difficulties. In one survey, for example, only 2 percent of psychiatrists, 2 percent of psychologists, and 4 percent of social workers said they were African Americans (Holzer et al., 1998). The number of mental health professionals who are representative of other minority groups is no better (USDHHS, 2001). The lack of trained therapists familiar with the issues important to different ethnic groups is a serious drawback, given the unique problems often associated with certain groups. This is illustrated in the following case, which concerns a Southeast Asian refugee woman in her mid-40s who was relocated to the United States.

A Khmer Woman

"I lost my husband, I lost my country, I lost every property/fortune we owned. And coming over here, I can't learn to speak English and the way of life here is different; my mother and oldest son are very sick: I feel crippled, I can do nothing. I can't control what's going on. I don't know what I'm going to do once my public assistance expires. I may feel safe in a way—there is no war here, no Communist to kill or torture you—but deep down inside me, I still don't feel safe or secure. I get scared. I get scared so easily." (From Rumbaut, 1985, p. 475.)

When specialized, culturally adapted interventions are made available in community settings, ethnic minority clients are less likely to drop out of treatment and often do well (Snowden & Yamada, 2005). However, such programs are still lacking in many communities. Also lacking are research investigations designed to understand how culture and ethnicity affect a person's ability to access and receive psychiatric and psychological treatments. Nonetheless, there are encouraging developments. For example, Weisman and colleagues (2006) are developing culturally informed treatments for the families of patients with schizophrenia. This approach considers the role of family cohesiveness as well as spirituality and religion in the therapy process. Researchers are also developing culturally informed psychotherapy for Hispanic patients with major depression (Markowitz et al., 2009), as well as for African American women who are suicidal and in abusive relationships (Kaslow et al., 2010).

in review

- Can psychotherapy ever be value free? Why or why not?
- What special issues do racial and ethnic minorities face when they seek therapy?

Biological Approaches to Treatment

16.6 Describe three biological approaches used to treat abnormal behavior.

In the following sections we discuss some of the major classes of medications that are now routinely used to help patients with a variety of mental disorders, as well as some additional treatment approaches (such as electroconvulsive therapy) that are less widely used but highly effective, especially for patients who fail to show a good clinical response to other treatments.

These drugs are sometimes referred to as psychoactive (literally, "mind-altering") medications, indicating that their major effects are on the brain. As we examine these medications, it is important to remember that people differ in how rapidly they metabolize drugs—that is, in how quickly their bodies break down the drugs once ingested. For example, many African Americans metabolize antidepressant and antipsychotic medications more slowly than European Americans do. What this means is that African Americans sometimes show a more rapid and greater response to these medications but also experience more side effects (see USDHHS, 2001, p. 67). Determining the correct dosage is critical because too little of a drug can be ineffective; on the other hand, too much medication can cause toxicity that may be life threatening, depending on the individual and the medication concerned.

Antipsychotic Drugs

As their name suggests, *antipsychotic drugs* (also called neuroleptics) are used to treat psychotic disorders such as schizophrenias. You have already read about these medications in Chapter 13. The key therapeutic benefit of antipsychotics derives from their ability to alleviate or reduce the intensity of delusions and hallucinations. They do this by blocking dopamine receptors. Table 16.1 lists some of the more commonly used neuroleptic drugs as well as information about typical dose ranges.

Studies have found that approximately 60 percent of patients with schizophrenia who are treated with traditional antipsychotic medications have a resolution of their positive symptoms within 6 weeks, compared to only about 20 percent of those treated with placebo (Sharif et al., 2007). These drugs are also useful in treating other disorders with psychotic symptoms such as mania, psychotic depression, and schizoaffective disorder, and they are occasionally used to treat transient psychotic symptoms when these occur in people with borderline personality disorder and schizotypal personality disorder (Koenigsberg et al., 2007). Finally, antipsychotic medications are sometimes used to treat the delusions, hallucinations,

Table 16.1 Commonly Prescribed Antipsychotic Medications

Drug Class	Generic Name	Trade Name	Dose Range (mg)
Second-Generation (Atypical)	clozapine	Clozaril	300–900
	risperidone	Risperdal	1–8
	olanzapine	Zyprexa	5–20
	quetiapine	Seroquel	100–750
	ziprasidone	Geodon	80–160
	aripiprazole	Abilify	15–30
	lurasidone	Latuda	40–120
First-Generation (Conventional)	chlorpromazine	Thorazine	75–900
	perphenazine	Trilafon	12–64
	molindone	Moban	50–200
	thiothixene	Navane	15–60
	trifluoperazine	Stelazine	6–40
	haloperidol	Haldol	2–100
	fluphenazine	Prolixin	2–20

SOURCES: Bezchlibnyk-Butler & Jeffries (2003); Buckley & Waddington (2000); and Sadock et al. (2009).

Note: A *generic name* is the name given to the drug compound and used by all makers of the drug. A *trade name* (or *brand name*) is the proprietary (and trademarked) name the specific drug companies give to that compound. For instance, clozapine is an antipsychotic medication that is called *Clozaril* by Novartis Pharmaceuticals (so that's the name that most people know from commercials and advertisements), but called other names (e.g., *Clopine, Denzapine, Zaponex*) by the other pharmaceutical companies that manufacture this compound.

paranoia, and agitation that can occur with Alzheimer's disease. However, antipsychotic medications pose great risks to patients with dementia because they are associated with increased rates of death (Sultzer et al., 2008). Because of this, there is now a "black box warning" about using these medications for patients with dementia. (A black box warning is a warning on the outside of a medication package about the potential dangers of that medication that literally appears inside a black box.)

Antipsychotic medications are usually administered daily in pill form. However, some patients are not able to remember to take their medications each day. In such cases, depot neuroleptics can be very helpful. These are neuroleptics that can be administered in a long-acting, injectable form. The clinical benefits of one injection can last for up to 4 weeks, which makes depot neuroleptics very valuable for patients who need medication but are unwilling or unable to take drugs every day. Research suggests that patients with schizophrenia who take depot medications do better than those who use oral compounds (Tiihonen et al., 2011).

One problematic side effect that can result from treatment with conventional antipsychotic medications such as chlorpromazine is **tardive dyskinesia** (see Chapter 13). Tardive (from *tardy*) dyskinesia is a movement abnormality that is a delayed result of taking antipsychotic medications. Because movement-related side effects are a little less common with atypical antipsychotic medications such as clozapine (Clozaril) and olanzapine (Zyprexa),

these medications are often preferred in the clinical management of schizophrenia. Clozapine also seems to be especially beneficial for patients with psychosis who are at high risk of suicide (Meltzer et al., 2003).

Even the atypical neuroleptics have side effects, however. Weight gain and diabetes are a major source of clinical concern (Sernyak et al., 2002). You may recall that an even more serious side effect of clozapine is a potentially life-threatening drop in white blood cell count called agranulocytosis, which occurs in 1 percent of patients (Sharif et al., 2007). Accordingly, patients must have their blood tested every week for the first 6 months of treatment and then every 2 weeks thereafter for as long as they are on the medication. Because of this, clozapine is best regarded as a medication to consider after other medications (e.g., some of the other atypical antipsychotic medications) have proved ineffective. Current thinking is that the atypical antipsychotics described above (with the exception of clozapine) are the first-choice treatments for psychosis and that clozapine and conventional antipsychotics (e.g., Haldol) are best considered as second-line therapies.

Antidepressant Drugs

Antidepressants are the most commonly prescribed psychiatric medications. More than 90 percent of patients being treated for depressive disorders will be given these medications (Olfson & Marcus, 2010).

Actress Brooke Shields is one of many public figures who have been open with the public about their experiences with depression.

SELECTIVE SEROTONIN REUPTAKE INHIBITORS As is the case for antipsychotic medications, the drugs that were discovered first (so-called classical antidepressants such as monoamine oxidase inhibitors [MAOIs] and tricyclic antidepressants [TCAs]) have now been replaced in routine clinical practice by "second-generation" treatments such as the SSRIs. In 1988 fluoxetine (Prozac) became the first SSRI to be released in the United States. Its pharmacological cousins include sertraline (Zoloft) and paroxetine (Paxil). More recent additions to the SSRI family are fluvoxamine (Luvox), which is used in the treatment of OCD; citalopram (Celexa); and escitalopram (Lexapro). All are equally effective. Table 16.2 lists some of the most widely used antidepressant medications.

Table 16.2 Commonly Prescribed Antidepressant Medications

Drug Class	Generic Name	Trade Name	Dose Range (mg)
SSRI	fluoxetine	Prozac	10–80
	sertraline	Zoloft	50–200
	paroxetine	Paxil	10–60
	fluvoxamine	Luvox	50–300
	citalopram	Celexa	10–60
	escitalopram	Lexapro	10–20
SNRI	venlafaxine	Effexor	75–375
	duloxetine	Cymbalta	40–60
Tricyclic	amitriptyline	Elavil	75–300
	clomipramine	Anafranil	75–300
	desipramine	Norpramin	75–300
	doxepin	Sinequan	75–300
	imipramine	Tofranil	75–300
	nortriptyline	Aventyl	40–200
	trimipramine	Surmontil	75–300
MAOI	phenelzine	Nardil	45–90
	tranylcypromine	Parnate	20–60
	isocarboxazid	Marplan	30–50
Atypical	bupropion	Wellbutrin	225–450
	trazodone	Desyrel	150–600

SOURCES: Bezchlibnyk-Butler & Jeffries (2003); Buckley & Waddington (2001); and Sadock et al. (2009).

SSRIs are chemically unrelated to the older TCAs and to the MAOIs. However, most antidepressants work by increasing the availability of serotonin, norepinephrine, or both. As their name implies, the SSRIs serve to inhibit the reuptake of the neurotransmitter serotonin following its release into the synapse. Unlike the tricyclics (which inhibit the reuptake of both serotonin and norepinephrine), SSRIs selectively inhibit the reuptake of serotonin (see Figure 16.2). They have become the preferred **antidepressant drugs**, in large part due to very aggressive advertising by the pharmaceutical companies. SSRIs are also easier to use, have

fewer side effects, and are generally not found to be fatal in overdose, as the tricyclics can be. However, there is no compelling evidence that they are more effective than other types of antidepressants (Sussman, 2009b).

Figure 16.2 SSRIs

Serotonin is synthesized from the amino acid tryptophan. After being released into the synaptic cleft, it binds to receptors on the postsynaptic neuron. A serotonin reuptake transporter then returns it to the presynaptic neuron. SSRI medications block this reuptake process, leaving more serotonin available in the synapse.

(From Ciccarelli, S. K., and White, J. N. Reprinted from *Psychology* (2nd ed.), © 2008, Pearson Education Inc., Upper Saddle River, New Jersey.)

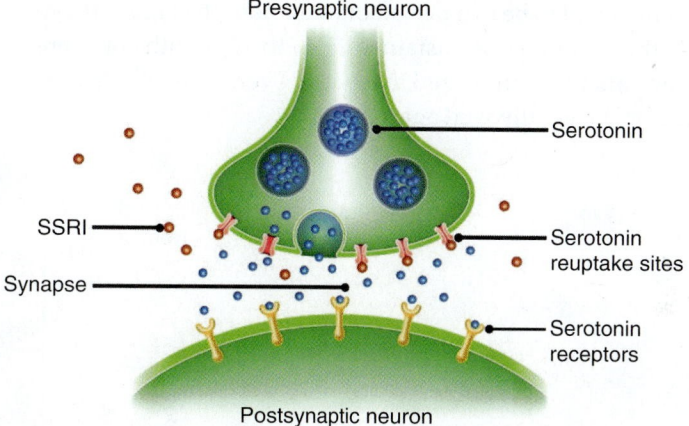

More recently, another class of medications has been introduced. These are called serotonin and norepinephrine reuptake inhibitors (SNRIs; Thase, 2009b). Examples of antidepressants in this drug family are venlafaxine (Effexor) and duloxetine (Cymbalta). SNRIs block the reuptake of both norepinephrine and serotonin. They have similar side effects to the SSRIs, and they are relatively safe in overdose. SNRIs seem to help a significant number of patients who have not responded well to other antidepressants, and they are slightly more effective than SSRIs in the treatment of major depression (Papakostas et al., 2007).

The newest antidepressant, which received FDA approval in 2011, is called Viibryd (vilazodone). It is a novel combination of an SSRI and a serotonin receptor agonist.

Watch SSRIs in Action

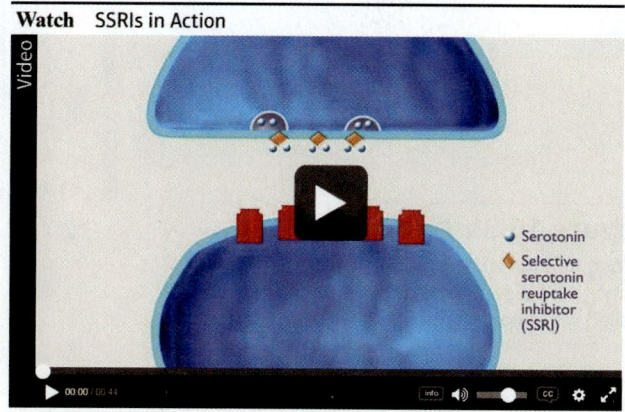

Studies suggest that vilazodone is safe and well tolerated by patients (Robinson et al., 2011) and that it works better than placebo for patients who are depressed (Khan et al., 2011; Reed et al., 2012). However, it remains to be learned how efficacious this medication is compared to other antidepressants in widespread use.

Clinical trials with the SSRIs indicate that patients tend to improve after about 3 to 5 weeks of treatment. Patients who show at least a 50 percent improvement in their symptoms are considered to have had a positive response to treatment (see Figure 16.3a). However, although considerably better, such patients are not fully well. When treatment removes all of a patient's symptoms, patients are considered to be in a period of remission (see Figure 16.3b). If this remission is sustained for 6 to 12 months or more, the patient is considered to have recovered. In other words, he or she is fully well again.

Side effects of the SSRIs include nausea, diarrhea, nervousness, insomnia, and sexual problems such as diminished sexual interest and difficulty with orgasm (Nemeroff & Schatzberg, 2007). After early reports linked Prozac with increased risk of suicide (e.g., Cole & Bodkin, 1990; Papp & Gorman, 1990), there was a decline in its use. However, Prozac is no more associated with suicide than are other antidepressants (Jick et al., 2004). Recently there has also been concern that, when used during pregnancy, fluoxetine (Prozac) and paroxetine (Paxil) may increase the risk of heart abnormalities in the baby (Diav-Citrin et al., 2008; Malm et al., 2011). For this reason these medications are not recommended as a first option for women planning to become pregnant. It is important to keep in mind, however, that all the risks we have just described are small when weighed against the risks associated with leaving people who are depressed without adequate treatment.

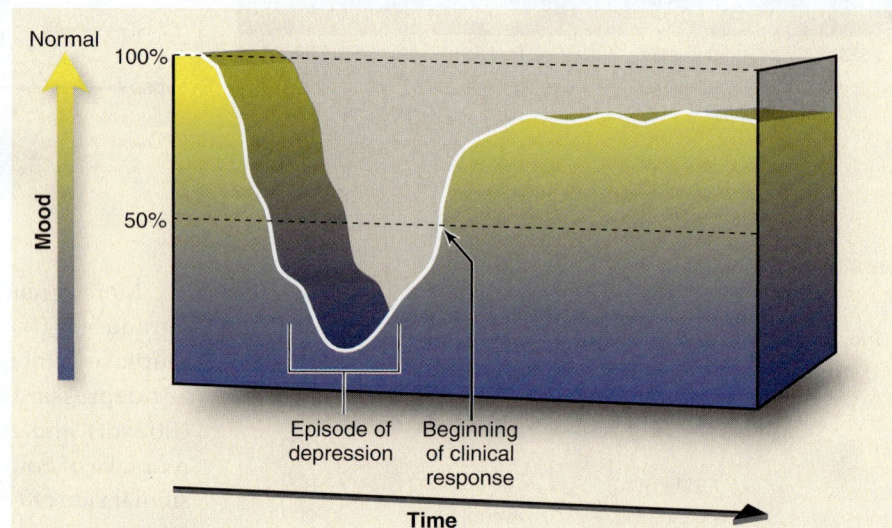

Figure 16.3a Defining a Positive Response

When treatment of depression results in at least a 50 percent improvement in symptoms, it is called a response. Such patients are better, but not well.

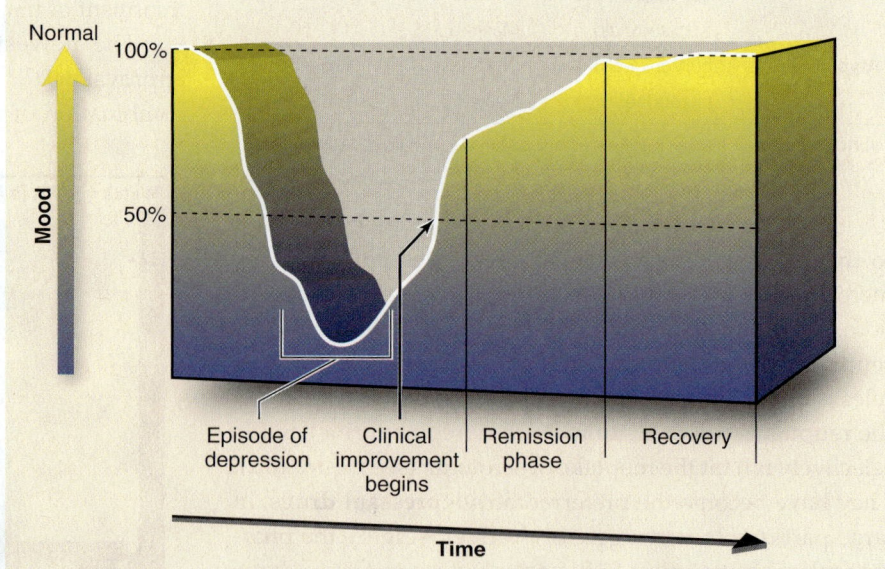

Figure 16.3b Defining Recovery

When treatment of depression results in removal of essentially all symptoms, it is called remission for the first several months, and then recovery if it is sustained for longer than 6 to 12 months. Such patients are not just better—they are well.

Although SSRIs help many people, some people have side effects that are so extreme that they are unable to continue to take their medication as prescribed. Researchers are now exploring the role that genes play in making some people especially susceptible to the adverse effects of specific medications (Hu et al., 2007).

MONOAMINE OXIDASE INHIBITORS Although they are used infrequently now, MAOIs were the first antidepressant medications to be developed, in the 1950s. These drugs were being studied for the treatment of tuberculosis when they were found to elevate the mood of patients (Stahl, 2000). They were later shown to be effective in treating depression. Monoamine oxidase inhibitors include isocarboxazid (Marplan), phenelzine (Nardil), tranylcypromine (Parnate), and selegiline (Eldepryl). They inhibit the activity of monoamine oxidase, an enzyme present in the synaptic cleft that helps break down the monoamine neurotransmitters (such as serotonin and norepinephrine) that have been released into the cleft. Patients taking MAOIs must avoid foods rich in the amino acid tyramine (such as salami and Stilton cheese). This limits the drugs' clinical usefulness. Nevertheless, MAOIs are used in certain cases of atypical depression that are characterized by hypersomnia and overeating and do not respond well to other classes of antidepressant medication (Nemeroff & Schatzberg, 2007).

TRICYCLIC ANTIDEPRESSANTS The TCAs operate to inhibit the reuptake of norepinephrine and (to a lesser extent) serotonin once these have been released into the synapse. Their discovery was also serendipitous in that the first TCA—imipramine—was being studied as a possible treatment for schizophrenia when it was found to elevate mood. The theory that these drugs work by increasing norepinephrine activity is now known to be oversimplified. It is also known that when the tricyclics are taken for several weeks, they alter a number of other aspects of cellular functioning including how receptors function and how cells respond to the activation of receptors and the synthesis of neurotransmitters. Because these alterations in cellular functioning parallel the time course for these drugs to exert their antidepressant effects, one or more of these changes are likely to be involved in mediating their antidepressant effects (refer back to Figure 16.3).

OTHER ANTIDEPRESSANTS Trazodone (Desyrel) was the first antidepressant to be introduced in the United States that was not lethal when taken in overdose. It specifically inhibits the reuptake of serotonin. Trazodone has heavy sedating properties that limit its usefulness. It is sometimes used in combination with SSRIs and taken at night to help counter the adverse effects the SSRIs often have on sleep. In rare cases, it can produce a condition in men called priapism (Nemeroff & Schatzberg, 2007). Priapism is prolonged erection in the absence of any sexual stimulation.

Bupropion (Wellbutrin) is an antidepressant that is not structurally related to other antidepressants. It inhibits the reuptake of both norepinephrine and dopamine. In addition to being an antidepressant medication, bupropion also reduces nicotine cravings and symptoms of withdrawal in people who want to stop smoking. One clinical advantage of bupropion is that, unlike some of the SSRIs, it does not inhibit sexual functioning (Nemeroff & Schatzberg, 2007).

USING ANTIDEPRESSANTS TO TREAT ANXIETY DISORDERS, BULIMIA NERVOSA, AND PERSONALITY DISORDERS In addition to their usefulness in treating depression, the antidepressant drugs are also widely used in the treatment of various other disorders. For example, SSRIs are often used in the treatment of panic disorder, social phobia, and generalized anxiety disorder, as well as OCD (Dougherty et al., 2007; Roy-Byrne & Cowley, 2007). However, some people with panic disorder are greatly bothered by the side effects of these drugs (which create some of the symptoms to which patients with panic disorder are hypersensitive), so they quickly discontinue the medication. SSRIs and TCAs are also used in the treatment of bulimia nervosa. Many studies have shown that these antidepressants are useful in reducing binge eating and purging (Wilson & Fairburn, 2007). Patients with Cluster B personality disorders such as borderline personality disorder may show a decrease in certain symptoms, most notably mood lability, if they take SSRIs (Rinne et al., 2002).

Antianxiety Drugs

Antianxiety drugs are used for conditions in which tension and anxiety are significant components. They do not provide a cure. However, these medications can keep symptoms under control until patients are able to receive

Antianxiety medications are widely prescribed. Why has this caused concern among some leaders in the medical and psychiatric fields?

other forms of effective psychological treatments. The fact that they are so widely prescribed has caused concern among some leaders in the medical and psychiatric fields because of these drugs' addictive potential and sedating effects. Antianxiety medications have little place in the treatment of psychosis. However, they are often used as supplementary treatments in certain neurological disorders to control such symptoms as convulsive seizures.

BENZODIAZEPINES   The most important and widely used class of antianxiety (or anxiolytic) drugs are the benzodiazepines. Another class of drugs, the barbiturates (e.g., phenobarbital), is seldom used today except to control seizures or as anesthetics during electroconvulsive therapy. The first benzodiazepines were released in the early 1960s. They are now the drugs of choice for the treatment of acute anxiety and agitation. They are rapidly absorbed from the digestive tract and start to work very quickly. At low doses they help quell anxiety; at higher doses they act as sleep-inducing agents and can be used to treat insomnia. For this reason, people taking these medications are cautioned about driving or operating machinery.

One problem with benzodiazepines is that patients can become psychologically and physiologically dependent on them (Roy-Byrne & Cowley, 2007). Patients taking these medications must be "weaned" from them gradually because of the risk of withdrawal symptoms, which include seizures in some cases. Moreover, relapse rates following discontinuation of these drugs are extremely high (Roy-Byrne & Cowley, 2007). For example, as many as 60 to 80 percent of patients with panic disorder relapse following discontinuation of Xanax. Table 16.3 lists some commonly prescribed antianxiety medications.

Table 16.3 Commonly Prescribed Antianxiety Medications

Drug Class	Generic Name	Trade Name	Dose Range (mg)
Benzodiazepines	alprazolam	Xanax	0.5–10
	clonazepam	Klonopin	1–6
	diazepam	Valium	4–40
	lorazepam	Ativan	1–6
	oxazepam	Serax	30–120
	clorazepate	Tranxene	15–60
	chlordiazepoxide	Librium	10–150
Other	buspirone	BuSpar	5–30

SOURCES: Bezchlibnyk-Butler & Jeffries (2003); Buckley & Waddington (2001); and Sadock et al. (2009).

Benzodiazepines and related anxiolytic medications are believed to work by enhancing the activity of GABA receptors (Stahl, 2000). GABA (gamma aminobutyric acid) is an inhibitory neurotransmitter that plays an important role in the way our brain inhibits anxiety in stressful situations. The benzodiazepines appear to enhance GABA activity in certain parts of the brain known to be implicated in anxiety such as the limbic system.

OTHER ANTIANXIETY MEDICATIONS   The only new class of antianxiety medication that has been released since the early 1960s is buspirone (Buspar), which is completely unrelated to the benzodiazepines and is thought to act in complex ways on serotonergic functioning rather than on GABA. It has been shown to be as effective as the benzodiazepines in treating generalized anxiety disorder (Roy-Byrne & Cowley, 2007), although patients who have previously taken benzodiazepines tend not to respond as well as patients who have never taken them. Buspar has a low potential for abuse, probably because it has no sedative or muscle-relaxing properties and so is less pleasurable for patients. It also does not cause any withdrawal effects. The primary drawback to the use of buspirone is that it takes 2 to 4 weeks to exert any anxiolytic effects. It is therefore not useful in acute situations. Because it is nonsedating, it cannot be used to treat insomnia.

Lithium and Other Mood-Stabilizing Drugs

In the late 1940s, John Cade in Australia discovered that lithium salts such as lithium carbonate were effective in treating manic disorders. One of Cade's (1949) own cases serves well as an illustration of the effects of lithium treatment.

Lithium Helps a Difficult Patient

Mr. W. B. was a 51-year-old man who had been in a state of chronic manic excitement for 5 years. So obnoxious and destructive was his behavior that he had long been regarded as the most difficult patient on his ward in the hospital.

He was started on treatment with a lithium compound, and within 3 weeks his behavior had improved so much that transfer to the convalescent ward was deemed appropriate. He remained in the hospital for another 2 months, during which time his behavior continued to be essentially normal. Prior to discharge, he was switched to another form of lithium salts because the one he had been taking had caused stomach upset.

He was soon back at his job and living a happy and productive life. In fact, he felt so good that, contrary to instructions, he stopped taking his lithium. Thereafter he steadily became more irritable and erratic; some 6 months following his discharge, he had to cease work. In another 5 weeks he was back at the hospital in an acute manic state.

Lithium therapy was immediately reestablished, with prompt positive results. In another month Mr. W. B. was pronounced ready to return to home and work, provided that he not fail to continue taking a prescribed dosage of lithium.

DSM-5 Thinking Critically about *DSM-5*

What Are Some of the Clinical Implications of the Recent Changes?

The recent publication of *DSM-5* has created a number of new diagnoses. It has also changed the diagnostic criteria for others. Of course, as a diagnostic manual, the *DSM* does not provide any information about treatment or make recommendations on that topic. However, changes in the *DSM* always have implications for treatment because a *DSM* diagnosis is necessary for clinical services to be covered by insurance. Here, we highlight some changes that are likely to have an impact on prevalence rates and medication usage in the years to come.

1. New to *DSM-5* is the diagnosis of disruptive mood dysregulation disorder. This disorder is characterized by temper tantrums in a child older than 6 years of age. In order for the diagnosis to be made, the angry outbursts must occur at least three times a week and be inconsistent with the child's developmental level. On the plus side, this diagnosis may allow children with very irritable temperaments to receive specialized help at an early age. However, there is also a risk that many children whose parents might benefit from parental skills training will instead receive powerful tranquilizing medications while their young brains are still maturing and developing.

2. To be diagnosed with attention-deficit/hyperactivity disorder (ADHD) in *DSM-IV-TR*, symptoms had to develop before the child reached the age of 7. In *DSM-5* this age of onset has been raised to age 12. Many children who would not have been eligible to be diagnosed with ADHD (because their symptoms developed when they were age 8, 9, or 10) will now receive the diagnosis. This simple change in the diagnostic criteria will dramatically increase the prevalence of ADHD. And, although it will allow many more children to receive treatment, it will undoubtedly result in many more children being medicated.

3. Another major change that was proposed for *DSM-5*, but not accepted, was to lower the threshold for the diagnosis of generalized anxiety disorder (GAD). In addition to excessive anxiety and worry, *DSM-IV-TR* required the presence of three additional symptoms. In *DSM-5* it was proposed that only one symptom (either muscle tension or a feeling of being on edge) should be required. This change would undoubtedly have led to a substantial increase in the number of people diagnosed with GAD. Had the change been approved, some people might have been relieved to learn that their worrying reflected a psychiatric disorder. However, had it been accepted, this change would likely have further increased the numbers of people who come to rely on anti-anxiety medications to get through the day.

What do you think about the changes that were made (or not made)? Are you in favor of relaxing diagnostic criteria and making more and more people eligible to receive clinical treatment? Or are you concerned that we are in danger of pathologizing normal life and increasing the inappropriate use of psychiatric medications?

Source: Data from the *Diagnostic and Statistical Manual of Mental Disorders*, Fifth Edition, (Copyright 2013). American Psychiatric Association.

Around 1970, about 20 years later, lithium treatment was introduced in the United States. There were at least two reasons for this delay. First, lithium had been used in the 1940s and 1950s as a salt substitute for patients with hypertension before its toxic side effects were known. Some tragic deaths resulted, making the medical community very wary of using it for any reason. Second, because it is a naturally occurring compound, it is unpatentable. This meant that drug companies did not find it profitable to investigate its effects. Nevertheless, lithium is still widely used for the treatment of bipolar disorder and is marketed as Eskalith and Lithobid. Although lithium has been used for many years, exactly how it brings about its therapeutic effect is still not certain (Stahl, 2000).

Even though we still do not know exactly how it works, there is no doubt about the effectiveness of lithium. As many as 70 to 80 percent of patients in a clear manic state show marked improvement after 2 to 3 weeks of taking lithium (Keck & McElroy, 2002). In addition, lithium sometimes relieves depression, although probably mainly in patients with bipolar depression (Stahl, 2000). There is

increasing evidence that lithium maintenance treatment may be less reliable at preventing future episodes of mania than was once thought. For example, several studies of patients with bipolar disorder maintained on lithium for 5 years or more found that only just over one-third remained in remission. Nevertheless, discontinuation of lithium is also very risky. The probability of relapse is estimated to be 28 times higher after withdrawal than when the patient is on lithium, with about 50 percent relapsing within 6 months (Keck & McElroy, 2007).

Side effects of lithium include increased thirst, gastro-intestinal difficulties, weight gain, tremor, and fatigue. In addition, lithium can be toxic if the recommended dose is exceeded or if the kidneys fail to excrete it from the body at a normal rate. Lithium toxicity is a serious medical condition. If not treated swiftly and appropriately, it can cause neuronal damage or even death.

Despite the clinical benefits of lithium, not all patients with bipolar disorder take it exactly as prescribed. Many seem to miss the "highs" and the abundance of energy associated with their hypomanic episodes, so when faced with unpleasant side effects and the loss of these highs they may stop taking the drug.

Although lithium is still widely used, other drugs are also considered first-line treatments for bipolar disorder (see Table 16.4). These include valproic acid (Depakote) and carbamazepine (Tegretol). Other drugs that are currently being researched and used clinically as treatments for rapid cycling bipolar disorders are gabapentin (Neurontin), lamotrigine (Lamictal), and topiramate (Topamax). Many of these drugs are also used in the treatment of epilepsy and are anticonvulsant agents (Keck & McElroy, 2007). Carbamazepine has been associated with significant side effects including blood problems, hepatitis, and serious skin conditions (Post & Frye, 2009). As with lithium, careful blood monitoring of patients is required. Valproate probably has the fewest and mildest side effects, which can include nausea, diarrhea, sedation, tremor, and weight gain. Abilify, an antipsychotic medication, is also now being marketed as a treatment for bipolar disorder.

Table 16.4 Commonly Prescribed Mood-Stabilizing Medications

Drug Class	Generic Name	Trade Name	Dose Range (mg)
Lithium	lithium	Eskalith	400–1200
Anticonvulsants	carbamazepine	Tegretol	300–1600
	valproic acid	Depakote	750–3000
	lamotrigine	Lamictal	100–500
	gabapentin	Neurontin	900–3600
	topiramate	Topamax	50–1300

SOURCES: Bezchlibnyk-Butler & Jeffries (2003); Buckley & Waddington (2001); and Sadock et al. (2009).

Nonmedicinal Biological Treatments

Psychotherapy attempts to change the brain by modifying a person's environment and experience (by using words, exposures, role-playing, etc.), whereas all of the biological changes discussed so far try to change the brain by introducing chemicals into the brain. Another type of biological intervention uses a third approach—changing the activity of the brain directly by using electrical activity and/or surgery. As we have discussed, the brain works using electrical signals. Guided by this fact, researchers have begun to use electrical activity to modify the electrical activity of the brain in ways they hope will alleviate mental disorder. Below we review several such approaches, as well as the use of neurosurgery to change the physical structure of the brain.

ELECTROCONVULSIVE THERAPY Using convulsions to treat mental disorders dates back to the Swiss physician and alchemist Paracelsus (1493–1541), who induced a

patient with "lunacy" to drink camphor until he experienced convulsions (Abrams, 2002; Mowbray, 1959). However, Ladislas von Meduna, a Hungarian physician, is generally regarded as the modern originator of this treatment approach. Von Meduna noted—erroneously, as it turned out—that schizophrenia rarely occurred in people with epilepsy. This observation caused him to infer that schizophrenia and epilepsy were somehow incompatible and to speculate that one might be able to cure schizophrenia by inducing convulsions. In an early treatment effort, von Meduna used camphor to induce convulsions in a patient with schizophrenia, who relatively quickly regained lucidity after the convulsive therapy. Later, von Meduna began to use a drug called Metrazol to induce convulsions because it operated more rapidly than camphor.

Another early approach, adopted by Manfred Sakel in the 1930s, was to cause convulsions by injecting patients with insulin (Fink, 2003). However, these chemical methods gave physicians no control over the induction and timing of the seizures. Then, in 1938, Italian physicians Ugo Cerletti and Lucio Bini tried the simplest method of all—passing an electric current through a patient's head. This method, which became known as **electroconvulsive therapy (ECT)**, is still used today (see Chapter 7). In the United States, about 100,000 patients are treated with ECT each year (Prudic, 2009).

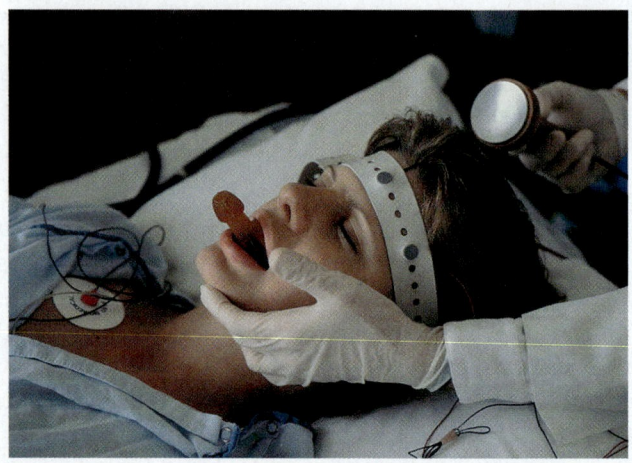

A patient who receives ECT today is given sedative and muscle-relaxant medications prior to the procedure to prevent violent contractions. In the days before such medication was available, the initial seizure was sometimes so violent as to fracture vertebrae.

The general public often views ECT as a horrific and primitive form of treatment, influenced no doubt by its depiction in movies such as *One Flew Over the Cuckoo's Nest*. Indeed, a number of malpractice lawsuits have been brought against psychiatrists who use ECT, primarily over the failure to obtain appropriate patient consent, which can be very difficult when patients may not be legally competent to give such consent due to their illness (Abrams, 2002; Leong & Eth, 1991). However, despite the distaste with which some people regard ECT, it is a safe and effective form of treatment. In fact, it is the only way of dealing with some patients who are severely depressed or suicidal—patients who may have failed to respond to other forms of treatment. In addition, it is often the treatment of choice for pregnant women who are severely depressed for whom taking antidepressants may be problematic, as well as for elderly people, who may have medical conditions that make taking antidepressant drugs dangerous (Pandya et al., 2007).

Reviews evaluating research on ECT have concluded that it is an effective treatment for patients with severe or psychotic-level depression, as well as for some patients with mania (Prudic, 2009). Properly administered, ECT is not thought to cause structural damage to the brain (Devanand et al., 1994), although this issue remains controversial (Reisner, 2003). Every neurotransmitter system is affected by ECT, and ECT is known to downregulate the receptors for norepinephrine, increasing the functional availability of this neurotransmitter. However, exactly how ECT works is still not fully clear (Abrams, 2002).

ECT can be administered in one of two ways. In bilateral ECT, electrodes are placed on either side of the patient's head (see Figure 16.4), and brief constant-current electrical pulses of either high or low intensity are passed from one side of the head to the other for up to about 1.5 seconds. In contrast, unilateral ECT (see Figure 16.4) involves limiting current flow to one side of the brain, typically the nondominant side (right side, for most people). A general anesthetic allows the patient to sleep through the procedure, and muscle relaxants are used to prevent the violent contractions that, in the early days of ECT, could be so severe as to cause the patient to fracture bones.

Figure 16.4 Electrode Placement for ECT

In unilateral ECT, current is limited to one side of the brain. In bilateral ECT, electrodes are placed on each side of the head. Bilateral ECT is more effective but is also associated with more cognitive side effects and memory problems.

(Based on Sadock & Sadock (2003, p. 1142).)

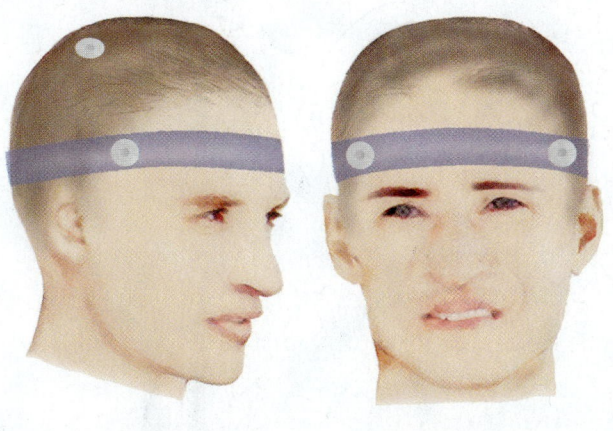

Unilateral   Bilateral

A bite block is also used to avoid injury to the teeth. Today, if you were to observe someone receiving ECT, all you might see would be a small twitch of the hand, perhaps, as the convulsions occurred.

After the ECT session is over, the patient has amnesia for the period immediately preceding the therapy and is usually somewhat confused for the next hour or so. Normally, a treatment series consists of fewer than a dozen sessions, although occasionally more are needed. Treatments are usually administered two or three times per week (Pandya et al., 2007).

Empirical evidence suggests that bilateral ECT is more effective than unilateral ECT. Unfortunately, bilateral ECT is also associated with more severe cognitive side effects and memory problems (Reisner, 2003). For instance, patients often have difficulty forming new memories (anterograde amnesia) for about 3 months after ECT ends. Physicians must therefore weigh the greater clinical benefits of bilateral ECT against its tendency to cause greater cognitive side effects. Some clinicians recommend starting with unilateral ECT and switching to bilateral after five or six treatments if no improvement is seen (Abrams, 2002).

A dramatic early example of successful ECT treatments is provided in the autobiographical account of Lenore McCall (1947/1961), who suffered a severe depressive disorder in her middle years.

Using ECT to Treat Severe Depression

Ms. McCall, a well-educated woman of affluent circumstances and the mother of three children, noticed a feeling of persistent fatigue as the first sign of her impending descent into depression. Too fearful to seek help, she at first attempted to fight off her increasingly profound apathy by engaging in excessive activity, a defensive strategy that accomplished little but the depletion of her remaining strength and emotional reserves.

In due course, she noticed that her mental processes seemed to be deteriorating—her memory appeared impaired and she could concentrate only with great difficulty. Emotionally, she felt an enormous loneliness, bleakness of experience, and increasingly intense fear about what was happening to her mind. She came to view her past small errors of commission and omission as the most heinous of crimes and increasingly withdrew from contact with her husband and children. Eventually, at her husband's and her physician's insistence, she was hospitalized despite her own vigorous resistance. She felt betrayed and shortly thereafter attempted suicide by shattering a drinking glass and ingesting its fragments. To her great disappointment, she survived.

Ms. McCall then spent nearly 4 years continuously in two separate mental hospitals, during which time she deteriorated further. She was silent and withdrawn, behaved in a mechanical fashion, lost an alarming amount of weight, and underwent a seemingly premature aging process. She felt that she emitted an offensive odor. At this time, ECT was introduced into the therapeutic procedures in use at her hospital.

A series of ECT treatments was given to Ms. McCall over about a 3-month period. Then one day, she woke up in the morning with a totally changed outlook: "I sat up suddenly, my heart pounding. I looked around the room and a sweep of wonder surged over me. God in heaven, I'm well. I'm myself. . . ." After a brief period of convalescence, she went home to her husband and children.

TRANSCRANIAL MAGNETIC STIMULATION A newer, more targeted approach that uses electricity to change brain functioning is **transcranial magnetic stimulation (TMS)**. TMS is a treatment in which the clinician positions a pulsed magnet over a carefully selected area of the patient's scalp and uses it to create an electrical field that increases or decreases neuronal activity in the brain (see Figure 16.5). Scientists have been using magnets to create electrical fields since the 1830s; however, it wasn't until 1985 that magnets were used for the purposes of brain stimulation (Barker et al., 1985). During the past 30 years, technological advances have led to the ability to carefully control the location, intensity, frequency, and pattern of the electrical currents directed at very specific parts of the brain. At this point, numerous studies have shown that TMS can be used to effectively treat major depression, with additional evidence supporting its use with other conditions (George & Post, 2011; Kravitz et al., 2015; Lefaucheur et al., 2014).

TMS is less invasive than surgical interventions and has fewer and less severe side effects than ECT. The most commonly reported side effects from repeated TMS sessions are mild headache and a small risk of seizure. However, there are no impairments in memory or concentration as there are with ECT. Although TMS has shown effectiveness for treating depression and other conditions, it is still a very new approach and typically is only considered after several courses of psychotherapy and antidepressant medication have proven ineffective.

NEUROSURGERY Although **neurosurgery** was used occasionally in the nineteenth century to treat mental disorders by relieving pressure in the brain (Berrios, 1990), it was not considered a treatment for psychological problems until the twentieth century. In 1935 in Portugal, Antonio Moniz introduced a neurosurgical procedure in which the frontal lobes of the brain were severed from the deeper centers underlying them. This technique eventually evolved into an operation known as prefrontal lobotomy, which stands as an infamous example of the extremes to which professionals have sometimes been driven in their search for effective treatments for the psychoses. In retrospect, it is ironic that this procedure—which results in permanent structural changes in the brain of the patient and has been highly criticized by many within the profession—won Moniz the 1949 Nobel Prize in medicine (although he was later shot by a former patient who was, presumably, less than grateful).

From 1935 to 1955 (when antipsychotic drugs became available), tens of thousands of psychiatric patients in the United States and abroad were subjected to prefrontal lobotomies and related neurosurgical procedures. In some settings, as many as 50 patients were treated in a single day (Freeman, 1959). Initial reports of results tended to be enthusiastic, downplaying complications (which included

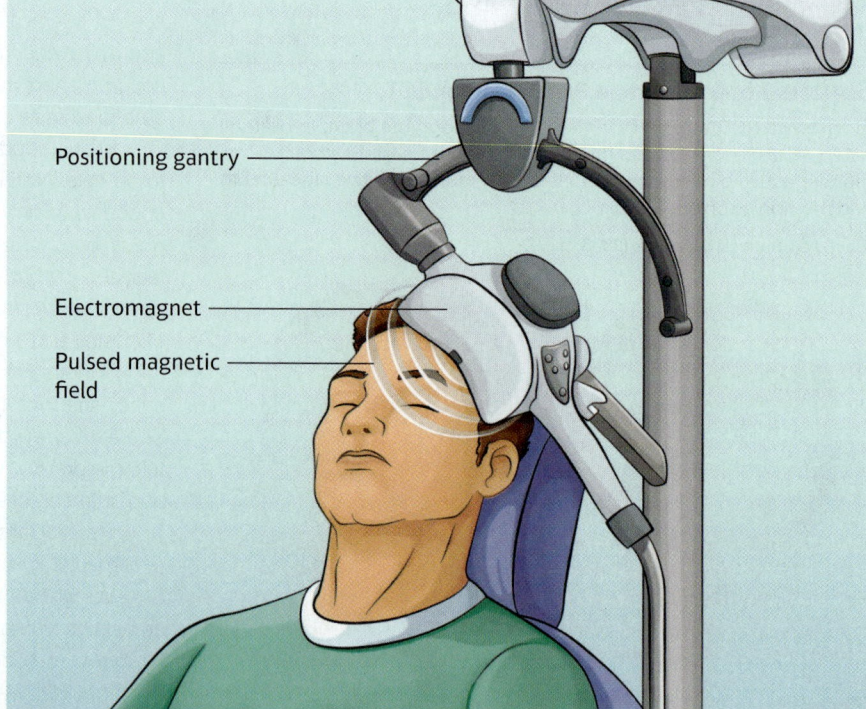

Figure 16.5 Transcranial Magnetic Stimulation

Positioning gantry

Electromagnet

Pulsed magnetic field

In TMS, a pulsed magnetic coil is carefully positioned on the patient's scalp and an electrical field is created to increase or decrease brain activity in specific brain regions or circuits. Treatment typically is repeated several days per week for 4 to 8 weeks.

(Adapted from National Institute of Mental Health.)

a 1 to 4 percent death rate) and undesirable side effects. It was eventually recognized, however, that the side effects of psychosurgery could be very undesirable indeed. In some instances they included a permanent inability to inhibit impulses, in others an unnatural "tranquility" with undesirable shallowness or absence of feeling.

Rosemary Kennedy, sister of former president John F. Kennedy, had developmental delays and behavioral problems. When she was 21, medical professionals recommended a prefrontal lobotomy. The surgery was a tragic failure, wiping out all her accomplishments and leaving little of her former personality. Rosemary is shown here on the right with her sister Kathleen (left) and mother Rose (center) before the surgery.

The introduction of the major antipsychotic drugs caused an immediate decrease in the widespread use of psychosurgery, especially prefrontal lobotomy. Such operations are rare today and are used only as a last resort for patients who have not responded to any other form of treatment for a period of 5 years and who are experiencing extreme and disabling symptoms.

Modern surgical techniques involve the selective destruction of minute areas of the brain. Psychosurgery is sometimes used for patients with debilitating OCD (Dougherty et al., 2007), treatment-resistant severe self-injury (Price et al., 2001), or even intractable anorexia nervosa (Morgan & Crisp, 2000). However, such approaches carry serious risks. In one study, 25 patients who had received brain lesions to treat severe OCD were followed up an average of 11 years later. Twelve of the 25 patients experienced significant relief from their OCD symptoms after the surgery. They also showed reductions in depression. However, 10 of the patients who showed clinical improvement also showed evidence of frontal lobe dysfunction at follow-up, including impaired executive functioning on cognitive tests, problems with apathy, and disinhibited behavior (Rück et al., 2008). These results highlight the risks of brain surgery even when it is effective in treating the symptoms of OCD.

Deep brain stimulation is a different treatment approach that involves surgery but does not result in a permanent lesion being made in the brain. As the World Around Us box describes, this innovative form of therapy is now being used to help patients get some relief from their unrelenting symptoms of depression.

in review

- What kinds of disorders can be treated with antipsychotic drugs? How do these drugs help patients? What are their drawbacks?
- Why have the SSRIs largely replaced MAO inhibitors and TCAs in routine clinical practice? What kinds of conditions can be treated with antidepressants?
- What kinds of medications can be used to treat acute anxiety and agitation? How are these medications believed to work?
- Do the clinical advantages of ECT outweigh its disadvantages?

The World Around Us

Deep Brain Stimulation for Treatment-Resistant Depression

An important development in the treatment of patients with severe and chronic mental health problems is deep brain stimulation. This involves stimulating patients' brains electrically over a period of several months. First, surgeons drill holes into the brain and implant small electrodes (see Figure 16.6). Because this procedure is done under local anesthetic, patients can talk to the doctors about what is happening to them and tell the doctors about the changes they experience. In an early study involving six patients, all reported a response to the electrical stimulation even though they had no cues to tell them when current was being passed through the electrodes or when the current was off (Mayberg et al., 2005). When current was flowing into an area of the brain that is thought to be metabolically overactive in

depression (the cingulate region), patients reported that they felt better and had experiences of "sudden calmness or lightness," "connectedness," or "disappearance of the void."

After the electrodes have been implanted, patients receive short sessions of deep brain stimulation in which current is passed through the implanted electrodes. Using the reports of the patients as a guide, the researchers can select the settings that will be used to provide stimulation through an implanted pulse device after the patients leave the hospital.

How effective is deep brain stimulation as a treatment for unrelenting depression? A total of 20 people who have received this treatment have now been followed up for an average of 3.5 years (Kennedy et al., 2011). The results suggest that this

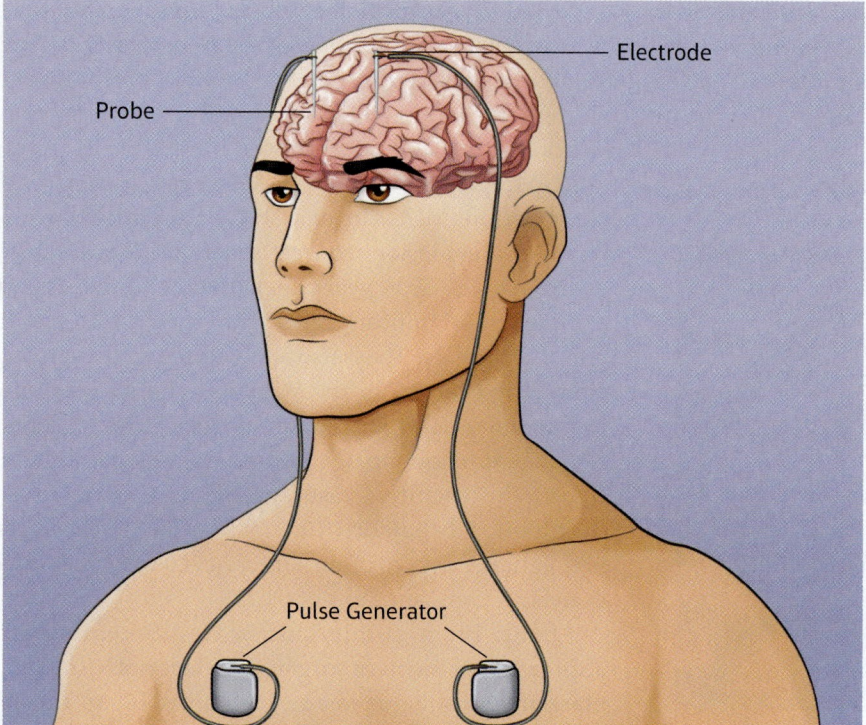

Figure 16.6 Deep Brain Stimulation
In deep brain stimulation, electrodes are implanted into the brain. These are stimulated by pulse generators implanted into the chest region.

(Adapted from National Institute of Mental Health.)

treatment is beneficial for approximately half of the patients. Many of those who responded also returned to work or began to volunteer in their communities. Although a 50 percent response rate may not strike you as very high, keep in mind that only the most chronically ill people are eligible to receive this treatment. Although it is invasive, deep brain stimulation may be able to help a small majority of patients who have failed to show improvement with any other methods.

What are the similarities and differences between lobotomy and deep brain stimulation? Why is deep brain stimulation less controversial than lobotomy?

Unresolved Issues

Do Psychiatric Medications Help or Harm?

Despite the benefits provided by evidence-based psychotherapies, an increasing number of mental health outpatients are now being treated solely with medications. Recent findings from a national survey show that, over the 10-year period from 1998 to 2007, the percentage of people being treated with medications and psychotherapy declined from 40 percent to 32 percent. In contrast, the number of people being treated with medications alone rose from 41 percent to 51 percent (Olfson & Marcus, 2010). This is a surprising trend because the number of people who receive therapy in a given year has remained stable at around 3 percent.

The trend may be related to the billions of dollars spent by the pharmaceutical industry to promote its products both to physicians and the general public alike. How many times have you seen a TV ad telling you to ask your doctor whether a certain medication is right for you? Because of this, many people are now receiving their psychiatric medications from their primary care physician and are never referred for (or do not seek) psychotherapy from a mental health specialist. Managed care organizations have also had financial incentives to get patients to substitute medications for psychotherapy because, in the short term, medications are cheaper (Druss, 2010).

But are we paying the price in a different currency? All of these changes are occurring at a time when serious concerns are being raised about psychiatric drugs and the harm that they may be causing in our society (Whitaker, 2010). Some observers believe that the pharmaceutical industry has made questionable claims about the biological causes of mental disorders in order to maximize profits (Wyatt & Midkiff, 2006). Although no one would argue that they do not provide benefits for patients, psychiatric medications are often less helpful than people think. There is also evidence that some of the drugs used in the treatment of mental disorders may actually make things worse for patients in the long run, creating chemical imbalances and chronic illnesses rather than curing them (Whitaker, 2010). In light of these concerns, it is important for all of us to be as informed as possible about the medications we take. This is especially so when children are involved. It also remains essential to preserve treatment options for patients and to improve access to evidence-based psychotherapies for all who need them.

Summary

16.1 Describe who seeks psychological treatment and what the most common goals are.

- People seek therapy for many reasons. These include stressful current circumstances, long-standing problems or chronic unhappiness, as well as a search for personal growth and insight into their own lives. In other cases, people are referred by their physician or required to seek treatment by a court.

- Psychological treatment is aimed at reducing abnormal behavior through psychological means. The goals of psychotherapy include changing maladaptive behavior, minimizing or eliminating stressful environmental conditions, reducing negative affect, improving interpersonal competencies, resolving personal conflicts, modifying people's inaccurate assumptions about themselves, and fostering a more positive self-image.

16.2 Explain how the success of psychological treatment is measured.

- Evaluation of the success of treatment can be based on the therapist's impression of change, the report of the client, reports of the client's family or friends, measures of change in specific target behaviors, or changes in scores from pretreatment to posttreatment on relevant measures or scales.

- Treatments that have been demonstrated to result in therapeutic change in controlled trials are referred to as evidence-based treatments.

16.3 Describe some of the factors that must be considered to provide optimal treatment.

- One must consider whether the treatment is evidence based or empirically supported by efficacy studies, whether the use of medication is appropriate, and whether a combination of treatments is the best option.

- A key element in all therapies is the development of an effective "working alliance." A principal social issue in psychotherapy is ensuring the development of a good therapeutic working alliance between client and therapist, even when they differ widely in cultural, ethnic, and/or socioeconomic backgrounds.

16.4 List the psychological approaches most often used to treat abnormal behavior.

- Behavior therapy is extensively used to treat many clinical problems. Behavior therapy approaches include exposure, aversion therapy, modeling, and reinforcement approaches.

- Cognitive or cognitive-behavioral therapy attempts to modify a person's self-statements and construal of events in order to change his or her behavior. Cognitive-behavioral methods have been used for a wide variety of clinical problems—from depression to anger control—and with a range of clinical populations. Much research attests to the efficacy of these approaches.

- Other psychological treatment approaches include humanistic-experiential therapies and gestalt therapy.

- Classical psychoanalysis dates back to Sigmund Freud. It is rarely practiced today, and there is little empirical support for its efficacy.

- Several variants of therapy have developed out of the psychoanalytic tradition. These diverge from classical psychoanalysis on matters such as the duration of therapy and the role of primitive psychosexual drives in personality dynamics. Many of the newer psychodynamic forms of treatment emphasize the way interpersonal processes are affected by early interactions with parents and other family members.

- In addition to their use in treating individuals, some psychological treatment methods are applied to problematic relationships through couple or family therapy. These approaches typically assume that a person's problems lie partly in his or her interactions with others. Consequently, the focus of treatment is on changing the ways in which members of the social or family unit interact.

16.5 Explain the roles that social values and culture play in psychological treatment.

- Although psychotherapy is a set of tools to be used in pursuit of a client's welfare, not an ethics system, therapists are often faced with moral dilemmas in the course of treatment.

- Racial and ethnic minorities are currently underserved by the mental health system.

16.6 Describe three biological approaches used to treat abnormal behavior.

- Medications are important in the treatment of many disorders. It is now common in clinical practice to combine medication and psychological treatments.

- The most commonly used antipsychotic medications are the atypical neuroleptics. These improve both positive and negative symptoms and have fewer extrapyramidal symptoms (unwanted side effects involving movement) than conventional (first-generation) antipsychotics.

- Some of the earlier antidepressant medications (e.g., tricyclics and MAOIs) have now been replaced by SSRIs and SNRIs. Although more widely used, there is no compelling evidence that these newer medications are more effective than the older antidepressants. In general, antidepressants work through their influence on the serotonin and norepinephrine neurotransmitter systems.

- Anxiolytic (antianxiety) medications work via their effect on the GABA system. They are widely prescribed.

- Lithium is an important medication in the treatment of mania. However, some of the newer mood-stabilizing drugs (which are also used to treat epilepsy) are now more frequently prescribed.

- Although not frequently used, ECT is a safe and effective treatment for depression and other disorders. It causes some short-term cognitive side effects, especially when administered bilaterally.

- Neurosurgery is used as a treatment of last resort. Even when patients improve clinically, they may have permanent, adverse side effects.

Key Terms

antianxiety drugs, p. 597
antidepressant drugs, p. 595
behavior therapy, p. 579
client-centered therapy, p. 585
countertransference, p. 589
couple therapy, p. 590
efficacy, p. 577
electroconvulsive
    therapy (ECT), p. 600
family therapy, p. 590
flooding, p. 579
gestalt therapy, p. 586
imaginal exposure, p. 579
in vivo exposure, p. 579

integrative behavioral couple
    therapy (IBCT), p. 590
latent content, p. 588
manifest content, p. 588
manualized therapies, p. 578
modeling, p. 580
motivational interviewing
    (MI), p. 585
neurosurgery, p. 602
psychodynamic therapy, p. 587
psychopharmacology, p. 578
psychotherapy, p. 571
randomized clinical
    trials (RCTs), p. 577

rational emotive behavior
    therapy (REBT), p. 582
resistance, p. 588
response shaping, p. 581
structural family therapy, p. 591
systematic desensitization, p. 579
tardive dyskinesia, p. 594
token economy, p. 581
traditional behavioral couple
    therapy (TBCT), p. 590
transcranial magnetic
    stimulation (TMS), p. 602
transference, p. 588

Chapter 17
Contemporary and Legal Issues in Abnormal Psychology

Learning Objectives

17.1 Describe the importance of prevention in mental health care, noting the major approaches to prevention.

17.2 Explain the contemporary issues of inpatient mental health treatment.

17.3 Discuss the controversial legal issues involving people with mental illness.

17.4 Describe national and international organizations that promote efforts for mental health.

17.5 Address the challenges that people face in advancing mental health improvement in contemporary societies.

A Tragic Case of Murder as an Outcome of Severe Mental Illness

On Mother's Day weekend in 2003, Deanna Laney, a very religious 39-year-old housewife and mother from Texas, began to see "signs from God" that she was supposed to do something drastic about her children. The first sign indicated to her that she was supposed to destroy her children when she saw her 14-month-old son, Aaron, playing with a spear. She hesitated because she was uncertain of exactly what the sign from God meant. Then she received another sign when Aaron handed her a rock that he was playing with. She then saw him squeezing a frog and began to conclude that she was supposed to kill her children, either by stoning them, strangling them, or stabbing them. She believed that God had given her three ways to kill them but concluded that killing them with rocks would be better than strangulation.

She killed two of her sons by beating them with a rock; her third son, Aaron, was severely injured but survived her attack. She called 911 and reported that she had killed her sons.

After she was arrested, she was very puzzled and behaved in an extreme manner, for example, lying in a fetal position and crying in the cell, walking around the cell singing gospel songs, and often praying and crying. The sheriff in the prison reported that "when she suddenly realizes what she's done she goes into an extreme blank stare and withdrawal." She was placed on a suicide watch because of her intense and psychotic behavior.

Laney had a history of serious mental illness including a prior psychotic experience in which she was hospitalized. During this episode, she reported that she had smelled sulfur and concluded that this was God's way of warning her that the devil was close. She was diagnosed with schizophrenia.

At her murder trial, Laney pleaded not guilty by reason of insanity (NGRI) (to be discussed later in the chapter). Her defense was based on her belief that God had told her the world was going to end and "she had to get her house in order," which included killing her children. The psychiatric evaluations of her mental health status prior to the trial reflected a strong consensus as to her condition. Psychiatrists who served as experts from both the defense and the prosecution in this case testified that Laney was psychotic at the time of the crime and met the criteria for NGRI. The evaluating psychiatrists concluded that Laney had crushed her sons' skulls with rocks because she was suffering from delusions and did not know right from wrong.

The jury acquitted her of all charges on grounds that she was insane at the time of the crime. Apparently, there was no premeditation, and Laney did not believe that she was doing wrong; thus, she was found not guilty by reason of insanity (Associated Press, 2004; Ramsland, 2005).

The final chapter of this book has traditionally been somewhat of a highlight for several important topics in abnormal psychology that have been noted only briefly in earlier chapters. These issues are very important to understanding the field of abnormal psychology and will give the reader a broader perspective on ways our society deals with, or in some cases fails to deal with, abnormal behavior or its consequences. We begin with the topic of prevention of mental disorders. Over the years, most mental health efforts have been geared toward helping people after they have already developed serious problems. If the goal is to reduce or eliminate emotional problems in our country or the world, then a major alteration in thinking is required. We need to expand efforts at prevention through early intervention (Breitborde et al., 2010; Tortolero, 2010).

Next, we describe inpatient mental health treatment and the state of mental hospitals in contemporary society, including a discussion of the prison system, which is where many mental health patients end up. We discuss changes that have taken place and some of the forces that have affected inpatient psychiatric care today. Following this, several legal issues pertinent to psychiatric care and the hospitalization of people with severe psychological problems are addressed. We then briefly survey the scope of organized efforts for mental health both in the United States and throughout the world. Finally, we consider what each of us can do to foster mental health.

Perspectives on Prevention

17.1 Describe the importance of prevention in mental health care, noting the major approaches to prevention.

In the early 1990s, the U.S. Congress directed the National Institute of Mental Health (NIMH) to work with the Institute of Medicine (IOM) to develop a report detailing a long-term prevention research program. Among other things, the IOM report focused attention on the distinction between prevention and treatment efforts (Dozois & Dobson, 2004; Munoz, 2001; Munoz et al., 1996). Prevention efforts are classified into three subcategories:

1. **Universal interventions**: These efforts are aimed at influencing the general population and include, for example, school-based efforts at preventing, rerating, and responding to suicide-related behavior (D'Arcy & Meng, 2014; Robinson et al., 2013).

2. **Selective interventions**: These efforts are aimed at a specific subgroup of the population considered at risk for developing mental health problems—for example, adolescents or ethnic minorities (Coie et al., 2000).

3. **Indicated interventions**: These efforts are directed toward high-risk individuals who are identified as having minimal but detectable symptoms of mental disorder but who do not meet criteria for clinical diagnosis—for example, individuals forced from their homes by a flood or some other disaster (see Reyes & Jacobs, 2006).

As shown in Figure 17.1, preventive efforts are clearly differentiated from treatment and maintenance interventions.

Figure 17.1 Classification of Prevention Strategies, Treatment, and Maintenance

The traditional terminology for describing general strategies of disease prevention in the field of public health has been revised to provide a more useful perspective on prevention efforts. The classification system for prevention (universal, selective, and indicated strategies) is shown in this context as distinct from treatment interventions and maintenance approaches to mental health problems

(From P. J. Mrazek & R. J. Haggerty (Eds.). (1994). *Reducing risks for mental disorders: Frontiers for preventive intervention research*. Copyright © 1994 by the National Academy of Sciences. Courtesy of the National Academy Press, Washington, DC.)

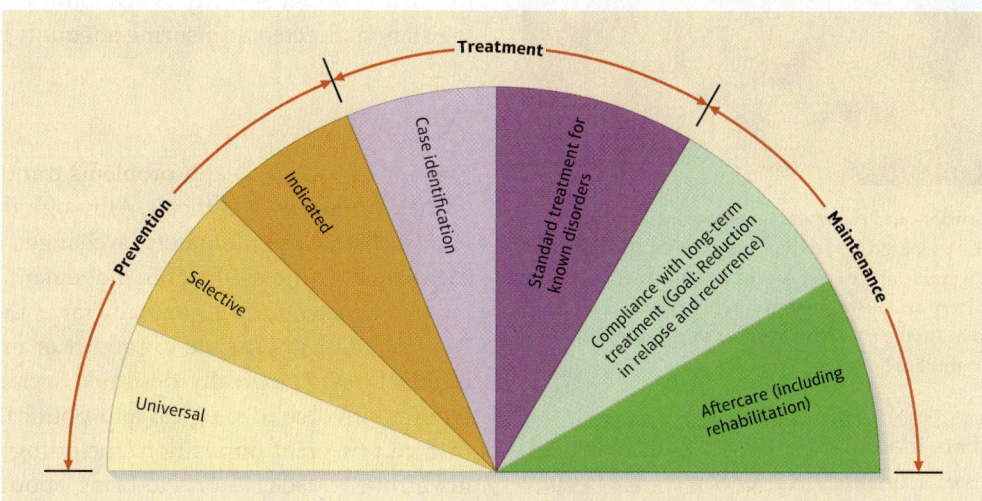

Universal Interventions

Universal interventions perform two key tasks: They (1) alter conditions that can cause or contribute to mental disorders (risk factors) and (2) establish conditions that foster positive mental health (protective factors). Epidemiologic studies help investigators obtain information about the incidence and distribution of various maladaptive behaviors (Dozois & Dobson, 2004) such as those seen in substance abuse disorders (Spoth et al., 2014). These findings can then be used to suggest what preventive efforts might be most appropriate. For example, various epidemiologic studies and reviews have shown that certain groups are at high risk for mental disorders: recently divorced people (Bulloch et al., 2009), people with physical disabilities (Goodheart & Rozensky, 2011), elderly people (Houtjes et al., 2010), those who have been physically abused (Panuzio & DiLillo, 2010), children experiencing natural disasters or terrorism (Pfefferbaum et al., 2014), victims of severe trauma (Jaranson et al., 2004), and adolescents who are potential victims of violence (Multisite Violence Prevention Project, 2014). Although findings such as these may be the basis for immediate selective or indicated prevention, they may also aid in universal prevention by telling us what to look for and where to look—in essence, by focusing our efforts in the right direction. Universal prevention is very broad and includes biological, psychosocial, and sociocultural efforts. Virtually any effort that is aimed at improving the human condition would be considered a part of universal prevention of mental disorder.

BIOLOGICAL STRATEGIES Biologically based universal strategies for prevention begin with promoting adaptive lifestyles. Many of the goals of health psychology can be viewed as universal prevention strategies. Efforts geared toward improving diet, establishing a routine of physical exercise, and developing overall good health habits can do much to improve physical well-being (Martins et al., 2010). Physical illness always produces some sort of psychological stress that can result in such problems as depression, so with respect to good mental health, maintaining good physical health is prevention.

PSYCHOSOCIAL STRATEGIES In viewing normality as optimal development and viewing high functioning (rather than the mere absence of pathology) as the goal, we imply that people need opportunities to learn physical, intellectual, emotional, and social competencies.

1. The first requirement for psychosocial health is that a person develop the skills needed for effective problem solving, for expressing emotions constructively, and for engaging in satisfying relationships with others. Failure to develop these protective skills places the individual at a serious disadvantage in coping with stresses and the unavoidable risk factors for mental disorder.

2. The second requirement for psychosocial health is that a person acquire an accurate frame of reference on which to build his or her identity. We have seen repeatedly that when people's assumptions about themselves

Preventing mental disorders and maintaining psychosocial health require that a person be prepared for the types of problems likely to be encountered during given life stages. For example, how might young people who want to marry and have children prepare themselves for the tasks of building a mutually satisfying relationship and helping children develop their abilities?

or their world are inaccurate, their behavior is likely to be maladaptive. Consider, for example, the young woman who believes that being thin can bring happiness and so becomes anorexic.

3. The third requirement for psychosocial health is that a person be prepared for the types of problems likely to be encountered during given life stages. For example, young people who want to marry and have children must be prepared for the tasks of building a mutually satisfying relationship and helping children develop their abilities. Similarly, a middle-aged adult needs to be prepared for problems that are likely to arise during retirement and old age.

In recent years, psychosocial measures aimed at prevention have received a great deal of attention. The field of behavioral medicine has been influential (Hunter et al., 2009), with efforts being made to change the psychological factors underlying unhealthy habits such as smoking, excessive drinking, and poor eating habits.

SOCIOCULTURAL STRATEGIES As has been demonstrated many times throughout this book, without a supportive community, individual development can be stifled. At the same time, without responsible, psychologically healthy individuals, the community will not thrive and, in turn, cannot be supportive. Individuals with psychosocial impairments as a result of exposure to disorganized communities lack the wherewithal to create better communities to protect and sustain the psychological health of those who come after them, and a persistently unprotective environment results. Sociocultural efforts toward universal prevention are focused on making the community as safe and attractive as possible for the individuals within it.

With our growing recognition of the role that pathological social conditions play in producing maladaptive behavior (in socially impoverished communities), increased attention must be devoted to creating social conditions that will foster healthy development and functioning in individuals. Efforts to create these conditions include a broad spectrum of measures—ranging from public education and Social Security to economic planning and social legislation directed at ensuring adequate health care for all.

Selective Interventions

Preventing mental health problems through social change in the community is difficult. Although the whole psychological climate can ultimately be changed by a social movement such as the civil rights movement of the 1960s, the payoff of such efforts is generally far in the future and may be difficult or impossible to predict or measure. Attempts to effect psychologically desirable social change are also likely to involve ideological and political issues that may inspire powerful opposition, including opposition from government itself. Efforts to bring about change through targeting a smaller segment of the population can have more effective results. For example, a review of the research in reducing depression in children concludes that selective intervention programs are more effective than universal programs (Horowitz & Garber, 2006) in reducing the extent of depressive disorders.

Though difficult to formulate, mobilize, and carry out, selective intervention can bring about major improvements. In this section, we look at the mobilization of prevention resources aimed at curtailing or reducing the problem of teenage alcohol and drug abuse. Prominent social forces such as advertising and marketing campaigns that are attractive to youth, the influence of peer groups, and the ready availability of alcohol, tobacco, and even many illicit drugs are instrumental in promoting the early use of alcohol in young people.

Although recent years have witnessed a decrease in the rate of adolescent substance use in the United States (Johnston et al., 2007), alcohol, tobacco, and other drug use by teenagers remains a persistent public health problem. Alcohol is the most commonly used drug among adolescents (Komro et al., 2008). Alcohol use among youth is related to many social, emotional, and behavioral problems (e.g., using illegal drugs, fighting, stealing, driving under the influence, having unplanned sex, and experiencing school problems). In fact, early alcohol use is a strong predictor of lifetime alcohol abuse or dependence (Grant & Dawson, 1997).

Because the factors that entice adolescents to begin using alcohol and drugs are influenced by social factors, it is tempting to think that if these forces could be counterbalanced with equally powerful alternative influences, the rate of substance abuse might radically decline. But this is easier said than done. The U.S. government has approached the drug abuse problem with three broad strategies for dealing with adolescent substance use, all of which have proved insufficient:

1. **Intercepting and/or reducing the supply of drugs available.** The reduction of supply by policing our borders has had minimal impact on the availability of drugs. These programs do little to affect the supply of the two drugs most abused by adolescents—alcohol and tobacco—which are, of course, available in corner stores and even in the adolescent's home. Reducing the supply of these drugs to adolescents is especially challenging given mass-media messages and other societal signals that these legal products can bring about social acceptance, are essential for celebrations, and can mark a young person's passage into adulthood, with limited cautions about their potential to damage health.

2. **Providing treatment services for those who develop drug problems.** Although much money is spent each year on treatment, treating substance abuse is perhaps the least effective way to reduce the problem. Addictive disorders are very difficult to overcome, and treatment failure or relapse is the rule rather than the exception. Therapeutic programs for those addicted to drugs or alcohol, though necessary, are not the answer to eliminating or even significantly reducing the problems in our society.

3. **Encouraging prevention.** By far the most desirable— and potentially the most effective—means of reducing the drug problem in our country is through prevention methods aimed at alerting citizens to the problems that surround drugs and teaching young people ways to avoid using them (Bloom & Gullotta, 2009). Although past efforts have had some limited success in discouraging adolescent drug use, many initially promising prevention efforts have failed to bring about the desired reduction in substance use. There are a number of reasons for this: The intervention typically has not been conducted for a long enough period to show the desired effect; the intervention efforts have not been powerful enough to make a sufficient impact on the participants; or the strategy may not have been well implemented.

In recent years prevention specialists have taken a more proactive position and have attempted to establish programs that prevent the development of abuse disorders before young people become so involved with drugs or alcohol that future adjustment becomes difficult, if not impossible. For example, one recent program has been devoted to assisting homeless children who are attending school to deal with the risks for problems of alcohol or drug abuse (Sulkowski & Michael, 2014). These recent prevention strategies have taken some diverse and encouraging directions. We examine several such efforts and then discuss the limitations of these prevention approaches.

SCHOOL-BASED INTERVENTIONS The most promising alcohol and drug use prevention curricula are based on behavioral theory; they target the risk (e.g., peer pressure, mass-media messages) and protective (e.g., alcohol-free activities, messages supporting "no use" norms) factors associated with adolescent use; include developmentally appropriate information about alcohol and other drugs; are skill based and interactive; and emphasize normative education that increases the awareness that most students do not use alcohol, tobacco, or other drugs (Komro & Toomey, 2002). Although several such programs exist, some have been evaluated more extensively than others; for example, the Drug Abuse Resistance Education Program, or D.A.R.E. (a program that uses local police officers who are invited by the local school districts to speak and work with students after undergoing special training), underwent an extensive number of evaluative studies that have generally concluded that the program has limited success at deterring substance use. In fact, a 10-year follow-up study reported no success for the D.A.R.E. program (Lynam et al., 2009).

Efforts to teach schoolchildren about the dangers of drugs before they reach the age of maximum risk are based on the premise that if children are made aware of the dangers of drugs and alcohol, they will choose not to use them. However, evaluative studies have cast doubt on the effectiveness of programs such as D.A.R.E. What do you think might account for D.A.R.E.'s lack of success?

INTERVENTION PROGRAMS FOR HIGH-RISK TEENS Intervention programs identify high-risk teenagers and take special measures to circumvent their further use of alcohol or other potentially dangerous drugs (Hawkins et al., 2004). Programs such as these are often school-based efforts and are not strictly prevention programs because they intervene with young people who have already developed problems. Programs for early intervention can be effective in identifying adolescents before their alcohol or drug problems become entrenched (Foley & Hochman, 2006).

Research Close-Up

Intervention Programs for High-Risk Populations

This research strategy involves identifying high-risk individuals and providing special approaches to circumvent their problems; for example, identifying adolescents at risk for abusing alcohol or committing suicide and implementing a program to prevent the problem behavior.

PARENT EDUCATION AND FAMILY-BASED INTERVENTION PROGRAMS Through their own drinking or positive verbalizations about alcohol, parents may encourage or sanction alcohol use among teens. Some research has shown that parental involvement and monitoring reduces substance use among adolescents (Becerra et al., 2014). Thus, many prevention programs focus on family interventions with good success.

EXTRACURRICULAR STRATEGIES Various extracurricular activities and youth programs have the potential to reduce problem behaviors like alcohol and drug use, school dropouts, violence, and juvenile delinquency (Scales & Leffert, 1999). These programs may be especially beneficial for high-risk teens who are unsupervised outside of school or who, because of poverty, may not have access to opportunities like sports, music, or other programs available to middle-class youth.

INTERNET-BASED INTERVENTION PROGRAMS One study (Schwinn et al., 2010) examined adolescent girls in seventh through ninth grade who were given an online test battery and 12 sessions of gender-specific drug prevention strategies. At follow-up, girls receiving the Internet intervention program reported lower rates of use for alcohol and drugs compared with the control sample.

COMPREHENSIVE PREVENTION STRATEGIES A consensus seems to be developing in the field that the most effective way to prevent complex problems like adolescent alcohol and other drug use is through the use of multicomponent programs that combine aspects of the various strategies described previously (Stigler et al., 2011). Typically, classroom curricula are used as the core component to which other strategies (e.g., parent programs, mass media, extracurricular activities, and community strategies to reduce access to alcohol via enforcement of age of drinking laws) are added.

Due to a scarcity of research on comprehensive prevention strategies, a team of University of Minnesota researchers developed Project Northland—an exemplary research-based set of interventions that aims to delay the onset of drinking in young adolescents, reduce alcohol use among those already drinking, and limit the number of alcohol-related problems during adolescence. Project Northland included multiple years of behavioral curricula, parental involvement and education, peer leadership opportunities, community task forces, and community-wide media campaigns (e.g., Perry et al., 1996, 2002). Interventions started with students in the sixth grade and continued until high school graduation. The program included peer-led and activity-driven learning strategies that involved students, parents, teachers, and community members in support of "no use" messages, while at the same time promoting alcohol-free norms for youth, providing fun alternatives to alcohol use, and reducing youth access to alcohol. Innovative activities and games were used to ensure high participation rates in the program, and comprehensive teacher and peer-leader

Why do you think peer programs, like those offered at the Boys and Girls Clubs, tend to be more successful than adult-driven programs in getting children and adolescents to avoid drug and alcohol abuse?

Recognizing the huge market potential of teenagers, advertisers exploit the tremendous value that the appearance of sophistication has for this age group. Some efforts have been aimed at deglamorizing these messages by showing ads that graphically depict the negative aspects of alcohol and drug use, like this antismoking billboard.

trainings were core features (see Hazelden Betty Ford Foundation, n.d., for descriptions of the program).

The success of prevention programs has come to the attention of educators, and a number of efforts are under way to "export" these laboratory programs for broader use in America's schools. Perhaps the most noteworthy is the National Registry of Evidence-based Programs and Practices (NREPP), a program of the U.S. Department of Health and Human Services' Substance Abuse and Mental Health Services Administration. However, the jury is still out on the relative success of the various substance abuse prevention programs at reducing alcohol and drug problems in adolescents. For example, an effort to implement Project Northland in a large Midwestern inner city where problems with gangs, violence, drug dealing, and housing were perceived as more pressing than underage drinking did not have the positive outcomes that were obtained in the more rural environment of northern Minnesota (Komro et al., 2008). It will take time and further research efforts to determine which of the strategies are superior to others in reducing alcohol and drug problems in adolescents, and in which settings.

Indicated Interventions

Indicated intervention emphasizes the early detection and prompt treatment of maladaptive behavior in a person's family and community setting. In some cases—for example, in a crisis or after a disaster (Garakani et al., 2004; see the discussion on crisis intervention in Chapter 5)—indicated prevention involves immediate and relatively brief intervention to prevent any long-term behavioral consequences of the traumatic events (Raphael & Wooding, 2004).

Watch **Prevention Programs**

in review

- What are some strategies for biological, psychosocial, and socio-cultural universal interventions?
- Define the term *selective intervention*. What selective intervention programs have shown promise in helping prevent teenage alcohol and drug abuse?
- What is indicated intervention?

Inpatient Mental Health Treatment in Contemporary Society

17.2 Explain the contemporary issues of inpatient mental health treatment.

Mental disorders are common in the United States. An estimated 18.6 percent of Americans ages 18 and older, or about one in five adults, suffer from a diagnosable mental disorder in a given year (NIMH, 2014). Over 19.6 percent of people ages 18 to 25, 21.2 percent between ages 26 and 49, and 15.8 percent of people age 50 or older have some diagnosable psychiatric disorder. Of these people with disorders, 16.3 percent are Hispanic, 19.3 percent are white, 18.6 percent are black, 13.9 percent are Asian, and 28.3 percent are American Indian or Alaska Native. While most people experiencing mental health problems seek or obtain help in an outpatient program, some individuals require admission to an inpatient treatment program because of perceived danger they experience in their daily lives. Inpatient admission to a psychiatric hospital can be a significant step that is taken as a means of protecting the individual or those close to her or him from harm by providing a secure environment to allow the patient to recover from her or his extreme symptoms.

The Mental Hospital as a Therapeutic Community

In cases where individuals might be considered dangerous to themselves or others (Richards et al., 1997) or where their symptoms are so severe that they are unable to care for themselves in the community, psychiatric hospitalization may be necessary in order to prevent the development of further problems and the individual's further psychological deterioration. Most of the traditional forms of therapy that we discussed in Chapter 16 may, of course, be used in a residential or inpatient hospital setting. In addition, in many mental hospitals, these techniques are supplemented by efforts to make the hospital environment itself a "therapeutic community" (Kennard, 2004). That is, the social environment is manipulated to provide the patient with the greatest benefit. All the ongoing activities of the hospital are brought into the total treatment program, and the environment, or milieu, is a crucial aspect of the therapy. This approach is thus often referred to as **milieu therapy** (Petti, 2010; Zimmerman, 2004). Three general therapeutic principles guide this approach to treatment:

1. Staff expectations are clearly communicated to patients. Both positive and negative feedback are used to encourage appropriate verbalizations and actions by patients.

2. Patients are encouraged to become involved in all decisions made, and in all actions taken, concerning them. A self-care, do-it-yourself attitude prevails.

3. All patients belong to social groups on the ward. The group cohesiveness that results gives the patients support and encouragement, and the related process of group pressure helps shape their behavior in positive ways.

In a therapeutic community, as few restraints as possible are placed on patients' freedom, and patients are encouraged to take responsibility for their behavior and participate actively in their treatment programs. Open wards permit patients to use the grounds and premises. Self-government programs give patients responsibility for managing their own affairs and those of the ward. All hospital personnel are expected to treat the patients as human beings who merit consideration and courtesy. The interaction among patients—whether in group therapy sessions, social events, or other activities—is planned in such a way as to be of therapeutic benefit. In fact, it is becoming apparent that often the most beneficial aspect of a therapeutic community is the interaction among the patients themselves. Differences in social roles and backgrounds may make empathy between staff and patients difficult, but fellow patients have been there—they have had similar problems and breakdowns and have experienced the anxiety and humiliation of being labeled "mentally ill" and being hospitalized. Constructive relationships frequently develop among patients in a supportive, encouraging milieu. However, although **residential treatment** has improved over time, such treatment for children and adolescents continues to face challenges.

Another successful method for helping patients take increased responsibility for their own behavior is the use of **social-learning programs**. Such programs normally make use of learning principles and techniques such as token economies (see Chapter 16) to shape more socially acceptable behavior (Corrigan, 1995, 1997; Mariotto et al., 2002; Paul et al., 1997).

Although a strong case can be made for the use of psychiatric hospitalization in stabilizing the adjustment of people living with psychiatric disorders (Glick & Tandon, 2009), a persistent concern about hospitalization is that the mental hospital may become a permanent refuge from the world. During the past four decades, considerable effort has been devoted to reducing the population of inpatients by closing hospitals and treating patients who have mental disorders as outpatients. This effort, which is often referred to as **deinstitutionalization**, was initiated to prevent the negative effects, for many psychiatric patients, of being confined to a mental hospital for long periods of time as well as to lower health care costs. To keep the focus on returning patients to the community and on preventing

their return to the institution, contemporary hospital staffs try to establish close ties with patients' families and communities and to provide them with positive expectations about the patients' recovery.

The rise of the biological therapies described in Chapter 16 has meant that between 70 and 90 percent of patients diagnosed with psychosis and admitted to mental hospitals can now be discharged within a few weeks, or at most a few months. Even where disorders have become chronic, effective treatment methods have been developed. In one of the most extensive and well-controlled studies of chronic hospitalized patients, Paul and Lentz (1977) compared the relative effectiveness of three treatment approaches:

1. Milieu therapy, which focuses on structuring a patient's environment to provide clear communication of expectations and to get the patient involved in the treatment. One major goal is to encourage the patient to participate in the therapeutic community through the group process.

2. A social-learning treatment program, organized around learning principles and using a rigorously programmed token economy system, with ward staff as reinforcing agents. Undesirable behavior was not reinforced, whereas the accumulation of many tokens through effective functioning made a patient eligible for attractive amenities not normally available in public mental hospitals.

3. Traditional mental hospital treatments including pharmacotherapy, occupational therapy, recreational therapy, activity therapy, and individual or group therapy. No systematic application of milieu therapy or the social-learning program was given to this group.

The treatment project covered a period of 6 years: an initial phase of staff training, patient assessment, and baseline recording; a treatment phase; an aftercare phase; and a long (year and a half) follow-up. The changes targeted included resocialization, learning new roles, and reducing or eliminating bizarre behavior. The 28 patients with chronic schizophrenia in each treatment group were matched for age, sex, socioeconomic level, symptoms, and duration of hospitalization. The results of the study were impressive. Both milieu therapy and the social-learning program produced significant improvement in overall functioning and resulted in more successful hospital releases than the traditional hospital care. The behaviorally based social-learning program, however, was clearly superior to the more diffuse program of milieu therapy, as evidenced by the fact that over 90 percent of the released patients from the social-learning program remained continuously in the community, compared with 70 percent of the released patients who had received milieu therapy. The figure for the traditional treatment program was less than 50 percent.

Despite the promise of the token economy approach, emulating as it does certain "real-world" principles of exchange that the patient will face outside the institution, it has not enjoyed wide public acceptance (Mariotto et al., 2002). Many feel that it is cruel and inhumane to expect patients with mental health challenges to govern their behavior in accordance with a prescribed schedule of reinforcements. One might ask, however, whether it is more humane to consign the patient to the status of a passive and helpless recipient of whatever the environment has to offer, which in many institutional settings is not very much. Is that truly the message we want to convey about the patient's relationship to his or her environment? Probably not, especially in light of the considerable evidence that most patients with chronic mental health challenges are surprisingly adept at making successful adaptations that are within their range of control.

Aftercare Programs

Even where hospitalization has successfully modified maladaptive behavior and a patient has learned needed occupational and interpersonal skills, readjustment in the community following release may still be difficult (Seidman, 2003; Thornicroft & Tansella, 2000). Many studies have shown that in the past, up to 45 percent of individuals with schizophrenia have been readmitted within the first year after their discharge. Community-based treatment programs, now referred to as *aftercare programs*, are live-in facilities that serve as a home base for former patients as they make the transition back to adequate functioning in the community. Typically, community-based facilities are run not by professional mental health personnel but by the residents themselves. Aftercare programs can help smooth the transition from institutional to community life and reduce the number of relapses. However, some individuals

Aftercare facilities do not always provide the safe refuge promised. Homeless people often live in large cities under austere conditions, as evidenced by this photograph, that resemble those seen in mental institutions several decades ago.

do not function well in aftercare programs. Owen and colleagues (1997) found that clients who were likely to hold unskilled employment, to have nonpsychotic symptoms, to have committed a crime, or to be more transient tended to be noncompliant in aftercare programs. The investigators concluded that many of the discharged patients did not "fit" the services typically offered to released psychiatric inpatients. Those with less severe symptoms may fail because they appear to aftercare staff as not needing much help; most services are geared to those patients who exhibit more extreme symptoms.

Sometimes aftercare includes a "halfway" period in which a released patient makes a gradual return to the outside world in what were formerly termed "halfway houses." Although some patients continue to have mental health problems including suicide attempts (Fenton et al., 1997), and many have trouble gaining the acceptance and support of the community (Fairweather, 1994; Seidman, 2003), efforts to treat patients who are severely disturbed in the community are often very successful. Recent research has shown that an intensive, holistic approach to recovery facilitation can be quite effective in reducing symptoms and restoring the client to living outside institutions (Young et al., 2014). However, Bromley and colleagues (2014) describe significant barriers to discharge and discuss the potential problems of clients "falling through the cracks" after being discharged from inpatient care. Moreover, some research has shown that aftercare programs do not always live up to their name. Levy and Kershaw (2001) disclose a number of problems in which relevant treatment was not made available and staff did not provide a secure environment.

Deinstitutionalization

The population of psychiatric patients in the United States has shrunk considerably during the past 40 years. Between 1967 and 2007, the number of people in state mental hospitals dropped 81 percent (Scott et al., 2008). The deinstitutionalization movement, which involves closing down mental hospitals and treating persons with severe mental disorders in community programs, has not been limited to the United States—the process of shifting the care of patients with mental disturbances from inpatient hospitals to community-based programs has been a worldwide trend (Emerson, 2004; Honkonen et al., 2003).

Deinstitutionalization has been a source of considerable controversy. Some authorities consider the emptying of mental hospitals a positive expression of society's desire to free previously confined persons, maintaining that deinstitutionalized patients show significant improvement compared with those who remain hospitalized (Newton et al., 2000; Reinharz et al., 2000). Others, however, speak of the "abandonment" of patients with chronic mental illness to a cruel and harsh existence (Grob, 2008), which for many includes homelessness, violent victimization (Walsh et al., 2003), or suicide (Goldney, 2003). Many citizens, too, complain of being harassed, intimidated, and frightened by obviously disturbed individuals wandering the streets of their neighborhoods. In an effort to address these concerns, some professionals and community members alike have lobbied to call attention to mental health challenges brought about by deinstitutionalization (Rosenberg & Rosenberg, 2006).

Some of the reduction in mental health services in recent years has come about because of changes in the health care system. (See the Unresolved Issues section at the end of this chapter.) The planned community efforts to fill the gaps in service never really materialized at effective levels (Lamb, 1998).

A number of factors have interacted to alter the pattern of mental hospital admissions and discharges in recent years. Antipsychotic drugs have made it possible for many patients who would otherwise have required confinement to live in the community, but not all mental health problems can be managed with medication. Kunitoh (2013) pointed out that much research has shown that even long-stay patients could achieve better functioning by being deinstitutionalized rather than remaining in hospitals. Moreover, changing treatment philosophies and the desire to eliminate mental institutions were bolstered by the assumption that society wanted and could afford to provide better community-based care for patients with chronic mental illness outside of large mental hospitals. In theory, closing the public mental hospitals seemed workable. The plan was to open many community-based mental health centers that would provide continuing care to the residents of hospitals after discharge. Residents would be given welfare funds (supposedly at less cost to the government than maintaining large mental hospitals) and would be administered medication to keep them stabilized until they could obtain continuing care. Many patients would be discharged to home and family; others would be placed in smaller, home-like board-and-care facilities or nursing homes.

Unforeseen problems arose, however, and in many cases, homeless shelters in metropolitan communities have become a "makeshift alternative" to inpatient mental health care (Haugland et al., 1997). Many residents of mental institutions have no families or homes to go to; board-and-care facilities are often substandard; and the community mental health centers have often been ill prepared and insufficiently funded to provide needed services for patients with chronic illness, particularly as national funding priorities shifted during the 1980s (Humphreys & Rappaport, 1993). Many patients are not carefully selected for discharge and are not ready for community living, and many of those who are discharged are not followed up sufficiently or often enough to ensure their successful

adaptation outside the hospital. In addition, some research has suggested that deinstitutionalization has increased the rates of suicide among people with mental illness (Yoon & Bruckner, 2009).

One important court case (*Albright v. Abington Memorial Hospital*, 1997) involved charges that the hospital failed to provide sufficient care for a seriously disturbed woman who later killed herself. Countless patients have been discharged to fates harsher than the conditions in any of the hospitals. The following case illustrates the situation.

From Institution to Homelessness

Dave B., 49 years old, had been hospitalized for 25 years in a state mental hospital. When the hospital was scheduled for phaseout, many of the patients, particularly those who were regressed or aggressive, were transferred to another state hospital. Dave was a borderline intellectually disabled man who had periodic episodes of psychosis. At the time of the hospital closing, however, he was not hallucinating and was "reasonably intact." Dave was considered to be one of the "less disturbed" residents because his psychotic behavior was less pronounced and he presented no dangerous problems. He was discharged to a board-and-care facility (actually an old hotel where most of the residents were former inpatients). At first, Dave seemed to fit in well at the facility; mostly he sat in his room or in the outside hallway, and he caused no trouble for the caretakers. Two weeks after he had arrived, however, he wandered off the hotel grounds and was missing for several days. The police eventually found him living in the city dump. He had apparently stopped taking his medication, and when he was discovered he was regressed and catatonic. He was readmitted to a state hospital.

Research on the effects of deinstitutionalization has been mixed. Some reports have noted positive benefits of briefer hospitalization (Honkonen et al., 2003; Rauktis, 2001), and some data suggest that deinstitutionalization appears not to be associated with an increased risk of homicide by people who are mentally ill (Simpson et al., 2004). However, others have reported problems with discharged patients and point to failures in programs to deinstitutionalize patients with mental disturbances (Chan et al., 2001; Leff, 2001).

Recent indications are that inpatient psychiatric hospitalization may now be increasing because of the failures to provide adequate mental health care for patients in need of mental health services in the community (Marcotty, 2004). A similar increase in the number of people being hospitalized has been reported in the United Kingdom (Priebe & Turner, 2003).

The full extent of problems created by deinstitutionalization is not precisely known, partly because there has been little rigorous follow-up on patients discharged from mental hospitals. Such research investigations are difficult to conduct because the patients are transient and hard to track over time. Certainly, not all homeless people are former patients with mental disorders, but deinstitutionalization has contributed substantially to the number of homeless people (Whitaker, 2009) and to the number of people with mental illness who are in prison (Lurigio, 2013; Markowitz, 2006). On the positive side, a study by Nelson and colleagues (2007) concluded that there has been a significant reduction in homelessness and significant improvements in "well-being" outcomes resulting from recent programs that provide permanent housing and support for the homeless. For example, Padgett and colleagues (2006) showed that assertive community treatment and programs to reduce harm can be successful in producing housing stability and reduction in the trauma of homelessness.

in review

- What is milieu therapy?
- What problems have resulted from deinstitutionalization?

Controversial Legal Issues and the Mentally Ill

17.3 Discuss the controversial legal issues involving people with mental illness.

A number of important issues are related to the legal status of people with mental illness—the subject matter of **forensic psychology or forensic psychiatry**—and they center on the rights of patients and the rights of members of society to be protected from individuals with mental disturbances (see Drogin et al., 2011, for a comprehensive overview). For a survey of some of the legal rights that people with mental illness have gained over the years, see the World Around Us box.

Civil Commitment

Individuals with psychological problems or behaviors that are so extreme and severe as to pose a threat to themselves or others may require protective confinement. Those who

The World Around Us

Important Court Decisions for Patient Rights

Several important court decisions have helped establish certain basic rights for individuals suffering from mental disorders. But they have also curtailed these rights, amid continuing controversy.

- *Right to treatment.* In 1972 a U.S. district court in Alabama rendered a landmark decision in the case of *Wyatt v. Stickney*. It ruled that a person with mental illness or a person with mental retardation had a right to receive treatment. Since that decision, the state of Alabama has increased its budget for the treatment of mental illness and mental retardation by 300 percent (see Winick, 1997).

- *Freedom from custodial confinement.* In 1975 the U.S. Supreme Court upheld the principle that patients have a right to freedom from custodial confinement if they are not dangerous to themselves or others and if they can safely survive outside of custody. In *Donaldson v. O'Connor*, the defendants were required to pay Donaldson $10,000 for having kept him in custody without providing treatment.

- *Right to compensation for work.* In 1973 a U.S. district court ruled in the case of *Souder v. Brennan* (the secretary of labor) that a patient in a nonfederal mental institution who performed work must be paid according to the Fair Labor Standards Act. Although a 1978 Supreme Court ruling nullified the part of the lower court's decision dealing with state hospitals, the ruling still applies to people with mental illness and patients with mental retardation in private facilities.

- *Right to live in a community.* In 1974 a U.S. district court decided, in the case of *Staff v. Miller*, that released state mental hospital patients have a right to live in "adult homes" in the community.

- *Right to less restrictive treatment.* In 1975 a U.S. district court issued a landmark decision in the case of *Dixon v. Weinberger*. The ruling established the right of individuals to receive treatment in less restrictive facilities than mental institutions.

- *Right to legal counsel at commitment hearings.* The Wisconsin State Supreme Court decided in 1976, in the case of *Memmel v. Mundy*, that an individual has the right to legal counsel during the commitment process.

- *Right to refuse treatment.* Several court decisions have provided rulings, and some states have enacted legislation, permitting patients to refuse certain treatments such as electroconvulsive therapy and psychosurgery.

- *The need for confinement must be shown by clear, convincing evidence.* In 1979 the U.S. Supreme Court ruled, in the case of *Addington v. Texas*, that a person's need to be kept in an institution must be based on demonstrable evidence.

- *Limitation on patients' rights to refuse psychotropic medication.* In 1990 the U.S. Supreme Court ruled, in *Washington v. Harper*, that a Washington State prison could override a disturbed prisoner's refusal of psychotropic medications. This decision was based on a finding that the prison's review process adequately protected the patient's rights. We see in this instance that changes in the national political climate can reverse prior trends that favored patients' rights.

Sources: Grounds (2000), Mrad & Watson (2011), Saks (2004), and Swartz, Swanson, & Elbogen (2004).

Which cases have been most helpful for establishing the rights of those suffering from mental disorders?

commit crimes, whether or not they have a psychological disorder, are dealt with primarily through the judicial system—arrest, court trial, and, if convicted, possible confinement in a penal institution. People who are judged to be potentially dangerous because of their psychological state may, after **civil commitment** procedures, be confined in a mental institution. The steps in the commitment process vary slightly depending on state law, the locally available community mental health resources, the nature of the problem, and the way in which the need for commitment is communicated to the court (Evans & Salekin, 2013). For example, commitment procedures for a person who is intellectually disabled are different from those for a person whose problem is alcohol abuse.

There is a distinction between voluntary hospitalization and involuntary commitment. In most cases, people accept the option of voluntary commitment or hospitalization. In these cases, they can, with sufficient notice, leave the hospital if they wish. But in cases where a person may be considered dangerous or unable to provide for her or his own care, the need for involuntary commitment may arise (Zerman & Schwartz, 1998).

Being mentally ill is not sufficient grounds for placing a person in a mental institution against his or her will. Although procedures vary somewhat from state to state, several conditions beyond mental illness usually must be met before formal involuntary commitment can occur (Simon & Aaronson, 1988). In brief, such individuals must be judged to be:

- Dangerous to themselves or to others and/or
- Incapable of providing for their basic physical needs and/or
- Unable to make responsible decisions about hospitalization and
- In need of treatment or care in a hospital

Typically, filing a petition for a commitment hearing is the first step in the process of committing a person involuntarily. This petition is usually filed by a concerned individual such as a relative, physician, or mental health professional. When such a petition is filed, a judge appoints two examiners to evaluate the proposed patient. In Minnesota, for example, one examiner must be a physician (not necessarily a psychiatrist); the other can be a psychiatrist or a psychologist. The patient is asked to appear voluntarily for psychiatric examination before the commitment hearing. The hearing must be held within 14 days of the original petition filing date, which can be extended to 30 more days if good cause for the extension can be shown. The law requires that the court-appointed examiners interview the patient before the hearing.

When a person is committed to a mental hospital for treatment, the hospital must report to the court within 60 days on whether the person needs to be confined even longer. If the hospital gives no report, the patient must be released. If the hospital indicates that the person needs further treatment, then the commitment period becomes indeterminate, subject to periodic reevaluations.

Because the decision to commit a person is based on the conclusions of others about the person's capabilities and her or his potential for dangerous behavior, the civil commitment process leaves open the possibility of the unwarranted violation of a person's civil rights. As a consequence, most states have stringent safeguards to ensure that any person who is the subject of a petition for commitment is granted due process, including rights to formal hearings with representation by legal counsel. If there is no time to get a court order for commitment or if there is imminent danger, however, the law allows emergency hospitalization without a formal commitment hearing. In such cases, a physician must sign a statement saying that an imminent danger exists. The patient can then be picked up (usually by the police) and detained under a "hold order," usually not to exceed 72 hours, unless a petition for commitment is filed within that period. As mentioned earlier, involuntary commitment in a psychiatric facility is largely contingent on a determination that a person is dangerous and requires confinement out of a need to protect himself or herself or society. Once committed, a patient may refuse treatment—a situation that mental health professionals working in psychiatric facilities often face.

We now turn to the important issue of evaluating patients in terms of potential dangerousness. (For a discussion of prisoners who are released from prison and then returned because of other offenses, see the World Around Us box.)

Assessment of "Dangerousness"

Although most psychiatric patients are not considered dangerous, some are violent and require close supervision—perhaps confinement until they are no longer dangerous. Rates of assaultiveness vary from setting to setting, but in all reported studies the overall number of assaultive patients is relatively low. An increasing number of clinical researchers in recent years have discovered that a history of violent behavior and some classes of mental disorder appear to be associated with violence (Pinard & Pagani, 2001). Although most people with mental disorders reportedly show no tendency toward violence (Lamberg, 1998), an increased risk of violence appears more likely among some who are experiencing symptoms of psychosis (Hodgins & Lalonde, 1999). The disorders that have an increased risk for violent behavior include schizophrenia, mania, personality disorder, substance abuse, and the rarer conditions of organic brain injury and Huntington's disease. One study from Finland (Eronen et al., 1996) reported

The World Around Us

Controversial Not Guilty Pleas: Can Altered Mind States or Personality Disorder Limit Responsibility for a Criminal Act?

If a person commits a capital offense when his or her consciousness and reason are impaired, as in an altered state, should he or she be held responsible for the crime? Can using psychotropic medicine such as Prozac or Zoloft "poison" a person's mind to such an extreme degree that she or he commits murder? If a murder is committed while someone is heavily "sedated"—for example, with Xanax or Halcion—should that person be released from criminal responsibility because he or she was involuntarily intoxicated with medications prescribed by a health professional? If a person experiences "multiple personalities" and a crime is committed by one personality, should all of the personalities suffer the consequences? These defense strategies are interesting and controversial challenges to today's legal system.

Altered States of Consciousness

In a civil trial, the jury failed to find the manufacturer of Prozac (Eli Lilly) liable in court action that resulted from a 1989 mass murder allegedly committed "under the influence" of Prozac. The murderer, Joseph Wesbecker, in a rage against his employer, killed 8 people and wounded 12 others before killing himself. Survivors and family members of several people who were killed in the incident filed a suit against Eli Lilly because the killer was taking the drug Prozac at the time of the murders and because the drug was alleged to be responsible for "intoxicating" the assassin and lowering his inhibitions. After a long trial, the jury found in favor of the manufacturer (*Fentress et al. v. Shea Communications et al.*, 1990).

Courts have generally not considered altered states of consciousness such as being intoxicated on drugs or alcohol sufficient grounds for an insanity defense because of the issue of volition— that is, that the perpetrator of the crime consciously chose to become intoxicated in the first place. However, the question of intoxication by drugs that were taken for the purpose of medication has added a new dimension to the defense. This issue has not been fully resolved in the court system.

Altered Personality States

Possibly the most fascinating of controversial insanity pleas are those raised by the phenomenon of dissociative identity disorder (DID), formerly known as multiple personality disorder, which has become a more common diagnosis in recent years (American Psychiatric Association, 2013; Brand et al., 2014). Although some professionals dispute even the existence of such a condition, others find it a credible and defensible diagnostic classification (Dorahy et al., 2014). Thus, this diagnostic disorder is, at times, used as a plausible argument for a plea of not guilty by reason of insanity.

The general nature of the problem can be stated quite succinctly: Within a legal system strongly oriented to the precise identification of individual responsibility for acts, what, if any, are the limits of the assignment of responsibility and sanctions for infractions of the law where the same physical space and body are occupied at different times by more than one distinct and legally recognizable person? Consider the following legal dilemmas:

- Who, among various copersonalities, is empowered to sign for withdrawals from a bank account?
- Are the provisions and obligations of a contract entered into by one constituent personality binding on all others regardless of their particular desires in the matter?
- Does the swearing of an oath, as in court, apply to the entire collection of personalities, or must each be sworn individually if she or he is to testify?
- In the case of a guilty verdict for the criminal act of a given personality, where other personalities did not acquiesce to the crime, how should punishment be fairly meted out?
- If no constituent personality meets a test of insanity, is it reasonable and lawful to declare DID itself an instance of insanity?
- Has rape occurred if the copersonalities of a 26-year-old woman who had acquiesced to intercourse included one or more personalities who had vehemently objected to it? (Such a case was prosecuted in Wisconsin in 1990.)
- And, of course, the most common real-life legal dilemma: Should an individual, as the primary personality, be held legally accountable for, say, a capital crime that evidence suggests may have actually been committed surreptitiously, so to speak, by an alter personality?

The scenario just mentioned has rather often been the contention underlying a plea of NGRI. Usually, as in the case of the "Hillside Strangler," Kenneth Bianchi (convicted of 12 rapes and murders in California and Washington States), and in the case of a woman who kidnapped a newborn from a hospital and later claimed that an alter personality had actually committed the crime (Appelbaum & Greer, 1994), the plea has failed. On a very few occasions, however, the NGRI plea has worked, as in the well-publicized 1978 case of Ohio resident Billy Milligan, who claimed to be host to 10 personalities and was accused of raping four women (*New York Times*, 1994).

The legal maneuvers inspired by the DID construct admittedly have a quality of whimsy about them. It is consequently difficult to convince most juries that the defendant was so taken over by an alter personality who perpetrated the crime that he or she should be absolved of guilt and responsibility.

Should individuals be able to use altered states of consciousness to explain the reason why he or she committed a crime and therefore get their sentence dropped or lessened? For example, can a person who committed a crime while taking a prescribed medication be found innocent then acquitted on grounds that he or she was not guilty by reason of insanity?

that homicidal behavior among former patients was considerably more frequent among patients with schizophrenia and even more common among patients with antisocial personality or alcoholism. In another study, psychiatric patients who abused alcohol (Steadman et al., 1998) were found to be notably violent.

Practitioners are often called on to evaluate the possibility that a patient might be dangerous, and there is some evidence that mental health professionals can contribute to such an assessment (Heilbrun & Holliday, 2013; Monahan, 2013), at least on a short-term basis (Binder, 1999). The determination that a patient is potentially dangerous can be difficult to make (Bauer et al., 2003), yet this is one of the most important responsibilities of professionals working in the fields of law and psychology (Larou, 2013). Scott and colleagues (2010) pointed out that the accuracy of a clinician's assessment of future violence is determined by many factors, such as the circumstances of the evaluation and the length of time over which violence is predicted. When asked to perform an evaluation of dangerousness in a client, a clinician has a clear responsibility to try to protect the public from potential violence or other uncontrolled behavior of dangerous patients.

ATTEMPTS TO PREDICT DANGEROUSNESS It is very difficult—for professionals and laypersons alike—to accurately appraise "dangerousness" in some individuals

Prediction of aggressive behavior is an important but not necessarily an easy task to accomplish in our society.

(Heilbrun, 2009). The complex problem of risk assessment or prediction of dangerousness can be likened to predicting the weather. "Ultimately, the goal of a warning system in mental health law is the same as the goal of a warning system in meteorology: to maximize the number of people who take appropriate and timely actions for the safety of life and property" (Monahan & Steadman, 1997, p. 937).

It is usually easy to determine, after the fact, that a person has demonstrated dangerous behavior, but how well do mental health professionals do in predicting the occurrence of dangerous acts? Not as well as we would like (Edens et al., 2005). Violent acts are particularly difficult to predict because they are apparently determined as much by situational circumstances (for example, whether a person is under the influence of alcohol) as by an individual's personality traits or violent predispositions. One obvious and significantly predictive risk factor is a past history of violence (Burke, 2010; Megargee, 2009), but clinicians are not always able to unearth this type of background information.

As already noted, some types of patients, particularly individuals with active schizophrenia and mania (Hodgins & Lalonde, 1999) and patients with well-entrenched delusions (de Pauw & Szulecka, 1988), are far more likely than others to commit violent acts. Martell and Dietz (1992) reported a study of persons convicted of pushing or attempting to push unsuspecting victims in front of New York City subway trains and found that most were both psychotic and homeless at the time of the act. Norko and Baranoski (2005) noted that although many studies point to a modest increased risk of violence associated with mental illness, particularly psychosis, other studies have not confirmed these findings.

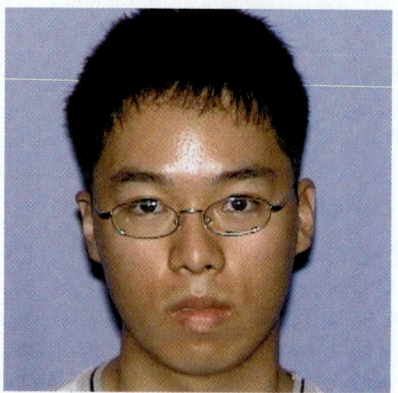

Student Seung Hui-Cho, the mass murderer responsible for the Virginia Tech massacre in 2007, was known to have severe mental health problems and was considered to be potentially dangerous.

Expert testimony to establish dangerousness or future violence in offenders has become an important part of the U.S. legal system. However, the prediction of dangerousness is often questionable (Krauss & Lieberman, 2007).

Mental health professionals typically overpredict violence and consider felons to be more dangerous than they actually are, and usually predict a greater percentage of clients to be dangerous than actually become involved in violent acts (Megargee, 2009). Such a tendency is, of course, understandable from the perspective of the practitioner, considering the potentially serious consequences of releasing a violent individual. It is likely, however, that many innocent patients thereby experience a violation of their civil rights. Given a certain irreducible level of uncertainty in the prediction of violence, it is not obvious how this dilemma can be completely resolved.

THE DUTY TO PROTECT: IMPLICATIONS OF THE *TARASOFF* DECISION

What should a therapist do upon learning that a patient is planning to harm another person? Can the therapist violate the legally sanctioned confidence of the therapy contract and take action to prevent the patient from committing the act? Today, in most states, the therapist not only can violate confidentiality with impunity but also may be required by law to take action to protect people from the threat of imminent violence against them. In its original form, this requirement was conceived as a duty to warn the prospective victim.

The duty-to-warn legal doctrine was given great impetus in a 1976 California court ruling in the case of *Tarasoff v. Regents of the University of California et al.* (Mills et al., 1987). In this case, Prosenjit Poddar was being seen in outpatient psychotherapy by a psychologist at the university mental health facility. During his treatment, Mr. Poddar indicated that he intended to kill his former girlfriend, Tatiana Tarasoff, when she returned from vacation. Concerned about the threat, the psychologist discussed the case with his supervisors, and they agreed that Poddar was dangerous and should be committed for further observation and treatment. They informed the campus police, who picked up Poddar for questioning, subsequently judged him to be rational, and released him after he promised to leave Ms. Tarasoff alone. Poddar then terminated treatment with the psychologist. About 2 months thereafter, he stabbed Ms. Tarasoff to death. Her parents later sued the University of California and staff members involved in the case for their failure to hospitalize Poddar and their failure to warn Tarasoff about the threat to her life. In due course, the California Supreme Court in 1974 ruled that the defendants were not liable for failing to hospitalize Poddar; it did, however, find them liable for failing to warn the victim. Ironically, Prosenjit Poddar, the criminal, served 5 years in prison but was released on a trial technicality and returned home to India. In a later analysis of the case, Knapp (1980) says that the court ruled that difficulty in determining dangerousness does not exempt a psychotherapist from attempting to protect others when a determination of dangerousness exists. The court acknowledged that confidentiality was important to the psychotherapeutic relationship but stated that the protection privilege ends where public peril begins.

The duty-to-warn ruling—which has come to be known as the *Tarasoff* decision—spelled out a therapist's responsibility in situations where there has been an explicit threat on a specific person's life, but it left other areas of application unclear. For example, does this ruling apply in cases where a patient threatens to commit suicide, and how might the therapist's responsibility be met in such a case? What, if anything, should a therapist do when the target of violence is not clearly named—for example, when global threats are made? Would the duty-to-warn ruling hold up in other states? Or might deleterious effects on patient–therapist relationships outweigh any public benefit to be derived from the duty to warn? Responding to mounting pressures for clarification, chiefly from professional mental health organizations, the California Supreme Court in 1976 issued a revised opinion called the "duty to warn doctrine." In this decision the court ruled that the duty was to protect, rather than specifically to warn, the prospective victim, but it left vague the question of how this duty might be discharged—presumably in order to give practitioners latitude in dealing with danger to third parties. Meanwhile, however, numerous other lawsuits in other jurisdictions have been filed and adjudicated in inconsistent and confusing ways (Mills et al., 1987).

The many perplexing issues for practitioners left in the wake of *Tarasoff* were partly resolved, at least in California, by the legislature's adoption in 1985 of a new state law essentially establishing that the duty to protect is discharged if the therapist makes "reasonable efforts" to inform potential victims and an appropriate law enforcement agency of the pending threat. The *Tarasoff* ruling was extended in 2004 (*Ewing v. Goldstein*, 2004) when the California Court of Appeals ruled that a communication from a patient's family member constitutes a "patient communication" that can trigger the therapist's duty to protect.

In other court jurisdictions, however, the inconsistent judicial fallout from *Tarasoff* has continued and has been a source of much anxiety and confusion among mental health professionals, many of whom continue to believe, on ethical and clinical grounds, that strict confidentiality is an absolute and inviolable trust. Some states—for example, Maryland, Texas, and Pennsylvania—have explicitly affirmed that position, abandoning *Tarasoff* altogether, while 33 U.S. jurisdictions impose a duty to warn, although the criteria for this typically vary (Barbee et al., 2007). Eleven states have made the duty to warn discretionary. There has been considerable debate over the need and utility of the *Tarasoff* ruling, and some authorities have raised questions about its survivability as a law (Bersoff, 2014; Quattrocchi & Schopp, 2005).

Official professional ethics codes, such as that of the American Psychological Association (2002), normally compel compliance with relevant laws regardless of one's personal predilections. Where the law is itself vague or equivocal, however, as it often is in this area, there is much room for individual interpretation (Kachigian & Felthous, 2004). Today there is considerable confusion among practitioners about their responsibility with regard to the rules of their state with respect to the *Tarasoff* ruling. One survey of clinicians found that 76 percent of practitioners failed to correctly identify their state's duty-to-protect law from a multiple-choice list (Pabian et al., 2009). Therapists are at great risk of a lawsuit for failing to deal with the risk of danger posed by some clients (Caudill, 2009).

The Insanity Defense

Some people who are being tried for murder use the **insanity defense**—also known as the **NGRI plea** ("not guilty by reason of insanity")—in an attempt to escape the legally prescribed consequences of their crimes (Chappell, 2010; Sadoff & Dattilio, 2011). These defendants claim that they

Jeffrey Dahmer was torturing and drowning cats and dogs by age 7. He never heard voices or broke with reality. He tricked his victims into being handcuffed (they thought it was part of a sexual game) and then dripped acid into their flesh and skulls, rendering them zombies. Then he would engage them sexually and would occasionally cannibalize them. Dahmer was charged with and later convicted of murder after body parts of several young men were found in his apartment. While serving his time in prison, he was bludgeoned to death by a psychotic killer in 1994.

were not legally responsible for their criminal acts. In technical legal terms, they invoke the ancient doctrine that their acts, while guilty ones (*actus rea*), lacked moral blameworthiness because they were not intentional since the defendants did not possess their full mental faculties at the time of the crime and did not "know what they were doing" (*mens rea*)—the underlying assumption being that "insanity" somehow precludes or absolves the harboring of a guilty intent. One of the most notorious uses of the not guilty by reason of insanity plea in American history was in the case of Jeffrey Dahmer, on trial for the murder, dismemberment, and cannibalization of 15 men in Milwaukee. In the Dahmer case, the planned insanity defense proved unsuccessful, which is the usual outcome (Steadman et al., 1993).

By contrast, attorneys for John Hinckley, who shot President Reagan and his press secretary, James Brady, in early 1981, successfully pleaded not guilty by reason of insanity (see the case study). The outcome of the Hinckley case was different from the Dahmer case in a number of important respects because the jury in this instance considered the defendant to be acting "outside of reason" and found him NGRI. At trial in June 1982, Hinckley was acquitted on those grounds. This verdict immediately unleashed a storm of public protest and generated widespread, often hasty attempts to reform the law to make the NGRI defense a less attractive option to defendants and their attorneys. Hinckley himself was committed to the care of a federally operated, high-security mental hospital, to be involuntarily detained there until such time as his disorder remits sufficiently that his release would not constitute a danger to himself or others. He remains incarcerated; however, under a 1999 federal appeals court ruling, Hinckley has been able to take supervised day trips off hospital grounds, and most recently was allowed to spend several weeks at his mother's home. However, his "recovery" continues to be questioned. Psychiatric testimony (Associated Press, 2003) has indicated that Hinckley still suffers from the same narcissistic personality disorder that drove him to shoot Reagan and three others in 1981.

Hinckley's Successful Insanity Plea

On March 30, 1981, in an apparent scheme to attract the attention of actress Jodie Foster, with whom he was obsessed, John Hinckley, Jr., shot six bullets at President Ronald Reagan in an assassination attempt. President Reagan was seriously injured, as was Press Secretary James Brady. At the end of his trial in 1982, Hinckley was found not guilty by reason of insanity. Since his trial, Hinckley has been confined to St. Elizabeth's Hospital in Washington, D.C. After what seemed to be significant improvement in his mental health, Hinckley was allowed unsupervised visits in April 2000, but these visits were revoked when guards discovered a smuggled book on Jodie Foster in his room.

Releasing Hinckley from custody would almost certainly bring forth another public outcry demanding abolition or limitation of the insanity defense. This unfortunate public outrage at all insanity defense pleas results from a persistent failure of legal scholars to examine critically and rigorously the guilt-absolving insanity construct and the *mens rea* doctrine from which it derives.

In recent years the use of the NGRI defense in trials where the defendant's life is at stake has been surrounded by controversy, largely owing to the uproar created by the outcome of the Hinckley trial (Steadman et al., 1993). Some have contended that the objection to the insanity defense in capital crimes might reflect negative social attitudes toward the insane (Perlin, 1996). There has been some concern, especially in cases of high visibility, that guilty defendants may feign mental disorder and hence avoid criminal responsibility. Good defense attorneys are of course aware of this public cynicism, which is likely to be shared by juries. They attempt to counteract it in various ways, often by portraying their purportedly "insane at the time of the act" clients as having been themselves victims of heinous and traumatic acts at an earlier time in their lives. Some of them undoubtedly were victimized, but the strategy of creating sympathy while offering a plausible explanation for the "insane" act would have a compelling attraction in any case. On the other hand, the insanity defense is often not employed where it is appropriate, as it would have been, for example, in two high-visibility cases: those of John Salvi (the abortion clinic assassin) and Theodore Kaczynski (the Unabomber). Apparently neither defendant wanted his mental state to be a part of the proceedings. Severe delusional disorder is likely to have played a significant role in both of their crimes. (There have been notable efforts to fake the insanity defense to avoid punishment; see the following case study.)

Detected Faking of the Insanity Defense

Michael McDermott testified that Michael the Archangel had sent him on a mission to prevent the Holocaust when he gunned down seven coworkers on December 26, 2000. McDermott also stated that he believed he was soulless and that by killing he would earn a soul. McDermott claimed to have been raped by a neighbor when he was a young boy and had a history of paranoia and suicide attempts. Despite this claim of insanity, a jury found McDermott guilty in the shooting deaths of his seven coworkers. The prosecution argued that McDermott was motivated to kill because his employer was about to deduct from his wages back taxes owed to the IRS. Evidence seized from his computer showed that McDermott had researched how to fake being mentally ill. McDermott is currently serving seven consecutive life sentences for his crimes.

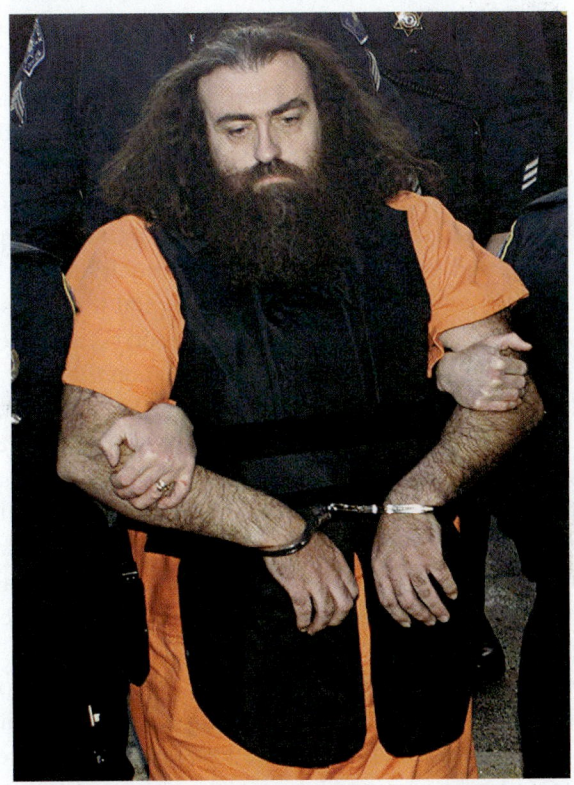

In some cases in some states, individuals with psychosis who fail to meet the standards set for the NGRI plea and are convicted of murder can receive the death sentence even though they were actually psychologically disturbed at the time of the crime and remain so as the execution approaches. An appeals process can be effective at showing that there may be extenuating circumstances that warrant softening the sentence on grounds that the death penalty would be cruel and unusual punishment because of the person's severe mental health problems or mental retardation (Ashford & Kupferberg, 2013). Pirelli and colleagues (2011) conducted an analysis of the results of 68 studies that compared competent and incompetent defendants on a number of variables. The most robust findings were that defendants who were diagnosed with a psychotic disorder were about eight times more likely to be found incompetent than defendants without a psychotic disorder diagnosis. The likelihood of being found incompetent was approximately double for unemployed defendants as compared to employed defendants. Defendants who had a previous psychiatric hospitalization were about twice more likely to be found not guilty by reason of insanity than those without a hospitalization history.

There have been cases in which a failed use of the NGRI plea led to greater punishment. In one recent case (*United States v. Batista*, 2007), a defendant in a murder trial intentionally feigned mental illness in an effort to avoid prison. His charade was discovered and he actually received an enhanced sentence after the trial because of his abuse of mental health protections in the legal system.

Despite some features that make it an appealing option to consider, especially when the undisputed facts are strongly aligned against the defendant, the NGRI defense has actually been employed quite rarely—in less than 2 percent of capital cases in the United States over time (Lymburner & Roesch, 1999; Steadman et al., 1993). Studies have confirmed, however, that in some jurisdictions, persons acquitted of crimes by reason of insanity spend less time, on the whole, in a psychiatric hospital than persons who are convicted of crimes spend in prison (Lymburner & Roesch, 1999) even though the determination that they are no longer dangerous might be difficult to ascertain. In addition, states differ widely in the amount of time that persons found not guilty by reason of insanity are actually confined. For example, one study by Callahan and Silver (1998) reported that in the states of Ohio and Maryland nearly all persons acquitted as NGRI have been released within 5 years, whereas in Connecticut and New York conditional release has been much more difficult to obtain. The rearrest rates for freed NGRI claimants vary, with some studies reporting rates as high as 50 percent (Callahan & Silver, 1998; Wiederanders et al., 1997), while lower rearrest rates can be obtained by carefully monitoring released inmates (Vitacco et al., 2014). Monson and colleagues (2001) conducted a follow-up of 125 NGRI acquittees and found a similarly high rearrest rate. These investigators reported that persons discharged to live with their family of origin or to live alone or in semi-independent living were more likely to maintain their conditional release and not reoffend. These investigators also reported that such factors as minority status, comorbid substance abuse, and prior criminal history were associated with return to custody after release. One study in which an active community treatment program was implemented reported low rearrest rates (1.4 percent) and moderate rehospitalization rates (14 percent) (G. F. Parker, 2004).

Up to this point in the discussion, we have used the term *insanity defense* loosely. We must now become more attentive to the many precise legal nuances involved. Established precedents that define the insanity defense are as follows:

1. **The *M'Naghten* rule (1843).** Under this ruling, which is often referred to as the "knowing right from wrong" rule, people are assumed to be sane unless it can be proved that at the time of committing the act they were laboring under such a defect of reason (from a disease of the mind) that they did not know the nature and quality of the act they were doing—or, if they did know they were committing the act, they did not know that what they were doing was wrong.

2. **The irresistible impulse rule (1887).** A second precedent in the NGRI defense is the doctrine of the "irresistible impulse." This view holds that accused persons might not be responsible for their acts—even when they knew that what they were doing was wrong (according to the *M'Naghten* rule)—if they had lost the power to choose between right and wrong. That is, they could not avoid doing the act in question because they were compelled beyond their will to commit the act.

3. **The Durham rule.** In 1954, Judge David Bazelon, in a decision of the U.S. Court of Appeals, broadened the insanity defense further. Bazelon did not believe that the previous precedents allowed for a sufficient application of established scientific knowledge of mental illness and proposed a test that would be based on this knowledge. Under this rule, which is often referred to as the "product test," the accused is not criminally responsible if her or his unlawful act was the product of mental disease or mental defect.

4. **The American Law Institute (ALI) standard (1962).** Often referred to as the "substantial capacity test" for insanity, this test combines the cognitive aspect of *M'Naghten* with the volitional focus of irresistible impulse in holding that the perpetrator is not legally responsible if at the time of the act he or she, owing to mental disease or defect, lacked "substantial capacity" either to appreciate the act's criminal character or to conform his or her behavior to the law's requirements.

5. **The federal Insanity Defense Reform ACT (IDRA).** Adopted by Congress in 1984 as the standard for the insanity defense to be applied in all federal jurisdictions, this act abolished the volitional element of the ALI standard and modified the cognitive standard to read "unable to appreciate," thus bringing the definition quite close to *M'Naghten*. IDRA also specified that the mental disorder involved must be a severe one and shifted the burden of proof from the prosecution to the defense. That is, the defense must clearly and convincingly establish the defendant's

insanity, in contrast to the prior requirement that the prosecution clearly and convincingly demonstrate the defendant to have been sane when the prohibited act was committed.

This shifting of the burden of proof for the insanity defense, by the way, had been instituted by many states in the wake of the Hinckley acquittal. The intent of this reform was to discourage use of the insanity defense, and it proved quite effective in altering litigation practices in the intended direction (Steadman et al., 1993).

At the present time, most states and the District of Columbia subscribe to a version of either the ALI or the more restrictive *M'Naghten* standard. New York is a special case. It uses a version of *M'Naghten* to define insanity, with the burden of proof on the defense, but an elaborate procedural code has been enacted to promote fairness in outcomes while ensuring lengthy and restrictive hospital commitment for defendants judged to be dangerous; this approach appears to have worked well (Steadman et al., 1993). In some jurisdictions, when an insanity plea is filed, the case is submitted for pretrial screening, which includes a psychiatric evaluation, review of records, and appraisal of criminal responsibility. In one study of 190 defendants who entered a plea of not criminally responsible, the following outcomes were obtained: 105 were judged to be criminally responsible, charges against 34 were dropped, and 8 defendants were agreed by both the prosecution and the defense to be insane and not responsible. A total of 134 withdrew their insanity pleas (Janofsky et al., 1996). The insanity defense was noted in this study to be somewhat of a "rich man's defense" in that such cases involved private attorneys rather than public defenders.

Silver (1995) found that the successful use of the NGRI defense varied widely among states. In addition, Silver reports that the length of confinement was related more to the judged seriousness of the crime than to whether the person was employing the NGRI defense. One study (Cirinclone et al., 1995) found that an NGRI plea was most likely to be successful if one or more of the following factors were present:

- A diagnosed mental disorder, particularly a major mental disorder
- A female defendant
- The violent crime was other than murder
- There had been prior mental hospitalizations

Three states—Idaho, Montana, and Utah—have entirely abolished the attribution of insanity as an acceptable defense for wrongdoing—a somewhat more harsh or severe solution that compensates in clarity for what some feel it lacks in compassion. As expected, with the disappearance of the insanity acquittals in Montana, there was a corresponding rise in the use of the "incompetent to stand trial" plea (see the following section), in which the charges were actually dismissed, largely negating the desired result (more effective prosecution) of doing away with the insanity defense (Callahan et al., 1995).

How, then, is guilt or innocence determined? Many authorities believe that the insanity defense sets the courts an impossible task—determining guilt or innocence by reason of insanity on the basis of psychiatric testimony. In some cases, conflicting testimony has resulted because both the prosecution and the defense have their own panel of expert psychiatric witnesses, who are in complete disagreement (see discussion by Lareau, 2007).

Finally, states have adopted the optional plea and verdict of **guilty but mentally ill (GBMI)**. In these cases, a defendant may be sentenced but placed in a treatment facility rather than in a prison. This two-part judgment serves to prevent the type of situation in which a person commits a murder, is found not guilty by reason of insanity, is turned over to a mental health facility, is found to be rational and in no further need of treatment by the hospital staff, and is unconditionally released to the community after only a minimal period of confinement. Under the two-part decision, such a person would remain in the custody of the correctional department until the full sentence has been served. Marvit (1981) has suggested that this approach might "realistically balance the interest of the mentally ill offender's rights and the community's need to control criminal behavior" (p. 23). However, others have argued that the GBMI defense is confusing to jurors and should be eliminated (Melville & Naimark, 2002). Interestingly, in Georgia, one of the states adopting this option, GBMI defendants receive longer sentences and longer periods of confinement than those who plead NGRI and lose. Overall, outcomes from the use of the GBMI standard, which is often employed in a plea-bargaining strategy, have been disappointing (Steadman et al., 1993).

Competence to Stand Trial

There is, in English common law, a principle that a person charged with a crime must be **competent to stand trial** (Fogel et al., 2013; Stafford & Sadoff, 2011). If someone is charged with a crime and is considered to be unable to understand the trial proceedings as a result of intellectual deficit or mental health problems, that person can be hospitalized until her or his mental state is judged to be improved sufficiently for the person to be considered competent to stand trial. Several factors can influence a court decision that the defendant in a case is not competent to stand trial. Both cognitive abilities (such as capability in making decisions, having a working memory, being able to attend to proceedings, and being able to process events successfully) and psychiatric symptoms (psychoticism, withdrawal, depression, hostility) can be crucial factors in a person being able to stand trial.

In May 2011, a federal court judge ruled that Jared Loughner was not competent to stand trial for shooting Congresswoman Gabrielle Giffords and killing six others (Harris, 2011). This court decision was based on the opinion of expert witness psychiatrists from both the defense and prosecution who examined Loughner. The defendant was held in a federal hospital for prisoners in Springfield, Illinois, until it was determined that he was able to stand trial. In August 2012, after treatment for mental health problems, Loughner was judged to be mentally able to stand trial. He pleaded guilty to the criminal charges (Santos, 2012). In exchange for his guilty plea, the government agreed not to seek the death penalty.

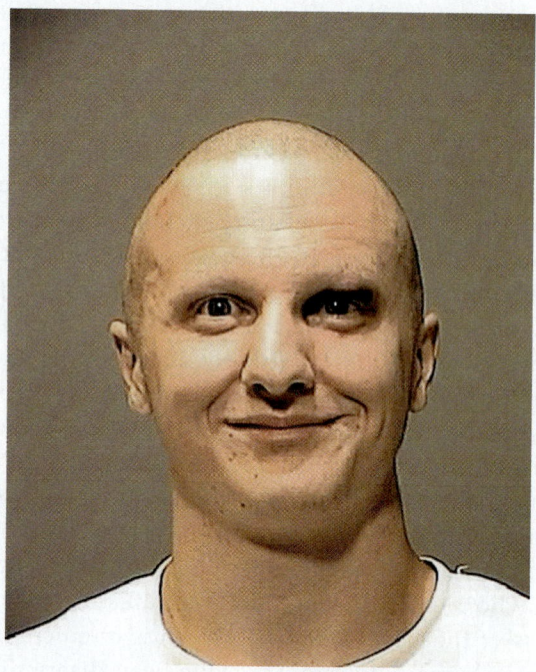

Jared Loughner, who killed six people and severely wounded Congresswoman Gabriel Giffords in May 2011, was determined to be not competent to stand trial as a result of his mental disorder. In August 2012, after treatment for mental health problems, Loughner was judged to be mentally able to stand trial. He pleaded guilty to the criminal charges. In exchange for his guilty plea, the government agreed not to seek the death penalty.

Research has underscored the role of cognitive deficits or mental health problems in determining a defendant's competence to stand trial. Ryba and Zapf (2011) recently reported that cognitive abilities accounted for higher scores for all three competence-related abilities than did the psychiatric symptoms, although there was an additive effect when these groups of variables were considered collectively. In a recent evaluation of the published literature on competence to stand trial, Pirelli and colleagues (2011) concluded that defendants who had been diagnosed as having a psychotic disorder were approximately eight times more

likely to be found incompetent than defendants without a psychotic disorder diagnosis. In addition, they found that defendants who had a previous psychiatric hospitalization, as compared with those never hospitalized, or had been unemployed, as compared to employed defendants, were more likely to be determined as incompetent to stand trial. Warren and colleagues (2013) found that about half of defendants who were being evaluated for competency to stand trial were likely to be restored to competency in the foreseeable future.

Does Having Mental Health Problems Result in Convicted Felons Being Returned to Prison After Being Released?

Given that many individuals with severe mental health problems are sentenced to prison terms and receive no mental health treatment while in prison, are they able to adjust to society once they are released? Are people with psychological disturbances who receive prison terms more vulnerable to maladjustment when they are freed from prison? Questions have been raised about the impact of mental health problems on the ability of convicted prisoners to successfully return to society if they are paroled, serve out their terms, or are released because they are believed to no longer be a threat to themselves or others in the case of a successful NGRI decision. Cloyes and colleagues (2010) evaluated parole violation rates among inmates who had significant mental health problems versus those who did not and found that there was a significant difference in return rates and community tenure for offenders with significant mental illness compared to inmates without mental health problems. They found that 23 percent of their sample of inmates with significant mental health problems returned to prison sooner than those without mental health problems.

Individuals who have been charged with a crime but found not guilty by reason of insanity can be released from confinement if or when they are no longer judged to be of danger to themselves or others. Although return to the community is not guaranteed for persons who are incarcerated after an NGRI plea, they can be released, and the state can determine explicit conditions for release, for example, follow-up mental health treatment, substance abuse treatment, and frequent monitoring. Some research has suggested that with conditional treatment and careful monitoring many people are able to return to society. However, the efficacy of treatment or careful monitoring has shown mixed results with many people being returned to confinement. Vitacco and colleagues (2008) found that 33.8 percent of inmates were returned to prison, with the majority of these being returned for failure to comply with treatment. When the amount of monitoring was taken into consideration, they found that those who were placed on higher restrictions and received closer monitoring had lower rates of return to confinement. Hiday and Burns (2010), in their evaluation of the role of mental illness in the criminal justice system, concluded that although the arrest rates and incarceration rates were higher for individuals with mental illness than the general population, most people with mental illness are not violent and only a small percentage of the population become violent.

in review

- What conditions must be met before an individual can be involuntarily committed to a mental institution? Describe the legal process that follows.
- What are the implications of the *Tarasoff* decision for practicing clinicians?
- What is the insanity (NGRI) defense in criminal cases?
- What is the federal Insanity Defense Reform Act? How does it differ from the *M'Naghten* rule?

Organized Efforts for Mental Health

17.4 Describe national and international organizations that promote efforts for mental health.

Public awareness of the magnitude of contemporary mental health problems and the interest of government, professional, and lay organizations have stimulated the development of programs directed at better understanding of mental health challenges, more effective treatment, and long-range prevention. Efforts to improve mental health are apparent not only in our society but also in many other countries, and they involve international as well as national and local organizations and approaches.

U.S. Efforts for Mental Health

In the United States in the eighteenth and nineteenth centuries, dealing with mental disorders was primarily the responsibility of state and local agencies. During World War II, however, the extent of mental disorders in the United States was brought to public attention when a large number of young men—two out of every seven recruits—were rejected for military service for psychiatric reasons. This discovery led to a variety of organized measures for taking care of people with mental illness.

THE FEDERAL GOVERNMENT AND MENTAL HEALTH In 1946, aware of the need for more research, training, and services in the field of mental health, Congress passed its first comprehensive mental health bill, the National Mental Health Act. In that same year, the NIMH was formed in Washington, D.C. The agency was to serve as a central research and training center and as headquarters for the administration of a grant-in-aid program designed to foster research and training elsewhere in the nation and to help state and local communities expand and improve their own mental health services. Congress authorized the institute to provide mental health project grants for experimental studies, pilot projects, surveys, and general research. Today the NIMH is a separate institute under the National Institutes of Health within the U.S. Department of Health and Human Services (NIMH, 2001).

The NIMH (1) conducts and supports research on the biological, psychosocial, and sociocultural aspects of mental disorders; (2) supports the training of professional and paraprofessional personnel in the mental health field; (3) helps communities plan, establish, and maintain more effective mental health programs; and (4) provides information on mental health to the public and the scientific community. Two companion institutes—the National Institute on Alcohol Abuse and Alcoholism (NIAAA) and the National Institute on Drug Abuse (NIDA)—perform comparable functions in these more specialized fields.

Although the federal government provides leadership and financial aid, the states and local organizations actually plan and run most NIMH programs. Most state and local governments, however, have not been able to fund programs and facilities because of cuts in federal support. As a result, many programs devoted to mental health training, research, and services have been greatly reduced or abandoned even as the need for them has increased. There is considerable uncertainty about the extent to which mental health problems will be included in forthcoming revisions of national health care policy and about the forms any such inclusion might take.

PROFESSIONAL ORGANIZATIONS AND MENTAL HEALTH A number of national professional organizations exist in the mental health field. These include the American Psychological Association (APA), the American Psychological Society (APS), the American Psychiatric Association (APA), the American Medical Association (AMA), the Association for Behavioral and Cognitive Therapies (ABCT), the International Association for Correctional and Forensic Psychology (IACFP), and the National Association of Social Workers (NASW).

A key function of professional organizations is the application of insights and methods to contemporary social problems—for example, by lobbying national and local government agencies to provide more services for underserved populations. Professional mental health organizations are in a unique position to serve as consultants on mental health problems and programs.

Another important function of these organizations is to set and maintain high professional and ethical standards within their specific areas. This function may include (1) establishing and reviewing training qualifications for professional and paraprofessional personnel; (2) setting standards and procedures for the accreditation of undergraduate and graduate training programs; (3) setting standards for the accreditation of clinics, hospitals, or other service operations and carrying out inspections to see that the standards are followed; and (4) investigating reported cases of unethical or unprofessional conduct and taking disciplinary action when necessary.

THE ROLE OF VOLUNTEER ORGANIZATIONS AND AGENCIES Although professional mental health personnel and organizations can give expert technical advice with regard to mental health needs and programs, informed citizens are essential in planning and implementing these programs. In fact, it is primarily concerned nonprofessionals who have blazed the trails in the mental health field.

Prominent among the many volunteer mental health agencies is the Mental Health America (formerly the National Mental Health Association). This organization was founded in 1909 by Clifford Beers as the National Association for Mental Health and has subsequently expanded through various mergers. Mental Health America works for the improvement of services in community clinics and mental hospitals; it helps recruit, train, and place volunteers for service in treatment and aftercare programs; and it works for enlightened mental health legislation and for the provision of needed facilities and personnel. It also offers special educational programs aimed at fostering positive mental health and helping people understand mental disorders. In addition, Mental Health America has been actively involved in many court decisions affecting patient rights (1997). In several cases, the organization has sponsored litigation or served as *amicus curiae* (friend of the court) in efforts to establish the rights of patients with mental illness to treatment, to freedom from custodial confinement, to freedom to live in the community, and to protection of their confidentiality.

The ARC, the largest national community-based organization advocating for people with intellectual and developmental disabilities, works to seek community and residential treatment centers and services for people with intellectual and developmental disabilities, and to carry on a program of education aimed at better public understanding of people with intellectual and developmental disabilities and greater support for legislation. The ARC also fosters scientific research into intellectual and developmental disabilities, recruitment and training of volunteer workers, and programs of community action.

These and other volunteer health organizations such as Alcoholics Anonymous and the National Alliance on Mental Illness (NAMI) need the backing of a wide constituency of knowledgeable and involved citizens in order to succeed.

MENTAL HEALTH RESOURCES IN PRIVATE INDUSTRY Personal problems—such as marital distress or other family problems, alcohol or drug abuse, financial difficulties, and job-related stress—can adversely affect employee morale and performance. Moreover, violence in the workplace has grown to be a common occurrence in our society (Kelloway et al., 2006) and often requires that employers take special steps to limit mental-health-related aggression.

Psychological difficulties among employees may result in numerous problems such as absenteeism, accident proneness, poor productivity, and high job turnover. The National Institute for Occupational Safety and Health (NIOSH) recognizes psychological disorders as 1 of the 10 leading work-related health problems, and work-related mental health risk factors may be increasing with changes in the economy, in technology, and in demographic factors in the workforce (Sauter et al., 1990). Research has shown, however, that persons with severe mental health problems can be integrated into the workplace if a supportive employment model is used to assist their involvement (Bond et al., 2007). Since the passage of the Americans with Disabilities Act, people with psychiatric problems cannot be discriminated against in the workplace. Employers are encouraged to alter the workplace as needed to accommodate the needs of individuals with mental illness. Although employers often object that it is too costly to hire people with psychiatric impairments, great benefits for society can result from integrating into productive jobs people who have disabilities but who also have appropriate skills (Kramer, 1998).

A great deal more research is needed to identify specific mental health risk factors in work situations. We already know (e.g., Harder et al., 2014) that serious, unrecognized problems may exist in the many areas of job design and conditions of work:

- *Workload and pace.* The critical factor here appears to be the degree of control the worker has over the pace of work rather than output demand. Machine-paced assembly work may be particularly hazardous to mental health.
- *Work schedule.* Rotating shifts and night work have been associated with elevated risk for psychological difficulties.
- *Role stressors.* Role ambiguity (such as uncertainty about who has responsibility for what), said to be common in many work situations, has a negative impact on mental and physical health, as does role conflict (incompatible role demands).

- *Career security factors.* Feelings of insecurity related to issues such as job future or obsolescence, career development, and encouragement of early retirement adversely affect mental and physical health.

- *Interpersonal relations.* Poor or unsupportive relationships among work colleagues significantly increase the risk of untoward psychological reactions.

- *Job content.* Poor mental health has been associated with work assignments involving fragmented, narrow, unvarying tasks that allow for little creativity and give the worker little sense of having contributed to the ultimate product.

Many corporations have recognized the importance of worker mental health and of enhancing mental health–promoting factors in the workplace, and some of them have acted on this knowledge. Some companies have expanded their "obligations" to employees to include appropriate psychological services. Employee assistance programs (EAPs) are means through which larger corporations can actively provide mental health services to employees and their family members (Finkel & Ryan, 2007; Sledge & Lazar, 2014).

International Efforts for Mental Health

Mental health is a major issue not only in the United States but also in the rest of the world. Indeed, many of the problems in this country with regard to the treatment of mental disorders are greatly magnified in poorer countries and countries with repressive governments. The severity of the world mental health problem is reflected in the World Health Organization's estimate that mental disorders affect more than 200 million people worldwide, partly because of the significant world refugee crisis (de Jong, 2002; Watters & Ingleby, 2004). Recognition of this great problem served to bring about the formation of several international organizations at the end of World War II. Here we will briefly discuss the World Health Organization (WHO) (2010) and the World Federation for Mental Health (WFMH).

THE WORLD HEALTH ORGANIZATION The WHO (2001) has always been keenly aware of the close interrelationships among biological, psychosocial, and sociocultural factors. Examples include the influence of rapid change and social disruption on both physical and mental health; the impossibility of major progress toward mental health in societies where a large proportion of the population suffers from malnutrition, parasites, and disease; and the frequent psychological and cultural barriers to successful programs in family planning and public health (Rutz, 2001).

Formed after World War II as part of the United Nations (UN) system, WHO's earliest focus was on physical diseases; it has helped make dramatic progress toward the conquest of such ancient scourges as smallpox and malaria. Over the years, mental health, too, has become an increasing concern among the member countries. WHO's goals are to integrate mental health resources to deal with the broad problems of overall health and socioeconomic development that many member countries face (WHO, 2010).

Another important contribution of WHO has been its *International Classification of Diseases* (ICD), which enables clinicians and researchers in different countries to use a uniform set of diagnostic categories. As discussed in Chapter 4, the American Psychiatric Association's diagnostic classification system has been coordinated with the WHO's *ICD-10* classification (Sartorius et al., 1993). Currently *ICD-10* is undergoing revision and is slated for publication in 2017.

THE WORLD FEDERATION FOR MENTAL HEALTH The WFMH was established in 1948 as an international congress of nongovernmental organizations and individuals concerned with mental health. Its purpose is to promote international cooperation among governmental and nongovernmental mental health agencies, and its membership now extends to more than 94 countries (Brody, 2004). The federation has been granted consultative status by WHO, and it assists UN agencies by collecting information on mental health conditions all over the world (World Federation for Mental Health, 2013).

The last century witnessed an amazing openness and a lowering of previously impassable barriers among nations. Along with this increased interchange of ideas and cooperation, we expect to see a broader mental health collaboration. It is vital that greater international cooperation in the sciences and in health planning continue, along with more sharing of information and views on mental health.

---

in review

- What is the role of the National Institute of Mental Health in providing care for people with mental illness?
- What is the Mental Health America group, and how does it contribute to improvement in mental health services?
- What major contributions has the World Health Organization made to improve mental health services?

Challenges for the Future

17.5 Address the challenges that people face in advancing mental health improvement in contemporary societies.

Even though international cooperation in efforts to understand and enhance mental health is encouraging, the media confront us daily with the stark truth that we have a long way to go before our dreams of a better world are realized. Many people question whether the United States or any other technologically advanced nation can achieve improvements in mental health for the majority of its citizens in our time. Racism, poverty, youth violence, terrorism, the uprooting of developing world populations, and other social problems that contribute to mental disorder sometimes seem insurmountable.

Other events in the rest of the world affect us also, both directly and indirectly. Worldwide economic instability and shortages and the possibility of the destruction of our planet's life ecology breed widespread anxiety about the future. The vast resources we have spent on military programs during the past half century to protect against perceived threats have absorbed funds and energy that otherwise might have been devoted to meeting human and social needs here and elsewhere in the world. The limited resources we are now willing to allocate to mental health problems prevent our solving major problems resulting from drug and alcohol abuse, homelessness, broken families, and squalid living conditions.

The Need for Planning

The Institute of Medicine (2006) recently reported that sweeping quality improvements are needed in the U.S. mental health care system. The report noted that only 20 percent of people with substance abuse or dependency and only 40 percent of people with serious mental illness actually receive treatment for their problems. If mental health problems are going to be reduced or eliminated, it is imperative that more effective planning be done at community, national, and international levels. Many challenges must be met if we are to create a better world for ourselves and future generations. Without slackening our efforts to meet needs at home, we will probably find it essential to participate more broadly in international measures aimed at reducing group tensions and promoting mental health and a better world for people everywhere. At the same time, we can expect that the measures we undertake to reduce international conflict and improve the general condition of humankind will make a significant contribution to our own nation's social progress and mental health. Both kinds of measures will require understanding and moral commitment from concerned citizens.

Within our own country and the rest of the industrialized world, progress in prolonging life has brought with it burgeoning problems in the prevalence of disorders associated with advanced age, particularly in the area of conditions such as Alzheimer's disease. Judging by the numbers of people already affected, it is not certain at this time that we will find the means of eradicating or arresting this threat before it has overwhelmed us. Planning and preparation would seem our only rational hope of forestalling a potential disaster of unprecedented magnitude; we need to make a beginning.

The Individual's Contribution

History provides clear examples of individuals whose efforts were instrumental in changing the way we think about mental health problems. Recall that Pinel took off the chains, Dorothea Dix initiated a movement to improve the conditions of asylums, and Clifford Beers inspired the modern mental health movement with his autobiographical account of his own experience with mental illness. Who will lead the next revolution in mental health is anyone's guess. What is clear is that a great deal can be accomplished by individual effort.

When students become aware of the tremendous scope of the mental health problem both nationally and internationally and of the woefully inadequate facilities for coping with it, they often ask, "What can I do?" Thus, it seems appropriate to suggest a few of the lines of action that interested students can take.

Many opportunities in mental health work are open to trained personnel, both professional and paraprofessional. Social work, clinical psychology, psychiatry, and other mental health occupations are personally fulfilling. In addition, many occupations, ranging from law enforcement to teaching and the ministry, can and do play key roles in the mental health and well-being of many people. Training in all these fields usually offers individuals opportunities to work in community clinics and related facilities, to gain experience in understanding the needs and problems of people in distress, and to become familiar with community resources.

Citizens can find many ways to be of direct service if they are familiar with national and international resources and programs and if they invest the effort necessary to learn about their community's special needs and problems. Whatever their roles in life—student, teacher, police officer, lawyer, homemaker, business executive, or trade unionist—their interests are directly at stake, for although the mental health of a nation may be manifested in many ways—in its purposes, courage, moral responsibility, scientific and cultural achievements, and quality of daily life—its health and resources derive ultimately from the individuals within it. In a participatory democracy, it is they who plan and implement the nation's goals.

Besides accepting some measure of responsibility for the mental health of others through the quality of one's own interpersonal relationships, there are several other constructive courses of action open to each citizen. These include (1) serving as a volunteer in a mental hospital, community mental health center, or service organization;

(2) supporting realistic measures for ensuring comprehensive health services for all age groups; and (3) working toward improved public education, responsible government, the alleviation of prejudice, and the establishment of a more sane and harmonious world.

Many of us are concerned with mental health for personal as well as altruistic reasons, for we want to overcome the nagging problems of contemporary living and find our share of happiness in a meaningful and fulfilling life. To do so, we may sometimes need the courage to admit that our problems are too much for us. When existence seems futile or the going becomes too difficult, it may help to remind ourselves of the following basic facts, which have been emphasized throughout this text: From time to time, each of us has serious difficulties in coping with the problems of living. During such crises, we may need psychological and related assistance. Such difficulties are not a disgrace; they can happen to anyone if the stress is severe enough. The early detection and treatment of maladaptive behavior are of great importance in preventing the development of more severe or chronic conditions. Preventive measures—universal, selective, and indicated—are the most effective long-range approach to the solution of both individual and group mental health problems.

in review

- What are national and international programs aimed at providing solutions to mental health problems?
- Describe several ways in which individuals can contribute to the advancement of mental health.

Unresolved Issues

The HMOs and Mental Health Care

A **health maintenance organization (HMO)** is a business or management corporation that provides a form of health care coverage in the United States that is fulfilled through contracts with hospitals, doctors, and other health providers. Unlike traditional health insurance, the health care is made available through agreements with health professionals to treat more patients and in return usually to provide services at a discount. This business arrangement allows the HMO to charge a lower monthly premium, which is an advantage over indemnity insurance, provided that its members are willing to abide by the additional restrictions (Frank et al., 2004). The HMO serves as a "gatekeeper" between the patient and the health provider. This arrangement has clearly affected access to mental health care in the United States in that business decisions often take precedence over treatment needs. Treatment, when it is allowed by the HMO, tends to be limited in both duration and quality. The disillusionment with HMOs in the 1990s led to the development of alternative health funding or **managed health care** products. Several programs emerged that were less restrictive, giving patients more treatment options. However, this has done little to reduce the anger toward managed care, and an alternative approach for providing more effective health care is still needed (Kominski & Melnick, 2007).

Mental health treatment is valuable for preventing as well as easing mental disorders. Yet mental health treatment has been less readily available than physical health treatment, and its cost has been less often reimbursed. HMO programs establish a treatment staff through systems of professionals, referred to as "panels," who are considered to have efficacy and efficiency in providing a wide range of services. Some HMOs—referred to as "open-panel systems"—have allowed patients some choice of health providers and allow any qualified professional in the community to participate. However, most are closed-panel systems, which limit the selection of available providers. The benefits vary from plan to plan and usually include limits on the problems covered or on the maximum amount of care provided or services available. To keep costs low, some HMOs have operated according to a system of "capitation," a method of payment in which a health care provider contracts to deliver all the health care services required by a population for a fixed cost or flat fee per enrolled member or employee (Sanchez & Turner, 2003). The HMO thus assumes some risk, but capitation allows for great profit if the subscriber's fees can be set higher than the cost of health services.

The need for comprehensive and effective mental health treatment is great. As noted earlier, about one in five adults, or about 18.6 percent of Americans ages 18 and older, suffer from a diagnosable mental disorder in a given year (NIMH, 2014). It has also been estimated that 70 percent of adults and 80 percent of children who require mental health services do not receive treatment, primarily because of discriminatory insurance practices (Sussman, 2009a). Many people with mental health problems seek medical treatment for their psychological symptoms, thereby increasing the cost of medical care. In one study, Hunkeler and colleagues (2003) point out a strong association between psychiatric symptoms, impaired functioning, and general medical care costs. About 75 percent of patients with depression seek treatment for physical symptoms (Unützer et al., 2006). Moreover, patients with other psychiatric conditions such as PTSD also present with physical symptoms (see Chapter 5). Health care costs in general are reportedly rising, and the presence of any psychiatric diagnosis increases the health care cost.

In response to these mental health needs, health care administrators have created a diverse array of programs in an attempt to provide services at a cost that the system can afford.

Mental Health Treatment—Who Decides What Kind and How Long?

In one common approach to reducing health care costs, the managed care agency negotiates a reduced price directly with the health service provider. The provider then bills the health service organization for the time spent, and the HMO can obtain "low-bid" services from the health professional. This approach poses little financial risk to the provider. As might be apparent even to the casual observer of managed care systems, the procedures for determining the amount of money paid to providers have frequently been a problem for mental health professionals—psychologists and psychiatrists (Resnick et al., 1994). The HMO representative or "gatekeeper" to reimbursement, often a medical generalist untrained in either psychiatric disorders or psychosocial interventions, controls access to therapy and sometimes the type of treatment to be provided (Resnick et al., 1994). In some systems of managed care, the gatekeeper might be a business professional who, in the view of the health service provider, is determining treatment by requiring that the clinician periodically justify treatment decisions to someone who has little or no background in mental health. Conflicts can develop in such situations, and patients may be deprived of appropriate and necessary care (Resnick et al., 1994). HMOs that are overly cost conscious have come to be viewed by some practitioners as simply tending to business and neglecting patients' needs (Karon, 1995).

Time-Limited Therapy

The mental health services typically covered by HMOs have favored less expensive and less labor-intensive approaches. As might be expected, pharmacotherapy is the most frequent mental health treatment provided by HMOs (Frank et al., 2005)—a situation that some research suggests actually reduces health care costs. Other research has shown that cost-containment measures that are intended to reduce drug costs by restricting access to medications can—and often do—wind up increasing total health care costs (Horn, 2003). Further, psychosocial interventions such as individual psychotherapy are discouraged or limited to relatively few sessions. Long-term psychotherapy has been substantially reduced for all but a small number of wealthy private clients (Lazarus, 1996). On the other hand, group psychotherapy is often promoted and encouraged because it is often thought of as cost effective. Many managed care corporations have adopted the model of providing focused, brief, intermittent mental health treatment for most problems. Many forms of behavioral health services such as counseling programs to teach patients how to manage their illness, how to use relaxation response methods, or how to reduce unhealthy behaviors such as smoking or drinking have been implemented to improve health care while reducing costs (Blount et al., 2007).

Patients who require longer treatments or need inpatient hospitalization are typically not well served in managed care organizations. In fact, long-term mental health treatment is usually discouraged by managed health care organizations. For example, most managed care groups approve only short inpatient stays (less than 10 days) and four to six sessions of outpatient mental health treatment at a time. Few if any of the decisions regarding the amount and type of services provided are directly guided by empirical criteria. Decisions whether to cover 8 or 20 sessions of psychotherapy, for example, are arbitrary and often seem capricious to both practitioner and patient (Harwood et al., 1997).

A clear divide has developed between health service providers and managers. Available services are often governed more by financial concerns than by a mental health professional's judgment. Critics of managed care argue that there is no convincing evidence that current efforts are actually controlling costs (Harwood et al., 1997) and that there is no scientific support for the limited-benefit options being exercised. Some researchers have pointed out that the administrative costs for managed care centers (including high salaries for HMO executives) are exorbitant. Gabbard (1994), for example, estimated that about one-fourth of the health care expenditures in the United States go for managed care administration.

The general lack of mental health care support has clearly created controversy in the field of psychotherapy, and the mental health field is being altered by economic considerations. Sanchez and Turner (2003) provide an overview of the impact of managed care on psychological practice and the provision of mental health services to clients in need. They point out that the economics of the mental health care system have greatly impacted the practice of behavioral health care by limiting treatment to time-limited and symptom-focused services. The most frequently cited problems include the remarkable shift of treatment decision-making power from the behavioral health care provider to policymakers. In addition, practitioners have experienced a reduction in income, which has likely impacted quality of care because less-well-trained (non-doctoral-level) therapists have taken on more responsibility and offer short-term therapeutic approaches instead of needed long-term therapy. The nature of the mental health professions is changing, and there is a growing discontent with HMOs in society today (Mechanic, 2004). Both clients and mental health professionals have long experienced a breakdown in trust of the managed care system (Shore, 2007).

Although discrimination against mental health care compared with medical or surgical treatment has long affected the provision of mental health treatment in the United States, recent attempts to provide parity for mental health care might bring about some much needed changes. A new law, referred to as the Paul Wellstone and Pete Domenici Mental Health Parity and Addiction Equity Act of 2008 (MHPAEA), requires that the annual or lifetime dollar caps on mental health benefits be no lower than the dollar limits for medical and surgical benefits (Sussman, 2009a). The parity act prohibits group health insurance plans, typically provided by employers, from restricting access to mental health care by limiting benefits and requiring higher patient costs than those that apply to general medical or surgical benefits.

It is difficult at this point to venture as to what impact the new health care plan and the parity bill will have on improving the quality and availability of mental health care in the United States. Any solutions to the long-standing problems are likely to be complex and require substantial change to the present system.

Summary

17.1 Describe the importance of prevention in mental health care, noting the major approaches to prevention.

- Many mental health professionals are trying not only to cure mental health problems but also to prevent them from occurring, or at least to reduce their effects.

- Prevention can be viewed as focusing on three levels: (1) universal interventions, which attempt to reduce the long-term consequences of having had a disorder; (2) selective interventions, which are aimed at reducing the possibility of disorder and fostering positive mental health efforts in subpopulations that are considered at special risk; and (3) indicated interventions, which attempt to reduce the impact or duration of a problem that has already occurred.

17.2 Explain the contemporary issues of inpatient mental health treatment.

- With the advent of many new psychotropic medications and changing treatment philosophies, there has been a major effort to discharge psychiatric patients into the community.

- There has been a great deal of controversy over deinstitutionalization and the failure to provide prompt and adequate follow-up of these patients in the community as soon as possible.

17.3 Discuss the controversial legal issues involving people with mental illness.

- Being mentally ill is not considered sufficient grounds for involuntary commitment. There must also be evidence that the individual either is dangerous to herself or himself or represents a danger to society.

- It is not an easy matter, even for trained professionals, to determine in advance whether a person is dangerous and likely to harm others. Nevertheless, professionals must sometimes make such judgments.

- Court rulings have found professionals liable when patients they were treating caused harm to others. The *Tarasoff* decision held that a therapist has a duty to protect potential victims if her or his patient has threatened to kill them.

- The insanity plea for capital crimes is an important issue in forensic psychology. Many mental health and legal professionals, journalists, and laypersons have questioned the present use of the not guilty by reason of insanity (NGRI) defense.

- The original legal precedent, the *M'Naghten* rule, held that at the time of committing the act the accused must have been laboring under such a defect of reason as not to know the nature and quality of the act or not to know that what he or she was doing was wrong.

- More recent broadenings of the insanity plea, as in the American Law Institute standard, leave open the possibility of valid NGRI pleas by persons who are not diagnosed to be psychotic.

- The successful use of the NGRI defense by John Hinckley, attempted assassin of President Reagan, set off a storm of protest. One effective and widely adopted reform was to shift the burden of proof (of insanity) to the defense.

17.4 Describe national and international organizations that promote efforts for mental health.

- Federal agencies such as the National Institute of Mental Health (NIMH), the National Institute on Drug Abuse (NIDA), and the National Institute on Alcohol Abuse and Alcoholism (NIAAA) are devoted to promoting research, training, and services to the mental health community.

- Several professional and mental health organizations, many corporations, and a number of volunteer associations are also active in programs to promote mental health.

- International organizations such as the World Health Organization and the World Federation for Mental Health have contributed to mental health programs worldwide.

17.5 Address the challenges that people face in advancing mental health improvement in contemporary societies.

- More effective planning needs to take place at community, national, and international levels in order to reduce or eliminate mental health problems.

- Many opportunities in mental health work, including social work, clinical psychology, and psychiatry, are open to trained personnel.

- Citizens can become involved in helping people with mental illness in their communities through volunteer work, supporting measures for ensuring comprehensive health services for all, and working toward improved public education, responsible government, and the alleviation of prejudice.

Key Terms

Glossary

Many of the key terms listed in the glossary appear in boldface when first introduced in the text discussion. A number of other terms commonly encountered in this or other psychology texts are also included; you are encouraged to make use of this glossary both as a general reference tool and as a study aid for the course in abnormal psychology.

A

1-year prevalence. The total number of cases of a health-related state or condition in a population for a given year.

ABAB design. An experimental design, often involving a single subject, wherein a baseline period (A) is followed by a treatment (B). To confirm that the treatment resulted in a change in behavior, the treatment is then withdrawn (A) and reinstated (B).

Abnormal behavior. Maladaptive behavior detrimental to an individual or a group.

Abnormal psychology. Field of psychology concerned with the study, assessment, treatment, and prevention of abnormal behavior.

Abstinence. Refraining altogether from the use of a particular addictive substance or from a particular behavior.

Accommodation. Cognitive process of changing existing cognitive frameworks to make possible the incorporation of discrepant information.

Acting out. Ego-defense mechanism of engaging in antisocial or excessive behavior without regard to negative consequences as a way of dealing with emotional stress.

Activation (arousal). Energy mobilization required for an organism to pursue its goals and meet its needs.

Actuarial approach. Application of probability statistics to human behavior.

Actuarial procedures. Methods whereby data about subjects are analyzed by objective procedures or formulas rather than by human judgments.

Acute. Term used to describe a disorder of sudden onset, usually with intense symptoms.

Acute stress disorder. Disorder that occurs within 4 weeks after a traumatic event and lasts for a minimum of 2 days and a maximum of 4 weeks.

Adderall. A habit-forming drug comprised of a combination of dextroamphetamine and amphetamine.

Addictive behavior. Behavior based on the pathological need for a substance or activity; it may involve the abuse of substances, such as nicotine, alcohol, or cocaine, or gambling.

Adjustment. Outcome of a person's efforts to deal with stress and meet his or her needs.

Adjustment disorder. A disorder in which a person's response to a common stressor is maladaptive and occurs within 3 months of the stressor.

Adjustment disorder with depressed mood. Moderately severe mood disorder that is similar to dysthymic disorder but has an identifiable, though not severe, psychosocial stressor occurring within 3 months before the onset of depression and does not exceed 6 months in duration.

Adoption method. Comparison of biological and adoptive relatives with and without a given disorder to assess genetic versus environmental influences.

Adrenal cortex. Outer layer of the adrenal glands; secretes the adrenal steroids and other hormones.

Adrenal glands. Endocrine glands located at the upper end of the kidneys; consist of inner adrenal medulla and outer adrenal cortex.

Adrenaline. Hormone secreted by the adrenal medulla during strong emotion; causes such bodily changes as an increase in blood sugar and a rise in blood pressure. Also called *epinephrine*.

Advocacy. Approach to meeting mental health needs in which advocates, often an interested group of volunteers, attempt to help children or others receive services that they need but often are unable to obtain for themselves.

Advocacy programs. Programs aimed at helping people in underserved populations to obtain aid with which to improve their situations.

Affect. Emotion or feeling.

Aftercare. Follow-up therapy after discharge from a hospital.

Aggression. Behavior aimed at hurting or destroying someone or something.

Agitation. Marked restlessness and psychomotor excitement.

Agoraphobia. Fear of being in places or situations where a panic attack may occur and from which escape would be physically difficult or psychologically embarrassing, or in which immediate help would be unavailable in the event that some mishap occurred.

AIDS-dementia complex (ADC). Generalized loss of cognitive functioning that eventually affects a substantial proportion of patients with AIDS.

AIDS-related complex (ARC). Pre-AIDS manifestation of HIV infection involving minor infections, various nonspecific symptoms (such as unexplained fever), blood cell count abnormalities, and sometimes cognitive difficulties.

AIDS-related dementia. See **HIV-associated dementia**.

Alarm and mobilization. Selye's first stage of responding to trauma, alerting and mobilizing a person's resources for coping with the trauma.

Alcohol amnestic disorder. Formerly known as Korsakoff's syndrome, is a condition characterized by a persisting memory deficit (particularly with regard to recent events) that is sometimes accompanied by falsification of events. This disorder is caused by malnutrition, specifically the lack of vitamin B (thiamine).

Alcohol withdrawal delirium. Acute delirium associated with withdrawal from alcohol after prolonged heavy consumption; characterized by intense anxiety, tremors, fever and sweating, and hallucinations.

Alexithymia. Term used to denote a personality pattern in which an individual has difficulty identifying and describing feelings.

Alienation. Lack or loss of relationships with others.

Allostatic load. The biological cost of adapting to stress. Under conditions of high stress our allostatic load is high. When we are calm, our allostatic load is low and our bodies are not experiencing any of the physiological consequences of stress (racing heart, high levels of cortisol, etc.).

Alogia. A term referring to poverty of speech; a symptom that often occurs in schizophrenia.

Alter identities. In a person with dissociative identity disorder, personalities other than the host personality.

Alzheimer's disease. A progressive and fatal neurodegenerative disorder that is characterized by deterioration in memory, cognition, and basic self-care skills.

Amnesia. Total or partial loss of memory.

Amnestic disorder. Striking deficit in the ability to recall ongoing events more than a few minutes after they have taken place, or the inability to recall the recent past. Now grouped into a new diagnostic category called neurocognitive disorders.

Amniocentesis. Technique that involves drawing fluid from the amniotic sac of a pregnant woman so that sloughed-off fetal cells can be examined for chromosomal irregularities, including that of Down syndrome.

Amphetamine. Drug that produces a psychologically stimulating and energizing effect.

Amygdala. A collection of nuclei that are almond shaped and that lie in front of the hippocampus in the limbic system of the brain. It is involved in the regulation of emotion and is critically involved in the emotion of fear.

Amyloid plaques. Found in the brains of people with Alzheimer's disease, these deposits of aluminum silicate and abnormal protein (beta amyloid) are believed to cause loss of neurons.

Anal stage. In psychoanalytic theory, stage of psychosexual development in which behavior is presumably focused on anal pleasure and activities.

Analogue studies. Studies in which a researcher attempts to emulate the conditions hypothesized as leading to abnormality.

Androgen. Hormone associated with the development and maintenance of male characteristics.

Anesthesia. Loss or impairment of sensitivity (usually to touch but often applied to sensitivity to pain and other senses as well).

Anhedonia. Inability to experience pleasure or joy.

Anorexia nervosa. Intense fear of gaining weight or becoming "fat" coupled with refusal to maintain adequate nutrition and with severe loss of body weight.

Anoxia. Lack of sufficient oxygen.

Antabuse. Drug used in the treatment of alcoholism.

Anterograde amnesia. Loss of memory for events that occur *following* trauma or shock.

Antianxiety drugs. Drugs that are used primarily for alleviating anxiety.

Antibody. Circulating blood substance coded for detection of and binding to a particular antigen.

Antidepressant drugs. Drugs that are used primarily to elevate mood and relieve depression. Often also used in the treatment of certain anxiety disorders, bulimia, and certain personality disorders.

Antigen. A foreign body (e.g., a virus or bacteria) or an internal threat (e.g., a tumor) that can trigger an immune response.

Antipsychotics (neuroleptics). Medications that alleviate or diminish the intensity of psychotic symptoms such as hallucinations or delusions.

Antisocial personality disorder (ASPD). Disorder characterized by continual violation of and disregard for the rights of others through deceitful, aggressive, or antisocial behavior, typically without remorse or loyalty to anyone.

Anxiety. A general feeling of apprehension about possible danger.

Anxiety disorder. An unrealistic, irrational fear or anxiety of disabling intensity. *DSM-5* recognizes 11 types of anxiety disorders: specific phobia, social phobia, panic disorder, agoraphobia, generalized anxiety disorder, separation anxiety disorder, selective mutism, substance/medication-induced anxiety disorder, anxiety disorder due to a medical condition, other specified anxiety disorder, and unspecified anxiety disorder.

Anxiety sensitivity. A personality trait involving a high level of belief that certain bodily symptoms may have harmful consequences.

Aphasia. Loss or impairment of ability to communicate and understand language symbols—involving loss of power of expression by speech, writing, or signs, or loss of ability to comprehend written or spoken language—resulting from brain injury or disease.

APOE-4 allele. Variant of a gene on chromosome 19 that significantly enhances risk for late-onset Alzheimer's disease.

Apraxia. Loss of ability to perform purposeful movements.

Arousal. See **Activation**.

Arteriosclerosis. Degenerative thickening and hardening of the walls of the arteries, occurring usually in old age.

Asperger's disorder. See **Autism spectrum disorder**. Asperger's disorder no longer exists in *DSM-5*. In *DSM-IV-TR*, Asperger's disorder referred to severe and sustained childhood impairment in social relationships and peculiar behaviors but without the language delays seen in autism. In *DSM-5*, Asperger's disorder is subsumed by autism spectrum disorders.

Assertive community treatment (ACT). Persistent and vigorous follow-up with and aid to patients in managing life problems.

Assertiveness therapy. Behavior therapy technique for helping people become more self-assertive in interpersonal relationships.

Assimilation. Cognitive process whereby new experiences tend to be worked into existing cognitive frameworks even if the new information has to be reinterpreted or distorted to make it fit.

Association studies. Genetic research strategy comparing frequency of certain genetic markers known to be located on particular chromosomes in people with and without a particular disorder.

Asylums. Historically, these were institutions meant solely for the care of people with mental illness.

At risk. Condition of being considered vulnerable to the development of certain abnormal behaviors.

Atrophy. Wasting away or shrinking of a bodily organ, particularly muscle tissue.

Attachment theory. Contemporary developmental and psychodynamic theory emphasizing the importance of early experience with attachment relationships in laying the foundation for later functioning throughout life.

Attention-deficit/hyperactivity disorder (ADHD). Disorder of childhood characterized by difficulties that interfere with task-oriented behavior, such as impulsivity, excessive motor activity, and difficulties in sustaining attention.

Attenuated psychosis syndrome. Characterized by psychotic-like symptoms that are less severe and more transient and that lie below the threshold for a full psychotic disorder.

Attribution. Process of assigning causes to things that happen.

Autism spectrum disorder. Pervasive developmental disorder beginning in infancy and involving a wide range of problematic behaviors, including deficits in language, perception, and motor development; defective reality testing; and social withdrawal.

Autogynephilia. Paraphilia characterized by sexual arousal in men at the thought or fantasy of being a woman.

Autonomic nervous system. Section of the nervous system that regulates the internal organs; consists primarily of ganglia connected with the brain stem and spinal cord; may be subdivided into the sympathetic and parasympathetic systems.

Autonomic reactivity. Individual's characteristic degree of emotional reactivity to stress.

Autonomy. Self-reliance; the sense of being an independent person.

Autosome. Any chromosome other than those determining sex.

Aversion therapy. Form of behavior therapy in which punishment or aversive stimulation is used to eliminate undesired responses.

Aversive stimulus. Stimulus that elicits psychic or physical pain.

Avoidance learning. Form of conditioning in which a subject learns to behave in a certain way in order to avoid an unpleasant stimulus.

Avoidant personality disorder. Extreme social inhibition and introversion, hypersensitivity to criticism and rejection, limited social relationships, and low self-esteem.

Avolition. Refers to a psychological state that is characterized by a general lack of drive or motivation to pursue meaningful goals.

Axes (of *DSM*). Evaluation of an individual according to five foci, the first three assessing the person's present clinical status or condition and the other two assessing broader aspects of the person's situation.

B

Barbiturates. Synthetic drugs that act as depressants to calm the individual and induce sleep.

Baseline. The initial level of responses emitted by an organism.

B-cell. A type of white blood cell, produced in the bone marrow, that is (along with T-cells) very important in the immune system. B-cells produce specific antibodies in response to specific antigens.

Behavior genetics. Field that studies the heritability of mental disorders and other aspects of psychological functioning such as personality and intelligence.

Behavior modification. Change of specific behaviors by learning techniques.

Behavior therapy. Use of therapeutic procedures based primarily on principles of classical and operant conditioning.

Behavioral activation treatment. Treatment for depression in which the patient and the therapist work together to help the patient find ways to become more active and engaged with life.

Behavioral contracting. Positive reinforcement technique using a contract, often between family members, to identify the behaviors to be changed and to specify privileges and responsibilities.

Behavioral medicine. Broad interdisciplinary approach to the treatment of physical disorders thought to have psychological factors as major aspects in their causation or maintenance.

Behavioral perspective. A theoretical viewpoint organized around the theme that learning is central in determining human behavior.

Behavioral sciences. Various interrelated disciplines, including psychology, sociology, and anthropology, that focus on human behavior.

Behaviorism. School of psychology that formerly restricted itself primarily to the study of overt behavior.

Benign. Of a mild, self-limiting nature; not malignant.

Bias. Observer bias occurs when the researcher has preconceived ideas and expectations that influence the observations he or she makes in the research study.

Binge. An out-of-control consumption of an amount of food that is far greater than what most people would eat in the same amount of time and under the same circumstances.

Binge-eating disorder (BED). Distinct from nonpurging bulimia nervosa, whereby binging is not accompanied by inappropriate compensatory behavior to limit weight gain.

Biofeedback. Treatment technique in which a person is taught to influence his or her own physiological processes that were formerly thought to be involuntary.

Biogenic amines. Chemicals that serve as neurotransmitters or modulators.

Biological clocks. Regular biological cycles of sleep, activity, hormone activity, and metabolism characteristic of each species.

Biological viewpoint. Approach to mental disorders emphasizing biological causation.

Biopsychosocial viewpoint. A viewpoint that acknowledges the interacting roles of biological, psychosocial, and sociocultural factors in the origins of psychopathology.

Bipolar disorder with a seasonal pattern. Bipolar disorder with recurrences in particular seasons of the year.

Bipolar disorders. Mood disorders in which a person experiences both manic and depressive episodes.

Bipolar I disorder. A form of bipolar disorder in which the person experiences both manic (or mixed) episodes and major depressive episodes.

Bipolar II disorder. A form of bipolar disorder in which the person experiences both hypomanic episodes and major depressive episodes.

Bisexuality. Sexual attraction to both females and males.

Blocking. Involuntary inhibition of recall, ideation, or communication (including sudden stoppage of speech).

Blood-injection-injury phobia. Persistent and disproportionate fear of the sight of blood or injury, or the possibility of having an injection. Afflicted persons are likely to experience a drop in blood pressure and sometimes faint.

Blunted affect. A reduction in the range of affective expression commonly found in patients with schizophrenia. The difference between blunted affect and flat affect is one of degree. When the reduction in affective range is more pronounced and extreme (such that the person is almost expressionless), the patient may be said to have flat affect.

Body dysmorphic disorder (BDD). Obsession with some perceived flaw or flaws in one's appearance.

Body mass index (BMI). An estimation of total body fat calculated as body weight (in kilograms) divided by height (in meters) squared.

Borderline personality disorder (BPD). Impulsivity and instability in interpersonal relationships, self-image, and moods.

Brain pathology. Diseased or disordered condition of the brain.

Brain waves. Minute oscillations of electrical potential given off by neurons in the cerebral cortex and measured by the electroencephalograph (EEG).

Brief Psychiatric Rating Scale (BPRS). Objective method of rating clinical symptoms that provides scores on 18 variables (e.g., somatic concern, anxiety, withdrawal, hostility, and bizarre thinking).

Brief psychotherapy. Short-term therapy, usually 8 to 10 sessions, focused on restoring an individual's functioning and offering emotional support.

Brief psychotic disorder. Brief episodes (lasting a month or less) of otherwise uncomplicated delusional thinking.

Bulimia nervosa. Frequent occurrence of binge-eating episodes accompanied by a sense of loss of control over eating and recurrent inappropriate behavior such as purging or excessive exercise to prevent weight gain.

C

Caffeine. A drug of dependence found in many commonly available drinks and foods.

Candidate genes. Genes that are of specific interest to researchers because they are thought to be involved in processes that are known to be aberrant in that disorder (e.g., serotonin transporter genes in depression, or dopamine receptor genes in schizophrenia).

Cardiovascular. Pertaining to the heart and blood vessels.

Case study (method). An in-depth examination of an individual or family that draws from a number of data sources, including interviews and psychological testing.

Castrating. Refers to any source of injury to the genitals, or, more broadly, to a threat to the masculinity of an individual.

Castration anxiety. As postulated by Freud, the anxiety a young boy experiences when he desires his mother while at the same time fearing that his father may harm him by cutting off his penis; this anxiety forces the boy to repress his sexual desire for his mother and his hostility toward his father.

CAT scan. See **Computerized axial tomography (CAT) scan**.

Catalepsy. Condition seen in some schizophrenic psychoses, and some psychotic mood disorders, in which body postures are waxy and semirigid, with the limbs maintaining for prolonged periods any position in which they are placed.

Catatonic schizophrenia. See **Schizophrenia, catatonic type**.

Catecholamines. Class of monoamine compounds sharing a similar chemical structure. Known to be neurotransmitters—norepinephrine and dopamine.

Categorical approach. Approach to classifying abnormal behavior that assumes that (1) all human behavior can be sharply divided into the categories normal and abnormal, and (2) there exist discrete, nonoverlapping classes or types of abnormal behavior, often referred to as mental illnesses or diseases.

Catharsis. Discharge of emotional tension associated with something, such as by talking about past traumas.

Causal pattern. In a cause-and-effect relationship, a situation in which more than one causal factor is involved.

Causal risk factor. A variable risk factor that, when changed, changes the likelihood of the outcome of interest (e.g., if effectively treating depression decreased the risk of suicide, we would call it a causal risk factor).

Causation. Relationship in which the preceding variable causes the other(s).

Central nervous system (CNS). The brain and spinal cord.

Cerebral arteriosclerosis. Hardening of the arteries in the brain.

Cerebral cortex. Surface layers of the cerebrum.

Cerebral hemorrhage. Bleeding into brain tissue from a ruptured blood vessel.

Cerebral laceration. Tearing of brain tissue associated with severe head injury.

Cerebral syphilis. Syphilitic infection of the brain.

Cerebral thrombosis. Formation of a clot or thrombus in the vascular system of the brain.

Cerebrovascular accident (CVA). Blockage or rupture of a large blood vessel in the brain leading to both focal and generalized impairment of brain function. Also called *stroke*.

Cerebrum. Main part of the brain; divided into left and right hemispheres.

Child abuse. Infliction of physical or psychological damage on a child by parents or other adults.

Child advocacy. Movement concerned with protecting rights and ensuring well-being of children.

Chorea. Pathological condition characterized by jerky, irregular, involuntary movements. See also **Huntington's disease**.

Chromosomal anomalies. Inherited defects or vulnerabilities caused by irregularities in chromosomes.

Chromosomes. Chain-like structures within cell nucleus that contain genes.

Chronic. Term used to describe a long-standing or frequently recurring disorder, often with progressing seriousness.

Chronic fatigue syndrome. A debilitating illness characterized by disabling fatigue that lasts 6 months or more and occurs with other symptoms.

Chronic major depressive disorder. A disorder in which a major depressive episode does not remit over a 2-year period.

Chronic schizophrenia. Term that can be used to describe a patient with this disorder whose clinical condition has deteriorated or remained stable over a very long period of time (years).

Circadian rhythms. The 24-hour rhythmic fluctuations in animals' sleep activity and in the metabolic processes of plants and animals. See also **Biological clocks**.

Civil commitment. Procedure whereby a person certified as mentally disordered can be hospitalized, either voluntarily or against his or her will.

Classical conditioning. A basic form of learning in which a neutral stimulus is paired repeatedly with an unconditioned stimulus (US) that naturally elicits an unconditioned response (UR). After repeated pairings, the neutral stimulus becomes a conditioned stimulus (CS) that elicits a conditioned response (CR).

Claustrophobia. Irrational fear of small enclosed places.

Client-centered (person-centered) therapy. Nondirective approach to psychotherapy, developed chiefly by Carl Rogers, that focuses on the natural power of the organism to heal itself; a key goal is to help clients accept and be themselves.

Clinical diagnosis. The process through which a clinician arrives at a general "summary classification" of the patient's symptoms by following a clearly defined system such as *DSM-5* or *ICD-10*.

Clinical picture. Diagnostic picture formed by observation of patient's behavior or by all available assessment data.

Clinical problem checklist. Computer-administered psychological assessment procedure for surveying the range of psychological problems a patient is experiencing.

Clinical psychologist. Mental health professional with Ph.D. degree or Psy.D. degree in clinical psychology and clinical experience in assessment and psychotherapy.

Clinical psychology. Field of psychology concerned with the understanding, assessment, treatment, and prevention of maladaptive behavior.

Cocaine. Stimulating and pain-reducing psychoactive drug.

Cognition. Act, process, or product of knowing or perceiving.

Cognitive dissonance. Condition of tension existing when several of one's beliefs and attitudes are inconsistent with each other.

Cognitive processes (cognition). Mental processes, including perception, memory, and reasoning, by which one acquires knowledge, solves problems, and makes plans.

Cognitive remediation. Training efforts designed to help patients improve their neurocognitive (e.g., memory, vigilance) skills. The hope is that this will also help improve patients' overall levels of functioning.

Cognitive restructuring. Cognitive-behavioral therapy techniques that aim to change a person's negative or unrealistic thoughts and attributions.

Cognitive-behavioral perspective. A theory of abnormal behavior that focuses on how thoughts and information processing can become distorted and lead to maladaptive emotions and behavior.

Cognitive-behavioral therapy (CBT). Therapy based on altering dysfunctional thoughts and cognitive distortions.

Collective unconscious. Term used by Carl Jung to refer to that portion of the unconscious that he considered common to all humanity, based on wisdom acquired by our predecessors.

Coma. Profound stupor with unconsciousness.

Community mental health. Application of psychosocial and sociocultural principles to the improvement of given environments.

Community psychology. Use of community resources in dealing with maladaptive behavior; tends to be more concerned with community intervention than with personal or individual change.

Comorbidity. Occurrence of two or more identified disorders in the same psychologically disordered individual.

Comparison or control group. Group of subjects who do not exhibit the disorder being studied but who are comparable in all other respects to the criterion group. Also, a comparison group of subjects who do not receive a condition or treatment the effects of which are being studied.

Competent to stand trial. The determination that a person who is charged with a crime has the mental health capability to participate in the proceedings.

Compulsions. Overt repetitive behaviors (such as hand washing or checking) or more covert mental acts (such as counting, praying, saying certain words silently, or ordering) that a person feels driven to perform in response to an obsession.

Compulsive gambling. See **Pathological gambling**.

Computer assessment. Use of computers to obtain or interpret assessment data.

Computerized axial tomography (CAT) scan. Radiological technique used to locate and assess the extent of organic damage to the brain without surgery.

Concordance rate. The percentage of twins sharing a disorder or trait.

Conduct disorders. Childhood and adolescent disorders that can appear by age 9 and are marked by persistent acts of aggressive or antisocial behavior that may or may not be against the law.

Confabulation. Filling in of memory gaps with false and often irrelevant details.

Confidentiality. Commitment on the part of a professional person to keep information he or she obtains from a client confidential.

Conflict. Simultaneous arousal of opposing impulses, desires, or motives.

Congenital. Existing at birth or before birth, but not necessarily hereditary.

Congenital defect. Genetic defect or environmental condition occurring before birth and causing a child to develop a physical or psychological anomaly.

Conjoint family therapy. Direct involvement of the family in improving communication, interaction, and relationships among family members and fostering a family system that better meets the needs of each member.

Consciousness. Awareness of inner or outer environment.

Constitution. Relatively constant biological makeup of an individual, resulting from the interaction of heredity and environment.

Consultation. Community intervention approach that aims at helping individuals at risk for disorder by working indirectly through caretaker institutions (e.g., police and teachers).

Contingency. Relationship, usually causal, between two events in which one is usually followed by the other.

Continuous reinforcement. Reward or reinforcement given regularly after each correct response.

Contributory cause. A condition that increases the probability of developing a disorder but that is neither necessary nor sufficient for it to occur.

Conversion disorder. Pattern in which symptoms of some physical malfunction or loss of control appear without any underlying organic pathology; originally called *hysteria*.

Convulsion. Pathological, involuntary muscle contractions.

Coping strategies. Efforts to deal with stress.

Coprolalia. Verbal tic in which an individual utters obscenities aloud.

Coronary heart disease (CHD). Potentially lethal blockage of the arteries supplying blood to the heart muscle, or myocardium.

Corpus callosum. Nerve fibers that connect the two hemispheres of the brain.

Correlate. A factor that co-varies with, or is associated with, some outcome of interest (e.g., height and weight).

Correlation. The tendency of two variables to change together. With positive correlation, as one variable goes up, so does the other; with negative correlation, one variable goes up as the other goes down.

Correlation coefficient. A statistic that ranges from +1.0 to –1.0 and reflects the degree of association between two variables. The magnitude of the correlation indicates the strength of the association, and the sign indicates whether the correlation is positive or negative.

Correlational research. A research strategy that examines whether and how variables go together (co-vary) without manipulating (changing) any variables.

Corticovisceral control mechanisms. Brain mechanisms that regulate autonomic and other bodily functions.

Cortisol. Human stress hormone released by the cortex of the adrenal glands.

Counseling psychology. Field of psychology that focuses on helping people with problems pertaining to education, marriage, or occupation.

Countertransference. Psychodynamic concept that the therapist brings personal issues, based on his or her own vulnerabilities and conflicts, to the therapeutic relationship.

Couple therapy. Treatment for disordered interpersonal relationships involving sessions with both members of the relationship present and emphasizing mutual need gratification, social role expectations, communication patterns, and similar interpersonal factors.

Covert. Concealed, disguised, not directly observable.

Covert sensitization. Behavioral treatment method for extinguishing undesirable behavior by associating noxious mental images with that behavior.

Criminal responsibility. Legal question of whether a person should be permitted to use insanity as a defense after having committed a crime.

Crisis. Stressful situation that approaches or exceeds the adaptive capacities of an individual or a group.

Crisis intervention. Provision of psychological help to an individual or a group in times of severe and special stress.

Criterion group. Group of subjects who exhibit the disorder under study.

Cross-gender identification. The desire to be, or the insistence that one is, of the opposite sex.

Cultural competence. Refers to a psychologist's need to be informed of the issues involved in multicultural assessment.

Cultural relativism. Position that one cannot apply universal standards of normality or abnormality to all societies.

Cyclothymic disorder. Mild mood disorder characterized by cyclical periods of hypomanic and depressive symptoms.

Cytokines. Small protein molecules that enable the brain and the immune system to communicate with each other. Cytokines can augment or enhance an immune system response or cause immunosuppression, depending on the specific cytokine that is released.

D

Day hospital. Community-based mental hospital where patients are treated during the day, returning to their homes at night.

Debriefing sessions. Psychological debriefing is a brief, directive treatment method that is used in helping people who have undergone a traumatic situation. Debriefing sessions are usually conducted with small groups of trauma victims shortly after the incident for the purpose of helping them deal with the emotional residuals of the event.

Defense mechanisms. See **Ego-defense mechanisms**.

Defense-oriented response. Behavior directed primarily at protecting the self from hurt and disorganization rather than at resolving the situation.

Deinstitutionalization. Movement to close mental hospitals and treat people with severe mental disorders in the community.

Delayed ejaculation disorder. Retarded ejaculation, or the inability to ejaculate following a normal sexual excitement phase.

Delinquency. Antisocial or illegal behavior by a minor.

Delirium. State of mental confusion characterized by relatively rapid onset of widespread disorganization of the higher mental processes, caused by a generalized disturbance in brain metabolism. May include impaired perception, memory, and thinking and abnormal psychomotor activity.

Delirium tremens. See **Alcohol withdrawal delirium**.

Delusion. False belief about reality maintained in spite of strong evidence to the contrary.

Delusion of grandeur. False belief that one is a noted or famous person, such as Napoleon or the Virgin Mary.

Delusion of persecution. False belief that one is being mistreated or interfered with by one's enemies.

Delusional disorder. Nurturing, giving voice to, and sometimes taking action on beliefs that are considered completely false by others; formerly called *paranoia*.

Delusional system. Internally coherent, systematized pattern of delusions.

Dementia. Progressive deterioration of brain functioning occurring after the completion of brain maturation in adolescence. Characterized by deficits in memory, abstract thinking, acquisition of new knowledge or skills, visuospatial comprehension, motor control, problem solving, and judgment. Now referred to as major neurocognitive disorder.

Dementia praecox. Older term for schizophrenia.

Demonology. Viewpoint emphasizing supernatural causation of mental disorder, especially "possession" by evil spirits or forces.

Denial of reality. Ego-defense mechanism that protects the self from an unpleasant reality by refusing to perceive or face it.

Dependence. Tendency to over-rely on others.

Dependent personality disorder. Extreme dependence on others, particularly the need to be taken care of, leading to clinging and submissive behavior.

Dependent variable. In an experiment, the factor that is observed to change with changes in the manipulated (independent) variables.

Depersonalization. Temporary loss of sense of one's own self and one's own reality.

Depersonalization/derealization disorder. Dissociative disorder in which episodes of depersonalization and derealization become persistent and recurrent.

Depression. Emotional state characterized by extraordinary sadness and dejection.

Depressive episode. Period of markedly depressed mood or loss of interest in formerly pleasurable activities (or both) for at least 2 weeks, accompanied by other symptoms such as changes in sleep or appetite or feelings of worthlessness.

Depressive personality disorder. Provisional category of personality disorder in *DSM-5* that involves a pattern of depressive cognitions and behaviors that begin by early adulthood and is pervasive in nature.

Depressogenic schemas. Dysfunctional beliefs that are rigid, extreme, and counterproductive and that are thought to leave one susceptible to depression when experiencing stress.

Derealization. Experience in which the external world is perceived as distorted and lacking a stable and palpable existence.

Desensitization. Therapeutic process by means of which reactions to traumatic experiences are reduced in intensity by repeatedly exposing a person to them in mild form, either in reality or in fantasy.

Desire phase. First phase of the human sexual response, consisting of fantasies about sexual activity or a sense of desire to have sexual activity.

Deterrence. Premise that punishment for criminal offenses will deter that criminal and others from future criminal acts.

Detox center. Center or facility for receiving and detoxifying alcohol- or drug-intoxicated individuals.

Detoxification. Treatment directed toward ridding the body of alcohol or other drugs.

Developmental disorder. Problem that is rooted in deviations in the development process itself, thus disrupting the acquisition of skills and adaptive behavior and often interfering with the transition to well-functioning adulthood.

Developmental psychopathology. Field of psychology that focuses on determining what is abnormal at any point in the developmental process by comparing and contrasting it with normal and expected changes that occur.

Developmental systems approach. Acknowledgment that genetic activity influences neural activity, which in turn influences behavior, which in turn influences the environment, and that these influences are bidirectional.

Deviant behavior. Behavior that deviates markedly from the average or norm.

Diagnosis. Determination of the nature and extent of a specific disorder.

Dialectical behavior therapy. A unique kind of cognitive and behavioral therapy specifically adapted for treating borderline personality disorder.

Diathesis. Predisposition or vulnerability to developing a given disorder.

Diathesis–stress model. View of abnormal behavior as the result of stress operating on an individual who has a biological, psychosocial, or sociocultural predisposition to developing a specific disorder.

Dimensional approach. Approach to classifying abnormal behavior that assumes that a person's typical behavior is the product of differing strengths or intensities of behavior along several definable dimensions, such as mood, emotional stability, aggressiveness, gender, identity, anxiousness, interpersonal trust, clarity of thinking and communication, social introversion, and so on.

Direct observation. Method of collecting research data that involves directly observing behavior in a given situation.

Direction of effect problem. Refers to the fact that, in correlational research, it cannot be concluded whether variable A causes variable B or whether variable B causes variable A.

Directive therapy. Type of therapeutic approach in which a therapist supplies direct answers to problems and takes much of the responsibility for the progress of therapy.

Disaster syndrome. Reactions of many victims of major catastrophes during the traumatic experience and the initial and long-lasting reactions after it.

Discordant marriage. Marriage in which one or both of the partners are not gaining satisfaction from the relationship and one spouse may express frustration and disillusionment in hostile ways, such as nagging, belittling, and purposely doing things to annoy the other.

Discrimination. Ability to interpret and respond differently to two or more similar stimuli.

Disintegration. Loss of organization or integration in any organized system.

Disorganization. Severely impaired integration.

Disorganized schizophrenia. See **Schizophrenia, disorganized type**.

Disorientation. Mental confusion with respect to time, place, or person.

Displacement. Ego-defense mechanism that discharges pent-up feelings, often of hostility, on objects less dangerous than those arousing the feelings.

Disrupted family. Family that is incomplete as a result of death, divorce, separation, or some other circumstance.

Dissociation. The human mind's capacity to mediate complex mental activity in channels split off from or independent of conscious awareness.

Dissociative amnesia. Psychogenically caused memory failure.

Dissociative disorders. Conditions involving a disruption in an individual's normally integrated functions of consciousness, memory, or identity.

Dissociative fugue. A dissociative amnesic state in which the person is not only amnesic for some or all aspects of his or her past but also departs from home surroundings.

Dissociative identity disorder (DID). Condition in which a person manifests at least two or more distinct identities or personality states that alternate in some way in taking control of behavior. Formerly called *multiple personality disorder*.

Distress. Negative stress, associated with pain, anxiety, or sorrow.

Disturbed family. Family in which one or both parents behave in grossly eccentric or abnormal ways and may keep the home in constant emotional turmoil.

Dizygotic (fraternal) twins. Twins that develop from two separate eggs.

DNA. Deoxyribonucleic acid; principal component of genes.

Dominant gene. A gene whose hereditary characteristics prevail, in offspring, over any recessive gene that affects the same trait.

Dopamine. Neurotransmitter from the catecholamine family that is initially synthesized from tyrosine, an amino acid common in the diet. Dopamine is produced from L-DOPA by the enzyme dopamine decarboxylase.

Dopamine hypothesis. Hypothesis that schizophrenia is the result of an excess of dopamine activity at certain synaptic sites.

Dopamine theory of addiction. Theory suggesting that addiction is the result of a dysfunction of the dopamine reward pathway.

Double bind. Situation in which a person will be disapproved for performing a given act and equally disapproved if he or she does not perform it.

Double-bind communication. Type of faulty communication in which one person (e.g., a parent) presents to another (e.g., a child) ideas, feelings, and demands that are mutually incompatible.

Double-blind study. Often used in studies examining drug treatment effects, a condition where neither the subject nor the experimenter has knowledge about what specific experimental condition (or drug) the subject is receiving.

Double depression. This condition is diagnosed when a person with dysthymia has a superimposed major depressive episode.

Down syndrome. Form of moderate-to-severe intellectual disability associated with a chromosomal abnormality and typically accompanied by characteristic physical features.

Dream analysis. Method involving the recording, description, and interpretation of a patient's dreams.

Drive. Internal conditions directing an organism toward a specific goal, often involving biological rather than psychological motives.

Drug abuse. Use of a drug to the extent that it interferes with health and/or occupational or social adjustment.

Drug addiction (dependence). Physiological or psychological dependence on a drug.

DSM-5. Current diagnostic manual of the American Psychiatric Association.

Dwarfism. Condition of arrested growth and very short stature.

Dyad. Two-person group.

Dynamic formulation. Integrated evaluation of an individual's personality traits, behavior patterns, environmental demands, and the like to describe the person's current situation and to hypothesize about what is driving the person to behave in maladaptive ways.

Dysfunction. Impairment or disturbance in the functioning of an organ or in behavior.

Dysfunctional beliefs. Negative beliefs that are rigid, extreme, and counterproductive.

Dyslexia. Impairment of the ability to read.

Dyspareunia. Painful coitus in a male or a female.

Dysrhythmia. Abnormal brain wave pattern.

Dysthymic disorder. Moderately severe mood disorder characterized by a persistently depressed mood most of the day for more days than not for at least 2 years. Additional symptoms may include poor appetite, sleep disturbance, lack of energy, low self-esteem, difficulty concentrating, and feelings of hopelessness.

E

Early-onset Alzheimer's disease. Form of Alzheimer's disease that appears in people who are younger than approximately 60 years of age. Thought to be caused by rare genetic mutations.

Eating disorder not otherwise specified (EDNOS). A diagnostic category reserved for disorders of eating that do not meet criteria for any other specific eating disorder.

Eating disorders. Disorders of food ingestion, regurgitation, or attitude that affect health and well-being, such as anorexia, bulimia, or binge eating.

Echolalia. Parrot-like repetition of a few words or phrases.

Ecstasy. A human manufactured drug that is taken orally and acts as both a stimulant and a hallucinogen. The drug effects include feelings of mental stimulation, emotional warmth, enhanced sensory perception, and increased physical energy.

Edema. Swelling of tissues.

EEG. See **Electroencephalogram**.

Effect size. A statistical term referring to the strength of the relationship between two variables in a statistical population.

Efficacy. In a situation where treatment is tested under ideal conditions (usually in a controlled clinical trial), efficacy is how well a given treatment improves clinical outcome compared to a control or comparison condition.

Ego. In psychoanalytic theory, the rational part of the personality that mediates between the demands of the id, the constraints of the superego, and the realities of the external world.

Ego psychology. Psychodynamic theory emphasizing the importance of the ego—the "executive branch of the personality"—in organizing normal personality development.

Egocentric. Preoccupied with one's own concerns and relatively insensitive to the concerns of others.

Ego-defense mechanisms. Psychic mechanisms that discharge or soothe anxiety rather than coping directly with an anxiety-provoking situation; usually unconscious and reality distorting. Also called *defense mechanisms.*

Electra complex. Excessive emotional attachment (love) of a daughter for her father; the female counterpart of the Oedipus complex.

Electroconvulsive therapy (ECT). Use of electricity to produce convulsions and unconsciousness; a treatment used primarily to alleviate depressive and manic episodes. Also known as *electroshock therapy.*

Electroencephalogram (EEG). Graphical record of the brain's electrical activity obtained by placing electrodes on the scalp and measuring the brain wave impulses from various brain areas.

Embolism. Lodgment of a blood clot in a blood vessel too small to permit its passage.

Emotion. Strong feeling accompanied by physiological changes.

Emotional disturbance. Psychological disorder.

Empathy. Ability to understand, and to some extent share, the state of mind of another person.

Encephalitis. Inflammation of the brain.

Encopresis. Disorder in children who have not learned appropriate toileting for bowel movements after age 4.

Encounter group. Small group designed to provide an intensive interpersonal experience focusing on feelings and group interactions; used in therapy or to promote personal growth.

Endocrine glands. Ductless glands that secrete hormones directly into the lymph or bloodstream.

Endogenous factors. Factors originating within an organism that affect behavior.

Endophenotypes. Discrete, measurable traits that are thought to be linked to specific genes that might be important in schizophrenia or other mental disorders.

Endorphins. Opiates produced in the brain and throughout the body that function like neurotransmitters to dampen pain sensations. They also play a role in the body's building up tolerance to certain drugs.

Enuresis. Bed-wetting; involuntary discharge of urine after the age of expected continence (age 5).

Environmental psychology. Field of psychology focusing on the effects of an environmental setting on an individual's feelings and behavior.

Epidemiologic studies. Attempts to establish the pattern of occurrence of certain (mental) disorders in different times, places, and groups of people.

Epidemiology. Study of the distribution of diseases, disorders, or health-related behaviors in a given population. Mental health epidemiology is the study of the distribution of mental disorders.

Epilepsy. Group of disorders varying from momentary lapses of consciousness to generalized convulsions.

Epinephrine. Hormone secreted by the adrenal medulla; also called *adrenaline*.

Episodic. Term used to describe a disorder that tends to abate and recur.

Equilibrium. Steady state; balance.

Erectile disorder. Sexual dysfunction in which a male is unable to achieve or maintain an erection sufficient for successful sexual gratification; formerly known as *impotence*.

Erotic. Pertaining to sexual stimulation and gratification.

Escape learning. Instrumental response in which a subject learns to terminate or escape an aversive stimulus.

Estrogens. Female hormones produced by the ovaries.

Ethnic group. Group of people who are treated as distinctive in terms of culture and group patterns.

Etiology. Factors that are related to the development (or cause) of a particular disorder.

Euphoria. Exaggerated feeling of well-being and contentment.

Eustress. Positive stress.

Evidence-based treatment. Treatment that has been demonstrated to be superior to a standard comparison treatment or to placebo in a randomized controlled trial.

Exacerbate. Intensify.

Excitement (arousal) phase. Second phase of the human sexual response, in which there is generally a subjective sense of sexual pleasure and physiological changes, including penile erection in the male and vaginal lubrication and enlargement in the female.

Exhaustion. Selye's third and final stage of responding to continued excessive trauma, in which a person's adaptive resources are depleted and the coping patterns developed during the resistance stage fail.

Exhibitionistic disorder. Intentional exposure of one's genitals to others under inappropriate circumstances and without their consent.

Existential anxiety. Anxiety concerning one's ability to find a satisfying and fulfilling way of life.

Existential neurosis. Disorder characterized by feelings of alienation, meaninglessness, and apathy.

Existential psychotherapy. Type of therapy that is based on existential thought and focuses on individual uniqueness and authenticity on the part of both client and therapist.

Existentialism. View of human beings that emphasizes an individual's responsibility for becoming the kind of person he or she should be.

Exogenous. Originating from or due to external causes.

Exorcism. Religiously inspired treatment procedure designed to drive out evil spirits or forces from a "possessed" person.

Experimental group. Group of subjects used to assess the effects of independent variables.

Experimental method. Rigorous scientific procedure by which hypotheses are tested.

Experimental research. Research that involves the manipulation of a given factor or variable with everything else held constant.

Exposure and response prevention. A method of treatment for obsessive-compulsive disorder that combines intense exposure of the patient to feared conditions and then they are asked not to respond by engaging in their usual rituals to the feared stimuli.

Exposure therapy. A technique in psychological treatment of anxiety disorders that involves exposing the patient to the feared object or context without any danger in order to overcome the anxiety.

Expressed emotion (EE). Type of negative communication involving excessive criticism and emotional overinvolvement directed at a patient by family members.

External validity. The extent to which the findings from a single study are relevant to other populations, contexts, or times.

Exteroceptive conditioning. Modifying the perception of environmental stimuli acting on the body.

Extinction. Gradual disappearance of a conditioned response when it is no longer reinforced.

Extraversion. Direction of interest toward the outer world of people and things rather than toward concepts and intellectual concerns.

F

Factitious disorder. Feigning of symptoms to maintain the personal benefits that a sick role may provide, including the attention and concern of medical personnel or family members.

Factitious disorder imposed on another. This diagnosis is given when a person deliberately falsifies medical or psychological symptoms in another adult, a child, or even a pet. This occurs in the absence of any external reward (e.g., insurance money). Methods might include fabrication, exaggeration of existing problems, or deliberate creation of illness or disease. The person who induces the injury or disease is given the diagnosis, not the victim who is made ill or impaired. Also called *factitious disorder by proxy* or *Munchausen's syndrome by proxy*.

Factor analysis. Statistical technique used for reducing a large array of intercorrelated measures to the minimum number of factors necessary to account for the observed overlap or associations among them.

Fading. Technique whereby a stimulus causing some reaction is gradually replaced by a previously neutral stimulus such that the latter acquires the property of producing the reaction in question.

False memories. "Memories" of events that did not actually happen, often produced by highly leading and suggestive techniques.

Familial. Pertaining to characteristics that tend to run in families and have a higher incidence in certain families than in the general population.

Family aggregation. The clustering of certain traits, behaviors, or disorders within a given family. Family aggregation may arise because of genetic or environmental similarities.

Family history method. Behavior genetic research strategy that examines the incidence of disorder in relatives of an index case to determine whether incidence increases in proportion to the degree of the hereditary relationship.

Family systems approach. Form of interpersonal therapy focusing on the within-family behavior of a particular family member and the assumption that it is largely influenced by the behaviors and communication patterns of other family members.

Family therapy. A treatment approach that includes all family members, not just the identified patient.

Fantasy. Daydream; also, an ego-defense mechanism by means of which a person escapes from the world of reality and gratifies his or her desires in fantasy achievements.

Fear. A basic emotion that involves the activation of the "fight-or-flight" response of the sympathetic nervous system.

Feedback. Explicit information pertaining to internal physiological processes or to the social consequences of one's overt behavior.

Female orgasmic disorder. Persistent or recurrent delay in, or absence of, orgasm after a normal sexual excitement phase.

Female sexual interest/arousal disorder. Sexual dysfunction involving an absence of sexual arousal and unresponsiveness to most or all forms of erotic stimulation.

Fetal alcohol syndrome. Observed pattern in infants born to mothers with alcoholism in which there is a characteristic facial or limb irregularity, low body weight, and behavioral abnormality.

Fetishism. Sexual variant in which sexual interest centers on some inanimate object or nonsexual part of the body.

Fetus. Embryo after the sixth week following conception.

Fixation. Ego-defense mechanism involving an unreasonable or exaggerated attachment to some person or arresting of emotional development on a childhood or adolescent level.

Fixed-interval schedule. Schedule of reinforcement based on a fixed period of time after the previous reinforced response.

Fixed marker. A risk factor that cannot change within a person (e.g., race cannot vary within a person, and white race is a marker of increased risk of suicide death).

Fixed-ratio schedule. Schedule of reinforcement based on reinforcement after a fixed number of nonreinforced responses.

Flashback. Involuntary recurrence of perceptual distortions or hallucinations weeks or months after taking a drug; in post-traumatic stress disorder, a dissociative state in which the person briefly relives the traumatic experience.

Flat affect. The lack of emotional expression.

Flooding. Anxiety-eliciting therapeutic technique involving having a client repeatedly experience the actual internal or external stimuli that had been identified as producing anxiety reactions.

Folie à deux. See **Shared psychotic disorder**.

Follow-up study. Research procedure in which people are studied over a period of time or are recontacted at a later time after an initial study.

Forensic. Pertaining to or used in a court of law.

Forensic psychology (forensic psychiatry). Branches of psychology and psychiatry dealing with legal problems related to mental disorders and the legal rights and protection of patients with mental disorders and members of society at large.

Fraternal twins. Dizygotic twins; fertilized by separate germ cells, thus not having the same genetic inheritance. May be of the same or of opposite sexes.

Free association. Method for probing the unconscious by having patients talk freely about themselves, their feelings, and their motives.

Free-floating anxiety. Anxiety not referable to any specific situation or cause.

Frontal lobe. Portion of the brain active in reasoning and other higher thought processes.

Frotteurism. A term that refers to interest in rubbing, usually one's pelvis or erect penis, against a nonconsenting person for sexual gratification.

Frustration. Thwarting of a need or desire.

Frustration tolerance. Ability to withstand frustration without becoming impaired psychologically.

Fugue. Dissociative disorder that entails loss of memory for personal information accompanied by actual physical flight from one's present life situation to a new environment or a less threatening former one.

Functional mental disorders. Outdated term used to refer to disorders that were not considered to have an organic basis.

Functional MRI (fMRI). Internal scanning technique that measures changes in local oxygenation (blood flow) to specific areas of brain tissue that in turn depend on neuronal activity in those specific regions, allowing the mapping of psychological activity such as sensations, images, and thoughts.

Functional psychoses. Severe mental disorders for which a specific organic pathology has not been demonstrated.

G

Gambling. Wagering on games or events in which chance largely determines the outcome.

Gender dysphoria. Persistent discomfort about one's biological sex or the sense that the gender role of that sex is inappropriate.

Gender identity. Individual's identification as being male or female.

Gender identity disorder. Identification with members of the opposite sex, persistent discomfort with one's biological sexual identity, and strong desire to change to the opposite sex.

General adaptation syndrome. A model that helps explain the course of a person's biological deterioration under excessive stress; consists of three stages (alarm reaction, stage of resistance, and exhaustion).

General paresis. Mental disorder associated with syphilis of the brain.

Generalizability. The extent to which the findings from a single study can be used to draw conclusions about other samples.

Generalization. Tendency of a response that has been conditioned to one stimulus to be elicited by other, similar stimuli.

Generalized anxiety disorder (GAD). Chronic excessive worry about a number of events or activities, with no specific threat present, accompanied by at least three of the following symptoms: restlessness, fatigue, difficulty concentrating, irritability, muscle tension, sleep disturbance.

Genes. Long molecules of DNA that are present at various locations on chromosomes and that are responsible for the transmission of hereditary traits.

Genetic code. Means by which DNA controls the sequence and structure of proteins manufactured within each cell and also makes exact duplicates of itself.

Genetic counseling. Counseling of prospective parents concerning the probability of their having impaired offspring as a result of genetic defects.

Genetic inheritance. Potential for development and behavior determined at conception by egg and sperm cells.

Genetics. Science of the inheritance of traits and the mechanisms of this inheritance.

Genital stage. In psychoanalytic theory, the final stage of psychosexual development, involving a shift from autoeroticism to heterosexual interest.

Genitalia. Organs of reproduction, especially the external organs.

Genito-pelvic pain/penetration disorder. Recurring difficulties of vaginal penetration or pelvic pain during intercourse.

Genome-wide association study (GWAS). This type of study allows researchers to scan the entire genomes of large numbers of individuals to search for genetic variants associated with specific diseases. DNA is usually obtained from blood or from cheek swab samples. The DNA is then placed on tiny chips and scanned on highly specialized automated machines. Genetic variations in people with and without the disease or disorder are then compared.

Genotype. A person's total genetic endowment.

Genotype–environment correlation. Genotypic vulnerability that can shape a child's environmental experiences.

Genotype–environment interaction. Differential sensitivity or susceptibility to their environments by people who have different genotypes.

Geriatrics. Science of the diseases and treatment of the older people.

Germ cells. Reproductive cells (female ovum and male sperm) that unite to produce a new individual.

Gerontology. Science dealing with the study of old age.

Gestalt psychology. School of psychology that emphasizes patterns rather than elements or connections, taking the view that the whole is more than the sum of its parts.

Gestalt therapy. Therapy designed to increase the integration of thoughts, feelings, and actions and to promote self-awareness and self-acceptance.

Ghrelin. Ghrelin is a hormone that is produced by the stomach. It stimulates appetite.

Glucocorticoids. Adrenocortical hormones involved in sugar metabolism but also having widespread effects on injury-repair mechanisms and resistance to disease; they include cortisol.

Glutamate. An excitatory neurotransmitter that is widespread throughout the brain.

Gonads. Sex glands.

Good premorbid schizophrenia. See **Reactive schizophrenia**.

Group therapy. Psychotherapy administered to several people at the same time.

Guilt. Feelings of culpability arising from behavior or desires contrary to one's ethical principles. Involves both self-devaluation and apprehension growing out of fears of punishment.

Guilty but mentally ill (GBMI). Plea and possible verdict that would provide an alternative to pleading not guilty by reason of insanity (NGRI) and would allow for placing a defendant in a treatment facility rather than in a prison.

H

Habituation. Automatic process whereby a person's response to the same stimulus lessens with repeated presentations.

Half-life. Time needed for the level of an active drug or medication in the body to be reduced to 50 percent of the original level.

Halfway house. Facility that provides aftercare following institutionalization, seeking to ease a person's adjustment to the community.

Hallucinations. False perceptions such as things seen or heard that are not real or present.

Hallucinogens. Drugs known to induce hallucinations; often referred to as *psychedelics*.

Hallucinosis. Persistent hallucinations in the presence of known or suspected organic brain pathology.

Hashish. Strongest drug derived from the hemp plant; a relative of marijuana that is usually smoked.

Health maintenance organization (HMO). Health plan that provides services to employers and individuals for a fixed, prepaid fee.

Health psychology. Subspecialty within behavioral medicine that deals with psychology's contributions to the diagnosis, treatment, and prevention of psychological components of physical dysfunction.

Hebephrenic schizophrenia. See **Schizophrenia, disorganized type**.

Hemiplegia. Paralysis of one lateral half of the body.

Heredity. Genetic transmission of characteristics from parents to their children.

Hermaphroditism. Anatomical sexual abnormality in which a person has some sex organs of both sexes.

Heroin. Powerful psychoactive drug, chemically derived from morphine, that relieves pain but is even more intense and addictive than morphine.

Heterosexuality. Sexual interest in a member of the opposite sex.

Hierarchy of needs. Concept, articulated by Maslow, that needs arrange themselves in a hierarchy in terms of importance from the most basic biological needs to those psychological needs concerned with self-actualization.

High-risk. Term applied to persons showing great vulnerability to physical or mental disorders.

Hikikomori. A disorder of acute social withdrawal in which young people remain in their room in their parents' house and refuse social interactions for at least 6 months, but often for many years.

Histrionic personality disorder. Excessive attention seeking, emotional instability, and self-dramatization.

HIV-associated dementia. A progressive brain deterioration that is caused by infection from the HIV virus.

HIV-associated neurocognitive impairment. Mild or major neurocognitive disorder caused by infection with the human immunodeficiency virus (HIV).

Hoarding disorder. A new *DSM-5* diagnosis characterized by long-standing difficulties discarding possessions, even those of little value.

Homeostasis. Tendency of organisms to maintain conditions that make possible a constant level of physiological functioning.

Homosexuality. Sexual preference for a member of one's own sex.

Hormones. Chemical messengers secreted by endocrine glands that regulate development of and activity in various parts of the body.

Host identity (personality). The identity in dissociative identity disorder that is most frequently encountered and carries the person's real name. This is not usually the original identity and it may or may not be the best adjusted identity.

Hostility. Emotional reaction or drive toward the destruction or damage of an object interpreted as a source of frustration or threat.

Humanistic-experiential therapies. Psychotherapies emphasizing personal growth and self-direction.

Humanistic perspective. Approach to understanding abnormal behavior that views basic human nature as good and emphasizes people's inherent capacity for growth and self-actualization.

Huntington's disease. A rare and fatal degenerative disorder that is manifested in jerking, twitching movements, and mental deterioration. Caused by a dominant gene on chromosome 4. Formerly called *Huntington's chorea*.

Hydrocephaly. Relatively rare condition in which the accumulation of an abnormal amount of cerebrospinal fluid within the cranium causes damage to the brain tissues and enlargement of the skull.

Hydrotherapy. Use of hot or cold baths, ice packs, and so on, in treatment.

Hyper-. Prefix meaning "increased" or "excessive."

Hyperactivity. See **Attention-deficit/hyperactivity disorder**.

Hyperobesity. Extreme overweight; 100 pounds or more above ideal body weight.

Hyperventilation. Rapid breathing associated with intense anxiety.

Hypesthesia. Partial loss of sensitivity.

Hypnosis. Trance-like mental state induced in a cooperative subject by suggestion.

Hypnotherapy. Use of hypnosis in psychotherapy.

Hypo-. Prefix meaning "decreased" or "insufficient."

Hypoactive sexual desire disorder. Sexual dysfunction in which either a man or a woman shows little or no sexual drive or interest.

Hypochondriacal delusions. Delusions concerning various horrible disease conditions, such as the belief that one's brain is turning to dust.

Hypochondriasis. Preoccupation, based on misinterpretations of bodily symptoms, with the fear that one has a serious disease.

Hypomania. Mild form of mania.

Hypomanic episode. A condition lasting at least 4 days in which a person experiences abnormally elevated, expansive, or irritable mood. At least three out of seven other designated symptoms similar to those in a manic episode must also be present but to a lesser degree than in mania.

Hypothalamic-pituitary-adrenal (HPA) axis/system. The HPA axis is a hormonal feedback system that becomes activated by stress and results in the production of cortisol.

Hypothalamus. Key structure at the base of the brain; important in emotion and motivation.

Hypothesis. Statement or proposition, usually based on observation, that is tested in an experiment; may be refuted or supported by experimental results but can never be conclusively proved.

Hypoxia. Insufficient delivery of oxygen to an organ, especially the brain.

Hysteria. Older term used for conversion disorders; involves the appearance of symptoms of organic illness in the absence of any related organic pathology.

I

Id. In psychoanalytic theory, the reservoir of instinctual drives and the first structure to appear in infancy.

Identical twins. Monozygotic twins; developed from a single fertilized egg.

Identification. Ego-defense mechanism in which a person identifies himself or herself with some person or institution, usually of an illustrious nature.

Ideology. System of beliefs.

Illusion. Misinterpretation of sensory data; false perception.

Imaginal exposure. Form of exposure therapy that does not involve a real stimulus. Instead, the patient is asked to imagine the feared stimulus or situation.

Immaturity. Pattern of childhood mal-adaptive behaviors suggesting lack of adaptive skills.

Immune reaction. Complex defensive reaction initiated on detection of an anti-gen invading the body.

Immune system. The body's principal means of defending itself against the intru-sion of foreign substances.

Immunosuppression. A downregulation or dampening of the immune system. This can be short or long term and can be triggered by injury, stress, illness, and other factors.

Implicit memory. Memory that occurs below the conscious level.

Implicit perception. Perception that occurs below the conscious level.

In vivo **exposure.** Exposure that takes place in a real-life situation as opposed to in a therapeutic or laboratory setting.

Incentive. External inducement to behave in a certain way.

Incest. Culturally prohibited sexual rela-tions between family members, such as a brother and sister or a parent and child.

Incidence. Occurrence (onset) rate of a given disorder in a given population.

Independent variable. Factor whose effects are being examined and which is manipulated in some way, while other variables are held constant.

Index case. See **Proband.**

Indicated intervention. Early detection and prompt treatment of maladaptive behavior in a person's family and com-munity setting.

Infantile autism. See **Autism spectrum disorder.**

Inhibition. Restraint of impulse or desire.

Innate. Inborn.

Inpatient. Hospitalized patient.

Insanity. Legal term for mental disorder, implying lack of responsibility for one's acts and inability to manage one's affairs.

Insanity defense. The not guilty by reason of insanity (NGRI) plea used as a legal defense in criminal trials.

Insight. Clinically, a person's understand-ing of his or her illness or of the motiva-tions underlying a behavior pattern; in general psychology, the sudden grasp or understanding of meaningful relationships in a situation.

Insight therapy. Type of psychotherapy that focuses on helping a client achieve greater self-understanding with respect to his or her motives, values, coping patterns, and so on.

Insomnia. Difficulty in sleeping.

Instinct. Inborn tendency to perform particular behavior patterns under certain conditions in the absence of learning.

Instrumental (operant) conditioning. Reinforcement of a subject for making a correct response that leads either to receipt of something rewarding or to escape from something unpleasant.

Insulin coma therapy. Physiological treatment for schizophrenia that is rarely used today; it involved administration of increasing amounts of insulin until the patient went into shock.

Integrative behavioral couple therapy (IBCT). Modification of traditional behavioral couple therapy that has a focus on acceptance of the partner rather than being solely change oriented.

Intellectual disability. Significant impair-ment in general intellectual functioning that is accompanied by significant limita-tions in adaptive functioning and is obvi-ous during the developmental period.

Intellectualization. Ego-defense mecha-nism by which a person achieves some measure of insulation from emotional hurt by cutting off or distorting the emotional charge that normally accompanies hurtful situations.

Intelligence. The ability to learn, reason, and adapt.

Intelligence quotient (IQ). Measurement of "intelligence" expressed as a number or position on a scale.

Intelligence test. Test used in establishing a subject's level of intellectual capability.

Intensive care management (ICM). Use of multidisciplinary teams with limited casel-oads to ensure that discharged patients do not get overlooked and "lost" in the system.

Interdisciplinary (multidisciplinary) approach. Integration of various scientific disciplines in understanding, assessing, treating, and preventing mental disorders.

Intermittent reinforcement. Reinforce-ment given intermittently rather than after every response.

Internal validity. The extent to which a study is free of confounds, is methodologi-cally sound, and allows the researcher to have confidence in the findings.

International Classification of Diseases (ICD-10). System of classification of disorders published by the World Health Organization.

Interoceptive conditioning. This term refers to a learning process that is similar to classic conditioning. It involves two conditioned stimuli and one uncondi-tioned response.

Interoceptive fears. Fear of various inter-nal bodily sensations.

Interpersonal accommodation. Process through which two people develop pat-terns of communication and interaction that enable them to attain common goals, meet mutual needs, and build a satisfying relationship.

Interpersonal perspective. Approach to understanding abnormal behavior that views much of psychopathology as rooted in the unfortunate tendencies we develop while dealing with our interper-sonal environments; it thus focuses on our relationships, past and present, with other people.

Interpersonal therapy (IPT). A time-limited psychotherapy approach that focuses on the interpersonal context and on building interpersonal skills.

Intrapsychic conflict. Inner mental struggles resulting from the interplay of the id, ego, and superego when the three subsystems are striving for different goals.

Introjection. Internal process by which a child incorporates symbolically, through images and memories, important people in his or her life.

Intromission. Insertion of the penis into the vagina or anus.

Introspection. Observing (and often reporting on) one's inner experiences.

Introversion. Direction of interest toward one's inner world of experience and toward concepts rather than external events and objects or people.

Ionizing radiation. Form of radiation; major cause of gene mutations.

Isolation. Ego-defense mechanism by means of which contradictory attitudes or feelings that normally accompany particu-lar attitudes are kept apart, thus prevent-ing conflict or hurt.

J

Juvenile delinquency. Legal term used to refer to illegal acts committed by minors.

Juvenile paresis. General paresis in chil-dren, usually of congenital origin.

K

Klinefelter's syndrome. Type of intellectual disability associated with sex chromosome anomaly.

Korsakoff's syndrome. This disorder, also referred to as *Korsakoff's dementia*, *Korsakoff's psychosis*, or *amnesic-confabulatory syndrome*, is a neurological condition resulting from chronic alcohol abuse and severe malnutrition (vitamin B).

L

La belle indifférence. The unconcern about serious illness or disability that is sometimes characteristic of conversion disorder.

Labeling. Assigning a person to a particular diagnostic category, such as schizophrenia.

Lability. Instability, particularly with regard to affect.

Latency stage. In psychoanalytic theory, a stage of psychosexual development during which sexual motivations recede in importance and a child is preoccupied with developing skills and other activities.

Latent. Inactive or dormant.

Latent content. In psychoanalytic theory, repressed actual motives of a dream that are seeking expression but are so painful or unacceptable that they are disguised by the manifest content of the dream.

Late-onset Alzheimer's disease. The occurrence of Alzheimer's disease in the more elderly. One gene thought to be involved in this form of Alzheimer's disease is the *APOE* gene.

Law of effect. Principle that responses that have rewarding consequences are strengthened and those that have aversive consequences are weakened or eliminated.

Learned helplessness. A theory that animals and people exposed to uncontrollable aversive events learn that they have no control over these events and this causes them to behave in a passive and helpless manner when later exposed to potentially controllable events. Later extended to become a theory of depression.

Learning. Modification of behavior as a consequence of experience.

Learning disorders. A set of disorders that reflect deficits in academic performance.

Leptin. Leptin is a hormone produced by fat cells that acts to reduce food intake.

Lesbian. Female homosexual person.

Lesion. Anatomically localized area of tissue pathology in an organ or a part of the brain.

Lethality scale. Criteria used to assess the likelihood of a person's committing suicide.

Leukocytes. See **Lymphocyte**.

Libido. In psychoanalytic theory, a term used to describe the instinctual drives of the id; the basic constructive energy of life, primarily sexual in nature.

Life crisis. Stress situation that approaches or exceeds a person's capacity to adjust.

Life history method. Technique of psychological observation in which the development of particular forms of behavior is traced by means of records of a subject's past or present behavior.

Lifestyle. General pattern of assumptions, motives, cognitive styles, and coping techniques that characterize a person's behavior and give it consistency.

Lifetime prevalence. The proportion of living persons in a population who have ever had a disorder up to the time of the epidemiologic assessment.

Linkage analysis. Genetic research strategy in which occurrence of a disorder in an extended family is compared with that of a genetic marker for a physical characteristic or biological process that is known to be located on a particular chromosome.

Lithium. A common salt that consists of a soft, silver-white metal; it has been found to reduce the symptoms of bipolar disorder although it has a number of negative side effects.

Lobotomy. See **Prefrontal lobotomy**.

Locomotor ataxia. Muscular incoordination usually resulting from syphilitic damage to the spinal cord pathways.

Longitudinal design. A research design in which people are followed over time.

LSD. Lysergic acid diethylamide, or LSD, is the most potent of the hallucinogens. It is odorless, colorless, and tasteless, and an amount smaller than a grain of salt can produce intoxication.

Lunacy. Old term roughly synonymous with *insanity*.

Lycanthropy. Delusion of being a wolf.

Lymphocyte. Generalized term for white blood cells involved in immune protection.

M

Macrocephaly. Rare type of intellectual disability characterized by an increase in the size and weight of the brain, enlargement of the skull, visual impairment, convulsions, and other neurological symptoms resulting from abnormal growth of glial cells that form the supporting structure for brain tissue.

Macrophage. Literally, "big eater." A white blood cell that destroys antigens by engulfment.

Magnetic resonance imaging (MRI). Internal scanning technique involving measurement of variations in magnetic fields that allows visualization of the anatomical features of internal organs, including the central nervous system and particularly the brain.

Mainstreaming. Placement of children with intellectual disabilities in regular school classrooms for all or part of the day.

Major depressive disorder. Moderate-to-severe mood disorder in which a person experiences only major depressive episodes but no hypomanic, manic, or mixed episodes. *Single episode* if only one; *recurrent episode* if more than one.

Major depressive episode. A mental condition in which a person must be markedly depressed for most of every day for most days for at least 2 weeks. In addition, a total of at least five out of nine designated symptoms must also be present during the same time period.

Major depressive episode with atypical features. A type of major depressive episode that includes a pattern of symptoms characterized by marked mood reactivity, as well as at least two out of four other designated symptoms.

Major depressive episode with catatonic features. A subset of major depressive disorders that is characterized by severe disturbances in motor function.

Major depressive episode with melancholic features. A type of major depressive episode that includes marked symptoms of loss of interest or pleasure in almost all activities, plus at least three of six other designated symptoms.

Major neurocognitive disorder. A new *DSM-5* diagnosis, this involves severe impairment in cognitive functioning that reflects a significant decline from the person's previous level of performance. The problems in cognitive functioning create problems for the person in terms of their ability to perform routine activities.

Major tranquilizers. Antipsychotic drugs, such as the phenothiazines.

Maladaptive (abnormal) behavior. Behavior that is detrimental to the well-being of an individual or a group.

Maladjustment. More or less enduring failure of adjustment; lack of harmony with self or environment.

Male hypoactive sexual desire disorder. Sexual dysfunction in which a man shows little or no sexual drive or interest.

Malingering. Consciously faking illness or symptoms of disability to achieve some specific nonmedical objective.

Managed health care. System of corporations that secures services from hospitals, physicians, and other providers for treating a designated population, with the goal of holding down health care costs.

Mania. Emotional state characterized by intense and unrealistic feelings of excitement and euphoria.

Manic episode. A condition in which a person shows markedly elevated, euphoric, or expansive mood, often interrupted by occasional outbursts of intense irritability or even violence that lasts for at least 1 week. In addition, at least three out of seven other designated symptoms must also occur.

Manic-depressive psychoses. Older term denoting a group of psychotic disorders characterized by prolonged periods of excitement and overactivity (mania) or by periods of depression and underactivity (depression) or by alternation of the two. Now known as *bipolar disorders*.

Manifest content. In psychoanalytic theory, the apparent (or obvious) meaning of a dream; masks the latent (or hidden) content.

Manualized therapy. Standardization of psychosocial treatments (as in development of a manual) to fit the randomized clinical paradigm.

Marijuana. Mild hallucinogenic drug derived from the hemp plant; often smoked in cigarettes called reefers or joints.

Masked disorder. "Masking" of underlying depression or other emotional disturbance by delinquent behavior or other patterns seemingly unrelated to the basic disturbance.

Masochism. Sexual stimulation and gratification from experiencing pain or degradation in relating to a lover.

Mass madness. Historically, widespread occurrence of group behavior disorders that were apparently cases of hysteria.

Masturbation. Self-stimulation of genitals for sexual gratification.

Maternal deprivation. Lack of adequate care and stimulation by the mother or mother surrogate.

Maturation. Process of development and body change resulting from heredity rather than learning.

Medical model. View of disordered behavior as a symptom of a disease process rather than as a pattern representing faulty learning or cognition.

Melancholic type. Subtype of major depression that involves loss of interest or pleasure in nearly all activities and other symptoms, including early morning awakenings, worse depression in the morning, psychomotor agitation or retardation, loss of appetite or weight, excessive guilt, and sadness qualitatively different from that usually experienced after a loss.

Meninges. Membranes that envelop the brain and spinal cord.

Mental age (MA). Scale unit indicating level of intelligence in relation to chronological age.

Mental disorder. Entire range of abnormal behavior patterns.

Mental hygiene movement. Movement that advocated a method of treatment focused almost exclusively on the physical well-being of hospitalized patients with mental disorders.

Mental illness. Serious mental disorder.

Mescaline. Hallucinogenic drug derived from the peyote cactus.

Mesmerism. Theory of "animal magnetism" (hypnosis) formulated by Anton Mesmer.

Mesocorticolimbic dopamine pathway (MCLP). Center of psychoactive drug activation in the brain. This area is involved in the release of dopamine and in mediating the rewarding properties of drugs.

Meta-analysis. A statistical method used to combine the results of a number of similar research studies. The data from each study are transformed into a common metric called the *effect size*. This allows the data from the various studies to be combined and then analyzed. You can think of a meta-analysis as being like research that you are already familiar with, except that the "participants" are individual research studies, not individual people.

Methadone. Synthetic narcotic related to heroin; used in the treatment of heroin addiction because it satisfies the craving for heroin without producing serious psychological impairment.

Microcephaly. Type of intellectual disability resulting from impaired development of the brain and a consequent failure of the cranium to attain normal size.

Migraine. Intensely painful, recurrent headache that typically involves only one side of the head and may be accompanied by nausea and other disturbances.

Mild (disorder). Disorder low in severity.

Mild neurocognitive disorder. A new *DSM-5* diagnosis that is characterized by a modest decline in cognitive functioning that does not interfere with the person's ability to perform the routine tasks.

Milieu. Immediate environment, physical or social or both.

Milieu therapy. General approach to treatment for hospitalized patients that focuses on making the hospital environment itself a therapeutic community.

Minnesota Multiphasic Personality Inventory (MMPI). Widely used and empirically validated personality scales.

Minor tranquilizers. Antianxiety drugs, such as the benzodiazepines.

Mixed episode. A condition in which a person is characterized by symptoms of both full-blown manic and major depressive episodes for at least 1 week, whether the symptoms are intermixed or alternate rapidly every few days.

Model. Analogy that helps a scientist order findings and see important relationships among them.

Modeling. Learning of skills by imitating another person who performs the behavior to be acquired.

Moderate (disorder). Disorder intermediate in severity.

Monoamine-oxidase inhibitors (MAOIs). Class of antidepressant drugs sometimes used for treating depression.

Monozygotic twins. Identical twins, developed from one fertilized egg.

Mood congruent. Delusions or hallucinations that are consistent with a person's mood.

Mood disorders. Disturbances of mood that are intense and persistent enough to be clearly maladaptive.

Mood incongruent. Delusional thinking that is inconsistent with a person's predominant mood.

Moral management. Wide-ranging method of treatment that focuses on a patient's social, individual, and occupational needs.

Moral therapy. Therapy based on provision of kindness, understanding, and favorable environment; prevalent during early part of the nineteenth century.

Morbid. Unhealthful, pathological.

Morphine. Addictive drug derived from opium that can serve as a powerful sedative and pain reliever.

Motivation. Often used as a synonym for *drive* or *activation*; implies that an organism's actions are partly determined in direction and strength by its own inner nature.

Motivational interviewing. A brief form of therapy, often used in areas of substance abuse and addiction, that allows clients to explore their desires, reasons, ability, and need for change.

Motive. Internal condition that directs action toward some goal; the term is generally used to include both the drive and the goal to which it is directed.

Multi-infarct dementia. See **Vascular dementia**.

Multiple personality disorder. See **Dissociative identity disorder**.

Mutant gene. Gene that has undergone some change in structure.

Mutation. Change in the composition of a gene, usually causing harmful or abnormal characteristics to appear in the offspring.

Mutism. Refusal or inability to speak.

N

Nancy School. Group of physicians in nineteenth-century Europe who accepted the view that hysteria was a sort of self-hypnosis.

Narcissism. Self-love.

Narcissistic personality disorder. Exaggerated sense of self-importance, preoccupation with being admired, and lack of empathy for the feelings of others.

Narcolepsy. Disorder characterized by transient, compulsive states of sleepiness.

Narcotic drugs. Drugs, such as morphine, that lead to physiological dependence and increased tolerance.

Natural killer cell. White blood cell that destroys antigens by chemical dissolution.

Necessary cause. A condition that must exist for a disorder to occur.

Need. Biological or psychological condition whose gratification is necessary for the maintenance of homeostasis or for self-actualization.

Negative affect. The experience of an emotional state characterized by negative emotions. Such negative emotions might include anger, anxiety, irritability, and sadness.

Negative automatic thoughts. Thoughts that are just below the surface of awareness and that involve unpleasant pessimistic predictions.

Negative cognitive triad. Negative thoughts about the self, the world, and the future.

Negative correlation. A relationship between two variables such that a high score on one variable is associated with a low score on another variable.

Negative-symptom schizophrenia. Schizophrenia characterized by an absence or deficit of normal behaviors, such as emotional expressiveness, communicative speech, and reactivity to environmental events.

Negative symptoms. Symptoms that reflect an absence or deficit in normal functions (e.g., blunted affect, social withdrawal).

Negativism. Form of aggressive withdrawal that involves refusing to cooperate or obey commands, or doing the exact opposite of what has been requested.

Neologisms. New words; a feature of language disturbance in schizophrenia.

Neonate. Newborn infant.

Neoplasm. Tumor.

Nervous breakdown. General term used to refer broadly to lowered integration and inability to deal adequately with one's life situation.

Neurodevelopmental disorders. A group of disorders in *DSM-5* that are typically manifested in early childhood.

Neurofibrillary tangles. Twisted and web-like nerve filaments that characterize the brains of patients with Alzheimer's disease.

Neurological examination. Examination to determine the presence and extent of organic damage to the nervous system.

Neurology. Field concerned with the study of the brain and nervous system and disorders thereof.

Neuron. Individual nerve cell.

Neurophysiology. Branch of biology concerned with the functioning of nervous tissue and the nervous system.

Neuropsychological assessment. Use of psychological tests that measure a person's cognitive, perceptual, and motor performance to obtain clues to the extent and locus of brain damage.

Neuropsychological disorders. Disorders that occur when there has been significant organic impairment or damage to a normal adolescent or adult brain.

Neuropsychological mood syndromes. Serious mood disturbances apparently caused by disruptions in the normal physiology of cerebral function.

Neuropsychological personality syndromes. Changes in an individual's general personality style or traits following brain injury of one or another type.

Neurosis. Term historically used to characterize maladaptive behavior resulting from intrapsychic conflict and marked by prominent use of defense mechanisms.

Neurosurgery. Surgery on the nervous system, especially the brain.

Neurosyphilis. Syphilis affecting the central nervous system.

Neurotic behavior. Anxiety-driven, exaggerated use of avoidance behaviors and defense mechanisms.

Neurotic disorders. Psychodynamic term for anxiety-driven mental health conditions that are manifest through avoidance patterns and defensive reactions.

Neuroticism. Personality pattern including the tendency to experience anxiety, anger, hostility, depression, self-consciousness, impulsiveness, and vulnerability.

Neurotransmitters. Chemical substances that are released into a synapse by a presynaptic neuron and that transmit nerve impulses from one neuron to another.

NGRI plea. The not guilty by reason of insanity plea, or NGRI, is a legal defense a defendant might use to claim that he or she was not guilty of a crime because of insanity.

Nicotine. Addictive alkaloid that is the chief active ingredient in tobacco and a drug of dependence.

Night hospital. Mental hospital in which an individual may receive treatment during all or part of the night while carrying on his or her usual occupation during the daytime.

Nihilistic delusion. Fixed belief that everything is unreal.

Nomenclature. A formalized naming system.

Nondirective therapy. Approach to psychotherapy in which a therapist refrains from giving advice or directing the therapy. See also **Client-centered (person-centered) psychotherapy**.

Nonsuicidal self-injury (NSSI) Direct, deliberate destruction of body tissue in the absence of any intent to die.

Norepinephrine. Catecholamine neurotransmitter substance.

Norm. Standard based on the measurement of a large group of people; used for comparing the scores of an individual with those of others in a defined group.

Normal. Conforming to the usual or norm; healthy.

Normal distribution. Tendency for most members of a population to cluster around a central point or average with respect to a given trait, with the rest spreading out to the two extremes in decreasing frequency.

NREM sleep. Stages of sleep not characterized by the rapid eye movements that accompany dreaming.

O

Obesity. The condition of having elevated fat masses in the body. Obesity is defined as having a body mass index (BMI) of 30 or higher.

Object-relations theory. In psychoanalytic theory, this viewpoint focuses on an infant or young child's interactions with "objects" (i.e., real or imagined people), as well as how they make symbolic representations of important people in their lives.

Objective personality tests. Structured tests, such as questionnaires, self-inventories, or rating scales, used in psychological assessment.

Observational learning. Learning through observation alone without directly experiencing an unconditioned stimulus (for classical conditioning) or a reinforcement (for instrumental conditioning).

Observational method. Systematic technique by which observers are trained to watch and record behavior without bias.

Observational research. In contrast to experimental research (which involves manipulating variables in some way and seeing what happens), in observational research the researcher simply observes or assesses the characteristics of different groups, learning about them without manipulating the conditions to which they are exposed. Sometimes called *correlational research*, although the former is the preferred term.

Obsessions. Persistent and recurrent intrusive thoughts, images, or impulses that a person experiences as disturbing and inappropriate but has difficulty suppressing.

Obsessive-compulsive disorder (OCD). Anxiety disorder characterized by the persistent intrusion of unwanted and intrusive thoughts or distressing images; these are usually accompanied by compulsive behaviors designed to neutralize the obsessive thoughts or images or to prevent some dreaded event or situation.

Obsessive-compulsive personality disorder (OCPD). Perfectionism and excessive concern with maintaining order, control, and adherence to rules.

Occipital lobe. Portion of cerebrum concerned chiefly with visual function.

Oedipus complex. Desire for sexual relations with a parent of opposite sex; specifically, the desire of a boy for his mother, with his father a hated rival.

Olfactory hallucinations. Hallucinations involving the sense of smell.

Operant (instrumental) conditioning. Form of learning in which if a particular response is reinforced, it becomes more likely to be repeated on similar occasions.

Operational definition. Definition of a concept on the basis of a set of operations that can be observed and measured.

Opium. Narcotic drug that leads to physiological dependence and the development of tolerance; derivatives are morphine, heroin, and codeine.

Oppositional defiant disorder (ODD). Childhood disorder that appears by age 6 and is characterized by persistent acts of aggressive or antisocial behavior that may or may not be against the law.

Oral stage. First stage of psychosexual development in Freudian theory, in which mouth or oral activities are the primary source of pleasure.

Organic mental disorders. Outdated term used to refer to disorders that resulted from some identifiable brain pathology.

Organic viewpoint. Concept that all mental disorders have an organic basis. See also **Biological viewpoint**.

Orgasm. Third phase of the human sexual response, during which there is a release of sexual tension and a peaking of sexual pleasure.

Outcome research. Studies of effectiveness of treatment.

Outpatient. Ambulatory client who visits a hospital or clinic for examination and treatment, as distinct from a hospitalized client.

Ovaries. Female gonads.

Overanxious disorder. Disorder of childhood characterized by excessive worry and persistent fears unrelated to any specific event; often includes somatic and sleeping problems.

Overcompensation. Type of ego-defense mechanism in which an undesirable trait is covered up by exaggerating a desirable trait.

Overloading. Subjecting an organism to excessive stress, for example, forcing the organism to handle or "process" an excessive amount of information.

Overprotection. Shielding a child to the extent that he or she becomes too dependent on the parent.

Overt behavior. Activities that can be observed by an outsider.

Ovum. Female gamete or germ cell.

P

Pain disorder. Experience of pain of sufficient duration and severity to cause significant life disruption in the absence of medical pathology that would explain it.

Panic. A basic emotion that involves activation of the "fight-or-flight" response of the sympathetic nervous system and that is often characterized by an overwhelming sense of fear or terror.

Panic attack. A severe, intense fear response that appears to come out of the blue; it has many physical and cognitive symptoms such as fear of dying or losing control.

Panic disorder. Occurrence of repeated unexpected panic attacks, often accompanied by intense anxiety about having another one.

Panic provocation procedures. A variety of biological challenge procedures that provoke panic attacks at higher rates in people with panic disorder than in people without panic disorder.

Paradigm. Model or pattern; in research, a basic design specifying concepts considered legitimate and procedures to be used in the collection and interpretation of data.

Paranoia. Symptoms of delusions and impaired contact with reality without the bizarreness, fragmentation, and severe personality disorganization characteristic of schizophrenia.

Paranoid personality disorder. Pervasive suspiciousness and distrust of others.

Paranoid schizophrenia. See **Schizophrenia, paranoid type**.

Paraphilic disorders. Persistent sexual behavior patterns in which unusual objects, rituals, or situations are required for full sexual satisfaction.

Paraprofessional. Person who has been trained in mental health services but not at the professional level.

Parasympathetic nervous system. Division of the autonomic nervous system that controls most of the basic metabolic functions essential for life.

Paresis. See **General paresis**.

Paresthesia. Exceptional sensations, such as tingling.

Parkinson's disease. A neurodegenerative disease characterized by motor problems (rigidity, tremors) and caused by destruction of dopamine neurons in the brain.

Passive-aggressive personality disorder. Provisional category of personality disorder in *DSM-IV-TR* characterized by a pattern of passive resistance to demands in social or work situations, which may take such forms as simple resistance to performing routine tasks, being sullen or argumentative, or alternating between defiance and submission.

Pathogenic. Pertaining to conditions that lead to pathology.

Pathological gambling. Progressive disorder characterized by loss of control over gambling, preoccupation with gambling and obtaining money for gambling, and irrational gambling behavior in spite of adverse consequences.

Pathology. Abnormal physical or mental condition.

PCP. Phencyclidine; developed as a tranquilizer but not marketed because of its unpredictability. Known on the street as "angel dust," this drug produces stupor and, at times, prolonged coma or psychosis.

Pedigree (family history) method. Observation of samples of relatives of each subject or each carrier of the trait or disorder in question.

Pedophilic disorder. A paraphilia in which an adult's preferred or exclusive sexual partner is a prepubertal child.

Pemoline. Drug, similar to Ritalin, used to treat ADHD.

Perception. Interpretation of sensory input.

Perceptual filtering. Processes involved in selective attention to aspects of the great mass of incoming stimuli that continually impinge on an organism.

Perfectionism. The need to get things exactly right. A personality trait that may increase risk for the development of eating disorders, perhaps because perfectionistic people may be more likely to idealize thinness.

Performance test. Test in which perceptual-motor rather than verbal content is emphasized.

Peripheral nervous system. Nerve fibers passing between the central nervous system and the sense organs, muscles, and glands.

Perseveration. Persistent continuation of a line of thought or activity once it is under way. Clinically inappropriate repetition.

Persistent depressive disorder (dysthymic disorder). A new *DSM-5* disorder that involves long-standing depressed mood (2 years or more). The disorder incorporates dysthymic disorder and chronic major depression from *DSM-IV-TR*.

Person-centered therapy. See **Client-centered therapy**.

Personality. Unique pattern of traits that characterize an individual.

Personality disorder. Gradual development of inflexible and distorted personality and behavioral patterns that result in persistently maladaptive ways of perceiving, thinking about, and relating to the world.

Personality or psychological decompensation. Inability to adapt to sustained or severe stressors.

Personality profile. Graphical summary that is derived from several tests or subtests of the same test battery or scale and that shows the personality configuration of an individual or group of individuals.

Personality tests. See **Objective personality tests** and **Projective personality tests**.

Pervasive developmental disorders (PDDs). Severely disabling conditions marked by deficits in language, perceptual, and motor development; defective reality testing; and inability to function in social situations.

Pessimistic attributional style. Cognitive style involving a tendency to make internal, stable, and global attributions for negative life events.

PET scan. See **Positron emission tomography (PET) scan**.

Phagocyte. Circulating white blood cell that binds to antigens and partially destroys them by engulfment.

Phallic stage. In psychoanalytic theory, the stage of psychosexual development during which genital exploration and manipulation occur.

Pharmacology. The science of drugs.

Pharmacotherapy. Treatment by means of drugs.

Phenomenological. Pertaining to the immediate perceiving and experiencing of an individual.

Phenotype. The observed structural and functional characteristics of a person that result from interaction between the genotype and the environment.

Phenylketonuria (PKU). Type of intellectual disability resulting from a baby's lack of a liver enzyme needed to break down phenylalanine, an amino acid found in many foods.

Phobia. Persistent and disproportionate fear of some specific object or situation that presents little or no actual danger.

Physiological dependence. Type of drug dependence involving withdrawal symptoms when drug is discontinued.

Pick's disease. Form of presenile dementia.

Pineal gland. Small gland at the base of the brain that helps regulate the body's biological clock and may also establish the pace of sexual development.

Pituitary gland. Endocrine gland associated with many regulatory functions.

Placebo effect. Positive effect experienced after an inactive treatment is administered in such a way that a person thinks he or she is receiving an active treatment.

Placebo treatment. An inert pill or otherwise neutral intervention that produces desirable therapeutic effects because of the subject's expectations that it will be beneficial.

Plaques. Abnormal accumulations of protein found in the brains of patients with Alzheimer's disease.

Play therapy. Use of play activities in psychotherapy with children.

Pleasure principle. Demand that an instinctual need be immediately gratified regardless of reality or moral considerations.

Point prevalence. The number of cases of a specific condition or disorder that can be found in a population at one given point in time.

Polygenic. Caused by the action of many genes together in an additive or interactive fashion.

Poor premorbid schizophrenia. See **Process schizophrenia**.

Positive correlation. A relationship between two variables such that a high score on one variable is associated with a high score on another variable.

Positive psychology. A new field that focuses on human traits (e.g., optimism) and resources that are potentially important for health and well-being.

Positive reinforcer. Reinforcer that increases the probability of recurrence of a given response.

Positive-symptom schizophrenia. Schizophrenia characterized by something added to normal behavior and experience, such as marked emotional turmoil, motor agitation, delusions, and hallucinations.

Positive symptoms. Symptoms that are characterized by something being added to normal behavior or experience. Includes delusions, hallucinations, motor agitation, and marked emotional turmoil.

Positron emission tomography (PET) scan. Scanning technique that measures metabolic processes to appraise how well an organ is functioning.

Posthypnotic amnesia. Subject's lack of memory for the period during which he or she was hypnotized.

Posthypnotic suggestion. Suggestion given during hypnosis to be carried out by a subject after he or she is brought out of hypnosis.

Postpartum depression. Depression occurring after childbirth. Most commonly it is mild and transient (postpartum blues) but can become a major depressive episode.

Posttraumatic stress disorder (PTSD). Disorder that occurs following an extreme traumatic event, in which a person reexperiences the event, avoids reminders of the trauma, and exhibits persistent increased arousal.

Posttraumatic theory (of DID). The view that DID starts from the child's attempt to cope with an overwhelming sense of hopelessness and powerlessness in the face of repeated traumatic abuse.

Predisposition. Tendency to develop certain symptoms under given stress conditions.

Prefrontal lobotomy. Surgical procedure used before the advent of antipsychotic drugs, in which the frontal lobes of the brain were severed from the deeper centers underlying them, resulting in permanent structural changes in the brain.

Prejudice. Emotionally toned conception favorable or unfavorable to some person, group, or idea—typically in the absence of sound evidence.

Premature ejaculation. Persistent and recurrent onset of orgasm and ejaculation with minimal sexual stimulation.

Prematurity. Birth of an infant before the end of a normal period of pregnancy.

Premorbid. Existing before the onset of mental disorder.

Prenatal. Before birth.

Prepared learning. The view that people are biologically prepared through evolution to more readily acquire fears of certain objects or situations that may once have posed a threat to our early ancestors. For example, people more readily develop fears of snakes and spiders if they are paired with aversive events, than they develop fears of knives or guns.

Presenile dementia. Mental disorders resulting from brain degeneration before old age.

Presenting problem. Major symptoms and behavior the client is experiencing.

Prevalence. In a population, the proportion of active cases of a disorder that can be identified at a given point in time or during a given period.

Primary gain. In psychodynamic theory it is the goal achieved by symptoms of conversion disorder by keeping internal intrapsychic conflicts out of awareness. In contemporary terms it is the goal achieved by symptoms of conversion disorder by allowing the person to escape or avoid stressful situations.

Primary prevention. Older term for preventive efforts aimed at reducing the incidence of a disease or disorder and fostering positive health.

Primary process thinking. Gratification of id demands by means of imagery or fantasy without the ability to undertake the realistic actions needed to meet those instinctual demands.

Proband. In a genetic study, the original individual who evidences the trait in which the investigator is interested. Same as *index case*.

Problem checklist. Inventory used in behavioral assessment to determine an individual's fears, moods, and other problems.

Problem drinker. Behavioral term referring to one who has serious problems associated with drinking.

Process schizophrenia. Schizophrenic pattern—marked by seclusiveness, gradual waning of interest in the surrounding world, diminished emotional responsivity, and mildly inappropriate responses—that develops gradually and tends to be long lasting; alternatively known as *poor premorbid schizophrenia* and *chronic schizophrenia.*

Prodromal. Considered to be an early (subclinical) stage of schizophrenia, characterized by very low-level symptoms or behavioral idiosyncrasies.

Prognosis. Prediction of the probable course and outcome of a disorder.

Projection. Ego-defense mechanism of attributing one's own unacceptable motives or characteristics to others.

Projective personality tests. Techniques that use various ambiguous stimuli that a subject is encouraged to interpret and from which the subject's personality characteristics can be analyzed.

Prolonged exposure. A behaviorally oriented treatment strategy in which a patient is asked to vividly recount the traumatic event over and over until the patient experiences a decrease in his or her emotional response.

Prospective research. Method that often focuses on individuals who have a higher-than-average likelihood of becoming psychologically disordered before abnormal behavior is observed.

Protective factors. Influences that modify a person's response to an environmental stressor, making it less likely that the person will experience the adverse effects of the stressor.

Prototypal approach. Approach to classifying abnormal behavior that assumes the existence of prototypes of behavior disorders that, rather than being mutually exclusive, may blend into others with which they share many characteristics.

Psilocybin. Hallucinogenic drug derived from a variety of mushrooms.

Psychedelic drugs. Drugs such as LSD that often produce hallucinations.

Psychiatric nursing. Field of nursing primarily concerned with mental disorders.

Psychiatric social worker. Professional who has had graduate training in social work with psychiatric specialization, typically leading to a master's degree.

Psychiatrist. Medical doctor who specializes in the diagnosis and treatment of mental disorders.

Psychiatry. Field of medicine concerned with understanding, assessing, treating, and preventing mental disorders.

Psychic trauma. Any aversive experience that inflicts serious psychological damage on a person.

Psychoactive substance. Drug that affects mental functioning.

Psychoactive substance abuse. Pathological use of a substance resulting in potentially hazardous behavior or in continued use despite a persistent social, psychological, occupational, or health problem.

Psychoactive substance dependence. Use of a psychoactive substance to the point where one has a marked physiological need for increasing amounts of the substance to achieve the desired effects.

Psychoanalysis. Methods Freud used to study and treat patients.

Psychoanalytic perspective. Theory of psychopathology, initially developed by Freud, that emphasizes the inner dynamics of unconscious motives.

Psychodrama. Psychotherapeutic technique in which the acting of various roles is an essential part.

Psychodynamic perspectives. Theories of psychopathology based on modification and revision of Freud's theories.

Psychodynamic therapy. Psychological treatment that focuses on individual personality dynamics, usually from a psychodynamic or psychodynamically derived perspective.

Psychogenic. Of psychological origin: originating in the psychological functioning of an individual.

Psychogenic amnesia. Amnesia of psychological origin, common in initial reactions to traumatic experiences.

Psychogenic illness. Psychologically induced or maintained disease.

Psychohistory. A field of study analyzing history according to psychoanalytic principles.

Psychological assessment. The use of psychological procedures such as behavioral observations, interview, and psychological tests to obtain a picture of a client's mental health symptoms and personality.

Psychological autopsy. Analytical procedure used to determine whether or not death was self-inflicted and, if so, why.

Psychological need. Need emerging out of environmental interactions, for example, the need for social approval.

Psychological screening. Use of psychological procedures or tests to detect psychological problems among applicants in preemployment evaluations.

Psychological test. Standardized procedure designed to measure a subject's performance on a specified task.

Psychomotor. Involving both psychological and physical activity.

Psychomotor retardation. Slowing down of psychological and motor functions.

Psychoneuroimmunology. Study of the interactions between the immune system and the nervous system and the influence of these factors on behavior.

Psychopathology. Abnormal behavior.

Psychopathy. A condition involving the features of antisocial personality disorder and such traits as lack of empathy, inflated and arrogant self-appraisal, and glib and superficial charm.

Psychopharmacology. Science of determining which drugs alleviate which disorders and why they do so.

Psychophysiological (psychosomatic) disorders. Physical disorders in which psychological factors are believed to play a major causal role.

Psychophysiological variables. Measures of biological functioning including heart rate, blood pressure, EEG, and so on.

Psychosexual development. Freudian view of development as involving a succession of stages, each characterized by a dominant mode of achieving libidinal pleasure.

Psychosexual stages of development. According to Freudian theory, there are five stages of psychosexual development, each characterized by a dominant mode of achieving sexual pleasure: the oral stage, the anal stage, the phallic stage, the latency stage, and the genital stage.

Psychosis. Severe impairment in the ability to tell what is real and what is not real.

Psychosocial deprivation. Lack of needed stimulation and interaction during early life.

Psychosocial viewpoints. Approaches to understanding mental disorders that emphasize the importance of early experience and an awareness of social influences and psychological processes within an individual.

Psychosurgery. Brain surgery used in the past with excessive frequency in the treatment of functional mental disorders.

Psychotherapy. Treatment of mental disorders by psychological methods.

Psychotropic drugs. Drugs whose main effects are mental or behavioral in nature.

Purge. Purging refers to the removal of food from the body by such means as self-induced vomiting or misuse of laxatives, diuretics, and enemas.

Q

Q-sort. Personality measure in which a subject, or a clinician, sorts a number of statements into piles according to their applicability to the subject.

R

Racism. Prejudice and discrimination directed toward individuals or groups because of their racial background.

Random assignment. A procedure used to create equivalent groups in which every research participant has an equal chance of being assigned to any group in the study.

Random sample. Sample drawn in such a way that each member of a population has an equal chance of being selected; it is hoped that such a sample will be fully representative of the population from which it is drawn.

Randomized clinical trials (RCTs). A clinical trial in which participants are randomly assigned to different treatments.

Randomized controlled trials. A randomized controlled trial involves a specific treatment group (the group the researchers are most interested in) as well as a control treatment group (against which the treatment group will be compared). Participants have an equal chance of being placed in either group because placement is determined randomly.

Rape. Sexual activity that occurs under actual or threatened forcible coercion of one person by another.

Rapid cycling. A pattern of bipolar disorder involving at least four manic or depressive episodes per year.

Rapport. Interpersonal relationship characterized by a spirit of cooperation, confidence, and harmony.

Rating scales. Formal structure for organizing information obtained from clinical observation and self-reports to encourage reliability and objectivity.

Rational emotive behavior therapy (REBT). Form of psychotherapy focusing on changing a client's maladaptive thought processes, on which maladaptive emotional responses and thus behavior are presumed to depend.

Rationalization. Ego-defense mechanism that involves the use of contrived "explanations" to conceal or disguise unworthy motives for a person's behavior.

Reaction formation. Ego-defense mechanism that prevents the awareness or expression of unacceptable desires via the exaggerated adoption of seemingly opposite behavior.

Reactive schizophrenia. Schizophrenia pattern—marked by confusion and intense emotional turmoil—that normally develops suddenly and has identifiable precipitating stressors; alternatively known as *good premorbid schizophrenia, Type I schizophrenia*, and *acute schizophrenia*.

Reality principle. Awareness of the demands of the environment and adjustment of behavior to meet these demands.

Reality testing. Behavior aimed at testing or exploring the nature of a person's social and physical environment; often used more specifically to refer to testing the limits of the permissiveness of the social environment.

Recessive gene. Gene that is effective only when paired with an identical gene.

Recidivism. Shift back to one's original behavior (often delinquent or criminal) after a period of treatment or rehabilitation.

Recompensation. Increase in integration or inner organization. Opposite of *decompensation.*

Recurrence. A new occurrence of a disorder after a remission of symptom.

Recurrent. Term used to describe a disorder pattern that tends to come and go.

Recurrent major depressive episode with a seasonal pattern. A form of major depression where the episodes of depression recur on a regular seasonal basis (fall/winter), but not at other times of the year.

Referral. Sending or recommending an individual or family for psychological assessment or treatment.

Regression. Ego-defense mechanism of retreat to an earlier developmental level involving less mature behavior and responsibility.

Rehabilitation. Use of reeducation rather than punishment to overcome behavioral deficits.

Reinforcement. The process of rewarding desired responses.

Relapse. Return of the symptoms of a disorder after a fairly short period of time.

Reliability. Degree to which a measuring device produces the same result each time it is used to measure the same thing or when two or more different raters use it.

REM sleep. Stage of sleep involving rapid eye movements (REM); associated with dreaming.

Remission. Marked improvement or recovery appearing in the course of a mental illness; may or may not be permanent.

Representative sample. Small group selected in such a way as to be representative of the larger group from which it is drawn.

Repression. Ego-defense mechanism that prevents painful or dangerous thoughts from entering consciousness.

Residential treatment. Out-of-home placements for children and adolescents with mental health problems.

Residual schizophrenia. See **Schizophrenia, residual type**.

Resilience. The ability to adapt successfully to even very difficult circumstances.

Resistance. Selye's second stage of responding to continuing trauma, involving finding some means to deal with the trauma and adjust to it. In psychodynamic treatment, the person's unwillingness or inability to talk about certain thoughts, motives, or experiences.

Resistance to extinction. Tendency of a conditioned response to persist despite lack of reinforcement.

Resolution. Final phase of the human sexual response, during which a person has a sense of relaxation and well-being.

Response shaping. Positive reinforcement technique used in therapy to establish, by gradual approximation, a response not initially in a person's behavioral repertoire.

Reticular activating system (RAS). Fibers going from the reticular formation to higher brain centers and presumably functioning as a general arousal system.

Reticular formation. Neural nuclei and fibers in the brain stem that apparently play an important role in arousing and alerting an organism and in controlling attention.

Retrograde amnesia. Loss of memory for events that occurred during a circumscribed period prior to brain injury or damage.

Retrospective research. Research approach that attempts to retrace earlier events in the life of a subject.

Retrospective strategy. Method of trying to uncover the probable causes of abnormal behavior by looking backward from the present.

Reward deficiency syndrome. A hypothesis suggesting that addiction is more likely to occur in individuals who have a genetic predisposition to be less satisfied by natural rewards, which leads them to overuse drugs as a way to adequately stimulate their reward pathway.

Rigidity. Tendency to follow established coping patterns, with failure to see alternatives or extreme difficulty in changing one's established patterns.

Risk factor. A correlate that occurs before some outcome of interest (e.g., depression is a risk factor for suicide).

Ritalin. Central nervous system stimulant often used to treat ADHD.

Role-playing. Form of assessment in which a person is instructed to play a part, enabling a clinician to observe a client's behavior directly.

Rorschach Inkblot Test. Use of 10 inkblot pictures to which a subject responds with associations that come to mind. Analysis of these responses enables a clinician to infer personality characteristics.

Rumination. Refers to the process of going over and over in one's mind or going over a thought repeatedly time and again.

S

Saint Vitus's dance. Name given to the dancing mania (and mass hysteria) that spread from Italy to Germany and the rest of Europe in the Middle Ages.

Sample. Group on which measurements are taken; should normally be representative of the population about which an inference is to be made.

Sampling. The process of selecting a representative subgroup from a defined population of interest.

Scapegoating. Displacement of aggression onto some object, person, or group other than the source of frustration.

Schedule of reinforcement. Program of rewards for requisite behavior.

Schema. An underlying representation of knowledge that guides current processing of information and often leads to distortions in attention, memory, and comprehension.

Schizoaffective disorder. Form of psychotic disorder in which the symptoms of schizophrenia co-occur with symptoms of a mood disorder.

Schizoid personality disorder. Inability to form social relationships or express feelings, and lack of interest in doing so.

Schizophrenia. Disorder characterized by hallucinations, delusions, disorganized speech and behavior, as well as problems in self-care and general functioning.

Schizophrenia, catatonic type. Sub-type of schizophrenia no longer included in *DSM-5* in which the central feature is pronounced motor symptoms, of either an excited or a stuporous type, which sometimes make for difficulty in differentiating this condition from a psychotic mood disorder.

Schizophrenia, disorganized type. Sub-type of schizophrenia no longer included in *DSM-5* that usually begins at an earlier age and represents a more severe disintegration of the personality than in the other types of schizophrenia.

Schizophrenia, paranoid type. Subtype of schizophrenia no longer included in *DSM-5* in which a person is increasingly suspicious, has severe difficulties in interpersonal relationships, and experiences absurd, illogical, and often changing delusions.

Schizophrenia, residual type. No longer included in *DSM-5,* this was a diagnostic category used for people who have experienced a schizophrenic episode from which they have recovered enough to not show prominent symptoms but are still manifesting some mild signs of their past disorder.

Schizophrenia, undifferentiated type. Subtype of schizophrenia no longer included in *DSM-5* in which a person meets the usual criteria for having schizophrenia—including (in varying combinations) delusions, hallucinations, thought disorder, and bizarre behavior—but does not clearly fit into one of the other types because of a mixed symptom picture.

Schizophreniform disorder. Category of schizophrenic-like psychosis less than 6 months in duration.

Schizophrenogenic. Schizophrenia-causing.

Schizotypal personality disorder. Disorder characterized by excessive introversion, pervasive social interpersonal deficits, cognitive and perceptual distortions, and eccentricities in communication and behavior.

Seasonal affective disorder. Mood disorder involving at least two episodes of depression in the past 2 years occurring at the same time of year (most commonly fall or winter), with remission also occurring at the same time of year (most commonly spring).

Secondary gain. External circumstances that tend to reinforce the maintenance of disability.

Secondary prevention. Older term for prevention techniques that typically involve emergency or crisis intervention, with efforts focused on reducing the impact, duration, or spread of a problem. See **Selective intervention**.

Secondary process thinking. Reality-oriented rational processes of the ego for dealing with the external world and the exercise of control over id demands.

Secondary reinforcer. Reinforcement provided by a stimulus that has gained reward value by being associated with a primary reinforcing stimulus.

Sedative. Drug used to reduce tension and induce relaxation and sleep.

Selective intervention. Mobilization of prevention resources to eliminate or reduce a particular type of problem (such as teenage pregnancy or alcohol or drug abuse).

Selective mutism. Condition that involves the persistent failure to speak in specific social situations and interferes with educational or social adjustment.

Selective serotonin reuptake inhibitors (SSRIs). A medication that inhibits serotonin and is used in the treatment of depression.

Self (ego). Integrating core of a personality that mediates between needs and reality.

Self-acceptance. Being satisfied with one's attributes and qualities while remaining aware of one's limitations.

Self-actualizing. Achieving one's full potentialities as a human being.

Self-concept. A person's sense of his or her own identity, worth, capabilities, and limitations.

Self-esteem. Feeling of personal worth.

Self-evaluation. Way in which an individual views the self, in terms of worth, adequacy, and so forth.

Self-ideal (ego-ideal). Person or "self" a person thinks he or she could and should be.

Self-identity. Individual's delineation and awareness of his or her continuing identity as a person.

Self-instructional training. Cognitive-behavioral method aimed at teaching a person to alter his or her covert behavior.

Self-monitoring. Observing and recording one's own behavior, thoughts, and feelings as they occur in various natural settings.

Self-reinforcement. Reward of self for desired or appropriate behavior.

Self-report data. Data collected directly from participants, typically by means of interviews or questionnaires.

Self-report inventory. Procedure in which a subject is asked to respond to statements in terms of their applicability to him or her.

Self-schema. Our view of what we are, what we might become, and what is important to us.

Self-statements. A person's implicit verbalizations of what he or she is experiencing.

Senile. Pertaining to old age.

Senile dementia. Mental disorders that sometimes accompany brain degeneration in old age.

Sensate focus learning. Learning to derive pleasure from touching one's partner and being touched by him or her; this training is used in sexual therapy to enhance sexual feelings and help overcome sexual dysfunction.

Sensory deprivation. Restriction of sensory stimulation below the level required for normal functioning of the central nervous system.

Sentence completion test. Projective technique utilizing incomplete sentences that a person is to complete, analysis of which enables a clinician to infer personality dynamics.

Separation anxiety disorder. Childhood disorder characterized by unrealistic fears, oversensitivity, self-consciousness, nightmares, and chronic anxiety.

Separation-individuation. According to Mahler, a developmental phase in which a child gains an internal representation of the self as distinct from representations of other objects.

Sequelae. Symptoms remaining as the aftermath of a disorder.

Serotonin. A neurotransmitter from the indolamine class that is synthesized from the amino acid tryptophan. Also referred to as 5-HT (5-hydroxytryptamine), this neurotransmitter is thought to be involved in a wide range of psychopathological conditions.

Set point. The tendency of our bodies to resist efforts to bring about a marked change (increase or decrease) in weight.

Severe (disorder). Disorder of a high degree of seriousness.

Severe major depressive episode with psychotic features. Major depression involving loss of contact with reality, often in the form of delusions or hallucinations.

Sex chromosomes. Pair of chromosomes inherited by an individual that determine sex and certain other characteristics.

Sexual abuse. Sexual contact that involves physical or psychological coercion or occurs when at least one individual cannot reasonably consent to the contact.

Sexual assault. Refers to acts, separate from rape, that involve unwanted sexual contact, such as groping or fondling another person without that person's consent.

Sexual aversion disorder. Sexual dysfunction in which a person shows extreme aversion to, and avoidance of, all genital sexual contact with a partner.

Sexual dysfunction. Impairment either in the desire for sexual gratification or in the ability to achieve it.

Sexual sadism disorder. Disorder in which an individual achieves sexual gratification by inflicting physical or psychic pain or humiliation on a sexual partner.

Shaping. Form of instrumental conditioning; at first, all responses resembling the desired one are reinforced, then only the closest approximations, until finally the desired response is attained. Also called *successive approximation.*

Shared psychotic disorder. Psychosis in which two or more people develop persistent, interlocking delusional ideas. Also known as *folie à deux.*

Sheltered workshops. Workshops where individuals with physical or mental disabilities can engage in constructive work in the community.

Short-term crisis therapy. Brief treatment that focuses on the immediate problem an individual or family is experiencing.

Siblings. Offspring of the same parents.

Sick role. Protected role provided by society via the medical model for a person suffering from a severe physical or mental disorder.

Significant others. In the interpersonal theory of psychological development, parents or others on whom an infant is dependent for meeting all physical and psychological needs.

Signs. Objective observations that suggest to a diagnostician a patient's physical or mental disorder.

Simple phobia. See **Specific phobia**.

Simple tension headaches. Common headaches in which stress leads to contraction of the muscles surrounding the skull; these contractions result in vascular constrictions that cause headache.

Single-case research design. An experimental research design (e.g., an ABAB design) that involves only one subject.

Situational test. Test that measures performance in a simulated life situation.

Sleepwalking disorder. Disorder of childhood that involves repeated episodes of leaving the bed and walking around without being conscious of the experience or remembering it later. Also known as *somnambulism.*

Social exchange view. Model of interpersonal relationships based on the premise that such relationships are formed for mutual gratification of needs.

Social introversion. Trait characterized by shy, withdrawn, and inhibited behavior.

Social-learning programs. Behavioral programs using learning techniques, especially token economies, to help patients assume more responsibility for their own behavior.

Social norms. Group standards concerning which behaviors are viewed as acceptable and which as unacceptable.

Social pathology. Abnormal patterns of social organization, attitudes, or behavior; undesirable social conditions that tend to produce individual pathology.

Social phobia. Fear of situations in which a person might be exposed to the scrutiny of others and fear of acting in a humiliating or embarrassing way.

Social recovery. Ability to manage independently as an economically effective and interpersonally connected member of society.

Social role. Behavior expected of a person occupying a given position in a group.

"Social" self. Façade a person displays to others, as contrasted with the private self.

Social work. Applied offshoot of sociology concerned with analyzing social environments and providing services that enhance the adjustment of a client in both family and community settings.

Social worker. Person in a mental health field with a master's degree in social work (MSW) plus supervised training in clinical or social service agencies.

Socialization. Process by which a child acquires the values and impulse controls deemed appropriate by his or her culture.

Sociocognitive theory (of DID). View that DID develops when a highly suggestible person learns to adopt and enact the roles of multiple identities, mostly because clinicians have inadvertently suggested, legitimized, and reinforced them and because these different identities are geared to the individual's own personal goals.

Sociocultural viewpoint. Perspective that focuses on broad social conditions that influence the development or behavior of individuals and groups.

Socioeconomic status. Position on social and economic scale in community; determined largely by income and occupational level.

Sociogenic. Having its roots in sociocultural conditions.

Sociopathic personality. See **Antisocial personality disorder**.

Sodium pentothal. Barbiturate drug sometimes used in psychotherapy to produce a state of relaxation and suggestibility.

Soma. Greek word for "body."

Somatic. Pertaining to the body.

Somatic symptom disorder. A new *DSM-5* diagnosis characterized by somatic (physical) symptoms and an excessive focus (in thoughts, feelings, or behavior) on these symptoms. Many people who would have been diagnosed with hypochondriasis in *DSM-IV-TR* will now be diagnosed with somatic symptom disorder.

Somatic weakness. Special vulnerability of given organ systems to stress.

Somatization disorder. Multiple complaints, over a long period beginning before age 30, of physical ailments that are inadequately explained by independent findings of physical illness or injury and that lead to medical treatment or to significant life impairment.

Somatoform disorders. Conditions involving physical complaints or disabilities that occur without any evidence of physical pathology to account for them.

Somnambulism. See **Sleepwalking disorder**.

Spasm. Intense, involuntary, usually painful contraction of a muscle or group of muscles.

Spasticity. Marked hypertonicity or continual overcontraction of muscles, causing stiffness, awkwardness, and motor incoordination.

Specific learning disorders. Developmental disorders involving deficits in language, speech, mathematical, or motor skills.

Specific phobia. Persistent or disproportionate fears of various objects, places, or situations, such as fears of situations (airplanes or elevators), other species (snakes, spiders), or aspects of the environment (high places, water).

Specifiers (in mood disorders). Different patterns of symptoms that sometimes characterize major depressive episodes that may help predict the course and preferred treatments for the condition.

Sperm. Male gamete or germ cell.

Split-brain research. Research associated with split-brain surgery, which cuts off the transmission of information from one cerebral hemisphere to the other by severing the corpus callosum.

Spontaneous recovery. The return of a learned response at some time after extinction has occurred.

Stage of exhaustion. Selye's third and final stage in the general adaptation syndrome, in which an organism is no longer able to resist continuing stress; may result in death.

Stage of resistance. Second stage of the general adaptation syndrome.

Standardization. Procedure for establishing the expected performance range on a test.

Stanford-Binet. Standardized intelligence test for children.

Startle reaction. Sudden involuntary motor reaction to intense unexpected stimuli; may result from mild stimuli if a person is hypersensitive.

Statistical significance. A measure of the probability that a research finding could have occurred by chance alone.

Statutory rape. Sexual intercourse with a minor.

Steady states (homeostasis). Tendency of an organism to maintain conditions that make possible a constant level of physiological functioning.

Stereotyping. The tendency to jump to conclusions (often negative) about what a person is like based on the beliefs about that group that exist (often incorrectly) in the culture (e.g., French people are rude, homosexuals have good taste in clothes, and patients with mental illness are dangerous).

Stereotypy. Persistent and inappropriate repetition of phrases, gestures, or acts.

Stigma. Negative labeling.

Stimulants. Drugs that tend to increase feelings of alertness, reduce feelings of fatigue, and enable a person to stay awake over sustained periods of time.

Stimulus generalization. Spread of a conditioned response to some stimulus similar to, but not identical with, the conditioned stimulus.

Strattera. A medication used in the treatment of ADHD.

Stress. Effects created within an organism by the application of a stressor.

Stress-inoculation therapy. Type of self-instructional training focused on altering self-statements that a person routinely makes in stress-producing situations.

Stress-inoculation training. Preventive strategy that prepares people to tolerate an anticipated threat by changing the things they say to themselves before the crisis.

Stress tolerance. A person's ability to withstand stress without becoming seriously impaired.

Stressors. Adjustive demands that require coping behavior on the part of an individual or group.

Stroke. See **Cerebrovascular accident**.

Structural family therapy. Treatment of an entire family by analysis of interaction among family members.

Structured assessment interview. Interview with a set introduction that follows a predetermined set of procedures and questions throughout.

Stupor. Condition of lethargy and unresponsiveness, with partial or complete unconsciousness.

Sublimation. Ego-defense mechanism that channels frustrated expression of sexual energy into substitutive activities.

Substance abuse. Maladaptive pattern of substance use manifested by recurrent and significant adverse consequences related to the use of the substance.

Substance dependence. Severe form of substance use disorder involving physiological dependence on the substance, tolerance, withdrawal, and compulsive drug taking.

Substance-related disorders. Patterns of maladaptive behavior centered on the regular use of a substance, such as a drug or alcohol.

Substitution. Acceptance of substitute goals or satisfactions in place of those originally sought or desired.

Successive approximation. See **Shaping**.

Sufficient cause. A condition that guarantees the occurrence of a disorder.

Suicide. Taking one's own life.

Suicidology. Study of the causes and prevention of suicide.

Superego. Conscience; ethical or moral dimensions (attitudes) of personality.

Suppression. Conscious forcing of desires or thoughts out of consciousness; conscious inhibition of desires or impulses.

Surrogate. Substitute for another person, such as a parent or mate.

Symbol. Image, word, object, or activity that is used to represent something else.

Symbolism. Representation of one idea or object by another.

Sympathetic-adrenomedullary (SAM) system. System designed to mobilize resources and prepare for a fight-or-flight response.

Sympathetic division. Division of the autonomic nervous system that is active in emergency conditions of extreme cold, violent effort, and emotions.

Symptoms. Patient's subjective description of a physical or mental disorder.

Synapse. Site of communication from the axon of one neuron to the dendrites or cell body of another neuron—a tiny filled space between neurons.

Syndrome. Group or pattern of symptoms that occur together in a disorder and represent the typical picture of the disorder.

Synthetic cannabinoids. Substances that mimic the effects of tetrahydrocannabinol (THC), the active plant-derived substance in marijuana.

Synthetic cathinones. Substances that mimic the effects of amphetamines and cocaine by activating the body's mono-amine system.

System. Assemblage of interdependent parts, living or nonliving.

Systematic desensitization. Behavior therapy technique for extinguishing maladaptive anxiety responses by teaching a person to relax or behave, while in the presence of the anxiety-producing stimulus, in some other way that is inconsistent with anxiety.

T

Tachycardia. Rapid heartbeat.

Tactual hallucinations. Hallucinations involving the sense of touch.

Tarantism. Dancing mania that occurred in Italy in the thirteenth century.

Tarasoff **decision.** Ruling by a California court (1974) that a therapist has a duty to warn a prospective victim of an explicit threat expressed by a client in therapy.

Tardive dyskinesia. Neurological disorder resulting from excessive use of antipsychotic drugs. Side effects can occur months to years after treatment has been initiated or has stopped. The symptoms involve involuntary movements of the tongue, lips, jaw, and extremities.

Task-oriented response. Making changes in one's self, one's surroundings, or both, depending on the situation.

Tay-Sachs disease. Genetic disorder of lipid metabolism usually resulting in death by age 3.

T-cell. A type of white blood cell that, when activated, can recognize specific antigens. T-cells play an important role in the immune system.

Telepathy. Communication from one person to another without use of any known sense organs.

Telomere. Human telomeres are the protective ends of our chromosomes. They are made up of repeated sequences of DNA. Their presence protects the genes close to them from being damaged and truncated during cell division. Telomeres shorten as we age. Stress also reduces the length of telomeres.

Temperament. Pattern of emotional and arousal responses and characteristic ways of self-regulation that are considered to be primarily hereditary or constitutional.

Temporal lobe. Portion of the cerebrum located in front of the occipital lobe and separated from the frontal and parietal lobes by the fissure of Sylvius.

Tension. Condition arising from the mobilization of psychobiological resources to meet a threat; physically, involves an increase in muscle tone and other emergency changes; psychologically, is characterized by feelings of strain, uneasiness, and anxiety.

Tertiary prevention. Older term for preventive techniques focused on reducing long-term consequences of disorders or serious problems.

Test validity. Degree to which a test actually measures what it was designed to measure.

Testes. Male reproductive glands or gonads.

Testosterone. Male sex hormone.

Test–retest reliability. Consistency with which a test measures a given trait on repeated administrations of the test to given subjects.

Thematic Apperception Test (TAT). Use of a series of simple pictures about which a subject is instructed to make up stories. Analysis of the stories gives a clinician clues about the person's conflicts, traits, personality dynamics, and the like.

Therapeutic. Pertaining to treatment or healing.

Therapeutic community. Hospital environment used for therapeutic purposes.

Therapy. Treatment; application of various treatment techniques.

Third variable problem. Refers to the problem of making causal inferences in correlational research, where the correlation between two variables could be due to their shared correlation with an unmeasured third variable.

Thyroid. Endocrine gland located in the neck that influences body metabolism, rate of physical growth, and development of intelligence.

Thyroxin. Hormone secreted by the thyroid glands.

Tic. Persistent, intermittent muscle twitch or spasm, usually limited to a localized muscle group, often of the facial muscles.

Token economies. Reinforcement techniques often used in hospital or institutional settings in which patients are rewarded for socially constructive behaviors with tokens that can then be exchanged for desired objects or activities.

Tolerance. Need for increased amounts of a substance to achieve the desired effects.

Tourette's disorder. Extreme tic disorder involving uncontrollable multiple motor and vocal patterns.

Toxic. Poisonous.

Traditional behavioral couple therapy (TBCT). Widely used form of therapy that uses behavioral approaches to bring about changes in the marital relationship.

Trait. Characteristic of a person that can be observed or measured.

Trance. Sleep-like state in which the range of consciousness is limited and voluntary activities are suspended; a deep hypnotic state.

Tranquilizers. Drugs used for reduction of psychotic symptoms (major tranquilizers) or reduction of anxiety and tension (minor tranquilizers).

Transcranial magnetic stimulation (TMS). A treatment in which the clinician positions a pulsed magnet over a carefully selected area of the patient's scalp and uses it to create an electrical field that increases or decreases neuronal activity in the brain.

Transference. In psychodynamic therapy, a process whereby clients project onto the therapist attitudes and feelings that they have had for a parent or others close to them.

Transsexualism. Individuals who identify with members of the opposite sex (as opposed to acceptance of their own biological sex) and who strongly desire to (and often do) change their sex. In most cases this is gender identity disorder in adults.

Transvestic disorder. Achievement of sexual arousal and satisfaction by dressing as a member of the opposite sex.

Trauma. Severe psychological or physiological stressor.

Traumatic. Pertaining to a wound or injury or to psychic shock.

Traumatic brain injury (TBI). Brain damage resulting from motor vehicle crashes, bullets, or other objects entering the brain, and other severe impacts to the head.

Traumatic childhood abuse. Mistreatment in childhood severe enough to cause psychological damage.

Treatment contract. Explicit arrangement between a therapist and a client designed to bring about specific behavioral changes.

Tremor. Repeated fine spastic movement.

Trichotillomania. Chronic pulling out of one's own hair.

Tricyclic antidepressants. Medications used to treat depression, and sometimes anxiety disorders, that are thought to block the reuptake of norepinephrine and serotonin at the synapse.

T-score distribution. A standard distribution of scores that allows for a comparison of scores on a test by comparing scores with a group of known values.

Twin method. The use of identical and nonidentical twins to study genetic influences on abnormal behavior.

Type A behavior pattern. Excessive competitive drive even when it is unnecessary, impatience or time urgency, and hostility.

Type D personality. Type D (for distressed) personality is characterized by high levels of negative emotions and social anxiety. Research suggests that Type D personality is linked to heart attacks.

Type I schizophrenia. Psychotic behavior of the positive syndrome variety thought to involve chiefly temporolimbic brain structures.

Type II schizophrenia. Psychotic behavior of the negative syndrome variety thought to involve chiefly frontal brain structures.

U

Unconscious. In psychoanalytic theory, a major portion of the mind, which consists of a hidden mass of instincts, impulses, and memories and is not easily available to conscious awareness, yet plays an important role in behavior.

Underarousal. Inadequate physiological response to a given stimulus.

Undifferentiated schizophrenia. See **Schizophrenia, undifferentiated type**.

Undoing. Ego-defense mechanism of atoning for or magically trying to dispel unacceptable desires or acts.

Unipolar depressive disorder. Mood disorder in which a person experiences only depressive episodes, as opposed to bipolar disorder, in which both manic and depressive episodes occur.

Universal intervention. The tasks of altering conditions that cause or contribute to mental disorders (risk factors) and establishing conditions that foster positive mental health (protective factors).

Unstructured assessment interviews. Typically subjective interviews that do not follow a predetermined set of questions. The beginning statements in the interview are usually general, and follow-up questions are tailored for each client. The content of the interview questions is influenced by the habits or theoretical views of the interviewer.

V

Vaginismus. Involuntary spasm of the muscles at the entrance to the vagina that prevents penetration and sexual intercourse.

Validity. Extent to which a measuring instrument actually measures what it purports to measure.

Variable. Characteristic or property that may assume any one of a set of different qualities or quantities.

Variable marker. A variable risk factor that, when changed, doesn't influence the outcome of interest (i.e., it can vary, but it is still a marker of increased risk for the outcome of interest).

Variable risk factor. A risk factor that can change within a person (e.g., level of depression can vary within a person).

Vascular dementia. A brain disorder in which a series of small strokes destroys neurons, leading to brain atrophy and behavioral impairments that are similar to Alzheimer's disease.

Vasomotor. Pertaining to the walls of the blood vessels.

Vegetative. Withdrawn or deteriorated to the point of leading a passive, vegetable-like existence.

Verbal test. Test in which a subject's ability to understand and use words and concepts is important in making the required responses.

Vertigo. Dizziness.

Virilism. Accentuation of masculine secondary sex characteristics, especially in a woman or young boy, caused by hormonal imbalance.

Viscera. Internal organs.

Voyeuristic disorder. Disorder in which an individual achieves sexual pleasure through clandestine "peeping," usually watching other people disrobe and/or engage in sexual activities.

Vulnerabilities. Factors that render a person susceptible to behaving abnormally.

W

Wechsler Intelligence Scale for Children (WISC). Standardized intelligence test for children.

Withdrawal. Intellectual, emotional, or physical retreat.

Withdrawal symptoms. Physical symptoms such as sweating, tremors, and tension that accompany abstinence from some drugs.

Word salad. Jumbled or incoherent use of words by individuals with psychosis or those who are disoriented.

X

X chromosome. Sex-determining chromosome; all female gametes contain X chromosomes, and if the fertilized ovum has also received an X chromosome from its father, it will be female.

XYY syndrome. Chromosomal anomaly in males (presence of an extra Y chromosome) possibly related to impulsive behavior.

Y

Y chromosome. Sex-determining chromosome found in half of the total number of male gametes; its uniting with an X chromosome provided by a female produces a male offspring.

Z

Zygote. Fertilized egg cell formed by the union of male and female gametes.

References

A

Aaronson, C. J., Katzman, G. P., & Gorman, J. M. (2007). Combination pharmacotherapy and psychotherapy for the treatment of depressive and anxiety disorders. In P. E. Nathan & J. M. Gorman (Eds.), *A guide to treatments that work* (pp. 681–710). New York: Oxford University Press.

Abbey, A., Zawacki, T., Buck, P. O., Clinton, A. M., & McAuslan, P. (2001). Alcohol and sexual assault. *Al. Res. Health, 25*(1), 43–51.

Abdul-Hamid, W, K., & Stein, G. (2013) The Surpu: Exorcism of antisocial personality disorder in ancient Mesopotamia. *Mental Health, Religion & Culture,* 16(7), 671–85. doi:10. 1080/13674676.2012.713337

Abel, G. G., & Rouleau, J. L. (1990). The nature and extent of sexual assault. In W. L. Marshall, D. R. Laws, & H. E. Barbaree (Eds.), *Handbook of sexual assault: Issues, theories, and treatment of the offender* (pp. 9–22). New York: Plenum.

Abel, K. M., Drake, R., & Goldstein, J. M. (2010). Sex differences in schizophrenia. *International Review of Psychiatry, 22,* 417–28.

Abela, J. R., Stolow, D., Mineka, S., Yao, S., Zhu, X. Z., & Hankin, B. L. (2011). Cognitive vulnerability to depressive symptoms in adolescents in urban and rural Hunan, China: A multiwave longitudinal study. *J. Abn. Psychol., 120*(4), 765–78. doi:10. 1037/a0025295

Abi-Saab, D., Beauvais, J., Mehm, J., Brody, M., Gottschalk, C., & Kosten, T. R. (2005). The effect of alcohol on the neuropsychological functioning of recently abstinent cocaine-dependent subjects. *Am. J. Addict., 14*(2), 166–78.

Abraham, H. D., & Wolf, E. (1988). Visual function in past users of LSD: Psychophysical findings. *J. Abn. Psychol., 97,* 443–47.

Abraham, K. (1927). *Selected papers on psychoanalysis* (International Psychoanalytical Library No. 13.) (Memoir by E. Jones; trans. by D. Bryan and A. Strachey.). Honolulu, HI: Hogarth Press.

Abrahamson, D. J., Barlow, D. H., Sakheim, D. K., Beck, J. G., & Athanasiou, R. (1985). Effects of distraction on sexual responding in functional and dysfunctional men. *Behav. Ther., 16,* 503–15.

Abramowitz, C., Kosson, D., & Seidenberg, M. (2004). The relationship between childhood attention deficit hyperactivity disorder and conduct problems and adult psychopathy in male inmates. *Personal. Indiv. Diff., 36,* 1031–47.

Abramowitz, J. S., Braddock, A. E., & Moore, E. L. (2009). Psychological treatment of obsessive-compulsive disorder. In M. M. Antony & M. B. Stein (Eds.), *Oxford handbook of anxiety and related disorders* (pp. 391–404). New York: Oxford University Press.

Abramowitz, J. S., Tolin, D. F., & Street, G. P. (2001). Paradoxical effects of thought suppression: A meta-analysis of controlled studies. *Clin. Psychol. Rev., 21*(5), 683–703.

Abrams, R. (2002). *Electroconvulsive therapy* (4th ed.). New York: Oxford University Press.

Abramson, L. Y., Alloy, L. B., Hankin, B. L., Haeffel, G. J., MacCoon, D. G., & Gibb, B. E. (2002). Cognitive vulnerability-stress models of depression in a self-regulatory and psychobiological context. In I. H. Gotlib & C. L. Hammen (Eds.), *Handbook of depression* (pp. 268–94). New York: Guilford Press.

Abramson, L., Alloy, L., & Metalsky, G. (1995). Hopelessness depression. In G. Buchanan & M. Seligman (Eds.), *Explanatory style* (pp. 113–34). Hillsdale, NJ: Erlbaum.

Abramson, L. Y., Metalsky, G. I., & Alloy, L. B. (1989). Hopelessness depression: A theory-based subtype of depression. *Psychol. Rev., 96,* 358–72.

Abramson, L. Y., & Seligman, M. E. P. (1977). Modeling psychopathology in the laboratory: History and rationale. In M. Maser & M. E. P. Seligman (Eds.), *Psychopathology: Experimental models.* San Francisco: Freeman.

Abramson, L. Y., Seligman, M. E. P., & Teasdale, J. D. (1978). Learned helplessness in humans: Critique and reformulation. *J. Abn. Psychol., 87,* 49–74.

Ackard, D. M., Fulkerson, J. A., & Neumark-Sztainer, D. (2007). Prevalence and utility of DSM-IV eating disorder diagnostic criteria among youth. *Int. J. Eat. Dis., 40,* 409–17.

AD2000 Collaborative Group. (2004, June 26). Long-term donepezil treatment in 565 patients with Alzheimer's disease (AD2000): Randomised double blind trial. *Lancet, 363,* 2105–15.

Adamis, D., Treloar, A., Martin, F. C., & Macdonald, A. J. D. (2007). A brief review of the history of delirium as a mental disorder. *Hist. Psychiatry, 18*(4), 459–69.

Adams, M. A., & Ferraro, F. R. (1997). Acquired immunodeficiency syndrome dementia complex. *J. Clin. Psychol., 53*(7), 767–78.

Addington, J., Cadenhead, K. S., Cannon, T. D., Cornblatt, B., McGlashan, T. H., Perkins, D. O., et al. (2007). North American Prodrome Longitudinal study: A collaborative multisite approach to prodromal schizophrenia research. *Schizo. Bull., 33,* 665–72.

Addington, J., Cornblatt, B. A., Cadenhead, K. S., Cannon, T. D., McGlashan, T. H., Perkins, D. O., et al. (2011). At clinical high risk for psychosis: Outcome for nonconverters. *Am. J. Psychiatry, 168,* 800–13.

Addis, M. E., & Krasnow, A. D. (2000). A national survey of practicing psychologists' attitudes toward psychotherapy treatment manuals. *J. Consult. Clin. Psychol., 68,* 331–39.

Addis, M. E., & Mahalik, J. R. (2003). Men, masculinity, and the contexts of help seeking. *Am. Psychol., 58,* 1, 5–1514.

Adler, A. B., Litz, B. T., Castro, C. A., Suvak, M., Thomas, J. L., Burrell, L., et al. (2008). A group randomized trial of critical incident stress debriefing provided to U.S. peacekeepers. *J. Trauma. Stress, 21,* 253–63.

Adler, T. (1994). Alzheimer's causes unique cell death. *Sci. News, 146*(13), 198.

Adriano, F., Caltagirone, C., & Spalletta, G. (2012). Hippocampal volume reduction in first-episode and chronic schizophrenia: A review and meta-analysis. *Neuroscientist, 18,* 180–200.

Afifi, T. O., Brownridge, D. A., MacMillan, H., & Sareen, J. (2010). The relationship of gambling to intimate partner violence and child maltreatment in a nationally representative sample. *J. Psychiatr. Res., 44*(5), 331–37.

Agras, W. S., Walsh, T., Fairburn, C. G., Wilson, T., & Kraemer, H. C. (2000). A multicenter comparison of cognitive-behavioral therapy and interpersonal therapy for bulimia nervosa. *Arch. Gen. Psychiat., 57*(5), 459–66.

Agrist, J. D., Chen, S. H., & Frandsen, B. R. (2010). Did Vietnam veterans get sicker in the 1990s? The complicated effects of military service on self-reported health. *J. Public Econ., 94,* 824–37.

Aiken, L. R. (1996). *Rating scales and checklists.* New York: Wiley.

Akiskal, H. S., & Benazzi, F. (2005). Atypical depression: A variant of bipolar II or a bridge between unipolar and bipolar II. *J. Affect. Dis., 84,* 209–17.

Akyuz, G., Dogan, O., Sar, V., Yargic, I. L., & Tutkin, H. (1999). Frequency of dissociative identity disorder in the general population of Turkey. *Compr. Psychiatry, 40*(2), 151–59.

Alanen, Y. O., González de Chávez, M., Silver, A. S., & Martindale, B. (Eds.). (2009). *Psychotherapeutic approaches to schizophrenic psychoses.* New York: Routledge/Taylor & Francis Group.

Alarcon, M., et al. (1997). A twin study of mathematics disability. *J. Learn. Dis., 30*(6), 617–23.

Alarcón, R. D., Becker, A. E., Lewis-Fernández, R., Like, R. C., Desai, P., Foulks, E., et al. (2009). Issues for DSM-V: The role of culture in psychiatric diagnosis. *J. Nerv. Ment. Dis., 197*(8), 559–60.

Alberini, C. M. (2009). Unwind: Chronic stress exacerbates the deficits of Alzheimer's disease. *Biol. Psychiatry, 65,* 916–17.

Albert, C. M., Chae, C. U., Rexrode, K. M., Manson, J. E., & Kawachi, I. (2005). Phobic anxiety and risk of coronary heart disease and sudden cardiac death among women. *Circulation, 111,* 480–87.

Albert, U., Maina, G., Forner, F., & Bogetto, F. (2004). DSM-IV obsessive-compulsive personality disorder: Prevalence in patients with anxiety disorders and in healthy comparison subjects. *Compr. Psychiatry, 45,* 325–32.

Albright v. Abington Memorial Hospital, 696 A. 2d 1159 (Pa 1997).

Alcántara, C., & Gone, J. P. (2014). Multicultural issues in the clinical interview and diagnostic process. In F. T. L. Leong, L. Comas-Díaz, G. C. Nagayama Hall, V. C. McLoyd, & J. E. Trimble (Eds.), *APA handbook of multicultural psychology, Vol. 2: Applications and training* (APA Handbooks in Psychology) (pp. 153–63). Washington, DC: American Psychological Association. doi:10.1037/14187-009

Alcoholics Anonymous. (2015). *A.A. fact file.* New York: Author.

Alden, L., Laposa, J., Taylor, C., & Ryder, A. (2002). Avoidant personality disorder: Current status and future directions. *J. Pers. Disord., 16,* 1–29.

Alderson, P. (2001). Down's syndrome: Cost, quality and value of life. *Soc. Sci. Med., 53,* 627–38.

Aldwin, C. M. (2007). *Stress, coping, and development: An integrative perspective* (2nd ed.). New York: Guilford Press.

Alegria, A. A., Petry, N. M., Hasin, D. S., Liu, S.-M., Grant, B. F., & Blanco, C. (2009). Disordered gambling among racial and ethnic groups in the U.S. : Results from the National Epidemiologic Survey on Alcohol and Related Conditions. *CNS Spectrums, 14,* 132–42.

Alegria, M., Woo, M., Cao, Z., Torres, M., Meng, X., & Striegel-Moore, R. (2007). Prevalence and correlates of eating disorders in Latinos in the United States. *Int. J. Eat. Dis., 40*(Suppl.), S15–S21.

Aleman, A., Kahn, R. S., & Selten, J. P. (2003). Sex differences in the risk of schizophrenia: Evidence from meta-analysis. *Arch. Gen. Psychiatry, 60,* 565–71.

Aleman, A., & Larøi, F. (2008). *Hallucinations: The science of idiosyncratic perception*. Washington, DC: American Psychological Association.

Alexander, N., Kuepper, Y., Schmitz, A., Osinsky, R., Kozyra, E., & Hennig, J. (2009). Gene–environment interactions predict cortisol responses after acute stress: Implications for the etiology of depression. *Psychoneuroendocrinology, 34*, 1294–303.

Alexopoulos, G. S., Borson, S., Cuthbert, B. N., Devanand, D. P., Mulsant, B. H., Olin, J. T., et al. (2002). Assessment of late life depression. *Biol. Psychiatry, 52*(3), 164–74.

Allen, A., & Hollander, E. (2004). Similarities and differences between body dysmorphic disorder and other disorders. *Psychiatr. Ann., 34*(12), 927–33.

Allen, L. A., & Woolfolk, R. L. (2012). Somatoform and factitious disorders. In P. Sturmey & M. Hersen (Eds.), *Handbook of evidence-based practice in clinical psychology, Volume 2: Adult disorders* (pp. 365–94). Hoboken, NJ: John Wiley & Sons.

Allen, P., Larøi, F., McGuire, P. K., & Aleman, A. (2008). The hallucinating brain: A review of structural and functional neuroimaging studies of hallucinations. *Neuroscience and Behavioral Reviews, 32*, 175–91.

Allik, J. (2005). Personality dimensions across cultures. *J. Pers. Disord., 19*, 212–32.

Allison, K. C., Grillo, C., Masheb, R. M., & Stunkard, A. J. (2005). Binge eating disorder and night eating syndrome: A comparative study of disordered eating. *J. Consult. Clin. Psychol., 73*, 1107–15.

Alloy, L. B., Abramson, L. Y., Gibb, B. E., Crossfield, A. G., Pieracci, A. M., Spasojevic, J., et al. (2004). Developmental antecedents of cognitive vulnerability to depression: Review of findings from the cognitive vulnerability to depression project. *J. Cog. Psychother., 18*(2), 115–33.

Alloy, L. B., Abramson, L. Y., Keyser, J., Gerstein, R. K., & Sylvia, L. G. (2008). Negative cognitive style. In K. S. Dobson & D. J. Dozois (Eds.), *Risk factors in depression*. Oxford, UK: Elsevier Press.

Alloy, L. B., Abramson, L. Y., Smith, J. M., Gibb, B. E., & Neeren, A. M. (2006). Role of parenting and maltreatment histories in unipolar and bipolar mood disorders: Mediation by cognitive vulnerability to depression. *Clin. Child. Fam. Psychol. Rev., 9*, 23–64.

Alloy, L. B., Abramson, L. Y., Walshaw, P. D., Gerstein, R. K., Keyser, J. D., Whitehouse, W. G., et al. (2009). Behavioral approach system (BAS)-relevant cognitive styles and bipolar spectrum disorders: Concurrent and prospective associations. *J. Abn. Psychol., 118*(3), 459–71. doi:10.1037/a0016604

Alloy, L. B., Abramson, L. Y., Walshaw, P. D., Keyser, J., & Gerstein, R. K. (2010). Adolescent onset bipolar spectrum disorders: A cognitive vulnerability–stress perspective informed by normative brain, cognitive, and emotional/motivational development. In D. Miklowitz & D. Cicchetti (Eds.), *Bipolar disorder: A developmental psychopathology approach* (pp. 282–330). New York: Guilford Press.

Alloy, L. B., Abramson, L. Y., Whitehouse, W. G., Hogan, M. E., Panzarella, C., & Rose, D. T. (2006). Prospective incidence of first onsets and recurrences of depression in individuals at high and low cognitive risk for depression. *J. Abn. Psychol., 115*(1), 145–57.

Alpert, J. E., Uebelacker, L. A., McLean, N. E., Nierenberg, A. A., Pava, J. A., Worthington III, J. J., et al. (1997). Social phobia, avoidant personality disorder and atypical depression: Co-occurrence and clinical implications. *Psychol. Med., 27*, 627–33.

Althof, S. E., Dean, J., Derogatis, L. R., Rosen, R. C., & Sisson, M. (2005). Current perspectives on the clinical assessment and diagnosis of female sexual dysfunction and clinical studies of potential therapies: A statement of concern. *J. Sex. Med., 2*, 146–53.

Althof, S. E., & Schreiner-Engel, P. (2000). The sexual dysfunctions. In M. G. Gelder, J. J. Lobez-Ibor, & N. Andreasen (Eds.), *New Oxford textbook of psychiatry*. New York: Oxford University Press.

Altshuler, L. L., Bauer, M., Frye, M. A., Gitlin, M. J., Mintz, J., Szuba, M. P., et al. (2001). Does thyroid supplementation accelerate tricyclic antidepressant response? A review and meta-analysis of the literature. *Am. J. Psychiatry, 158*, 1617–22.

Alzheimer's Association (2015). Alzheimer's Association report: 2015 Alzheimer's disease facts and figures. *Alzheimer's and Dementia, 11*, 332–84.

Amad, A., Ramoz, N., Thomas, P., Jardri, R., & Gorwood, P. (2014). Genetics of borderline personality disorder: Systematic review and proposal of an integrative model. *Neuroscience and Biobehavioral Reviews, 40*, 6–19.

Amato, P. R. (2000). The consequences of divorce for adults and children. *J. Marr. Fam., 62*, 1269–87.

Amato, P. R. (2001). Children of divorce in the 1990s: An update of the Amato and Keith (1991) meta-analysis. *J. Fam. Psychol., 15*, 355–70.

Amato, P. R. (2006). Marital discord, divorce, and children's well-being: Results from a 20-year longitudinal study of two generations. In A. Clarke-Stewart & J. Dunn (Eds.), *Families count: Effects on child and adolescent development* (pp. 179–202). New York: Cambridge University Press.

Amato, P. R. (2010). Research on divorce: Continuing trends and new developments. *J. Marr. Fam., 72*(3), 650–66. doi:10.1111/j.1741-3737.2010.00723.x

Amato, P. R., & Booth, A. (2001). The legacy of parents' marital discord: Consequences for children's marital quality. *J. Pers. Soc. Psychol., 81*, 627–38.

Amato, P. R., & Cheadle, J. (2005). The long reach of divorce: Divorce and child well-being across three generations. *J. Marr. Fam., 67*(1), 191–206.

Amato, P. R., & Hohmann-Marriott, B. (2007). A comparison of high and low-distress marriages that end in divorce. *J. Marr. Fam., 69*(3), 621–38.

Amato, P. R., & Keith, B. (1991a). Parental divorce and adult well-being: A meta-analysis. *J. Marr. Fam., 53*, 43–58.

Amato, P. R., & Keith, B. (1991b). Parental divorce and the well-being of children: A meta-analysis. *Psychol. Bull., 110*, 26–46.

Ambrogne, J. A. (2002). Reduced-risk drinking as a treatment goal: What clinicians need to know. *J. Sub. Abuse Treat., 22*(1), 45–53.

American Medical Association Committee on Human Sexuality. (1972). *Human sexuality* (p. 40). Chicago: Author.

American Psychiatric Association (APA). (1968). *Diagnostic and statistical manual of mental disorders* (2nd ed.). Washington, DC: Author.

American Psychiatric Association (APA). (1994). *Diagnostic and statistical manual of mental disorders (DSM-IV)* (4th ed.). Washington, DC: American Psychiatric Association.

American Psychiatric Association (APA). (2000). *Diagnostic and statistical manual of mental disorders* (4th ed., revised text). Washington, DC: Author.

American Psychiatric Association (APA). (2013). *Diagnostic and statistical manual of mental disorders (DSM-5)* (5th ed.). Washington, DC: Author.

American Psychological Association. (2002). Ethical principles of psychologists and code of conduct. *Am. Psychol., 57*, 1060–73.

American Psychological Association. (2014). *Standards for educational and psychological testing* (2014 ed.). Washington, DC: Author.

Ammerman, R. T., Kane, V. R., Slomka, G. T., Reigel, D. H., Franzen, M. D., & Gadow, K. D. (1998). Psychiatric symptomatology and family functioning in children and adolescents with spina bifida. *J. Clin. Psychol. Med. Set., 5*(4), 449–65.

Anderluh, M. B., Tchanturia, K., Rabe-Hesketh, S., & Treasure, J. (2003). Childhood obsessive-compulsive personality traits in adult women with eating disorders: Defining a broader eating disorder phenotype. *Am. J. Psychiatry, 160*, 242–47.

Anderson, V., Catroppa, C., Godfrey, C., & Reosenfeld, J. V. (2012). Intellectual ability 10 years after traumatic brain injury in infancy and childhood: What predicts outcome? *J. Neurotrauma, 29*, 143–53.

Andersson, E., Hedman, E., Enander, J., Radu Djurfeldt, D., Ljótsson, B., Cervenka, S., et al. (2015). d-Cycloserine vs placebo as adjunct to cognitive behavioral therapy for obsessive-compulsive disorder and interaction with antidepressants: A randomized clinical trial. *JAMA Psychiatry, 72*, 659–67.

Andrade, L., Caraveo-Anduaga, J. J., Berglund, P., Bijl, R. V., DeGraaf, R., Vollerbergh, W., et al. (2004). The epidemiology of major depressive episodes: Results from the International Consortium of Psychiatric Epidemiology (ICPE) surveys. *Int. J. Meth. Psychiat. Res., 12*(1), 3–21.

Andreasen, N. C. (1984). *The broken brain: The biological revolution in psychiatry*. New York: Harper & Row.

Andreasen, N. C. (1985). Positive vs. negative schizophrenia: A critical evaluation. *Schizo. Bull., 11*, 380–89.

Andreasen, N. C., Liu, D., Ziebell, S., Vora, A., & Ho, B.-C. (2013). Relapse duration, treatment intensity, and brain tissue loss in schizophrenia: A prospective longitudinal MRI study. *Am. J. Psychiatry, 170*, 609–15.

Andreescu, C., & Aizenstein, H. J. (2009). Amnestic disorders and mild cognitive impairment. In B. J. Sadock, A. A. Sadock, & P. Ruiz (Eds.), *Kaplan and Sadock's comprehensive textbook of psychiatry* (9th ed., pp. 1198–207). Philadelphia, PA: Lippincott Williams & Wilkins.

Andrews, B., Brewin, C. R., Philpott, R., & Stewart, L. (2007). Delayed-onset posttraumatic stress disorder: A systematic review of the evidence. *Am. J. Psychiatry, 164*, 1319–26.

Andrews, G., Hobbs, M. J., Borkovec, T. D., Beesdo, K., Craske, M. G., Heimberg, R. G., et al. (2010). Generalized worry disorder: A review of DSM-IV generalized anxiety disorder and options for DSM-V. *Depression and Anxiety, 27*(2), 134–47. doi:10.1002/da.20658

Andrews, G. G., Pine, D. S., Hobbs, M. J., Anderson, T. M., & Sunderland, M. M. (2009). Neurodevelopmental disorders: Cluster 2 of the proposed meta-structure for DSM-V and ICD-11. *Psychological Med., 39*(12), 2013–23. doi:10.1017/S0033291709990274

Andrews, J., & Hops, H. (2010). The influence of peers on substance use. In L. Scheier (Ed.), *Handbook of drug use etiology: Theory, methods, and empirical findings* (pp. 403–20). Washington, DC: American Psychological Association.

Anglin, D. M., Cohen, P. R., & Chen, H. (2008). Duration of early maternal separation and prediction of schizotypal symptoms from early adolescence to midlife. *Schizo. Res., 103*, 143–50.

Angst, J., Gamma, A., Rössler, W., Ajdacic, V., & Klein, D. (2011). Childhood adversity and chronicity of mood disorders. *Eur. Arch. Psychiat. Clin. Neurosci., 261*(1), 21–27. doi:10.1007/s00406-010-0120-3

Angst, J., & Sellaro, R. (2000). Historical perspectives and natural history of bipolar disorder. *Biol. Psychiatry, 48*, 445–57.

Ansell, E., Pinto, A., Edelen, M., & Grilo, C. (2008). Structure of *Diagnostic and Statistical Manual of Mental Disorders*, Fourth Edition, criteria for obsessive-compulsive personality disorder in patients with binge eating disorder. *Can. J. Psychiatry, 53*, 863–67.

Antony, M. M., & Barlow, D. H. (2002). Specific phobias. In D. H. Barlow (Ed.), *Anxiety and its disorders* (2nd ed., pp. 380–417). New York: Guilford Press.

Antony, M., Downie, F., & Swinson, R. (1998). Diagnostic issues and epidemiology in obsessive-compulsive disorder. In R. Swinson, M. Antony, S. Rachman, & M. Richter (Eds.), *Obsessive-compulsive disorder: Theory, research, and treatments* (pp. 3–32). New York: Guilford Press.

Appelbaum, P. S., & Greer, A. (1994). Who's on trial? Multiple personalities and the insanity defense. *Hosp. Comm. Psychiat., 45*(10), Spec. Issue 965–66.

Aragona, M., Bancheri, L., Perinelli, D., Tarsitani, L., Pizzimenti, A., Conte, A., & Inghilleri, M. (2005). Randomized double-blind comparison of serotonergic (citalopram) versus noradrenergic (reboxetine) reuptake inhibitors in outpatients with somatoform, DSM-IV-TR pain disorder. *Eur. J. Pain, 9*(1), 33–38.

Arcelus, J., Mitchell, A. J., Wales, J., & Nielsen, S. (2011). Mortality rates in patients with anorexia nervosa and other eating disorders. *Arch. Gen. Psychiat., 68*, 724–31.

Arcelus, J., Witcomb, G. L., & Mitchell, A. (2014). Prevalence of eating disorders amongst dancers: A systematic review and meta-analysis. *European Eating Disorders Review, 22*, 92–101.

Arch, J., & Craske, M. G. (2008). Panic disorder. In W. E. Craighead, D. J. Miklowitz, & L. W. Craighead (Eds.), *Psychopathology: History, diagnosis, and empirical foundations* (pp. 115–58). Hoboken, NJ: John Wiley & Sons.

Arch, J. J., & Craske, M. G. (2009). First-line treatment: A critical appraisal of cognitive behavioral therapy developments and alternatives. *Psychiatr. Clin. North Am., 32*(3), 525–47. doi:10.1016/j.psc.2009.05.001

Archer, R. P., Buffington-Vollum, J. K., Stredny, R. V., & Handel, R. W. (2006). A survey of psychological test use patterns among forensic psychologists. *J. Pers. Assess., 87*, 84–94.

Armbruster, D., Mueller, A., Strobel, A., Lesch, K. P., Brocke, B., & Kirschbaum, C. (2012). Children under stress–COMT genotype and stressful events predict cortisol increase in an acute social stress paradigm. *Int. J. Neuropsychop., 15*, 1229–39.

Arndt, R. (1878). Zur electrotherapie der psychischen krankheiten. *Allg. Z. Psychiat., 134*, 483–574.

Arnold, M. B. (1962). *Story sequence analysis: A new method of measuring motivation and predicting achievement.* New York: Columbia University Press.

Arnold, S. E. (2000). Hippocampal pathology. In P. J. Harrison & G. W. Roberts (Eds.), *The neuropathology of schizophrenia* (pp. 57–80). Oxford, UK: Oxford University Press.

Arnold, S. E., & Trojanowski, J. Q. (1996). Recent advances in defining the neuropathology of schizophrenia. *Acta Neuropathologie, 92*, 217–31.

Arntz, A., Bernstein, D., Gielen, D., Nieuwenhuyzen van, M., Penders, K., Haslam, N., et al. (2009). Taxometric evidence for the dimensional structure of cluster-C, paranoid, and borderline personality disorders. *J. Pers. Disord., 23*(6), 606–28.

Arntz, A., Weertman, A., & Salet, S. (2011). Behaviour research and therapy interpretation bias in cluster-C and borderline personality disorders. *Behav. Res. Ther., 49*(8), 472–81. doi:10.1016/j.brat.2011.05.002

Arrindell, W. A. (2003). Cultural abnormal psychology. *Beh. Res. Ther., 41*, 749–53.

Arsenault, L., Cannon, M., Poulton, R., Murray, R., Caspi, A., & Moffitt, T. E. (2002). Cannabis use in adolescence and risk for adult psychosis: A longitudinal prospective study. *BMJ, 325*, 1212–13.

Arthur, C., Hickling, F. W., Robertson-Hickling, H., Haynes-Robinson, T., Abel, W., & Whitley, R.

(2010). "Mad, sick, head nuh good": Mental illness stigma in Jamaican communities. *Transcult. Psychiat., 47*, 252–75.

Asarnow, J. R. (2005). Childhood-onset schizotypal disorder: A follow-up study and comparison with childhood-onset schizophrenia. *J. Child Adol. Psychopharmacol., 15*, 395–402.

Ashford, J. B., & Kupferberg, M. (2013). *Death penalty mitigation: A handbook for mitigation specialists, investigators, social scientists, and lawyers.* New York: Oxford University Press.

Ashton, A. K., Hamer, R., & Rosen, R. C. (1997). Serotonin reuptake inhibitor-induced sexual dysfunction and its treatment: A large-scale retrospective study of 596 psychiatric outpatients. *J. Sex Marit. Ther., 23*, 165–75.

Askew, C., & Field, A. P. (2007). Vicarious learning and the development of fears in childhood. *Behav. Res. Ther., 45*(11), 2616–27.

Askew, C., & Field, A. P. (2008). The vicarious learning pathway to fear 40 years on. *Clin. Psychol. Rev., 28*(7), 1249–65. doi:10. 1016/j.cpr.2008.05. 003

Askin-Edgar, S., White, K. E., & Cummings, J. L. (2002). Neuropsychiatric aspects of Alzheimer's disease and other dementing illnesses. In S. C. Yudofsky & R. E. Hales (Eds.), *The American Psychiatric Publishing textbook of neuropsychiatry and clinical neurosciences* (pp. 953–88). Washington, DC: American Psychiatric Publishing.

Asnaani, A., Chelmonski, I., Young, D., & Zimmerman, M. (2007). Heterogeneity of borderline personality disorder: Do the number of criteria met make a difference? *J. Personality Disorders, 21*, 615–15.

Associated Press. (2001, August 7). Fire in asylum in southern India kills 25 mentally ill patients, many chained to beds. *Daily Star International News*, p. 3.

Associated Press. (2003, November 18). Psychiatrist disputes Hinckley's recovery. *Free Republic.* Retrieved from http://www.freerepublic.com/focus/f-news/1025164/posts

Associated Press. (2004, March 31). Doctor says mom who killed sons mentally ill. *Associated Press.*

Astley, S., Aylward, E. H., Olson, H. C., Kerns, K., Brooks, A., Coggins, T. E., et al. (2009). Functional magnetic resonance imaging outcomes from a comprehensive magnetic resonance study of children with fetal alcohol spectrum disorders. *J. Neuredevelop. Disord., 1*(1), 61–80.

Atkins, D. C., Berns, S. B., George, W., Doss, B., Gattis, K., & Christensen, A. (2005). Prediction of response to treatment in a randomized clinical trial of marital therapy. *J. Consult. Clin. Psychol., 73*, 893–903.

Atkinson, J. W. (1992). Motivational determinants of thematic apperception. In C. P. Smith, J. W. Atkinson, & J. Veroff (Eds.), *Motivation and personality: Handbook of thematic content analysis* (pp. 21–48). New York: Cambridge University Press.

Atlis, M. M., Hahn, J., & Butcher, J. N. (2006). Computer-based assessment with the MMPI-2. In J. N. Butcher (Ed.), *MMPI-2: The practitioner's handbook* (pp. 445–76). Washington, DC: American Psychological Association.

Attia, E., & Roberto, C. A. (2009). Should amenorrhea be a diagnostic criterion for anorexia nervosa? *Int. J. Eat. Dis., 42*, 581–89.

Attia, E., & Walsh, B. T. (2007). Anorexia nervosa. *Am. J. Psychiatry, 164*, 1805–10.

Autism Genome Project (AGP). (2007, February 18). Consortium mapping autism risk loci using genetic linkage and chromosomal rearrangements. *Nature Genetics.* doi:10.1038/ng1985.

Avants, S. K., Margolin, A., Kosten, T. R., Rounsaville, B. J., & Schottenfeld, R. S. (1998). When is less treatment better? The role of social anxiety in matching methadone patients to psychosocial treatments. *J. Consult. Clin. Psychol., 66*, 924–31.

Avenevoli, S., Knight, E., Kessler, R. C., & Merikangas, K. R. (2008). Epidemiology of depression in children and adolescents. In J. R. Z. Abela & B. L. Hankin (Eds.), *Handbook of depression in children and adolescents* (pp. 6–32). New York: Guilford Press.

Avery, J., Francois, D., Martins, O., Park, S., & Roth, S. (2012). An updates model for the first-time hospitalization of patients with borderline personality disorder: Two illustrative case reports. *Psychiatric Quarterly, 83*, 391–96.

Ayala, E. S., Meuret, A. E., & Ritz, T. (2009). Treatments for blood-injury-injection phobia: A critical review of current evidence. *J. Psychiatr. Res., 43*(15), 1235–42. doi:10.1016/j.jpsychires.2009.04.008

Aycicegi-Dinn, A., Caldwell-Harris, C. L., & Dinn, W. M. (2009). Obsessive-compulsive personality traits: Compensatory response to executive function deficit? *Int. J. Neurosci., 119*, 600–08.

Azar, B. (1997). Researchers debunk myth of crack baby. *Monitor, 29*(12), 14–15.

Azari, N. P., Horwitz, B., Pettigrew, K. D., & Grady, C. L. (1994). Abnormal pattern of glucose metabolic rates involving language areas in young adults with Down syndrome. *Brain Lang., 46*(1), 1–20.

Azim, H. F. (2001). Partial hospitalization programs. In W. J. Livesley (Ed.), *Handbook of personality disorders* (pp. 527–40). New York: Guilford Press.

B

Baaré, F. C., van Oel, C. J., Hulshoff Pol, H. E., Schnack, H. G., Durston, S., Sitkoorn, M. M., et al. (2001). Volumes of brain structures in twins discordant for schizophrenia. *Arch. Gen. Psychiatry, 58*, 33–40.

Babcock, Q., & Byrne, T. (2000). Student perceptions of methylphenidate abuse at a public liberal arts college. *J. American College of Health, 49*, 143–45.

Babiak, P., Neumann, C. S., & Hare, R. D. (2010). Corporate psychopathy: Taking the walk. *Behavioral Science and the Law, 28*, 174–93.

Bach, A. K., Barlow, D. H., & Wincze, J. P. (2004). The enhancing effects of manualized treatment for erectile dysfunction among men using sildenafil: A preliminary investigation. *Behav. Ther., 35*, 55–73.

Bagge, C., Nickell, A., Stepp, S., Durrett, C., Jackson, K., & Trull, T. (2004). Borderline personality disorder features predict negative outcomes 2 years later. *J. Abn. Psychol., 113*(2), 279–88.

Bagner, D. M., Pettit, J. W., Lewinsohn, P. M., & Seeley, J. R. (2010). Effect of maternal depression on child behavior: A sensitive period? *J. Am. Acad. Child Adoles. Psychiat., 49*(7), 699–707.

Bailer, U. F., & Kaye, W. H. (2011). Serotonin: Imaging findings in eating disorders. *Curr. Topics Behav. Neurosci., 6*, 59–79.

Bailey, J. M. (1999). Homosexuality and mental illness. *Arch. Gen. Psychiatry, 56*, 883–84.

Bailey, J. M. (2003). *The man who would be queen.* Washington, DC: Joseph Henry Press.

Bailey, J. M., & Greenberg, A. S. (1998). The science and ethics of castration: Lessons from the Morse case. *Northwestern Law Rev., 92*, 1225–45.

Bailey, J. M., & Triea, K. (2007). What many transgender activists don't want you to know and why you should know it anyway. *Persp. Biol. Med., 50*(4), 521–34.

Bailey, S. (2000). Juvenile delinquency and serious antisocial behavior. In M. G. Gelder, J. J. Lopez-Ibor, Jr., & N. C. Andreasen (Eds.), *New Oxford textbook of psychiatry* (pp. 1859–73). Oxford, UK: Oxford University Press.

Baio, J. (2014). Prevalence of autism spectrum disorder among children aged 8 years—Autism and developmental disabilities monitoring network, 11 sites, United States, 2010. *Morbidity and Mortality Weekly Report, 63*, 1–21.

Baker, A., & Lee, N. K. (2003). A review of psychosocial interventions for amphetamine use. *Drug Alcohol Rev., 22*(3), 323–35.

Baker, D., Hunter, E., Lawrence, E., Medford, N., Patel, M., Senior, C., et al. (2003). Depersonalization disorder: Clinical features of 204 cases. *Brit. J. Psychiatry, 182*, 428–33.

Baker, L. A., Jacobson, K. C., Raine, A., Lozano, D. I., & Bezdjian, S. (2007). Genetic and environmental bases of childhood antisocial behavior: A multi-informant twin study. *J. Abn. Psychol., 116*(2), 219–23.

Baker, R. R., Stenger, C., Gurel, L., & Goldstein, G. (2012). Patient care by VA psychologists in the 1950s and 1960s. *Psychological Services, 9*(4), 417–26. doi:10.1037/a0029515

Baker, T. B., McFall, R. M., & Shoham, V. (2008). Current status and future prospects of clinical psychology: Toward a scientifically principled approach to mental and behavioral health care. *Psychological Science in the Public Interest, 9*, 67–103.

Bakkevig, J. F., & Karterud, S. (2010). Is the *Diagnostic and Statistical Manual of Mental Disorders,* Fourth Edition, histrionic personality disorder category a valid construct? *Compr. Psychiatry, 51*(5), 462–70. doi:10.1016/j.comppsych.2009.11. 009

Baldessarini, R. J., & Hennen, J. (2004). Genetics of suicide. *Harv. Rev. Psychiatry, 12*(1), 1–13.

Baldessarini, R. J., Salvatore, P., Khalsa, H.-M. K., & Tohen, M. (2010). Dissimilar morbidity following initial mania versus mixed-states in type-I bipolar disorder. *J. Affect. Dis., 126*(1–2), 299–302. doi:10.1016/j.jad.2010.03.014

Ball, S. A., Martino, N. C., Frankforter, T. L., Van Horn, D., Crits-Cristoph, P., & Carroll, K. M. (2007). Site matters: Multi-site randomized trial of motivational enhancement therapy in community drug abuse clinics. *J. Consult. Clin. Psychol., 75*, 556–67.

Ballard, C., Gauthier, S., Corbett, A., Brayne, C., Aarsland, D., & Jones, E. (2011). Alzheimer's disease. *Lancet, 377*, 1019–31.

Bancroft, J., Carnes, L., Janssen, E., Goodrich, D., & Long, J. S. (2005). Erectile and ejaculatory problems in gay and heterosexual men. *Arch. Sex. Behav., 34*(3), 285–97.

Bancroft, J., Loftus, J., & Long, J. S. (2003). Distress about sex: A national survey of women in heterosexual relationships. *Arch. Sex. Behav., 32*, 193–208.

Bandettini, P. (2007). Functional MRI today. *Int. J. Psychophysiol., 63*(2), 138–45.

Bandura, A. (1964). The stormy decade: Fact or fiction? *Psychol. Sch., 1*, 224–31.

Bandura, A. (1969). *Principles of behavior modification.* New York: Holt, Rinehart & Winston.

Bandura, A. (1974). Behavior theory and the models of man. *Am. Psychol., 29*(12), 859–69.

Bandura, A. (1977). Self-efficacy: Toward a unifying theory of behavioral change. *Psychol. Rev., 84*(2), 191–215.

Bandura, A. (1986). *Social foundations of thought and action: A social cognitive theory.* Englewood Cliffs, NJ: Prentice Hall.

Bandura, A. (1997). *Self-efficacy: The exercise of control.* New York: W. H. Freeman/Times Books/Henry Holt & Co.

Banjo, O. C., Nadler, R., & Reiner, P. B. (2010). Physician attitudes towards pharmacological cognitive enhancement: Safety concerns are paramount. *PLoS ONE, 5*(12): e14322. doi:10.1371/journal.pone.0014322

Bannon, S., Gonsalvez, C. J., & Croft, R. J. (2008). Processing impairments in OCD: It is more than inhibition! *Behav. Res. Ther., 46*(6), 689–700. doi:10.1016/j.brat.2008.02.006

Barbaree, H. E., & Blanchard, R. (2008). Sexual deviance over the lifespan: Reduction in deviant sexual behavior in the aging sex offender. In D. R.

Laws & W. T. O'Donohue (Eds.), *Sexual deviance: Theory, assessment, and treatment* (2nd ed., pp. 37–60). New York: Guilford Press.

Barbaree, H. E., & Seto, M. C. (1997). Pedophilia: Assessment and treatment. In D. R. Laws & W. O'Donohue (Eds.), *Sexual deviance: Theory, assessment, and treatment* (pp. 175–93). New York: Guilford Press.

Barbee, P. W., Combs, D. C., Ekleberry, F., & Villalobos, S. (2007). Duty to warn and protect: Not in Texas. *J. Profession. Counsel. Prac. Theory Res., 35*(1), 18–25.

Barch, D. M. (2005). The cognitive neuroscience of schizophrenia. *Annu. Rev. Clin. Psychol., 1*, 12.1–12.33.

Barch, D. M. (2013). The CAINS: Theoretical and practical advances in the assessment of negative symptoms in schizophrenia. *Am. J. Psychiatry, 170*, 133–35.

Bardone-Cone, A. M., & Cass, K. M. (2007). What does viewing a pro-anorexia website do? An experimental examination of website exposure and moderating effects. *Int J. Eat. Disorder, 40*, 537–48.

Bardone-Cone, A. M., Wonderlich, S. A., Frost, R. O., Bulik, C. M., Mitchell, J. E., Uppala, S., & Simonich, H. (2007). Perfectionism and eating disorders: Current status and future directions. *Clin. Psychol. Rev., 27*, 384–405.

Barker, A., Freeston, I., Jalinous, R., & Jarrat, J. (1985). Noninvasive magnetic stimulation of the human motor cortex. *Lancet, 2*, 1106–07.

Barkley, R. A. (1997). Behavioral inhibition, sustained attention, and executive function: Constructing a unified theory of ADHD. *Psychol. Bull., 121*, 65–94.

Barlow, D. H. (Ed.). (2002). *Anxiety and its disorders: The nature and treatment of anxiety and panic* (2nd ed.). New York: Guilford Press.

Barlow, D. H. (2004). Psychological treatments. *Am. Psychol., 59*(9), 869–78.

Barlow, D. H. (2008). *Clinical handbook of psychological disorders: A step-by-step treatment manual* (4th ed.). New York: Guilford Press.

Barlow, D. H., Allen, L. B., & Basden, S. L. (2007). Psychological treatments for panic disorder, phobias, and generalized anxiety disorder. In P. E. Nathan and J. M. Gorman (Eds.), *A guide to treatments that work* (pp. 351–94). New York: Oxford University Press.

Barlow, D. H., Raffa, S. D., & Cohen, E. M. (2002). Psychosocial treatments for panic disorders, phobias and generalized anxiety disorders. In P. E. Nathan & J. M. Gorman (Eds.), *A guide to treatments that work* (2nd ed., pp. 301–36). New York: Oxford University Press.

Barlow, D. H., Sakheim, D. K., & Beck, J. G. (1983). Anxiety increases sexual arousal. *J. Abn. Psychol., 92*, 49–54.

Barnett, D., Ganiban, J., & Cicchetti, D. (1999). Maltreatment, negative expressivity, and the development of type D attachments from 12 to 24 months of age. *Monogr. Soc. Res. Child Develop., 64*, 97–118.

Baron, I. S., & Goldberger, E. (1993). Neuropsychological disturbances of hydrocephalic children with implications for special education and rehabilitation. *Neuropsychological Rehabilitation, 3*(4), 389–410.

Baron-Kuhn, E. A., & Segraves, R. T. (2007). Iatrogenic causes of female sexual disorders. In S. F. Owens and M. S. Tepper (Eds.), *Sexual health, Volume 4: State-of the art treatments and research* (pp. 329–48). Westport, CT: Praeger.

Barringer, T. A., & Weaver, E. M. (2002). Does long-term bupropion (Zyban) use prevent smoking relapse after initial success at quitting smoking? *J. Fam. Pract., 51*, 172.

Barry, H., III. (1982). Cultural variations in alcohol abuse. In I. Al-Issa (Ed.), *Culture and psychopathology.* Baltimore: University Park Press.

Barsetti, I., Earls, C. M., Lalumiere, M. L., & Belanger, N. (1998). The differentiation of intrafamilial and extrafamilial heterosexual child molesters. *J. Interpers. Violen., 13*(2), 275–86.

Barsky, A. J., & Ahern, D. K. (2004). Cognitive behavior therapy for hypochondriasis: A randomized controlled trial. *JAMA, 291*(12), 1464–70.

Barsky, A. J., Wool, C., Barnett, M. C., & Cleary, P. D. (1994). Histories of childhood trauma in adult hypochondriacal patients. *Am. J. Psychiatry, 151*(3), 397–401.

Bartak, A., Andrea, H., Spreeuwenberg, M. D., Ziegler, U. M., Dekker, J., Rossum, B. V., et al. (2011). Effectiveness of outpatient, day hospital, and inpatient psychotherapeutic treatment for patients with cluster B personality disorders. *Psychother. Psychosom., 80*(1), 28–38. doi:10.1159/000321999

Bartak, A., Spreeuwenberg, M. D., Andrea, H., Holleman, L., Rijnierse, P., Rossum, B. V., et al. (2010). Effectiveness of different modalities of psychotherapeutic treatment for patients with cluster C personality disorders: Results of a large prospective multicentre study. *Psychother. Psychosom., 79*(1), 20–30. doi:10.1159/000254902

Bartholme, L. T., Raymond, N. C., Lee, S. S., Peterson, C. B., & Warren, C. S. (2006). Detailed analysis of binges in obese women with binge eating disorder: Comparisons using multiple methods of data collection. *Int. J. Eating Disorders, 36*, 685–93.

Bartholomew, K., Kwong, M. J., & Hart, S. D. (2001). Attachment. In W. J. Livesley (Ed.), *Handbook of personality disorders* (pp. 196–230). New York: Guilford Press.

Bartholow, B. D., Sher, K. J., & Krull, J. L. (2003). Changes in heavy drinking over the third decade of life as a function of collegiate fraternity and sorority involvement: A prospective, multilevel analysis. *Health Psychol., 22*, 618–26.

Bartzokis, G., Lu, P. H., Turner, J., Mintz, J., & Saunders, C. S. (2005). Adjunctive risperidone in the treatment of chronic combat-related posttraumatic stress disorder. *Biol. Psychiat., 57*(5), 474–79.

Baskin-Sommers, A. R., Wallace, J. F., MacCoon, D. G., Curtin, J. J., & Newman, J. P. (2010). Clarifying the factors that undermine behavioral inhibition system functioning in psychopathy. *Personality Disorders: Theory, Research and Treatment, 1*, 203–17.

Başoğlu, M., Mineka, S., Paker, M., Aker, T., Livanou, M., & Gok, S. (1997). Psychological preparedness for trauma as a protective factor in survivors of torture. *Psychol. Med., 27*, 1421–33.

Başoğlu, M., Paker, M., Paker, O., Ozmen, E., Marks, I., Sahin, D., et al. (1994). Psychological effects of torture: A comparison of tortured with nontortured political activists in Turkey. *Am. J. Psychiatry, 151*, 76–81.

Başoğlu, M., Salcioglu, E., & Livanou, M. (2007). A randomized controlled study of single-session behavioral treatment of earthquake-related post traumatic stress disorder using an earthquake simulator. *Psychol. Med., 37*, 203–13.

Bass, E., & Davis, L. (1988). *The courage to heal.* New York: Harper & Row.

Basson, R. (2003). Biopsychosocial models of women's sexual response: Applications to management of "desire disorders. " *Sexual Relation. Ther., 18*, 107–15.

Basson, R. (2005). Women's sexual dysfunction: Revised and expanded definitions. *Can. Med. Assoc. J., 172*, 1327–33.

Basson, R. (2010). Sexual function of women with chronic illness and cancer. *Women's Health, 6*, 407–29.

Basson, R., McInnes, R., Smith, M. D., Hodgson, G., & Koppiker, N. (2002). Efficacy and safety of sildenafil citrate in women with sexual dysfunction associated with female sexual arousal disorder. *J. Women's Health & Gender-Based Medicine, 11*(4), 367–77.

Bateman, A., & Fonagy, P. (2008). 8-year follow-up of patients treated for borderline personality disorder: Mentalization-based treatment versus treatment as usual. *Am. J. Psychiatry, 165,* 631–38.

Bateman, A., & Fonagy, P. (2010). Mentalization based treatment for borderline personality disorder. *World Psychiatry, 9,* 11–15.

Bateman, A. W., Gunderson, J., & Mulder, R. (2015). Treatment of personality disorder. *Lancet, 385,* 735–43.

Bateson, G. (1959). Cultural problems posed by a study of schizophrenic process. In A. Auerbach (Ed.), *Schizophrenia: An integrated approach.* New York: Ronald Press.

Bateson, G. (1960). Minimal requirements for a theory of schizophrenia. *Arch. Gen. Psychiat., 2,* 477–91.

Bath, E. P. J., & Billick, S. B. (2010). Overview of juvenile law. In E. P. Benedek, P. Ash, & C. L. Scott (Eds.), *Principles and practice of child and adolescent forensic mental health* (pp. 337–45). Arlington, VA: American Psychiatric Publishing.

Battle, C. L., Shea, M. T., Johnson, D. M., Yen, S., Zlotnick, C., Zanarini, M. C., et al. (2004). Childhood maltreatment associated with adult personality disorders: Findings from the collaborative longitudinal personality disorders study. *J. Pers. Disord., 18*(2), 193–211.

Batstra, L., & Frances, A. (2012a). Diagnostic inflation: Causes and a suggested cure. *J. Nerv. Mental Dis., 200,* 474–79.

Batstra, L., & Frances, A. (2012b). DSM-5 further inflates attention deficit hyperactivity disorder. *J. Nerv. Ment. Dis., 200*(6), 486–488.

Battaglia, M., Pesenti-Gritti, P., Medland, S. E., Ogliari, A., Tambs, K., & Spatola, C. A. M. (2009). A genetically informed study of the association between childhood separation anxiety, sensitivity to CO_2, panic disorder, and the effects of childhood parental loss. *Arch. General Psychiatry, 66,* 64–71.

Bauer, A., Rosca, P., Khawalled, R., Gruzniewski, A., & Grinshpoon, A. (2003). Dangerousness and risk assessment: The state of the art. *Israel J. Psychiatry Related Sci., 40*(3), 182–90.

Bauer, A. M., & Shea, T. M. (1986). Alzheimer's disease and Down syndrome: A review and implications for adult services. *Education and Training of the Mentally Retarded, 21,* 144–50.

Bauer, S. M., Schanda, H., Karakula, H., Olajossy-Hilkesberger, L., Rudaleviciene, P., Okribelashvili, N., et al. (2011). Culture and the prevalence of hallucinations in schizophrenia. *Compr. Psychiat., 52,* 319–25.

Bauermeister, J. J., Canino, G., Polanczyk, G., & Rohde, L. A. (2010). ADHD across cultures: Is there evidence for a bidimensional organization of symptoms? *J. Clin. Child Adol. Psych., 39*(3), 362–72.

Baumann, M. H., Solis, E., Watterson, L. R., Marusich, J. A., Fantegrossi, W. E., & Wiley, J. L. (2014). Bath salts, spice, and related designer drugs: The science behind the headlines. *J. Neuroscience, 34,* 15150–58.

Baumeister, R. F., & Butler, J. L. (1997). Sexual masochism: Deviance without pathology. In D. R. Laws & W. O'Donohue (Eds.), *Sexual deviance: Theory, assessment, and treatment.* New York: Guilford Press.

Baumrind, D. (1967). Child care practices anteceding three patterns of preschool behavior. *Genetic Psychology Monographs, 75,* 43–88.

Baumrind, D. (1971). Current patterns of parental authority. *Develop. Psychol., 4*(1), 1–103.

Baumrind, D. (1975). *Early socialization and the discipline controversy.* Morristown, NJ: General Learning Press.

Baumrind, D. (1991). Effective parenting during the early adolescent transition. In P. A. Cowan & E. M. Hetherington (Eds.), *Family transitions* (pp. 111–64). Hillsdale, NJ: Erlbaum.

Baumrind, D. (1993). The average expectable environment is not good enough: A response to Scarr. *Child Develop., 64,* 1299–317.

Baxter, L. R., Jr., Ackermann, R. F., Swerdlow, N. R., Brody, A., Saxena, S., Schwartz, J. M., et al. (2000). Specific brain system mediation of obsessive-compulsive disorder responsive to either medication or behavior therapy. In W. K. Goodman & M. V. Rudorfer (Eds.), *Obsessive-compulsive disorder: Contemporary issues in treatment. Personality and clinical psychology series* (pp. 573–609). Mahwah, NJ: Erlbaum.

Baxter, L. R., Jr., Schwartz, J. M., Bergman, K. S., Szuba, M. P., Guze, B. H., Mazziota, J. C., et al. (1992). Caudate glucose metabolic rate changes with both drug and behavior therapy for obsessive-compulsive disorder. *Arch. Gen. Psychiat., 49,* 681–89.

Baxter, L. R., Jr., Schwartz, J. M., & Guze, B. H. (1991). Brain imaging: Toward a neuroanatomy of OCD. In J. Zohar, T. Insel, & S. Rasmussen (Eds.), *The psychobiology of obsessive-compulsive disorder.* New York: Springer.

Bayer, R. (1981). *Homosexuality and American psychiatry.* New York: Basic Books.

Bazargan, M., Bazargan, S., & Akanda, M. (2001). Gambling habits among aged African Americans. *Clin. Geron., 22*(3–4), 51–62.

Bazarian, J. J., Zhu, T., Zhong, J., Janigro, D., Rozen, E., Roberts, A., et al. (2014). Persistent, long-term cerebral white matter changes after sports-related repetitive head impacts. *PLoS ONE, 9,* e94734.

Beach, S. R. H., & Jones, D. J. (2002). Marital and family therapy for depression in adults. In I. H. Gotlib & C. L. Hammen (Eds.), *Handbook of depression* (pp. 422–40). New York: Guilford Press.

Beaton, A. A. (1997). The relation of planum temporale asymmetry and morphology of the corpus callosum to handedness, gender, and dyslexia: A review of the evidence. *Brain Lang., 60*(2), 255–322.

Beauchaine, T. P., Hinshaw, S. P., & Pang, K. L. (2010). Comorbidity of attention-deficit/hyperactivity disorder and early-onset conduct disorder: Biological, environmental, and developmental mechanisms. *Clinical Psychology: Science and Practice, 17*(4), 327–36. doi:10.1111/j.1468-2850.2010.01224.x

Beaumont, P. J. V. (2002). Clinical presentation of anorexia nervosa and bulimia nervosa. In C. G. Fairburn & K. D. Brownell (Eds.), *Eating disorders and obesity: A comprehensive handbook* (2nd ed.). New York: Guilford Press.

Becerra, D., Castillo, J. T., Ayón, C., & Blanchard, K. N. (2014). The moderating role of parental monitoring on the influence of peer pro-drug norms on alcohol and cigarette use among adolescents in Mexico. *J. Child & Adolescent Substance Abuse, 23*(5), 297–306. doi:http://dx.doi.org/10.1080/1067828X.2013.869138

Beck, A. T. (1967). *Depression: Causes and treatment.* Philadelphia, PA: University of Pennsylvania Press.

Beck, A. T. (2005). The current state of cognitive therapy: A 40-year retrospective. *Arch. Gen. Psychiat., 62,* 953–59.

Beck, A. T., Emery, G., & Greenberg, R. L. (1985). *Anxiety disorders and phobias: A cognitive perspective.* New York: Basic Books.

Beck, A. T., Emery, G., & Greenberg, R. L. (2005). *Anxiety disorders and phobias: A cognitive perspective.* New York: Basic Books.

Beck, A. T., Freeman, A., et al. (1990). *Cognitive therapy of personality disorders.* New York: Guilford Press.

Beck, A. T., Freeman, A., & Davis, D. D. (2004). *Cognitive therapy of personality disorders* (2nd ed.). New York: Guilford Press.

Beck, A. T., & Rector, N. A. (2005). Cognitive approaches to schizophrenia: Theory and therapy. *Annu. Rev. Clin. Psychol., 1,* 577–606.

Beck, A. T., Rush, A. J., Shaw, B., & Emery, G. (1979). *Cognitive therapy of depression: A treatment manual.* New York: Guilford Press.

Beck, A. T., Wright, F., Newman, C., & Liese, B. (1993). *Cognitive therapy of substance abuse.* New York: Guilford Press.

Beck, J. G., & Barlow, D. H. (1984). Current conceptualizations of sexual dysfunction: A review and an alternative perspective. *Clin. Psychol. Rev., 4*(4), 363–78.

Becker, A., Burwell, R. A., Gilman, S., Herzog, D. B., & Hamburg, P. (2002). Eating behaviors and attitudes following prolonged exposure to television among ethnic Fijian adolescent girls. *Brit. J. Psychiatry, 180,* 509–14.

Becker, J. B., Monteggia, L. M., Perrot-Sinal, T. S., Romeo, R. D., Taylor, J. R., Yehuda, R., et al. (2007). Stress and disease: Is being female a predisposing factor? *J. Neurosci., 27*(44), 11851–11855. doi:10.1523/jneurosci.3565-07.2007

Beckett, C., Maughan, B., Rutter, M., Castle, J., Colvert, E., Groothues, C., et al. (2006). Do the effects of early severe deprivation on cognition persist into early adolescence? Findings from the English and Romanian Adoptees Study. *Child Develop., 77*(3), 696–711.

Beech, A. R., & Harkins, L. (2012). DSM-IV paraphilia: Descriptions, demographics and treatment interventions. *Aggression Violent Behav., 17*(6). doi:10.1016/j.avb.2012.07.008

Beevers, C. G., & Miller, I. W. (2004). Depression-related negative cognition: Mood-state and trait dependent properties. *Cog. Ther. Res., 28*(3), 293–307.

Beevers, C. G., Rohde, P., Stice, E., & Nolen-Hoeksema, S. (2007). Recovery from manor depressive disorder among female adolescents: A prospective test of the scar hypothesis. *J. Consult. Clin. Psychol., 75,* 888–900.

Begemann, M. J. H., Dekker, C. F., van Lunenburg, M., & Sommer, I. E. (2012). Estrogen augmentation in schizophrenia: A quantitative review of current evidence. *Schizophrenia Res., 141,* 179–84.

Behan, J., & Carr, A. (2000). Oppositional defiant disorder. In A. Carr (Ed.), *What works with children and adolescents? A critical review of psychological interventions with children, adolescents and their families* (pp. 102–30). Florence, KY: Taylor & Francis/Routledge.

Behar, E., & Borkovec, T. D. (2006). The nature and treatment of generalized anxiety disorder. In B. O. Rothbaum (Ed.), *Pathological anxiety: Emotional processing in etiology and treatment* (pp. 181–96). New York: Guilford Press.

Behar, E., DiMarco, I. D., Hekler, E. B., et al. (2008). Current theoretical models of GAD: Conceptual review and treatment implications. *J. Anx. Dis., 23,* 1011–23.

Bekker, M. H. (1996). Agoraphobia and gender: A review. *Clin. Psychol. Rev., 16*(2), 129–46.

Belanoff, J. K., Gross, K., Yager, A., & Schatzberg, A. F. (2001). Corticosteroids and cognition. *J. Psychiatr. Res., 35*(3), 127–45.

Bellack, A. S., & Mueser, K. T. (1993). Psychosocial treatment for schizophrenia. *Schizo. Bull., 19,* 317–36.

Bender, R. E., & Alloy, L. B. (2011). Life stress and kindling in bipolar disorder: Review of the evidence and integration with emerging biopsychosocial theories. *Clin. Psychol. Rev., 31*(3), 383–98. doi:10.1016/j.cpr.2011.01.004

Benes, F. M., & Berretta, S. (2001). GABAergic interneurons: Implications for understanding schizophrenia and bipolar disorder. *Neuropsychopharmacol., 25,* 1–27.

Benjamin, L. S. (2004). An interpersonal family-oriented approach to personality disorder. In M. M. MacFarlane (Ed.), *Family treatment of personality disorders: Advances in clinical practice* (pp. 41–69). Binghamton, NY: Haworth Clinical Practice Press.

Benjamin, L. S. (2005). Interpersonal theory of personality disorders: The structural analysis of social behavior and interpersonal reconstructive therapy. In M. F. Lezenweger & J. F. Clarkin (Eds.), *Major theories of personality disorder* (2nd ed., pp. 157–230). New York: Guilford Press.

Benjamin, L. (2014). *A brief history of modern psychology* (2nd ed.). New York: Blackwell Publishers.

Bennett, D., Sharpe, M., Freeman, C., & Carson, A. (2004). Anorexia nervosa among female secondary students in Ghana. *Brit. J. Psychiatry, 185,* 312–17.

Bennett, J. B., & Lehman, W. E. K. (1996). Alcohol, antagonism, and witnessing violence in the workplace: Drinking climates and social alienation-integration. In G. R. Vandenbos & E. Q. Bulatao (Eds.), *Violence in the workplace* (pp. 105–52). Washington, DC: American Psychological Association.

Bennett, T. L., Dittmar, C., & Ho, M. R. (1997). The neuropsychology of traumatic brain injury. In A. M. Horton, D. Wedding, & J. Webster (Eds.), *The neuropsychology handbook* (Vol. 2, pp. 123–72). New York: Springer.

Benros, M. E., Pederson, M. G., Rasmussen, H., Eaton, W. W., Nordentoft, M., & Mortensen, P. B. (2014). A nationwide study on the risk of autoimmune diseases in individuals with a personal or family history of schizophrenia and related psychosis. *Am. J. Psychiatry, 171,* 218–26.

Bentley, K. H., Gallagher, M. W., Boswell, J. F., Gorman, J. M., Shear, M. K., Woods, S. W., & Barlow, D. H. (2013). The interactive contributions of perceived control and anxiety sensitivity in panic disorder: A triple vulnerabilities perspective. *J. Psychopathology and Behavioral Assessment, 35,* 57–64.

Berenbaum, H., Thompson, R. J., Milanek, M. E., Boden, T. M., & Bredmeier, K. (2008). Psychological trauma and schizotypal personality disorder. *J. Abn. Psych., 117*(3), 502–19.

Berenson, K. R., Downey, G., Rafaeli, E., Coifman, K. G., & Paquin, N. L. (2011). The rejection-rage contingency in borderline personality disorder. *J Abn. Psychol., 120*(3), 681–90. doi:10.1037/a0023335

Bergem, A. L. M., Engedal, K., & Kringlen, E. (1997). The role of heredity in late-onset Alzheimer disease and vascular dementia. *Arch. Gen. Psychiat., 54*(3), 264–70.

Bergemann, N., Oarzer, P., Runnebaum, B., Resch, F., & Mundt, C. (2007). Estrogen, menstrual cycle phases, and psychopathology in women suffering from schizophrenia. *Psychological Medicine, 37,* 1427–36.

Bergeron, S., Binik, T., Khalife, S., Pagidas, K., Glazer, H. I., Meana, M., et al. (2001). A randomized comparison of group cognitive-behavioral therapy, surface electromyographic biofeedback, and vestibulectomy in the treatment of dyspareunia resulting from vulvar vestibules. *Pain, 91,* 297–306.

Bergner, D. (2009). *The other side of desire: Four journeys into the far realms of lust and longing.* New York: HarperCollins.

Berk, L. E. (2003). *Child development* (6th ed.). Boston: Allyn & Bacon.

Berkman, L. F., Blumenthal, J., Burg, M., Carney, R. M., Catellier, D., Cowan, M. J., et al. (2003). Effects of treating depression and low perceived social support on clinical events after myocardial infarction: The enhancing recovery in coronary

heart diseases patients (ENRICHD) randomized trial. *JAMA, 289,* 3106–16.

Berkman, L. F., Leo-Summers, L., & Horwitz, R. I. (1992). Emotional support and survival after myocardial infarction: A prospective population-based study of the elderly. *Ann. Int. Med., 117,* 1003–09.

Berle, D., & Starcevic, V. (2005). Thought-action fusion: Review of the literature and future directions. *Clin. Psych. Rev., 25*(3), 263–84.

Berlin, F. S. (1994, May). The case for castration, part 2. *Washington Monthly, 26,* 28–29.

Berlin, F. S. (2003). Sex offender treatment and legislation. *J. Am. Acad. Psychiat. Law, 31*(4), 510–13.

Bermpohl, F., Kahnt, T., Dalanay, U., Hägele, C., Sajonz, B., Wegner, T., et al. (2010). Altered representation of expected value in the orbitofrontal cortex in mania. *Human Brain Mapping, 31,* 958–69.

Berney, T. P. (2000). Methods of treatment. In M. G. Gelder, J. J. Lopez-Ibor, Jr., & N. C. Andreason (Eds.), *New Oxford textbook of psychiatry* (Vol. 2, pp. 1989–94). Oxford, UK: Oxford University Press.

Bernstein, A., Zvolensky, M. J., Sachs-Ericsson, N., Schmidt, N. B., & Bonn-Miller, M. O. (2006). Associations between age of onset and lifetime history of panic attacks and alcohol use, abuse, and dependence in a representative sample. *Compr. Psychiat., 47*(5), 342–49.

Bernstein, D. P., Arntz, A., & Travaglini, L. (2009). Schizoid and avoidant personality disorders. In P. H. Blaney & T. Millon (Eds.), *Oxford textbook of psychopathology* (2nd ed., pp. 586–601). New York: Oxford University Press.

Bernstein, D. P., & Travaglini, L. (1999). Schizoid and avoidant personality disorders. In T. Millon, P. H. Blaney, & R. D. Davis (Eds.), *Oxford textbook of psychopathology* (pp. 523–34). New York: Oxford University Press.

Bernstein, D. P., & Useda, D. J. (2007). Paranoid personality disorder. In W. O'Donohue, K. A. Fowler, & S. C. Lilienfeld (Eds.), *Personality disorders: Toward the DSM-V* (pp. 41–62). Thousand Oaks, CA: Sage Publications.

Bernstein, G. A., & Layne, A. E. (2006). Separation anxiety disorder and generalized anxiety disorder. In M. K. Dulcan & J. M. Wiener (Eds.), *Essentials of child and adolescent psychiatry* (pp. 415–39). Washington, DC: American Psychiatric Publishing.

Berntsen, D., & Rubin, D. C. (2015). Pretraumatic stress reactions in soldiers deployed to Afghanistan. *Clinical Psychological Science, 3,* 663–74.

Berridge, K. C., & Kringelbach, M. L. (2015). Pleasure systems in the brain. *Neuron, 86,* 646–64.

Berrios, G. (1990). A British contribution to the history of functional brain surgery. Special issue: History of psychopharmacology. *J. Psychopharm., 4,* 140–44.

Bersoff, D. N. (2014). Protecting victims of violent patients while protecting confidentiality. *American Psychologist, 69*(5), 461–67. doi:10.1037/a0037198

Berthold, T., & Ellinger, M. (2009). Conducting initial client interviews. In T. Berthold, J. Miller, & A. Avila-Esparza (Eds.), *Foundations for community health workers* (pp. 197–219). San Francisco: Jossey-Bass.

Berthoud, H.-R., & Morrison, C. (2008). The brain, appetite, and obesity. *Annu. Rev. Psych., 59,* 55–92.

Beutler, L. E., Malik, M., Alimohamed, S., Harwood, T. M., Talebi, H., Noble, S., et al. (2004). In M. J. Lambert (Ed.), *Bergin and Garfield's handbook of psychotherapy and behavior change* (pp. 227–306). New York: John Wiley & Sons.

Beveridge, A. (1997). Voices of the mad: Patients' letters from the Royal Edinburgh Asylum, 1873–1908. *Psychol. Med., 27,* 899–908.

Bezchlibnyk-Butler, K. Z., & Jeffries, J. J. (2003). *Clinical handbook of psychotropic drugs.* Seattle, WA: Hogrefe & Huber.

Bhattacharjee, S., & Lukiw, W. J. (2013, September 17). Alzheimer's disease and the microbiome. *Frontiers in Cellular Neuroscience.* http://dx.doi.org/10.3389/fncel.2013.00153

Bickel, W. K., Amass, L., Higgins, S. T., Badger, G. J., & Esch, R. A. (1997). Effects of adding behavioral treatment to opioid detoxification with buprenorphine. *J. Consult. Clin. Psychol., 65*(5), 803–10.

Bieber, I., Dain, H. J., Dince, P. R., Drellich, M. G., Grand, H. G., Gundlach, R. H., et al. (1962). *Homosexuality: A psychoanalytic study of male homosexuals.* New York: Basic Books.

Biederman, J., Monteaux, M. C., Doyle, A. E., Seidman, L. J., Wilens, T. E., Ferraro, F., et al. (2004). Impact of executive function deficits and attention deficit/hyperactivity disorder (ADHD) on academic outcomes in children. *J. Consult. Clin. Psychol., 72,* 757–76.

Biederman, J., Petty, C. R., Faraone, S. V., Hirshfeld-Becker, D. R., Henin, A., Brauer, L., et al. (2006). Antecedents to panic disorder in nonreferred adults. *J. Clin. Psychiat., 67*(8), 1179–86.

Bienvenu, O. J., Hettema, J. M., Neale, M. C., Prescott, C. A., & Kendler, K. S. (2007). Low extraversion and high neuroticism as indices of genetic and environmental risk for social phobia, agoraphobia, and animal phobia. *Am. J. Psychiatry, 164*(11), 1714–21. doi:10.1176/appi.ajp.2007.06101667

Bijttebier, P., & Goethals, E. (2006). Parental drinking as a risk factor for children's maladjustment: The mediating role of family environment. *Psych. Addict. Behav., 20*(2), 126–30.

Billioti de Gage, S., Moride, Y., Ducruet, T., Kurth, T., Verdoux, H., Tournier, M., et al. (2014). Benzodiazepine use and risk of Alzheimer's disease: Case-control study. *BMJ, 349,* g5205.

Binder, R. L. (1999). Are the mentally ill dangerous? *J. Am. Acad. Psychiatry Law, 27*(2), 189–201.

Binik, Y. M. (2005). Should dyspareunia be retained as a sexual dysfunction in DSM-V? A painful classification decision. *Arch. Sex. Behav., 34*(1), 11–21.

Binik, Y. M. (2010a). The DSM diagnostic criteria for vaginismus. *Arch. Sexual Behavior, 39*(2), 278–91.

Binik, Y. M. (2010b). The DSM diagnostic criteria for dyspareunia. *Arch. Sexual Behavior, 39*(2), 292–303.

Binik, Y. M., Bergeron, S., Khalifé, S., & Leiblum, S. R. (2007). Dyspareunia and vaginismus: So-called sexual pain. *Principles and practice of sex therapy* (4th ed., pp. 124–56). New York: Guilford Press.

Binks, C. A., Fenton, M., McCarthy, L., Lee, T., Adams, C. E., & Duggan, C. (2006). Psychological therapies for people with borderline personality disorder. *Cochrane Database Syst. Rev.,* CD005652.

Birbaumer, N., Veit, R., Lotze, M., Erb, M., Hermann, C., Grodd, W., et al. (2005). Deficient fear conditioning in psychopathy: A functional magnetic resonance imaging study. *Arch. Gen. Psychiat., 62*(7), 799–805.

Birkeland, S. F. (2013). Paranoid personality disorder and organic brain injury: A case report. *J. Neuropsychiatry and Clinical Neuroscience, 25,* E52.

Bisson, J. I., McFarlane, A. C., Rose, S., Ruzek, J. I., & Watson, P. J. (2009). Psychological debriefing for adults. In E. B. Foa, T. M. Keane, M. J. Friedman, & J. A. Cohen (Eds.), *Effective treatments for PTSD: Practice guidelines from the International Society for Traumatic Stress Studies* (2nd ed., pp. 83–105). New York: Guilford Press.

Bittles, A. H., Bower, C., Hussain, R., & Glasson, E. J. (2007). The four ages of Down syndrome. *European J. Public Health, 17*(2), 121–225.

Bjorklund, D. F. (2000). *False-memory creation in children and adults: Theory, research and implications.* Mahway, NJ: Erlbaum.

Black, D. W., & Andreasen, N. C. (2014). *Introductory textbook of psychiatry* (6th ed.). Arlington, VA: American Psychiatric Publishing.

Blackburn, I. M., & Davidson, K. (1990). *Cognitive therapy for depression and anxiety.* Oxford, UK: Blackwell Scientific.

Blagov, P. S., Fowler, K. A., & Lilienfeld, S. O. (2007). Histrionic personality disorder. In W. O'Donohue, K. A. Fowler, & S. O. Lilienfeld (Eds.), *Personality disorders: Toward the DSM-V* (pp. 203–32). Thousand Oaks, CA: Sage Publications.

Blagov, P. S., & Westen, D. (2008). Questioning the coherence of histrionic personality disorder: Borderline and hysterical personality subtypes in adults and adolescents. *J. Nerv. Ment. Dis., 196*(11), 785–97. doi:10.1097/NMD.0b013e31818b502d

Blair, K., Geraci, M., Devido, J., McCaffrey, D., Chen, G., Vythilingam, M., et al. (2008). Neural response to self and other referential praise and criticism in generalized social phobia. *Arch. Gen. Psychiat., 65*(10), 1176–84. doi:10.1001/archpsyc.65.10.1176

Blair, R. J. (2007). The amygdala and ventromedial prefrontal cortex in morality and psychopathy. *Trends in Cognitive Sciences, 11*(9), 387–92.

Blair, R. J. R. (2006). The subcortical brain systems in psychopathy: The amygdala and associated structures. In C. J. Patrick (Ed.), *Handbook of the psychopathy* (pp. 296–312). New York: Guilford Press.

Blair, R. J. R., Jones, L., Clark, F., & Smith, M. (1997). The psychopathic individual: A lack of responsiveness to distress cues? *Psychophysiology, 34*, 192–98.

Blanchard, R. (1989). The classification and labeling of nonhomosexual gender dysphorias. *Arch. Sex. Behav., 18*, 315–34.

Blanchard, R. (1991). Clinical observations and systematic study of autogynephilia. *J. Sex Marit. Ther., 17*, 235–51.

Blanchard, R. (1993). Varieties of autogynephilia and their relationship to gender dysphoria. *Arch. Sex. Behav., 22*, 241–51.

Blanchard, R. (1994). A structural equation model for age at clinical presentation in nonhomosexual male gender dysphorics. *Arch. Sex. Behav., 23*, 311–32.

Blanchard, R. (2010). The fertility of hebephiles and the adaptationist argument against including hebephilia in *DSM-5. Arch. Sexual Behavior, 39*, 817–18.

Blanchard, R., & Hucker, S. J. (1991). Age, transvestitism, bondage, and concurrent paraphilic activities in 117 fatal cases of autoerotic asphyxia. *Brit. J. Psychiatry, 159*, 371–77.

Blanco, C., Cohen, O., Luján, J. J., & Wulfert, E. (2010). Pathological gambling among patients with substance use disorders. In E. V. Nunes, J. Selzer, P. Levounis, & C. A. Davies (Eds.), *Substance dependence and co-occurring psychiatric disorders: Best practices for diagnosis and treatment* (pp. 1–15). Kingston, NJ: Civic Research Institute.

Blashfield, R. K., Keeley, J. W., Flanagan, E. H., & Miles, S. R. (2014). The cycle of classification: DSM-1 through DSM-5. *Annu. Rev. Clin. Psychology, 10*, 25–51.

Blashfield, R. K., & Livesley, W. J. (1999). Classification. In T. Millon, P. H. Blaney, & R. D. Davis (Eds.), *Oxford textbook of psychopathology* (pp. 3–28). New York: Oxford University Press.

Blashfield, R., Reynolds, S. M., & Stennett, B. (2012). The death of histrionic personality disorder. In T. Widiger (Ed.), *The Oxford handbook of personality disorders* (pp. 603–27). Oxford, UK: Oxford University Press.

Blaszczynski, A., McConaghy, N., & Frankova, A. (1989). Crime, antisocial personality and pathological gambling. *J. Gambling Behavior, 5*, 137–52.

Blazer, D. G., & Hybels, C. F. (2009). Depression in later life: Epidemiology, assessment, impact, and treatment. In I. H. Gotlib & C. L. Hammen (Eds.), *Handbook of depression* (2nd ed., pp. 492–509). New York: Guilford Press.

Bleiberg, K. L., & Markowitz, J. C. (2008). Interpersonal psychotherapy for depression. In D. H. Barlow (Ed.), *Clinical handbook of psychological disorders: A step-by-step treatment manual* (4th ed., pp. 306–27). New York: Guilford Press.

Bleichhardt, G., & Hiller, W. (2006). Pathological features, medical consulting behaviour and media consume in outpatients with health anxiety. *Verhaltenstherapie & Verhaltensmedizin, 21*(1), 29–41.

Bleichhardt, G., Timer, B., & Rief, W. (2004). Cognitive-behavioural therapy for patients with multiple somatoform symptoms: A randomised controlled trial in tertiary care. *J. Psychosomat. Res., 56*, 449–54.

Bleuler, E. (1950). *Dementia praecox or the group of schizophrenias.* New York: International Universities Press. (Originally published in 1911.)

Bloch, H. S. (1969). Army clinical psychiatry in the combat zone—1967–1968. *Am. J. Psychiatry, 126*, 289.

Bloch, M. H., Landeros-Weisenberger, A., Kelmendi, B., Coric, V., Bracken, M. B., & Leckman, J. F. (2006). A systematic review: Antipsychotic augmentation with treatment refractory obsessive-compulsive disorder. *Molecular Psychiatry, 11*, 622–32.

Blonigen, D. M., Carlson, S. R., Krueger, R. F., & Patrick, C. J. (2003). A twin study of self-reported psychopathic personality traits. *Personal. Indiv. Diff., 35*(1), 179–97.

Blonigen, D. M., Hicks, B. M., Krueger, R. F., Patrick, C. J., & Iacono, W. G. (2006). Continuity and change in psychopathic traits as measured via normal-range personality: A longitudinal-biometric study. *J. Abn. Psych., 115*(1), 85–95.

Bloom, M., & Gullotta, T. P. (2009). Primary prevention in adolescent substance abuse. In C. G. Leukefeld, T. P. Gullotta, & M. Staton-Tindall (Eds.), *Adolescent substance abuse: Evidence-based approaches to prevention and treatment, issues in children's and families' lives* (pp. 155–70). New York: Springer.

Blount, A., Schoenbaum, M., Kathol, R., Rollman, B. L., Thomas, M., O'Donohue, W., et al. (2007). The economics of behavioral health services in medical settings: A summary of the evidence. *Prof. Psychol. Res. Pract., 38*(3), 290–97.

Blum, K., Cull, J. G., Braverman, E. R., & Comings, D. E. (1996). Reward deficiency syndrome. *American Scientist, 84*, 132–45.

Blum, K., Febo, M., McLaughlin, R., Cronjé, F. J., Han, D., & Gold, S. M. (2015). Hatching the behavioral addiction egg: Reward Deficiency Solution System (RDSS)™ as a function of dopaminergic neurogenetics and brain functional connectivity linking all addictions under a common rubric. *J. Behavioral Addictions, 3*, 149–56.

Blum, N., St. John, D., Pfohl, B., Stuart, S., McCormick, B., Allen, J., et al. (2008). Systems training for emotional predictability and problem solving (STEPPS) for outpatients with borderline personality disorder: A randomized controlled trial and 1-year follow-up. *Am. J. Psychiatry, 165*, 468–78.

Blum, R. (1969). *Society and drugs* (Vol. 1). San Francisco: Jossey-Bass.

Blumenthal, J. A., Sherwood, A., Gullette, E. C. D., Georgiades, A., & Tweedy, D. (2002). Biobehavioral approaches to the treatment of essential hypertension. *J. Consult. Clin. Psychol., 70*, 569–89.

Bockhoven, J. S. (1972). *Moral treatment in community mental health.* New York: Springer.

Bodenhausen, G. V., & Morales, J. R. (2013). Social cognition and perception. In I. Weiner (Ed.), *Handbook of psychology* (2nd ed., Vol. 5, pp. 225–246). Hoboken, NJ: Wiley.

Boehm, G. (1968). At last—A nonaddicting substitute for morphine? *Today's Health, 46*(4), 69–72.

Bogaerts, K., Rayen, L., Lavrysen, A., Van Diest, I., Janssens, T., Schruers, K., & Van den Bergh, O. (2015). Unraveling the relationship between trait negative affectivity and habitual symptom reporting. *PLoS ONE, 10*(1), e0115748. doi:10.1371/journal.pone.0115748

Boland, R. J., & Keller, M. B. (2002). Course and outcome of depression. In I. H. Gotlib & C. L. Hammen (Eds.), *Handbook of depression* (pp. 43–57). New York: Guilford Press.

Boland, R. J., & Keller, M. B. (2009). Course and outcome of depression. In I. H. Gotlib & C. L. Hammen (Eds.), *Handbook of depression* (2nd ed., pp. 23–43). New York: Guilford Press.

Bolinskey, P. K., James, A. V., Cooper-Bolinskey, D., Novi, J. H., Hunter, H. K., Hudak, D. V., et al. (2015). Revisiting the blurry boundaries of schizophrenia; Spectrum disorders in psychometrically identified schizotypes. *Psychiatry Res., 225*, 335–40.

Bonanno, G. A., & Kaltman, S. (1999). Toward an integrative perspective on bereavement. *Psychol. Bull., 125*(6), 760–76.

Bonanno, G. A., Moskowitz, J. T., Papa, A., & Folkman, S. (2005). Resilience to loss in bereaved spouses, bereaved parents, and bereaved gay men. *J. Pers. Soc. Psychol., 88*(5), 827–43.

Bonanno, G. A., Westphal, M., & Mancini, A. D. (2011). Resilience to loss and potential trauma. *Annu. Rev. Clin. Psychol., 7*, 511–35.

Bonanno, G. A., Wortman, C. B., & Nesse, R. M. (2004). Prospective patterns of resilience and maladjustment during widowhood. *Psychol. Aging, 19*(2), 260–71.

Bondi, M. W., & Lange, K. L. (2001). Alzheimer's disease. In H. S. Friedman (Ed.), *The disorders: Specialty articles from the encyclopedia of mental health.* San Diego, CA: Academic Press.

Bookheimer, S. Y., Strojwas, M. H., Cohen, M. S., Saunders, A. M., Pericak-Vance, M. A., Mazziotta, J. C., et al. (2000). Patterns of brain activation in people at risk for Alzheimer's disease. *N. Engl. J. Med., 343*, 450–56.

Bora, E., Yücel, M., & Pantelis, C. (2010). Cognitive impairment in affective psychoses: A meta-analysis. *Schizo. Bull., 36*(1), 112–25. doi:10.1093/schbul/sbp093

Bora, E., Yücel, M., Pantelis, C., & Berk, M. (2011). Meta-analytic review of neurocognition in bipolar II disorder. *Acta Psychiatr. Scand., 123*, 165–74.

Boraska, V., Franklin, C. S., Floyd, J. A. B., Thornton, L. M., Huckins, L. M., Southam, L., et al. (2014). A genome-wide association study of anorexia nervosa. *Molecular Psychiatry, 19*(10), 1085–94.

Borch-Jacobsen, M. (2009). *Making minds and madness: From hysteria to depression.* Cambridge, UK: Cambridge University Press.

Borges, G., Nock, M. K., Haro Abad, J. M., Hwang, I., Sampson, N. A., Alonso, J., et al. (2010). Twelve-month prevalence of and risk factors for suicide attempts in the World Health Organization World Mental Health Surveys. *J. Clin. Psychiat., 71*, 1617–28.

Borkovec, T. D. (1985). The role of cognitive and somatic cues in anxiety and anxiety disorders. In A. Tuma & J. D. Maser (Eds.), *Anxiety and the anxiety disorders* (pp. 463–78). Hillsdale, NJ: Erlbaum.

Borkovec, T. D. (1994). The nature, functions, and origins of worry. In G. L. C. Davey & F. Tallis (Eds.), *Worrying, perspectives on theory, assessment, and treatment* (pp. 5–34). Sussex, UK: Wiley.

Borkovec, T. D. (2006). Applied relaxation and cognitive therapy for pathological worry and generalized anxiety disorder. In G. C. L. Davey & A. Wells (Eds.), *Worry and its psychological disorders: Theory, assessment and treatment* (pp. 273–87). Hoboken, NJ: John Wiley & Sons.

Borkovec, T. D., Abel, J. L., & Newman, H. (1995). Effects of psychotherapy on comorbid conditions in generalized anxiety disorder. *J. Consult. Clin. Psychol., 63*(3), 479–83.

Borkovec, T. D., Alcaine, O. M., & Behar, E. (2004). Avoidance theory of worry and generalized anxiety disorder. In R. G. Heimberg, C. L. Turk, & D. S. Mennin (Eds.), *Generalized anxiety disorder: Advances in research and practice.* (pp. 77–108). New York: Guilford Press.

Bornstein, R. F., Denckla, C. A., & Chung, W.-J. (2015). Dependent and histrionic personality disorders. In P. H. Blaney, R. F. Krueger, & T. Millon (Eds.), *Oxford textbook of psychopathology* (pp. 659–80). New York: Oxford University Press.

Bornstein, R. F., & Malka, I. L. (2009). Dependent and histrionic personality disorders. In P. H. Blaney & T. Millon (Eds.), *Oxford textbook of psychopathology* (2nd ed., pp. 602–21). New York: Oxford University Press.

Borthwick, A., Holman, C., Kennard, D., McFetridge, M., Messruther, K., & Wilkes, J. (2001). The relevance of moral treatment to contemporary mental health care. *J. Ment. Health, 10,* 427–39.

Bos, K., Zeanah, C. H., Fox, N. A., Drury, S. S., McLaughlin, K. A., & Nelson, C. A. (2011). Psychiatric outcomes in young children with a history of institutionalization. *Harv. Rev. Psychiat., 19*(1), 15–24. doi:10.3109/10673229.2011.549773

Bosshard, G., Broeckaert, B., Clark, D., Materstvedt, L. J., Gordijn, B., & Muller-Busch, H. C. (2008). A role for doctors in assisted dying? An analysis of legal regulations and medical professional positions in six European countries. *J. Med. Ethics, 34*(1), 28–32.

Bostic, J. Q., Biederman, J., Spencer, T. J., Wilens, T. E., Prince, J. B., Monuteaux, M. C., et al. (2000). Pemoline treatment of adolescents with attention deficit hyperactivity disorder: A short-term controlled trial. *J. Child. Adoles. Psychopharm., 10*(3), 205–16.

Bostwick, W. B., Boyd, C. J., Hughes, T. L., & McCabe, S. E. (2010). Dimensions of sexual orientation and the prevalence of mood and anxiety disorders in the United States. *Journal Information, 100*(3), 468–75.

Bouchard, T. J., & Propping, P. (Eds.). (1993). *Twins as a tool of behavioral genetics.* New York: Wiley.

Bouchard, T. J., Jr., & Loehlin, J. C. (2001). Genes, evolution, and personality. *Behav. Gen., 31*(3), 243–73.

Bouma, E. M., Ormel, J., Verhulst, F. C., & Oldehinkel, A. J. (2008). Stressful life events and depressive problems in early adolescent boys and girls: The influence of parental depression, temperament and family environment. *J. Affect. Dis., 105,* 185–93.

Bouman, T. K. (2015). Somatic symptom and related disorders. In Blaney, P. H., Krueger, R. F., & Millon, T. (Eds.), *Oxford textbook of psychopathology* (3rd ed., pp. 540–65). New York: Oxford University Press.

Bourque, F., van der Ven, E., & Malla, A. (2011). A meta-analysis of the risk for psychotic disorders among first- and second-generation immigrants. *Psychological Medicine, 41,* 897–910.

Bouton, M. E. (1994). Conditioning, remembering, and forgetting. *J. Exper. Psychol. Animal Behavior Processes, 20,* 219–31.

Bouton, M. E. (2002). Context, ambiguity, and unlearning: Sources of relapse after behavioral extinction. *Biol. Psychiat., 52*(10), 976–86.

Bouton, M. E. (2005). Behavior systems and the contextual control of anxiety, fear, and panic. In L. F. Barrett, P. M. Niedenthal, & P. Winkielman (Eds.), *Emotion and consciousness* (pp. 205–27). New York: Guilford Press.

Bouton, M. E. (2007). *Learning and behavior: A contemporary synthesis.* Sunderland, MA: Sinauer Associates.

Bouton, M. E., Mineka, S., & Barlow, D. H. (2001). A modern learning theory perspective on the etiology of panic disorder. *Psychol. Rev., 108,* 4–32.

Bouton, M. E., Westbrook, R. F., Corcoran, K. A., & Maren, S. (2006). Contextual and temporal modulation of extinction: Behavioral and biological mechanisms. *Biol. Psychiat., 60*(4), 352–60.

Bovet, P., Perret, F., Cornuz, J., Quilindo, J., & Paccaud, F. (2002). Improved smoking cessation in smokers given ultrasound photographs of their own atherosclerotic plaques. *Preventive Medicine, 34*(2), 215–20.

Bowlby, J. (1960). Separation anxiety. *Int. J. Psychoanal., 41,* 89–93.

Bowlby, J. (1969). *Attachment and loss* (Vol. 1). New York: Basic Books.

Bowlby, J. (1973). Separation: Anxiety and anger. *Psychology of attachment and loss series* (Vol. 3). New York: Basic Books.

Bowlby, J. (1980). *Attachment and loss, III: Loss, sadness, and depression.* New York: Basic Books.

Bowler, J. V., Eliasziw, M., Steenhuis, R., Munoz, D. G., Fry, R., Merskey, H., & Hachinski, V. C. (1997). Comparative evolution of Alzheimer disease, vascular dementia, and mixed dementia. *Arch. Neurol., 54*(6), 697–703.

Bowman, E. S., & Markand, O. N. (2005). Diagnosis and treatment of pseudoseizures. *Psychiat. Ann., 35*(4), 306–16.

Boyce, W. T., Essex, M. J., Alkon, A., Goldsmith, H. H., Kraemer, H. C., & Kupfer, D. J. (2006). Early father involvement moderates biobehavioral susceptibility to mental health problems in middle childhood. *J. Am. Acad. Child Adoles. Psychiatry, 45*(12), 1510–20.

Boylan, K., Georgiades, K., & Szatmari, P. (2010). The longitudinal association between oppositional and depressive symptoms across childhood. *J. Am. Acad. Child Adoles. Psychiat., 49*(2), 152–61.

Boys, A., Marsden, J., & Strang, J. (2001). Understanding reasons for drug use amongst young people: A functional perspective. *Health Ed. Res., 16*(4), 457–69.

Boysen, G. A., & VanBergen, A. (2013). A review of published research on adult dissociative identity disorder 2000–2010. *J. Nervous and Mental Disease, 201,* 5–11.

Boysen, G. A., & VanBergen, A. (2014). Simulation of multiple personalities: A review of research comparing diagnosed and simulated dissociative identity disorder. *Clinical Psychology Review, 34,* 14–28.

Braaten, E. B. (2011). Mood disorders. In E. B. Braaten (Ed.), *How to find mental health care for your child, APA lifetools imprint* (pp. 87–99). Washington, DC: American Psychological Association.

Bradford, J. M. W., & Greenberg, D. M. (1996). Pharmacological treatment of deviant sexual behaviour. *Annu. Rev. Sex Res., 7,* 283–306.

Brand, B. L., Myrick, A. C., & Ducharme, E. (2014). Dissociative disorders. In L. Grossman & S. Walfish (Eds.), *Translating psychological research into practice* (pp. 167–73). New York: Springer.

Brand, M., Fujiwara, E., Kalbe, E., Steingrass, H. P., Kessler, J., & Markowitsch, H. J. (2003). Cognitive estimation and affective judgments in alcoholic Korsakoff patients. *J. Clini. Exper. Neuropsych., 25*(3), 324–34.

Brans, R. G. H., Van Haren, N. E. M., van Baal, G. C., Schnack, H. G., Kahn, R. S., & Hulsoff Pol, H. E. (2008). Heritability of changes in brain volume over time in twin pairs discordant for schizophrenia. *Arch. Gen. Psychiat., 65,* 1259–68.

Branson, R., Potoczna, N., Kral, J. G., Lentes, K.-U., Hoehe, M. R., & Horber, F. F. (2003). Binge eating as a major phenotype of melanocortin 4 receptor gene mutation. *N. Engl. J. Med., 348,* 1096–103.

Braun, S. (1996). *Buzz* (Vol. 1). New York: Oxford University Press.

Braus, D., Ende, G., Weber-Fahr, W., Sartorius, A., Krier, A., Hubrich-Ungureanu, P., et al. (1999).

Antipsychotic drug effects on motor activation measured by functional magnetic resonance imaging in schizophrenic patients. *Schiz. Res., 39*(1), 19–29.

Brecht, M. L., O'Brien, A., Mayrhauser, C., & Anglin, M. D. (2004). Methamphetamine use behaviors and gender differences. *Add. Behav., 29*(1), 89–106.

Brecht, M., von Mayrhauser, C., & Anglin, M. D. (2000). Predictors of relapse after treatment for methamphetamine use. *J. Psychoact. Drugs, 32*(2), 211–20.

Breitborde, N. J. K., Srihari, V. H., Pollard, J. M., Addington, D. N., & Woods, S. W. (2010). Mediators and moderators in early intervention research. *Early Intervention in Psychiatry, 4*(2), 143–52.

Breitner, J. C. S., Gatz, M., Bergem, A. L. M., Christian, J. C., Mortimer, J. A., McClearn, G. E., et al. (1993). Use of twin cohorts for research in Alzheimer's disease. *Neurol., 43,* 261–67.

Breitner, J. C., Gau, B. A., Welsh, K. A., et al. (1994). Inverse association of anti-inflammatory treatments and Alzheimer's disease: Initial results of a co-twin control study. *Neurol., 44,* 227–32.

Brennan, P. A., Le Brocque, R., & Hammen, C. (2003). Maternal depression, parent–child relationships, and resilient outcomes in adolescence. *J. Am. Acad. Child Adoles. Psychiat., 42*(12), 1469–77.

Brent, D. A., Melhem, N. M., Oquendo, M., Burke, A., Birmaher, B., Stanley, B., et al. (2015). Familial pathways to early-onset suicide attempt: A 5.6-year prospective study. *JAMA Psychiatry* [Epub ahead of print].

Breslau, J., Aguilar-Gaxiola, S., Kendler, K. S., Su, M., Williams, D., & Kessler, R. C. (2006). Specifying race-ethnic differences in risk for psychiatric disorder in a USA national sample. *Psychol. Med., 36*(1), 57–68.

Breslau, J., Miller, E., Sampson, N. A., Alonso, J., Andrade, L. H., et al. (2011). A multinational study of mental disorders, marriage, and divorce. *Acta Psychiatrica Scandanavica, 124,* 474–86.

Breslau, N., Davis, G. C., & Andreski, P. (1995). Risk factors for PTSD-related traumatic events: A prospective analysis. *Am. J. Psychiatry, 152,* 529–35.

Breslau, N., Davis, G. C., Andreski, P., & Peterson, E. (1991). Traumatic events and posttraumatic stress disorder in an urban population of young adults. *Arch. Gen. Psychiat., 48,* 216–22.

Breslau, N., Lucia, V. C., & Alvarado, G. F. (2006). Intelligence and other predisposing factors in exposure to trauma and posttraumatic stress disorder: A followup study at age 17 years. *Arch. Gen. Psychiatry, 63,* 1238–45.

Breslow, R. A., Faden, V. B., & Smothers, B. (2003). Alcohol consumption by elderly Americans. *J. Stud. Alcoh., 64,* 884–92.

Brewerton, T. D., Lydiard, R. B., Herzog, D. B., Brotman, A. W., O'Neil, P. M., & Ballenger, J. C. (1995). Comorbidity of Axis I psychiatric disorders in bulimia nervosa. *J. Clin. Psychiat., 56,* 77–80.

Brewin, C., & Holmes, E. A. (2003). Psychological theories of posttraumatic stress disorder. *Clin. Psychol. Rev., 23*(3), 339–76.

Brezo, J., Bureau, A., Merette, C., Jomphe, V., Barker, E. D., Vitaro, F., et al. (2010). Differences and similarities in the serotonergic diathesis for suicide attempts and mood disorders: A 22-year longitudinal gene-environment study. *Molec. Psychiat., 15*(8), 831–43. doi:10.1038/mp.2009.19

Bridge, J. A., Greenhouse, J. B., Weldon, A. H., Campo, J. V., & Kelleher, K. J. (2008). Suicide trends among youths aged 10 to 19 years in the United States, 1996–2005. *JAMA, 300,* 1025–26.

Bridge, J. A., Iyengar, S., Salary, C. B., Barbe, R. P., Birmaher, B., Pincus, H. A., et al. (2007). Clinical response and risk for reported suicidal ideation and suicide attempts in pediatric antidepressant treatment: A meta-analysis of randomized controlled trials. *JAMA, 297,* 1683–96.

Brock, A. J. (1979). *Galen. On the natural faculties* (English translation, Loeb Classical Library). Cambridge, MA: Harvard University Press.

Brodaty, H., & Arasaratnam, C. (2012). Meta-analysis of nonpharmacological interventions for neuropsychiatric symptoms of dementia. *Am. J. Psychiatry, 169,* 946–53.

Brody, A. L., Saxena, S., Mandelkern, M. A., Fairbanks, L. A., Ho, M. L., & Baxter, L. R., Jr. (2001). Brain metabolic changes associated with symptom factor improvement in major depressive disorder. *Biol. Psychiat., 50,* 171–78.

Brody, E. B. (2004). The World Federation for Mental Health: Its origins and contemporary relevance to WHO and WPA policies. *J. Nerv. Ment. Dis., 3*(1), 54–55.

Brokate, B., Hildebrandt, H., Eling, P., Fichtner, H., Runge, K., & Timm, C. (2003). Frontal lobe dysfunctions in Korsakoff's syndrome and chronic alcoholism: Continuity or discontinuity? *Neuropsych., 17*(3), 420–28.

Bromley, E., Mikesell, L., Armstrong, N. P., & Young, A. S. (2014). "You might lose him through the cracks": Clinicians' views on discharge from assertive community treatment. *Adm. Policy Ment. Health.* doi:10.1007/s10488-014-0547-3

Bronte-Tinkew, J., Moore, K. A., & Carrano, J. (2006). The father–child relationship, parenting styles, and adolescent risk behaviors in intact families. *J. Family Issues, 27*(6), 850–81.

Broome, M., & Bortolotti, L. (2010). What's wrong with mental disorders? *Psychol. Med., 40,* 1783–85.

Brotto, L. A. (2010). The DSM diagnostic criteria for hypoactive sexual desire disorder in men. *J. Sexual Medicine, 7*(6), 2015–30.

Brown, A. S. (2011). The environment and susceptibility to schizophrenia. *Prog. Neurobiol., 11,* 23–58.

Brown, A. S., Begg, M. D., Gravenstein, S., Schaefer, C. A., Wyatt, R. J., Bresnahan, M., et al. (2004). Serologic evidence of prenatal influenza in the etiology of schizophrenia. *Arch. General Psychiatry, 61,* 774–80.

Brown, D. W., Anda, R. F., Tiemeier, H., Felitti, V. J., Edwards, V. J., Croft, J. B., & Giles, W. H. (2009). Adverse childhood experiences and the risk of premature mortality. *Am. J. Preventive Medicine, 37,* 389–96.

Brown, E. S., Vornik, L. A., Khan, D. A., & Rush, A. J. (2007). Bupropion in the treatment of outpatients with asthma and major depressive disorder. *Int. J. Psychiatry in Medicine, 37*(1), 23–28.

Brown, G. K., Have, T. T., Henriques, G. R., Xie, S. X., Hollander, J. E., & Beck, A. T. (2005). Cognitive therapy for the prevention of suicide attempts: A randomized controlled trial. *JAMA, 294*(5), 563–70.

Brown, G. W. (1985). The discovery of expressed emotion: Induction or deduction? In J. Leff & C. Vaughn (Eds.), *Expressed emotion in families* (pp. 7–25). New York: Guilford Press.

Brown, G. W., Carstairs, G. M., & Topping, G. (1958). Post hospital adjustment of chronic mental patients. *Lancet, 2,* 685–89.

Brown, G. W., & Harris, T. O. (1978). *Social origins of depression.* London: Tavistock.

Brown, J. F., & Menninger, K. A. (1940). *Psychodynamics of abnormal behavior.* New York: McGraw-Hill.

Brown, L. M., Frahm, K. A., & Bongar, B. (2013). In G. Stricker, T. A. Widiger, & I. B. Weiner (Eds.), *Handbook of psychology, Vol. 8: Clinical psychology* (2nd ed., pp. 408–30). Hoboken, NJ: John Wiley & Sons.

Brown, P. (1994). Toward a psychobiological model of dissociation and posttraumatic stress disorder. In S. J. Lynn & J. W. Rhue (Eds.), *Dissociation:*

Clinical and theoretical perspectives (pp. 94–122). New York: Guilford Press.

Brown, R. D., Goldstein, E., & Bjorklund, D. F. (2000). The history and Zeitgeist of the repressed-false-memory debate: Scientific and sociological perspectives on suggestibility and childhood memory. In D. F. Bjorklund (Ed.), *False-memory creation in children and adults: Theory, research, and implications* (pp. 1–30). Mahwah, NJ: Erlbaum.

Brown, R. J. (2004). Psychological mechanisms of medically unexplained symptoms: An integrative model. *Psychological Bull., 130,* 793–812.

Brown, R. J. (2006). Dissociation and conversion in psychogenic illness. In M. Hallett, S. Fahn, J. Jankovic, A. E. Lang, C. R. Cloninger, & S. C. Yudofsky (Eds.), *Psychogenic movement disorders: Neurology and neuropsychiatry* (pp. 131–43). Philadelphia, PA: Lippincott Williams & Wilkins.

Brown, R., & Lo, R. (2000). The physical and psychosocial consequences of opioid addiction: An overview of changes in opioid treatment. *Austral. NZ J. Mental Health Nursing, 9,* 65–74.

Brown, R., Taylor, J., & Matthews, B. (2001). Quality of life: Aging and Down syndrome. *Down Syndrome: Research & Practice, 6,* 111–16.

Brown, T. A., & Barlow, D. H. (2001). *Casebook in abnormal psychology* (2nd ed.). Belmont, CA: Wadsworth/Thomson Learning.

Brown, T. A., & Barlow, D. H. (2009). A proposal for a dimensional classification system based on the shared features of the DSM-IV anxiety and mood disorders: Implications for assessment and treatment. *Psychol. Assess., 21*(3), 256–71. doi:10.1037/a0016608

Brown, T. A., & Keel, P. K. (2012a). The impact of relationships on the association between sexual orientation and disordered eating in men. *Int. J. Eat. Disorder, 45,* 792–99.

Brown, T. A., & Keel, P. K. (2012b). Current and emerging directions in the treatment of eating disorders. *Subst. Abuse: Res. Treatment, 6,* 33–61.

Browne, E. G. (1921). *Arabian medicine.* New York: Macmillan.

Brownell, K. (2003). *Food fight: The inside story of the food industry.* New York: McGraw-Hill.

Brownmiller, S. (1975). *Against our will: Men, women, and rape.* New York: Simon & Schuster.

Bruce, S. E., Yonkers, K. A., Otto, M. W., Eisen, J. L., Weisberg, R. B., Pagano, M., et al. (2005). Influence of psychiatric comorbidity on recovery and recurrence in generalized anxiety disorder, social phobia, and panic disorder: A 12-year prospective study. *Am. J. Psychiat, 162*(6), 1179–87.

Bruch, H. (1973). *Eating disorders: Obesity, anorexia nervosa and the person within.* New York: Basic Books.

Bruder, G. E., Tenke, C. E., Warner, V., & Weissman, M. M. (2007). Grandchildren at high and low risk for depression differ in EEG measures of regional brain asymmetry. *Biological psychiatry, 62*(11), 1317–31.

Bruffaerts, R., Demyttenaere, K., Borges, G., Haro, J. M., Hwang, I., Karam, E. G., et al. (2010). Childhood adversities as risk factors for the onset and persistence of suicidal behaviour. *Brit. J. Psychiatry, 197,* 20–27. doi:10.1192/bjp. bp.109.074716

Bruffaerts, R., Demyttenaere, K., Hwang, I., Chiu, W. T., Sampson, N., Kessler, R. C., et al. (2011). Treatment of suicidal persons around the world. *Brit. J. Psychiatry, 199,* 64–70.

Bryant, R. A., & Das, P. (2012). The neural circuitry of conversion disorder and its recovery. *J. Abn. Psychol., 121,* 289–96.

Bryant, R. A., O'Donnell, M. L., Creamer, M., McFarlane, A. C., Clark, C. R., & Silove, D. (2010). The psychiatric sequelae of traumatic injury. *Am. J. Psychiatry, 167*(3), 312–20.

Bryant-Waugh, R., & Lask, B. (2002). Childhood-onset eating disorders. In C. G. Fairburn & K. D. Brownell (Eds.), *Eating disorders and obesity: A comprehensive handbook* (2nd ed., pp. 210–14). New York: Guilford Press.

Bryden, D. P., & Grier, M. M. (2013). The search for rapists' "real" motives. *J. Crim. Law & Criminology, 101,* 171–278.

Buchsbaum, M. S., Haier, R. J., Potkin, S. G., Nuechterlein, K., Bracha, H. S., Katz, M., et al. (1992). Frontostriatal disorder of cerebral metabolism in never-medicated schizophrenics. *Arch. Gen. Psychiatry, 49*(12), 935–41.

Buckholtz, J. W. (2015). Social norms, self-control, and the value of antisocial behavior. *Curr. Opin. Behavioral Sciences, 3,* 122–29.

Buckholtz, J. W., & Faigman, D. L. (2014). Promises, promises for neuroscience and law. *Current Biology, 24*(18). doi:10.1016/j.cub.2014.07.057

Buckholtz, J. W., & Meyer-Lindenberg, A. (2013). MAOA and the bioprediction of antisocial behavior: Science fact and science fiction. In I. Singh and W. Sinnott-Armstrong (Eds.), *Bioprediction of antisocial behavior* (pp. 131–52). Oxford, UK: Oxford University Press.

Buckley, M. A., & Zimmermann, S. H. (2003). *Mentoring children and adolescents: A guide to the issues.* Westport, CT: Praeger Publishers.

Buckley, P. F., & Waddington, J. L. (Eds.). (2000). *Schizophrenia and mood disorders: The new drug therapies in clinical practice.* Oxford, UK: Oxford University Press.

Budman, C. L., Braun, R. D., Park, K. S., Lesser, M., & Olson, M. (2000). Explosive outbursts in children with Tourette's disorder. *J. Am. Acad. Child Adoles. Psychiat., 39*(10), 1270–76.

Budney, A. J., Moore, B. A., Vandrey, R. G., & Hughes, J. R. (2003). The time course and significance of cannabis withdrawal. *J. Abn. Psychol., 112,* 393–402.

Buhlmann, U., Glaesmer, H., Mewes, R., Fama, J. M., Wilhelm, S., & Rief, W. (2010). Updates on the prevalence of body dysmorphic disorder: A population-based survey. *Psychiatry Research, 178*(1), 171–75.

Buhlmann, U., & Wilhelm, S. (2004). Cognitive factors in body dysmorphic disorder. *Psychiat. Ann., 34*(12), 922–26.

Bulik, C. M., & Allison, D. B. (2002). Constitutional thinness and resistance to obesity. In C. G. Fairburn & K. D. Brownell (Eds.), *Eating disorders and obesity: A comprehensive handbook* (2nd ed., pp. 22–25). New York: Guilford Press.

Bulik, C. M., & Kendler, K. S. (2000). "I am what I (don't) eat": Establishing an identity independent of an eating disorder. *Am. J. Psychiatry, 157*(11), 1755–60.

Bulik, C. M., Sullivan, P. F., & Kendler, K. S. (2003). Genetic and environmental contributions to obesity and binge eating. *Int. J. Eat. Dis., 33,* 293–98.

Bulik, C. M., Sullivan, P. F., Tozzi, F., Furberg, H., Lichenstieb, P., & Pedersen, N. L. (2006). Prevalence, heritability, and prospective factors for anorexia nervosa. *Arch. Gen. Psychiat., 63,* 305–12.

Bulloch, A. G., Williams, J. V., Lavorato, D. H., & Patten, S. B. (2009). The relationship between major depression and martial disruption is bidirectional. *Depression and Anxiety, 26*(12), 1172–77.

Bult, M. J. F., van Dalen, T., & Muller, A. (2008). Surgical treatment of obesity. *European J. Endocrinology, 158,* 135–45.

Burd, L., & Christensen, T. (2009). Treatment of fetal alcohol spectrum disorders: Are we ready yet? *J. Clin. Psychopharmacol., 29*(1), 1–4.

Bureau of Labor Statistics. (2013, April 5). *The employment situation—March 2013* (News Release USDL-13-0581). Washington, DC: U.S. Department of Labor.

Burke, M. J., Ghaffar, O., Staines, W. R., Downar, J., & Feinstein, A. (2014). Functional neuroimaging of conversion disorder: The role of ancillary activation. *Neuroimage: Clinical, 6*, 333–39.

Burke, T. (2010). Psychiatric disorder: Understanding violence. In A. Bartlett & G. McGauley (Eds.), *Forensic mental health: Concepts, systems, and practice* (pp. 35–51). New York: Oxford University Press.

Burks, V. S., Dodge, K. A., & Price, J. M. (1995). Models of internalizing outcomes of early rejection. *Develop. Psychopath., 7*, 683–95.

Burt, K. B., Van Dulmen, M. H. M., Carlivati, J., Egeland, B., Sroufe, L. A., Forman, D. R., et al. (2005). Mediating links between maternal depression and offspring psychopathology: The importance of independent data. *J. Child Psychol. Psychiat., 46*(5), 490–99.

Burton, G. (2001). The tenacity of historical misinformation: Titchner did not invent the Titchner illusion. *History of Psychology, 4*, 228–44.

Burton, R. (1621). *Anatomy of melancholia.* London: Oxford.

Busch, K. A., Fawcett, J., & Jacobs, D. G. (2003). Clinical correlates of inpatient suicide. *J. Clin. Psychiat., 64*(1), 14–19.

Bushman, B., Bonacci, A., Baumeister, R., & van Dijk, M. (2003). Narcissism, sexual refusal, and aggression: Testing a narcissistic model of sexual coercion. *J. Pers. Soc. Psychol., 84*, 1027–40.

Buss, D. M. (1989). Sex differences in human mate preferences: Evolutionary hypotheses tested in 37 cultures. *Behavioral and Brain Sciences, 12*, 1–49.

Bustillo, J. R., Lauriello, J., Horan, W. P., & Keith, S. J. (2001). The psychosocial treatment of schizophrenia: An update. *Am. J. Psychiatry, 158*, 163–75.

Butcher, J. N. (Ed.). (1996). *International applications of the MMPI-2: A handbook of research and clinical applications.* Minneapolis: University of Minnesota Press.

Butcher, J. N. (2005). Exploring universal personality characteristics: An objective approach. *Int. J. Clinical and Health Psychology, 5*, 553–66.

Butcher, J. N. (2010). Personality assessment from the 19th to the early 21st century: Past achievements and contemporary challenges. *Annu. Rev. Clin. Psychol., 6*, 1–20.

Butcher, J. N. (2011). *A beginner's guide to the MMPI-2* (3rd ed.). Washington, DC: American Psychological Association.

Butcher, J. N. (2013). Computerized psychological assessment. In J. R. Graham & J. Naglieri (Eds.), *Handbook of psychology, Vol. 10* (2nd ed., pp. 165–91). New York: Wiley Press.

Butcher, J. N., Bubany, S., & Mason, S. N. (2013). Assessment of personality and psychopathology with self-report inventories. In Geisinger, K. F., Bracken, B. A., Carlson, J. F., Hansen, J. C., Kuncel, N. R., Reise, S. P., & Rodriguez, M C. (Eds.), *APA handbook of testing and assessment in psychology, Vol. 2: Testing and assessment in clinical and counseling psychology* (pp. 171–92). Washington, DC: American Psychological Association. doi:10.1037/14048-011

Butcher, J. N., Cabiya, J., Lucio, E. M., & Garrido, M. (2007). *Assessing Hispanic clients using the MMPI-2 and MMPI-A.* Washington, DC: American Psychological Association.

Butcher, J. N., Graham, J. R., Ben-Porath, Y. S., Tellegen, A., Dahlstrom, W. G., & Kaemmer, B. (2001). *Minnesota Multiphasic Personality Inventory-2 (MMPI-2): Manual for administration and scoring* (2nd ed.). Minneapolis: University of Minnesota Press.

Butcher, J. N., & Han, K. (1996). Methods of establishing cross-cultural equivalence. In J. N. Butcher (Ed.), *International adaptations of the MMPI-2* (pp. 44–66). Minneapolis: University of Minnesota Press.

Butcher, J. N., Hass, G. A., Greene, R. L., & Nelson, L. D. (2015). *Using the MMPI-2 in forensic assessment.* Washington, DC: American Psychological Association.

Butcher, J. N., Perry, J., & Dean, B. L. (2009). Computer-based assessment. In J. N. Butcher (Ed.), *Oxford handbook of personality assessment* (pp. 163–82). New York: Oxford University Press.

Butcher, J. N., Perry, J., & Hahn, J. (2004). Computers in clinical assessment: Historical developments, present status, and future challenges. *J. Clin. Psychol., 60*, 331–46.

Butcher, J. N., Tsai, J., Coelho, S., & Nezami, E. (2006). Cross cultural applications of the MMPI-2. In J. N. Butcher (Ed.), *MMPI-2: The practitioner's handbook* (pp. 505–37). Washington, DC: American Psychological Association.

Butcher, J. N., & Williams, C. L. (2009). Personality assessment with the MMPI-2: Historical roots, international adaptations, and current challenges. *Applied Psychology: Health and Well-Being, 2*, 105–35.

Butler, A. C., Chapman, J. E., Forman, E. M., & Beck, A. T. (2006). The empirical status of cognitive-behavioral therapy: A review of meta-analyses. *Clin. Psychol. Rev., 26*(1), 17–31.

Butler, L. D., Duran, R. E., Jasiukaitis, P., Koopman, C., & Spiegel, D. (1996). Hypnotizability and traumatic experience: A diathesis–stress model of dissociative symptomatology. *Am. J. Psychiatry, 153*, 42–63.

Butow, P., Beumont, P., & Touyz, S. (1993). Cognitive processes in dieting disorders. *Int. J. Eat. Dis., 14*, 319–30.

Butzlaff, R. L., & Hooley, J. M. (1998). Expressed emotion and psychiatric relapse: A meta-analysis. *Arch. Gen. Psychiat., 55*(6), 547–52.

C

Cacioppo, J. T., Hughes, M. E., Waite, L. J., Hawkley, L. C., & Thisted, R. A. (2006). Loneliness as a specific risk factor for depressive symptoms: Cross-sectional and longitudinal analyses. *Psychology and Aging, 21*(1), 140–51.

Cade, J. F. J. (1949). Lithium salts in the treatment of psychotic excitement. *Med. J. Austral., 36*(Part II), 349–52.

Cadenhead, K. S., Light, G. A., Geyer, M. A., & Braff, D. L. (2000). Sensory gating deficits assessed by the P50 event-related potential in subjects with schizotypal personality disorder. *Am. J. Psychiatry, 157*(1), 55–59.

Cadenhead, K. S., Swerdlow, N. R., Shafer, K. M., Diaz, M., & Braff, D. L. (2000). Modulation of the startle response and startle laterality in relatives of schizophrenic patients and in subjects with schizotypal personality disorder: Evidence of inhibitory deficits. *Am. J. Psychiatry, 157*(10), 1660–67.

Cadoret, R. J., Yates, W. R., Troughton, E., Woodworth, G., & Stewart, M. A. (1995). Genetic–environmental interaction in the genesis of aggressivity and conduct disorders. *Arch. Gen. Psychiat., 52*, 916–24.

Cahn, W., Hulsoff Pol, H. E., Lems, E. B. T. E., van Haren, N. E. M., Schnack, H. G., van der Linden, J. A., et al. (2002). Brain volume changes in first-episode schizophrenia: A 1-year follow-up study. *Arch. Gen. Psychiat., 59*, 1002–10.

Cain, N. M., Pincus, A. L., & Ansell, E. B. (2008). Narcissism at the crossroads: Phenotypic description of pathological narcissism across clinical theory, social/personality psychology, and psychiatric diagnosis. *Clin. Psychol. Rev., 28*, 638–56.

Cale, E. M., & Lilienfeld, S. O. (2002a). Histrionic personality disorder and antisocial personality disorder: Sex-differentiated manifestations of psychopathy. *J. Pers. Disord., 16*(1), 52–72.

Cale, E. M., & Lilienfeld, S. O. (2002b). Sex differences in psychopathy and antisocial personality disorder: A review and integration. *Clin. Psychol. Rev., 22*, 1179–207.

Calhoun, F., & Warren, K. (2007). Fetal alcohol syndrome: Historical perspectives. *Neuroscience & Biobehavioral Reviews, 31*(2), 168–71.

Callahan, J. (2009). Emergency intervention and crisis intervention. In P. E. Kleespies (Ed.), *Behavioral emergencies: An evidence-based resource for evaluating and managing risk of suicide, violence, and victimization* (pp. 13–32). Washington, DC: American Psychological Association.

Callahan, L. A., Robbins, P. C., Steadman, H., & Morrissey, J. P. (1995). The hidden effects of Montana's "abolition" of the insanity defense. *Psychiatr. Q., 66*(2), 103–17.

Callahan, L. A., & Silver, E. (1998). Factors associated with the conditional release of persons acquitted by reason of insanity: A decision tree approach. *Law and Human Behavior, 22*, 147–63.

Calvo, R., Lazaro, L., Castro-Fornieles, J., Font, E., Moreno, E., & Toro, J. (2009). Obsessive-compulsive personality disorder traits and personality dimensions in parents of children with obsessive-compulsive disorder. *Eur. Psychiat., 24*, 201–06.

Campbell, D. (1926). *Arabian medicine and its influence on the Middle Ages.* New York: Dutton.

Campbell, H. C., Knox, T. W., & Byrnes, T. (1892). *Darkness and daylight; or, lights and shadows of New York life.* Hartford: A. D. Worthington & Co.

Campbell, M., & Cueva, J. E. (1995). Psychopharmacology in child and adolescent psychiatry: A review of the past seven years. Part 1. *J. Am. Acad. Child Adoles. Psychiatry, 34*(9), 1124–32.

Campbell, N. D. (2010). Multiple paths to partial truths: A history of drug use etiology. In L. Scheier (Ed.), *Handbook of drug use etiology: Theory, methods, and empirical findings* (pp. 29–50). Washington, DC: American Psychological Association.

Campbell-Sills, L., & Barlow, D. H. (2007). Incorporating emotion regulation into conceptualizations and treatments of anxiety and mood disorders. In J. J. Gross (Ed.), *Handbook of emotion regulation* (pp. 542–59). New York: Guilford Press.

Canetta, S., Sourander, A., Surcel, H.-M., Leviskä, J., Kellendonk, C., McKeague, I. W., & Brown, A. S. (2014). Elevated C-reactive protein and increased risk of schizophrenia in a national birth sample. *Am. J. Psychiatry, 171*, 960–68.

Canetti, L., Bachar, E., & Berry, E. M. (2002). Food and emotion. *Behavioural Processes, 60*, 157–64.

Canetti, L., Bachar, E., Bonne, O., Agid, O., Lerer, B., de-Nour, A. K., et al. (2000). The impact of parental death versus separation from parents on the mental health of Israeli adolescents. *Compr. Psychiat., 41*, 360–68.

Canino, G., & Alegria, M. (2008). Psychiatric diagnosis—Is it universal or relative to culture? *J. Child Psychology and Psychiatry, 49*, 237–50.

Cannon, M., Jones, P. B., & Murray, R. M. (2002). Obstetric complications and schizophrenia: Historical and meta-analytic review. *Am. J. Psychiatry, 159*(7), 1080–92.

Cannon, M. C., Clarke, M. C., & Cotter, D. R. (2014). Priming the brain for psychosis: Maternal inflammation during fetal development and the risk of later psychiatric disorder. *Am. J. Psychiatry, 171*, 901–05.

Cannon, T. D., Cadenhead, K., Cornblatt, B., Woods, S. W., Addington, J., Walker, E., et al. (2008). Prediction of psychosis in youth at high clinical risk: A multisite longitudinal study in North America. *Arch. Gen. Psychiat., 65*(1), 28–37.

Cannon, T. D., Cornblatt, B., & McGorry, P. (2007). Editor's introduction: The empirical status of the ultra high-risk (prodromal) research paradigm. *Schizo. Bull., 33*, 661–64.

Cannon, T. D., Glahn, D. C., Kim, J., Van Erp, T. G. M., Karlsgodt, K., Cohen, M. S., et al. (2005). Dorsolateral prefrontal cortex activity during maintenance and manipulation of information in working memory in patients with schizophrenia. *Arch. Gen. Psychiatry, 62*(10), 1071–80.

Cannon, T. D., Kaprio, J., Lönnqvist, J., Huttunen, M., & Koskenvuo, M. (1998). The genetic epidemiology of schizophrenia in a Finnish twin cohort. *Arch. Gen. Psychiat., 55*(1), 67–74.

Cannon, T. D., Mednick, S. A., Parnas, J., Schulsinger, F., Praestholm, J., & Verstergaard, A. (1993). Developmental brain abnormalities in the offspring of schizophrenic mothers. *Arch. Gen. Psychiat., 50*, 551–64.

Cantor, J. M., Blanchard, R., Robichaud, L. K., & Christensen, B. K. (2005). Quantitative reanalysis of aggregate data on IQ in sexual offenders. *Psych. Bull., 131*(4), 555–68.

Cantor, J. M., Kabani, N., Christensen, B. K., Zipursky, R. B., Barbaree, H. E., Dickey, R., et al. (2008). Cerebral white matter deficiencies in pedophilic men. *J. Psychiatr. Res., 42*, 167–83.

Cantor, J. M., Klassen, P. E., Dickey, R., Christensen, B. K., Kuban, M. E., Blak, T., et al. (2005). Handedness in pedophilia and hebephilia. *Arch. Sex. Behav., 34*(4), 447–59.

Cantor-Graae, E., & Selten, J.-P. (2005). Schizophrenia and migration: A meta-analysis and review. *Am. J. Psychiatry, 162*, 12–24.

Cantwell, D. P., & Baker, L. (1989). Stability and natural history of DSM III childhood diagnoses. *J. Am. Acad. Child Adoles. Psychiat., 28*, 691–700.

Capaldi, D. M., & Patterson, G. R. (1994). Interrelated influences of contextual factors on antisocial behavior in childhood and adolescence for males. In D. C. Fowles, P. Sutker, & S. H. Goodman (Eds.), *Progress in experimental personality and psychopathology research*. New York: Springer.

Capron, C., & Duyme, M. (1989). Assessment of effects of socioeconomic status on IQ in a full cross-fostering study. *Nature, 340*, 552–54.

Caracci, G., & Mezzich, J. E. (2001). Culture and urban mental health. *Psychiatr. Clin. N. Am., 24*(3), 581–93.

Cardeña, E., & Carlson, E. (2011). Acute stress disorder revisited. *Annu. Rev. Clin. Psychol., 7*, 245–67.

Carey, B. (2011, June 23). Expert on mental illness reveals her own fight. *New York Times*.

Carey, G. (2003). *Human genetics for the social sciences*. London: Sage Publications.

Carey, G., & Goldman, D. (1997). The genetics of antisocial behavior. In D. M. Stoff, J. Breiling, & J. D. Maser (Eds.), *Handbook of antisocial behavior* (pp. 243–54). New York: Wiley.

Carey, K. B., Henson, J. M., Carey, M. B., & Maisto, S. A. (2007). Which heavy drinking college students benefit from Brief Motivational Intervention? *J. Consult. Clin. Psych., 75*, 663–69.

Carlat, D. J., Carmargo, C. A., & Herzog, D. B. (1997). Eating disorders in males: A report on 135 patients. *Am. J. Psychiatry, 154*, 1127–32.

Carlson, E. A., Sampson, M. C., & Sroufe, L. A. (2003). Implications of attachment theory and research for developmental-behavioral pediatrics. *J. Dev. Behav. Ped., 24*(5), 364–79.

Carlson, E. A., & Sroufe, L. A. (1995). Contribution of attachment theory to developmental psychopathology. In D. Cicchetti & D. J. Cohen (Eds.), *Developmental psychopathology: Vol. 1, Theory and methods* (pp. 581–617). New York: Wiley.

Carlson, M. (2001). Child rights and mental health. *Child Adoles. Psychiatr. Clin. North Am., 10*, 825–39.

Carlson, N. R. (2007). *Foundations of physiological psychology*. Boston: Allyn & Bacon.

Carlson, R. (1997, April). *Sildenafil: An effective oral drug for impotence. In Pharma, 1085*, 11–12.

Carlsson, K., Petersson, K. M., Lundqvist, D., Karlsson, A., Ingvar, M., & Öhman, A. (2004). Fear and the amygdale: Manipulation of awareness generates differential cerebral responses to phobic and fear-relevant (but nonfeared) stimuli. *Emotion, 4*(4), 340–53.

Carmona, R. H. (2005). Advisory on alcohol use in pregnancy: A 2005 message to women from the U.S. Surgeon General.

Carpenter, P. K. (1989). Descriptions of schizophrenia in the psychiatry of Georgian Britain: John Haslam and James Tilly Matthews. *Compr. Psychiatry, 30*, 332–38.

Carpenter, W. T., & van Os, J. (2011). Should attenuated psychosis be a DSM-5 diagnosis? *Am. J. Psychiatry, 168*, 1–4.

Carr, A., O'Reilly, G., Walsh, P. N., & McEvoy, J. (Eds.). (2007). *The handbook of intellectual disability and clinical psychology practice*. New York: Routledge/Taylor & Francis Group.

Carr, D., & Friedman, M. A. (2005). Is obesity stigmatizing? Body weight, perceived discrimination, and psychological well-being in the United States. *J. Health. Soc. Behav., 46*(3), 244–59.

Carroll, B. J. (2009). Clomipramine and glucocorticoid receptor function. *Neuropsychopharmacol., 34*(9), 2192–93.

Carroll, K. M., Fenton, L. R., Ball, S. A., Nich, C., Frankforter, T. L., Shi, J., et al. (2004). Efficacy of disulfiram and cognitive behavior therapy in cocaine-dependent outpatients. *Arch. Gen. Psychiat., 61*(3), 264–72.

Carroll, K. M., Kiluk, B. D., Nich, C., Gordon, M. A., Portnoy, G. A., Marino, D. R., & Ball, S. A. (2014). Computer-assisted delivery of cognitive-behavioral therapy: Efficacy and durability of CBT4CBT among cocaine-dependent individuals maintained on methadone. *Am. J. Psychiatry, 171*, 436–44.

Carstairs, G. M., & Kapur, R. L. (1976). *The great universe of Kota: Stress, change and mental disorder in an Indian village*. Berkeley: University of California Press.

Carter, A. S., Garrity-Rokous, F. E., Chazan-Cohen, R., Little, C., & Briggs-Gowan, M. J. (2001). Maternal depression and comorbidity: Predicting early parenting, attachment security, and toddler social-emotional problems and competencies. *J. Am. Acad. Child Adoles. Psychiat., 40*(1), 18–26.

Carter, M. M., Hollon, S. D., Carson, R., & Shelton, R. C. (1995). Effects of a safe person on induced distress following a biological challenge in panic disorder with agoraphobia. *J. Abn. Psychol., 104*, 156–63.

Carter, S. A., & Wu, K. D. (2010). Relations among symptoms of social phobia subtypes, avoidant personality disorder, panic, and depression. *Behav. Ther., 41*(1), 2–13. doi:10.1016/j.beth.2008.10.002

Case, B. G., Olfson, M., Marcus, S. C., & Siegel, C. (2007). Trends in inpatient mental health treatment of children and adolescents in US community hospitals between 1990 and 2000. *Arch. Gen. Psychiat., 64*, 89–96.

Casey, L. M., Newcombe, P. A., & Oei, T. P. S. (2005). Cognitive mediation of panic severity: The role of catastrophic misinterpretation of bodily sensations and panic self-efficacy. *Cognitive Therapy and Research, 29*(2), 187–200.

Caspi, A., Hariri, A. R., Holmes, A., Uher, R., & Moffitt, T. E. (2010). Genetic sensitivity to the environment: The case for the serotonin transporter gene and its implications for studying complex disease and traits. *Am. J. Psychiatry, 167*, 509–27.

Caspi, A., McClay, J., Moffitt, T., Mill, J., Martin, J., Craig, I. W., et al. (2002). Role of genotype in the cycle of violence in maltreated children. *Science, 297*, 851–54.

Caspi, A., Moffitt, T. E., Cannon, M., McClay, J., Murray, R., Harrington, H., et al. (2005). Moderation of the effect of adolescent-onset cannabis use on adult psychosis by a functional polymorphism in the catechol-O-methyltransferase gene: Longitudinal evidence of a gene x environment interaction. *Biol. Psychiat., 57*, 1117–27.

Caspi, A., Sugden, K., Moffitt, T. E., Taylor, A., Craig, I. W., Harrington, H., et al. (2003). Influence of life stress on depression: Moderation by a polymorphism in the 5HTT gene. *Science, 301*, 386–89.

Cassady, J. D., Kirschke, D. L., Jones, T. F., Craig, A. S., Bermudez, O. B., & Schaffner, W. (2005). Case series: Outbreak of conversion disorder among Amish adolescent girls. *J. Am. Acad. Child Adoles. Psychiat., 44*(3), 291–97.

Cassidy, C., O'Connor, R. C., Howe, C., & Warden, D. (2004). Perceived discrimination and psychological distress: The role of personal and ethnic self-esteem. *J. Couns. Psychol., 51*(3), 329–39.

Cassin, S. E., & von Ranson, K. M. (2005). Personality and eating disorders: A decade in review. *Clinical Psychology Review, 25*, 895–916.

Castellanos, F. X., Lee, P. P., Sharp, W., Jeffries, N. O., Greenstein, D. K., Clasen, L. S., et al. (2002). Developmental trajectories of brain volume abnormalities in children and adolescents with attention-deficit/hyperactivity disorder. *JAMA, 288*(14), 1740–48.

Castellini, G., Lo Sauro, C., Mannucci, E., Ravaldi, C., Rotella, C. M., Faravelli, C., et al. (2011). Diagnostic crossover and outcome predictors in eating disorders according to DSM-IV and DSM-V proposed criteria. A 6-year follow-up study. *Psychosomat. Med., 73*, 270–79.

Castiglioni, A. (1924). *Adventures of the mind*. New York: Dutton.

Castonguay, L. G., Reid, J. J., Halperin, G. S., & Goldfried, M. R. (2003). Psychotherapy integration. In G. Stricker, T. A. Widiger, & I. B. Weiner (Eds.), *Handbook of psychology: Clinical psychology* (Vol. 8, pp. 327–66). Hoboken, NJ: John Wiley & Sons.

Castro, F. G., Barrington, E. H., Walton, M. A., & Rawson, R. A. (2000). Cocaine and methamphetamine: Differential addiction rates. *Psych. Addict. Behav., 14*(4), 390–96.

Cato, C., & Rice, B. D. (1982). *Report from the study group on rehabilitation of clients with specific learning disabilities*. St. Louis, MO: National Institute of Handicapped Research.

Catroppa, C., Crossley, L., Hearps, S. J. C., Yeates, K. O., Beauchamp, M., Rogers, K., & Anderson, V. (2015). Social and behavioral outcomes: Pre-injury to six months following childhood traumatic brain injury. *J. Neurotrauma, 32*, 109–15.

Cauce, A. M., Paradise, M., Ginzler, J. A., Embry, L., Morgan, C. J., Lohr, Y., et al. (2000). The characteristics and mental health of homeless adolescents: Age and gender differences. *J. Emotional & Behavioral Disorders, 8*, 230–39.

Caudill, O. B., Jr. (2009). When a mental health professional is in litigation. In S. F. Bucky, J. E. Callan, & G. Stricker (Eds.), *Ethical and legal issues for mental health professionals in forensic settings* (pp. 127–40). New York: Routledge/Taylor & Francis Group.

Cavaco, S., Anserson, S. W., Allen, J. S., Castro-Caldas, A., & Damasio, H. (2004). The scope of preserved procedural memory in amnesia. *Brain, 127*, 1853–67.

Cavanagh, J. T. O., Carson, A. J., Sharpe, M., & Lawrie, S. M. (2003). Psychological autopsy studies of suicide: A systematic review. *Psychological Medicine, 33*, 395–405.

CBS News. (2003, August 5). *Autistic boy dies during exorcism*. New York: Author.

Centers for Disease Control and Prevention (CDC). (2009). *Prevalence of autism spectrum disorders—Autism and Developmental Disabilities Monitoring Network, United States* (MMWR Surveillance Summaries 209), *58*(SS–20).

Centers for Disease Control and Prevention (CDC). (2010). *Survivor stories.* Retrieved from http://www.cdc.gov/concussion/sports/stories.html

Centers for Disease Control and Prevention (CDC). (2015a). *Fetal alcohol spectrum disorders: Alcohol use in pregnancy.* Retrieved from http://www.cdc.gov/ncbddd/fasd/alcohol-use.html

Centers for Disease Control and Prevention (CDC). (2015b). *Chronic liver disease and cirrhosis.* Retrieved from http://www.cdc.gov/nchs/fastats/liver-disease.htm

Centers for Disease Control and Prevention (CDC). (2015c). Fatal injury reports, 1999–2012. Retrieved from http://www.cdc.gov/injury/wisqars/fatal_injury_reports.html

Cerletti, U., & Bini, L. (1938). Un Nuevo metodo di shockterapie "L'electroshock" (A new method of shock therapy "the electroshock"). *Bolletino Academia Medicino Roma, 64,* 136–38.

Cha, C. B., & Nock, M. K. (2009). Emotional intelligence is a protective factor for suicidal behavior. *J. Am. Academy of Child and Adolescent Psychiatry, 48,* 422–30.

Chaffin, M., Silvosky, J. F., Funderburk, B., Valle, L. A., Brestan, E. V., Balachova, T., et al. (2004). Parent–child interaction therapy with physically abusive parents: Efficacy for reducing future abuse reports. *J. Consult. Clin. Psychol., 72,* 500–10.

Chakraborty, A., McManus, S., Brugha, T. S., Bebbington, P., & King, M. (2011). Mental health of the non-heterosexual population of England. *Brit. J. Psychiatry, 2,* 143–48.

Chamberlin, N. L., & Saper, C. B. (2009). The agony of the ecstasy: Serotonin and obstructive sleep apnea. *Neurol., 73*(23), 1947–48.

Chambers, R. A., & Potenza, M. N. (2003). Neurodevelopment, impulsivity, and adolescent gambling. *J. Gambling Studies, 19*(1), 53–84.

Chambless, D. L., Frydrich, T., & Rodenabugh, T. (2008). Generalized social phobia and avoidant personality disorder: Meaningful distinction or useless duplication? *Depression and Anxiety, 25*(1), 8–19.

Chambless, D. L., & Ollendick, T. H. (2001). Empirically supported psychological interventions: Controversies and evidence. *Annu. Rev. Psychol., 52,* 685–716.

Champion, H. R., Holcomb, J. B., & Young, L. A. (2009). Injuries from explosions. *J. Trauma, 66,* 1468–76.

Chan, G. W. L. (2001). Residential services for psychiatric patients in Hong Kong. *Hong Kong J. Psychiatry, 11*(3), 13–17.

Chan, G. W. L., Ungvari, G. S., & Leung, J. P. (2001). Residential services for psychiatric patients in Hong Kong. *Hong Kong J. Psychiatry, 11*(3), 13–17.

Chang, C.-K., Hayes, R. D., Perera, G., Broadbent, M. T. M., Fernandes, A. C., Lee, W. F., et al. (2011). Life expectancy at birth for people with serious mental illness and other major disorders from a secondary mental health care case register in London. *PLoS ONE, 6,* e19590.

Chang, L., Alicata, D., Ernst, T., & Volkow, N. (2007). Structural and metabolic changes in the stratum associated with methamphetamine abuse. *Addiction, 102,* 16–32.

Chang, S. W., Piacentina, J., & Walkup, J. T. (2007). Behavioral treatment of Tourette syndrome. *Clin. Psychol. Sci. Prac., 14,* 268–73.

Chang, Z., Lichtenstein, P., D'Onofrio, B. M., Sjölander, A., & Larsson, H. (2014). Serious transport accidents in adults with attention-deficit/hyperactivity disorder and the effect of medication: A population-based study. *JAMA Psychiatry, 71,* 319–25.

Chapman, L. J., Chapman, J. P., & Miller, E. N. (1982). Reliabilities and intercorrelations of eight measures of proneness to psychosis. *J. Consult. Clin. Psychol., 50,* 187–95.

Chapman, L. J., Chapman, J. P., Kwapil, T. R., Eckblad, M., & Zinzer, M. (1994). Putatively psychosis prone subjects ten years later. *J. Abn. Psychol., 103,* 171–83.

Chapman, L. J., Chapman, J. P., & Raulin, M. L. (1978). Body-image aberration in schizophrenia. *J. Abn. Psychology, 87,* 399–407.

Chappell, D. (2010). Victimization and the insanity defense: Coping with confusion, conflict and conciliation. *Psychiatry, Psychology and Law, 17*(1), 39–51.

Chaput, J. P., Després, J. P., Bouchard, C., & Tremblay, A. (2008). The association between sleep duration and weight gain in adults: A 6-year prospective study from the Quebec Family Study. *Sleep, 31,* 517–23.

Charach, A., Ickowicz, A., & Schachar, R. (2004). Stimulant treatment over five years: Adherence, effectiveness, and adverse effects. *J. Am. Acad. Child Adoles. Psychiat., 43,* 559–67.

Charney, D., Grillon, C., & Bremner, J. D. (1998). The neurobiological basis of anxiety and fear: Circuits, mechanisms, and neurochemical interactions (part I). *The Neuroscientist, 4,* 35–44.

Chartier, M. J., Walker, J. R., & Stein, M. B. (2001). Social phobia and potential childhood risk factors in a community sample. *Psychol. Med., 31,* 307–15.

Charuvastra, A., & Cloitre, M. (2008). Social bonds and posttraumatic stress disorder. *Annu. Rev. Psychol., 59,* 301–28.

Chase-Lansdale, P. L., Cherlin, A. J., & Kieran, K. E. (1995). The long-term effects of parental divorce on the mental health of young adults: A developmental perspective. *Child Develop., 66,* 1614–34.

Chassin, L., Pillow, D. R., Curran, P. J., Molina, B. S., & Barrera, M. (1993). Relation of parental alcoholism in early adolescent substance use: A test of three mediating mechanisms. *J. Abn. Psychol., 102,* 3–19.

Chaudhuri, K. R., Odin, P., Antonini, A., & Martinez-Martin, P. (2011). Parkinson's disease: The non-motor issues. *Parkinsonism and Related Disorders* [Epub ahead of print].

Chavira, D., Grilo, C., Shea, M. T., Yen, S., Gunderson, J., Morey, L., et al. (2003). Ethnicity and four personality disorders. *Compr. Psychiat., 44,* 483–91.

Chavira, D. A., Stein, M. B., & Roy-Byrne, P. (2009). Managing anxiety in primary care. In M. M. Antony & M. B. Stein (Eds.), *Oxford handbook of anxiety and related disorders* (pp. 512–22). New York: Oxford University Press.

Chen, C. C., & Yeh, E. K. (1997). Population differences in ALDH levels and flushing response. In G. Y. San (Ed.), *Molecular mechanisms of alcohol.* New York: Humana.

Chen, C. H., Suckling, J., Lennox, B. R., Ooi, C., & Bullmore, E. T. (2011). A quantitative meta-analysis of fMRI studies in bipolar disorder. *Bipolar Dis., 13*(1), 1–15. doi:10.1111/j.1399-5618.2011.00893.x

Chen, E. Y., & Safer, D. (2010). Dialectical behavior therapy. In W. A. Agras (Ed.), *The Oxford Handbook of Eating Disorders* (pp. 402–16). New York: Oxford University Press.

Chen, M. C., Hamilton, J. P., & Gotlib, I. H. (2010). Decreased hippocampal volume in healthy girls at risk of depression. *Arch. Gen. Psychiat., 67*(3), 270–76. doi:10.1001/archgenpsychiatry.2009.202

Chen, Q., Sjölander, A., Runeson, B., D'Onofrio, B. M., Lichtenstein, P., & Larsson, H. (2014). Drug treatment for attention-deficit/hyperactivity disorder and suicidal behavior: Register based study. *Brit. Med. J., 348,* g3769.

Chentsova-Dutton, Y. E., & Tsai, J. L. (2009). Understanding depression across cultures. In I. H. Gotlib & C. L. Hammen (Eds.), *Handbook of depression and its treatment* (2nd ed.). New York: Guilford Press.

Cherpitel, C. J. (1997). Alcohol and injuries resulting from violence: A comparison of emergency room samples from two regions of the U.S. *J. Addict. Dis., 16*(1), 25–40.

Chesney, M. (1996). New behavioral risk factors for coronary heart disease: Implications for intervention. In K. Orth-Gomer & N. Schneider-man (Eds.), *Behavioral medicine approaches to cardiovascular disease prevention* (pp. 169–82). Mahwah, NJ: Erlbaum.

Chételat, G., Desgranges, B., Sayette, V., Viader, F., Berkouk, K., Landeau, B., et al. (2003). Dissociating atrophy and hypometabolism impact on episodic memory in mild cognitive impairment. *Brain, 126,* 1955–67.

Cheung, A., Dewa, C., Michalak, E. E., Browne, G., Levitt, A., Levitan, R. D., et al. (2012). Direct health care costs of treating seasonal affective disorder: a comparison of light therapy and fluoxetine. *Depression Research and Treatment, 2012,* 628343.

Chida, Y., & Steptoe, A. (2009). The association of anger and hostility with future coronary heart disease: A meta-analytic review of the prospective evidence. *J. Am. College of Cardiology, 53,* 936–46.

Choca, J. (2004). *Interpretive guide to the Millon Multiaxial Personality Inventory.* Washington, DC: American Psychological Association.

Choca, J. P. (2012). *The Rorschach Inkblot Test: An interpretive guide for clinicians.* Washington, DC: American Psychological Association.

Chorpita, B. F. (2001). Control and the development of negative emotion. In M. W. Vasey & M. R. Dadds (Eds.), *The developmental psychopathology of anxiety* (pp. 112–42). New York: Oxford University Press.

Chou, S. P., Dawson, D. A., Stinson, F. S., Huang, B., Pickering, R. P., Zhou, Y., et al. (2006). The prevalence of drinking and driving in the United States, 2001–2002: Results from the national epidemiological survey on alcohol and related conditions. *Drug Alc. Depend., 83*(2), 137–46.

Choy, Y., Fyer, A. J., & Lipsitz, J. D. (2007). Treatment of specific phobia in adults. *Clin. Psychol. Rev., 27*(3), 266–86.

Christakis, N. A., & Fowler, J. H. (2007). The spread of obesity in a large social network over 32 years. *New Eng. J. Med., 357,* 370–79.

Christensen, A., & Pike, C. J. (2015). Menopause, obesity and inflammation: Interactive risk factors for Alzheimer's disease. *Frontiers in Aging Neuroscience, 7,* 130. doi:10.3389/fnagi.201500130

Christensen, A., Wheeler, J. G., & Jacobson, N. S. (2007). Couple distress. In D. H. Barlow (Ed.), *Clinical handbook of psychological disorders* (4th ed., pp. 662–89). New York: Guilford Press.

Chu, B. C., & Kendall, P. C. (2004). Positive association of child involvement and treatment outcome within a manual-based cognitive-behavioral treatment for children with anxiety. *J. Consult. Clin. Psychol., 72,* 821–29.

Chu, J. A., Frey, L. M., Ganzel, B. L., & Matthews, J. A. (1999). Memories of childhood abuse: Dissociation, amnesia, and corroboration. *Am. J. Psychiatry, 156,* 749–55.

Chung, M. C., Symons, C., Gilliam, J., & Kaminski, E. R. (2010). Stress, psychiatric comorbidity and coping in patients with chronic idiopathic urticaria. *Psychology & Health, 25*(4), 477–90.

Chutko, L. S., Yur'eva, R. G., Surushkina, S. Y., Niki-shena, I. S., Yakovenko, I. S., Anisimova, T. I., et al. (2010). Principles of medical care for children with attention deficit hyperactivity disorder. *Neuroscience and Behavioral Physiology, 40*(3), 351–55.

Cicchetti, D., & Lynch, M. (1995). Failures in the expectable environment and their impact on individual development: The case of child maltreatment. In D. Cicchetti & D. J. Cohen (Eds.), *Developmental psychopathology: Vol. 2. Risk, disorder, and adaptation* (pp. 32–72). New York: Wiley.

Cicchetti, D., & Toth, S. L. (1995a). Developmental psychopathology and disorders of affect. In D. Cicchetti & D. J. Cohen (Eds.), *Developmental psychopathology Vol. 2: Risk, disorder, and adaptation* (pp. 369–420). New York: Wiley.

Cicchetti, D., & Toth, S. L. (1995b). A developmental psychopathology perspective on child abuse and neglect. *J. Am. Acad. Child Adoles. Psychiat., 34*(5), 541–65.

Cicchetti, D., & Toth, S. L. (2005). Child maltreatment. *Annu. Rev. Clin. Psychol., 1*(1), 409–38.

Cirinclone, C., Steadman, H., & McGreevy, M. A. (1995). Rates of insanity acquittals and the factors associated with successful insanity pleas. *Bull. Am. Acad. Psychiat. Law, 23*(3), 399–409.

Clark, D. A. (1997). Twenty years of cognitive assessment: Current status and future directions. *J. Consult. Clin. Psychol., 65*(6), 996–1000.

Clark, D. A. (2005). Focus on 'cognition' in cognitive behavior therapy for OCD: Is it really necessary? *Cognitive Behaviour Therapy, 34*(3), 131–39.

Clark, D. A., & Beck, A. T. (2010). Cognitive theory and therapy of anxiety and depression: Convergence with neurobiological findings. *Trends in Cognitive Sciences, 14*(9), 418–24. doi:10.1016/j.tics.2010.06.007

Clark, D. A., Beck, A. T., & Alford, B. A. (1999). *Scientific foundations of cognitive theory and therapy of depression.* New York: Wiley.

Clark, D. M. (1986). A cognitive approach to panic. *Behav. Res. Ther., 24*, 461–70.

Clark, D. M. (1997). Panic disorder and social phobia. In C. G. Fairburn (Ed.), *Science and practice of cognitive behaviour therapy* (pp. 119–53). New York: Oxford University Press.

Clark, D. M., Ehlers, A., Hackmann, A., McManus, F., Fennell, M., Grey, N., et al. (2006). Cognitive therapy versus exposure and applied relaxation in social phobia: A randomized controlled trial. *J. Consult. Clin. Psychol., 74*(3), 568–78.

Clark, D. M., Ehlers, A., McManus, F., Hackmann, A., Fennell, M., Campbell, H., et al. (2003). Cognitive therapy versus fluoxetine in generalized social phobia: A randomized placebo-controlled trial. *J. Consult. Clin. Psychol., 71*(6), 1058–67.

Clark, D. M., & McManus, F. (2002). Information processing in social phobia. *Biol. Psychiat., 51*, 92–100.

Clark, D. M., Salkovskis, P. M., Hackmann, A., Middleton, H., Anastasiades, P., & Gelder, M. (1994). A comparison of cognitive therapy, applied relaxation, and imipramine in the treatment of panic disorder. *Brit. J. Psychiatry, 164*, 759–69.

Clark, D. M., Salkovskis, P. M., Hackmann, A., Wells, A., Ludgate, J., & Gelder, M. (1999). Brief cognitive therapy for panic disorder: A randomized controlled trial. *J. Consult. Clin. Psychol., 67*, 583–89.

Clark, D. M., & Wells, A. (1995). A cognitive model of social phobia. In R. G. Heimberg, M. R. Liebowitz, D. A. Hope, & F. R. Schneier (Eds.), *Social phobia: Diagnosis, assessment, and treatment* (pp. 69–93). New York: Guilford Press.

Clark, L. A. (2005). Temperament as a unifying basis for personality and psychopathology. *J. Abn. Psych., 114*, 505–21.

Clark, L. A. (2007). Assessment and diagnosis of personality disorder: Perennial issues and an emerging reconceptualization. *Annu. Rev. Psych., 58*, 227–57.

Clark, L. A., & Harrison, J. A. (2001). Assessment instruments. In W. J. Livesley (Ed.), *Handbook of personality disorders* (pp. 277–306). New York: Guilford Press.

Clark, L. A., & Watson, D. (1991). Theoretical and empirical issues in differentiating depression from anxiety. In J. Becker & A. Kleinman (Eds.), *Psychosocial aspects of depression.* Hillsdale, NJ: Erlbaum.

Clark, L. A., Watson, D., & Mineka, S. (1994). Temperament, personality, and the mood and anxiety disorders. *J. Abn. Psychol., 103*, 103–16.

Clarke-Flory, T. (2012, June 30). Meet pedophiles who mean well: The men behind VirtuousPedophiles.com are attracted to children but devoted to denying their desires. *Salon.com.* Retrieved from http://www.salon.com/2012/07/01/meet_pedophiles_who_mean_well

Clarkin, J. F., & Levy, K. N. (2004). The influence of client variables on psychotherapy. In M. J. Lambert (Ed.), *Bergin and Garfield's handbook of psychotherapy and behavior change* (pp. 194–226). New York: John Wiley & Sons.

Clarkin, J., Levy, K., Lenzenweger, M., & Kernberg, O. (2004). The personality disorders institute/borderline personality disorder research foundation randomized controlled trial for borderline personality disorder: Rationale, methods, and patient characteristics. *J. Pers. Disord., 18*, 52–72.

Clarkin, J. F., Levy, K. N., Lenzenweger, M. F., & Kernberg, O. F. (2007). Evaluating three treatments for borderline personality disorder: A multiwave study. *Am. J. Psychiatry, 164*, 922–28.

Classen, T. J., & Dunn, R. A. (2011, February 14). The effect of job loss and unemployment duration on suicide risk in the United States: A new look using mass-layoffs and unemployment duration. *Health. Econ.* [Epub ahead of print]. doi:10.1002/hec.1719

Claxton, A., Baker, L. D., Hanson, A., Trittschuh, E. H., Cholerton, B., Morgan, A., et al. (2015). Long-acting intranasal insulin detemir improves cognition for adults with mild cognitive impairment or early-stage Alzheimer's disease dementia. *J. Alzheimer's Disease, 41*, 897–906.

Cleckley, H. M. (1941). *The mask of sanity* (1st ed.). St. Louis, MO: Mosby.

Cleckley, H. (1988). *The mask of sanity* (5th ed.). Augusts, GA: Emily S. Cleckley.

Clément, F., & Belleville, S. C. (2010). Compensation and disease severity on the memory-related activations in mild cognitive impairment. *Biol. Psychiatry, 68*, 894–902.

Clement, S., Schauman, O., Graham, T., Maggionni, F., Evans-Lacko, S. E., Bezborodovs, N., et al. (2015). What is the impact of mental health-related stigma on help-seeking? A systematic review of quantitative and qualitative studies. *Psychological Medicine, 45*, 11–27.

Clementz, B. A., Geyer, M. A., & Braff, D. L. (1998). Poor P50 suppression among schizophrenia patients and their first-degree biological relatives. *Am. J. Psychiatry, 155*, 1691–702.

Cloitre, M. (2009). Effective psychotherapies for post-traumatic stress disorder: A review and critique. *CNS Spectrums, 14*(1 Suppl. 1), 32–43.

Cloninger, C. R. (1987). A systematic method for clinical description and classification of personality invariants. *Arch. Gen. Psychiat., 44*, 161–67.

Cloninger, C. R., Bayon, C., & Pszybeck, T. R. (1997). Epidemiology and Axis I comorbidity of antisocial personality. In D. M. Stoff, J. Breiling, & J. D. Maser (Eds.), *Handbook of antisocial behavior* (pp. 12–21). New York: Wiley.

Cloninger, C. R., Reich, T., Sigvardsson, S., von Knorring, A. L., & Bohman, M. (1986). The effects of changes in alcohol use between generations on the inheritance of alcohol abuse. In *Alcoholism: A medical disorder: Proceedings of the 76th Annual Meeting of the American Psychopathological Association.*

Cloyes, K. G., Wong, B., Latimer, S., & Abarca, J. (2010). Time to prison return for offenders with serious mental illness released from prison: A survival analysis. *Crim. Just. Behav., 37*(2), 175–87.

Coccaro, E. F. (2001). Biological and treatment correlates. In W. J. Livesley (Ed.), *Handbook of personality disorders* (pp. 124–35). New York: Guilford Press.

Cochran, S. D., & Mays, V. M. (2011). Sexual orientation and mortality among US men aged 17 to 59 years: Results from the National Health and Nutrition Examination Survey III. *Am. J. Public Health, 101*(6), 1133.

Cochran, S. D., & Mays, V. M. (2012). Sexual orientation and mental health. In C. J. Patterson & A. R. D'Augelli (Eds.), *Handbook of psychology and sexual orientation* (pp. 204–22). New York: Oxford University Press.

Cockayne, T. O. (1864–1866). Leechdoms, wort cunning, and star craft of early England. London: Longman & Green.

Coffey, B. J., & Zwilling, A. L. (2012). Anxiolytics. In D. R. Rosenberg & S. Gershon (Eds.), *Pharmacotherapy of child and adolescent psychiatric disorders* (3rd ed., pp. 301–40): New York: John Wiley & Sons.

Cohen, A. N., Hammen, C., Henry, R. M., & Daley, S. E. (2004). Effects of stress and social support on recurrence in bipolar disorder. *J. Affect. Dis., 82*(1), 143–47.

Cohen, F., Kemeny, M. E., Zegans, L. S., Johnson, P., Kearney, K. A., & Stites, D. P. (2007). Immune function declines with unemployment and recovers after stressor termination. *Psychosom. Med., 69*, 225–34.

Cohen, J. A., Mannarino, A. P., & Deblinger, E. (2006). *Treating trauma and traumatic grief in children and adolescents.* New York: Guilford Press.

Cohen, L. J., & Galynker, I. I. (2002). Clinical features of pedophilia and implications for treatment. *J. Psychiatry Pract., 8*(5), 276–89.

Cohen, P., Chen, H., Gordon, K., Johnson, J., Brook, J., & Kasen, S. (2008). Socioeconomic background and the developmental course of schizotypal and borderline personality disorder symptoms. *Develop. Psychopath., 20*, 633–50.

Cohen, S. (2005). The Pittsburgh common cold studies: Psychosocial predictors of susceptibility to respiratory infectious illness. *Int. J. Behavioral Medicine, 12*, 123–31.

Cohen-Kettenis, P. T. (2010). Psychosocial and psychosexual aspects of disorders of sex development. *Best Practice & Research: Clinical Endocrinology & Metabolism, 24*, 325–34.

Cohen-Kettenis, P. T., Dillen, C. M., & Gooren, L. J. G. (2000). Treatment of young transsexuals in the Netherlands. *Nederlands Tijdschrift voor Geneeskunde, 144*, 698–702.

Cohen-Kettenis, P. T., & Gooren, L. J. G. (1999). Trans-sexualism: A review of etiology, diagnosis, and treatment. *J. Psychosom. Res., 46*, 315–33.

Cohen-Kettenis, P. T., & Klink, D. (2015). Adolescents with gender dysphoria. *Best Practice & Research: Clinical Endocrinology & Metabolism, 29*, 485–95.

Cohen-Kettenis, P. T., Owen, A., Kaijser, V. G., Bradley, S. J., & Zucker, K. J. (2003). Demographic characteristics, social competence, and behavior problems in children with gender identity disorder: A cross-national, cross-clinic comparative analysis. *J. Abn. Child Psych., 31*(1), 41–53.

Cohen-Kettenis, P. T., & Pfafflin, F. (2010). The DSM diagnostic criteria for gender identity disorder in adolescents and adults. *Arch. Sexual Behavior, 39*, 499–513.

Cohen-Kettenis, P. T., Wallien, M., Johnson, L. L., Owen-Anderson, A. F. H., Bradley, S. J., & Zucker, K. J. (2006). A parent-report gender identity questionnaire for children: A cross-national, cross-clinic comparative analysis. *Clin. Child Psych. Psychiat., 11*(3), 397–405.

Cohler, B. J., Stott, F. M., & Musick, J. S. (1995). Adversity, vulnerability, and resilience: Cultural and developmental perspectives. In D. Cicchetti & D. J. Cohen (Eds.), *Developmental psychopathology: Vol. 2. Risk, disorder, and adaptations* (pp. 753–800). New York: Wiley.

Coid, J., Yang, M., Bebbington, P., Moran, P., Brugha, T., Jenkins, R., et al. (2009). Borderline personality disorder: Health service use and social functioning among a national household population. *Psychol. Med., 39*, 1721–31.

Coie, J. D. (1990). Toward a theory of peer rejection. In S. R. Asher & J. D. Coie (Eds.), *Peer rejection in childhood* (pp. 365–402). New York: Cambridge University Press.

Coie, J. D., Dodge, K. A., Terry, R., & Wright, V. (1991). The role of aggression in peer relations: An analysis of aggression episodes in boys' play groups. *Child Develop., 62*, 812–26.

Coie, J. D., Miller-Johnson, S., & Bagwell, C. (2000). Prevention science. In A. J. Sameroff & M. Lewis et al. (Eds.), *Handbook of developmental psychopathology* (2nd ed., pp. 93–112). New York: Kluwer/Plenum.

Cole, J. O., & Bodkin, J. A. (1990). Antidepressant drug side effects. *J. Clin. Psychiat., 51*, 21–26.

Coles, M. E., Phillips, K. A., Menard, W., Pagano, M. E., Fay, C., Weisberg, R. B., et al. (2006). Body dysmorphic disorder and social phobia: Cross-sectional and prospective data. *Depression and Anxiety, 23*(1), 26–33.

Collacott, R. A., et al. (1998). Behavior phenotype for Down's syndrome. *Brit. J. Psychiatry, 172*, 85–89.

Collins, N. L., Dunkel-Schetter, C., Lobel, M., & Scrimshaw, S. C. M. (2004). Social support in pregnancy: Psychosocial correlates of birth outcomes and postpartum depression. In H. T. Reis & C. E. Rusbult (Eds.), *Close relationships: Key readings* (pp. 35–55). Philadelphia, PA: Taylor & Francis.

Collishaw, S., Pickles, A., Messer, J., Rutter, M., Shearer, C., & Maughan, B. (2007). Resilience to adult psychopathology following childhood maltreatment: Evidence from a community sample. *Child Ab. Negl., 31*, 211–29.

Conduct Problems Prevention Research Group. (2011). The effects of the Fast Track preventive intervention on the development of conduct disorder across childhood. *Child Development, 82*(1), 331.

Conger, R. D., & Donnellan, M. B. (2007). An interactionist perspective on the socioeconomic context of human development. *Annu. Rev. Psychol., 58*, 175–99.

Conklin, H. M., & Iacono, W. G. (2002). Schizophrenia: A neurodevelopmental perspective. *Curr. Dis. Psychol. Sci., 11*(1), 33–37.

Conley, R. W. (2003). Supported employment in Maryland: Successes and issues. *Mental Retardation, 41*(4), 237–49.

Conley, C. S., & Rudolph, K. D. (2009). The emerging sex difference in adolescent depression: Interacting contributions of puberty and peer stress. *Developmental Psychopathology, 21*, 593–620.

Conlon, L., & Fahy, T. J. (2001). Psychological debriefing for acute trauma—A welcome demise? *Int. J. Psychological Medicine, 18*(2), 43–44.

Connell, P. (1958). *Amphetamine psychosis* (Maudsley Monographs No. 5). London: Oxford University Press.

Connors, G. J., & Walitzer, K. S. (2001). Reducing alcohol consumption among heavily drinking women: Evaluating the contributions of life-skills training and booster sessions. *J. Consult. Clin. Psychol., 69*(3), 447–56.

Constantino, M. J., Castonguay, L. G., & Schut, A. J. (2001). The working alliance. In G. S. Tryon (Ed.),

Counseling based on process research: Applying what we know. Boston: Allyn and Bacon.

Constantinou, E., Bogaerts, K., Van Diest, I., & Van den Bergh, O. (2013). Inducing symptoms in high symptom reporters via emotional pictures: The interactive effects of valence and arousal. *J. Psychosomatic Research, 74*, 191–96.

Cook, M., & Mineka, S. (1989). Observational conditioning of fear to fear-relevant versus fear-irrelevant stimuli in rhesus monkeys. *J. Abn. Psychol., 98*, 448–59.

Cook, M., & Mineka, S. (1990). Selective associations in the observational conditioning of fear in monkeys. *J. Exper. Psychol. Animal Behavior Processes, 16*, 372–89.

Cooke, D. J. (1996). Psychopathic personality in different cultures: What do we know? What do we need to find out? *J. Person. Dis., 10*(1), 23–40.

Cooke, D. J., & Michie, C. (1999). Psychopathy across cultures: North America and Scotland compared. *J. Abn. Psychol., 108*(1), 58–68.

Cooke, D. J., Michie, C., Hart, S. D., & Clark, D. (2005). Searching for the pan-cultural core of psychopathic personality disorder. *Personal. Indiv. Diff., 39*, 283–95.

Cooley-Quille, M., Boyd, R., Frantz, E., & Walsh, J. (2001). Emotional and behavioral impact of exposure to community violence in inner-city adolescents. *J. Clin. Child Psychol., 30*, 199–206.

Coons, P. M., & Bowman, E. S. (2001). Ten-year follow-up study of patients with dissociative identity disorder. *J. Trauma & Dissociation, 2*, 73–89.

Coons, P. M., Bowman, E. S., & Milstein, V. (1988). Multiple personality disorder. A clinical investigation of 50 cases. *J. Nervous and Mental Dis., 176*, 519–27.

Cooper, C. I., & Dewe, P. (2007). In A. Monat, R. S. Lazarus, & G. Reevy (Eds.), *The Praeger handbook of stress and coping* (pp. 7–31). Westport, CT: Praeger Publishers.

Cooper, M., Todd, G., & Wells, A. (2000). *Bulimia nervosa: A cognitive therapy programme for clients.* London: Jessica Kingsley Publishers.

Cooper, S.-A., Smiley, E., Allan, L. M., Jackson, A., Finlayson, J., Mantry, D., et al. (2009). Adults with intellectual disabilities: Prevalence, incidence and remission of self-injurious behaviour, and related factors. *J. Intell. Dis. Res., 53*(3), 200–16.

Cooper, S.-A., & van der Speck, R. (2009). Epidemiology of mental ill health in adults with intellectual disabilities. *Curr. Opin. Psychiat., 22*(5), 431–36.

Cooper, Z., Doll, H. A., Hawker, D. M., Byrne, S., Bonner, G., Eeley, E., et al. (2010). Testing a new cognitive behavioral treatment for obesity: A randomized controlled trial with three-year follow up. *Behav. Res. Ther., 48*, 706–13.

Copeland, W. E., Miller-Johnson, S., Keeler, G., Angold, A., & Costello, E. J. (2007). Childhood psychiatric disorders and young crime: A prospective population-based study. *Am. J. Orthopsychiat., 164*, 1668–75.

Corcoran, J. (2011). *Mental health treatment for children and adolescents.* New York: Oxford University Press.

Corigliano, V., De Carolis, A., Trovini, G., Dehning, J., Di Pietro, S., Curto, M., et al. (2014). Neurocognition in schizophrenia: From prodrome to multi-episode illness. *Psychiatry Research, 220*, 129–34.

Cornblatt, B. A., Green, M. F., & Walker, E. F. (2008). Schizophrenia: Etiology and neurocognition. In T. Millon, P. H. Blaney, & R. D. Davis (Eds.), *Oxford textbook of psychopathology* (2nd ed.). New York: Oxford University Press.

Cornblatt, B. A., Lenzenweger, M. F., Dworkin, R. H., & Erlenmeyer-Kimling, L. (1992). Childhood attentional dysfunctions predict social deficits in unaffected adults at risk for schizophrenia. *Brit. J. Psychiat., 16*(Suppl. 18), 59–64.

Cornblatt, B. A., Lenzenweger, M. F., & Erlenmeyer-Kimling, L. (1989). The Continuous Performance Test, identical pairs version: II. Contrasting attentional profiles in schizophrenic and depressed patients. *Psychiat. Res., 29*, 65–85.

Cororve, M. B., & Gleaves, D. H. (2001). Body dysmorphic disorder: A review of conceptualizations, assessment, and treatment strategies. *Clin. Psychol. Rev., 21*, 949–70.

Corrigan, P. W. (1995). Use of token economy with seriously mentally ill patients: Criticisms and misconceptions. *Psychiatr. Serv., 46*(12), 1258–63.

Corrigan, P. W. (1997). Behavior therapy empowers persons with severe mental illness. *Behav. Mod., 21*(1), 45–61.

Corrigan, P. W., Druss, B. G., & Perlick, D. A. (2014). The impact of mental health stigma on seeking and participating in mental health care. *Psychological Science in the Public Interest, 15*, 38–70.

Corrigan, P. W., & Watson, A. C. (2005). Mental illness and dangerousness: Fact or misperception and implications for stigma. In P. W. Corrigan (Ed.), *On the stigma of mental illness: Practical strategies for research and social change* (pp. 165–79). Washington, DC: American Psychological Association.

Cortina, L. M., & Kubiak, S. P. (2006). Gender and post-traumatic stress: Sexual violence as an explanation for women's increased risk. *J. Abn. Psychol., 115*, 753–59.

Coryell, W., Endicott, J., Maser, J. D., Mueller, T., Lavori, P., & Keller, M. (1995). The likelihood of recurrence in bipolar affective disorder: The importance of episode recency. *J. Affect. Dis., 33*, 201–06.

Coryell, W., Solomon, D., Turvey, C., Keller, M., Leon, A. C., Endicott, J., et al. (2003). The long-term course of rapid-cycling bipolar disorder. *Arch. Gen. Psychiat., 60*(9), 914–20.

Coryell, W., & Winokur, G. (1992). Course and outcome. In E. S. Paykel (Ed.), *Handbook of affective disorders* (2nd ed.). New York: Guilford Press.

Costa, P. T., & Widiger, T. A. (2002). *Personality disorders and the five-factor model of personality* (2nd ed.). Washington, DC: American Psychological Association.

Costello, E. J., Erkanli, A., & Angold, A. (2006). Is there an epidemic of child or adolescent depression? *J. Child Psychol. Psychiat., 47*(12), 1263–71.

Cota, D., Tschop, M. H., Horvath, T. L., & Levine, A. S. (2006). Cannabinoids, opioids, and eating behavior: The molecular face of hedonism? *Brain Res. Rev., 51*, 85–107.

Cote, G., O'Leary, T., Barlow, D. H., Strain, J. J., Salkovskis, P. M., Warwick, H. M. C., et al. (1996). Hypochondriasis. In T. A. Widiger, A. J. Frances, H. A. Pincus, R. Ross, M. B. First, & W. W. Davis (Eds.), *DSM-IV sourcebook* (Vol. 2, pp. 933–47). Washington, DC: American Psychiatric Association.

Cotton, N. S. (1979). The familial incidence of alcoholism. *J. Stud. Alcoh., 40*, 89–116.

Cottraux, J., & Blackburn, I. M. (2001). Cognitive therapy. In W. J. Livesley (Ed.), *Handbook of personality disorders* (pp. 377–99). New York: Guilford Press.

Cougle, J. R., Salkovskis, P. M., & Wahl, K. (2007). Perception of memory ability and confidence in recollections in obsessive-compulsive checking. *J. Anxiety Dis., 21*(1), 118–30.

Cousins, D. A., Butts, K., & Young, A. H. (2009). The role of dopamine in bipolar disorder. *Bipolar Disorder, 11*, 787–806.

Couture, S., & Penn, D. L. (2003). Interpersonal contact and the stigma of mental illness: A review of the literature. *J. Ment. Health, 12*, 291–305.

Couzin-Frankel, J. (2010, August 17). Brain scans not acceptable for detecting lies, says judge. *AAAS Science Insider.*

Covey, H. C. (Eds.). (2007). *The methamphetamine crisis: Strategies to save addicts, families, and communities.* Westport, CT: Praeger.

Coyne, J. C. (1976). Depression and the response of others. *J. Abn. Psychol., 55*(2), 186–93.

Coyne, J. C., Rohrbaugh, M. J., Shoham, V., Sonnega, J. S., Nicklas, J. M., & Cranford, J. A. (2001). Prognostic importance of marital quality for survival of congestive heart failure. *Am. J. Cardio., 88,* 526–29.

Craig, R. (2009). The clinical interview. In J. N. Butcher (Ed.), *Oxford handbook of personality and clinical assessment* (pp. 201–25). New York: Oxford University Press.

Craighead, W. E., Sheets, E. S., Brosse, A. L., & Ilardi, S. S. (2007). Psychosocial treatments for major depressive disorder. In P. E. Nathan & J. M. Gorman (Eds.), *A guide to treatments that work* (3rd ed., pp. 289–307). New York: Oxford University Press.

Craske, M. G. (1999). *Anxiety disorders: Psychological approaches to theory and treatment.* Boulder, CO: Westview.

Craske, M. G., & Barlow, D. H. (2008). Panic disorder and agoraphobia. In D. H. Barlow (Ed.), *Clinical handbook of psychological disorders* (4th ed., pp. 1–64). New York: Guilford Press.

Craske, M. G., Lang, A. J., Mystowski, J. L., Zucker, B. G., Bystritsky, A., & Yango, F. (2002). Does nocturnal panic represent a more severe form of panic disorder? *J. Nerv. Ment. Dis., 190*(9), 611–18.

Craske, M. G., & Mystkowski, J. L. (2006). Exposure therapy and extinction: Clinical studies. In M. G. Craske, D. Hermans, & D. Vansteenwegen (Eds.), *Fear and learning: Basic science to clinical application* (pp. 217–233). Washington, DC: APA Books.

Craske, M. G., & Rowe, M. K. (1997). A comparison of behavioral and cognitive treatments of phobias. In G. C. L. Davey (Ed.), *Phobias: A handbook of theory, research and treatment* (pp. 247–80). Chichester, UK: Wiley.

Craske, M. G., & Waters, A. M. (2005). Panic disorders, phobias, and generalized anxiety disorder. *Annu. Rev. Clin. Psychol., 1,* 197–225.

Creed, F., & Barsky, A. (2004). A systematic review of the epidemiology of somatisation disorder and hypochondriasis. *J. Psychosom. Res., 56,* 391–408.

Crerand, C. E., Sarwer, D. B., Magee, L., Gibbons, L. M., Lowe, M. R., Bartlett, S. P., et al. (2004). Rate of body dysmorphic disorder among patients seeking facial plastic surgery. *Psychiat. Ann., 34*(12), 958–65.

Cretzmeyer, M., Sarrazin, M. V., Huber, D. L., Block, R. I., & Hall, J. A. (2003). Treatment of methamphetamine abuse: Research findings and clinical directions. *J. Sub. Abuse Treat., 24*(3), 267–77.

Crews, F. (1995). *The memory wars: Freud's legacy in dispute.* New York: Granta.

Crick, N. R., & Dodge, K. A. (1994). A review and reformulation of social information-processing mechanisms in children's social adjustment. *Psychol. Bull., 115*(1), 74–101.

Crisp, A. H., Douglas, J. W. B., Ross, J. M., & Stonehill, E. (1970). Some developmental aspects of disorders of weight. *J. Psychosom. Res., 14,* 313–20.

Crisp, A., Gowers, S., Joughin, N., McClelland, L., Rooney, B., Nielsen S., et al. (2006). Death, survival and recovery in anorexia nervosa: A thirty-five-year study. *Eur. Eat. Dis. Rev., 14,* 168–75.

Crits-Christoph, P., & Barber, J. P. (2002). Psychosocial treatments for personality disorders. In P. E. Nathan & J. M. Gorman (Eds.), *A guide to treatments that work* (pp. 544–53). New York: Oxford University Press.

Crits-Christoph, P., & Barber, J. P. (2007). Psychological treatments for personality disorders. In P. E. Nathan & J. M. Gorman (Eds.), *A guide to treatments that work* (pp. 641–58). New York: Oxford University Press.

Crits-Christoph, P., Gibbons, M. C., & Crits-Christoph, K. (2004). Supportive-expressive psychodynamic therapy. In R. G. Heimberg, C. L. Turk, & D. S. Mennin (Eds.), *Generalized anxiety disorder: Advances in research and practice* (pp. 293–319). New York: Guilford Press.

Cromer, K. R., Schmidt, N. B., & Murphy, D. L. (2007). An investigation of traumatic life events and obsessive-compulsive disorder. *Behaviour Research and Therapy, 45,* 1683–91.

Cross-Disorder Group of the Psychiatric Genomics Consortium. (2014). Genetic relationship between five psychiatric disorders estimated from genome-wide SNPs. *Nature Genetics, 45,* 984–94.

Crouter, A. C., & Booth, A. (2003). *Children's influence on family dynamics: The neglected side of family relationships.* Mahwah, NJ: Lawrence Erlbaum Associates.

Crow, T. J. (2007). Genetic hypotheses for schizophrenia. *Brit. J. Psychiatry, 191,* 180–81.

Crowther, J. H., Armey, M., Luce, K. H., Dalton, G. R., & Leahey, T. (2008). The point prevalence of bulimic disorders from 1990–2004. *Int. J. Eat. Dis., 41*(6), 491–97. doi:10.1002/eat.20537

Crowther, J. H., Kichler, J. C., Sherwood, N., & Kuhnert, M. E. (2002). The role of family factors in bulimia nervosa. *Eat. Dis., 10,* 141–51.

Cruts, M., van Duijn, C. M., Backhovens, H., van den Broeck, M., Serneels, S., Sherrington, R., et al. (1998). Estimations of the genetic contribution of presenilin-1 and presenilin-2 mutations in a population-based study of presenile Alzheimer disease. *Human Molecular Genetics, 7,* 43–51.

Cuellar, A. K., Johnson, S. L., & Winters, R. (2005). Distinctions between bipolar and unipolar depression. *Clin. Psychol. Rev., 25,* 307–39.

Cui, M., & Fincham, F. E. (2010). The differential effects of parental divorce and marital conflict on young adult romantic relationships. *Personal Relationships, 17*(3), 331–43. doi:10.1111/j.1475-6811.2010.01279.x

Cuijpers, P., Andersson, G., Donker, T., & van Straten, A. (2011). Psychological treatment of depression: Results of a series of meta-analyses. *Nordic J. Psychiatry, 65,* 354–64.

Cummings, E. M., Goeke-Morey, M. C., & Papp, L. M. (2004). Everyday marital conflict and child aggression. *J. Abn. Psychol., 32*(2), 191–202.

Cunningham, R. M., Chermack, S. T., Shope, J. T., Bingham, C. R., Zimmerman, M. A., Blow, F. C., & Walton, M. A. (2010). Effects of a brief intervention for reducing violence and alcohol misuse among adolescents: A randomized controlled trial. *JAMA, 304,* 527–35. doi:10.1001/jama.2010.1066

Curlin, F. A., Nwodim, C., Vance, J. L., Chin, M. H., & Lantos, J. D. (2008). To die, to sleep: US physicians' religious and other objections to physician-assisted suicide, terminal sedation, and withdrawal of life support. *Am. J. Hospice & Palliative Medicine, 25*(2), 112–20.

Currie, J., & Widom, C. S. (2010). Long-term consequences of child abuse and neglect on adult economic well-being. *Child Maltreatment, 15*(2), 111–20.

Currier, G. (2000). Datapoints: Psychiatric bed reductions and mortality among persons with mental disorders. *Psychiatr. Serv., 51,* p. 851.

Custers, K., & Van den Bulck (2009). Viewership of pro-anorexia websites in seventh, ninth and eleventh graders. *Eur. Eat. Disord. Rev., 17,* 214–19.

Cutolo, M., & Straub, R. H. (2006). Stress as a risk factor in the pathogenesis of rheumatoid arthritis. *Neuroimmunomodulation, 13,* 277–82.

Cutting, J. (1995). Descriptive psychopathology. In S. R. Hirsch & D. R. Weinberger (Eds.), *Schizophrenia* (pp. 15–27). Cambridge, UK: Cambridge University Press.

Cutting, J., & Murphy, D. (1990). Impaired ability of schizophrenics, relative to manics or depressives, to appreciate social knowledge about their culture. *Brit. J. Psychiatry, 157,* 355–58.

Czajkowski, N., Kendler, K. S., Tambs, K., Roysamb, E. & Reichborn-Kjennerud, T. (2011). The structure of genetic and environmental risk factors for phobias in women. *Psychological Medicine, 41,* 1987–95.

D

Dadds, M. R., Spence, S. H., Holland, D. E., Barren, P. M., & Laurens, K. R. (1997). Prevention and early intervention for anxiety disorders: A controlled study. *J. Consult. Clin. Psychol., 65*(4), 627–35.

Dager, A. D., Jamadar, S., Stevens, M. C., Rosen, R., Jiantonio-Kelly, R. E., Sisante, J. F., et al. (2014). fMRI response during figural memory task performance in college drinkers. *Psychopharmacology, 231,* 167–179. doi:10.1007/s00213-013-3219-1

Dahl, R. E. (1992). The pharmacologic treatment of sleep disorders. *Psychiat. Clin. North Am., 15,* 161–78.

Dahlkamp, J., Kraske, M., von Mittelstaedt, J., Robel,S., & von Roohr, M. (2008, May 5). How Josef Fritzl created his regime of terror. *Spiegel Online.* Retrieved from http://www.spiegel.de/international/europe/constructing-hell-how-josef-fritzl-created-his-regime-of-terror-a-551451.html

Dahllöf, O., & Öst, L.-G. (1998). The diphasic reaction in blood phobic situations: Individually or stimulus bound? *Scandinavian J. Behaviour Therapy, 27*(3), 97–104.

Dain, N. (1964). *Concepts of insanity in the United States: 1789–1865.* New Brunswick, NJ: Rutgers University Press.

Dallman, M. F., Pecorano, N., Akana, S. F., la Fleur, S. E., Gomez, F., Houshyar, H., et al. (2003, September 30). Chronic stress and obesity: A new view of "comfort food. " *Proceedings of the National Academy of Sciences, 100*(20), 11696–701.

Dallam, S. J., Gleaves, D. H., Cepeda-Benito, A., Silberg, J. L., Kraemer, H. C., & Spiegel, D. (2001). The effects of child sexual abuse: Comment on Rind, Tromovitch, and Bauserman (1998). *Psych. Bull., 127,* 715–33.

Daly, M., & Wilson, M. (1988). *Homicide.* New York: Aldine de Gruyter.

Daly, M., & Wilson, M. I. (1996). Violence against stepchildren. *Curr. Dir. Psychol. Sci., 5*(3), 77–81.

Daniel, M., & Gurczynski, J. (2010). Mental status examination. In D. L. Segal & M. Hersen (Eds.), *Diagnostic interviewing* (pp. 61–88). New York: Springer.

Danoff-Burg, S., Agee, J. D., Romanoff, N. R., Kremer, J. M., & Strosberg, J. M. (2006). Benefit finding and expressive writing in adults with lupus or rheumatoid arthritis. *Psychology and Health, 21,* 651–65.

Dantzer, R., & Kelley, K. W. (2007). Twenty years of research on cytokine-induced sickness behavior. *Brain, Behavior, and Immunity, 21,* 153–60.

Dantzer, R., O'Connor, J. C., Freund, G. G., Johnson, R. W., & Kelley, K. W. (2009). From inflammation to sickness and depression: When the immune system subjugates the brain. *Nature Reviews Neuroscience, 9,* 46–57.

Dar, R., Rish, S., Hermesh, H., Taub, M., & Fux, M. (2000). Realism of confidence in obsessive-compulsive checkers. *J. Abn. Psychol., 109*(4), 673–78.

D'Arcy, C., & Meng, X. (2014). Prevention of common mental disorders: Conceptual framework and effective interventions. *Curr. Opin. Psychiatry, 27*(4), 294–301. doi:http://dx.doi.org/10.1097/YCO.0000000000000076

Dare, C., & Eisler, I. (2002). Family therapy and eating disorders. In C. G. Fairburn & K. D. Brownell (Eds.), *Eating disorders and obesity: A comprehensive handbook* (2nd ed., pp. 314–19). New York: Guilford Press.

Darke, S., & Ross, J. (2001). The relationship between suicide and heroin overdose among methadone maintenance patients in Sydney, Australia. *Addiction, 96,* 1443–53.

Daskalakis, Z. J., Christensen, B. K., Chen, R., Fitzgerald, P. B., Zipursky, R. B., & Kapus, S. (2002). Evidence for impaired cortical inhibition in schizophrenia using transcranial magnetic stimulation. *Arch. Gen. Psychiat., 59,* 347–54.

Dattilio, F. M., & Freeman, A. (2007). *Cognitive behavioral strategies in crisis intervention.* New York: Guilford Press.

D'Avanzo, B., Barbato, A., Barbui, C., Battino, R. N., Civenti, G., & Frattura, L. (2003). Discharges of patients from public psychiatric hospitals in Italy between 1994 and 2000. *Inter. J. Soc. Psychiat., 49*(1), 27–34.

Daversa, M. T., & Knight, R. A. (2007). A structural examination of the predictors of sexual coercion against children in adolescent sexual offenders. *Crim. Just. Behav., 34*(10), 1313–33.

David, D., De Faria, L., Lapeyra, O., & Mellman, T. A. (2004). Adjunctive risperidone treatment in combat veterans with chronic PTSD. *J. Clin. Psychopharm., 24*(5), 556–58.

David, D., Szentagotai, A., Eva, K., & Macavei, B. (2005). A synopsis of rational-emotive behavior therapy (REBT): Fundamental and applied research. *J. Rational-Emotive and Cognitive-Behavior Therapy, 23,* 175–21.

Davidson, K. W., Burg, M. M., Kronish, I. M., Shimbo, D., Dettenborn, L., Mehran, R., et al. (2010). *Arch. Gen. Psychiat., 67,* 480–88.

Davidson, L., Shahar, G., Stayner, D. A., et al. (2004). Supported socialization for people with psychiatric disabilities: Lessons from a random-ized controlled trial. *J. Comm. Psychol., 32,* 453–77.

Davidson, M. C., Thomas, K. M., & Casey, B. J. (2003). Imaging the developing brain with fMRI. *Men. Retard. Devel. Res. Rev., 9,* 161–67.

Davidson, R. J., Pizzagalli, D., & Nitschke, J. B. (2002). The representation and regulation of emotion in depression: Perspectives from affective neuroscience. In I. H. Gotlib & C. L. Hammen (Eds.), *Handbook of depression* (pp. 219–44). New York: Guilford Press.

Davidson, R. J., Pizzagalli, D., & Nitschke, J. B. (2009). The representation and regulation of emo-tion in depression: Perspectives from affective neuroscience. In I. H. Gotlib & C. L. Hammen (Eds.), *Handbook of depression* (2nd ed., pp. 218–48). New York: Guilford Press.

Davis, A. A., & Nguyen, M. (2014). A case study of anorexia nervosa driven by religious sacrifice. *Case Reports in Psychiatry,* 512764. doi:10.1155/2014/512764

Davis, J. O., Phelps, J. A., & Bracha, H. S. (1995). Prenatal development of monozygotic twins and concordance for schizophrenia. *Schizo. Bull., 21*(3), 357–66.

Davis, M. (2002). Role of NMDA receptors and MAP kinase in the amygdala in extinction of fear: Clinical implications for exposure therapy. *Europ. J. Neurosci., 16*(3), 395–98.

Davis, M. (2006). Neural systems involved with anxiety and fear measured with fear-potentiated startle. *Am. Psychol., 61,* 441–756.

Davis, M., Myers, K. M., Ressler, K. J., & Rothbaum, B. O. (2005). Facilitation of extinction of conditioned fear by d-cycloserine: Implications for psychotherapy. *Curr. Dis. Psychol. Sci., 14*(4), 214–19.

Davis, M., Ressler, K., Rothbaum, B. O., & Richardson, R. (2006). Effects of D-cycloserine on extinction: Translation from preclinical to clinical work. *Biol. Psychiat., 60*(4), 369–75.

Dawkins, M. P. (1997). Drug use and violent crime among adolescents. *Adolescence, 32,* 395–405.

Dawson, G., Jones, E. J., Merkle, K., Venema, K., Lowy, R., Faja, S., et al. (2012). Early behavioral intervention is associated with normalized brain activity in young children with autism. *J. Am. Acad. Child Adolesc. Psychiatry, 51*(11), 1150–59. doi:10.1016/j.jaac.2012.08.018

Dawson, G., Panagiotides, H., Klinger, L. G., & Spieker, S. (1997). Infants of depressed and nondepressed mothers exhibit differences in frontal brain electrical activity during the expression of negative emotions. *Develop. Psychol., 33*(5), 650–56.

Dawson, G., Rogers, S., Munson, J., Smith, M., Winter, J., Greenson, J., et al. (2010). Randomized, controlled trial of an intervention for toddlers with autism: The Early Start Denver Model. *Pediatrics, 125*(1), e17–23. doi:10.1542/peds.2009-0958

Day, N. (2007). Critical incident stress management and TIR. In V. R. Volkman (Ed.), *Traumatic incident reduction and critical incident stress management.* Ann Arbor, MI: Loving Healing Press.

de Graaf, R., Kessler, R. C., Fayyad, J., ten Have, M., Alonso, J., Angermeyer, M., et al. (2008). The prevalence and effects of adult attention-deficit/hyperactivity disorder (ADHD) on the perfor-mance of workers: Results from the WHO World Mental Health Survey Initiative. *Occup. Environ. Med., 65*(12), 835–42. doi:10.1136/oem.2007.038448

de Jong, J. (Ed.). (2002). *Trauma, war, and violence: Public health in socio-cultural context.* New York: Kluwer Academic/Plenum.

De Kloet, C. S., Vermetten, E., Geuze, E., Kavelaars, A., Heijnen, C. J., & Westenberg, H. G. M. (2006). Assessment of HPA-axis function in post-traumatic stress disorder: Pharmacological and non-pharmacological challenge tests, a review. *J. Psychiatr. Res., 40,* 550–67.

De Leon, M. J., Desanti, S., Zinkowski, R., Mehta, P. D., Pratico, D., Segal, S., et al. (2004). MRI and CSF studies in the early diagnosis of Alzheimer's disease. *J. Int. Med., 256,* 205–23.

de Mello, M. F., de Jesus Mari, J., Bacaltchuk, J., Verdeli, H., & Neugebauer, R. (2005). A systematic review of research findings on the efficacy of interpersonal therapy for depressive disorders. *Eur. Arch. Psychiat. Clin. Neurosci., 255*(2), 75–82.

de Pauw, K. W., & Szulecka, T. K. (1988). Dangerous delusions: Violence and misidentification syndromes. *Brit. J. Psychiatry, 152,* 91–96.

De Santi, S., de Leon, M. J., Rusinek, H., Convit, A., Tarshish, C. Y., Roche, A., et al. (2001). Hippocam-pal formation, glucose metabolism and volume losses in MCI and AD. *Neurobiol. Aging, 22,* 529–39.

De Silva, P., Rachman, S. J., & Seligman, M. E. P. (1977). Prepared phobias and obsessions: Therapeutic outcomes. *Behav. Res. Ther., 15,* 65–78.

Deb, S., & Ahmed, Z. (2000). Specific conditions leading to mental retardation. In M. G. Gelder, J. J. Lopez-Ibor, Jr., & N. Andreason (Eds.), *New Oxford textbook of psychiatry* (pp. 1954–63). New York: Oxford University Press.

Debbané, M., Glaser, B., David, M. K., Feinstein, C., & Eliez, S. (2006). Psychotic symptoms in children and adolescents with 22q11.2 deletion syndrome: Neuropsychological and behavioral implications. *Schiz. Res., 84,* 187–93.

Decety, J., Chen, C., Harenski, C., & Kiehl, K. A. (2013). An fMRI study of affective perspective taking in individuals with psychopathy: Imagining another in pain does not evoke empathy. *Frontiers in Human Neuroscience, 7,* 489.

Declercq, F., Vanheule, S., Markey, S., & Willemsen, J. (2007). Posttraumatic distress in security guards and the various effects of social support. *J. Clinical Psychology, 63,* 1239–46.

Deecher, D., Andree, T. H., Sloan, D., & Schechter, L. E. (2008). From menarche to menopause: Exploring the underlying biology of depression in women experiencing hormonal changes. *Psychoneuroendocrinology, 33*(1), 3–17. doi:10.1016/j.psyneuen.2007.10.006

Deep-Soboslay, A., Benes, F. M., Haroutunian, V., Ellis, J. K., Kleinman, J. E., & Hyde, T. M. (2011). Psychiatric brain banking: Three perspectives on current trends and future directions. *Biological Psychiatry, 69,* 104–12.

Degenhardt, L., Bruno, R., & Topp, L. (2010). Is ecstasy a drug of dependence? Drug Alcohol Dep., 107(1), 1–10.

Degenhardt, L., Chiu, W.-T., Sampson, N., Kessler, R. C., Anthony, J. C. Angermeyer, M., et al. (2008). Toward a global view of alcohol, tobacco, cannabis, and cocaine use: Findings from the WHO World Mental Health Surveys. *PLoS Medicine, 5,* 1053–67.

Del-Ben, C. M., & Graeff, F. G. (2009). Panic disorder: Is the PAG involved? *Neural Plasticity, 2009,* Article ID 108135.

DeLuca, N. L., Moser, L. L., & Bond, G. R. (2008). Assertive community treatment. In K. T. Mueser & D. V. Jeste (Eds.), *Clinical handbook of schizophre-nia* (pp. 329–38). New York: Guilford Press.

den Heijer, T., Geerlings, M. I., Hoebeek, F. E., Hofman, A., Koudstaal, P. J., & Breteler, M. M. B. (2006). Use of hippocampal and amygdalar volumes on magnetic resonance imaging to predict dementia in cognitively intact elderly people. *Arch. Gen. Psychiat., 63,* 57–62.

Dennis, C. (2004). Asia's tigers get the blues. *Nature, 429,* 696–98.

Denollet, J., Vaes, J., & Brutsaert, D. L. (2000). Inadequate response to treatment in coronary heart disease: Adverse effects of Type D personality and younger age on 5-year prognosis and quality of life. *Circulation, 102,* 630–35.

Depue, R. A. (2009). Genetic, environmental, and epigenetic factors in the development of personality disturbance. *Develop. Psychopath., 21*(4), 1031–63. doi:10.1017/S0954579409990034

Depue, R. A., & Lenzenweger, M. F. (2001). A neurobehavioral dimensional model. In W. J. Livesley (Ed.), *Handbook of personality disorders* (pp. 136–76). New York: Guilford Press.

Depue, R. A., & Lenzenweger, M. F. (2005). A neurobehavioral model of personality disturbance. In M. F. Lenzenweger & J. F. Clarkin (Eds.), *Major theories of personality disorder* (2nd ed., pp. 391–453). New York: Guilford Press.

Depue, R. A., & Lenzenweger, M. F. (2006). A multidimensional neurobehavioral model of personality disturbance. In R. F. Krueger & J. L. Tackett (Eds.), *Personality and psychopathology.* New York: Guilford Publications.

Derr, R. F., & Gutmann, H. R. (1994). Alcoholic liver disease may be prevented with adequate nutrients. *Medical Hypotheses, 42,* 1–4.

DeRubeis, R. J., Gelfand, L. A., Tang, T. Z., & Simons, A. D. (1999). Medications versus cognitive behavior therapy for severely depressed outpatients: Meta-analysis of four randomized comparisons. *Am. J. Psychiatry, 156*(7), 1007–13.

DeRubeis, R. J., Hollon, S. D., Amsterdam, J. D., Shelton, R. C., Young, P. R., Salomon, R. M., et al. (2005). Cognitive therapy vs medications in the treatment of moderate to severe depression. *Arch. Gen. Psychiatry, 62,* 409–16.

Deters, P. B., Novins, D. K., Fickenscher, A., & Beals, J. (2006). Trauma and posttraumatic stress disorder symptomatology: Patterns among American Indian adolescents in substance abuse treatment. *Am. J. Orthopsychiat., 76*(3), 335–45.

Deutsch, A. (1944). Military psychiatry: The Civil War 1860–65. In J. K. Hall (Ed.), *One hundred years of American psychiatry.* New York: Columbia University Press.

Deutsch, A. (1948). *The shame of the states*. New York: Harcourt, Brace.

Devanand, D. P., Dwork, A. J., Hutchinson, E. R., Bolwig, T. G., & Sackeim, H. A. (1994) Does ECT alter brain structure? *Am. J. Psychiatry, 151*, 957–70.

Devanand, D. P., Pradhanab, G., Liu, X., Khandji, A., De Santi, S., Segal, S., et al. (2007). Hippocampal and entorhinal atrophy in mild cognitive impairment. *Neurol., 68*, 828–36.

Deveci, A., Aydemir, O., Taskin, O., Tanelli, F., & Esen-Danaci, A. (2007). Serum brain derived neurotropic factor levels in conversion disorder: Comparative study with depression. *Psychiat. Clin. Neurosci., 61*, 571–73.

Devilly, G. J., Gist, R., & Cotton, P. (2006). Fire! Aim! The status of psychological debriefing and therapeutic interventions: In the workplace and after disasters. *Rev. Gen. Psychol., 10*, 318–45.

DeVito, E. E., Babuscio, T. A., Nich, C., Ball, S. A., & Carroll, K. M. (2014). Gender differences in clinical outcomes for cocaine dependence: Randomized clinical trials of behavioral therapy and disulfiram. *Drug and Alcohol Dependence, 145*, 156–67.

Dew, M. A., Bromet, E. J., & Schulberg, H. C. (1987). A comparative analysis of two community stressors' long-term mental health effects. *Am. J. Community Psychol., 15*, 167–84.

Dew, M. A., Penkower, L., & Bromet, E. J. (1991). Effects of unemployment on mental health in the contemporary family. *Behav. Mod., 15*, 501–44.

Dhejne, C., Lichtenstein, P., Boman, M., Johansson, A. L. V., Långström, N., & Landén, M. (2011). Long-term follow-up of transsexual persons undergoing sex reassignment surgery: Cohort study in Sweden. *PLoS ONE, 6*(2), e16885.

Diana, M. (2011). The dopamine hypothesis of drug addiction and its potential therapeutic value. *Frontiers in Psychiatry, 2*(64), 1–7.

Diav-Citrin, O., Shechtman, S., Wienbaum, D., Wajnberg, R., Avgil, M., Di Gianantonio, E., et al. (2008). Paroxetine and fluoxetine in pregnancy: A prospective, multicentre, controlled, observational study. *Br. J. Clin. Pharmacol., 66*, 695–705.

Dickey, C. C., Morocz, I. A., Niznikiewicz, M. A., Voglmaier, M., Tone, S., Khan, U., et al. (2008). Auditory processing abnormalities in schizotypal personality disorder: An fMRI experiment using tones of deviant pitch and duration. *Schiz. Res., 103*, 26–39.

Dickey, R., Nussbaum, D., Chevolleau, K., & Davidson, H. (2002). Age as a differential characteristic of rapists, pedophiles, and sexual sadists. *J. Sex Marit. Ther., 28*, 211–18.

DiClemente, C. C. (1993). Changing addictive behaviors: A process perspective. *Curr. Dis. Psychol. Sci., 2*, 101–06.

Didie, E. R., Tortolani, C. C., Pope, C. G., Menard, W., Fay, C., & Phillips, K. A. (2006). Childhood abuse and neglect in body dysmorphic disorder. *Child Ab. Negl., 30*, 1105–15.

Diefenbach, G. J., Abramowitz, J. S., Norberg, M. M., & Tolin, D. F. (2007). Changes in quality of life following cognitive-behavioral therapy for obsessive-compulsive disorder. *Behav. Res. Ther., 45*(12), 3060–68.

Dietz, P. E., Hazelwood, R. R., & Warren, J. (1990). The sexually sadistic criminal and his offenses. *Bull. Am. Acad. of Psychiatry & the Law, 18*(2), 163–78.

Difede, J., Malta, L. S., Best, S., Henn-Haase, C., Metzler, T., Bryant, R., et al. (2007). A randomized controlled clinical treatment trial for World Trade Center attack-related PTSD in disaster workers. *J. Nerv. Ment. Dis., 195*, 861–65.

DiGrande, L., Neria, Y., Brackbill, R. M., Pulliam, P., & Galea, S. (2011). Long-term post-traumatic stress symptoms among 3,271 civilian survivors of the September 11, 2011, terrorist attacks on the World Trade Center. *Am. J. Epidemiol, 173*, 271–81.

Dikmen, S. S., Temkin, N. R., Machamer, J. E., & Holubkov, A. L. (1994). Employment following traumatic head injuries. *Arch. Neurol., 51*(2), 177–86.

Diller, L., & Gordon, W. A. (1981). Interventions for cognitive deficits in brain-injured adults. *J. Consult. Clin. Psychol., 49*, 822–34.

Dimberg, U., & Öhman, A. (1996). Behold the wrath: Psychophysiological responses to facial stimuli. *Motivation & Emotion, 20*, 149–82.

Dimidjian, S., Barrera, M., Martell, C., Munoz, R. F., & Lewinsohn, P. M. (2011). The origins and current status of behavioral activation treatments for depression. *Annu. Rev. Clin. Psychol., 7*, 1–38.

Dimidjian, S., Hollon, S. D., Dobson, K. S., Schmaling, K. B., Kohlenberg, R. J., Addis, M. E., et al. (2006). Randomized trial of behavioral activation, cognitive therapy, and antidepressant medication in the acute treatment of adults with major depression. *J. Consult. Clin. Psychol., 74*(4), 658–70.

Dimsdale, J. E. (2011). Medically unexplained symptoms: A treacherous foundation for somatoform disorders? *Psychiatric Clin. North Am., 34*, 511–13.

Dingfelder, S. F. (2010). Time capsule: The first modern psychology study. *Monitor on Psychology, 41*(7), 30–31.

DiPietro, L., Mossberg, H.-O., & Stunkard, A. J. (1994). A 40-year history of overweight children in Stockholm: Lifetime overweight, morbidity, and mortality. *Int. J. Obesity, 18*, 585–90.

Dishion, T. J., & Stormshak, E. A. (2007). *Intervening in children's lives: An ecological, family-centered approach to mental health care*. Washington, DC: American Psychological Association.

Disner, S. G., Beevers, C. G., Haigh, E. A., & Beck, A. T. (2011). Neural mechanisms of the cognitive model of depression. *Nature Reviews Neuroscience, 12*(8), 467–77. doi:10.1038/nrn3027

Disner, S. G., Beevers, C. G., Lee, H.-J., Ferrell, R. E., Hariri, A. R., & Telch, M. J. (2013). War zone stress interacts with the 5-HTTLPR polymorphism to predict the development of sustained attention for negative emotion stimuli in soldiers returning from Iraq. *Clinical Psychological Science, 1*, 413–25.

Doane, L. S., Feeny, N. C., & Zoellner, L. A. (2010). A preliminary investigation of sudden gains in exposure therapy for PTSD. *Behav. Res. Ther., 48*(6), 555–60.

Dobson, K. S., Hollon, S. D., Dimidjian, S., Schmaling, K. B., Kohlenberg, R. J., Gallop, R. J., et al. (2008). Randomized trail of behavioral activation, cognitive therapy, and antidepressant medications in the prevention of relapse and recurrence in major depression. *J. Consult. Clin. Psychol., 76*, 468–77.

Docter, R. F., & Prince, V. (1997). Transvestism: A survey of 1032 cross-dressers. *Arch. Sex. Behav., 26*, 589–605.

Dodd, S., Kulkarni, J., Berk, L., Ng, F., Fitzgerald, P. B., de Castella, A. R., et al. (2010). A prospective study of the impact of subthreshold mixed states on the 24-month clinical outcomes of bipolar I disorder or schizoaffective disorder. *J. Affect. Disord., 124*(1–2), 22–28. doi:10.1016/j.jad.2009.10.027

Dodge, K. A. (2006). Translational science in action: Hostile attributional style and the development of aggressive behavior problems. *Develop. Psychopath., 18*(3), 791–814.

Dodge, K. A., Laird, R., Lochman, J., & Zelli, A. (2002). Multidimensional latent-construct analysis of children's social information processing patterns: Correlations with aggressive behavior problems. *Psychol. Assess., 14*, 60–73.

Dodge, K. A., Lochman, J. E., Harnish, J. D., Bates, J. E., & Pettit, G. S. (1997). Reactive and proactive aggression in school children and psychiatrically impaired chronically assaultive youth. *J. Abn. Psychol., 106*(1), 37–51.

Doering, S., Katzberger, F., Rumpold, G., Roessler, S., Hofstoeetter, B., Schatz, D. S., et al. (2000). Videotape preparation of patients before hip replacement surgery reduces stress. *Psychosom. Med., 62*, 365–73.

Doherty, J. L., O'Donovan, M. C., & Owen, M. J. (2012). Recent genomic advances in schizophrenia. *Clinical Genetics, 81*, 103–09.

Dohrenwend, B. P. (2000). The role of adversity and stress in psychopathology: Some evidence and its implications for theory and research. *J. Health & Social Behavr., 41*(1), 1–19.

Dohrenwend, B. P. (2006). Inventorying stressful life events as risk factors for psychopathology: Toward resolution of the problem of intracategory variability. *Psych. Bull., 132*(3), 477–95.

Dohrenwend, B. P., Shrout, P. E., Link, B. G., Skodol, A. E., & Stueve, A. (1995). A case-control study of life events and other possible psychosocial risk factors for episodes of schizophrenia and major depression. In C. M. Mazure (Ed.), *Does stress cause psychiatric illness?* Washington, DC: American Psychiatric Press.

Dohrenwend, B. P., Yager, T. J., Wall, M. M., & Adams, B. G. (2013). The roles of combat exposure, personal vulnerability, and involvement in harm to civilians of prisoners in Vietnam-war-related posttraumatic stress disorder. *Clinical Psychological Science, 1*, 223–38.

Dolan-Sewell, R. T., Krueger, R. F., & Shea, M. T. (2001). Co-occurrence with syndrome disorders. In W. J. Livesley (Ed.), *Handbook of personality disorders* (pp. 84–104). New York: Guilford Press.

Dolberg, O. T., Iancu, I., Sasson, Y., & Zohar, J. (1996). The pathogenesis and treatment of obsessive-compulsive disorder. *Clinical Neuropharmacology, 19*(2), 129–47.

Dolberg, O. T., Sasson, Y., Marazziti, D., Kotler, M., Kendler, S., & Zohar, J. (1996). New compounds for the treatment of obsessive-compulsive disorder. In H. G. Westenberg, J. A. Den Boer, & D. L. Murphy (Eds.), *Advances in the neurobiology of anxiety disorders* (pp. 299–311). Chichester, UK: Wiley.

Domjan, M. (2005). Pavlovian conditioning: A functional perspective. *Annu. Rev. Psychol., 56*, 179–206.

Domjan, M. P. (2009). *The principles of learning and behavior: Active learning edition* (6th ed.). Stamford, CT: Wadsworth.

D'Onofrio, B. M., Rickert, M. E., Frans, E., Kuja-Halkola, R., Almqvist, C., Sjölander, A., et al. (2014). Paternal age at childbearing and offspring psychiatric and academic morbidity. *JAMA Psychiatry, 71*(4), 432–38. doi:10.1001/jamapsychiatry.2013.4525

Dooley, D., & Prause, J. (2004). *The social costs of underemployment: Inadequate employment as disguised unemployment*. New York: Cambridge University Press.

Dooley, D., & Prause, J. (2007). Predictors of early alcohol drinking onset. *J. Child & Adolescent Substance Abuse, 16*(2), 1–29.

Dooley, D., Prause, J., & Ham-Rowbottom, K. A. (2000). Underemployment and depression: Longitudinal relationships. *J. Health Soc. Behav., 41*(4), 421–36.

Doornbos, B., Fekkes, D., Tanke, M. A. C., de Jonge, P., & Korf, J. (2008). Sequential serotonin and noradrenalin associated processes involved in postpartum blues. *Prog. Neuropsychopharmacol. Biol. Psychiatry, 32*(5), 1320–25.

Dorahy, M. J., Brand, B. L., Şar, V., Krüger, C., Stavropoulos, P., Martínez-Taboas, et al. (2014). Dissociative identity disorder: An empirical overview. *Austral. NZ J. Psychiatry, 48*(5), 402–17. doi:http://dx.doi.org/10.1177/0004867414527523

Dorahy, M. J., Middleton, W., Seager, L., Williams, & Chambers, R. (2015, August 14). Child abuse and neglect in complex dissociative disorder, abuse-related chronic PTSD and mixed psychiatric samples. *J. Trauma and Dissociation* [Epub ahead of print].

dos Reis, S., Zito, J. M., Safer, D. J., & Soeken, K. L. (2001). Mental health services for youths in foster care and disabled youths. *Am. J. Pub. Health, 91,* 1094–99.

Doss, B. D., Benson, L. A., Georgia, E. J., & Christensen, A. (2013). Translation of integrative behavioral couple therapy to a web-based intervention. *Family Process, 52,* 139–53.

Doss, B. D., Simpson, L. E., & Christensen, A. (2004). Why do couples seek marital therapy? *Professional Psychology: Research and Practice, 35,* 608–14.

Dougherty, D. D., Baer, L., Cosgrove, G. R., Cassem, E. H., Price, B. H., Nierenberg, A. A., et al. (2002). Prospective long-term follow-up of 44 patients who received cingulotomy for treatment-refractory obsessive-compulsive disorder. *Am. J. Psychiat., 159*(2), 269–75.

Dougherty, D. D., Rauch, S. L., & Jenike, M. A. (2002). Pharmacological treatments for obsessive compulsive disorder. In P. E. Nathan & J. M. Gorman (Eds.), *A guide to treatments that work* (2nd ed., pp. 387–410). New York: Oxford University Press.

Dougherty, D. D., Rausch, S. L., & Jenike, M. A. (2007). Pharmacological treatments for obsessive-compulsive disorder. In P. E. Nathan & J. M. Gorman (Eds.), *A guide to treatments that work* (pp. 447–74). New York: Oxford University Press.

Dougherty, L. R., Klein, D. N., & Davila, J. (2004). A growth curve analysis of the course of dysthymic disorder: The effects of chronic stress and moderation by adverse parent-child relationships and family history. *J. Consult. Clin. Psychol., 72*(6), 1012–21.

Douglas, K. R., Chan, G., Gelernter, J., Arias, A. J., Anton, R. F., Weiss, R. D., et al. (2010). Adverse childhood events as risk factors for substance dependence: Partial mediation by mood and anxiety disorders. *Addict. Behav., 35*(1), 7–13.

Douglas, K. S., Vincent, G. M., & Edens, J. F. (2006). Risk for criminal recidivism: The role of psychopathy. In C. J. Patrick (Ed.), *Handbook of the psychopathy* (pp. 533–54). New York: Guilford Press.

Dowlati, Y., Herrmann, N., Swardfager, W., Liu, H., Sham, L., Reim, E. K., et al. (2010). A meta-analysis of cytokines in major depression. *Biol. Psychiat., 67*(5), 446–57. doi:10.1016/j.biopsych.2009.09.033

Dozois, D. J. A., & Dobson, K. S. (Eds.). (2004). *The prevention of anxiety and depression: Theory, research, and practice.* Washington, DC: American Psychological Association.

Draguns, J. G. (2001). Toward a truly international psychology: Beyond English only. *Am. Psychol., 56,* 1019–30.

Draguns, J. G., & Tanaka-Matsumi, J. (2003). Assessment of psychopathology across and within cultures: Issues and findings. *Behav. Res. Ther., 41,* 755–76.

Dreger, A. D. (2008). The controversy surrounding The Man Who Would Be Queen: A case history of the politics of science, identity, and sex in the Internet age. *Arch. Sexual Behavior, 37*(3), 366–421.

Drogin, E. Y., Dattilio, F. M., Sadoff, R. L., & Gutheil, T. G. (2011). *Handbook of forensic assessment: Psychological and psychiatric perspectives.* Hoboken, NJ: Wiley.

Drtikova, I., Balastikova, B., Lemanova, H., & Zak, J. (1996). Clonazepam, clonidine and tiapride in children with tic disorder. *Homeostasis in Health & Disease, 37*(5), 216.

Drug Enforcement Administration, U.S. Department of Justice. (1979). *Controlled substance inventory list.* Washington, DC: Author.

Drummond, K. D., Bradley, S. J., Peterson-Badali, M., & Zucker, K. J. (2008). A follow-up study of girls with gender identity disorder. *Develop. Psych., 44*(1), 34–45.

Druss, B. G. (2010). The changing face of U.S. mental health care. *Am. J. Psychiatry, 167,* 1419–21.

D'Souza, D. C., Abi-Saab, W. M., Madonick, S., Forse-lius-Bielen, K., Doersch, A., Braley, G., et al. (2005). Delta-9-tetrahydrocannabinol effects in schizophrenia: Implications for cognition, psychosis, and addiction. *Biol. Psychiat., 57,* 594–608.

Du Rocher Schudlich, T. D., Shamir, H., & Cummings, E. M. (2004). Marital conflict, children's representations of family relationships, and children's dispositions towards peer conflict strategies. *Soc. Develop., 13,* 171–92.

Dubner, A. E., & Motta, R. W. (1999). Sexually and physically abused foster care children and post-traumatic stress disorder. *J. Consult. Clin. Psychol., 67,* 367–73.

Dugas, M. J., Buhr, K., & Ladouceur, R. (2004). The role of intolerance of uncertainty in etiology and maintenance. In R. G. Heimberg, C. L. Turk, & D. S. Mennin (Eds.), *Generalized anxiety disorder: Advances in research and practice* (pp. 143–63). New York: Guilford Press.

Dugas, M. J., Marchand, A., & Ladouceur, R. (2005). Further validation of a cognitive-behavioral model of generalized anxiety disorder: Diagnostic and symptom specificity. *J. Anxiety Dis., 19*(3), 329–43.

Dugas, M. J., Savard, P., Gaudet, A., Turcotte, J., Laugesen, N., Robichaud, M., et al. (2007). Can the components of a cognitive model predict the severity of generalized anxiety disorder? *Behav. Ther., 38*(2), 169–78.

Duinkerke, A., Williams, M. A., Rigamonti, D., & Hillis, A. E. (2004). Cognitive recovery in idiopathic normal pressure hydrocephalus after shunt. *Cog. Behav. Neurol., 17*(3), 179–84.

Dunai, J., Labuschagne, I., Castle, D. J., Kyrios, M., & Rossell, S. L. (2010). Executive function in body dysmorphic disorder. *Psychological Medicine, 40,* 1541–48.

Dunmore, E., Clark, D. M., & Ehlers, A. (2001). A prospective investigation of the role of persistent posttraumatic stress disorder (PTSD) after physical and sexual assault. *Behav. Res. Ther., 39,* 1063–84.

Dunne, E. J. (1992). Following a suicide: Postvention. In B. Bongar (Ed.), *Suicide: Guidelines for assessment, management and treatment.* New York: Oxford University Press.

DuPaul, G. J., Stoner, G., et al. (1998). *Classroom interventions for ADHD.* New York: Guilford Press.

Durbin, C. E., Klein, D. N., Hayden, E. P., Buckley, M. E., & Moerk, K. C. (2005). Temperamental emotionality in preschoolers and parental mood disorders. *J. Abn. Psych., 114*(1), 28–37.

Durkin, K. (2010). Videogames and young people with developmental disorders. *Rev. Gen. Psychol., 14*(2), 122–40.

Duterte, E., Segraves, T., & Althof, S. (2007). Psychotherapy and pharmacotherapy for sexual dysfunctions. In P. E. Nathan & J. M. Gorman (Eds.), *A guide to treatments that work* (3rd ed., pp. 531–60). New York: Oxford University Press.

Dutra, L., et al. (2008). A meta-analytic review of psychosocial interventions for substance abuse disorders. *Am. J. Psychiatry, 165,* 179–87.

Dutta, R., Murray, R. M., Hotopf, M., Allardyce, J., Jones, P. B., & Boydell, J. (2010). Reassessing the long-term risk of suicide after a first episode of psychosis. *Arch. Gen. Psychiat., 67,* 1230–37.

Duyme, M., Arseneault, L., & Dumaret, A.-C. (2004). Environmental influences on intellectual abilities in childhood: Findings from a longitudinal adoption study. In *Human development across lives and generations: The potential for change* (pp. 278–92). New York: Cambridge University Press.

Dworkin, R. H., Lewis, J. A., Cornblatt, B. A., & Erlenmeyer-Kimling, L. (1994). Social competence deficits in adolescents at risk for schizophrenia. *J. Nerv. Ment. Dis., 182*(2), 103–08.

d'Ydewalle, G., & Van Damme, I. (2007). Memory and the Korsakoff syndrome: Not remembering what is remembered. *Neuropsychologia, 45*(5), 905–20.

Dyer, C. A. (1999). Pathophysiology of phenylketon-uria. *Ment. Retard. Dev. Dis. Res. Rev., 5,* 104–12.

E

Eagly, A. H., & Carli, L. L. (2007). *Through the labyrinth: The truth about how women become leaders.* Boston: Harvard Business School Press.

Eagly, A. H., & Karau, S. J. (2002). Role congruity theory of prejudice toward female leaders. *Psychol. Rev., 109,* 573–98.

Earleywine, M. (2002). *Understanding marijuana.* New York: Oxford University Press.

Earleywine, M., & Finn, P. R. (1990, March). *Personality, drinking habits, and responses to cues for alcohol.* Paper presented at the 5th Congress of the International Society for Biomedical Research on Alcoholism and the Research Society on Alcoholism, Toronto, Canada.

Eaton, N. R., Krueger, R. F., Keyes, K. M., Skodol, A. E., Markon, K. E., Grant, B. F., et al. (2011). Borderline personality disorder co-morbidity: Relationship to the internalizing-externalizing structure of common mental disorders. *Psychol. Med., 41*(5), 1041–50. doi:10.1017/S0033291710001662

Eaton, W. W., Kessler, R. C., Wittchen, H. U., & Magee, W. J. (1994). Panic and panic disorder in the United States. *Am. J. Psychiat., 151*(3), 413–20.

Eaton, W. W., Pedersen, M. G., Nielsen, P. R., & Mortensen, P. B. (2010). Autoimmune diseases, bipolar disorder and non-affective psychosis. *Bipolar Disorders, 12,* 638–46.

Ebigbo, P. O. (1982). Development of a culture specific (Nigeria) screening scale of somatic complaints indicating psychiatric disturbance. *Cult. Med. Psychiatr., 6,* 29–43.

Eckblad, M., & Chapman, L. J. (1983). Magical ideation as an indicator of schizotypy. *J. Consulting and Clinical Psychology, 51,* 215–25.

Eckhardt, C. I. (2007). Effects of alcohol intoxication on anger experience and expression among partner assaultive men. *J. Consult. Clin. Psychol., 75,* 61–71.

Eddy, K. T., Dorer, K. T., Franko, D. L., Tahilani, K., Thompson-Brenner, H., & Herzog, D. B. (2008). Diagnostic cross over in anorexia nervosa and bulimia nervosa: Implications for DSM-V. *Am. J. Psychiat., 165,* 245–50.

Eddy, K. T., Doyle, A. C., Hoste, R. R., Herzog, B. B., & le Grange, D. (2008). Eating disorder not otherwise specified in adolescents. *J. Amer. Acad. Child Adoles. Psychiat., 47*(2), 156–64.

Edens, J. F., Buffington-Vollum, J. K., Keilen, A., Roskamp, P., & Anthony, C. (2005). Predictions of future dangerousness in capital murder trials: Is it time to "disinvent the wheel"? *Law & Human Behavior, 29*(1), 55–86.

Edwards, L. Y., & Edwards, C. L. (2010). Psychosocial treatments in pain management of sickle cell disease. *J. National Medical Association, 102*(11), 1084–94.

Egeland, B., & Sroufe, L. A. (1981). Attachment and early maltreatment. *Child Develop., 52,* 44–52.

Egger, H. L., Costello, E. J., & Angold, A. (2003). School refusal and psychiatric disorders: A community study. *J. Am. Acad. Child Adoles. Psychiat., 42*(7), 797–807.

Egley, A., Howell, J. C., & Moore, P. (2010). *Highlights of the 2008 National Youth Gang Survey* (Fact Sheet NCJ 229249). Washington, DC: U.S. Department of Justice.

Egliston, K.-A., & Rapee, R. M. (2007). Inhibition of fear acquisition in toddlers following positive modelling by their mothers. *Behav. Res. Ther., 45*(8), 1871–82.

Ehlers, A., & Clark, D. M. (2008). Post-traumatic stress disorder: The development of effective psychological treatments. *Nordic J. Psychiatry, 62,* S47, 11–18.

Ehlers, A., Clark, D. M., Hackman, A., McManus, F., & Fennell, M. (2005). Cognitive therapy for post-traumatic stress disorder: Development and evaluation. *Behav. Res. Ther., 43,* 413–31.

Eisen, J. L., Phillips, K. A., Coles, M. E., & Rasmussen, S. A. (2003). Insight in obsessive compulsive disorder and body dysmorphic disorder. *Compr. Psychiatry, 45*(1), 10–15.

Eisenberger, N. J., Lieberman, M. D., & Williams, K. D. (2003). Does rejection hurt? An fMRI study of social exclusion. *Science, 302,* 290–92.

El-Bassel, N., Simoni, J. M., Cooper, D. K., Gilbert, L., & Schilling, R. F. (2001). Sex trading and psychological distress among women on methadone. *Psych. Addict. Behav., 15,* 177–84.

El-Hai, J. (2005). *The lobotomist: A maverick genius and his tragic quest to rid the world of mental illness.* New York: John Wiley & Sons.

El Khoury, M. A., Gorgievski, V., Moutsimilli, L., Giros, B., & Tzavara, E. T. (2012). Interactions between the cannabinoid and dopaminergic systems: Evidence from animal studies. *Progress in Neuro-Psychopharmacology and Biological Psychiatry, 2,* 36–50.

Eldaief, M. C., Press, D. Z., & Pascual-Leone, A. (2013). Transcranial magnetic stimulation in neurology. *Neurology: Clinical Practice, 3,* 519–26.

Ellason, J. W., & Ross, C. A. (1997). Two-year follow-up of inpatients with dissociative disorder. *Am. J. Psychiatry, 154,* 832–39.

Elliott, A. N., Alexander, A. A., Pierce, T. W., Aspelmeier, J. E., & Richmond, J. M. (2009). Childhood victimization, poly-victimization, and adjustment to college in women. *Child Maltreat., 14*(4), 330–43.

Elliot, R., Greenberg, L. S., & Lietaer, G. (2004). Research on experiential psychotherapies. In M. J. Lambert (Ed.), *Bergin and Garfield's handbook of psychotherapy and behavior change* (pp. 493–539). New York: John Wiley & Sons.

Ellis, A. (1989). The history of cognition in psychotherapy. In A. Freeman, K. M. Simon, L. E. Beutler, & H. Arkowitz (Eds.), *Comprehensive handbook of cognitive therapy* (pp. 5–19). New York: Plenum.

Ellis, A., & Dryden, W. (1997). *The practice of rational emotive behavior therapy* (2nd ed.). New York: Springer.

Ellis, B. H., Fisher, P. A., & Zaharie, S. (2004). Predictors of disruptive behavior, developmental delays, anxiety, and affective symptomology among institutionally reared Romanian children. *J. Am. Acad. Child Adoles. Psychiatry, 43*(10), 1283–92.

Else-Quest, N. M., Hyde, J. S., Goldsmith, H. H., & Van Hulle, C. A. (2006). Gender differences in temperament: A meta-analysis. *Psychol. Bull., 132*(1), 33–72.

Embury, J. E., Charron, C. E., Martynyuk, A., Zori, A. G., Liu, B., Ali, S. F., et al. (2007). PKU is a reversible neurodegenerative process within the nigrostriatum that begins as early as 4 weeks of age in Pah-super(enu2) mice. *Brain Res., 1127*(1), 136–50.

Emerson, E. (2004). Deinstitutionalisation in England. *J. Intell Dev. Dis., 29*(1), 79–84.

Emery, R. E., & Laumann-Billings, L. (1998). An overview of the nature, causes, and consequences of abusive relationships: Toward differentiating maltreatment and violence. *Am. Psychol., 53*(2), 121–35.

Emmelkamp, P. M. G. (1994). Behavior therapy with adults. In A. E. Bergin & S. L. Garfield (Eds.), *Handbook of psychotherapy and behavior change* (4th ed., pp. 379–427). New York: Wiley.

Emmelkamp, P. M. G. (2004). Behavior therapy with adults. In M. J. Lambert (Ed.), *Bergin and Garfield's handbook of psychotherapy and behavior change* (pp. 393–446). New York: John Wiley & Sons.

Emmelkamp, P. M. G., & Wessels, H. (1975). Flooding in imagination vs. flooding in vivo: A comparison with agoraphobics. *Behav. Res. Ther., 13*(1), 7–15.

Emmers-Sommer, T. M., Allen, M., Bourhis, J., Sahlstein, E., Laskowski, K., Falato, W. L., et al. (2004). A meta-analysis of the relationship between social skills and sexual offenders. *Commun. Rep., 17,* 1–10.

Emslie, G. J., Croarkin, P., & Mayes, T. L. (2010). Antidepressants. In M. K. Dulcan (Ed.), *Dulcan's textbook of child and adolescent psychiatry* (pp. 701–23). Arlington, VA: American Psychiatric Publishing.

Engel, S. G., Wonderlich, S. A., Crosby, R. D., Mitchell, J. E., Crow, S., Peterson, C. B., et al. (2013). The role of affect in the maintenance of anorexia nervosa: Evidence from a naturalistic assessment on momentary behaviors and emotion. *J. Abn. Psychol., 122,* 709–19.

Engelhard, I. M., Van Den Hout, M. A., Weerts, J., Arntz, A., Hox, J. C. M., & McNally, R. J. (2007). Deployment-related stress and trauma in Dutch soldiers returning from Iraq. *Brit. J. Psychiatry, 191,* 140–45.

Engelhardt, C. R., Mazurek, M. O., & Sohl, K. (2013). Media use and sleep among boys with autism spectrum disorder, ADHD, or typical development. *Pediatrics, 132*(6), 1081–88. doi:10.1542/peds.2013-2066

Epel, E. S., Blackburn, E. H., Lin, J., Dhabhar, F. S., Adler, N. E., Morrow, J. D., & Cawthon, R. M. (2004). Accelerated telomere shortening in response to life stress. *Proc. Natl. Acad. Sci. USA, 101,* 17312–15.

Epstein, J., & Klinkenberg, W. D. (2001). From Eliza to Internet: A brief history of computerized assessment. *Comput. Human Behav., 17,* 295–314.

Erblich, J., Earleywine, M., & Erblich, B. (2001). Positive and negative associations with alcohol and familial risk for alcoholism. *Psych. Addict. Behav., 15*(3), 204–09.

Erikson, K. I., Raji, C. A., Lopez, O. L., Becker, J. T., Rosano, C., Newman, A. B., et al. (2010). Physical activity predicts gray matter volume in late adulthood. *Neurol., 75,* 1415–22.

Erikson, K. I., Voss, M. W., Prakash, R. S., Basak, C., Szabo, A., Chaddock, L., et al. (2011). Exercise training increases size of hippocampus and improves memory. *PNAS, 108,* 3017–22.

Eriksson, M., Glader, E-L., Norrving, B., & Asplund, K. (2015). Poststroke suicide attempts and completed suicides. *Neurology, 84,* 1732–38.

Erlenmeyer-Kimling, L., & Cornblatt, B. A. (1992). A summary of attentional findings in the New York High-Risk Project. *J. Psychiatr. Res., 26,* 405–26.

Erlenmeyer-Kimling, L., Roberts, S. A., Rock, D., Adamo, U. H., Shapiro, B. M., & Pape, S. (1998). Prediction from longitudinal assessments of high-risk children. In M. F. Lenzenweger & R. H. Dworkin (Eds.), *Origins and development of schizophrenia.* Washington, DC: American Psychological Association.

Eronen, M., Hakola, P., & Tiihonen, J. (1996). Mental disorders and homicidal behavior in Finland. *Arch. Gen. Psychiatry, 53*(6), 497–501.

Ershler, W. B., & Keller, E. T. (2000). Age-associated increased interleukin-6 gene expression, late-life diseases, and frailty. *Annu. Rev. Medicine, 51,* 245–70.

Eskridge, W. N. (2008). *Dishonorable passions: Sodomy laws in America 1861–2003.* New York: Viking Press.

ESPAD. (2000). *The 1999 ESPAD Report: Alcohol and other drug use among students in 30 European countries.* Stockholm, Sweden: European School Survey Project on Alcohol and Other Drugs.

Essau, C. A., Lewinsohn, P. M., Seeley, J. R., & Sasagawa, S. (2010). Gender differences in the developmental course of depression. *J. Affective Disorders, 127,* 185–90.

Esterberg, M. L., Goulding, S. M., & Walker, E. F. (2010). Cluster A personality disorders: Schizotypal, schizoid and paranoid personality disorders in childhood and adolescence. *J. Psychopath. Behav. Assess., 32*(4), 515–28. doi:10.1007/s10862-010-9183-8

Estruch, R., Bono, G., Laine, P., Antunez, E., Petrucci, A., Morocutti, C., et al. (1998). Brain imaging in alcoholism. *Eur. J. Neurol., 5*(2), 119–35.

Etkin, A. (2010). Functional neuroanatomy of anxiety: A neural circuit perspective. *Behavioral neurobiology of anxiety and its treatment.* New York: Springer.

Evans, D. W., King, R. A., & Leckman, J. F. (1996). Tic disorders. In E. J. Mash & R. A. Barkley (Eds.), *Child psychopathology* (pp. 436–56). New York: Guilford Press.

Evans, D. W., Lewis, M. D., & Iobst, E. (2004). The role of the orbitofrontal cortex in normally developing compulsive like behaviors and obsessive compulsive disorder. *Brain & Cognition, 55*(1), 220–34.

Evans, E., Hawton, K., & Rodham, K. (2004). Factors associated with suicidal phenomena in adolescents: A systematic review of population-based studies. *Clin. Psychol. Rev., 24,* 957–79.

Evans, G., & Stecker, R. (2004). Motivational consequences of environmental stress. *J. Environ. Psych., 24*(2), 143–65.

Evans, S. A., & Salekin, K. L. (2014). Involuntary civil commitment: Communicating with the court regarding "danger to other." *Law and Human Behavior, 38*(4), 325–36. doi:10.1037/lhb0000068

Everett, C. A., & Everett, S. V. (2001). *Family therapy for ADHD.* New York: Guilford Press.

Evers, A. W. M., Kraaimaat, F. W., van Riel, P. L. C. M., & De Jong, A. J. L. (2002). Tailored cognitive-behavioral therapy in early rheumatoid arthritis for patients at risk: A randomized controlled trial. *Pain, 100,* 141–53.

Ewing v. Goldstein. (2004). Cal. App. 4th (No. B163112. Second Dist., Div. Eight. July 16, 2004).

Exline, J. J., Baumeister, R. F., Bushman, B. J., Campbell, W. K., & Finkel, E. J. (2004). Too proud to let go: Narcissistic entitlement as a barrier to forgiveness. *J. Pers. Soc. Psych., 87*(6), 894–912.

Exner, J. E. (1987). Computer assistance in Rorschach interpretation. In J. N. Butcher (Ed.), *Computerized psychological assessment: A practitioner's guide.* New York: Basic Books.

Exner, J. E. (1995). Why use personality tests? A brief historical view. In J. N. Butcher (Ed.), *Clinical personality assessment: Practical considerations* (10th ed., pp. 10–18). New York: Oxford University Press.

Exner, J. E., Jr., & Erdberg, P. (2002). Why use personality tests? A brief history and some comments. In J. N. Butcher (Ed.), *Clinical personality assessment: Practical approaches* (2nd ed., pp. 7–12). London: Oxford University Press.

Eysenck, M. W., Mogg, K., May, J., Richards, A., & Mathews, A. (1991). Bias in interpretation of ambiguous sentences related to threat in anxiety. *J. Abn. Psychol., 100,* 144–50.

F

Fabrega, H., Jr. (2001). Culture and history in psychiatric diagnosis and practice. *Cultural Psychiatry: International Perspectives, 24,* 391–405.

Fabricatore, A. N., & Wadden, T. A. (2006). Obesity. *Annu. Rev. Clin. Psych., 2*, 357–77.

Fagundes, C. P., Glaser, R., & Kiecolt-Glaser, J. K. (2013). Stressful early life experiences and immune dysregulation across the lifespan. *Brain, Behavior, and Immunity, 27*, 8–12.

Faigel, H., & Heiligenstein, E. (1996). Medication for attention deficit hyperactivity disorder: Commentary and response. *J. Am. Coll. Health, 45*, 40–42.

Fairburn, C. G. (1995). *Overcoming binge eating*. New York: Guilford Press.

Fairburn, C. G., Bailey-Straebler, S., Basden, S., Doll, H. A., Jones, R., Murphy, R., et al. (2015). A transdiagnostic comparison of enhanced cognitive behavior therapy (CBT-E) and interpersonal psychotherapy in the treatment of eating disorders. *Behavior Research and Therapy, 70*, 64–71.

Fairburn, C. G., & Bohn, K. (2005). Eating disorder NOS (EDNOS): An example of the troublesome "not otherwise specified" (NOS) category in DSM-IV. *Behav. Res. Ther., 43*, 691–701.

Fairburn, C. G., Cooper, Z., Bohn, K., O'Connor, M. E., Doll, H. A., & Palmer, R. L. (2007). The severity and status of eating disorder NOS: Implications for DSM-V. *Behav. Res. Ther., 45*, 1705–15.

Fairburn, C. G., Cooper, Z., Doll, H. A., O'Connor, M. E., Bohn, K., Hawker, D. M., et al. (2009). Trans-diagnostic cognitive-behavioral therapy for patients with eating disorders: A two-site trial with a 60 week follow-up. *Am. J. Psychiatry, 166*, 311–19.

Fairburn, C. G., Cooper, Z., Shafran, R., & Wilson, G. T. (2008). Eating disorders: A transdiagnostic protocol. In D. H. Barlow (Ed.), *Clinical handbook of psychological disorders* (4th ed., pp. 578–614). New York: Guilford Press.

Fairburn, C. G., & Harrison, P. J. (2003, February). Eating disorders. *Lancet, 361*, 407–16.

Fairburn, C. G., Jones, R., Peveler, R. C., Hope, R. A., & O'Connor, M. (1993). Psychotherapy and bulimia nervosa: Long-term effects of interpersonal psychotherapy, behavior therapy, and cognitive behavior therapy. *Arch. Gen. Psychiatry, 50*(6), 419–28.

Fairburn, C. G., Welch, S. L., Doll, H. A., Davies, B. A., & O'Connor, M. E. (1997). Risk factors for bulimia nervosa: A community-based case-control study. *Arch. Gen. Psychiatry, 54*(6), 509–17.

Fairweather, G. W. (1994). *Keeping the balance: A psychologist's story*. Austin, TX: Fairweather Publishing.

Fales, C. L., Barch, D. M., Rundle, M. M., Mintun, M. A., Mathews, J., Snyder, A. Z., & Sheline, Y. I. (2009). Antidepressant treatment normalizes hypoactivity in dorsolateral prefrontal cortex during emotional interference processing in major depression. *J. Affective Disorders, 112*, 206–11.

Fallon, A. E., & Rozin, P. (1985). Sex differences in perceptions of desirable body shape. *J. Abn. Psychol., 94*, 102–05.

Falloon, I. R. H., Boyd, J. L., McGill, C. W., Williamson, M., & Razani, J. (1985). Family management in the prevention of morbidity of schizophrenia: Clinical outcome of a two-year longitudinal study. *Arch. Gen. Psychiatry., 42*, 887–96.

Fals-Stewart, W., & Lam, W. K. K. (2010). Computer-assisted cognitive rehabilitation for the treatment of patients with substance use disorders: A randomized clinical trial. *Exper. Clin. Psychopharmacol., 18*(1), 87–98.

Fanselow, M. S., & Ponnusamy, R. (2008). The use of conditioning tasks to model fear and anxiety. In R. J. Blanchard, D. C. Blanchard, G. Griebel, & D. Nutt (Eds.), *Handbook of anxiety and fear* (pp. 29–48). San Diego, CA: Elsevier Academic Press.

Faraone, S. V., Biederman, J., Lehman, B. F., Spencer, T., Norman, T., Seidman, L. J., et al. (1993). Intellectual performance and school failure in children with attention deficit hyperactivity disorder and in their siblings. *J. Abn. Psychol., 102*, 616–23.

Farkas, M. A., & Stichman, A. (2002). Sex offender laws: Can treatment, punishment, incapacitation, and public safety be reconciled? *Crim. Just. Rev., 27*(2), 256–83.

Farmer, A., Eley, T. C., & McGuffin, P. (2005). Current strategies for investigating the genetic and environmental risk factors for affective disorders. *Brit. J. Psychiatry, 186*(3), 179–81.

Farooqi, I. S., Matarese, G., Lord, G. M., Keogh, J. M., Lawrence, E., Agwu, C., et al. (2002). Beneficial effects of leptin on obesity, T cell hyporesponsiveness, and neuroendocrine/metabolic dysfunction of human congenital leptin deficiency. *J. Clinical Investigation, 110*, 1093–103.

Farrington, D. P. (2006). Family background and psychopathy. In C. J. Patrick (Ed.), *Handbook of the psychopathy* (pp. 229–50). New York: Guilford Press.

Farronato, N. S., Dursteler-MacFarland, K. M., Wiesbeck, G. A., & Petitjean, S. A. (2013). A systematic review comparing cognitive-behavioral therapy and contingency management for cocaine dependence. *J. Addictive Diseases, 32*, 274–87.

Faul, M., Xu, L., Wald, M. M., & Coronado, V. G. (2010). *Traumatic brain injury in the United States: Emergency department visits, hospitalizations, and deaths*. Atlanta, GA: Centers for Disease Control and Prevention, National Center for Injury Prevention and Control.

Fava, M. (1997). Psychopharmacologic treatment of pathologic anger. *Psychiatr. Clin. North Am., 20*, 427–52.

Fava, M., & Rosenbaum, J. F. (1995). Pharmacotherapy and somatic therapies. In E. E. Beckham & W. R. Leber (Eds.), *Handbook of depression* (2nd ed., pp. 280–301). New York: Guilford Press.

Fawcett, J. (2004). Is BDD culturally induced? *Psychiatr. Ann., 34*(12), 900.

Feczer, D., & Bjorklund, P. (2009). Forever changed: Posttraumatic stress disorder in female military veterans, a case report. *Perspectives in Psychiatric Care, 45*, 278–91.

Fedoroff, J. P., Fishell, A., & Federoff, B. (1999). A case series of women evaluated for paraphilic sexual disorders. *Canadian J. Human Sexuality, 8*, 127–40.

Fedoroff, P. (2009). Review of *Principles and practice of sex therapy*, 4th ed. *Canadian J. Psychiatry/La Revue Canadienne de Psychiatrie, 54*(2), 135–36.

Feeney, L., Kelly, B. D., Whitty, P., & O'Callaghan, E. (2002). Mental illness in migrants: Diagnostic and therapeutic challenges. *Irish J. Psychiatric Medicine, 19*(1), 29–31.

Feinstein, A. (2011). Conversion disorder: advances in our understanding. *Canadian Medical Assoc. J., 183*, 915–20.

Feldman, M. B., & Meyer, I. H. (2007). Eating disorders in diverse lesbian, gay, and bisexual populations. *Int. J. Eat. Dis., 40*, 218–26.

Felsman, J. K., & Valliant, G. E. (1987). Resilient children as adults: A 40-year study. In E. J. Anthony & B. J. Cohler (Eds.), *The invulnerable child* (pp. 289–314). New York: Guilford Press.

Fennell, M. J. V. (1989). Depression. In K. Hawton, P. M. Salkovskis, J. Kirk, & D. M. Clark (Eds.), *Cognitive behaviour therapy for psychiatric problems: A practical guide*. Oxford, UK: Oxford University Press.

Fenton, W. S., McGlashan, T. H., Victor, B. J., & Blyler, C. R. (1997). Symptoms, subtype, and suicidality in patients with schizophrenia spectrum disorders. *Am. J. Psychiatry, 154*(2), 199–204.

Fentress et al. v. Shea Communications et al. (1990). Jefferson Circuit Court, No 90-CI-06033.

Fergusson, D. M., Horwood, L. J., & Swain-Campbell, N. R. (2003). Cannabis dependence and psychotic symptoms in young people. *Psychol. Med., 33*, 15–22.

Fernald, P. S., & Fernald, L. D. (2010). The Sentence Completion Test: Assessing personality. In L. T. Benjamin, Jr. (Ed.), *Favorite activities for the teaching of psychology* (pp. 196–200). Washington, DC: American Psychological Association.

Fernandez, F., Ringholz, G. M., & Levy, J. K. (2002). Neuropsychiatric aspects of human immunodeficiency virus infection of the central nervous system. In S. Yudofsky & R. E. Hales (Eds.), *The American Psychiatric Association Publishing textbook of neuropsychiatry and clinical sciences* (4th ed., pp. 783–812). Washington, DC: American Psychiatric Publishing.

Ferri, C. P., Prince, M., Brayne, C., Brodaty, H., Fratiglioni, L., Ganguli, M., et al. (2005). Global prevalence of dementia: A Delphi consensus study. *Lancet, 366*, 2112–17.

Ferri, M., Amato, L., & Davoli, M. (2006). Alcoholics Anonymous and other 12-step programmes for alcohol dependence. *Cochrane Database Syst. Rev., 19*, CD005032.

Ferster, C. B. (1974). Behavioral approaches to depression. In R. J. Friedman & M. M. Katz (Eds.), *The psychology of depression: Contemporary theory and research*. Washington, DC: Hemisphere.

Feusner, J. D., Moody, T., Hembacher, E., Townsend, J., McKinley, M, Moller, H., & Bookheimer, S. (2010). Abnormalities of visual processing and frontostriatal systems in body dysmorphic disorder. *Arch. General Psychiatry, 67*, 197–205.

Feusner, J. D., Townsend, J., Bystritsky, A., & Bookheimer, S. (2007). Visual information processing of faces in body dysmorphic disorder. *Arch. Gen. Psychiatry, 64*(12), 1417–26.

Few, L. R., Miller, J. D., Grant, J. D., Maples, J., Trull, T. J., Nelson, E. C., et al. (2015, May 18). Trait-based assessment of borderline personality disorder using the NEO Five-Factor Inventory: Phenotypic and genetic support. *Psychological Assessment* [Epub ahead of print].

Fichter, M. M., & Quadflieg, N. (2007). Long-term stability of eating disorder diagnoses. *Int. J. Eat. Dis., 40*, S61–S66.

Field, T., Hernandez-Reif, M., & Diego, M. (2006). Intrusive and withdrawn depressed mothers and their infants. *Developmental Review, 26*, 15–30.

Fields, J. Z., Turk, A., Durkin, M., Ravi, N. V., & Keshavarzian, A. (1994). Increased gastrointestinal symptoms in chronic alcoholics. *Am. J. Gastroenterology, 89*, 382–86.

Finger, S., & Zaromb, F. (2006). Benjamin Franklin and shock-induced amnesia. *Am. Psychol., 61*, 240–48.

Fink, M. (2003). A beautiful mind and insulin coma: Social constraints on psychiatric diagnosis and treatment. *Harv. Rev. Psychiatry, 11*, 284–90.

Fink, M., & Taylor, M. A. (2006). Catatonia: Subtype in DSM. *Am. J. Psychiatry, 163*(11), 1875–76.

Fink, P., Ørnbøl, E., & Christensen, K. S. (2010). The outcome of health anxiety in primary care. A two-year follow-up study on health care costs and self-rated health. *PLoS ONE, 5*(3), e9873. doi:10.1371/journal.pone.0009873

Fink, P., Ørnbøl, E., Toft, T., Sparle, K. C., Frostholm, L., & Olesen, F. (2004). A new empirically established hypochondriasis diagnosis. *Am. J. Psychiatry, 161*(9), 1680–91.

Finkel, A. M., & Ryan, P. B. (2007). Risk in the workplace: Where analysis began and problems remain unsolved. In M. G. Robson & W. A. Toscano (Eds.), *Risk assessment for environmental health* (pp. 187–237). San Francisco, CA: Jossey-Bass.

Finkenbine, R., & Miele, V. J. (2004). Globus hystericus: A brief review. *Gen. Hosp. Psychiatry, 26*, 78–82.

Finn, J., Garner, M. D., & Wilson, J. (2010, September 29). Volunteer and user evaluation of the National Sexual Assault Online Hotline. *Eval. Program. Plann.* [Epub ahead of print].

Finn, P. R., Sharkansky, E. J., Viken, R., West, T. L., Sandy, J., & Bufferd, S. (1997). Heterogeneity in the families of sons of alcoholics: The impact of familial vulnerability type on offspring characteristics. *J. Abn. Psychol.*, 106(1), 26–36.

Finn, S. E., & Kamphuis, J. H. (2006). Therapeutic assessment with the MMPI-2. In J. N. Butcher (Ed.), *MMPI-2: The practitioner's handbook* (pp. 165–91). Washington, DC: American Psychological Association.

First, M. B. (2005). Desire for amputation of a limb: Paraphilia, psychosis, or a new type of identity disorder. *Psychol. Med.*, 35, 919–28.

First, M. B., & Wakefield, J. C. (2010). Defining mental disorder in DSM-V. *Psychol. Med.*, 40, 1779–82.

Fischer, J. L., Pidcock, B. W., Munsch, J., & Forthun, L. (2005). Parental abusive drinking and sibling role differences. *Al. Treat. Quart.*, 23(1), 79–97.

Fischer, M. (1971). Psychoses in the offspring of schizophrenic monozygotic twins and their normal co-twins. *Brit. J. Psychiatry*, 118, 43–52.

Fischer, M. (1973). Genetic and environmental factors in schizophrenia: A study of schizophrenic twins and their families. *Acta Psychiatr. Scandin.*, Suppl. No. 238.

Fiske, S., & Taylor, S. (1991). *Social cognition* (2nd ed.). New York: McGraw-Hill.

Fleming, S. K., Blasey, C., & Schatzberg, A. F. (2004). Neuropsychological correlates of psychotic features in major depressive disorders: A review and meta-analysis. *J. Psychiatr. Res.*, 38, 27–35.

Fletcher, P. C. (2004). Functional neuroimaging of psychiatric disorders: Exploring hidden behavior. *Psychol. Med.*, 34, 577–81.

Flier, J. S., Underhill, L. H., & Lieber, C. S. (1995). Medical disorders of alcoholism. *N. Engl. J. Med.*, 333(6), 1058–65.

Flint, J., & Munafò, M. (2014, July 24). Genesis of a complex disease. *Nature*, 511, 412–13.

Flor, H., Birbaumer, N., Hermann, C., Ziegler, S., & Patrick, C. J. (2002). Aversive Pavlovian conditioning in psychopaths: Peripheral and central correlates. *Psychophysiology*, 39(4), 505–18.

Flores, B. H., & Schatzberg, A. F. (2006). Psychotic depression. In D. J. Stein & D. J. Kupfer (Eds.), *The American Psychiatric Publishing textbook of mood disorders* (pp. 561–71). Arlington, VA: American Psychiatric Publishing.

Foa, E. B., & Kozak, M. J. (1995). DSM-IV field trial: Obsessive-compulsive disorder. *Am. J. Psychiatry*, 152, 90–96.

Foa, E. B., Liebowitz, M. R., Kozak, M. J., Davies, S., Campeas, R., Franklin, M. E., et al. (2005). Randomized, placebo-controlled trial of exposure and ritual prevention, clomipramine, and their combination in the treatment of obsessive-compulsive disorder. *Am. J. Psychiatry*, 162(1), 151–61.

Foa, E. B., & Rauch, S. A. M. (2004). Cognitive changes during prolonged exposure versus prolonged exposure plus cognitive restructuring in female assault survivors with posttraumatic stress disorder. *J. Cons. Clin. Psychol.*, 72, 879–84.

Fogel, M. F., Schiffman, W., Mumley, D., Tillbrook, C., & Thomas Grisso, T. (2013). Ten-year research update (2001–2010): Evaluations for competence to stand trial (adjudicative competence). *Behav. Sci. Law*, 31, 165–91. doi:10.1002/bsl.2051

Foley, D., Wormley, B., Silberg, J., Maes, H., Hewitt, J., Eaves, L., et al. (2004). Childhood adversity, MAO-A genotype, and risk for conduct disorder. *Arch. Gen. Psychiatry*, 61, 738–44.

Foley, G. M., & Hochman, J. D. (2006). *Mental health in early intervention: Achieving unity in principles and practice*. Baltimore, MD: Brookes Publishing.

Folino, J. O., & Abait, P. E. (2009). Pathological gambling and criminality. *Curr. Opin. Psychiatry*, 22(5), 477–81.

Fombonne, E. (2005). Epidemiological Studies of Pervasive Developmental Disorders. In F. R. Volkmar, P. Rhea, A. Klin, & D. Cohen (Eds.), *Handbook of autism and pervasive developmental disorders, Vol. 1: Diagnosis, development, neurobiology, and behavior* (3rd ed., pp. 42–69). Hoboken, NJ: John Wiley & Sons.

Fonagy, P., & Luyten, P. (2012). Psychodynamic models of personality disorders. In T. A. Widiger (Ed.). *The Oxford handbook of personality disorders* (pp. 345–71). New York: Oxford University Press.

Fontaine, K. R., Redden, D. T., Wang, C., Westfall, A. O., & Allison, D. B. (2003). Years of life lost due to obesity. *JAMA*, 289(2), 187–93.

Forchetti, C. M. (2005). Treating patients with moderate to severe Alzheimer's disease: Implications of recent pharmacologic studies. *Primary Care Companion J. Clinical Psychiatry*, 7, 155–61.

Fournier, J. C., DeRubeis, R. J., Hollon, S. D., Dimidjian, S., Amsterdam, J. D., Shelton, R. C., et al. (2010). Antidepressant drug effects and depression severity: A patient-level meta-analysis. *JAMA*, 303(1), 47–53. doi:10.1001/jama.2009.1943

Fowles, D. C. (2001). Biological variables in psychopathology: A psychobiological perspective. In P. D. Sutker & H. E. Adams (Eds.), *Comprehensive handbook of psychopathology* (3rd ed., pp. 85–104). New York: Kluwer Academic.

Fowles, D. C., & Dindo, L. (2006). A dual-deficit model of psychopathy. In C. J. Patrick (Ed.), *Handbook of the psychopathy* (pp. 14–34). New York: Guilford Press.

Fox, E. R., Young, J. H., Li, Y., Dreisbach, A. W., Keating, B. J., et al. (2011). Association of genetic variation with systolic and diastolic blood pressure among African Americans: The Candidate Gene Association Resource Study. *Human Molecular Genetics*, 20(11), 2273–84. doi:10.1093/hmg. ddr092

Fox, M. J. (2002). *Lucky man*. New York: Hyperion Press.

Fox, S. E., Levitt, P., & Nelson III, C. A. (2010). How the timing and quality of early experiences influence the development of brain architecture. *Child Dev.*, 81(1), 28–40. doi:10.1111/j.1467-8624.2009.01380.x

Fraley, R. C., & Shaver, P. R. (2008). Attachment theory and its place in contemporary personality theory and research. In O. P. John, R. W. Robins, & L. A. Pervin (Eds.), *Handbook of personality: Theory and research* (3rd ed., pp. 518–41). New York: Guilford Press.

Frances, A. (2010a, February 11). Opening Pandora's box: The 19 worst suggestions for DSM5. *Psychiatric Times*, pp. 1–2.

Frances, A. (2010b, August 14). Good grief. *New York Times*.

Frances, A. (2013a). DSM-5 somatic symptom disorder. *J. Nervous and Mental Disease*, 201, 530–31.

Frances, A. (2013b). The new somatic symptom disorder in DSM-5 risks mislabeling many people as mentally ill. *Brit. Med. J.*, 13(346), f1580.

Frances, A., & Chapman, S. (2013). DSM-5 somatic symptom disorder mislabels medical illness as mental disorder. *Austral. NZ J. Psychiatry*, 47, 483–84.

Francis, A. N., Bhojraj, T. S., Prasad, K. M., Kulkami, S., Montrose, D. M., Eack, S. M., et al. (2011). Abnormalities of the corpus callosum in non-psychotic high-risk offspring of schizophrenia patients. *Psychiatry Res. Neuroimag.*, 191, 9–15.

Frances, A., & Widiger, T. (2012). Psychiatric diagnosis: Lessons from the DSM-IV past and cautions for the DSM-5 future. *Annu. Rev. Clinical Psychology*, 8, 109–30.

Frank, E., Kupfer, D. J., Perel, J. M., Cornes, C., Jarett, D. B., Mallinger, A. G., et al. (1990).

Three-year outcomes for maintenance therapies in recurrent depression. *Arch. Gen. Psychiatry*, 47, 1093–99.

Frank, E., Prien, R. F., Jarrett, R. B., Keller, M. B., Kupfer, D. J., Lavori, P. W., et al. (1991). Conceptualization and rationale for consensus definitions of terms in major depressive disorder: Remission, recovery, relapse, and recurrence. *Arch. Gen. Psychiatry*, 48, 851–55.

Frank, R. G., Conti, R. M., & Goldman, H. H. (2005). Mental health policy and psychotropic drugs. *Milbank Quarterly*, 83(2), 271–98.

Frank, R. G., McDaniel, S. H., Bray, J. H., & Heldring, M. (Eds.). (2004). *Primary care psychology*. Washington, DC: American Psychological Association.

Frankenburg, F. R. (1994). History of the development of antipsychotic medications. *Psychiatr. Clin. North Am.*, 17(3), 531–41.

Franklin, M. E., & Foa, E. B. (1998). Cognitive-behavioral treatments for obsessive-compulsive disorder. In P. E. Nathan & J. M. Gorman (Eds.), *A guide to treatments that work* (pp. 339–57). New York: Oxford University Press.

Franklin, M. E., & Foa, E. B. (2002). Cognitive behavioral treatments for obsessive compulsive disorder. In P. E. Nathan & J. M. Gorman (Eds.), *A guide to treatments that work* (2nd ed., pp. 367–86). London: Oxford University Press.

Franklin, M. E., & Foa, E. B. (2007). Cognitive behavioral treatment of obsessive compulsive disorder. In P. E. Nathan & J. M. Gorman (Eds.), *A guide to treatments that work* (pp. 431–46). New York: Oxford University Press.

Franklin, M. E., & Foa, E. B. (2008). Obsessive-compulsive disorder. In D. H. Barlow (Ed.), *Clinical handbook of psychological disorders: A step-by-step treatment manual* (4th ed., pp. 164–215). New York: Guilford Press.

Franko, D. L., & Keel, P. K. (2006). Suicidality in eating disorders: Occurrence, correlates, and clinical implications. *Clin. Psych. Rev.*, 26, 769–82.

Franko, D. L., Keel, P. K., Dorer, D. J., Blais, M. A., Delinsky, S. S., Eddy, K. T., et al. (2004). What predicts suicide attempts in women with eating disorders? *Psychol. Med.*, 34, 843–53.

Frattarolli, J. (2006). Experimental disclosure and its moderators: A meta-analysis. *Psychological Bull.*, 132, 823–65.

Freedman, D., Deicken, R., Kegeles, L. S., Vinogradov, S., Bao, Y., & Brown, A. S. (2011). Maternal-fetal blood incompatibility and neuromorphic anomalies in schizophrenia: Preliminary findings. *Prog. Neuropsychopharmacol Biol. Psychiatry*, 35, 1525–29.

Freeman, A., Freeman, S. M., & Rosenfield, B. (2005). Histrionic personality disorder. In G. O. Gabbard, J. S. Beck, & J. Holmes (Eds.), *Oxford textbook of psychotherapy* (pp. 305–10). New York: Oxford University Press.

Freeman, W. (1959). Psychosurgery. In S. Arieti (Ed.), *American handbook of psychiatry* (Vol. 2, pp. 1521–40). New York: Basic Books.

Freidenfelt, J., & Klinteberg, B. (2007). Exploring adult personality and psychopathy tendencies in former childhood hyperactive delinquent males. *J. Indiv. Diff.*, 28(1), 27–36.

Freud, A. (1946). *The ego and the mechanisms of defence*. Ann Arbor, MI: International Universities Press.

Freud, S. (1909). Analysis of a phobia in a five-year-old boy. *Standard edition* (Vol. 10). London: Hogarth Press (1955). (First German edition 1909.)

Freud, S. (1917). Mourning and melancholia. In W. Gaylin (Ed.), *The meaning of despair: Psychoanalytic contributions to the understanding of depression*. New York: Science House.

Freud, S. (1935). Letter to an American mother. Reprinted in Paul Friedman (1959), Sexual deviations. In S. Arieti (Ed.), *American Handbook of Psychiatry* (Vol. 1, pp. 606–7). New York: Basic Books.

Freund, K., & Seto, M. C. (1998). Preferential rape in the theory of courtship disorder. *Arch. Sex. Behav., 27*, 433–43.

Friborg, O., Martinussen, M., Kaiser, S., Øvergård, K., Martinsen, E. W., Schmierer, & Rosenvinge, J. H. (2014). Personality disorders in eating disorder not otherwise specified and binge eating disorder. *J. Nervous and Mental Disease, 202*, 119–25.

Fricchione, G. L., Nejad, S. H., Esses, J. A., Cummings, T. J., Querques, J., Cassem, N. H., et al. (2008). Postoperative delirium. *Am. J. Psychiatry, 165*, 803–12.

Frick, P. J. (1998). *Conduct disorders and severe antisocial behavior.* New York: Plenum.

Frick, P. J., Cornell, A., Bodin, S., Dane, H., Barry, C., & Loney, B. (2003). Callous-unemotional traits and developmental pathways to severe conduct problems. *Develop. Psychol., 39*, 246–60.

Frick, P. J., & Marsee, M. A. (2006). Psychopathy and developmental pathways to antisocial behavior in youth. In C. J. Patrick (Ed.), *Handbook of the psychopathy* (pp. 353–74). New York: Guilford Press.

Frick, P. J., & Morris, A. S. (2004). Temperament and developmental pathways to conduct problems. *J. Clin. Child. Adol. Psych., 33*, 54–68.

Frick, P. J., & Nigg, J. T. (2012). Current issues in the diagnosis of attention deficit hyperactivity disorder, oppositional defiant disorder, and conduct disorder. *Annu. Rev. Clin. Psychol., 8*, 77–107. doi:10.1146/annurev-clinpsy-032511-143150

Friedlander, L., & Desrocher, M. (2006). Neuroimaging studies of obsessive-compulsive disorder in adults and children. *Clin. Psychol. Rev., 26*(1), 32–49.

Friedman, A. F., Bolinskey, P. K., Levak, R., & Nichols, D. S. (2015). *Psychological assessment with the MMPI-2/RF* (3rd ed.). New York: Routledge/Taylor & Francis.

Friedman, J. M. (2003). A war on obesity, not the obese. *Science, 299*(5608), 856–58.

Friedman, J. M. (2004). Modern science versus the stigma of obesity. *Nature Medicine, 10*(6), 563–69.

Friedman, M., & Rosenman, R. H. (1959). Association of specific overt behavior pattern with blood and cardiovascular findings. *JAMA, 169*, 1286.

Fries, J. (2001, November 14). Mother drowned daughter, 4, in exorcism rite. *New York Times.*

Friesen, M. D., Woodward, L. J., Horwood, L. J., & Fergusson, D. M. (2010). Childhood exposure to sexual abuse and partnership outcomes at age 30. *Psychological Medicine: A J. Research in Psychiatry and the Allied Sciences, 40*(4), 679–88.

Friman, P. C., Resetar, J., & DeRuyk, K. (2008). Encopresis: Biobehavioral treatment. In W. T. O'Donohue & J. E. Fisher (Eds.), *Cognitive behavior therapy: Applying empirically supported techniques in your practice* (2nd ed., pp. 187–96). Hoboken, NJ: John Wiley & Sons.

Frohlich, P. F., & Meston, C. M. (2005). Fluoxetine-induced changes in tactile sensation and sexual functioning among clinically depressed women. *J. Sex & Marital Therapy, 31*, 113–28.

Fromm-Reichmann, F. (1948). Notes on the development of treatment of schizophrenics by psychoanalytic psychotherapy. Reprinted in D. M. Bullard (Ed.), *Psychoanalysis and psychotherapy: Selected papers of Freida Fromm-Reichmann.* Chicago: University of Chicago Press, 1959.

Frone, M. R. (2003). Predictors of overall and on-the-job substance use among young workers. *J. Occup. Health Psych., 8*, 39–54.

Frone, M. R. (2006). Prevalence and distribution of illicit drug use in the workforce and in the workplace: Findings and implications from a U.S. national survey. *J. Appl. Psych., 91*(4), 856–69.

Frueh, B. C., Elhai, J. D., Grubaugh, A. L., Monnier, J., Kashdan, T. B., Sauvageot, J. A., et al. (2005). Documented combat exposure of US veterans seeking treatment for combat-related post-traumatic stress disorder. *Brit. J. Psychiatry, 186*, 467–72.

Fryers, T. (2000). Epidemiology of mental retardation. In M. G. Gelder, J. J. Lopez-Ibor, Jr., & N. Andreason (Eds.), *New Oxford textbook of psychiatry* (pp. 1941–45). New York: Oxford University Press.

Fugelstad, A., Stenbacka, M., Leifman, A., Nylander, M., & Thiblin, I. (2007). Methadone maintenance treatment: The balance between life-saving treatment and fatal poisoning. *Addiction, 102*, 406–12.

Fukutake, T., Mine, S., Yamakami, I., Yamaura, A., & Hattori, T. (2000). Rollercoaster headache and subdural hematoma. *Neurol., 54*, 264.

Fulmer, R. H., & Lapidus, L. B. (1980). A study of professed reasons for beginning and continuing heroin use. *Int. J. Addiction, 15*, 631–45.

Fusar-Poli, P., Bonoldi, I., Yung, A. R., Borgwardt, S., Kempton, M. J., Valmaggia, L., Barale, F., Caverzasi, E., & McGuire, P. (2012). Predicting psychosis: Meta-analysis of transition outcomes in individuals at high clinical risk. *Arch. General Psychiatry, 69*, 220–29.

Fusar-Poli, P., Carpenter, W. T., Woods, S. W., & McGlashan, T. H. (2014). Attenuated psychosis syndrome: Ready for DSM-5.1? *Annu. Rev. Clinical Psychology, 10*, 155–92.

Fusar-Poli, P., & Meyer-Lindberg, A. (2012). Striatal presynaptic dopamine in schizophrenia, Part II: Meta-analysis of [^{18}F^{11}C]-DOPA PET studies. *Schizophrenia Bulletin, 39*, 33–42.

Fusar-Poli, P., Perez, J., Broome, M., Borgwardt, S., Placentino, A., Caverzasi, E., et al. (2007). Neurofunctional correlates of vulnerability to psychosis: A systematic review and meta-analysis. *Neuroscience and Biobehavioral Reviews, 31*, 465–84.

G

Gabbard, G. O. (1994). Inpatient services: The clinician's view. In R. K. Schreter, S. S. Sharfstein, & C. A. Schreter (Eds.), *Allies and adversaries* (pp. 22–30). Washington, DC: American Psychiatric Press.

Gabbard, G. O., Gunderson, J. G., & Fonagy, P. (2002). The place of psychoanalytic treatments within psychiatry. *Arch. Gen. Psychiatry, 59*, 505–10.

Gabbard, G. O., & Kay, J. K. (2001). The fate of integrated treatment: Whatever happened to the bio-psychosocial psychiatrist? *Am. J. Psychiatry, 158*, 1956–63.

Gabriel, R. A. (1987). *No more heroes. Madness and psychiatry in war.* New York: Hill and Wang.

Galanter, M., Hayden, F., Castañeda, R., & Franco, H. (2005). Group therapy, self-help groups, and network therapy. In R. J. Frances, S. I. Miller, & A. H. Mack, Avram (Eds.), *Clinical textbook of addictive disorders* (3rd ed., pp. 502–27). New York: Guilford Publications.

Gallup. (2010). *Gay and lesbian rights.* Retrieved from http://www.gallup.com/poll/1651/gay-lesbian-rights.aspx

Galton, F. (1879). Psychometric experiments. *Brain, 2*, 179–85.

Gan, Y., Gong, Y., Tong, X., Sun, H., Cong, Y., Dong, X., et al. (2014). Depression and the risk of coronary heart disease: A meta-analysis of prospective cohort studies. *BMC Psychiatry, 14*, 371. doi:10.1186/s12888-014-0371-z

Ganzini, L., Nelson, H. D., Lee, M. A., Kraemer, D. F., Schmidt, T. A., & Delorit, M. A. (2001). Oregon physicians' attitudes about and experiences with end-of-life care since passage of the Oregon death with dignity act. *JAMA, 285*(18), 2362–69.

Garakani, A., Hirschowitz, J., & Katz, C. I. (2004). General disaster psychiatry. *Psychiatr. Clin. North Am., 27*, 391–406.

Garb, H. N. (2007). Computer-administered interviews and rating scales. *Psychological Assessment, 19*(1), 4–13.

Garb, H. N., Florio, C. M., & Grove, W. M. (1998). The validity of the Rorschach and the Minnesota Multiphasic Personality Inventory: Results from metaanalyses. *Psychol. Sci., 9*(5), 402–04.

Garber, J., Gallerini, G. M., & Frankel, S. A. (2009). Depression in children. In I. H. Gotlib & C. L. Hammen (Eds.), *Handbook of depression and its treatment* (2nd ed.). New York: Guilford Press.

Garber, J., & Weersing, V. R. (2010). Comorbidity of anxiety and depression in youth: Implications for treatment and prevention. *Clinical Psychology, 17*, 293–306.

Garcia, F. D., & Thibaut, F. (2010). Sexual addictions. *Am. J. Drug Alcohol Abuse, 36*, 254–260.

Gardner, C. D., Kiazand, A., Alhassan, S., Kim, S., Stafford, R. S., Balise, R. R., et al. (2007). Comparison of the Atkins, Zone, Ornish, and LEARN diets for change in weight and related risk factors among overweight pre-menopausal women. *JAMA, 297*, 969–77.

Garlow, S. J., & Nemeroff, C. B. (2003). Neurobiology of depressive disorders. In R. J. Davidson, K. R. Scherer, & H. H. Goldsmith (Eds.), *Handbook of affective sciences* (pp. 1021–43). New York: Oxford Press.

Garner, D. M. (1997). Psychoeducational principles in treatment. In D. M. Garner & P. E. Garfinkel (Eds.), *Handbook of treatment for eating disorders* (pp. 145–77). New York: Guilford Press.

Garner, D. M., & Garfinkel, P. E. (Eds.). (1997). *Handbook of treatment for eating disorders* (2nd ed.). New York: Guilford Press.

Garner, D. M., Vitousek, K. M., & Pike, K. M. (1997). Cognitive-behavioral therapy for anorexia nervosa. In D. M. Garner & P. E. Garfinkel (Eds.), *Handbook of treatment for eating disorders* (pp. 94–144). New York: Guilford Press.

Garratt, G., Ingram, R. E., Rand, K. L., & Sawalani, G. (2007). Cognitive processes in cognitive therapy: Evaluation of the mechanisms of change in the treatment of depression. *Clinical Psychology Science and Practice, 14*, 224–39.

Gass, C. (2009). Use of the MMPI-2 in neuropsychological evaluations. In J. N. Butcher (Ed.), *Oxford handbook of personality and clinical assessment* (pp. 432–56). New York: Oxford University Press.

Gath, A. (2000). Families with a mentally retarded member and their needs. In M. G. Gelder, J. J. Lopez-Ibor, Jr., & N. C. Andreason (Eds.), *New Oxford textbook of psychiatry* (Vol. 2, pp. 2002–05). Oxford, UK: Oxford University Press.

Gatz, M. (2007). Genetics, dementia, and the elderly. *Curr. Dir. Psych. Sci., 16*, 123–27.

Gaugler, T., Klei, L., Sanders, S. J., Bodea, C. A., Goldberg, A. P., Lee, A. B., et al. (2014). Most genetic risk for autism resides with common variation. *Nature Genetics, 46*(8), 881–85.

Gazdzinski, S., Durazzo, T., & Meyerhoff, D. J. (2005). Temporal dynamics and determinants of whole brain tissue volume changes during recovery from alcohol dependence. *Drug Al. Dep., 78*(3), 263–73.

Gearhardt, A., N., Bragg, M. A., Pearl, R. L., Schvey, N. A., Roberto, C. A., & Brownell, K. D. (2012). Obesity and public policy. *Annu. Rev. Clin. Psychol., 8*, 405–30.

Gearhardt, A. N., Grilo, C. M., DiLeone, R. J., Brownell, K. D., & Potenza, M. N. (2011). Can food be addictive? Public health and policy implications. *Addiction, 106*, 1208–12.

Gejman, P. V., Sanders, A. R., & Kendler, K. S. (2011). *Annu. Rev. Genomics Hum. Genet.* Genetics of schizophrenia: New findings and challenges.

Gelehrter, T. F., Collins, F. S., & Ginsburg, D. (Eds.). (1998). Principles of medical genetics. Philadelphia, PA: Lippincott Williams & Wilkins.

Geller, B., & DelBello, M. P. (Eds.). (2008). *Treatment of bipolar disorder in children and adolescents.* New York: Guilford Press.

Geller, B., Tillman, R., Bolhofner, K., & Zimerman, B. (2008). Child bipolar I disorder: Prospective continuity with adult bipolar I disorder; characteristics of second and third episodes; predictors of 8-year outcome. *Arch Gen Psychiatry, 65*(10), 1125–33. doi:10.1001/archpsyc.65.10.1125

Gentile, B. F., & Miller, B. O. (2009). *Foundations of psychological thought: A history of psychology.* Thousand Oaks, CA: Sage Publications.

George, M. S., & Post, R. M. (2011). Daily left prefrontal repetitive transcranial magnetic stimulation for acute treatment of medication-resistant depression. *Am. J. Psychiatry, 168*(4), 356–64. doi:10.1176/appi.ajp.2010.10060864

George, M. S., Taylor, J. J., & Short, B. (2013). Treating the depressions with superficial brain stimulation methods. in A. M. Lozano & M. Hallett (Eds.), *Handbook of clinical neurology* (3rd series, pp. 399–413). New York: Elsevier.

Geraerts, E., Schooler, J. W., Merckelbach, H., Jelicic, M., Hauner, B., & Ambadar, Z. (2007). The reality of recovered memories. *Psychological Science, 18*(7), 564–68.

Gerardi, M., Rothbaum, B. O., Ressler, K., Heekin, M., & Rizzo, A. (2008). Virtual reality exposure therapy using a virtual Iraq: Case Report. *J. Trauma. Stress., 21*, 209–13.

Gettinger, M., & Koscik, R. (2001). Psychological services for children with learning disabilities. In J. N. Huges, A. W. La Greca, & J. C. Conoley (Eds.), *Handbook of psychological services for children and adolescents* (pp. 421–35). Oxford, UK: Oxford University Press.

Ghaddar, A., Elsouri, G., & Abboud, Z. (2014, November 6). Torture and long-term health effects among Lebanese female political prisoners. *J. Interpersonal Violence* [Epub ahead of print].

Ghaderi, A. (2006). Does individualization matter? A randomized trial of standard (focused) versus individualized (broader) cognitive behavior therapy for bulimia nervosa. *Behav. Res. Ther., 44*, 273–88.

Ghaemi, S. N., Hsu, D. J., Soldani, F., & Goodwin, F. K. (2003). Antidepressants in bipolar disorder: The case for caution. *Bipolar Disorders, 5*, 421–33.

Ghaffar, O., Staines, W. R., & Reinstein, A. (2006). Unexplained neurologic symptoms: An fMRI study of sensory conversion disorder. *Neurology, 67*, 2036–38.

Ghosh, S., Tamuli, K. K., & Dihingia, S. (2007). A case presented with "as if" phenomenon. *Indian J. Psychiatry, 49*, 292–93.

Gibbons, M. B. C., Crits-Christoph, P., & Hearon, B. (2008). The empirical status of psychodynamic therapies. *Annu. Rev. Clin. Psychol., 4*, 93–108.

Gibbons, R. D., Brown, C. H., Hur, K., Davis, J. M., & Mann, J. J. (2012). Suicidal thoughts and behavior with antidepressant treatment: Reanalysis of the randomized placebo-controlled studies of fluoxetine and venlafaxine. *Arch. General Psychiatry, 69*, 580–87.

Giesbrecht, T., Lynn, S. J., Lilienfeld, S. O., & Merckelbach, H. (2008). Cognitive processes in dissociation: An analysis of core theoretical assumptions. *Psychol. Bull., 134*, 617–47. doi:10.1037/0033-2909.134.5.617

Giesbrecht, T., Merckelbach, H., van Oorsouw, K., & Simeon, D. (2010). Skin conductance and memory fragmentation after exposure to an emotional clip

in depersonalization disorder. *Psychiatr. Res., 177*, 342–49. doi:10.1016/j.psychres.2010.03.010

Gilbertson, M. W., Shenton, M. E., Ciszewski, A., Kasai, K., Lasko, N. B., Orr, S. P., et al. (2002). Smaller hippocampal volume predicts pathologic vulnerability to psychological trauma. *Nature Neuroscience, 5*, 1242–47.

Gilboa, A., Winocur, G., Rosenbaum, R. S., Poreh, A., Gao, F., Black, S., et al. (2006). Hippocampal contributions to recollection in retrograde and anterograde amnesia. *Hippocampus, 16*, 966–80.

Gill, K., Eagle Elk, M., Liu, Y., & Deitrich, R. A. (1999). An examination of ALDH2 genotypes, alcohol metabolism and the flushing response in Native Americans. *J. Stud. Alcoh., 60*(2), 149–58.

Gillespie, C. F., & Nemeroff, C. B. (2007). Corticotropin releasing factor and the psychobiology of early life stress. *Curr. Dis. Psychol. Sci., 16*, 85–89.

Gilley, D. W., et al. (1997). Psychotic symptoms and physically aggressive behavior in Alzheimer's disease. *J. Am. Geriat. Soc., 45*(9), 1074–79.

Gillman, M. W., Rifas-Shiman, S. L., Kleinman, K., Oken, E., Rich-Edwards, J. W., & Taveras, E. M. (2008). Developmental origins of childhood overweight: Potential public health impact. *Obesity, 16*(7), 1651–56. doi:10.1038/oby.2008.260

Gilman, S. E., Ni, M. Y., Dunn, E.C., Breslau, J., McLaughlin, K. A., Smoller, J. W., & Perlis, R. H. (2015). Contributions of the social environment to first-onset and recurrent mania. *Molecular Psychiatry, 20*, 329–36.

Gilmer, W. S., Trivedi, M. H., Rush, A. J., Wisniewski, S. R., Luther, J., Howland, R. H., et al. (2005). Factors associated with chronic depressive episodes: A preliminary report from the STAR-D project. *Acta Psychiatrica Scandinavica, 112*(6), 425–33.

Gilmore, J. H. (2010). Understanding what causes schizophrenia: A developmental perspective. *Am. J. Psychiatry, 167*, 8–10.

Gilovich, T. (1991). *How do we know what isn't so: The fallibility of human reason in everyday life.* New York: Free Press.

Giotakos, O., Vaidakis, N., Markianos, M., Spandoni, P., & Christodoulou, G. N. (2004). Temperament and character dimensions of sex offenders in relation to their parental rearing. *Sexual and Relationship Therapy, 19*, 141–50.

Gitlin, L. N., Kales, H. C., & Lyketsos, C. G. (2012). Nonpharmacologic management of behavioral symptoms in dementia. *JAMA, 308*, 2020–29.

Gitlin, M. J. (1996). *The psychotherapist's guide to psychopharmacology* (2nd ed.). New York: Free Press.

Gitlin, M. J. (2002). Pharmacological treatment of depression. In I. H. Gotlib & C. L. Hammen (Eds.), *Handbook of depression* (pp. 360–82). New York: Guilford Press.

Gjerde, L. C., Czajkowski, N., Roysamb, E., Orstavik, R. E., Knudsen, G. P., Ostby, K., et al. (2012). The heritability of avoidant and dependent personality disorder assessed by personal interview and questionnaire. *Acta Psychiatrica Scandinavica, 126*, 448–57.

Glassman, A. H. (2005). Commentary: Does treating postmyocardial infarction depression reduce medical mortality? *Arch. Gen. Psychiatry, 62*(7), 711–12.

Glassman, A. H. (2007). Depression and cardiovascular comorbidity. *Dialog. Clin. Neurosci., 9*, 9–17.

Gleaves, D. H. (1996). The sociocognitive model of dissociative identity disorder: A reexamination of the evidence. *Psychol. Bull., 120*, 42–59.

Gleaves, D. H., May, M. C., & Cardena, E. (2001). Examination of the diagnostic validity of dissociative identity disorder. *Clin. Psychol. Rev., 21*, 577–608.

Gleaves, D. H., Smith, S. M., Butler, L. D., & Spiegel, D. (2004). False and recovered memories in the laboratory and clinic: A review of experimental and clinical evidence. *Clin. Psychol. Sci. Prac., 11*(1), 3–28.

Gleaves, D. H., & Williams, T. L. (2005). Critical questions: Trauma, memory, and dissociation. *Psychiatr. Ann., 35*(8), 649–54.

Glenn, A. L., Johnson, A. K., & Raine, A. (2013). Antisocial personality disorder: A current review. *Current Psychiatry Reports, 15*, 427.

Glick, I. D., & Tandon, R. (2009). The acute crisis stabilization unit for adults. In S. S. Sharfstein, F. B. Dickerson, & J. M. Oldham (Eds.), *Textbook of hospital psychiatry* (pp. 23–35). Arlington, VA: American Psychiatric Association.

Glidden, L. M., & Schoolcraft, S. A. (2007). From diagnosis to adaptation: Optimizing family and child functioning when a genetic diagnosis is associated with mental retardation. In M. M. Mazzocco & J. L. Ross (Eds.), *Neurogenetic developmental disorders: Variation of manifestation in childhood* (pp. 391–413). Cambridge, MA: The MIT Press.

Glisky, E. L., Ryan, L., Reminger, S., Hardt, O., Hayes, S. M., & Hupbach, A. (2004). A case of psychogenic fugue: I understand, aber ich verstehe nichts. *Neuropsychologia, 42*, 1132–47.

Glover, M. R. (1984). *The York retreat: An early Quaker experiment in the treatment of mental illness.* York, UK: William Sessions Ltd.

Goddard, A. W., Mason, G. F., Almai, A., Rothman, D. L., Behar, K. L., Petroff, O., et al. (2001). Reductions in occipital cortex GABA levels in panic disorder detected with superscript 1H-magnetic resonance spectroscopy. *Arch. Gen. Psychiatry, 58*(6), 556–61.

Goddard, A. W., Mason, G. F., Rothman, D. L., Behar, K. L., Petroff, O., & Krystal, J. H. (2004). Family psychopathology and magnitude of reductions in occipital cortex GABA levels in panic disorder. *Neuropsychopharmacol., 29*(3), 639–40.

Goddard, A. W., Narayan, M., Woods, S. W., Germine, M., Gerald, L., Kramer, L. L., et al. (1996). Plasma levels of gamma-aminobutyric acid and panic disorder. *Psych. Res., 63*(2–3), 223–25.

Goel, M. S., McCarthy, E. P., Phillips, R. S., & Wee, C. C. (2004). Obesity among US immigrant subgroups by duration of residence. *JAMA, 292*, 2860–67.

Goff, D. C., & Coyle, J. T. (2001). The emerging role of glutamate in the pathophysiology and treatment of schizophrenia. *Am. J. Psychiatry, 158*, 1367–77.

Goffman, E. (1961). *Asylums.* New York: Doubleday.

Goin, R. P. (1998). Nocturnal enuresis in children. *Child: Care, Health, and Development, 24*, 277–88.

Goldberg, L. R. (1990). An alternative "description of personality": The big-five factor structure. *J. Pers. Soc. Psychol., 59*(6), 1216. Retrieved from http://psycnet.apa.org/psycinfo/1991-09869-001

Golden, R. N., Gaynes, B. N., Ekstrom, R. D., Hamer, R. M., Jacobsen, F. M., Suppes, T., et al. (2005). The efficacy of light therapy in the treatment of mood disorders: A review and meta-analysis of the evidence. *Am. J. Psychiatry, 162*(4), 656–62.

Goldin, P. R., Manber, T., Hakimi, S., Canli, T., & Gross, J. J. (2009). Neural bases of social anxiety disorder: Emotional reactivity and cognitive regulation during social and physical threat. *Arch. Gen. Psychiatry, 66*(2), 170–80. doi:10.1001/archgenpsychiatry.2008.525

Goldman-Rakic, P. S., & Selemon, L. D. (1997). Functional and anatomical aspects of prefrontal pathology in schizophrenia. *Schizo. Bull., 23*, 437–58.

Goldney, R. D. (2003). Deinstitutionalization and suicide. *J. Crisis Int. Suicide Prev., 24*, 39–40.

Goldschmidt, A. B., Wall, M., Loth, K. A., Le Grange, D., & Neumark-Sztainer, D. (2012). Which dieters are at risk for the onset of binge eating? A prospective study of adolescents and young adults. *J. Adolescent Health, 51*, 86–92.

Goldsmith, D. F., & Rogoff, B. (1997). Mother's and toddler's coordinated joint focus of attention: Variations with maternal dysphoric symptoms. *Develop. Psychol., 33*, 113–19.

Goldsmith, H. H. (2003). Genetics of emotional development. In R. J. Davidson, K. R. Scherer, & H. H. Goldsmith (Eds.), *Handbook of affective sciences* (pp. 300–19). New York: Oxford University Press.

Goldsmith, R., Joanissse, D. R., Gallagher, D., Pavlovich, K., Shamoon, E., Leibel, R. L., et al. (2010). Effects of experimental weight perturbation on skeletal work efficiency, fuel utilization, and biochemistry in human subjects. *Am. J. Physiology–Regulatory, Integrative and Comparative Physiology, 298*, R79–R88.

Goldstein, I., Lue, T. F., Padma-Nathan, H., Rosen, R. C., Steers, W. D., & Wicker, P. A. (1998). Oral sildenafil in the treatment of erectile dysfunction. *N. Engl. J. Med., 338*, 20, 1397–1404.

Goldstein, R. B., Grant, B. F., Ruan, W. J., Smith, S. M., & Saha, T. D. (2006). Antisocial personality disorder with childhood vs adolescence-onset conduct disorder: Results from the national epidemiologic survey on alcohol and related conditions. *J. Nerv. Ment. Dis., 194*(9), 667–75.

Good, B. J., & Kleinman, A. M. (1985). Culture and anxiety: Cross-cultural evidence for the patterning of anxiety disorders. In A. H. Tuma & J. D. Master (Eds.), *Anxiety and the anxiety disorders*. Hillsdale, NJ: Erlbaum.

Goodheart, C. D., & Rozensky, R. H. (2011). Health and medical conditions. In J. C. Norcross, G. R. VandenBos, & D. K. Freedheim (Eds.), *History of psychotherapy: Continuity and change* (2nd ed., pp. 467–74). Washington, DC: American Psychological Association.

Goodman, S. H. (2007). Depression in mothers. *Annu. Rev. Clin. Psych., 3*, 107–35.

Goodman, S. H., & Brand, S. R. (2009). Depression and early adverse experiences. In I. H. Gotlib & C. L. Hammen (Eds.), *Handbook of depression and its treatment* (2nd ed.). New York: Guilford Press.

Goodman, S. H., & Gotlib, I. H. (1999). Risk for psychopathology in the children of depressed mothers: A developmental model for understanding mechanisms of transmission. *Psychol. Rev., 106*, 458–90.

Goodman, W. K. (2004). Selecting pharmacotherapy for generalized anxiety disorder. *J. Clin. Psychiatry, 65*(113), 8–13.

Goodwin, C. J. (2011). *A history of modern psychology* (4th ed.). New York: Wiley & Sons.

Goodwin, D. W., Schulsinger, F., Hermansen, L., Guze, S. B., & Winokur, G. (1973). Alcohol problems in adoptees raised apart from alcoholic biological parents. *Arch. Gen. Psychiatry, 28*(2), 238–43.

Goodwin, D. W., Schulsinger, F., Moller, N., Hermansen, L., Winokur, G., & Guze, S. B. (1974). Drinking problems in adopted and nonadopted sons of alcoholics. *Arch. Gen. Psychiatry, 31*(2), 164–69.

Goodwin, F. K., Fireman, B., Simon, G. E., Hunkeler, E. M., Lee, J., & Revicki, D. (2003). Suicide risk in bipolar disorder during treatment with lithium and divalproex. *JAMA, 290*(11), 1467–73.

Goodwin, F. K., & Jamison, K. R. (2007). *Manic-depressive illness: Bipolar disorders and recurrent depression* (2nd ed.). New York: Oxford University Press.

Goodwin, J. (2014). The horror of stigma: Psychosis and mental healthcare environments in twenty-first-century horror film (part II). *Perspectives in Psychiatric Care, 50*, 224–34.

Gordis, E. (1997). Patient-treatment matching. *Alcohol Alert, 36*, 1–4.

Gordis, E. (2001). Cognitive impairment and recovery from alcoholism. *Alcohol Alert* (National Institute on Alcohol Abuse and Alcoholism, No. 53). Washington, DC: U.S. Department of Health and Human Services.

Gordis, E., Dufour, M. C., Warren, K. R., Jackson, R. J., Floyd, R. L., & Hungerford, D. W. (1995). Should physicians counsel patients to drink alcohol? *JAMA, 273*, 1–12.

Gordon, I., Pierce, M. D., Bartlett, M. S., & Tanaka, J. W. (2014). Training facial expression production in children on the autism spectrum. *J Autism Dev Disord, 44*(10), 2486–98. doi:10.1007/s10803-014-2118-6

Gordon, R. A. (2000). *Eating disorders: Anatomy of a social epidemic* (2nd ed.). London: Blackwell.

Gorenstein, E. E. (1992). *The science of mental illness*. San Diego, CA: Academic Press.

Gorman, J. M., Battista, D., Goetz, R. R., Dillon, D. J., Liebowitz, M. R., Fyer, A. J., et al. (1989). A comparison of sodium bicarbonate and sodium lactate infusion in the induction of panic attacks. *Arch. Gen. Psychiatry, 46*, 145–50.

Gorman, J. M., Kent, J. M., Sullivan, G. M., & Coplan, J. D. (2000). Neuroanatomical hypothesis of panic disorder, revised. *Am. J. Psychiatry, 157*, 493–505.

Gortner, E. T., Gollan, J. K., & Jacobson, N. S. (1997). Psychological aspects of perpetrators of domestic violence and their relationships with the victims. *Psychiatr. Clin. North Am., 20*(2), 327–52.

Gosselin, P., Ladouceur, R., Morin, C. M., Dugas, M. J., & Baillargeon, L. (2006). Benzodiazepine discontinuation among adults with GAD: A randomized trial of cognitive-behavioral therapy. *J Consult. Clin. Psychol., 74*(5), 908–19.

Gothelf, D., Feinstein, C., Thompson, T., Gu, E., Penniman, L., Van Stone, E., et al. (2007). Risk factors for the emergence of psychotic disorders in adolescents with 22q11.2 deletion syndrome. *Am. J. Psychiatry, 164*, 663–69.

Gotlib, I. H., & Abramson, L. Y. (1999). Attributional theories of emotion. In T. Dalgleish & M. J. Power (Eds.), *Handbook of cognition and emotion* (pp. 613–36). Chichester, UK: Wiley.

Gotlib, I. H., & Hammen, C. L. (1992). *Psychological aspects of depression: Toward a cognitive-interpersonal integration*. Chichester, UK: Wiley.

Gotlib, I. H., & Joormann, J. (2010). Cognition and depression: Current status and future directions. *Annu. Rev. Clin. Psychol., 6*, 285–312. doi:10.1146/annurev.clinpsy.121208.131305

Gottesman, I. I. (1991). *Schizophrenia genesis: The origins of madness*. New York: Freeman.

Gottesman, I. I. (2001). Psychopathology through a life span-genetic prism. *Am. Psychol., 56*, 867–78.

Gottesman, I. I., & Bertelson, A. (1989). Confirming unexpressed genotypes for schizophrenia: Risks in the offspring of Fischer's Danish identical and fraternal discordant twins. *Arch. Gen. Psychiatry, 46*, 867–72.

Gottesman, I. I., & Gould, T. D. (2003). The endophenotype concept in psychiatry: Etymology and strategic intentions. *Am. J. Psychiatry, 160*, 636–45.

Gottesman, I. I., & Hanson, D. R. (2005). Human development: Biological and genetic processes. *Annu. Rev. Psychol., 56*, 263–86.

Gottlieb, G. (1992). *Individual development and evolution: The genesis of novel behavior*. New York: Oxford University Press.

Gottlieb, G., & Halpern, C. T. (2002). A relational view of causality in normal and abnormal development. *Develop. Psychopath., 14*(3), 421–35.

Götz, J., Chen, F., van Dorpe, J., & Nitsch, R. M. (2001). Formation of neurofibrillary tangles in P301L tau transgenic mice induced by A(42) fibrils. *Science, 293*, 1491–96.

Gouin, J.-P., & Kiecolt-Glaser, J. K. (2011). The impact of psychological stress on wound healing: Methods and mechanisms. *Immunology and Allergy Clinics of North America, 31*, 81–93.

Gould, L. N. (1949). Auditory hallucinations and sub-vocal speech. *J. Nerv. Ment. Dis., 109*, 418–27.

Gouvier, W. D., et al. (1997). Cognitive retraining with brain-damaged patients. In A. M. Horton, D. Wedding, & J. Webster (Eds.), *The neuropsychology handbook* (Vol. 2, pp. 3–46). New York: Springer.

Grabe, H. J., Ruhrmann, S., Ettelt, S., Buhtz, F., Hochrein, A., Schulze-Rauschenbach, S., et al. (2006). Familiality of obsessive-compulsive disorder in nonclinical and clinical subjects. *Am. J. Psychiatry, 163*(11), 1986–92.

Grabe, S., & Hyde, J. (2006). Ethnicity and body dissatisfaction among women in the United States: A meta-analysis. *Psych. Bull., 132*, 622–40.

Graeff, F. G., & Del-Ben, C. M. (2008). Neurobiology of panic disorder: From animal models to brain neuroimaging. *Neuroscience and Biobehavioral Reviews, 32*(7), 1326–35. doi:10.1016/j.neubiorev.2008.05.017

Graham, C. A. (2010). The DSM diagnostic criteria for female orgasmic disorder. *Arch. Sexual Behavior, 39*(2), 256–70.

Granato, P., Weill, S., & Revillon, J. J. (1997). Ecstasy and dementia in a young subject. *European Psychiatry, 12*(7), 369–71.

Grandin, L. D., Alloy, L. B., & Abramson, L. Y. (2006). The social Zeitgeber theory, circadian rhythms, and mood disorders: Review and evaluation. *Clin. Psych. Rev., 26*(6), 679–94.

Granic, I., & Patterson, G. R. (2006). Toward a comprehensive model of antisocial development: A dynamic systems approach. *Psych. Rev., 113*(1), 101–31.

Grant, B. F., Chou, S. P., Goldstein, R. B., et al. (2008). Prevalence, correlates, disability, and comorbidity of DSM-IV borderline personality disorder: Results from the Wave 2 National Epidemiologic Survey on Alcohol and Related Conditions. *J. Clin. Psychiatry, 69*, 533–45.

Grant, B. F., & Dawson, D. A. (1997). Age at onset of alcohol use and its association with DSM-IV alcohol abuse and dependency: Results from the National Longitudinal Alcohol Epidemiologic Survey. *J. Subst. Abuse, 9*, 103–10.

Grant, B. F., Hasin, D. S., Stinson, F. S., Dawson, D. A., Chou, S. P., Ruan, W. J., & Pickering, R. P. (2004). Prevalence, correlates, and disability of personality disorders in the US: Results from the National Epidemiologic Survey on Alcohol and Related Conditions. *J. Clinical Psychiatry, 65*, 948–58.

Grant, B. F., Stinson, F. S., Dawson, D. A., Chou, P., Dufour, M., Compton, W., et al. (2004). Prevalence and co-occurrence of substance use disorders and independent mood and anxiety disorders: Results from the national epidemiologic survey on alcohol and related conditions. *Arch. Gen. Psychiatry, 61*(8), 807–16.

Grant, B. F., Stinson, F. S., Dawson, D. A., Chou, S. P., & Ruan, W. J. (2005). Co-occurrence of DSM-IV personality disorders in the United States: Results from the national epidemiologic survey on alcohol and related conditions. *Compr. Psychiatry, 46*, 1–5.

Grant, J. E., & Potenza, M. N. (2010). Impulse control disorders. In J. E. Grant & M. N. Potenza (Eds.), *Young adult mental health* (pp. 335–51). New York: Oxford University Press.

Grant, M. (1956). *Tacitus: The annals of Imperial Rome* (Michael Grant, Trans.). New York: Penguin Books.

Grant, S. J., & Sonti, G. (1994). Buprenorphine and morphine produce equivalent increases in extracellular single unit activity of dopamine neurons in the ventral tegmental area in vivo. *Synapse, 16*, 181–87.

Graves, R. E., Cassisi, J. E., & Penn, D. L. (2005). Psychophysiological evaluation of stigma toward schizophrenia. *Schizo. Res., 76*, 315–27.

Gray, J. A. (1987). *The psychology of fear and stress* (2nd ed.). New York: Cambridge University Press.

Gray, J. A., & McNaughton, N. (2000). *The neuropsychology of anxiety* (2nd ed.). Oxford, UK: Oxford University Press.

Gray-Little, B. (2009). The assessment of psychopathology in racial and ethnic Minorities. In J. N. Butcher (Ed.), *Oxford handbook of personality and clinical assessment* (pp. 396–414). New York: Oxford University Press.

Graziottin, A., & Althof, S. (2011). What does premature ejaculation mean to the man, the woman, and the couple? *J. Sexual Medicine, 8*(Suppl. 4), 304–09.

Green, B. A. (2009). Culture and mental health assessment. In S. Eshun & R. A. Gurung (Eds.), *Culture and mental health: Sociocultural influences, theory, and practice* (pp. 19–33). New York: Wiley-Blackwell.

Green, B. L., Lindy, J. D., Grace, M. C., & Leonard, A. C. (1992). Chronic posttraumatic stress disorder and diagnostic comorbidity in a disaster sample. *J. Nerv. Ment. Dis., 180*, 760–66.

Green, J. G., McLaughlin, K. A., Berglund, P. A., Gruber, M. J., Sampson, N. A., Zaslavsky, A. M., & Kessler, R. C. (2010). Childhood adversities and adult psychiatric disorders in the National Comorbidity Survey Replication I: Associations with first onset of *DSM-IV* disorders. *Arch. General Psychiatry, 67*, 113–23.

Green, M. F. (2001). *Schizophrenia revealed: From neurons to social interactions*. New York: Norton.

Green, M. F. (2007). Stimulating the development of drug treatments to improve cognition in schizophrenia. *Annu. Rev. Clin. Psych., 3*, 159–80.

Green, R. M. (1951). *Galen's hygiene*. Springfield, IL: Charles C. Thomas.

Green, R. (1987). *The "sissy boy syndrome" and the development of homosexuality*. New Haven, CT: Yale University Press.

Green, R. (1992). *Sexual science and the law*. Cambridge, MA: Harvard University Press.

Green, R., & Fleming, D. (1990). Transsexual surgery followup: Status in the 1990's. In J. Bancroft, C. Davis, & H. Ruppel (Eds.), *Annual review of sex research*. Mt. Vernon, IA: Society for the Scientific Study of Sex.

Greenberg, P. E., Sisitsky, T., Kessler, R. C., Finkelstein, S. N., Berndt, E. R., Davidson, J. R. T., et al. (1999). The economic burden of anxiety disorders in the 1990s. *J. Clin. Psychiatry, 60*, 427–35.

Greene, R. L. (2011). *The MMPI-2/MMPI-2-RF: An interpretive manual*. Boston: Allyn & Bacon.

Greene, R. L., Robin, R. W., Albaugh, B., Caldwell, A., & Goldman, D. (2003). Use of the MMPI-2 in American Indians: II. Empirical correlates. *Psychol. Assess., 15*(3), 360–69.

Greenfield, S. F., Back, S. E., Lawson, K., & Brady, K. T. (2010). Substance abuse in women: Contribution of early environmental stress to alcoholism vulnerability. *Psychiatr. Clin. North Am., 33*(2), 339–55.

Gregg, C., & Hoy, C. (1989). Coherence: The comprehension and production abilities of college writers who are normally achieving, learning disabled, and underprepared. *J. Learn. Dis., 22*, 370–72.

Gretton, H. M., Hare, R. D., & Catchpole, R. E. H. (2004). Psychopathy and offending from adolescence to adulthood: A 10-year follow-up. *J. Cons. Clin. Psych., 72*(4), 636–45.

Greysmith, D. (1979). *Richard Dadd: The rock and castle of seclusion*. London, U. K. : Tate Gallery.

Griffiths, M. (2003). Internet gambling: Issues, concerns, and recommendations. *Cyber Psychology & Behavior, 6*(6), 557–68.

Griffiths, M. D. (2012). The use of online methodologies in studying paraphilias—A review. *J. Behavioral Addictions, 1*, 143–50.

Grillon, C. (2008). Models and mechanisms of anxiety: Evidence from startle studies. *Psychopharmacol., 199*(3), 421–37. doi:10.1007/s00213-007-1019-1

Grilo, C. M. (2002). Binge eating disorder. In C. G. Fairburn & K. D. Brownell (Eds.), *Eating disorders and obesity: A comprehensive handbook* (2nd ed., pp. 178–82). New York: Guilford Press.

Grilo, C. M., Skodol, A., Gunderson, J., Sanislow, C., Stout, R., Shea, M., et al. (2004). Longitudinal diagnostic efficiency of DSM-IV criteria for obsessive-compulsive personality disorder: A 2-year prospective study. *Acta Psychiatr. Scandin., 110*, 64–68.

Grimes, K., & Walker, E. F. (1994). Childhood emotional expressions, educational attainment, and age at onset of illness in schizophrenia. *J. Abn. Psychol., 103*(4), 784–90.

Grisham, J. R., Anderson, T. M., & Perminder, S. S. (2008). Genetic and environmental influences on obsessive-compulsive disorder. *Eur. Arch. Psychiatr. Clin. Neurosci., 258*(2), 107–16. doi:10.1007/s00406-007-0789-0

Grob, C. S. (2000). Deconstructing ecstasy: The politics of MDMA research. *Addiction Research, 8*(6), 549–88.

Grob, G. N. (1994). Mad, homeless, and unwanted: A history of the care of the chronically mentally ill in America. *Psychiatr. Clin. North Am., 17*(3), 541–58.

Grob, G. N. (2008). Mental health policy in the liberal state: The example of the United States. *Int. J. Law and Psychiatry, 31*(2), 89–100.

Grodin, M., & Laurie, G. T. (2000). Susceptibility genes and neurological disorders: Learning the right lessons from the Human Genome Project. *Arch. Neurol., 57*, 1569–74.

Gropalis, M., Bleichardt, G., Hiller, W., & Witthöft, M. (2013). Specificity and modifiability of cognitive biases in hypochondriasis. *J. Consulting and Clinical Psychology, 81*, 558–65.

Grossman, J. B., & Ruiz, P. (2004). Shall we make a leap-of-faith to disulfiram (Antabuse)? *Addictive Disorders & Their Treatment, 3*(3), 129–32.

Grossmann, K. E., Grossmann, K., & Waters, E. (2005). *Attachment from infancy to adulthood: The major longitudinal studies*. New York: Guilford Publications.

Grounds, A. (2000). The psychiatrist in court. In M. G. Gelder, J. J. Lopez-Ibor, Jr., & N. C. Andreason (Eds.), *New Oxford textbook of psychiatry* (pp. 2089–96). Oxford, UK: Oxford University Press.

Grove, W. M., Zald, D. H., Lebow, B., Snitz, E., & Nelson, C. (2000). Clinical versus mechanical prediction: A meta-analysis. *Psychol. Assess., 12*, 19–30.

Grover, K. E., Carpenter, L. L., Price, L. H., Gagne, G. G., Mello, A. F., Mello, M. F., et al. (2007). The relationship between childhood abuse and adult personality disorder symptoms. *J. Pers. Disord., 21*, 442–47.

Groza, V., Maschmeier, C., Jamison, C., & Piccola, T. (2003). Siblings and out-of-home placement: Best practices. *Families in Society, 84*(4), 480–90.

Gruber, S. A., Tzilos, G. K., Silveri, M. M., Pollack, M., Renshaw, P. F., Kaufman, M. J., et al. (2006). Methadone maintenance improves cognitive performance after two months of treatment. *Exp. Clin. Psychopharm., 14*(2), 157–64.

Grzywacz, J. G., & Dooley, D. (2003). "Good jobs" to "bad jobs": Replicated evidence of an employment continuum from two large surveys. *Soc. Sci. Med., 56*, 1749–60.

Guarnaccia, P. J., Lewis-Fernandez, R., Pincay, I. M., Shrout, P., Guo, J., Torres, M., et al. (2010). Ataque de nervios as a marker of social and psychiatric vulnerability: Results from the NLAAS. *Int. J. Soc. Psychiatry, 56*(3), 298–309. doi:10.1177/0020764008101636

Guarnaccia, P. J., Martinez, I., Ramirez, R., & Canino, G. (2005). Are ataques de nervios in Puerto Rican children associated with psychiatric disorder? *J. Am. Acad. Child Adoles. Psychiatry, 44*(11), 1184–92.

Guastella, A. J., Richardson, R., Lovibond, P. F., Rapee, R., Gaston, J. E., Mitchell, P., et al. (2008). A randomized controlled trial of D-cycloserine enhancement of exposure therapy for social anxiety disorder. *Biol. Psychiat, 63*, 544–49.

Gueorguieva, R., Wu, R., Pittman, B., Cramer, J., Rosenheck, R. A., O'Malley, S. S., et al. (2007). New insights into the efficacy of naltrexone based on trajectory-based reanalyses of two negative clinical trials. *Biol. Psychiatry, 61*(11), 1290–95.

Guerra, F. (1971). *The pre-Columbian mind*. New York: Seminar Press.

Guerreiro, R. J., Gustafson, D. R., & Hardy, J. (2012). The genetic architecture of Alzheimer's disease: Beyond APP, PSENs and APOE. *Neurobiology of Aging, 33*, 437–56.

Guerrero-Pedrazza, A., McKenna, P. J., Gomar, J. J., Sarró, S., Salvador, R., Amman, B., et al. (2011). First-episode psychosis is characterized by failure of deactivation but not by hyper- or hypofrontality. *Psych. Med., 42*, 73–84.

Gull, W. (1888). Anorexia nervosa. *Lancet, I*, 516–17.

Gunderson, J. G., Zanarini, M. C., Choi-Kain, L. W., Mitchell, K. S., Lang, K. L., & Hudson, J. I. (2011). Family study of borderline personality disorder and its sectors of psychopathology. *Arch. General Psychiatry, 68*, 753–62.

Gunderson, J. G., Zanarini, M. C., & Kisiel, C. L. (1995). Borderline personality disorder. In W. J. Livesley (Ed.), *The DSM-IV personality disorders* (pp. 141–57). New York: Guilford Press.

Gunn, J. (1993). Castration is not the answer. *Brit. Med. J., 307*, 790–91.

Gunnar, M., & Quevedo, K. (2007). The neurobiology of stress and development. *Annu. Rev. Psychol., 58*, 145–73.

Gupta, B. P., Murad, M. H., Clifton, M. M., Prokop, L., Nehra, A., & Kopecky, S. L. (2011). The effect of lifestyle modification and cardiovascular risk factor reduction on erectile dysfunction: A systematic review and meta-analysis. *Arch. Internal Medicine, 171*, 1797–1803.

Gupta, J. C., Deb, A. K., & Kahali, B. S. (1943). Preliminary observations on the use of *Rauwolfia serpentina* benth in the treatment of mental disorder. *Indian Medical Gazette, 78*, 547–49.

Gupta, S., & Bonanno, G. A. (2010). Trait self-enhancement as a buffer against potentially traumatic events: A prospective study. *Psychological Trauma, 2*, 83–92.

Gureje, O., Oladeji, B., Borges, G., Bruffaerts, R., Haro, J. M., Hwang, I., et al. (2011). Parental psychopathology and the risk of suicidal behavior in their offspring: Results from the WHO World Mental Health Surveys. *Molecular Psychiatry, 16*, 1221–33.

Guskiewicz, K. M., Marshall, S. W., Bailes, J., McCrea, M., Cantu, R. C., Randolph, C., et al. (2005). Association between recurrent concussion and late-life cognitive impairment in retired professional footballers. *Neurosurgery, 57*, 719–26.

H

Haaga, D. A., & Davison, G. C. (1989). Outcome studies of rational-emotive therapy. In M. Bernard & R. DeGiuseppe (Eds.), *Inside rationale-motive therapy*. New York: Academic Press.

Haber, S. N., & Knutson, B. (2010). The reward circuit: Linking primate anatomy and human imaging. *Neuropsychopharmacol., 35*(1), 4–26. doi:10.1038/npp.2009.129

Hackmann, A., Clark, D. M., & McManus, F. (2000). Recurrent images and early memories in social phobia. *Behav. Res. Ther., 38*, 601–10.

Hackmann, A., Ehlers, A., Speckens, A., & Clark, D. M. (2004). Characteristics and content of intrusive memories in PTSD and their changes with treatment. *Characteristics and Traumatic Stress, 17*, 231–40.

Hadley, S. J., Kim, S., Priday, L., & Hollander, E. (2006). Pharmacologic treatment of body dysmorphic disorder. *Primary Psychiatry, 13*(7), 61–69.

Haeffel, G. J., Abramson, L. Y., Brazy, P. C., & Shah, J. Y. (2008). Hopelessness theory and the approach system: Cognitive vulnerability predicts decreases in goal-directed behavior. *Cognitive Therapy and Research, 32,* 281–90.

Haffner, H., et al. (1998). Causes and consequences of the gender difference in age at onset of schizophrenia. *Schizo. Bull., 24*(1), 99–114.

Haijma, S. V., Van Haren, N., Cahn, W., Koolschijn, P. C. M. P., Hulsoff pol, H. E., & Kahn, R. S. (2013). Brain volumes in schizophrenia: A meta-analysis in over 18000 subjects. *Schizophrenia Bulletin, 39,* 1129–38.

Haldane, M., & Frangou, S. (2004). New insights help define the pathophysiology of bipolar affective disorder: Neuroimaging and neuropathology findings. *Prog. Neuropsychopharmacol. Biol. Psychiatry, 28,* 943–60.

Hall, D. E., Eubanks, L., Meyyazhagan, S., Kenney, R. D., & Johnson, S. C. (2000). Evaluation of covert video surveillance in the diagnosis of Munchausen syndrome by proxy: Lessons from 41 cases. *Pediatrics, 105*(6), 1305–11.

Hall, G. (1994). Pavlovian conditioning: Laws of association. In N. J. Mackintosh (Ed.), *Animal learning and cognition* (pp. 15–43). San Diego, CA: Academic Press.

Hall, G. C., Bansal, A., & Lopez, I. R. (1999). Ethnicity and psychopathology: A meta-analytic review of 31 years of comparative MMPI/MMPI-2 research. *Psychol. Assess., 11,* 186–97.

Hall, J. R., & Benning, S. D. (2006). The "successful" psychopath: Adaptive and subclinical manifestations of psychopathy in the general population. In C. J. Patrick (Ed.), *Handbook of the psychopathy* (pp. 459–78). New York: Guilford Press.

Halligan, S. L., Murray, L., Martins, C., & Cooper, P. J. (2007). Maternal depression and psychiatric outcomes in adolescent offspring: A 13-year longitudinal study. *J. Affect. Disord., 97*(1–3), 145–54.

Halmi, K. A. (2010). Psychological comorbidity of eating disorders. In W. A. Agras (Ed.), *The Oxford handbook of eating disorders* (pp. 292–303). New York: Oxford University Press.

Halmi, K. A., Bellace, D., Berthod, S., Ghosh, S., Berrettini, W., Brandt, H. A., et al. (2012). An examination of early childhood perfectionism across anorexia nervosa subtypes. *Int. J. Eat. Disorder, 45,* 800–07.

Halmi, K. A., Eckert, E., Marchi, P., Sampugnaro, V., Apple, R., & Cohen, J. (1991). Comorbidity of psychiatric diagnoses in anorexia nervosa. *Arch. Gen. Psychiatry, 48,* 712–18.

Halmi, K. A., Sunday, S. R., Strober, M., Kaplan, A., Woodside, D. B., Fichter, M., et al. (2000). Perfectionism in anorexia nervosa: Variation by clinical subtype, obsessionality, and pathological eating behavior. *Am. J. Psychiatry, 157*(11), 1799–805.

Halpern, S. (2008, May 19). Virtual Iraq. *The New Yorker*, pp. 32–37.

Hammen, C. (1995). Stress and the course of unipolar disorders. In C. M. Mazure (Ed.), *Does stress cause psychiatric illness?* Washington, DC: American Psychiatric Press.

Hammen, C. (2005). Stress and depression. In *Annu. Rev. Clin. Psychol.* (Vol. 1, pp. 293–319). Palo Alto, CA: Annual Reviews.

Hammen, C. (2009). Children of depressed parents. In I. H. Gotlib & C. L. Hammen (Eds.), *Handbook of depression and its treatment* (2nd ed.). New York: Guilford Press.

Hammen, C., Brennan, P. A., & Le Brocque, R. (2011). Youth depression and early childrearing:

Stress generation and intergenerational transmission of depression. *J. Cons. Clin. Psychol., 79*(3), 353–63. doi:10.1037/a0023536

Hammen, C., Shih, J. H., & Brennan, P. A. (2004). Intergenerational transmission of depression: Test of an interpersonal stress model in a community sample. *J. Cons. Clin. Psychol., 72,* 511–22.

Hampton, T. (2011). Traumatic brain injury a growing problem among troops serving in today's wars. *JAMA, 306,* 477–79.

Hance, M., Carney, R., Freedland, K., & Skala, J. (1996). Depression in patients with coronary heart disease: A 12 month follow-up. *Gen. Hosp. Psychiatry, 18,* 61–65.

Haney, B., & Gold, M. (1973). The juvenile delinquent nobody knows. *Psych. Today, 7*(4), 48–52, 55.

Hankin, B. L. (2006). Adolescent depression: Description, causes, and interventions. *Epilepsy & Behavior, 8*(1), 102–14.

Hankin, B. L., & Abramson, L. Y. (2001). Development of gender differences in depression: An elaborated cognitive vulnerability-transactional stress theory. *Psychol. Bull., 127,* 773–96.

Hankin, B. L., Abramson, L. Y., Miller, N., & Haeffel, G. J. (2004). Cognitive vulnerability-stress theories of depression: Examining affective specificity in the prediction of depression versus anxiety in three prospective studies. *Cog. Ther. Res., 28*(3), 309–45.

Hankin, B. L., Wetter, E., & Cheely, C. (2008). Sex differences in child and adolescent depression: A developmental psychopathological approach. In J. R. Z. Abela & B. L. Hankin (Eds.), *Handbook of depression in children and adolescents* (pp. 377–414). New York: Guilford Press.

Hanna, G. L. (2000). Clinical and family-genetic studies of childhood obsessive-compulsive disorder. In W. K. Goodman & M. V. Rudorfer (Eds.), *Obsessive-compulsive disorder: Contemporary issues in treatment. Personality and clinical psychology series* (pp. 87–103). Mahwah, NJ: Erlbaum.

Hansen, R. A., Gartlehner, G., Lohr, K. N., & Kaufer, D. I. (2007). Functional outcomes of drug treatment in Alzheimer's disease. *Drugs Aging, 24,* 155–67.

Hanson, R. K., Bourgon, G., Helmus, L., & Hodgson, S. (2009). The principles of effective correctional treatment also apply to sexual offenders: A meta-analysis. *Criminal Justice and Behavior, 36*(9), 865–91.

Harder, H. G., Wagner, S. L., & Rash, J. A. (2014). *Mental illness in the workplace: Psychological disability management. Psychological and behavioral aspects of risk series.* Brookfield, VT: Gower Publishing.

Hare, E. H. (1962). Masturbatory insanity: The history of an idea. *J. Ment. Sci., 108,* 1–25.

Hare, R. D. (1970). *Psychopathy: Theory and research.* New York: Wiley.

Hare, R. D. (1980). A research scale for the assessment of psychopathy in criminal populations. *Personal. Indiv. Diff., 1,* 111–19.

Hare, R. D. (1991). *The Hare psychopathy checklist—revised.* Toronto: Multi-Health Systems.

Hare, R. D. (1998). Psychopathy, affect and behavior. In D. J. Cooke, A. E. Forth, & R. D. Hare (Eds.), *Psychopathy: Theory, research, and implications for society* (pp. 105–37). Dordrecht, Netherlands: Kluwer Academic Publishers.

Hare, R. D. (2003). *The Hare Psychopathy Checklist Revised* (2nd ed.). Toronto, ON, Canada: Multi-Health Systems.

Hare, R. D., Cooke, D. J., & Hart, S. D. (1999). Psychopathy and sadistic personality disorder. In T. Millon, P. H. Blaney, & R. D. Davis (Eds.), *Oxford textbook of psychopathology* (pp. 555–84). New York: Oxford University Press.

Hare, R. D., McPherson, L. M., & Forth, A. E. (1988). Male psychopaths and their criminal careers. *J. Cons. Clin. Psychol, 56,* 710–14.

Hare, R. D., Nuemann, C. S., & Widiger, T. A. (2012). Psychopathy. In T. A. Widiger (Ed.). *The Oxford Handbook of personality disorders* (pp. 478–504). New York: Oxford University Press.

Harkness, K. L., & Lumley, M. N. (2008). Child abuse and neglect and the development of depression in children and adolescents. In J. R. Z. Abela & B. L. Hankin (Eds.), *Handbook of depression in children and adolescents* (pp. 466–88). New York: Guilford Press.

Harkness, K. L., & Monroe, S. M. (2002). Childhood adversity and the endogenous versus nonendogenous distinction in women with major depression. *Am. J. Psychiatry, 159*(3), 387–93.

Harlow, J. M. (1868). Recovery from the passage of an iron bar through the head. *Publication of the Massachusetts Medical Society, 2,* 327.

Harpur, T. J., Hart, S. D., & Hare, R. D. (1993). The personality of the psychopath. In P. T. Costa & T. A. Widiger (Eds.), *Personality disorders and the five-factor model of personality* (pp. 149–73). Washington, DC: American Psychological Association.

Harrington, R., & Clark, A. (1998). Prevention and early intervention for depression in adolescence and early adult life. *Eur. Arch. Psychiatr. Clin. Neurosci., 248*(1), 32–45.

Harris, B. (1979). Whatever happened to Little Albert? *Am. Psychol., 34,* 151–60.

Harris, C. (2011, May 25). Judge: Loughner not competent to stand trial. *The Arizona Republic.*

Harris, G. T., & Rice, M. E. (2006). Treatment of psychopathy: A review of empirical findings. In C. J. Patrick (Ed.), *Handbook of the psychopathy* (pp. 555–72). New York: Guilford Press.

Harris, J. C. (2006). *Intellectual disability: Understanding its development, causes, classification, evaluation, and treatment.* New York: Oxford University Press.

Harris, J. L., Bargh, J. A., & Brownell, K. D. (2009). Priming effects of television food advertising on eating behavior. *Health Psych., 28,* 404–13.

Harrison, B. J., Soriano-Mas, C., Pujol, J., Ortiz, H., López-Solà, M., Hernández-Ribas, R., et al. (2009). Altered corticostriatal functional connectivity in obsessive-compulsive disorder. *Arch. Gen. Psychiatry, 66*(11), 1189–200. doi:10.1001/archgenpsychiatry.2009.152

Harrison, G., Amin, S., Singh, S. P., Croudace, T., & Jones, P. (1999). Outcome of psychosis in people of Afro-Caribbean family origin. *Brit. J. Psychiatry, 175,* 43–49.

Harrison, G., Hopper, K., Craig, T., Laska, E., Siegel, C., Wanderling, J., et al. (2001). Recovery from psychotic illness: A 15- and 25-year international follow-up study. *Brit. J. Psychiatry, 178,* 506–17.

Harrop, E. N., & Marlatt, G. A. (2010). The comorbidity of substance use disorders and eating disorders in women: Prevalence, etiology, and treatment. *Addictive Behaviors, 35,* 392–98.

Harrow, M., Grossman, L. S., Herbener, E. S., & Davies, E. W. (2000). Ten-year outcome: Patients with schizoaffective disorders, schizophrenia, affective disorders and mood incongruent psychotic symptoms. *Brit. J. Psychiatry, 177,* 421–26.

Harrow, M., Jobe, T. H., & Fall, R. N. (2012). Do all schizophrenia patients need antipsychotic treatment continuously throughout their lifetime? A 20 year longitudinal study. *Psychological Medicine, 42,* 2145–55.

Hartmann, D. P., Barrios, B. A., & Wood, D. D. (2004). Principles of behavioral observation. *Comprehensive handbook of psychological assessment* (Vol. 3, pp. 108–27). New York: John Wiley & Sons.

Hartz, S. M., & Bierut, L. J. (2010). Genetics of addictions. *Psychiatr. Clin. North Am., 33*(1), 107–24.

Harvey, A. G. (2008). Sleep and circadian rhythms in bipolar disorder: Seeking synchrony, harmony, and regulation. *Am. J. Psychiatry, 165*(7), 820–29. doi:10.1176/appi. ajp.2008.08010098

Harvey, A. G., Schmidt, D. A., Scarna, A., Semler, C. N., & Goodwin, G. M. (2005). Sleep-related functioning in euthymic patients with bipolar disorder, patients with insomnia, and subjects without sleep problems. *Am. J. Psychiatry, 162,* 50–57.

Harvey, P. D. (2014). What is the evidence for changes in cognition and functioning over the lifespan in patients with schizophrenia? *J. Clinical Psychiatry, 74*(Suppl. 2), 34–38.

Harvey, P. D., Reichenberg, A., & Bowie, C. R. (2006). Cognition and aging in psychopathology: Focus on schizophrenia and depression. *Annu. Rev. Clin. Psych., 2,* 389–409.

Harvey, S. T., & Taylor, J. E. (2010). A meta-analysis of the effects of psychotherapy with sexually abused children and adolescents. *Clin. Psychol. Rev., 30*(5), 517–35.

Harwood, M., & Beutler, L. (2009). Assessment of clients in pretreatment planning. In J. N. Butcher (Ed.), *Oxford handbook of personality and clinical assessment* (pp. 643–56). New York: Oxford University Press.

Harwood, T. M., Beutler, L. E., Fisher, D., Sandowicz, M., Albanese, A. L., & Baker, M. (1997). Clinical decision making in managed health care. In J. N. Butcher (Ed.), *Personality assessment in managed health care: Using the MMPI-2 in treatment planning* (pp. 15–41). New York: Oxford University Press.

Hasegawa, S., et al. (1997). Physical aging in persons with Down syndrome: Bases on external appearance and diseases. *Japanese J. Special Education, 35*(2), 43–49.

Hasin, D. S., Goodwin, R. D., Stinson, F. S., & Grant, B. F. (2005). Epidemiology of major depressive disorder: Results from the national epidemiologic survey on alcoholism and related conditions. *Arch. Gen. Psychiatry, 62*(10), 1097–106.

Hasin, D. S., Stinson, F. S., Ogburn, E., & Grant, B. F. (2007). Prevalence, correlates, disability, and comorbidity of DSM-IV alcohol abuse and dependence in the United States: Results from the National Epidemiologic Study on Alcohol and Related Conditions. *Arch. General Psychiatry, 64,* 830–42.

Hasler, G., Drevets, W. C., Manji, H. K., & Charney, D. S. (2004). Discovering endophenotypes for major depression. *Neuropsychopharmacol., 29*(10), 1765–81.

Hathaway, S. R. (1965). Personality inventories. In B. B. Wolman (Ed.), *Handbook of clinical psychology* (pp. 451–76). New York: McGraw-Hill.

Haug Schnabel, G. (1992). Daytime and nighttime enuresis: A functional disorder and its ethological decoding. *Behaviour, 120,* 232–61.

Haugland, G., Sigel, G., Hopper, K., & Alexander, M. J. (1997). Mental illness among homeless individuals in a suburban county. *Psychiatr. Serv., 48*(4), 504–09.

Haukkala, A., Konttinen, H., Laatikainen, T., Kawachi, I., & Uutela, A. (2010). Hostility, anger control, and anger expression as predictors of cardiovascular disease. *Psychosom. Med., 72,* 556–62.

Havermans, R., Nicolson, N. A., & DeVries, M. W. (2007). Daily hassles, uplifts, and time use in individuals with bipolar disorder in remission. *J. Nerv. Ment. Dis., 195,* 861–65.

Hawkins, E. H., Cummins, L. H., & Marlatt, G. A. (2004). Preventing substance abuse in American Indian and Alaska Native youth: Promising strategies for healthier communities. *Psychol. Bull., 130,* 304–23.

Hawton, K., & Williams, K. (2002). Influences of the media on suicide. *Brit. Med. J., 325,* 1374–75.

Hay, P. J., Mond, J., Buttner, P., & Darby, A. (2008). Eating disorder behaviors are increasing: Findings from two sequential community surveys in South Australia. *PLoS ONE, 3*(2), e1541.

Hayama, T. (1999). Trial of the new psychological test MMPI-2 on the chronic schizophrenic patients: Investigation of the basic and content scales. *Kitasato Medicine, 29*(5), 281–97.

Hayden, M. F. (1998). Civil rights litigation for institutionalized persons with mental retardation: A summary. *Mental Retardation, 36*(1), 75–83.

Hayden, M. R. (2000). Predictive testing for Huntington's disease: The calm after the storm. *Lancet, 356,* 1944–45.

Hayes, S. C. (1998). Single case experimental design and empirical clinical practice. In A. E. Kazdin (Ed.), *Methodological issues and strategies in clinical research* (pp. 419–49). Washington, DC: American Psychological Association.

Hayes, S. C., Villatte, M., Levin, M., & Hildebrandt, M. (2011). Open, aware, and active: Contextual approaches as an emerging trend in the behavioral and cognitive therapies. *Annu. Rev. Clin. Psychol., 7,* 141–68.

Haynes, S., Yoshioka, D. T., Kloezeman, K., & Bello, I. (2009). Behavioral assessment. In J. N. Butcher (Ed.), *Oxford handbook of personality and clinical assessment* (pp. 226–48). New York: Oxford University Press.

Hays, J. T., Hurt, R. D., Rigotti, N. A., Niaura, R., Gonzales, D., Durcan, M. J., et al. (2001). Sustained-release bupropion for pharmacologic relapse prevention after smoking cessation. *Ann. Int. Med., 135*(6), 423–33.

Hays, P. A. (2008). *Addressing cultural complexities in practice: Assessment, diagnosis, and therapy* (2nd ed.). Washington, DC: American Psychological Association.

Hayward, C. (2003). Methodological concerns in puberty-related research. In C. Hayward (Ed.), *Gender differences at puberty* (pp. 1–14). New York: Cambridge University Press.

Hayward, C., Killen, J. D., Kraemer, H. C., & Taylor, C. B. (1998). Linking self-reported childhood behavioral inhibition to adolescent social phobia. *J. Am. Acad. Child Adoles. Psychiatry, 37,* 1308–16.

Hazelden Betty Ford Foundation. (n. d.). *Project Northland and class action: Alcohol and drug prevention for teens.* Retrieved from http://www.hazelden.org/web/go/projectnorthland

Hazell, P. (2007). Pharmacological management of attention-deficit hyperactivity disorder in adolescents: Special considerations. *CNS Drugs, 21*(1), 37–46.

Hazlett, E. A., Levine, J., Buchsbaum, M. S., Silverman, J. M., New, A., & Sevin, E. M. (2003). Deficient attentional modulation of the startle response in patients with schizotypal personality disorder. *Am. J. Psychiatry, 160,* 1621–26.

Heck, A. M., Yanovski, J. A., & Calis, K. A. (2000). Orlistat, a new lipase inhibitor for the management of obesity. *Pharmacotherapy, 20,* 270–79.

Hedman, E., Andersson, G., Andersson, E., Ljótsson, B., Rück, C., Asmundson, G. J. G., & Lindefors, N. (2011). Internet-based cognitive-behavioural therapy for severe health anxiety: Randomised controlled trial. *Brit. J. Psychiatry, 198*(3), 230–36.

Hefez, A. (1985). The role of the press and the medical community in the epidemic of "mysterious gas poisoning" in the Jordan West Bank. *Am. J. Psychiatry, 142,* 833–37.

Heijnen, W. T., Birkenhäger, T. K., Wierdsma, A. I., & van den Broek, W. W. (2010). Antidepressant pharmacotherapy failure and response to subsequent electroconvulsive therapy: A meta-analysis. *J. Clinical Psychopharmacology, 30,* 616–19.

Heilbron, N., & Prinstein, M. J. (2010). Adolescent peer victimization, peer status, suicidal ideation, and nonsuicidal self-injury. *Merrill-Palmer Quarterly: J. Developmental Psychology, 56*(3), 388–419.

Heilbrun, K. (2009). *Evaluation for risk of violence in adults.* New York: Oxford University Press.

Heilbrun, K., & Holliday, S. B. (2013). Psychological assessment in forensic contexts. In K. Geisinger (Ed.), *APA handbook of testing and assessment in psychology* (Vol. 2). Washington, DC: American Psychological Association. doi:10.1037/14048-016

Heim, C., & Nemeroff, C. B. (2001). The role of childhood trauma in the neurobiology of mood and anxiety disorders: Preclinical and clinical studies. *Biol. Psychiatry, 49*(12), 1023–39.

Heim, C., Newport, J., Heit, S., Graham, Y., Wilcox, M., Bonsall, R., et al. (2000). Pituitary adrenal and autonomic responses to stress in women after sexual and physical abuse in childhood. *JAMA, 284,* 592–96.

Heimberg, R. G. (2002). Cognitive-behavioral therapy for social anxiety disorder: Current status and future directions. *Biol. Psychiatry, 51,* 101–08.

Heinrichs, R. W. (2001). *In search of madness: Schizophrenia and neuroscience.* New York: Oxford University Press.

Heinrichs, R. W. (2005). The primacy of cognition in schizophrenia. *American Psychologist, 60,* 229–42.

Heinrichs, R. W., & Zakanis, K. K. (1998). Neurocognitive deficits in schizophrenia: a quantitative review of the evidence. *Neuropsychology, 12,* 426–45.

Helfling, K. (2011, April 16). Iraq, Afghan war veteran who epitomized recovery kills self. *Boston Globe.*

Heller, T., Miller, A. B., & Factor, A. (1997). Adults with mental retardation as supports to their parents: Effects on parental caregiving appraisal. *Mental Retardation, 35*(5), 338–46.

Helmchen, H., & Sartorius, N. (Eds.). (2010). *Ethics in psychiatry: European contributions.* Berlin: Springer.

Helzer, J. E., Canino, G. J., Yeh, E. K., Bland, R., et al. (1990). Alcoholism—North America and Asia: A comparison of population surveys with the Diagnostic Interview Schedule. *Arch. Gen. Psychiatry, 47*(4), 313–19.

Hendrie, H. C. (1998). Epidemiology of dementia and Alzheimer's disease. *Am. J. Geriat. Psychiatry, 6,* 3–18.

Hengartner, M. P., Ajdacic-Gross, V., Rodgers, S., Müller, M., & Rössler, W. (2013). Childhood adversity in association with personality disorder dimensions: New findings in an old debate. *European Psychiatry, 28,* 476–82.

Hengartner, M. P., Cohen, L. J., Rodgers, S., Müller, M., Rössler, W., & Ajdacic-Gross, V. (2015). Association between childhood maltreatment and normal adult personality traits: Exploration of an understudied field. *Journal of Personality Disorders, 29,* 1–14.

Henggeler, S. W. (2011). Efficacy studies to large-scale transport: The development and validation of multisystemic therapy programs. *Annu Rev Clin Psychol, 7,* 351–81. doi:10.1146/annurev-clinpsy-032210-104615

Henriques, J. B., & Davidson, R. J. (1990). Regional brain electrical asymmetries discriminate between previously depressed and healthy control subjects. *J. Abn. Psychol., 99,* 22–31.

Henshaw, C., Foreman, D., & Cox, J. (2004). Postnatal blues: A risk factor for postnatal depression. *J. Psychosom. Obst. Gyn., 25*(3–4), 267–72.

Herdt, G. (2000). Why the Sambia initiate boys before age 10. In J. Bancroft (Ed.), *The role of theory in sex research* (pp. 82–109). Bloomington: Indiana University Press.

Herdt, G., & Stoller, R. G. (1990). *Intimate communications: Erotics and the study of a culture.* New York: Columbia University Press.

Herek, G. M. (2010). Sexual orientation differences as deficits: Science and stigma in the history of American psychology. *Perspectives on Psychological Science, 5,* 693–99.

Herek, G. M., & Garnets, L. D. (2007). Sexual orientation and mental health. *Annu. Rev. Clin. Psych., 3*, 353–75.

Herman, J. L. (1993, March/April). The abuses of memory. *Mother Jones, 18*, 3–4.

Herman-Stahl, M., & Peterson, A. C. (1999). Depressive symptoms during adolescence: Direct and stress-buffering effects of coping, control beliefs, and family relationships. *J. Applied Developmental Psychology, 120*, 45–62.

Hertel, P. T., & Brozovich, F. (2010). Cognitive habits and memory distortions in anxiety and depression. *Curr. Dir. Psychol. Sci., 19*(3), 155–60. doi:10.1177/0963721410370137

Hertel, P. T., Brozovich, F., Joormann, J., & Gotlib, I. H. (2008). Biases in interpretation and memory in generalized social phobia. *J. Abn. Psychol., 117*(2), 278–88. doi:10.1037/0021-843x.117. 2. 278

Heshka, S., Anderson, J. W., Atkinson, R. L., Greenway, F. L., Hill, J. O., et al. (2003). Weight loss with self-help compared with a structured commercial program: A randomized trial. *JAMA, 289*, 1792–98.

Heshka, S., Greenway, F., Anderson, J. W., Atkinson, R. L., Hill, J. O., Phinney, S. D., et al. (2000). Self-help weight loss versus a structured commercial program after 26 weeks: A random-ized controlled study. *Am. J. Med., 109*, 282–87.

Heston, L. (1966). Psychiatric disorders in foster home reared children of schizophrenic mothers. *Brit. J. Psychiatry, 112*, 819–25.

Hetherington, E. M. (1991). The role of individual differences and family relationships in children's coping with divorce and remarriage. In P. S. Cowan & E. M. Hetherington (Eds.), *Family transitions* (pp. 165–94). Hillsdale, NJ: Erlbaum.

Hetherington, E. M. (2003a). Intimate pathways: Changing patterns in close personal relationships across time. *Family Relations: Interdisciplinary J. Applied Family Studies, 52*(4), 318–31.

Hetherington, E. M. (2003b). Social support and the adjustment of children in divorced and remarried families. *Childhood: Global J. Child Research, 10*(2), 217–36.

Hetherington, E. M., Bridges, M., & Insabella, G. (1998). What matters? What does not? Five perspectives on the association between marital transitions and children's adjustment. *Am. Psychol., 53*, 167–84.

Hetherington, E. M., & Parke, R. D. (1993). *Child psychology: A contemporary viewpoint* (4th ed.). New York: McGraw-Hill.

Hettema, J. M. (2008). What is the genetic relationship between anxiety and depression. *Am. J. Medical Genetics, 148C*, 140–46.

Hettema, J. M., Annas, P., Neale, M. C., Kendler, K. S., & Fredrikson, M. (2003). A twin study of the genetics of fear conditioning. *Arch. Gen. Psychiatry, 60*(7), 702–08.

Hettema, J. M., Kettenmann, B., Ahluwalia, V., McCarthy, C., Kates, W. R., Schmitt, J. E., et al. (2012). Pilot multimodal twin imaging study of generalized anxiety disorder. *Depression and Anxiety, 29*, 202–09.

Hettema, J. M., Neale, M. C., & Kendler, K. S. (2001). A review and meta-analysis of the genetic epidemiology of anxiety disorders. *Am. J. Psych., 158*(10), 1568–78.

Hettema, J. M., Prescott, C. A., & Kendler, K. S. (2001). A population-based twin study of generalized anxiety disorder in men and women. *J. Nerv. Ment. Dis., 189*, 413–20.

Hettema, J. M., Prescott, C. A., & Kendler, K. S. (2004). Genetic and environmental sources of covariation between generalized anxiety disorder and neuroticism. *Am. J. Psych., 161*(9), 1581–87.

Hettema, J. M., Prescott, C. A., Myers, J. M., Neale, M. C., & Kendler, K. S. (2005). The structure of genetic and environmental risk factors for anxiety disorders in men and women. *Arch. Gen. Psychiatry, 62*(2), 182–89.

Hettema, J., Steele, J., & Miller, W. R. (2005). Motivational interviewing. *Annu. Rev. Clin. Psychol., 1*, 91–111.

Heyman, A., Wilkinson, W. E., Stafford, J. A., Helms, M. J., Sigmon, A. H., & Weinberg, T. (1984). Alzheimer's disease: A study of epidemiological aspects. *Ann. Neurol., 15*, 335–41.

Heymsfield, S. B., Allison, D. B., Heshka, S., & Pierson, R. N. (1995). Assessment of human body composition. In D. B. Allison et al. (Eds.), *Handbook of assessment methods for eating behaviors and weight-related problems: Measures, theory, research* (pp. 515–60). Thousand Oaks, CA: Sage Publications.

Hibar, D. P., Stein, J. L., Renteria, M. E., Arias-Vasquez, A., Desrivieres, S., et al. (2015). Common genetic variants influence human subcortical brain structures. *Nature, 520*, 224–29.

Hibbard, S. (2003). A critique of Lilienfeld et al.'s "The scientific status of projective techniques." *J. Pers. Assess., 80*, 260–71.

Hibell, B., Anderson, B., Ahlstrom, S., Balakireva, O., Bjaranson, T., Kokkevi, A., et al. (2000). *The 1999 ESPAD Report: Alcohol and other drugs among students in 30 European countries.* Stockholm: Swedish Council for Information on Alcohol and Drug Abuse.

Hicks, B., Krueger, R., Iacono, W., McGue, M., & Patrick, C. (2004). Family transmission and heritability of externalizing disorders: A twin family study. *Arch. Gen. Psychiatry, 61*, 922–28.

Hiday, V. A., & Burns, P. J. (2010). Mental illness and the criminal justice system. In T. L. Scheid & T. N. Brown (Eds.), *A handbook for the study of mental health: Social contexts, theories, and systems* (2nd ed., pp. 478–98). New York: Cambridge University Press.

Higgins, J. W., Williams, R. L., & McLaughlin, T. F. (2001). The effects of a token economy employing instructional consequences for a third-grade student with learning disabilities: A data-based case study. *Education and Treatment of Children, 24*, 99–106.

Higgins, S. T., Wong, C. J., Badger, G. J., Haug Ogden, D. E. H., & Dantona, R. L. (2000). Contingent reinforcement increases cocaine abstinence during outpatient treatment and 1 year of follow-up. *J. Cons. Clin. Psychol., 68*(1), 64–72.

Higuci, S. S., Matsushita, H., Imazeki, T., Kinoshita, T., Takagi, S., & Kono, H. (1994). Aldehyde dehydrogenase genotypes in Japanese alcoholics. *Lancet, 343*, 741–42.

Hijii, T., et al. (1997). Life expectancy and social adaptation in individuals with Down syndrome with and without surgery for congenital heart disease. *Clin. Pediat., 36*(6), 327–32.

Hill, A. J. (2002). Prevalence and demographics of dieting. In C. G. Fairburn & K. D. Brownell (Eds.), *Eating disorders and obesity: A comprehensive handbook* (2nd ed., pp. 80–83). New York: Guilford Press.

Hill, C. E., & Lambert, M. J. (2004). Methodological issues in studying psychotherapy process and outcomes. In M. J. Lambert (Ed.), *Bergin and Garfield's handbook of psychotherapy and behavior change* (pp. 84–135). New York: John Wiley & Sons.

Hill, J. M., Bhattacharjee, S., Pogue, A., & Lukiw, W. J. (2014, April 4). The gastrointestinal tract microbiome and potential link to Alzheimer's disease. *Frontiers in Neurology.* Retrieved from http://dx.doi.org/10.3389/fneur.2014.00043

Hill, J. O., Wyatt, H. R., Reed, G. W., & Peters, J. C. (2003, February 7). Obesity and the environment: Where do we go from here? *Science, 299*, 853–55.

Hiller, W., Kroymann, R., Leibbrand, R., Cebulla, M., Korn, H. J., Rief, W., et al. (2004). Effects and cost-effectiveness analysis of inpatient treatment for somatoform disorders. *Fortschritte Der Neurologie, Psychiatrie, 72*(3), 136–46.

Hiller, W., Rief, W., & Brähler, E. (2006). Somatization in the population: From mild bodily misperceptions to disabling symptoms. *Social Psychiatry and Psychiatric Epidemiology, 41*, 704–12.

Hillman, J., Snyder, S., & Neubrander, J. (2007). *Childhood autism: A clinician's guide to early diagnosis and integrated treatment.* New York: Routledge/Taylor & Francis Group.

Hines, L. A., Sundin, J., Rona, R. J., Wessely, S., & Fear, N. T. (2014). Posttraumatic stress disorder post Iraq and Afghanistan: Prevalence among military subgroups. *Canadian J. Psychiatry, 59*, 468–79.

Hines, M. (2004). *Brain gender.* New York: Oxford University Press.

Hing, N., & Breen, H. (2001). Profiling lady luck: An empirical study of gambling and problem gambling amongst female club members. *J. Gambling Studies, 17*(1), 47–69.

Hinshaw, S. P. (1994). Conduct disorder in childhood: Conceptualization, diagnosis, comorbidity, and risk status for antisocial functioning in adulthood. In D. C. Fowles, P. Sutker, & S. H. Goodman (Eds.), *Progress in experimental personality and psychopathology research.* New York: Springer.

Hinton, D. E., Chong, R., Pollack, M. H., Barlow, D. H., & McNally, R. J. (2008). Ataque de nervios: Relationship to anxiety sensitivity and dissociation predisposition. *Depression and Anxiety, 25*(6), 489–95. doi:10.1002/da. 20309

Hinton, D. E., Hufford, D. J., & Kirmayer, L. J. (2005). Culture and sleep paralysis. *Transcult. Psychiatry, 42*(1), 5–10.

Hinton, D. E., Lewis-Fernández, R., & Pollack, M. H. (2009). A model of the generation of ataque de nervios: The role of fear of negative affect and fear of arousal symptoms. *CNS Neurosci. Therap., 15*(3), 264–75. doi:10.1111/j.1755-5949.2009.00101.x

Hinton, D. E., Park, L., Hsia, C., Hofmann, S., & Pollack, M. H. (2009). Anxiety disorder presentations in Asian populations: A review. *CNS Neurosci. Ther., 15*(3), 295–303. doi:10.1111/j.1755-5949.2009.00095.x

Hiroto, D. S., & Seligman, M. E. P. (1975). Generality of learned helplessness in man. *J. Pers. Soc. Psychol., 31*(2), 311–27.

Hirsch, C. R., Clark, D. M., & Mathews, A. (2006). Imagery and interpretations in social phobia: Support for the combined cognitive biases hypothesis. *Behavior Therapy, 37*(3), 223–36.

Hirsch, C., Clark, D. M., Mathews, A., & Williams, R. (2003). Self-images play a causal role in social phobia. *Behav. Res. Ther., 41*(8), 909–21.

Hirsch, C. R., Meynen, T., & Clark, D. M. (2004). Negative self-imagery in social anxiety contaminates social interactions. *Memory, 12*(4), 496–506.

Hirsch, S. R., & Leff, J. P. (1975). *Abnormalities in parents of schizophrenics.* London: Oxford University Press.

Hirschfeld, M. (1948). *Sexual anomalies* (p. 167). New York: Emerson.

Hirshfeld-Becker, D. R., Biederman, J., Henin, A., Faraone, S. V., Davis, S., Harrington, K., et al. (2007). Behavioral inhibition in preschool children at risk is a specific predictor of middle childhood social anxiety: A five-year follow-up. *J. Develop-mental & Behavioral Pediatrics, 28*(3), 225–33.

Hirshfeld-Becker, D. R., Masek, B., Henin, A., Blakely, L. R., Pollock-Wurman, R. A., McQuade, J., et al. (2010). Cognitive behavioral therapy for 4- to 7-year-old children with anxiety disorders: A randomized clinical trial. *J. Cons. Clin. Psychol., 78*(4), 498–510.

Ho, B.-C., Andreasen, N. C., Ziebell, S., Pierson, R., & Magnotta, V. (2011). Long-term antipsychotic treatment and brain volumes: A longitudinal study of first-episode schizophrenia. *Arch. Gen. Psychiatry, 68,* 128–37.

Hobfoll, S., Ritter, C., Lavin, J., Hulsizer, M., et al. (1995). Depression prevalence and incidence among inner-city pregnant and postpartum women. *J. Cons. Clin. Psychol., 3,* 445–53.

Hodgins, D. C., & el-Guebaly, N. (2004). Retrospective and prospective reports of precipitants to relapse in pathological gambling. *J. Cons. Clin. Psychol., 72,* 72–80.

Hodgins, S., & Lalonde, N. (1999). Major mental disorders and crime: Changes over time? In P. Cohen & C. Slomkowski et al. (Eds.), *Historical and geographical influences on psychopathology* (pp. 57–83). Mahwah, NJ: Erlbaum.

Hoek, H. W. (2002). Distribution of eating disorders. In C. G. Fairburn & K. D. Brownell (Eds.), *Eating disorders and obesity: A comprehensive handbook* (2nd ed., pp. 233–37). New York: Guilford Press.

Hoeppner, B. B., Barnett, N. P., Jackson, K. M., Colby, S. M., Kahler, C. W., Monti, P. M, et al. (2012). Daily college student drinking patterns across the first year of college. *J. Stud. Alcohol Drugs, 73,* 613–624.

Hoeve, M., Dubas, J. S., Eichelsheim, V. I., van der Laan, P. H., Smeenk, W., & Gerris, J. R. M. (2009). The relationship between parenting and delinquency: A meta-analysis. *J. Abn. Child Psychol., 37*(6), 749–75. doi:10.1007/s10802-009-9310-8

Hofer, S. M., Christensen, H., Mackinnon, A., Korten, A. E., Jorm, A. F., Henderson, A. F., et al. (2002). Change in cognitive functioning associated with ApoE genotype in a community sample of older adults. *Psychol. Aging, 17*(2), 194–208.

Hoffman, D. L., Dukes, E. M., & Wittchen, H. U. (2008). Human and economic burden of generalized anxiety disorder. *Depression and Anxiety, 25,* 72–90.

Hoffman, R. E., Gueorguieva, R., Hawkins, K. A., Varanko, M., Boutros, N. N., Wu, Y.-T., et al. (2005). Temporoparietal transcranial magnetic stimulation for auditory hallucinations: Safety, efficacy and moderators in a fifty patient sample. *Biol. Psychiatry, 58,* 97–104.

Hoffmann, H. (2012). Considering the role of conditioning in sexual orientation. *Arch. Sexual Behavior,* pp. 1–9.

Hofman, S. G., Meuret, A. E., Smits, J. A., Simon, N. M., Pollack, M. H., Eisenmenger, K., et al. (2006). Augmentation of exposure therapy with D-cycloserine for social anxiety disorder. *Arch. Gen. Psychiatry, 63,* 298–304.

Hofmann, A. (1971). LSD discoverer disputes "chance" factor in finding. *Psychiatr. News, 6*(8), 23–26.

Hofmann, S. G., Otto, M. W., Pollack, M. H., & Smits, J. A. (2015). D-cycloserine augmentation of cognitive behavioural therapy for anxiety disorders: An update. *Current Psychiatry Reports, 17,* 532.

Hogarty, G. E., et al. (1997a). Three-year trials of personal therapy among schizophrenic patients living with or independent of family: I. Description of study and effects on relapse rate. *Am. J. Psychiatry, 154*(11), 1504–13.

Hogarty, G. E., et al. (1997b). Three-year trials of personal therapy among schizophrenic patients living with or independent of family, II: Effects on adjustment of patients. *Am. J. Psychiatry, 154*(11), 1514–24.

Hogarty, G. E., Anderson, C. M., Reiss, D. J., Kornblith, S. J., Greenwald, D. P., Javna, C. D., et al. (1986). Family psychoeducation, social skills training, and maintenance chemotherapy in the aftercare treatment of schizophrenia. *Arch. Gen. Psychiatry, 43,* 633–42.

Hoge, C. W., Castro, C. A., Messer, S. C., McGurk, D., Cotting, D. I., & Koffman, R. L. (2004). Combat duty in Iraq and Afghanistan, mental health problems, and barriers to care. *N. Engl. J. Med., 351,* 13–32.

Hoge, C. W., McGurk, T. D., Thomas, J. L., Cox, A. L., Engel, C. C., & Castro, C. A. (2008). Mild traumatic brain injury in soldiers returning from Iraq. *New England J. Medicine, 358,* 453–63.

Hoiseth, G., Fosen, J. T., Liane, V., Bogstrand, S. T., & Morland, J. (2015). Alcohol hangover as a cause of impairment in apprehended drivers. *Traffic Injury Prevention, 16,* 323–28.

Holliday, J., Wall, E., Treasure, J., & Weinman, J. (2005). Perceptions of illness in individuals with anorexia nervosa: A comparison with lay men and women. *Int. J. Eat. Dis., 37,* 50–56.

Hollister, J. M., Laing, P., & Mednick, S. A. (1996). Rhesus incompatibility as a risk factor for schizophrenia in male adults. *Arch. Gen. Psychiatry, 53,* 19–24.

Hollon, S. D. (2011). Cognitive and behavior therapy in the treatment and prevention of depression. *Depression and Anxiety, 28,* 263–66.

Hollon, S. D., & Beck, A. T. (1994). Cognitive and cognitive-behavioral therapies. In A. E. Bergin & S. L. Garfield (Eds.), *Handbook of psychotherapy and behavior change* (4th ed., pp. 428–66). New York: Wiley.

Hollon, S. D., & Beck, A. T. (2004). Cognitive and cognitive behavioral therapies. In M. J. Lambert (Ed.), *Bergin and Garfield's handbook of psychotherapy and behavior change* (pp. 447–52). New York: John Wiley & Sons.

Hollon, S. D., DeRubeis, R. J., Shelton, R. C., Amsterdam, J. D., Salomon, R. M., O'Reardon, J. P., et al. (2005). Prevention of relapse following cognitive therapy vs medications in moderate to severe depression. *Arch. Gen. Psychiatry, 62,* 417–22.

Hollon, S. D., & Dimidjian, S. (2009). Cognitive and behaviors treatment of depression. In I. H. Gotlib & C. L. Hammen (Eds.), *Handbook of depression and its treatment* (2nd ed.). New York: Guilford Press.

Hollon, S. D., & Fawcett, J. (1995). Combined medication and psychotherapy. In G. O. Gabbard (Ed.), *Treatments of psychiatric disorders* (2nd ed., Vol. 1, pp. 1221–36). Washington, DC: American Psychiatric Press.

Hollon, S. D., Haman, K. L., & Brown, L. L. (2002). Cognitive-behavioral treatment of depression. In I. H. Gotlib & C. L. Hammen (Eds.), *Handbook of depression* (pp. 383–403). New York: Guilford Press.

Hollon, S. D., & Ponniah, K. (2010). A review of empirically supported psychological therapies for mood disorders in adults. *Depression and Anxiety, 27*(10), 891–832. doi:10.1002/da. 20741

Hollon, S. D., Stewart, M. O., & Strunk, D. (2006). Enduring effects for cognitive behavior therapy in the treatment of depression and anxiety. *Annu. Rev. Psychol., 57,* 285–315.

Hollon, S. D., Thase, M. E., & Markowitz, J. C. (2002). Treatment and prevention of depression. *Psychol. Sci. in the Pub. Int., 3*(2, suppl.), 39–77.

Holmes, E. A., James, E. L., Coode-Bate, T., & Deeprose, C. (2009). Can playing the computer game "Tetris" reduce the build-up of flashbacks for trauma? A proposal from cognitive science. *PLoSONE, 4*(1), e4153. doi:10.1371/journal.pone.0004153

Holmes, E. A., James, E. L., Kilford, E. J., & Deeprose, C. (2010). Key steps in developing a cognitive vaccine against traumatic flashbacks: Visuospatial Tetris versus verbal pub quiz. *PLoS ONE, 5,* e13706.

Holmes, T. H., & Rahe, R. H. (1967). The social readjustment rating scale. *J. Psychosom. Res., 11*(2), 213–18.

Holroyd, K. A. (2002). Assessment and psychological management of recurrent headache disorders. *J. Cons. Clin. Psychol., 70*(3), 656–77.

Holsboer, F. (1992). The hypothalamic-pituitary-adreno-cortical system. In E. S. Paykel (Ed.), *Handbook of affective disorders* (2nd ed.). New York: Guilford Press.

Holsinger, T., Steffens, D. C., Helms, P. C., Havlik, R. J., Bretiner, J. C., Guralnik, J. M., et al. (2002). Head injury in early adulthood and the lifetime risk of depression. *Arch. Gen. Psychiatry, 59*(1), 17–22.

Holvey, D. N., & Talbott, J. H. (Eds.). (1972). *The Merck manual of diagnosis and therapy* (12th ed.). Rahway, NJ: Merck, Sharp, & Dohme Research Laboratories.

Holzer, C. E., Goldsmith, H. F., & Ciarlo, J. A. (1998). Effects of rural-urban county type on the availability of health and mental health care providers. In R. W. Manderscheid & M. J. Henderson (Eds.), *Mental health, United States.* Rockville, MD: Center for Mental Health Services.

Honkonen, T., Karlsson, H., Koivisto, A. M., Stengård, E., & Salokangas, R. K. R. (2003). Schizophrenic patients in different treatment settings during the era of deinstitutionalization: Three-year follow-up of three discharge cohorts in Finland. *Austral. NZ J. Psychiatry, 37*(2), 160–68.

Hooker, C., & Park, S. (2002). Emotion processing and its relationship to social functioning in schizophrenia patients. *Psychiatry Research, 112,* 41–50.

Hooker, E. (1957). The adjustment of the male overt homosexual. *J. Projective Techniques, 21,* 18–30.

Hooley, J. M. (2007). Expressed emotion and relapse of psychopathology. *Annu. Rev. Clin. Psychol., 3,* 329–52.

Hooley, J. M. (2010). Social factors in schizophrenia. *Curr. Dir. Psych. Sci., 19,* 238–42.

Hooley, J. M. (2015). Social functioning and schizophrenia. In T. Millon, P. Blaney, & R. Davis (Eds.), *Oxford textbook of psychopathology* (3rd ed.). New York: Oxford University Press.

Hooley, J. M., & Campbell, C. (2002). Control and controllability: Beliefs and behavior in high and low expressed emotion relatives. *Psychol. Med., 32*(6), 1091–99.

Hooley, J., Cole, S., & Gironde, S. (2012). Borderline personality disorder. In T. Widiger (Ed.), *The Oxford handbook of personality disorders* (pp. 409–36). Oxford, UK: Oxford University Press.

Hooley, J. M., Franklin, J. C., & Nock, M. K. (2014). Chronic pain and suicide: Understanding the association. *Current Pain and Headache Reports, 18,* 435.

Hooley, J. M., & Gotlib, I. H. (2000). A diathesis-stress conceptualization of expressed emotion and clinical outcome. *App. Prev. Psychol., 9,* 135–51.

Hooley, J. M., Gruber, S. A., Parker, H., Guillaumot, J., Rogowska, J., & Yurgelun-Todd, D. A. (2009). Cortico-limbic response to personally-challenging emotional stimuli after complete recovery from major depression. *Psychiatry Research: Neuroimaging, 171*(2), 106–19.

Hooley, J. M., Gruber, S. A., Parker, H. A., Guillaumot, J., Rogowska, J., & Yurgelun-Todd, D. A. (2010). Neural processing of emotional overinvolvement in borderline personality disorder. *J. Clin. Psychiatry, 71,* 1017–24.

Hooley, J. M., & Hiller, J. B. (2001). Family relationships and major mental disorder: Risk factors and preventive strategies. In B. R. Sarason & S. Duck (Eds.), *Personal relationships: Implications for clinical and community psychology* (pp. 61–87). New York: Wiley.

Hooley, J. M., Ho, D. T., Slater, J., & Lockshin, A. (2010). Pain perception and nonsuicidal self-injury: A laboratory investigation. *Personality Disorders: Theory, Research, and Treatment, 1,* 170–79.

Hooley, J. M., Rosen, L. R., & Richters, J. E. (1995). Expressed emotion: Toward clarification of a critical construct. In G. Miller (Ed.), *The behavioral high-risk paradigm in psychopathology* (pp. 88–120). New York: Springer.

Hopfer, C., Mendelson, B., Van Leeuwen, J. M., Kelly, S., & Hooks, S. (2006). Club drug use among youths in treatment for substance abuse. *Am. J. Addictions, 15*(1), 94–99.

Hopwood, C. J., & Thomas, K. T. (2012). Paranoid and schizoid personality disorders. In T. Widiger (Ed.), *The Oxford handbook of personality disorders* (pp. 582–602). Oxford, UK: Oxford University Press.

Horn, S. D. (2003). Limiting access to psychiatric services can increase total health care costs. *Drug Benefit Trends, 15*(Suppl. I), 12–18.

Hornish, G. G., & Leonard, K. E. (2007). The drinking partnership and marital satisfaction: The longitudinal influence of discrepant drinking. *J. Cons. Clin. Psych., 75*, 43–51.

Horowitz, J. L., & Garber, J. (2006). The prevention of depressive symptoms in children and adolescents: A meta-analytic review. *J. Cons. Clin. Psychol., 74*, 401–15.

Horowitz, M. J., Merluzzi, R. V., Ewert, M., Ghannam, J. H., Harley, D., & Stinson, C. H. (1991). Role-relationship models of configuration (RRMC). In M. Horowitz (Ed.), *Person schemas and maladaptive interpersonal patterns* (pp. 115–54). Chicago: University of Chicago Press.

Horton, A. M., Jr. (2008). The Halstead-Reitan Neuro-psychological Test Battery: Past, present, and future. In A. M. Horton, Jr. & D. Wedding (Eds.), *The neuropsychology handbook* (3rd ed., pp. 251–78). New York: Springer.

Horton, R. S., Bleau, G., & Drwecki, B. (2006). Parenting narcissus: What are the links between parenting and narcissism? *J. Pers., 74*, 345–76.

Hoskins, M., Pearce, J., Bethell, A., Dankova, L., Barbui, C., Tol, W. A., et al. (2015). Pharmacotherapy for post-traumatic stress disorder: Systematic review and meta-analysis. *Brit. J. Psychiatry, 206*, 93–100.

Hoste, R. R., Hewell, K., & le Grange, D. (2007). Family interaction among white and ethnic minority adolescents with bulimia nervosa and their parents. *European Eating Disorders Review, 15*, 152–58.

Houtjes, W., van Meijel, B., Deeg, D. J. H., & Beekman, A. T. F. (2010). Major depressive disorder in late life: A multifocus perspective on care needs. *Aging & Mental Health, 14*(7), 874–80.

Houts, A. C., Berman, J. S., & Abramson, H. (1994). Effectiveness of psychological and pharmacological treatments for nocturnal enuresis. *J. Cons. Clin. Psychol., 62*, 737–45.

Howes, O. D., Kambeitz, J., Kim, E., Stahl, D., Slifstein, M., Abi-Dargham, A., & Kapur, S. (2012). The nature of dopamine dysfunction in schizophrenia and what this means for treatment. *Arch. General Psychiatry, 69*, 776–86.

Howland, R. H., & Thase, M. E. (1999). Affective disorders: Biological aspects. In T. Millon & P. H. Blaney et al. (Eds.), *Oxford textbook of psychopathology. Oxford textbooks in clinical psychology* (Vol. 4, pp. 166–202). New York: Oxford University Press.

Hoza, B., Mrug, S., Gerdes, A. C., Hinshaw, S. P., Bukowski, W. M., Gold, J. A., et al. (2005). What aspects of peer relationships are impaired in children with Attention Deficit/Hyperactivity Disorder? ? *J. Cons. Clin. Psychol., 73*, 411–23.

Hsu, L. K., Benotti, P. N., Dwyer, J., Roberts, S. B., Saltzman, E., Shikora, S., et al. (1998). Nonsurgical factors that influence the outcome of bariatric surgery: A review. *Psychosom. Med., 60*, 338–46.

Hsu, W.-Y., Ku, Y., Zanto, T. P., & Gazzaley, A. (2015). Effects of noninvasive brain stimulation on cognitive function in healthy aging and Alzheimer's disease: A systematic review and meta-analysis. *Neurobiology of Aging, 36*, 2348–59.

Hu, X.-Z., Rush, A. J., Charney, D., Wilson, A. F., Sorant, A. J. M., Papanicolaou, G. J., et al. (2007). Association between a functional serotonin transporter promoter polymorphism and citalopram treatment in adult outpatients with major depression. *Arch. Gen. Psychiatry, 64*, 783–92.

Huber, K., & Tamminga, C. A. (2007). Fragile X syndrome: Molecular mechanisms of cognitive dysfunction. *Am. J. Psychiatry, 164*(4), 556.

Hucker, S. J. (1997). Sexual sadism: Psychopathology and theory. In D. R. Laws & W. O'Donohue (Eds.), *Sexual deviance: Theory, assessment, and treatment* (pp. 210–24). New York: Guilford Press.

Hucker, S. J. (2011). Hypoxyphilia. *Arch. Sexual Behavior, 40*, 1323–26.

Hudson, J. I., Hiripi, E., Pope, H. G., & Kessler, R. C. (2007). The prevalence and correlates of eating disorders in the National Comorbidity Survey Replication. *Biol. Psychiatry, 61*(3), 348–58.

Hudson, J. L., & Rapee, R. M. (2001). Parent-child interactions and anxiety disorders: An observational study. *Behav. Res. Ther., 39*(12), 1411–27.

Hudson, J. L., & Rapee, R. M. (2009). Familial and social environments in the etiology and maintenance of anxiety disorders. In M. M. Antony & M. B. Stein (Eds.), *Oxford handbook of anxiety and related disorders* (pp. 173–89). New York: Oxford University Press.

Hudson, S. M., & Ward, T. (1997). Rape: Psychopathology and theory. In D. R. Laws & W. O'Donohue (Eds.), *Sexual deviance: Theory, assessment and treatment* (pp. 332–55). New York: Guilford Press.

Hughes, J. R. (2007). Measurement of the effects of abstinence from tobacco: A qualitative review. *Psych. Addict. Behav., 21*(2), 127–37.

Hulshoff Pol, H. E., & Kahn, R. S. (2008). What happens after the first episode? A review of progressive brain changes in chronically ill patients with schizophrenia. *Schizo. Bull., 34*, 354–66.

Hummelen, B., Wilberg, T., Pedersen, G., & Karterud, S. (2007). The relationship between avoidant personality disorder and social phobia. *Compr. Psychiatry, 48*, 348–56.

Humphreys, K., & Rappaport, J. (1993). From community mental health movement to the war on drugs: A study of the definition of social problems. *Am. Psychol., 48*(8), 892–901.

Humphry, D., & Wickett, A. (1986). *The right to die: Understanding euthanasia.* New York: Harper & Row.

Hunkeler, E. M., Spector, W. D., Fireman, B., Rice, D. P., & Weisner, C. (2003). Psychiatric symptoms, impaired function, and medical care costs in an HMO setting. *General Hospital Psychiatry, 2*, 178–84. doi:http://dx.doi.org/10.1016/S0163-8343(03)00018-5

Hunsley, J., & Bailey, J. M. (1999). The clinical utility of the Rorschach: Unfulfilled promises and an uncertain future. *Psychol. Assess., 11*(3), 266–77.

Hunter, C. L., Goodie, J. L., Oordt, M. S., & Dobmeyer, A. C. (2009). *Integrated behavioral health in primary care: Step-by-step guidance for assessment and intervention.* Washington, DC: American Psychological Association.

Hunter, E. C. M., Phillips, M. L., Chalder, T., Sierra, M., & David, A. S. (2003). Depersonalization disorder: A cognitive-behavioural conceptualisation. *Behav. Res. Ther., 41*, 1451–67.

Huntjens, R. J. C., Peters, M. L., Postma, A., Woertman, L., Effting, M., & van der Hart, O. (2005). Transfer of newly acquired stimulus valence between identities in dissociative identity disorder (DID). *Behav. Res. Ther., 43*, 243–55.

Husain, M., & Mehta, M. A. (2011). Cognitive enhancement by drugs in health and disease. *Trends in Cognitive Sciences, 15*, 28–36.

Hussong, A. M., Hicks, R. E., Levy, S. A., & Curran, P. J. (2001). Specifying the relations between affect and heavy alcohol use among young adults. *J. Abn. Psychol., 110*(3), 449–61.

Hutchins, E. C., Frank, R. G., & Glied, S. A. (2011). The evolving private psychiatric inpatient market. *The J. Behavioral Health Services & Research, 38*(1), 122–31.

Hyman, S. E. (2011). Cognitive enhancement: Promise and perils. *Neuron, 69*, 595–98.

I

Iacono, W. G., Moreau, M., Beiser, M., Fleming, J. A., & Lin, T. (1992). Smooth-pursuit eye tracking in first-episode psychotic patients and their relatives. *J. Abn. Psychol., 101*(1), 104–16.

Iancu, I., Dannon, P. N., Lustig, M., Sasson, Y., & Zohar, J. (2000). Preferential efficacy of serotonergic medication in obsessive-compulsive disorder: From practice to theory. In W. K. Goodman & M. V. Rudorfer et al. (Eds.), *Obsessive-compulsive disorder: Contemporary issues in treatment. Personality and clinical psychology series* (pp. 303–13). Mahwah, NJ: Erlbaum.

Ibarra-Rovillard, M. S., & Kuiper, N. A. (2011). Social support and social negativity findings in depression: Perceived responsiveness to basic psychological needs. *Clin. Psychol. Rev., 31*(3), 342–52. doi:10.1016/j.cpr.2011.01.005

Igwe, M. (2103). Dissociative fugue symptoms in a 28-year-old male Nigerian medical student: A case report. *J. Medical Case Reports, 7*, 143.

Ilechukwu, S. T. (1992). Magical penis loss in Nigeria: Report of a recent epidemic of a koro-like syndrome. *Trans. Cult. Psych. Res. Rev., 29*(2), 91–108.

Ilott, N., Saudino, K. J., Wood, A., & Asherson, P. (2010). A genetic study of ADHD and activity level in infancy. *Genes, Brain & Behavior, 9*(3), 296–304.

Ingram, R. E., & Luxton, D. D. (2005). Vulnerability-stress models. In B. J. Hankin & J. R. Z. Abela (Eds.), *Development of psychopathology: A vulnerability-stress perspective* (pp. 32–46). Thousand Oaks, CA: Sage Publications.

Ingram, R. E., Miranda, J., & Segal, Z. (2006). Cognitive vulnerability to depression. In L. B. Alloy & J. H. Riskind (Eds.), *Cognitive vulnerability to emotional disorders* (pp. 63–91). Mahwah, NJ: Lawrence Erlbaum Associates.

Ingram, R. E., & Price, J. M. (Eds.). (2001). *Vulnerability to psychopathology: Risk across the lifespan.* New York: Guilford Press.

Ingram, R. E., Scott, W., & Siegle, G. (1999). Depression: Social and cognitive aspects. In T. Millon & P. H. Blaney et al. (Eds.), *Oxford textbook of psychopathology* (pp. 203–26). New York: Oxford University Press.

Insel, T. R. (2010). Rethinking schizophrenia. *Nature, 468*(11 November), 187–93.

Insel, T. R. (2014). Mental disorders in childhood: Shifting the focus from behavioral symptoms to neurodevelopmental trajectories. *JAMA, 311*(17), 1727–28. doi:10.1001/jama.2014.1193

Institute of Medicine. (2006). *Improving the quality of health care for mental and substance abuse conditions.* Washington, DC: National Academies Press.

in't Veld, B. A., Ruitenberg, A., Hofman, A., Launer, L. J., van Duijn, C. M., Stijnen, T., Breteler, M. M. B., & Stricker, B. H. C. (2001). Nonsteroidal anti-inflammatory drugs and the risk of Alzheimer's disease. *N. Engl. J. Med., 345*, 1515–21.

Ipser, J. C., Kariuki, C. M., & Stein, D. J. (2008). Pharmacotherapy for social anxiety disorder: A systematic review. *Expert Review of Neurotherapeutics, 8*(2), 235–57.

Irie, F., Masaki, K. H., Petrovitch, H., Abbott, R. D., Ross, G. W., Taaffe, D. R., et al. (2008). Apolipoprotein E Σ4 allele genotype and the effect of depressive symptoms on the risk of dementia in men. *Arch. Gen. Psychiatry, 65*, 906–12.

IsHak, W. W., Bolton, M. A., Bensoussan, J. C., Dous, G. V., Nguyen, T. T., Powell-Hicks, A. L., et al. (2012). Quality of life in body dysmorphic disorder. *CNS Spectrums, 17,* 167–75.

Ishikawa, S. S., Raine, A., Lencz, T., Bihrle, S., & Lacasse, L. (2001). Autonomic stress reactivity and executive functions in successful and unsuccessful criminal psychopaths from the community. *J. Abn. Psychol., 110*(3), 423–32.

Isohanni, M., Jones, P., Moilanen, K., Veijola, J., Oja, H., Koiranen, M., et al. (2001). Early developmental milestones in adult schizophrenia and other psychoses. A 31-year follow-up of the North Finland 1966 birth cohort. *Schiz. Res., 52,* 1–19.

Ivan, C. S., Seshadri, S., Beiser, A., Au, R., Kase, C., Kelly-Hayes, M., et al. (2004). Dementia after stroke: The Framingham study. *Stroke, 35,* 1264–68.

Iversen, A. C., van Staden, L., Hughes, J. H., Browne, T., Hull, L., Hall, J., et al. (2009). The prevalence of common mental disorders and PTSD in the UK military: Using data from a clinical interview-based study. *BMC Psychiatry, 9,* 68. doi:10.1186/1471-244X-9-68

J

Jääskeläinen, E., Juola, P., Hirvonen, N., McGrath, J. J., Saga, S., Isohanni, M., et al. (2013). A systematic review and meta-analysis of recovery in schizophrenia. *Schizophrenia Bulletin.* doi:10.1093/schbul/sbs130

Jablensky, A., et al. (1992). Schizophrenia: Manifestations, incidence, and course in different cultures. A World Health Organization ten-country study. *Psychological Medicine Monograph Supplement, 20,* 1–97.

Jackson, A. P., & Huang, C. C. (2000). Parenting stress and behavior among single mothers of preschoolers: The mediating role of self-efficacy. *J. Social Service Research, 26,* 29–42.

Jackson, D. B., & Beaver, K. M. (2015). A shared pathway of antisocial risk: A path model of parent and child effects. *Journal of Criminal Justice, 43,* 154–63.

Jacob, T., & Johnson, S. L. (2001). Sequential interactions in the parent-child communications of depressed fathers and depressed mothers. *J. Fam. Psychol., 15*(1), 38–52.

Jacobi, C., Hayward, C., de Zwaan, M., Kraemer, H. C., & Agras, W. S. (2004). Coming to terms with risk factors for eating disorders: Application of risk terminology and suggestions for a general taxonomy. *Psych. Bull., 130*(1), 19–65.

Jacobs, T. L., Epel, E. S., Lin, J., Blackburn, E. H., Wolkowitz, O. M., Bridwell, D. A. et al., (2011). Intensive meditation training, immune cell telomerase activity, and psychological mediators. *Psychoneuroendocrinology, 36,* 664–81.

Jacobson, N. S., & Addis, M. E. (1993). Research on couples and couple therapy: What do we know? Where are we going? *J. Cons. Clin. Psychol., 61,* 85–93.

Jacobson, N. S., Christensen, A., Prince, S. E., Cordova, J., & Eldridge, K. (2000). Integrative behavioral couple therapy: An acceptance-based, promising new treatment for couple discord. *J. Cons. Clin. Psychol., 68,* 351–55.

Jacobson, N. S., Dobson, K. S., Truax, P. A., Addis, M. E., Koerner, K., Gollan, J. K., et al. (1996). A component analysis of cognitive behavioral treatment for depression. *J. Cons. Clin. Psychol., 64,* 295–304.

Jacobson, N. S., Martell, C. R., & Dimidjian, S. (2001). Behavioral activation treatment for depression: Returning to contextual roots. *Clin. Psychol. Sci. Prac., 8*(3), 255–70.

Jacobson, N. S., Schmaling, K. B., & Holtzworth-Monroe, A. (1987). A component analysis of behavioral marital therapy: Two-year follow-up and prediction of relapse. *J. Marit. Fam. Ther., 13,* 187–95.

Jaffee, S., Caspi, A., Moffitt, T., Dodge, K., Rutter, M., Taylor, A., et al. (2005). Nature x nurture: Genetic vulnerabilities interact with physical maltreatment to promote conduct problems. *Develop. Psychopath., 17,* 67–84.

Jalbert, J. J., Daiello, L. A., & Lapane, K. L. (2008). Dementia of the Alzheimer type. *Epidemiol Rev, 30,* 15–34.

Jamieson, J. P., Koslov, K., Nock, M. K., & Mendes, W. B. (2013). Experiencing discrimination increases risk-taking. *Psychological Science, 24,* 131–39.

Jamieson, R., & Wells, C. (1979). Manic psychosis in a patient with multiple metastatic brain tumors. *J. Clin. Psychiatry, 40,* 280–83.

Jamison, K. R. (1993). *Touched with fire.* New York: Free Press.

Jamison, K. R. (1999). *Night falls fast: Understanding suicide.* New York: Vintage Books.

Janet, P. (1901). *The mental state of hystericals: A study of mental stigmata and mental accidents.* New York: Putnam.

Janet, P. (1907). *The major symptoms of hysteria.* New York: Macmillan.

Jang, K. L., Thordarson, D. S., Stein, M. B., Cohan, S. L., & Taylor, S. (2007). Coping styles and personality: A biometric analysis. *Anxiety, Stress and Coping: An International Journal, 20,* 17–24.

Jang, K. L., Woodward, T., Lang, D., Honer, W., & Livesley, W. J. (2005). The genetic and environmental basis of the relationship between schizotypy and personality: A twin study. *J. Nerv. Ment. Dis., 193,* 153–59.

Janicak, P. G., Dowd, S. M., Strong, M. J., Alam, D., & Beedle, D. (2005). The potential role of repetitive transcranial magnetic stimulation in treating severe depression. *Psychiatr. Ann., 35*(2), 138–45.

Janicki, M. P., & Dalton, A. J. (1993). Alzheimer disease in a select population of older adults with mental retardation. *Irish J. Psychology: Special Issue, Psychological Aspects of Aging, 14*(1), 38–47.

Jankovic, J. (1997). Phenomenology and classification of tics. *Neurologic Clinics, 15*(2), 267–75.

Janofsky, J. S., Dunn, M. H., Roskes, E. J., Briskin, J. K., & Rudolph, M. S. (1996). Insanity defense pleas in Baltimore city: An analysis of outcome. *Am. J. Psychiatry, 153*(11), 1464–68.

Janowsky, D. S., Addario, D., & Risch, S. C. (1987). *Pharmacology case studies.* New York: Guilford Press.

Janssen, I., Hanssen, M., Bak, M., Bijl, R. V., De Graaf, R., Vollebergh, W., et al. (2003). Discrimination and delusional ideation. *Brit. J. Psychiatry, 182,* 71–76.

Jaranson, J., Butcher, J. N., Halcón, L., Johnson, D. R., Robertson, C., Savik, K., et al. (2004). Somali and Oromo refugees: Correlates of torture and trauma. *Am. J. Pub. Health, 94,* 591–97.

Jaremka, L. M., Lindgren, M. E., & Kiecolt-Glaser, J. K. (2013). Synergistic relationships among stress, depression, and troubled relationships: Insights from psychoneuroimmunology. *Depression and Anxiety, 30,* 288–96.

Jarvik, M. E. (1967). The psychopharmacological revolution. *Psych. Today, 1*(1), 51–58.

Jasper, F., & Witthöft, M. (2011). Health anxiety and attentional bias: The time course of vigilance and avoidance in light of pictorial illness information. *J. Anxiety Disorders, 25*(8), 1131–38.

Javaras, K. N., Laird, N. M., Reichborn-Kjennerud, T., Bulik, C. M., Pope, H. R., & Hidson, J. I. (2008). Familiarity and heritability of binge eating disorder: Results of a case-control family study and a twin study. *Int. J. Eat. Dis., 41,* 174–79.

Javitt, D. C. (2012). Twenty-five years of glutamate in schizophrenia: Are we there yet? *Schizophrenia Bulletin, 38,* 911–13.

Jeffrey, R. W., Adlis, S. A., & Forster, J. L. (1991). Prevalence of dieting among working men and women: The healthy worker project. *Health Psychol., 10,* 274–81.

Jenike, M. A. (2000). Neurosurgical treatment of obsessive-compulsive disorder. In W. K. Goodman & M. V. Rudorfer et al. (Eds.), *Obsessive-compulsive disorder: Contemporary issues in treatment. Personality and clinical psychology series* (pp. 457–82). Mahwah, NJ: Erlbaum.

Jenkins, J. H., & Carpenter-Song, E. A. (2008). Awareness of stigma among persons with schizophrenia. *J. Nerv. Ment. Dis., 197,* 520–29.

Jensen, C. D., Cushing, C. C., Aylward, B. S., Craig, J. T., Sorell, D. M., & Steele, R. G. (2011). Effectiveness of motivational interviewing interventions for adolescent substance use behavior change: A meta-analytic review. *J. Cons. Clin. Psychol., 79,* 433–40.

Jick, H., Kaye, J. A., & Jick, S. S. (2004). Antidepressants and the risk of suicidal behaviors. *JAMA, 292*(3), 338–43.

Jobe, T. H., & Harrow, M. (2010). Schizophrenia course, long-term outcome, recovery, and prognosis. *Curr. Dir. Psych. Sci., 19,* 220–25.

Johansson, P., Høgland, P., Ulberg, R., Amlo, S., Marble, A., Bøgwald, K.-P., et al. (2010). The mediating role of insight for long-term improvements in psychodynamic therapy. *J. Cons. Clin. Psychol., 78,* 438–48.

John, O., & Naumann, L. (2008). Paradigm shift to the integrative Big-Five trait taxonomy: History, measurement, and conceptual issues. In O. P. John, R. Robins, & L. Pervin (Eds.), *Handbook of personality: Theory and Research* (3rd ed., pp. 114–58). New York: Guilford Press.

Johnsen, T. J., & Friborg, O. (2015). The effects of cognitive behavioral therapy as an antidepressive treatment is falling: A meta-analysis. *Psychological Bulletin, 141,* 747–68.

Johnson, C. L., Stuckey, M. K., Lewis, L. D., & Schwartz, D. M. (1982). Bulimia: A descriptive survey of 316 cases. *Int. J. Eat. Dis., 2,* 3–16.

Johnson, D. E. (2000). Medical and developmental sequelae of early childhood institutionalization in Eastern European adoptees. In C. A. Nelson (Ed.), *The Minnesota symposia on child psychology: The effects of early adversity on neurobehavioral development. Minnesota symposia on child psychology* (Vol. 31, pp. 113–62). Mahwah, NJ: Erlbaum.

Johnson, F., & Wardle, J. (2005). Dietary restraint, body dissatisfaction, and psychological distress: A prospective analysis. *J. Abn. Psychol., 114,* 119–25.

Johnson, J. D., O'Connor, K. A., Deak, T., Spencer, R. L., Watkins, L. R., & Maier, S. F. (2002). Prior stressor exposure primes the HPA axis. *Psychoneuroimmunology, 27,* 353–65.

Johnson, J. G., Cohen, P., Brown, J., Smailes, E. M., & Bernstein, D. P. (1999). Childhood maltreatment increases risk for personality disorders during early adulthood. *Arch. Gen. Psychiatry, 56,* 600–06.

Johnson, J. G., Cohen, P., Kasen, S., & Brook, J. S. (2006). Dissociative disorders among adults in the community, impaired functioning, and axis I and II comorbidity. *J. Psychiatr. Res., 40,* 131–40.

Johnson, J. G., Cohen, P., Smailes, E., Kasen, S., Oldham, J. M., & Skodol, A. E. (2000). Adolescent personality disorders associated with violence and criminal behavior during adolescence and early childhood. *Am. J. Psychiatry, 157,* 1406–12.

Johnson, P. M., & Kenny, P. J. (2010). Dopamine D2 receptors in addiction-like reward dysfunction and compulsive eating in obese rats. *Nat. Neurosci., 13*(5), 635–41.

Johnson, S. L., Cuellar, A. K., & Miller, C. (2009). Bipolar and unipolar depression: A comparison of clinical phenomenology, biological vulnerability, and psychosocial predictors. In I. H. Gotlib & C. L.

Hammen (Eds.), *Handbook of depression* (2nd ed., pp. 142–62). New York: Guilford Press.

Johnston, L. D., O'Malley, P. M., Bachman, J. G., & Schulenberg, J. E. (2007). *Monitoring the future national results on adolescent drug use: Overview of key findings, 2006* (NIH Publication No. 07-6202). Bethesda, MD: National Institute on Drug Abuse.

Johnston, L. D., O'Malley, P. M., Bachman, J. G., & Schulenberg, J. E. (2009). *Monitoring the Future National Survey results on drug use, 1975–2008: Volume I, Secondary school students* (NIH Publication No. 09-7402). Bethesda, MD: National Institute on Drug Abuse.

Joiner, T. (2005). *Why people die by suicide*. Cambridge, MA: Harvard University Press.

Joiner, T. E. (2002). Depression in its interpersonal context. In I. H. Gotlib & C. L. Hammen (Eds.), *Handbook of depression* (pp. 295–313). New York: Guilford Press.

Joiner, T. E., & Metalsky, G. I. (1995). A prospective test of an integrative interpersonal theory of depression: A naturalistic study of college roommates. *J. Pers. Soc. Psychol., 69*(4), 778–88.

Joiner, T. E., Jr., & Timmons, K. A. (2009). Depression in its interpersonal context. In I. H. Gotlib & C. L. Hammen (Eds.), *Handbook of depression* (2nd ed., pp. 322–39). New York: Guilford Press.

Jonas, D. E., et al. (2014). Pharmacotherapy for adults with alcohol use disorders in outpatient settings: A systematic review and meta-analysis. *JAMA, 311*, 1889–1900.

Jones, E., Thomas, A., & Ironside, S. (2007). Shell shock: An outcome study of a First World War "PIE" unit. *Psychol. Med., 37*, 215–23.

Jones, E., & Wessely, S. (2002). Psychiatric battle casualties: An intra- and interwar comparison. *Brit. J. Psychiatry, 178*, 242–47.

Jones, E., & Wessely, S. (2007). A paradigm shift in the conceptualization of trauma in the 20th century. *J. Anxiety Dis., 21*, 164–75.

Jones, K. D. (2012). A critique of the DSM-5 field trials. *J. Nervous and Mental Disease, 200*, 517–19.

Jones, L. (1992). Specifying the temporal relationship between job loss and consequences: Implication for service delivery. *J. Applied Social Sciences, 16*, 37–62.

Jones, M. C. (1924). A laboratory study of fear: The case of Peter. *Pedagogical Seminary, 31*, 308–15.

Jones, P. B., Rodgers, B., Murray, R., & Marmot, M. (1994). Child developmental risk factors for adult schizophrenia in the British 1946 birth cohort. *Lancet, 344*, 1398–402.

Jones, R. S. P., Zahl, A., & Huws, J. C. (2001). First hand accounts of emotional experiences in autism: A qualitative analysis. *Disability & Society, 16*, 393–401.

Jones, S. R., & Fernyhough, C. (2009). Caffeine, stress, and proneness to psychosis-like experiences. *Pers. Indiv. Diff., 46*, 562–64.

Jones, W., & Klin, A. (2013). Attention to eyes is present but in decline in 2-6-month-old infants later diagnosed with autism. *Nature, 504*(7480), 427–31. doi:10.1038/nature12715

Jones, W. R., & Morgan, J. F. (2010). Eating disorders in men: A review of the literature. *J. Pub. Ment. Health, 9*, 23–31.

Joormann, J. (2009). Cognitive aspects of depression. In I. H. Gotlib & C. L. Hammen (Eds.), *Handbook of depression and its treatment* (2nd ed., pp. 298–321). New York: Guilford Press.

Joormann, J., & Quinn, M. E. (2014). Cognitive processes and emotion regulation in depression. *Depression and Anxiety, 301*, 308–15.

Jordaan, G. P., & Emsley, R. (2014). Alcohol-induced psychotic disorder: A review. *Metabolic Brain Disease, 29*, 231–43.

Jordan, B. D., Relkin, N. R., Ravdin, L. D., Jacobs, A. R., Bennett, A., & Gandy, S. (1997). Apolipoprotein

E 4 associated with chronic traumatic brain injury in boxing. *JAMA, 278*, 136–40.

Joseph, J. E., Zhu, X., Corbly, C. R., DeSantis, S., Lee, D. C., Baik, G., et al. (2014, September 23). Influence of neurobehavioral incentive valence and magnitude on alcohol drinking behavior. *NeuroImage*. doi:http://dx.doi.org/10.1016/j.neuroimage.2014.09.037

Joyce, K. A. (2008). *Magnetic appeal: MRI. and the myth of transparency*. Ithaca, NY, and London: Cornell University Press.

Judd, L. L., Akiskal, H. S., Maser, J. D., Zeller, P. J., Endicott, J., Coryell, W., et al. (1998). A prospective 12-year study of subsyndromal and syndromal depressive symptoms in unipolar major depressive disorders. *Arch. Gen. Psychiatry, 55*, 694–700.

Judd, L. L., Akiskal, H. S., Schettler, P. J., Endicott, J., Maser, J., Solomon, D. A., et al. (2002). The long-term natural history of the weekly symptomatic status of bipolar I disorder. *Arch. Gen. Psychiatry, 59*(6), 530–37.

Judd, L. L., Paulus, M. P., Zeller, P., Fava, G. A., Rafanelli, C., Grandi, S., et al. (1999). The role of residual subthreshold depressive symptoms in early episode relapse in unipolar major depressive disorder. *Arch. Gen. Psychiatry, 56*(8), 764–65.

Judd, L. L., Schettler, P. J., Akiskal, H. S., Maser, J., Coryell, W., Solomon, D., et al. (2003). Long-term symptomatic status of bipolar I vs. bipolar II disorders. *Int. J. Neuropsychopharm., 6*(2), 127–37.

K

Kachigian, C., & Felthous, A. R. (2004). Court responses to Tarasoff statutes. *J. Am. Acad. Psychiatr. Law, 32*(3), 263–73.

Kafka, M. P. (2010). The DSM diagnostic criteria for fetishism. *Arch. Sexual Behavior, 39*, 357–62.

Kagan, J. (1997). Temperament and the reactions to un-familiarity. *Child Develop., 68*(1), 139–43.

Kagan, J. (2003). Biology, context and developmental inquiry. *Annu. Rev. Psychol., 54*, 1–23.

Kagan, J., & Fox, N. A. (2006). Biology, culture, and temperamental biases. In N. Eisenberg, W. Damon, & R. M. Lerner (Eds.), *Handbook of child psychology: Social, emotional, and personality development* (6 ed., Vol. 3, pp. 167–225). Hoboken, NJ: John Wiley & Sons.

Kagan, J., Snidman, N., McManis, M., & Woodward, S. (2001). Temperamental contributions to the affect family of anxiety. *Psychiatr. Clin. North Am., 2*, 677–88.

Kahlem, P. (2006). Gene-dosage effect on chromosome 21 transcriptome in trisomy 21: Implication in Down syndrome cognitive disorders. *Behav. Genet., 36*(3), 416–28.

Kalant, O. J. (1966). *The amphetamines: Toxicity and addiction*. Brookside Monographs, No. 5. Toronto: University of Toronto Press.

Kalarchian, M. A., Wilson, G. T., Brolin, R. E., & Bradley, L. (1998). Binge eating in bariatric surgery patients. *Int. J. Eat. Dis., 23*(1), 89–92.

Kalat, J. W. (2001). *Biological psychology* (7th ed.). Belmont, CA: Wadsworth.

Kalus, P., Senitz, D., & Beckmann, H. (1997). Cortical layer I changes in schizophrenia: A marker for impaired brain development? *J. Neural Transmission, 104*, 549–59.

Kamphaus, R. W., & Kroncke, A. P. (2004). "Back to the future" of the Stanford-Binet Intelligence Scales. In *Comprehensive handbook of psychological assessment* (pp. 77–86). New York: John Wiley & Sons.

Kamphaus, R. W., Reynolds, C. R., & Dever, B. V. (2014). Behavioral and mental health screening. In R. J. Kettler, T. A. Glover, C. A. Albers, & K. A. Feeney-Kettler (Eds.), *Universal screening in educational settings: Evidence-based decision making for schools* (pp. 249–73). Washington, DC:

American Psychological Association. doi:10.1037/14316-010

Kang, H. K., Natelson, B. H., Mahan, C. M., Lee, K. Y., & Murphy, F. (2003). Post-traumatic stress disorder and chronic fatigue syndrome-like illness among Gulf War veterans: A population-based survey of 30,000 veterans. *Am. J. Epidemiol., 157*, 141–48.

Kannel, W. B., Wolf, P. A., Garrison, R. J., Cupples, L. A., & D'Agostino, R. B. (1987). *The Framingham study: An epidemiological investigation of cardiovascular disease*. Bethesda, MD: National Heart, Lung and Blood Institute.

Kanner, L. (1943). Autistic disturbances of effective content. *Nervous Child, 2*, 217–40.

Kaplan, H. S. (1979). *Disorders of sexual desire*. New York: Brunner/Mazel.

Kaplan, H. S. (1987). *The illustrated manual of sex therapy* (2nd ed.). New York: Brunner/Mazel.

Kaplan, M. S., & Krueger, R. B. (1997). Voyeurism: Psychopathology and theory. In D. R. Laws & W. O'Donohue (Eds.), *Sexual deviance: Theory, assessment, and treatment* (pp. 297–310). New York: Guilford Press.

Kaplan, R. M., & Stone, A. A. (2013). Bringing the laboratory and clinic to the community: Mobile technologies for health promotion and disease prevention. *Annu. Rev. Psychology, 64*, 471–98.

Kapner, D. A. (2003). Recreational use of Ritalin on college campuses. *Info Fact Resources*. Washington, DC: U.S. Department of Justice.

Kapur, N. (1999). Syndromes of retrograde amnesia: A conceptual and empirical synthesis. *Psychol. Bull., 125*, 800–25.

Kapur, S. (2003). Psychosis as a state of aberrant salience: A framework linking biology, phenomenology, and pharmacology in schizophrenia. *Am. J. Psychiatry, 160*, 13–23.

Kapur, S., Arenovich, T., Agid, O., Zipursky, R., Lindborg, S., & Jones, B. (2005). Evidence for the onset of antipsychotic effects within the first 24 hours of treatment. *Am. J. Psychiatry, 162*, 939–46.

Karavasilis, L., Doyle, A. B., & Markiewicz, D. (2003). Associations between parenting style and attachment to mother in middle childhood and adolescence. *Int. J. Behavioral Development, 27*(2), 153–64.

Karch, C., Cruchaga, C., & Goate, A. M. (2014). Alzheimer's disease genetics: From the bench to the clinic. *Neuron, 83*, 11–26.

Karg, K., Burmeister, M., Shedden, K., & Sen, S. (2011). The serotonin transporter promoter variant (5-HTTLPR), stress, and depression meta-analysis revisited. *Arch. Gen. Psychiatry, 68*(5), 444–54.

Kario, K., & Ohashi, T. (1997). Increased coronary heart disease mortality after the Hanshin-Awaji earthquake among the older community on Awaji Island. Tsuna Medical Association. *J. Am. Geriat. Soc., 45*, 610–13.

Karlsgodt, K. H., Niendam, T. A., Bearden, C. E., & Cannon, T. D. (2009). White matter integrity and prediction of social role functioning in subjects at ultra-high risk for psychosis. *Biol. Psychiatry, 66*, 562–69.

Karlsgodt, K. H., Sun, D., & Cannon, T. D. (2010). Structural and functional brain abnormalities in schizophrenia. *Curr. Dir. Psych. Sci., 19*, 226–31.

Karnesh, L. J. (with collaboration of Zucker, E. M.). (1945). *Handbook of psychiatry*. St. Louis, MO: Mosby.

Karno, M., Jenkins, J. H., de la Selva, A., Santana, F., Telles, C., Lopez, S., et al. (1987). Expressed emotion and schizophrenic outcome among Mexican-American families. *J. Nerv. Ment. Dis., 175*(3), 143–51.

Karon, B. P. (1995). Provision of psychotherapy under managed health care: A growing crisis and national nightmare. *Professional Psychology: Research & Practice, 26*(1), 5–9.

Karran, E., Mercken, M., & De Strooper, B. (2011). The amyloid cascade hypothesis for Alzheimer's disease: An appraisal for the development of therapeutics. *Nat. Rev. Drug Discov., 10*, 698–712.

Karver, C. L., Wade, S. L., Cassedy, A., Taylor, H. G., Stancin, T., Yeates, K. O., & Walz, N. C. (2012). Age at injury and long-term behavioral problems after traumatic brain injury in young children. *Rehabilitation Psychology, 57*, 256–65.

Kaski, M. (2000). Aetiology of mental retardation: General issues and prevention. In M. G. Gelder, J. J. Lopez-Ibor, Jr., & N. Andreason (Eds.), *New Oxford textbook of psychiatry* (pp. 1947–52). New York: Oxford University Press.

Kaslow, N. J., Leiner, A. S., Reviere, S., Gantt, M.-J., Senter, H., Jackson, E., et al. (2010). Suicidal, abused African-American women's response to a culturally-informed intervention. *J. Cons. Clin. Psychol., 78*, 449–58.

Kato, T., Knopman, D., & Liu, H. Y. (2001). Dissociation of regional activation in mild AD during visual encoding—A functional MRI Study. *Neurol., 57*, 812–16.

Katon, W. J. (2006). Panic disorder. *New Eng. J. Med., 354*(22), 2360–67.

Katon, W. J., Roy-Byrne, P., Russo, J., & Cowley, D. (2002). Cost effectiveness and cost offset of a collaborative care intervention for primary care patients with panic disorder. *Arch. Gen. Psychiatry, 59*, 1098–104.

Katz, E. C., Brown, B. S., Schwartz, R. P., Weintraub, E., Barksdale, W., & Robinson, R. (2004). Role induction: A method for enhancing early retention in outpatient drug-free treatment. *J. Cons. Clin. Psychol., 72*, 227–34.

Katz, L. F., & Gottman, J. M. (1997). Buffering children from marital conflict and dissolution. *J. Clin. Child Psychol., 26*(2), 157–71.

Katz, S., Kravetz, S., & Marks, Y. (1997). Parents' and doctors' attitudes toward plastic facial surgery for persons with down syndrome. *J. Intell. Develop. Dis., 22*(4), 265–73.

Katzmarzyk, P. T., & Davis, C. (2001). Thinness and body shape of Playboy centerfolds from 1978 to 1998. *Int. J. Obesity and Related Metabolic Disorders, 25*(4), 590–92.

Kaufman, J., Yang, B., Douglas-Palumberi, H., Crouse-Artus, M., Lipschitz, D., Krystal, J. H., et al. (2007). Genetic and environmental predictors of early alcohol use. *Biol. Psychiatry, 61*(11), 1228–34.

Kaufman, J., & Zigler, E. (1989). The intergenerational transmission of child abuse. In D. Cicchetti & V. Carlson (Eds.), *Child maltreatment: Theory and research on the causes and consequences of child abuse and neglect* (pp. 129–50). Cambridge, UK: Cambridge University Press.

Kaul, M., Zheng, J., Okamoto, S., Gendelman, H. E., & Lipton, S. A. (2005). HIV-1 infection and AIDS: Consequences for the central nervous system. *Cell Death and Differentiation, 12*, 878–92.

Kausch, O. (2003). Patterns of substance abuse among treatment-seeking pathological gamblers. *J. Sub. Abuse Treat., 25*(4), 263–70.

Kawachi, I., Colditz, G., Ascherio, A., et al. (1994). Prospective study of phobic anxiety and risk of coronary heart disease in men. *Circulation, 89*, 1992.

Kawachi, I., Sparrow, D., Vokonas, P., et al. (1994). Symptoms of anxiety and risk of coronary heart disease: The normative aging study. *Circulation, 90*, 2225.

Kawachi, I., Sparrow, D., Vokonas, P., et al. (1995). Decreased heart rate variability in men with phobic anxiety (data from the normative aging study). *Am. J. Cardiol., 75*, 882.

Kaye, W. (2008). Neurobiology of anorexia and bulimia nervosa. *Physiology and Behavior, 94*, 121–35.

Kaye, W. H., Bulik, C. M., Thornton, L., Barbarich, N., Masters, K., & Price Foundation Collaborative Group. (2004). Comorbidity of anxiety disorders with anorexia and bulimia nervosa. *Am. J. Psychiatry, 161*, 2215–21.

Kazdin, A. E. (1995). Conduct disorder. In F. C. Verhulst & H. M. Koot (Eds.), *The epidemiology of child and adolescent psychopathology* (pp. 258–90). New York: Oxford University Press.

Kazdin, A. E. (1998). *Research designs in clinical psychology.* Needham, MA: Allyn and Bacon.

Kazdin, A. E. (2007). Psychosocial treatments for conduct disorder in children and adolescents. In P. E. Nathan & J. M. Gorman (Eds.), *A guide to treatments that work* (pp. 71–104). New York: Oxford University Press.

Kazdin, A. E. (2008a). Evidence-based treatment and practice: New opportunities to bridge clinical research and practice, enhance the knowledge base, and improve patient care. *Am. Psychol., 63*, 146–59.

Kazdin, A. E. (2008b). *The Kazdin method for parenting the defiant child: With no pills, no therapy, no contest of wills.* Boston: Houghton Mifflin.

Kazdin, A. E., & Blase, S. L. (2011). Rebooting psychotherapy research and practice to reduce the burden of mental illness. *Perspectives on Psychological Science, 6*, 21–37.

Kazdin, A. E., Holland, L., & Crowley, M. (1997). Family experience of barriers to treatment and premature termination from child therapy. *J. Cons. Clin. Psychol., 65*(3), 453–63.

Kazdin, A. E., & Nock, M. K. (2003). Delineating mechanisms of change in child and adolescent therapy: Methodological issues and research recommendations. *J. Child Psychol. Psychiatry, 44*(8), 1116–29.

Kean, S. (2014, May 6). Phineas Gage, neuroscience's most famous patient. Retrieved from http://www.slate.com/articles/health_and_science/science/2014/05/phineas_gage_neuroscience_case_true_story_of_famous_frontal_lobe_patient.html

Kearney, C. A., Sims, K. E., Pursell, C. R., & Tillotson, C. A. (2003). Separation anxiety disorder in young children: A longitudinal and family analysis. *J. Clin. Child & Adol. Psych., 32*(4), 593–98.

Keck, P. E., Jr., & McElroy, S. L. (2002). Pharmacological treatments for bipolar disorder. In P. E. Nathan & J. M. Gorman (Eds.), *A guide to treatments that work* (2nd ed., pp. 277–300). New York: Oxford University Press.

Keck, P. E., & McElroy, S. L. (2007). Pharmacological treatments for bipolar disorder. In P. E. Nathan & J. M. Gorman (Eds.), *A guide to treatments that work* (3rd ed., pp. 323–50). New York: Oxford University Press.

Keefe, R. S. E. (2014). The longitudinal course of cognitive impairment in schizophrenia: An examination of data from premorbid through post-treatment phases of illness. *J. Clinical Psychiatry, 75*(Suppl. 2), 8–13.

Keel, P. K. (2010). Epidemiology and course of eating disorders. In W. S. Agras (Ed.), *The Oxford handbook of eating disorders* (pp. 25–46). New York: Oxford University Press.

Keel, P. K., Heatherton, T. F., Dorer, D. J., Joiner, T. E., & Zalta, A. K. (2006). Point prevalence of bulimia in 1982, 1992, and 2002. *Psych. Med., 36*, 119–27.

Keel, P. K., & Klump, K. L. (2003). Are eating disorders culture-bound syndromes? Implications for conceptualizing their etiology. *Psychol. Bull., 129*(5), 747–69.

Keel, P. K., Mitchell, J. E., Miller, K. B., Davis, T. L., & Crow, S. J. (1999). Long-term outcome of bulimia nervosa. *Arch. Gen. Psychiatry, 56*(1), 63–69.

Keeley, J. W., Morton, H. E., & Blashfield, R. K. (2015). Classification. In Blaney, P. H., Krueger, R. F., & Millon, T. (Eds.). *Oxford textbook of psychopathology* (3rd ed., pp. 42–70). New York: Oxford University Press.

Keeley, M. L., Graziano, P., & Geffken, G. R. (2009). Nocturnal enuresis and encopresis: Empirically supported approaches for refractory cases. In D. McKay & E. A. Storch (Eds.), *Cognitive-behavior therapy for children: Treating complex and refractory cases* (pp. 445–73). New York: Springer.

Keller, J., Schatzberg, A. F., & Maj, M. (2007). Current issues in the classification of psychotic major depression. *Schizophrenia Bulletin, 33*(4), 877–85.

Keller, M. B. (2004). Remission versus response: The new gold standard of antidepressant care. *J. Clin. Psychiatry, 65*(Suppl. 4), 53–59.

Keller, M. B., Hirschfeld, R. M. A., & Hanks, D. (1997). Double depression: A distinctive subtype of unipolar depression. *J. Affect. Dis., 45*(1–2), 65–73.

Keller, M. B., McCullough, J. P., Klein, D. N., Arnow, B., Dunner, D. L., Gelenberg, A. J., et al. (2000). A comparison of nefazodone, the cognitive behavioral-analysis system of psychotherapy, and their combination for the treatment of chronic depression. *N. Engl. J. Med., 342*, 1462–70.

Keller, M. C., & Nesse, R. M. (2005). Is low mood an adaptation? Evidence for subtypes with symptoms that match precipitants. *J. Affect. Dis., 86*, 27–35.

Kellner, R. (1985). Functional somatic symptoms and hypochondriasis: A survey of empirical studies. *Arch. Gen. Psychiatry, 42*, 821–33.

Kelloway, E. K., Barling, J., & Hurrell, J. J. (2006). *Handbook of workplace violence.* Thousand Oaks, California: Sage Publications.

Kelly-Irving, M., Lepage, B., Dedieu, D., Bartley, M., Blane, D., Grosclaude, P., et al. (2013). Adverse childhood experiences and premature all-cause mortality. *European J. Epidemiology, 28*, 721–34.

Kelsoe, J. R. (1997). The genetics of bipolar disorder. *Moskovskogo Nauchno-Issledovatel'Skogo Instituta Psikhiatrii, 27*(4), 285–92.

Kempner, J. (2008). The chilling effect: How do researchers react to controversy? *PLoS Medicine, 5*, e222.

Kenardy, J., Arnow, B., & Agras, S. W. (1996). The aversiveness of specific emotional states associated with binge eating in obese patients. *Austral. NZ J. Psychiatry, 30*(6), 839–44.

Kendall, P. C. (1990). Cognitive processes and procedures in behavior therapy. In C. M. Franks, G. T. Wilson, P. C. Kendall, & J. P. Foreyt (Eds.), *Review of behavior therapy: Theory and practice* (pp. 103–37). New York: Guilford Press.

Kendall, P. C., & Braswell, L. (1985). *Cognitive-behavioral therapy for impulsive children.* New York: Guilford Press.

Kendall, P. C., Compton, S. N., Walkup, J. T., Birmaher, B., Albano, A. M., Sherrill, J., et al. (2010). Clinical characteristics of anxiety disordered youth. *J. Anxiety Dis., 24*(3), 360–65.

Kendall, P. C., Holmbeck, G., & Verduin, T. (2004). Methodology, design, and evaluation in psychotherapy research. In M. J. Lambert (Ed.), *Bergin and Garfield's handbook of psychotherapy and behavior change* (5th ed., pp. 16–43). New York: John Wiley & Sons.

Kendler, K. S. (1997). The diagnostic validity of melancholic major depression in a population-based sample of female twins. *Arch. Gen. Psychiatry, 54*, 299–304.

Kendler, K. S. (1999). Long-term care of an individual with schizophrenia: Pharmacological, psychological, and social factors. *Am. J. Psychiatry, 156*, 124–28.

Kendler, K. S. (2005). "A gene for": The nature of gene action in psychiatric disorders. *Am. J. Psychiat, 162*(7), 1243–52.

Kendler, K. S., Aggen, S. H., Czajkowski, N., Røysamb, E., Tambs, K., Torgersen, S., et al. (2008). The structure of genetic and environmental risk factors for DSM-IV personality disorders. *Arch. Gen. Psychiatry, 65*(12), 1438–46. doi:10.1017/S0033291710002436

Kendler, K. S., Aggen, S. H., Knudsen, G. P., Røysamb, E., Neale, M. C., & Reichborn-Kjennerud, T. (2011). The structure of genetic and environmental risk factors for syndromal and subsyndromal common DSM-IV axis I and all axis II disorders. *Am. J. Psychiatry, 168*(1), 29–39. doi:10.1176/appi. ajp.2010.10030340

Kendler, K. S., Czajkowski, N., Tambs, K., Torgersen, S., Aggen, S. H., Neale, M. C., & Reichborn-Kjennerud T. (2006). Dimensional representations of DSM-IV cluster A personality disorders in a population-based sample of Norwegian twins: A multivariate study. *Psychol Med., 36*(11), 1583–91.

Kendler, K. S., & Gardner, C. O. (1997) The risk for psychiatric disorders in relatives of schizophrenic and control probands: A comparison of three independent studies. *Psychol. Med., 27*, 411–19.

Kendler, K. S., Gardner, C. O., Gatz, M., & Pedersen, N. L. (2007). The sources of comorbidity between major depression and generalized anxiety disorder in a Swedish national twin sample. *Psychol. Med., 37*(3), 453–62.

Kendler, K. S., Gardner, C. O., & Prescott, C. A. (2002). Toward a comprehensive developmental model for major depression in women. *Am. J. Psychiatry, 159*(7), 1133–45.

Kendler, K. S., Gardner, C. O., & Prescott, C. A. (2003). Personality and the experience of environmental adversity. *Psychol. Med., 33*, 1193–202.

Kendler, K. S., & Gruenberg, A. M. (1984). An independent analysis of the Danish adoption study of schizophrenia: VI. The relationship between psychiatric disorders as defined by DSM-III in the relatives and adoptees. *Arch. Gen. Psychiat, 41*, 555–64.

Kendler, K. S., Gruenberg, A. M., & Kinney, D. K. (1994). Independent diagnoses of adoptees and relatives as defined by DSM-III in the provincial and national samples of the Danish adoption study of schizophrenia. *Arch. Gen. Psychiatry, 51*(6), 456–68.

Kendler, K. S., Hettema, J. M., Butera, F., Gardner, C. O., & Prescott, C. A. (2003). Life event dimensions of loss, humiliation, entrapment, and danger in the prediction of onsets of major depression and generalized anxiety. *Arch. Gen. Psychiatry, 60*, 789–96.

Kendler, K. S., Karkowski, L. M., & Prescott, C. A. (1999a). Causal relationship between stressful life events and the onset of major depression. *Am. J. Psychiatry, 156*(6), 837–41.

Kendler, K. S., Karkowski, L. M., & Prescott, C. A. (1999b). Fears and phobias: Reliability and heritability. *Psychol. Med., 29*, 539–53.

Kendler, K. S., Kuhn, J., & Prescott, C. A. (2004). The interrelationship of neuroticism, sex, and stressful life events in the prediction of episodes of major depression. *Am. J. Psychiatry, 161*(4), 631–36.

Kendler, K. S., Kuhn, J. W., Vittum, J., Prescott, C. A., & Riley, B. (2005). The interaction of stressful life events and a serotonin transporter polymorphism in the prediction of episodes of major depression. *Arch. Gen. Psychiatry, 62*(5), 529–35.

Kendler, K. S., Myers, J., Torgersen, S., Neale, M. C., & Reichborn-Kjennerud, T. (2007). The heritability of cluster A personality disorders assessed by both personal interview and questionnaire. *Psychological Medicine, 37*, 655–65.

Kendler, K. S., Neale, M. C., Kessler, R. C., Heath, A. C., & Eaves, L. J. (1992). Generalized anxiety disorder in women: A population-based twin study. *Arch. Gen. Psychiatry, 49*, 267–72.

Kendler, K. S., Ohlsson, H., Sundquist, J., & Sundquist, K. (2015). IQ and schizophrenia in a Swedish national sample: Their causal relationship and the interaction of IQ with genetic risk. *Am. J. Psychiatry, 172*, 259–65.

Kendler, K. S., Sundquist, K., Ohlsson, H., Palmer, K., Maes, H., Winkleby, M. A., & Sundquist, J. (2012). Genetic and familial environmental influences on the risk for drug abuse: A National Swedish Adoption Study. *Arch. Gen. Psychiat., 69*(7), 690–97.

Kendler, K. S., Thornton, L. M., & Gardner, C. O. (2000). Stressful life events and previous episodes in the etiology of major depression in women: An evaluation of the "kindling" hypothesis. *Am. J. Psychiatry, 157*, 1243–51.

Kendler, K. S., Walters, E. E., Neale, M. C., Kessler, R. C., Heath, A. C., & Eaves, L. J. (1995). The structure of the genetic and environmental risk factors for six major psychiatric disorders in women: Phobia, generalized anxiety disorder, panic disorder, bulimia, major depression, and alcoholism. *Arch. Gen. Psychiatry, 52*, 374–83.

Kennard, D. (2004). The therapeutic community as an adaptable treatment modality across different settings. *Psychiatr. Q., 75*(3), 295–307.

Kennedy, S. H., Giacobbe, P., Rivzi, S. J., Placenza, F. M., Nishikawa, Y., Mayberg, H. S., et al. (2011). Deep brain stimulation for treatment-resistant depression: Follow-up after 3 to 6 years. *Am. J. Psychiatry, 168*, 502–10.

Kenrick, D. T., & Luce, C. L. (2004). *The functional mind: Readings in evolutionary psychology.* Auckland, New Zealand: Pearson Education New Zealand.

Kernberg, O. F. (1985). *Borderline conditions and pathological narcissism.* Northvale, NJ: Jason Aronson.

Kernberg, O. F. (1996). A psychoanalytic theory of personality disorders. In J. F. Clarkin & M. F. Lenzenweger (Eds.), *Major theories of personality disorder* (pp. 106–40). New York: Guilford Press.

Kernberg, O. F., & Michels, R. (2009). Borderline personality disorder. *Am. J. Psychiatry, 166*(5), 505–08. doi:10.1176/appi. ajp.2009.09020263

Kernberg, O. F., Yeomans, F. E., Clarkin, J. F., & Levy, K. N. (2008). Transference focused psychotherapy: Overview and update. *Int. J. Psychoanalysis, 89*, 601–20.

Keshavan, M., Shad, M., Soloff, P., & Schooler, N. (2004). Efficacy and tolerability of olanzapine in the treatment of schizotypal personality disorder. *Schiz. Res, 71*, 97–101.

Keshavan, M. S., Tandon, R., Boutros, N. N., & Nasrallah, H. A. (2008). Schizophrenia, "just the facts": What we know in 2008. Part 3: Neurobiology. *Schiz. Res., 106*, 89–107.

Keshaviah, A., Edkins, K., Hastings, E. R., Krishna, M., Franko, D. L., Herzog, D. B., et al. (2014). Re-examining premature mortality in anorexia nervosa: A meta-analysis redux. *Comprehensive Psychiatry, 55*, 1773–84.

Kessler, R. C., Adler, L. A., Barkley, R. A., Biederman, J., Conners, C. K., Demler, O., et al. (2006). The prevalence and correlates of adult ADHD in the United States: Results from the National Comorbidity Survey Replication. *Am. J. Psychiatry, 163*, 716–23. doi:10.1176/appi. ajp.163.4.716

Kessler, R. C., Adler, L. A., Berglund, P., Green, J. G., McLaughlin, K. A., Fayyad, J., et al. (2014). The effects of temporally secondary co-morbid mental disorders on the associations of DSM-IV ADHD with adverse outcomes in the US National Comorbidity Survey Replication Adolescent Supplement (NCS-A). *Psychol. Med., 44*(8), 1779–92. doi:10.1017/S0033291713002419

Kessler, R. C., Aguilar-Gaxiola, S., Alonso, J., Chatterji, S., Lee, S., Ormel, J., et al. (2009). The global burden of mental disorders: An update from the WHO World Mental Health (WMH) Surveys. *Epidemiology and Psychiatric Services, 18*, 23–33.

Kessler, R. C., Avenevoli, S., Costello, J., Green, J. G., Gruber, M. J., McLaughlin, K. A., et al. (2012). Severity of 12-month DSM-IV disorders in the National Comorbidity Survey Replication Adolescent Supplement. *Archives of General Psychiatry, 69*, 381–89.

Kessler, R. C., Berglund, P., Borges, G., Nock, M., & Wang, P. S. (2005). Trends in suicide ideation, plans, gestures, and attempts in the United States. *JAMA, 293*(20), 2487–95.

Kessler, R. C., Berglund, P. A., Chiu, W. T., Deitz, A. C., Hudson, J. I., Shahly, V., et al. (2013). The prevalence and correlated of binge eating disorder in the World Health Organization World Mental Health Surveys. *Biol. Psychiatry.* doi:http://dx. doi.org/10.1016/j.biopsych.2012.11.020

Kessler, R. C., Berglund, P., Chiu, W. T., Demler, O., Heeringa, S., Hiripi, E., et al. (2004). The US National Comorbidity Survey Replication (NCS-R): Design and field procedures. *Int. J. Method. Psych. Res., 13*(2), 69–92.

Kessler, R. C., Berglund, P., Demler, O., Jin, R., Koretz, D., Merikangas, K. R., et al. (2003). The epidemiology of major depressive disorder: Results from the National Comorbidity Survey Replication. *JAMA, 289*(23), 3095–105.

Kessler, R. C., Berglund, P., Demler, O., Jin, R., Merikangas, K. R., & Walters, E. E. (2005). Lifetime prevalence and age-of-onset distributions of DSM-IV disorders in the National Comorbidity Survey Replication. *Arch. Gen. Psychiatry, 62*, 593–602.

Kessler, R. C., Birnbaum, H., Bromet, E., Hwang, I., Sampson, N., & Shahly, V. (2010). Age differences in major depression: Results from the National Comorbidity Survey Replication (NCS-R). *Psychol. Med., 40*(02), 225–37. doi:10.1017/S0033291709990213

Kessler, R. C., Chiu, W. T., Demler, O., & Walters, E. E. (2005). Prevalence, severity, and comorbidity of 12-month DSM-IV disorders in the National Comorbidity Survey Replication. *Arch. Gen. Psychiatry, 62*, 617–27.

Kessler, R. C., Chiu, W. T., Jin, R., Ruscio, A. M., Shear, K., & Walters, E. E. (2006). The epidemiology of panic attacks, panic disorder, and agoraphobia in the national comorbidity survey replication. *Arch. Gen. Psychiatry, 63*(4), 415–24.

Kessler, R. C., Green, J. G., Adler, L. A., Barkley, R. A., Chatterji, S., Faraone, S. V., et al. (2010). Structure and diagnosis of adult attention-deficit/hyperactivity disorder: Analysis of expanded symptom criteria from the Adult ADHD Clinical Diagnostic Scale. *Arch Gen Psychiatry, 67*(11), 1168–78. doi:10.1001/archgenpsychiatry.2010.146

Kessler, R. C., McGonagle, K. A., Zhao, S., Nelson, C. B., Hughes, M., Eshleman, S., et al. (1994). Lifetime and 12-month prevalence of DSM-III-R psychiatric disorders in the United States: Results from the National Comorbidity Survey. *Arch. Gen. Psychiatry, 51*, 8–19.

Kessler, R. C., McLaughlin, K. A., Green, J. G., Gruber, M. J., Sampson, N. A., Zaslavsky, A. M., et al. (2010). Childhood adversities and adult psychopathology in the WHO World Mental Health Surveys. *Brit. J. Psychiatry, 197*, 378–85. doi:10.1192/bjp.bp.110.080499

Kessler, R. C., Merikangas, K. R., & Wang, P. S. (2007). Prevalence, comorbidity, and service utilization for mood disorders in the United States at the beginning of the twenty-first century. *Annu. Rev. Clin. Psych., 3*, 137–58.

Kessler, R. C., Rubinow, D. R., Holmes, C., Abelson, J. M., & Zhao, S. (1997). The epidemiology of DSM-III-R bipolar 1 disorder in a general population survey. *Psych. Med., 27*, 1079–89.

Kessler, R. C., Ruscio, A. M., Shear, K., & Wittchen, H.-U. (2009). Epidemiology of anxiety disorders. In M. M. Antony & M. B. Stein (Eds.), *Oxford handbook of anxiety and related disorders* (pp. 19–33). New York: Oxford University Press.

Kessler, R. C., & Ustun, T. B. (Eds.). (2008). The WHO World Mental Health Surveys: Global perspectives on the epidemiology of mental disorders. Cambridge, UK: Cambridge University Press.

Kessler, R. C., & Zhao, S. (1999). Overview of descriptive epidemiology of mental disorders. In C. S. Aneshensel & J. C. Phelan (Eds.), *Handbook of sociology of mental health. Handbook of sociology and social research* (pp. 127–50). New York: Kluwer/Plenum.

Kety, S. S. (1974). From rationalization to reason. *Am. J. Psychiatry, 131,* 957–63.

Kety, S. S., Rosenthal, D., Wender, P. H., Schulsinger, F., & Jacobsen, B. (1978). The biologic and adoptive families of adopted individuals who became schizophrenic: Prevalence of mental illness and other characteristics. In L. C. Wynne, R. L. Cromwell, & S. Matthyse (Eds.), *The nature of schizophrenia: New approaches to research and treatment* (pp. 25–37). New York: Wiley.

Kety, S. S., Wender, P. H., Jacobsen, B., Ingraham, L. J., Jansson, L., Faber, B., et al. (1994). Mental illness in the biological and adoptive relatives of schizophrenic adoptees: Replication of the Copenhagen study in the rest of Denmark. *Arch. Gen. Psychiatry, 51*(6), 442–55.

Keys, A., Brozek, J., Henschel, A., Mickelson, O., & Taylor, H. L. (1950). *The biology of human starvation.* Minneapolis: University of Minnesota Press.

Khalifa, N., & von Knorring, A. L. (2004). Prevalence of tic disorders and Tourette syndrome in a Swedish school population. *J. Am. Acad. Child Adoles. Psychiatry, 43*(2), 206–14.

Khan, A., Cowan, C., & Roy, A. (1997). Personality disorders in people with learning disabilities: A community survey. *J. Intell. Dis. Res., 41*(4), 324–30.

Khan, A., Cutler, A. J., Kajdasz, D. K., Gallipoli, S., Athanasiou, M., Robinson, D. S., et al. (2011). A randomized, double-blind, placebo-controlled, 8-week study of vilazodone, a serotonergic agent for the treatment of major depressive disorder. *J. Clin. Psychiatry, 72,* 441–47.

Khandaker, G. M., Zimbon, J., Lewis, G., & Jones, P. B. (2013). Prenatal maternal infection, neurodevelopment and adult schizophrenia: A systematic review of population-based studies. *Psychological Medicine, 43,* 239–57.

Khashan, A. S., Abel, K. M., Mc Namee, R., Pedersen, M. G., Webb, R. T., Baker, P. N., et al. (2008). Higher risk of offspring schizophrenia following antenatal maternal exposure to severe adverse life events. *Arch. Gen. Psychiat, 65,* 146–52.

Khazaal, Y., Zimmerman, & Zullino, D. F. (2005). Depersonalization—Current data. *Canad. J. Psychiatry, 50*(2), 101–07.

Kici, G., & Westhoff, K. (2004). Evaluation of requirements for the assessment and construction of interview guides in psychological assessment. *Europ. J. Psychol. Assess., 20,* 83–98.

Kiecolt-Glaser, J. K., Loving, T. J., Stowell, J. R., Malarkey, W. B., Lemeshow, S., Dickinson, S. L., & Glaser, R. (2005). Hostile marital interactions, proinflammatory cytokine production, and wound healing. *Arch. General Psychiatry, 62,* 1377–84.

Kiecolt-Glaser, J. K., McGuire, L., Robles, T. F., & Glaser, R. (2002). Emotion, morbidity, and mortality: New perspectives from psychoneuroimmunology. *Annu. Rev. Psychol., 53,* 83–107.

Kiehl, K. A. (2006). A cognitive neuroscience perspective on psychopathy: Evidence for paralimbic system dysfunction. *Psychiatry Research, 142,* 107–28.

Kihlstrom, J. F. (2001). Dissociative disorders. In P. B. Sutker & H. E. Adams (Eds.), *Comprehensive handbook of psychopathology* (3rd ed., pp. 259–76). New York: Kluwer Academic/Plenum.

Kihlstrom, J. F. (2002). To honor Kraepelin . . . : From symptoms to pathology in the diagnosis of mental illness. In L. E. Beutler & M. L. Malik (Eds.), *Rethinking the DSM: A psychological perspective* (pp. 279–303). Washington, DC: American Psychological Association.

Kihlstrom, J. F. (2005). Dissociative disorders. *Annu. Rev. Clin. Psych., 1,* 227–53.

Kihlstrom, J. F., Glisky, M. L., & Angiulo, M. J. (1994). Dissociative tendencies and dissociative disorders. *J. Abn. Psychol., 103*(1), 117–24.

Kihlstrom, J. F., & Schacter, D. L. (2000). Functional amnesia. In L. S. Cermak (Ed.), *Handbook of neuropsychology, Volume 2: Memory and its disorders* (2nd ed., pp. 409–27). Amsterdam: Elsevier Science.

Kihlstrom, J. F., Tataryn, D. J., & Hoyt, I. P. (1993). Dissociative disorders. In P. B. Sutker & H. E. Adams (Eds.), *Comprehensive handbook of psychopathology* (pp. 203–34). New York: Plenum.

Kilpatrick, D. G., Koenan, K. C., Ruggiero, K. J., Acierno, R., Galea, S., Resnick, H. S., et al. (2007). The serotonin transporter genotype and social support and moderation of posttraumatic stress disorder and depression in hurricane-exposed adults. *Am. J. Psychiatry, 164,* 1693–99.

Kiluk, B. D., Nich, C., Witkiewitz, K., Babuscio, T. A., & Carroll, K. M. (2014). What happens in treatment doesn't stay in treatment: Cocaine abstinence during treatment is associated with fewer problems at follow-up. *J. Consulting and Clinical Psychology, 82,* 619–27.

Kiluk, B. D., Serafini, K., Malin-Mayor, B., Babuscio, T. A., Nich, C., & Carroll, K. M. (2015). Prompted to treatment by the criminal justice system: Relationships with treatment retention and outcome among cocaine abusers. *Am. J. Addiction, 24,* 225–32.

Kilzieh, N., & Akiskal, H. S. (1999). Rapid-cycling bipolar disorder: An overview of research and clinical experience. *Psychiatr. Clin. North Am., 22,* 585–607.

Kim, J., Rapee, R. M., & Gaston, J. E. (2008). Symptoms of offensive type Taijin-Kyofusho among Australian social phobics. *Depression and Anxiety, 25*(7), 601–08. doi:10.1002/da. 20345

Kim-Cohen, J., Caspi, A., Moffitt, T. E., Harrington, H., Milne, B. J., & Poulton, R. (2003). Prior juvenile diagnoses in adults with mental disorder: Developmental follow-back of a prospective-longitudinal cohort. *Arch Gen Psychiatry, 60*(7), 709–17. doi:10.1001/archpsyc.60.7.709

Kim-Cohen, J., Caspi, A., Taylor, A., Williams, B., Newcombe, R., Craig, I. W., et al. (2006). MAOA, maltreatment, and gene-environment interaction predicting children's mental health: New evidence and a meta-analysis. *Molecular Psychiatry, 11*(10), 903–13.

King, S., St-Hilaire, A., & Heidkamp, D. (2010). Prenatal factors in schizophrenia. *Curr. Dis. Psychol. Sci., 19,* 209–13.

Kingston, D. A., Seto, M. C., Firestone, P., & Bradford, J. M. (2010). Comparing indicators of sexual sadism as predictors of recidivism among adult male sexual offenders. *J. Consulting and Clinical Psychology, 78*(4), 574–84.

Kinney, D. K., Holzman, P. S., Jacobsen, B., Jansson, L., Faber, B., Hildebrand, W., et al. (1997). Thought disorder in schizophrenic and control adoptees and their relatives. *Arch. Gen. Psychiatry, 54*(5), 475–79.

Kinsey, A. C., Pomeroy, W. B., & Martin, C. E. (1948). *Sexual behavior in the human male.* Philadelphia, PA: Sanders.

Kinsey, A. C., Pomeroy, W. B., Martin, C. E., & Gebhard, P. H. (1953). *Sexual behavior in the human female.* Philadelphia, PA: Saunders.

Kirk, S. A., & Kutchins, H. (1992). *The selling of DSM: The rhetoric of science in psychiatry.* Hawthorne, NY: Aldine de Gruyter.

Kirkbridge, J. B., Fearon, P., Morgan, C., Dazzan, P., Morgan, K., Tarrant, J., et al. (2006). Heterogeneity in incidence rates of schizophrenia and other psychotic syndromes. *Arch. Gen. Psychiatry, 63,* 250–58.

Kirkland, G. (1986). *Dancing on my grave.* New York: Doubleday.

Kirmayer, L. J. (1991). The place of culture in psychiatric nosology: Taijin Kyofusho and DSM III-R. *J. Nerv. Ment. Dis., 179,* 19–28.

Kirmayer, L. J., & Taillefer, S. (1997). Somatoform disorders. In S. M. Turner & M. Hersen (Eds.), *Adult psychopathology and diagnosis* (pp. 333–83). New York: Wiley.

Kirmayer, L. J., Young, A., & Hayton, B. C. (1995). The cultural context of anxiety disorders. *Cultur. Psychiatry, 18*(3), 503–21.

Kirsch, L. G., & Becker, J. V. (2007). Emotional deficits in psychopathy and sexual sadism: Implications for violent and sadistic behavior. *Clinical Psychology Review, 27,* 904–22.

Klauke, B., Deckert, J., Reif, A., Pauli, P., & Domschke, K. (2010). Life events in panic disorder—An update on candidate stressors. *Depression and Anxiety, 27,* 715–30.

Klaus, K., Rief, W., Brahler, E., Martin, A., Glaesmer, H., & Mewes, R. (2013). The distinction between "medically unexplained" and "medically explained" in the context of somatoform disorders. *Int. J. Behavioral Medicine, 20,* 161–71.

Kleim, B., Ehlers, A., & Glucksman, E. (2007). Early predictors of chronic post-traumatic stress disorder in assault survivors. *Psychol. Med., 37,* 1457–67.

Kleim, B., Grey, N., Wild, J., Nussbeck, F. W., Stott, R., Hackmann, A., et al. (2013). Cognitive change predicts symptom reduction with cognitive therapy for posttraumatic stress disorder. *J. Consulting and Clinical Psychology, 81,* 383–93.

Klein, D. F. (1981). Anxiety reconceptualized. In D. F. Klein & J. Rabkin (Eds.), *Anxiety: New research and changing concepts.* New York: Raven Press.

Klein, D. N. (2008). Dysthymia and chronic depression. In W. E. Craighead, D. J. Miklowitz, & L. W. Craighead (Eds.), *Psychopathology: History, theory, and diagnosis* (pp. 329–65). Hoboken, NJ: John Wiley & Sons.

Klein, D. N. (2010). Chronic depression: Diagnosis and classification. *Curr. Dir. Psychol. Sci., 19*(2), 96–100. doi:10.1177/0963721410366007

Klein, D. N., Durbin, C. E., & Shankman, S. A. (2009). Personality and mood disorders. In I. H. Gotlib & C. L. Hammen (Eds.), *Handbook of depression* (2nd ed., pp. 93–112). New York: Guilford Press.

Klein, D. N., Shankman, S. A., & Rose, S. (2006). Ten-year prospective follow-up study of the naturalistic course of dysthymic disorder and double depression. *Am. J. Psychiat, 163*(5), 872–80.

Kleinknecht, R. A., Dinnel, D. L., & Kleinknecht, E. E. (1997). Cultural factors in social anxiety: A comparison of social phobia symptoms and Taijin Kyofusho. *J. Anxiety Dis., 11*(2), 157–77.

Kleinman, A. (1988). *Rethinking psychiatry: From cultural category to personal experience.* New York: Free Press.

Kleinman, A. (2004). Culture and depression. *N. Engl. J. Med., 351*(10), 951–53.

Kleinman, A. M. (1986). *Social origins of distress and disease: Depression, neurasthenia and pain in modern China.* New Haven, CT: Yale University Press.

Kleinman, A. M., & Good, B. J. (1985). *Culture and depression.* Berkeley: University of California Press.

Klerman, G. L., Weissman, M. M., Rounsaville, B. J., & Chevron, E. S. (1984). *Interpersonal psychotherapy of depression.* New York: Basic Books.

Klinger, E. (1979). Modes of normal conscious flow. In K. S. Pope & J. L. Singer (Eds.), *The stream of consciousness: Scientific investigations into the flow of human experience.* New York: Plenum.

Klingman, A. (1993). School-based intervention following a disaster. In C. F. Saylor (Ed.), *Children and disasters* (pp. 187–210). New York: Plenum.

Kloner, R. A. (2006). Natural and unnatural triggers of myocardial infarction. *Prog. Cardiovascular Diseases, 48* (4), 285–300.

Kloner, R. A., Leor, J., Poole, W. K., & Perritt, R. (1997). Population-based analysis of the effect of the Northridge earthquake on cardiac death in Los Angeles County, California. *J. Am. College of Cardiology, 30,* 1174–80.

Kloner, R. A., McDonald, S. A., Leeka, J., & Poole, W. K. (2011). Role of age, sex, and race on cardiac and total mortality associated with Super Bowl wins and losses. *Clinical Cardiology, 34,* 102–07.

Kluft, R. P. (1993). Basic principles in conducting the treatment of multiple personality disorder. In R. P. Kluft & C. G. Fine (Eds.), *Clinical perspectives on multiple personality disorder* (pp. 53–73). Washington, DC: American Psychiatric Press.

Kluft, R. P. (1999). Dissociative identity disorder. In N. Miller & K. Magruder (Eds.), *Cost-effectiveness of psychotherapy: A guide for practitioners, researchers, and policymakers* (pp. 306–13). New York: Oxford University Press.

Kluft, R. P. (2005). Diagnosing dissociative identity disorder. *Psychiatr. Ann., 35*(8), 633–43.

Klump, K. L., Burt, A., McGue, M., & Iocono, W. G. (2007). Changes in genetic and environmental influences on disordered eating across adolescence. *Arch. Gen. Psychiatry, 64*(12), 1409–15.

Klump, K. L., Strober, M., Bulik, C. M., Thornton, L., Johnson, C., Devlin, B., et al. (2004). Personality characteristics of women before and after recovery from an eating disorder. *Psychol. Med., 34,* 1407–18.

Klump, K. L., Suisman, J. L., Culbert, K. M., Kashy, D. A., & Sisk, C. L. (2011). Binge eating proneness emerges during puberty in female rats: A longitudinal study. *J. Abn. Psych.*

Knapp, S. (1980). A primer on malpractice for psychologists. *Profess. Psychol., 11*(4), 606–12.

Knight, R. A., & Guay, J.-P. (2006). The role of psychopathy in sexual coercion against women. In C. J. Patrick (Ed.), *Handbook of the psychopathy* (pp. 512–32). New York: Guilford Press.

Knight, R., & Prentky, R. (1990). Classifying sexual offenders: The development and corroboration of taxonomic models. In W. L. Marshall, D. R. Laws, & H. E. Barbaree (Eds.), *Handbook of sexual assault: Issues, theories, and treatment of the offender* (pp. 23–52). New York: Plenum.

Knight, R., Prentky, R., & Cerce, D. (1994). The development, reliability, and validity of an inventory for the multidimensional assessment of sex and aggression. *Crim. Just. Behav., 21,* 72–94.

Koenigsberg, H. W., Kernberg, O. F., Stone, M. H., Appelbaum, A. H., Yeomans, F. E., & Diamond, D. (2000). *Borderline patients: Extending the limits of treatability.* New York: Basic Books.

Koenigsberg, H. W., Woo-Ming, A. M., & Siever, L. J. (2002). Pharmacological treatments for personality disorders. In P. E. Nathan & J. M. Gorman (Eds.), *A guide to treatments that work* (2nd ed., pp. 625–54). New York: Oxford University Press.

Koenigsberg, H. W., Woo-Ming, M., & Siever, J. (2007). Pharmacological treatments of personality disorders. In P. Nathan & J. Gorman (Eds.), *Treatments that work* (3rd ed., pp. 659–80). New York: Oxford University Press.

Koerner, N., & Dugas, M. J. (2008). An investigation of appraisals in individuals vulnerable to excessive worry: The role of intolerance of uncertainty. *Cog. Ther. Res., 32*(5), 619–38. doi:10.1007/s10608-007-9125-2

Kohler, C. G., Walker, J. B., Martin, E. A. Healy, K. M., & Moberg, P. J. (2010). Facial emotion perception in schizophrenia: A meta-analytic review. *Schizophrenia Bulletin, 36,* 1009–19.

Kohut, H., & Wolff, E. (1978). The disorders of the self and their treatment: An outline. *Inter. J. Psychoanal., 59,* 413–26.

Kolb, B., Gibb, R., & Robinson, T. E. (2003). Brain plasticity and behavior. *Curr. Dis. Psychol. Sci., 12*(1), 1–5.

Kolen, M. J., & Hendrickson, A. B. (2013). Scaling, norming and equating. In K. F. Geisinger, B. A. Bracken, J. F. Carlson, J. C. Hansen, N. R. Kuncel, S. P. Reise, & M. C. Rodriguez (Eds.), *APA handbook of testing and assessment in psychology, Vol. 2: Testing and assessment in clinical and counseling psychology* (pp. 201–21). Washington, DC: American Psychological Association. doi:10.1037/14048-011

Kominski, G. F., & Melnick, G. A. (2007). Managed care and the growth of competition. In R. M. Andersen, T. H. Rice, & G. F. Kominski (Eds.), *Changing the U.S. health care system: Key issues in health services policy and management* (3rd ed., pp. 551–68). San Francisco, CA: Jossey-Bass.

Komro, K., Perry, C. L., Veblen-Mortenson, S., Farbakhsh, K., Toomey, T. L., Stigler, M. H., et al. (2008). Outcomes from a randomized controlled trial of a multi-component alcohol use preventive intervention for Urban Youth Project Northland Chicago. *Addiction, 103*(4), 606–18.

Komro, K. A., & Toomey, T. L. (2002). Strategies to prevent underage drinking. *Alcohol Research & Health, 26*(1), 5–14.

Konarski, J. Z., McIntyre, R. S., Kennedy, S. H., Rafi-Tari, S., Soczynska, J. K., & Ketter, T. A. (2008). Volumetric neuroimaging investigations in mood disorders: Bipolar disorder versus major depressive disorder. *Bipolar Disorders, 10*(1), 1–37. doi:10.1111/j.1399-5618.2008.00435.x

Konrad, K., Gunther, T., Hanisch, C., & Herpertz-Dahlmann, B. (2004). Differential effects of methylphenidate on attentional functions in children with attention-deficit/hyperactivity disorder. *J. Am. Acad. Child Adoles. Psychiat., 43*(2), 191–98.

Koob, G. F., Mason, B. J., De Witte, P., Littleton, J., & Siggins, G. R. (2002). Potential neuroprotective effects of acamprosate. *Alcoholism: Clinical & Experimental Research, 26*(4), 586–92.

Koolschijn, P. C., van Haren, N. E., Lensvelt-Mulders, G. J., Hulshoff Pol, H. E., & Kahn, R. S. (2009). Brain volume abnormalities in major depressive disorder: A meta-analysis of magnetic resonance imaging studies. *Human Brain Mapping, 30*(11), 3719–35. doi:10.1002/hbm.20801

Kopelowicz, A., Liberman, R. P., & Zarate, R. (2007). Psychosocial treatments for schizophrenia. In P. E. Nathan & J. M. Gorman (Eds.), *A guide to treatments that work* (pp. 243–70). New York: Oxford University Press.

Koponen, S., Taiminem, T., Portin, R., Himanen, L., Isoniemi, H., Heinonen, H., et al. (2002). Axis I and Axis II psychiatric disorders after traumatic brain injury: A 30-year follow up study. *Am. J. Psychiatry, 159,* 1315–21.

Korbel, J. O., Tirosh-Wagner, T., Urban, A. E., Chen, X. N., Kasowski, M. D. L., et al. (2009). *Proc. Natl. Acad. Sci. USA, 106*(29), 12031–36.

Korczak, D. J., Goldstein, B. I., & Levitt, A. J. (2007). Panic disorder, cardiac diagnosis and emergency department utilization in an epidemiologic community sample. *General Hospital Psychiatry, 29*(4), 335–39.

Korkeila, J., Lehtinen, V., Tuori, T., & Helenius, H. (1998). Patterns of psychiatric hospital service use in Finland: A national register study of hospital discharges in the early 1990's. *Soc. Psychiatry Psychiatr. Epidemiol., 33,* 218–23.

Kornstein, S. G. (2010). Gender issues and DSM-V. *Arch. Women's Mental Health, 13*(1), 11–13.

Koschwanez, H. E., Kerse, N., Darragh, M., Jarrett, P., Booth, R. J., & Broadbent, E. (2013). Expressive writing and wound healing in older adults. A randomized controlled trial. *Psychosomatic Medicine, 75,* 581–90.

Kosten, T. R. (1997). Substance abuse and schizophrenia. *Schizo. Bull., 23,* 181–86.

Kovacs, M., Devlin, B., Pollack, M., Richards, C., & Mukerji, P. (1997). A controlled family history study of childhood- onset depressive disorder. *Arch. Gen. Psychiatry, 54,* 613–23.

Kraemer, H. C., Kazdin, A. E., Offord, D. R., Kessler, R. C., Jensen, P. S., & Kupfer, D. J. (1997). Coming to terms with the terms of risk. *Arch. General Psychiatry, 54,* 337–43.

Kraepelin, E. (1883). *Compendium der psychiatrie.* Leipzig: Abel.

Kraepelin, E. (1896). Dementia praecox. In J. Cutting & M. Shepherd (1987), *The clinical roots of the schizophrenia concept: Translation of seminal European contributions on schizophrenia* (pp. 13–24). Cambridge, UK: Cambridge University Press.

Kraepelin, E. (1919). *Dementia praecox and paraphrenia* (R. M. Barclay, Trans.). Edinburgh, Scotland: E and S Livingstone.

Kraft, S. (2011, March). DEA Ban: Faux marijuana "Imminent threat to public safety. " *Medical News Today,* pp. 1–2.

Kramer, R. A., Warner, V., Olfson, M., Ebanks, C. M., Chaput, F., & Weissman, M. M. (1998). General medical problems among the offspring of depressed parents: A 10-year follow-up. *J. Am. Acad. Child Adoles. Psychiatry, 37*(6), 602–11.

Kramer, R. M. (1998). Paranoid cognition in social systems: Thinking and acting in the shadow of doubt. *Personal. Soc. Psychol. Rev., 2*(4), 251–75.

Kranzler, H. R., Del Boca, F. K., & Rounsaville, B. (1997). Comorbid psychiatric diagnosis predicts three-year outcomes in alcoholics: A posttreatment natural history study. *J. Stud. Alcoh., 57*(6), 619–26.

Kraus, L., & Pope, K. (2010). Juvenile justice. In M. K. Dulcan (Ed.), *Dulcan's textbook of child and adolescent psychiatry* (pp. 987–96). Arlington, VA: American Psychiatric Publishing.

Krauss, D., & Lieberman, J. (2007). Expert testimony on risk and future dangerousness. In M. Costanzo, D. Krauss, & D. K. Pezdek (Eds.), *Expert psychological testimony for the courts* (pp. 227–49). Mahwah, NJ: Lawrence Erlbaum Associates.

Kravitz, A. V., et al. (2015, April 9). Cortico-striatal circuits: Novel therapeutic targets for substance use disorders. *Brain Research* [Epub ahead of print]. doi:10.1016/j.brainres.2015.03.048

Kreek, M. J., Borg, L., Ducat, E., & Ray, B. (2010). Pharmacotherapy in the treatment of addiction: Methadone. *J. Addict. Dis., 29*(2), 200–16.

Kremen, W. S., Koenen, K. C., Boake, C., Purcell, S., Eisen, S. A., Franz, C. E., et al. (2007). Pretrauma cognitive ability and risk for posttraumatic stress disorder: A twin study. *Arch. Gen. Psychiatry, 64,* 361–68.

Kreppner, J. M., Rutter, M., Beckett, C., Castle, J., Colvert, E., Groothues, C., et al. (2007). Normality and impairment following profound early institutional deprivation: A longitudinal follow-up into early adolescence. *Developmental Psychology, 43*(4), 931–46.

Krieg, A., & Dickie, J. R. (2013). Attachment and hikikomori: A psychosocial developmental model. *Int. J. Social Psychiatry, 59,* 61–72.

Kring, A. M., Gur, R. E., Blanchard, J. J., Horan, W., & Reise, S. P. (2013). The Clinical Assessment Interview for Negative Symptoms (CAINS): Final development and validation. *Am. J. Psychiatry, 170,* 165–72.

Kring, A. M., & Neale, J. M. (1996). Do schizophrenic patients show a disjunctive relationship among expressive, experiential, and psychophysiological correlates of emotion? *J. Abn. Psychol., 105,* 249–57.

Krippner, S. (1994). Cross-cultural treatment perspectives on dissociative disorders. In S. J. Lynn & J. W. Rhue (Eds.), *Dissociation: Clinical and theoretical perspectives* (pp. 338–64). New York: Guilford Press.

Krippner, S., Pitchford, D. B., & Jeannine Davies, J. (2012). *Post-traumatic stress disorder*. Santa Barbara, CA: Greenwood/ABC-CLIO.

Krishna, R., Grinn, M., Giordano, N., Thirunanuk-karasu, M., Tadi, P., & Das, S. (2012). Diagnostic confirmation of mild traumatic brain injury by diffusion tensor imaging: A case report. *J. Medical Case Reports, 6*(66). doi:10.1186/1752-1947-6-66

Krishnan, C., Santos, L., Peterson, M. D., & Ehinger, M. (2015). Safety of noninvasive brain stimulation in children and adolescents. *Brain Stimulation, 8*, 76–87.

Krishnan, V., & Nestler, E. J. (2010). Linking molecules to mood: New insight into the biology of depression. *Am. J. Psychiatry, 167*(11), 1305–20. doi:10.1176/appi. ajp.2009.10030434

Kroenke, K. (2003). Patients presenting with somatic complaints: epidemiology, psychiatric comorbidity and management. *Int. J. Methods in Psychiatric Research, 12*, 34–43.

Kroes, M. C., Rugg, M. D., Whalley, M. G., & Brewin, C. R. (2011). Structural brain abnormalities common to posttraumatic stress disorder and depression. *J. Psychiatry Neurosci, 256*–65.

Kroll, J., & Bachrach, B. (1984). Sin and mental illness in the Middle Ages. *Psychol. Med., 14*, 507–14.

Kronfol, Z., & Remick, D. G. (2000). Cytokines and the brain: Implications for clinical psychiatry. *Am. J. Psychiatry, 157*(5), 683–94.

Krueger, R. B. (2010). The DSM diagnostic criteria for sexual masochism. *Arch. Sexual Behavior., 39*(2), 325–45.

Krueger, R. F., & Eaton, N. R. (2010). Personality traits and the classification of mental disorders: Toward a more complete integration in DSM-5 and an empirical model of psychopathology. *Personality Disorders: Theory, Research, and Treatment, 1*(2), 97–118. doi:10.1037/a0018990

Krueger, R. F., Eaton, N. R., Derringer, J., Markon, K. E., Watson, D., & Skodol, A. E. (2011). Personality in DSM-5: Helping delineate personality disorder content and framing the metastructure. *J. Pers. Assess., 93*(4), 325–31. doi:10.1080/00223891.2011.577478

Krueger, R. F., Hicks, B. M., Patrick, C. J., Carlson, S. R., Iacono, W. G., & McGue, M. (2002). Etiologic connections among substance dependence, antisocial behavior, and personality: Modeling the externalizing spectrum. *J. Abn. Psychol., 111*(3), 411–24.

Krueger, R. F., Markon, K. E., Patrick, C. J., Benning, S. D., & Kramer, M. D. (2007). Linking antisocial behavior, substance use, and personality: An integrative quantitative model of the adult externalizing spectrum. *J. Abn. Psych., 116*(4), 645–66.

Krystal, J. H., Perry, E. B., Gueorguieva, R., Belger, A., Madonick, S. H., Abi-Dargham, A., et al. (2005). Comparative and interactive psychopharmacologic effects of ketamine and amphetamine. *Arch. Gen. Psychiatry, 62*, 985–95.

Kubicki, M., McCarley, R., Westin, C. F., Park, H. J., Maier, S., Kikinis, R., et al. (2007). A review of diffusion tensor imaging studies in schizophrenia. *J. Psychiatr. Res., 41*, 15–30.

Kubota, T., Ushijima, Y., Yamada, K., Okuyama, C., Kizu, O., & Nishimura, T. (2005). Diagnosis of Alzheimer's disease using brain perfusion SPECT and MRI Imaging: Which modality achieves better diagnostic accuracy? *European J. Nuclear Medicine and Molecular Imaging, 32*, 414–21.

Kubzansky, L. D., Park, N., Peterson, C., Vokonas, P., & Sparrow, D. (2011). Healthy psychological functioning and incident coronary heart disease. *Arch. Gen. Psychiatry, 68*, 400–08.

Kulhara, P., & Chakrabarti, S. (2001). Culture and schizophrenia and other psychotic disorders. *Cultural Psychiatry: International Perspectives, 24*, 449–64.

Kulkarni, J., de Castella, A., Fitzgerald, P. B., Gurvich, C. T., Bailey, M., Bartholomeusz, C., et al. (2008). Estrogen in severe mental illness: A potential new treatment approach. *Arch. Gen. Psychiatry, 65*, 955–60.

Kumar, C. N., Andrade, C., & Murthy, P. (2015). A randomized, double-blind comparison of lorazepam and chlordiazepoxide in patients with uncomplicated alcohol withdrawal. *J. Studies on Alcohol and Drugs, 70*, 467–74.

Kunda, Z. (1999). *Social cognition: Making sense of people*. Cambridge, MA: The MIT Press.

Kunitoh, N. (2013). From hospital to the community: The influence of deinstitutionalization on discharged long-stay psychiatric patients. *Psychiatry and Clinical Neurosciences, 67*, 384–96. doi:10.1111/pcn.12071

Kupka, R. W., Altshuler, L. L., Nolen, W. A., Suppes, T., Luckenbaugh, D. A., Leverich, G. S., et al. (2007). Three times more days depressed than manic or hypomanic in both bipolar I and bipolar II disorder. *Bipolar Disorders, 9*(5), 531–35.

Kupka, R. W., Luckenbaugh, D. A., Post, R. M., Suppes, T., Altshuler, L. L., Keck, P. E., Jr., et al. (2005). Comparison of rapid-cycling and non-rapid-cycling bipolar disorder based on prospective mood ratings in 539 outpatients. *Am. J. Psychiatry, 162*(7), 1273–80.

Kupper, N., & Denollet, J. (2007). Type D personality as a prognostic factor in heart disease: Assessment and mediating mechanisms. *J. Personality Assessment, 98*(3) 265–76.

Kurlan, R. (1997). Treatment of tics. *Neurologic Clin., 15*(2), 403–09.

Kurtz, M. M., & Mueser, K. T. (2008). A meta-analysis of controlled research on social skills training for schizophrenia. *J. Cons. Clin. Psych., 76*, 491–504.

Kurtz, M. M., & Richardson, C. L. (2012). Social cognitive training for schizophrenia: A meta-analytic investigation of controlled research. *Schizophrenia Bulletin, 38*, 1092–1104.

Kwapil, T., & Barrantes-Vidal, N. (2012). Schizotypal personality disorder: An integrative review. In T. Widiger (Ed.), *The Oxford handbook of personality disorders* (pp. 437–77). Oxford, UK: Oxford University Press.

Kwoh, L. (2010). Stress of long-term unemployment takes a toll on thousands of Jerseyans who are out of work. *Star-Ledger*, Sunday, June 13.

L

Ladd, C. O., Huot, R. L., Thrivikraman, K. V., Nermeroff, C. B., Meaney, M. J., & Plotsky, P. M. (2000). Long-term behavioral and neuroendocrine adaptations to adverse early experience. In E. A. Meyer & C. B. Saper (Eds.), *Progress in brain research: Volume 122, The biological basis for mind–body interactions*. Amsterdam: Elsevier.

Ladd, G. T., & Petry, N. M. (2003). A comparison of pathological gamblers with and without substance abuse treatment histories. *Exper. Clin. Psychopharm., 11*, 202–09.

Ladd, G. W. (2006). Peer rejection, aggressive or withdrawn behavior, and psychological maladjustment from ages 5 to 12: An examination of four predictive models. *Child Develop., 77*(4), 822–46.

LaFrance Jr., W. C., Miller, I. W., Ryan, C. E., Blum, A. S., Solomon, D. A., Kelley, J. E., & Keitner, G. I. (2009). Cognitive behavioral therapy for psychogenic nonepileptic seizures. *Epilepsy & Behavior, 14*(4), 591–96.

Lahey, B. B. (2009). Public health significance of neuroticism. *Am. Psychol., 64*(4), 241–56. doi:10.1037/a0015309

Lahey, B. B., Loeber, R., Burke, J. D., & Applegate, B. (2005). Predicting future antisocial personality disorder in males from a clinical assessment in childhood. *J. Cons. Clin. Psychol., 73*, 389–99.

Lahey, B. B., McBurnett, K., & Loeber, R. (2000). Are attention-deficit/hyperactivity disorder and oppositional defiant disorder developmental precursors to conduct disorder? In A. J. Sameroff & M. Lewis et al. (Eds.), *Handbook of developmental psychopathology* (2nd ed., pp. 431–46). New York: Kluwer.

Lally, S. J. (2003). What tests are acceptable for use in forensic evaluations? A survey of experts. *Prof. Psychol: Res. Pract., 34*, 434–47.

Lalumière, M. L., Harris, G. T., Quinsey, V. L., & Rice, M. E. (2005a). Rape across cultures and time. In *The causes of rape: Understanding individual differences in male propensity for sexual aggression* (pp. 9–30). Washington, DC: American Psychological Association.

Lalumière, M. L., Harris, G. T., Quinsey, V. L., & Rice, M. E. (2005b). Sexual interest in rape. In *The causes of rape: Understanding individual differences in male propensity for sexual aggression* (pp. 105–28). Washington, DC: American Psychological Association.

Lam, D. H., Watkins, E. R., Hayward, P., Bright, J., Wright, K., Kerr, N., et al. (2003). A randomized controlled study of cognitive therapy for relapse prevention for bipolar affective disorder: Outcome of the first year. *Arch. Gen. Psychiatry, 60*(2), 145–52.

Lamb, H. R. (1998). Deinstitutionalization at the beginning of the new millennium. *Harv. Rev. Psychiatry, 6*, 1–10.

Lamb H. R., & Weinberger, L. E. (2005). The shift of psychiatric inpatient care from hospitals to jails and prisons. *J. Am. Acad. Psychiatry and Law, 33*, 529–34.

Lamberg, L. (1998). Mental illness and violent acts: Protecting the patient and the public. *JAMA, 280*, 407–08.

Lambert, K. G., & Kinsley, C. H. (2005). *Clinical neuroscience: The neurobiological foundations of mental health*. New York: Worth.

Lambert, M. J., Hansen, N. B., & Finch, A. E. (2001). Patient-focused research: Using patient outcome data to enhance treatment. *J. Cons. Clin. Psychol., 69*(2), 159–72.

Lambert, M. J., & Ogles, B. M. (2004). The efficacy and effectiveness of psychotherapy. In M. J. Lambert (Ed.), *Bergin and Garfield's handbook of psychotherapy and behavior change* (pp. 139–93). New York: John Wiley & Sons.

Lambrou, C., Veale, D., & Wilson, G. (2011). The role of aesthetic sensitivity in body dysmorphic disorder. *J. Abn. Psychol., 120*(2), 443–53.

Landgraf, D., McCarthy, M. J., & Welsh, D. K. (2014). Circadian clock and stress interactions in the molecular biology of psychiatric disorders. *Current Psychiatry Reports, 16*, 483.

Lane, H.-Y., Liu, Y.-C., Huang, C.-L., Chang, Y.-C., Liau, C.-H., Perng, C.-H., et al. (2008). Sarcosine (N-methylglycine) treatment for acute schizophrenia: A randomized, double-blind study. *Biol. Psychiatry, 63*, 9–19.

Lane, S. D., Cherek, D. R., Pietras, C. J., & Steinberg, J. L. (2005). Performance of heavy marijuana-smoking adolescents on a laboratory measure of motivation. *Add. Behav., 30*(2), 815–28.

Lang, P. J. (1985). The cognitive psychophysiology of emotion: Fear and anxiety. In A. H. Tuma & J. D. Maser (Eds.), *Anxiety and the anxiety disorders*. Hillsdale, NJ: Erlbaum.

Lang, P. J., Davis, M., & Öhman, A. (2000). Fear and anxiety: Animal modes and human cognitive psychophysiology. *J. Affec. Dis., 61*, 137–59.

Langan, C., & McDonald, C. (2009). Neurobiological trait abnormalities in bipolar disorder. *Molecular Psychiatry, 14*, 833–46.

Langevin, R., Curnoe, S., Fedoroff, P., Bennett, R., Langevin, M., Peever, C., et al. (2004). Lifetime sex offender recidivism: A 25-year follow-up study. *Canadian J. Criminology and Criminal Justice, 46*(5), 531–52.

Langleben, D. D., Loughead, J. W., Bilker, W. B., Ruparel, K., Childress, A. R., Busch, S. I., et al. (2005). Telling truth from lie in individual subjects with fast event-related fMRI. *Human Brain Mapping, 26,* 262–72.

Langstrom, N. (2010). The *DSM* diagnostic criteria for exhibitionism, voyeurism, and frotteurism. *Arch. Sexual Behavior, 39,* 317–324.

Langstrom, N., & Seto, M. C. (2006). Exhibitionistic and voyeuristic behavior in a Swedish national population survey. *Arch. Sex. Behav., 35,* 427–35.

Langstrom, N., & Zucker, K. J. (2005). Transvestic fetishism in the general population: Prevalence and correlates. *J. Sex Mar. Ther., 31,* 87–95.

Lanni, C., Lenzken, S. C., Pascale, A., Del Vecchio, I., Racchi, M., Pistoia, F., et al. (2008). Cognition enhancers between treating and doping the mind. *Pharmacological Research, 57,* 196–213.

Lansford, J. E., Malone, P. S., Dodge, K. A., Crozier, J. C., Pettit, G. S., & Bates, J. E. (2006). A 12-year prospective study of patterns of social information-processing problems and externalizing behaviors. *J. Abnorm. Child Psychol., 34*(5), 715–24.

Lapham, S. C., Smith, E., Baca, J. C., Chang, L., Skipper, B. J., Baum, G., et al. (2001). Prevalence of psychiatric disorders among persons convicted of driving while impaired. *Arch. Gen. Psychiatry, 58,* 943–49.

Lara, C., Fayyad, J., de Graaf, R., Kessler, R. C., Aguilar-Gaxiola, S., Angermeyer, M., et al. (2009). Childhood predictors of adult attention-deficit/hyperactivity disorder: results from the World Health Organization World Mental Health Survey Initiative. *Biol. Psychiatry, 65*(1), 46–54. doi:10.1016/j.biopsych.2008.10.005

Lareau, C. R. (2007). Violence risk assessment in release decisions for NGRI aquittees: Awareness of practical realities. *J. Foren. Psychol. Pract., 7*(3), 113–24.

Large, M., Sharma, S., Compton, M. T., Slade, T., & Nielssen, O. (2011). Cannabis use and earlier onset of psychosis: A systematic meta-analysis. *Arch. Gen. Psychiatry, 68,* 555–61.

Larou, C. R. (2013). Civil Commitment and Involuntary Hospitalization of the Mentally Ill. In I. B. Weiner (Ed.) *Handbook of Psychology, Second Edition* (308–331), New York: John Wiley & Sons.

Larson, S. L., Eyerman, J., Foster, M. S., & Gfroerer, J. G. (2007). *Worker substance use and workplace policies and programs.* Rockville, MD: Substance Abuse and Mental Health Services Administration, Office of Applied Studies.

Larsson, H., Andershed, H., & Lichtenstein, P. (2006). A genetic factor explains most of the variation in the psychopathic personality. *J. Abn. Psychol., 115,* 221–30.

Larsson, H., Viding, E., & Plomin, R. (2008). Callous-unemotional traits and antisocial behavior: genetic, environmental, and early parenting characteristics. *Criminal Justice Behavior, 35,* 197–211.

Last, C. G., & Perrin, S. (1993). Anxiety disorders in African-American and white children. *J. Abnorm. Child Psychol., 21,* 153–64.

Latner, J. D., & Stunkard, A. (2003). Getting worse: The stigmatization of obese children. *Obesity Research, 11*(3), 452–56.

Latt, N., & Dore, G. (2014). Thiamine in the treatment of Wernicke encephalopathy in patients with alcohol use disorders. *Internal Medicine J., 44,* 911–15.

Laumann, E. O., Gagnon, J. H., Michael, R. T., & Michaels, S. (1994). *The social organization of sexuality: Sexual practices in the United States.* Chicago: University of Chicago Press.

Laumann, E., Paik, A., Glasser, D. B., Jeong, H. K., Wang, T., Levinson, B., et al. (2005). A cross-national study of subjective well-being among older women and men: Findings from the global study of sexual attitudes and behaviors. *Arch. Sex. Behav., 35,* 143–59.

Laumann, E. O., Paik, A., & Rosen, R. C. (1999). Sexual dysfunction in the United States: Prevalence and predictors. *JAMA, 281,* 537–44.

Lawrence, A. A. (2006). Patient-reported complications and functional outcomes of male-to-female sex reassignment surgery. *Arch. of Sex. Behav., 35,* 717–27.

Lawrence, A. A. (2007). Becoming what we love: Auto-gynephilic transsexualism conceptualized as an expression of romantic love. *Persp. Biol. Med., 50*(4), 506–20.

Lawrence, A. A. (2013). *Men trapped in men's bodies.* New York: Springer.

Lawrence, A. A., Latty, E. M., Chivers, M. L., & Bailey, J. M. (2005). Measurement of sexual arousal in postoperative male-to-female transsexuals using vaginal photoplethysmography. *Arch. Sex. Behav., 34*(2), 135–45.

Lawrie, S. M., & Abukmeil, S. S. (1998). Brain abnormality in schizophrenia. *Brit. J. Psychiatry, 172,* 110–20.

Laws, D. R., & O'Donohue, W. T. (2008). *Sexual deviance: Theory, assessment, and treatment* (2nd ed.). New York: Guilford Press.

Lawson, W. B. (2008). Schizophrenia in African Americans. In K. T. Mueser & D. V. Jeste (Eds.), *Clinical handbook of schizophrenia* (pp. 616–23). New York: Guilford Press.

Lay, B., Nordt, C., & Rössler, W. (2007). Trends in psychiatric hospitalization of people with schizophrenia: A register-based investigation over the last three decades. *Schizo. Res., 97,* 68–78.

Lazarus, A. A. (Ed.). (1996). *Controversies in managed mental health care.* Washington, DC: American Psychiatric Press.

Lazarus, A. A. (1997). *Brief but comprehensive psychotherapy: The multimodal way.* New York: Springer.

Le Blanc, L. A., Hagopian, L. P., & Maglieri, K. A. (2000). Use of a token economy to eliminate excessive inappropriate social behavior in an adult with developmental disabilities. *Behavioral Interventions, 15,* 135–43.

le Grange, D., & Lock, J. (2005). The dearth of psychological treatment studies for anorexia nervosa. *Int. J. Eat. Dis., 37,* 79–91.

le Grange, D., Telch, C. F., & Tibbs, J. (1998). Eating attitudes and behaviors in 1,435 South African Caucasian and non-Caucasian college students. *Am. J. Psychiatry, 155*(2), 250–54.

Leahy, R. L., & McGinn, L. (2012). Cognitive therapy for personality disorders. In T. Widiger (Ed.), *The Oxford Handbook Of Personality Disorders* (pp. 727–50). Oxford, UK: Oxford University Press.

Leas, L., & Mellor, D. (2000). Prediction of delinquency: The role of depression, risk-taking, and parental attachment. *Behavior Change, 17*(3), 155–66.

LeBlond, R. F., DeGowin, R. L., & Brown, D. D. (2004). *DeGowin's diagnostic examination.* New York: McGraw-Hill.

LeDoux, J. E. (2000). Emotion circuits in the brain. *Annu. Rev. Neurosci., 23,* 155–84.

LeDoux, J. E. (2002). *Synaptic self: How our brains become who we are.* New York: Penguin, Putnam.

Lee, J., Altshuler, L., Glahn, D. C., Miklowitz, D. J., Ochsner, K., & Green, M. F. (2013). Social and nonsocial cognition in bipolar disorder and schizophrenia: Relative levels of impairment. *Am. J. Psychiatry, 170,* 334–41.

Lee, P. E., Gill, S. S., Freedman, M., Bronskill, S. E., Hillmer, M. P., & Rochon, P. A. (2004). Atypical antipsychotic drugs in the treatment of behavioral and psychological symptoms of dementia. *BMJ, 329,* 75–78.

Lee, S., Ho, T. P., & Hsu, L. K. (1993). Fatphobic and nonfatphobic anorexia nervosa: A comparative study of 70 Chinese patients in Hong Kong. *Psychol. Med., 23*(4), 999–1017.

Lee, S., & Katzman, M. A. (2002). Cross-cultural perspectives on eating disorders. In C. G. Fairburn & K. D. Brownell (Eds.), *Eating disorders and obesity: A comprehensive handbook* (2nd ed., pp. 260–64). New York: Guilford Press.

Lee, S., Tsang, A., Ruscio, A. M., Haro, J. M., Stein, D. J., Alonso, J., et al. (2009). Implications of modifying the duration requirement of generalized anxiety disorder in developed and developing countries. *Psychological Medicine, 39,* 1163–76.

Lees-Roitman, S. E., Cornblatt, B. A., Bergman, A., Obuchowski, M., Mitropoulou, V., Keefe, R. S. E., et al. (1997). Attentional functioning in schizotypal personality disorder. *Am. J. Psychiatry, 154*(5), 655–60.

Lefaucheur, J. P., et al. (2014). Evidence-based guidelines on the therapeutic use of repetitive transcranial magnetic stimulation (rTMS). *Clinical Neurophysiology, 125,* 2150–206.

Leff, J. (2001). Can we manage without the mental hospital? *Austral. NZ J. Psychiatry, 35*(4), 421–27.

Leff, J., Kuipers, L., Berkowitz, R., Eberlein-Fries, R., & Sturgeon, D. (1982). A controlled trial of social intervention in the families of schizophrenic patients. *Brit. J. Psychiatry, 141,* 121–34.

Leff, J., Wig, N. N., Ghosh, A., Bedi, H., Menon, D. K., Kuipers, L., et al. (1987). Influence of relatives' expressed emotion in the course of schizophrenia in Chandigarh. *Brit. J. Psychiatry, 151,* 166–73.

Legerstee, J. S., Tulen, J. H. M., Dierckx, B., Treffers, P. D. A., Verhulst, F. C., & Utens, E. M. (2010). CBT for childhood anxiety disorders: Differential changes in selective attention between treatment responders and non-responders. *J. Child Psychol. Psychiatry, 51*(2), 162–17.

Lehman, A. F., Steinwachs, D. M., Dixon, L. B., Postrado, L., Scott, J. E., Fahey, M., et al. (1998). Patterns of usual care for schizophrenia: Initial results from the Schizophrenia Patient Outcomes Research Team (PORT) Client Survey. *Schizo. Bull., 24*(1), 11–20.

Leichsenring, F., Leibing, E., Kruse, J., New, A. S., & Leweke, F. (2011). Borderline personality disorder. *Lancet, 377*(9759), 74–84. doi:10.1016/S0140-6736(10)61422-5

Leichtman, M. (2009). Behavioral observations. In J. N. Butcher (Ed.), *Oxford handbook of personality and clinical assessment* (pp. 187–99). New York: Oxford University Press.

Leistico, A.-M. R., Salekin, R. T., DeCsoter, J., & Rogers, R. (2008). A large-scale meta-analysis relating the Hare measures of psychopathy to antisocial conduct. *Law and Human Behavior, 32,* 28–45.

Lemche, E., Surguladze, S., Giampietro, V. P., Anilkumar, A., Brammer, M. J., Sierria, M., et al. (2007). Limbic and prefrontal responses to facial emotion expressions in depersonalization. *Neuroreport, 18*(5), 473–77.

Lemmer, B. (2007). The sleep–wake cycle and sleeping pills. *Physiology & Behavior, 90*(2–3), 285–93.

LeMoult, J., Joormann, J., Sherdell, L., Wright, Y., & Gotlib, I. H. (2009). Identification of emotional facial expressions following recovery from depression. *J. Abn. Psychol., 118*(4), 828–33. doi:10.1037/a0016944

Lengweiler, M. (2003). Psychiatry beyond the asylum: The origins of German military psychiatry before World War I. *History of Psychiatry, 14,* 14–62.

Lennon, M. C., & Limonic, L. (2010). Work and unemployment as stressors. In T. L. Scheid & T. N. Brown (Eds.), *A handbook for the study of mental health: Social contexts, theories, and systems* (2nd ed., pp. 213–25). New York: Cambridge University Press.

Lenz, G., & Demal, U. (2000). Quality of life in depression and anxiety disorders: An explanatory follow-up study after intensive cognitive behaviour therapy. *Psychopath., 33,* 297–302.

Lenzenweger, M. F. (2008). Epidemiology of personality disorders. *Psychiatr. Clinics North Am., 31,* 395–403.

Lenzenweger, M. F. (2009). Schizotypic psychopathology: Theory, evidence, and future directions. In P. H. Blaney & T. Millon (Eds.), *Oxford textbook of psychopathology* (2nd ed., pp. 692–722). New York: Oxford University Press.

Lenzenweger, M. F. (2010). *Schizotypy and schizophrenia: The view from experimental psychopathology.* New York: Guilford Press.

Lenzenweger, M. F., Lane, M. C., Loranger, A. W., & Kessler, R. C. (2007). DSM-IV personality disorders in the national comorbidity survey replication. *Biol. Psychiatry, 62,* 553–64.

Leon, D. E., & McCambridge, J. (2006). Liver cirrhosis mortality rates in Britain from 1950 to 2002: An analysis of routine data. *Lancet, 367*(9504), 52–56.

Leon, G. R., Keel, P. K., Klump, K. L., & Fulkerson, J. A. (1997). The future of risk factor research in understanding the etiology of eating disorders. *Psychopharm. Bull., 33*(3), 405–11.

Leonard, K. E., & Eiden, R. D. (2007). Marital and family processes in the context of alcohol use and alcohol disorders. *Annu. Rev. Clin. Psychol., 3,* 285–310.

Leonard, L. M., & Follette, V. M. (2002). Sexual functioning in women reporting a history of child sexual abuse: Review of the empirical literature and clinical implications. *Annu. Rev. Sex Res., 13,* 346–88.

Leonardo, E. D., & Hen, R. (2006). Genetics of affective and anxiety disorders. *Annu. Rev. Psych., 57,* 117–37.

Leong, G. B., & Eth, S. (1991). Legal and ethical issues in electroconvulsive therapy. *Psychiatr. Clin. North Am., 14,* 1007–16.

Leor, J., Poole, W. K., & Kloner, R. A. (1996). Sudden cardiac death triggered by an earthquake. *New England J. Medicine, 334*(7), 413–19.

Lepore, S. J., Revenson, T. A., Roberts, K. J., Pranikoff, J. R., & Davey, A. (2015). Randomised controlled trial of expressive writing and quality of life in men and women treated for colon or rectal cancer. *Psychology and Health, 30,* 284–300.

Lerman, P. (1981). *Deinstitutionalization: A cross-problem analysis.* Rockville, MD: U.S. Department of Health and Human Services.

Leserman, J., Pence, B. W., Whetten, K., Mugavero, M. J., Thielman, N. M., Schwartz, M. S., et al. (2007). Relation of lifetime trauma and depressive symptoms to mortality in HIV. *Am. J. Psychiatry, 164,* 1707–13.

Lesperance, F., Frasure-Smith, N., Talajic, M., & Bourassa, M. G. (2002). Five-year risk of cardiac mortality in relation to initial severity and one-year changes in depression symptoms after myocardial infarction. *Circulation, 105,* 1049–53.

Lester, B. M., Masten, A., & McEwen, B. (2006). *Resilience in children.* Malden, MA: Blackwell Publishing.

Leucht, S. (2014). Measurement of response, remission, and recovery in schizophrenia and examples for their clinical application. *J. Clinical Psychiatry, 75*(Suppl. 1), 8–14. doi:http://dx.doi.org/10.4088/JCP.13049su1c.02

Leukefeld, C. G., Logan, P. R., Clayton, C., Martin, R., Zimmerman, A., Milch, R., et al. (1998). Adolescent drug use, delinquency, and other behaviors. In T. P. Gullotta, G. R. Adams, & R. Montemayor (Eds.), *Advances in adolescent development: An annual book series* (Vol. 9, pp. 98–128). Thousand Oaks, CA: Sage Publications.

Leung, A., & Chue, P. (2000). Sex differences in schizophrenia: A review of the literature. *Acta Psychiatr. Scandin., 101,* 3–38.

Leung, A. W., & Heimberg, R. G. (1996). Homework compliance, perceptions of control, and outcome of cognitive-behavioral treatment of social phobia. *Behav. Res. Ther., 34*(5), 423–32.

Leung, C. W., Laraia, B. A., Needham, B. L., Rehkopf, D. H., Adler, N. E., Lin, J., et al. (2014). Soda and cell aging: Associations between sugar-sweetened beverage consumption and leukocyte telomere length I healthy adults from the National Health and Nutrition Examination Surveys. *Am. J. Public Health, 104,* 2425–31.

Levav, I., Kohn, R., Golding, J. M., & Weisman, M. M. (1997). Vulnerability of Jews to affective disorders. *Am. J. Psychiatry, 154*(7), 941–47.

LeVay, S., & Baldwin, J. (2012). *Human sexuality* (4th ed.). Sunderland, MA: Sinauer Associates.

Levenson, J. S., D'Amora, D. A., & Hern, A. L. (2007). Megan's Law and its impact on community reentry for sex offenders. *Behavioral Sciences and the Law, 25,* 587–602.

Levine, R. E., & Gaw, A. C. (1995). Culture-bound syndromes. *Psychiatr. Clin. North Am. Cultural Psychiatry, 18*(3), 523–36.

Levinson, D. F. (2006). The genetics of depression: A review. *Biol. Psychiatry, 60*(2), 84–92.

Levinson, D. F. (2009). Genetics of major depression. In I. H. Gotlib & C. L. Hammen (Eds.), *Handbook of depression* (2nd ed., pp. 165–86). New York: Guilford Press.

Levy, C., & Kershaw, S. (2001, April 18). *New York Times,* p. A20.

Levy, D. L., Holzman, P. S., Matthysse, S., & Mendell, N. R. (1993). Eye tracking dysfunction and schizophrenia: A critical perspective. *Schizo. Bull., 19*(3), 461–536.

Levy, D. L., Sereno, A. B., Gooding, D. C., & O'Driscoll, G. A. (2010). Eye tracking dysfunction in schizophrenia: Characterization and pathophysiology. *Current Topics in Behavioral Neuroscience, 4,* 311–47.

Levy, K. N., & Wasserman, R. H. (2009). Psychodynamic model of depression. In R. Ingram (Ed.), *The international encyclopedia of depression* (pp. 457–60). New York: Springer.

Lewinsohn, P. M., & Essau, C. A. (2002). Depression in adolescents. In I. H. Gotlib & C. L. Hammen (Eds.), *Handbook of depression* (pp. 541–59). New York: Guilford Press.

Lewinsohn, P. M., & Gotlib, I. H. (1995). Behavioral theory and treatment of depression. In E. E. Beckham & W. R. Leber (Eds.), *Handbook of depression* (2nd ed., pp. 352–75). New York: Guilford Press.

Lewinsohn, P. M., Joiner, T. E., & Rohde, P. (2001). Evaluation of cognitive diathesis-stress models in predicting major depressive disorder in adolescents. *J. Abn. Psychol., 110*(2), 203–15.

Lewinsohn, P. M., Rohde, P., Seely, J. R., Klein, D. N., & Gotlib, I. H. (2003). Psychosocial functioning of young adults who have experienced and recovered from major depressive disorder during adolescence. *J. Abn. Psychol., 112*(3), 353–63.

Lewis, D. A. (2011). Antipsychotic medications and brain volume: Do we have cause for concern? *Arch. Gen. Psychiatry, 68,* 126–27.

Lewis, D. O., Yeager, C. A., Swica, Y., Pincus, J. H., & Lewis, M. (1997). Objective documentation of child abuse and dissociation in 12 murderers with dissociative identity disorder. *Am. J. Psychiatry, 154*(12), 1703–10.

Lewis, J., Dickson, D. W., Lin, W.-L., Chisholm, L., Corral, A., Jones, G., et al. (2001). Enhanced neurofibrillary degeneration in transgenic mice expressing mutant tau and APP. *Science, 293,* 1487–91.

Lewis, T. T., Aiello, A. E., Leurgans, S., Kelly, J., & Barnes, L. L. (2010). Self-reported experiences of everyday discrimination are associated with elevated C-reactive protein levels in older African-America adults. *Brain, Behavior, and Immunity, 24,* 438–43.

Lezak, M. D., Howieson, D. B., & Loring, D. W. (2004). *Neuropsychological assessment* (4th ed.). New York: Oxford University Press.

Li, G., Wang, L. Y., Shofer, J. B., Thompson, M. L., Peskind, E. R., McCormick, W., et al. (2011). Temporal relationship between depression and dementia. *Arch. Gen. Psychiatry, 68,* 970–77.

Li, Q. (2007). New bottle but old wine: A research of cyberbullying in schools. *Computers in Human Behavior, 23*(4), 1777–91.

Li, S., Jin, M., Zhang, D., Yang, T., Koeglsperger, T., Fu., H., & Selkoe, D. J. (2013). Environmental novelty activates b$_2$-adrenergic signaling to prevent the impairment of hippocampal LTP by Ab oligomers. *Neuron, 77,* 929–41.

Li, W., & Zinbarg, R. E. (2007). Anxiety sensitivity and panic attacks: A 1-year longitudinal study. *Behav. Mod., 31*(2), 145–61.

Liberman, R. P. (1982). Assessment of social skills. *Schizophrenia Bulletin, 8,* 62–83.

Lichtenberger, E. O., & Kaufman, A. S. (2009). *Essentials of WAIS-IV assessment.* New York: John Wiley.

Lidz, T., Fleck, S., & Cornelison, A. R. (1965). *Schizophrenia and the family.* New York: International Universities Press.

Lieb, K., Zanarini, M., Schmahl, C., Linehan, M., & Bohus, M. (2004). Borderline personality disorder. *Lancet, 364,* 453–61.

Lieb, R., Schuetz, C. G., Pfister, H., von Sydow, K., & Wittchen, H. (2002). Mental disorders in ecstasy users: A prospective-longitudinal investigation. *Drug & Alcohol Dependence, 68,* 195–207.

Lieb, R., Wittchen, H.-U., Hofler, M., Fuetsch, M., Stein, M., & Merikangas, K. R. (2000). Parental psychopathology, parenting styles, and the risk of social phobia in offspring: A prospective-longitudinal community study. *JAMA, 57,* 859–66.

Lieberman, J. A., & Stroup, T. S. (2011). The NIMH-CATIE schizophrenia study: What did we learn? *Am. J. Psychiatry, 168,* 770–75.

Liem, J. H. (1974). Effects of verbal communications of parents and children: A comparison of normal and schizophrenic families. *J. Cons. Clin. Psychol., 42,* 438–50.

Lieverse, R., Van Someren, E. J., Nielen, M. M., Uitdehaag, B. M., Smit, J. H., & Hoogendijk, W. J. (2011). Bright light treatment in elderly patients with nonseasonal major depressive disorder: A randomized placebo-controlled trial. *Arch. Gen. Psychiatry, 68*(1), 61–70. doi:10.1001/archgenpsychiatry.2010.183

Lilenfeld, L. R. R., Wonderlich, S., Riso, L. P., Crosby, R., & Mitchell, J. (2006). Eating disorders and personality: A methodological and empirical review. *Clin. Psych. Rev., 26,* 299–320.

Lilenfeld, L. R., Kaye, W. H., Greeno, C. G., Merikangas, K. R., Plotnicov, K., Pollice, C., et al. (1998). A controlled family study of anorexia nervosa and bulimia nervosa. *Arch. Gen. Psychiatry, 55,* 603–10.

Lilienfeld, S. O. (2002). When worlds collide: Social science, politics, and the Rind et al. (1998) child sexual abuse meta-analysis. *Am. Psychol., 57,* 176–88.

Lilienfeld, S. O. (2007). Psychological treatments that cause harm. *Perspectives on Psychological Science, 2,* 53–70. doi:10.1111/j.1745-6916.2007.00029.x

Lilienfeld, S. O., & Lynn, S. J. (2003). Dissociative identity disorder: Multiple personalities, multiple controversies. In S. O. Lilienfeld & S. J. Lynn (Eds.), *Science and pseudoscience in clinical psychology* (pp. 109–42). New York: Guilford Press.

Lilienfeld, S. O., Lynn, S. J., Kirsch, I., Chaves, J. F., Sarbin, T. R., Ganaway, G. K., et al. (1999). Dissociative identity disorder and the sociocognitive model: Recalling lessons of the past. *Psychol. Bull., 125*, 507–23.

Lilienfeld, S. O., Marshall, J., Todd, J. T., & Shane, H. C. (2014). The persistence of fad interventions in the face of negative scientific evidence: Facilitated communication for autism as a case example. *Evidence-Based Communication Assessment and Intervention, 8*, 62–101.

Lilienfeld, S. O., Smith, S. F., & Watts, A. L. (2013). Issues in diagnosis: Conceptual issues and controversies. In W. E. Craighead, D. J. Miklowitz, & L. W. Craighead (Eds.), *Psychopathology: History, diagnosis and empirical foundations* (2nd ed., pp. 334–63). Hoboken, NJ: John Wiley & Sons.

Lilienfeld, S. O., Wood, J. M., & Garb, H. N. (2001, May). What's wrong in this picture? *Scientific American*, 81–87.

Lim, S.-L., & Kim, J.-H. (2005). Cognitive processing of emotional information in depression, panic, and somatoform disorder. *J. Abn. Psych., 114*(1), 50–61.

Lin, C. C. H., Kuo, P. H., Su, C. H., & Chen, W. J. (2006). The Taipei Adolescent Twin/Sibling Family Study I: Behavioral problems, personality features, and neuropsychological performance. *International Society for Twin Studies, 9*, 890–94.

Lin, C. C. H., Su, C. H., Kuo, P. H., Hsiao, C. K., Soong, W. T., & Chen, W. (2007). Genetic and environmental influences on schizotypy among adolescents in Taiwan: A multivariate twin/sibling analysis. *Behav. Gen., 37*, 334–44.

Lin, P.-Y., & Tsai, G. (2004). Association between serotonin transporter gene promoter polymorphism and suicide: Results of a meta-analysis. *Biol. Psychiatry, 55*(10), 1023–30.

Lincoln, A. E., Caswell, S. V., Almquist, J. L., Dunn, R. E., Norris, J. B., & Hinton, R. Y. (2011). Trends in concussion incidence in high school sports: A prospective 11-year study. *Am. J. Sports Med., 39*, 958–63.

Lindau, S. T., Schumm, L. P., Laumann, E. O., Levinson, W., O'Muircheartaigh, C. A., & Waite, L. J. (2007). A study of sexuality and health among older adults in the United States. *N. Eng. J. Med., 357*(8), 762–74.

Lindman, R. E., & Lang, A. R. (1994). The alcohol-aggression stereotype: A cross-cultural comparison of beliefs. *Inter. J. Addict., 29*, 1–13.

Linehan, M. M. (1993). *Cognitive-behavioral treatment of borderline personality disorder: The dialectics of effective treatment*. New York: Guilford Press.

Linehan, M. M., Comtois, K. A., Murray, A. M., Brown, M. Z., Gallop, R. J., Heard, H. L., et al. (2006). Two-year randomized controlled trial and follow-up of dialectical behavior therapy vs therapy by experts for suicidal behaviors and borderline personality disorder. *Arch. Gen. Psychiatry, 63*, 757–66.

Ling, W., Jacobs, P., Hillhouse, M., Hasson, A., Thomas, C., Freese, T., et al. (2010). From research to the real world: Buprenorphine in the decade of the clinical trials network. *J. Subst. Abuse Treat., 38* (Suppl. 1), S53–60.

Link, B. G. (2001). Stigma: Many mechanisms require multifaceted responses. *Epidemiologia e Psichi-Atria Sociale, 10*, 8–11.

Links, P. S., Ansari, J. Y., Fazalullasha, F., & Shah, R. (2012). The relationship of personality disorders and Axis I clinical disorders. In T. A. Widiger (Ed.), *The Oxford handbook of personality disorders* (pp. 237–59). New York: Oxford University Press.

Lintzeris, N., Holgate, F., & Dunlop, A. (1996). Addressing dependent amphetamine use: A place for prescription. *Drug and Alcohol Review, 15*(2), 189–95.

Lipp, O. V. (2006). Human fear learning: Contemporary procedures and measurement. In M. G. Craske, D. Hermans, & D. Vansteenwegen (Eds.), *Fear and learning: From basic processes to clinical implications* (pp. 37–51). Washington, DC: American Psychological Association.

Lissek, S., Levenson, J., Biggs, A. L., Johnson, L. L., Ameli, R., Pine, D. S., et al. (2008). Elevated fear conditioning to socially relevant unconditioned stimuli in social anxiety disorder. *Am. J. Psychiatry, 165*(1), 124–32. doi:10.1176/appi. ajp.2007.06091513

Lissek, S., Rabin, S., Heller, R. E., Lukenbaugh, D., Geraci, M., Pine, D. S., et al. (2010). "Overgeneralization of conditioned fear as a pathogenic marker of panic disorder": Correction. *Am. J. Psychiatry, 167*(1), doi:10.1176/appi.ajp.2009.09030410.

Litt, M. D., Kadden, R. M., Kabele-Cormier, E., & Petry, N. (2007). Changing network support for drinking initial findings from the Network Support Project. *J. Cons. Clin. Psych., 75*, 542–55.

Littrell, J. (2001). What neurobiology has to say about why people abuse alcohol and other drugs. *J. Social Work Practice in the Addictions, 1*(3), 23–40.

Liu, R. T., & Alloy, L. B. (2010). Stress generation in depression: A systematic review of the empirical literature and recommendations for future study. *Clin. Psychol. Rev., 30*(5), 582–93. doi:10.1016/j.cpr. 2010.04.010

Livesley, W. J. (2001). Conceptual and taxonomic issues. In W. J. Livesley (Ed.), *Handbook of personality disorders* (pp. 3–38). New York: Guilford Press.

Livesley, W. J. (2003). Diagnostic dilemmas in classifying personality disorder. In K. A. Phillips, M. B. First, & H. A. Pincus (Eds.), *Advancing DSM: Dilemmas in psychiatric diagnosis* (pp. 153–90). Washington, DC: American Psychiatric Association.

Livesley, W. J. (2005). Behavioral and molecular genetic contributions to a dimensional classification of personality disorders. *J. Pers. Disord., 19*, 131–55.

Livesley, W. J. (2008). Toward a genetically-informed model of borderline personality disorder. *J. Pers. Disord., 22*, 42–71.

Livesley, W. J. (2011). The current state of personality disorder classification: Introduction to the special feature on the classification. *J. Pers. Disord., 25*(3), 269–78. doi:10.1521/pedi.2011.25.3.269

Livesely, W. J., & Jang, K. L. (2000). Toward an empirically based classification of personality disorders. *J. Personality Disorders, 14*, 137–51.

Livesley, W. J., & Jang, K. L. (2008). The behavioral genetics of personality disorder. *Annu. Rev. Clin. Psych., 4*, 247–74.

Lizardi, D., Oquendo, M., & Graver, R. (2009). Clinical pitfalls in the diagnosis of ataque de nervios: A case study. *Transcult. Psychiatry, 46*, 463–86.

Lobbestael, J., & Arntz, A. (2012). Cognitive contributions to personality disorders. In T. Widiger (Ed.), *The Oxford handbook of personality disorders* (pp. 325–44). Oxford, UK: Oxford University Press.

Lochner, C., & Stein, D. J. (2003). Heterogeneity of obsessive-compulsive disorder: A literature review. *Har. Rev. Psychiatry, 11*(3), 113–32.

Lock, J., le Grange, D., Agras, W. S., & Dare, C. (2001). *Treatment manual for anorexia nervosa: A family-based approach*. New York: Guilford Press.

Lock, J., le Grange, D., Agras, W. S., Moye, A., Bryson, S. W., & Jo, B. (2010). Randomized clinical trial comparing family-based treatments with adolescent-focused individual therapy for adolescents with anorexia nervosa. *Arch. Gen. Psychiatry, 67*, 1025–32.

Locke, A. E., Kahali, B., Berndt, S., Justice, A. E., Pers, T. H., et al. (2015). Genetic studies of body mass index yield new insights for obesity biology. *Nature, 518*, 197–206.

Loeb, T. B., Williams, J. K., Carmona, J. V., Rivkin, I., Wyatt, G. E., Chin, D., et al. (2002). Child sexual abuse: Associations with the sexual functioning of adolescents and adults. *Annu. Rev. Sex Res., 13*, 307–45.

Loewenthal, K., Goldblatt, V., Gorton, T., Lubitsch, G., Bicknell, H., Fellowes, D., et al. (1995). Gender and depression in Anglo-Jewry. *Psychol. Med., 25*, 1051–63.

Loewenthal, K. M., MacLeod, A. K., Cook, S., Lee, M., & Goldblatt, V. (2003). Beliefs about alcohol among UK Jews and Protestants: Do they fit the alcohol depression hypothesis? *Soc. Psychiatry Psychiatr. Epidemiol., 38*, 122–27.

Loftus, E. F., & Bernstein, D. M. (2005). Rich false memories: The royal road to success. In A. F. Healy (Ed.), *Experimental cognitive psychology and its applications: Decade of behavior* (pp. 101–13). Washington, DC: American Psychological Association.

Loftus, E. F., & Davis, D. (2006). Recovered memories. *Annu. Rev. Clin. Psych., 2*(2006), 469–98.

Loftus, E. F., Feldman, J., & Dashiell, R. (1995). The reality of illusory memories. In D. Schacter, J. Coyle, L. Sullivan, M. Mesulam, & G. Fischbach (Eds.), *Memory distortions: Interdisciplinary perspectives*. Cambridge, MA: Harvard University Press.

Lohr, B. A., Adams, H. E., & Davis, J. M. (1997). Sexual arousal to erotic and aggressive stimuli in sexually coercive and noncoercive men. *J. Abn. Psychol., 106*, 230–42.

Lomax, C. L., Oldfield, V. B., & Salkovskis, P. M. (2009). Clinical and treatment comparisons between adults with early- and late-onset obsessive-compulsive disorder. *Behav. Res. Ther., 47*(2), 99–104.

London, K., Bruck, M., Ceci, S. J., & Shuman, D. W. (2005). Disclosure of child sexual abuse: What does the research tell us about the ways that children tell? *Psychology, Public Policy, and Law, 11*(1), 194–226.

Long, J. V. F., & Valliant, G. E. (1984). Natural history of male psychological health, XI: Escape from the underclass. *Am. J. Psychiatry, 141*, 341–46.

Longe, O., Maratos, F. A., Gilbert, P., Evans, G., Volker, F., Rockliff, H., et al. (2010). Having a word with yourself: Neural correlates of self-criticism and self-reassurance. *NeuroImage, 49*(2), 1849–56.

Longin, E., Chammat, M., Chapouthier, G., & Jouvent, R. (2010). Physical versus social fear: A fundamental dichotomy. *Activitas Nervosa Superior, 52*(2), 62–70.

Lonsdorf, T. B., & Kalisch, R. (2011). A review on experimental and clinical genetic associations studies on fear conditioning, extinction and cognitive-behavioral treatment. *Translational Psychiatry, 1*, e41.

Lonsdorf, T. B., Weike, A. I., Nikamo, P., Schalling, M., Hamm, A. O., & Öhman, A. (2009). Genetic gating of human fear learning and extinction: Possible implications for gene-environment interaction in anxiety disorder. *Psychol. Science, 20*(2), 198–206. doi:10.1111/j.1467-9280.2009.02280.x

Looper, K. J., & Kirmayer, L. J. (2002). Behavioral medicine approaches to somatoform disorders. *J. Cons. Clin. Psychol., 70*, 810–27.

Lopez, S. R., & Guarnaccia, P. J. (2005). Cultural dimensions of psychopathology: The social world's impact on mental illness. In J. E. Maddux & B. A. Winstead (Eds.), *Psychopathology: Foundations for a contemporary understanding*. Mahwah, NJ: Lawrence Erlbaum Associates.

Lopez, S. R., Lopez, A. A., & Fong, K. T. (1991). Mexican Americans' initial preferences for counselors: The role of ethnic factors. *J. Couns. Psychol., 38,* 487–96.

López-Muñoz, F., Ucha-Udabe, R., & Alamo, C. (2005). The history of barbiturates a century after their clinical introduction. *Neuropsychiatr. Dis. Treat., 1*(4), 329–43.

López-Solà, C., Fontenelle, L. F., Alonso, P., Cuadras, D., Foley, D., Pantelis, C., et al. (2014). Prevalence and heritability of obsessive-compulsive spectrum and anxiety disorder symptoms: A survey of the Australian twin registry. *Am J Med Genet Part B, 165B,* 314–25.

Lord, C., Risi, S., DiLavore, P. S., Shulman, C., Thurm, A., & Pickles, A. (2006). Autism from 2 to 9 years of age. *Arch. Gen. Psychiatry, 63*(6), 694–701.

LoSasso, G. L., Rapport, L. J., & Axelrod, B. N. (2001). Neuropsychological symptoms associated with low-level exposure to solvents and (meth) acrylates among nail technicians. *Neuropsychiatry Neuropsychol. Behav. Neurol., 14*(3), 183–89.

LoSasso, G. L., Rapport, L. J., Axelrod, B. N., & Whitman, R. D. (2002). Neurocognitive sequelae of exposure to organic solvents and (meth) acrylates among nail-studio technicians. *Neuropsychiatry Neuropsychol. Behav. Neurol., 15*(1), 44–55.

Lovaas, O. I. (1987). Behavioral treatment and normal educational and intellectual functioning in young autistic children. *J. Consulting and Clinical Psychology, 55,* 3–9.

Lovett, B. J. (2006). The new history of psychology: A review and critique. *History of Psychology, 9*(1), 17–37.

Löwe, B., Zipfel, S., Buchholz, C., Dupont, Y., Reas, D. L., & Herzog, W. (2001). Long-term outcome of anorexia nervosa in a prospective 21-year follow-up study. *Psychol. Med., 31,* 881–90.

Lowe, J. R., Edmundson, M., & Widiger, T. A. (2009). Assessment of dependency, agreeableness, and their relationship. *Psychol. Assess., 21,* 543–53.

Lozano, B. E., & Johnson, S. L. (2001). Can personality traits predict increases in manic and depressive symptoms? *J. Affect. Dis., 63*(1–3), 103–11.

Lubke, G. H., Laurin, C., Amin, N., Hottenga, J. J., Willemsen, G., van Grootheest, G., et al. (2014). Genome-wide analyses of borderline personality features. *Molecular Psychiatry, 19,* 923–29.

Luborsky, L., & Barrett, M. S. (2006). The history and empirical status of key psychoanalytic concepts. *Annu. Rev. Clin. Psychol., 2,* 1–19.

Lucas, B. R., et al. (2014). Gross motor deficits in children prenatally exposed to alcohol: A meta-analysis. *Pediatrics, 134,* e192–e209.

Lucey, M. R., Mathurin, P., & Morgan, T. R. (2009). Alcoholic hepatitis. *N. Engl. J. Med., 360*(26), 2758–69.

Luchins, A. S. (1989). Moral treatment in asylums and general hospitals in 19th-century America. *J. Psychol. Interdisciplinary & Applied, 123*(6), 585–607.

Luckasson, R., Coulter, D. L., Polloway, E. A., Reiss, S., Schalock, R. L., Snell, M. E., et al. (1992). *Mental retardation: Definition, classification, and systems of supports* (9th ed.). Washington, DC: American Association on Mental Retardation.

Ludewig, S., Geyer, M. A., Ramseier, M., Vollenweider, F. X., Rechsteiner, E., & Cattapan-Ludewig, K. (2005). Information-processing deficits and cognitive dysfunction in panic disorder. *J. Psychiatr. Neurosci., 30*(1), 37–43.

Lukas, C., & Seiden, H. M. (1990). *Silent grief: Living in the wake of suicide.* New York: Bantam Books.

Lukas, S. E. (2015). Substance abuse: Drugs. In H. S. Friedman (Ed.), *Encyclopedia of mental health* (2nd ed., pp. 249–62). Oxford, UK: Elsevier Press.

Lundgren, J. D., Danoff-Burg, S., & Anderson, D. A. (2004). Cognitive-behavior therapy for bulimia nervosa: An empirical analysis of clinical significance. *Int. J. Eat. Dis., 35,* 262–74.

Luntz, B. K., & Widom, C. S. (1994). Antisocial personality disorder in abused and neglected children grown-up. *Am. J. Psychiatry, 151,* 670–74.

Luo, Y., Parish, W. L., & Laumann, E. O. (2008). A population-based study of childhood sexual contact in China: Prevalence and long-term consequences. *Child Ab. Negl., 32*(7), 721–31.

Lupien, S. J., McEwen, B. S., Gunnar, M. R., & Heim, C. (2009). Effects of stress throughout the lifespan on the brain, behavior and cognition. *Nature Reviews: Neuroscience, 10,* 434–45.

Lurigio, A. J. (2013). Forty years after Abramson: Beliefs about the criminalization of people with serious mental illnesses. *Int. J. Offender Therapy Comparative Criminol, 57,* 763.

Lutgendorf, S., Garand, L., Buckwalter, K. C., Reimer, T. T., Hong, S., & Lubaroff, D. (1999). Life stress, mood disturbance, and elevated interleukin-6 in healthy older women. *J. Gerontol. Series A, Biological Sciences and Medical Sciences, 54A,* M434–39.

Luxton, D. D., Pruitt, L. D., & Osenbach, J. E. (2014). Best practices for remote psychological assessment via telehealth technologies. *Professional Psychology: Research and Practice, 45*(1), 27–35. doi:10.1037/a0034547

Lyketsos, C. G., Steinberg, M., Tschanz, J. T., Norton, M. C., Steffens, D. C., & Breitner, J. C. S. (2000). Mental and behavioral disturbances in dementia: Findings from the Cache County study on memory and aging. *Am. J. Psychiatry, 157*(5), 708–14.

Lykken, D. T. (1957). A study of anxiety in the sociopathic personality. *J. Abn. Soc. Psychol., 55*(1), 6–10.

Lykken, D. T. (1995). *The antisocial personalities.* Hillsdale, NJ: Erlbaum.

Lymburner, J. A., & Roesch, R. (1999). The insanity defense: Five years of research (1993–1997). *Int. J. Law and Psychiatry, 22,* 213–40. doi:http://dx.doi.org/10.1016/S0160-2527(99)00006-0

Lynam, D. R., Milich, R., Zimmerman, R., Novak, S. P., Logan, T. K., Martin, C., et al. (2009). Project DARE: No effects at 10-year follow-up. In G. A. Marlatt & K. Witkiewitz (Eds.), *Addictive behaviors: New readings on etiology, prevention, and treatment* (pp. 187–96). Washington, DC: American Psychological Association.

Lynam, D. R., & Widiger, T. A. (2007). Using a general model of personality to understand sex differences in the personality disorders. *J. Pers. Disord., 21*(6), 583–602.

Lynch, D., Laws, K. R., & McKenna, P. J. (2010). Cognitive behavioral therapy for major psychiatric disorder: Does it really work? A meta-analytical review of well-controlled trials. *Psychol. Med., 40,* 9–24.

Lynch, P. S., Kellow, J. T., & Willson, V. L. (1997). The impact of deinstitutionalization on the adaptive behavior of adults with mental retardation. *Education & Training in Mental Retardation & Developmental Disabilities, 32*(3), 255–61.

Lynch, T., & Cuper, P. (2012). Dialectical behavior therapy of borderline and other personality disorders. In T. Widiger (Ed.), *The Oxford handbook of personality disorders* (pp. 785–96). Oxford, UK: Oxford University Press.

Lynch, T. R., Trost, W. T., Salsman, N., & Linehan, M. M. (2007). Dialectical behavior therapy for borderline personality disorder. *Annu. Rev. Clin. Psych., 3,* 181–205.

Lynn, S. J., Knox, J. A., Fassler, O., Lilienfeld, S. O., & Loftus, E. F. (2004). Memory, trauma, and dissociation. In G. M. Rosen (Ed.), *Posttraumatic stress disorder: Issues and controversies* (pp. 163–86). New York: John Wiley & Sons.

Lynn, S. J., Merckelbach, H., Lilienfeld, S. O., Condon, L., van Heugten, D., & Giesbrecht, T. (2015). Dissociative disorders. In H. S. Friedman (Ed.), *Encyclopedia of mental health, Volume 1* (2nd ed., pp. 75–78). Oxford, UK: Elsevier Press.

Lytton, H. (1980). *Parent–child interaction: The socialization process observed in twin and singleton families.* New York: Plenum.

Lyubomirsky, S., Caldwell, N. D., & Nolen-Hoeksema, S. (1998). Effects of ruminative and distracting responses to depressed mood on retrieval of autobiographical memories. *J. Pers. Soc. Psychol., 75,* 166–77.

Lyvers, M. (2000). "Loss of control" in alcoholism and drug addiction: A neuroscientific interpretation. *Exp. Clin. Psychopharm., 8*(2), 225–45.

M

Maat, A., Fett, A-K., Derks, E., & GROUP Investigators (2012). Social cognition and quality of life in schizophrenia. *Schizophrenia Research, 137,* 212–18.

MacCulloch, T. (2010). Constructions of truth, gate-keeping and the power of diagnostic labels. *Issues in Mental Health Nursing, 31*(2), 151–52.

MacDonald, A. W., & Jones, J. A. (2009). Functional imaging in clinical assessment: The rise of neurodiagnostics with fMRI. In J. N. Butcher (Ed.), *Oxford handbook of personality assessment* (pp. 364–74). New York: Oxford University Press.

Macgowan, M., & Engle, B. (2010). Evidence for optimism: Behavior therapies and motivational interviewing in adolescent substance abuse treatment. *Child Adol. Psychiatr. Clin. North Am., 19*(3), 527–45.

MacGregor, J. M. (1989). *The discovery of the art of the insane.* Princeton, NJ: Princeton University Press.

Maciejewski, P. K., Zhang, B., Block, S. D., & Prigerson, H. G. (2007). An empirical examination of the stage theory of grief. *JAMA, 297*(7), 716–23.

Mackay, L. E. (1994). Benefits of a formalized traumatic brain injury program within a trauma center. *J. Head Trauma Rehab., 9*(1), 11–19.

Mackenzie, C. S., Reynolds, K. Chou, K. L., Pagura, J., & Sareen, J. (2011). Prevalence and correlates of generalized anxiety disorder in a national sample of older adults. *Am. J. Geriatric Psychiatry, 19*(4), 305–15.

MacLean, H. N. (1992). *Once upon a time.* New York: HarperCollins.

Maclean, W. E., Jr. (Ed.). (1997). *Ellis' handbook of mental deficiency: Psychological theory and research.* Mahwah, NJ: Erlbaum.

MacLeod, A. K. (1999). Prospective cognitions. In T. Dalgleish & M. J. Power (Eds.), *Handbook of cognition and emotion* (pp. 267–80). Chichester, UK: Wiley.

MacLeod, C., Campbell, L., Rutherford, E., & Wilson, E. (2004). The causal status of anxiety-linked attentional and interpretive bias. In J. Yiend (Ed.), *Cognition, emotion and psychopathology: Theoretical, empirical and clinical directions* (pp. 172–89). New York: Cambridge University Press.

MacLeod, C., & Mathews, A. (2012). Cognitive bias modification approaches to anxiety. *Annu. Rev. Clinical Psychology, 8,* 189–217.

MacLeod, C., Rutherford, E., Campbell, L., Ebsworthy, G., & Holker, L. (2002). Selective attention and emotional vulnerability: Assessing the causal basis of their association through the experimental manipulation of attentional bias. *J. Abn. Psychol., 111*(1), 107–23. doi:10.1037/0021-843x.111.1.107

MacManus, D., Laurens, K. R., Walker, E. F., Brasfield, J. L., Riaz, M., & Hodgkins, S. (2011). Movement abnormalities and psychotic-like experiences in childhood: Markers of developing schizophrenia. *Psych. Med., 42*(1), 99–109.

MacMillan, P. J., Hart, R., Martelli, M., & Zasler, N. (2002). Pre-injury status and adaptation following traumatic brain injury. *Brain Injury, 16*(1), 41–49.

MacMullan, J. (2007, February 7). "I don't want anyone to end up like me. " *Boston Globe.*

Macpherson, K., Charlop, M. H., & Miltenberger, C. A. (2014, February 27). Using portable video modeling technology to increase the compliment behaviors of children with autism during athletic group play. *J. Autism and Developmental Disorders* [Epub ahead of print]. doi:10.1007/s10803-014-2072-3.

Maddock, R. J., Buonocore, M. H., Kile, S. J., & Garrett, A. S. (2003). Brain regions showing increased activation by threat-related words in panic disorder. *Neuroreport, 14*(3), 325–28.

Magee, W. J., Eaton, W. W., Wittchen, H., McGonagle, K. A., & Kessler, R. C. (1996). Agoraphobia, simple phobia, and social phobia in the National Comorbidity Survey. *Arch. Gen. Psychiatry, 53,* 159–68.

Magid, D. J., Houry, D., Koepsell, T. D., Ziller, A. A., Soules, M. R., & Jenny, C. (2004). The epidemiology of female rape victims who seek immediate medical care: Temporal trends in the incidence of sexual assault and acquaintance rape. *J. Interpers. Violen., 19,* 3–12.

Magill, M., & Ray, L. A. (2009). Cognitive-behavioral treatment with adults alcohol and illicit drug users: A meta-analysis of randomized controlled trials. *J. Studies on Alcohol and Drugs, 70,* 516–27.

Maguen, S., Lucenko, B. A., Reger, M. A., Gahm, G. A., Litz, B. T., Seal, K. H., et al. (2010). The impact of reported direct and indirect killing on mental health symptoms in Iraq War veterans. *J. Trauma. Stress., 23*(1), 86–90.

Maher, B. A., & Maher, W. R. (1985). Psychopathology: 1. From ancient times to the eighteenth century. In G. A. Kimble & K. Schlesinger (Eds.), *Topics in the history of psychology* (pp. 251–94). Hillsdale, NJ: Erlbaum.

Maher, B. A., & Maher, W. R. (1994). Personality and psychopathology: A historical perspective. *J. Abn. Psychol., 103,* 72–77.

Mahoney, M., & Arnkoff, D. (1978). Cognitive and self-control therapies. In S. Garfield & A. Bergin (Eds.), *Handbook of psychotherapy and behavior change: An empirical analysis.* New York: Wiley.

Mai, F. (2004). Somatization disorder: A practical review. *Canad. J. Psychiatry, 49*(10), 652–62.

Maier, S., Seligman, M., & Solomon, R. (1969). Pavlovian fear conditioning and learned helplessness. In B. A. Campbell & R. M. Church (Eds.), *Punishment and aversive behavior.* New York: Appleton-Century-Crofts.

Maier, S. F., & Watkins, L. R. (2005). Stressor controllability and learned helplessness: The roles of the dorsal raphe nucleus, serotonin, and corticotropin-releasing factor. *Neurosci. Biobehav. Rev., 29*(4), 829–41.

Maier, S. F., & Watkins, L. R. (2010). Role of the medial prefrontal cortex in coping and resilience. *Brain Research, 1355,* 52–60.

Maier, S. F., Watkins, L. R., & Fleshner, M. (1994). Psychoneuroimmunology: The interface between behavior, brain, and immunity. *Am. Psychol., 49*(12), 1004–17.

Maj, M., Pirozzi, R., Formicola, A. M., Bartoli, L., & Bucci, P. (2000). Reliability and validity of the DSM-IV diagnostic category of schizoaffective disorder: Preliminary data. *J. Affect. Disord., 57*(1–3), 95–98.

Malaspina, D., Corcoran, C., & Hamilton, S. P. (2002). Epidemiologic and genetic aspects of neuropsychiatric disorders. In S. C. Yudofsky & R. E. Hales (Eds.), *The American Psychiatric Publishing textbook of neuropsychiatry and clinical neurosciences* (pp. 323–415). Washington, DC: American Psychiatric Publishing.

Malcolm, R. (2003). Pharmacologic treatments manage alcohol withdrawal, relapse prevention. *Psychiatry Ann., 33*(9), 593–601.

Maldonado, J. R., Butler, L. D., & Spiegel, D. (2002). Treatments for dissociative disorders. In P. E. Nathan & J. M. Gorman (Eds.), *A guide to treatments that work* (2nd ed., pp. 463–96). New York: Oxford University Press.

Maldonado, J. R., & Spiegel, D. (2001). Somatoform and factitious disorders. *Review of Psychiatry Series, 20,* 95–128.

Maldonado, J. R., & Spiegel, D. (2007). Dissociative disorders. In J. A. Bourgeois, R. H. Hales, & S. C. Yudofsky (Eds.), *The American Psychiatric Publishing board prep and review guide for psychiatry* (pp. 251–58). Washington, DC: American Psychiatric Publishing.

Maletzky, B. M. (1998). The paraphilias: Research and treatment. In P. E. Nathan & J. M. Gorman (Eds.), *A guide to treatments that work* (pp. 472–500). New York: Oxford University Press.

Maletzky, B. M. (2002). The paraphilias: Research and treatment. In P. E. Nathan & J. M. Gorman (Eds.), *A guide to treatments that work* (pp. 525–58). New York: Oxford University Press.

Maletzky, B. M., & Field, G. (2003). The biological treatment of dangerous sex offenders: A review and preliminary report of the Oregon pilot depo-Provera program. *Aggression & Violent Behavior, 8,* 391–412.

Maletzky, B. M., & Steinhauser, C. (2002). A 25-year follow-up of cognitive/behavioral therapy with 7,275 sexual offenders. *Behav. Mod., 26,* 123–47.

Maletzky, B. M., Tolan, A., & McFarland, B. (2006). The Oregon Depo-Provera program: A five-year follow-up. *Sex Abuse, 18,* 303–16.

Malhi, G. S., Ivanovski, B., Szekeres, V., & Olley, A. (2004). Bipolar disorder: It's all in your mind: The neuropsychological profile of a biological disorder. *Can. J. Psychiatry, 49*(12), 813–19.

Malhi, G. S., Lagopoulos, J., Owen, A. M., & Yatham, L. N. (2004). Bipolaroids: Functional imaging in bipolar disorder. *Acta Psychiatr. Scandin., 110,* 46–54.

Malin, D. H. (2001). Nicotine dependence: Studies with a laboratory model. *Pharmacology, Biochemistry, & Behavior, 70*(4), 551–59.

Malla A., & Payne, J. (2005). First-episode psychosis: Psychopathology, quality of life, and functional outcome. *Schizophrenia Bulletin, 31,* 650–71.

Malm, H., Artama, M., Gissler, M., & Ritvanen, A. (2011). Selective serotonin reuptake inhibitors and risk for major congenital abnormalities. *Obstet. Gynecol., 118,* 111–20.

Malnick, S. D., & Knobler, H. (2006). The medical complications of obesity. *QJM, 99,* 565–79.

Mancebo, M. C., Eisen, J. L., Pinto, A., Greenberg, B. D., Dyck, I. R., & Rasmussen, S. A. (2006). The Brown Longitudinal Obsessive Compulsive Study: Treatments received and patient impressions of improvement. *J. Clin. Psychiatry, 67*(11), 1713–20.

Mangweth, B., Hudson, J. I., Pope, H. G., Hausman, A., De Col, C., Laird, N. M., et al. (2003). Family study of the aggregation of eating disorders and mood disorders. *Psychol. Med., 33,* 1319–23.

Maniglio, R. (2009). The impact of child sexual abuse on health: A systemic review of reviews. *Clinical Psychology Review, 29,* 647–57.

Manji, H. K., & Lenox, R. H. (2000). The nature of bipolar disorder. *J. Clin. Psychiatry, 61,* 42–57.

Mann, A. (2004). *Cocaine abusers' cognitive deficits compromise treatment.* Washington, DC: NIDA.

Mann, J. J., Waternaux, C., Haas, G. L., & Malone, K. M. (1999). Toward a clinical model of suicidal behavior in psychiatric patients. *Am. J. Psychiatry, 156,* 181–89.

Mann, R. E., Hanson, R. K., & Thornton, D. (2010). Assessing risk for sexual recidivism: Some proposals on the nature of psychologically meaningful risk factors. *Sexual Abuse: J. Research and Treatment, 22*(2), 191–217.

Mann, T., Tomiyama, J., Westling, E., Lew, A.-M., Samuels, B., & Chatman, J. (2007). Medicare's search for effective obesity treatments. *Am. Psychol., 62,* 220–33.

Manson, S. M. (1995). Culture and major depression: Current challenges in the diagnosis of mood disorders. *Psychiatr. Clin. North Am. Cultural Psychiatry, 18*(3), 487–501.

Mantovani, A., Simeon, D., Urban, N., Bulow, P., Allart, A., & Lisanby, S. (2011). Temporo-parietal junction stimulation in the treatment of depersonalization disorder. *Psychiatry Res., 186,* 138–40. doi:10.1016/j.psychres.2010.08.022

Manzeske, D. P., & Stright, A. D. (2009). Parenting styles and emotion regulation: The role of behavioral and psychological control during young adulthood. *J. Adult Devel., 16*(4), 223–29. doi:10.1007/s10804-009-9068-9

Mapou, R. L. (2009). *Adult learning disabilities and ADHD.* New York: Oxford University Press.

March, J. S., & Franklin, M. E. (2006). Cognitive-behavioral therapy for pediatric obsessive-compulsive disorder. In B. O. Rothbaum (Ed.), *Pathological anxiety: Emotional processing in etiology and treatment* (pp. 147–65). New York: Guilford Press.

Marcotty, J. (2004). Outpatient psychiatric care is scarce: One result has been an increase in psychiatric admissions in Minnesota. *Minneapolis Star and Tribune, Section B,* pp. 1–2.

Marcus, D. K., Gurley, J. R., Marchi, M. M., & Bauer, C. (2007). Cognitive and perceptual variables in hypochondriasis and health anxiety: A systematic review. *Clin. Psych. Rev., 27,* 127–39.

Marcus, S. C., & Olfson, M. (2010). National trends in the treatment for depression from 1998 to 2007. *Arch. Gen. Psychiatry, 67*(12), 1265–73. doi:10.1001/archgenpsychiatry.2010.151

Marcus, S. M., Gorman, J., Shea, M. K., Lewin, D., Martinez, J., Ray, S., et al. (2007). A comparison of medication side effect reports by panic disorder patients with and without concomitant cognitive behavior therapy. *Am. J. Psychiatry, 164*(2), 273–75.

Margallo, L. M. L., Moore, P. B., Kay, D. W. K., Perry, R. H., Reid, B. E., Berney, T. P., et al. (2007). Fifteen-year follow-up of 92 hospitalized adults with Down's syndrome: Incidence of cognitive decline, its relationship to age and neuropathology. *J. Intellectual Disability Research, 51*(6), 463–77.

Margolis, A., Donkervoort, M., Kinsbourne, M., & Peterson, B. S. (2006). Interhemispheric connectivity and executive functioning in adults with Tourette syndrome. *Neuropsychol., 20*(1), 66–76.

Margolis, R. D., & Zweben, J. E. (1998). *Treating patients with alcohol and other drug problems: An integrated approach.* Washington, DC: American Psychological Association.

Marijuana Treatment Project Research Group. (2004). Brief treatments for cannabis dependence: Findings from a randomized multi-site trial. *J. Cons. Clin. Psychol., 72,* 455–66.

Mariotto, M. J., Paul, G. L., & Licht, M. H. (2002). Assessment in inpatient and residential settings. In J. N. Butcher (Ed.), *Clinical personality assessment* (2nd ed., pp. 466–90). New York: Oxford University Press.

Maris, R. W., Berman, A. L., & Silverman, M. M. (2000). *Comprehensive textbook of suicidology.* New York: Guilford Press.

Markel, H. (2011). *An anatomy of addiction: Sigmund Freud, William Halsted, and the miracle drug, cocaine.* Vintage Books: NY.

Markham, D. (2003). Attitudes towards patients with a diagnosis of "borderline personality disorder": Social rejection of dangerousness. *J. Ment. Health, 12,* 595–612.

Markovitz, P. (2001). Pharmacotherapy. In W. J. Livesley (Ed.), *Handbook of personality disorders* (pp. 475–93). New York: Guilford Press.

Markovitz, P. J. (2004). Recent trends in the pharmacotherapy of personality disorders. *J. Pers. Disord., 18*(1), 90–101.

Markowitsch, H. J. (1999). Functional neuroimaging correlates of functional amnesia. *Memory, 7,* 561–83.

Markowitz, F. E. (2006). Psychiatric hospital capacity, homelessness, and crime and arrest rates. *Criminology, 44,* 45–72.

Markowitz, J. C., Patel, S. R., Balan, I. C., Blanco, C., Yellow Horse Brave Heart, M., Sosa, S. B., et al. (2009). Toward an adaptation of interpersonal psychotherapy for Hispanic patients with DSM-IV major depressive disorder. *J. Clin. Psychiatry, 70,* 214–22.

Markowitz, J. C., Skodol, A. E., & Bleiberg, K. (2006). Interpersonal psychotherapy for borderline personality disorder: Possible mechanisms of change. *J. Cons. Clin. Psychol., 62,* 431–44.

Marks, I., & Nesse, R. M. (1991). *Fear and fitness: An evolutionary analysis of anxiety disorders.* Paper presented at the Eleventh National Conference on Anxiety Disorders, Chicago, IL.

Marks, I., Swinson, R. P., Başoğlu, M., & Kunch, K. (1993). Alprazolam and exposure alone and combined in panic disorder with agoraphobia: A controlled study in London and Toronto. *Brit. J. Psychiatry, 162,* 776–87.

Marlatt, G. A. (1985). Cognitive assessment and intervention procedures for relapse prevention. In G. A. Marlatt & J. R. Gordon (Eds.), *Relapse prevention.* New York: Guilford Press.

Marlatt, G. A., Baer, J. S., Kivahan, D. R., Dimeoff, L. A., Larimer, M. E., Quigley, L. A., et al. (1998). Screening and brief intervention for high-risk college student drinkers: Results from a 2-year follow up assessment. *J. Cons. Clin. Psychol., 66*(4), 604–15.

Marmorstein, N. R., Iacono, W. G., & McGue, M. (2009). Alcohol and illicit drug dependence among parents: Associations with offspring externalizing disorders. *Psychol. Med., 39*(1), 149–55. doi:10.1017/s0033291708003085

Maron, E., Hettema, J. M., & Shilk, J. (2010). Advances in the molecular genetics of panic disorder. *Molecular Psychiatry, 15,* 681–701.

Marsella, A. J. (1980). Depressive experience and disorder across cultures. In H. C. Triandis & J. Draguns (Eds.), *Handbook of cross-cultural psychology* (Vol. 6). Boston: Allyn and Bacon.

Marsh, A. A., & Blair, R. J. R. (2008). Deficits in facial affect recognition among antisocial populations: A meta-analysis. *Neuroscience and Biobehavioral Reviews, 32,* 454–65.

Marsh, A. A., Finger, E. C., Mitchell, D. G., Derek, G. V., Reid, M. E., Sims, C., et al. (2008). Reduced amygdala response to fearful expressions in children and adolescents with callous-unemotional traits and disruptive behavior disorders. *Am. J. Psychiatry, 165*(6), 712–20.

Marsh, L., & Margolis, R. L. (2009). Neuropsychiatric aspects of movement disorders. In B. J. Sadock, A. A. Sadock, & P. Ruiz (Eds.), *Kaplan and Sadock's comprehensive textbook of psychiatry* (9th ed., pp. 481–506). PA: Lippincott Williams & Wilkins.

Marshall, C., Denny, E., Cadenhead, K. S., Cannon, T. D., Cornblatt, B. A., McGlashan, T. H., et al. (2014). The content of attenuated psychotic symptoms in those at clinical high risk for psychosis. *Psychiatry Research, 219,* 506–12.

Marshall, M., Lewis, S., Lockwood, A., Drake, R., Jones, P., & Croudace, T. (2005). Association between duration of untreated psychosis and outcome in cohorts of first-episode patients. *Arch. Gen. Psychiatry, 62,* 975–83.

Marshall, R. D. (2006). Learning from 9/11: Implications for disaster research and public health. In Y. Neria, R. Gross, R., Marshall, & E. Susser (Eds.), *9/11 Mental health in the wake of terrorists attacks* (pp. 617–39). Cambridge, UK: Cambridge University Press.

Marshall, R. D., Bryant, R. A., Amsel, L., Suh, E. J., Cook, J. M., & Neria, Y. (2007). The psychology of ongoing threat: Relative risk appraisal, the September 11 attacks, and terrorism-related fears. *Am. Psych., 62*(4), 304–16.

Marshall, W. L. (1998). Adult sexual offenders. In N. N. Singh (Ed.), *Comprehensive clinical psychology: Volume 9: Applications in diverse populations.* Oxford, UK: Elsevier.

Marshall, W. L., Jones, R., Ward, T., Johnston, P., & Barbaree, H. E. (1991). Treatment outcome with sex offenders. *Clin. Psychol. Rev., 11,* 465–85.

Marsman, A., van den Heuvel, M. P., Klopm, D. W. J., Kahn, R. S., Luitjen, P. R., & Hulsoff Pol, H. E. (2011). Glutamate in schizophrenia: A focused review and meta-analysis of 1H-MRS studies. *Schizo. Bull., 39*(1), 120–29.

Martell, C. R. (2009). Behavioral activation for depression. In W. T. O'Donohue & J. E. Fisher (Eds.), *General principles and empirically supported techniques of cognitive behavior therapy* (pp. 138–43). Hoboken, NJ: John Wiley & Sons.

Martell, D. A., & Dietz, P. E. (1992). Mentally disordered offenders who push or attempt to push victims onto subway tracks in New York City. *Arch. Gen. Psychiatry, 49*(6), 472–75.

Martin, D. J., Garske, J. P., & Davis, M. K. (2000). Relation of the therapeutic alliance with outcome and other variables: A meta-analytic review. *J. Cons. Clin. Psychol., 68,* 438–50.

Martin, P. R., Forsyth, M. R., & Reece, J. (2007). Cognitive-behavioral therapy versus temporal pulse amplitude biofeedback training for recurrent headache. *Behav. Ther., 38,* 350–63.

Martins, A., Ramalho, N., & Morin, E. (2010). A comprehensive meta-analysis of the relationship between emotional intelligence and health. *Personal. Indiv. Diff., 49*(6), 554–64.

Marucha, P. T., Kiecolt-Glaser, J. K., & Favagehi, M. (1998). Mucosal wound healing is impaired by examination stress. *Psychosomatic Medicine, 60,* 362–65.

Marvit, R. C. (1981). Guilty but mentally ill—An old approach to an old problem. *Clin. Psychol., 34*(4), 22–23.

Marziano, V., Ward, T., Beech, A. R., & Pattison, P. (2006). Identification of five fundamental implicit theories underlying cognitive distortions in child abusers: A preliminary study. *Psychology, Crime & Law, 12*(1), 97–105.

Marzuk, P. M., Nock, M. K., Leon, A. C., Portera, L., & Tardiff, K. (2002). Suicide among New York City police officers, 1977–1996. *Am. J. Psychiatry, 159,* 2069–71.

Mascia, J. (2010, August 28). Medical use of marijuana costs some a job. *New York Times.*

Mash, E. J., & Barkley, R. A. (2006). *Treatment of childhood disorders* (3rd ed.). New York: Guilford Press.

Mason, F. L. (1997). Fetishism: Psychopathology and theory. In D. R. Laws & W. O'Donohue (Eds.), *Sexual deviance: Theory, assessment, and treatment* (pp. 75–91). New York: Guilford Press.

Mason, W. A., Kosterman, R., Hawkins, J. D., Herrenkohl, T. I., Lengua, L. J., & McCauley, E. (2004). Predicting depression, social phobia, and violence in early adulthood from childhood behavior problems. *J. Am. Acad. Child Adoles. Psychiatry, 43*(3), 307–15.

Masten, A. S. (2001). Ordinary magic: Resilience processes in development. *Am. Psychol., 56,* 227–38.

Masten, A. S. (2006). Developmental psychopathology: Pathways to the future. *Int. J. Behavioral Development, 30*(1), 47–54.

Masten, A. S. (2007). Resilience in developing systems: Progress and promise as the fourth wave rises. *Develop. Psychopath., 19*(3), 921–30.

Masten, A. S., & Coatsworth, J. D. (1995). Competence, resilience, and psychopathology. In D. Cicchetti & D. J. Cohen (Eds.), *Psychopathology: Vol. 2. Risk, disorder, and adaptation* (pp. 715–52). New York: Wiley.

Masten, A. S., & Coatsworth, J. D. (1998). The development of competence in favorable and unfavorable environments: Lessons from research on successful children. *Am. Psychol., 53,* 205–20.

Masters, W. H., & Johnson, V. E. (1966). *Human sexual response.* Boston: Little, Brown.

Masters, W. H., & Johnson, V. E. (1970). *Human sexual inadequacy.* Boston: Little, Brown.

Masters, W. H., & Johnson, V. E. (1975). *The pleasure bond: A new look at sexuality and commitment.* Boston: Little, Brown.

Masters, W. H., Johnson, V. E., & Kolodny, R. C. (1992). *Human sexuality.* New York: HarperCollins.

Mataix-Cols, D., Frost, R. O., Pertusa, A., Clark, L. A., Saxena, S., Leckman, J. F., et al. (2010). Hoarding disorder: A new diagnosis for DSM-V? *Depression and Anxiety, 27*(6), 556–72. doi:10.1002/da. 20693

Mataix-Cols, D., Rauch, S. L., Baer, L., Eisen, J. L., Shera, D. M., Goodman, W. K., et al. (2002). Symptom stability in adult obsessive-compulsive disorder: Data from a naturalistic two-year follow-up study. *Am. J. Psychiatry, 159*(2), 263–68.

Mataix-Cols, D., Wooderson, S., Lawrence, N., Brammer, M. J., Speckens, A., & Phillips, M. L. (2004). Distinct neural correlates of washing, checking, and hoarding symptom dimensions in obsessive-compulsive disorder. *Arch. Gen. Psychiatry, 61*(6), 564–76.

Materro, M., Junque, C., Poca, M. A., & Sahuquillo, J. (2001). Neuropsychological findings in congenital and acquired childhood hydrocephalus. *Neuropsych., 11,* 169–78.

Mathalondolf, D. H., Sullivan, E. V., Lim, K. O., & Pfefferbaum, A. (2001). Progressive brain volume changes and the clinical course of schizophrenia in men: A longitudinal magnetic resonance imaging study. *Arch. Gen. Psychiatry, 58,* 48–157.

Matheson, S. L., Shepherd, A. M., & Carr, V. J. (2014). How much do we know about schizophrenia and how well do we know it? Evidence from the Schizophrenia Library. *Psychological Medicine, 44*(16), 3387–405. doi:10.1017/S0033291714000166

Mathew, S. J., Amiel, J. M., & Sackeim, H. A. (2005). Electroconvulsive therapy in treatment-resistant depression. *Prim. Psychiatry, 12,* 52–56.

Mathew, S. J., Coplan, J. D., & Gorman, J. M. (2001). Neurobiological mechanisms of social anxiety disorder. *Am. J. Psychiatry, 158,* 1558–67.

Mathews, A., & MacLeod, C. (2002). Induced processing biases have causal effects on anxiety. *Cog. Emo., 16*(3), 331–54.

Mathews, A., & MacLeod, C. (2005). Cognitive vulnerability to emotional disorders. *Annu. Rev. Clin. Psychol., 1*(1), 167–95.

Mathews, C. A. (2009). Phenomenology of obsessive-compulsive disorder. In M. M. Antony & M. B. Stein (Eds.), *Oxford handbook of anxiety and related disorders* (pp. 56–64). New York: Oxford University Press.

Matthews, K. A., & Gump, B. B. (2002). Chronic work stress and marital dissolution increase risk of post-trial mortality in men from the Multiple Risk Factor Intervention Trial. *Arch. Int. Med., 162,* 309–15.

Mattia, J. I., & Zimmerman, M. (2001). Epidemiology. In W. J. Livesley (Ed.), *Handbook of personality disorders* (pp. 107–23). New York: Guilford Press.

Matza, L. S., Revicki, D. A., Davidson, J. R., & Stewart, J. W. (2003). Depression with atypical features in the national comorbidity survey. *Arch. Gen. Psychiatry, 60*, 817–26.

Max, J. E., Wilde, E. A., Bigler, E. D., Hanten, G., Dennis, M., Schachar, R. J., Saunders, A. E., Ewing-Cobbs, L., Chapman, S.B., Thompson, W. K., Yang, T. T., & Levin, H. S. (2015). Personality change due to traumatic brain injury in children and adolescents: Neurocognitive correlates. *Journal of Neuropsychiatry and Clinical Neuroscience, 27*, 272–79.

Mayberg, H. S., Lozano, A. M., Voon, V., McNeely, H. E., Seminowicz, D., Hamani, C., et al. (2005, March 3). Deep brain stimulation for treatment-resistant depression. *Neuron, 45*, 651–60.

Mazzucchelli, T., Kane, R., & Rees, C. (2009). Behavioral activation treatments for depression in adults: A meta-analysis. *Clinical Psychology: Science and Practice, 16*, 383–411.

McAnulty, R. D., Adams, H. E., & Dillon, J. (2001). Sexual disorders: The paraphilias. In P. B. Sutker & H. E. Adams (Eds.), *Comprehensive handbook of psychopathology* (pp. 749–73). New York: Kluwer/ Plenum.

McCabe, M. P., & Wauchope, M. (2005). Behavioral characteristics of men accused of rape: Evidence for different types of rapists. *Arch. Sex. Behav., 34*, 241–53.

McCabe, R. E., Antony, M. M., Summerfield, L. J., Liss, A., & Swinson, R. P. (2003). Preliminary examination of the relationship between anxiety disorders in adults and self-reported history of teasing or bullying experiences. *Cog. Behav. Ther., 32*(4), 187–93.

McCabe, R. E., & Gifford, S. (2009). Psychological treatment of panic disorder and agoraphobia. In M. M. Antony & M. B. Stein (Eds.), *Oxford handbook of anxiety and related disorders* (pp. 308–20). New York: Oxford University Press.

McCall, L. (1961). *Between us and the dark. Originally published in 1947. Summary in W. C. Alvarez, (1961) Minds that came back.* Philadelphia, PA: J. B. Lippincott.

McCann, J. T. (1999). Obsessive-compulsive and negativistic personality disorders. In T. Millon, P. H. Blaney, & R. D. Davis (Eds.), *Oxford textbook of psychopathology* (pp. 585–604). New York: Oxford University Press.

McCann, U. D., Sgambati, F. P., Schwartz, A. R., & Ricaurte, G. A. (2009). Sleep apnea in young abstinent recreational MDMA ("ecstasy") consumers. *Neurol., 73*(23), 2011–17.

McCarthy, B. W. (1989). Cognitive-behavioral strategies and techniques in the treatment of early ejaculation. In S. R. Leiblum & R. C. Rosen (Eds.), *Principles and practice of sex therapy* (2nd ed., pp. 141–67). New York: Guilford Press.

McCarthy, J. J., & Flynn, N. (2001). Hepatitis C in methadone maintenance patients. Prevalence and public policy implications. *J. Addict. Dis., 20*, 19–31.

McCleery, A., Ventura, J., Subotnik, K. L., Gretchen-Doorly, D., Green, M. F., Hellemann, G. S., & Nuechterlein, K. H. (2014). Cognitive functioning in first-episode schizophrenia: MATRICS Consensus Battery (MCCB) profile of impairment. *Schizophrenia Research, 157*, 33–39.

McClellan, J., Susser, E., & King, M.-C. (2007). Schizophrenia: A common disease caused by multiple rare alleles. *Brit. J. Psychiatry, 190*, 194–99.

McClelland, G. M., & Teplin, L. (2001). Alcohol intoxication and violent crime: Implications for public health policy. *American Journal on Addictions, 10*(Suppl.), 70.

McClelland, L., & Crisp, A. (2001). Anorexia nervosa and social class. *Int. J. Eat. Dis., 29*, 150–56.

McCloud, A., Barnaby, B., Omu, N., Drummond, C., & Aboud, A. (2004). Relationship between alcohol use disorders and suicidality in a psychiatric population: In-patient prevalence study. *Brit. J. Psychiatry, 184*, 439–45.

McComb, J. L., Lee, B. K., & Sprenkle, D. H. (2009). Conceptualizing and treating problem gambling as a family issue. *J. Marital Fam. Ther., 35*(4), 415–31.

McCrady, B. S., Owens, M. D., Borders, A. Z., & Brovko, J. M. (2014). Psychosocial approaches to alcohol use disorders since 1940: A review. *J. Studies on Alcohol and Drugs, Suppl. 17*, 68–78.

McCrae, R. R., & Costa, P. T. (2008). The five-factor theory of personality. In O. P. John, R. W. Robins, & L. A. Pervin (Eds.), *Handbook of personality: Theory and research* (3rd ed., pp. 159–81). New York: Guilford Press.

McElroy, S. L., Guerdjikova, A. I., O'Melia, A. M., Mori, N., & Keck, P. E. (2010). Pharmacotherapy of the eating disorders. In W. A. Agras (Ed.), *The Oxford Handbook Of Eating Disorders* (pp. 417–51). New York: Oxford University Press.

McFall, R. M. (1990). The enhancement of social skills: An information-processing analysis. In W. L. Marshall, D. R. Laws, & H. E. Barbaree (Eds.), *Handbook of sexual assault: Issues, theories, and treatment of the offender* (pp. 311–30). New York: Plenum.

McFarlane, W. R., Lukens, E., Link, B., Dushay, R., Deakins, S. A., Newmark, M., et al. (1995). Multiple-family groups and psychoeducation in the treatment of schizophrenia. *Arch. Gen. Psychiatry, 52*, 679–87.

McGlashan, T. H., Grilo, C. M., Sanislow, C. A., Ralevski, E., Morey, L. C., et al. (2005). Two-year prevalence and stability of individual DSM-IV criteria for schizotypal, borderline, avoidant, and obsessive-compulsive personality disorders: Toward a hybrid model of axis II disorders. *Am. J. Psychiatry, 162*, 883–89.

McGrath, M., & Turvey, B. E. (2008). Sexual asphyxia. In B. E. Turvey (Ed.), *An introduction to behavioral evidence analysis* (3rd ed., pp. 605–28). San Diego, CA: Elsevier Academic Press.

McGuffin, P., Cohen, S., & Knight, J. (2007). Honing in on depression genes. *Am. J. Psychiatry, 164*(2), 195–97.

McGuffin, P., Rijsdijk, F., Andrew, M., Sham, P., Katz, R., & Cardno, A. (2003). The heritability of bipolar affective disorder and the genetic relationship to unipolar depression. *Arch. Gen. Psychiatry, 60*, 497–502.

McGuire, W. J. (1994). Uses of historical data in psychology: Comments on Munsterberg (1899). *Psychol. Rev., 101*, 243–47.

McHugh, P. F., & Kreek, M. J. (2004). In J. Brick (Ed.), *Handbook of the medical consequences of alcohol and drug abuse* (pp. 219–55). New York: Haworth Press.

McKenna, K., Gordon, C. T., & Rapoport, J. L. (1994). Childhood-onset schizophrenia: Timely neurobiological research. *J. Am. Acad. Child Adoles. Psychiatry, 33*(6), 771–81.

McKnight Investigators. (2003). Risk factors for the onset of eating disorders in adolescent girls: Results of the McKnight Longitudinal Risk Factor Study. *Am. J. Psychiatry, 160*, 248–54.

McLaughlin, K. A., Borkovec, T. D., & Sibrava, N. J. (2007). The effects of worry and rumination on affect states and cognitive activity. *Behavior Therapy, 38*(1), 23–38.

McLaughlin, K. A., Costello, E. J., Leblanc, W., Sampson, N. A., & Kessler, R. C. (2012). Socioeconomic status and adolescent mental disorders. *Am. J. Public Health, 102*, 1742–50.

McLaughlin, K. A., Fox, N. A., Zeanah, C. H., Sheridan, M. A., Marshall, P., & Nelson, C. A. (2010). Delayed maturation in brain electrical activity partially explains the association between early environmental deprivation and symptoms of attention-deficit/ hyperactivity disorder. *Biol. Psychiatry, 68*(4), 329–36. doi:10.1016/j.biopsych.2010.04. 005

McLaughlin, K. A., Green, J. G., Gruber, M. J., Sampson, N. A., Zaslavsky, A. M., & Kessler, R. C. (2012). Childhood adversities and first onset of psychiatric disorders in a national sample of U.S. adolescents. *Arch. General Psychiatry, 69*, 1151–60. doi:10.1001/archgenpsychiatry.2011.2277

McLaurin, J., Cecal, R., Kierstead, M. E., Tian, X., Phinney, A. L., Manea, M., et al. (2002). Therapeutically effective antibodies against amyloid-â peptide target amyloid-â residues 4–10 and inhibit cytotoxicity and fibrillogenesis. *Nature Medicine, 8*(11), 1263–69.

McLean, C. P., & Anderson, E. R. (2009). Brave men and timid women? A review of the gender differences in fear and anxiety. *Clin. Psychol. Rev., 29*(6), 496–505. doi:10.1016/j.cpr.2009.05. 003

McMinn, M. R., Buchanan, T., Ellens, B. M., & Ryan, M. K. (1999). Technology, professional practice, and ethics: Survey findings and implications. *Profess. Psychol. Res. and Prac., 30*(2), 165–72.

McMurran, M., Huband, N., & Overton, E. (2010). Non-completion of personality disorder treatments: A systematic review of correlates, consequences, and interventions. *Clin. Psychol. Rev., 30*(3), 277–87. doi:10.1016/j.cpr.2009.12. 002

McMurray, R. G., Newbould, E., Bouloux, G. M., Besser, G. M., & Grossman, A. (1991). High-dose naloxone modifies cardiovascular and neuroendocrine function in ambulant subjects. *Psychoneuroendocrinology, 16*, 447–55.

McNally, K. (2007). Schizophrenia as split personality/Jekyll and Hyde: The origins of the informal usage in the English language. *J. History of the Behavioral Sciences, 43*(1), 69–79.

McNally, R. F., & Reese, H. E. (2009). Information-processing approaches to understanding anxiety disorders. In M. M. Antony & M. B. Stein (Eds.), *Oxford handbook of anxiety and related disorders* (pp. 136–52). New York: Oxford University Press.

McNally, R. J. (2000). Information-processing abnormalities in obsessive-compulsive disorder. In W. K. Goodman & M. V. Rudorfer et al. (Eds.), *Obsessive-compulsive disorder: Contemporary issues in treatment. Personality and clinical psychology series* (pp. 106–16). Mahwah, NJ: Erlbaum.

McNally, R. J. (2002). Anxiety sensitivity and panic disorder. *Biol. Psychiatry, 51*, 938–46.

McNally, R. J. (2008). Posttraumatic stress disorder. In P. H. Blaney, T. Millon, & S. Grossman (Eds.), *Oxford textbook of psychiatry* (2nd ed.). Oxford, UK: Oxford University Press.

McNally, R. J. (2009). Can we fix PTSD in DSM-V? *Depression and Anxiety, 26*, 597–600.

McNally, R. J. (2013). Posttraumatic stress disorder and dissociative disorders. In P. H. Blaney, T. Millon, & S. Grossman (Eds.). *Oxford textbook of Psychopathology* (3rd ed.). Oxford, UK: Oxford University Press.

McNally, R. J. (2015). Posttraumatic stress disorder and dissociative disorders. In P. H. Blaney, R. F. Kreuger, & T. Millon, (Eds.), *Oxford textbook of psychopathology* (3rd ed., pp. 191–221). New York: Oxford University Press.

McNally, R. J., Bryant, R. A., & Ehlers, A. (2003). Does early intervention promote recovery from post-traumatic stress? *Psychol. Sci. in the Pub. Int., 4*, 45–79.

McNally, R. J., & Geraerts, E. (2009). A new solution to the recovered memory debate. *Perspectives on Psychological Science, 4*, 126–34. doi:10.1111/j.1745-6924.2009.01112.x

McNaughton, N. (2008). The neurobiology of anxiety: Potential for comorbidity of anxiety and substance use disorders. In S. H. Stewart & P. J. Conrod (Eds.), *Anxiety and substance use disorders: The vicious cycle of comorbidity* (pp. 19–33). New York: Springer Science + Business Media.

McNicholas, F., Slonims, V., & Cass, H. (2000). Exaggeration of symptoms or psychiatric Munchausen's syndrome by proxy? *Child Psych. Psychiatry Rev., 5*, 69–75.

McNulty, J. P. (2004). Commentary: Mental illness, society, stigma, and research. *Schizo. Bull., 30*(3), 573–75.

McRae-Clark, A. L., Carter, R. E., Killeen, T. K., Carpenter, M. J., Wahlquist, A. E., Simpson, S. A., et al. (2009). A placebo-controlled trial of buspirone for the treatment of marijuana dependence. *Drug Alcohol Depend., 105*(1–2), 132–38.

McReynolds, P. (1996). Lightner Witmer: Little-known founder of clinical psychology. *Am. Psychol., 51*, 237–40.

McReynolds, P. (1997). Lightner Witmer: The first clinical psychologist. In W. G. Bringmann, H. E. Luck, R. Miller, & C. E. Early (Eds.), *A pictorial history of psychology* (pp. 465–70). Chicago: Quintessence Books.

Mechanic, D. (2004). The rise and fall of managed care. *J. Health Soc. Behav., 45*(Suppl.), 76–86.

Mednick, S. A., Machon, R. A., Huttunen, M. O., & Bonnet, D. (1988). Adult schizophrenia following prenatal exposure to an influenza epidemic. *Arch. Gen. Psychiatry, 45*, 189–92.

Mednick, S. A., & Schulsinger, F. (1968). Some premorbid characteristics related to breakdown in children with schizophrenic mothers. In D. Rosenthal & S. S. Kety (Eds.), *The transmission of schizophrenia* (pp. 267–91). Oxford, UK: Pergamon.

Meehl, P. E. (1962). Schizotaxia, schizotypy, schizophrenia. *Am. Psychol., 17*, 827–38.

Meewisse, M.-L., Reitsma, J. B., de Vries, G.-J., Gersons, B. P. R., & Olff, M. (2007). Cortisol and post-traumatic stress disorder in adults. *Brit. J. Psychiatry, 191*, 387–92.

Megargee, E. I. (2009). Understanding and assessing aggression and violence. In J. N. Butcher (Ed.), *Oxford handbook of personality and clinical assessment* (pp. 542–66). New York: Oxford University Press.

Meier, B. R., & Patkar, A. A. (2007). Buprenorphine treatment: Factors and first-hand experiences for providers to consider. *J. Addict. Dis., 26*(1), 3–14.

Meier, M. H., Caspi, A., Reichenberg, A., Keefe, S. E., Fisher, H. L., Harrington, H., et al. (2014). Neuropsychological decline in schizophrenia from the premorbid to the postonset period: Evidence from a population-representative longitudinal study. *Am. J. Psychiatry, 171*, 91–101.

Meinzer, M., Obleser, J., Flaisch, T., Eulitz, C., & Rockstroh, B. (2007). Recovery from aphasia as a function of language therapy in an early bilingual patient demonstrated by fMRI. *Neuropsychologia, 45*(6), 1247–56.

Mellon, M. W., & McGrath, M. L. (2000). Empirically supported treatments in pediatric psychology: Nocturnal enuresis. *J. Pediat. Psychol., 25*, 193–214.

Meltzer, H. Y., Alphs, L., Green, A. I., Altamura, A. C., Anand, R., Bertoldi, A., et al., for the InterSePT Study Group. (2003). Clozapine treatment for suicidality in schizophrenia. *Arch. Gen. Psychiatry, 60*, 82–91.

Melville, J. D., & Naimark, D. (2002). Punishing the insane: The verdict of guilty but mentally ill. *J. Am. Acad. Psychiatry Law, 30*, 553–55.

Mendelson, J. H., & Mello, N. (1992). Human laboratory studies of buprenorphine. In J. D. Blaine (Ed.), *Buprenorphine: An alternative treatment for opiate dependence* (pp. 38–60). Washington, DC: U.S. Department of Health and Human Services.

Mendes, W. B., Major, B., McCoy, S., & Blascovich, J. (2008). How attributional ambiguity shapes physiological and emotional responses to social rejection and acceptance. *J. Personality and Social Psychology, 94*, 278–91.

Merbaum, M. (1977). Some personality characteristics of soldiers exposed to extreme war stress: A follow-up study of post-hospital adjustment. *J. Clin. Psychol., 33*, 558–62.

Mercer, C. H., Fenton, K. A., Johnson, A. M., et al. (2003). Sexual function problems and help seeking behaviour in Britain: National probability sample survey. *BMJ, 327*, 426–27.

Merikangas, K. R., Akiskal, H. S., Angst, J., Greenberg, P. E., Hirschfeld, R. M., Petukhova, M., & Kessler, R. C. (2007). Lifetime and 12-month prevalence of bipolar spectrum disorder in the National Comorbidity Survey replication. *Arch. General Psychiatry, 64*, 543–52.

Merikangas, K. R., He, J. P., Burstein, M., Swanson, S. A., Avenevoli, S., Cui, L., et al. (2010). Lifetime prevalence of mental disorders in U.S. adolescents: Results from the National Comorbidity Survey Replication–Adolescent Supplement (NCS-A). *J. Am. Acad. Child Adolesc. Psychiatry, 49*(10), 980–89. doi:10.1016/j.jaac.2010.05. 017

Merikangas, K. R., He, J. P., Burstein, M., Swendsen, J., Avenevoli, S., Case, B., et al. (2011). Service utilization for lifetime mental disorders in U.S. adolescents: Results of the National Comorbidity Survey–Adolescent Supplement (NCS-A). *J. Am. Acad. Child Adolesc. Psychiatry, 50*(1), 32–45. doi:10.1016/j.jaac. 2010.10.006

Merikangas, K. R., Zhang, H., Avenevoli, S., Acharya, S., Neuenschwander, M., & Angst, J. (2003). Longitudinal trajectories of depression and anxiety in a prospective community study. *Arch. Gen. Psychiatry, 60*(10), 993–1000.

Merkler, A. E., Parikh, N., Chaudhry, S., Chait, A., Allen, N. C., Navi, B. B., & Kamel, H. (2015, April 8). Hospital revisit rate after a diagnosis of conversion disorder. *J. Neurology and Neurosurgical Psychiatry* [Epub ahead of print]. doi:10.1136/jnnp-2014-310181

Mervielde, I., De Clercq, B., De Fruyt, F., & Van Leeuwen, K. (2005). Temperament, personality, and developmental psychopathology as childhood antecedents of personality disorders. *J. Pers. Disord., 19*, 171–201.

Mesholam-Gately, R., Guiliano, A. J., Goff, K. P., Faraone, S. V., & Seidman, L. J. (2009). Neurocognition in first-episode schizophrenia: A meta-analytic review. *Neuropsychology, 23*, 315–36.

Meston, C. M., & Bradford, A. (2007). Sexual dysfunctions in women. *Annu. Rev. Clin. Psych., 3*, 233–56.

Meston, C. M., & Rellini, A. (2008). Sexual dysfunction. In W. E. Craighead, D. J. Miklowitz, & L. W. Craighead (Eds.), *Psychopathology: History, diagnosis, and empirical foundations* (pp. 544–64). Hoboken, NJ: John Wiley & Sons.

Mestre, J. I., Rossi, P. C., & Torrens, M. (2013). The assessment interview: A review of structured and semi-structured clinical interviews available for use among Hispanic clients. In L. T. Benuto (Ed.), *Guide to psychological assessment with Hispanics* (pp. 33–48). New York: Springer Science. doi:http://dx.doi.org/10.1007/978-1-4614-4412-1_3

Metz, M. E., Pryor, J. L., Nesvacil, L. J., Abuzzahab, F., & Koznar, J. (1997). Premature ejaculation: A psychophysiological review. *J. Sex Marit. Ther., 23*, 3–23.

Meyer, B., & Pilkonis, P. A. (2005). An attachment model of personality disorders. In M. F. Lenzenweger & J. F. Clarkin (Eds.), *Major theories of personality disorder* (2nd ed., pp. 231–81). New York: Guilford Press.

Meyer, B., Pilkonis, P. A., Krupnick, J. L., Egan, M. K., Simmens, S. J., & Sotsky, S. M. (2002). Treatment expectancies, patient alliance, and outcome: Further analyses from the National Institute of Mental Health Treatment of Depression Collaborative Research Program. *J. Cons. Clin. Psychol., 70*, 1051–55.

Meyer, G. J., Mihura, J. L., & Smith, B. L. (2005). The interclinician reliability of Rorschach interpretation in four data sets. *J. Pers. Assess., 84*, 296–314.

Meyer, G., Finn, S. E., Eyde, L. D., Kay, G. G., Moreland, K. L., Dies, R. R., et al. (2001). Psychological testing and psychological assessment: A review of evidence and issues. *Am. Psychol., 56*, 128–65.

Meyer, G. J., Viglione, D. J., Mihura, J. L., Erard, R. E., & Erdberg, P. (2011). *Rorschach performance assessment system: Administration, coding, interpretation, and technical manual.* Toledo, OH: Rorschach Performance Assessment System.

Meyer, J. K. (1995). Paraphilias. In H. I. Kaplan & J. B. Sadock (Eds.), *Comprehensive textbook of psychiatry* (6th ed., pp. 1334–47). Baltimore, MD: Williams and Wilkins.

Meyer, P. T., Rijntjes, M, & Weiller, C. (2012). Neuroimaging: Functional neuroimaging. In R. B. Daroff, G. M. Fenichel, J. Jankovic , J. C. Mazziotta (Eds.), *Bradley's neurology in clinical practice* (6th ed.) Philadelphia, PA: Elsevier Saunders.

Meyer-Bahlburg, H. F. L. (2011). Transsexualism ("gender identity disorder")—A CNS-limited form of intersexuality? *Advances in Experimental Medicine and Biology, 707*, 75–79.

Mezulis, A. H., Abramson, L. Y., Hyde, J. S., & Hankin, B. L. (2004). Is there a universal positivity bias in attributions? A meta-analytic review of individual, developmental, and cultural differences in the self-serving attributional bias. *Psychol. Bull., 130*(5), 711–47.

Michael, T., Blechert, J., Vriends, N., Margraf, J. R., & Wilhelm, F. H. (2007). Fear conditioning in panic disorder: Enhanced resistance to extinction. *J. Abn. Psych., 116*(3), 612–17.

Miczek, K. A., Covington, H. E., Nikulna, E. M., & Hammer, R. P. (2004). Aggression and defeat: Persistent effects on cocaine self-administration and gene expression in peptidergic and aminergic mesocorticolimbic circuits. *Neuroscience and Biobehavioral Reviews, 27*, 787–802.

Mihura, J. L., Meyer, G. J., Dumitrascu, N., Bombel, G., & Dumitrascu, N. (2015). Standards, accuracy, and questions of bias in Rorschach meta-analyses: Reply to Wood, Garb, Nezworski, Lilienfeld, and Duke (2015). *Psychological Bulletin, 141*(1), 250–60. Retrieved from http://dx.doi.org/10.1037/a0038445

Miklowitz, D. J. (2009). Pharmacotherapy and psychosocial treatments for bipolar disorder. In I. H. Gotlib & C. L. Hammen (Eds.), *Handbook of depression and its treatment* (2nd ed.). New York: Guilford Press.

Miklowitz, D. J., & Craighead, W. E. (2007). Psychosocial treatments for bipolar disorder. In P. E. Nathan & J. M. Gorman (Eds.), *A guide to treatments that work* (pp. 309–22). New York: Oxford University Press.

Miklowitz, D. J., & Stackman, D. (1992). Communication deviance in families of schizophrenic and other psychiatric patients: Current state of the construct. In E. F. Walker, R. H. Dworkin, & B. A. Cornblatt (Eds.), *Progress in experimental personality and psychopathology research* (Vol. 15). New York: Springer.

Milde-Busch, A., Blaschek, A., Heinen, F., Borggräfe, I., Koerte, I., Straube, A., et al. (2011). Associations between stress and migraine and tension-type headache: Results from a school-based study in adolescents from grammar schools in Germany. *Cephalgia, 31*, 774–85.

Milev, P., Ho, B.-C., Arndt, S., & Andreasen, N. C. (2005). Predictive values of neurocognition and negative symptoms on functional outcome in schizophrenia: A longitudinal first-episode study with 7-year followup. *Am. J. Psychiatry, 162*, 495–506.

Millar, A., Espie, C. A., & Scott, J. (2004). The sleep of remitted bipolar outpatients: A controlled naturalistic study using actigraphy. *J. Affect. Dis., 80*, 145–53.

Miller, B., Messias, E., Miettunen, J., Alaräisänen, A., Järvelin, M. R., Koponen, H., et al. (2011). Meta-analysis of paternal age and schizophrenia risk in male versus female offspring. *Schizophrenia Bulletin, 37*, 1039–47.

Miller, G. (2011, July 29). Healing the brain, healing the mind. *Science, 333*, 514–17.

Miller, G. E., & Blackwell, E. (2006). Turning up the heat: Inflammation as a mechanism linking chronic stress, depression, and heart disease. *Curr. Dis. Psychol. Sci., 15*(6), 269–72.

Miller, J. D., & Campbell, W. K. (2008). Comparing clinical and social personality conceptualizations of narcissism. *J. Personality, 76*, 449–76.

Miller, J. D., Reynolds, S. K., & Pilkonis, P. A. (2004). The validity of the five-factor model prototypes for personality disorders in two clinical samples. *Psychol. Assess., 16*, 310–33.

Miller, J. D., Widiger, T. A., & Campbell, W. K. (2010). Narcissistic personality disorder and the DSM-V. *J. Abn. Psychol., 119*(4), 640–49. doi:10.1037/a0019529

Miller, L. (2007). Traumatic stress disorders. In F. M. Dattilio & A. Freeman (Eds.), *Cognitive behavioral strategies in crisis intervention.* (pp. 494–530). New York: Guilford Press.

Miller, L. J. (2002). Postpartum depression. *JAMA, 287*(6), 762–65.

Miller, M. B., Useda, J. D., Trull, T. J., Burr, R. M., & Minks-Brown, C. (2001). Paranoid, schizoid, and schizotypal personality disorders. In H. E. Adams & P. B. Sutker (Eds.), *Comprehensive handbook of psychopathology* (pp. 535–58). New York: Kluwer Academic.

Miller, N., & Lyon, D. (2003). Biology of opiates affects prevalence of addiction, options for treatment. *Psychiatr. Ann., 33*, 559–64.

Miller, W. R. (1983). Motivational interviewing with problem drinkers. *Behav. Psychotherapy, 11*, 147–72.

Miller, W. R., Leckman, A. L., Tinkcom, M., & Rubenstein, J. (1986). *Long-term follow-up of controlled drinking therapies.* Paper given at the Ninety-Fourth Annual Meeting of the American Psychological Association, Washington, DC.

Miller, W. R., & Rollnik, S. (2002). *Motivational interviewing: Preparing people to change addictive behavior* (2nd ed.). New York: Guilford Press.

Miller, W. R., & Rollnick, S. (2012). *Motivational interviewing: Helping people change* (3rd ed.). New York: Guilford Press.

Miller, W. R., Walters, S. T., & Bennett, M. E. (2001). How effective is alcoholism treatment in the United States? *J. Stud. Alcoh., 62*(2), 211–20.

Miller-Horn, J. W., Kaleyias, J., Valencia, I., Melvin, J. J., Khurana, D. S., Hardison, H. H., et al. (2008). Efficacy and tolerability of ADHD medications in a clinical practice. *J. Ped. Neurol., 6*(1), 5–10.

Milliken, C. S., Aucherlonie, J. L., & Hoge, C. W. (2007). Longitudinal assessment of mental health problems among active and reserve component soldiers returning from the Iraq war. *JAMA, 298*, 2141–48.

Millon, T., & Davis, R. D. (1995). The development of personality disorders. In D. Cicchetti & D. J. Cohen (Eds.), *Developmental psychopathology: Vol. 2. Risk, disorder, and adaptation* (pp. 633–76). New York: Wiley.

Millon, T., & Martinez, A. (1995). Avoidant personality disorder. In W. J. Livesley (Ed.), *The DSM-IV personality disorders* (pp. 218–33). New York: Guilford Press.

Mills, M. J., Sullivan, G., & Eth, S. (1987). Protecting third parties: A decade after Tarasoff. *Am. J. Psychiatry, 144*(1), 68–74.

Milne, J. M., Edwards, J. K., & Murchie, J. C. (2001). Family treatment of oppositional defiant disorder: Changing views and strength-based approaches. *Family Journal—Counseling & Therapy for Couples & Families, 9*(1), 17–28.

Milns, R. D. (1986). Squibb academic lecture: Attitudes towards mental illness in antiquity. *Austral. NZ J. Psychiatry, 20*, 454–62.

Milos, G., Spindler, A., Ruggiero, G., Klaghofer, R., & Schnyder, U. (2002). Comorbidity of obsessive compulsive disorders and duration of eating disorders. *Int. J. Eat. Dis., 31*, 284–89.

Mindus, P., Rasmussen, S. A., & Lindquist, C. (1994). Neurosurgical treatment for refractory obsessive-compulsive disorder: Implications for understanding frontal lobe function. *J. Neuropsychiat. Clin. Neurosci., 6*, 467–77.

Mineka, S. (1985). Animal models of anxiety-based disorders: Their usefulness and limitations. In A. H. Tuma & J. D. Maser (Eds.), *Anxiety and the anxiety disorders.* Hillsdale, NJ: Erlbaum.

Mineka, S. (2004). The positive and negative consequences of worry in the aetiology of generalized anxiety disorder: A learning theory perspective. In J. Yiend (Ed.), *Cognition, emotion and psychopathology: Theoretical, empirical and clinical directions* (pp. 29–48). New York: Cambridge University Press.

Mineka, S., Gunnar, M., & Champoux, M. (1986). Control and early socioemotional development: Infant rhesus monkeys reared in controllable versus uncontrollable environments. *Child Develop. 57*, 1241–56.

Mineka, S., & Oehlberg, K. (2008). The relevance of recent developments in classical conditioning to understanding the etiology and maintenance of anxiety disorders. *Acta Psychologica, 127*(3), 567–80.

Mineka, S., & Öhman, A. (2002). Phobias and preparedness: The selective, automatic, and encapsulated nature of fear. *Biol. Psychiatry, 52*(10), 927–37.

Mineka, S., Rafaeli, E., & Yovel, I. (2003). Cognitive biases in emotional disorders: Social-cognitive and information processing perspectives. In R. Davidson, H. Goldsmith, & K. Scherer (Eds.), *Handbook of affective science.* Amsterdam: Elsevier.

Mineka, S., & Sutton, J. (2006). Contemporary learning theory perspectives on the etiology of fears and phobias. In M. G. Craske, D. Hermans, & D. Vansteenwegen (Eds.), *Fear and learning: From basic processes to clinical implications* (pp. 75–97). Washington, DC: American Psychological Association.

Mineka, S., Watson, D., & Clark, L. A. (1998). Comorbidity of anxiety and unipolar mood disorders. In J. T. Spence, J. M. Darley, & D. J. Foss (Eds.), *Annu. Rev. Psychol., 49*, 377–412.

Mineka, S., Yovel, I., & Pineles, S. (2002). Toward a psychological model of the etiology of generalized anxiety disorder. In D. J. Nutt, K. Rickels, & D. J. Stein (Eds.), *Generalized anxiety disorder: Symptomatology, pathogenesis and management.* London: Martin Dunitz.

Mineka, S., & Zinbarg, R. (1995). Conditioning and ethological models of social phobia. In R. Heimberg, M. Liebowitz, D. Hope, & F. Schneier (Eds.), *Social phobia: Diagnosis, assessment, and treatment.* New York: Guilford Press.

Mineka, S., & Zinbarg, R. (1996). Conditioning and ethological models of anxiety disorders: Stress-in-Dynamic context anxiety models. In D. Hope (Ed.), *Perspectives on anxiety, panic, and fear: Nebraska symposium on motivation.* Lincoln: University of Nebraska Press.

Mineka, S., & Zinbarg, R. (2006). A contemporary learning theory perspective on the etiology of anxiety disorders: It's not what you thought it was. *Am. Psychol., 61*, 10–26.

Minnis, H., Everett, K., Pelosi, A. J., Dunn, J., & Knapp, M. (2006). Children in foster care: Mental health, service use and costs. *European Child & Adolescent Psychiatry, 15*(2), 63–70.

Minuchin, S. (1974). *Families and family therapy.* Cambridge, MA: Harvard University Press.

Miranda, J., Bernal, G., Lau, A., Kohn, L., Hwang, W.-C., & LaFramboise, T. (2005). State of the science on psychosocial interventions for ethnic minorities. *Annu. Rev. Clin. Psychol., 1*(1), 113–42.

Mirsky, A. F., & Quinn, O. W. (1988). The Genain quadruplets. *Schizo. Bull., 14*, 595–612.

Mishara, B. L., Chagnon, F., Daigle, M., Balan, B., Raymond, S., Marcoux, I., et al. (2007). Which helper behaviors and intervention styles are related to better short-term outcomes in a telephone crisis intervention? Results from a silent monitoring study of calls to the U.S. 1-800-SUICIDE network. *Suicide Life Threat. Behav., 37*, 308–21.

Mishler, E. G., & Waxler, N. E. (1968). *Interaction in families: An experimental study of family processes and schizophrenia.* New York: Wiley.

Mishra, S. K., & Singh, P. (2010). History of neuroimaging: The legacy of William Oldendorf. *J. Child Neurology, 25*(4), 508–17.

Mitchell, J. E., & Crow, S. J. (2010). Medical complications of eating disorders. In W. A. Agras (Ed.), *The Oxford handbook of eating disorders* (pp. 259–66). New York: Oxford University Press.

Mittal, V. A., Kalus, O., Bernstein, D. P., & Siever, L. J. (2007). Schizoid personality disorder. In W. O'Donohue, K. A. Fowler, & S. O. Lilienfeld (Eds.), *Personality disorders: Toward the DSM-V* (pp. 63–79). Thousand Oaks, CA: Sage Publications.

Mittal, V. A., Neumann, C., Saczawa, M., & Walker, E. F. (2008). Longitudinal progression of movement abnormalities in relation to psychotic symptoms in adolescents at high risk of schizophrenia. *Arch. Gen. Psychiatry, 65*, 165–71.

Mitte, K. (2005). A meta-analysis of the efficacy of psycho- and pharmacotherapy in panic disorder with and without agoraphobia. *J. Affect. Dis., 88*(1), 27–45.

Mittelman, M. S., Roth, D. L., Coon, D. W., & Haley, W. E. (2004). Sustained benefit of supportive intervention for depressive symptoms in the caregivers of patients with Alzheimer's disease. *Am. J. Psychiatry, 161*, 850–56.

Mizrahi, R., Rusjan, P., Agidm, O., Graff, A., Mamo, D. C., Zipursky, R. B., et al. (2007). Adverse subjective experience with antipsychotics and its relationship to striatal and extrastriatal D_2 receptors: A PET study in schizophrenia. *Am. J. Psychiatry, 164*, 630–37.

Moeller, F. G., & Dougherty, D. M. (2001). Antisocial personality disorder, alcohol and aggression. *Alc. Res. Health, 25*(1), 5–11.

Moene, F. C., Spinhoven, P., Hoogduin, K., & Dyck, R. V. (2003). A randomized controlled clinical trial of a hypnosis-based treatment for patients with conversion disorder, motor type. *Int. J. Clin. Exp. Hypn., 51*(1), 29–50.

Moffatt, M. E. (1997). Nocturnal enuresis: A review of the efficacy of treatments and practical advice for clinicians. *Developmental and Behavioral Pediatrics, 18*(1), 49–56.

Moffitt, T. E. (2005). The new look of behavioral genetics in developmental psychopathology: Gene-environment interplay in antisocial behaviors. *Psych. Bull., 131*(4), 533–54.

Moffitt, T. E. (2006). Life-course-persistent versus adolescence-limited antisocial behavior. In D. Cicchetti & D. J. Cohen (Eds.), *Developmental psychopathology: Volume 3, Risk, disorder, and adaptation* (2nd ed., pp. 570–98). Hoboken, NJ: John Wiley & Sons.

Moffitt, T. E., Caspi, A., Harrington, H., & Milne, B. J. (2002). Males on the life-course-persistent and adolescence limited antisocial pathways: Follow-up at age 26 years. *Develop. Psychopath., 14,* 179–207.

Moffitt, T. E., Caspi, A., & Rutter, M. (2005). Strategy for investigating interactions between measured genes and measured environments. *Arch. Gen. Psychiatry, 62*(5), 473–81.

Moffitt, T. E., & Lynam, D. (1994). The neuropsychology of conduct disorder and delinquency: Implications for understanding antisocial behavior. In D. C. Fowles, P. Sutker, & S. H. Goodman (Eds.), *Progress in experimental personality and psychopathology research.* New York: Springer.

Mohler-Kuo, M., Dowdall, G. W., Koss, M. P., & Wechsler, H. (2004). Correlates of rape while intoxicated in a national sample of college women. *J. Studies on Alcohol, 65*(1), 37–45.

Mold, F., & Forbes, A. (2011). Patients' and professionals' experiences and perspectives of obesity in health-care settings: A synthesis of current research. *Health Expect.* doi:10.1111/j.1369-7625.2011.00699.x

Moldin, S. O., & Rubenstein, J. L. (2006). *Understanding autism: From basic neuroscience to treatment.* Boca Raton, FL: CRC Press.

Moldovan, A. R., & David, D. (2011). Effect of obesity treatments on eating behavior: Psychosocial interventions versus surgical interventions. A systematic review. *Eating Behaviors, 12,* 161–67.

Molina, P. E., Gardner, J. D., Souza-Smith, F. M., & Whitaker, A. M. (2014). Alcohol abuse: Critical pathophysiological processes and contribution to disease burden. *Physiology, 29,* 203–15.

Monahan, J. (2013). Violence risk assessment. In R. K. Otto & I. B. Weiner (Eds.), *Handbook of psychology, Vol. 11: Forensic psychology* (2nd ed., pp. 541–55). Hoboken, NJ: John Wiley & Sons.

Monahan, J., & Steadman, H. J. (1997). Violent storms and violent people: How meteorology can inform risk communication in mental health law. *Am. Psychol., 51*(9), 931–38.

Money, J. (1985). *The destroying angel* (pp. 17–31, 51–52, 61–68, 83–90, 107–20, 137–48). Buffalo, NY: Prometheus Books.

Money, J. (1986). *Lovemaps: Clinical concepts of sexual/erotic health and pathology, paraphilia, and gender transposition.* New York: Irvington.

Monroe, S. M. (2008). Modern approaches to conceptualizing and measuring human life stress. *Annu. Rev. Clin. Psychol., 4,* 33–52.

Monroe, S. M., & Hadjiyannakis, K. (2002). The social environment and depression: Focusing on severe life stress. In I. H. Gotlib & C. L. Hammen (Eds.), *Handbook of depression* (pp. 314–40). New York: Guilford Press.

Monroe, S. M., & Harkness, K. L. (2005). Life stress, the "kindling" hypothesis, and the recurrence of depression: Considerations from a life stress perspective. *Psychol. Rev., 112*(2), 417–45.

Monroe, S. M., & Harkness, K. L. (2011). Recurrence in major depression: A conceptual analysis. *Psychol. Rev.* doi:10.1037/a0025190.

Monroe, S. M., & Simons, A. D. (1991). Diathesis-stress theories in the context of life stress research: Implications for the depressive disorders. *Psychol. Bull., 110,* 406–25.

Monroe, S. M., Slavich, G. M., & Georgiades, K. (2009). The social environment and life stress in depression. In I. H. Gotlib & C. L. Hammen (Eds.), *Handbook of depression and its treatment* (2nd ed., pp. 340–60). New York: Guilford Press.

Monroe, S. M., Slavich, G. M., Torres, L. D., & Gotlib, I. H. (2007). Major life events and major

chronic difficulties are differentially associated with history of major depressive episodes. *J. Abn. Psych., 116*(1), 116–24.

Monson, C. M., Gunnin, D. D., Fogel, M. H., & Kyle, L. L. (2001). Stopping (or slowing) the revolving door: Factors related to NGRI acquittees' maintenance of a conditional release. *Law and Human Behavior, 25*(3), 257–66.

Montague, C. T., Farooqi, I. S., Whitehead, J. P., Soos, M. A., Rau, H., Wareham, N. J., et al. (1997, June 26). Congenital leptin deficiency is associated with severe early-onset obesity in humans. *Nature, 387,* 903–08.

Montenigro, P. H., Corp, D. T., Stein, T. D., Cantu, R. C., & Stern, R. A. (2015). Chronic traumatic encephalopathy: Historical origins and current perspective. *Annu. Rev. Clinical Psychology, 11,* 309–30.

Monzani, B., Rijsdijk, F., Anson, M., Iervolino, A. C., Cherkas, L., Spector, T., & Mataix-Cols, D. (2012). A twin study of body dysmorphic concerns. *Psychological Medicine, 42*(9), 1949–55.

Moore, S. (2009). Prison term for a seller of medical marijuana. *New York Times, 158*(54), 704.

Mora, G. (1967). Paracelsus' psychiatry. *Am. J. Psychiatry, 124,* 803–14.

Moran, P., Coffey, C., Chanen, A., Mann, A., Carlin, J. B., & Patton, G. C. (2010). Childhood sexual abuse and abnormal personality: A population-based study. *Psychol. Med.,* 1–8. doi:10.1017/S0033291710001789

Morein-Zamir, S., Fineberg, N. A., Robbins, T. W., & Sahakian, B. J. (2010). Inhibition of thoughts and actions in obsessive-compulsive disorder: Extending the endophenotype? *Psychol. Med., 40*(2), 263–72. doi:10.1017/s003329170999033x

Moreno, C., Laje, G., Blanco, C., Jiang, H., Schmidt, A. B., & Olfson, M. (2007). National trends in the outpatient diagnosis and treatment of bipolar disorder in youth. *Arch. Gen. Psychiatry, 64,* 1032–39. doi:10.1001/archpsyc.64.9.1032

Morey, L. C. (1988). Personality disorders in DSM-III and DSM-III-R: Convergence, coverage, and internal consistency. *Am. J. Psychiatry, 145,* 573–77.

Morgan, J. F., & Crisp, A. H. (2000). Use of leucotomy for intractable anorexia nervosa: A long-term follow-up study. *Int. J. Eat. Dis., 27,* 249–58.

Morgan, M. J. (1998). Recreational use of "ecstasy" (MDMA) is associated with elevated impulsivity. *Neuropsychopharmacol., 19*(4), 252–64.

Morgan, W. G. (2002). Origin and history of the earliest Thematic Apperception Test pictures. *J. Pers. Assess., 79*(3), 422–45.

Morganstern, J., Langenbucher, J., Labouvie, E., & Miller, K. J. (1997). The comorbidity of alcoholism and personality disorders in a clinical population. *J. Abn. Psychol., 106*(1), 74–84.

Mori, E., et al. (1997a). Medial temporal structures relate to memory impairment in Alzheimer's disease: An MRI volumetric study. *J. Neurol. Neurosurg. Psychiatry, 63*(2), 214–21.

Mori, E., et al. (1997b). Premorbid brain size as a determinant of reserve capacity against intellectual decline in Alzheimer's disease. *Am. J. Psychiatry, 154*(1), 18–24.

Moriarty, J. C., Langleben, D. D. & Provenzale, J. M. (2013). Brain trauma, PET scans and forensic complexity. *Behavioral Sciences and the Law, 31,*702–720. doi:10.1002/bsl.2089

Moriarty, K. M., Alagna, S. W., & Lake, C. R. (1984). Psychopharmacology: An historical perspective. *Psychiatr. Clin. North Am., 7*(3), 411–33.

Morissette, S. B., Tull, M. T., Gulliver, S. B., Kamholtz, B. W., & Zimering, R. T. (2007). Anxiety, anxiety disorders, tobacco use, and nicotine: A critical review of interrelationships. *Psychol. Bull., 133,* 245–72.

Morley, T. E., & Moran, G. (2011). The origins of cognitive vulnerability in early childhood: Mechanisms linking early attachment to later depression. *Clin. Psychol. Rev., 31*(7), 1071–82. doi:10.1016/j.cpr.2011.06.006

Morris, D., & Turnbull, P. (2007). A survey-based exploration of the impact of dyslexia on career progression of UK registered nurses. *J. Nursing Management, 15*(1), 97–106.

Morris, T. L. (2001). Social phobia. In M. W. Vasey & M. R. Dadds (Eds.), *The developmental psychopathology of anxiety* (pp. 435–58). New York: Oxford University Press.

Morrison, J. (1995). *DSM-IV made easy: The clinicians guide to diagnosis.* New York: Guilford Press.

Morrison, B. F., & Burnett, A. L. (2011). Priapism in haematological and coagulative disorders: An update. *Nature Reviews Urology, 8,* 223–30.

Mörtberg, E., Clark, D. M., Sundin, Ö., & Wistedt, A. Å. (2007). Intensive group cognitive treatment and individual cognitive therapy vs. Treatment as usual in social phobia: A randomized controlled trial. *Acta Psychiatr. Scand., 115*(2), 142–54. doi:10.1111/j.1600-0447.2006.00839.x

Moser, P. W. (1989, January). Double vision: Why do we never match up to our mind's ideal? *Self,* pp. 51–52.

Morton, W. A., Gwendolyn G., & Stockton, G. G. (2000, October). Methylphenidate abuse and psychiatric side effects. *Prim. Care Companion J. Clin. Psychiat., 2*(5), 159–164.

Mote, J., Stuart, B. K., & Kring, A. M. (2014). Diminished emotion expressivity but not experience in men and women with schizophrenia. *J. Abn. Psych., 123*(4), 796–801.

Mott, F. W. (1919). *War neuroses and shell shock.* Oxford, UK: Oxford Medical Publications.

Mott, T. F., & Leach, L. (2004). Is methylphenidate useful for treating adolescents with ADHD? *J. Fam. Pract., 53*(8), 659–61.

Mowbray, R. M. (1959). Historical aspects of electric convulsant therapy. *Scott Medical Journal, 4,* 373–78.

Mowrer, O. H. (1947). On the dual nature of learning—A reinterpretation of "conditioning" and "problem-solving." *Harvard Educational Rev., 17,* 102–48.

Mowrer, O. H., & Mowrer, W. M. (1938). Enuresis—A method for its study and treatment. *Am. J. Orthopsychiat., 8,* 436–59.

Mrad, D. H., & Watson, C. (2011). Civil commitment. In E. Y. Drogin, F. M. Dattilio, R. L. Sadoff, & T. G. Gutheil (Eds.), *Handbook of forensic assessment: Psychological and psychiatric perspectives* (pp. 479–501). Hoboken, NJ: Wiley.

Mrazek, P. J., & Haggerty, R. J. (Eds.). (1994). *Reducing risks for mental disorders: Frontiers for prevention intervention research.* Washington, DC: National Academy Press.

Mueser, K. T., & Berenbaum, H. (1990). Psychodynamic treatment of schizophrenia. Is there a future? *Psychol. Med., 20,* 253–62.

Mueser, K. T., Deavers, F., Penn, D. L., & Cassisi, J. E. (2013). Psychosocial treatments for schizophrenia. *Annu. Rev. Clinical Psychology, 9,* 465–97.

Muhlberger, A., Wiedemann, G., Herrmann, M. J., & Pauli, P. (2006). Phylo- and ontogenetic fears and the expectation of danger: Differences between spider- and flight-phobic subjects in cognitive and physiological responses to disorder-specific stimuli. *J. Ab. Psych., 115*(3), 580–89.

Mula, M., Pini, S., & Giovanni, B. C. (2007). The neurobiology and clinical significance of depersonalization in mood and anxiety disorders: A critical reappraisal. *J. Affect. Dis., 99,* 91–99.

Multisite Violence Prevention Project. (2014). Targeting high-risk, socially influential middle school students to reduce aggression: Universal versus selective preventive intervention effects.

J. Res. Adolescence, 24(2), 364–82. doi:http://dx.doi.org/10.1111/jora.12067

Mulugeta, S., Tesfay, K., Frank, R., & Gruber-Frank, C. (2015). Acute loss of vision in a young woman: A case report on psychogenic blindness. *Ethiopian J. Health Science, 25,* 99–104.

Mundo, E., Zanoni, S., & Altamura, A. C. (2006). Genetic issues in obsessive-compulsive disorder and related disorders. *Psychiatr. Ann., 36*(7), 495–512.

Munoz, R. F. (2001). How shall we ensure that the prevention of onset of mental disorders becomes a national priority? *Prevention & Treatment, 4,* n.p.

Munoz, R. F., Mrazek, P. J., & Haggerty, R. J. (1996). Institute of Medicine report on prevention of mental disorders: Summary and commentary. *Am. Psychol., 51*(11), 1116–22.

Munsey, C. (2007). A long road back. *Monitor on Psychology, 38,* 34–36.

Murphy, C. C., Boyle, C., Schendel, D., Decoufle, P., & Yeargin-Allsopp, M. (1998). Epidemiology of mental retardation in children. *Ment. Retard. Dev. Dis. Res. Rev., 4,* 6–13.

Murphy, G. C., & Athanasou, J. A. (1999). The effect of unemployment on mental health. *J. Occup. Org. Psychol., 72,* 83–99.

Murphy, J. M. (1976). Psychiatric labeling in cross-cultural perspective. *Science, 191,* 1019–28.

Murphy, W. D. (1997). Exhibitionism: Psychopathology and theory. In D. R. Laws & W. O'Donohue (Eds.), *Sexual deviance: Theory, assessment, and treatment* (pp. 22–39). New York: Guilford Press.

Murray, G., & Harvey, A. (2010). Circadian rhythms and sleep in bipolar disorder. *Bipolar Disorder, 12,* 459–72.

Murray, G., & Johnson, S. L. (2010). The clinical significance of creativity in bipolar disorder. *Clinical Psychology Review, 30,* 721–32.

Murray, G. K., Leeson, V., & McKenna, P. J. (2004). Spontaneous improvement in severe, chronic schizophrenia and its neurological correlates. *Brit. J. Psychiatry, 184,* 357–58.

Murray, J. B. (2001). Ecstasy is a dangerous drug. *Psychol. Rep., 88*(3), 895–902.

Musante, G. J., Costanzo, P. R., & Friedman, K. E. (1998). The comorbidity of depression and eating dysregulation processes in a diet-seeking obese population: A matter of gender specificity. *Int. J. Eat. Dis., 23*(1), 65–75.

Mussell, M. P., Mitchell, J. E., Crosby, R. D., Fulkerson, J. A., Hoberman, H. M., & Romano, J. L. (2000). Commitment to treatment goals in prediction of group cognitive-behavioral therapy treatment outcome for women with bulimia nervosa. *J. Cons. Clin. Psychol., 68,* 432–37.

Musselman, D. L., Lawson, D., Gumnick, J. F., Manatunga, A., Penna, S., Goodkin, R. S., et al. (2001). Paroxetine for the prevention of depression induced by high dose interferon-alpha. *New Engl. J. Med., 344,* 961–66.

Myers, R. H., Schaefer, E. J., Wilson, P. W., D'Agostino, R., Ordovas, J. M., Espino, A., et al. (1996). Apolipoprotein E epsilon4 association with dementia in a population-based study: The Framingham study. *Neurol., 46,* 673–77.

Mystkowski, J. L., & Mineka, S. (2007). Behavior therapy for specific fears and phobias: Context specificity of fear extinction. In T. A. Treat, R. R. Bootzin, & T. B. Baker (Eds.), *Psychological clinical science: Papers in honor of Richard Mcfall* (pp. 197–222). New York: Psychology Press.

N

Nabeyama, M., Nakagawa, A., Yoshiura, T., Nakao, T., Nakatani, E., Togao, O., et al. (2008). Functional MRI Study of brain activation alterations in patients with obsessive-compulsive disorder after symptom improvement. *Psychiatry Research Neuroimaging, 163,* 236–47.

Naeem, F., Ayub, M., Masood, K., Gul, H., Khalid, M., Farrukh, A., et al. (2011). Prevalence and psychosocial risk factors of PTSD; 18 months after Kashmir earthquake in Pakistan. *J. Affect. Dis., 130,* 268–74.

Nagata, T., van Vliet, I., Yamada, H., Kataoka, K., Iketani, T., & Kiriike, N. (2006). An open trial of paroxetine for the "offensive subtype" of taijin kyofusho and social anxiety disorder. *Depression and Anxiety, 23*(3), 168–74.

Nagayama Hall, G. C. (2001). Psychotherapy research with ethnic minorities: Empirical, ethical, and conceptual issues. *J. Cons. Clin. Psychol., 69*(3), 502–10.

Nakao, T., Nakagawa, A., Yoshiura, T., Nakatani, E., Nabeyama, M., Yoshizato, C., et al. (2005). Brain activation of patients with obsessive-compulsive disorder during neuropsychological and symptom provocation tasks before and after symptom improvement: A functional magnetic resonance imaging study. *Biol. Psychiatry, 57,* 901–10.

Naninck, E. F. G., Lucassen, P. J., & Bakker, J. (2011). Sex differences in adolescent depression: Do sex hormones determine vulnerability? *J. Neuroendocrin., 23*(5), 383–92. doi:10.1111/j.1365-2826.2011.02125.x

Naqvi, N. H., Rudrauf, D., Damasio, H., & Bechara, A. (2007). Damage to the insula disrupts addiction to cigarette smoking. *Science, 315*(5811), 531–34.

Naragon-Gainey, K., Watson, D., & Markon, K. E. (2009). Differential relations of depression and social anxiety symptoms to the facets of extraversion/positive emotionality. *J. Abn. Psych., 118,* 299–310.

Narby, J. (1982). The evolution of attitudes towards mental illness in preindustrial England. *Orthomolecular Psychiatry, 11,* 103–10.

Narrow, W. E., Regier, D. A., Rae, D. S., Manderscheld, R. W., & Locke, B. Z. (1993). Use of services by persons with mental and addictive disorders: Findings from the National Institute of Mental Health Epidemiologic Catchment Area Program. *Arch. Gen. Psychiatry, 50,* 95–107.

Nash, M. R., Hulsey, T. L., Sexton, M. C., Harralson, T. L., & Lambert, W. (1993). Long-term sequelae of childhood sexual abuse: Perceived family environment, psychopathology, and dissociation. *J. Cons. Clin. Psychol., 61*(2), 276–83.

Nathan, D. (2011). *Sybil exposed: The extraordinary story behind the famous multiple personality case.* New York: Free Press.

Nathan, P. E., & Gorman, J. M. (2007). *A guide to treatments that work.* New York: Oxford University Press.

National Institute on Alcohol Abuse and Alcoholism (NIAAA). (1997). *Monitoring the future.* National Institutes of Mental Health. Washington, DC: Author.

National Institute on Alcohol Abuse and Alcoholism (NIAAA). (2015). *College drinking.* Retrieved from http://www.niaaa.nih.gov/alcohol-health/special-populations-co-occurring-disorders/college-drinking

National Institute of Mental Health (NIMH). (2007). *NIMH perspective on diagnosing and treating bipolar disorder in children.* Washington, DC: Author.

National Institute of Mental Health (NIMH). (2001). *Facts about the National Institute of Mental Health.* Washington, DC: Author.

National Institute of Mental Health (NIMH). (2014). *Prevalence of any mental illness among U.S. Adults, 2012.* Retrieved from http://www.nimh.nih.gov/health/statistics/prevalence/serious-mental-illness-smi-among-us-adults.shtml

National Institutes of Health. (2001). Special Issue: Alcohol and disease interaction. *Alcohol Research & Health, 25,* 241–306.

National Mental Health Association. (1997). *Working for America's mental health.* Alexandria, VA: Author.

Natsuaki, M. N., Cicchetti, D., & Rogosch, F. A. (2009). Examining the developmental history of child maltreatment, peer relations, and externalizing problems among adolescents with symptoms of paranoid personality disorder. *Develop. Psychopath., 21*(4), 1181–93. doi:10.1017/S0954579409990101

Natsuaki, M. N., Ge, X., Leve, L. D., Neiderhiser, J. M., Shaw, D. S., Conger, R. D., et al. (2010). Genetic liability, environment, and the development of fussiness in toddlers: The roles of maternal depression and parental responsiveness. *Devel. Psychol., 46*(5), 1147–58. doi:10.1037/a0019659

Nattala, P., Leung, K. S., & Nagarajaiah, M. P. (2010). Family member involvement in relapse prevention improves alcohol dependence outcomes: A prospective study at an addiction treatment facility in India. *J. Stud. Alcohol Drugs, 71*(4), 581–87.

Nayani, T. H., & David, A. S. (1996). The auditory hallucination: A phenomenological survey. *Psychol. Med., 26*(1), 177–89.

Neacsiu, A. D., & Linehan, M. M. (2014). Borderline personality disorder. In D. H. Barlow (Ed.) *Clinical Handbook of Psychological Disorders* (5th ed., pp. 394–461). New York: Guilford Press.

Neale, J. M., & Oltmanns, T. F. (1980). *Schizophrenia.* New York: Wiley.

Neighbors, C., Larimer, M. E., & Lewis, M. A. (2004). Targeting misperceptions of descriptive drinking norms: Efficacy of a computer-delivered personalized normative feedback intervention. *J. Cons. Clin. Psychol., 72,* 202–17.

Neisser, U. (1967). *Cognitive psychology.* New York: Appleton Century Crofts.

Neisser, U. (Ed.). (1982). *Memory observed: Remembering in natural contexts.* San Francisco: Freeman.

Nelson, C. A., & Bloom, F. E. (1997). Child development and neuroscience. *Child Develop., 68*(5), 970–87.

Nelson, G., Aubry, T., & Lawrence, A. (2007). A review of the literature on the effectiveness of housing and support, assertive community treatment, and intensive case management interventions for persons with mental illness who have been homeless. *Am. J. Orthopsychiat., 77,* 350–61.

Nemeroff, C. B. (2003). Anxiolytics: Past, present, and future agents. *J. Clin. Psychiatry, 64*(Suppl. 3), 3–6.

Nemeroff, C. B., & Shatzberg, A. F. (2007). Pharmacological treatments for unipolar depression. In P. E. Nathan & J. M. Gorman (Eds.), *A guide to treatments that work* (pp. 217–88). New York: Oxford University Press.

Neria, Y., Nandi, A., & Galea, S. (2008). Post-traumatic stress disorder following disasters: A systematic review. *Psychol. Med., 38,* 467–80.

Nesse, R. M. (2000). Is depression an adaptation? *Arch. Gen. Psychiatry, 57*(1), 14–20.

Nestadt, G., Grados, M., & Samuels, J. F. (2010). Genetics of obsessive-compulsive disorder. *Psychiatr. Clin. North Am., 33*(1), 141–58.

Nestoriuc, Y., Rief, W., & Martin, A. (2008). Meta-analysis of biofeedback for tension type headache: Efficacy, specificity, and treatment moderators. *J. Consult. Clin. Psychol., 76,* 379–96.

Neumeister, A., Bain, E., Nugent, A. C., Carson, R. E., Bonne, O., Luckenbaugh, D. A., et al. (2004). Reduce serotonin type 1-sub(a) receptor binding in panic disorder. *J. Neurosci., 24*(3), 589–91.

Neutze, J., Seto, M. C., Schaefer, G. A., Mundt, I. A., Beier, K. M. (2011). Predictors of child pornography offenses and child sexual abuse in a community sample of pedophiles and hebephiles. *Sexual Abuse: J. Res. Treatment, 23*(2), 212–42.

New York Times. (1994, May 9). Multiple personality cases perplex legal system, p. A1.

Newman, J. P., & Lorenz, A. R. (2003). Response modulation and emotion processing: Implications for psychopathy and other dysregulatory psychopathology. In R. J. Davidson, K. R. Scherer, & H. H. Goldsmith (Eds.), *Handbook of affective sciences* (pp. 904–29). New York: Oxford Press.

Newschaffer, C. J., Croen, L. A., Daniels, J., Giarelli, E., Grether, J. K., Levy, S. E., (2007). The epidemiology of autism spectrum disorders. *Annu. Rev. Public Health, 28,* 235–58. doi:10.1146/annurev.publhealth.28.021406.144007

Newsom, J. T., Mahan, T. L., Rook, K. S., & Krause, N. (2008). Stable negative social exchanges and health. *Health Psychology, 27,* 78–86.

Newton, L., Rosen, A., Tennant, C., Hobbs, C., Lapsley, H. M., & Tribe, K. (2000). Deinstitutionalisation for long-term mental illness: An ethnographic study. *Austral. NZ J. Psychiatry, 34,* 484–90.

Neziroglu, F., Roberts, M., & Yaryura-Tobias, J. (2004). A behavioural model for body dysmorphic disorder. *Psychiatr. Ann., 34*(12), 915–20.

Ng, D. M., & Jeffery, R. W. (2003). Relationships between perceived stress and health behaviors in a sample of working adults. *Health Psychol., 22*(6), 638–42.

Nierenberg, A. A., Akiskal, H. S., Angst, J., Hirschfeld, R. M., Merikangas, K. R., Petukhova, M., et al. (2010). Bipolar disorder with frequent mood episodes in the national comorbidity survey replication (NCS-R). *Molec. Psychiat, 15*(11), 1075–87. doi:10.1038/mp.2009.61

Nitschke, J., Istrefi, S., Osterheider, M., & Mokros, A. (2012). Empathy in sexually sadistic offenders: An experimental comparison with non-sadistic sexual offenders. *Int. J. Law Psychiatry, 35*(3), 165–167.

Nisbett, R. E., & Wilson, T. D. (1977). Telling more than we can know: Verbal reports on mental processes. *Psychol. Rev., 84,* 231–59.

Nixon, R. D., & Bryant, R. A. (2005). Are negative cognitions associated with severe acute trauma responses? *Behav. Chng., 22*(1), 22–28.

Nobakht, M., & Dezhkam, M. (2000). An epidemiological study of eating disorders in Iran. *Int. J. Eat. Dis., 28,* 265–71.

Nobre, P. J. (2010). Psychological determinants of erectile dysfunction: Testing a cognitive-emotional model. *J. Sexual Medicine, 7,* 1429–37.

Nock, M. K. (2009). Why do people hurt themselves? New insights into the nature and functions of self-injury. *Current Directions in Psychological Science, 18,* 78–83.

Nock, M. K. (2010). Self-injury. *Annu. Rev. Clinical Psychology, 6,* 339–63.

Nock, M. K., Borges, G., Bromet, E. J., Alonso, J., Angermeyer, M., Beautrais, A., et al. (2008). Cross-national prevalence and risk factors for suicidal ideation, plans and attempts. *Brit. J. Psychiatry, 192*(2), 98–105.

Nock, M. K., Borges, G., Bromet, E., Cha, C. B., Kessler, R. C., & Lee, S. (2008). The epidemiology of suicide and suicidal behaviors. *Epidemiologic Reviews, 30,* 133–54.

Nock, M. K., Green, J. G., Hwang, I., McLaughlin, K. A., Sampson, N. A., Zaslavsky, A. M., & Kessler, R. C. (2013). Prevalence, correlates and treatment of lifetime suicidal behavior among adolescents: Results from the National Comorbidity Survey Replication–Adolescent Supplement (NCS-A). *JAMA Psychiatry, 70,* 300–10. doi:10.1001/2013. jamapsychiatry.55

Nock, M. K., Hwang, I., Sampson, N., Kessler, R. C., Angermeyer, M., Beautrais, A., et al. (2009). Cross-national analysis of the associations among mental disorders and suicidal behavior: Findings from the WHO World Mental Health Surveys. *PLoS Med., 6*(8), e1000123.

Nock, M. K., Hwang, I., Sampson, N. A., & Kessler, R. C. (2010). Mental disorders, comorbidity and suicidal behavior: Results from the National Comorbidity Survey Replication. *Molec. Psychiatry, 15*(8), 868–76. doi:10.1038/mp.2009.29

Nock, M. K., Kazdin, A. E., Hiripi, E., & Kessler, R. C. (2006). Prevalence, subtypes, and correlates of DSM-IV conduct disorder in the National Comorbidity Survey Replication. *Psychol. Med., 36*(5), 699–710. doi:10.1017/S0033291706007082

Nock, M. K., Kazdin, A. E., Hiripi, E., & Kessler, R. C. (2007). Lifetime prevalence, correlates, and persistence of oppositional defiant disorder: Results from the national comorbidity survey replication. *J. Child Psych. Psychiatry, 48*(7), 703–13. doi:10.1111/j.1469-7610.2007.01733.x

Nock, M. K., Prinstein, M. J., & Sterba, S. (2009). Revealing the form and function of self-injurious thoughts and behaviors: A real-time ecological assessment study among adolescents and young adults. *J. Abn. Psych., 118,* 816–27.

Nock, M. K., Stein, M. B., Heeringa, S. G., Ursano, R. J., Colpe, L. J., Fullerton, C. S., et al. (2014). Prevalence and correlates of suicidal behavior among soldiers: Results from the Army Study to Assess Risk and Resilience in Service Members (Army STARRS). *JAMA Psychiatry, 71,* 514–22.

Nolan, E. E., & Gadow, K. D. (1997). Children with ADHD and tic disorder and their classmates: Behavioral normalization with methylphenidate. *J. Am. Acad. Child Adoles. Psychiatry, 36*(5), 597–604.

Nolen-Hoeksema, S. (1991). Responses to depression and their effects on the duration of depressive episodes. *J. Abn. Psych., 100*(4), 569–82.

Nolen-Hoeksema, S. (2000). The role of rumination in depressive disorders and mixed anxiety/ depressive symptoms. *J. Abn. Psych., 109*(3), 504–11.

Nolen-Hoeksema, S. (2012). Emotion regulation and psychopathology: The role of gender. *Annu. Rev. Clinical Psychology, 8,* 161–187.

Nolen-Hoeksema, S., & Aldao, A. (2011). Gender and age differences in emotion regulation strategies and their relationship to depressive symptoms. *Pers. Indiv. Diff., 51*(6), 704–08. doi:10.1016/j.paid.2011.06. 012

Nolen-Hoeksema, S., & Corte, C. (2004). Gender and self-regulation. In R. F. Baumeister & K. D. Vohs (Eds.), *Handbook of self-regulation: Research, theory, and applications* (pp. 411–21). New York: Guilford Press.

Nolen-Hoeksema, S., & Hilt, L. (2009). Gender differences in depression. In I. H. Gotlib & C. L. Hammen (Eds.), *Handbook of depression and its treatment* (2nd ed.). New York: Guilford Press.

Nolen-Hoeksema, S., Larson, J., & Grayson, C. (1999). Explaining the gender difference in depressive symptoms. *J. Person. Soc. Psychol., 77*(5), 1061–72.

Nolen-Hoeksema, S., Wisco, B. E., & Lyubomirsky, S. (2008). Rethinking rumination. *Perspectives on Psychological Science, 3,* 400–24.

Norberg, M. M., Krystal, J. H., & Tolin, D. F. (2008). A meta-analysis of D-cycloserine and the facilitation of fear extinction and exposure therapy. *Biol. Psychiatry, 63*(12), 1118–26. doi:10.1016/j.biopsych.2008.01.012

Nordstrom, B. R., & Levin, F. R. (2007). Treatment of cannabis use disorders: A review of the literature. *Am. J. Addictions, 16,* 331–42.

Norko, M., & Baranoski, M. V. (2005). The state of contemporary risk assessment research. *Canad. J. Psychiatry, 50*(1), 18–26.

Norrholm, S. D., & Ressler, K. J. (2009). Genetics of anxiety and trauma-related disorders. *Neuroscience, 164*(1), 272–87. doi:10.1016/j.neuroscience.2009.06.036

Norris, D. M., Gutheil, T. G., & Strasburger, L. H. (2003). This couldn't happen to me: Boundary problems and sexual misconduct in the psychotherapy relationship. *Psychiatr. Serv., 54,* 517–22.

Norup, A., & Mortensen, E. L. (2015). Prevalence and predictors of personality change after severe brain injury. *Arch. Physical Med. Rehab., 96,* 56–62.

Novak, N. L., & Brownell, K. D. (2011). Taxation as prevention and as a treatment for obesity: The case of sugar-sweetened beverages. *Curr. Pharm. Des., 17,* 1218–22.

Nuechterlein, K. H. (1977). Reaction time and attention in schizophrenia: A critical evaluation of the data and theories. *Schizo. Bull., 3,* 373–428.

Nuechterlein, K. H., Green, M. F., Kern, R. S., Baade, L. E., Barch, D. M., Cohen, J. D., et al. (2008). The MATRICS consensus cognitive battery, Part 1: Test selection, reliability, and validity. *Am. J. Psychiatry, 165,* 203–13.

Nuechterlein, K. H., Snyder, K. S., & Mintz, J. M. (1992). Paths to relapse: Possible transactional processes connecting patient illness onset, expressed emotion, and psychotic relapse. *Brit. J. Psychiatry, 161*(Suppl. 18), 88–96.

Nuechterlein, K. H., Ventura, J., Subotnik, K. L., & Bartzokis, G. (2014). The early longitudinal course of cognitive deficits in schizophrenia. *J. Clinical Psychiatry, 75*(Suppl. 2), 25–29.

Nusslock, R., Shackman, A. J., Harmon-Jones, E., Alloy, L. B., Coan, J. A., & Abramson, L. Y. (2011). Cognitive vulnerability and frontal brain asymmetry: Common predictors of first prospective depressive episode. *J. Abn. Psychol., 120*(2), 497–503. doi:10.1037/a0022940

Nutt, D. J. (2010). Rationale for, barriers to, and appropriate medication for the long-term treatment of depression. *J. Clinical Psychiatry, 71*(Suppl. E1), e02.

Nutt, D., Argyropoulos, S., Hood, S., & Potokar, J. (2006). Generalized anxiety disorder: A comorbid disease. *European Neuropsychopharmacology, 16*(2), 109–18.

Nutt, D. J., Lingford-Hughes, A., Erritzoe, D., & Stokes, P. R. A. (2015). The dopamine theory of addiction: 40 years of highs and lows. *Nature Reviews Neuroscience, 16,* 305–12.

O

O'Brien, K. M., & Vincent, N. K. (2003). Psychiatric comorbidity in anorexia and bulimia nervosa: Nature, prevalence, and causal relationships. *Clin. Psychol. Rev., 23,* 57–74.

Ochsner, K. N., Silvers, J. A., & Buhle, J. T. (2012). Functional imaging studies of emotion regulation: A synthetic review and evolving model of the cognitive control of emotion. *Ann. NY Acad. Sci., 1251,* E1–E24.

O'Connor, B. P., McGuire, S., Reiss, D., Hetherington, E. M., & Plomin, R. (1998). Co-occurrence of depressive symptoms and antisocial behavior in adolescence: A common genetic liability. *J. Abn. Psychol., 107*(1), 27–37.

O'Connor, M. J. (2001). Prenatal alcohol exposure and infant negative affect as precursors of depressive features in children. *Infant Mental Health Journal, 22*(3), 291–99.

O'Connor, R. C., & Nock, M. K. (2014). The psychology of suicidal behaviour. *Lancet Psychiatry, 1,* 73–85.

Odlaug, B. L., & Grant, J. E. (2012). Pathologic skin picking. In J. E. Grant, D. J. Stein, D. W. Woods & N. J. Keuthen (Eds.), *Trichotillomania, skin picking, and other body-focused repetitive behaviors* (pp. 21–41). Arlington, VA: American Psychiatric Publishing.

O'Donnell, C. R. (Eds.). (2004). *Culture, peers and delinquency.* Binghamton, NY: Haworth Press.

O'Donnell, R., Rome, D., Godin, M., & Fulton, P. (2000). Changes in inpatient utilization and quality of care performance measures in a capitated HMO population, 1989–1999. *Psychiatr. Clin. North Am., 23*(2), 319–33.

O'Donoghue, E. G. (1914). *The story of Bethlehem Hospital from its foundation in 1247.* London: Adelphi Terrace.

O'Donohue, W., Fowler, K. A., & Lilienfeld, S. O. (Eds.). (2007). *Personality disorders: Toward the DSM-V.* Thousand Oaks, CA: Sage Publications.

O'Donovan, A., Lin, J., Tillie, J., Dhabhar, F. S., Wolkowitz, O. M., Blackburn, E. H., & Epel, E. S. (2009). Pessimism correlates with leukocyte telomere shortness and elevated interkeukin-6 in post-menopausal women. *Brain, Behavior and Immunity, 23*, 446–49.

Oehlberg, K. A., & Mineka, S. (2011). Fear conditioning and attention to threat: An integrative approach to understanding the etiology of anxiety disorders. In T. R. Schachtman & S. Reilly (Eds.), *Associative learning and conditioning theory: Human and non-human applications* (pp. 44–78). New York: Oxford University Press.

Office of Technology Assessment. (1993). *Biological components of substance abuse and addiction.* Washington, DC: Author.

Ogden, C. L., Carroll, M. D., Kit, B. K., & Flegal, K. M. (2014). Prevalence of childhood and adult obesity in the United States, 2011–2012. *JAMA, 311*, 806–14.

Ogden, C. L., Fryar, C. D., Carroll, M. D., & Felgal, K. M. (2004). Mean body weight, height, and body mass index, United States 1960–2002 (Advance data from *Vital and Health Statistics*, No. 347). Hyattsville, MD: National Center for Health Statistics.

O'Hara, M., & Gorman, L. L. (2004). Can postpartum depression be predicted. *Prim. Psychiatry, 11*(3), 42–47.

O'Hara, M., Schlecte, J., Lewis, D., & Varner, M. (1991). Controlled prospective study of postpartum mood disorders: Psychological, environmental, and hormonal variables. *J. Abn. Psychol., 100*, 63–73.

O'Hara, M. W., & Swain, A. M. (1996). Rates and risk of postpartum depression-A meta-analysis. *Intern. Rev. Psychiatry, 8*(1), 37–54.

Öhman, A. (1996). Preferential preattentive processing of threat in anxiety: Preparedness and attentional biases. In R. M. Rapee (Ed.), *Current controversies in the anxiety disorders* (pp. 253–90). New York: Guilford Press.

Öhman, A. (2009). Of snakes and faces: An evolutionary perspective on the psychology of fear. *Scand. J. Psychol., 50*(6), 543–52. doi:10.1111/j.1467-9450.2009.00784.x

Öhman, A., Carlsson, K., Lundqvist, D., & Ingvar, M. (2007). On the unconscious subcortical origin of human fear. *Physiology & Behavior, 92*(1), 180–85.

Öhman, A., Dimberg, U., & Öst, L. G. (1985). Animal and social phobias: Biological constraints on learned fear responses. In S. Reiss & R. Bootzin (Eds.), *Theoretical issues in behavior therapy* (pp. 123–75). New York: Academic Press.

Öhman, A., & Mineka, S. (2001). Fears, phobias, and preparedness: Toward an evolved module of fear and fear learning. *Psychol. Rev., 108*, 483–22.

Öhman, A., & Soares, J. (1993). On the automatic nature of phobic fear: Conditioned electrodermal responses to masked fear-relevant stimuli. *J. Abn. Psychol., 102*, 121–32.

Okasha, A., & Okasha, T. (2000). Notes on mental disorders in Pharaonic Egypt. *History of Psychiatry, 11*, 413–24.

Okazaki, S., Okazaki, M., & Sue, S. (2009). Clinical personality assessment with Asian Americans. In J. N. Butcher (Ed.), *Oxford handbook of personality assessment* (pp. 377–95). New York: Oxford University Press.

Oken, B. S., Chamine, I., & Wakeland, W. (2015). A systems approach to stress, stressors and resilience in humans. *Behavioural Brain Research, 282*, 144–54.

Okuda, M., Balán, I., Petry, N. M., Oquendo, M., & Blanco, C. (2009). Cognitive-behavioral therapy for pathological gambling: Cultural considerations. *Am. J. Psychiatry, 166*(12), 1325–30.

Olatunji, B. O., Kauffman, B. Y., Meltzer, S., Davis, M. L., Smits, J. A. J., & Powers, M. B. (2014). Cognitive-behavioral therapy for hypochondriasis/health anxiety: A meta-analysis of treatment outcome and moderators. *Behaviour Research and Therapy, 58*, 65–74.

Oldehinkel, A. J., Veenstra, R., Ormel, J., de Winter, A. F., & Verhulst, F. C. (2007). Temperament, parenting, and depressive symptoms in a population sample of preadolescents. *J. Child Psychol. Psychiatry, 47*(7), 684–95.

Oldham, J. M. (2006). Borderline personality disorder and suicidality. *Am. J. Psychiatry, 163*(1), 20–26.

Olds, J., & Milner, P. (1954). Positive reinforcement produced by electrical stimulation of septal area and other regions of rat brain. *J. Comparative Physiology and Psychology, 47*, 419–27.

O'Leary, D. S., Block, R. I., Turner, B. M., Koeppel, J., Magnotta, V. A., Ponto, B., et al. (2003). Marijuana alters the human cerebellar clock. *NeuroReport: For Rapid Commun. Neurosci. Res., 14*(8), 1145–51.

Olfson, M., & Marcus, S. C. (2009). National patterns in antidepressant medication treatment. *Arch. Gen. Psychiatry, 66*, 848–56.

Olfson, M., & Marcus, S. C. (2010). National trends in outpatient psychotherapy. *Am. J. Psychiatry, 167*, 1456–63.

Ollendick, T. H., Öst, L.-G., Reuterskiöld, L., Costa, N., Cederlund, R., Sirbu, C., et al. (2009). One-session treatment of specific phobias in youth: A randomized clinical trial in the United States and Sweden. *J. Cons. Clin. Psychol., 77*(3), 504–16. doi:10.1037/a0015158

Ollendick, T. H., Yang, B., King, N. J., Dong, Q., et al. (1996). Fears in American, Australian, Chinese, and Nigerian children and adolescents: A cross-cultural study. *J. Child Psychology & Psychiatry & Allied Sciences, 37*(2), 213–20.

Olney, J. W., & Farber, N. B. (1995). Glutamate receptor dysfunction and schizophrenia. *Arch. Gen. Psychiatry, 52*, 998–1007.

Olson, K. R. (2001). Computerized psychological test usage in APA accredited training programs. *J. Clin. Psychol., 57*, 727–36.

Oltmanns, T. F., & Okada, M. (2006). Paranoia. In J. E. Fisher & W. T. O'Donohue (Eds.), *Practitioner's guide to evidence-based psychotherapy* (pp. 503–13). New York: Springer Science and Business Media.

O'Mahony, J. F., & Ward, B. G. (2003). Differences between those who panic by day and those who also panic by night. *J. Behav. Ther. Exper. Psychiatry, 34*, 239–49.

Ondersma, S. J., Chaffin, M., Berliner, L., Cordon, I., & Goodman, G. S. (2001). Sex with children is abuse: Comment on Rind, Tromovitch, and Bauserman (1998). *Psychol. Bull., 127*, 707–14.

O'Neil, K. A., Podell, J. L., Benjamin, C. L., & Kendall, P. C. (2010). Comorbid depressive disorders in anxiety-disordered youth: Demographic, clinical, and family characteristics. *Child Psychiatr. Human Devel., 41*(3), 330–41.

Onishi, N. (2002, October 3). Globalization of beauty makes slimness trendy. *New York Times*, p. A4.

O'Regan, N. A., Ryan, D. J., Boland, E., Connolly, W., McGlade, C., Leonard, M., et al. (2014). Attention! A good bedside test for delirium? *J. Neurol. Neurosurg. Psychiatry, 85*, 1122–31.

Oren, D. A., & Rosenthal, N. E. (1992). Seasonal affective disorders. In E. S. Paykel (Ed.), *Handbook of affective disorders* (2nd ed., pp. 551–67). New York: Guilford Press.

Orlovska, S., Pedersen, M. K., Benros, M. E., Mortensen, P. B., Agerbo, E., & Nordentoft, M. (2014). Head injury as a risk factor for psychiatric disorders: A nationwide register-based follow-up study of 113,906 persons with head injury. *Am. J. Psychiatry, 171*, 463–69.

Orne, M. T., Dinges, D. F., & Orne, E. C. (1984). On the differential diagnosis of multiple personality in the forensic context. *Int. J. Clin. Exp. Hypn., 32*, 118–69.

Öst, L.-G. (1987). Age of onset of different phobias. *J. Abn. Psychol., 96*, 223–29.

Öst, L.-G. (1997). Rapid treatment of specific phobias. In G. C. L. Davey (Ed.), *Phobias. A handbook of theory, research and treatment* (2nd ed., pp. 227–46). Chichester, UK: Wiley.

Öst, L.-G., Alm, T., Brandberg, M., & Breitholtz, E. (2001). One vs. five sessions of exposure and five sessions of cognitive therapy in the treatment of claustrophobia. *Behav. Res. Ther., 39*(2), 167–83.

Öst, L.-G., & Hellström, K. (1997). Blood-injury-injection phobia. In G. C. L. Davey (Ed.), *Phobias. A handbook of theory, research and treatment* (pp. 63–80). Chichester, UK: Wiley.

Öst, L.-G., & Hugdahl, K. (1981). Acquisition of phobias and anxiety response patterns in clinical patients. *Behav. Res. Ther., 19*, 439–47.

Otto, M. W., Teachman, B. A., Cohen, L. S., Soares, C. N., Vitonis, A. F., & Harlow, B. L. (2007). Dysfunctional attitudes and episodes of major depression: Predictive validity and temporal stability in never depressed, depressed, and recovered women. *J. Abn. Psych., 116*(3), 475–83.

Otway, L. J., & Vignoles, V. L. (2006). Narcissism and childhood recollections: A quantitative test of psychoanalytic predictions. *Pers. Social Psychol. Bull., 32*, 104–16.

Ouimet, A. J., Gawronski, B., & Dozois, D. J. A. (2009). Cognitive vulnerability to anxiety: A review and an integrative model. *Clin. Psychol. Rev., 29*(6), 459–70. doi:10.1016/j.cpr.2009.05.004

Overall, J. E., & Hollister, L. E. (1982). Decision rules for phenomenological classification of psychiatric patients. *J. Cons. Clin. Psychol., 50*(4), 535–45.

Overbeek, T., van Diest, R., Schruers, K., Kruizinga, F., & Griez, E. (2005). Sleep complaints in panic disorder patients. *J. Nerv. Ment. Dis., 193*(7), 488–93.

Overmier, J. B., & Seligman, M. E. P. (1967). Effects of inescapable shock upon subsequent escape and avoidance learning. *J. Comparative and Physiological Psychology, 63*, 23–33.

Owen, C., Rutherford, M. J., Jones, M., Tennant, C., & Smallman, A. (1997). Noncompliance in psychiatric aftercare. *Comm. Ment. Health J., 33*, 25–34.

Ownby, R. L., Crocco, E., Acevedo, A., John, V., & Loewenstein, D. (2006). Depression and risk for Alzheimer disease. *Arch. Gen. Psychiatry, 63*, 530–38.

P

Pabian, Y. L., Welfel, E., & Beebe, R. S. (2009). Psychologists' knowledge of their states' laws pertaining to Tarasoff-type situations. *Prof. Psychol. Res. Pract., 40*, 8–14.

Pachter, H. M. (1951). *Magic into science: The story of Paracelsus.* New York: Schumen.

Padela, A. I., & Heisler, M. (2010). The association of perceived abuse and discrimination after September 11, 2001, with psychological distress, level of happiness, and health status among Arab Americans. *Am. J. Pub. Health, 100*(2), 284–91. doi:10.2105/ajph.2009.164954

Padgett, D. K., Hawkins, R. L., Abrams, C., & Davis, A. (2006). In their own words: Trauma and substance abuse in the lives of formerly homeless women with serious mental illness. *Am. J. Ortho-Psychiatry, 76*, 461–67.

Padma-Nathan, H., McMurray, J. G., Pullman, W. E., Whitaker, J. S., Saoud, J. B., Ferguson, K. M., et al. (2001). On-demand IC351 (Cialis) enhances erectile function in patients with erectile dysfunction. *Int. J. Impotence Research, 13,* 2–9.

Page, A. C., & Tan, B. J. (2009). Disgust and blood-injury-injection phobia. In B. O. Olatunji & D. McKay (Eds.), *Disgust and its disorders: Theory, assessment, and treatment implications* (pp. 191–209). Washington, DC: American Psychological Association.

Pagura, J., Cox, B. J., & Enns, M. W. (2009). Personality factors in the anxiety disorders. In M. M. Antony & M. B. Stein (Eds.), *Oxford handbook of anxiety and related disorders* (pp. 190–208). New York: Oxford University Press.

Pagura, J., Stein, M. B., Bolton, J. M., Cox, B. J., Grant, B., & Sareen, J. (2010). Comorbidity of borderline personality disorder and posttraumatic stress disorder in the U.S. population. *J. Psychiatr. Res., 44,* 1190–98.

Pail, G., Huf, W., Pjrek, E., Winkler, D., Willeit, M., Praschak-Rieder, N., et al. (2011). Bright-light therapy in the treatment of mood disorders. *Neuropsychobiol., 64*(3), 152–62. doi:10.1159/000328950

Palace, E. M., & Gorzalka, B. B. (1990). The enhancing effects of anxiety on arousal in sexually dysfunctional and functional women. *J. Abn. Psychol., 99,* 403–11.

Pandya, M., Pozuelo, L., & Malone, D. (2007). Electroconvulsive therapy: What the internist needs to know. *Cleveland Clinic J. Medicine, 74,* 679–85.

Pankratz, L. (2006). Persistent problems with the Munchausen syndrome by proxy label. *J. Am. Acad. Psychiatr. Law, 34,* 90–95.

Panuzio, J., & DiLillo, D. (2010). Physical, psychological, and sexual intimate partner aggression among newlywed couples: Longitudinal prediction of marital satisfaction. *J. Family Violence, 25*(7), 689–99.

Paolacci, G., & Chandler, J. (2014). Inside the Turk: Understanding Mechanical Turk as a participant pool. *Current Directions in Psychological Science, 23,* 184–88.

Papadimitriou, G. N., & Linkowski, P. (2005). Sleep disturbance in anxiety disorders. *Int. Rev. Psychiatry, 17*(4), 229–36.

Papakostas, G. I., Thase, M. E., Fava, M., Nelson, J. C., & Shelton, R. C. (2007). Are antidepressant drugs that combine serotonergic and noradrenergic mechanisms of action more effective than the selective serotonin reuptake inhibitors in treating major depressive disorder? A meta-analysis of studies of newer agents. *Biol. Psychiatry, 62,* 1217–27.

Papp, L., & Gorman, J. M. (1990). Suicidal preoccupation during fluoxetine treatment. *Am. J. Psychiatry, 147,* 1380.

Paris, J. (1999). Borderline personality disorder. In T. Millon, P. H. Blaney, & R. D. Davis (Eds.), *Oxford textbook of psychopathology* (pp. 628–52). New York: Oxford University Press.

Paris, J. (2001). Psychosocial adversity. In W. J. Livesley (Ed.), *Handbook of personality disorders* (pp. 231–41). New York: Guilford Press.

Paris, J. (2005). Neurobiological dimensional models of personality: A review of the models of Cloninger, Depue, and Siever. *J. Pers. Disord., 19,* 156–70.

Paris, J. (2007). The nature of borderline personality disorder: Multiple dimensions, multiple symptoms, but one category. *J. Pers. Disord., 21*(5), 457–73.

Paris, J. (2009). The treatment of borderline personality disorder: Implications of research on diagnosis, etiology, and outcome. *Annu. Rev. Clin. Psychol., 5,* 277–90. doi:10.1146/annurev. clinpsy.032408.153457

Paris, J. (2012a). Modernity and narcissistic personality disorder. *Personality Disorders: Theory, Research, and Treatment, 5*(2), 220–26

Paris, J. (2012b). Pathology of personality disorder: An integrative conceptualization. In T. Widiger (Ed.), *The Oxford handbook of personality disorders* (pp. 399–408). Oxford, UK: Oxford University Press.

Paris, J. (2012c). The rise and fall of dissociative identity disorder. *J. Nervous and Mental Disease, 200,* 1076–79.

Park, S., Holzman, P. S., & Goldman-Rakic, P. S. (1995). Spatial working memory deficits in the relatives of schizophrenic patients. *Arch. Gen. Psychiatry, 52,* 821–28.

Parke, R. D. (2004). Development in the family. *Annu. Rev. Psychol., 55,* 365–99.

Parker, G. F. (2004). Outcomes of assertive community treatment in an NGRI conditional release program. *J. Am. Acad. Psychiatr. Law, 32*(3), 291–303.

Parker, G., Gladstone, G., & Chee, K. T. (2001). Depression in the planet's largest ethnic group: The Chinese. *Am. J. Psychiatry, 158*(6), 857–64.

Parker, I. (2004, August 2). The gift. *The New Yorker,* pp. 54–63.

Parker, K. J., Buckmaster, C. L., Schatzberg, A. F., & Lyons, D. M. (2004). Prospective investigation of stress inoculation in young monkeys. *Arch. Gen. Psychiatry, 61*(9), 933–41.

Parra, C., Esteves, F., Flykt, A., & Öhman, A. (1997). Pavlovian conditioning to social stimuli: Backward masking and the dissociation of implicit and explicit cognitive processes. *Europ. Psychol., 2*(2), 106–17.

Parrott, A. C. (2001). Human psychopharmacology of Ecstasy (MDMA): A review of 15 years of empirical research. *Human Psychopharmacology Clinical & Experimental, 16*(8), 557–77.

Parrott, A. C., Lees, A., Garnham, N. J., Jones, M., & Wesnes, K. (1998). Cognitive performance in recreational users of MDMA or "ecstasy": Evidence for memory deficits. *J. Psychopharml., 12*(1), 79–83.

Parsons, T. D., & Rizzo, A. A. (2008). Affective outcomes of virtual reality exposure therapy for anxiety and specific phobias: A meta-analysis. *J. Behav. Ther. Exper. Psychiatry, 39*(3), 250–61. doi:10.1016/j.jbtep.2007.07.007

Pary, R. J. (2004). Behavioral and psychiatric disorders in children and adolescents with Down syndrome. *Ment. Health Asp. Dev. Dis., 7,* 69–76.

Patel, V., & Kim, Y.-R. (2007). Contribution of low- and middle-income countries to research published in leading general psychiatry journals, 2002–2004. *Brit. J. Psychiatry, 190,* 77–78.

Patel, V., & Sumathipala, A. (2001). International representation in psychiatric literature: Survey of six leading journals. *Brit. J. Psychiatry, 178,* 406–09.

Patrick, C., & Drislane, L. E. (2015). Antisocial personality disorder and psychopathy. In P. H. Blaney, R. F. Krueger, & T. Millon (Eds.). *Oxford textbook of psychopathology* (pp. 681–706). New York: Oxford University Press.

Patrick, C. J. (1994). Emotion and psychopathy: Startling new insights. *Psychophysiology, 31*(4), 319–30.

Patrick, C. J. (2005). Getting to the heart of psychopathy. In H. Herve & J. C. Yuille (Eds.), *Psychopathy: Theory, research, and social implications.* Hillsdale, NJ: Erlbaum.

Patrick, C. J. (2006). Back to the future: Cleckley as a guide to the next generation of psychopathy research. In C. J. Patrick (Ed.), *Handbook of the psychopathy* (pp. 605–17). New York: Guilford Press.

Patrick, C. J., Bradley, M. M., & Lang, P. J. (1993). Emotion in the criminal psychopath: Startle reflex modulation. *J. Abn. Psychol., 102*(1), 82–92.

Patterson, D., & Lott, I. (2008). Etiology, diagnosis, and development in Down syndrome. In J. E. Roberts, R. S. Chapman, S. F. Warren, & F. Steven (Eds.), *Speech and language development and intervention in Down syndrome and fragile X syndrome, communication and language intervention series* (pp. 3–25). Baltimore, MD: Paul H. Brookes Publishing.

Patterson, G. R., Capaldi, D., & Bank, L. (1991). An early starter model for predicting delinquency. In D. Pepler & K. H. Rubin (Eds.), *The development and treatment of childhood aggression* (pp. 139–68). Hillsdale, NJ: Erlbaum.

Patterson, G. R., DeGarmo, D. S., & Knutson, N. (2000). Hyperactivity and antisocial behaviors: Comorbid or two points in the same process? *Develop. Psychopath., 12*(1), 91–106.

Patterson, G. R., Reid, J. B., & Dishion, T. J. (1998). Antisocial boys. In J. M. Jenkins & K. Oatley (Eds.), *Human emotions: A reader* (pp. 330–36). Malden, MA: Blackwell.

Patton, G. C., Johnson-Sabine, E., Wood, K., Mann, A. H., & Wakeling, A. (1990). Abnormal eating attitudes in London schoolgirls—A prospective epidemiological study: Outcome at twelve month follow-up. *Psychol. Med., 20*(2), 383–94.

Paul, G. L. (1982). *The development of a "transportable" system of behavioral assessment for chronic patients.* Invited address. University of Minnesota, Minneapolis.

Paul, G. L., & Lentz, R. J. (1977). *Psychosocial treatment of chronic mental patients: Milieu versus social-learning programs.* Cambridge, MA: Harvard University Press.

Paul, G. L., Stuve, P., & Cross, J. V. (1997). Real-world inpatient programs: Shedding some light—A critique. *App. Prev. Psychol., 6*(4), 193–204.

Paul, T., Schroeter, K., Dahme, B., & Nutzinger, D. O. (2002). Self-injurious behavior in women with eating disorders. *Am. J. Psychiatry, 159*(3), 408–11.

Paulesu, E., Sambugaro, E., Torti, T., Danelli, L., Ferri, F., Scialfa, G., et al. (2010). Neural correlates of worry in generalized anxiety disorder and in normal controls: A functional MRI Study. *Psychol. Med., 40*(1), 117–24.

Pauli, P., & Alpers, G. W. (2002). Memory bias in patients with hypochondriases and somatoform pain disorder. *J. Psychom. Res., 52,* 42–53.

Paulik, G. (2011). The role of social schema in the experience of auditory hallucinations: A systematic review and a proposal for the inclusion of social schema in a cognitive behavioral model of voice hearing. *Clin. Psych. Psychother.,* doi:10.1002/cpp.768

Pauls, D. L., Alsobrooke, J. P., Goodman, W., Rasmussen, S., & Leckman, J. F. (1995). A family study of obsessive-compulsive disorder. *Am. J. Psychiatry, 152*(1), 76–84.

Pauls, D. L., Raymond, C. L., & Robertson, M. (1991). The genetics of obsessive-compulsive disorder: A review. In J. Zohar, T. Insel, & S. Rasmussen (Eds.), *The psychobiology of obsessive-compulsive disorder.* New York: Springer.

Pauls, D. L., Towbin, K. E., Leckman, J. F., Zahner, G. E., & Cohen, D. J. (1986). Gilles de la Tourette's syndrome and obsessive-compulsive disorder. *Arch. Gen. Psychiatry, 43,* 1180–82.

Paulussen-Hoogeboom, M. C., Stams, G. J. J. M., Hermanns, J. M. A., & Peetsma, T. T. D. (2007). Child negative emotionality and parenting from infancy to preschool: A meta-analytic review. *Developmental Psychology, 43*(2), 438–53.

Pavlov, I. P. (1927). *Conditioned reflexes.* London: Oxford University Press.

Pavone, L., Meli, C., Nigro, F., & Lisi, R. (1993). Late diagnosed phenylketonuria patients: Clinical presentation and results of treatment. *Developmental Brain Dysfunction, 6*(1–3), 184–87.

Pederson, C. B., & Mortensen, P. B. (2001). Evidence of a dose-response relationship between urbanicity during upbringing and schizophrenia risk. *Arch. Gen. Psychiatry, 58,* 1039–46.

Pediatric OCD Treatment Study. (2004). Cognitive-behavior therapy, sertraline, and their combination for children and adolescents with obsessive-compulsive disorder: The pediatric OCD treatment study (POTS) randomized controlled trial. *JAMA, 292*(16), 1969–76.

Peeke, P. M., & Chrousos, G. P. (1995). Hypercortisolism and obesity. In G. P. Chrousos & R. McCarty et al. (Eds.), *Stress: Basic mechanisms and clinical implications* (pp. 515–60). New York: New York Academy of Sciences.

Pelham, W. E., Burrows-MacLean, L., Gnagy, E. M., Fabiano, G. A., Coles, E. K., Tresco, K. E., et al. (2005). Transdermal methylphenidate, behavioral, and combined treatment for children with ADHD. *Exper. Clin. Psychopharmacol., 13*(2), 111–26.

Pelham, W. E., Jr., & Fabiano, G. A. (2008). Evidence-based psychosocial treatments for attention-deficit/hyperactivity disorder. *J. Clin. Child Adol. Psych., 37*(1), 184–214.

Pelham, W. E., Jr., Hoza, B., Pillow, D. R., Gnagy, E., Kipp, H. L., Greiner, D. R., et al. (2002). Effects of methylphenidate and expectancy on children with ADHD behavior, academic performance, and attributions in a summer treatment program and regular classroom setting. *J. Cons. Clin. Psychol., 70,* 320–25.

Pelletier, A. R., & Gilchrist, J. (2005). Roller coaster related fatalities, United States, 1994–2004. *Injury Prevention, 11,* 309–12.

Pennebaker, J. W. (1997). *Opening up: The healing power of expressing emotions.* New York: Guilford Press.

Penning, R., van Nuland, M., Fliervoet, L. A., Olivier, B., & Verster, J. C. (2010). The pathology of alcohol hangover. *Current Drug Abuse Reviews, 3,* 68–75.

Perkins, D. O., Lieberman, J. A., Gu, H., Tohen, M., McEvoy, J., Green, A. I., et al. (2004). Predictors of antipsychotic treatment response in patients with first-episode schizophrenia, schizoaffective disorder and schizophreniform disorders. *Brit. J. Psychiatry, 185,* 18–24.

Perl, D. P. (1999). Abnormalities in brain structure on postmortem analysis of dementias. In D. S. Charney, E. J. Nestler, & B. S. Bunney (Eds.), *Neurobiology of mental illness.* New York: Oxford University Press.

Perlin, M. L. (1996). Myths, realities, and the political world: The anthropology of insanity defense attitudes. *Bull. Am. Acad. Psychiatr. Law, 24*(1), 5–25.

Perls, F. S. (1969). *Gestalt therapy verbatim.* Lafayette, CA: Real People Press.

Perreira, K. M., & Sloan, F. A. (2001). Life events and alcohol consumption among mature adults: A longitudinal analysis. *J. Stud. Alcoh., 62*(4), 501–08.

Perrin, M. A., DiGrande, L., Wheeler, K., Thorpe, L., Farfel, M., & Brackbill, R. (2007). Differences in PTSD prevalence and associated risk factors among World Trade Center disaster rescue and recovery workers. *Am. J. Psychiatry, 164,* 1385–94.

Perrin, M. C., Opler, M. G., Harlap, S., Harkavy-Friedman, J., Kleinhaus, K., Nahon, D., et al. (2007). Tetrachloroethylene exposure and risk of schizophrenia: Offspring of dry cleaners in a population birth cohort, preliminary findings. *Schizo. Res., 90,* 251–54.

Perris, C. (1992). Bipolar-unipolar distinction. In E. S. Paykel (Ed.), *Handbook of affective disorders* (2nd ed.). New York: Guilford Press.

Perry, C., Williams, C. L., Komro, K. A., Veblen-Mortenson, S., Stigler, M. H., Munson, K. A., et al. (2002). Project northland: Long-term outcomes of community action to reduce adolescent alcohol use. *Health Education Research, 17*(1), 117–32.

Perry, C. L., Williams, C. L., Veblen-Mortenson, S., Toomey, T. L., et al. (1996). Project Northland: Outcomes of a community wide alcohol use prevention program during early adolescence. *Am. J. Public Health, 86*(7), 956–65.

Perry, J. N. (2009). Assessment of treatment resistance via questionnaire. In J. N. Butcher (Ed.), *Oxford handbook of personality assessment* (pp. 667–82). New York: Oxford University Press.

Pertusa, A., Frost, R. O., Fullana, M. A., Samuels, J., Steketee, G., Tolin, D., et al. (2010). Refining the diagnostic boundaries of compulsive hoarding: A critical review. *Clin. Psychol. Rev., 30*(4), 371–86. doi:10.1016/j.cpr.2010.01.007

Pescosolido, B. A., Martin, J. K., Long, J. S., Medina, T. R., Phelan, J. C., & Link, B. G. (2010). "A disease like any other"? A decade of change in public reactions to schizophrenia, depression, and alcohol dependence. *Am. J. Psychiatry, 167,* 1321–30.

Peter, R., & Siegrist, J. (2000). Psychosocial work environment and the risk of coronary heart disease. *Int. Arch. Occupational and Environmental Health, 73,* S41–S45.

Peterson, P. L., Baer, J. S., Wells, E. A., Ginzler, J. A., & Garrett, S. B. (2006). Short-term effects of a brief motivational intervention to reduce alcohol and drug risk among homeless adolescents. *Psych. Addict. Behav., 20*(3), 254–64.

Petrie, A., & Sabin, C. (2000). *Medical statistics at a glance.* Oxford, UK: Blackwell Science.

Petronis, A., Gottesman, I. I., Kan, P., Kennedy, J. L., Basile, V. S., Patterson, A. D., et al. (2003). Monozygotic twins exhibit numerous epigenetic differences: Clues to twin discordance? *Schizo. Bull., 29,* 169–78.

Petrovic, V. (2004). Level of psychopathology in children with war related trauma. *Psychiatry Today, 36*(1), 17–28.

Petrovich, G. (2011). Learning and motivation to eat: Forebrain circuitry. *Physiology & Behavior, 104,* 582–89.

Petry, N. (2005). *Pathological gambling: Etiology, comorbidity and treatment.* Washington, DC: American Psychological Association Press.

Petry, N. M., Alessi, S. M., Barry, D., & Carroll, K. M. (2014). Standard magnitude prize reinforcers can be as efficacious as larger magnitude reinforcers in cocaine-dependent methadone patients. *J. Consulting and Clinical Psychology, 83*(3), 464–72.

Petry, N. M., Barry, D., Pietrzak, R. H., & Wagner, J. A. (2008). Overweight and obesity are associated with psychiatric disorders: Results from the National Epidemiologic Survey on Alcohol and Related Conditions. *Psychosom. Med., 70,* 288–97.

Petry, N. M., & Madden, G. J. (2010). Discounting and pathological gambling. In G. J. Madden & W. K. Bickel (Eds.), *Impulsivity: The behavioral and neurological science of discounting* (pp. 273–94). Washington, DC: American Psychological Association.

Pettersson-Yeo, W., Alen, P., Benetti, S., McGuire, P., & Mechelli, A. (2011). Dysconnectivity in schizophrenia: Where are we now? *Neuroscience and Biobehavioral Reviews, 35,* 1110–24.

Petti, T. A. (2010). Milieu treatment: Inpatient, partial hospitalization, and residential programs. In M. K. Dulcan (Ed.), *Dulcan's textbook of child and adolescent psychiatry* (pp. 939–53). Arlington, VA: American Psychiatric Publishing.

Pew Research Center. (2013). *The global divide on homosexuality: Greater acceptance in more secular and affluent countries.* Retrieved from http://www.pewglobal.org/files/2014/05/Pew-Global-Attitudes-Homosexuality-Report-REVISED-MAY-27-2014.pdf

Pfammatter, M., Junghan, U. M., & Brenner, H. D. (2006). Efficacy of psychological therapy in schizophrenia: Conclusions from meta-analyses. *Schizo. Bull., 32*(S1), S64–S80.

Pfefferbaum, B., Varma, V., Nitiéma, P., & Newman, E. (2014). Targeting high-risk, socially influential middle school students to reduce aggression: Universal versus selective preventive intervention effects. *Child and Adolescent Psychiatric Clinics of North America, 23*(2), 363–82.

Phan, K. L., Fitzgerald, D. A., Nathan, P. J., & Tancer, M. E. (2006). Association between amygdala hyper-activity to harsh faces and severity of social anxiety in generalized social phobia. *Biol. Psychiat, 59*(5), 424–29.

Phares, V., Duhig, A. M., & Watkins, M. M. (2002). Family context: Fathers and other supporters. In S. H. Goodman & I. H. Gotlib (Eds.), *Children of depressed parents: Mechanisms of risk and implications for treatment* (pp. 203–25). Washington DC: American Psychological Association.

Phillippi, S. W., & DePrato, D. K. (2010). Assessment and treatment of juvenile offenders. In E. P. Benedek, P. Ash, & C. L. Scott (Eds.), *Principles and practice of child and adolescent forensic mental health* (pp. 361–88). Arlington, VA: American Psychiatric Publishing.

Phillips, K. (2001). Body dysmorphic disorder. In K. Phillips (Ed.), *Somatoform and factitious disorders* (pp. 67–94). Washington, DC: American Psychiatric Association.

Phillips, K. A. (2004). Treating body dysmorphic disorder using medication. *Psychiatr. Ann., 34*(12), 945–53.

Phillips, K. A. (2005). *The broken mirror: Understanding and treating body dysmorphic disorder* (2nd ed.). New York: Oxford University Press.

Phillips, K. A., & Diaz, S. F. (1997). Gender differences in body dysmorphic disorder. *J. Nerv. Ment. Dis., 185,* 570–77.

Phillips, K. A., Grant, J., Siniscalchi, J., & Albertini, R. S. (2001). Surgical and nonpsychiatric medical treatment of patients with body dysmorphic disorder. *Psychosomatics, 42,* 504–10.

Phillips, K. A., & Menard, W. (2006). Suicidality in body dysmorphic disorder: A prospective study. *Am. J. Psychiatry, 163*(7), 1280–82.

Phillips, K. A., Menard, W., & Fay, C. (2006). Gender similarities and differences in 200 individuals with body dysmorphic disorder. *Compr. Psychiatry, 47*(2), 77–87.

Phillips, K. A., Pagano, M. E., & Menard, W. (2006). Pharmacotherapy for body dysmorphic disorder: Treatment received an illness severity. *Ann. Clin. Psych., 18*(4), 251–57.

Phillips, M. L., Drevets, W. C., Rauch, S. L., & Lane, R. (2003). Neurobiology of emotion perception II: Implications for major psychiatric disorders. *Biol. Psychiatry, 54,* 515–28.

Phillips, M. L., & Sierra, M. (2003). Depersonalization disorder: A functional neuroanatomical perspective. *Stress, 6*(3), 157–65.

Phillips, S. (2002). Free to speak: Clarifying the legacy of witch hunts. *J. Psychology and Christianity, 21,* 25–37.

Phillips, W., Shannon, K. M., & Barker, R. A. (2008). The current clinical management of Huntington's disease. *Movement Disorders, 23,* 1491–504.

Pickworth, W. B., Rohrer, M. S., & Fant, R. V. (1997). Effects of abused drugs on psychomotor performance. *Exp. Clin. Psychopharm., 5*(3), 235–41.

Piet, J., & Hougaard, E. (2011). The effect of mindfulness-based cognitive therapy for prevention of relapse in recurrent major depressive disorder: A systematic review and meta-analysis. *Clin. Psychol. Rev., 31*(6), 1032–40. doi:10.1016/j.Cpr.2011.05.002

Pietrzak, R. H., Morasco, B. J., Blanco, C., Grant, B. F., & Petry, N. M. (2007). Gambling level and psychiatric and medical disorders in older adults: Results from the National Epidemiologic Survey on Alcohol and Related Conditions. *Am. J. Ger. Psychiatry, 15*(4), 301–13.

Pijl, Y., Kluiter, H., & Wiersma, D. (2001). Deinstitutionalisation in the Netherlands. *Eur. Arch. Psychiatr. Clin. Neurosci., 25*, 124–29.

Pike, K. M., & Mizushima, H. (2005). The clinical presentation of Japanese women with anorexia nervosa and bulimia nervosa: A study of the Eating Disorders Inventory-2. *Int. J. Eat. Dis., 37*, 26–31.

Pike, K. M., Dohm, F., Striegel-Moore, R. H., Wilfley, D. E., & Fairburn, C. G. (2001). A comparison of black and white women with binge eating disorder. *Am. J. Psychiatry, 158*(9), 1455–60.

Pike, K. M., Walsh, B. T., Vitousek, K., Wilson, G. T., & Bauer, J. (2003). Cognitive behavioral therapy in the posthospitalization treatment of anorexia nervosa. *Am. J. Psychiatry, 160*(11), 2046–49.

Pilkonis, P. A. (2001). Treatment of personality disorders in association with symptom disorders. In W. J. Livesley (Ed.), *Handbook of personality disorders* (pp. 541–54). New York: Guilford Press.

Pinard, G. F., & Pagani, L. (Eds.). (2001). *Clinical assessment of dangerousness: Empirical contributions.* New York: Cambridge University Press.

Pincus, A. L., & Lukowitsky, M. R. (2010). Pathological narcissism and narcissistic personality disorder. *Annu. Rev. Clin. Psychol., 6*(8), 1–28. doi:10.1146/annurev. clinpsy.121208.131215

Pineles, S. L., & Mineka, S. (2005). Attentional biases to internal and external sources of potential threat in social anxiety. *J. Abn. Psychol., 114*(2), 314–18.

Pinkham, A. E. (2014). Social cognition in schizophrenia. *J. Clinical Psychiatry, 74*(Suppl. 2), 14–19.

Piotrowski, C., Belter, R. W., & Keller, J. M. (1998). The impact of "managed care" on the practice of psychological testing: Preliminary findings. *J. Pers. Assess., 70*, 441–47.

Piper, A. (1998). Repressed memories from World War II: Nothing to forget. Examining Karon and Widener's (1997) claim to have discovered evidence for repression. *Profess. Psychol. Res. Prac., 29*, 476–78.

Piper, A., & Merskey, H. (2004a). The persistence of folly: A critical examination of dissociative identity disorder. Part I. The excesses of an improbable concept. *Canad. J. Psychiatry, 49*(9), 592–600.

Piper, A., & Merskey, H. (2004b). The persistence of folly: A critical examination of dissociative identity disorder. Part II. The defence and decline of multiple personality or dissociative identity disorder. *Canad. J. Psychiatry, 49*(10), 678–83.

Pirelli, G., Gottdiener, W. H., & Zapf, P. A. (2011). A meta-analytic review of competency to stand trial research. *Psychology, Public Policy, and Law, 17*(1), 1–53.

Pithouse, A., & Crowley, A. (2007). National standards in children's advocacy—What do young people say? *Child Care in Practice, 13*(1), 17–32.

Pittman, R. K., Rasmusson, A. M., Koenen, K. C., Shin, L. M., Orr, S. P., Gilbertson, M. W., et al. (2012). Biological studies of post-traumatic stress disorder. *Nature Reviews: Neuroscience, 13*(11), 769–87.

Pizzagalli, D. A., Nitschke, J. B., Oakes, T. R., Hendrick, A. M., Horras, K. A., Larson, C. L., et al. (2002). Brain electrical tomography in depression: The importance of symptom severity, anxiety, and melancholic features. *Biol. Psychiatry, 52*, 73–85.

Planty, M., Langton, L., Krebs, C., Berzofsky, M., & Smiley-McDonald, H. (2013). Female victims of sexual violence, 1994–2010 (Special Report NCJ 240655). Washington, DC: . U.S. Department of Justice.

Platte, P., Zelten, J. F., & Stunkard, A. J. (2000). Body image in the Old Order Amish: A people separate from "the world." *Int. J. Eat. Dis., 28*, 408–14.

Pleis, J. R., Lucas, J. W., & Ward, B. W. (2009). Summary health statistics for U.S. adults: National Health Interview Survey, 2008. National Center for Health Statistics. *Vital Health Stat., 10*(242).

Plomin, R. (1986). *Development, genetics and psychology.* Hillsdale, NJ: Erlbaum.

Plomin, R., & DeFries, J. C. (Eds.). (2003). *Behavioral genetics in the postgenomic era.* Washington, DC: American Psychological Association.

Plomin, R., DeFries, J. C., Knopik, V., & Neiderhiser, J. M. (2013). *Behavioral genetics* (6th ed.). New York: Worth.

Pogarell, O., Hamann, C., Popperl, G., Juckel, G., Chouker, M., Zaudig, M., et al. (2003). Elevated brain serotonin transporter availability in patients with obsessive-compulsive disorder. *Biol. Psychiatry, 54*(12), 1406–13.

Pogue-Geile, M. F., & Yokley, J. L. (2010). Current research on the genetic contributors to schizophrenia. *Curr. Dis. Psychol. Sci., 19*, 214–19.

Polich, J. M., Armor, D. J., & Braiker, H. B. (1981). *The course of alcoholism: Four years after treatment.* New York: Wiley Interscience.

Polivy, J., Herman, C. P., & Boivin, M. (2005). Eating disorders. In J. E. Maddux & B. A. Winstead (Eds.), *Psychopathology: Foundations for a contemporary understanding.* Mahwah, NJ: Lawrence Erlbaum Associates.

Pollack, M. H., & Simon, N. M. (2009). Pharmacotherapy for panic disorder and agoraphobia. In M. M. Antony & M. B. Stein (Eds.), *Oxford handbook of anxiety and related disorders* (pp. 295–307). New York: Oxford University Press.

Polo, C. (1997). *Del Padre Jofre al jofrismo. La Locura y sus instruciones* (pp. 125–40). Valencia: Disputacion de Valencia.

Polvan, N. (1969). Historical aspects of mental ills in Middle East discussed. *Roche Reports, 6*(12), 3.

Pomeranz, J. L., & Brownell, K. D. (2014). Can government regulate portion sizes? *New Engl. J. Med., 371*(121), 1956–58.

Ponce, F. Q., & Atkinson, D. R. (1989). Mexican-American acculturation, counselor ethnicity, counseling style, and perceived counselor credibility. *J. Couns. Psychol., 36*, 203–08.

Pope, H. G., Jr., Gruber, A. J., Hudson, J. I., Huestis, M. A., & Yurgelun-Todd, D. (2001). Neuropsychological performance in long-term cannabis users. *Arch. Gen. Psychiatry, 58*, 909–15.

Pope, H. G., Hudson, J. I., Bodkin, J. A., & Oliva, P. (1998). Questionable validity of "dissociative amnesia" in trauma victims: Evidence from prospective studies. *Brit. J. Psychiatry, 172*, 210–15.

Pope, K. W., & McNally, R. J. (2002). Nonspecific placebo effects explain the therapeutic benefits of magnets. *Scientific Review of Alternative Medicine, 6*, 10–14.

Popkin, J. (1994, September 19). Sexual predators. *U.S. News and World Report*, 65–73.

Popma, A. (2007). Assessing and managing violence risk in juveniles. *J. Am. Acad. Child Adoles. Psychiatry, 46*(9), 1231–32.

Porst, H. (2011). An overview of pharmacotherapy in premature ejaculation. *J. Sexual Medicine, 8*(Suppl. 4), 335–41.

Posner, M. I., & Rothbart, M. K. (2007). Temperament and learning. In *Educating the human brain* (pp. 121–46). Washington, DC: American Psychological Association.

Post, R. M., & Frye, M. A. (2009). Carbamazepine. In B. J. Sadock, A. A. Sadock, & P. Ruiz (Eds.), *Kaplan and Sadock's comprehensive textbook of psychiatry* (9th ed., pp. 3073–89). PA: Lippincott Williams & Wilkins.

Potash, J. B., & DePaulo, J. R. (2000). Searching high and low: A review of the genetics of bipolar disorder. *Bipolar Disorders, 2*, 8–26.

Potenza, M. N. (2002). A perspective on future directions in the prevention, treatment, and research of pathological gambling. *Psychiatr. Ann., 32*(3), 203–07.

Potochnick, S. R., & Perreira, K. M. (2010). Depression and anxiety among first-generation immigrant Latino youth. *J. Nerv. Ment. Dis., 198*(7), 470–77.

Potter, D., Summerfelt, A., Gold, J., & Buchanan, R. W. (2006). Review of clinical correlates of P50 sensory gating abnormalities in patients with schizophrenia. *Schizophrenia Bulletin, 32*, 692–700.

Poulton, R., Grisham, J. R., & Andrews, G. (2009). Developmental approaches to understanding anxiety disorders. In M. M. Antony & M. B. Stein (Eds.), *Oxford handbook of anxiety and related disorders* (pp. 123–35). New York: Oxford University Press.

Powell, L. H., Calvin, J. E., & Calvin, J. E. (2007). Effective obesity treatments. *Am. Psychol., 62*, 234–46.

Powell, L. M., Harris, J. L., & Fox, T. (2013). Food marketing expenditures aimed at youth: Putting the numbers in to context. *Am. J. Preventive Medicine, 45*, 453–61.

Powers, M. B., & Emmelkamp, P. M. G. (2008). Virtual reality exposure therapy for anxiety disorders. *J. Anx. Disord., 22*, 561–69.

Powers, M. B., Halpern, J. M., Ferenschak, M. P., Gillihan, S. J., & Foa, E. B. (2010). A meta-analytic review of prolonged exposure for posttraumatic stress disorder. *Clin. Psychol. Rev.*, n.p. doi:10.1016/j.cpr.2010.04.007

Practice guideline for the treatment of patients with Alzheimer's disease and other dementias. (2007). *Am. J. Psychiatry, 164*(Suppl.), 1–56.

Prasher, V. P., & Kirshnan, V. H. (1993). Age of onset and duration of dementia in people with Down syndrome: Integration of 98 reported cases in the literature. *Int. J. Geriat. Psychiatry, 8*(11), 915–22.

Pratchett, L. C., Pelcovitz, M. R., & Yehuda, R. (2010). Trauma and violence: Are women the weaker sex? *Psychiatr. Clin. North Am., 33*(2), 465–74.

Preiss, J., & Preiss, M. (2013). Assessing neuropsychological impairment using Reitan and Wolfson's screening battery. *Arch. Clinical Neuropsychology 28*, 492–98.

Prenoveau, J. M., Zinbarg, R. E., Craske, M. G., Mineka, S., Griffith, J. W., & Epstein, A. M. (2010). Testing a hierarchical model of anxiety and depression in adolescents: A tri-level model. *J. Anxiety Disorders, 24*, 334–44.

Prentky, R. A. (1997). Arousal reduction in sexual offenders: A review of antiandrogen interventions. *Sexual Abuse: J. Research and Treatment, 9*, 335–47.

Presnell, K., & Stice, E. (2003). An experimental test of the effect of weight-loss dieting on bulimic pathology: Tipping the scales in a different direction. *J. Abn. Psychol., 112*, 166–70.

Pretzer, J. L., & Beck, A. T. (1996). A cognitive theory of personality disorders. In J. F. Clarkin & M. F. Lenzenweger (Eds.), *Major theories of personality disorder* (pp. 36–105). New York: Guilford Press.

Pretzer, J. L., & Beck, A. T. (2005). A cognitive theory of personality disorders. In M. F. Lenzenweger & J. F. Clarkin (Eds.), *Major theories of personality disorder* (2nd ed., pp. 43–113). New York: Guilford Press.

Price, B. H., Baral, I., Cosgrove, G. R., Rauch, S. L., Nierenberg, A. A., Jenike, M. A., et al. (2001). Improvement in severe self-mutilation following limbic leucotomy: A series of 5 consecutive cases. *J. Clin. Psychiatry, 62*, 925–32.

Price, L. H., Kao, H-T., Burgers, D. E., Carpenter, L. L., & Tyrka, A. R. (2013). Telomeres and early-life stress: An overview. *Biological Psychiatry, 73*, 15–23.

Priebe, S., & Turner, T. (2003). Reinstitutionalisation in mental health care: This largely unnoticed process requires debate and evaluation. *Brit. Med. J., 326*(7382), 175–76.

Prigatano, G. P. (1992). Personality disturbances associated with traumatic brain injury. *J. Cons. Clin. Psychol., 60*(3), 360–68.

Prinstein, M. J., Borelli, J. L., Cheah, C. S. L., Simon, V. A., & Aikins, J. W. (2005). Adolescent girls' interpersonal vulnerability to depressive symptoms: A longitudinal examination of reassurance-seeking and peer relationships. *J. Abn. Psych., 114*(4), 676–88.

Prizant, B. M. (1983). Language acquisition and communicative behavior in autism: Toward an understanding of the "whole" of it. *J. Speech Hear. Dis., 46*, 241–49.

Prochaska, J. O., & Norcross, J. C. (2003). *Systems of psychotherapy* (5th ed.). Pacific Grove, CA: Brooks/Cole.

Prokopetz, J. J., & Lehmann, L. S. (2012). Redefining physicians' role in assisted dying. *New Engl. J. Med., 367*, 97–99.

Prout, H. T., & Brown, D. T. (Eds.). (2007). *Counseling and psychotherapy with children and adolescents: Theory and practice for school and clinical settings* (4th ed.). Hoboken, NJ: John Wiley & Sons.

Prudic, J. (2009). Electroconvulsive therapy. In B. J. Sadock, A. A. Sadock, & P. Ruiz (Eds.), *Kaplan and Sadock's comprehensive textbook of psychiatry* (9th ed., pp. 3285–301). PA: Lippincott Williams & Wilkins.

Pucci, A., & Finer, N. (2015). New medications for treatment of obesity: Metabolic and cardiovascular effects. *Canadian J. Cardiology, 31*, 142–52.

Purcell, R., Pathé, M., & Mullen, P. E. (2001). A study of women who stalk. *Am. J. Psychiatry, 158*(12), 2056–60.

Purdon, C. (2004). Empirical investigations of thought suppression in OCD. *J. Behav. Ther. Exper. Psychiatry, 35*(2), 121–36.

Purdon, C. (2009). Psychological approaches to understanding obsessive-compulsive disorder. In M. M. Antony & M. B. Stein (Eds.), *Oxford handbook of anxiety and related disorders* (pp. 238–49). New York: Oxford University Press.

Purdon, C., Rowa, K., & Antony, M. M. (2007). Diary records of thought suppression by individuals with obsessive-compulsive disorder. *Behavioural and Cognitive Psychotherapy, 35*(1), 47–59.

Purvis, T. E. (2012). Debating death: Religion, politics, and the Oregon Death with Dignity Act. *Yale J. Biology and Medicine, 85*, 271–84.

Puterman, E., Lin, J., Blackburn, E., O'Donovan, A., Adler, N., & Epel, E. (2010). The power of exercise: Buffering the effect of chronic stress on telomere length. *PLoS ONE, 5*(5), e10837. doi:10.10.1371/journal.pone.0010837

Putnam, F. W. (1997). *Dissociation in children and adolescents: A developmental perspective*. New York: Guilford Press.

Putnam, F. W., Gurff, J. J., Silberman, E. K., Barban, L., & Post, R. M. (1986). The clinical phenomenology of multiple personality disorder: Review of 100 recent cases. *Journal of Clinical Psychiatry, 47*, 285–93.

Puzzanchera, C. (2009, December). Juvenile arrests 2008 (Juvenile Justice Bulletin). Washington, DC: U.S. Department of Justice.

Q

Quale, A. J., & Schanke, A.-K. (2010). Resilience in the face of coping with a severe physical injury: A study of trajectories of adjustment in a rehabilitation setting. *Rehabilitation Psychology, 55*, 12–22.

Quattrocchi, M. R., & Schopp, R. F. (2005). Tarasaurus Rex: A standard of care that could not adapt. *Psychology, Public Policy, and Law, 11*(1), 109–37.

Quilty, L. C., Sellbom, M., Tackett, J. L., & Bagby, R. M. (2009). Personality trait predictors of bipolar disorder symptoms. *Psychiatr. Res., 169*(2), 159–63. doi:10.1016/j.psychres.2008.07.004

Quinsey, V. L., & Earls, C. M. (1990). The modification of sexual preferences. In W. L. Marshall, D. R. Laws, & H. E. Barbaree (Eds.), *Handbook of sexual assault: Issues, theories, and treatment of the offender* (pp. 279–95). New York: Plenum.

Quinsey, V. L., Lalumiere, M. L., Rice, M. E., & Harris, G. T. (1995). Predicting sexual-offenses. In J. C. Campbell (Ed.),*Assessing dangerousness: Violence by sexual offenders, batterers, and child abusers* (pp. 114–37). Thousand Oaks, CA: Sage Publications.

R

Rabbitt, S. M., Kazdin, A. E., & Scassellati, B. (2015). Integrating socially assistive robotics into mental healthcare interventions: Applications and recommendations for expanded use. *Clinical Psychology Review, 35*, 35–46.

Rabin, L. A., Spadaccini, A. T., Brodale, D. L., Grant, K. S., Elbulok-Charcape, M. M., & Barr, W. B. (2014). Utilization rates of computerized tests and test batteries among clinical neuropsychologists in the United States and Canada. *Professional Psychology: Research and Practice, 45*(5), 368–77. http://dx.doi.org/10.1037/a0037987

Rachman, J. G., & Hodgson, R. (1980). *Obsessions and compulsions*. Englewood Cliffs, NJ: Prentice Hall.

Rachman, S. J. (1997). Claustrophobia. In G. C. L. Davey (Ed.), *Phobias: A handbook of theory, research and treatment* (pp. 163–81). Chichester, UK: Wiley.

Rachman, S., Radomsky, A. S., & Shafran, R. (2008). Safety behaviour: A reconsideration. *Behav. Res. Ther., 46*(2), 163–73. doi:10.1016/j.brat.2007.11. 008

Rachman, S., & Shafran, R. (1998). Cognitive and behavioral features of obsessive-compulsive disorder. In R. Swinson, M. Antony, S. Rachman, & M. Richter (Eds.), *Obsessive-compulsive disorder: Theory, research, and treatment* (pp. 51–78). New York: Guilford Press.

Rachman, S. J., Shafran, R., & Riskind, J. (2006). Cognitive vulnerability to obsessive-compulsive disorders. In L. B. Alloy & J. H. Riskind (Eds.), *Cognitive vulnerability to emotional disorders* (pp. 235–49). Hillsdale, NJ: Lawrence Erlbaum Associates.

Radden, J. (Ed.). (2000). *The nature of melancholy: From Aristotle to Kristeva*. New York: Oxford University Press.

Rado, S. (1962). *Psychoanalysis of behavior II* (p. 96). New York: Grune & Stratton.

Rahm, C., Schulz-Juergensen, S., & Eggert, P. (2010). Effects of desmopressin on the sleep of children suffering from enuresis. *Acta Paediatrica, 99*(7), 1037–41.

Raine, A. (2006). Schizotypal personality: Neurodevelopmental and psychosocial trajectories. *Annu. Rev. Clin. Psych., 2*, 291–326.

Rais, M., Cahn, W., Van Haren, N., Schnack, H., Caspers, E., Hulshoff, H., et al. (2008). Excessive brain volume loss over time in cannabis-using first episode patients. *Am. J. Psychiatry, 165*, 490–96.

Rajan, K. B., Wilson, R. S., Skarupski, K. A., Mendes de Leon, C. F., & Evans, D. A. (2014). Gene–behavior interaction of depressive symptoms and the apolipoprotein E epsilon4 allele on cognitive decline. *Psychosomatic Medicine, 76*, 101–08.

Ramchandani, P., Stein, A., Evans, J., & O'Connor, T. G. (2005). Paternal depression in the postnatal period and child development: A prospective population study. *Lancet, 365*(9478), 2201–05.

Ramey, C. H., & Weisberg, R. W. (2004). The "poetical activity" of Emily Dickinson: A further test of the hypothesis that affective disorders foster creativity. *Creativity Research Journal, 16*(2–3), 173–85.

Ramseyer, F., Kupper, Z., Caspar, F., Znoj, H., & Tschacher, W. (2014). Time-series panel analysis (TSPA): Multivariate modeling of temporal associations in psychotherapy process. *J. Consult. Clin. Psychol., 82*(5), 828–38.

Ramsland, K. (2005). *Inside the minds of mass murderers: Why they kill*. Westport, CT: Praeger.

Rao, V., & Lyketsos, C. (2002). Psychiatric aspects of traumatic brain injury. *Psychiatr. Clin. North Am., 25*(1), 43–69.

Rapee, R. M. (1996). Information-processing views of panic disorder. In R. M. Rapee (Ed.), *Current controversies in the anxiety disorders* (pp. 77–93). New York: Guilford Press.

Raphael, B., & Wooding, S. (2004). Debriefing: Its evolution and current status. *Psychiatr. Clin. North Am., 27*, 407–23.

Raphael, B., Wooding, S., Stevens, G., & Connor, J. (2005). Comorbidity: Cannabis and complexity. *J. Psychiatr. Pract., 11*(3), 161–76.

Rapoport, J. (1989). *The boy who couldn't stop washing: The experience and treatment of obsessive-compulsive disorder*. New York: Penguin.

Rapp, J. T., Miltenberger, R. G., Galensky, T. L., Ellingson, S. A., Stricker, J., Garlinghouse, M., et al. (2000). Treatment of hair pulling and hair manipulation maintained by digital-tactile stimulation. *Behav. Ther., 31*, 381–93.

Rasmussen, H. N., Scheier, M. F., & Greenhouse, J. B. (2009). Optimism and physical health: A meta-analytic review. *Ann. Beh. Med., 37*, 239–56.

Rasmussen, P. R. (2005a). The histrionic prototype. In *Personality-guided cognitive-behavioral therapy* (pp. 147–66). Washington, DC: American Psychological Association.

Rasmussen, P. R. (2005b). *Personality-guided cognitive-behavioral therapy*. Washington, DC: American Psychological Association.

Rassovsky, Y., Levi, Y., Agranov, E., Seal-Kaurfan, M., Sverdlik, A., & Vakin, E. (2015). Predicting long-term outcome following traumatic brain injury (TBI). *J. Clinical and Experimental Neuropsychology, 37*, 354–66.

Rauch, S. L., Phillips, K. A., Segal, E., Makris, N., Shin, L. M., Whalen, P. J., et al. (2003). A preliminary morphometric resonance imaging study of regional brain volumes in body dysmorphic disorder. *Psych. Res. Neuroimag., 122*, 13–19.

Rauch, S. L., & Savage, C. R. (2000). Investigating cortico-striatal pathophysiology in obsessive-compulsive disorders: Procedural learning and imaging probes. In W. K. Goodman & M. V. Rudorfer et al. (Eds.), *Obsessive-compulsive disorder: Contemporary issues in treatment. Personality and clinical psychology series* (pp. 133–54). Mahwah, NJ: Erlbaum.

Rauktis, M. (2001). The impact of deinstitutionalization on the seriously and persistently mentally ill elderly: A one-year follow-up. *J. Mental Health & Aging, 7*(3), 335–48.

Raulin, M. L., & Lilienfeld, S. O. (2015). Conducting research in the field of psychopathology. In P. H. Blaney, R. F. Krueger, & T. Millon (Eds.), *Oxford textbook of psychopathology* (3rd ed., pp. 100–30). New York: Oxford University Press.

Ravussin, Y., Leibel, R. L., & Ferrante, A. W. (2014). A missing link in body weight homeostasis: The catabolic signal of the overfed state. *Cell Metabolism, 20*(4), 565–72.

Rawson, R. A., Huber, A., McCann, M., Shoptaw, S., Farabee, D., Reiber, C., et al. (2002). A comparison of contingency management and cognitive-behavioral approaches during methadone maintenance treatment for cocaine dependence. *Arch. Gen. Psychiatry., 59*(9), 817–24.

Raylu, N., & Oei, T. P. (2004). Role of culture in gambling and problem gambling. *Clinical Psychology Review, 23*, 1087–14.

Razzak, M. (2012). Paediatrics: Understanding pubertal precocity—Are kids growing up faster? *Nature Reviews Urology, 9*(12), 668–668.

Read, J. P., Wood, M. D., Kahler, C. W., Maddock, J. E., & Palfai, T. P. (2003). Examining the role of drinking motives in college student alcohol use and problems. *Psych. of Addict. Beh., 17*, 13–23.

Reardon, M. L., Lang, A. R., & Patrick, C. J. (2002). An evaluation of relations among antisocial behavior, psychopathic traits, and alcohol problems in incarcerated men. *Alcoholism, 26*(8), 1188–97.

Reck, C., Stehle, E., Reinig, K., & Mundt, C. (2009). Maternity blues as a predictor of DSM-IV depression and anxiety disorders in the first three months postpartum. *J. Affect. Disord., 113*(1–2), 77–87. doi:10.1016/j.jad.2008.05. 003

Ready, R. E., & Veague, H. B. (2014). Training in psychological assessment: Current practices of clinical psychology programs. *Professional Psychology: Research and Practice, 45*(4), 278–82. doi:10.1037/a0037439

Reed, C. R., Kajdasz, D. K., Whalen, H., Athanasiou, M. C., Gallipoli, S., & Thase, M. E. (2012). The efficacy profile of vilazodone, a novel antidepressant for the treatment of major depressive disorder. *Current Medical Research and Opinion, 28*(1), 27–39.

Reger, G., & Gahm, G. A. (2008). Virtual reality exposure therapy for active duty soldiers. *J. Clinical Psychology: In Session, 64*, 1–7.

Rehman, U.S. , Gollan, J., & Mortimer, A. R. (2008). The marital context of depression: Research, limitations, and new directions. *Clin. Psychol. Rev., 28*(2), 179–98. doi:10.1016/j.cpr.2007.04.007

Reichborn-Kjennerud, T., Czajkowski, N., Neale, M. C., Orstavik, R. E., Togersen, S., Tmabs, K., et al. (2007). Genetic and environmental influences on dimensional representations of DSM-IV cluster C personality disorders: A population-based multivariate twin study. *Psych. Med., 37*, 645–53.

Reichborn-Kjennerud, T., Czajkowski, N., Torgersen, S., Neale, M. C., Orstavik, R. E., Tambs, K., et al. (2007). The relationship between avoidant personality disorder and social phobia: A population-based twin study. *Am. J. Psychiatry, 164*, 1722–28.

Reichborn-Kjennerud, T., & Knudsen, G. P. (2015). Obsessive-compulsive personality disorder. In P. H. Blaney, R. F., Krueger, & T. Millon (Eds.), *Oxford textbook of psychopathology* (pp. 707–28). New York: Oxford University Press.

Reijntjes, A., Thomaes, S., Kamphuis, J. H., Bushman, B. J., de Castro, B. O., & Telch, M. J. (2011). Explaining the paradoxical rejection-aggression link: The mediating effects of hostile intent attributions, anger, and decreases in state self-esteem on peer rejection-induced aggression in youth. *Pers. Soc. Psychol. Bull., 37*(7), 955–63. doi:10.1177/0146167211410247

Reilly-Harrington, N. A., Alloy, L. B., Fresco, D. M., & Whitehouse, W. G. (1999). Cognitive styles and life events interact to predict bipolar and unipolar symptomatology. *J. Abn. Psychol., 108*(4), 567–78.

Reinharz, D., Lesage, A. D., & Contandriopoulos, A. P. (2000). II. Cost-effectiveness analysis of psychiatric deinstitutionalization. *Canad. J. Psychiatry, 45*, 533–38.

Reinherz, H. Z., Tanner, J. L., Berger, S. R., Beardslee, W. R., & Fitzmaurice, G. M. (2006). Adolescent suicidal ideation as predictive of psychopathology, suicide behavior, and compromised functioning at age 30. *Am. J. Psychiatry, 163*, 1226–32.

Reisberg, B., Doody, R., Stöffler, A., Schmitt, F., Ferris, S., & Möbius, H. J. (2003). Memantine in moderate-to-severe Alzheimer's disease. *New Engl. J. Med., 348*(14), 1333–41.

Reisner, A. D. (2003). The electroconvulsive therapy controversy: Evidence and ethics. *Neuropsychol. Rev., 13*, 199–219.

Reissing, E. D., Binik, Y. M., Khalife, S., Cohen, D., & Amsel, R. (2003). Etiological correlates of vaginismus: Sexual and physical abuse, sexual knowledge sexual self-schema and relationship adjustment. *J. Sex Mar. Ther., 29*(1), 47–59.

Reitan, R. M., & Wolfson, D. (1985). *The Halstead-Reitan Neuropsychological Test Battery: Theory and clinical interpretation*. Tucson, AZ: Neuropsychology Press.

Ren, W., Lui, S., Deng, W., Li, F., Li, M., Huang, X., et al. (2013). Anatomical and functional brain abnormalities in drug-naïve first-episode schizophrenia. *Am. J. Psychiatry, 170*, 1308–16.

Renner, M. J., & Mackin, R. S. (1998). A life stress instrument for classroom use. *Teaching of Psychology, 25*, 46–48.

Rescorla, R. A. (1988). Pavlovian conditioning: It's not what you think it is. *Am. Psychol., 43*, 151–60.

Resnick, R. J., Bottinelli, R., Puder-York, M., Harris, H. B., & O'Keffe, B. E. (1994). Basic issues in managed mental health services. In R. L. Lowman & R. J. Resnick (Eds.), *The mental health professional's guide to managed care*. Washington, DC: American Psychological Association.

Ressler, K. J., Rothbaum, B. O., Tannenbaum, L., Anderson, P., Graap, K., et al. (2004). Cognitive enhancers as adjuncts to psychotherapy: Use of d-cycloserine in phobic individuals to facilitate extinction of fear. *Arch. Gen. Psychiatry, 61*, 1136–44.

Reutens, S., Nielsen, O., & Sachdev, P. (2010). Depersonalization disorder. *Curr. Opin. Psychiatry, 23*(3), 278–83.

Reyes, G., & Jacobs, G. A. (Eds.). (2006). *Handbook of international disaster psychology: Interventions with special needs populations* (Vol. 4). Westport, CT: Praeger Publishers.

Ricciuti, H. N. (1993). Nutrition and mental development. *Curr. Dir. Psychol. Sci., 2*(2), 43–46.

Rice, M. E., & Harris, G. T. (2011). Is androgen deprivation therapy effective in the treatment of sex offenders? *Psychology, Public Policy, and Law, 17*, 315–32.

Rice, M. E., Quinsey, V. L., & Harris, G. T. (1991). Sexual recidivism among child molesters released from a maximum security psychiatric institution. *J. Cons. Clin. Psychol., 59*, 381–86.

Richards, J., Smith, D. J., Harvey, C. A., & Pantelis, C. (1997). Characteristics of the new long-stay population in an inner Melbourne acute psychiatric hospital. *Austral. NZ J. Psychiatry, 31*(4), 488–95.

Richards, S. R., & Sweet, R. A. (2009). Dementia. In B. J. Sadock, A. A. Sadock, & P. Ruiz (Eds.), *Kaplan and Sadock's comprehensive textbook of psychiatry* (9th ed., pp. 1167–98). PA: Lippincott Williams & Wilkins.

Richards, T., Berninger, V., Nagy, W., Parsons, A., Field, K., & Richards, A. (2005). Brain activation during language task contrasts in children with and without dyslexia: Inferring mapping processes and assessing response to spelling instruction. *Educational and Child Psychology, 22*(2), 62–80.

Riebel, K., Egloff, B., & Witthöft, M. (2013). The implicit health-related self-concept in somatoform disorders. *J. Behavior Therapy and Experimental Psychiatry, 44*, 335–42.

Rieber, R. W. (2006). *Bifurcation of the self: The history and theory of dissociation and its disorders*. New York: Springer.

Rief, W., & Barsky, A. J. (2005). Psychobiological perspectives on somatoform disorders. *Psychoneuroendocrinology, 30*, 996–1002.

Rief, W., Buhlman, U., Wilhelm, S., Borkenhagan, A., & Brahler, E. (2006). The prevalence of body dysmorphic disorder: A population-based survey. *Psych. Med., 36*(6), 877–85.

Rief, W., Hiller, W., & Margraf, J. (1998). Cognitive aspects of hypochondriasis and the somatization syndrome. *J. Abn. Psychol., 107*, 587–95.

Rief, W., & Martin, A. (2014). How to use the new DSM-5 somatic symptom disorder diagnosis in research and practice: A critical evaluation and a proposal for modifications. *Annu. Rev. Clinical Psychology, 10*, 339–67.

Riggins-Caspers, K. M., Cadoret, R. J., Knutson, J. F., & Langbehn, D. (2003). Biology-environment interaction and evocative biology-environment correlation: Contributions of harsh discipline and parental psychopathology to problem adolescent behaviors. *Behav. Gen., 33*, 205–20.

Rigozzi, C., Rossier, J., Dahourou, D., Adjahouisso, M., Ah-Kion, J., Amoussou-Yeye, D., et al. (2009). A cross-cultural study of the higher-order structures underlying personality disorders in French-speaking Africa and Switzerland. *J. Pers. Disord., 23*(2), 175–86. doi:10.1521/pedi.2009.23.2.175

Rind, B. (2003). Adolescent sexual experiences with adults: Pathological or functional? *J. Psychology & Human Sexuality, 15*(1), 5–22.

Rind, B. (2004). An empirical examination of sexual relations between adolescents and adults: They differ from those between children and adults and should be treated separately. *J. Psychology & Human Sexuality, 16*(2), 55–62.

Rind, B., Bauserman, R., & Tromovitch, P. (2000). Science versus orthodoxy: Anatomy of the congressional condemnation of a scientific article and reflections on remedies for future ideological attacks. *App. Prev. Psychol., 9*, 211–26.

Rind, B., & Tromovitch, P. (1997). A meta-analytic review of findings from national samples on psychological correlates of child sexual abuse. *J. Sex Res., 34*, 237–55.

Rind, B., & Tromovitch, P. (2007). National samples, sexual abuse in childhood, and adjustment in adulthood: A commentary on Najman, Dunne, Purdie, Boyle, and Coxeter (2005). *Arch. Sexual Behavior, 36*, 101–06.

Rind, B., Tromovitch, P., & Bauserman, R. (1998). A meta-analytic examination of assumed properties of child sexual abuse using college samples. *Psychological Bulletin, 124*, 22–53.

Rind, B., Tromovitch, P., & Bauserman, R. (2001). The validity and appropriateness of methods, analyses, and conclusions in Rind et al. (1998): A rebuttal of victimological critique from Ondersma et al. (2001) and Dallam et al. (2001). *Psychol. Bull., 127*, 734–58.

Rind, B., & Yuill, R. (2012). Hebephilia as mental disorder? A historical, cross-cultural, sociological, cross-species, non-clinical empirical, and evolutionary review. *Arch. Sexual Behav.*, pp. 1–33.

Ringwalt, C. L., Greene, J. M., Robertson, M., & McPheeters, M. (1998). The prevalence of homelessness among adolescents in the United States. *Am. J. Pub. Health, 88*(9), 1325–29.

Rinne, T., van der Brink, W., Wouters, L., & van Dyck, R. (2002). SSRI treatment of borderline personality disorder: A randomized, placebo-controlled clinical trial for female patients with borderline personality disorder. *Am. J. Psychiatry, 159*, 2048–54.

Risacher, S. L., & Saykin, A. J. (2013). Neuroimaging and other biomarkers for Alzheimer's disease: The changing landscape of early detection. *Annu. Rev. Clin. Psychol., 9*, 621–648.

Risch, N., Herrell, R., Lehner, T., Liang, K.-Y., Eaves, L., Hoh, J., et al. (2009). Interaction between the serotonin transporter gene (5-HTTLPR), stressful life events, and risk of depression: A meta-analysis. *JAMA, 301*(23), 2462–71. doi:10.1001/jama.2009.878

Ritchie, E. C. (2007). Update on combat psychiatry: From the battle front to the home front and back again. *Military Medicine, 172*, 11–14.

Rø, O., Martinsen, E. W., Hoffart, A., & Rosenvinge, J. (2005). Two-year prospective study of personality disorders in adults with longstanding eating disorders. *Int. J. Eat. Dis., 37*, 112–18.

Roberto, C. A., Larsen, P. D., Agnew, H., Baik, J., & Brownell, K. D. (2010). Evaluating the impact of menu labeling on food choices and intake. *Am. J. Pub. Health, 100*, 312–18.

Roberts, A. (1981). *The lunacy commission.* London: Middlesex University. Retrieved from http://www.mdx.ac.uk/www/study/01.htm

Roberts, G. M. P., Nestor, L., & Garavan, H. (2009). Learning and memory deficits in ecstasy users and their neural correlates during a face-learning task. *Brain Res., 1292*, 71–81.

Robin, R. W., Greene, R. L., Albaugh, B., Caldwell, A., & Goldman, D. (2003). Use of the MMPI-2 in American Indians: I. Comparability of the MMPI-2 between two tribes and with the MMPI-2 normative group. *Psychological Assessment, 15*(3), 351–59.

Robins, L. N. (1978). Aetiological implications in studies of childhood histories relating to antisocial personality. In R. D. Hare & D. Schalling (Eds.), *Psychopathic behavior: Approaches to research* (pp. 255–71). Chichester, UK: Wiley.

Robins, L. N. (1991). Conduct disorder. *J. Child Psychol. Psychiatry, 32*, 193–212.

Robins, P. M., Smith, S. M., Glutting, J. J., & Bishop, C. T. (2005). A randomized controlled trial of a cognitive-behavioral family intervention for pediatric recurrent abdominal pain. *J. Pediatric Psychology, 30*, 397–408.

Robinson, D. S., Kajdasz, D. K., Gallipoli, S., Whalen, H., Wamil, A., & Reed, C. R. (2011). A 1-year, open-label study assessing the safely and tolerability of vilazodone in patients with major depressive disorder. *J. Clin. Pharmacol., 31*, 643–46.

Robinson, E. B., Samocha, K. E., Kosmicki, J. A., McGrath, L., Neale, B. M., Perlis, R. H., & Daly, M. J. (2014). Autism spectrum disorder severity reflects the average contribution of de novo and familial influences. *Proc. Natl. Acad. Sci. USA.* doi:10.1073/pnas.1409204111

Robinson, J., Cox, G., Malonn, A., Wlliamson, M., Baldwin, G., Fletcher, K., and O'Brien, M. (2013). Treating, and responding to suicide- related behavior in young people. *Crisis, 34*(3),164–82. doi:10.1027/0227-5910/a000168

Robinson, M. S., & Alloy, L. B. (2003). Negative cognitive styles and stress-reactive rumination interact to predict depression: A prospective study. *Cog. Ther. Res., 27*(3), 275–92.

Robinson, R. G., & Downhill, J. E. (1995). Lateralization of psychopathology in response to focal brain injury. In R. J. Davidson & K. Hugdahl (Eds.), *Brain asymmetry* (pp. 693–711). Cambridge, MA: The MIT Press.

Robles, T. F., Glaser, R., & Kiecolt-Glaser, J. K. (2005). Out of balance: A new look at chronic stress, depression, and immunity. *Curr. Dis. Psychol. Sci., 14*(2), 111–15.

Rodewald, F., Wilhelm-Gobling, C., Emrich, H. M., Reddemann, L., & Gast, U. (2011). Axis-I comorbidity in female patients with dissociative identity disorder and dissociative identity disorder not otherwise specified. *J. Nerv. Ment. Dis., 199*, 122–31.

Rodin, J. (1993). *Body traps.* New York: Norton.

Roeleveld, N., Zielhuis, G. A., & Gabreels, F. (1997). The prevalence of mental retardation: A critical review of recent literature. *Develop. Med. Child Neurol., 39*(2), 125–32.

Roelofs, K., Spinhoven, P., Sandijck, P., Moene, F. C., & Hoogduin, A. L. (2005). The impact of early trauma and recent life-events on symptom severity in patients with conversion disorder. *J. Nerv. Ment. Dis., 193*, 508–14.

Roemer, L., Molina, S., & Borkovec, T. D. (1997). An investigation of worry content among generally anxious individuals. *J. Nerv. Ment. Dis., 185*(5), 314–19.

Roemer, L., Orsillo, S. M., & Barlow, D. H. (2002). Generalized anxiety disorder. In D. H. Barlow (Ed.), *Anxiety and its disorders* (2nd ed., pp. 477–15). New York: Guilford Press.

Roerrig, J. L., Steffen, K. J., Mitchelle, J. E., & Zunker, C. (2010). Laxative abuse: Epidemiology, diagnosis and management. *Drugs, 70*, 1487–503.

Rogers Wood, N. A., & Petrie, T. A. (2010). Body dissatisfaction, ethnic identity and disordered eating among African American women. *J. Couns. Psychol., 57*, 141–53.

Rogers, C. R. (1951). *Client-centered therapy.* Boston: Houghton Mifflin.

Rogers, C. R. (1959). A theory of therapy, personality, and interpersonal relationships as developed in the client-centered framework. In S. Koch (Ed.), *Psychology: A study of a science* (Vol. 3, pp. 184–256). New York: McGraw-Hill.

Rogers, C. R. (1961). The process equation of psychotherapy. *Am. J. Psychother., 15*, 27–45.

Rogers, R. (2004). Diagnostic, explanatory, and detection models of Munchausen by proxy: Extrapolations from malingering and deception. *Child Ab. Negl., 28*, 225–39.

Rogosch, F. A., Cicchetti, D., & Toth, S. L. (2004). Expressed emotion in multiple subsystems of the families of toddlers with depressed mothers. *Develop. Psychopath., 16*(3), 689–706.

Roizen, N. J. (2007). Complementary and alternative therapies for Down syndrome. *Mental Retardation and Developmental Disabilities Research Reviews, 11*(2), 149–55.

Rolak, L. A. (2001). *Neurology secrets* (3rd ed.). Philadelphia, PA: Hanley and Belfus.

Romer, D., & Walker, E. F. (2007). *Adolescent psychopathology and the developing brain.* New York: Oxford University Press.

Ronningstam, E. F. (2005). Narcissistic personality disorder: A review. In M. Maj, H. S. Akiskal, J. E. Mezzich, & A. Okasha (Eds.), *Evidence and experience in psychiatry, Vol. 8: Personality disorders* (pp. 277–27). New York: Wiley.

Ronningstam, E. F. (2009). Narcissistic personality disorder: Facing DSM-V. *Psychiatr. Ann., 39*, 111–21.

Ronningstam, E. (2012). Narcissistic personality disorder: The diagnostic process. In T. Widiger (Ed.), *The Oxford handbook of personality disorders* (pp. 527–48). Oxford, UK: Oxford University Press.

Root, T. L., Szatkiewicz, J. P., Jonassaint, C. R., Thornton, L. M., Pinheiro, A. P., Strober, M., et al. (2011). Association of candidate genes with phenotypic traits relevant to anorexia nervosa. *Eur. Eat. Disord. Rev., 19*, 487–93.

Rorvik, D. M. (1970, April 7). Do drugs lead to violence? *Look*, 58–61.

Rosema, S., Crowe, L., & Anderson, V. (2012). Social function in children and adolescents after traumatic brain injury: A systematic review 1989–2011. *J. Neurotrauma, 29*, 1277–91.

Rosen, R. C. (1996). Erectile dysfunction: The medicalization of male sexuality. *Clin. Psychol. Rev., 16*, 497–519.

Rosen, R. C., & Marin, H. (2003). Prevalence of antidepressant-associated erectile dysfunction. *J. Clin. Psychiatry, 64*, 5–10.

Rosenberg, J., & Rosenberg, S. (2006). *Community mental health: Challenges for the 21st century.* New York: Routledge.

Rosenberg, L. A., Brown, J., & Singer, H. S. (1995). Behavioral problems and severity of tics. *J. Clin. Psychol., 51*(6), 760–67.

Rosendal, M., Flemming, B., Sokolowski, I., Fink, P., Toft, T., & Olesen, F. (2005). A randomised controlled trial of brief training in assessment and treatment of somatisation: Effects on GPs' attitudes. *Family Practice, 22*, 419–27.

Rosenfarb, I. S., Goldstein, M. J., Mintz, J., & Nuechterlein, K. H. (1995). Expressed emotion and sub-clinical psychopathology observable within the transactions between schizophrenic patients and their family members. *J. Abn. Psychol., 104*, 259–67.

Rosenman, R. H., Brand, R. J., Jenkins, C. D., Friedman, M., & Straus, R. (1975). Coronary heart disease in the Western Collaborative Group study: Final follow-up experience of 8 1/2 years. *JAMA, 233*, 872–77.

Rosenthal, D. (Eds.). (1963). *The Genain quadruplets.* New York: Basic Books.

Rosenvinge, J. H., Martinussen, M., & Ostensen, E. (2000). The comorbidity or eating disorders and personality disorders: A meta-analytic review of studies published between 1983 and 1998. *Eating and Weight Disorders, 5*, 52–61.

Rosenzweig, M. R., Breedlove, S. M., & Leiman, A. L. (2002). *Biological psychology: An introduction to behavioral, cognitive, and clinical neuroscience* (3rd ed.). Sunderland, MA: Sinauer Associates.

Rosin, H. (2008, November). A boy's life. *The Atlantic.*

Rosler, A., & Witztum, E. (1998). Treatment of men with paraphilia with a long-acting analogue of gonadotropin-releasing hormone. *New Engl. J. Med., 338*, 416–22.

Ross, C. A. (1997). *Dissociative identity disorder: Diagnosis, clinical features, and treatment of multiple personality* (2nd ed.). New York: Wiley.

Ross, C. A. (1999). Dissociative disorders. In T. Millon & P. Blaney (Eds.), *Oxford textbook of psychopathology* (pp. 466–81). New York: Oxford University Press.

Ross, C. A., Miller, S. D., Bjornson, L., Reagor, P., Fraser, G. A., & Anderson, G. (1991). Abuse histories in 102 cases of multiple personality disorder. *Canadian Journal of Psychiatry, 36*, 97–101.

Ross, C. A., Norton, G. R., & Wozney, K. (1989). Multiple personality disorder: An analysis of 236 cases. *Canadian Journal of Psychiatry, 34*, 413–18.

Rossini, E. D., & Moretti, R. J. (1997). Thematic Apperception Test (TAT) interpretation: Practice recommendations from a survey of clinical psychology doctoral programs accredited by the American Psychological Association. *Profess. Psychol. Res. Prac., 28*(4), 393–98.

Rost, K., Kashner, T. M., & Smith, G. R. (1994). Effectiveness of psychiatric intervention with somatization disorder patients: Improved outcomes at reduced costs. *Gen. Hospit. Psychiatry, 16*, 381–87.

Rothbart, M. K., Ahadi, S. A., & Evans, D. E. (2000). Temperament and personality: Origins and outcomes. *J. Pers. Soc. Psychol., 78*, 122–35.

Rothbart, M. K., & Bates, J. E. (2006). Temperament. In W. Damon, R. Lerner, & N. Eisenberg (Eds.), *Handbook of child psychology, Vol. 3, Social, emotional, and personality development* (6th ed., pp. 99–106). New York: Wiley.

Rothbart, M. K., Derryberry, D., & Hershey, K. (2000). Stability of temperament in childhood: Laboratory infant assessment to parent report at seven years. In V. J. Molfese & D. L. Molfese (Eds.), *Temperament and personality development across the life span*, (pp. 85–119). Hillsdale, NJ: Erlbaum.

Rothbaum, B. O., Anderson, P., Zimand, E., Hodges, L., Lang, D., & Wilson, J. (2006). Virtual reality exposure therapy and standard (in vivo) exposure therapy in the treatment of fear of flying. *Behav. Ther., 37*(1), 80–90.

Rothbaum, B. O., & Foa, E. B. (1993). Subtypes of post-traumatic stress disorder and duration of symptoms. In J. R. T. Davidson & E. B. Foa (Eds.), *Posttraumatic stress disorder: DSM-IV and beyond* (pp. 23–35). Washington, DC: American Psychiatric Press.

Rothbaum, B. O., Hodges, L., Smith, S., Lee, J. H., & Price, L. (2000). A controlled study of virtual reality exposure therapy for the fear of flying. *J. Cons. Clin. Psychol., 68,* 1020–26.

Rothbaum, F., Weisz, J., Pott, M., Miyake, K., & Morelli, G. (2000). Attachment and culture security in the United States and Japan. *Am. Psychol., 55,* 1093–104.

Rothbaum, F., Weisz, J., Pott, M., Miyake, K., & Morelli, G. (2001). Deeper into attachment and culture. *Am. Psychol., 56,* 827–29.

Rothman, R. B., Paratilla, J. S., Dersch, C. M., Carroll, F. I., Rice, K. C., & Baumann, M. H. (2000). Methamphetamine dependence: Medication development efforts based on the dual deficit model of stimulant addiction. *Ann. NY Acad. Sci., 914,* 71–81.

Rothschild, A. J., Langlais, P. J., Schatzberg, A. F., Walsh, F. X., Cole, J. O., & Bird, E. D. (1985). The effects of a single dose of dexamethasone on monoamine and metabolite levels in rat brains. *Life Sciences, 36,* 2491.

Rothschild, A. J., Williamson, D. J., Tohen, M. F., Schatzberg, A., Andersen, S. W., Van Campen, L. E., et al. (2004). A double-blind, randomized study of olanzapine and olanzapine/fluoxetine combination for major depression with psychotic features. *J. Clin. Psychopharm., 24*(4), 365–73.

Roussos, P., & Siever, L. J. (2012). Neurobiological contributions. In T. Widiger (Ed.), *The Oxford handbook of personality disorders* (pp. 299–324). Oxford, UK: Oxford University Press.

Roy, P. K. (2014). Efficacy of combined cognitive-behavior therapy and hypnotherapy in anorexia nervosa: A case study. *Int. J. Clinical and Experimental Hypnosis, 62,* 224–30.

Roy-Byrne, P. P., & Cowley, D. S. (2002). Pharmacological treatments for panic disorder, generalized anxiety disorder, specific phobia, and social anxiety disorder. In P. E. Nathan & J. M. Gorman (Eds.), *A guide to treatments that work* (2nd ed., pp. 337–66). New York: Oxford University Press.

Roy-Byrne, P. P., & Cowley, D. S. (2007). Pharmacological treatments for panic disorder, generalized anxiety disorder, specific phobia, and social anxiety disorder. In P. E. Nathan & J. M. Gorman (Eds.), *A guide to treatments that work* (pp. 395–430). New York: Oxford University Press.

Roy-Byrne, P. P., Craske, M. G., & Stein, M. B. (2006). Panic disorder. *Lancet, 368*(9540), 1023–32.

Roy-Byrne, P. P., Davidson, K. W., Kessler, R. C., Asmundson, G. J. G., Goodwin, R. D., Kubzansky, L., et al. (2008). Anxiety disorders and comorbid medical illness. *Gen. Hosp. Psychiatry, 30*(3), 208–25. doi:10.1016/j.genhosppsych.2007.12.006

Rozin, P., Kabnick, K., Pete, E., Fischler, C., & Shields, C. (2003). The ecology of eating: Smaller portion sizes in France than in the United States help explain the French paradox. *Psychol. Sci., 14*(5), 450–54.

Rubio, R. G., & Lopez-Ibor, J. (2007). Generalized anxiety disorder: A 40-year follow-up study. *Acta Psychiatr. Scand., 115,* 372–79.

Rück, C., Karlsson, A., Steele, D., Edman, G., Meyerson, B. A., Ericson, K., et al. (2008). Capsulotomy for obsessive compulsive disorder. Long terms follow up of 25 patients. *Arch. Gen. Psychiatry, 65,* 914–21.

Rudd, M. D., Berman, A. L., Joiner, T. E., Nock, M. K., Silverman, M. M., Mandrusiak, M., et al. (2006). Warning signs for suicide: Theory, research, and clinical applications. *Suicide and Life-Threatening Behavior, 36,* 255–62.

Rudolph, K. (2008). Developmental influences on interpersonal stress generation in depressed youth. *J. Abn. Psychol., 117,* 673–79.

Rumbaut, R. (1985). Mental health and the refugee experience: A comparative study of Southeast

Asian refugees. In T. C. Owan (Ed.), *Southeast Asian mental health: Treatment, prevention, services, training, and research* (pp. 443–86). Washington, DC: National Institute of Mental Health.

Rurup, M. L., Muller, M. T., Onwuteaka-Philipsen, B. D., Van Der Heide, A., Van Der Wal, G., & Van Der Maas, P. J. (2005). Requests for euthanasia or physician-assisted suicide from older persons who do not have a severe disease: An interview study. *Psychol. Med., 35*(5), 665–71.

Ruscio, A. M., Brown, T. A., Chiu, W. T., Sareen, J., Stein, M. B., & Kessler, R. C. (2008). Social fears and social phobia in the USA: Results from the National Comorbidity Survey Replication. *Psychol. Med., 38*(1), 15–28. doi:10.1017/s0033291707001699

Ruscio, A. M., Lane, M., Roy-Byrne, P., Stang, P. E., Stein, D. J., Wittchen, H.-U., et al. (2005). Should excessive worry be required for a diagnosis of generalized anxiety disorder? Results from the US National Comorbidity Survey Replication. *Psychol. Med., 35,* 1761–72.

Ruscio, A. M., Stein, D. J., Chiu, W. T., & Kessler, R. C. (2010). The epidemiology of obsessive-compulsive disorder in the National Comorbidity Survey Replication. *Molec. Psychiatry, 15*(1), 53–63. doi:10.1038/mp.2008.94

Ruscio, J. (2004). Diagnoses and the behaviors they denote: A critical evaluation of the labeling theory of mental illness. *Scientific Review of Mental Health Practice, 3,* 5–22.

Rush, B. (1812). *Medical inquiries and observations upon diseases of the mind.* Philadelphia, PA: Grigg and Elliot.

Russell, G. F. M. (1997). The history of bulimia nervosa. In D. M. Garner & P. E. Garfinkel (Eds.), *Handbook of treatment for eating disorders* (2nd ed., pp. 11–24). New York: Guilford Press.

Russo, J., Vitaliano, P. P., Brewer, D. D., Katon, W., & Becker, J. (1995). Psychiatric disorders in spouse caregivers of care recipients with Alzheimer's disease and matched controls: A diathesis-stress model of psychopathology. *J. Abn. Psychol., 104,* 197–204.

Rutledge, P. C., & Sher, K. J. (2001). Heavy drinking from the freshman year into early young adulthood: The roles of stress, tension-reduction drinking motives, gender and personality. *J. Stud. Alcoh., 62*(4), 457–66.

Rutter, M. (1987). Psychosocial resilience and protective mechanisms. *Am. J. Orthopsychiat., 51,* 316–31.

Rutter, M. (1991). Nature, nurture, and psychopathology: A new look at an old topic. *Develop. Psychopath., 3,* 125–36.

Rutter, M. (1996). Introduction: Concepts of antisocial behavior, of cause, and of genetic influences. In G. R. Bock & J. A. Goode (Eds.), *Genetics of criminal and antisocial behavior* (Vol. 194, pp. 1–20). Chichester, UK, and New York: Wiley.

Rutter, M. (2006a). *Genes and behavior: Nature-nurture interplay explained.* Oxford, UK: Blackwell.

Rutter, M. (2006b). Review of attachment from infancy to adulthood. The major longitudinal studies. *J. Child Psychology and Psychiatry, 47*(9), 974–77.

Rutter, M. (2007). Resilience, competence, and coping. *Child Ab. Negl., 31*(3), 205–09.

Rutter, M., Kreppner, J., & Sonuga-Barke, E. (2009). Emanuel Miller lecture: Attachment insecurity, disinhibited attachment, and attachment disorders: Where do research findings leave the concepts? *J. Child Psychol. Psychiatry, 50*(5), 529–43. doi:10.1111/j.1469-7610.2009.02042.x

Rutz, W. (2001). Mental health in Europe—The World Health Organization's perspective: Diversities, possibilities, shortcomings and challenges. *Primary Care Psychiatry, 7*(3), 117–19.

Ryan-Krause, P., Yetman, R. J., & Cromwell, P. F. (2010). Attention deficit hyperactivity disorder: Part I. *J. Pediatric Health Care, 24*(3), 194–98.

Ryba, N. L., & Zapf, P. A. (2011). The influence of psychiatric symptoms and cognitive abilities on competence-related abilities. *Int. J. Forensic Mental Health, 10*(1), 29–40.

Ryder, A. G., Yang, J., Zhu, X., Yao, S., Yi, J., Heine, S. J., & Bagby, R. M. (2008). The cultural shaping of depression: Somatic symptoms in China, psychological symptoms in North America? *J. Abn. Psychol., 117,* 300–13.

Ryff, C. D., Keyes, C. L. M., & Hughes, D. L. (2003). Status inequalities, perceived discrimination, and eudiamonic well-being: Do the challenges of minority life hone purpose and growth? *J. Health Soc. Behav., 44*(3), 275–91.

S

Sacco, P., Cunningham-Williams, R. M., Ostmann, E., & Spitznagel, E. L. (2008). The association between gambling pathology and personality disorders. *J. Psychiatr. Res., 42,* 1122–30.

Sackeim, H. A., Dillingham, E. M., Prudic, J., Cooper, T., McCall, W. V., Rosenquist, P., et al. (2009). Effect of concomitant pharmacotherapy on electroconvulsive therapy outcomes: Short-term efficacy and adverse effects. *Arch. General Psychiatry, 66,* 729–37.

Sackeim, H. A., Prudic, J., Fuller, R., Keilp, J., Lavori, P. W., & Olfson, M. (2007). The cognitive effects of electroconvulsive therapy in community settings. *Neuropsychopharmacology, 32,* 244–54.

Sacks, F. M., Bray, G. A., Carey, V. J., Smith, S. R., Ryan, D. H., Anton, S. D., et al. (2009). Comparison of weight-loss diets with different compositions of fat, protein, and carbohydrates. *New Engl. J. Med., 360*(9), 859–73.

Sadock, B. J., & Sadock, V. A. (2003). *Kaplan & Sadock's synopsis of psychiatry* (8th ed.). Philadelphia, PA: Wolters Kluwer.

Sadock, B. J., Sadock, V. A., & Ruz, P. (Eds.). (2009). *Kaplan & Sadock's comprehensive textbook of psychiatry* (9th ed.). Philadelphia, PA: Wolters Kluwer.

Sadoff, R. L., & Dattilio, F. M. (2011). Competence to stand trial. In E. Y. Drogin, F. M. Dattilio, R. L. Sadoff, & T. G. Gutheil (Eds.), *Handbook of forensic assessment: Psychological and psychiatric perspectives* (pp. 3–24). Hoboken, NJ: Wiley.

Safer, D. L., Telch, C. F., & Agras, W. S. (2001). Dialectical behavior therapy for bulimia nervosa. *Am. J. Psychiatry, 158,* 632–34.

Saha, S., Chant, D., Welham, J., & McGrath, J. (2005). A systematic review of the prevalence of schizophrenia. *PLoS Med., 2,* 413–33.

Saj, A., Raz, N., Levin, N., Ben-Hur, T., & Arzy, S. (2014). Disturbed mental imagery of affected-body parts in patients with hysterical conversion paraplegia correlates with pathological limbic activity. *Brain Sciences, 4,* 396–404.

Sakai, Y., Kumano, H., Nishikawa, M., Sakano, Y., Kaiya, H., Imabayashi, E., et al. (2005). Cerebral glucose metabolism associated with a fear network in panic disorder. *Neuroreport, 16*(9), 927–31.

Saks, E. R. (2004). Refusing care: Forced treatment and the use of psychiatric advance directives. *J. Foren. Psychol. Pract., 4*(4), 35–50.

Salekin, R. T. (2006). Psychopathy in children and adolescents: Key issues in conceptualization and assessment. In C. J. Patrick (Ed.), *Handbook of the psychopathy* (pp. 389–414). New York: Guilford Press.

Salekin, R., Neumann, C., Leistico, A., & Zalot, A. (2004). Psychopathy in youth and intelligence: An investigation of Cleckley's hypothesis. *J. Clin. Child. Adol. Psych., 33,* 731–42.

Salem-Pickartz, J., & Donnelly, J. (2007). The family as a source of strength and life skill: The role of authoritative parenting in building resilience. In A. S. Loveless & T. B. Holman (Eds.), *The family in the new millennium: World voices supporting the "natural" clan* (Vol. 1, pp. 363–68). Westport, CT: Praeger Publishers/Greenwood Publishing Group.

Salkovskis, P. M. (1989). Cognitive-behavioural factors and the persistence of intrusive thoughts in obsessional problems. *Behav. Res. Ther., 27,* 677–82.

Salkovskis, P. M., & Bass, C. (1997). Hypochondriasis. In D. M. Clark & C. G. Fairburn (Eds.), *Science and practice of cognitive behaviour therapy* (pp. 313–39). Oxford, UK: Oxford University Press.

Salkovskis, P. M., Clark, D. M., & Gelder, M. G. (1996). Cognition-behavior links in the persistence of panic. *Behav. Res. Ther., 34*(5/6), 453–58.

Salkovskis, P. M., & Kirk, J. (1997). Obsessive-compulsive disorder. In D. M. Clark & C. G. Fairburn (Eds.), *Science and practice of cognitive behaviour therapy* (pp. 179–208). New York: Oxford University Press.

Salkovskis, P. M., & Wahl, K. (2003). Treating obsessional problems using cognitive behavioral therapy. In M. Reinecke & D. A. Clark (Eds.), *Cognitive therapy across the life span: Theory, research, and practice* (pp. 138–71). Cambridge, UK: Cambridge University Press.

Salkovskis, P. M., & Warwick, M. C. (2001). Meaning, misinterpretations, and medicine: A cognitive-behavioral approach to understanding health anxiety and hypochondriasis. In V. Starcevic & D. Lipsitt (Eds.), *Hypochondriasis: Modern perspectives on an ancient malady* (pp. 202–22). New York: Oxford University Press.

Salmivalli, C. (2010). Bullying and the peer group: A review. *Aggression and Violent Behavior, 15*(2), 112–20. doi:10.1016/j.avb.2009.08.007

Salmivalli, C., & Nieminen, E. (2002). Proactive and reactive aggression among school bullies, victims, and bully victims. *Aggr. Behav., 28,* 30–44.

Salmivalli, C., & Voeten, M. (2004). Connections between attitudes, group norms, and behavior in bullying situations. *Int. J. Behavioral Adjustment, 28*(3), 246–58.

Salter, A. (1949). *Conditioned reflex therapy.* New York: Creative Age Press.

Samelson, F. (1980). J. B. Watson's Little Albert, Cyril Burt's twins, and the need for a critical science. *Am. Psychol., 35,* 619–25.

Samuel, D. B., & Widiger, T. A. (2011). Conscientiousness and obsessive-compulsive personality disorder. *Personality Disorders: Theory, Research, and Treatment, 2*(3), 161–74. doi:10.1037/a0021216

Samuels, J., & Costa, P. T. (2012). Obsessive-compulsive personality disorder. In T. Widiger (Ed.), *The Oxford handbook of personality disorders* (pp. 566–81). Oxford, UK: Oxford University Press.

Samuels, J., Shugart, Y. Y., Grados, M. A., Willour, V. L., Bienvenu, O. J., Greenberg, B. D., et al. (2007). Significant linkage to compulsive hoarding on chromosome 14 in families with obsessive-compulsive disorder: Results from the OCD Collaborative Genetics Study. *Am. J. Psychiatry, 164*(3), 493–99.

Sanborn, K., & Hayward, C. (2003). Hormonal changes at puberty and the emergence of gender differences in internalizing disorders. In C. Hayward (Ed.), *Gender differences at puberty* (pp. 29–58). Cambridge, UK: Cambridge University Press.

Sanchez, L., & Turner, S. M. (2003, February). Practicing psychology in the era of managed care: Implications for practice and training. *Am. Psychol., 58*(2), 116–29.

Sanderson, W. C., Rapee, R. M., & Barlow, D. H. (1989). The influence of an illusion of control on panic attacks induced via inhalation of 5. 5%-carbon dioxide-enriched air. *Arch. Gen. Psychiatry, 46,* 157–62.

Sandfort, T. G. M., de Graaf, R., Bijl, R. V., & Schnabel, P. (2001). Same-sex sexual behavior and psychiatric disorders: Findings from the Netherlands mental health survey and incidence study (NEMESIS). *Arch. Gen. Psychiatry, 58,* 85–91.

Sandnabba, N. K., Santtila, P., Alison, L., & Nordling, N. (2002). Demographics, sexual behaviour, family background and abuse experiences of practitioners of sadomasochistic sex: A review of recent research. *Sexual and Relationship Therapy, 17*(1), 39–55.

Sandweiss, D. A., Slymen, D. J., Leard-Mann, C. A., Smith, B., White, M. R., Boyko, E. J., et al. (2011). Preinjury psychiatric status, injury severity, and post-deployment posttraumatic stress disorder. *Arch. Gen. Psychiatry, 68,* 496–504.

Sanislow, C. A., da Cruz, K., Gianoli, M. O., & Reagan, E. (2012). Avoidant personality disorder, traits and type. In T. Widiger (Ed.), *The Oxford handbook of personality disorders* (pp. 549–65). Oxford, UK: Oxford University Press.

Sansone, R., Schumacher, D., Wiederman, M., & Routsong-Weichers, L. (2008). The prevalence of binge eating disorder and borderline symptomatology among gastric surgery patients. *Eating Behaviors, 9*(2), 197–202.

Santos, F. (2012, August 7). Loughner pleads guilty in 2011 Tucson shootings. *New York Times.*

Sapienza, J. K., & Masten, A. S. (2011). Understanding and promoting resilience in children and youth. *Curr. Opin. Psychiatry, 24*(4), 267–73.

Sapolsky, R. M. (2000). Glucocorticoids and hippocampal atrophy in neuropsychiatric disorders. *Arch. Gen. Psychiatry, 57,* 925–35.

Sar, V., Akyüz, G., Kundakçi, T., Kiziltan, E., & Dogan, O. (2004). Childhood trauma, dissociation, and psychiatric comorbidity in patients with conversion disorder. *Am. J. Psychiatry, 161*(12), 2271–76.

Sarbin, T. R. (1997). On the futility of psychiatric diagnostic manuals (DSMs) and the return of personal agency. *App. Prev. Psychol., 6*(4), 233–43.

Sartorius, N., Kaelber, C. T., Cooper, J. E., Roper, M. T., Rae, D. S., Gulbinat, W., et al. (1993). Progress toward achieving a common language in psychiatry: Results from the field trial of the clinical guidelines accompanying the WHO classification of mental and behavioral disorders in ICD-10. *Arch. Gen. Psychiatry, 50,* 115–24.

Sarwer, D. B., Brown, G. K., & Evans, D. L. (2007). Cosmetic breast augmentation and suicide. *Am. J. Psychiatry, 164,* 1006–13.

Sarwer, D. B., Gibbons, L. M., & Crerand, C. E. (2004). Treating body dysmorphic disorder with cognitive-behavior therapy. *Psychiatr. Ann., 34,* 934–41.

Sashidharan, S. P. (1993). Afro-Caribbeans and schizophrenia: The ethnic vulnerability hypothesis re-examined. *Int. Rev. Psychiatry, 5,* 129–43.

Satel, S. (2007). The trouble with traumatology. *The Weekly Standard, 12*(22), 14–15.

Sauter, S. L., Murphy, L. R., & Hurrell, J. J., Jr. (1990). Prevention of work-related psychological disorders: A national strategy proposed by the National Institute for Occupational Safety and Health (NIOSH). *Am. Psychol., 45*(10), 1146–58.

Savin-Williams, R. C. (2006). Who's gay? Does it matter? *Curr. Dis. Psychol. Sci., 15*(1), 40–44.

Saxena, S. (2007). Is compulsive hoarding a genetically and neurobiologically discrete syndrome? Implications for diagnostic classification. *Am. J. Psychiatry, 164*(3), 380–84.

Saxena, S. (2008). Recent advances in compulsive hoarding. *Curr. Psychiatr. Reports, 10*(4), 297–303. doi:10.1007/s11920-008-0048-8

Saxena, S., Ayers, C. R., Maidment, K. M., Vapnik, T., Wetherell, J. L., & Bystritsky, A. (2011). Quality of life and functional impairment in compulsive hoarding. *J. Psychiatric Research, 45,* 475–80.

Saxena, S., Brody, A. L., Ho, M. L., Alborzian, S., Maidment, K. M., Zohrabi, N., et al. (2002). Differential cerebral metabolic changes with paroxetine treatment of obsessive-compulsive disorder vs major depression. *Arch. Gen. Psychiatry, 59,* 250–61.

Saxena, S., & Feusner, J. D. (2006). Toward a neurobiology of body dysmorphic disorder. *Primary Psychiatry, 13*(7), 41–48.

Saxena, S., Gorbis, E., O'Neill, J., Baker, S. K., Mandelkern, M. A., Maidment, K. M., et al. (2009). Rapid effects of brief intensive cognitive-behavioral therapy on brain glucose metabolism in obsessive-compulsive disorder. *Molec. Psychiatry, 14*(2), 197–205. doi:10.1038/sj. mp.4002134

Saxena, S., & Rauch, S. L. (2000). Functional neuro-imaging and the neuroanatomy of obsessive-compulsive disorder. *Psychiatr. Clin. North Am., 23*(3), 563–86.

Saykin, A. J., Wishart, H. A., Rabin, L. A., Santulli, R. B., Flashman, L. A., West, J. D., et al. (2006). Older adults with cognitive complaints show brain atrophy similar to that of amnestic MCI. *Neurology, 67*(5), 834–42.

Sbarra, D. A., Boals, A., Mason, A. E., Larson, G. M., & Mehl, M. R. (2013). Expressive writing can impede emotional recover following marital separation. *Clinical Psychological Science, 1,* 120–34.

Sbrocco, T., & Barlow, D. H. (1996). Conceptualizing the cognitive component of sexual arousal: Implications for sexuality research and treatment. In P. M. Salkovskis (Ed.), *Frontiers of cognitive therapy* (pp. 419–49). New York: Guilford Press.

Scales, P. C., & Leffert, N. (1999). Developmental assets. *A synthesis of the scientific research on adolescent development.* Minneapolis, MN: Search Institute.

Scannell, E. D., Quirk, M. M., Smith, K., Maddern, R., & Dickerson, M. (2000). Females' coping styles and control over poker machine gambling. *J. Gambling Studies, 16*(4), 417–32.

Scepkowski, L. A., Wiegel, M., Bach, A. K., Weisberg, R. B., Brown, T. A., & Barlow, D. H. (2004). Attributions for sexual situations in men with and without erectile disorder: Evidence from a sex-specific attributional style measure. *Arch. Sex. Behav., 33,* 559–69.

Schacter, D. L., Norman, K. A., & Koutstaal, W. (2000). The cognitive neuroscience of constructive memory. In D. F. Bjorklund (Ed.), *False-memory creation in children and adults* (pp. 129–68). Mahwah, NJ: Erlbaum.

Schafer, I., & Najavits, L. M. (2007). Clinical challenges in the treatment of patients with posttraumatic stress disorder and substance abuse. *Current Opinions in Psychiatry, 20,* 614–18.

Schapiro, M. B., & Rapoport, S. I. (1987). "Pathological similarities between Alzheimer's disease and Down's syndrome: Is there a genetic link?": Commentary. *Integr. Psychiatry, 5,* 167–69.

Scharnberg, K. (2007). As bullies go online, schools crack down. *Chicago Tribune,* pp. 1.1–1.20.

Scher, C. D., Ingram, R. E., & Segal, Z. V. (2005). Cognitive reactivity and vulnerability: Empirical evaluation of construct activation and cognitive diatheses in unipolar depression. *Clin. Psychol. Rev., 25,* 487–510.

Scherrer, J. F., Xian, H., Kapp, J. M. K., Waterman, B., Shah, K. R., Volberg, R., et al. (2007). Association between exposure to childhood and lifetime traumatic events and lifetime pathological gambling in a twin cohort. *J. Nerv. Ment. Dis., 195*(1), 72–78.

Scheurich, A. (2005). Neuropsychological functioning and alcohol dependence. *Curr. Opin. Psychiatry, 18*(3), 319–23.

Schildkraut, J. J. (1965). The catecholamine hypothesis of affective disorders: A review of supporting evidence. *Am. J. Psychiatry, 122,* 509–22.

Schilt, T., Koeter, M. W., Smal, J. P., Gouwetor, M. N., van den Brink, W., & Schmand, B. (2010). Long-term neuropsychological effects of ecstasy in middle-aged ecstasy/polydrug users. *Psychopharmacology, 207*(4), 583–91.

Schiltz, K., Witzel, J., Northoff, G., Zierhut, K., Gubka, U., Fellmann, H., et al. (2007). Brain pathology in pedophilic offenders. *Arch. Gen. Psychiatry, 64*, 737–46.

Schizophrenia Working Group of the Psychiatric Genomics Consortium. (2014). Biological insights from 108 schizophrenia-associated genetic loci. *Nature, 511*, 421–26.

Schliebs, R., & Arendt, T. (2006). The significance of the cholinergic system in the brain during aging and Alzheimer's disease. *J. Neural Transmission, 113*, 1625–44.

Schmand, B., et al. (1997). The effects of intelligence and education on the development of dementia: A test of the brain reserve hypothesis. *Psychol. Med., 27*(6), 1337–44.

Schmidt, N. B., Lerew, D. R., & Jackson, R. J. (1997). The role of anxiety sensitivity in the pathogenesis of panic: Prospective evaluation of spontaneous panic attacks during acute stress. *J. Abn. Psychol., 106*, 355–65.

Schmidt, N. B., Richey, J. A., Buckner, J. D., & Timpano, K. R. (2009). Attention training for generalized social anxiety disorder. *J. Abn. Psychol., 118*(1), 5–14. doi:10.1037/a0013643

Schmidt, N. B., Richey, J. A., Maner, J. K., & Woolaway-Bickel, K. (2006). Differential effects of safety in extinction of anxious responding to a CO_2 challenge in patients with panic disorder. *J. Abn. Psych., 115*(2), 341–50.

Schmidt, U., Magill, N., Renwick, B., Keyes, A., Kenyon, M., Dejong, H., et al. (2015). The Maudsley Outpatient Study of Treatments for Anorexia Nervosa and Related Conditions (MOSAIC): Comparison of the Maudsley Model of Anorexia Nervosa Treatment for Adults (MANTRA) with Specialist Supportive Clinical Management (SSCM) in outpatients with broadly defined anorexia nervosa: A randomized controlled trial. *J. Consulting and Clinical Psychology, 83*, 796–807.

Schmit, D. (2005). Re-visioning antebellum American psychology: The dissemination of Mesmerism, 1836–1854. *History of Psychology, 8*, 403–34.

Schmitz, J. M., Stotts, A. L., Sayre, S. L., DeLaune, K. A., & Grabowski, J. (2004). Treatment of cocaine-alcohol dependence with naltrexone and relapse prevention therapy. *Journal on Addictions, 13*(4), 333–41.

Schneider, F., Backes, V., & Mathiak, K. (2009, November). Brain imaging: On the way toward a therapeutic discipline. *Eur. Arch. Psychiatr. Clin. Neurosci., 259*(Suppl. 2), S143–47.

Schneider, M. L. (1992). The effects of mild stress during pregnancy on birthweight and neuromotor maturation in Rhesus monkey infants (Macaca mulatta). *Inf. Behav. Develop., 15*, 389–403.

Schneider, R. H., Alexander, C. N., Staggers, F., Orme-Johnson, D. W., Rainforth, M., Salerno, J. W., et al. (2005). A randomized controlled trial of stress reduction in African-Americans treated for hypertension for over one year. *Am. J. Hypertension, 18*, 88–98.

Schneiderman, N., Ironson, G., & Siegel, S. D. (2005). Stress and health: Psychological, behavioral, and biological determinants. *Annu. Rev. Clinical Psychology, 1*, 607–28.

Shneidman, E. S. (1996). *The suicidal mind*. Oxford University Press: New York.

Schnurr, P. P., Friedman, M. J., Engel, C. C., Foa, E. B., Shea, M. T., Chow, B. K., et al. (2007). Cognitive behavioral therapy for posttraumatic stress disorder in women. A randomized clinical trial. *JAMA, 297*, 820–30.

Schoeneman, T. J. (1984). The mentally ill witch in textbooks of abnormal psychology: Current status and implications of a fallacy. *Profess. Psychol., 15*(3), 299–314.

Schonberg, M. A., & Shaw, D. S. (2007). Risk factors for boy's conduct problems in poor and lower-middle-class neighborhoods. *J. Abn. Child Psychol., 35*(5), 759–72.

Schotte, D. E., & Clum, G. A. (1987). Problem solving skills in suicidal psychiatry patients. *J. Consulting and Clinical Psychology, 55*, 49–54.

Schreiber, F. R. (1973). *Sybil*. New York: Warner Paperback.

Schroeder, C. S., & Gordon, B. N. (2002). *Assessment and treatment of childhood problems: A clinician's guide* (2nd ed.). New York: Cambridge University Press.

Schudson, M. (1995). Collective memory and modes of distortion. In D. Schachter, J. Coyle, L. Sullivan, M. Mesulam, & G. Fishbach (Eds.), *Memory distortion: Interdisciplinary perspectives*. Cambridge, MA: Harvard University Press.

Schulte-Koerne, G. (2001). Genetics of reading and spelling disorder. *J. Child Psychol. Psychiatry & Allied Disciplines, 42*(8), 985–97.

Schultz, S. K. (2008). Atypical antipsychotic medications in Alzheimer's disease: Effectiveness versus expectations. *Am. J. Psychiatry, 165*, 787–89.

Schulz, R., Drayer, R. A., & Rollman, B. L. (2002). Depression as a risk factor for the non-suicide mortality in the elderly. *Biol. Psychiatry, 52*(3), 205–25.

Schulze-Rauschenbach, S. C., Harms, U., Schlaepfer, T. E., Maier, W., Falkai, P., & Wagner, M. (2005). Distinctive neurocognitive effects of repetitive transcranial magnetic stimulation and electroconvulsive therapy in major depression. *Brit. J. Psychiatry, 186*, 410–16.

Schupf, N., Kapell, D., Lee, J. H., Ottman, R., & Mayeux, R. (1994). Increased risk of Alzheimer's disease in mothers of adults with Down's syndrome. *Lancet, 344*(8919), 353–56.

Schupf, N., Kapell, D., Nightingale, B., Lee, J. H., Mohlenhoff, J., Bewley, S., et al. (2001). Specificity of the fivefold increase in AD in mothers with Down syndrome. *Neurology, 57*(6), 979–84.

Schupp, H. T., Öhman, A., Junghofer, M., Weike, A. I., Stockburger, J., & Hamm, A. O. (2004). The facilitated processing of threatening faces: An ERP analysis. *Emotion, 4*(2), 189–200.

Schvey, N. A., Puhl, R. M., & Brownell, K. D. (2011). The impact of weight stigma on caloric consumption. *Obesity (Silver Spring), 19*(10), 1957–62.

Schvey, N. A., Puhl, R. M., Levandoski, K. A., & Brownell, K. D. (2013). The influence of a defendant's body weight on perceptions of guilt. *Int. J. Obesity, 37*, 1275–81.

Schwarte, A. R. (2008). Fragile x syndrome. *School Psychology Quarterly, 23*(2), 290–300.

Schwartz, C. E., Snidman, N., & Kagan, J. (1996). Early childhood temperament as a determinant of externalizing behavior in adolescence. *Develop. Psychopath., 8*(3), 527–37.

Schwartz, D., Dodge, K. A., & Coie, J. D. (1993). The emergence of chronic peer victimization in boys' play groups. *Child Develop., 64*, 1755–72.

Schwinn, T. M., Schinke, S. P., & Di Noia, J. (2010). Preventing drug abuse among adolescent girls: Outcome data from an Internet-based intervention. *Prevention Science, 11*(1), 24–32.

Scott, C. L. (Ed.). (2010). *Handbook of correctional mental health* (2nd ed.). Arlington, VA: American Psychiatric Publishing.

Scott, C. L., & Holmberg, T. (2003). Castration of sex offenders: Prisoner's rights versus public safety. *J. Am. Acad. Psychiatr. Law, 31*, 502–09.

Scott, J., Varghese, D., & McGrath, J. (2010). As the twig is bent, the tree inclines: Adult mental health consequences of childhood adversity. *Arch. Gen. Psychiatry, 67*(2), 111–12.

Scott, M. J., & Stradling, S. G. (2006). *Counseling for posttraumatic stress disorder* (3rd ed.). Thousand Oaks, CA: Sage Publications.

Scott, N., Lakin, C., & Larson, S. A. (2008). The 40th anniversary of deinstitutionalization in the United States: Decreasing state institutional populations, 1967–2007. *Trends and Milestones, 46*, 402–05.

Scull, A. (1996). *The most solitary of afflictions: Madness and society in Britain*. New Haven, CT: Yale University Press.

Scull, A. (2005). *Madhouse: A tragic tale of megalomania and modern medicine*. New Haven, CT: Yale University Press.

Seal, K. H., Metzler, T. J., Gima, K. S., Bertenthal, D., Maguen, S., & Marmar, C. R. (2009). Trends and risk factors for mental health diagnoses among Iraq and Afghanistan veterans using Department of Veterans Affairs health care, 2002–08. *Am. J. Public Health, 99*, 1651–58.

Sears, S. R., & Stanton, A. L. (2001). Physician-assisted dying: Review of issues and roles for health psychologists. *Health Psychol., 20*(4), 302–10.

Seawell, A. H., Toussaint, L. L., & Cheadle, A. C. D. (2014). Prospective associations between unforgivingness and physical health and positive mediating mechanisms in a nationally representative sample of older adults. *Psychology and Health, 29*, 375–89.

Seedat, S., Scott, K. M., Angermeyer, M. C., Berglund, P., Bromet, E. J., Brugha T. S., et al. (2009). Cross-national associations between gender and mental disorders in the World Health Organization World mental health surveys. *Arch. General Psychiatry, 66*, 785–95.

Seeley, M. F. (1997). The role of hotlines in the prevention of suicide. In R. W. Maris, M. M. Silverman, & S. S. Canetton (Eds.), *Review of suicidology, 1997* (pp. 251–70). New York: Guilford Press.

Seeman, P. (2011). All roads to schizophrenia lead to dopamine supersensitivity and elevated dopamine D_2 high receptors. *CNS Neuroscience and Therapeutics, 17*, 118–32.

Segal, N. L. (2005). Twins reared apart design. In B. Everitt & D. C. Howell (Eds.), *Encyclopedia of statistics in behavioral science* (pp. 2072–76). Chester, UK: John Wiley & Sons.

Segal, Z. V., Williams, J. M. G., & Teasdale, J. T. (2002). *Mindfulness-based cognitive therapy for depression: A new approach to preventing relapse*. New York: Guilford Press.

Segerstrom, S. C., & Miller, G. E. (2004). Psychological stress and the human immune system: A meta-analytic study of 30 years of inquiry. *Psychol. Bull., 130*, 610–30.

Segraves, R., & Woodard, T. (2006). Female hypoactive sexual desire disorder: History and current status. *J. Sexual Medicine, 3*, 408–18.

Segraves, T., & Althof, S. (2002). Psychotherapy and pharmacotherapy for sexual dysfunctions. In P. E. Nathan & J. M. Gorman (Eds.), *A guide to treatments that work* (pp. 497–524). New York: Oxford University Press.

Seidman, E. (2003). Fairweather and ESID: Contemporary impact and a legacy for the twenty-first century. *Am. J. Community Psychol., 32*(3–4), 371–75.

Seifert, K. (2003). Childhood trauma: Its relationship to behavioral and psychiatric disorders. *Forensic Examiner, 12*, 27–33.

Selassie, A. W., Zaloshnja, E., Langlois, J. A., Miller, T., Jones, P., & Steiner, C. (2008). Incidence of long-term disability following traumatic brain injury hospitalization, United States, 2003. *J. Head Trauma Rehabilitation, 23*, 123–31.

Selby, E. A., Bender, T. W., Gordon, K. H., Nock, M. K., & Joiner, T. E., (2012). Non-suicidal self-injury NNSSI) disorder: A preliminary study. *Personality Disorders: Theory, Research, and Treatment, 3*, 167–75.

Selemon, L. D. (2004). Increased cortical neuronal density in schizophrenia. *Am. J. Psychiatry, 161,* 9.

Selemon, L. D., Rajkowska, G., & Goldman-Rakic, P. S. (1995). Abnormally high neuronal density in the schizophrenic cortex. *Arch. Gen. Psychiatry, 52,* 805–18.

Seligman, M. E. P. (1971). Phobias and preparedness. *Behav. Ther., 2,* 307–20.

Seligman, M. E. P. (1974). Depression and learned helplessness. In R. J. Friedman & M. M. Katz (Eds.), *The psychology of depression: Contemporary theory and research.* Washington, DC: Hemisphere.

Seligman, M. E. P. (1975). *Helplessness: On depression, development, and death.* San Francisco: Freeman.

Selkoe, D. J. (2012). Preventing Alzheimer's disease. *Science, 337,* 1488–92.

Selling, L. S. (1943). *Men against madness.* New York: Garden City Books.

Selye, H. (1956). *The stress of life.* New York: McGraw-Hill.

Selye, H. (1976). *Stress in health and disease.* Woburn, MA: Butterworth.

Senft, R. A., Polen, M. R., Freeborn, D. K., & Hollis, J. F. (1997). Brief intervention in a primary care set ting for hazardous drinkers. *Am. J. Prev. Med., 13*(6), 464–70.

Sentse, M., Lindenberg, S., Omvlee, A., Ormel, J., & Veenstra, R. (2010). Rejection and acceptance across contexts: Parents and peers as risks and buffers for early adolescent psychopathology. The TRAILS study. *J. Abn. Child Psychol., 38*(1), 119–30. doi:10.1007/s10802-009-9351-z

Serbin, L. A., & Karp, J. (2004). The intergenerational transfer of psychosocial risk: Mediators of vulnerability and resilience. *Annu. Rev. Psychol., 55,* 333–63.

Sernyak, D. L., Leslei, D. L., Alarcon, R. D., Losonczy, M. F., & Rosenheck, R. (2002). Association of diabetes mellitus with use of atypical neuroleptics in the treatment of schizophrenia. *Am. J. Psychiatry, 159,* 561–66.

Serretti, A., & Chiesa, A. (2009). Treatment-emergent sexual dysfunction related to antidepressants: A meta-analysis. *J. Clinical Psychopharmacology, 29,* 259–66.

Seto, M. (2004). Pedophilia and sexual offenses against children. *Annu. Rev. Sex Res., 15,* 329–69.

Seto, M. C. (2012). Is pedophilia a sexual orientation? *Arch. Sexual Behavior, 41,* 231–36.

Seto, M. C., Cantor, J. M., & Blanchard, R. (2006). Child pornography offenses area valid diagnostic indicator of pedophilia. *J. Abn. Psych., 115*(3), 610–15.

Seto, M. C., Lalumiere, M. L., & Kuban, M. (1999). The sexual preferences of incest offenders. *J. Abn. Psychol., 108,* 267–72.

Seto, M. C., Marques, J. K., Harris, G. T., Chaffin, M., Lalumiere, M. L., Miner, M. H., et al. (2008). Good science and progress in sex offender treatment are intertwined: A response to Marshall and Marshall (2007). *Sexual Abuse: J. Research and Treatment, 20*(3), 247–55.

Sewell, D. W., Jeste, D. V., Atkinson, J. H., Heaton, R. K., Hesselink, J. R., Wiley, C., et al. (1994). HIV-associated psychosis: A study of 20 cases. *Am. J. Psychiatry, 151*(2), 237–42.

Shadish, W. R., Matt, G. E., Navarro, A. M., & Phillips, G. (2000). The effects of psychological therapies under clinically-representative conditions: A meta-analysis. *Psychol. Bull., 126,* 512–29.

Shaffer, T. W., Erdberg, P., & Haroian, J. (1999). Current nonpatient data for the Rorschach, WAIS-R and MMPI-2. *J. Pers. Assess., 73,* 305–16.

Shalev, A. Y. (2009). Posttraumatic stress disorder and stress-related disorders. *Psychiatr. Clin. North Am., 32*(3), 687–704.

Shalev, A. Y., & Freedman, S. (2005). PTSD following terrorist attacks: A prospective evaluation. *Am. J. Psychiatry, 162,* 1118–91.

Shapiro, D. N., Chandler, J., & Mueller, P. A. (2013). Using Mechanical Turk to study clinical populations. *Clinical Psychological Science, 2,* 213–20.

Shapiro, F. (1996). Eye movement desensitization and reprocessing (EMDR): Evaluation of controlled PTSD research. *J. Behav. Ther. Exper. Psychiatry, 27,* 209–18.

Sharif, Z., Bradford, D., Stroup, S., & Lieberman, J. (2007). Pharmacological treatment of schizophrenia. In P. E. Nathan & J. M. Gorman (Eds.), *A guide to treatments that work* (pp. 203–42). New York: Oxford University Press.

Sharma, V., Burt, V. K., & Ritchie, H. L. (2009). Bipolar II postpartum depression: Detection, diagnosis, and treatment. *Am. J. Psychiatry, 166*(11), 1217–21. doi:10.1176/appi. ajp.2009.08121902

Sharp, K. L., Williams, A. J., Rhyner, K. T. & Ilardi, S. S. (2013). The clinical interview. In K. F. Geisinger, B. A. Bracken, J. F. Carlson, J.-I. Hansen, N. R. Kuncel, S. P. Reise, & M. C. Rodriguez (Eds.), *APA handbook of testing and assessment in psychology, Vol. 2: Testing and assessment in clinical and counseling psychology* (APA handbooks in psychology) (pp. 103–17). Washington, DC: American Psychological Association. doi:10.1037/14048-007

Sharp, S. I., McQuillin, A., & Gurling, H. M. (2009). Genetics of attention-deficit hyperactivity disorder (ADHD). *Neuropharmacol., 57*(7–8), 590–600.

Shaw, J. A. (2003). Children exposed to war/terrorism. *Clin. Child Fam. Psych. Rev., 6*(4), 237–46.

Shaw, P., Eckstrand, K., Sharp, W., Blumenthal, J., Lerch, J. P., Greenstein, D., et al. (2007). Attention-deficit/hyperactivity disorder is characterized by a delay in cortical maturation. *Proc. Natl. Acad. Sci. USA, 104*(49), 19649–54. doi:10.1073/pnas.0707741104

Shedler, J. (2010). The efficacy of psychodynamic psychotherapy. *Am. Psychol., 65*(2), 98–109. doi:10.1037/a0018378

Sheehan, D. Z. (1982). Panic attacks and phobias. *New Engl. J. Med., 307,* 156–58.

Sheehan, D. Z. (1983). *The anxiety disease.* New York: Bantam Books.

Sheets, E., & Craighead, W. E. (2007). Toward an empirically based classification of personality pathology. *Clin. Psychol. Sci. Prac., 14*(2), 77–93.

Shenton, M. E., Dickey, C. C., Frumin, M., & McCarley, R. W. (2001). A review of MRI findings in schizophrenia. *Schizophrenia Research, 49,* 1–52.

Sheppard, D. P., Iudicello, J. E., Bondi, M. W., Doyle, K. L., Morgan, E. E., Massman, P. J., et al. (2015, July 3). Elevated rates of mild cognitive impairment in HIV disease. *J. Neurovirol.* [Epub ahead of print]. doi:10.1007/s13365-0366-7

Sheps, D. S., McMahon, R. P., Becker, L., Camey, R. M., Freeland, K. E., Cohen, J. D., et al. (2002). Mental stress-induced ischemia and all-cause mortality in patients with coronary artery disease. *Circulation, 105,* 1700–84.

Sher, K. J., Bartholow, B. D., & Nanda, S. (2001). Short and long term effects of fraternity and sorority membership on heavy drinking: A social norms perspective. *Psychol. Addict. Behav., 15,* 42–51.

Sher, K., Grekin, E. R., & Williams, N. A. (2005). The development of alcohol use disorders. *Annu. Rev. Clin. Psychol., 1*(1), 493–523.

Sher, K. J., Wood, M. D., Wood, P. D., & Raskin, G. (1996). Alcohol outcome expectancies and alcohol use: A latent variable cross-lagged panel study. *J. Abn. Psychol., 105*(4), 561–74.

Shergill, S. S., Brammer, M. J., Williams, S. C. R., Murray, R. M., & McGuire, P. K. (2000). Mapping auditory hallucinations in schizophrenia using functional magnetic resonance imaging. *Arch. Gen. Psychiatry, 57,* 1033–38.

Sheridan, M. A., Fox, N. A., Zeanah, C. H., McLaughlin, K. A., & Nelson, C. A. (2012). Variation in neural development as a result of exposure to institutionalization early in childhood. *Proc. Natl. Acad. Sci. USA, 109,* 12927–32.

Shields, A., Ryan, R. M., & Cicchetti, D. (2001). Narrative representations of caregivers and emotion dysregulation as predictors of maltreated children's rejection by peers. *Develop. Psychol., 37,* 321–37.

Shif, J. I. (2006). Conditions of successful task solving in high school students with mental retardation (on the material of grammar task). *Cultural-Historical Psychology, 3,* 93–100.

Shiffman, S., Ferguson, S. G., Gwaltney, C. J., Balabanis, M. H., & Shadel, W. G. (2006). Reduction of abstinence-induced withdrawal and craving using high-dose nicotine replacement therapy. *Psychopharmacology, 184*(3–4), 637–44.

Shim, Y. S., & Morris, J. C. (2011). Biomarkers predicting Alzheimer's disease in cognitively normal aging. *J. Clin. Neurol, 7,* 60–68.

Shimada-Sugimoto, M., Otowa, T., & Hettema, J. M. (2015, March 12). Genetics of anxiety disorders: Genetic epidemiological and molecular studies in humans. *Psychiatry and Clinical Neurosciences, 69*(7), 388–401. doi:10.1111/pcn.12291

Shin, L. M., & Liberzon, I. (2009). The neurocircuitry of fear, stress, and anxiety disorders. *Neuropsychopharmacol., 35*(1), 169–91. doi:10.1038/npp.2009.83

Shiner, R. L. (2009). The development of personality disorders: Perspectives from normal personality development in childhood and adolescence. *Develop. Psychopath., 21*(3), 715–34. doi:10.1017/S0954579409000406

Shively, C. A., Clarkson, T. B., & Kaplan, J. R. (1989). Social deprivation and coronary artery atherosclerosis in female cynomolgus monkeys. *Atherosclerosis, 77,* 69–76.

Shonk, S. M., & Cicchetti, D. (2001). Maltreatment, competency deficits, and risk for academic and behavioral maladjustment. *Develop. Psychol., 37,* 3–17.

Shore, D. A. (Ed.). (2007). *The trust crisis in healthcare: Causes, consequences, and cures.* New York: Oxford University Press.

Shoulson, I., & Young, A. B. (2011). Milestones in Huntington disease. *Movement Disorders, 26,* 1127–33.

Shriver, E. (2015). *A history of psychology: A global perspective.*: Thousand Oaks, CA: Sage Publications.

Shulman, R. G. (2013). *Brain imaging: What it can (and cannot) tell us about consciousness.* New York: Oxford University Press.

Sibrava, N. J., & Borkovec, T. D. (2006). The cognitive avoidance theory of worry. In G. C. L. Davey & A. Wells (Eds.), *Worry and its psychological disorders: Theory, assessment, and treatment.* West Sussex, UK: John Wiley & Sons.

Sidebotham, P., Fraser, J., Covington, T., Freemantle, J., Petrou, S., Pulikottil-Jacob, R., et al. (2014). Understanding why children die in high-income countries. *Lancet, 384*(9946), 915–27. doi:10.1016/S0140-6736(14)60581-X

Siegle, G. J., Thompson, W. K., Collier, A., Berman, S. R., Feldmiller, J., Thase, M. E., et al. (2012). Toward clinically useful neuroimaging in depression treatment. *Arch. General Psychiatry, 69,* 913–24.

Siegler, R., DeLoache, J., & Eisenberg, N. (2003). *How children develop.* New York: Worth Publishers.

Siever, L. J., Bernstein, D. P., & Silverman, J. M. (1995). Schizotypal personality disorder. In W. J. Livesley (Ed.), *The DSM-IV personality disorders* (pp. 71–90). New York: Guilford Press.

Siever, L., & Davis, K. (2004). The pathophysiology of schizophrenia disorders: Perspectives from the spectrum. *Am. J. Psychiatry, 161,* 398–413.

Sigman, M., Spence, S. J., & Wang, A. T. (2006). Autism from developmental and neuropsychological perspectives. *Annu. Rev. Clin. Psychol., 2,* 327–55. doi:10.1146/annurev.clinpsy.2.022305.095210

Signorini, A., De Filippo, E., Panico, S., De Caprio, C., Pasanisi, F., & Contaldo, F. (2007). Long-term mortality in anorexia nervosa: A report after an 8-year follow-up and review of the most recent literature. *Eur. J. Clin. Nutr., 61,* 119–22.

Silberg, J. L., Pickles, A., Rutter, M., Hewitt, J., Simonoff, E., Maes, H., et al. (1999). The influence of genetic factors and life stress on depression among adolescent girls. *Arch. Gen. Psychiatry, 56,* 225–32.

Silk, J. S., Nath, S. R., Siegel, L. R., & Kendall, P. C. (2000). Conceptualizing mental disorders in children: Where have we been and where are we going? *Develop. Psychopathol., 12,* 713–35.

Silk, K., & Feurino, L. (2012). Psychopharmacology of personality disorders. In T. Widiger (Ed.), *The Oxford handbook of personality disorders* (pp. 713–26). Oxford, UK: Oxford University Press.

Silver, E. (1995). Punishment or treatment? Comparing the lengths of confinement of successful and unsuccessful insanity defendants. *Law and Human Behavior, 19*(4), 375–88.

Silverman, J. A. (1997). Anorexia nervosa: Historical perspective on treatment. In D. M. Garner & P. E. Garfinkel (Eds.), *Handbook of treatment for eating disorders* (2nd ed., pp. 3–10). New York: Guilford Press.

Silverman, K., Higgins, S. T., Brooner, R. K., & Montoya, I. D. (1996). Sustained cocaine abstinence in methadone maintenance patients through voucher-based reinforcement therapy. *Arch. Gen. Psychiatry, 53*(3), 409–15.

Silverman, M. M., & Felner, R. D. (1995). The place of suicide prevention in the spectrum of intervention: Definitions of critical terms and constructs. *Suicide and Life-Threatening Behavior, 25,* 70–81.

Simeon, D., Guralnik, O., Schmeidler, J., & Knutelska, M. (2004). Fluoxetine therapy in depersonalization disorder: Randomised controlled trial. *Brit. J. Psychiatry, 185*(1), 31–36.

Simeon, D., Kozin, D. S., Segal, K., Lerch, B., Dujour, R., & Giesbrecht, T. (2008). Deconstructing depersonalization: Further evidence for symptom clusters. *Psychiatr. Res., 157,* 303–06. doi:10.1016/j.psychres.2007.07. 007

Simon, G. E. (2002). Management of somatoform and factitious disorders. In P. E. Nathan & J. M. Gorman (Eds.), *A guide to treatments that work* (2nd ed., pp. 447–61). New York: Oxford University Press.

Simon, R. J., & Aaronson, D. E. (1988). *The insanity defense.* New York: Praeger.

Simon, W. (2009). Follow-up psychotherapy outcome of patients with dependent, avoidant and obsessive-compulsive personality disorders: A meta-analytic review. *Int. J. Psychiatr. Clin. Prac., 13*(2), 153–65. doi:10.1080/13651500802570972

Simonoff, E. (2001). Gene-environment interplay in oppositional defiant and conduct disorder. *Child Adoles. Psychiatr. Clin. North Am., 10*(2), 351–74.

Simons, R. L., Simons, L. G., Burt, C. H., Brody, G. H., & Cutrona, C. (2005). Collective efficacy, authoritative parenting and delinquency: A longitudinal test of a model integrating community- and family-level processes. *Criminology, 43*(4), 989–1029.

Simpson, A. I. F., McKenna, B., Moskowitz, A., Skip-worth, J., & Barry-Walsh, J. (2004). Homicide and mental illness in New Zealand, 1970–2000. *Brit. J. Psychiatry, 185*(5), 394–98.

Simpson, G., & Tate, R. (2002). Suicidality after traumatic brain injury: Demographic, injury and clinical correlates. *Psychol. Med., 32,* 687–97.

Simpson, H. B., & Liebowitz, M. R. (2006). Best practice in treating obsessive-compulsive disorder: What the evidence says. In B. Rothbaum (Ed.), *Pathological anxiety: Emotional processing in etiology and treatment* (pp. 147–65). New York: Guilford Press.

Singer, D. G., & Singer, J. L. (Eds.). (2000). *Handbook of children and the media.* Thousand Oaks, CA: Sage Publications.

Singh, R., Meier, T. B., Kuplicki, R., Savitz, J., Mukai, I., Cavanagh, L., et al. (2014). Relationship of collegiate football experience and concussion with hippocampal volume and cognitive outcomes. *JAMA, 311,* 1883–88.

Sinha, M. (2011). Resurgence of Koro: Perception of mankind. *Asian J. Psychiatry, 4*(2), 153–54. doi:10.1016/j.ajp.2011.04.005

Sink, M. (2004, November 8). Drinking deaths draw attention to old campus problem. *New York Times,* p. A14.

Skinner, B. F. (1951). How to teach animals. *Scientif. Am., 185,* 26–29.

Skinner, B. F. (1990). Can psychology be a science of mind? *Am. Psychol., 45,* 1206–10.

Skodol, A. E., Clark, L. A., Bender, D. S., Krueger, R. F., Morey, L. C., Verheul, R., et al. (2011). Proposed changes in personality and personality disorder assessment and diagnosis for DSM-5 Part I: Description and rationale. *Personality Disorders: Theory, Research, and Treatment, 2*(1), 4–22. doi:10.1037/a0021891

Skodol, A., Gunderson, J., Pfohl, B., Widiger, T., Livesely, W. J., & Siever, L. (2002). The borderline diagnosis I: Psychopathology, comorbidity, and personality structure. *Biol. Psychiatry, 51,* 936–50.

Slater, E. (1986). First person account: A parent's view on enforcing medication. *Schizo. Bull., 12,* 291–92.

Slavich, G. M., Monroe, S. M., & Gotlib, I. H. (2011). Early parental loss and depression history: Associations with recent life stress in major depressive disorder. *J. Psychiatr. Res., 45*(9), 1146–52.

Sledge, W. H., & Lazar, S. G. (2014). Workplace effectiveness and psychotherapy for mental, substance abuse, and subsyndromal conditions. *Psychodynamic Psychiatry, 42*(3), 497–556. doi:http://dx.doi.org/10.1521/pdps.2014.42.3.497

Slicker, E. K., & Thornberry, I. (2002). Older adolescent well-being and authoritative parenting. *Adolescent & Family Health, 3*(1), 9–19.

Sloan, D. M., Lee, D. J., Litwack, S. D., Sawyer, A. T., & Marx, B. P. (2013). Written exposure therapy for veterans diagnosed with PTSD: A pilot study. *J. Traumatic Stress, 26,* 776–79.

Slotema, C. W., Blom, J. D., van Lutterveld, R., Hoek, H. W., & Sommer, I. E. C. (2014). Review of the efficacy of transcranial magnetic stimulation for auditory verbal hallucinations. *Biological Psychiatry, 76,* 101–10.

Slovenko, R. (2001). The stigma of psychiatric discourse. *J. Psychiatry & Law, 29,* 5–29.

Slutske, W. S., Heath, A. C., Dinwiddie, S. H., Madden, P. A., & Bucholz, K. K. (1998). Common genetic risk factors for conduct disorder and alcohol dependence. *J. Abn. Psychol., 107*(3), 363–74.

Slutske, W. S., Zhu, G., Meier, M. H., & Martin, N. G. (2010). Genetic and environmental influences on disordered gambling in men and women. *Arch. Gen. Psychiatry, 67*(6), 624–30.

Smith, A. R., Hawkeswood, S. E., Bodell, L. P., & Joiner, T. E. (2011). Muscularity versus leanness: An examination of body ideals and predictors of disordered eating in heterosexual and gay college students. *Body Image, 8,* 232–36.

Smith, C. D., Andersen, A. H., Kryscio, R. J., Schmitt, F. A., Kindy, M. S., Blonder, L. X., et al. (2002). Women at risk for AD show increased parietal activation during a fluency task. *Neurol., 58,* 1197–202.

Smith, G. T., Goldman, M. S., Greenbaum, P. E., & Christiansen, B. A. (1995). Expectancy for social facilitation from drinking: The divergent paths of high-expectancy and low-expectancy adolescents. *J. Abn. Psychol., 104,* 32–40.

Smith, I. M., & Bryson, S. (1994). Imitation and action in autism: A critical review. *Psychol. Bull., 116*(2), 259–73.

Smith, J. P., & Smith, G. C. (2010). Long-term economic costs of psychological problems during childhood. *Soc. Sci. Med., 71*(1), 110–15.

Smith, K. S., & Berridge, K. C. (2007). Opioid limbic circuit for reward: Interaction between hedonic hotspots of nucleus accumbens and ventral pallidum. *J. Neuroscience, 27,* 1594–605.

Smith, P. M., Reilly, K. R., Miller, N. H., DeBusk, R. F., & Taylor, C. B. (2002). Application of a nurse-managed inpatient smoking cessation program. *Nicotine & Tobacco Research, 4*(2), 211–22.

Smith, T. W., & Ruiz, J. M. (2002). Psychosocial influences on the development and course of coronary heart disease: Current status and implications for research and practice. *J. Cons. Clin. Psychol., 70*(3), 548–68.

Smith-Spark, J. H., & Fisk, J. E. (2007). Working memory functioning in developmental dyslexia. *Memory, 15*(1), 34–56.

Smolak, L., & Murnen, S. K. (2002). A meta-analytic examination of the relationship between child sexual abuse and eating disorders. *Int. J. Eat. Dis., 31*(2), 136–50.

Smoller, J. W. (2013). Disorders and borders: Psychiatric genetics and nosology. *Am. J. Medical Genetics B, 162B,* 559–78.

Smoller, J. W., & Cross-Disorder Group of the Psychiatric Genomics Consortium. (2013). Identification of risk loci with shared effects on five major psychiatric disorders: A genome-wide analysis. *Lancet, 381*(9875), 1371–79.

Smoller, J. W., Gardner-Schuster, E., & Misiaszek, M. (2008). Genetics of anxiety: Would the genome recognize the DSM? *Depression and Anxiety, 25*(4), 368–77. doi:10.1002/da.20492

Smyke, A. T., Koga, S. F., Johnson, D. E., Fox, N. A., Marshall, P. J., Nelson, C. A., et al. (2007). The caregiving context in institution-reared and family-reared infants and toddlers in Romania. *J. Child Psychology and Psychiatry, 48*(2), 210–18.

Snider, W. D., Simpson, D. M., Nielsen, S., Gold, J. W., Metroka, C. E., & Posner, J. B. (1983). Neurological complications of acquired immune deficiency syndrome: Analysis of 50 patients. *Ann. Neurol., 14*(4), 403–18.

Snitz, B. E., Hellinger, A., & Daum, I. (2002). Impaired processing of affective prosody in Korsakoff's syndrome. *Cortex, 38*(5), 797–803.

Snowden, L. R., & Yamada, A.-M. (2005). Cultural differences in access to care. *Annu. Rev. Clin. Psychol., 1,* 143–66.

Snyder, D. K., Castellani, A. M., & Whisman, M. A. (2006). Current status and future directions in couple therapy. *Annu. Rev. Psychol., 57,* 317–44.

Snyder, P. J., Nussbaum, P. D., & Robins, D. L. (Eds.). (2006). *Clinical neuropsychology: A pocket handbook for assessment* (2nd ed.). Washington, DC: American Psychological Association.

Soar, K., Turner, J. J. D., & Parrott, A. C. (2001). Psychiatric disorders in Ecstasy (MDMA) users: A literature review focusing on personal predisposition and drug history. *Human Psychopharmacology Clinical & Experimental, 16,* 641–45.

Sobell, M. B., & Sobell, L. C. (1995). Controlled drinking after 25 years: How important was the great debate? *Addiction, 90*(9), 1149–53.

Solomon, D. A., Leon, A. C., Coryell, W. H., Endicott, J., Li, C., Fiedorowicz, J. G., et al. (2010). Longitudinal course of bipolar I disorder: Duration of mood episodes. *Arch. Gen. Psychiatry, 67*(4), 339–47. doi:10.1001/archgenpsychiatry.2010.15

Solomon, D. A., Leon, A. C., Endicott, J., Coryell, W. H., Mueller, T. I., Posternak, M. A., et al. (2003). Unipolar mania over the course of a 20-year follow-up study. *Am. J. Psychiatry, 160*(11), 2049–51.

Solomon, D. A., Leon, A. C., Endicott, J., Mueller, T. I., Coryell, W., Shea, M. T., et al. (2004). Psychosocial impairment and recurrence of major depression. *Compr. Psychiatry, 45*(6), 423–30.

Solomon, D. A., Leon, A. C., Mueller, T. I., Coryell, W., Teres, J. J., Posternak, M. A., et al. (2005). Tachyphylaxes in unipolar major depressive disorder. *J. Clin. Psychiatry, 66*(3), 283–90.

Solomon, Z., & Mikulincer, M. (2007). Posttraumatic intrusion, avoidance, and social functioning: A 20 year longitudinal study. *J Consult. Clin. Psychol., 75*, 336–24.

Soong, W. T. (2006). Psychiatry in Taiwan: Past, present and future. *International Medical Journal, 13*, 21–28.

South, S., Reichborn-Kjennerud, T., Eaton, N., & Krueger, R. F. (2012). Behavior and molecular genetics of personality disorders. In T. Widiger (Ed.), *The Oxford handbook of personality disorders* (pp. 143–65). Oxford, UK: Oxford University Press.

Southall, A. (2010). Washington, D.C., approves medical use of marijuana. *New York Times, 159*(55), 31.

Southwick, S. M., Vythilingam, M., & Charney, D. S. (2005). The psychobiology of depression and resilience to stress: Implications for prevention and treatment. *Annu. Rev. Clin. Psych., 1*(1), 255–91.

Spadoni, A. D., McGee, C. L., Fryer, S. L., & Riley, E. P. (2007). Neuroimaging and fetal alcohol spectrum disorders. *Neuroscience & Biobehavioral Reviews, 31*(2), 239–45.

Spanos, A., Klump, K. L., Burt, S. A., McGue, M., & Iacono, W. G. (2010). A longitudinal investigation of the relationship between disordered eating attitudes and behaviors and parent-child conflict: A monozygotic twin differences design. *J. Abn. Pysch., 119*, 293–99.

Spanos, N. P. (1994). Multiple identity enactments and multiple personality disorder: A sociocognitive perspective. *Psychol. Bull., 116*, 143–65.

Spanos, N. P. (1996). *Multiple identities and false memories: A sociocognitive perspective.* Washington, DC: American Psychological Association.

Spanos, N. P., Weekes, J. R., & Bertrand, L. D. (1985). Multiple personality: A social psychological perspective. *J. Abn. Psychol., 94*, 362–76.

Spataro, J., Mullen, P. M., Burgess, P. M., Wells, D. L., & Moss, S. A. (2004). Impact of child sexual abuse on mental health: Prospective study in males and females. *Brit. J. Psychiatry, 184*, 416–21.

Speck, C. E., Kukull, W. A., Brenner, D. E., Bowen, J. D., McCormick, W. C., Teri, L., et al. (1995). History of depression as a risk factor for Alzheimer's disease. *Epidemiology, 6*, 366–69.

Speed, J. (1996). Behavioral management of conversion disorder: Retrospective study. *Arch. Physical Medicine and Rehabilitation, 77*, 435–54.

Spencer, J. P., Blumberg, M. S., McMurray, B., Robinson, S. R., Samuelson, L. K., & Tomblin, J. B. (2009). Short arms and talking eggs: Why we should no longer abide the nativist-empiricist debate. *Child Development Perspectives, 3*(2), 79–87. doi:10.1111/j.1750-8606.2009.00081.x

Spencer, T. J. (2004b). Non stimulant treatment of adult attention deficit hyperactivity disorder. *Psychiatr. Clin. North Am., 27*, 373–83.

Spiegel, D. (2006). Recognizing traumatic dissociation. *Am. J. Psychiatry, 163*, 566–68.

Spiegel, D., Lewis-Fernandez, R., Lanius, R., Vermetten, E., Simeon, D., & Friedman, M. (2013). Dissociative disorders in DSM-5. *Annu. Rev. Clinical Psychology, 9*, 299–26

Spiegel, D., Loewenstein, R. J., Lewis-Fernández, R., Şar, V., Simeon, D., Vermetten, E., et al. (2011a). Dissociative disorders in DSM-5. *Depression and Anxiety, 28*, 824–52.

Spiegel, D., Loewenstein, R. J., Lewis-Fernández, R., Şar, V., Simeon, D., Vermetten, E., et al. (2011b). Dissociative disorders in DSM-5. *Depression and Anxiety, 28*, E17–45.

Spirito, A., Esposito-Smythers, C., Wolff, J., & Uhl, K. (2011). Cognitive-behavioral therapy for adolescent depression and suicidality. *Child Adolesc Psychiatr Clin N Am, 20*(2), 191–204. doi:10.1016/j.chc.2011.01.012

Spitzer, R. L., Gibbon, M., Skodol, A. E., Williams, J. B. W., & First, M. B. (Eds.). (2002). *DSM-IV-TR casebook: A learning companion to the diagnostic and statistical manual of mental disorders, fourth edition, text revision.* Washington, DC: American Psychiatric Press.

Sporn, A., Greenstein, D., Gogtay, N., Sailer, F., Hommer, D. W., Rawlings, R., et al. (2005). Childhood-onset schizophrenia: Smooth pursuit eye-tracking dysfunction in family members. *Schiz. Res., 73*, 243–52.

Spoth, R., Trudeau, L., Redmond, C., & Shin, C. (2014, May 12). Replication RCT of early universal prevention effects on young adult substance misuse. *J. Consulting and Clinical Psychology, 82*(6), 949–63. http://dx.doi.org/10.1037/a0036840

Sridhar, G. R., Lakshmi, G., & Nagamani, G. (2015). Emerging links between type 2 diabetes and Alzheimer's disease. *World J. Diabetes, 6*, 744–51.

Srisurapanont, M., Ali, R., Marsden, J., Sunga, A., Wada, K., & Monteiro, M. (2003). Psychotic symptoms in methamphetamine psychotic in-patients. *Int. J. Neuropsychopharm., 6*(4), 347–52.

Srivareerat, M., Tran, T. T., Alzoubi, K. H., & Alkadhi, K. A. (2009). Chronic psychosocial stress exacerbates impairment of cognition and long-term potentiation in beta amyloid rat model of Alzheimer's disease. *Biol. Psychiatry, 65*, 918–26.

Sroufe, L. A., Duggal, S., Weinfeld, N., & Carlson, E. (2000). Relationships, development, and psychopathology. In A. J. Sameroff & M. Lewis (Eds.), *Handbook of developmental psychopathology* (2nd ed., pp. 75–91). New York: Kluwer/Plenum.

St. Clair, D. (2009). Copy number variation and schizophrenia. *Schiz. Bull., 35*, 9–12.

Staebler, K., Helbing, E., Rosenbach, C., & Renneberg, B. (2011). Rejection sensitivity and borderline personality disorder. *Clinical Psychology and Psychotherapy, 18*, 275–83.

Stafford, K. P., & Sadoff, R. L. (2011). Competence to stand trial. In E. Y. Drogin, F. M. Dattilio, R. L. Sadoff, & T. G. Gutheil (Eds.), *Handbook of forensic assessment: Psychological and psychiatric perspectives* (pp. 3–24). Hoboken, NJ: Wiley.

Stahl, S. M. (2000). *Essential psychopharmacology: Neuroscientific basis and practical applications* (2nd ed.). Cambridge, UK: Cambridge University Press.

Staley, D., Wand, R., & Shady, G. (1997). Tourette disorder: A cross-cultural review. *Compr. Psychiatry, 38*(1), 6–16.

Stamm, J. M., Bourlas, A. P., Baugh, C. M., Fritts, N. G., Daneshvar, D. H., Martin, B. M., et al. (2015). Age of first exposure to football and later-life cognitive impairment in former NFL players. *Neurology, 84*, 1114–20.

Stangier, U., Schramm, E., Heidenreich, T., Berger, M., & Clark, D. M. (2011). Cognitive therapy vs interpersonal psychotherapy in social anxiety disorder. *Am. J. Psychiatry, 68*, 692–700.

Staniloiu, A., & Markowitsch, H. J. (2010). Searching for the anatomy of dissociative amnesia. *Zeitschrift fur Psychologie/J. Psychology, 218*, 96–108. doi:10.1027/0044-3409/a000017

Stanley, B., Brodsky, B., Nelson, J., & Dulit, R. (2007). Brief dialectical behavior therapy for suicidality and self-injurious behaviors. *Arch. Suicide Res., 11*, 337–41.

Stanley, B., Brown, G., Brent, D. A., Wells, K., Poling, K., Curry, J., et al. (2009). Cognitive-behavioral therapy for suicide prevention (CBT-SP): Treatment model, feasibility, and acceptability. *J Am. Acad. Child Adol. Psychiat., 48*(10), 1005–13. doi:10.1097/CHI.0b013e3181b5dbfe

Starcevic, V., Latas, M., Kolar, D., Vucinic-Latas, D., Bogojevic, G., & Milovanovic, S. (2008). Cooccurrence of Axis I and Axis II disorders in female and male patients with panic disorder with agoraphobia. *Compr. Psychiatry, 49*(6), 537–43. doi:10.1016/j.comppsych.2008.02.009

Stark, S., Sachse, R., Liedl, T., Hensen, J., Rohde, G., Wensing, G., et al. (2001). Vardenafil increases penile rigidity and tumescence in men with erectile dysfunction after a single oral dose. *European Urology, 40*, 181–88.

State, M. W., & Sestan, N. (2012). Neuroscience. The emerging biology of autism spectrum disorders. *Science, 337*(6100), 1301–03. doi:10.1126/science.1224989

Stattin, H., & Klackenberg-Larsson, I. (1993). Early language and intelligence development and their relationship to future criminal behavior. *J. Abn. Psychol., 102*(3), 369–78.

Steadman, H. J., McGreevy, M. A., Morrissey, J. P., Callahan, L. A., Robbins, P. C., & Cirincione, C. (1993). *Before and after Hinckley: Evaluating insanity defense reform.* New York: Guilford Press.

Steadman, H. J., Mulvey, E. P., Monahan, J., Robbins, P. C., Appelbaum, P. S., Grisso, T., et al. (1998). Violence by people discharged from acute psychiatric inpatient facilities and by others in the same neighborhoods. *Arch. Gen. Psychiatry, 55*, 393–401.

Steen, R. G., Mull, C., McClure, R., Hamer, R. M., & Lieberman, J. A. (2006). Brain volume in first-episode schizophrenia: Systematic review and meta-analysis of magnetic resonance imaging studies. *Brit. J. Psychiat, 188*, 510–18.

Steensma, T. D., Biemond, R., de Boer, F., & Cohen-Kettenis, P. T. (2011). Desisting and persisting gender dysphoria after childhood: A qualitative follow-up study. *Clinical Child Psychology and Psychiatry, 16*(4), 499–516.

Stefanoff, P., Wolanczyk, T., Gawrys, A., Swirszcz, K., Stefanoff, E., Kaminska, A., et al. (2008). Prevalence of tic disorders among schoolchildren in Warsaw, Poland. *European Child and Adolescent Psychiatry, 17*, 171–78.

Steiger, A. (2007). Neurochemical regulation of sleep. *J. Psychiatr. Res., 41*(7), 537–52.

Stein, D. J., Denys, D., Gloster, A. T., Hollander, E., Leckman, J. F., Rauch, S. L., & Phillips, K. A. (2009). Obsessive-compulsive disorder: Diagnostic and treatment issues. *Psychiatric Clin. North Am., 32*, 665–85.

Stein, D. J., Phillips, K. A., Bolton, D., Fulford, K. W. M., Sadler, J. Z., & Kendler, K. S. (2010). What is a mental/psychiatric disorder? From DSM-IV to DSM-V. *Psychol. Med., 40*, 1759–65.

Stein, D. J., & Simeon, D. (2009). Cognitive-affective neuroscience of depersonalization. *CNS Spectrums, 14*, 467–71.

Stein, M. B. (2004). Public health perspectives on generalized anxiety disorder. *J. Clin. Psychiatry, 65*(113), 3–7.

Stein, M. B., Jang, K. L., & Livesley, W. J. (2002). Heritability of social anxiety-related concerns and personality characteristics: A twin study. *J. Nerv. Ment. Dis., 190*(4), 219–24.

Stein, M. B., & Stein, D. J. (2008). Social anxiety disorder. *Lancet, 371*(9618), 1115–25.

Steinberg, H. (2013). A pioneer work on electric brain stimulation in psychotic patients: Rudolph Gottfried Arndt and his 1870s studies. *Brain Stimulation, 6*, 477–81.

Steinberg, L., Blatt-Eisengart, I., & Cauffman, E. (2006). Patterns of competence and adjustment among adolescents from authoritative, authoritarian, indulgent, and neglectful homes: A replication in a sample of serious juvenile offenders. *J. Research on Adolescence, 16*(1), 47–58.

Steinbrecher, N., Koerber, S., Frieser, D., & Hiller, W. (2011). The prevalence of medically unexplained symptoms in primary care. *Psychosomatics, 52,* 263–71.

Steinhausen, H. C. (2002). The outcome of anorexia nervosa in the 20th century. *Am. J. Psychiatry, 159,* 1284–93.

Steketee, G. S. (1993). *Treatment of obsessive-compulsive disorder.* New York: Guilford Press.

Steketee, G., & Barlow, D. H. (2002). Obsessive-compulsive disorder. In D. H. Barlow (Ed.), *Anxiety and its disorders* (2nd ed., pp. 516–50). New York: Guilford Press.

Steketee, G., & Frost, R. (2004). Compulsive hoarding: Current status of research. *Clin. Psychol. Rev., 23,* 905–27.

Stene, J., Stene, E., Stengel-Rutkowski, S., & Murken, J. D. (1981). Paternal age and Down's syndrome, data from prenatal diagnoses (DFG). *Human Genet., 59,* 119–24.

Stermac, L. E., Segal, Z. V., & Gillis, R. (1990). Social and cultural factors in sexual assault. In W. L. Marshall, D. R. Laws, & H. E. Barbaree (Eds.), *Handbook of sexual assault* (pp. 143–60). New York: Plenum.

Stetler, C., & Miller, G. E. (2011). Depression and hypothalamic-pituitary-adrenal activation: A quantitative summary of four decades of research. *Psychosom. Med., 73*(2), 114–26. doi:10.1097/PSY.0b013e31820ad12b

Stevens, A. H., & Schaller, J. (2009). *Short-run effects of parental job loss on children's academic achievement* (National Bureau of Economic Research Working Paper 15480). Retrieved from http://www.nber.org/papers/w15480

Stewart, J. L., Bismark, A. W., Towers, D. N., Coan, J. A., & Allen, J. J. B. (2010). Resting frontal EEG asymmetry as an endophenotype for depression risk: Sex-specific patterns of frontal brain asymmetry. *J. Abn. Psychol., 119*(3), 502–12. doi:10.1037/a0019196

Stewart, J. L., Coan, J. A., Towers, D. N., & Allen, J. J. (2011). Frontal EEG asymmetry during emotional challenge differentiates individuals with and without lifetime major depressive disorder. *J. Affective Disorders, 129,* 167–74.

Stewart, S. E., Jenike, E., & Jenike, M. A. (2009). Biological treatment for obsessive-compulsive disorder. In M. M. Antony & M. B. Stein (Eds.), *Oxford handbook of anxiety and related disorders* (pp. 375–90). New York: Oxford University Press.

Stewart, S. E., Platko, J., Fagerness, J., Birns, J., Jenike, E., Smoller, J. W., et al. (2007). A genetic family-based association study of OLIG2 in obsessive-compulsive disorder. *Arch. Gen. Psychiatry, 64*(2), 209–15.

Stewart, S. H., Finn, P. R., & Pihl, R. O. (1990, March). *The effects of alcohol on the cardiovascular stress response in men at high risk for alcoholism: A dose response study.* Paper presented at the annual meeting of the Canadian Psychological Association, Ottawa.

Stewart, S. M., Kennard, B. D., Lee, P. W. H., Hughes, C. W., Mayes, T., Emslie, G. J., et al. (2004). A cross-cultural investigation of cognitions and depressive symptoms in adolescents. *J. Abn. Psychol., 113*(2), 248–57.

Stice, E. (2001). A prospective test of the dual-pathway model of bulimic pathology: Mediating effects of dieting and negative affect. *J. Abn. Psychol., 110*(1), 124–35.

Stice, E. (2002). Risk and maintenance factors for eating pathology: A meta-analytic review. *Psychol. Bull., 128*(5), 825–48.

Stice, E., Marti, C. N., & Durant, S. (2011). Risk factors for onset of eating disorders: Evidence of multiple risk pathways from an 8-year prospective study. *Behav. Res. Ther., 49*(10), 622–27. doi:10.1016/j.brat.2011.06.009

Stice, E., Presnell, K., & Spangler, D. (2002). Risk factors for binge eating onset in adolescent girls. A 2-year prospective study. *Health Psychol., 21*(2), 131–38.

Stigler, M. H., Neusel, E., & Perry, C. L. (2011). School based programs to prevent and reduce alcohol use among youth. *Alcohol Research & Health, 34,* 157–62.

Stiglmayr, C. E., Ebner-Priemer, U. W., Bretz, J., Behm, R., Mohse, M., Lammers, C.-H., et al. (2008). Dissociative symptoms are positively related to stress in borderline personality disorder. *Acta Psychiatrica Scandinavica, 117,* 139–47.

Stolberg, R., & Bongar, B. (2009). *Oxford handbook of personality and clinical assessment.* New York: Oxford University Press.

Stolberg, R. A., Clark, D. C., & Bongar, B. (2002). Epidemiology, assessment, and management of suicide in depressed patients. In I. H. Gotlib & C. L. Hammen (Eds.), *Handbook of depression* (pp. 581–601). New York: Guilford Press.

Stone, J., LaFrance, W. C., Brown, R., Spiegel, D., Levenson, J. L., & Sharpe, M. (2011). Conversion disorder: Current problems and potential solutions for DSM-5. *J. Psychosomatic Research, 71,* 369–76.

Stone, J., Smyth, R., Carson, A., Lewis, S., Prescott, R., Warlow, C., et al. (2005). Systematic review of misdiagnosis of conversion symptoms and "hysteria." *Brit. Med. J., 33,* 989.

Stone, J., Smythe, R., Carson, A., Warlow, C., & Shapre, M. (2006). La belle indifference in conversion symptoms and hysteria: Systematic review. *Brit. J. Psychiatry, 188,* 204–09.

Stone, S. (1937). Psychiatry through the ages. *J. Abnorm. Soc. Psychol., 32,* 131–60.

Stonnington, C. M., Barry, J. J., & Fisher, R. S. (2006). Conversion disorder. *Am. J. Psychiatry, 163*(9), 1510–17.

Storandt, M. (2008). Cognitive deficits in the early stages of Alzheimer's disease. *Curr. Dis. Psychol. Sci., 17,* 198–202.

Strain, J. J., & Newcorn, J. (2007). Adjustment disorder. In J. A. Bourgeois, R. A. Hales, & S. C. Yudofsky (Eds.), *The American Psychiatric Publishing board prep and review guide for psychiatry.* Washington, DC: American Psychiatric Association.

Stranahan, A. M., Khalil, D., & Gould, E. (2007). Running induces widespread structural alterations in the hippocampus and entorhinal cortex. *Hippocampus, 17,* 1017–22.

Strauss, R. S., & Pollack, H. A. (2003). Social marginalization of overweight children. *Arch. Pediatric and Adolescent Medicine, 157*(8), 746–53.

Strawn, J. R., Keck, P. E., & Caroff, S. N. (2007). Neuroleptic malignant syndrome. *Am. J. Psychiatry, 164,* 870–76.

Striegel-Moore, R. H., & Bulik, C. M. (2007). Risk factors for eating disorders. *Am. Psychol., 62,* 181–98.

Striegel-Moore, R. H., Dohm, F. A., Kraemer, H. C., Taylor, C. B., Daniels, S., Crawford, P. B., et al. (2003). Eating disorders in white and black women. *Am. J. Psychiatry, 160,* 1326–31.

Strober, M. (2004). Managing the chronic, treatment-resistant patient with anorexia nervosa. *Int. J. Eat. Dis., 36,* 245–55.

Strober, M., Freeman, R., Lampert, C., Diamond, J., & Kaye, W. (2000). Controlled family study of anorexia nervosa and bulimia nervosa: Evidence of shared liability and transmission of partial syndromes. *Am. J. Psychiatry, 157*(3), 393–401.

Strohschein, L. (2005). Parental divorce and child mental health trajectories. *J. Marr. Fam., 7*(5), 1286–300.

Strote, J., Lee, J. E., & Wechsler, H. (2002). Increasing MDMA use among college students: Results of a national survey. *J. Adol. Health, 30*(1), 64–72.

Stroud, C. B., Davila, J., Hammen, C., & Vrshek-Schallhorn, S. (2011). Severe and nonsevere events in first onsets versus recurrences of depression: Evidence for stress sensitization. *J. Abn. Psychol., 120,* 142–54.

Strug, L. J., Suresh, R., Fyer, A. J., Talati, A., Adams, P. B., Li, W., et al. (2010). Panic disorder is associated with the serotonin transporter gene (SLC6A4) but not the promoter region (5-HTTLPR). *Molec. Psychiatry, 15*(2), 166–76. doi:10.1038/mp.2008.79

Strunk, D. R., Brotman, M. A., DeRubeis, R. J., & Hollon, S. D. (2010). Therapist competence in cognitive therapy for depression: Predicting subsequent symptom change. *J. Cons. Clin. Psychol., 78,* 429–37.

Stueve, A., Dohrenwend, B. P., & Skodol, A. E. (1998). Relationships between stressful life events and episodes of major depression and nonaffective psychotic disorders: Selected results from a New York risk factor study. In B. P. Dohrenwend (Ed.), *Adversity, stress, and psychopathology* (pp. 341–57). New York: Oxford University Press.

Stuss, D. T., Gow, C. A., & Hetherington, C. R. (1992). "No longer Gage": Frontal lobe dysfunction and emotional changes. *J. Cons. Clin. Psychol., 60*(3), 349–59.

Suárez, L. M., Bennett, S. M., Goldstein, C. R., & Barlow, D. H. (2009). Understanding anxiety disorders from a "triple vulnerability" framework. In M. M. Antony & M. B. Stein (Eds.), *Oxford handbook of anxiety and related disorders* (pp. 153–72). New York: Oxford University Press.

Substance Abuse and Mental Health Services Administration. (2013). *Drug abuse warning network, 2011: National estimates of drug-related emergency department visits* (DHHS Publication No. SMA 13-4760, DAWN Series D-39). Rockville, MD: Author.

Substance Abuse and Mental Health Services Administration. (2014, September 4). *The NSDUH report: Substance use and mental health estimates from the 2013 National Survey on Drug Use and Health: Overview of findings.* Rockville, MD: Author.

Substance Abuse and Mental Health Services Administration, Office of Applied Studies. (2009). *Results from the 2008 National Survey on Drug Use and Health: National findings* (NSDUH Series H-36, DHHS Publication No. SMA 09-4434). Rockville, MD: Author.

Sue, S., & Chang, J. (2003). The state of psychological assessment in Asia. *Psychol. Assess., 15*(3), 306–10.

Sue, S., Zane, N., & Young, K. (1994). Research on psychotherapy with culturally diverse populations. In A. E. Bergin & S. L. Garfield (Eds.), *Handbook of psychotherapy and behavior change* (pp. 783–820). New York: Wiley.

Sulkowski, M., & Michael, K. (2014). Meeting the mental health needs of homeless students in schools: A multi-tiered system of support framework. *Children and Youth Services Review, 44,* 145–51. doi:http://dx.doi.org/10.1016/j.childyouth.2014.06.014

Sullivan, E. A., & Kosson, D. S. (2006). Ethnic and cultural variations in psychopathy. In C. J. Patrick (Ed.), *Handbook of the psychopathy* (pp. 437–58). New York: Guilford Press.

Sullivan, E. V., Deshmukh, A., Desmond, J. E., Lim, K. O., & Pfefferbaum, A. (2000). Cerebellar volume decline in normal aging, alcoholism, and Korsakoff's syndrome relation to ataxia. *Neuropsych., 14*(3), 341–52.

Sullivan, J., & Chang, P. (1999). Review: Emotional and behavioral functioning in phenylketonuria. *J. Pediat. Psychol., 24,* 281–99.

Sullivan, P. F. (2002). Course and outcome of anorexia nervosa and bulimia nervosa. In C. G. Fairburn & K. D. Brownell (Eds.), *Eating disorders and obesity: A comprehensive handbook* (2nd ed., pp. 226–30). New York: Guilford Press.

Sullivan, P. F., Neale, M. C., & Kendler, K. S. (2000). Genetic epidemiology of major depression: Review and meta-analysis. *Am. J. Psychiatry, 157*(10), 1552–62.

Sultzer, D. L., Davis, S. M., Tariot, P. N., Dagerman, K. S., Lebowitz, B. D., Lyketsos, C. G., et al. (2008). Clinical symptom response to atypical antipsychotic medications in Alzheimer's disease: Phase 1 outcomes from the CATIE-AD effectiveness trial. *Am. J. Psychiatry, 165,* 844–54.

Sundin, J., Fear, N. T., Iversen, A., Rona, R. J., & Wessely, S. (2010). PTSD after deployment to Iraq: Conflicting rates, conflicting claims. *Psychol, Med., 40*(3), 367–82.

Sundquist, K., Frank, G., & Sundquist, J. (2004). Urbanisation and incidence of psychosis and depression. Follow-up study of 4. 4 million women and men in Sweden. *Brit. J. Psychiatry, 184,* 293–98.

Sunjic, S., & Zabor, D. (1999). Methadone syrup-related deaths in New South Wales, Australia, 1990–95. *Drug Al. Rev., 18,* 409–15.

Susser, E., Moore, R., & Link, B. (1993). Risk factors for homelessness. *Am. J. Epidemiol., 15,* 546–66.

Sussman, N. (2009a). Mental Health Parity Act becomes the law on October 3, 2009. *Prim. Psychiatry, 16*(10), 10–11.

Sussman, N. (2009b). Selective serotonin reuptake inhibitors. In B. J. Sadock, A. A. Sadock, & P. Ruiz (Eds.), *Kaplan and Sadock's comprehensive textbook of psychiatry* (9th ed., pp. 3190–205). Philadelphia, PA: Lippincott Williams & Wilkins.

Sutin, A. R., Beason-Held, L. L., Dotson, V. M., Resnick, S. M., & Costa, P. T., Jr. (2010). The neural correlates of neuroticism differ by sex prospectively mediate depressive symptoms among older women. *J. Affective Disorders, 127,* 241–47.

Sutker, P. B., & Allain, A. N. (2001). Antisocial personality disorder. In H. E. Adams & P. B. Sutker (Eds.), *Comprehensive handbook of psychopathology* (pp. 445–90). New York: Kluwer Academic.

Suzuki, M., Zhou, S. Y., Hagino, H., Takahashi, T., Kawasaki, Y., Nohara, S., et al. (2004). Volume reduction of the right anterior limb of the internal capsule in patients with schizotypal disorder. *Psychiatry Research: Neuroimaging, 130*(3), 213–25.

Svensson, L., Larsson, A., & Oest, L.-G. (2002). How children experience brief-exposure treatment of specific phobias. *J. Comm. Psychol., 31*(1), 80–89.

Swami, V., Frederick, D. A., Aavik, T., Alcalay, L., Allik, J., Anderson, D., et al. (2010). The attractive female body weight and female body dissatisfaction in 26 countries across 10 world regions: Results of the International Body Project I. *Personality and Social Psychology Bull., 36,* 309–25.

Swannell, S. V., Martin, G. E., Page, A., Hasking, P., & St John, N. J. (2014). Prevalence of nonsuicidal self-injury in nonclinical samples: Systematic review, meta-analysis and meta-regression. *Suicide and Life-Threatening Behavior, 44*(3), 273–303.

Swartz, M. W. (2014). *Textbook of physical diagnosis.* Philadelphia, PA: Elsevier.

Swartz, M., Swanson, J. W., & Elbogen, E. B. (2004). Psychiatric advance directives: Practical, legal, and ethical issues. *J. Foren. Psychol. Pract., 4*(4), 97–107.

Swartz, R. (2010). Medical marijuana users in substance abuse treatment. *Harm Reduction Journal, 7,* article 3. doi:10.1186/1477-7517-7-3

Sylvain, C., Ladouceur, R., & Boisvert, J. M. (1997). Cognitive and behavioral treatment of pathological gambling: A controlled study. *J. Cons. Clin. Psychol., 65*(5), 727–32.

Sypeck, M. F., Gray, J. J., & Ahrens, A. H. (2004). No longer just a pretty face: Fashion magazines' depictions of ideal female beauty from 1959–1999. *Int. J. Eat. Dis., 36,* 342–47.

Sysko, R., Sha, N., Wang, Y., Duan, N., & Walsh, B. T. (2010). Early response to antidepressant treatment in bulimia nervosa. *Psych. Med., 40,* 999–1005.

Szasz, T. S. (1999). *Fatal freedom: The ethics and politics of suicide.* Westport, CT: Praeger.

Szeszko, P. R., MacMillan, S., McMeniman, M., Chen, S., Baribault, K., Lim, K. O., et al. (2004). Brain structural abnormalities in psychotropic drug-naive pediatric patients with obsessive-compulsive disorder. *Am. J. Psychiatry, 161*(6), 1049–56.

T

Taber, D. R., Chriqui, J. F., Perna, F. M., Powell, L. M., & Cgaloupka, F. J. (2012). Weight status among adolescents in states that govern competitive food nutritional content. *Pediatrics, 130,* 437–44.

Takei, N., Persaud, R., Woodruff, P., Brockington, I., & Murray, R. M. (1998). First episodes of psychosis in Afro-Caribbean and white people: An 18-year follow-up population-based study. *Brit. J. Psychiatry, 172,* 147–54.

Takeshita, T. K., Morimoto, X., Mao, Q., Hashimoto, T., & Furyuama, J. (1993). Phenotypic differences in low Km aldehyde dehydrogenase in Japanese workers. *Lancet, 341,* 837–38.

Tandon, R., Nasrallah, H. A., & Keshavan, K. (2009). Schizophrenia, "just the facts" 4. Clinical features and conceptualization. *Schizophrenia Research, 110,* 1–23.

Tandon, R., Nasrallah, H. A., & Keshavan, M. S. (2010). Schizophrenia, "just the facts" 5. Treatment and prevention past, present, and future. *Schizophrenia Research, 122,* 1–21.

Tang, T. Z., & DeRubeis, R. J. (1999). Sudden gains and critical sessions in cognitive-behavioral therapy for depression. *J. Cons. Clin. Psychol., 67,* 894–904.

Tang, T. Z., Luborsky, L., & Andrusyna, T. (2002). Sudden gains in recovering from depression: Are they also found in psychotherapies other than cognitive-behavioral therapy? *J. Cons. Clin. Psychol., 70,* 444–47.

Tareen, A., Hodes, M., & Rangel, L. (2005). Non-fat phobic anorexia nervosa in British South Asian adolescents. *Int. J. Eat. Dis., 37,* 161–65.

Tarrier, N., Lowson, K., & Barrowclough, C. (1991). Some aspects of family interventions in schizophrenia, II: Financial considerations. *Brit. J. Psychiatry, 159,* 481–84.

Tateno, A., Murata, Y., & Robinson, R. G. (2002). Comparison of cognitive impairment associated with major depression following stroke versus traumatic brain injury. *Psychosomatics, 43*(4), 295–301.

Tatetsu, S. (1964). Methamphetamine psychosis. *Folia Psychiatrica et Neurologica Japonica* (Suppl. 7), 377–80.

Taveras, E. M., Rifas-Shiman, S. L., Oken, E., Gunderson, E. P., & Gillman, M. W. (2008). Short sleep duration in infancy and risk of childhood overweight. *Arch. Pediatric and Adolescent Medicine, 162,* 305–11.

Taylor, C., Laposa, J., & Alden, L. (2004). Is avoidant personality disorder more than just social avoidance? *J. Pers. Disord., 18,* 571–94.

Taylor, C., & Meux, C. (1997). Individual cases: The risk, the challenge. *Int. Rev. Psychiatry, 9*(2), 285–302.

Taylor, C. B., Youngblood, M. E., Catellier, D., Veith, R. C., Carney, R. M., Burg, M. M., et al. (2005). Effects of antidepressant medication on morbidity and mortality in depressed patients after myocardial infarction. *Arch. Gen. Psychiatry, 62,* 792–98.

Taylor, J., & Lang, A. R. (2006). Psychopathy and substance use disorders. In C. J. Patrick (Ed.), *Handbook of psychopathy* (pp. 495–511). New York: Guilford Press.

Taylor, R. L. (2000). *Distinguishing psychological from organic disorders: Screening for psychological masquerade* (2nd ed.). New York: Springer.

Taylor, S. (2010). Posttraumatic stress disorder. In D. McKay, J. Abramowitz, & S. Taylor (Eds.), *Cognitive-behavioral therapy for refractory cases: Turning failure into success* (pp. 139–53). Washington, DC: American Psychological Association.

Taylor, S. E., & Stanton, A. L. (2007). Coping resources, coping processes, and mental health. *Annu. Rev. Clin. Psychol., 3,* 377–401.

Taylor, W. S., & Martin, M. F. (1944). Multiple personality. *J. Abnorm. Soc. Psychol., 39,* 281–300.

Teachman, B. A., & Saporito, J. (2009). I am going to gag: Disgust cognitions in spider and blood-injury-injection fears. *Cognition and Emotion, 23*(2), 399–414. doi:10.1080/02699930801961731

Teachman, B. A., Smith-Janik, S. B., & Saporito, J. (2007). Information processing biases and panic disorder: Relationships among cognitive and symptom measures. *Behav. Res. Ther., 45*(8), 1791–811.

Teachman, B. A., Woody, S. R., & Magee, J. C. (2006). Implicit and explicit appraisals of the importance of intrusive thoughts. *Behav. Res. Ther., 44*(6), 785–805.

Teasdale, G. M., Nicoll, J. A. R., Murray, G., et al. (1997). Association of apolipoprotein E polymorphism with outcome after head injury. *Lancet, 350,* 1069–71.

Teasdale, J. (1988). Cognitive vulnerability to persistent depression. *Cognition and Emotion, 2,* 247–74.

Teasdale, J. D. (1996). Clinically relevant therapy: Integrating clinical insight with cognitive science. In P. M. Salkovskis (Ed.), *Frontiers of cognitive therapy* (pp. 26–47). New York: Guilford Press.

Teasdale, J. D. (2004). Mindfulness-based cognitive therapy. In J. Yiend (Ed.), *Cognition, emotion and psychopathology: Theoretical, empirical and clinical directions* (pp. 270–89). Cambridge, UK: Cambridge University Press.

Teglasi, H. (2010). *Essentials of TAT and other storytelling assessments* (2nd ed.). Hoboken, NJ: John Wiley & Sons.

Ten Berge, M., Veerkamp, J. S., & Hoogstraten, J. (2002). The etiology of childhood dental fear: The role of dental and conditioning experiences. *J. Anxiety Disorders, 16,* 321–29.

Tessner, K. D., Mittal, V., & Walker, E. F. (2011). Longitudinal study of stressful life events and daily stressors among adolescents at high risk for psychotic disorders. *Schizo. Bull., 37*(2), 432–41. doi:10.1093/schbul/sbp087

Testa, M., Livingston, J. A., Vanzile-Tamsen, C., & Frone, M. R. (2003). The role of women's substance use in vulnerability to forcible and incapacitated rape. *J. Studies on Alcohol, 64*(6), 756–64.

Thapar, A., Langley, K., O-Donovan, M., & Owen, M. (2006). Refining the attention-deficit hyperactivity disorder phenotype for molecular genetic studies. *Molec. Psychiatry, 11,* 714–20.

Thase, M. E. (2009a). Neurobiological aspects of depression. In I. Gotlib & C. Hammen (Eds.), *Handbook of depression* (2nd ed.). New York: Guilford Press.

Thase, M. E. (2009b). Selective serotonin-norepinephrine reuptake inhibitors. In B. J. Sadock, A. A. Sadock, & P. Ruiz (Eds.), *Kaplan and Sadock's comprehensive textbook of psychiatry* (9th ed., pp. 3184–90). Philadelphia, PA: Lippincott Williams & Wilkins.

Thase, M. E., & Denko, T. (2008). Pharmacotherapy of mood disorders. *Annu. Rev. Clin. Psych., 4,* 53–91.

Thase, M. E., Jindal, R., & Howland, R. H. (2002). Biological aspects of depression. In I. H. Gotlib & C. L. Hammen (Eds.), *Handbook of depression* (pp. 192–218). New York: Guilford Press.

Theodorou, S., & Haber, P. S. (2005). The medical complications of heroin use. *Curr. Opin. Psychiatry, 18*(3), 257–63.

Thibodeau, R., Jorgensen, R. S., & Kim, S. (2006). Depression, anxiety, and resting frontal EEG asymmetry: A meta-analytic review. *J. Abn. Psychol., 115*(4), 715–29.

Thomas, A. K., & Loftus, E. F. (2002). Creating bizarre false memories through imagination. *Memory and Cognition, 30,* 423–31.

Thomas, C., Benzeval, M., & Stansfeld, S. (2007). Psychological distress after employment transitions: The role of subjective financial position as a mediator. *J. Epidemiology & Community Health, 61*(1), 48–52.

Thomas, J. L., Wilk, J. E., Riviere, L. A., McGurk, D., Castro, C. A., & Hoge, C. W. (2010). Prevalence of mental health problems and functional impairment among active component and National Guard soldiers 3 and 12 months following combat in Iraq. *Arch. General Psychiatry, 67,* 614–23.

Thomas, S. P. (2006). From the editor—The phenomenon of cyberbullying. *Issues in Mental Health Nursing, 27*(10), 1015–16.

Thompson, R. A., & Nelson, C. A. (2001). Developmental science and the media: Early brain development. *Am. Psychol., 56,* 5–15.

Thompson, R. F. (2000). *The brain: A neuroscience primer* (3rd ed.). New York: Worth.

Thompson, S. B. N. (2003). Rate of decline in social and cognitive abilities in dementing individuals with Down's syndrome and other learning disabilities. *Clin. Geron., 26*(3–4), 145–53.

Thompson, W. W., Gottesman, I. I., & Zalewski, C. (2006). Reconciling disparate prevalence rates of PTSD in large samples of US male Vietnam veterans and their controls. *BMC Psychiatry, 6,* 19. Retrieved from http://www.biomedcentral.com/1471-244X/6/19

Thornhill, R., & Palmer, C. T. (2000). *A natural history of rape: Biological bases of sexual coercion.* Cambridge, MA: The MIT Press.

Thornicroft, G., Rose, D., Kassam, A., & Sartorius, N. (2007). Stigma: Ignorance, prejudice or discrimination? *Brit. J. Psychiatry, 190,* 192–93.

Thornicroft, G., & Tansella, M. (2000). Planning and providing mental health services for a community. In M. G. Gelder, J. J. Lopez-Ibor, Jr., & N. C. Andreason (Eds.), *New Oxford textbook of psychiatry* (pp. 1547–58). Oxford, UK: Oxford University Press.

Thurston, R. C., & Kubzansky, L. D. (2009). Women, loneliness, and incident coronary heart disease. *Psychosomatic Medicine, 71,* 836–42.

Tidey, J. W., & Miczek, K. A. (1996). Social defeat stress selectively alters mesocorticolimbic dopamine release: An in vivo micro-dialysis study. *Brain Research, 721,* 140–49.

Tienari, P., Lahti, I., Sorri, A., Naarala, M., Moring, J., Wahlberg, K.-E., et al. (1987). The Finnish adoptive family study of schizophrenia. *J. Psychiatr. Res., 21,* 437–45.

Tienari, P., Wynne, L. C., Läksy, K., Moring, J., Nieminen, P., Sorri, A., et al. (2003). Genetic boundaries of the schizophrenia spectrum: Evidence from the Finnish adoptive family study. *Am. J. Psychiatry, 160,* 1587–94.

Tienari, P., Wynne, L. C., Moring, J., Läksy, K., Nieminen, P., Sorri, A., et al. (2000). Finnish adoptive family study: Sample selection and adoptee DSM-III-R diagnoses. *Acta Psychiatr. Scandin., 101,* 433–43.

Tienari, P., Wynne, L. C., Sorri, A., Lahti, I., Läksy, K., Moring, J., et al. (2004). Genotype-environment interaction in schizophrenia-spectrum disorder. *Brit. J. Psychiatry, 184,* 216–22.

Tignol, J., Biraben-Gotzamanis, L., Martin-Guehl, C., Grabot, D., & Aouizerate, B. (2007). Body dysmorphic disorder and cosmetic surgery: Evolution of 24 subjects with a minimal defect in appearance 5 years after their request for cosmetic surgery. *European Psychiatry, 22*(8), 520–24.

Tiihonen, J., Haukka, J., Taylor, M., Haddad, P. M., Patel, M. X., & Korhonen, P. (2011). A nationwide cohort study of oral and depot antipsychotics after first hospitalization for schizophrenia. *Am. J. Psychiatry, 168,* 603–09.

Tillfors, M. (2004). Why do some individuals develop social phobia? A review with emphasis on the neurobiological influences. *Nord. J. Psychiatry, 58*(4), 267–76.

Tillfors, M., Furmark, T., Ekselius, L., & Fredrikson, M. (2004). Social phobia and avoidant personality disorder: One spectrum disorder? *Nord. J. Psychiatry, 58,* 147–52.

Tizard, J. (1975). Race and IQ: The limits of probability. *New Behaviour, 1,* 6–9.

Tolin, D. F. (2010). Is cognitive-behavioral therapy more effective than other therapies? A metaanalytic review. *Clin. Psychol. Rev., 30*(6), 710–20.

Tolin, D. F., & Foa, E. B. (2006). Sex differences in trauma and posttraumatic stress disorder: A quantitative review of 25 years of research. *Psychological Bulletin, 132,* 959–92.

Tolin, D. F., Frost, R. O., Steketee, G., Gray, K. D., & Fitch, K. E. (2008). The economic and social burden of compulsive hoarding. *Psychiatr. Res., 160*(2), 200–11. doi:10.1016/j.psychres.2007.08.008

Tomko, R. L., Trull, T. J., Wood, P. K., & Sher, K. J. (2014). Characteristics of borderline personality disorder in a community sample: Comorbidity, treatment utilization, and general functioning. *J. Personality Disorders, 28,* 734–50.

Tong, J., Miao, S. J., Wang, J., Zhang, J. J., Wu, H. M., Li, T., et al. (2005). Five cases of male eating disorders in Central China. *Int. J. Eat. Dis., 37,* 72–75.

Took, K. J., & Buck, B. L. (1996). Enuresis with combined risperidone and SSRI use. *J. Am. Acad. Child Adoles. Psychiatry, 35*(7), 840–41.

Torgersen, S. (1993). Genetics. In A. S. Bellack & M. Hersen (Eds.), *Psychopathology in adulthood.* Needham Heights, MA: Allyn and Bacon.

Torgersen, S. (2012). Epidemiology. In T. Widiger (Ed.), *The Oxford handbook of personality disorders* (pp. 186–205). Oxford, UK: Oxford University Press.

Torgersen, S., Lygren, S., Oien, P. A., Skre, I., Onstad, S., Edvardsen, J., et al. (2000). A twin study of personality disorders. *Compr. Psychiatry, 41*(6), 416–25.

Torres, A. R., Prince, M. J., Bebbington, P. E., Bhugra, D., Brugha, T. S., Farrell, M., et al. (2006). Obsessive-compulsive disorder: Prevalence, comorbidity, impact, and help-seeking in the British National Psychiatric Morbidity survey of 2000. *Am. J. Psychiatry, 163*(11), 1978–85.

Torrey, E. F., Bower, A. E., Taylor, E. H., & Gottesman, I. I. (1994). *Schizophrenia and manic-depressive disorder: The biological roots of mental illness as revealed by the landmark study of identical twins.* New York: Basic Books.

Tortolero, S. (2010). New leadership, new directions, new format. *J. Primary Prevention, 31*(3), 97–98.

Toulouse, A., & Sullivan, A. M. (2008). Progress in Parkinson's disease—Where do we stand? *Progress in Neurobiology, 85,* 376–92.

Toussaint, L., Shields, G. S., Dorn, G., & Slavich, G. M. (2015). Effects of lifetime stress exposure on mental and physical health in young adulthood" How stress degrades and forgiveness protects health. *J. Health Psychology* [Epub ahead of print].

Townsley, R., Turner, S., Beidel, D., & Calhoun, K. (1995). Social phobia: An analysis of possible developmental factors. *J. Abn. Psychol., 104,* 526–31.

Tozzi, F., Sullivan, P. F., Fear, J. L., McKenzie, J., & Bulik, C. M. (2003). Causes and recovery in anorexia nervosa: The patient's perspective. *Int. J. Eat. Dis., 33,* 143–54.

Treadway, M. T., & Pizzagalli, D. A. (2014). Imaging the pathophysiology of major depressive disorder—From localist models to circuit-based analysis. *Biology of Mood & Anxiety Disorders, 4,* 5.

Treatment for Adolescents with Depression Study Team, U.S. (2004). Fluoxetine, cognitive-behavioral therapy, and their combination for adolescents with depression: Treatment for Adolescents with Depression Study (TADS) randomized controlled trial. *JAMA, 292*(7), 807–20.

Tredget, J., Kirov, A., & Kirov, G. (2010). Effects of chronic lithium treatment on renal function. *J. Affect. Disord., 126*(3), 436–40. doi:10.1016/j.Jad.2010.04.018

Trevisan, L. A., Boutros, N., Petrakis, I. L., & Krystal, J. (1998). Complications of alcohol withdrawal: Pathophysiological insights. *Alcohol Health and Research World, 22,* 61–66.

Trim, R. S., & Chassin, L. (2004). Drinking restraint, alcohol consumption and alcohol dependence among children of alcoholics. *J. Stud. Alcoh., 65*(1), 122–25.

Tronick, E. Z., & Cohn, J. F. (1989). Infant-mother face-to-face interaction: Age and gender differences in coordination and miscoordination. *Child Develop., 59,* 85–92.

Trope, H. (1997). *Locura y sociedad en la valencia de los siglos XV al XVII: Los locos del Hospital de los Inocentes sus instituciones La Locura y sus instuciones* (pp. 141–54). Valencia: Diputacion de Valencia.

Trull, T. J. (2015). Borderline personality disorder: Contemporary approaches to conceptualization and etiology. In P. H. Blaney, R. F. Krueger, & T. Millon (Eds.), *Oxford textbook of psychopathology* (pp. 768–90). New York: Oxford University Press.

Trull, T. J., & Durrett, C. A. (2005). Categorical and dimensional models of personality disorder. *Annu. Rev. Clin. Psychol., 1,* 355–80.

Trull, T. J., Sheiderer, E., & Tomko, R. (2012). Axis II comorbidity. In T. Widiger (Ed.), *The Oxford handbook of personality disorders* (pp. 219–36). Oxford, UK: Oxford University Press.

Trzepacz, P. T., Meagher, D. J., & Wise, M. G. (2002). Neuropsychiatric aspects of delirium. In S. C. Yudofsky & R. E. Hales (Eds.), *The APA textbook of neuropsychiatry and clinical neurosciences* (pp. 525–64). Washington, DC: American Psychiatric Publishing.

Tsai, A., Loftus, E., & Polage, D. (2000). Current directions in false-memory research. In D. Bjourkund (Ed.), *False-memory creation in children and adults: Theory, research, and implications* (pp. 31–44). Mahwah, NJ: Erlbaum.

Tsai, J. L., Butcher, J. N., Munoz, R. F., & Vitousek, K. (2001). Culture, ethnicity, and psychopathology. In P. B. Sutker & H. E. Adams (Eds.), *Comprehensive handbook of psychopathology* (3rd ed., pp. 105–27). New York: Kluwer/Plenum.

Tsai, J. L., & Chentsova-Dutton, Y. (2002). Understanding depression across cultures. In I. H. Gotlib & C. L. Hammen (Eds.), *Handbook of depression* (pp. 467–91). New York: Guilford Press.

Tseng, W. (2001). *Handbook of cultural psychiatry.* San Diego, CA: Academic Press.

Tseng, W. S. (1973). The development of psychiatric concepts in traditional Chinese medicine. *Arch. Gen. Psychiatry, 29*(4), 569–75.

Tsuang, M. T., Taylor, L., & Faraone, S. V. (2004). An overview of the genetics of psychotic mood disorders. *J. Psychiatr. Res., 38,* 3–15.

Tsuno, N., Besset, A., & Ritchie, K. (2005). Sleep and depression. *J. Clinical Psychiatry, 66,* 1254–69.

Tucker, G. J. (1998). Editorial: Putting DSM-IV in perspective. *Am. J. Psychiatry, 155*(2), 159–61.

Tuke, D. H. (1882). *History of the insane in the British Isles.* London: Kegan, Paul, Trench.

Tully, P. J., Pedersen, S. S., Winefield, H. R., Baker, R. A., Turnbull, D. A., & Denollet, J. (2011). Cardiac morbidity risk and depression and anxiety: A disorder, symptom, and trait analysis among cardiac surgery patients. *Psychol Health Med, 16,* 333–45.

Turan, M., & Senol, S. (2000). Tic disorders in children and adolescents. *Psikiyatri Psikoloji Psikofarmakoloji Dergisis, 8,* 215–20.

Turner, R. J., Lloyd, D. A., & Taylor, J. (2006). Physical disability and mental health: An epidemiology of psychiatric and substance disorders. *Rehabilitation Psychology, 51*(3), 214–23.

Turrisi, R. (1999). Cognitive and attitudinal factors in the analysis of alternatives to binge drinking. *J. Applied Social Psychology, 29,* 1510–33.

Turrisi, R., Wiersma, K. A., & Hughes, K. K. (2000). Binge-drinking-related consequences in college students: Role of drinking beliefs and mother–teen communications. *Psych. Addict. Behav., 14*(4), 342–55.

Twenge, J. M., & Campbell, W. K. (2002). Self-esteem and socioeconomic status: A meta-analytic review. *Personal. Soc. Psychol. Rev., 6*(1), 59–71.

Tyrer, P., & Baldwin, D. (2006). Generalised anxiety disorder. *Lancet, 368*(9553), 2156–66.

Tyrer, S. P. (2011). Review of Behavioral and psychopharmacologic pain management. *Brit. J. Psychiatry, 199*(5), 435–36.

Tyrka, A. R., Cannon, T. D., Haslam, N., Mednick, S. A., Schulsinger, F., Schulsinger, H., et al. (1995). The latent structure of schizotypy: I. Premorbid indicators of a taxon of individuals at risk for schizophrenia-spectrum disorders. *J. Abn. Psychol., 104*(1), 173–83.

U

Uc, E. Y., Doerschug, K. C., Magnotta, V., Dawson, J. D., Thomsen, T. R., Kline, J. N., et al. (2014). Phase I/II randomized trial of aerobic exercise in Parkinson disease in a community setting. *Neurology, 83,* 413–25.

Udry, J. R. (1993). The politics of sex research. *J. Sex Res., 30,* 103–10.

Uecker, A., Mangan, P. A., Obrzut, J. E., & Nadel, L. (1993). Down syndrome in neurobiological perspective: An emphasis on spatial cognition. *J. Clin. Child Psychol., 22*(2), 266–76.

Uhde, T. W. (1990). Caffeine provocation of panic: A focus on biological mechanisms. In J. C. Ballenger (Ed.), *Neurobiology of panic disorder* (pp. 219–42). New York: Wiley-Liss.

Uher, R., & McGuffin, P. (2010). The moderation by the serotonin transporter gene of environmental adversity in the etiology of depression: 2009 update. *Molec. Psychiatry, 15*(1), 18–22. doi:10.1038/mp.2009.123

Uher, R., & Treasure, J. (2005). Brain lesions and eating disorders. *J. Neurol. Neurosurg. Psychiatry, 76,* 852–57.

Uliaszek, A. A., Zinbarg, R. E., Mineka, S., Craske, M. G., Griffith, J. W., Sutton, J. M., et al. (2012). A longitudinal examination of stress generation in depressive and anxiety disorders. *J. Abn. Psychol., 121,* 4–15.

Ulmer, S., & Jansen. U. (Eds.). (2010). *fMRI: Basics and clinical applications.* New York: Springer.

Ungar, M. (2015). Diagnosing childhood resilience: A systematic approach to the diagnosis of adaptation in adverse social and physical ecologies. *J. Child Psychology and Psychiatry, 56,* 4–17.

United States v. Batista, 483 F. 3d 193 (3rd Cir. 2007).

Unützer, J., Schoenbaum, M., Druss, B. G., & Katon, W. J. (2006). Transforming mental health care at the interface with general medicine: Report for the president's commission. *Psychiatric Services, 57*(1), 37–47. doi:http://dx.doi.org/10.1176/appi.ps.57.1.37

U.S. Census Bureau. (2009). *Annual demographic supplement to the March 2002 Current Population Survey.* Retrieved from http://www.census.gov

U.S. Census Bureau. (2014). *United States Census, 2013.* Washington, DC: Author.

U.S. Department of Defense. (2010, August). *The challenge and the promise: Strengthening the force, preventing suicide and saving lives. Final report of the Department of Defense Task Force on the Prevention of Suicide by Members of the Armed Forces.* Washington, DC: Author.

U.S. Department of Defense. (2014). Department of Defense suicide event report: Calendar year 2013 annual report. Retrieved from http://www.suicideoutreach.org/SuicideData/DoDSER_Reports.htm

U.S. Department of Health and Human Services. (1994). *Preventing tobacco use among young people: A report of the Surgeon General.* Atlanta, GA: Author.

U.S. Department of Health and Human Services. (2001). *Mental health: Culture, race, and ethnicity—A supplement to mental health: A report of the surgeon general.* Rockville, MD: Author.

U.S. Department of Health and Human Services. (2006). *Intermediate care facilities for the retarded.* Rockville, MD: Author.

U.S. Department of Health and Human Services, Administration for Children and Families, Administration on Children, Youth and Families, Children's Bureau. (2013). *Child maltreatment 2012.* Retrieved from http://www.acf.hhs.gov/programs/cb/research-data-technology/statistics-research/child-maltreatment

U.S. Food and Drug Administration (FDA). (2002). *The FDA approved Strattera.* Washington, DC: U.S. Department of Health and Human Services.

U.S. Food and Drug Administration (FDA). (2004). *FDA talk paper: Warning about Strattera.* Washington, DC: U.S. Department of Health and Human Services.

Üstün, T. B., Bertelsen, A., Dilling, H., van Drimmelen, J., Pull, C., Okasha, A., et al. (1996). *ICD-10 casebook: The many faces of mental disorders: Adult case histories according to ICD-10.* Washington, DC: American Psychiatric Press.

V

Vaillant, G. E., Gale, L., & Milofsky, E. S. (1982). Natural history of male alcoholism: II. The relationship between different diagnostic dimensions. *J. Stud. Alcoh., 43*(3), 216–32.

Valmaggia, L. R., Tabraham, P., Morris, E., & Bouman, T. K. (2008). Cognitive-behavioral therapy across stages of psychosis: Prodromal, first episode, and chronic schizophrenia. *Cognitive and Behavioral Practice, 15,* 179–93.

Van Amsterdam, J., Brunt, T., & van den Brink, W. (2015). The adverse health effects of synthetic cannabinoids with emphasis on psychosis-like effects. *J. Psychopharmacology, 29,* 254–63.

van der Leeuw, G., Gerrits, M. J., Terluin, B., Numans, M. E., van der Feltz-Cornelis, C. M., van der Horst, H. E., et al. (2015). The association between somatization and disability in primary care patients. *J. Psychosomatic Res., 79*(2), 117–22. doi:10.1016/j.jpsychores.2015.03.001

van der Stouwe, T., Asscher, J. J., Stams, G. M., Deković, M., & van der Laan, P. H. (2014). The effectiveness of multisystemic therapy (MST): A meta-analysis. *Clin. Psychology Rev., 34*(6), 468–81. doi:10.1016/j.cpr.2014.06.006

Van Doren, C. V. (1938). *Benjamin Franklin.* New York: Penguin.

van Grootheest, D. S., Bartels, M., Cath, D. C., Beekman, A. T., Hudziak, J. J., & Boomsma, D. I. (2007). Genetic and environmental contributions underlying stability in childhood obsessive-compulsive behavior. *Biological Psychiatry, 61,* 308–15.

Van Kampen, J., & Katz, M. (2001). Persistent psychosis after a single ingestion of "ecstasy." *Psychosomatics: J. Consultation Liaison Psychiatry, 42*(6), 525–27.

Van Kuyck, K., Gérard, N., Van Laere, K., Casteels, C., Pieters, G., Gabriëls, L., et al. (2009). Towards a neurocircuitry in anorexia nervosa: Evidence from functional neuroimaging studies. *J. Psychiatr. Res., 43,* 1133–45.

Van Lier, P. A. C., Muthen, B. O., van der Sar, R. M., & Crijnen, A. A. M. (2004). Preventing disruptive behavior in elementary school children: Impact of a universal classroom-based intervention. *J. Cons. Clin. Psychol., 72,* 467–78.

van Os, J., Bak, M., Hanssen, M., Bijl, R. V., de Graaf, R., & Verdoux, H. (2002). Cannabis use and psychosis: A longitudinal population-based study. *Am. J. Epidemiol., 156,* 319–27.

Van Winkel, R., & Kuepper, R. (2014). Epidemiological, neurobiological, and genetic clues to the mechanisms linking cannabis abuse to risk for nonaffective psychosis. *Annu. Rev. Clin. Psychol., 10,* 767–91.

Vandereycken, W. (2002). History of anorexia nervosa and bulimia nervosa. In C. G. Fairburn & K. D. Brownell (Eds.), *Eating disorders and obesity* (2nd ed., pp. 151–52). New York: Guilford Press.

Vanhala, M., Korpelained, R., Tapanainen, P., Kaikkonen, K., Kaikkonen, H., Saukkonen, T., et al. (2009). Lifestyle risk factors for obesity in 7-year-old children. *Obesity Research and Clinical Practice, 3,* 99–107.

Vasey, P. L., & Bartlett, N. H. (2007). What can the Samoan "fa'afafine" teach us about the Western concept of gender identity disorder in childhood? *Persp. Biol. Med., 50*(4), 481–90.

Veague, H. B., & Hooley, J. M. (2014). Enhanced sensitivity and response bias for male anger in women with borderline personality disorder. *Psychiatry Research, 215,* 687–93.

Veale, D., & Riley, S. (2001). Mirror, mirror on the wall, who is the ugliest of them all? The psychopathology of mirror gazing in body dysmorphic disorder. *Behav. Res. Ther., 39,* 1381–93.

Veale, J. F., Clarke, D. E., & Lomax, T. C. (2008). Sexuality of male-to-female transsexuals. *Arch. Sex. Behav., 37,* 586–97.

Velasquez, M. M., Maurer, G. G., Crouch, C., & DiClemente, C. C. (2001). *Group treatment of substance abuse.* New York: Guilford Press.

Velting, D. M., & Gould, M. S. (1997). Suicide contagion. In R. W. Maris, M. M. Silverman, & S. S. Canetton (Eds.), *Review of suicidology, 1997* (pp. 96–137). New York: Guilford Press.

Ventura, J., Nuechterlein, K. H., Hardesty, J. P., & Gitlin, M. (1992). Life events and schizophrenic relapse after withdrawal of medication. *Brit. J. Psychiatry, 161,* 615–20.

Ventura, J., Nuechterlein, K. H., Lukoff, D., & Hardesty, J. P. (1989). A prospective study of stressful life events and schizophrenic relapse. *J. Abn. Psychol., 98,* 407–11.

Verdejo, A., Toribio, I., Orozco, C., Puente, K. L., & Pérez-García, M. (2005). Neuropsychological functioning in methadone maintenance patients versus abstinent heroin abusers. *Drug Al. Dep., 78*(3), 283–88.

Verghese, J., Lipton, R. B., Hall, C. B., Kuslansky, G., Katz, M. J., & Buschke, H. (2002). Abnormality of gait as a predictor of non-Alzheimer's dementia. *New Engl. J. Med., 347,* 1761–68.

Verheul, R., Bartak, A., & Widiger, T. (2007). Prevalence and construct validity of personality disorder not otherwise specified (PDNOS). *J. Pers. Disord., 21,* 359–70.

Verheul, R., & Widiger, T. (2004). A meta-analysis of the prevalence and usage of the personality disorder not otherwise specified (PDNOS) diagnosis. *J. Pers. Disord., 18,* 309–19.

Verhoeven, J. E., Revesz, D., Epel, E. S., Lin, J., Wolkowitz, O. M., & Penninx, B. W. (2014). Major depressive disorder and accelerated cellular aging: Results from a large psychiatric cohort study. *Molecular Psychiatry, 19,* 895–910.

Verkerk, A. J. M. H., Pieretti, M., et al. (1991). Identification of a gene (FMR-1) containing a CGG repeat coincident with a breakpoint cluster region exhibiting length variation in fragile X syndrome. *Cell, 65,* 905–14.

Vermetten, E., Schmahl, C., Lindner, S., Loewenstein, R. J., & Bremner, J. D. (2006). Hippocampal and amygdalar volumes in dissociative disorder. *Am. J. Psychiatry, 163*, 630–36.

Verona, E., Patrick, C. J., & Joiner, T. E. (2001). Psychopathy, antisocial personality, and suicide risk. *J. Abn. Psychol., 110*(3), 462–70.

Verster, J. C., Stephens, R., Penning, R., Rohsenow, D., McGeary, J., Levy, D., et al. (2010). The Alcohol Hangover Research Group consensus statement on best practice in alcohol hangover research. *Current Drug Abuse Reviews, 3*, 116–126.

Verster, J. C., Van Herwijnen, J., Olivier, B., & Kahler, C. W. (2009). Validation of the Dutch Brief Young Adult Alcohol Consequences Questionnaire (B-YAACQ). *Addict Behav., 34*, 411–14.

Vickers, K., & McNally, R. J. (2004). Panic disorder and suicide attempt in the National Comorbidity Survey. *J. Abn. Psychol., 113*(4), 582–91.

Viding, E., Blair, R. J., Moffitt, T. E., & Plomin, R. (2005). Evidence for substantial genetic risk for psychopathy in 7-year-olds. *J. Child Psychol. Psychiatry, 46*(6), 592–97.

Vidovic, V., Juresa, V., Begovac, I., Mahnik, M., & Tocilj, G. (2005). Perceived family cohesion, adaptability and communication in eating disorders. *European Eating Disorders Review, 13*, 19–28.

Villanueva, M., Tonigan, J. S., & Miller, W. R. (2003). A retrospective study of client-treatment matching: Differential treatment response of Native American alcoholics in project MATCH. *Alcohol. Clin. Exp. Res., 26*(Suppl.), A83.

Villasante, O. (2003). The unfulfilled project of the model mental hospital in Spain: Fifty years of the Santa Isabel Madhouse, Leganis (1851–1900). In T. Dening (Ed.), *Hist. Psychiatry 14*(53, Pt. 1), pp. 3–23.

Viney, W. (1996). Dorothea Dix: An intellectual conscience for psychology. In G. A. Kimble, C. A. Boneau, & M. Wertheimer (Eds.), *Portraits of pioneers in psychology* (pp. 15–33). Washington, DC: American Psychological Association.

Vita, A., De Peri, L., Silenzi, C., & Dieci, M. (2006). Brain morphology in first episode schizophrenia: A meta-analysis of quantitative magnetic resonance imaging studies. *Schiz. Res., 82*, 75–88.

Vitacco, M. J., Van Rybroek, G. J., Erickson, S. K., Rogstad, J. E., Tripp, A., Harris, L., et al. (2008). Developing services for insanity acquittees conditionally released into the community: Maximizing success and minimizing recidivism. *Psychological Services, 5*(2), 118–25.

Vitacco, M. J., Vauter, R., Erickson, S. K., & Ragatz, L. (2014). Evaluating conditional release in not guilty by reason of insanity acquittees: A prospective follow-up study in Virginia. *Law and Human Behavior, 38*,, 346–56. doi:10.1037/lhb0000071

Vitale, J. E., & Newman, J. P. (2013). Psychopathy as psychopathology: Key developments in assessment, etiology and treatment. In W. E. Craighead, D. J. Miklowitz, & L. W. Craighead (Eds.), *Psychopathology* (2nd ed., pp. 583–615). Hoboken, NJ: John Wiley & Sons.

Vitiello, B., & Waslick, B. (2010). Pharmacotherapy for children and adolescents with anxiety disorders. *Psychiatr. Ann., 40*(4), 185–91.

Vitousek, K. B. (2002). Cognitive-behavioral therapy for anorexia nervosa. In C. G. Fairburn & K. D. Brownell (Eds.), *Eating disorders and obesity: A comprehensive handbook* (2nd ed., pp. 308–13). New York: Guilford Press.

Vögele, C., & Gibson, E. L. (2010). Moods, emotions, and eating disorders. In W. S. Agras (Ed.), *The Oxford handbook of eating disorders* (pp. 180–205). New York: Oxford University Press.

Vogeltanz-Holm, N. D., Wonderlich, S. A., Lewis, B. A., Wilsnack, S. C., Harris, T. R., Wilsnack, R. W., et al. (2000). Longitudinal predictors of binge eating, intense dieting, and weight concerns in a national sample of women. *Behav. Ther., 31*, 221–35.

Voglmaier, M. M., Seidman, L. J., Niznikiewicz, M. A., Dickey, C. C., Shenton, M. E., & McCarley, R. W. (2005). A comparative profile analysis of neuropsychological function in men and women with schizotypal personality disorder. *Schiz. Res., 74*(1), 43–49.

Voight, K., Wollburg, E., Weinmann, N., Herzog, A., Meyer, B., Langs, G., & Löwe, B. (2012). Predictive validity and clinical utility of DSM-5 somatic symptom disorder—Comparison with DSM-IV somatoform disorders and additional criteria for consideration. *J. Psychosomatic Res., 73*, 345–50.

Volk, H. E., Scherrer, J. F., Bucholz, K. K., Todorov, A., Heath, A. C., Jacob, T., et al. (2007). Evidence for specificity of transmission of alcohol and nicotine dependence in an offspring of twins design. *Drug and Alcohol Dependence, 87*(2–3), 225–32.

Volkow, N. D., Ding, Y. S., Fowler, J. S., Ashby, C., Liebermann, J., Hitzemann, R., et al. (1995). Is methylphenidate like cocaine? Studies on their pharmacokinetics and distribution in the human brain. *Arch. Gen. Psychiatry, 52*, 456–63.

Volkow, N. D., & O'Brien, C. P. (2007). Issues for DSM-V: Should obesity be included as a brain disorder? *Am. J. Psychiatry, 164*(5), 708–10.

Vollmer-Larsen, A., Jacobsen, T. B., Hemmingsen, R., & Parnas, J. (2006). Schizoaffective disorder: The reliability of its clinical diagnostic use. *Acta Psych. Scand., 113*(5), 402–07.

von der Hagen, M., Pivarcsi, M., Liebe, J., von Bernuth, H., Didonato, N., Hennermann, J. B., et al. (2014). Diagnostic approach to microcephaly in childhood: A two-center study and review of the literature. *Dev. Med. Child Neurol., 56*(8), 732–41. doi:10.1111/dmcn.12425

Vreugdenhil, A., Cannell, J., Davies, D., & Razay, G. (2012). A community-based exercise programme to improve functional ability in people with Alzheimer's disease: A randomized controlled trial. *Scandinavian J. Caring Sciences, 26*, 12–19.

Vrshek-Schallhorn, S., Mineka, S., Zinbarg, R. E., Craske, M. G., Griffith, J. W., Sutton, J., et al. (2013). Refining the candidate environment: Interpersonal stress, the serotonin transporter polymorphism, and gene–environment interactions in major depression. *Clin. Psychological Sci., 2*, 235–48.

W

Waddington, J. L., O'Callaghan, E., Youssef, H. A., Buckley, P., Lane, A., Cotter, D., et al. (1999). Schizophrenia: Evidence for a "cascade" process with neurodevelopmental origins. In E. Z. Susser, A. S. Brown, & J. M. Gorman (Eds.), *Prenatal exposures in schizophrenia* (pp. 3–34). Washington, DC: American Psychiatric Press.

Wade, K., Sharman, S., Garry, M., Memon, M., Garry, M., et al. (2007). False claims about false memory research. *Consciousness and Cognition, 16*, 118–28.

Wade, T. D. (2010). Genetic influences on eating and the eating disorders. In W. A. Agras (Ed.), *The Oxford handbook of eating disorders* (pp. 103–22). New York: Oxford University Press.

Wade, T. D., Tiggerman, M., Bulik, C. M., Fairburn, C. G., Wray, N. R., & Martin, N. G. (2008). Shared temperament risk factors for anorexia nervosa: A twin study. *Psychosomat. Med., 70*, 239–44.

Wahlberg, K.-E., Wynne, L. C., et al. (1997). Gene-environment interaction in vulnerability to schizophrenia: Findings from the Finnish adoptive family study of schizophrenia. *Am. J. Psychiatry, 154*(3), 355–62.

Wakefield, J. C. (2012). The DSM-5's proposed new categories of sexual disorder: The problem of false positives in sexual diagnosis. *Clin. Soc. Work J., 40*(2), 213–223.

Wakefield, J. C., Schmitz, M. F., First, M. B., & Horwitz, A. V. (2007). Extending the bereavement exclusion for major depression to other losses: Evidence from the National Comorbidity Survey. *Arch. Gen. Psychiatry, 64*(4), 433–40.

Waldman, I. D., & Rhee, S. H. (2006). Genetic and environmental influences on psychopathy and antisocial behavior. In C. Patrick (Ed.), *Handbook of psychopathy* (pp. 205–29). New York: Guilford Press.

Waldman, I. D., & Slutske, W. S. (2000). Antisocial behavior and alcoholism: A behavioral genetic perspective on comorbidity. *Clin. Psychol. Rev., 20*(2), 255–87.

Walford, E. (1878). *Old and new London: A narrative of its history, its people, and its places* (Vol. VI). London: Cassell, Petter, & Galpin.

Walker, E. F., & Diforio, D. (1997). Schizophrenia: A neural diathesis-stress model. *Psychol. Rev., 104*, 667–85.

Walker, E. F., Grimes, K. E., Davis, D. M., & Smith, A. J. (1993). Childhood precursors of schizophrenia: Facial expressions of emotion. *Am. J. Psychiatry, 150*(11), 1654–60.

Walker, E., Kestler, L., Bollini, A., & Hochman, K. M. (2004). Schizophrenia: Etiology and course. *Annu. Rev. Psychol., 55*, 401–30.

Walker, E. F., Savoie, T., & Davis, D. (1994). Neuro-motor precursors of schizophrenia. *Schizo. Bull., 20*(3), 441–51.

Walker, E., Shapiro, D., Esterberg, M., & Trotman, H. (2010). Neurodevelopment and schizophrenia: Broadening the focus. *Curr. Dis. Psychol. Sci., 19*, 204–08.

Walker, E. F., & Tessner, K. (2008). Schizophrenia. *Perspectives on Psychological Science, 3*, 30–37.

Walker, H. (2008). Breaking free: My life with dissociative identity disorder. New York: Touchstone and Howard Books.

Walker, J., Archer, J., & Davies, M. (2005). Effects of rape on men: A descriptive analysis. *Arch. Sex. Behav., 34*, 69–80.

Wallace, J., Schneider, T., & McGuffin, P. (2002). Genetics of depression. In I. H. Gotlib & C. L. Hammen (Eds.), *Handbook of depression* (pp. 169–91). New York: Guilford Press.

Wallen, K., & Lloyd, E. A. (2011). Female sexual arousal: Genital anatomy and orgasm in intercourse. *Hormones and Behavior, 59*, 780–92.

Wallenstein, M. B., & Nock, M. K. (2007). Physical exercise as a treatment for non-suicidal self injury: Evidence from a single case study. *Am. J. Psychiatry, 164*, 350–51.

Wallien, M. S., & Cohen-Kettenis, P. T. (2008). Psychosexual outcome of gender-dysphoric children. *J. Am. Acad. Child and Adolescent Psychiatry, 47*, 1413–23.

Wallin, A., & Blennow, K. (1993). Heterogeneity of vascular dementia: Mechanisms and subgroups. *J. Geriatric Psychiatry and Neurology, 6*(3), 177–88.

Wallwiener, C. W., Wallwiener, L. M., Seeger, H., Mück, A. O., Bitzer, J., & Wallwiener, M. (2010). Prevalence of sexual dysfunction and impact of contraception in female German medical students. *J. Sexual Medicine, 7*(6), 2139–48.

Walsh, E., Moran, P., Scott, C., McKenzie, K., Burns, T., Creed, F., et al. (2003). Prevalence of violent victimization in severe mental illness. *Brit. J. Psychiatry, 183*, 233–38.

Walters, J. (2006, November 3). National Public Health official issues statement regarding South Dakota's proposed "medical" marijuana initiative. *News & Public Affairs.*

Wang, P. S., Berglund, P., Olfson, M., Pincus, H. A., Wells, K. B., & Kessler, R. C. (2005). Failure and delay in initial treatment contact after the first onset of mental disorders in the National Comorbidity Survey Replication. *Arch. Gen. Psychiatry, 62*, 603–13.

Wang, P. S., Lane, M., Olfson, M., Pincus, H. A., Wells, K. B., & Kessler, R. C. (2005). Twelve-month use of mental health services in the United States. *Arch. Gen. Psychiatry, 62*, 629–40.

Wang, Y., Beydoun, M. A., Liang, L., Caballero, B., & Kumanyika, S. K. (2008). Will all Americans become overweight or obese? Estimating the progression and cost of the US obesity epidemic. *Obesity, 16,* 2323–30.

Ward, C. L., & Laughlin, J. E. (2003). Social contexts, age and juvenile delinquency: A community perspective. *J. Child and Adolescent Mental Health, 15,* 13–26.

Ward, T., McCormack, J., Hudson, S. M., & Polaschek, D. (1997). Rape: Assessment and treatment. In D. R. Laws & W. O'Donohue (Eds.), *Sexual deviance: Theory, assessment, and treatment* (pp. 356–93). New York: Guilford Press.

Ware, A. L., O'Brien, J. W., Crocker, N., Deweese, B. N., Roesch, S. C., Coles, C. D., et al. (2012, August). The effects of prenatal alcohol exposure and attention-deficit/hyperactivity disorder on psychopathology. *Alcoholism: Clin. Exper. Res., 36*(8), 1431–41.

Wargo, E. (2007). Understanding the have-knots: The role of stress in just about everything. *APS Observer, 20*(11), 18–23.

Warren, J. I., Chauhan, P., Kois, L., Dibble, A., & Knighton, J. (2013). Factors influencing 2,260 opinions of defendants' restorability to adjudicative competency. *Psychology, Public Policy, and Law, 19*(4), 498–508. doi:10.1037/a0034740

Warren, J. I., Dietz, P. E., & Hazelwood, R. R. (1996). The sexually sadistic serial killer. *J. Forensic Sciences, 41,* 970–74.

Wasserman, D. R., & Leventhal, J. M. (1993). Maltreatment of children born to cocaine-dependent mothers. *Arch. Pediatrics and Adolescent Medicine, 147,* 1324–28.

Wasserman, J. D. (2003). Assessment of intellectual functioning. *Handbook of psychology* (Vol. 10, pp. 417–42). New York: John Wiley & Sons.

Wassink, T. H., Piven, J., & Patil, S. R. (2001). Chromosomal abnormalities in a clinic sample of individuals with autistic disorder. *Psychiatric Genetics, 11*(2), 57–63.

Watanabe, H., Kawauchi, A., Kitamori, T., & Azuma, Y. (1994). Treatment system for nocturnal enuresis according to an original classification system. *European Urology, 25,* 43–50.

Waters, R. J., & Nicoll, A. R. (2005). Genetic influences on outcome following acute neurological insults. *Curr. Opin. Critical Care, 11,* 105–10.

Watkins, S. S., Koob, G. F., & Markou, A. (2000). Neural mechanisms underlying nicotine addiction: Acute positive reinforcement and withdrawal. *Nicotine & Tobacco Res., 2,* 19–37.

Watson, D. (2005). Rethinking the mood and anxiety disorders: A quantitative hierarchical model for DSM-V. *J. Abn. Psych., 114*(4), 522–36.

Watson, D., Clark, L. A., & Chmielewski, M. (2008). Structures of personality and their relevance to psychopathology: II. Further articulation of a comprehensive unified trait structure. *J. Pers., 76*(6), 1545–86. doi:10.1111/j.1467-6494.2008.00531.x

Watson, D., Clark, L. A., & Harkness, A. R. (1994). Structures of personality and their relevance to psychopathology. *J. Abn. Psychol., 103,* 18–31.

Watson, D., Gamez, W., & Simms, L. J. (2005). Basic dimensions of temperament and their relation to anxiety and depression: A symptom-based perspective. *J. Res. Person., 39*(1), 46–66.

Watson, D., Kotov, R., & Gamez, W. (2006). Basic dimensions of temperament in relation to personality and psychopathology. In R. F. Krueger & J. L. Tackettt (Eds.), *Personality and psychopathology* (pp. 7–38). New York: Guilford Press.

Watson, J. (1924). *Behaviorism.* New York: The People's Institute Publishing Co.

Watson, S. J., Benson, J. A., Jr., & Joy, J. E. (2000). Marijuana and medicine: Assessing the science base: A summary of the 1999 Institute of Medicine Report. *Arch. Gen. Psychiatry, 57,* 347–52.

Watson, S., Gallagher, P., Ritchie, J. C., Ferrier, I. N., & Young, A. H. (2004). Hypothalamic-pituitary-adrenal axis function in patients with bipolar disorder. *Brit. J. Psychiatry, 184,* 496–502.

Watson, T. L., Bowers, W. A., & Andersen, A. E. (2000). Involuntary treatment of eating disorders. *Am. J. Psychiatry, 157*(11), 1806–10.

Watt, N. F., Anthony, E. J., Wynne, L. C., & Rolf, J. E. (Eds.). (1984). *Children at risk for schizophrenia: A longitudinal perspective.* Cambridge, UK: Cambridge University Press.

Watters, C., & Ingleby, D. (2004). Locations of care: Meeting the mental health and social care needs of refugees in Europe. *Int. J. Law & Psychiatry, 27*(6), 549–70.

Watts-English, T., Fortson, B. L., Gibler, N., Hooper, S. R., & DeBellis, M. D. (2006). The psychobiology of maltreatment in childhood. *J. Social Issues, 62*(4), 717–36.

Webb, C. A., DeRubeis, R. J., & Barber, J. P. (2010). Therapist adherence/competence and treatment outcome: A meta-analytic review. *J. Cons. Clin. Psychol., 78,* 200–11.

Weck, F., Gropalis, M., Hiller, W., & Bleichhardt, G. (2015). Effectiveness of cognitive behavioral group therapy for patients with hypochondriasis. *J. Anxiety Disorders, 30,* 1–7.

Weggen, S., Eriksen, J. L., Das, P., Sagi, S. A., Wang, R., Pietrzik, C. U., et al. (2001). A subset of NSAIDs lower amyloidogenic A(42) independently of cyclooxygenase activity. *Nature, 414,* 212–16.

Wegman, H. L., & Stetler, C. (2009). A meta-analytic review of the effects of childhood abuse on medical outcomes in adulthood. *Psychosom. Med., 71*(8), 805–12. doi:10.1097/PSY.0b013e3181bb2b46

Wegner, D. M. (1994). Ironic processes of mental control. *Psychol. Rev., 101*(1), 34–52.

Wehman, P. (2003). Workplace inclusion: Persons with disabilities and coworkers working together. *J. Vocational Rehabilitation, 18*(2), 131–41.

Weinberger, D. R. (1987). Implications of normal brain development for the pathogenesis of schizophrenia. *Arch. Gen. Psychiatry, 44,* 660–69.

Weinberger, L. E., Sreenivasan, S., Garrick, T., & Osran, H. (2005). The impact of surgical castration on sexual recidivism risk among sexually violent predatory offenders. *J. Am. Acad. Psychiatr. Law, 33,* 16–36.

Weiner, D. N., & Rosen, R. C. (1999). Sexual dysfunctions and disorders. In T. Millon, P. H. Blaney, & R. D. Davis (Eds.), *Oxford textbook of psychopathology* (pp. 410–43). New York: Oxford University Press.

Weiner, I. B. (Ed.) (2013). *Handbook of psychology, Vol. 12: Industrial and organizational psychology* (2nd ed.). Hoboken, NJ: John Wiley & Sons.

Weiner, I. B., & Greene, R. L. (2008). *Handbook of personality assessment.* Hoboken, NJ: John Wiley & Sons.

Weiner, L. A. B., & Meyer, G. (2009). Personality assessment with the Rorschach inkblot method. In J. N. Butcher (Ed.), *Oxford handbook of personality and clinical assessment* (pp. 277–98). New York: Oxford University Press.

Weinstock, J., Rash, C. J., & Petry, N. M. (2010). Contingency management for cocaine use in methadone maintenance patients: When does abstinence happen? *Psych. Addict. Behav., 24*(2), 282–91.

Weir, K. (2012). Big kids. *Monit. Psychol., 43,* 58–63.

Weiser, M. (2011). Early intervention for schizophrenia: The risk-benefit ratio of antipsychotic treatment in the prodromal phase. *Am. J. Psychiatry, 168,* 761–63.

Weisman, A., Duarte, E., Koneru, V., & Wasserman, S. (2006). The development of a culturally informed, family-focuses treatment for schizophrenia. *Fam. Process, 45,* 171–86.

Weiss, B., Weisz, J. R., & Bromfield, R. (1986). Performance of retarded and nonretarded persons on information processing tasks: Further tests of the similar structure hypothesis. *Psychol. Bull., 100,* 157–75.

Weiss, L. G., Keith, T. G., Zhu, J. & Chen, H. (2013). WAIS-IV and clinical validation of the four- and five-factor interpretative approaches. *J. Psychoeducational Assessment, 31.* doi:10.1177/0734282913478030

Weiss, L. G., Saklofske, D. H., Prifitera, A., & Holdnack, J. A. (Eds.). (2006). *WISC-IV advanced clinical interpretation.* Burlington, MA: Elsevier Academic Press, 2006.

Weissman, M. M., Fendrich, M., Warner, V., & Wickramaratne, P. (1992). Incidence of psychiatric disorder in offspring at high and low risk for depression. *J. Am. Acad. Child Adoles. Psychiatry, 31,* 640–48.

Weissman, M. M., Klerman, G. L., Markoqitz, J. S., & Ouellette, R. (1989). Suicidal ideation and suicide attempts in panic disorder and attacks. *New Engl. J. Med., 321,* 1209–14.

Weissman, M. M., & Markowitz, J. C. (2002). Interpersonal psychotherapy for depression. In I. H. Gotlib & C. L. Hammen (Eds.), *Handbook of depression* (pp. 404–21). New York: Guilford Press.

Weisz, J. R., McCarty, C. A., Eastman, K. L., Chaiyasit, W., & Suwanlert, S. (1997). Developmental psychopathology and culture: Ten lessons from Thailand. In S. Luthar, J. Burack, D. Cicchetti, & J. Weisz (Eds.), *Developmental psychopathology: Perspectives on adjustment, risk, and disorder* (pp. 568–92). Cambridge, UK: Cambridge University Press.

Weisz, J. R., McCarty, C. A., & Valeri, S. M. (2006). Effects of psychotherapy for depression in children and adolescents: A meta-analysis. *Psychol. Bull., 132*(1), 132–49. doi:10.1037/0033-2909.132.1.132

Weisz, J. R., Suwanlert, S., Chaiyasit, W., & Walter, B. R. (1987). Over and undercontrolled clinic-referral problems among Thai and American children and adolescents: The wat and wai of cultural differences. *J. Cons. Clin. Psychol., 55,* 719–26.

Weisz, J. R., Suwanlert, S., Chaiyasit, W., Weiss, B., Achenbach, T. M., & Eastman, K. L. (1993). Behavior and emotional problems among Thai and American adolescents: Parent reports for ages 12–16. *J. Abn. Psychol., 102,* 395–403.

Weisz, J. R., & Weiss, B. (1991). Studying the referability of child clinical problems. *J. Cons. Clin. Psychol., 59,* 266–73.

Weisz, J. R., Weiss, B., Suwanlert, S., & Chaiyasit, W. (2003). Syndromal structure of psychopathology in children of Thailand and the United States. *J. Cons. Clin. Psychol., 71*(2), 375–85.

Weisz, J. R., Weiss, B., Suwanlert, S., & Chaiyasit, W. (2006). Culture and youth psychopathology: Testing the Syndromal Sensitivity Model in Thai and American adolescents. *J Consult. Clin. Psychol., 74*(6), 1098–107.

Welin, C., Lappas, G., & Wilhelmsen, L. (2000). Independent importance of psychological factors for prognosis after myocardial infarction. *J. Internal Medicine, 247,* 629–39.

Wells, A. (1999). A cognitive model of generalized anxiety disorder. *Behav. Mod., 23,* 526–55.

Wells, A., & Butler, G. (1997). Generalized anxiety disorder. In D. M. Clark & C. G. Fairburn (Eds.), *Science and practice of cognitive behaviour therapy* (pp. 155–78). New York: Oxford University Press.

Wells, A., & Clark, D. M. (1997). Social phobia: A cognitive perspective. In G. C. L. Davey (Ed.), *Phobias: A handbook of description, treatment, and theory.* Chichester, UK: Wiley.

Wells, A., & Papageorgiou, C. (1995). Worry and the incubation of intrusive images following stress. *Behav. Res. Ther., 33,* 579–83.

Wells, D. L., & Ott, C. A. (2011, March). The "new" marijuana. *Ann. Psychiatry, 45*(3), 414–17. doi:10.1345/aph.1P580.

Welte, J. W., Barnes, G. M., Wieczorek, W. F., Tidwell, M. C., & Parker, J. C. (2004). Risk factors for pathological gambling. *Add. Behav., 29*(2), 323–35.

Wen-Shing, T., & Streltzer, J. (2008). *Cultural competence in health care: A guide for professionals.* New York: Springer.

West, J. R., Perotta, D. M., & Erickson, C. K. (1998). Fetal alcohol syndrome: A review for texas physicians. *Medical J. Texas, 94*, 61–67.

West, S. G., & Friedman, S. H. (2008). These boots are made for stalking: Characteristics of female stalkers. *Psychiatry, 5*, 37–42.

Westen, D., Shedler, J., & Bradley, R. (2006). A prototype approach to personality disorder diagnosis. *Am. J. Psychiatry, 163*, 846–56.

Westermeyer, J. (2001). Personal communication to J. N. Butcher.

Westermeyer, J., & Janca, A. (1997). Language, culture and psychopathology: Conceptual and methodological issues. *Transcult. Psychiatry, 34*, 291–311.

Westermeyer, J., & Kroll, J. (1978). Violence and mental illness in a peasant society: Characteristics of violent behaviors and "folk" use of restraints. *Brit. J. Psychiatry, 133*, 529–41.

Whalley, H. C., Simonotto, E., Flett, S., et al. (2004). fMRI correlates of state and trait effects in subjects at genetically enhanced risk of schizophrenia. *Brain, 127*, 478–91.

Whang, W., Kubzansky, L. D., Kawachi, I., Rexrode, K. M., Kroenke, C. H., Glynn, R. J., et al. (2009). Depression and risk of sudden cardiac death and coronary heart disease in women: Results from the Nurses' Health Study. *J. Am. Coll. Cardiol., 53*(11), 950–58. doi:10.1016/j.jacc.2008.10. 060

Wheeler, J. G., Christensen, A., & Jacobson, N. S. (2001). Couple distress. In D. H. Barlow (Ed.), *Clinical handbook for psychological disorders* (3rd ed., pp. 609–30). New York: Guilford Press.

Whipple, J. L., & Lambert, M. J. (2011). Outcome measures for practice. *Annu. Rev. Clin. Psychol., 7*, 87–111.

Whisman, M. A. (2007). Marital distress and DSM-IV psychiatric disorders in a population-based national survey. *J. Abn. Psych., 116*(3), 63843.

Whitaker, R. (2009). Deinstitutionalization and neuroleptics: The myth and reality. In Y. O. Alanen, M. González de Chávez, A. S. Silver, & B. Martindale (Eds.), *Psychotherapeutic approaches to schizophrenic psychoses: Past, present and future (International Society for the Psychological Treatments of the Schizophrenias and Other Psychoses)* (pp. 346–56). New York: Routledge/Taylor & Francis Group.

Whitaker, R. (2010). *Anatomy of an epidemic: Magic bullets, psychiatric drugs, and the astonishing rise of mental illness in America.* New York: Crown Publishers.

White, A. G., Birnbaum, H. G., Mareva, M. N., et al. (2005). Direct costs of opioid abuse in an insured population in the United States. *J. Managed Care Pharm., 11*(6), 469–79.

White, B. P., Becker-Blease, K., & Grace-Bishop, K., (2006). Stimulant medication use, misuse, and abuse in an undergraduate and graduate student sample. *J. Am. College of Health, 54*, 261–68.

White, K. S., & Barlow, D. H. (2002). Panic disorder and agoraphobia. In D. H. Barlow (Ed.), *Anxiety and its disorders* (2nd ed., pp. 328–79). New York: Guilford Press.

White, K. S., Brown, T. A., Somers, T. J., & Barlow, D. H. (2006). Avoidance behavior in panic disorder: The moderating influence of perceived control. *Behav. Res. Ther., 44*(1), 147–57.

Whiteford, H. A., Degenhardt, L., Rehm, J., Baxter, A. J., Ferrari, A. J., Charlson, F. J., et al. (2013). Global burden of disease attributable to mental and substance use disorders: Findings from the Global Burden of Disease Study 2010. *Lancet, 382*, 1575–86.

Whitfield-Gabrieli, S., Thermenos, H. W., Milanovic, S., Tsuang, M. T., Faraone, S. V., McCarley, R. W., et al. (2009). Hyperactivity and hyperconnectivity of the default network in schizophrenia and in first-degree relatives of persons with schizophrenia. *Proc. Natl. Acad. Sci. USA, 106*, 1279–84.

Whittington, C. J., Kendall, T., Fonagy, P., Cottrell, D., Cotgrove, A., & Boddington, E. (2004). Selective serotonin reuptake inhibitors in childhood depression: Systematic review of published versus unpublished data. *Lancet, 363*, 1341–45.

Whittington, C. J., Kendall, T., & Pilling, S. (2005). Are the SSRIs and atypical antidepressants safe and effective for children and adolescents? *Curr. Opin. In Psychiatry, 18*, 21–25.

WHO World Mental Health Survey Consortium. (2004). Prevalence, severity, and unmet need for treatment of mental disorders in the World Health Organization World Mental Health Surveys. *JAMA, 291*, 2581–90.

Whoriskey, P. (2013, January 2). Rising painkiller addiction shows damage from drugmaker's role in shaping medical opinion. *Washington Post.*

Whybrow, P. C. (1997). *A mood apart.* New York: Basic Books.

Widiger, T. A. (2006). Psychopathy and DSM-IV psychopathology. In C. J. Patrick (Ed.), *Handbook of the psychopathy* (pp. 156–71). New York: Guilford Press.

Widiger, T. A., & Bornstein, R. F. (2001). Histrionic, dependent, and narcissistic personality disorders. In H. E. Adams & P. B. Sutker (Eds.), *Comprehensive handbook of psychopathology* (pp. 509–34). New York: Kluwer Academic.

Widiger, T. A., & Boyd, S. E. (2009). Personality disorder assessment instruments. In J. N. Butcher (Ed.), *Oxford handbook of personality and clinical assessment* (pp. 336–62). New York: Oxford University Press.

Widiger, T. A., & Frances, A. J. (1994). Toward a dimensional model for the personality disorders. In P. T. Costa, Jr. & T. A. Widiger (Eds.), *Personality disorders and the five-factor model of personality* (pp. 19–39). Washington, DC: American Psychological Association.

Widiger, T. A., Frances, A. J., Pincus, H. A., Davis, W. W., & First, M. B. (1991). Toward an empirical classification for the DSM-IV. *J. Abn. Psychol., 100*(3), 280–88.

Widiger, T. A., Livesley, W. J., & Clark, L. A. (2009). An integrative dimensional classification of personality disorder. *Psychol. Assess., 21*(3), 243–55. doi:10.1037/a0016606

Widiger, T. A., & Mullins-Sweatt, S. N. (2005). Categorical and dimensional models of personality disorders. In J. M. Oldham, A. E. Skodol, & D. Bender (Eds.), *The APA textbook of personality disorders* (pp. 35–53). Washington, DC: American Psychiatric Publishing.

Widiger, T. A., & Rogers, J. (1989). Prevalence and comorbidity of personality disorders. *Psychiatr. Ann., 19*, 132–36.

Widiger, T. A., Samuel, D. B., Mullins-Sweatt, S., Gore, W. L., & Crego, C. (2012). An integration of normal and abnormal personality structure: The five-factor model. In T. A. Widiger (Ed.). *The Oxford handbook of personality disorders* (pp. 82–107). New York: Oxford University Press.

Widiger, T. A., & Sanderson, C. J. (1995). Toward a dimensional model of personality disorders. In W. J. Livesley (Ed.), *The DSM-IV personality disorders* (pp. 433–58). New York: Guilford Press.

Widiger, T. A., & Trull, T. J. (2007). Plate tectonics in the classification of personality disorder: Shifting to a dimensional model. *Am. Psychol., 62*(2), 71–83.

Widiger, T. A., Trull, T. J., Clarkin, J. F., Sanderson, C. J., & Costa, P. T. (2002). A description of the DSM-IV personality disorders with the five-factor model of personality. In P. T. Costa, Jr. & T. A. Widiger (Eds.), *Personality disorders and the five-factor model of personality* (pp. 89–102). Washington, DC: American Psychological Association.

Widom, C. S. (1977). A methodology for studying non-institutionalized psychopaths. *J. Cons. Clin. Psychol., 45*, 674–83.

Widom, C. S., Czaja, S. J., & Paris, J. (2009). A prospective investigation of borderline personality disorder in abused and neglected children followed up into adulthood. *J. Pers. Disord., 23*, 433–46.

Wiederanders, M. R., Bromley, D. L., & Choate, P. A. (1997). Forensic conditional release programs and outcomes in three states. *Int. J. Law and Psychiatry, 20*, 249–57.

Wiik, K. L., Loman, M. M., Van Ryzin, M. J., Armstrong, J. M., Essex, M. J., Pollak, S. D., et al. (2011). Behavioral and emotional symptoms of post-institutionalized children in middle childhood. *J. Child Psychol. Psychiatry, 52*(1), 56–63. doi:10.1111/j.1469-7610. 2010.02294.x

Wilbert-Lampen, U., Leistner, D., Greven, S., Pohl, T., Sper, S., Völker, C., et al. (2008). Cardiovascular events during World Cup soccer. *New Engl. J. Med., 358*, 475–83.

Wilder, D. A., et al. (1997). A simplified method of toilet training adults in residential settings. *J. Behav. Ther. Exper. Psychiatry, 28*(3), 241–46.

Wildes, J. E., Emery, R. E., & Simons, A. D. (2001). The roles of ethnicity and culture in the development of eating disturbance and body dissatisfaction: A meta-analytic review. *Clin. Psychol. Rev., 21*(4), 521–51.

Wilfley, D. E., Friedman, M. A., Dounchis, J. Z., Stein, R. I., Welch, R. R., & Ball, S. A. (2000). Comorbid psychopathology in binge eating disorder: Relation to eating disorder severity at baseline and following treatment. *J. Cons. Clin. Psychol., 68*(4), 641–49.

Wilhelm, S., Peterson, A. L., Piacentini, J., Woods, D. W., Deckersbach, T., Sukhodolsky, D. G., et al. (2012). Randomized trial of behavior therapy for adults with Tourette syndrome. *Arch. General Psychiatry, 69*, 795–803.

Wilk, J. E., Bliese, P. D., Kim, P. Y., Thomas, J. L., McGurk, D., & Hoge, C. W. (2010). Relationship of combat experiences to alcohol misuse among U.S. soldiers returning from the Iraq war. *Drug Alcohol Depend., 108*(1–2), 115–21.

Wilkinson, B. J., Newman, M. G., Shytle, R. D., Silver, A. A., Sandberg, P. R., & Sheehan, D. (2001). Family impact of Tourette's syndrome. *J. Child Fam. Stud., 10*, 477–83.

Wilkinson, P., Kelvin, R., Roberts, C., Dubicka, B., & Goodyear, I. (2011). Clinical and psychosocial predictors of suicide attempts and nonsuicidal self-injury in the adolescent depression antidepressants and psychotherapy trial (ADAPT). *Am. J. Psychiatry, 168*, 495–501.

Willard, N. E. (2007). *Cyberbullying and cyberthreats: Responding to the challenge of online social aggression, threats, and distress.* Champaign, IL: Research Press.

Willcutt, E., & McQueen, M. (2010). Genetic and environmental vulnerability to bipolar spectrum disorders. In D. J. Miklowitz & D. Cicchetti (Eds.), *Understanding bipolar disorder: A developmental psychopathology perspective* (pp. 225–58). New York: Guilford Press.

Williams, C. L., & Butcher, J. N. (2011). *A beginner's guide to the MMPI-A.* Washington, DC: American Psychological Association.

Williams, D. R., Gonzalez, H. M., Neighbors, H., Nesse, R., Abelson, J. M., Sweetman, J., et al. (2007). Prevalence and distribution of major depressive disorder in African Americans, Caribbean blacks, and non-Hispanic whites: Results from the National Survey of American Life. *Arch. Gen. Psychiatry, 64*(3), 305–15. doi:10.1001/archpsyc.64.3.305

Williams, J. G., Higgins, J. P., & Brayne, C. E. (2006). Systematic review of prevalence studies of autism spectrum disorders. *Arch. Disease in Childhood, 91,* 8–15.

Williams, J. M. G., Russell, I., & Russell, D. (2008). Mindfulness-based cognitive therapy: Further issues in current evidence and future research. *J. Cons. Clin. Psych., 76*(3), 524–29.

Williams, L. R., Degnan, K. A., Perez-Edgar, K. E., Henderson, H. A., Rubin, K. H., Pine, D. S., et al. (2009). Impact of behavioral inhibition and parenting style on internalizing and externalizing problems from early childhood through adolescence. *J. Abn. Child Psychol., 37*(8), 1063–75. doi:10.1007/s10802-009-9331-3

Williams, R. B., Jr., Barefoot, J. C., Califf, R. M., Haney, T. L., Saunders, W. B., Pryor, D. B., et al. (1992). Prognostic importance of social and economic resources among medically treated patients with angiographically documented coronary artery disease. *JAMA, 267,* 520–24.

Wilson, E. J., MacLeod, C., Mathews, A., & Rutherford, E. M. (2006). The causal role of interpretive bias in anxiety reactivity. *J. Abn. Psych., 115*(1), 103–11.

Wilson, G. T. (1998). Manual-based treatment and clinical practice. *Clin. Psychol. Sci. Prac., 5,* 363–75.

Wilson, G. T. (2005). Psychological treatment of eating disorders. *Annu. Rev. Clin. Psychol., 1,* 439–65.

Wilson, G. T. (2010). Cognitive behavior therapy for eating disorders. In W. A. Agras (Ed.), *The Oxford handbook of eating disorders* (pp. 331–47). New York: Oxford University Press.

Wilson, G. T., & Fairburn, C. G. (2007). Treatments for eating disorders. In P. E. Nathan & J. M. Gorman (Eds.), *A guide to treatments that work* (3rd ed., pp. 579–609). New York: Oxford University Press.

Wilson, G. T., Grilo, C. M., & Vitousek, K. M. (2007). Psychological treatment of eating disorders. *Am. Psychol., 3,* 199–216.

Wilson, G. T., Wilfley, D. E., Agras, W. S., & Bryson, S. W. (2010). Psychological treatments of binge eating disorder. *Arch. Gen. Psychiatry, 67,* 94–101.

Wilson, K. G., Chochinov, H. M., McPherson, C. J., Skirko, M. G., Allard, P., Chary, S., et al. (2007). Desire for euthanasia or physician-assisted suicide in palliative cancer care. *Health Psych., 26*(3), 314–23.

Wilson, K., Sinclair, I., & Gibbs, I. (2000). The trouble with foster care: The impact of stressful events on foster care. *Brit. J. Social Work, 30,* 193–209.

Wilson, R. F. (2004). Recognizing the threat posed by an incestuous parent to the victim's siblings: Part I: Appraising the risk. *J. Child and Family Studies, 13*(2), 143–62.

Wilson, R. S., Arnold, S. E., Beck, T., Bienias, J. L., & Bennett, D. A. (2008). Changes in depressive symptoms during the prodromal phase of Alzheimer disease. *Arch. Gen. Psychiatry, 65,* 439–46.

Wilson, R. S., Krueger, K. R., Arnold, S. E., Schneider, J. A., Kelly, J. F., Barnes, L. L., et al. (2007). Loneliness and risk of Alzheimer disease. *Arch. Gen. Psychiatry, 64,* 234–40.

Wilson, T. D. (2009). Know thyself. *Perspectives on Psychological Science, 4,* 384–89.

Winblad, B., Engedal, K., Sioininen, H., Verhey, F., Waldeman, G., Wimo, A., et al. (2001). A 1-year, randomized, placebo-controlled study of donepezil in patients with mild to moderate AD. *Neurology, 57*(3), 489–95.

Wincze, J. P., Bach, A. K., & Barlow, D. H. (2008). Sexual dysfunction. In D. H. Barlow (Ed.), *Clinical handbook of psychological disorders: A step-by-step treatment manual* (4th ed., pp. 615–61). New York: Guilford Press.

Windhaber, J., Maierhofer, D., & Dantendorfer, K. (1998). Panic disorder induced by large doses of 3,4-methylenedioxymethamphetamine resolved by paroxetine. *J. Clin. Psychopharmacol., 18*(1), 95–96.

Winick, B. J. (1997). *The right to refuse mental health treatment.* Washington, DC: American Psychological Association.

Wink, P. (1991). Two faces of narcissism. *J. Pers. Soc. Psychol., 61,* 590–97.

Winokur, G., & Tsuang, M. T. (1996). *The natural history of mania, depression, and schizophrenia.* Washington, DC: American Psychiatric Press.

Winslow, J. T., & Insel, T. R. (1991). Neuroethological models of obsessive-compulsive disorder. In J. Zohar, T. Insel, & S. Rasmussen (Eds.), *The psychobiology of obsessive-compulsive disorder.* New York: Springer.

Winston, A. P., Jamieson, C. P., Madira, W., Gatward, N. M., & Palmer, R. L. (2000). Prevalence of thiamin deficiency in anorexia nervosa. *Int. J. Eat. Dis., 28,* 451–54.

Winston, A., Laikin, M., Pollack, J., Samstag, L. W., McCullough, L., & Muran, C. (1994). Short-term psychotherapy of personality disorders. *Am. J. Psychiatry, 151,* 190–94.

Wirdefeldt, K., Adami, H.-O., Cole, P., Trichopoulos, D., & Mandel, J. (2011). Epidemiology and etiology of Parkinson's disease: A review of the evidence. *Eur. J. Epidemiol, 26,* S1–S58.

Wise, R. A. (1980). The dopamine synapse and the notion of "pleasure centers" in the brain. *Trends in Neuroscience, 3,* 91–95.

Wise, R. A. (1996). Addictive drugs and brain stimulation reward. *Annu. Rev. Neurosci., 19,* 319–40.

Wise, R. A., & Munn, E. (1995). Withdrawal from chronic amphetamine elevates baseline intracranial self-stimulation thresholds. *Psychopharmacology, 117*(2), 130–36.

Wiseman, C. V., Gray, J. J., Mosimann, J. E., & Ahrens, A. (1992). Cultural expectations of thinness in women: An update. *Int. J. Eat. Dis., 11,* 85–89.

Wisniewski, T., Dowjat, W. K., Buxbaum, J. D., Khorkova, O., Efthimiopoulos, S., Kulczycki, J., et al. (1998). A novel Polish presenilin-2 mutation (p117l0 is associated with familial Alzheimer's disease and leads to death as early as the age of 28 years). *Neuroreport, 9,* 217–21.

Witkiewitz, K., & Marlatt, G. A. (2004). Relapse prevention for alcohol and drug problems: That was Zen, this is Tao. *Am. Psychol., 59*(4), 224–35.

Witkiewitz, K., & Marlatt, G. A. (2007). Modeling the complexity of post-treatment drinking: It's a rocky road to relapse. *Clin. Psych. Rev., 27*(6), 724–38.

Witlox, J., Eurelings, L. S., de Jonghe, J. F., Kalisvaart, K. J., Eikelenboom, P., & van Gool, W. A. (2010). Delirium in elderly patients and the risk of post-discharge mortality, institutionalization, and dementia: A meta-analysis. *JAMA, 304,* 443–51.

Witt, S. H., Kleindienst, N., Frank, J., Treutlein, J., Mühleisen, T., Degenhardt, F., et al. (2014). Analysis of genome-wide significant bipolar disorder genes in borderline personality disorder. *Psychiatric Genetics, 24,* 262–65.

Witthöft, M., & Hiller, W. (2010). Psychological approaches to origins and treatments of somatoform disorders. *Annu. Rev. Clin. Psychol., 6,* 2010, 257–83.

Witvliet, C. V., Ludwig, T. E., & Vander Laan, K. L. (2001). Granting forgiveness or harboring grudges: Implications for emotion, physiology, and health. *Psychol. Sci., 12*(2), 117–23.

Wobrock, T., Falkai, P., Schneider-Axmann, T., Frommann, N., Wölwer, W., & Gaebel, W. (2009). Effects of abstinence on brain morphology in alcoholism: A MRI study. *Eur. Arch. Psychiatr. Clin. Neurosci., 259*(3), 143–50.

Wojtyna, E., & Popiolek, K. (2015). The pain of a heart being broken: Pain experience and use of analgesics by caregivers of patients with

Alzheimer's disease. *BMC Psychiatry, 15,* 176. doi:10.1186/s12888-015-0571-1

Wolitzky-Taylor, K. B., Horowitz, J. D., Powers, M. B., & Telch, M. J. (2008). Psychological approaches in the treatment of specific phobias: A meta-analysis. *Clin. Psychol. Rev., 28*(6), 1021–37. doi:10.1016/j.cpr.2008.02.007

Wollburg, E., Voigt, K., Braukhaus, C., Herzog, A., & Löwe, B. (2013). Construct validity and descriptive validity of somatoform disorders in light of proposed changes for the DSM-5. *J. Psychosomatic Research, 74,* 18–24.

Wolpe, J. (1958). *Psychotherapy by reciprocal inhibition.* Stanford, CA: Stanford University Press.

Wolpe, J. (1988). *Life without fear. Anxiety and its cure.* Oakland, CA: New Harbinger Publications.

Wolpe, J. (1993). Commentary: The cognitivist oversell and comments on symposium contributions. *J. Behav. Ther. Exper. Psychiatry, 24*(2), 141–47.

Wolpe, J., & Rachman, S. J. (1960). Psychoanalytic evidence: A critique based on Freud's case of Little Hans. *J. Nerv. Ment. Dis., 131,* 135–45.

Wonderlich, S. A., Gordon, K. H., Mitchell, J. E., Crosby, R. D., & Engel, S. G. (2009). The validity and clinical utility of binge eating disorder. *Int. J. Eat. Dis., 42,* 687–705.

Wong, J. M., Na, B., Regan, M. C., & Whooley, M. A. (2013). Hostility, health behaviors, and risk of recurrent events in patients with stable coronary heart disease: Findings from the Heart and Soul Study. *J. Am. Heart Assoc., 2,* e000052. doi:10.1161/JAHA.113.000052

Woo, M., & Oei, T. P. S. (2007). MMPI-2 profiles of Australian and Singaporean psychiatric patients. *Psychiatr. Res., 150*(2), 153–61. doi:10.1016/j.psychres.2006.04.007

Wood, J. M., Garb, H. N., Nezworski, M. T., Lilienfeld, S. O., & Duke, M. C. (2015). A second look at the validity of widely used Rorschach indices: Comment on Mihura, Meyer, Dumitrascu, and Bombel (2013). *Psychological Bulletin, 141,* 236–49. http://dx.doi.org/10.1037/a0036005

Woodruff-Borden, J., Morrow, C., Bourland, S., & Cambron, S. (2002). The behavior of anxious parents: Examining mechanisms of transmission of anxiety from parent to child. *J. Clin. Child Adol. Psych., 31*(3), 364–74.

Woods, C. G. (2004). Human microcephaly. *Curr. Opin. Neurobiol., 14*(1), 112–17. doi:10.1016/j.conb.2004.01.003

Woods, D. W., & Miltenberger, R. G. (2001). *Tic disorder, trichotillomania, and other repetitive disorders.* New York: Kluwer.

Woods, S. W., Charney, D. S., Goodman, W. K., & Heninger, G. R. (1987). Carbon dioxide-induced anxiety: Behavioral, physiologic, and biochemical effects of 5% CO_2 in panic disorder patients and 5 and 7. 5% CO_2 in healthy subjects. *Arch. Gen. Psychiatry, 44,* 365–75.

Woodside, D. B., Bulik, C. M., Halmi, K. A., Fichter, M. M., Kaplan, A., Berrettini, W. H., et al. (2002). Personality, perfectionism, and attitudes toward eating in parents of individuals with eating disorders. *Int. J. Eat. Dis., 31*(3), 290–99.

Woodside, D. B., Bulik, C. M., Thornton, L., Klump, K. L., Tozzi, F., Fichter, M., et al. (2004). Personality in men with eating disorders. *J. Psychosom. Res., 57,* 273–78.

Woon, F. L., Sood, S., & Hedges, D. W. (2010). Hippocampal volume deficits associated with exposure to psychological trauma and posttraumatic stress disorder in adults: A meta-analysis. *Prog. Neuropsychopharmacology and Biological Psychiatry, 34,* 1181–88.

World Federation for Mental Health. (2013). *Mental health and older adults.* Retrieved from http://wfmh.com/wp-content/uploads/2013/11/2013_wmhday_english.pdf

World Health Organization (WHO). (1994). *Schedules for clinical assessment in neuropsychiatry.* Geneva: Author.

World Health Organization (WHO). (2001). *The world health report 2001. Mental health: New understanding, new hope.* Geneva: Author.

World Health Organization (WHO). (2003). *International and statistical classification of diseases and related health problems* (10th rev. ed.). Geneva: Author.

World Health Organization (WHO). (2010). *The world health report 2010.* Retrieved from http://www.who.int.en

World Health Organization (WHO). (2014a). *Global status report on alcohol and health 2014.* Geneva: Author.

World Health Organization (WHO). (2014b). WHODAS 2.0. Retrieved from http://www.who.int/classifications/icf/whodasii/en/index4.html

World Health Organization (WHO). (2015a). *Disease and injury mortality estimates, 2000–2012.* Retrieved from http://www.who.int/healthinfo/global_burden_disease/estimates/en/index1.html

World Health Organization (WHO). (2015b). *International statistical classification of diseases and related health problems, 10th revision (ICD-10)-2015-WHO, Chapter V: Mental and behavioural disorders (F00–F99).* Retrieved from http://apps.who.int/classifications/icd10/browse/2015/en#/V

World Health Organization (WHO). (2015c, January). *Fact sheet no. 311: Obesity and overweight.* Geneva: Author.

World Health Organization (WHO). (2015d, July). *Fact sheet no. 360: HIV/AIDS.* Retrieved from http://www.who.int/mediacentre/factsheets/fs360/en

Wright, J. H., Basco, M. R., & Thase, M. E. (2006). *Learning cognitive-behavior therapy.* Washington, DC: American Psychiatric Publishing.

Wright, M. J., & Jackson, R. C. (2007). Brain regions concerned with perceptual skills in tennis: An fMRI study. *Int. J. Psychophysiology, 63*(2), 214–20.

Wyatt, W. J., & Midkiff, D. M. (2006). Biological psychiatry: A practice in search of a science. *Behavior and Social Issues, 15,* 132–51.

Wykes, T., Huddy, V., Cellard, C., McGurk, S. R., & Czobor, P. (2011). A meta-analysis of cognitive remediation for schizophrenia: Methodology and effect sizes. *Am. J. Psychiatry, 168,* 472–85.

Wykes, T., Reeder, C., Landau, S., Everitt, B., Knapp, M., Patel, A., & Romeo, R. (2007). Cognitive remediation therapy in schizophrenia: Randomised controlled trial. *Brit. J. Psychiatry, 190,* 421–27.

X

Xia, J., Merinder, L. B., & Belgamwar, M. R. (2011). Psychoeducation for schizophrenia. *Cochran Database of Systematic Reviews, 6,* CD002831. doi:10.1002/14651858.CD002831.pub2

Xiao, Z., Yan, H., Wang, Z., Zou, Z., Xu, Y., Chen, J., et al. (2006). Trauma and dissociation in China. *Am. J. Psychiatry, 163,* 1388–91.

Xiong, W., Phillips, R., Hu, X., Wang, R., Dai, Q., Kleinman, J., et al. (1994). Family-based intervention for schizophrenic patients in China. *Brit. J. Psychiatry, 165,* 239–247.

Y

Yamada, T., & Meng, E. (2011). *Practical guide for clinical neurophysiologic testing.* Philadelphia, PA: Lippincott Williams & Wilkins.

Yang, L. R., Anglin, D. M., Wonpat-Borja, A. J., Opler, M. G., Greenspoon, M., & Corcoran, C. M. (2013). Public stigma associated with psychosis risk syndrome in a college population: Implications for peer intervention. *Psychiatric Services, 63,* 284–88.

Yang, Y., & Raine, A. (2009). Prefrontal structural and functional brain imaging findings in antisocial, violent, and psychopathic individuals: A meta-analysis. *Psychiatry Research: Neuroimaging, 174,* 81–88.

Yang, Y., Raine, A., Colletti, P., Toga, A. W., & Narr, K. L. (2010). Morphological alterations in the prefrontal cortex and the amygdala in unsuccessful psychopaths. *J. Abn. Psychol., 119,* 546–54.

Yanovski, S. Z., & Yanovski, J. A. (2002). Obesity. *New Engl. J. Med., 346,* 591–602.

Yapko, M. D. (1994). *Suggestions of abuse: True and false memories of childhood sexual trauma.* New York: Simon & Schuster.

Yardley, W. (2010). Violence prompts debate over medical marijuana. *New York Times, 159*(54), 982.

Ye, X., Scott, T., Gao, X., Maras, J. E., Bakun, P. J., & Tucker, K. L. (2013). Mediterranean diet, healthy eating index 2005, and cognitive function in middle-aged and older Puerto Rican adults. *J. Acad. Nutrition and Dietetics, 113,* 276–81.

Yeates, K. O., et al. (1997). Preinjury family environment as a determinant of recovery from traumatic brain injuries in school-age children. *J. Int. Neuropsycholog. Soc., 3*(6), 617–30.

Yegambaram, M., Mannivannan, B., Beach, T. G., & Halden, R. U. (2015). Role of environmental contaminants in the etiology of Alzheimer's disease: A review. *Curr. Alzheimer Res., 12,* 116–46.

Yen, S., Shea, M. T., Sanislow, C. A., Skodol, A. E., Grilo, C. M., Edelen, M. O., et al. (2009). Personality traits as prospective predictors of suicide at tempts. *Acta Psychiatr. Scand., 120*(3), 222–29. doi:10.1111/j.1600-0447.2009.01366.x

Yeomans, F. E., Levy, K. N., & Caligor, E. (2013). Transference-focused psychotherapy. *Psychotherapy, 50,* 449–53.

Yeung, A. C., Vekshtein, V. I., Krantz, D. S., Vita, J. A., Ryan, T. J., Ganz, P., et al. (1991). The effects of atherosclerosis on the vasomotor response of coronary arteries to mental stress. *New Engl. J. Med., 325,* 1551–56.

Yoder, K. A., Whitlock, L. B., & Hoyt, D. R. (2003). Gang involvement and membership among homeless and runaway youth. *Youth and Society, 34,* 441–67.

Yokum, S., Gearhardt, A. N., Harris, J. L., Brownell, K. D., & Stice, E. (2014). Individual differences in striatum activity to food commercials predict weight gain in adolescents. *Obesity, 22,* 2544–51.

Yoo, S. Y., Jang, J. H., Shin, Y. W., Kim, D. J., Park, H. J., Moon, W. J., et al. (2007). White matter abnormalities in drug-naïve patients with obsessive-compulsive disorder: A diffusion tensor study before and after citalopram treatment. *Acta Psychiatrica Scandinavica, 116*(3), 211–19.

Yoon, J., & Bruckner, T. A. (2009). Does deinstitutionalization increase suicide? *Health Services Research, 44*(4), 1385–405.

Yoshimoto, S., Minabe, Y., Kawai, M., Suzuki, K., Iyo, M., Isoda, H., et al. (2002). Metabolite alterations in basal ganglia associated with methamphetamine-related psychiatric symptoms: A proton MRS study. *Neuropsychopharmacol., 27*(3), 453–61.

Young, E. A., & Breslau, N. (2004). Cortisol and catecholamines in posttraumatic stress disorder. An epidemiological community study. *Arch. Gen. Psychiatry, 61,* 394–401.

Young, J. E., Weinberger, A. D., & Beck, A. T. (2008). Cognitive therapy for depression. In D. H. Barlow (Ed.), *Clinical handbook of psychological disorders* (4th ed., pp. 250–305). New York: Guilford Press.

Young, S., Schactman, L., & Snyder, M. (2014). Early report on the effectiveness of a recovery model oriented therapeutic community for individuals with complex and persistent recovery challenges. *Psychiatr. Quarterly.* doi:10.1007/s11126-014-9292-8

Yovel, I., Revelle, W., & Mineka, S. (2005). Who sees trees before forest: The obsessive-compulsive style of visual attention. *Psychol. Sci., 16,* 123–29.

Yung, A. R., Phillips, L. J., Yuen, H. P., & McGorry, P. D. (2004). Risk factors for psychosis in an ultra high-risk group: Psychopathology and clinical features. *Schizo. Res., 67,* 131–42.

Z

Zahniser, D. (2012, July 31), Pot backers rally support for allies on L. A. council. *Los Angeles Times.*

Zammit, S., Allebeck, P., Andréasson, S., Lundberg, I., & Lewis, G. (2002). Self-reported cannabis use as a risk factor for schizophrenia: Further analysis of the 1969 Swedish conscript cohort. *BMJ, 325,* 1199–201.

Zanarini, M. C., Barison, L. K., Frankenburg, F. R., Reich, D. B., & Hudson, J. I. (2009). Family history study of the familial coaggregation of borderline personality disorder with Axis I and nonborderline dramatic cluster Axis II disorders. *J. Personality Disorders, 23,* 357–69.

Zanarini, M. C., Frankenburg, F. R., Hennen, J., Reich, D. B., & Silk, K. R. (2005). The McLean Study of Adult Development (MSAD): Overview and implications of the first six years of prospective follow-up. *J. Personal. Disord., 19,* 505–23.

Zanarini, M. C., Williams, A. A., Lewis, R. E., Reich, R. B., Vera, S. C., Marino, M. F., et al. (1997). Reported pathological childhood experiences associated with the development of borderline personality disorder. *Am. J. Psychiatry, 154*(8), 1101–06.

Zapata-Sola, A., Kreuch, T., Landers, R. N., Hoyt, T., & Butcher, J. N. (2009). Personality assessment in personnel selection using the MMPI-2: A cross-cultural comparison. *Int. J. Clin. Health Psychology, 9*(2), 287–98.

Zellner, D. A., Harner, D. E., & Adler, R. L. (1989). Effects of eating abnormalities and gender on perceptions of desirable body shape. *J. Abn. Psychol., 98,* 93–96.

Zerman, P. M., & Schwartz, H. I. (1998). Hospitalization: Voluntary and involuntary. In R. Rosner (Ed.), *Principles and practice of forensic psychiatry* (pp. 111–17). London: Oxford University Press.

Zerwas, S., Larsem, J. T., Petersen, L., Thornton, L. M., Mortensen, P. B., & Bulik, C. M. (2014). The incidence of eating disorders in a Danish register study: Associations with suicide risk and mortality. *J. Psychiatric Research, 65,* 16–22.

Zettergreen, P. (2003). School adjustment in adolescence for previously rejected, average and popular children. *Brit. J. Educational Psychology, 73*(2), 207–21.

Zgoba, K. M., & Levenson, J. (2008). Variations in the recidivism of treated and nontreated sexual offenders in New Jersey: An examination of three time frames. *Victims & Offenders, 3*(1), 10–30.

Zhang, L. D., & Lu, M. K. (2006). Psychiatry in China: Past, present and future. *Int. Medical J., 13,* 44–51.

Zhang, L., Plotkin, R. C., Wang, G., Sandel, E., & Lee, S. (2004). Cholinergic augmentation with donepezil enhances recovery in short-term memory and sustained attention after traumatic brain injury. *Arch. Physical and Medical Rehabilitation, 85,* 1050–55.

Zhao, Y., & Lukiw, W. J. (2015). Microbiome-generated amyloid and potential impact on amyloidogenesis in Alzheimer's disease (AD). *J. Nature and Science, 1*(7), e138.

Zhou, T. X., Zhang, S. P., Jiang, Y. Q., & Wang, J. M. (2000). Epidemiology of neuroses in a Shanghai community. *Chinese Mental Health Journal, 14,* 332–34.

Zickler, P. (2002). *Study demonstrates that marijuana smokers experience significant withdrawal*. Washington, DC: National Institute on Drug Abuse.

Zilboorg, G., & Henry, G. W. (1941). *A history of medical psychology*. New York: Norton.

Zimmerman, D. P. (2004). Psychotherapy in residential treatment: Historical development and critical issues. *Child Adoles. Psychiatr. Clin. North Am., 13*(2), 347–61.

Zimmerman, M., & Coryell, W. (1989). DSM-III personality disorder diagnoses in a nonpatient sample: Demographic correlates and comorbidity. *Arch. Gen. Psychiatry, 46*, 682–89.

Zimmerman, M., Rothchild, L., & Chelminski, I. (2005). The prevalence of DSM-IV personality disorders in psychiatric outpatients. *Am. J. Psychiatry, 162*, 1911–18.

Zimmermann, P., Brückl, T., Nocon, A., Pfister, H., Lieb, R., Wittchen, H.-U., et al. (2009). Heterogeneity of DSM-IV major depressive disorder as a consequence of subthreshold bipolarity. *Arch. Gen. Psychiatry, 66*(12), 1341–52. doi:10.1001/archgenpsychiatry.2009.158

Ziolko, H. U. (1996). Bulimia: A historical outline. *Int. J. Eat. Dis., 20*, 345–58.

Zipfel, S., Wild, B., Gross, Friederich, H-C., Teufel, M., et al., on behalf of the ANTOP study group (2014). Focal psychodynamic therapy, cognitive behaviour therapy, and optimised treatment as usual in outpatients with anorexia nervosa (ANTOP study): Randomised controlled trial. *Lancet, 383*, 127–37.

Zoccolillo, M., Meyers, J., & Assiter, S. (1997). Conduct disorder, substance dependence, and adolescent motherhood. *Am. J. Orthopsychiat., 67*(1), 152–57.

Zubin, J., & Spring, B. J. (1977). Vulnerability: A new view of schizophrenia. *J. Abn. Psychol., 86*, 103–26.

Zucker, K. J. (2005). Gender identity disorder in children and adolescents. *Annu. Rev. Clin. Psychol., 1*, 467–92.

Zucker, K. J., & Bradley, S. J. (1995). *Gender identity disorder and psychosexual problems in children and adolescents*. New York: Guilford Press.

Zucker, K. J., Bradley, S. J., Owen-Anderson, A., Kibblewhite, S. J., & Cantor, J. M. (2008). Letter to the editor: Is gender identity disorder in adolescents coming out of the closet? *J. Sex Mar. Ther., 34*, 287–90.

Zucker, K. J., Owen, A., Bradley, S. J., & Ameeriar, L. (2002). Gender-dysphoric children and adolescents: A comparative analysis of demographic characteristics and behavioral problems. *Clin. Child Psych. Psychiatry, 7*, 398–411.

Zuckerman, M. (2007). *Sensation seeking and risky behavior*. Washington, DC: American Psychological Association.

Zuvekas, S. H., & Vitiello, B. (2012). Stimulant medication use in children: A 12-year perspective. *Am. J. Psychiatry, 169*(2), 160–66.

Zvolensky, M. J., & Bernstein, A. (2005). Cigarette smoking and panic psychopathology. *Curr. Dis. Psychol. Sci., 14*(6), 301–05.

Zvolensky, M. J., Cougle, J. R., Johnson, K. A., Bonn-Miller, M. O., & Bernstein, A. (2010). Marijuana use and panic psychopathology among a representative sample of adults. *Exper. Clin. Psychopharmacol., 18*(2), 139–34.

Zvolensky, M. J., Eiffert, G. H., Lejeuz, C. W., & McNeil, D. W. (1999). The effects of offset control over 20% carbon-dioxide-enriched air on anxious response. *J. Abn. Psychol., 108*, 624–32.

Zvolensky, M. J., Lejeuz, C. W., & Eifert, G. H. (1998). The role of offset control in anxious responding: An experimental test using repeated administrations of 20%-carbon-dioxide-enriched air. *Behav. Ther., 29*, 193–209.

Zwelling, S. S. (1985). *Quest for a cure*. Williamsburg, VA: The Colonial Williamsburg Foundation.

Credits

Photo Credits

Page 492: Eric Audras/PhotoAlto/Alamy; **Page 493:** Ellen McKnight/Alamy; **Page 499:** Jean gill/E+/Getty images.

Chapter 14   Page 503: Tetra Images/Alamy; **Page 506:** Zero Creatives/Getty Images; **Page 508 (left):** Pearson Education; **Page 508 (right):** Pearson Education; **Page 514:** Allstar Picture Library/Alamy; **Page 518:** Thomas Deerinck, Ncmir/Science Source; **Page 520:** Image courtesy of Dr. Mony de Leon Professor of Psychiatry and Director of the Center for Brain Health at the NYU School of Medicine, New York, NY; **Page 521:** Fredfroese/E+/Getty Images; **Page 524:** Chip Somodevilla/Getty Images; **Page 525 (top):** Christian Müller/Fotolia; **Page 525 (bottom):** Talyaona/123RF; **Page 527:** From H. Damasio, T. Grabowski, R. Frank, A. M. Galaburda & A. R. Damasio (1994), The Return of Phineas Gage: clues about the brain from a skull of a famous patent, *Science, 264,* 1102–1105. Dornsife Cognitive Neuroimaging Center and Brain and Creativity Institute, University of Southern California; **Page 528:** Jerome Davis/Icon Sportswire/Newscom.

Chapter 15   Page 532: Nina Shannon/Getty Images; **Page 534:** Matthew Nock; **Page 535:** Kelly Redinger/Design Pics Inc/Alamy; **Page 538:** Ili/Juice Images/Alamy; **Page 539:** Michaela Begsteiger/Getty Images; **Page 541:** Anna Nahabed/123RF; **Page 544:** Photo courtesy of www.dri-sleeper.com; **Page 547:** Marlin Levison/Zuma Press/Newscom; **Page 550:** Warren Jones and Ami Klin, Attention to Eyes is Present But in Decline in 2–6 Month-Olds Later Diagnosed with Autism, *Nature.* 2013 Dec 19; 504(7480): 427–431. Permission by Copyright Clearance Center; **Page 555:** Alamy; **Page 557:** BSIP SA/Alamy; **Page 559:** Marcel Jancovic/Shutterstock; **Page 560:** SPL/CNRI/Science Source; **Page 561:** Taro Yamasaki/Getty Images; **Page 563:** Vilevi/Fotolia.

Chapter 16   Page 570: Buena Vista Images/Photodisc/Getty Images; **Page 573:** Design Pics/Alamy; **Page 574:** Lisa F. Young/Alamy; **Page 580 (left):** Steven May/Alamy; **Page 580 (right):** Rob/Fotolia; **Page 582:** Image Source/Getty Images; **Page 586:** Af archive/Alamy; **Page 587:** SuperStock; **Page 590:** Moviestore collection Ltd/Alamy; **Page 594:** Eli Winston/Everett Collection/Newscom; **Page 597:** Alamy; **Page 600:** Will Mcintyre/Science Source; **Page 603:** Keystone/Hulton Archive/Getty Images.

Chapter 17   Page 607: Cusp/Superstock; **Page 610:** Blend Images/Alamy; **Page 611:** Sarah J. Glover/Krt/Newscom; **Page 612 (left):** John Minchillo/AP Images; **Page 612 (right):** Bill Aron/PhotoEdit; **Page 615:** Rafael Ben-Ari/Fotolia; **Page 620 (left):** lukasvideo/Fotolia; **Page 620 (right):** Zuma Press/Newscom; **Page 622:** Reuters; **Page 623 (left):** Department of Justice/Zuma Press/Newscom; **Page 623 (right):** STR New/Reuters; **Page 626:** AFP PHOTO/Pima County Sheriff's Department/Getty.

Text Credits

Chapter 1   Pages 3 to 6: "Subjective distress: If people suffer or experience . . ." Corrigan, P. W., & Watson, A. C. (2005). Findings from the National Comorbidity Survey on the frequency of dangerous behavior in individuals with psychiatric disorders. *Psychiatry Research, 136* (2-3) 153–162; **Page 6:** "World Around Us" Taken from Parker, G. F. (2004). Outcomes of assertive community treatment in an NGRI conditional release program. *J. Am. Acad. Psychiatr. Law, 32*(3), 291–303; **Page 9:** "I have lived with bipolar disorder . . ." McNulty, J. P. (2004). Commentary: Mental illness, society, stigma, and research. *Schizo. Bull., 30*(3), 573–75 by permission of Oxford University Press; **Page 9:** "We treat them as in a sense second class citizens . . ." Arthur, C., Hickling, F. W., Robertson-Hickling, H., Haynes-Robinson, T., Abel, W., & Whitley, R. (2010, p. 263). "Mad, sick, head nuh good": Mental illness stigma in Jamaican communities. *Transcult. Psychiat., 47,* 252–75; **Pages 9 to 10:** "There is a mad lady on the road named . . ." Arthur, C., Hickling, F. W., Robertson-Hickling, H., Haynes-Robinson, T., Abel, W., & Whitley, R. (2010, p. 261). "Mad, sick, head nuh good": Mental illness stigma in Jamaican communities. *Transcult. Psychiat., 47,* 252–75; **Page 10:** "you are fearful even . . ." Arthur, C., Hickling, F. W., Robertson-Hickling, H., Haynes-Robinson, T., Abel, W., & Whitley, R. (2010, p. 262). "Mad, sick, head nuh good": Mental illness stigma in Jamaican communities. *Transcult. Psychiat., 47,* 252–75; **Page 11:** "Depression in a Native American Elder . . ." Manson, S. M. (1995, p. 488). Culture and major depression: Current challenges in the diagnosis of mood disorders. *Psychiatr. Clin. North Am.: Cultural Psychiatry, 18*(3), 487–501; **Page 13:** Table 1.1: Based on Kessler, R. C., Berglund, P., Borges, G., Nock, M., & Wang, P. S. (2005a). Trends in suicide ideation, plans, gestures, and attempts in the United States. *JAMA, 293*(20), 2487–95.; Kessler, R. C., Chiu, W. T., Demler, O., & Walters, E. E. (2005c). Prevalence, severity, and comorbidity of 12-month DSM-IV disorders in the National Comorbidity Survey Replication. *Arch. Gen. Psychiatry, 62,* 617–27; **Page 13:** Table 1.2: Based on Kessler, R. C., Berglund, P., Borges, G., Nock, M., & Wang, P. S. (2005a). Trends in suicide ideation, plans, gestures, and attempts in the United States. *JAMA, 293*(20), 2487–95.; Kessler, R. C., Chiu, W. T., Demler, O., & Walters, E. E. (2005c). Prevalence, severity, and comorbidity of 12-month DSM-IV disorders in the National Comorbidity Survey Replication. *Arch. Gen. Psychiatry, 62,* 617–27; **Page 14:** Figure 1.1: Data courtesy of SAMHSA; **Page 15:** Figure 1.2: Adapted from Whiteford, H. A., Degenhardt, L., Rehm, J., Baxter, A. J., Ferrari, A. J., Charlson, F. J., Norman, R. E., Flaxman, A. D., Johns, N., Burstein, R., Murray, C. J. L., & Vos, T. (2013). *Global burden of disease attributable to mental and substance use disorders: findings from the Global Burden of Disease Study 2010. Lancet, 382,* 1580. (Figure 3 from that paper.); **Page 17:** "methodology is not merely a compilation . . ." Kazdin, A. E. (1998b, p. x). *Research design in clinical psychology.* Needham, MA: Allyn and Bacon; **Page 18:** Figure 1.3: © Pearson Education, Inc.; **Page 22:** Figure 1.4: Adapted from Petrie & Sabin, 2000. *Medical Statistics at a Glance.* Oxford, UK: Blackwell Science Ltd.; **Page 23:** Figure 1.5: © Pearson Education, Inc.; **Page 26:** Figure 1.6: Adapted from Petrie & Sabin, 2000. *Medical Statistics at a Glance.* Oxford, UK: Blackwell Science Ltd.; **Page 28:** Figure 1.7: Data adapted from Rapp et al., 2000. Treatment of hair pulling and hair manipulation maintained by digital-tactile stimulation. *Behavior Therapy, 31,* pp. 381–93.

Chapter 2   Page 34: "The Lord shall smite thee with madness . . ." Deuteronomy 28:28; **Page 37:** "The person suffering from excited insanity initially . . ." Tseng, W. S. (1973, p. 570). The development of psychiatric concepts in traditional Chinese medicine. *Arch. Gen. Psychiatry, 29*(4), 569–75; **Page 37:** "Prince of physicians" Campbell, D. (1926). *Arabian medicine and its influence on the Middle Ages.* New York: Dutton; **Pages 38 to 39:** "A certain prince was afflicted with melancholia and suffered . . ." Browne, E. G. (1921, pp. 88–89). *Arabian medicine.* New York: Macmillan; **Page 39:** "For a fiend-sick man: When a devil possesses a man . . ." Cockayne, T. O. (1864–1866). *Leechdoms, wort cunning, and star craft of early England.* London: Longman, Green, Longman, Roberts & Green; **Page 39:** "the typical accused witch was not a mentally ill person . . ." Schoeneman, T. J. (1984, p. 301). The mentally ill witch in textbooks of abnormal psychology: Current status and implications of a fallacy. *Profess. Psychol., 15*(3), 299–314; **Page 39:** "witchcraft was, in fact, never considered a variety of possession . . ." Schoeneman, T. J. (1984, p. 306). The mentally ill witch in textbooks of abnormal psychology: Current status and implications of a fallacy. *Profess. Psychol., 15*(3), 299–314; **Page 40:** "Mental disease is no different than bodily disease and Christianity . . ." Castiglioni, A. (1924). *Adventures of the mind.* New York: Dutton; **Pages 40 to 41:** "Accordingly we were admitted in thro' an iron gate . . ." Tuke, D. H. (1882, pp. 76–77). *History of the insane in the British Isles.* London: Kegan, Paul, Trench; **Page 42:** "Paupers and lunatics" Scull, A. (1996). *The most solitary of afflictions: Madness and society in Britain.* New Haven, CT: Yale University Press; **Page 44:** "more than 9000 idiots, epileptics and insane . . ." Zilboorg, G., & Henry, G. W. (1941, pp. 583–584). *A history of medical psychology.* New York: Norton; **Page 44:** "among the noblest examples of humanity in all history" Karnesh, L. J. (with collaboration of Zucker, E. M.). (1945, p. 18). *Handbook of psychiatry.* St. Louis: Mosby; **Page 50:** "The Search for Medications to Cure Mental Disorders" Based on Frankenburg, F. R. (1994). History of the development of antipsychotic medications. *Psychiatr. Clin. North Am., 17*(3), 531–41; Green, R. M. (1951). Galen's hygiene. Springfield, IL: Charles C. Thomas; Moriarty, K. M., Alagna, S. W., & Lake, C. R. (1984). Psychopharmacology: An historical perspective. *Psychiatr. Clin. North Am., 7*(3), 411–33; Pachter, H. M. (1951). *Magic into science: The story of Paracelsus.* New York: Schumen; **Page 54:** "to shape an animal's behavior almost as a sculptor shapes a lump of clay" Skinner, B. F. (1951, pp. 26–27). How to teach animals. *Scientif. Am., 185,* 26–29; **Pages 55 to 56:** Table 2.1: © Pearson Education, Inc.; **Page 57:** "a fur pelt, . . . a man's beard, . . . a cat, a pup, a fur muff . . ." Harris, B. (1979, p. 153). Whatever happened to Little Albert? *Am. Psychol., 34,* 151–60; **Page 57:** "Collective memory, more than individual memory . . ." Schudson, M. (1995, p. 16). Collective memory and modes of distortion. In D. Schachter, J. Coyle, L. Sullivan, M. Mesulam, & G. Fishbach (Eds.), *Memory distortion: Interdisciplinary perspectives.* Cambridge: Harvard University Press.

Chapter 3   Page 62: Figure 3.1: Adapted from Kraemer, H. C., Kazdin, A. E., Offord, D. R., Kessler, R. C., Jensen, P. S., & Kupfer, D. J. (1997). Coming to terms with the terms of risk. *Archives of General Psychiatry, 54,* 337–343; **Page 64:** Figure 3.2: Adapted from S. M. Monroe & A. D. Simons (1991). Diathesis-stress theories in the context of life stress research: Implications for the depressive disorders. *Psychological Bulletin, 110,* 406–25; **Page 64:** "some individuals have a relatively good outcome despite . . ." Rutter, M. (2007). Resilience, competence, and coping. *Child Ab. Negl., 31*(3), 205–09. p. 205; **Page 71:** "In the great majority of cases, both psychological traits . . ." Rutter, M. (2006a, p. 29). *Genes and behavior: Nature-nurture interplay explained.* Oxford: Blackwell; **Page 72:** Figure 3.4: From Gilbert Gottlieb. 1992. *Individual Development and Evolution: The Genesis of Novel Behavior.* New York: Oxford University Press. Reprinted by permission of Lawrence Erlbaum Associates; **Page 78:** Table 3.1: Based on A. Freud (1946) and DSM-IV-TR (American Psychiatric Association, 2000); **Page 82:** "Each individual exists in a private world . . ." Rogers, C. R. (1951). *Client-centered therapy.* Boston: Houghton Mifflin; **Page 86:** "a capacity for self-direction" Bandura, A. (1974, p. 861). Behavior theory and the models of man. *Am. Psychol., 29*(12), 859–69; **Page 91:** Figure 3.8: Sheridan, M. A., Fox, N. A., Zeanah, C. H., McLaughlin, K. A., & Nelson, C. A. (2012). Variation in neural development as a result of exposure to institutionalization early in childhood. *Proceedings of the National Academy of Science, 109,* 12927–12932; **Page 94:**

Figure 3.9: McLaughlin, K. A., Costello, E. J., Leblanc, W., Sampson, N. A., & Kessler, R. C. (2012). Socioeconomic status and adolescent mental disorders. *American Journal of Public Health, 102*, 1742–1750.

Chapter 4 Page 118: "Vocabulary (verbal): This subtest consists . . ." Lichtenberger & Kaufman, *Essentials of WAIS-IV Assessment* (John Wiley & Sons, 2009); **Page 119:** "People may see many different things in these inkblot pictures . . ." Exner, J. E. (1993). *The Rorschach: A comprehensive system. Vol. 1: Basic Foundations*. New York: Wiley; **Page 125:** Figure 4.1: Excerpted from *The Minnesota Report™: Adult Clinical System-Revised*, 4th Edition by James N. Butcher; **Page 125:** Figure 4.2: Excerpted from *The Minnesota Report™: Adult Clinical System-Revised*, 4th Edition by James N. Butcher; **Pages 126 to 127:** "Computer-Based MMPI-2 Report for Andrea C." Excerpted from *The Minnesota Report™: Adult Clinical System-Revised*, 4th Edition by James N. Butcher; **Page 133:** "Imperfect, but it is indispensable" Frances, A., & Widiger, T. (2012, p. 111). Psychiatric Diagnosis: Lessons from the DSM-IV Past and Cautions for the DSM-5 Future. *Annual Review of Clinical Psychology*, 8, 109–130.

Chapter 5 Page 137: "I was working one evening . . ." Based on Feczer, D., & Bjorklund, P. (2009). Forever changed: Posttraumatic stress disorder in female military veterans, a case report. *Perspectives in Psychiatric Care, 45*, 278–91; **Page 140:** Figure 5.1: Renner, M. J., & Mackin, R. S. (1998). A life stress instrument for classroom use. *Teaching of Psychology, 47*; **Page 142:** Figure 5.2: Leor et al., 1996. *The New England Journal of Medicine, 334*(7), February 15, 1996, p. 415; **Page 143:** Figure 5.3: Based on KALAT. *Biological Psychology* (Non-InfoTrac Version), 7th ed. © 2001 Wadsworth, a part of Cengage Learning, Inc.; **Page 144:** Figure 5.4: From Kalat. *Biological Psychology* (with CD- ROM and InfoTrac), 7E. © 2001 South-Western, a part of Cengage Learning, Inc. All rights reserved. Reproduced by permission. Text/images may not be modified or reproduced in any way without prior written permission of the publisher. www.cengage.com/permissions; **Page 145:** Figure 5.5: P. T. Marucha et al., *Psychosomatic Medicine 60*: 364 (1998). This is Fig 2 from p. 364 of Marucha et al. Source: Philip T. Marucha, Janice Kiecolt-Glaser, and Mehrdad Favagehi, *Mucosal Wound Healing is Impaired by Examination Stress*, copyright 1998 by the American Psychosomatic Society; **Page 149:** Figure 5.6: Based on Johan Denollet. 1998 Personality and coronary heart disease: The type-D Scale-16 (DS16). *Annals of Behavioral Medicine, 20* (3) 209–215, and N. Kupper and J. Denollet (2007). Type D Personality as a prognostic factor in heart disease: Assessment and mediating mechanisms. *Journal of Personality Assessment, 89*(3) 265–276; **Page 150:** Figure 5.7: Miller & Blackwell. 2006, Dec. Turning Up the Heat: Inflammation as a Mechanism Linking Chronic Stress, Depression and Heart Disease. *Current Directions in Psychological Science, 15*, (6): 269–272(4). Copyright © 2006. Reproduced with permission of Blackwell Publishing Ltd.; **Page 156:** "Tony wakes up at 5:30 every morning and makes coffee . . ." Based on Kwoh, L. (2010). Stress of long-term unemployment takes a toll on thousands of Jerseyans who are out of work. *Star-Ledger*, Sunday, June 13; **Page 159:** "Criteria for Posttraumatic Stress Disorder DSM-5" Reprinted with permission from the *Diagnostic and Statistical Manual of Mental Disorders*, Fifth Edition, (Copyright 2013). American Psychiatric Association; **Page 161:** "Clay was a handsome and friendly 28-year-old . . ." Based on Helfling, K. (2011, April 16). Iraq, Afghan war veteran who epitomized recovery kills self. *Boston Globe*; **Page 169:** "'I didn't want it put on my military record that I was crazy" Halpern, S. (2008, May 19). Virtual Iraq. *The New Yorker*, pp. 32–37; **Page 170:** "minimization or outright denial of human suffering" Marshall, R. D. (2006, p. 629). Learning from 9/11: Implications for disaster research and public health. In Y. Neria, R. Gross, R., Marshall, & E. Susser (Eds.), *9/11 Mental health in the wake of terrorists attacks* (pp. 617–39). Cambridge, UK: Cambridge University Press.

Chapter 6 Page 175: Table 6.1: Author created; **Page 177:** "Specific Phobia DSM-5" Reprinted with permission from the *Diagnostic and Statistical Manual of Mental Disorders*, Fifth Edition (Copyright 2013). American Psychiatric Association; **Page 178:** Table 6.2: Data from the *Diagnostic and Statistical Manual of Mental Disorders*, Fifth Edition, (Copyright 2013). American Psychiatric Association; **Page 184:** "criticized for having an anxiety symptom . . ." Hackmann, A., Clark, D. M., & McManus, F. (2000, p. 606). Recurrent images and early memories in social phobia. *Behav. Res. Ther.*, 38, 601–10; **Page 184:** "Social Anxiety Disorder (Social Phobia)" Reprinted with permission from the *Diagnostic and Statistical Manual of Mental Disorders*, Fifth Edition (Copyright 2013). American Psychiatric Association; **Page 188:** "Panic Disorder DSM-5" Reprinted with permission from the *Diagnostic and Statistical Manual of Mental Disorders*, Fifth Edition (Copyright 2013). American Psychiatric Association; **Pages 188 to 189:** "John D. was a 45-year-old married European . . ." Adapted from Brown, T. A., & Barlow, D. H. (2001, pp. 19–22). *Casebook in abnormal psychology* (2nd ed.). Belmont, CA: Wadsworth/Thomson Learning; **Page 189:** "Agoraphobia DSM-5" Reprinted with permission from the *Diagnostic and Statistical Manual of Mental Disorders*, Fifth Edition (Copyright 2013). American Psychiatric Association; **Page 190:** Table 6.3: WHO World Mental Health Survey Initiative (Seedat et al. [2009]. Cross-national associations between gender and mental disorders in the World Health Organization World Mental Health

Surveys. *Archives of General Psychiatry, 66*, 785–795.); **Page 191:** Figure 6.1: Gorman (2000); **Page 193:** Figure 6.2: Adapted from Clark, D. M. (1986). A cognitive approach to panic. *Behav. Res. Ther., 24*, 461–70.; Clark, D. M. (1997). Panic disorder and social phobia. In C. G. Fairburn (Ed.), *Science and practice of cognitive behaviour therapy* (pp. 119–53). New York: Oxford University Press; **Page 198:** "Generalized Anxiety Disorder DSM-5" Reprinted with permission from the *Diagnostic and Statistical Manual of Mental Disorders*, Fifth Edition (Copyright 2013). American Psychiatric Association; **Page 198:** "The result is that they fail to escape the illusory world created in their thoughts . . ." Behar, E., & Borkovec, T. D. (2006, p. 184). The nature and treatment of generalized anxiety disorder. In B. O. Rothbaum (Ed.), *Pathological anxiety: Emotional processing in etiology and treatment* (pp. 181–96). New York: Guilford Press; **Page 203:** "the highly stereotyped, driven, repetitive, and nonfunctional quality . . ." Stein, D. J., Phillips, K. A., Bolton, D., Fulford, K. W. M., Sadler, J. Z., & Kendler, K. S. (2010, p. 497). What is a mental/psychiatric disorder? From DSM-IV to DSM-V. *Psychol. Med., 40*, 1759–65; **Page 205:** "Obsessive-Compulsive Disorder DSM-5" Reprinted with permission from the *Diagnostic and Statistical Manual of Mental Disorders*, Fifth Edition (Copyright 2013). American Psychiatric Association; **Page 212:** Table 6.4: *The Broken Mirror: Understanding and Treating Dysmorphic Disorder* by Phillips (1996) Tab. 8 pp. 119 © 1996, 2005 Katharine A. Phillips, M. D. By permission of Oxford University Press, USA; **Page 213:** "Body Dysmorphic Disorder DSM-5" Reprinted with permission from the *Diagnostic and Statistical Manual of Mental Disorders*, Fifth Edition (Copyright 2013). American Psychiatric Association; **Page 214:** "If my appearance is defective, then I am worthless" Buhlmann, U., & Wilhelm, S. (2004, p. 924). Cognitive factors in body dysmorphic disorder. *Psychiat. Ann., 34*(12), 922–26; **Page 217:** "I have the feeling of something like water in my brain . . ." Ebigbo, P. O. (1982). Development of a culture specific (Nigeria) screening scale of somatic complaints indicating psychiatric disturbance. *Cult. Med. Psychiatr., 6*, 29–43.

Chapter 7 Page 222: "Major Depressive Disorder DSM-5 " Reprinted with permission from the *Diagnostic and Statistical Manual of Mental Disorders*, Fifth Edition (Copyright 2013). American Psychiatric Association; **Page 223:** "Manic Episode DSM-5" Reprinted with permission from the *Diagnostic and Statistical Manual of Mental Disorders*, Fifth Edition (Copyright 2013). American Psychiatric Association; **Page 223:** Figure 7.1: WHO World Mental Health Survey Consortium. (2004). Prevalence, severity, and unmet need for treatment of mental disorders in the World Health Organization World Mental Health Surveys. *JAMA, 291*, 2581–2590; **Page 228:** "Persistent Depressive Disorder DSM-5" Reprinted with permission from the *Diagnostic and Statistical Manual of Mental Disorders*, Fifth Edition (Copyright 2013). American Psychiatric Association; **Page 230:** "I wasn't simply emotional or weepy, like I had been told I might be . . ." Brook Shields, *Down Came the Rain* (New York: Hyperion, 2005); **Page 231:** Figure 7.2: Caspi et al., 2003. Influence of life stress on depression: Moderation with a polymorphism in the 5-HTT gene. *Science, 301*, 386–89. Reprinted with permission from *Science*, 18 July 2003, Vol. 301. Copyright © 2003 AAAS; **Page 234:** Figure 7.3: From R. J. Davidson, Diego Pizzagalli, and Jack Nitschke. (2002). The representation and regulation of emotion in depression. In I. H. Gotlib and C. L. Hammen (Eds.), *Handbook of Depression* (pp. 219–44). New York: Guilford; **Page 238:** Figure 7.4: Adapted from Fennell, M. J. V. (1989). Depression. In K. Hawton, P. M. Salkovskis, J. Kirk, & D. M. Clark (Eds.), *Cognitive behaviour therapy for psychiatric problems: A practical guide*. Oxford, UK: Oxford University Press; **Page 239:** "This therapy will never work for me" Fennell, M. J. V. (1989, p. 193). Depression. In K. Hawton, P. M. Salkovskis, J. Kirk, & D. M. Clark (Eds.), *Cognitive behaviour therapy for psychiatric problems: A practical guide*. Oxford, UK: Oxford University Press; **Page 245:** Figure 7.6: Based on Hooley, J. M., Gruber, S. A., Parker, H., Guillaumot, J., Rogowska, J., & Yurgelun-Todd, D. A. (2009). Cortico-limbic response to personally-challenging emotional stimuli after complete recovery from major depression. *Psychiatry Research: Neuroimaging, 171*(2), 106–19; **Page 248:** Figure 7.7: Adapted From Frederick K. Goodwin and Kay R. Jamison. (2009). *Manic Depressive Illness*. Copyright © 1990. Oxford University Press, Inc. Used by permission of Oxford University Press, Inc.; **Page 254:** Figure 7.9: Fournier J. C., DeRubeis R. J., Hollon S. D., Dimidjian S., Amsterdam J. D., Shelton R. C., and Fawcett J. (2010). Antidepressant drug effects and depression severity: A patient-level meta-analysis. *JAMA, 303*, 47–53; **Page 256:** "Therapy Session: "My Husband Doesn't Love Me Anymore . . ." From Fennell, M. J. V. (1989). Depression. In K. Hawton, P. M. Salkovskis, J. Kirk, & D. M. Clark (Eds.), *Cognitive behaviour therapy for psychiatric problems: A practical guide*. Oxford University Press; **Page 257:** Figure 7.10: From Hollon, et al. (2005, April). Prevention of relapse following cognitive therapy vs. medications in moderate to severe depression. *Arch. Gen. Psychiat., 62*(4), 417–26. © 2005 American Medical Association. Reprinted with permission; **Page 259:** Figure 7.11: World Health Organization, http://www.who.int/mental_health/suicide-prevention/en; **Page 260:** "is one of the greatest burdens individuals and families may endure . . ." Dunne, E. J. (1992, p. 222). Following a suicide: Postvention. In B. Bongar (Ed.), *Suicide: Guidelines for assessment, management* *and treatment.* New York: Oxford University Press; **Page 261:** Figure 7.12: Nock, M. K., Green, J. G., Hwang, I., McLaughlin, K. A., Sampson, N. A., Zaslavsky, A. M., & Kessler, R. C. (2013). Prevalence, correlates and treatment of lifetime suicidal behavior among adolescents: Results from the National Comorbidity Survey Replication – Adolescent Supplement (NCS-A). *JAMA Psychiatry, 70,* 300–310; **Page 262:** "Consensus Warning Signs for Suicide . . ." Rudd et al., Warning signs for suicide: theory, research, and clinical applications, *Suicide Life Threat Behav.* 2006 Jun; *36*(3):255–62; **Page 262:** "In almost every case suicide is . . ." Shneidman, E. S. (1997, pp. 23, 24, 29). The suicidal mind. In R. W. Maris, M. M. Silverman, & S. S. Canetton (Eds.), *Review of suicidology,* 1997 (pp. 22–41). New York: Guilford; **Page 264:** Figure 7.13: Joiner, T. (2005). *Why people die by suicide.* Harvard University Press: Cambridge, MA.

Chapter 8 Page 271: "Somatic Symptom Disorder DSM-5" Reprinted with permission from the *Diagnostic and Statistical Manual of Mental Disorders,* Fifth Edition (Copyright 2013). American Psychiatric Association; **Page 272:** Table 8.1: Frances (2013b). DSM-5 Somatic Symptom Disorder, *Journal of Nervous and Mental Disease, 2013,* 530-531; **Page 273:** Figure 8.1: Author created; **Page 273:** "Bodily changes are usually a sign of serious disease, because every symptom has to have an identifiable physical cause . . ." Salkovskis, P. M., & Bass, C. (1997, p.318). Hypochondriasis. In D. M. Clark & C. G. Fairburn (Eds.), *Science and practice of cognitive behaviour therapy* (pp. 313–39). Oxford: Oxford University Press; **Page 276:** "Illness Anxiety Disorder DSM-5" Reprinted with permission from the *Diagnostic and Statistical Manual of Mental Disorders,* Fifth Edition (Copyright 2013). American Psychiatric Association; **Pages 276 to 277:** "Unable To See For Seven Days . . ." Taken from Mulugeta, S., Tesfay, K., Frank, R., & Gruber-Frank, C. (2015). Acute loss of vision in a young woman: A case report on psychogenic blindness. *Ethiopian Journal of Health Science, 25,* 99–104; **Page 277:** "functional neurological symptom disorder" Stone et al., 2011, Stimulation of Entorhinal Cortex Promotes Adult Neurogenesis and Facilitates Spatial Memory, *The Journal of Neuroscience,* September 21, 2011, *31*(38): 13469 –13484; **Page 277:** "Conversion Disorder DSM-5" Reprinted with permission from the *Diagnostic and Statistical Manual of Mental Disorders,* Fifth Edition (Copyright 2013). American Psychiatric Association; **Page 280:** Figure 8.2: Feinstein, A. (2011). Conversion disorder: advances in our understanding. *Canadian Medical Association Journal, 183,* 915–920; **Pages 282:** "Factitious Disorder DSM-5" Reprinted with permission from the *Diagnostic and Statistical Manual of Mental Disorders,* Fifth Edition (Copyright 2013). American Psychiatric Association; **Page 283:** "a disruption of and/or discontinuity in the normal, subjective integration of one or more aspects of psychological functioning . . ." Spiegel, D., Loewenstein, R. J., Lewis-Fernandez, R., Sar, V., Simeon, D., Vermetten, E., Cardena, E., & Dell, P.F. (2011a, p. 826). Dissociative disorders in DSM-5. *Depression and Anxiety, 28,* 824–852; **Page 283:** "perceived as disruptive, invoking a loss of needed information, as producing discontinuity of experience . . ." Spiegel, D., Loewenstein, R. J., Lewis-Fernandez, R., Sar, V., Simeon, D., Vermetten, E., Cardena, E., & Dell, P. F. (2011b, p. E19). Dissociative disorders in DSM-5. *Depression and Anxiety, 28,* 824–852; **Page 284:** Serenity Programme™, www.serene.me.uk; **Page 285:** "Living in a Dream . . ." Based on Ghosh et al., 2007; **Page 285:** "the feeling puzzles the experiencers: the changed condition is perceived as unreal . . ." Kihlstrom, J. F. (2001, p. 267). Dissociative disorders. In P. B. Sutker & H. E. Adams (Eds.), *Comprehensive handbook of psychopathology* (3rd ed., pp. 259–76). New York: Kluwer Academic/Plenum; **Page 286:** "Depersonalization/Derealization Disorder DSM-5" Reprinted with permission from the *Diagnostic and Statistical Manual of Mental Disorders,* Fifth Edition (Copyright 2013). American Psychiatric Association; **Page 288:** "Dissociative Amnesia DSM-5 "Reprinted with permission from the *Diagnostic and Statistical Manual of Mental Disorders,* Fifth Edition (Copyright 2013). American Psychiatric Association; **Page 288:** "How did I get here? . . ." Based on Igwe, 2013; **Page 291:** "The problem is not having more than one personality, it is having less than one" Spiegel, 2006, p. 567; **Page 291:** "Dissociative Identity Disorder DSM-5" Reprinted with permission from the *Diagnostic and Statistical Manual of Mental Disorders,* Fifth Edition (Copyright 2013). American Psychiatric Association; **Page 295:** "Have you had anyone confirm these events?" Chu, J. A., Frey, L. M., Ganzel, B. L., & Matthews, J. A. (1999, p. 751). Memories of childhood abuse: Dissociation, amnesia, and corroboration. *Am. J. Psychiatry, 156,* 749–55; **Page 298:** "I knew my father could get some of me, but he couldn't get all of me . . ." Maldonado, J. R., & Spiegel, D. (2007, p. 781). Dissociative disorders. In J. A. Bourgeois, R. H. Hales, & S. C. Yudofsky (Eds.), *The American Psychiatric Publishing board prep and review guide for psychiatry* (pp. 251–58). Washington, DC: American Psychiatric Publishing.

Chapter 9 Page 305: "Criteria for Anorexia Nervosa DSM-5" Reprinted with permission from the *Diagnostic and Statistical Manual of Mental Disorders,* Fifth Edition (Copyright 2013). American Psychiatric Association; **Page 305:** "without apparent cause, to evince a repugnance to food . . ." Gull, W. (1888). Anorexia nervosa. *Lancet,* pp. i, 516–17; **Page 305:** Figure 9.1: Gull, W. (1888). Anorexia nervosa. *Lancet,* pp. i, 516–17; **Page 306:** "Eisha" Based on Roy, P. K. (2014). Efficacy of combined cognitive-behavior therapy and hypnotherapy in anorexia nervosa: A case study. *International Journal of Clinical and Experimental*

Hypnosis, 62, 224-230; **Page 307:** "must see the bones" Kirkland, G. (1986, pp. 55–56). *Dancing on my grave.* New York: Doubleday; **Page 307:** "Criteria for Bulimia Nervosa DSM-5" Reprinted with permission from the *Diagnostic and Statistical Manual of Mental Disorders,* Fifth Edition (Copyright 2013). American Psychiatric Association; **Page 308:** "Catherine: Distressed by Her Weight" Adapted from Cooper, Todd, & Wells, (2000). *Bulimia Nervosa: A Cognitive Therapy Programme.* London: Reproduced by permission of Jessica Kingsley Publishers; **Page 309:** "Criteria for Binge-Eating Disorder DSM-5" Reprinted with permission from the *Diagnostic and Statistical Manual of Mental Disorders,* Fifth Edition (Copyright 2013). American Psychiatric Association; **Page 312:** Table 9.3: Reproduced by special permission of the Publisher, Psychological Assessment Resources, Inc., 16204 North Florida Avenue, Lutz, Florida 33549, from the *Eating Disorder Inventory-3* by David M. Garner, PhD, Copyright 1984, 1991, 2004, by Psychological Assessment Resources, Inc. (PAR). Further reproduction is prohibited without permission of PAR; **Page 314:** Figure 9.3: Adapted from Fichter, M. M., & Quadflieg, N. (2007). Long-term stability of eating disorder diagnoses. *Int. J. Eat. Dis., 40,* S61–S66., and Eddy, K. T., Dorer, K. T., Franko, D. L., Tahilani, K., Thompson-Brenner, H., & Herzog, D. B. (2008). Diagnostic cross over in anorexia nervosa and bulimia nervosa: Implications for DSM-V. *Am. J. Psychiat., 165,* 245–50; **Page 327:** Figure 9.4: Data from M. Cooper, G. Todd, and A. Wells, *Bulimia Nervosa: A Cognitive Therapy Programme for Clients* with permission from Jessica Kingsley Publishers. Copyright © 2000 Myra Cooper, Gillian Todd, and Adrian Wells; **Page 328:** Figure 9.5: Behavioral Risk Factor Surveillance Systems (BRFSS), Centers for Disease Control and Prevention; **Page 329:** Table 9.5: Ogden, C. L., Carroll, M. D., Kit, B. K., & Flegal, K. M. (2014). Prevalence of childhood and adult obesity in the United States, 2011-2012. *JAMA, 311,* 806-814; **Page 332:** Table 9.6: Gearhardt, A. N., Grilo, C. M., DiLeone, R. J., Brownell, K. D., & Potenza, M. N. (2011). Can food be addictive? Public health and policy implications. *Addiction, 106,* 1208–12.

Chapter 10 Page 343: Table 10.1: Torgersen, S. (2012). Epidemiology. In T. A. Widiger (Ed.). *The Oxford Handbook of Personality Disorders.* New York: Oxford University Press, pp 186–205; **Page 346:** Table 10.2: Adapted from Widiger, Trull et al. (2002). A description of the DSM-IV personality disorders with the five-factor model of personality. In P. T. Costa & T. A. Widiger (Eds.), *Personality Disorders and the Five-Factor Model of Personality* (2nd ed.) (p. 90). Washington, DC: APA Books; **Page 349:** "Paranoid Personality Disorder" Taken from Birkeland, S. F. (2013). Paranoid personality disorder and organic brain injury: A case report. *Journal of Neuropsychiatry and Clinical Neuroscience, 25,* E52; **Page 349:** "Criteria for Paranoid Personality Disorder DSM-5" Reprinted with permission from the *Diagnostic and Statistical Manual of Mental Disorders,* Fifth Edition (Copyright © 2013). American Psychiatric Association; **Page 350:** "Criteria for Schizoid Personality Disorder DSM-5" Reprinted with permission from the *Diagnostic and Statistical Manual of Mental Disorders,* Fifth Edition (Copyright © 2013). American Psychiatric Association; **Page 351:** Beck, A. T., Freeman, A., et al. (1990, p. 51). *Cognitive therapy of personality disorders.* New York: Guilford; **Page 351:** "Relationships are messy . . ." Pretzer, J. L., & Beck, A. T. (1996, p. 60). A cognitive theory of personality disorders. In J. F. Clarkin & M. F. Lenzenweger (Eds.), *Major theories of personality disorder* (pp. 36–105). New York: Guilford; **Page 352:** "Criteria for Schizotypal Personality Disorder DSM-5" Reprinted with permission from the *Diagnostic and Statistical Manual of Mental Disorders,* Fifth Edition (Copyright © 2013). American Psychiatric Association; **Page 353:** "Criteria for Histrionic Personality Disorder DSM-5" Reprinted with permission from the *Diagnostic and Statistical Manual of Mental Disorders,* Fifth Edition (Copyright © 2013). American Psychiatric Association; **Page 354:** "Unless I captivate people, I am nothing" and "If I can't entertain people, they will abandon me" Beck, A. T., Freeman, A., et al. (1990, p. 51). *Cognitive therapy of personality disorders.* New York: Guilford; **Page 354:** "Criteria for Narcissistic Personality Disorder DSM-5" Reprinted with permission from the *Diagnostic and Statistical Manual of Mental Disorders,* Fifth Edition (Copyright © 2013). American Psychiatric Association; **Page 355:** "The strongest impairment associated . . ." J. D. Miller, Narcissistic Personality Disorder: Relations with distress and functional impairment, *Compr. Psychiatry.* 2007; 48(2): 170–177. p. 176; **Page 355:** "bossy, intolerant, cruel, argumentative, dishonest . . ." Wink, P. (1991). Two faces of narcissism. *J. Pers. Soc. Psychol., 61,* 590–97. p. 595; **Page 356:** "Criteria for Antisocial Personality Disorder DSM-5" Reprinted with permission from the *Diagnostic and Statistical Manual of Mental Disorders,* Fifth Edition (Copyright © 2013). American Psychiatric Association; **Page 357:** Figure 10.1: Reprinted with permission from Caspi et al. (2002), *Science, 297,* 851–54. Copyright © 2002 AAAS; **Page 358:** "Life-course-persistent" antisocial behavior originates . . ." Moffitt, T. E., Caspi, A., Harrington, H., & Milne, B. J. (2002). Males on the life-course-persistent and adolescence limited antisocial pathways: Follow-up at age 26 years. *Develop. Psychopath., 14,* 179–207. p. 180; **Page 359:** Figure 10.2: Capaldi & Patterson, 1994. Interrelated influences of contextual factors on antisocial behavior. In D. C. Fowles et al. (Eds.), *Progress in Experimental Personality and Psychopathology Research.* Springer Publishing Company; **Page 360:** "may regard suffering and pain as something they deserve" Hooley, J. M., Gruber, S. A., Parker, H. A., Guillaumot, J.,

Rogowska, J., & Yurgelun-Todd, D. A. (2010). Neural processing of emotional overinvolvement in borderline personality disorder. *J. Clin. Psychiatry, 71,* 1017–24; **Page 361:** "Criteria for Borderline Personality Disorder DSM-5" Reprinted with permission from the *Diagnostic and Statistical Manual of Mental Disorders,* Fifth Edition (Copyright © 2013). American Psychiatric Association; **Page 361:** "Ms. R: Borderline Personality Disorder" From Avery, J., Francois, D., Martins, O., Park, S., & Roth, S. (2012). An updates model for the first-time hospitalization of patients with borderline personality disorder: Two illustrative case reports. *Psychiatric Quarterly, 83,* 391–396; **Page 363:** Figure 10.3: Paris, J. (1999). Borderline personality disorder. In T. Millon, P. H. Blaney, & R. D. Davis (Eds.), *Oxford textbook of psychopathology* (pp. 628–52). New York: Oxford University Press; **Page 365:** "Criteria for Avoidant Personality Disorder DSM-5" Reprinted with permission from the *Diagnostic and Statistical Manual of Mental Disorders,* Fifth Edition (Copyright © 2013). American Psychiatric Association; **Page 366:** "Criteria for Dependent Personality Disorder DSM-5" Reprinted with permission from the *Diagnostic and Statistical Manual of Mental Disorders,* Fifth Edition (Copyright © 2013). American Psychiatric Association; **Page 367:** "I am completely helpless . . ." Beck, A. T., Freeman, A., et al. (1990, p. 60). *Cognitive therapy of personality disorders.* New York: Guilford; **Page 368:** "Criteria for Obsessive-Compulsive Personality Disorder DSM-5" Reprinted with permission from the *Diagnostic and Statistical Manual of Mental Disorders,* Fifth Edition (Copyright © 2013). American Psychiatric Association; **Page 370:** Table 10.3: Beck, Freeman & Davis (2004). *Cognitive Therapy of Personality Disorders,* New York: Guildford Press; **Page 372:** Table 10.4: Cleckley, 1988. *The Mask of Sanity,* 5th Edition; Emily S. Cleckley: Augusta, Georgia, pp. 337–338; **Page 373:** "Are you adventurous? Psychologist studying adventurous . . ." Widom, C. S. (1977). A methodology for studying non-institutionalized psychopaths. *J. Cons. Clin. Psychol., 45,* 674–83. p. 675; **Page 373:** "Are you looking for hookers or trying to make a listing of all the sociopaths in Boston?" Widom, C. S. (1977). A methodology for studying non-institutionalized psychopaths. *J. Cons. Clin. Psychol., 45,* 674–83. p. 675; **Page 374:** Figure 10.4: From Gretton et al. (2004). Psychopathy and offending from adolescence to adulthood: A 10-year follow-up. *Journal of Consulting and Clinical Psychology, 72,* 636–45. Copyright © 2004 by the American Psychological Association. Reproduced with permission; **Page 375:** Figure 10.5: Yang, Y., Raine, A., Colletti, P., Toga, A. W., & Narr, K. L. (2010). Morphological alterations in the prefrontal cortex and the amygdala in unsuccessful psychopaths. *Journal of Abnormal Psychology, 119,* 546–554; **Page 376:** "Conceptualizing psychopaths as remorseless . . ." Hare, R. D. (1998, pp. 128–29). Psychopathy, affect and behavior. In D. J. Cooke, A. E. Forth, & R. D. Hare (Eds.), *Psychopathy: Theory, research, and implications for society* (pp. 105–37). Dordrecht, Netherlands: Kluwer Academic Publishers; **Pages 376 to 377:** "A Psychopath in Action" Reprinted with permission of Robert D. Hare, *PSYCHOPATHY Theory and Research,* Wiley NY 1970, University of British Columbia, rhare@mail.ubc.ca; **Page 378:** "It is the emotionally charged thought, images, and internal dialogue that give the 'bite' to conscience, account . . ." Hare, R. D. (1998, p. 112). Psychopathy, affect and behavior. In D. J. Cooke, A. E. Forth, & R. D. Hare (Eds.), *Psychopathy: Theory, research, and implications for society* (pp. 105–37). Dordrecht, Netherlands: Kluwer Academic Publishers; **Page 380:** "grandiosity, glibness and superficiality, promiscuity . . . as well as a lack of responsibility for others . . ." Cooke, D. J., & Michie, C. (1999, p. 65). Psychopathy across cultures: North America and Scotland compared. *J. Abn. Psychol., 108*(1), 58–68.

Chapter 11 **Pages 385 to 386:** "drinking that causes detrimental health . . ." World Health Organization. (2014, p. 2). *Global status report on alcohol and health 2014.* Geneva, Switzerland; **Page 388:** "Alcohol Use Disorder DSM-5" Reprinted with permission from the *Diagnostic and Statistical Manual of Mental Disorders,* Fifth Edition (Copyright © 2013). American Psychiatric Association; **Page 388:** Table 11.2: Verster J. C., Van Herwijnen J., Olivier B., Kahler C. W. Validation of the Dutch Brief Young Adult Alcohol Consequences Questionnaire (B-YAACQ) *Addict Behav.* 2009; *34*:411–414; **Page 389:** Figure 11.1: Penning, R., van Nuland, M., Fliervoet, L. A., Olivier, B., & Verster, J. C. (2010). The pathology of alcohol hangover. *Current Drug Abuse Reviews, 3,* 68-75; **Page 390:** "There is no safe amount of alcohol use during pregnancy or while trying to get pregnant . . ." Center for Disease Control. (Retrieved May 4, 2015). http://www.cdc.gov/ncbddd/fasd/alcohol-use.html; **Page 392:** Figure 11.2: Office of Technology Assessment, 1993; **Page 396:** "having a few drinks to celebrate special occasions" Turrisi, R. (1999). Cognitive and attitudinal factors in the analysis of alternatives to binge drinking. *Journal of Applied Social Psychology, 29,* 1510–33; **Page 397:** "diseases of denial" DiClemente, C. C. (1993). Changing addictive behaviors: A process perspective. *Curr. Dis. Psychol. Sci., 2,* 101–06; **Page 403:** "It resists poison and venomous bites . . ." Brock, A. J. (1979). Galen. *On the natural faculties.* (English translation). Loeb Classical Library. Cambridge, MA: Harvard University Press; **Page 412:** "Last Friday, April 16, 1943, I was forced . . ." Hoffman, A. (1971, p. 23). LSD discoverer disputes "chance" factor in finding. *Psychiatr. News, 6*(8), 23–26; **Page 417:** "Gambling Disorder DSM-5" Reprinted with permission from the *Diagnostic and Statistical Manual of Mental Disorders,* Fifth Edition (Copyright © 2013). American Psychiatric Association.

Chapter 12 **Page 423:** "almost literally, as anti-masturbation food" Money, J. (1986, p. 186). *Lovemaps: Clinical concepts of sexual/ erotic health and pathology, paraphilia, and gender transposition.* New York: Irvington; **Page 424:** "the detestable and abominable vice of buggery [anal sex]" King Henry VIII of England, in the sixteenth century; **Page 425:** "Dear Mrs. . . .I gather from your letter that your son is a homosexual . . ." Freud, Sigmund, "Letter to an American mother", *American Journal of Psychiatry, 107* (1951): p. 787; **Page 427:** "Criteria for Fetishistic Disorder" Reprinted with permission from the *Diagnostic and Statistical Manual of Mental Disorders,* Fifth Edition (Copyright 2013). American Psychiatric Association; **Page 427:** "Criteria for Transvestic Disorder" Reprinted with permission from the *Diagnostic and Statistical Manual of Mental Disorders,* Fifth Edition (Copyright 2013). American Psychiatric Association; **Page 427:** "Criteria for Voyeuristic Disorder" Reprinted with permission from the *Diagnostic and Statistical Manual of Mental Disorders,* Fifth Edition (Copyright 2013). American Psychiatric Association; **Page 427:** "Criteria for Exhibitionistic Disorder" Reprinted with permission from the *Diagnostic and Statistical Manual of Mental Disorders,* Fifth Edition (Copyright 2013). American Psychiatric Association; **Page 427:** "Criteria for Sexual Sadism Disorder" Reprinted with permission from the *Diagnostic and Statistical Manual of Mental Disorders,* Fifth Edition (Copyright 2013). American Psychiatric Association; **Page 427:** "Criteria for Sexual Masochism Disorder" Reprinted with permission from the *Diagnostic and Statistical Manual of Mental Disorders,* Fifth Edition (Copyright 2013). American Psychiatric Association; **Page 427:** "Criteria for Pedophilic Disorder" Reprinted with permission from the *Diagnostic and Statistical Manual of Mental Disorders,* Fifth Edition (Copyright 2013). American Psychiatric Association; **Page 427:** "Criteria for Frotteuristic Disorder" Reprinted with permission from the *Diagnostic and Statistical Manual of Mental Disorders,* Fifth Edition (Copyright 2013). American Psychiatric Association; **Page 428:** "They feel attracted not by the women outside them, but by the woman inside them" Hirschfeld, M. (1948, p. 167). *Sexual anomalies* (p. 167). New York: Emerson; **Page 433:** "Gender Dysphoria in Children DSM-5" Reprinted with permission from the *Diagnostic and Statistical Manual of Mental Disorders,* Fifth Edition (Copyright 2013). American Psychiatric Association; **Page 434:** "Gender Dysphoria in Adolescents and Adults DSM-5" Reprinted with permission from the *Diagnostic and Statistical Manual of Mental Disorders,* Fifth Edition (Copyright 2013). American Psychiatric Association; **Page 439:** "to believe that she was a member of a satanic cult, that she was sexually abused by multiple men . . ." Brown, R. D., Goldstein, E., & Bjorklund, D. F. (2000, p. 3). The history and Zeitgeist of the repressed-false-memory debate: Scientific and sociological perspectives on suggestibility and childhood memory. In D. F. Bjorklund (Ed.), *False-memory creation in children and adults: Theory, research, and implications* (pp. 1–30). Mahwah, NJ: Erlbaum; **Page 439:** "If you are unable to remember any specific instances [of sexual abuse] . . ." Bass, E., & Davis, L. (1988, p. 21). *The courage to heal.* New York: Harper & Row; **Page 441:** Figure 12.1: Planty et al., 2013; **Page 448:** "Criteria for Delayed Ejaculation" Reprinted with permission from the *Diagnostic and Statistical Manual of Mental Disorders,* Fifth Edition (Copyright 2013). American Psychiatric Association; **Page 448:** "Criteria Erectile Disorder" Reprinted with permission from the *Diagnostic and Statistical Manual of Mental Disorders,* Fifth Edition (Copyright 2013). American Psychiatric Association; **Page 448:** "Criteria for Premature (early) Ejaculation" Reprinted with permission from the *Diagnostic and Statistical Manual of Mental Disorders,* Fifth Edition (Copyright 2013). American Psychiatric Association; **Page 448:** "Criteria for Male Hypoactive Sexual Disorder" Reprinted with permission from the *Diagnostic and Statistical Manual of Mental Disorders,* Fifth Edition (Copyright 2013). American Psychiatric Association; **Page 448:** "Criteria for Female Sexual Interest/Arousal Disorder" Reprinted with permission from the *Diagnostic and Statistical Manual of Mental Disorders,* Fifth Edition (Copyright 2013). American Psychiatric Association; **Page 449:** "Criteria for Female Orgasmic Disorder" Reprinted with permission from the *Diagnostic and Statistical Manual of Mental Disorders,* Fifth Edition (Copyright 2013). American Psychiatric Association; **Page 449:** "Criteria for Genito-Pelvic Pain/Penetration Disorder" Reprinted with permission from the *Diagnostic and Statistical Manual of Mental Disorders,* Fifth Edition (Copyright 2013). American Psychiatric Association; **Page 449:** "Criteria for Substance/Medication-Induced Sexual Dysfunction" Reprinted with permission from the *Diagnostic and Statistical Manual of Mental Disorders,* Fifth Edition (Copyright 2013). American Psychiatric Association.

Chapter 13 **Page 460:** "Emilio is a 40-year-old man who looks . . ." Modified from Spitzer, R. L., Gibbon, M., Skodol, A. E., Williams, J. B. W., & First, M. B. (Eds.). (2002, pp. 189–90.). *DSM-IV-TR casebook: A learning companion to the diagnostic and statistical manual of mental disorders,* fourth edition, text revision. Washington, DC: American Psychiatric Press; **Pages 460 to 461:** "becomes suspicious of those around him . . ." Kraepelin, E. (1896). Dementia praecox. In J. Cutting & M. Shepherd (1987), *The clinical roots of the schizophrenia concept: Translation of seminal European contributions on schizophrenia* (pp. 13–24). Cambridge: Cambridge University Press; **Page 461:** Figure 13.1: From Haffner, H., et al. (1998). Causes and consequences of the gender difference in age at onset of schizophrenia. *Schizophrenia Bulletin, 24*(1), 99–114; **Page 463:** "Schizophrenia DSM-5" Reprinted with permission from the *Diagnostic and Statistical Manual of Mental Disorders*, Fifth Edition (Copyright 2013). American Psychiatric Association; **Page 467:** "Schizoaffective Disorder DSM-5" Reprinted with permission from the *Diagnostic and Statistical Manual of Mental Disorders*, Fifth Edition (Copyright 2013). American Psychiatric Association; **Page 468:** "Schizophreniform Disorder DSM-5" Reprinted with permission from the *Diagnostic and Statistical Manual of Mental Disorders*, Fifth Edition (Copyright 2013). American Psychiatric Association; **Page 468:** "Delusional Disorder DSM-5" Reprinted with permission from the *Diagnostic and Statistical Manual of Mental Disorders*, Fifth Edition (Copyright 2013). American Psychiatric Association; **Page 469:** "Brief Psychotic Disorder DSM-5" Reprinted with permission from the *Diagnostic and Statistical Manual of Mental Disorders*, Fifth Edition (Copyright 2013). American Psychiatric Association; **Page 469:** "Four Days of Symptoms and Rapid Recovery . . ." Based on Janowsky, D. S., Addario, D., & Risch, S. C. (1987). *Pharmacology case studies*. New York: Guilford; **Page 470:** Figure 13.2: Compiled from family and twin studies in European populations between 1920 and 1987. From Gottesman, I. I. (1991). *Schizophrenia Genesis: The Origins of Madness* (p. 96). Copyright © 1991 by Irving I. Gottesman. Used with permission of W. H. Freeman and Company/ Worth Publishers; **Page 475:** Figure 13.4: Haller C. S., Padmanabhan, J. L., Lizano, P., Torous, J., Keshavan, M. (2014). Recent advances in understanding schizophrenia. *F1000Prime Reports 2014, 6*:57 (doi:10.12703/P6-57); **Page 475:** Table 13.1: Based on Eckbald & Chapman (1983); Chapman et al. (1978); **Page 476:** "infections in the years of development might have a causal significance . . ." Kraepelin, E. (1919). *Dementia praecox and paraphrenia* (R. M. Barclay, Trans.). Edinburgh, Scotland: E. and S. Livingstone; **Page 478:** Figure 13.5: From Davis, J. O., Phelps, J. A., & Bracha, H. S. (1995). Prenatal development of monozygotic twins and concordance for schizophrenia. *Schizophrenia Bulletin, 21*(3), 357–66. Used with permission of Oxford University Press; **Page 482:** Figure 13.6: Figure from Levy et al. (1993). Eye tracking dysfunction and schizophrenia: A critical perspective. *Schizophrenia Bulletin, 19*(3), 461–536. Used with permission of Oxford University Press; **Page 482:** "I have trouble concentrating and keeping my mind . . ." Liberman, R. P. (1982). Assessment of Social Skills. *Schizophrenia Bulletin, 8*, 62–83; **Page 486:** Figure 13.9: Figure 7.1 from Heinrichs R. W. (2001). *In search of madness: Schizophrenia and neuroscience* (p. 196). Oxford University Press. Adapted from Arnold, S. E., & Trojanowski, J. Q. (1996). Recent advances in defining the neuropathology of schizophrenia. *Acta Neuropathologie, 92*, 217–31 and Kolb, B., & Wishaw, I. Q. (1996). *Fundamentals of human neuropsychology* (4th ed.). New York: Freeman; **Page 491:** "the range of feelings and emotions to be found in ordinary families" Brown, G. W. (1985, p. 22). The discovery of expressed emotion: Induction or deduction? In J. Leff & C. Vaughn (Eds.), *Expressed emotion in families* (pp. 7–25). New York: Guilford; **Page 492:** "Schizophrenia in an Immigrant from China" Based on Feeney, L., Kelly, B. D., Whitty, P., & O'Callaghan, E. (2002). Mental illness in migrants: Diagnostic and therapeutic challenges. *Irish Journal of Psychiatric Medicine, 19*(1), 29–31; **Page 494:** Figure 13.10: Data from Rais, M., Cahn, W., Van Haren, N., Schnack, H., Caspers, E., Hulshoff, H., et al. (2008). Excessive brain volume loss over time in cannabis using first episode patients. *Am. J. Psychiatry, 165*, 490–96; **Page 494:** Table 13.2: Author-created; **Page 494:** "Schizophrenia may be the uniquely human price we pay as a species . . ." Gilmore, J. H. (2010, p. 9). Understanding what causes schizophrenia: A developmental perspective. *Am. J. Psychiatry, 167*, 8–10; **Page 496:** "From Impairment to Improvement" Adapted from Murray, G. K., Leeson, V., & McKenna, P. J. (2004). Spontaneous improvement in severe, chronic schizophrenia and its neurological correlates. *Brit. J. Psychiatry, 184*, 357–58; **Page 497:** Figure 13.12: Figure 3 from Kulkarni et al. (2008). *Archives of General Psychiatry, 65*(8), 958 (Copyright © 2008). American Medical Association. Reprinted with permission; **Page 498:** "As a parent I also know that medication is not perfect . . ." From Slater, E. (1986). First person account: A parent's view on enforcing medication. *Schizo. Bull., 12*, 291–92; **Page 500:** "The use of neuroleptics is a trap . . ." Whitaker, R. (2010, pp. 107). *Anatomy of an epidemic: Magic bullets, psychiatric drugs, and the astonishing rise of mental illness in America*. New York: Crown Publishers.

Chapter 14   Page 504: "A Simple Case of Mania?" Adapted from Jamieson, R., & Wells, C. (1979). Manic psychosis in a patient with multiple metastatic brain tumors. *J. Clin. Psychiatry, 40*, 280–83; **Page 505 to 506:** "Memory Impairment Following a Car Accident" Based on Krishna, R., Grinn, M., Giordano, N., Thirunanukkarasu, M., Tadi, P., & Das, S. (2012). Diagnostic confirmation of mild traumatic brain injury by diffusion tensor imaging: a case report. *Journal of Medical Case Reports, 6*:66, doi:10.1186/1752-1947-6-66; **Page 506:** Figure 14.1: Based on Dr. Steven Warach, National Institute of Neurological Disorders and Stroke; American Heart Association; **Page 509:** Figure 14.3: Adapted with permission from the *American Psychiatric Publishing Textbook of Neuropsychiatry and Behavioral Neurosciences*, Fifth Edition (Copyright © 2008). American Psychiatric Publishing; **Page 509:** "Delirium Following a Routine Operation" Based on Üstün et al., 1996; **Page 510:** "Criteria for Delirium" Reprinted with permission from the *Diagnostic and Statistical Manual of Mental Disorders*, Fifth

Edition (Copyright 2013). American Psychiatric Association; **Page 511:** "Criteria for Major Neurocognitive Disorder" Reprinted with permission from the *Diagnostic and Statistical Manual of Mental Disorders*, Fifth Edition (Copyright 2013). American Psychiatric Association; **Page 513:** "The Forgetful Mail Carrier" Based on Üstün et al., 1996; **Page 513:** Figure 14.5: Figure 1 on Page 198 from Martha Storandt. (2008). Cognitive deficits in the early stages of Alzheimer's disease. *Current Directions in Psychological Science, 17*(3), 198–202 (Copyright © 2008). Association for Psychological Science. Reproduced with permission of Blackwell Publishing Ltd.; **Page 524:** "He Forgot the Name of His Daughter" Based on Morrison, J. (1995). *DSM-IV made easy: The clinicians guide to diagnosis*. New York: Guilford; **Page 526:** "Zack's Story" Adapted from Centers for Disease Control and Prevention, 2010; **Page 526:** Figure 14.7: Singh et al. (2014), Relationship of Collegiate Football Experience and Concussion With Hippocampal Volume and Cognitive Outcomes, *JAMA*. 2014; *311*(18):1883-1888. doi:10.1001/jama.2014.3313; **Page 527:** "He is fitful, irreverent, indulging at times in the grossest . . ." Harlow, J. M. (1868). Recovery from the passage of an iron bar through the head. *Publication of the Massachusetts Medical Society, 2, 327*; **Page 529:** Table 14.6: Based on Bennett, T. L., Dittmar, C., & Ho, M. R. (1997). The neuropsychology of traumatic brain injury. In A. M. Horton, D. Wedding, & J. Webster (Eds.), *The neuropsychology handbook* (Vol. 2, pp. 123–72). New York: Springer. Dikmen, S. S., Temkin, N. R., Machamer, J. E., & Holubkov, A. L. (1994). Employment following traumatic head injuries. *Arch. Neurol., 51*(2), 177–86. Diller, L., & Gordon, W. A. (1981). Interventions for cognitive deficits in brain-injured adults. *J. Consult. Clin. Psychol., 49*, 822–34. Mackay, L. E. (1994). Benefits of a formalized traumatic brain injury program within a trauma center. *J. Head Trauma Rehab., 9*(1), 11–19. MacMillan, P. J., Hart, R., Martelli, M., & Zasler, N. (2002). Pre-injury status and adaptation following traumatic brain injury. *Brain Injury, 16*(1), 41–49.

Chapter 15   Page 533: Figure 15.1: Based on Merikangas et al., 2010; Merikangas, K., Jin, R., He, J. P., Kessler, R. C., Lee, S., et al. (2011). *Archives of General Psychiatry, 68*, 241–51; **Page 536:** Figure 15.2: Based on Merikangas et al., 2010, Lifetime Prevalence of Mental Disorders in US Adolescents: Results from the National Comorbidity Study-Adolescent Supplement (NCS-A), *J. Am. Acad. Child. Adolesc Psychiatry*. 2010 October; *49*(10): 980–989; **Page 539:** Figure 15.3: Moreno, C., Laje, G., Blanco, C., Jiang, H., Schmidt, A. B., & Olfson, M. (2007). National trends in the outpatient diagnosis and treatment of bipolar disorder in youth. *Arch. Gen. Psychiatry, 64*, 1032–39; **Page 541:** "Conduct Disorder DSM-5" Reprinted with permission from the *Diagnostic and Statistical Manual of Mental Disorders*, Fifth Edition (Copyright 2013). American Psychiatric Association; **Page 543:** Figure 15.4: Conduct Problems Research Group, 2011, The Effects of the Fast Track Preventive Intervention on the Development of Conduct Disorder Across Childhood, *Child Dev*. 2011 Jan–Feb; *82*(1): 331–345; **Page 546:** "Attention-Deficit/Hyperactivity Disorder DSM-5" Reprinted with permission from the *Diagnostic and Statistical Manual of Mental Disorders*, Fifth Edition (Copyright 2013). American Psychiatric Association; **Page 548:** Figure 15.5: Based on Zuvekas, S. H., & Vitiello, B. (2012). Stimulant medication use in children: a 12-year perspective. *Am. J. Psychiatry, 169*(2), 160–166; **Page 550:** Figure 15.6: Warren Jones and Ami Klin, Attention to Eyes is Present But in Decline in 2–6 Month-Olds Later Diagnosed with Autism, *Nature*. 2013 Dec 19; *504*(7480): 427–431; **Page 551:** "Autism Spectrum Disorder DSM-5" Reprinted with permission from the *Diagnostic and Statistical Manual of Mental Disorders*, Fifth Edition (Copyright 2013). American Psychiatric Association; **Page 553:** Figure 15.7: Based on Gordon et al. 2014, Quantifying narrative ability in autism spectrum disorder: a computational linguistic analysis of narrative coherence, *J. Autism Dev. Disord*. 2014 Dec; *44*(12):3016–25; **Page 556:** "(b) INDIVIDUALS WITH DISABILITIES . . ." Second Session of the 111 Congress of the United States in 2010; **Page 559:** Table 15.2: Based on American Psychiatric Association. (2013). *Diagnostic and statistical manual of mental disorders* (DSM-5) (5th ed.). Washington, DC: American Psychiatric Association; Harris, J. C. (2006). *Intellectual disability: Understanding its development, causes, classification, evaluation, and treatment*. New York: Oxford University Press.

Chapter 16   Page 572: Figure 16.1: Based on WHO World Mental Health Survey Consortium, 2004, *JAMA*; **Pages 573 to 574:** "a sense of working collaboratively on the problem . . ." Constantino, M. J., Castonguay, L. G., & Schut, A. J. (2001). The working alliance. In G. S. Tryon (Ed.), *Counseling based on process research: Applying what we know*. Boston: Allyn and Bacon; **Page 579:** "Pharmacotherapy appears to provide rapid . . ." Hollon, S. D. and Fawcett, J. (1995) *Combined medication and psychotherapy in treatments of psychiatric disorders* (2nd ed.). Washington: American Psychiatric Press; **Page 583:** "Cognitive Therapy" From I. M. Blackburn and K. M. Davidson. (1990). *Cognitive therapy for depression and anxiety: A practitioner's guide* (pp. 106–7). Copyright © 1995 Blackwell Science, in the format republish in a book via Copyright Clearance Center; **Page 584:** "CBT has been an effective treatment for depression . . ." Johnsen, T. J., & Friborg, O. (2015). "The effects of cognitive behavioral therapy as an anti-depressive treatment is falling: A meta-analysis." *Psychological Bulletin, 141*, 747–768; **Page 586:** "Gestalt Therapy" Adapted from Prochaska, J. O., & Norcross, J. C. (2003). *Systems of psychotherapy* (5th ed.). Pacific Grove,

CA: Brooks/Cole; **Page 587:** "Psychodynamic Therapy" Adapted from Prochaska, J. O., & Norcross, J. C. (2003). *Systems of psychotherapy* (5th ed.). Pacific Grove, CA: Brooks/Cole; **Page 593:** "A Khmer Woman" Rumbaut, R. (1985). Mental health and the refugee experience: A comparative study of Southeast Asian refugees. In T. C. Owan (Ed.), *Southeast Asian mental health: Treatment, prevention, services, training, and research* (pp. 443–86). Washington, DC: National Institute of Mental Health; **Page 594:** Table 16.1: Based on Bezchlibnyk-Butler, K. Z., & Jeffries, J. J. (2003). *Clinical handbook of psychotropic drugs*. Seattle: Hogrefe & Huber. Buckley & Waddington (2001); and Sadock et al. (2009); **Page 595:** Table 16.2: Based on Bezchlibnyk-Butler, K. Z., & Jeffries, J. J. (2003). *Clinical handbook of psychotropic drugs*. Seattle: Hogrefe & Huber. Buckley & Waddington (2001); and Sadock et al. (2009); **Page 595:** Figure 16.2: Based on Ciccarelli, S. K., and White, J. N. Reprinted from *Psychology* (2nd ed.), © 2008, Pearson Education Inc., Upper Saddle River, New Jersey; **Page 598:** Table 16.3: Based on Bezchlibnyk-Butler, K. Z., & Jeffries, J. J. (2003). *Clinical handbook of psychotropic drugs*. Seattle: Hogrefe & Huber. Buckley & Waddington (2001); and Sadock et al. (2009); **Page 599:** "THINKING CRITICALLY about DSM-5" Data from the *Diagnostic and Statistical Manual of Mental Disorders*, Fifth Edition (Copyright 2013). American Psychiatric Association; **Page 600:** Table 16.4: Based on Bezchlibnyk-Butler, K. Z., & Jeffries, J. J. (2003). *Clinical handbook of psychotropic drugs*. Seattle: Hogrefe & Huber. Buckley & Waddington (2001); and Sadock et al. (2009); **Page 601:** Figure 16.4: Based on Sadock & Sadock (2003, p. 1142); **Page 602:** Figure 16.5: National Institute of Mental Health; **Page 604:** Figure 16.6: National Institute of Mental Health.

Chapter 17   Page 608: "A Tragic Case of Murder as an Outcome of Severe Mental Illness" Based on Associated Press. (2004, March 31). Doctor says mom who killed sons mentally ill. Associated Press.; Ramsland, K. (2005). *Inside the minds of mass murderers: Why they kill*. Westport, CT: Praeger; **Page 609:** Figure 17.1: From P. J. Mrazek & R. J. Haggerty (Eds.). (1994). *Reducing risks for mental disorders: Frontiers for preventive intervention research*. Copyright © 1994 by the National Academy of Sciences. Courtesy of the National Academy Press, Washington, DC; **Page 614:** "Milieu therapy focuses on structuring a patient's . . ." Paul, G. L., & Lentz, R. J. (1977). *Psychosocial treatment of chronic mental patients: Milieu versus social-learning programs*. Cambridge, MA: Harvard University Press; **Page 617:** "Important Court Decisions for Patient Rights" Based on Grounds, A. (2000). The psychiatrist in court. In M. G. Gelder, J. J. Lopez-Ibor, Jr., & N. C. Andreason (Eds.), *New Oxford textbook of psychiatry* (pp. 2089–96). Oxford: Oxford University Press; Mental Health Law Project (1987), Mrad, D. H., & Watson, C. (2011). Civil commitment. In E. Y. Drogin, F. M. Dattilio, R. L. Sadoff, & T. G. Gutheil (Eds.), *Handbook of forensic assessment: Psychological and psychiatric perspectives* (pp. 479–501). Hoboken, NJ: Wiley.; Saks, E. R. (2004). Refusing care: Forced treatment and the use of psychiatric advance directives. *J. Foren. Psychol. Pract.*, 4(4), 35–50. and Swartz, M., Swanson, J. W., & Elbogen, E. B. (2004). Psychiatric advance directives: Practical, legal, and ethical issues. *J. Foren. Psychol. Pract.*, 4(4), 97–107; **Page 620:** "Ultimately, the goal of a warning system in mental health law . . ." Monahan, J., & Steadman, H. J. (1997, p. 937). Violent storms and violent people: How meteorology can inform risk communication in mental health law. *Am. Psychol.*, 51(9), 931–38; **Page 625:** "realistically balance the interest of the mentally ill offender's rights . . ." Marvit, R. C. (1981, p. 23). Guilty but mentally ill—an old approach to an old problem. *Clin. Psychol.*, 34(4), 22–23.

Name Index

Subject Index

Note: Page numbers followed by *f* indicate figures; and those followed by *t* indicate tables.